ECONOMICS

SECOND EDITION

MICHAEL PARKIN

UNIVERSITY
OF
WESTERN ONTARIO

ADDISON-WESLEY
PUBLISHING COMPANY

Reading, Massachusetts ◆ Menlo Park, California ◆ New York
Don Mills, Ontario ◆ Wokingham, England ◆ Amsterdam
Bonn ◆ Sydney ◆ Singapore ◆ Tokyo
Madrid ◆ San Juan ◆ Milan ◆ Paris

Library of Congress Cataloging-in-Publication Data

Parkin, Michael, 1939–
Economics / Michael Parkin.—2nd ed.
p. cm.
Includes index.
ISBN 0-201-54697-3
1. Economics. I. Title.
HB171.5.P313 1992
330—dc20 92-15707
CIP

Printed in the United States of America.
1 2 3 4 5 6 7 8 9-DO-9695949392

Executive Editor: **Barbara Rifkind**
Senior Sponsoring Editor: **Marjorie Williams**
Senior Development Editor: **Marilyn R. Freedman**
Production Supervisor: **Loren Hilgenhurst Stevens**
Managing Editor: **Kazia Navas**
Cover Design Director: **Peter M. Blaiwas**
Cover Design Associate: **Eileen R. Hoff**
Cover and Interior Designer: **Karen Gourley-Lehman**
Art and Design Coordinator: **Meredith Nightingale**
Art Development Editor: **Kelley Hersey, Focus Design**
Technical Art Supervisor: **Joseph Vetere**
Technical Art Consultants: **Loretta Bailey and Dick Morton**
Art Coordinators: **Janice Alden Mello and Connie Hulse**
Illustrators: **TSI Graphics**
Electronic Vignettes: **Frank Mazzola, Jr., Raffaele Delicata Design, and Thomas Vanin-Bishop, Ampersand Studios**
Photo Researchers: **Pembroke Herbert and Sandi Rygiel, Picture Research Consultants**
Prepress Services Manager: **Sarah McCracken**
Assistant Editor: **Kari Heen**
Special Project Manager: **Cindy Johnson**
Copyeditor: **Barbara Willette**
Production Services: **Jane Hoover, Lifland et al., Bookmakers, and Sarah Hallet Corey**
Layout Artists: **Jane Hoover and Karen Gourley-Lehman**
Permissions Editor: **Mary Dyer**
Indexer: **Alexandra Nickerson**
Manufacturing Supervisor: **Roy Logan**
Senior Marketing Manager: **David Theisen**
Creative Services Manager: **Eileen Spingler**
Compositor: **Black Dot Graphics**
Color Separator: **Black Dot Graphics**
Printer: **R. R. Donnelley & Sons Company**

Text and photo credits appear on page 1088, which constitutes a continuation of the copyright page.

To Robin

About Michael Parkin

Michael Parkin received his training as an economist at the Universities of Leicester and Essex in England. Currently in the Department of Economics at the University of Western Ontario, Canada, Professor Parkin has held faculty appointments at Brown University, the University of Manchester, and the University of Essex. He has served on the editorial boards of the *American Economic Review* and the *Journal of Monetary Economics* and as managing editor of the *Canadian Journal of Economics*. He is the author of *Macroeconomics* (Prentice-Hall). Professor Parkin's research on macroeconomics, monetary economics, and international economics has resulted in 160 publications in journals and edited volumes, including the *American Economic Review,* the *Journal of Political Economy,* the *Review of Economic Studies,* the *Journal of Monetary Economics,* and the *Journal of Money, Credit and Banking.* It became most visible to the

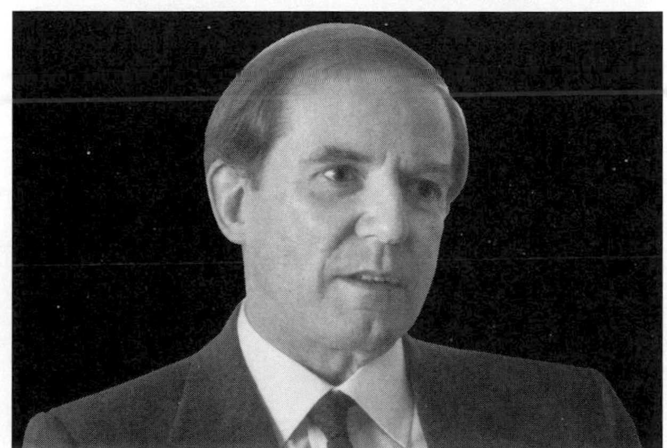

public with his work on inflation that discredited the use of wage and price controls. Michael Parkin also spearheaded the movement toward European monetary union. Professor Parkin is an experienced and dedicated teacher of introductory economics.

PREFACE

To change the way students see the world—this is my purpose in teaching economics and has remained my goal in preparing this revision. There is no greater satisfaction for a teacher than sharing the joy of students who have come to understand the powerful lessons of the economic approach. But these lessons are not easy to master. Every day in my classroom, I relearn the challenges of gaining the insights that we call the economist's way of thinking and recall my own early struggles to master this discipline. In preparing this revision, I have been able to draw on the experiences not only of my own students, but also of hundreds of users of the first edition, both instructors and their students.

Three assumptions have guided the choices that faced me in writing this book. First, students are eager to learn, but they are overwhelmed by the seemingly endless claims on their time and energy. Therefore they want to know why they are being asked to study a particular body of material and require demonstration of its relevance to their own everyday experience. Second, students expect thoughtful and straightforward explanations, so they can begin to apply the principles they are learning. Third, today's students are more interested in the present and the future than in the past. They want to learn the economics of the 1990s so that, as they enter the twenty-first century, uncertain of the future and what it holds, they will be equipped with the useful principles that will help them understand apparently unpredictable events.

Approach

The core of the principles course has been around for more than 100 years, and other important elements, especially parts of the theory of the firm and Keynesian macroeconomics, have been with us for more than 50 years. But economics has also been developing and changing rapidly during the past few decades. All principles texts pay some attention to these more recent developments, but none has succeeded in integrating the new and traditional. My goal has been to incorporate new ideas—game theory, the modern theory of the firm, information, and public choice—into the body of timeless principles.

The presence of modern topics does not translate into "high level"; nor does it translate into "bias." At every point, I have striven to make recent developments in economics thoroughly accessible to beginning students. Where these modern theories are controversial, alternative approaches are presented, evaluated, and compared.

But this book does have a point of view. It is that economics is a serious, lively, and evolving science—a science that seeks to develop a body of theory powerful enough to explain the economic world around us and that pursues its task by building, testing, and rejecting economic models. In some areas the science has succeeded at its task, but in others it has some way to go and controversy persists. Where matters are settled, I present what we know; where controversy persists, I present the alternative viewpoints. This positive approach to economics is, I believe, especially valuable for students as they prepare to function in a world in which simple ideologies have become irrelevant and in which familiar patterns in the economic landscape have shifted and blurred.

Microeconomics and Changes in the Second Edition

The structure of the microeconomics presentation remains consistent with the first edition, but I have made many important changes. I have simplified but vastly increased the range of application of the demand and supply model (Chapter 6) to deal with such issues as who pays a sales tax and trading in prohibited goods. I have expanded the treatment of the marginal utility theory of consumer choice (Chapter 7) to give a stronger graphical derivation of consumer equilibrium and the demand curve. The modern theory of the firm, including principal and agent issues, is given a much simplified treatment in Chapter 9, and isoquants are covered in the appendix to Chapter 10. My presentation of the game theory approach to understanding oligopoly has been well received for its simple yet serious treatment. In revising the oligopoly chapter (Chapter 13), I recognized that students can gain additional insights from the traditional oligopoly models and included these. A completely new chapter (Chapter 17) deals with the issues arising from uncertainty and incomplete information and illustrates these issues with examples drawn from markets for used cars, insurance, credit, and risky assets. My approach in this chapter is the same as in the rest of the book—to explain a difficult (and in this case relatively new) topic in a clear and accessible way that fits naturally into the core principles sequence. Finally, the discussion of income distribution issues in Chapter 18 now contains a much expanded treatment of income redistribution policies, including the negative income tax.

Macroeconomics and Changes in the Second Edition

My goals in revising the macroeconomics coverage have been to extend and improve the positive, fact-driven approach of the first edition, to make the complexities of macroeconomic models and events relevant and understandable to students, and to address the global macroeconomic issues of the 1990s. I have changed the balance of the coverage of national income accounting (Chapter 23), giving greater prominence to a discussion of the validity of GDP as a measure of economic well-being. Since the aggregate demand–aggregate supply model is inherently more subtle than the microeconomic demand and supply model, it needs to be explained carefully and clearly. I have simplified and streamlined the initial presentation of aggregate demand–aggregate supply model (Chapter 24) so that students can make effective and immediate use of it. I have also clarified the discussion of the components and workings of the aggregate demand model (in Chapters 25 and 26). In light of the 1991 recession and the ongoing federal deficit, it has become increasingly apparent that an understanding of both fiscal and monetary policy is essential. The role of fiscal policy is thoroughly discussed throughout the text (especially in Chapters 24, 26, 29, and 32) and is illustrated through issues drawn from the 1991 recession. And the role of financial deregulation in the macroeconomy is given enhanced prominence in Chapter 27. The extended coverage of aggregate supply issues has also been thoroughly revised. Today's students care about the issues of productivity and growth, and they will find information on these in Chapter 30. The discussion of inflation as an issue and subject of analysis is now separated from the thorough discussion of expectations (Chapter 31). The coverage of stabilization policy has been revised and extended to include a discussion of the political business cycle. Finally, the coverage of economies in transition has necessarily been completely revised. Chapter 38 provides a framework for understanding events in Eastern Europe, the former Soviet Union, and China as these countries change their economic systems and open their markets to international influences.

Special Features

This second edition, like its predecessor, is packed with special features designed to enhance the learning process.

Art Program

A highly successful innovation in the first edition was the outstanding art program. The art not only was visually attractive and engaging but also communicated the economic principles unambiguously and clearly. We received enormously positive feedback on the art program, confirming our belief that one of the most important tools for economists is graphical analysis and also that this is precisely an area that gives many students much difficulty. In the second edition, we have further refined the data-based art by deriving a style that clearly reveals the data and trends. In addition, diagrams that illustrate economic processes now consistently distinguish key economic players (firms, households, governments, and markets).

Our goal is to show clearly "where the economic action is." To achieve this, we observe a consistent protocol in style, notation, and use of color, including:

- Highlighting shifted curves, points of equilibrium, and the most important features in red
- Using arrows in conjunction with color to lend directional movement to what are usually static presentations
- Pairing graphs with data tables from which the curves have been plotted

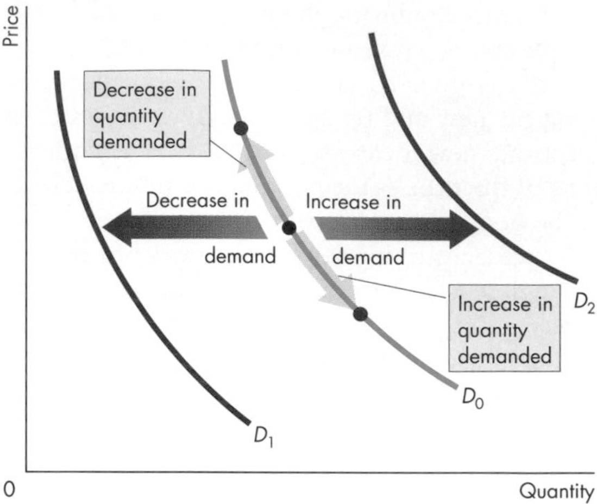

- Using color consistently to underscore the content and referring to such use of color in the text and captions
- Labeling key pieces of information in graphs with boxed notes
- Rendering each piece electronically so that precision is achieved

The entire art program has been developed with the study and review needs of the student in mind. We have retained the following features:

- Marking the most important figures and tables with a red key and listing them at the end of the chapter under "Key Figures and Tables"
- Using complete, informative captions that encapsulate major points in the graph so that students can preview or review the chapter by skimming through the art

The Interviews

Substantive interviews with famous economists constituted another popular feature in the first edition. I am continuing the tradition and have included all new interviews—fourteen in total—each with an economist who has contributed significantly to advancing the thinking and practice in our discipline. Four of the interviews are with Nobel laureates: Kenneth Arrow, Ronald H. Coase, Franco Modigliani, and Robert Solow. The interviews encourage students to participate in the conversations as the economists discuss their areas of specialization, their unique contributions to economics, and also their general insights that are relevant to beginning students.

Each interview opens one of the book's fourteen parts and has been carefully edited to be self-contained. Since each interview discusses topics that are introduced formally in the subsequent chapters, students can use it as a preview to some of the terminology and theory they are about to encounter. A more careful reading afterwards will give students a fuller appreciation of the discussion. Finally, the whole series of interviews can be approached as an informal symposium on the subject matter of economics as it is practiced today.

Reading Between the Lines

Another feature of the previous edition that was well received was "Reading Between the Lines." These news article spreads help students to build critical thinking skills and to interpret daily news events (and their coverage in the media) using economic principles. I have updated all of the news articles in this edition and have selected topics that appeal to students, such as falling SAT scores, Nintendo rentals, and the environmental debate over the spotted owl. Each "Reading Between the Lines" spread contains three passes at a story. It begins with a facsimile (usually abbreviated) of an actual newspaper or magazine article. It then presents a digest of the article's essential points. Finally, it provides an economic analysis of the article, based on the economic methods presented in that chapter.

Our Advancing Knowledge

The fully revised "Our Advancing Knowledge" features help students trace the evolution of path-breaking economic ideas and recognize the universality of their application, not only to the past but to the present. For example, Adam Smith's powerful ideas about the division of labor apply to the creation of a computer chip as well as to the pin factory of the eighteenth century. And Dionysius Lardner's 1850s application of demand and supply theory to railroad pricing applies equally to airline pricing today. A new visual design brings excitement and vitality to these inserts, much in the way that the ideas have brought excitement and vitality to economics.

Learning Aids

We have refined our careful pedagogical plan to ensure that this book complements and reinforces classroom learning. Each chapter contains the following pedagogical elements:

Objectives Each chapter opens with a list of objectives that enable students to set their goals as they begin the chapter.

Chapter Openers Intriguing puzzles, paradoxes, or metaphors frame the important questions that are unraveled and resolved as the chapter progresses.

Highlighted In-Text Reviews Succinct summaries for review are interspersed throughout the chapter at the ends of sections.

Key Terms Highlighted within the text, these concepts form the first part of a three-tiered review of economic vocabulary. These terms are repeated with page references at chapter ends and compiled in the end-of-book glossary.

Key Figures and Tables The most important figures and tables are identified with the red key and listed at chapter end.

End-of-Chapter Study Material Chapters conclude with summaries organized around major headings, lists of key terms with page references, lists of key figures and tables with page references, review questions, and problems. In the second edition, we have added many new problems.

Flexibility

I have chosen to present microeconomics first, but the book has been written to accommodate courses that are sequenced with either microeconomics or macroeconomics first. The microeconomics and macroeconomics chapters do not depend on each other; concepts and terms are defined and ideas are developed independently in each of the two halves.

I have tried to accommodate a wide range of teaching approaches by building flexibility and optionality into the book. There are several optional sections, which are indicated by footnote. These may be omitted with no loss of continuity.

The Teaching and Learning Package

Our fully integrated text and supplements package provides

students and professors with a seamless teaching and learning experience. The authors of the components are outstanding educators and scholars and have brought their own human capital (and that of their students!) to the job of improving the quality and value of the ancillaries for the second edition.

Study Guide Now available in microeconomics and macroeconomics split versions, the revised Study Guide was prepared by David Spencer of Brigham Young University. Carefully coordinated with the main textbook, each chapter of the Study Guide contains: Chapter in Perspective; Learning Objectives; Helpful Hints; Self-Test (concepts review, true/false, multiple-choice, and short-answer questions, and problems) and Answers to Self-Test; and Key Figures and Tables.

Economics in the News with Video Selections Updated with all new articles, this unique workbook extends the "Reading Between the Lines" feature of the textbook. Prepared by Saul Pleeter (U.S. Department of Defense) and Philip Way of the University of Cincinnati, the supplement includes eighty-five recent news articles organized according to the topical outline of the textbook. An introductory paragraph, learning objectives, and preview precede a facsimile of each article, which is accompanied by analytical questions that give students practice in developing their ability to think like economists. In this edition we have also incorporated ten video excerpts from the MacNeil-Lehrer Business Reports. Just as for the print articles, Pleeter and Way provide a series of probing questions to help students dissect the economic principles that underlie the issues illustrated in the video news clips.

Instructor's Manual for Economics in the News The solutions to questions and problems in Economics in the News are available to instructors upon request from the Business and Economics Group at Addison-Wesley.

Test Item File Thoroughly revised test items were prepared by David Denslow of the University of Florida and Barbara Haney Martinez of the Center for Economic Education at the University of Alaska, Fairbanks. The file includes over 4,000 multiple choice questions, about half of which are new to this edition. All questions have been reviewed carefully for accuracy by Robert Horn and Sharon O'Hare at James Madison University. Each chapter includes a section of questions that are directly from the Study Guide and a section of questions that parallel those in the Study Guide.

Computerized Test Item File Testing software with graphics capability for IBM-PC and compatible microcomputers or Macintosh microcomputers is available to qualified adopters.

Instructor's Manual A brand new Instructor's Manual has been prepared by Mark Rush of the University of Florida. It includes detailed chapter outlines and teaching suggestions; cross-references to the color acetates, videos, and software; answers to all review questions and problems in the textbook; additional discussion questions; information on material new to the second edition; explanations of how each chapter relates to the rest of the book; and a flexibility guide for different course sequences.

Acetates and Overlays Key figures from the text are rendered in full color on the acetates. There are 180 acetates, of which 70 have overlays. The acetates are available to qualified adopters of the textbook (contact your Addison-Wesley sales representative).

MacNeil-Lehrer Business Reports Videos An exclusive from Addison-Wesley, these videos illustrate economic principles in action via highly topical news stories. Ten video selections, split evenly between macroeconomic and microeconomic concepts, can be used in conjunction with either the textbook or the Economics in the News supplement. The videos are free to adopters.

Video Guide to MacNeil-Lehrer Business Reports Helpful teaching notes and discussion questions for using videos in the classroom, as well as relevant graphics prepared as transparency masters, are provided free to adopters.

"Economics in Action" Software New to this edition is truly interactive tutorial software available for both IBM-compatible and Macintosh computers. This software was created specifically for this text by Douglas McTaggart (co-author of the Australian edition of this book) and David Gould of Bond University, Paul Davies of the University of Melbourne, and myself, with a great deal of help from the many people thanked below. The software includes modules on core concepts such as graphing, production possibilities and opportunity cost, demand and supply, elasticity, utility and demand, product curves and cost curves, perfect competition, monopoly, macroeconomic performance, aggregate demand and aggregate supply, expenditure multipliers, money and banking, and international trade.

Three interactive modes take full advantage of the computer's capability to facilitate critical thinking skills. First, a tutorial mode walks students through the central concepts. Second, a quiz mode enables guided self-testing. Third, a free mode allows students and professors to interact with economic models by changing parameters and observing the effects on the graphs. For professors, a special disk is available that extends this capability to generating electronic transparencies for dynamic use in the classroom.

In addition to its emphasis on interaction, the software is also closely integrated with the text. The art style is the same, the terminology is consistent, and supporting material in the text is cross-referenced in the software.

The software has its own authoring language that enables professors to customize tutorials, quizzes, and graphs to fit their own course material. The software has been fully tested and reviewed for accuracy. An Economics in Action Instructor's Guide is available.

Acknowledgments

The endeavor of creating a principles textbook involves the creative collaboration and contribution of many individuals. Although the extent of my debts cannot be fully acknowledged here, it is nevertheless a joy to record my gratitude to the many people who have helped, some without realizing just how helpful they were.

I want to thank those of my colleagues at the University of Western Ontario who have taught me a great deal that can be found in these pages: Jim Davies, Jeremy Greenwood, Ig Horstmann, Peter Howitt, Greg Huffman, David Laidler, Phil Reny, Chris Robinson, John Whalley, and Ron Wonnacott. I want to extend a special thanks to Glenn MacDonald, who worked well beyond the call of duty discussing this project with me from its outset, helping me develop many of the pedagogical features and reading and commenting in detail on all the micro chapters. Special thanks also go to Doug McTaggart of Bond University and Christopher Findlay of the University of Adelaide, co-authors of the Australian edition, and David King, co-author of the European edition. Their suggestions arising from their adaptations of the first edition have been extremely helpful in fine-tuning this edition. More than that, Doug and I worked together on the early drafts of the new chapter on uncertainty and information in the perfect Queensland winter of 1991.

I also want to acknowledge my debt to those who have had a profound influence on my whole view of and approach to economics and whose influence I can see in these pages. Although I never sat in their classrooms, they are in a very real sense my teachers. I am especially grateful to John Carlson (Purdue University), Carl Christ (Johns Hopkins University), Robert Clower (University of South Carolina), Ed Feige (University of Wisconsin at Madison), Herschel Grossman (Brown University), and Sam Wu (University of Iowa). I also want to place on record my enormous debt to the late Karl Brunner. The energy, drive, and entrepreneurship of this outstanding economist provided me and my generation of economists with incredible opportunities to interact and learn from each other in a wide variety of conference settings, in both the United States and Europe.

It is also a pleasure to acknowledge my debt to the several thousand students to whom I have been privileged to teach introductory economics. The instant feedback that comes from the look of puzzlement or enlightenment has taught me, more than anything else, how to teach economics.

Producing a text such as this is a team effort, and the members of the Addison-Wesley "Parkin Team" are genuine co-producers of this book. I am especially grateful to and have been truly inspired by Barbara Rifkind, an extraordinary editor who, as executive editor, created and directed the team with whom it has been a privilege to work. I am also deeply indebted to my development editor, Marilyn Freedman. The personal dedication and professional skill that she brought to the task of crafting the book's broad thrust and fine details and her commitment to making the book as interesting, effective, and error-free as possible were extraordinary. High praise and great thanks go to Loren Hilgenhurst Stevens, who, as production supervisor, coordinated the entire production process, coping calmly and decisively with the cascading crises that daily crossed her desk as she brought all the many complex elements together. Sincere thanks also to Marjorie Williams, who, as senior economics editor, managed and coordinated all the interviews and devised the weekly workload memo that kept my nose pointed firmly in the desired direction; Dave Theisen, business and economics marketing manager, who devised and managed the marketing plan; Kari Heen, assistant editor, whose cheery voice and friendly faxes lifted the sagging spirits in just the right way at just the right time; and especially Cindy Johnson, project manager of the supplements, whose outstanding editorial and managerial skills and personal commitment have brought together a state-of-the-art teaching and learning package. Great thanks go to Loretta Bailey, Janice Mello, Sherry Berg, Sharon Cogdill, Phyllis Coyne, Kelley Hersey, Jane Hoover, Karen Lehman, Stephanie Magean, Dick Morton, Kazia Navas, Meredith Nightingale, and Barbara Willette.

I also wish to express my gratitude to Bob McGough, a superb financial and economics journalist, who provided a thorough and creative edit of an early draft of the first edition and who taught me a great deal about how to write more clearly and effectively. Mark Rush, David Denslow, Barbara Haney Martinez, David Spencer, Saul Pleeter, Phillip Way, Paul Davis, and David Gould were the primary authors of the supplements package and graciously shared their professional insights and teaching expertise with me. I also want to thank my secretary, Barbara Craig, who helped at various stages of this book, typing and retyping its countless drafts and redrafts.

I have left until last four people to whom I want to give special thanks. First, my wife, colleague, best friend, and co-author of the Canadian edition, Robin Bade, has been almost a co-author of this work. She has read every word that I have written, commented in detail on every draft, and helped manage the project from its conception to its conclusion. Without the anticipation of her help and its availability, I could not have contemplated embarking on this project. Finally, I want to acknowledge the help and inspiration of my children, Catherine, Richard, and Ann. Through the years when I was developing and writing the first edition, they were going through various stages of high school and college. They forced me to craft a book that they could understand and found interesting. In preparing this edition, I have been especially helped by Richard, who became a Harvard Graphics wizard and created the entire art manuscript.

The empirical test of this textbook's value continues to be made in the classroom. I would appreciate hearing from instructors and students about how I might continue to improve the book in future editions.

Michael Parkin
Department of Economics
University of Western Ontario
London, Ontario N6A 5C2

Reviewers

Manuscript Reviews

Ronald M. Ayers, University of Texas at San Antonio; **Mohsen Bahmani-Oskooee**, University of Wisconsin–Milwaukee; **Charles L. Ballard**, Michigan State University; **Vanessa Craft**, Bentley College; **Ronald E. Crowe**, University of Central Florida; **Shirley J. Gedeon**, The University of Vermont; **James Robert Gillette**, Texas A&M University; **John W. Graham**, Rutgers—The State University of New Jersey, Newark Campus; **James H. Holcomb**, The University of Texas at El Paso; **Robert N. Horn**, James Madison University; **Noreen E. Lephardt**, Marquette University; **Steven J. Matusz**, Michigan State University; **J. M. Pogodzinski**, San Jose State University; **James E. Price**, Syracuse University; **Jonathan B. Pritchett**, Tulane University; **Christine Rider**, St. John's University; **Richard Rosenberg**, Pennsylvania State University; **Peter Rupert**, State University of New York at Buffalo

Planning Reviews

Mary E. Allender, University of Portland; **Philip J. Grossman**, Wayne State University; **Bruce Herrick and members of the Department of Economics**, Washington and Lee University; **Andrew Kliman**, New York Institute of Technology; **M. L. Livingston**, University of Northern Colorado; **Nan Maxwell**, California State University–Hayward; **Henry McCarl**, University of Alabama at Birmingham; **Augustus Shackelford**, El Camino

College; **Eleanor T. von Ende**, Texas Tech University; **Larry Wimmer**, Brigham Young University; **Gary Zinn**, East Carolina University

Accuracy Reviews

William Aldridge, Shelton State Community College; **Donald H. Dutkowsky**, Syracuse University; **Mark Rush**, University of Florida; **David Spencer**, Brigham Young University

Telephone Interviews

David Abel, Mankato State University; **Richard Adelstein**, Wesleyan University; **Marjorie Baldwin**, East Carolina University; **Maurice Ballabon**, City University of New York, Bernard M. Baruch College; **Scott Benson, Jr.**, Idaho State University; **Steven Berry**, Yale University; **Scott Bloom**, North Dakota State University; **Mary O. Borg**, University of North Florida; **Michael Boyd**, University of Vermont; **Jim Bradley**, University of South Carolina; **Habtu Braha**, Coppin State College; **Michael Brun**, Illinois State University; **Gregory Bush**, Suffolk County Community College; **Rupert Caine**, Onondaga Community College; **Fred Carstensen**, University of Connecticut; **Shirley Cassing**, University of Pittsburgh; **Cleveland A. Chandler, Sr.**, Howard University; **Larry Chenault**, Miami University; **Edward Christ**, Cabrini College; **Donald Coffin**, Indiana University; **Walter Coleman**, Shaw University; **James Perry Cover**, University of Alabama; **Anthony Davies**, State University of New York at Albany; **Edward A. Day**, University of Central Florida; **Larry DeBrock**, University of Illinois at Urbana-Champaign; **David Denslow**, University of Florida; **Johan Deprez**, Texas Tech University; **Frances Durbin**, University of Delaware; **John Eastwood**, Northern Arizona University; **David H. Feldman**, College of William and Mary; **David Ferrell**, Central College; **Warren Ford**, North Shore Community College; **Joseph Fosu**, Western Illinois University; **Alwyn Fraser**, Atlantic Union College; **Arthur Friedberg**, Mohawk Valley Community College; **Joseph Fuhrig**, Golden Gate University; **Ena Garland**, Babson College; **Gasper Garofalo**, University of Akron; **Maria Giuili**, Diablo Valley College; **Marsha Goldfarb**, University of Maryland, Baltimore County; **Mary Goldschmid**, College of Mount Saint Vincent; **Lawrence Gwinn**, Wittenberg University; **Anthony Gyapong**, Wayne State University; **Ahsan Habib**, Adrian College; **Steven Henson**, Western Washington University; **Carter Hill**, Louisiana State University; **Basawaraj Hiremath**, Fisk University; **Chris W. Holmes**, Bainbridge College; **Soloman Honig**, Montclair State College; **Esmail Hossein-zadeh**, Drake University; **Sheng Hu**, Purdue University; **M. G. Inaba**, Hofstra University; **Wasfy B. Iskander**, Rhodes College; **Rebecca Janski**, Indiana State University; **Nancy Jianakoplos**, Colorado State University; **Holorin Jones**, Empire State College; **Allen Kelly**, Duke University; **Jyoti Khanna**, Cleveland State University; **Shin Kim**, Chicago State University; **John J. Klein**, Georgia State University; **Ghanbar Kooti**, Albany State College; **Julia Lane**, American University; **Stanley J. Lawson**, St. John's University; **Dennis Patrick Leyden**, University of North Carolina; **Y. Joseph Lin**, University of California–Riverside; **Colin Linsley**, St. John Fisher College; **Ashley Lyman**, University of Idaho; **Kathryn Marshall**, Ohio University; **Robert Marshall**, Duke University; **Therese McCarty**, Union College; **David Mirza**, Loyola University; **Richard Moss**, Ricks College; **Archontis Pantsios**, State University of New York at Binghamton; **Sanjay Paul**, State University of New York at Buffalo; **Richard Payne**, Boise State University; **Pegg Pelt**, Gulf Coast Community College; **Robert Pugh**, Surry Community College; **Jack Railey**, Illinois Central College; **Victor Rieck**, Miami Dade Community College; **Debra Rose**, Gordon College; **Gary Santoni**, Ball State University; **Phillip Sarver**, University of Southern Colorado; **George Sawdy**, Providence College; **Ralph Scott**, Hendrix College; **Chiqurupati Rama Seshu**, State University of New York at New Paltz; **Michael Sesnowitz**, Kent State University; **Larry G. Sgontz**, University of Iowa; **Steve Shapiro**, University of North Florida; **B. Ted Stecker**, North Hennepin Community College; **Andrew Stern**, California State University–Long Beach; **Gerard Stockhauser**, Creighton University; **Sue Stockly**, University of Texas at Austin; **Michael Stoller**, State University of New York at Plattsburgh; **Scot Stradley**, University of North Dakota; **Fredrick Tiffany**, Wittenberg University; **James Vincent**, University of St. Thomas; **Arthur Welsh**, Pennsylvania State University; **Bert Wheeler**, Liberty University; **Chuck Whiteman**, University of Iowa; **Peter Wilanoski**, University of Portland; **Patricia Wiswell**, Columbia-Greene Community College; **Craig Witt**, University of Louisville

BRIEF CONTENTS

CONTENTS

PART 1

INTRODUCTION

Summary, Key Elements, Review Questions, and Problems appear at the end of each chapter.

PART 2

How Markets Work

PART 4

Firms' Choices

Chapter 8 Possibilities, Preferences, and Choices 178

Chapter 9 Organizing Production 207

CHAPTER 12 Monopoly 312

CHAPTER 13 Monopolistic Competition and Oligopoly 340

PART 6

Markets for Factors of Production

PART 7

MARKETS, UNCERTAINTY, AND DISTRIBUTION

CHAPTER 16 Capital and Natural Resource Markets 427

CHAPTER 17 Uncertainty and Information 458

PART 9

Introduction to Macroeconomics

PART 10

Aggregate Demand Fluctuations

Chapter 24 Aggregate Demand and Aggregate Supply 636

Chapter 25 Expenditure Decisions and GDP 668

CHAPTER 26 Expenditure Fluctuations and Fiscal Policy 699

CHAPTER 27 Money, Banking, and Prices 726

CHAPTER 28 The Federal Reserve, Money, and Interest Rates 758

CHAPTER 29 Fiscal and Monetary Influences on Aggregate Demand 786

PART 11

Aggregate Supply, Inflation, and Recession

PART 12

MACROECONOMIC POLICY

PART 1

INTRODUCTION

Talking with Robert Solow

Robert M. Solow was born in New York City in 1924. He was an undergraduate and graduate student at Harvard University, where he obtained his Ph.D. in 1951. Professor Solow is an Institute Professor at MIT and has received all the honors possible for his outstanding contributions, including the John Bates Clark Medal (awarded to the best economist under 40) in 1961, President of the Econometrics Society, and President of the American Economics Association. In 1987, he was awarded the Nobel Memorial Prize in Economics. Professor Solow has studied a wide range of problems, including the links between unemployment and inflation, the theory of long-run economic growth, and the role of nonrenewable natural resources. Michael Parkin talked with Professor Solow about some of these issues and the economic landscape of the 1990s.

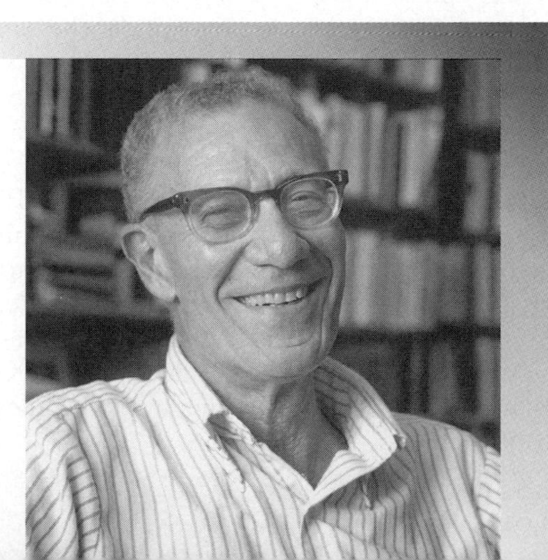

Professor Solow, why and how did you get into economics?

I grew up during the Depression of the 1930s and went to college in 1940 just before the outbreak of the Second World War. Our economy and our society were functioning badly, so it was hard *not* to be interested in economics. As a freshman and sophomore, I studied a little of all the social sciences. Then I joined the Army. When I came back to the university, I had to choose an area of study. I chose economics because it combined analytical precision with a focus on what seemed the central social problems.

Today there is a lot of anxiety about the prospects for income growth in the United States in the 1990s. Is the anxiety justified?

There is plenty of reason to be anxious about income growth in the 1990s. You only have to look at the 1970s and 1980s to understand why. So far nothing has happened to suggest that the near stagnation of the past two decades will give way to something better. There are no signs of greater investment and no partic-

> "It is a fantasy . . . that a handful of space-age engineers simply have to apply themselves . . . to revolutionize civilian technology."

ular reasons to expect the rate of technological progress to improve. Perhaps we will be able to release much of the first-class science and engineering talent that has been used in weapons systems and divert it to advancing civilian technology. But that hasn't happened yet; and when it does happen, there will not be some instantaneous golden age. Good people will eventually produce good results, but it is a fantasy to believe that a handful of space-age engineers simply have to apply themselves in order to revolutionize civilian technology. They will have some old habits to unlearn and new ones to acquire. My guess is that we will scrape along in the 1990s.

Does the same prediction hold true for jobs in the 1990s?

Jobs present an altogether more complicated question. An economy can grow slowly and generate plenty of jobs, and I expect that our economy will do so. There is a lot of talk about whether it will produce "good" jobs. In a sense, the answer is no, if by good jobs one means jobs with good wages and rising wages. On average, incomes will follow productivity. For example, if productivity rises only very slowly, then incomes will also rise only very slowly on the average. I doubt that the range of unemployment rates will be very different from the recent past. So there will be about the usual number of jobs, paying about what productivity will permit.

Remember that it is not quite right to speak of "jobs" as if they are all the same. In the 1980s, Americans with good education and advanced skills did well, even if not quite as well as earlier. It is the uneducated with limited skills who find themselves falling behind, forced to compete with low-wage labor elsewhere.

Does creating jobs inevitably create more inflation? Or can we have steady growth *and* stable prices?

We can probably have reasonably steady growth and reasonably stable prices. The harder question is whether we can do it with a low unemployment rate. I am something of a pessimist here. It seems to me that no one has yet found a way to achieve price stability in an economy that runs along with very little unemployment and excess industrial capacity. Japan may be an exception, but I don't pretend to understand how the Japanese economy works in this respect. Anyway, there is no guarantee that the Japanese secret, if there is one, could be transferred elsewhere. The tendency of modern macroeconomics is to define the problem away, I fear: "low unemployment" *is* whatever is compatible with stable prices. To my mind, the "natural rate of unemployment" is an analytically and empirically flimsy concept. There is room for different models of the way the labor market works, with quite different implications for the understanding of inflation. This is an active subject of research right now.

How should we view international competition from Japan?

I think there are two sides to the Japan problem. The important thing to keep in mind is that no one is forced to buy a Japanese car or VCR. Many Americans do so because they prefer the combination of price and quality. North American manufacturing can get a lot better. It has already started to do so. From that point of view, competition from Japan and Europe is a good thing. Eliminate it and there is danger that our own producers will backslide. Between exchange rate movements and productivity improvements at home, we will come to an equilibrium.

"The various scenarios in which the world economy runs out of resources and then falls into a tailspin are neither valid nor helpful."

I also think that evidence suggests that the Japanese do not play completely by the free-trade rules. I suspect that Japanese institutions, policies, and habits contribute to the large Japanese trade surplus. Of course, a country that saves a lot more than it can invest at home is bound to have a current-account surplus. We should keep pressuring Japan, hard, to abide by the norms. But we should not kid ourselves: the main part of the problem and its solution lie at home.

Has the federal government deficit got in the way of using tax cuts to stimulate our economy?

It certainly has. You can make a case that the Reagan administration intended the massive tax cuts of 1981–1983 to do just that, to leave the federal government without the resources to undertake any positive action at all. There is no doubt that the Congress today feels that there is no elbow room. Some may think that was a good idea. I have no doubt that micromanagement by government is a loser. But I think that passive macroeconomic policy will occasionally get us what we have now—three years of stagnation, apparently to be followed by a period of weak growth.

What is an appropriate goal of macroeconomic policy?

Prolonged budget deficits that persist even when the economy is doing well present a real problem. They are a drain on the national saving, and they imply some combination of low investment and large current-account deficits. So it should be a goal of macroeconomic policy to move toward budget balance or even a surplus, depending on how much we value investment and growth compared with current consumption. But when the economy is weak, when there is plenty of idle labor and capacity, the situation is different. There is no need for investment to displace consumption. There is room for both, and consumption spending stimulates investment. Both fiscal and monetary policy stimuli would be a good thing, even at the expense of a temporary increase in the deficit.

Are there any limits to economic growth? Are we going to run Spaceship Earth out of fuel?

Finding a route to sustainable growth or sustainable development or even to a sustainable state will not be easy. First of all, I think the various scenarios in which the world economy runs

out of resources and then falls into a tailspin are neither valid nor helpful. My reading is that they are poor science and poor economics. We are more likely to experience rising costs of fuel and materials than to run out. We simply cannot know what tastes and technology will be like 50 or 100 years from now.

“It may be a mistake to think in terms of Great Unsolved Problems and Sensational Breakthroughs.”

There are, however, plenty of things that people and policy should be concerned with now. Ensure that full environmental costs are reckoned into economic decision making. Impose the taxes or regulations that are needed for efficient long-run use of fish stocks and other renewable resources. Subsidize scientific and technological research that can find or create new materials and energy sources. Help and induce poor countries to control their populations. I really don't think that Doomsday scenarios move us in these directions.

What are the most important economic questions that have not been answered and that the next generation of economists will work on and possibly solve?

It may be a mistake to think in terms of Great Unsolved Problems and Sensational Breakthroughs. Instead, the next generation of economists would be wise to direct themselves toward slowly coming to understand the way the economy works. I have already mentioned the behavior of the labor market as a fertile field for research: flows into and out of employment, how they and the stocks of employed and unemployed workers relate to the level of wages. Those are traditional questions. But more and more data accumulate, and models are improved. A lot of purely technical finger exercises get done on the way.

Another, less traditional, set of questions emerges from growth theory. Once upon a time, it was customary to treat technological change as exogenous. No one believed that, of course, but economics seemed to have little to say about the pace and direction of invention and innovation. It is now fashionable to go a step further and try to understand the allocation of resources to research and development and the payoff to resources invested. It is far from clear that this work will get very far. But it is obviously important, so the effort has to be made.

How would you advise a student to prepare for a career in economics today? What subjects are the most important to study while an undergraduate? Math? History? Politics?

Certainly an undergraduate interested in economics has no choice but to learn a little mathematics. Better to get it done before graduate school. Then some probability, statistics, and econometrics. Those are indispensable research tools. Then what? Almost anything, I would say. These days you meet too many economists who don't seem to know anything else—not history, not literature, not anything. I think anyone would be a better economist for knowing that there are other things in the world. My own favorite, I will admit, is history, especially social history and economic history. What I am hoping for is some grasp of the many ways in which people have managed to organize themselves and their societies, to give some insight into our own.

CHAPTER 1

WHAT IS ECONOMICS?

After studying this chapter, you will be able to:

- State the kinds of questions that economics tries to answer
- Explain why all economic questions and economic activity arise from scarcity
- Explain why scarcity forces people to make choices
- Define opportunity cost
- Describe the function and the working parts of an economy
- Distinguish between positive and normative statements
- Explain what is meant by an economic theory and how economic theories are developed by building and testing economic models

Choice and Change

IF YOU WANTED TO WATCH A MOVIE IN YOUR HOME IN 1975, you had to rent a movie projector and screen—as well as the movie itself. The cost of such entertainment was as high as that incurred by a theater showing the same movie to several hundred people. Only the rich chose to watch movies in the comfort of their own homes. ◆◆ In 1976, the video cassette recorder (VCR) became available to consumers. Its typical price tag was $2,000 ($4,000 in today's dollars). Even at such a high price, the VCR slashed the cost of home movie watching. Since that time, the price of VCRs has steadily fallen so that today you can buy a reliable machine for $200. A video can be rented for a dollar a day and can be bought for less than $30. In just a few years, watching a movie at home changed from a luxury available to the richest few to an event enjoyed by millions. ◆◆ Advances in technology affect the way we consume. We now watch far more movies at home than we did a decade ago because new technologies have lowered the cost. ◆◆ We hear a great deal these days about lasers. Their most dramatic use is in weapons systems such as those used in "Desert Storm" in 1991. They are also used to guide the machines that bore tunnels and lay pipelines and to align the jigs that build the wings and bodies of modern jet aircraft. But lasers affect us every day. They scan prices at the supermarket checkout. They create holograms on credit cards, making them harder to forge. Neurosurgeons and eye surgeons use them in our hospitals. These advances in technology affect the way we produce.

Ever-changing technology raises the first big economic question:

How do people choose what to consume and how to produce and how are these choices affected by the discovery of new technologies?

Wages and Earnings

On a crisp, bright winter day on the ski slopes at Aspen, a bronzed 23-year-old instructs some beginning skiers in the snowplow turn. For this pleasant and uncomplicated work, the young man, who quit school after eleventh grade, is paid $10 an hour.

In a lawyer's office in the center of a busy city, a 23-year-old secretary handles a large volume of correspondence, filing, scheduling, and meetings. She arrives home most evenings exhausted. She has a bachelor's degree in English and has taken night courses in computer science and word processing. She receives $8 an hour for her work.

On September 7, 1991, Monica Seles and Martina Navratilova played a superb tennis match in the final of the Women's U.S. Open Championship. At the end of the hard-fought match, the winner, Monica Seles, received $400,000; Ms. Navratilova collected only half that amount. A similar phenomenon can be seen in the headquarters of large corporations. Chief executive officers who work no harder (and in some cases even less hard) than the people immediately beneath them receive far higher salaries than their subordinates.

Situations like these raise the second big economic question:

What determines people's incomes and why do some people receive much larger rewards than others whose efforts appear to be similar?

Government, Environment, and Economic Systems

At the beginning of this century, government economic activity was limited to little more than providing law and order. Over the years, the scope of government in the United States has expanded to include the provision of health care, social insurance, education, national defense and international security, the regulation of food and drug production, nuclear energy, and agriculture.

Also, over the years, we've become more aware of our fragile environment. Chlorofluorocarbons (CFCs), used in a wide variety of products from coolants in refrigerators and air conditioners to plastic phones and cleaning solvents for computer circuits, are believed to damage the atmosphere's protective ozone layer. Burning fossil fuels—coal and oil—adds carbon dioxide and other gases to the atmosphere, which prevents infrared radiation from escaping, resulting in what has been called the "greenhouse effect."

We've been hearing a lot recently about alternative economic systems and the proper role of government in economic life. The former Soviet Union and the countries of Eastern Europe have been shaking off decades of central economic planning and public ownership of their farms and factories. Bit by bit, they are moving toward the type of economic system and organization that is familiar to you in the United States—an economic system in which the government does not plan all the details of what is produced and does not own the nation's farms and factories. Instead, each individual farmer and business owner decides what to produce and seeks out better and better profit opportunities.

These facts about government, the environment, and the dramatic changes taking place in Eastern Europe raise the third big economic question:

What is the most effective role for government in economic life and can government help us protect our environment and do as effective a job as private enterprise at producing goods and services?

Unemployment

During the Great Depression, the four years from 1929 to 1933, unemployment afflicted almost one fifth of the labor force in the industrial world. For months and in some cases years on end, many families had no income other than meager payments from the government or from private charities. In the 1950s and 1960s, unemployment rates stayed below 5 percent in most countries and, in some, below 2 percent. During the 1970s and early 1980s, unemployment steadily increased so that by late 1982 and early 1983 almost 11 percent of the U.S. labor force was looking for work. But in 1989, the U.S. unemployment rate had fallen to 5 percent.

Unemployment hurts different groups unequally. When the average unemployment rate in the United States was 5 percent—as it was in 1989—the unemployment rate among young people 16 to 19 years old was 19 percent. But for young blacks it was 43 percent. These facts raise the fourth big economic question:

What are the causes of unemployment and why are some groups more severely affected than others?

Inflation

Between August 1945 and July 1946, prices in Hungary rose by an average of 20,000 percent per month. In the worst month, July 1946, they rose 419 quadrillion percent (a quadrillion is the number 1 followed by 15 zeros).

In 1985, the cost of living in Bolivia rose by 11,750 percent. This meant that in downtown La Paz a McDonald's hamburger that cost 20 bolivianos on January 1 cost 2,370 bolivianos by the end of the year. That same year, prices rose only 3.2 percent in the United States. But in the late 1970s, prices in the United States were rising at a rate well in excess of 10 percent a year. These facts raise the fifth big economic question:

Why do prices rise and why do some countries sometimes experience rapid price increases while others have stable prices?

International Trade

In the 1960s, almost all the cars and trucks on the highways of the United States were Fords, Chevrolets, and Chryslers. By the 1980s, Toyotas, Hondas, Volkswagens, and BMWs were a common sight on these same highways. As a matter of fact, in 1990, more than one third of all new cars sold in the United States were imported; in 1950, less than 1 percent were.

Cars are not exceptional. The same can be said of television sets, clothing, and computers.

Governments regulate international trade in cars and in most other commodities. They impose taxes on imports, called tariffs, and also establish quotas, which restrict the quantities that may be imported. These facts raise the sixth big economic question:

What determines the pattern and the volume of trade between nations and what are the effects of tariffs and quotas on international trade?

Wealth and Poverty

At the mouth of the Canton River in southeast China is a small rocky peninsula and a group of islands with virtually no natural resources. But this bare land supports more than five million people who, though not excessively rich, live in rapidly growing abundance. They produce much of the world's fashion goods and electronic components. They are the people of Hong Kong.

On the eastern edge of Africa, bordering the Red Sea, a tract of land a thousand times larger supports a population of 34 million people—only seven times that of Hong Kong. Its people suffer such abject poverty that in 1985 rock singers from Europe and North America organized one of the most spectacular worldwide fund-raising efforts ever seen—Live Aid—to help them. These are the desperate and dying people of Ethiopia.

Hong Kong and Ethiopia, two extremes in income and wealth, are not isolated examples. The poorest two thirds of the world's population consumes less than one fifth of all the things produced. A middle income group accounts for almost one fifth of the world's population and consumes almost one fifth of the world's output. A further one fifth of the world's population—living in rich countries such as the United States, Canada, Western Europe, Japan, Australia, and New Zealand—consumes two thirds of the world's output.

These facts raise the seventh big economic question:

What causes differences in wealth among nations, making the people in some countries rich and those in other countries poor?

These seven big questions provide an overview of economics. They are *big* questions for two reasons. First, they have an enormous influence on the quality of human life. Second, they are hard questions to answer. They generate passionate argument and debate, and just about everybody has an opinion about them. One of the hardest things for students of economics, whether beginners or seasoned practitioners, is to stand clear of the passion and emotion and to approach their work with the detachment, rigor, and objectivity of a scientist.

Later in this chapter, we'll explain how economists try to find answers to economic questions. But before doing that, let's go back to the big questions.

What do these questions have in common? What makes them *economic* questions? What distinguishes them from non-economic questions?

Scarcity

All economic questions arise from a single and inescapable fact: you can't always get what you want. We live in a world of scarcity. An economist defines **scarcity** to mean that wants always exceed the resources available to satisfy them. A child wants a 75¢ can of soft drink and a 50¢ pack of gum but has only $1.00 in her pocket. She experiences scarcity. A student wants to go to a party on Saturday night but also wants to spend that same night catching up on late assignments. He also experiences scarcity. The rich and the poor alike face scarcity. The U.S. government with its $1.4 trillion budget faces scarcity. The total amount that the federal government wants to spend on defense, health, education, welfare, and other services exceeds what it collects in taxes. Even parrots face scarcity—there just aren't enough crackers to go around.

Wants do not simply exceed resources; they are unlimited. People want good health and a long life, material comfort, security, physical and mental recreation, and, finally, an awareness and understanding of themselves and their environment.

None of these wants are satisfied for everyone; and everyone has some unsatisfied wants. While many Americans have all the material comfort they want, many do not. No one feels entirely satisfied with his or her state of health and length of life. No one feels entirely secure, even in this post–Cold War era, and no one—not even the wealthiest person—has the time to enjoy all the travel, vacations, and art that he or she would like. Not even the wisest and most knowledgeable philosopher or scientist knows as much as he or she would like to know.

We can imagine a world that satisfies people's wants for material comfort and perhaps even security. But we cannot imagine a world in which people live as long and in as good a state of health as they would like. Nor can we imagine people having all the time, energy, and resources to enjoy all the sports, travel, vacations, and art that they would like. Natural resources and human resources—in the form of time, muscle-power, and brain-power—as well as all the dams, highways, buildings, machinery, tools, and other equipment that have been built by past human efforts amount to an enormous heritage, but they are limited. Our unlimited wants will always outstrip the limited resources available to satisfy them.

"Not only do I want a cracker—we all want a cracker!"

Drawing by Modell; © 1985 The New Yorker Magazine, Inc.

Economic Activity

The confrontation of unlimited wants with limited resources results in economic activity. **Economic activity** is what people do to cope with scarcity. And **economics** is the study of how people use their limited resources to try to satisfy unlimited wants. Defined in this way, economic activity and economics deal with a wide range of issues and problems. The seven big questions posed earlier are examples of the more important problems that economists study. Let's see how those questions could not arise if resources were infinitely abundant and scarcity did not exist.

With unlimited resources there would be no need to devise better ways of producing more goods. Studying how we all spend our time and effort would not be interesting because we would simply do what we enjoyed without restriction. We would do only the things that we enjoyed because there would be enough goods and services to satisfy everyone without effort. Unemployment would not be an issue because no one would work—except for people who wanted to work simply for the pleasure that it gave them. There would be no wages. Inflation—rising prices—would not be a problem because no one would care about prices. Questions about government intervention in economic life would not arise because there would be no need for government-provided goods and no taxes. We would simply take whatever we wanted from the infinite resources available. There would be no international trade since, with complete abundance, it would be pointless to transport things from one place to another. Finally, differences in wealth among nations would not arise because we would all have as much as we wanted. There would be no such thing as rich and poor countries—all countries would be infinitely wealthy.

You can see that this science fiction world of complete abundance would have no economic questions. It is the universal fact of scarcity that produces economic questions.

Choice

Faced with scarcity, people must make *choices*. When we cannot have everything that we want, we have to choose among the available alternatives. Because scarcity forces us to choose, economics is sometimes called the science of choice—the science that explains the choices that people make and predicts how changes in circumstances affect their choices.

To make a choice, we balance the benefits of having more of one thing against the costs of having less of something else. The process of balancing benefits against costs and doing the best within the limits of what is possible is called **optimizing**. There is another word that has a similar meaning—*economizing*. **Economizing** is making the best use of the resources available. Once people have made a choice and have optimized, they cannot have more of *everything*. To get more of one thing means having less of something else. Expressed in another way: in making choices, we face costs. Whatever we choose to do, we could always have chosen to do something else instead.

Opportunity Cost

Economists use the term *opportunity cost* to emphasize that making choices in the face of scarcity implies a cost. The **opportunity cost** of any action is the best alternative forgone. If you cannot have everything that you want, then you have to choose among the alternatives. The best thing that you choose not to do—the forgone alternative—is the cost of the thing that you choose to do.

Dollar Cost We often express opportunity cost in terms of dollars. But this is just a convenient unit of measure. The dollars spent on a book are not available for spending on a CD. The opportunity cost of the book is not the dollars spent on it, but the CD forgone.

Time Cost The opportunity cost of a good includes the value of the time spent obtaining it. If it takes an hour to visit your dentist, the value of that hour must be added to the amount you paid your dentist. We can convert time into a dollar cost by using a person's hourly wage rate. If you take an hour off work to visit your dentist, the opportunity cost of that visit (expressed in units of dollars) is the amount that you paid to your dentist plus the wages that you lost by not being at work. Again, it's important to keep reminding yourself that the opportunity cost is not the dollars involved but the goods that you could have bought with those dollars.

External Cost Not all of the opportunity costs that you incur are the result of your own choices. Sometimes others make choices that impose opportunity costs on you. And your own choices can impose opportunity costs on others. For example, when you enjoy a cold drink from your refrigerator, part of its opportunity cost (borne by others) is the increased carbon dioxide in the atmosphere resulting from burning coal to generate the electricity that powers the refrigerator.

Best Alternative Forgone In measuring opportunity cost, we value only the *best* alternative forgone. To make this clear, consider the following example. You are supposed to attend a lecture at 8:30 on a Monday morning. There are two alternatives to attending this lecture: stay in bed for an hour or go jogging for an hour. You cannot stay in bed *and* go jogging for that same hour. The opportunity cost of attending the lecture is not the cost of an hour in bed *and* the cost of jogging for an hour. If these are the only two alternatives that you would contemplate, then you have to decide which one you would do if you did not go to the lecture. The opportunity cost of attending a lecture for a jogger is an hour of exercise; the opportunity cost of attending a lecture for a late sleeper is an hour in bed.

Scarcity implies cost—opportunity cost. It also implies one other fundamental feature of human life—competition.

Competition and Cooperation

Competition If wants exceed resources, wants must compete against each other for what is available. **Competition** is a contest for command over scarce resources. In the case of the child with $1.00 in pocket money who wants a soft drink and gum that add up to $1.25, the soft drink and gum compete for the $1.00 in her pocket. For the student who has allowed assignments to accumulate, the party and the assignments compete with each other for Saturday night. For the government, defense and social services compete with each other for limited tax dollars.

Scarcity also implies competition between people. Because it is not possible to have everything that you want, you must compete with others for what is available. In modern societies, competition has been organized within a framework of almost universally accepted rules that have evolved. This evolution of rules is itself a direct response to the problem of scarcity. Not all societies, even modern societies, employ identical rules to govern competition. For example, the way in which economic life is organized in the United States differs greatly from that in the former Soviet Union. In Chapter 38, we examine these differences and compare alternative economic systems. For now, we'll focus on the rules that govern competition in the United States.

A key rule of economic competition in the United States is that people own what they have acquired through voluntary exchange. People can compete with each other by offering more favorable exchanges—for example, selling something for a lower price or buying something for a higher price. But they cannot compete with each other by simply taking something from someone else.

Cooperation Perhaps you are thinking that scarcity does not make competition inevitable and that cooperation would better solve economic problems. **Cooperation** means working with others to achieve a common end. If instead of competing with each other we cooperated, wouldn't that solve our economic problems? Unfortunately, cooperation does not eliminate economic problems, because it does not eliminate economic scarcity. But cooperation is part of the solution to scarcity. We cooperate, for example, when we agree to rules of the game that limit competition to avoid violence and when we agree to participate in an economic system based on the rule of law and voluntary exchange.

Other examples of solving economic problems through cooperation abound. Marriage partners cooperate. Most forms of business also entail cooperation. Workers cooperate with each other on the production line; members of a management team cooperate with each other to design, produce, and market their products; management and workers cooperate; business partners cooperate.

Common as it is, cooperative behavior neither solves the economic problem nor eliminates competition. Almost all cooperative behavior implies some prior competition to find the best individuals with whom to cooperate. Marriage provides a good example. Although marriage is a cooperative affair, unmarried people compete intensely to find a marriage partner. Similarly, although workers and management cooperate with each other, firms compete for the best workers and workers compete for the best employers. Professionals such as lawyers and doctors compete with each other for the best business partners.

Competition does not end when a partner has been found. Groups of people who cooperate together compete with other groups. For example, although a group of lawyers may have formed a partnership and may work together, they will be in competition with other lawyers.

REVIEW

Scarcity is the confrontation of unlimited wants with limited resources. Scarcity forces people to make choices. To make choices, people evaluate the costs of alternative actions. We call these opportunity costs, to emphasize that doing one thing removes the opportunity to do something else. Scarcity also implies that people must compete with each other. Economics studies the activities arising from scarcity. ◆

You now know the types of questions that economists try to answer and that all economic questions and economic activity arise from scarcity. In the following chapters, we are going to study economic activity and discover how a modern economy such as that of the United States works. But before we do that, we need to stand back and take an overview of the economy.

The Economy

What do we mean by "the economy"? How does an economy work? Rather than trying to answer these questions directly, let's begin by asking similar questions about a more familiar subject. What is an airplane? How does an airplane work?

Without delving into the detail that would satisfy an aeronautical engineer, most of us could take a shot at answering these two questions. We would describe an airplane as a flying machine that transports people and cargo. To explain how an airplane works, we would describe its key components—fuselage (or body), wings, and engines, and also perhaps its flaps, rudder, and control and navigation systems. We would also explain that as powerful engines move the machine forward, its wings create an imbalance in air pressure that lifts it into the air.

This example nicely illustrates four things. First, it is hard to explain what something is without saying what it does. To say that an airplane is a machine does not tell us much. We have to go beyond that and say what the machine is for and how it works.

Second, it is hard to explain how something works without being able to divide it up into components. Once we have described something in terms of its components, we can explain how those components work and how they interact with each other.

Third, it is hard to explain how something works without leaving out some details. Notice that we did not describe an airplane in all its detail. Instead, we isolated the most important parts in order to explain how the whole works. We did not mention the in-flight movie system, the seat belts, or the color of the paint on the wings. We supposed that these things were irrelevant to an explanation of how an airplane works.

Fourth, and finally, there are different levels of understanding how something works. We gave a superficial account of how an airplane works. An aeronautical engineer would have given a deeper explanation, and experts in the individual components—engines, navigation systems, control system, and so on—would have given even more detailed and precise explanations than a general engineer.

Now let's return to questions about the economy. What is the economy? How does it work?

What Is the Economy?

The **economy** is a mechanism that allocates scarce resources among competing uses. This mechanism achieves three things:

- What
- How
- For whom

1. *What* goods and services will be produced and in *what* quantities? Will more VCRs be made or will more movie theaters be built? Will young professionals vacation in Europe or live in large houses? Will more high-performance sports cars or more trucks and station wagons be built?
2. *How* will the various goods and services be produced? Will a supermarket operate with three checkout lines and clerks using laser scanners or six checkout lines and clerks keying in prices by hand? Will workers weld station wagons by hand or will robots do the job? Will farmers keep track of their livestock feeding schedules and inventories by using paper and pencil records or personal computers? Will credit card companies use computers to read charge slips in New York or ship paper records to Barbados for hand processing?
3. *For whom* will the various goods and services be produced? The distribution of economic benefits depends on the distribution of income. People with high incomes are able to consume more goods and services than people with low incomes. Who gets to consume what thus depends on income. Will the ski instructor consume more than the lawyer's secretary? Will the people of Hong Kong consume more than the people of Ethiopia?

FIGURE 1.1

A Picture of the Economy

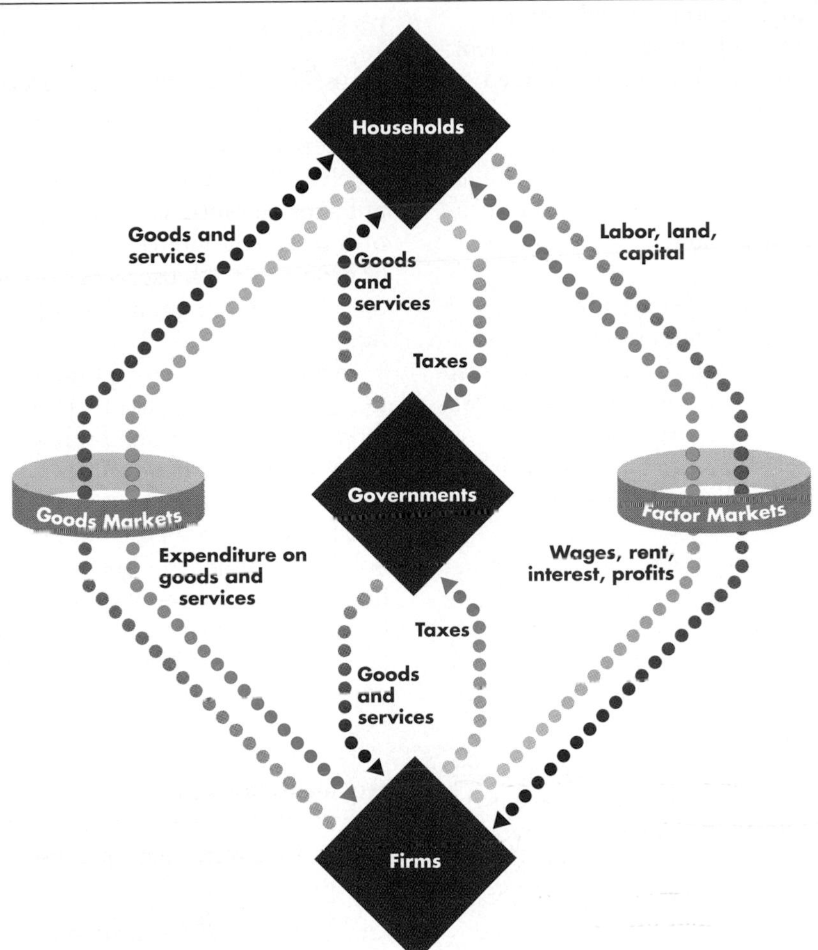

Households, firms, and governments make economic decisions. Households decide how much of their labor, land, and capital to supply in exchange for wages, rent, interest, and profits. They also decide how much of their income to spend on the various types of goods and services available. Firms decide how much labor, land, and capital to hire and how much of the various types of goods and services to produce. Governments decide which goods and services they will provide and the taxes that households and firms will pay.

These decisions by households, firms, and governments are coordinated in markets—the goods markets and factor markets. In these markets, prices constantly adjust to keep buying and selling plans consistent.

To understand how an economy achieves its objectives, we must identify its main components and then study the way in which these components interact with each other. Figure 1.1 shows a picture of the economy. It contains two types of components:

- Decision makers
- Markets

Decision Makers

Decision makers are the economic actors. They make the economizing choices. Figure 1.1 identifies three types of decision makers:

1. Households
2. Firms
3. Governments

A **household** is any group of people living together as a decision-making unit. Every individual in the economy belongs to a household. Some households consist of a single person, while others consist either of families or of groups of unrelated individuals, such as two or three students sharing an apartment. Each household has unlimited wants and limited resources.

A **firm** is an organization that uses resources to produce goods and services. All producers are called firms, no matter how big they are or what they produce. Car makers, farmers, banks, and insurance companies are all firms.

A **government** is an organization that provides goods and services and redistributes income and wealth. The most important of the services provided by government is a framework of laws and a mechanism for their enforcement (courts and police forces). But governments also provide such services as national defense, public health, transportation, and education.

Markets

In ordinary speech, the word *market* means a place where people buy and sell goods such as fish, meat, fruits, and vegetables. In economics, *market* has a more general meaning. A **market** is any arrangement that facilitates buying and selling. An example is the market in which oil is bought and sold—the world oil market. The world oil market is not a place. It is the arena in which the many firms—oil producers, oil users, wholesalers, and brokers—who buy and sell oil interact. In this market, decision makers do not meet physically. They make deals by telephone, fax, and direct computer link.

Figure 1.1 identifies two types of market: goods markets and factor markets. **Goods markets** are those in which goods and services are bought and sold. **Factor markets** are those in which factors of production are bought and sold.

Factors of production are the economy's productive resources. They are classified under three headings:

1. Labor
2. Land
3. Capital

Labor is the brain-power and muscle-power of human beings; **land** includes natural resources of all kinds; **capital** is all the equipment, buildings, tools, and other manufactured goods that can be used in production.

Decisions

Households and firms make decisions that result in the transactions in the goods markets and factor markets shown in Fig. 1.1. Households decide how much of their labor, land, and capital to sell or rent in factor markets. They receive incomes in the form of wages, rent, interest, and profit from these factors of production. Households also decide how to spend their incomes on goods and services produced by firms.

Firms decide the quantities of factors of production to hire, how to use them to produce goods and services, what goods and services to produce, and in what quantities. They sell their output in goods markets.

The flows resulting from these decisions by households and firms are shown in Fig. 1.1. The red flows are the factors of production that go from households to firms and the goods and services that go from firms to households. The green flows in the opposite direction are the payments made in exchange for these items.

Governments decide what goods and services to provide to households and firms, as well as the rates of taxes that create the funds to pay for them. These actions by governments are also shown in Fig. 1.1.

Coordination Mechanisms

Perhaps the most striking thing about the choices made by households, firms, and governments is that they surely must come into conflict with each other. For example, households choose how much work to do and what type of work to specialize in, but firms choose the type and quantity of labor to employ in the production of various goods and services. In other words, households choose the types and quantities of labor to sell, and firms choose the types and quantities of labor to buy. Similarly, in markets for goods and services, households choose the types and quantities of goods and services to buy, while firms choose the types and quantities to sell. Government choices regarding taxes and the provision of goods and services also enter the picture. Taxes taken by the government affect the amount of income that households and firms have available for spending. Also, decisions by firms and households depend on the types and quantities of goods and services that governments make available. For example, if the government provides excellent highways but a dilapidated railroad system, households will allocate more of their income to buying motor vehicles and less to buying train rides.

How is it possible for the millions of individual decisions made by households, firms, and governments to be consistent with each other? What makes households want to sell the same types and quantities of labor that firms want to buy? What happens if the number of households wanting to work as economics professors exceeds the number that universities want to hire? How do firms know what to produce so that households will buy their output? What happens if firms want to sell more hamburgers than households want to buy?

Markets Coordinate Decisions Markets coordinate individual decisions through price adjustments. To see how, think about the market for hamburgers in your local area. Suppose that the quantity of hamburgers being offered for sale is less than the quantity that people would like to buy. Some people who want to buy hamburgers will not be able to do so. To make the choices of buyers and sellers compatible, buyers will have to scale down their appetites and more hamburgers will have to be offered for sale. An increase in the price of hamburgers will produce this outcome. A higher price will encourage producers to offer more hamburgers for sale. It will also curb the appetite for hamburgers and change some lunch plans. Fewer people will buy hamburgers and more will buy hot dogs (or some other alternative to hamburgers). More hamburgers (and more hot dogs) will be offered for sale.

Now imagine the opposite situation. More hamburgers are available than people want to buy. In this case, the price is too high. A lower price will discourage the production and sale of hamburgers and encourage their purchase and consumption. Decisions to produce and sell, and to buy and consume, are continuously adjusted and kept in balance with each other by adjustments in prices.

In some cases, prices get stuck or fixed. When this happens, some other adjustment has to make the plans and choices of individuals consistent. Customers waiting in lines and inventories of goods operate as a temporary safety valve when the market price is stuck. If people want to buy more than the quantity that firms have decided to sell, and if the price is temporarily stuck, then one of two things can happen. Sometimes, firms wind up selling more than they would like and their inventories shrink. At other times, lines of customers develop and only those who get to the head of the line before the goods run out are able to make a purchase. The longer the line or the bigger the decline in inventories, the more prices adjust to keep buying and selling decisions in balance.

We have now seen how the market solves the question of *what* quantity to produce—how many hamburgers to make. The market also solves the question of *how* to produce in similar fashion. For example, hamburger producers can use gas, electric power, or charcoal to cook their hamburgers. Which fuel is used depends in part on the flavor that the producer wants to achieve and on the cost of the different fuels. If a fuel becomes very expensive, as did oil in the 1970s, less of it is used and more of other fuels are used in its place. By substituting one fuel for another as the costs of the different fuels change, the market solves the question of how to produce.

Finally, the market helps solve the question of *for whom* to produce. Skills, talents, and resources that are in very short supply command a higher price than those in greater abundance. The owners of rare resources and skills obtain a larger share of the output of the economy than the owners of resources that are in abundant supply.

Alternative Coordination Mechanisms The market is one of two alternative coordination mechanisms. The other is a command mechanism. A **command mechanism** is a method of determining *what, how,* and *for whom* goods and services are produced, using an hierarchical organization structure in which people carry out the instructions given to them. The best example of an hierarchical organization structure is the military. Commanders make decisions requiring actions that are passed down a chain of command. Soldiers and marines on the front line take the actions they are ordered to take.

An economy that relies on a command mechanism is called a **command economy.** Examples of command economies in today's world are China, North Korea, Vietnam, and Cambodia. Before they embarked on programs of reform in the late 1980s, the former Soviet Union and other countries of Eastern Europe also had command economies.

In a command economy, a central planning bureau makes decisions about *what, how,* and *for whom* goods and services are to be produced. We will study command economies and compare them with other types of economies at the end of our study of economics, in Chapter 38.

An economy that determines *what, how,* and *for whom* goods and services are produced by coordinating individual choices through markets is called a **market economy.** But most real-world economies use both markets and commands to coordinate economic activity. An economy that relies on both markets and command mechanisms is called a **mixed economy.**

The U.S. economy relies extensively on the market as a mechanism for coordinating the decisions of individual households and firms. But the U.S. economy also uses command mechanisms. The economy of the armed forces is a command economy. Command mechanisms are also employed in other government organizations and also within large firms. There is also a command element in our legal system. By enacting laws and establishing regulations and agencies to monitor the market economy, governments influence the economic decisions of households and firms and change our economic course.

Thus *what, how,* and *for whom* goods and services are produced in the United States depends mainly on the market mechanism, but also partly on a command mechanism, so the U.S. economy is a mixed economy.

FIGURE 1.2
International Linkages

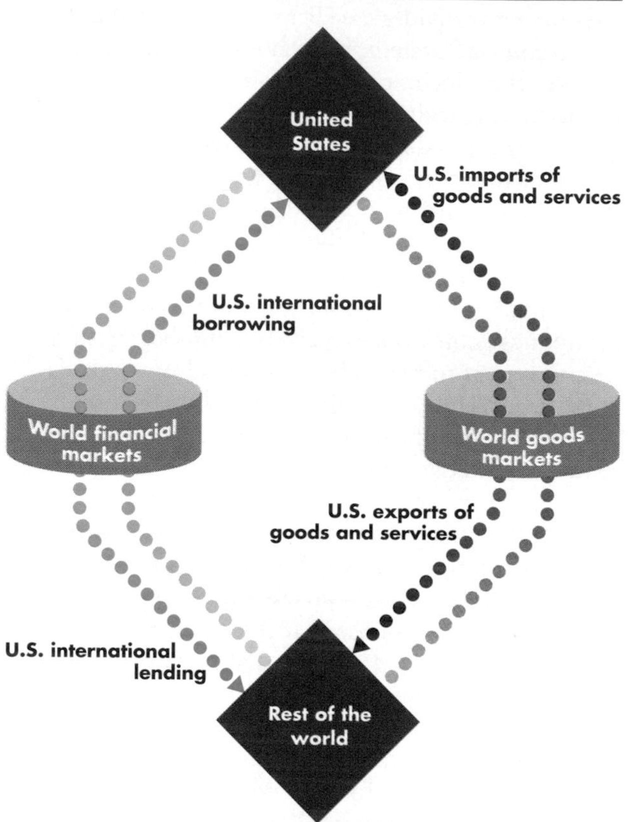

The U.S. economy buys and sells goods and services in world goods markets. What it buys are U.S. imports, and what it sells are U.S. exports. The U.S. economy also borrows from and lends to the rest of the world. These transactions take place in the world financial markets.

The Global Economy

A **closed economy** is one that has no links with any other economy. The only closed economy is that of the entire world. The U.S. economy is an **open economy,** an economy that has economic links with other economies.

The economic links between the U.S. economy and the rest of the world are illustrated in Fig. 1.2. Firms in the open U.S. economy sell some of their production to the rest of the world. These sales are U.S. exports of goods and services. Also, firms, households, and governments in the United States buy goods and services from firms in other countries. These purchases are U.S. imports of goods and services. Both types of transactions take place in world goods markets and are illustrated in the figure.

The total values of exports and imports are not necessarily equal to each other. When U.S. exports exceed U.S. imports, we have a surplus. When U.S. imports exceed U.S. exports, we have a deficit. A country with a surplus lends to the rest of the world, and a country with a deficit borrows from the rest of the world. These international lending and borrowing transactions take place in the world financial markets and are also illustrated in Fig. 1.2.

The United States has had an international deficit in recent years. As a consequence, by the mid-1980s, foreigners had larger investments in the United States than we had in the rest of the world. Other countries, notably those of the European Community and Japan, have international surpluses and are using those surpluses to invest in businesses in the United States.

During the 1980s, the global economy became a highly integrated mechanism for allocating scarce resources and deciding *what* will be produced, *how* it will be produced, and *for whom* it will be produced. It is also a mechanism deciding *where* the various goods and services will be produced and consumed.

REVIEW

An economy is a mechanism that determines what is produced, how it is produced, and for whom it is produced. Choices are made by households, firms, and government, that are coordinated through markets—markets for goods and services and markets for factors of production—or by command mechanisms. The U.S. economy relies mainly on markets but to a degree on command mechanisms. The U.S. economy and the global economy became highly integrated during the 1980s. ◆

We have now described an economy in about as much detail as we described an airplane. But we're about to become the economic equivalent of aeronautical engineers! We're going to build economies that fly! To do that, we have to understand the principles of economics as thoroughly as aeronautical engineers understand the principles of flight. To discover these principles, economists approach their work with the rigor and objectivity of natural scientists—they do economic science.

Economic Science

Economic science, like the natural sciences (such as physics and biology) and the other social sciences (such as political science, psychology, and sociology), is an attempt to find a body of laws. All sciences have two components:

1. Careful and systematic observation and measurement
2. Development of a body of theory to direct and interpret observations

All sciences are careful to distinguish between two types of statements:

- Statements about what *is*
- Statements about what *ought* to be

What Is and What Ought To Be

Statements about what *is* are **positive statements.** Statements about what *ought* to be are **normative statements.** Let's illustrate the distinction between positive and normative statements with two examples.

First, consider the controversy over global warming. Some scientists believe that the burning of coal and oil is increasing the carbon dioxide content of the earth's atmosphere and leading to higher temperatures that eventually will have devastating consequences for life on this planet. "Our planet is warming because of an increased carbon dioxide buildup in the atmosphere" is a positive statement. "We ought to cut back on our use of carbon-based fuels such as coal and oil" is a normative statement. Second, consider the economic controversy over tax cuts and cutbacks on social programs. "Lower taxes and less generous social programs will make people work harder" is a positive statement. "Taxes and social programs should be cut" is a normative statement.

Positive statements may be true or false. It is the task of science—whether natural, social, or economic—to discover and catalog positive statements that are true, that is, consistent with what we observe in the world. Normative statements are matters of opinion. You agree or disagree with them. Science is silent on normative questions. It is not that such questions are unimportant. On the contrary, they are often the most important questions of all. Nor is it that scientists as people do not have opinions on such questions. It is simply that the activity of doing science cannot settle a normative matter, and the possession of scientific knowledge does not equip a person with superior morals or norms. A difference of opinion on a positive matter can ultimately be settled by careful observation and measurement. A difference of opinion on a normative matter cannot be settled in that way. In fact, there are no well-defined rules for settling a normative dispute, and sometimes reasonable people simply have to agree to disagree. When they cannot, political and judicial institutions intervene so that decisions can be made. We settle normative disagreements in the political, not the scientific, arena. The scientific community can, and often does, contribute to the normative debates of political life. But science is a distinct activity. Even though scientists have opinions about what ought to be, those opinions have no part in science itself.

Now let's see how economists attempt to discover and catalog positive statements that are consistent with their observations and that enable them to answer economic questions.

Observation and Measurement

Economic phenomena can be observed and measured in great detail. We can catalog the amounts and locations of natural and human resources. We can describe who does what kind of work, for how many hours, and how they are paid. We can catalog the things that people produce, consume, and store and their prices. We can describe in detail who borrows and who lends and at what interest rates. We can also catalog the things that government taxes and at what rates, the programs it finances and at what cost.

These are examples of the array of things that economists can describe through careful observation and measurement of economic activity.

In today's world, computers have given us access to an enormous volume of economic description. Government agencies around the world, national statistical bureaus, private economic consultants, banks, investment advisors, and research economists working in universities generate an astonishing amount of information about economic behavior.

But economists do more than observe and measure economic activity, crucial as that is. Describing something is not the same as understanding it. You can describe your digital watch in great detail, but that does not mean you can explain what makes it work. Understanding what makes things work requires the discovery of laws. That is the main task of economists—the discovery of laws governing economic behavior. How do economists go about this task?

Economic Theory

We can describe in great detail the ups and downs, or cycles, in unemployment, but can we explain *why* unemployment fluctuates? We can describe the fall in the price of a VCR or a pocket calculator and the dramatic increase in its use, but can we explain the low price and popularity of such items? Did the fall in the price lead more people to use pocket calculators, or did their popularity lower the costs of production and make it possible to lower the price? Or did something else cause both the fall in the price and the increase in use?

Questions like these can be answered only by developing a body of economic theory. An **economic theory** is a general rule or principle that enables us to understand and predict the economic choices that people make. We develop economic theories by building and testing economic models. What is an economic model?

Economic Model

You have just seen an economic model. To answer the question "What is an economy and how does it work?" we built a model of an economy. We did not describe in all their detail all the economic actions that take place in the United States. We concentrated our attention only on those features that seemed important for understanding economic choices, and we ignored everything else. You will perhaps better appreciate what we mean by an economic model if you think about more familiar models.

We have all seen model trains, cars, and airplanes. Although we do not usually call dolls and stuffed animals "models," we can think of them in this way. Architects make models of buildings, and biologists make models of DNA (the double helix carrier of the genetic code).

A model is usually smaller than the real thing that it represents. But models are not always smaller in scale (think of a biologist's model of the components of cells), and in any case, the scale of a model is not its most important feature. A model also shows less detail than its counterpart in reality. For example, all the models that we have mentioned resemble the real thing in *appearance,* but they are not usually made of the same substance, nor do they work like the real thing that they represent. The architect's model of a new high-rise shows us what the building will look like and how it will conform with the buildings around it—but it does not contain plumbing, telephone cables, elevator shafts, air conditioning plants, and other interior workings.

All the models that we have discussed (including those that are typically used as toys) represent something that is real, but they lack some key features and deliberately so. The model abstracts from the detail of the real thing. It includes only those features that are needed for the purpose at hand. It leaves out the inessential or unnecessary. What a model includes and leaves out is not arbitrary; it results from a conscious and careful decision.

The models that we have just considered are all physical models. We can see the real thing and we can see the model. Indeed, the purpose of those models is to enable us to visualize the real thing. Some models, including economic models, are not physical. We cannot look at the real thing and look at the model and simply decide whether the model is a good or bad representation of the real thing. But the idea of a model as an abstraction from reality still applies to an economic model.

An economic model has two components:

1. Assumptions
2. Implications

Assumptions form the foundation on which a model is built. They are propositions about what is important and what can be ignored. **Implications** are the outcome of a model. The link between a model's assumptions and its implications is a process of logical deduction.

Let's illustrate these components of a model by building a simple model of your daily journey to school. The model has three assumptions:

1. You want to be in class when it begins at 9:00 A.M.
2. The bus ride to school takes 30 minutes.
3. The walk from the bus to class takes 5 minutes.

The implication of this model is that you will be on the bus no later than 8:25 A.M. With knowledge of the bus timetable, we could use this model to predict the bus that you would catch to school.

The assumptions of a model depend on the model's purpose. The purpose of an economic model is to understand how households, firms, and governments make choices in the face of scarcity. Thus in building an economic model, we abstract from the rich detail of human life and focus only on behavior that is relevant for coping with scarcity. Everything else is ignored. Economists know that people fall in love and form deep friendships, that they experience great joy and security or great pain and anxiety. But economists assume that in seeking to understand economic behavior, they may build models that ignore many aspects of life. They focus on one and only one feature of the world: people have wants that exceed their resources and so, by their choices, have to make the best of things.

Assumptions of an Economic Model Economic models are based on four key assumptions:

1. *People have preferences.* Economists use the term **preferences** to denote likes and dislikes and the intensity of those likes and dislikes. People can judge whether one situation is better, worse, or just as good as another one. For example, you can judge whether, for you, one loaf of bread and no cheese is better, worse, or just as good as a half a loaf of bread and four ounces of cheese.
2. *People are endowed with a fixed amount of resources and a technology that can transform those resources into goods and services.* Economists use the term **endowment** to refer to the resources that people have and the term **technology** to describe the methods of converting those endowments into goods and services.
3. *People economize.* People choose how to use their endowments and technologies in order to make themselves as well-off as possible. Such a choice is called a rational choice. A **rational choice** is one which, among all possible choices, best achieves the goals of the person making the choice. Each choice, no matter what it is or how foolish it may seem to an observer, is interpreted, in an economic model, as a rational choice. Choices are made on the basis of the information available. With hindsight, and with more information, people may well feel that some of their past choices were bad ones. This fact does not make such choices irrational. Again, a rational choice is the best possible course of action, from the point of view of the person making the choice, given that person's preferences and *given the information available when the choice is made.*
4. *People's choices are coordinated.* One person's choice to buy something must be matched by another person's choice to sell that same thing.

One person's choice to work at a particular job must be matched by another person's choice to hire someone to do that job. The coordination of individual choices is made by either a market mechanism or a command mechanism.

Implications of an Economic Model The implications of an economic model are the equilibrium values of various prices and quantities. An **equilibrium** is a situation in which everyone has economized—that is, all individuals have made the best possible choices in the light of their own preferences and given their endowments, technologies and information—and in which those choices have been coordinated and made compatible with the choices of everyone else. Equilibrium is the solution or outcome of an economic model.

The term *equilibrium* conjures up the picture of a balance of opposing forces. For example, a balance scale can be said to be in equilibrium if a pound of butter is placed on one side of the balance and a one-pound weight is placed on the other side. The two weights exactly equal each other and so offset each other, leaving the balance arm horizontal. A soap bubble provides another excellent physical illustration of equilibrium. The delicate spherical film of soap is held in place by a balance of forces of the air inside the sphere and the air outside it.

This second physical analogy illustrates a further important feature of an equilibrium. An equilibrium is not necessarily static but may be dynamic—constantly changing. By squeezing or stretching the bubble, you can change its shape, but its shape is always determined by the balance of the forces acting upon it (including the forces that you exert upon it).

An economic equilibrium has a great deal in common with that of the soap bubble. First, it is in a constant state of motion. At each point in time, each person makes the best possible choice, given the endowments and actions of others. But changing circumstances alter those choices. For example, on a busy day in Manhattan, there are more cars looking for parking spaces than the number of spaces available. But people do get to park. Individual cars are leaving and arriving at a steady pace. As soon as one car vacates a parking space, another instantly fills it. In this situation, the equilibrium number of free spaces is zero. But being in equilibrium does not mean that everyone gets to park instantly. There is an equilibrium amount of time spent finding a vacant space. People hunting for a space are frustrated and experience rising blood pressure and increased anger. But there is still an equilibrium in the hunt for available parking spaces.

"And now a traffic update: A parking space has become available on Sixty-fifth Street between Second and Third. Hold it! A bulletin has just been handed me. That space has been taken."

Drawing by H. Martin; © 1987 The New Yorker Magazine, Inc.

Similarly, an economic equilibrium does not mean that everyone is experiencing economic prosperity. The constraints may be such that some people are very poor. Nevertheless, given their preferences, their endowments, the available technologies, and the actions of everyone else, each person has made the best possible choice and sees no advantage in modifying his or her current action.

Microeconomic and Macroeconomic Models

Economic models fall into two categories: microeconomic and macroeconomic. **Microeconomics** is the branch of economics that studies the decisions of individual households and firms. Microeconomics also studies the way in which individual markets work and the detailed way in which regulation and taxes affect the allocation of labor and of goods and services.

Macroeconomics is the branch of economics that studies the economy as a whole. It seeks to understand the big picture rather than the detailed individual choices. In particular, it studies the determination of the overall level of economic activity—of unemployment, aggregate income, average prices, and inflation.

Of the seven big economic questions, those dealing with technological change, production and consumption, and wages and earnings are microeconomic. Those dealing with unemployment, inflation, and differences in wealth among nations are macroeconomic.

Model, Theory, and Reality

People who build models often get carried away and start talking as if their model *is* the real world—as if their model is reality. No matter how useful it is, there is no sense in which a model can be said to be reality.

A model is abstract. It lists assumptions and their implications. When economists talk about people who have made themselves as well-off as possible, they are not talking about real people. They are talking about artificial people in an economic model. Do not lose sight of this important but easily misunderstood fact.

Economic theory is the bridge between economic models and the real world. Economic theory is a catalog of models that seem to work—that seem to enable us to understand and interpret the past and to predict some aspects of the future. Economic theory evolves from a process of building and testing economic models.

To test an economic model, its implications are matched against actual events in the real world. That is, the model is used to make predictions about the real world. The model's predictions may correspond to or be in conflict with the facts. It is by comparing the model's predictions with the facts that we are able to test a model. The process of developing economic theories by using models is illustrated in Fig. 1.3. We begin by building a model. The model's implications are used to generate predictions about the world. These predictions and their test form the basis of a theory. When predictions are in conflict with the facts, either a theory is discarded in favor of a superior alternative or we return to the model-building stage, modifying our assumptions and creating a new model. Economics itself provides guidance on how we might discover a better model. It prompts us to look for some aspect

FIGURE 1.3

How Theories Are Developed

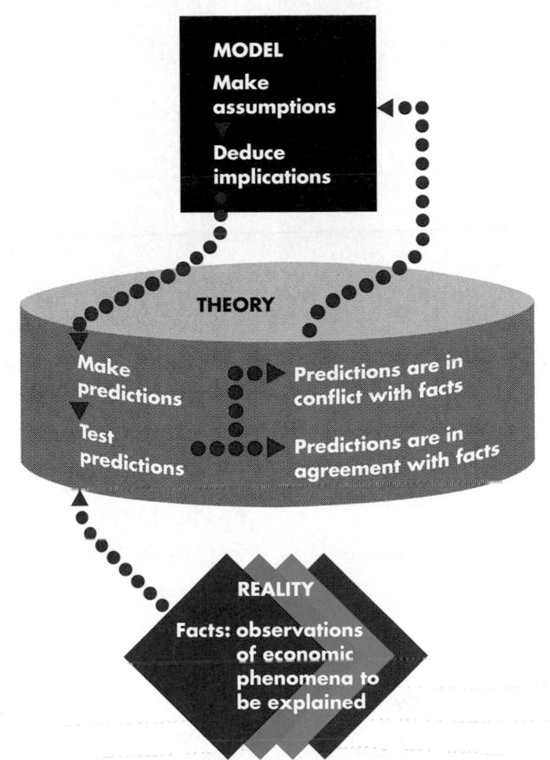

Economic theories are developed by building and testing economic models. An economic model is a set of *assumptions* about what is important and what can be ignored and the *implications* of those assumptions. The implications of a model form the basis of *predictions* about the world. These predictions are tested by being checked against the facts. If the predictions are in conflict with the facts, the model-building process begins again with new assumptions. Only when the predictions are in agreement with the facts has a useful theory been developed.

of preferences, endowments, technology, or the coordination mechanism that has been overlooked.

Economics is a young science and a long way from having achieved its goal of explaining and understanding economic activity. Its birth can be dated fairly precisely in the eighteenth century with the publication of Adam Smith's *The Wealth of Nations* (see Our Advancing Knowledge, pp. 22–23). In the closing years of the twentieth century, economic science has managed to discover a sizable

UNDERSTANDING the Sources of ECONOMIC WEALTH

In 1776, new technologies were being invented and applied to the manufacture of cotton and wool, iron, transportation, and agriculture in what came to be called the "Industrial Revolution."

Adam Smith was keenly interested in these events. He wanted to understand the sources of economic wealth, and he brought his acute powers of observation and abstraction to bear on this question. His answer:

- The division of labor
- Free domestic and international markets

Smith identified the division of labor as the source of "the greatest improvement in the productive powers of labor." The division of labor became even more productive when applied to creating new technologies. Scientists and engineers, trained in extremely narrow fields, became specialists at inventing. Their powerful skills speeded the advance of technology so that by the 1850s we could make machines that could make consumer goods and other machines by performing repetitive operations faster, more accurately, and for longer than people.

But, said Smith, the fruits of the division of labor are limited by the extent of the market. To make the market as large as possible, there must be no impediments to free trade both within a country and among countries. Smith argued that when each person makes the best possible economic choice based on self-interest, that choice leads as if by "an invisible hand" to the best outcome for society as a whole.

"It is not from the benevolence of the butcher, the brewer, or the baker, that we expect our dinner, but from their regard to their own interest."

ADAM SMITH
The Wealth of Nations

Adam Smith speculated that one person, working hard, using the hand tools available in the 1770s, might possibly make 20 pins a day. Yet by using those same hand tools but breaking the process into a number of individually small operations in which people specialize—by the division of labor—he observed that ten people could make a staggering 48,000 pins a day. One draws out the wire, another straightens it, a third cuts it, a fourth points it, a fifth grinds it. Three specialists make the head and a fourth attaches it. Finally, the pin is polished and wrapped in paper.

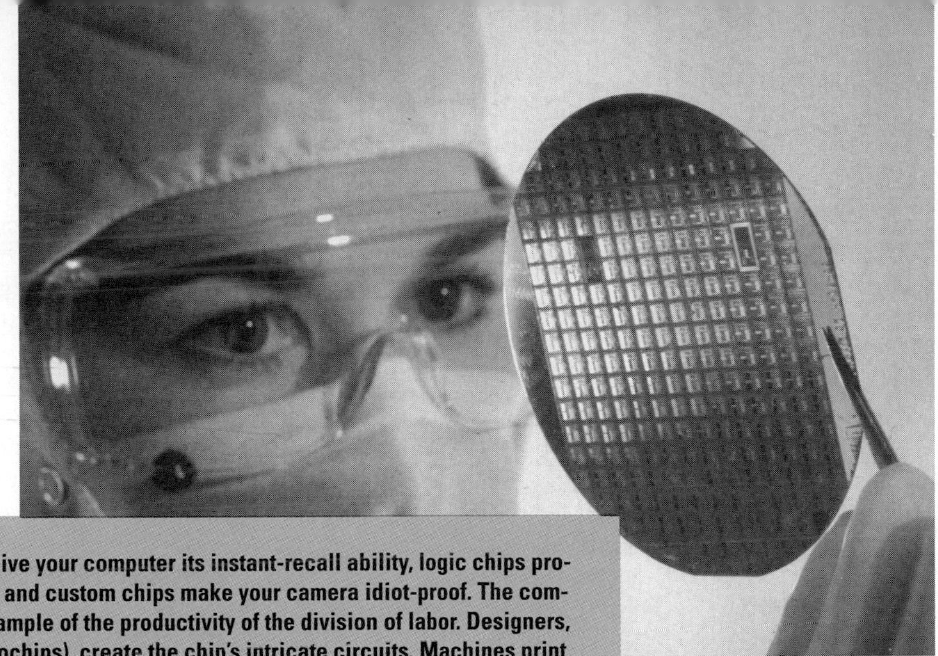

Memory chips give your computer its instant-recall ability, logic chips provide its number-crunching power, and custom chips make your camera idiot-proof. The computer chip is an extraordinary example of the productivity of the division of labor. Designers, using computers (made from microchips), create the chip's intricate circuits. Machines print the design on paper and photograph it on glass plates called masks that work like stencils. Workers prepare silicon wafers on which the circuits are printed. Some slice the wafers, others polish them, others bake them, and yet others coat them with a light-sensitive chemical. Technicians put masks and wafers into a machine that shines light through the mask, imprinting a copy of the circuit onto the wafer. Chemicals eat the unexposed portion of the wafer. A further series of passes through gas-filled ovens deposits atoms that act as transistors. Aluminum is deposited on the wafer to connect the transistors. Finally, a diamond saw or laser separates the hundreds of chips on the wafer.

ADAM SMITH AND THE *Wealth of Nations*

Adam Smith, born in 1723 in Kirkcaldy, a small fishing town near Edinburgh, Scotland, and only child of the town's customs officer (who died before his son was born), was a giant of a scholar who made extraordinary contributions in ethics and jurisprudence as well as economics.

His first academic appointment, at age 28, was as Professor of Logic at the University of Glasgow. He subsequently became tutor to a wealthy Scottish duke whom he accompanied on a two-year European grand tour, following which he received a pension of £300 a year—ten times the average income at that time.

With the financial security of his pension, Smith devoted ten years to writing the treatise that founded economic science, *An Inquiry into the Nature and Causes of The Wealth of Nations,* which was published to great acclaim in 1776.

Many had written on economic issues before Adam Smith, but it was he who made economics a science. His account of what was then known was so broad and authoritative that no subsequent writer on economics could advance his own ideas while ignoring the state of general knowledge.

number of useful generalizations. In many areas, however, we are still going around the circle—changing assumptions, performing new logical deductions, generating new predictions, and getting wrong answers yet again. The gradual accumulation of correct answers gives most practitioners some faith that their methods will eventually provide usable answers to the big economic questions.

As we make progress, though, more and more things become clearer and seem to fit together. Theoretical advances lead to deeper understanding. This feature of economics is shared with scientists in all fields. As Albert Einstein, the great physicist, said, "Creating a new theory is not like destroying an old barn and erecting a skyscraper in its place. It is rather like climbing a mountain, gaining new and wider views, discovering new connections between our starting point and its rich environment. But the point from which we started still exists and can be seen, although it appears smaller and forms a tiny part of our broad view gained by the mastery of the obstacles on our adventurous way up."[1]

◆ ◆ ◆ ◆ In the next chapter, we will study some of the tools that economists use to build economic models. Then, in Chapter 3, we will build an economic model and use that model to understand the world around us and to start to answer some of the seven big economic questions.

[1] These words are attributed to Einstein in a letter by Oliver Sacks to *The Listener*, 88, No. 2279, November 30, 1972, 756.

SUMMARY

Scarcity

All economic questions arise from the fundamental fact of scarcity. Scarcity means that wants exceed resources. Human wants are effectively unlimited, but the resources available to satisfy them are finite.

Economic activity is what people do to cope with scarcity. Scarcity forces people to make choices. Making the best choice possible from what is available is called optimizing or economizing. To make the best possible choice, a person weighs the costs and benefits of the alternatives—optimizes.

Opportunity cost is the cost of one choice in terms of the best forgone alternative. The opportunity cost of any action is the best alternative action that could have been undertaken in its place. Attending class instead of staying in bed has an opportunity cost—the cost of one hour of rest.

Scarcity forces people to compete with each other for scarce resources. People may cooperate in certain areas, but all economic activity ultimately results in competition among individuals acting alone or in groups. (pp. 9–11)

The Economy

People have unlimited wants but limited resources or factors of production—labor, land, and capital. The economy is a mechanism that allocates scarce resources among competing uses, determining *what, how,* and *for whom* the various goods and services will be produced.

The economy's two key components are decision makers and markets. Economic decision makers are households, firms, and governments. Households decide how much of their labor, land, and capital to sell or rent and how much of the various goods and services to buy. Firms decide what factors of production to hire and which goods and services to produce. Governments decide what goods and services to provide to households and firms and how much to raise in taxes.

The decisions of households, firms, and governments are coordinated through markets in which prices adjust to keep buying plans and selling plans consistent. Alternatively, coordination can be achieved by a command mechanism. The U.S. economy relies mainly on markets, but there is a command element in the actions taken by governments that also influences the allocation of scarce resources. The U.S. economy is therefore a mixed economy. (pp. 12–17)

Economic Science

Economic science, like the natural sciences and the other social sciences, attempts to find a body of laws. Economic science makes only *positive* statements—statements about what is. It does not make *normative* statements—statements about what ought to be. Economists try to find economic laws by developing a body of economic theory, and economic theory, in turn, is developed by building and testing economic models. Economic models are abstract, logical constructions that contain two components: assumptions and implications. An economic model has four key assumptions:

1. People have preferences.
2. People have a given endowment of resources and technology.
3. People economize.
4. People's choices are coordinated through market or command mechanisms.

The implications of an economic model are the equilibrium values of various prices and quantities that result from each individual doing the best that is possible, given the individual's preferences, endowments, information, and technology and given the coordination mechanism. (pp. 17–24)

KEY ELEMENTS

Key Terms

Assumptions, 19
Capital, 14
Closed economy, 16
Command economy, 15
Command mechanism, 15
Competition, 11
Cooperation, 11
Economic activity, 9
Economic theory, 18
Economics, 9
Economizing, 10
Economy, 12
Endowment, 19
Equilibrium, 20
Factor market, 14
Factors of production, 14
Firm, 14
Goods market, 14
Government, 14
Household, 14
Implications, 19
Labor, 14
Land, 14
Macroeconomics, 20
Market, 14
Market economy, 16
Microeconomics, 20
Mixed economy, 16
Normative statement, 17
Open economy, 16
Opportunity cost, 10
Optimizing, 10
Positive statement, 17
Preferences, 19
Rational choice, 19
Scarcity, 9
Technology, 19

Key Figure

Figure 1.1 A Picture of the Economy, 13

REVIEW QUESTIONS

1 Give two examples, different from those in the chapter, that illustrate each of the seven big economic questions.

2 Why does scarcity force us to make choices?

3 What do we mean by "rational choice"? Give examples of rational and irrational choices.

4 Why does scarcity force us to economize?

5 Why does optimization require us to calculate costs?

6 Why does scarcity imply competition?

7 Why can't we solve economic problems by cooperating with each other?

8 Name the main economic decision makers.

9 List the economic decisions made by households, firms, and governments.

10 What is the difference between a command mechanism and a market?

11 Distinguish between positive and normative statements by listing three examples of each type of statement.

12 What are the four key assumptions of an economic model?

13 Explain the difference between a model and a theory.

PROBLEMS

1 You plan to go to school this summer. If you do, you won't be able to take your usual job that pays $6,000 for the summer and you won't be able to live at home for free. The cost of your tuition will be $2,000, textbooks $200, and living expenses $1,400. What is the opportunity cost of going to summer school?

2 On Valentine's Day, Bernie and Catherine exchanged gifts: Bernie sent Catherine red roses and Catherine bought Bernie a box of chocolate. They each spent $15. They also spent $50 on dinner and split the cost evenly. Did either Bernie or Catherine incur any opportunity costs? If so, what were they? Explain your answer.

3 Nancy asks Beth to be her maid-of-honor at her wedding. Beth accepts. Which of the following are part of her opportunity cost of being Nancy's maid-of-honor? Explain why they are or are not.

- **a** The $200 Beth spent on a new outfit for the occasion
- **b** The $50 she spent on a party for Nancy's friends
- **c** The money she spent on a haircut a week before the wedding
- **d** The weekend visit she missed for her grandmother's 75th birthday—the same weekend as the wedding
- **e** The $10 she spent on lunch on the way to the wedding

4 The local mall has free parking, but the mall is always very busy, and it usually takes 30 minutes to find a parking space. Today when you found a vacant spot, Harry also wanted it. Is parking really free at this mall? If not, what did it cost you to park today? When you parked your car today, did you impose any costs on Harry? Explain your answers.

5 Which of the following statements are positive and which are normative?

- **a** A cut in wages will reduce the number of people willing to work.
- **b** High interest rates prohibit many young people from buying their first home.
- **c** No family ought to pay more than 25 percent of its income in taxes.
- **d** The government should reduce the number of minorities in the military and increase the number of whites.
- **e** The government ought to supply a medical insurance scheme for everyone free of charge.

6 You have been hired by Soundtrend, a company that makes and markets tapes, records, and compact discs (CDs). Your employer is going to start selling these products in a new region that has a population of 10 million people. A survey has indicated that 50 percent of people buy only popular music, 10 percent buy only classical music, and no one buys both types of music. Another survey suggests that the average income of a pop music fan is $10,000 a year and that of a classical fan is $50,000 a year. Based on a third survey, it appears that, on the average, people with low incomes spend one quarter of 1 percent of their income on tapes, records, and CDs, while people with high incomes spend 2 percent of their income on these products.

Build a model to enable Soundtrend to predict how much will be spent on pop music and classical music in this region in one year. In doing so:

- **a** List your assumptions.
- **b** Work out the implications of your assumptions.
- **c** Highlight the potential sources of errors in your predictions.

CHAPTER 2

MAKING AND USING GRAPHS

After studying this chapter, you will be able to:

- Make and interpret a scatter diagram and a time-series graph
- Distinguish between linear and nonlinear relationships and relationships that have a maximum and a minimum
- Define and calculate the slope of a line
- Graph relationships among more than two variables

Three Kinds of Lies

Benjamin Disraeli, British prime minister in the late nineteenth century, is reputed to have said that there are three kinds of lies: lies, damned lies, and statistics. One of the most powerful ways of conveying statistical information is in the form of a picture—a graph. Thus graphs, too, like statistics, can tell lies. But the right graph does not lie. Indeed, it reveals data and helps its viewer to see and think about relationships that would otherwise be obscure. ◆◆ Graphs are a surprisingly modern invention. The first graphs appeared in the late eighteenth century, long after the discovery of mathematically sophisticated ideas such as logarithms and calculus. But today, especially in the age of the personal computer and the video display, graphs have become almost more important than words. The ability to make and use graphs is as important as the ability to read and write. ◆◆ How do economists use graphs? What are the different types of graphs that economists use? What do economic graphs reveal and what can they hide? What are the main pitfalls that can result in a graph that lies? ◆◆ The seven big questions that you studied in Chapter 1—the problems that economics seeks to solve—are difficult ones. They involve relationships among a large number of variables. Hardly anything in economics has a single cause. Instead, a large number of variables interact with each other. It is often said that in economics, everything depends on everything else. Well, maybe not everything else, but lots of things. Variations in the quantity of ice cream consumed are caused not merely by variations in the air temperature or in the price of cream, but by at least these two factors and probably several others as well. How can we draw graphs of relationships that involve several variables, all of which vary simultaneously? How can we interpret such relationships?

◆ ◆ ◆ ◆ In this chapter, we are going to look at the different kinds of graphs that are used in economics. We are going to learn how to make them and read them. We are going to look at examples of useful graphs as well as misleading graphs. We are also going to study how we can calculate the strength of the effect of one variable on another. ◆ ◆ There are no graphs or techniques used in this book that are more complicated than those explained and described in this chapter. If you are already familiar with graphs, you may want to skip or at least only skim this chapter. Whether you study this chapter thoroughly or give it a quick pass, you should regard it as a handy reference chapter to which you can return if you feel that you need additional help understanding the graphs that you encounter in your study of economics.

FIGURE 2.1

Graphing a Single Variable

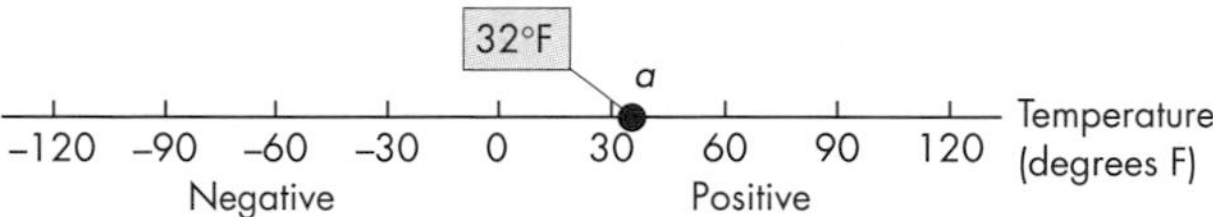

(a) Temperature

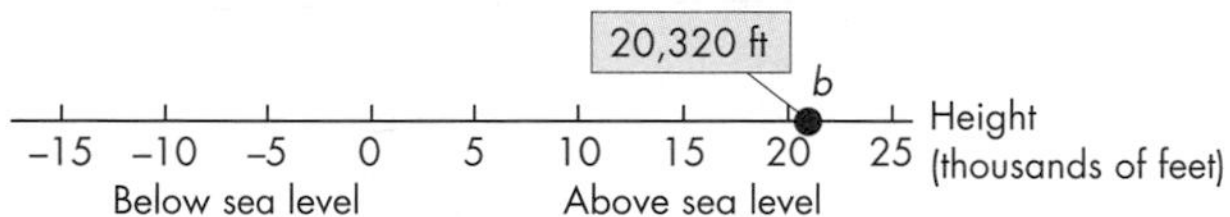

(b) Height

All graphs have a scale that measures a quantity as a distance. The two scales here measure temperature and height. Numbers to the right of zero are positive. Numbers to the left of zero are negative.

Graphing Data

Graphs represent a quantity as a distance. Figure 2.1 gives two examples. Part (a) shows temperature, measured in degrees Fahrenheit, as the distance on a scale. Movements from left to right represent increases in temperature. Movements from right to left represent decreases in temperature. The point marked 0 represents zero degrees Fahrenheit. To the right of zero, the temperatures are positive. To the left of zero, the temperatures are negative (as indicated by the minus sign in front of the numbers).

Figure 2.1(b) provides another example. This time altitude, or height, is measured in thousands of feet above sea level. The point marked 0 represents sea level. Points to the right of zero represent feet above sea level. Points to the left of zero (indicated by a minus sign) represent depths below sea level. There are no rigid rules about the scale for a graph. The scale is determined by the range of the variable being graphed and the space available for the graph.

The two graphs in Fig. 2.1 show just a single variable. Marking a point on either of the two scales indicates a particular temperature or a particular height. Thus the point marked *a* represents 32°F, the freezing point of water. The point marked *b* represents 20,320 feet, the height of Mount McKinley, the highest mountain in North America.

Graphing a single variable as we have done does not usually reveal much. Graphs become powerful when they show how two variables are related to each other.

Two-Variable Graphs

To construct a two-variable graph, we set two scales perpendicular to each other. Let's continue to use the same two variables as those in Fig. 2.1. We will measure temperature in exactly the same way, but we will turn the height scale to a vertical position. Thus temperature is measured exactly as it was before, but height is now represented by movements up and down a vertical scale.

The two scale lines in Fig. 2.2 are called **axes.** The vertical line is called the ***y*-axis,** and the horizontal line is called the ***x*-axis.** The letters *x* and *y* appear on the axes of Fig. 2.2. Each axis has a zero point that is shared by the two axes. The zero point, common to both axes, is called the **origin.**

FIGURE 2.2

Graphing Two Variables

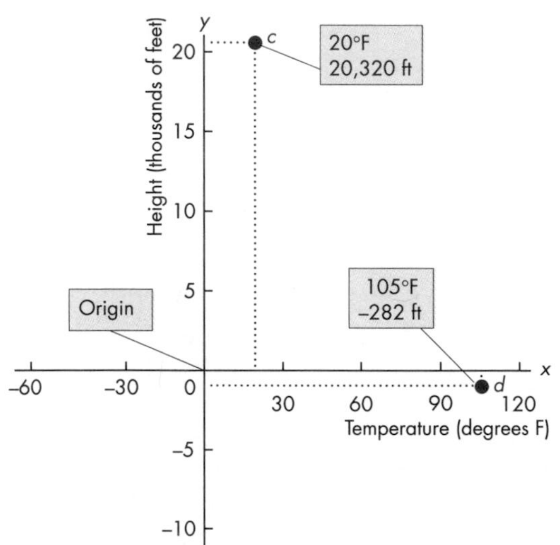

The relationship between two variables is graphed by drawing two axes perpendicular to each other. Height is measured here on the *y*-axis and temperature on the *x*-axis. Point *c* represents the top of Mt. McKinley, 20,320 feet above sea level (measured on the *y*-axis), with a temperature of 20°F (measured on the *x*-axis). Point *d* represents Death Valley, 282 feet below sea level, with a temperature of 105°F.

To represent something in a two-variable graph, we need two pieces of information. For example, Mount McKinley is 20,320 feet high and, on a particular day, the temperature at its peak is 20°F. We can represent this information in Fig. 2.2 by marking the height of the mountain on the *y*-axis at 20,320 feet and the temperature on the *x*-axis at 20°F. We can now identify the values of the two variables that appear on the axes by marking point *c*.

Two lines, called coordinates, can be drawn from point *c*. **Coordinates** are lines running from a point on a graph perpendicularly to an axis. The line running from *c* to the *x*-axis is the ***y*-coordinate,** because its length is the same as the value marked off on the *y*-axis. Similarly, the line running from *c* to the vertical axis is the ***x*-coordinate,** because its length is the same as the value marked off on the *x*-axis.

Now let's leave the top of Mount McKinley, at 20,320 feet and 20°F, and go to Death Valley in the Mojave Desert, the lowest point in the United States at 282 feet *below* sea level. Death Valley is represented by point *d*, which shows that we are 282 feet below sea level (the *y*-coordinate) and the temperature is 105°F (the *x*-coordinate).

Economists use graphs similar to this one in a variety of ways. Let's look at two examples.

Scatter Diagrams

Economists use graphs to reveal and describe the relationship between two economic variables. The most important type of graph used for these purposes is the scatter diagram, an example of which is shown in Fig. 2.3. A **scatter diagram** plots the value of one economic variable associated with the value

FIGURE 2.3

A Scatter Diagram: Consumption and Income

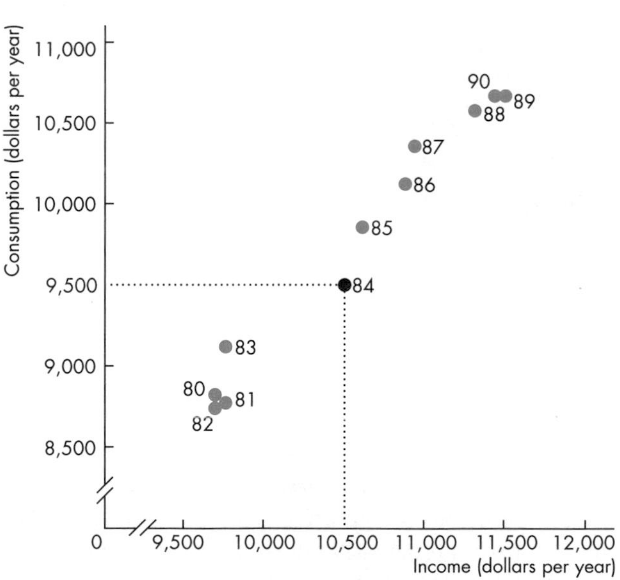

A scatter diagram shows the relationship between two variables. This scatter diagram shows the relationship between average consumption and average income during the years 1980 to 1990. Each point shows the values of the two variables in a specific year, and the year is identified by the two-digit number. For example, in 1984 average consumption was $9,500 and average income was $10,500. The pattern formed by the points shows that as income increases, so does consumption.

of another. It measures one of the variables on the x-axis and the other variable on the y-axis.

The Relationship Between Consumption and Income Figure 2.3 uses a scatter diagram to show the relationship between consumption and income. The x-axis measures average income, and the y-axis measures average consumption. Each point represents average consumption and average income in the United States in a given year between 1980 and 1990. The points for all ten years are "scattered" within the graph. Each point is labeled with a two-digit number that tells us its year. For example, the point marked 84 tells us that in 1984, average consumption was $9,500 and average income was $10,500.

This graph reveals that a relationship *does* exist between average income and average consumption. The pattern formed by the points in Fig. 2.3 tells us that when income increases, consumption also increases.

Breaks in the Axes Notice that each axis in Fig. 2.3 has a break in it—illustrated by the small gaps. The breaks indicate that there are jumps from the origin, 0, to the first values recorded. The breaks are used because in the period covered by the graph average consumption was never less than $8,500 and average income was never less than $9,500. With no breaks in the axes of this graph, there would be a lot of empty space, all the points would be crowded into the top right corner, and we would not be able to see whether a relationship existed between these two variables. By using axis breaks, we are able to bring the relationship into view. In effect, we use a zoom lens to bring the relationship into the center of the graph and magnify it so that it fills the graph.

The range of the variables plotted on the axes of a graph are an important feature of a graph, and it is a good idea to get into the habit of always looking closely at the axis values—and labels—before you start to interpret a graph.

Other Relationships Figure 2.4 shows two other scatter diagrams. In part (a), the x-axis shows the percentage of households owning a video cassette recorder, and the y-axis shows its average price. Each point with its two-digit number represents a year. Thus the point marked 81 tells us that the

FIGURE 2.4

More Scatter Diagrams

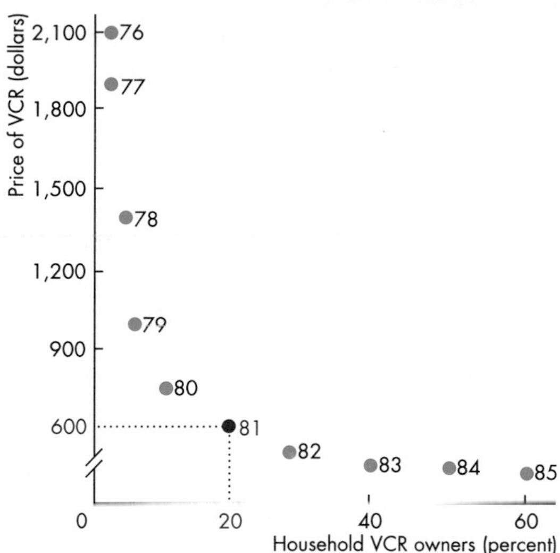

(a) VCR ownership and price

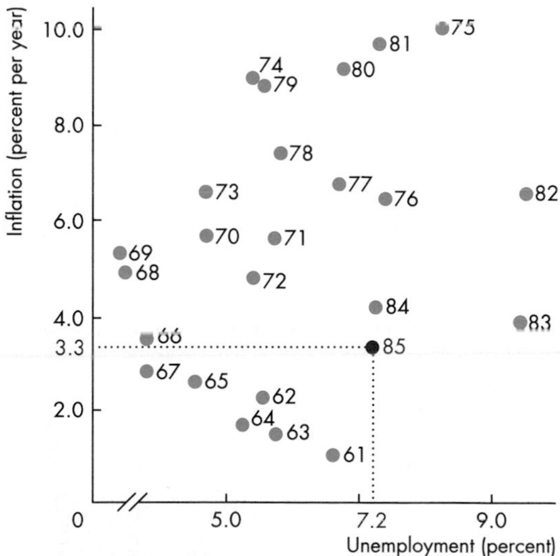

(b) Unemployment and inflation

Part (a) is a scatter diagram showing the relationship between the percentage of households owning a VCR and the average price of a VCR. It shows that as the price of a VCR has fallen, the percentage of households owning a VCR has increased. Part (b) is a scatter diagram showing inflation and unemployment. It shows that there is no clear relationship between these two variables.

average price of a VCR in 1981 was $600 and that VCRs were owned by 20 percent of all households. The pattern formed by the points in part (a) tells us that as the price of a VCR falls, a larger percentage of households own one.

In part (b), the *x*-axis measures unemployment in the United States, and the *y*-axis measures inflation. Again, each point with its two-digit number represents a year. The point marked 85 tells us that in 1985 unemployment was 7.2 percent and inflation was 3.3 percent. The pattern formed by the points in part (b) does not reveal a clear relationship between the two variables. The graph thus informs us, by its lack of a distinct pattern, that there is no relationship between these two variables.

A scatter diagram enables us to see the relationship between two economic variables. But it does not give us a clear picture of how those variables evolve over time. To see the evolution of economic variables, we use a different but common kind of graph—the time-series graph.

Time-Series Graphs

A **time-series graph** measures time (for example, years or months) on the *x*-axis and the variable or variables in which we are interested on the *y*-axis.

Figure 2.5 illustrates a time-series graph. Time is measured in years on the *x*-axis. The variable that we are interested in—the U.S. unemployment rate (the percentage of the labor force unemployed)—is measured on the *y*-axis. The time-series graph conveys an enormous amount of information quickly and easily:

1. It tells us the *level* of the unemployment rate—when it is *high* and *low*. When the line is a long way from the *x*-axis, the unemployment rate is high. When the line is close to the *x*-axis, the unemployment rate is low.
2. It tells us how the unemployment rate *changes*—whether it *rises* or *falls*. When the line slopes upward, as in the early 1930s, the unemployment rate is rising. When the line slopes downward,

FIGURE 2.5

A Time-Series Graph

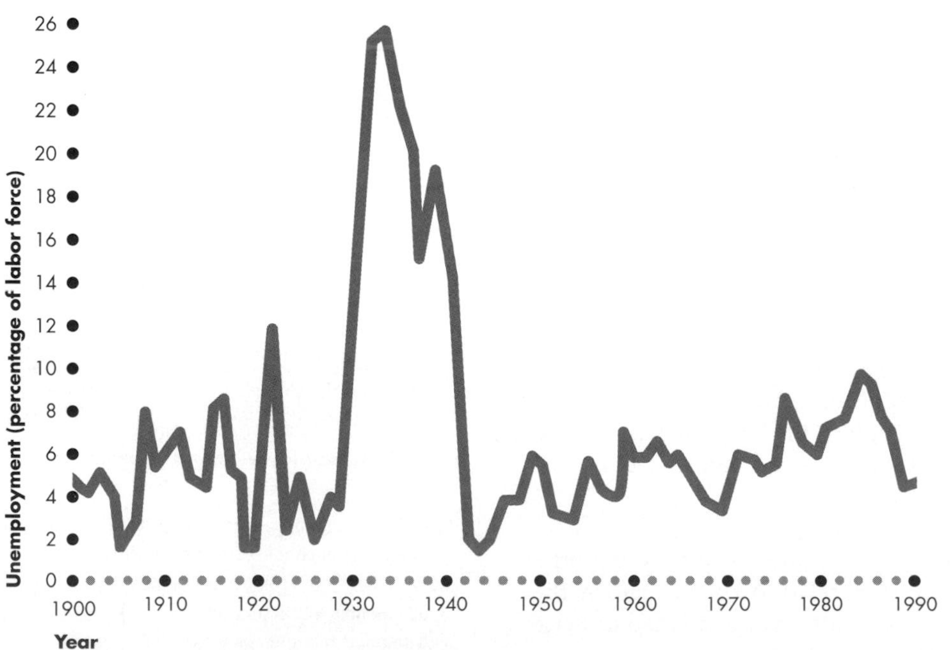

A time-series graph plots the level of a variable on the *y*-axis against time (day, week, month, or year) on the *x*-axis. This graph shows the U.S. unemployment rate each year from 1900 to 1990.

Source: Economic Report of the President.

as in the early 1940s, the unemployment rate is falling.

3. It tells us the *speed* with which the unemployment rate is *changing*—whether it is rising or falling *quickly* or *slowly*. If the line rises or falls very steeply, then unemployment is changing quickly. If the line is not steep, unemployment is rising or falling slowly. For example, unemployment rose very quickly between 1930 and 1932. Unemployment went up again in 1933 but more slowly. Similarly, when unemployment was falling in the early 1950s, it fell quickly between 1950 and 1951, but then it began to fall much more slowly in 1952 and 1953.

A time-series graph can also be used to depict a trend. A **trend** is a general tendency for a variable to rise or fall. You can see that unemployment had a general tendency to rise from the mid-1940s to the mid-1980s. That is, although there were ups and downs in the unemployment rate, there was an upward trend.

Graphs also allow us to compare different periods quickly. It is apparent, for example, that the 1930s were different from any other period in the twentieth century because of exceptionally high unemployment. You can also see that unemployment fluctuated more violently in the years before 1920 than it did in the years after 1950. The sawtooth pattern is more jagged in the period from 1900 to 1930 than it is in the period after 1950.

Thus we can see that Fig. 2.5 conveys a wealth of information, and it does so in much less space than we have used to describe only some of its features.

Misleading Time-Series Graphs Although time-series graphs are powerful devices for conveying a large amount of information, they can also be used to distort data and to create a misleading picture. The two most commonly used ways of distorting data are stretching and squeezing the scales on the y-axis and omitting the origin—the zero point—on the y-axis.

Figure 2.6 illustrates the first of these devices. It contains exactly the same information as Fig. 2.5, but the information is packaged in a different way. In part (a) the scale on the y-axis has been compressed; in part (b) it has been expanded. When we look at these two parts as a whole, they suggest that unemployment was pretty stable during the first half of this century, but that it has trended upward dramatically in the last 40 years or so.

You might think that this graphical way of distorting data is so outrageous that no one would ever

FIGURE 2.6

Misleading Graphs: Squeezing and Stretching Scales

(a) 1900–1944

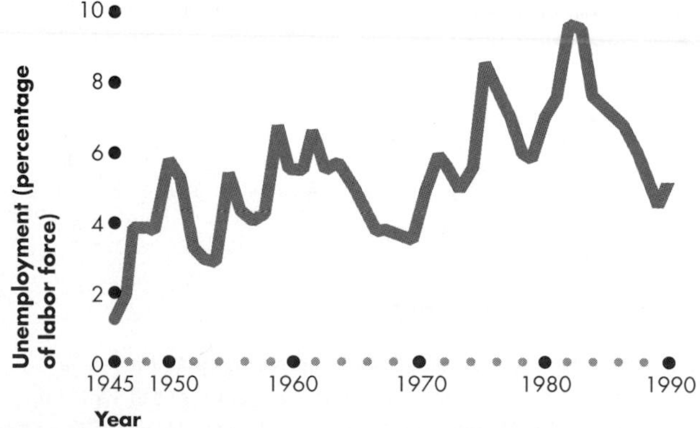

(b) 1945–1990

Graphs can mislead by squeezing and stretching the scales. These two graphs show exactly the same thing as Fig. 2.5—U.S. unemployment from 1900 to 1990. Part (a) has squeezed the y-axis, while part (b) has stretched that axis. The result appears to be a low and stable unemployment rate before 1945 and a rising, highly volatile unemployment rate after that date. Contrast the lie of Fig. 2.6 with the truth of Fig. 2.5.

attempt to use it. If you scrutinize the graphs that you see in newspapers and magazines, you will be surprised how common this device is.

Figure 2.7 illustrates the effect of omitting the origin on the *y*-axis. Sometimes, omitting the origin is precisely the correct thing to do, as it enables the graph to reveal its information. But there are also times when omitting the origin is misleading. In parts (a) and (b), you can see a graph of the unemployment rate between 1970 and 1990. Part (a) includes the origin, and part (b) does not. The graph in part (a) provides a clear account of what hap-

FIGURE 2.7

Omitting the Origin

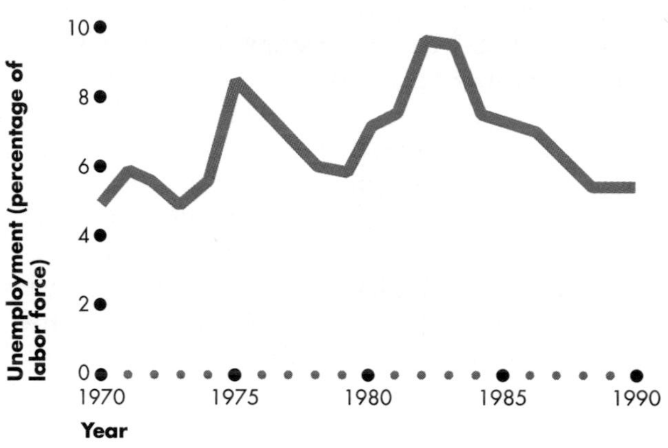

(a) Revealing graph with origin

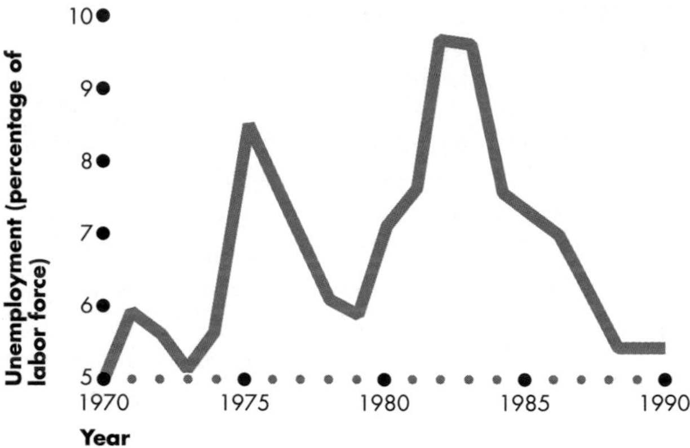

(b) Misleading graph with origin omitted

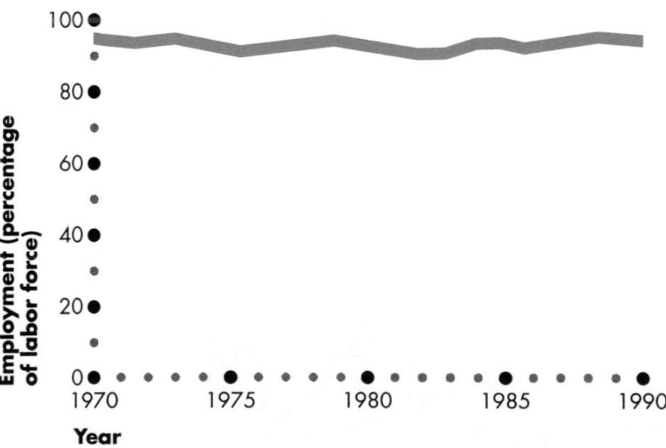

(c) Uniformative graph with origin

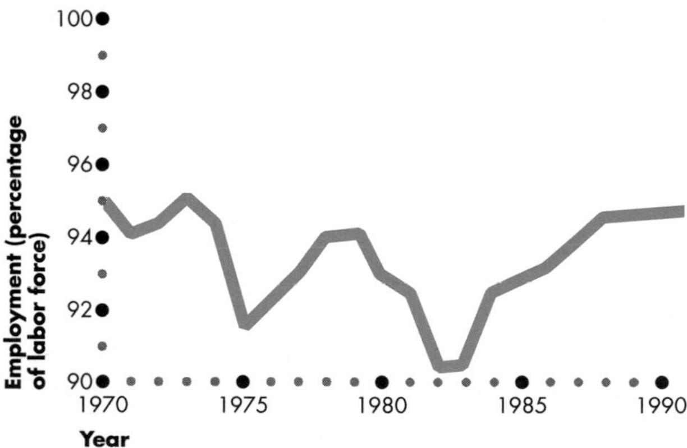

(d) Revealing graph with origin omitted

Sometimes the origin is omitted from a graph. This practice can be either revealing or misleading, depending on how it is used. Parts (a) and (b) graph the U.S. unemployment rate between 1970 and 1990. Part (a) is graphed with the origin on the *y*-axis, and part (b) without it. Part (a) reveals a large amount of information about the level and changes in the unemployment rate over this time period. Part (b) overdramatizes the rises and falls in unemployment and gives no direct visual information about its level.

Parts (c) and (d) graph the employment rate. Part (c) contains an origin on the *y*-axis, and part (d) does not. In this case the graph in part (c) with the origin on the *y*-axis is uninformative and shows virtually no variation in the employment rate. The graph in part (d) gives a clear picture of fluctuations in the employment rate and is more informative than part (c) about those fluctuations.

pened to unemployment over the time period in question. You can use that graph in the same way that we used Fig. 2.5 to describe all the features of unemployment during that time period. But the graph in part (b) is less revealing and distorts the picture. It fails to reveal the *level* of unemployment. It focuses only on, and exaggerates, the magnitude of the increases and decreases in the unemployment rate. In particular, the increases in the unemployment rate in 1974–1975 and in 1981–1982 look enormous when compared with the increases that appear in part (a). With the origin omitted, small percentage changes in unemployment look like many hundredfold changes. Another example of this device is shown in Reading Between the Lines, on pp. 36–37.

Parts (c) and (d) of Fig. 2.7 graph the employment rate—the percentage of the labor force employed. Part (c) includes the origin, and part (d) omits it. As you can see, the graph in part (c) reveals very little about movements in the employment rate. It seems to suggest that the employment rate was pretty constant and lying between 90 and 95 percent. The main feature of part (c) is an enormous amount of empty space and an inefficient use of the space available. Part (d) shows the same information but with the origin omitted. The scale begins at 90 percent. In this case, we can see very clearly the ups and downs in the employment rate. This graph does not provide a visual impression of the level of employment, but it does provide a clear picture of variations in its rate.

The decision about whether to include or exclude the origin of the graph depends on what the graph is designed to reveal. To convey information about the level of employment and unemployment and variations in their rates, the graphs in parts (a) and (d) of Fig. 2.7 are almost equally revealing. By comparison, the graphs in parts (b) and (c) convey almost no information.

Comparing Two Time Series Sometimes we want to use a time-series graph to compare two different variables. For example, suppose you wanted to know how the balance of the government's budget—its surplus or deficit—fluctuated and how those fluctuations compared with fluctuations in the unemployment rate. You can examine two such series by drawing a graph of each of them in the manner shown in Fig. 2.8(a). The scale for the unemployment rate appears on the left side of the figure, and

FIGURE 2.8

Time-Series Relationships

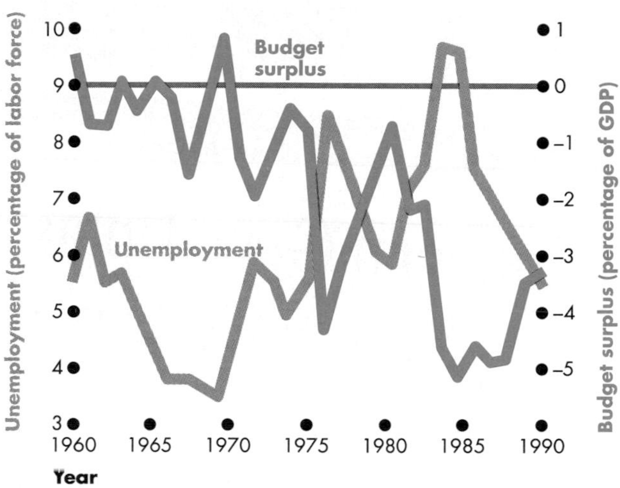

(a) Unemployment and budget surplus

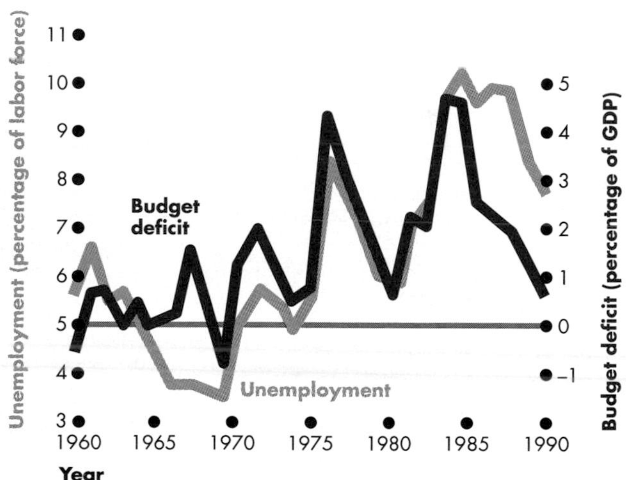

(b) Unemployment and budget deficit

A time-series graph can be used to reveal relationships between two variables. These two graphs show the unemployment rate and the balance of the government's budget between 1960 and 1990. The unemployment line is identical in the two parts. In part (a), the budget balance is shown measuring surpluses upward and deficits downward (as negative numbers) on the right scale. It looks as if the budget goes into a bigger deficit when unemployment rises, but not much else is shown by part (a). Part (b) inverts the scale on which the budget is measured. Now a deficit is measured in the up direction and a surplus in the down direction on the right scale. The relationship between the budget deficit and unemployment is now easier to see.

Graphs in Action

The Wall Street Journal, August 27, 1991

Concern Goes Up as SAT Scores Go Down

By Gary Putka

Scholastic Aptitude Test scores declined despite increased course loads and higher grades in U.S. high schools, suggesting that efforts to reform education are being hampered by falling academic standards. . . .

The average composite score on the SAT, the most-taken college-admissions test, fell to 896 from 900 out of a maximum 1,600. The average score has fallen four years in a row and is at its lowest point since 1983's 893. The verbal score, which fell two points to 422, is the lowest on record at the College Board, the New York organization that gives the test on behalf of U.S. colleges. The score in mathematics, the test's other part, slipped two points to 474, also the lowest since 1984. . . .

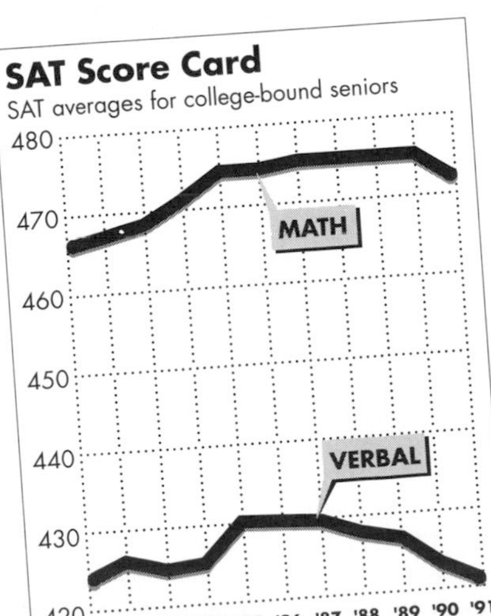

Need for a New Strategy

"You either have to say it's too early and reforms haven't been in place long enough, or all the things we put in the schools were wrong and we need a radical new strategy," said Albert Shanker, president of the American Federation of Teachers. "My own view is the latter is the case." . . .

Mr. Shanker said that his analysis of federal test scores indicate that only 4% of high-school graduates "really know algebra," although 96% of those who took the SAT reported taking an algebra class. Ninety-three percent took geometry. Yet on the math section of the SAT, which is largely a test of algebra and geometry, students got an average of only 26 of 60 questions correct. . . .

Not all of the SAT data pointed to educational setbacks. The total number of test takers, which stayed about flat at one million, represented 42% of this year's high-school graduates, up from 40% in 1990 and an indication of rising educational aspirations. . . .

The Essence of the Story

The average composite SAT score has fallen for four years in a row.

The verbal score in 1991 was the lowest on record, and the mathematics score in 1991 was at its lowest level since 1984.

The 1980s have been years of major reforms in education and of large increases in expenditure on education.

Many people read these facts as a sign of "falling academic standards" and of the failure of the reforms.

The percentage of high school graduates taking the SAT increased from 40 percent in 1990 to 42 percent in 1991.

This last fact is seen as a sign of "rising educational aspirations."

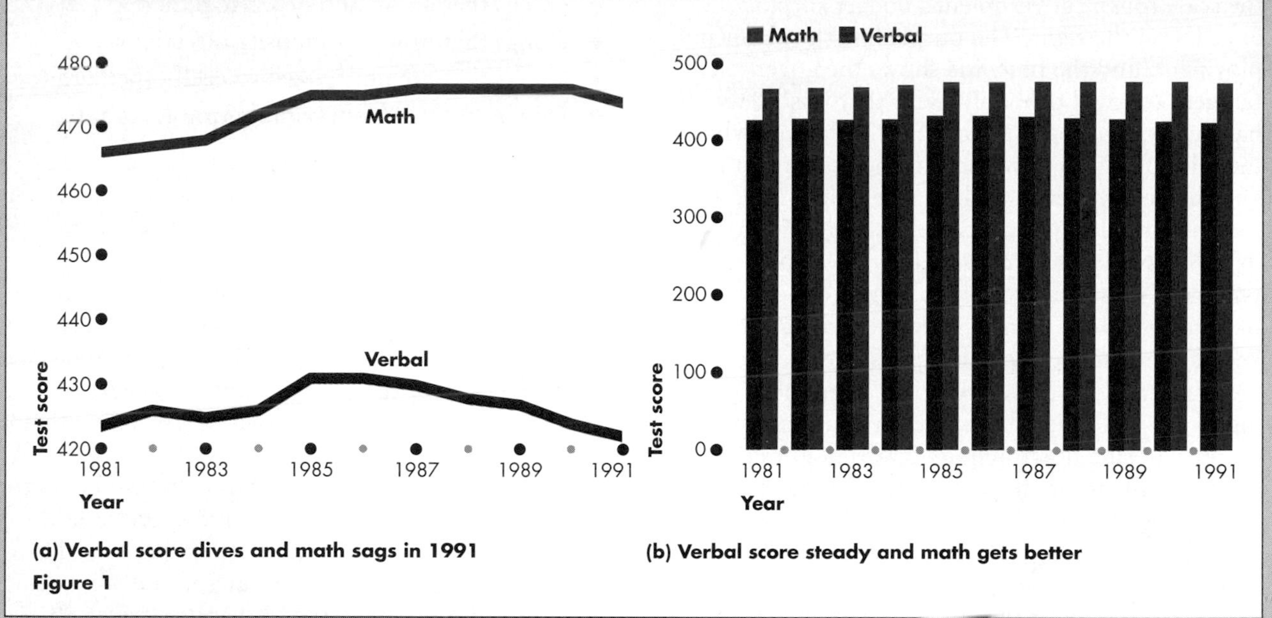

(a) Verbal score dives and math sags in 1991

(b) Verbal score steady and math gets better

Figure 1

Background and Analysis

A 2 percent fall in the SAT verbal score is shown in both parts of Fig. 1, but the false impression of a large fall is created in part (a)—as in the news story—by omitting the origin.

During the 1980s, the number of students taking the SAT increased and the college entry age population decreased. The percentage of the college entry age population taking the SAT increased from 23 percent in 1981 to 29 percent in 1991.

Other things being equal, the larger the percentage of the population taking *any* test, the lower the average score.

Figure 2 gives a third view of the falling SAT scores that shows the relationship between the SAT scores and the percentage of the college entry age population taking the test.

Despite the increased percentage taking the test, the math score increased throughout the 1980s and dipped only in 1991. These facts suggest remarkable improvements in mathematical achievement.

The verbal score increased between 1981 and 1985 but declined as the percentage taking the test increased after 1985. It continued to decline in 1990 and 1991, even though the percentage of the population taking the test stabilized.

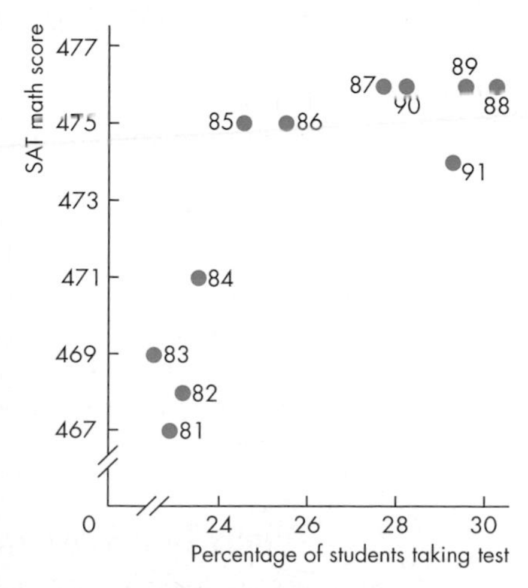

(a) SAT math score and percentage taking test

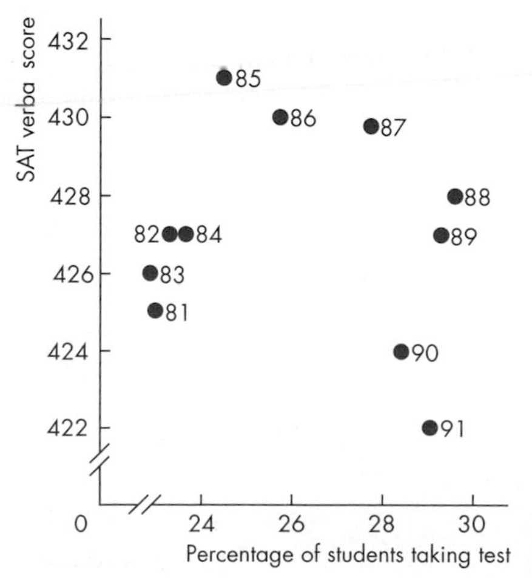

(b) SAT verbal score and percentage taking test

Figure 2

the scale for the government's budget surplus appears on the right. The purple line shows unemployment, and the blue line shows the government's budget. You will probably agree that it is pretty hard work figuring out from Fig. 2.8(a) just what the relationship is between the unemployment rate and the government's budget. But it does look as if there is a tendency for the budget to go into a bigger deficit (blue line goes downward) when the unemployment rate increases (purple line goes upward). In other words, it seems as if these two variables have a tendency to move in opposite directions.

In a situation such as this, it is often more revealing to flip the scale of one of the variables over and graph it upside-down. Figure 2.8(b) does this. The unemployment rate in part (b) is graphed in exactly the same way as in part (a). But the government's budget has been flipped over. Now, instead of measuring the deficit (a negative number) in the down direction and the surplus (a positive number) in the up direction, we measure the deficit upward and the surplus downward. You can now "see" very clearly the relationship between these two variables. There is indeed a tendency for the government's deficit to get bigger when the unemployment rate gets higher. But the relationship is by no means an exact one. There are significant periods, clearly revealed in the graph, when the deficit and the unemployment rate move apart. You can "see" these periods as those in which the gap between the two lines widens.

Now that we have seen how we can use graphs in economics to represent economic data and to show the relationship between variables, let us examine how economists use graphs in a more abstract way to construct and analyze economic models.

Graphs Used in Economic Models

Although you will encounter many different kinds of graphs in economics, there are some patterns that, once you have learned to recognize them, will instantly convey to you the meaning of a graph. There are graphs that show each of the following:

- Things that go up and down together
- Things that move in opposite directions
- Things that are not related to each other at all
- Things that have a maximum or a minimum

Let's look at these four cases.

Things That Go Up and Down Together

Graphs that show the relationship between two variables that move up and down together are shown in Fig. 2.9. The relationship between two variables that move in the same direction is called a **positive relationship.** Such a relationship is shown by a line that slopes upward.

Part (a) shows the relationship between the number of miles traveled in 5 hours and speed. For example, the point marked *a* tells us that we will travel 200 miles in 5 hours if our speed is 40 miles an hour. If we double our speed and travel at 80 miles an hour, we will cover a distance of 400 miles in 5 hours. The relationship between the number of miles traveled in 5 hours and speed is represented by an upward-sloping straight line. A relationship depicted by a straight line is called a **linear relationship.**

Part (b) shows the relationship between distance sprinted and exhaustion (exhaustion being measured by the time it takes the heart rate to return to normal). This relationship is an upward-sloping one depicted by a curved line that starts out with a gentle slope but then becomes steeper as we move along the curve away from the origin.

Part (c) shows the relationship between the number of problems worked by a student and the amount of study time. This relationship is illustrated by an upward-sloping curved line that starts out with a steep slope but then becomes more gentle as we move away from the origin.

There are three types of upward-sloping lines in the graphs in Fig. 2.9: one straight and two curved. But they are all called curves. Any line on a graph—no matter whether it is straight or curved—is called a **curve.**

Things That Move in Opposite Directions

Figure 2.10 shows relationships between things that move in opposite directions. A relationship between variables that move in opposite directions is called a **negative relationship.**

FIGURE 2.9

Positive Relationships

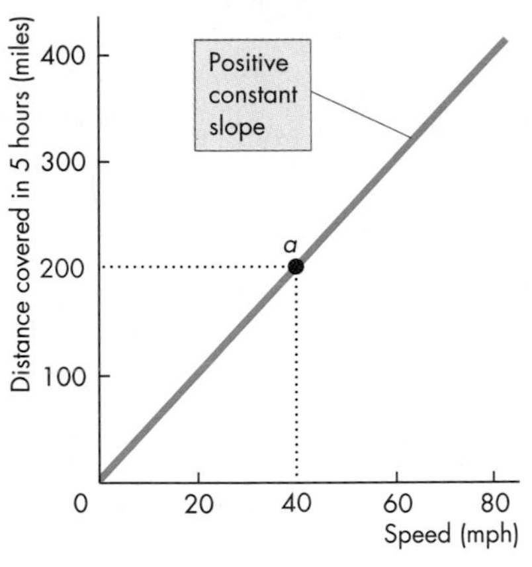

(a) Positive constant slope

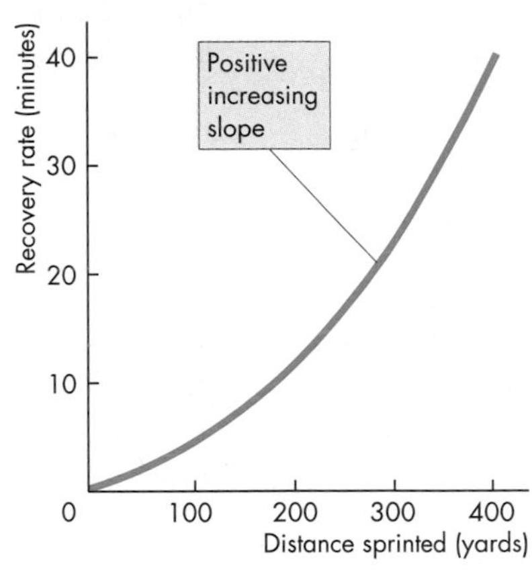

(b) Positive increasing slope

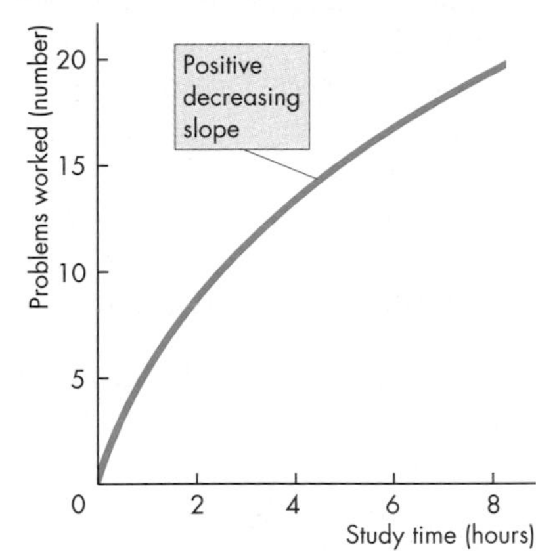

(c) Positive decreasing slope

Each part of this figure shows a positive relationship between two variables. That is, as the value of the variable measured on the *x*-axis increases, so does the value of the variable measured on the *y*-axis. Part (a) illustrates a linear relationship—a relationship whose slope is constant as we move along the curve. Part (b) illustrates a positive relationship whose slope becomes steeper as we move along the curve away from the origin. It is a positive relationship with an increasing slope. Part (c) shows a positive relationship whose slope becomes flatter as we move away from the origin. It is a positive relationship with a decreasing slope.

FIGURE 2.10

Negative Relationships

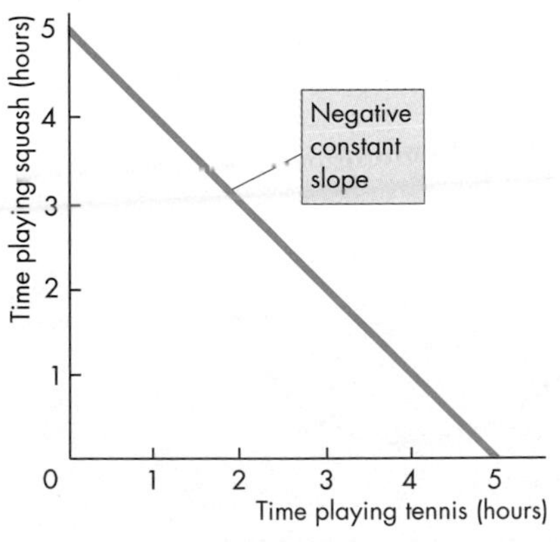

(a) Negative constant slope

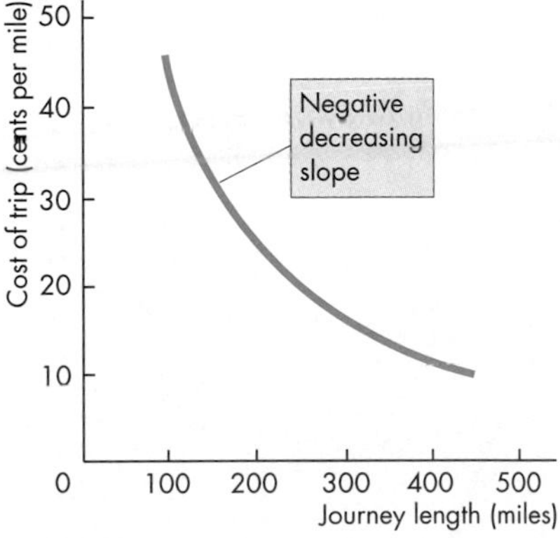

(b) Negative decreasing slope

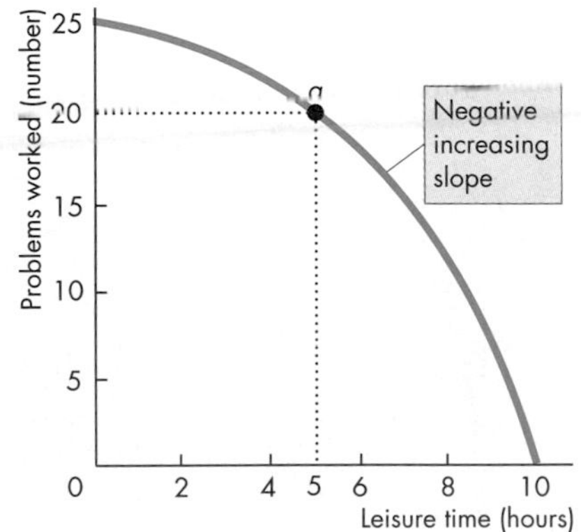

(c) Negative increasing slope

Each part of this figure shows a negative relationship between two variables. Part (a) shows a linear relationship—a relationship whose slope is constant as we travel along the curve. Part (b) shows a negative relationship of decreasing slope. That is, the slope of the relationship gets less steep as we travel along the curve from left to right. Part (c) shows a negative relationship of increasing slope. That is, the slope becomes steeper as we travel along the curve from left to right.

Part (a) shows the relationship between the number of hours available for playing squash and the number of hours for playing tennis. One extra hour spent playing tennis means one hour less playing squash and vice versa. This relationship is negative and linear.

Part (b) shows the relationship between the cost per mile traveled and the length of a journey. The longer the journey, the lower is the cost per mile. But as the journey length increases, the cost per mile decreases at a decreasing rate. This feature of the relationship is illustrated by the fact that the curve slopes downward, starting out steep at a short journey length and then becoming flatter as the journey length increases.

Part (c) shows the relationship between the amount of leisure time and the number of problems worked by a student. If the student takes no leisure, 25 problems can be worked. If the student takes 5 hours of leisure, only 20 problems can be worked (point *a*). Increasing leisure time beyond 5 hours produces a large reduction in the number of problems worked, and if the student takes 10 hours of leisure a day, no problems get worked. This relationship is a negative one that starts out with a gentle slope at a low number of leisure hours and becomes increasingly steep as leisure hours increase.

Things That Have a Maximum and a Minimum

Economics is about optimizing, or doing the best with limited resources. Examples of optimizing include making the highest possible profits and achieving the lowest possible costs of production. Economists make frequent use of graphs depicting relationships that have a maximum or a minimum. Figure 2.11 illustrates such relationships.

Part (a) shows the relationship between rainfall and wheat yield. When there is no rainfall, wheat will not grow, so the yield is zero. As the rainfall increases up to 10 days a month, the wheat yield also increases. With 10 rainy days each month, the wheat yield reaches its maximum at 40 bushels an acre (point *a*). Rain in excess of 10 days a month starts to lower the yield of wheat. If every day is rainy, the wheat suffers from a lack of sunshine and the yield falls back almost to zero. This relationship

FIGURE 2.11

Maximum and Minimum Points

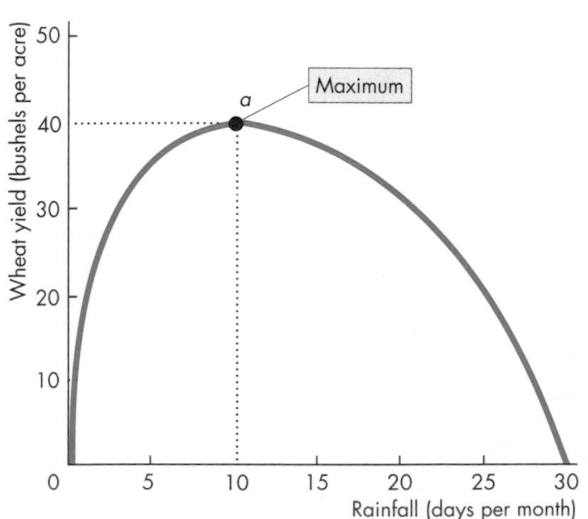

(a) Maximum

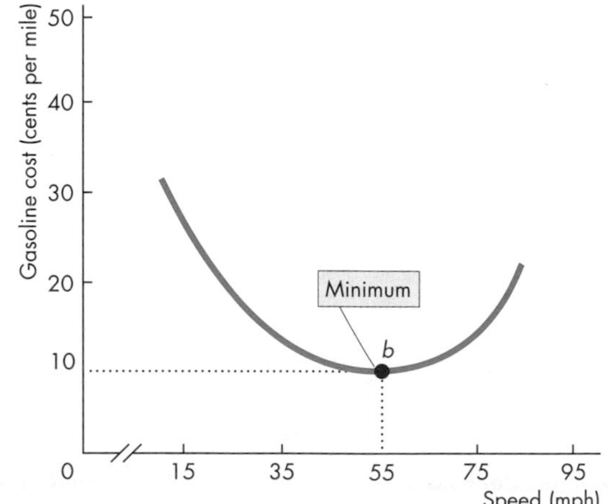

(b) Minimum

Part (a) shows a relationship that has a maximum point, *a*. The curve rises at first, reaches its highest point, and then falls. Part (b) shows a relationship with a minimum point, *b*. The curve falls to its minimum and then rises.

is one that starts out positive, reaches a maximum, and then becomes negative.

Part (b) shows the reverse case—a relationship that begins with a negative slope, falls to a minimum, and then becomes positive. An example of such a relationship is the gasoline cost per mile as the speed of travel varies. At low speeds, the car is creeping along in a traffic snarl-up. The number of miles per gallon is low, so the gasoline cost per mile is high. At very high speeds, the car is operated beyond its most efficient rate, and again the number of miles per gallon is low and the gasoline cost per mile is high. At a speed of 55 miles an hour, the gasoline cost per mile traveled is at its minimum (point *b*).

Things That Are Independent

There are many situations in which one variable is independent of another. No matter what happens to the value of one variable, the other variable remains constant. Sometimes we want to show the independence between two variables in a graph. Figure 2.12 shows two ways of achieving this. In part (a), your grade in economics is shown on the vertical axis against the price of bananas on the horizontal axis. Your grade (75 percent in this example) does not depend on the price of bananas. The relationship between these two variables is shown by a horizontal straight line. In part (b), the output of French wine is shown on the horizontal axis and the number of rainy days a month in California is shown on the vertical axis. Again, the output of French wine (3 billion gallons a year in this example) does not change when the number of rainy days in California changes. The relationship between these two variables is shown by a vertical straight line.

Figures 2.9 through 2.12 illustrate ten different shapes of graphs that we will encounter in economic models. In describing these graphs, we have talked about curves that slope upward or slope downward and slopes that are steep or gentle. The concept of slope is an important one. Let's spend a little time discussing exactly what we mean by slope.

FIGURE 2.12

Variables with No Relationship

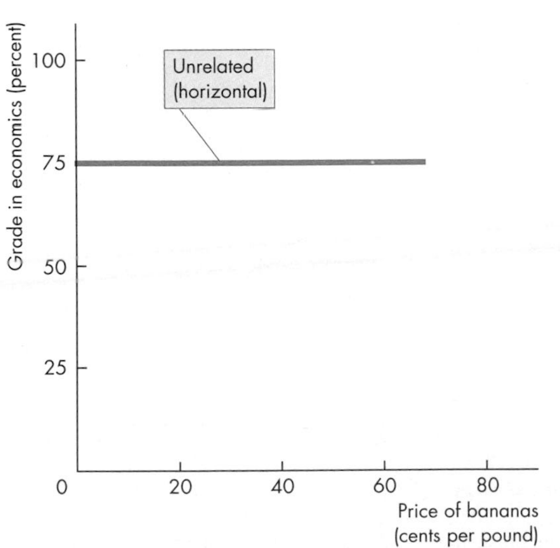

(a) Unrelated: horizontal

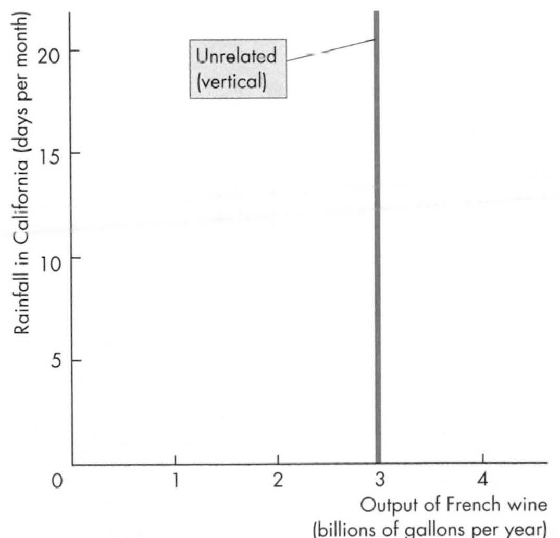

(b) Unrelated: vertical

This figure shows how we can graph two variables that are unrelated to each other. In part (a), a student's grade in economics is plotted at 75 percent regardless of the price of bananas on the *x*-axis. In part (b), the output of the vineyards of France does not vary with the rainfall in California.

The Slope of a Relationship

The **slope** of a relationship is the change in the value of the variable measured on the *y*-axis divided by the change in the value of the variable measured on the *x*-axis. We use the Greek letter Δ to represent "change in." Thus Δy means the change in the value of the variable measured on the *y*-axis, and Δx means the change in the value of the variable measured on the *x*-axis. Therefore the slope of the relationship is

$$\Delta y/\Delta x.$$

If a large change in the variable measured on the *y*-axis (Δy) is associated with a small change in the variable measured on the *x*-axis (Δx), the slope is large and the curve is steep. If a small change in the variable measured on the *y*-axis (Δy) is associated with a large change in the variable measured on the *x*-axis (Δx), the slope is small and the curve is flat.

We can make the idea of slope sharper by doing some calculations.

Calculating Slope of a Straight Line

The slope of a straight line is the same regardless of where on the line you calculate it. Thus the slope of a straight line is constant. Let's calculate the slopes of the lines in Fig. 2.13. In part (a), when x increases from 2 to 6, y increases from 3 to 6. The change in x is +4—that is, Δx is 4. The change in y is +3—that is, Δy is 3. The slope of that line is

$$\frac{\Delta y}{\Delta x} = \frac{3}{4}.$$

FIGURE 2.13
The Slope of a Straight Line

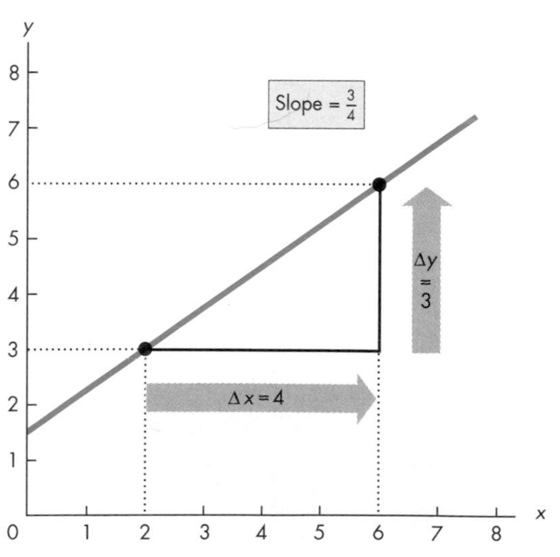

(a) Positive slope

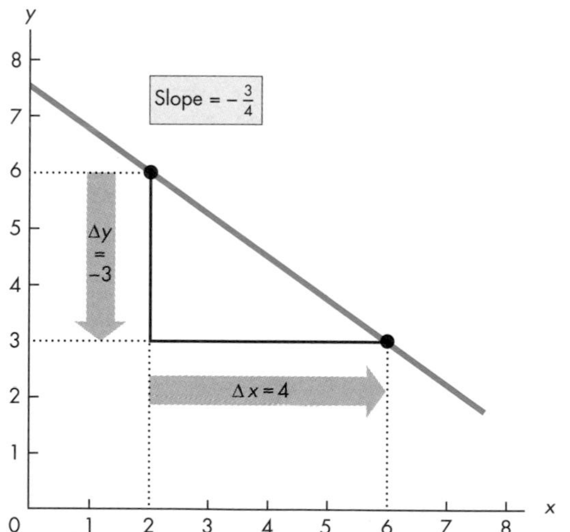

(b) Negative slope

To calculate the slope of a straight line, we divide the change in the value of the variable measured on the *y*-axis by the change in the value of the variable measured on the *x*-axis. Part (a) shows the calculation of a positive slope (when *x* goes up, *y* goes up). When *x* goes up from 2 to 6, the change in *x* is 4—that is, Δx equals 4. That change in *x* brings about an increase in *y* from 3 to 6, so Δy equals 3. The slope ($\Delta y/\Delta x$) equals ¾. Part (b) shows a negative slope (when *x* goes up, *y* goes down). When *x* goes up from 2 to 6, Δx equals 4. That change in *x* brings about a decrease in *y* from 6 to 3, so Δy equals −3. The slope ($\Delta y/\Delta x$) equals −¾.

In part (b), when x increases from 2 to 6, y decreases from 6 to 3. The change in y is *minus* 3—that is, Δy is −3. The change in x is *plus* 4—that is, Δx is +4. The slope of the curve is

$$\frac{\Delta y}{\Delta x} = \frac{-3}{4}.$$

Notice that the two slopes have the same magnitude (3/4), but the slope of the line in part (a) is positive (+3/+4 = 3/4), while that in part (b) is negative (−3/+4 = −3/4). The slope of a positive relationship is positive; the slope of a negative relationship is negative.

Calculating Slope of a Curved Line

Calculating the slope of a curved line is trickier. The slope of a curved line is not constant. Its slope depends on where on the line we calculate it. There are two ways to calculate the slope of a curved line: you can calculate the slope at a point on the line, or you can calculate the slope across an arc of the line. Let's look at the two alternatives.

Slope at a Point To calculate the slope at a point on a curved line, you need to construct a straight line that has the same slope as the curve at the point in question. Figure 2.14 shows how such a calculation is made. Suppose you want to calculate the

FIGURE 2.14

The Slope of a Curve

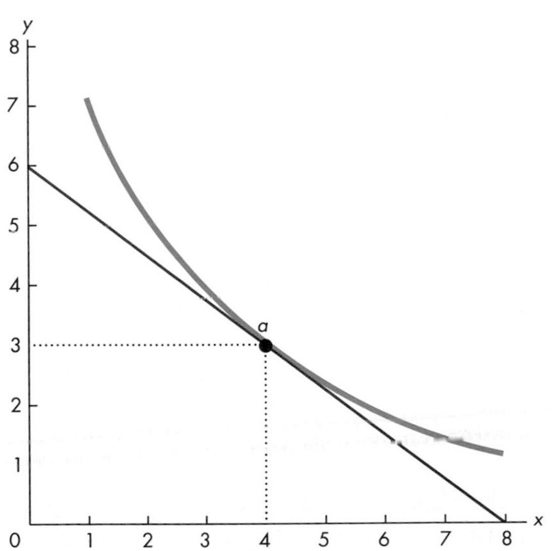

(a) Slope at a point

The slope of a curve can be calculated either at a point, as in part (a), or across an arc, as in part (b). The slope at a point is calculated by finding the slope of a straight line that touches the curve only at one point. One such straight line touches the curve at point *a*. The slope of that straight line is calculated by dividing the change in y by the change in x. When x increases from 0 to 8, Δx equals 8. That change in x is associated with a fall in y from 6 to 0, so Δy equals −6. The slope of the line is −6⁄8, or −3⁄4.

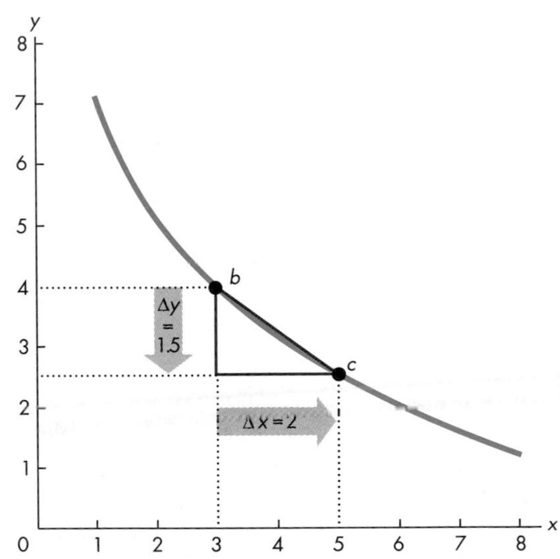

(b) Slope across an arc

To calculate the slope across an arc, we place a straight line across the curve from one point to another and then calculate the slope of that straight line. One such line is that from *b* to *c* in part (b). The slope of the straight line *bc* is calculated by dividing the change in y by the change in x. In moving from *b* to *c*, x goes up by 2, Δx equals 2, and y goes down by 1½, Δy equals −1½. The slope of the line *bc* is −1½ divided by 2, or −3⁄4.

slope of the curve at the point marked *a*. Place a ruler on the graph so that it touches point *a* and no other point on the curve; then draw a straight line along the edge of the ruler. The straight red line in part (a) is such a line. If the ruler touches the curve only at point *a*, then the slope of the curve at point *a* must be the same as the slope of the edge of the ruler. If the curve and the ruler do not have the same slope, the line along the edge of the ruler will cut the curve instead of just touching it.

Having now found a straight line with the same slope as the curve at point *a*, you can calculate the slope of the curve at point *a* by calculating the slope of the straight line. We already know how to calculate the slope of a straight line, so the task is straightforward. In this case, as x increases from 0 to 8 ($\Delta x = 8$), y decreases from 6 to 0 ($\Delta y = -6$). Therefore the slope of the straight line is

$$\frac{\Delta y}{\Delta x} = \frac{-6}{8} = \frac{-3}{4}.$$

Thus the slope of the curve at point *a* is –3/4.

Slope across an Arc Calculating a slope across an arc is similar to calculating an average slope. In Fig. 2.14(b), we are looking at the same curve as in part (a), but instead of calculating the slope at point *a*, we calculate the slope for a change in x from 3 to 5. As x increases from 3 to 5, y decreases from 4 to 2½. The change in x is +2 ($\Delta x = 2$). The change in y is –1½ ($\Delta y = -1\frac{1}{2}$). Therefore the slope of the line is

$$\frac{\Delta y}{\Delta x} = \frac{-1\frac{1}{2}}{2} = \frac{-3}{4}.$$

This calculation gives us the slope of the line between points *b* and *c*. In this particular example, the slope of the arc *bc* is identical to the slope of the curve at point *a* in part (a). Calculating the slope does not always work out so neatly. You might have some fun constructing counterexamples.

Graphing Relationships among More Than Two Variables

e have seen that we can graph a single variable as a point on a straight line and we can graph the relationship between two variables as a point formed by the x- and y-coordinates in a two-dimensional graph. You might be suspecting that although a two-dimensional graph is informative, most of the things in which you are likely to be interested involve relationships among many variables, not just two.

Examples of relationships among more than two variables abound. For example, consider the relationship between the price of ice cream, the air temperature, and the amount of ice cream eaten. If ice cream is expensive and the temperature is low, people eat much less ice cream than when ice cream is inexpensive and the temperature is high. For any given price of ice cream, the quantity consumed varies with the temperature; for any given temperature, the quantity of ice cream consumed varies with its price.

Other Things Being Equal

Figure 2.15 illustrates such a situation. The table shows the number of gallons of ice cream that will be eaten each day at various temperatures and ice cream prices. How can we graph all these numbers? To graph a relationship that involves more than two variables, we consider what happens if all but two of the variables are held constant. This device is called ceteris paribus. **Ceteris paribus** is a Latin phrase that means "other things being equal." For example, in Fig. 2.15(a), you can see what happens to the quantity of ice cream consumed when the price of ice cream varies while the temperature is held constant. The line labeled 70°F shows the relationship between ice cream consumption and the price of ice cream when the temperature stays at 70°F. The numbers used to plot that line are those in the third column of the table in Fig. 2.15. For example, when the temperature is 70°F, 18 gallons are consumed when the price is 30¢ a scoop and 13 gallons are consumed when the price is 45¢. The curve labeled 90°F shows the consumption of ice cream when the price varies and the temperature is 90°F.

Alternatively, we can show the relationship between ice cream consumption and temperature while holding the price of ice cream constant, as is shown in Fig. 2.15(b). The curve labeled 30¢ shows how the consumption of ice cream varies with the temperature when ice cream costs 30¢, and a second curve shows the relationship when ice cream costs 15¢. For example, at 30¢ a scoop, 12 gallons are

FIGURE 2.15

Graphing a Relationship among Three Variables

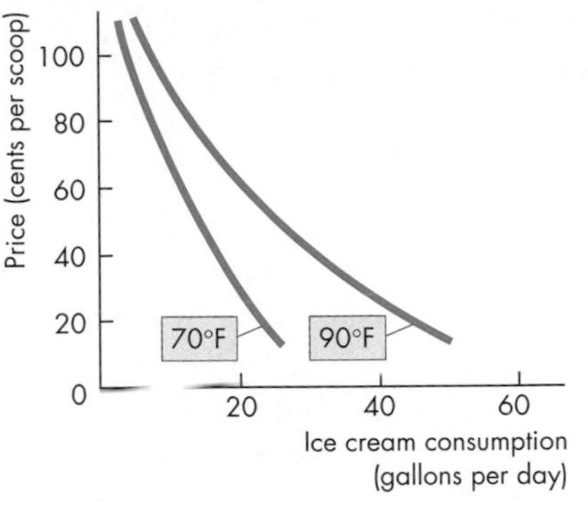

(a) Price and consumption at a given temperature

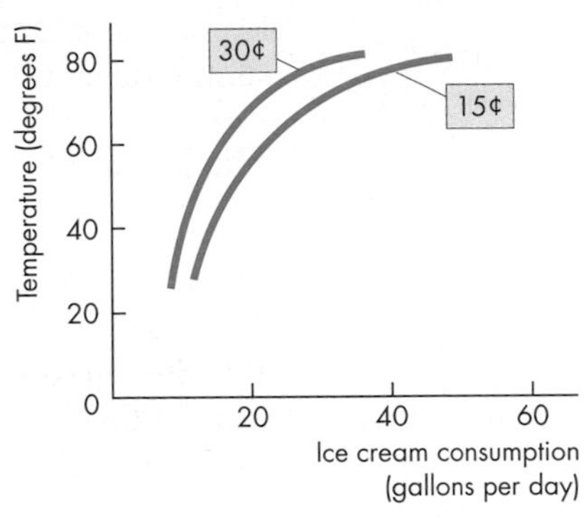

(b) Temperature and consumption at a given price

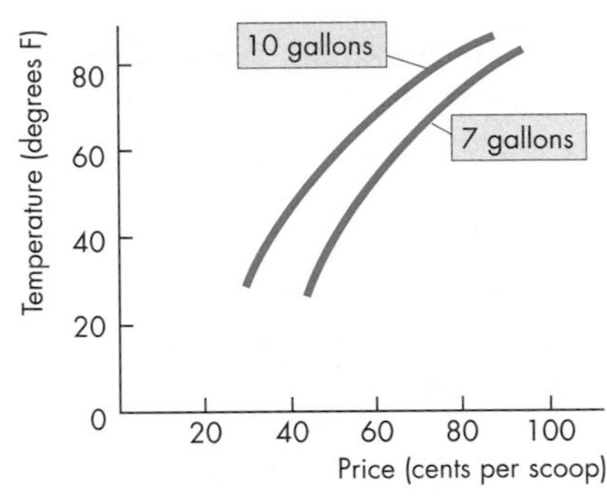

(c) Temperature and price at a given consumption

Price (cents per scoop)	Ice cream consumption (gallons per day)			
	30°F	50°F	70°F	90°F
15	**12**	**18**	**25**	**50**
30	**10**	**12**	**18**	**37**
45	**7**	**10**	**13**	**27**
60	**5**	**7**	**10**	**20**
75	**3**	**5**	**7**	**14**
90	**2**	**3**	**5**	**10**
105	**1**	**2**	**3**	**6**

The quantity of ice cream consumed (one variable) depends on its price (a second variable) and the air temperature (a third variable). The table provides some hypothetical numbers that tell us how many gallons of ice cream are consumed each day at different prices and different temperatures. For example, if the price is 45¢ per scoop and the temperature is 50°F, 10 gallons of ice cream will be consumed. To graph a relationship among three variables, the value of one variable must be held constant.

Part (a) shows the relationship between price and consumption, holding temperature constant. One curve holds temperature constant at 90°F and the other at 70°F. Part (b) shows the relationship between temperature and consumption, holding price constant. One curve holds the price at 30¢ and the other at 15¢. Part (c) shows the relationship between temperature and price, holding consumption constant. One curve holds consumption constant at 10 gallons and the other at 7 gallons.

consumed when the temperature is 50°F and 18 gallons when the temperature is 70°F.

Figure 2.15(c) shows the combinations of temperature and price that result in a constant consumption of ice cream. One curve shows the combination that results in 10 gallons a day being consumed, and the other shows the combination that results in 7 gallons a day being consumed. A high price and a high temperature lead to the same consumption as a lower price and lower temperature. For example, 7 gallons are consumed at 30°F and 45 cents per scoop and at 70°F and 75 cents per scoop.

◆ ◆ ◆ ◆ With what you have now learned about graphs, you can move forward with your study of economics. There are no graphs in this book that are more complicated than those that have been explained here.

SUMMARY

Graphing Data

There are two main types of graphs used to represent economic data: scatter diagrams and time-series graphs. A scatter diagram plots the value of one economic variable associated with the value of another. Such a diagram reveals whether or not there is a relationship between two variables and, if there is a relationship, its nature.

A time-series graph plots the value of one or more economic variables on the vertical axis (y-axis) and time on the horizontal axis (x-axis). A well-constructed time-series graph quickly reveals the level, direction of change, and speed of change of a variable. It also reveals trends. Graphs sometimes mislead, especially when the origin is omitted or when the scale is stretched or squeezed to exaggerate or understate a variation. (pp. 29–38)

Graphs Used in Economic Models

Graphs are used in economic models to illustrate relationships between variables. There are four cases: positive relationships, negative relationships, relationships that have a maximum or a minimum, and variables that are not related to each other. Examples of these different types of relationships are summarized in Figs. 2.9 through 2.12. (pp. 38–41)

The Slope of a Relationship

The slope of a relationship is calculated as the change in the value of the variable measured on the y-axis divided by the change in the value of the variable measured on the x-axis, that is, $\Delta y/\Delta x$. A straight line has a constant slope, but a curved line has a varying slope. To calculate the slope of a curved line, we calculate the slope either at a point or across an arc. (pp. 42–44)

Graphing Relationships among More Than Two Variables

To graph a relationship among more than two variables, we hold constant the values of all the variables except two. We then plot the value of one of the variables against the value of another. Holding constant all the variables but two is called the ceteris paribus assumption—the assumption of other things being equal. (pp. 44–45)

KEY ELEMENTS

Key Terms

Axes, 29
Ceteris paribus, 44
Coordinates, 30
Curve, 38
Linear relationship, 38
Negative relationship, 38
Origin, 29
Positive relationship, 38
Scatter diagram, 30
Slope, 42
Time-series graph, 32
Trend, 33
x-axis, 29
x-coordinate, 30
y-axis, 29
y-coordinate, 30

Key Figures

Figure 2.9 Positive Relationships, 39
Figure 2.10 Negative Relationships, 39
Figure 2.11 Maximum and Minimum Points, 40
Figure 2.12 Variables with No Relationship, 41
Figure 2.13 The Slope of a Straight Line, 42
Figure 2.14 The Slope of a Curve, 43
Figure 2.15 Graphing a Relationship among Three Variables, 45

REVIEW QUESTIONS

1 Why do we use graphs?

2 What are the two scale lines on a graph called?

3 What is the origin on a graph?

4 What do we mean by the *y*-coordinate and the *x*-coordinate?

5 What is a scatter diagram?

6 What is a time-series graph?

7 List three things that a time-series graph shows quickly and easily.

8 What do we mean by trend?

9 Sketch some graphs to illustrate the following:

a Two variables that move up and down together

b Two variables that move in opposite directions

c A relationship between two variables that has a maximum

d A relationship between two variables that has a minimum

10 Which of the relationships in question 9 is a positive relationship and which a negative relationship?

11 What is the definition of the slope of a relationship?

12 What are the two ways of calculating the slope of a curved line?

13 How do we graph relationships among more than two variables?

PROBLEMS

1 The inflation rate in the United States between 1970 and 1990 was as follows:

Year	Inflation rate (percent per year)
1970	5.7
1971	4.4
1972	3.2
1973	6.2
1974	11.0
1975	9.1
1976	5.8
1977	6.5
1978	7.6
1979	11.3
1980	13.5
1981	10.3
1982	6.2
1983	3.2
1984	4.3
1985	3.6
1986	1.9
1987	3.6
1988	4.1
1989	4.8
1990	5.4

Draw a time-series graph of these data, and use your graph to answer the following questions:

a In which year was inflation highest?

b In which year was inflation lowest?

c In which years did inflation rise?

d In which years did inflation fall?

e In which year did inflation rise/fall the fastest?

f In which year did inflation rise/fall the slowest?

g What have been the main trends in inflation?

2 Interest rates on treasury bills in the United States between 1970 and 1990 were as follows:

Year	Interest rate (percent per year)
1970	6.5
1971	4.3

Year	Interest rate (percent per year)
1972	4.1
1973	7.0
1974	7.9
1975	5.8
1976	5.0
1977	5.3
1978	7.2
1979	10.0
1980	11.5
1981	14.0
1982	10.7
1983	8.6
1984	9.6
1985	7.5
1986	6.0
1987	5.8
1988	6.7
1989	8.1
1990	7.5

Use these data together with those in problem 1 to draw a scatter diagram showing the relationship between inflation and the interest rate. Use this diagram to determine whether there is a relationship between inflation and the interest rate and whether it is positive or negative.

3 Use the following information to draw a graph showing the relationship between two variables x and y:

x	0	1	2	3	4	5	6	7	8
y	0	1	4	9	16	25	36	49	64

a Is the relationship between x and y positive or negative?

b Does the slope of the relationship rise or fall as the value of x rises?

4 Using the data in problem 3:

a Calculate the slope of the relationship between x and y when x equals 4.

b Calculate the slope of the arc when x rises from 3 to 4.

c Calculate the slope of the arc when x rises from 4 to 5.

d Calculate the slope of the arc when x rises from 3 to 5.

e What do you notice that is interesting about your answers to (b), (c), and (d) compared with your answer to (a)?

5 Calculate the slopes of the following two relationships between two variables x and y:

a

x	0	2	4	6	8	10
y	20	16	12	8	4	0

b

x	0	2	4	6	8	10
y	0	8	16	24	32	40

6 Draw a graph showing the following relationship between two variables x and y:

x	0	1	2	3	4	5	6	7	8	9
y	0	2	4	6	8	10	8	6	4	2

a Is the slope positive or negative when x is less than 5?

b Is the slope positive or negative when x is greater than 5?

c What is the slope of this relationship when x equals 5?

d Is y at a maximum or at a minimum when x equals 5?

7 Draw a graph showing the following relationship between two variables x and y:

x	0	1	2	3	4	5	6	7	8	9
y	10	8	6	4	2	0	2	4	6	8

a Is the slope positive or negative when x is less than 5?

b Is the slope positive or negative when x is greater than 5?

c What is the slope of this relationship when x equals 5?

d Is y at a maximum or at a minimum when x equals 5?

CHAPTER 3

PRODUCTION, SPECIALIZATION, AND EXCHANGE

After studying this chapter, you will be able to:

- Define the production possibility frontier
- Calculate opportunity cost
- Explain why economic growth and technological change do not provide free gifts
- Explain comparative advantage
- Explain why people specialize and how they gain from trade
- Explain why property rights and money have evolved

E LIVE IN A STYLE THAT MOST OF OUR GRANDPARENTS could not even have imagined. Advances in medicine have cured diseases that terrified them. Most of us live in better and more spacious homes. We eat more, we grow taller, we are even born larger than they were. Our parents are amazed at the matter-of-fact way in which we handle computers. We casually use products—microwave ovens, graphite tennis rackets, digital watches—that didn't exist in their youth. Economic growth has made us richer than our parents and grandparents. ◆◆ But economic growth and technological change, and the wealth they bestow, have not liberated us from scarcity. Why not? Why, despite our immense wealth, do we still have to face costs? Why are there no "free lunches"? ◆◆ We see an incredible amount of specialization and trading in the modern world. Each one of us specializes in a particular job—as lawyer, car maker, homemaker. Countries and regions also specialize—Florida in orange juice, Idaho in potatoes, Detroit in cars, and the Silicon Valley in computer-related products. We have become so specialized that one farm worker can feed 100 people. Only one in five of us works in manufacturing. More than half of us work in wholesale and retail trade, banking and finance, other services, and government. Why do we specialize? How do we benefit from specialization and exchange? ◆◆ Over many centuries, institutions and social arrangements have evolved that today we take for granted. One of them is private property rights, together with the legal system that protects them. Another is money. Why have these institutions evolved? And how do they extend our ability to specialize and increase production?

Making the Most of It

◆ ◆ ◆ ◆ These are the questions that we tackle in this chapter. We will begin by making the idea of scarcity more precise. Then we will go on to see how we can measure opportunity cost. We will also see how, when each individual tries to get the most out of scarce resources, specialization and exchange occur. That is, people specialize in doing what they do best and exchange their products with other specialists. We are also going to see why such institutions as private property and money exist and how they arise from people's attempts to make the most of their limited resources.

The Production Possibility Frontier

What do we mean by production? **Production** is the conversion of *land, labor,* and *capital* into goods and services. We defined the factors of production in Chapter 1. Let's briefly recall what they are.

Land is all the gifts of nature. It includes the air, the water, and the land surface, as well as the minerals that lie beneath the surface of the earth. *Labor* is all the muscle-power and brain-power of human beings. The voices and artistry of singers and actors, the strength and coordination of athletes, the daring of astronauts, the political skill of diplomats, as well as the physical and mental skills of the many millions of people who make cars and cola, gum and glue, wallpaper and watering cans are included in this category.

Capital is all the goods that have been produced and can now be used in the production of other goods and services. Examples include the interstate highway system, the fine buildings of great cities, dams and power projects, airports and jumbo jets, car production lines, shirt factories, and cookie shops. A special kind of capital is called human capital. **Human capital** is the accumulated skill and knowledge of human beings, which arise from their training and education.

Goods and services are all the valuable things that people produce. Goods are tangible—cars, spoons, VCRs, and bread. Services are intangible—haircuts, amusement park rides, and telephone calls. There are two types of goods: capital goods and consumption goods. **Capital goods** are goods that are used in the production process and can be used many times before they eventually wear out. Examples of capital goods are buildings, computers, automobiles, and telephones. **Consumption goods** are goods that can be used just once. Examples are dill pickles and toothpaste. **Consumption** is the process of using up goods and services.

Our limited resources and the technologies available for transforming those resources into goods and services limit what can be produced. That limit is described by the production possibility frontier. The **production possibility frontier** (PPF) marks the boundary between those combinations of goods and services that can be produced and those that cannot. It is important to understand the production possibility frontier in the real world, but to achieve that goal more easily, we will first study an economy that is simpler than the one in which we live— a model economy.

A Model Economy

Instead of looking at the real-world economy with all its complexity and detail, we will build a model of an economy. The model will have features that are essential to understanding the real economy, but we will ignore most of reality's immense detail. Our model economy will be simpler in three important ways:

1. Everything that is produced is also consumed so that in our model, capital resources neither grow nor shrink. (Later we will examine what happens if we consume less than we produce and add to capital resources.)
2. There are only two goods, corn and cloth. (In the real world we use our scarce resources to produce countless goods and services.)
3. There is only one person, Jane, who lives on a deserted island and has no dealings with other people. (Later we will see what happens when Jane's island economy has links with another economy. Also, we'll extend our view to the real world with its five billion people.)

Jane uses all the resources of her island economy to produce corn and cloth. She works 10 hours each day. The amount of corn and cloth that Jane produces depends on how many hours she devotes to

TABLE 3.1

Jane's Production Possibilities

Hours worked (per day)		Corn grown (pounds per month)		Cloth produced (yards per month)
0	either	0	or	0
2	either	6	or	1
4	either	11	or	2
6	either	15	or	3
8	either	18	or	4
10	either	20	or	5

If Jane does no work, she produces no corn or cloth. If she works for 2 hours per day and spends the entire amount of time on corn production, she produces 6 pounds of corn per month. If that same time is used for cloth production, 1 yard of cloth is produced but no corn. The last four rows of the table show the amounts of corn or cloth that can be produced per month as more hours are devoted to each activity.

producing them. Table 3.1 sets out Jane's production possibilities for corn and cloth. If she does no work, she produces nothing. Two hours a day devoted to corn farming produces 6 pounds of corn per month. Devoting more hours to corn increases the output of corn, but there is a decline in the extra amount of corn that comes from extra effort. The reason for this decline is that Jane has to use increasingly unsuitable land for growing corn. At first, she plants corn on a lush, flat plain. Eventually, when she has used all the arable land, she has to start planting on the rocky hills and the edge of the beach. The numbers in the second column of the table show how the output of corn rises as the number of hours devoted to cultivating it rises.

To produce cloth, Jane gathers wool from sheep that live on the island. As she devotes more hours to collecting wool and making cloth, her output rises. The numbers in the third column of Table 3.1 show how the output of cloth rises as the number of hours devoted to this activity rises.

If Jane devotes all her time to growing corn, she can produce 20 pounds of corn in a month. In that case, however, she cannot produce any cloth. Conversely, if she devotes all her time to making cloth, she can produce 5 yards a month but will have no time left for growing corn. Jane can devote some of her time to corn and some to cloth but not more than 10 hours a day total. Thus she can spend 2 hours growing corn and 8 hours making cloth or 6 hours on one and 4 hours on the other (or any other combination of hours that add up to 10 hours).

We have defined the production possibility frontier as the boundary between what is attainable and what is not attainable. You can calculate Jane's production possibility frontier by using the information in Table 3.1. These calculations are summarized in the table in Fig. 3.1 and graphed in that figure as Jane's production possibility frontier. To see how we calculated that frontier, let's concentrate first on the table in Fig. 3.1.

Possibility *a* shows Jane devoting no time to cloth and her entire 10-hour working day to corn. In this case, she can produce 20 pounds of corn per month and no cloth. For possibility *b*, she spends 2 hours a day making cloth and 8 hours growing corn, to produce a total of 18 pounds of corn and 1 yard of cloth a month. The pattern continues on to possibility *f*, where she devotes 10 hours a day to cloth and no time to corn. These same numbers are plotted in the graph shown in Fig. 3.1. Yards of cloth are measured on the horizontal axis and pounds of corn on the vertical axis. Points *a*, *b*, *c*, *d*, *e*, and *f* represent the numbers in the corresponding row of the table.

Of course, Jane does not have to work in blocks of 2 hours, as in our example. She can work 1 hour or 1 hour and 10 minutes growing corn and devote the rest of her time to making cloth. All other feasible allocations of Jane's 10 hours enable her to produce the combinations of corn and cloth described by the line that joins points *a*, *b*, *c*, *d*, *e*, and *f*. This line shows Jane's production possibility frontier. She can produce at any point on the frontier or inside it, within the orange area. These are attainable points. Points outside the frontier are unattainable. To produce at points beyond the frontier, Jane needs more time than she has—more than 10 hours a day. By working 10 hours a day producing both corn and cloth, Jane can choose any point she wishes on the frontier. And by working less than 10 hours a day, or by not putting her resources to their best possible use—by wasting some of her resources—she can produce at a point inside the frontier.

FIGURE 3.1

Jane's Production Possibility Frontier

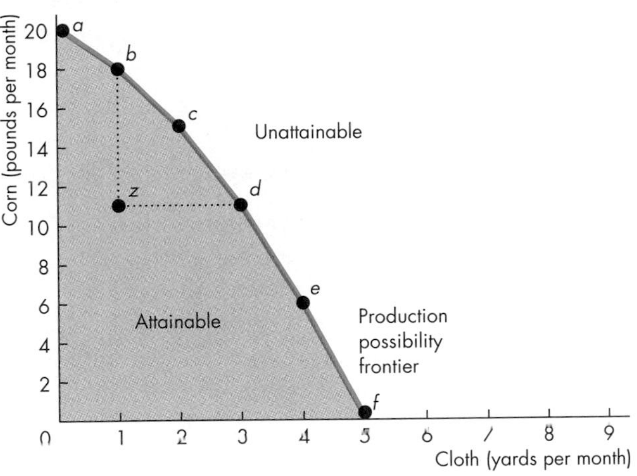

Possibility	Corn (pounds per month)		Cloth (yards per month)
a	20	and	0
b	18	and	1
c	15	and	2
d	11	and	3
e	6	and	4
f	0	and	5

The table lists six points on Jane's production possibility frontier. Row *e* tells us that if Jane produces 6 pounds of corn, the maximum cloth production that is possible is 4 yards. These same points are graphed as points *a, b, c, d, e,* and *f* in the figure. The line passing through these points is Jane's production possibility frontier, which separates the attainable from the unattainable. The attainable orange area contains all the possible production points. Jane can produce anywhere inside this area or on the production possibility frontier. Points outside the frontier are unattainable. Jane prefers points on the frontier to any point inside. She prefers points between *b* and *d* on the frontier to point *z* inside the frontier because they give her more of both goods.

Jane's Preferences

Jane produces corn and cloth not for the fun of it, but so that she can eat and keep warm. She wants much more corn and cloth than she can produce, and the more of each she has, the better she likes it. Because Jane wants as much as possible of both corn and cloth, the best she can do is to produce—and therefore consume—at a point *on* her production possibility frontier. To see why, consider a point such as *z* in the attainable region. At point *z*, Jane is wasting resources. She may be taking time off work, but leisure time on the island is not worth anything to Jane. Or she may not be using her sheep and her cornfields as effectively as possible. Jane can improve her situation at *z* by moving to a point such as *b* or *d* or to a point on the frontier between *b* and *d*, such as point *c*. Jane can have more of both goods on the frontier than at points inside it. At point *b*, she can consume more corn and no less cloth than at point *z*. At point *d*, she can consume more cloth and no less corn than at point *z*. At point *c*, she can consume more corn and more cloth than at point *z*. Jane will never choose points such as *z* because preferred points, such as *b*, *c*, and *d*, are available to her. That is, Jane prefers some point on the frontier to a point inside it.

We have just seen that Jane wants to produce at some point on her production possibility frontier, but she is still faced with the problem of choosing her preferred point. In choosing between one point and another, Jane is confronted with opportunity costs. At point *c*, for example, she has less cloth and more corn than at point *d*. If she chooses point *d*, she does so because she figures that the extra cloth is worth the corn forgone. Let's go on to explore opportunity cost more closely and see how we can measure it.

REVIEW

The production possibility frontier is the boundary between the attainable and the unattainable. There is always a point on the frontier that is preferred to any point inside it. But moving from one point on the frontier to another involves an opportunity cost—having less of one good to get more of another. ◆

Opportunity Cost

We've defined opportunity cost as the best alternative forgone: for a late sleeper, the opportunity cost of attending an early morning class is an hour in bed; for a jogger, it is an hour of exercise. The concept of opportunity cost can be made more precise by using a production possibility frontier such as the one shown in Fig. 3.1. Let's see what that curve tells us.

The Best Alternative Forgone

The production possibility frontier in Fig. 3.1 traces the boundary between attainable and unattainable combinations of corn and cloth. Since there are only two goods, there is no difficulty in working out what is the best alternative forgone. More corn can be grown only by paying the price of having less cloth, and more cloth can be made only by bearing the cost of having less corn. Thus the opportunity cost of an additional yard of cloth is the amount of corn forgone, and the opportunity cost of producing an additional pound of corn is the amount of cloth forgone. Let's put numerical values on the opportunity costs of corn and cloth.

Measuring Opportunity Cost

We are going to measure opportunity cost by using Jane's production possibility frontier. We will calculate how much cloth she has to give up to get more corn and how much corn she has to give up to get more cloth.

If all Jane's time is used to produce corn, she produces 20 pounds of corn and no cloth. If she decides to produce 1 yard of cloth, how much corn does she have to give up? You can see the answer in Fig. 3.2. To produce 1 yard of cloth, Jane moves from *a* to *b* and gives up 2 pounds of corn. Thus the opportunity cost of the first yard of cloth is 2 pounds of corn. If she decides to produce an additional yard of cloth, how much corn does she give up? This time, Jane moves from *b* to *c* and gives up 3 pounds of corn to produce the second yard of cloth.

These opportunity costs are set out in the table of Fig. 3.2. The first two rows set out the opportunity costs that we have just calculated. The table also lists the opportunity costs of moving between points *c*, *d*, *e*, and *f* on Jane's production possibility frontier of Fig. 3.1. You might want to work out another example on your own to be sure that you understand what is going on. Calculate Jane's opportunity cost of moving from *e* to *f*.

Increasing Opportunity Cost

As you can see, opportunity cost varies with the quantity produced. The first yard of cloth costs 2 pounds of corn. The next yard of cloth costs 3 pounds of corn. The last yard of cloth costs 6 pounds of corn. Thus the opportunity cost of cloth increases as Jane produces more cloth. Figure 3.2(a) illustrates the increasing opportunity cost of cloth.

The Shape of the Frontier

Pay special attention to the shape of the production possibility frontier in Fig. 3.1. When a large amount of corn and not much cloth is produced—between points *a* and *b*—the frontier has a gentle slope. When a large amount of cloth and not much corn is produced—between points *e* and *f*—the frontier is steep. The whole frontier bows outward. These features of the production possibility frontier are a reflection of increasing opportunity cost. You can see the connection between increasing opportunity cost and the shape of the production possibility frontier in Fig. 3.2(b). Between points *a* and *b*, 1 yard of cloth can be obtained by giving up a small amount of corn. Here the opportunity cost of cloth is low, and the opportunity cost of corn is high. Between points *e* and *f*, a large amount of corn must be given up to produce 1 extra yard of cloth. In this region, the opportunity cost of cloth is high, and the opportunity cost of corn is low.

Everything Has an Increasing Opportunity Cost

We've just worked out the opportunity cost of cloth. But what about the opportunity cost of corn? Does it also increase as more of it is produced? You can see the answer in Fig. 3.2. By giving up 1 yard of

FIGURE 3.2

Jane's Opportunity Costs of Corn and Cloth

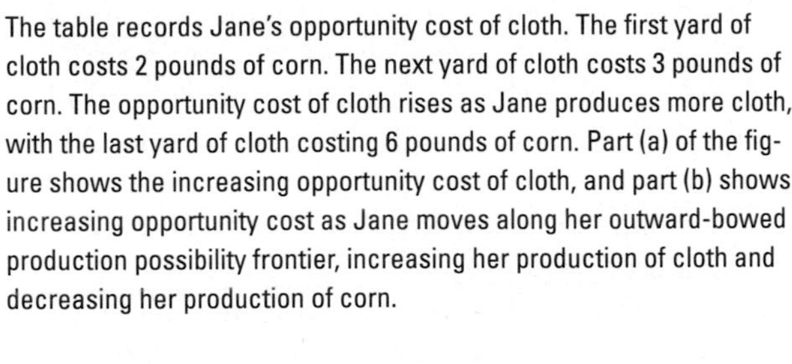

The table records Jane's opportunity cost of cloth. The first yard of cloth costs 2 pounds of corn. The next yard of cloth costs 3 pounds of corn. The opportunity cost of cloth rises as Jane produces more cloth, with the last yard of cloth costing 6 pounds of corn. Part (a) of the figure shows the increasing opportunity cost of cloth, and part (b) shows increasing opportunity cost as Jane moves along her outward-bowed production possibility frontier, increasing her production of cloth and decreasing her production of corn.

As Jane increases her cloth production:

First **1** yard of cloth costs **2** pounds of corn
Next **1** yard of cloth costs **3** pounds of corn
Next **1** yard of cloth costs **4** pounds of corn
Next **1** yard of cloth costs **5** pounds of corn
Last yard of cloth costs **6** pounds of corn

Opportunity cost of cloth (pounds of corn per yard of cloth)
8
6
4
2
0
1 2 3 4 5
Cloth (yards per month)

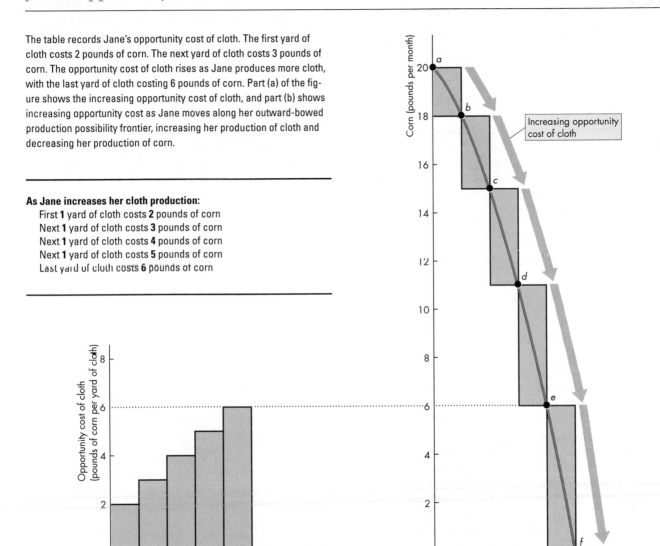

(a) Opportunity cost of cloth

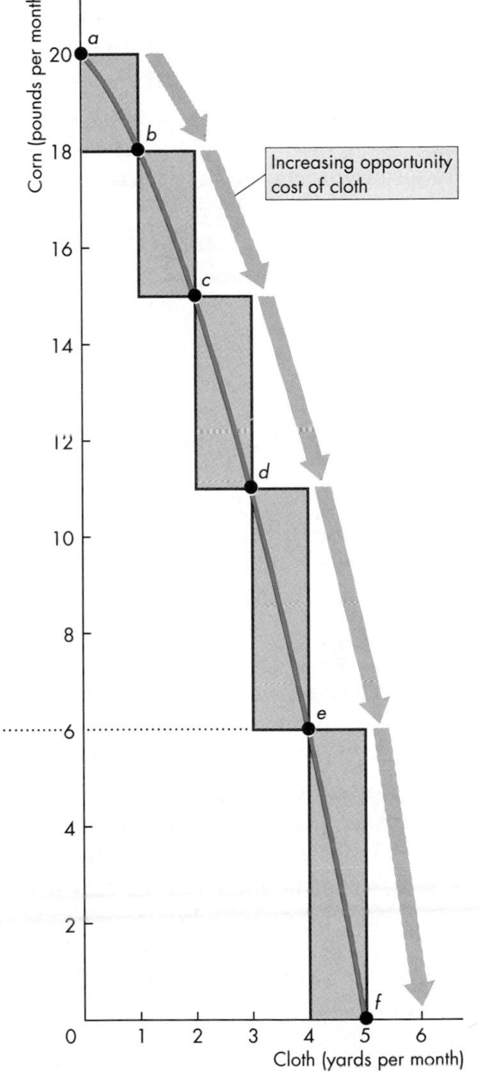

(b) Opportunity cost along the PPF

cloth to produce some corn, Jane moves from *f* to *e* and produces 6 pounds of corn. Thus the opportunity cost of the first 6 pounds of corn is 1 yard of cloth. Moving from *e* to *d*, you can see that the next 5 pounds of corn cost 1 yard of cloth. Thus the opportunity cost of corn also increases as Jane makes more corn.

Increasing opportunity cost and the outward bow of the production possibility frontier arise from the fact that scarce resources are not equally useful in all activities. For instance, some of the land on Jane's island is extremely fertile and produces a high crop yield, while other land is rocky and barren. The sheep on the island, however, prefer the rocky, barren land.

Jane uses the most fertile land for growing corn and the most barren areas for raising sheep. Only if she wants a larger amount of corn does she try to cultivate relatively barren areas. If she uses all her time to grow corn, she has to use some very unsuitable, low-yielding land. Devoting some time to making cloth, and reducing the time spent growing corn by the same amount, produces a small drop in corn production but a large increase in the output of cloth. Conversely, if Jane uses all her time to make cloth, a small reduction in woolgathering yields a large increase of corn production.

Production Possibilities in the Real World

Jane's island is dramatically different from the world that we live in. The fundamental lesson it teaches us, however, applies to the real world. The world has a fixed number of people endowed with a given amount of human capital and limited time. The world also has a fixed amount of land and capital equipment. These limited resources can be employed, using the available but limited technology to produce goods and services. But there is a limit to the goods and services that can be produced, a boundary between what is attainable and what is not attainable. That boundary is the real-world economy's production possibility frontier. On that frontier, producing more of any one good requires producing less of some other good or goods.

For example, a presidential candidate who promises better welfare and education services must at the same time, to be credible, promise either cuts in defense spending or higher taxes. Higher taxes mean less money left over for vacations and other consumption goods and services. The cost of better welfare and educational services is less of other goods. On a smaller scale but equally important, each time you decide to rent a video, you decide not to use your limited income to buy soda, popcorn, or some other good. The cost of one more video is one less of something else.

On Jane's island, we saw that the opportunity cost of a good increased as the output of the good increased. Opportunity costs in the real world increase for the same reasons that Jane's opportunity costs increase. Consider, for example, two goods vital to our well-being: food and health care. In allocating our scarce resources, we use the most fertile land and the most skillful farmers to produce food. We use the best doctors and the least fertile land for health care. If we shift fertile land and tractors away from farming and ask farmers to do surgery, the production of food drops drastically and the increase in the production of health care services is small. The opportunity cost of health care services rises. Similarly, if we shift our resources away from health care toward farming, we have to use more doctors and nurses as farmers and more hospitals as hydroponic tomato factories. The drop in health care services is large, but the increase in food production small. The opportunity cost of producing more food rises.

This example is extreme and unlikely, but these same considerations apply to any pair of goods that you can imagine: guns and butter, housing for the needy and diamonds for the rich, wheelchairs and golf carts, television programs and breakfast cereals. We cannot escape from scarcity and opportunity cost. Given our limited resources, more of one thing always means less of something else, and the more of anything that we have or do, the higher is its opportunity cost.

REVIEW

Opportunity cost is the value of the best alternative forgone. It is measured along the production possibility frontier by calculating the number of units of one good that must be given up to obtain one more unit of the other good. The production possibility frontier is bowed outward because not all resources are equally useful for producing all goods. The most useful resources are employed first. Because the frontier is bowed outward, the opportunity cost of each good increases as more of it is produced. ◆

Economic Growth

Although the production possibility frontier defines the boundary between what is attainable and what is unattainable, that boundary is not static. It is constantly changing. Sometimes the production possibility frontier shifts *inward,* reducing our production possibilities. For example, droughts or other extreme climatic conditions shift the frontier inward. Sometimes the frontier moves outward. For example, excellent growing and harvest conditions have this effect. Sometimes the frontier shifts outward because we get a new idea. It suddenly occurs to us that there is a better way of doing something that we never before imagined possible—we invent the wheel.

Over the years, our production possibilities have undergone enormous expansion. The expansion of our production possibilities is called **economic growth.** As a consequence of economic growth, we can now produce much more than we could a hundred years ago and quite a bit more than even ten years ago. By the late 1990s, if the same pace of growth continues, our production possibilities will be even greater. By pushing out the frontier, can we avoid the constraints imposed on us by our limited resources? That is, can we get our free lunch after all?

The Cost of Economic Growth

We are going to discover that although we can and do increase our production possibilities, we cannot have economic growth without incurring costs. The faster the pace of economic growth, the less we can consume at the present time. Let's investigate the costs of growth by examining why economies grow and prosper.

Two key activities generate economic growth: capital accumulation and technological progress. **Capital accumulation** is the growth of capital resources. **Technological progress** is the development of new and better ways of producing goods and services. As a consequence of capital accumulation and technological progress, we have an enormous quantity of cars and airplanes that enable us to produce more transportation than when we had only horses and carriages; we have satellites that make transcontinental communications possible on a scale much larger than that produced by the earlier cable technology. But accumulating capital and developing new technology are costly. To see why, let's go back to Jane's island economy.

Capital Accumulation and Technological Change

So far, we've assumed that Jane's island economy can produce only two goods, corn and cloth. But let's now suppose that while pursuing some of the sheep, Jane stumbles upon an outcrop of flint stone and a forest that she had not known about before. She realizes that she can now make some flint tools and start building fences around the corn and sheep, thereby increasing production of both of these goods. But to make tools and build fences, Jane has to devote time to these activities. Let's continue to suppose that there are only 10 hours of working time available each day. Time spent making tools and building fences is time that could have been spent growing corn and making cloth. Thus to expand her future production, Jane must produce less corn and cloth today so that some of her time can be devoted to making tools and building fences. The decrease in her output of corn and cloth today is the opportunity cost of expanding her production of these two goods in the future.

Figure 3.3 provides a concrete example. The table sets out Jane's production possibilities for producing capital—tools and fences—as well as current consumption goods—corn and cloth. If she devotes all her working hours to corn and cloth production (row *e*), she produces no capital—no tools or fences. If she devotes enough time to producing one unit of capital each month (row *d*), her corn and cloth production is cut back to 90 percent of its maximum possible level. She can devote still more time to capital accumulation, and as she does so, her corn and cloth production falls by successively larger amounts.

The numbers in the table are graphed in Fig. 3.3. Each point, *a* through *e*, represents a row of the

FIGURE 3.3

Economic Growth on Jane's Island

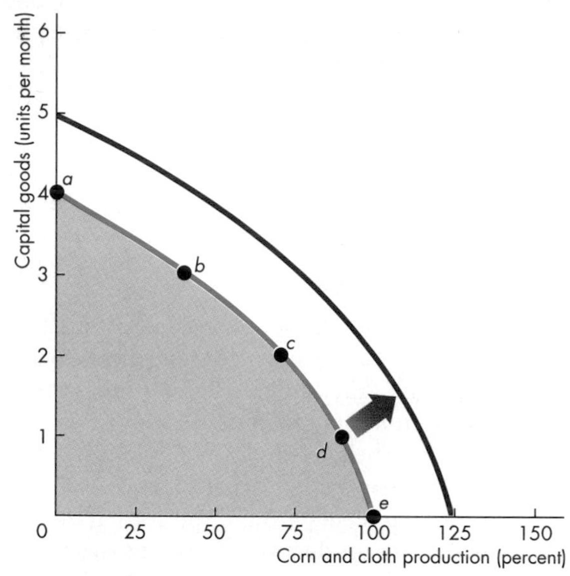

Possibility	Capital (units per month)	Corn and cloth production (percent)
a	4	0
b	3	40
c	2	70
d	1	90
e	0	100

If Jane devotes all her time to corn and cloth production, she produces no capital equipment (row *e* of the table). If she devotes more time to capital accumulation, she produces successively smaller amounts of corn and cloth. The curve *abcde* is Jane's production possibility frontier for capital and consumption goods (tools and fence versus corn and cloth). If Jane produces no capital (point *e*), her production possibility frontier remains fixed at *abcde*. If she cuts her current production of corn and cloth and produces one unit of capital (point *d*), her future production possibility frontier lies outside her current frontier. The more time Jane devotes to accumulating capital and the less to producing corn and cloth, the farther out her frontier shifts. The decreased output of corn and cloth is the opportunity cost of increased future production possibilities.

table. Notice the similarity between Fig. 3.3 and Fig. 3.1. Each shows a production possibility frontier. In the case of Fig. 3.3, the frontier is that between producing capital equipment—tools and fences—and producing current consumption goods—corn and cloth. If Jane produces at point *e* in Fig. 3.3, she produces no capital goods and remains stuck on the production possibility frontier for corn and cloth shown in Fig. 3.1. But if she moves to point *d* in Fig. 3.3, she can produce one unit of capital each month. To do so, Jane reduces her current production of corn and cloth to 90 percent of what she can produce if all her time is devoted to those activities. In terms of Fig. 3.1, Jane's current production possibility frontier for corn and cloth shifts to the left as less time is devoted to corn and cloth production and some of her time is devoted to producing capital goods.

By decreasing her production of corn and cloth and producing tools and building fences, Jane is able to increase her future production possibilities. An increasing stock of tools and fences makes her more productive at growing corn and producing cloth. She can even use tools to make better tools. As a consequence, Jane's production possibility frontier shifts outward as shown by the shift arrow. Jane experiences economic growth.

But the amount by which Jane's production possibility frontier shifts out depends on how much time she devotes to accumulating capital. If she devotes no time to this activity, the frontier remains at *abcde*—the original production possibility frontier. If she cuts back on current production of corn and cloth and produces one unit of capital each month (point *d*), her frontier moves out in the future to the position shown by the red curve in Fig. 3.3. The less time she devotes to corn and cloth production and the more time to capital accumulation, the farther out the frontier shifts.

But economic growth is not a free gift for Jane. To make it happen, she has to devote more time to producing tools and building fences and less to producing corn and cloth. Economic growth is no magic formula for abolishing scarcity.

Economic Growth in the Real World

The ideas that we have explored in the setting of Jane's island also apply to our real-world economy. If we devote all our resources to producing food, clothing, housing, vacations, and the many other consumer goods that we enjoy and none to research, development, and accumulating capital, we will have no more capital and no better technologies in the future than we have at present. Our production possibilities in the future will be exactly the same as those we have today. If we are to expand our production possibilities in the future, we must produce fewer consumption goods today. The resources that we free up today will enable us to accumulate capital and to develop better technologies for producing consumption goods in the future. The cut in the output of consumption goods today is the opportunity cost of economic growth.

The recent experience of the United States and Japan provides a striking example of the effects of our choices on the rate of economic growth. In 1965, the production possibilities per person in the United States were much larger than those in Japan (see Fig. 3.4). The United States devoted one fifth of its resources to producing capital goods and the other four fifths to producing consumption goods, as illustrated by point *a* in Fig. 3.4(a). But Japan devoted one third of its resources to producing capital goods and only two thirds to producing consumption goods, as illustrated by point *a* in Fig. 3.4(b). Both countries experienced economic growth, but the growth in Japan was much more

FIGURE 3.4

Economic Growth in the United States and Japan

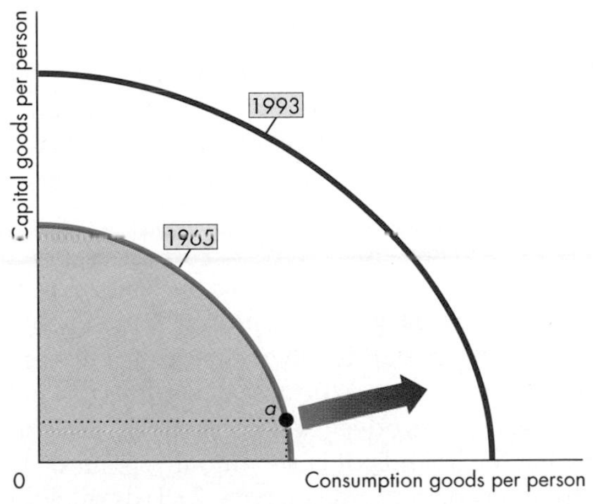

(a) United States

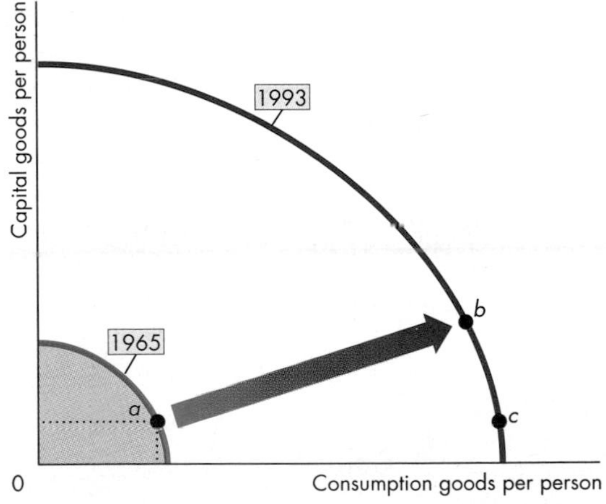

(b) Japan

In 1965, the production possibilities per person in the United States, part (a), were much larger than those in Japan, part (b). But Japan devoted one third of its resources to producing capital goods, while the United States devoted only one fifth—point *a* in each part of the figure. Japan's more rapid increase in capital resources resulted in its production possibility frontier shifting out more quickly than that of the United States. The two production possibilities per person in 1993 are similar. If Japan produces at point *b* on its 1993 frontier, it will continue to grow more quickly than the United States. If Japan increases consumption and produces at point *c* on its 1993 frontier, its growth rate will slow down to that of the United States.

rapid than the growth in the United States. Because Japan devoted a bigger fraction of its resources to producing capital goods, its stock of capital equipment grew more quickly than ours, and its production possibilities expanded more quickly. As a result, Japanese production possibilities per person are now so close to those in the United States that it is hard to say which country has the larger per person production possibilities. If Japan continues to devote a third of its resources to producing capital goods (at point *b* on its 1993 production possibility frontier), it will continue to grow much more rapidly than the United States, and its frontier will move out beyond our own. If Japan increases its production of consumption goods and reduces its production of capital goods (moving to point *c* on its 1993 production possibility frontier), then its rate of economic expansion will slow down to that of our own.

REVIEW

Economic growth results from the accumulation of capital and the development of better technologies. To reap the fruits of economic growth, we must incur the cost of fewer goods and services for current consumption. By cutting the current output of consumption goods, we can devote more resources to accumulating capital and to the research and development that lead to technological change—the engines of economic growth. Thus economic growth does not provide a free lunch. It has an opportunity cost—the fall in the current output of consumption goods. ◆

Gains from Trade

No one excels at everything. One person is more athletic than another; another person has a quicker mind or a better memory. What one person does with ease, someone else finds difficult.

Comparative Advantage: Jane Meets Joe

Differences in individual abilities mean that there are also differences in individual opportunity costs of producing various goods. Such differences give rise to **comparative advantage**—we say that a person has a comparative advantage in producing a particular good if that person can produce the good at a lower opportunity cost than anyone else.

People can produce for themselves all the goods that they consume, or they can concentrate on producing one good (or perhaps a few goods) and then exchange some of their own products for the output of others. Concentrating on the production of only one good or a few goods is called **specialization.** We are going to discover how people can gain by specializing in the good at which they have a comparative advantage and trading their output with others.

Let's return again to our island economy. Suppose that Jane has discovered another island very close to her own and that it too has only one inhabitant—Joe. Jane and Joe each have access to a simple boat that is adequate for transporting themselves and their goods between the two islands.

Joe's island, too, can produce only corn and cloth, but its terrain differs from that on Jane's island. While Jane's island has a lot of fertile corn-growing land and a small sheep population, Joe's island has little fertile corn-growing land and plenty of hilly land and sheep. This important difference between the two islands means that Joe's production possibility frontier is different from Jane's. Figure 3.5 illustrates these production possibility frontiers. Jane's frontier is labeled "Jane's PPF," and Joe's frontier is labeled "Joe's PPF."

Jane and Joe can be self-sufficient in corn and cloth. **Self-sufficiency** is a situation in which people produce only enough for their own consumption. Suppose that Jane and Joe are each self-sufficient. Jane chooses to produce and consume 3 yards of cloth and 11 pounds of corn a month, point *d*. Joe chooses to produce and consume 2 yards of cloth and 7 pounds of corn a month, point *b*'. These choices are identified on their respective production possibility frontiers in Fig. 3.5. (Each could have chosen any other point on his or her own production possibility frontier.) Total production of corn and cloth is the sum of Jane's and Joe's production: 18 pounds of corn and 5 yards of cloth. Point *n* in the figure represents this total production.

FIGURE 3.5

The Gains from Specialization and Exchange

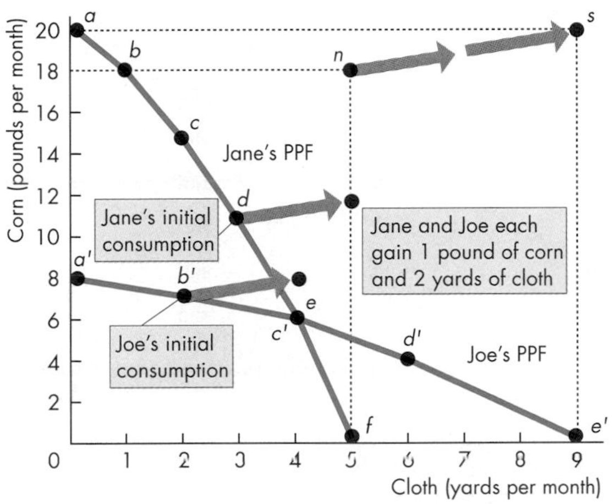

When Jane and Joe are each self-sufficient, Joe consumes 7 pounds of corn and 2 yards of cloth (point *b´*), and Jane consumes 11 pounds of corn and 3 yards of cloth (point *d*). Their total production is 18 pounds of corn and 5 yards of cloth (point *n*). Joe and Jane can do better by specialization and exchange. Jane, whose comparative advantage is in corn production, specializes in that activity, producing 20 pounds a month (point *a*). Joe, whose comparative advantage is in cloth production, specializes in that activity, producing 9 yards of cloth a month (point *e´*). Total production is then 20 pounds of corn and 9 yards of cloth (point *s*). If Jane gives Joe 8 pounds of corn in exchange for 5 yards of cloth, they each enjoy increased consumption of both corn and cloth. They each gain from specialization and exchange.

Jane's Comparative Advantage In which of the two goods does Jane have a comparative advantage? We have defined comparative advantage as a situation in which one person's opportunity cost of producing a good is lower than another person's opportunity cost of producing that same good. Jane, then, has a comparative advantage in producing whichever good she produces at a lower opportunity cost than Joe. What is that good?

You can answer the question by looking at the production possibility frontiers for Jane and Joe in Fig. 3.5. At the points at which they are producing and consuming, Jane's production possibility frontier is much steeper than Joe's. To produce one more pound of corn, Jane gives up less cloth than Joe. Hence Jane's opportunity cost of a pound of corn is lower than Joe's. This means that Jane has a comparative advantage in producing corn.

Joe's Comparative Advantage Joe's comparative advantage is in producing cloth. His production possibility frontier at his consumption point is flatter than Jane's. This means that Joe has to give up less corn to produce one more yard of cloth than Jane does. Joe's opportunity cost of a yard of cloth is lower than Jane's, so Joe has a comparative advantage in cloth production.

Achieving the Gains from Trade

Can Jane and Joe do better than be self-sufficient? In particular, what would happen if each were to specialize in producing the good at which each has a comparative advantage and then trade with the other?

If Jane, who has a comparative advantage in corn production, puts all her time into growing corn, she can grow 20 pounds. If Joe, who has a comparative advantage in cloth production, puts all his time into making cloth, he can make 9 yards. By specializing, Jane and Joe together can produce 20 pounds of corn and 9 yards of cloth (the amount labeled *s* in the figure). Point *s* shows the production of 20 pounds of corn (all produced by Jane) and 9 yards of cloth (all produced by Joe). Clearly, Jane and Joe produce more cloth and corn at point *s* than they were producing at point *n*, when each took care of only his or her own requirements. Jane and Joe prefer point *s* to point *n* because, between them, they have more of both corn and cloth at point *s* than at point *n*. They have an additional 2 pounds of corn and 4 yards of cloth.

To obtain the gains from trade, Jane and Joe must do more than specialize in producing the good at which each has a comparative advantage. They must exchange the fruits of their specialized production. Suppose that Jane and Joe agree to exchange 5 yards of cloth for 8 pounds of corn. Jane has 20 pounds of corn, and Joe has 9 yards of cloth before any exchange takes place. After the exchange takes place, Joe consumes 8 pounds of corn and Jane 12 pounds of corn; Joe consumes 4 yards of cloth and Jane 5 yards of cloth. Compared to the time when they were each self-sufficient, Jane now has 1 extra pound of corn and 2 extra yards of cloth, and Joe has 1 extra pound of corn and 2 extra yards of cloth. The gains from trade are represented by the increase in consumption of both goods that each obtains. Each consumes at a point outside their individual production possibility frontier.

Productivity and Absolute Advantage

Productivity is defined as the amount of output produced per unit of inputs used to produce it. For example, Jane's productivity in making cloth is measured as the amount of cloth she makes per hour of work. If one person has greater productivity than another in the production of all goods, that person is said to have an **absolute advantage.** In our example, neither Jane nor Joe has an absolute advantage. Jane is more productive than Joe in growing corn, and Joe is more productive than Jane in making cloth.

It is often suggested that people and countries that have an absolute advantage can outcompete others in the production of all goods. For example, it is often suggested that the United States cannot compete with Japan because the Japanese are more productive than we are. This conclusion is wrong, as you are just about to discover. To see why, let's look again at Jane and Joe.

Suppose that a volcano engulfs Jane's island, forcing her to search for a new one. And suppose further that this disaster leads to good fortune. Jane stumbles onto a new island that is much more productive than the original one, enabling her to produce twice as much of either corn or cloth with each hour of her labor. Jane's new production possibilities appear in Table 3.2. Notice that she now has an absolute advantage.

We have already worked out that the gains from trade arise when each person specializes in producing the good in which he or she has a comparative advantage. Recall that a person has a comparative advantage in producing a particular good if that person can produce it at a lower opportunity cost than anyone else. Joe's opportunity costs remain exactly the same as they were before. What has happened to Jane's opportunity costs now that she has become twice as productive?

You can work out Jane's opportunity costs by using exactly the same calculation that was used in the table of Fig. 3.2. Start by looking at Jane's

TABLE 3.2

Jane's New Production Possibilities

Possibility	Corn (pounds per month)		Cloth (yards per month)
a	40	and	0
b	36	and	2
c	30	and	4
d	22	and	6
e	12	and	8
f	0	and	10

opportunity cost of corn. The first 12 pounds of corn that Jane grows cost her 2 yards of cloth. So the opportunity cost of 1 pound of corn is ⅙ of a yard of cloth—the same as Jane's original opportunity cost of corn. If you calculate the opportunity costs for Jane's production possibilities *a* through *f*, you will discover that each of them has remained the same.

Since the opportunity cost of cloth is the inverse of the opportunity cost of corn, Jane's opportunity costs of cloth also have remained unchanged. Let's work through one example. If Jane moves from *a* to *b* to make 2 yards of cloth, she will have to reduce her corn production by 4 pounds—from 40 to 36 pounds. Thus the first 2 yards of cloth cost 4 pounds of corn. The cost of 1 yard of cloth is therefore 2 pounds of corn—exactly the same as before.

When Jane becomes twice as productive as before, each hour of her time produces more output, but her opportunity costs remain the same. One more unit of corn costs the same in terms of cloth forgone as it did previously. Since Jane's opportunity costs have not changed and Joe's have not changed, Joe continues to have a comparative advantage in producing cloth. Both Jane and Joe can have more of both goods if Jane specializes in corn production and Joe in cloth production.

The key point to recognize is that it is *not* possible for a person having an absolute advantage to have a comparative advantage in everything.

REVIEW

Gains from trade come from comparative advantage. A person has a comparative advantage in producing a good if that person can produce the good at a lower opportunity cost than anyone else. Thus differences in opportunity cost are the source of gains from specialization and exchange. Each person specializes in producing the good in which he or she has a comparative advantage and then exchanges some of that output for the goods produced by others. ◆◆ If a person can produce a good with fewer inputs than someone else—is more productive—that person has an absolute advantage but not necessarily a comparative advantage. Even a person with an absolute advantage gains from specialization and exchange. ◆

Exchange in the Real World

In the real world, countries can gain by specializing in the production of those goods and services in which they have a comparative advantage. An example is given in Reading Between the Lines on pp. 64–65. But to obtain the gains from trade in the real world, where billions of people specialize in millions of different activities, trade has to be organized. To organize trade, we have evolved rules of conduct and mechanisms for enforcing those rules. One such mechanism is private property rights. Another is the institution of money. In the island economy of Jane and Joe, direct exchange of one good with another is feasible. In the real-world economy, direct exchange of one good for another would be very cumbersome. To lubricate the wheels of exchange, societies have created money—a medium that enables indirect exchange of goods for money and money for goods. Let's examine these two aspects of exchange arrangements in more detail.

Property Rights

Property rights are social arrangements that govern the ownership, use, and disposal of property. **Property** is anything of value: it includes land and buildings—the things that we call property in ordinary speech; it also includes stocks and bonds, durable goods, and plant and equipment; it also includes intellectual property. **Intellectual property** is the intangible product of creative effort, protected by copyrights and patents. This type of property includes books, music, computer programs, and inventions of all kinds.

What if property rights did not exist? What would such a social science fiction world be like?

A World Without Property Rights Without property rights, people could take possession of whatever they had the strength to obtain for themselves. In such a world, people would have to devote a good deal of their time, energy, and resources to protecting what they had produced or acquired.

In a world without property rights, it would not be possible to reap all the gains from specialization and exchange. People would have little incentive to specialize in producing those goods at which they each had a comparative advantage. In fact, the more of a particular good someone produced, the bigger the chance that others would simply help themselves to it. Also, if a person could take the goods of others without giving up something in exchange, then there would be no point to specializing in producing something for exchange. In a world without property rights, no one would enjoy the gains from specialization and exchange, and everyone would specialize only in unproductive acts of piracy.

It is to overcome the problems that we have just described that property rights have evolved. Let's examine these property rights as they operate to govern economic life in the United States today.

Property Rights in Private Enterprise Capitalism The U.S. economy operates for the most part on the principles of private enterprise capitalism. **Private enterprise** is an economic system that permits individuals to decide on their own economic activities. **Capitalism** is an economic system that permits private individuals to own the capital resources used in production.

The Gains from Specialization and Exchange

The New York Times, February 21, 1991

Bush Asserts Need for Foreign Oil

BY MATTHEW L. WALD

Saying he was committed to "the power of the marketplace," President Bush presented an energy policy today that he asserted would save energy, increase domestic production of fuels and improve the environment without new taxes or harsh Government edicts. . . .

The plan gives considerable attention to oil. In contrast to the energy policy initiatives undertaken by Presidents Richard Nixon and Jimmy Carter in the oil crises that occurred during their terms, the Bush proposal asserts that the United States will have to live with a high level of dependence on foreign oil. . . .

The Energy Secretary, James D. Watkins, defended the policy's approach to energy efficiency, saying that its critics "want Government control of how you run your life."

FORTUNE, DECEMBER 31, 1990

America's Hottest Export: Pop Culture

BY JOHN HUEY

Industrial hard guys like Henry Ford, Andrew Carnegie, and George Westinghouse probably wouldn't take much heart from what we're about to report, but there is good news for the U.S. these days on the export front. Around the globe, folks just can't get enough of America. They may not want our *hardware* any more—our cars, steel, or television sets. But when they want a jolt of popular culture—and they want more all the time—they increasingly turn to American *software*—our movies, music, TV programming, and home video, which together now account for an annual trade surplus of some $8 billion. Only aerospace—aircraft and related equipment—outranks pop culture as an export.

Like it or not, Mickey Mouse, Michael Jackson, and Madonna—her overseas sales are 2½ times her domestic numbers—prop up what's left of our balance of trade. Radio Free Europe and Radio Moscow are out; international broadcasts of CNN and MTV are in.

Essence of the Stories

The Bush Administration energy policy is one that relies on a large amount of oil imports from other countries.

The Energy Secretary claims this approach delivers energy efficiently.

One of the major U.S. exports is pop culture—movies, music, TV programming, and home videos.

Only aerospace equipment outranks pop culture as an export.

Madonna's overseas sales are 2½ times her domestic sales.

Background and Analysis

Holding the production of all other goods and services constant, the United States can produce pop culture and oil along the production possibility frontier, U.S. PPF in the figure.

With no specialization and exchange, we could consume 3 million hours of pop culture and 6 billion barrels of oil a day at point *a* in the figure (the numbers are hypothetical).

By specializing in the production of pop culture and cutting back our domestic production of oil, we can produce 8 million hours of fun a day and 3 billion barrels of oil at point *b* in the figure.

We can exchange pop culture for oil with the rest of the world along the red line in the figure. This line shows our international trading possibilities.

At point *b*, our opportunity cost of producing oil—the hours of fun we must give up to produce one more barrel—exceeds its opportunity cost in the rest of the world—the amount of fun we must give up to get one more barrel of foreign oil. By specializing in pop culture and selling it to the rest of the world in exchange for oil, we can increase our consumption of both pop culture and oil and consume at point *c* in the figure.

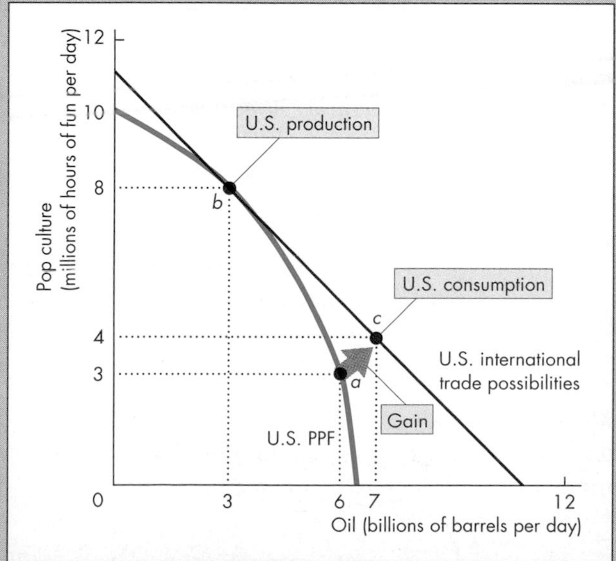

Under the property rights in such an economic system, individuals own what they have made, what they have acquired in a voluntary exchange with others, or what they have been given. Any attempt to remove someone's property against that person's will is considered theft, a crime that is punished by a sufficiently severe penalty to deter most people from becoming thieves.

It is easy to see that property rights based on these ideas can generate gainful trade: people can specialize in producing those goods that, for them, have the least opportunity cost. Some people will specialize in enforcing and maintaining property rights (for example, politicians, judges, and police officers), and all individuals will have the incentive to trade with each other, offering the good in which they have a comparative advantage in exchange for the goods produced by others.

The U.S. economic system is based on private property rights and voluntary exchange. But there are important ways in which private property rights are modified in our country.

Taxes Modify Private Property Rights Taxes on expenditure, income, and wealth transfer property from individuals to governments. Such transfers limit people's efforts to create more property and reduce their gains from specialization and exchange. But the taxes themselves are not arbitrary. Everyone faces the same rules and can calculate the effects of their own actions on the taxes for which they will be liable.

Regulation Modifies Private Property Rights Some voluntary exchanges are prohibited or regulated. For example, food and drug manufacturers cannot place a product on the market without first obtaining approval from a government agency. The government controls or prohibits the sale of many types of drugs and also restricts trading in human beings and their component parts—that is, it prohibits the selling of slaves, children, and human organs.

These restrictions on the extent of private property and on the legitimacy of voluntary exchange, though important, do not, for the most part, seriously impede specialization and gainful trade. Most people take the view that the benefits of regulation—for example, prohibiting the sale of dangerous drugs—far outweigh the costs imposed on the sellers.

Let's now turn to the other social institution that permits specialization and exchange—the development of an efficient means of exchange.

Money

We have seen that well-defined property rights based on voluntary exchange allow individuals to specialize and exchange their output with each other. In our island economy, we studied only two people and two goods. Exchange in such a situation was a simple matter. In the real world, however, how can billions of people exchange the millions of goods that are the fruits of their specialized labor?

Barter Goods can be simply exchanged for other goods. The direct exchange of one good for another is known as **barter.** However, barter severely limits the amount of trading that can take place. Imagine that you have roosters but you want to get roses. First, you must look for someone with roses who wants roosters. Economists call this a **double coincidence of wants**—when person A wants to sell exactly what person B wants to buy, and person B wants to sell exactly what person A wants to buy. As the term implies, such occurrences are coincidences and will not arise frequently. A second way of trading by barter is to undertake a sequence of exchanges. If you have oranges and you want apples, you might have to trade oranges for plums, plums for pomegranates, pomegranates for pineapples, and then eventually pineapples for apples.

Cumbersome though it is, quite a large amount of barter trade does take place. For example, when British rock star Rod Stewart played in Budapest, Hungary, in 1986, he received part of his $30,000 compensation in Hungarian sound equipment, electrical cable, and the use of a forklift truck. And before the recent changes in Eastern Europe, hairdressers in Warsaw, Poland, obtained their barbershop equipment from England in exchange for hair clippings that they supplied to London wigmakers.

Although barter exchange does occur, it is an inefficient means of exchanging goods. Fortunately, a better alternative has been invented.

Monetary Exchange An alternative to barter is **monetary exchange**—a system in which some commodity or token serves as the medium of exchange.

A **medium of exchange** is anything that is generally acceptable in exchange for goods and services. **Money** can also be defined as a medium of exchange—something that can be passed on to others in exchange for goods and services.

Money lowers the cost of transacting and makes millions of transactions possible that simply would not be worth undertaking by barter. Can you imagine the chain of barter transactions you'd have to go through every day to get your coffee, Coke, textbooks, professor's time, video, and all the other goods and services you consume? In a monetary exchange system, you exchange your time and effort for money and use that money to buy the goods and services you consume, cutting out the incredible hassle you'd face each day in a world of barter.

Metals such as gold, silver, and copper have long served as money. Most commonly, they serve as money by being stamped as coins. Primitive societies have traditionally used various commodities, such as seashells, as money. During the Civil War and for several years after, people used postage stamps as money. Prisoners of war in German camps in World War II used cigarettes as money. Using cigarettes as a medium of exchange should not be confused with barter. When cigarettes play the role of money, people buy and sell goods by using cigarettes as a medium of exchange.

In modern societies, governments provide paper money. The banking system also provides money in the form of checking accounts. Checking accounts can be used for settling debts simply by writing an instruction—writing a check—to the bank requesting that funds be transferred to another checking account. Electronic links between bank accounts, now becoming widespread, enable direct transfers between different accounts without any checks being written.

◆ ◆ ◆ ◆ You have now begun to see how economists go about the job of trying to answer some important questions. The simple fact of scarcity and the associated concept of opportunity cost allow us to understand why people specialize, why they trade with each other, why they have social conventions that define and enforce private property rights, and why they use money. One simple idea—scarcity and its direct implication, opportunity cost—explains so much!

SUMMARY

The Production Possibility Frontier

The production possibility frontier is the boundary between what is attainable and what is not attainable. Production can take place at any point inside or on the production possibility frontier, but it is not possible to produce outside the frontier. There is always a point on the production possibility frontier that is better than a point inside it. (pp. 51–53)

Opportunity Cost

The opportunity cost of any action is the best alternative action forgone. The opportunity cost of acquiring one good is equivalent to the amount of another good that must be given up. The opportunity cost of a good increases as the quantity of it produced increases. (pp. 54–56)

Economic Growth

Although the production possibility frontier marks the boundary between the attainable and the unattainable, that boundary does not remain fixed. It changes over time, partly because of natural forces (for example, changes in climate and the accumulation of ideas about better ways of producing) and partly because of the choices that we make (choices about consumption and saving). If we use some of today's resources to produce capital goods and for research and development, we will be able to produce more goods and services in the future. The economy will grow. But growth cannot take place without incurring costs. The opportunity cost of more goods and services in the future is consuming fewer goods and services today. (pp. 57–60)

Gains from Trade

A person has a comparative advantage in producing a good if that person can produce the good at a lower opportunity cost than anyone else. People can gain from trade if each specializes in the activity at which he or she has a comparative advantage. Each person produces the good for which his or her opportunity cost is lower than everyone else's. They then exchange part of their output with each other. By this activity, each person is able to consume at a point *outside* his or her individual production possibility frontier.

When a person is more productive than another person—is able to produce more output from fewer inputs—that person has an absolute advantage. But having an absolute advantage does not mean that there are no gains from trade. Even if someone is more productive than other people in all activities, as long as the other person has a lower opportunity cost of some good, then gains from specialization and exchange are available. (pp. 60–63)

Exchange in the Real World

Exchange in the real world involves the specialization of billions of people in millions of different activities. To make it worthwhile for each individual to specialize and to enable societies to reap the gains from trade, institutions and mechanisms have evolved. The most important of these are private property rights, with a political and legal system to enforce them, and a system of monetary exchange. These institutions enable people to specialize, exchanging their labor for money and their money for goods, thereby reaping the gains from trade. (pp. 63–67)

KEY ELEMENTS

Key Terms

Absolute advantage, 62
Barter, 66
Capital accumulation, 57
Capital goods, 51
Capitalism, 63
Comparative advantage, 60
Consumption, 51
Consumption goods, 51
Double coincidence of wants, 66
Economic growth, 57
Goods and services, 51
Human capital, 51
Intellectual property, 63
Medium of exchange, 67
Monetary exchange, 66
Money, 67
Private enterprise, 63
Production, 51
Production possibility frontier, 51
Productivity, 62
Property, 63
Property rights, 63
Self-sufficiency, 60
Specialization, 60
Technological progress, 57

Key Figures

REVIEW QUESTIONS

1 How does the production possibility frontier illustrate scarcity?

2 How does the production possibility frontier illustrate opportunity cost?

3 Explain what shifts the production possibility frontier outward and what shifts it inward.

4 Explain how our choices influence economic growth. What is the cost of economic growth?

5 Why does it pay people to specialize and trade with each other?

6 What are the gains from trade? How do they arise?

7 Why do social contracts such as property rights and money become necessary?

8 What is money? Give some examples of money. In the late 1980s, people in Rumania could use Kent cigarettes to buy almost anything. Was this monetary exchange or barter? Explain your answer.

9 What are the advantages of monetary exchange over barter?

PROBLEMS

1 Suppose that there is a change in the weather conditions on Jane's island that makes the corn yields much higher. This enables Jane to produce the following amounts of corn:

Hours worked (per day)	Corn (pounds per month)
0	0
2	60
4	100
6	120
8	130
10	140

Her cloth production possibilities are the same as those that appeared in Table 3.1.

a What are six points on Jane's new production possibility frontier?

b What are Jane's opportunity costs of corn and cloth? List them at each of the five levels of output.

c Compare Jane's opportunity cost of cloth with that in the table in Fig. 3.2. Has her opportunity cost of cloth gone up, gone down, or remained the same? Explain why.

2 Amy lives with her parents and attends the local college. The college is operated by the state government, and tuition is free. Jobs that pay $7 an hour are available to high school graduates in the town. Amy's mother, a high school graduate, takes a part-time job so that Amy can go to school. Amy's textbooks cost $280, and Amy gets an allowance of $140 a month from her mother. List the items that make up the opportunity cost of Amy attending college.

3 Suppose that Leisureland produces only two goods—food and suntan oil. Its production possibilities are

Food (pounds per month)		Suntan oil (gallons per month)
300	and	0
200	and	50
100	and	100
0	and	150

Busyland also produces only food and suntan oil, and its production possibilities are

Food (pounds per month)		Suntan oil (gallons per month)
150	and	0
100	and	100
50	and	200
0	and	300

a What are the opportunity costs of food and suntan oil in Leisureland? List them at each output given in the table.

b Why are the opportunity costs the same at each output level?

c What are the opportunity costs of food and suntan oil in Busyland? List them at each output given in the table.

4 Suppose that in problem 3 Leisureland and Busyland do not specialize and trade with each other—each country is self-sufficient. Leisureland produces and consumes 50 pounds of food and 125 gallons of suntan oil per month. Busyland produces and consumes 150 pounds of food per month and no suntan oil. The countries then begin to trade with each other.

a Which good does Leisureland export, and which good does it import?

b Which good does Busyland export, and which good does it import?

c What is the maximum quantity of food and suntan oil that the two countries can produce if each country specializes in the activity at which it has the lower opportunity cost?

5 Suppose that Busyland becomes three times as productive as in problem 3.

a Show, on a graph, the effect of the increased productivity on Busyland's production possibility frontier.

b Does Busyland now have an absolute advantage in producing both goods?

c Can Busyland gain from specialization and trade with Leisureland now that it is twice as productive? If so, what will it produce?

d What are the total gains from trade? What do these gains depend on?

6 Andy and Bob work at Mario's Pizza Palace. In an 8-hour day, Andy can make 240 pizzas or 100 ice cream sundaes, and Bob can make 80 pizzas or 80 ice cream sundaes. Who does Mario get to make the ice cream sundaes? Who makes the pizzas? Explain your answer.

CHAPTER 4

DEMAND AND SUPPLY

After studying this chapter, you will be able to:

- Construct a demand schedule and a demand curve
- Construct a supply schedule and a supply curve
- Explain how prices are determined
- Explain how quantities bought and sold are determined
- Explain why some prices rise, some fall, and some fluctuate
- Make predictions about price changes using the demand and supply model

SLIDE, ROCKET, AND ROLLER COASTER—DISNEYLAND rides? No. Commonly used descriptions of the behavior of prices. There are lots of examples of price slides. One particular example is probably very familiar to you. In 1979, Sony began to market a pocket-sized cassette player that delivered its sound through tiny earphones. Sony named its new product the Walkman and gave it a price tag of around $300—more than $500 in today's money. Today Sony has been joined by many other producers of Walkman clones, and you can buy a Walkman (or its equivalent) that's even better than the 1979 prototype for less than one tenth of the original price. During the time that the Walkman has been with us, the quantity bought has increased steadily each year. Why has there been a long and steady slide in the price of the Walkman? Why hasn't the increase in the quantity bought kept its price high? ◆◆ Rocketing prices are also a familiar phenomenon. An important recent example is that of rents paid for apartments and houses, especially in central locations in big cities. Huge increases in rents and house prices have not deterred people from living in the centers of cities—on the contrary, their numbers have increased slightly in recent years. Why do people continue to seek housing in city centers when rents have rocketed so sharply? ◆◆ There are lots of price roller coasters—cases in which prices rise and fall from season to season or year to year. Prices of coffee, strawberries, and many other agricultural commodities fit this pattern. Why does the price of coffee roller-coaster even when people's taste for coffee hardly changes at all? ◆◆ Though amusement

Slide, Rocket, and Roller Coaster

park rides provide a vivid description of the behavior of prices, many of the things that we buy have remarkably steady prices. The audiocassette tapes that we play in a Walkman are an example. The price of a tape has barely changed over the past ten years. Nevertheless, the number of tapes bought has risen steadily year after year. Why do firms sell more and more tapes, even though they're not able to get higher prices for them, and why do people willingly buy more tapes, even though their price is no lower than it was a decade ago?

◆ ◆ ◆ ◆ We will discover the answers to these and similar questions by studying the theory of demand and supply. This powerful theory enables us to analyze many important economic events that affect our lives. It even enables us to make predictions about future prices.

Demand

The **quantity demanded** of a good or service is the amount that consumers plan to buy in a given period of time at a particular price. Demands are different from wants. **Wants** are the unlimited desires or wishes that people have for goods and services. How many times have you thought that you would like something "if only you could afford it" or "if it weren't so expensive"? Scarcity guarantees that many—perhaps most—of our wants will never be satisfied. Demand reflects a decision about which wants to satisfy. If you demand something, then you've made a plan to buy it.

The quantity demanded is not necessarily the same amount as the quantity actually bought. Sometimes the quantity demanded is greater than the amount of goods available, so the quantity bought is less than the quantity demanded.

The quantity demanded is measured as an amount per unit of time. For example, suppose a person consumes one cup of coffee a day. The quantity of coffee demanded by that person can be expressed as 1 cup per day or 7 cups per week or 365 cups per year. Without a time dimension, we cannot tell whether a particular quantity demanded is large or small.

What Determines Buying Plans?

The amount that consumers plan to buy of any particular good or service depends on many factors. Among the more important ones are

- The price of the good
- The prices of related goods
- Income
- Expected future prices
- Population
- Preferences

The theory of demand and supply makes predictions about prices and quantities bought and sold. Let's begin by focusing on the relationship between the quantity demanded and the price of a good. To study this relationship, we hold constant all other influences on consumers' planned purchases. We can then ask: how does the quantity demanded of the good vary as its price varies?

The Law of Demand

The law of demand states:

> Other things being equal, the higher the price of a good, the lower is the quantity demanded.

Why does a higher price reduce the quantity demanded? The key to the answer lies in *other things being equal.* Because other things are being held constant, when the price of a good rises, it rises *relative* to the prices of all other goods. Although each good is unique, it has substitutes—other goods that serve almost as well. As the price of a good climbs higher, relative to the prices of its substitutes, people buy less of that good and more of its substitutes.

Let's consider an example—blank audiocassette tapes, which we'll refer to as "tapes." Many different goods provide a service similar to that of a tape; for example, records, compact discs, prerecorded tapes, radio and television broadcasts, and live concerts. Tapes sell for about $3 each. If the price of a tape doubles to \$6 while the prices of all the other goods remain constant, the quantity of tapes demanded will fall. People will buy more compact discs and prerecorded tapes and fewer blank tapes. If the price of a tape falls to \$1 while the prices of all the other goods stay constant, the quantity of tapes demanded will rise, and the demand for compact discs and prerecorded tapes will fall.

Demand Schedule and Demand Curve

A **demand schedule** lists the quantities demanded at each different price when all the other influences on consumers' planned purchases—such as the prices of related goods, income, expected future prices, population, and preferences—are held constant.

The table in Fig. 4.1 sets out a demand schedule for tapes. For example, if the price of a tape is \$1, the quantity demanded is 9 million tapes a week. If the price of a tape is \$5, the quantity demanded is 2 million tapes a week. The other rows of the table show us the quantities demanded at prices between \$2 and \$4.

A demand schedule can be illustrated by drawing a demand curve. A **demand curve** graphs the relationship between the quantity demanded of a good and its price, holding constant all other influences on consumers' planned purchases. The graph in Fig. 4.1 illustrates the demand curve for tapes. By convention, the quantity demanded is always measured on the horizontal axis, and the price is measured on the vertical axis. The points on the demand curve labeled *a* through *e* represent the rows of the demand schedule. For example, point *a* on the graph represents a quantity demanded of 9 million tapes a week at a price of \$1 a tape.

Willingness to Pay

There is another way of looking at the demand curve: it shows the highest price that people are willing to pay for the last unit bought. If a large quantity is available, that price is low; but if only a small quantity is available, that price is high. For example, if 9 million tapes are available each week, the highest price that consumers are willing to pay for the 9 millionth tape is \$1. But if only 2 million tapes are available each week, consumers are willing to pay \$5 for the last tape available.

FIGURE 4.1

The Demand Curve and the Demand Schedule

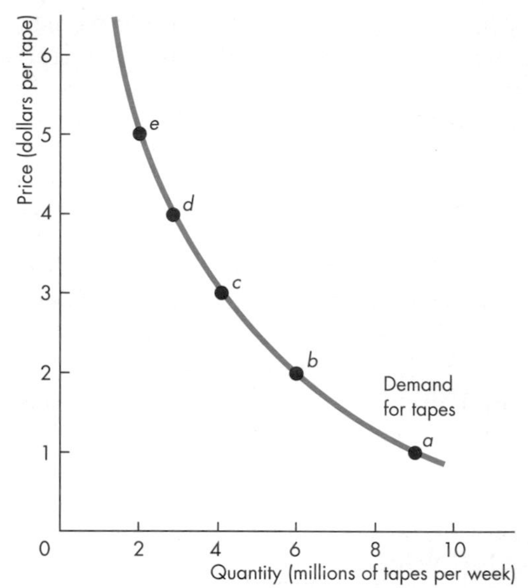

	Price (dollars per tape)	Quantity (millions of tapes per week)
a	**1**	**9**
b	**2**	**6**
c	**3**	**4**
d	**4**	**3**
e	**5**	**2**

The table shows a demand schedule listing the quantity of tapes demanded at each price if all other influences on buyers' plans are held constant. At a price of \$1 a tape, 9 million tapes a week are demanded; at a price of \$3 a tape, 4 million tapes a week are demanded. The demand curve shows the relationship between quantity demanded and price, holding everything else constant. The demand curve slopes downward: as price decreases, the quantity demanded increases. The demand curve can be read two ways. For a given price, it tells us the quantity that people plan to buy. For example, at a price of \$3 a tape, the quantity demanded is 4 million tapes a week. For a given quantity, the demand curve tells us the maximum price that consumers are willing to pay for the last tape bought. For example, the maximum price that consumers will pay for the 6 millionth tape is \$2.

This view of the demand curve may become clearer if you think about your own demand for tapes. If you are given a list of possible prices of tapes, you can write down alongside each price your planned weekly purchase of tapes—your demand schedule for tapes. Alternatively, if you are told that there is just one tape available each week, you can say how much you are willing to pay for it. If you are then told that there is one more tape available, you can say the maximum price that you will be willing to pay for that second tape. This process can continue—you are told that there is one more tape available, and you say how much you are willing to pay for each extra tape. The schedule of prices and quantities arrived at is your demand schedule.

A Change in Demand

The term **demand** refers to the entire relationship between the quantity demanded and the price of a good. The demand for tapes is described by both the demand schedule and the demand curve in Fig. 4.1. To construct a demand schedule and demand curve, we hold constant all the other influences on consumers' buying plans. But what are the effects of each of those other influences?

1. Prices of Related Goods The quantity of tapes that consumers plan to buy does not depend only on the price of tapes. It also depends in part on the prices of related goods. These related goods fall into two categories: substitutes and complements.

A **substitute** is a good that can be used in place of another good. For example, a bus ride substitutes for a train ride; a hamburger substitutes for a hot dog; a pear substitutes for an apple. As we have seen, tapes have many substitutes—records, prerecorded tapes, compact discs, radio and television broadcasts, and live concerts. If the price of one of these substitutes increases, people economize on its use and buy more tapes. For example, if the price of compact discs doubles, fewer compact discs are bought, and the demand for tapes increases—there is much more taping of other people's compact discs. Conversely, if the price of one of these substitutes decreases, people use the now cheaper good in larger quantities, and they buy fewer tapes. For example, if the price of prerecorded tapes decreases, people play more of these tapes and make fewer of their own tapes—the demand for blank tapes falls.

The effects of a change in the price of a substitute occur no matter what the price of a tape. Whether tapes have a high or a low price, a change in the price of a substitute encourages people to make the substitutions that we've just reviewed. As a consequence, a change in the price of a substitute changes the entire demand schedule for tapes and shifts the demand curve.

A **complement** is a good that is used in conjunction with another good. Some examples of complements are hamburgers and french fries, party snacks and drinks, spaghetti and meat sauce, running shoes and jogging pants. Tapes also have their complements: Walkmans, tape recorders, and stereo tape decks. If the price of one of these complements increases, people buy fewer tapes. For example, if the price of a Walkman doubles, fewer Walkmans are bought and, as a consequence, fewer people are interested in buying tapes—the demand for tapes decreases. Conversely, if the price of one of these complements decreases, people buy more tapes. For example, if the price of the Walkman halves, more Walkmans are bought, and a larger number of people buy tapes—the demand for tapes increases.

2. Income Another influence on demand is consumer income. Other things remaining the same, when income increases, consumers buy more of most goods, and when income decreases, they buy less of most goods. Consumers with higher incomes demand more of most goods. Consumers with lower incomes demand less of most goods. Rich people consume more food, clothing, housing, art, vacations, and entertainment than do poor people.

Although an increase in income leads to an increase in the demand for most goods, it does not lead to an increase in the demand for all goods. Goods that do increase in demand as income increases are called **normal goods.** Goods that decrease in demand when income increases are called **inferior goods.** Examples of inferior goods are rice and potatoes. These two goods are a major part of the diet of people with very low incomes. As incomes increase, the demand for these goods declines as more expensive meat and dairy products are substituted for them.

3. Expected Future Prices If the price of a good is expected to rise, it makes sense to buy more of the good today and less in the future, when its price is higher. Similarly, if its price is expected to fall, it pays to cut back on today's purchases and buy more later, when the price is expected to be lower. Thus the higher the expected future price of a good, the larger is today's demand for the good.

4. Population Demand also depends on the size of the population. Other things being equal, the larger the population, the greater is the demand for all goods and services, and the smaller the population, the smaller is the demand for all goods and services.

5. Preferences Finally, demand depends on preferences. *Preferences* are an individual's attitudes toward goods and services. For example, a rock music fanatic has a much greater preference for tapes than does a tone-deaf workaholic. As a consequence, even if they have the same incomes, their demands for tapes will be very different.

There is, however, a fundamental difference between preferences and all the other influences on demand. Preferences cannot be directly observed. We can observe today's price of a good and the prices of its substitutes and complements. We can observe income and population size. We can observe economic forecasts of future prices. But we cannot observe people's preferences. Economists assume that *changes* in preferences occur only slowly and so are not an important influence on *changes* in demand.

A summary of influences on demand and the direction of those influences is presented in Table 4.1.

TABLE 4.1
The Demand for Tapes

THE LAW OF DEMAND

The quantity of tapes demanded

Decreases if:	*Increases if:*
◆ The price of a tape rises	◆ The price of a tape falls

CHANGES IN DEMAND

The demand for tapes

Decreases if:	*Increases if:*
◆ The price of a substitute falls	◆ The price of a substitute rises
◆ The price of a complement rises	◆ The price of a complement falls
◆ Income falls*	◆ Income rises*
◆ The price of a tape is expected to fall in the future	◆ The price of a tape is expected to rise in the future
◆ The population decreases	◆ The population increases

*A tape is a normal good

Movement along the Demand Curve versus a Shift in the Curve

Changes in the influences on buyers' plans cause either a movement along the demand curve or a shift in it. Let's discuss each case in turn.

Movement along the Demand Curve If the price of a good changes but everything else remains the same, there is a movement along the demand curve. For example, if the price of a tape changes from $3 to $5, the result is a movement along the demand curve, from point *c* to point *e* in Fig. 4.1.

A Shift in the Demand Curve If the price of a good remains constant but some other influence on buyers' plans changes, we say that there is a change in demand for that good. We illustrate the change in demand as a shift in the demand curve. For example, a fall in the price of the Walkman—a complement of tapes—increases the demand for tapes. We illustrate this increase in demand for tapes with a new demand schedule and a new demand curve. Consumers demand a larger quantity of tapes at each and every price.

The table in Fig. 4.2 provides some hypothetical numbers that illustrate such a shift. The table sets out the original demand schedule when the price of a Walkman is $200 and the new demand schedule when the price of a Walkman is $50. These numbers record the change in demand. The graph in Fig. 4.2 illustrates the corresponding shift in the demand

FIGURE 4.2

A Change in the Demand Schedule and a Shift in the Demand Curve

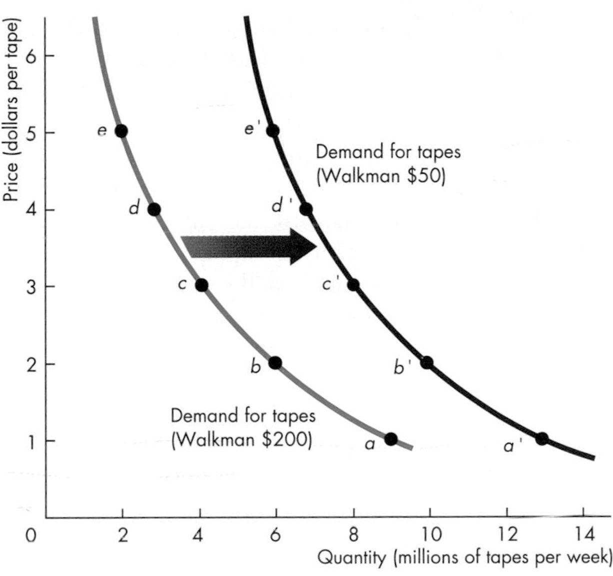

	Original demand schedule (Walkman $200)			New demand schedule (Walkman $50)	
	Price (dollars per tape)	Quantity (millions of tapes per week)		Price (dollars per tape)	Quantity (millions of tapes per week)
a	**1**	**9**	***a′***	**1**	**13**
b	**2**	**6**	***b′***	**2**	**10**
c	**3**	**4**	***c′***	**3**	**8**
d	**4**	**3**	***d′***	**4**	**7**
e	**5**	**2**	***e′***	**5**	**6**

A change in any influence on buyers other than the price of the good itself results in a new demand schedule and a shift in the demand curve. Here, a fall in the price of a Walkman—a complement of tapes—increases the demand for tapes. At a price of $3 a tape (row *c* of table), 4 million tapes a week are demanded when the Walkman costs $200 and 8 million tapes a week are demanded when the Walkman costs only $50. A fall in the price of a Walkman increases the demand for tapes. The demand curve shifts to the right, as shown by the shift arrow and the resulting red curve.

curve. When the price of the Walkman falls, the demand curve for tapes shifts to the right.

A Change in Demand versus a Change in Quantity Demanded A point on the demand curve shows the quantity demanded at a given price. A movement along the demand curve shows a **change in the quantity demanded.** The entire demand curve shows demand. A shift in the demand curve shows a **change in demand.**

Figure 4.3 illustrates and summarizes these distinctions. If the price of a good falls but nothing else

FIGURE 4.3

A Change in Demand versus a Change in the Quantity Demanded

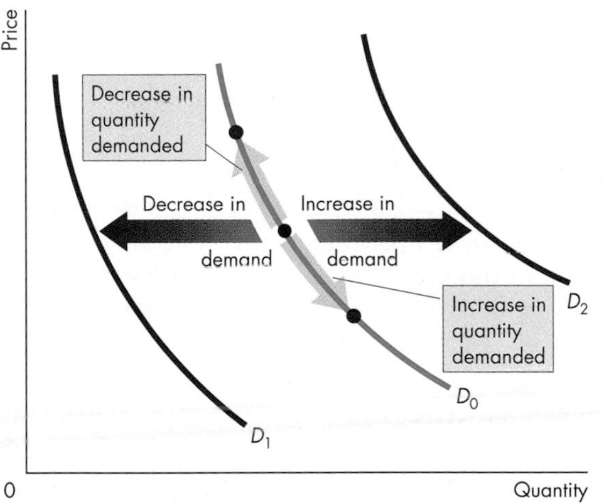

When the price of a good changes, there is a movement along the demand curve and a *change in the quantity of the good demanded.* For example, if the demand curve is D_0, a rise in the price of the good produces a decrease in the quantity demanded and a fall in the price of the good produces an increase in the quantity demanded. The blue arrows on demand curve D_0 represent these movements along the demand curve. If some other influence on demand changes, which increases the quantity that people plan to buy, there is a shift in the demand curve to the right (from D_0 to D_2) and an *increase in demand.* If some other influence on demand changes, which reduces the quantity people plan to buy, there is a shift in the demand curve to the left (from D_0 to D_1) and a *decrease in demand.*

changes, then there is an increase in the quantity demanded of that good (a movement down the demand curve D_0). If the price rises but nothing else changes, then there is a decrease in the quantity demanded (a movement up the demand curve D_0). When any other influence on buyers' planned purchases changes, the demand curve shifts and there is a *change* (an increase or a decrease) *in demand.* A rise in income (for a normal good), in population, in the price of a substitute, or in the expected future price of the good or a fall in the price of a complement shifts the demand curve to the right (to the red demand curve D_2). This represents an *increase in demand.* A fall in income (for a normal good), in population, in the price of a substitute, or in the expected future price of the good or a rise in the price of a complement shifts the demand curve to the left (to the red demand curve D_1). This represents a *decrease in demand.* For an inferior good, the effects of changes in income are in the opposite direction to those described above.

REVIEW

The quantity demanded is the amount of a good that consumers plan to buy in a given period of time. Other things being equal, the quantity demanded of a good increases if its price falls. Demand can be represented by a schedule or curve that sets out the quantity demanded at each price. Demand describes the quantity that consumers plan to buy at each possible price. Demand also describes the highest price that consumers are willing to pay for the last unit bought. Demand increases if the price of a substitute rises, if the price of a complement falls, if income rises (for a normal good), or if the population increases; demand decreases if the price of a substitute falls, if the price of a complement rises, if income falls (for a normal good), or if the population decreases. ◆ ◆ If the price of a good changes but all other influences on buyers' plans are held constant, there is a change in the quantity demanded and a movement along the demand curve. All other influences on consumers' planned purchases shift the demand curve. ◆

Supply

The **quantity supplied** of a good is the amount that producers plan to sell in a given period of time at a particular price. The quantity supplied is not the amount a firm would like to sell but the amount it definitely plans to sell. However, the quantity supplied is not necessarily the same as the quantity actually sold. If consumers do not want to buy the quantity a firm plans to sell, the firm's sales plans will be frustrated. Like quantity demanded, the quantity supplied is expressed as an amount per unit of time.

What Determines Selling Plans?

The amount that firms plan to sell of any particular good or service depends on many factors. Among the more important ones are

- The price of the good
- The prices of factors of production
- The prices of related goods
- Expected future prices
- The number of suppliers
- Technology

Because the theory of demand and supply makes predictions about prices and quantities bought and sold, we focus first on the relationship between the price of a good and the quantity supplied. To study this relationship, we hold constant all the other influences on the quantity supplied. We ask: how does the quantity supplied of a good vary as its price varies?

The Law of Supply

The law of supply states:

Other things being equal, the higher the price of a good, the greater is the quantity supplied.

Why does a higher price lead to a greater quantity supplied of a good? It is because the cost of producing an additional unit of the good increases (at least eventually) as the quantity produced increases. To induce them to incur a higher cost and increase production, firms must be compensated with a higher price.

Supply Schedule and Supply Curve

A **supply schedule** lists the quantities supplied at each different price when all other influences on the amount firms plan to sell are held constant. Let's construct a supply schedule. To do so, we examine how the quantity supplied of a good varies as its price varies, holding constant the prices of other goods, the prices of factors of production used to produce it, expected future prices, and the state of technology.

The table in Fig. 4.4 sets out a supply schedule for tapes. It shows the quantity of tapes supplied at each possible price. For example, if the price of a tape is $1, no tapes are supplied. If the price of a tape is $4, 5 million tapes are supplied each week.

A supply schedule can be illustrated by drawing a supply curve. A **supply curve** graphs the relationship between the quantity supplied and the price of a good, holding everything else constant. Using the numbers listed in the table, the graph in Fig. 4.4 illustrates the supply curve for tapes. For example, point *d* represents a quantity supplied of 5 million tapes a week at a price of $4 a tape.

FIGURE 4.4

The Supply Curve and the Supply Schedule

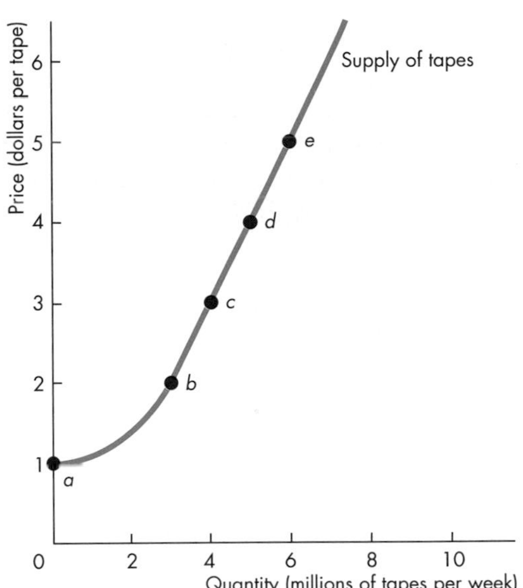

	Price (dollars per tape)	Quantity (millions of tapes per week)
a	1	0
b	2	3
c	3	4
d	4	5
e	5	6

The table shows the supply schedule of tapes. For example, at $2 a tape, 3 million tapes a week are supplied; at $5 a tape, 6 million tapes a week are supplied. The supply curve shows the relationship between the quantity supplied and price, holding everything else constant. The supply curve usually slopes upward: as the price of a good increases, so does the quantity supplied. A supply curve can be read in two ways. For a given price, it tells us the quantity that producers plan to sell. For example, at a price of $3 a tape, producers plan to sell 4 million tapes a week. The supply curve also tells us the minimum acceptable price at which a given quantity will be offered for sale. For example, the minimum acceptable price that will bring forth a supply of 4 million tapes a week is $3 a tape.

Minimum Supply Price

Just as the demand curve has two interpretations, so too does the supply curve. So far we have thought about the supply curve and the supply schedule as showing the quantity that firms will supply at each possible price. But we can also think about the supply curve as showing the minimum price at which the last unit will be supplied. Looking at the supply schedule in this way, we ask: what is the minimum price that brings forth a supply of a given quantity? For firms to supply the 3 millionth tape each week, the price has to be at least $2 a tape. For firms to supply the 5 millionth tape each week, they have to get at least $4 a tape.

A Change in Supply

The term **supply** refers to the entire relationship between the quantity supplied of a good and its price. The supply of tapes is described by both the supply schedule and the supply curve in Fig. 4.4. To construct a supply schedule and supply curve, we hold constant all the other influences on suppliers' plans. Let's now consider these other influences.

1. Prices of Factors of Production The prices of the factors of production used to produce a good exert an important influence on its supply. For example, an increase in the prices of the labor and the capital equipment used to produce tapes increases the cost of producing tapes, so the supply of tapes decreases.

2. Prices of Related Goods The supply of a good can be influenced by the prices of related goods. For example, if an automobile assembly line can produce either sports cars or sedans, the quantity of sedans produced will depend on the price of sports cars and the quantity of sports cars produced will depend on the price of sedans. These two goods are *substitutes in production*. An increase in the price of a substitute in production lowers the supply of the good. Goods can also be complements in production. *Complements in production* arise when two things are, of necessity, produced together. For example, extracting chemicals from coal produces coke, coal tar, and nylon. An increase in the price of any one of these by-products of coal increases the supply of the other by-products.

Tapes have no obvious complements in production, but they do have substitutes in production: prerecorded tapes. Suppliers of tapes can produce blank tapes and prerecorded tapes. An increase in the price of prerecorded tapes encourages producers to increase the supply of prerecorded tapes and decrease the supply of blank tapes.

3. Expected Future Prices If the price of a good is expected to rise, it makes sense to sell less of the good today and more in the future, when its price is higher. Similarly, if its price is expected to fall, it pays to expand today's supply and sell less later, when the price is expected to be lower. Thus, other things being equal, the higher the expected future price of a good, the smaller is today's supply of the good.

4. The Number of Suppliers Other things being equal, the larger the number of firms supplying a good, the larger is the supply of the good.

5. Technology New technologies that enable producers to use fewer factors of production will lower the cost of production and increase supply. For example, the development of a new technology for tape production by companies such as Sony and Minnesota Mining and Manufacturing (3M) has lowered the cost of producing tapes and increased their supply.

A summary of influences on supply and the directions of those influences is presented in Table 4.2. Over the long term, changes in technology are the most important influence on supply.

TABLE 4.2

The Supply of Tapes

THE LAW OF SUPPLY

The quantity of tapes supplied

Decreases if:	***Increases if:***
◆ **The price of a tape falls**	◆ **The price of a tape rises**

CHANGES IN SUPPLY

The supply of tapes

Decreases if:	***Increases if:***
◆ **The price of a factor of production used to produce tapes increases**	◆ **The price of a factor of production used to produce tapes decreases**
◆ **The price of a substitute in production rises**	◆ **The price of a substitute in production falls**
◆ **The price of a complement in production falls**	◆ **The price of a complement in production rises**
◆ **The price of a tape is expected to rise in the future**	◆ **The price of a tape is expected to fall in the future**
◆ **The number of firms supplying tapes decreases**	◆ **The number of firms supplying tapes increases**
	◆ **More efficient technologies for producing tapes are discovered**

Movement along the Supply Curve versus a Shift in the Curve

Changes in the influences on producers cause either a movement along the supply curve or a shift in it.

Movement along the Supply Curve If the price of a good changes but everything else influencing suppliers' planned sales remains constant, there is a movement along the supply curve. For example, if the price of tapes increases from $3 to $5 a tape, there will be a movement along the supply curve from point *c* (4 million tapes a week) to point *e* (6 million tapes a week) in Fig. 4.4.

A Shift in the Supply Curve If the price of a good remains constant but another influence on suppliers' planned sales changes, then there is a change in supply and a shift in the supply curve. For example, as we have already noted, technological advances lower the cost of producing tapes and increase their supply. As a result, the supply schedule changes. The table in Fig. 4.5 provides some hypothetical numbers that illustrate such a change. The table contains two supply schedules: the original, based on "old" technology, and one based on "new" technology. With the new technology, more tapes are supplied at each price. The graph in Fig. 4.5 illustrates the resulting shift in the supply curve. When tape-producing technology improves, the supply curve of tapes shifts to the right, as shown by the shift arrow and the red supply curve.

A Change in Supply versus a Change in Quantity Supplied A point on the supply curve shows the quantity supplied at a given price. A movement along the supply curve shows a **change in the quantity supplied.** The entire supply curve shows supply. A shift in the supply curve shows a **change in supply.**

Figure 4.6 illustrates and summarizes these distinctions. If the price of a good falls but nothing else changes, then there is a decrease in the quantity supplied of that good (a movement down the supply curve S_0). If the price of a good rises but nothing else changes, there is an increase in the quantity supplied (a movement up the supply curve S_0). When any other influence on sellers changes, the supply curve

FIGURE 4.5

A Change in the Supply Schedule and a Shift in the Supply Curve

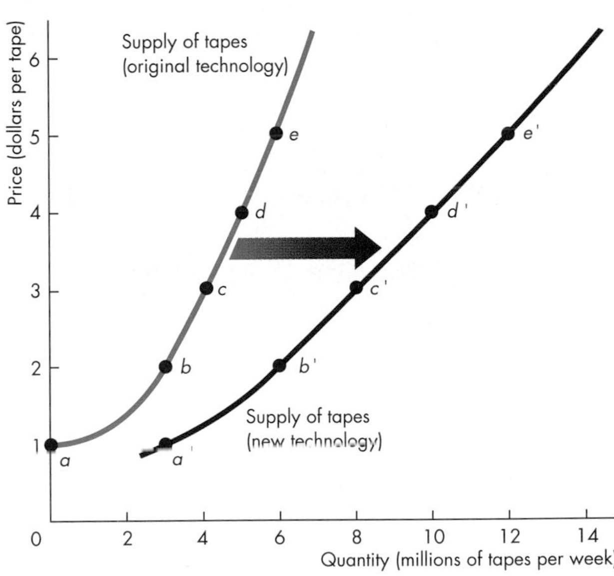

	Original technology			New technology	
	Price (dollars per tape)	Quantity (millions of tapes per week)		Price (dollars per tape)	Quantity (millions of tapes per week)
a	1	0	*a'*	1	3
b	2	3	*b'*	2	6
c	3	4	*c'*	3	8
d	4	5	*d'*	4	10
e	5	6	*e'*	5	12

If the price of a good remains constant but another influence on its supply changes, there will be a new supply schedule and the supply curve will shift. For example, if Sony and 3M invent a new, cost-saving technology for producing tapes, the supply schedule changes, as shown in the table. At $3 a tape, producers plan to sell 4 million tapes a week with the old technology and 8 million tapes a week with the new technology. Improved technology increases the supply of tapes and shifts the supply curve for tapes to the right.

FIGURE 4.6

A Change in Supply versus a Change in the Quantity Supplied

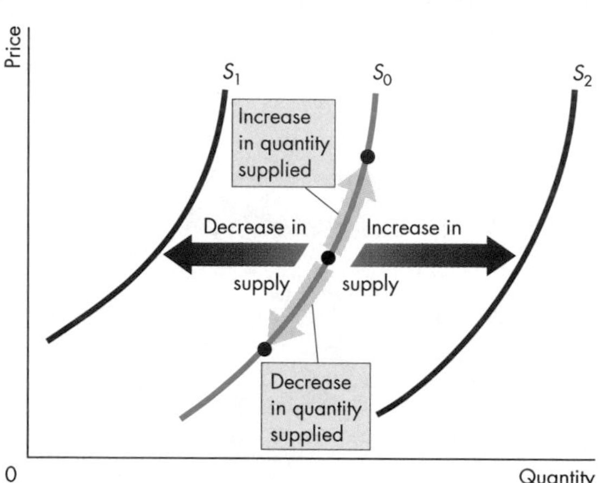

When the price of a good changes, there is a movement along the supply curve and a *change in the quantity of the good supplied.* For example, if the supply curve is S_0, a rise in the price of the good produces an increase in the quantity supplied, and a fall in the price produces a decrease in the quantity supplied. The blue arrows on curve S_0 represent these movements along the supply curve. If some other influence on supply changes, increasing the quantity that producers plan to sell, there is a shift in the supply curve to the right (from S_0 to S_2) and an *increase in supply.* If some other influence on supply changes, reducing the quantity the producers plan to sell, there is a shift to the left in the supply curve (from S_0 to S_1) and a *decrease in supply.*

shifts and there is a *change in supply.* If the supply curve is S_0 and there is, say, a technological change that reduces the amounts of the factors of production needed to produce the good, then supply increases and the supply curve shifts to the red supply curve S_2. If production costs rise, supply decreases and the supply curve shifts to the red supply curve S_1.

REVIEW

The quantity supplied is the amount of a good that producers plan to sell in a given period of time. Other things being equal, the quantity supplied of a good increases if its price rises. Supply can be represented by a schedule or a curve that shows the relationship between the quantity supplied of a good and its price. Supply describes the quantity that will be supplied at each possible price. Supply also describes the lowest price at which producers will supply the last unit. Supply increases if the prices of the factors of production used to produce the good fall, the prices of substitutes in production fall, the prices of complements in production rise, the expected future price of the good falls, or technological advances lower the cost of production. If the price of a good changes but all other influences on producers' plans are held constant, there is a change in the quantity supplied and a movement along the supply curve but *no change in supply.* A change in any other influence on producers' plans changes supply and shifts the supply curve. Changes in the prices of factors of production, in the prices of substitutes in production and complements in production, in expected future prices, or in technology shift the supply curve and are said to change supply. ◆

Let's now bring the two concepts of demand and supply together and see how prices are determined.

Price Determination

We have seen that when the price of a good rises, the quantity demanded decreases and the quantity supplied increases. We are now going to see how adjustments in price coordinate the choices of buyers and sellers.

Price as a Regulator

The price of a good regulates the quantities demanded and supplied. If the price is too high, the quantity supplied exceeds the quantity demanded. If the price is too low, the quantity demanded exceeds the quantity supplied. There is one price, and only one price, at which the quantity demanded equals the quantity supplied. We are going to work out what that price is. We are also going to discover that natural forces operating in a market move the price toward the level that makes the quantity demanded equal the quantity supplied.

The demand schedule shown in the table in Fig. 4.1 and the supply schedule shown in the table in Fig. 4.4 appear together in the table in Fig. 4.7. If the price of a tape is $1, the quantity demanded is 9 million tapes a week, but no tapes are supplied. The quantity demanded exceeds the quantity supplied by 9 million tapes a week. In other words, at a price of $1 a tape, there is a shortage of 9 million tapes a week. This shortage is shown in the final column of the table. At a price of $2 a tape, there is still a shortage but only of 3 million tapes a week. If the price of a tape is $5, the quantity supplied exceeds the quantity demanded. The quantity supplied is 6 million tapes a week, but the quantity demanded is only 2 million. There is a surplus of 4 million tapes a week. There is one price and only one price at which there is neither a shortage nor a surplus. That price is $3 a tape. At that price the quantity demanded is equal to the quantity supplied—4 million tapes a week.

The market for tapes is illustrated in the graph in Fig. 4.7. The graph shows both the demand curve of Fig. 4.1 and the supply curve of Fig. 4.4. The demand curve and the supply curve intersect when the price is $3 a tape. At that price, the quantity demanded and supplied is 4 million tapes a week. At each price *above* $3 a tape, the quantity supplied exceeds the quantity demanded. There is a surplus of tapes. For example, at $4 a tape, the surplus is 2 million tapes a week, as shown by the blue arrow in the figure. At each price *below* $3 a tape, the quantity demanded exceeds the quantity supplied. There is a shortage of tapes. For example, at $2 a tape, the shortage is 3 million tapes a week, as shown by the red arrow in the figure.

Equilibrium

We defined *equilibrium* in Chapter 1 as a situation in which opposing forces balance each other and in which no one is able to make a better choice given the available resources and actions of others. In an equilibrium, the price is such that opposing forces exactly balance each other. The **equilibrium price** is the price at which the quantity demanded equals the

FIGURE 4.7
Equilibrium

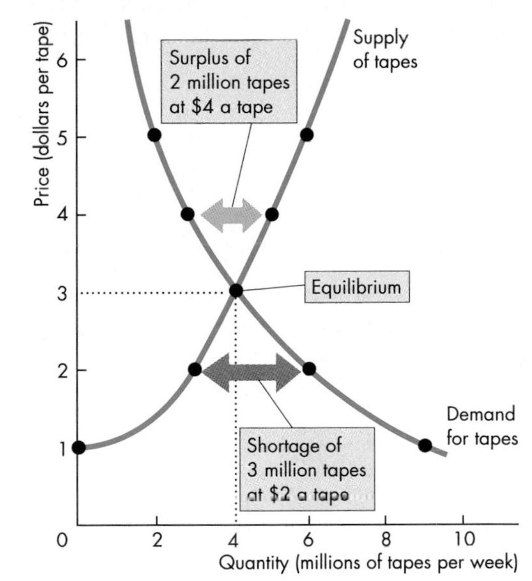

Price (dollars per tape)	Quantity demanded (millions of tapes per week)	Quantity supplied (millions of tapes per week)	Shortage (–) or surplus (+) (millions of tapes per week)
1	9	0	–9
2	6	3	–3
3	4	4	0
4	3	5	+2
5	2	6	+4

The table lists the quantities demanded and quantities supplied as well as the shortage or surplus of tapes at each price. If the price of a tape is $2, 6 million tapes a week are demanded and 3 million are supplied. There is a shortage of 3 million tapes a week, and the price rises. If the price of a tape is $4, 3 million tapes a week are demanded but 5 million are supplied. There is a surplus of 2 million tapes a week, and the price falls. If the price of a tape is $3, 4 million tapes a week are demanded and 4 million are supplied. There is neither a shortage nor a surplus. Neither buyers nor sellers have any incentive to change the price. The price at which the quantity demanded equals the quantity supplied is the equilibrium price.

quantity supplied. The **equilibrium quantity** is the quantity bought and sold at the equilibrium price. To see why equilibrium occurs where the quantity demanded equals the quantity supplied, we need to examine the behavior of buyers and sellers a bit more closely. First, let's look at the behavior of buyers.

The Demand Curve and the Willingness to Pay
Suppose the price of a tape is $2. In such a situation, producers plan to sell 3 million tapes a week. Consumers cannot force producers to sell more than they want to sell, so the quantity sold is also 3 million tapes a week. What is the highest price that buyers are willing to pay for the 3 millionth tape each week? The answer can be found on the demand curve in Fig. 4.7—it is $4 a tape.

If the price remains at $2 a tape, the quantity of tapes demanded is 6 million tapes a week—3 million tapes more than are available. In such a situation, the price of a tape does not remain at $2. Because people want more tapes than are available at that price and because they are willing to pay up to $4 a tape, the price rises. If the quantity supplied stays at 3 million tapes a week, the price rises all the way to $4 a tape.

In fact, the price doesn't have to rise by such a large amount because at higher prices, the quantity supplied increases. The price will rise from $2 a tape to $3 a tape. At that price, the quantity supplied is 4 million tapes a week, and $3 a tape is the highest price that consumers are willing to pay. At $3 a tape, buyers are able to make their planned purchases and producers are able to make their planned sales. Therefore no buyer has an incentive to bid the price higher.

The Supply Curve and the Minimum Supply Price
Suppose that the price of a tape is $4. In such a situation, the quantity demanded is 3 million tapes a week. Producers cannot force consumers to buy more than they want, so the quantity bought is 3 million tapes a week. Producers are willing to sell 3 million tapes a week for a price lower than $4 a tape. In fact, you can see on the supply curve in Fig. 4.7 that suppliers are willing to sell the 3 millionth tape each week at a price of $2. At $4 a tape, they would like to sell 5 million tapes each week. Because they want to sell more than 3 million tapes a week at $4 a tape, and because they are willing to sell the 3 millionth tape for as little as $2, they will continuously undercut each other to get a bigger share of the market. They will cut their price all the way to $2 a tape if only 3 million tapes a week can be sold.

In fact, producers don't have to cut their price to $2 a tape because the lower price brings forth an increase in the quantity demanded. When the price falls to $3, the quantity demanded is 4 million tapes a week, which is exactly the quantity that producers want to sell at that price. So when the price reaches $3 a tape, producers have no incentive to cut the price any further.

The Best Deal Available for Buyers and Sellers Both situations that we have just examined result in price changes. In the first case, the price starts out at $2 and is bid upward. In the second case, the price starts out at $4 and producers undercut each other. In both cases, prices change until they hit the price of $3 a tape. At that price, the quantity demanded and the quantity supplied are equal, and no one has any incentive to do business at a different price. Consumers are paying the highest acceptable price and producers are selling at the lowest acceptable price.

When people can freely make bids and offers and when they seek to buy at the lowest price and sell at the highest price, the price at which they trade is the equilibrium price—the quantity demanded equals the quantity supplied.

REVIEW

The equilibrium price is the price at which the plans of buyers and sellers match each other —the price at which the quantity demanded equals the quantity supplied. If the price is below equilibrium, the quantity demanded exceeds the quantity supplied, buyers offer higher prices, sellers ask for higher prices, and the price rises. If the price is above equilibrium, the quantity supplied exceeds the quantity demanded, buyers offer lower prices, sellers ask for lower prices, and the price falls. Only when the price is such that the quantity demanded and the quantity supplied are equal are there no forces acting on the price to make it change. Therefore that price is the equilibrium price. At that price, the quantity actually bought and sold is also equal to the quantity demanded and the quantity supplied. ◆

The theory of demand and supply that you have just studied is now a central part of economics. But that was not always so. Only 100 years ago, the best economists of the day were quite confused about these matters, which today even students in introductory courses find relatively easy to get right (see Our Advancing Knowledge on pp. 86–87).

As you'll discover in the rest of this chapter, the theory of demand and supply enables us to understand and make predictions about changes in prices —including the price slides, rockets, and roller coasters described in the chapter opener.

Predicting Changes in Price and Quantity

The theory we have just studied provides us with a powerful way of analyzing influences on prices and the quantities bought and sold. According to the theory, a change in price stems from either a change in demand or a change in supply, or a change in both. Let's look first at the effects of a change in demand.

A Change in Demand

What happens to the price and quantity of tapes if demand for tapes increases? We can answer this question with a specific example. If the price of a Walkman falls from $200 to $50, the demand for tapes will increase as is shown in the table in Fig. 4.8. The original demand schedule and the new one are set out in the first three columns of the table. The table also shows the supply schedule.

The original equilibrium price was $3 a tape. At that price, 4 million tapes a week were demanded and supplied. When demand increases, the price that makes the quantity demanded equal the quantity supplied is $5 a tape. At this price, 6 million tapes are bought and sold each week. When demand increases, both the price and the quantity increase.

We can illustrate these changes in the graph in Fig. 4.8. The graph shows the original demand for and supply of tapes. The original equilibrium price is $3 a tape and the quantity is 4 million tapes a week. When demand increases, the demand curve shifts to the right. The equilibrium price rises to $5 a tape and the quantity supplied increases to 6 million tapes a week, as is highlighted in the figure. There is an increase in the quantity supplied but *no change in supply.*

FIGURE 4.8

The Effect of a Change in Demand

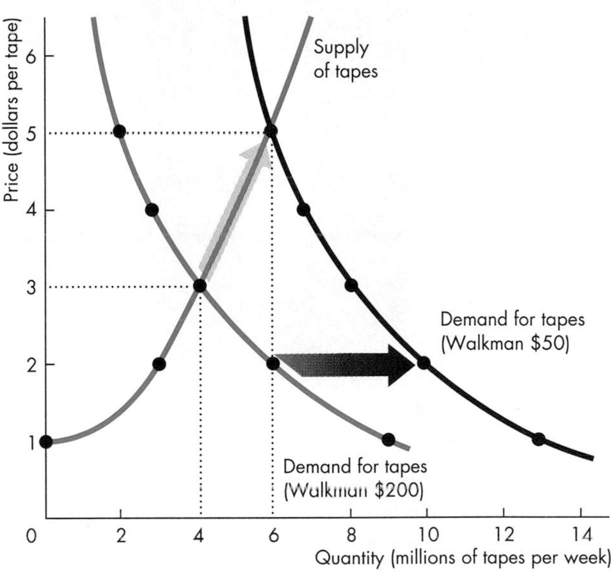

Price (dollars per tape)	Quantity demanded (millions of tapes per week)		Quantity supplied (millions of tapes per week)
	Walkman $200	Walkman $50	
1	9	13	0
2	6	10	3
3	4	8	4
4	3	7	5
5	2	6	6

With the price of a Walkman at $200, the demand for tapes is the blue curve. The equilibrium price is $3 a tape and the equilibrium quantity is 4 million tapes a week. When the price of a Walkman falls from $200 to $50, there is an increase in the demand for tapes and the demand curve shifts to the right—the red curve. At $3 a tape, there is now a shortage of 4 million tapes a week. The quantities of tapes demanded and supplied are equal at a price of $5 a tape. The price rises to this level and the quantity supplied increases. But there is no change in supply. The increase in demand increases the equilibrium price to $5 and increases the equilibrium quantity to 6 million tapes a week.

DISCOVERING the Laws of DEMAND AND SUPPLY

Railroads in the 1850s were as close to the cutting edge of technology as airlines are today. Railroad investment was profitable, but as in the airline industry today, competition was fierce.

The theory of demand and supply was being developed at the same time as the railroads were expanding, and it was their economic problems that gave the newly emerging theory its first practical applications.

In France, Jules Dupuit worked out how to use demand theory to calculate the value of railroad bridges. His work was the forerunner of what is today called *cost-benefit analysis*. Working with the very same principles invented by Dupuit, economists today calculate the costs and benefits of highways, airports, dams, and power stations.

In England, Dionysius Lardner showed railroad companies how they could increase their profits by cutting rates on long-distance business, where competition was fiercest, and raising rates on short-haul business, where they had less to fear from other suppliers. The principles first worked out by Lardner in the 1850s are used by economists working for the major airline companies today to work out the freight rates and passenger fares that will give the airline the largest possible profit. And the rates that result have a lot in common with those railroad rates of the nineteenth century. The airlines have local routes that feed like the spokes of a wheel into a hub on which there is little competition and on which they charge high fares (per mile), and they have long-distance routes between hubs on which they compete fiercely with other airlines and on which fares per mile are lowest.

"When demand and supply are in stable equilibrium, if any accident should move the scale of production from its equilibrium position, there will be instantly brought into play forces tending to push it back to that position; just as, if a stone hanging by a string is displaced from its equilibrium position, the force of gravity will at once tend to bring it back to its equilibrium position."

ALFRED MARSHALL
Principles of Economics

Dupuit used the law of demand to determine whether a bridge or canal would be valued enough by its users to justify the cost of building it, and Lardner first worked out the relationship between the cost of production and supply and used demand and supply theory to explain the costs, prices, and profits of railroad operations and to discover ways of increasing revenue by raising rates on short-haul business and lowering them on long-distance freight.

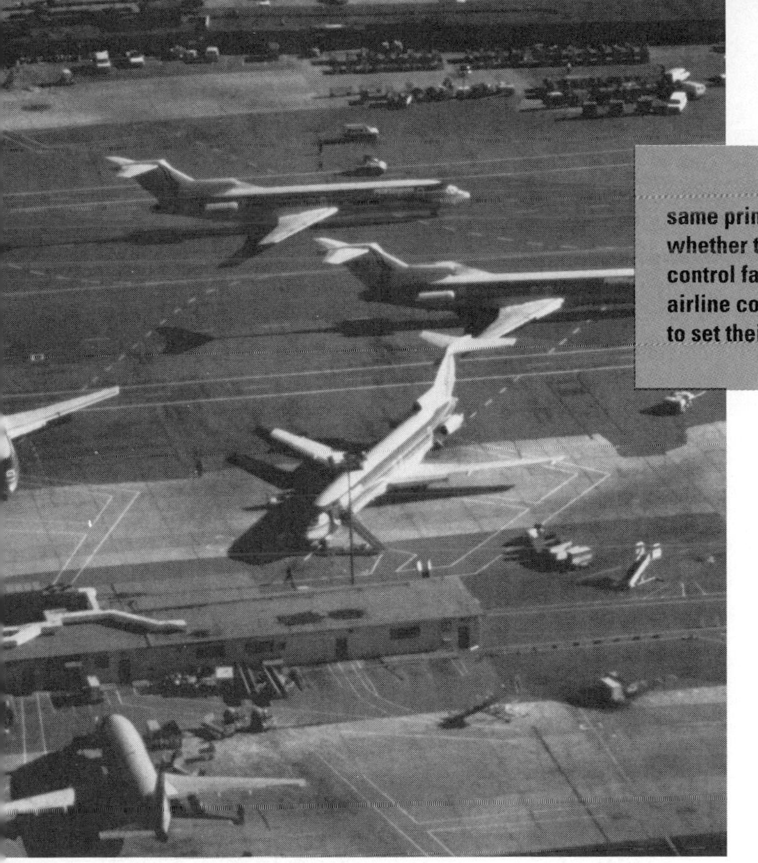

Today, using the same principles devised by Dupuit, economists calculate whether the benefits of expanding airports and air traffic control facilities are sufficient to cover their costs, and airline companies use the principles developed by Lardner to set their prices and to decide when to offer "seat sales."

The law of demand was discovered by Antoine-Augustin Cournot (1801–1877), pictured right, professor of mathematics at the University of Lyon, France, and it was he who drew the first demand curve in the 1830s. The first practical application of demand theory, by Jules Dupuit (1804–1966), a French engineer/economist, was the calculation of the benefits from building a bridge—and, given that a bridge had been built, of the correct toll to charge for its use.

THE DISCOVERERS OF THE *Laws of Demand and Supply*

The laws of demand *and* supply and the connection between the costs of production and supply were first worked out by Dionysius Lardner (1793–1859), an Irish professor of philosophy at the University of London. Known satirically among scientists of the day as "Dionysius Diddler," Lardner worked on an amazing range of problems from astronomy to railway engineering to economics. A colorful character, he would have been a regular guest of Arsenio Hall, Phil Donahue, and Oprah Winfrey if their talk shows had been around in the 1850s. He visited the École des Ponts et Chaussées (the School of Bridges and Roads) in Paris and must have learned a great deal from Dupuit, who was doing his major work on economics at the time.

Many others had a hand in refining the theory of demand and supply, but the first thorough and complete statement of the theory as we know it today was that of Alfred Marshall (1942–1924), pictured left, professor of political economy at the University of Cambridge, who, in 1890, published a monumental treatise—*Principles of Economics*—a work that became *the* textbook on economics for almost half a century. Marshall was an outstanding mathematician, but he kept mathematics and even diagrams in the background. His own supply and demand diagram (reproduced here at its original size) appears only in a footnote.

The exercise that we've just conducted can easily be reversed. If we start at a price of $5 a tape, trading 6 million tapes a week, we can then work out what happens if demand falls back to its original level. You can see that the fall in demand decreases the equilibrium price to $3 a tape and decreases the equilibrium quantity to 4 million tapes a week. Such a fall in demand could arise from a decrease in the price of compact discs or of CD players.

We can now make our first two predictions. Holding everything else constant:

- When demand increases, both the price and the quantity increase.
- When demand decreases, both the price and the quantity decrease.

A Change in Supply

Suppose that Sony and 3M have just introduced a new cost-saving technology in their tape-production plants. The new technology changes the supply. The new supply schedule (the same one that was shown in Fig. 4.5) is presented in the table in Fig. 4.9. What is the new equilibrium price and quantity? The answer is highlighted in the table: the price falls to $2 a tape and the quantity rises to 6 million a week. You can see why by looking at the quantities demanded and supplied at the old price of $3 a tape. The quantity supplied at that price is now 8 million tapes a week, and there is a surplus of tapes. The price falls. Only when the price is $2 a tape does the quantity supplied equal the quantity demanded.

Figure 4.9 illustrates the effect of an increase in supply. It shows the demand curve for tapes and the original and new supply curves. The initial equilibrium price is $3 a tape and the original quantity is 4 million tapes a week. When the supply increases, the supply curve shifts to the right. The equilibrium price falls to $2 a tape and the quantity demanded increases to 6 million tapes a week, highlighted in the figure. There is an increase in the quantity demanded but *no change in demand.*

The exercise that we've just conducted can easily be reversed. If we start out at a price of $2 a tape with 6 million tapes a week being bought and sold, we can work out what happens if the supply curve shifts back to its original position. You can see that the fall in supply increases the equilibrium price to $3 a tape and decreases the equilibrium quantity to 4 million tapes a week. Such a fall in supply could arise from an increase in the cost of labor and raw materials.

FIGURE 4.9

The Effect of a Change in Supply

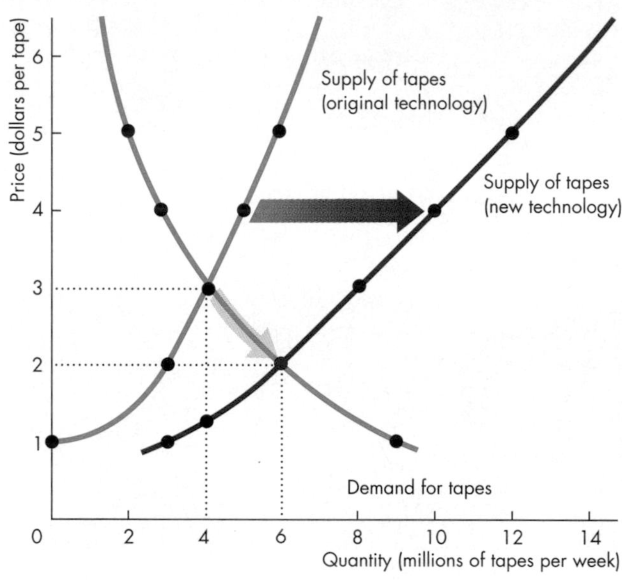

Price (dollars per tape)	Quantity demanded (millions of tapes per week)	Quantity supplied (millions of tapes per week) Original technology	New technology
1	9	0	3
2	6	3	6
3	4	4	8
4	3	5	10
5	2	3	12

With the original technology, the supply of tapes is shown by the blue curve. The equilibrium price is $3 a tape and the equilibrium quantity is 4 million tapes a week. When the new technology is adopted, there is an increase in the supply of tapes. The supply curve shifts to the right—the red curve. At $3 a tape, there is now a surplus of 4 million tapes a week. The quantities of tapes demanded and supplied are equal at a price of $2 a tape. The price falls to this level and the quantity demanded increases. But there is no change in demand. The increase in supply lowers the price of tapes to $2 and increases the quantity to 6 million tapes a week.

We can now make two more predictions. Holding everything else constant:

- When supply increases, the quantity increases and the price falls.
- When supply decreases, the quantity decreases and the price rises.

Reading Between the Lines on pp. 90–91 shows the effects of a decrease in the supply of oil in the summer of 1990 on the price of oil and on the quantities supplied and demanded.

Changes in Both Supply and Demand

In the above exercises, either demand or supply changed, but only one at a time. If just one of these changes, we can predict the direction of change of the price and the quantity. If both demand and supply change, we cannot always say what will happen to both the price and the quantity. For example, if both demand and supply increase, we know that the quantity increases, but we cannot predict whether the price rises or falls. To make such a prediction, we need to know the relative magnitude of the increase in demand and supply. If demand increases and supply decreases, we know that the price rises, but we cannot predict whether the quantity increases or decreases. Again, to be able to make a prediction about the change in the quantity, we need to know the relative magnitudes of the changes in demand and supply.

As an example of a change in both supply and demand, let's take one final look at the market for tapes. We've seen how demand and supply determine the price and quantity of tapes, how an increase in demand resulting from a fall in the price of a Walkman both raises the price of tapes and increases the quantity bought and sold, and how an increase in the supply of tapes resulting from an improved technology lowers the price of tapes and increases the quantity bought and sold. Let's now examine what happens when both of these changes —a fall in the price of a Walkman (which increases the demand for tapes) and an improved production technology (which increases the supply of tapes)— occur together.

The table in Fig. 4.10 brings together the numbers that describe the original quantities demanded and supplied and the new quantities demanded and supplied after the fall in the price of the Walkman and the improved tape production technology. These same numbers are illustrated in the graph. The original demand and supply curves intersect at a price of $3 a tape and a quantity of 4 million tapes a week.

FIGURE 4.10

The Effect of a Change in Both Demand and Supply

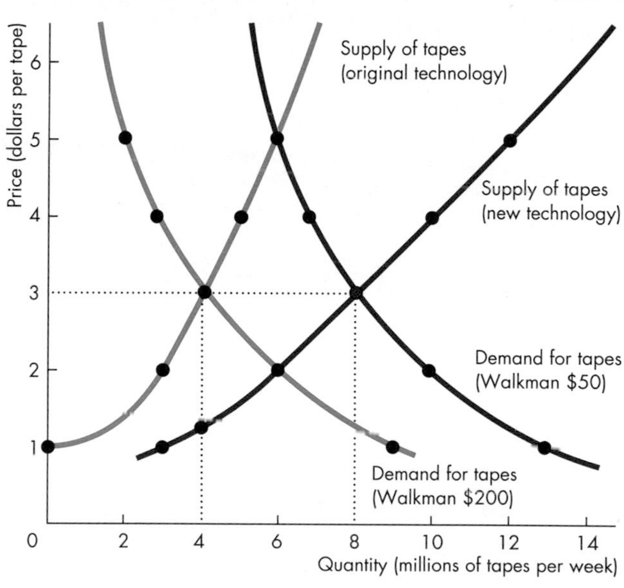

Price (dollars per tape)	Original quantities (millions of tapes per week): Quantity demanded (Walkman $200)	Quantity supplied (original technology)	New quantities (millions of tapes per week): Quantity demanded (Walkman $50)	Quantity supplied (new technology
1	9	0	13	3
2	6	3	10	6
3	4	4	8	8
4	3	5	7	10
5	2	6	6	12

When a Walkman costs $200, the price of a tape is $3 and the equilibrium quantity is 4 million tapes a week. A fall in the price of a Walkman increases the demand for tapes, and improved technology increases the supply of tapes. The new technology supply curve intersects the higher demand curve at $3, the same price as before, but the quantity increases to 8 million tapes a week. The increase in both demand and supply increases the quantity but leaves the price unchanged.

Demand and Supply: The Gulf Crisis and World Oil Market

The New York Times, August 31, 1990

Oil Shortage by Year-End

BY STEVEN GREENHOUSE
SPECIAL TO THE NEW YORK TIMES

PARIS, Aug. 30—Officials at the International Energy Agency, which represents 21 oil-consuming nations, predict that a substantial oil shortage will develop late this year. At present, however, daily worldwide demand for oil is only slightly greater than supply, despite the embargo on Iraqi and Kuwaiti crude.

As the energy agency's governing board prepared for a meeting on Friday, an official said the worldwide shortage in September would be only 100,000 barrels a day, despite the loss of some 4.3 million barrels a day from Iraq and Kuwait. . . .

But a senior agency economist said that . . . the worldwide shortage could rise to 200,000 barrels a day in October and to more than 500,000 barrels a day in December as demand swells with cold weather and as oil companies and some countries feel they should stop drawing down their stocks. . . .

"A shortage of 100,000 barrels a day is manageable, but uncomfortable, but a shortage of 500,000 barrels a day is unmanageable," said an agency official. "If it gets up above that level, then the shoe really starts to pinch."

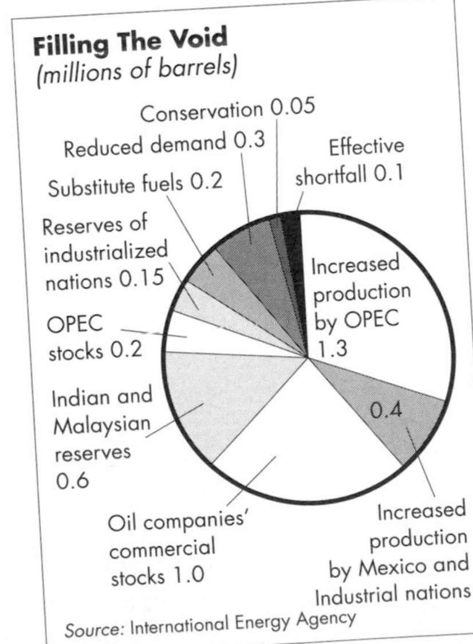

The Essence of the Story

In August 1990, an embargo on oil exports from Iraq and Kuwait decreased the worldwide supply of crude oil by 4.3 million barrels a day.

Officials at the International Energy Agency said that despite this decrease in supply, the worldwide demand for oil exceeded supply by only 100,000 barrels a day in September 1990.

But they predicted a shortage of 500,000 barrels a day by the end of 1990.

Background and Analysis

On August 2, 1990, Iraq invaded Kuwait, and the United Nations imposed sanctions on Iraq that included an embargo on oil exports from both Iraq and Kuwait.

Figure 1 illustrates the effects of these events in the world oil market. At the end of July 1990, the price of a barrel of crude oil was $23 and approximately 60 million barrels a day were being bought and sold. This situation is shown as the point at which the demand curve *D* intersects the supply curve S_0.

The loss of oil from Iraq and Kuwait decreased the world supply of crude oil by 4.3 million barrels a day. This decrease in supply is shown as the shift in the supply curve from S_0 to S_1 in Fig. 1.

The decrease in supply increased the price of oil from $23 a barrel to $32 a barrel.

The higher price induced a movement along the demand curve—a *decrease in the quantity demanded*—and along the new supply curve—an *increase in the quantity supplied*. These changes are also shown in Fig. 1 and in Fig. 2.

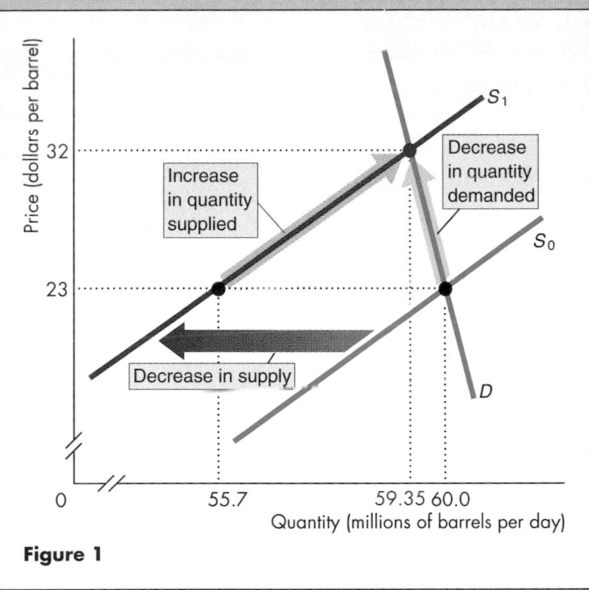

Figure 1

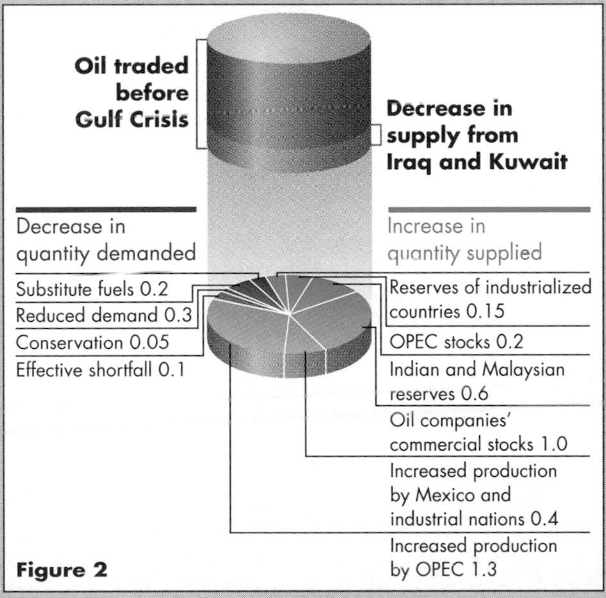

Figure 2

The pie chart in the story identifies "reduced demand" of 0.3 million barrels a day. Actually, there was no "reduced demand" but a *decrease in the quantity demanded.* That decrease in the quantity demanded is made up of what the story calls reduced demand, substitute fuels, conservation, and the "effective shortfall" shown in the pie chart in the story and in Fig. 2.

The story says that following these events, the "demand for oil" exceeded the "supply." The words "demand" and "supply" are misused here and should be replaced with "quantity demanded" and "quantity supplied."

It is difficult to make sense of the reported shortage of oil and even more difficult to make sense of the predicted larger "shortage" in the ensuing winter. Oil is traded on a world market, and its price is adjusted by market forces to keep the quantities demanded and supplied equal to each other. The so-called "effective shortfall" or "shortage" is most likely made up of unidentified decreases in the quantity demanded. Only if prices were controlled—virtually impossible in the worldwide oil market—would a shortage develop.

The new supply and demand curves also intersect at a price of $3 a tape but at a quantity of 8 million tapes a week. In this example, the increases in demand and supply are such that the rise in price brought about by an increase in demand is offset by the fall in price brought about by an increase in supply—so the price does not change. An increase in either demand or supply increases the quantity. Therefore when both demand and supply increase, so does quantity. Note that if demand had increased slightly more than shown in the figure, the price would have risen. If supply had increased by slightly more than shown in the figure, the price would have fallen. But in both cases, the quantity would have increased.

Walkmans, Apartments, and Coffee

At the beginning of this chapter, we looked at some facts about prices and quantities of Walkmans, apartments, and coffee. Let's use the theory of demand and supply to explain the movements in the prices and the quantities of those goods. Figure 4.11 illustrates the analysis.

FIGURE 4.11

More Changes in Supply and Demand

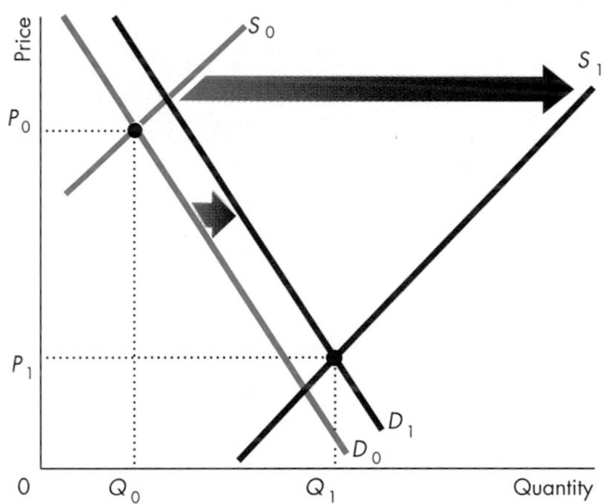

(a) Walkmans

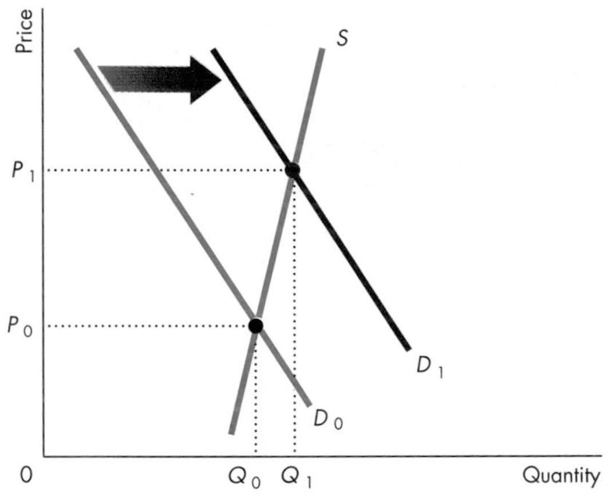

(b) Apartments

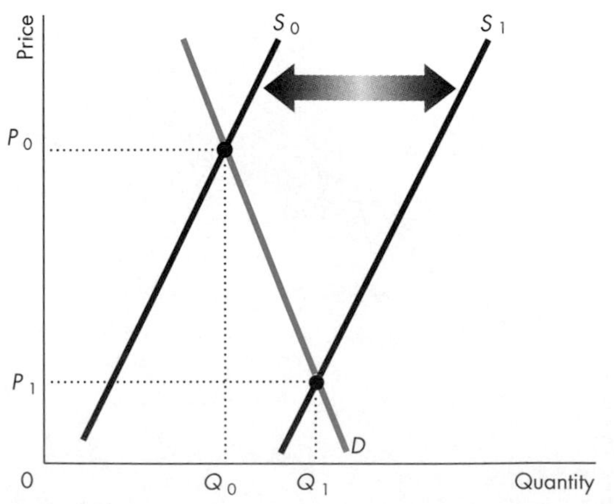

(c) Coffee

A large increase in the supply of Walkmans, from S_0 to S_1, combined with a small increase in demand, from D_0 to D_1, results in a fall in the price of the Walkman, from P_0 to P_1, and an increase in the quantity, from Q_0 to Q_1 (part a). An increase in the demand for apartments produces a large increase in the price, from P_0 to P_1, but only a small increase in the quantity, from Q_0 to Q_1 (part b). Variations in the weather and in growing conditions lead to fluctuations in the supply of coffee, between S_0 and S_1, which produce fluctuations in the price of coffee, between P_0 and P_1, and in the quantity, between Q_0 and Q_1 (part c).

First, let's consider the Walkman, shown in part (a). In 1980, using the original technology, the supply of Walkmans is described by the supply curve S_0. The 1980 demand curve is D_0. The quantities supplied and demanded in 1980 are equal at Q_0, and the price is P_0. Advances in technology and the building of additional production plants increase supply and shift the supply curve from S_0 to S_1. At the same time, increasing incomes increase the demand for Walkmans but not by nearly as much as the increase in supply. The demand curve shifts from D_0 to D_1. With the new demand curve D_1 and supply curve S_1, the equilibrium price is P_1 and the quantity is Q_1. The large increase in supply combined with a smaller increase in demand results in an increase in the quantity of Walkmans and a dramatic fall in their price.

Next, let's consider apartments in the center of the city, as in part (b). The supply of apartments is described by supply curve S. The supply curve is steep, reflecting the fact that there is a fixed number of apartment buildings. As the number of young urban professionals increases and the number of two-income families increases, the demand for city apartments increases sharply. The demand curve shifts from D_0 to D_1. As a result, the price increases from P_0 to P_1 and the quantity also increases, but not as much as the price.

Finally, let's consider the market for coffee, shown in part (c). The demand for coffee is described by curve D. The supply of coffee fluctuates between S_0 and S_1. When growing conditions are good, the supply curve is S_1. When there are adverse growing conditions such as frost, the supply decreases and the supply curve is S_0. As a consequence of fluctuations in supply, the price of coffee fluctuates between P_0 (the maximum price) and P_1 (the minimum price). The quantity fluctuates between Q_0 and Q_1.

◆ ◆ ◆ ◆ By using the theory of demand and supply, you will be able to explain past fluctuations in prices and quantities and also make predictions about future fluctuations. But you will want to do more than predict whether prices are going to rise or fall. In your study of microeconomics, you will learn to predict *by how much* they will change. In your study of macroeconomics you will learn to explain fluctuations in the economy as a whole. In fact, the theory of demand and supply can help answer almost every economic question.

SUMMARY

Demand

The quantity demanded of a good or service is the amount that consumers plan to buy in a given period of time at a particular price. Demands are different from wants. Wants are unlimited, whereas demands reflect decisions to satisfy specific wants. The quantity that consumers plan to buy of any good depends on:

- The price of the good
- The prices of related goods—substitutes and complements
- Income
- Expected future prices
- Population
- Preferences

Other things being equal, the higher the price of a good, the smaller is the quantity of that good demanded. The relationship between the quantity demanded and price, holding constant all other influences on consumers' planned purchases, is illustrated by the demand schedule or demand curve. A change in the price of a good produces movement along the demand curve for that good. Such a movement is called a change in the quantity demanded.

Changes in all other influences on buying plans are said to change demand. When demand changes, there is a new demand schedule and the demand curve shifts. When there is an increase in demand, the demand curve shifts to the right; when there is a decrease in demand, the demand curve shifts to the left. (pp. 73–78)

Supply

The quantity supplied of a good or service is the amount that producers plan to sell in a given period of time. The quantity that producers plan to sell of any good or service depends on:

- The price of the good
- The prices of factors of production
- The prices of related goods
- Expected future prices
- The number of suppliers
- Technology

Other things being equal, the higher the price of a good, the larger is the quantity of that good supplied. The relationship between the quantity supplied and price, holding constant all other influences on firms' planned sales, is illustrated by the supply schedule or supply curve. A change in the price of a good produces movement along the supply curve for that good. Such a movement is called a change in the quantity supplied.

Changes in all other influences on selling plans are said to change supply. When supply changes, there is a new supply schedule and the supply curve shifts. When there is an increase in supply, the supply curve shifts to the right; when there is a decrease in supply, the supply curve shifts to the left. (pp. 78–82)

Price Determination

Price regulates the quantities supplied and demanded. The higher the price, the greater is the quantity supplied and the smaller is the quantity demanded. At high prices, there is a surplus—an excess of the quantity supplied over the quantity demanded. At low prices, there is a shortage—an excess of the quantity demanded over the quantity supplied. There is one price and only one price at which the quantity demanded equals the quantity supplied. That price is the equilibrium price. At that price, buyers have no incentive to offer a higher price and suppliers have no incentive to sell at a lower price. (pp. 82–84)

Predicting Changes in Price and Quantity

Changes in demand and supply lead to changes in price and in the quantity bought and sold. An increase in demand leads to a rise in price and to an increase in quantity. A decrease in demand leads to a fall in price and to a decrease in quantity. An increase in supply leads to an increase in quantity and to a fall in price. A decrease in supply leads to a decrease in quantity and to a rise in price. A simultaneous increase in demand and supply increases the quantity bought and sold but can raise or lower the price. If the increase in demand is larger than the increase in supply, the price rises. If the increase in demand is smaller than the increase in supply, the price falls. (pp. 85–93)

KEY ELEMENTS

Key Terms

Key Figures and Tables

REVIEW QUESTIONS

1 Define the quantity demanded of a good or service.

2 Define the quantity supplied of a good or service.

3 List the more important factors that influence the amount that consumers plan to buy and say whether an increase in each factor increases or decreases consumers' planned purchases.

4 List the more important factors that influence the amount that firms plan to sell and say whether an increase in each factor increases or decreases firms' planned sales.

5 State the law of demand and the law of supply.

6 If a fixed amount of a good is available, what does the demand curve tell us about the price that consumers are willing to pay for that fixed quantity?

7 If consumers are willing to buy only a certain fixed quantity, what does the supply curve tell us about the price at which firms will supply that quantity?

8 Distinguish between:

- **a** A change in demand and a change in the quantity demanded
- **b** A change in supply and a change in the quantity supplied

9 Why is the price at which the quantity demanded equals the quantity supplied the equilibrium price?

10 Describe what happens to the price of a tape and the quantity of tapes sold if:

- **a** The price of CDs increases.
- **b** The price of a Walkman increases.
- **c** The supply of live concerts increases.
- **d** Consumers' incomes increase and firms producing tapes switch to new cost-saving technology.
- **e** The prices of the factors of production used to make tapes increase.
- **f** A new good comes onto the market that makes tapes obsolete.

PROBLEMS

1 Suppose that one of the following events occurs:

- **a** The price of gasoline rises.
- **b** The price of gasoline falls.
- **c** All speed limits on highways are abolished.
- **d** A new fuel-effective engine that runs on cheap alcohol is invented.
- **e** The population doubles.
- **f** Robotic production plants lower the cost of producing cars.
- **g** A law banning car imports from Japan is passed.
- **h** The rates for auto insurance double.
- **i** The minimum age for drivers is increased to 19 years.
- **j** A massive and high-grade oil supply is discovered in Mexico.
- **k** The environmental lobby succeeds in closing down all nuclear power stations.
- **l** The price of cars rises.
- **m** The price of cars falls.
- **n** The summer temperature is 10 degrees lower than normal, and the winter temperature is 10 degrees higher than normal.

State which of the above events will produce:

1 A movement along the demand curve for gasoline
2 A shift of the demand curve for gasoline to the right
3 A shift of the demand curve for gasoline to the left
4 A movement along the supply curve of gasoline
5 A shift of the supply curve of gasoline to the right
6 A shift of the supply curve of gasoline to the left
7 A movement along the demand curve for cars
8 A movement along the supply curve of cars
9 A shift of the demand curve for cars to the right
10 A shift of the demand curve for cars to the left
11 A shift of the supply curve of cars to the right
12 A shift of the supply curve of cars to the left
13 An increase in the price of gasoline
14 A decrease in the quantity of oil bought and sold

2 The demand and supply schedules for gum are as follows:

Price (cents per pack)	Quantity demanded (millions of packs per week)	Quantity supplied (millions of packs per week)
10	200	0
20	180	30
30	160	60
40	140	90
50	120	120
60	100	140
70	80	160
80	60	180
90	40	200

a What is the equilibrium price of gum?
b How much gum is bought and sold each week?

Suppose that a huge fire destroys one half of the gum-producing factories. Supply decreases to one half of the amount shown in the above supply schedule.

c What is the new equilibrium price of gum?
d How much gum is now bought and sold each week?
e Has there been a shift in or a movement along the supply curve of gum?
f Has there been a shift in or a movement along the demand curve for gum?
g As the gum factories destroyed by fire are rebuilt and gradually resume gum production, what will happen to:
  (1) The price of gum
  (2) The quantity of gum bought
  (3) The demand curve for gum
  (4) The supply curve of gum

3 Suppose the demand and supply schedules for gum are those in problem 2. An increase in the teenage population increases the demand for gum by 40 million packs per week.

a Write out the new demand schedule for gum.
b What is the new quantity of gum bought and sold each week?
c What is the new equilibrium price of gum?
d Has there been a shift in or a movement along the demand curve for gum?
e Has there been a shift in or a movement along the supply curve of gum?

4 Suppose the demand and supply schedules for gum are those in problem 2. An increase in the teenage population increases the demand for gum by 40 million packs per week, and simultaneously the fire described in problem 2 occurs, wiping out one half of the gum-producing factories.

a Draw a graph of the original and new demand and supply curves.
b What is the new quantity of gum bought and sold each week?
c What is the new equilibrium price of gum?

PART 2

How Markets Work

Talking with Herbert Stein

Herbert Stein was born in Detroit in 1916. He obtained his A.B. degree from Williams College in 1935 and his Ph.D. from the University of Chicago in 1958. Herbert Stein has made a profession of analyzing and advising on national economic policy and has spent his entire career in Washington. He was Chairman of the Council of Economic Advisors to President Nixon from 1972 to 1974 and is currently a Senior Fellow at the American Enterprise Institute in Washington. He is a regular contributor to the national public debate on economic policy through his many writings and especially through his regular columns in the *Wall Street Journal*. His latest book, written with Murray Foss, is *An Illustrated Guide to the American Economy,* published in 1992 by the American Enterprise Institute.

Dr. Stein, what attracted you to economics?

I was in college during the Great Depression. That experience surely focused my attention on economics. But there were other, more direct factors at work. As a student, my two best subjects were English and economics. But I could not see how I would make a living out of English. Moreover, at my college there was a $500 prize for an essay in the field of economics. The prize had been awarded only about four times in the previous 50 years, but still it was there as an incentive. And indeed, I won it.

Yours has been an unusual career path for an economist. Why did you choose a Washington-based policy advisory role over the opportunity to teach or do economic research?

In 1938, while still working toward my Ph.D. at the University of Chicago, I went to work in Washington, D.C. From 1940 to 1945, during World War II, many economists moved to Washington. During this period, I learned that I was good at, and that I enjoyed, applying a little list

"The best economists . . . keep foremost in their minds . . . that economic actions have important indirect and long-run effects."

of economic principles to a body of data in order to produce a policy statement or options paper that the educated public could understand. There have always been other economists who would be better teachers or writers of journal articles than I, but few who would be better at what I did. This comparative advantage provided me with employment opportunities superior in many respects to what I could have obtained in a university. By the way, it wasn't until 1958 that I finished my dissertation, but by then it no longer had a major impact on my career.

You are reported to have said that economists don't know very much but that politicians know even less. What do economists know that politicians don't know?

I did say that economists know more about economics than politicians do. But that may not have been a precise statement. The difference is probably less in knowledge than in objectives. What the best economists, unlike most politicians, keep foremost in their minds is that economic actions have important indirect and long-run effects. Most of the more specific things economists know—about markets, for example—are really specific cases of these indirect and long-run effects. Of course, politicians are capable of obtaining whatever knowledge they need, but in general they do not find this specialized knowledge of economists very useful.

We usually think of economic policy as being either pro-business and conservative or pro-labor and liberal. Is this the right distinction?

I do not find these terms—"conservative," "liberal," "pro-business," and "pro-labor"—useful any more, if they ever have been. Fifteen years ago, conservatism included support for strong defense against communism, resistance to inflation, and fiscal prudence. But the communist threat has evaporated; inflation, at least for the time, is not an issue; and practicing conservatives have given up their claim to being champions of fiscal prudence.

No one can be unflinchingly pro-labor any more, in the sense of pro–labor-union, because the union movement is withering away. At the same time, everyone has to be at least somewhat pro-labor, because labor is the great affluent American middle class.

> "Everyone has to be at least somewhat pro-labor, because labor is the great affluent American middle-class."

Similarly, neither can anyone be totally pro- or anti-business. Some have adopted a position that they call pro-business but that I prefer to call "pro-businesses." They want to promote particular industries and businesses that the government would select. That is, they want to supplant or supplement the operation of market forces in determining the direction of investment, research, and production by adopting policies that are favorable to chosen businesses. In principle, conservatives object to this approach as inefficient and as unnecessary expansions of the government's power. The difference between conservatives and liberals in devotion to market processes is unlikely to become a major issue. Neither side will be either pure in adherence to the market or thoroughgoing in rejecting it. Therefore, as conditions change and as distinctions blur, such shorthand labels are more and more uninformative and misleading.

Why are so many politicians, whether conservative or liberal, so anti-market?

Politicians in general are not anti-market. They are just not devoted to it. The benefits from interfering with the market generally are prompt, clear, and evident to the beneficiaries. The costs are diffused and perhaps delayed.

The classic case of anti-market economic policy is interference with international trade through tariffs, quotas, voluntary agreements, and similar devices. In the short run, these measures benefit certain protected industries. The U.S. auto industry, for example, benefited from the Japanese agreement to limit auto exports to the United States. Likewise, American textile producers benefited from an international textile agreement limiting exports to the United States. Voters accepted such arrangements because those who were injured, either by higher prices for the products that might have been obtained more cheaply abroad or because their own export sales were hurt, did not fully realize what was happening to them. Still, government interference with foreign trade has diminished greatly over the past sixty years, which is some evidence that people are becoming more aware of the damage that such interference does to particular sectors and to the country in general.

> "Politicians in general are not anti-market. They are just not devoted to it."

"It's possible that the market may result in a distribution of income that society legitimately considers inappropriate."

Is it possible to be too pro-market?

No. Now, it's possible that the market may result in a distribution of income that the society legitimately considers inappropriate. And calculations of private market participants may exclude some social costs or benefits that are important, as in the case of pollution. The problem is to try to make an objective assessment of the claims that the market is not yielding the best solution and that some government action would be superior. The proper role of economists is to be skeptical about such claims but not dogmatically to deny the possibility that they may be justified in some cases.

What are the sorts of issues that the Council of Economic Advisors addresses, and what in your opinion is the appropriate role for economic advisors?

In the past 46 years or so since the Council of Economic Advisors to the President was established, it has concentrated on two main issues. The first, which was dominant in the early period, was the problem of economic stabilization—avoiding large-scale unemployment and inflation. Economic advice in this area followed the trend of thinking in the profession. Initially very committed to active, fine-tuning fiscal policy, the Council later gave more weight to monetary policy and, still later, became much more reserved about activism and more concerned with the long-run consequences of short-run stabilization measures. The second major problem addressed by the Council was the evaluation of the performance of markets and of the possible effects of proposed interventions in markets. The whole arsenal of microeconomic theory has been brought to bear on these issues, and that has been a valuable contribution.

On most subjects, what is called for from advisors is not a recommendation but an option paper evaluating the likely consequences of the different policy choices that are available. That is psychologically difficult to produce because it requires an objective appraisal of one's own preferences. I wish more economists were trained in writing such papers.

What advice would you give to a student embarking on the study of economics today?

I assume that an economics student will be fully exposed to economic analysis, both micro and macro. I would suggest that economics students try to add three other subject to their studies.

First, become familiar with some body of economic data, such as national income data or international economic data, to learn about the problems in creating and using statistical representations of the real world. Second, study some economic history for a more realistic understanding of the applicability of economics to policy. And third, learn about other social sciences—notably political science and sociology—since the lines between them and economics are increasingly blurring.

CHAPTER 5

ELASTICITY

After studying this chapter, you will be able to:

- Define and calculate the price elasticity of demand
- Explain what determines the elasticity of demand
- Distinguish between short-run demand and long-run demand
- Use elasticity to determine whether a price change will increase or decrease revenue
- Define and calculate other elasticities of demand
- Define and calculate the elasticity of supply
- Distinguish among momentary supply, long-run supply, and short-run supply

OPEC's Dilemma

IF THE SUPPLY OF A GOOD DECREASES, ITS PRICE RISES. But by how much? To answer this question, you will have to don a flowing caftan: you have just been named chief economic strategist for OPEC—the Organization of Petroleum Exporting Countries. You want to bring more money into OPEC. Would you restrict the supply of oil to raise prices? Or would you produce more oil? ◆◆ You know that a higher price will bring in more dollars per barrel, but lower production means that fewer barrels will be sold. Will the price rise high enough to offset the smaller quantity that OPEC will sell? ◆◆ As OPEC's economic strategist, you need to know about the demand for oil in great detail. For example, as the world economy grows, how will that growth translate into an increasing demand for oil? What about substitutes for oil? Will we discover inexpensive methods to convert coal and tar sands into usable fuel? Will nuclear energy become safe and cheap enough to compete with oil? ◆◆ A bumper grape crop is good news for wine consumers. It brings plentiful supplies at lower prices. But is it good news for grape growers? Do they make a bigger income? Or does the lower price more than wipe out their gains from larger quantities sold? ◆◆ Looking for greater tax revenues, the government decides to increase the tax rates on tobacco and alcohol. Does the higher tax rate bring in more tax revenue? Or do people switch to substitutes for tobacco and alcohol on such a massive scale that the higher tax rate brings in less tax revenue?

◆ ◆ ◆ ◆ In this chapter you will learn how to tackle questions such as the ones just posed. You will learn how we can measure in a precise way the responsiveness of the quantities bought and sold to changes in prices and other influences on buyers or sellers.

Elasticity of Demand

Let's begin by looking a bit more closely at your task as OPEC's economic strategist. You are trying to decide whether to advise a cut in output to shift the supply curve and raise the price of oil. To make this decision, you need to know how the quantity of oil demanded responds to a change in price. You also need some way to measure that response.

Two Possible Scenarios

To understand the importance of the responsiveness of the quantity of oil demanded to a change in its price, let's compare two possible scenarios in the oil industry, shown in Fig. 5.1. In the two parts of the figure, the supply curves are identical, but the demand curves differ.

The supply curve labeled S_0 in each part of the figure shows the initial supply. It intersects the demand curve, in both cases, at a price of $10 a barrel and a quantity of 40 million barrels a day. Suppose that you contemplate a cut in supply that shifts the supply curve from S_0 to S_1. In part (a), the new supply curve S_1 intersects the demand curve D_a at a price of $30 a barrel and a quantity of 23 million barrels a day. In part (b), with demand curve D_b, the same supply curve shift increases the price to $15 a barrel and decreases the quantity to 15 million barrels a day.

You can see that in part (a) the price increases by more and the quantity decreases by less than it does in part (b). What happens to the revenue of the oil producers in these two cases? The revenue from the sale of a good equals the price of the good multiplied by the quantity sold. An increase in price has

FIGURE 5.1

Demand, Supply, and Revenue

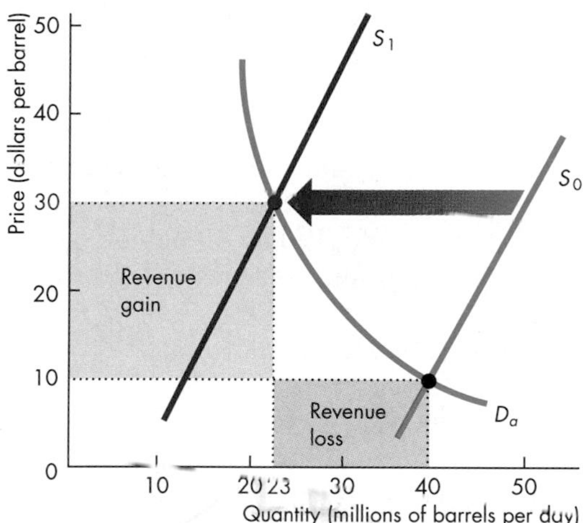

(a) More revenue

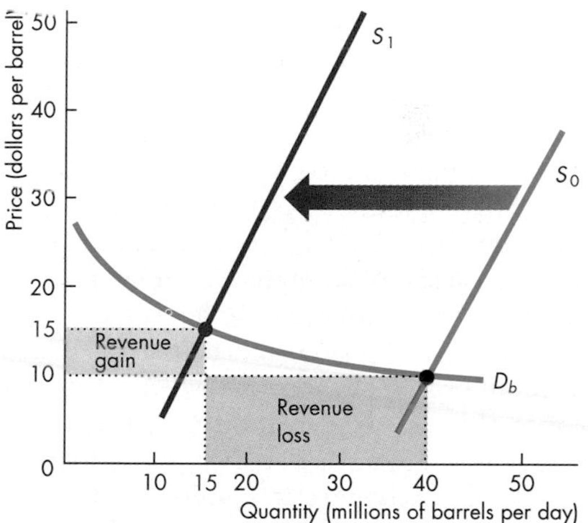

(b) Less revenue

If supply is cut from S_0 to S_1, the price rises and the quantity bought decreases. In part (a), revenue—the quantity multiplied by price—increases from $400 million to $690 million a day. The increase in revenue from a higher price (blue area) exceeds the decrease in revenue from lower sales (red area). In part (b), revenue decreases from $400 million to $225 million a day. The increase in revenue from a higher price (blue area) is smaller than the decrease in revenue from lower sales (red area). These two different responses in revenue arise from different responses of the quantity demanded to a change in price.

two opposing effects on revenue. The higher price brings in more revenue on each unit sold (blue area) but also leads to a decrease in the quantity sold, which in turn results in less revenue (red area). In case (a), the first effect is larger (blue area exceeds red area), so revenue increases. In case (b), the second effect is larger (red area exceeds blue area), so revenue decreases.

You can confirm these results by calculating the original and new revenues and comparing them. In both cases, the original revenue was $400 million a day ($10 a barrel multiplied by 40 million barrels a day). In case (a), revenue increases to $690 million a day ($30 a barrel multiplied by 23 million barrels a day). In case (b), revenue decreases to $225 million a day ($15 a barrel multiplied by 15 million barrels a day).

Slope Depends on Units of Measurement

The difference between these two cases is the responsiveness of the quantity demanded to a change in price. Demand curve D_a is steeper than demand curve D_b. But we can't compare two demand curves simply by their slopes, because the slope of a demand curve depends on the units in which we measure the price and quantity.

Also, we often need to compare the demand curves for different goods and services. For example, when deciding by how much to change tax rates, the government needs to compare the demand for oil and the demand for tobacco. Which is more responsive to price? Which can be taxed at an even higher rate without decreasing the tax revenue? Comparing the slopes of these two demand curves has no meaning, since oil is measured in gallons and tobacco in pounds—completely unrelated units.

To overcome these problems, we need a measure of response that is independent of the units of measurement of prices and quantities. Elasticity is such a measure.

Calculating Elasticity

The **price elasticity of demand** measures the responsiveness of the quantity demanded of a good to a change in its price. It is calculated by using the formula

$$\text{Price elasticity of demand} = \frac{\text{Percentage change in quantity demanded}}{\text{Percentage change in price}}$$

To use this formula to calculate the elasticity of demand, we need to know the quantities demanded at different prices, holding constant all the other influences on consumers' buying plans. As an example, let's assume that we have the relevant data on prices and quantities demanded of oil and calculate the elasticity of demand for oil. The calculations are illustrated in Fig. 5.2 and summarized in Table 5.1.

At $9.50 a barrel, 41 million barrels a day are sold. If the price increases to $10.50 a barrel, the quantity demanded decreases to 39 million barrels a day. When the price increases by $1 a barrel, the quantity demanded decreases by 2 million barrels a day. To calculate the elasticity of demand, we have to express changes in price and quantity demanded as percentage changes. But there are two prices and two quantities—the original and the new. Which price and which quantity do we use for calculating the percentage change? By convention, we use the *average price* and the *average quantity*. By using the average price and average quantity, we are actually

FIGURE 5.2

Calculating the Elasticity of Demand

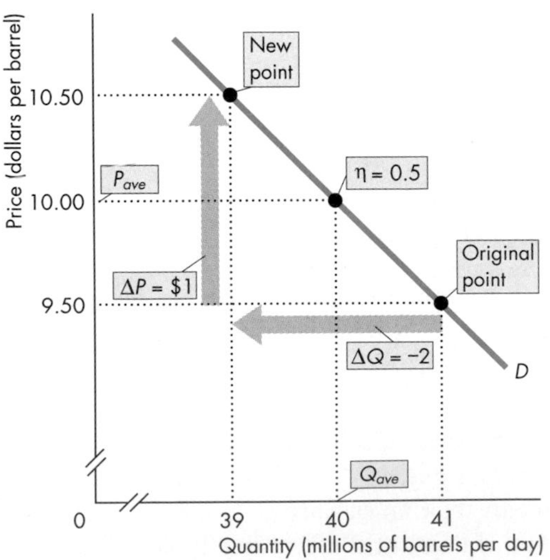

The elasticity of demand (η) is calculated midway between the original price-quantity point and the new price-quantity point as $(\Delta Q/Q_{ave})/(\Delta P/P_{ave})$. This calculation measures the elasticity at an average price of $10 per barrel and an average quantity of 40 million barrels.

calculating elasticity at a point on the demand curve midway between the original price-quantity point and the new price-quantity point, as shown in Fig. 5.2. The original price was \$9.50 and the new price is \$10.50, so the average price is \$10. A \$1 price change is 10 percent of the average price. The original quantity was 41 million barrels and the new quantity is 39 million barrels, so the average quantity demanded is 40 million barrels. A change in quantity of –2 million barrels a day is –5 percent of the average quantity.

The price elasticity of demand is

$$\frac{-5\%}{10\%} = -0.5$$

Minus Sign and Elasticity

When the price of a good *increases* along a demand curve, the quantity demanded *decreases*. Because a *positive* price change results in a *negative* change in the quantity demanded, the price elasticity of demand is negative. But it is the *absolute value* of the price elasticity of demand that tells us how responsive—how elastic—demand is. To make it easier to compare elasticities, we drop the minus sign and use the term **elasticity of demand** to mean the *absolute value* of the *price* elasticity of demand, and we denote it by the Greek letter *eta* (η). In this example, the elasticity of demand (η) is 0.5.

Why Average Price and Quantity?

We use the *average* price and *average* quantity to avoid having two values for the elasticity of demand, depending on whether the price increases or decreases. A price increase of \$1 is 10.5 percent of \$9.50, and 2 million barrels is 4.9 percent of 41 million barrels. If we use these numbers to calculate the elasticity, we get 0.47. A price decrease of \$1 is 9.5 percent of \$10.50, and 2 million barrels is 5.1

TABLE **5.1**

Calculating the Elasticity of Demand

	Numbers	Symbols and formulas*
Prices (dollars per barrel)		
Original price	**\$ 9.50**	P_0
New price	**\$10.50**	P_1
Change in price	**\$ 1.00**	$\Delta P = P_1 - P_0$
Average price	**\$10.00**	$P_{ave} = (P_0 + P_1)/2$
Percentage change in price	**10%**	$(\Delta P/P_{ave}) \times 100$
Quantities (millions of barrels per day)		
Original quantity demanded	**41**	Q_0
New quantity demanded	**39**	Q_1
Change in quantity demanded	**–2**	$\Delta Q = Q_1 - Q_0$
Average quantity demanded	**40**	$Q_{ave} = (Q_0 + Q_1)/2$
Percentage change in quantity demanded	**–5%**	$(\Delta Q/Q_{ave}) \times 100$
Percentage change in quantity demanded divided by the percentage change in price	**–0.5**	$[(\Delta Q/Q_{ave}) \times 100]/[(\Delta P/P_{ave}) \times 100] = (\Delta Q/Q_{ave})/(\Delta P/P_{ave})$
Elasticity of demand	**0.5**	η

*The Greek letter *delta* (Δ) stands for "change in."

percent of 39 million barrels. Using these numbers to calculate the elasticity, we get 0.54. If we use the average price and average quantity demanded, the elasticity is 0.5 regardless of whether the price increases or decreases.

Percentages and Proportions

Although elasticity is the ratio of the *percentage* change in the quantity demanded to the *percentage* change in the price, it is also, equivalently, the *proportionate* change in the quantity demanded divided by the *proportionate* change in the price. In Table 5.1, notice that although the formula multiplies both the proportionate change in price ($\Delta P/P_{ave}$) and the proportionate change in quantity demanded ($\Delta Q/Q_{ave}$) by 100 to create the percentage change, those hundreds cancel when we divide.

Elastic and Inelastic Demand

The elasticity that we have just calculated is 0.5. Is that a large or a small elasticity? The elasticity of demand can range between zero and infinity. The elasticity of demand is zero if the quantity demanded does not change when the price changes. An example of a good that has a very low elasticity of demand (perhaps zero) is insulin. This commodity is of such importance to many diabetics that they will buy the quantity that keeps them healthy at almost any price.

If a price rise causes a decrease in the quantity demanded, the elasticity is greater than zero. When the percentage change in the quantity demanded is less than the percentage change in price, the elasticity is less than 1 (the example that we calculated in Table 5.1 is such a case). If the percentage change in the quantity demanded equals the percentage change in price, the elasticity of demand is 1. If the percentage change in the quantity demanded exceeds the percentage change in price, the elasticity is greater than 1.

In an extreme case, the quantity demanded may be infinitely sensitive to price changes. At a particular price, people demand any quantity of a good, but if the price rises by 1¢, then the quantity demanded drops to zero. In this case, an almost zero percentage change in the price produces an infinite percentage change in the quantity demanded, so the elasticity of demand is infinity. An example of a good that has a very high elasticity of demand (almost infinite) is marker pens at the campus bookstore. If the price of marker pens increases at the campus bookstore, while all other prices, including the price of marker pens at the local supermarket, remain constant, there will be a large decrease in the quantity of marker pens bought at the campus bookstore. Marker pens at the local supermarket are almost perfect substitutes for marker pens at the campus bookstore.

For elasticities between zero and 1, demand is called **inelastic;** for elasticities greater than 1, demand is called **elastic.** The dividing line between inelastic and elastic demand is called **unit elastic demand.** When elasticity is equal to infinity, demand is called **perfectly elastic;** when elasticity is equal to zero, demand is called **perfectly inelastic.**

Table 5.2 shows examples of inelastic, unit elastic, and elastic demands. We can see in this table the changes in quantities demanded for a 10 percent change in price. The first row simply reproduces the calculations that you worked through in Table 5.1.

TABLE 5.2

Elastic and Inelastic Demand

Effects of a 10 percent price change

	Original quantity demanded	New quantity demanded	Average quantity demanded	Change in quantity demanded	Percentage change in quantity demanded	Elasticity of demand
Inelastic demand	41	39	40	–2	–5	0.5
Unit elastic demand	42	38	40	–4	–10	1.0
Elastic demand	50	30	40	–20	–50	5.0

The second row shows the case of a unit elastic demand. The initial quantity demanded was 42 million barrels a day, and the new quantity demanded is 38. Thus the average quantity demanded is 40, and the change in the quantity demanded is –4. The percentage change in the quantity demanded is –10 percent. Therefore the elasticity of demand is 1. The final case is one in which the original quantity demanded was 50 and the new quantity demanded is 30. The average quantity demanded is still 40, but the change in quantity demanded is now –20. The percentage change in the quantity demanded is –50 percent. In this case, the elasticity is 5.

Elasticity along a Straight-Line Demand Curve

Elasticity is not the same as slope, but the two are related. To understand how they are related, let's look at elasticity along a straight-line demand curve—a demand curve that has a constant slope.

Figure 5.3 illustrates the calculation of elasticity along such a demand curve. Let's start with a price of \$50 a barrel. What is the elasticity if we lower the price from \$50 to \$40? The change in the price is –\$10 and the average price is \$45 (average of \$50 and \$40), which means that the proportionate change in price is

$$\frac{\Delta P}{P_{ave}} = \frac{-10}{45}$$

The original quantity demanded is zero and the new quantity demanded is 10 million barrels a day, so the change in the quantity demanded is 10 million barrels a day and the average quantity is 5 million barrels a day (the average of 10 million and zero). Thus the proportionate change in the quantity demanded is

$$\frac{\Delta Q}{Q_{ave}} = \frac{10}{5}.$$

Dividing the proportionate change in the quantity demanded by the proportionate change in the price gives

$$\frac{\Delta Q/Q_{ave}}{\Delta P/P_{ave}} = \frac{10/5}{-10/45} = -9.$$

Then taking the absolute value gives us the elasticity of demand:

$$\eta = 9.$$

FIGURE 5.3

Elasticity along a Straight-Line Demand Curve

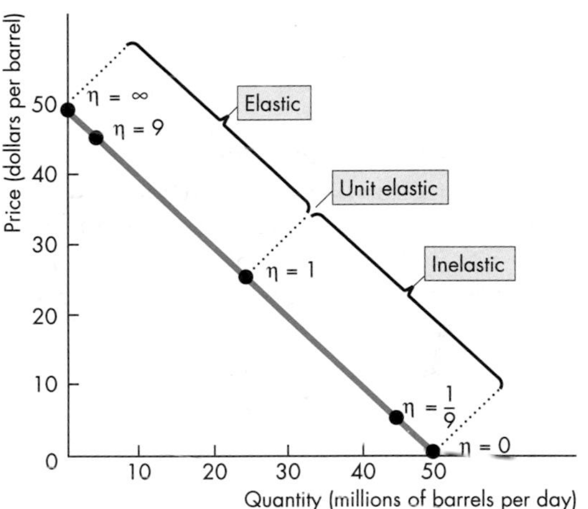

On a straight-line demand curve, elasticity decreases as the price falls and the quantity demanded increases. Demand is unit elastic at the midpoint of the demand curve (elasticity is 1). Above the midpoint, demand is elastic (elasticity is greater than 1); below the midpoint, demand is inelastic (elasticity is less than 1).

Using this same method, we can calculate the elasticity of demand when the price of a barrel is cut repeatedly by \$10—from \$45 to \$35, from \$40 to \$30, from \$35 to \$25, and so on. You can verify the elasticity of demand at other points on the demand curve in Fig. 5.3. On a straight-line demand curve, the elasticity decreases as the price falls.

At the midpoint of the demand curve, where the price is \$25 a barrel and the quantity demanded is 25 million barrels a day, elasticity is exactly 1. Above the midpoint, the elasticity is greater than 1 and it increases as the price rises. Below the midpoint, the elasticity is less than 1 and it decreases as the price falls. Elasticity is infinity when the price is \$50 a barrel and the quantity demanded is zero, and elasticity is zero when the quantity demanded is 50 million barrels a day and the price is zero.

Why Elasticity Is Smaller at Lower Prices

Why is elasticity smaller at lower prices along a straight-line demand curve? It is because the *levels* of price and quantity demanded affect their *percentage* changes. For a given change in price, the percentage change is small at a high price and large at a low price. Similarly, for a given change in quantity demanded, the percentage change is small at a large quantity and large at a small quantity. So for a given change in price, the lower the initial price, the larger is the percentage change in price, the smaller is the percentage change in the quantity demanded, and the smaller is the elasticity.

Constant Elasticity Demand Curves

A demand curve can have a constant elasticity. A perfectly inelastic demand curve has a constant elasticity of zero ($\eta = 0$) and is vertical. A perfectly elastic demand curve has a constant elasticity of infinity ($\eta = \infty$) and is horizontal. Other constant elasticity demand curves are *curved*. Figure 5.4 illustrates three constant elasticity demand curves—the cases of zero, unity, and infinity.

The example that we gave earlier, of a good with very low elasticity of demand (shown as zero in part a of the figure) is insulin. Regardless of the price, the quantity demanded remains constant in part (a). An example of a good whose elasticity is close to 1 (part b) is electricity. As its price increases, the quantity demanded decreases by the same percentage amount. The example that we gave of a good whose elasticity is (almost) infinite (part c) is marker pens at the campus bookstore. Marker pens are bought from the campus bookstore only if their price doesn't exceed that of marker pens at the local supermarket. If the price of marker pens at the campus bookstore exceeds the price at the local supermarket, the quantity of marker pens bought from the bookstore is zero. If the price of marker pens at the local supermarket exceeds that at the campus bookstore, marker pens are bought only from the bookstore. When the prices are equal, there is no unique quantity demanded.

Real-World Elasticities

Actual values of elasticities of demand have been estimated from the average spending patterns of consumers, and some examples are set out in Table 5.3. But elasticity is not just a number calculated by economists. Whether demand is elastic or inelastic is of enormous importance to each of us. In the 1970s, when OPEC did in fact cut back on the supply of oil, Americans discovered that their demand for oil was inelastic. Despite the smaller supplies, we still demanded a lot of oil and gasoline, which led to cuts

FIGURE 5.4

Demand Curves with Constant Elasticity

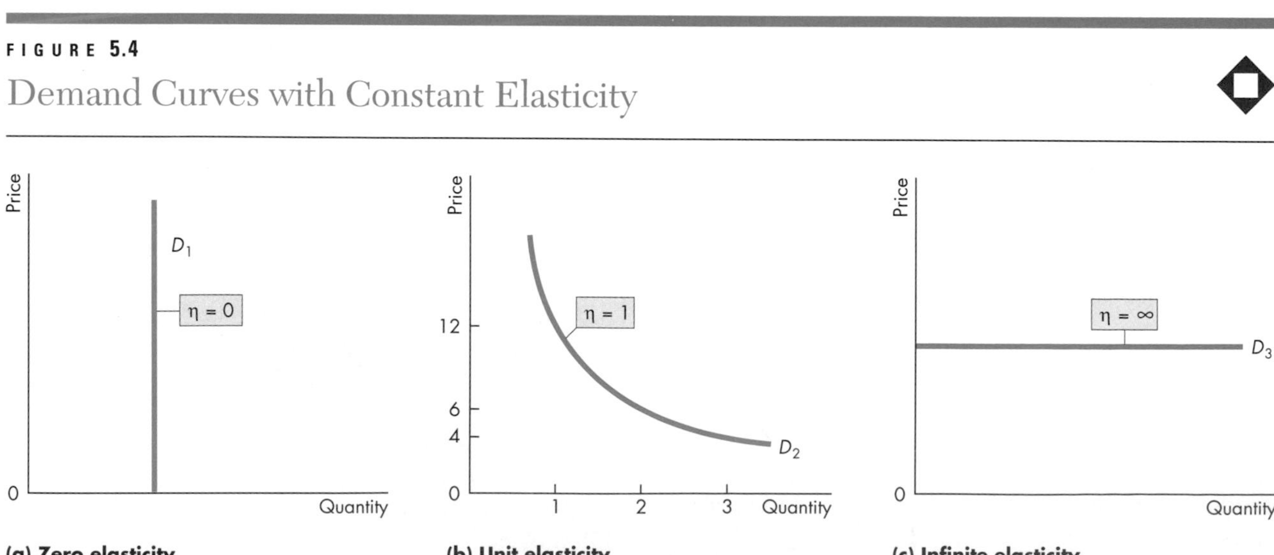

(a) Zero elasticity **(b) Unit elasticity** **(c) Infinite elasticity**

Each demand curve shown here has a constant elasticity. The demand curve in part (a) has zero elasticity. The demand curve in part (b) has unit elasticity. The demand curve in part (c) has infinite elasticity.

TABLE 5.3
Some Price Elasticities in the U.S. Economy

Industry	Elasticity
Elastic demand	
Metals	**1.52**
Electrical engineering products	**1.39**
Mechanical engineering products	**1.30**
Furniture	**1.26**
Motor vehicles	**1.14**
Instrument engineering products	**1.10**
Professional services	**1.09**
Transportation services	**1.03**
Inelastic demand	
Gas, electricity, and water	**0.92**
Oil	**0.91**
Chemicals	**0.89**
Beverages (all types)	**0.78**
Tobacco	**0.61**
Food	**0.58**
Banking and insurance services	**0.56**
Housing services	**0.55**
Clothing	**0.49**
Agricultural and fish products	**0.42**
Books, magazines, and newspapers	**0.34**
Coal	**0.32**

Source: Ahsan Mansur and John Whalley, "Numerical Specification of Applied General Equilibrium Models: Estimation, Calibration, and Data," in *Applied General Equilibrium Analysis,* eds. Herbert E. Scarf and John B. Shoven (New York: Cambridge University Press, 1984), 109.

in spending on other things—people took fewer vacations; vast companies were thrown into a panic as they tried to adjust; schools had to cut the salaries of teachers so that they could pay for heating oil; speed restrictions were imposed; and angry car owners had to face the premature obsolescence of their gas guzzlers.

What makes the demand for some goods elastic and the demand for others inelastic? Elasticity depends on:

- The ease with which one good can be substituted for another
- The proportion of income spent on the good
- The amount of time elapsed since the price change

Substitutability

Substitutability depends on the nature of the good itself. For example, oil, a good with an inelastic demand, certainly has substitutes but none that are very close (imagine a steam-driven, coal-fueled car or a nuclear-powered jetliner). On the other hand, metals, a group of goods with elastic demands, have very good substitutes in the form of plastics.

The degree of substitutability between two goods depends on how narrowly (or broadly) we define them. For example, even though oil does not have a close substitute, different types of oil substitute for each other without much difficulty. Oils from different parts of the world differ in weight and chemical composition. Let's consider a particular kind of oil—called Saudi Arabian Light. Its elasticity will be relevant if you happen to be the economic advisor to Saudi Arabia (as well as the OPEC economic strategist!). Suppose Saudi Arabia is contemplating a unilateral price rise, which means that prices of other types of oil will stay the same. Although Saudi Arabian Light has unique characteristics, other oils can easily substitute for it, and most buyers will be very sensitive to its price relative to the prices of other types of oil. Demand in this case is highly elastic.

This example, which distinguishes between oil in general and different types of oil, has broad applications. For example, the elasticity of demand for meat is low, but the elasticity of demand for beef, lamb, or pork is high. The elasticity of demand for personal computers is low, but the elasticity of demand for an IBM, Zenith, or Apple is high.

Proportion of Income Spent on a Good

Other things being equal, the higher the proportion of income spent on a good, the higher is the elasticity. If only a small fraction of income is spent on a good, then a change in its price will have little impact on the consumer's overall budget. In contrast, even a small rise in the price of a good that commands a large part of a consumer's budget will induce the consumer to undertake a radical reappraisal of expenditures.

To appreciate the importance of the proportion of income spent on a good, consider your own elasticity of demand for textbooks and chewing gum. If the price of textbooks doubles (increases 100 percent), there will be an enormous decrease in the quantity of textbooks bought. There will be an increase in sharing and in illegal photocopying. If the price of chewing gum doubles (also a 100 percent increase), there will be almost no change in the quantity of gum demanded. Why the difference? Textbooks take a large proportion of your budget, while gum takes only a tiny portion. You don't like either price increase, but you hardly notice the effects of the increased price of gum, while the increased price of textbooks blows you away!

Time Frame for Demand

Elasticity also depends on the amount of time that has elapsed since a price change. In general, the greater the lapse of time, the higher the elasticity of demand. The reason is related to substitutability. The greater the passage of time, the more it becomes possible to develop substitutes for a good whose price has increased. Thus at the moment of a price increase, the consumer often has little choice but to continue consuming similar quantities of a good. However, given enough time, the consumer finds alternatives or cheaper substitutes and gradually lowers the rate of purchase of items that have become more expensive. To take account of the importance of time on the elasticity of demand, we distinguish between two time frames for demand:

1. Short-run demand
2. Long-run demand

Short-Run Demand The **short-run demand curve** describes the initial response of buyers to a change in the price of a good. The short-run response depends on whether the price change is seen as permanent (or at least long-lasting) or temporary. A price change that is believed to be temporary produces a highly elastic buyer response. Why would you pay a higher price now if you believe you can get the same thing for a lower price a few days from now? And if the price is temporarily low, why wouldn't you take advantage of it and buy a lot before the price goes up again?

For example, you can make telephone calls at lower rates on weekends than during the week. The fall in price on Saturday and the rise in price on Monday produce a large change in the quantity demanded—demand is highly elastic. Of course, many calls are made during normal business hours, but the lower price on the weekend induces a large switch from business day calling to weekend calling. Other examples are seasonal variations in the price of travel and of certain fresh fruits and vegetables.

When a price change is believed to be permanent, the quantity bought does not change much in the short run. That is, short-run demand is inelastic. The reason is that people find it hard to change their buying habits. More importantly, they often have to adjust their consumption of other complementary goods, an expensive and time-consuming undertaking.

An example of a permanent, or at least a long-lasting, price change occurred in the market for oil in the early 1970s. At the end of 1973 and the beginning of 1974, the price of oil increased fourfold, leading in turn to a sharp rise in the costs of home heating and of gasoline. Initially, consumers had little choice but to accept the price increases and maintain consumption at more or less their original levels. Home heating equipment and cars might not have been very energy-efficient, but nothing else was available. Drivers could lower their average speed and economize on gasoline. Thermostats could be turned down, but that too imposed costs—costs of discomfort. As a consequence, there were severe limits on the extent to which people felt it worthwhile to cut back on their consumption of the now much more costly fuel. The short-run buyer response in the face of this sharp price increase was inelastic.

Long-Run Demand The **long-run demand curve** describes the response of buyers to a change in price after all possible adjustments have been made. Long-run demand is more elastic than short-run demand. The 1974 rise in the price of oil and gasoline produced a clear demonstration of the distinction between long-run and short-run demand. Initially, buyers responded to higher gasoline and oil prices by using their existing capital equipment—furnaces and gas guzzlers—in a way that economized on the more expensive fuel. With a longer time to respond, people bought more energy-efficient capital equipment. Cars became smaller and more fuel-efficient, and car engines also became more efficient.

Two Demand Curves The short-run and long-run demand curves for oil in 1974 looked like those in Fig. 5.1. Look back at that figure and refresh your memory about the two demand curves in parts (a) and (b). The short-run demand curve is D_a, and the long-run demand curve is D_b. The price of a barrel of oil in 1974 was $10, and 40 million barrels a day were bought and sold. At that price and quantity, long-run demand, D_b, is much more elastic than short-run demand, D_a.

REVIEW

The elasticity of demand is a measure of the response of a change in the quantity demanded to a change in price that is independent of the units of measurement. It is calculated as the absolute value of the percentage change in the quantity demanded divided by the percentage change in price. The elasticity of demand ranges between zero and infinity. Goods that have a high elasticity of demand are those that have close substitutes and on which a large proportion of income is spent. Goods that have a low elasticity of demand are those that do not have good substitutes and on which a small portion of income is spent. Elasticity is also higher the longer the time lapse since a price change. ◆

Elasticity, Revenue, and Expenditure

Revenue is the price of a good multiplied by the quantity *sold*. Expenditure is the price of a good multiplied by the quantity *bought*. Thus revenue and expenditure are two sides of the same coin—revenue is the receipts of the sellers, while expenditure is the outlays of the buyers. When the price of a good rises along a demand curve, the quantity sold decreases. What happens to revenue (and expenditure) depends on the extent to which the quantity sold decreases as the price rises. If a 1 percent rise in the price reduces the quantity sold by less than 1 percent, revenue increases. If a 1 percent rise in price reduces the quantity sold by more than 1 percent, revenue decreases. If a 1 percent rise in price reduces the quantity sold by 1 percent, the price rise and the quantity decrease just offset each other and revenue stays constant. But we now have a precise way of linking the percent change of the quantity sold to the percent change in price—the elasticity of demand. When the price of a good rises, the size of the elasticity of demand determines whether revenue increases or decreases. Table 5.4 gives some examples based on the three cases in Table 5.2.

In case *a*, the elasticity of demand is 0.5. When the price rises from $9.50 to $10.50, the quantity sold decreases from 41 million to 39 million barrels a day. Revenue, which is equal to price multiplied by quantity sold, was originally $9.50 multiplied by 41 million, which is $389.50 million a day. After the price rises, revenue increases to $409.50 million a day. Thus a rise in the price leads to an *increase* in revenue of $20 million a day.

In case *b*, the elasticity of demand is 1. The quantity sold decreases from 42 million to 38 million barrels a day as the price rises from $9.50 to $10.50. Revenue in this case is the same at each price, $399 million a day. Thus when the price changes and the elasticity of demand is 1, revenue *does not change*.

In case *c*, the elasticity of demand is 5. When the price rises from $9.50 to $10.50, the quantity sold decreases from 50 million to 30 million barrels a day. The original revenue was $475 million a day, but the new revenue is $315 million a day. Thus in this case, a rise in the price leads to a *decrease* in revenue of $160 million a day.

Elasticity and revenue are closely connected. When the elasticity of demand is greater than 1, the percentage decrease in the quantity demanded exceeds the percentage rise in price and therefore revenue decreases. When the elasticity of demand is less than 1, the percentage decrease in the quantity demanded is less than the percentage rise in price and therefore revenue increases. When the elasticity of demand is 1, the percentage decrease in the quantity demanded equals the percentage rise in price and revenue remains constant. The extra revenue from a higher price is exactly offset by the loss in revenue from the smaller quantities sold.

TABLE 5.4

Elasticity of Demand, Revenue, and Expenditure

		Price (dollars per barrel)		Quantity demanded (millions of barrels per day)		Revenue/expenditure (millions of dollars per day)		
	Elasticity	Original	New	Original	New	Original	New	Change
a	0.5	9.50	10.50	41	39	389.50	409.50	+20
b	1.0	9.50	10.50	42	38	399.00	399.00	0
c	5.0	9.50	10.50	50	30	475.00	315.00	–160

As we have seen, long-run demand curves are more elastic than short-run demand curves. It is possible, therefore, that an increase in price will result in an increase in revenue in the short run but not in the long run. If the short-run elasticity is less than 1 but the long-run elasticity is greater than 1, this outcome will occur. Reading Between the Lines on pp. 116–117 is a practical application of the relationship between the elasticity of demand and revenue in the timber industry.

So far, we've studied the most important elasticity—the price elasticity of demand. But there are other useful elasticities. Let's see what they are.

More Demand Elasticities

The quantity demanded of any good (or service or factor of production) is influenced by many things other than its price. It depends on, among other things, incomes and the prices of other goods. We can calculate elasticities of demand with respect to these other variables as well. Let's now examine some of these additional elasticities.

Income Elasticity of Demand

As income grows, how will the demand for a particular good change? The answer depends on the income elasticity of demand for the good. The **income elasticity of demand** is the percentage change in the quantity demanded divided by the percentage change in income. It is represented by η_y. That is,

$$\eta_y = \frac{\text{Percentage change in quantity demanded}}{\text{Percentage change in income}}.$$

Income elasticities of demand can be positive or negative; however, there are three interesting ranges for the income elasticity of demand:

1. Greater than 1 (income elastic)
2. Between zero and 1 (income inelastic)
3. Less than zero (negative income elasticity)

These three cases are illustrated in Fig. 5.5, and some real-world examples are shown in Table 5.5. Part (a) of the figure shows an income elasticity of demand that is greater than 1. As income increases, the quantity demanded increases, but the quantity demanded increases faster than income. The curve slopes upward and has an increasing slope. Goods that fall into this category include ocean cruises, custom clothing, international travel, jewelry, and works of art.

Part (b) shows an income elasticity of demand that is between zero and 1. In this case, the quantity demanded increases as income increases, but income increases faster than the quantity demanded. The curve slopes upward, but the slope declines as income increases. Goods that fall into this category include food, clothing, furniture, newspapers, and magazines.

Part (c) illustrates a third category of goods that is a bit more complicated. For these goods, as income increases, the quantity demanded increases until it reaches a maximum at income *m*. Beyond that point, as income continues to increase, the

FIGURE 5.5
Income Elasticity of Demand

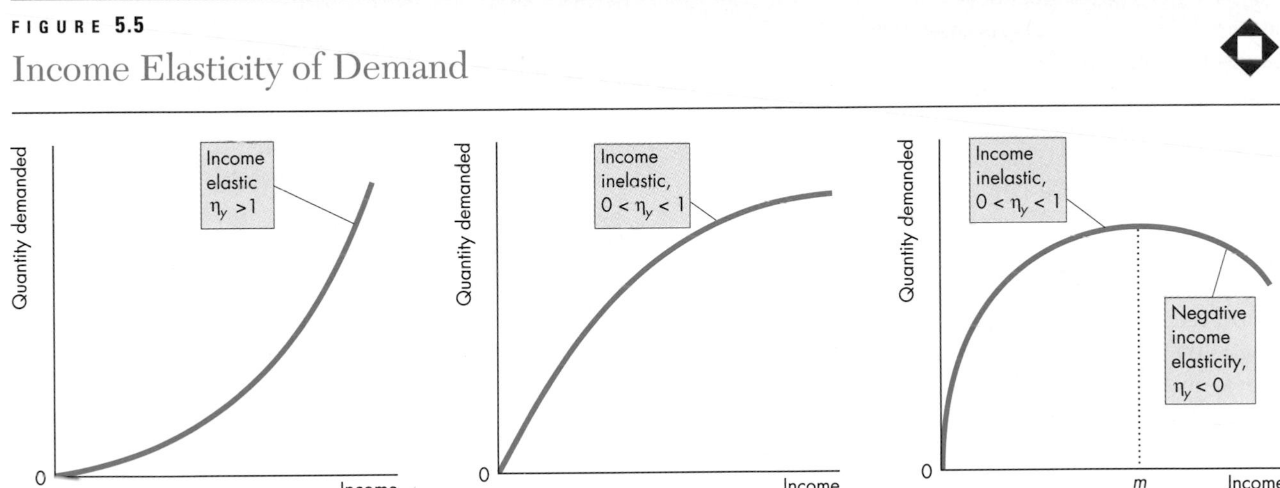

(a) Elasticity greater than 1 **(b) Elasticity between zero and 1** **(c) Elasticity less than 1 and becomes negative**

There are three ranges of values for income elasticity of demand. In part (a), income elasticity of demand is greater than 1. In this case, as income increases, the quantity demanded increases but by a bigger percentage than the increase in income. In part (b), income elasticity of demand is between zero and 1. In this case, as income increases, the quantity demanded increases but by a smaller percentage than the increase in income. In part (c), the income elasticity of demand is positive at low incomes but becomes negative as income increases above level *m*. Maximum consumption occurs at the income *m*.

TABLE 5.5
Some Income Elasticities of Demand

Industry	Elasticity	Industry	Elasticity
Elastic demand		**Unit Elastic demand**	
Airline travel	**5.82**	**Dentists' services**	**1.00**
Movies	**3.41**	**Inelastic demand**	
Foreign travel	**3.08**	**Shoes and other footwear**	**0.94**
Housing services	**2.45**	**Tobacco**	**0.86**
Electricity	**1.94**	**Alcoholic beverages**	**0.62**
Restaurant meals	**1.61**	**Water**	**0.59**
Local buses and trains	**1.38**	**Clothing**	**0.51**
Gasoline and oil	**1.36**	**Newspapers and magazines**	**0.38**
Haircutting	**1.36**	**Telephone**	**0.32**
Cars	**1.07**		

Source: H. S. Houthakker and Lester D. Taylor, *Consumer Demand in the United States* (Cambridge, Mass.: Harvard University Press, 1970).

quantity demanded declines. The elasticity of demand is positive but less than 1 up to income *m*. Beyond income *m*, the income elasticity of demand is negative. Examples of goods in this category include one-speed bicycles, small motorbikes, potatoes, and rice. Low income consumers buy most of these goods. At low-income levels, the demand for such goods increases as income increases. Eventually, income reaches a level (at point *m*) at which consumers replace these goods with superior alternatives. For example, a small car replaces the motorbike, and fruit, vegetables, and meat begin to appear in a diet that was heavy in rice or potatoes.

Goods whose income elasticities of demand are positive are called *normal goods.* Goods whose income elasticities of demand are negative are called *inferior goods.*

Real-World Income Elasticities of Demand

Estimates of income elasticities of demand in the United States are shown in Table 5.5. By using estimates of income elasticity of demand, we can translate projections of average income growth rates into growth rates of demand for particular goods and services. For example, if average incomes grow by 3 percent a year, the demand for gasoline and oil will grow by 4 percent a year (3 percent multiplied by the income elasticity of demand for gasoline and oil, which, as shown in Table 5.5, is 1.36).

Cross Elasticity of Demand

The quantity of any good demanded depends on the prices of its substitutes and complements. The responsiveness of the quantity demanded of a particular good to the prices of its substitutes and complements is measured by cross elasticity of demand, which is represented by η_x. The **cross elasticity of demand** is calculated as the percentage change in the quantity demanded of one good divided by the percentage change in the price of another good (a substitute or a complement). That is,

$$\eta_x = \frac{\text{Percentage change in quantity demanded of one good}}{\text{Percentage change in the price of another good}}.$$

The cross elasticity of demand with respect to the price of a substitute is positive. The cross elasticity of demand with respect to the price of a complement is negative. Figure 5.6 makes it clear why. In part (a), when the price of coal (a substitute for oil) rises, the demand for oil increases. In part (b), when the price of cars (a complement of oil) rises, the demand for oil decreases. The more easily two goods substitute for or complement each other, the larger is the magnitude of their cross elasticity.

Table 5.6 provides a compact summary of all the different kinds of demand elasticities you've just studied.

FIGURE 5.6

Cross Elasticities: Substitutes and Complements

(a) Substitutes

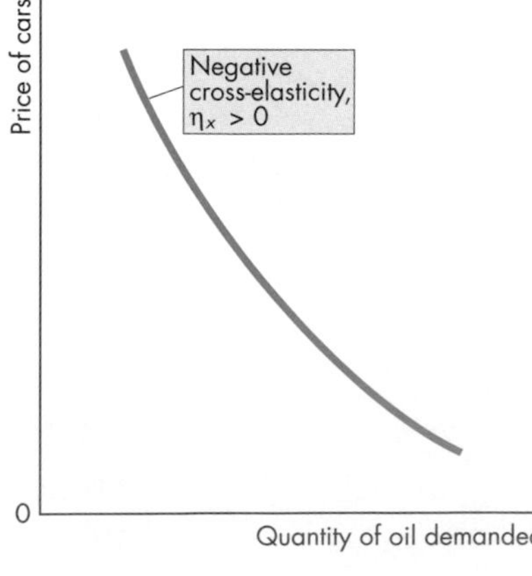

(b) Complements

Part (a) shows the cross elasticity of demand with respect to the price of a substitute. When the price of coal increases, the quantity of oil demanded also increases. Part (b) shows the cross elasticity of demand with respect to the price of a complement. When the price of cars increases, the quantity of oil demanded decreases.

TABLE 5.6

A Compact Glossary of Elasticities of Demand

Price elasticities (η)

A relationship is described as:	When η is:	Which means that:
Perfectly elastic or infinitely elastic	**Infinity**	**The smallest possible increase (decrease) in price causes an infinitely large decrease (increase) in the quantity demanded**
Elastic	**Less than infinity but greater than 1**	**The percentage decrease (increase) in the quantity demanded exceeds the percentage increase (decrease) in price**
Unit elastic	**1**	**The percentage decrease (increase) in the quantity demanded equals the percentage increase (decrease) in price**
Inelastic	**Greater than zero but less than 1**	**The percentage decrease (increase) in the quantity demanded is less than the percentage increase (decrease) in price**
Perfectly inelastic or completely inelastic	**Zero**	**The quantity demanded is the same at all prices**

Income elasticities (η_y)

A relationship is described as:	When η_y is:	Which means that:
Income elastic (normal good)	**Greater than 1**	**The percentage increase (decrease) in the quantity demanded is greater than the percentage increase (decrease) in income**
Income inelastic (normal good)	**Less than 1 but greater than zero**	**The percentage increase (decrease) in the quantity demanded is less than the percentage increase (decrease) in income**
Negative income-elastic (inferior good)	**Less than zero**	**When income increases (decreases), quantity demanded decreases (increases)**

Cross elasticities (η_x)

A relationship is described as:	When η_x is:	Which means that:
Perfect substitutes	**Infinity**	**The smallest possible increase (decrease) in the price of one good causes an infinitely large increase (decrease) in the quantity demanded of the other good**
Substitutes	**Positive, less than infinity**	**If the price of one good increases (decreases), the quantity demanded of the other good also increases (decreases)**
Independent	**Zero**	**The quantity demanded of one good remains constant regardless of the price of the other good.**
Complements	**Less than zero (negative)**	**The quantity demanded of one good decreases (increases) when the price of the other good increases (decreases)**

Elasticity in Action

THE WASHINGTON POST, AUGUST 4, 1991

The Owl's Golden Egg

Environmentalism Could Boost Lumber Profits and Prices

BY JOHN M. BERRY

It is sometimes hard to tell the winners and the losers, and why each is winning or losing, in the war over timber cutting on federal land in the Pacific Northwest.

The regional timber industry has sought to portray itself as a clear loser if environmentalists get their way and the timber harvest is sharply curtailed to protect recreational uses, scenic vistas, water quality, fisheries and wildlife such as the officially endangered spotted owl.

Nevertheless, a few weeks ago Mark S. Rogers, a wood industry analyst at Prudential Securities Inc. in New York, declared in a headline on a research paper, "What's Good for the Spotted Owl Is Great for the Wood-Products Industry."

"No tonic could be better for the depressed wood-products industry than a decrease in capacity coinciding with an increase in demand," Rogers wrote. "Thanks to the controversy over the spotted owl, industry capacity is almost certain to be cut just as the housing recovery begins to stimulate demand."

Rogers said the lumber industry has been plagued for more than a decade with too much production capacity, a condition that has kept profits low. Reduced harvests in this region will lead to a cut in industry capacity of 5 percent to 10 percent and a rebound in profits, he predicted.

This follows a decade in which national lumber production surged, rising from 31.8 billion board feet in 1981 to 49 billion board feet in 1989, as construction boomed around the country.

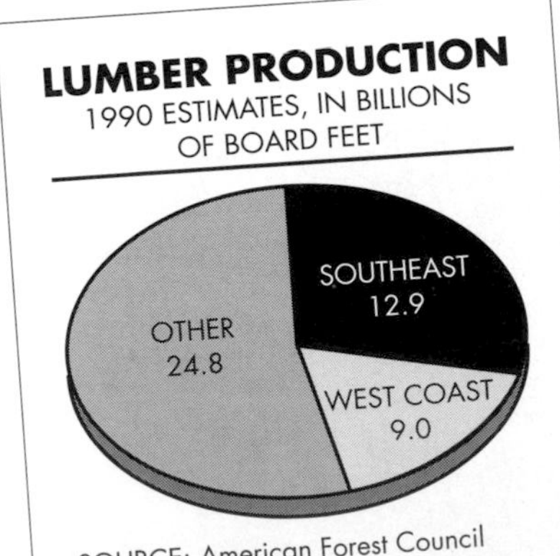

The Essence of the Story

The timber industry has experienced a large increase in production during the 1980s, but its profits have been low.

The demand for timber products is predicted to increase, and so are industry profits.

Environmentalists are seeking cuts in timber production in the Pacific Northwest.

Regional timber producers believe that they will lose from these cuts.

A timber industry analyst believes that the industry's profits will increase as a result of lower production in the Northwest.

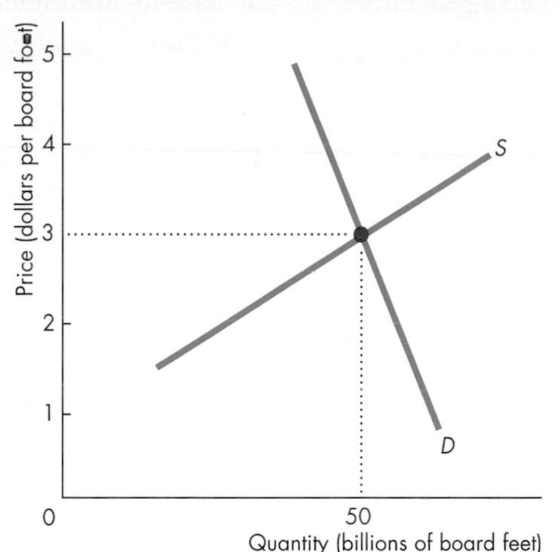

Figure 1

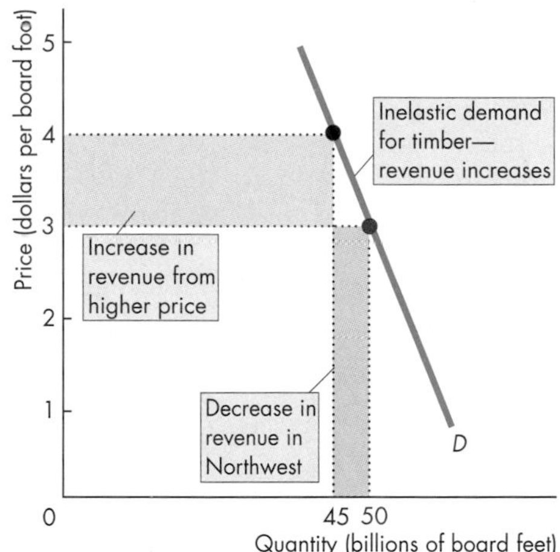

Figure 2

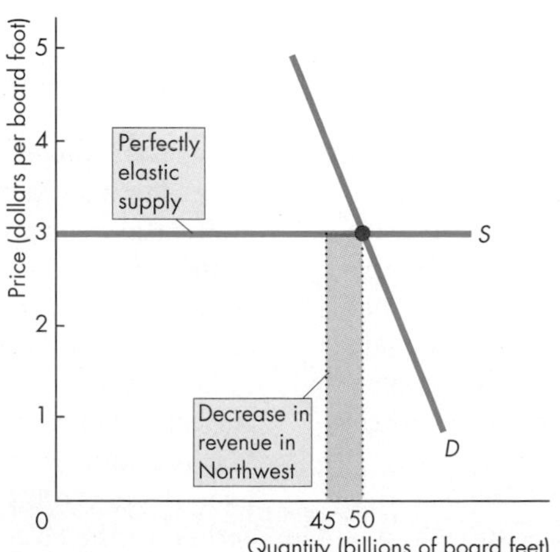

Figure 3

Background and Analycic

Timber is bought and sold on an unregulated national and international market in which the price is determined by demand and supply as shown in Fig. 1.

Timber has substitutes, but in the short run, none of them are very close and the demand for timber is inelastic.

Because the demand for timber is inelastic, a decrease in supply will increase price and increase industry revenue, as shown in Fig. 2. Mark S. Rogers predicts this outcome as the consequence of cutting Northwest production.

But Northwest timber has perfect substitutes on the production side—timber from the Southeast, other regions, and other parts of the world—and the supply of timber is possibly perfectly elastic.

If the supply of timber is perfectly elastic, a decrease in production in the Northwest will be offset by an increase in production in other places—as shown in Fig. 3. The price of timber will be unchanged by the lower production in the Northwest, and the Northwest producers will lose, as they predict and fear.

Let's now turn our attention to the supply curve and study the elasticity of supply.

Elasticity of Supply

We've seen how the concept of elasticity of demand may be used to determine the extent of a change in the quantity demanded when there is a change in price. As Fig. 5.1 illustrates, such changes result from a change in supply that shifts the supply curve and leads to a movement along a demand curve. There is a change in the quantity demanded but no change in demand.

But suppose we want to predict the effects on price and quantity of a change in demand. A change in demand shifts the demand curve and leads to a movement along the supply curve. To make such a prediction, we need to know how responsive the quantity supplied is to the price of a good. That is, we need to know the elasticity of supply.

The **elasticity of supply** is the percentage change in the quantity supplied of a good divided by the percentage change in its price. It is represented by η_s. That is,

$$\eta_s = \frac{\text{Percentage change in quantity supplied}}{\text{Percentage change in price}}.$$

The supply curves that we have considered in this chapter (and those in Chapter 4) all slope upward. When the price increases, the quantity supplied increases. Upward-sloping supply curves have a positive elasticity.

There are two interesting cases of the elasticity of supply. If the quantity supplied is fixed regardless of the price, the supply curve is vertical. In this case, the elasticity of supply is zero. An increase in price leads to no change in the quantity supplied. Supply is perfectly inelastic. If there is a price below which nothing will be supplied but at which suppliers are willing to sell any quantity demanded, the supply curve is horizontal. In this case, the elasticity of supply is infinite. The small fall in price reduces the quantity supplied from an indefinitely large amount to zero. Supply is perfectly elastic.

The magnitude of the elasticity of supply depends on:

- The technological conditions governing production
- The amount of time elapsed since the price change

Technological Conditions

The importance of technological conditions can be illustrated by considering two extreme examples. Some goods, such as a painting by Georgia O'Keeffe, are unique. There is just one of each of her paintings. Its supply curve is vertical, and its elasticity of supply is zero. At the other extreme, a good such as sand for making silicon chips is available in indefinitely large quantities at a virtually constant cost of production. Its supply curve is horizontal, and its elasticity of supply is infinity. The supply of internationally produced goods to an individual country—even a large country such as the United States—is also highly elastic. An example of such a good is timber, the market for which is featured in Reading Between the Lines on pp. 116–117.

The supply of most goods and services lies between the two extremes. The quantity produced can be increased, but only by incurring a higher cost. If a higher price is offered, the quantity supplied increases. Such goods and services have an elasticity of supply between zero and infinity.

Time Frame for Supply

To study the influence of the length of time elapsed since a price change, we distinguish three time frames for supply:

1. Momentary supply
2. Short-run supply
3. Long-run supply

Momentary Supply When the price of a good rises or falls in a sudden, unforeseen way, we use the momentary supply curve to describe the initial change in the quantity supplied. The **momentary supply curve** shows the response of the quantity supplied immediately following a price change.

Some goods, such as fruits and vegetables, have a perfectly inelastic momentary supply—which means that the supply curve is vertical. The quantities supplied depend on the crop-planting decisions made earlier. In the case of oranges, for example, planting decisions have to be made many years in advance of the crop being available.

Other goods, an example of which is electric power, have an elastic momentary supply. When we all turn on our TV sets and air conditioners simultaneously, there is a big surge in the demand for electricity and the quantity bought increases, but the price remains constant. Electricity producers usually anticipate fluctuations in demand and bring more generators into operation to ensure that the quantity supplied equals the quantity demanded without raising the price.

Long-Run Supply The **long-run supply curve** shows the response of the quantity supplied to a change in price after all the technologically possible ways of adjusting supply have been exploited. In the case of oranges, the long run is the time it takes new plantings to grow to full maturity—about 15 years. In some cases, the long-run adjustment occurs only after a completely new production plant has been built and workers have been trained to operate it—typically a process that may take several years.

Short-Run Supply The **short-run supply curve** shows how the quantity supplied responds to a price change when only *some* of the technologically possible adjustments to production have been made. The first adjustment that is usually made is in the amount of labor employed. To increase output in the short run, firms work their labor force overtime and perhaps hire additional workers. To decrease their output in the short run, firms lay off workers or reduce their hours of work. With the passage of more time, firms can make additional adjustments, perhaps training additional workers or buying additional tools and other equipment. The short-run response to a price change, unlike the momentary and long-run responses, is not a unique response but a sequence of adjustments.

Three Supply Curves Three supply curves corresponding to the three time frames are illustrated in Fig. 5.7. They are the supply curves in the world market for coal in a year in which the price is $70 a ton and the quantity of coal produced is 3 billion tons. The three supply curves all pass through that point. Momentary supply is perfectly inelastic at 3 billion tons, as shown by the light blue curve labeled *MS*. Long-run supply, as shown by the dark blue curve labeled *LS*, is the most elastic of the three supplies. Short-run supply, as shown by the curve labeled *SS*, lies between the other two. In fact, there is a series of short-run supply curves between the momentary and long-run curves. Each supply is successively more elastic. As more time elapses following a price change, more changes can be made in the method of production to increase output. The short-run supply curve *SS* shown in Fig. 5.7 is an example of one of these short-run supply curves.

The momentary supply curve (*MS*) is vertical because, at a given moment in time, no matter what the price of coal, producers cannot change their output. They have a certain labor force and a certain amount of coal-mining equipment in place, and there is a given amount of output that can be produced. But as time elapses, coal-producing companies can increase their capacity. They can hire and train more miners and buy more equipment. In the long run, they can sink new mines, discover more accessible coal deposits, and increase the quantity supplied even more in response to a given price rise.

FIGURE 5.7

Supply: Momentary, Short-Run, and Long-Run

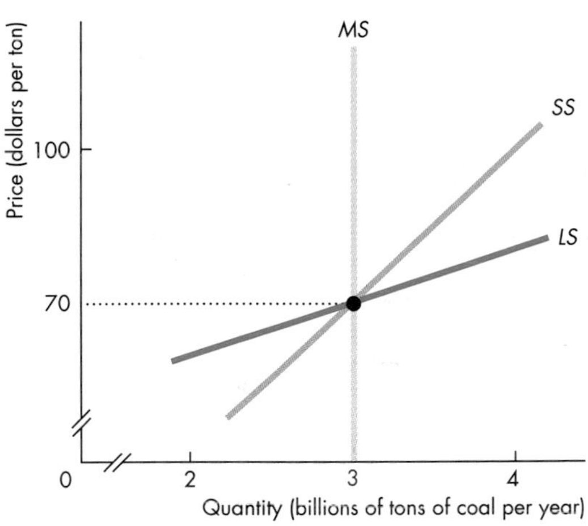

The momentary supply curve (*MS*) shows how quantity supplied responds to a price change the moment that it occurs. The very light blue momentary supply curve shown here is perfectly inelastic. The medium blue short-run supply curve (*SS*) shows how the quantity supplied responds to a price change after some adjustments to production have been made. The dark blue long-run supply curve (*LS*) shows how the quantity supplied responds to a price change when all the technologically possible adjustments to the production process have been made.

◆ ◆ ◆ ◆ You have now studied the theory of demand and supply, and you have learned how to measure the responsiveness of the quantities demanded to changes in prices and income. You have also learned how to measure the responsiveness of the quantity supplied to a change in the price. In the next chapters we are going to use what we have learned about demand, supply, and elasticity to study the ways in which some real-world markets work—markets in action.

SUMMARY

Elasticity of Demand

Elasticity of demand is a measure of the responsiveness of the quantity demanded of a good to a change in its price. It enables us to calculate the effect of a change in supply on price, quantity bought, and revenue. Elasticity of demand (η) is the absolute value of the percentage change in the quantity demanded divided by the percentage change in price.

The larger the elasticity, the greater is the responsiveness of the quantity demanded to a given change in price. When the percentage change in the quantity demanded is smaller than the percentage change in price, elasticity is between zero and 1 and demand is inelastic. When the percentage change in the quantity demanded equals the percentage change in price, elasticity is 1 and demand is unit elastic. When the percentage change in the quantity demanded is larger than the percentage change in price, elasticity is greater than 1 and demand is elastic.

Along a straight-line demand curve, elasticity declines as the price falls and the quantity demanded increases.

The size of the elasticity depends on how easily one good may serve as a substitute for another, on the proportion of income spent on the good, and on the time that has elapsed since the price change.

We use two time frames to analyze demand: short-run and long-run. Short-run demand describes the initial response of buyers to a price change. Long-run demand describes the response of buyers to a price change after all possible adjustments have been made. Short-run demand is usually less elastic than long-run demand. (pp. 103–111)

Elasticity, Revenue, and Expenditure

If the elasticity of demand is less than 1, a decrease in supply leads to an increase in revenue—the percentage increase in price is greater than the percentage decrease in the quantity bought. If the elasticity of demand is greater than 1, a decrease in supply leads to a decrease in revenue—the percentage increase in price is less than the percentage decrease in the quantity bought. (pp. 111–112)

More Demand Elasticities

Income elasticity of demand measures the responsiveness of demand to a change in income. Income elasticity of demand is calculated as the percentage change in the quantity bought divided by the percentage change in income. The larger the income elasticity of demand, the greater is the responsiveness of the quantity bought to a given change in income. When income elasticity is between zero and 1, demand is income inelastic. In this case, as income increases, the quantity bought increases but the percentage of income spent on a good decreases. When income elasticity is greater than 1, demand is income elastic. In this case, as income increases, the quantity bought increases and the percentage of income spent on the good also increases. When income elasticity is less than zero, demand is negative income-elastic. In this case, as income increases, the quantity bought decreases. Income elasticities are greater than 1 for items that are typically consumed by the rich; they are positive but less than 1 for more basic consumption items. Income elasticities are less than zero for inferior goods—goods that are consumed only at low incomes and that disappear as budgets increase.

Cross elasticity of demand measures the responsiveness of demand for one good to a change in the price of another good (a substitute or a complement). Cross elasticity of demand is calculated as the percentage change in the quantity demanded of one good divided by the percentage change in the price of another good. The cross elasticity of demand with respect to the price of a substitute is positive. The cross elasticity of demand with respect to the price of a complement is negative. (pp. 112–118)

Elasticity of Supply

The elasticity of supply measures the responsiveness of the quantity supplied to a change in price. Elasticity of supply is calculated as the percentage change in the quantity supplied of a good divided by the percentage change in its price. Supply elasticities are usually positive but range between zero (vertical supply curve) and infinity (horizontal supply curve).

We classify supply according to three different time frames: momentary, long-run, and short-run. Momentary supply refers to the response of suppliers to a price change at the instant that it happens. Long-run supply refers to the response of suppliers to a price change when all the technologically feasible adjustments in production have been made. Short-run supply refers to the response of suppliers to a price change after some adjustments in production have been made. For many goods, momentary supply is perfectly inelastic. Supply becomes more elastic as suppliers have more time to respond to price changes. (pp. 118–119)

KEY ELEMENTS

Key Terms

Cross elasticity of demand, 114
Elastic demand, 106
Elasticity of demand, 105
Elasticity of supply, 118
Income elasticity of demand, 112
Inelastic demand, 106
Long-run demand curve, 110
Long-run supply curve, 119
Momentary supply curve, 118
Perfectly elastic demand, 106
Perfectly inelastic demand, 106
Price elasticity of demand, 104
Short-run demand curve, 110
Short-run supply curve, 118
Unit elastic demand, 106

Key Figures and Tables

REVIEW QUESTIONS

1 Define the price elasticity of demand.

2 Why is elasticity a more useful measure of responsiveness than slope?

3 Draw a graph of, or describe the shape of, a demand curve that along its whole length has an elasticity of:

a Infinity
b Zero
c Unity

4 What three factors determine the size of the elasticity of demand?

5 What do we mean by short-run demand and long-run demand?

6 Explain why the short-run demand curve is usually less elastic than the long-run demand curve.

7 What is the connection between elasticity and revenue? If the elasticity of demand is 1, by how much does a 10 percent price increase change revenue?

8 Define the income elasticity of demand.

9 Give an example of a good whose income elasticity is

a Greater than 1
b Positive but less than 1
c Less than zero

10 Define the cross elasticity of demand. Is the cross elasticity of demand positive or negative?

11 Define the elasticity of supply. Is the elasticity of supply positive or negative?

12 Give an example of a good whose elasticity of supply is

a Zero
b Greater than zero but less than infinity
c Infinity

13 What do we mean by momentary, short-run, and long-run supply?

14 Why is momentary supply perfectly inelastic for many goods?

15 Why is long-run supply more elastic than short-run supply?

PROBLEMS

1 The demand schedule for videotape rentals is

Price (dollars per videotape)	Quantity demanded (videotapes per day)
0	150
1	125
2	100
3	75
4	50
5	25
6	0

a At what price is the elasticity of demand equal to:
 (1) 1
 (2) Infinity
 (3) Zero
b What price brings in the most revenue per day?
c Calculate the elasticity of demand for a rise in price from \$4 to \$5.

2 Assume that the demand for videotape rentals in problem 1 increases by 10 percent at each price.
a Draw the old and new demand curves.
b Calculate the elasticity of demand for a rise in the rental price from \$4 to \$5. Compare your answer with that of problem 1(c).

3 Which item in each of the following pairs has the larger price elasticity of demand?
a *People* magazine or all magazines
b Vacations in Florida or vacations in North America
c Broccoli or vegetables

4 You have been hired as an economic consultant by OPEC and given the following schedule showing the world demand for oil:

Price (dollars per barrel)	Quantity demanded (millions of barrels per day)
10	60,000
20	50,000
30	40,000
40	30,000
50	20,000

Your advice is needed on the following questions:
a If the supply of oil is cut back so that the price rises from \$20 to \$30 a barrel, will the revenue from oil sales increase or decrease?
b What will happen to revenue if the supply of oil is cut back further and the price rises to \$40 a barrel?
c What is the price that will achieve the highest revenue?
d What quantity of oil will be sold at the price that answers part (c)?
e What are the values of the price elasticity of demand for price changes of \$10 a barrel at average prices of \$15, \$25, \$35, and \$45 a barrel?
f What is the elasticity of demand at the price that maximizes revenue?
g Over what price range is the demand of oil inelastic?

5 State the sign (positive or negative) and, where possible, the range (less than 1, 1, greater than 1) of the following elasticities:

- **a** The elasticity of demand for ice cream at the point of maximum revenue
- **b** The cross elasticity of demand for ice cream with respect to the price of frozen yogurt
- **c** The income elasticity of demand for Caribbean cruises
- **d** The income elasticity of demand for toothpaste
- **e** The elasticity of supply of Irish salmon
- **f** The cross elasticity of demand for corn ready to be popped with respect to the price of popcorn machines

6 The following table gives some data on the demand for chocolate chip cookies:

Price (cents per cookie)	Quantity demanded (thousands per day)	
	Short-run	Long-run
10	700	1,000
20	500	500
30	300	0

At a price of 20¢ a cookie:

- **a** Calculate the elasticity of short-run demand.
- **b** Calculate the elasticity of long-run demand.
- **c** Is the demand for cookies more elastic in the short run or the long run?

7 The following table gives some data on the supply of chocolate chip cookies:

Price (cents per cookie)	Quantity supplied (thousands per day)		
	Momentary	Short-run	Long-run
10	500	300	0
20	500	500	500
30	500	700	10,000

At a price of 20¢ a cookie, calculate the elasticity of:

- **a** Momentary supply
- **b** Short-run supply
- **c** Long-run supply

8 In problem 7, which supply is most elastic and which is most inelastic? Compare the elasticities of supply when the average price of a cookie is 15¢. Compare them when the average price of a cookie is 25¢.

CHAPTER 6

MARKETS IN ACTION

After studying this chapter, you will be able to:

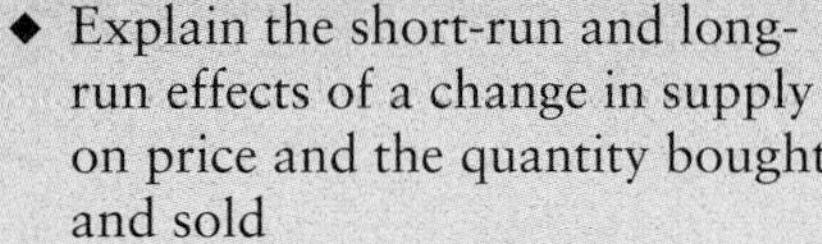

- Explain the short-run and long-run effects of a change in supply on price and the quantity bought and sold
- Explain the short-run and long-run effects of a change in demand on price and the quantity bought and sold
- Explain the effects of price controls
- Explain why price controls can lead to black markets
- Explain how sales taxes affect prices
- Explain how the prohibition of a good affects its price and quantity consumed
- Explain why farm prices and revenues fluctuate
- Explain how inventories and speculation limit price fluctuations

Turbulent Times

IN 1906, SAN FRANCISCO SUFFERED A DEVASTATING earthquake that destroyed countless buildings but killed very few people. The population somehow had to fit into a vastly smaller number of houses and apartments. How did the San Francisco housing market cope with this enormous shock? What happened to rents and to the quantity of housing services available? Did rents have to be controlled to keep housing affordable? ◆◆ Almost every day, new machines are invented that save labor and increase productivity. The simplest tasks performed by the least skilled people are the most easily mechanized, so the march of technological change brings a persistent decrease in the demand for unskilled workers. But ever more sophisticated equipment needs ever more sophisticated management and maintenance and brings a steady increase in the demand for skilled workers. How do labor markets cope with the changing patterns in the demand for labor? Is it necessary to have minimum wage laws to prevent the wages of the unskilled from falling? ◆◆ Almost everything we buy is taxed. Do taxes increase prices by the full amount of the tax so that we, the buyers, pay? ◆◆ Trading in some goods, such as drugs, automatic firearms, and enriched uranium, is prohibited. How does the prohibition of trade affect the actual amounts of prohibited goods consumed? And how does it affect the prices paid by those who trade illegally? ◆◆ Grain yields in 1991 were high, but those in 1988 were extremely low because crops were devastated by drought. How do farm prices and revenues react to such output fluctuations? How do the actions of speculators and official agencies influence farm revenues?

◆ ◆ ◆ ◆ In this chapter, we use the theory of demand and supply (of Chapter 4) and the concept of elasticity (of Chapter 5) to answer questions such as those that we have just posed. Let's begin by studying how a market responds to a severe supply shock.

Housing Markets and Rent Ceilings

To see how an unregulated market copes with a massive supply shock, let's transport ourselves to the city of San Francisco in April 1906, as the city is facing the effects of its massive earthquake and fire. You can sense the enormity of San Francisco's problems by reading some headlines from the *New York Times* about the first days of the crisis. On April 19, 1906:

Over 500 Dead, $200,000,000 Lost in San Francisco Earthquake

Nearly Half the City Is in Ruins and 50,000 Are Homeless

On April 20, 1906:

Army of Homeless Fleeing from Devastated City

200,000 Without Shelter and Facing Famine

And again on April 21, 1906:

San Francisco's New Peril; Gale Drives Fire Ferryward

Fighting Famine and Disease Among the 200,000 Refugees

San Francisco Multitudes Camped Out Shelterless and in Want

The commander of federal troops in charge of the emergency described the magnitude of the problem:

> Not a hotel of note or importance was left standing. The great apartment houses had vanished . . . two hundred and twenty-five thousand people were . . . homeless.[1]

Almost overnight, more than half the people in a city of 400,000 had lost their homes. Temporary shelters and camps alleviated some of the problem, but it was also necessary to utilize the apartment buildings and houses left standing. As a consequence, they had to accommodate 40 percent more people than they had before the earthquake.

The *San Francisco Chronicle* was not published for more than a month after the earthquake. When the newspaper reappeared on May 24, 1906, the city's housing shortage—what would seem like a major news item that would still be of grave importance—was not mentioned. Milton Friedman and George Stigler describe the situation:

> *There is not a single mention of a housing shortage!* The classified advertisements listed sixty-four offers of flats and houses for rent, and nineteen of houses for sale, against five advertisements of flats or houses wanted. Then and thereafter a considerable number of all types of accommodation except hotel rooms were offered for rent.[2]

How did San Francisco cope with such a devastating reduction in the supply of housing?

The Market Response to an Earthquake

We can work out how the unregulated San Francisco housing market responded to the earthquake of 1906 by using the theory of demand and supply that we studied in Chapters 4 and 5. Figure 6.1 analyzes this market. Part (a) shows the situation before the earthquake and parts (b) and (c), after the earthquake. The horizontal axis of each part measures the quantity of housing units, and the vertical axis measures the monthly rent of a unit of housing.

Look first at the situation before the earthquake (part a). The demand curve for housing is *D*. There are two supply curves: the short-run supply curve, which is labeled *SS*, and the long-run supply curve, which is labeled *LS*. The short-run supply curve shows how the quantity of housing supplied varies as the price (rent) varies, while the number of houses and apartment buildings remains constant. This supply response arises from a variation in the intensity with which existing buildings are used. The quantity

[1]Reported in Milton Friedman and George J. Stigler, "Roofs or Ceilings? The Current Housing Problem," in *Popular Essays on Current Problems,* vol. 1, no. 2 (New York: Foundation for Economic Education, 1946), 3–15.

[2]Ibid., 3.

FIGURE 6.1

The San Francisco Housing Market in 1906

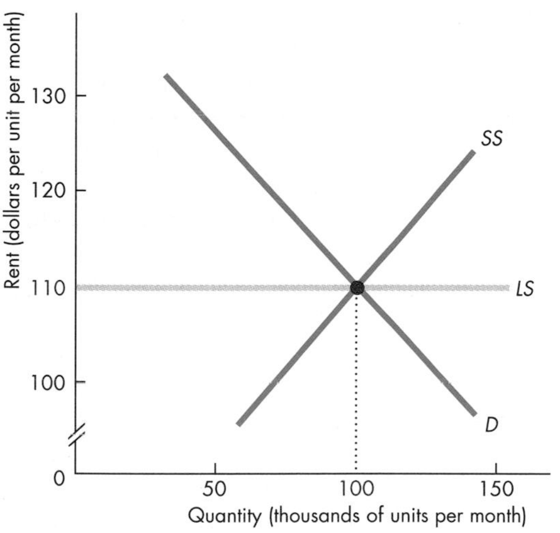

(a) Before earthquake

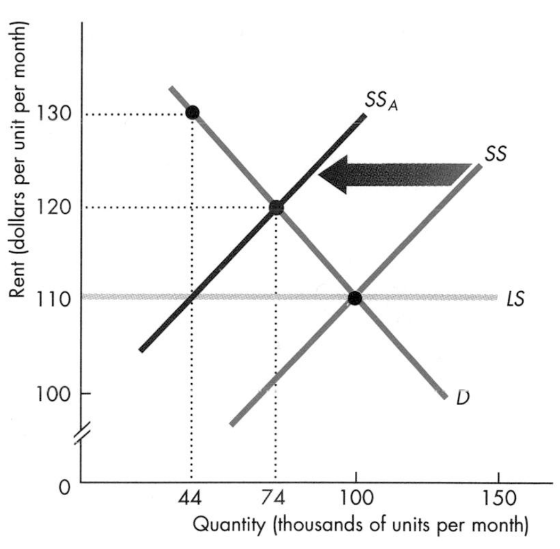

(b) After earthquake

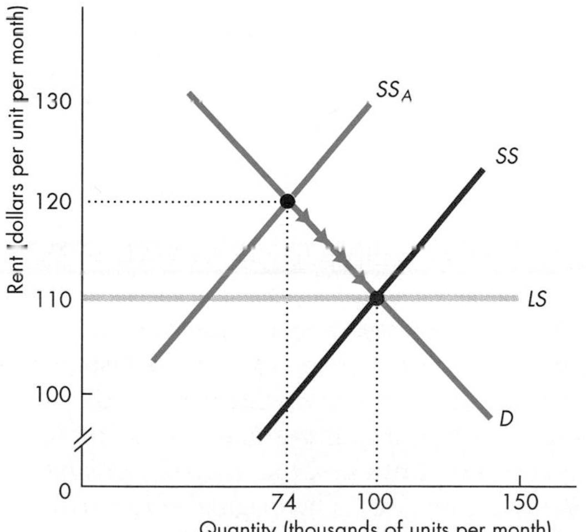

(c) Long-run adjustment

Before the earthquake, the San Francisco housing market is in equilibrium; 100,000 housing units are traded each month at an average rent of $110 a month. This equilibrium is at the intersection of demand curve *D*, short-run supply curve *SS*, and long-run supply curve *LS* (part a). After the earthquake, the short-run supply curve shifts from *SS* to SS_A (part b). The equilibrium rent rises to $120 a month and the number of housing units available falls to 74,000 a month. The rent rises because only 44,000 units of housing will be supplied at the old rent of $110 a month, and the price that demanders will willingly pay for the 44 thousandth unit is $130 a month. With rents at $120 a month, there is profit in building new apartments and houses. As the building program proceeds, the short-run supply curve shifts to the right. As it does so (part c), rents gradually fall back to $110 a month and the number of housing units available increases gradually to 100,000. Note that we use a special arrowed line to indicate such gradual movements along a curve.

of housing supplied increases as families rent out rooms or parts of their houses and apartments to others, and the quantity supplied decreases as families occupy a larger number of the rooms that are under their control.

The long-run supply curve shows how the quantity supplied varies after enough time has elapsed for new apartment buildings and houses to be erected or existing buildings to be destroyed. The long-run supply curve is shown as being perfectly elastic. We do not actually know that the long-run supply curve is perfectly elastic, but it is a reasonable assumption. It implies that the cost of building an apartment is pretty much the same regardless of whether there are 50,000, 100,000, or 150,000 apartments in existence.

The equilibrium price and quantity traded are determined at the point of intersection of the short-run supply curve and the demand curve. Before the earthquake, that equilibrium rent is $110 a month, and the quantity of housing units traded is 100,000 as shown in Fig. 6.1(a). In addition (for simplicity), the housing market is on its long-run supply curve, *LS*. Let's now look at the situation immediately after the earthquake.

After the Earthquake

After the earthquake and the subsequent fires, housing for 56 percent of the population is destroyed. Figure 6.1(b) reflects the new situation by shifting the short-run supply curve *SS* to the left by 56,000 units to become the short-run supply curve SS_A (*A* for after the earthquake). If people use the remaining housing units with the same intensity as before the earthquake and if the rent remains at $110 a month, only 44,000 units of housing are available.

But rents do not remain at $110. With only 44,000 units of housing available, the maximum rent that will willingly be paid for the last available apartment is $130 a month. Since people value the available housing more highly than the long-run price of $110 a month, they offer to pay higher rents. At higher rents, people with accommodations economize on their use of space and make their spare rooms, attics, and basements available to others. Thus the quantity of housing units offered increases. The market achieves a new, short-run equilibrium at a rent of $120 a month, where 74,000 units of housing are available. In this new short-run equilibrium, approximately 20 percent of the population has left the city and a further 6 percent has been housed in temporary camps.[3]

You've now seen how the housing market reacts, almost overnight, to a devastating shock. When supply decreases, the intersection point of the new short-run supply curve and the demand curve determines the price and the quantity bought and sold. The price rises; people who are willing to pay the higher price find housing, and those who have housing are willing to economize on its use. People who are unwilling or unable to pay the higher rents either leave the city or are housed in temporary shelters.

[3]Ibid., 3.

Long-Run Adjustments

The new equilibrium depicted in Fig. 6.1(b) is not the end of the story. The long-run supply curve tells us that with sufficient time for new apartment buildings and houses to be constructed, housing will be supplied at a rent of $110 a month. Since the current rent of $120 a month is higher than the long-run supply price of housing, there will be a rush to build and supply new apartments and houses. As time passes, more apartments and houses are built, and the short-run supply curve starts moving back gradually to the right.

Figure 6.1(c) illustrates the long-run adjustment. As the short-run supply curve shifts back to the right, it intersects the demand curve at lower rents and higher quantities. The market follows the arrows down the demand curve. The process ends when there is no further profit in building new housing units. Such a situation occurs at the original rent of $110 a month and the original quantity of 100,000 units of housing.

REVIEW

An earthquake reduces the short-run supply, raising rents and lowering the quantity traded. Higher rents immediately bring forth an increase in the quantity of housing supplied as people economize on their own use of space and make rooms available for rent to others. High rents also lead to increased building activity, which causes the short-run supply curve to shift gradually back to the right. As this process continues, the price of housing falls and the quantity rises. The original (pre-earthquake) equilibrium eventually is restored (because nothing has happened in the meantime to shift the long-run supply curve or the demand curve). ◆

A Regulated Housing Market

We've just seen how the housing market of San Francisco coped with a massive supply shock. One of the things that happened was that rents increased sharply. Let's now suppose that the San Francisco city government imposed a rent ceiling. A **rent ceiling** is a regulation making it illegal to charge a rent higher than a specified level. What would have happened if a rent ceiling of $110 a month—the rent before the earthquake—had been imposed? This question is answered in Fig. 6.2.

First, let's work out what will happen to the quantities supplied and demanded. The quantity supplied at the controlled rent of $110 a month is 44,000 units. The quantity demanded at that rent is 100,000 units. When the quantity demanded exceeds the quantity supplied, what determines the quantity actually bought and sold? The answer is the smaller of the quantities demanded and supplied. At a monthly rent of $110, the suppliers of housing want to supply only 44,000 units. They cannot be forced to supply more. The demanders would like to rent 100,000 units at that price, but they cannot do so. The difference between the quantity demanded and the quantity supplied is called the excess quantity demanded.

FIGURE 6.2

A Rent Ceiling

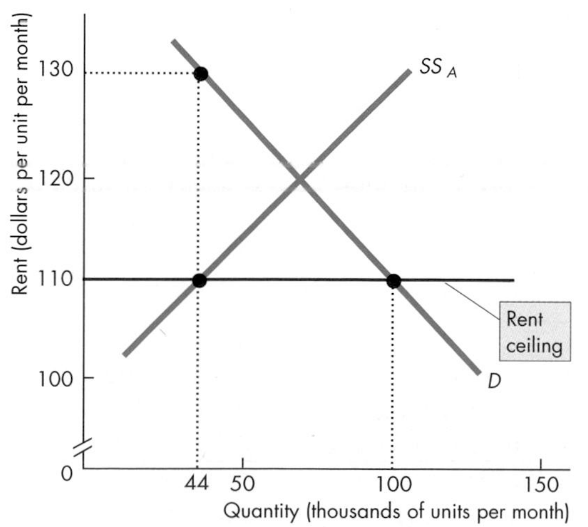

If there had been a rent ceiling of $110 a month after the earthquake, the quantity of housing supplied would have been stuck at 44,000 units. People would willingly pay $130 a month for the 44 thousandth unit. The difference between the rent ceiling and the maximum price that will willingly be paid is the value of the time used up in searching for an available apartment. The individuals doing the searching are those with the lowest opportunity cost of time. Those whose value of time is high avoid search costs by buying on an illegal black market.

When a rent ceiling of $110 a month is imposed, the quantity of housing available falls to 44,000 units, but the quantity demanded remains constant at 100,000 units. There is an excess demand of 56,000 units. Is that the end of the story? Is this situation an equilibrium? To answer this question, we need to explore a bit more closely what the demanders are doing.

If the rent really is $110 a month, a lot of people who would like to rent more housing will not be able to do so. Moreover, some people would be willing to pay much more than $110 a month to get an apartment. To understand why, recall that there are two ways of interpreting a demand curve. One interpretation is that the curve tells us the quantities demanded at each price. But the demand curve also tells us the highest price that demanders will pay for the last unit available. What is the highest price that people will pay for the last apartment available? The answer, which can be read from the demand curve, is $130 a month. Since the people who are not able to find housing are willing to pay more than the rent ceiling, the situation that we have just described is not an equilibrium. Two mechanisms come into play in an unbalanced situation such as this one to achieve equilibrium. They are search activity and black markets.

Search Activity

Even when the quantity demanded exceeds the quantity supplied, some suppliers have goods available. But many are sold out. In these circumstances, buyers spend time looking for a supplier with whom they can do business. The time and effort spent in searching for someone with whom to do business is called **search activity.** Even in markets in which prices are permitted to fluctuate to bring equality between the quantities demanded and supplied, search activity takes place. But when price is regulated, search activity increases.

The time spent searching for available supplies imposes costs on buyers. Adjustments in the time spent searching bring about an equilibrium. You can see why by thinking about the total amount that the demanders are willing to pay for the last unit of housing available. With only 44,000 housing units available, demanders are willing to pay $130 a month. But the rent is restricted to $110. How does the buyer spend another $20? The answer is by using $20 worth of time in the business of searching for an available apartment. That is, the total cost of housing—the price actually paid for housing obtained—is equal to the rent paid to the owner plus the opportunity cost of time spent searching for the available supply.

Black Markets

Opportunity cost (the value of the best opportunity forgone) enables us to predict *who* will search for available housing. Some people earn high wages, and others earn low wages. If it takes one hour to find an apartment, the total price paid is higher for a high-wage earner than for a low-wage earner. Therefore the lowest-paid people will be those who devote the most time to searching out available supplies. High-wage earners will devote time to search activity only if they place a much higher value on the good than do low-wage earners.

A person with a high opportunity cost of time has another way of obtaining a good—buying it from someone whose opportunity cost of time is lower. The person with a low wage can devote time to searching out the available supplies and then resell to someone whose opportunity cost of searching is higher. Buying goods in this way is illegal and creates what is known as a black market. A **black market** is an illegal trading arrangement in which buyers and sellers do business at a price that is higher than the legally imposed price ceiling. The functioning of a black market depends on how tightly the government polices its price regulations, on the chances of being caught violating them, and on the scale of the penalties imposed for violations.

At one extreme, the chance of being caught violating a rent ceiling is small. In this case, the black market will function similarly to an unregulated market, and the black market rent and quantity bought and sold will be close to the unregulated equilibrium. At the other extreme, policing is highly effective and large penalties are imposed on violators. In this case, the rent ceiling will restrict the quantity bought and sold to 44,000 units. The small number of black marketeers operating in the market will buy at the controlled rent of $110 a month and sell at $130 a month. The government will constantly try to detect and punish such people. The equilibrium in the black market will be such that anyone can obtain an apartment for $130 a month, and the profit for the black marketeer is just sufficient compensation for the risk of being caught and punished.

There are many examples of markets other than housing markets that are regulated in some way and in which economic forces result in black market trading. One example is the market for bread in Rumania before the recent dramatic changes in that country (see Reading Between the Lines, pp. 132–133).

We've just looked at what would have happened in a hypothetical situation if there had been rent ceilings after the San Francisco earthquake. But San Francisco actually did have rent ceilings 45 years later—after World War II—so we can see how rent ceilings operated in practice. Let's take a look at that episode in the history of the San Francisco housing market.

Rent Ceilings in Practice

By 1940, the population of San Francisco had increased to 635,000. At that time, only 93 percent of the city's houses and apartments were occupied. The situation stayed much the same throughout World War II. Then, after the war, the population increased by 30 percent, but the number of houses and apartments increased by only 20 percent. As a result, each dwelling unit had to house 10 percent more people in 1946 than one year earlier. The housing problems that San Francisco suffered in 1946 were only a quarter of the magnitude of the problems that followed the earthquake in 1906. Yet the 1946 housing shortage was a major political problem:

> On January 8 [1946] the California State Legislature was convened, and the Governor listed the housing shortage as "the most critical problem facing California." During the first five days of the year there were altogether only four advertisements offering houses or apartments for rent . . . [and] . . . there were thirty advertisements per day by persons wanting to rent houses or apartments.[4]

The key difference between San Francisco in 1906 and in 1946 was the way in which scarce

[4]Ibid., 4.

housing was rationed. In 1906, the scarce housing was allocated by an unregulated market. Rent increases achieved an equilibrium between the quantity of housing supplied and the quantity demanded and resulted in a steady increase in the quantity of housing available. In 1946, rent ceilings were in place. Scarce housing was allocated by people devoting time and effort to searching out and advertising for available houses and apartments. The actual cost of housing—taking account of the frustration and effort involved in finding accommodation—exceeded the controlled rent level and even exceeded the rents that would have prevailed in an unregulated market.

We've now studied the way in which a market responds, in both the short run and the long run, to a change in supply and how a regulated market would work in the face of such a supply shock. Let's now study how a market responds, in both the short run and the long run, to a change in demand. We'll study how an unregulated market handles such a shock and the effects of government intervention to limit price movements.

The Labor Market and Minimum Wage Regulation

Labor-saving technology is constantly being invented, and as a result, the demand for certain types of labor, usually the least skilled types, is constantly decreasing. How does the labor market cope with this continuous decrease in the demand for unskilled labor? Doesn't it mean that the wages of the unskilled will constantly be falling? To study this question, let's examine the market for unskilled labor.

Figure 6.3(a) shows this market. The quantity of labor (millions of hours per year) is measured on the horizontal axis and the wage rate (dollars per hour) on the vertical axis. The demand curve for unskilled labor is D. There are two supply curves for unskilled labor: the upward-sloping short-run supply curve SS and the horizontal long-run supply curve LS.

The short-run supply curve shows how the hours of labor supplied by a given number of workers vary as the wage rate varies. To get workers to work longer hours, firms have to offer higher wages, so the short-run supply curve is upward sloping.

The long-run supply curve shows the relationship between the quantity of labor supplied and the wage rate after enough time has passed for people to have acquired new skills and moved to new types of jobs. The number of people in the unskilled labor market depends on the wage in this market compared with other opportunities. If the wage is high enough, people will enter this market. If the wage is too low, people will leave it and seek training to enter the skilled labor market. Because people can freely enter and leave the unskilled labor market, the long-run supply curve is highly elastic. Here (for simplicity) it is assumed to be perfectly elastic (horizontal).

The labor market is initially in equilibrium at a wage rate of $4 an hour and with 30 million hours of labor being supplied. We're now going to analyze what happens in the labor market if the demand for this particular type of labor falls as a result of the invention of some labor-saving technology. Figure 6.3(b) shows the short-run effects of such a change. The demand curve before the new technology is introduced is D. After the introduction of the new technology, the demand curve shifts to the left, to D_A. The wage rate falls to $3 an hour and the quantity of labor employed falls to 20 million hours. This short-run effect on wages and employment is not the end of the story.

People who are now earning only $3 an hour look around for other opportunities. They see, for example, that the new labor-saving equipment doesn't always work properly, and when it breaks down, it is maintained by more highly paid, highly skilled workers. There are many other jobs (in markets for other types of skills) paying higher wages than $3 an hour. One by one, workers decide to quit this particular market for unskilled labor. They go back to school, or they take jobs that pay less but offer on-the-job training. As a result of these decisions, the short-run supply curve begins to shift to the left.

Figure 6.3(c) shows the long-run adjustment. As the short-run supply curve shifts to the left, it intersects the demand curve D_A at higher wage rates and lower levels of employment. In the long run, the

Supply and Demand Returns in Eastern Europe

TIME, JANUARY 15, 1990

In Rumania, Supply and Demand Redux

BY JOHN BORRELL

Pushing his long flat shovel deep into a coal-fired oven, Sachie Lazar draws out five crusty brown loaves, each weighing just over 4 lbs. He glazes them quickly with practiced brushstrokes and tips them into plastic containers, which fill up rapidly. Then the baker starts kneading and shaping a new batch of bread on a flour-dusted table, as a rivulet of perspiration makes its way down his forehead beneath a clean white cap.

Brushing away the sweat, Lazar acknowledges that his working hours at the village bakery in Buciumi (pop. 1900) have doubled since the overthrow of dictator Nicolae Ceausescu. But Lazar is not complaining. "I am now working with my heart as well as my hands," he says, a grin exploding across his thin face. Before the overthrow, rationing allowed a bit more than 8 oz. of bread per person per day. Even before the shooting stopped in Bucharest, Buciumi abandoned the system, and the tiny bakery's production doubled to 4,000 loaves a week. When asked who ordered the increase in production, Lazar grins again. "The revolution demanded it," he says. "I am producing as much as people want to buy."

For almost as long as anyone can remember, the laws of supply and demand were suspended in Buciumi, as in the rest of Rumania. Economics was governed by harsh dictates that affected everything from electricity consumption to local supplies of bread and meat. "How we suffered under Ceausescu, how we suffered," laments Gheorghe Moldovan, a Buciumi electrician. "It was better here than in the cities, but even here it was like living in the Middle Ages."

The Essence of the Story

In December 1989, the Rumanian people overthrew the socialist dictatorship of Nicolae Ceausescu.

Under the Ceausescu regime, the government determined almost all aspects of economic life, down to how much electricity, bread, and meat people could consume.

Life was likened to that in the Middle Ages.

Within one month of the overthrow of Ceausescu, the laws of supply and demand had returned to Rumania.

As an example, Sachie Lazar's bakery in Buciumi, a village of 1,900 people, doubled its bread production, and Sachie doubled his hours of work.

Background and Analysis

Before December 1989, Rumania operated a socialist economy in which the quantities of goods and services produced and their prices were determined by the dictates of the government and not by the forces of supply and demand.

But the forces of supply and demand cannot be eradicated. Even in a socialist dictatorship, the supply curve tells us the quantity that will be supplied at each price and the minimum price necessary to call forth a given quantity. The demand curve tells us the quantity that will be demanded at each price and the maximum price that people are willing to pay for a given quantity.

The figure illustrates the bread market in Buciumi, Rumania. The demand curve *D* tells us the quantities of bread that people are willing to buy at various prices.

At the price *P*, Sachie Lazar can produce all the bread demanded in Buciumi. But if he raises his price above *P*, someone else will come into the market, undercut his price, and take his market. Thus someone is always willing to supply bread at the price *P*. In this market, the supply curve *S* is horizontal: any quantity will be supplied, provided the price is *P*, and this price is the minimum one at which anyone will produce and sell bread.

In the socialist economy, the government rationed the amount of bread produced in Buciumi to 2,000 loaves a week, making the supply curve vertical. It probably enforced this ration by restricting the amount of flour and other ingredients that it made available to the bakery.

The government also determined the price of bread in the socialist economy, but the news item does not tell us what the price was. The price could have been anything between *P* and P_{max}. *P* is the lowest price at which anyone would produce bread. P_{max} is the highest price that anyone would pay for the 2 thousandth loaf each week.

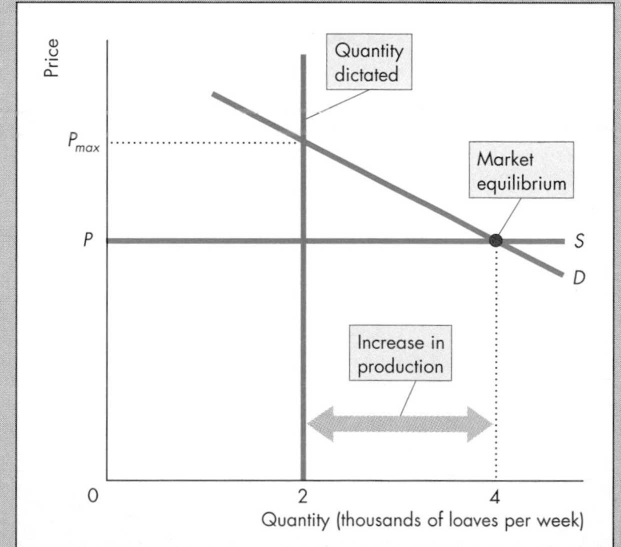

In a socialist economy, at a price of P_{max}, the quantity demanded would equal the quantity produced. There would be no waiting lines. At a price lower than P_{max}, the quantity demanded would exceed the quantity produced. A waiting line would form, and a black market would develop

The government had to pay a price of *P* to the baker to bring forth any supply at all. If the price of bread exceeds *P*, the difference between the price charged to consumers and *P* is a tax on bread—and a profit for the government. If the price of bread is below *P*, the difference between *P* and the price charged to consumers is a subsidy on bread—and a loss for the government.

When the socialist dictatorship was abandoned, the forces of supply and demand began to operate. Those forces resulted in an equilibrium quantity of bread produced of 4,000 loaves a week and a price of *P*. The baker worked longer hours to produce this larger output.

The return of market forces eliminated the waiting line and the black market and lowered the price of bread.

FIGURE 6.3

A Market for Unskilled Labor

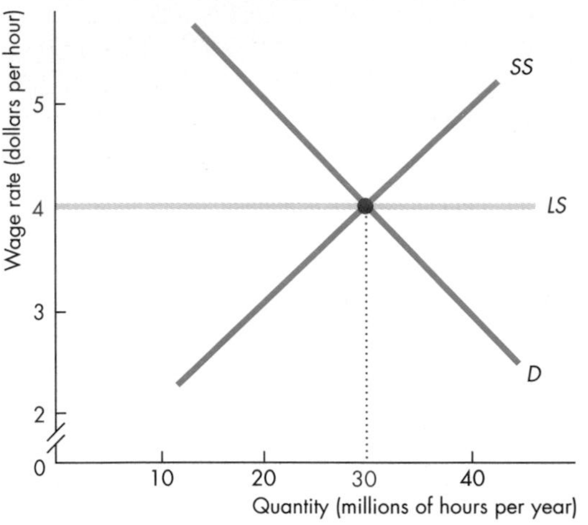

(a) Before invention

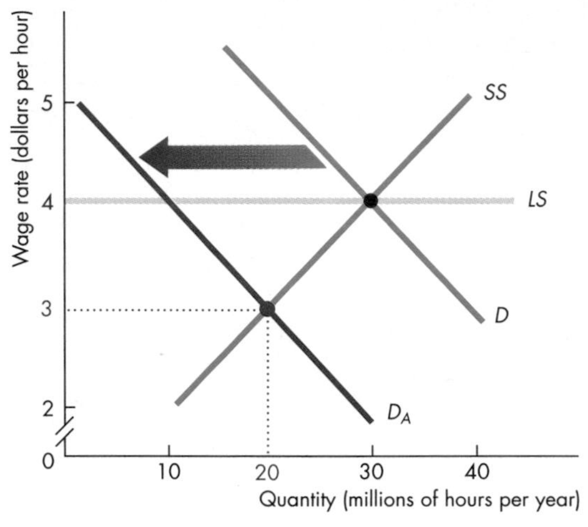

(b) After invention

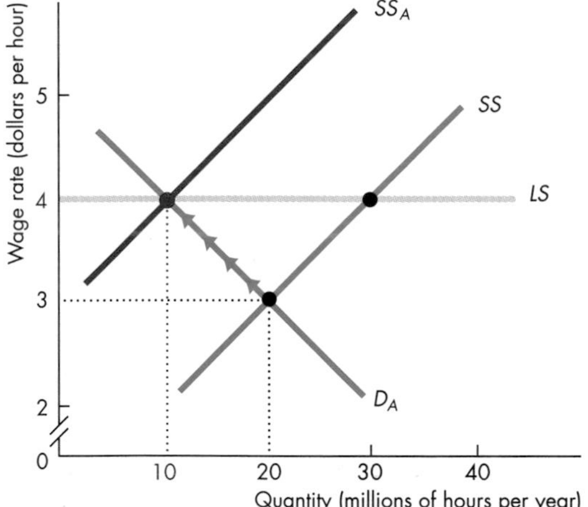

(c) Long-run adjustment

A market for unskilled labor is in equilibrium (part a) at a wage rate of \$3 an hour with 30 million hours of labor a year being traded. The short-run supply curve (*SS*) slopes upward because employers have to pay a higher wage to get more hours out of a given number of workers. The long-run supply curve (*LS*) is perfectly elastic because workers will eventually enter this labor market if the wage rate is above \$3 an hour or leave it if the wage rate is below \$3 an hour. The invention of a labor-saving machine shifts the demand curve from *D* to D_A (part b). The wage rate falls to \$2 an hour, and employment falls to 20 million hours a year. With the lower wage, workers begin to leave this market to undertake training for other types of work. As they do so, the short-run supply curve shifts to SS_A (part c). As the supply curve shifts, the wage rate gradually increases, and the employment level decreases. Ultimately, wages return to \$3 an hour, and employment falls to 10 million hours a year.

short-run supply curve will have shifted all the way to SS_A. At this point, the wage has returned to \$4 an hour, and the level of employment has fallen to 10 million hours.

Sometimes, the adjustment process that we have just described will take place quickly. At other times, it will be a long drawn-out affair. If the adjustment process is long and drawn out and wages remain low for a prolonged period, there will be a temptation on the part of government to intervene in the market, setting a minimum wage to protect the incomes of the lowest-paid workers. What are the effects of imposing a minimum wage?

The Minimum Wage

Suppose that when the demand for labor decreases from *D* to D_A, as illustrated in Fig. 6.3(b), and the wage falls to \$3 an hour, the government passes a minimum wage law. A **minimum wage law** is a regulation that makes trading labor below a specified wage illegal. In particular, suppose that the government declares that the minimum wage is $4 an hour. What are the effects of this law? The answer can be found by studying Fig. 6.4. In that figure, the minimum wage is shown as the horizontal red line labeled "Minimum wage." At the minimum wage, only 10 million hours of labor are demanded (point *a*). But 30 million hours of labor are available at that wage (point *b*). Because the number of hours demanded is less than the number of hours supplied, 20 million hours of available labor go unemployed.

What are the workers doing with their unemployed hours? They are looking for work. It pays to spend a lot of time searching for work. With only 10 million hours of labor being employed, there are many people willing to supply their labor for wages much lower than the minimum wage. In fact, the 10 millionth hour of labor will be supplied for as little as $2.

FIGURE 6.4

The Minimum Wage and Unemployment

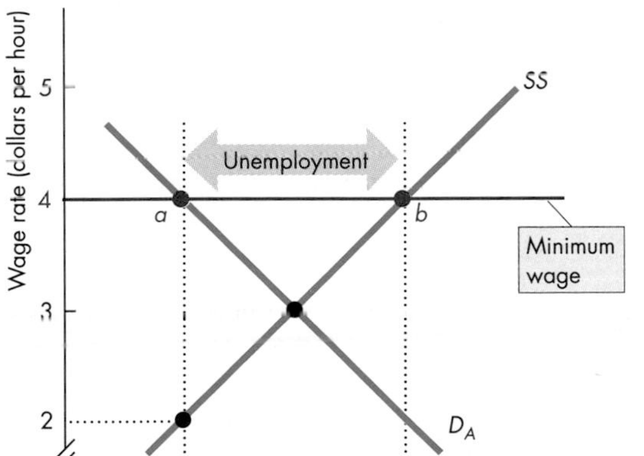

The demand curve for labor is D_A and the supply curve is *SS*. In an unregulated market, the wage rate is $3 an hour and 20 million hours of labor a year are employed. If a minimum wage of $4 an hour is imposed, only 10 million hours of labor are hired, but 30 million hours are available. This results in unemployment—*ab*—of 20 million hours of labor a year. With only 10 million hours of labor being demanded, workers will willingly supply that ten millionth hour for $2. It will pay such suppliers to spend the difference between the minimum wage and the wage for which they are willing to work—$2 an hour—in time and effort looking for a job.

How do we know that there are people willing to work for as little as $2 an hour? Look again at Fig. 6.4. As you can see, when only 10 million hours of work are available, the lowest wage at which workers will supply that 10 millionth hour—read off from the supply curve—is $2. Someone who manages to find a job will earn $4 an hour—$2 an hour more than the lowest wage at which someone is willing to work. It pays the unemployed, therefore, to spend a considerable amount of time and effort looking for work. Even though only 10 million hours of labor actually find employment, each person will spend time and effort searching for one of the scarce jobs.

The severity of the unemployment generated by a minimum wage depends on the demand for and supply of labor. You can see that if the supply curve were farther to the left, unemployment would be less. In fact, if the supply curve cut the demand curve at point *a*, the minimum wage would be the same as the unregulated wage. In such a situation, there would be no unemployment. Also, the farther to the right the demand for labor, the smaller is the amount of unemployment. If the demand curve cut the supply curve at point *b*, then, again, the minimum wage would be the same as the unregulated wage, and there would be no unemployment.

The Minimum Wage in Reality

The **Fair Labor Standards Act** makes it illegal to hire an adult worker for less than $4.25 an hour. Economists are not in agreement on the effects of the minimum wage or on how much unemployment it causes. However, they do agree that minimum wages bite hardest on the unskilled. Since there is a preponderance of unskilled workers among the young—the young have had less opportunity to obtain work experience and acquire skills—we would expect the minimum wage to cause more unemployment among young workers than among older workers. That is exactly what happens. The unemployment rate for teenagers is more than twice the average. Although many factors other than the minimum wage influence unemployment among young people, it is almost certain that part of the higher unemployment among the young arises from the impact of minimum wage laws.

REVIEW

Governments intend minimum wages to protect the incomes of the lowest paid. But a minimum wage lowers the quantity of labor demanded and hired. Some people will want to work, but they will be unemployed and will spend time searching for work. The young and the unskilled are hit hardest by the minimum wage. ◆

We've now seen how price ceilings and minimum wages affect prices and the quantities produced and consumed. Taxes are another important influence on markets. Let's look at their effects.

FIGURE 6.5

A Sales Tax

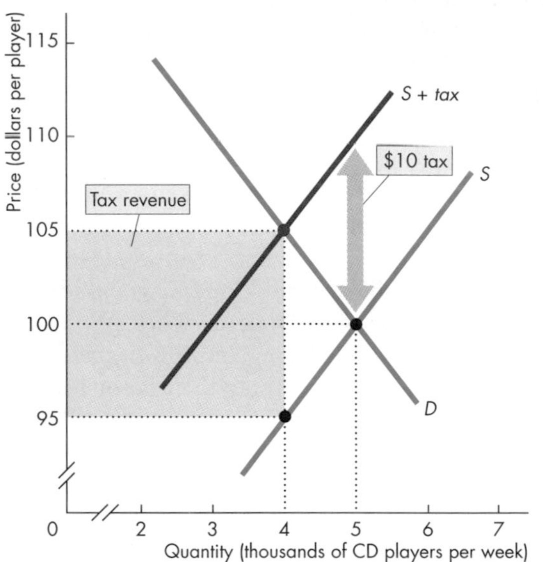

The demand curve for CD players is *D* and the supply curve is *S*. With no taxes, the price is $100 per player and 5,000 players a week are bought and sold. Imposing a sales tax increases the minimum price that sellers are willing to accept. The curve *S + tax* shows the terms on which sellers will make CD players available. The vertical distance between the supply curve *S* and the new supply curve *S + tax* equals the tax—$10 a player. The new equilibrium is at a price of $105 with 4,000 CD players a week bought and sold. The sales tax increases the price by less than the tax, decreases the price received by the supplier, and decreases the quantity bought and sold. It brings in revenue to the government equal to the blue area.

Taxes

One reason the demand and supply model was developed in the nineteenth century was to enable predictions to be made about the effects of taxes on prices and on the quantities produced and consumed. (See Our Advancing Knowledge, pp. 140–141.) Here, we'll look at the effects of sales taxes.

Do the prices of the goods and services that you buy increase by the full amount of a sales tax? Sales tax is added to the price of a good or service when you pay for it at the cash register, so isn't it obvious that *you* pay the entire tax? Isn't the price higher than it otherwise would be by an amount equal to the tax? It can be, but usually it isn't. And it is even possible that you, the consumer, actually pay none of the sales tax, forcing the seller to pay it for you. Let's see how we can make sense of these apparently absurd statements.

Who Pays a Sales Tax?

To study the effect of a sales tax, we need to start by looking at a market in which there is no such tax. We'll then introduce a sales tax and see the changes it brings.

The market for CD players is shown in Fig. 6.5. The demand curve is *D*, and the supply curve is *S*. With no sales tax, the equilibrium occurs at a price of $100 per player and 5,000 players a week bought and sold.

A sales tax of $10 a player is now imposed. When a CD player is sold, the $10 tax must be added to its price. Does the price increase by $10 from $100 to $110? It doesn't, because at a price of $110 the quantity of CD players demanded decreases to 3,000 a week, a quantity smaller than that supplied.

When a sales tax is imposed on a good, it is offered for sale at a higher price than in a no-tax situation. To determine that higher price, we must add the tax to the minimum price that suppliers are willing to accept for each quantity sold. To do this, we construct the new curve $S + tax$. The vertical distance between the supply curve S and the curve $S + tax$ equals the tax. The curve $S + tax$ describes the terms on which the good is available to buyers. A new equilibrium is determined where this new supply curve intersects the demand curve. This equilibrium is at a price of $105 and a quantity of 4,000 CD players a week.

The $10 sales tax has increased the price paid by the consumer by less than $10 and has decreased the price received by the supplier. The $10 tax paid is made up of the higher price to the buyer and the lower price to the seller.

The tax brings in tax revenue to the government equal to the tax per item multiplied by the items sold. It is illustrated by the blue area in the figure. The $10 tax on CD players brings in a tax revenue of $40,000 a week.

In this example, the buyer and the seller split the tax equally; the buyer pays $5 a player, and so does the seller. This equal sharing of the tax is a special case and does not usually occur. But some split of the tax between the buyer and seller is usual. And cases in which either the buyer or the seller pays the entire tax can occur. Let's look at these.

Tax Division and Elasticity of Supply

The division of the burden of a tax between buyers and sellers depends, in part, on the elasticity of supply. There are two extreme cases:

- Perfectly inelastic supply—seller pays
- Perfectly elastic supply—buyer pays

Perfectly Inelastic Supply Figure 6.6(a) shows the market for water from a mineral spring that flows at

FIGURE **6.6**

Sales Tax and the Elasticity of Supply

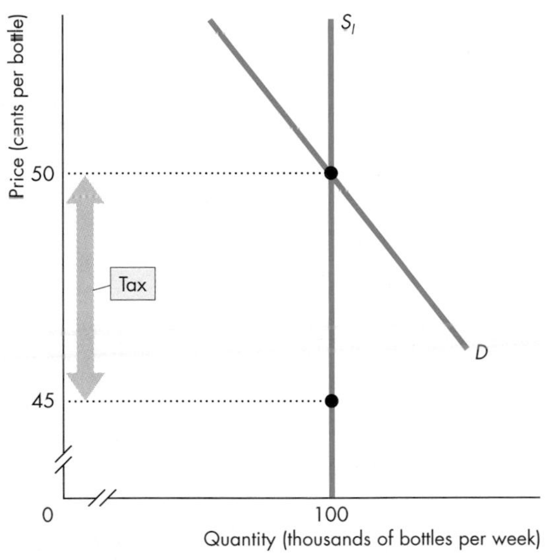

(a) Inelastic supply

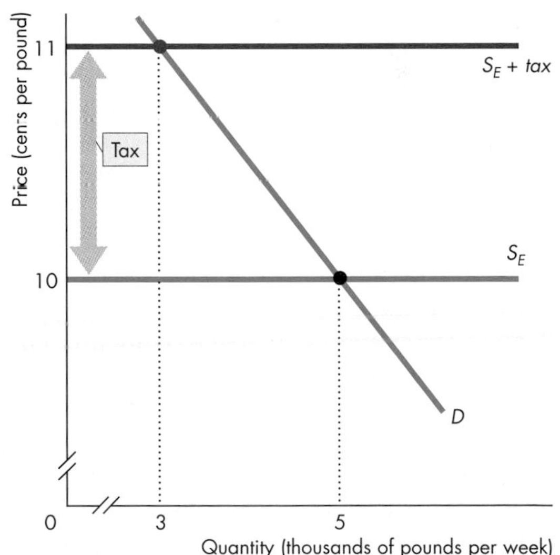

(b) Elastic supply

Part (a) shows the market for water from a mineral spring. Supply is perfectly inelastic and the supply curve is S_I. The demand curve is D. With no tax, the price is 50¢ a bottle. A sales tax of 5¢ decreases the price received by sellers, but the price remains at 50¢ a bottle and the number of bottles bought remains the same. Suppliers pay the entire tax.

Part (b) shows the market for sand from which silicon is extracted. Supply is perfectly elastic at a price of 10¢ a pound. The supply curve is S_E and the demand curve is D. With no tax, the price is 10¢ a pound and 5,000 pounds a week are bought. A sales tax of 1¢ a pound increases the minimum price at which sellers are willing to supply to 11¢ a pound. The supply curve shifts to S_E + *tax*. The price increases to 11¢ a pound, the quantity decreases to 3,000 pounds a week, and buyers pay the entire tax.

a constant rate that can't be controlled. The quantity supplied is 100,000 bottles a week, regardless of the price. The supply is perfectly inelastic and the supply curve is S_I. The demand curve for the water from this spring is D. With no tax, the price is 50¢ a bottle and the 100,000 bottles that flow from the spring are bought at that price.

If this spring water is taxed at 5¢ a bottle, we must add the tax to the minimum price at which the spring owners are willing to sell the water to determine the terms on which this water will be available to consumers. But the spring owners are able to supply only one quantity—100,000 bottles a week—at any price (greater than zero). Consumers, on the other hand, are willing to buy the 100,000 bottles available each week only if the price is 50¢ a bottle. So the price remains at 50¢ a bottle, and the suppliers pay the entire tax. A sales tax of 5¢ a bottle reduces the price received by suppliers to 45¢ a bottle.

Perfectly Elastic Supply Figure 6.6(b) shows the market for sand from which computer-chip makers extract silicon. There is a virtually unlimited quantity of this sand available, and its owners are willing to supply any quantity at a price of 10¢ a pound. The supply is perfectly elastic and the supply curve is S_E. The demand curve for sand is D in Fig. 6.6(b). With no tax, the price is 10¢ a pound and 5,000 pounds a week are bought at that price.

If this sand is taxed at 1¢ a pound, we must add the tax to the minimum price at which the owners are willing to sell the sand to determine the terms on which this sand will be available to computer-chip makers. Since without the tax the suppliers of sand are willing to supply any quantity at 10¢ a pound, with the 1¢ tax they are willing to supply any quantity at 11¢ a pound along the curve $S_E + tax$. A new equilibrium is determined where this new supply curve intersects the demand curve. This equilibrium is at a price of 11¢ a pound and 3,000 pounds a week are bought and sold. The sales tax has increased the price paid by consumers by the full amount of the tax—1¢ a pound—and has decreased the quantity sold.

We've seen that when supply is perfectly inelastic, the seller pays the tax, and when supply is perfectly elastic, the buyer pays it. In the usual case, supply is neither perfectly inelastic nor perfectly elastic, and the tax is split between the seller and the buyer. But the division depends on the elasticity of supply. The more elastic the supply, the larger is the portion of the tax paid by the buyer.

Tax Division and Elasticity of Demand

The division of the burden of a tax between buyers and sellers also depends on the elasticity of demand. Again, there are two extreme cases:

- Perfectly inelastic demand—buyer pays
- Perfectly elastic demand—seller pays

Perfectly Inelastic Demand Figure 6.7(a) shows the market for insulin, a vital daily medication of diabetics. The quantity demanded is 100,000 doses a day, regardless of the price. That is, a diabetic would sacrifice almost all other goods and services rather than not consume the insulin dose that provides good health and survival. The demand for insulin reflects this fact and is perfectly inelastic. It is shown by the vertical curve D. The supply curve of insulin is S. With no tax, the price is \$2 a dose, and the 100,000 doses a day that keep the population of diabetics healthy are bought.

If insulin is taxed at 20¢ a dose, we must add the tax to the minimum price at which the drug companies are willing to sell insulin to determine the terms on which it will be available to consumers. The result is a new supply curve $S + tax$. The new equilibrium occurs at a price of \$2.20 a dose, but the quantity bought does not change. The buyer pays the entire sales tax of 20¢ a dose.

Perfectly Elastic Demand Figure 6.7(b) shows the market for pink marker pens. Aside from a few pink freaks, people don't care whether they use a pink, blue, yellow, or green marker pen. If pink markers are less expensive than the others, everyone will use pink. If pink markers are more expensive than the others, no one will use them. The demand for pink marker pens is perfectly elastic at the price of other colored marker pens—\$1 a pen in Fig. 6.7(b). The demand curve for pink markers is the horizontal curve D. The supply curve is S. With no tax, the price of a pink marker is \$1 and 4,000 a week are bought at that price.

If a sales tax of 10¢ a pen is levied on pink—and only pink—marker pens, we must add the tax to the minimum price at which suppliers are willing to sell them to determine the terms on which pink marker

FIGURE 6.7

Sales Tax and the Elasticity of Demand

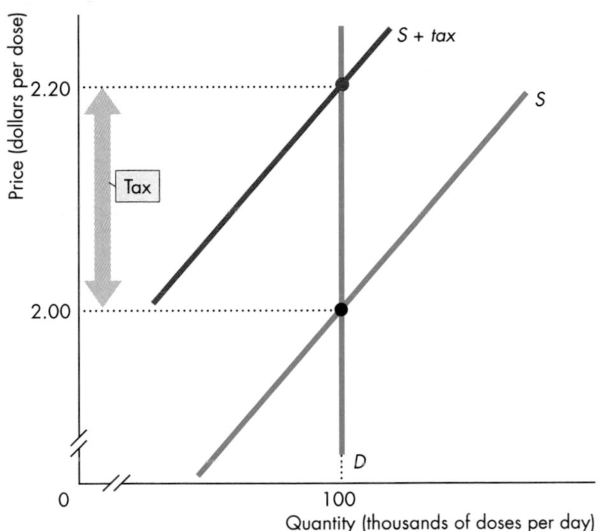

(a) Inelastic demand

Part (a) shows the market for insulin. The demand for insulin is perfectly inelastic, as shown by the curve *D*. The supply curve of insulin is *S*. With no tax, the price is $2 a dose and 100,000 doses a day are bought. A sales tax of 20¢ a dose increases the price at which sellers are willing to make insulin available and shifts the supply curve to *S + tax*. The price rises to $2.20 a dose, but the quantity bought does not change, and buyers pay the entire tax.

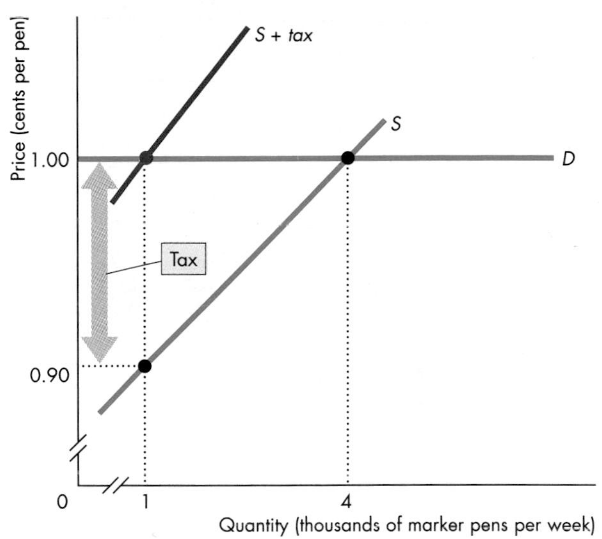

(b) Elastic demand

Part (b) shows the market for pink marker pens. The demand for pink marker pens is perfectly elastic at the price of other colored marker pens—$1 a pen. The demand curve is *D* and the supply curve is *S*. With no tax, the price of a pink marker pen is $1 and 4,000 a week are bought. A sales tax of 10¢ a pink pen decreases the supply of pink marker pens, shifting the supply curve to *S + tax*. The price remains at $1 a pen and the quantity of pink markers sold decreases to 1,000 a week. Suppliers pay the entire tax.

pens will be available to consumers. The new supply curve is *S + tax*. The new equilibrium is at a price of $1 a pen, the same as before, and the quantity of pink markers sold decreases to 1,000 a week. The 10¢ sales tax has left the price paid by the consumer unchanged but has decreased the amount received by the supplier by the full amount of the sales tax—10¢ a pen. As a result, sellers decrease the quantity offered for sale. (In the case of pink marker pens, it is likely that once sellers have run down their inventories, supply will also be perfectly elastic. In this case, pink marker pens will disappear!)

We've seen that when demand is perfectly inelastic, the buyer pays the entire tax, and when demand is perfectly elastic, the supplier pays it. In the usual case, demand is neither perfectly inelastic nor perfectly elastic, and the tax is split. But the division depends on the elasticity of demand. The more inelastic the demand, the larger is the portion of the tax paid by the buyer.

REVIEW

The effect of a sales tax depends on the elasticities of supply and demand. The more elastic the supply, the larger is the price increase, the larger is the quantity decrease, and the larger is the portion of the tax paid by the buyer. The less elastic the demand, the larger is the price increase, the smaller is the quantity decrease, and the larger is the portion of the tax paid by the buyer. ◆

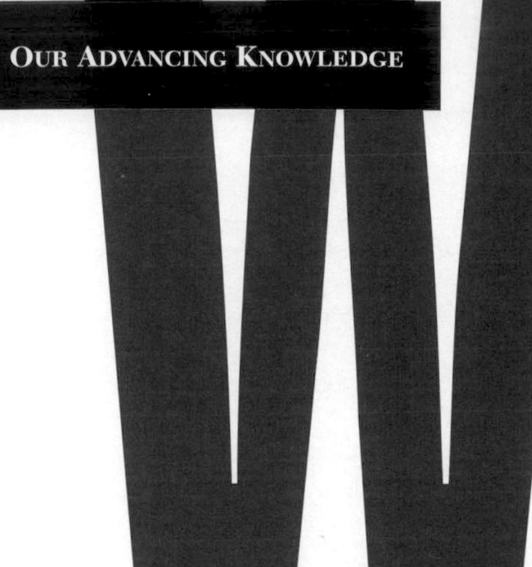

WHO Pays the Taxes?

Taxes increase the price paid by the buyer and decrease the price received by the seller. As a result, they decrease the quantities bought and sold and inflict costs on both buyers and sellers. These costs must be weighed against the benefits of the things on which the government spends the taxes it collects.

In the late nineteenth century, economists worked out how to measure the costs of taxes and to determine who bears those costs. At this time, most of the taxes were those on international trade—like the taxes we impose on imported Japanese automobiles today. It was discovered that a critical factor determining the effects of taxes is what we now call the *elasticity of demand*. Taxing goods that have an inelastic demand has a bigger effect on the price than on the quantity and brings in a large tax revenue. The smaller the effect of a tax on the quantity bought, the less the tax decreases consumption and the lower is its cost. So it pays to tax items—sometimes luxuries such as boats and expensive cars and sometimes necessities such as gasoline—that have an inelastic demand.

It was also discovered that the *elasticity of supply* plays an important role in determining the effects of taxes. Taxing goods that have an inelastic supply lowers the price received by the seller but has a small effect on the quantity sold and brings in a large tax revenue. The smaller the effect of a tax on the quantity sold, the less the tax decreases consumption and the lower is its cost. So it also pays to tax items that have an inelastic supply. This explains why land is a common item to tax.

"Thus, although the French may tax our goods, and so inflict a loss on themselves and on us, this is no reason for our inflicting an additional loss on the two communities by taxing the import of their goods."

Fleeming Jenkin
"On the Principles which Regulate the Incidence of Taxes"

Taxes are the revenue source that enables governments to provide a wide range of valuable public services. But taxes also impose a burden on those who pay them. When those who pay get none of the benefits, the seeds of a tax revolt are sown. Such was the situation in 1773 when the British Parliament imposed a tea tax on its American colonists. Rather than buy tea and pay this tax, the colonists held a tea party of a different kind, dumping valuable cargoes of British tea into the waters of Boston harbor.

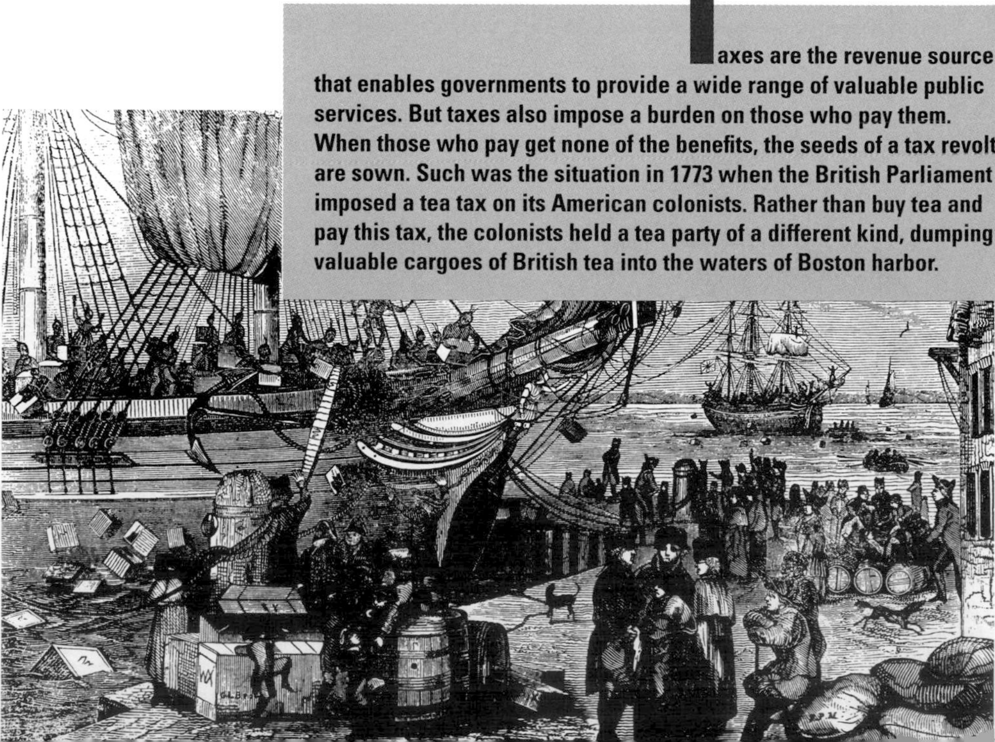

Every time you buy a gallon of gas, the government collects part of what you pay as a tax. And these taxes are large. They average 17½ cents a gallon. Even the lowest rate, in Georgia, is 7½ cents a gallon and the highest rate, in Rhode Island, is 26 cents a gallon. Who really pays these high gas taxes? Do the buyers pay? Does the seller pay? Or do the buyer and seller share the burden of the tax? If they share it, in what proportions?

Fleeming Jenkin: An *Engineer's Contribution to Economics*

Fleeming Jenkin (1833–1885) was a distinguished engineer who put his clear mind to work on a wide range of problems. Jenkin was not a famous economist in his own day, and his contributions to economic science were subsequently rediscovered by others. But he was a remarkable person who made a remarkable contribution to economics.

Jenkin worked on submarine cables, electrical standards, urban sanitation, and developing an electrical monorail transportation system. Between all these engineering projects, he was one of the first people to work out the laws of supply and demand and to put them to work on practical questions. One of these questions was: Who pays the taxes imposed on the sale of goods and services—the buyer or the seller or a combination of the two? The answer he came up with is the right one and is explained in this chapter.

Markets for Prohibited Goods

The markets for many goods and services are regulated, and buying or selling some goods is prohibited—the goods and services are illegal. The best-known example of such goods is illegal drugs.

Despite the fact that drugs are illegal, trade in drugs does take place. In fact, it is a multibillion-dollar business. Such trade can be understood by using the same economic models and principles that explain trading in markets for legal goods and services. Also, economic models can help us to understand the debate about drugs. They can help to answer questions such as: What would happen if drugs are legalized? Would they become less expensive? Would their consumption increase?

A Reminder about the Limits of Economics

Before we begin to study the market for drugs, let's remind ourselves that economics is a science that tries to answer questions about how the economic world works. It neither condones nor condemns the activities that it seeks to explain. It is vital that as a well-informed citizen, you have an opinion about drugs and about public policy toward them. What you learn about the economics of markets for illegal goods is one input into developing your opinion. But it is not a substitute for your moral judgments and does not help you to develop those judgments. What follows contains no moral judgments. It is a value-free analysis of how markets for prohibited goods work, not an argument about how they ought to be regulated and controlled.

To study the market for prohibited goods, we're first going to examine the prices and quantities that would prevail if these goods were not prohibited. Next, we'll see how prohibition works. Then we'll see how a tax might be used to limit the consumption of these goods.

A Free Market for Drugs

The demand for drugs is determined by the same forces that determine the demand for other goods. Other things being equal, the lower the price of drugs, the larger is the quantity of drugs demanded. The demand curve for drugs, *D*, is shown in Fig. 6.8. The supply of drugs is also determined in a similar way to the supply of other goods and is shown as the supply curve *S* in the figure. If drugs were not prohibited, the quantity bought and sold would be Q_c and the price would be P_c.

Prohibition on Drugs

When trading in a good is prohibited, the cost of undertaking such trading increases. By how much

FIGURE 6.8

The Market for a Prohibited Good

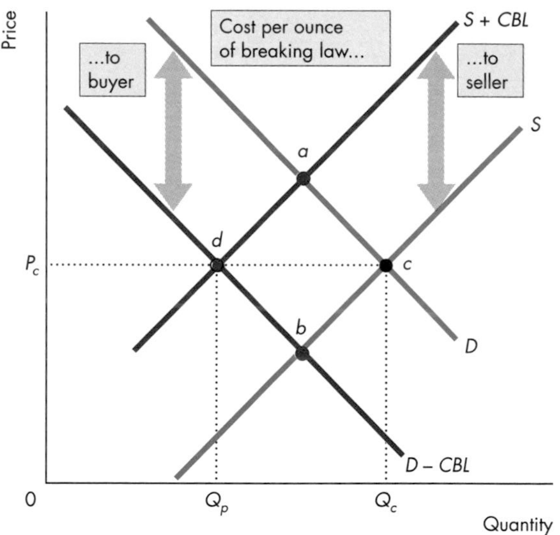

The demand curve for drugs is *D*, and the supply curve is *S*. With no prohibition on drugs, the quantity consumed is Q_c at a price P_c—point *c*. If selling drugs is illegal, the cost of breaking the law by selling drugs (*CBL*) is added to the other costs, and supply decreases to *S* + *CBL*. The price rises and the quantity consumed decreases—point *a*. If buying drugs is illegal, the cost of breaking the law is subtracted from the maximum price that buyers are willing to pay, and demand decreases to *D* – *CBL*. The price falls and the quantity consumed decreases—point *b*. If both buying and selling are illegal, both the supply curve and the demand curve shift, and the quantity consumed decreases even more, but (in this example) the price remains at its unregulated level—point *d*.

the cost increases and on whom the cost falls depend on the penalties for violating the law and the effectiveness with which the law is enforced. The larger the penalties for violation and the more effective the policing, the higher are the costs. Penalties may be imposed on sellers, buyers, or both.

Penalties on Sellers When sellers of illegal goods such as drugs are penalized, the cost of selling increases. Supply decreases and the supply curve shifts. In Fig. 6.8, the cost of breaking the law by selling drugs (*CBL*) is added to the other costs, and the supply decreases, shifting the supply curve to $S + CBL$. If penalties are imposed only on sellers, the market moves from point *c* to point *a*. The price increases and the quantity bought decreases.

Penalties on Buyers When buyers of illegal goods are penalized, the goods have less value to buyers. The cost of breaking the law must be subtracted from the value of the good to determine the maximum price that buyers are willing to pay. Demand decreases and the demand curve shifts. In Fig. 6.8, the demand curve shifts to $D - CBL$. If penalties are imposed only on buyers, the market moves from point *c* to point *b*. The price and the quantity bought decrease.

Penalties on Both Sellers and Buyers If penalties are imposed on sellers *and* buyers, both supply and demand decrease, and both the supply curve and demand curve shift. If the costs of breaking the law are the same for both buyers and sellers, both curves shift by the same amounts. This is the case in Fig. 6.8. The market moves to point *d*. The price remains at the competitive market price, but the quantity bought decreases to Q_p. But other distributions of penalties are possible. The larger the penalty and greater the degree of law enforcement, the larger is the decrease in demand and/or supply and the greater the shift of the demand and/or supply curve.

With high enough penalties and effective law enforcement, it is possible to decrease demand and supply to the point at which the quantity bought is zero. But in reality, such an outcome is unusual. It does not happen in the case of illegal drugs. The key reason is the high cost of law enforcement and insufficient resources for the police to achieve effective enforcement. Because of this situation, some people suggest that drugs (and other illegal goods) should be legalized and sold openly but should also be taxed at a high rate in the same way that legal drugs such as alcohol are taxed. How would such an arrangement work?

Legalizing and Taxing Drugs

If drugs were legalized, there would be no costs of law breaking. With no taxes on drugs, the quantity Q_c in Fig. 6.8 would be consumed. But suppose that drugs were taxed at a high rate. Figure 6.9 shows the effects of such an arrangement. Here, the tax rate has been chosen to make the quantity bought the same as with a prohibition. The tax added to the supply price shifts the supply curve to $S + tax$. Equilibrium occurs at a quantity of Q_p. The price paid by consumers increases to P_b and the price received by suppliers decreases to P_s. The government collects a tax revenue equal to the blue area in the figure.

FIGURE 6.9

Legalizing and Taxing Drugs

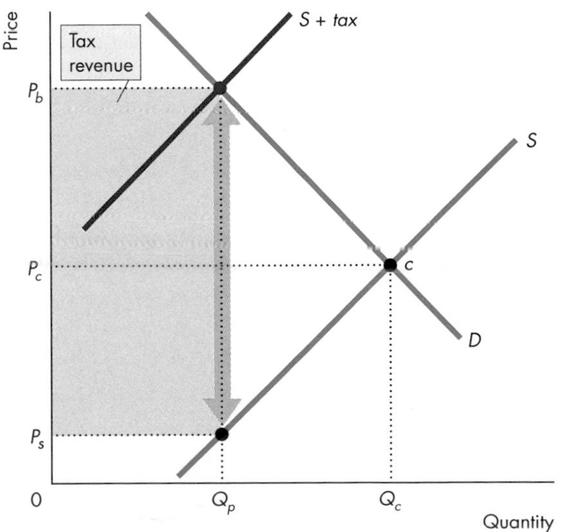

Drugs are legalized but taxed at a high rate. The tax added to the supply price shifts the supply curve from S to $S + tax$. The quantity bought decreases to Q_p, the price paid by consumers increases to P_b, and the price received by suppliers decreases to P_s. The government collects a tax revenue equal to the blue area.

Illegal Trading to Evade the Tax It is likely that an extremely high tax rate would be needed to cut drug consumption to the level that would prevail with a prohibition. It is also likely that many drug dealers and consumers would try to cover up their activities to evade the tax. If they did act in this way, they would face the cost of breaking the law—the tax law. If the penalty for tax law violation was as severe and as effectively policed as drug dealing laws, the analysis that we've already conducted would also apply to this case. The quantity of drugs consumed would remain at Q_p. But to the extent that the tax was successfully evaded, the tax revenue would fall short of the area highlighted in Fig. 6.9.

Some Pros and Cons of Taxes versus Prohibition So which works more effectively, prohibition or taxing? The comparison we've just made suggests that the two methods can be made to be equivalent if the taxes and penalties are set at the appropriate levels. But there are some differences. In favor of taxes and against prohibition is the fact that the tax revenue can be used to make law enforcement more effective. It can also be used to run a more effective education campaign against drugs. In favor of prohibition and against taxes is the fact that a prohibition sends a signal that may influence preferences, decreasing the demand for drugs. Also, some people intensely dislike the idea of the government profiting from trade in harmful substances.

REVIEW

Penalizing dealers for the sale of an illegal good increases the cost of selling the good and decreases the supply of it. Penalizing buyers for the consumption of an illegal good decreases the willingness to pay for the good and decreases the demand for it. The quantity bought decreases and the price increases if penalties for selling are higher than those for buying, and the price decreases if penalties for buying are higher than those for selling. Taxing a good at a sufficiently high rate can achieve the same consumption level as prohibition. ◆

Stabilizing Farm Revenue

Farm revenue fluctuates a great deal because of variations in harvests and prices. Sometimes, the combination of rainfall, sunshine, and temperature throughout the growing and harvesting seasons is all wrong, resulting in low crop yields. Sometimes the climate is ideal, resulting in bumper harvests. At other times the climate is average, resulting in normal crop yields. How do variations in crop yields affect farm revenue? And how might those revenues be stabilized?

No Stabilization Program

Figure 6.10 illustrates the market for wheat. In both parts, the demand curve for wheat is *D*. Once farmers have harvested their crop, they have no control over the quantity supplied and supply is inelastic along a *momentary supply curve*. In normal climate conditions, the momentary supply curve is MS_0 (in both parts of the figure).

The price is determined at the point of intersection of the momentary supply curve and the demand curve. In normal conditions, the price is $3 a bushel. The quantity of wheat produced is 16 billion bushels, and farm revenue is $48 billion. Suppose the opportunity cost to farmers of producing wheat is also $48 billion. Then in normal conditions, farmers just cover their opportunity cost.

Poor Harvest Suppose there is a bad growing season, resulting in a poor harvest. What happens to the price of wheat and the revenue of farmers? These questions are answered in Fig. 6.10(a). Supply decreases to 14 billion bushels and the momentary supply curve shifts to the left to MS_1. With a decrease in supply, the price increases to $4 a bushel.

What happens to total farm revenue? It *increases* to $56 billion. A decrease in supply has brought an increase in price and an increase in farm revenue. The reason is that the demand for wheat is *inelastic*. The percentage decrease in the quantity demanded is

FIGURE 6.10

Harvests, Farm Prices, and Farm Revenue

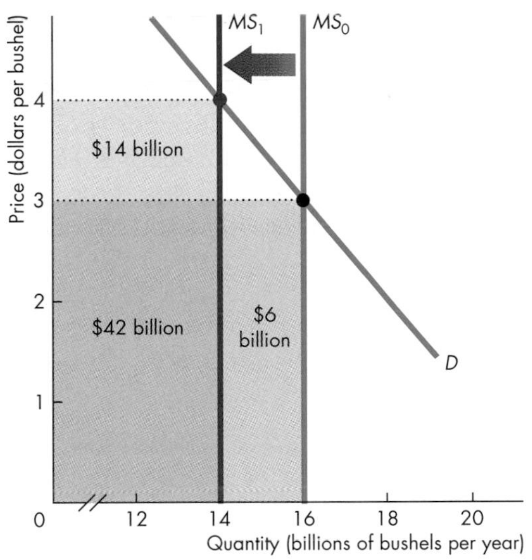

(a) Poor harvest: revenue increases

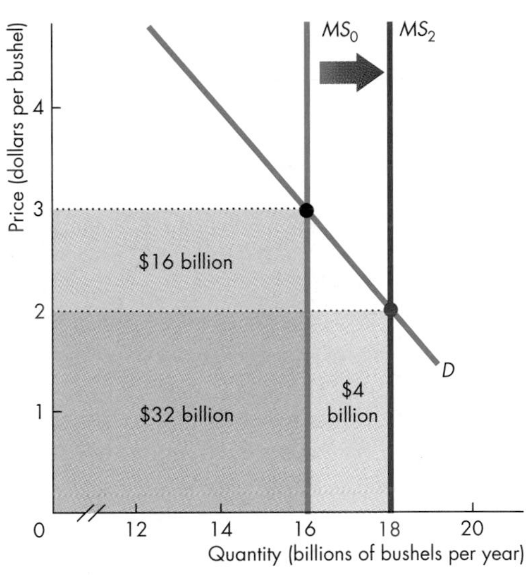

(b) Bumper harvest: revenue decreases

In both parts, the demand curve for wheat is D, in normal times the momentary supply curve is MS_0, and 16 billion bushels are sold for \$3 a bushel. In part (a), a poor growing season decreases supply, shifting the momentary supply curve to MS_1. The price increases to \$4 a bushel, and farm revenue *increases* from \$48 billion to \$56 billion—the increase in revenue from the higher price (\$14 billion light blue area) exceeds the decrease in revenue from the smaller quantity (\$6 billion red area). In part (b), a bumper harvest increases supply, shifting the momentary supply curve to MS_2. The price decreases to \$2 a bushel, and farm revenue *decreases* to \$36 billion—the decrease in revenue from the lower price (\$16 billion red area) exceeds the increase in revenue from the increase in the quantity sold (\$4 billion light blue area).

less than the percentage increase in price. You can verify this fact by noticing in Fig. 6.10(a) that the increase in revenue from the higher price (\$14 billion light blue area) exceeds the decrease in revenue from the smaller quantity (\$6 billion red area). Farmers are now making a profit in excess of their opportunity cost.

Although total farm revenue increases when there is a poor harvest, some farmers, whose entire crop is wiped out, suffer a fall in revenue. Others, whose crop is unaffected, make an enormous gain.

Bumper Harvest Figure 6.10(b) shows what happens in the opposite situation, when there is a bumper harvest. Now supply increases to 18 billion bushels and the momentary supply curve shifts to the right to MS_2. With the increased quantity supplied, the price falls to \$2 a bushel. Farm revenues also decline—to \$36 billion. They do so because the demand for wheat is inelastic. To see this fact, notice in Fig. 6.10(b) that the decrease in revenue from the lower price (\$16 billion red area) exceeds the increase in revenue from the increase in the quantity sold (\$4 billion light blue area). Farmers are now not covering their opportunity cost.

Elasticity of Demand In the example we've just worked through, demand is inelastic. If demand is elastic, the price fluctuations go in the same directions as those we've worked out, but revenues fluctuate in the opposite directions. Bumper harvests increase revenue, and poor harvests decrease it. But the demand for most agricultural products is inelastic, and the case we've studied is the relevant one.

Because farm revenues fluctuate, institutions have evolved to stabilize them. There are two types of institutions:

- Speculative markets in inventories
- Farm price and revenue stabilization agencies

Speculative Markets in Inventories

Many goods, including a wide variety of agricultural products, can be stored. These inventories provide a cushion between production and consumption. If production decreases, goods can be sold from inventory; if production increases, goods can be put into inventory.

In a market that has inventories, we must distinguish production from supply. The quantity produced is not the same as the quantity supplied. The quantity supplied exceeds the quantity produced when goods are sold from inventory, and the quantity supplied is less than the quantity produced when goods are put into inventory. The supply curve therefore depends on the behavior of inventory holders. Let's see how they behave.

The Behavior of Inventory Holders Inventory holders speculate. They buy at a low price and sell at a high price. That is, they buy goods and put them into inventory when the price is low and sell them from inventory when the price is high. They make a profit equal to the difference between their buying price and selling price, minus the cost of storage.[5]

But how do inventory holders know when to buy and when to sell? How do they know whether the price is high or low? To decide whether a price is high or low, inventory holders make their best forecast of future prices.[6] If the price is above its expected future level, they sell goods from inventory. If the price is below its expected future level, they buy goods to put into inventory. Even if the price is just a penny above or below the inventory holder's expected price, goods are supplied from or put into inventory. This behavior by inventory holders makes the supply curve perfectly elastic at the price expected by inventory holders.

Let's work out what happens to price and quantity in a market in which inventories are held when production fluctuates. Let's look again at the wheat market.

Fluctuations in Production In Fig. 6.11 the demand curve for wheat is *D*. Inventory holders expect the future price to be $3 a bushel. The supply curve is *S*—supply is perfectly elastic at the future price expected by inventory holders. Production fluctuates between Q_1 and Q_2.

When production fluctuates and there are no inventories, the price and the quantity fluctuate. Price falls when production increases and rises when

FIGURE 6.11

How Inventories Limit Price Changes

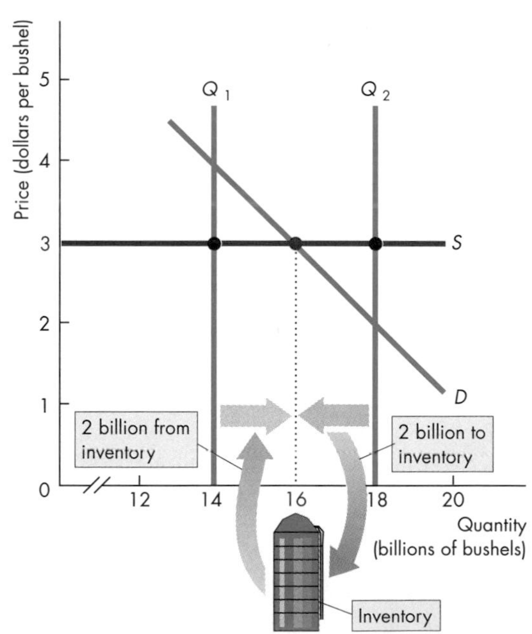

Inventory holders supply from inventory if the price rises above $3 a bushel and take wheat into inventory if the price falls below $3 a bushel, making supply perfectly elastic along the supply curve *S*. When production decreases to Q_1, 2 billion bushels are supplied from inventory; when production increases to Q_2, 2 billion bushels are added to inventory. The price remains constant at $3 a bushel.

[5]We will suppose that the cost of storage is so small that we can ignore it. This assumption, though not essential, enables us to see more sharply the effects of inventory holders' decisions on prices.

[6]The process of making the best possible forecast—a *rational expectation*—is explained in Chapter 17, pp. 478–479.

production decreases. We saw this result in Fig. 6.10. But if there are inventories, the price does not fluctuate. When production is low, at Q_1 or 14 billion bushels, inventory holders sell 2 billion bushels from inventory and the quantity bought by consumers is 16 billion bushels. The price remains at $3 a bushel. When production is high, at Q_2 or 18 billion bushels, inventory holders buy 2 billion bushels and consumers continue to buy 16 billion bushels. Again, the price remains at $3 a bushel.

Inventories in Reality The model of a market with inventories that we've just reviewed is the simplest possible. But it shows how inventories and inventory holders' expectations about future prices reduce price fluctuations. In the above example, the price fluctuations are entirely eliminated. When there are costs of carrying inventories and when inventories become almost depleted, some price fluctuations do occur, but these fluctuations are smaller than those occurring in a market without inventories.

Farm Revenue Even if inventory speculation succeeds in stabilizing prices, it does not stabilize farm revenue. With the price stabilized, farm revenue fluctuates as production fluctuates. But the direction in which revenue fluctuates is now reversed. Bumper harvests bring larger revenues than poor harvests. The reason is that now farmers, in effect, face a perfectly elastic demand curve for their output.

Stabilizing Farm Revenue

Every country has regulatory agencies that intervene in agricultural markets. The most extensive such agencies are in the European Community. But they are also present in the United States, where they stabilize the prices of many agricultural products, such as grains, dairy products, tobacco, rice, peanuts, and cotton.

These agencies operate at an enormous cost to taxpayers. Usually, they set price floors—similar to the minimum wage that we studied earlier—above the production cost of efficient farms. The result is persistent excess supply, which the stabilization agency must mop up. The stabilization agency buys more than it sells and winds up with a large inventory. Such has been the outcome in Europe, where agencies have mountains of butter and lakes of wine! The cost of buying and storing the inventory falls on taxpayers, and the main gainers are the large, efficient farms.

REVIEW

The demand for most farm products is inelastic. With no inventory, a poor harvest (a decrease in supply) increases price and increases farm revenue, and a bumper harvest (an increase in supply) decreases price and decreases farm revenue. Inventory holders speculate, buying at a low price and selling at a high price, reducing price fluctuations. Farm stabilization agencies also limit price fluctuations but usually create surpluses. ◆

◆ ◆ ◆ ◆ We've now completed our study of demand and supply and its applications. You've seen how this powerful model enables us to make predictions about prices and quantities traded and also how it enables us to understand a wide variety of markets and situations. ◆ ◆ We're now going to start digging a bit more deeply into people's economic choices. In the next part we'll study the economic choices of households.

SUMMARY

Housing Markets and Rent Ceilings

A sudden decrease in the supply of housing shifts the short-run supply curve to the left. Rents increase. In the short run, higher rents bring forth an increase in the quantity of housing supplied as people economize on the available space. In the long run, the higher rents stimulate building activity, resulting in a shift to the right in the short-run supply curve. Through this process, rents gradually decrease, and the quantity of housing available gradually increases.

If a rent ceiling prevents rents from increasing, the quantity of housing supplied is lower, in both the short run and the long run, than it would be in an unregulated market. There is no inducement to economize on space in the short run and no incentive to build new houses and apartments in the long run. Equilibrium is achieved by people spending time searching for housing and by the development of a black market. The total cost of housing, including the value of the time spent searching, exceeds the cost in an unregulated market. (pp. 126–131)

The Labor Market and Minimum Wage Regulation

A decrease in the demand for unskilled labor lowers wages and reduces employment in the short run. Low wages encourage people to quit a particular market and to acquire skills and seek different, more highly paid work. As they do so, the short-run supply curve for unskilled labor shifts to the left. As it does so, it intersects the demand curve at higher wages and lower levels of employment. Eventually, the wage will return to its previous level but at a much lower employment level.

If the government imposes a minimum wage, a decrease in the demand for labor will result in an increase in unemployment and an increase in the amount of time spent searching for a job. Minimum wages bite hardest on people having the fewest skills, and such workers tend to be young people. The unemployment rate among such people is more than twice the average rate. (pp. 131–136)

Taxes

When a sales tax is imposed on a good or service, the item in question is offered for sale at a higher price than in a no-tax situation. Usually, the quantity traded decreases, and the price of the good increases but by less than the amount of the tax. The tax is borne partly by the buyer and partly by the seller. The division of the burden of a tax between buyers and sellers depends on the elasticity of supply and the elasticity of demand. There are four extreme cases:

1. If supply is perfectly inelastic, the quantity and price remain constant, and the seller pays the entire tax.
2. If supply is perfectly elastic, the quantity decreases, the price increases by the full amount of the tax, and the buyer pays the entire tax.
3. If demand is perfectly inelastic, the quantity remains constant, the price increases by the full amount of the tax, and the buyer pays the entire tax.
4. If demand is perfectly elastic, the quantity decreases, the price remains constant, and the seller pays the entire tax.

The more elastic the supply and the less elastic the demand, the greater is the price increase, the smaller is the quantity decrease, and the larger is the portion of the tax paid by the buyer. (pp. 136–139)

Markets for Prohibited Goods

Other things being equal, the lower the price of drugs, the larger is the quantity of drugs demanded, and the higher the price, the larger is the quantity of drugs supplied. Penalties for selling an illegal good increase the cost of selling it and decrease its supply. Penalties on buyers decrease their willingness to pay and decrease the demand for the good. The higher the penalties and the more effective the law enforcement, the smaller is the quantity bought. The price is higher or lower than the unregulated price, depending on whether penalties for sellers or buyers are higher. Effective law enforcement and high enough penalties will decrease demand and supply to the point at which the good disappears.

A tax set at a sufficiently high rate will also decrease the quantity of drug consumption, but there will be a tendency for the tax to be evaded. If the penalty for tax law violation is as severe and as effectively policed as drug dealing laws, the quantity of drugs consumed will remain at the prohibition level but the tax revenue will be lower. Tax revenue from a drug tax could be used to make law enforcement more effective and to pay for a campaign against drugs. But prohibiting drugs sends a signal that may influence preferences, decreasing the demand for drugs. (pp. 142–144)

Stabilizing Farm Revenue

Farm revenues fluctuate because climatic conditions bring fluctuations in crop yields. The demand for most farm products is inelastic, so a decrease in supply brings an increase in price and an increase in farm revenue, and a bumper harvest brings a decrease in price and a decrease in farm revenues. Inventory holders and official agencies act to stabilize farm prices and revenues.

Inventory holders speculate, buying at a low price and selling at a high price. As a consequence (and ignoring storage costs), the supply curve is perfectly elastic at the future price expected by inventory holders. When production is low, inventory holders sell from inventory, preventing the price from rising. When production is high, inventory holders buy, preventing the price from falling.

Farm stabilization agencies set minimum prices that create persistent surpluses. (pp. 144–147)

KEY ELEMENTS

Key Terms

Key Figures

REVIEW QUESTIONS

1 Describe what happens to the rent and to the quantity of housing available if an earthquake suddenly and unexpectedly reduces the supply of housing. Trace the evolution of the rent and the quantity traded over time.

2 In the situation described in question 1, how will things be different if a rent ceiling is imposed?

3 Describe what happens to the price and quantity bought and sold in a market in which there is a sudden and unforeseen increase in supply. Trace the evolution of the price and quantity bought and sold in the market over time.

4 Describe what happens to the price and quantity bought and sold in a market in which there is a sudden and unforeseen increase in demand. Trace the evolution of the price and quantity bought and sold in the market over time.

5 Describe what happens to the wage rate and quantity of labor employed when there is a sudden and unforeseen decrease in demand for labor. Trace the evolution of the wage rate and employment over time.

6 In the situation described in question 5, how are things different if a minimum wage is introduced?

7 Why does a minimum wage create unemployment?

8 When a government regulation prevents a price from changing, what forces come into operation to achieve an equilibrium?

9 How does the imposition of a sales tax on a good influence the supply of and demand for that good? How does it influence the price of the good and the quantity bought?

10 How does a prohibition of the sale of a good affect the demand for and supply of the good? How does it affect the price of the good and the quantity bought?

11 How does a prohibition of the consumption of a good affect the demand for and supply of the good? How does it affect the price of the good and the quantity bought?

12 Explain the alternative ways in which the consumption of harmful drugs can be controlled. What are the arguments for and against each method?

13 Why do farm revenues fluctuate?

14 Do farm revenues increase or decrease when there is a bumper crop and there are no inventories? Why?

15 Explain why speculation can stabilize the price of a storable commodity but does not stabilize the revenues of the producers of such a commodity.

16 How can an official agency stabilize farm revenues? Is such stabilization profitable?

PROBLEMS

You will find it easier to answer these problems by drawing the supply and demand curves on graph paper.

1 You have been given the following information about the market for rental housing in your town:

Rent (dollars per month)	Quantity demanded	Quantity supplied
100	20,000	0
150	15,000	5,000
200	10,000	10,000
250	5,000	15,000
300	2,500	20,000
350	1,500	25,000

a What is the equilibrium rent?
b What is the equilibrium quantity of housing bought and sold?

2 Now suppose that a rent ceiling of $150 a month is imposed in the housing market described in problem 1.

a What is the quantity of housing demanded?
b What is the quantity of housing supplied?
c What is the excess quantity of housing demanded?
d What is the maximum price that demanders will be willing to pay for the last unit available?
e Suppose that the average wage rate is $10 per hour. How many hours a month will a person spend looking for housing?

3 The demand for and supply of teenage labor are as follows:

Wage rate (dollars per hour)	Hours demanded	Hours supplied
2	3,000	1,000
3	2,500	1,500
4	2,000	2,000
5	1,500	2,500
6	1,000	3,000

a What is the equilibrium wage rate?
b What is the level of employment?
c What is the level of unemployment?
d If the government imposes a minimum wage of $3 an hour for teenagers, how many hours do teenagers work?
e If the government imposes a minimum wage of $5 an hour for teenagers, what are the employment and unemployment levels?
f If there is a minimum wage of $5 an hour and demand increases by 500 hours, what is the level of unemployment?

4 The following table illustrates three supply curves for train travel:

Price (cents per passenger mile)	Quantity supplied (billions of passenger miles)		
	Momentary	Short-run	Long-run
10	500	300	100
20	500	350	200
30	500	400	300
40	500	450	400
50	500	500	500
60	500	550	600

Price (cents per passenger mile)	Quantity supplied (billions of passenger miles)		
	Momentary	Short-run	Long-run
70	500	600	700
80	500	650	800
90	500	700	900
100	500	750	1,000

a If the price is 50¢ per passenger mile, what is the quantity supplied in
(1) The long run
(2) The short run

b Suppose that the price is initially 50¢ but that it then rises to 70¢. What will be the quantity supplied
(1) Immediately following the price rise
(2) In the short run
(3) In the long run

5 Suppose that the supply of train travel is the same as in problem 4. The following table gives two demand schedules—original and new:

Price (cents per passenger mile)	Quantity demanded (billions of passenger miles)	
	Original	New
10	10,000	10,300
20	5,000	5,300
30	2,000	2,300
40	1,000	1,300
50	500	800
60	400	700
70	300	600
80	200	500
90	100	400
100	0	300

a What is the original equilibrium price and quantity?

b After the increase in demand has occurred, what is
(1) The momentary equilibrium price and quantity
(2) The short-run equilibrium price and quantity
(3) The long-run equilibrium price and quantity

6 The short-run and long-run demand for train travel are as follows:

Price (cents per passenger mile)	Quantity demandod (billions of passenger miles)	
	Short-run	Long-run
10	700	10,000
20	650	5,000
30	600	2,000
40	550	1,000
50	500	500
60	450	400
70	400	300
80	350	200
90	300	100
100	250	0

The supply of train travel is as given in problem 4.

a What is the long-run equilibrium price and quantity of train travel?

b Serious floods destroy one fifth of the trains and train tracks. Supply falls by 100 billion passenger miles. What happens to the price and the quantity of train travel in:
(1) The short run
(2) The long run

7 The following are the demand and supply schedules for chocolate brownies:

Price (cents per brownie)	Quantity demanded (millions per day)	Quantity supplied (millions per day)
90	1	7
80	2	6
70	3	5
60	4	4
50	5	3
40	6	2

a If there is no tax on brownies, what is their price and how many are produced and consumed?

b If a tax of 20¢ per brownie is introduced, what happens to the price of a brownie and the number produced and consumed?

c How much tax does the government collect and who pays it?

8 Calculate the elasticity of demand in Fig. 6.10 when the price of wheat changes from \$2 to \$4 a bushel. Does its magnitude imply that farm revenues fluctuate in the same direction as price fluctuations or in the opposite direction?

PART 3

HOUSEHOLDS' CHOICES

Talking with Richard Easterlin

Born in Ridgefield Park, New Jersey, in 1926, Richard Easterlin received his first degree from the Stevens Institute of Technology in Philadelphia. He followed that with graduate work at the University of Pennsylvania, where he obtained his Ph.D. in 1953. Professor Easterlin spent most of his career at the University of Pennsylvania but moved to the University of Southern California in 1982. Professor Easterlin's work has been at the interface of economics and demography, studying the implications of the choices that people make about marriage and children for the evolution of populations as a whole.

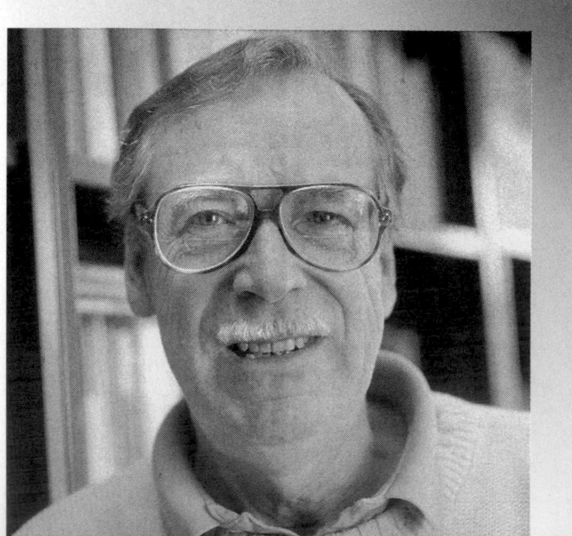

What attracted you to economics?

My first encounter with an economics course was in the graduate MBA curriculum at the University of Pennsylvania. There was a great air of excitement in the field at that time, the late 1940s. The Keynesian revolution was afoot, and the use of fiscal policy as a tool for avoiding another Great Depression had powerful appeal. Methodologically, I found economics appealing because it involved problem-solving techniques much like those of engineering, which was my undergraduate major. The difference was that the problems economics was dealing with were great social concerns.

What attracted you to questions of demography?

The truth is, I was not initially attracted to demography. My view of population was unfortunately like that of many graduate economics students today, that it is not a proper subject for economic analysis. But I was invited to join an empirical research project on population redistribution and economic growth in the United States. Although my work

"The difference was that the problems economics was dealing with were great social concerns."

related to economic aspects of the project—estimating trends in income, agriculture, and manufacturing—some demography started to rub off on me. I never had any formal demographic training, but I benefited from frequent contact with collaborators in demographic economics and sociology. I soon developed a fairly good grip on the subject matter and techniques of the field.

What is special about the way *economists* study demographic issues?

Economists bring to bear a systematic theoretical framework of great potential value in a field where emphasis on statistical techniques and measurement has dominated. Unfortunately, however, economists too often have little knowledge of the field of demography and little respect for non-economists. Early in my career, I was prone to the latter shortcoming and wrote a draft of an arrogant article about the American baby boom, demeaning the work of demographers. I received feedback that it was a good article but had benefited enormously from prior work by demographers. I was asked, "Why put them down?" Ever since, I've tried to have a more balanced appreciation of demographers and their work and, more generally, that of disciplines other than economics.

At the University of Pennsylvania in the 1970s, you were the intellectual leader of what came to be called the "Pennsylvania School." Was there in fact such a school? What were the principal views that characterized it?

The Pennsylvania School comprised a fairly small group of scholars who, at least in the area of childbearing behavior, were willing to expand the limits of economic theory to take into account systematic changes in preferences and the real-world existence of natural fertility (the latter came to be called "supply-side" considerations in fertility behavior). In contrast, the opposing Chicago School more or less adamantly pursued a demand theory that focused on prices and income alone. In considering sources of demand change, they ignored the possibility of preference change due to differences among generations in their socialization experience.

"The question is whether this fertility upswing will resume once the current recession ends."

What were the intellectual roots of your Pennsylvania School perspective?

I had found economic theory to be useful in understanding demographic behavior. Indeed, early on, when Gary Becker (who is closely associated with the Chicago School) and I were fellow researchers at the National Bureau of Economic Research in New York, we had many fruitful discussions. But while Becker tended to put theory first (though not without concern for its value in interpreting real-world problems), I tended to put real-world problems first and see economic theory as merely one tool for understanding them.

My foremost concern at the time was the causes of the post–World War II American baby boom and subsequent baby bust. As I studied the data, I increasingly felt that economic theory as usually applied failed to supply an answer. Like most economists, I was reluctant to consider the effect of changing tastes or preferences as a possible causal influence. Eventually, however, I changed my views, as I came to see the relevance of what sociologists call socialization and reference group theory to the determination of preferences. This changed view of tastes was also influenced by demographers' empirical work on childbearing preferences. Later, when I started working on the transition from high to low fertility in less developed countries, I benefited greatly from demographers' empirical work on natural fertility. This means fertility is not deliberately regulated, a concept many economists, especially those of the Chicago School, find hard to swallow.

Has there been a convergence of the Pennsylvania and Chicago Schools, or do sharp differences remain between them?

There has been some convergence. With regard to the demand for children, Becker's work on child endowments is a step in the direction of recognizing how one's home environment may influence behavior. But it still carefully avoids the idea of preference change. There has also been limited recognition by Chicago School economists of what are called supply-side constraints on fertility, but in the Chicago view, these remain purely biological, for example, subfertility or infertility.

How can these differences be resolved?

On the theoretical side, I'm afraid there is unlikely to be much further convergence. Chicago-trained economists are distinctive in their preference for what I consider to be a fairly narrow theoretical paradigm. Their approach means either rejecting or rewriting the theoretical contributions of other disciplines, such as sociology. It also means rejecting much of the survey evidence on attitudes collected by demographers.

In a broader sense, time will help resolve the differences between the two views. For example, so far as I'm aware, Chicago theorists see the future of American fertility and that of developed countries generally as one of continued fertility decline. The Pennsylvania School is more prone to accept the likelihood of longer-term fertility swings—up and down. The 1990s should be of special interest in this regard.

> "Demographic policies are not important or appropriate ways to promote economic growth in either developed or less developed countries."

American fertility moved up sharply from 1986 to 1990, contrary to what Chicago-type theory would lead one to expect. The question is whether this fertility upswing will resume once the current recession ends. If it continues, it would have direct bearing on the relative merits of the Chicago and Pennsylvania School theories.

Two of the world's biggest countries, China and India, are struggling under the burden of huge and rapidly growing populations. How can economics help design effective population programs for countries such as these?

I'm not a population alarmist. Rapid population growth in less developed countries is due to dramatic mortality decline. Hand in hand with mortality decline goes major health improvement, which in turn means more vigorous labor and less labor time lost due to the debilitating effects of disease. There is no empirical evidence that rapid population growth has caused significantly slower economic growth. Moreover, historical experience—and, I might add, the theory of the Pennsylvania School—shows that the phase of rapid population growth is a temporary one. Fertility decline follows mortality decline, and this is currently going on in both China and India.

In the 1970s, I was a member of a United Nations team that visited India to study its family planning program. I saw first-hand the harmful effects of family planning programs being pushed by both Indians and Americans who feared population explosion. The worst effect of their programs was disregard of basic human rights. I feel that the case for family planning programs should rest not on unfounded population explosion theories but on concern for maternal, child, and family welfare. If programs are concerned with this goal, then economists could usefully contribute to them via cost-benefit analysis, a notion that is frequently absent in these programs.

Some populations decline. Currently, there are concerns about possible adverse effects of declining population growth in a number of countries, such as Canada, the United States, and those in Western and Northern Europe. Why does population growth decline, and is it a problem?

I am also not an alarmist about the problems of declining population growth in developed countries. This development reflects the long-term shift in fertility from high to low, which, as I previously mentioned, lags a corresponding movement in mortality. Neither historical experience nor a properly conceived theory of economic growth warrants concern that declining population growth will seriously impede economic growth. Prospective population changes in the developed countries are not greatly out of line with historical experience. The policies needed to raise the rate of economic growth are those relating to stimulation of aggregate demand, promotion of international trade and monetary cooperation, and the design of appropriate education, science, research, and development programs. Demographic policies are not important or appropriate ways to promote economic growth, in either developed or less developed countries.

What are the central principles of economics that you find most useful in your work as an economic demographer?

The traditional micro and macro principles of economic theory. But, as I indicated, economic theory is not enough. The incorporation of sociological theory, especially on reference groups and socialization, is important, as are contributions from a variety of other social and natural science disciplines. Economic theory needs to be informed by the wide range of survey evidence generated by researchers in other disciplines. In my experience, training in economics is a good starting point for the study of human behavior, but no more than that.

CHAPTER 7

UTILITY AND DEMAND

After studying this chapter, you will be able to:

- Explain the connection between individual demand and market demand
- Define total utility and marginal utility
- Explain the marginal utility theory of consumer choice
- Use the marginal utility theory to predict the effects of changing prices
- Use the marginal utility theory to predict the effects of changing income
- Define and calculate consumer surplus
- Explain the paradox of value

Water, Water, Everywhere

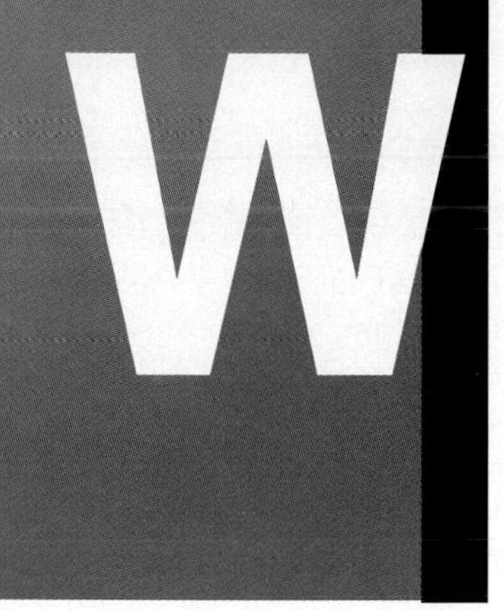

E NEED WATER TO LIVE. WE DON'T NEED DIAMONDS FOR much besides decoration. If the benefits of water far outweigh the benefits of diamonds, why, then, does water cost practically nothing while diamonds are terribly expensive? ◆◆ When OPEC restricted its sale of oil in 1973, it created a dramatic rise in price, but people continued to use almost as much oil as they had before. Our demand for oil was inelastic. But why? ◆◆ When Sony introduced the Walkman in 1979, it cost about $300, and consumers didn't buy very many. Since then, the price has decreased dramatically, and people are buying Walkmans in enormous quantities. Our demand for portable audio headsets is elastic. What makes the demand for some things elastic while the demand for others is inelastic? ◆◆ Over the past 15 years, after removing the effects of inflation, incomes have increased by 40 percent. Over that same period, expenditure on electricity has increased by 66 percent, while expenditure on transportation has increased by only 18 percent. Thus the proportion of income spent on electricity has increased while the proportion spent on transportation has decreased. Why, as incomes rise, does the proportion of income spent on some goods rise and that spent on others fall?

◆◆◆◆ In the last three chapters, we've seen that demand has an important effect on the price of a good. But we have not analyzed what exactly shapes a person's demand. This chapter explains why demand is elastic for some goods and inelastic for others. It also explains why the prices of some things, such as diamonds and water, are so out of proportion to their benefits.

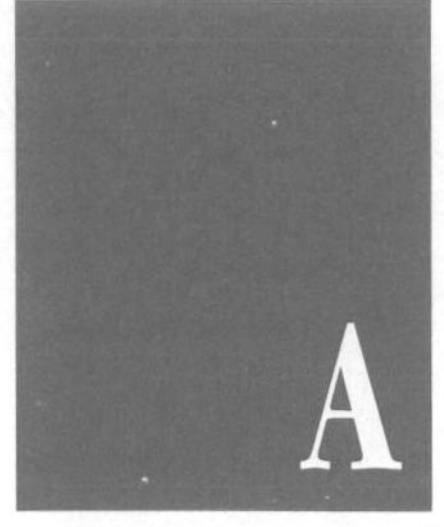

Individual Demand and Market Demand

The relationship between the total quantity of a good demanded and its price is called **market demand.** But goods and services are demanded by individuals. The relationship between the quantity of a good demanded by a single individual and its price is called **individual demand.** Market demand is the sum of all individual demands.

The table in Fig. 7.1 illustrates the relationship between individual demand and market demand. In this example, Lisa and Chuck are the only people. The market demand is the total demand of Lisa and Chuck. At \$3 a movie, Lisa demands 5 movies and Chuck demands 2, so the total quantity demanded by the market is 7 movies. Figure 7.1 illustrates the relationship between individual and market demand curves. Lisa's demand curve for movies in part (a) and Chuck's in part (b) sum *horizontally* to the market demand curve in part (c).

The market demand curve is the horizontal sum of the individual demand curves and is formed by adding the quantities demanded by each individual at each price.

FIGURE 7.1
Individual and Market Demand Curves

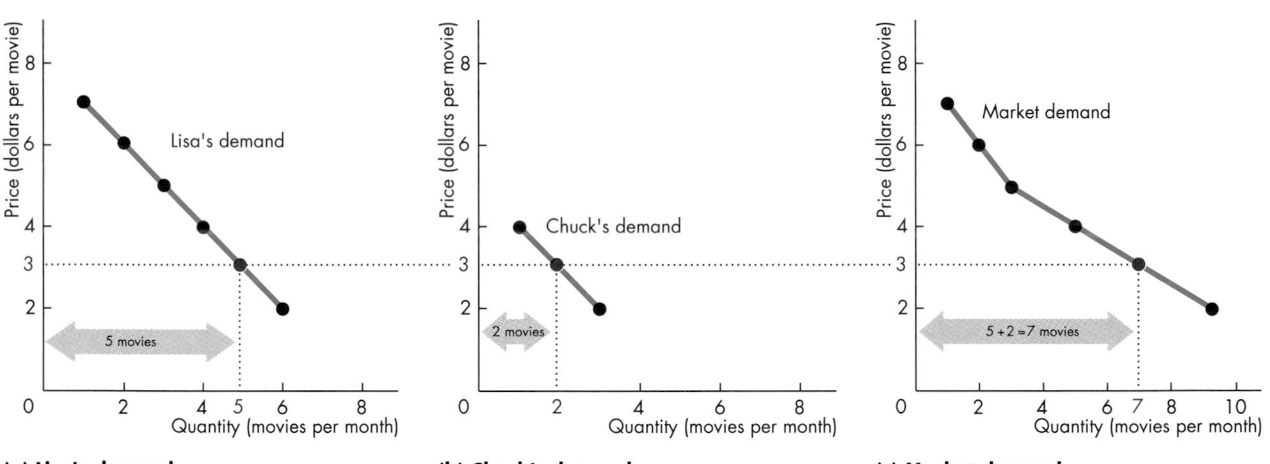

Price of a movie (dollars)	Quantity of movies demanded		
	Lisa	Chuck	Market
7	**1**	**0**	**1**
6	**2**	**0**	**2**
5	**3**	**0**	**3**
4	**4**	**1**	**5**
3	**5**	**2**	**7**
2	**6**	**3**	**9**

The table and diagram illustrate how the quantity of movies demanded varies as the price of a movie varies. In the table, the market demand is the sum of the individual demands. For example, at a price of \$3, Lisa demands 5 movies and Chuck demands 2 movies, so the total quantity demanded in the market is 7 movies. In the diagram, the market demand curve is the horizontal sum of the individual demand curves. Thus when the price is \$3, the market demand curve shows that the quantity demanded is 7 movies, the sum of the quantities demanded by Lisa and Chuck.

Let's investigate an individual demand curve by studying how a household makes its consumption choices.

Household Consumption Choices

A household's consumption choice is determined by two factors:

- Constraints
- Preferences

Constraints

A household's choices are constrained by its income and the prices of the goods and services that it buys. Marginal utility theory assumes that the household has a given income to spend and that it can't influence the prices of the goods and services that it buys.

To study marginal utility theory, we'll examine Lisa's consumption choices. Lisa has a monthly income of $30 and spends it on only two goods—movies and soda. Movies cost $6 each, and soda costs 50¢ a can or $3 for a six-pack. Figure 7.2 illustrates Lisa's possible consumption levels of movies and soda. Rows *a* through *f* in the table show six possible ways of allocating $30 to these two goods. For example, Lisa can buy 2 movies for $12 and 6 six-packs for $18 (row *c*). The same possibilities are represented by the points *a* through *f* in the figure. The line passing through those points is a boundary between what Lisa can afford and cannot afford. Her choices must lie inside the orange area or along the line *af*.

Preferences

How does Lisa divide her $30 between these two goods? The answer depends on her likes and dislikes—on her *preferences*. Marginal utility theory uses the concept of utility to describe preferences. The benefit or satisfaction that a person gets from the consumption of a good or service is called **utility**. But what exactly is utility and in what units can we measure it? Utility is an abstract concept, and the units of utility are chosen arbitrarily.

FIGURE 7.2

Consumption Possibilities

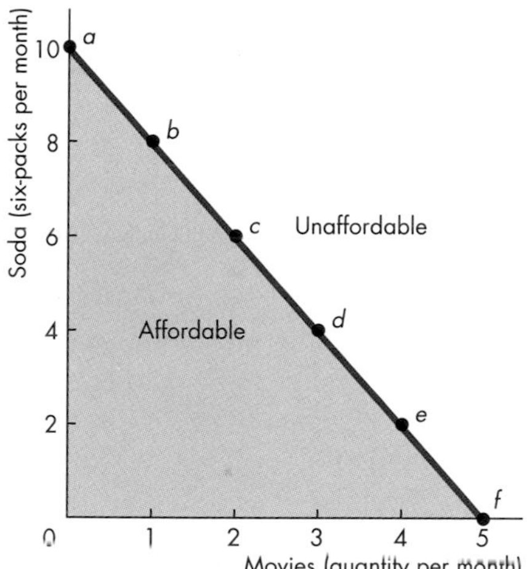

	Expenditure			
	Movies		Soda	
Possibility	Quantity	Expenditure (dollars)	Six-packs	Expenditure (dollars)
a	0	0	10	30
b	1	6	8	24
c	2	12	6	18
d	3	18	4	12
e	4	24	2	6
f	5	30	0	0

Six possible ways of allocating $30 to movies and soda are shown as rows *a* through *f* in the table. For example, Lisa can buy 2 movies and 6 six-packs (row *c*). Each row shows a combination of movies and soda that costs $30. These possibilities are points *a* through *f* in the figure. The line through those points is a boundary between what Lisa can and cannot afford. Her choices must lie inside the orange area or along the line *af*.

Temperature—An Analogy

Temperature is an abstract concept, and the units of temperature are chosen arbitrarily. You know when you feel hot, and you know when you feel cold. But you can't *observe* temperature. You can observe water turning to steam if it is hot enough or turning to ice if it is cold enough. You can construct an instrument, called a thermometer, that will predict when such changes will occur. The scale on the thermometer is what we call temperature. But the units in which we measure temperature are arbitrary. For example, we can accurately predict that when a Celsius thermometer shows a temperature of 0°, water will turn to ice. But the units of measurement do not matter because this same event also occurs when a Fahrenheit thermometer shows a temperature of 32°.

The concept of utility helps us make predictions about consumption choices in much the same way that the concept of temperature helps us make predictions about physical phenomena. It has to be admitted, though, that the marginal utility theory is not as precise as the theory that enables us to predict when water will turn to ice or steam.

Let's now see how we can use the concept of utility to describe preferences.

Total Utility and Consumption

Total utility is the total benefit or satisfaction that a person gets from the consumption of goods and services. Total utility depends on the person's level of consumption—more consumption gives more total utility. Table 7.1 shows Lisa's total utility from consuming different quantities of movies and soda. If she sees no movies, she gets no utility from movies. If she sees 1 movie in a month, she gets 50 units of utility. As the number of movies she sees in a month increases, her total utility increases, so if she sees 10 movies a month, she gets 250 units of total utility. The other part of the table shows Lisa's total utility from soda. If she drinks no soda, she gets no utility. As the amount of soda she drinks rises, her total utility increases.

Marginal Utility

Marginal utility is the change in total utility resulting from a one-unit increase in the quantity of a good consumed. The table in Fig. 7.3 shows the calculation of Lisa's marginal utility of movies. When her consumption of movies increases from 4 to 5 movies a month, her total utility from movies increases from 150 units to 175 units. Thus for Lisa, the marginal utility of seeing a fifth movie each month is 25 units. Notice that marginal utility appears midway between the quantities of consumption. It does so

TABLE 7.1
Lisa's Total Utility from Movies and Soda

Movies		Soda	
Quantity per month	Total utility	Six-packs per month	Total utility
0	0	0	0
1	50	1	75
2	88	2	117
3	121	3	153
4	150	4	181
5	175	5	206
6	196	6	225
7	214	7	243
8	229	8	260
9	241	9	276
10	250	10	291

because the *change* in consumption from 4 to 5 movies is what produces the *marginal* utility of 25 units. The table displays calculations of marginal utility for each level of movie consumption.

Figure 7.3(a) illustrates the total utility that Lisa gets from movies. As you can see, the more movies Lisa sees in a month, the more total utility she gets. Part (b) illustrates her marginal utility. This graph tells us that as Lisa sees more movies, the marginal utility she gets from watching movies decreases. For example, her marginal utility from the first movie is 50 units, from the second, 38 units, and from the third, 33 units. We call this decrease in marginal utility as the consumption of a good increases the principle of **diminishing marginal utility.**

Marginal utility is positive but diminishes as the consumption of a good increases. Why does marginal utility have these two features? In Lisa's case, she likes movies, and the more she sees, the better. That's why marginal utility is positive. The benefit that Lisa gets from the last movie seen is its marginal utility. To see why marginal utility diminishes, think about how you'd feel in the following two sit

FIGURE 7.3

Total Utility and Marginal Utility

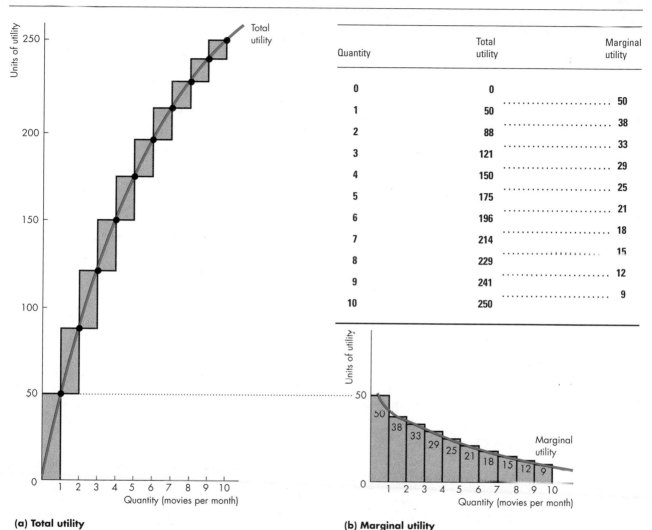

Quantity	Total utility	Marginal utility
0	0	
		50
1	50	
		38
2	88	
		33
3	121	
		29
4	150	
		25
5	175	
		21
6	196	
		18
7	214	
		15
8	229	
		12
9	241	
		9
10	250	

(a) Total utility

(b) Marginal utility

The table shows that as Lisa's consumption of movies increases, so does the utility she derives from movies. For example, 4 movies give 150 units of utility, while 5 movies give 175 units. The table also shows her marginal utility—the change in utility resulting from the last movie seen. Marginal utility declines as consumption increases. For example, the marginal utility from the fourth movie is 29 units, while that from the fifth movie is 25 units. Lisa's utility and marginal utility from movies are graphed in the figure. Part (a) shows the extra utility gained from each additional movie as a bar. Part (b) shows the marginal utility of each new movie as a declining series of steps.

uations. In one, you've just been studying for 29 evenings in a row. An opportunity arises to see a movie. The utility you get from that movie is the marginal utility from seeing one movie in a month. In the second situation, you've been on a movie binge. For the past 29 nights, you have not even seen an assignment or test. You are up to your eyeballs in movies. You are happy enough to go to a movie on yet one more night. But the thrill that you get out of that thirtieth movie in 30 days is not very large. It is the marginal utility of the thirtieth movie in a month.

REVIEW

Lisa divides her income of $30 a month between movies that cost $6 each and soda that costs $3 a six-pack. Lisa's preferences are described by using the concept of utility: the more movies Lisa sees in a given month, the more total utility she gets; the more cans of soda she drinks in a month, the more total utility she gets. The increase in total utility that results from the last unit of a good consumed is called marginal utility. As the quantity of a good consumed increases, marginal utility decreases. ◆

Utility Maximization

Utility maximization is the attainment of the greatest possible utility. A household's income and the prices that it faces limit the utility that it can obtain. We assume that a household consumes in a way that maximizes its total utility, taking into consideration its income and the prices that it faces. In Lisa's case, we examine how she allocates her spending between movies and soda to maximize her total utility, assuming that movies cost $6 each, soda costs $3 a six-pack, and Lisa has only $30 a month to spend.

The Utility-Maximizing Choice

Let's calculate how Lisa spends her money to maximize her total utility by constructing a table. Table 7.2 considers the same affordable combinations of movies and soda that are shown in Fig. 7.2. It records three things: first, the number of movies consumed and the total utility derived from them (the left side of the table); second, the number of six-packs of soda consumed and the total utility derived from them (the right side of the table); and third, the total utility derived from both movies and soda (the middle column of the table).

Consider, for example, the first row of Table 7.2. It shows Lisa watching no movies, getting no utility from them, but getting 291 units of total utility from drinking 10 six-packs of soda. Her total utility from movies and soda is 291 units. The rest of the table is constructed in exactly the same way.

The consumption of movies and soda that maximizes Lisa's total utility is highlighted in the table.

TABLE 7.2

Lisa's Utility-Maximizing Combinations of Movies and Soda

Movies		Total utility from movies and soda	Soda	
Quantity	Total utility		Total utility	Six-packs
0	0	291	291	10
1	50	310	260	8
2	88	313	225	6
3	121	302	181	4
4	150	267	117	2
5	175	175	0	0

When Lisa consumes 2 movies and 6 six-packs of soda, she gets 313 units of total utility. This is the best Lisa can do, given that she has only $30 to spend and given the prices of movies and six-packs. If she buys 8 six-packs of soda, she can see only 1 movie and gets 310 units of total utility, 3 less than the maximum attainable. If she sees 3 movies and drinks only 4 six-packs, she gets 302 units of total utility, 11 less than the maximum attainable.

We've just described a consumer equilibrium. A **consumer equilibrium** is a situation in which a consumer has allocated his or her income in the way that maximizes total utility.

In finding Lisa's consumer equilibrium, we measured her total utility from the consumption of movies and soda. There is a better way of determining a consumer equilibrium that does not involve measuring total utility at all. Let's look at this alternative.

Equalizing Marginal Utility per Dollar Spent

Another way to find out the allocation that maximizes a consumer's total utility is to make the marginal utility per dollar spent on each good equal for all goods. The **marginal utility per dollar spent** is the marginal utility obtained from the last unit of a good consumed divided by the price of the good. For example, Lisa's marginal utility from consuming the first movie is 50 units of utility. The price of a movie is $6, which means that the marginal utility per dollar spent on movies is 50 units divided by $6, or 8.33 units of utility per dollar.

Total utility is maximized when all the consumer's income is spent and when the marginal utility per dollar spent is equal for all goods.

Lisa maximizes total utility when she spends all her income and consumes movies and soda such that

$$\frac{\text{Marginal utility from movies}}{\text{Price of movies}} = \frac{\text{Marginal utility from soda}}{\text{Price of soda}}.$$

Call the marginal utility from movies MU_m, the marginal utility from soda MU_s, the price of movies P_m, and the price of soda P_s. Then Lisa's utility is maximized when she spends all her income and when

$$\frac{MU_m}{P_m} = \frac{MU_s}{P_s}.$$

Let's use this formula to find Lisa's utility-maximizing allocation of her income.

Table 7.3 sets out Lisa's marginal utilities per dollar spent for both movies and soda. For example, in row *b*, Lisa's marginal utility from movies is 50 units and, since movies cost $6 each, her marginal utility per dollar spent on movies is 8.33 units per dollar (50 units divided by $6). Each row contains an allocation of Lisa's income that uses up her $30. You can see that Lisa's marginal utility per dollar spent on each good, like marginal utility itself, decreases as consumption of the good increases.

Total utility is maximized when the marginal utility per dollar spent on movies is equal to the marginal utility per dollar spent on soda—possibility *c*, with Lisa consuming 2 movies and 6 six-packs—the same allocation as we calculated in Table 7.2.

Figure 7.4 shows why the rule "equalize marginal utility per dollar spent on all goods" works. Suppose that instead of consuming 2 movies and 6 six-packs

TABLE 7.3

Maximizing Utility by Equalizing Marginal Utilities per Dollar Spent

	Movies ($6 each)			Soda ($3 per six-pack)		
	Quantity	Marginal utility	Marginal utility per dollar spent	Six-packs	Marginal utility	Marginal utility per dollar spent
a	0	0		10	15	5.00
b	1	50	8.33	8	17	5.67
c	2	38	6.33	6	19	6.33
d	3	33	5.50	4	28	9.33
e	4	29	4.83	2	42	14.00
f	5	25	4.17	0	0	

FIGURE 7.4

Equalizing Marginal Utility per Dollar Spent

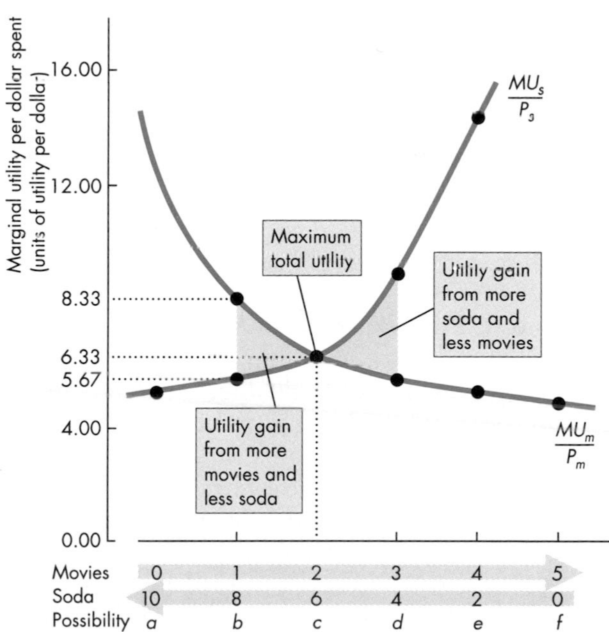

If Lisa consumes 1 movie and 8 six-packs of soda (possibility *b*), she gets 8.33 units of utility from the last dollar spent on movies and 5.67 units of utility from the last dollar spent on soda. She can get more total utility by buying one more movie. If she consumes 4 six-packs and 3 movies (possibility *d*), she gets 5.50 units of utility from the last dollar spent on movies and 9.33 units of utility from the last dollar spent on soda. She can get more total utility by buying one fewer movie. When Lisa's marginal utility per dollar spent on both goods is equal, her total utility is maximized.

(possibility *c*), Lisa consumes 1 movie and 8 six-packs (possibility *b*). She then gets 8.33 units of utility from the last dollar spent on movies and 5.67 units from the last dollar spent on soda. In this situation, it pays Lisa to spend less on soda and more on movies. If she spends a dollar less on soda and a dollar more on movies, her total utility from soda decreases by 5.67 units and her total utility from movies increases by 8.33 units. Lisa's total utility increases if she spends less on soda and more on movies.

Or suppose that Lisa consumes 3 movies and 4 six-packs (possibility *d*). In this situation, her marginal utility per dollar spent on movies is less than her marginal utility per dollar spent on soda. Lisa can now get more total utility by cutting her spending on movies and increasing her spending on soda. When Lisa's marginal utility per dollar spent on both goods is equal, she cannot get more total utility by spending differently. Her total utility is maximized.

Units of Utility

In calculating the utility-maximizing allocation of income in Table 7.3 and Fig. 7.4, we have not used the concept of total utility at all. All the calculations have been performed by using marginal utility and price. By making the marginal utility per dollar spent equal for both goods, we know that Lisa has maximized her total utility.

This way of viewing maximum utility is important; it means that the units in which utility is measured do not matter. We could double or halve all the numbers measuring utility, or multiply them by any other positive number, or square them, or take their square roots. None of these transformations of the units used to measure utility make any difference to the outcome. It is in this respect that utility is analogous to temperature. Our prediction about the freezing of water does not depend on the temperature scale; our prediction about maximizing utility does not depend on the units of utility.

REVIEW

A consumer allocates his or her income to maximize total utility by making the marginal utility per dollar spent on each good equal. Once the marginal utilities per dollar spent are equal, the consumer cannot reallocate spending to get more total utility from a given income. The units in which utility is measured are irrelevant—all that matters is that the marginal utility per dollar spent is equal for all goods. ◆

Predictions of Marginal Utility Theory

Let's now use marginal utility theory to make some predictions. What happens to Lisa's consumption of movies and soda when their prices change and when her income changes?

A Fall in the Price of Movies

To determine the effect of a change in price on consumption requires three steps. First, determine the combinations of movies and soda that can be bought at the new prices. Second, calculate the new marginal utilities per dollar spent. Third, determine the consumption of each good that makes the marginal utility per dollar spent on each good equal and that just exhausts the money available for spending.

Table 7.4 shows the combinations of movies and soda that exactly exhaust Lisa's $30 of income when movies cost $3 each and soda costs $3 a six-pack. Lisa's preferences do not change when prices change, so her utility schedule remains the same as that in Table 7.1. But now we divide her marginal utility from movies by $3, the new price of a movie, to get the marginal utility per dollar spent on movies.

What is the effect of the fall in the price of a movie on Lisa's consumption? You can find the answer by comparing her new utility-maximizing allocation (Table 7.4) with her original allocation (Table 7.3). Lisa responds to a fall in the price of a movie by watching more movies (up from 2 to 5 a month) and drinking less soda (down from 6 to 5 six-packs a month). That is, Lisa substitutes movies for soda when the price of a movie falls. Figure 7.5

TABLE 7.4

How a Change in the Price of Movies Affects Lisa's Choices

Movies ($3 each)		Soda ($3 per six-pack)	
Quantity	Marginal utility per dollar spent	Six-packs	Marginal utility per dollar spent
0		10	5.00
1	16.67	9	5.33
2	12.67	8	5.67
3	11.00	7	6.00
4	9.67	6	6.33
5	8.33	5	8.33
6	7.00	4	9.33
7	6.00	3	12.00
8	5.00	2	14.00
9	4.00	1	25.00
10	3.00	0	

illustrates these effects. In part (a), a fall in the price of movies produces a movement along Lisa's demand curve for movies, and in part (b), it shifts her demand curve for soda.

A Rise in the Price of Soda

Table 7.5 shows the combinations of movies and soda that exactly exhaust Lisa's $30 of income when movies cost $3 each and soda costs $6 a six-pack. Now we divide her marginal utility from soda by $6, the new price of a six-pack, to get the marginal utility per dollar spent on soda.

The effect of the rise in the price of soda on Lisa's consumption is seen by comparing her new utility-maximizing allocation (Table 7.5) with her previous allocation (Table 7.4). Lisa responds to a rise in the price of soda by drinking less soda (down from 5 to 2 six-packs a month) and watching more movies (up from 5 to 6 a month). That is, Lisa substitutes

FIGURE 7.5

A Fall in the Price of Movies

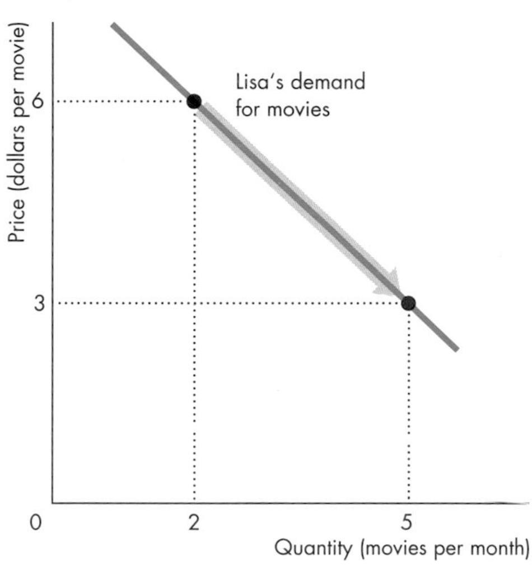

(a) Movies

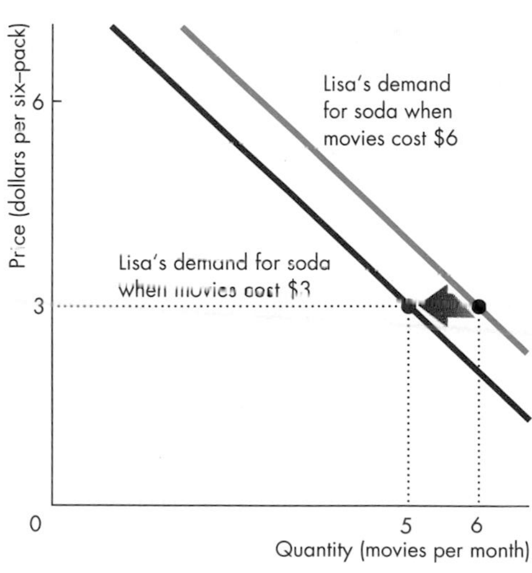

(b) Soda

When the price of movies falls and the price of soda remains constant, the quantity of movies demanded by Lisa increases and, in part (a), Lisa moves along her demand curve for movies. Also, Lisa's demand for soda decreases and, in part (b), her demand curve for soda shifts to the left.

TABLE 7.5

How a Change in the Price of Soda Affects Lisa's Choices

Movies ($3 each)		Soda ($6 per six-pack)	
Quantity	Marginal utility per dollar spent	Six-packs	Marginal utility per dollar spent
0		5	4.17
2	12.67	4	4.67
4	9.67	3	6.00
6	7.00	2	7.00
8	5.00	1	12.50
10	3.00	0	

movies for soda when the price of soda rises. Figure 7.6 illustrates these effects. In part (a), a rise in the price of soda produces a movement along Lisa's demand curve for soda, and in part (b), it shifts her demand curve for movies.

REVIEW

When the price of a movie falls but the price of soda stays constant, Lisa increases her consumption of movies and reduces her consumption of soda. There is a movement along her demand curve for movies and a shift in her demand for soda. When the price of a movie stays constant but the price of soda increases, Lisa reduces her consumption of soda and increases her consumption of movies. There is a movement along her demand curve for soda and a shift in her demand for movies.

FIGURE 7.6

A Rise in the Price of Soda

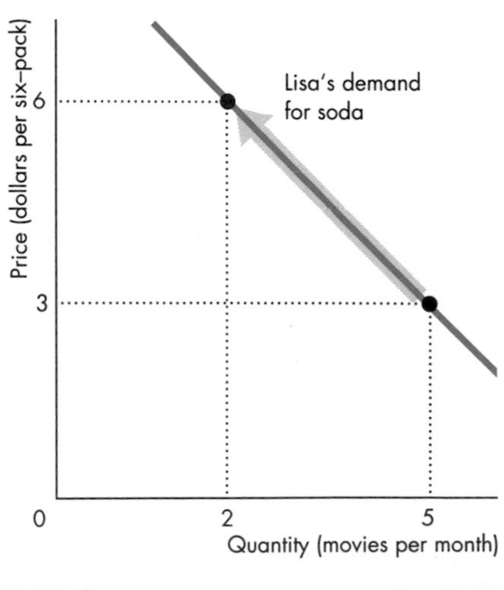

(a) Soda

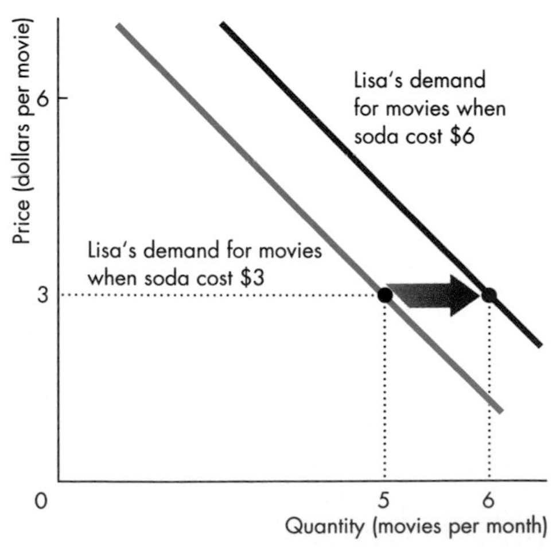

(b) Movies

When the price of soda rises and the price of movies remains constant, the quantity of soda demanded by Lisa decreases and, in part (a), Lisa moves along her demand curve for movies. Also, Lisa's demand for movies increases and, in part (b), her demand curve for movies shifts to the right.

When the price of a movie falls or the price of soda rises, and Lisa does not change her consumption, her marginal utility per dollar spent on movies exceeds that spent on soda. To restore the equality of the marginal utility per dollar spent on each good, she must increase her consumption of movies and decrease her consumption of soda. ◆

Marginal utility theory predicts these two results: when the price of a good rises, the quantity demanded of that good decreases; if the price of one good rises, the demand for another good that can serve as a substitute increases. Does this sound familiar? It should. These predictions of marginal utility theory correspond to the assumptions that we made about consumer demand in Chapter 4. There we *assumed* that the demand curve for a good sloped downward, and we *assumed* that a rise in the price of a substitute increased demand. Marginal utility theory predicts these responses to price changes. In doing so, it makes four assumptions: first, consumers have a given income and face given prices; second, they maximize total utility; third, they get more utility as they consume more of a good; fourth, as consumption increases, marginal utility declines.

Next let's see the effects of a change in income on consumption.

The Effects of a Rise in Income

Let's suppose that Lisa's income increases to $42 a month and that movies cost $3 each and a six-pack costs $3 (as in Table 7.4). We saw, in Table 7.4, that with these prices and with an income of $30 a month, Lisa consumes 5 movies and 5 six-packs a month. We want to compare this consumption of movies and soda with Lisa's consumption at an income of $42. The calculations for the comparison are shown in Table 7.6. With $42, Lisa can buy 14 movies a month and no soda, or 14 six-packs a month and no movies, or any combination of the two goods as shown in the rows of the table. We calculate the marginal utility per dollar spent in exactly the same way as we did before and find the quantities at which the marginal utilities per dollar spent on movies and on soda are equal. With an income of $42, the marginal utility per dollar spent on each good is equal when Lisa watches 7 movies and drinks 7 six-packs of soda a month.

TABLE 7.6

Lisa's Choices with an Income of $42 a Month

Movies ($3 each)		Soda ($3 per six-pack)	
Quantity	Marginal utility per dollar spent	Six-packs	Marginal utility per dollar spent
0		14	
1	16.67	13	
2	12.67	12	
3	11.00	11	
4	9.67	10	5.00
5	8.33	9	5.33
6	7.00	8	5.67
7	6.00	7	6.00
8	5.00	6	6.33
9	4.00	5	8.33
10	3.00	4	9.33
11		3	12.00
12		2	14.00
13		1	25.00
14		0	

By comparing this situation with that in Table 7.4, we see that with an additional $12 a month, Lisa consumes 2 more six-packs and 2 more movies. This response arises from Lisa's preferences, as described by her marginal utilities. Different preferences produce different quantitative responses. But, for normal goods, a higher income always brings a larger consumption of all goods. For Lisa, soda and movies are normal goods. When her income increases, Lisa buys more of both goods.

Marginal Utility and the Real World

The marginal utility theory is summarized in Table 7.7. This theory can be used to answer a wide range of questions about the real world. An example, described in Reading Between the Lines on pp. 168–169, is its ability to explain the fluctuations in

Marginal Utility Theory in Action

The New York Times, July 7, 1991

Wood Makes a Baseball Comeback

By Eric N. Berg

LOUISVILLE, KY.—As recently as 1985, the wooden baseball bat seemed doomed in all but professional leagues, done in by aluminum bats that not only were far more durable but also seemed to contain more base hits.

Never mind that no fan ever preferred the ping of aluminum striking the ball to the resounding crack of a wooden bat. Or that every great slugger has made his name using wood.

But now wooden bats are making a comeback, to the joy of everyone who insists that baseball is meant to be played on grass instead of a rug, with an organist instead of recorded disco tunes, while fans eat peanuts and hot dogs instead of taco chips and frozen yogurt.

Aluminum bats still outsell wooden ones, but sales of wooden bats are up 50 percent in the last two years, bat companies say.

Behind the comeback are several factors, including thrift, changes in retailing, a growth in the memorabilia business and wishful thinking about a career in Major League Baseball.

There is no debate that aluminum bats are far more durable—almost impossible to break. But they cost at least twice as much as wooden bats, sometimes far more. At discount stores, aluminum bats start at $20, while the best sell for up to $70; wooden bats, for children and adults, sell for $10 to $15. Some parents have decided they would rather buy the less expensive wooden bat and take their chances on its breaking. Bats are unlikely to snap in the relatively tame games of young children. . . .

Other parents, stars in their eyes, say they buy wooden bats to give their children a better chance at the long odds of becoming professional players. . . .

Of all the reasons for the return of the wooden bat, perhaps the most important is the growth of discount chains. Before a new Wal-Mart opens, bat makers say, it will be stocked with hundreds of bats, both aluminum and wood. The same is true at other rapidly growing discounters, like K Mart and Target Stores. . . .

The growing appetite for players' autographs, baseball cards and souvenirs has also helped wooden bat makers. Some Major League players order 100 to 1,000 bats each, which they autograph and then sell at baseball memorabilia shows.

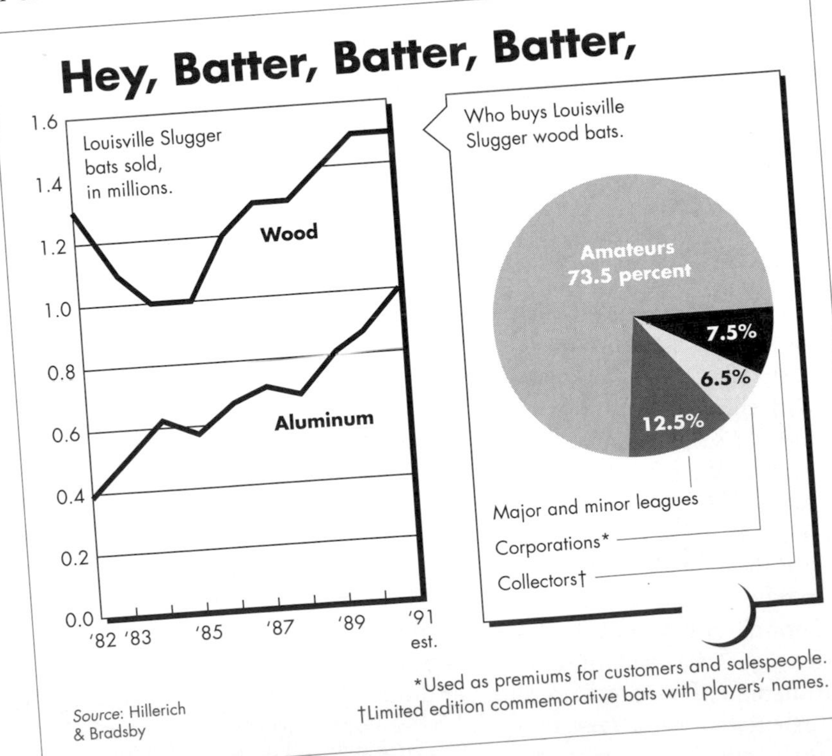

The Essence of the Story

Aluminum baseball bats outsell wood ones.

But sales of wood bats, after falling for many years, are growing again.

Reasons for increased sales include:

- Thrift
- Changes in retailing
- Growth in the memorabilia business
- Wishful thinking about a career in Major League Baseball

Aluminum bats are unbreakable but cost \$20 to \$70; wooden bats are breakable but not by small children and cost \$10 to \$15.

Major League players buy wooden bats, which they autograph and sell at baseball memorabilia shows.

Discount chains such as Wal-Mart, Kmart, and Target Stores are well stocked with both aluminum and wooden bats.

Wooden bats give children a better chance at the long odds of becoming professional players.

Background and Analysis

Consumers make the marginal utility per dollar spent equal across all goods—including wooden and aluminum baseball bats.

Call the marginal utility of wooden bats MU_w, the marginal utility of aluminum bats MU_a, the price of wooden bats P_w, and the price of aluminum bats P_a. Total utility is maximized when

$$\frac{MU_w}{P_w} = \frac{MU_a}{P_a}.$$

The quantity of wooden bats bought has increased rapidly, but so has the quantity of aluminum bats bought.

The data in the story (and in Fig. 1) show that sales of aluminum Louisville Sluggers grew from 25 percent to 40 percent of total sales between 1982 and 1991—a fact that is different from the impression given by the story.

The proportion of wooden Louisville Sluggers increased between 1985 and 1988 but declined after 1988—another fact that is different from the impression given by the story.

The prices of aluminum bats increased in relation to the prices of wooden bats from 1985 to 1988 and decreased after 1988—see Fig. 1.

The movements in the prices and quantities shown in Fig. 1 are consistent with the marginal utility theory. When the price of aluminum bats increases relative to the price of wooden bats, the percentage of bats that are aluminum decreases; when the price of aluminum bats decreases relative to the price of wooden bats, the percentage of bats that are aluminum increases.

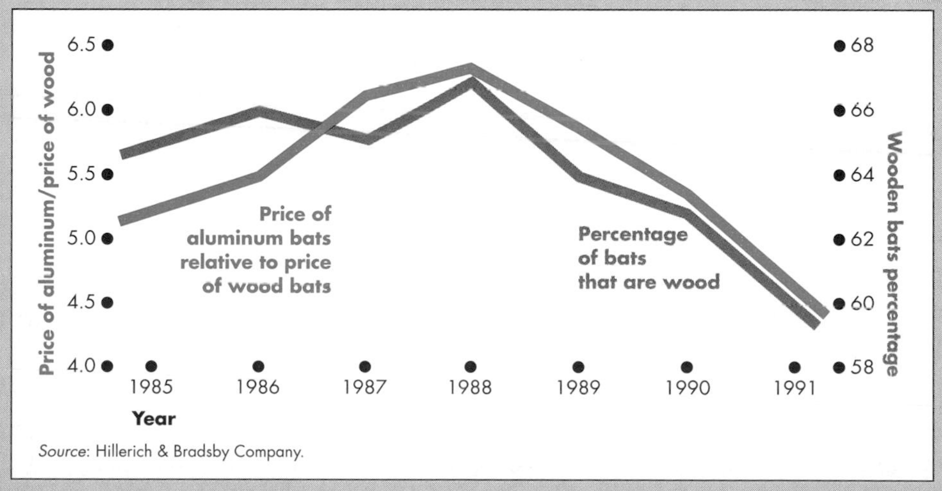

Source: Hillerich & Bradsby Company.

TABLE 7.7

Marginal Utility Theory

Assumptions

(a) **A consumer has a given income and faces given prices.**

(b) **A consumer derives utility from the goods consumed.**

(c) **Each additional unit of consumption yields additional utility; marginal utility is positive.**

(d) **As the quantity of a good consumed increases, marginal utility decreases.**

Implication

Utility is maximized when the marginal utility per dollar spent is equal for all goods and all income is spent.

Predictions

(a) **Other things being equal, the higher the price of a good, the lower is the quantity bought (the law of demand).**

(b) **The higher the price of a good, the higher is the consumption of substitutes for that good.**

(c) **The higher the consumer's income, the greater is the quantity demanded of normal goods.**

the relative popularity of wooden and aluminum baseball bats. Other examples are the ability of the theory to answer the questions posed at the beginning of this chapter: why is the demand for audio headsets elastic and the demand for oil inelastic; and why, as income increases, does the proportion of income spent on electricity increase while the proportion spent on transportation decreases? These patterns in our spending result from the speed with which our marginal utility for each good diminishes as its consumption is increased. Goods whose marginal utility diminishes rapidly have inelastic demands and small income effects; goods whose marginal utility diminishes slowly have elastic demands and large income effects.

But the marginal utility theory can do much more than explain households' consumption choices. It can be used to explain *all* household choices. One of these choices, the allocation of time between work in the home, office, or factory and leisure is the theme of Our Advancing Knowledge on pp. 172–173.

Criticisms of Marginal Utility Theory

Marginal utility theory helps us to understand the choices people make, but there are some criticisms of this theory. Let's look at them.

Utility Can't Be Observed or Measured

Agreed—we can't observe utility. But we don't need to observe it to use it. We can and do observe the quantities of goods and services that people consume, the prices of those goods and services, and people's incomes. Our goal is to understand the consumption choices that people make and to predict the effects of changes in prices and incomes on these choices. To make such predictions, we *assume* that people derive utility from their consumption, that more consumption yields more utility, and that marginal utility diminishes. From these assumptions, we make predictions about the directions of change in consumption when prices and incomes change. As we've already seen, the actual numbers that we use to express utility do not matter. Consumers maximize utility by making the marginal utility per dollar spent on each good equal. As long as we use the same scale to express utility for all goods, we'll get the same answer regardless of the units on our scale. In this regard, utility is similar to temperature—water freezes when it's cold enough, and that occurs independently of the temperature scale used.

"People Aren't That Smart"

Some critics maintain that marginal utility theory assumes that people are supercomputers. It requires people to look at the marginal utility of every good at every different quantity they might consume, divide those numbers by the prices of the goods, and then calculate the quantities so as to equalize the marginal utility of each good divided by its price.

Such criticism of marginal utility theory confuses the actions of people in the real world with those of people in a model economy. A model economy is no more an actual economy than a model railway is an actual railway. The people in the model economy perform the calculations that we have just described. People in the real world just consume. We observe their consumption choices, not their mental gymnastics. The marginal utility theory proposes that the consumption patterns that we observe in the real world are similar to those implied by the model economy in which people do compute the quantities of goods that maximize utility. We test how closely the marginal utility model resembles reality by checking the predictions of the model against observed consumption choices.

Marginal utility theory also has some broader implications that provide an interesting way of testing its usefulness. Let's examine two of these.

Some Implications of Marginal Utility Theory

We all love bargains—paying less for something than its usual price. One implication of the marginal utility theory is that we almost *always* get a bargain when we buy something. That is, we place a higher total value on the things we buy than on the amount they cost us. Let's see why.

Consumer Surplus and the Gains from Trade

In Chapter 3, we saw how people can gain by specializing in the things at which they have a comparative advantage and then trading with each other. Marginal utility theory provides a precise way of measuring the gains from trade.

When Lisa buys movies and soda, she exchanges her income for them. Does Lisa profit from this exchange? Are the dollars she has to give up worth more or less than the movies and soda are worth to her? As we are about to discover, the principle of diminishing marginal utility guarantees that Lisa, and everyone else, gets more value from the things they buy than the amount of money they give up in exchange.

Calculating Consumer Surplus

The **value** that a consumer places on a good is the maximum amount that person would be willing to pay for it. The amount actually paid for a good is its price. **Consumer surplus** is the difference between the value of a good and its price. Diminishing marginal utility guarantees that a consumer always makes some consumer surplus. To understand why, let's look again at Lisa's consumption choices.

As before, let's assume that Lisa has $30 a month to spend, that movies cost $3 each, and that she watches 5 movies each month. Now let's look at Lisa's demand curve for movies, shown in Fig. 7.7. We can see from Lisa's demand curve that if she were able to watch only 1 movie a month, she

FIGURE 7.7
Consumer Surplus

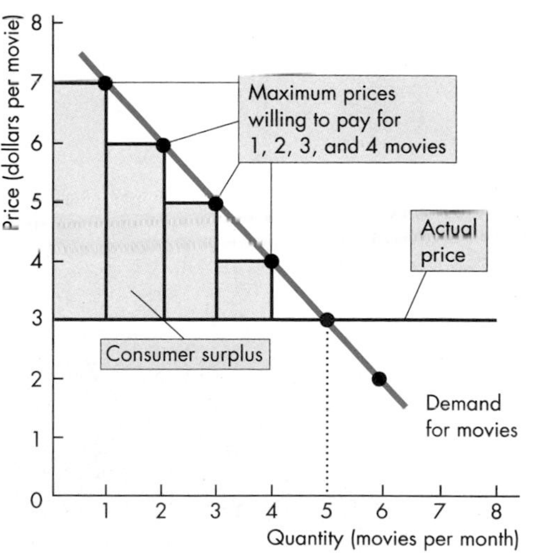

Lisa is willing to pay $7 to watch her first movie, $6 to watch her second, $5 to watch her third, and $4 to watch her fourth. She actually has to pay only $3 for each movie. At that price, she sees 5 movies. She has a consumer surplus on the first four movies equal to $10—the difference between the highest price she is willing to pay and the price actually paid ($4 + $3 + $2 + $1).

Understanding Human Behavior

The economic analysis of human behavior, in the workplace, in the markets for goods and services, in the markets for labor services, in financial markets, and in transactions with each other in social as well as economic situations, is based on the idea that our behavior can be understood as a response to scarcity. Everything we do can be understood as a choice that maximizes utility subject to the constraints imposed by our limited resources and technology. If people's preferences are stable in the face of changing constraints, then we have a chance of predicting how they will respond to an evolving environment.

The incredible change that has occurred over the past 100 years in the way women allocate their time can be explained as the consequence of changing constraints. Technological advances have equipped the nation's factories with machines that have increased the productivity of both women and men, thereby raising the wages they can earn. The increasingly technological world has increased the return to education for both women and men and has led to a large increase in the number of high-school and college graduates of both sexes. And equipped with a wide array of gadgets and machines that cut the time of household jobs, women have increasingly allocated their time to work outside the home.

This economic view might not be correct, but it is a powerful one. And if it is correct, the changing attitudes toward women are a consequence, not a cause, of their economic advancement.

"Economy is the art of making the most of life."

George Bernard Shaw
"Man and Superman"

Economists explain people's actions as the consequence of choices that maximize utility subject to constraints. In the 1890s, fewer than 5 percent of women chose paid employment and most of those who did had low-paying and unattractive jobs. The other 95 percent of women chose unpaid work in the home. What were the constraints that led to these choices?

By 1990, more than 60 percent of women had paid work and, although many had low-paying jobs, more and more women were found in the professions and in executive positions. What brought about this dramatic change compared with 100 years earlier? Was it a change in preferences or a change in the constraints that women face?

BENTHAM, JEVONS, & BECKER:

UNDERSTANDING

People's Choices

Many economists have contributed to our understanding of human behavior, but three stand out from the rest. They are Jeremy Bentham (1748–1832), pictured left, William Stanley Jevons (1835–1882), pictured right, and Gary Becker (1930–).

Bentham, who lived in London (and whose embalmed body is preserved to this day in a glass cabinet in the University of London), was the first to use the concept of utility to explain and prescribe human choices. The distinction between explanation and prescription was not a sharp one in Bentham's day. He was a founder of social security and advocated guaranteed employment, minimum wages, and social benefits such as free education and free medical care.

Jevons' main claim to fame in his own day was his proposal—wrong as it turned out—that economic fluctuations are caused by sun spots. He was a co-discoverer of the concept of *marginal utility,* and it was he who developed the theory explained in this chapter.

Gary Becker teaches both economics and sociology at the University of Chicago. He has used the ideas of Bentham and Jevons to explain a wide range of human choices, including the choices made by women about how many children to bear and how much and what type of work to do.

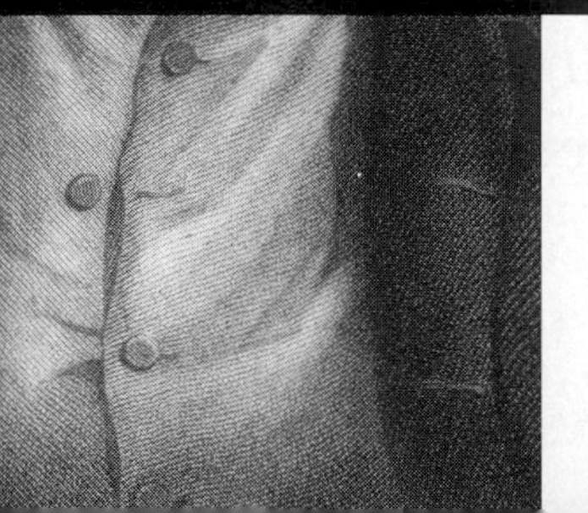

would be willing to pay $7 to see it. She would be willing to pay $6 to see a second movie, $5 to see a third, and so on.

Luckily for Lisa, she has to pay only $3 for each movie she sees—the market price of a movie. Although she values the first movie she sees in a month at $7, she pays only $3, which is $4 less than she would be willing to pay. The second movie she sees in a month is worth $6 to her. The difference between the value that she places on the movie and what she has to pay is $3. The third movie she sees in a month is worth $5 to her, which is $2 more than she has to pay for it, and the fourth movie is worth $4, which is $1 more than she has to pay for it. You can see this progression in Fig. 7.7, which highlights the difference between the price she pays ($3) and the higher value she places on the first, second, third, and fourth movies. These differences are a gain to Lisa. Let's calculate her total gain.

The total amount that Lisa is willing to pay for the 5 movies she sees is $25 (the sum of $7, $6, $5, $4, and $3). She actually pays $15 (5 movies multiplied by $3). The extra value that she receives from the movies is therefore $10. This amount is the value of Lisa's consumer surplus. From watching 5 movies a month, she gets $10 worth of value in excess of what she has to spend to see them.

Let's now look at another implication of the marginal utility theory.

The Paradox of Value

More than 200 years ago, Adam Smith posed a paradox that we also raised at the start of this chapter. Water, which is essential to life itself, costs little, but diamonds, which are useless in comparison to water, are expensive. Why? Adam Smith could not solve the paradox. Not until the theory of marginal utility had been invented could anyone give a satisfactory answer.

You can solve Adam Smith's puzzle by distinguishing between total utility and marginal utility. The total utility that we get from water is enormous. But remember, the more we consume of something, the smaller is its marginal utility. We use so much water that the marginal utility—the benefit we get from one more glass of water—diminishes to a tiny value. Diamonds, on the other hand, have a small total utility relative to water, but because we buy few diamonds, they have a high marginal utility.

Our theory also tells us that consumers spend their income in a way that makes the marginal utility from each good divided by its price equal for all goods. This also holds true for their spending on diamonds and water: diamonds have a high marginal utility divided by a high price, while water has a low marginal utility divided by a low price. In each case, the marginal utility per dollar spent is the same.

◆ ◆ ◆ ◆ We've now completed our study of the marginal utility theory of consumption. We've used that theory to examine how Lisa allocates her income between the two goods that she consumes—movies and soda. We've also seen how the theory can be used to resolve the paradox of value. Furthermore, we've seen how the theory can be used to explain our real-world consumption choices. ◆ ◆ In the next chapter, we're going to study an alternative theory of household behavior. To help you see the connection between the marginal utility theory of this chapter and the more modern theory of consumer behavior of the next chapter, we'll continue with the same example. We'll meet Lisa again and discover another way of understanding how she gets the most out of her $30 a month.

SUMMARY

Individual Demand and Market Demand

Individual demand represents the relationship between the price of a good and the quantity demanded by a single individual. Market demand is the sum of all individual demands. (pp. 158–159)

Household Consumption Choices

The marginal utility theory explains how people divide their spending between goods and services. The theory is based on a model that assumes certain characteristics about the consumer. The consumer has a given income and faces given prices. The consumer derives utility from the goods consumed, and the consumer's total utility increases as consumption of the good increases. The change in total utility resulting from a one-unit increase in the consumption of a good is called marginal utility. Marginal utility declines as consumption increases. The consumer's goal is to maximize total utility, which occurs when the marginal utility per dollar spent on each good is equal and all income is spent. (pp. 159–164)

Predictions of Marginal Utility Theory

Marginal utility theory predicts how prices and income affect the amounts of each good consumed. First, it predicts the law of demand. That is, other things being equal, the higher the price of a good, the lower is the quantity demanded of that good. Second, it predicts that, other things being equal, the higher the consumer's income, the greater is the consumption of all normal goods. (pp. 164–170)

Criticisms of Marginal Utility Theory

Some people criticize marginal utility theory because utility cannot be observed or measured. However, the size of the units of measurement of utility does not matter. All that matters is that the ratio of the marginal utility from each good to its price is equal for all goods. Any units of measure that are consistently applied will do. The concept of utility is analogous to the concept of temperature—it cannot be directly observed, but it can be used to make predictions about events that are observable.

Another criticism of marginal utility theory is that consumers can't be as smart as the theory implies. In fact, the theory makes no predictions about the thought processes of consumers. It makes predictions only about their actions and assumes that people spend their income in what seems to them to be the best possible way. (pp. 170–171)

Some Implications of Marginal Utility Theory

Marginal utility theory implies that every time we buy goods and services, we get more value for our expenditure than the money we spend. We benefit from consumer surplus, which is equal to the difference between the maximum amount that we are willing to pay for a good and the price that we actually pay.

Marginal utility theory resolves the paradox of value: water is extremely valuable but cheap, while diamonds are less valuable though expensive. When we talk loosely about value, we are thinking of total utility. The total utility of water is higher than the total utility of diamonds. But, at the quantities consumed, the marginal utility of water is lower than the marginal utility of diamonds. People choose the amounts of water and diamonds to consume so as to maximize total utility. In maximizing total utility, they make the marginal utility per dollar spent the same for water as for diamonds. (pp. 171–174)

KEY ELEMENTS

Key Terms

Consumer equilibrium, 162
Consumer surplus, 171
Diminishing marginal utility, 160
Individual demand, 158
Marginal utility, 160
Marginal utility per dollar spent, 162
Market demand, 158
Total utility, 160
Utility, 159
Utility maximization, 162
Value, 171

Key Figures and Tables

REVIEW QUESTIONS

1 What is the relationship between individual demand and market demand?

2 How do we construct a market demand curve from individual demand curves?

3 What do we mean by utility?

4 Distinguish between total utility and marginal utility.

5 How does marginal utility change as the level of consumption of a good changes?

6 Susan is a consumer. When is Susan's utility maximized?

a When she has spent all her income

b When she has spent all her income and marginal utility is equal for all goods

c When she has spent all her income and the marginal utility per dollar spent is equal for all goods

Explain your answer.

7 What does the marginal utility theory predict about the effect of a change in price on the quantity of a good consumed?

8 What does the marginal utility theory predict about the effect of a change in the price of one good on the consumption of another good?

9 What does the marginal utility theory predict about the effect of a change in income on consumption of a good?

10 How would you answer someone who says that the marginal utility theory is useless because utility cannot be observed?

11 How would you respond to someone who tells you that the marginal utility theory is useless because people aren't smart enough to compute a consumer equilibrium in which the marginal utility per dollar spent is equal for all goods?

12 What is consumer surplus? How is consumer surplus calculated?

13 What is the paradox of value? How does the marginal utility theory resolve it?

PROBLEMS

1 Shirley's demand for yogurt is given by the following:

Price (dollars per pound)	Quantity (cartons per week)
1	12
2	9
3	6
4	3
5	1

a Draw a graph of Shirley's demand for yogurt.

Dan also likes yogurt. His demand for yogurt is given by the following:

Price (dollars per pound)	Quantity (cartons per week)
1	6
2	5
3	4
4	3
5	2

b Draw a graph of Dan's demand curve.

c If Shirley and Dan are the only two individuals, construct the market demand schedule for yogurt.
Draw a graph of the market demand for yogurt.

e Draw a graph to show that the market demand curve is the horizontal sum of Shirley's demand curve and Dan's demand curve.

2 Calculate Lisa's marginal utility from soda from the numbers given in Table 7.1. Draw two graphs, one of her total utility and the other of her marginal utility from soda. Make your graphs look similar to those in Fig. 7.3.

3 Max enjoys windsurfing and snorkeling. He obtains the following utility from each of these sports:

Half-hours per month	Utility from windsurfing	Utility from snorkeling
1	60	20
2	110	38
3	150	53
4	180	64
5	200	70
6	206	75
7	211	79
8	215	82
9	218	84

a Draw graphs showing Max's utility from windsurfing and from snorkeling.
b Compare the two utility graphs. Can you say anything about Max's preferences?
c Draw graphs showing Max's marginal utility from windsurfing and from snorkeling.
d Compare the two marginal utility graphs. Can you say anything about Max's preferences?

4 Max has $35 to spend. Equipment for windsurfing rents for $10 a half-hour, while snorkeling equipment rents for $5 a half-hour. Use this information together with that given in problem 3 to answer the following questions.

a What is the marginal utility per dollar spent on snorkeling if Max snorkels for:
(1) Half an hour
(2) One and a half hours

b What is the marginal utility per dollar spent on windsurfing if Max windsurfs for:
(1) Half an hour
(2) One hour

c How long can Max afford to snorkel if he windsurfs for:
(1) Half an hour
(2) One hour
(3) One and a half hours

d Will Max choose to snorkel for one hour and windsurf for one and a half hours?
e Will he windsurf for more or less than one and a half hours?
f How long will Max choose to windsurf and to snorkel?

5 Max's sister gives him $20 to spend on his leisure pursuits, so he now has $55 to spend. How long will Max now windsurf and snorkel?

6 If Max has only $55 to spend and the rent on windsurfing equipment halves to $5 a half hour, how will Max now spend his time windsurfing and snorkeling?

7 Does Max's demand curve for windsurfing slope downward or upward?

8 Max takes a Club Med holiday, the cost of which includes unlimited sports activities—including windsurfing, snorkeling, and tennis. There is no extra charge for any equipment. Max decides to spend three hours each day on both windsurfing and snorkeling. How long does he windsurf? How long does he snorkel?

9 Sara's demand for windsurfing is given by:

Price (dollars per half-hour)	Time windsurfing (half-hours per month)
12.50	8
15.00	6
17.50	4
20.00	2

a If windsurfing costs $17.50 a half-hour, what is Sara's consumer surplus?
b If windsurfing costs $12.50 a half-hour, what is Sara's consumer surplus?

CHAPTER 8

Possibilities, Preferences, and Choices

After studying this chapter, you will be able to:

- Calculate and graph a household's budget line
- Work out how the budget line changes when prices and income change
- Make a map of preferences by using indifference curves
- Calculate a household's optimal consumption plan
- Predict the effects of price and income changes on the pattern of consumption
- Explain why the workweek gets shorter as wages rise
- Explain how budget lines and indifference curves can be used to understand all household choices

LIKE THE CONTINENTS FLOATING ON THE EARTH'S mantle, our spending patterns change steadily over time. On such subterranean movements, business empires rise and fall. Goods such as home videos and microwave popcorn now appear on our shopping lists, while Davy Crockett coonskin caps and horse-drawn carriages have disappeared. Miniskirts appear, disappear, and reappear in cycles of fashion. ◆◆ But the glittering surface of our consumption obscures deeper and slower changes in how we spend. In the last few years, we've seen a proliferation of gourmet food shops and designer clothing boutiques. Yet we spend a smaller percentage of our income today on food and clothing than we did in 1950. Despite the growth of jet travel and interstate highways, we spend about the same percentage of our income on transportation today as we did 40 years ago. At the same time, the percentage of our income spent on fuel, housing, and medical care has grown steadily. Why does consumer spending change over the years? How do people react to changes in income and changes in the prices of the things they buy? ◆◆ Similar subterranean movements govern the way we spend our time. For example, the workweek has fallen steadily from 70 hours a week in the nineteenth century down to 35 hours a week today. Why has the average workweek declined? Similarly, there have been trends in fertility, marriage, education, crime, and social interactions. Why do the habits and social mores of one generation become the old-fashioned ideas of another?

Subterranean Movements

◆ ◆ ◆ ◆ We're going to study a model of household choice that predicts the effects of changes in prices and incomes on what people buy, on how much work they do, on how much they borrow and lend, and even on how many children they have and how much crime they commit.

Consumption Possibilities

How does a household divide its income among the goods and services available? We are going to study a model of household choice that can answer this question and that predicts how consumption patterns change when income and prices change. Our first step is to examine the constraint on the household's possible choices.

Constraint

A household's consumption choices are constrained by the household's income and by the prices of the goods and services available. We're going to study a household that has a given amount of income to spend and that cannot influence the prices of the goods and services it buys. It has to take those prices as given.

The limits to a household's consumption choices are described by its **budget line.** To make the concept of the household's budget line as clear as possible, we'll consider the example of Lisa, who has an income of $30 a month to spend.[1] She buys two goods—movies and soda. Movies cost $6 each; soda costs $3 for a six-pack. If Lisa spends all of her income, she will reach the limits to her consumption of movies and soda.

In Fig. 8.1, each row of the table shows an affordable way for Lisa to consume movies and soda. Row *a* indicates that she can buy 10 six-packs of soda and see no movies. You can see that this combination of movies and soda exhausts her monthly income of $30. Now look at row *f*. It says

FIGURE 8.1

The Budget Line

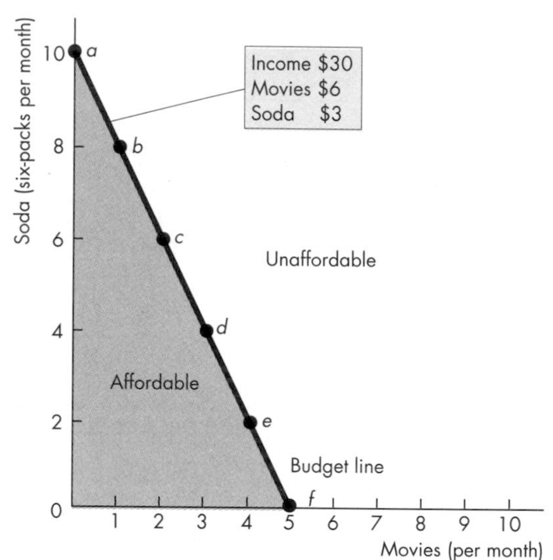

Consumption possibility	Movies (per month)	Soda (six-packs per month)
a	**0**	**10**
b	**1**	**8**
c	**2**	**6**
d	**3**	**4**
e	**4**	**2**
f	**5**	**0**

Lisa's budget line shows the boundary between what Lisa can and cannot afford. The table lists Lisa's affordable combinations of movies and soda when she has an income of $30 and when soda costs $3 a six-pack and movies cost $6 each. For example, row *a* tells us that Lisa can buy 10 six-packs and see no movies—a combination that exhausts her $30 income. The figure graphs Lisa's budget line. Points *a* through *f* on the graph represent rows of the table. For divisible goods, the budget line is the continuous line *af*.

[1]If you have read the preceding chapter on marginal utility theory, you have already met Lisa. This tale of her thirst for soda and zeal for movies will sound familiar to you—up to a point. But in this chapter, we're going to use a different method for representing preferences—one that does not require us to resort to the idea of utility.

that Lisa can watch 5 movies and drink no soda—another combination that exhausts the $30 available. Each of the other rows in the table also exhausts Lisa's income. (Check that each of the other rows costs exactly $30.) The numbers in the table define Lisa's consumption possibilities. We can graph Lisa's consumption possibilities as points *a* through *f* in Fig. 8.1.

Divisible and Indivisible Goods

Some goods can be bought in any quantity desired. Such goods are called divisible. Examples of divisible goods are gasoline and electricity, both of which can be bought in almost any quantity at all. Other goods—called indivisible goods—can be bought only in whole units. Movies are an example of an indivisible good. Although you can watch a fraction of a movie (as presumably you've done when you've picked a loser), you can buy movies only in whole units.

We can best understand the model of household choice that we're about to study if we suppose that all goods and services are divisible. In this case, the consumption possibilities are not just the points *a* through *f* shown in Fig. 8.1, but those points plus all the intermediate points that form a continuous straight line running from *a* to *f*. Such a line is a budget line. Thus, for example, if instead of movies and soda, we measure gallons of gasoline on the vertical axis and yards of cloth on the horizontal axis, Lisa can buy at any point along the line, consuming any fraction of a gallon or a yard.

Though Lisa can consume at only one of the six points represented by the rows of the table in our example, we'll develop the model so that it can deal with the case in which goods are divisible into any desired units.

Lisa's budget line is a constraint on her choices. It marks the boundary between what is affordable and what is unaffordable. She can afford all the points on the line and inside it. She cannot afford points outside the line. The constraint on her consumption depends on prices and on her income, and the constraint changes when prices and her income change.

The Budget Equation

To discover how the constraint on consumption changes when prices and income change, we need to describe the budget line in the form of an equation. Such an equation is called the budget equation. The **budget equation** states the limits to consumption for a given income and for given prices. We're going to work out such an equation and, to keep things tidy, we'll summarize our calculations in Table 8.1.

The left side of the table works out the budget equation by using symbols that apply to any consumer; the right side of the table works out the equation by using numbers that describe Lisa's situation. The first section of the table lists the variables that affect a household's budget. Those variables are income, the prices of the goods consumed, and the quantities consumed. To make our calculations clear, we have assigned symbols to each of these variables. In Lisa's case, her income is $30, the prices are $6 for movies and $3 for soda, and Lisa will choose the quantities of movies and soda to consume.

The consumer's budget is set out in the second section of the table. It states that expenditure (on the

TABLE 8.1

Calculating the Budget Equation

In general		In Lisa's case
	1. The variables	
Income $= y$		$y = \$30$
Price of movies $= P_m$		$P_m = \$6$
Price of soda $= P_s$		$P_s = \$3$
Quantity of movies $= Q_m$		$Q_m =$ **Lisa's choice**
Quantity of soda $= Q_s$		$Q_s =$ **Lisa's choice**
	2. The budget	
$P_sQ_s + P_mQ_m = y$		$(\$3)Q_s + (\$6)Q_m = \$30$
	3. Calculating the budget equation	
◆ **Divide by P_s to obtain** $Q_s + \frac{P_m}{P_s}Q_m = \frac{y}{P_s}$.		◆ **Divide by $3 to obtain** $Q_s + 2Q_m = 10$.
◆ **Subtract $(P_m/P_s)Q_m$ from both sides to obtain** $Q_s = \frac{y_m}{P_s}Q_m - \frac{P_m}{P_s}Q_m$.		◆ **Subtract $2Q_m$ from both sides to obtain** $Q_s = 10 - 2Q_m$.

left side of the equation) equals income (on the right side of the equation). Look at the elements of expenditure. Expenditure is equal to the sum of the expenditures on each of the goods. Expenditure on any one good equals its price multiplied by the quantity consumed. In Lisa's case, income (on the right side) is \$30, and the most that she can spend (on the left side of the equation) is the amount of soda consumed (Q_s) multiplied by the price of a soda (\$3) plus the number of movies consumed (Q_m) multiplied by their price (\$6).

The third section of the table shows you how to derive the budget equation from the consumer's budget equation. There are just two steps. First, divide both sides by the price of soda. Second, subtract $(P_m/P_s)Q_m$ from both sides of the resulting equation. The result is the budget equation shown in the last line of the table. The budget equation is

$$Q_s = \frac{y}{P_s} - \frac{P_m}{P_s} Q_m.$$

This equation tells us how the consumption level of one good varies as consumption of the other good varies. To interpret the equation, let's go back to the budget line of Fig. 8.1.

Let's first check that the budget equation that we have derived in Table 8.1 delivers the graph of the budget in Fig. 8.1. Begin by setting Q_m equal to zero. In this case, the budget equation tells us that Q_s will be 10. This combination of Q_s and Q_m is the same as that shown in row *a* of the table in Fig. 8.1. Setting Q_m equal to 5 makes Q_s equal to zero (row *f* of the table in Fig. 8.1). Check that you can derive the other rows of the table in Fig. 8.1.

The budget equation contains two variables under the control of the individual (Q_m and Q_s) and two numbers outside the individual's control. Let's look more closely at the two numbers outside the individual's control (y/P_s and P_m/P_s).

The first number, y/P_s, or 10 in Lisa's case, is the maximum number of six-packs that can be bought. It is called real income in terms of soda. **Real income** is income expressed in units of goods. Real income in terms of a particular good is income divided by the price of that good. In Lisa's case, her real income is 10 six-packs. In Fig. 8.1, the budget line intersects the vertical axis at Lisa's real income in terms of soda. That is, if Lisa spends all her income on soda, she can buy 10 six-packs.

Let's now look at the second number in the budget equation that is outside the consumer's control, P_m/P_s, or 2 in Lisa's case. This number shows the relative price of the two goods. A **relative price** is the price of one good divided by the price of another good. In the equation, P_m/P_s is the relative price of movies in terms of soda. For Lisa, that relative price is 2. That is, in order to see one more movie, she has to give up 2 six-packs.

You can see the relative price of movies to soda in Fig. 8.1 as the magnitude of the slope of the budget line. To calculate the slope of the budget line, recall the formula for slope that was introduced in Chapter 2: the slope of a line equals the change in the variable measured on the *y*-axis divided by the change in the variable measured on the *x*-axis as we move along the line. In this case, the variable measured on the *y*-axis is the quantity of soda, and the variable measured on the *x*-axis is the quantity of movies. Along Lisa's budget line, as soda decreases from 10 to 0, movies increase from 0 to 5. Therefore the slope of the budget line is $-10/5$, or -2. The flatter the budget line, the less expensive is the good measured on the horizontal axis relative to the good measured on the vertical axis. The steeper the line, the more expensive is the good measured on the horizontal axis relative to the one on the vertical axis. In other words, the slope of the budget line is the relative price of the good whose quantity appears on the horizontal axis.

The relative price of one good in terms of another is the opportunity cost of the first good in terms of the second. In Lisa's case, the opportunity cost of 1 movie is 2 six-packs of soda. Equivalently, the opportunity cost of 2 six-packs of soda is 1 movie.

Changes in Prices and Income

Let's now work out what happens to the budget line when prices and income change. We'll begin with a change in the price of one good.

A Change in the Price of Movies Suppose that the price of movies rises. What happens to Lisa's budget line? To make things vivid, let's suppose that the price of movies falls to \$3 a movie. By working through the calculations in Table 8.1, you can work out Lisa's budget line with the new price of movies. Recall that the budget equation is

$$Q_s = \frac{y}{P_s} - \frac{P_m}{P_s} Q_m.$$

Nothing has happened to income (y) or the price of soda (P_s). Lisa's real income in terms of soda remains 10. But the price of movies has fallen and is now equal to the price of soda. Therefore the relative price of movies (P_m/P_s) has decreased to 1. Lisa's new budget equation is

$$Q_s = 10 - Q_m.$$

Let's check that this new budget equation works. With movies costing $3 each, Lisa can see as many as 10 movies with her income. Using Lisa's new budget equation, you will see that substituting 10 for Q_m results in zero for Q_s. We know that this answer is correct because if Lisa sees 10 movies, she spends all her income on movies and has nothing left to spend on soda.

Figure 8.2(a) shows how the fall in the price of movies affects the budget line. Because the price of movies has gone down, the new budget line is flatter than budget line *af*. But notice that point *a* has not changed. If Lisa spends all her income on soda, she can still buy 10 six-packs. In other words, Lisa's real income in terms of soda has not changed. Only the price of movies has changed. Movies have become cheaper in terms of soda. Previously, 1 movie was worth 2 six-packs. In the new situation, the relative price or opportunity cost of 1 movie is 1 six-pack.

Let's see what happens to the budget line when the price of soda changes.

A Change in the Price of Soda Let's go back to the original situation in which movies cost $6 each and soda $3 a six-pack. What happens to Lisa's budget line if the price of a six-pack rises? Let's suppose that the price goes up from $3 to $6. If Lisa spends all her income on soda, she can buy 5 six-packs. Her real income in terms of soda has gone down. Since movies cost $6 each and soda costs $6 a six-pack, the relative price of movies is 1, the same as in the previous example. The opportunity cost of 1 movie is 1 six-pack of soda. We can work out the new budget line by using the budget equation:

$$Q_s = \frac{y}{P_s} - \frac{P_m}{P_s} Q_m.$$

FIGURE 8.2

Prices, Income, and the Budget Line

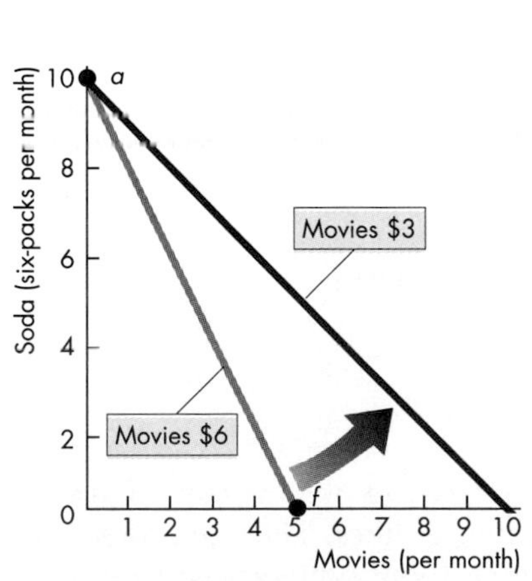

(a) A fall in the price of movies

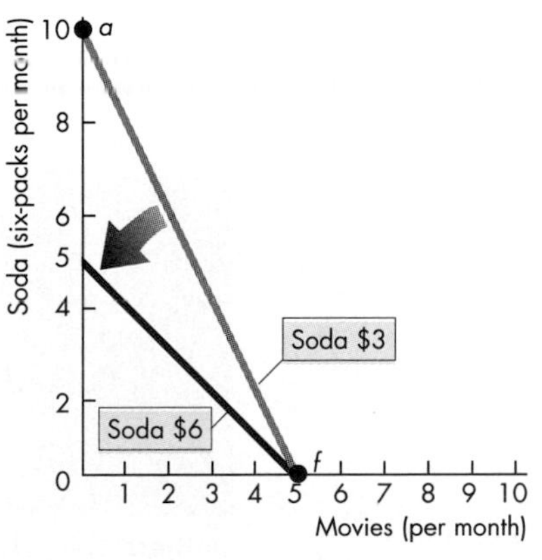

(b) A rise in the price of soda

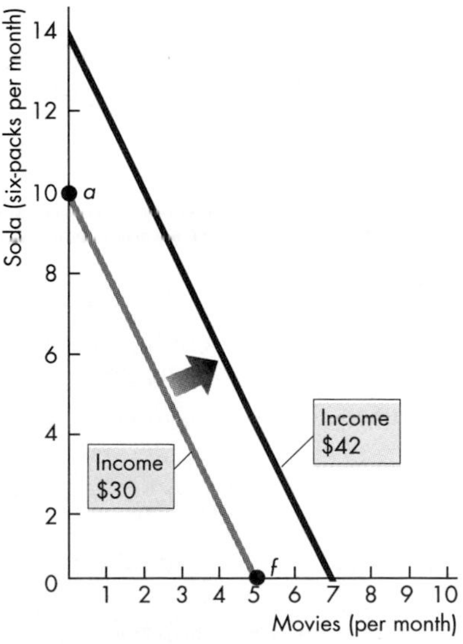

(c) A rise in income

In part (a), the price of a movie falls from $6 to $3. In part (b), the price of a six-pack of soda increases from $3 to $6. In part (c), income increases from $30 to $42, but prices remain constant. The arrow in each part indicates the shift in the budget line.

The price of a soda (P_s) is now \$6. Lisa's income is still \$30, and the price of a movie is still \$6. So Lisa's budget equation is

$$Q_s = \frac{30}{6} - \frac{6}{6}Q_m,$$

or

$$Q_s = 5 - Q_m.$$

Figure 8.2(b) shows the new budget line. Notice this time that point *f* has not moved. If Lisa spends all her income on movies, she can still see only 5 movies. Her real income in terms of movies has not changed.

Look at the new budget lines in parts (a) and (b) of Fig. 8.2. In part (a), both movies and soda cost \$3; in part (b), they both cost \$6. Lisa earns \$30 in both cases. Therefore in part (b), she can consume less of everything than in part (a), but movies have the same opportunity cost in the two cases—to see 1 more movie, she must give up 1 six-pack of soda. Notice that the new budget line in part (b) has the same slope as the new budget line in part (a).

Let's now see what happens to the budget line when income changes.

A Change in Income If prices remain constant and income increases, a person can then consume more of all goods. Go back to the initial situation in which Lisa had an income of \$30, movies cost \$6 each, and a six-pack costs \$3. Keeping the prices of the two goods constant, let's work out what happens if Lisa's income goes up from \$30 to \$42. Again, recall the budget equation:

$$Q_s = \frac{y}{P_s} - \frac{P_m}{P_s}Q_m.$$

Let's put into this equation the numbers for prices and for the new income. The price of soda (P_s) is \$3, and the price of movies (P_m) is \$6. Income (y) is \$42. Putting these numbers into the equation gives

$$Q_s = \frac{42}{3} - \frac{6}{3}Q_m,$$

or

$$Q_s = 14 - 2Q_m.$$

Lisa's real income has gone up because her income has gone up, while the prices of movies and soda have stayed the same. Her real income in terms of soda has gone up from 10 to 14. That is, if she spends all her income on soda, she can now buy 14 six-packs. Her real income in terms of movies has also gone up. If she spends all her income on movies, she can see 7 movies.

The shift in Lisa's budget line is shown in Fig. 8.2(c). The initial budget line is the same one we began with in parts (a) and (b), when Lisa's income was \$30. The new budget line shows Lisa able to consume more of each good. The new line is parallel to the old one but farther out. The two budget lines are parallel, or have the same slope, because the relative price is the same in both cases. With movies costing \$6 each and a six-pack costing \$3, Lisa must give up 2 six-packs to see 1 movie. The new budget line is farther out than the initial one because her real income has increased.

REVIEW

The budget line describes the maximum amounts of consumption that a household can undertake, given its income and the prices of the goods it buys. A change in the price of one good changes the slope of the budget line. If the price of the good measured on the horizontal axis rises, the budget line gets steeper. A change in income makes the budget line shift, but its slope does not change. ◆

Let's now leave the budget line and look at the second ingredient in the model of household choice—preferences.

Preferences

Preferences are a person's likes and dislikes. There are three fundamental assumptions about preferences:

- Preferences do not depend on the prices of goods.
- Preferences do not depend on income.
- More of any good is preferred to less of that good.

The first two assumptions amount to the proposition that people's likes and dislikes do not depend on what they can afford to buy. This assumption does *not* mean that people's preferences do not change over time. Nor does it mean that their preferences are not influenced by the things that they have consumed and experienced. It *does* mean that just because income increases or the price of a good decreases, people do not, *for one of those reasons*, suddenly decide that they like a particular good more than they did before.

The third assumption—more of any good is preferred to less of that good—is just a different way of saying that wants are unlimited. Of course, in reality, you can imagine having enough of any one good to want no more of it, but there will always be something that you will prefer to have more of.

We are going to discover in this section a very neat idea—that of drawing a map of a person's preferences.

A Preference Map

Let's see how we can draw a map of a person's preferences by constructing a map of Lisa's preferences for movies and soda. This map, which appears in Fig. 8.3, measures the number of movies seen on the horizontal axis and the number of six-packs consumed on the vertical axis. Let's start with Fig. 8.3(a) and focus on point *c*, where Lisa sees 2 movies and consumes 6 six-packs of soda. We will use this point as a reference and ask how Lisa likes all the other points in relation to point *c*.

Figure 8.3(b) takes us to the next step. It is divided into four areas. The area shaded yellow has, at each point, more movies and more soda than at point *c*. Lisa prefers all the points in this area to point *c*. The area shaded gray has, at each point, fewer movies and less soda than at point *c*. She prefers point *c* to all the points in this area. Points in the two white areas have either more movies and

FIGURE 8.3

Mapping Preferences

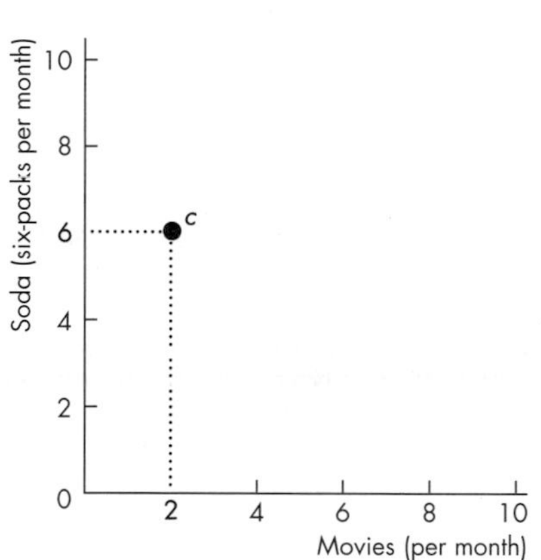

(a) A consumption point

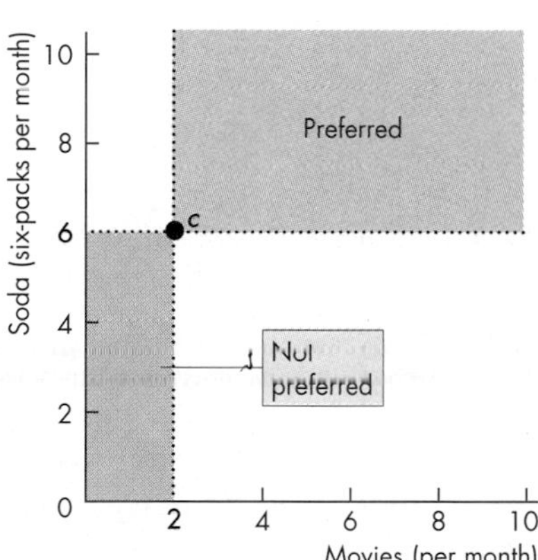

(b) Preference relations

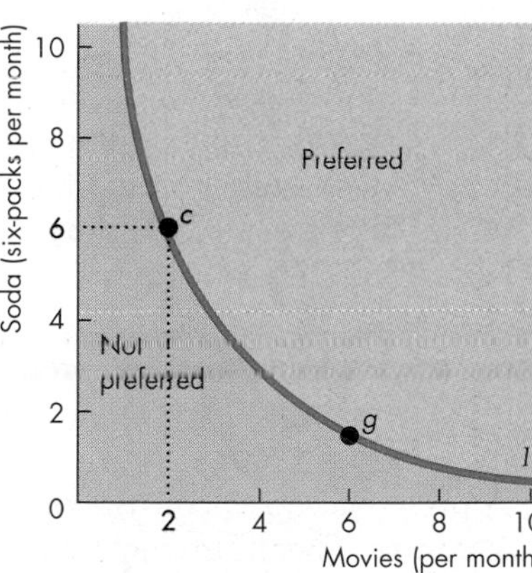

(c) Indifference curve

If Lisa consumes 6 six-packs of soda and 2 movies, she consumes at point *c* in part (a). Lisa prefers more goods to fewer goods. This fact is illustrated in part (b). She prefers any point at which she consumes more of both soda and movies to point *c* (all the points in the yellow area). She prefers point *c* to any point at which fewer movies and six-packs are consumed (all the points in the gray area). Whether she prefers seeing more movies but having less soda than at point *c* depends on how many more movies and how much less soda she has. Similarly, if she consumes more soda and sees fewer movies than at point *c*, whether she prefers that situation to *c* depends on how much more soda and how many fewer movies she has. The boundary between points that she prefers to point *c* and those to which *c* is preferred is shown in part (c). That boundary is called an indifference curve. Lisa is indifferent between points such as *g* and *c* on the indifference curve. She prefers any point above the indifference curve (yellow area) to any point on it, and she prefers any point on the indifference curve to any point below it (gray area).

less soda than point *c* or more soda and fewer movies than point *c*. How does Lisa rank points in these areas against point *c*? To answer this question, we need to take the final step in constructing a map of Lisa's preferences.

Figure 8.3(c) takes the final step. It contains a line—I_1—passing through point *c* and through what were the two white areas. That line defines the boundary between points that Lisa prefers to point *c* and points she regards as inferior to point *c*. Lisa is indifferent between point *c* and the other points on the line I_1, such as point *g*. The line is called an indifference curve. An **indifference curve** is a line that shows all combinations of two goods that give the consumer equal satisfaction. The indifference curve in Fig. 8.3(c) shows all the combinations of movies and soda that give Lisa equal satisfaction.

The indifference curve shown in Fig. 8.3(c) is just one of a whole family of such curves. This indifference curve appears again in Fig. 8.4. It is labeled I_1 and passes through points *c* and *g*. Two other indifference curves are I_0 and I_2. Lisa prefers any point on indifference curve I_2 to those on indifference curve I_1, and she prefers any point on I_1 to those on I_0. We refer to I_2 as being a higher indifference curve than I_1 and I_1 as higher than I_0.

Indifference curves never intersect each other. To see why, consider indifference curves I_1 and I_2 in Fig. 8.4. We know that point *j* is preferred to point *c*. We also know that all points on indifference curve I_2 are preferred to all points on indifference curve I_1. If these indifference curves did intersect, the consumer would be indifferent between the combination of goods at the intersection point and combinations *c* and *j*. But we know that *j* is preferred to *c*, so such a point cannot exist. Thus the indifference curves never intersect.

A preference map consists of a series of indifference curves. The indifference curves shown in Fig. 8.4 are only a part of Lisa's preference map. Her entire map consists of an infinite number of indifference curves, all of them sloping downward and none of them intersecting. They resemble the contour lines on a map measuring the height of mountains. An indifference curve joins points representing combinations of goods among which a consumer is indifferent in much the same way that contour lines on a map join points of equal height above sea level. By looking at the shape of the contour lines on a map, we can draw conclusions about the terrain. In the same way, by looking at the shape of a person's indifference curves, we can draw conclusions about preferences. But interpreting a preference map requires a bit of work. It also requires some way of describing the shape of the indifference curves. In the next two sections, we'll learn how to "read" a preference map.

FIGURE 8.4

A Preference Map

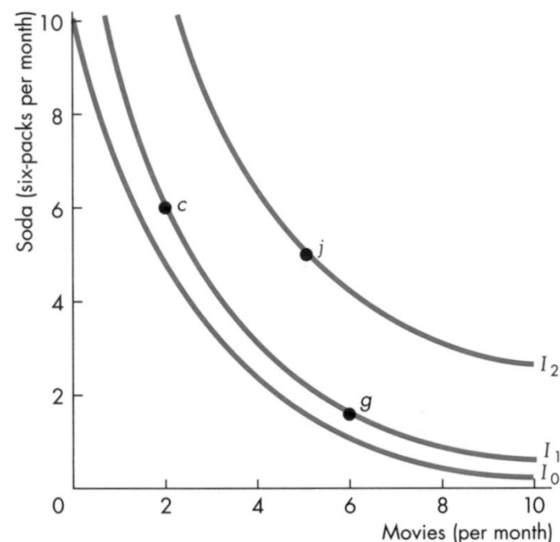

A preference map consists of an infinite number of indifference curves. Here, we show just three—I_0, I_1, and I_2—that are part of Lisa's preference map. Each indifference curve shows points among which Lisa is indifferent. For example, she is indifferent between point *c* and point *g* on indifference curve I_1. But points on a higher indifference curve are preferred to points on a lower indifference curve. For example, Lisa prefers all the points on indifference curve I_2 to all the points on indifference curve I_1; she prefers point *j* to points *c* or *g*.

Indifference Curves and Preferences

We use the concept of the marginal rate of substitution to describe the shape of an indifference curve. The **marginal rate of substitution** (or MRS) is the rate at which a person will give up good *y* in order to get more of good *x* and at the same time remain indifferent. The marginal rate of substitution is measured from the slope of an indifference curve. If the indifference curve is steep, the marginal rate of substitution is high. The person is willing to give up a large quantity of good y (the good measured on the y-axis) in exchange for a small quantity of good x (the good measured on the x-axis) while remaining indifferent. If the indifference curve is flat, the marginal rate of substitution is low. The person is willing to give up only a small amount of good y and must be compensated with a large amount of good x to remain indifferent.

Let's work out the marginal rate of substitution in two cases, both illustrated in Fig. 8.5. The curve labeled I_1 is one of Lisa's indifference curves. Suppose that Lisa drinks 6 six-packs of soda and watches 2 movies (point c in the figure). What is her marginal rate of substitution at this point? It is calculated by measuring the magnitude of the slope of the indifference curve at that point. To measure the slope, place a straight line against, or tangential to, the indifference curve at that point. The slope of that line is the change in the quantity of soda divided by the change in the quantity of movies as we move along the line. As soda consumption decreases by 10 six packs, movie consumption increases by 5. The slope of the line is –2. Thus when Lisa is consuming 2 movies and 6 six packs of soda, her marginal rate of substitution is 2.

FIGURE 8.5

The Marginal Rate of Substitution

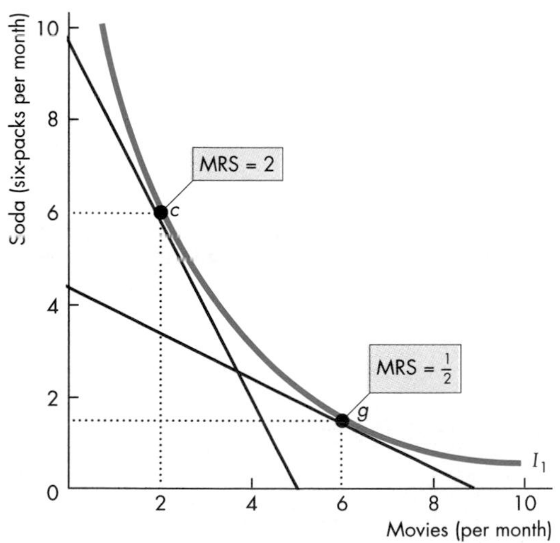

The magnitude of the slope of an indifference curve is called the marginal rate of substitution, or MRS. The marginal rate of substitution tells us how much of one good a person is willing to give up to gain more of another good while remaining indifferent. The marginal rate of substitution at point c is 2; at point g it is ½.

Now, suppose that Lisa is consuming 6 movies and 1½ six-packs (point g in Fig. 8.5). What is her marginal rate of substitution at this point? The answer is found by calculating the slope of the indifference curve at that point. That slope is the same as the slope of the straight line that is drawn tangential to the point. Here, as soda consumption decreases by 4½ six-packs, movie consumption increases by 9. Hence the slope equals –½. Her marginal rate of substitution is ½. Thus when Lisa sees 6 movies and consumes 1½ six-packs of soda a month, she is willing to substitute movies for soda at the rate of half a six-pack per movie while remaining indifferent.

Notice that if Lisa drinks a lot of soda and does not see many movies, her marginal rate of substitution is high. If she watches a lot of movies and does not drink much soda, her marginal rate of substitution is low. This feature of the marginal rate of substitution is the central assumption of the theory of consumer behavior and is referred to as the diminishing marginal rate of substitution. The assumption of **diminishing marginal rate of substitution** is a general tendency for the marginal rate of substitution to diminish as the consumer moves along an indifference curve, increasing consumption of good x and decreasing consumption of good y.

You may be able to appreciate why we assume the principle of a diminishing marginal rate of substitution by thinking about your own preferences. Imagine two situations: in one, you are watching 3 movies a night but have no soda; in the other, you have 6 six-packs of soda and no movies. In the first situation, you will probably willingly give up seeing 1 movie if you can get just a small amount of soda in exchange. In the second situation, you will probably be willing to give up quite a lot of soda to watch just 1 movie. Your preferences satisfy the principle of diminishing marginal rate of substitution.

The shape of the indifference curves incorporates the principle of the diminishing marginal rate of substitution because the curves are bowed toward the origin. The tightness of the bend of an indifference curve tells us how willing a person is to substitute one good for another while remaining indifferent. Let's look at some examples that will clarify this point.

Degree of Substitutability

Most of us would not regard movies and soda as being close substitutes for each other. We probably have some fairly clear ideas about how many movies we want to see each month and how many cans of soda we want to drink. Nevertheless, to some degree, we are willing to substitute between these two goods. No matter how big a soda freak you are, there is surely some increase in the number of movies you can see that will compensate you for being deprived of a can of soda. Similarly, no matter how addicted you are to the movies, surely some number of cans of soda will compensate you for being deprived of seeing one movie. A person's indifference curves for movies and soda might look something like those shown in Fig. 8.6(a).

Close Substitutes Some goods substitute so easily for each other that most of us do not even notice which we are consuming. A good example concerns different brands of personal computers. Zenith, Leading Edge, and Tandy are all clones of the IBM PC, but most of us can't tell the difference between the three clones and indeed the IBM machine itself. The same holds true for marker pens. Most of us don't care whether we use a marker pen from the campus bookstore or the local supermarket. When two goods are perfect substitutes for each other, their indifference curves are straight lines that slope downward, as illustrated in Fig. 8.6(b). The marginal rate of substitution between perfect substitutes is constant.

Complements Some goods cannot substitute for each other at all. Instead, they are complements. The complements in Fig. 8.6(c) are left and right running shoes. Indifference curves of perfect complements are L-shaped. One left running shoe and one right running shoe are as good as one left shoe and two right ones. Two of each is preferred to one of each, but two of one and one of the other is no better than one of each.

The extreme cases of perfect substitutes and perfect complements shown here don't often happen in

FIGURE 8.6

The Degree of Substitutability

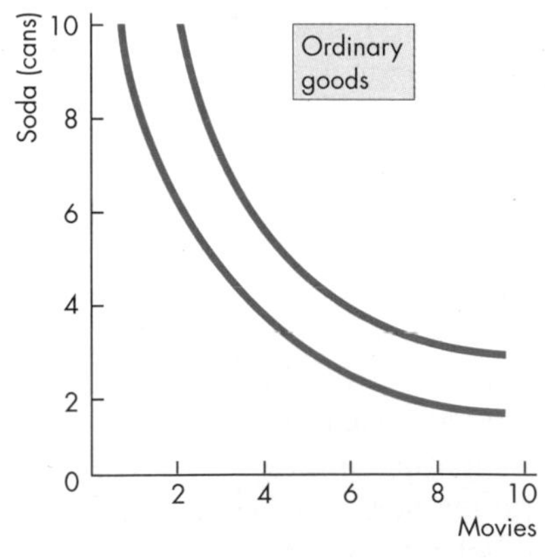

(a) Ordinary goods

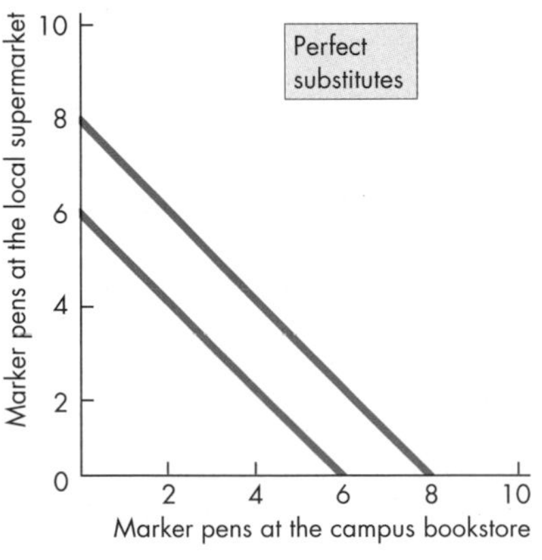

(b) Perfect substitutes

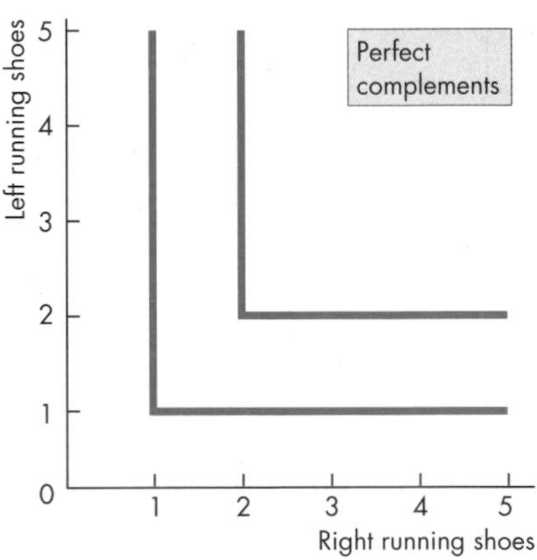

(c) Perfect complements

The shape of the indifference curves reveals the degree of substitutability between two goods. Part (a) shows the indifference curves for two ordinary goods: movies and soda. To remain indifferent as less soda is consumed, one must see more movies. The number of movies that compensates for a reduction in soda increases as less soda is consumed. Part (b) shows the indifference curves for two perfect substitutes. For the consumer to remain indifferent, one fewer marker pen from the local supermarket must be replaced by one extra marker pen from the campus bookstore. Part (c) shows two perfect complements—goods that cannot be substituted for each other at all. Two left running shoes with one right running shoe is no better than one of each. But two of each is preferred to one of each.

"With the pork I'd recommend an Alsatian white or a Coke."

reality. They do, however, illustrate that the shape of the indifference curve shows the degree of substitutability between two goods. The more perfectly substitutable the two goods, the more nearly are their indifference curves straight lines and the less quickly does the marginal rate of substitution fall. Poor substitutes for each other have tightly curved indifference curves, approaching the shape of those shown in Fig. 8.6(c).

As you can see in the cartoon, according to the waiter's preferences, Coke and Alsatian white wine are perfect substitutes for each other and each is a complement with pork. We hope the customers agree with him.

REVIEW

A person's preferences can be represented by a preference map. A preference map consists of a series of indifference curves. Indifference curves slope downward, bow toward the origin, and do not intersect each other. The magnitude of the slope of an indifference curve is called the marginal rate of substitution. The marginal rate of substitution falls as a person consumes less of the good measured on the *y*-axis and more of the good measured on the *x*-axis. The tightness of an indifference curve tells us how well two goods substitute for each other. Indifference curves that are almost straight lines indicate that the goods are close substitutes. Indifference curves that are tightly curved and that approach an L-shape indicate that the two goods complement each other. ◆

The two components of the model of household choice are now in place: the budget line and the preference map. We will now use these two components to work out the consumer's choice.

Choice

Recall that Lisa has $30 to spend and she buys only two goods: movies (at $6 each) and soda (at $3 a six-pack). We've learned how to construct Lisa's budget line, which summarizes what she can buy, given her income and the prices of movies and soda (Fig. 8.1). We've also learned how to characterize Lisa's preferences in terms of her indifference curves (Fig. 8.4). We are now going to bring Lisa's budget line and indifference curves together and discover her best affordable way of consuming movies and soda.

The analysis is summarized in Fig. 8.7. You can see in that figure the budget line from Fig. 8.1 and the indifference curves from Fig. 8.4. Let's first focus on point *h* on indifference curve I_0. That point is on Lisa's budget line, so we know that she can afford it. But does she prefer this combination of movies and soda over all the other affordable combinations? The answer is no, she does not. To see why not, consider point *c*, at which she consumes 2 movies and 6 six-packs. Point *c* is also on Lisa's budget line, so we know that she can afford to consume at this point. But point *c* is on indifference curve I_1, a higher indifference curve than I_0. Therefore we know that Lisa prefers point *c* to point *h*.

Are there any affordable points that Lisa prefers to point *c*? The answer is that there are not. All Lisa's other affordable consumption points—all the other points on or below her budget line—lie on indifference curves that are below I_1. Indifference curve I_1 is the highest indifference curve on which Lisa can afford to consume.

FIGURE 8.7
The Best Affordable Point

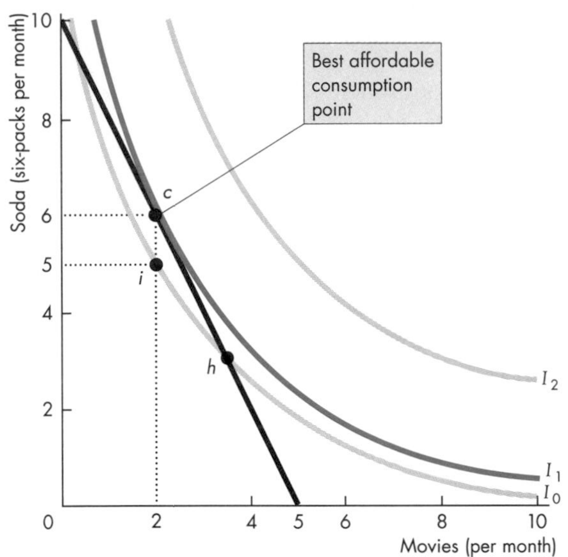

Lisa's best affordable consumption point is *c*. At that point, she is on her budget line and so spends her entire income on the two goods. She is also on the highest attainable indifference curve. Higher indifference curves (such as I_2) do not touch her budget line, and so she cannot afford any point on them. At point *c*, the marginal rate of substitution (the magnitude of the slope of the indifference curve) equals the relative price of movies (the magnitude of the slope of the budget line). A point such as *h* on the budget line is not Lisa's best affordable consumption point because at that point she is willing to give up more movies in exchange for soda than she has to. She can move to a point such as *i*, which she regards as being just as good as point *h* and which allows her to still have some income left over. She can spend that income and move to *c*, a point that she prefers to point *i*.

Let's look more closely at Lisa's best affordable choice.

Properties of the Best Affordable Point

The best affordable point—point *c* in this example—has two properties. It is *on:*

- The budget line
- The highest attainable indifference curve

On the Budget Line The best affordable point is *on* the budget line. If Lisa consumes at a point inside her budget line, there are affordable points on the budget line at which she can consume more of both goods. Lisa prefers any of these points to the one inside the budget line. The best affordable point cannot be outside the budget line because Lisa cannot afford such a point.

On the Highest Attainable Indifference Curve The chosen point is *on* the highest attainable indifference curve where that curve has the same slope as the budget line. Stated another way, the marginal rate of substitution between the two goods (the magnitude of the slope of the indifference curve) equals their relative price (the magnitude of the slope of the budget line).

To see why this condition describes the best affordable point, consider point *h*, which Lisa regards as inferior to point *c*. At point *h*, Lisa's marginal rate of substitution is less than the relative price—indifference curve I_0 is flatter than Lisa's budget line. As Lisa gives up movies for soda and moves up indifference curve I_0, she moves inside her budget line and has some money left over. She can move to point *i*, for example, where she consumes 2 movies and 5 six-packs and has $3 to spare. She is indifferent between the combination of goods at point *i* and that at point *h*. But she prefers point *c* to point *i*, since at *c* she has more soda than at *i* and sees the same number of movies.

By moving along her budget line from point *h* toward point *c*, Lisa passes through a whole array of indifference curves (not shown in the figure) located between indifference curves I_0 and I_1. All of these indifference curves are higher than I_0, and therefore any point on them is preferred to point *h*. Once she gets to point *c*, Lisa has reached the highest attainable indifference curve. If she keeps moving along the budget line, she will start to encounter indifference curves that are lower than I_1.

REVIEW

The consumer has a given income and faces fixed prices. The consumer's problem is to allocate that fixed income in the best possible way. Affordable combinations of goods are described by the consumer's budget line. The consumer's preferences are represented by indifference curves. The consumer's best allocation of income occurs when all income is spent (on the budget line) and when the marginal rate of substitution (the magnitude of the slope of the indifference curve) equals the relative price (the magnitude of the slope of the budget line). ◆

We will now use this model of household choice to make some predictions about changes in consumption patterns when income and prices change.

Predicting Consumer Behavior

Let's examine how consumers respond to changes in prices and income. We'll start by looking at the effect of a change in price. By studying the effect of a change in price on a consumer's choice, holding all other effects constant, we are able to derive a consumer's demand curve.

A Change in Price

The effect of a change in price on the quantity of a good consumed is called the **price effect.** We will use Fig. 8.8(a) to work out the price effect of a fall in the price of movies. We start with movies costing $6 each, soda costing $3 a six-pack, and Lisa's income at $30 a month. In this situation, she consumes at point *c*, where her budget line is tangential to her highest attainable indifference curve, I_1. She consumes 6 six-packs and 2 movies a month.

Now suppose that the price of a movie falls to $3. We've already seen how a change in price (in Fig. 8.2a) affects the budget line. With a lower price of movies, the budget line moves outward and becomes less steep. The new budget line is the dark red one in Fig. 8.8(a). Lisa's best affordable point is *j*, at which she consumes 5 movies and 5 six-packs of soda. As you can see, Lisa drinks less soda and watches more movies now that movies cost less. She reduces her soda consumption from 6 to 5 six-packs and increases her movie consumption from 2 to 5. Lisa substitutes movies for soda when the price of movies falls and the price of soda and her income remain constant.

FIGURE 8.8

Price Effect and Demand Curve

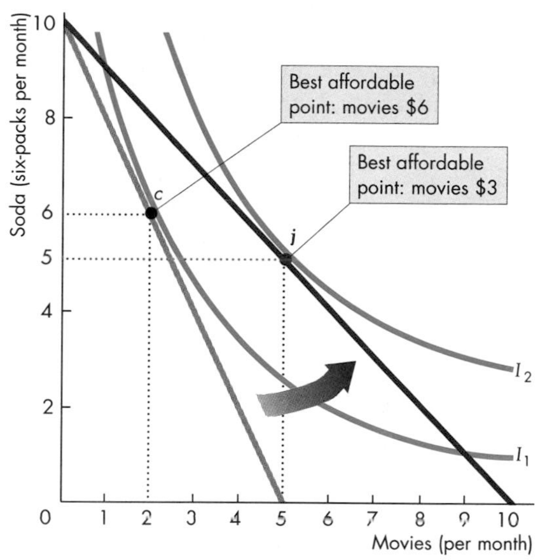

(a) Price effect

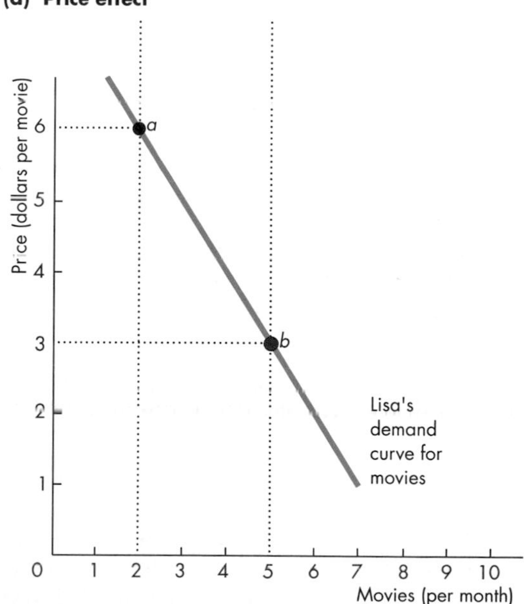

(b) Demand curve

Initially, Lisa consumes at point *c* (part a). If the price of a movie falls from $6 to $3, she consumes at point *j*. The increase in the consumption of movies from 2 to 5 per month is the price effect. When the price of a movie falls, Lisa consumes more movies. She also consumes less soda. Lisa's demand curve for movies is shown in part (b). When the price of movies is $6, she consumes 2 a month, at point *a*. When the price of movies falls to $3, she consumes 5 a month, at point *b*. The demand curve is traced by varying the price of movies and calculating Lisa's best affordable consumption of movies for each different price.

The Demand Curve

This analysis of the effect of a change in the price of movies enables us to derive Lisa's demand curve for movies. Recall that the demand curve graphs the relationship between the quantity demanded of a good and its price, holding constant all other influences on the quantity demanded. We can derive Lisa's demand curve for movies by gradually lowering the price of movies and working out how many movies she sees by finding her best affordable point at each different price. Figure 8.8(b) highlights just two prices and two points that lie on Lisa's demand curve for movies. When the price of movies is $6, Lisa consumes 2 movies a month at point *a*. When the price falls to $3, she increases her consumption to 5 movies a month at point *b*. The entire demand curve is made up of these two points plus all the other points that tell us Lisa's best affordable consumption of movies at each price—more than $6, between $6 and $3, and less than $3—given the price of soda and Lisa's income. As you can see, Lisa's demand curve for movies slopes downward—the lower the price of a movie, the more she watches each month. This is the law of demand.

Next, let's examine what happens when Lisa's income changes.

A Change in Income

The effect of a change in income on consumption is called the **income effect.** Let's work out the income effect by examining how consumption changes when income changes with constant prices. We've already seen, earlier in this chapter, how a change in income shifts the budget line. We worked out and illustrated (in Fig. 8.2c) that an increase in income shifts the budget line outward, with its slope unchanged.

It will be clear to you that, as income increases, a person can consume more of all goods. But being able to consume more of all goods does not mean that a person will do so. Goods are classified into two groups: normal goods and inferior goods. *Normal goods* are goods whose income effect is positive—consumption increases as income increases. *Inferior goods* are goods whose income effect is negative—consumption decreases as income increases.

As the name implies, most goods are normal goods. But a few are inferior goods. Rice and potatoes are perhaps the most obvious. People with low incomes have a heavy rice or potato component to their diet. As incomes increase, people substitute chicken and beef for rice and potatoes. Thus as income increases, the consumption of chicken and beef increases but that of rice and potatoes decreases. Therefore chicken and beef are normal goods, while rice and potatoes are inferior goods.

Figure 8.9 illustrates the two types of income effect. Part (a) shows the income effect for normal goods, using Lisa's consumption as an example. With an income of $30 and with movies costing $6 each and soda costing $3 for a six-pack, she consumes at point *c*—2 movies and 6 six-packs. If her income goes up to $42, she consumes at point *k*—consuming 3 movies and 8 six-packs. Thus with a higher income, Lisa consumes more of both goods. These income effects are marked on the axes of Fig. 8.9(a). As you can see, both income effects are positive. In Lisa's case, as her income increases, she consumes more movies and more soda. For Lisa, both movies and soda are normal goods.

Figure 8.9(b) shows the income effect for an inferior good—rice. At the initial income level, the household consumes at point *a*—2 ounces of chicken and 6 ounces of rice a day. When income increases, chicken consumption increases to 6 ounces a day, but rice consumption decreases to 4 ounces a day, at point *b*. The income effect for an inferior good is negative.

A Change in Price: Income and Substitution Effects

We've now worked out the effects of a change in the price of movies and the effects of a change in Lisa's income on the consumption of movies and soda. We've discovered that when her income increases, she increases her consumption of both goods. Movies and soda are *normal goods.* When the price of movies falls, Lisa increases her consumption of movies and decreases her consumption of soda. A fall in the price of a normal good leads to an increase in the consumption of that good, as well as to a decrease in the consumption of the substitutes for that good. In this example, a fall in the price of movies leads to an increase in the consumption of movies and to a decrease in the consumption of soda, a substitute for movies. To see why these changes in spending patterns occur when there is a change in price, we separate the effect of the change into two parts. One part is called the substitution effect; the other part is called the income effect. The price effect and its separation into a substitution

FIGURE 8.9

The Income Effect

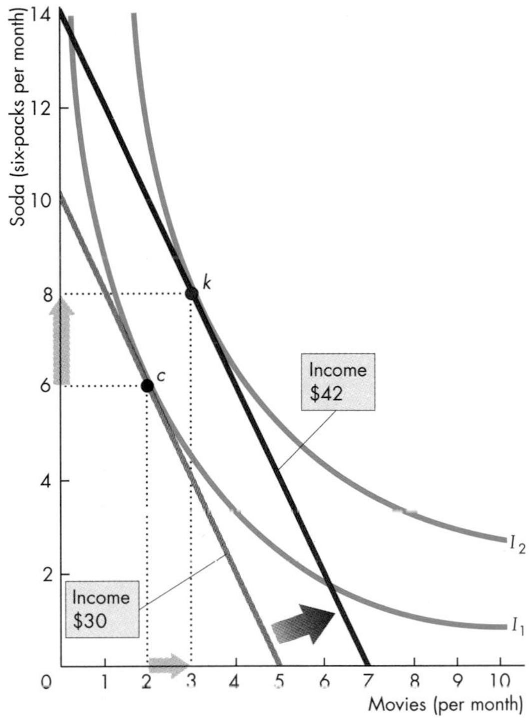

(a) Normal goods

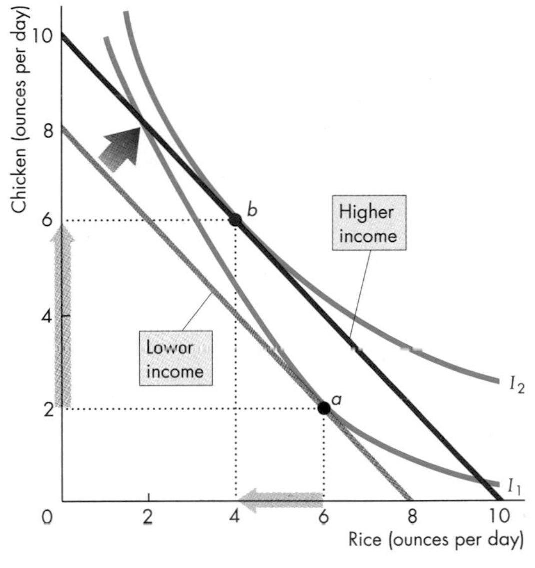

(b) Inferior good

An increase in income increases the consumption of most goods. These goods are normal goods. In part (a), Lisa consumes more of both soda and movies (as shown by the orange arrows) as her income increases. Soda and movies are normal goods, but some goods are inferior goods. The consumption of inferior goods decreases as income increases. In part (b), as income increases, the consumption of rice decreases and more chicken is consumed (again shown by orange arrows). For this consumer, rice is an inferior good.

effect and an income effect are illustrated in Fig. 8.10. Part (a) shows the price effect we've already worked out in Fig. 8.8. Let's see how that price effect comes about, first by isolating the substitution effect.

The Substitution Effect The **substitution effect** is the effect of a change in price on the quantities consumed when the consumer (hypothetically) remains indifferent between the original and the new combinations of goods consumed. To work out Lisa's substitution effect, we have to imagine that when the price of movies falls, Lisa's income also decreases by an amount that is just enough to leave her on the same indifference curve as before.

The substitution effect is illustrated in Fig. 8.10(b). When the price of movies falls from $6 to $3, let's suppose (hypothetically) that Lisa's income decreases to $21. What's special about $21? It is the income that is just enough, at the new price of movies, to keep Lisa's best affordable point on the same indifference curve as her initial consumption point *c*. Lisa's budget line in this situation is the light red line shown in Fig. 8.10(b). With the new price of movies and the new lower income, Lisa's best affordable point is *l* on indifference curve I_1. The move from *c* to *l* isolates the substitution effect of a price change. The substitution effect of the fall in the price of movies is an increase in the consumption of movies from 2 to 4 and a decrease in the consumption of soda from 6 to 3 six-packs. The direction of the substitution effect never varies: when the relative price of a good falls, the consumer substitutes more of that good for the other good.

FIGURE 8.10

Price Effect, Substitution Effect, and Income Effect

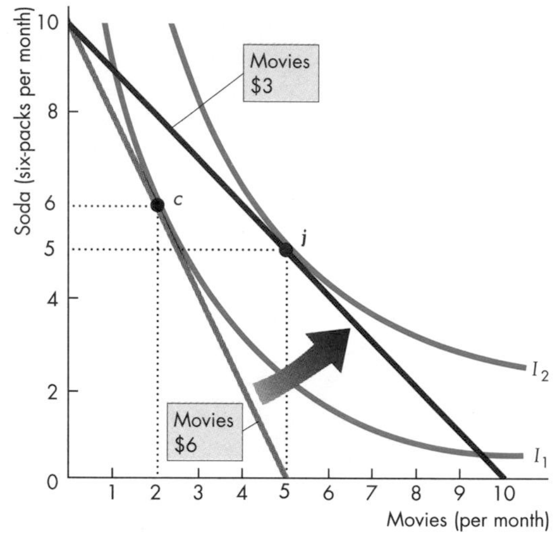

(a) Price effect

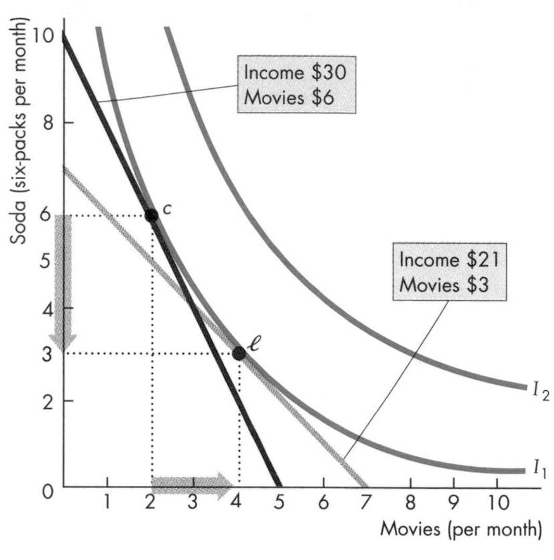

(b) Substitution effect

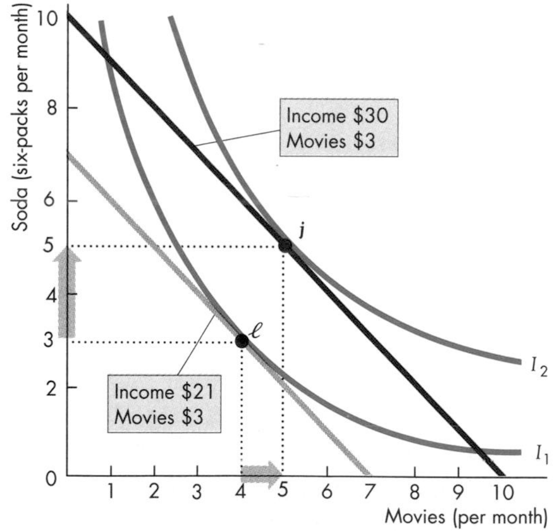

(c) Income effect

The price effect can be separated into a substitution effect and an income effect. The price effect is shown in part (a) and is the same as that in Fig. 8.8(a).

The substitution effect in part (b) is calculated by imagining that Lisa's income decreases at the same time as the fall in the price of a movie, so that when she chooses her best affordable point, she is indifferent between that and the original situation. The move from *c* to *l* is the substitution effect. The substitution effect of a price change always results in more consumption of the good whose price has fallen. The orange arrows show the changes in consumption.

The income effect (part c) is calculated by reversing the imaginary pay cut. Income is increased by holding prices constant at their new level. The budget line moves outward and more of both goods is consumed, as shown by the orange arrows. The move from *l* to *j* is the income effect.

Income Effect To calculate the substitution effect, we gave Lisa a $9 pay cut. Now let's give Lisa her money back. This means shifting Lisa's budget line, as shown in Fig. 8.10(c). That move does not involve any change in prices. The budget line moves outward, but its slope does not change. This change in the budget is similar to the one that occurs in Fig. 8.9, where we studied the effect of income on consumption. As Lisa's budget line shifts outward, her consumption possibilities expand, and her best affordable point becomes *j* on indifference curve I_2. The move from *l* to *j* isolates the income effect of a price change. The increase in income increases the consumption of both movies and soda; they are normal goods.

Price Effect As Fig. 8.10 illustrates, we have separated the effect of a change in price, shown in part (a), into two parts: part (b) keeps the consumer indifferent between the two situations (by making a hypothetical income change at the same time) and looks at the substitution effect of the price change; part (c) keeps prices constant and (hypothetically) restores the original income. It looks at the income effect. The substitution effect always works in the same direction—the consumer slides along an indifference curve, buying more of the good whose price has fallen. The direction of the income effect depends on whether the good is normal or inferior. By definition, normal goods are ones whose consumption increases as income increases. In our example, movies and soda are normal goods because the income effect increases their consumption. Both the income effect and the substitution effect increase Lisa's consumption of movies.

The substitution and income effects of a price change are marked off on the axes in parts (b) and (c) of Fig. 8.10. The move from point *c* to point *l* is the substitution effect, and the move from point *l* to point *j* is the income effect. For movies, the income effect reinforces the substitution effect, with the result that Lisa's consumption of movies increases. For soda, the substitution effect and the income effect work in opposite directions, with the result that Lisa's consumption of soda decreases.

The example that we have just studied is that of a change in the price of a normal good. For an inferior good—a good whose consumption decreases as income increases—the income effect is negative. Thus for an inferior good, it is not always the case that a lower price leads to an increase in the quantity demanded of the good. The lower price has a substitution effect that tends to increase the quantity demanded. But the lower price also has a negative income effect, which reduces the demand for the inferior good. Thus the income effect offsets the substitution effect to some degree.[2]

[2]It has been suggested that the negative income effect for some goods is so large that it dominates the substitution effect. As a result, a lower price leads to a decrease in the quantity demanded for such a good. Goods of this type are called "Giffen goods," named after Sir Robert Giffen, an Irish economist. During a potato famine in Ireland in the nineteenth century, Giffen noticed that when the price of potatoes increased, the quantity of potatoes consumed also increased. Potatoes made up such a large part of the diets of these impoverished people that when the price of potatoes rose, consumers couldn't afford to buy meat or other substitutes, which were all even more expensive.

Model, Theory, and Reality

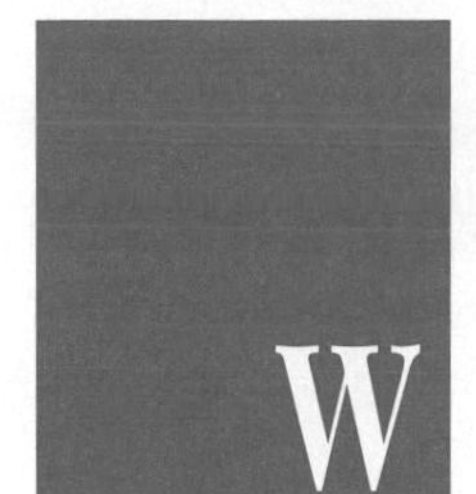

We have built a model of household choice that makes predictions about consumption choices and how those choices are affected by changes in income and prices. This model leads to a theory of household choice that helps us to understand past spending patterns and to predict future ones. Let's summarize this model.

The Model

All models begin with assumptions. By using logic, we work out the implications of those assumptions. Let's look at the assumptions and implications in the model of household choice.

Assumptions The assumptions of the model of household choice are as follows:

- A household has a fixed income to allocate among various goods.
- The prices of goods cannot be influenced by the household.
- The household has preferences and can compare alternative combinations of goods as preferred, not preferred, or indifferent.
- Preferences can be represented by indifference curves.
- Indifference curves bow toward the origin—the marginal rate of substitution falls as consumption of the good measured on the x-axis increases and consumption of the good measured on the y-axis decreases.
- The household chooses its best affordable combination of goods.
- Preferences do not change when prices and incomes change. *Choices* change, but the new choices result from given preferences and changed constraints.

Implications The implications of the model of household choice are as follows:

- The chosen consumption point is affordable and is *on* the budget line.

- The chosen consumption point is on the highest attainable indifference curve.
- At the chosen consumption point, the slope of the indifference curve equals the slope of the budget line. Expressed in another way, the marginal rate of substitution equals the relative price of the two goods.
- For normal goods, an increase in income increases demand.
- For inferior goods, an increase in income decreases demand.
- For any good, a rise in its price has a substitution effect that decreases the quantity demanded of it.
- For a normal good, a rise in its price decreases the quantity demanded of it—the income effect and the substitution effect reinforce each other. This is the law of demand.

The above is, in a nutshell, the model of household choice we have studied in this chapter. That model provides a basis for developing a theory that explains the patterns of consumption.

The Theory

The theory of consumer choice can be summarized as follows:

- The choices made by real people resemble the choices made by the artificial people in the model economy.
- Spending patterns in the model look like the actual spending patterns in the real world.

What the Theory Is Not The theory of consumer choice does *not* say that people compute marginal rates of substitution and then set them equal to relative prices to decide how much of each good to buy. Economists do not have a theory about the mental processes that people use to arrive at their choices.

Back to the Facts

We started this chapter by observing how consumer spending has changed over the years. The theory of consumption choice studied in this chapter can be used to explain those changes. Spending patterns are interpreted as being the best choices that households can make, given their preferences and incomes and given the prices of the goods they consume. Changes in prices and in income lead to changes in the best possible choice—changes in consumption patterns.

Models based on the same ideas you've studied here are used to explain the actual changes that occur and to measure the response of consumption to changes in prices and in income—the price and income elasticities of demand. You met some measures of these elasticities in Chapter 5. Most of those elasticities were measured by using models of exactly the same type that we've studied here (but models that have more than two goods).

But the model of household choice can do much more than explain consumption choices. It can be used to explain a wide range of other household choices. Let's look at some of these.

Other Household Choices

Households make many choices other than those about how to spend their income on the various goods and services available. But we can use the model of consumer choice to understand many other household choices. Some of these are discussed in Our Advancing Knowledge on pp. 172–173. Here, we'll study the two key choices that households make. They are

- How many hours to work
- How much to save

Work Hours and Labor Supply

Every day, we have to allocate our 24 hours among leisure, working for ourselves, and working for someone else. When we work for someone else, we are supplying labor.

We can understand our labor supply decisions by using the theory of household choice. Supplying more labor is exactly the same thing as consuming less leisure. Leisure is a good, just like movies and soda. Other things being equal, a situation that has more leisure is preferred to one that has less leisure. We have indifference curves for leisure and consumption goods that are similar to those we've already studied. For example, we can relabel the axes of Fig. 8.4 so that instead of soda, we measure all consumption goods on the *y*-axis, and instead of movies, we measure leisure on the *x*-axis.

We can't have as much leisure and consumption as we'd like. Our choices are constrained by the wages that we can earn. For a given hourly wage rate, increasing our consumption of goods and services is possible only if we decrease our leisure time and increase our supply of labor. The wage rate that we can earn determines how much extra consumption we can undertake by giving up an extra hour of leisure. The magnitude of the slope of our indifference curve tells us the marginal rate of substitution—the rate at which we will be willing to give up consumption of goods and services to get one more hour of leisure while remaining indifferent. Our best choice of consumption and leisure has exactly the same properties as our best choice of movies and soda. We get onto the highest possible indifference curve by making the marginal rate of substitution between consumption and leisure equal to the wage rate relative to the price of consumption goods.

Changes in wages affect our choice of consumption and leisure in a similar way to that in which a change in the price of movies affects our consumption of movies and soda. A higher wage rate makes leisure more expensive. There is a substitution effect encouraging us to take less leisure and work longer hours, thereby consuming more goods and services. But a higher wage rate also has an income effect. A higher wage leads to a higher income, and with a higher income, we consume more of all normal goods. Leisure is a normal good. Other things being equal, the higher the income, the more leisure we take. In Reading Between the Lines, pp. 198–199, Elizabeth Cook's high income has perhaps encouraged her to take more leisure.

People who can earn only a very low hourly wage rate tend to work fewer hours, or perhaps not at all. As the wage rate increases, the substitution effect encourages less leisure and more work to be undertaken. But as the wage rate keeps on increasing, the income effect eventually comes to dominate the substitution effect. The higher wage leads to higher consumption of goods and services and to additional leisure. It is the ultimately dominant role of the income effect that has resulted in a steadily shorter workweek despite the fact that wages have increased.

Saving

We don't have to spend all our income here and now. Nor are we constrained to consuming only our current income. We can consume less than our current income, saving the difference for future consumption. Or we can consume more than our current income, borrowing the difference and repaying our loan by consuming less later. Choosing when to consume, how much to save, and how much to borrow can also be understood by using the same theory of household choice that explained Lisa's allocation of her income to movies and soda.

Other things being equal, more consumption today is preferred to less. Also, other things being equal, more consumption in the future is preferred to less. As a consequence, we have indifference curves for consumption now and in the future that are similar to our indifference curves for any pair of goods. Of course, we cannot consume as much as we'd like to today or in the future. Our choices are constrained. The constraint on our choices depends on our income and the interest rate that we can earn on our savings or that we have to pay on our borrowing. The interest rate is a relative price—the relative price of consumption today versus consumption in the future. We choose the timing of consumption (and the amount of saving or borrowing to undertake) by making the marginal rate of substitution between current and future consumption equal to the interest rate. Thus high interest rates will discourage borrowing and lead to lower current consumption and higher future consumption.

◆ ◆ ◆ ◆ We've now completed our study of household choices. We've seen how we can derive the law of demand from a model of household choice. We've also seen how that same model can be applied to a wide range of other choices, including the demand for leisure and the supply of labor. ◆ ◆ In Part 4, we're going to study the choices made by firms. We'll see how, in the pursuit of profit, firms make choices governing the supply of goods and services and the demand for factors of production (inputs). ◆ ◆ After completing these chapters, we'll then bring the analysis of households and firms back together again, studying their interactions in markets for goods and services and factors of production.

Household Choice Theory in Action

The Wall Street Journal, August 5, 1991

Trading Fat Paychecks for Free Time

By Carol Hymowitz

What's the point of a six-figure salary with no time to enjoy it?

That's what Elizabeth Cook asked herself recently before she quit her Manhattan law job just to unwind. She traveled to Maine, where she learned how to make goat cheese.

"My life consisted of going to work and coming home for a few hours to catch some sleep," says Ms. Cook, a 33-year-old attorney, who routinely put in 14-hour days. "Friends stopped calling because I was always canceling on them at the last moment. And I began to realize if I didn't get off this treadmill, at 50 I'd be in the same spot, in the office at midnight faxing documents." Ms. Cook hopes to find a new job in September, but not one that requires such long hours—no matter how high the pay.

In companies around the country, a growing number of managers and professionals are balking at schedules that don't reflect their true priorities and values. They're admitting that the emphasis they have placed on career success and making lots of money hasn't made them very happy. Instead, they want time for family, friends and fun—even at a sizable income loss.

"Leisure time—not money—is becoming the status symbol of the 1990s," says John P. Robinson, who directs the Americans' Use of Time Project at the University of Maryland. "A large segment of Americans say they feel a significant time crunch—and the more time needy they feel, the stronger their desire to take time off."

So Much to Do, So Little Time

Americans' attitudes about their goals and the time pressures in their lives.

GOALS FOR THE 1990s	
77%	Spend time with family and friends.
74%	Improve yourself Intellectually, emotionally or physically.
72%	Save money.
66%	Have free time to spend any way you please.
61%	Make money.
59%	Pursue personal experiences such as traveling and hobbies.

Illustration by Chris Demarest

SUMMARY

Consumption Possibilities

A household's budget line shows the limits to consumption given the household's income and the prices of goods. The budget line is the boundary between what the consumer can and cannot afford.

Changes in prices and changes in income produce changes in the budget line. The magnitude of the slope of the budget line equals the relative price of the two goods. The point at which the budget line intersects each axis marks the consumer's real income in terms of the good measured on that axis. (pp. 180–184)

Preferences

A consumer's preferences can be represented by indifference curves. An indifference curve joins all the combinations of goods among which the consumer is indifferent. A consumer prefers points above an indifference curve to the points on it and prefers points on an indifference curve to all points below it. Indifference curves bow toward the origin.

The magnitude of the slope of an indifference curve is called the marginal rate of substitution. A key assumption is that of a diminishing marginal rate of substitution. In other words, the marginal rate of substitution diminishes as consumption of the good measured on the y-axis decreases and consumption of the good measured on the x-axis increases. The more perfectly two goods substitute for each other, the straighter are the indifference curves. The less easily they substitute, the more tightly curved are the indifference curves. Goods that are always consumed together are complements and have L-shaped indifference curves. (pp. 184–189)

Choice

A household consumes at the best affordable point. Such a point is on the budget line and on the highest attainable indifference curve. At that point, the indifference curve and the budget line have the same slope—the marginal rate of substitution equals the relative price. (pp. 189–191)

Predicting Consumer Behavior

Goods are classified into two groups: normal goods and inferior goods. Most goods are normal. When income increases, a consumer buys more normal goods and fewer inferior goods. If prices are held constant, the change in consumption resulting from a change in income is called the income effect.

The change in consumption resulting from a change in the price of a good is called the price effect. The price effect can be divided into a substitution effect and an income effect. The substitution effect is calculated as the change in consumption resulting from the change in price accompanied by a (hypothetical) change in income that leaves the consumer indifferent between the initial situation and the new situation. The substitution effect of a price change always results in an increase in consumption of the good whose price has decreased. The income effect of a price change is the effect of (hypothetically) restoring the consumer's original income but keeping the price of the good constant at its new level. For a normal good, the income effect reinforces the substitution effect. For an inferior good, the income effect offsets the substitution effect. (pp. 191–195)

Model, Theory, and Reality

A model of household choice is based on the assumption that households' preferences can be represented by indifference curves that bow toward the origin (that have a diminishing marginal rate of substitution). The model has the implication that the household will choose to consume on its budget line at a point at which the marginal rate of substitution and relative price are equal. A change in price leads to a new choice that corresponds to the law of demand: when the price of a good falls, the quantity consumed increases; when income increases, the demand for (normal) goods increases.

The Essence of the Story

According to John P. Robinson, director of a time-use research project, a large number of people are placing more emphasis on leisure time and less on money in the 1990s.

One such person is Elizabeth Cook, a former Manhattan attorney, who quit a job with long hours to unwind and hopes to find a new job with shorter hours—no matter how high the pay.

Managers and professionals in growing numbers say that making lots of money hasn't made them happy, and they want more time for family, friends, and fun—even at a sizable income loss.

Background and Analysis

People value both leisure time and consumption goods and prefer more of both to less of both. The amount of leisure that is willingly given up to get more consumption goods (measured in dollars) is described by an indifference curve such as I_0 in Fig. 1.

An unskilled worker whose wage is low has the budget line in Fig. 1 and makes the best choice possible by working 8 hours, taking 16 hours of leisure, and earning $40 a day.

An attorney whose wage is high has the budget line in Fig. 2 and makes the best choice possible by working 14 hours, taking 10 hours of leisure, and earning $1,400 a day.

An attorney who has been earning $1,400 a day for 10 years may have saved a large part of that income and is earning a large amount of interest on the saving. The interest income shifts the attorney's budget line rightward, as shown in Fig. 3. Now the best choice possible is to work only 8 hours and take 16 hours of leisure.

Much of the concern about leisure time is a reflection of the fact that we are becoming more wealthy and can afford more free time.

But high wages have an income effect—inducing more leisure and less work—and a substitution effect—inducing more work and less leisure. Each individual balances these forces and chooses her or his own best possible time allocation.

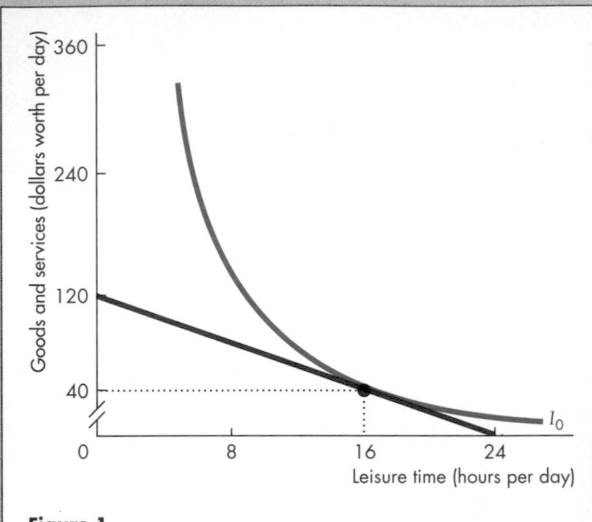

Figure 1

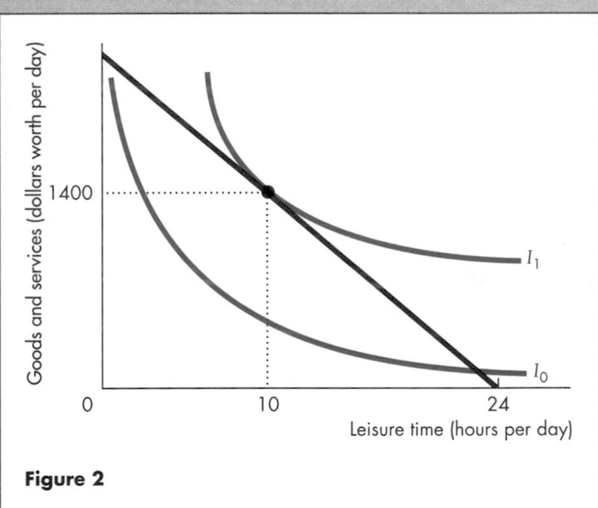

Figure 2

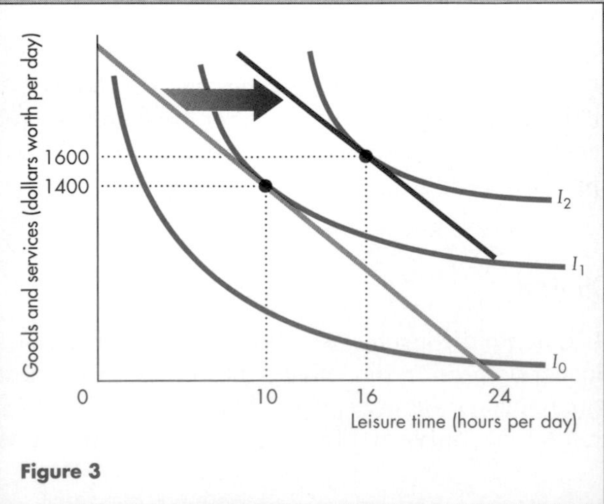

Figure 3

less soda than point c or more soda and fewer movies than point c. How does Lisa rank points in these areas against point c? To answer this question, we need to take the final step in constructing a map of Lisa's preferences.

Figure 8.3(c) takes the final step. It contains a line—I_1—passing through point c and through what were the two white areas. That line defines the boundary between points that Lisa prefers to point c and points she regards as inferior to point c. Lisa is indifferent between point c and the other points on the line I_1, such as point g. The line is called an indifference curve. An **indifference curve** is a line that shows all combinations of two goods that give the consumer equal satisfaction. The indifference curve in Fig. 8.3(c) shows all the combinations of movies and soda that give Lisa equal satisfaction.

The indifference curve shown in Fig. 8.3(c) is just one of a whole family of such curves. This indifference curve appears again in Fig. 8.4. It is labeled I_1 and passes through points c and g. Two other indifference curves are I_0 and I_2. Lisa prefers any point on indifference curve I_2 to those on indifference curve I_1, and she prefers any point on I_1 to those on I_0. We refer to I_2 as being a higher indifference curve than I_1 and I_1 as higher than I_0.

Indifference curves never intersect each other. To see why, consider indifference curves I_1 and I_2 in Fig. 8.4. We know that point j is preferred to point c. We also know that all points on indifference curve I_2 are preferred to all points on indifference curve I_1. If these indifference curves did intersect, the consumer would be indifferent between the combination of goods at the intersection point and combinations c and j. But we know that j is preferred to c, so such a point cannot exist. Thus the indifference curves never intersect.

A preference map consists of a series of indifference curves. The indifference curves shown in Fig. 8.4 are only a part of Lisa's preference map. Her entire map consists of an infinite number of indifference curves, all of them sloping downward and none of them intersecting. They resemble the contour lines on a map measuring the height of mountains. An indifference curve joins points representing combinations of goods among which a consumer is indifferent in much the same way that contour lines on a map join points of equal height above sea level. By looking at the shape of the contour lines on a map, we can draw conclusions about the terrain. In the same way, by looking at the shape of a person's indifference curves, we can draw conclusions about preferences. But interpreting a preference map requires a bit of work. It also requires some way of describing the shape of the indifference curves. In the next two sections, we'll learn how to "read" a preference map.

FIGURE 8.4

A Preference Map

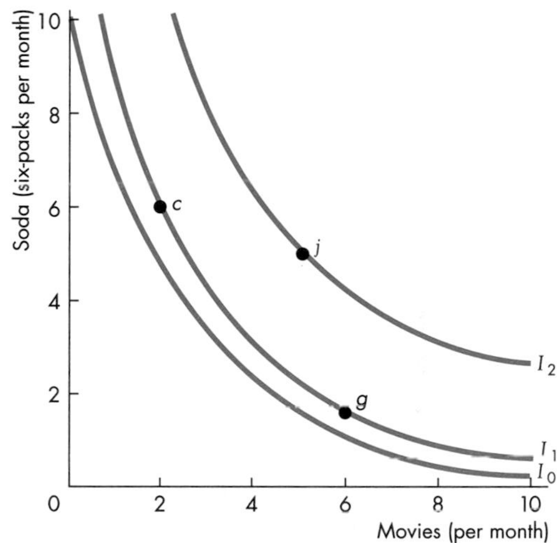

A preference map consists of an infinite number of indifference curves. Here, we show just three—I_0, I_1, and I_2—that are part of Lisa's preference map. Each indifference curve shows points among which Lisa is indifferent. For example, she is indifferent between point c and point g on indifference curve I_1. But points on a higher indifference curve are preferred to points on a lower indifference curve. For example, Lisa prefers all the points on indifference curve I_2 to all the points on indifference curve I_1; she prefers point j to points c or g.

Indifference Curves and Preferences

We use the concept of the marginal rate of substitution to describe the shape of an indifference curve. The **marginal rate of substitution** (or MRS) is the rate at which a person will give up good y in order to get more of good x and at the same time remain indifferent. The marginal rate of substitution is measured from the slope of an indifference curve. If the indifference curve is steep, the marginal rate of substitution is high. The person is willing to give up a large

The first two assumptions amount to the proposition that people's likes and dislikes do not depend on what they can afford to buy. This assumption does *not* mean that people's preferences do not change over time. Nor does it mean that their preferences are not influenced by the things that they have consumed and experienced. It *does* mean that just because income increases or the price of a good decreases, people do not, *for one of those reasons*, suddenly decide that they like a particular good more than they did before.

The third assumption—more of any good is preferred to less of that good—is just a different way of saying that wants are unlimited. Of course, in reality, you can imagine having enough of any one good to want no more of it, but there will always be something that you will prefer to have more of.

We are going to discover in this section a very neat idea—that of drawing a map of a person's preferences.

A Preference Map

Let's see how we can draw a map of a person's preferences by constructing a map of Lisa's preferences for movies and soda. This map, which appears in Fig. 8.3, measures the number of movies seen on the horizontal axis and the number of six-packs consumed on the vertical axis. Let's start with Fig. 8.3(a) and focus on point *c*, where Lisa sees 2 movies and consumes 6 six-packs of soda. We will use this point as a reference and ask how Lisa likes all the other points in relation to point *c*.

Figure 8.3(b) takes us to the next step. It is divided into four areas. The area shaded yellow has, at each point, more movies and more soda than at point *c*. Lisa prefers all the points in this area to point *c*. The area shaded gray has, at each point, fewer movies and less soda than at point *c*. She prefers point *c* to all the points in this area. Points in the two white areas have either more movies and

FIGURE 8.3

Mapping Preferences

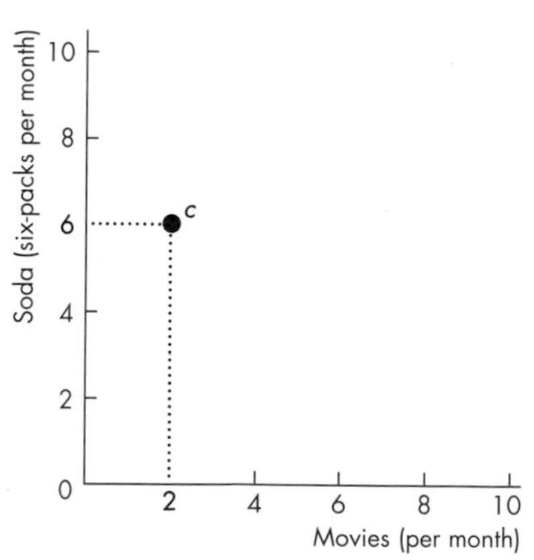

(a) A consumption point

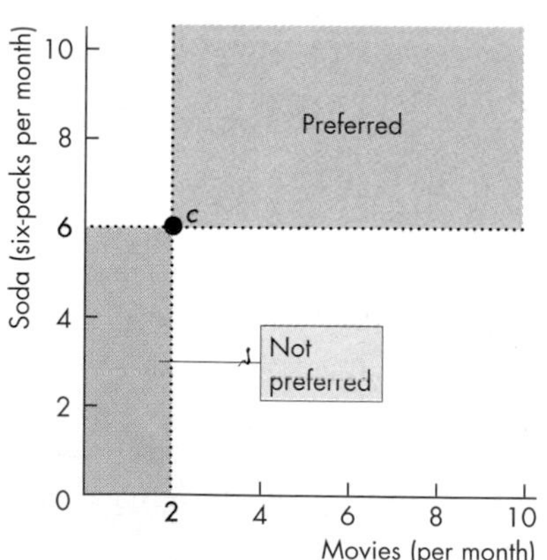

(b) Preference relations

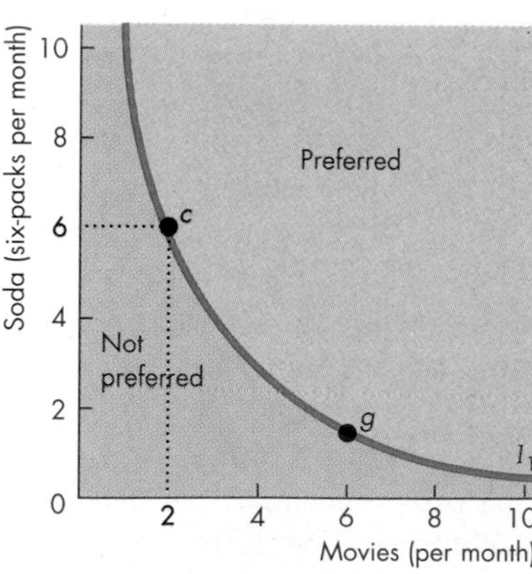

(c) Indifference curve

If Lisa consumes 6 six-packs of soda and 2 movies, she consumes at point *c* in part (a). Lisa prefers more goods to fewer goods. This fact is illustrated in part (b). She prefers any point at which she consumes more of both soda and movies to point *c* (all the points in the yellow area). She prefers point *c* to any point at which fewer movies and six-packs are consumed (all the points in the gray area). Whether she prefers seeing more movies but having less soda than at point *c* depends on how many more movies and how much less soda she has. Similarly, if she consumes more soda and sees fewer movies than at point *c*, whether she prefers that situation to *c* depends on how much more soda and how many fewer movies she has. The boundary between points that she prefers to point *c* and those to which *c* is preferred is shown in part (c). That boundary is called an indifference curve. Lisa is indifferent between points such as *g* and *c* on the indifference curve. She prefers any point above the indifference curve (yellow area) to any point on it, and she prefers any point on the indifference curve to any point below it (gray area).

The theory of household choice based on this model is that the choices made in the real world correspond to choices made in the model economy. Such a model is used to measure the response of consumption to changes in price and income—the price and income elasticities of demand that appeared in Chapter 5. (pp. 195–196)

Other Household Choices

The model of household choice also enables us to understand households' choices regarding the allocation of time between leisure and work, the allocation of consumption over time, and decisions regarding borrowing and saving. (pp. 196–199)

KEY ELEMENTS

Key Terms

Budget equation, 181
Budget line, 180
Diminishing marginal rate of substitution, 187
Income effect, 192
Indifference curve, 186
Marginal rate of substitution, 186
Price effect, 191
Real income, 182
Relative price, 182
Substitution effect, 193

Key Figures and Tables

Figure 8.1 The Budget Line, 180
Figure 8.3 Mapping Preferences, 185
Figure 8.4 A Preference Map, 186
Figure 8.7 The Best Affordable Point, 190
Table 8.1 Calculating the Budget Equation, 181

REVIEW QUESTIONS

1 What determines the limits to a household's consumption choices?

2 What is the budget line?

3 What determines the intercept of the budget line on the y-axis?

4 What determines the intercept of the budget line on the x-axis?

5 What determines the slope of the budget line?

6 What do all the points on an indifference curve have in common?

7 What is the marginal rate of substitution?

8 How can you tell how closely two goods substitute for each other according to the preferences of a consumer by looking at the consumer's indifference curves?

9 What two conditions are satisfied when a consumer makes the best possible consumption choice?

10 What is the effect of a change in income on consumption?

11 What is the effect of a change in price on consumption?

12 Define and distinguish between the income effect and the substitution effect of a price change.

PROBLEMS

1 Sara has an income of $9 a week. Popcorn costs $1 a bag, and cola costs $1.50 a can.

a What is Sara's real income in terms of cola?
b What is her real income in terms of popcorn?
c What is the relative price of cola in terms of popcorn?
d What is the opportunity cost of a can of cola?
e What is Sara's budget equation?
f Calculate the equation for Sara's budget line (placing cans of cola on the left side).
g Draw a graph of Sara's budget line with popcorn on the x-axis.
h In part (g), what is the slope of Sara's budget line? What is it equal to?

2 Suppose that with the same income and prices as in problem 1, Sara chooses to consume 4 cans of cola and 3 bags of popcorn each week.

a Is Sara on her budget line?
b What is her marginal rate of substitution of cola for popcorn?

3 Now suppose that the price of cola doubles to $3 a can and the price of popcorn doubles to $2 a bag. At the same time, Sara's income doubles to $18 a week.

a Can Sara still buy the same quantities of cola and popcorn as before if she wants to?
b What is Sara's real income now? What is the relative price? Describe how Sara's budget line has changed.

4 In problem 3, what are your answers if only:

a The price of cola changed
b The price of popcorn changed
c Sara's income changed

5 Jerry buys cookies that cost $1 each and comic books that cost $2 each. Each month, Jerry buys 20 cookies and 10 comic books. He spends all of his income. Next month, the price of cookies will fall to 50¢, but the price of a comic book will rise to $3.

a Will Jerry be able to buy 20 cookies and 10 comic books next month?
b Will he want to?
c If he changes his consumption, which good will he buy more of and which less of?
d Which situation does Jerry prefer—cookies at $1 and comic books at $2 or cookies at 50¢ and comic books at $3?
e When the prices change next month, will there be an income effect and a substitution effect at work or just one of them? If there is only one effect at work, which one will it be?

6 Now suppose that the prices of cookies and comic books are at their original levels—$1 and $2, respectively. Jerry gets a pay raise of $10 a month. He now buys 16 comic books and 18 cookies. For Jerry, are cookies and comic books normal goods or inferior goods?

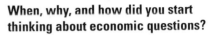

PART 4

Firms' Choices

Talking with Ronald H. Coase

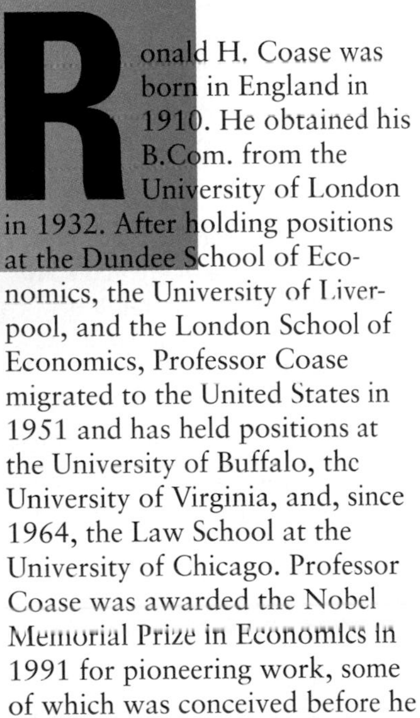

Ronald H. Coase was born in England in 1910. He obtained his B.Com. from the University of London in 1932. After holding positions at the Dundee School of Economics, the University of Liverpool, and the London School of Economics, Professor Coase migrated to the United States in 1951 and has held positions at the University of Buffalo, the University of Virginia, and, since 1964, the Law School at the University of Chicago. Professor Coase was awarded the Nobel Memorial Prize in Economics in 1991 for pioneering work, some of which was conceived before he received his bachelor's degree (see Our Advancing Knowledge, pp. 256–257).

When, why, and how did you start thinking about economic questions?

When I was an undergraduate at the London School of Economics, I did not take courses in economic theory. Most of my courses, such as those in accounting, statistics, and law, had nothing to do with economics. Arnold Plant had been appointed Professor of Commerce at the London School of Economics in 1930. Only five months before the final examinations in 1931, I took a seminar of his. It was a revelation to me to hear Plant explain Adam Smith's Invisible Hand and how the whole economic system was coordinated by a pricing mechanism that led producers to produce things that consumers valued most highly and to produce at the lowest cost. I was no doubt also influenced by the fact that I was very friendly with a number of fellow students who were economics specialists and we often talked about economics. The London School of Economics at that time was a very active place, and all sorts of ideas were being developed, such as the opportunity cost approach. While Plant's seminar got me going, it got me going in a place where economics

> "We should begin by taking a walk into the street and studying the real problems of the economic system."

was very much in the air. Even though I wasn't taking economics courses, I still talked about economics with other people. It was in this rather indirect way that I got interested in economics.

How did Plant's seminars shape your interest in the place of the firm and help lead to the incredible insights that provided the explanation of why firms exist?

Plant left me with a puzzle. It was the time of the Great Depression. Unemployment was everywhere, and people were producing all sorts of schemes for economic planning and coordinating the economic system. Plant was very much opposed to all these schemes for economic planning, and he pointed out that if you want coordination, the pricing mechanism acting through competition would give all the coordination necessary. This was a puzzle to me. If pricing did it all, why do we have management—the function of which is to coordinate? You must realize it seems a simpler question now that we know the answer than it was at that time.

So you had this puzzle, and you answered the puzzle. But how did such a young, untrained person come to have the insights that you had concerning the fundamental theory of the firm?

In fact, it is only an untrained person who could. If you receive thorough training in economics, you're trained in thinking in a particular way, and that means there are things you do not think about. After all, when did economists start taking an interest in the firm? Most still haven't. And yet most resources are employed within the firm. Certain questions never arise in their minds because they supposedly have all the answers.

There was one other important contributing factor. I went to the London School of Economics as a student in 1929, and I finished in 1931. The Russian Revolution had started in 1917, but it wasn't until 1928 that Stalin came to power and they had the first five-year plan. There was a lot of discussion going on at the time I was a student about planning in a communist society, with almost no experience of what it would be. Some economists in the West said that it was impossible to have a centrally planned economy. Lenin had said that the Russian economic system would be run as one big factory. Since we had factories in the West, some extremely large, why was it that you can't run society as one large factory? Anyway, those thoughts were flitting through my mind. It must be remembered that I was a socialist at that time.

You are on record as favoring plain English for the most part as the tool of analysis rather than mathematical and formal methods in economics. What is the place of those methods versus careful verbal, logical reasoning? And what do you think of the way we are training young economists today?

I've certainly been very critical of the way in which mathematics has been used in economics. I've been critical, for example, of how some economists develop very elaborate systems of analysis that are difficult to learn and use in order to study imaginary systems. I have no doubt at all that if ever we start to analyze the *actual* economic system, about which we currently know very little, then ultimately a mathematical approach will be needed. Just as in the natural sciences, interrelations in the economic system are so complex that mathematical analysis will be essential to understand them. But at the moment, we turn economic analysis into a game. Unable or unwilling to analyze the real economic system, we invent imaginary ones that we can study with the techniques we have at our disposal. There is no end to the work that can be done along these lines, but it's useless.

We start our work as economists by studying the work of other economists. Instead, we should begin by taking a walk into the street and studying the real problems of the economic system. When students focus their learning on what economists have said and are trained in the techniques of what economists do, they come out very well trained in certain techniques of analysis, and they then want to apply them. For example, nothing is bigger at the moment than game theory. Well, I think at present it's largely useless. People say, "Ah, but it must apply somewhere!" Maybe eventually we'll find that in certain areas and for certain problems the game theoretic techniques that have been developed are just what we need. But it's no good starting off with your techniques and then looking around for a problem to use them on.

Okay, let's take a walk into the street, so to speak, and discuss a major real-world problem: the way in which we allocate that scarce resource, the frequency spectrum. You wrote about this problem many years ago, and of course the frequency spectrum is an even more valuable resource today than it was then. What was behind your thinking on this issue?

What I suggested over 30 years ago was that instead of allocating use of the radiofrequency spectrum by means of administrative decisions—which are carried out in the United States in a very imperfect and inefficient way—we should use pricing. But pricing requires one to discuss what the highest bidder would actually purchase, and that led me to a discussion of the rationale of a property rights system.

The interesting thing is that these ideas that I put forward over 30 years ago are now being treated seriously. I know that they are being discussed within the

"But it's no good starting off with your techniques and then looking around for a problem to use them on."

"I don't start with the idea that there is an economic solution."

"Start by trying to frame the problem well and then learn along the way what techniques of analysis you will need to know to solve it."

Federal Communications Commission, for example. I've also learned that there are similar discussions going forward in France. There is no doubt work going on elsewhere that I don't know about.

Let's take a problem with a bigger global externality, such as the warming of the planet and increased carbon dioxide buildup. Do you see an economic solution to the problem of global warming based on your ideas about property rights?

Well, the answer is that I don't ever have an economic solution. That's what economists always have—that price should equal marginal cost, and things like that.

Many people think human beings have certain rights. That is not my position. The rights for me follow after you've discovered which ones promote the best sort of society. I try to look at the problem, make sure that it's correctly stated, ask what the real alternative institutional arrangements are for handling it, and then discuss which seems on the whole best. So I don't start with the idea that there is an economic solution. Rather, there's a choice among institutional arrangements.

But in a fundamental sense, that is economics, is it not?

It's what I'd like economics to be. One of the problems with economics is that we're so close to public policy, and the closer we are to public policy, the less solid the analysis tends to be. People are trying to promote certain solutions, and therefore they are less concerned with finding the truth than with producing studies that support their conclusions. Nowhere is it clearer to me that this happens than in subjects like global warming or the effects of radiation. Yet, it is very difficult to formulate or critique policy recommendations without first establishing the basic facts. The basic scientific facts about global warming are not at all clear. For example, the variation in temperature historically has been extremely great, ranging from Ice Ages to conditions that produce tropical forests. It's not clear whether that is due to something happening in the sun or some other cause. One of the difficulties in dealing with public policy questions is that the data are often so contaminated by the desire to promote certain positions that it is extraordinarily difficult to know what the basic facts really are.

What advice do you have for today's students of economics?

To look at the world and find problems they'd like to work on. I think the way to start is to look for problems, things for which we don't have a decent answer.

What tools of reasoning and what tools of analysis do you recommend they bring to bear on the problems?

The ones necessary to solve it! Don't bother too much about learning the methods of analysis, but start by trying to frame the problem well and then learn along the way what techniques of analysis you will need to know to solve it.

CHAPTER 9

ORGANIZING PRODUCTION

After studying this chapter, you will be able to:

- Explain what a firm is and describe the economic problems that *all* firms face
- Describe and distinguish between different forms of business organization
- Explain how firms raise the money to finance their operations
- Calculate and distinguish between a firm's historical costs and its opportunity costs
- Define technological efficiency and economic efficiency and distinguish between them
- Explain why firms solve some economic problems and markets solve others

An Apple a Day

On a July day in 1977, a tiny new firm was born that grew into a giant—Apple Computer. But that day was not unusual. Every day a new successful firm is born. Apple began its life when Steven Jobs and Stephen Wozniak, two Stanford University students working out of a garage, bought a few components and produced the world's first commercially successful personal computer. From that modest start, Apple Computer has grown into a giant. Apple Computer is one of some 20 million firms that operate in the United States today. They range from multinational giants, such as IBM and Sony, to small family restaurants and corner stores. Three quarters of all firms are operated by their owners, as Apple once was. But corporations (like Apple today) account for 90 percent of all business sales. What are the different forms a firm can take? Why do some firms remain small, while others become giants? Why are most firms owner-operated, while most business is undertaken by corporations? ◆◆ Firms spend billions of dollars on buildings and production lines and on developing and marketing new products. How does a firm get the finances needed to pay for all these activities? What do investors expect in return when they put money into a firm? And how do we measure a firm's economic health? ◆◆ The market is an amazing mechanism for coordinating the economic actions of millions of individuals. Firms are another type of coordination mechanism. Why do firms coordinate some activities and markets others? Why don't people simply buy everything they need from each other in markets?

◆ ◆ ◆ ◆ In this chapter we are going to learn about the many different types of firms, but we'll understand better the behavior of all firms if we focus first on the things they have in common.

The Firm and Its Economic Problem

The 20 million firms in the United States differ enormously in size and in what they do. What do they have in common? What is the distinguishing characteristic of a firm? What are the different ways in which firms are organized? Why are there different forms of organization? These are the questions we'll tackle first.

What Is a Firm?

A **firm** is an institution that hires factors of production and *organizes* them to produce and sell goods and services. To organize production, a firm enters into a wide range of relationships with a large number of individuals and other firms.

One of these relationships is that between the firm and its owner (or owners), since a firm has a separate legal identity from the individuals who own it. For example, if you buy a share in the stock of the Bank of America, you are a part owner of that company. You have a relationship with the company that defines your obligations if the company cannot meet its debts and that defines your rights to a share in the company's profits.

Other relationships are those between a firm and its managers and other workers. For example, if you get a job at the Bank of America as a teller, you are an employee of the company. You have a relationship with the company that defines your obligations to perform certain tasks in exchange for a compensation and benefits package.

A firm also has relationships with other firms. For example, if you run a window-cleaning company and get a contract with the Bank of America to clean its office windows, you have a relationship with the bank that defines your agreement to perform a specific service for a specific price.

Principal-Agent Relationships

The relationships between a firm and its owners, managers, and workers and between a firm and other firms are called **agency relationships.** In an agency relationship an *agent* undertakes an action that affects a *principal.* An **agent** is a person (or firm) hired by a firm (or another person) to do a specified job. A **principal** is a firm (or person) that hires a person (or firm) to undertake a specified job. For example, as a stockholder of the Bank of America, you are a principal and the managers are your agents. Your profit depends on how good a job the managers do. As a teller, your manager is a principal and you are an agent. Your performance determines whether the bank gains a new valued customer, helping the manager to meet her operating targets. As the window cleaner, you are also an agent and the bank is the principal. The bank wants clean windows, but the quality of your work determines whether it gets them.

The Firm's Decisions

Firms exist because of scarcity. They enable us to get more out of our scarce resources than would be possible if we didn't use the rich array of relationships that they embody. But each firm has to solve its own economic problem. That is, each firm has to get the most it can out of the scarce resources under its control. To do so, a firm has to decide on the following:

- Which goods and services to produce and in what quantities
- Which of its inputs to produce itself and which to buy from other firms
- Which techniques of production to use
- Which factors of production to employ and in what quantities
- How to organize its management structure
- How to compensate its factors of production and suppliers

A firm's receipts from the sale of goods and services are called *revenue.* The total payment that a firm makes for the services of factors of production is called *cost.* The difference between a firm's revenue and cost is its *profit* (if revenue exceeds cost) or its *loss* (if cost exceeds revenue). A firm's revenue, cost, and profits (or losses) are obviously affected by the choices it makes to solve its economic problem.

The goal of a firm's owners is to make the largest possible profit. But running a firm is not just a matter of giving orders and getting them obeyed. In most firms, it isn't possible for the shareholders to monitor the managers or even for the managers to monitor the workers and the other firms who supply it with goods and services. To achieve their goal, the firm's owners (principals) must induce its managers (agents) to pursue the maximum possible profit. And the managers (principals) must induce the workers and other firms (agents) to work efficiently. Each principal attempts to do this by creating incentives that induce each agent to work in the interests of the firm. For example, managers often share in a firm's profits, and workers get bonuses for meeting production targets.

But the perfect incentive scheme does not exist. Managers pursue their own goals, and so do workers. Nonetheless, firms constantly strive to find ways of improving performance and increasing profits.

Although all firms face common problems, they do not solve their problems in the same way. In particular, the management structure and the arrangements for compensating factors of production vary from firm to firm and lead to different forms of business organization. Let's look at these different forms.

The Forms of Business Organization

There are three main forms of business organization:

- Proprietorship
- Partnership
- Corporation

Which form a firm takes influences its management structure, how it compensates factors of production, how much tax its owners pay, and who receives its profits and is liable for its debts if it goes out of business.

Proprietorship A **proprietorship** is a firm with a single owner—a proprietor—who has unlimited liability. *Unlimited liability* is the legal responsibility for all the debts of a firm up to an amount equal to the entire wealth of the owner. If a proprietorship cannot pay its debts, the personal property of the owner can be claimed by those to whom the firm owes money. Corner stores, computer programmers, professional athletes, and artists are all examples of proprietorships.

The proprietor makes the management decisions and is the firm's sole residual claimant. A firm's *residual claimant* is the person who receives the firm's profits and is responsible for its losses.

The profits of a proprietorship are part of the income of the proprietor. They are added to any other income that the proprietor has and are taxed as personal income.

Partnership A **partnership** is a firm with two or more owners who have unlimited liability. Partners must agree on an appropriate management structure and on how to divide the firm's profits among themselves. As in a proprietorship, the profits of a partnership are taxed as the personal income of the owners. But each partner is legally liable for all the debts of the partnership (only limited by the wealth of an individual partner). Liability for the full debts of the partnership is called *joint unlimited liability.* Most law firms and accounting firms are partnerships.

Corporation A **corporation** is a firm owned by one or more limited liability stockholders. *Limited liability* means the owners have legal liability only for the value of their initial investment. The stock of a corporation is divided into shares. A *share* is a fraction of the stock of a corporation. Shares in most corporations can be bought and sold on stock markets such as the New York Stock Exchange.

Some corporations, no bigger than a proprietorship, have just one effective owner and are managed in the same way as a proprietorship. Large corporations have elaborate management structures headed by a chief executive officer and senior vice-presidents responsible for such areas as production, finance, marketing, and research. These senior executives are in turn served by a series of specialists. Each layer in the management structure knows enough about what happens in the layer below to exercise control, but the entire management consists of specialists who concentrate on a narrow aspect of the corporation's activities.

The corporation receives its financial resources from its owners (the stockholders) and by issuing bonds (loans on which it pays a fixed interest rate).

If a corporation makes a profit, the residual claimants to that profit are the stockholders. If a corporation incurs a loss on such a scale that it becomes bankrupt, the residual loss is absorbed by the banks and other corporations to which the troubled corporation is in debt. The stockholders themselves, by virtue of their limited liability, are responsible for the debt of the corporation only up to the value of their initial investment.

The profits of a corporation are taxed independently of the incomes of its stockholders, so corporate profits are, in effect, taxed twice. After the corporation has paid tax on its profits, the stockholders themselves pay taxes on their dividend income.

The Relative Importance of Different Types of Firms

Figure 9.1(a) shows the relative importance of the three main types of firms for the economy as a whole. The figure also shows that the revenue of corporations is much larger than that of the other two types of firms. Although only 20 percent of all firms are corporations, they generate 90 percent of revenue.

Figure 9.1(b) shows the percentage of total revenue accounted for by the different types of firms in various industries. Proprietorships account for a large percentage of revenue in agriculture, forestry, and fishing and in the service sector. They also account for a large percentage in construction and retail trades. Partnerships are more prominent in agriculture, forestry and fishing, services, mining, and finance, insurance, and real estate than in other sectors of the economy. Corporations are important in all sectors and have the manufacturing field almost to themselves.

Why do corporations dominate the business scene? Why do the other forms of business survive? And why are proprietorships and partnerships more prominent in some sectors? The answer to these questions lies in the pros and cons of the various different forms of business organization.

The Pros and Cons of Different Types of Firms

Since each of the three main types of firms exists in large numbers, each type obviously has advantages in particular situations. Each type also has its disadvantages, which explains why it has not driven out the other two. These pros and cons of each type of firm are summarized in Table 9.1.

FIGURE 9.1

The Relative Importance of the Three Main Types of Firms

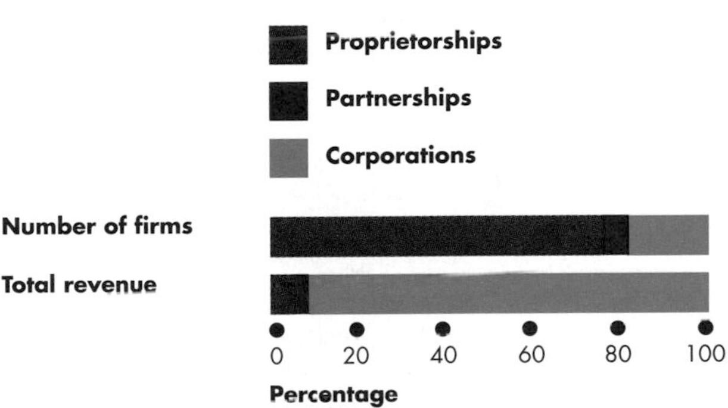

(a) Number of firms and total revenue

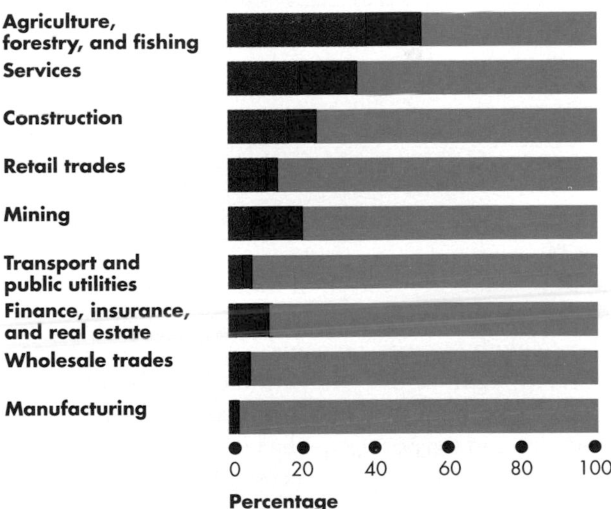

(b) Total revenue in various industries

Three quarters of all firms are proprietorships, a fifth are corporations, and only a twentieth are partnerships. Corporations account for 90 percent of business revenue (part a). But proprietorships and partnerships account for a significant percentage of business revenue in some industries (part b). These types of firms are especially significant in agriculture and services.

Source: U.S. Bureau of the Census, *Statistical Abstract of the United States: 1990,* 110th ed. (Washington, D.C.: 1990): 521, 641.

TABLE 9.1

The Pros and Cons of Different Types of Firms

Type of firm	Pros	Cons
Proprietorship	◆ Easy to set up ◆ Simple decision making ◆ Profits taxed only once as owner's income	◆ Bad decisions not checked by need for consensus ◆ Owner's entire wealth at risk ◆ Firm dies with owner ◆ Capital is expensive ◆ Labor is expensive
Partnership	◆ Easy to set up ◆ Diversified decision making ◆ Can survive withdrawal of partner ◆ Profits taxed only once as owners' incomes	◆ Achieving consensus may be slow and expensive ◆ Owners' entire wealth at risk ◆ Withdrawal of partner may create capital shortage ◆ Capital is expensive
Corporation	◆ Owners have limited liability ◆ Large-scale, low-cost capital available ◆ Professional management not restricted by ability of owners ◆ Perpetual life ◆ Long-term labor contracts cut labor costs	◆ Complex management structure can make decisions slow and expensive ◆ Profits bear corporation tax and dividends are taxed as income of stockholders

REVIEW

A firm is an institution that enters into a wide range of relationships—agency relationships—with owners, managers, workers, and other firms to organize the production of goods and services. Each main type of firm—proprietorship, partnership, and corporation—has its advantages and each plays a role in every sector of the economy. ◆

Business Finance

Every year firms raise billions of dollars to enable them to buy buildings, plant, and equipment and to finance their inventory holdings. Let's see how they do it.

How Firms Raise Capital

All firms get some of their capital from their owners. The owner's stake in a business is called **equity** or **equity capital**. Proprietorships and partnerships raise additional money by borrowing from the bank or from friends. This limits the amount of money that they can raise. Corporations raise much more money than partnerships and proprietorships. For example, an airline may raise hundreds of millions of dollars to buy a bigger fleet of jets. A steel manufacturer may raise hundreds of millions of dollars to build a new plant. The more permanent structure of corporations gives them two important ways of raising large sums of money that are not generally available to households and unincorporated businesses. They are

- Selling bonds
- Issuing stock

Let's look at these two ways in which corporations raise billions of dollars each year.

Selling Bonds A **bond** is a legally enforceable obligation to pay specified sums of money at specified future dates. Usually a corporate bond specifies that a certain sum of money called the *redemption value* of the bond will be paid at a certain future date called the *maturity date*. In addition, another sum will be paid each year between the date of issue of the bond and the maturity date. The sum of money paid each year is called the *coupon payment*.

An example of bond financing is shown in Fig. 9.2. On June 25, 1987, the General Cinema Corporation raised more than $100 million by selling bonds. On that day, General Cinema obligated itself to make a payment on the maturity date, July 1, 1997, of $125 million plus the interest then owing. It also committed itself to making a coupon payment of 9⅜ percent on July 1 each year. General Cinema did not get $125 million on July 1, 1987. The bonds were sold for 99¼ percent of the redemption value. That is, General Cinema received $99.25 for every $100 that it promised to pay back.

FIGURE 9.2

Selling Bonds

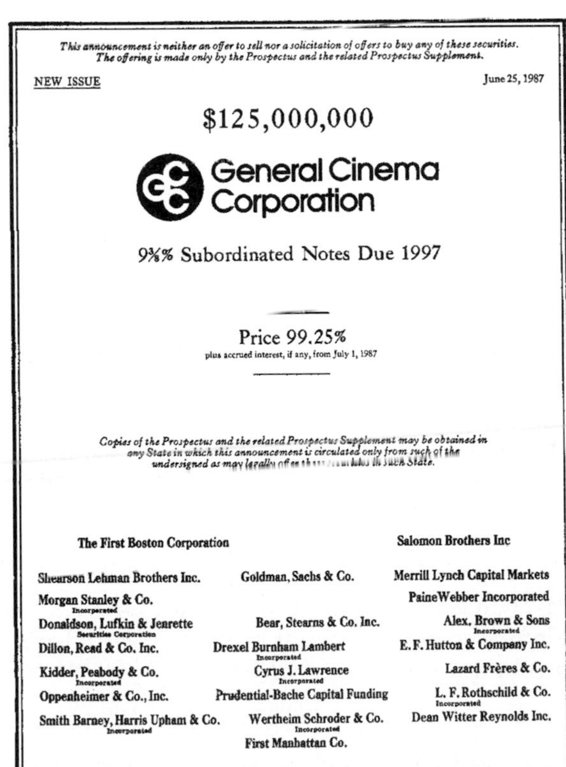

This announcement is neither an offer to sell nor a solicitation of offers to buy any of these securities. The offering is made only by the Prospectus and the related Prospectus Supplement.

NEW ISSUE June 25, 1987

$125,000,000

General Cinema Corporation

9⅜% Subordinated Notes Due 1997

Price 99.25%
plus accrued interest, if any, from July 1, 1987

Copies of the Prospectus and the related Prospectus Supplement may be obtained in any State in which this announcement is circulated only from such of the undersigned as may legally [illegible] in such State.

The First Boston Corporation
Salomon Brothers Inc

Shearson Lehman Brothers Inc.
Goldman, Sachs & Co.
Merrill Lynch Capital Markets
Morgan Stanley & Co. Incorporated
PaineWebber Incorporated
Donaldson, Lufkin & Jenrette Securities Corporation
Bear, Stearns & Co. Inc.
Alex. Brown & Sons Incorporated
Dillon, Read & Co. Inc.
Drexel Burnham Lambert Incorporated
E. F. Hutton & Company Inc.
Kidder, Peabody & Co. Incorporated
Cyrus J. Lawrence Incorporated
Lazard Frères & Co.
Oppenheimer & Co., Inc.
Prudential-Bache Capital Funding
L. F. Rothschild & Co. Incorporated
Smith Barney, Harris Upham & Co. Incorporated
Wertheim Schroder & Co. Incorporated
Dean Witter Reynolds Inc.
First Manhattan Co.

A bond is an obligation to make coupon payments and a redemption payment. General Cinema issued bonds promising to pay 9⅜ percent each year as a coupon payment. For each $100 of redemption value, General Cinema received $99.25.

Issuing Stock The second major way in which corporations raise money is by issuing stock. Money raised in this way is the corporation's *equity capital* because the stockholders of a corporation are its owners. They have bought shares of the corporation's stock.

There are three types of corporate stock:

- Common stock
- Preferred stock
- Convertible stock

Common stock entitles its holder to vote at stockholders' meetings and to participate in the election of directors. The holder of common stock is entitled to claim a dividend only if the directors vote to pay one. Such a dividend is paid at a variable rate, determined by the directors and varying according to the firm's profits.

Preferred stock gives no voting rights but gives a prior claim on dividends at a fixed rate, regardless of the profit level. If the corporation cannot meet all its obligations, preferred stockholders are paid before common stockholders but after bondholders.

Convertible stock entitles its holder to a fixed coupon payment together with the privilege of being able to convert the stock into a fixed number of shares of common stock. Thus convertible stock is not quite a bond and not quite a stock.

Corporations issue billions of shares of their stock, and these shares regularly trade on stock exchanges. A **stock exchange** is an organized market for trading in stock. The most important stock exchanges in the United States are the New York Stock Exchange (NYSE) and the American Stock Exchange (ASE) in New York City. Although only the NYSE is physically located on Wall Street, in the parlance of finance they are both "on Wall Street." Other major U.S. stock exchanges are in Boston, Philadelphia, Chicago, and San Francisco.

FIGURE 9.3

Issuing Stock

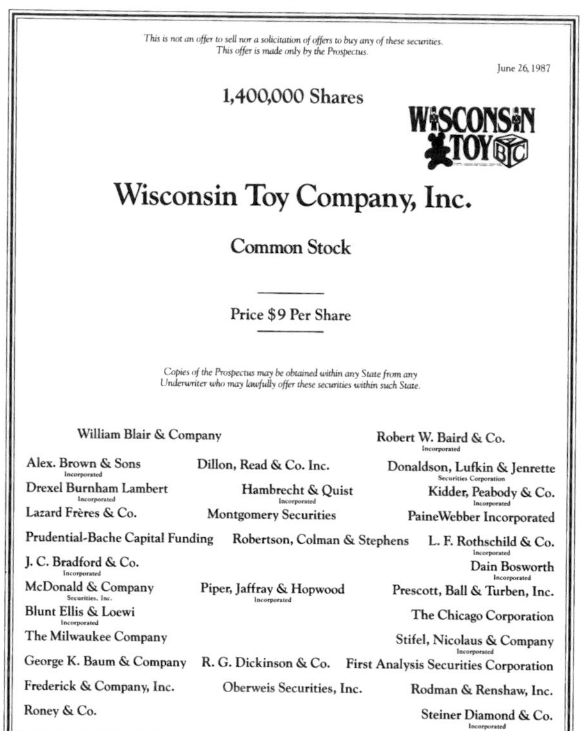

This is not an offer to sell nor a solicitation of offers to buy any of these securities. This offer is made only by the Prospectus.

June 26, 1987

1,400,000 Shares

Wisconsin Toy Company, Inc.

Common Stock

Price $9 Per Share

Copies of the Prospectus may be obtained within any State from any Underwriter who may lawfully offer these securities within such State.

William Blair & Company
Robert W. Baird & Co. Incorporated
Alex. Brown & Sons Incorporated
Dillon, Read & Co. Inc.
Donaldson, Lufkin & Jenrette Securities Corporation
Drexel Burnham Lambert Incorporated
Hambrecht & Quist Incorporated
Kidder, Peabody & Co. Incorporated
Lazard Frères & Co.
Montgomery Securities
PaineWebber Incorporated
Prudential-Bache Capital Funding
Robertson, Colman & Stephens
L. F. Rothschild & Co. Incorporated
J. C. Bradford & Co. Incorporated
Dain Bosworth Incorporated
McDonald & Company Securities, Inc.
Piper, Jaffray & Hopwood Incorporated
Prescott, Ball & Turben, Inc.
Blunt Ellis & Loewi Incorporated
The Chicago Corporation
The Milwaukee Company
Stifel, Nicolaus & Company Incorporated
George K. Baum & Company
R. G. Dickinson & Co.
First Analysis Securities Corporation
Frederick & Company, Inc.
Oberweis Securities, Inc.
Rodman & Renshaw, Inc.
Roney & Co.
Steiner Diamond & Co. Incorporated

Common stock is stock in a company that entitles its holder to vote at stockholders' meetings, to participate in the election of directors, and to receive a dividend (if the directors vote to pay one). Wisconsin Toy issued 1,400,000 shares of common stock at $9 a share, thereby raising $12,600,000 of additional capital.

An example of a firm raising capital by issuing stock is illustrated in Fig. 9.3. In June 1987, Wisconsin Toy Company, Inc. sold 1.4 million shares of common stock for $9 a share, thereby raising $12.6 million. Unlike the case of a bond, there is no obligation to make payments to stockholders. But there is an expectation of such payments—otherwise no one would buy the shares.

Financing Decisions and Stock Prices

A firm's financing decision has an important influence on its profits. Let's see how by looking a bit more closely at General Cinema and Wisconsin Toy. Was the bond issue a good deal for General Cinema? And did Wisconsin Toy get the right price for its stock?

Bond Sales and Cash Flows When General Cinema sold its bonds in 1987, it received $124 million (99.25 percent of $125 million). But it was then committed to making coupon payments of almost $11.7 million (9⅜ percent of $125 million) each year through 1996. Also, it is obliged to pay another $11.7 million (the final coupon payment) plus $125 million (the redemption value) in 1997. At that time, General Cinema will have paid out a total of $242 million, $118 million more than it received in 1987.

On the face of it, this appears to be a terrible way of doing business. Why would General Cinema find that a worthwhile deal? To answer this question, we need to understand a fundamental principle of business (and personal) finance.

Discounting and Present Value When a firm raises capital by selling a bond, it takes on an obligation to make a series of *future* payments. Cash flows into General Cinema in 1987 and out in 1988 through 1997.

If you are given a choice between a dollar today and a dollar a year from today, you will choose a dollar today. The same is true for General Cinema. A dollar in 1987 is worth more to General Cinema than that same dollar in 1988 and even more still than that same dollar in 1997. A dollar today is worth more than a dollar in the future because today's dollar can be invested to earn interest.

To compare an amount of money in the future with an amount of money today, we must calculate today's value—the present value—of the future amount of money. The **present value** of a future amount of money is the amount that, if invested today, will grow as large as that future amount, taking into account the interest that it will earn. Let's express this idea with an equation:

$$\text{Future amount} = \text{Present value} \times (1 + r).$$

If you have $100 today and the interest rate (r) is 10 percent a year ($r = 0.1$), one year from today you will have $110. Check that the above formula delivers that answer. One hundred dollars multiplied by 1.1 equals $110.

The formula that we have just used calculates a future amount from the present value and an interest rate. To calculate the present value, we just have to work backward. Instead of multiplying the present value by $(1 + r)$, we divide the future amount by $(1 + r)$. That is,

$$\text{Present value} = \frac{\text{Future amount}}{(1 + r)}.$$

You can use this formula to calculate present value. Calculating present value is called discounting. **Discounting** is the conversion of a future amount of money to its present value. Let's check that we can use the present value formula by calculating the present value of $110 one year from now if the interest rate is 10 percent a year. You'll be able to guess that the answer is $100 because we just calculated that $100 invested today at 10 percent a year becomes $110 in one year. Thus it follows immediately that the present value of $110 in one year's time is $100. But let's use the formula. Putting the numbers into the above formula, we have

$$\begin{aligned}\text{Present value} &= \frac{\$110}{(1 + 0.1)}\\ &= \frac{\$110}{(1.1)}\\ &= \$100.\end{aligned}$$

Calculating the present value of an amount of money one year from now is the easiest case. But we can also calculate the present value of an amount any number of years in the future. As an example, let's see how we calculate the present value of an amount of money available two years from now.

Suppose that you invest $100 today for two years at an interest rate of 10 percent a year. The money will earn $10 in the first year, which means that by the end of the first year you will have $110. If the interest of $10 is invested, then the interest earned in the second year will be a further $10 on the original $100 plus $1 on the $10 interest. Thus the total interest earned in the second year will be $11. The total interest earned overall will be $21 ($10 in the first year and $11 in the second year). After two years, you will have $121. From the definition of present value, you can see that the present value of $121 two years hence is $100. That is, $100 is the present amount that, if invested at 10 percent interest, will grow to $121 two years from now.

To calculate the present value of an amount of money two years in the future, we use the formula

$$\text{Present value} = \frac{\text{Amount of money two years in future}}{(1 + r)^2}$$

Let's see if the formula works by calculating the present value of $121 two years in the future if the rate of interest is 10 percent a year. Putting these numbers into the above formula gives

$$\begin{aligned}\text{Present value} &= \frac{\$121}{(1 + 0.1)^2}\\ &= \frac{\$121}{(1.1)^2}\\ &= \frac{\$121}{1.21}\\ &= \$100.\end{aligned}$$

We can calculate the present value of an amount of money any number of years in the future by using a formula based on the two that we've already used. The general formula is

$$\text{Present value} = \frac{\text{Amount of money available } n \text{ years in future}}{(1 + r)^n}$$

For example, if the rate of interest is 10 percent a year, $100 received 10 years from now will have a present value of $38.55. That is, if $38.55 is invested today at an interest rate of 10 percent, it will accumulate to $100 in 10 years. (You may want to check that calculation on your pocket calculator.)

Let's now return to the main question: why does it pay General Cinema to borrow $124 million in 1987 and pay out $242 million over the next 10 years?

The Present Value of a Bond First, General Cinema isn't planning to pay out $242 million on a $124 million loan just for fun. It plans to use the money for its business. Let's suppose that General Cinema plans to build $124 million worth of movie theaters in college towns across the country. It doesn't have $124 million in its pocket to spare. It can borrow the money from the bank at 9.5 percent interest. Alternatively, it can sell the bonds that we have just been describing. Let's suppose it sells the bonds.

You know from what you have learned about discounting that a sum of money paid two or five or 10 years in the future is worth a smaller sum today. Discounting tells you that the money General Cinema pays in future years to its bondholders is worth less today. How much less? To find out, let's calculate the present value of the bond payments.

We will use the formulas that we have just learned. To begin, we need to list the cash that General Cinema is going to receive and to pay out. Such a list appears in Table 9.2, in the column headed "Cash flow." A plus sign (+) means that money flows into General Cinema, and a minus sign (–) means that money flows out from General Cinema. In 1987, General Cinema receives $99.25 on each $100 worth of bonds. Between 1988 and 1996, the company makes coupon payments of $9.375. In 1997, the company makes a final coupon payment of $9.375 and redeems each bond for $100, so it makes a total payment of $109.375. To calculate the present value of this stream of receipts and payments, we divide each item by $(1 + r)^n$. The variable n is the number of years in the future that the money is paid, and r is the interest rate. Since General Cinema could have borrowed the money that it needs from the bank for 9.5 percent, that is the interest rate we will use for calculating the present value of a bond. The interest rate (r) is 0.095.

The results of our calculations are set out in Table 9.2 in the column headed "Present value." The present value of a sum of money today is the sum itself. So for 1987, the present value of the cash flow is $99.25. The present value of $9.375 one year hence is $8.562. How did we arrive at that figure? We used our formula:

$$\text{Present value} = \frac{\$9.375}{(1 + 0.095)} = \frac{\$9.375}{1.095} = \$8.562.$$

You can use your pocket calculator to verify this calculation. The further out we go into the future, the smaller are the present values. In the final year, when General Cinema makes a $100 payment to redeem the bond plus the coupon payment of $9.375 for the last year, the present value of that payment is $44.134.

The sum of the present values is called the net present value. The **net present value** of a stream of future payments is the sum of the present values of the payments in each year. As you can see, the net present value per $100 worth of bonds is $0.035 (or 3.5 cents) when the interest rate is 9.5 percent a year. The net present value of General Cinema's entire bond issue of $124,000,000 is $43,400 ($124,000,000 multiplied by $0.035 divided by $100). That is, the present value of the payments is $43,400 less than the amount received in the first place.

Now you can see that General Cinema was not so crazy to take in $124 million in 1987 and pay out $242 million over the next 10 years. The present value of its future payments is far smaller than $242 million. In our example, we used an interest rate of 9.5 percent to calculate the present value. Using other interest rates will yield different results. But if a bank loan at an interest rate of 9.5 percent is the alternative, issuing the bond is better than borrow-

TABLE 9.2

General Cinema Corporation Bonds: Cash Flow per $100 of Redemption Value

Year	Cash flow (dollars)	Present value at 9½% (dollars)
1987	**+99.250**	**+99.250**
1988	**–9.375**	**–8.562**
1989	**–9.375**	**–7.819**
1990	**–9.375**	**–7.141**
1991	**–9.375**	**–6.521**
1992	**–9.375**	**–5.955**
1993	**–9.375**	**–5.439**
1994	**–9.375**	**–4.967**
1995	**–9.375**	**–4.536**
1996	**–9.375**	**–4.141**
1997	**–109.375**	**–44.134**
Net	**–94.500**	**0.035**

ing from the bank. The wisdom of borrowing at all will finally depend on the profits of the new college town movie theaters. General Cinema will want the theaters to earn enough profits to meet the payments on the bonds.

The Price of a Share of Stock We've seen how one firm, General Cinema, lowered the cost of raising capital by selling bonds. But often firms issue new stock, such as the Wisconsin Toy Company did in 1987. That company raised $12.6 million by issuing 1.4 million shares of common stock for $9 a share. What determined the price for the shares of Wisconsin Toy's common stock? Why couldn't it get $10 a share? Why were people willing to pay more than $8 a share?

To answer these questions, we need to examine common stock as an investment. The holder of a share receives a dividend each year. Suppose that a corporation is expected to pay a dividend of $110 a share one year from now and nothing thereafter. What will such a share be worth? You probably guessed it: the share will be worth the present value of $110 one year from now. If the interest rate is 10 percent a year, the present value of $110 one year from now is $100. People will be willing to pay $100 for the share today. If the share sells for less than $100, there will be a strong demand for it, since the expected return on the share will exceed 10 percent, the prevailing interest rate. For example, if you can buy the stock for $90, and you receive $110 next year, you will have earned $20, or 22 percent, on your initial $90 investment. If someone tries to sell the share for more than $100, no one will buy it. No one will pay more than $100 for a claim to $110 one year from now if the interest rate is 10 percent. You will do better by simply putting $100 in the bank and collecting $110 in one year's time.

In general, the price of a share is the present value of its expected future dividends. To drive this fact home, let's consider another example. Suppose that investors expect a corporation to pay a dividend of $10 a share each and every year into the indefinite future. Suppose also that the interest rate is 10 percent a year. What will that corporate share be worth? The answer is $100. An investment of $100 in the share will produce $10 a year, or a return of 10 percent a year. That is the same as the interest rate available on other investments. The net present value of $10 a year forever, discounted at a 10 percent interest rate, is $100.[1]

Investors can estimate future dividends, but they cannot know them for sure, and their estimates can change. These changing expectations cause share prices to fluctuate dramatically. Because corporations pay dividends out of their profits, news about a corporation's profitability can change investors' expectations of future dividends.

One number that investors pay attention to is called the price-earnings ratio. The *price-earnings ratio* is the current price of a share divided by the current profit per share. A high price-earnings ratio means that investors are willing to pay a high price for a share compared to the profits that the share is currently earning. Such a situation arises when the firm's future profits are expected to be high relative to its current profits. A low price-earnings ratio means that investors are willing to pay only a low price for a share relative to its current earnings. This situation arises when future profits are expected to be low compared with current profits.

In this example, we have worked out how the price of a share of common stock is determined. The prices of preferred stock and convertible stock are determined in a similar manner and depend on the expected future stream of payments that will be made to the holders of those stocks.

---

[1]If you like algebra, you might find the following demonstration of this result helpful. First, write out the formula for the present value of $10 forever, at an interest rate of 10 percent (0.1):

$$PV = \frac{\$10}{1.1} + \frac{\$10}{(1.1)^2} + \ldots + \frac{\$10}{(1.1)^n} + \ldots.$$

The dots stand for the years between year 2 and year n and the years beyond year n. Next, divide this equation by 1.1 to give

$$\frac{PV}{1.1} = \frac{\$10}{(1.1)^2} + \ldots + \frac{\$10}{(1.1)^n} + \ldots.$$

Now subtract the second equation from the first to give

$$PV - \frac{PV}{1.1} = \frac{\$10}{(1.1)}.$$

Multiply both sides of this equation by 1.1 to give

$$(1.1)\,PV - PV = \$10, \quad \text{or} \quad (0.1)\,PV = \$10.$$

Finally, divide both sides of the last equation by 0.1 to give

$$PV = \frac{\$10}{0.1} = \$100.$$

So the present value of $10 forever at an interest rate of 10 percent is $100.

REVIEW

Firms finance purchases of buildings, plant, and equipment by selling bonds (promises of a fixed income independent of the firm's profit) and issuing stock (opportunities to share in the firm's profit). Firms borrow if doing so increases the net present value of their cash flow. The stock market value of a firm is equal to the present value of its expected future profits. ◆

Let's now turn to another aspect of a firm's finances—the measurement of its costs and profits.

Cost and Profit

Cost is the total payment made by a firm for the services of factors of production. There are two ways of measuring cost—the accountant's way and the economist's way.

Accountants measure historical cost. **Historical cost** values factors of production at the prices actually paid for them. Economists measure opportunity cost. *Opportunity cost* is the best alternative forgone. For example, the opportunity cost of an hour in the classroom is an hour of swimming if that is the best alternative forgone.

Although opportunity cost is a real alternative forgone, it is convenient, when measuring the costs of firms, to express opportunity cost in dollars. But don't lose sight of the fact that this measure is just a convenience. When we calculate the opportunity cost of producing something, we state what was given up to produce the good.

Historical cost sometimes equals opportunity cost. It does so when a firm pays for a factor of production at the same time as it uses it. The historical cost is the amount paid for the factor of production. But this same amount could have been spent on goods, so it is also the opportunity cost (expressed in dollars) of using this factor of production. For example, if a pizza restaurant hires a waiter, the wages paid are both the historical cost and the opportunity cost of the waiter—the firm pays the waiter at the same time as it uses the waiter. Labor is the most important factor of production whose historical cost typically equals its opportunity cost.

Historical cost and opportunity cost diverge when a firm pays for a factor of production and uses it some time later and when it uses a factor of production that it does not pay for.

Pay Now, Use Later

Factors of production that are not entirely used up in a single production period are called **durable inputs**. When a firm uses a durable input, it usually pays for the input long before it finishes using it. For example, GM buys an assembly line and then uses it over a period of a few years. Similarly, a firm may carry inventories of raw materials and semifinished products that it uses over a prolonged period. For example, GM keeps an inventory of steel sheets from which it presses car bodies. It may use sheets in production that it bought a year earlier. What is the opportunity cost of using equipment bought several years earlier? What is the opportunity cost of taking items from inventory?

Buildings, Plant, and Machinery Costs

The cost of buildings, plant, and machinery has two components:

- ◆ Depreciation
- ◆ Interest

Depreciation The fall in the value of a durable input over a given period of time is **depreciation.** Accountants assess this fall in value by applying a conventional depreciation rate to the original purchase price. For buildings, a conventional depreciation allowance is 5 percent a year. Thus, if a firm builds a factory for $100,000, the accountant regards 5 percent of that amount, $5,000, as a cost of production in the first year. At the end of the first year, the accountant records the value of the building as $95,000 (the original cost minus the 5 percent depreciation). In the next year, the accountant regards $4,750 as a cost of production (5 percent of the remaining $95,000 value of the building), and so on. The accountant uses different depreciation rates for different types of inputs. Fifteen percent is a common rate for plant and equipment.

Interest If a firm borrows money to buy a building, plant, or equipment, the accountant counts the interest on the borrowing as a cost of production. So, in this case, if the firm borrows the entire $100,000 and if the interest rate is 10 percent a year, the accountant treats the $10,000 interest payment as a cost of production. If the firm has not borrowed anything to build the factory but has instead used its own previously earned profits, the accountant regards the interest cost incurred in production as zero.

Next, let's see how economists determine these costs. Like accountants, economists also look at depreciation and interest costs to assess the cost of buildings, plant, and machinery, but economists calculate both as opportunity cost.

Economic Depreciation The change in the market price of a durable input over a given period is **economic depreciation.** For example, economic depreciation over a year is calculated as the market price of the input at the beginning of the year minus its market price at the end of the year. That amount is part of the implicit cost of using the input. The original cost of the equipment is not directly relevant to this calculation. The equipment could have been sold at the beginning of the year for the market price then prevailing. The opportunity cost of hanging onto the equipment, therefore, is the value lost by not selling it. If a firm has kept the equipment for a year and used it, the difference between its market prices at the beginning of the year and at the end of the year tells us how much of its value has been used up in production.

Sunk Costs A situation sometimes arises in which a firm has bought some equipment and the equipment is in place, functioning well, but has no resale value. The historical cost of buying that equipment is called a sunk cost. A **sunk cost** is the historical cost of buying plant and machinery that have no current resale value. The opportunity cost of using such equipment is zero.

Interest Costs The other cost of using durable inputs is interest. Whether a firm borrows to buy its buildings, plant, and equipment or uses previously earned profits to pay for them, it makes no difference to the opportunity cost of the funds tied up in the productive assets. If a firm borrowed the money, then the company made an interest payment. (That's the payment the accountant picks up using the historical cost method.) If the firm uses its own funds, then the opportunity cost is the amount that could have been earned by using those funds for something else. The firm could have sold the equipment at the beginning of the year and used the funds from the sale for some other purpose. At the very least, the firm could have put the money in the bank and earned interest. The interest passed up is the opportunity cost of the funds tied up in equipment, regardless of whether that money is borrowed or not. So the economist's measure of the interest cost of a durable resource—its opportunity cost—is the value of the input at the beginning of the year multiplied by the current year's interest rate.

Inflation Inflation complicates the calculation of opportunity cost. A change in prices that results purely from inflation—a rise in all prices—does not affect opportunity cost. To avoid being misled by inflation, we measure opportunity cost in terms of the prices prevailing in a single year. As a result of the high inflation rates experienced in the 1970s and early 1980s, accountants also have begun to pay attention to the distortions that inflation can cause in measuring historical cost and comparing costs between one year and another.

Implicit Rental Rate To measure the opportunity cost of using buildings, plant, and equipment, we calculate the sum of economic depreciation and interest costs. Another way of looking at this opportunity cost is as the income that the firm forgoes by not renting out its assets to another firm and instead renting the assets to itself. When a firm rents assets to itself, it pays an **implicit rental rate** for their use. You are familiar with the idea of renting equipment. People commonly rent houses, apartments, cars, televisions, VCRs, and videotapes; firms commonly rent earth-moving equipment, satellite launching services, and so on. When someone rents a piece of equipment, that person pays an *explicit* rent. When an owner uses a piece of equipment rather than renting it out, the economist notes that the owner could have rented the equipment out instead. By not doing so, owners *implicitly* rent from themselves. Another term that is sometimes used to describe an implicit cost or rent is an imputed cost. An **imputed cost** is an opportunity cost that does not require an actual expenditure of cash.

Next, let's examine inventory costs.

Inventory Costs

Inventories are stocks of raw materials, semifinished goods, and finished goods held by firms. Some firms have small inventories or inventories that turn over very quickly. In such cases, the accountant's historical cost and the economist's opportunity cost are the same. When a production process requires inventories to be held for a long time, the two measurements differ and possibly in important ways.

Historical Cost Measures To measure the cost of using inventories, accountants use a historical cost method called FIFO, which stands for "First In, First Out." This method of pricing the use of inventories assumes, as a convenient fiction, that the first item placed into the inventory is literally the first one out. An alternative accountant's measure that is used in some cases is called LIFO, which stands for "Last In, First Out." This measure, though not quite opportunity cost, is sometimes close to it, since it measures the cost of an inventory item at the price most recently paid. If prices are constant, the price most recently paid is the same as the price that will have to be paid to replace the used item and therefore is precisely its opportunity cost. But so is FIFO. When prices are changing, LIFO gets closer to the opportunity cost than FIFO.

Opportunity Cost Measures The opportunity cost of using an item from inventory is its current replacement cost. If an item is taken out of inventory, it will have to be replaced by a new item. The cost of that new item is the opportunity cost of using the item taken from inventory.

Inputs Not Paid For

A firm's owner often uses her or his own factors of production, and the firm doesn't directly pay for these factors. But they do have opportunity costs. Let's see what they are.

Owners' Wages The owner of a firm often puts a great deal of time and effort into working for the firm but rarely takes an explicit wage payment for this work. Instead, the owner withdraws cash from the business to meet living expenses. Accountants regard such withdrawals of cash as part of the owner's profit from the business rather than as a measure of the cost of the owner's time. But the owner could have worked at some other activity and earned a wage. The opportunity cost of the owner's time is the income forgone by the owner by not working in the best alternative job.

Patents, Trademarks, and Names Many firms have patents, trademarks, or a name that has come to be associated with reliability, service, or some other desirable characteristic. Sometimes firms have acquired these things by their own past efforts. In other cases, they have bought them. A firm always has the option of selling its patents, trademarks, or name to other firms.

In calculating historical cost, these items are ignored unless the firm actually bought them. But they have an opportunity cost regardless of whether they were bought. The opportunity cost of a firm's patents, trademarks, or name used in this year's production is the change in their market value—the change in the best price for which they could be sold. If their value falls over the year, there is an additional opportunity cost of production. If their value rises, there is a negative opportunity cost, or a reduction in the opportunity cost of production.

The Bottom Line

What does all this add up to? Is the historical measure of cost higher or lower than the opportunity cost measure? And what about the bottom line—the profit or loss of the firm? Does the accountant come up with the same answer as the economist, or is there a difference in the measurement of profit as well?

Profit is the difference between revenue and cost. There is no difference in the accountant's measure and the economist's measure of a firm's receipts or revenue. However, the two measures of cost generally differ. Opportunity cost generally includes more things than historical cost, so the historical measure of cost understates the opportunity cost of production. Thus profit as measured by economists is generally less than profit as measured by accountants. Profit as measured by economists is called economic profit. **Economic profit** is revenue minus costs, when the opportunity costs of production are included in costs.

To see how this works out, let's look at an example. Rocky owns a shop that sells bikes. His revenue, costs, and profit appear in Table 9.3. The historical view is on the left side, and the economic view on the right side.

TABLE 9.3

Rocky's Mountain Bikes' Revenue, Cost, and Profit Statement

The accountant

Item	Amount
Sales revenue	**$300,000**
Costs:	
Wholesale cost of bikes	**150,000**
Utilities and other services	**20,000**
Wages	**50,000**
Depreciation 10%	**22,000**
Bank interest	**12,000**
Total costs	**$254,000**
Profit	**$46,000**

The economist

Item	Amount
Sales revenue	**$300,000**
Costs:	
Wholesale cost of bikes	**150,000**
Utilities and other services	**20,000**
Wages	**50,000**
Rocky's wages (imputed)*	**40,000**
Fall in market value of assets†	**10,000**
Bank interest	**12,000**
Interest on Rocky's money‡ invested in firm (imputed)	**11,500**
Total costs	**$293,500**
Profit	**$6,500**

*Rocky could have worked elsewhere for $40 an hour, but he worked 1,000 hours on the firm's business, which means that the opportunity cost of his time is $40,000.

†The fall in the market value of the assets of the firm gives the opportunity cost of not selling them one year ago. That is part of the opportunity cost of using them for the year.

‡Rocky has invested $115,000 in the firm. If the current rate of interest is 10 percent a year, the opportunity cost of those funds is $11,500.

Rocky sold $300,000 worth of bikes during the year. This amount appears as his revenue. The wholesale cost of bikes was $150,000, he bought $20,000 worth of utilities and other services, and he paid out $50,000 in wages to his mechanic and sales clerk. Rocky also paid $12,000 in interest to the bank. All of the items just mentioned appear in both the accountant's and the economist's statement. The remaining items differ between the two statements; some notes at the foot of the table explain the differences.

The only additional cost taken into account by the accountant is depreciation, which the accountant calculates as a fixed percentage of Rocky's assets. The economist imputes a cost to Rocky's time and money invested in the firm and also calculates economic depreciation. The historical cost method puts Rocky's cost at $254,000 and his profit at $46,000. In contrast, the opportunity cost of Rocky's year in business was $293,500 and his economic profit was $6,500.

REVIEW

A firm's economic profit is the difference between its revenue and the opportunity cost of production. Opportunity cost differs from historical cost. Historical cost measures cost as the dollars spent to buy inputs. Opportunity cost measures cost as the value of the best alternative forgone. The most important differences between the two measures arise when assessing the cost of durable inputs and of inputs that the firm does not directly buy, such as the labor of the owner. ◆

We are interested in measuring the opportunity cost of production, not for its own sake, but so that we can compare the efficiency of alternative methods of production. What do we mean by efficiency?

Economic Efficiency

How does a firm choose among alternative methods of production? What is the most efficient way of producing? There are two concepts of efficiency: technological efficiency and economic efficiency. **Technological efficiency** occurs when it is not possible to increase output without increasing inputs. **Economic efficiency** occurs when the cost of producing a given output is as low as possible.

Technological efficiency is an engineering matter. Given what is technologically feasible, something can or cannot be done. Economic efficiency depends on the prices of the factors of production. Something that is technologically efficient is not necessarily economically efficient. But something that is economically efficient is always technologically efficient. Let's study technological efficiency and economic efficiency by looking at an example.

Suppose that there are four methods of making TV sets:

a. Robot production. One person monitors the entire computer-driven process.

b. Production line. Workers specialize in a small part of the job as the emerging TV set passes them on a production line.

c. Human production. Workers specialize in a small part of the job but walk from bench to bench to perform their tasks.

d. Hand-tool production. A single worker uses a few hand tools to make a TV set.

Table 9.4 sets out the amount of labor and capital required to make 10 TV sets a day by each of these four methods. Are all of these alternative methods technologically efficient? By inspecting the table you will be able to see that method *c* is not technologically efficient. It requires 100 workers and 10 units of capital to produce 10 TV sets. Those same 10 TV sets can be produced by method *b* with 10 workers and the same 10 units of capital. Therefore method *c* is not technologically efficient.

TABLE 9.4

Four Ways of Making 10 TV Sets a Day

Method	Quantities of inputs: Labor	Capital
a **Robot production**	**1**	**1,000**
b **Production line**	**10**	**10**
c **Human production**	**100**	**10**
d **Hand-tool production**	**1,000**	**1**

Of the four ways of making 10 TV sets a day shown here, only three are technologically efficient—methods *a, b,* and *d.* Method *c* is technologically inefficient because it uses the same amount of capital as method *b* but more labor.

Are any of the other methods not technologically efficient? The answer is no: each of the other three methods is technologically efficient. Method *a* uses less labor and more capital than method *b*, and method *d* uses more labor and less capital than method *b*.

What about economic efficiency? Are all three methods economically efficient? To answer that question, we need to know the labor and capital costs. Let's suppose that labor costs $75 per person-day and that capital costs $250 per machine-day. Recall that economic efficiency occurs with the least expensive production process. Table 9.5 calculates the costs of using the four different methods of production. As you can see, the least expensive method of producing a TV set is *b*. Method *a* uses less labor but more capital. The combination of labor and capital needed for method *a* winds up costing much more than that for method *b*. Method *d*, the other technologically efficient method, uses much more labor and hardly any capital. Like method *a*, it winds up costing far more to make a TV set using method *d* than method *b*.

Method *c* is technologically inefficient. It uses the same amount of capital as method *b* but 10 times as

TABLE 9.5

The Costs of Four Ways of Making 10 TV Sets a Day

Method	Labor cost ($75 per day)		Capital cost ($250 per day)		Total cost	Cost per TV set
a	**$75**	**+**	**$250,000**	**=**	**$250,075**	**$25,007.50**
b	750	+	2,500	=	3,250	325.00
c	**7,500**	**+**	**2,500**	**=**	**10,000**	**1,000.00**
d	**75,000**	**+**	**250**	**=**	**75,250**	**7,525.00**

much labor. It is interesting to notice that although method *c* is technologically inefficient, it costs less to produce a TV set using method *c* than it does using methods *a* and *d*. But method *b* dominates method *c*. Because method *c* is not technologically efficient, there is always a lower cost-method available. That is, a technologically inefficient method is never economically efficient.

Although *b* is the economically efficient method in this example, method *a* or *d* could be economically efficient in other circumstances. Let's see when.

First, suppose that labor costs $150 a person-day and capital only $1 a machine-day. Table 9.6 now shows the costs of making a TV set. In this case, method *a* is economically efficient. Capital is now sufficiently cheap relative to labor that the method using the most capital is the economically efficient method. Firms substitute capital for labor to take advantage of the low cost of capital.

Now, suppose that labor costs only $1 a day while capital costs $1,000 a day. Table 9.7 shows the costs in this case. As you can see, method *d*, which uses a lot of labor and little capital, is now the economically efficient method. Firms now substitute labor for capital.

A firm that does not use the economically efficient method of production makes a smaller profit. Natural selection favors firms that choose the economically efficient method of production and goes against firms that do not. In extreme cases, an inefficient firm may go bankrupt or be taken over by another firm that can see the possibilities for lower cost and greater profit. Efficient firms will be stronger and better able to survive temporary adversity than inefficient ones.

TABLE 9.6

The Costs of Three Ways of Making 10 TV Sets: High Labor Costs

Method	Labor cost ($150 per day)		Capital cost ($1 per day)		Total cost	Cost per TV set
a	$150	+	$1,000	=	$1,150	$115.00
b	**1,500**	**+**	**10**	**=**	**1,510**	**151.00**
d	**150,000**	**+**	**1**	**=**	**150,001**	**15,000.10**

TABLE 9.7

The Costs of Three Ways of Making 10 TV Sets: High Capital Costs

Method	Labor cost ($1 per day)		Capital cost ($1,000 per day)		Total cost	Cost per TV set
a	$1	+	$1,000,000	=	$1,000,001	$100,000.10
b	10	+	10,000	=	10,010	1,001.00
d	1,000	+	1,000	=	2,000	200.00

Firms and Markets

At the beginning of this chapter, we defined a firm as an institution that buys or hires factors of production and organizes these resources to produce and sell goods and services. In organizing production, firms coordinate the economic activities of many individuals. But a firm is not the only institution that coordinates economic activity. Coordination can also be achieved by using the market. In Chapter 1, we defined the market as a mechanism for coordinating people's buying and selling plans. By buying inputs and services in many individual markets, each one of us can organize the production of the goods and services that we consume. Consider, for example, two ways in which you might get your creaking car fixed:

- *Firm coordination.* You take the car to the garage. Parts and tools as well as the mechanic's time are coordinated by the garage owner, and your car gets fixed. You pay one bill for the entire job.
- *Market coordination.* You hire a mechanic who diagnoses the problems and makes a list of the parts and tools needed to fix them. You buy the parts from the local wrecker's yard and rent the tools from ABC Rentals. You hire the mechanic again to fix the problems. You return the tools and pay your bills—wages to the mechanic, rental to ABC, and the cost of the parts used to the wrecker.

What determines the method that you use? The answer is cost. Taking account of the opportunity cost of your own time as well as the costs of the other inputs that you'd have to buy, you will use the method that costs least. In other words, you will use the economically efficient method.

Firms coordinate economic activity when they can perform a task more efficiently than markets. In such a situation, it will pay someone to set up a firm. If markets can perform a task more efficiently than a firm, people will use markets and any attempt to set up a firm to replace such market coordination will be doomed to failure.

Why Firms?

There are three key reasons why, in many instances, firms are more efficient than markets as coordinators of economic activity. Firms achieve:

- Lower transactions costs
- Economies of scale
- Economies of team production

Transactions Costs The idea that firms exist because there are activities in which they are more efficient than markets was first suggested by Nobel Prize–winning University of Chicago economist

Ronald Coase.[2] Coase focused on the firm's ability to reduce or eliminate transactions costs. **Transactions costs** are the costs arising from finding someone with whom to do business, of reaching an agreement about the price and other aspects of the exchange, and of ensuring that the terms of the agreement are fulfilled. *Market* transactions require buyers and sellers to get together and negotiate the terms and conditions of their trading. Sometimes lawyers have to be hired to draw up contracts. A broken contract leads to still more expenses. A *firm* can lower such transactions costs by reducing the number of individual transactions undertaken.

Consider, for example, the two ways of getting your car fixed that we've just described. The first method requires that you undertake only one transaction with one firm. It's true that the firm has to undertake several transactions—hiring the labor and buying the parts and tools required to do the job. But the firm doesn't have to undertake those transactions simply to fix your car. One set of such transactions enables the firm to fix hundreds of cars. Thus there is an enormous reduction in the number of individual transactions that take place if people get their cars fixed at the garage rather than going through the elaborate sequence of market transactions that we described above.

Economies of Scale When the cost of producing a unit of a good falls as its output rate increases, **economies of scale** exist. Many industries experience economies of scale, and automobile and television manufacturing are two examples. Economies of scale can be reaped only by a large organization; thus they give rise to firm coordination rather than market coordination.

Team Production A production process in which individuals work in a group and each individual specializes in mutually supportive tasks is **team production.** Sport provides the best example of team activity. Some team members specialize in pitching and some in batting, some in defense and some in offense. The production of goods and services offers many examples of team activity. For example, production lines in automobile and TV manufacturing plants work most efficiently when individual activity is organized in teams, each specializing in a small task. You can also think of an entire firm as being a team. The team has buyers of raw material and other inputs, production workers, and salespeople. There are even specialists within these various groups. Each individual member of the team specializes, but the value of the output of the team and the profit earned depend on the coordinated activities of all the team's members.

The idea that firms arise as a consequence of the economies of team production was first suggested by Armen Alchian and Harold Demsetz of the University of California at Los Angeles.[3]

Because firms can economize on transactions costs, reap economies of scale, and organize efficient team production, it is firms rather than markets that coordinate most of our economic activity. There are, however, limits to the economic efficiency of firms. If firms become too big or too diversified in the things they seek to do, the cost of management and monitoring per unit of output begins to rise, and, at some point, the market becomes more efficient at coordinating the use of resources.

Sometimes firms enter into long-term relationships with each other that effectively cut out ordinary market transactions and make it difficult to see where one firm ends and another begins. For example, GM has long-term relationships with suppliers of windows, tires, and other parts. Wal-Mart Stores has long-term relationships with a wide variety of suppliers—see Reading Between the Lines, pp. 226–227. Such relationships make transactions costs lower than they would be if the firms went shopping on the open market each time they wanted new supplies. At the same time, a firm avoids diseconomies of scale that can arise if it becomes too big and its management becomes unresponsive to changing conditions.

◆ ◆ ◆ ◆ In the next chapter, we are going to study the choices of firms. We will study their production decisions, how they minimize costs, and how they choose the amounts of the various inputs to employ.

---

[2]Ronald H. Coase, "The Nature of the Firm," *Economica* (November 1937): 386–405.

[3]Armen Alchian and Harold Demsetz, "Production, Information Costs, and Economic Organization," *American Economic Review* 57, 5 (December 1972): 777–795.

Cutting Coordination Costs

The New York Times, July 1, 1991

Behind Wal-Mart's Surge, a Web of Suppliers

BY THOMAS C. HAYES

BIRMINGHAM, ALA. – The phenomenal success of Wal-Mart Stores can be traced in large part to the workrooms and factories of many of its suppliers, including the Liberty Trouser Company, a once-sleepy maker of work and hunting clothes.

Its marriage with Wal-Mart has given Liberty a hot new business in Liberty-brand children's wear for Wal-Mart. . . . Four Liberty sewing plants have been opened in northern Alabama in the last four years. . . .

Many suppliers and retailing experts think the close ties that Wal-Mart has with Liberty and its other suppliers is a reason the discounter has been able to continue its rapid growth. . . .

For Wal-Mart's hundreds of suppliers, which include Procter & Gamble, J. P. Stevens and Nintendo, demonstrating that they can keep the goods flowing can mean a long and lucrative partnership with Wal-Mart. . . .

There are many reasons for Wal-Mart's success. Customers like the prices. Suppliers like the fact that Wal-Mart's sophisticated computers spew out sales data regularly and alert them to coming orders, right down to the colors and sizes that are most neeed; with this order system, goods are rushed to stores, sometimes in as few as nine days. . . .

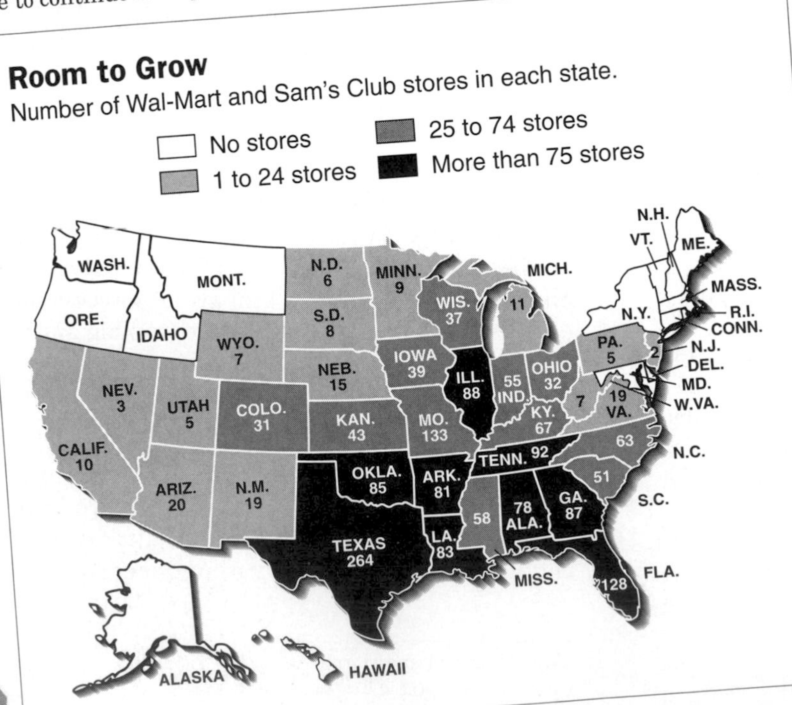

Wal-Mart has "a zealous approach," to cost containment, efficient buying, product knowledge and consumer buying habits, says Andrew S. Patti, president of the Dial Corporation, which makes soap and other consumer goods. "Under Sam Walton's direction," he said, "this company has changed the way companies like ours do business." . . .

. . . Four years ago, Mr. Walton wondered if Liberty's brand of railroad-style coveralls for children could be broadened into a line of tops and bottoms.

Knowing little then about children's fashion, the president of Liberty, Mitchell Ives, hired a New Jersey designer to whip up some fresh drawings.

Now Mr. Ives spends several hours a week on the phone with Wal-Mart executives, reviewing sales trends in their children's wear department to determine what fashions could be winners for the next season. By continually monitoring styles and prices at rivals like K Mart, Sears and Target stores, Wal-Mart knows the retail price it can charge for any item that Liberty makes.

When Liberty's production costs for any design appear too steep for the retail price Wal-Mart wants to charge, Mr. Ives and the Wal-Mart buyer will whittle away at the design. . . .

Once Liberty and Wal-Mart have agreed on a final design, cloth and acceptable pricing, Mr. Ives aims to ship the goods within four weeks. . . .

The Essence of the Story

Wal-Mart Stores, under the direction of Sam Walton, is able to sell high-quality goods at competitive prices by forming long-term relationships with manufacturers such as the Liberty Trouser Company, Procter & Gamble, J. P. Stevens, and Nintendo.

Retailing experts and suppliers think a key reason Wal-Mart has grown so quickly and been so profitable is its close ties with its suppliers.

Liberty has had rapid growth in the past four years as a result of its close relationship with Wal-Mart.

Four years ago, Mr. Walton asked Liberty to broaden its railroad-style coveralls for children into a line of tops and bottoms. Liberty's president, Mitchell Ives, responded by hiring a designer and coming up with the required range of clothes.

Mr. Ives and Wal-Mart executives monitor sales trends and predict next season's winners in children's fashions.

Wal-Mart continually monitors styles and prices at rival stores to determine the retail price it can charge for the items that Liberty makes.

If Liberty's production costs for a design are too high, Mr. Ives and the Wal-Mart buyer adjust the design until they have a product that can be priced to sell.

Once Liberty and Wal-Mart have agreed on a final design, Mr. Ives sets up a production schedule that will enable goods to be shipped within four weeks.

Wal-Mart's computers generate sales data and alert Liberty to coming orders—down to details such as colors and sizes—enabling goods to be rushed to stores, sometimes in as few as nine days.

Background and Analysis

In less than ten years, Wal-Mart has grown from 400 stores to become the nation's largest retailer with almost 1,800 stores, selling $33 billion worth of merchandise, and making an annual profit of $1.2 billion—see the figure.

It has stores in all regions except the Northeast and Northwest—see the map in the news story.

Wal-Mart is a spectacular example of a firm coordinating the economic activities of many individuals and firms.

Wal-Mart economizes on transactions and achieves economies of scale and team production by entering into long-term relationships with other firms.

Being a retailer, Wal-Mart stands between the consumer and the producer. It monitors the demands of consumers and the activities of its competitors and translates this information into a set of demands for specific products at specific prices.

Wal-Mart monitors the activities of suppliers, identifies which suppliers are capable of meeting its demands, and enters into long-term relationships with them.

By giving suppliers detailed information about future demand, Wal-Mart obtains its supplies at the least possible cost, and, because of the forces of competition, it passes on these low costs to its own customers.

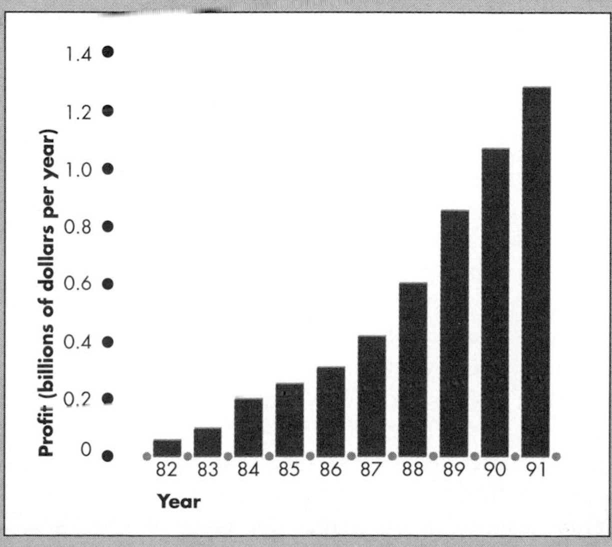

SUMMARY

The Firm and Its Economic Problem

A firm is an institution that enters into a wide range of agency relationships to hire factors of production that it organizes to produce and sell goods and services. In an agency relationship an agent undertakes an action that affects a principal and the principal sets the terms of the relationship to best achieve her or his ends. Firms decide what to produce and in what quantities, the techniques of production to use, the quantities of each factor of production to employ, the organization and management structure, and the arrangements for compensating the factors of production.

There are three main forms of business organization: proprietorship, partnership, and corporation. Each has its advantages and disadvantages. Proprietorships are easy to set up and face lower taxes than corporations, but they are risky and face higher costs of capital and labor. Partnerships can draw on diversified expertise, but they can also involve decision conflicts. Corporations have limited liability, so they can obtain large-scale capital at relatively low cost. They can hire professional management, but complex management structures can slow down decisions. Corporations pay taxes on profits, and their stockholders pay taxes on dividends. Proprietorships are the most common form of business organization, but corporations account for most of the economy's production. (pp. 209–212)

Business Finance

Firms raise money to finance their purchases of plant and equipment by selling bonds and issuing stock. When a firm sells bonds, it promises its bondholders a fixed payment that is independent of the firm's profit. When a firm issues stock, it offers stockholders an opportunity to become part owners of the firm but with limited liability for the firm's debts.

Firms take actions that are expected to increase the net present value of their cash flow. In deciding whether to raise money by issuing bonds, firms calculate the present value of the payments that they will obligate themselves to make to bondholders and compare that present value with that of some alternative method of financing. The value of a firm's stock is determined on the stock market by the present value of the expected future stream of dividends that the firm will pay from its profits. The value of a firm's stock is *not* determined by its *current profit,* although, to the extent that current profit is an indicator of future profit, it is a relevant factor. For this reason, the price-earnings ratios of firms vary considerably. (pp. 212–218)

Cost and Profit

Business profit is calculated as the difference between revenue and cost. Accountants and economists measure cost in different ways. Accountants measure historical cost; economists measure opportunity cost. Opportunity cost usually exceeds historical cost because it includes imputed costs that are not counted as part of historical cost. The different measures of cost lead to different measures of profit. Economic profit equals revenue minus opportunity cost. (pp. 218–221)

Economic Efficiency

There are two concepts of efficiency: technological efficiency and economic efficiency. A method of production is technologically efficient when, to produce a given output, it is not possible to use less of one factor of production without at the same time using more of another. A method of production is economically efficient when the cost of producing a given output is as low as possible. Economic efficiency requires technological efficiency. Economic efficiency also takes into account the relative prices of inputs. Economically efficient firms have a better chance of surviving than do inefficient ones. (pp. 222–224)

Firms and Markets

Firms coordinate economic activities when they are able to achieve lower costs than coordination through markets. Firms are able to economize on transactions costs and to achieve the benefits of economies of scale and of team production. (pp. 224–227)

KEY ELEMENTS

Key Terms

Agency relationship, 209
Agent, 209
Bond, 213
Corporation, 210
Depreciation, 218
Discounting, 215
Durable input, 218
Economic depreciation, 219
Economic efficiency, 222
Economic profit, 220
Economies of scale, 225
Equity, 212
Equity capital, 212
Firm, 209
Historical cost, 218
Implicit rental rate, 219
Imputed cost, 219
Inventories, 220
Net present value, 216
Partnership, 210
Present value, 214
Principal, 209
Proprietorship, 210
Stock exchange, 213
Sunk costs, 219
Team production, 225
Technological efficiency, 222
Transactions costs, 225

Key Figures and Tables

REVIEW QUESTIONS

1 What is a firm?

2 What are the economic problems that all firms face? List the main forms of business organization and the advantages and disadvantages of each.

3 What are the main ways in which firms can raise money?

4 What is a bond?

5 What is a stock?

6 What do we mean by net present value?

7 What determines the value of a bond?

8 What determines the value of a stock?

9 Distinguish between historical cost and opportunity cost. What are the main items of opportunity cost that don't get counted as part of historical cost?

10 Define economic efficiency.

11 Distinguish between economic efficiency and technological efficiency.

12 Why do firms, rather than markets, coordinate such a large amount of economic activity?

PROBLEMS

1 Soap Bubbles, Inc. has a bank loan of $1 million on which it is paying an interest rate of 10 percent a year. The firm's financial advisor suggests paying off the loan by selling bonds. Soap Bubbles, Inc. has to offer bonds with a redemption value two years in the future of $1,050,000 and with a coupon payment of 9 percent to raise $1 million.

a Does it pay Soap Bubbles to sell the bonds to repay the bank loan?

b What is the present value of the profit or loss that would result from repaying the bank loan and selling the bonds?

2 One year ago, Jack and Jill set up a vinegar bottling firm (called JJVB).

- Jack and Jill put $50,000 of their own money into the firm.
- They bought equipment for $30,000 and an inventory of bottles and vinegar for $15,000.
- They hired one employee to help them for an annual wage of $20,000.
- JJVB's sales for the year were $100,000.
- Jack gave up his previous job, at which he earned $30,000, and spent all his time working for JJVB.
- Jill kept her old job, which paid $30 an hour, but gave up 10 hours of leisure each week (for 50 weeks) to work for JJVB.
- The cash expenses of JJVB were $10,000 for the year.
- The inventory at the end of the year was worth $20,000.
- The market value of the equipment at the end of the year was $28,000.
- JJVB's accountant depreciated the equipment by 20 percent a year.

a Construct JJVB's profit and loss account as recorded by its accountant.

b Construct JJVB's profit and loss account based on opportunity cost rather than historical cost concepts.

3 There are three methods you can use for doing your tax return: a personal computer, a pocket calculator, or a pencil and paper. With a PC, you complete the job in an hour; with a pocket calculator, it takes 12 hours; and with a pencil and paper, it takes two days. The PC and its software cost $1,000, the pocket calculator costs $10, and the pencil and paper cost $1. Assume there is no depreciation.

a Which, if any, of the above methods are technologically efficient?

b Suppose that your wage rate is $5 an hour. Which of the above methods is economically efficient?

c Suppose that your wage rate is $50 an hour. Which of the above methods is economically efficient?

d Suppose that your wage rate is $500 an hour. Which of the above methods is economically efficient?

CHAPTER 10

Output and Costs

After studying this chapter, you will be able to:

- Explain the objective of a firm
- Explain what limits a firm's profitability
- Explain the relationship between a firm's output and its costs
- Derive a firm's short-run cost curves
- Explain how cost changes when a firm's plant size changes
- Derive a firm's long-run average cost curve
- Explain why some firms operate with excess capacity and others overutilize their plants

Survival of the Fittest

SIZE DOES NOT GUARANTEE SURVIVAL IN BUSINESS. OF the 100 largest companies in the United States in 1917, only 22 still remained in that league in 1991. But remaining small does not guarantee survival either. Every year, millions of small businesses close down. Call a random selection of restaurants and fashion boutiques from *last* year's yellow pages and see how many have vanished. What does a firm have to do to be one of the survivors? ◆◆ Firms differ in lots of ways—from Mom-and-Pop's convenience store to multinational giants producing hi-tech goods. But regardless of their size or what they produce, all firms must decide what to produce, how much to produce, and how to produce it. How do firms make these decisions? ◆◆ Most auto makers in the United States can produce far more cars than they can sell. Why do auto makers have expensive equipment lying around that isn't fully used? Many electric utilities in the United States don't have enough production equipment on hand to meet demand on the coldest and hottest days and have to buy power from other producers. Why don't such firms have a bigger production plant and supply the market themselves?

◆◆◆◆ We are going to answer these questions in this chapter. To do so, we are going to study the economic decisions of a small, imaginary firm—Swanky, Inc., a producer of knitted sweaters. The firm is owned and operated by Sidney. By studying Swanky's economic problems and the way Sidney solves them, we will be able to get a clear view of the problems that face all firms—small ones like Swanky as well as the giants.

Firms' Objectives and Constraints

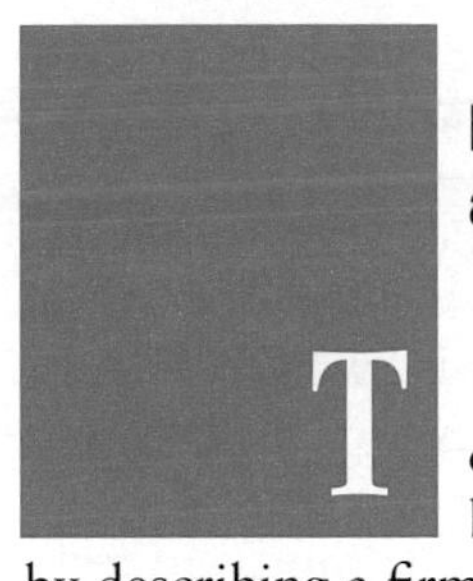

To understand and predict the behavior of firms, we will start by describing a firm's objectives—what it is trying to achieve.

The Objective: Profit Maximization

The firm that we will study has a single objective: profit maximization. **Profit maximization** is striving for the largest possible profit. As you know, the fundamental problem from which all economic activity springs is scarcity. Profit maximization is a direct consequence of scarcity. Seeking to make the best possible use of scarce resources is the same thing as trying to make the highest possible profit. A firm that tries to maximize profit has the best chance of surviving in a competitive environment and of avoiding being the target of a successful takeover by another firm.

Sidney is constantly striving to make the highest possible profits, but there are limits to, or constraints on, the profits that a firm can make. What are they?

Constraints

There are two types of constraints that limit the profits a firm can make. They are

- Market constraints
- Technology constraint

Market Constraints A firm's **market constraints** are the conditions under which it can buy its inputs and sell its output. On the output side, people have a limited demand for each good or service and will buy additional quantities only at lower prices. Firms have to recognize this constraint on how much they can sell. A small firm competing with many other firms in a large market has no choice but to sell its output at the same price as everyone else. It cannot, through its own actions, influence the market price. A large firm that dominates the market for a particular good can manipulate the price to its own advantage. But in so doing, it has to accept the fact that at higher prices it will sell lower quantities.

On the input side, people have a limited supply of the factors of production that they own and will supply additional quantities only at higher prices. Most firms, even large ones, compete with many other firms in the markets for factors of production and have no choice but to buy their inputs at the same prices as everyone else. Except in rare circumstances, firms cannot manipulate the market prices of their factors of production through their own actions.

We will study the output market constraints on firms more thoroughly in Chapters 11 through 13 and the input market constraints in Chapters 14 through 16. Swanky, the firm that we will study in this chapter, is small and cannot influence the prices at which it sells its sweaters or at which it buys the inputs used to make them.

Technology Constraint Firms use inputs to produce outputs. Any feasible way in which inputs can be converted into output is called a **technique.** For example, one technique that Swanky can adopt to produce sweaters uses workers equipped with knitting needles. A second technique uses labor and hand-operated knitting machines. A third technique uses automated knitting machines that require a small amount of labor to set them going and to reset them for different sizes and styles of sweaters. A fourth technique uses robotic knitting machines controlled by computers that automatically adjust the size, type, and color of the sweaters with human intervention only at the point of programming the computer. These different techniques use different amounts of labor and capital. But they are all capable of producing the same total output.

Some techniques are capital-intensive and some are labor-intensive. A **capital-intensive technique** uses a relatively large amount of capital and a relatively small amount of labor. A computer-controlled automated knitting machine is an example of a capital-intensive technique. A **labor-intensive technique** uses a relatively large amount of labor and a relatively small amount of capital. Knitting sweaters by hand—where the only capital equipment used is knitting needles—is an example of a labor-intensive technique.

To maximize profit, a firm will choose a technologically efficient production method. Recall the definition of technological efficiency that you encountered in Chapter 9—a state in which no more output can be produced without using more inputs.

Technological efficiency does not necessarily require the use of up-to-date or sophisticated equipment. When knitters are working flat out, even if they are using only needles, sweaters are being produced in a technologically efficient way. To produce more sweaters will require more knitters. No resources are being wasted. Similarly, when a computerized automated knitting plant is operating flat out, sweaters are also being produced in a technologically efficient way.

A firm can do no better than use a technologically efficient technique. But it must determine which technique to employ, since not all technologically efficient methods of production are economically efficient. Furthermore, the possibilities that are open to the firm will depend on the length of the planning period over which the firm is making its decisions. A firm that wants to change its output rate overnight has far fewer options than one that can plan ahead and change its output rate several months in the future. In studying the way a firm's technology constrains its actions, we distinguish between two planning horizons—the short run and the long run.

The Short Run and the Long Run

The **short run** is a period of time in which the quantity of at least one input is fixed and the quantities of the other inputs can be varied. The **long run** is a period of time in which the quantities of all inputs can be varied. Inputs whose quantity can be varied in the short run are called **variable inputs.** Inputs whose quantity cannot be varied in the short run are called **fixed inputs.**

There is no fixed time that can be marked on the calendar to separate the short run from the long run. The short-run and long-run distinction varies from one industry to another. For example, if an electric power company decides that it needs a bigger production plant, it will take several years to implement its decision. If United Airlines decides that it needs 100 additional Boeing 767s, it will take a few years for Boeing to turn out the new planes needed to accommodate United's demand. The short run for these firms is several years in length. At the other extreme, a laundromat or a copying service has a short run of just a month or two. New premises can be acquired and new machines installed and made operational quickly.

Swanky has a fixed amount of capital equipment in the form of knitting machines, and to vary its output in the short run, it has to vary the quantity of labor that it uses. For Swanky, labor is the variable input. The quantity of knitting machinery is fixed in the short run, and this equipment is Swanky's fixed input. In the long run, Swanky can vary the quantity of both knitting machines and labor employed.

Let's look a bit more closely at the short-run technology constraint.

Short-Run Technology Constraint

To increase output in the short run, a firm must increase the quantity of a variable input[1]. The firm's short-run technology constraint determines how much additional variable input is needed to produce a given amount of additional output. A firm's short-run technology constraint is described by using three related curves that show the relationship between the quantity of a variable input and:

- Total product
- Marginal product
- Average product

Total Product

The total quantity produced is called **total product.** The **total product curve** shows the maximum output attainable with a given amount of capital as the amount of labor employed is varied. Equivalently, the relationship between total product and the amount of labor employed can be described by a schedule that lists the amounts of labor required to produce given amounts of output. Swanky's total product schedule and curve are shown in Fig. 10.1.

[1]If you are anxious to move more quickly to a study of costs, you may omit this section and jump immediately to the section entitled "Short-Run Cost."

FIGURE 10.1
Total Product

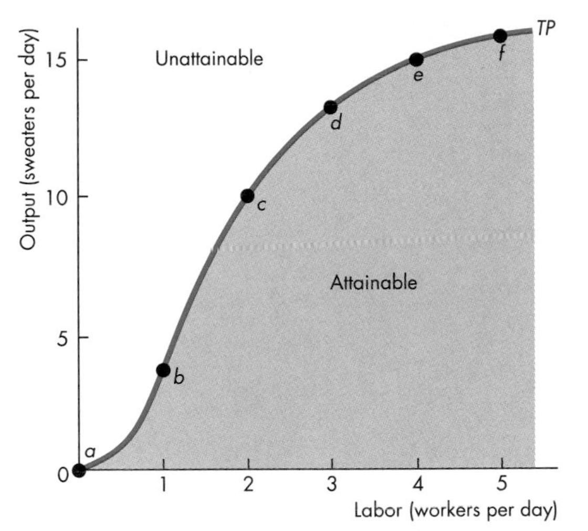

	Labor (workers per day)	Output (sweaters per day)
a	0	0
b	1	4
c	2	10
d	3	13
e	4	15
f	5	16

The numbers in the table show how, with one knitting machine, Swanky can vary the total output of sweaters by varying the amount of labor it employs. For example, 1 worker (row *b*) produces 4 sweaters a day; 2 workers (row *c*) produce 10 sweaters a day. The short-run production function is graphed here as the total product curve *TP*. Points *a* through *f* on the curve correspond to the rows of the table. The total product curve separates the attainable output from the unattainable.

As you can see, when employment is zero, no sweaters are knitted. As employment increases, so does the number of sweaters knitted. The total product curve for Swanky, labeled *TP*, is based on the schedule in the figure. Points *a* through *f* on the curve correspond to the same rows in the table.

The total product curve has a lot in common with the *production possibility frontier* you met in Chapter 3. It separates the attainable output levels from those that are unattainable. All the points that lie above the curve are unattainable. Points that lie below the curve, in the orange area, are attainable. But they are technologically inefficient—they use more labor than is necessary to produce a given output. Only the points *on* the total product curve are technologically efficient.

Marginal Product

The **marginal product** of any input is the increase in total product resulting from an increase of one unit of that input. The **marginal product of labor** is the change in total product resulting from a one-unit increase in the quantity of labor employed, holding the quantity of capital constant. It is calculated as the change in output divided by the change in the quantity of labor employed. In Swanky's case, the marginal product of labor is the additional number of sweaters knitted each day that results from hiring one additional worker each day. The magnitude of that marginal product depends on how many workers Swanky is employing. Swanky's marginal product of labor is calculated in the table of Fig. 10.2. The first two columns of the table are the same as the table in Fig. 10.1. The last column shows the calculation of marginal product. For example, when the quantity of labor increases from 1 to 2 workers, total product increases from 4 to 10 sweaters. The change in total product—6 sweaters—is the marginal product of the second worker.

Swanky's marginal product of labor is illustrated in the two parts of Fig. 10.2. Part (a) reproduces the total product curve that you met in Fig. 10.1. Part (b) shows the marginal product curve (labeled *MP*). In part (a), the marginal product of labor is illustrated by the orange bars. The height of each bar measures marginal product. Marginal product is also measured by the slope of the total product curve. Recall that the slope of a curve is the change in *y*—output—divided by the change in *x*—labor input—as we move along the curve. A 1-unit increase in labor input, from 1 to 2 workers, increases output from 4 to 10 sweaters, so the slope from point *b* to point *c* is 6, exactly the same as the marginal product that we've just calculated.

FIGURE 10.2

Total Product and Marginal Product

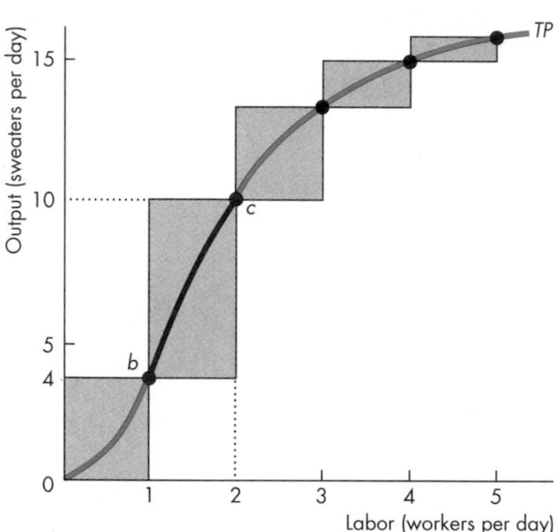

(a) Total product

	Labor (workers per day)	Output (sweaters per day)	Marginal product (sweaters per worker)
a	**0**	**0**	
			4
b	**1**	**4**	
			6
c	**2**	**10**	
			3
d	**3**	**13**	
			2
e	**4**	**15**	
			1
f	**5**	**16**	

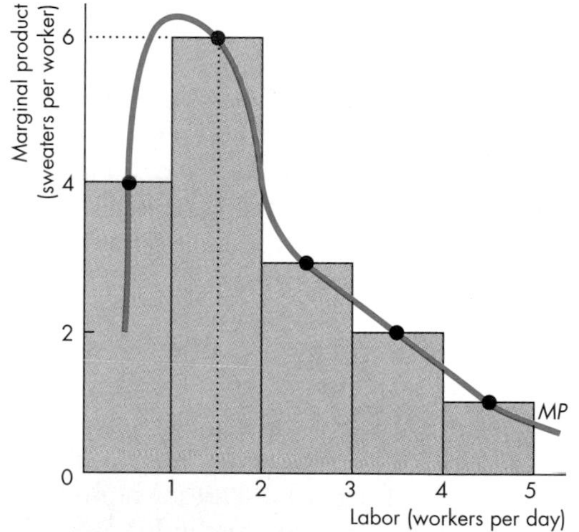

(b) Marginal product

The table calculates marginal product as the change in total product resulting from a 1-unit increase in labor input. For example, when labor increases from 1 to 2 workers a day (row *b* to row *c*), total product increases from 4 to 10 sweaters a day. The marginal product of the second worker is 6 sweaters. (Marginal product is shown midway between the rows to emphasize that it is the result of *changing* inputs—moving from one row to the next.)

Marginal product is illustrated in both parts of the figure by the orange bars. The height of a bar indicates the size of the marginal product. For example, when labor increases from 1 to 2, marginal product is the orange bar whose height is 6 sweaters (visible in each part of the figure). The steeper the slope of the total product curve (*TP*) in part (a), the higher is marginal product (*MP*) in part (b). Marginal product increases to a maximum (when 1 worker is employed in this example) and then declines—diminishing marginal product.

Notice the relationship between the total and marginal product curves. The steeper the *slope* of the total product curve, the higher is the *level* of the marginal product curve. The total product curve in part (a) of Fig. 10.2 shows that an increase in employment from 1 to 2 workers increases output from 4 to 10 sweaters (an increase of 6). The increase in output of 6 sweaters appears on the vertical axis of part (b) as the marginal product of the second worker. We plot that marginal product at the midpoint between 1 and 2 workers per day. Notice that marginal product shown in Fig. 10.2(b) reaches a peak at 1 unit of labor and at that point marginal product is more than 6. The peak occurs at 1 unit of labor because the total product curve is steepest at 1 unit of labor.

FIGURE 10.3

Total Product, Marginal Product, and Average Product

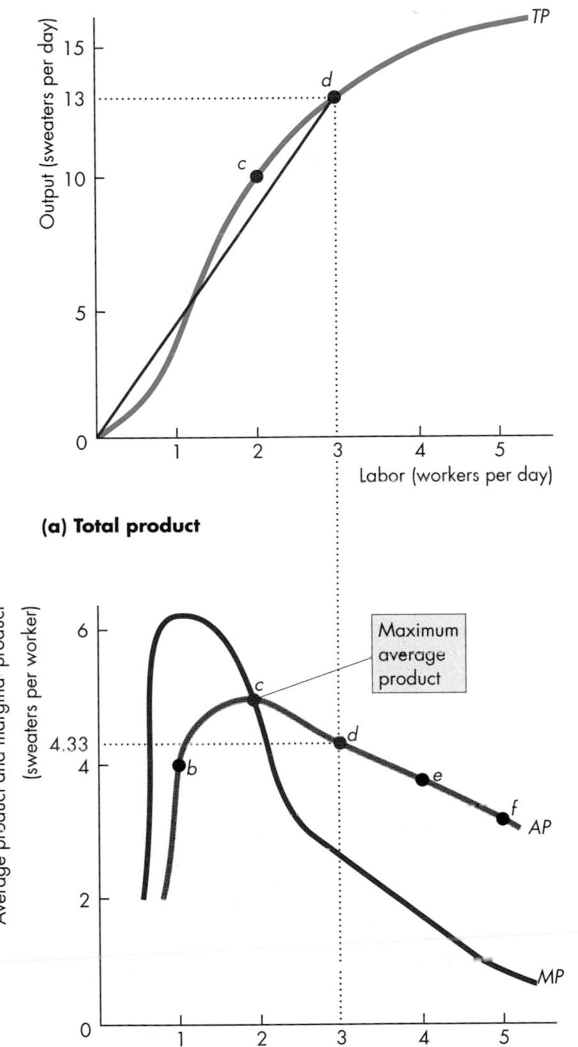

	Labor (workers per day)	Output (sweaters per day)	Average product (sweaters per worker)
b	**1**	**4**	**4.00**
c	**2**	**10**	**5.00**
d	**3**	**13**	**4.33**
e	**4**	**15**	**3.75**
f	**5**	**16**	**3.20**

Average product—total product per unit of labor—is calculated in the table by dividing total product by the quantity of labor employed. For example, in a day, 3 workers produce 13 sweaters, so the average product of 3 workers is 4.33 sweaters per worker.

The two parts of the figure show two ways of representing average product on a graph. In part (a), average product is measured as the slope of a straight line from the origin to a point on the total product curve. The straight line to point *d* is such a line. The slope of that line is 4.33 (13 sweaters divided by 3 workers). Part (b) graphs average product. Points *b* through *f* on the average product curve, *AP*, correspond to the rows of the table. Part (b) also shows the connection between the average product and marginal product curves. When marginal product exceeds average product, average product is increasing. When marginal product is less than average product, average product is decreasing. When marginal product and average product are equal, average product is at its maximum. Part (b) shows that marginal product increases from 0 to 1 worker and decreases thereafter and that average product increases from 0 to 2 workers and decreases thereafter.

Average Product

Total product per unit of variable input is called **average product.** In Swanky's case, average product is the total number of sweaters produced each day, divided by the number of workers employed each day. Swanky's average product is calculated in the table in Fig. 10.3. For example, 3 workers can knit 13 sweaters a day, so the average product is 13 divided by 3, which is 4.33 sweaters per worker.

Average product is illustrated in the two parts of Fig. 10.3. First, average product can be measured in part (a) as the slope of a line from the origin to a point on the total product curve. For example, at point *d*, 3 workers knit 13 sweaters. The slope of the line from the origin to point *d* is equal to the output—13 sweaters—divided by the quantity of labor used—3 workers. The result is an average product for 3 workers of 4.33 sweaters per worker. You can use this method of calculating average product to check that point *c* is the point of maximum average product. The steepest line from the origin that touches the total product curve touches only at *c*. Place a ruler on the curve and check that. Since the slope of such a line measures average product and this line is steepest when 2 workers are employed, average product is at a maximum at that point.

Part (b) graphs the average product curve, *AP*, and also shows the relationship between average product and marginal product. Points *b* through *f* on the average product curve correspond to those same rows in the table. Average product increases from 1 to 2 workers (its maximum value at point *c*) but then decreases as yet more workers are employed. Notice also that the highest average product occurs where average and marginal product are equal to each other. That is, the marginal product curve cuts the average product curve at the point of maximum average product. When marginal product exceeds average product, average product is increasing. When marginal product is less than average product, average product is decreasing.

Why does Swanky care about marginal product and average product? Because they have an important influence on the costs of producing sweaters and the way those costs vary as the production rate varies. We will examine these matters soon, but first we will take one more look at how marginal product and average product are related. You will meet this type of relationship many times in your study of economics and in your everyday life.

Relationship Between Marginal and Average Values

We have seen, in Fig. 10.3, that when marginal product exceeds average product, average product is increasing, and when marginal product is less than average product, average product is decreasing. We have also seen that when marginal product equals average product, average product is neither increasing nor decreasing—it is at its maximum and is constant. These relationships between the average and marginal product curves are a general feature of the relationship between the average and marginal values of any variable. Let's look at a familiar example.

Sidney (the owner of Swanky) attends an introductory economics class with his friends Steve and Sam. Each receives a grade of 70 percent in the course the first semester, but each achieved this in a different way. Table 10.1 illustrates how. They took four tests, each worth a quarter of the final mark. Sidney, preoccupied with managing Swanky, started out disastrously with 55 percent but then steadily improved. Steve started out brilliantly but then nosedived, while Sam scored 70 percent on every test.

We can calculate the average and the marginal scores of these three students. The average score is simply the total marks obtained divided by the number of tests written. After two tests, Sidney has an aggregate score of 55 percent plus 65 percent, which is 120 percent, so his average score is 60 percent. A student's marginal score is the score on the last test written. After two tests, Sidney's marginal score was 65 percent.

Over the four tests, Sidney's marginal score rises, Steve's falls, and Sam's is constant. But notice what the average scores are doing. For Sidney, the average is rising. His marginal score is higher than his average score, and his average rises. For Steve, the marginal score falls. So, too, does his average. Steve's marginal score is always below his average score and pulls his average down. Sam's marginal score equals his average score, so his average stays constant.

These examples of an everyday relationship between marginal and average values agree with the relationship between marginal and average products that we have just discovered. Average product increases when marginal product exceeds average product (Sidney). Average product decreases when marginal product is below average product (Steve). Average product is at a maximum and constant (it neither rises nor falls) when marginal product equals average product (Sam).

The Shapes of the Product Curves

Now let's get back to studying production. The total, marginal, and average product curves are different for different firms and different types of goods. Ford Motor Company's production function is different from that of Jim's Burger Stand, which in turn is different from that of Sidney's sweater factory. But the shapes of the product curves are similar, because almost every production process incorporates two features:

TABLE 10.1
Average and Marginal Test Scores

	Test	Test score	Aggregate score	Average score	Marginal score
Sidney					
	1	55	55	55	
					65
	2	65	120	60	
					75
	3	75	195	65	
					85
	4	85	280	70	
Steve					
	1	85	85	85	
					75
	2	75	160	80	
					65
	3	65	225	75	
					55
	4	55	280	70	
Sam					
	1	70	70	70	
					70
	2	70	140	70	
					70
	3	70	210	70	
					70
	4	70	280	70	

On the second test, Sidney scores 65 percent. After the first two tests, he has an average score of 60 percent. On the third test, Sidney scores 75 percent. His marginal score is the change in his aggregate score as the result of doing one more test. The marginal score after three tests is 75 percent. This score is located midway between the scores for the second and third tests to emphasize that it is associated with doing one more test. His marginal score now exceeds his previous average (60 percent), so his average after three tests is higher (65 percent). Steve's marginal score is below his average score, so his average falls. Sam's marginal score equals his average score, so his average remains constant.

- Increasing marginal returns initially
- Diminishing marginal returns eventually

Increasing Marginal Returns **Increasing marginal returns** occur when the marginal product of an additional worker exceeds the marginal product of the previous worker. If Sidney employs just one worker at Swanky, that person has to learn all the different aspects of sweater production—running the knitting machines, fixing breakdowns, packaging and mailing sweaters, buying and checking the type and color of the wool. All of these tasks have to be done by that one person. If Sidney hires a second person, the two workers can specialize in different parts of the production process. As a result, two workers produce more than twice as much as one. This is the range over which marginal returns are increasing.

Diminishing Marginal Returns *Increasing* marginal returns do not always occur, but all production processes eventually reach a point of *diminishing* marginal returns. **Diminishing marginal returns** occur when the marginal product of an additional worker is less than the marginal product of the previous worker. If Sidney hires a third worker, output increases but not by as much as it did when he added the second worker. With a third worker, the factory produces more sweaters, but the equipment is being operated closer to its limits. Furthermore, there are times when the third worker has nothing to do because the plant is running without the need for further attention. Adding yet more and more workers continues to increase output but by successively smaller amounts. This is the range over which marginal returns are diminishing. This phenomenon is such a pervasive one that it is called "the law of diminishing returns." The **law of diminishing returns** states that:

As a firm uses more of a variable input, with the quantity of fixed inputs constant, its marginal product eventually diminishes.

Because marginal product eventually diminishes, so does average product. Recall that average product decreases when marginal product is less than average product. If marginal product is diminishing, it must eventually become less than average product, and when it does so, average product declines.

The product and technology concepts we've just studied are summarized in a compact glossary in Table 10.2.

TABLE 10.2

A Compact Glossary on Product

Term	Symbol	Equation	Definition
Fixed input			**An input whose quantity used cannot be varied in the short run**
Variable input	L		**An input (labor in our examples) whose quantity used can be varied in the short run**
Total product	TP		**Output produced**
Marginal product	MP	$MP = \Delta TP \div \Delta L$	**Change in total product resulting from a one-unit rise in variable input (equals change in total product divided by change in variable factor)**
Average product	AP	$AP = TP \div L$	**Total product per unit of variable input (equals total product divided by number of units of variable factor)**
Point of maximum average product			**Output rate above which average product diminishes**
Point of maximum marginal product			**Output rate above which marginal product diminishes**

REVIEW

Three curves—total product, marginal product, and average product—show how the output rate of a given plant varies as the input of labor is varied. Initially, as the amount of labor increases, average product and marginal product increase. But eventually, average product and marginal product decline. When marginal product exceeds average product, average product increases. When marginal product is below average product, average product decreases. When marginal product and average product are equal, average product is at its maximum. ◆

Short-Run Cost

To produce more output in the short run, a firm must employ more labor. But if it employs more labor, its costs increase. Thus, to produce more output, a firm must increase its costs. We're going to examine how a firm's costs vary as it varies its output by studying Swanky's costs.

Swanky cannot influence the prices of its inputs and has to pay the market price for them. Given the prices of its inputs, Swanky's lowest attainable cost of production for each output level is determined by its technology. Let's see how.

Total Cost

A firm's **total cost** is the sum of the costs of all the inputs it uses in production. It includes the cost of renting land, buildings, and equipment and the wages paid to the firm's work force. Total cost is divided into two categories: fixed cost and variable cost. A **fixed cost** is a cost that is independent of the output level. A **variable cost** is a cost that varies with the output level. **Total fixed cost** is the cost of the fixed inputs. **Total variable cost** is the cost of the variable inputs. We call total cost *TC*, total fixed cost *TFC*, and total variable cost *TVC*.

Swanky's total cost and its division into total fixed cost and total variable cost appear in the table of Fig. 10.4. Swanky has one knitting machine, and

FIGURE 10.4

Short-Run Costs

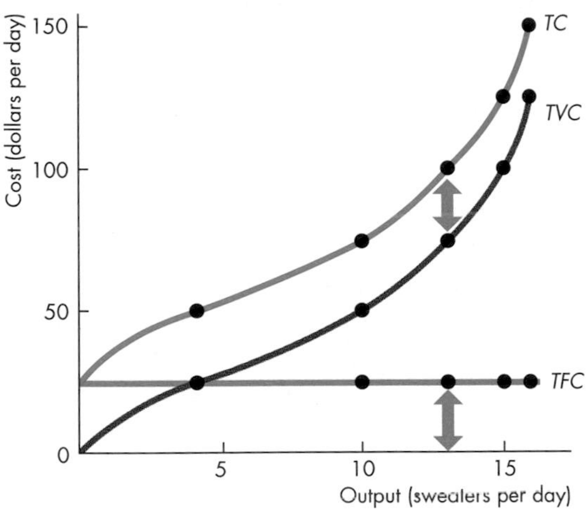

(a) Total costs

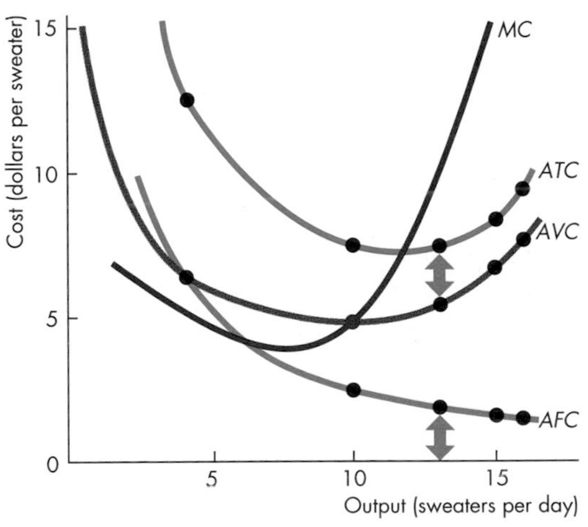

(b) Marginal and average costs

Labor (workers per day)	Output (sweaters per day)	Total fixed cost (*TFC*)	Total variable cost (*TVC*)	Total cost (*TC*)	Marginal cost (change in dollars per change in output) (*MC*)	Average fixed cost (*AFC*)	Average variable cost (*AVC*)	Average total cost (*ATC*)
		(dollars per day)			(dollars per sweater)			
0	**0**	**25**	**0**	**25**		**—**	**—**	**—**
					6.25			
1	**4**	**25**	**25**	**50**		**6.25**	**6.25**	**12.50**
					4.17			
2	**10**	**25**	**50**	**75**		**2.50**	**5.00**	**7.50**
					8.33			
3	**13**	**25**	**75**	**100**		**1.92**	**5.77**	**7.69**
					12.50			
4	**15**	**25**	**100**	**125**		**1.67**	**6.67**	**8.33**
					25.00			
5	**16**	**25**	**125**	**150**		**1.56**	**7.81**	**9.38**

Short-run costs are calculated in the table and illustrated in the graphs. At each level of employment and output in the table, total variable cost (*TVC*) is added to total fixed cost (*TFC*) to give total cost (*TC*). The change in total cost per unit change in output gives marginal cost (*MC*). Average costs are calculated by dividing the total costs by output.

The firm's total cost curves are shown in part (a). Total cost (*TC*) increases as output increases. Total fixed cost (*TFC*) is constant—it graphs as a horizontal line—and total variable cost (*TVC*) increases in a similar way to total cost. The vertical distance between the *TC* and *TVC* curves equals total fixed cost (*TFC*).

The average and marginal cost curves are shown in part (b). Average fixed cost (*AFC*) decreases as the constant total fixed cost is divided by ever higher output levels. The curves showing average total cost (*ATC*) and average variable cost (*AVC*) are U-shaped. The vertical distance between them is equal to average fixed cost, which becomes smaller as output increases. The marginal cost curve (*MC*) is also U-shaped. It cuts the average variable cost curve and the average total cost curve at their minimum points.

this is its fixed input. To produce more sweaters, Sidney must hire more labor, and the first two columns of the table show how many sweaters can be produced at each level of employment. This is Swanky's technology constraint.

Let's suppose that Swanky rents its knitting machine for $25 a day. This amount is Swanky's total fixed cost. Let's suppose that Swanky can hire workers at a wage rate of $25 a day. Total variable cost depends on the quantity of labor hired. For example, when Swanky employs 3 workers, total variable cost is $75 (3 multiplied by $25). Total cost is the sum of total fixed cost and total variable cost. For example, when Swanky employs 3 workers, total variable cost is $75, total fixed cost is $25, and total cost is $100.

Marginal Cost

A firm's **marginal cost** is the increase in total cost resulting from a one-unit increase in output. To calculate marginal cost, we find the change in total cost and divide it by the change in output. For example, when output increases from 4 to 10 sweaters, total cost increases from $50 to $75. The change in output is 6 sweaters, and the change in total cost is $25. The marginal cost of one of those 6 sweaters is $4.17 ($25 divided by 6).

Notice that when Swanky hires a second worker, marginal cost decreases from $6.25 for the first worker to $4.17 for the second worker. But when a third, fourth, and fifth worker are employed, marginal cost successively increases. Marginal cost increases because each additional worker produces a successively smaller addition to output—*the law of diminishing returns.*

Average Cost

Average cost is the cost per unit of output. There are three average costs:

1. Average fixed cost
2. Average variable cost
3. Average total cost

Average fixed cost (*AFC*) is total fixed cost per unit of output. **Average variable cost** (*AVC*) is total variable cost per unit of output. **Average total cost** (*ATC*) is total cost per unit output. Average fixed cost plus average variable cost equals average total cost. For example, in the table in Fig. 10.4, when output is 10 sweaters, average fixed cost is $2.50 ($25 divided by 10), average variable cost is $5.00 ($50 divided by 10), and average total cost is $7.50 ($75 divided by 10 or, equivalently, $2.50 average fixed cost plus $5.00 average variable cost).

Short-Run Cost Curves

We can illustrate Swanky's short-run costs as short-run cost curves (Fig. 10.4a). Total fixed cost is a constant $25. It appears in the figure as the horizontal green curve labeled *TFC*. Total variable cost and total cost both increase with output. They are graphed in the figure as the purple total variable cost curve (*TVC*) and the blue total cost curve (*TC*). The vertical distance between those two curves is equal to total fixed cost—as indicated by the green arrows.

The average cost curves appear in Fig. 10.4(b). The green average fixed cost curve (*AFC*) slopes downward. As output increases, the same constant fixed cost is spread over a larger output: when Swanky produces only 4 sweaters, average fixed cost is $6.25; when it produces 16 sweaters, average fixed cost is $1.56.

The blue average total cost curve (*ATC*) and the purple average variable cost curve (*AVC*) are U-shaped curves. The vertical distance between the average total cost and average variable cost curves is equal to average fixed cost—as indicated by the green arrows. That distance shrinks as output increases, since average fixed cost declines with increasing output.

Figure 10.4(b) also illustrates the marginal cost curve. It is the red curve labeled *MC*. That curve is also U-shaped. It cuts the average variable cost curve and the average total cost curve at their minimum points. That is, when marginal cost exceeds average cost, average cost is increasing, and when marginal cost is less than average cost, average cost is decreasing. This relationship holds for both the *ATC* and the *AVC* curves. You might wonder why the marginal cost curve cuts both the average total cost curve and the average variable cost curve at their minimum points. It does so because the source of the change in total cost, from which we calculate marginal cost, is variable cost. For average variable cost to decrease, marginal cost must be less than average variable cost, and for average variable cost to increase, marginal cost must exceed average variable cost. Similarly, for average total cost to decrease, marginal cost must be less than average total cost, and for average total cost to increase, marginal cost must exceed average total cost. This is exactly the same relationship we found when studying students' grades in Table 10.1.

Why the Average Total Cost Curve Is U-Shaped

The U-shape of the average total cost curve arises from the influence of two opposing forces:

- Decreasing average fixed cost
- Eventually increasing average variable cost

Because total fixed cost is constant, as output increases, average fixed cost decreases—the average fixed cost curve is downward sloping. But at low output levels the average fixed cost curve is steep, while at high output levels it is relatively flat. Because of diminishing returns, average variable cost eventually increases—the average variable cost curve eventually slopes upward and gets steeper.

Since average total cost is the sum of average fixed cost and average variable cost, the average total cost curve combines these two effects. At first the average total cost curve slopes downward because the effect of spreading fixed costs over larger output levels is the dominant influence on average total cost. But as output increases, diminishing returns bring ever higher average variable cost, and the average total cost curve slopes upward. At the point at which these two opposing influences on average total cost are balanced, average total cost is at its minimum.

The cost concepts we've just studied are summarized in a compact glossary in Table 10.3.

TABLE **10.3**

A Compact Glossary on Cost

Term	Symbol	Equation	Definition
Fixed cost			**Cost that is independent of the output level**
Variable cost			**Cost that varies with the output level**
Total fixed cost	***TFC***		**Cost of the fixed inputs (equals their number times their unit price)**
Total variable cost	***TVC***		**Cost of the variable inputs (equals their number times their unit price)**
Total cost	***TC***	$TC = TFC + TVC$	**Cost of all inputs (equals fixed costs plus variable costs)**
Marginal cost	***MC***	$MC = \Delta TC \div \Delta TP$	**Change in total cost resulting from a one-unit rise in total product (*TP*) (equals the change in total cost divided by the change in total product)**
Average fixed cost	***AFC***	$AFC = TFC \div TP$	**Total fixed cost per unit of output (equals total fixed cost divided by total product)**
Average variable cost	***AVC***	$AVC = TVC \div TP$	**Total variable cost per unit of output (equals total variable cost divided by total product)**
Average total cost	***ATC***	$ATC = AFC + AVC$	**Total cost per unit of output (equals average fixed cost plus average variable cost)**

Cost Curves and the Technology Constraint[2]

The shapes of a firm's cost curves are determined by its technology, and there are some interesting relationships between its cost curves and its product curves.

First, there is a relationship between the total variable cost curve in Fig. 10.4(a) and the total product curve in Fig. 10.1. They both slope upward, but look closely at their shapes. Initially, as more labor is employed, the total product curve gets steeper and the total variable cost curve gets less steep. This is the range over which marginal product is increasing. Once diminishing returns set in, as more labor is employed, the total variable cost curve gets steeper and the total product curve gets less steep.

Second, there is a relationship between the marginal product curve in Fig. 10.2 and the marginal cost curve in Fig. 10.4(b). The marginal cost curve is like the flip side of the marginal product curve. Marginal cost is at a minimum at the same output at which marginal product is at a maximum. The output range over which marginal cost is decreasing is the same as that over which marginal product is increasing. Similarly, the output range over which marginal cost is increasing is the same as that over which marginal product is decreasing—the range of diminishing marginal product.

Third, there is a relationship between the average product curve in Fig. 10.3(b) and the average cost curve in Fig. 10.4(b). It is similar to the relationship between the marginal curves that we've just described. The average cost curve is like the flip side of the average product curve. Average variable cost is at a minimum at the same output at which average product is at a maximum (10 sweaters). The output range over which average variable cost is decreasing is the same as that over which average product is increasing. Similarly, the output range over which average variable cost is increasing is the same as that over which average product is decreasing.

[2]If you skipped the section entitled "Short-Run Technology Constraint," you will also want to skip this short section.

FIGURE 10.5

NEPOOL's Output and Cost

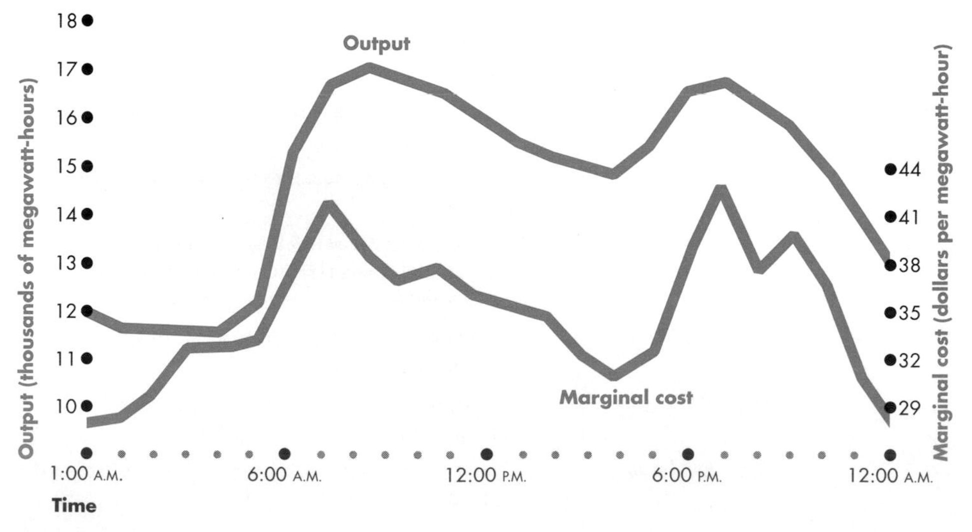

During a 24-hour period, electric power production fluctuated between 11,500 and 17,000 megawatt-hours. Over the same period, marginal cost fluctuated between \$29 and \$44 per megawatt-hour. The empirical relationship between output and marginal cost is not exact because of maintenance scheduling and uncontrollable factors such as plant breakdowns.

Real-World Short-Run Costs

Swanky's costs are a lot like the costs of a real-world firm. Let's confirm this fact by looking at the costs of a group of real firms, the New England Power Pool (NEPOOL). NEPOOL is an association of 92 electric power companies serving more than 5 million customers in the six New England states.

NEPOOL's production fluctuates between 11,500 and 17,000 megawatt-hours, depending partly on the time of day, partly on the day of the week, and partly on the temperature. To vary their output in the short run, the power producers vary the amount of fuel that they use. Fuel is the variable input of a power producer. The power source with the lowest fuel cost in the New England system is nuclear. Large coal-burning and oil-burning generators come next. The power sources with the highest fuel cost are small gas-turbine generators that use the same kind of fuel as jet aircraft.

On a cold winter day, the hour-by-hour output of the NEPOOL producers and the marginal cost per 1,000 megawatt-hours fluctuated in the manner shown in Fig. 10.5. As you can see, there are two cycles over a 24-hour period in electric power production. From 1:00 A.M. to 6:00 A.M., output (shown by the blue curve) is between 11,500 and 12,000 megawatt-hours. Then between 6:00 A.M. and 7:00 A.M., output increases as we all turn on morning TV shows, toasters, and coffeemakers. Output reaches a peak at 9:00 A.M. and then falls off slightly during the day to a low point at 4:00 P.M. In the early evening, there is another TV viewing and meal-preparation peak and then a gradual fall through to midnight as people go to bed. The marginal cost of production follows a similar cycle and fluctuates between $29 a megawatt-hour at the trough and $44 a megawatt-hour at the peak.

The relationship between output and marginal cost is not perfect because mechanical failure and maintenance shutdowns make it impossible always to use the generator with the lowest marginal cost. But it is pretty close, as Fig. 10.6 shows. Here, each point represents the marginal cost and output at a particular hour. For example, you can see in Fig. 10.5 that, between 10:00 P.M. and 11:00 P.M., 14,000 megawatt-hours were produced at a marginal cost of $32 a megawatt-hour. That output and marginal cost generate point *a* in Fig. 10.6. The continuous red curve labeled *MC* is the marginal cost curve for NEPOOL.

FIGURE 10.6

NEPOOL's Marginal Cost Curve

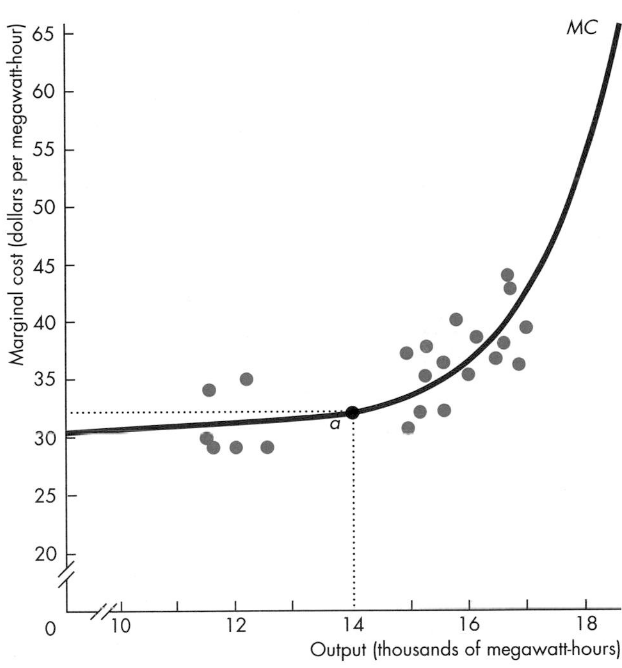

Each point in the figure represents marginal cost at a particular hour on a particular day. For example, point *a* represents a marginal cost of $32 per megawatt-hour and an output rate of 14,000 megawatt-hours. The marginal cost curve for electric power in New England rises steeply as output approaches the physical limits of the generating plant.

Notice the similarity between the marginal cost curves for NEPOOL and Swanky. All production processes experience diminishing returns and have marginal cost curves that (eventually) slope upward.

Swanky adjusts its rate of sweater production by varying the amount of labor it employs and varying the extent to which it utilizes its fixed amount of knitting machinery—its physical plant. NEPOOL meets fluctuations in the production of electric power by varying the fuel input and varying the output of a fixed physical generating plant. All types of firms face cost curves such as the ones you've just studied. Another example—that of General Motors' cost curves—is given in Reading Between the Lines on pp. 246–247.

Auto Plant Cost Curves

The New York Times, July 3, 1991

G.M.'s Plan for a Nearly Nonstop Auto Plant

BY DORON P. LEVIN

DETROIT The General Motors Corporation and a local chapter of the United Automobile Workers union have tentatively agreed to begin near-nonstop assembly operations at G.M.'s Lordstown, Ohio, plant starting next summer. The step would enable G.M. to effectively produce as many cars at one plant as the company can now assemble in two.

The move represents a growing trend among American auto makers to cut costs by wringing more use from existing plants. The Chrysler Corporation, for example, has an agreement with the U.A.W. to step up mini-van production, if needed, by using three shifts instead of the usual two. . . .

Under the G.M. and union proposal for Lordstown, the plant would operate with two 10-hour shifts Monday through Friday, one 10-hour shift on Saturday and one 10-hour shift on Sunday, for a total of 120 hours of production weekly.

G.M.'s push to trim production and labor costs at its Baltimore plant, which makes midsized vans, precipitated a strike last week because workers complained that the faster pace was causing too many accidents. . . .

Beyond the pace of work, some manufacturing experts are concerned that near-nonstop assembly operations do not allow enough time for routine maintenance and repairs. . . .

Although G.M. declined to comment on its production capacity at Lordstown, [Bill] Alli [the U.A.W. shop chairman] said the company had told him that the plant would be able to build 480,000 cars annually. A G.M. spokesman said that in the latest year the plant produced 360,000 cars on two shifts, plus overtime.

In the new Lordstown arrangement, three crews of workers would each work four days a week, 10 hours a day. Two crews would receive 44 hours of pay for a 40-hour workweek. The third crew, working Friday though Monday, would receive 48 hours of pay.

The Essence of the Story

General Motors and the United Automobile Workers union have tentatively agreed to operate G.M.'s Lordstown, Ohio, plant for twelve 10-hour shifts—120 hours—each week.

Under the deal, weekday workers receive 44 hours of pay for a 40-hour workweek and weekend workers receive 48 hours of pay for a 40-hour workweek.

The plant will be able to build 480,000 cars annually compared with 360,000 cars under the previous arrangement of two 8-hour shifts plus overtime.

The deal is part of a trend to cut costs by squeezing more from existing plants.

Workers say that the faster pace causes too many accidents, and experts say that near-nonstop operations do not allow enough time for maintenance and repairs.

Background and Analysis

By increasing output, auto producers are able to spread their fixed cost over a larger quantity produced and lower their average fixed cost (*AFC*)—for example, from *A* to *B* in Fig. 1.

But with two 8-hour shifts plus overtime, the cost of the additional labor that is needed to increase output increases average variable cost by more than the decrease in average fixed cost. As a result, average total cost (*ATC*) increases—for example, from *C* to *D* in Fig. 1.

By introducing 10-hour shifts, the cost of the first 80 crew hours—Monday through Thursday crews—increases to 88 crew hours of pay—a 10 percent increase on the cost with 8-hour shifts. But the next 40 crew hours—Friday through Sunday crews—cost only 48 crew hours of pay, a lower amount than the overtime wage rate.

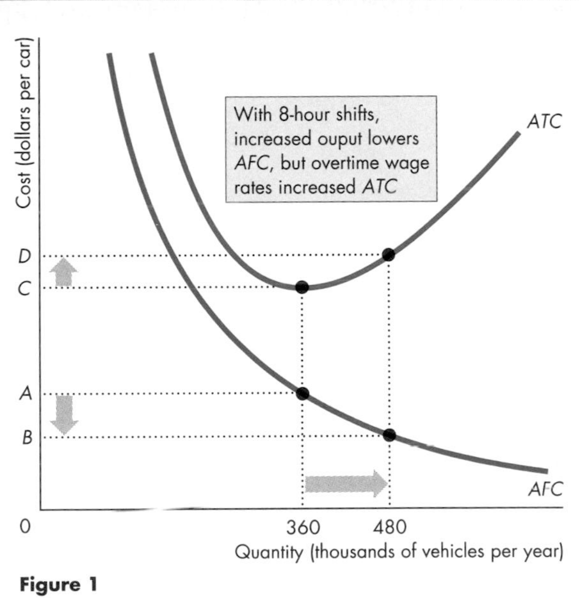

Figure 1

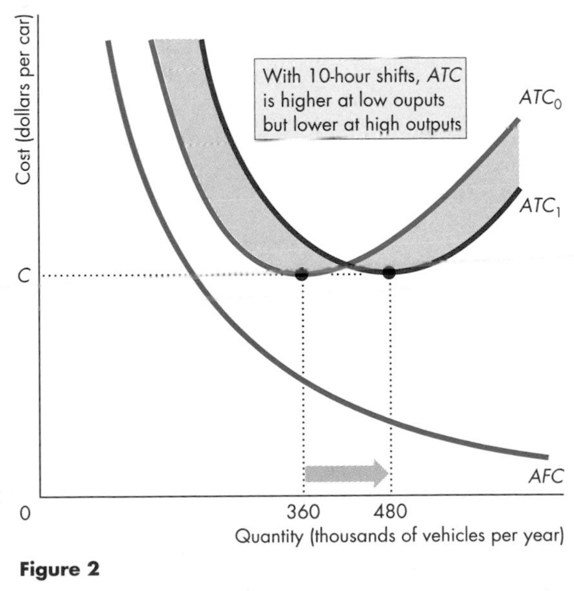

Figure 2

Because the 10-hour shift arrangement *increases* the cost of the first 80 crew hours but *decreases* the cost of the next 40 crew hours, it increases *ATC* at low outputs but decreases *ATC* at high outputs, as shown in Fig. 2. With 8-hour shifts plus overtime, the average total cost curve is ATC_0, and with 10-hour shifts it is ATC_1.

With the output rate of 360,000 cars per year, it does not pay to switch to 10-hour shifts because average total cost is higher. But with the higher output rate of 480,000 cars per year, average total cost is lower with 10-hour shifts.

Figure 2 shows the average total cost of producing 480,000 cars with a 10-hour shift to be the same as that of producing 360,000 cars with 8-hour shifts—*C* dollars per car. We do not know from the article whether this assumption is correct. It is possible, because of the faster and more intense pace of plant operation, that higher maintenance costs reduce the benefits of the 10-hour shift arrangement.

As the demand grows, firms such as Swanky, electric power utilities, and auto makers install new plant and equipment. When does it pay Swanky to install new knitting machines, the New England power producers to install new and larger generators, and GM to install new assembly lines? Let's now answer these questions.

Plant Size, Cost, and Capacity

We have studied how the cost of production varies for a given sweater plant when different quantities of labor are used. The output rate at which a plant's average total cost is at a minimum is called the **capacity** of the plant. If a plant's output is below the point of minimum average total cost—that is, if it produces a lower amount than its capacity—it is said to have **excess capacity.** If a plant's output is above the point of minimum average total cost—that is, if it produces a higher amount than its capacity—it is said to have **overutilized capacity.**

The economist's use of the word *capacity* differs from the everyday use. It seems more natural to talk about a plant operating at capacity when it cannot produce any more. However, when we want to refer to the maximum output that a plant can produce, we call that output the **physical limits** of the plant.

The cost curves that were shown in Fig. 10.4 apply to a plant size of one knitting machine that has a fixed cost of $25. There is a set of short-run cost curves like those shown in Fig. 10.4 for each different plant size. In the short run, a firm will be economically efficient if it produces at a point on the short-run cost curve for its given plant. In the long run, though, the firm can do better. It can choose its plant size and therefore can create a different short-run cost curve on which it will operate.

The Capacity Utilization Puzzle

NEPOOL sometimes operates its plants at outputs above capacity and close to their physical limits. This situation is not uncommon. High-quality gardeners, plumbers, electricians, painters, and other suppliers of services often work so hard that they produce at an average total cost that is higher than their minimum average cost. To get the work done, they have to hire extra help at overtime wage rates and work evenings and weekends, thereby incurring a high average cost of production.

Operating with increasing average total cost looks uneconomic. Why don't such firms buy more capital equipment and increase the scale of their business to meet the obvious high demand for their output? Is there an economic reason why they don't?

In contrast, it is not uncommon in many industries to have an almost permanent excess capacity. Steel production is an example. Excess capacity also occurs in the auto industry, in many mining operations, and in a host of other industries. These producers claim that they could increase their output if the demand for their product was higher and, as a result, could produce at a lower average total cost.

It sounds as if these firms have invested in too big a production plant. It seems as if the steel producers and auto makers would be better off if they had smaller plants so that they could produce closer to the point of minimum average total cost. Is this in fact the case? Or is there some economic explanation for why firms in such industries persistently have excess capacity? This section provides a large part of the answers to these questions.

You have already studied how a firm's costs change when it varies its use of labor while holding constant the size of its production plant. This cost behavior is described by the firm's short-run cost curves. Now we are going to study how a firm's costs vary when all its inputs vary—labor and the scale of the production plant. These variations in costs are described by the firm's long-run cost curves.

Although we want to understand the behavior of real firms, we will, as before, spend most of our time studying the long-run costs of our imaginary firm—Swanky, Inc. We will then use the insights that we get from this sweater factory to make sense of the behavior of real firms.

Short-Run Cost and Long-Run Cost

Short-run cost is made up of the fixed cost of a fixed plant and the variable cost of labor. The behavior of short-run cost depends on the short-run production function. **Long-run cost** is the cost of production when a firm uses the economically efficient plant size. The behavior of long-run cost depends on the firm's production function. A **production function** is the relationship between the maximum output attainable and the quantities of inputs used.

The Production Function

Swanky's production function is shown in Fig. 10.7. In the table, we look at four different plant sizes and five different quantities of labor input. Perhaps you will recognize the numbers in the column for a plant size of one knitting machine. This is the sweater factory whose short-run product and cost curves we have just studied. With one knitting machine, output varies as the labor input is varied, as described by the numbers in that column. The table also shows three other plant sizes: two, three, and four times the size of the original one. If Sidney doubles the plant size (to 2 knitting machines), the various amounts of labor can produce the outputs shown in the second column of the table. The other two columns show the outputs of yet larger plants. Each of the columns of the table is a short-run production function. The production function itself is just the collection of all the short-run production functions.

The total product curves for these four different plant sizes appear in Fig. 10.7. As you can see, each total product curve has the same basic shape, but the bigger the sweater plant, the larger is the number of sweaters knitted each day by a given number of workers. One of the fundamental technological facts reflected in the shape of a total product curve is the law of diminishing returns.

FIGURE 10.7

The Production Function

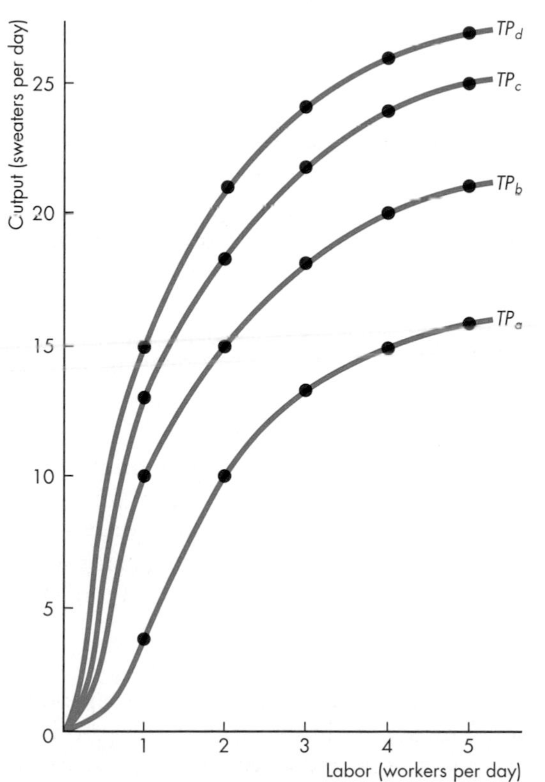

Labor (workers per day)	Output (sweaters per day) Plant *a*	Plant *b*	Plant *c*	Plant *d*
1	**4**	10	13	15
2	10	**15**	18	21
3	13	18	**22**	24
4	15	20	24	**26**
5	16	21	25	27
Knitting machines (number)	1	2	3	4

The table shows four short-run production functions for four plant sizes. These production functions are plotted in the graph and are labeled TP_a (1 knitting machine), TP_b (2 knitting machines), TP_c (3 knitting machines), and TP_d (4 knitting machines). Each total product curve displays diminishing marginal product. The bigger the plant, the higher is the total product for any given amount of labor employed. The highlighted numbers in the table show what happens as the firm changes its scale of production. Doubling the scale from 1 machine and 1 worker to 2 machines and 2 workers more than doubles the output—increasing returns to scale. Increasing the scale again from 2 workers and 2 machines to 3 workers and 3 machines and to 4 workers and 4 machines increases output by a smaller percentage than the increase in inputs—decreasing returns to scale.

Diminishing Returns

Diminishing returns occur in all four plants as the labor input increases. You can check that fact by doing calculations for the larger plants similar to those done in Fig. 10.2. Regardless of the size of the plant, the larger the labor input, the lower (eventually) is its marginal product.

Just as we can calculate the marginal product of labor for each plant size, we can also calculate the marginal product of capital for each quantity of labor. The **marginal product of capital** is the change in total product resulting from a one-unit increase in the quantity of capital employed, holding the quantity of labor constant. It is calculated in a similar way to the marginal product of labor. Also, it behaves in a similar way to the marginal product of labor. That is, if the labor input is held constant as the capital input is increased, the marginal product of capital diminishes.

The law of diminishing returns tells us what happens to output when a firm changes one input, either labor or capital, and holds the other input constant. What happens to output if a firm changes both labor and equipment?

Returns to Scale

A change in scale occurs when there is an equal percentage change in the use of all the firm's inputs. For example, if Swanky has been employing one worker and has one knitting machine and then doubles its use of both inputs (to use two workers and two knitting machines), the scale of the firm will double. **Returns to scale** are the increases in output that result from increasing all inputs by the same percentage. There are three possible cases:

- Constant returns to scale
- Increasing returns to scale
- Decreasing returns to scale

Constant Returns to Scale **Constant returns to scale** occur when the percentage increase in a firm's output is equal to the percentage increase in its inputs. If constant returns to scale are present, when a firm doubles all its inputs, its output exactly doubles. Constant returns to scale occur if an increase in output is achieved by replicating the original production process. For example, General Motors can double its production of Cavaliers by doubling its production facility for those cars. It can build an identical production line and hire an identical number of workers. With the two identical production lines, GM will produce exactly twice as many cars.

Increasing Returns to Scale **Increasing returns to scale** (also called **economies of scale**) occur when the percentage increase in output exceeds the percentage increase in inputs. If economies of scale are present when a firm doubles all its inputs, its output more than doubles. Economies of scale occur in production processes in which increased output enables a firm to use a more productive technology. For example, if GM produces only 100 cars a week, it will not pay to install an automated assembly line. The cost per car will be lower if instead GM uses skilled, but expensive, workers equipped only with inexpensive hand tools. But at an output rate of a few thousand cars a week, it will pay GM to install an automated assembly line. Each worker will specialize in a small number of tasks and will become highly proficient in them. General Motors may use 100 times more capital and labor, but the number of cars it can make will increase much more than a hundredfold. It will experience increasing returns to scale.

Decreasing Returns to Scale **Decreasing returns to scale** (also called **diseconomies of scale**) occur when the percentage increase in output is less than the percentage change in inputs. For example, if inputs double and output increases by 50 percent, diseconomies of scale are present. Diseconomies of scale occur in all production processes at some output rate, but perhaps at a very high one. The most common source of diseconomies of scale is the increasingly complex management and organizational structure required to control a large firm. The larger the organization, the larger are the number of layers in the management pyramid and the greater are the costs of monitoring and maintaining control of all the various stages in the production and marketing process.

Scale Economies at Swanky Swanky's production possibilities, set out in Fig. 10.7, display both economies of scale and diseconomies of scale. If Sidney has 1 knitting machine and employs 1 worker, his factory will produce 4 sweaters a day. If he doubles the firm's inputs to 2 knitting machines and 2 workers, the factory's output increases almost fourfold to 15 sweaters a day. If he increases his inputs another 50 percent to 3 knitting machines and 3 workers, output increases to 22 sweaters a day—an increase of less than 50 percent. Doubling the scale of Swanky from 1 to 2 units of each input gives rise to economies of scale, but the further increase from 2 to 3 units of each input gives rise to diseconomies of scale.

Whether a firm experiences increasing, constant, or decreasing returns to scale has an important effect on its long-run costs. Let's see how.

Plant Size and Cost

Earlier in this chapter, we worked out Swanky's short-run costs when it has a fixed amount of capital—one knitting machine—and a variable number of workers. We can also work out the short-run costs of different plant sizes. It takes longer to change the size of the production plant than to change the size of the plant's work force. That is why we speak of a short run for each different plant size. But Sidney can buy another knitting machine and put it into his existing factory. He will then have a different size of plant. He can vary the amount of labor employed in that plant, and as he does so, we can trace the short-run cost curves associated with those different levels of variable input.

Let's look at the short-run costs for different plants and see how plant size itself affects the short-run cost curves.

Four Different Plants

We've already studied the costs of a plant with 1 knitting machine. We'll call that Plant *a*. The table in Fig. 10.8 sets out the costs for Plant *a* and for three other plants—what we will call Plants *b*, *c*, and *d*. Plant *b* has 2 knitting machines; Plant *c* has 3 knitting machines; and Plant *d* has 4 knitting machines.

The average total cost curves associated with the original plant and these three larger plants appear in Fig. 10.8(a). The average total cost curve for each of the four plant sizes has the same basic U-shape. Which of these cost curves Swanky operates on depends on its plant size. For example, if Swanky has Plant *a*, then its average total cost curve will be ATC_a and it will cost $7.69 per sweater to knit 13 sweaters a day. But Swanky can produce 13 sweaters a day with any of these four different plant sizes. If it uses Plant *b*, the average total cost curve is ATC_b and the average total cost of a sweater will be $6.80. And if it uses Plant *d*, the average total cost of a sweater will be $9.50. If Swanky wants to produce 13 sweaters a day, the economically efficient plant is Plant *b*—the one with the lowest average total cost of production.

The Long-Run Average Cost Curve

The **long-run average cost curve** traces the relationship between the lowest attainable average total cost and output when both capital and labor inputs can be varied. This curve is illustrated in Fig. 10.8(b) as *LRAC*. The curve is derived directly from the four short-run average total cost curves that we have just reviewed in Fig. 10.8(a). As you can see, from either part (a) or part (b), Plant *a* has the lowest average total cost for all output rates up to 10 sweaters a day. Plant *b* has the lowest average total cost for output rates between 10 and 18 sweaters a day. Between output rates of 18 and 24 sweaters a day, Plant *c* has the lowest average total cost. Finally, for output rates above 24 sweaters a day, Plant *d* has the lowest average total cost. The segments of the four average total cost curves for which each plant has the lowest average total cost are highlighted in Fig. 10.8(b). The scallop-shaped curve made up of these four segments is the long-run average cost curve.

Swanky will be on its long-run average cost curve if it does the following: to produce up to 10 sweaters a day, it uses 1 machine; to produce between 11 and 18 sweaters a day, it uses 2 machines; to produce between and 19 and 24 sweaters, it uses 3 machines; and, finally, to produce more than 24 sweaters, it uses 4 machines. Within these ranges, it varies its output by varying the amount of labor employed.

FIGURE 10.8

Short-Run and Long-Run Costs

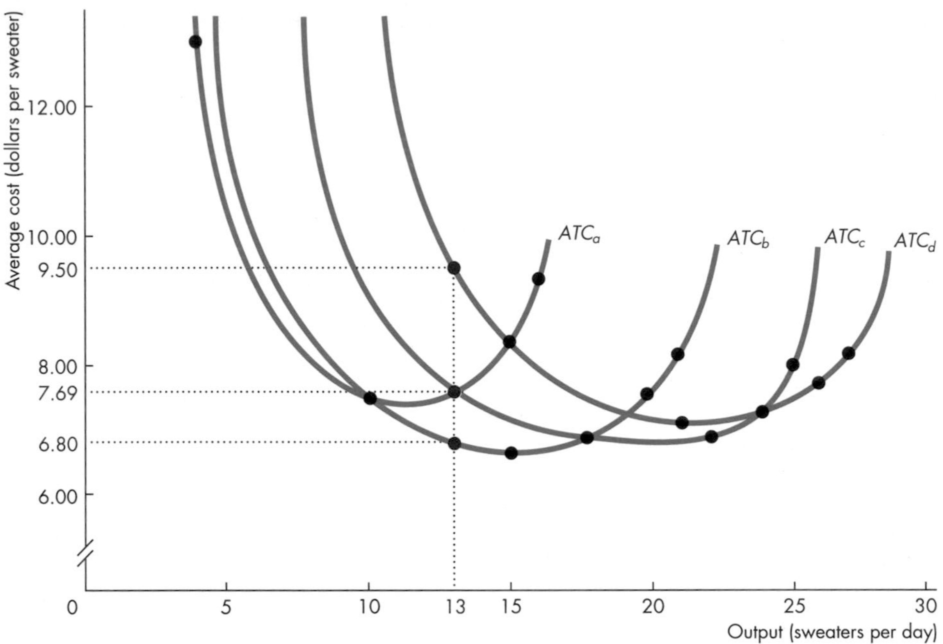

(a) Short-run average cost

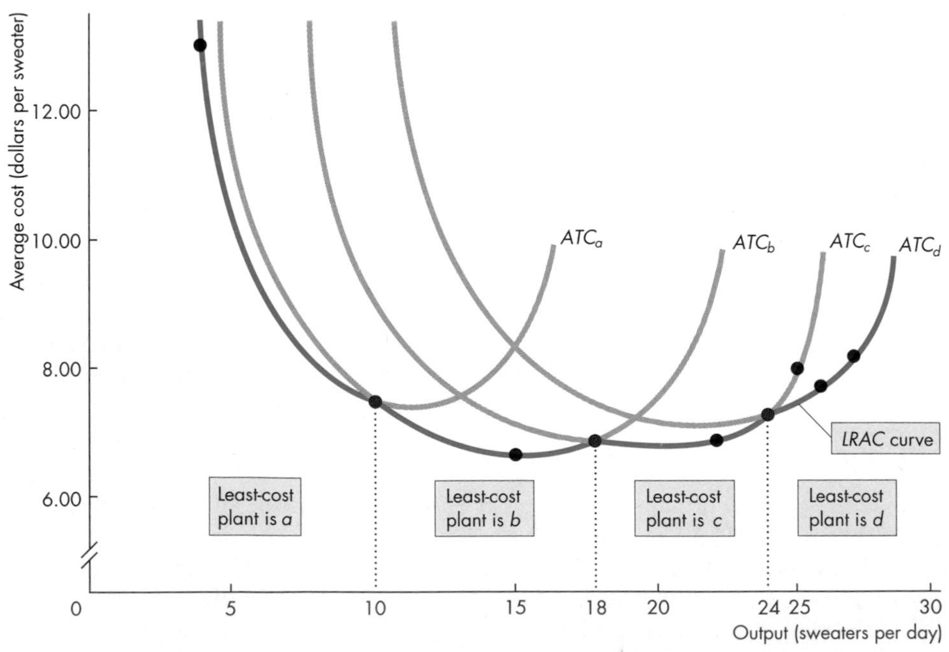

(b) Long-run average cost

Labor (workers per day)	Output (sweaters per day)	Total fixed cost	Total variable cost	Total cost	Average total cost (dollars per sweater)
		(dollars per day)			
Plant *a*: 1 unit of capital—total cost of capital = $25					
1	4	25	25	50	12.50
2	10	25	50	75	7.50
3	13	25	75	100	7.69
4	15	25	100	125	8.33
5	16	25	125	150	9.38
Plant *b*: 2 units of capital—total cost of capital = $50					
1	10	50	25	75	7.50
2	15	50	50	100	6.67
3	18	50	75	125	6.94
4	20	50	100	150	7.50
5	21	50	125	175	8.33
Plant *c*: 3 units of capital—total cost of capital = $75					
1	13	75	25	100	7.69
2	18	75	50	125	6.94
3	22	75	75	150	6.82
4	24	75	100	175	7.29
5	25	75	125	200	8.00
Plant *d*: 4 units of capital—total cost of capital = $100					
1	15	100	25	125	8.33
2	21	100	50	150	7.14
3	24	100	75	175	7.29
4	26	100	100	200	7.69
5	27	100	125	225	8.33

The table shows the short-run costs of four different plants. Each plant has a different fixed cost. Plant *a* has 1 knitting machine and a fixed cost of $25; Plant *b* has 2 knitting machines and a fixed cost of $50; Plant *c* has 3 knitting machines and a fixed cost of $75; and Plant *d* has 4 knitting machines and a fixed cost of $100. The short-run average total cost curve for each plant is graphed in part (a). Part (b) illustrates the construction of the long-run average cost curve. The curve traces the lowest attainable costs of production at each output when both capital and labor inputs are varied. On the long-run average cost curve, Swanky uses Plant *a* to produce up to 10 sweaters a day, Plant *b* to produce between 11 and 18 sweaters a day, Plant *c* to produce between 19 and 24 sweaters a day, and Plant *d* to produce more than 24 sweaters a day.

Long-Run Cost and Returns to Scale There is a connection between the long-run average cost curve and returns to scale. Figure 10.9 shows this connection. When long-run average cost is decreasing, there are increasing returns to scale (or economies of scale). When long-run average cost is increasing, there are decreasing returns to scale (or diseconomies of scale). At outputs up to 15 sweaters a day, Swanky experiences economies of scale; at 15 sweaters a day, long-run average cost is at a minimum. When output increases above 15 sweaters a day, Swanky experiences diseconomies of scale.

The long-run average cost curve that we have derived for Swanky has two special features that will not always be found in a firm's long-run cost curve. First, Swanky is able to adjust its plant size only in big jumps. In contrast, we can imagine varying the plant size in tiny increments so that there is an infinite number of plant sizes. In such a situation, there is an infinite number of short-run average total cost curves, one for each plant. Second, Swanky's long-run average cost curve is U-shaped—it slopes either downward (economies of scale) or upward (disceconomies of scale). In contrast, many production processes have constant returns to scale over some intermediate range of output, and long-run average cost is constant. The long-run average cost curve is horizontal.

Figure 10.10 illustrates this situation. Here, there is an infinite number of plant sizes, so the long-run average cost curve is smooth, not scalloped like Swanky's. For outputs up to Q_1, there are increasing returns to scale and long-run average cost is decreasing. For outputs between Q_1 and Q_2, there are constant returns to scale and long-run average cost is constant. And for outputs that exceed Q_2, there are decreasing returns to scale and long-run average cost is increasing.

To keep the figure clear, only one of the infinite number of short-run average total cost curves, labeled *SRAC*, is shown. Each short-run average total cost curve touches the long-run average cost curve, *LRAC*, at a single point (1 output). Thus, for each output, there is a unique, economically efficient

FIGURE 10.9

Returns to Scale

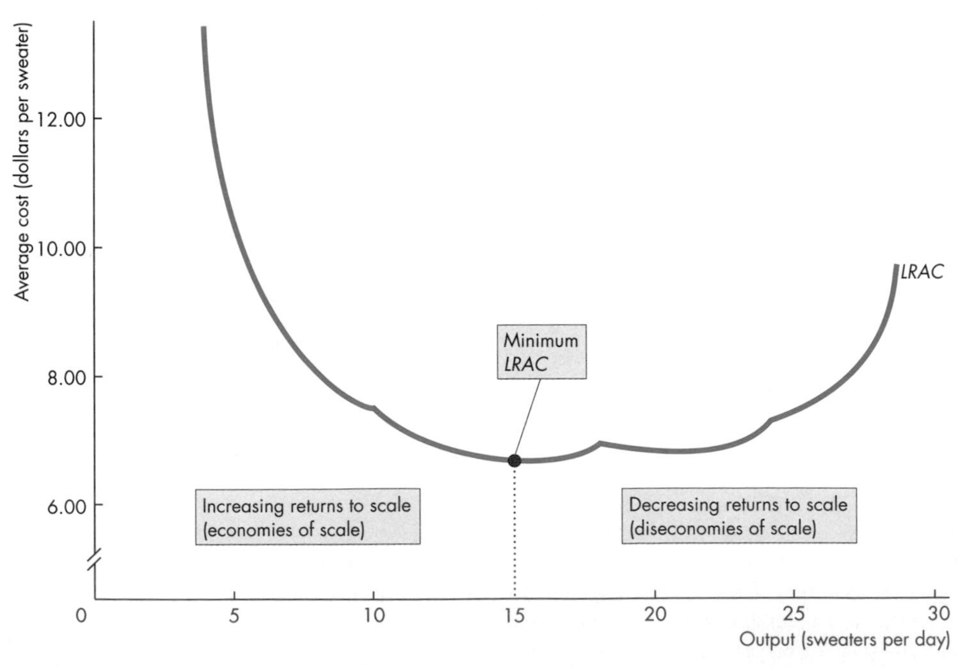

When the long-run average cost curve (*LRAC*) slopes downward, there are increasing returns to scale (or economies of scale). When the long-run average cost curve slopes upward, there are decreasing returns to scale (or diseconomies of scale).

FIGURE 10.10
Short-Run and Long-Run Average Costs

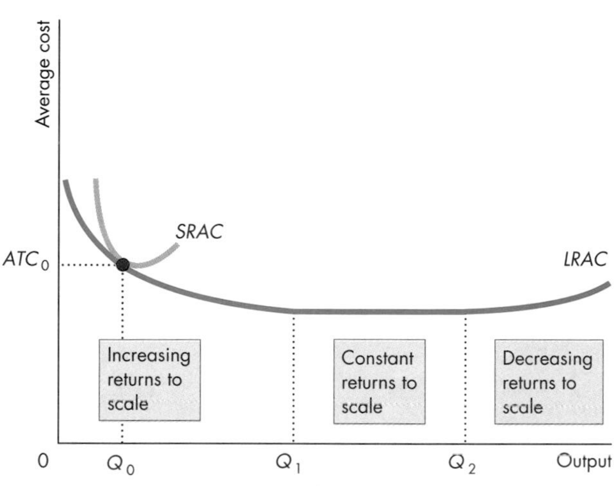

If capital can be varied in small units, there are an infinitely large number of plant sizes and an infinitely large number of short-run average total cost curves. Each short-run average total cost curve touches the long-run average cost curve at a single point. For example, the short-run average total cost curve (*SRAC*) touches the long-run average cost curve (*LRAC*) at the output rate Q_0 and average total cost ATC_0. The short-run average total cost curve shown is representative of the infinite number of others, each with only one point touching the long-run average cost curve. For outputs up to Q_1, there are increasing returns to scale; for outputs between Q_1 and Q_2, there are constant returns to scale; and for outputs greater than Q_2, there are decreasing returns to scale.

plant size. The short-run average total cost curve shown in Fig. 10.10 is for the plant that can produce output rate Q_0 at minimum average total cost, ATC_0.

The first time the long-run average cost curve appeared in print, it was drawn incorrectly. Take a look at Our Advancing Knowledge (pp. 256–257) to see why. You will understand the connection between short-run and long-run average cost curves more thoroughly after you have studied this material.

Long-Run Costs Are Total Costs When we examine short-run costs, we distinguish between fixed, variable, and total costs. We make no such distinctions for long-run costs. All inputs vary in the long run, so there are no long-run fixed costs. Since there are no long-run fixed costs, long-run total cost and long-run variable cost are the same thing. The long-run average variable cost is the long-run average cost.

There is a long-run marginal cost curve that goes with the long-run average cost curve. The relationship between the long-run average cost curve and the long-run marginal cost curve is similar to that between the short-run average cost curve and the short-run marginal cost curve. When long-run average cost is decreasing, long-run marginal cost is less than long-run average cost. When long-run average cost is increasing, long-run marginal cost exceeds long-run average cost, and when long-run average cost is constant, long-run marginal cost is equal to long-run average cost.

Shifts in Cost Curves

Both short-run and long-run cost curves depend on two things: the production function and input prices. A change in technology shifts the production function and thus shifts the cost curves. Technological advances increase the output that can be produced from given inputs. They also shift the total product curve as well as the average and the marginal product curves upward, and they shift the cost curves downward. For example, advances in genetic engineering are making it possible to increase the milk production of a cow without increasing the amount of food that it eats—a technological advance that lowers the cost of milk production.

Resource or input prices also affect the cost curves. If the price of an input increases, it directly increases cost and shifts the cost curves upward.

Returns to Scale in Reality

Let's close this chapter by looking at some real-world examples and see why there is a great deal of excess capacity in some industries while in others firms are operating flat out.

FIRMS and COSTS

Why do firms exist? Ronald H. Coase was the first to ask and answer this question. Firms exist, he said, because they enable us to avoid costs arising from market transactions. Without firms, each individual would have to find the best way of selling her or his own resources in a wide range of markets. The time cost of these activities would be extremely large. With firms, each person sells her or his resources to just one firm—the one offering the highest price—and managers direct the resources hired by the firm to their highest-value uses.

How are firm's costs related to their output? Jacob Viner answered this question, showing how a firm's short-run and long-run cost curves are related to each other. But he didn't get it quite right, and his mistake can reinforce your understanding of the short-run average cost curve (*SRAC*) and the long-run average cost curve (*LRAC*). (Viner's mistake is contained in an article that has been reprinted many times. One of its most accessible sources is in Kenneth E. Boulding and George J. Stigler (eds.), *Readings in Price Theory* (Chicago: Richard D. Irwin, 1952), 198–232. The article was first published in *Zeitschrift für Nationalkonomie,* vol. III (1931): 23–46.)

"Outside the firm, price movements direct production, which is co-ordinated through a series of exchange transactions on the market. Within a firm, these market transactions are eliminated..."

Ronald H. Coase
"The Nature of the Firm"

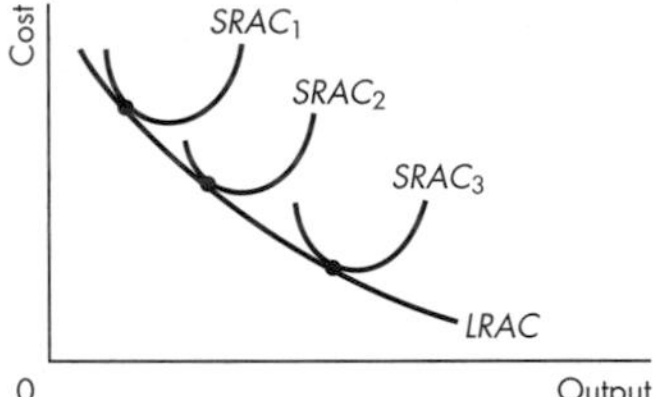

Figure 1 Long-run average cost curve

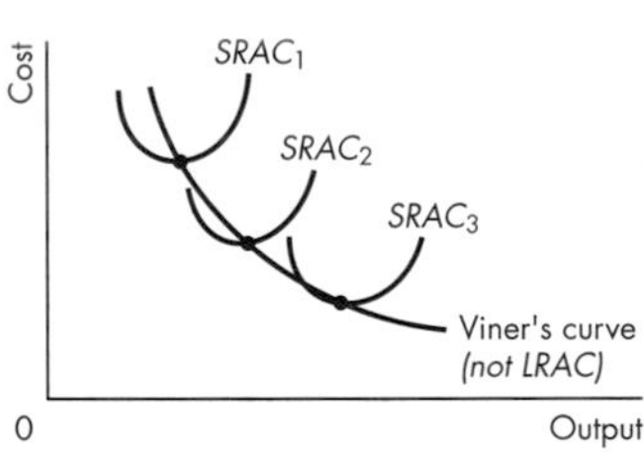

Figure 2 Viner's error

Viner asked his draftsman to draw a long-run average cost curve that satisfied two conditions:

- Not rise above any *SRAC* curve at any point
- Pass through the minimum point of each *SRAC* curve

The *SRAC* curve in Fig. 1 is never below the *LRAC* and thus satisfies Viner's first condition—that the *LRAC* not rise above any *SRAC* at any point. But it does not satisfy the second—that the *LRAC* pass through the minimum points of each *SRAC*. Viner's wrong version of a long-run average cost curve is shown in Fig. 2. That curve does pass through the minimum points of the *SRAC* curves and so satisfies the second condition but not the first.

It is not possible to draw a curve that satisfies both of Viner's conditions (except when there are constant returns to scale and *LRAC* is horizontal). The curve in Fig. 1 is a long-run average cost curve, and Viner's curve in Fig. 2 is not.

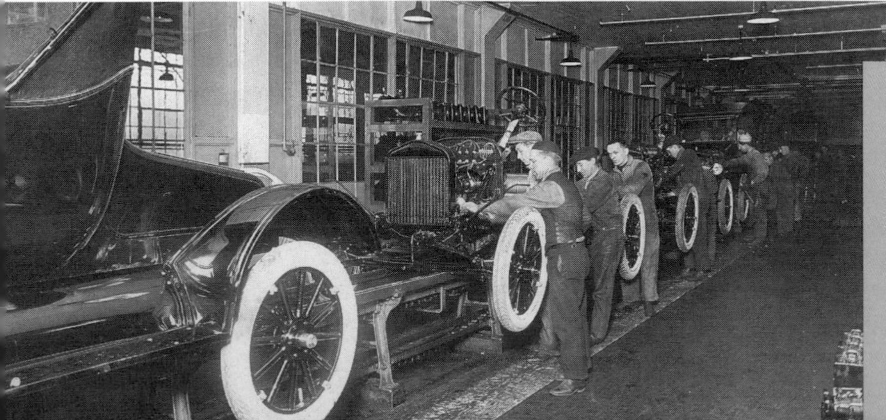

Factories employing hundreds of workers using specialized machinery became common in the industrial revolution of the eighteenth century. By organizing production on a large scale and by allocating resources directly rather than indirectly through markets, firms were able to cut the costs of production. This process saw a further advance with the development of the production line method in the automobile industry of the 1920s.

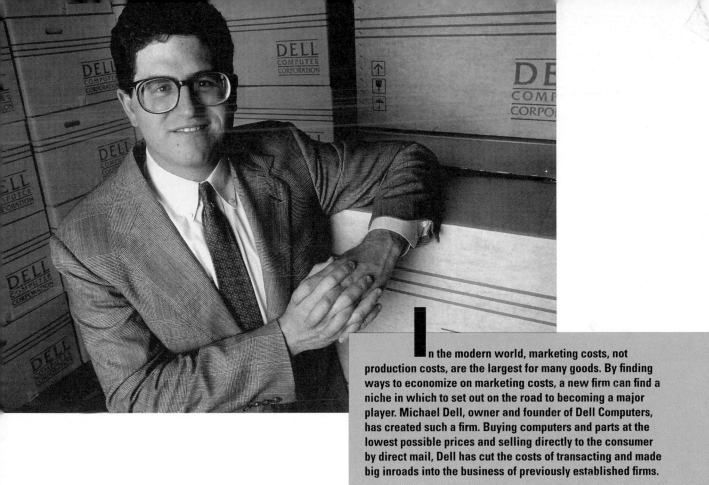

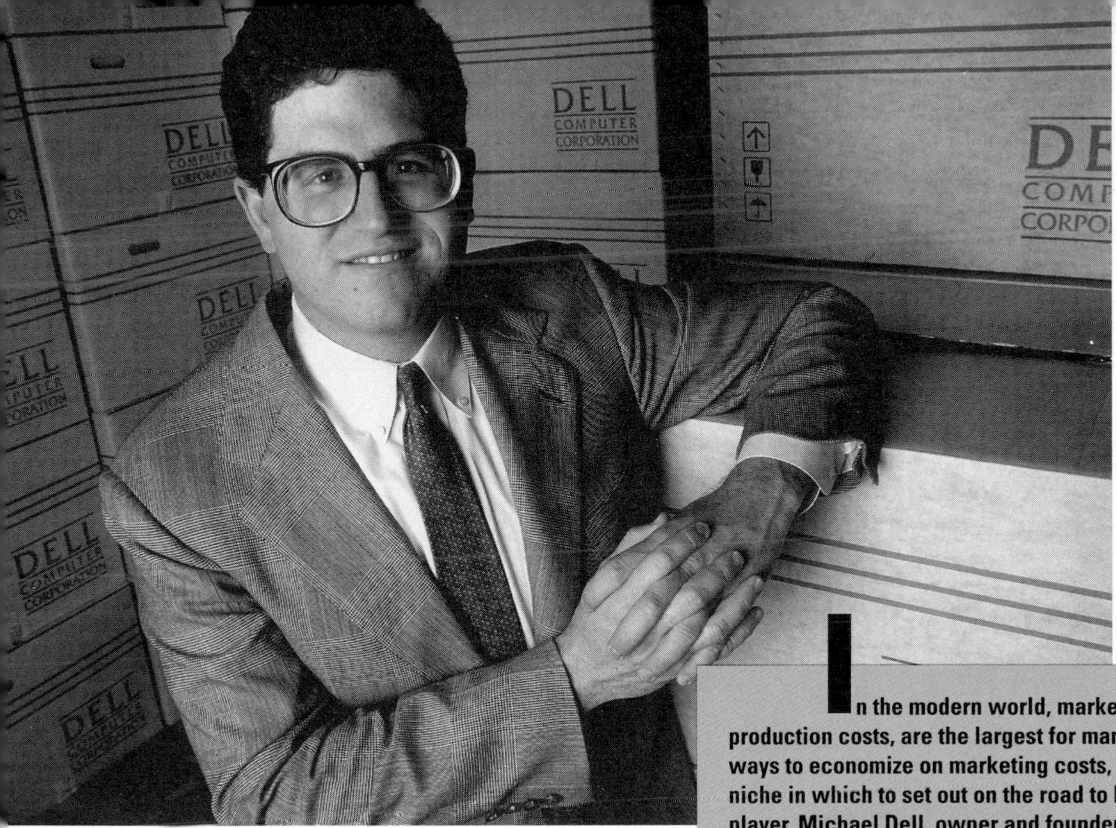

In the modern world, marketing costs, not production costs, are the largest for many goods. By finding ways to economize on marketing costs, a new firm can find a niche in which to set out on the road to becoming a major player. Michael Dell, owner and founder of Dell Computers, has created such a firm. Buying computers and parts at the lowest possible prices and selling directly to the consumer by direct mail, Dell has cut the costs of transacting and made big inroads into the business of previously established firms.

Ronald Coase & Jacob Viner: Understanding *How Firms Work*

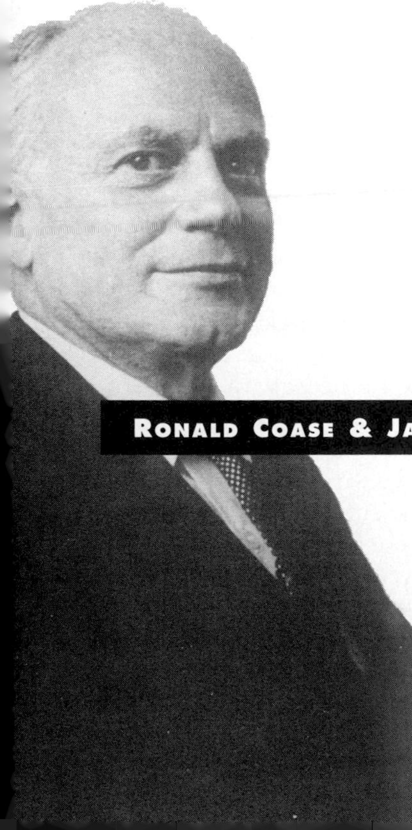

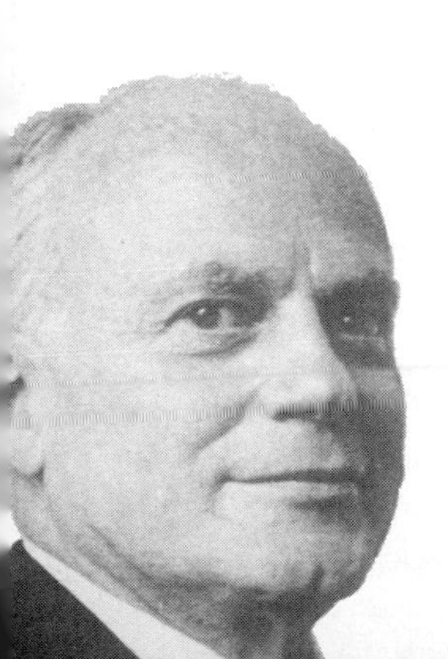

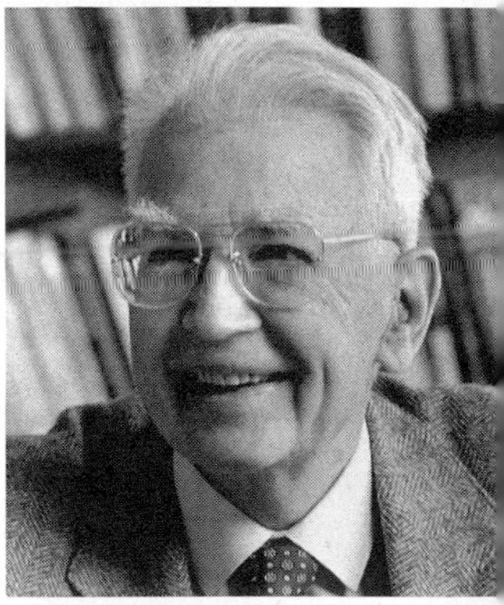

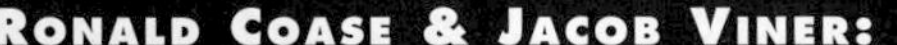

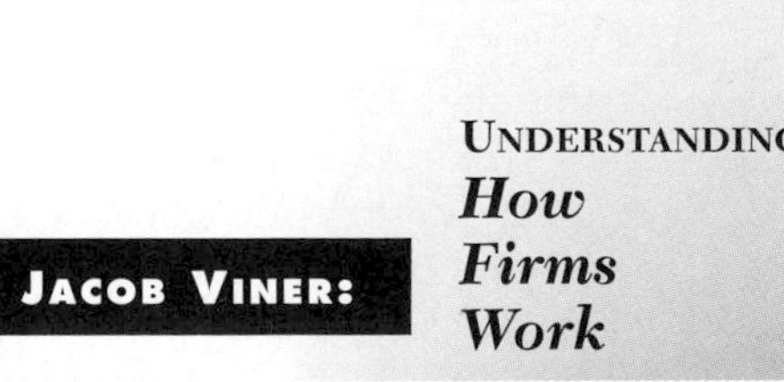

Our understanding of the working of firms was developed in the 1930s, and many economists contributed to our advancing knowledge. Two important contributers were Ronald H. Coase (1910–), pictured right, and Jacob Viner (1892–1970), pictured left.

Coase was born in England but has lived in the United States since 1951, which he first visited as a 20-year-old on a traveling scholarship during the depths of the Great Depression. It was on that visit, and before he had completed his bachelor's degree, that he conceived the ideas for his paper, "The Nature of the Firm," cited 60 years later by the Swedish Academy of Sciences as his main contribution to economics when awarding him the Nobel Prize for Economic Science.

Viner was born in Montreal, Canada, the son of a poor immigrant family from Eastern Europe. He was educated at McGill and Harvard Universities and taught at Chicago and Princeton. Viner's main contribution was to explain the nature of a firm's costs, and it was he who first described the firm's cost curves that are explained in this chapter.

Excess Capacity

It has been estimated that one vacuum cleaner factory can produce a quarter of all the vacuum cleaners produced in the United States before its long-run average cost reaches its minimum.[3] But there are more than four vacuum cleaner factories in the United States, so each factory is operating at an output rate below that at which long-run average cost is at a minimum. The situation also holds for TV picture tubes and for steel, cars, and petroleum refining. Economies of scale also exist in the market for typewriters, cigarettes, semiconductors, and matches.

Figure 10.11 illustrates the situation that prevails in those industries that can lower their average production costs if the market is big enough to permit them to expand to their most efficient scale. Output, limited by the extent of the market, is Q_0. The firm is producing efficiently at an average total cost of ATC_0. But the firm has excess capacity. It can lower its costs to ATC_{min} even with its existing plant if output can be increased to Q_c, and it can lower its costs even more by switching to a bigger plant. But the firm can't sell more than Q_0. So, even when it is operating as efficiently as possible, the firm has excess capacity. The production of vacuum cleaners, TV picture tubes, steel, cars, and the other products mentioned above are examples of industries in which the situation shown in Fig. 10.11 prevails.

FIGURE 10.11

Excess Capacity

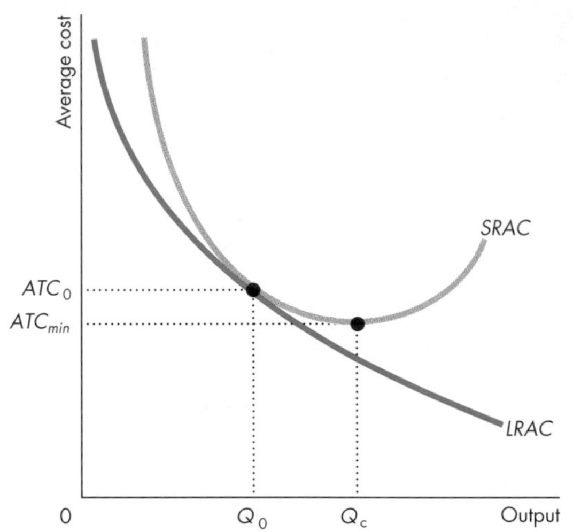

The size of the market limits a firm's output to Q_0. At output Q_0, the long-run average cost curve is downward sloping—there are economies of scale. To produce Q_0 at least cost, the firm installs a plant with a capacity of Q_c and operates the plant below capacity. This situation prevails in many industries, including those manufacturing vacuum cleaners, TV picture tubes, steel, cars, refined petroleum, typewriters, cigarettes, semiconductors, and matches.

Operating Flat Out

When we examined the short-run marginal cost of NEPOOL, we discovered that its marginal cost increases as it produces more power. As we saw in Fig. 10.6, NEPOOL's marginal cost curve slopes upward and becomes extremely steep at output rates in excess of 17,000 megawatt-hours. Why don't the companies in NEPOOL build additional plants? We can answer this question by applying the lessons that you've just learned about the relationship between short-run and long-run costs.

Figure 10.12 shows NEPOOL's short-run marginal cost curve (*MC*) as well as its short-run average total cost curve (*ATC*). Two points are marked on the *x*-axis. Point *C* is NEPOOL's capacity. (The word *capacity* is being used here in its economic sense as the output rate that minimizes average total cost.) The other point marked is *L*, the physical limits of the output of the existing plant.

NEPOOL's marginal cost curve slopes upward very steeply because as its output approaches its physical limits, generators are brought into operation that use very expensive fuel (similar to that used by jet aircraft). But the average total cost curve has a much more gentle slope. Why? Because the bulk of NEPOOL's costs are not variable fuel costs at all but fixed costs. NEPOOL's fixed resources—equipment and skilled labor—cannot be varied to meet hourly shifts in demand for power. The great proportion of total costs coming from these fixed resources smooths out NEPOOL's average total cost. NEPOOL's output fluctuates between 11,500 and 17,000 megawatt-hours (see Fig. 10.6), a range over which the marginal cost curve is upward sloping but the average total cost curve is downward sloping.

[3] James V. Koch, *Industrial Organization and Prices*, 2nd ed. (Englewood Cliffs, N.J.: Prentice-Hall, 1980), 123–134.

FIGURE 10.12

Overutilizing Capacity

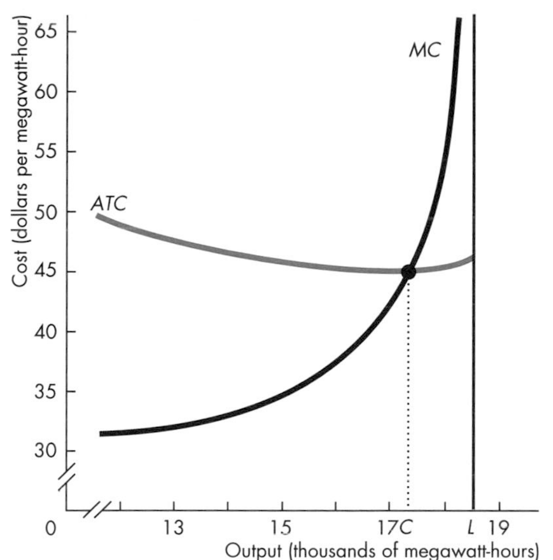

Although NEPOOL faces a steeply increasing marginal cost, its average total cost declines up to output *C*. The capacity (minimum cost) of NEPOOL's plant is output *C*. Output *L* is the physical limit of its plant. Between *C* and *L*, average total cost rises. When demand increases so that NEPOOL is producing in the range between *C* and *L* for a significant amount of time, it will be efficient to increase plant size to meet the additional demand. It will not be efficient to build a bigger plant to meet current demand even though at peak demand NEPOOL is operating flat out. Although marginal cost can be lowered with a larger plant, average total cost will rise.

Occasionally, output increases above capacity and therefore moves into the range in which average total cost is increasing. But such cases are rare—occurring only at the peak of demand for the year.

As the demand for electric power gradually increases, the NEPOOL producers will be able to achieve greater economic efficiency by increasing their plant size. Currently, output fluctuates between 11,500 megawatt-hours and 17,000 megawatt-hours. If demand fluctuates between 17,000 and 19,000 megawatt-hours, production will be taking place on the upward-sloping part of the short-run average total cost curve, and on some occasions, it will be necessary for NEPOOL to operate flat out—at its physical limits—and to import power from neighboring power pools to meet the demand. It will pay NEPOOL producers to increase their production capacity to meet the additional demand.

It does not pay to increase capacity to meet demand fluctuations in the range currently being experienced. An increased plant will increase the fixed costs and shift the average total cost curve upward. The new average total cost curve will be below the current one only at higher outputs than can be sold. Thus it pays the NEPOOL power companies to stick with their existing plants and operate them flat out to meet the peak demand.

◆ ◆ ◆ ◆ We've now studied the way in which a firm's costs vary as it varies its inputs and output rate. We've seen how the fact that marginal product eventually diminishes gives rise to eventually increasing average and marginal cost. We've also seen how long-run cost curves take their shape from economies and diseconomies of scale—long-run average cost decreasing as output increases with economies of scale and long-run average cost increasing as output increases with diseconomies of scale. ◆ ◆ Our next task is to study the interactions of firms and households in markets for goods and services and see how prices, output levels, and profits are determined.

SUMMARY

Firms' Objectives and Constraints

Firms aim to maximize profit. Profit maximization stems directly from scarcity. Only firms that maximize profits can survive in a competitive environment.

Constraints are imposed on profit maximization by the market and by technology. Some firms operate in such competitive markets that they have no choice but to sell their output at the going price. In other cases the firm can choose the price of its output. However, at higher prices, it will sell less. Most firms are unable to influence the markets for their inputs and have to buy them at the going prices. Technology limits the production process of firms. If firms are technologically efficient, then they can increase their output only by using more inputs.

In the short run, some inputs cannot be changed. In most cases, the capital input is fixed in the short run while labor can be varied. (pp. 233–234)

Short-Run Technology Constraint

The short-run production function describes the limits to output as a firm changes the quantity of a variable input such as labor. The short-run production function is described by the total, marginal, and average product curves. Total product is the output produced in a given period. Average product is total product per unit of variable input. Marginal product is the change in total product resulting from a one-unit increase in the variable input. As the variable input is increased, marginal product increases at first until it reaches a peak, and thereafter it declines—diminishing returns begin. When marginal product exceeds average product, average product is increasing. When marginal product is less than average product, average product is decreasing. When marginal product equals average product, average product is at its maximum. (pp. 234–240)

Short-Run Cost

Total cost is divided into total fixed cost and total variable cost. As output increases, total cost increases because total variable cost increases. Marginal cost is the additional cost of producing one more unit of output. Average total cost is total cost per unit of output.

Costs depend on how much a firm produces. Average fixed cost decreases as output increases. Average variable cost and average total cost are U-shaped curves. Marginal cost is also U-shaped. When marginal cost is less than average cost, average cost is decreasing, and when marginal cost exceeds average cost, average cost is increasing. When average product is at a maximum, average variable cost is at a minimum. When average product is increasing, average variable cost is decreasing, and when average product is decreasing, average variable cost is increasing. (pp. 240–248)

Plant Size, Cost, and Capacity

Plant capacity is the output rate with the lowest average total cost. Firms that produce a smaller amount than their capacity are said to have excess capacity; those that produce a larger amount than their capacity are said to have overutilized their capacity. Firms choose their plant size to minimize long-run cost.

Long-run cost is the cost of production when all inputs—labor as well as plant and equipment—have been adjusted to their economically efficient levels. The behavior of long-run cost depends on the firm's production function. As a firm uses more labor while holding capital constant, it eventually experiences diminishing returns. When it uses more capital while holding labor constant, it also experiences diminishing returns. When it varies all its inputs in equal proportions, it experiences returns to scale. Returns to scale can be constant, increasing, or decreasing. (pp. 248–251)

Plant Size and Cost

There is a set of short-run cost curves for each different plant size. There is one least-cost plant for each output. The higher the output, the larger is the plant that will minimize average total cost.

The long-run average cost curve traces out the relationship between the lowest attainable average total cost and output when both capital and labor inputs can be varied. With increasing returns to scale, the long-run average cost curve slopes downward. With decreasing returns to scale, the long-run average cost curve slopes upward.

There is no distinction between fixed cost and variable cost in the long run. Since all inputs are variable, all costs are also variable.

Short-run and long-run cost curves shift when either input prices or technology changes. An improvement in technology increases the output from a given set of inputs and shifts the cost curves downward. A rise in input prices shifts the cost curves upward. (pp. 251–255)

Returns to Scale in Reality

Some firms, including those that make vacuum cleaners, TV picture tubes, and cars, have increasing returns to scale (economies of scale). Usually economies of scale exist when the total market is too small to allow the efficient scale of production. In such industries, firms operate efficiently with excess capacity.

Some firms overutilize their plants, operating them at an output rate that exceeds capacity. NEPOOL is a good example. Though the marginal cost of electric power increases as output increases, only rarely does NEPOOL produce so much power that it is operating on the upward-sloping section of its short-run average total cost curve. Only if a firm persistently operates on the upward-sloping part of its short-run average total cost curve will it be efficient to increase its plant size. (pp. 255–259)

KEY ELEMENTS

Key Terms

Average fixed cost, 242
Average product, 237
Average total cost, 242
Average variable cost, 242
Capacity, 248
Capital-intensive technique, 233
Constant returns to scale, 250
Decreasing returns to scale, 250
Diminishing marginal returns, 239
Diseconomies of scale, 250
Economies of scale, 250
Excess capacity, 248
Fixed cost, 240
Fixed inputs, 234
Increasing marginal returns, 239
Increasing returns to scale, 250
Labor-intensive technique, 233
Law of diminishing returns, 239
Long run, 234
Long-run average cost curve, 251
Long-run cost, 248
Marginal cost, 242
Marginal product, 235
Marginal product of capital, 250
Marginal product of labor, 235
Market constraints, 233
Overutilized capacity, 248
Physical limits, 248
Production function, 249
Profit maximization, 233
Returns to scale, 250
Short run, 234
Technique, 233
Total cost, 240
Total fixed cost, 240
Total product, 234
Total product curve, 234
Total variable cost, 240
Variable cost, 240
Variable inputs, 234

Key Figures and Tables

REVIEW QUESTIONS

1 Why do we assume that firms maximize profit?

2 What are the main constraints on a firm's ability to maximize profit?

3 Distinguish between the short run and the long run.

4 Define total product, average product, and marginal product. Explain the relationships between a total product curve, average product curve, and marginal product curve.

5 State the law of diminishing returns. What does this law imply about the shapes of the total, marginal, and average product curves?

6 Define total cost, total fixed cost, total variable cost, average total cost, average fixed cost, average variable cost, and marginal cost.

7 What is the relationship between the average total cost curve, the average variable cost curve, and the marginal cost curve?

8 Define the long-run average cost curve. What is the relationship between the long-run average cost curve and the short-run average total cost curve?

9 What does the long-run average cost curve tell us?

10 Define economies of scale. What effects do economies of scale have on the shape of the long-run average cost curve?

11 When does the long-run average cost curve touch the minimum point of a short-run average total cost curve?

12 When does the long-run average cost curve touch a point on the short-run average total cost curve to the left of its minimum point?

13 When does the long-run average cost curve touch a point on the short-run average total cost curve to the right of its minimum point?

14 Why might long-run average cost decline? Why might long-run average cost increase?

15 What makes the short-run cost curves shift

a upward
b downward

PROBLEMS

1 The total product schedule of Rubber Duckies, Inc., a firm making rubber boats, is described by the following:

Labor (number of workers employed per week)	Output (rubber boats per week)
1	1
2	3
3	6
4	10
5	15
6	21
7	26
8	30
9	33
10	35

a Draw the total product curve.
b Calculate average product and draw the average product curve.
c Calculate marginal product and draw the marginal product curve.
d What is the relationship between average product and marginal product at output rates below 30 boats a week? Why?
e What is the relationship between average product and marginal product at outputs above 30 boats a week? Why?

2 Suppose that the price of labor is $400 a week, the total fixed cost is $10,000 a week, and the total product schedule is the same as in problem 1.

a Calculate the firm's total cost, total variable cost, and total fixed costs for each of the outputs given.
b Draw the total cost, total variable cost, and total fixed cost curves.
c Calculate the firm's average total cost, average fixed cost, average variable cost, and marginal cost at each of the outputs given.
d Draw the following cost curves: average total cost, average variable cost, average fixed cost, and marginal cost.

3 Suppose that total fixed cost increases to $11,000 a week. How will this affect the firm's average total cost, average fixed cost, average variable cost, and marginal cost curves in problem 2?

4 Suppose that total fixed cost remains at $10,000 a week but that the price of labor increases to $450 a week. Using these new costs, rework problems 2(a) and 2(b) and draw the new cost curves.

APPENDIX

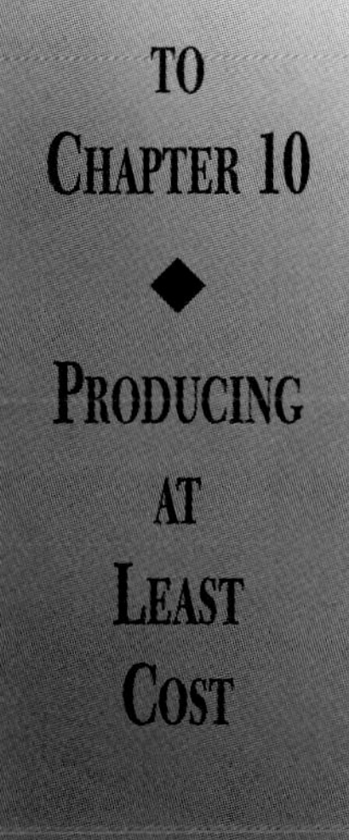

Input Substitution

You would be hard-pressed to think of many goods that can be produced in only one way. Just about every good and service can be produced by using a capital-intensive technique or a labor-intensive technique. For example, cars can be made with computer-controlled robotic assembly lines that use enormous amounts of capital and hardly any labor, a capital-intensive technique, or they can be built by skilled labor using only hand tools, a labor-intensive technique.

The firm's technically feasible range of production possibilities is described by its production function. For example, Swanky, Inc.'s production function tells us the maximum daily output of sweaters that can be produced by using different combinations of labor and capital. Figure A10.1 shows Swanky's production function. It tells us, for example, that when Sidney hires 2 workers a day and rents 2 machines, the output produced is 15 sweaters a day. The figure highlights that Swanky can use three different techniques to produce 15 sweaters a day and two different techniques to produce 10 and 21 sweaters a day.

The production function in Fig. A10.1 can be used to calculate the marginal product of labor and the marginal product of capital. The *marginal product of labor* is the change in total product per unit change of labor, holding the amount of capital constant. We've already learned how to calculate the marginal product of labor, so we'll not repeat the calculations here. The marginal product of capital is the change in total product per unit change in capital, holding the amount of labor constant. Although we have not calculated the marginal product of capital, it is done in exactly the same way as the calculation of the marginal product of labor. Furthermore, the law of diminishing returns applies to capital just as it does to labor. That is, holding labor input constant, the marginal product of capital diminishes as the capital input increases.

It's easy to see why the law of diminishing returns applies to capital by imagining this scene in Swanky's knitting factory. Suppose that there is 1 worker with 1 machine. Output (as shown in Fig. A10.1) is 4 sweaters a day. If an extra machine is installed, the 1 worker can still easily handle the 2 machines. One machine can be set to knit blue sweaters and the other, red sweaters. There's no need to stop the machines to change the wool color. Output more than doubles to 10 sweaters a day. But if a third machine is added, a single worker finds it hard to cope with the increasingly complex factory. For example, there are now three times as many

FIGURE A10.1

Swanky's Production Function

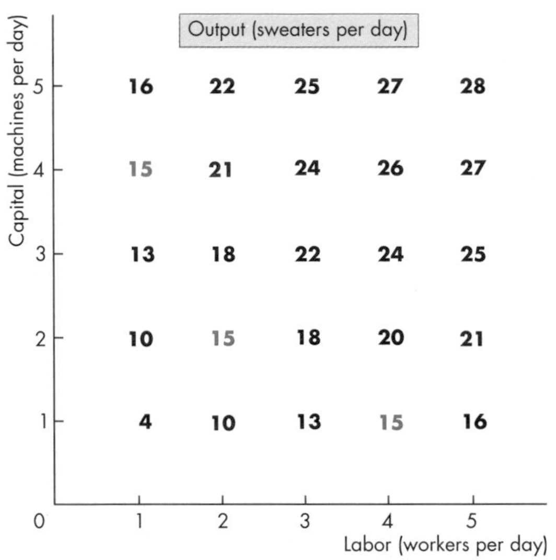

The figure shows how many sweaters can be produced per day by various combinations of labor and capital inputs. For example, by using 1 worker and 2 knitting machines, Swanky can produce 10 sweaters a day; and by using 4 workers and 2 machines, Swanky can produce 20 sweaters.

TABLE A10.1

Substituting Between Capital and Labor to Produce 15 Sweaters a Day

Method	Capital (K)	Labor (L)	Fall in capital ($-\Delta K$)	Rise in labor (ΔL)	Marginal rate of substitution of labor for capital ($-\Delta K/\Delta L$)
a	4	1			
			2	1	2
b	2	2			
			1	2	½
c	1	4			

Switching from method *a* to method *b* involves cutting capital ($-\Delta K$) by 2 machines and raising labor (ΔL) by 1 worker. The marginal rate of substitution of labor for capital—which is the ratio of the fall in capital ($-\Delta K$) to the rise in labor (ΔL)—is 2. Switching from method *b* to method *c* involves cutting capital by 1 machine and raising labor by 2 workers, which means that the marginal rate of substitution of labor for capital is ½.

breakdowns as there were with just one machine. The worker has to spend an increasing amount of time fixing problems. Output increases to only 13 sweaters a day.

Although all goods and services can be produced by using a variety of alternative methods of production, the ease with which capital and labor can be substituted for each other varies from industry to industry. The production function reflects the ease with which inputs can be substituted for each other. Also, the production function can be used to calculate the degree of substitutability between inputs. Such a calculation involves a new concept—that of the marginal rate of substitution of capital for labor.

The Substitutability of Capital and Labor

The **marginal rate of substitution of labor for capital** is the decrease in capital needed per unit increase in labor that keeps output constant. Table A10.1 illustrates how to calculate the marginal rate of substitution of labor for capital. As we saw in Fig. A10.1, an output of 15 sweaters a day can be produced with 4 knitting machines and 1 worker, 2 units of each input, or 1 knitting machine and 4 workers. Let's call those methods *a*, *b*, and *c*.

We can calculate the marginal rate of substitution of labor for capital by changing the method of producing 15 sweaters a day and calculating the ratio of the fall in capital to the rise in labor. Switching the method from *a* to *b* reduces the capital input by 2 machines and increases the labor input by 1 worker. The marginal rate of substitution is 2. Switching from method *b* to *c* reduces capital by 1 machine and increases labor by 2 workers. The marginal rate of substitution is ½.

The marginal rates of substitution we've just calculated obey the **law of diminishing marginal rate of substitution,** which states that:

The marginal rate of substitution of labor for capital falls as the amount of capital decreases and the amount of labor increases.

You can see that the law of diminishing marginal rate of substitution makes sense by considering Swanky's sweater factory. With 1 worker racing among 4 knitting machines, desperately trying to keep them all operating, coping with breakdowns, and keeping the wool from tangling, output can be held constant at 15 sweaters a day by getting rid of 1 machine and hiring only a small additional amount of labor. The marginal rate of substitution is high. At the other extreme, 4 workers are falling over each other to operate 1 machine. In this situation, output can be kept constant at 15 sweaters a day by laying off 2 workers and installing 1 additional machine. The marginal rate of substitution is low. The principle of the diminishing marginal rate of substitution applies to (almost) all production processes.

FIGURE A10.2

An Isoquant Map

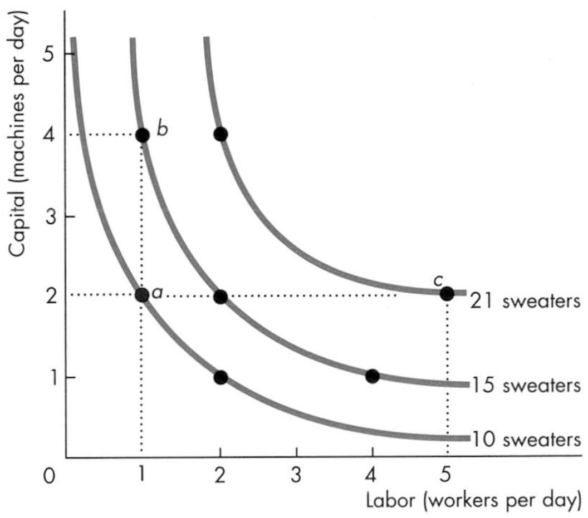

The figure illustrates an isoquant map, but one that shows only three isoquants—those for 10, 15, and 21 sweaters a day. These curves correspond to the production function shown in Fig. A10.1. If Swanky uses 2 machines and 1 worker (point *a*), it produces 10 sweaters. If it uses 4 machines and 1 worker (point *b*), it produces 15 sweaters. And if it uses 2 machines and 5 workers, it produces 21 sweaters.

Isoquants

A graph of the different combinations of labor and capital that produce 15 sweaters a day is called an isoquant. An **isoquant** is a curve that shows the different combinations of labor and capital required to produce a given quantity of output. The word *isoquant* means "equal quantity"—*iso* meaning equal and *quant* meaning quantity. There is an isoquant for each output level. The series of isoquants is called an **isoquant map.** Figure A10.2 shows an isoquant map. It has three isoquants: one for 10 sweaters, one for 15 sweaters, and one for 21 sweaters. Each isoquant shown is based on the production function presented in Fig. A10.1. But Fig. A10.2 does not show all the isoquants. For example, Swanky's isoquant for 10 sweaters shows all the techniques of production—the combinations of workers and knitting machines—that can produce 10 sweaters a day. Isoquants for larger outputs are farther from the origin. That is because for any given capital input, to produce more output Swanky needs more labor, and for any given labor input, to produce more output Swanky needs more capital. For example, if Sidney hires 1 worker and rents 2 machines (point *a*), Swanky's output is 10 sweaters a day. But if Sidney rents 2 more machines (point *b*), Swanky's output increases to 15 sweaters a day. Or if Sidney hires 4 more workers (point *c*), Swanky's output increases to 21 sweaters a day.

Marginal Rate of Substitution

The marginal rate of substitution equals the magnitude of the slope of the isoquant. Figure A10.3 illustrates this relationship. The figure shows the isoquant for 13 sweaters a day. Pick any point on this isoquant and imagine increasing labor by the smallest conceivable amount and decreasing capital by the amount necessary to keep output constant at 13 sweaters. As we reduce the capital input and increase the labor input, we travel along the isoquant. If the isoquant is steep (as at point *a*), the capital input decreases by a large amount relative to the increase in the labor input. The marginal rate of substitution is high. But if the isoquant has a gentle slope (as at point *b*), the capital input decreases by a small amount relative to the increase in labor, and the marginal rate of substitution is small.

FIGURE A10.3

The Marginal Rate of Substitution

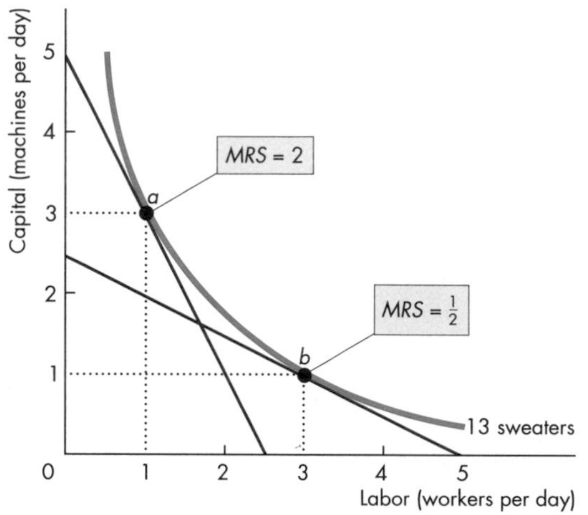

The marginal rate of substitution is measured by the magnitude of the slope of the isoquant. To calculate the marginal rate of substitution at point *a*, use the red line that is tangential to the isoquant at point *a*. Calculate the slope of that line to find the slope of the isoquant at point *a*. The magnitude of the slope at point *a* is 2. Thus at a point *a*, the marginal rate of substitution of labor for capital is 2. The marginal rate of substitution at point *b* is found from the slope of the line tangential to the isoquant at that point. That slope is ½. Thus the marginal rate of substitution of labor for capital at point *b* is ½.

The marginal rate of substitution at point *a* is the magnitude of the slope of the straight red line that is tangent to the isoquant at point *a*. The slope of the isoquant at point *a* is the same as the slope of the line. To calculate that slope, let's move along the red line from 5 knitting machines and no workers to 2.5 workers and no knitting machines. Capital decreases by 5 knitting machines, and labor increases by 2.5 workers. The magnitude of the slope is 5 divided by 2.5, which equals 2. Thus at point *a*, the marginal rate of substitution of labor for capital is 2.

The marginal rate of substitution at point *b* is the magnitude of the slope of the straight red line that is tangent to the isoquant at point *b*. This line has the same slope as the isoquant at point *b*. Along this red line, if capital falls by 2.5 knitting machines, labor increases by 5 workers. The magnitude of the slope is 2.5 knitting machines divided by 5 workers, which equals ½. Thus at point *b*, the marginal rate of substitution of labor for capital is ½.

You can now see that the law of diminishing marginal rate of substitution is embedded in the shape of the isoquant. When the capital input is large and the labor input is small, the isoquant is steep. As the capital input decreases and the labor input increases, the slope of the isoquant diminishes. Only curves that are bowed toward the origin have this feature; thus isoquants are always bowed toward the origin.

Isoquants are very nice, but what do we do with them? The answer is that we use them to work out a firm's least-cost technique of production. But to do so, we need to illustrate the firm's costs in the same sort of diagram that contains the isoquants.

Isocost Lines

An **isocost line** shows all the combinations of capital and labor that can be bought for a given total cost. To make the concept of the isocost line as clear as possible, we'll consider the following example. Swanky is going to spend a total of $100 a day producing sweaters. Knitting-machine operators can be hired for $25 a day, and knitting machines can be rented for $25 a day. The points *a*, *b*, *c*, *d*, and *e* in Fig. A10.4 show five possible combinations of labor and capital that Swanky can employ for a total cost of $100. For example, point *b* shows that Swanky can use 3 machines (costing $75) and 1 worker (costing $25). If Swanky can employ workers and machines for fractions of a day, then any of the combinations along the line *ae* can be employed for a total cost of $100. This line is Swanky's isocost line for a total cost of $100.

The Isocost Equation

The isocost line can be described by an isocost equation. An **isocost equation** states the relationship between the quantities of inputs that can be hired for a given total cost. We'll work out the isocost

FIGURE A10.4

Swanky's Input Possibilities

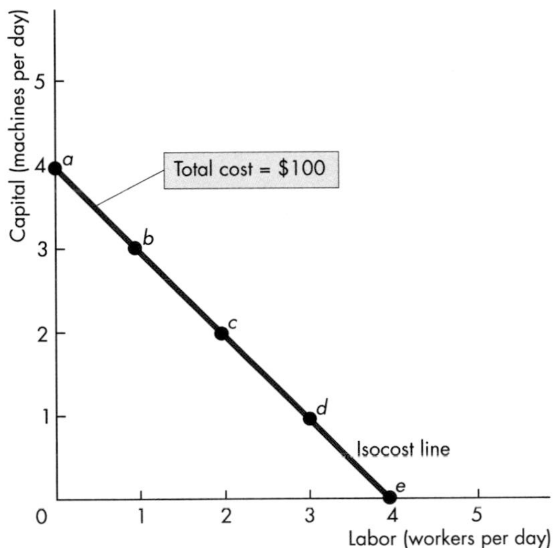

For a given total cost, Swanky's input possibilities depend on input prices. If labor and capital cost $25 a day each, for a total cost of $100 Swanky can employ the combinations of capital and labor shown by the points *a* through *e*. The line passing through these points is an isocost line. It shows the combinations of capital and labor, when each costs $25 a day, that have a total cost of $100.

equation by using symbols that apply to any firm and numbers that describe Swanky's situation.

The variables that affect the firm's total cost (TC) are the prices of the inputs—the price of labor (P_L) and the price of capital (P_K)—and the quantities of the inputs employed—labor (L) and capital (K). In Swanky's case, we're going to look at the amount of labor and capital that can be employed when each input costs $25 a day and when total cost is $100. The cost of the labor employed ($P_L \times L$) plus the cost of the capital employed ($P_K \times K$) is the firm's total cost (TC). That is,

$$P_L L + P_K K = TC,$$

and, in Swanky's case,

$$25L + 25K = 100.$$

To calculate the isocost equation, divide the firm's total cost by the price of capital and then subtract $(P_L/P_K)L$ from both sides of the resulting equation. The isocost equation is

$$K = TC/P_K - (P_L/P_K)L.$$

It tells us how the capital input varies as the labor input varies, holding total cost constant. Swanky's isocost equation is

$$K = 4 - L.$$

This equation corresponds to the isocost line in Fig. A10.4.

The Effect of Input Prices

Along the isocost line that we have just calculated, capital and labor cost $25 a day each. Because these input prices are the same, in order to increase labor by 1 unit, capital must be decreased by 1 unit. The magnitude of the slope of the isocost line shown in Fig. A10.4 is 1. The slope tells us that 1 unit of labor costs 1 unit of capital.

Next, let's consider some different prices, as shown in the table for Fig. A10.5. If the daily wage rate is $50 and the daily rental rate for knitting machines remains at $25, then 1 worker costs the same as 2 machines. Holding total cost constant at $100, to use 1 more worker now requires using 2 fewer machines. With the wage rate double that of the machine rental rate, the isocost line is line *B* in Fig. A10.5(a), and the magnitude of its slope is 2. That is, in order to hire 1 more worker and keep total cost constant, Swanky must give up 2 knitting machines.

If the daily wage rate remains at $25 and the daily rental rate of a knitting machine rises to $50, then 2 workers cost the same as 1 machine. In this case, in order to hire 1 more worker and keep total cost constant, Swanky must give up only half a knitting machine. The magnitude of the slope of the isocost line is now ½, as shown by line *C* in Fig. A10.5(b).

The higher the relative price of labor, the steeper is the isocost line. The magnitude of the slope of the isocost line measures the relative price of labor in terms of capital—that is, the price of labor divided by the price of capital.

FIGURE A10.5

Input Prices and the Isocost Line

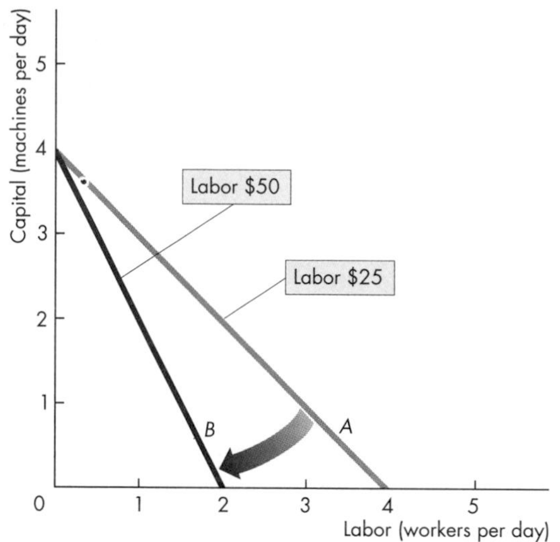

(a) An increase in the price of labor

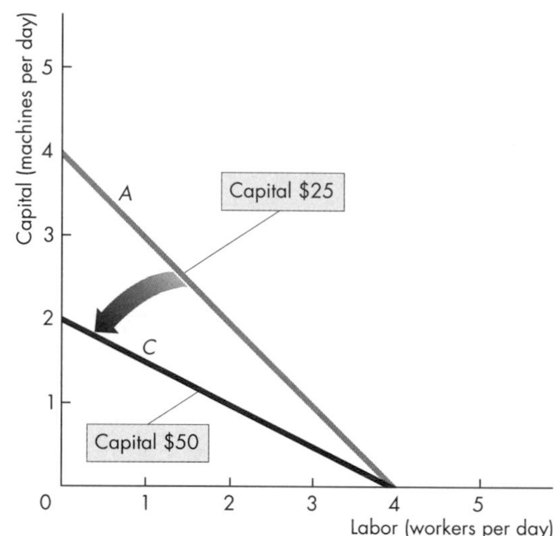

(b) An increase in the price of capital

Isocost line	Price of capital (rental rate per day)	Price of labor (wage per day)	Isocost equation for $TC = \$100$
A	**$25**	**$25**	$K = 4 - L$
B	**$25**	**$50**	$K = 4 - 2L$
C	**$50**	**$25**	$K = 2 - (1/2)L$

The slope of the isocost line depends on the relative input prices. Three cases are set out in the table (each for a total cost of $100). In case *A*, both labor and capital have a price of $25 a day and the isocost line is that labeled *A*. In case *B*, the price of labor rises to $50 but the price of capital remains $25 and the isocost line becomes that labeled *B*. Its slope is twice that of *A*. In case *C* the price of capital rises to $50 and the price of labor remains constant at $25 and the isocost line becomes that labeled *C*. Its slope is half that of *A*.

The Isocost Map

An **isocost map** shows a series of isocost lines, each for a different level of total cost. The larger the total cost, the larger are the quantities of all inputs that can be employed. Figure A10.6 illustrates an isocost map. In that figure, the middle isocost line is the original one that appears in Fig. A10.4. It is the isocost line for a total cost of $100 when both capital and labor cost $25 a day each. The other two isocost lines in Fig. A10.6 are for a total cost of $125 and $75, holding the prices of the inputs constant at $25 each.

The Least-Cost Technique

The **least-cost technique** is the combination of inputs that minimizes total cost of producing a given output. Let's suppose that Swanky wants to produce 15 sweaters a day. What is the least-cost way of doing this? The answer can be seen in Fig. A10.7. The isoquant for 15

FIGURE A10.6
An Isocost Map

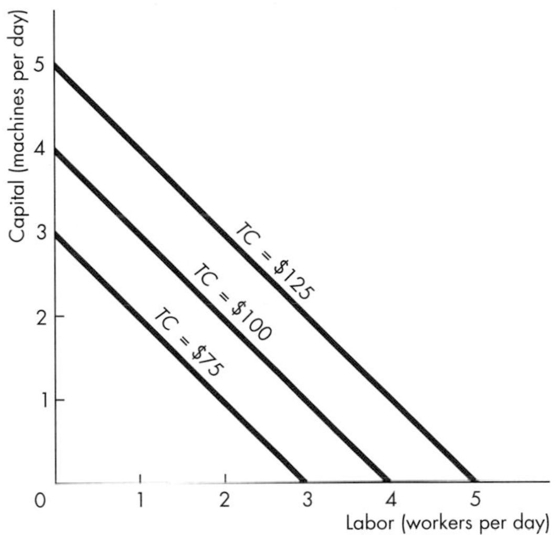

There is an isocost line for each level of cost, and the lines shown here are just a sample. This isocost map shows three isocost lines: one for a total cost of $75, one for $100, and one for $125. For each isocost line, the prices of capital and labor are $25 each. The magnitude of the slope of the lines in an isocost map is determined by the relative price of the two inputs—the price of labor divided by the price of capital. The higher the total cost, the further is the isocost line from the origin.

FIGURE A10.7
The Least-Cost Technique of Production

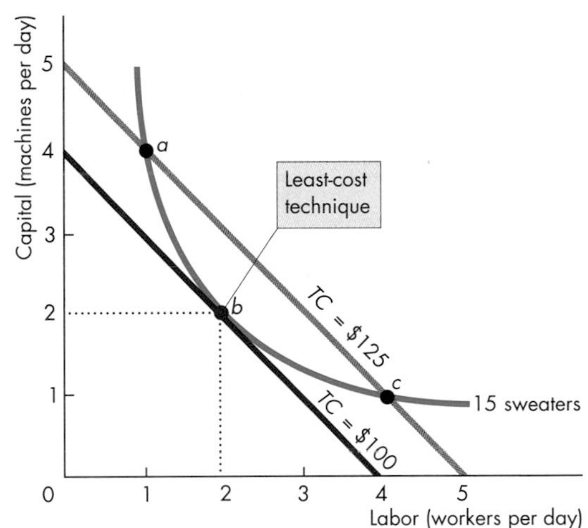

The least-cost technique of producing 15 sweaters occurs when 2 machines and 2 workers are employed at point *b*. An output of 15 sweaters can be produced with the technique illustrated by point *a* (4 machines and 1 worker) or with the technique illustrated by point *c* (1 machine and 4 workers). With either of these techniques, the total cost is $125 and exceeds the total cost at *b* of $100. At *b*, the isoquant for 15 sweaters is tangential to the isocost line for $100. The isocost line and the isoquant have the same slope. If the isoquant intersects the isocost line—for example at *a* and *c*—the least-cost technique has not been found. With the least-cost technique, the marginal rate of substitution (the magnitude of the slope of isoquant) equals the relative price of the inputs (the magnitude of the slope of isocost line).

sweaters is shown, and the three points on that isoquant (marked *a*, *b*, and *c*) illustrate the three techniques of producing 15 sweaters that were shown earlier in Fig. A10.1. The figure also contains two isocost lines—each drawn for a price of capital and a price of labor of $25. One isocost line is for a total cost of $125, and the other is for a total cost of $100.

First, consider point *a*, which is on the isoquant for 15 sweaters and also on the isocost line with a total cost of $125. Swanky can produce 15 sweaters at point *a* by using 1 worker and 4 machines. The total cost, using this technique of production, is $125. Point *c*, which uses 4 workers and 1 machine, is similar to point *a*, except that it shows another technique by which the firm can produce 15 sweaters for a cost of $125.

Next look at point *b*. At this point, Swanky uses 2 machines and 2 workers to produce 15 sweaters at a total cost of $100. Point *b* is the *least-cost technique*, or the *economically efficient technique,* for producing 15 sweaters when knitting machines and workers each cost $25 a day. At those input prices, there is no way that Swanky can produce 15 sweaters for less than $100.

There is an important feature of point *b*, the least-cost technique. At that point, the isoquant on which Swanky is producing (the isoquant for 15 sweaters) has a slope equal to that of the isocost line. The isocost line (for a total cost of $100) is tangential to the isoquant (for 15 sweaters).

Notice that although there is only one way that Swanky can produce 15 sweaters for $100, there are several ways of producing 15 sweaters for more than \$100. Techniques shown by points *a* and *c* are two examples. All the points between *a* and *b* and all the points between *b* and *c* are also ways of producing 15 sweaters for a cost that exceeds \$100 but is less than \$125. That is, there are isocost lines between those shown, for total costs falling between \$100 and \$125. Those isocost lines cut the isoquant for 15 sweaters at the points between *a* and *b* and between *b* and *c*. Swanky can also produce 15 sweaters for a cost that even exceeds \$125. That is, the firm can change its technique of production by moving to a point on the isoquant higher than point *a* and using a more capital-intensive technique than at point *a*. Or the firm could move to a point on the isoquant lower than point *c* and use a more labor-intensive technique than at point *c*. All of these ways of producing 15 sweaters are economically inefficient.

You can see that Swanky cannot produce 15 sweaters for less than \$100 by imagining the isocost line for \$99. That isocost line will not touch the isoquant for 15 sweaters. That is, the firm cannot produce 15 sweaters for \$99. At \$25 for a unit of each input, \$99 will not buy the inputs required to produce 15 sweaters.

Marginal Rate of Substitution Equals Relative Input Price

When a firm is using the least-cost technique of production, the marginal rate of substitution between the inputs equals their relative price. Recall that the marginal rate of substitution is the magnitude of the slope of an isoquant. Relative input prices are measured by the magnitude of the slope of the isocost line. We've just seen that producing at least cost means producing at a point where the isocost line is tangential to the isoquant. Since the two curves are tangential, their slopes are equal. Hence the marginal rate of substitution (the magnitude of the slope of isoquant) equals the relative input price (the magnitude of the slope of isocost line).

You will perhaps better appreciate the importance of relative input prices if we examine what happens to the least-cost technique when those prices change.

Changes in Input Prices

The least-cost technique of production depends in an important way on the relative prices of the inputs. The case that we've just studied is one in which capital and labor cost \$25 a day each. Let's look at two other cases: one in which capital costs twice as much as labor and another in which labor costs twice as much as capital.

If knitting machines cost \$25 a day and a worker is paid \$50 a day, the isocost line becomes twice as steep as the one in Fig. A10.7. That is, to hire one more worker while holding total cost constant, Swanky has to operate two fewer knitting machines. Let's see how this change in input prices changes the least-cost production technique. Figure A10.8(a) illustrates this. You can see in that figure the isoquant for 15 sweaters a day and the initial inputs of 2 knitting machines and 2 workers. When wages are \$50 a day and knitting machines cost \$25 a day, the isocost line becomes steeper. Also, to continue producing 15 sweaters a day, total cost has to rise. That is, the minimum total cost for producing 15 sweaters is higher than originally. The new, steeper isocost line in the figure is that for the minimum cost at which 15 sweaters can be produced at the new input prices. Along that isocost line, Swanky is spending \$140. This is the least-cost method of producing 15 sweaters a day; it is achieved by using 3 machines and 1.3 workers a day. (These inputs cost \$140: 3 machines × \$25 = \$75 and 1.3 workers × \$50 = \$65.)

Next, let's see what happens if wages stay constant but the cost of a machine increases. In particular, suppose that knitting machines cost \$50 a day while wages stay at \$25 a day. In this case, the isocost line becomes less steep. Swanky now has to give up only half a worker-day to get one more machine. The effect of this change on the least-cost technique is illustrated in Fig. A10.8(b). Again, the initial isocost line and least-cost technique are shown in the figure. When the cost of capital increases, the isocost line flattens. The least-cost method of producing 15 sweaters a day now uses 1.3 machines and 3 workers a day. This combination again costs Swanky \$140 a day, but it is the least-cost method of producing 15 sweaters a day when machines cost \$50 and labor \$25 a day.

A change in input prices leads to input substitution. Less of the input whose price has increased and more of the other input are used to produce a given output level. The size of this substitution depends on the technology itself. If the inputs are very close substitutes for each other, the isoquants will be almost straight lines and substitution will be large. If the

FIGURE A10.8

Changes in Input Prices

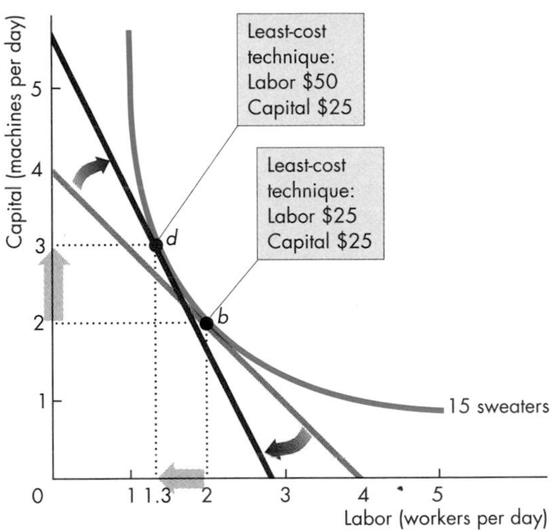

(a) An increase in wages

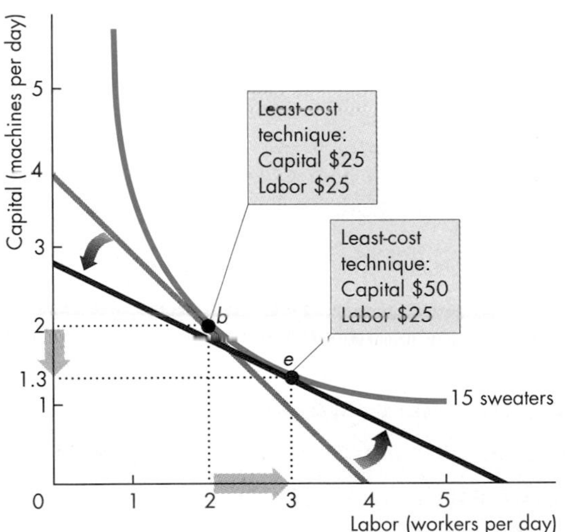

(b) An increase in the price of capital

If the price of labor doubles while the price of capital is held constant, the isocost line becomes twice as steep (part a). The least-cost method of producing 15 sweaters a day changes from point *b* to point *d* (using 1 more machine and 0.7 fewer workers per day). If the price of capital doubles while the price of labor is held constant, the isocost line becomes half as steep (part b). The least-cost method of producing 15 sweaters a day now changes from point *b* to point *e*. One additional worker is hired, and 0.7 fewer machines are used.

inputs are not close substitutes for each other, the isoquants will be curved very tightly and quite large changes in input prices will lead to only small substitution effects.

Marginal Product and Marginal Cost

When we studied short-run and long-run cost in the chapter, we learned about the connection between the marginal product curve of a variable input and the marginal cost curve. In the output range over which marginal product increases, marginal cost decreases; in the output range over which marginal product decreases, marginal cost increases. We also learned in the chapter that it pays a firm to change its plant size if a different plant can produce the firm's desired output at a lower short-run cost than the existing plant. In this appendix, we learned how to calculate the firm's cost-minimizing combination of capital (plant) and labor. Thus our discussion of product curves and cost curves in the chapter and of isocost lines, isoquants, and least-cost techniques of production in this appendix are both dealing with the same problem. But they're looking at the problem from different viewpoints. Let's examine the connection between these two approaches to the firm's cost minimization problem.

First, we're going to learn about the relationship between the marginal rate of substitution and marginal products.

Marginal Rate of Substitution and Marginal Products

The marginal rate of substitution and the marginal products are linked together in a simple formula:

The marginal rate of substitution of labor for capital equals the marginal product of labor divided by the marginal product of capital.

A few steps of reasoning are needed to establish this fact. First, we know that output changes when a firm changes the amount of labor and capital employed. Furthermore, we know that the effect on output of a change in one of the inputs is determined by the marginal product of the input. That is,

$$\text{Change in output} = MP_L \times \Delta L + MP_K \times \Delta K.$$

That is, the change in output is equal to the change in the labor input multiplied by its marginal product plus the change in the capital input multiplied by its marginal product.

Suppose now that the firm wants to remain on an isoquant—that is, Swanky wants to produce the same number of sweaters when it changes its labor and capital inputs. To remain on an isoquant, the change in output must be zero. We can make the change of output zero in the above equation, and doing so yields the equation

$$MP_L \times \Delta L = -MP_K \times \Delta K.$$

This equation tells us what must happen to the capital and labor inputs for Swanky to stay on an isoquant. If the labor input increases, the capital input must decrease, or, equivalently, if the labor input decreases, the capital input must increase. Thus we can write this equation in a slightly different way:

$$MP_L \times \Delta L = MP_K \times -\Delta K.$$

If we divide both sides of the above equation by the increase in the labor input (ΔL) and also divide both sides by the marginal product of capital (MP_K), we get

$$-\Delta K/\Delta L = MP_L/MP_K.$$

This equation tells us that when Swanky remains on an isoquant, the decrease in its capital input ($-\Delta K$) divided by the increase in its labor input (ΔL) is equal to the marginal product of labor (MP_L) divided by the marginal product of capital (MP_K). But we have defined the marginal rate of substitution of labor for capital as the decrease in capital divided by the increase in labor when we remain on a given isoquant. What we have discovered, then, is that the marginal rate of substitution of labor for capital is the ratio of the marginal product of labor to the marginal product of capital.

Marginal Cost

We can use the fact that we have just discovered—that the marginal rate of substitution of labor for capital equals the ratio of the marginal product of labor to the marginal product of capital—to work out an important implication of cost minimization. A few steps are needed, and Table A10.2 provides a guide to those steps.

Part (a) defines some symbols. Part (b) reminds us that the marginal rate of substitution of labor for capital is the slope of the isoquant, which in turn equals the ratio of the marginal product of labor (MP_L) to the marginal product of capital (MP_K). Part (b) also reminds us that the magnitude of the slope of the isocost line equals the ratio of the price of labor (P_L) to the price of capital (P_K). Part (c) of the table summarizes some propositions about a firm that is using the least-cost technique of production.

TABLE **A10.2**

The Least-Cost Technique

(a) Symbols	
Marginal rate of substitution of labor for capital	***MRS***
Marginal product of labor	MP_L
Marginal product of capital	MP_K
Price of labor	P_L
Price of capital	P_K
(b) Definitions	
The magnitude of the slope of the isoquant (*MRS*)	MP_L/MP_K
The magnitude of the slope of the isocost line	P_L/P_K
(c) The least-cost technique	
Slope of the isoquant = Slope of the isocost line	
Therefore:	$MP_L/MP_K = P_L/P_K$
Equivalently:	$MP_L/P_L = MP_K/P_K$
That is,	
Total cost is minimized when the marginal product per dollar spent on labor equals the marginal product per dollar spent on capital.	
Equivalently, flipping the last equation over:	$P_L/MP_L = P_K/MP_K$
That is,	
When total cost is minimized, marginal cost with fixed capital and a change in labor input equals marginal cost with fixed labor and a change in capital input.	

The first of these propositions is that when the least-cost technique is employed, the slope of the isoquant and the isocost line are the same. That is,

$$MP_L/MP_K = P_L/P_K.$$

The second proposition is that total cost is minimized when the marginal product per dollar spent on labor equals the marginal product per dollar spent on capital. To see why, just rearrange the above equation in the following way. First, multiply both sides by the marginal product of capital and then divide both sides by the price of labor. We then get

$$MP_L/P_L = MP_K/P_K.$$

This equation says that the marginal product of labor per dollar spent on labor is equal to the marginal product of capital per dollar spent on capital. In other words, the extra output from the last dollar spent on labor equals the extra output from the last dollar spent on capital. This makes sense. If the extra output from the last dollar spent on labor exceeds the extra output from the last dollar spent on capital, it will pay the firm to use less capital and use more labor. By doing so, the firm can produce the same output at a lower total cost. Conversely, if the extra output from the last dollar spent on capital exceeds the extra output from the last dollar spent on labor, it will pay the firm to use less labor and use more capital. Again, by doing so, the firm lowers the cost of producing a given output. A firm achieves the least-cost technique of production only when the extra output from the last dollar spent on all the inputs is the same.

The third proposition is that with the least-cost technique for producing a given output, marginal cost with fixed capital and variable labor equals marginal cost with fixed labor and variable capital. To see this proposition, simply flip the last equation over and write it as

$$P_L/MP_L = P_K/MP_K.$$

Expressed in words, this equation says that the price of labor divided by its marginal product must equal the price of capital divided by its marginal product. But what is the price of an input divided by its marginal product? The price of labor divided by the marginal product of labor is marginal cost when the capital input is held constant. To see why this is so, first recall the definition of marginal cost: *marginal cost* is the change in total cost resulting from a unit increase in output. If output increases because one more unit of labor is employed, total cost rises by the cost of the extra labor and output increases by the marginal product of the labor. So marginal cost is the price of labor divided by the marginal product of labor. For example, if labor costs $25 a day and if the marginal product of labor is 2 sweaters, then the marginal cost of a sweater is $12.50 ($25 divided by 2).

The price of capital divided by the marginal product of capital has a similar interpretation. The price of capital divided by the marginal product of capital is marginal cost when the labor input is constant. As you can see from the above equation, with the least-cost technique of production, marginal cost is the same regardless of whether the capital input is constant and more labor is used or the labor input is constant and more capital is used.

PART 5

MARKETS FOR GOODS AND SERVICES

Talking with Kenneth Arrow

Kenneth Arrow was born in New York City in 1921. He was an undergraduate at City College and a graduate student at Columbia, where he obtained his Ph.D. in 1951. He has been a professor at Harvard University but since 1979 has been at Stanford University. Professor Arrow has made fundamental contributions to economic theory, especially in areas dealing with uncertainty, information, and organization. He was awarded the Nobel Prize for Economic Science in 1972.

Professor Arrow, what drew you to economics?

My path into economics exemplifies one of my guiding observations on life—that it is highly uncertain. Being brought up during the Great Depression in a family not immune to it, I was deeply concerned about economic conditions. My main bent was clearly for mathematics, but I did take an unusual number of courses in history and some in economics at college. Largely on my own, I became fascinated with mathematical statistics, a field that was undergoing rapid development at the time. In retrospect, my strongest interest was in the foundations of statistical inference. When I entered graduate study in mathematics at Columbia University, I wanted to study statistics with Harold Hotelling, who was actually in the Department of Economics. Under his influence, I eventually enrolled in economics. Hotelling taught a course in mathematical economics, which excited me intensely—though a recent review of my lecture notes leaves me somewhat puzzled as to the basis of my enthusiasm. The course covered only the theory of the firm and of the household.

"My path into economics exemplifies one of my guiding observations on life—that it is highly uncertain."

What did your study of economics involve?

Columbia in the early 1940s was dominated by an institutionalist heritage and a dislike of formal theory. There was no general course in economic theory, but instead a year-long course in the history of economic theory. It crowded the whole curriculum, apart from statistics, into a single year. I also read a good deal on my own, notably American economic history, which I enjoyed greatly, and economic theory, mostly on the then-fashionable topic of imperfect competition and on the exciting work of Hicks and Samuelson, as well as Hotelling's important papers on natural resource economics and general welfare. Looking back, I consider the fact that I did most of my learning on my own to have been a great advantage.

What's your view of the role of mathematics in economics?

Mathematics is a tool that has turned out to be very useful in economics. While there are many issues in economics for which verbal reasoning enables one to see through the issues, there are many others, particularly those which emphasize complex interactions, that can be understood only with the aid of mathematics. This is equally true whether one is trying to get a theoretical understanding or seeking a basis for empirical analysis. An undergraduate who aspires to further study in economics should certainly study calculus with many variables and linear algebra, some elements at least of differential equations, and, if possible, real analysis. Beyond that, quantity is more important than specialization. It is practice at mathematics that counts rather than specific courses.

You are known for your work in general equilibrium theory. Why is this branch of economics important?

In many ways, general equilibrium theory is the underlying premise of all economic reasoning, even when it is not explicitly invoked. Briefly, it emphasizes the interconnection of markets. The demand for any one product depends not only on the price of that product but also on the prices of the other products that the consumer buys, as well as on the prices of the products that he

"I consider the fact that I did most of my learning on my own to have been a great advantage."

or she sells—labor, capital, or whatever. Similarly, the output of a product by a firm depends not only on the price for that product but also on the prices of the other products the firm might sell and on the prices of the firm's inputs.

A tenet of economic theory is that markets clear, at least over time. That is, prices are such that the supply of cotton cloth will equal the demand. But both supply and demand depend not only on the price of cotton cloth but also on wages, interest rates, and the prices of other goods bought by consumers or used by firms. Hence the condition of market clearing has to be interpreted as a large number of equations—each saying supply equals demand in some markets—which *simultaneously* determine a large number of unknowns, such as the prices in each of the markets.

General equilibrium theory as now developed has many limitations. It assumes perfect competition, although there are obvious departures from competition in many parts of the economy. Further, many economists argue that the economy overall does not tend toward equilibrium. But I would contend that that line of reasoning argues for developing general equilibrium theory further. Analysis of individual parts of the economy can never be complete without understanding the wider implications and feedbacks.

Can you give an example of how general equilibrium theory has given a useful description of real events?

The sharp increases in oil prices in 1973 and 1979 and the accompanying decrease in supplies gave rise to great public fears, usually motivated by failure to understand that the economy will react by changing behavior in many industries. Industrial users of oil for heating found ways of conserving, industries that used oil contracted, automobiles were redesigned to reduce gasoline consumption, and the search for oil and oil substitutes, especially natural gas, was intensified. Hence the system as a whole, not just the oil market, reacted in ways that could be understood only when the economy as a whole was considered, not merely the oil market.

"We have made great progress in developing tools of analysis but much less in understanding how to interpret them in the real world."

Why do we spend so much time in the principles course studying perfect competition and the other extreme case of monopoly?

Competition is important to study because it does occur in many markets and because it serves as a useful guideline. Pure monopoly is very rare. But in fact the theory of the intermediate cases of monopolistic competition and oligopoly is much less understood than that of monopoly, so at least some picture, some insight, can be obtained from the study of monopoly.

Have we at least made some progress in understanding oligopoly?

There has been a good deal of study, especially through the development of game theory. But the very foundations of this theory are still not understood. What in fact are the strategies available to the oligopolists? Do they choose prices, or do they choose quantities? More progress has been made on competition in other dimensions, such as quality. In short, we have made great progress in developing tools of analysis but much less in understanding how to interpret them in the real world.

What do you regard as the place of theory in the science of economics?

Most empirical analysis in applied fields today starts with a theoretically inspired model and then fits theory to the real world by econometrics. It is also true that good policymaking depends on some theoretical understanding of the economy. Economic theory is very limited in its ability to predict accurately and in some cases is misleading. But it provides the basis for both empirical analysis and policy formation, even if events in the real world move in a different direction.

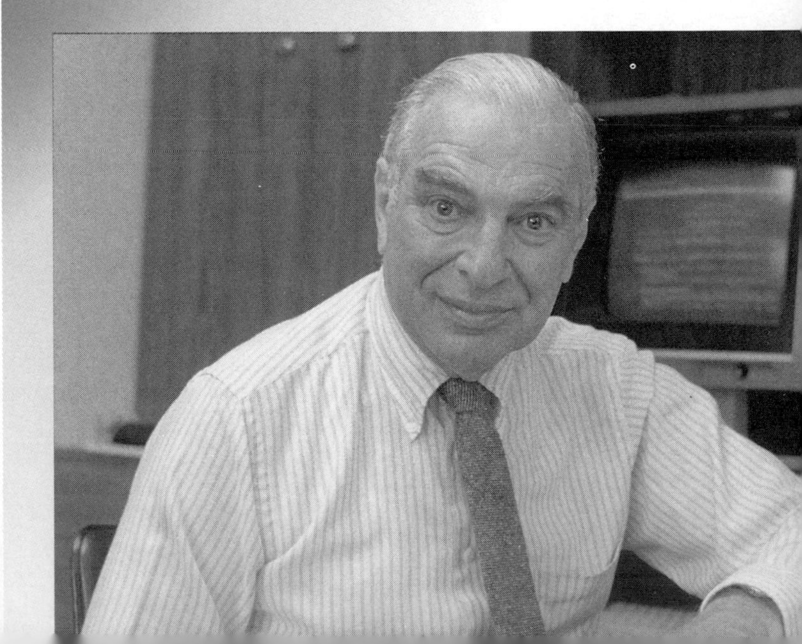

CHAPTER 11

COMPETITION

After studying this chapter, you will be able to:

- Define perfect competition
- Explain why a perfectly competitive firm cannot influence the market price
- Explain how a competitive industry's output changes when price changes
- Explain why firms sometimes shut down temporarily and lay off workers
- Explain why firms enter and leave an industry
- Predict the effects on an industry and on a typical firm of a change in demand and of a technological advance
- Explain why farmers have had such a bad time in recent years
- Explain why perfect competition is efficient

Hot Rivalry in Ice Cream

ICE CREAM IS BIG BUSINESS. IN 1988, CLOSE TO 1 BILLION gallons were bought—an average of four gallons per person—at a cost of more than $7 billion. Competition in the ice cream industry is fierce. National names, such as Häagen-Dazs and Frusen Glädjé, are competing with other national, regional, and local brands. Ben and Jerry's, Bart's, and Annabel's are all battling for a place in a crowded market. ◆◆ In this fiercely competitive environment, new firms are entering and trying their luck while other firms are being squeezed out of the business. Some are growing and disappearing in a matter of months. One example is Steve's Homemade Ice Cream, Inc. of Bloomfield, New Jersey. After growing 56 percent in 1987, sales became stagnant in 1988. Steve's moved into microwave sundaes and other products. Many other ice cream producers have moved into frozen yogurt. How does competition affect prices and profits? What causes some firms to leave an industry and others to enter it? What are the effects on profits and prices of new firms entering and old firms leaving an industry? ◆◆ In 1990 and 1991, more than 10 million people were unemployed. Of these, 6 million were unemployed because they had been laid off by firms seeking to trim their costs and avoid bankruptcy. Ice cream producers, computer manufacturers, and firms in almost every sector of the economy laid off workers on a massive scale. Those years were unusually harsh ones, but even in a typical year, more than 3 million people are laid off. Why do firms lay off workers? When will a firm temporarily shut down, laying off its workers? ◆◆ Over the past few years, there has been a dramatic fall in the prices of all kinds of consumer goods, such as

VCRs, Walkmans, and personal computers. What exactly goes on in an industry when the price of its output falls dramatically? What happens to the profits of the firms producing such goods? ◆◆ American farms have been in the news a great deal in recent years. Most farmers have fallen on very hard times. Many of them have gone out of business. What is happening in the farm sector that is creating such serious problems?

◆◆◆◆ To tackle the questions just posed, we have to look beyond the individual firm standing in isolation and think about how firms interact with each other. Most goods are produced by more than one firm, so the firms compete with each other. Each firm tries to outdo its rivals by producing at a lower cost and by selling a larger output, thereby making the biggest possible profit. In this chapter we'll study markets in which firms are locked together in such stiff competition that the best a firm can do is to match its rivals in terms of quality and price.

Perfect Competition

In order to study competitive markets, we are going to build a model of a market in which competition is as fierce and extreme as possible. Economists call the most extreme form of competition perfect competition. **Perfect competition** occurs in a market in which:

- There are many firms, each selling an identical product.
- There are many buyers.
- There are no restrictions on entry into the industry.
- Firms in the industry have no advantage over potential new entrants.
- Firms and buyers are completely informed about the prices of the products of each firm in the industry.

Therefore in perfect competition, no single firm can exert a significant influence on the market price of a good. Firms in such markets are said to be price takers. A **price taker** is a firm that cannot influence the price of its product.

Perfect competition does not occur frequently in the real world, but in many industries, competition is so fierce that the model of perfect competition we're about to study is of enormous help in predicting the behavior of the firms in these industries. Ice cream making and retailing, farming, fishing, wood pulping and paper milling, the manufacture of paper cups and plastic shopping bags, grocery retailing, photo finishing, lawn service, plumbing, painting, and dry cleaning and the provision of laundry services are all examples of industries that are highly competitive.

When a Firm Can't Influence Price

Perfectly competitive or, equivalently, price-taking behavior occurs in markets in which a single firm produces a small fraction of the total output of a particular good. Imagine for a moment that you are a wheat farmer in Kansas. You have a thousand acres under cultivation—which sounds like a lot. But then you go on a drive, first heading west. The flat lands turn into rolling hills as you head toward the Rocky Mountains, but everywhere you look you see thousands and thousands of acres of wheat. The sun goes down in the west behind millions of acres of golden plants. The next morning, it rises in the east above the same scene. Driving to Colorado, Oklahoma, Texas, and back up to Nebraska and the Dakotas reveals similar vistas. You also find unbroken stretches of wheat in Canada, Argentina, Australia, and the former Soviet Union. Your thousand acres is a drop in the bucket.

You are a price taker. Nothing makes your wheat any better than any other farmer's. If everybody else sells their wheat for $3 a bushel, and you want $3.10, why would people buy from you? They can simply go to the next farmer, and the one after that, and the next and buy all they need for $3.

Elasticity of Industry and Firm Demand

A price-taking firm faces a demand curve that is perfectly elastic. To see why this is so, let's consider an example. Suppose that there are 1,000 firms of equal size producing a good. Even if one firm doubles its output (a big change for an individual firm), indus-

try output will rise by only 0.1 percent (one thousandth is 0.1 percent). If the elasticity of industry demand for the good is 0.5, then this increase in industry output results in a 0.2 percent fall in price. To put things in perspective, a price change of this magnitude is $1 on a $500 television set, 10¢ on a $50 dress, or 1¢ on a $5 movie ticket. But these price changes, although small, are much larger than the ones that result from changes in output of a magnitude that a firm might actually make. Therefore when a firm changes its output rate, the effect of that change on price is tiny and the firm ignores it. The firm behaves as if its own actions have no effect on the market price.

Table 11.1 works through a real-world example—the market for fish—and shows the relationship between the elasticity of demand facing an individual competitive fishery and the fish market as a whole. The elasticity of the market demand for fish is 0.42, but the elasticity of an individual producer's demand is almost 40,000.

When we studied the concept of elasticity in Chapter 5, we discovered that a horizontal demand curve has an elasticity of infinity. An elasticity of 40,000 is not quite infinity, but it is very large. A firm whose demand has such an elasticity has, for all practical purposes, an infinitely elastic demand. Such a firm's demand curve is horizontal. The firm is a price taker.

Competition in Everyday Life

We have defined perfect competition as a market in which a firm has no choice but to be a price taker. Even massive percentage changes in a firm's own output have only a negligible effect on the market price. In such a situation, there is little point in a firm attempting to set its own price at a level different from the market. If a firm tries to charge a higher price, no one will buy its output; if it offers its goods for a lower price, it will sell them, but it can sell them for the market price, so there is no point in price cutting.

The inability of a perfectly competitive firm to compete by price cutting makes it seem as if a perfectly competitive market is not, in fact, very competitive at all. If firms don't compete on price, in what sense are they competing with each other?

Firms compete with each other in much the same way as athletes or football teams do. Firms try to

TABLE **11.1**

A Fishery's Elasticity of Demand

(a) Data

- **World output of fish is 169 billion pounds a year.**
- **The average U.S. fishery produces 1.8 million pounds a year.**
- **The average price of fish is 37.5¢ a pound.**
- **The elasticity of demand for fish and fish products (η_m) is 0.42.**

(b) Effect on world price

- **If an average U.S. fishery raises output by 100 percent, world output rises by 1.8 million pounds—0.00107 percent.**
- **To calculate change in world price, use the formula**

$$\eta_m = \frac{\text{Percentage change in quantity}}{\text{Percentage change in price}},$$

which means that

$$\text{Percentage change in price} = \frac{\text{Percentage change in quantity}}{\eta_m}.$$

- **To find the fall in price, use the formula**

$$\text{Percentage change in price} = \frac{0.00107}{0.42} = 0.00254 \text{ percent}$$

So a price fall of 0.00254 percent is a fall of 0.00095¢.

- **When a firm doubles its output, the price falls by 0.00095¢.**

(c) Elasticity of a fishery's demand

- **The elasticity of a firm's demand (η_f) is given by**

$$\eta_f = \frac{\text{Percentage change in firm's output sold}}{\text{Percentage change in price}} = \frac{100}{0.00254} = 39{,}370$$

Part (a) provides some data about the market for fish. Most fish is sold frozen, and the market for fish is a worldwide market. Part (b) calculates the effects on the world market price of fish if one U.S. fishery doubles its output. If one fishery doubles its output, world output will rise by 1.8 million pounds, or change by approximately 0.001 percent. As a result of this increase in output, the world price of fish falls by 0.00254 percent, or 0.00095¢ a pound. Part (c) calculates the elasticity of the individual producer's demand, η_f. That elasticity is almost 40,000!

find new tricks that will give them the edge over their competitors and enable them to win. Sometimes, though, the competition that they face is so stiff that they are left with little room to maneuver. This happens in sporting events, too. For example, when two wrestlers are closely matched, they compete with each other, but neither of them has much room to maneuver. They are locked in such fierce competition that the best they can do is to match each other's moves, try not to make a mistake, and accept the inevitable—that the outcome will be close and may even be a tie.

Like evenly matched athletes, firms in perfect competition are locked in such a fierce competitive struggle with each other that they have no choice but to mimic each other's actions and put up with an outcome analogous to a tie. They produce comparable quality goods at comparable prices.

Let's now study the behavior of a perfectly competitive industry, beginning with an examination of the choices made by a typical firm in such an industry.

Firms' Choices in Perfect Competition

A perfectly competitive firm has to make three key decisions:

- Whether to stay in the industry or to leave it
- If the decision is to stay in the industry, whether to produce or to temporarily shut down
- If the decision is to produce, how much to produce

In studying the competitive firm's choices, we will continue to look at a model firm whose single objective is to maximize its profit. We'll first consider a situation in which a firm decides to produce. We will then look at the other cases—firms that decide to shut down production temporarily or to leave the industry altogether.

Profit and Revenue

Profit is the difference between a firm's total revenue and total cost. We defined and studied the behavior of total cost in the last two chapters. But what is total revenue? Let's begin by looking at the concepts of revenue.

Total revenue is the value of a firm's sales. It equals the price of the firm's output multiplied by the number of units of output sold (price × quantity). **Average revenue** is total revenue divided by the total quantity sold—revenue per unit sold. Since total revenue is price times quantity sold, average revenue (total revenue divided by quantity sold) equals price. **Marginal revenue** is the change in total revenue resulting from a one-unit increase in the quantity sold. Since, in the case of perfect competition, the price remains constant when the quantity sold changes, the change in total revenue is equal to price multiplied by the change in quantity. Therefore in perfect competition, marginal revenue equals price.

An example of these revenue concepts is set out for Swanky, Inc. in Fig. 11.1. The table shows three different quantities of sweaters sold. For a price taker, as the quantity sold varies, the price stays constant—in this example at $25. Total revenue is equal to price multiplied by quantity. For example, if Swanky sells 8 sweaters, total revenue is 8 times $25, which equals $200. Average revenue is total revenue divided by quantity. Again, if Swanky sells 8 sweaters, average revenue is total revenue ($200) divided by quantity (8), which equals $25. Marginal revenue is the change in total revenue resulting from a one-unit change in quantity. For example, when the quantity sold rises from 7 to 8, total revenue rises from $175 to $200, so marginal revenue is $25. (Notice that in the table, marginal revenue appears *between* the lines for the quantities sold. This arrangement presents a visual reminder that marginal revenue results from the *change* in the quantity sold.)

Suppose that Swanky is one of a thousand similar small producers of sweaters. The demand and supply curves for the entire sweater industry are shown in Fig. 11.1(a). Demand curve *D* intersects supply curve *S* at a price of $25 and a quantity of 7,000 sweaters. Figure 11.1(b) shows Swanky's demand curve. Since the firm is a price taker, its demand curve is perfectly elastic—the horizontal line at $25. The figure also illustrates Swanky's total, average, and marginal revenues, calculated in the table. The average revenue curve and marginal revenue curve are the same as the firm's demand curve. That is, the

FIGURE 11.1

Demand, Price, and Revenue in Perfect Competition

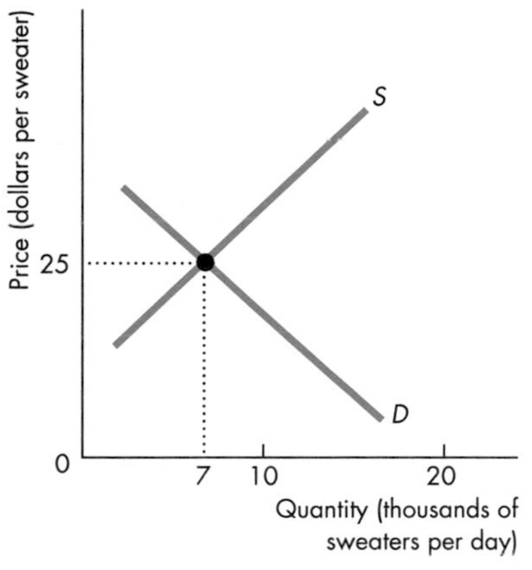

(a) Sweater industry

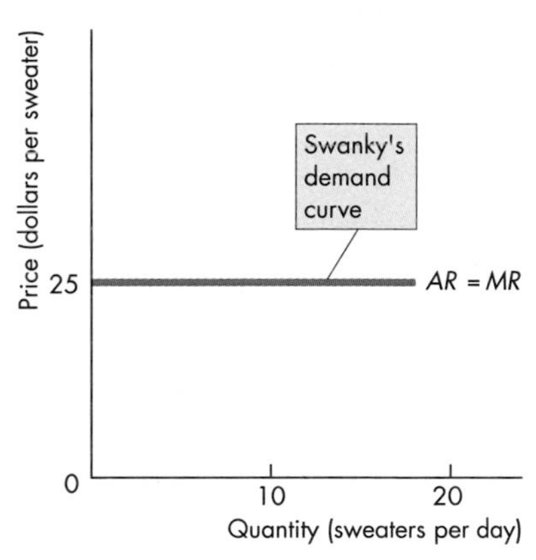

(b) Swanky's demand, average revenue, and marginal revenue

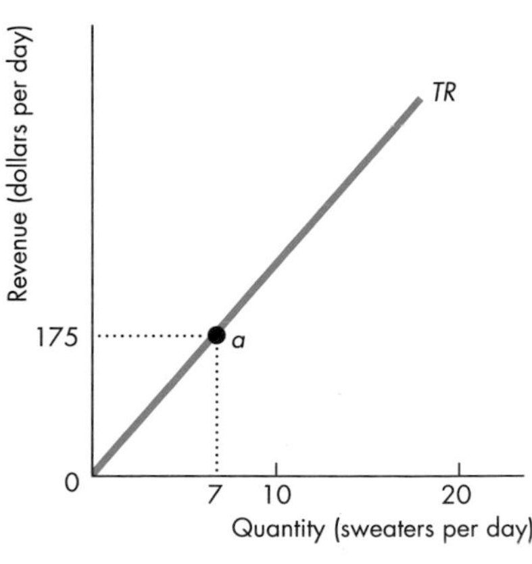

(c) Swanky's total revenue

Quantity sold (Q) (sweaters per day)	Price (P) (dollars per sweater)	Total revenue ($TR = P \times Q$) (dollars)	Average revenue ($AR = TR/Q$) (dollars per sweater)	Marginal revenue ($MR = \Delta TR/\Delta Q$) (dollars per sweater)
7	**25**	**175**	**25**	
				25
8	**25**	**200**	**25**	
				25
9	**25**	**225**	**25**	

In perfect competition, price is determined where the industry demand and supply curves intersect. Such an equilibrium is illustrated in part (a), where the price is $25 and 7,000 sweaters are bought and sold. Swanky, a perfectly competitive firm, faces a fixed price, $25 in this example, regardless of the quantity it produces. The table calculates Swanky's total, average, and marginal revenues. For example, when 7 sweaters are sold, total revenue is $175, and average revenue is $25. When sales increase from 7 sweaters to 8 sweaters, marginal revenue equals $25. The demand curve faced by Swanky is perfectly elastic at the market price and is shown in part (b) of the figure. Swanky's demand curve is also its average revenue curve and marginal revenue curve ($AR = MR$). Swanky's total revenue curve (TR) is shown in part (c). Point *a* on the total revenue curve corresponds to the first row of the table.

firm's demand curve tells us the revenue per sweater sold and the change in total revenue that results from selling one more sweater. Swanky's total revenue curve (part c) shows the total revenue for each quantity sold. For example, when Swanky sells 7 sweaters, total revenue is $175 (point *a*). Since each additional sweater sold brings in a constant amount—in this case $25—the total revenue curve is an upward-sloping straight line with a constant slope equal to the price of a sweater.

REVIEW

A firm in a perfectly competitive market is a price taker. The firm's demand curve is perfectly elastic at the market price. The firm's average revenue and marginal revenue are each equal to price, so the marginal revenue and average revenue curves are the same as the firm's demand curve. Total revenue rises as the quantity sold rises. ◆

Profit-Maximizing Output

Profit is the difference between a firm's total revenue and total cost. Maximizing profit is the same thing as maximizing the difference between total revenue and total cost. Even though a perfectly competitive firm cannot influence its price, it can influence its profit by choosing its level of output. As we have just seen, a perfectly competitive firm's total revenue changes when its output changes. Also, as we discovered in Chapter 10, a firm's total cost varies as its output varies. By changing its inputs and its output, a firm can change its total cost. In the *short run*, a firm can change its output by changing its variable inputs and by changing the intensity with which it operates its fixed inputs. In the *long run*, a firm can vary all its inputs. Let's work out how a firm maximizes profit in the short run.

Total Revenue, Total Cost, and Profit Figure 11.2 shows Swanky's total revenue, total cost, and profit both as numbers (in the table) and as curves (in the graphs). Part (a) of the figure shows Swanky's total revenue and total cost curves. These curves are graphs of the numbers shown in the first three columns of the table. The total revenue curve (*TR*) is the same as that in Fig. 11.1(c). The total cost curve (*TC*) is similar to the one that you met in Chapter 10. Notice that Swanky's total cost is $25 when output is zero. This amount is Swanky's fixed cost—the cost that is incurred even if nothing is produced and sold. As output increases, so does total cost.

The difference between total revenue and total cost is profit. As you can see in Fig. 11.2(b), Swanky will make a profit at any output above 4 and below 12 sweaters a day. At outputs below 4 sweaters, Swanky makes a loss. A loss is also made if output exceeds 12 sweaters a day. At outputs of 4 sweaters and 12 sweaters, total cost equals total revenue. Swanky makes zero profit. An output at which total cost equals total revenue is called a **break-even point**.

Swanky's profit, calculated in the final column of the table, is graphed in part (b) of the figure. Notice the relationship between the total revenue, total cost, and profit curves. Profit is measured by the vertical distance between the total revenue and total cost curves. When the total revenue curve in part (a) is above the total cost curve, between 4 and 12 sweaters, the firm is making a profit and the profit curve in part (b) is above the horizontal axis. At the break-even point, where the total cost and total revenue curves intersect, the profit curve cuts the horizontal axis.

When the profit curve is at its highest, the distance between *TR* and *TC* is greatest. In this example, profit maximization occurs at an output of 9 sweaters a day. At this output, profit is $40 a day.

Marginal Calculations In working out Swanky's profit-maximizing output, we examined its cost and revenue schedules and, from all the possibilities, picked out the point at which profit is at a maximum. There is a quicker, neater, and more powerful way of figuring out the profit-maximizing output. All Swanky has to do is to calculate its marginal cost and marginal revenue and compare the two. If marginal revenue exceeds marginal cost, it pays to produce more. If marginal revenue is less than marginal cost, it pays to produce less. When marginal revenue and marginal cost are equal, profit is maximized. Let's convince ourselves that this rule works.

Look at the table in Fig. 11.3. It records Swanky's marginal revenue and marginal cost. Recall that marginal revenue is the change in revenue per unit change in the quantity sold and is, for a perfectly competitive firm, the same as its price. In this case, marginal revenue is $25. Marginal cost is the change in total cost per unit change in output. For example, when output rises from 8 to 9 sweaters, total cost rises from $163 to $185, a rise of $22, which is the marginal cost of changing the output rate from 8 to 9 sweaters a day. The marginal revenue and marginal cost curves corresponding to the table appear in Fig. 11.3.

Now focus on the highlighted row of the table. When output rises from 8 to 9 sweaters, marginal cost is $22. Since marginal revenue is $25, the rise in total revenue exceeds the rise in total cost. Profit goes up by the difference—$3. By looking at the last column of the table, you can see that profit does indeed rise by $3. Because marginal revenue exceeds marginal cost, it pays to expand output from 8 to 9 sweaters. At 8 sweaters a day profit is $37, and at 9 sweaters a day it is $40—$3 more.

Suppose that output is expanded yet further to 10 sweaters a day. Marginal revenue is still $25, but marginal cost is now $27. Marginal cost exceeds marginal revenue by $2. So expanding output to 10 sweaters increases total cost by $2 more than total revenue, and profit falls by $2. So, to maximize

FIGURE 11.2

Total Revenue, Total Cost, and Profit

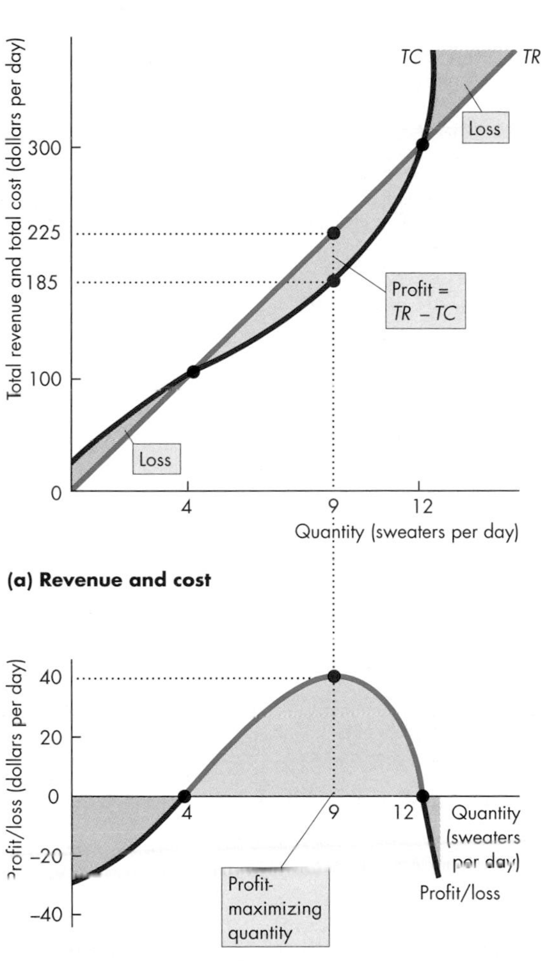

(a) Revenue and cost

(b) Profit and loss

Quantity (Q) (sweaters per day)	Total revenue (TR) (dollars)	Total cost (TC) (dollars)	Profit ($TR - TC$) (dollars)
0	0	25	–25
1	25	49	–24
2	50	69	–19
3	75	86	–11
4	100	100	0
5	125	114	11
6	150	128	22
7	175	144	31
8	200	163	37
9	225	185	40
10	250	212	38
11	275	246	29
12	300	300	0
13	325	360	–35

The table lists Swanky's total revenue, total cost, and profit. Part (a) graphs the total revenue and total cost curves. Profit is seen in part (a) as the blue area between the total cost and total revenue curves. The maximum profit, $40 a day, occurs when 9 sweaters are produced where the vertical distance between the total revenue and total cost curves is at its largest. At outputs of 4 sweaters a day and 12 sweaters a day, Swanky makes zero profit—these are break-even points. At outputs below 4 sweaters a day and above 12 sweaters a day, Swanky makes a loss. Part (b) of the figure shows Swanky's profit curve. The profit curve is at its highest when profit is at a maximum and cuts the horizontal axis at the break-even points.

profit, all Swanky has to do is to compare marginal cost and marginal revenue. As long as marginal revenue exceeds marginal cost, it pays to increase output. Swanky keeps increasing output until the cost of producing one more sweater equals the price at which the sweater can be sold. At that point, it is making maximum profit. If Swanky makes one more sweater, that sweater will cost more to produce than the revenue it will bring in, so Swanky will not produce it.

Profit in the Short Run

We've just seen that we can calculate a firm's profit-maximizing output by comparing marginal revenue

FIGURE 11.3

Marginal Revenue, Marginal Cost, and Profit-Maximizing Output

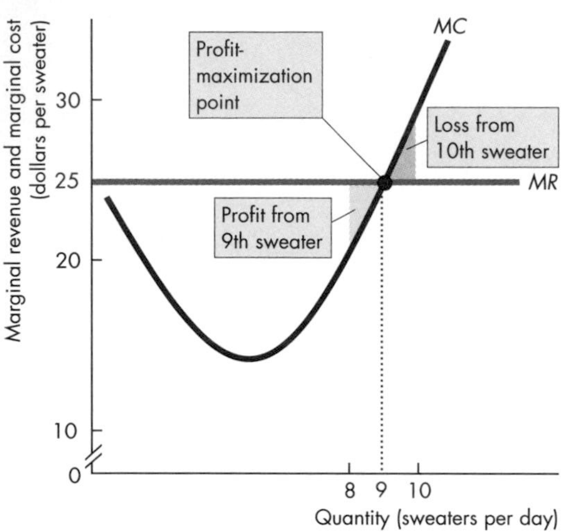

Quantity (Q) (sweaters per day)	Total revenue (TR) (dollars)	Marginal revenue (MR) (dollars per sweater)	Total cost (TC) (dollars)	Marginal cost (MC) (dollars per sweater)	Profit ($TR - TC$) (dollars)
0	0		25		–25
		25		24	
1	25		49		–24
		25		20	
2	50		69		–19
		25		17	
3	75		86		–11
		25		14	
4	100		100		0
		25		14	
5	125		114		11
		25		14	
6	150		128		22
		25		16	
7	175		144		31
		25		19	
8	200		163		37
		25		22	
9	225		185		40
		25		27	
10	250		212		38
		25		34	
11	275		246		29
		25		54	
12	300		300		0
		25		60	
13	325		360		–35

Another way of finding the profit-maximizing output is to determine the output at which marginal revenue equals marginal cost. The table shows that if output rises from 8 to 9 sweaters, marginal cost is $22, which is less than the marginal revenue of $25. If output rises from 9 to 10 sweaters, marginal cost is $27, which exceeds the marginal revenue of $25. The figure shows that marginal cost and marginal revenue are equal when Swanky produces 9 sweaters a day. If marginal revenue exceeds marginal cost, an increase in output increases profit. If marginal revenue is less than marginal cost, an increase in output lowers profit. If marginal revenue equals marginal cost, profit is maximized.

with marginal cost. But maximizing profit is not the same thing as *making* a profit. Maximizing profit can mean minimizing loss. We cannot tell whether a firm is actually making a profit only by comparing the marginal revenue and marginal cost curves. To check whether a firm is making a profit, we need to look at total revenue and total cost, as we did before, or we need to compare average total cost with price. When a firm makes a profit, average total cost is lower than price. If average total cost exceeds price, the firm makes a loss. When average total cost equals price, the firm breaks even.

Three Possible Profit Outcomes The three possible profit outcomes in the short run are illustrated in Fig. 11.4. In part (a), Swanky is making an economic profit. At a price of $25, marginal revenue equals marginal cost at an output of 9 sweaters a day. That is, the profit-maximizing output is 9 sweaters a day. Average total cost is lower than the market price, and economic profit is represented by the blue rectangle. The height of that rectangle is the gap between price and average total cost, or economic profit per sweater. Its length shows the quantity of sweaters produced. So the rectangle's area measures Swanky's economic profit: profit per sweater (the rectangle's height—$4.44 a sweater) multiplied by the number of sweaters produced (its length—9 sweaters) equals total profit (its area—$40).

In part (b), Swanky breaks even. At a price of $20, Swanky's profit-maximizing output is 8 sweaters. The average total cost of producing this

FIGURE 11.4

Three Possible Profit Outcomes in the Short Run

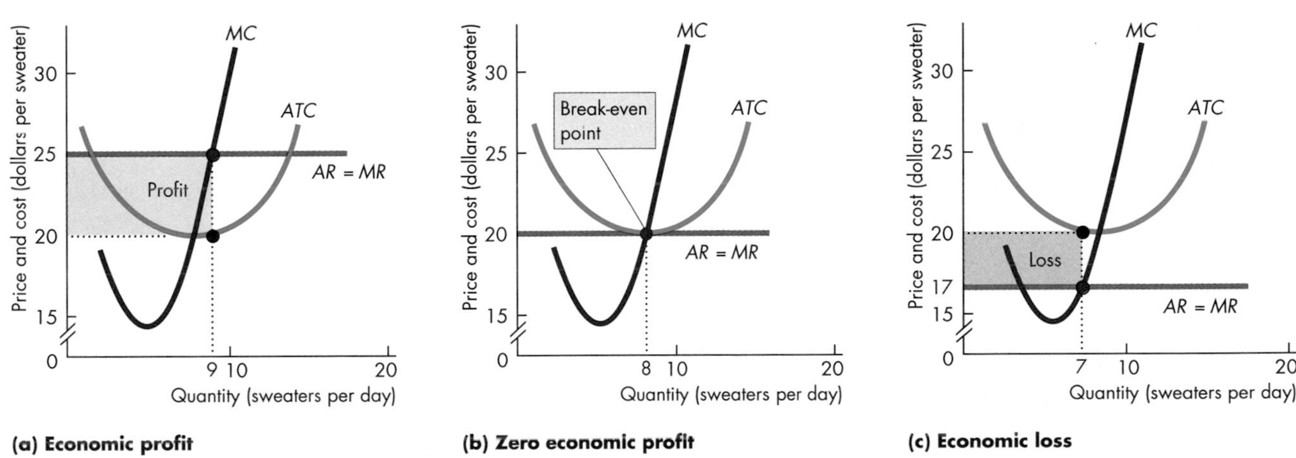

(a) Economic profit **(b) Zero economic profit** **(c) Economic loss**

In the short run, a firm's economic profit may be positive, zero (break even), or negative (a loss). If the market price is greater than the average total cost of producing the profit-maximizing output, the firm makes a profit (part a). If price equals minimum average total cost, the firm breaks even (part b). If the price is below minimum average total cost, the firm makes a loss (part c). The firm's profit is shown as the blue rectangle, and the firm's loss is the red rectangle.

output level is \$20, the same as its price. It is also the minimum average total cost. The economic profit that Swanky makes in this case is zero.

In part (c), Swanky incurs an economic loss. At a price of \$17, the profit-maximizing output is 7 sweaters. At that output, average total cost is \$20.57, so the firm is losing \$3.57 a sweater and incurring a total loss of \$25.

Temporary Plant Shutdown There are some situations in which a firm's profit-maximizing decision is to shut down temporarily, lay off its workers, and produce nothing. A firm's **shutdown point** is the level of output and price at which the firm is just covering its total *variable* cost. If the price is so low that total revenue is not enough to cover total variable cost, the firm shuts down.

A firm cannot escape its fixed costs. These costs are incurred even at zero output. A firm that shuts down and produces no output makes a loss equal to its total fixed cost. If the price just equals average variable cost, total revenue equals total variable cost and the firm's loss equals its total fixed cost. But if price is below average variable cost, total revenue does not cover total variable cost, and if the firm produces just one unit of output, its loss exceeds total fixed cost. It is in such a situation that the firm minimizes its loss by shutting down. Its loss then equals total fixed cost.

The shutdown point is reached when the market price falls to a level equal to the minimum average variable cost. Table 11.2 illustrates what happens at the shutdown point. The table has two parts: part (a) shows a case in which it just pays the firm to keep producing, and part (b) shows a case in which it just pays the firm to shut down. The table shows Swanky's total fixed cost, total variable cost, and total cost of producing 6, 7, and 8 sweaters. It also shows the average variable cost and marginal cost. The cost data are the same in both parts (a) and (b) of the table.

Next let's look at the revenue. In part (a), the price of a sweater is \$17. To find Swanky's total revenue, multiply the price by the quantity sold. We calculate the profit or loss (and they are all losses in this case) by subtracting total cost from total revenue. For example, if Swanky sells 7 sweaters at \$17 each, then total revenue is \$119. Total cost is \$144,

TABLE 11.2

The Shutdown Point

(a) *Swanky keeps on producing*

Output (sweaters per day)	Total fixed cost (dollars)	Total variable cost (dollars)	Total cost (dollars)	Average variable cost (dollars per sweater)	Marginal cost (dollars per sweater)	Price (dollars per sweater)	Total revenue (dollars)	Marginal revenue (dollars per sweater)	Profit (+) or loss (–) (dollars)
6	25	103	128	17.17		17	102		–26
					16			17	
7	25	119	144	17.00		17	119		–25
					19			17	
8	25	138	163	17.25		17	136		–27

(b) *Swanky shuts down*

Output (sweaters per day)	Total fixed cost (dollars)	Total variable cost (dollars)	Total cost (dollars)	Average variable cost (dollars per sweater)	Marginal cost (dollars per sweater)	Price (dollars per sweater)	Total revenue (dollars)	Marginal revenue (dollars per sweater)	Profit (+) or loss (–) (dollars)
6	25	103	128	17.17		16.99	101.94		–26.06
					16			16.99	
7	25	119	144	17.00		16.99	118.93		–25.07
					19			16.99	
8	25	138	163	17.25		16.99	135.92		–27.08

The shutdown point occurs at the point of minimum average variable cost. If price equals minimum average variable cost, Swanky is indifferent between producing at the shutdown point and producing nothing. If price falls below minimum average variable cost, Swanky produces nothing. Minimum average variable cost is $17 and occurs at 7 units of output. If the price is $17 and Swanky produces 7 sweaters, its loss equals its total fixed cost of $25 (part a). If the price falls to $16.99, even when it produces at the point of minimum average variable cost, the firm makes a loss that is bigger than its total fixed cost, and so it shuts down (part b).

so the loss equals $144 minus $119, which is $25. We calculate the loss from producing 6 sweaters or 8 sweaters in a similar way.

The minimum loss occurs when 7 sweaters are produced. You can see that fact directly by looking at the profit or loss column. You can also check that the loss is minimized by looking at marginal cost and marginal revenue. Increasing output from 6 to 7 sweaters has a marginal cost of $16 but a marginal revenue of $17, so total revenue rises by more than total cost. Increasing output still further, from 7 to 8 sweaters, has a marginal cost of $19, which exceeds marginal revenue, so profit falls (loss rises).

Swanky's loss when producing 7 sweaters exactly equals its total fixed costs—$25. Alternatively, if Swanky produces nothing, it will also lose its $25 of total fixed cost. So, at a price of $17, Swanky is indifferent between producing and shutting down—it makes a loss equal to its fixed cost.

In part (b), the price is $16.99—a lower price but by just a penny. Costs are unchanged. We calculate total revenue and profit in the same way as before. The output that maximizes profit (minimizes loss) is still 7 sweaters, but in this case the minimum possible loss is $25.07. Swanky loses 7¢ more than it would if it produced nothing at all. The firm will shut down. Its minimum average variable cost is $17. At $17 it just pays to produce, and at $16.99 it just pays to shut down. The minimum output that Swanky produces is 7 sweaters.

Real-World Shutdowns Shutdowns occur in the real world either because of a fall in price or because of a rise in costs. Shutdowns occur most frequently in raw material–producing sectors as a result of fluctuating prices. For example, if the price of gold falls, gold mines temporarily stop producing. If the price of nickel falls, nickel mines shut down. Shutdowns also occur in many industries—such as those producing ice cream, cars, and transportation services.

A famous example of an airline shutdown occurred in 1982. Braniff, a Dallas-based airline, had grown rapidly following the deregulation of the airline business in 1978. When 1,000 new domestic routes became available, Braniff's aggressive chairman, Harding Lawrence, applied for 624 of them, spreading over the Southwest and the Southeast. The company also added routes to Asia, Europe, and the Middle East. If airfares had remained stable, the company's expansion plans would have been highly profitable. But the airlines became embroiled in a fare-cutting orgy, and at a time when fuel prices were rising sharply. Braniff, vastly overextended, lost more than $40 million in 1979, and by 1981 it was losing $160 million. In May 1982, after 54 years in the airline business, Braniff laid off all its workers and stopped flying. Because the firm was losing more than its total variable cost and because it saw no prospect of the situation improving, it shut down.

REVIEW

In perfect competition, a firm's marginal revenue equals its price. A firm maximizes profit by producing the output at which marginal cost equals marginal revenue (equals price). The lowest output a firm will produce is that at which average variable cost is at a minimum. If price falls below the minimum of average variable cost, the best a firm can do is to stop producing and make a loss equal to its total fixed cost. Maximizing profit is not the same thing as making a profit. In the short run, a firm can make a profit, break even, or make a loss. The maximum loss that a firm will make is equal to its total fixed cost. ◆

The Firm's Supply Curve

A **perfectly competitive firm's supply curve** shows how a firm's profit-maximizing output varies as the market price varies, other things remaining constant. We are now going to derive Swanky's supply curve. Actually, we have already calculated three points on Swanky's supply curve. We discovered that when the price is $25, Swanky produces 9 sweaters a day; when the price is $20, Swanky produces 8 sweaters a day; and when the price is $17, Swanky is indifferent between producing 7 sweaters a day and shutting down. We are now going to derive Swanky's entire supply curve. Figure 11.5 illustrates the analysis.

Figure 11.5(a) shows Swanky's marginal cost and average variable cost curves, and Fig. 11.5(b) shows its supply curve. There is a direct connection between the marginal cost and average variable cost curves and the supply curve. Let's see what that connection is.

The smallest quantity that Swanky will supply is at the shutdown point. When the price is equal to the minimum average variable cost, the marginal revenue curve is MR_0 and the firm produces the output at its shutdown point—point *s* in the figure. If the price falls below minimum average variable cost, Swanky produces nothing. As the price rises above its minimum average variable cost, Swanky's output rises. Since Swanky maximizes profit by producing the output at which marginal cost equals price, we can determine from its marginal cost curve how much the firm produces at each price. At a price of $25, the marginal revenue curve is MR_1. Swanky maximizes profit by producing 9 sweaters. At a price of $31, the marginal revenue curve is MR_2 and Swanky produces 10 sweaters. The supply curve, shown in Fig. 11.5(b), has two separate parts. First, in the range of prices that exceed the minimum of average variable cost, the supply curve is the same as the marginal cost curve—above the shutdown point (*s*). Second, at prices below minimum average variable cost, Swanky shuts down and produces nothing, and its supply curve runs along the vertical axis.

FIGURE 11.5

Swanky's Supply Curve

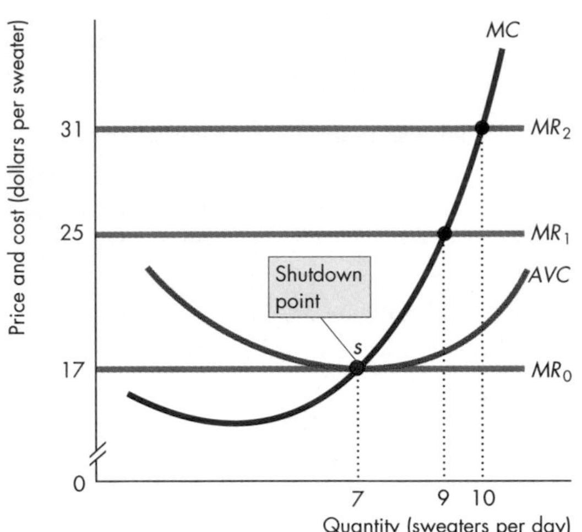

(a) Marginal cost and average variable cost

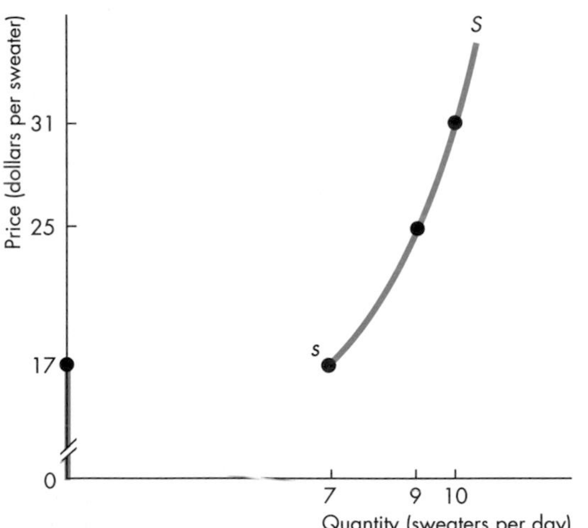

(b) Firm's supply curve

Part (a) shows Swanky's profit-maximizing output at each market price. At $25 a sweater, Swanky produces 9 sweaters. At $17 a sweater, Swanky produces 7 sweaters. At any price below $17 a sweater, Swanky produces nothing. Swanky's shutdown point is *s*. Part (b) shows Swanky's supply curve—the number of sweaters Swanky will produce at each price. Swanky's supply curve is made up of its marginal cost curve (part a) at all points above the average variable cost curve and the vertical axis at all prices below minimum average variable cost.

So far, we have studied a single firm in isolation. We have seen that the firm's profit-maximizing actions depend on the market price—which the firm takes as given. The higher the price, the larger is the quantity that the firm will choose to produce—the firm's supply curve is upward sloping. But how is the market price determined? To answer this question, we need to study not one firm in isolation but the market as a whole.

Output, Price, and Profit in the Short Run

Market price is determined by industry demand and industry supply. It is the price that makes the quantity demanded equal the quantity supplied. But the quantity supplied depends on the supply decisions of all the individual firms in the industry. Those supply decisions, in turn, depend on the market price.

A short-run equilibrium prevails in a competitive market when each firm operates its plant to produce the profit-maximizing output level and when the total quantity produced by all the firms in the market equals the quantity demanded at that price. To find the short-run equilibrium, we first need to construct the short-run industry supply curve.

Short-Run Industry Supply Curve

The **short-run industry supply curve** shows how the total quantity supplied in the short run by all firms in an industry varies as the market price varies. The quantity supplied in the short run by the industry at a given price is the sum of the quantities supplied in the short run by all firms in the industry at that price. To construct the industry supply curve, we sum horizontally the supply curves of the individual firms. Let's see how we do that.

Suppose that the competitive sweater industry consists of 1,000 firms exactly like Swanky. The relationship between a firm's supply curve and the industry supply curve for this case is illustrated in Fig. 11.6. Each of the 1,000 firms in the industry has a supply schedule like Swanky's, set out in the table.

At a price below $17, every firm in the industry will shut down production so that the industry will supply nothing. At $17, each firm is indifferent between shutting down and producing 7 sweaters. Since each firm is indifferent, some firms will produce and others will shut down. Industry supply can be anything between 0 (all firms shut down) and 7,000 (all firms producing 7 sweaters a day each). Thus at $17, the industry supply curve is horizontal—it is perfectly elastic. As the price rises above $17, each firm increases its quantity supplied and the industry quantity supplied also increases, but by 1,000 times that of each individual firm.

The supply schedules set out in the table form the basis of the supply curves that are graphed in Fig. 11.6. Swanky and every other firm has the supply curve S_F shown in Fig. 11.6(a); the industry supply curve S_I is shown in Fig. 11.6(b). Look carefully at the units on the horizontal axes of parts (a) and (b), and note that in part (a) the units are individual sweaters while in part (b) they are thousands of sweaters. There are two important differences. First, at each price, the quantity supplied by the industry is 1,000 times the quantity supplied by a single firm. Second, at a price of $17, the firm supplies either nothing or 7 sweaters a day. There is no individual firm supply curve between those two numbers. But for the industry, any quantity between zero and 7,000 will be produced, so the industry supply curve is perfectly elastic over that range.

FIGURE 11.6

Firm and Industry Supply Curves

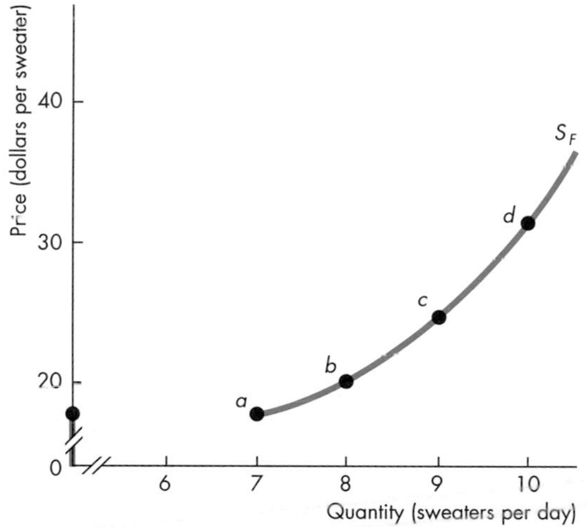

(a) Swanky, Inc.

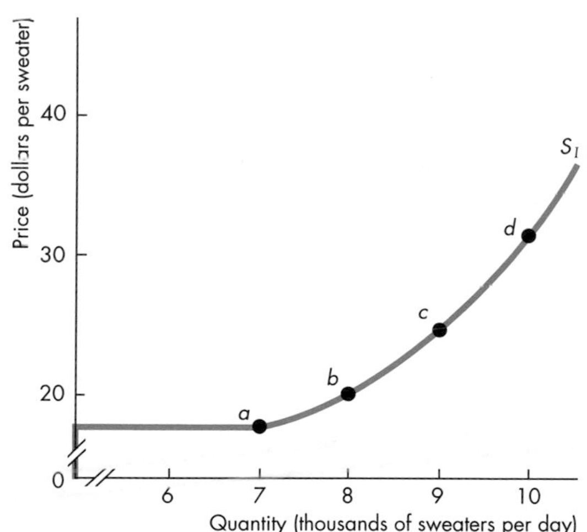

(b) Sweater industry

The industry supply schedule is the sum of the supply schedules of all individual firms. An industry that consists of 1,000 identical firms has a supply schedule similar to that of the individual firm. But the quantity supplied by the industry is 1,000 times as large as that of the individual firm (see the table). At the shutdown price, the firm produces either 0 or 7 sweaters per day. The industry supply curve is perfectly elastic at the shutdown price. Part (a) shows Swanky's supply curve, S_F, and part (b) shows the sweater industry supply curve, S_I. Points *a*, *b*, *c*, and *d* correspond to the rows of the table. Note that the unit of measurement on the horizontal axis for the industry supply curve is 1,000 times the unit for Swanky.

	Price (dollars per sweater)	Quantity supplied by Swanky, Inc. (sweaters per day)	Quantity supplied by industry (sweaters per day)
a	**17**	**0 or 7**	**0 to 7,000**
b	**20**	**8**	**8,000**
c	**25**	**9**	**9,000**
d	**31**	**10**	**10,000**

Short-Run Competitive Equilibrium

Price and industry output are determined by industry demand and supply. Three different possible short-run competitive equilibrium positions are shown in Fig. 11.7. The supply curve (S) is the same as S_I, which we derived in Fig. 11.6. If the demand curve is D_1, the equilibrium price is \$25 and industry output is 9,000 sweaters a day. If the demand curve is D_2, the price is \$20 and industry output is 8,000 sweaters a day. If the demand curve is D_3, the price is \$17 and industry output is 7,000 sweaters a day.

To see what is happening to each individual firm and its profit in these three situations, you need to check back to Fig. 11.4. With demand curve D_1, the price is \$25 a sweater, each firm produces 9 sweaters a day and makes a profit as shown in Fig. 11.4(a); if the demand curve is D_2, the price is \$20 a sweater, each firm produces 8 sweaters a day and makes a zero profit, as shown in Fig. 11.4(b); and if the demand curve is D_3, the price is \$17 a sweater, each firm is indifferent between producing 7 sweaters a day and shutting down and, in either event, is making a loss equal to total fixed cost, as shown in Fig. 11.4(c). If the demand curve shifts farther to the left than D_3, the price will remain constant at \$17, since the industry supply curve is horizontal at that price. Some firms will continue to produce 7 sweaters a day, and others will shut down. Firms will be indifferent between these two activities and, whichever they choose, will make a loss equal to their total fixed cost. The number of firms continuing to produce will just be enough to satisfy the market demand at a price of \$17.

FIGURE 11.7

Three Short-Run Equilibrium Positions for a Competitive Industry

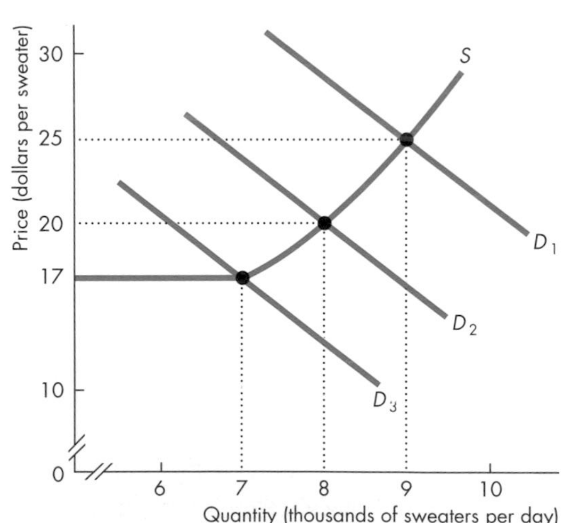

The competitive sweater industry's supply curve is S. If demand is D_1, the price is \$25 and the industry produces 9,000 sweaters. If demand is D_2, the price is \$20 and industry output is 8,000 sweaters. If demand is D_3, the price is \$17 and industry output is 7,000 sweaters. To see what is happening to the individual firms, look back at Fig. 11.4. When the price is \$25, the firms are making a profit; when the price is \$20, they are breaking even (making zero profit); and when the price is \$17, they are incurring a loss. Even when they make a loss, the firms are maximizing profit (minimizing loss).

REVIEW

In a competitive industry, the price and quantity sold are determined by industry supply and industry demand. Industry supply is the sum of the supplies of all the individual firms. The price determined by industry demand and industry supply cannot be influenced by the actions of any one individual firm. Each firm takes the market price and, given that price, maximizes profit. The firm maximizes its profit by producing the output at which marginal cost equals marginal revenue (equals price), as long as price is not lower than minimum average variable cost. If the price falls below minimum average variable cost, the firm shuts down and incurs a loss equal to its total fixed cost. ◆

Output, Price, and Profit in the Long Run

We have seen that in short-run equilibrium a firm might make a profit, make a loss, or break even. Though each of these three situations is a short-run equilibrium, only one of them is a long-run equilibrium. To see why, we need to examine the dynamic forces at work in a competitive industry. An industry adjusts over time in two ways. First, the number of firms in the industry changes; second, the existing firms change the scale of their plants, thereby shifting their short-run cost curves. Let's study the effects of these two dynamic forces in a competitive industry.

Entry and Exit

Entry is the act of setting up a new firm in an industry. **Exit** is the act of closing down a firm and leaving an industry. When will a new firm enter an industry or an existing one leave? How do entry and exit affect the market price, profit, and output in an industry? Let's first look at the causes of entry and exit.

Profits and Losses as Signals What triggers entry and exit? The prospect of profit triggers entry, and the prospect of continuing losses triggers exit. Temporary profits and temporary losses that are purely random, like the winnings and losings at a casino, do not trigger entry or exit, but the prospect of profits or losses for some foreseeable future period does. An industry making economic profits attracts new entrants; one making economic losses induces exits; and an industry in which neither economic losses nor economic profits are being made stimulates neither entry nor exit. Thus profits and losses are the signals to which firms respond in making entry and exit decisions.

What are the effects of entry and exit on price and profits?

Effects of Entry and Exit on Price and Profits The immediate effect of entry and exit is to shift the industry supply curve. If more firms enter an industry, the industry supply curve shifts to the right: supply increases. If firms exit an industry, the industry supply curve shifts to the left: supply falls. The effects of entry and exit on price and on the total quantity sold in the sweater industry are shown in Fig. 11.8.

FIGURE 11.8

Entry and Exit

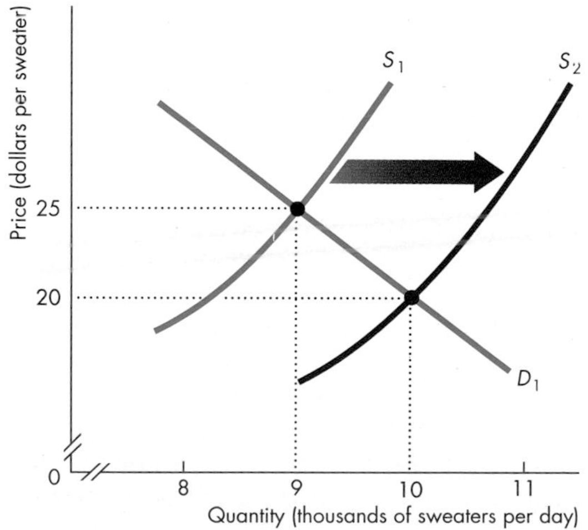

(a) Effect of entry

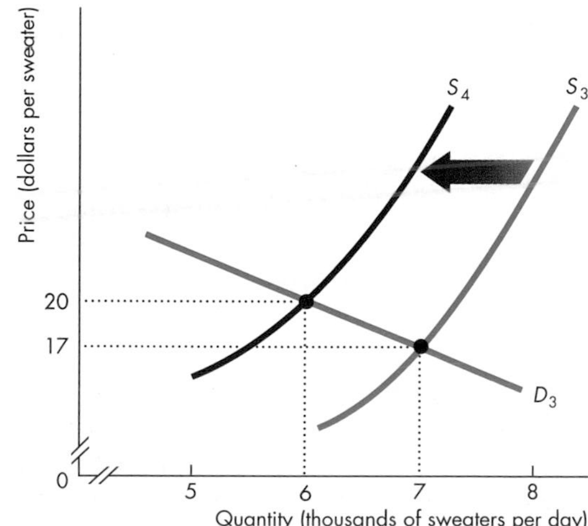

(b) Effect of exit

When new firms enter the sweater industry, the industry supply curve shifts to the right, from S_1 to S_2 (part a). The equilibrium price falls from \$25 to \$20, and the quantity sold increases from 9,000 to 10,000 sweaters. When firms exit the sweater industry, the industry supply curve shifts to the left, from S_3 to S_4 (part b). The equilibrium price rises from \$17 to \$20, and the quantity sold decreases from 7,000 to 6,000 sweaters.

Entry First, let's look at what happens when new firms enter an industry. Suppose that the demand curve for sweaters is D_1 and the industry supply curve is S_1, so sweaters sell for $25 and 9,000 sweaters are being bought and sold. Now suppose that some new firms enter the industry. As they do so, the industry supply curve shifts to the right to become S_2. With the higher supply and unchanged demand, the price falls from $25 to $20 a sweater and the quantity increases from 9,000 to 10,000.

As the price falls, Swanky and the other firms in the industry will react by lowering their output. That is, for each existing firm in the industry, its profit-maximizing output falls. Since the price falls, and since each firm sells less, profit falls for each firm. You can see this reduction of profit by glancing back at Fig. 11.4. Initially, when the price is $25, each firm makes a profit and is in the situation shown in Fig. 11.4(a). When the price falls to $20, the firm's profit disappears and the firm is in the situation shown in Fig. 11.4(b).

You have just discovered an important result:

As new firms enter an industry, the price falls and the profit of each existing firm falls.

A good example of this process has occurred in the last few years in the personal computer industry. When IBM introduced its first personal computer in the early 1980s, the price of PCs gave IBM a big profit. Very quickly thereafter, new firms such as Compaq, Zenith, Leading Edge, and a host of others entered the industry with machines technologically identical to the IBM. In fact, they were so similar that they came to be called "clones." The massive wave of entry into the personal computer industry shifted the supply curve to the right and lowered the price and the profits for all firms.

Exit Let's see what happens when firms leave an industry. Again, the impact of a firm leaving is to shift the industry supply curve, but this time to the left. Figure 11.8(b) illustrates. Suppose that initially the demand curve is D_3 with an industry supply curve S_3, so the market price is $17 and 7,000 sweaters are being sold. As firms leave the industry, the supply curve shifts to the left and becomes S_4. With the fall in supply, industry output falls from 7,000 to 6,000 sweaters and the price rises from $17 to $20.

To see what is happening to Swanky, go back again to Fig. 11.4. With the demand curve D_3 and a price of $17, Swanky is in a situation like that illustrated in Fig. 11.4(c). Price is lower than average total cost, and Swanky is making a loss. Some firms exit, and Swanky (and some others) hang in. As firms exit, the price rises from $17 to $20, so the firms that remain increase their output, and their losses vanish. They are then back in a situation like that illustrated in Fig. 11.4(b).

You have just worked out the second important result:

As firms leave an industry, the price rises and so do the profits of the remaining firms.

An example of a firm leaving an industry is International Harvester, a manufacturer of farm equipment. For decades, people associated the name "International Harvester" with tractors, combines, and other farm machines. But International Harvester wasn't the only maker of farm equipment. The industry became intensely competitive, and the firm began losing money. Now the company has a new name, Navistar International, and it doesn't make tractors anymore. After years of losses and shrinking revenues, it got out of the farm business in 1985. Now it makes trucks. Another example is Singer sewing machines. The name "Singer" still means sewing machines to millions of people, but Singer no longer makes these machines. It makes electronic equipment for jet aircraft and the like.

Both Singer and International Harvester exited because they were losing money on their operations. Their exits lowered supply and made it possible for the remaining firms in those two industries to break even.

Long-Run Equilibrium We've seen that the prospect of profit triggers entry and the prospect of continuing loss triggers exit. We have also seen that entry into an industry lowers the profits of the existing firms and that exit from an industry increases the profits of the remaining firms. Long-run equilibrium results from the interaction of profits and losses as signals to entry and exit and the effects of entry and exit on profits and losses.

Long-run equilibrium occurs in a competitive industry when economic profits are zero. If an industry makes economic profits, firms enter the industry and the supply curve shifts to the right. As a result, the market price falls and so do profits. Firms continue to enter and profits continue to fall as long as the industry is earning positive economic profits.

In an industry with economic losses, some firms will exit. As those firms leave the industry, the supply curve shifts to the left and the market price rises. As the price rises, the industry's losses shrink. As long as losses continue, some firms will leave the industry. Only when losses have been eliminated and zero economic profits are being made will firms stop exiting.

Let's now examine the second way in which the competitive industry adjusts in the long run—by existing firms changing their plant size.

FIGURE 11.9

Changes in Plant Size

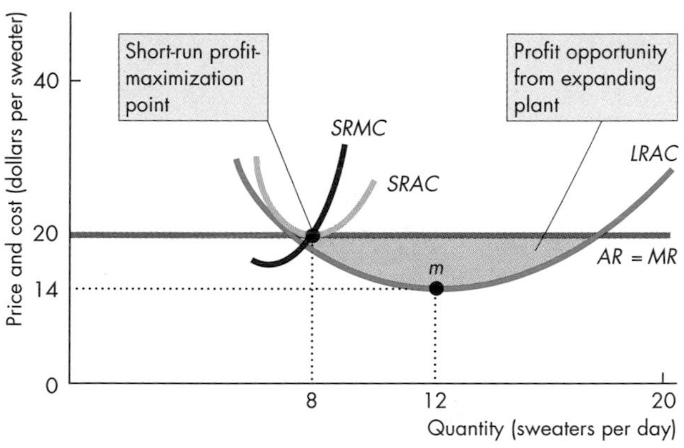

Swanky has a plant whose short-run cost curves are *SRMC* and *SRAC*. The price of a sweater is $20, so average revenue and marginal revenue (*AR* = *MR*) are $20. The profit-maximizing short-run output is 8 sweaters a day. Swanky's long-run costs are described by the long-run average cost curve (*LRAC*). The firm will want to expand its plant to take advantage of lower average costs and make a bigger profit—it will want to move into the blue area. As firms expand, the industry supply increases and the price falls.

Changes in Plant Size

A firm will change its plant size whenever it can increase its profit by doing so. A situation in which a firm can profitably expand its output by increasing its plant is illustrated in Fig. 11.9. In that figure the price (and marginal revenue) is $20. With its current plant, Swanky's marginal and average total cost—its short-run costs—are shown by the curves *SRMC* and *SRAC*. Swanky maximizes profit by producing 8 sweaters a day, but with its existing plant, Swanky makes zero economic profit.

Swanky's long-run average cost curve is *LRAC*. By installing more knitting machines—increasing its plant size—Swanky can lower its costs and operate at a positive economic profit. For example, if Swanky increases its plant size so that it operates at point *m*, the minimum of its long-run average cost, it lowers its average cost from $20 to $14 and makes a profit of $6 a sweater. Since Swanky is a price taker, expanding output from 8 to 12 sweaters does not lower the market price and so would be a profitable thing for Swanky to do. Because it takes time to change the production plant, the short-run equilibrium prevails. Nevertheless, over time, the firm will gradually expand its plant.

As firms expand their plants, the short-run industry supply curve starts to shift to the right. (Recall that the industry supply curve is the sum of the supply curves of all the individual firms.) With increases in supply and a given demand, the price gradually falls. As the price falls, so do profits. It will pay firms to expand as long as expansion increases profits. Only when no economic profits are being made will firms stick with their existing plant size. There is only one possible plant size that is consistent with long-run equilibrium in a competitive industry, and that is the one associated with the minimum long-run average cost (point *m* in Fig. 11.9).

Figure 11.10 illustrates the long-run competitive equilibrium. It occurs at a price of $14 with each firm producing 12 sweaters a day. Each firm in the industry has the plant size such that its marginal cost and average total cost curves are *SRMC* and *SRAC*. Each firm produces the output at which its short-run marginal cost equals price. No firm can change its output in the short run and make more profit. As each firm is producing at minimum long-run average cost (point *m* on *LRAC*), no firm has an incentive to expand or contract its production plant—a bigger plant or a smaller plant will lead to a higher long-run average cost and an economic loss. Finally, no firm has an incentive to leave the industry or to enter it.

FIGURE 11.10

The Long-Run Equilibrium of a Firm

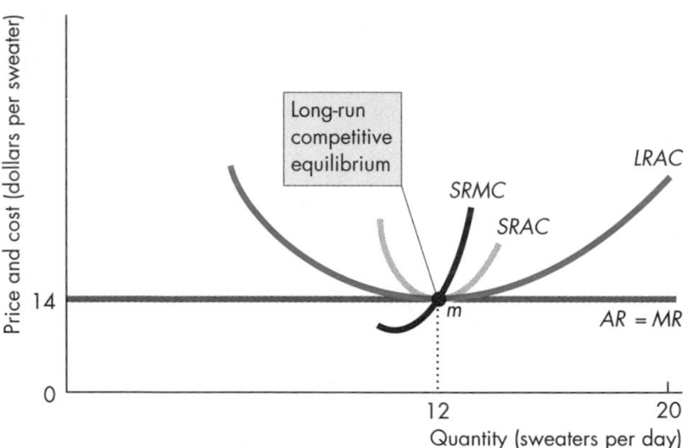

As firms expand their plants, industry supply increases and the price falls. Long-run equilibrium occurs when the price equals $14 and each firm is producing at point *m*, its point of minimum long-run average cost.

REVIEW

Long-run competitive equilibrium is described by three conditions:

- Firms maximize short-run profit, so marginal cost equals marginal revenue (equals price).
- Economic profits are zero, so no firm has an incentive to enter or to leave the industry.
- Long-run average cost is at a minimum, so no firm has an incentive to expand or to contract its plant. ◆

Responding to Changing Tastes and Advancing Technology

Increased awareness of the health hazards of smoking has caused a decrease in the demand for tobacco and cigarettes. The development of inexpensive car and air transportation has caused a huge decrease in the demand for long-distance trains and buses. Solid-state electronics have caused a large decrease in the demand for TV and radio repair. There has been a decrease in the demand for American-made cars as a result of high-quality alternatives from Japan. What happens in a competitive industry when there is a permanent decrease in the demand for its products?

The development of the microwave oven has produced an enormous increase in the demand for paper, glass, and plastic cooking utensils and for plastic wrap. The demand for almost all products is steadily increasing as a result of increasing population and increasing incomes. What happens in a competitive industry when the demand for its product increases?

Advances in technology are constantly lowering the costs of production. New biotechnologies have dramatically lowered the costs of many food and pharmaceutical products. New electronics technologies have lowered the cost of producing just about every good and service. What happens in a competitive industry when technological change lowers its production costs?

Let's use the theory of perfect competition to answer these questions.

A Permanent Decrease in Demand

Suppose that an industry starts out in long-run competitive equilibrium, shown in Fig. 11.11(a). The demand curve labeled D_0 and the supply curve labeled S_0 represent the initial demand and supply in the market. The price initially is P_0, and the total industry output is Q_0. A single firm is shown in Fig. 11.11(b). Initially, it produces the quantity q_0 and makes zero economic profit.

Now suppose that demand decreases to D_1, as shown in part (a). This decrease in demand causes the price to drop to P_1. At this lower price, each firm produces a smaller output (q_1), and the quantity supplied by the industry decreases from Q_0 to Q_1 as the industry slides down its short-run supply curve (S_0). The industry is now in short-run equilibrium but not long-run equilibrium. It is in short-run equilibrium because each firm is maximizing profit. But it is not in long-run equilibrium because each firm is making an economic loss—its average total cost exceeds the price.

FIGURE 11.11

A Decrease in Demand

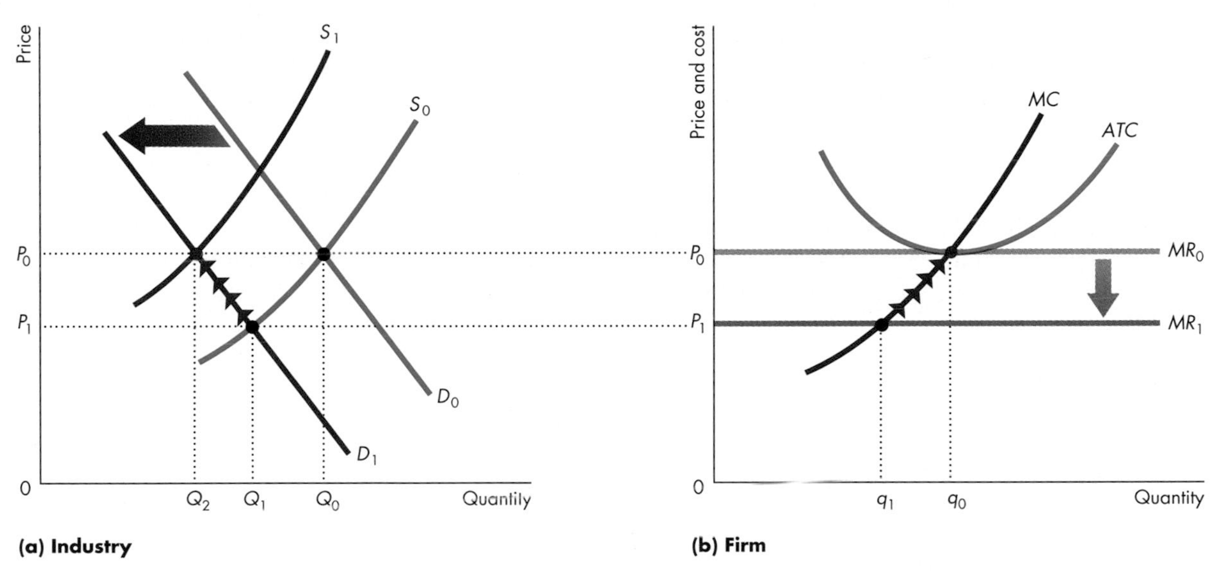

An industry starts out in long-run competitive equilibrium. Part (a) shows the industry demand curve D_0 and the industry supply curve S_0, the equilibrium quantity Q_0, and the market price P_0. Each firm sells at price P_0, so its marginal revenue curve is MR_0 in part (b). Each firm produces q_0 and makes a zero profit. Demand decreases from D_0 to D_1 (part a). The equilibrium price falls to P_1, each firm lowers its output to q_1 (part b), and industry output falls to Q_1. In this new situation, firms are making losses and some firms will leave the industry. As they do so, the industry supply curve gradually shifts to the left, from S_0 to S_1. This shift gradually raises the industry price from P_1 back to P_0. While the price is below P_0, firms are making losses and some are leaving the industry. Once the price has returned to P_0, the smaller number of firms whose supply curves add up to the industry supply curve (S_1) will each be making a zero profit. There will be no further incentive for any firm to leave the industry. Each firm produces q_0, and industry output is Q_2.

In this situation, firms will leave the industry. As they do so, the industry supply curve starts shifting to the left, the quantity supplied shrinks, and the price gradually rises. At each higher price, the profit-maximizing output is higher, so the firms remaining in the industry raise their output as the price rises. Each slides up its marginal cost or supply curve (part b). Eventually, enough firms will have left the industry for the supply curve to have shifted to S_1 (part a). When that has happened, the price will have returned to its original level (P_0). At that price, the firms remaining in the industry will produce the same amount as they did before the fall in demand (q_0). No firms will want to leave the industry because of losses, and none will want to enter. The industry supply curve settles down at S_1, and total industry output is Q_2. The industry is again in long-run equilibrium.

In the long-run equilibrium following a permanent decrease in demand, fewer firms remain in the industry. Each remaining firm produces the same output in the new long-run equilibrium as it did initially. While moving from the original equilibrium to the new one, firms that remain in the industry suffer losses. But they keep their losses to a minimum because they adjust their output to keep price equal to marginal cost.

A Permanent Increase in Demand

What happens in a competitive industry when the demand for its product increases? Let's begin the story again in long-run equilibrium, as shown in Fig. 11.12(a). With demand curve D_0 and supply curve S_0, the market price is P_0 and quantity Q_0 is sold by the industry. Figure 11.12(b) shows a single firm. At price P_0, the firm is making zero economic profit and producing an output of q_0. Now suppose that the demand for the industry's output increases from D_0 to D_1. The increased demand raises the price to P_1. The quantity supplied by the industry rises from Q_0 to Q_1 as each firm increases its output from q_0 to q_1 (part b). At price P_1 and quantity Q_1, the industry is in short-run equilibrium but not in long-run equilibrium. Firms in the industry are making economic profits. These economic profits will attract new firms into the industry.

As new firms enter, the industry supply curve starts shifting to the right, and as it does so, it intersects the demand curve at lower and lower prices and higher and higher quantities. Firms in the industry react to the falling price by cutting their output. That is, in Fig. 11.12(b) each firm slides back down its marginal cost curve in order to maximize profit at each successively lower price. Eventually, enough new firms enter the industry to shift the industry supply curve all the way to S_1. By that time, the market price falls to P_0, the original price, and the industry output is Q_2. At a price of P_0, each firm cuts its output back to its original level, q_0. Each firm is again making zero economic profit, and no firms enter or exit the industry. This new situation is a long-run equilibrium. During the adjustment process from the initial long-run equilibrium to the new one, all firms—both those firms that were in the industry originally and those that entered—make economic profits.

The process that we've just described goes on in

FIGURE 11.12

An Increase in Demand

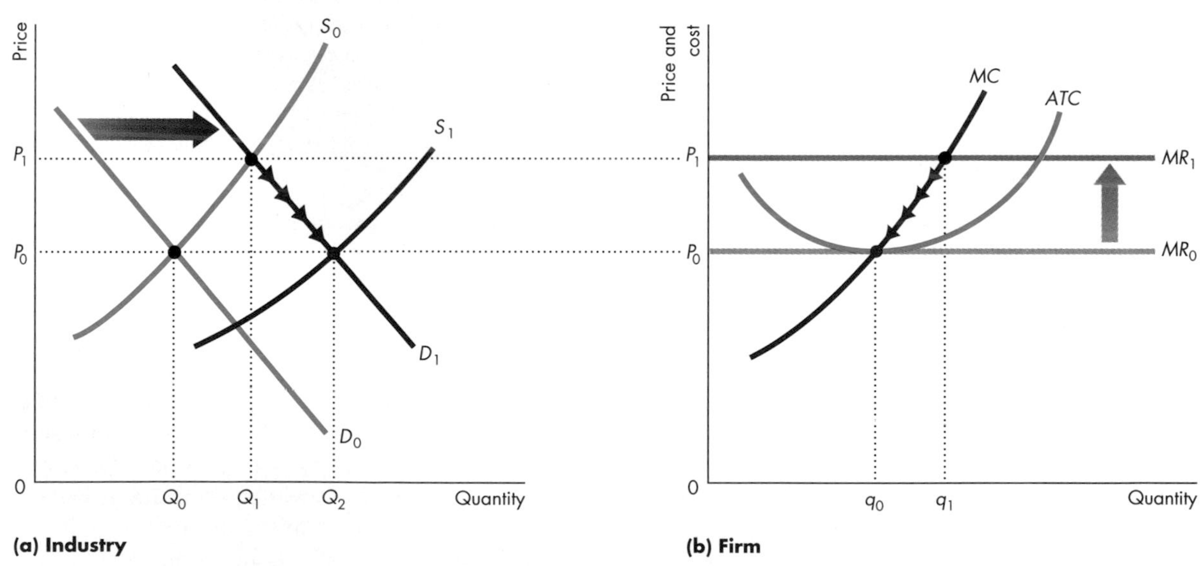

(a) Industry

(b) Firm

A competitive industry is in long-run equilibrium. The demand curve is D_0, and the supply curve is S_0 (part a). The industry's output is Q_0, and the market price is P_0. Each firm faces the marginal revenue curve MR_0 and maximizes profit by producing q_0 (part b). Demand increases from D_0 to D_1. The price rises to P_1, and industry output increases to Q_1. Each firm increases its output to q_1. In this situation, firms are making a profit (price is greater than average total cost). New firms will enter the industry, and as they do so, the industry supply curve shifts to the right. As the supply curve shifts to the right, the price gradually falls and each individual firm gradually cuts its output from q_1 back to q_0. Since firms are entering the industry, total industry output increases even though each firm's output is cut back. The new equilibrium occurs when enough firms have entered the industry for the supply curve to have moved to S_1 with the price restored to its original level, P_0, and with each firm making zero profit. At this point, industry output is at Q_2. Since each firm is making a zero profit, there is no further tendency for new firms to enter the industry, so the supply curve remains stationary at S_1.

many real-world markets. An example is the market for pizza, which experienced strong expansion throughout the 1980s—see Reading Between the Lines, pp. 300–301.

External Economies and Diseconomies

One feature of the predictions that we have just generated seems odd: in the long run, regardless of whether demand increases or decreases, the price returns to its original level. Is that outcome inevitable? In fact, it is not. It is possible for the long-run equilibrium price to rise, fall, or stay the same. Figure 11.13 illustrates these three cases. In part (a), the long-run supply curve (LS_A) is perfectly elastic. In this case, an increase in demand from D_0 to D_1 (or a decrease in demand from D_1 to D_0) results in a change in the quantity sold but an

FIGURE 11.13

Long-Run Changes in Price and Quantity

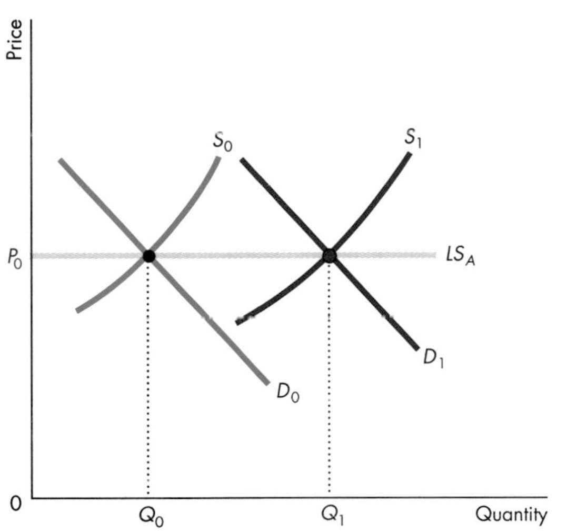

(a) Constant cost industry

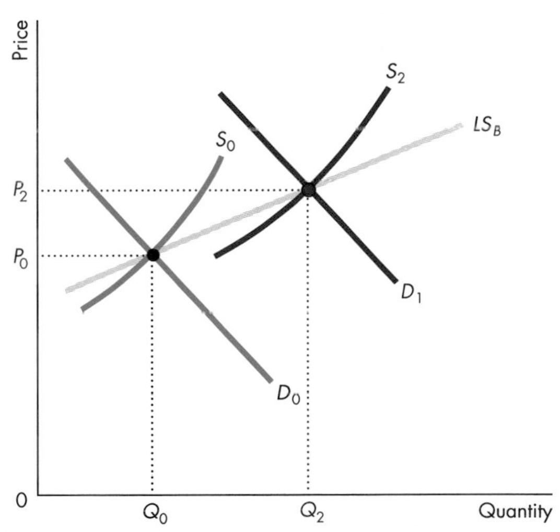

(b) Increasing cost industry

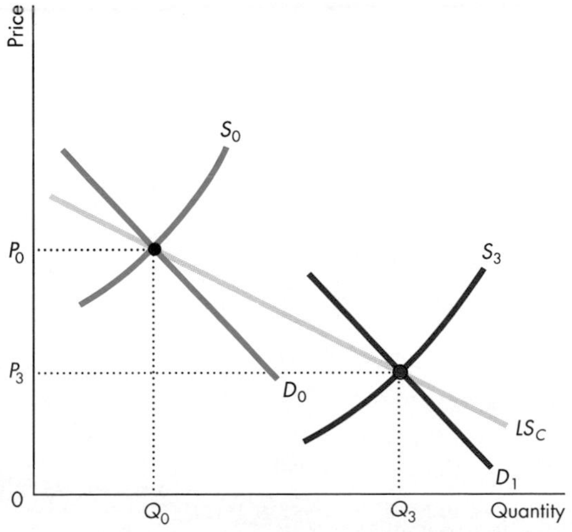

(c) Decreasing cost industry

Three possible long-run changes in price and quantity are illustrated. When demand increases from D_0 to D_1, entry occurs and the industry supply curve shifts from S_0 to S_1. In part (a), the long-run supply curve, LS_A, is horizontal. The quantity increases from Q_0 to Q_1, and the price remains constant at P_0. In part (b), the long-run supply curve is LS_B; the price increases to P_2, and the quantity increases to Q_2. This case occurs in industries with external diseconomies. In part (c), the long-run supply curve is LS_C; the price decreases to P_3, and the quantity increases to Q_3. This case occurs in an industry with external economies.

Competition in Action

THE POST-STANDARD, JULY 8, 1991

The Pizza War Mushrooms

As Big Chains Battle, Little Shops Fight for Slice of the Pie

BY ELIZABETH DORAN

When the pizza shops battle over who gets the biggest slice of the pie, they bring out their heavy artillery.

Their weapons include pepperoni, mushrooms and extra cheese, two-for-one deals and deep discounts. Toss in the ultimate ingredient—home delivery—and the pizza wars are cooking.

Local pizza chains are following the national trend—each one trying to better the other with mouth-watering deals.

The Big Three—Pizza Hut Inc., Domino's Pizza Inc. and Little Caesar's Pizza—are waging the war on the front lines, but the foot soldiers, from regional chains down to the neighborhood ma-and-pa pizzerias, also are in the thick of the battle.

Healthy competition, however, may not bode well for the smaller pizza shops.

"There's an old saying: 'When the elephants fight, the ants take a beating,' " Correll added. "When the Big Three do war, they trample on the little guys who are competing in the same arena. If they're healthy, they survive. If they're marginal, they sink."

The Big Three's passion for promotions has driven the price of pizza down. To stay afloat, the little guy may have to follow suit, however reluctantly.

Ronald Ross, owner of two of the Twin Trees restaurants in Syracuse, finds himself in that position. Although he'd rather avoid it, Ross said he's had to issue coupons "a bit more than we want to" to stay competitive, even though it lowers the company's profits. . . .

"We're a small company, and so it's tough to compete with the big chains," he said. . . .

. . . There are more than 130 establishments listed under "pizza" in the 1991–1992 Syracuse Yellow Pages, compared with just under 70 in the 1981–1982 telephone book.

Other small shops which have opened in recent years, such as Severino's in Fayetteville, match their competitors' prices. Severino's does that in part by accepting coupons from both Pizza Hut and Domino's, said Jim Harriger, assistant manager. . . .

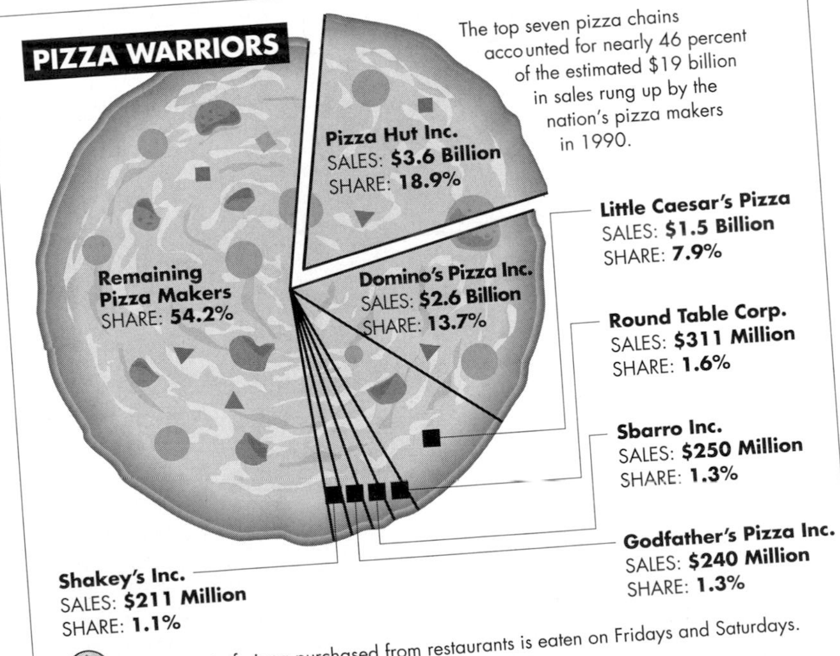
PIZZA WARRIORS
The top seven pizza chains accounted for nearly 46 percent of the estimated $19 billion in sales rung up by the nation's pizza makers in 1990.
Pizza Hut Inc. SALES: $3.6 Billion SHARE: 18.9%
Little Caesar's Pizza SALES: $1.5 Billion SHARE: 7.9%
Domino's Pizza Inc. SALES: $2.6 Billion SHARE: 13.7%
Remaining Pizza Makers SHARE: 54.2%
Round Table Corp. SALES: $311 Million SHARE: 1.6%
Sbarro Inc. SALES: $250 Million SHARE: 1.3%
Godfather's Pizza Inc. SALES: $240 Million SHARE: 1.3%
Shakey's Inc. SALES: $211 Million SHARE: 1.1%
45 percent of pizza purchased from restaurants is eaten on Fridays and Saturdays.
Almost half of all pizza eaten is by customers in the 25-to-50 age bracket. Customers over 50 are least likely to order pizza, while teenagers prefer pizza two-to-one over restaurant food.
Source: Nation's Restaurant News; National Restaurant Association CREST survey
The Post-Standard

The Essence of the Story

More than 130 establishments produce pizza in the area covered by the Syracuse Yellow Pages in 1991–1992, compared with under 70 a decade earlier.

The Big Three pizza chains—Pizza Hut Inc., Domino's Pizza Inc., and Little Caesar's Pizza—and the smaller regional and local pizza producers are locked in a fierce competitive battle.

The competition is especially tough for the smaller pizza shops. They must match the prices and quality of the big producers. Only the healthy survive; the marginal ones fail.

Background and Analysis

The pizza market in large cities can be explained by the model of perfect competition. Some pizza producers are large, and some are small. But no firm is large enough to control the price of pizza.

In 1980, the demand for pizza was D_0 and the supply was S_0 (see Fig. 1a). Competition among a large number of suppliers keeps the price at its equilibrium level, which in 1980 was P_0. The quantity sold was Q_0.

The demand for pizza increased through the 1980s and by 1991 was D_1. Increased demand brought profits that induced the entry of new firms and the expansion of existing ones. As a result, supply increased and by 1991 was S_1. The price decreased to P_1, and the quantity of pizza sold increased to Q_1.

Some pizza producers have lower average costs than others. The Big Three are low-cost producers. But so are many of the smaller firms. A low-cost producer's average total cost curve, ATC_L, and marginal cost curve, MC_L, are shown in Fig. 1(b).

The demand curve facing a low-cost producer is perfectly elastic at the market-determined price, P_1. The profit-maximizing output is q_l, the quantity that makes marginal cost equal to price, as shown in Fig. 1(b). The firm makes an economic profit shown by the blue rectangle. Such firms enter and expand as long as profit opportunities exist.

Some producers—most likely small ones and firms in a poor location—have high average costs, shown by the average total cost curve ATC_M in Fig. 1(c). Such a firm's marginal cost curve is MC_M, and it maximizes profit by producing q_M, the quantity at which marginal cost equals the market-determined price.

The firm shown makes zero economic profit and is a marginal producer. Firms with average costs higher than those shown in Fig. 1(c) have gone out of business. The firm in Fig. 1(c) will go out of business as low-cost firms enter and expand, increasing supply and lowering the price below P_1.

As the demand for pizza increased throughout the 1980s, the forces we have described shifted the supply curve of pizza in Fig. 1(a) to the right, keeping prices low and bringing new resources into the pizza industry in response to changing consumer demands.

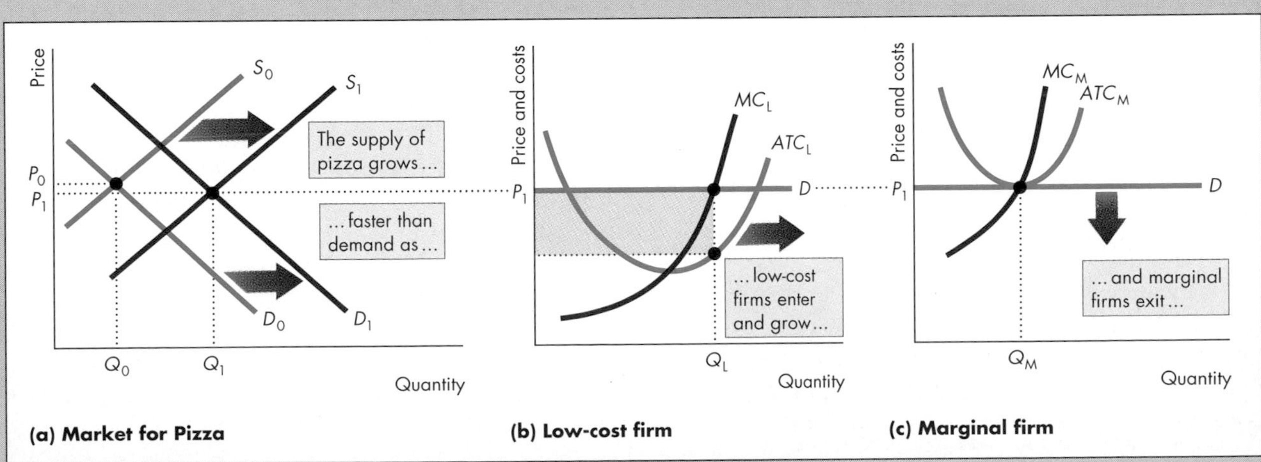

unchanged price. This is the case that we have just analyzed. In part (b), the long-run supply curve (LS_B) slopes upward. In this case, when demand increases from D_0 to D_1, the price increases, and when demand decreases from D_1 to D_0, the price decreases. Finally, part (c) shows a case in which the long-run supply curve (LS_C) slopes downward. In this case, an increase in demand from D_0 to D_1 results in a fall in the price in the long run. A decrease in demand from D_1 to D_0 results in a higher price in the long run.

Which outcome occurs depends on external economies and external diseconomies. **External economies** are factors beyond the control of an individual firm that lower its average total cost as industry output rises. **External diseconomies** are factors outside the control of a firm that raise its average total cost as industry output rises. There are many examples of external economies and diseconomies.

One of the best examples of external economies is the growth of specialist support services for an industry as it expands. As farm output increased in the nineteenth and early twentieth centuries, the services available to farmers expanded and their costs fell. Farm machinery, fertilizers, transportation networks, storage, and marketing facilities all improved—lowering farm costs. Farms enjoyed the benefits of external economies. As a consequence, as the demand for farm products increased, the quantity produced increased but the price fell (as in Fig. 11.13c).

One of the best examples of external diseconomies is congestion. The airline industry provides a good illustration. With bigger airline industry output, there is greater congestion of both airports and airspace, which results in longer delays and extra waiting time for passengers and airplanes. These external diseconomies mean that as the demand for air transportation continues to increase, eventually (in the absence of further technological change), prices will rise (as in Fig. 11.13b).

Technological Change

Industries are constantly discovering lower-cost techniques of production. Most cost-saving production techniques cannot be implemented, however, without investing in new plant and equipment. As a consequence, it takes time for a technological advance to spread through an industry. Some firms whose plants are on the verge of being replaced will be quick to adopt the new technology, while other firms whose plants have recently been replaced will continue to operate with older technology until they can no longer cover their average variable cost. Once average variable cost cannot be covered, it pays a firm to scrap even a relatively new plant (embodying the original technology) in favor of a plant with the new technology.

Let's work out exactly what happens to the output and profit of each firm in an industry reshaped by a new technology. Figure 11.14(a) shows the demand curve for an industry (D) and an initial supply curve (S_0). The price is P_0, and the quantity is Q_0. Initially, there are only original technology firms in existence (Fig. 11.14b). Each firm has a marginal cost curve MC_O and an average total cost curve ATC_O. At the market price (P_0), each firm faces a marginal revenue curve MR_0, produces an output q_0^O, and makes zero economic profit. The industry is in long-run competitive equilibrium.

New technology allows firms to produce at substantially lower cost than with the existing technology. The cost curves of firms with the new technology are shown in Fig. 11.14(c). Suppose that one firm with the new technology enters the industry. Since the industry is competitive, this one firm will be a negligible part of the total industry and will hardly affect the industry supply, so the supply curve remains at S_0. The price remains at P_0, and the new technology firm produces a profit-maximizing output of q_0^N and makes a positive economic profit.

Gradually, more new technology firms enter the industry, and after a period, enough have entered to shift the industry supply curve to S_1 in part (a). By this time, the market price has fallen to P_1 and the industry output has risen to Q_1. Each firm takes the price P_1 and maximizes its profit. Each new technology firm, in part (c), maximizes profit by producing the output q_1^N and continues to make a positive economic profit. Each original technology firm, in part (b), minimizes its loss by producing the output q_1^O.

More new technology firms will continue to enter, since the new technology is profitable. Original technology firms will begin to leave the industry or switch to the new technology because the original technology is unprofitable. Eventually, all the firms in the industry will be new technology firms, and by this time, the industry supply curve will have moved

FIGURE 11.14

Technological Change in a Competitive Industry

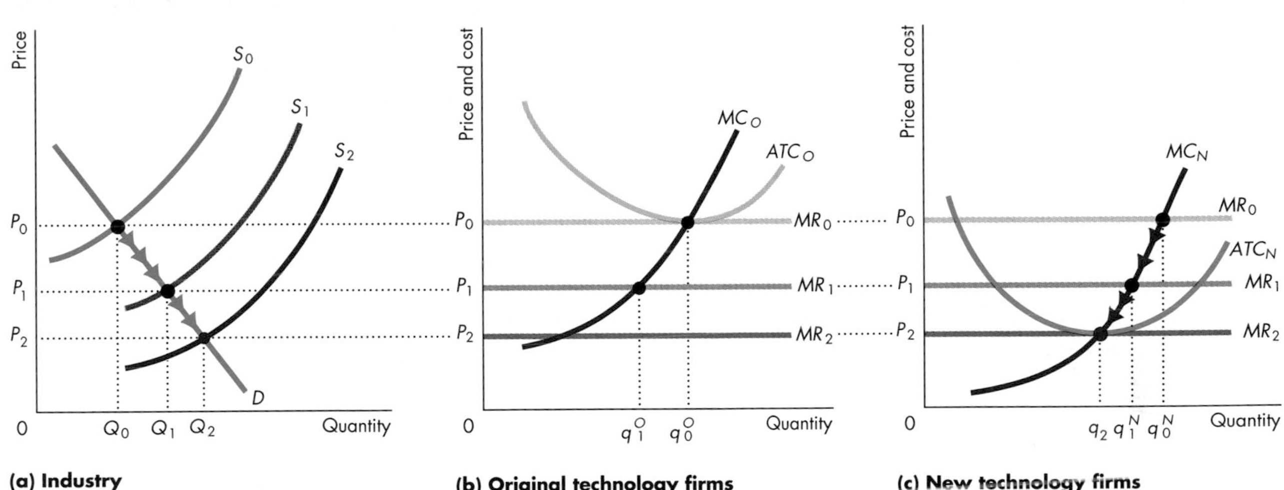

Initially, the industry supply curve is S_0 and the demand curve is D, so the equilibrium price is P_0, and quantity Q_0 is traded (part a). Each individual firm, shown in part (b), produces q_0^O and makes a zero profit. A new technology is developed. The costs associated with the new technology (ATC_N and MC_N) are shown in part (c) and are lower than those for the original technology. A new technology firm, faced with the price P_0, produces a profit-maximizing output of q_0^N and makes a profit. Since the new technology is profitable, more and more firms will use it. As they do so, the industry supply curve begins to shift to the right, from S_0 to S_1. With an increase in industry supply, industry output increases to Q_1, but the price falls to P_1. As a result, new technology firms will cut their output from q_0^N to q_1^N, but they will still be making a profit. Original technology firms will cut their output from q_0^O to q_1^O. They will be making losses. As firms with the original technology begin to close down and more new technology firms enter the industry, the industry supply curve continues to shift to the right, from S_1 to S_2. At S_2, the price is P_2 and industry output is Q_2. Each new technology firm is now producing q_2 and making a zero profit, and there are no firms using the original technology.

The effect of the introduction of the new technology has been to increase industry output and lower price. In the process, firms that adopted the new technology early made profits, while firms that stuck with the original technology for too long incurred losses.

to S_2. The supply curve S_2 is based on the marginal cost curves of the new technology firms. The supply curve S_0 is based on the marginal cost curves of the original technology firms. The supply curve S_1 is based on the marginal cost curves for both original technology and new technology firms. With supply curve S_2, the market price is P_2 and the industry output is Q_2. At price P_2, the new technology firms produce a profit-maximizing output of q_2, making zero profits. The industry long-run equilibrium price is P_2.

The process that we have just analyzed is one in which some firms experience economic profits and others experience economic losses. It is a period of dynamic change for an industry. Some firms do well, and others do badly. Often a change of the kind that we have just examined will have a geographical dimension to it. For example, the new technology firms might be located in a new industrial region of a country, while the original technology firms might be located in a traditional industrial region. Alternatively, the new technology firms might be in a foreign country, while the original technology firms are in the domestic economy. The struggles of the American textile industry to keep up with the fierce competition from Hong Kong and Taiwan is a good example of this phenomenon. Another example is the dairy industry, which is undergoing a major technological change arising from the use of hormones.

REVIEW

When the demand for a competitive industry's product declines, firms begin to incur losses and leave the industry. Exiting firms decrease supply, and the price begins to increase. Eventually, enough firms exit, and the remaining firms just cover their costs. When the demand for a competitive industry's product increases, firms make profits and new firms enter. Entry increases the industry supply, and the price begins to fall. Eventually, enough firms enter to compete away all the economic profit. ◆ ◆ When a new technology lowers costs, the industry supply increases and price falls. Firms that adopt the new technology make a profit, and those sticking with the old technology incur a loss. Old technology firms either adopt the new technology or exit. Eventually, all firms remaining in the industry have adopted the new technology and are just covering their costs. ◆

Farms in Distress

In 1981, there were 2.4 million farms in the United States. The average farm had 425 acres. The population of farms has steadily declined over the years. In the five years between 1976 and 1981, that decline was close to 1 percent a year. But in the five years between 1981 and 1986, 220,000 farms (9 percent of the total) disappeared—more than three times the number that went out of business in the preceding five years. At the same time, the average size of farms increased by 7 percent to 455 acres. Through the early to mid-1980s, there were many indications of financial distress in the farm sector. By 1985, more than 5 percent of farms were unable to meet their bank loan repayment schedules; almost 40 percent had borrowed up to their loan limits; close to 5 percent a year were going out of business; and close to 4 percent were in bankruptcy. Why have American farms gone through a period of such tremendous financial distress? Why have so many farms gone out of business? Why, after such a shakeout, is the remaining farm larger, on the average?

The farm problem is a complex one. In fact, there is no single "farm problem" but many individual problems, varying from region to region and from crop to crop. But there is a single, common problem that affected all farmers to some degree during the early 1980s. It's on this problem that we'll focus.

Although some farmers are wealthy, many are not. They have to buy their land and farm buildings and equipment by borrowing from the bank. In the early 1980s, the cost of bank borrowing increased on an unprecedented scale. Bank loans that in the 1970s had cost an average of 7 or 8 percent a year suddenly were costing an average of 13 percent and climbed briefly to 20 percent in 1981. The cost remained high at 15 percent a year through 1982. This massive increase in the cost of borrowing represented an increase in the fixed costs of a farm. Recall that fixed costs are those incurred independently of the volume of output. Even if a farm produces nothing, it has to pay the bank the interest on its loans.

We can analyze the effects of an increase in fixed costs in the farm sector by using the model of a perfectly competitive industry that we've just been studying. Figure 11.15 shows you what happens. In part (a), a farm's average total cost curve is *ATC* and its marginal cost curve is *MC*. The market price is P_0, and the farm's marginal revenue curve is *MR*. The farm's profit-maximizing output is q_0. The initial situation shown in part (a) is a long-run equilibrium with the farm making zero economic profit.

An increase in total fixed cost shifts the average total cost curve upward but does not change the marginal cost curve. (Recall that marginal cost is the cost of producing one additional unit of output. Since the increase in interest charges increases fixed cost but not variable cost, marginal cost is unchanged.) Suppose that the increased fixed cost shifts the average total cost curve to *ATC*'. If the price remains P_0, the farm's profit-maximizing output remains at q_0. But the farm is now losing money. In Fig. 11.15(a), the loss is equal to the red rectangle.

The size of a farm's loss depends on its financial situation. Farms with large debts make the largest losses. During the 1980s, 9 percent of farms had loans that exceeded 70 percent of the value of their land and buildings. It is these farms that incur the largest losses. These are the farms that will begin to leave the industry. As farms go out of business, the supply curve for farm products starts to shift to the left and the price of farm products begins to increase. Figure 11.15(b) shows what happens in the long run. When enough farms have left the industry, the price will have increased from P_0 to P_1. At the

FIGURE 11.15

The Effects of High Interest Rates on Farm Profits and Prices

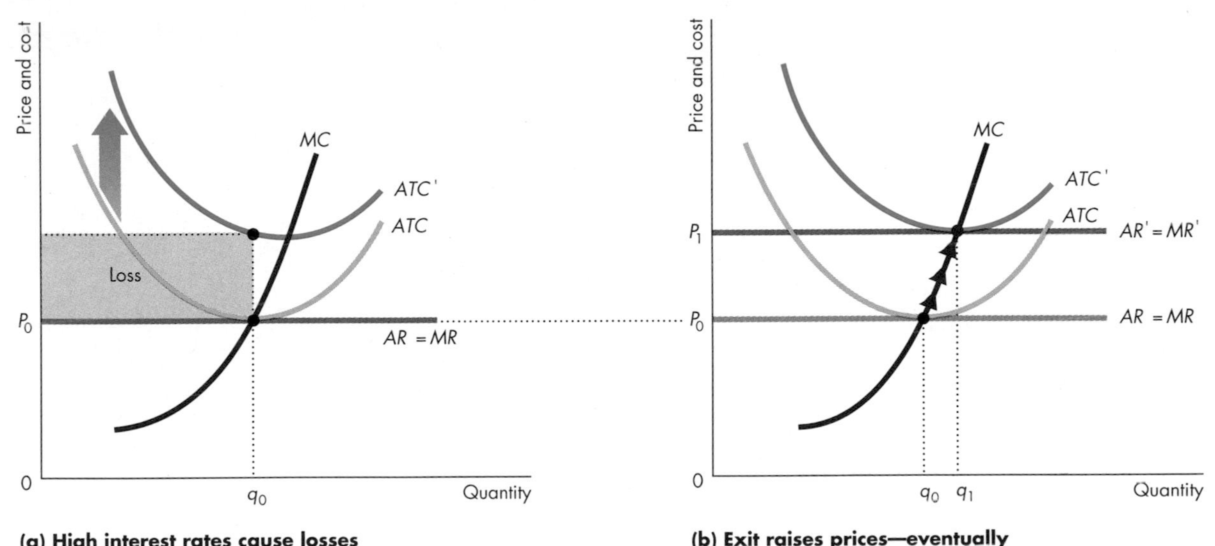

(a) High interest rates cause losses

(b) Exit raises prices—eventually

Initially, an individual farm has an average total cost curve *ATC*, and at a price of P_0 its profit-maximizing output is q_0 (part a). Fixed costs increase, shifting the average total cost curve upward to *ATC'*. Marginal cost and price remain constant, and so does the profit-maximizing output. Farms now make a loss shown by the red rectangle. As some farms exit, the industry supply curve shifts to the left and the price begins to rise from P_0 to P_1. The profit-maximizing output increases from q_0 to q_1 (part b). The process of adjustment is not instantaneous, and farms make losses for a prolonged period.

higher price, farm output increases from q_0 to q_1 and farms are no longer losing money. Individual farm outputs are now bigger than before, which means that the average farm uses more inputs—more labor, machines, and land.

But the situation shown in part (b) takes a long time to come about. The price does not rise quickly from P_0 to P_1. The main factor slowing the rise in price is the fact that even with a large exit of U.S. farms, these farms produce but a small fraction of the world supply of most agricultural products. As a consequence, farms make losses for a prolonged period of time, during which the adjustment process takes place.

You've now studied how a competitive market works and have used the model of perfect competition to interpret and explain a variety of aspects of real-world economic behavior. The last topic that we'll study in this chapter is the efficiency of perfect competition.

Competition and Efficiency

In perfect competition, freedom of entry ensures that firms produce at the least possible cost. Also, the fact that each firm is a price taker, facing a perfectly elastic demand curve, results in firms producing a quantity such that marginal cost equals price. These features of a perfectly competitive market have important implications for the efficiency of such a market.

Allocative Efficiency

Allocative efficiency occurs when no resources are wasted—when no one can be made better off without someone else being made worse off. If someone can be made better off without making someone else worse off, a more efficient allocation of resources can be achieved. Three conditions must be satisfied to achieve allocative efficiency:

- Economic efficiency
- Consumer efficiency
- Equality of marginal social cost and marginal social benefit

We defined economic efficiency in Chapter 9 as a situation in which the cost of producing a given output is minimized. Economic efficiency involves technological efficiency—producing the maximum possible output from given inputs—as well as using inputs in their cost-minimizing proportions. Economic efficiency occurs whenever firms maximize profit. Since firms in perfect competition maximize profit, perfect competition is economically efficient.

Consumer efficiency occurs when consumers cannot make themselves better off by reallocating their budgets. A consumer's best possible budget allocation is summarized in the consumer's demand curves. That is, a demand curve tells us the quantity demanded at a given price when the consumer has made the best possible use of a given budget. Thus when the quantity bought at a given price is a point on the demand curve, the allocation satisfies consumer efficiency.

The third condition occurs in perfect competition if there are no external costs and benefits. **External costs** are those costs not borne by the producer but borne by other members of society. Examples of such costs are the costs of pollution and congestion. **External benefits** are those benefits accruing to people other than the buyer of a good. Examples of such benefits are the pleasure we get from well-designed buildings and beautiful works of art. As long as *someone* buys these things, *everyone* can enjoy them.

Marginal social cost is the cost of producing one additional unit of output, including external costs. **Marginal social benefit** is the dollar value of the benefit from one additional unit of consumption, including any external benefits. Allocative efficiency occurs when marginal social cost equals marginal social benefit. Figure 11.16 illustrates such a situation. The marginal social benefit curve is *MSB*, and the marginal social cost curve is *MSC*. Allocative efficiency occurs at a quantity Q^* and a price P^*. In this situation, there is no waste. No one can be made better off without someone else being made worse off. If output is above Q^*, marginal social cost will exceed marginal social benefit. The cost of producing the last unit will exceed its benefit. If output is below Q^*, marginal social benefit will exceed marginal social cost. Producing one more unit will bring more benefit than it costs.

There are some circumstances in which perfect competition delivers allocative efficiency, as shown in Fig. 11.16. Those circumstances are ones in which there are no external costs and benefits. In such a case, all the benefits accrue to the buyers of a good and the costs are borne by its producer. In that case, the marginal social benefit curve is the same as the industry demand curve. Also, the marginal social cost curve is the industry supply curve. With perfect competition, price and quantity are determined at

FIGURE 11.16

Allocative Efficiency

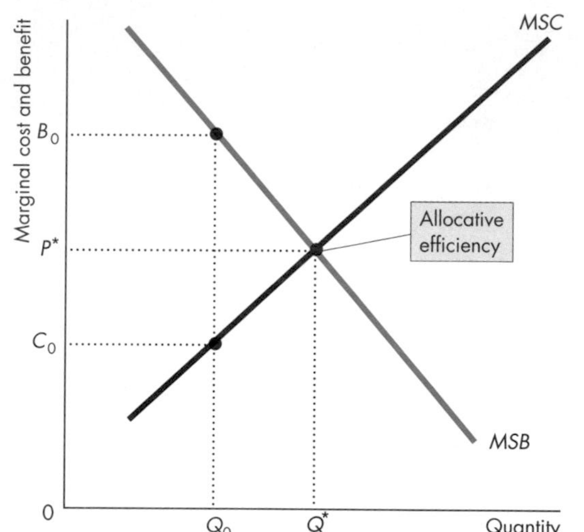

Allocative efficiency, which occurs when no resources are wasted, requires that marginal social cost (*MSC*) be equal to marginal social benefit (*MSB*). Allocative efficiency occurs at output Q^*. If output is Q_0, marginal social cost (C_0) will be less than marginal social benefit (B_0). The benefit from one additional unit of output exceeds its cost. A perfectly competitive market delivers allocative efficiency when there are no external costs and benefits. In such a situation, the marginal social cost curve is the industry supply curve and the marginal social benefit curve is the industry demand curve. The price is P^*, and the quantity traded is Q^*.

the point of intersection of the demand and supply curves. Hence a perfectly competitive market produces an output Q^* at a price P^*. Perfect competition delivers allocative efficiency.

To check that in this situation no resources are being wasted—no one can be made better off without someone being made worse off—consider what will happen if output is restricted to Q_0. At that output, marginal social cost is C_0 but marginal social benefit is B_0. Everyone can be made better off by increasing output. Producers will willingly supply more of the good for a price higher than C_0. Consumers will willingly buy more of the good for a price lower than B_0. Everyone would like to trade more. But once output has increased to Q^*, there are no further available gains from increasing the output of this good. The benefit to the consumer of the last unit produced exactly equals the cost to the producer of the last unit.

The Invisible Hand

The founder of economic science, Adam Smith, suggested that a competitive market acts like an invisible hand to guide buyers and sellers to achieve the best possible social outcome. Each participant in a competitive market is, according to Smith, "led by an invisible hand to promote an end which was no part of his intention." You can see the invisible hand at work in the cartoon. Adam Smith was not able to work out his conclusion with the clarity and precision with which we are able to do so today. It is the work of Léon Walras and Vilfredo Pareto and, more recently, of Nobel Prize–winning American economists Kenneth Arrow and Gérard Debreu that demonstrated the precise conditions under which perfect competition and maximum social welfare coincide.

Drawing by M. Twohy; © 1985 The New Yorker Magazine, Inc.

Obstacles to Efficiency

There are two main obstacles to allocative efficiency:

- External costs and external benefits
- Monopoly

External costs and external benefits mean that many goods cannot be efficiently produced even in perfectly competitive markets. Such goods as national defense, the enforcement of law and order, the provision of clean drinking water, and the disposal of sewage and garbage are all examples of goods in which there are enormous external benefits. Left to competitive markets, we would have too small a production of such goods. There are also many examples of goods that impose high external costs. The production of steel and chemicals generates air and water pollution. Perfect competition will result in an overproduction of such goods. One of the key functions of government is to modify the outcome of competitive markets in cases such as these. Government institutions (which we study in Chapters 19 through 21) arise, in part, because of external costs and benefits.

Another obstacle to allocative efficiency is the existence of monopoly. Monopoly, which we study in the next chapter, results in the restriction of output below its competitive level in order to increase price and make a larger profit. Precisely how monopoly achieves this outcome is the subject of the next chapter.

◆ ◆ ◆ ◆ We have now completed our study of perfect competition. We have seen how a firm in a perfectly competitive market chooses its profit-maximizing output. We have seen how the actions of all the firms in a market combine to determine the market supply curve and how the market supply and demand curves determine the price and quantity. We have seen how a competitive industry operates in the short run, and we have studied the dynamic forces that move such a market to a long-run equilibrium. We have used the model of perfect competition to understand several important features of real-world markets. Finally, we have seen that under some specific circumstances, perfect competition delivers an economically efficient allocation of resources.

◆ ◆ Although many markets approximate the model of perfect competition, many do not. Our next task, in Chapters 12 and 13, is to study markets that depart from perfect competition. When we have completed this study, we'll have a toolkit of alternative models of markets that will enable us to study all the possible situations that arise in the real world. We begin, in the next chapter, by going to the opposite extreme of perfect competition—pure monopoly. Then, in Chapter 13, we'll study the markets between perfect competition and pure monopoly—monopolistic competition and oligopoly (competition among a few producers).

SUMMARY

Perfect Competition

Perfect competition occurs in a market in which a large number of firms produce an identical good, there are many buyers, firms face competition from potential new entrants, and all firms and buyers are fully informed about the prices charged by each firm. In perfect competition, each firm sells its good for the same price and no single firm can influence the market price. Even if one firm doubles its output, the industry output will change by a tiny percentage and the market price will hardly be affected at all. (pp. 280–282)

Firms' Choices in Perfect Competition

A competitive firm takes the market price and has to choose how much to produce, when to temporarily shut down, and when to permanently leave an industry. The firm's choices are motivated by its desire to maximize profit. Firms maximize profit by producing the output that makes marginal cost equal to marginal revenue.

A firm's maximum profit is not necessarily a positive profit. If price is above average total cost, the firm makes a profit. If price equals average total cost, the firm breaks even. If price is below average total cost, the firm makes a loss. If price is low enough, the firm maximizes profit by temporarily shutting down and laying off its workers. It pays to shut down production if price is below minimum average variable cost. When price equals minimum average variable cost, the firm makes a loss equal to its total fixed costs whether it produces the profit-maximizing output or shuts down.

The firm's supply curve is the upward-sloping part of its marginal cost curve at all points above the point of minimum average variable cost and runs along the vertical axis at all prices below minimum average variable cost. (pp. 282–290)

Output, Price, and Profit in the Short Run

The short-run industry supply curve shows how the total quantity supplied in the short run by all the firms in an industry varies as the market price varies.

The market price occurs where the quantity supplied and the quantity demanded are equal. Each firm takes the market price as given and chooses the output that maximizes profit. In short-run equilibrium, each firm can make an economic profit, make an economic loss, or break even. (pp. 290–292)

Output, Price, and Profit in the Long Run

If the firms in an industry make positive economic profits, existing firms will expand and new firms will enter the industry. If the firms in an industry make economic losses, some firms will leave the industry and the remaining firms will produce less. Entry and exit shift the industry supply curve. As firms enter, the industry supply curve shifts to the right. As firms leave, the industry supply curve shifts to the left. Entry causes profits of existing firms to fall, and exit causes profits of existing firms to rise (or losses to fall). In long-run equilibrium, firms make zero economic profit. No firm wants to enter or leave the industry, and no firm wants to expand or contract its production plant. Long-run competitive equilibrium occurs when each firm maximizes its short-run profit, economic profit is zero so there is no entry or exit, and each firm produces at the point of minimum long-run average cost, so it has no incentive to change its plant size. (pp. 292–296)

Responding to Changing Tastes and Advancing Technology

In a perfectly competitive market, a permanent decrease in demand leads to a lower industry output and a smaller number of firms in the industry. A permanent increase in demand leads to a rise in industry output and an increase in the number of firms in the industry. If there are no external economies or diseconomies, the market price remains constant in the long run as demand changes. If there are external economies, price falls in the long run as demand increases. If there are external diseconomies, price rises in the long run as demand increases.

New technology increases the industry supply, and in the long run the market price falls and the quantity sold increases. The number of firms in the industry falls. Firms that are slow to change to the new technology will make losses and eventually will go out of business. Firms that are quick to adopt the new technology will make economic profits initially, but in the long run they will make zero economic profit.

The farm problem of the 1980s can be interpreted by using the model of perfect competition. A large increase in interest rates—a fixed cost—increased average total cost and brought losses. These losses, in turn, forced many farms out of business. As the number of farms declines, the supply curve of farm products shifts to the left and prices increase. But this process takes time—time during which persistent losses occur in the farm sector. Eventually, after the adjustment process is complete, a smaller number of farms will break even. (pp. 296–305)

Competition and Efficiency

Allocative efficiency occurs when no one can be made better off without making someone else worse off. Three conditions for allocative efficiency—economic efficiency, consumer efficiency, and equality of marginal social cost and marginal social benefit—occur in perfect competition when there are no external costs and benefits. It is this situation that Adam Smith was describing when he talked of the economy being led by an "invisible hand."

There are two main obstacles to the achievement of allocative efficiency—the existence of external costs and external benefits and the existence of monopoly. (pp. 305–308)

KEY ELEMENTS

Key Terms

Allocative efficiency, 305
Average revenue, 282
Break-even point, 284
Entry, 293
Exit, 293
External benefits, 306
External costs, 306
External diseconomies, 302
External economies, 302
Marginal revenue, 282
Marginal social benefit, 306
Marginal social cost, 306
Perfect competition, 280
Perfectly competitive firm's supply curve, 289
Price taker, 280
Short-run industry supply curve, 290
Shutdown point, 287

Key Figures

REVIEW QUESTIONS

1 What are the main features of a perfectly competitive industry?

2 Why can't a perfectly competitive firm influence the industry price?

3 List the three key decisions that a firm in a perfectly competitive industry has to make in order to maximize profit.

4 Why is marginal revenue equal to price in a perfectly competitive industry?

5 When will a perfectly competitive firm temporarily stop producing?

6 What is the connection between a competitive firm's supply curve and its marginal cost curve?

7 What is the relationship between a firm's supply curve and the short-run industry supply curve in a perfectly competitive industry?

8 Why do firms enter an industry?

9 What happens to the short-run industry supply curve when firms enter a competitive industry?

10 What is the effect of entry on the price and quantity produced?

11 What is the effect of entry on profit?

12 Trace the effects of a permanent increase in demand on price, quantity sold, number of firms, and profit.

13 Trace the effects of a permanent decrease in demand on price, quantity sold, number of firms, and profit.

14 Under what circumstances will a perfectly competitive industry have:

a A perfectly elastic long-run supply curve

b An upward-sloping long-run supply curve

c A downward-sloping long-run supply curve

15 Use the model of a perfectly competitive industry to explain why such a large number of farms went out of business in the 1980s.

16 What is allocative efficiency and under what circumstances does it arise?

PROBLEMS

1 Suppose that a firm produces one hundredth of an industry's output. The elasticity of the industry's demand is 4. What is the elasticity of the firm's demand?

2 Why have the prices of pocket calculators and VCRs fallen?

3 What has been the effect of a rise in world population on the wheat market and the individual wheat farmer?

4 Pat's Pizza Kitchen is a price taker. It has the following hourly costs:

Output (pizzas per hour)	Total cost (dollars per hour)
0	10
1	21
2	30
3	41
4	54
5	69
6	86

a If pizzas sell for $14, what is Pat's profit-maximizing output per hour? What is his profit?

b What is Pat's shutdown point?
c Derive Pat's supply curve.
d What price will cause Pat to leave the pizza industry?
e What price will cause other firms with costs identical to Pat's to enter the industry?
f What is the long-run equilibrium price of pizzas?

5 How has the diaper service industry been affected by the fall in the U.S. birth rate and the development of disposable diapers?

6 The market demand schedule for record albums is as follows:

Price (dollars per album)	Quantity demanded (albums per week)
3.65	500,000
4.40	475,000
5.20	450,000
6.00	425,000
6.80	400,000
7.60	375,000
8.40	350,000
9.20	325,000
10.00	300,000
10.80	275,000
11.60	250,000
12.40	225,000
13.20	200,000
14.00	175,000
14.80	150,000

The market is perfectly competitive, and each firm has the same cost structure, described by the following table:

Output (albums per week)	Marginal cost (dollars per album)	Average variable cost (dollars per album)	Average total cost (dollars per album)
150	6.00	8.80	15.47
200	6.40	7.80	12.80
250	7.00	7.00	11.00
300	7.65	7.10	10.43
350	8.40	7.20	10.06
400	10.00	7.50	10.00
450	12.40	8.00	10.22
500	12.70	9.00	11.00

There are 1,000 firms in the industry.
a What is the industry price?
b What is the industry's output?
c What is the output of each firm?
d What is the economic profit of each firm?
e What is the shutdown point?
f What is the long-run equilibrium price?
g What is the number of firms in the long run?

7 The same demand conditions as those in problem 6 prevail and there are still 1,000 firms in the industry, but fixed costs increase by $980.
a What is the short-run profit-maximizing output for each firm?
b Do firms enter or exit the industry in the long run?
c What is the new long-run equilibrium price?
d What is the new long-run equilibrium number of firms in the industry?

8 The same cost conditions as those in problem 6 prevail and there are 1,000 firms in the industry, but the falling price of compact discs decreases the demand for record albums and the demand schedule becomes as follows:

Price (dollars per album)	Quantity demanded (albums per week)
2.95	500,000
3.54	475,000
4.13	450,000
4.71	425,000
5.30	400,000
5.89	375,000
6.48	350,000
7.06	325,000
7.65	300,000
8.24	275,000
8.83	250,000
9.41	225,000
10.00	200,000
10.59	175,000
11.18	150,000

a What is the short-run profit-maximizing output for each firm?
b Do firms enter or exit the industry in the long run?
c What is the new long-run equilibrium price?
d What is the new long-run equilibrium number of firms in the industry?

CHAPTER 12

MONOPOLY

After studying this chapter, you will be able to:

- Define monopoly
- Explain the conditions under which monopoly arises
- Distinguish between legal monopoly and natural monopoly
- Explain how a monopoly determines its price and output
- Define price discrimination
- Explain why price discrimination leads to a bigger profit
- Compare the performance of a competitive and a monopolistic industry
- Define rent seeking and explain why it arises
- Explain the conditions under which monopoly is more efficient than competition

OU HAVE BEEN READING A LOT IN THIS BOOK ABOUT firms that want to maximize profit. But perhaps you've been looking around at some of the places where you do business and wondering whether they are really so intent on profit. After all, don't you get a student's discount when you get a haircut? Don't museums and movie theaters give discounts to students, too? And what about the airline that gives a discount for buying a ticket in advance? Are your barber and movie theater owner, as well as the museum and airline operators, simply generous folks to whom the model of profit-maximizing firms does not apply? Aren't they simply throwing profit away by cutting ticket prices and offering discounts? ◆◆ When you want a phone line installed, you really have only one choice—you have to call the local phone company. If you live in New York City and want to buy cable TV service, you have only one option: buy from Manhattan Cable. Regardless of where you live, you have no choice about the supplier of your local phone service, gas, electricity, or water. If you want to mail a letter, there is only one producer of letter-carrying services (aside from expensive couriers), the U.S. Postal Service. These are all examples of a single producer of a good or service controlling its supply. Such firms are obviously not like firms in perfectly competitive industries. They don't face a market-determined price. They can choose their own price. How do such firms behave? How do they choose the quantity to produce and the price at which to sell it? How does their behavior compare with that of firms in perfectly competitive industries? Do such firms charge prices that are too high and that damage the interests of consumers? And do such firms bring any benefits?

The Profits of Generosity

◆ ◆ ◆ ◆ In this chapter we study markets in which individual firms can influence the quantity of goods supplied and, as a consequence, exert an influence on price. We analyze the price and quantity decisions of such firms when they sell all their output at the same price to all their customers. After that, we study markets in which a firm can charge a higher price to some customers than others. We also compare the performance of a firm in such an industry with that of a competitive firm and examine whether monopoly is as efficient as competition.

How Monopoly Arises

A **monopoly** is an industry in which there is one supplier of a good, service, or resource that has no close substitutes and in which there is a barrier preventing the entry of new firms. The supply of local phone services, gas, electricity, and water are examples of local monopolies—monopolies restricted to a given location. The U.S. Postal Service is an example of a national monopoly—a sole supplier of letter-carrying service.

Barriers to Entry

The key feature of a monopoly is the existence of barriers preventing the entry of new firms. **Barriers to entry** are legal or natural impediments protecting a firm from competition from potential new entrants.

Legal Barriers to Entry Legal barriers to entry give rise to legal monopoly. **Legal monopoly** occurs when a law, license, or patent restricts competition by preventing entry.

The first type of legal barrier to entry is a public franchise. A **public franchise** is an exclusive right granted to a firm to supply a good or service. An example of a public franchise is the U.S. Postal Service, which has the exclusive right to carry first-class mail. Another common form of public franchise occurs on freeways and turnpikes where particular firms are given exclusive rights to sell gasoline and food services.

A second legal barrier is a government license. A **government license** controls entry into particular occupations, professions, and industries. Government licensing in the professions is the most important example of this type of barrier to entry. For example, a license is required to practice medicine, law, dentistry, schoolteaching, architecture, and a variety of other professional services and industries. Licensing does not create monopoly, but it does restrict competition.

A third legal restriction on entry is a patent. A **patent** is an exclusive right granted by the government to the inventor of a product or service. A patent is valid for a limited time period that varies from country to country. In the United States, a patent is valid for 17 years. Patents protect inventors by creating a property right and thereby encourage invention by preventing others from copying an invention until sufficient time has elapsed for the inventor to have reaped some benefits. They also stimulate *innovation*—the use of new inventions—by increasing the incentives for inventors to publicize their discoveries and offer them for use under license.

Natural Barriers to Entry Natural barriers to entry give rise to natural monopoly. **Natural monopoly** occurs when there is a unique source of supply of a raw material or when one firm can supply the entire market at a lower price than two or more firms can. As the definition of natural monopoly implies, natural barriers to entry take two forms. First, a single firm may own and control the entire supply of a mineral or natural resource. This type of monopoly occurs in the production of particular types of mineral water for which there is just a single, unique source and for some raw materials such as diamonds and chromium. De Beers, a South African company, for example, owns and controls four fifths of the world's diamond mines. Also, all the sources of chromium, again concentrated in southern Africa, are controlled by a small number of producers.

Natural monopoly can also arise because of economies of scale. When a single producer can supply the entire market at a lower average total cost of production than can two or more firms, then only a single firm can survive in the industry. Examples of natural monopoly arising from economies of scale are public utilities, such as the distribution of electricity, natural gas, and water.

Most monopolies in the real world, whether legal or natural, are regulated in some way by government or by government agencies. We will study such regulation in Chapter 21. Here we will consider an

unregulated monopoly for two important reasons. First, we can better understand why governments regulate monopolies and the effects of regulation if we also know how an unregulated monopoly would behave. Second, even in industries with more than one producer, firms often have a degree of monopoly power, arising from locational advantages or from important differences in product quality protected by patents. The theory of monopoly sheds important light on the behavior of such firms and industries.

We will begin by studying the behavior of a single-price monopoly. A **single-price monopoly** is a monopoly that charges the same price for each and every unit of its output. How does a single-price monopoly determine the quantity to produce and the price to charge for its output?

Single-Price Monopoly

The starting point for understanding how a single-price monopoly chooses its price and output is to work out the relationship between the demand for the good produced by the monopoly and the monopoly's revenue.

Demand and Revenue

Since in a monopoly there is only one firm, the demand curve facing that firm is the industry demand curve. Let's look at an example—Bobbie's Barbershop, the sole supplier of haircuts in Cairo, Nebraska. The demand schedule that Bobbie faces is set out in Table 12.1. At a price of $20, Bobbie sells no haircuts. The lower the price, the more haircuts per hour Bobbie is able to sell. For example, at a price of $12, consumers demand 4 haircuts per hour (row *e*), and at a price of $4, they demand 8 haircuts per hour (row *i*).

Total revenue (*TR*) is the price (*P*) multiplied by the quantity sold (*Q*). For example, in row *d*, Bobbie sells 3 haircuts at $14 each, so total revenue is $42. *Marginal revenue* (*MR*) is the change in total revenue (Δ*TR*) resulting from a one-unit rise in the quantity sold. For example, if the price falls from $18 (row *b*) to $16 (row *c*), the quantity sold rises from 1 to 2 haircuts. Total revenue rises from $18 to

TABLE 12.1

Single-Price Monopoly's Revenue

	Price (*P*) (dollars per haircut)	Quantity demanded (*Q*) (haircuts per hour)	Total revenue ($TR = P \times Q$) (dollars)	Marginal revenue ($MR = \Delta TR/\Delta Q$) (dollars per haircut)
a	20	0	0	
				18
b	18	1	18	
				14
c	16	2	32	
				10
d	14	3	42	
				6
e	12	4	48	
				2
f	10	5	50	
				–2
g	8	6	48	
				–6
h	6	7	42	
				–10
i	4	8	32	
				–14
j	2	9	18	
				–18
k	0	10	0	

The table shows Bobbie's demand schedule—the number of haircuts demanded per hour at each price. Total revenue (*TR*) is price multiplied by quantity sold. For example, row *c* shows that when the price is $16 a haircut, two haircuts are sold for a total revenue of $32. Marginal revenue (*MR*) is the change in total revenue resulting from a one-unit increase in the quantity sold. For example, when the price falls from $16 to $14 a haircut, the quantity sold increases from 2 to 3 haircuts and total revenue increases by $10. The marginal revenue from the third haircut is $10. Total revenue rises through row *f*, where 5 haircuts are sold for $10, and it falls thereafter. In the output range over which total revenue is increasing, marginal revenue is positive; in the output range over which total revenue is decreasing, marginal revenue is negative.

$32, so the change in total revenue is $14. Since the quantity sold rises by 1 haircut, marginal revenue equals the change in total revenue and is $14. When recording marginal revenue, we write it between two rows to emphasize that marginal revenue relates to the *change* in the quantity sold.

Figure 12.1 shows Bobbie's demand curve (*D*). Each row of Table 12.1 corresponds to a point on the demand curve. For example, row *d* in the table and point *d* on the demand curve tell us that at a price of $14, Bobbie sells 3 haircuts. The figure also

FIGURE 12.1

Demand and Marginal Revenue for a Single-Price Monopoly

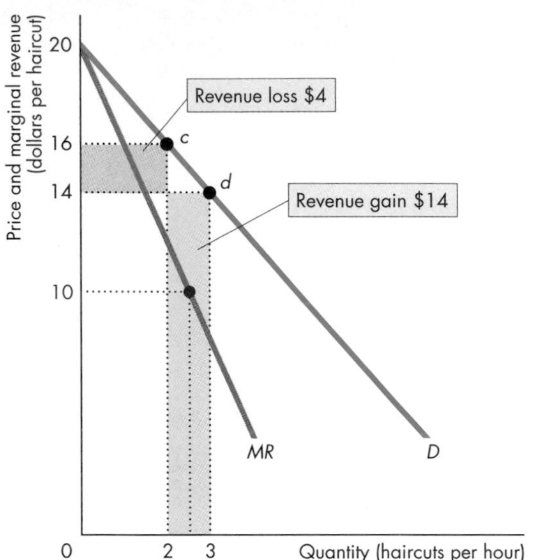

The monopoly demand curve (*D*) is based on the numbers in Table 12.1. At a price of $16 a haircut, Bobbie sells 2 haircuts an hour. If she lowers the price to $14, she sells 3 haircuts an hour. The sale of the third haircut brings a revenue gain of $14 (the price charged for the third haircut). But there is a revenue loss of $4 ($2 per haircut) on the 2 haircuts that she could have sold for $16 each. The marginal revenue (extra total revenue) from the third haircut is the difference between the revenue gain and the revenue loss—$10. The marginal revenue curve (*MR*) shows the marginal revenue at each level of sales. Marginal revenue is lower than price.

shows Bobbie's marginal revenue curve (*MR*). Notice that the marginal revenue curve is below the demand curve. That is, at each level of output, marginal revenue is less than price. Why is marginal revenue less than price? It is because when the price is lowered to sell one more unit, there are two opposing effects on total revenue. The lower price results in a revenue loss, and the increased quantity sold results in a revenue gain. For example, at a price of $16, Bobbie sells 2 haircuts (point *c*). If she reduces the price to $14, she sells 3 haircuts and has a revenue gain of $14 on the third haircut. But she receives only $14 on the first two as well—$2 less than before—so her revenue loss on the first 2 haircuts is $4. She has to deduct this amount from the revenue gain of $14. Marginal revenue—the difference between the revenue gain and the revenue loss—is $10.

Figure 12.2 shows Bobbie's demand curve (*D*), marginal revenue curve (*MR*), and total revenue curve (*TR*) and illustrates the connections between them. Again, each row in Table 12.1 corresponds to a point on the curves. For example, row *d* in the table and point *d* on the graphs tell us that when 3 haircuts are sold for $14 each (part a), total revenue is $42 (part b). Notice that as the quantity sold rises, total revenue rises to a peak of $50 (point *f*) and then declines. To understand the behavior of total revenue, notice what happens to marginal revenue as the quantity sold increases. Over the range 0 to 5 haircuts, marginal revenue is positive. When more than 5 haircuts are sold, marginal revenue becomes negative. The output range over which marginal revenue is positive is the same as that over which total revenue is rising. The output range over which marginal revenue is negative is the same as that over which total revenue declines. When marginal revenue is zero, total revenue is at a maximum.

Revenue and Elasticity

When we studied elasticity in Chapter 5, we discovered a connection between the elasticity of demand and the effect of a change in price on total expenditure or total revenue. Let's refresh our memories of that connection.

Recall that the elasticity of demand is the percentage change in the quantity demanded divided by the percentage change in price. If a 1 percent decrease in price results in a greater than 1 percent increase in the quantity demanded, the elasticity of demand is greater than 1 and demand is *elastic.* If a 1 percent decrease in price results in a less than 1 percent increase in the quantity demanded, the elasticity of demand is less than 1 and demand is *inelastic.* If a 1 percent decrease in price results in a 1 percent increase in the quantity demanded, the elasticity of demand is 1 and demand is *unit elastic.*

The elasticity of demand influences the change in total revenue. If demand is elastic, total revenue increases when the price decreases; if demand is inelastic, total revenue decreases when the price decreases; and if demand is unit elastic, total revenue does not change when the price changes.

The output range over which total revenue increases when the price decreases is the same as

FIGURE 12.2

A Single-Price Monopoly's Revenue Curves

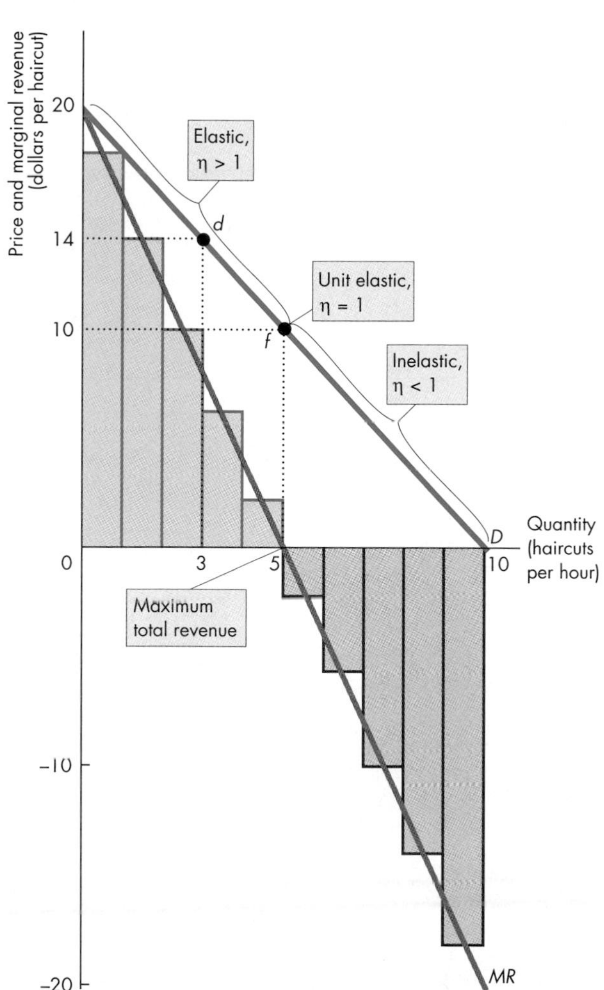

(a) Demand and marginal revenue curves

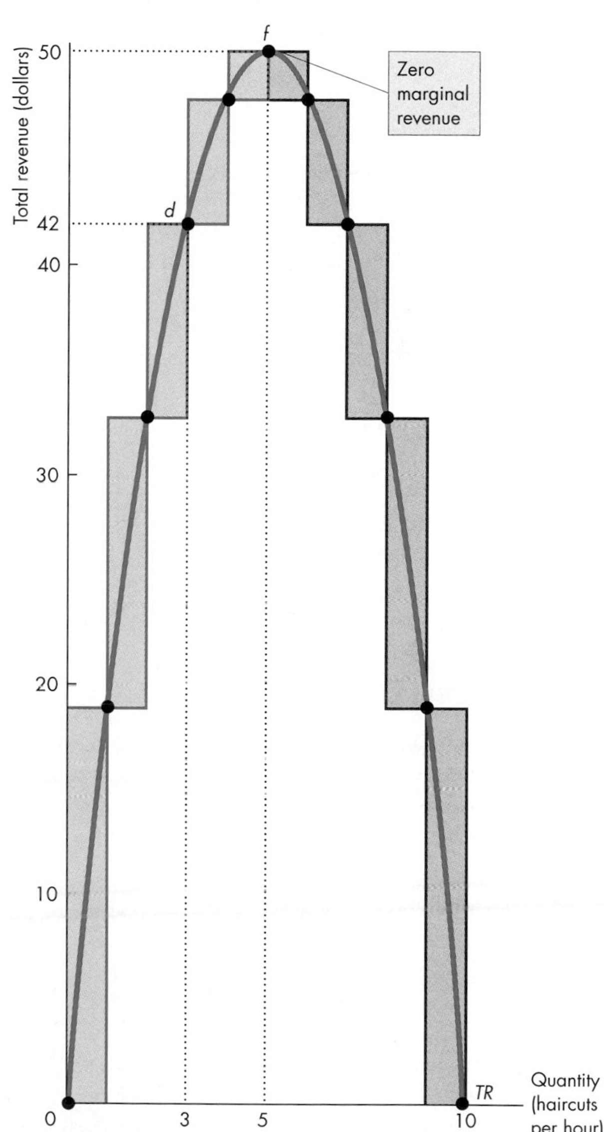

(b) Total revenue curve

Bobbie's demand curve (*D*) and marginal revenue curve (*MR*), shown in part (a), and total revenue curve (*TR*), shown in part (b), are based on the numbers in Table 12.1. For example, at a price of $14, Bobbie sells 3 haircuts an hour (point *d* in part a) for a total revenue of $42 (point *d* in part b). Over the range 0 to 5 haircuts an hour, total revenue is increasing and marginal revenue is positive, as shown by the blue bars. Over the range 5 to 10 haircuts an hour, total revenue declines—marginal revenue is negative, as shown by the red bars. Over the output range for which marginal revenue is positive, demand is elastic. Over the output range for which marginal revenue is negative, demand is inelastic. At the output at which marginal revenue is zero, demand is unit elastic.

that over which marginal revenue is positive—shown in Fig. 12.2. Thus the output range over which marginal revenue is positive is also the output range over which demand is elastic—over which the elasticity of demand is greater than 1. The output range over which total revenue decreases when price decreases is the same as that over which marginal revenue is negative. Thus the output range over which marginal revenue is negative is also the output range over which demand is inelastic—over which the elasticity of demand is less than 1. The output at which total revenue remains constant when price decreases is that at which marginal revenue is zero. Thus the output at which marginal revenue is zero is also the output at which demand is unit elastic—at which the elasticity of demand is 1.

The relationship that you have just discovered has an important implication: a profit-maximizing monopoly never produces an output in the inelastic range of its demand curve. If it did so, marginal revenue would be negative—each additional unit sold would lower total revenue. In such a situation, it always pays to charge a higher price and sell a smaller quantity. But exactly what price and quantity does a profit-maximizing monopoly firm choose?

Price and Output Decision

Profit is the difference between total revenue and total cost. To determine the output level and price that maximize a monopoly's profit, we need to study the behavior of both revenue and costs as output varies.

A monopoly faces the same types of technology and cost constraints as a competitive firm. The monopoly has a production function that is subject to diminishing returns. The monopoly buys its inputs in competition with other firms at prices that it cannot influence. The sole difference between the monopoly that we'll study here and a perfectly competitive firm lies in the market constraint for the output that each firm faces. The competitive firm is a price taker, whereas the monopoly supplies the entire market. Because the monopoly supplies the entire market, its output decision affects the price at which that output is sold. It is this fact that gives rise to the difference between the decisions faced by these two types of firm.

We have already looked at Bobbie's revenue in Table 12.1 and Figs. 12.1 and 12.2. The revenue information contained in Fig. 12.3 is extracted from

FIGURE 12.3

A Monopoly's Output and Price

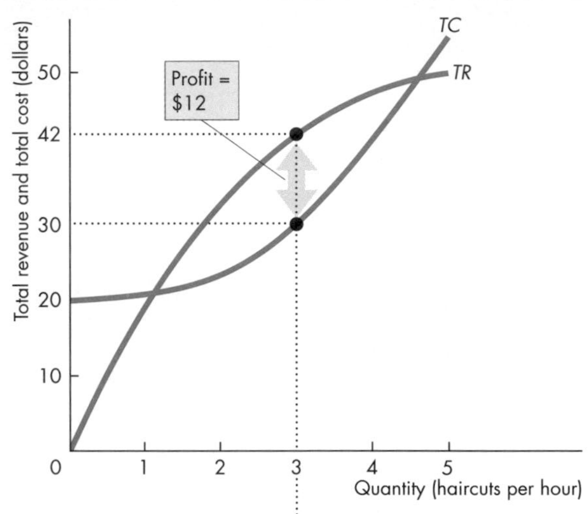

(a) Total revenue and total cost curves

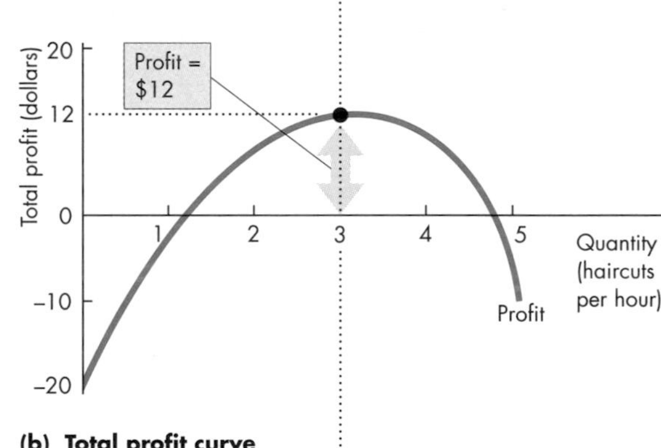

(b) Total profit curve

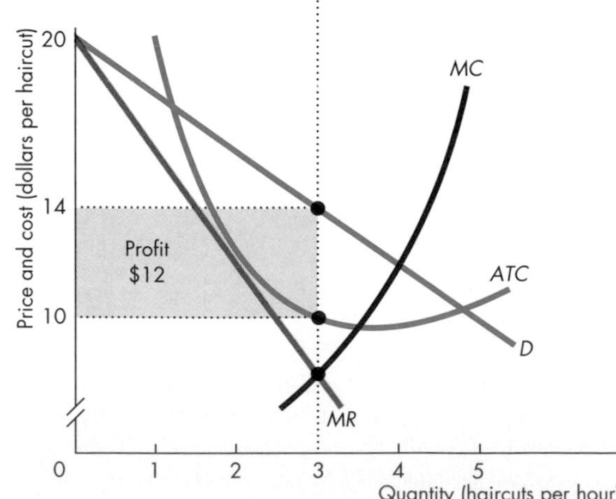

(c) Demand and marginal revenue and cost curves

FIGURE 12.3 (continued)

Price (P) (dollars per haircut)	Quantity demanded (Q) (haircuts per hour)	Total revenue ($TR = P \times Q$) (dollars)	Marginal revenue ($MR = \Delta TR/\Delta Q$) (dollars per haircut)	Total cost (TC) (dollars)	Marginal cost ($MC = \Delta TC/\Delta Q$) (dollars per haircut)	Profit ($TR - TC$) (dollars)
20	0	0		20		–20
			18		1	
18	1	18		21		–3
			14		3	
16	2	32		24		+8
			10		6	
14	3	42		30		+12
			6		10	
12	4	48		40		+8
			2		15	
10	5	50		55		–5

The table adds information about total cost (TC), marginal cost (MC), and profit ($TR - TC$) to the information on demand and revenue in Table 12.1. For example, at a price of $16, 2 haircuts will be sold for a total revenue of $32. The total cost of producing 2 haircuts is $24, so profit equals $8 ($32 – $24). Profit is at a maximum in the row highlighted in red in the table.

The numbers in the table are graphed in the three parts of the figure. The total cost and total revenue curves appear in part (a). The vertical distance between total revenue (TR) and total cost (TC) equals total profit. Maximum profit occurs at 3 haircuts an hour. Part (b) shows the total profit curve. This curve reaches a maximum at 3 haircuts an hour. The total profit curve is at a maximum (part b) when the vertical distance between the total revenue and total cost curves is also at a maximum (part a). Where total revenue equals total cost (in part a), the total profit curve cuts the horizontal axis (in part b). Part (c) shows that at the profit-maximizing output of 3 haircuts, marginal cost (MC) equals marginal revenue (MR). The monopoly sells the output for the maximum possible price as determined by its demand curve. In this case, that price is $14. The monopoly's profit is illustrated in part (c) by the blue rectangle. That profit is $12—the profit per haircut ($4) multiplied by 3 haircuts.

Table 12.1. The figure also contains information on Bobbie's costs and profit.

Total cost (*TC*) rises as output increases, and so does total revenue (*TR*). Profit equals total revenue minus total cost. As you can see in the table in Fig. 12.3, the maximum profit ($12) occurs when Bobbie sells 3 haircuts for $14 each. If she sells 2 haircuts for $16 each or 4 haircuts for $12 each, her profit will be only $8.

You can see why 3 haircuts is the profit-maximizing output by looking at the marginal revenue and marginal cost columns. When Bobbie increases output from 2 to 3 haircuts, she generates a marginal revenue of $10 and incurs a marginal cost of $6. Profit increases by the difference—$4. If Bobbie increases output yet further, from 3 to 4 haircuts, she generates a marginal revenue of $6 and a marginal cost of $10. In this case, marginal cost exceeds marginal revenue by $4, so profit falls by $4. It always pays to produce more if marginal revenue exceeds marginal cost and to produce less if marginal cost exceeds marginal revenue. It pays to produce neither more nor less when marginal cost and marginal revenue are equal to each other. Thus the profit-maximizing output occurs when marginal revenue equals marginal cost.

The information set out in the table is shown graphically in Fig. 12.3. Part (a) shows Bobbie's total revenue curve (*TR*) and total cost curve (*TC*). Profit is the vertical distance between *TR* and *TC*. Bobbie maximizes her profit at 3 haircuts an hour—profit is $42 minus $30, or $12. Part (b) shows how her profit varies with the number of haircuts sold.

Figure 12.3(c) shows the demand curve (*D*) and the marginal revenue curve (*MR*) along with the marginal cost curve (*MC*) and average total cost curve (*ATC*). The profit-maximizing output is 3 haircuts, where marginal cost equals marginal revenue. The price charged is found by reading from the demand curve the highest price at which 3 haircuts can be sold. That price is $14. When Bobbie produces 3 haircuts, average total cost is $10 (read from the *ATC* curve). Her profit per haircut is $4 ($14 minus $10). Bobbie's total profit is indicated by the blue rectangle, which equals the profit per haircut ($4) multiplied by the number of haircuts (3), for a total profit of $12. Since price always *exceeds* marginal revenue and, at the profit-maximizing output, marginal revenue equals marginal cost, price always exceeds marginal cost. (The theory of monopoly price determination shown in Fig. 12.3c was first worked out by the brilliant Joan Robinson—see Our Advancing Knowledge on pp. 322–323.)

Bobbie makes a positive profit. But there is nothing to guarantee that a monopoly will be able to make a profit. A monopoly can make a zero profit or even, in the short run, a loss. Figure 12.4 shows the conditions under which these other two outcomes will occur.

If Bobbie's average total cost is ATC_a, as shown in Fig. 12.4(a), then the profit-maximizing output, where marginal revenue equals marginal cost, will be 3 haircuts. At this output, average cost just equals price, so both the profit per haircut and total profit are zero. If Bobbie's average total cost curve is ATC_b, as shown in Fig. 12.4(b), then marginal cost equals marginal revenue at 3 haircuts and average total cost is $16. But 3 haircuts can only be sold for $14 each, so Bobbie makes a loss of $2 a haircut. That loss, however, is the minimum possible loss, so Bobbie is still maximizing profit. A monopoly that makes a loss will do so only in the short run. If the situation shown in Fig. 12.3(b) were permanent, Bobbie would go out of business.

When we studied a competitive firm, we checked to see whether price was higher or lower than average variable cost. With a price below average variable cost, it pays a firm to shut down temporarily and produce nothing. It makes a loss equal to total fixed cost. Like a competitive firm, Bobbie also needs to check average variable cost to see whether it pays to shut down temporarily. There is no point in any firm—competitor or monopoly—making a loss that exceeds total fixed cost.

FIGURE 12.4

Short-Run Profit, Costs, and Demand

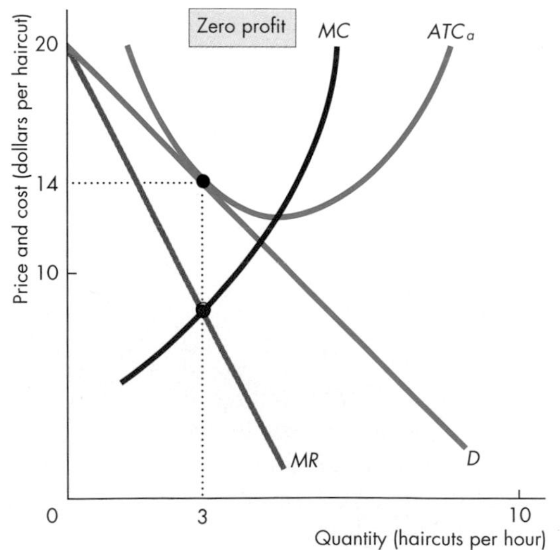

(a) Zero profit

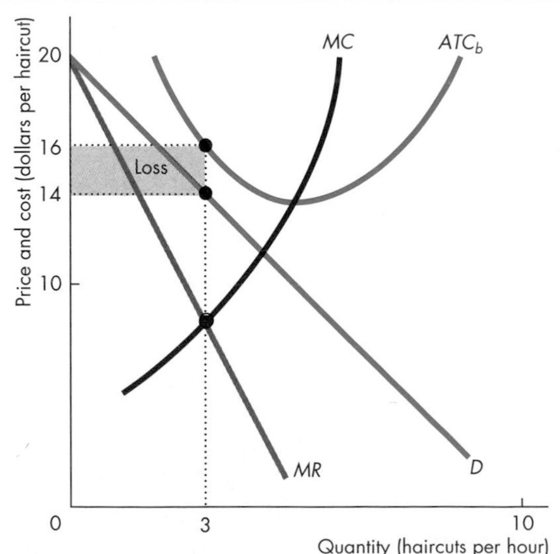

(b) Loss

In the short run, a monopoly can make zero profit or even a loss. Part (a) shows a monopoly making zero profit. At the profit-maximizing output—3 haircuts an hour—average total cost and price are $14 each. Part (b) shows a monopoly making a short-run loss. In this case, at the profit-maximizing output (again 3 haircuts an hour), average total cost is $16 and price is $14, so the firm incurs a loss of $6. The loss is represented by the red rectangle.

If firms in a perfectly competitive industry are making a positive economic profit, new firms enter. That does not happen in a monopoly industry. Barriers to entry prevent new firms from entering. So a firm can make a positive economic profit and continue to do so indefinitely in a monopoly industry. Sometimes that profit is large, as in the cable TV industry.

No Monopoly Supply Curve

Unlike a perfectly competitive firm, a monopoly does not have a supply curve. Recall that a supply curve shows the quantity supplied at each price. A change in demand in a competitive industry results in the industry moving along its supply curve and each firm moving along its marginal cost curve. A change in demand in a monopoly also produces a change in price and quantity, but the monopoly does not slide along a supply curve. Instead, given the new demand conditions, the monopoly picks the combination of output and price that maximizes profit, given its cost curves. As in competitive conditions, the monopoly chooses to sell a quantity such that marginal revenue equals marginal cost. But the relationship between price and marginal revenue, and that between price and marginal cost, depends on the shape of the demand curve. For a given profit-maximizing quantity, the steeper the demand curve, the higher is the price at which that quantity is sold. It is for this reason that there is no unique relationship between the monopoly's profit-maximizing quantity and price and therefore no such thing as a monopoly's supply curve.

REVIEW

A single-price monopoly maximizes profit by producing an output at which marginal cost equals marginal revenue. At that output, the monopoly charges the highest price that consumers are willing to pay. Since a monopoly's price exceeds its marginal revenue, its price also exceeds its marginal cost. But there is no guarantee that a monopoly will make a profit in the short run. Depending on its cost curves and the demand for its output, the monopoly might make a positive economic profit, make a zero profit, or incur a loss. But a monopoly can make a positive economic profit even in the long run, since there are barriers to the entry of new firms. There is no unique relationship between the quantity that a monopoly produces and its price—there is no monopoly supply curve. ◆

Price Discrimination

Price discrimination is the practice of charging some customers a higher price than others for an identical good or of charging an individual customer a higher price on a small purchase than on a large one. An example of price discrimination is the practice of charging children or students a lower price than adults to see a movie. Another example is the common practice of barbers and hairdressers giving discounts to senior citizens and students. Price discrimination can be practiced in varying degrees. **Perfect price discrimination** occurs when a firm charges a different price for each unit sold and charges each consumer the maximum price that he or she is willing to pay for each unit. Though perfect price discrimination does not happen in the real world, it shows the limit to which price discrimination can be taken.

Not all price *differences* imply price *discrimination*. In many situations, goods that are similar but not identical have different costs and sell for different prices *because* they have different costs. For example, we saw in Chapter 10 that the marginal cost of producing electricity depends on the time of day. If an electric power company charges a higher price for consumption between 7:00 and 9:00 in the morning and between 4:00 and 7:00 in the evening than it does at other times of the day, this practice is not called price discrimination. Price discrimination charges varying prices to consumers, not because of differences in the cost of producing the good but because different consumers have different demands for the good.

At first sight, it appears that price discrimination contradicts the assumption of profit maximization. Why would a movie operator charge children half price? Why would a hairdresser or barber charge students and senior citizens less? Aren't these producers losing profit by being nice guys?

UNDERSTANDING Monopoly POWER

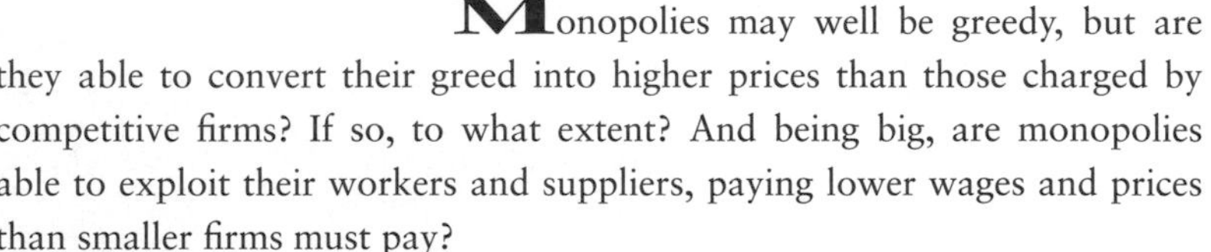

Monopolies may well be greedy, but are they able to convert their greed into higher prices than those charged by competitive firms? If so, to what extent? And being big, are monopolies able to exploit their workers and suppliers, paying lower wages and prices than smaller firms must pay?

These questions puzzled generations of economists. Adam Smith said, "The price of a monopoly is upon every occasion the highest which can be got." But Smith was wrong. The questions were first answered correctly by Antoine-August Cournot, although his answer was not appreciated until almost a century later when Joan Robinson explained how monopolies behave.

Questions about monopoly behavior took on an urgent and practical tone during the 1870s, a time when rapid technological change and falling transportation costs enabled huge monopolies to emerge in the United States. Monopolies dominated oil, steel, railroads, tobacco, and even sugar, and industrial empires grew ever larger.

The success of the nineteenth-century monopolies led to the creation of our antitrust laws—laws that limit the use of monopoly power. Those laws have been used to prevent monopolies from being set up and to break up existing monopolies. They were used in the 1960s to break up a conspiracy between General Electric and Westinghouse when they colluded to fix their prices instead of competing against each other. The laws were also used in the 1980s to bring greater competition in long-distance telecommunications. But in spite of antitrust laws, monopolies still exist. One of the most prominent is cable television. Like their notorious forerunners, the cable television companies use their monopoly power and make large profits.

"People in the same trade seldom meet together, even for merriment and diversion, but the conversation ends in . . . some contrivance to raise prices."

Adam Smith
The Wealth of Nations

Ruthless greed, exploitation of both workers and customers—these are the traditional images of monopolies and the effects of their power. And these images appeared to be an accurate description in the 1880s, when monopolies were at their peak of power and influence. One monopolist, John D. Rockefeller, Sr., had built his giant Standard Oil Company, which, by 1879, was refining 90 percent of the nation's oil and controlling its entire pipeline capacity.

In spite of antitrust laws that regulate monopolies, they still exist. One of the most prominent is that in cable television. In most cities, one firm decides which channels viewers will receive and the price they will pay. During the 1980s, with the advent of satellite technology and specialist cable program producers such as CNN and HBO, the cable companies expanded their offerings. At the same time, they steadily increased prices and their businesses became very profitable. Are the local cable companies exploiting their customers? What would happen to their prices if they were regulated? And what would happen to the number of channels and to the quality and variety of the programs they offered?

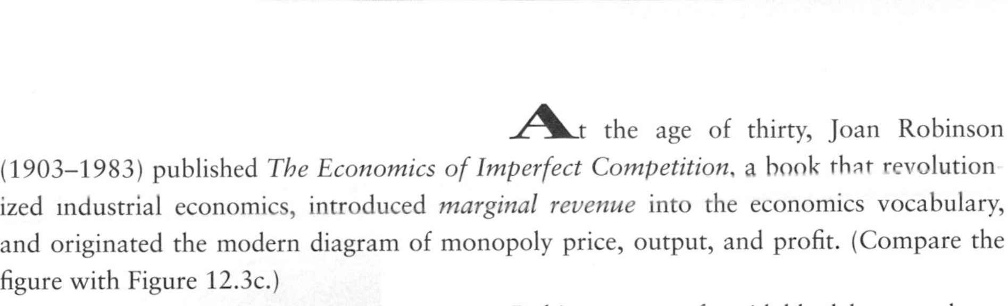

JOAN ROBINSON:

DISCOVERING ***the Limits to Monopoly Power***

At the age of thirty, Joan Robinson (1903–1983) published *The Economics of Imperfect Competition*, a book that revolutionized industrial economics, introduced *marginal revenue* into the economics vocabulary, and originated the modern diagram of monopoly price, output, and profit. (Compare the figure with Figure 12.3c.)

Robinson was a formidable debater and reveled in verbal battles, a notable one of which was with the famous MIT economist Paul Samuelson. Anxious to make a point on the blackboard, Samuelson asked Robinson for the chalk. Monopolizing the chalk and board, the unyielding Robinson snapped, "Say it in words, young man."

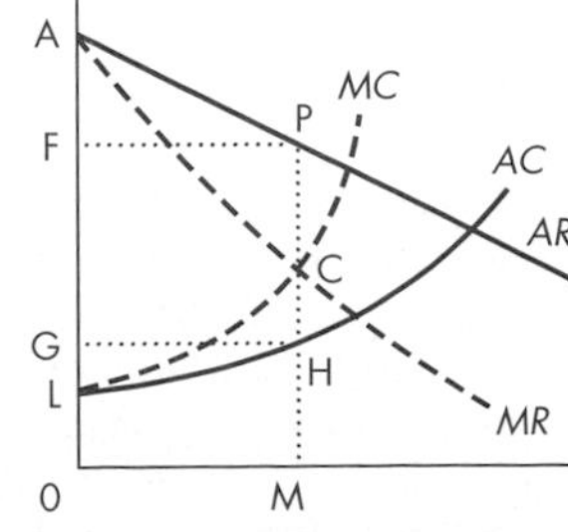

This story illustrates Joan Robinson's approach to economics: work out the answers to economic problems using the most powerful methods of logic available, but then "say it in words." Don't be satisfied with a formal argument if you don't *understand* it.

Deeper investigation shows that far from losing profit, price discriminators actually make a bigger profit than they would otherwise. Thus a monopoly has an incentive to try to find ways of discriminating among groups of consumers and charging each group the highest possible price. Some people may pay less with price discrimination, but others pay more. How does price discrimination bring in more total revenue?

Price Discrimination and Total Revenue

The total revenue received by a single-price monopoly equals the quantity sold multiplied by the single price charged. That revenue is illustrated in Fig. 12.5(a). Suppose that Bobbie sells 4 haircuts for a single price of $12 each. Bobbie's total revenue, $48, is the area of the blue rectangle—the quantity sold, 4 haircuts, multiplied by the price, $12.

Now suppose that Bobbie can sell some haircuts for one price and some for another, higher price. Figure 12.5(b) illustrates this case. The first 2 haircuts are sold for $16 each, and then two more are sold for the original price, $12. In this case, Bobbie has greater total revenue than when she charges a single price. The extra revenue earned on the first 2 haircuts sold has to be added to the original revenue. Total revenue, the blue area shown in part (b), is $56 (2 at $12 plus 2 at $16).

What will happen if Bobbie can perfectly price discriminate? The answer is shown in Fig. 12.5(c). Each haircut is sold for the maximum possible price. The first haircut sells for $18, the next for $16, the third for $14, and the fourth for $12. Total revenue, the blue area in part (c), is $60.

Price Discrimination and Consumer Surplus

Demand curves slope down because the value that an individual places on a good falls as the quantity consumed of that good rises. When all the units consumed can be bought for a single price, consumers benefit. We call this benefit *consumer surplus.* (If you need to refresh your understanding of consumer

FIGURE 12.5

Total Revenue and Price Discrimination

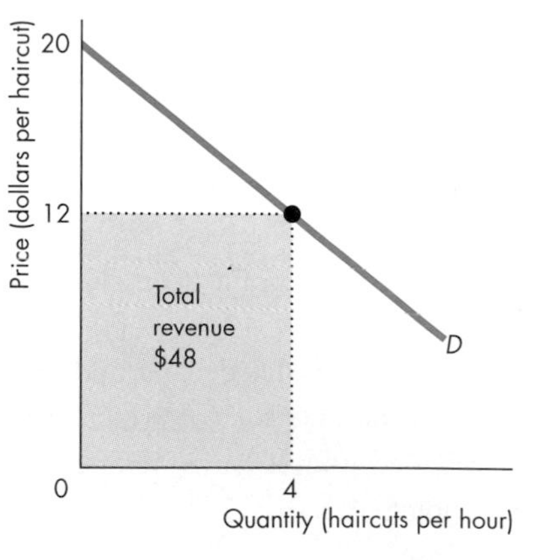

(a) One price

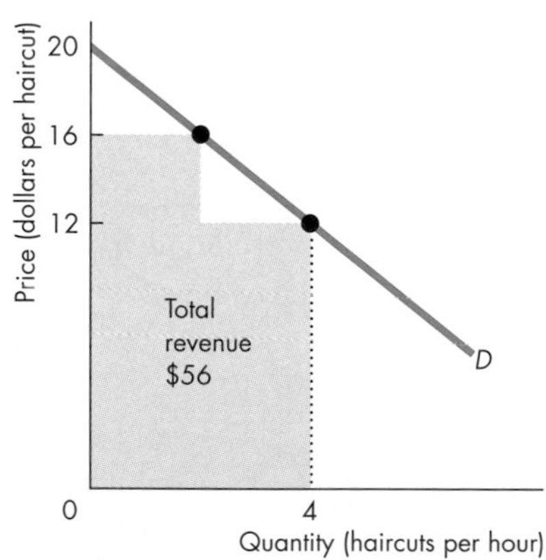

(b) Two prices

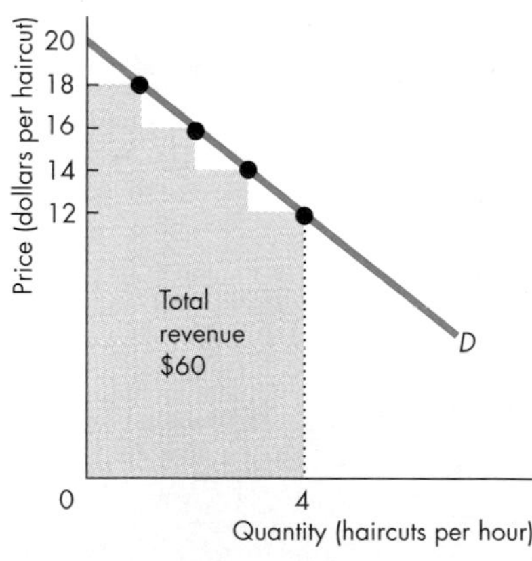

(c) Many prices

If Bobbie sells 4 haircuts for the same price—$12 each—her total revenue is $48, as shown by the blue rectangle in part (a). If she charges two prices—$16 each for the first 2 haircuts and $12 each for the next 2—her total revenue will be $56, as shown by the blue area in part (b). If Bobbie charges four different prices—$18 for the first haircut, $16 for the second haircut, $14 for the third haircut, and $12 for the fourth haircut—her total revenue will be $60, as shown by the blue area in part (c). The more finely a monopoly can discriminate, the larger is the total revenue from a given level of sales.

surplus, flip back to Chapter 7, p. 171.) Price discrimination can be seen as an attempt by a monopoly to capture the consumer surplus (or as much of the surplus as possible) for itself.

Discriminating among Units of a Good One form of price discrimination charges each single buyer a different price on each unit of a good bought. An example of this type of discrimination is a discount for bulk buying. The larger the order, the larger is the discount—and the lower is the price. This type of price discrimination works because each individual's demand curve slopes downward. For example, suppose that Lisa is willing to pay $7 to see one movie a month, $6 to see two, and $5 to see three. If movies cost $5, she sees three and pays $5 for each. But the value to her of the first movie is $7—$2 more than she pays for it. And the value to her of the second movie is $6—$1 more than she pays for it. Lisa's consumer surplus is $3.

Now imagine that a movie theater offers the following monthly subscription. For $7, you can see one movie a month; for $13, you can see two movies a month; for $18, you can see three movies a month. If Lisa opts for the three-movie package, the movie theater extracts from Lisa her entire consumer surplus. But to extract every dollar of consumer surplus from every buyer, the monopolist would have to offer each individual customer a separate contract based on that customer's own demand curve. Clearly, such price discrimination cannot be carried out in practice because a firm does not have sufficient information about each individual consumer's demand curve to be able to do the necessary calculations. But by making arrangements of the type just described that extract most of the consumer surplus of a typical customer, firms can move somewhere toward perfect price discrimination.

Discriminating among Individuals Even when it is not possible to charge each individual a different price for each unit bought, it might still be possible to discriminate among individuals. This possibility arises from the fact that some people place a higher value on consuming one more unit of a good than do other individuals. By charging such an individual a higher price, the producer can obtain some of the consumer surplus that would otherwise accrue to its customers.

Let's look a bit more closely at the price and output decisions of a monopoly that practices price discrimination.

Price and Output Decisions with Price Discrimination

Price discrimination often takes the form of discriminating between different groups of consumers on the basis of age, employment status, or other easily distinguished characteristics. Price discrimination works only if each group has a different price elasticity of demand for the product. If one group has a high elasticity and the other a low elasticity, then a firm can increase profit by charging a lower price to the group with the high elasticity and a higher price to the group with a low elasticity.

Let's stick with the example of haircuts. Bobbie suspects that the students and the elderly of Cairo have a higher elasticity of demand for haircuts than do other people—they do not seem to care as much about getting a bit shaggy as do the business people and homemakers. Let's see how Bobbie exploits these differences in demand and raises her profit by price discriminating. Until now, Bobbie has sold 3 haircuts an hour at $14 a haircut, for a total revenue of $42. With a total cost of $30 an hour, Bobbie makes an hourly profit of $12. Bobbie's costs, revenues, and profit are shown in the table in Fig. 12.3.

Bobbie has noticed that students and elderly customers come in less frequently than other clients. In fact, of the 3 haircuts she does each hour, 2 are for business people or homemakers and only 1 for an elderly customer or a student. Bobbie also suspects that the business people and homemakers will still turn up for haircuts at the rate of 2 an hour even if she charges them a higher price. She knows that to get more students and seniors, she has to lower the price she charges them. Bobbie decides to try price discriminating between the two groups. But she has to figure out what price to charge each group to maximize her profit.

Table 12.2 sets out the calculations that Bobbie performs. It shows Bobbie's estimates of the demand schedules for her two groups of customers. It also shows the total revenue and marginal revenue calculations for the two separate groups. Bobbie's marginal costs are the same for both groups—hair is hair, whether it belongs to a student or a homemaker. But marginal revenue differs between the two

TABLE 12.2

Profiting from Price Discrimination

	Students and the elderly			Others		
Price (P) (dollars per haircut)	Quantity demanded (Q) (haircuts per hour)	Total revenue (TR) (dollars)	Marginal revenue (MR) (dollars per haircut)	Quantity demanded (Q) (haircuts per hour)	Total revenue (TR) (dollars)	Marginal revenue (MR) (dollars per haircut)
20	**0**	**0**		**0**	**0**	
			0			**18**
18	**0**	**0**		**1**	**18**	
			0			**14**
16	**0**	**0**		**2**	**32**	
			14			**–4**
14	**1**	**14**		**2**	**28**	
			10			**–4**
12	**2**	**24**		**2**	**24**	
			6			**–4**
10	**3**	**30**		**2**	**20**	

Profit calculation:

Profit = $TR - TC$ = (\$12 × 2) + (\$16 × 2) – \$40 = \$16.

As a single-price monopoly, Bobbie sells 3 haircuts an hour for \$14 each and makes a maximum profit of \$12, as was shown in Fig. 12.3. By discriminating between two groups of customers—the first group consisting of students and the elderly and the second group consisting of all other customers—Bobbie is able to make a bigger profit. She raises the price of regular haircuts to \$16 and lowers the price for students and the elderly to \$12. Her sales increase to 4 haircuts an hour, and her profit rises to \$16.

groups of customers. For example, when the price falls from \$18 to \$16, the marginal revenue from students and the elderly is zero, while for others it is \$14. When the price falls from \$16 to \$14, the marginal revenue from students and the elderly is \$14, while that from others is *minus* \$4.

Bobbie calculates her profit-maximizing prices and output in the following way. She knows that the marginal cost of the third haircut is \$6. (To see this, look back at the table for Fig. 12.3.) If her output increases, the marginal cost of the fourth haircut is \$10. She looks at her marginal revenues and compares them with this \$10 marginal cost. She notices that if she charges her business and homemaking customers \$16, this group buys 2 haircuts an hour for a marginal revenue of \$14. If she charges her students and elderly customers \$12, that group buys 2 haircuts an hour and brings in a marginal revenue of \$10. Thus when she sells a total of 4 haircuts (2 to students and elderly and 2 to other customers), the marginal revenue from the students and elderly, \$10, equals the marginal cost of the fourth haircut.

But she can see that if she lowers the price to either group, marginal revenue will fall short of marginal cost. Marginal cost will climb to \$15 for a fifth haircut, and marginal revenue will fall to \$6 if an extra haircut is sold to students and the elderly. Other customers have an inelastic demand curve and will not buy any more than 2 haircuts, so marginal revenue from lowering the price to that group is negative. Thus Bobbie can make no more profit than that arising from charging students and the elderly \$12 and other customers \$16 and producing 4 haircuts an hour. The profit from such price discrimination is \$16. (The calculation is set out at the foot of Table 12.2.)

Perfect Price Discrimination

Suppose that Bobbie is able to devise a means of being a perfect price discriminator. How much profit can she make in this case? Bobbie's demand and cost curves are shown in Fig. 12.6. As a single-price monopoly, she produces 3 haircuts, sells them for $14 each, and makes a profit of $12—the light blue rectangle. (Refresh your memory if necessary by referring back to Fig. 12.3c.) If Bobbie can get each of her customers to pay the maximum price that each is willing to pay for a haircut, then she can sell the first haircut for $18. She makes an extra profit of $4 ($18 minus $14) from that first haircut sold. She can sell the second haircut for $16, $2 more than before. She will still sell the third for $14, since that is the maximum price that the third customer is willing to pay for a haircut. If Bobbie continues to produce 3 haircuts, her profit rises to $18, an increase of $6.

But Bobbie will not stop at 3 haircuts an hour. To see why, consider the marginal revenue from selling a fourth haircut and the marginal cost of producing it. The fourth haircut can be sold for $12. The marginal cost of the fourth haircut, from the table in Fig. 12.3, is only $10. So by producing a fourth haircut and selling it for $12, Bobbie makes a further $2 profit. The maximum profit with perfect price discrimination occurs when Bobbie sells 4 haircuts, each for the maximum price that the consumers are willing to pay. That profit is $20. It is illustrated in the figure as the sum of the light blue and the three dark blue rectangles. The table in Fig. 12.6 summarizes this calculation.

When a firm practices perfect price discrimination, its output exceeds that of a single-price monopoly. It produces up to the point at which the marginal cost curve cuts the demand curve. The less perfect the price discrimination, the smaller is the additional output produced.

FIGURE 12.6

Output and Profit with Perfect Price Discrimination

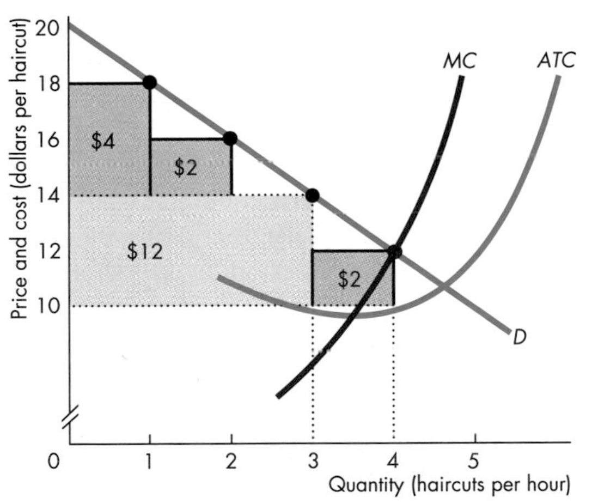

Maximum profit with single price:		$12	Quantity: 3 haircuts
add	extra profit from 1st haircut	+4	
add	extra profit from 2nd haircut	+2	
add	extra profit from 4th haircut (extra revenue is $12 and the marginal cost is $10)	+2	
equals	maximum profit with price discrimination	$20	Quantity: 4 haircuts

Bobbie's profit as a single-price monopoly, shown by the light blue area, is $12. With perfect price discrimination, Bobbie charges $18 for the first haircut, $16 for the second, $14 for the third, and $12 for the fourth. Marginal revenue equals price in each case because, with perfect price discrimination, the marginal revenue curve is the same as the demand curve. Profit is maximized when the demand curve intersects the marginal cost curve. It does not pay Bobbie to sell a fifth haircut because its marginal revenue (price) is less than its marginal cost. Bobbie's additional profit as a perfect price discriminator, shown by the dark blue areas, is $8. Her maximum total profit with perfect price discrimination is $20. The calculation is summarized in the table.

REVIEW

Price discrimination increases a monopoly's profit by increasing its total revenue. By charging the highest price for each unit of the good that each person is willing to pay, a monopoly perfectly price discriminates and captures all of the consumer surplus. Much price discrimination takes the form of discriminating among different groups of customers, charging a higher price to some and a lower price to others. Such price discrimination increases total revenue and profit, but it is possible only if the two groups have different elasticities of demand. A price-discriminating monopoly produces a larger output than a single-price monopoly. ◆

Discrimination among Groups

You can now see why it pays to price discriminate. The sign in Bobbie's window—"Haircuts $16: special for students and seniors, only $12"—is no generous gesture. It is profit-maximizing behavior. The model of price discrimination that you have just studied explains a wide variety of familiar pricing practices, even by firms that are not pure monopolies. For example, airlines offer lower fares for advance-purchase tickets than for last-minute travel. Last-minute travelers usually have a low elasticity of demand, while vacation travelers who can plan ahead have a higher elasticity of demand. Retail stores of all kinds hold seasonal "sales" when they reduce their prices, often by substantial amounts. These sales are a form of price discrimination. Each season, the newest fashions carry a high price tag, but retailers do not expect to sell all their stock at such high prices. At the end of the season, they sell off what is left at a discount. Thus such stores discriminate between buyers who have an inelastic demand (for example, those who want to be instantly fashionable) and buyers who have an elastic demand (for example, those who pay less attention to up-to-the-minute fashion and more attention to price).

Limits to Price Discrimination

Since price discrimination is profitable, why don't more firms do it? Why don't we see senior citizen discounts on speeding tickets? What are the limits to price discrimination?

Profitable price discrimination can take place only under certain conditions. First, it is possible to price discriminate only if the good cannot be resold. If a good can be resold, then customers who get the good for the low price can resell it to someone willing to pay a higher price. Price discrimination breaks down. It is for this reason that price discrimination usually occurs in markets for services rather than in markets for storable goods. One major exception, price discrimination in the sale of fashion clothes, works because at the end of the season when the clothes go on sale, the fashion plates are looking for next season's fashions. People buying on sale have no one to whom they can resell the clothes at a higher price.

Second, a price-discriminating monopoly must be able to identify groups with different elasticities of demand. The characteristics used for discrimination must also be within the law. These requirements usually limit price discrimination to cases based either on age or employment status or on the timing of the purchase.

Despite these limitations, there are some ingenious criteria used for discriminating. For example, American Airlines Inc. discriminates among many different passenger groups on many of its international flights. Five economy class alternatives between New York and London in March 1992 were

- $2,084—no restrictions
- $918—no stopovers, mid-week only
- $599—21-day advance purchase, mid-week only
- $439—14-day advance purchase, no refund
- $379—21-day advance purchase, mid-week only, no refund

These different prices discriminate between different groups of customers with different elasticities of demand.

"Yoo-hoo! My husband gets the senior-citizen discount! Yoo-hoo, Officer, yoo-hoo!"

Comparing Monopoly and Competition

We have now studied a variety of ways in which firms and households interact in markets for goods and services. In Chapter 11, we saw how perfectly competitive firms behave and discovered the price and output at which they operate. In this chapter, we have studied the price and output of a single-price monopoly and a monopoly that price discriminates. How do the quantities produced, prices, and profits of these different types of firms compare with each other?

To answer this question, let's imagine an industry made up of a large number of identical competitive firms. We will work out what the price charged and quantity produced will be in that industry. Then we will imagine that a single firm buys out all the individual firms and creates a monopoly. We will then work out the price charged and quantity produced by the monopoly, first when it charges a single price and second when it price discriminates.

Price and Output

We will conduct the analysis by using Fig. 12.7. The industry demand curve is D, and the industry supply curve is S. In perfect competition, the market equilibrium occurs where the supply curve and the demand curve intersect. The quantity produced by the industry is Q_C, and the price is P_C.

Each firm takes the price P_C and maximizes its profit by producing the output at which its own marginal cost equals the price. Since each firm is a small part of the total industry, there is no incentive for any firm to try to manipulate the price by varying its output.

Now suppose that this industry is taken over by a single firm. No changes in production techniques occur, so the new combined firm has costs identical to those of the original separate firms. The new single firm recognizes that by varying output, it can influence price. It also recognizes that its marginal revenue curve is MR. To maximize profit, the firm chooses an output at which marginal revenue equals marginal cost. But what is the monopoly's marginal cost curve? To answer this question, you need to recall the relationship between the marginal cost curve and the supply curve of a competitive firm. The supply curve of an individual competitive firm is its marginal cost curve. The supply curve of a competitive industry is the sum of the supply curves of individual firms. The industry supply curve tells us how the sum of the quantities supplied by each firm varies as the price varies. Thus the industry supply curve is also the industry's marginal cost curve. (The supply curve has also been labeled MC to remind you of this fact.) Therefore, when the industry is taken over by a single firm, that firm's marginal cost curve is the same as what used to be the competitive industry's supply curve.

FIGURE 12.7

Monopoly and Competition Compared

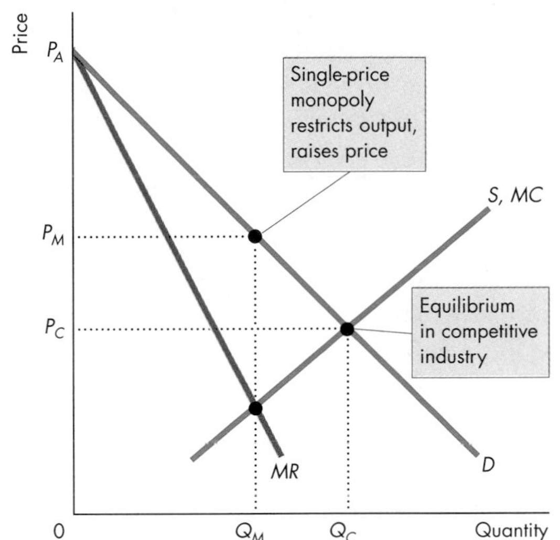

A competitive industry has a demand curve D and a supply curve S. Equilibrium occurs where the quantity demanded equals the quantity supplied at quantity Q_C and price P_C. If all the firms in the industry are taken over by a single producer that sells the profit-maximizing output for a single price, marginal revenue is MR and the supply curve of the competitive industry (S) becomes the monopoly's marginal cost curve (MC). The monopoly produces the output at which marginal revenue equals marginal cost. A single-price monopoly produces Q_M and sells that output for the price P_M. A perfectly price-discriminating monopoly produces Q_C and charges a different price for each unit sold. The prices charged range from P_A to P_C.

Monopoly restricts output and raises the price. But the more perfectly a monopoly can price discriminate, the closer its output gets to the competitive output.

We have seen that a competitive industry always operates at the point of intersection of its supply and demand curves. In Fig. 12.7, this is the point at which price is P_C and the industry produces the quantity Q_C. In contrast, the single-price monopoly maximizes profit by restricting output to Q_M, so that marginal revenue equals marginal cost. Since the marginal revenue curve is below the demand curve, output Q_M will always be smaller than output Q_C. The monopoly charges the highest price for which output Q_M can be sold, and that price is P_M.

If the monopoly can perfectly price discriminate, it will charge a different price on each unit sold and increase output to Q_C. The highest price charged is P_A, and the lowest price charged is P_C, the price in a competitive market. The price P_A is the highest that is charged because at yet higher prices, nothing can be sold. The price P_C is the lowest charged because when a monopoly perfectly price discriminates, its marginal revenue curve is the same as the demand curve and at prices below P_C marginal cost exceeds marginal revenue.

The key price and output differences between competition and monopoly are the following:

- Monopoly price exceeds the competitive price.
- Monopoly output is less than competitive output.
- The more perfectly the monopoly can price discriminate, the closer its output gets to the competitive output.

Allocative Efficiency

Monopoly is less efficient than competition. It prevents some of the gains from trade from being achieved. To see why, look at Fig. 12.8. The maximum price that consumers are willing to pay for each unit is shown by the demand curve. The difference between the maximum price that they are willing to pay for each unit bought and the price that they do pay is *consumer surplus*. Under perfect competition (part a), consumers have to pay only P_C for each unit bought and obtain a consumer surplus represented by the green triangle.

A single-price monopoly (part b) restricts output to Q_M and sells that output for P_M. Consumer surplus is reduced to the smaller green triangle. Consumers lose partly by having to pay more for what is available and partly by getting less of the good. But is the consumers' loss equal to the monopoly's gain? Is there simply a redistribution of the gains from trade? A closer look at Fig. 12.8(b) will convince you that there is a reduction in the gains from trade. It is true that some of the loss in consumer surplus does accrue to the monopoly—the monopoly gets the difference between the higher price (P_M) and P_C on the quantity sold (Q_M). So the monopoly has taken the blue rectangle part of the consumer surplus.

What, though, has become of the rest of the consumer surplus? The answer is that because output has been restricted, it is lost. But more than that has

FIGURE 12.8

Allocative Inefficiency of Monopoly

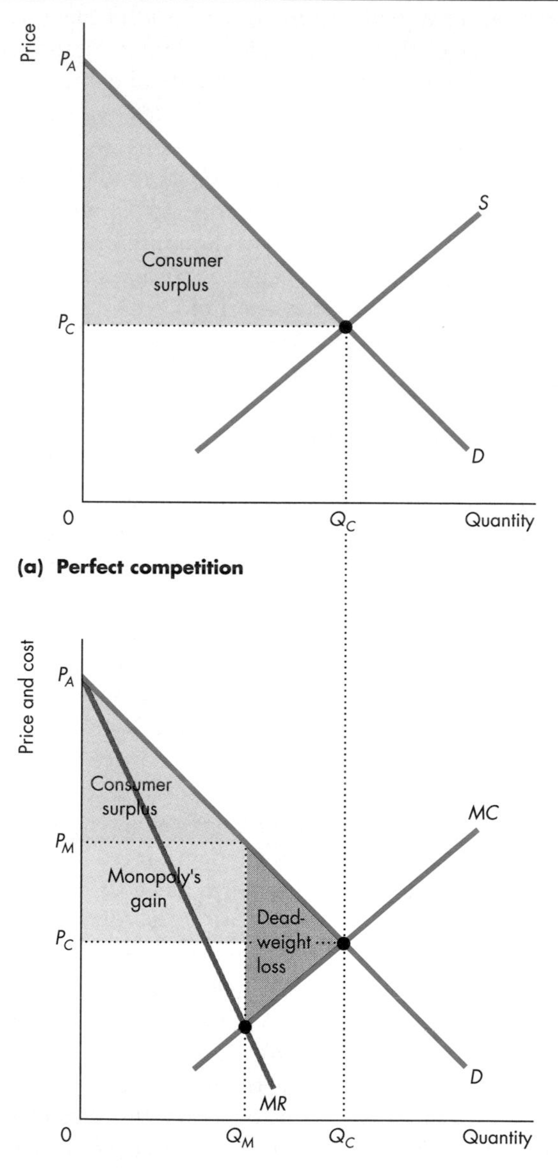

In perfect competition (part a), demand curve D intersects supply curve S at quantity Q_C and price P_C. Consumer surplus is represented by the green triangle. With free entry, firms' profits in long-run equilibrium are zero. Consumer surplus is maximized. Under a single-price monopoly (part b), output is restricted to Q_M and the price increases to P_M. Consumer surplus is reduced to the smaller green triangle. The monopoly takes the blue rectangle for itself, but the gray triangle is a deadweight loss. Part of the deadweight loss (above P_C) is a loss of consumer surplus, and part of it (below P_C) is a loss of producer surplus.

been lost. The total loss resulting from the lower monopoly output (Q_M) is the gray triangle in Fig. 12.8(b). The part of the gray triangle above P_C is the loss of consumer surplus, and the part of the triangle below P_C is a loss to the producer—a loss of producer surplus. **Producer surplus** is the difference between a producer's revenue and the opportunity cost of production. It is calculated as the sum of the differences between price and the marginal cost of producing each unit of output. Under competitive conditions, the producer sells the output between Q_M and Q_C for a price of P_C. The marginal cost of producing each extra unit of output through that range is shown by the marginal cost (supply) curve. Thus the vertical distance between the marginal cost curve and the price represents a producer surplus. Part of the producer surplus is lost when a monopoly restricts output below its competitive level.

The gray triangle, which measures the total loss of both consumer and producer surplus, is called the deadweight loss. **Deadweight loss** measures allocative inefficiency as the reduction in consumer and producer surplus resulting from a restriction of output below its efficient level. The combination of a monopoly's reduced output and higher price results in the monopoly capturing some of the consumer surplus. It also results in the elimination of the producer surplus and the consumer surplus on the output that a competitive industry would have produced but that the monopoly does not.

We have seen that a single-price monopoly creates a deadweight loss by restricting output. What is the deadweight loss if the monopoly practices perfect price discrimination? The answer is zero. A perfect price discriminator produces the same output as the competitive industry. The last item sold costs P_C, the same as its marginal cost. Thus from the point of view of allocative efficiency, a perfect price-discriminating monopoly achieves the same result as perfect competition.

Redistribution

Under perfect competition, the consumer surplus is the green triangle in Fig. 12.8(a). With free entry, the long-run equilibrium economic profit of each perfectly competitive firm is zero. We've just seen that the creation of monopoly reduces consumer surplus. Further, in the case of a single-price monopoly, a deadweight loss arises. But what happens to the distribution of surpluses between producers and consumers? The answer is that the monopoly always wins. In the case of a single-price monopoly (Fig. 12.8b), the monopoly gains the blue rectangle at the expense of the consumer. It has to offset against that gain its loss of producer surplus—its share of the deadweight loss. But there is always a net positive gain for the monopoly and a net loss for the consumer. We also know that because there is a deadweight loss, the consumer loses more than the monopoly gains.

In the case of a perfect price-discriminating monopoly, there is no deadweight loss but there is an even larger redistribution away from consumers to the monopoly. In this case, the monopoly captures the entire consumer surplus, the green triangle in Fig. 12.8(a).

An example of these possible effects of monopoly is given in Reading Between the Lines on pp. 332–333, which looks at the market for low-calorie sweeteners.

REVIEW

The creation of a monopoly results in a redistribution of economic gains away from consumers to the monopoly producer. If the monopoly can perfectly price discriminate, it produces the same output as a competitive industry and achieves allocative efficiency but captures the entire consumer surplus. If the monopoly cannot perfectly price discriminate, it restricts output below the level that a competitive industry would produce and creates a deadweight loss. The monopoly gains and the consumer loses, but the loss of the consumer exceeds the gain of the monopoly. In this case, monopoly creates allocative inefficiency. ◆

Rent Seeking

Operating a monopoly is more profitable than operating a firm in a perfectly competitive industry. Economic profit can be made in a competitive industry in the short run but not in the long run. Freedom of entry brings new firms into a profitable industry and results in economic profit being competed away. Barriers to entry prevent this process in a monopoly industry, so a monopoly can enjoy economic profit even in the long run. Because monopoly is more

The End of a Sweet Arrangement

THE CHICAGO TRIBUNE, July 28, 1991

As NutraSweet patent expires, consumers may benefit most

BY NANCY RYAN

As NutraSweet Co. celebrated a decade of unprecedented growth and brand-name recognition on its 10th anniversary this month, the aspartame producer faces a not-so-sweet competitive environment in the next 10 years.

Its exclusive patent on the sugar substitute, which helped revolutionize the diet-soda industry, expires in December 1992—a milestone most experts agree will dramatically change the carbonated beverage industry and the Deerfield, Ill.-based manufacturer.

But "the winner in all of this is going to be the consumer," said Jesse Meyers, publisher of Beverage Digest newsletter. "We're going to have the technology of Monsanto (NutraSweet's parent company) and its competitors giving the consumers better products at lower retail prices."

Several businesses are expected to attempt to sell aspartame as a generic commodity or under their own brand names, and several major manufacturers have come up with other sweeteners that may end up replacing aspartame for some products.

"Over the next two to five years, as the FDA approves more products, there will be better and improved sweeteners," said Tom Pirko, head of BevMark, a Los Angeles-based consultant to the beverage industry.

Johnson & Johnson's McNeil Specialty Products is awaiting Food and Drug Administration approval of its sucralose, which can be used in baked goods and other foods currently off limits to NutraSweet, and the government agency already has approved acesulfame-k, made by the German manufacturer Hoechst Celanese, for limited use.

FDA approvals for Pfizer Inc.'s alitame and NutraSweet's Sweetener 2000, which is 10,000 times sweeter than sugar, also are pending.

"They will chip away at NutraSweet as companies try out new blends. But NutraSweet is going to hang around for a long time," Pirko said. "It's part of the landscape."

No other food ingredient has gained the kind of brand identity that NutraSweet has. Its trademark red swirl has helped make the name known to almost 98 percent of Americans, according to NutraSweet's president and chief operating officer, Lauren S. Williams.

Though NutraSweet, which is part of Monsanto's G. D. Searle division, also produces the tabletop sweetener Equal and is included in foods and other beverages, Coke and Pepsi make up some two-thirds of the company's sales.

The Essence of the Story

NutraSweet Co., a subsidiary of Monsanto Company, makes NutraSweet, the brand name of the aspartame used to sweeten diet sodas, and Equal, a table sweetener.

The NutraSweet used in Coke and Pepsi makes up two thirds of the company's sales and is protected by a patent that expires in 1992.

When the NutraSweet patent expires, several firms are expected to offer aspartame as a generic commodity or under their own brand names.

Other firms have developed substitutes for aspartame. One is sucralose, made by McNeil Specialty Products, a subsidiary of Johnson & Johnson. This sweetener can be used in baked goods and other foods for which NutraSweet is unsuitable.

Other substitutes are acesulfame-k, made by the German manufacturer Hoechst Celanese; alitame, made by Pfizer Inc.; and Sweetener 2000—a sweetener that is 10,000 times sweeter than sugar—made by NutraSweet.

Background and Analysis

NutraSweet Co. produces aspartame in three large plants in Augusta, Georgia; Harbor Beach, Michigan; and University Park, Illinois. In 1990, its sales were $933 million and its profit was $183 million.

The average total cost curve *ATC* and marginal cost curve *MC* of a typical plant are illustrated in Fig. 1(a).

To expand output, NutraSweet can add plants like the one in Fig. 1(a). It can increase output by *q*, the capacity of a plant, at a marginal cost of *C*, so marginal cost for the firm and the industry that it controls is the horizontal line shown in Fig. 1(b).

Protected by a patent, NutraSweet is the sole supplier of aspartame, which it markets under the brand name NutraSweet. The demand curve for NutraSweet is *D* shown in Fig. 1(b).

If NutraSweet Co. sells aspartame for a single price, its marginal revenue curve is *MR* and it maximizes profit by producing an output of Q_M and selling it for P_M per unit. Its economic profit is shown by the blue rectangle. The gray triangle shows the resulting deadweight loss, and the green triangle shows the consumer surplus.

If NutraSweet price discriminates—and it probably does—its output exceeds Q_M and the deadweight loss is smaller than that shown in Fig. 1(b).

When patent protection expires at the end of 1992 and there is free entry into the sweetener industry, competition will drive the price down to its competitive level.

If perfect competition arises, the price will be driven down to equal minimum average total cost, P_C, as shown in Fig. 2(a). Industry output increases to Q_C, and consumer surplus also increases, as shown in Fig. 2(b).

Each individual plant produces its least-cost output of *q*, but the number of plants (of both NutraSweet Co. and its competitors) increases to produce the larger total output.

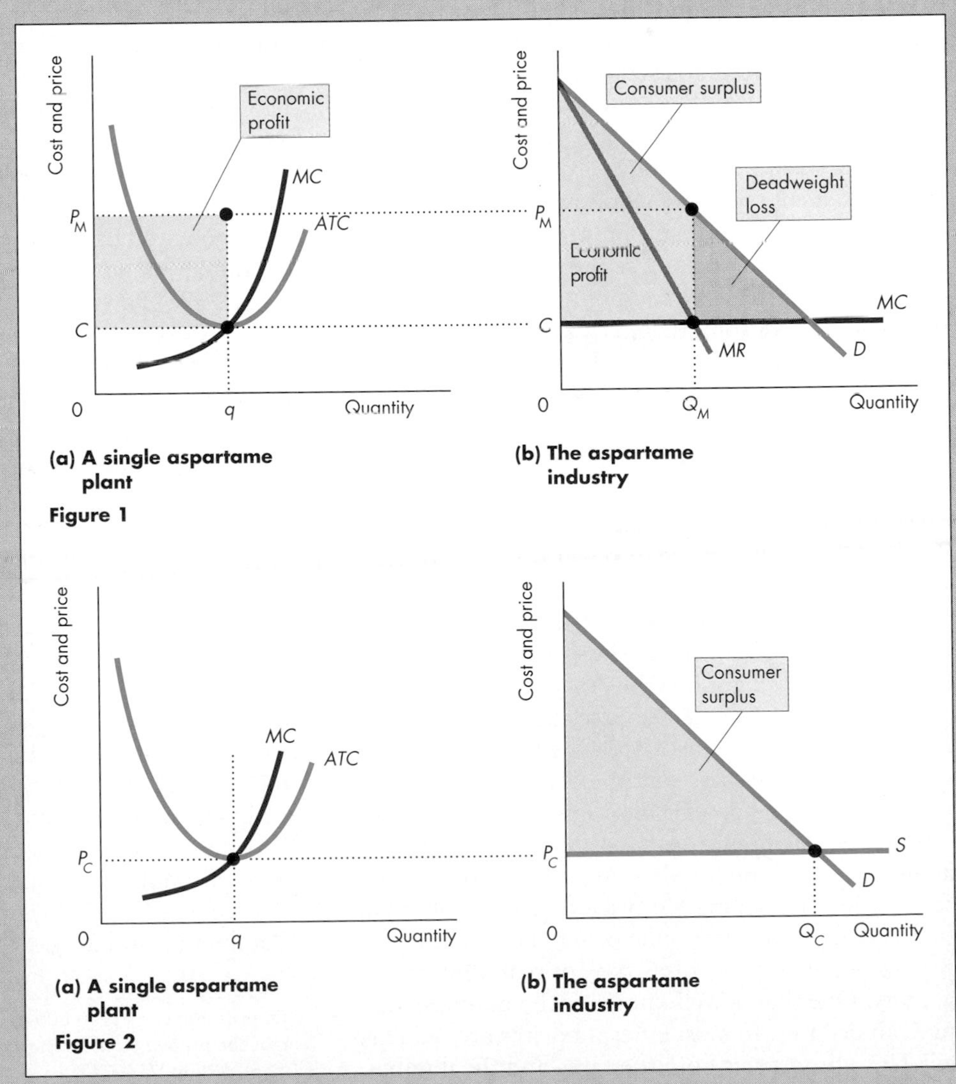

(a) A single aspartame plant

(b) The aspartame industry

Figure 1

(a) A single aspartame plant

(b) The aspartame industry

Figure 2

profitable than perfect competition, there is an incentive to attempt to create monopoly. The activity of creating monopoly is called **rent seeking.** The name *rent seeking* arises from the fact that another name for consumer surplus and producer surplus is *rent.* We've just seen that a monopoly makes its profit by diverting part of the consumer surplus to itself. Thus pursuing maximum monopoly profit is the same thing as diverting consumer surplus, or rent seeking.

Rent seeking is not a costless activity. To obtain a monopoly right, resources have to be used. Furthermore, everyone has an incentive to seek monopoly power, so there will be competition for monopoly rights. There are two ways in which people compete for monopoly rights—they buy an existing right or they create a new one. But existing monopoly rights had to be created at some time, so, ultimately, competition for monopoly rights is a process that uses productive resources to establish a monopoly right. What is the value of the resources that a person will use to obtain a monopoly right? The answer is any amount up to the monopoly's profit. If the value of resources spent trying to acquire a monopoly exceeds the monopoly's profit, the net result is an economic loss. But as long as the value of the resources used to acquire a monopoly falls short of the monopoly's profit, there is a profit to be earned. If there is no barrier to entry, the value of the resources used up in rent seeking will, in equilibrium, equal the monopoly's profit.

Because of rent seeking, monopoly imposes costs that exceed the deadweight loss that we calculated earlier. To calculate that cost, we must add to the deadweight loss the value of resources used in rent seeking. That amount equals the entire monopoly profit, since that is the value of the resources that it pays to use in rent seeking. Thus the cost of monopoly is the deadweight loss plus monopoly profit.

What exactly are the resources used in rent seeking? What do rent seekers do? One form of rent seeking is the searching out of existing monopoly rights that can be bought for a lower price than the monopoly's economic profit—that is, seeking to acquire existing monopoly rights. This form of rent seeking results in a market price for monopoly rights that is close to the economic profit. There are many real-world examples of this type of rent-seeking activity. One that is well known is the purchase of taxicab licenses. In most cities, taxicabs are regulated. The city restricts both the fares and the number of taxis that are permitted to operate. Operating a taxi is profitable—resulting in economic profit or rent being earned by the operator. A person who wants to operate a taxi has to buy the right to do so from someone who already has that right. Competition for that right leads to a price sufficiently high to eliminate long-run economic profit. For example, in New York City, the price that has to be paid for the right to operate a taxi is close to $100,000.[1]

Rent seeking is also big business among airlines. In 1986, United Airlines bought the rights to all the international air routes across the Pacific Ocean that had previously been owned and operated by Pan American Airlines. United paid Pan Am $500 million for the exclusive rights to these routes. Pan Am had originated these Pacific routes, and other U.S. airlines were prohibited from competing on them by an international air transportation agreement entered into by the United States and other governments. To acquire these routes, United had to pay Pan Am a price that provided as much profit as Pan Am would have made by hanging onto the rights and operating the routes itself. Competition for these rights among airlines resulted in the most efficient potential operator buying them, because that operator was willing to offer the highest price.

By 1991, Pan Am was in deep trouble and its entire assets went on the block. An incredible bidding war broke out for its domestic shuttle, European, and Latin American routes and equipment. At one point in the battle, four airlines—American, Delta, Northwest, and TWA—were competing with bids exceeding $300 billion for these valuable monopoly rights.

Although a great deal of rent-seeking activity involves searching out existing monopoly rights that can be profitably bought, much of it is devoted to the creation of monopoly. This type of rent-seeking activity takes the form of lobbying and seeking to influence the political process. Such influence is sometimes sought by making campaign contributions in exchange for legislative support or by indirectly seeking to influence political outcomes through publicity in the media or more direct contacts with politicians and bureaucrats. (This type of rent seeking is discussed and explained more fully in Chapters 20 and 21.)

[1]Taxis do not earn $100,000 in a single year. The $100,000 price tag is the *present value* of the expected future profits—see Chapter 9, pp. 214–217.

REVIEW

When rent seeking is taken into account, there are no guaranteed long-run profits, even from monopoly. Competition for monopoly rights results in the use of resources to acquire those rights that are equal in value to the potential monopoly profit. As a consequence, monopoly imposes costs equal to the deadweight loss plus the monopoly's economic profit. ◆

Gains from Monopoly

In our comparison of monopoly and competition, monopoly comes out in a pretty bad light. If monopoly is so bad, why do we put up with it? Why don't we have laws that crack down on monopoly so hard that it never rears its head? As we'll see in Chapter 21, we do indeed have laws that limit monopoly power. We also have laws that regulate those monopolies that exist. But monopoly is not all bad. Let's look at its potential advantages and some of the reasons for its existence.

The main reasons for the existence of monopoly are

- Economies of scale and economies of scope
- Incentive to innovate

Economies of Scale and Scope You met economies of scale in Chapters 9 and 10. There we defined *economies of scale* as decreases in average total cost resulting from increasing a firm's scale. The scale of a firm increases when it increases all its inputs—capital, labor, and materials—in the same proportions. For example, if all inputs double, total cost also doubles. If output more than doubles, average total cost declines or, equivalently, the firm has economies of scale.

Economies of scope are decreases in average total cost made possible by increasing the number of different goods produced. Economies of scope are important when highly specialized (and expensive) technical inputs can be shared by different goods. For example, McDonald's can produce both hamburgers and french fries at an average total cost that is lower than what it would cost two separate firms to produce the same goods. McDonald's can do so because the hamburgers and fries share the use of specialized food storage and preparation facilities. Firms producing a wide range of products can hire specialist computer programmers, designers, and marketing experts whose skills can be used across the product range, thereby spreading their costs and lowering the cost of production of each of the goods.

Large-scale firms that have control over supply and can influence price—and that therefore behave like the monopoly firm we've been studying in this chapter—can reap these economies of scale and scope. Small, competitive firms cannot. As a consequence, there are situations in which the comparison of monopoly and competition that we made earlier in this chapter is not a valid one. Recall that we imagined the takeover of a large number of competitive firms by a single monopoly firm. But we also assumed that the monopoly would use exactly the same technology as the small firms and have the same costs. But if one large firm can reap economies of scale and scope, its marginal cost curve will lie below the supply curve of a competitive industry made up of thousands of small firms. It is possible for such economies of scale and scope to be so large as to result in a higher output and lower price under monopoly than a competitive industry would achieve.

Figure 12.9 illustrates such a situation. Here the demand curve and the marginal revenue curve are the same regardless of whether the industry is a competitive one or a monopoly. With a competitive industry, the supply curve is S, the quantity produced is Q_C, and the price is P_C. With a monopoly that can exploit economies of scale and scope, the marginal cost curve is MC_M. The monopoly maximizes profit by producing the output (Q_M) at which marginal revenue equals marginal cost. The price that maximizes profit is P_M. By exploiting a superior technology not available to each of the large number of small firms, the monopoly is able to achieve a higher output and lower price than the competitive industry.

There are many examples of industries in which economies of scale are so important that they lead to an outcome similar to that shown in Fig. 12.9. Public utilities such as gas, electric power, water, and local telephone service are all such cases. There are also many examples of industries in which a combination of economies of scale and economies of scope is important. Examples are the brewing of beer, the manufacture of refrigerators and other household appliances, the production of pharmaceuticals, and the refining of petroleum.

FIGURE 12.9

When Economies of Scale and Scope Make Monopoly More Efficient

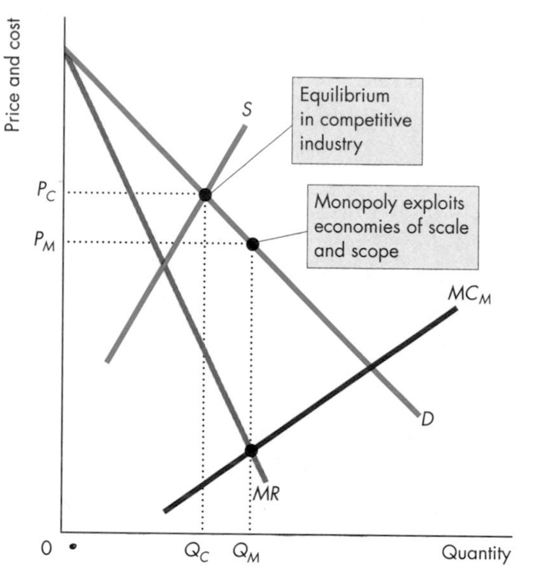

In some industries, economies of scale and economies of scope result in the monopoly's marginal cost curve (MC_M) lying below the competitive industry supply curve (S). In such a case, it is possible that the single-price monopoly output (Q_M) exceeds the competitive output (Q_C) and that the monopoly price (P_M) is below the competitive price (P_C).

Innovation Innovation is the first-time application of new knowledge in the production process. Innovation may take the form of developing a new product or a lower-cost way of making an existing product. Controversy has raged among economists over whether large firms with monopoly power or small competitive firms lacking such monopoly power are the most innovative. It is clear that some temporary monopoly power arises from innovation. A firm that develops a new product or process and patents it obtains exclusive right to that product or process for the term of the patent.

But does the granting of a monopoly, even a temporary one, to an innovator increase the pace of innovation? One line of reasoning suggests that it does. With no protection, an innovator is not able to enjoy the profits from innovation for very long. Thus the incentive to innovate is weakened. A contrary argument is that monopolies can afford to be lazy while competitive firms cannot. Competitive firms must strive to innovate and cut costs even though they know that they cannot hang onto the benefits of their innovation for long. But that knowledge spurs them on to greater and faster innovation.

A matter such as this one cannot be resolved by listing arguments and counterarguments. It requires a careful empirical investigation. Many such investigations have been conducted. But the evidence that they bring to bear on this question is mixed. They show that large firms do much more research and development than do small firms. They also show that large firms are significantly more prominent at the development end of the research and development process. But measuring research and development is measuring the volume of inputs into the process of innovation. What matters is not input but output. Two measures of the output of research and development are the number of patents and the rate of productivity growth. On these measures, there is no clear evidence that big is best. But there is a clear pattern in the process of diffusion of technological knowledge. After innovation, a new process or product spreads gradually through the industry. Whether an innovator is a small firm or a large firm, large firms jump on the bandwagon more quickly than do small firms. Thus large firms are important in speeding the process of diffusion of technological advances.

In determining public policy toward monopoly (matters discussed in Chapter 21), laws and regulations are designed that balance these positive aspects of monopoly (economies of scale and scope and innovation) against the deadweight loss and redistribution that they also generate.

◆ ◆ ◆ ◆ We've now studied two models of market structure—perfect competition and monopoly. We've used these two models to make predictions about allocative efficiency and the effects on prices and quantities of changing cost and demand conditions. ◆ ◆ Although there are examples of markets in the U.S. economy that are highly competitive or highly monopolistic, the markets for most goods and services lie somewhere between these two extremes. In the next chapter, we're going to study this middle ground between monopoly and competition. We're going to discover that many of the lessons we have learned from these two extreme models are still relevant and useful in understanding behavior in real-world markets.

SUMMARY

How Monopoly Arises

Monopoly arises because of barriers to entry that prevent competition. Barriers to the entry of new firms may be legal or natural. Legal barriers take the form of public franchise, government license, or patent. Natural barriers exist when a single firm possesses total control of a mineral or natural resource or when economies of scale are so large that a single firm can supply an entire market at a lower average total cost than can several firms. (pp. 314–315)

Single-Price Monopoly

A monopoly is an industry in which there is a single supplier of a good, service, or resource. A single-price monopoly is a firm that charges the same price for each unit of output. The monopoly's demand curve is the market demand curve for the good. For a single-price monopoly, marginal revenue is less than price. Total revenue rises at first, but above some output level it begins to decline. When total revenue is rising, marginal revenue is positive. When total revenue is falling, marginal revenue is negative. When marginal revenue is positive (total revenue rising), the elasticity of demand is greater than 1. The elasticity of demand equals 1 when total revenue is at a maximum.

A monopoly's technology and costs behave in a way similar to those of any other type of firm. The monopoly maximizes profit by producing the output that makes marginal revenue equal to marginal cost and by charging the maximum price that consumers are willing to pay for that output. The price charged always exceeds marginal cost. A monopoly has no supply curve. (pp. 315–321)

Price Discrimination

Price discrimination is the practice of charging some consumers a higher price than others for an identical item or charging an individual customer a higher price on a small purchase than on a large one. Price discrimination is an attempt by the monopoly to convert consumer surplus into profit. Perfect price discrimination extracts all the consumer surplus. Such a monopoly charges a different price for each unit sold and obtains the maximum price that each consumer is willing to pay for each unit bought. With perfect price discrimination, the monopoly's marginal revenue curve is the same as its demand curve and the monopoly produces the same output as would a perfectly competitive industry.

A monopoly can discriminate between different groups of customers on the basis of age, employment status, or other distinguishable characteristics. Such price discrimination increases the monopoly's profit if each group has a different elasticity of demand for the product. To maximize profit with price discrimination, the monopoly produces an output such that marginal cost equals marginal revenue but then charges each group the maximum price that it is willing to pay.

Price discrimination can be practiced only when it is impossible for a buyer to resell the good and when consumers with different elasticities can be identified. (pp. 321–328)

Comparing Monopoly and Competition

If a monopoly takes over all the firms in a perfectly competitive industry and if the technology and input prices in the industry remain unchanged, the monopoly charges a higher price and produces a lower quantity than would prevail in a perfectly competitive industry. If the monopoly can perfectly price discriminate, it produces the competitive quantity and sells the last unit for the competitive price.

Monopoly is less efficient than competition because it prevents some of the gains from trade from being achieved. A monopoly captures some part of the consumer surplus. But to do so, it restricts output and creates a deadweight loss. The more a monopoly is able to price discriminate, the smaller is the deadweight loss but the larger is the monopoly profit and the smaller is the consumer surplus.

Monopoly always redistributes the gains from trade away from consumers toward the producer. The more perfectly a monopoly can price discriminate, the smaller is the deadweight loss but the larger is the reallocation of surpluses from consumers to the producer.

Monopoly imposes costs that equal its deadweight loss plus the cost of the resources devoted to rent seeking—searching out profitable monopoly opportunities. It pays to use resources that are equal in value to the entire monopoly profit that might be attained. As a result, the cost of monopoly equals its deadweight loss plus the entire monopoly profit.

There are some industries in which a monopoly is more efficient than a large number of perfectly competitive firms. Such industries are those in which economies of scale and scope are so large that the monopoly's output is higher and its price is lower than those that would arise if the industry had a large number of firms. There are also situations in which monopoly may be more innovative than competition, resulting in a faster pace of technological change. (pp. 328–336)

KEY ELEMENTS

Key Terms

Barriers to entry, 314
Deadweight loss, 331
Economies of scope, 335
Government license, 314
Legal monopoly, 314
Monopoly, 314
Natural monopoly, 314
Patent, 314
Perfect price discrimination, 321
Price discrimination, 321
Producer surplus, 331
Public franchise, 314
Rent seeking, 334
Single-price monopoly, 315

Key Figures

Figure 12.1 Demand and Marginal Revenue for a Single-Price Monopoly, 316
Figure 12.2 A Single-Price Monopoly's Revenue Curves, 317
Figure 12.3 A Monopoly's Output and Price, 318
Figure 12.7 Monopoly and Competition Compared, 329

REVIEW QUESTIONS

1 What is a monopoly? What are some examples of monopoly in your state?

2 How does monopoly arise?

3 Distinguish between a legal monopoly and a natural monopoly. Give examples of each type.

4 Explain why marginal revenue is always less than average revenue for a single-price monopoly.

5 Why does a monopoly's profit increase as output rises initially but eventually decrease when output gets too big?

6 Explain how a monopoly chooses its output and price.

7 Does a monopoly operate on the inelastic part of its demand curve? Explain why it does or does not.

8 Explain why a monopoly produces a smaller output than an equivalent competitive industry.

9 Is monopoly as efficient as competition?

10 What is deadweight loss?

11 Can any monopoly price discriminate? If yes, why? If no, why not?

12 Show graphically the deadweight loss under perfect price discrimination.

13 As far as allocative efficiency is concerned, is single-price monopoly better or worse than perfect price discrimination? Why?

14 Explain why people indulge in rent-seeking activities.

15 When taking account of the cost of rent seeking, what is the social cost of monopoly?

16 What are economies of scale and economies of scope? What effects, if any, do they have on the allocative efficiency of monopoly?

17 Explain why the consumer loses more under perfect price discrimination than under single-price monopoly.

PROBLEMS

1 Minnie's Mineral Springs, a single-price monopoly, has the following demand schedule and total cost for bottled mineral water:

Quantity (bottles)	Price (dollars per bottle)	Total cost (dollars)
0	10	1
1	8	3
2	6	7
3	4	13
4	2	21
5	0	31

a Calculate Minnie's total revenue schedule.
b Calculate its marginal revenue schedule.
c At what price is the elasticity of demand equal to 1?

2 Calculate Minnie's profit-maximizing levels of:
a Output
b Price
c Marginal cost
d Marginal revenue
e Profit

3 Suppose that Minnie's can perfectly price discriminate. What is its profit-maximizing:
a Output
b Total revenue
c Profit

4 How much would someone be willing to pay Minnie's for a license to operate its mineral spring?

5 Two demand schedules for round-trip flights between New York and Los Angeles are set out below.

Weekday travelers		Weekend travelers	
Price (dollars per round-trip)	Quantity demanded (thousands of round-trips)	Price (dollars per round-trip)	Quantity demanded (thousands of round-trips)
1,500	0	500	0
1,000	10	250	10
500	20	125	20
250	30	0	30
125	40		
0	50		

The schedule for weekday travelers is for those making round-trips on weekdays and returning within the same week. The schedule for weekend travelers is for those who stay through the weekend. (The former tend to be business travelers, and the latter tend to be vacation and pleasure travelers.) The marginal cost of a round-trip is a constant $125. If a single-price monopoly airline controls the New York–Los Angeles route, use a graph to find out the following:
a What price is charged?
b How many passengers travel?
c What is the consumer surplus?

6 If the airline in problem 5 discriminates between round-trips within a week and round-trips through the weekend:
a What is the price for the round-trip within the week?
b What is the price of the airline ticket with a weekend stay?
c What is the consumer surplus?

7 Barbara runs a truck stop on the prairie, miles from anywhere. She has a monopoly and faces the following demand schedule for meals:

Price (dollars per meal)	Quantity demanded (meals per week)
1.00	160
1.50	140
2.00	120
2.50	100
3.00	80
3.50	60
4.00	40
4.50	20
5.00	10

Barbara's marginal cost and average total cost are a constant $2 per meal.
a If Barbara charges all customers the same price for a meal, what price is it?
b What is the consumer surplus of all the customers who buy a meal from Barbara?
c What is the producer surplus?
d What is the deadweight loss?

CHAPTER 13

MONOPOLISTIC COMPETITION AND OLIGOPOLY

After studying this chapter, you will be able to:

- Describe and distinguish among market structures that lie between perfect competition and monopoly
- Define monopolistic competition and oligopoly
- Explain how price and output are determined in a monopolistically competitive industry
- Explain why the price may be sticky in an oligopolistic industry
- Explain how price and output are determined when there is one dominant firm and several small firms in an industry
- Explain duopoly and oligopoly as games that firms play
- Predict the price and output behavior of duopolists
- Make predictions about price wars and competition among small numbers of firms

EVERY WEEK, WE RECEIVE A NEWSPAPER STUFFED WITH supermarket fliers describing this week's "specials," providing coupons and other enticements, all designed to grab our attention and persuade us that A&P, Kroger, Safeway, Alpha Beta, Winn Dixie, Stop & Shop, Shop 'n' Save, and H.E.B.'s have the best deals in town. One claims the lowest price, another the best brands, yet another the best value for the money even if its prices are not the lowest. How do firms locked in fierce competition with other firms set their prices, pick their products, and choose the quantities to produce? How are the profits of such firms affected by the actions of other firms? ◆◆ Suddenly, in 1973, the prices that people paid for gasoline, heating oil, and other petroleum products depended on the whims of the Organization of Petroleum Exporting Countries (OPEC). In that year, OPEC raised the price of oil from $3 to $12 a barrel. And it kept on increasing prices to $35 a barrel by 1982. Then, equally suddenly and to the surprise of millions of people, OPEC fell apart. By 1986 the price of oil had collapsed to one half of its 1982 level. Headlines screamed, "The Price War Is Here" and "Frenzied Gas Wars Push Down Pump Prices." How did OPEC increase the price of oil in the 1970s? And why did OPEC's stranglehold on oil prices disappear?

Fliers and War Games

◆◆◆◆ The theories of monopoly and perfect competition do not predict the kind of behavior that we've just described. There are no fliers and coupons, best brands, or price wars in perfect competition because each firm produces an identical product and is a price taker. And there are none in monopoly because each monopoly firm has the entire market to itself. To understand coupons, fliers, and price wars, we need richer models of the behavior of firms in markets than those of perfect competition and monopoly. This chapter presents such models. But before turning to these models, we are going to describe the characteristics of different types of markets so that we can identify those to which each model applies.

Varieties of Market Structure

We have studied two types of market structure—perfect competition and monopoly. In perfect competition, a large number of firms produce identical goods and there are no barriers to the entry of new firms into the industry. In this situation, each firm is a price taker and, in the long run, there is no economic profit. In monopoly, there is one firm that is protected by barriers preventing the entry of new firms. The firm sets its price to maximize profit and enjoys economic profit even in the long run.

Many real-world industries are not well described by the models of perfect competition and monopoly. They lie somewhere between these two cases. There are many situations in which firms are in fierce competition with a large number of other firms but they do have some power to set prices. There are other cases in which the industry consists of very few firms and each firm has considerable power in price determination.

Measures of Concentration

In order to tell how close to the competitive or monopolistic extreme an industry comes, economists have developed measures of industrial concentration. These measures are designed to indicate the degree of control that a small number of firms have over a market.

The most commonly used measure of concentration is called the four-firm concentration ratio. The **four-firm concentration ratio** is the percentage of the value of sales accounted for by the largest four firms in an industry. (Concentration ratios are also defined and measured for the largest 8, 20, and 50 firms in an industry.) Table 13.1 sets out two hypothetical concentration ratio calculations, one for tires and one for printing. In this example, there are 14 firms in the tire industry. The biggest four have 80 percent

TABLE **13.1**

Concentration Ratio Calculations

Tiremakers		Printers	
Firm	Sales (millions of dollars)	Firm	Sales (millions of dollars)
Top, Inc.	**200**	**Fran's**	**2.5**
ABC, Inc.	**250**	**Ned's**	**2.0**
Big, Inc.	**150**	**Tom's**	**1.8**
XYZ, Inc.	**100**	**Jill's**	**1.7**
Top 4 sales	**700**	**Top 4 sales**	**8.0**
Other 10 firms	**175**	**Other 1,000 firms**	**1,592.0**
Industry sales	**875**	**Industry sales**	**1,600.0**

Four-firm concentration ratios:

Tiremakers: 700/875 = 80% **Printers: 8/1,600 = 0.5%**

of the sales of the industry, so the four-firm concentration ratio for that industry is 80 percent. In the printing industry, with 1004 firms, the top four firms account for only 0.5 percent of total industry sales. In that case, the four-firm concentration ratio is 0.5 percent.

Another commonly used measure of concentration is the Herfindahl-Hirschman (H-H) Index. The **Herfindahl-Hirschman Index** is calculated as the square of market share (percentage) of each firm summed over the largest 50 firms (or summed over all the firms if there are fewer than 50) in a market. For example, if a market is shared equally by two firms, the H-H Index is equal to $50^2 + 50^2 = 5{,}000$. If each of the largest 50 firms has a market share of 0.5 percent, the H-H Index is equal to $0.5^2 \times 50 = 12.5$.

Concentration in the U.S. Economy

The Department of Commerce uses data on individual firms' sales to calculate concentration ratios for a large number of industry groups. A selection of their calculations is shown in Fig. 13.1. As you can

FIGURE 13.1

Some Concentration Measures in the United States

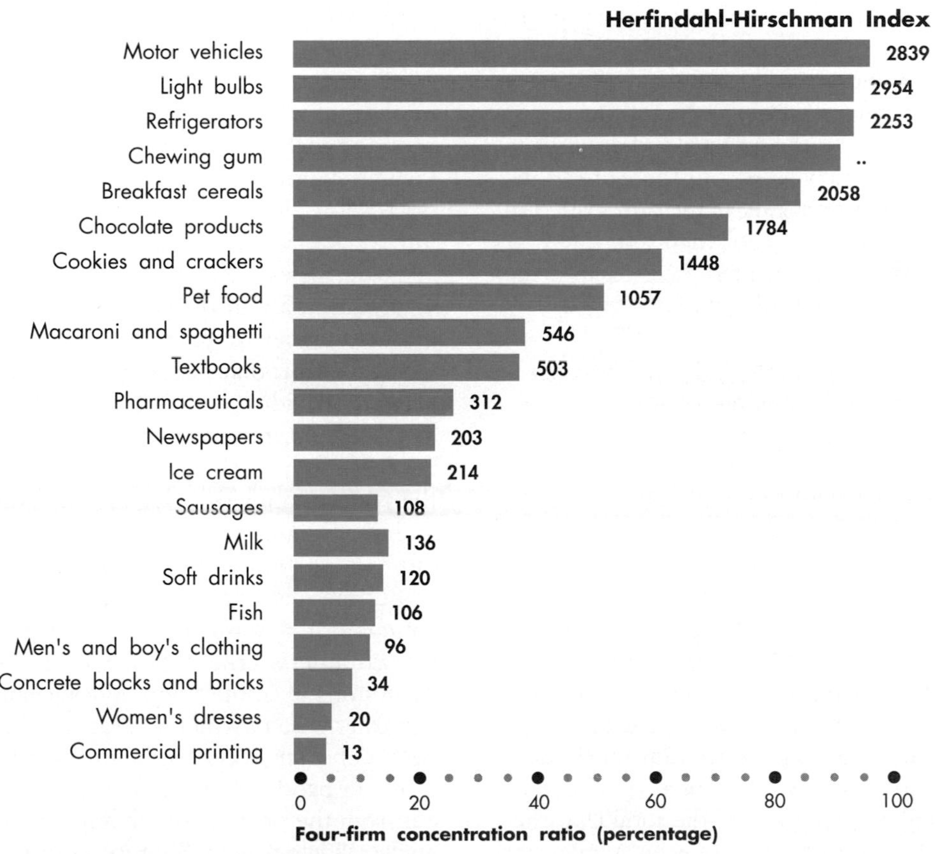

Measured by the four-firm concentration ratio and the Herfindahl-Hirschman Index, the industries producing motor vehicles, light bulbs, and refrigerators are highly concentrated, while the commercial printing, women's dresses, and concrete blocks and bricks industries are highly competitive. The industries producing macaroni, spaghetti, and textbooks have an intermediate degree of concentration.

Source: U.S. Department of Commerce, *Concentration Ratios in Manufacturing,* MC82-S-7, Washington D.C., 1986.

see, some industries—from pharmaceuticals to commercial printing and including ice cream and soft drinks—have low concentration ratios. These industries are highly competitive. At the other extreme are industries with a high concentration ratio, such as motor vehicles, light bulbs, refrigerators, chewing gum, and breakfast cereals. These are industries in which there is competition but among a small number of firms, each of which has considerable control over its price. Medium concentration ratios are found for such products as pet foods and textbooks.

Limitations of Measures of Concentration

The idea behind calculating concentration ratios is to provide information about the degree of competitiveness of a market. A low concentration ratio indicates a high degree of competition, and a high concentration ratio indicates an absence of competition. In the extreme case of monopoly, the four-firm concentration ratio is 100—the largest (and only) firm makes the entire industry sales. But there are problems with concentration ratios as measures of competitiveness. Although the ratios themselves are useful, they have to be supplemented by other information. There are three key problems.

1. Geographical Scope of the Market Concentration ratio data are based on a national view of the market. Many goods are indeed sold in a national market, but some are sold in a regional market and some in a global one. The newspaper industry is a good example of one in which the local market is more important than the national market. Thus, although the concentration ratio for newspapers is not high, there is nevertheless a high degree of concentration in the newspaper industry in most cities. The automobile industry is an example of one for which there is a global market. Thus, although the biggest four U.S. car producers account for 92 percent of all cars sold by U.S. producers, they account for a much smaller percentage of the total U.S. car market (including imports) and an even smaller percentage of the global market for cars.

2. Barriers to Entry and Turnover Measures of concentration do not tell us how severe are the barriers to entry in an industry. Some industries, for example, are highly concentrated but have virtually free entry and experience an enormous amount of turnover of firms. A good example is the market in local restaurants. Many small towns have few restaurants. But there are no restrictions on entering the restaurant industry, and indeed firms do enter and exit with great regularity.

3. Market and Industry The classifications used to calculate concentration ratios allocate every firm in the U.S. economy to a particular industry. But markets for particular goods do not always correspond exactly to particular industries. For example, Westinghouse is classified by the Department of Commerce as being in the electrical goods and equipment industry. That is indeed the main product line of Westinghouse. But Westinghouse also produces, among other things, gas-fired incinerators and plywood. Thus this one firm operates in three quite separate markets. Furthermore, the market or markets in which a firm operates depend on the profit opportunities that exist. There are many spectacular examples of firms that have built their initial organization on one product but then diversified into a wide variety of others.

Nevertheless, concentration ratios combined with information about the geographical scope of the market, barriers to entry, and the extent to which large, multiproduct firms straddle a variety of markets do provide the basis for classifying industries. The less concentrated an industry and the lower its barriers to entry, the more closely it approximates the perfect competition case. The more concentrated an industry and the higher the barriers to entry, the more it approximates the monopoly case.

But there is a great deal of space between perfect competition and monopoly. That space is occupied by two other market types. The first of these is monopolistic competition. **Monopolistic competition** is a market type in which a large number of firms compete with each other by making similar but slightly different products. Making a product slightly different from the product of a competing firm is called **product differentiation.** Because of product differentiation, a monopolistically competitive firm has an element of monopoly power. The firm is the sole producer of the particular version of the good in question. For example, in the market for microwave popcorn, only Nabisco makes Planters Premium Select. Only General Mills makes Pop Secret. And only American Popcorn makes Jolly Time. Each of these firms has a monopoly on a particular brand of microwave popcorn. Differentiated products are not necessarily different in an objective sense. For example, the different brands of microwave popcorn might actually be only different ways of packaging an identical commodity. What matters is that consumers perceive products to be differentiated. In fact, there are claims that the different brands of microwave popcorn are different in ways other than their packaging—for example, in "popability."

Oligopoly is a market type in which a small number of producers compete with each other. There are hundreds of examples of oligopolistic industries. Oil and gasoline production, the manufacture of electrical equipment, and international air transportation are but a few. In some oligopolistic industries, each firm produces an almost identical product, while in others, products are differentiated. For example, oil and gasoline are essentially the same whether they are produced by Texaco or Exxon. But Chrysler's Acclaim is a differentiated commodity from Chevrolet's Lumina and Ford's Mercury Topaz.

Table 13.2 summarizes the characteristics of the two market types that we're going to study in this chapter, monopolistic competition and oligopoly, along with those of perfect competition and monopoly.

Market Types in the U.S. Economy

Three quarters of the value of goods and services bought and sold in the United States is traded in markets that are essentially competitive—markets that have almost perfect competition or monopolistic competition. Monopoly is rare—accounting for less than 3 percent of the value of goods and services in the United States—and is found mainly in public utilities and public transportation. A similarly small number of markets—accounting for less than 3 percent of the value of sales—are dominated by one or two firms but are not monopolies. These, too, are in the public utilities and transportation sectors. Oligopoly, found mainly in manufacturing, accounts for about 18 percent of sales.

Over the years, the U.S. economy has become increasingly competitive. This trend and the percentages of each market type are shown in Fig. 13.2.

TABLE 13.2
Market Structure

Characteristics	Perfect competition	Monopolistic competition	Oligopoly	Monopoly
Number of firms in industry	**Many**	**Many**	**Few**	**One**
Product	**Identical**	**Differentiated**	**Either identical or differentiated**	**No close substitutes**
Barriers to entry	**None**	**Some**	**Scale and scope economies**	**Scale and scope economies or legal barriers**
Firm's control over price	**None**	**Some**	**Considerable**	**Considerable or regulated**
Concentration ratio (0 to 100)	**0**	**Low**	**High**	**100**
Examples	**Wheat, corn**	**Food, clothing**	**Automobiles, cereals**	**Local phone service, electric and gas utilities**

FIGURE 13.2

The Market Structure of the U.S. Economy

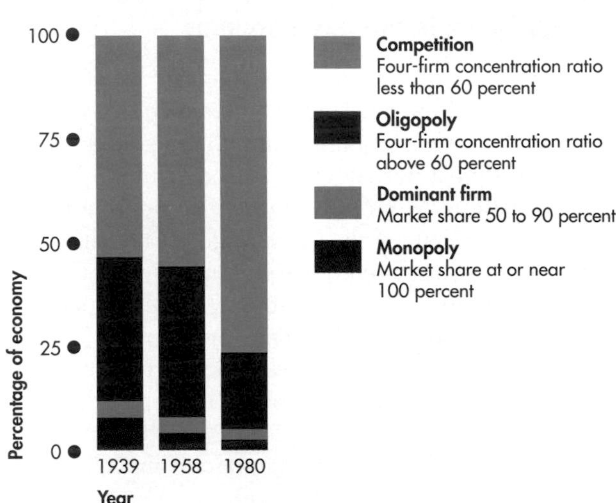

Three quarters of the U.S. economy is effectively competitive (perfect competition or monopolistic competition), one fifth is oligopolistic, and the rest is dominated by a few firms or is monopolistic. The economy has been getting more competitive over the years.

Source: William G. Shepherd, "Causes of Increased Competition in the U.S. Economy, 1939–1980," *Review of Economics and Statistics*, November, 1982, pp. 613–626.

Monopolistic Competition

Three conditions define a monopolistically competitive industry:

- Each firm faces a downward-sloping demand curve.
- There is free entry.
- There are a large number of firms in the industry.

Because each firm faces a downward-sloping demand curve, it has to choose its price as well as its output. Also the firm's marginal revenue curve is different from its demand curve. These features of monopolistic competition are also present in monopoly. The important difference between monopoly and monopolistic competition lies in free entry.

In monopoly, there is no entry. In monopolistic competition, there is free entry. As a consequence, though monopolistic competition enables economic profits to occur in the short run, they cannot persist forever. When profits are available, new firms will enter the industry. Such entry will result in lower prices and lower profits. When losses are being incurred, firms will leave the industry. Such exit will increase prices and increase profits. In long-run equilibrium, firms will neither enter nor leave the industry, and firms will be making a zero economic profit.

Because the industry consists of a large number of firms, no one firm can effectively influence what other firms will do. That is, if one firm changes its price, that firm is such a small part of the total industry that it will have no effect on the actions of the other firms in the industry.

Price and Output in Monopolistic Competition

To see how price and output are determined by a firm in a monopolistically competitive industry, let's look at Fig. 13.3. Part (a) deals with the short run, and part (b) with the long run. To keep things simple, we will suppose that the industry consists of a large number of firms with a differentiated product and that all firms in the industry have identical demand and cost curves. Let's concentrate initially on the short run. The demand curve D is the demand curve for the firm's own variety of the product. For example, it is the demand for Bayer aspirin rather than for painkillers in general or for McDonald's hamburgers rather than for hamburgers in general. The curve MR is the marginal revenue curve associated with the demand curve. The firm's average total cost (ATC) and marginal cost (MC) are also shown in the figure. A firm maximizes profit in the short run by producing output Q_S, where marginal revenue equals marginal cost, and charging the price P_S. The firm's average total cost is C_S, and the firm makes a short-run profit, as measured by the blue rectangle.

So far, the monopolistically competitive firm looks just like a monopoly. It produces the quantity at which marginal revenue equals marginal cost and then charges the highest possible price for that quan-

FIGURE 13.3
Monopolistic Competition

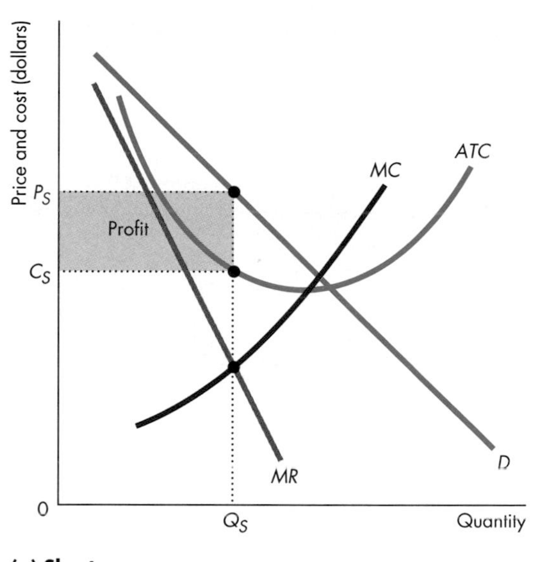

(a) Short run

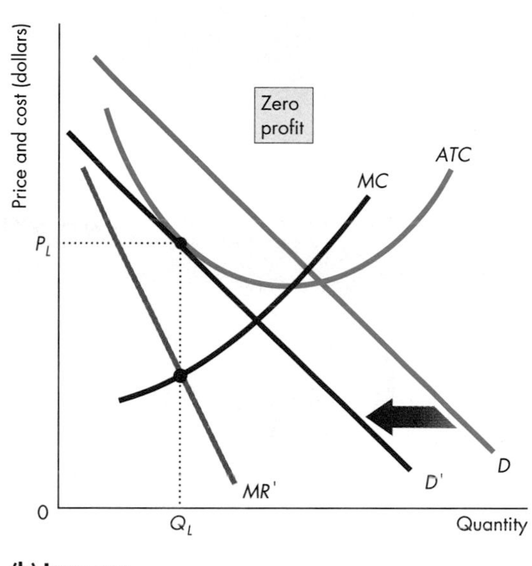

(b) Long run

Under monopolistic competition, a firm faces a downward-sloping demand curve and so has to choose its price and the quantity to produce. Profit is maximized where marginal revenue equals marginal cost. Part (a) of the figure shows a short-run profit-maximizing situation. The quantity produced is Q_S, the price is P_S, average total cost is C_S, and profit is represented by the blue rectangle.

Profit encourages new entrants, and so the firm's demand curve begins to shift to the left, as shown in part (b). As the demand curve shifts to the left, so too does the firm's marginal revenue curve (only the new marginal revenue curve is shown). When the demand curve has shifted all the way from *D* to *D'*, the marginal revenue curve is *MR'* and the firm is in long-run equilibrium. The output that maximizes profit is Q_L, and the price is P_L. Profit, in long-run equilibrium, is zero. There is no further entry into the industry.

tity. The key difference between monopoly and monopolistic competition lies in what happens next.

There is no restriction on entry in monopolistic competition, so with economic profit being earned, new firms enter the industry and take some of the market away from the existing firms. As they do so, the firm's demand curve starts to shift to the left. The marginal revenue curve also starts to shift to the left. At each point in time, the firm will seek to maximize its short-run profit. That is, it chooses its output so that marginal revenue equals marginal cost, and it charges the highest possible price for the good. But as the demand curve shifts to the left, the profit-maximizing quantity and price fall. In long-run equilibrium, shown in Fig. 13.3(b), the firm produces Q_L and sells it at a price of P_L. In this situation, the firm is making a zero economic profit. Average total cost exactly equals price. There is no incentive for firms to enter or exit.

A process similar to the one that we've just described seems to be going on in the video game industry at the present time, as you can see by studying Reading Between the Lines on pp. 348–349.

Excess Capacity

Recall that a firm's capacity output is the output produced when average total cost is at its minimum point—the output at the bottom of the U-shaped *ATC* curve. In monopolistic competition, in the long run, firms always have excess capacity. That is, they produce a lower output than that which minimizes average total cost. As a consequence, the consumer pays more than the minimum average total cost.

Monopolistic Competition in Action

The Wall Street Journal, September 18, 1990

Nintendo Tries to Zap Game Rentals by Video Stores

by Michael W. Miller

Nintendo Co. is trying to stomp a new enemy that's sprouting up faster than the dread Micro-Goombas in Super Mario Brothers 3: video stores that rent Nintendo games.

With game prices in the range of $40 to $50, rental has become an increasingly popular way for Nintendo addicts to get a quick fix. Game rentals make up an estimated 5% to 15% of the revenue of the nation's roughly 25,000 video stores, up from virtually nothing three years ago.

Nintendo, based in Kyoto, Japan, and the companies that make games for the Nintendo system are lobbying Congress for a law to ban game rental, which the House Judiciary Committee is scheduled to vote on today. They argue that the rental boom is cutting into Nintendo game sales, which they project will total 70 million units this year.

Both sides can claim legal precedent thanks to the patchwork of federal regulations covering rental of published works. For instance, videos can be rented whereas records cannot. Congress seems likely to pass a bill that would ban the rental of personal-computer software. Game makers point out that some titles are available both for PCs and Nintendo machines, and say it makes no sense to ban rental of one format and not the other.

The video-store industry argues that movie rentals haven't damaged the movie business, despite Hollywood's anguished predictions that they would. Even though video stores typically don't pay royalties on rentals, the movie industry makes huge revenue from sales to the stores.

In fact, some video-store owners say they ultimately help Nintendo and the game-makers, who also don't earn royalties from rentals. "I sell games mainly through rentals—people come in here, try a game, like it, and buy it," says Franklin Sellars, owner of Videotape Home Systems Inc., a Pasadena, Texas, store.

Nintendo and its allies deride this argument: They say kids are renting games over and over again, not just once to try them out. "Consumers can obtain complete use and enjoyment of many video games through rental without purchasing them, creating lost sales to the copyright owner," said Bruce Davis, chairman of game-maker Mediagenic, in testimony to Congress this summer.

The video-store lobby argues that the rationale for anti-rental laws should be to prevent copying. It is easy for consumers to copy records and PC software, but there is no simple way to duplicate a Nintendo game (although Nintendo has been circulating advertisements for a game-copying device marketed overseas by a Taiwanese concern, Baelih Co.). . . .

The Essence of the Story

Nintendo games cost from $40 to $50, and renting has become increasingly popular—making up an estimated 5% to 15% of the revenue of the nation's roughly 25,000 video stores.

Nintendo Co., based in Kyoto, Japan, wants a law to ban video game rentals, which, it argues, cut into game sales.

The video-store industry says that it helps Nintendo and the game-makers—much as video rentals help the movie industry—because people try games, like them, and then buy them.

Nintendo disagrees, arguing that people are renting games over and over again, not just once to try them out.

Both sides can claim legal precedent for a rental ban: videos can be rented, but records cannot. There is also support for a ban on the rental of personal-computer software.

The video-store lobby argues that the rationale for anti-rental laws should be to prevent copying. Records and PC software are easily copied, but Nintendo games are not—although a game-copying device apparently does exist.

Background and Analysis

If Nintendo could get a ban on game rentals and if it could keep other competitors out of the business, it would have a monopoly as shown in Fig. 1.

In that figure, the demand curve for Nintendo games is *D*, the marginal revenue curve is *MR*, the average total cost curve is *ATC*, and the marginal cost curve is *MC*. Profit is maximized by producing Q_M games per week at a price of P_M per game. Economic profit is shown by the blue rectangle.

Profit leads to entry. Video stores get into the game rental business, and other game-makers such as Camerica and Game Genie compete for business with Nintendo.

Video games for rent and games made by other producers are substitutes for Nintendo games, and their availability decreases the demand for Nintendo games.

The demand for Nintendo games falls, and the demand curve and marginal revenue curves shift to those shown in Fig. 2. Nintendo is in the position shown in that figure. The price of video games has fallen to P_C, and Nintendo is sharing the market with other firms producing Q_C games a week.

It is likely that the situation in the real-world video-games market lies between the two shown in Figs. 1 and 2. Nintendo is certainly not a monopolist, but it is making an economic profit, and entry into the industry continues.

It clearly pays Nintendo to try to get a ban on game rentals, since such a ban pushes the market toward that shown in Fig. 1 and away from that of Fig. 2.

It pays consumers of games to support rentals, since rentals lower the cost of games and increase their availability.

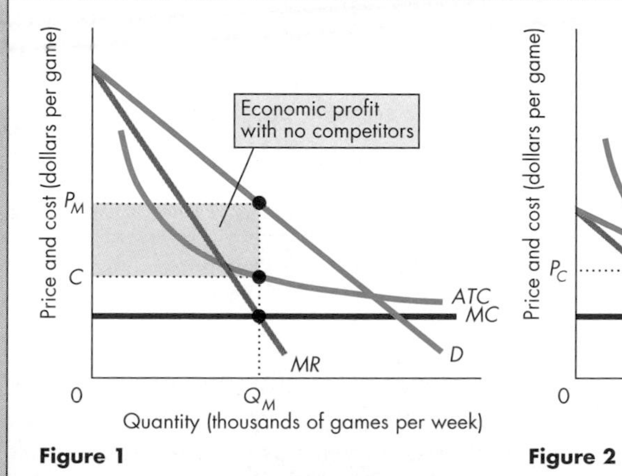

Figure 1

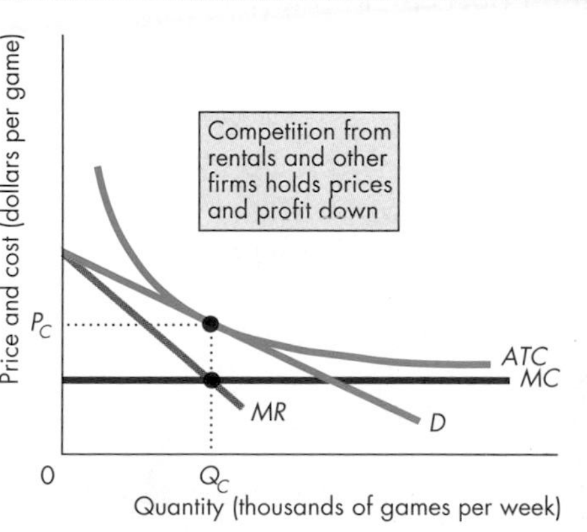

Figure 2

This result arises from the fact that the firm faces a downward-sloping demand curve. Only if the demand curve facing the firm is perfectly elastic is the long-run equilibrium at the point of minimum average total cost. The demand curve slopes down because of product differentiation. If each firm produces an identical product, each firm's output will be a perfect substitute for the outputs of all other firms and so the demand curve will be perfectly elastic. Thus it is product differentiation that produces excess capacity.

Efficiency of Monopolistic Competition

When we studied a perfectly competitive industry, we discovered that in some circumstances, such an industry achieves allocative efficiency. A key feature of allocative efficiency is that price equals marginal cost. Recall that price measures the value placed on the last unit bought by the consumer and marginal cost measures the opportunity cost of producing the last unit. We also discovered that monopoly is allocatively inefficient because it restricts output below the level at which price equals marginal cost. As we have just discovered, monopolistic competition shares this feature with monopoly. Even though there is zero economic profit in long-run equilibrium, the monopolistically competitive industry produces an output at which price equals average total cost and exceeds marginal cost.

Does this feature of monopolistic competition mean that this market structure, like monopoly, is allocatively inefficient? It does not. It is true that if the firms in a monopolistically competitive industry all produce identical products, products that are perfect substitutes, then each firm will face a perfectly elastic demand curve. In the long run, such firms will produce at the point of minimum average total cost and charge a price equal to marginal cost. But achieving that outcome will itself have a cost. The cost is the absence of product differentiation. Variety is valued by consumers, but variety is achievable only if firms make differentiated products. The loss in allocative efficiency that occurs in monopolistic competition has to be weighed against the gain of greater product variety.

Product Innovation

Another source of gain from monopolistically competitive industries is product innovation. Monopolistically competitive firms are constantly seeking out new products that will provide them with a competitive edge, even if only temporarily. A firm that manages to introduce a new and differentiated variety will temporarily face a steeper demand curve than before and will be able to temporarily increase its price. Entry of new firms will eventually compete away the profit arising from this initial advantage.

Advertising

Monopolistically competitive firms seek to differentiate their products partly by designing and introducing products that actually are different from those of the other firms in the industry. But they also attempt to differentiate the consumer's perception of the product. Advertising is the principal means whereby firms seek to achieve this end. But advertising increases the monopolistically competitive firm's costs above those of a competitive firm or a monopoly that does not advertise.

To the extent that advertising provides consumers with information about the precise nature of the differentiation of products, it serves a valuable purpose to the consumer, enabling a better product choice to be made. But the opportunity cost of the additional information provided through advertising has to be offset against the gain to the consumer from making a better choice.

The bottom line on the question of allocative efficiency of monopolistic competition is ambiguous. In some cases, the gains from extra product variety unquestionably offset the costs in the form of advertising and excess capacity. The tremendous varieties of books and magazines, clothing, food, and drink are examples of such gains. It is less easy to see the gains from being able to buy brand name drugs that have a chemical composition identical to that of a generic alternative. But some people do willingly pay more for the brand name alternative.

REVIEW

A firm in a monopolistically competitive industry faces a downward-sloping demand curve and so has to choose its price as well as the quantity to produce. Such firms also compete on product variety and by advertising. A lack of barriers to entry into such industry ensures that economic profit is competed away. In long-run equilibrium, firms make zero economic profit, charging a price equal to average total cost. But price exceeds marginal cost, and the quantity produced is below that which minimizes average total cost. The cost of monopolistic competition is excess capacity and high advertising expenditure; the gain is a wide product variety. ◆

Oligopoly

We have defined oligopoly as a market in which a small number of producers compete with each other. In such a market, each producer is interdependent. The sales of any one producer depend upon that producer's price and the prices charged by the other producers. To see this interplay between prices and sales, suppose that you run one of the three gas stations in a small town. If you lower your price and your two competitors don't lower theirs, your sales increase but the sales of the other two firms decrease. In such a situation, the other firms will, most likely, lower their prices too. If they do cut their prices, your sales and profits will take a tumble. So, before deciding to cut your price, you try to predict how the other firms will react and you attempt to calculate the effects of those reactions on your own profit.

A variety of models have been developed to explain the determination of price and quantity in oligopoly markets, and no one theory has been found that can explain all the different types of behavior that we observe in such markets. The models fall into two broad groups: traditional models and game theory models. We'll look at examples of both types, starting with the traditional models.

Traditional Models of Oligopoly

Economists have studied oligopoly and duopoly since the time of Cournot in the 1830s. The earliest models were based on assumptions about the beliefs of each firm concerning the reactions of another firm (or firms) to its own actions. A particularly influential model was proposed in the 1930s by Paul M. Sweezy (editor of the *Monthly Review* for the past 40 years). It is known as the kinked demand curve model.

The Kinked Demand Curve Model

Sweezy's concern was to explain why prices did not fall more quickly during the years of the Great Depression—why prices were sticky. He proposed a theory based on the following propositions about the beliefs held by firms:

- ◆ If I increase my price, I will be on my own—others will not follow me.
- ◆ If I decrease my price, so will everyone else.

If these beliefs are correct, a firm faces a demand curve for its product that has a kink occurring at the current price, *P*, as shown in Fig. 13.4. At prices above *P*, the demand curve is relatively elastic. It reflects the belief that if the firm increases its price, it will be out of line with all other firms and so will experience a large fall in the quantity demanded. At prices below *P*, the demand curve is less elastic. It reflects the belief that if the firm cuts its price, all other firms will match the price cut and so will experience a small increase in the quantity demanded. This increase in the quantity demanded will not be as large as the decrease in the quantity demanded resulting from a price rise.

The kink in demand curve *D* creates a break in the marginal revenue curve (*MR*). To maximize profit, the firm produces the quantity that makes marginal cost and marginal revenue equal. But that output, *Q*, is where the marginal cost curve passes through the discontinuity in the marginal revenue curve—the gap *ab*. If marginal cost fluctuates between *a* and *b*, an example of which is shown in the figure with the marginal cost curves MC_0 and MC_1, the firm will change neither its price nor its quantity of output. Only if marginal cost fluctuates outside the range *ab* will the firm change its price and quantity produced.

Thus the kinked demand curve model predicts that price and quantity will be insensitive to small cost changes but will respond if cost changes are large enough. But there are two problems with the

FIGURE 13.4
The Kinked Demand Curve Model

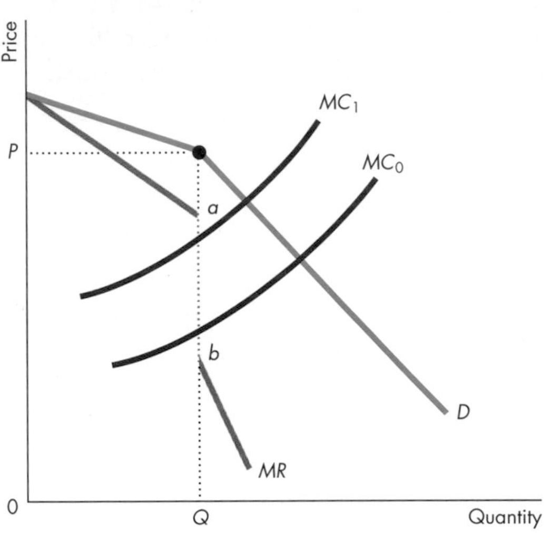

The price in an oligopoly market is *P*. Each firm believes that it faces the demand curve *D*. At prices above *P*, demand is highly elastic because the firm believes that its price increases will not be matched by other firms. At prices below *P*, demand is less elastic because the firm believes that its price cuts will be matched. Because the demand curve is kinked, the marginal revenue curve, *MR*, has a break, *ab*. Profit is maximized by producing *Q*. The marginal cost curve passes through the break in the marginal revenue curve. Marginal cost changes inside the range *ab* leave the price and quantity unchanged.

kinked demand curve model:

- It does not tell us how the price, *P*, is determined.
- It does not tell us what happens if firms discover that their belief about the demand curve is incorrect.

Suppose, for example, that marginal cost increases by enough to cause the firm to increase its price and that all firms experience the same increase in marginal cost so they all increase their prices together. Each firm bases its action on the belief that other firms will not match its price increase, but that belief is incorrect. The firm's beliefs are inconsistent with reality, and the demand and marginal revenue curves that summarize those beliefs are not the correct ones for the purpose of calculating the new profit-maximizing price and output. A firm that bases its actions on beliefs that are wrong does not maximize profit and might well end up incurring a loss leading to its eventual exit from the industry.

The kinked demand curve model is an attempt to understand price and output determination in an oligopoly in which the firms are of similar size. Another traditional model deals with the case in which firms differ in size and one firm dominates the industry.

Dominant Firm Oligopoly

Suppose there are eleven firms operating gas stations in a city. Big-G is huge and controls 50 percent of all the city's gas sales. The others are small, accounting for only 5 percent of the city's gas sales each. The market for gas in this city is a type of oligopoly, but one with a dominant firm.

To see how the price and quantity of gas sales are determined, look at Fig. 13.5. Here, in part (a), the demand curve *D* tells us how the total quantity of gas demanded in the city is influenced by its price. The supply curve S_{10} is the supply curve of the ten small price-taking suppliers all added together.

Part (b) shows the situation facing Big-G, the dominant firm. Big-G's marginal cost curve is *MC*. The demand curve for gasoline facing Big-G is *XD*. This curve is found by working out the amount of excess demand arising from the rest of the market. It graphs the difference between the quantity demanded and the quantity supplied in the rest of the market at each price. Thus, for example, at a price of $1 a gallon, there is an excess demand in the rest of the market measured by the distance *ab* in part (a). That same distance *ab* at the price $1 a gallon, in part (b), provides us with one point, point *b*, on Big-G's demand curve, *XD*.

If Big-G sold gasoline in a perfectly competitive city gas market, it would be willing to supply the gas at the prices indicated by its marginal cost curve. The city market would operate at the point of intersection of Big-G's marginal cost curve and its demand curve. But Big-G can do better for itself than that. Because it controls 50 percent of the city's gas market, it can restrict its sales, decreasing the amount of gas available and increasing its price.

To maximize its profit, Big-G operates like a monopoly. It calculates the extra revenue obtained from selling one more gallon of gas—its marginal

FIGURE 13.5

A Dominant Firm Oligopoly

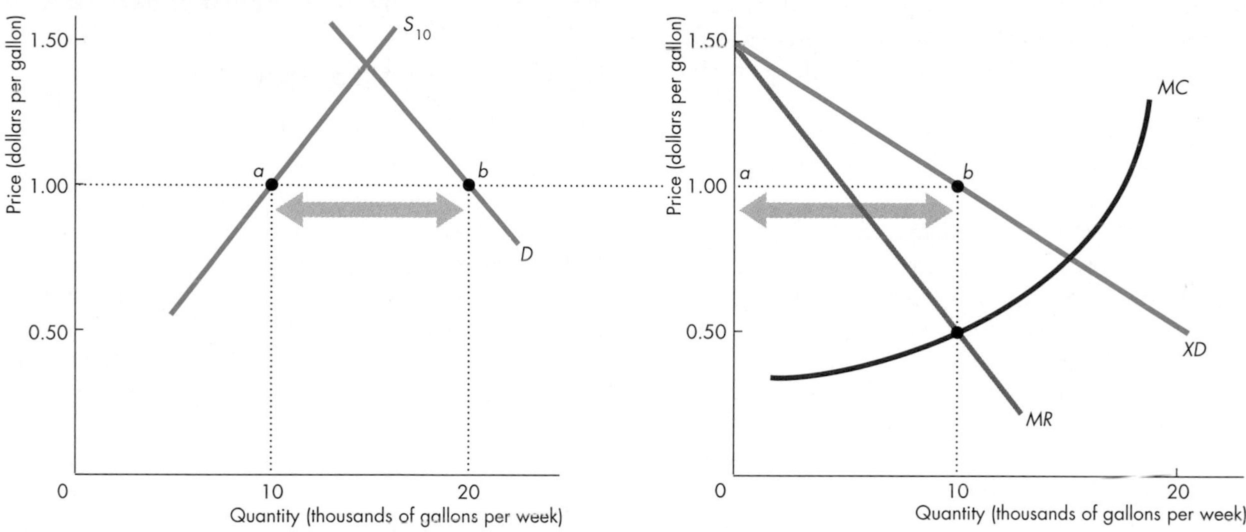

The demand curve for gas in a city is *D* in part (a). There are ten small firms that (taking all ten together) have a supply curve of S_{10} in part (a). In addition there is one large firm, Big-G, shown in part (b). Big-G faces the demand curve, *XD*, determined as market demand *D* minus the supply of the other firms, S_{10}—the excess demand not satisfied by the small firms. Big-G's marginal revenue is *MR* and marginal cost is *MC*. Big-G sets the price to maximize profit by equating marginal cost, *MC*, and marginal revenue, *MR*. The price is $1 a gallon. Big-G sells 10 thousand gallons, and the other 10 firms sell 1 thousand gallons each.

revenue curve. It then sells the quantity that makes its marginal revenue equal to its marginal cost. Thus it sells 10 thousand gallons of gas for $1 a gallon. This combination of price and quantity of sales gives Big-G the biggest possible profit. The quantity of gas demanded in the entire city at $1 a gallon is 20 thousand gallons, as shown in part (a). The additional 10 thousand gallons are sold by 10 small firms that sell 1 thousand gallons each.

REVIEW

Oligopoly is a market in which a small number of interdependent producers compete with each other. The profit of any one producer depends on the prices charged by that producer and all the other producers. So any theory of oligopoly must contain an account of how firms react to each other's price changes. One traditional theory is based on the kinked demand curve model. This model assumes that if a firm increases its price, no other firm will follow, while if a firm decreases its price, so will all the other firms. Given these assumptions, each firm faces a kinked demand curve for its product and the kink occurs at the current price and quantity. The kink creates a break in the marginal revenue curve and a range over which marginal cost can vary without causing a change in the profit-maximizing price. Hence prices are sticky. Another traditional oligopoly model deals with an industry in which one firm dominates. The dominant firm acts like a monopoly and sets its profit-maximizing price. The other firms take this price as given and act like competitive firms. ◆

The dominant firm model of oligopoly works for some markets in which there really is a dominant producer. But even in such markets, it does not explain why sometimes the dominant firm tries to drive the smaller firms out of business rather than just putting up with their competition. Also it is of no help in predicting prices and quantities in markets in which firms are of similar size. The kinked demand curve model is an attempt to deal with this alternative case. But, as we've seen, that model has some weaknesses.

The weaknesses of traditional theories and a widespread dissatisfaction with them are the main forces leading to the development of new oligopoly models based on game theory.

The situation faced by firms in an oligopolistic industry is not unlike that faced by military planners. For example, in deciding whether to launch an attack on Iraq in the winter of 1991, U.S. military planners had to take into account the effects of U.S. actions on the behavior of Iraq. Would Iraq counter with chemical-laden SCUD missiles against Israel? Similarly, in making its plans, Iraq had to take into account the reactions of the United States—and in this case Israel. Neither side can assume that its rival's behavior will be independent of its own actions.

Whether we're studying price wars or star wars, we need a method of analyzing choices that takes into account the interactions between agents. Such a method has been developed and is called game theory.

Oligopoly and Game Theory

A **game theory** is a method of analyzing strategic behavior. Acting in a way that takes into account the expected behavior of others and the mutual recognition of interdependence is called **strategic behavior**. Game theory was invented by John von Neumann in 1937 and extended by von Neumann and Oskar Morgenstern in 1944. It is the topic of a massive amount of current research in economics.

Game theory seeks to understand oligopoly as well as political and social rivalries by using a method of analysis specifically designed to understand games of all types, including the familiar games of everyday life. We will begin our study of game theory, and its application to the behavior of firms, by considering those familiar games.

Familiar Games: What They Have in Common

What is a game? At first thought, the question seems silly. After all, there are many different games. There are ball games and parlor games, games of chance and games of skill. What do games of such diversity and variety have in common? In answering this question, we will focus on those features of games that are relevant and important for game theory and for analyzing oligopoly as a game. All games have three things in common:

- Rules
- Strategies
- Payoffs

Let's see how these common features of ordinary games apply to oligopoly.

Rules of the Oligopoly Game

The rules of the oligopoly game have not been written down by the "National Oligopoly League." They arise from the economic, social, and political environment in which the oligopolists operate.

One rule of the oligopoly game is the number of players—the number of firms in the market. Another rule is the method of calculating the score. This rule states that the score of each player is the player's economic profit or loss. The goal of each player of the oligopoly game is to make the largest possible profit. The remaining rules of the oligopoly game are determined by the framework of laws within which the oligopolists are operating. Oligopolists' actions are restricted only by the legal code.

Strategies in the Oligopoly Game

In game theory as in ordinary games, **strategies** are all the possible actions of each player. A comprehensive list of strategies in the oligopoly game would be very long, but it would include, for each player, such actions as:

- Raise price, lower price, hold price constant

- Raise output, lower output, hold output constant
- Increase advertising, cut advertising, hold advertising constant
- Enhance features of product, simplify product, leave product unchanged

Payoffs in the Oligopoly Game

In game theory, the score of each player is called the **payoff.** In the oligopoly game, the payoffs are the profits and losses of the players. These payoffs are determined by the oligopolists' strategies and by the constraints that they face. Constraints come from customers who determine the demand curve for the product of the oligopoly industry, from the technology available, and from the prices of the resources used by the oligopolists.

To understand how an oligopoly game works, it is revealing to study a special case of oligopoly called duopoly. **Duopoly** is a market structure in which there are two producers of a commodity competing with each other. There are few cases of duopoly on a national and international scale but many cases of local duopolies. For example, in some communities, there are two suppliers of milk, two local newspapers, two taxi companies, or two car rental firms. But the main reason for studying duopoly is not its "realism" but the fact that it captures all the essential features of oligopoly and yet is more manageable to analyze and understand. Furthermore, there is a well-known game called "the prisoners' dilemma" that captures some of the essential features of duopoly. It provides a good illustration of how game theory works and how it leads to predictions about the behavior of the players. Let's now turn our attention to studying a duopoly game, beginning with the prisoners' dilemma.

The Prisoners' Dilemma

Abe and Bob have been caught red-handed stealing a car. Facing airtight cases, they will receive a sentence of 2 years each for their crime. During his interviews with the two prisoners, the district attorney begins to suspect that he has stumbled on the two people who were responsible for a multimillion-dollar bank robbery some months earlier. The district attorney also knows, however, that this is just a suspicion. He has no evidence on which he can convict them of the greater crime unless he can get each of them to confess. The district attorney comes up with the following idea.

He places the prisoners in separate rooms so that they cannot communicate with each other. Each prisoner is told that he is suspected of having carried out the bank robbery and that if he and his accomplice both confess to that crime, each will receive a sentence of 3 years. Each is also told that if he alone confesses and his accomplice does not, he will receive an even shorter sentence of 1 year while his accomplice will receive a 10-year sentence. The prisoners know that if neither of them confesses, then they will be tried for and convicted of only the lesser offense of car theft, which carries a 2-year prison term. How do the prisoners respond to the district attorney?

First, notice that the prisoners' dilemma is a game with two players. Each player has two strategies: to confess to the multimillion-dollar bank robbery or to deny the charge. Because there are two players, each with two strategies, there are four possible outcomes:

1. Neither player confesses.
2. Both players confess.
3. Abe confesses but Bob does not.
4. Bob confesses but Abe does not.

Each prisoner can work out exactly what will happen to him—his payoff—in each of these four situations. We can tabulate the four possible payoffs for each of the prisoners in what is called a payoff matrix for the game.

The Payoff Matrix A **payoff matrix** is a table that shows the payoffs for every possible action by each player for every possible action by each other player.

Table 13.3 shows a payoff matrix for Abe and Bob. The squares show the payoffs for each prisoner—the red triangle in each square shows Abe's and the blue triangle shows Bob's. If both prisoners confess (top left), each gets a prison term of 3 years. If Bob confesses but Abe denies (top right), Abe gets a 10-year sentence and Bob gets a 1-year sentence. If Abe confesses and Bob denies (bottom left), Abe gets a 1-year sentence and Bob gets a 10-year sentence. Finally, if both of them deny (bottom right), neither can be convicted of the bank robbery charge but both are sentenced for the car theft—a 2-year sentence.

TABLE 13.3

Prisoners' Dilemma Payoff Matrix

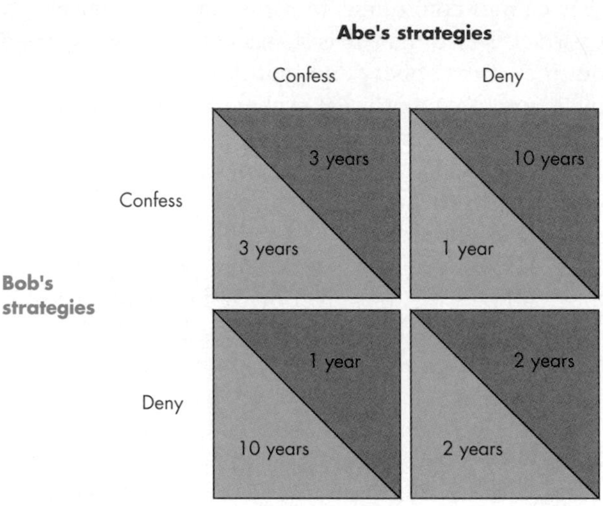

Each square shows the payoffs for the two players, Abe and Bob, for each possible pair of actions. In each square, Abe's payoff is shown in the red triangle and Bob's in the blue triangle. For example, if both confess, the payoffs are in the top left square. Abe reasons as follows: If Bob confesses, it pays me to confess because then I get 3 years rather than 10. If Bob denies, it pays me to confess because then I get 1 year rather than 2. Regardless of what Bob does, it pays me to confess. Thus Abe's dominant strategy is to confess. Bob reasons similarly: If Abe confesses, it pays me to confess and get 3 years rather than 10. If Abe denies, it pays me to confess and get 1 year rather than 2. Thus Bob's dominant strategy is to confess. Since each player's dominant strategy is to confess, the equilibrium of the game is for both players to confess and to get 3 years each.

The Dilemma The dilemma is seen by considering the consequences of confessing and not confessing. Each prisoner knows that if he and his accomplice remain silent about the bank robbery, they will be sentenced to only 2 years for stealing the car. Neither prisoner, however, has any way of knowing that his accomplice will remain silent and refuse to confess. Each knows that if the other confesses and he denies, the other will receive only a 1-year sentence while the one denying will receive a 10-year sentence. Each poses the following questions: Should I deny and rely on my accomplice to deny so that we may both get only 2 years? Or should I confess in the hope of getting just 1 year (provided that my accomplice denies) but knowing that if my accomplice does confess, we will both get 3 years in prison? Resolving the dilemma involves finding the equilibrium for the game.

Equilibrium The equilibrium of a game is called a Nash equilibrium; it is so named because it was first proposed by John Nash. A **Nash equilibrium** occurs when player *A* takes the best possible action given the action of player *B* and player *B* takes the best possible action given the action of player *A*. In the case of the prisoners' dilemma, the equilibrium occurs when Abe makes his best choice given Bob's choice and when Bob makes his best choice given Abe's choice.

The prisoners' dilemma is a game that has a special kind of Nash equilibrium called a dominant strategy equilibrium. A **dominant strategy** is a strategy that is the same regardless of the action taken by the other player. In other words, there is a unique best action regardless of what the other player does. A **dominant strategy equilibrium** occurs when there is a dominant strategy for each player. In the prisoners' dilemma, no matter what Bob does, Abe's best strategy is to confess; and no matter what Abe does, Bob's best strategy is to confess. Thus the equilibrium of the prisoners' dilemma is that each player confesses.

If each prisoner plays the prisoners' dilemma game in his own individual best interest, the outcome of the game will be that each confesses. To see why each player confesses, let's consider again their strategies and the payoffs from the alternative courses of action.

Strategies and Payoffs Look at the situation from Abe's point of view. Abe realizes that his outcome depends on the action Bob takes. If Bob confesses, it pays Abe to confess also, because in that case, he will be sentenced to 3 years rather than 10 years. But if Bob does not confess, it still pays Abe to confess, because in that case he will receive 1 year rather than 2 years. Abe reasons that regardless of Bob's action, his own best action is to confess.

The dilemma from Bob's point of view is identical to Abe's. Bob knows that if Abe confesses, he will receive 10 years if he does not confess or 3 years if he does. Therefore, if Abe confesses, it pays Bob to confess. Similarly, if Abe does not confess, Bob will receive 2 years for not confessing and 1 year if he confesses. Again, it pays Bob to confess. Bob's best action, regardless of Abe's action, is to confess.

Each prisoner sees that regardless of what the other prisoner does, his own best action is to confess. Since each player's best action is to confess, each confesses, each gets a 3-year prison term, and the district attorney has solved the bank robbery. This is the equilibrium of the game.

A Bad Outcome For the prisoners, the equilibrium of the game, with each confessing, is not the best outcome. If neither of them confesses, each will get only 2 years for the lesser crime. Isn't there some way in which this better outcome can be achieved? It seems that there is not, because the players cannot communicate with each other. Each player can put himself in the other player's place, and so each player can figure out that there is a dominant strategy for each of them. The prisoners are indeed in a dilemma. Each knows that he can serve 2 years only if he can trust the other not to confess. Each prisoner also knows, however, that it is not in the best interest of the other to not confess. Thus each prisoner knows that he has to confess, thereby delivering a bad outcome for both.

Let's now see how we can use the ideas we've just developed to understand price fixing, price wars, and the behavior of duopolists.

A Duopoly Game

To study a duopoly game, we're going to build a model of a duopoly industry.[1] Suppose that only two firms, Trick and Gear, make a particular kind of electric switchgear. Our goal is to make predictions about the prices charged and the outputs produced by each of the two firms. We are going to pursue that goal by constructing a duopoly game that the two firms will play. To set out the game, we need to specify the strategies of the players and the payoff matrix.

We will suppose that the two firms enter into a collusive agreement. A **collusive agreement** is an agreement between two (or more) producers to restrict output in order to raise prices and profits. Such an agreement is illegal and is undertaken in secret. A group of firms that has entered into a collusive agreement to restrict output and increase prices and profits is called a **cartel**. The strategies that firms in a cartel can pursue are to:

- Comply
- Cheat

Complying simply means sticking to the agreement. Cheating means breaking the agreement in a manner designed to benefit the cheating firm and harm the other firm.

Since each firm has two strategies, there are four possible combinations of actions for the two firms:

- Both firms comply.
- Both firms cheat.
- Trick complies and Gear cheats.
- Gear complies and Trick cheats.

We need to work out the payoffs to each firm from each of these four possible sets of actions. To do that, we need to explore the costs and demand conditions in the industry.

Cost and Demand Conditions

The cost of producing switchgears is the same for both Trick and Gear. The average total cost curve (*ATC*) and the marginal cost curve (*MC*) for each firm are shown in Fig. 13.6(a). The market demand curve for switchgears (*D*) is shown in Fig. 13.6(b). Each firm produces an identical switchgear product, so one firm's switchgear is a perfect substitute for the other's. The market price of each firm's product, therefore, is identical. The quantity demanded depends on that price—the higher the price, the lower is the quantity demanded.

Notice that in this industry, there is room for only two firms. For each firm, the *minimum efficient scale* of production is 3,000 switchgear units a week. When the price equals the average total cost of production at the minimum efficient scale, total industry demand is 6,000 switchgear units a week. Thus there is no room for three firms in this industry. If there were only one firm in the industry, it would make an enormous profit and invite competition. If there were three firms, at least one of them would make a loss. Thus the number of firms that an

[1]The model is inspired by a real-world case known as "the incredible electrical conspiracy," which we examine below. But don't lose sight of the fact that what follows is a *model*. It is not a description of a real historical episode.

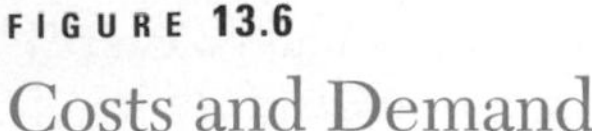

FIGURE 13.6

Costs and Demand

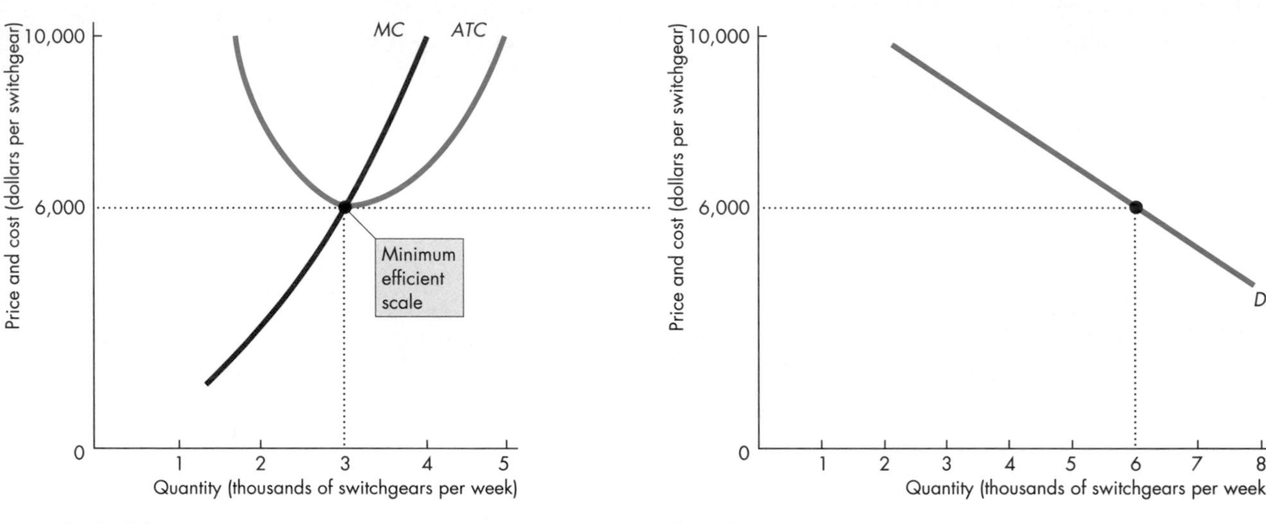

Part (a) shows the costs facing Trick and Gear, two duopolists that make switchgears. Each firm faces identical costs. The average total cost curve for each firm is *ATC*, and the marginal cost curve is *MC*. For each firm, the minimum efficient scale of production is 3,000 units per week and the average total cost of producing that output is $6,000 a unit. Part (b) shows the industry demand curve. At a price of $6,000, the quantity demanded is 6,000 units per week. There is room for only two firms in this industry.

industry can sustain depends on the relationship between cost and the industry's demand conditions.

In the model industry that we're studying here, the particular cost and demand conditions assumed are designed to generate an industry in which two firms can survive in the long run. In real-world oligopoly and duopoly, barriers to entry may arise from economies of scale of the type featured in our model industry, but there are other possible barriers as well (as discussed in Chapter 12, p. 314).

Colluding to Maximize Profits

Let's begin by working out the payoffs to the two firms if they collude to make the maximum industry profit—the profit that would be made by a single monopoly. The calculations that the two firms will perform are exactly the same calculations that a monopoly performs. (You have already studied such calculations in Chapter 12, pp. 314–315.) The only additional thing that the duopolists have to do is to agree on how much of the total output each of them will produce.

The price and quantity that maximize industry profit for the duopolists are shown in Fig. 13.7. Part (a) shows the situation for each firm, and part (b) for the industry as a whole. The curve labeled *MR* is the industry marginal revenue curve. The curve labeled MC_I is the industry marginal cost curve if each firm produces the same level of output. That curve is constructed by adding together the outputs of the two firms at each level of marginal cost. That is, at each level of marginal cost, industry output is twice as much as the output of each individual firm. Thus the curve MC_I in part (b) is twice as far to the right as the curve *MC* in part (a).

To maximize industry profit, the duopolists agree to restrict output to the rate that makes the industry marginal cost and marginal revenue equal. That output rate, as shown in part (b), is 4,000 switchgear units a week. The highest price for which the 4,000 units can be sold is $9,000 each. Let's suppose that

FIGURE 13.7

Colluding to Make Monopoly Profits

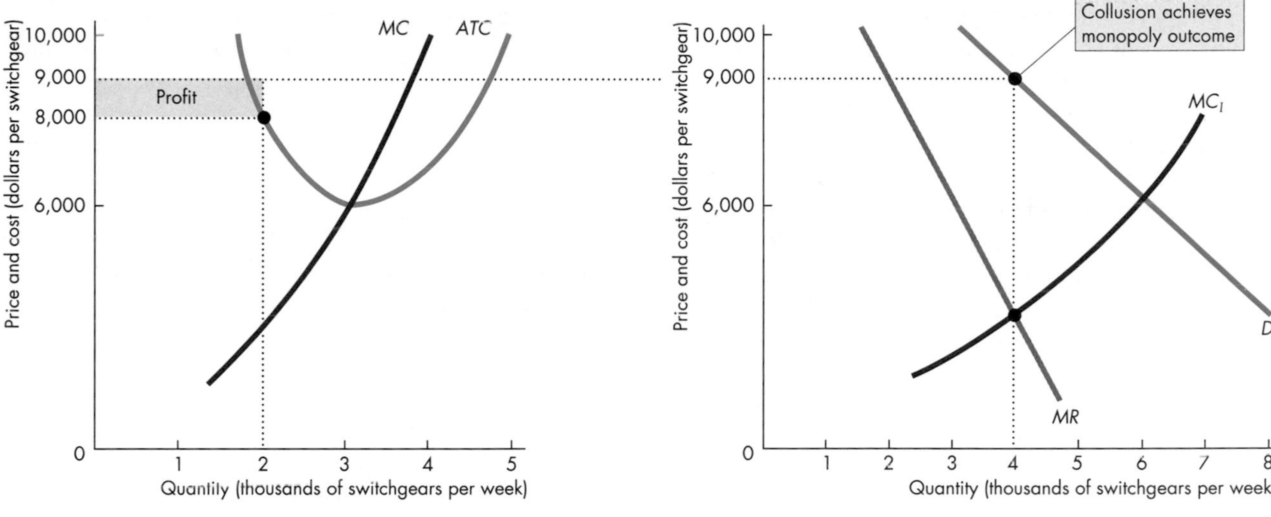

(a) Individual firm

(b) Industry

If Trick and Gear come to a collusive agreement, they can act as a single monopolist and maximize profit. Part (a) shows the consequences of reaching such an agreement for each firm, and part (b) shows the situation in the industry as a whole.

To maximize profit, the firms first calculate the industry marginal cost curve (MC_I) shown in part (b)—the horizontal sum of the two firms' marginal cost curves (MC) in part (a). Next they calculate the industry marginal revenue, MR in part (b). They then choose the output rate that makes marginal revenue equal to marginal cost (4,000 units per week). They agree to sell that output for a price of $9,000, the price at which 4,000 switchgear units are demanded.

The costs and profit of each firm are seen in part (a). Each firm produces half the total output—2,000 units per week. Average total cost is $8,000 per unit, so each firm makes a profit of $2 million (blue rectangle)—2,000 units multiplied by $1,000 profit per unit.

Trick and Gear agree to split the market equally so that each firm produces 2,000 switchgear units a week. The average total cost (ATC) of producing 2,000 units a week is $8,000, so the profit per unit is $1,000 and the total profit is $2 million (2,000 units × $1,000 per unit). The profit of each firm is represented by the blue rectangle in Fig. 13.7(a).

We have just described one possible outcome for the duopoly game: the two firms collude to produce the monopoly profit-maximizing output and divide that output equally between themselves. From the industry point of view, this solution is identical to a monopoly. A duopoly that operates in this way is indistinguishable from a monopoly. The profit that is made by a monopoly is the maximum profit that can be made by colluding duopolists.

Cheating on a Collusive Agreement

Under a collusive agreement, the colluding firms restrict output to make their joint marginal revenue equal to their joint marginal cost. They set the highest price for which the quantity produced can be sold—a price higher than marginal cost. In such a situation, each firm recognizes that if it cheats on the agreement and raises its output, even though the price will fall below that agreed to, more will be added to revenue than to cost, so its profit will increase. Since each firm recognizes this fact, there is a temptation for each firm to cheat. There are two possible cheating situations: one in which one firm cheats and one in which both firms cheat. What happens if one of the firms cheats on the agreement?

One Firm Cheats What is the effect of one firm cheating on a collusive agreement? How much extra profit does the cheating firm make? What happens to the profit of the firm that sticks to the agreement in the face of cheating by the other firm? Let's work out the answers to these questions.

There are many different ways for a firm to cheat. We will work out just one possibility. Suppose that Trick convinces Gear that there has been a fall in industry demand and that it cannot sell its share of the output at the agreed price. It tells Gear that it plans to cut its price in order to sell the agreed 2,000 switchgear units each week. Since the two firms produce a virtually identical product, Gear has no alternative but to match the price cut of Trick.

In fact, there has been no fall in demand, and the lower price has been calculated by Trick to be exactly the price needed to sell the additional output that it plans to produce. Gear, though lowering its price in line with that of Trick, restricts its output to the previously agreed level.

Figure 13.8 illustrates the consequences of Trick cheating in this way: part (a) shows what happens to Gear (the complier), part (b) shows what happens to Trick (the cheat), and part (c) shows what is happening in the industry as a whole.

Suppose that Trick decides to raise output from 2,000 to 3,000 units a week. It recognizes that if Gear sticks to the agreement to produce only 2,000 units a week, total output will be 5,000 a week and, given demand in part (c), the price will have to be cut to $7,500 a unit.

Gear continues to produce 2,000 units a week at a cost of $8,000 a unit and incurs a loss of $500 a unit, or $1 million a week. This loss is represented by the red rectangle in part (a). Trick produces 3,000 units a week at an average total cost of $6,000 each. With a price of $7,500, Trick makes a profit of $1,500 a unit and therefore a total profit of $4.5 million. This profit is the blue rectangle in part (b).

We have now described a second possible outcome for the duopoly game—one of the firms cheats on the collusive agreement. In this case, the industry output is larger than the monopoly output and the industry price is lower than the monopoly price. The

FIGURE 13.8

Cheating on a Collusive Agreement

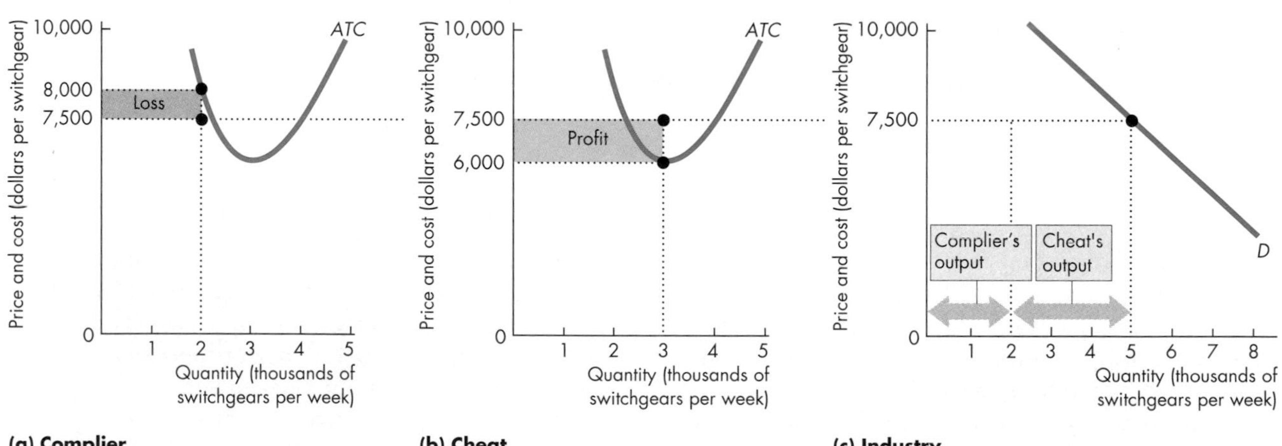

(a) Complier **(b) Cheat** **(c) Industry**

In part (a), one firm complies with the agreement. In part (b), the other firm cheats by raising output above the agreed limit to 3,000 switchgears per week. Either firm can be the complier and the other the cheat. In part (c), the effect on the industry price of the actions of the cheat is shown. As a result of cheating, industry output rises to 5,000 units a week and the market price falls to $7,500—the price at which 5,000 switchgear units can be sold.

Part (a) describes the complier's situation. Output remains at 2,000 units, and average total cost remains at $8,000 per unit. The firm loses $500 per switchgear and makes a total loss of $1 million (red rectangle). Part (b) describes the cheat's situation. Average total cost is $6,000 per unit, and profit per switchgear is $1,500, so the cheat's total profit is $4.5 million (blue rectangle).

total profit made by the industry is also smaller than the monopoly's profit. Trick (the cheat) makes a profit of $4.5 million, and Gear (the complier) incurs a loss of $1 million. The industry makes a profit of $3.5 million. Thus the industry profit is $0.5 million less than the maximum profit would be with a monopoly outcome. But that profit is distributed unevenly. Trick makes an even bigger profit than it would under the collusive agreement, while Gear makes a loss.

We have just worked out what happens if Trick cheats and Gear complies with the collusive agreement. There is another similar outcome that would arise if Gear cheated and Trick complied with the agreement. The industry profit and price would be the same, but in this case, Gear (the cheat) would make a profit of $4.5 million and Trick (the complier) would incur a loss of $1 million.

There is yet another possible outcome—both firms cheat on the agreement.

Both Firms Cheat Suppose that instead of just one firm cheating on the collusive agreement, both firms cheat. In particular, suppose that each firm behaves in exactly the same way as the cheating firm that we have just analyzed. Each firm tells the other that it is unable to sell its output at the going price and that it plans to cut its price. But since both firms cheat, each will propose a successively lower price. They will stop proposing lower prices only when the price has reached $6,000. That is the price that equals minimum average cost. At a price of less than $6,000, each firm will make a loss. At a price of $6,000, each firm will cover all its costs and make zero economic profit. Also, at a price of $6,000, each firm will want to produce 3,000 units a week, so the industry output will be 6,000 units a week. Given the demand conditions, 6,000 units can be sold at a price of $6,000 each.

The situation just described is illustrated in Fig. 13.9. Each firm, shown in part (a) of the figure, is

FIGURE 13.9

Both Firms Cheat

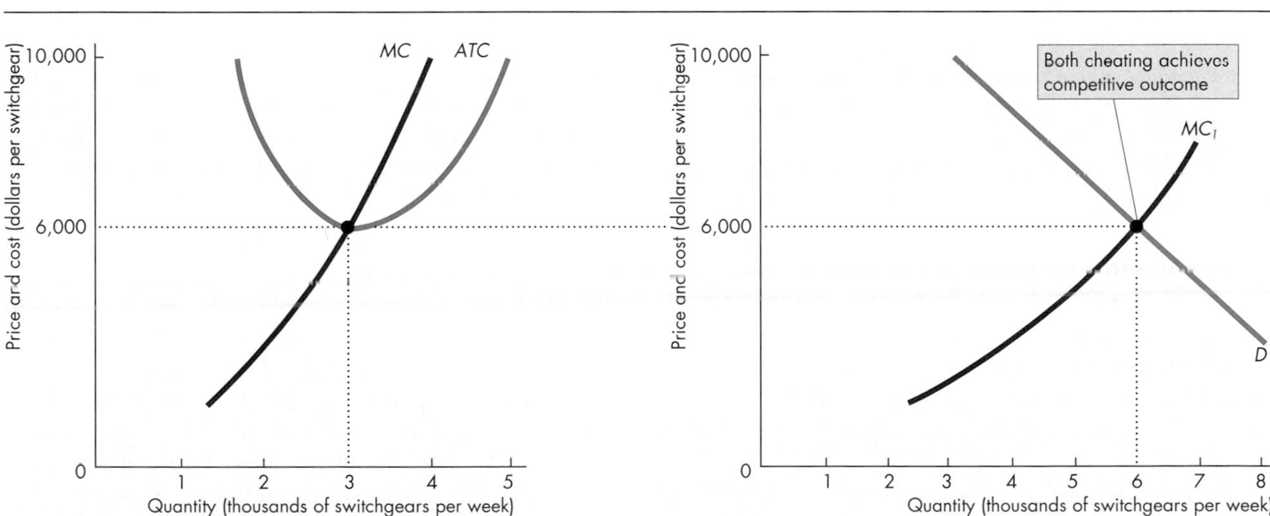

(a) Individual firm

(b) Industry

If both firms cheat by raising their output and lowering the price, the collusive agreement completely breaks down. The limit to the breakdown of the agreement is the competitive equilibrium. Neither firm will want to cut the price below $6,000 (minimum average total cost), because to do so will result in losses. Part (a) shows the situation facing each firm. At a price of $6,000, the firm's profit-maximizing output is 3,000 units per week. At that output rate, price equals marginal cost, and it also equals average total cost. Economic profit is zero. Part (b) describes the situation in the industry as a whole. The industry marginal cost curve (MC_I)—the horizontal sum of the individual firms' marginal cost curves (MC)—intersects the demand curve at 6,000 switchgear units per week and at a price of $6,000. This output and price are the ones that would prevail in a competitive industry.

producing 3,000 units a week, and this output level occurs at the point of minimum average total cost ($6,000 per unit). The market as a whole, shown in part (b), operates at the point at which the demand curve (*D*) intersects the industry marginal cost curve. This marginal cost curve is constructed as the horizontal sum of the marginal cost curves of the two firms. Each firm has lowered its price and increased its output in order to try to gain an advantage over the other firm. They have pushed this process as far as they can without incurring losses.

We have now described a third possible outcome of this duopoly game—both firms cheat. If both firms cheat on the collusive agreement, the output of each firm is 3,000 units a week and the price is $6,000. Each firm makes zero profit.

The Payoff Matrix and Equilibrium

Now that we have described the strategies and the payoffs in the duopoly game, let's summarize the strategies and the payoffs in the form of the game's payoff matrix and then calculate the equilibrium.

Table 13.4 sets out the payoff matrix for this game. It is constructed in exactly the same way as the payoff matrix for the prisoners' dilemma in Table 13.3. The squares show the payoffs for the two firms—Gear and Trick. In this case, the payoffs are profits. (In the case of the prisoners' dilemma, the payoffs were losses.)

The table shows that if both firms cheat (top left), they achieve the perfectly competitive outcome—each firm makes zero economic profit. If both firms comply (bottom right), the industry makes the monopoly profit and each firm earns a profit of $2 million. The top right and bottom left squares show what happens if one firm cheats while the other complies. The firm that cheats collects a profit of $4.5 million, and the one that complies makes a loss of $1 million.

This duopoly game is, in fact, the same as the prisoners' dilemma that we examined earlier in this chapter; it is a duopolist's dilemma. You will see this once you have determined what the equilibrium of this game is.

To find the equilibrium, let's look at things from the point of view of Gear. Gear reasons as follows: Suppose that Trick cheats. If we comply with the agreement, we make a loss of $1 million. If we also cheat, we make a zero profit. Zero profit is better than a $1 million loss, so it will pay us to cheat. But suppose Trick complies with the agreement. If we cheat, we will make a profit of $4.5 million, and if we comply, we will make a profit of $2 million. A $4.5 million profit is better than a $2 million profit, so it would again pay us to cheat. Thus, regardless of whether Trick cheats or complies, it pays us to cheat. Gear's dominant strategy is to cheat.

Trick comes to the same conclusion as Gear. Therefore both firms will cheat. The equilibrium of this game, then, is that both firms cheat on the agreement. Although there are only two firms in the industry, the price and quantity are the same as in a competitive industry. Each firm makes zero profit.

Although we have done this analysis for only two firms, it would not make any difference (other than to increase the amount of arithmetic) if we were to

TABLE 13.4

Duopoly Payoff Matrix

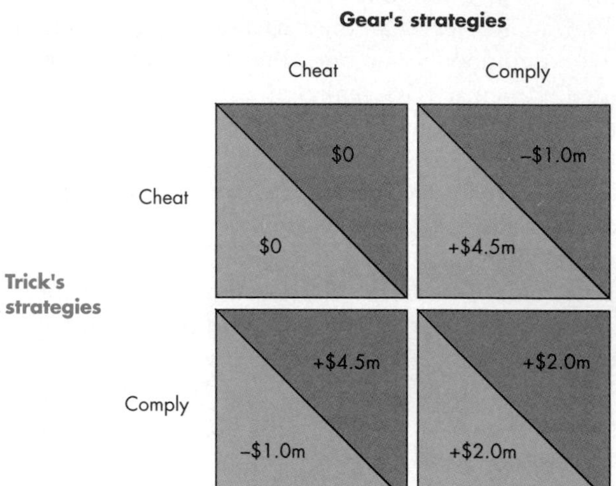

Each square shows the payoffs from a pair of actions. For example, if both firms comply with the collusive agreement, the payoffs are recorded in the square at the bottom right corner of the table. Gear's payoff is shown in the red triangle and Trick's in the blue triangle. Gear reasons as follows: If Trick cheats, it pays me to cheat and make a zero economic profit rather than a $1 million loss. If Trick complies, it pays me to cheat and make a $4.5 million profit rather than a $2 million profit. Thus cheating is Gear's dominant strategy. Trick reasons similarly: If Gear cheats, it pays me to cheat and make a zero profit rather than a $1 million loss. If Gear complies, it pays me to cheat and make a $4.5 million profit rather than a $2 million profit. The equilibrium is a Nash equilibrium in which both firms cheat.

play the game with three, four, or more firms. In other words, though we have analyzed duopoly, the game theory approach can also be used to analyze oligopoly. The analysis of oligopoly is much harder, but the essential ideas that we have learned apply to oligopoly.

Repeated Games

The first game that we studied, the prisoners' dilemma, was played just once. The prisoners did not have an opportunity to observe the outcome of the game and then play it again. The duopolist game just described was also played only once. But real-world duopolists do get opportunities to play repeatedly against each other. This fact suggests that real-world duopolists might find some way of learning to cooperate so that their efforts to collude are more effective.

If a game is played repeatedly, one player always has the opportunity to penalize the other player for previous "bad" behavior. If Trick refuses to cooperate this week, then Gear can refuse to cooperate next week (and vice versa). If Gear cheats this week, won't Trick cheat next week? Before Gear cheats this week, shouldn't it take account of the possibility of Trick cheating next week?

What is the equilibrium of this more complicated prisoners' dilemma game when it is repeated indefinitely? Actually, there is more than one possibility. One is the Nash equilibrium that we have just analyzed. Both players cheat, and each makes zero profit forever. In such a situation, it will never pay one of the players to start complying unilaterally, because to do so would result in a loss for that player and a profit for the other. The price and quantity will remain at the competitive levels forever.

But another equilibrium is possible—one in which the players make and share the monopoly profit. How might this equilibrium come about? Why wouldn't it always pay each firm to try to get away with cheating? The key to answering this question is the fact that when a prisoners' dilemma game is played repeatedly, the players have an increased array of strategies. Each player can punish the other player for previous actions.

There are two extremes of punishment. The smallest penalty that one player can impose on the other is what is called "tit for tat." A **tit-for-tat strategy** is one in which a player cooperates in the current period if the other player cooperated in the previous period but cheats in the current period if the other player cheated in the previous period. The most severe form of punishment that one player can impose on the other arises in what is called a trigger strategy. A **trigger strategy** is one in which a player cooperates if the other player cooperates but plays the Nash equilibrium strategy forever thereafter if the other player cheats. Since a tit-for-tat strategy and a trigger strategy are the extremes of punishment—the most mild and most severe—there are evidently other intermediate degrees of punishment. For example, if one player cheats on the agreement, the other player could punish by refusing to cooperate for a certain number of periods. In the duopoly game between Gear and Trick, it turns out that a tit-for-tat strategy keeps both players cooperating and earning monopoly profits. Let's see why.

Table 13.5 sets out the profits that each firm will make in each period of play under two sets of condi-

TABLE 13.5

Repeated Duopoly Game

	Collude		Cheat with tit-for-tat strategy	
Period of play	Trick's profit (millions of dollars)	Gear's profit (millions of dollars)	Trick's profit (millions of dollars)	Gear's profit (millions of dollars)
1	**2**	**2**	**2.0**	**2.0**
2	**2**	**2**	**4.5**	**–1.0**
3	**2**	**2**	**–1.0**	**4.5**
4	**2**	**2**	**2.0**	**2.0**
.	.	.	.	.
.	.	.	.	.
.	.	.	.	.

If duopolists repeatedly play the "cooperate" strategy, each makes $2 million in each period. If one player cheats in one period, the other player cheats in the following period—tit for tat. The profit from cheating can be made only for a single period. In the following period, the other player cheats and the first player must cooperate if the cooperative agreement is to be restored in period 4. The profit from cheating, calculated over four periods of play, is lower than that from colluding. Under collusion, each player makes $8 million; with a single cheat responded to with a tit for tat, each makes a profit of $7.5 million. It pays each player to cooperate, so cooperation is an equilibrium.

tions: first, if they cooperate, and second, if cheating is responded to with a tit-for-tat strategy. As you can see, as long as both firms stick to the collusive agreement, they make the monopoly profit ($2 million per period each). Suppose that Trick contemplates cheating in period 2. The cheating produces a quick $4.5 million profit and inflicts a $1 million loss on Gear. The next period, Gear will hit Trick with its tit-for-tat response and cheat. If Trick reverts to cooperating (to induce Gear to cooperate in period 4), Gear now makes a profit of $4.5 million and Trick makes a loss of $1 million. Adding up the profits over two periods of play, Trick comes out ahead by cheating ($6.5 million compared with $4 million). But if we run the game forward for four periods, Trick would be better off having cooperated. In that case, it would have made $8 million in profit compared with $7.5 million from cheating and generating Gear's tit-for-tat response.

Though we have just worked out what happens if Trick cheats, we can turn the tables and perform the same thought experiment for Gear cheating. We will come up with the same conclusion—it pays Gear to collude. Since it pays both firms to stick with the collusive agreement, both firms will do so and the monopoly price, quantity, and profit will prevail in the industry. This equilibrium is called a **cooperative equilibrium**—an equilibrium resulting from each player responding rationally to the credible threat of the other player to inflict heavy damage if the agreement is broken. But in order for this strategy to work, the threat must be credible—that is, each player must recognize that it is in the interest of the other player to respond with a "tit for tat." The tit-for-tat strategy is credible because if one player cheats, it clearly does not pay the other player to continue complying. So the threat of cheating next period is credible and sufficient to support the monopoly equilibrium outcome.

REVIEW

Game theory, a method of analyzing actions that takes into account the expected reactions of others, is a tool that can be used to explain the behavior of oligopolists. A classic game, the prisoners' dilemma, explains the behavior of duopolists. Two firms form a cartel to charge the same price as a monopoly would charge and share the monopoly profit. Each firm may either comply with the agreement or break it. If the game is played just once, both firms break the agreement. The price is competed down to the competitive level and profits are competed away. If the game is played repeatedly, cheating can be punished and this threat enables the duopolists to make the monopoly price stick and share the monopoly profit. ◆

Uncertainty

In reality, there are random fluctuations in demand and in costs that make it impossible for one firm to detect whether the other firm is cheating. For example, a fall in demand can lower the industry price. One firm increasing its output can also lower the industry price. If a firm observes only that the industry price has fallen, it cannot tell which of these forces caused it. If it knows that the price has fallen because of a fall in demand, its profit-maximizing action will be to continue cooperating with the other firm to maintain the monopoly agreement. But if the price fall resulted from the other firm cheating and increasing its output, the profit-maximizing response will be to hit the other firm with a tit for tat in the next period. Yet by observing only the price fall, neither firm can tell whether the other firm has cheated. What can the firms do in a situation such as this one?

If each always *assumes* that whenever the price falls it is because the other firm has cheated, the monopoly agreement will repeatedly break down and the firms will fail to realize the potentially available monopoly profits. If, on the other hand, one firm assumes that the other firm is always cooperating and that any price falls have resulted from market forces beyond the control of either firm, then that other firm will have an incentive to cheat. (Recall that with one firm cheating and the other cooperating, the cheat makes even bigger profits than when they both cooperate.) To remove that incentive to cheat, each firm will assume that the other is cooperating, provided that the price does not fall by more than a certain amount. If the price does fall below that predetermined amount, each firm will react as if the other firm had cheated. When market forces take the price back up above the critical level, the firms will cooperate again.

Games and Price Wars

Let's see whether the theory of price and output determination under duopoly can help us understand real-world behavior and, in particular, price wars. Suppose that two (or more) producers reach a collusive agreement and set their prices at the monopoly profit-maximizing level. Let's also suppose that the agreement is enforced by each firm pursuing a strategy that involves cooperating unless the price falls below a certain critical level, as described above. Fluctuations in demand will lead to fluctuations in the industry price and output. Most of the time, these fluctuations are small, and the price does not fall far enough to make either firm depart from the agreement. When the price falls below the critical level, each firm responds by abandoning the agreement. What happens looks exactly like a price war. It is extremely unlikely that each firm abandons the agreement and lowers its price at exactly the same moment. But it appears as if one firm abandons the agreement and then the other abandons it in retaliation. But what is actually happening is that each firm is reacting to the large price fall in a manner that maintains the credibility of the threat to the other firm and that preserves the monopoly cooperative equilibrium in normal demand conditions. When demand increases again and market forces increase the price, the firms revert to their cooperative behavior, reaping the monopoly profit.

Thus there will be cycles of price wars and the restoration of collusive agreements. The behavior of prices and outputs in the oil industry can be explained by the type of game that you have just studied. The market for crude oil is dominated by the OPEC cartel. From time to time, to increase the price of oil, the cartel has agreed to production limits for each member. But also, from time to time, the agreements have broken down. Members of the cartel have exceeded their agreed production levels, and prices have fallen.

The Incredible Electrical Conspiracy

Price-fixing arrangements such as those we've just studied are illegal in the United States. This means that any conspiracies by firms to fix prices have to be undertaken in secrecy. As a result, we get to know about such agreements only after they have been cracked by the Justice Department.

One famous price-fixing arrangement, involving almost 30 firms, has been called "the incredible electrical conspiracy."[2] For most of the 1950s, 30 producers of electrical equipment, including such giants as General Electric and Westinghouse, fixed prices "on items ranging from $2 insulators to huge turbine generators costing several million dollars."[3]

Although the electrical equipment pricing conspiracy operated throughout the entire decade of the 1950s, the individual firms conspiring often changed. In particular, General Electric sometimes participated in the price-fixing agreement and sometimes dropped out, undercutting the agreed price and dragging down the industry price and profit in much the way that the model we've studied predicts.

Preserving Secrecy

Because collusion is illegal, one special problem that colluding firms face is hiding the fact of their collusion and preserving secrecy. "The incredible electrical conspiracy" provides a fascinating view of one way in which this problem has been solved. The particular device used in this conspiracy was called the "phases of the moon" pricing formula.

> [These pricing formulas were listed on] sheets of paper, each containing a half dozen columns of figures. . . . One group of columns established the bidding order of the seven switchgear manufacturers—a different company, each with its own code number, phasing into the priority position every two weeks (hence "phases of the moon"). A second group of columns, keyed into the company code numbers, established how much each company was to knock off the agreed-upon book price. For example, if it were No 1's (G.E.'s) turn to be low bidder at a certain number of dollars off book, then all Westinghouse (No 2), or Allis-Chalmers (No 3) had to do was look for their code number in the second group of columns to find how many dollars they were to bid *above* No 1. These bids would then

---

[2]Richard A. Smith, "The Incredible Electrical Conspiracy," Part I, *Fortune* (April 1961): 132; Part II, (May 1961): 161.

[3]James V. Koch, *Industrial Organization and Prices,* 2nd ed. (Englewood Cliffs, N.J.: Prentice-Hall, 1980): 423.

be fuzzed up by having a little added to them or taken away by companies 2, 3, etc. Thus, there was not even a hint that the winning bid had been collusively arrived at.[4]

Before stumbling on the "phases of the moon" papers, the Justice Department was having a very hard time proving conspiracy, but, with the formula in hand, it was able to put the conspiracy under the spotlight and end it.

Other Strategic Variables

We have focused here on firms that play a simple game and consider only two possible strategies (complying and cheating) concerning two variables (price and quantity produced). However, the approach that we have used can be extended to deal with a much wider range of choices facing firms. For example, a firm has to decide whether to enter or leave an industry; whether to mount an expensive advertising campaign; whether to modify its product; how reliable to make its product (the more reliable a product, usually, the more expensive it is to produce); whether to price discriminate and, if so, among which groups of customers and to what degree; and whether to undertake a large research and development (R&D) effort aimed at lowering production costs. All of these choices that firms make can be analyzed by using game theory. The basic method of analysis that you have studied can be applied to these problems by working out the payoff for each of the alternative strategies and then finding the equilibrium of the game. Let's look at an example—based on an important real-world case—of an R&D game.

An R&D Game in the Disposable Diaper Industry

Disposable diapers were first marketed in 1966. The two market leaders from the start of this industry have been Procter & Gamble (makers of Pampers) and Kimberly-Clark (makers of Huggies). Procter & Gamble has 60 to 70 percent of the total market, while Kimberly-Clark has 25 percent. The disposable diaper industry is fiercely competitive. When the product was first introduced in 1966, it had to be cost-effective in competition against reusable, laundered diapers. A massive research and development effort resulted in the development of machines that could make disposable diapers at a low enough cost to achieve that initial competitive edge. But, as the industry has matured, a large number of firms have tried to get into the business and take market share away from the two industry leaders, and the industry leaders themselves have battled against each other to maintain or increase their own market share.

The disposable diaper industry is one in which technological advances that result in small decreases in the average total cost of production can provide an individual firm with an enormous competitive advantage. The current machines can produce disposable diapers at a rate of 3,000 an hour—a rate that represents a tenfold increase on the output rate of just a decade earlier. The firm that develops and uses the least-cost technology gains a competitive edge, undercutting the rest of the market, increasing its market share, and increasing its profit. But the research and development effort that has to be undertaken to achieve even small cost reductions is itself very costly. This cost of research and development has to be deducted from the profit resulting from the increased market share that lower costs achieve. If no firm does R&D, every firm can be better off, but if one firm initiates the R&D activity, all must.

Each firm is in a research and development dilemma situation. Table 13.6 illustrates the dilemma (with hypothetical numbers) for the R&D game that Kimberly-Clark and Procter & Gamble are playing. Each firm has two strategies: to spend $25 million a year on R&D or to spend nothing on R&D. If neither firm spends on R&D, they make a joint profit of $100 million, $30 million for Kimberly-Clark and $70 million for Procter & Gamble (bottom right square in payoff matrix). If each firm conducts R&D, market shares are maintained but each firm's profit is lower, by the amount spent on R&D (top right square of payoff matrix). If Kimberly-Clark pays for R&D but Procter & Gamble does not, Kimberly-Clark gains a large part of Procter &

[4]Richard A. Smith, "The Incredible Electrical Conspiracy," Part II, *Fortune* (May 1961): 210.

TABLE 13.6
Pampers versus Huggies: An R&D Game

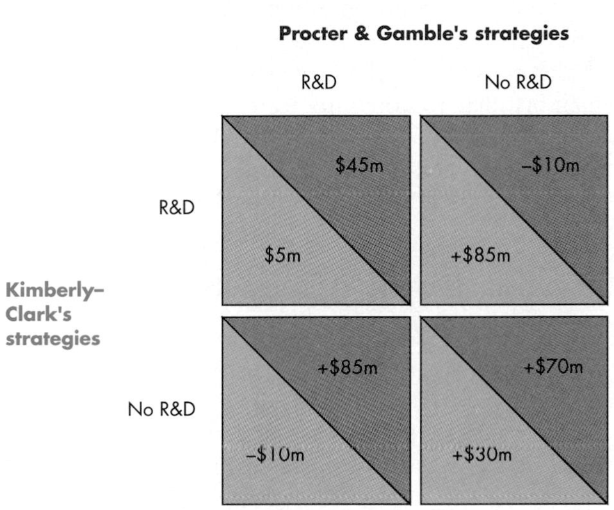

If both firms undertake R&D, their payoffs are those shown in the top left square. If neither firm undertakes R&D, their payoffs are in the bottom right square. When one firm undertakes R&D and the other one does not, their payoffs are in the top right and bottom left squares. The dominant strategy equilibrium for this game is for both firms to undertake R&D. The structure of this game is the same as that of the prisoners' dilemma.

Gamble's market. Kimberly-Clark profits, and Procter & Gamble loses (top right square of payoff matrix). Finally, if Procter & Gamble invests in R&D and Kimberly-Clark does not, Procter & Gamble gains market share from Kimberly-Clark, increasing its profit while Kimberly-Clark makes a loss.

Confronted with the payoff matrix in Table 13.6, the two firms calculate their best strategies. Kimberly-Clark reasons as follows: If Procter & Gamble does not undertake R&D, we make $85 million if we do and $30 million if we do not; therefore it pays to conduct R&D. If Procter & Gamble conducts R&D, we lose $10 million if we don't and make $5 million if we do. Again, R&D pays off. Thus conducting R&D is a dominant strategy for Kimberly-Clark. Doing it pays regardless of Procter & Gamble's decision.

Procter & Gamble reasons similarly: If Kimberly-Clark does not undertake R&D, we make $70 million if we follow suit and $85 million if we conduct R&D. It therefore pays to conduct R&D. If Kimberly-Clark does undertake R&D, we make $45 million by doing the same and lose $10 million by not doing R&D. Again, it pays to conduct R&D. So, for Procter & Gamble, R&D is also a dominant strategy.

Since R&D is a dominant strategy for both players, it is the Nash equilibrium. The outcome of this game is that both firms conduct R&D. They make lower profits than they would if they could collude to achieve the cooperative outcome of no R&D.

The real-world situation has more players than Kimberly-Clark and Procter & Gamble. There are a large number of other firms sharing a small portion of the market, all of them ready to eat into the market share of Procter & Gamble and Kimberly-Clark. So the R&D effort by these two firms not only serves the purpose of maintaining shares in their own battle, but also helps to keep barriers to entry high enough to preserve their joint market share.

◆ ◆ ◆ ◆ We have now studied the four main market types—perfect competition, monopolistic competition, oligopoly, and monopoly—and discovered how prices and outputs, revenue, cost, and profit are determined in these industries. We have used the various models to make predictions about behavior and to assess the efficiency of alternative market structures. ◆ ◆ A key element in our analysis of the markets for goods and services is the behavior of costs. Costs are determined partly by technology and partly by the prices of factors of production. We have treated those factor prices as given. We are now going to see how factor prices are themselves determined. Factor prices interact with the goods market that we have just studied in two ways. First, they determine the firm's production costs. Second, they determine household incomes and therefore influence the demand for goods and services. Factor prices also have an important effect upon the distribution of income. The firms that we've been studying in the past four chapters decide *how* to produce; the interactions of households and firms in the markets for goods and services decide *what* will be produced. But the factor prices determined in the markets for factors of production determine *for whom* the various goods and services are produced.

SUMMARY

Varieties of Market Structure

Most real-world industries lie between the extremes of perfect competition and monopoly. The degree of competition is sometimes measured by the four-firm concentration ratio—the percentage of the value of the sales of an industry accounted for by its four largest firms—or by the Herfindahl-Hirschman Index. High concentration ratios indicate a relatively low degree of competition, and vice versa, with some important qualifications. Three problems with concentration ratios are: (1) they refer to the national market, but some industries are local while others are international; (2) they do not tell us about the degree of turnover of firms and the ease of entry; and (3) some firms classified in one particular industry operate in several others. In the United States, most industries are effectively competitive, but there are important non-competitive elements.

Two models of industries that lie between monopoly and perfect competition are monopolistic competition and oligopoly. Monopolistic competition is a market type in which a large number of firms compete, each making a slightly differentiated product from the others by competing on price, quality, and advertising. Oligopoly is a market type in which a small number of firms compete with each other and in which the actions of any one firm have an important impact on the profit of the others. (pp. 342–346)

Monopolistic Competition

Monopolistic competition occurs when a large number of firms compete with each other by making slightly different products. Under monopolistic competition, each firm faces a downward-sloping demand curve and so has to choose its price as well as its output level. Because there is free entry, in long-run equilibrium zero economic profit is earned. When profit is maximized, with marginal cost equal to marginal revenue, average cost also equals price in the long run. But average cost is not at its minimum point. That is, in monopolistic competition, firms operate with excess capacity. (pp. 346–351)

Oligopoly

Oligopoly is a situation in which a small number of producers compete with each other. The key feature of oligopoly is that the firms strategically interact. Each firm has to take into account the effects of its own actions on the behavior of other firms and the effects of the actions of other firms on its own profit. (p. 351)

Traditional Models of Oligopoly

The kinked demand curve model of oligopoly is based on the assumption that each firm believes that its price cuts will be matched by its rivals but its price increases will not be matched. If these beliefs are correct, each firm faces a kinked demand curve for its product, the kink occurring at the current price, and has a break in its marginal revenue curve. To maximize profit, the firm produces the quantity that makes marginal cost and marginal revenue equal, an output level such that the marginal cost curve passes through the break in the marginal revenue curve. Fluctuations in marginal cost inside the range of the break in marginal revenue have no effects on either price or output.

The dominant firm model of oligopoly assumes that an industry consists of one large firm and a large number of small firms. The large firm acts like a monopoly and sets a profit-maximizing price. The small firms take this price as given and act like perfectly competitive firms. (pp. 351–354)

Oligopoly and Game Theory

Game theory is a method of analyzing strategic behavior. Game theory focuses on three aspects of a game:

- Rules
- Strategies
- Payoffs

The rules of the oligopoly game specify the permissible actions by the players. These actions are limited only by the legal code and involve such things as raising or lowering prices, raising or lowering output, increasing or cutting advertising, and enhancing or not enhancing the product. The strategies in the oligopoly game are all the possible actions that each player can take given the action of the other player. The payoff of the oligopoly game is the player's profit or loss. It depends on the actions of each player and on the constraints imposed by the market, technology, and input costs.

Duopoly is a market structure in which there are two producers of a good competing against each other. Duopoly is a special case of oligopoly. The duopoly game is similar to the prisoners' dilemma game. Two prisoners are faced with the problem of deciding whether or not to confess to a crime. If neither confesses, they are tried for a lesser crime and receive a light penalty. If both confess, they receive a higher penalty. If one confesses and the other does not confess, the one confessing receives the lightest of all penalties and the one not confessing receives a very heavy penalty.

The prisoners' dilemma has a dominant strategy Nash equilibrium. That is, regardless of the action of the other player, there is a unique best action for each player—to confess. (pp. 354–357)

A Duopoly Game

A duopoly game can be constructed in which two firms contemplate the consequences of colluding to achieve a monopoly profit or of cheating on the collusive agreement to make a bigger profit at the expense of the other firm. Such a game is identical to the prisoners' dilemma. The equilibrium of the game is one in which both firms cheat on the agreement. The industry output is the same in this case as it would be if the industry were perfectly competitive. The industry price is also the competitive price, and firms make zero economic profit. If the firms are able to enforce the collusive agreement, the industry looks exactly like a monopoly industry. Price, output, and profit are the same as in a monopoly.

If a game is repeated indefinitely, there is an opportunity for one player to punish another player for previous "bad" behavior. In such a situation, a tit-for-tat strategy can produce an equilibrium in which both firms stick to the agreement. A tit-for-tat strategy is one in which the players begin by colluding. If one player cheats, the other player responds at the next play by also cheating. Since each knows that it pays the other to respond in this manner, no one cheats. This equilibrium is a cooperative equilibrium—one in which each player cooperates because such behavior is a rational response to the credible threat of the other to inflict damage if the agreement is broken. Uncertainty makes it possible for such an equilibrium to break down from time to time. (pp. 357–364)

Games and Price Wars

Price wars can be interpreted as the outcome of a repeated duopoly game. The competing firms comply with the agreement unless market forces bring about a sufficiently large fall in price. A large fall in price is responded to as if it had resulted from the other firm cheating. Only by responding in this manner can each firm maintain the credible threat that it will punish a cheat and thereby ensure that the ever-present temptation to cheat is held in check and the monopoly agreement is maintained. When market conditions bring about an increase in price, the firms revert to their cooperative behavior. Industries will go through cycles, starting with a monopoly price and output and occasionally, when demand falls by enough, temporarily pursuing noncooperative actions. At these times, the industry price and output will be the competitive ones. (pp. 365–366)

Other Strategic Variables

Firms in oligopolistic industries have to make a large range of decisions: whether to enter or leave an industry; how much to spend on advertising; whether to modify its product; whether to price discriminate; whether to undertake research and development. All these choices result in payoffs for the firm and the other firms in the industry, and a game can be constructed to predict the outcome of such choices.

An interesting real-world example is the research and development game played between producers of disposable diapers. The equilibrium of that game results in a large amount of research and development being undertaken and lower profits than would emerge if the firms could collude somehow to keep out new entrants and undertake less research and development. Thus that game is similar to the prisoners' dilemma. (pp. 366–367)

KEY ELEMENTS

Key Terms

Cartel, 357
Collusive agreement, 357
Cooperative equilibrium, 364
Dominant strategy, 356
Dominant strategy equilibrium, 356
Duopoly, 355
Four-firm concentration ratio, 342
Game theory, 354
Herfindahl-Hirschman Index, 343
Monopolistic competition, 344
Nash equilibrium, 356
Oligopoly, 345
Payoff, 355
Payoff matrix, 355
Product differentiation, 344
Strategic behavior, 354
Strategies, 354
Tit-for-tat strategy, 363
Trigger strategy, 363

Key Figures and Tables

Figure 13.3 Monopolistic Competition, 347
Figure 13.6 Costs and Demand, 358
Figure 13.7 Colluding to Make Monopoly Profits, 359
Figure 13.9 Both Firms Cheat, 361
Table 13.2 Market Structure, 345
Table 13.4 Duopoly Payoff Matrix, 362

REVIEW QUESTIONS

1 What are the main varieties of market structure? What are the main characteristics of each of those market structures?

2 What is a four-firm concentration ratio? If the four-firm concentration ratio is 90 percent, what does that mean?

3 Give some examples of U.S. industries that have a high concentration ratio and of U.S. industries that have a low concentration ratio.

4 What is the Herfindahl-Hirschman Index, and what does a large value of that index indicate?

5 What are barriers to entry? Give some examples of barriers to entry that exist in the U.S. economy.

6 Explain how a firm can differentiate its product.

7 What is the difference between monopolistic competition and perfect competition?

8 Is monopolistic competition more efficient or less efficient than perfect competition?

9 What is the difference between duopoly and oligopoly?

10 Why might the demand curve facing an oligopolist be kinked, and what happens to a firm's marginal revenue curve if its demand curve is kinked?

11 In what circumstances might the dominant firm model of oligopoly be relevant?

12 What is the essential feature of both duopoly and oligopoly?

13 List the key features that all games have in common.

14 What are the features of duopoly that make it reasonable to treat duopoly as a game between two firms?

15 What is the prisoners' dilemma?

16 What is a dominant strategy equilibrium?

17 What is meant by a repeated game?

18 Explain what a tit-for-tat strategy is.

19 What is a price war? What is the effect of a price war on the profit of the firms in the industry and on the profitability of the industry itself?

PROBLEMS

1 A monopolistically competitive industry is in long-run equilibrium as illustrated in Fig. 13.3(b). Demand for the industry's product increases, increasing the demand for each firm's output. Using diagrams similar to those in Fig. 13.3, analyze the short-run and long-run effects of this increase in demand on price, output, and profit.

2 Another monopolistically competitive industry is in long-run equilibrium, as illustrated in Fig. 13.3(b), when it experiences a large increase in wages. Using diagrams similar to those in Fig. 13.3, analyze the short-run and long-run effects of this increase in wages on price, output, and profit.

3 A firm with a kinked demand curve experiences an increase in its fixed cost. Explain the effects on the firm's price, output, and profit/loss.

4 An industry with one very large firm and a hundred very small firms experiences an increase in the demand for its product. Explain the effects on:

- **a** The price, output, and profit of the large firm
- **b** The price, output, and profit of a typical small firm

5 Describe the game known as the prisoners' dilemma. In describing the game:

- **a** Make up a story that motivates the game.
- **b** Work out a payoff matrix.
- **c** Describe how the equilibrium of the game is arrived at.

6 Consider the following game. There are two players, each isolated from the other. They are asked a question. They can answer the question honestly, or they can lie. If both answer honestly, each receives a payoff of $100. If one answers honestly and the other lies, the liar gains at the expense of the honest player. In that event, the liar receives a profit of $500 and the honest player gets nothing. If both lie, then each receives a payoff of $50.

- **a** Describe this game in terms of its players, strategies, and payoffs.
- **b** Construct the payoff matrix.
- **c** What is the equilibrium for this game?

7 Explain the behavior of world oil prices since 1973 by using a repeated prisoners' dilemma game. Describe the types of strategy that individual countries of OPEC have adopted.

8 Two firms, Soapy and Suddies Inc., are the only two producers of laundry detergent. They collude and agree to share the market equally. If neither firm cheats on the agreement, each can make $1 million profit. If either firm cheats, the cheater can increase its profit to $1.5 million, while the firm that abides by the agreement makes a loss of $0.5 million. Neither firm has any way of policing the actions of the other.

- **a** Describe the best strategy for each firm in a game that is played once.
- **b** What is the payoff matrix and what is the equilibrium of a game that is played just once?
- **c** If the buyers of laundry detergent lobby successfully for government regulation of the laundry detergent industry, explain what happens to the price and the profits made by the industry.
- **d** If this duopolist game can be played many times, describe some of the strategies that each firm may adopt.

9 Use the model of oligopoly to explain why, in the disposable diaper industry, Procter & Gamble and Kimberly-Clark spend so much on R&D.

PART 6

MARKETS FOR FACTORS OF PRODUCTION

Talking with Claudia Goldin

Born in New York City, Claudia Goldin was an undergraduate at Cornell University and a graduate student at the University of Chicago, where she obtained her Ph.D. in 1972. Now Professor of Economics at Harvard University and Program Director at the National Bureau of Economic Research, Claudia Goldin has made important contributions to our understanding of the evolution of modern labor markets. Michael Parkin talked with Professor Goldin about some of the problems facing U.S. labor markets in the 1990s.

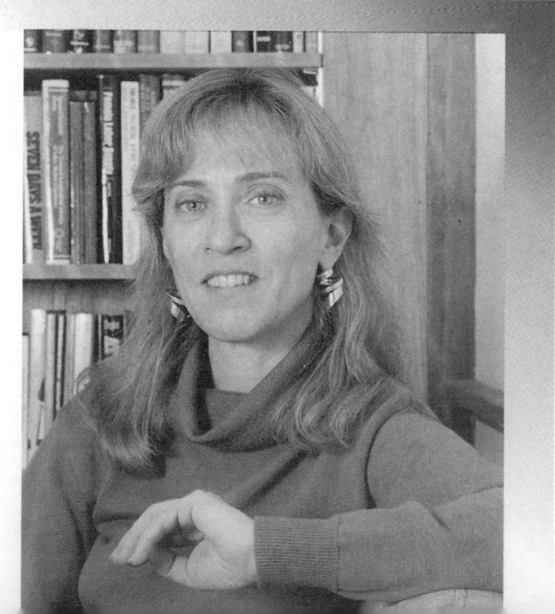

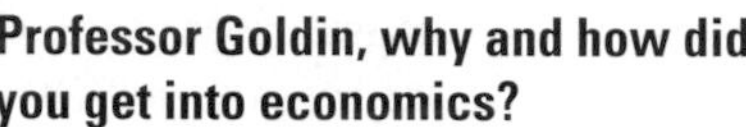

Professor Goldin, why and how did you get into economics?

I entered Cornell University from the Bronx High School of Science intending to be a microbiologist, but I first wanted to acquire a strong liberal arts education. Economics appealed to me because of its rigor, its internal consistency, and, most of all, its relevance. But only after I took economics from Fred Kahn (who later, as head of the Civil Aeronautics Board, deregulated the airline industry) did I decide to major in the subject. I traded the laboratory of the scientist for that of the social scientist. Ours, I should add, is more challenging because we have to devise controlled experiments from already existing data.

In 1890, 18 percent of women were in the labor force; in 1990, 58 percent were in the labor force. What have been the driving forces behind this substantial change?

In 1890, most of the 18 percent were young, single, foreign-born, and black. Women generally worked for pay only before they married, although black women and poor women worked regardless of their marital status and age. Less than 5 percent of all married women in 1890 were in the paid labor force. Thus the question is why married and adult women entered the labor force in such large numbers in the past 100 years. Contrary to popular opinion, the first large increase in married women's employment did not occur during the resurgence of feminism in the late 1960s, nor did it occur among the younger age groups. The large initial movement into the labor force occurred during the 1940s and 1950s among women older than 40 years. A host of long-run factors had been operating to reduce the time demands of women in their homes. These include the markedly reduced birth rate and the appearance of market goods substituting for those produced within the home, such as factory-made bread and clothing.

How do you explain the timing and the extent of the explosion in women's employment?

It was rooted in two changes earlier in the century. Between 1915 and 1930, the proportion of all Americans graduating from high school vastly increased, and at the same time there was a surge in the demand for educated labor in the burgeoning clerical and sales sectors. Young women entered these jobs in droves in the 1920s but generally exited when they married. After World War II, rising wages and an increased demand for labor drew these women back into the labor force. Younger married women were raising the baby boom of the 1950s and were less willing to trade the household for the marketplace. The shift of employment from manufacturing to office and sales work from 1920 to 1950 was an important factor in enabling adult and married women to work for pay. And the generation of older women in the 1950s, who had the requisite education for these jobs, was ripe for this monumental change in employment. They, not the young women of their era, were the real pioneers in women's employment. But the trailblazers did not view these changes as part of a larger social movement.

In the 1970s and 1980s, younger women greatly increased their participation in the labor force, and in the 1980s, even women with infants expanded their employment. In short, rising real wages, falling relative prices of market substitutes for home-produced goods, a declining demand for goods within the home, and a shift of jobs from blue collar to white collar led women to enter the labor force. But the timing of the changes suggests that various norms and institutional rigidities had to be broken down for the long-run forces to operate. These were accomplished first during the 1940s and 1950s.

What have we learned from your work and the work of other labor economists about the sources of persistent wage differences between men and women?

From the mid-1950s to 1980, the ratio of female to male full-time, year-round earnings was constant at about 0.60. Women as a group made little if any noticeable progress relative to men. But from 1981 to the present, the ratio increased by approximately 10 percentage points to 0.70. The analysis of the period of stability and the subsequent period of a narrowing gap reveals much about the sources of gender differences in earnings.

The factors that economists group under the heading of "human capital" are most relevant. When working women's job experience and education advanced on those of men, their relative earnings increased, and when these factors remained constant compared with those of men, women's relative earnings were stable. The aspirations and expectations of teenaged girls are another factor. These young women formed far more realistic expectations in the 1970s than in the 1960s, when they severely underestimated their future participation in the labor force. Young women today are in a much better position to prepare themselves for a lifetime of labor market work than were their elders.

We also know that in the 1980s the returns to education and job experience increased for women relative to men. We aren't certain why this has been the case. Some of the increase could be due to better education or women's greater willingness to undertake more demanding jobs. But we cannot dismiss the notion that the labor market became more gender-neutral in the 1980s, and we also cannot dismiss the role of policy interventions in making it so.

What trend do we observe in the wage differences between blacks and whites?

Similar forces have operated over the long run to narrow differences in earnings between white and black males and between white and black females. In 1940, the ratio of the earnings of black men to white men was astoundingly low—0.43—but by 1980 it was 0.73. Among college graduate men about 35 years old, the increase was even greater—from 0.45 in 1940 to 0.81 in 1980. On average, black women have made greater progress relative to white women than have black men relative to white men.

What caused these extraordinary changes?

There were two compelling factors—educational changes, including advances in the quality of the education of black Americans, and the movement of blacks from the low-wage South to the higher-wage North. But there were critical junctures in this history. Two occurred during World Wars I and II and led to the greater integration of blacks into the white-dominated manufacturing sector and to an enormous migration to the North. The third occurred during the mid-1960s, when the Civil Rights Act led to further inroads by blacks into the higher-wage manufacturing sector. Unfortunately, some of the gains made since World War I were reversed in the 1980s. I don't mean that we have turned the clock back with regard to education and prejudice. The 1980s were a period a widening inequality in which the lower-educated and the manufacturing sector in particular lost a tremendous amount of ground, and black Americans are still disproportionately represented in these two groups.

What do minimum wage laws do?

The minimum wage sets a floor for covered workers below which the hourly wage cannot fall. If the minimum wage is set very high, as it is, for example, in Puerto Rico, which is covered by the U.S. minimum wage, it can create substantial unemployment. In the United States, the current minimum wage, which was recently increased after nine years, is about 38 percent of the average wage in manufacturing. But in Puerto Rico it was 70 to 90 percent of the average at its inception and has remained extremely high by Puerto Rican standards. Not surprisingly, the unemployment rate in Puerto Rico, particularly among young and inexperienced workers, is enormous, running in the double-digit range for some time. Surely we do not want a minimum wage that is so much higher than the average wage that the supply of labor greatly exceeds the demand. If the demand for labor is very inelastic, there will be an increase in income from a minimum wage, but the decrease in employment will be small. Many researchers believe that the U.S. minimum wage is currently in this range. The employment effects appear to be small while the income effects appear moderate.

What is your view of comparable-worth laws?

Comparable worth is a doctrine that says jobs that use comparable skills should get paid the same amount per unit time. Therefore if a nurse uses 10 units of skill and a truck driver also uses 10 units of skill, there should be no difference in their earnings per hour if the jobs don't differ in other important dimensions, such as benefits or intensity of work.

The first question is why a competitive labor market doesn't produce such an outcome. If identical levels of skill are used in two jobs that do not differ in any other manner (except that one is nursing and one is truck driving), then workers should be indifferent between the two. If workers are indifferent between the two, firms would be forced to pay nurses and truck drivers the same wage. If truck drivers received more than nurses, the nurses would become truck drivers. The champions of comparable worth claim that women are segregated into particular jobs. Because they were denied access to various higher-paying jobs, like being a physician, they "crowd" into nursing, thereby depressing the wages of nurses. Because they were denied access to becoming a truck driver, they cannot equalize wages between the two occupations. The result is lower wages for nurses than for truck drivers. The proponents of comparable worth see it as a means of increasing the wages of nurses relative to, say, truck drivers and bringing about the free market solution that would exist had there been no discrimination.

The question is how the researcher can evaluate whether two occupations use comparable skills and thus ought to have the same wages in a competitive and discrimination-free labor market. The answer is that the researcher cannot. None of us is so all-knowing that we can assess all the skills required in a job and all the attributes of a job that are valued or devalued by workers. I would much rather see the energies of legislatures channeled into ensur-

ing that women and minorities are afforded equal access to positions such as truck driver and physician, among others. We can try to guarantee equality of opportunity, and we can try to remedy past inequities through affirmative action. But we cannot easily dictate market prices.

What have been the main effects of affirmative action programs? Have they helped or hindered the progress of women and minorities?

Affirmative action is a complex doctrine under which federal contractors, that is, firms that sell goods or services to the federal government, have target levels for the hiring and promotion of women and minorities. There are direct effects from affirmative action programs and, possibly, indirect effects. Most scholarly work has been focused on the direct effects and finds that affirmative action programs have increased the employment and earnings of minorities. There is little evidence, however, that the programs have served to increase the employment and earnings of women. The indirect effects are more difficult to quantify.

Let's look at the economics profession, for example. Far fewer women than men major in economics, so it isn't surprising that women are vastly underrepresented as teachers and researchers in the field. If we want to know whether having more women economics professors would encourage more female undergraduates to major in economics—that is, if there is a "role model effect"—we could test whether female enrollments increase when women teach the basic economics courses, such as principles. If so, we can make a case for affirmative action as a means of increasing the pool of candidates for a field and thus increasing the future employment of the group even in the absence of further affirmative action. Another possible indirect effect has been the subject of considerable controversy and forms the conservative attack on the programs. It is that women and minorities get hired or promoted under affirmative action when they should not have been. Such actions will then reinforce discriminatory views of women and minorities as being incompetent at particular jobs and can, in addition, make both groups more complacent and less competitive. I know of no hard evidence to substantiate such claims.

What are the most important labor market problems that we don't understand and that the next generation of economists will work on and possibly solve?

A pressing problem today is why the wage structure and distribution of earnings widened so substantially during the past 10 or 15 years. We need to know more about the interaction among education, inherent ability, and new technologies, such as the computer revolution. What makes some individuals more able to adapt while others are left behind? What types of educational and training interventions will help workers make the transition?

Returning to gender differences in the workplace, I wonder whether the gap in earnings can ever be eliminated, given the structure of jobs and the division of labor in the home. If women are still expected to raise children

"Even if individual husbands and wives would like to create the egalitarian home, the husband is likely to confront considerable problems . . ."

and do a disproportionate share of household work, they will not advance with men in the labor market. Even if individual husbands and wives would like to create the egalitarian home, the husband is likely to confront considerable problems if he asks his employer for family leave, shorter hours, or a flexible schedule, even at greatly reduced pay. The labor market isn't yet structured or ready for the egalitarian family. I see this restructuring of the workplace as a major issue facing the next generation of labor economists.

CHAPTER 14

Pricing and Allocating Factors of Production

After studying this chapter, you will be able to:

- Explain how firms choose the quantities of labor, capital, and land to employ in their production activities
- Explain how households choose the quantities of labor, capital, and land to supply
- Explain how wages, interest, and rent are determined in competitive factor markets
- Explain the concept of economic rent
- Distinguish between economic rent and transfer earnings

Many Happy Returns

IT MIGHT NOT BE YOUR BIRTHDAY, AND EVEN IF IT IS, chances are you are spending most of it working. But at the end of the week or month (or, if you're devoting all your time to college, when you graduate), you will receive the *returns* from your labor. Those returns vary a lot. Pedro Lopez, who spends his chilly winter days in a small container suspended from the top of Chicago's John Hancock Tower cleaning windows, makes a happy return of $12 an hour. Dan Rather, who puts on a 30-minute news show each weekday evening, makes a very happy return of $3.6 million a year. Students working at McDonald's and in the fields of southern California labor away for just a few dollars an hour. What determines the jobs we do and the wages we are paid? ◆◆ Most of us have little trouble spending our pay. But most of us do manage to save some of what we earn. What determines the amount of saving that people do and the returns that they make on that saving? How do the returns on saving influence the allocation of savings across the many industries and activities that use our capital resources? ◆◆ Some people receive income from renting land, but the amount earned varies enormously with its location and quality. For example, an acre of farmland in Iowa rents for about $1,000 a year, while a block on Chicago's Magnificent Mile rents for several million dollars a year. What determines the rent that people are willing to pay for different blocks of land? Why are rents so enormously high in big cities and so relatively low in the great farming regions of the country?

◆ ◆ ◆ ◆ In this chapter we deal with the kinds of questions that we have just posed. We study markets for factors of production—labor, capital, and land—and learn how their prices and people's incomes are determined.

Factor Prices and Incomes

Factors of production are the inputs into production. They are divided into three broad categories: *labor, capital,* and *land.* (We defined these factors of production in Chapter 1, p. 14.) The owners of factors of production receive an income from the firms that use those factors as inputs into their production activities. These incomes are *wages* paid for labor, *interest* paid for capital, and *rent* paid for land. Wages include all labor income including salaries, commissions, bonuses, and benefits paid in compensation for labor. Interest includes all forms of capital income including dividends paid by firms. Rent is the income paid for the use of land and natural resources. Apartment rents include an element of rent and also an element of interest—a payment for the use of capital.

Labor is by far the most important factor of production and generates about 70 percent of all income, and that percentage has been steadily increasing over the years.

In the rest of this chapter, we're going to build a model of a factor market, a model that determines factor prices, the quantities of factors used, and the incomes that factors of production earn.

An Overview

Factor prices are determined in factor markets, and we can understand those prices by using the model of demand and supply. The quantity of a factor of production demanded depends on the factor's price. That is, the quantity of labor demanded depends on the wage rate, the quantity of capital demanded depends on the interest rate, and the quantity of land demanded depends on the rent. The law of demand applies to factors of production just as it applies to all other economic entities. Thus as the price of a factor of production decreases, the quantity of the factor demanded increases. The demand curve for a factor of production is shown in Fig. 14.1 as the curve labeled *D*.

The quantity supplied of a factor of production depends on its price. With some exceptions that we'll identify later in this chapter, the law of supply applies to factors of production: as the price of a factor of production increases, the quantity of the factor supplied increases. The supply of a factor of production is shown in Fig. 14.1 as the curve labeled *S*.

The equilibrium factor price is determined at the point of intersection of the factor demand and factor supply curves. Figure 14.1 shows such an equilibrium—*QF* is the quantity of the factor of production used and *PF* is the factor price.

FIGURE 14.1

Demand and Supply in a Factor Market

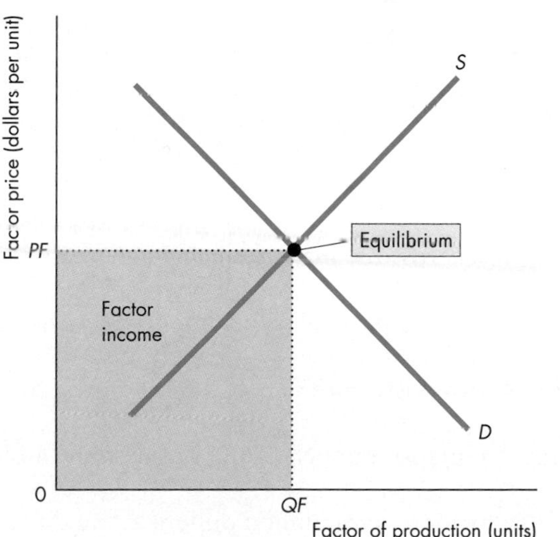

The demand curve for a factor of production (*D*) slopes downward, and the supply curve (*S*) slopes upward. Where the demand and supply curves intersect, the factor price (*PF*) and the quantity of a factor used (*QF*) are determined. The factor income is the product of the factor price and the quantity of the factor, as represented by the blue rectangle.

The income earned by a factor of production is its price multiplied by the quantity used. In Fig. 14.1, the price is measured by the distance from the origin to *PF*, and the quantity used is measured by the distance from the origin to *QF*. The factor income is the product of these two distances and is equivalent to the blue area in the figure.

All the influences on the quantity of a factor bought other than its price result in a shift in the factor demand curve. We'll study what those influences are in the next section. For now, let's simply work out the effects of a change in the demand for a factor of production. An increase in demand for a factor of production, as illustrated in Fig. 14.2(a), shifts the demand curve to the right, leading to an increase in the quantity of the factor used and an increase in its price. Thus when the demand curve shifts from D_0 to D_1, the quantity used increases from QF_0 to QF_1 and the price increases from PF_0 to PF_1. An increase in the demand for a factor of production increases that factor's income. The dark blue area in Fig. 14.2(a) illustrates the increase in income.

When the demand for a factor of production decreases, its demand curve shifts to the left. Figure 14.2(b) illustrates the effects of a decrease in demand. The demand curve shifts to the left from D_0 to D_2, the quantity used decreases from QF_0 to QF_2, and the price decreases from PF_0 to PF_2. When the demand for a factor of production decreases, the income of that factor also decreases. The light blue area in Fig. 14.2(b) illustrates the decrease in income.

The extent to which a change in the demand for a factor of production changes the factor price and the quantity used depends on the elasticity of supply. If the supply curve is very flat (supply is elastic), the change in the quantity used is large and the change in price is small. If the supply curve is very steep (supply is inelastic), the change in the price is large and the change in the quantity used is small.

A change in the supply of a factor of production also changes the price and quantity used as well as the income earned by those supplying the factor. An increase in supply results in an increase in the quantity used and a decrease in the factor price. A decrease in supply results in a decrease in the quantity used and an increase in the factor price. But whether a change in supply increases or decreases income depends on the elasticity of demand for the factor.

FIGURE 14.2

Changes in Demand

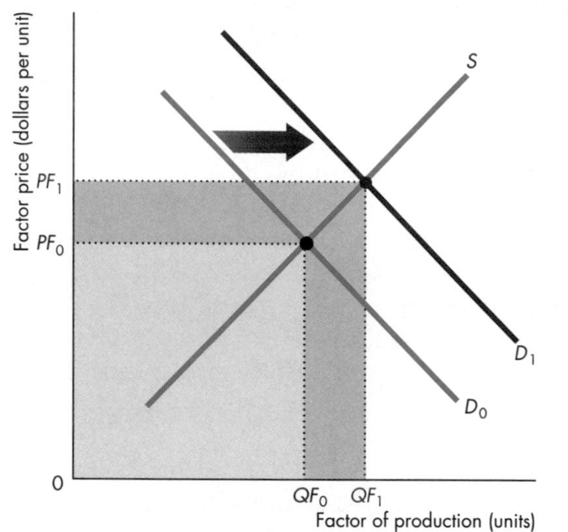

(a) An increase in demand

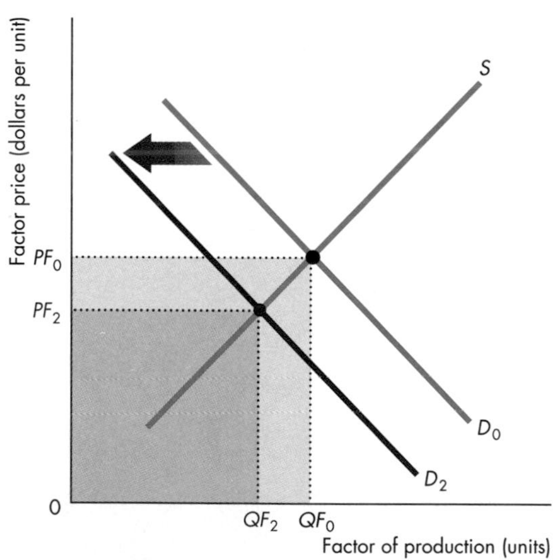

(b) A decrease in demand

An increase in the demand for a factor of production (part a) shifts its demand curve to the right—from D_0 to D_1. The quantity used increases from QF_0 to QF_1, and the price increases from PF_0 to PF_1. The factor income increases, and that income increase is shown by the dark blue area. A decrease in the demand for a factor of production from D_0 to D_2 results in a decrease in the quantity used from QF_0 to QF_2, and a decrease in the factor price from PF_0 to PF_2. The decrease in demand results in a decrease in the factor income. That decrease in income is illustrated by the light blue area.

Suppose that the quantity used of the factor of production illustrated in Fig. 14.3 decreases from 3 units to 2 units. Initially, the price is $10 a unit. If the demand curve is D_0, the decrease in supply results in an increase in the price of the factor but a decrease in the income of the suppliers of this factor of production. You can see that income decreases by multiplying the factor price by the quantity used. Initially, when the quantity is 3 units and the price is $10, the income earned by the suppliers of this factor of production is $30 (the $20 light blue area plus the $10 red area). When the quantity decreases to 2 units and the price increases to $14, income decreases by the $10 red area but increases by the $8 dark blue area for a net decrease to $28. Over the range of the price change that we've just considered, the demand curve D_0 is elastic—its elasticity is greater than 1.

Conversely, suppose that the demand curve is D_1. In this case, when the quantity decreases to 2 units, the price increases to $20 a unit. Income increases to $40. The smaller quantity lowers income by $10 (red area), but the higher factor price increases income by $20 (dark blue plus green areas). Over the range of the price change that we've just considered, the demand curve D_1 is inelastic—its elasticity is less than 1.

FIGURE 14.3

Factor Income and Demand Elasticity

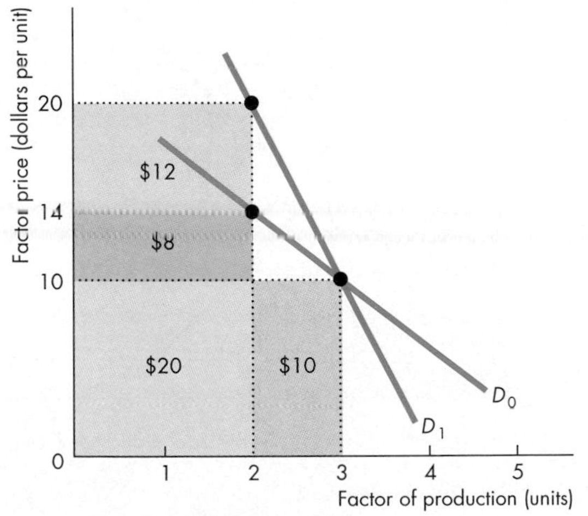

A decrease in the quantity used of a factor of production may result in a decrease or an increase in the factor's income. If the demand curve is D_0 (an elastic demand curve over the relevant range), a decrease in the quantity from 3 to 2 results in a decrease in the factor income from $30 to $28. If the demand curve is D_1 (an inelastic demand curve over the relevant range), a decrease in the quantity from 3 to 2 results in an increase in the factor's income from $30 to $40.

The markets for factors of production determine factor prices in much the same way as goods markets determine the prices of goods and services. Factor markets also determine factor incomes. Factor income is the factor price multiplied by the quantity of the factor used. Thus to work out the influences on factor incomes, we have to pay attention simultaneously to the determination of the prices and the quantities used of the factors of production.

We're going to spend the rest of this chapter exploring more closely the influences on the demand for and supply of factors of production. We're also going to discover what determines the elasticities of supply of and demand for factors. These elasticities are important because of their effects on factor prices and the incomes earned. Let's begin by studying the demand for inputs.

Demand for Factors

The demand for any factor of production is a derived demand. A **derived demand** is a demand for an input not for its own sake but in order to use it in the production of goods and services. A firm's derived demand for inputs depends on the constraints the firm faces—its technology constraint and its market constraint. It also depends on the firm's objective. The objective of the model firms that we have studied is to maximize profit. We'll continue to study the behavior of such firms.

A firm's demand for factors stems from its profit-maximization decision. *What* to produce and *how* to produce it are the questions that the firm must answer in order to make maximum profit. Those choices have implications for the firm's demand for inputs, which we'll now investigate.

Profit Maximization

A firm's inputs fall into two categories: fixed and variable. In most industries, the fixed inputs are capital (plant, machinery, and buildings) and land, and the variable input is labor. A firm meets permanent changes in output by changing the scale of its inputs of capital and land. It meets short-run variations in output by varying its input of labor.

Profit-maximizing firms produce the output at which marginal cost equals marginal revenue. This principle holds true whether the firm is in a perfectly competitive industry, in monopolistic competition, in oligopoly, or in a monopoly. If one more unit of output adds less to total cost than it adds to total revenue, the firm can increase its profit by producing more. A firm maximizes profit by producing the output at which the additional cost of producing one more unit of output equals the additional revenue from selling it. If we shift our perspective slightly, we can also state the condition for maximum profit in terms of the marginal cost of an input and the marginal revenue that input generates. Let's see how.

Marginal Revenue Product and Factor Price

The change in total revenue resulting from employing one more unit of any factor is called the factor's **marginal revenue product.** The concept of marginal revenue product sounds a bit like the concept of marginal revenue that you have met before. These concepts are indeed related, but there is an important distinction between the two. *Marginal revenue product* is the extra revenue generated as a result of employing one extra unit of a factor; *marginal revenue* is the extra revenue generated as a result of selling one additional unit of output.

A profit-maximizing firm hires the quantity of a factor that makes the marginal revenue product of the factor equal to the marginal cost of the factor. For a firm that buys its factors of production in competitive factor markets, the marginal cost of a factor is the factor's price. That is, in a competitive factor market, each firm is such a small demander of the factor that the firm has no influence on the factor's price. The firm simply has to pay the going factor price—market wage rate for labor, interest rate for capital, and rent for land.

Factor Price as Opportunity Cost You might be wondering why the interest rate is the factor price for capital. It looks different from the other two factor prices. Why isn't the factor price for capital the price of a piece of machinery—the price of a knitting machine for Swanky's sweater factory, the price of a computer for a tax consultant, or the price of an automobile assembly line for GM? The answer is that these prices do not represent the opportunity cost of *using* capital equipment. They are the prices at which a piece of capital can be bought. A firm can buy or sell a piece of capital equipment at its going market price. The opportunity cost of *using* the equipment is the interest rate that has to be paid on the funds tied up in its purchase. These funds may be borrowed, in which case there is an explicit payment of interest to the bank or other lender. Or the funds may be owned by the firm, in which case there is an implicit interest cost—the interest that could have been earned by using those funds in some other way.

Quantity of Factor Demanded We have defined the additional revenue resulting from employing one more unit of a factor as the factor's marginal revenue product. We have seen that in competitive factor markets, the marginal cost of a factor equals its price. Therefore a profit-maximizing firm—a firm that makes the marginal revenue product equal to the marginal cost of each input—hires each factor up to the point at which its marginal revenue product equals the factor's price. As the price of a factor varies, the quantity demanded of it also varies. The lower the price of a factor, the larger is the quantity demanded of that factor. Let's illustrate this proposition by working through an example—that of labor.[1]

The Firm's Demand for Labor

Labor is a variable input. A firm can change the quantity of labor it employs in both the short run

[1]The principles governing the demand for factors of production are the same for all factors—labor, capital, and land. There are some interesting special features concerning the demand for capital, however, that are explained in greater detail in Chapter 16. That part of Chapter 16 is relatively self-contained and may be studied at the same time as the material that you are now studying in this chapter.

and the long run. Let's focus first on a firm's short-run demand for labor.

A firm's short-run technology constraint is described by its *total product schedule*. Table 14.1 sets out the total product schedule for a car wash operated by Max's Wash 'n' Wax. (This total product schedule is similar to the one we studied in Chapter 10, Fig. 10.1.) The numbers in the first two columns of the table tell us how the maximum number of car washes each hour varies as the amount of labor employed varies. The third column shows the *marginal product of labor*—the change in output resulting from a one-unit increase in labor input.

Max's market constraint is the demand curve for his product. If, in the goods market, a firm is a monopoly or engaged in monopolistic competition or oligopoly, it faces a downward-sloping demand curve for its product. If a firm is perfectly competitive, it faces a fixed price for its product regardless of its output level and therefore faces a horizontal demand curve for its product. We will assume that Max operates his car wash in a perfectly competitive market and can sell as many washes as he chooses at a constant price of $4 a wash. Given this information, we can calculate Max's total revenue (fourth column) by multiplying the number of cars washed per hour by $4. For example, if 9 cars are washed each hour (row *c*), total revenue is $36.

The fifth column of Table 14.1 shows the calculation of the marginal revenue product of labor—the change in total revenue per unit change in labor input. For example, if Max hires a second worker (row *c*), total revenue increases from $20 to $36, so the marginal revenue product is $16. There is an alternative way of calculating the marginal revenue product of labor—multiply marginal product by marginal revenue. To see that this method gives the same answer, multiply the marginal product of hiring a second worker—4 cars an hour—by marginal

TABLE 14.1

Marginal Revenue Product and Average Revenue Product at Max's Wash 'n' Wax

	Quantity of labor *(L)* (workers)	Output *(Q)* (cars washed per hour)	Marginal product $(MP = \Delta Q/\Delta L)$ (washes per worker)	Total revenue $(TR = P \times Q)$ (dollars)	Marginal revenue product $(MRP = \Delta TR/\Delta L)$ (dollars per worker)	Average revenue product $(ARP = TR/L)$ (dollars per worker)
a	0	0		0		
			5		20	
b	1	5		20		20
			4		16	
c	2	9		36		18
			3		12	
d	3	12		48		16
			2		8	
e	4	14		56		14
			1		4	
f	5	15		60		12

The marginal revenue product of labor is the change in total revenue that results from a one-unit increase in labor input. To calculate marginal revenue product, first work out total revenue. If Max hires 1 worker (row *b*), output is 5 washes an hour and total revenue, at $4 a wash, is $20. If he hires 2 workers (row *c*), output is 9 washes an hour and total revenue is $36. By hiring the second worker, total revenue rises by $16—the marginal revenue product of labor is $16. The average revenue product of labor is total revenue per unit of labor employed. For example, when Max employs 2 workers, total revenue is $36 and average revenue product is $18 ($36 divided by 2).

revenue—\$4 a car—and notice that the answer is the same (\$16).

Total revenue divided by the quantity of the factor hired is called the **average revenue product** of the factor. Thus average revenue product is the average contribution of each unit of an input to the firm's total revenue. The last column of Table 14.1 shows the average revenue product of labor. For example, when Max employs 3 workers (row *d*), total revenue is \$48. Thus the average revenue product of labor is \$48 divided by 3 workers, which is \$16 per worker.

Notice that as the quantity of labor rises, the marginal revenue product of labor falls. When Max hires the first worker, the marginal revenue product of labor is \$20. If Max hires a second worker, the marginal revenue product of labor is \$16. Marginal revenue product of labor continues to decline as Max hires more workers.

Marginal revenue product diminishes as Max hires more workers because of the principle of diminishing returns that we first studied in Chapter 10. With each additional worker hired, the marginal product of labor falls and so brings in a smaller marginal revenue product. Because Max's Wash 'n' Wax is a perfectly competitive firm, the price of each additional car wash is the same and brings in the same marginal revenue. If instead Max had a monopoly, he would have to lower his price to sell more washes. In such a case, the marginal revenue product of labor diminishes even more quickly than in perfectly competitive conditions. Marginal revenue product diminishes because of diminishing marginal product of labor and also because of diminishing marginal revenue. Table 14.2 provides a compact glossary of factor market terms.

TABLE 14.2

A Compact Glossary of Factor Market Terms

Term	Definition
Factors of production	**Labor, capital, and land (including raw materials)**
Factor prices	**Wages—price of labor; interest—price of capital; rent—price of land**
Marginal product	**Output produced by last unit of input hired; for example, the marginal product of labor is additional output produced by employing one more person**
Average product	**Output per unit of input; for example, average product of labor is output divided by labor input**
Marginal revenue	**Revenue resulting from selling one additional unit of output**
Marginal revenue product	**Revenue resulting from hiring one additional unit of a factor of production; for example, marginal revenue product of labor is the additional revenue resulting from selling the output produced by employing one more person**
Average revenue product	**Total revenue per unit of input; calculated as total revenue divided by labor input**

We can illustrate the average revenue product and marginal revenue product of labor as curves. The **average revenue product curve** shows the average revenue product of a factor at each quantity of the factor hired. The **marginal revenue product curve** shows the marginal revenue product of a factor at each quantity of the factor hired.

Figure 14.4(a) shows the marginal revenue product and average revenue product curves for workers employed by Max. The horizontal axis measures the number of workers that Max hires, and the vertical axis measures the average and marginal revenue product of labor. The curve labeled *ARP* is the average revenue product curve and is based on the numbers in Table 14.1. For example, point *d* on the *ARP* curve represents row *d* in the table. Max employs 3 workers, and the average revenue product of labor is \$16 a worker. The blue bars show the marginal revenue product of labor as Max employs more workers. These bars correspond to the numbers in Table 14.1. The curve *MRP* is the marginal revenue product curve.

The firm's demand for labor curve is based on its marginal revenue product curve. You can see Max's demand for labor curve (*D*) in Fig. 14.4(b). The horizontal axis measures the number of workers hired—the same as part (a). The vertical axis measures the wage rate in dollars per hour. The demand for labor curve is exactly the same as the firm's marginal revenue product curve. For example, when Max employs 3 workers an hour, his marginal revenue product is \$10 an hour, as in Fig. 14.4(a); and

FIGURE 14.4

The Demand for Labor at Max's Wash 'n' Wax

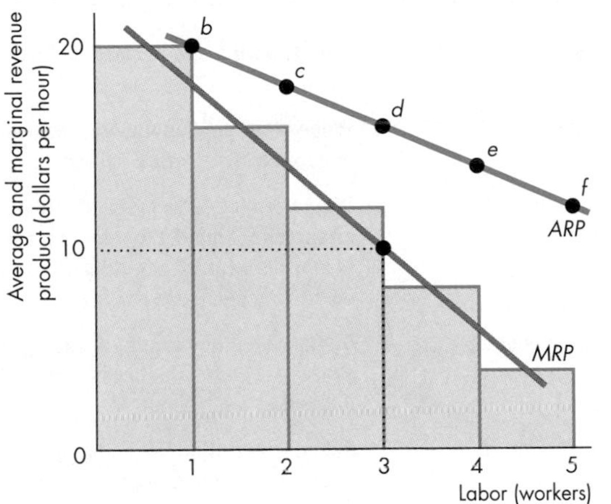

(a) Average and marginal revenue product

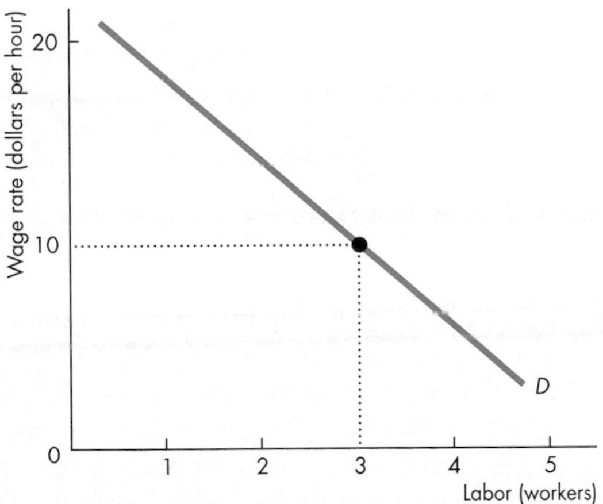

(b) Demand for labor

Part (a) shows the average and marginal revenue product curves for Max's Wash 'n' Wax. Points *b* through *f* on the average revenue product curve correspond to the rows of Table 14.1. The blue bars representing marginal revenue product are also based on the numbers in that table. (Each point is plotted midway between the labor inputs used in its calculation.) Average revenue product and marginal revenue product decline, and the marginal revenue product curve is always below the average revenue product curve. Part (b) shows Max's demand for labor curve. It is identical to his marginal revenue product curve. Max demands labor up to the point at which the wage rate (the worker's marginal cost) equals marginal revenue product.

at a wage rate of $10 an hour, Max hires 3 workers an hour, as in Fig. 14.4(b).

But why is the demand for labor curve identical to the marginal revenue product curve? Because the firm hires the profit-maximizing quantity of labor. If the cost of hiring one more worker—the wage rate—is less than the additional revenue that worker will bring in—the marginal revenue product of labor—then it pays the firm to employ one more worker. Conversely, if the cost of hiring one more worker is greater than the additional revenue that worker will bring in—the wage rate exceeds the marginal revenue product—then it does not pay the firm to employ one more worker. When the cost of the last worker hired equals the revenue brought in by that worker, the firm is making the maximum possible profit. Such a situation occurs when the wage rate equals the marginal revenue product. Thus the quantity of labor demanded by the firm is such that the wage rate equals the marginal revenue product of labor.

REVIEW

A firm chooses the quantity of labor to hire so that its profit is maximized. The additional total revenue generated by hiring one additional worker is called the marginal revenue product of labor. It is the change in total revenue generated by a one-unit change in labor input. In a competitive labor market, the marginal cost of labor is the wage rate. Profit is maximized when the marginal revenue product of labor equals the wage rate. The marginal revenue product of labor curve is the firm's demand for labor curve. The lower the wage rate, the higher is the quantity of labor demanded. ◆

Two Conditions for Profit Maximization When we studied firms' output decisions, we discovered that a condition for maximum profit is that marginal revenue equals marginal cost. We've now discovered another condition for maximum profit—marginal revenue product of a factor equals the factor's price. How can there be two conditions for a maximum profit? It is because they are equivalent to each other. When marginal revenue equals marginal cost,

TABLE 14.3

Two Conditions for Maximum Profit

Symbols

Marginal product	***MP***
Marginal revenue	***MR***
Marginal cost	***MC***
Marginal revenue product	***MRP***
Factor price	***PF***

Two conditions for maximum profit

1. **MR = *MC***	2. **MRP = *PF***

Equivalence of conditions

1. *MRP/MP* = ***MR*** = ***MC*** = *PF/MP*

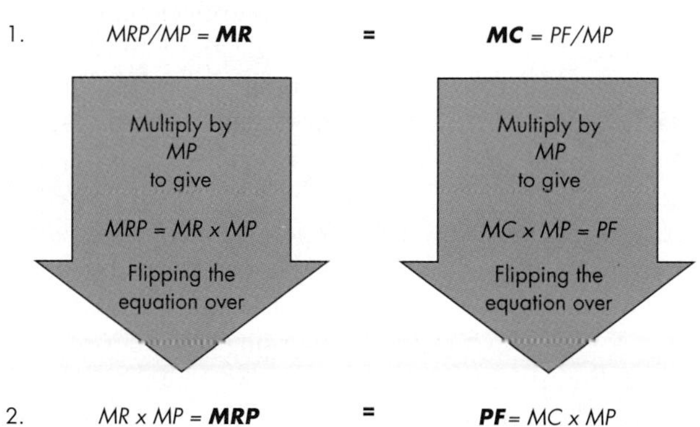

2. *MR* x *MP* = ***MRP*** = ***PF*** = *MC* x *MP*

Marginal revenue (*MR*) equals marginal cost (*MC*), and marginal revenue product (*MRP*) equals the price of the factor (*PF*). The two conditions for maximum profit are equivalent because marginal revenue product (*MRP*) equals marginal revenue (*MR*) multiplied by marginal product (*MP*) and the factor price (*PF*) equals marginal cost (*MC*) multiplied by marginal product (*MP*).

the marginal revenue product of a factor equals the factor's price. The equivalence of these two conditions is set out in Table 14.3.

We have just derived the law of demand as it applies to the labor market. And we've discovered that the same principles that apply to the demand for goods and services apply here as well. The demand for labor curve slopes downward. Other things being equal, the lower the wage rate (the price of labor), the greater is the quantity of labor demanded. Let's now study the influences that result in a change in the demand for labor and therefore in a shift in the demand for labor curve.

Shifts in the Firm's Demand for Labor Curve The position of the demand for labor curve depends on three factors:

- The price of the firm's output
- The prices of other inputs
- Technology

The higher the price of a firm's output, the greater is the quantity of labor demanded by the firm, other things being equal. The price of output affects the demand for labor through its influence on marginal revenue product. A higher price for the firm's output increases marginal revenue, which, in turn, increases the marginal revenue product of labor. A change in the price of a firm's output leads to a shift in the firm's demand for labor curve. If the output price increases, the demand for labor increases.

The other two influences on the demand for labor have their main effects not in the short run but in the long run. The **short-run demand for labor** is the relationship between the wage rate and the quantity of labor demanded when the firm's capital is fixed and labor is the only variable input. The **long-run demand for labor** is the relationship between the wage rate and the quantity of labor demanded when all inputs can be varied. A change in the relative price of inputs—such as the relative price of labor and capital—leads to a substitution away from the input whose relative price has increased and toward the input whose relative price has decreased. Thus, if the price of using capital decreases relative to that of using labor, the firm substitutes capital for labor, increasing the quantity of capital demanded and decreasing its demand for labor.

Finally, a technological change that influences the marginal product of labor also affects the demand for labor. For example, the development of electronic telephones with memories and a host of clever features decreased the marginal product of and the demand for telephone operators. At the same time, it increased the marginal product of and the demand for telephone engineers trained in the installation and maintenance of the new telephones. Again, these effects are felt in the long run when the firm adjusts all its inputs and incorporates new technologies into its production process. Table 14.4 summarizes the influences on a firm's demand for labor.

As we saw earlier, Fig. 14.2 illustrates the effects of a change in the demand for a factor. If that factor is labor, then Fig. 14.2 shows the effects of a change in the demand for labor on the wage rate and the quantity of labor hired. But we can now say why the demand for labor curve shifts. For example, an increase in the price of the firm's output, an increase in the price of capital, or a technological change that increases the marginal product of labor shifts the demand for labor curve from D_0 to D_1 in Fig. 14.2(a). Conversely, a decrease in the price of the firm's output, a decrease in the price of capital, or a technological change that lowers the marginal product of labor shifts the demand curve for labor from D_0 to D_2 in Fig. 14.2(b).

TABLE 14.4

A Firm's Demand for Labor

The law of demand

The quantity of labor demanded by a firm

Decreases if:	*Increases if:*
◆ **The wage rate increases**	◆ **The wage rate decreases**

Changes in demand

A firm's demand for labor

Decreases if:	*Increases if:*
◆ **The firm's output price decreases**	◆ **The firm's output price increases**
◆ **The prices of other inputs decrease**	◆ **The prices of other inputs increase**
◆ **A technological change decreases the marginal product of labor**	◆ **A technological change increases the marginal product of labor**

Market Demand

So far, we've studied only the demand for labor by an individual firm. Let's now look at the market demand. The market demand for a factor of production is the total demand for that factor by all firms. The market demand curve for a given factor is obtained by adding up the quantities demanded of that factor by each firm at each given factor price. Thus the concept of the market demand for labor curve is exactly like the concept of the market demand curve for a good or service. The market demand curve for a good or service is obtained by adding together the quantities demanded of that good by all households at each price. The market demand curve for labor is obtained by adding together the quantities of labor demanded by all firms at each wage rate.

Elasticity of Demand for Labor

The elasticity of demand for labor measures the responsiveness of the quantity of labor demanded to the wage rate. We calculate this elasticity in the same way that we calculate a price elasticity. The elasticity of demand for labor equals the percentage change in the quantity of labor demanded divided by the percentage change in the wage rate. The elasticity of demand for labor depends on the elasticity of demand for the good that the firm is producing and on the properties of the firm's total product curve—on how rapidly the marginal product of labor diminishes. There is, however, a slight difference in the things that affect the elasticity of demand for labor in the short run and in the long run.

Short-Run Elasticity The **short-run elasticity of demand for labor** is the magnitude of the percentage change in the quantity of labor demanded divided by the percentage change in the wage rate when labor is the only variable input. The short-run elasticity of demand for labor depends on three things:

1. *Labor intensity.* The proportion of labor in the production of a good—the labor intensity of the production process—also affects the elasticity of demand for labor. Suppose that the cost of labor is 90 percent of the total cost of producing a good. In such a situation, a 10 percent change in the cost of labor generates a 9 percent change in

total cost. Conversely, if the cost of labor is only 10 percent of the total cost, then a 10 percent change in the cost of labor produces only a 1 percent change in total cost. The larger the percentage change in total cost, the larger is the percentage change in price and, for a given elasticity of demand for the product, the larger is the percentage change in output. The larger the change in output, the larger is the change in labor input. So the larger the proportion of total cost coming from labor (labor intensity), the more elastic is the demand for labor, other things being equal.

2. *The slope of the marginal product of labor curve.* The slope of the marginal product of labor curve depends on the production technology. In some activities marginal product diminishes quickly. For example, the marginal product of one bus driver is high, but the marginal product of a second driver on the same bus is close to zero. In other activities marginal product is fairly constant. For example, hiring a second window cleaner on a team almost doubles the amount of glass that can be cleaned in an hour—the marginal product of the second window cleaner is almost the same as the first. The steeper the slope of the marginal product curve, the more responsive is marginal revenue product to a change in labor input and the less responsive is the quantity of labor demanded to a change in the wage rate—the less elastic is the firm's demand for labor.
3. *The short-run elasticity of demand for the product.* If a wage rate changes, so does the supply of the good produced by the labor whose wage has changed. A change in supply changes the price of the good and changes the quantity of the good demanded. The greater the elasticity of demand for the good, the larger is the change in the quantity demanded of both the good and the labor used to produce it.

Long-Run Elasticity The **long-run elasticity of demand for labor** is the magnitude of the percentage change in the quantity of labor demanded divided by the percentage change in the wage rate when all inputs are varied. The long-run elasticity of demand for labor depends on *labor intensity* and on the long-run elasticity of demand for the product. In addition, it depends on the *substitutability of capital for labor.* The more easily capital can be substituted for labor in production, the more elastic is the long-run demand for labor. For example, it is fairly easy to substitute robots for assembly line workers in car factories and to substitute automatic picking machines for labor in vineyards and orchards. At the other extreme, it is difficult (though not impossible) to substitute robots for newspaper reporters, bank loan officers, and stockbrokers. The more readily capital can be substituted for labor, the more elastic is the firm's demand for labor in the long run.

REVIEW

The short-run elasticity of demand for labor depends on three factors:

- Labor intensity of the production process
- The slope of the marginal product of labor curve
- The short-run elasticity of demand for the product

The long-run elasticity of demand for labor also depends on three factors:

- Labor intensity of the production process
- Substitutability of capital for labor
- The long-run elasticity of demand for the product ◆

Supply of Factors

The supply of factors is determined by the decisions of households. Households allocate the factors of production they own to their most rewarding uses. The quantity supplied of any factor of production depends on its price. Usually, the higher the price of a factor of production, the larger is the quantity supplied. There is an important possible exception to this general law of supply concerning the supply of labor. It arises from the fact that labor is the single most important factor of production and the source of the largest portion of household income.

Let's examine household factor supply decisions, beginning with the supply of labor.

Supply of Labor

A household chooses how much labor to supply as part of its time allocation decision. Time is allocated between two broad activities:

- Market activity
- Nonmarket activity

Market activity is the same thing as supplying labor. **Nonmarket activity** consists of leisure and nonmarket production activities including housework, education, and training. The household obtains an immediate return from market activities in the form of an income. Nonmarket activities generate a return in the form of goods and services produced in the home, in the form of a higher future income, or in the form of leisure, which is valued for its own sake and which is classified as a good.

In deciding how to allocate its time between market activity and nonmarket activity, a household weighs the returns that it can get from the different activities. We are interested in the effects of the wage rate on the household's allocation of its time and on how much labor it supplies.

Wages and Quantity of Labor Supplied To induce a household to supply labor, it must be offered a high enough wage rate. Nonmarket activities are valued by households either because the time is used in some productive activity or because of the value they attach to leisure. In order for it to be worthwhile to supply labor, a household has to be offered a wage rate that is at least equal to the value it places on the last hour it spends in nonmarket activities. This wage rate—the lowest one for which a household will supply labor to the market—is called its **reservation wage**. At wage rates below the reservation wage, the household supplies no labor. Once the wage rate reaches the reservation wage, the household begins to supply labor. As the wage rate rises above the reservation wage, the household varies the quantity of labor that it supplies. But a higher wage rate has two offsetting effects on the quantity of labor supplied—a *substitution effect* and an *income effect*.

Substitution Effect Other things being equal, the higher the wage rate, the more will people economize on their nonmarket activities and increase the time they spend working. As the wage rate rises, the household will discontinue any nonmarket activity that yields a return that is less than the wage rate; instead, the household will switch to market activity. For example, a household might use some of its time to cook meals and do laundry—nonmarket activities—that can, alternatively, be bought for $10 an hour. If the wage rate available to the household is less than $10 an hour, the household will cook and wash for itself. If the household's wage rate rises above $10 an hour, it will be worthwhile for the household to work more hours and use part of its income ($10) to buy laundry services and to eat out. The higher wage rate induces a switch of time from nonmarket activities to market activities.

Income Effect The higher the household's wage rate, the higher is its income. A higher income, other things being equal, induces an increase in demand for most goods. Leisure, a component of nonmarket activity, is one of those goods. Since an increase in income creates an increase in the demand for leisure, it also creates a decrease in the amount of time allocated to market activities and therefore a fall in the quantity of labor supplied.

Backward-Bending Household Supply of Labor Curve The substitution effect and the income effect work in opposite directions. The higher the wage rate, the higher is the quantity of labor supplied via the substitution effect but the lower is the quantity of labor supplied via the income effect. At low wage rates, the substitution effect is larger than the income effect. As the wage rate rises, the household supplies more labor. But as the wage rate continues to rise, there comes a point at which the substitution effect and the income effect just offset each other. At that point, a change in the wage rate has no effect on the quantity of labor supplied. If the wage rate continues to rise, the income effect begins to dominate the substitution effect and the quantity of labor supplied declines. The household's supply of labor curve does not slope upward throughout its entire length but begins to bend back on itself. It is called a backward-bending supply curve.

Three individual household labor supply curves are shown in Fig. 14.5(a). Each household has a

FIGURE 14.5

The Supply of Labor

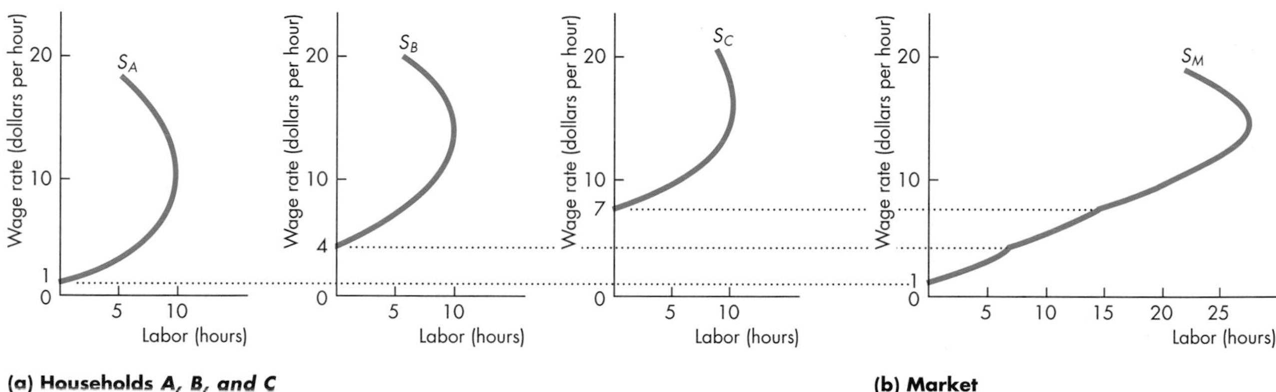

(a) Households *A, B, and C*

(b) Market

Part (a) shows the labor supply curves of three households (S_A, S_B, and S_C). Each household has a reservation wage below which it will supply no labor. As the wage rises above the reservation wage, the quantity of labor supplied rises to a maximum. If the wage continues to rise, the quantity of labor supplied begins to decline. Each household's supply curve eventually bends backward. When the quantity of labor supplied increases as the wage increases, the substitution effect dominates the income effect. When the quantity of labor supplied begins to fall as the wage rate increases, the income effect (which leads people to demand more leisure) dominates the substitution effect.

Part (b) shows how, by adding together the quantities of labor supplied by the individual households at each wage rate, we derive the market supply curve of labor (S_M). The market supply curve also eventually bends backward but, in the real world, at a higher wage rate than that currently experienced. The upward-sloping part of the labor supply curve before it bends backward is the part along which the market operates.

different reservation wage. Household A has a reservation wage of $1 an hour, household B of $4 an hour, and household C of $7 an hour. Each household's labor supply curve is backward bending.

Market Supply The quantity of labor supplied to the entire market is the total quantity supplied by all households. The market supply of labor curve is the sum of the supply curves of all the individual households. Figure 14.5(b) shows the market supply curve (S_M) derived from the supply curves of the three households (S_A, S_B, and S_C) in Fig. 14.5(a). At wage rates of less than $1 an hour, the three households do laundry and cook but they do not supply any market labor. The household most eager to supply market labor has a reservation wage of $1 an hour. As the wage rate rises to $4 an hour, household *A* increases the quantity of labor that it supplies to the market. The reservation wage of household *B* is $4 an hour, so as the wage rate rises above $4 an hour, the quantity of labor supplied in the market is the sum of the labor supplied by households *A* and *B*. When the wage rate reaches $7 an hour, household *C* begins to supply some labor to the market. At wage rates above $7 an hour, the quantity supplied in the market is equal to the sum of the quantities supplied by the three households.

Notice that the market supply curve S_M, like the individual household supply curves, eventually bends backward. But the market supply curve has a long upward-sloping section. The reason why the market supply curve slopes up for such a long stretch is that the reservation wages of individual households are not equal and, at higher wage rates, additional households are confronted with their reservation wage and so begin to supply labor.

Although the market supply curve eventually bends backward, no real-world wage rate is so high that the economy operates on the backward-bending portion of its labor supply curve. But many individual households are on the backward-bending portion of their own labor supply curve. Thus as wage rates rise, some people work fewer hours. But higher wage rates induce those workers who are on the upward-sloping part of their labor supply curve to supply more hours and induce additional workers to enter the work force. The response of these workers to higher wage rates dominates that of the workers whose work hours decline as wage rates rise. Therefore, for the economy as a whole, the labor supply curve slopes upward. For this reason, we will restrict our attention to the upward-sloping part of the labor supply curve in Fig. 14.5(b).

Supply to Individual Firms We've studied the labor supply decisions of individual households and seen how those decisions add up to the total market supply. But how is the supply of labor to each individual firm determined? The answer to this question depends on the degree of competitiveness in the labor market. In a perfectly competitive labor market, each firm faces a perfectly elastic supply of labor curve. This situation arises because the individual firm is such a small part of the total labor market that it has no influence on the wage rate.

Some labor markets are noncompetitive in the sense that firms can and do influence the price of the labor that they hire. In these cases, firms face an upward-sloping supply of labor curve. The more labor they wish to employ, the higher is the wage rate they have to offer. We examine how this type of labor market operates in Chapter 15. Here, we deal only with the case of perfectly competitive input markets.

REVIEW

At wage rates above the household's reservation wage, the household supplies labor to the market. An increase in the wage has two opposing effects on the quantity of labor supplied: a substitution effect (higher wage, more work) and an income effect (higher wage, less work). At low wages, the substitution effect is the more powerful and the labor supply curve slopes upward. At high wages, the income effect is the more powerful and the labor supply curve bends backward. The market supply of labor curve is the sum of the supply curves of individual households. Actual economies operate on the upward-sloping part of the market supply of labor curve. The supply of labor curve faced by each individual firm depends on the degree of competitiveness of the labor market. In a perfectly competitive labor market, each firm faces a perfectly elastic supply curve. ◆

Supply of Capital

Capital—the physical plant, buildings, and equipment used in production—is purchased by firms using funds borrowed from households. These funds are channeled through a complex network of financial institutions (banks, insurance companies, and others) and financial markets (bond and stock markets). But the amount of capital that firms can buy depends on the amount of saving that households undertake. Ultimately, households supply capital to firms by consuming less than their income. Thus the scale on which a household supplies capital depends on how much of its income the household saves.

The most important factors determining a household's saving are

- Its current income in relation to its expected future income
- The interest rate

Current and Future Income A household with a current income that is low in comparison with its expected future income saves little and might even have negative saving. A household with a current income that is high in comparison with its expected future income saves a great deal in the present in order to be able to consume more in the future. The stage in the household's life cycle is the main factor influencing whether current income is high or low in comparison with expected future income. Young households typically have a current income that is low in comparison with their expected future income, while older households have a current income that is high relative to their expected future income. The consequence of this pattern in income over the life cycle is that young people have negative saving and older people have positive saving. Thus the young incur debts (such as mortgages and consumer credit) to acquire durable goods and to consume more than their income, while older people save and accumulate assets (often in the form of pension and life insurance arrangements) to provide for their later retirement years.

Interest Rate and Capital Supply Curve A household's supply of capital is the stock of capital that it has accumulated as a result of its past saving. The household's supply curve of capital shows the relationship between the quantity of capital supplied and the interest rate. Other things being equal, a higher interest rate encourages people to economize on current consumption in order to take advantage of the higher return available from saving. Thus the higher the interest rate, the greater is the quantity of capital supplied.

Market Supply The market supply of capital is the sum of the supplies of all the individual households. The market supply curve of capital shows how the quantity of capital supplied varies as the interest rate varies. In the short run, the supply of capital is inelastic and might even be perfectly inelastic. Such a case is illustrated in Fig. 14.6 by the vertical supply curve *SS*. The long-run supply of capital is elastic. Such a case is illustrated in Fig. 14.6 by the supply curve *LS*.

Supply to Individual Firms In the short run, a firm can vary its labor input but not its capital. Thus in the short run, the firm's supply of capital is fixed. It has a specific set of capital assets. For example, an auto producer has a production assembly line; a laundromat operator has a number of washing machines and dryers; the campus print shop has a number of photocopying and other printing machines. These pieces of capital cannot be quickly disposed of or added to.

In the long run, a firm can vary all its inputs—capital as well as labor. A firm operating in a competitive capital market can obtain any amount of capital it chooses at the going market interest rate. Thus it faces a perfectly elastic supply of capital.

The fact that the short-run supply of capital is inelastic and the long-run supply is elastic has important implications for the returns obtained from different types of capital. We'll explore those implications later in this chapter when we study equilibrium in the capital market. But before that, let's complete our analysis of the supply of factors of production by examining the supply of land.

FIGURE 14.6

The Short-Run and Long-Run Supply of Capital

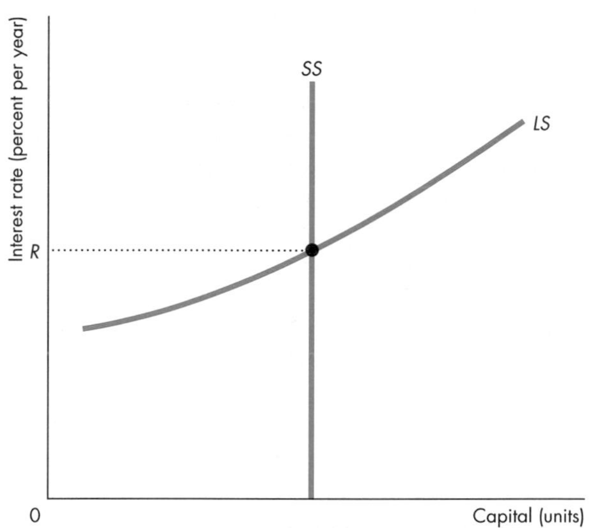

The long-run supply of capital (*LS*) is highly elastic. If the interest rate is above *R*, households increase their saving and increase the total amount of capital supplied. If the interest rate is below *R*, households decrease their saving and reduce the amount of capital supplied. The short-run supply of capital (*SS*) is highly inelastic (perfectly inelastic in the figure). For the economy as a whole and for individual firms in the short run, once capital is put in place, it is difficult to vary its quantity easily and quickly. Thus no matter what the interest rate, at a given point in time there is a given amount of capital supplied.

Supply of Land

Land is the stock of natural resources, and its aggregate quantity supplied cannot be changed by any individual decisions. Individual households can vary the amount of land they own, but whatever land is acquired by one household is sold by another, so the aggregate quantity of land supplied of any particular type and in any particular location is fixed regardless of the decisions of any individual household. This fact means that the supply of each particular piece of land is perfectly inelastic. Figure 14.7 illustrates such a supply. Regardless of the rent available, the quantity of land supplied on Chicago's Magnificent Mile is a fixed number of square feet.

Expensive land can be, and is, used more intensively than inexpensive land. For example, high-rise buildings enable land to be used more intensively. However, to use land more intensively, it has to be combined with another factor of production—capital. Increasing the amount of capital per block of land does nothing to change the supply of land itself.

Although the supply of each type of land is fixed and its supply is inelastic, each individual firm, operating in competitive land markets, faces an elastic supply of land. That is, each firm can acquire the land that it demands at the going rent, as determined in the marketplace. Thus provided that land markets are highly competitive, firms are price takers in these markets, just as they are in the markets for other factors of production.

FIGURE 14.7

The Supply of Land

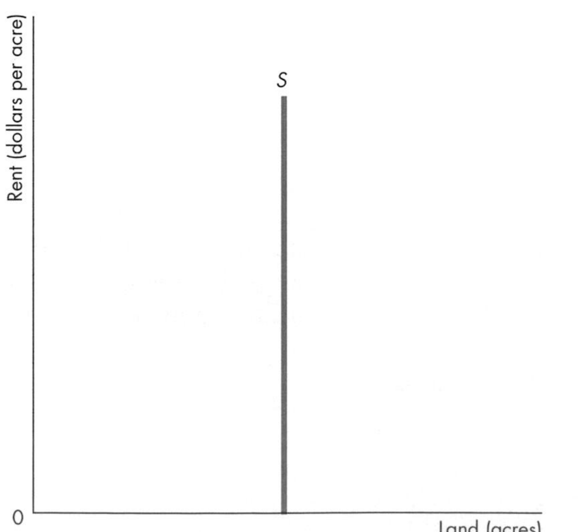

The supply of a given piece of land is perfectly inelastic. No matter what the rent, no more land than exists can be supplied.

REVIEW

The supply of capital is determined by households' saving decisions. Other things being equal, the higher the interest rate, the greater is the amount of capital supplied. The supply of capital to individual firms is highly inelastic in the short run but elastic in the long run. ◆ Individual households can vary the amount of land that they supply, but the aggregate supply of land is determined by the fact that there is a given, fixed quantity of it available. Thus the supply of each particular piece of land is perfectly inelastic. In a competitive land market, each firm faces an elastic supply of land at the going rent. ◆

Let's now see how factor prices and quantities are determined.

Competitive Equilibrium

The price of a factor of production and the quantity of it used are determined by the interaction of the demand for the factor and its supply. We'll illustrate competitive equilibrium by looking at the markets for labor, capital, and land and by looking at two examples of each.

Labor Market Equilibrium

Figure 14.8 shows two labor markets. That in part (a) is the labor market for national news anchors. Such people have a very high marginal revenue product, and this is reflected in the demand curve for their services, curve D_N. The supply of individuals with the required talents for this kind of job is low, and this fact is reflected in supply curve S_N. Equilibrium occurs at a high hourly wage rate ($500 in this example) and a low quantity employed, Q_N.

Figure 14.8(b) shows another market, that for babysitters. Although people value the output of

FIGURE 14.8
Labor Market Equilibrium

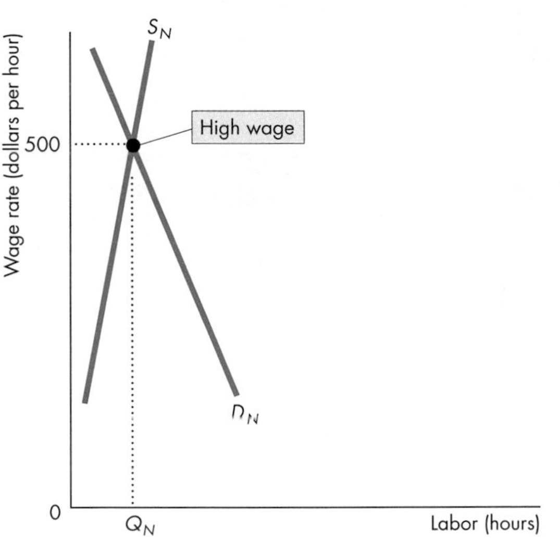

(a) News anchors

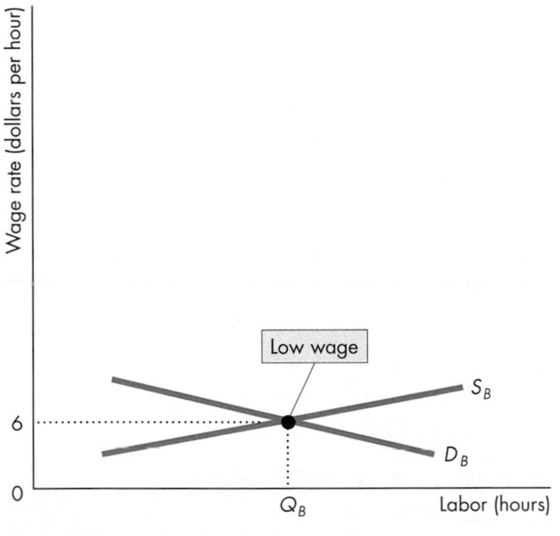

(b) Babysitters

News anchors (part a) have a high marginal revenue product, which is reflected in the high demand for their services—curve D_N. The number of people with the talents required for this job is few, and the supply curve is S_N. Equilibrium occurs at a high hourly wage rate of $500 and a low quantity employed, Q_N. The marginal revenue product of babysitters (part b) is low, so the demand curve is D_B. There is a huge supply of babysitters, and the supply curve is S_B. Equilibrium occurs at a low wage rate of $6 an hour and a high quantity employed, Q_B.

babysitters, the marginal revenue product of these services is low, a fact reflected in demand curve D_B. There are many households, typically those with high school students, willing to supply these services, and the supply curve is S_B. This market achieves an equilibrium at a low wage rate ($6 an hour in this example) and at a relatively high quantity employed, Q_B.

If there is an increase in the demand for news anchors, the demand curve D_N in Fig. 14.8(a) shifts to the right, increasing their wage rate and increasing the quantity employed. The higher wage rate will induce more households to offer their services in this activity. If there is an increase in demand for babysitters, the demand curve D_B in Fig. 14.8(b) shifts to the right, increasing their wage rate and increasing the quantity employed. Again, a higher wage rate will induce an increase in the quantity supplied. Movements in wage rates occur to achieve a balance between the quantities demanded and supplied in each individual labor market. Changes in demand result in changes in the wage rate that achieve a reallocation of the labor force.

There have been some important changes in recent years in the demand for a highly paid part of the labor force—senior executives. Reading Between the Lines on pp. 394–395 looks at this market.

Capital Market Equilibrium

Figure 14.9 shows capital market equilibrium. In Fig. 14.9(a), we illustrate that part of the capital market in the steel industry—the market for steel mills. The long-run supply of capital to the steel industry is shown as the perfectly elastic supply curve *LS*. But the actual quantity of steel mills in place is Q_1, and the short-run supply curve is SS_1. The demand curve for steel mills, determined by their marginal revenue product, is D_1. The interest rate earned by the owners of steel mills—the stockholders of USX and similar firms—is R_1.

Figure 14.9(b) shows that part of the capital market in the computer industry. Again, the long-run supply curve is *LS*, the same curve as in the steel industry. That is, in the long run, capital is supplied to each of these industries at an interest rate *R*. But the amount of computer-producing capital in place is Q_3, and the short-run supply curve is SS_3 in part (b). The demand curve for computer-producing capital, determined by its marginal revenue product, is

The Market for CEOs

The Wall Street Journal, April 17, 1991

Hard Times Trim CEO Pay Raises

by Amanda Bennett

For Barry F. Sullivan, chairman of First Chicago Corp., last year's hard times brought both good and bad pay news.

The bad news: a pay cut. Because of slumping profits at the Chicago-based bank-holding company, Mr. Sullivan did without a bonus last year, thus cutting his cash compensation by 50%, to $735,632. The good news: Last year, the company gave him 65,000 stock options, as well as 25,000 restricted shares valued at $662,500.

"Our senior people took a significant zap in terms of annual pay," says Paul Knuti, vice president of human-resources policy at First Chicago. But in bad times and good, he adds, "we want to provide them significant long-term opportunities. Then our shareholders will be happy, and we will create some nice wealth for our senior management."

As Mr. Sullivan and others are discovering, hard times cut into many executives' pay last year. Overall, chief executives' salary and bonuses still rose, but the rate of increase slid for the second year in a row, to its lowest rate in five years. Many executives saw annual bonuses slip away altogether as corporate profits faded.

But don't weep for anyone just yet. Behind the scenes, many companies continue to fatten executive stock plans. That may not have boosted pay for 1990, but it set the stage for huge pay gains in the future.

"It is very safe to predict that if the stock market remains strong, the gains reaped from [these] stock plans will yield dramatic numbers in the mid- to late-1990s," says Michael Halloran, head of the executive-compensation practice at compensation consultants Towers Perrin.

Of course, stock ownership implies risk, since stock prices go down as well as up. But most of these stock and option grants represent net additions to executives' compensation packages, and their sheer size means that even very small stock-price gains will translate into big paper profits. . . .

The Essence of the Story

Chief executives' salaries and bonuses increased in 1990 but at their lowest rate in five years, and many annual bonuses were eliminated entirely.

At the same time, many executives received increased compensation in the form of stock plans.

An example is Barry F. Sullivan, chairman of First Chicago Corp., who, because of slumping profits, took a cash pay cut of 50 percent in 1990. But he also received 65,000 stock options as well as 25,000 restricted shares valued at $662,500.

Paul Knuti, vice-president of human-resources policy at First Chicago, says that the company's senior executives took a significant cut in annual pay but the company wants to provide them with significant long-term rewards.

Stock ownership is risky, since stock prices go both down and up. But if the stock market remains strong, executives stand to make large gains later in the 1990s.

Background and Analysis

In 1989, the demand curve for top executives at First Chicago was D_{89} in part (a) of the figure. The short-run supply curve of senior executives was *SS*, and an executive's wage was $500,000 a year. (The numbers are hypothetical.)

In 1990, the marginal productivity of top executives declined and the demand curve for their services shifted to the left to D_{90} in part (a) of the figure. Their wages fell to $300,000.

First Chicago is a small buyer in the large nationwide market for senior executives, and in the long run, if it does not offer a compensation package comparable with those of other firms, it will lose its executives. It faces a long-run supply curve that is perfectly elastic, shown as *LS* in part (b) of the figure.

If the demand for executives at First Chicago remains at D_{90}, the company will decrease the number of executives employed to L_1 and pay that smaller number the going market rate of $500,000 a year.

But First Chicago wants its executives to become more productive, so it offers them stock in the company, the value of which depends on the effectiveness of the executives.

If the plan works, the marginal productivity of executives increases, and the demand curve shifts back to the right to D_{95}. First Chicago continues to employ the same number of executives as before—*L*—and an executive's pay package—wage plus income from stocks—returns to $500,000.

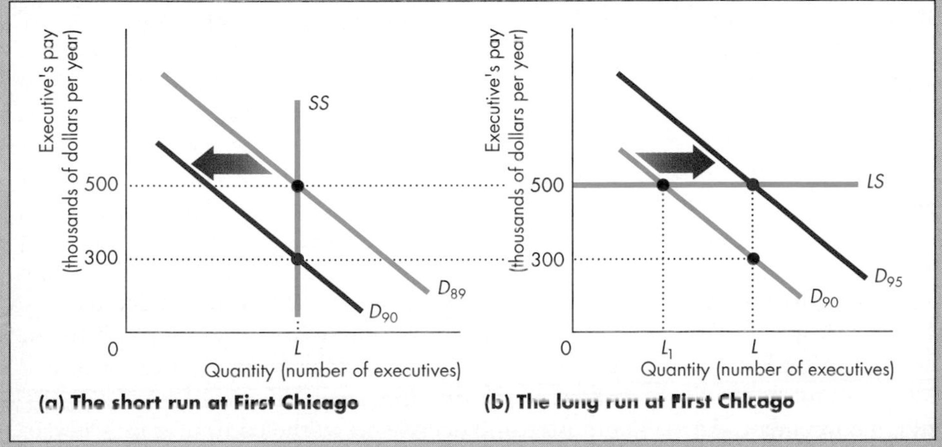

(a) The short run at First Chicago

(b) The long run at First Chicago

FIGURE 14.9

Capital Market Equilibrium

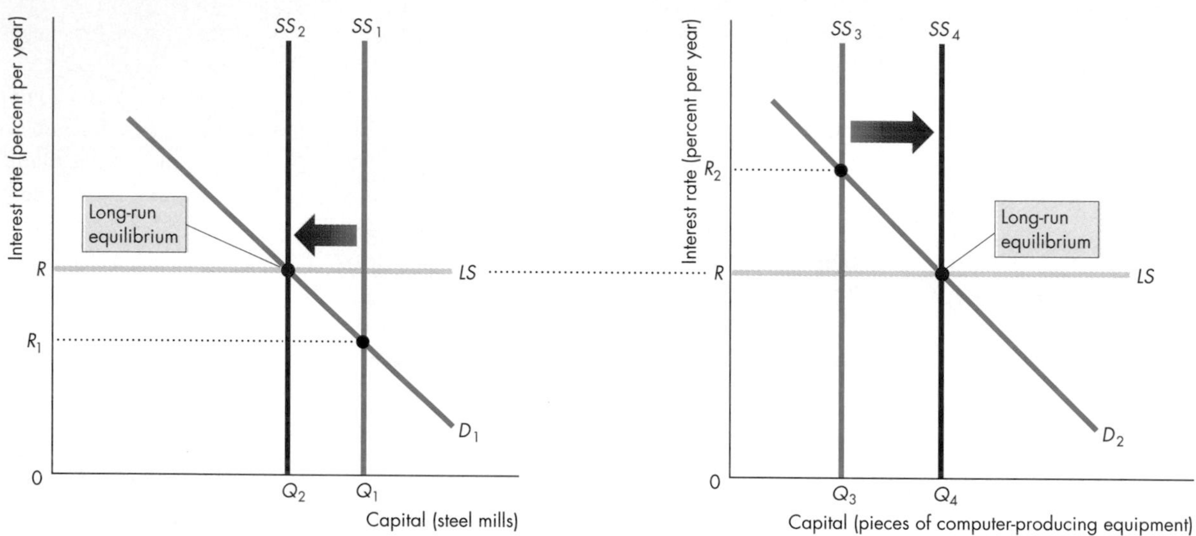

(a) Steel industry

(b) Computer industry

The long-run supply curve of capital (*LS*) in the steel industry (part a) and the computer industry (part b) is perfectly elastic. The number of steel mills in place is fixed at Q_1, so the short-run supply curve in the steel industry is SS_1. The demand curve for steel mills is D_1. The interest rate on capital invested in steel is R_1. The amount of computer-producing equipment in place is fixed at Q_3, so the short-run supply curve in the computer industry is SS_3. The demand curve for computer-producing equipment is D_2. The interest rate in the computer industry is R_2.

With a higher interest rate in the computer industry, capital leaves the steel industry and goes into the computer industry. The short-run supply curves shift. In the steel industry, the short-run supply curve shifts to the left, to SS_2, and the interest rate rises. In the computer industry, the short-run supply curve shifts to the right, to SS_4, and the interest rate falls. In long-run equilibrium, interest rates are the same in both industries.

D_2. The interest rate earned by the owners of computer production equipment—the stockholders of IBM and similar firms—is R_2.

You can see that the interest rate paid to owners of capital in the steel industry is lower than that in the computer industry. This inequality of interest rates on capital sets up an interesting dynamic adjustment process that gradually lowers the stock of capital in the steel industry and increases the stock of capital in the computer industry. With a low interest rate on capital in the steel industry and a high interest rate on capital in the computer industry, it pays people to take their investments out of the steel industry and to put them into the computer industry. But physical plant and equipment have been built in the steel industry and cannot be readily transformed into computer-making equipment. An individual steel producer could sell off its unwanted capital or operate it until it has worn out. Even if the producer does sell off the equipment, the firm that buys it will be willing to pay only a low price for it and that firm also will not replace the equipment when it is finally worn out. Whether the equipment is operated by its present owner or a new owner that buys it for a low price, the equipment continues to be operated. But it gradually wears out and is not replaced, so the capital stock in the steel industry declines. The short-run supply curve shifts to the left, to SS_2. Conversely, as additional saving is made, it is directed toward the computer industry, so the short-run supply curve in that industry shifts to the right, to SS_4. During this process, interest rates adjust in the two industries, increasing in the steel industry and decreasing in the computer industry.

Eventually, in long-run equilibrium, the interest rate on capital in the two industries will have equalized at R.

The Stock Market In the story of a contracting steel industry and an expanding computer industry that we have just worked through, you might be wondering why people are willing to own shares in the steel industry when the rate of return on steel mills is below that on computer-producing equipment. The answer is that the stock market reacts by lowering the value of steel shares relative to computer shares. The fall in the price of steel shares increases the interest rate that people expect to earn on steel shares to equal that expected on computer shares. That is, during the period in which the steel industry is declining and its capital stock is decreasing, the stock market lowers the value of the steel industry to equalize the return expected on shares in that industry and in all other industries.

Next, let's see how rents are determined in the market for land.

Land Market Equilibrium

Equilibrium in the land market occurs at rents that allocate the fixed amounts of land available to their highest-value uses. Figure 14.10 illustrates two land markets. Part (a) shows the market for land on Chicago's Magnificent Mile. Its marginal revenue product gives rise to the demand curve D_M. There are a fixed number of square feet of land, Q_M, so the supply is inelastic, as shown by the curve S_M. Equilibrium occurs at a rent of $10,000 a square foot a year.

Figure 14.10(b) illustrates the market for farmland in Iowa. Here, the marginal revenue product produces the demand curve D_I. There is a vast amount of land available but, again, only a fixed quantity—in this case Q_I. Thus the supply curve lies a long way to the right but is vertical—perfectly inelastic—at S_I. Here, the equilibrium rent occurs at $1,000 an acre a year.

The explanation of land rents given here can be extended to the rents and prices of all natural resources, and a discussion of some of these broader issues is found in Our Advancing Knowledge on pp. 398–399.

We've now studied the markets for the three factors of production and seen how wages, interest, and rent are determined. We now turn to our final task in this chapter—defining and distinguishing between economic rent and transfer earnings.

FIGURE 14.10

Land Market Equilibrium

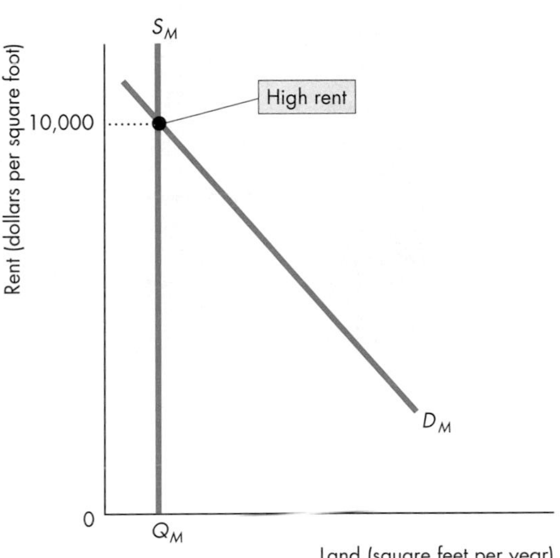

(a) Magnificent Mile

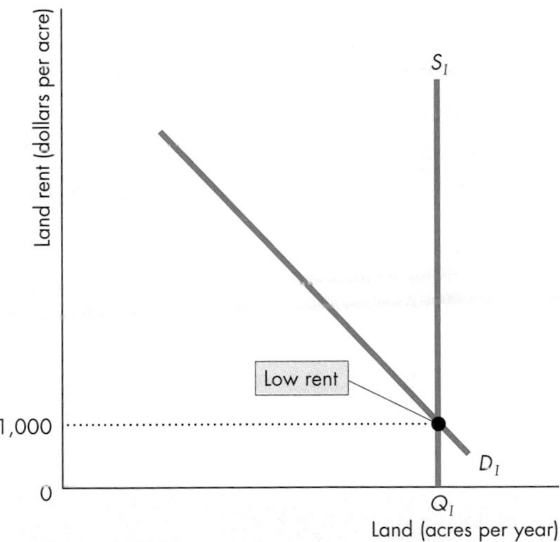

(b) Iowa farmland

The marginal revenue product of land on Chicago's Magnificent Mile gives rise to the demand curve D_M (part a). The quantity of land on the Magnificent Mile is fixed at Q_M, so the supply curve is S_M. Equilibrium occurs at an annual rent of $10,000 a square foot. The marginal revenue product of farmland in Iowa (part b) gives rise to a demand curve D_I. The quantity of farmland in Iowa is fixed at Q_I, and the supply curve is S_I. Equilibrium occurs at an annual rent of $1,000 an acre.

Running out of Space?

Is there a limit to economic growth, or can we expand production and population without effective limit? One of the most influential answers to these questions was given by Thomas Malthus in 1798. He reasoned that population, unchecked, would grow at a geometric rate—1, 2, 4, 8, 16, . . .—while the food supply would grow at an arithmetic rate—1, 2, 3, 4, 5, ... To prevent the population from outstripping the available food supply, there would be periodic wars, famines, and plagues. In Malthus's view, only "moral restraint" could prevent such periodic disasters.

As industrialization proceeded through the nineteenth century, Malthus's idea came to be applied to all natural resources, especially those that are exhaustible. A modern day Malthusian, ecologist Paul Ehrlich, believes that we are sitting on a "population bomb" and that the government must limit both population growth and the resources that may be used each year.

"Men, like all animals, naturally multiply in proportion to the means of their subsistence."

Adam Smith
The Wealth of Nations

In 1931, Harold Hotelling developed a theory of natural resources with different predictions from those of Malthus. The Hotelling Principle is that the relative price of an exhaustible natural resource will rise steadily, bringing a decline in the quantity used and an increase in the use of substitute resources.

Julian Simon, a contemporary economist, has challenged both the Malthusian gloom and the Hotelling Principle. He believes that *people* are the "ultimate resource" and predicts that a rising population *lessens* the pressure on natural resources. A bigger population provides a larger number of resourceful people who can work out more efficient ways of using scarce resources. As these solutions are found, the prices of exhaustible resources actually fall. To demonstrate his point, in 1980 Simon bet Ehrlich that the prices of five metals—copper, chrome, nickel, tin, and tungsten—would fall during the 1980s. Simon won the bet!

No matter whether it is agricultural land, an exhaustible natural resource, or the space in the center of Chicago and no matter whether it is 1992 or, as shown here, 1909, there is a limit to what is available, and we persistently push against that limit. Economists see urban congestion as a consequence of the value of doing business in the city center relative to the cost. They see the price mechanism, bringing ever higher rents and prices of raw materials, as the means of allocating and rationing scarce natural resources. Malthusians, in contrast, explain congestion as the consequence of population pressure, and they see the solution as population control.

In Tokyo, the pressure on space is so great that in some residential neighborhoods, a parking space costs $1,700 a month. To economize on this expensive space—and to lower the cost of car ownership and hence boost the sale of cars—Honda, Nissan, and Toyota, three of Japan's big car producers, have developed a parking machine that enables two cars to occupy the space of one. The most basic of these machines costs a mere $10,000—less than 6 months of parking fees.

A Parson & a Mathematician

Probe ***the Pressure on Resources***

Thomas Robert Malthus (1766–1834), pictured right, an English parson and professor, was an extremely influential social scientist. In his best-selling *Essay on the Principle of Population,* published in 1798, he argued that population growth would outstrip food production. Modern-day Malthusians believe that his basic idea was right and that it applies to all natural resources.

The most profound work on the economics of natural resources is that of Harold Hotelling (1895–1973), pictured left. Hotelling worked as a journalist, schoolteacher, and mathematical consultant before becoming an economics professor at Columbia University. He explained how the price mechanism allocates exhaustible resources, making them progressively more expensive. Their higher price encourages the development of new technologies, the discovery of new sources of supply, and the development of substitutes.

Economic Rent and Transfer Earnings

The total income of a factor of production is made up of its economic rent and its transfer earnings. **Economic rent** is an income received by the owner of a factor over and above the amount required to induce that owner to offer the factor for use. The income required to induce the owner to offer the factor for use is called **transfer earnings.**

These concepts of economic rent and transfer earnings are illustrated in Fig. 14.11. The figure shows the market for a factor of production. It could be *any* factor of production—labor, capital, or land. The demand curve for the factor of production is *D*, and its supply curve is *S*. The factor price is *PF* and the quantity of the factor used is *QF*. The income of the factor is the sum of the yellow and green areas. The yellow area below the supply curve measures transfer earnings, and the green area below the factor price but above the supply curve measures economic rent.

FIGURE 14.11

Economic Rent and Transfer Earnings

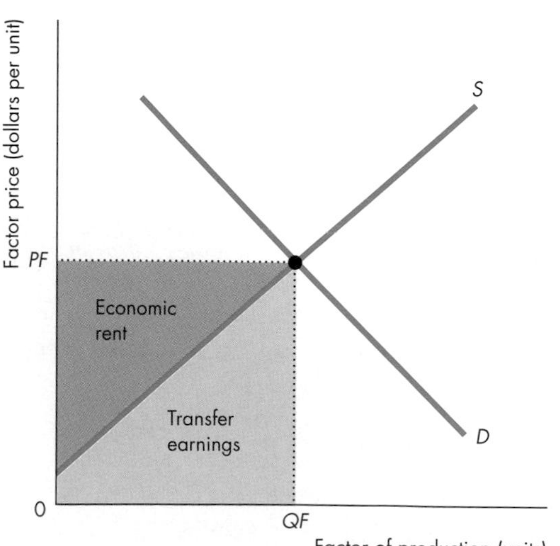

The total income of a factor of production is made up of its economic rent and its transfer earnings. Transfer earnings are measured by the yellow area under the supply curve, and economic rent is measured by the green area above the supply curve and below the factor price.

To see why the area below the supply curve measures transfer earnings, recall that a supply curve can be interpreted in two different ways. The standard interpretation is that a supply curve indicates the quantity supplied at a given price. But the alternative interpretation of a supply curve is that it shows the minimum price at which a given quantity is willingly supplied. If suppliers receive only the minimum amount required to induce them to supply each unit of the factor of production, they will be paid a different price for each unit. The prices will trace the supply curve, and the income received is entirely transfer earnings—the yellow area in Fig. 14.11.

The concept of economic rent is similar to the concept of consumer surplus that you met in Chapter 7, p. 171. Consumer surplus, recall, is the difference between the price the household pays for a good and the maximum price it would be willing to pay, as indicated by the demand curve. In a parallel sense, economic rent is the difference between the factor price a household actually receives and the minimum factor price at which it would be willing to supply a given amount of a factor of production.

It is important to distinguish between *economic rent* and *rent*. Rent is the price paid to the factor of production land. Economic rent is a component of the income received by every factor of production.

The portion of the income of a factor of production that consists of economic rent depends on the elasticity of the supply of the factor of production. When the supply of a factor of production is inelastic, its entire income is economic rent. Most of Peter Jennings's and Joe Montana's incomes are economic rent. When the supply of a factor of production is perfectly elastic, none of its income is economic rent. Most of the income of a babysitter is transfer earnings. In general, when the supply curve is neither perfectly elastic nor perfectly inelastic (like that illustrated in Fig. 14.11), some part of the factor income is economic rent and the other part is transfer earnings.

Figure 14.12 illustrates the three possibilities. Part (a) of the figure shows the market for a particular parcel of land in New York City. The land is fixed in size at *L* square yards. Therefore the supply

FIGURE 14.12

Economic Rent and Supply Elasticity

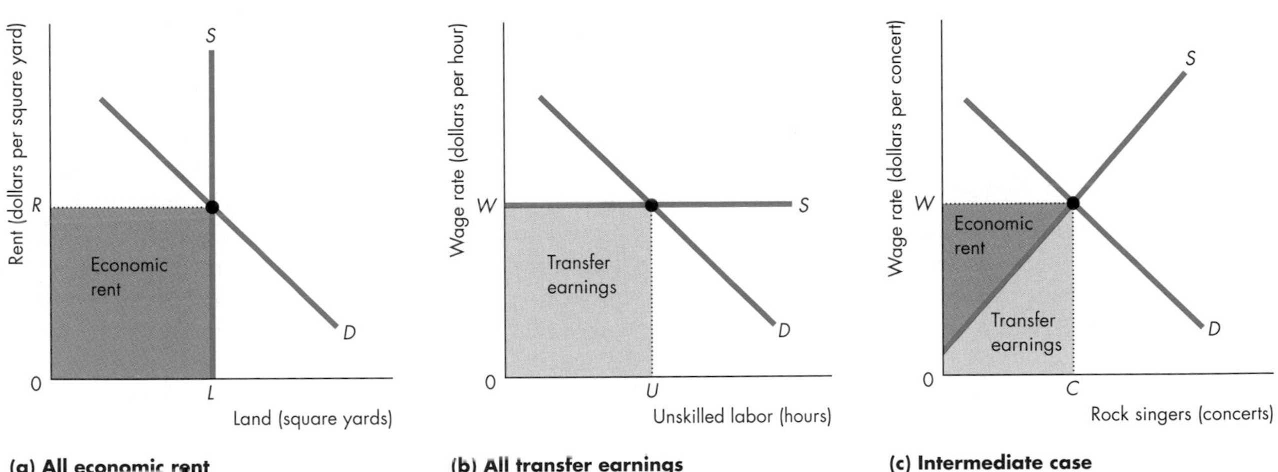

(a) All economic rent **(b) All transfer earnings** **(c) Intermediate case**

When the supply of the factor of production is perfectly inelastic (the supply curve is vertical), as in part (a), the entire factor income is economic rent. When the supply of the factor of production is perfectly elastic, as in part (b), the factor's entire income is transfer earnings. When a factor supply curve slopes upward, as in part (c), part of the factor income is economic rent and part is transfer earnings. Land is the example shown in part (a); unskilled labor in poor countries such as India and China in part (b); and rock singers in part (c).

curve of the land is vertical—perfectly inelastic. No matter what the rent on the land is, there is no way of increasing the quantity that can be supplied.

The demand for that block of land is determined by its marginal revenue product. The marginal revenue product in turn depends on the uses to which the land can be put. In a central business district such as Manhattan, the marginal revenue product is high because a large number of people are concentrated in that area, making it a prime place for conducting valuable business. Suppose that the marginal revenue product of this block of land is shown by the demand curve in Fig. 14.12(a). Then it commands a rent of *R*. The entire income accruing to the owner of the land is the green area in the figure. This income is *economic rent.* The rent charged for this piece of land depends entirely on its marginal revenue product—on the demand curve. If the demand curve shifts to the right, the rent rises. If the demand curve shifts to the left, the rent falls. The quantity of land supplied remains constant at *L*.

Is coffee expensive in New York City because rents are high, or are rents high because people in New York City are willing to pay a high price for coffee? The conclusion we've just reached answers this question. We've seen that the rent of a New York City block is determined entirely by the demand for it and that the demand, in turn, is determined by the marginal revenue product. Land has a high marginal revenue product only if people are willing to pay a high price to use the land. Of course, from the point of view of McDonald's, it feels that it has to charge a high price for coffee at its 57th Street restaurant because of the high rent it pays there. But the rent wouldn't be high if McDonald's (and other potential users) did not have a high marginal revenue product "attached" to that land, making it willing to pay those high rents.

Figure 14.12(b) shows the market for a factor of production that is in perfectly elastic supply. An example of such a market might be that for unskilled labor in a poor country such as India or China. In those countries, large amounts of labor flock to the cities and are available for work at the going wage rate (in this case, *W*). Thus in these situations, the supply of labor is almost perfectly elastic. The entire income earned by this labor is transfer earnings. It receives no economic rent.

Figure 14.12(c) shows the market for rock singers. To induce a rock singer to sing at a larger number of concerts, a higher income has to be offered—the rock singer's supply curve is upward sloping. The demand curve—measuring the marginal revenue product of the rock singer—is labeled *D* in the figure. Equilibrium occurs where the rock singer receives a wage of *W* and sings in *C* concerts. The green area above the rock singer's supply curve is economic rent, and the yellow area below the supply curve is the rock singer's transfer earnings. If the rock singer is not offered at least the amount of the transfer earnings, then the singer will withdraw from the rock concert market and perform an alternative activity.

◆ ◆ ◆ ◆ We've now studied the market for the three factors of production—labor, capital, and land—and we've seen how the returns to these factors of production—wages, interest, and rent—are determined. We've seen the crucial role played in determining the demand for a factor of production by the factor's marginal revenue product. We've seen how the interaction of demand and supply determines factor prices and factor incomes. We've also seen how changes in these prices and incomes come about from changes in demand and supply. Finally, we've distinguished between economic rent and transfer earnings. ◆ ◆ In the next chapter, we're going to examine some detailed features of the labor market more closely, explaining differences in wage rates among the skilled and the unskilled, males and females, and racial and ethnic minorities.

SUMMARY

Factor Prices and Incomes

The factors of production—labor, capital, and land—earn a return—wages, interest, and rent. Labor is the most important source of income. Factor prices are determined by the demand for and supply of factors of production. Incomes are determined by the prices of factors of production and the quantities used. An increase in the demand for a factor of production increases the factor's price and income; a decrease in the demand for a factor of production decreases its price and income. An increase in supply increases the quantity used of a factor of production but decreases its price. A decrease in supply decreases the quantity used and increases the factor's price. Whether an increase in supply leads to an increase or a decrease in the income of a factor of production depends on the elasticity of demand for the factor. When elasticity of demand is greater than 1, an increase in supply leads to an increase in the factor's income. When the elasticity of demand for a factor is less than 1, an increase in supply leads to a decrease in the factor's income. (pp. 378–380)

Demand for Factors

A firm's demand for a factor stems from its desire to maximize profit. The extra revenue generated by hiring one more unit of a factor is called the marginal revenue product of the factor. A firm's demand curve for a factor is derived from that factor's marginal revenue product curve. A firm demands an input up to the point at which the marginal revenue product of the factor equals the factor's price.

A firm's labor input is variable in both the short run and the long run. The firm's capital input may be varied only in the long run. The elasticity of the demand for labor in the short run depends on the short-run elasticity of demand for the firm's product, on the labor intensity of the production process, and on the slope of the marginal product of labor curve. The long-run elasticity of a firm's demand for labor depends on the long-run elasticity of demand for the product, on labor intensity, and on the ease with which capital can be substituted for labor.

The market demand for labor is the sum of the demands by each individual firm. (pp. 380–387)

Supply of Factors

The supply of factors is determined by households' decisions on the allocation of their time and the division of their income between consumption and saving. In choosing how much time to allocate to market activities, each household compares the wage rate that can be earned with the value of its time in other nonmarket activities. The household will supply no market labor at wage rates below its reservation wage. At wage rates above the household's reservation wage, the quantity of labor supplied rises as long as the substitution effect of the higher wage rate is larger than the income effect. As the wage rate continues to rise, the income effect, which leads to more time taken for leisure, becomes larger than the substitution effect, and the quantity of labor supplied by the household falls.

The market supply curve of labor is the sum of the supply curves of all households. Like the household's labor supply curve, the market supply curve of labor eventually bends backward. However, the response to higher wage rates of households on the upward-sloping part of their labor supply curve dominates the response of those on the backward-bending part, and the market supply curve slopes upward over the range of wage rates that we experience.

Households supply capital by saving. Saving increases as the interest rate increases. The supply of capital to an individual firm is highly inelastic in the short run but highly elastic in the long run.

The supply of land is fixed and independent of its rent. (pp. 387–392)

Competitive Equilibrium

In a competitive factor market, the factor price and quantity used are determined at the point of intersection of the demand and supply curves. High factor prices occur for factors of production that have a high marginal revenue product and a low supply. Low factor prices occur for factors of production with a low marginal revenue product and a high supply. (pp. 392–399)

Economic Rent and Transfer Earnings

Economic rent is that part of the income received by a factor owner over and above the amount needed to induce the owner to supply the factor of production for use. The rest of a factor's income is transfer earnings. When the supply of a factor is perfectly inelastic, its entire income is made up of economic rent. Factors that have a perfectly elastic supply receive only transfer earnings. In general the supply curve of a factor is upward sloping, and part of its income received is transfer earnings (below the supply curve) and part is economic rent (above the supply curve but below the factor price). (pp. 400–402)

KEY ELEMENTS

Key Terms

Average revenue product, 383
Average revenue product curve, 383
Derived demand, 380
Economic rent, 400
Long-run demand for labor, 385
Long-run elasticity of demand for labor, 387
Marginal revenue product, 381
Marginal revenue product curve, 383
Market activity, 388
Nonmarket activity, 388
Reservation wage, 388
Short-run demand for labor, 385
Short-run elasticity of demand for labor, 386
Transfer earnings, 400

Key Figures and Tables

REVIEW QUESTIONS

1 Explain what happens to the price of a factor of production and its income if the following occurs:

a There is an increase in demand for the factor.
b There is an increase in supply of the factor.
c There is a decrease in demand for the factor.
d There is a decrease in supply of the factor.

2 Explain why the effect of a change in supply of a factor on a factor's income depends on the elasticity of demand for the factor.

3 Define marginal revenue product and distinguish between marginal revenue product and marginal revenue.

4 Why does marginal revenue product decline as the quantity of a factor employed increases?

5 What is the relationship between the demand curve for a factor of production and its marginal revenue product curve? Why?

6 Show that the condition for maximum profit in the product market—marginal cost equals marginal revenue—is equivalent to the condition for maximum profit in the factor market—marginal revenue product equals marginal cost of factor (equals factor price in a competitive factor market).

7 Review the main influences on the demand for a factor of production—the influences that shift the demand curve for a factor.

8 What determines the short-run and long-run elasticity of demand for labor?

9 What determines the supply of labor?

10 Why might the supply of labor curve bend backward at a high enough wage rate?

11 What determines the supply of capital?

12 Define economic rent and transfer earnings and distinguish between these two components of income.

13 Suppose that a factor of production is in perfectly inelastic supply. If the marginal revenue product of the factor decreases, what happens to the price, quantity used, income, transfer earnings, and rent of the factor?

PROBLEMS

1 Wanda owns a fish shop. She employs students to sort and pack the fish. Students can pack the following amounts of fish in an hour:

Number of students	Quantity of fish (pounds)
1	20
2	50
3	90
4	120
5	145
6	165
7	180
8	190

a Draw the average and marginal product curves of these students.
b If Wanda can sell her fish for 50¢ a pound, draw the average and marginal revenue product curves.
c Draw Wanda's demand for labor curve.
d If all fish packers in Wanda's area pay their packers $7.50 an hour, how many students will Wanda hire?

2 The price of fish falls to 33.33¢ a pound, and fish packers' wages remain at $7.50 an hour.

a What happens to Wanda's average and marginal product curves?
b What happens to her average and marginal revenue product curves?
c What happens to her demand for labor curve?
d What happens to the number of students that she hires?

3 Fish packers' wages increase to $10 an hour, but the price of fish remains at 50¢ a pound.

a What happens to the average and marginal revenue product curves?
b What happens to Wanda's demand curve?
c How many packers does Wanda hire?

4 Using the information provided in problem 1, calculate Wanda's marginal revenue and marginal cost, marginal revenue product, and marginal cost of labor. Show that when Wanda is making maximum profit, marginal cost equals marginal revenue and marginal revenue product equals the marginal cost of labor.

5 You are given the following information about the labor market in an isolated town in the Amazon rainforest. Everyone works for logging companies, but there are many logging companies in the town. The market for logging workers is perfectly competitive. The town's labor supply is given as follows:

Wage rate (cruzados per hour)	Quantity of labor supplied (hours)
2	120
4	160
6	200
8	240
10	280
12	320
14	360

The market demand for labor from all the logging firms in the town is as follows:

Wage rate (cruzados per hour)	Quantity of labor demanded (hours)
2	400
4	360
6	320
8	280
10	240
12	200
14	160

a What is the competitive equilibrium wage rate?
b What is the quantity of labor employed?
c What is total labor income?
d How much of that labor income is economic rent and how much is transfer earnings? (You might find it easier to answer this question by drawing graphs of the demand and supply curves and then finding the economic rent and transfer earnings as areas on the graph in a manner similar to what was done in Fig. 14.11.)

CHAPTER 15

LABOR MARKETS

After studying this chapter, you will be able to:

- Explain why skilled workers earn more, on. the average, than unskilled workers
- Explain why college graduates earn more, on the average, than high school graduates
- Explain why union workers earn higher wages than nonunion workers
- Explain why, on the average, men earn more than women and whites earn more than minorities
- Predict the effects of a comparable-worth program

The Sweat of Our Brows

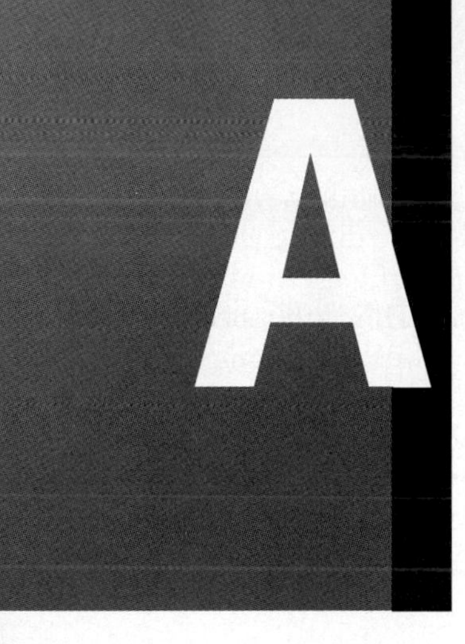

S YOU WELL KNOW, COLLEGE IS NOT JUST A BALL. THOSE exams and problem sets require a lot of hard work. Are they worth the effort that goes into them? What is the payoff? Is it sufficient to make up for the years of tuition, room and board, and lost wages? (You could, after all, be washing dishes now instead of slogging through this economics course.) ◆◆ Many workers belong to labor unions. Usually, union workers earn a higher wage than nonunion workers in comparable jobs. Why? How are unions able to get higher wages for their members than the wages that nonunion workers are paid? ◆◆ Among the most visible and persistent differences in earnings are those between men and women and between whites and minorities. White men, on the average, earn incomes that are one third higher than the incomes earned by black men. Black men earn more, in descending order, than Hispanic men, white women, black women, and Hispanic women, who earn only 56 cents for each dollar earned by the average white man. Certainly a lot of individuals defy the averages. But why do minorities and women so consistently earn less than white men? Is it because of discrimination and exploitation? Or is it because of economic factors? Or is it a combination of the two? ◆◆ Equal pay legislation has resulted in comparable-worth programs, which try to ensure that jobs of equivalent value receive the same pay regardless of the pay set by the market. Can comparable-worth programs bring economic help to women and minorities?

◆ ◆ ◆ ◆ In this chapter, we study the way labor markets work and answer questions such as these. We begin by using the competitive labor market model developed in Chapter 14 to analyze the effects on wages of differences in education and training. We then extend the model to explain differences in union and nonunion wages, to explain differences in pay among men, women, and minorities, and to analyze the effects of comparable-worth laws.

Skill Differentials

Differences in earnings between workers with varying levels of education and training can be explained by using a model of competitive labor markets. In the real world, there are many different levels and varieties of education and training. To keep our analysis as clear as possible, we'll study a model economy in which there are just two different levels that result in two types of labor, what we will call skilled labor and unskilled labor. We'll study the demand for and supply of these two types of labor and see why there is a difference in their wages and what determines that difference. Let's begin by looking at the demand for the two types of labor.

The Demand for Skilled and Unskilled Labor

Skilled workers can perform a wide variety of tasks that unskilled workers would perform badly or perhaps could not even perform at all. Imagine an untrained, inexperienced person performing surgery or piloting an airplane. Because skilled workers perform complex tasks, they have a higher marginal revenue product than unskilled labor. As we learned in Chapter 14, the demand for labor curve is derived from the marginal revenue product curve. The higher the marginal revenue product of labor, the higher is the demand for labor.

Figure 15.1(a) shows the demand curves for skilled and unskilled labor. At any given level of employment, firms are willing to pay a higher wage to a skilled worker than to an unskilled worker. The gap between the two wages is the difference between the marginal revenue products of a given number of skilled and unskilled workers. This difference is the marginal revenue product of skill. For example, at an employment level of 2,000 hours, firms are willing to pay $12.50 for a skilled worker and only $5 for an unskilled worker. The difference in the marginal revenue product of the two workers is $7.50 an hour. Thus the marginal revenue product of skill is $7.50 an hour.

The Supply of Skilled and Unskilled Labor

Skills are costly to acquire. Furthermore, a worker pays the cost of acquiring a skill before benefiting from a higher wage. For example, attending college usually leads to a higher income, but the higher income is not earned until after graduation. These facts make the acquisition of skills similar to investment. To emphasize the investment nature of acquiring a skill, we call that activity an investment in human capital. **Human capital** is the accumulated skill and knowledge of human beings. The value of a person's human capital is the present value of the extra earnings received as a result of acquiring skill and knowledge. (The concept of present value is explained in Chapter 9.) It is equivalent to a sum of money that, if invested today at the average interest rate, will yield a stream of income equivalent to the extra earnings resulting from a person's acquired knowledge and skills.

The cost of acquiring a skill includes actual expenditures on such things as tuition and room and board and also includes costs in the form of lost or reduced earnings while the skill is being acquired. When a person goes to school full-time, that cost is the total earnings forgone. However, some people acquire skills on the job. Such skill acquisition is called on-the-job training. Usually, a worker undergoing on-the-job training is paid a lower wage than one doing a comparable job but not undergoing training. In such a case, the cost of acquiring the skill is the difference between the wage paid to a person not being trained and that paid to a person being trained.

Supply Curves of Skilled and Unskilled Labor The position of the supply curve of skilled workers

FIGURE 15.1
Skill Differentials

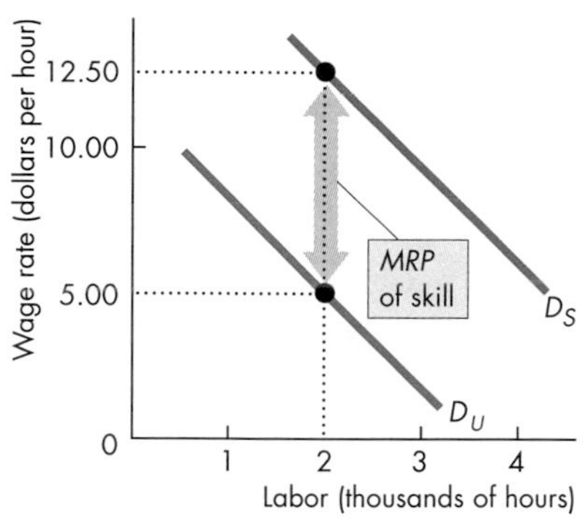

(a) Demand for skilled and unskilled labor

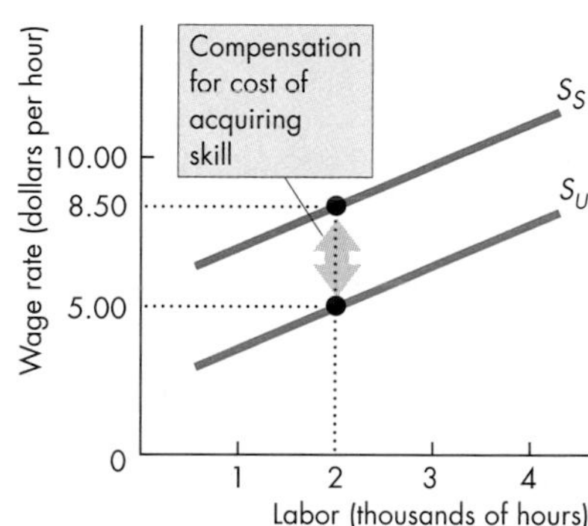

(b) Supply of skilled and unskilled labor

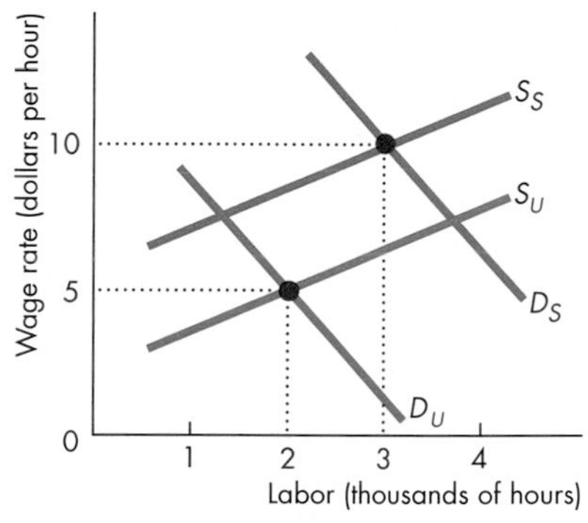

(c) Markets for skilled and unskilled labor

Part (a) illustrates the marginal revenue product of skill. Unskilled workers have a marginal revenue product that gives rise to the demand curve marked D_U. Skilled workers have a higher marginal revenue product than unskilled workers. Therefore the demand curve for skilled workers, D_S, lies to the right of D_U. The vertical distance between these two curves is the marginal revenue product of the skill.

Part (b) shows the effects of the cost of acquiring skills on the supply curves of labor. The supply curve for unskilled workers is S_U. Skilled workers have to incur costs in order to acquire their skills. Therefore they would supply labor services only at a wage rate that exceeds that of unskilled labor. The supply curve for skilled workers is S_S. The vertical distance between these two curves is the required compensation for the cost of acquiring a skill.

Part (c) shows the determination of the equilibrium levels of employment and the skilled-unskilled wage differential. Unskilled workers earn the wage rate $5 an hour where the quantities demanded and supplied of unskilled workers are equal. The employment level of unskilled workers is 2,000 hours. Skilled workers earn the wage rate $10 an hour, where the quantities demanded and supplied of skilled workers are equal. The employment level of skilled workers is 3,000 hours. Wages for skilled workers are always greater than those for unskilled workers.

reflects the cost of acquiring the skill. Figure 15.1(b) shows two supply curves, one for skilled workers and the other for unskilled workers. The supply curve for skilled workers is S_S, and that for unskilled workers is S_U.

The skilled worker's supply curve lies above the unskilled worker's supply curve. The vertical distance between the two supply curves is the compensation for the cost of acquiring the skill. (The difference is the amount that has a present value equal to the cost of acquiring the skill.) For example, suppose that the quantity of unskilled labor supplied is 2,000 hours at a wage rate of $5 an hour. This wage rate compensates the unskilled workers purely for their time on the job. Consider next the supply of skilled workers. To induce 2,000 hours of skilled labor to be supplied, firms have to pay a wage rate of $8.50 an hour. This wage rate for skilled labor is higher than that for unskilled labor, since skilled labor must be compensated not only for the time on the job but also for the time and other costs of acquiring the skill.

Wage Rates of Skilled and Unskilled Labor

To work out the wage rates of skilled and unskilled labor, all we have to do is bring together the effects of skill on the demand for and supply of labor. Figure 15.1(c) shows the demand curves and the supply curves for skilled and unskilled labor. These curves are exactly the same as those plotted in parts (a) and (b). Equilibrium occurs in the market for unskilled labor where the supply and demand curves for unskilled labor intersect. The equilibrium wage rate is $5 an hour, and the quantity of unskilled labor employed is 2,000 hours. Equilibrium in the market for skilled workers occurs where the supply and demand curves for skilled workers intersect. The equilibrium wage rate is $10 an hour, and the quantity of skilled labor employed is 3,000 hours.

As you can see in part (c), the equilibrium wage rate of skilled labor is higher than that of unskilled labor. There are two reasons why this occurs: first, skilled labor has a higher marginal revenue product than unskilled labor, so at a given wage rate the demand for skilled labor is greater than the demand for unskilled labor; second, skills are costly to acquire, so at a given wage rate the supply of skilled labor is less than the supply of unskilled labor. The wage differential (in this case $5 an hour) depends on both the marginal revenue product of the skill and the cost of acquiring it. The higher the marginal revenue product of the skill, the larger is the vertical distance between the demand curves for skilled and unskilled labor. The more costly it is to acquire a skill, the larger is the vertical distance between the supplies of skilled and unskilled labor. The higher the marginal revenue product of the skill and the more costly it is to acquire, the larger is the wage differential between skilled and unskilled workers.

Do Education and Training Pay?

There are large and persistent differences in earnings based on the degree of education and training. An indication of those differences can be seen in Fig. 15.2. This figure highlights two important sources of earnings differences. The first is the degree of education itself. The higher the level of education, other things being equal, the higher are a person's earnings. The second source of earnings differences apparent in Fig. 15.2 is age. Age is strongly correlated with experience and the degree of on-the-job training a person has had. Thus as a person gets older, up to middle age, earnings increase.

We can see, from Fig. 15.2, that going through high school, college, and postgraduate education leads to higher incomes. But does education pay in the sense of yielding a higher income that compensates for its cost and for the delay in the start of earnings? For most people, education does indeed pay. Rates of return have been calculated suggesting that a college degree is a better investment than almost any other that a person can undertake. Rates of return as high as 15 percent, after allowing for inflation, are not uncommon.

FIGURE 15.2

Education and Earnings

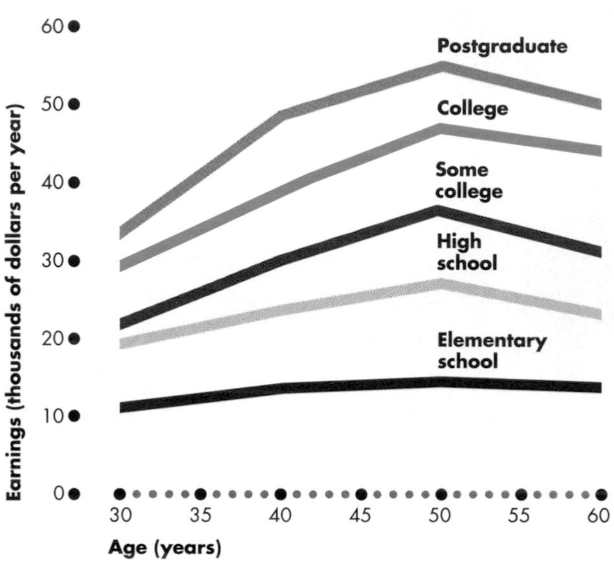

Earnings of male employees at various ages and with varying school levels are shown. Earnings increase with length of education and also with age, but only up to the middle forties. Beyond that age, earnings decrease. These differences show the importance of experience and education in influencing skill differentials.

Source: U.S. Bureau of the Census, *Money Income in 1981 of Families and Persons in the United States,* Current Population Reports, Series P-60, No. 137 (1983), Table 48.

Differences in education and training are an important source of differences in earnings. But they are not the only source. Another is the activities of labor unions. Let's see how unions affect wages and why, on the average, union wages exceed nonunion wages.

Union-Nonunion Wage Differentials

A **labor union** is an organized group of workers whose purpose is to increase wages and influence other job conditions. A labor union acts in the labor market like a monopo-

TABLE 15.1

A Compact Glossary on Unions

Labor union	**An organized group of workers that attempts to increase wages and improve other conditions of employment**
AFL-CIO	**A federation of unions formed in 1955 by a merger of the American Federation of Labor (AFL) and the Congress of Industrial Organizations (CIO); acts as the voice of organized labor in media and political arenas**
Craft union	**A union in which workers have a similar range of skills but work for many firms and in many different industries**
Industrial union	**A union in which workers have a variety of skills and job types but work in the same industry**
Local	**A subunit of a union that organizes individual workers; in craft unions, the local is geographical, and in industrial unions, the local is based on a plant or a company**
Open shop	**A place of work that has no union restriction on who can work in the shop; here, the union bargains for its members but not for nonmembers**
Closed shop	**A place of work where only union members may be employed; illegal since 1947, when Congress passed the Labor-Management Relations Act (the Taft-Hartley Act)**
Union shop	**A place of work that may hire nonunion workers but only if they join the union within a specified period; illegal in the 20 states where "right-to-work" legislation has been passed**
Right-to-work law	**A law that protects the right of an individual to work without joining a union**
Collective bargaining	**Negotiations between representatives of employers and unions on wages and other employment conditions**
Strike	**A group decision to refuse to work under prevailing conditions**
Lockout	**A firm's refusal to allow its labor force to work**
Binding arbitration	**Determination of wages and other employment conditions by a third party (an arbitrator) acceptable to both parties**

list in the product market. The union seeks to restrict competition and, as a result, raises the price at which labor is traded. A compact glossary on unions can be found in Table 15.1.

There are two main types of union: craft unions and industrial unions. A **craft union** is a group of workers who have a similar range of skills but work for many different firms in many different industries and regions. Examples are the carpenters' union and the electrical workers' union (IBEW). An **industrial union** is a group of workers who have a variety of skills and job types but work for the same firm or industry. The United Auto Workers (UAW) and the United Steelworkers of America are examples of industrial unions.

Most unions are members of the AFL-CIO. The AFL-CIO was created in 1955 when two labor organizations combined: the American Federation of Labor (AFL), which was founded in 1886 to organize craft unions, and the Congress of Industrial Organizations (CIO), founded in 1938 to organize industrial unions. The AFL-CIO acts as the national voice of organized labor in the media and in politics.

Unions vary enormously in size. Craft unions are the smallest, and industrial unions are the biggest. The 12 largest unions in the United States—measured by number of members—are shown in Fig. 15.3.

Union strength peaked in the 1950s, when 35 percent of the work force belonged to unions. That percentage has declined steadily since 1955 and is now less than 20 percent. Changes in union membership, however, have been uneven. Some unions have declined dramatically, while others, especially those in the government sector, such as the American Federation of State, County, and Municipal Employees, have increased in strength.

Union organization is based on a subdivision known as the local. The **local** is a subunit of a union that organizes the individual workers. In craft unions the local is based on a geographical area, while in industrial unions the local is based on a plant or an individual firm.

There are three possible forms of organization for a local: an open shop, a closed shop, or a union shop. An **open shop** is an arrangement in which

FIGURE 15.3
Unions with the Largest Membership

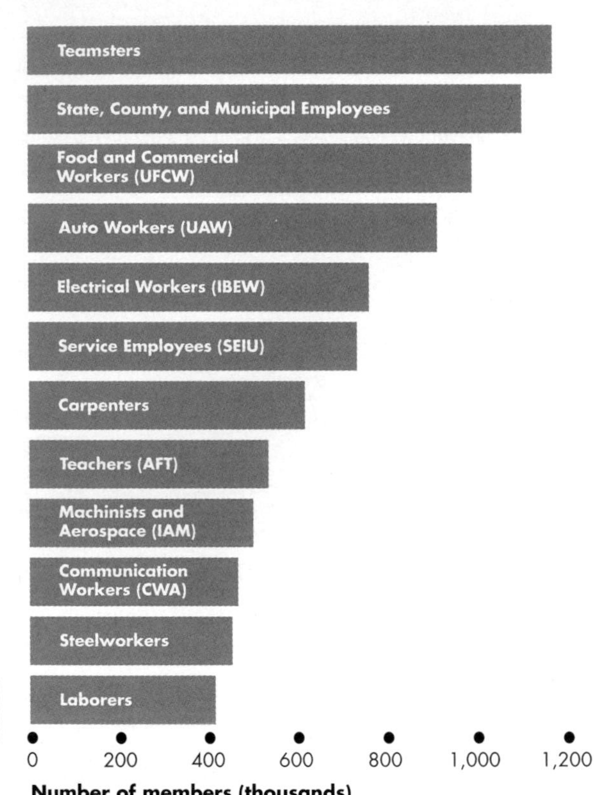

Each of the 12 largest labor unions in the United States, shown here, have more than 400,000 members.

Source: U.S. Bureau of the Census, *Statistical Abstract of the United States: 1991,* 111th edition, 424–425.

workers have a right to be employed without joining the union—there is no union restriction on who can work in the "shop." A **closed shop** is an arrangement in which only union members may be employed by a firm. Closed shops have been illegal since the passage of the Taft-Hartley Act in 1947. A **union shop** is an arrangement in which a firm may hire nonunion workers, but in order for such workers to remain employed they must join the union within a brief period specified by the union. Union shops are illegal in the 20 states that have passed "right-to-work" laws. A **right-to-work law** allows an individual to work at any firm without joining a union.

Unions negotiate with employers or their representatives in a process called **collective bargaining.** The main weapons available to the union and the employer in collective bargaining are the strike and the lockout. A **strike** is a group decision to refuse to work under prevailing conditions. A **lockout** is a firm's refusal to operate its plant and employ its workers. Each party uses the threat of a strike or a lockout to try to get an agreement in its own favor. Sometimes, when the two parties in the collective bargaining process cannot agree on wages and other conditions of employment, they agree to put their disagreement to binding arbitration. **Binding arbitration** is a process in which a third party—an arbitrator—determines wages and other employment conditions on behalf of the negotiating parties and the decision is final.

Though not labor unions in a legal sense, professional associations act, in many ways, like labor unions. A **professional association** is an organized group of professional workers such as lawyers, dentists, or doctors (an example of which is the American Medical Association—AMA). Professional associations control entry into the professions and license practitioners, ensuring the adherence to minimum standards of competence. But they also influence the compensation and other labor market conditions of their members.

Unions' Objectives and Constraints

A union has three broad objectives:

- Increasing compensation
- Improving working conditions
- Expanding job opportunities

Each of these objectives contains a series of more detailed goals. For example, in seeking to increase its members' compensation, a union operates on a variety of fronts: wages, fringe benefits, retirement pay, and such things as vacation allowances. In seeking to improve working conditions, a union is concerned with occupational health and safety as well as the environmental quality of the workplace. In seeking to expand job opportunities, a union tries to obtain greater job security for existing union members and to find ways of creating additional jobs for existing and new members.

A union's ability to pursue its objectives is restricted by two sets of constraints—one on the supply side and the other on the demand side of the labor market. On the supply side, the union's activities are limited by how well it can restrict nonunion workers from offering their labor. The larger the fraction of the work force controlled by the union, the more effective the union can be. For example, unions find it difficult to be effective in markets for unskilled farm labor in southern California because of their inability to control the flow of nonunion, often illegal, labor from Mexico. At the other extreme, unions in the construction industry can better pursue their goals because they can influence the number of people obtaining skills as electricians, plasterers, and carpenters. The unions that are best able to restrict supply are the professional associations for such groups as lawyers, dentists, and doctors. These groups control the number of qualified workers by controlling the examinations that new entrants must pass.

On the demand side of the labor market, the constraint facing a union is the fact that it cannot force firms to hire more labor than they demand. Anything that raises wages or other employment costs decreases the quantity of labor demanded. Unless the union can take actions that shift the demand curve for the labor that it represents, it has to accept the fact that a higher wage can be obtained only at the price of lower employment. Recognizing the importance of the demand for labor curve, unions try to make the demand for their labor inelastic and to increase the demand for union labor. Here are some of the methods that they employ:

- Encouraging import restrictions
- Supporting minimum wage laws
- Supporting immigration restrictions
- Increasing product demand
- Increasing the marginal product of union members

One of the best examples of import restrictions is the support by the United Auto Workers union (UAW) for import restrictions on foreign cars. Unions support minimum wage laws in order to increase the cost of unskilled labor. An increase in the wage rate of unskilled labor leads to a decrease in the quantity demanded of unskilled labor and to an increase in demand for skilled union labor, a substitute for unskilled labor. Restrictive immigration laws decrease the supply and increase the wage rate of unskilled workers. As a result, the demand for skilled union labor increases. Increasing product demand indirectly increases the demand for union labor. The best examples of attempts by unions in this activity are in the textile and auto industries. The garment workers union urges us to buy union-made clothes, and the UAW urges us to buy only American cars made by union workers. Increasing the marginal product of union members directly shifts the demand curve for their services. Unions use apprenticeship, training, and professional certification to increase the marginal product of their members.

Unions in a Competitive Labor Market

When a union operates in an otherwise competitive labor market, it seeks to raise wages and other compensation and to limit employment reductions by increasing demand for the labor of its members.

Figure 15.4 illustrates a labor market. The demand curve is D_C, and the supply curve is S_C. If the market is a competitive one with no union, the wage rate is \$4 an hour and 100 hours of labor will be employed. Suppose that a union is formed to organize the workers in this market and that the union has sufficient control over the supply of labor to be able to artificially restrict that supply below its competitive level—to S_U. If that is all the union does, employment will fall to 62.5 hours of labor and the wage rate will rise to \$10 an hour. If the union can also take steps that increase the demand for labor to D_U, it can achieve an even bigger rise in the wage rate with a smaller fall in employment. By maintaining the restricted labor supply at S_U, the union raises the wage rate to \$16 an hour and achieves an employment level of 75 hours of labor.

Because they restrict the supply of labor in the markets in which they operate, labor unions increase the supply of labor in nonunion markets. Workers who can't get union jobs must look elsewhere for work. This increase in supply in nonunion markets lowers the wage rate in those markets and further widens the union-nonunion differential. But low nonunion wages decrease the demand for union labor and limit the increase in wages that unions can achieve. For this reason, unions are strong supporters of minimum wage laws that keep nonunion

FIGURE 15.4

A Union in a Competitive Labor Market

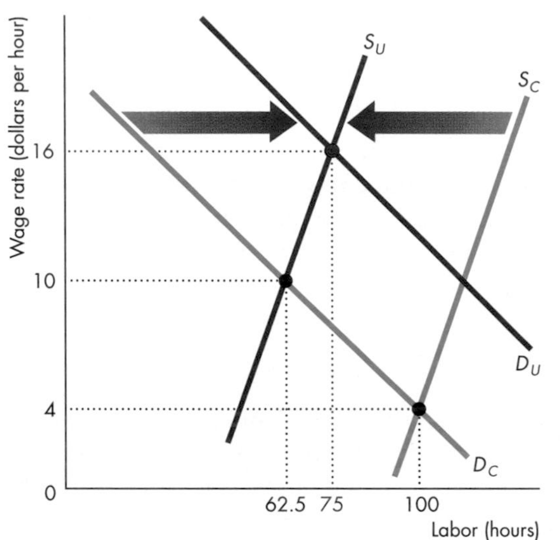

In a competitive labor market, the demand curve is D_C and the supply curve is S_C. Competitive equilibrium occurs at a wage rate of $4 an hour with 100 hours employed. By restricting employment below its competitive level, the union shifts the supply of labor to S_U. If the union can do no more than that, the wage rate will rise to $10 an hour, but employment will fall to 62.5 hours. If the union can increase the demand for labor (by increasing the demand for the good produced by the union members or by raising the price of substitute labor) and shift the demand curve to D_U, then it can raise the wage rate still higher, to $16 an hour, and achieve employment of 75 hours.

wages high and limit the incentive to use nonunion labor (see Reading Between the Lines, pp. 416–417).

We next turn our attention to the case in which employers have considerable influence in the labor market.

Monopsony

A **monopsony** is a market structure in which there is just a single buyer. With the growth of large-scale production over the last century, large manufacturing plants such as coal mines, steel and textile mills, and car manufacturers became the major employer of labor in some regions, and in some places a single firm employed almost all the labor. Such a firm is a monopsonist in the labor market.

A monopsonist can make a bigger profit than a group of firms that have to compete with each other for their labor. Figure 15.5 illustrates how a monopsonist operates. The monopsonist's marginal revenue product curve is *MRP*. This curve tells us the extra revenue from selling the output produced by the last hour of labor hired. The curve labeled *S* is the supply curve of labor. This curve tells us how many hours are supplied at each wage rate. It also tells us the minimum wage that is acceptable at each level of labor supplied.

In deciding how much labor to hire, the monopsonist recognizes that to hire more labor it must pay a higher wage, or, equivalently, by hiring less labor the monopsonist can get away with paying a lower wage. The monopsonist takes account of this fact when calculating its marginal cost of labor. The marginal cost of labor is shown by the curve *MCL*. The relationship between the marginal cost of labor curve and the supply curve is similar to the relationship between the marginal cost and average total cost curves that you studied in Chapter 10. The supply curve is like the average total cost of labor curve.

FIGURE 15.5

A Monopsony Labor Market

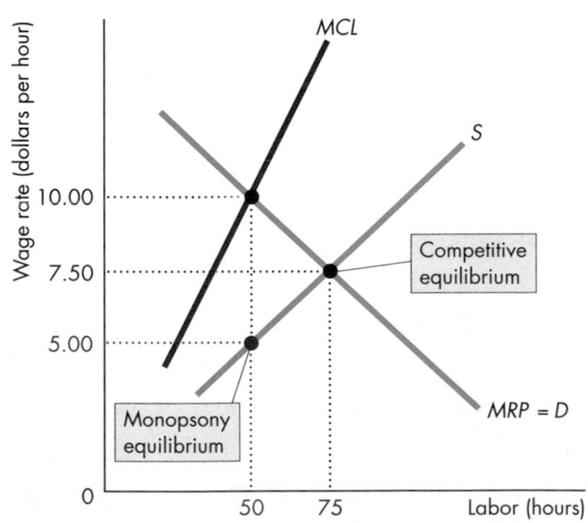

A monopsony is a market structure in which there is a single buyer. A monopsonist who has marginal revenue product curve *MRP* faces a labor supply curve *S*. The marginal cost of labor curve is *MCL*. Profit is maximized by making the marginal cost of labor equal to marginal revenue product. The monopsonist hires 50 hours of labor and pays the lowest wage for which that labor will work, $5 an hour.

For example, in Fig. 15.5 the firm can hire 50 hours of labor at $5 an hour, so its average total cost is $5 an hour. The total cost of labor is $5 an hour multiplied by 50 hours, which equals $250. But suppose that the firm hires slightly less than 50 hours of labor, say 49 hours. The wage rate at which 49 hours of labor can be hired is $4.90 an hour. The firm's total labor cost is 49 multiplied by $4.90, which equals $240.10. Hiring the 50th hour of labor raises the total cost of labor from $240.10 to $250, which is almost $10. The curve *MCL* shows the $10 marginal cost of hiring the 50th hour of labor.

To calculate the profit-maximizing quantity of labor to hire, the firm sets the marginal cost of labor equal to the marginal revenue product of labor. That is, the firm wants the cost of the last worker hired to equal the extra revenue brought in. In Fig. 15.5, this outcome occurs when the monopsony employs 50 hours of labor. To hire 50 hours of labor, the firm has to pay $5 an hour. The marginal revenue product of labor, however, is $10 an hour, which means that the firm makes an economic profit of $5 on the last hour of labor that it hires. Each worker gets paid $5, and marginal revenue product is $10. So the firm gets an extra $5 economic profit out of the last hour of labor hired.

The ability of a monopsonist to make an economic profit depends on the elasticity of labor supply. The more elastic the supply of labor, the less opportunity a monopsonist has to make an economic profit. If this labor market is competitive, the wage rate will be $7.50 and the level of employment will be 75 hours. Compared with a competitive labor market, employment and the wage rate are lower under monopsony.

Monopsony Tendencies With today's low costs of transportation, it is unlikely that many pure monopsonists remain. Workers can easily commute long distances to a job, and so for most people there is not just one potential employer. Nevertheless, many firms face an upward-sloping supply of labor curve and so have a problem similar to that of a monopsonist. To attract more workers, they must offer higher wages. Firms compete with each other for labor by offering wages that compensate their workers not only for time on the job but also for commuting time. The more workers a firm hires, the larger is the area from which it must recruit and the longer is the commute for the marginal worker. Therefore, as a firm hires more workers, the higher is the wage it must pay to attract that worker. How strong such a monopsony tendency is depends on the size and density of the urban area in which the labor market is situated.

Next, let's see the effects of minimum wage laws and unions in a monopsonistic labor market.

Monopsony, Minimum Wage, and Unions

In Chapter 6, we saw how a minimum wage usually decreases employment. However, if a firm is a monopsonist, minimum wage regulations can actually raise both the wage rate and employment. A union can also raise the wage rate and employment. Let's see how.

Minimum Wages and Monopsony Suppose that the labor market is that shown in Fig. 15.6 and that the wage rate is $5 an hour with 50 hours of labor

FIGURE 15.6

Minimum Wage in Monopsony

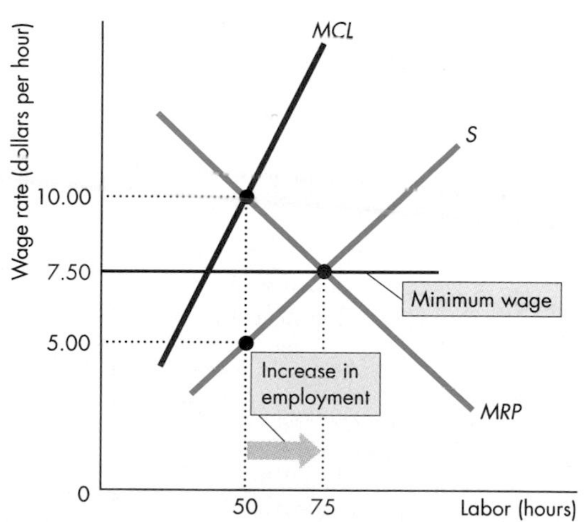

In a monopsony labor market the wage rate is $5 an hour. If a minimum wage law raises the wage rate to $7.50 an hour, employment rises to 75 hours. Equivalently, if a union enters the market, it will attempt to increase the wage rate to above $5 an hour. If the union is all powerful, the highest wage rate it can achieve is $10 an hour. If the union and the firm are equally powerful, they will bargain and agree to a wage rate of $7.50 an hour—the wage rate that splits in half the difference between marginal revenue product and the lowest wage for which labor will work.

Wage Laws versus Laws of Supply and Demand

The New York Times, February 5, 1991

Business Groups Fight Laws in California on Wage Scales

BY ANDREW POLLACK

Several communities in the San Francisco Bay area have enacted what labor lawyers say are the nation's first local laws that specify the wages to be paid to employees of private businesses.

The ordinances require that workers on private construction projects be paid what is called the prevailing wage. That wage, determined by a state agency, is usually close to union wages.

Prevailing-wage laws have been applied to Federal and some state public works projects, starting with the Federal Davis-Bacon Act in 1931. But the ordinances in the Bay Area are the first in the nation to cover private construction projects.

The difference in wages can be striking. A study commissioned by construction unions showed that on one project nonunion workers were paid an average of $12.39 an hour, including benefits, while the average prevailing wage would have been $27.97. And in an affidavit filed in one of the lawsuits challenging the laws, the president of a company that provides maintenance and repair service for industry said that under prevailing wages he would have to pay $25.03 an hour, including benefits, to workers who now receive $11.27.

Supporters of the laws argue that they prevent businesses from using low-paid, poorly trained workers who pose a workplace safety hazard and do construction of poor quality.

"If someone thinks that all you do is hire someone off the street and they know what they are doing, that's not the way it works," said Robert Gilmore, business manager for the Building and Construction Trades Council in San Mateo County, which is immediately south of San Francisco.

Often, he and other supporters say, such workers are brought in from other parts of the country in migrations reminiscent of *The Grapes of Wrath*, overloading local schools and hospitals and hurting the local economy.

Union officials concede that the laws help the unions. While the ordinances do not require union labor, the fact that high wages must be paid removes a big incentive for private businesses to use nonunion workers. . . .

The Essence of the Story

Some San Francisco Bay area communities have enacted laws that require that workers on private construction projects be paid the "prevailing wage."

The prevailing wage is determined by a state agency and is usually close to the union wage.

Prevailing-wage laws have been applied to federal and state public works projects, but the Bay Area laws are the first in the nation to cover private construction projects.

The laws will increase wages (including benefits) from $11 and $12 an hour to $25 to $27 an hour.

Unions agree that the laws benefit them because they decrease the incentive to hire nonunion labor.

Background and Analysis

With no unions, all workers (of a given ability) receive the same wage—illustrated in Fig. 1. In both part (a) and part (b), the demand for labor is D_0, the supply of labor is S_0, the quantity of labor employed is L_0, and the wage rate is W_0.

A union restricts the supply of labor in the union sector, and the supply curve in part (b) shifts to S_1.

Workers who can't get a union job supply their labor to the nonunion sector. The supply curve in part (a) shifts to the right to S_1. The nonunion wage falls to $12 an hour. L_N workers are employed in nonunion jobs.

The low nonunion wage decreases the demand for union workers—the demand curve in part (b) shifts to D_1. With the decreased demand for union workers but a larger decrease in supply, the union wage rises and is $28 an hour.

The prevailing-wage law increases the nonunion wage—in Fig. 2(a) to $25 an hour. The quantity of nonunion labor employed falls to L_D, and the quantity supplied increases to L_S. Unemployment arises—illustrated in part (a).

With a higher nonunion wage, the demand for union labor increases to D_2 in part (b). The union wage increases to W_U, and the number of union workers employed increases to L_U.

Union workers benefit from the prevailing-wage law. Nonunion workers who get jobs also benefit. But the law creates unemployment.

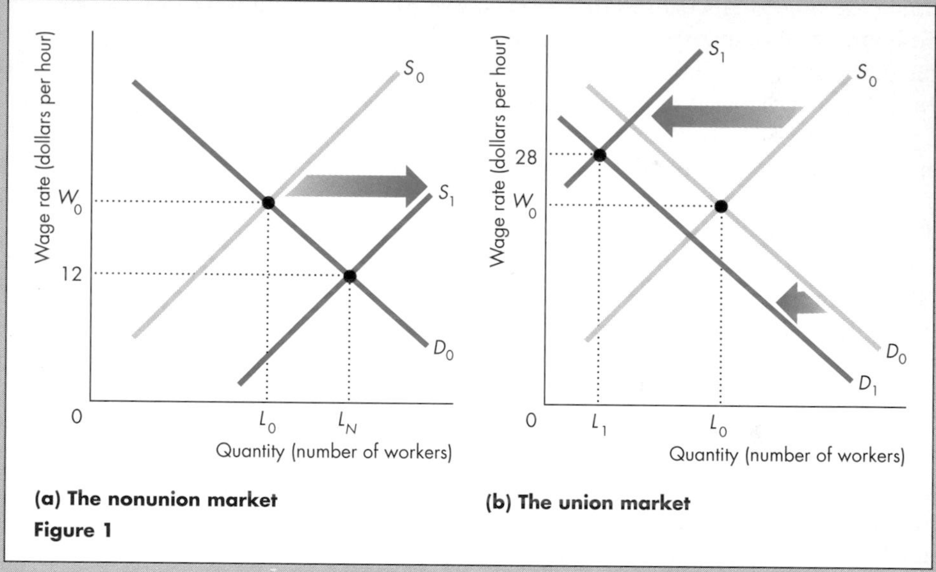

(a) The nonunion market

(b) The union market

Figure 1

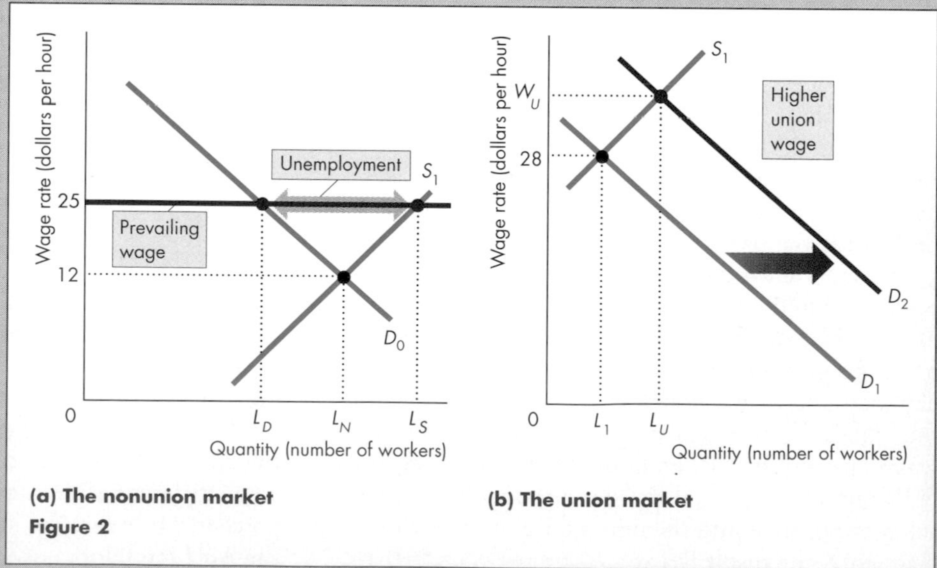

(a) The nonunion market

(b) The union market

Figure 2

being employed. The government now passes a minimum wage law that prohibits anyone from hiring labor for less than $7.50 an hour. Firms can hire labor for $7.50 an hour or more but not for less than that wage. The monopsonist in Fig. 15.6 now faces a perfectly elastic supply of labor at $7.50 an hour up to 75 hours. Above 75 hours, a higher wage than $7.50 an hour has to be paid to hire additional hours of labor. Since the wage rate is a fixed $7.50 an hour up to 75 hours, the marginal cost of labor is also constant at $7.50 up to 75 hours. Beyond 75 hours, the marginal cost of labor rises above $7.50 an hour. To maximize profit, the monopsonist sets the marginal cost of labor equal to its marginal revenue product. That is, the monopsonist hires 75 hours of labor at $7.50 an hour. The minimum wage law has made the supply of labor perfectly elastic and made the marginal cost of labor the same as the wage rate up to 75 hours. The law has not affected the supply of labor curve or the marginal cost of labor at employment levels above 75 hours. The minimum wage law has succeeded in raising wages by $2.50 an hour and raising the amount of labor employed by 25 hours.

Monopsony and Unions When we studied monopoly in Chapter 12, we discovered that a single seller in a market is able to determine the price in that market. We have just studied monopsony—a market with a single buyer—and discovered that in such a market the buyer is able to determine the price. Suppose that a union starts to operate in a monopsony labor market. A union is like a monopoly. It controls the supply of labor and acts like a single seller of labor. If the union (monopoly seller) faces a monopsony buyer, the situation is one of **bilateral monopoly.** In bilateral monopoly, the wage rate is determined by bargaining between the two traders. Let's study the bargaining process.

We saw that if the monopsony in Fig. 15.5 is free to determine the wage rate and the level of employment, it hires 50 hours of labor for a wage rate of $5 an hour. If a union that represents the workers can maintain employment at 50 hours but charge the highest wage rate acceptable to the employer, the wage rate will be $10 an hour. That is, the wage rate will equal the marginal revenue product of labor. If the monopsonist and the union bargain over the wage rate, the result is a wage rate between $10 an hour (the maximum that the union can get) and $5 an hour (the minimum that the firm can pay).

The actual outcome of the bargaining depends on the costs that each party can inflict on the other as a result of a failure to agree on the wage rate. The firm can shut down the plant and lock out its workers, and the workers can shut down the plant by striking. Each party knows the strength of the other and knows what it has to lose if it does not agree to the demands of the other. If the two parties are equally strong, and they realize it, they will split the difference and agree to a wage rate of $7.50 an hour. If one party is stronger than the other—and both parties know that—the agreed wage will favor the stronger party. Usually, an agreement is reached without a strike or a lockout. The threat—the knowledge that such an event can occur—is usually enough to bring the bargaining parties to an agreement. When strikes or lockouts do occur, it is because one party has misjudged the situation.

The Scale of Union-Nonunion Wage Differentials

We have seen that unions can influence the wages of their members partly by restricting the supply of labor and partly by increasing the demand for labor. How much of a difference to wage rates do unions make in practice?

Union wage rates are, on the average, 33 percent higher than nonunion wage rates. In mining and financial services, union and nonunion wages are similar, and in services, manufacturing, and transportation the differential is between 11 and 19 percent. But in the wholesale and retail trades the differential is 42 percent, and in construction it is 77 percent.

These union-nonunion wage differentials do not give a true measure of the effects of unions on wages, however. In some industries, union wages are higher than nonunion wages because union members do jobs that involve greater skill. Even without a union, those who perform such tasks receive a higher wage. To calculate the effects of unions, we have to examine the wages of unionized and nonunionized workers who do nearly identical work. The evidence suggests that after allowing for the effects of skill differentials, the union-nonunion wage differential lies between 10 percent and 25 percent. For example, airline pilots who belong to the Air Line Pilots Association earn about 25 percent more than nonunion pilots with the same level of skill.

REVIEW

Differences in earnings based on skill or education level arise because skilled labor has a higher marginal revenue product than unskilled labor and because skills are costly to acquire. Union workers have higher wages than nonunion workers because unions are able to control the supply of labor and, indirectly, influence the marginal revenue product of their members. ◆

Wage Differentials Between Sexes and Races

There are persistent earnings differences between the sexes and the races. Figure 15.7 provides a snapshot of these differences in 1989. The wages of each race and sex group are expressed as a percentage of the wages of white men. By definition, then, the wages of white men are 100. As you can see, the wages of each group fall progressively from 72 percent for black men down to 56 percent for women of Hispanic origin.

FIGURE 15.7
Sex and Race Differentials

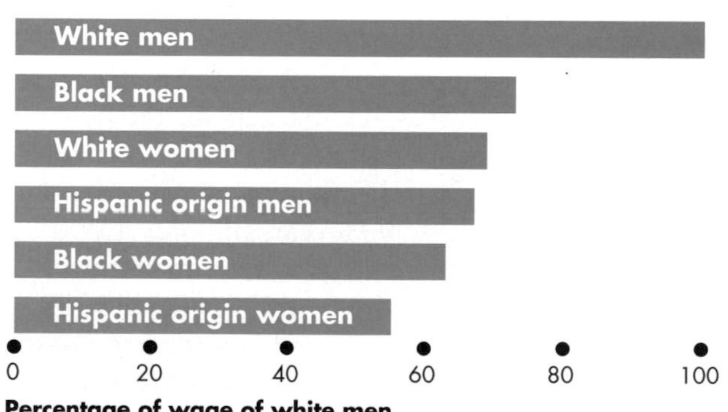

Wages of different race and sex groups in the labor market are shown as percentages of white male wages. These differentials have persisted over many years.

Source: U.S. Bureau of the Census, *Statistical Abstract of the United States: 1991,* 111th edition, 415.

Why do the differentials shown in Fig. 15.7 exist, and why do they persist? Do they arise because there is discrimination against women and members of minority races, or is there some other explanation? These controversial questions generate an enormous amount of passion. It is not my intention to make you angry, but that might happen as an unintended consequence of this discussion. The objective of this section is to show you how to use economic analysis to address controversial and emotionally charged issues.

We are going to examine three possible explanations for these earnings differences:

- Discrimination
- Differences in human capital
- Differences in degree of specialization

Discrimination

To see how discrimination can affect earnings, let's look at an example—the market for investment advisors. Suppose that there are two groups of investment advisors who are identical in terms of picking good investments. One group consists of black females, and the other of white males. The supply curve of black females, S_{BF}, is shown in Fig. 15.8(a). The supply curve of white males, S_{WM}, is shown in Fig. 15.8(b). These supply curves are identical. The marginal revenue product of investment advisors, whether they are black female or white male, is also identical and is shown by the two curves labeled *MRP* in parts (a) and (b). (Their revenues are the fees their customers pay for investment advice.)

Suppose that everyone in this society is free of prejudice about color and sex. The market for black female investment advisors determines a wage rate of $40,000 a year, and there are 2,000 black female investment advisors. The white male investment advisor market also clears at a wage rate of $40,000 a year, and there are 2,000 white male investment advisors.

In contrast to the previous situation, suppose that the customers of investment houses are prejudiced against women and against members of racial

FIGURE 15.8

Discrimination

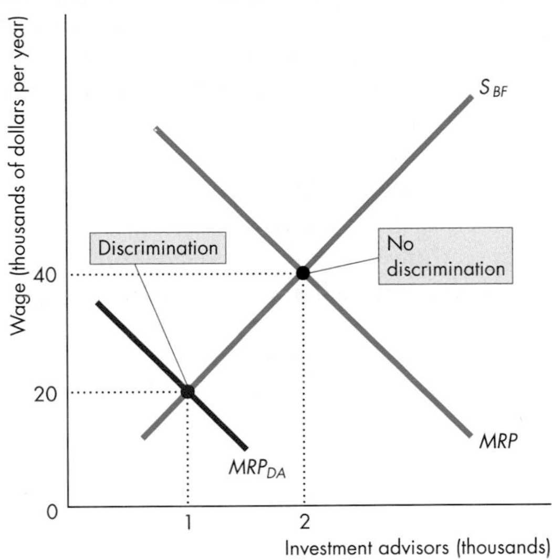

(a) Black females

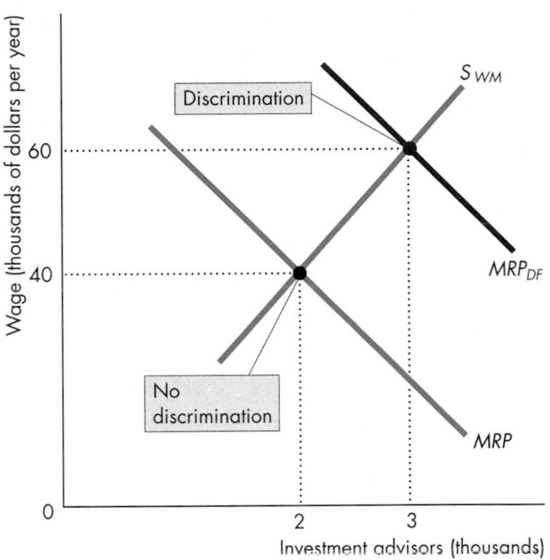

(b) White males

The supply curve for black female investment advisors is S_{BF} in part (a), and the supply curve for white male investment advisors is S_{WM} in part (b). If the marginal revenue product of both groups of investment advisors is *MRP* (the same curve in each part), then the equilibrium wage rate for each group is \$40,000 a year and 2,000 of each type of advisor are employed. If there is discrimination against blacks and women, the marginal revenue product curve is to the left of the original curve. It is the curve labeled MRP_{DA}—*DA* standing for discriminated against. There is discrimination in favor of white males, so their marginal revenue product curve is MRP_{DF}—*DF* standing for discriminated in favor of. The wage rate for black women falls to \$20,000 a year, and only 1,000 are employed. The wage rate for white males rises to \$60,000 a year, and 3,000 are employed.

minorities. The two groups are equally able, as before, but the degree of prejudice is so strong that the customers are not willing to pay as much for investment advice given by a black female as they will pay for advice from a white male. Because of the differences in the amounts that people are willing to pay, based purely on their prejudices, the marginal revenue products of the two groups are different. The ability of the two groups is the same, but the value that prejudiced consumers place on their outputs is not the same. Suppose that the marginal revenue product of the black females, when discriminated against, is the line labeled MRP_{DA}—*DA* standing for discriminated against. Suppose that the marginal revenue product for white males, the group discriminated in favor of, is MRP_{DF}—*DF* standing for discriminated in favor of. Given these marginal revenue product curves, the markets for the two groups of investment advisors will now determine very different wages and employment levels. Black females will earn \$20,000 a year, and only 1,000 will work as investment advisors. White males will earn \$60,000 a year, and 3,000 of them will work as investment advisors. Thus, purely on the basis of the prejudice of the demanders of investment advice, black women will earn one third the wages of white men, and three quarters of all investment advisors will be white men and only one quarter will be black women.

The case that we have just examined is a hypothetical example of how prejudice can produce differences in earnings. But economists disagree about

whether or not prejudice actually causes wage differentials for a simple but difficult reason: you can recognize prejudice when you see it, but you cannot easily measure it. Our model shows that sex and race differentials might come from prejudice. But without a way of measuring prejudice in the real world, we cannot easily test that model to see whether it is true.

We need to make another point as well. Our model of prejudice, like all economic models, is in an equilibrium, albeit an unhappy one. But simply because a model is in equilibrium does not mean that such a real situation is either desirable or inevitable. Economic theory makes predictions about the way things will be, not moral statements about the way things ought to be. Policies designed to bring equal wages and employment prospects to women and minorities can be devised. But to be successful, such policies must be based on careful economic analysis. Good intentions are not enough to bring about equality.

Human Capital Differences

As we saw above (pp. 408–410), wages are compensation, in part for time spent on the job and in part for the cost incurred in acquiring skill—in acquiring human capital. The more human capital a person supplies, the higher is that person's earnings, other things being equal. Measuring human capital with any precision is difficult. But there are some rough indicators. One such indicator is the number of years of schooling that a person has had. A second indicator is the number of years of work experience. The most recent figures indicate that the median years in school for all races and both sexes are almost equal at about 12½ years. But this equality in median years of schooling is recent. In 1960, whites, on the average, spent about 11 years in school, while blacks, on the average, had about 8 years of schooling. By 1970, that differential had been cut to 2 years, and today it has virtually disappeared.

A third possible indicator of human capital is the number of job interruptions. Interruptions to a career disrupt and reduce the effectiveness of job experience and slow down the accumulation of human capital. Also, during a job interruption, it is possible that human capital depreciates through lack of use. Traditionally, women's careers have been interrupted more frequently than men's, usually for bearing and rearing children. This factor is a possible source of lower wages, on the average, for women. Just as education differences are virtually disappearing, so career interruptions for women are becoming less severe. Maternity leave and day-care facilities are providing an increasing number of women with uninterrupted employment that makes their human capital accumulation indistinguishable from that of men.

Thus it seems that human capital differences possibly can account for earnings differentials among races and sexes in the past and some of the differentials that still remain. The trends, however, suggest that wage differentials from this source will eventually disappear.

Degrees of Specialization

People undertake two kinds of production activities: they supply labor services to the market (market activities), and they undertake household production (nonmarket activities). **Household production** creates goods and services to be consumed within the household rather than to be supplied to the market. Such activities include cooking, cleaning, minor repair work, education, and various organizational services such as arranging vacations and other leisure activities. Bearing and rearing children are other important nonmarket activities.

In Chapter 3, we discovered that people can gain from specializing in particular activities and trading their output with each other. Specialization and the gains from trade do not operate exclusively in the marketplace. They also operate within the household and among its members. It is not uncommon for one member of a household to specialize in shopping, another in cleaning, another in laundry, and so on. Specialization in bearing children is a biological necessity, although rearing them is not.

Consider, for example, a household that has two members—Bob and Sue. Bob and Sue have to decide how they will allocate their time between various nonmarket household production activities and market activity. One solution is for Bob to specialize in market activity and Sue to specialize in nonmarket activity. Another solution is to reverse the roles and have Sue specialize in market activity and Bob in nonmarket activity. Alternatively, one or both of them can become diversified, doing some market

and some nonmarket activity. A completely egalitarian allocation will have them share the nonmarket tasks equally and each devote the same amount of time and energy to market activity. But unequal allocations of time are also possible, with one of the household members specializing in market activity and the other being diversified.

In deciding which of the many alternative time allocations to choose, Bob and Sue will take into consideration their future plans for having children. The particular allocation chosen by Bob and Sue will depend on their preferences and on the market earning potential of each of them. An increasing number of households are choosing the egalitarian allocation with each person diversified between nonmarket household production and market activity. Most households, however, still choose an allocation that would have Bob almost fully specialized in market activity and Sue covering a greater diversity of tasks in both the job market and the household. What are the effects of this more common assignment of market and nonmarket tasks? Though there will always be exceptions, on the average, it seems likely that if Bob specializes in market production and Sue diversifies between market and nonmarket production, Bob will have higher earning potential in the marketplace than Sue. If Sue is devoting a great deal of productive effort to ensuring Bob's mental and physical well-being, the quality of Bob's market labor will be higher than if he were undertaking his household production tasks on his own. If the roles were reversed, Sue would be able to supply market labor capable of earning more than Bob.

Economists have attempted to test whether the degree of specialization can account for earnings differentials between the sexes by examining the wages of men and women where, as far as possible, the degree of specialization is held constant. For example, if the degree of specialization is an important factor influencing a person's wage, then men and women of identical ages and educational backgrounds in identical occupations will be paid different wages depending on whether they are single, married to a spouse who specializes in household production, or married to a spouse who works. Single men and women who live alone and who are equally specialized in household and market production and who have the same amounts of human capital and who do similar jobs will be paid the same wage. To make nonmarket factors as similar as possible, two groups have been chosen for analysis. They are "never married" men and women. The available evidence suggests that, on the average, when they have the same amount of human capital—measured by years of schooling, work experience, and career interruptions—the wages of these two groups are not identical but are much closer than the difference between *average* wages for men and women. The average wage differential between women and men exceeds 30 percent. But, when allowance is made for degree of specialization and human capital, this wage differential comes down to between 5 and 10 percent, by some estimates. Some economists suspect that the remaining discrepancy stems from discrimination against women, although the difficulty of measuring such discrimination makes this hypothesis hard to test.

Most of the difference in men's and women's wages arises from the fact that men and women do different jobs, and, for the most part, men's jobs are better paid than women's jobs. There are, however, an increasing number of women entering areas that were traditionally the preserve of men. This trend is particularly clear in professions such as architecture, medicine, economics, law, accounting, and pharmacology. The percentage of total enrollments in university courses in these subjects for women has increased from less than 20 percent in 1970 to approaching, and in some cases exceeding, 50 percent today.

Comparable-Worth Laws

In 1963, Congress passed the Equal Pay Act, and in 1964 it passed the Civil Rights Act. These acts require equal pay for equal work. They are attempts to remove the most blatant forms of discrimination between men and women and between whites and minorities. But many people believe that these acts do not go far enough. In their view, getting paid the *same* wage for doing the *same* job is just the first tiny step that has to be taken. What's important is that *comparable* jobs receive the *same* wages regardless of whether they are done by men or women or by

blacks or whites. Paying the same wage for different jobs that are judged to be comparable is called **comparable worth.**

Advocates of comparable-worth laws argue that wages should be determined by analyzing the characteristics of jobs and determining their worth on objective grounds. However, such a method of determining wage rates does not achieve the objectives sought by supporters of wage equality. Let's see why.

Figure 15.9 shows two markets: that for oil rig operators in part (a) and that for school teachers in part (b). The marginal revenue product curves (MRP_R and MRP_T) and the supply curves (S_R and S_T) are shown for each type of labor. Competitive equilibrium generates a wage rate W_R for oil rig operators and W_T for teachers.

Suppose that the knowledge and skills required in those two occupations—the mental and physical demands, the responsibilities, and the working conditions—result in a judgment that these two jobs are of comparable worth. The wage rate that is judged to apply to each of them is W_C, and the courts enforce this wage rate. What happens? First, there is a shortage of oil rig operators. Oil rig companies are able to hire only S_r workers at the wage rate W_C. They cut back their production or build more expensive labor-saving oil rigs. There is also a decrease in the number of teachers employed. But this decrease occurs because school boards demand fewer teachers. At the higher wage W_C, school boards demand only D_t teachers. The quantity of teachers supplied is S_t and the difference between S_t and D_t is the number of unemployed teachers looking for jobs. These teachers eventually accept nonteaching jobs (which they don't like as much as teaching jobs) at a lower rate of pay than that of teachers.

Thus legislated comparable wages for comparable work may have serious and costly unintended consequences.

FIGURE 15.9

The Problem with Comparable Worth

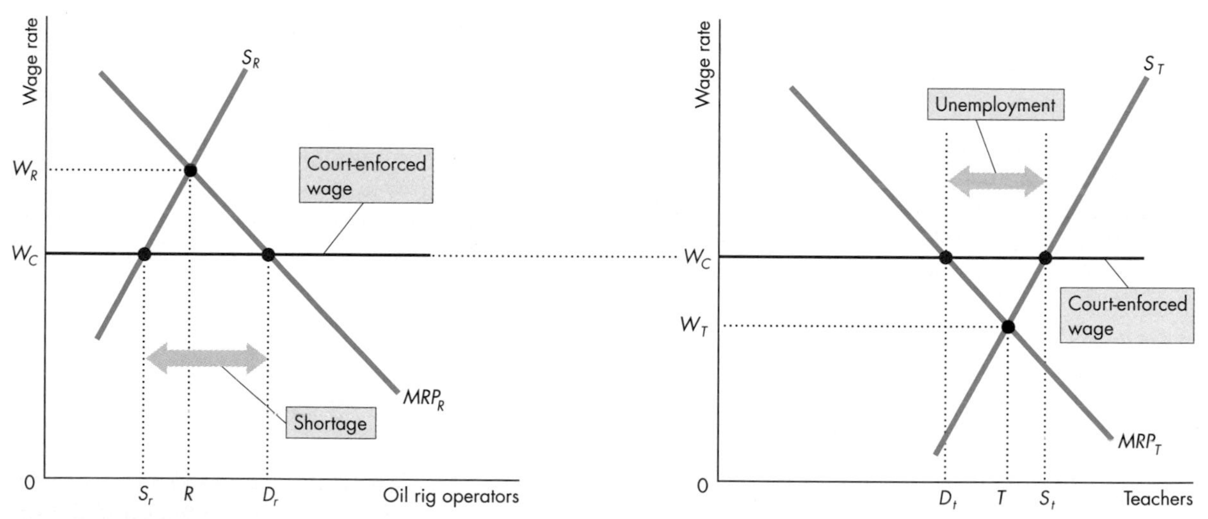

(a) Market for oil rig operators

(b) Market for teachers

The demand for and supply of oil rig operators, MRP_R and S_R, are shown in part (a), and those for schoolteachers, MRP_T and S_T, in part (b). The competitive equilibrium wage rate for oil rig operators is W_R and for teachers is W_T. If an evaluation of the two jobs finds that they have comparable worth and rules that the wage rate W_C be paid to both types of workers, there is an excess of demand for oil rig operators and an excess supply of teachers. There are $S_t - D_t$ teachers unemployed and a shortage of $D_r - S_r$ oil rig operators. Oil producers have to find other labor-saving ways of producing oil (that are more expensive), and teachers have to find other jobs (that are less desirable to them and less well paid).

REVIEW

Wage differences between the sexes and the races may arise from discrimination and from differences in human capital. Sex differentials may also in part arise from differences in the degree of specialization. Comparable-worth law cannot, on its own, eliminate wage differentials. Differentials will be reduced only if differences in marginal revenue product are reduced. The process of equalization of human capital and of the degree of specialization will lead to lower differentials and possibly will eliminate them. ◆

◆ ◆ ◆ ◆ In this chapter, we extended and applied the factor markets model to understand a variety of phenomena in labor markets, such as wage differentials. In the next chapter, we apply and extend the factor markets model to deal with markets for capital and for natural resources.

SUMMARY

Skill Differentials

Skill differentials arise partly because skilled labor has a higher marginal product than unskilled labor and partly because skills are costly to acquire. The higher marginal product of skilled workers results in a higher marginal revenue product. Since the demand for labor curve is derived from the marginal revenue product curve, the higher the marginal revenue product of skilled labor, the greater is the demand for skilled labor.

Skills are costly to acquire because households have to invest in human capital to become skilled. Investment sometimes means direct payments such as tuition and other training fees and sometimes means working for a lower wage during on-the-job training. Because skills are costly to acquire, households supply skilled labor on terms that compensate them for both the time spent on the job and the costs of acquiring the skills. Thus the supply curve of skilled labor lies above the supply curve of unskilled labor.

Wage rates of skilled and unskilled labor are determined by demand and supply in the two labor markets. The equilibrium wage rate for skilled labor exceeds that for unskilled labor. The difference in wages reflects the higher marginal product of skill and the cost to acquire skill. (pp. 408–410)

Union-Nonunion Wage Differentials

Labor unions influence wages by controlling the supply of labor. In competitive labor markets, unions obtain higher wages only at the expense of lower employment. Unions in competitive industries also attempt to influence the marginal revenue product of their members—and the demand for their members' labor—by restricting imports, raising minimum wages, supporting immigration restrictions, increasing demand for their product, and increasing the marginal product of their members.

In a monopsony—a market in which there is a single buyer—unions increase wages without sacrificing employment. Bilateral monopoly occurs when the union is a monopoly seller of labor, the firm is a monopsony buyer of labor, and the wage rate is determined by bargaining between the two parties.

In practice, union workers earn an estimated 10–25 percent more than comparable nonunion workers. (pp. 410–419)

Wage Differentials Between Sexes and Races

There are persistent differentials in earnings between men and women and between whites and minorities. Three possible explanations for these differentials are discrimination, differences in human capital, and differences in degree of specialization.

Discrimination results in lower wage rates and lower employment for workers who are discriminated against and higher wage rates and higher employment levels for those discriminated in favor of. Human capital differences result from differences in schooling and work experience. Differentials based

on schooling have been falling and have almost been eliminated. Differentials based on work experience have kept women's pay below that for men because women's careers have traditionally been interrupted more frequently than those of men, resulting, on the average, in a smaller accumulation of human capital. This difference is less important today than in the past. Differentials arising from different degrees of specialization are probably important and may persist. Men have traditionally been more specialized in market activity, on the average, than women. Women have traditionally undertaken both nonmarket (household production) activities and market activities. Attempts to test for the importance of the degree of specialization suggest that it is an important source of the difference between the earnings of men and women. (pp. 419–422)

Comparable-Worth Laws

Comparable-worth laws determine wages by assessing the value of different types of jobs according to objective characteristics rather than what the market will pay. Determining wages through comparable worth results in a decrease in the number of people employed in those jobs on which the market places a lower value and shortages of those workers that the market values more highly. Thus the attempt to achieve comparable wages for comparable work has costly, unintended consequences. (pp. 422–424)

KEY ELEMENTS

Key Terms

Bilateral monopoly, 418
Binding arbitration, 412
Closed shop, 412
Collective bargaining, 412
Comparable worth, 423
Craft union, 411
Household production, 421
Human capital, 408
Industrial union, 411
Labor union, 410
Local, 411
Lockout, 412
Monopsony, 414
Open shop, 411
Professional association, 412
Right-to-work law, 412
Strike, 412
Union shop, 412

Key Figures and Tables

Figure 15.1 Skill Differentials, 409
Figure 15.4 A Union in a Competitive Labor Market, 414
Figure 15.8 Discrimination, 420
Table 15.1 A Compact Glossary on Unions, 411

REVIEW QUESTIONS

1 Explain why skilled workers are paid more than unskilled workers.

2 What are the main types of labor union?

3 How does a labor union try to influence wages?

4 What can a union do in a competitive labor market?

5 How might a union increase the demand for its members' labor?

6 Under what circumstances will the introduction of a minimum wage increase employment?

7 How big are the union-nonunion wage differentials in the United States today?

8 What are the three main reasons why sex and race differentials in earnings exist?

9 How do comparable-worth laws work, and what are their predicted effects?

PROBLEMS

1 The demand for and supply of unskilled laborers are given by the following schedules:

Hourly wage rate (dollars per hour)	Quantity supplied (hours)	Quantity demanded (hours)
9	9,000	1,000
8	8,000	2,000
7	7,000	3,000
6	6,000	4,000
5	5,000	5,000
4	4,000	6,000
3	3,000	7,000
2	2,000	8,000

a What is the wage rate of unskilled labor?
b What is the quantity of unskilled labor employed?

2 The workers in problem 1 can be trained—can obtain a skill—and their marginal productivity doubles. (The marginal product at each employment level is twice the marginal product of an unskilled worker.) But the compensation for the cost of acquiring a skill adds $2 an hour to the wage that must be offered to attract skilled labor.

a What is the wage rate of skilled labor?
b What is the quantity of skilled labor employed?

3 Suppose that skilled workers become unionized and the union restricts entry into skilled work to 1,000 workers. What is the wage rate of skilled workers? How do unskilled workers react to the new situation?

4 In a small, isolated town in the Rocky Mountains, the only firm hiring workers is a logging company. The firm's demand for labor and the town's supply of labor are as follows:

Wage rate (dollars per hour)	Quantity supplied (hours per day)	Quantity demanded (hours per day)
1	20	220
2	40	200
3	60	180
4	80	160
5	100	140
6	120	120
7	140	100
8	160	80
9	180	60
10	200	40

a What is the wage rate?
b How much labor does the firm hire?

5 The townspeople in problem 4 form a union. The union and the firm agree that the level of employment will not change and the union gets the highest wage rate acceptable to the firm. What is that wage rate?

6 A nationwide investigation determines that on the basis of comparable worth, a logger should be paid $7 an hour. In the logging village in problem 4 before the union described in problem 5 is formed:

a What is the actual hourly wage rate paid?
b How much labor does the logging company hire at this wage?
c How much labor is unemployed?

CHAPTER 16

CAPITAL AND NATURAL RESOURCE MARKETS

After studying this chapter, you will be able to:

- Define and distinguish among financial and physical assets, capital, and investment
- Define and distinguish between saving and portfolio choice
- Describe the structure of capital markets in the United States today
- Explain how interest rates and stock prices are determined and why the stock market fluctuates
- Define natural resources and explain how their prices are determined
- Explain how markets regulate the pace at which we use exhaustible resources such as oil

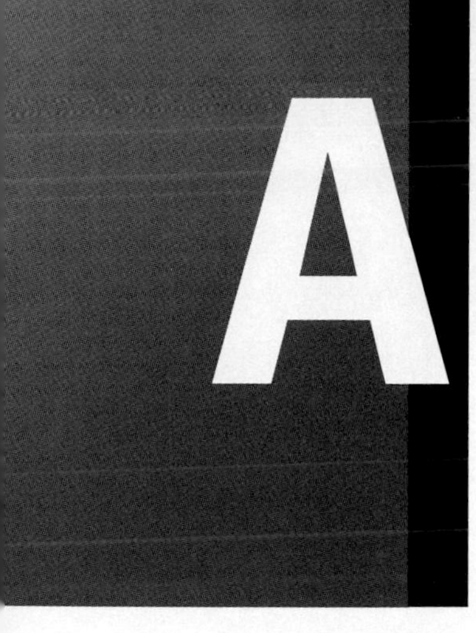

N AIR OF PANIC FILLED THE CAVERNOUS NEW YORK Stock Exchange on Monday, October 19, 1987. It had taken five years, from August 1982, for the average price of a common stock to climb 200 percent. But on that single day, stock prices fell an unheard of 22 percent—knocking billions of dollars off the value of people's investments. The crash touched off other stock market plunges from Tokyo to London. Why does the stock market boom for several years and then crash suddenly and spectacularly? ◆◆ The New York Stock Exchange, large as it is, is only a part of the enormous capital market of the United States and the even more enormous worldwide capital market. Every year, billions of dollars are saved and flow into these capital markets. Savings flow through banks, insurance companies, and stock exchanges and end up financing the purchases of machinery, factory and office buildings, cars, and homes. How does a dollar saved and placed on deposit in a bank enable Pepsi-Cola to open a new bottling plant? ◆◆ Many of our natural resources are exhaustible, yet we are using them up at a rapid rate. Every year we burn billions of cubic feet of natural gas, billions of gallons of petroleum, and millions of tons of coal. We extract bauxite to make aluminum and iron ore to make steel. Aren't we one day going to run out of these and other natural resources? And long before that day, aren't they going to become too expensive to use? How are the prices of natural resources determined? And do their prices adjust to encourage conservation, or does the market need help to ensure that we do not pillage nature's exhaustible endowments?

Boom and Bust

◆ ◆ ◆ ◆ In this chapter, we study capital and natural resource markets. We'll find out what determines the amount of saving and purchases of new capital equipment and how interest rates and stock values are determined. In our study of natural resource markets, we'll discover how market forces encourage conservation.

Capital, Investment, and Saving

Let's begin with some capital market vocabulary and define three key terms:

- Asset
- Liability
- Balance sheet

An **asset** is anything of value that a household, firm, or government *owns*. A **liability** is a debt—something that a household, firm, or government *owes*. A **balance sheet** is a list of assets and liabilities.

Table 16.1 shows an example of a balance sheet—that for Rocky's Mountain Bikes. It lists three assets—cash in the bank, an inventory of bikes, and fixtures and fittings—that add up to $243,000. The balance sheet contains two liabilities—a bank loan of $120,000 and Rocky's equity of $123,000. Rocky's equity is his personal stake in the company—equivalently, it is the amount the company owes to Rocky.

TABLE **16.1**

Balance Sheet of Rocky's Mountain Bikes

Assets		Liabilities	
Cash in bank	**$ 18,000**	**Bank loan**	**$120,000**
Inventory of bikes	**15,000**	**Rocky's equity**	**123,000**
Fixtures and fittings	**210,000**		
Total assets	**$243,000**	**Total liabilities**	**$243,000**

Financial Assets and Physical Assets

Assets fall into two broad classes: financial and physical. **Financial assets** are sophisticated IOUs—pieces of paper that represent a claim against another household, firm, or government. When you hold an IOU, it means that somebody else owes you money. Similarly, if you own a financial asset, someone else has a financial liability—owes you money. For example, the savings deposit that you own (your asset) is a liability of your bank. The difference between financial assets and financial liabilities is called **net financial assets**. Net financial assets are the net value of the paper claims that one household, firm, or government has against everyone else.

Physical assets are buildings, plant and equipment, inventories, and consumer durable goods. Physical assets are also called capital. **Capital** is the physical assets owned by a household, firm, or government.

Table 16.2 illustrates the distinction between financial assets and physical assets by again presenting the information contained in the balance sheet of Rocky's Mountain Bikes. But this time the informa-

TABLE **16.2**

Financial Assets and Physical Assets of Rocky's Mountain Bikes

Financial assets	
Cash in bank	**$ 18,000**
Bank loan	**–120,000**
Rocky's equity	**–123,000**
Net financial assets	**–$225,000**
Physical assets	
Inventory of bikes	**$ 15,000**
Fixtures and fittings	**210,000**
Capital	**$225,000**

tion is sorted into financial and physical items. The financial items in the balance sheet are the cash in bank (an asset) and the bank loan (a liability). To calculate net financial assets, we have to subtract financial liabilities from financial assets, so the bank loan and Rocky's equity appear with negative signs. The net financial assets of Rocky's Mountain Bikes are –$225,000. The physical assets are the inventory of bikes and the fixtures and fittings—the firm's capital—which add up to $225,000.

Capital and Investment

Capital is the value of buildings, plant and equipment, and inventories in existence at a given point in time. **Investment** is the value of new capital equipment purchased in a given time period. **Depreciation** is the decrease in the value of capital resulting from its use in a given time period. Investment is an addition to capital; depreciation is a subtraction from capital. The net change in capital is investment minus depreciation. To emphasize this fact, we distinguish between **gross investment,** the value of all the new capital purchased in a given time period, and **net investment,** which equals gross investment minus depreciation.

Capital, gross investment, and depreciation are similar to the water in Lake Powell and the San Juan and Colorado Rivers. Capital is like the water in Lake Powell at a given point in time. Gross investment is like the water flowing from the San Juan and Colorado Rivers into Lake Powell. It adds to the water in the lake. Depreciation is like the water flowing out of Lake Powell into the Colorado River. That flow lowers the water in the lake. The lake level (the amount of capital) rises by an amount equal to the inflow (gross investment) minus the outflow (depreciation).

Saving and Portfolio Choice

The quantity of capital supplied results from people's saving decisions. Saving is the opposite of consuming. **Saving** is income minus consumption. The current market value of a household's past saving, together with any inheritances it has received, is the household's **wealth.** Wealth is allocated across a variety of financial assets such as stocks, bonds, and bank deposits and physical assets such as houses, cars, and other consumer durable goods. These assets together with the household's liabilities are described by its balance sheet.

A household's choice regarding how much to hold in various assets and how much to owe in various liabilities is called a **portfolio choice.** For example, if a household decides to borrow $100,000 from a bank and to use that $100,000 to buy stock in a corporation, the household is making a portfolio choice. It is choosing the amount of an asset (the equity in a corporation) and the amount of a liability (the bank loan).

In everyday language, we often refer to the purchase of stocks and bonds as investment. That everyday use of the word *investment* can cause confusion in economic analysis. It is to avoid that confusion that we use the term *portfolio choice* to refer to the choices that households make in allocating their wealth across the various assets available to them. *Investment* is the purchases of new physical assets by firms and households.

We can illustrate the concepts of saving, wealth, and portfolio choice by looking at Rocky's *personal* situation—at Rocky's household balance sheet. Rocky has an initial wealth of $150,000 (see Table 16.3). During year 1, Rocky earns an income of $58,000, consumes $50,000, and saves $8,000. His wealth rises to $158,000.

How has Rocky allocated his wealth among the various assets and liabilities? Table 16.4 separates out Rocky's financial assets and liabilities from his physical assets. His financial assets include, first of all, his equity in Rocky's Mountain Bikes. Second, Rocky has some cash in the bank. This is his own personal bank account and is completely separate

TABLE **16.3**

Rocky's Income, Consumption, Saving, and Wealth

	Income	Consumption	Saving	Wealth
Initial net worth				**150,000**
Year 1	**58,000**	**50,000**	**8,000**	**158,000**

TABLE 16.4

Rocky's Financial Assets and Physical Assets at End of Year 1

Financial assets	
Equity in Rocky's Mountain Bikes	**$123,000**
Cash in bank	**10,000**
Mortgage	**–140,000**
Car loan	**–10,000**
Net financial assets	**–$17,000**
Physical assets	
House	**$160,000**
Car	**15,000**
Capital	**$175,000**
Wealth	**$158,000**

from the cash in the bike business. Third, Rocky has a mortgage on his home of $140,000 and a bank loan of $10,000 secured by the value of his car. Rocky's personal net financial assets are –$17,000. Note the minus sign. It tells us that, ignoring his physical assets, Rocky *owes* $17,000 more than he owns—his net *financial* assets are negative.

Rocky's physical assets are his house (valued at $160,000) and his car (valued at $15,000), so his capital stock is $175,000. Rocky's wealth is the sum of his capital stock and his net financial assets. Since Rocky's net financial assets are negative (he owes more than he owns), his wealth is his capital stock minus what he owes—$158,000.

With exactly the same saving, investment, and wealth, Rocky could have chosen a different portfolio allocation. For example, he could have used his bank deposit to pay off part of his bank loan or part of his mortgage. Alternatively, he could have taken a bigger mortgage and a smaller bank loan. Saving and investment decisions determine how much wealth a person has. Portfolio decisions determine how that wealth is held and financed.

REVIEW

There are two kinds of assets: financial and physical. Financial assets are the claims that lenders have on borrowers. One person's financial asset is another person's financial liability. Physical assets are buildings, plant and equipment, and inventories. Physical capital is the value of physical assets in existence at a point in time. Additions to capital are called investment. Capital wears out over time. This process is called depreciation. The quantity of capital supplied results from people's saving decisions. Saving is income minus consumption. The accumulated value of past saving is wealth. The allocation of wealth among the different assets is called portfolio choice. ◆

Capital Markets in the United States Today

Capital markets are the channels through which savings flow into firms to finance investment—the purchase of new capital. Figure 16.1 illustrates the structure of the capital markets and the financing of investment.

The actors in the capital markets are households, firms, and financial intermediaries.[1] You've met *households* and *firms* before. **Financial intermediaries** are institutions whose principal business is taking deposits, making loans, and buying securities. The best-known type of financial intermediary is a commercial bank. Other important types of financial intermediaries are insurance companies and savings and loan associations.

[1]Other actors in capital markets are governments and foreigners. We ignore these actors so that we can concentrate on the links between households' saving and firms' investment. These additional actors change the details of the story but not its main point.

FIGURE 16.1

Capital Market Flows

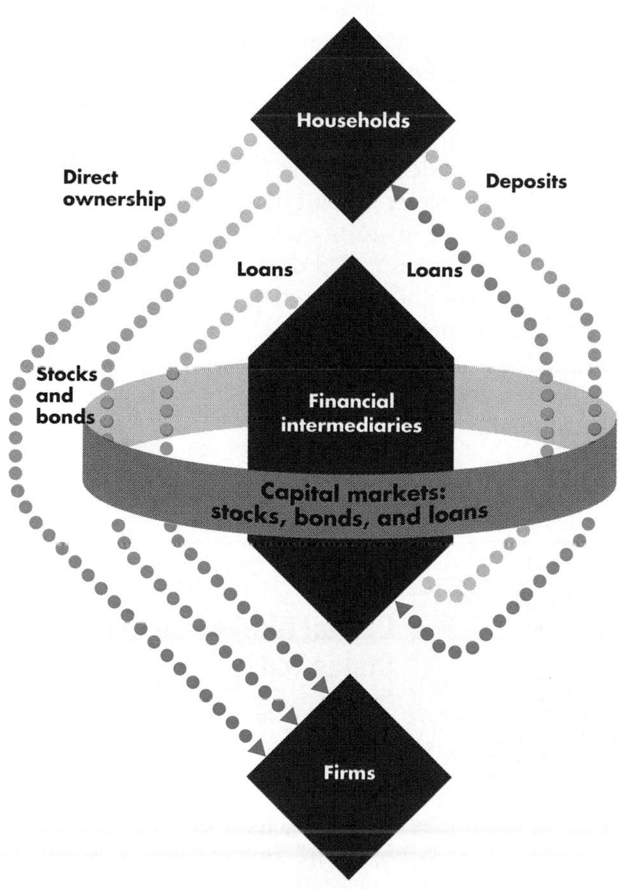

Households, firms, and financial intermediaries have extensive interactions in capital markets. Households purchase stocks and bonds, make deposits in financial intermediaries, and own firms directly. These flows are shown by the green dotted lines. Financial intermediaries lend to both households and firms.

The main types of capital market are

- The **stock market,** in which the equities of firms are traded
- The **bond market,** in which the bonds issued by firms are traded[2]
- The **loans market,** in which households and firms borrow and lend

These markets coordinate the decisions of households, firms, and financial intermediaries.

Investment takes place as a result of:

- Households buying capital directly and financing it either with their own resources or by borrowing from financial intermediaries
- Firms buying capital and financing it by selling stocks and bonds to households
- Firms buying capital and financing it by loans from financial intermediaries who in turn borrow from households

These financial transactions are illustrated by the green dotted lines in Fig. 16.1. Households use their savings to buy capital for their own firms (proprietorships and partnerships), to buy stocks or bonds issued by firms, and to make deposits with financial intermediaries. Financial intermediaries make loans to households and firms.

The Nation's Balance Sheet

How large are the U.S. capital markets? How big a role do the various elements play? The borrowing and lending pictured in Fig. 16.1 can be measured in the nation's balance sheet. This balance sheet lists the assets and liabilities of each of the major groups of agents in the economy—households, financial intermediaries, firms, and governments. Figure 16.2 provides a picture of those balance sheets. The data, in trillions of dollars, are from December 31, 1989 and are the most recent available. Assets are shown in blue and liabilities in red. The green arrows show the direction of the flow of funds.

First look at the households. They have financial assets in the form of deposits with financial intermediaries, savings in life insurance and pension funds, and holdings of equity and bonds. The total of these items is \$10.3 trillion. Households have financial liabilities in the form of mortgages and consumer credit, totaling \$3.3 trillion. Total financial assets of households exceed their liabilities by \$7 trillion, that is, \$10.3 trillion minus \$3.3 trillion. Households own physical assets in the form of houses and consumer durable goods valued at a total of \$6.4 trillion (\$4.5 trillion houses plus \$1.9 trillion consumer durables). Total household wealth is the sum of financial and physical assets and is \$13.4 trillion.

[2]The distinction between stocks and bonds is explained in Chapter 9, p. 16–32

FIGURE 16.2

The Nation's Balance Sheet

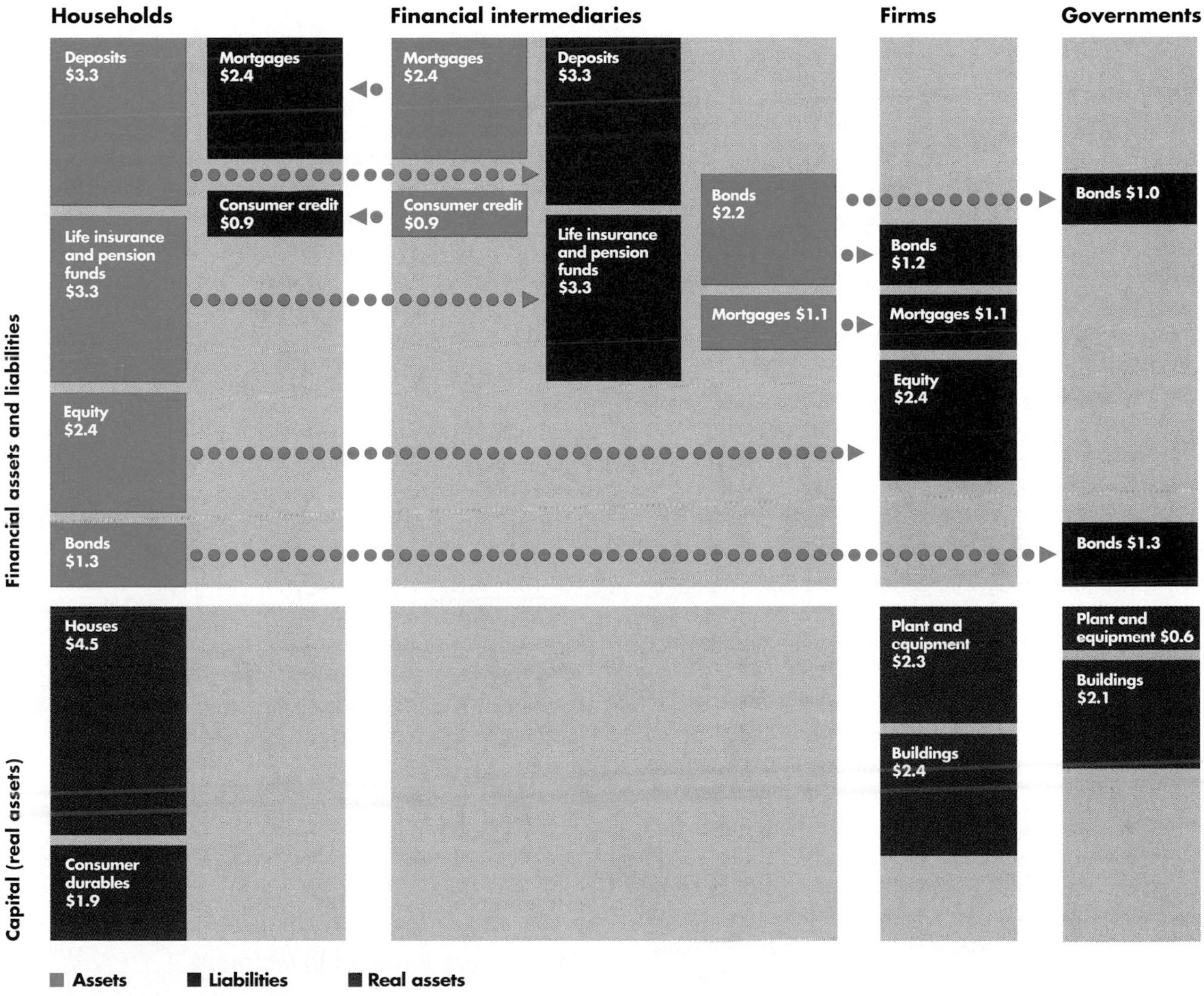

The nation's balance sheet records the indebtedness between the sectors of the economy—households, financial intermediaries, firms, and governments. The financial assets (blue) and liabilities (red) are shown in the top part of the figure, and capital (physical assets—purple) appears in the bottom part. All numbers are in trillions of dollars.

Households' financial assets are deposits with financial intermediaries, life insurance and pension funds, equity, and bonds. These assets are the liabilities of financial intermediaries, firms, and governments. Financial intermediaries take deposits and life insurance and pension fund contributions from households. Then they lend some of these funds back to households as mortgages and consumer credit; the remainder is lent to firms and governments in the form of bonds and mortgages. Both firms and governments borrow from financial intermediaries and households.

Capital (physical assets) consists of houses and consumer durables owned by households and of plant and equipment and buildings owned by firms and governments.

Source: *Statistical Abstract of the United States: 1991,* 111th edition, U.S. Bureau of the Census, Washington, D.C., p. 496; *Survey of Current Business,* 70 (9), September 1990, pp. 99–106; and my calculations.

Next look at the financial intermediaries. Their liabilities are the deposits and life insurance and pension funds, which we have just seen as the assets of households. They are liabilities of financial intermediaries because the financial intermediaries "owe" them to households. The assets of financial intermediaries represent loans by these institutions to households, firms, and governments. Financial intermediaries make loans to households in the form of mortgages and consumer credit. The financial intermediaries make loans to firms and governments as a result of purchasing bonds issued by these institutions. Financial intermediaries also make mortgage loans to firms. These bond sales provide firms and governments with funds to buy physical assets. The financial assets and liabilities of financial intermediaries are each $6.6 trillion.

The financial liabilities of firms—bonds ($1.2 trillion), mortgages ($1.1 trillion), and equity ($2.4 trillion)—totaling $4.7 trillion, are matched by their capital—plant and equipment ($2.3 trillion) and buildings ($2.4 trillion).

Government financial liabilities (bonds) generate funds to finance the purchase of plant and equipment and buildings. The value of the government sector's physical assets exceeds the value of its liabilities, and the difference is the wealth of the government sector.

The numbers in Fig. 16.2 give you an idea of the scale of the operations of the various elements in the capital markets. But they do not provide a flavor of the huge volume of transactions that take place—the flow of activity each day—or of the dynamic change over time in the scale of capital market transactions. The daily turnover in the ownership of stocks and bonds is enormous. On a typical day more than 200 million individual stocks change hands on the New York Stock Exchange. On what has come to be called Black Monday—October 19, 1987—a record 605 million shares were traded.

Demand for Capital

The demand for capital, like the demand for any other input, stems from firms' profit-maximization choices. As a firm increases the quantity of capital employed, other things being equal, the marginal revenue product of capital eventually diminishes. To maximize profit, a firm uses additional amounts of capital until the marginal revenue product of capital equals the opportunity cost of a unit of capital. That is, the firm increases its capital stock until the additional total revenue generated by one extra unit of capital equals the opportunity cost of one unit of capital. When a firm rents capital equipment, its calculations are identical to those made to choose its labor input. The firm faces an hourly rate for renting a machine, and it calculates the marginal revenue product of the machine per hour and compares that number with the hourly rental rate. Many machines are rented—for example, earth-moving equipment, cars, and airplanes—so these calculations are relevant in such cases.

But most capital is not rented. Firms *buy* buildings, plant, and equipment and operate them for several years. To decide how much capital equipment to buy, the firm has to compare the price of the equipment to be paid, here and now, with the returns—the marginal revenue products—that the equipment will generate over its entire life. To see how a firm decides how much capital to buy, we need to convert the future stream of marginal revenue products into its present value so that it can be directly compared with the price of buying a new piece of capital equipment. You have already met the concept of present value in Chapter 9 (pp. 214–217), and you might like to flip back to it to refresh your memory before moving on.

Net Present Value of Investment

Let's calculate the present value of the marginal revenue product of a capital input and see how we can use the result to make an investment decision. Table 16.5(a) summarizes the data that we'll use.

Tina runs a firm called Taxfile, Inc. The firm sells advice to taxpayers designed to minimize the taxes that they have to pay. Tina is considering buying a new computer that will cost $10,000. The computer has a life of two years, after which it will be worthless. Although Tina works hard all year studying tax law and writing sophisticated computer programs that will enable her to corner a good share of the

TABLE 16.5

Net Present Value of an Investment—Taxfile, Inc.

(a) Data

Price of computer	$10,000
Life of computer	2 years
Marginal revenue product	$5,900 at end of each year
Interest rate	4% a year

(b) Present value of the flow of marginal revenue product

$$PV = \frac{MRP}{1+r} + \frac{MRP}{(1+r)^2}$$
$$= \frac{\$5{,}900}{1.04} + \frac{\$5{,}900}{(1.04)^2}$$
$$= \$5{,}673 + \$5{,}455$$
$$= \$11{,}128$$

(c) Net present value of investment

$$NPV = PV \text{ of Marginal revenue product} - \text{Cost of computer}$$
$$= \$11{,}128 - \$10{,}000$$
$$= \$1{,}128$$

market, she generates an income only once each year—at tax filing time. If she buys the computer that she is now evaluating, Tina expects to be able to sell tax advice in each of the next two years that will bring in $5,900 at the end of each year. The interest rate that she has to pay is 4 percent a year.

We can calculate the present value of the marginal revenue product of Taxfile's computer by using a formula similar to the one that you met on p. 215. The formula is set out in Table 16.5(b). The present value (*PV*) of $5,900 one year in the future is $5900 divided by 1.04 (1 plus the interest rate expressed as a proportion—4 percent as a proportion is 0.04). The present value of $5,900 two years in the future is $5,900 divided by $(1.04)^2$. Working out those two present values and then adding them gives the present value of the flow of marginal revenue product from the machine as $11,128.

To decide whether or not to buy the computer, Tina compares the present value of its stream of marginal revenue products with its price. She makes this comparison by calculating the net present value (*NPV*) of the investment. The **net present value of an investment** is the present value of the stream of marginal revenue products generated by the investment minus the cost of the investment. If the net present value of the investment is positive, it pays her to buy the computer. If the net present value of the investment is negative, it does not pay her to buy the computer. In such a case, the cost of the computer exceeds the present value of the stream of income that it generates. Table 16.5(c) shows the calculation of the net present value of Tina's investment in a computer. The net present value is $1,128. Therefore Tina buys the computer.

Whenever the net present value of an investment is positive, a firm will increase its net worth by making the investment. Like all other inputs, capital is subject to diminishing marginal returns. The more capital is added, the lower is its marginal product and the lower is its marginal revenue product. We have seen in the above example that it pays the firm to buy one machine because that investment yields a positive net present value. Should Tina invest in two computers or three? To answer this question, she must do more calculations similar to those summarized in Table 16.5.

Suppose, in particular, that Taxfile's investment opportunities are as set out in Table 16.6. Tina can buy any number of computers. Each computer costs $10,000 and has a life of two years. The marginal revenue product generated by each computer depends on how many computers Taxfile operates. If it operates just one computer, it has a marginal revenue product of $5,900 a year (the case just reviewed). If Taxfile uses a second computer, marginal revenue product falls to $5,600 a year, and in the case of a third computer it falls to $5,300 a year. Part (b) of the table calculates the present value of the marginal revenue product of each of these three levels of investment in computers.

We have seen that with an interest rate of 4 percent it pays to invest in the first computer—the net present value of that computer is positive. It also pays to invest in a second computer. The present value of the marginal revenue product resulting

TABLE 16.6

Taxfile's Investment Decision

(a) Data

Price of computer	**$10,000**
Life of computer	**2 years**
Marginal revenue product:	
Using one computer	**$5,900 a year**
Using two computers	**$5,600 a year**
Using three computers	**$5,300 a year**

(b) Present value of the stream of marginal revenue products

If r = 0.04 (4% a year):

Using one computer, $PV = \frac{\$5{,}900}{1.04} + \frac{\$5{,}900}{(1.04)^2} = \$11{,}128$

Using two computers, $PV = \frac{\$5{,}600}{1.04} + \frac{\$5{,}600}{(1.04)^2} = \$10{,}562$

Using three computers, $PV = \frac{\$5{,}300}{1.04} + \frac{\$5{,}300}{(1.04)^2} = \$9{,}996$

If r = 0.08 (8% a year):

Using one computer, $PV = \frac{\$5{,}900}{1.08} + \frac{\$5{,}900}{(1.08)^2} = \$10{,}521$

Using two computers, $PV = \frac{\$5{,}600}{1.08} + \frac{\$5{,}600}{(1.08)^2} = \$9{,}986$

If r = 0.12 (12% a year):

Using one computer, $PV = \frac{\$5{,}900}{1.12} + \frac{\$5{,}900}{(1.12)^2} = \$9{,}971$

from using two computers, $10,562, exceeds the cost of the second machine by $562. You can also see that it does not pay to invest in a third computer. The present value of the marginal revenue product resulting from using three computers is $9,996. But the computer costs $10,000, so the net present value of the third computer is –$4. Tina buys a second computer but does not buy a third one. If she does, the net worth of Taxfile will fall by $4.

We have just discovered that at an interest rate of 4 percent a year it pays Tina to buy two computers but not three. Suppose that the interest rate is higher than 4 percent a year—say, 8 percent a year. In this case, the present value of one machine (see the calculations in Table 16.6b) is $10,521. Therefore it still pays to buy the first machine. But its net present value is smaller when the interest rate is 8 percent than at the lower rate of 4 percent. At an 8 percent interest rate, the net present value resulting from using two machines is negative. The present value of the marginal revenue product, $9,986, is less than the $10,000 that the second computer costs. Therefore at an interest rate of 8 percent it pays Tina to buy one computer but not two.

Suppose that the interest rate is even higher, say, 12 percent a year. In this case the present value of the marginal revenue product of one computer is $9,971 (see Table 16.6b). At this interest rate, it does not pay to buy even one computer.

The calculations that you have just reviewed trace out Taxfile's demand schedule for capital. The demand schedule for capital shows the value of computers demanded by Taxfile at each interest rate. As the interest rate falls, the value of capital demanded increases. At an interest rate of 12 percent a year, the firm demands no computers. At an interest rate of 8 percent a year, one computer or $10,000 of capital is demanded; at 4 percent a year, $20,000 of capital is demanded (two computers). (Although we have stopped our calculations at two computers, at lower interest rates Tina would buy yet more machines and demand more capital.)

Demand Curve for Capital

A firm's demand curve for capital relates the quantity of capital demanded to the interest rate. Figure 16.3 illustrates the demand for computers (D_F) by Tina's firm. The horizontal axis measures the value of computers that Taxfile owns, and the vertical axis measures the interest rate. Points *a*, *b*, and *c* correspond to the example that we have just worked through. At an interest rate of 12 percent a year, it does not pay Tina to buy any computers—point *a*. At an interest rate of 8 percent, it pays to buy 1 computer worth $10,000—point *b*. At an interest rate of 4 percent, it pays to buy 2 computers worth $20,000—point *c*.

In our example, we've only considered one type of computer—that which costs exactly $10,000. In practice, Tina could consider buying a different type of computer, the power of which could be expressed as a multiple or fraction of one of the $10,000 computers that we've been considering here. For example, there might be a $5,000 computer that has half

FIGURE 16.3

A Firm's Demand for Capital

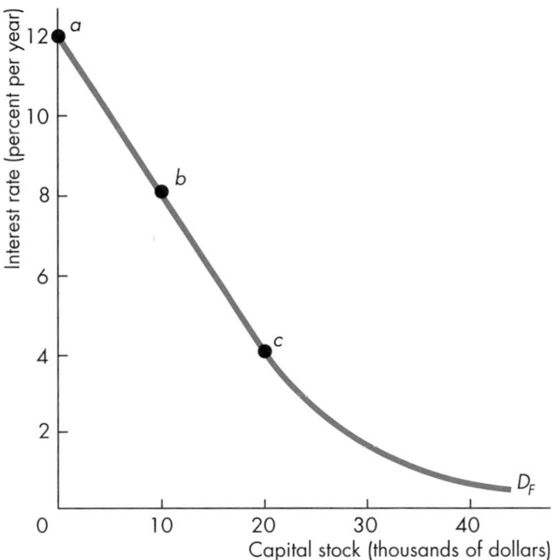

Taxfile demands capital (computers) until the present value of the stream of marginal revenue products of computers equals the price of a computer. The present value depends on the interest rate. The lower the interest rate, the higher is the number of computers demanded. At an interest rate of 12 percent a year, Taxfile demands no computers (point *a*). At an interest rate of 8 percent, the firm demands 1 computer worth $10,000 (point *b*). At an interest rate of 4 percent, the firm demands 2 computers worth $20,000 (point *c*). If computers of different types (fractions of a $10,000 computer) can be bought, a demand curve that passes through points *a*, *b*, and *c* is generated.

FIGURE 16.4

The Market Demand for Capital

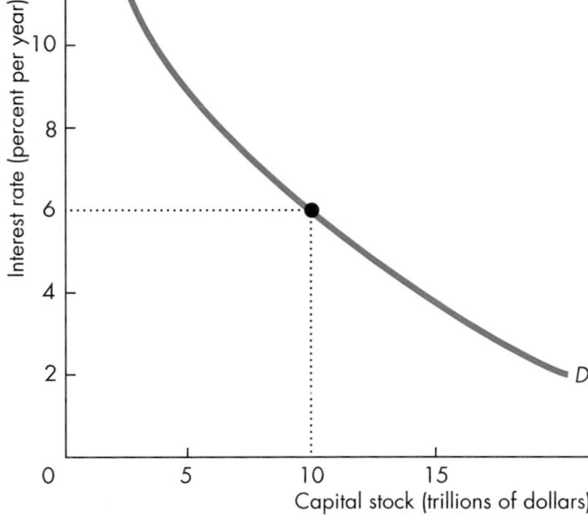

The market demand curve for capital is obtained by adding together the demand curves for capital of all the firms in the economy. An example of a market demand curve is *D*. On this demand curve, quantity of capital demanded is $10 trillion when the interest rate is 6 percent a year and the quantity of capital demanded falls as the interest rate rises, other things being equal.

the power of a $10,000 machine or a bigger machine costing $12,500 that has one and a quarter times the power of a $10,000 machine. If we consider all the different types of computers that Tina can buy, we will generate not just the three points, *a*, *b*, and *c*, but an entire demand curve like that shown in the figure.

The market demand curve for capital is shown in Fig. 16.4. It measures the total quantity of capital demanded (in trillions of dollars) on the horizontal axis and the interest rate on the vertical axis. On that curve, at an interest rate of 6 percent per year the quantity of capital demanded is $10 trillion. Like the firm's demand curve, the market demand curve slopes down.

Changes in the Demand for Capital

The demand for capital is constantly changing, and the demand curve for capital is constantly shifting. Also, the composition of the demand for capital is constantly changing; the demand for some types of capital increases, while the demand for other types decreases. Technological change is the main force generating these changes in the demand for capital. For example, the development of diesel engines for railroad transportation resulted in a decrease in demand for steam engines, an increase in demand for diesel engines, and not much change in the overall demand for capital in the railroad industry. In contrast, the development of desktop computers has led to a large increase in demand for office and research computing equipment.

The general trend resulting from the development of new technology and its exploitation through innovation is for the demand for capital to steadily increase over time with a steady rightward shift of the demand curve for capital.

REVIEW

The demand for capital is determined by firms' profit-maximization choices. The marginal product of capital declines as the amount of capital used rises. As a consequence, the marginal revenue product of capital declines as more capital is used. Capital is demanded up to the point where the present value of its stream of marginal revenue products equals its price. The interest rate is an important factor in the present value calculation. The higher the interest rate, the lower is the present value of the stream of marginal revenue products. ◆◆ The demand curve for capital is the relationship between the quantity of capital demanded and the interest rate. The higher the interest rate, the lower is the present value of the stream of marginal products and the smaller is the quantity of capital demanded by a firm. The demand curve for capital slopes downward. The demand for capital changes as a result of technological change. There is a general tendency for the demand for capital to increase over time with the demand curve for capital shifting to the right. ◆

The Supply of Capital

The quantity of capital supplied results from the saving decisions of households.[3] The most important factors determining a household's saving are

- ◆ The household's current income in relation to its expected future income
- ◆ The interest rate

[3]We ignore the government and foreign sectors so that we can focus on essentials without making things too complicated. The basic story is not changed by the existence of foreign and government sources of saving.

The stage in the household's life cycle is the major factor influencing whether current income is high or low in comparison with expected future income. Households typically smooth their consumption over the life cycle. Consumption smoothing is one of the main influences on the saving of a household. As we saw in Chapter 14 (pp. 390–391), young households typically have current income that is low in comparison with their expected future income, and older households have income that is high relative to expected future income; young people incur debts, while older people save, pay off earlier debts, and accumulate assets. A household's saving depends on how much it smooths its consumption over the life cycle.

Interest Rate

There are two distinct effects of interest rates on the level of saving:

- ◆ Substitution effect
- ◆ Income effect

Substitution Effect A higher interest rate increases the future payoff from today's saving. It therefore increases the opportunity cost of current consumption. Thus a higher interest rate encourages people to economize on current consumption and take advantage of the higher interest rate available on savings. As the interest rate rises, people substitute higher future consumption for current consumption, and saving increases.

Income Effect A change in the interest rate changes people's incomes. Other things being equal, the higher a person's income, the higher is the level of current consumption and the higher are the levels of future consumption and of saving.

The effect of a change in the interest rate on income depends on whether a person is a borrower or a lender. For a lender—a person with positive net financial assets—an increase in interest rates increases income, so the income effect is positive. The income effect reinforces the substitution effect, and a higher interest rate results in higher saving.

For a borrower—a person with negative net financial assets—an increase in interest rates decreases the income available for consumption. In this case, the income effect is negative—higher interest rates lower consumption and saving. The income effect works in a direction opposite to that of the substitution effect, and saving may decrease.

Supply Curve of Capital

The quantity of capital supplied is the total value of accumulated savings. The supply curve of capital shows the relationship between the quantity of capital supplied and the interest rate. We've seen that this relationship depends on the relative strengths of the income effect and the substitution effect and, for an individual household, may be either positive or negative. For the economy as a whole, however, the substitution effect is stronger than the income effect, so a higher interest rate encourages saving and the supply curve of capital is upward sloping. Figure 16.5 illustrates the supply curve of capital. On that curve, at an interest rate of 6 percent per year, the quantity of capital supplied is $10 trillion.

FIGURE 16.5

The Supply of Capital

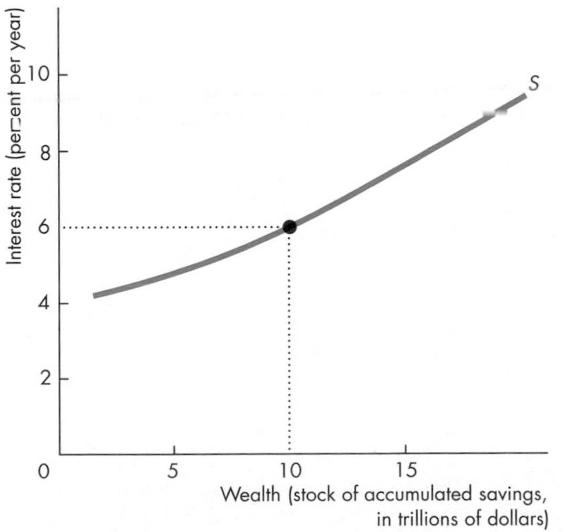

The higher the interest rate, the more capital households supply—the supply curve of capital slopes upward. At an interest rate of 6 percent a year, the quantity of capital supplied is $10 trillion.

Changes in the Supply of Capital

The supply of capital changes constantly. The main influences on the supply of capital are demographic. As the population changes and as its age distribution changes, so does the supply of capital. A population with a larger proportion of young people has a smaller supply of capital than a population with a larger proportion of middle-aged people. The age distribution of the population affects the supply of capital as a result of the life-cycle consumption smoothing described above.

Another influence on the supply of capital is the average income level. The higher the level of income, the larger is the supply of capital. A growing population and steadily rising income result in the supply of capital curve shifting to the right over time.

REVIEW

The quantity of capital supplied is determined by households' saving decisions. Saving depends on the amount of consumption smoothing the household undertakes over its life cycle and the interest rate. The more the household smooths its consumption and the higher the interest rate, the larger is the amount people save. The supply curve of capital is the relationship between the interest rate and the quantity of capital supplied. It slopes upward—the higher the interest rate, the larger is the quantity of capital supplied, other things being equal. The supply of capital changes as a result of changes in the population and its age composition and the level of income. Increasing population and increasing income result in a steady increase in the supply of capital—with the supply curve shifting steadily to the right. ◆

Now that we have studied the demand for and supply of capital, we can bring these two sides of the capital market together and study the determination of interest rates and asset prices. We'll then be able to answer some of the questions posed at the beginning of this chapter about the stock market and understand the forces that produce stock market booms and crashes.

Interest Rates and Asset Prices

Households' saving plans and firms' investment plans are coordinated through capital markets. Asset prices and interest rates adjust to make these plans compatible. We are now going to study the way in which these market forces work. And we are going to discover what determines the stock market value of a firm.

Two Sides of the Same Coin

Interest rates and asset prices can be viewed as two sides of the same coin. We'll look first at interest rates, then at asset prices, and finally at the connection between them. Some assets, such as bank deposits, earn a guaranteed interest rate. Other assets, such as bonds and shares in the stocks of firms, do not. The interest rates on these assets are usually called bond yields and stock yields. A **bond yield** is the interest on a bond, expressed as a percentage of the price of the bond. A **stock yield** is the income from a share in the stock of a firm, expressed as a percentage of the price of the share—the stock market price. A bond earns a guaranteed dollar income, but its market price fluctuates and hence its yield also fluctuates. A share in the stock of a firm earns a dividend based on the profitability of the firm. Also the stock market value of the share fluctuates. Thus a stock yield fluctuates for two reasons—fluctuations in the dividend and fluctuations in its stock market price.

Let's now look at the two sides of the same coin—the price of an asset and its yield or interest rate. To calculate a bond yield or stock yield, we divide the earnings of the asset by the price paid for it. For example, if Taxfile, Inc. pays a dividend of $5 a share and if a share can be bought for $50, the stock yield will be 10 percent ($5 divided by $50, expressed as a percentage). It follows from this calculation that for a given amount of earnings, the higher the price of an asset, the lower is its yield. For example, if the price of a share in Taxfile is $100 but its dividend remains constant at $5, its yield falls to 5 percent. This connection between the price of an asset and its yield or interest rate means that we can study the market forces in capital markets as simultaneously determining asset yields (interest rates) and asset prices. We will look at capital market equilibrium first in terms of interest rate (or yield) determination and then in terms of the stock market value of a particular firm.

Equilibrium Interest Rate

Figure 16.6 brings together the relevant parts of the previous analysis of the demand for and supply of capital. The diagram shows the entire capital market. The horizontal axis measures the total quantity of capital. Notice that the axis is labeled "Capital stock and wealth." This label emphasizes the fact that the value of the capital stock and wealth are equivalent. The vertical axis measures the interest rate. The demand curve (D) is the market demand for capital that you met in Fig. 16.4. The supply curve (S) is the market supply of capital shown in Fig. 16.5.

FIGURE 16.6

Capital Market Equilibrium

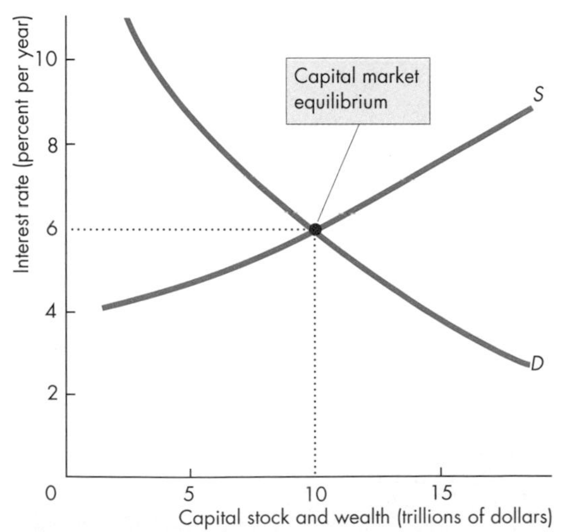

Capital market equilibrium occurs when the interest rate is such that the quantity of capital demanded equals the quantity of capital supplied. The demand curve is D, and the supply curve is S. These curves intersect at an interest rate of 6 percent a year and a capital stock of $10 trillion.

Capital market equilibrium occurs where the quantity of capital supplied equals the quantity of capital demanded. In Fig. 16.6, this equilibrium is at an interest rate of 6 percent a year and $10 trillion of capital is supplied and demanded. The market forces that bring about the equilibrium are exactly the same as those that we studied in the markets for goods and services.

If the interest rate exceeds 6 percent, the quantity of capital demanded is less than the quantity supplied. There is an excess supply of funds in the capital markets. In such a situation, financial intermediaries, anxious to increase their loans, lower the interest rates. The quantity demanded increases as firms increase their borrowing and buy additional capital. The interest rate continues to fall until financial institutions are able to lend all they wish to at the going rate. Conversely, if the interest rate is below 6 percent, the quantity of capital supplied is less than the quantity demanded. Financial intermediaries, unable to find enough funds to lend, increase interest rates. Rates increase until there are no unsatisfied borrowers. The end point of either of these situations is an interest rate of 6 percent, the equilibrium interest rate. The institutions that trade most heavily in capital markets—banks, insurance companies, and specialized dealers—handle millions of dollars of business every day and maintain a near continuous equality between the quantity of capital demanded and the quantity supplied.

These same competitive forces ensure that the interest rate is the same in all parts of the capital market, both across the regions of the nation and around the world. A further description of how these forces work to keep interest rates the same in all parts of the world can be seen in Reading Between the Lines on pp. 442–443.

The interest rate determined in Fig. 16.6 (and in Reading Between the Lines) is the *average* interest rate. Interest rates on individual assets will be distributed around that average, based on the relative degree of riskiness of individual assets. An asset with a high degree of risk will earn an interest rate that exceeds the average, and a very safe asset will earn an interest rate that is below the average. For example, if the average interest rate is 6 percent a year as shown in Fig. 16.6, the interest rate on a safe asset, such as a bank deposit, might be 4 percent a year and that on a riskier asset, such as a stock, could be 8 percent a year.

We've now seen how asset yields or interest rates are determined. Let's look at the other side of the coin—asset prices. To determine asset prices, we will change our focus and look not at the capital market in aggregate but at the stock market value of an individual firm.

Stock Market Value of a Firm

We've seen that there is a connection between an asset's yield (or interest rate) and that asset's price. The yield is the earnings on the asset divided by its price (expressed as a percentage). Let's use this fact to work out the stock market value of a firm. Suppose that a firm finances its purchases of capital by selling shares of its stock. What determines the price of a share? What determines the total value of all the shares sold?

The value of a share depends on the total value of the firm and on the number of shares sold. The value of one share is equal to the value of a firm divided by the number of shares sold, or, equivalently, the value of the firm is equal to the value of one share multiplied by the number of shares sold. So for a firm with a given number of shares, asking what determines the price of a share is the same as asking what determines the value of the firm.

When a person buys a share in the stock of a firm, that person becomes entitled to receive a profit each year. The price of a share depends on the expected future profit to be paid out by the firm. As we discovered in Chapter 9 (pp. 214–217) when we looked at the value of a share in Wisconsin Toy, the price of a share is the present value of its expected future profit. If a firm is expected to pay out no profits at all in the future, its shares will be worthless. If it is expected to pay out $10 a year on a share and if the interest rate is 10 percent a year, its shares will be worth $100 each. If it is expected to pay out $20 a year on a share and the interest rate is 10 percent, its shares will be worth $200 each.

Price-Earnings Ratio

A commonly used measure to describe the performance of a firm's stock is its price-earnings ratio. A *price-earnings ratio* is the current price of a share in a firm's stock divided by the most recent year's profit per share. In 1982, the average price-earnings ratio of the stocks that formed the Dow Jones Industrial

The Global Capital Market

THE ECONOMIST, November 16, 1991

The Surprising Emergence of Distant Shares

"Emerging markets" once seemed an optimistic term. Now it is really happening. The stock markets of Asia and Latin America, plus a handful of others classified as "emerging" by the International Finance Corporation (IFC, the private-sector arm of the World Bank), have collectively grown fourfold since 1985. Last year they provided $22 billion of fresh money for companies. . . . The IFC reckons that foreigners' stake in the young markets has grown from next to nothing a decade ago to around $17 billion.

By the end of the decade, this sum may seem paltry. For reasons unconnected with the individual charms of these markets, the world's biggest savings institutions—pension and mutual funds, insurance companies—are keener to spread their assets internationally; Salomon Brothers, an American investment bank, reckons that the value of cross-border equity flows increased 20 times during the 1980s. As they diversify, fund managers establish benchmarks to guide their asset allocation. A popular solution is to allocate money in proportion to the capitalisation of each market. If this were applied to the developing world, the result would be a deluge of foreign capital.

Each year the rich world's savers invest something like $1 trillion of new money in equities. Together the emerging markets represent 5% of world stockmarket capitalisation, so the benchmark would imply an annual transfer of $50 billion. If the savings institutions also began to shift existing funds to reflect that proportion, the transfers could be even bigger—perhaps amounting to $100 billion a year. . . .

Next consider the scope for issuing international equity. The new rival to the growth of cross-border equity flows is "cross-exchange" trading. . . . Salomon Brothers calculates that the volume of cross-exchange equity trading jumped from $583 billion in 1989 to $874 billion last year.

Developing countries have recently begun to exploit investors' appetite for international listings. The most noted example is Telmex, Mexico's telephone company, whose listing on the New York Stock Exchange in May [1991] raised $2.2 billion; on October 28th [1991] Telmex was the exchange's most actively traded stock. South Korean, Indonesian and Thai companies issued $1.6 billion of international equity and convertible bonds between them during the 18 months from January 1990. Indian and Brazilian rivals are tipped to join in next.

The Essence of the Story

The stock markets of Asia and Latin America (plus a few others) have grown fourfold since 1985. In 1990, $22 billion of savings were channeled through these markets, $17 billion of which were foreign savings.

The world's pension and mutual funds and insurance companies have spread their assets internationally, resulting in a twenty-fold increase in the value of cross-border equity flows during the 1980s.

If these institutions also shift existing funds in proportion to market size, the transfers will be $100 billion a year.

An alternative to allocating funds to foreign stock markets is for investors to buy foreign shares in their own countries—cross-exchange trading—which increased from $583 billion in 1989 to $874 billion in 1990.

Developing countries are taking advantage of cross-exchange equities. Telmex, Mexico's telephone company, raised $2.2 billion on the New York Stock Exchange, and South Korean, Indonesian, and Thai companies raised $1.6 billion. Indian and Brazilian companies are expected to be next.

Background and Analysis

The world capital market is made up of thousands of local markets, but it is a single integrated market. People with funds to lend supply them where they can get the highest interest rate. People borrowing funds to buy capital demand them where they can get the lowest interest rate. As a result, each local capital market has the same interest rate.

The figure shows how the world capital market for equity capital—shares in companies—works. Part (a) illustrates the Asian and Latin American "emerging" markets, and part (b) illustrates the New York market. Initially, the demand and supply curves are D_0 and S_0. The interest rate is r_N, and the quantities of equity capital are K_N in New York and zero in the emerging markets.

Then the demand for equity capital increases in Asia and Latin America, and the demand curve for capital shifts to the right, to D_1. (Such an increase occurred in Asia and Latin America during the 1980s partly because the number of profitable business opportunities increased and partly because banks stopped lending to companies in these regions.)

Other things remaining equal, the interest rate rises in the emerging markets to r_E and the quantity of equity capital increases to K_E.

But other things do not remain equal. With the interest rate in the emerging markets higher than that in New York, U.S. institutions with funds to lend move them from the New York market to the emerging markets. The supply curves shift to S_2 (in both markets). These are the "cross-border equity flows" in the story.

Also, borrowers in Asia and Latin America switch their borrowing from their local market to the New York market. The demand curves shift to D_2 in both markets. This is the "cross-exchange trading" in the story.

As a consequence of these changes in supply and demand, the interest rate rises in the New York market and falls in the emerging markets. When the two rates are equal at r_W, the demand and supply curves stop shifting and a single interest rate prevails in both markets.

The capital markets of Asia and Latin America are "emerging" and "cross-exchange" trading is expanding because, if they did not, interest rates in the two markets would diverge and profits could be made simply by borrowing in the market that has the low interest rate and lending in the other market.

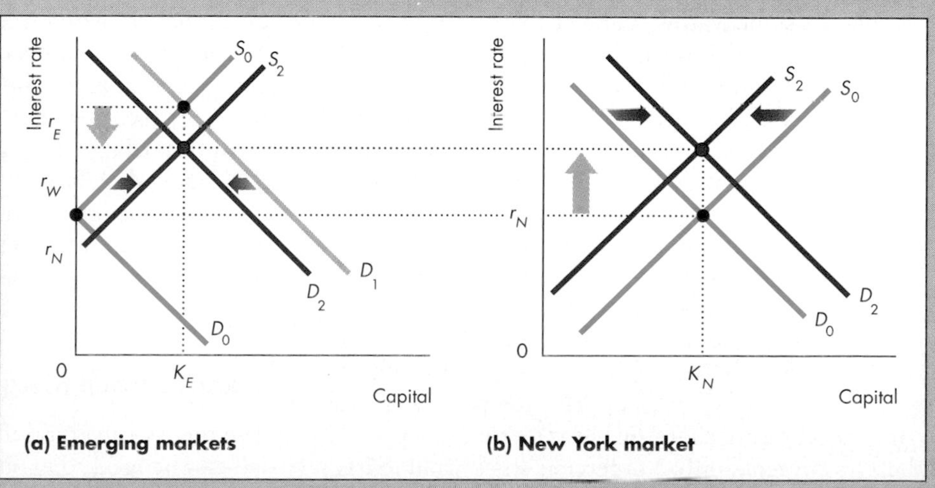

Average was 8.1. By 1987, the price-earnings ratio had risen to 20.5, but that was a peak year. The ratio then fell off and, at the beginning of 1989, stood at about 12.

What determines a price-earnings ratio? Why, at the beginning of 1989, was Ford's price-earnings ratio only 5 while Sony's was 33?

We have seen that the price of a share of stock is determined by the present value of the expected future profit of the firm. The higher the *expected future* profit, the higher is *today's* price. The price-earnings ratio of a firm depends on its current profit in relation to its expected future profit. When expected future profit is high relative to current profit, the price-earnings ratio is high. When expected future profit is low relative to current profit, the price-earnings ratio is low. Fluctuations in the price-earnings ratio arise from fluctuations in expected future profit relative to current profit.

Stock Market Volume and Prices

Sometimes the prices quoted on the stock market rise or fall with little trading taking place. At other times, stock market prices rise or fall with an enormous volume of trading. On yet other occasions, there is little change in the stock prices but there is an enormous volume of trading. Why do stock prices rise or fall, and what determines the volume of trading on the stock market?

Stock prices rise and fall because of changes in expectations of future profit. Consider the firm whose profit per share is $1. Suppose that the interest rate on assets that are as risky as a share of this firm's stock is 8 percent a year. Further suppose that the firm's profit in each future year is expected to be exactly the same as this year's. The price of the firm's stock will adjust until a share can be bought for the price that makes the stock yield equal to 8 percent a year. That price is $12.50. People will buy shares in this company for $12.50 and expect, on the average, to make $1 a share each year, or a stock yield of 8 percent ($1 is 8 percent of $12.50). The price-earnings ratio will be 12.5—today's price ($12.50) divided by last year's profit ($1 per share).

Suppose that market conditions change and people now expect the firm's profit to double to $2 per share starting next year. With an expected profit of $2 a share the stock market price jumps to $25. It's true that at $25 a share this year's profit ($1 per share) represents only a 4 percent stock yield ($1 is 4 percent of $25), but with profit expected to be $2 per share next year and every year thereafter, the expected yield is 8 percent a year—the interest rate available on other assets of similar risk. This price jump to $25 occurs with no change in the current year's profitability of the firm. It occurs entirely because people observe some event today that leads them to expect higher profit in the future.

Suppose that the change in market conditions leading to expected higher future profit is so obvious that everyone can see it and everyone agrees that this firm's earnings are indeed going to double next year. In such a situation, the market value of the firm's shares rises to $25 but no one buys or sells shares. Stockholders are happy with the shares that they already hold. If the price does not rise to $25, everyone will want to buy some shares. If the price rises to more than $25, everyone will want to sell some shares. If the price rises to exactly $25, everyone will be indifferent between hanging onto those shares or buying some other shares that are currently yielding 8 percent a year.

On the other hand, suppose that the event that changed expectations about this firm's profitability is difficult to interpret. Some people think the event will lead to a rise in the firm's profit, and others think it will not have any effect on profit. Let's call the first group optimists and the second group pessimists. The optimists will want to buy the stock and will be willing to do so as long as its price is less than $25. The pessimists will sell the stock as long as its price is above $12.50. In such a situation, the pessimists will sell out and the optimists will buy in. The price will not necessarily change, but there will be a large volume of trading activity. What causes the trading activity is the disagreement, not the event that triggered the change in expected profitability. High volume of trading on the stock market implies a large amount of disagreement. Large price changes with low volume of trading imply a great deal of agreement that something fundamental has changed. A large volume of trading with hardly any price change means that the underlying changes are difficult to interpret: some people predict that things will move in one direction, while others predict the opposite.

Takeovers and Mergers

The theory of capital markets that you've now studied can be used to explain why takeovers and mergers occur. A **takeover** is the purchase of the stock of one firm by another firm. A takeover occurs when the stock market value of a firm is lower than the present value of the expected future profits from operating the firm. For example, suppose that Taxfile, Inc. has a stock market value of $120,000. But suppose also that the present value of the future profit of the firm is $150,000. It will pay for someone to try to take over the firm. Takeover activity affects the price of a firm, and often the threat of a takeover drives the price to the point at which the takeover is no longer profitable.

There are other takeover situations in which the expected future profit of a firm depends on the firm taking it over. A recent example illustrates this point very well. The Atari Computer Company was having difficulty in breaking into the retail computer market on the scale that it desired. To overcome its problems, Atari searched out, surprisingly, a retail chain that was losing money. The present value of a firm that is making a loss is less than the value of its plant and equipment. So Atari was able to buy retail outlets for a lower price from their current owners than it could have done by starting afresh. Atari believed that by buying the firm and using its retail stores to sell Atari computers, Atari could convert that firm's loss into a profit.

A **merger** is the combining of the assets of two firms to form a single new firm. Mergers take place when two firms perceive that by combining their assets, they can increase their combined stock market values. For example, the merger of Piedmont and USAir enabled the resulting firm to increase its profit by integrating their routes and schedules.

REVIEW

Saving plans and investment plans are coordinated through capital markets. Adjustments in asset prices and interest rates make the saving plans and investment plans compatible. Interest rates and asset prices are two sides of the same coin. The interest rate on an asset is the income on the asset divided by its price. The average interest rate makes the quantity of capital demanded equal to the quantity of savings supplied. ◆ ◆ The value of a share of a firm's stock is determined by the firm's current and expected future profit. Expected future profit is based on expectations of future prices, costs, and technologies that the firm will face. The stock market value of a firm is often expressed as a ratio of the firm's current profit per share—the price-earnings ratio. The price-earnings ratio depends on expected profit growth. ◆ ◆ Stock market prices sometimes move dramatically, and the volume of trading on the stock market is sometimes high and sometimes low. Prices change quickly when everyone expects changes in future profitability. The volume of stock market trading rises when people disagree about the future. ◆ ◆ Mergers and takeovers occur when the stock market value of a firm is lower than the present value of the future profit stream that another firm believes it could generate with the first firm's assets. ◆

The lessons that we've just learned about capital markets have wider application than explaining fluctuations in the stock market. They also help us to understand how natural resource markets work. Let's now examine these important markets.

Natural Resource Markets

N**atural resources** are the nonproduced factors of production with which we are endowed. Natural resources fall into two categories: exhaustible and nonexhaustible. **Exhaustible natural resources** are natural resources that can be used only once and that cannot be replaced once used. Examples of exhaustible natural resources are coal, natural gas, and oil—the so-called hydrocarbon fuels. **Nonexhaustible natural resources** are natural resources that can be used repeatedly without depleting what's available for future use. Examples of nonexhaustible natural resources are land, sea, rivers and lakes, rain, and sunshine. Plants and animals are also examples of nonexhaustible natural resources. By careful cultivation and husbandry, more of these natural resources can be produced to replace those used up in production and consumption activities.

Natural resources have two important economic dimensions—a stock dimension and a flow dimension. There is a stock of each natural resource determined by nature and by the previous rate of use of the resource. The flow of a natural resource is the rate at which it is being used. This flow is determined by human choices, and those choices determine whether a given stock of natural resources is used up quickly, slowly, or not at all. In studying the operation of natural resource markets, we'll begin by considering the stock dimension of a natural resource.

Supply and Demand in a Natural Resource Market

The stock of a natural resource supplied is the amount of the resource in existence. For example, the stock of oil supplied is the total volume of oil lying beneath the earth's surface. This amount is fixed independently of the price of the resource. Its supply is perfectly inelastic, and the position of its supply curve depends on the amount of the resource available initially and on the rate at which it has been used up in the past.[4] The smaller the initial stock and the faster the rate of use, the smaller is the stock of a resource available.

Demand for a Stock The demand for a stock of a natural resource is one aspect of portfolio choice. People own stocks of natural resources as an alternative to owning equities in corporations, other financial assets such as bonds, or other physical assets such as plant, equipment, and buildings.

The demand for a stock of a natural resource is determined in the same way as the demand for any other asset—by the income that it is expected to earn, expressed as a percentage yield or interest rate.

But what is the interest rate on a natural resource? It is the rate of change in the price of the resource. If you buy a stock of a natural resource, you buy it at today's price. If you sell your natural resource stock a year later, you sell it at the price prevailing at that time. The percentage change in the price of the resource over the year is the interest rate you make from holding the stock of the natural resource over the year. Thus the more rapid the increase in the price of a natural resource, other things being equal, the larger is the interest rate on that natural resource.

If the expected interest rate on a stock of a natural resource exceeds that on other assets (with comparable risk), people allocate more of their net worth to owning the natural resource and less to other assets. Conversely, if the expected interest rate on a natural resource falls short of that on other assets (with comparable risk), portfolios are reallocated by selling the stock of a natural resource and buying other assets.

Stock Equilibrium Equilibrium occurs in the market for a stock of a natural resource when the interest rate on owning a natural resource stock equals that on other comparably risky assets. In such a situation, there is no tendency for people to either buy or sell stocks of natural resources or other assets. They are satisfied with their existing portfolio allocation and with the quantity of the stock of the natural resource that they are holding.

Since the interest rate on a natural resource stock is the rate at which the price of the natural resource rises, the expected interest rate is the rate at which the price of the resource is *expected* to rise over time. That rate equals the interest rate on other assets. This proposition is known as the **Hotelling Principle.**[5]

Why is the price of a natural resource expected to grow at a rate equal to the interest rate on other assets? It is to make the expected interest rate on the natural resource equal to the interest rate on other comparably risky assets.

The supply of and demand for the stock of a natural resource determine the interest rate from owning that stock. But the supply of and demand for the stock of the resource do not determine the current *level* of the price—only its future expected rate of

[4]The actual quantity is not the same as the *known* (or proven) quantity. The known quantity of a natural resource in existence is larger the higher its price, other things being equal. For example, the known reserves of oil in 1973, when the price of oil was $3 a barrel, were 580 billion barrels. By 1990, after we had consumed 350 billion barrels but by which time the price of oil had increased to $30 a barrel, known reserves had *increased* to more than 1 trillion barrels.

[5]The Hotelling Principle, discovered by Harold Hotelling, first appeared in "Economics of Exhaustible Resources," *Journal of Political Economy* 39 (April 1931): 137–175.

change. To determine the level of the price of a natural resource, we have to consider not only the supply of and demand for the stock of the resource but also the demand for its flow.

Price of a Natural Resource

To determine the price of a natural resource, we first consider the influences on the demand for the flow of the natural resource and then we study the equilibrium that emerges from the interaction of the demand for the flow with the available stock.

Demand for a Flow The demand for a flow of a natural resource is determined in the same way as the demand for any other input. It arises from firms' profit-maximization decisions. A firm maximizes profit when the marginal revenue product of an input equals the marginal cost of the input. In a perfectly competitive market, the marginal cost of an input equals the factor price. The quantity demanded of a flow of a natural resource is the amount that makes the marginal revenue product of that flow equal to the price of the resource. As in the case of all other inputs, the marginal revenue product of a natural resource diminishes as the quantity of the resource used increases. Thus the lower the price of a resource, the greater is the quantity demanded of the flow of the natural resource—as illustrated in Fig. 16.7.

For any resource, there is a price that is so high that it does not pay anyone to use the resource. The price at which it no longer pays to use a natural resource is called the **choke price**. Figure 16.7 shows a choke price of P_C. Everything has substitutes, and at a high enough price, a substitute is used. For example, we do not have to use aluminum to make cans for soft drinks; we can use plastic instead. We do not have to use oil as the fuel for cars; we can use alcohol or electric cars instead. We do not have to use gas and electric power to heat our homes; we can use solar energy instead. The natural resources that we *do* use are the least expensive resources available. They cost us less than the next best alternatives would.

FIGURE 16.7

Demand for a Flow of a Natural Resource

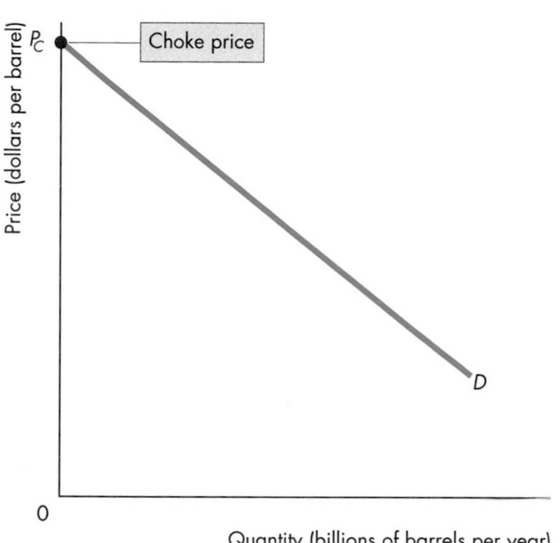

Natural resources have substitutes. If the price of a natural resource is too high, then a substitute will be used. At a price below P_C, the quantity demanded is positive, and the lower the price, the larger is the quantity demanded. The price P_C is called the choke price. At P_C, none of this resource is demanded and a substitute will be used.

Equilibrium Stock and Flow

The price and the flow of a natural resource depend on three things:

- The interest rate
- The demand for the flow
- The stock of the resource remaining

Figure 16.8 shows how these three factors combine to determine the price of a natural resource: the expected path of that price, the rate at which the resource is used up, and the stock of the resource remaining. Let's take the figure one part at a time.

In part (a), you can see the expected price path of the natural resource. That path is determined by the interest rate r. The line with a slope of $1 + r$ shows the relationship between the price in the current year and the price next year if the price rises at a rate equal to the interest rate. Suppose that initially the price is P_0. Next year, the price will rise to P_1, the price that is r percent higher than P_0. You can see the rise in price by following the steps between the 45° line and the line with a slope of $1 + r$. Each step represents a price increase. The steps become larger,

FIGURE 16.8
The Market for an Exhaustible Natural Resource

The expected rate of increase in the price of a natural resource equals the interest rate. Starting at P_0, in part (a), the price increases at first to P_1 and eventually to P_C. The price path follows the steps shown, with each step bigger than the previous one. Part (b) shows the rate at which the resource is used up. Its demand curve (D) determines the quantity demanded for use (a flow) at each price. Initially, when the price is P_0, that flow is Q_0. As the price increases, the flow decreases. When the price reaches P_C, the choke price, the flow is zero. Part (c) illustrates the remaining stock after each year. The initial stock is used up in decreasing amounts until, after six years, the stock is exhausted. The price P_0 is the equilibrium price because it achieves equality between the sum of the flows in each year and the initial stock.

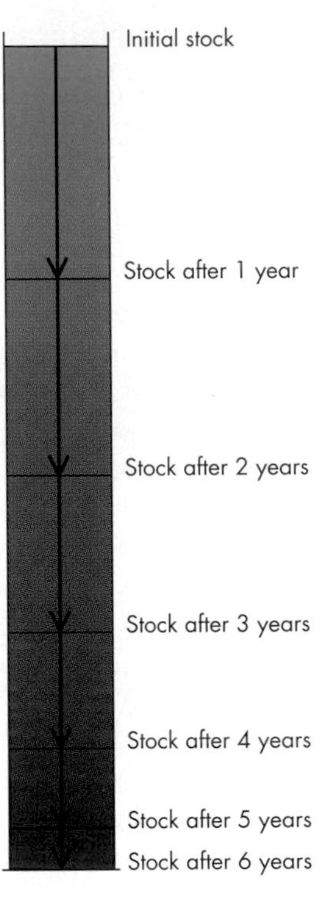

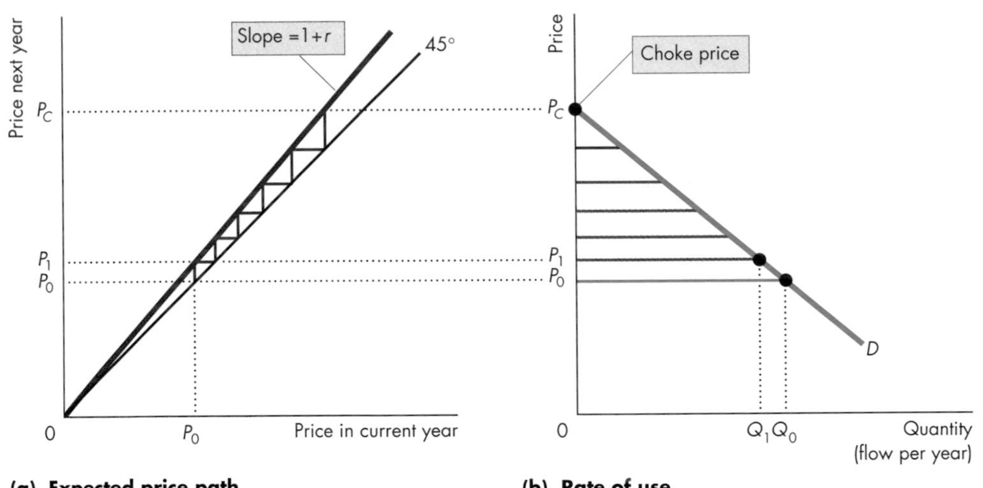

(a) Expected price path **(b) Rate of use** **(c) Remaining stock**

but the height of each step is a constant percentage of the previous year's price. Since the price keeps rising, eventually it reaches the choke price, identified as P_C in the figure.

Next, consider Fig. 16.8(b), which shows the rate at which the resource is used up. The demand for the flow, based on the marginal revenue product of the natural resource, is illustrated by the curve D. In the initial year, at a price of P_0, the quantity Q_0 is used. In the following year, we know from part (a) that the price increases to P_1. At this price, the quantity used up is Q_1. As the price increases each year, the quantity used each year decreases.

Figure 16.8(c) shows the remaining stock. The initial stock is identified in the figure, and the stock remaining after each year is also identified. For example, the stock after one year is the initial stock minus Q_0, the amount used up in the first year. In this example, after six years there is no stock left. The price has increased from P_0 to the choke price P_C, and the quantity used in each year has declined until, in the final year, it has become zero—the quantity of the flow of natural resources demanded at the choke price.

How do we know that P_0 is the current price? It is because it is the price that achieves an equilibrium between the remaining stock and the current year's flow and the future years' expected flows. That is, it is the only current price that leads to a sequence of future prices (growing at the interest rate) that generate a sequence of flows such that the stock is exhausted in the same year that the choke price is reached. If the current price is higher than P_0 and if the future prices are expected to rise at the interest rate, the choke price will be reached before the stock is exhausted. If the current price is below P_0 and, again, if the future prices are expected to rise at the interest rate, the stock will be exhausted before the choke price is reached.

We can now see how the current price is determined by the three factors that we identified above. First, the higher the interest rate, the lower is the current price of a natural resource. The higher interest rate means that the price is going to increase more quickly. Thus starting from the same initial price, the choke price will be reached sooner. But if the choke price is reached sooner, the stock available will not be used up at that point in time. Thus the initial price has to be lower when the interest rate is higher to ensure that by the time the price does reach the choke price, the total stock available has been used.

Second, the higher the marginal revenue product of the natural resource—the higher the demand for the flow of the natural resource—the higher is the current price of the resource. You can see why this relationship exists by looking again at Fig. 16.8(b). If the demand for the flow of the resource were higher than that shown in this figure, the demand curve would lie to the right of the demand curve shown. In this case, the current price would be higher than P_0.

Third, the larger the initial stock of the natural resource, the lower is the current price. You can also see why this relationship holds by considering Fig. 16.8(c). If the initial stock is larger than that shown in the figure, P_0 cannot be the equilibrium price, because it leads to a sequence of prices that generate a sequence of quantities demanded that do not exhaust the stock by the time the choke price is reached. Thus the initial price would have to be below P_0 to ensure that the larger stock is exhausted by the time that the choke price is reached.

Equilibrium in the market for a natural resource determines the current price of the natural resource and the expected path of future prices. But the price path actually followed is rarely the same as its expected path. For example, in 1984, expectations about the future price of oil were that it would rise at a rate equal to the interest rate. Opinions differed about the long-term average interest rate, so projections ranged from a low growth rate of 1.8 percent a year to a high growth rate of 7.1 percent a year. But, as events have turned out, the price of oil fell after 1984 (see Fig. 16.9).

FIGURE 16.9
Unfulfilled Expectations

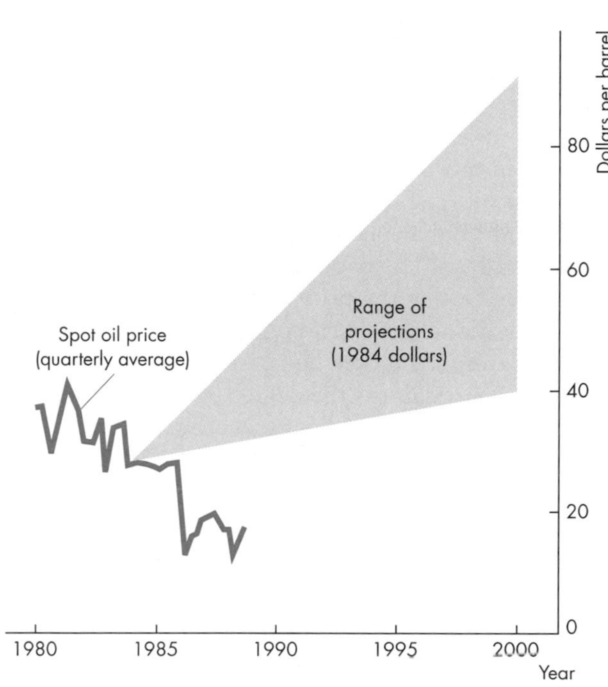

In 1984, the price of oil was expected to increase at a rate equal to the interest rate. There were different views of the future interest rate, so there was a range of expected price increases. The events of the 1980s unfolded in a way that was different from what had been expected in 1984. Higher interest rates, the discovery of increased reserves, and new energy-saving technologies all contributed to a falling price of oil. The breakup of the OPEC cartel also contributed significantly to falling oil prices.

Source: "Future Imperfect," *The Economist:* Feb. 4, 1989, p. 67. © 1989, The Economist Newspaper Limited. Reprinted with permission.

Why do natural resource prices change unexpectedly, sometimes even falling rather than following their expected path?

Unexpected Price Changes

The price of a natural resource depends on expectations about future events. It depends on expectations about the interest rate, the future demand for the flow of the resource, and the size of the remaining stock. Natural resource markets are constantly being bombarded by new information that leads to new expectations. For example, new information about the stock of a resource or the technologies available for its use can lead to sudden and perhaps quite large changes in the price of a natural resource.

All of these forces have been at work in many of the markets for exhaustible natural resources in recent years. The market for oil illustrates these effects very well. The discovery of new sources of supply and of new extraction technologies has resulted in previously unforeseen increases in the supply of oil. The development of energy-efficient automobile and airplane engines has decreased the demand for oil. The combination of these factors has led to a fall in the price of oil.

An additional force leading to price changes in natural resource markets in general and in the oil market in particular is the degree of competitiveness in the markets. The model market that we have been studying is a perfectly competitive one. But the real-world market for oil is dominated by the OPEC cartel, an oligopoly similar to that analyzed in Chapter 14 (pp. 351–354). The breakup of the OPEC cartel contributed significantly to the decline in the price of oil during the 1980s.

In forecasting the future price of a natural resource, it is necessary to forecast future changes in market structure. Adding this complication to an already complex forecasting problem makes it clear that the fluctuations in prices of natural resources such as oil are, for the most part, unforecastable.

Conservation and Doomsday

The analysis that you have just reviewed concerning the price of a natural resource and its expected change over time has important implications for the popular debate concerning natural resources and their use. Many people fear that we are using the earth's exhaustible natural resources at such a rapid pace that we shall eventually (and perhaps in the not very distant future) run out of important sources of energy and of other crucial raw materials. Such people urge a slowing down in the rate of use of exhaustible natural resources so that the limited stocks available will last longer.

This topic is an emotional one and generates passionate debate. It is also a matter that involves economic issues that can be understood by using the economic model of a depletable natural resource that you have just studied.

The economic analysis of an exhaustible natural resource market predicts that doomsday—the using up of the entire stock of a natural resource—will eventually arise if our use of natural resources is organized in competitive markets. The economic model also implies that a competitive market will provide an automatic conservation program arising from a steadily rising price. As a natural resource gets closer and closer to being depleted, its price gets closer to the choke price—the price at which no one wants to use the resource anymore. Each year, as the price rises, the quantity demanded of the flow declines.

But what if the resource gets completely used up? Don't we have a real problem then? We have the problem of scarcity but in no more acute a form than we had it before. The resource that is no longer available was used because to use it was more efficient than to use some alternative. Once that resource is completely used up, then and only then does it pay to turn to using a more expensive substitute. So the market economy handles the depleting stocks of natural resources by persistently forcing up their prices. Higher prices cause us to ration our use and eventually drive the quantity demanded of the flow to zero when the supply of the stock disappears.

There is an important economic issue as to whether or not a competitive market leads us to use our scarce exhaustible natural resources at an efficient rate. Recall that we studied the allocative efficiency of a perfectly competitive market in Chapter 11 (pp. 305–308). There we discovered that perfectly competitive markets achieve allocative efficiency if there are no external costs and benefits. The same conclusion applies to markets for natural resources. If there are no external costs or benefits impinging upon these markets, then the rate of use determined in a perfectly competitive exhaustible natural resource market is the allocatively efficient rate of use. But if there are external costs associated with the use of the natural resource, allocative efficiency will result from a slowdown in the rate of use of the resource compared with that arising in the competitive market. For example, if burning hydrocarbon fuels increases the carbon dioxide in the atmosphere and a warming of the earth's atmosphere results—the so-called greenhouse effect—the costs associated with this atmospheric change have to be added to the costs of using oil and coal as fuels. When these costs are taken into account, the allocatively efficient rate of use of these fuels is lower than that resulting from a perfectly competitive market. We examine ways in which government intervention can achieve allocative efficiency in such a situation in Chapter 19 (pp. 519–520).

◆ ◆ ◆ ◆ We have now studied the way in which factor markets allocate scarce productive resources —labor, capital, and land—and the determination of factor prices and factor incomes. The outcome of the operation of the factor markets is the distribution of income among individuals and families that determines *for whom* goods and services are produced. But that outcome is uncertain. People decide what type of work to do, how much to save, and what to do with their savings with no sure knowledge of the payoffs from their decisions. In the next part we study uncertainty and its consequences in a more systematic way. And we examine the distribution of income that emerges from our choices about work, saving, and investment. We discover the ways in which we cope with uncertainty and the main sources of income and wealth inequality in our economy.

SUMMARY

Capital, Investment, and Saving

There are two kinds of assets: financial and physical. Financial assets are all the paper claims of one economic agent against another. Physical assets, or capital, are the stock of all the productive assets owned by households and firms. Investment is the flow of additions to the stock of capital. Depreciation is the flow reduction in the stock of capital through use or the passage of time.

The quantity of capital supplied results from people's saving decisions. Saving equals income minus consumption. People allocate their savings to a variety of alternative financial and physical assets. (pp. 429–431)

Capital Markets in the United States Today

Capital markets provide the link between the saving decisions of households and the investment decisions of firms and governments. Households finance firms' investment by buying equity and bonds or by making deposits in financial intermediaries that in turn make loans to firms. Households also make loans to governments by buying bonds and indirectly through deposits with financial intermediaries. (pp. 431–434)

Demand for Capital

The demand for capital is determined—like the demand for factors—by firms' profit-maximization choices. The quantity of capital demanded by a firm is such that the marginal revenue product of capital equals its opportunity cost. A firm can make the comparison between marginal revenue product and cost by calculating the present value of marginal revenue product and comparing that present value with the price of a new piece of capital.

The quantity of capital demanded by a firm depends on the interest rate. The higher the interest rate, the lower is the present value of the future stream of marginal revenue products and the smaller is the quantity of capital equipment a firm buys. The lower the interest rate, the greater is the quantity of capital demanded—the demand curve for capital is downward sloping. The demand curve for capital shifts steadily to the right as a result of technological change and the general tendency to exploit innovations over time. (pp. 434–438)

The Supply of Capital

The quantity of capital supplied results from the saving decisions of households. Savings depend on how much households smooth their consumption over the life cycle and on the interest rate. The supply curve for capital is upward sloping—as interest rates rise, the quantity of capital supplied increases. The supply curve of capital shifts over time as a result of changes in the population and its age composition and the level of income. (pp. 438–439)

Interest Rates and Asset Prices

Interest rates and asset prices can be viewed as two sides of the same coin. Interest rates and asset prices adjust to achieve equality between the quantity of capital demanded and the quantity supplied. Interest rates on particular assets are distributed around the average rate according to the degree of riskiness of different types of assets.

The stock market value of a firm depends on the firm's current profit and expectations of its future profit. The higher the expected growth rate of a firm's profit, the higher is the price of a share of its stock. The price-earnings ratio is the ratio of the price of a share in a firm's stock to its profit per share. That ratio depends on the expected growth rate of profit.

The volume of trading on the stock market is determined by the extent of the divergence of expectations of the future. When everyone agrees about the future, volume of trading is low. When there is widespread disagreement, volume of trading is high. There can be large changes in prices with low or high volume of trading. Price changes occur when there is a change in expectations about profit growth.

Mergers and takeovers occur as part of the process of maximizing profit. If a firm's stock market value is lower than the value of its assets when used by another firm, it will pay that other firm to take over the first firm. Mergers occur when there is a mutually agreed benefit from combining the assets of two (or more) firms. (pp. 440–445)

Natural Resource Markets

Natural resources are the nonproduced factors of production with which we are endowed. The price of a natural resource is determined by the interest rate, its marginal revenue product (which determines the demand for its flow), and the quantity remaining of the natural resource (the supply of its stock). The price of a natural resource is such that its future price is expected to rise at a rate equal to the interest rate and to reach the choke price at the time at which the resource is exhausted. The actual price is constantly changing to take into account new information. Even though the future price is expected to increase, the actual price often decreases as a result of new information leading to an increase in the estimate of the remaining stock or to a decrease in the demand for the flow of the resource. (pp. 445–451)

KEY ELEMENTS

Key Terms

Asset, 429
Balance sheet, 429
Bond market, 432
Bond yield, 440
Capital, 429
Choke price, 447
Depreciation, 430
Exhaustible natural resources, 445
Financial assets, 429
Financial intermediary, 431
Gross investment, 430
Hotelling Principle, 446
Investment, 430
Liability, 429
Loans market, 432
Merger, 445
Natural resources, 445
Net financial assets, 429
Net investment, 430
Net present value of an investment, 435
Nonexhaustible natural resources, 445
Physical assets, 429
Portfolio choice, 430
Saving, 430
Stock market, 432
Stock yield, 440
Takeover, 445
Wealth, 430

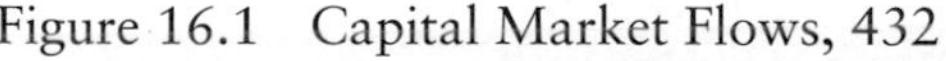

REVIEW QUESTIONS

1 Why does the quantity of capital demanded by a firm rise as the interest rate falls?

2 Set out the key reasons for differences in interest rates on different types of assets.

3 What is the relationship between interest rates and asset prices?

4 Explain how the stock market value of a firm is determined.

5 Define the price-earnings ratio and explain how it is determined.

6 Why are there some occasions when stock market prices change a lot but with little trading and other times when prices are stable but trading volumes are high?

7 Why do mergers and takeovers occur?

Distinguish between the stock and the flow of an exhaustible natural resource.

9 Explain why the price of an exhaustible natural resource is expected to rise at a rate equal to the interest rate.

10 What determines the price of a natural resource?

11 Why are most of the fluctuations in the price of a natural resource unforecastable?

PROBLEMS

1 At the end of 1991 a firm had a production plant worth $1,000,000. The plant depreciated during 1992 by 10 percent. During the same year, the firm also bought new capital equipment for $250,000. What is the value of the firm's stock of capital at the end of 1992? What was the firm's gross investment during 1992? What was the firm's net investment during 1992?

2 You earn $20,000 per year (after paying your taxes) for three years, and you spend $16,000 each year. How much do you save each year? What happens to your wealth during this three-year period?

3 What are the different ways in which a holder of wealth can channel capital into firms?

4 Why is a deposit in a financial intermediary less risky than buying equity or bonds?

5 A firm is considering buying a new machine. It is estimated that the marginal revenue product of the machine will be $10,000 a year for five years. The machine will have a scrap value at the end of five years of $10,000. The interest rate is 10 percent a year.

a What is the maximum price that the firm will pay for the machine?

b If the machine costs $40,000, would the firm buy the machine at an interest rate of 10 percent?

c What is the highest interest rate at which the firm would buy the machine?

PART 7

Markets, Uncertainty, and Distribution

Talking with Tony Atkinson

Tony Atkinson was born in Caerleon, Wales, in 1944. He studied economics at Cambridge University, has been a professor at the University of Essex and the London School of Economics, and has recently returned to Cambridge. Professor Atkinson's major contributions have been in the area of taxation and the distribution of income.

How did you get interested in economics?

Like many other economists, I began as a mathematics student and then became interested in social problems. In the 1960s, we believed that we could change the world for the better—and I am not sure that we were wrong.

What are the key principles of economics that you have repeatedly found useful in your work?

I should say that I am suspicious of "general principles" in economics. When I hear people say "economic theory tells us X," I am immediately on my guard. Increasingly, I have become impressed with the importance of blending economic theory with the institutional realities of particular countries and particular time periods. Historical, cultural, and social factors mean that an economic model that is applicable to the United States might not be equally relevant to Europe or Japan. Too often, economic theory is applied without regard to such institutional features. The standard economic treatment of unemployment insurance, for example, ignores important fea-

"**W**hat I believe economics can teach is not a set of universally applicable tools, like a wrench that will always undo a nut, but an *approach*."

tures of real-world unemployment insurance schemes, which may change its economic impact.

Why is a background in economics useful today?

What I believe economics can teach is not a set of universally applicable tools, like a wrench that will always undo a nut, but an *approach*. After receiving an economics degree, a student should not expect to have the answers but to be able to ask the right questions. When considering a particular policy change, for example, an economist will ask how the new policy might affect the behavior of different groups and will ask who gains and who loses from its introduction.

One particular question that I have found useful to ask is "What is the quantitative importance of different phenomena? Is the effect under discussion large or small?" One major contribution that economists can make is in evaluating and providing statistical information. I was once a member of a multidisciplinary group investigating the transmission of deprivation from generation to generation. It turned out that there was, at the time, no information at all about the proportion of children from poor families who went on to create poor families themselves. This led to a fascinating piece of research in which we traced the children of families who had been poor when studied a generation earlier. From this detective work, we were able to quantify the extent to which these children faced a greater risk of poverty.

Of course, everyone knows that statistics can be misused, and one should certainly not treat numbers in statistical yearbooks with undue reverence. At the same time, one cannot discuss applied economic problems without a view of their quantitative importance. A first reaction of the good economist should be to reach for some numbers.

What drew you to work on problems of poverty and the distribution of income?

There were two important influences that affected the direction of my first research. The first were the lectures and writing of James Meade, who later won the Nobel Prize. From him, I learned both that economic analysis could contribute to understanding issues of inequality and that explaining the distribution of income was an intellectual challenge. The second was reading *The Poor and the Poorest* by Brian Abel-Smith and Peter Townsend, two British experts on social policy. Published in 1965, the book described the poverty in Britain despite the welfare state and despite—at that time—full employment. It also demonstrated the potential impact of careful empirical research, just as the writing of economists in the United States was at the same time influential in leading to the launching of Lyndon Johnson's War on Poverty.

How does the study of income distribution relate to the main body of economics?

For classical economists, such as Adam Smith or David Ricardo, the distribution of income was central to the study of economics. Today, on the other hand, the distribution of income is often treated as a special subject—one that sits uneasily between macroeconomics and microeconomics.

This seems to me a great pity, since distributional issues are at the heart of economics. Aggregate objectives, such as the growth of GDP, are only a means of achieving the more fundamental goal of

"The degree of inequality is influenced by the particular traditions and history of the country and . . . can be affected by government policy."

improving the welfare of individuals. The welfare of individuals in turn depends on how total GDP is distributed. By this, I do not just mean the distribution of money income, but also the provision of public goods and the quality of the environment. It is paradoxical that Western democratic societies, with their emphasis on individual liberty, should be preoccupied with macroeconomic aggregates and show much less interest in measuring individual welfare.

Which economic systems stand out as having achieved the greatest measure of equality and which as having determined the greatest inequity?

I recently finished a research project with John Micklewright of the European University Institute at Florence in which we looked at the distribution of income under communism in Eastern Europe and the former Soviet Union. When we started work on this, we found that opinion was sharply divided. Some people pointed to the absence of property income and to the compression of wage differentials and concluded that Communist governments had succeeded in reducing income inequality. Others argued that inequality was in fact no different under communism than under capitalism, citing the privileged position of the political elite, the so-called *nomenklatura*, and suggesting that old inequalities had simply been replaced by new ones.

In the case of the former Soviet Union, it used to be very difficult to obtain firm evidence about income inequality, which appeared on the list of censored subjects along with alcoholism and drug addiction. With *glasnost*, however, much information has been made available. It now appears that under Khrushchev, wage dispersion was indeed reduced below that in Britain, particularly because of the minimum wage. But in the 1980s, there was little difference, and Gorbachev's wage reform actually widened differentials. On the other hand, the distribution of *income*, taking into account transfer payments and capital income and including those not in the labor force, did appear to be significantly less unequal in the USSR than in Britain in the mid-1980s. This conclusion might be modified if a value could be placed on the nonmonetary advantages of the elite, but, on the other hand, fringe benefits for executives add to inequality in Western countries.

However, these conclusions cannot be attributed simply to the differences in economic systems, since the situation in the Central European communist countries appears to be distinctly different from that in the former Soviet Union. In particular, Czechoslovakia has a much lower recorded degree of earnings dispersion and of income inequality than Western countries. From our research, I conclude that the degree of inequality is influenced by the particular traditions and history of the country and that it can be affected by government policy.

A grand solution to the redistribution problem is the negative income tax. What are its major attractions to economists? And what are the major impediments in the political arena to its introduction?

A negative income tax means different things to different people. In its least radical form, it would involve the Internal Revenue Service paying to people below the tax threshold a proportion of the extent to which their income falls below that amount. As such, it appears to some economists as a better targeted form of redistribution, being directly related to income, rather than paid on the basis of unemployment, sickness, family size, or other criteria. The effectiveness of such a proposal depends on the level of the tax threshold and on the proportion of the gap filled, but it does not seem realistic to suppose that it would allow existing social security programs to be dismantled.

A more radical proposal, which has attracted more support in Europe, is for a *basic income policy*. In its pure form, this would replace all income tax exemptions and social security and welfare benefits by a basic income payable at so many dollars a week to every citizen. This would provide a comprehensive guaranteed minimum income and would greatly simplify the benefit system. The problem is that the abolition of tax exemptions means that income tax would be due on every dollar of income. Moreover, to finance an adequate basic income, the tax rate would have to be set at a level that frightens politicians. The electorate has not been asked whether it would support such a plan, but politically it might be easier to redistribute by other means.

If you could start from scratch to write the tax code for a large country like the United States, or an emerging political grouping such as the European Community, what would the code contain?

I have difficulty answering this question, since I do not believe in immutable principles of economic policy. Economists have, for example, stongly advocated an expenditure tax in place of the income tax, and I can see the attractions. However, I do not believe that an expenditure tax is necessarily better in all circumstances. Similarly, economists have objected to the use of earmarked taxes, but again there may be occasions when they are desirable.

My conception of the proper role of the public finance economist is that of illuminating the choices open to democratically elected governments and to the voters who elect them. To this end, I would be happy to draw up a menu of choices—to draft two or three alternative tax codes—as the basis for political discussion and to advise on their possible implications.

This gives the central role to the political authority, which is where it belongs in a democratic country. But one has to recognize that governments change, and one general principle that I will accept is that any tax code should ideally be sustainable in the face of changes in public opinion. No doubt rates of tax will be different with different governments, but a hallmark of a successful tax code is one that can accommodate different political preferences.

"Any tax code should ideally be sustainable in the face of changes in public opinion."

CHAPTER 17

UNCERTAINTY AND INFORMATION

After studying this chapter, you will be able to:

- Explain how people make decisions when they are uncertain about the consequences
- Explain why people buy insurance and how insurance companies make a profit
- Explain why buyers search and sellers advertise
- Explain why private information can limit the gains from exchange and how markets attempt to overcome these problems with warranties and other devices
- Explain how people use financial markets to lower risk

Lotteries and Lemons

LIFE IS LIKE A LOTTERY. YOU WORK HARD IN SCHOOL, but what will the payoff be? Will you get an interesting, well-paying job or a miserable, low-paying one? You set up a small summer business and work hard at it. But will you make enough profit to keep you in school next year, or will you get wiped out? How do people make a decision when they don't know its consequences? ◆◆ As you cross an intersection on a green light, you see a car on your left that's still moving. Will it stop, or will it run the red light? You buy insurance against such a risk, and insurance companies profit from your business. Why are we willing to buy insurance at prices that leave insurance companies with a profit? ◆◆ Buying a new car—or a used car—is fun, but it's also scary. You could get stuck with a lemon. And cars are not unique. Just about every complicated product you buy could be defective. How do car dealers and retailers induce us to buy what might turn out to be a lemon? ◆◆ People keep some of their wealth in the bank, some in bonds, and some in stocks; and they hold a diversity of stocks. Some of these ways of holding wealth have a high return, and some a low return. Why don't people put all their wealth in the place that has the highest return? Why does it pay to diversify?

◆◆◆◆ In this chapter we answer questions such as these. We'll begin by explaining how people make decisions when they're uncertain about the consequences. We'll see how it pays to buy insurance, even if its price leaves the insurance company with a profit. We'll explain why we use scarce resources to generate and disseminate information. And we'll look at transactions in a wide variety of markets in which uncertainty and the cost of acquiring information play important roles.

Coping with Uncertainty

Although we live in an uncertain world, it rarely occurs to us to ask what uncertainty is. Yet to explain how we make decisions and do business with each other in an uncertain world, we need to think a bit more deeply about uncertainty. What exactly is uncertainty? We also live in a risky world. Is risk the same as uncertainty? Let's begin by defining uncertainty and risk and distinguishing between them.

Uncertainty and Risk

Uncertainty is a state in which more than one event may occur but we don't know which one. Usually, the event that does occur affects our economic well-being. For example, when farmers plant their crops, they are uncertain about the weather during the growing season, but their profits depend on the weather.

To describe uncertainty, we use the concepts of probability and risk. A **probability** is a number between zero and 1 that measures the chance of some possible event occurring. A zero probability means the event will not happen. A probability of 1 means the event will occur for sure—with certainty. A probability of 0.5 means that half the time the event will occur and half the time it will not. An example is the probability of a tossed coin falling heads. In a large number of tosses, half of them will most likely be heads and the other half tails.

In ordinary speech, risk is the probability of incurring a loss (or some other misfortune). In economics, **risk** is a state in which more than one outcome may occur and the *probability* of each possible outcome can be estimated. Sometimes the probabilities can be measured. For example, the probability that a tossed coin will come down heads is based on the fact that, in a large number of tosses, half are heads and half are tails; the probability that a woman will give birth to twins is determined from the records of births in previous years; the probability of an automobile in Chicago in 1992 being involved in an accident is based on police and insurance records of previous accidents.

Some situations cannot be described by using probabilities based on observed events. These situations may be unique events, such as the introduction of a new product. How much will sell and at what price? This question cannot be answered by looking at the previous occasions on which *this particular* new product was introduced. But it can be answered by looking at past experience with *similar* new products, supported by some judgments. Such judgments are called *subjective probabilities*.

Regardless of whether the probability of some event occurring is based on actual data or judgments—or even guesses—we can use probability to study the way in which people make decisions in the face of uncertainty. The first step in doing this is to describe how people assess the cost of risk.

Utility of Wealth

Some people are more willing to take chances than others, but everyone prefers less risk to more, other things being equal. We measure people's attitudes toward risk by using their utility of wealth schedules and curves. A **utility of wealth schedule (or curve)** describes how much utility a person attaches to each level of wealth. The greater a person's wealth, other things being equal, the higher is the person's utility. The utility of wealth is based on the same concept of utility that you studied in Chapter 7. Not only does greater wealth bring higher utility, but as wealth increases, each additional unit of wealth increases utility by a smaller amount. That is, the *marginal utility of wealth diminishes*.

Figure 17.1 sets out Tania's utility of wealth schedule and curve. Each point *a* through *e* on Tania's utility of wealth curve corresponds to the row of the table identified by the same letter. You can see that as her wealth increases, her utility of wealth also increases. You can also see that her marginal utility of wealth diminishes. When wealth increases from $3,000 to $6,000, utility increases by 20 units and her marginal utility is 6.7. But when wealth increases by a further $3,000, to $9,000, utility increases by only 10 units and her marginal utility falls to 3.3.

FIGURE 17.1

The Utility of Wealth Curve

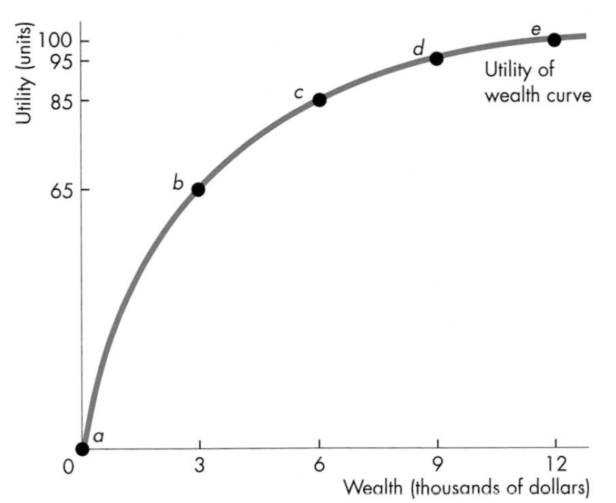

	Wealth (thousands of dollars)	Utility (units)	Marginal utility (units: change in utility ÷ change in wealth)
a	**0**	**0**	
			21.7
b	**3**	**65**	
			6.7
c	**6**	**85**	
			3.3
d	**9**	**95**	
			1.7
e	**12**	**100**	

The level of utility increases as wealth increases, but there is diminishing marginal utility of wealth—each increment in wealth brings a smaller increment in utility. Tania's utility of wealth schedule is set out in the table and shown in the figure. Each row of the table corresponds to a point in the figure.

Measuring the Cost of Risk

We can use Tania's utility of wealth curve to measure the cost of risk. The bigger the risk Tania faces, the worse off she is and the less she likes it. To measure the cost of risk to Tania, let's see how she evaluates two alternative summer jobs that involve different amounts of risk.

One job, working as a painter, pays enough for her to save $5,000 by the end of the summer. There is no uncertainty about the income from this job. If Tania takes this job, by the end of the summer her wealth will be $5,000. The other job, as a telemarketer selling subscriptions to a magazine, is risky. If she takes this job, her wealth at the end of the summer depends entirely on her success at selling. She might be a good salesperson or a poor one. A good salesperson makes $9,000 in a summer, and a poor one makes $3,000. Tania has never tried this line of business before, and she doesn't know how successful she'll be. She assumes that there is an equal chance—a probability of 0.5—of making either $3,000 or $9,000. Which outcome does Tania prefer, $5,000 for sure from the painting job or a 50 percent chance of either $3,000 or $9,000 from the telemarketing job?

When there is uncertainty, people do not know how much utility they will end up with from taking a particular action. The amount of utility they get is called *actual* utility. But it is possible to calculate the utility they expect to get. And they take the action that gives them the highest expected utility. **Expected utility** is the average utility arising from all the possible outcomes. Equivalently, it is the average utility the person would get if the action could be repeated a large number of times. So, to choose her summer job, Tania must calculate the expected utility arising from painting and telemarketing. Figure 17.2 shows how she does this.

If Tania takes the painting job, she has $5,000 of wealth and 80 units of utility, as shown in Fig. 17.2(a). There is only one possible outcome in this case. Her expected utility, which also equals her actual utility, is 80 units. Figure 17.2(b) shows the value to Tania of the risky alternative. If she makes $9,000, her utility is 95 units. If she makes only $3,000, her utility is 65 units. Her *expected utility* is the average of these two possible outcomes and is 80 units—calculated as $(95 \times 0.5) + (65 \times 0.5)$.

Tania does the best she can by maximizing expected utility. In this case, the two alternatives give the same expected utility—80 units—so she is indifferent between them. She is equally likely to take either job. The difference between Tania's expected wealth of $6,000 from the risky job and $5,000 from the no-risk job—$1,000—is just large enough to offset the additional risk that Tania faces.

FIGURE 17.2

Choice in a Risky Situation

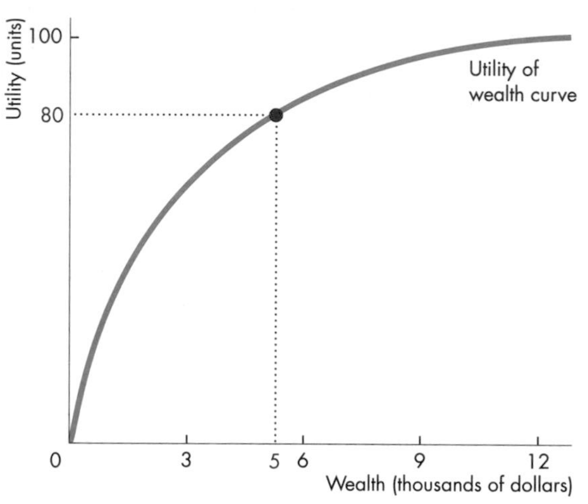

(a) No risk

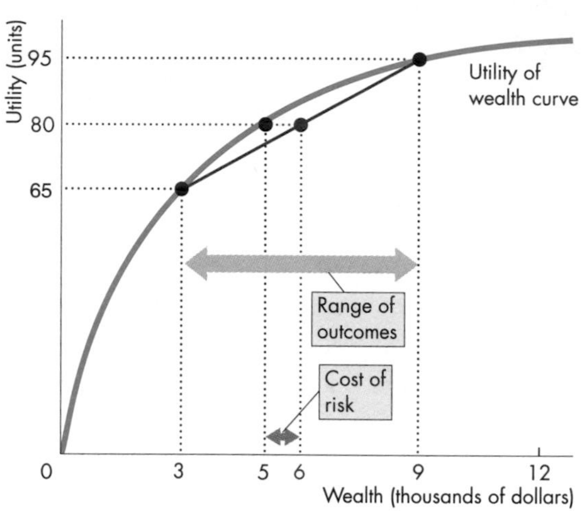

(b) Risk

To make a choice in the face of uncertainty, a person maximizes expected utility. In part (a), Tania's wealth is $5,000 and her utility is 80 units. In part (b), she faces an equal probability of having $9,000 with a utility of 95 units or $3,000 with a utility of 65 units. Her expected wealth is $6,000—$1,000 more than in part (a)—but her expected utility is 80 units, the same as in part (a). Tania is indifferent between these two alternatives. The extra $1,000 of expected wealth is just sufficient to offset the risk associated with it.

The calculations that we've just done enable us to measure Tania's cost of risk. The cost of risk is the amount by which expected wealth must be increased to give the same expected utility as a no-risk situation. In Tania's case, the cost of the risk arising from an uncertain income is $1,000.

If the amount Tania can make from painting falls to only $3,000, the extra income from the risky job will be more than sufficient to cover her cost of the risk, and she will take the risky alternative of telemarketing. An income of $3,000 for sure gives only 65 units of utility, an amount less than the 80 units expected from the telemarketing job.

If the amount Tania can make from painting remains at $5,000 and the expected income from telemarketing also remains constant while its range of uncertainty increases, Tania will take the painting job. To see this conclusion, suppose that good telemarketers make $12,000, and poor ones make nothing. The average income from telemarketing is unchanged at $6,000, but the range of uncertainty has increased. Looking at the table in Fig. 17.1 you can see that Tania gets 100 units of utility from a wealth of $12,000 and zero units of utility from a wealth of zero. Thus in this case Tania's expected utility from telemarketing is 50 units—calculated as $(100 \times 0.5) + (0 \times 0.5)$. Since the expected utility from telemarketing is now less than that from painting, she chooses painting.

Risk Aversion and Risk Neutrality

There is an enormous difference between Bill Parcells, former coach of the New York Giants, who favors a cautious running game, and Jim Kelley, quarterback of the Buffalo Bills, who favors a risky passing game. They have different attitudes toward risk. Bill is much more *risk averse* than is Jim. Tania is also *risk averse*—other things being equal, she prefers situations with less risk. The shape of a person's utility of wealth curve tells us about his or her attitude toward risk—about the person's degree of *risk aversion.* The more rapidly a person's marginal utility of wealth diminishes, the more the person dislikes risk—the more risk-averse the person is. You can see this fact best by considering an extreme case, that of *risk neutrality.* A risk-neutral person is one for whom risk is costless. Such a person cares only about *expected wealth* and does not mind how much uncertainty there is.

Figure 17.3 shows the utility of wealth curve of a risk-neutral person. It is a straight line, and the marginal utility of wealth is constant. If this person has an expected wealth of $6,000, expected utility is 50 units regardless of the range of uncertainty around that average. An equal probability of having $3,000 or $9,000 gives the same expected utility as an equal probability of having $0 or $12,000, which is also the expected utility of a certain $6,000. Real people are risk averse, and their utility of wealth curves look like Tania's. But the extreme case of risk neutrality illustrates the importance and the consequences of the shape of the utility of wealth curve for a person's degree of risk aversion.

FIGURE 17.3

Risk Neutrality

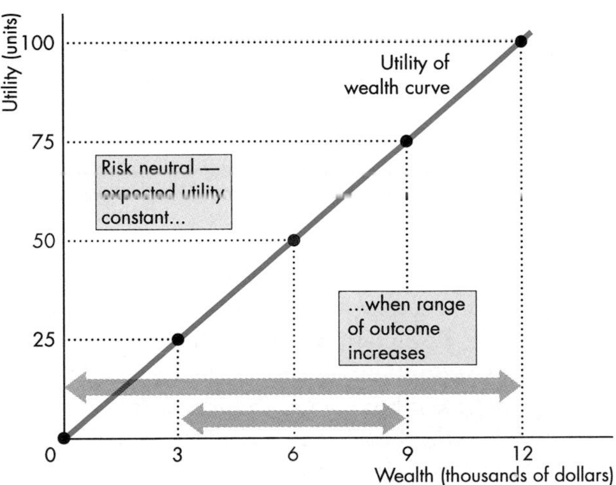

People dislike risk because they have diminishing marginal utility of wealth. A (hypothetical) risk-neutral person has a linear utility of wealth curve. Expected utility is constant, regardless of the range of uncertainty.

REVIEW

Uncertainty, a state in which the outcome is unknown, is described by using the concepts of probability and risk. Risk is a state of uncertainty in which the probability of each possible outcome can be estimated. The probability of each outcome may be estimated by using data or making judgments—called a subjective probability. Faced with uncertainty, people make decisions to maximize *expected utility.* Greater wealth gives higher utility, but the marginal utility of wealth diminishes. Because the marginal utility of wealth diminishes, greater risk with constant expected wealth gives smaller expected utility. To choose a riskier action, a person must expect a sufficiently higher expected wealth to compensate for bearing the higher risk. ◆

Insurance

One way of reducing the risk we face is to buy insurance. How does insurance reduce risk? Why does it pay people to insure? And how much of our incomes do we spend on insurance? Let's answer this last question first and take a look at the insurance industry in the United States today.

Insurance Industry in the United States

We spend close to 15 percent of our income, on the average, on insurance. That's as much as we spend on housing and more than we spend on cars and food. When we buy insurance, we enter into an agreement with an insurance company to pay an agreed price—called a *premium*—in exchange for benefits to be paid to us if some specified event occurs. There are three main types of insurance:

- Life insurance
- Health insurance
- Property and casualty insurance

Life Insurance Life insurance reduces the risk of financial loss in the event of death. More than 80 percent of households in the United States have life insurance, and the average amount of coverage is $110,000 per household. More than 2,400 companies supply life insurance, and the total premiums paid in a year are around $300 billion. As you can see in Fig. 17.4, life insurance has been the greatest source of the insurance industry's business in recent years and has generated most of the industry's profit.

Health Insurance Health insurance reduces the risk of financial loss in the event of illness. It can provide funds to cover both lost earnings and the cost of medical care. This type of insurance is growing rapidly, but in recent years it has not been highly profitable. Figure 17.4 illustrates its scale and relative importance.

Property and Casualty Insurance Property and casualty insurance reduces the risk of financial loss in the event of an accident involving damage to persons or property. It includes auto insurance—its biggest component—workers' compensation, fire, earthquake, professional malpractice, and a host of other, smaller items. Figure 17.4 shows that we spend more on this type of insurance than on health insurance but not as much as on life insurance.

FIGURE 17.4

The Insurance Industry

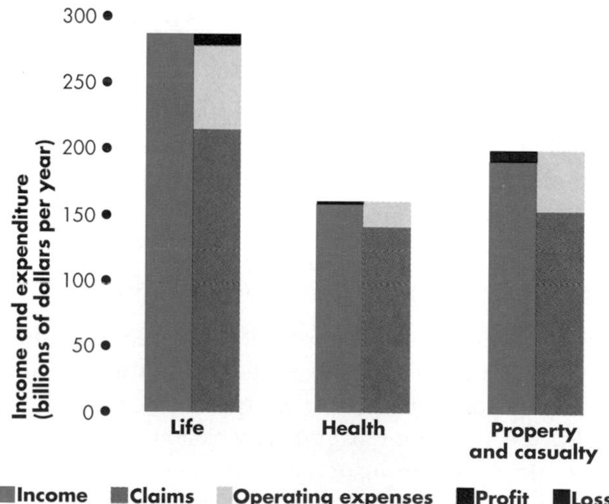

Total expenditure on insurance is more than $600 billion a year. Most is spent on life insurance, and in recent years this type of insurance has also been the most profitable.

Source: U.S. Bureau of the Census, *Statistical Abstract of the United States: 1991*, 111th edition (1991), 518–521.

How Insurance Works

Insurance works by pooling risks. It is possible and profitable because people are risk averse. The probability of any one person having a serious auto accident is small, but the cost to that person in the event of an accident is enormous. For a large population, the probability of one person having an accident is the proportion of the population that does have an accident. Since this probability can be estimated, the total cost of accidents can be predicted. An insurance company can pool the risks of a large population and share the costs. It does so by collecting premiums from everyone and paying out benefits to those who suffer a loss. If the insurance company does its calculations right, it collects at least as much in premiums as it pays out in benefits and operating costs.

Why It Pays to Insure

To see why insurance pays and why it is profitable, let's consider an example. Dan has the utility of wealth curve shown in Fig. 17.5. He owns a car worth $10,000, and that is his only wealth. If there is no risk of his having an accident, his utility will be 100 units. But there is a 10 percent chance (a probability of 0.1) that he will have an accident within a year. Suppose Dan does not buy insurance. If he does have an accident, his car is worthless, and with no insurance, he has no wealth and no utility. Because the probability of an accident is 0.1, the probability of *not* having an accident is 0.9. Dan's expected wealth, therefore, is $9,000—calculated as ($10,000 × 0.9) + ($0 × 0.1)—and his expected utility is 90 units—calculated as (100 × 0.9) + (0 × 0.1).

Given his utility of wealth curve, Dan has 90 units of utility if his wealth is $7,000 and he faces no uncertainty. That is, Dan is just as well off, in his own opinion, if he has a guaranteed wealth of $7,000 as he is with a 90 percent chance of having wealth of $10,000 and a 10 percent chance of hav-

FIGURE 17.5

Insurance

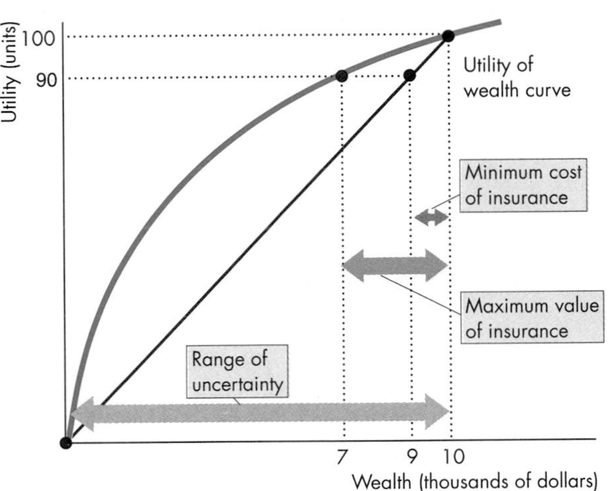

Dan has a car valued at $10,000, which gives him a utility of 100 units, but there is a 0.1 probability that he will have an accident, making his car worthless (wealth and utility equal to zero). With no insurance, his expected utility is 90 units and he is willing to pay up to $3,000 for insurance. An insurance company (with no operating expenses) can offer insurance to Dan and the rest of the community for $1,000. Hence there is a gain from insurance for both Dan and the insurance company.

ing nothing. If Dan can buy, for less than $3,000 ($10,000 minus $7,000), insurance that pays out in the event of an accident, he will be better off. Thus Dan has a demand for insurance at premiums less than $3,000.

Suppose there are lots of people like Dan, each with a $10,000 car and each with a 10 percent chance of having an accident within the year. If an insurance company agrees to pay each person who has an accident $10,000, the company will pay out $10,000 to one tenth of the population, or an average of $1,000 per person. This amount is the insurance company's minimum premium for such insurance. It is a smaller amount than the value of insurance to Dan because Dan is risk averse. He is willing to pay something to reduce the risk he faces.

Suppose the insurance company's operating expenses are a further $1,000 and that it offers insurance for $2,000. The company now covers all its costs—the amounts paid out to policyholders for their losses plus the company's operating expenses. But Dan—and all the other people who are similar to Dan—are better off with this insurance deal than without it. The calculations in Table 17.1 summarize the gain each makes. With no insurance, expected utility is 90 units. But with insurance costing $2,000, expected utility is 95 units, a gain of 5 units.

TABLE 17.1

Risk Taking versus Insurance

(a) Possible outcomes	No accident Probability 0.9		Accident Probability 0.1	
	Wealth	Utility	Wealth	Utility
No insurance	**$10,000**	**100**	**$ 0**	**0**
Insurance	**$ 8,000**	**95**	**$8,000**	**95**

(b) Expected outcomes	Expected wealth	Expected utility
No insurance	**($10,000 x 0.9) + ($0 x 0.1) = $9,000**	**(100 x 0.9) + (0 x 0.1) = 90**
Insurance	**($8,000 x 0.9) + ($8,000 x 0.1) = $8,000**	**(95 x 0.9) + (95 x 0.1) = 95**

With no insurance, Dan's expected wealth is $9,000 and his expected utility is 90 units. By buying insurance for $2,000, Dan's expected wealth falls to $8,000, but he has no uncertainty and his expected utility increases to 95 units.

REVIEW

Americans spend 15 percent of their income, on the average, on life, health, and property and casualty insurance. Insurance works by pooling risks. Every insured person pays in, but only those who suffer a loss are compensated. Insurance pays and insurance is profitable because people are risk averse and are willing to pay for lower risk. ◆

Much of the uncertainty we face arises from ignorance. We just don't know all the things we could benefit from knowing. But knowledge or information is not free. We must make decisions about how much information to acquire. Let's now study the choices we make about obtaining information and see how incomplete information affects some of our economic transactions.

Information

We spend a huge quantity of our scarce resources on economic information. **Economic information** includes data on the prices, quantities, and qualities of goods and services and factors of production.

In the models of perfect competition, monopoly, and monopolistic competition, information is free. Everyone has all the information they need. Households are completely informed about the prices of the goods and services they buy and the factors of production they sell. Similarly, firms are completely informed.

In contrast, information is scarce in the real world. If it were not, we wouldn't need *The Wall Street Journal* and CNN. And we wouldn't need to shop around for bargains or spend time looking for a job. The opportunity cost of economic information—the cost of acquiring information on prices, quantities, and qualities of goods and services and factors of production—is called the **information cost.** The fact that many economic models ignore information costs does not make those models useless. They give us insights into the forces generating trends in prices and quantities over periods long enough for information limits not to be important. But to understand how markets work hour by hour and day by day, we must take information problems into account, because people economize on their use of information just like they economize on their use of other productive resources.

We'll look at some examples, starting with a buyer's problem of searching for the lowest available price.

Searching for Price Information

In real-world markets, when many firms offer an identical good for sale, it is unusual for their prices to be identical. Usually, there is a range of prices and buyers want to find the lowest price. But searching takes time and is costly, so the buyer must balance the expected gain from further search against its additional cost. Let's see how buyers perform this balancing act, deciding when to buy and at what price.

You've decided to buy a used Mazda Miata, but you want to pay the lowest possible price. How will you find it? You can't just look at the advertisements in the Friday newspaper. They tell you the prices but not the qualities of the cars available at those prices. You're looking for a car in mint condition, so you need to check the dealers and do some test driving. It takes half a day to visit a dealer and check out a car. And you don't know enough about cars to trust your own judgment, so you take an expert along. The value of your time plus the cost of your expert's time is your opportunity cost. Let's call it $C per visit.

Thirty dealers are offering used Miatas at prices that range between $6,000 and $9,000. You know this is the range of prices, but you don't know which dealer is offering the lowest price for a car in mint condition. You are about to start your search, but how will you know when it's time to stop looking and to buy?

You need a decision rule. The *optimal-search rule*—also called the *optimal-stopping rule*—is to search for a lower price until the expected marginal benefit of search equals the marginal cost of search.

FIGURE 17.6

Optimal-Search Rule

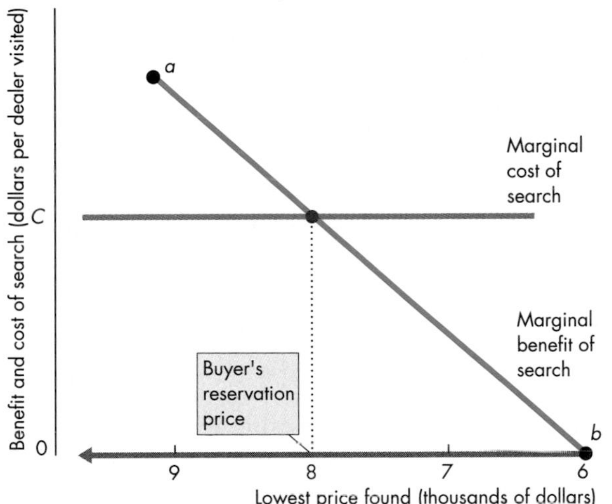

The marginal cost of search is constant at $C. As a lowest price found (measured from right to left on the horizontal axis) declines, the expected marginal utility of further search diminishes. The lowest price found at which the marginal cost equals the expected marginal benefit is the reservation price. The optimal-search rule is to search until the reservation price (or lower) is found and then buy at that lowest found price.

When the expected marginal benefit equals the marginal cost, stop searching and buy.

Your marginal cost is constant, $C, and is illustrated in Fig. 17.6 as the horizontal line. Your expected marginal benefit is not constant; it depends on the lowest price that you've found. Let's see how the marginal benefit curve is constructed. To do this, we'll go on an imaginary car shopping trip, not a real one. We'll do the real trip after we've discovered the stopping rule.

An Imaginary Car Shopping Trip Suppose the lowest price that you've found for a used car in top condition is $9,000. You know that this is the highest price dealers are offering and that if you visit another dealer, there is a good chance that you'll find a lower price. If you do find a lower price, you will gain the difference between $9,000 and the price found. This amount is your marginal benefit. You won't find a lower price for sure. So you must multiply this marginal benefit by the probability of obtaining it to calculate your *expected* marginal benefit. We'll suppose that this expected marginal benefit is greater than your marginal cost of search, as shown by point *a* in Fig. 17.6.

Next, suppose that the lowest price you've found is $6,000. You know that $6,000 is the lowest price at which cars are being offered, and since you've now found such a car, you can't do any better. Your expected marginal benefit from further search is zero. This fact is shown by point *b* on the marginal benefit curve in Fig. 17.6.

Lying between these two prices are all the other possible prices that dealers are offering. For any given price found, except for the lowest ($6,000), there is some chance that you'll find an even lower one. But the lower the price you've found, the less likely it is that you'll find an even lower price. Because it is less likely that you'll find a lower price, the *expected* marginal benefit from additional search diminishes as the lowest price found declines. That is, the marginal benefit curve slopes downward as shown in Fig. 17.6 when the lowest price found measured on the horizontal axis runs from *right to left*.

There is a particular lowest price found that makes the expected marginal benefit equal to the marginal cost of visiting one more dealer. It is called the buyer's reservation price. The **buyer's reservation price** is the highest price that the buyer is willing to pay for a good. The buyer will happily buy for a lower price than the reservation price but will continue to search for a lower price if the lowest price found exceeds the reservation price. At the buyer's reservation price, the expected marginal benefit of search equals the marginal cost of search.

We can now state the **optimal-search rule**: search until an item is found at or below the buyer's reservation price and then stop searching and buy.

A Real Car Shopping Trip Real car shoppers are confronted with a much bigger problem than the one we've just studied. They probably don't even know the range of prices being offered. Also, there are many more dimensions of the car they are looking for than its price. They could spend almost forever gathering information about the alternatives. But at some point in their search, they decide they've done enough looking and make a decision to buy. The imaginary shopping trip rationalizes their decision. Real shoppers are saying, the benefits I expect from further search are insufficient to make it worth going on with the process. They don't do the calculations we've just done—at least, not explicitly—but their actions can be explained by those calculations.

Real shoppers differ in their marginal cost of search and so have different buyer's reservation prices. As a result, similar items can be found selling for a wide range of prices. Such a case is described in Reading Between the Lines on pp. 470–471.

Buyers are not alone in creating information. Sellers do a lot of it too—in the form of advertising. Let's see what the effects of advertising are.

Advertising

Advertising constantly surrounds us—on television, radio, or billboards and in newspapers or magazines—and costs billions of dollars. How do firms decide how much to spend on advertising? And what are the effects of advertising? Does it create information, or does it just persuade us to buy things that we don't really want? What does it do to prices?

Advertising for Profit Maximization A firm's advertising decision is part of its overall profit maximization strategy. Firms in perfect competition don't advertise, because everyone has all the information there is. But firms selling differentiated products in monopolistic competition and firms locked in the struggle of survival in oligopoly advertise a great deal.

The amount of advertising undertaken by firms in monopolistic competition is such that the marginal revenue from advertising equals the marginal cost of advertising. The amount of advertising undertaken by firms in oligopoly is determined by the game they are each playing. If that game is a *prisoners' dilemma,* they might end up spending amounts that lower their combined profits but that they can't avoid spending without being wiped out by other firms in the industry.

Persuasion or Information Much advertising is designed to persuade us that the product being advertised is the best in its class. For example, the Pepsi advertisement tells us that Pepsi is really better than Coke. The Coca-Cola advertisement tells us that Coke is really better than Pepsi. But advertising also informs. It provides information about the quality and price of a good or service.

Does advertising mainly persuade or mainly inform? The answer varies for different goods and different types of markets. Goods whose quality can be assessed *before* they are bought are called *search goods*. Typically, the advertising of search goods mainly informs—gives information about price, quality, and location of suppliers. Examples of such goods are gasoline, basic foods, and household goods. Goods whose quality can be assessed only *after* they are bought are called *experience goods.* Typically, the advertising of experience goods is light on information and mainly persuades—is designed to encourage the consumer to buy now and make a judgment later about quality, based on experience with the good. Cigarettes and alcoholic beverages are in this category.

Because most advertising involves experience goods, it is likely that advertising is more often persuasive rather than merely informative. But persuasive advertising doesn't necessarily harm the consumer. It might result in lower prices.

Advertising and Prices Advertising is costly, but does it increase the price of the good advertised? Since firms advertise to increase their profits, it makes sense for them to do so only if the consumer is willing to pick up the advertising tab.

But two lines of reasoning tell us that advertising can actually lower prices. The first is that to the extent that advertising is informative, it *increases* competition. By informing potential buyers about alternative sources of supply, informative advertising forces firms to keep their prices and profit margins low. There is evidence of such effects, especially in retailing. The second is that if advertising—even persuasive advertising—enables firms to increase their output and reap economies of scale, it is possible that the price of the good will be lower with advertising than without it, provided that competition prevents monopoly pricing. There are certainly economies of scale in advertising itself. That is, the effect of advertising on sales is much larger for large firms than for small firms. So, provided that a large firm does not become so large that it is able to extract monopoly profits, consumers will benefit from the greater preponderance of large firms made possible by advertising.

The final cost-benefit calculation on advertising is not yet available, and whether these pro-consumer aspects of advertising are the largest ones is not known.

REVIEW

Information on the prices, quantities, and qualities of goods and services and factors of production—economic information—is scarce, and people economize on its use. Buyers searching for price information stop when they find their reservation price, the price that makes the expected marginal benefit of search equal to the marginal cost of search. Sellers advertise to inform potential buyers of the good or to persuade them to buy it. Informative advertising can increase competition. If advertising enables economies of scale to be reaped, it is possible that it lowers the price of the advertised good. ◆

Private Information

So far we have looked at situations in which information is available to everyone and can be obtained with an expenditure of resources. But not all situations are like this. For example, it might be the case that one person has information that is too costly for anyone else to obtain. Such information is called private information. **Private information** is information that is available to one person but is too costly for anyone else to obtain.

There are many examples of private information that affects economic transactions. One is your knowledge about your driving. You know much more than your auto insurance company does about how carefully and defensively you drive. Another is your knowledge about your work effort. You know far more than your employer about how hard you work. Yet another is your knowledge about the quality of your car. You know whether it's a lemon. But the person to whom you are about to sell it does not and can't find out until after he or she has purchased it from you, and then it's too late.

Private information creates two problems:

- Moral hazard
- Adverse selection

Moral hazard exists when one of the parties to an agreement has an incentive, *after the agreement is made,* to act in a manner that brings additional benefits to himself or herself at the expense of the other party. It arises because it is too costly for the injured party to monitor the actions of the advantaged party. For example, Jackie hires Mitch as a salesperson and pays him a fixed wage regardless of the level of sales. Mitch faces a moral hazard. He has an incentive to put in the least possible effort, benefiting himself and lowering Jackie's profits. For this reason, salespeople are not paid a fixed wage. Instead, they receive an income that depends in some way on the volume (or value) of their sales.

Adverse selection is the tendency for the people who accept contracts to be those with private information that they plan to use to their own advantage and to the disadvantage of the less informed party. For example, if Jackie really offers the type of contract we've just described, it will attract lazy salespeople. Hardworking salespeople will prefer *not* to work for Jackie because they can do better working for someone who pays by results. The fixed wage contract adversely selects those with private information (knowledge about their work habits) who can use that knowledge to their own advantage and to the disadvantage of the other party.

A variety of devices have evolved that enable markets to function in the face of moral hazard and adverse selection. We've just seen one, the use of incentive payments for salespeople. Let's look at some more and also see how moral hazard and adverse selection influence three real-world markets:

- Markets for cars
- Markets for credit
- Markets for insurance

Markets for Cars

When a person buys a new car, it might turn out to be a lemon. If the car is a lemon, it is worth less to the person who bought it and to everyone else than if it has no defects. Does the used car market have two prices reflecting these two values—a low price for lemons and a higher price for cars without defects? It does not. To see why, let's look at a used car market, first with no dealer warranties and second with warranties.

Cars Without Warranties To make the points as clearly as possible, we'll make some extreme

Profiting from Information

FORTUNE, December 2, 1991

Reading the Customer Right

By Susan Caminiti

We're at Galeries Lafayette, a chic new Parisian clothing store in midtown Manhattan. A stylish woman in her 30s is speaking rapid French to a friend in front of a display of denim jeans. Spotting a pricetag, she turns to her companion and says in pristine English: "Are they kidding—$110 for a pair of *jeans*? I'm sticking with the Gap."

So are legions of other shoppers, which is why analysts who follow the Gap's stock closely are estimating the San Francisco retailer's earnings will grow around 20% a year during each of the next several years. Says Joseph Ellis of Goldman Sachs: "The Gap continues to be *the* apparel specialty-store leader in terms of product integrity and quality and fastidious attention to color, style, and detail."

The company has floated above the general misery in retailing by offering reasonably priced casual clothing that doesn't go out of style in a season but changes enough to keep shoppers interested. For example, fans of the Gap's popular $10.50 cotton T-shirt might find it in a dozen bright colors one month and pastels the next. Explains Millard—everyone calls him Mickey—Drexler, 47, the Gap's Bronx-born, fast-talking president: "We just keep trying to figure out what people wear on a regular basis. Our business is reading signals from the customer day in and day out."

The merchandise, all with a Gap label, draws customers back again and again. Plenty of retailers offer private-label goods, but few have elevated their name to the dignity of a brand the way the Gap has. Tight cost controls help pump up profits: The company has goods made exclusively for it, mainly in the U.S. and Hong Kong, and large production runs keep unit costs low.

Drexler likes to boast that almost anybody can wear the Gap's clothes. That's because the company has wisely realized that those anybodies' bodies are changing. The Gap division now has four cuts of jeans for women and three for men. With names like Relaxed Fit ("loose-fitting, very relaxed leg") and Reverse Fit ("full at the top, tapered at the bottom"), the sizes recognize that baby-boom customers can no longer squeeze into the slim-cut jeans they wore to Woodstock. But they still want to wear jeans.

Drexler & Co. also understand that customers' lifestyles are changing with their figures. So there are now 213 GapKids stores, some with babyGap boutiques in them, selling tiny T-shirts, jeans, and sweaters for the under-12 set. While the Gap doesn't break out results for its divisions, Edward Weller, a retail analyst at Montgomery Securities in San Francisco, estimates GapKids made $13 million on sales of $125 million last year. To attract working moms and other shoppers too tired to trek out to the mall after work or on the weekends, new Gap stores are opening in busy downtown locations.

If imitation is the sincerest form of you-know-what, then the Gap is in the middle of an outright lovefest. Superfashionable—and superexpensive—designers such as Donna Karan and Giorgio Armani are selling their versions of the Gap's T-shirts, khakis, and jeans, priced mostly under $100. Is Drexler worried? "Sure," he says, "but, hey look, there aren't too many secrets in this business. It's just going to make us run a little harder." Talk like that makes the Gap's competitors worried too.

The Essence of the Story

The Gap is expanding quickly, and its earnings are forecast to grow by 20 percent a year during each of the next several years.

The Gap sells only its own label and has a big reputation for quality; attention to color, style, and detail; and reasonable prices.

The company keeps sales high by "reading signals from the customer day in and day out," making clothes that fit most people and locating downtown as well as in suburban malls.

The Gap keeps unit costs low by having goods made for it in the United States and Hong Kong in large production runs.

Fashionable and expensive designers such as Donna Karan and Giorgio Armani are copying the Gap's product range but offering their versions at higher prices—sometimes as high as $110 for a pair of jeans.

The Gap's president, Mickey Drexler, says there are no secrets in clothes retailing and competition just makes the Gap run harder.

Background and Analysis

Clothes retailing is a highly competitive industry, but many different types of firms compete.

Some jeans sell for very high prices (at designer boutiques); some sell for average prices (at the Gap); and some sell for very low prices (at discount chains).

A key reason for the diversity of prices is that buyers lack complete information on quality, and to get information, valuable time must be spent searching.

But the cost of searching for information is not the same for everyone. A person's opportunity cost of time spent searching depends on his or her wage rate. For people with very high wage rates, the opportunity cost is high. For people with low wage rates, the opportunity cost is low.

Suppose that everyone gets the same benefit from finding a pair of jeans of given quality, color, fit, and price. To find the "best buy," time must be spent searching. Other things being equal, the longer the time spent searching (shopping), the better is the buy found. But the marginal benefit from finding a better pair of jeans diminishes as shown in the figure by the marginal benefit of search curve *MB*.

The figure illustrates how differences in the marginal cost of search can lead to a variety of types and prices of the same product.

For high wage earners, the marginal cost of search is MC_H, for average wage earners it is MC_A, and for low wage earners it is MC_L.

High wage earners confine their search to the boutiques that sell expensive designer items, average wage earners go to the Gap, and low wage earners check out all the discount stores and keep looking until they've found the best buy in town.

The Gap is profitable and growing quickly because it incurs the cost of identifying the preferences of mid-range wage earners and produces the items demanded by this group at the least possible cost.

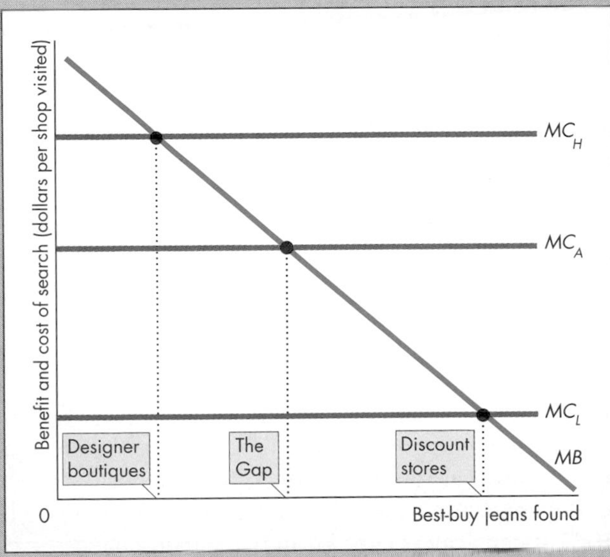

assumptions. There are just two kinds of cars, lemons and those without defects. A lemon is worth $1,000 both to its current owner and to anyone who buys it. A car without defects is worth $5,000 to its current and potential future owners. Whether a car is a lemon is private information to the person who owns it and has spent enough time driving it to discover its quality. Buyers of used cars can't tell whether they are buying a lemon until *after* they have bought the car and learned as much about it as its current owner knows. There are no dealer warranties.

The first thing to notice is that because buyers can't tell the difference between a lemon and a good car, they are willing to pay only one price for a used car. What is that price? Are they willing to pay $5,000, the value of a good car? They are not, because there is at least some probability that they are buying a lemon worth only $1,000. If buyers are not willing to pay $5,000 for a used car, are the owners of good cars willing to sell? They are not because a good car is worth $5,000 to them, so they hang onto their cars. Only the owners of lemons are willing to sell—as long as the price is $1,000 or higher. But, reason the buyers, if only the owners of lemons are selling, all the used cars available are lemons, so the maximum price worth paying is $1,000. Thus the market for used cars is a market for lemons, and the price is $1,000.

Moral hazard exists in the car market because sellers have an incentive to claim that lemons are good cars. But, given the assumptions in the above description of the car market, no one believes such claims. Adverse selection exists, resulting in only lemons actually being traded.

The market for used cars is not working well. Good used cars just don't get bought and sold, but people want to be able to exchange good used cars. How can they do so? The answer is by introducing warranties into the market.

Cars with Warranties Car dealers perform two economic functions: they are intermediaries between buyers and sellers, and they do auto maintenance work (usually on the cars they have sold). The information they get from their auto maintenance business is useful in helping them make the market for used cars operate more efficiently than the market for lemons that we've just described.

Buyers of used cars can't tell a lemon from a good car, but car dealers can. From their maintenance records, they have as much information about a car's quality as its owner has. They know, therefore, whether they are buying a lemon or a good car and can offer $1,000 for lemons and $5,000 for good cars.[1] But how can they convince buyers that it is worth paying $5,000 for what might be a lemon? The answer is by giving a guarantee in the form of a warranty. The dealer *signals* which cars are good ones and which are lemons. A **signal** is an action taken outside a market that conveys information that can be used by that market. In this case, the dealer takes an action in the market for car repairs that can be used by the market for cars. For each good car sold, the dealer agrees to pay the costs of repairing the car if it turns out to have a defect. Cars with a warranty are good; cars without a warranty are lemons.

Why do buyers believe the signal? It is because the cost of sending a false signal is high. A dealer who gives a warranty on a lemon ends up paying the high cost of repairs—and risks gaining a bad reputation. A dealer who gives a warranty only on good cars has no repair costs and a reputation that gets better and better. It pays the dealer to send an accurate signal. It is rational, therefore, for buyers to believe the signal. Warranties break the lemon problem and enable the used car market to function with two prices, one for lemons and one for good cars.

Markets for Credit

When a bank or other financial institution makes a loan, it is uncertain about whether the loan will be repaid. Some people always repay their debts and are better risks than others. But the lender has no way of knowing who is a good risk and who is a bad risk until after the loan has been repaid, and by then it is too late. Lending to low-risk people is much less costly than lending to high-risk people.

Faced with this situation, banks and other financial institutions use a variety of devices to minimize the risk they face. They check the credit worthiness of borrowers. And for large loans, they monitor the borrower's activities. They also often require the borrower to pledge assets that are valued more high-

[1]In this example, to keep the numbers simple, we'll ignore dealers' profit margins and other costs of doing business and suppose that dealers buy cars for the same price as they sell them. The principles are the same with dealers' profit margins.

ly than the loan to secure a loan. A secured loan, in effect, puts the risk back on the borrower. But many loans are unsecured. They are made to people on the basis of a promise to repay, and their ultimate worth depends on the value of that promise.

What determines the interest rate paid on unsecured loans? To see the problem, look at Fig. 17.7. "No-risk borrowers" in part (a) are those who always repay their loans and "risky borrowers" in part (b) are those who attempt to evade loan repayments and impose higher costs on the lender. The demand curves in the two markets are D_n and D_r. If the bank can sort borrowers into no-risk borrowers and risky ones, its supply curve of loans to no-risk borrowers is S_n and its supply curve to risky borrowers is S_r. The high interest rate at which loans are offered to risky borrowers reflects the high cost of lending to them. The bank lends Q_n to no-risk borrowers at an interest rate r_n and Q_r to risky borrowers at an interest rate of r_r.

But the problem is that the bank has no way of knowing who is risky when a loan is made, so the arrangement just described can't be implemented. Instead, the bank must charge the same interest rate to all borrowers. If it lends to all borrowers at r_n, no-risk borrowers borrow Q_n. The opportunity cost of these loans is reflected in the supply curve of no-risk loans, so the bank just covers its opportunity cost on these loans and makes no profit on them. Risky customers borrow Q'_r (in part b). But to get their money back from risky borrowers, banks incur a great deal of expense chasing borrowers, bringing lawsuits, and enforcing their claims. These costs are built into the supply curve for risky loans, so the banks incur a loss recovering these loans equal to the red rectangle in part (b). It's clear that banks would not be in business for long if this is how they operated.

Suppose the banks make loans available to everyone at the interest rate that covers the cost of lend-

FIGURE 17.7

Low- and High-Risk Borrowers

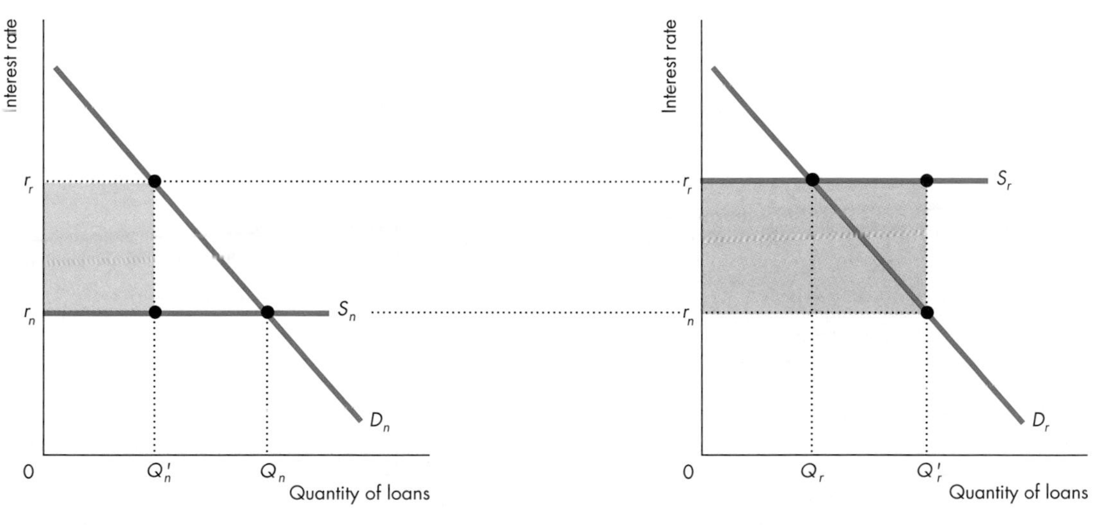

(a) No-risk borrowers **(b) Risky borrowers**

Banks can't distinguish between borrowers with differing risk characteristics. If they could, they would lend to "no-risk borrowers" at interest rate r_n (part a) and to "risky borrowers" at interest rate r_r (part b). If they lend to all borrowers at r_n, they incur a loss on "risky borrowers" (part b) equal to the red area. If they lend to all borrowers at interest rate r_r, they make a profit equal to the blue area in part (a). But they have an incentive to find ways of lending more to "no-risk borrowers," and competition among banks forces interest rates down below r_r.

ing to risky borrowers—r_r. In this case, the quantity of loans to risky borrowers is Q_r (part b), and the banks break even on these loans. No-risk customers borrow Q'_n at the interest rate r_r, and banks make a profit on these loans equal to the blue rectangle in part (a). If this is how banks operate, they will make huge profits and there will be a scramble to get into the banking business. Banks will also have an incentive to find ways of identifying no-risk customers and do even more business with them at lower interest rates.

Figure 17.8 shows what happens to resolve these problems. First, competition among banks for loan business forces interest rates down below the rate on risky loans. In the absence of any further changes, the interest rate will fall until the banks are incurring losses on risky loans and making profits on no-risk loans that balance out to a zero economic profit. At such a point there is no further entry into the loan business.

But banks use *signals* to discriminate between borrowers, and they ration or limit loans to amounts below those demanded. Using signals such as length of time in a job, ownership of a home (even if mortgaged), marital status, and age, banks restrict the amounts they are willing to lend to each type of borrower. These loan limits are shown in each part of Fig. 17.8. The factors used to determine loan limits have a bigger impact on risky borrowers than on no-risk borrowers, so the amounts that the two groups can borrow based on these rationing devices are L_n and L_r. Competition between banks lowers the interest rate to r and shifts the supply curve to S. The profit on loans made to no-risk borrowers (the blue rectangle in part a) equals the loss made on loans to risky borrowers (the red rectangle in part b). Both no-risk borrowers and risky borrowers would like to borrow more. Both types of borrowers have an excess demand for loans. But these amounts of excess demand are efficient as far as the banks are concerned. They cannot increase their profits made on loans because they can't identify the type of borrower taking out the loan. And because far more risky borrowers are unsatisfied

FIGURE 17.8

The Market for Loans

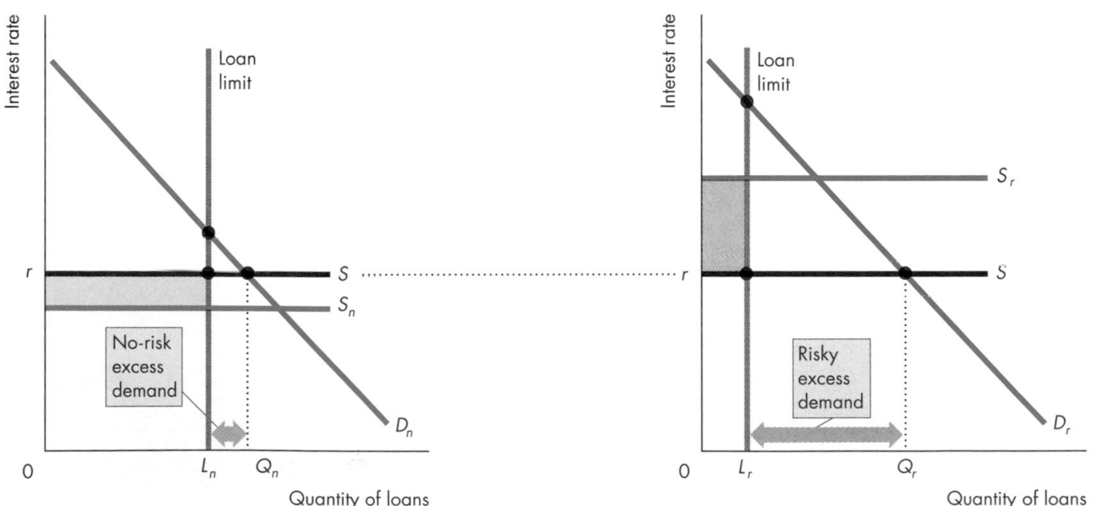

(a) No-risk borrowers

(b) Risky borrowers

Competition among banks forces the interest rate down until the profit on loans to "no-risk borrowers"—the blue area in part (a)—is equal to the losses on loans to "risky borrowers"—the red area in part (b). In an attempt to discriminate in favor of "no-risk borrowers" the banks use signals and ration loans, imposing limits on the amounts that may be borrowed based on characteristics of their borrowers. The excess demand does not force interest rates up because banks can't tell the quality of potential borrowers.

than no-risk borrowers, it is likely that any new business will be biased toward high-risk lending.

Markets for Insurance

When we studied Dan's auto insurance, earlier in this chapter, we looked at problems that can arise from private information. People who buy insurance face a moral hazard problem, and insurance companies face an adverse selection problem.

The moral hazard problem is that a person with insurance coverage for a loss has less of an incentive to avoid such a loss than an uninsured person. While nobody goes out looking for an accident, the risk of an auto accident certainly depends on how carefully and defensively a person drives. Similarly, the risk of poor health and large medical bills depends on a person's decisions about exercise and diet.

In the absence of some means of overcoming moral hazard problems, insurance premiums are higher than they would otherwise be. Thus safe, defensive drivers and people who pursue healthy exercise and diets contribute more to the insurance fund than they receive from it, while the less careful drivers and less health-conscious individuals receive more than they pay in. As a result there is an adverse selection problem. Insurance companies attract high-risk people rather than low-risk people. That is, high-risk people tend to buy insurance, and low-risk people tend not to buy insurance but to self-insure—to bear more of the risk themselves.

Real-world insurance markets have developed a variety of devices for overcoming or at least moderating these private information problems. One device is that of using signals, much like banks do and based on similar criteria.

One of the clearest signals a person can give an auto insurance company is her or his accident record. Suppose that Dan is a good driver and rarely has an accident. If he can demonstrate to the insurance company that his driving record is impeccable over a long enough period, then the insurance company will recognize him as a good driver. It reasons that there is only a slim chance that a bad driver could have such a good accident record. If Dan has established a long and unblemished driving record, then he is most likely a good driver. It pays Dan to work at establishing a reputation as a good driver because he will be able to get his insurance at a lower price.

If all drivers, good and bad alike, can establish good records, then simply having a good record will not convey any information. For the signal to be informative, it must be the case that the cost of sending the signal increases with increasing risk. Thus it must be difficult for bad drivers to fake low risk by having a good record. These types of signals are used in car insurance in the form of "no-claim" bonuses that drivers accumulate the more years they go without making an insurance claim.

Another device used by insurance companies is the deductible. A deductible is the amount of a loss that the insured person agrees to bear. For example, most auto insurance policies have the insurer paying the first few hundred dollars worth of damage. The size of the premium varies with the size of the deductible and in a significant way. That is, the decrease in the premium is more than proportionate to the increase in the size of the deductible. By offering insurance with full coverage on terms attractive only to the highest-risk people and then by offering coverage with a deductible on more favorable terms, insurance companies can do profitable business with everyone. High-risk people fully cover at the full cost of their risk, and lower-risk people cover partially at a cost commensurate with their risk.

REVIEW

Private information, a situation in which one party to an exchange has information that is not available to the other party, creates moral hazard and adverse selection. In many markets, such as those for cars, loans, and insurance, methods have been devised to limit the problems caused by private information. Warranties, loan limits, no-claim bonuses, and deductibles are examples. ◆

Managing Risk in Financial Markets

Risk is a dominant feature of markets for stocks and bonds—indeed for any asset whose price fluctuates and is determined by demand and supply in a market. One thing people do to cope with risky asset prices is diversify their asset holdings.

Diversification to Lower Risk

The idea that diversification lowers risk is very natural. It is just an application of not putting all one's eggs into the same basket. How exactly does diversification reduce risk? The best way to answer this question is to consider an example.

Suppose there are two risky projects that you can undertake. Each involves investing $100,000. The two projects are independent of each other, but both promise the same degree of risk and return.

Project 1 will either lose $25,000 or make $50,000, and the chance that either of these things will happen is 50 percent. The expected return is (–$25,000 × 0.5) + ($50,000 × 0.5), which is $12,500.

Project 2 also holds out the same promise of return—a 50 percent chance of losing $25,000 and a 50 percent chance of making $50,000. But the two projects are completely independent. The outcome of one project in no way influences or is related to the outcome of the other.

Undiversified Suppose you put all your eggs in one basket—investing the $100,000 in either project 1 or project 2. Your returns are illustrated in the frequency distribution shown in Fig. 17.9(a). You expect to make $12,500, which is an expected return of 12.5 percent. But there is no chance that you will actually make a return of 12.5 percent. You will either lose $25,000, a return of –25 percent, or make $50,000, a return of 50 percent, and the probability of each of these outcomes is 50 percent.

Diversified Suppose instead that you diversify by putting 50 percent of your money into project 1 and 50 percent into project 2. (Someone else is putting up the other money in these two projects.) What now are your possible returns? If both projects lose, your loss is $12,500 on each project, or a total loss of $25,000. Your return is –25 percent. If project 1 turns out to be a winner and project 2 a loser, you

FIGURE 17.9
The Gains from Diversification

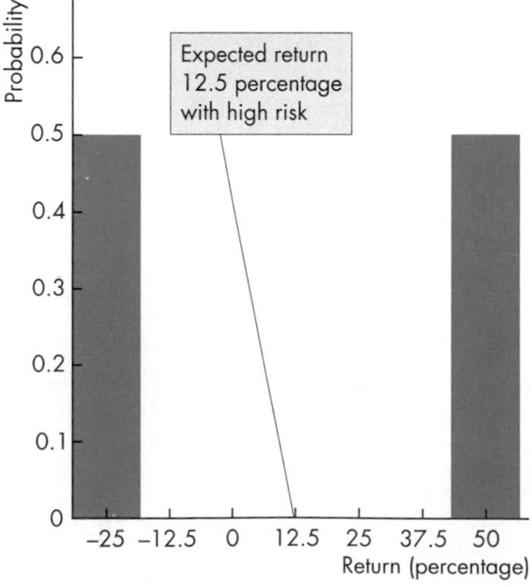

(a) Not diversified

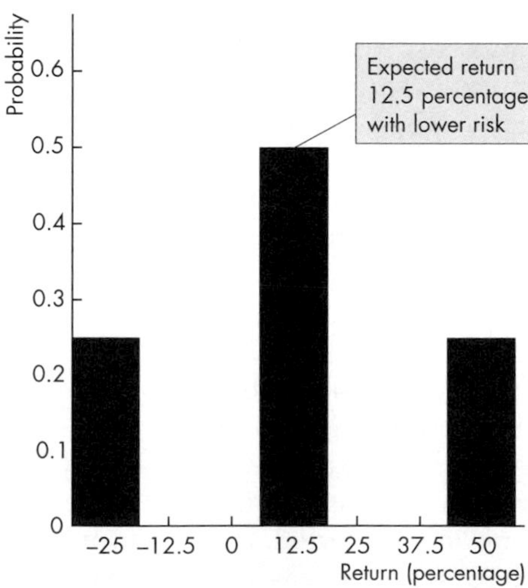

(b) Diversified

With no diversification (part a), returns are equally likely to be –25 percent and +50 percent with an expected return of 12.5 percent. But with diversification (part b), the probability of the extremes falls and the probability of the expected return increases. Diversification lowers risk.

lose $12,500 on project 1 and make $25,000 on project 2, or in total you make $12,500. Your return is 12.5 percent. Also if project 1 turns out to be a loser and project 2 a winner, you make $12,500—a 12.5 percent return. If both projects turn out to be winners, you make $50,000—a 50 percent return. There are now four possible outcomes, and each is equally probable. Each outcome has a 25 percent chance of occurring. The frequency distribution for your returns is now that shown in Fig. 17.9(b). Your expected return is still 12.5 percent, and there is now an excellent chance—a 50 percent chance, in fact—that your return will be 12.5 percent. There is now only a 25 percent chance that you will lose $25,000 and make a –25 percent return. Also there is now only a 25 percent chance that you will make $50,000, or a 50 percent return. By diversifying portfolio assets you have reduced its riskiness while maintaining an expected return of 12.5 percent.

If you are risk averse—that is, if your utility of wealth curve looks like Tania's, which you studied earlier in this chapter—you'll prefer the diversified portfolio to the one that is not diversified. That is, your *expected utility* with a diversified set of assets is greater.

A further consequence of risk in asset markets is the development of market institutions that enable people to avoid risk. One of these is the establishment of forward and futures markets.

Forward and Futures Markets

Producers are especially concerned about two uncertainties: the price at which they will be able to sell their product and the conditions affecting how much of their product will be produced. Farmers provide a clear illustration of the importance of these two uncertainties. First, when farmers decide how many acres of corn to plant, they do not know the price at which the corn will be sold. Knowing the price of corn today does not help them make decisions about how much seed to sow today. Today's planting becomes tomorrow's crop, and so tomorrow's price determines how much revenue farmers get from today's sowing decisions. Second, when farmers plant corn, they do not know what the growing conditions will turn out to be. Conditions might be excellent, producing a high yield and a bumper crop, or conditions such as drought and inadequate sunshine might lead to a low crop yield and disaster.

Uncertainty about the future price of a good can arise from uncertainty about its future demand or its future supply. We have just considered some uncertainties about supply. There are also many uncertainties about demand. We know that demand for a good depends on the prices of its substitutes and complements, income, population, and preferences. Demand varies as a result of fluctuations in all these influences on buyers' plans. Since these influences *do* fluctuate and are impossible to predict exactly, the level of future demand is always uncertain.

Forward Markets Uncertainties about future supply and demand make future prices uncertain. But producers must make decisions today even though they do not know the price at which their output will be sold. In making such decisions, farmers are able to take advantage of special types of markets—forward markets. A **forward market** is a market in which a commitment is made at a price agreed here and now to exchange a specified quantity of a particular commodity at a specified future date.

Forward markets are very useful for farmers and others whose production decisions yield an output with a time lag. By engaging in a forward transaction it is possible to know the price at which the output will be sold even though the output is not yet available.

Futures Markets Forward contracts enable farmers and others engaging in transactions for the future to reduce their risk arising from price variations. But they don't eliminate risk altogether. The person holding the contract has to stand ready to deliver or make delivery at the agreed price. In some situations it might not be convenient to actually deliver goods. In such a case the person holding a promise to deliver might want to sell that promise. To facilitate such exchanges, futures markets have been developed. A **futures market** is an organized market operated on a futures exchange in which large-scale contracts for the future delivery of goods can be exchanged. Rarely do futures contracts result in an actual delivery taking place. All futures contracts are liquidated through subsequent resale of the future promise before the delivery date becomes due. The existence of futures markets enables people to diversify risk in much the same way as holding a range of assets in a portfolio enables risks to be diversified.

Rational Expectations

To decide whether to engage in a forward or futures transaction, traders and producers must make forecasts of future prices. How do they do that?

Making Forecasts The amount of time and effort devoted to making forecasts varies considerably from one individual to another. Most people devote hardly any time to this activity at all. Instead, they follow rules of thumb that, most of the time, seem to work well. But in important matters that directly affect their incomes, people will try to do better than that. One way of doing better is to simply imitate the actions of others who have a track record of success. Another way of doing better is to buy forecasts from specialists. A large number of forecasting agencies exist—from investment advisors and stock and commodity brokers to professional economic forecasting agencies. Such agencies have a strong incentive to make their forecasts correct, at least on the average.

The particular methods used to make forecasts are, of course, highly diverse, but our task is not to describe all of the actual methods used to make forecasts. Instead, our task is to build a model of forecasting. To build such a model, we use the fundamental assumption of economics—the assumption that people are seeking to get the most they can out of their scarce resources. In pursuit of that goal, forecasts will be correct on the average, and forecasting errors will be as small as possible. If any information is available that can improve a forecast, that information will be used. The forecast that uses all of the relevant information available about past and present events and that has the least possible error is called a **rational expectation.**

How does an economist go about calculating a rational expectation? The answer is by using an economic model. The economic model that explains prices is the model of demand and supply. Therefore, we use the demand and supply model to forecast prices—to calculate a rational expectation of a future price. We know that the point at which next year's demand curve intersects next year's supply curve determines next year's price. Until next year arrives, we don't know where those demand and supply curves will be located. However, we do know the factors that determine their position, and by forecasting those factors we can forecast next year's demand and supply curves and forecast their point of intersection—next year's price. Let's work out a rational expectation of the future price of corn.

Expected Demand and Expected Supply Our goal is to make the best forecast we can of the future price of corn. To make that forecast, we must forecast the positions of next year's demand and supply curves for corn. We learned earlier that the position of the demand curve for a good depends on the prices of its substitutes and complements, income, population, and preferences. The expected position of a demand curve, therefore, depends on the expected values of all these variables. In order to form an expectation about the future position of the demand curve of corn, it is necessary to forecast the future prices of corn's substitutes and complements, income, population, and current trends that might influence tastes. By taking into account every conceivable piece of available information that helps forecast such variables, farmers—or the specialists from whom farmers buy forecasts—can form a rational expectation of next year's demand for corn.

We also learned earlier that the position of the supply curve of a good depends on the prices of its substitutes and complements in production, the prices of the resources used to produce the good, and technology. An important part of the technology of farming is the biological process that converts seed to crop. That process, of course, depends in an important way on the temperature, the amount of sunshine, and the amount of rain. Expected supply depends on the expected values of all these variables. In order to form an expectation about the future supply of corn, it is necessary to forecast the future prices of corn's substitutes and complements in production, the prices of the resources used to produce the corn (the wages of farm workers and the prices of seed and fertilizers), and any current trends in weather patterns that might influence growing conditions. By taking into account every available piece of information that helps forecast such variables, people can form a rational expectation of the next year's corn supply.

Calculating a Rational Expectation A rational expectation of next year's price of corn can be

FIGURE 17.10

A Rational Expectation of Price

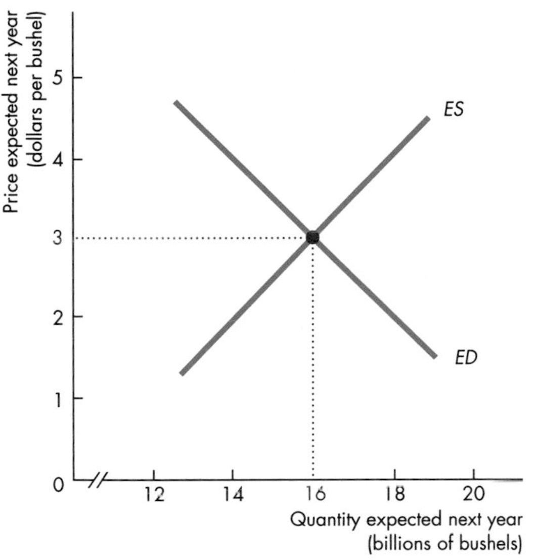

Since actual price is determined by actual supply and demand, expected price is determined by expected supply and expected demand. The point where expected demand, *ED*, cuts expected supply, *ES*, determines the rational expectation of the price ($3 a bushel) and quantity traded (16 billion bushels).

formed by bringing together expectations about next year's demand and supply. Figure 17.10 illustrates how to accomplish this. The quantities measured on the two axes are expectations of next year's price and quantity. The curve labeled *ED* is the best forecast available of next year's demand for corn. The curve labeled *ES* is the best forecast available of next year's supply of corn.

What do people expect the price of corn to be next year? They expect it to be $3 a bushel. That is the price at which expected quantity demanded equals the expected quantity supplied. People also can forecast next year's quantity traded. That forecast is 16 billion bushels. The price of $3 a bushel is the rational expectation of next year's price of corn. It is the forecasted price based on all the available relevant information. Producers use that forecast of the price to decide how many acres of corn to plant.

REVIEW

Gisk can be lowered by diversifying asset holdings. Diversification works by combining the returns on projects that are independent of each other. Risk can also be lowered by trading in forward markets. Such trading enables producers to know the future price at which their output will be sold. The existence of futures markets provides even greater opportunities for risk reduction. They enable people to take positions in forward markets without necessarily having to take delivery of goods. Decisions to engage in a forward or futures transaction are based on rational expectation of future prices. All organized asset markets determine a price that embodies all the available information about the future price. ◆

What are the implications of rational expectations for the way in which competitive asset markets work? Let's answer this question by looking at the stock market.

The Stock Market The stock market is the market on which the stocks of corporations are traded. Figure 17.11 illustrates how a stock price is determined. The horizontal axis measures the quantity expected next period. The vertical axis measures the price expected next period and the actual price this period. This period's expectations of next period's demand and supply curves are shown as *ED* and *ES*. The intersection point of those curves determines the rational expectation of next period's price, *EP*. If the actual price rises above the expected price, people sell stocks. If the price falls below the expected price, people buy stocks. Thus the *current period supply curve* is the perfectly elastic supply curve *S* at the price level that is rationally expected for next period. The actual price (*P*) is equal to the expected price (*EP*).

We have seen that a rational expectation is an expectation that uses all the available information that is relevant for forecasting a future price. Since the actual stock price is equal to the rational expectation of the future stock price, that stock price also

FIGURE 17.11
The Stock Market

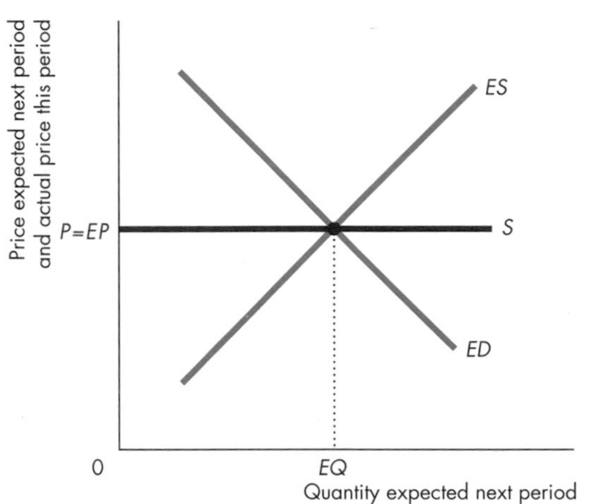

Holders of stocks form a rational expectation of the future price of a stock, *EP*, at the point of intersection of the expected demand curve (*ED*) and the expected supply curve (*ES*). If the price is above their expectation of the future price, stockholders sell. If the price is below their expectation of the future price, they buy. As a consequence, the current supply curve (*S*) is horizontal at the expected price (*EP*). These transactions keep the actual price (*P*) equal to the expected future price. Such a market is called an efficient market. In an efficient market, it is not possible to forecast a future price change and profit from that forecast. A foreseen price change is acted on immediately, and the actual price adjusts to eliminate the profit opportunity.

embodies all the relevant information that is available. A market in which the actual price embodies all currently available relevant information is called an **efficient market.** In an efficient market, it is impossible to forecast changes in price. Why? If your forecast is that the price is going to rise next period, you will buy now (since the price is low today in comparison with what you predict it is going to be in the future). Your action of buying today acts like an increase in demand today and increases today's price. It's true that your action—the action of a single trader—is not going to make much difference to a huge market like the New York Stock Exchange. But if traders in general expect a higher price next period and they all act today on the basis of that expectation, then today's price will rise. It will keep on rising until it reaches the expected future price. Only at that price do traders see no profit in buying more stock today.

There is an apparent paradox about efficient markets. Markets are efficient because people try to make a profit. They seek a profit by buying at a low price and selling at a high price. But the very act of buying and selling to make a profit means that the market price moves to its expected future value. Having done that, no one, not even those who are seeking to profit, can *predictably* make a profit. Every profit opportunity seen by a trader leads to an action that produces a price change that removes the profit opportunity for others. Even the possibility of an intergalactic attack on New York City is taken into account in determining stock market prices—see the cartoon.

Thus an efficient market has two features:

- Its price equals the expected future price and embodies all the available information.
- There are no forecastable profit opportunities available.

The key thing to understand about an efficient market such as the stock market is that if something can be anticipated, it will be, and the anticipation will be acted upon.

Volatility in Stock Prices If the price of a stock is always equal to its expected future price, why is the stock market so volatile? The answer must be that expectations themselves are subject to fluctuation. Expectations depend on the information available. As new information becomes available, stock traders form new expectations about the future state of the economy and, in turn, new expectations of future stock prices. Expectations about the economy are of crucial importance: Is the economy going to enjoy sustained rapid expansion? Or is it going to suffer a recession? Macroeconomic events, such as expansion and recession, influence stock prices. Individual stock prices are influenced by technological change, which in turn influences the supply of and demand for particular goods and services. Since new information is being accumulated daily about all these matters, expectations about the future price of a stock are constantly being re-evaluated. It is this

"Drat! I suppose the market has already discounted this, too."

process of re-evaluation that leads to high volatility in the stock market. As expectations change from being optimistic to pessimistic, the stock market can plunge many percentage points—as it did dramatically on October 19, 1987. On the other hand, a sustained period of increasing optimism can produce a long upswing in stock prices. The five-year run from mid-1982 to mid-1987 is an example of such stock market behavior.

◆ ◆ ◆ ◆ We've studied the way people cope with uncertainty and how markets work when there are important information problems. In the next chapter we're going to see how the market economy solves one of its biggest problems—determining the distribution of the gains from economic activity. We'll also see how government programs modify the outcome of a pure market economy.

SUMMARY

Coping with Uncertainty

Uncertainty is a state in which more than one event may occur but we don't know which one. To describe uncertainty, we use concepts of probability and risk. A probability is a number between zero and 1 that measures the chance of some possible event occurring. Risk is a state of uncertainty in which the probability of each possible outcome can be estimated. Sometimes the probabilities can be measured, and sometimes they cannot. When they cannot be measured, they are subjective probabilities.

People's attitudes toward risk are described by their utility of wealth schedules and curves. Greater wealth brings higher utility, but as wealth increases, the marginal utility of wealth diminishes. The cost of risk is measured as the dollar change in expected wealth necessary to keep expected utility constant in the face of a given increase in risk. Faced with uncertainty, people choose the action that gives them the greatest expected utility. (pp. 460–463)

Insurance

We spend 15 percent of our income on insurance, one of the most important ways in which we reduce risk. The three main types of insurance are life, health, and property and casualty. Insurance works by pooling risks, and it pays people to insure because they are risk averse—they value risk reduction. By pooling risks, insurance companies can eliminate the risks people face (from insured activities) and at a low cost in terms of reduced expected wealth. The lower risk is valued much more highly than the lower expected wealth. (pp. 463–466)

Information

Economic information is data on the prices, quantities, and qualities of goods and services and factors of production. Information is scarce, and people economize on their use of information just like they economize on their use of other productive resources.

Buyers search for price information—looking for the source of supply with the lowest cost. In doing so, they use the optimal-search rule of searching for a lower price until the expected marginal benefit of search equals the marginal cost of search. When the expected marginal benefit equals the marginal cost, stop searching and buy. There is a reservation price at which the expected marginal benefit of search equals the marginal cost of search. When a price equal to (or less than) the reservation price is found, the search ends and the item is bought.

Sellers advertise, sometimes to persuade and sometimes to inform. Advertising is part of a firm's profit maximization strategy. The general presumption is that advertising increases prices. But advertising can increase competition and enable economies of scale to be experienced, in which case it is possible that some prices are lower because of advertising. (pp. 466–469)

Private Information

Private information is the knowledge that one person has that is just too costly for anyone else to discover. Private information creates the problems of moral hazard—the use of private information to the advantage of the informed and the disadvantage of the uninformed—and adverse selection—the tendency for the people who accept contracts to be those with private information that can be used to their own advantage and to the disadvantage of the uninformed person or firm. Devices that enable markets to function in the face of moral hazard and adverse selection are incentive payments, guarantees and warranties, and signals. (pp. 469–475)

Managing Risk in Financial Markets

Risk can be lowered by diversifying asset holdings, thereby combining the returns on projects that are independent. Risk can also be lowered by trading in forward markets, which enables producers to know the future price at which their output will be sold. Futures markets provide yet further opportunities for risk reduction, enabling people to take positions in forward markets without necessarily taking delivery of goods. Decisions to engage in a forward or futures transaction are based on rational expectation of future prices. A rational expectation is one that uses all the available and relevant information. It is correct on the average and has the smallest possible range of forecast error. Asset markets determine a price that embodies a rational expectation of the future price and are efficient. The stock market is an example of such a market. In such markets there are no forecastable price changes or profit opportunities. (pp. 475–481)

KEY ELEMENTS

Key Terms

Adverse selection, 469
Buyer's reservation price, 467
Economic information, 466
Efficient market, 480
Expected utility, 461
Forward market, 477
Futures market, 477
Information cost, 466
Moral hazard, 469
Optimal-search rule, 467
Private information, 469
Probability, 460
Rational expectation, 478
Risk, 460
Signal, 472
Uncertainty, 460
Utility of wealth schedule (or curve), 460

Key Figures

REVIEW QUESTIONS

1 What is the difference between uncertainty and risk?

2 How do we measure a person's attitude toward risk? How do these attitudes vary from one person to another?

3 Why do people buy insurance, and why do insurance companies make a profit?

4 Why is information valuable?

5 What determines the amount of searching you do for a bargain?

6 Why do firms advertise?

7 What are moral hazard and adverse selection, and how do they influence the way credit and insurance markets work?

8 Explain how the used car market works.

9 Why do firms give warranties and guarantees?

10 How do deductibles make insurance more efficient and enable insurance companies to discriminate between high-risk and low-risk customers?

11 How does diversification lower risk?

12 What is the difference between a forward market and a futures market?

13 What is a rational expectation? How is such an expectation arrived at?

14 What is an efficient market? What types of markets are efficient?

PROBLEMS

1 Jimmy and Zenda have the following utility of wealth schedules:

Wealth	Jimmy's utility	Zenda's utility
0	0	0
100	200	512
200	300	640
300	350	672
400	375	678
500	387	681
600	393	683
700	396	684

Who is more risk averse, Jimmy or Zenda?

2 Suppose that Jimmy and Zenda have $400 each and that each sees a business project that involves committing the entire $400 to the project. They reckon that the project could return $600 (a profit of $200) with a probability of 0.85 or $200 (a loss of $200) with a probability of 0.15. Who goes for the project and who hangs onto the initial $400?

3 Who is more likely to buy insurance, Jimmy or Zenda, and why?

4 There are two independent investment projects: Project 1 is expected to give the investor a wealth of $200 with a probability of 0.5 and a wealth of zero with a probability of 0.5. Project 2 is expected to give a wealth of $300 with a probability of 0.5 and a wealth of zero with a probability of 0.5.

- **a** Which project would a risk-neutral person invest in?
- **b** How much would Jimmy (from problem 1) be willing to invest in project 1? In project 2?
- **c** How much would Zenda (from problem 1) be willing to invest in project 1? In project 2?
- **d** Draw a diagram similar to Fig. 17.9 illustrating the wealth resulting from investing in project 1, investing in project 2, and investing equal amounts in both projects.

5 Explain how the rational expectation of next year's wheat price is arrived at.

CHAPTER 18

THE DISTRIBUTION OF INCOME AND WEALTH

After studying this chapter, you will be able to:

- Describe the distribution of income and wealth in the United States today
- Explain the effects of income redistribution policies
- Explain why the wealth distribution shows greater inequality than the income distribution
- Explain how the distribution of income arises from the prices of productive resources and the distribution of endowments
- Explain how the distribution of income and wealth is affected by individual choices
- Explain the different views about fairness in the distribution of income and wealth

Riches and Rags

FIFTY-THREE STORIES ABOVE MANHATTAN IS A PENTHOUSE with unobstructed views of Central Park, the Hudson River, and the city skyline: its price? $4 million. "Now, you can be one of the enviable few to fly Around the World by Supersonic Concorde . . . for just $26,800 per person," trumpets an advertisement in the *New Yorker.* Obviously, only the very richest Americans can afford homes and vacations as costly as these. Not quite within view of the $4 million penthouse, but not far from it, is Fort Washington Armory in Upper Manhattan. What was opened as a temporary shelter in 1981 permanently houses 850 men sleeping in one huge room. "As the men at Fort Washington stretch out on cots on the coarse wooden drill floor in a room the size of a football field, there is pervasive fear—fear of AIDS and tuberculosis, fear for physical survival. And there is widespread despair over the future. . . . There, side by side, are predators and their prey, the mentally ill, alcoholics, men with limbs thinned by disease and malnutrition, others with muscles trained through exercise in prison."[1] ◆◆ Why are some people exceedingly rich while others earn very little and own almost nothing? Are the rich getting richer and the poor getting poorer? Is it fair that some people are incredibly rich while others live in miserable poverty? And what do we mean by fairness?

[1]*New York Times* (February 18, 1988): 1, 42.

◆ ◆ ◆ ◆ In this chapter, we study the sources of income and wealth inequality. We'll also study the connection between income and wealth and discover why the distribution of wealth is much more uneven than that of income. We'll see how factor prices and the quantities of factors hired, as determined in factor markets, result in unequal incomes. We'll also see how inequality results in part from the choices that people make. ◆ ◆ Most of the chapter deals with positive issues—with trying to understand the world as it is—and not normative matters—commenting on or making judgments about what is desirable. Nevertheless, the final section reviews some of the key contributions to the unending search for a widely acceptable concept of fairness. ◆ ◆ Let's begin by looking at some facts about the distributions of income and wealth.

Distributions of Income and Wealth in the United States Today

The incomes earned by the factors of production are the wages (including salaries and other forms of compensation) paid to labor, the interest (and dividend) income paid to the owners of capital, and the rental incomes received by the owners of land and minerals. Labor earns the largest share of total income, and that share has increased slightly over the years.

The distribution of income among individuals and families depends on the amount of labor, capital, and natural resources that they supply and on the wage rates, interest and dividend rates, and rental rates that they receive. The resource that everyone has in identical amounts is time. But the price at which a person can sell his or her time, the wage rate, depends on the individual's marginal product. That marginal product in turn depends partly on natural ability, partly on luck or chance, and partly on the amount of human capital that the individual has built up. The income from working is a mixture of a return on human capital and a compensation for forgoing leisure.

There is a great deal of inequality in the distribution of ownership of all other factors of production. We will more closely examine that inequality shortly. For now, let's just note that the total income of a family depends on its labor income (including its returns on human capital) as well as its income from other assets.

In 1989, the average U.S. family income was $41,506. But there was considerable inequality around that average. Figure 18.1 shows the percentage of total income received by each of five equal-sized groups from the poorest 20 percent to the richest 20 percent of families in 1989. The 20 percent of families with the lowest incomes received less than 5 percent of total income. The second lowest 20 percent received less than 11 percent of total income. You can continue reading across the figure to see the percentages of income received by families that are increasingly better off. The 20 percent of families with the highest incomes received almost 45 percent of total income.

Although the distribution of income shows considerable inequality, the distribution of wealth shows even greater inequality. Wealth and income are

FIGURE 18.1

Family Income Shares

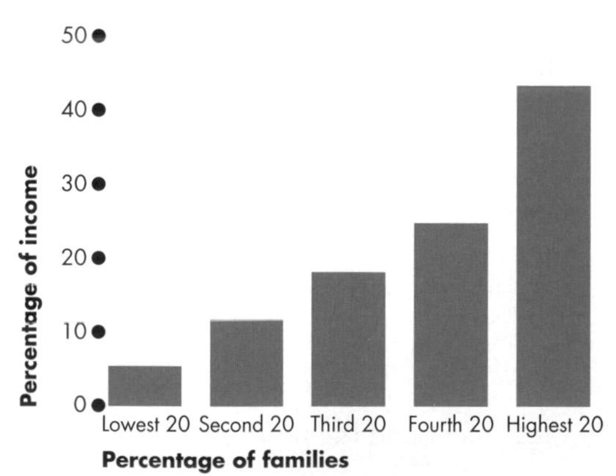

One way of measuring income inequality is to calculate the percentage of total income earned by a given percentage of families, starting with the poorest. The figure shows us that in 1989, the poorest 20 percent of families earned only 5 percent of total income while the richest 20 percent earned 44 percent of total income. On the average, the incomes of the richest 20 percent of families were almost nine times the incomes of the poorest 20 percent of families.

Source: Current Population Reports, Consumer Income, Series P-60, Nos. 167 and 168 (1990) (Washington, D.C.: U.S. Department of Commerce, Bureau of the Census).

linked in a way that we will examine shortly, but it's important to remember the distinction: income is what you earn, wealth is what you own. Wealth is measured as the value of an individual's or family's holdings of real estate and financial assets. Average family wealth in 1988 was $36,000. The range about that average was enormous. The poorest 90 percent of families owned about one third of total wealth. The next 9 percent owned another third of total wealth. And the wealthiest 1 percent of families owned the remaining one third of total wealth.

Lorenz Curves

Another way of describing the distributions of income and wealth is presented in Fig. 18.2. The table divides families into five groups arranged from the lowest income (row *a*) to highest income (row *e*) and shows the percentages of income of each of these groups. For example, row *a* tells us that the lowest 20 percent of families receives 5 percent of total income; row *e* tells us that the highest 20 percent of families receives 44 percent of total income. The table also shows the cumulative percentages of families and income. For example, row *b* tells us that the lowest 40 percent of families receives 16 percent of total income.

The data on cumulative income shares are illustrated in the figure by a Lorenz curve. A **Lorenz curve** graphs the cumulative percentage of income (or wealth) against the cumulative percentage of families. The horizontal axis of the figure measures the cumulative percentages of families ranked from the lowest to the highest income. For example, the point marked 40 on the horizontal axis represents the 40 percent of families with the lowest income. The vertical axis measures the cumulative percentages of income. For example, the point marked 40 indicates 40 percent of total income.

If each family had the same amount of income, the cumulative percentages of income received by the cumulative percentages of families would fall along the straight line labeled "Line of equality." The actual distribution of income is shown by the curve labeled "Income." The points on the income distribution curve labeled *a* through *e* correspond to the family income shares shown in the table.

The horizontal axis of the figure also measures the cumulative percentage of families ranked from the lowest to the highest wealth, and the vertical axis also measures the cumulative percentage of

FIGURE 18.2

Lorenz Curves for Income and Wealth

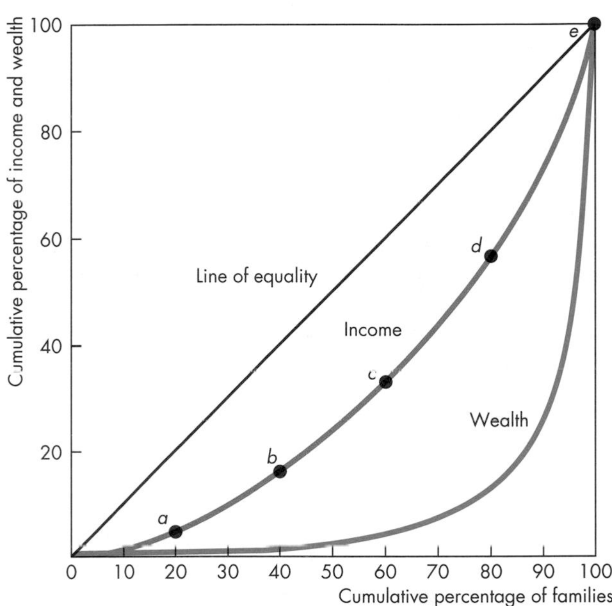

	Families		Income	
	Percentage	Cumulative percentage	Percentage	Cumulative percentage
a	**Lowest 20**	**20**	**5**	**5**
b	**Second 20**	**40**	**11**	**16**
c	**Third 20**	**60**	**16**	**32**
d	**Fourth 20**	**80**	**24**	**56**
e	**Highest 20**	**100**	**44**	**100**

The cumulative percentages of income and wealth are graphed against the cumulative percentage of families. If income and wealth were distributed equally, each 20 percent of families would have 20 percent of the income and wealth—the line of equality. Points *a* through *e* on the Lorenz curve for income correspond to the rows of the table showing family income. The Lorenz curve for wealth is based on the fact that the top 1 percent, the next 9 percent, and the bottom 90 percent of families each own about one third of total wealth.

Source: Income: *Current Population Reports, Consumer Income,* Series P-60, Nos. 167 and 168 (1990) (Washington, D.C.: U.S. Department of Commerce, Bureau of the Census). Wealth: Robert D. Avery and Arthur B. Kennickell, "Measurement of Household Saving Obtained from First Differencing Wealth Estimates" (Washington, D.C.: Federal Reserve Board, February 1990).

wealth. Plotting the cumulative percentage of wealth against the cumulative percentage of families gives the Lorenz curve for wealth—the curve labeled "Wealth." This curve is based on the distribution described above in which total wealth is divided approximately equally between the bottom 90 percent, the next 9 percent, and the top 1 percent of families.

The advantage of using Lorenz curves to describe the distributions of income and wealth is that they provide a graphic illustration of the degree of inequality. The closer the Lorenz curve is to the line of equality, the more equal is the distribution. As you can see from the two Lorenz curves in Fig. 18.2, the distribution of wealth is much more unequal than the distribution of income. That is, the Lorenz curve for the wealth distribution is much farther away from the line of equality.

Inequality over Time

Figure 18.3 shows how the distribution of income has changed over the years. The first impression gained from this figure is that the distribution has been remarkably constant. But a closer look reveals that from 1950 to about 1967 the distribution was becoming more equal—the richest 20 percent were becoming slightly less rich, the poorest 20 percent were becoming slightly less poor, and the three middle groups were not changing much. Since 1967, the trends have been reversed and the distribution of income has become less equal. All three of the lower groups have lost ground, and the two richest groups have gained. We do not have a good explanation for these trends at the present time.

These trends are apparent in other data and apply not only to the population in total but also to each major group. Reading Between the Lines on pp. 490–491 examines these trends for black families during the 1980s.

Who Are the Rich and the Poor?

We have seen that there is a great deal of inequality in income and wealth. But *who* are the rich and *who* are the poor? What are the key characteristics of rich and poor families?

The poorest person in the United States today is most likely to be a black woman living on her own, probably widowed, who is over 65 years of age, has had less than eight years of elementary school, and lives in the South. The highest-income family in the United States today is likely to be a married couple, between ages 45 and 54, with two children. The adult household members in this family have had four years or more of college education, are white, and live in the Northeast. These snapshot profiles are the extremes in Fig. 18.4. That figure illustrates the importance of education, marital status, size of household, age of householder, race, and region of residence in influencing the size of a family's income.

Education is the single most important factor. On the average, people with eight years or less of elementary school earn $12,700 a year, while those with four years or more of college earn almost $50,000 a year. Marital status is also important.

FIGURE 18.3

Trends in the Distribution of Income: 1950–1990

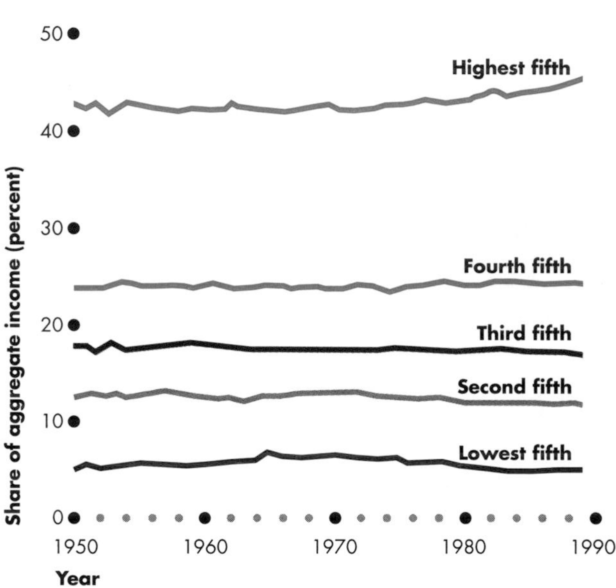

The distribution of income in the United States became more equal between 1950 and 1967 and less equal after 1967. The main change was in the percentage of income earned by the highest fifth.

Source: Current Population Reports, Consumer Income, Series P-60, Nos. 162 (1989), 167, and 168 (1990) (Washington, D.C.: U.S. Department of Commerce, Bureau of the Census).

FIGURE 18.4

Distribution of Income by Selected Family Characteristics in 1989

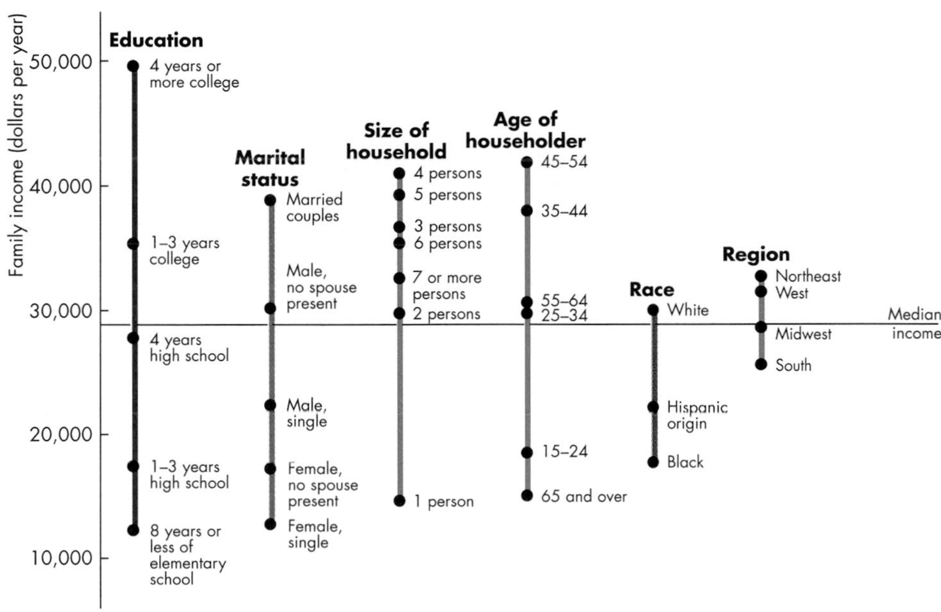

Education is the single biggest factor affecting family income distribution, but marital status, size of household, and age of householder are also important. Race and region of residence also play a role.

Source: Statistical Abstract of the United States: 1991, 111th edition (Washington D.C.: 1991), 450.

Single females, on the average, have incomes of less than $14,000 a year, while married couples earn an average income of $39,000 a year. Household size has an obvious effect on household income, but the household size at which income is highest is four persons. Age also is important, with the oldest and youngest households having the lowest incomes and middle-aged households the highest. Race and region of residence also influence the income distribution but on a smaller scale than the other characteristics that we have just examined. Black families have a median income of $18,000, while white families have a median income of slightly more than $30,000. The family with the median income is located in the middle of the income distribution—50 percent of families have higher incomes and 50 percent have lower incomes than the median income. Incomes are lowest in the South and highest in the Northeast, with those in the West fairly close to those in the Northeast and incomes in the Midwest lying midway between these two.

Poverty

Families at the bottom end of the income distribution are so poor that they are considered to be living in poverty. **Poverty** is an income level measured by a poverty index first calculated by the Social Security Administration in 1964. The index is based on Department of Agriculture assessments of the minimum consumption requirements of families based on their size and composition. In 1989, the poverty level for a two-person family was an income of $8,076. For a four-person family, it was $12,675. In 1989, 28 million Americans, 11.4 percent of the population, had incomes below the poverty level. The distribution of poverty is very unequal by race, with 6.8 percent of white families, 20.9 percent of Hispanic origin families, and 25.4 percent of black families being below the poverty level. Poverty is also heavily influenced by family status. More than 30 percent of families in which the householder is a female and no husband is present are below the

Black Inequality

THE SAN FRANCISCO CHRONICLE, AUGUST 9, 1991

Income Gap Widens Among U.S. Blacks, New Report Says

As the income gap widens between rich and poor in the black community, blacks may define themselves more by economic status than by race, demographic researchers reported yesterday.

"The middle-class blacks of the future may feel little in common with poor blacks because their experiences will have been dramatically different in so many ways," said the report, "African Americans in the 1990s." The study is the work of the Population Reference Bureau, a nonprofit educational organization that reports on demographic trends.

Researchers found two black communities: "one of middle-class and affluent blacks who took advantage of the increased opportunities provided by the civil rights movement; the other poor, largely urban blacks who remain socially and economically isolated from the American mainstream."

The study documents the plight of the so-called black underclass but also shows that the number of black families with annual incomes of more than $50,000 doubled during the 1980s.

"In families headed by younger blacks, especially those with a college degree, average income is almost as high for blacks as it is for whites," said the report. "Among married-couple families where the head of household is 25 to 44 years old and a college graduate, the median income of blacks ($54,400) is 93 percent that of whites ($58,800)."

Dismal Findings

Overall, however, the report's findings are dismal.

"Economically, blacks fare poorly compared to whites," said Taynia Mann, one of four researchers who prepared the profile of black society in the 1990s from federal and academic statistics.

"They are more than twice as likely to be unemployed, much less likely to work in managerial and professional jobs, and earn 56 percent of whites' incomes. They are three times more likely to live in poverty and have an average net worth only 10 percent that of whites."

Single Parents Hit Hard

The report says that economic problems among black families can be linked "foremost" to the growth in households headed by women. In 1989, the average female-headed black family had only one-third the annual income ($11,600) of the average black family with both a husband and wife ($30,700).

"While most of the 10 million African households are family households, only half of them are headed by a married couple, compared to four-fifths of white families," Mann said.

Mann warned that African Americans cannot be sterotyped as a "monolithic" group.

"The report indicates in general that the black population is changing," said Mann. "In fact, there's an increasing amount of social and economic diversity within the African American population." . . .

The Essence of the Story

A report, "African Americans in the 1990s," identified two black communities, an affluent middle class and a poor "black underclass."

The number of black families with annual incomes of more than $50,000 doubled during the 1980s, and young, college-educated, black married couples earned a median income of $54,400, 93 percent of that of similar white couples.

But compared to white families, poor black families are more than twice as likely to be unemployed, less likely to have managerial and professional jobs, and three times more likely to live in poverty. These families earn 56 percent of whites' incomes and have an average net worth only 10 percent that of whites.

Black families headed by women are among the poorest. They earn one third of the income of the average black married couple, and while four fifths of white families are married couples, only half of black families are.

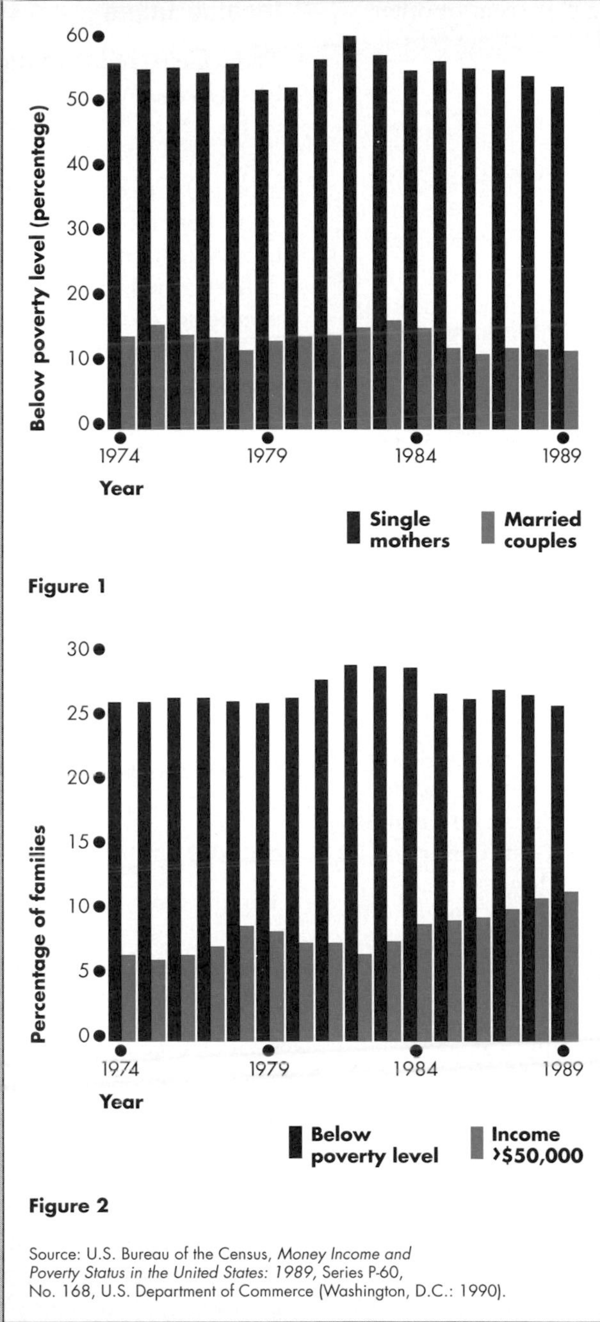

Figure 1

Figure 2

Source: U.S. Bureau of the Census, *Money Income and Poverty Status in the United States: 1989*, Series P-60, No. 168, U.S. Department of Commerce (Washington, D.C.: 1990).

Background and Analysis

The findings of the report "African Americans in the 1990s" are similar to the official U.S. Department of Commerce current population reports.

But the Commerce Department's numbers reveal no simple trends during the 1980s.

Figure 1 shows the percentage of black families living below the poverty level. That percentage increased sharply between 1979 and 1982. After 1983, the percentage declined for both married couples and single mothers.

Figure 2 shows the percentages of all black families at the two ends of the income distribution. The percentage living below the poverty level increased through 1982 and then declined, and the percentage earning an annual income in excess of $50,000 (1989 dollars) declined through 1982 and then steadily increased.

poverty level, while fewer than 5 percent of other families are.

Extreme Wealth

We've seen that there are a large number of very poor families—families living in poverty. Are there a similarly large number of extremely rich families? The answer is no. Extremely rich families are rare in comparison with extremely poor families. For example, in 1985 there were only 32,000 families in the United States whose wealth exceeded $5 million, and those families had an average wealth of $10 million each. There were, in that same year, only 375,000 families with wealth of more than $1 million but less than $5 million. These families have an average wealth of almost $2 million.

REVIEW

There is a great deal of inequality of income and wealth. The degree of inequality is illustrated by the Lorenz curve. The closer the Lorenz curve is to the line of equality, the more equal is the distribution. From 1950 to 1967, the distribution of income became more equal, and after 1967 it became less equal. The main influences on a family's income (in decreasing order of importance) are education, marital status, family size, age of householder, race, and region of residence. ◆

Income Redistribution

There are three main ways in which governments redistribute income in the United States today:

- Income taxes
- Income maintenance programs
- Provision of goods and services below cost

Income Taxes

The scale of redistribution of income achieved through income taxes depends on the form that the income taxes take. Income taxes may be progressive, regressive, or proportional. A **progressive income tax** is one that taxes income at a marginal rate that rises with the level of income. The term *marginal,* applied to income tax rates, refers to the fraction of the last dollar earned that is paid in taxes. A **regressive income tax** is one that taxes income at a marginal rate that falls with the level of income. A **proportional income tax** (also called a *flat-rate income tax*) is one that taxes income at a constant rate regardless of the level of income.

The income tax rates that apply in the United States are composed of two parts: federal and state taxes. Some cities also have an income tax—for example, New York City. There is variety in the detailed tax arrangements in the individual states, but the tax system, at both the federal and state levels, is progressive. The poorest families pay no federal income tax, the middle-income families pay 15 percent of their taxable income, and successively richer families pay 28 percent and 33 percent.

Income Maintenance Programs

Three main types of programs redistribute income by making direct payments (in cash, services, or vouchers) to people in the lower part of the income distribution. They are

- Social security programs
- Unemployment compensation
- Welfare programs

Social Security The main social security program is OASDHI—Old Age, Survivors, and Disability Health Insurance. Monthly cash payments to retired or disabled workers or their surviving spouses are paid for by compulsory payroll taxes on both employers and employees. In 1990, total social security expenditure was $236 billion, and 39 million people received an average monthly social security check of $550.

The other component of social security is Medicare, which provides hospital and health insurance for the elderly and disabled.

Unemployment Compensation To provide an income to unemployed workers, every state has established an unemployment compensation program. Under these programs, a tax is paid based on the income of each covered worker and a benefit is received by such a worker when he or she becomes unemployed. The details of the benefits vary from state to state. In 1990, more than 2 million people benefited from unemployment compensation programs and received a total of $15 billion.

Welfare Programs Four state-administered federal welfare programs provide income maintenance for families and persons who do not qualify for social security or unemployment compensation. They are

- Supplementary Security Income (SSI) program, designed to help the neediest elderly, disabled, and blind people
- Aid to Families with Dependent Children (AFDC) program, designed to help families in which a single parent (usually a mother) has no other source of financial support
- Food Stamp program, designed to help the poorest families obtain a basic diet
- Medicaid, designed to cover the costs of medical care for families receiving help under the SSI or AFDC programs

Provision of Goods and Services below Cost

A great deal of redistribution takes place in the United States through the provision of goods and services by the government that the consumer pays for through taxes rather than as a fee-for-service. One of the most important of these services is education, especially college and university education. For example, in 1991, students enrolled in the University of California system who were state residents paid annual tuition fees of around $3,000. The cost of a year's education at Berkeley or San Diego in 1991 was close to $15,000. Thus California families with a member enrolled in these institutions received a benefit from the state government of $12,000 a year. Those with several college or university students received proportionately higher benefits.

The Scale of Income Redistribution

A person's income in the absence of government redistribution is called **market income**. One way of measuring the scale of income redistribution is to calculate the percentage of market income paid in taxes and the percentage received in benefits at each income level. Making such a calculation in a way that takes into account the value of government-provided services is almost impossible. The only calculations available ignore this aspect of redistribution and focus on taxes and cash benefits.

The most recent year for which such a calculation has been done is 1980, and the results are shown in Fig. 18.5. This figure shows that the poorest 32 percent of the population receive more benefits than they pay in taxes—they receive net benefits. For example, people at the tenth percentile point (the

FIGURE 18.5

The Effect of Taxes and Income Maintenance Programs on the Distribution of Income in 1980

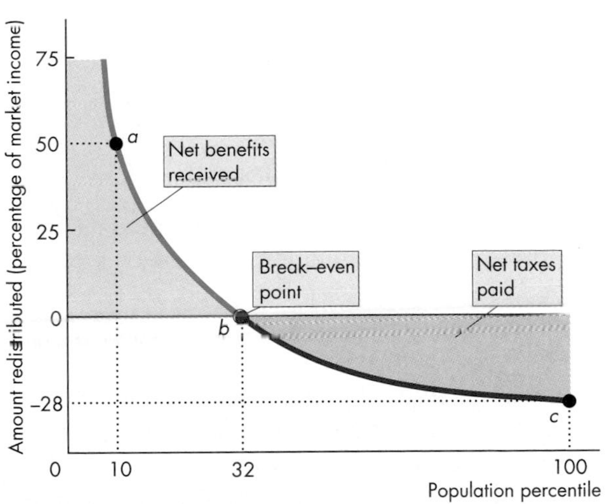

Taxes and income maintenance programs reduce the degree of inequality that the market generates. In 1980, the 32 percent of families with the lowest incomes received net benefits and the 68 percent of families with the highest incomes paid net taxes. Families at the 10th percentile received 50 percent of their income from income maintenance programs, those at the 32nd percentile broke even, and those at the top of the income distribution paid 28 percent of their incomes in taxes.

Source: Joseph A. Pechman, *Who Paid the Taxes, 1966–85?* (Washington, D.C.: Brookings Institution, 1985), 54.

point at which 10 percent are poorer and 90 percent are richer) receive benefits equal to 50 percent of their market incomes, on the average (point *a* in the figure). In contrast, the richest 68 percent of the population pay more in taxes than they receive in benefits—they pay net taxes. For example, the very richest people, on the average, pay 28 percent of their market incomes to the government in net taxes (point *c* in the figure). Those at the dividing line between these two groups break even, paying as much in taxes as they receive in benefits, on the average (point *b* in the figure).

Another measure of the scale of redistribution is provided by an examination of the sources of income of families at different points on the income distribution scale. The poorest 20 percent of families receive almost two thirds of their income in the form of payments from the government—called transfer income. Even the second 20 percent receive a third of their income in government transfers. In contrast, the richest 20 percent receive hardly anything from the government but receive a third of their income from capital—interest and dividends from financial assets. The fraction of income from that source for the other 80 percent of families is remarkably constant at about 8 percent.

Problems and Reform Proposals

Our complex and piecemeal income maintenance programs create several important problems and have led to a variety of reform proposals.

Problems

1. *Discourage work.* For many families, the income from not working and receiving benefits under programs such as Supplementary Security Income and Aid to Families with Dependent Children is larger than the income they can earn from working. In such a family, when a person gets a job and benefits are withdrawn, the family in effect pays a tax of more than 100 percent on the earnings. This marginal tax rate is higher than that paid by the wealthiest Americans, and it locks poor families in a welfare trap.
2. *Break up families and increase number of illegitimate children.* For many families, benefits are larger if the family breaks up or if a young mother is unmarried. The result is a kind of poverty trap—the limited opportunities for the children in such families increase the probability that they will become low-income earners and join the next generation of welfare recipients.
3. *Create social tensions and unfairness.* Social tensions arise because the poor often believe they should receive larger benefits, and some people, especially those who work for low incomes, resent the payment of benefits to those who don't work. Unfairness arises because, ignorant of their entitlements, some poor families miss out on benefits.
4. *Create a costly administrative superstructure.* The cost of administering welfare programs is large, there being close to half a million people employed in the public welfare departments of federal, state, and local governments.

Reform Proposals Several proposals have been made for the reform of income maintenance programs. One of these is the negative income tax. A **negative income tax** gives every family a *guaranteed annual income* and decreases the family's benefit at a specified *benefit-loss rate* as its market income increases. For example, suppose the guaranteed annual income is $10,000 and the benefit-loss rate is 25 percent. A family with no earnings receives the $10,000 guaranteed income. A family with earnings of $8,000 loses 25 percent of that amount—$2,000—and receives a total income of $16,000 ($8,000 earnings plus $10,000 guaranteed income minus $2,000 benefit loss). A family earning $40,000 receives an income of $40,000 ($40,000 earnings plus $10,000 guaranteed income minus $10,000 benefit loss). Such a family is at the break-even income level. Families with earnings exceeding $40,000 pay more in taxes than they receive in benefits.

A negative income tax is illustrated and compared with our current arrangements in Fig. 18.6. In both parts of the figure, the horizontal axis measures *market income*—that is, income *before* taxes are paid and benefits received—and the vertical axis measures income *after* taxes are paid and benefits received. The 45° line shows the hypothetical case of "no redistribution."

Part (a) shows the current redistribution arrangements—the blue line. Benefits of *G* are paid to families with no income. As incomes increase from zero to *A*, benefits are withdrawn, lowering income after redistribution below *G*. This arrangement creates a *welfare trap*—it does not pay a person to work if the

FIGURE 18.6

Comparing Current Income Maintenance Programs and a Negative Income Tax

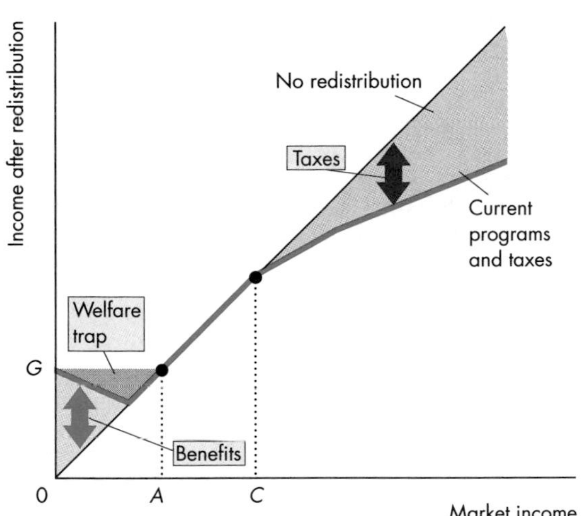

(a) Current redistribution arrangements

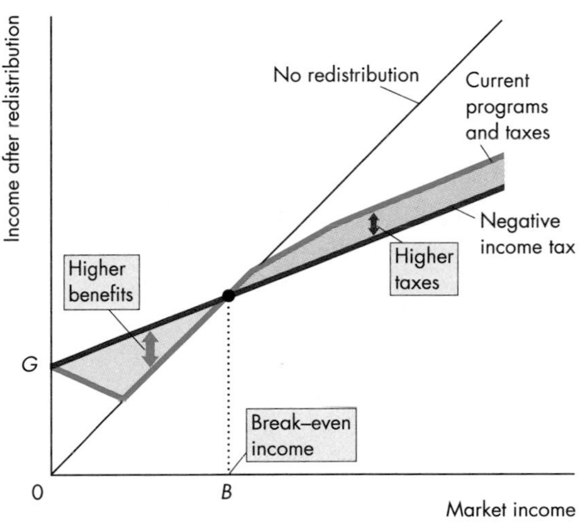

(b) A negative income tax

The 45° line shows the hypothetical case of no redistribution. Part (a) shows the current redistribution arrangements—the blue line. Benefits of *G* are paid to people with no income. As incomes increase from zero to *A*, benefits are withdrawn, *lowering* income after redistribution below *G* and creating a welfare trap—the gray triangle in the figure. In the range *A* to *C*, there is no redistribution. As incomes rise above *C*, income taxes are paid at successively higher rates.

In part (b), a negative income tax gives a guaranteed annual income of *G* and decreases benefits at the same rate as the tax rate on incomes. The red line shows how market incomes translate into income after redistribution. Families with market incomes below *B*, the break-even income, receive benefits. Those with market incomes above *B* pay taxes.

income he or she can earn is less than *A*. The welfare trap is shown as the gray triangle in the figure. Over the income range *A* to *C*, each additional dollar of market income increases income after redistribution by a dollar. At incomes greater than *C*, income taxes are paid, at successively higher rates, and income after redistribution is smaller than market income.

Part (b) shows the negative income tax. The guaranteed annual income is *G*, and the break-even income is *B*. Families with market incomes below *B* receive a net benefit (blue area), and those with incomes above *B* pay taxes (red area). You can see why such a scheme is called a negative income tax. Every family receives a guaranteed minimum income, and every family pays a tax on its earnings—losing benefits is like paying a tax—but families whose income lies below the break-even income level receive more than they pay and so, in total, pay a negative amount of tax.

A negative income tax removes the welfare trap (the gray triangle) and gives greater encouragement to low-income families to seek additional employment, even at a low wage. It also overcomes many of the other problems arising from existing income maintenance programs.

So why don't we have a negative income tax scheme? The main reason is cost. The guaranteed annual income that puts a family of four on the official *poverty* level is \$12,675. With a benefit-loss rate equal to 20 percent—a rate similar to the income tax rate for most families—the break-even income level is \$63,375. This income level is much higher than the average income, and the taxes on families with incomes above this level would increase substantially (as shown in Fig. 18.6b). Less generous negative income tax schemes are feasible, but most welfare experts believe that a better job can be done by a more piecemeal approach to reform.

The critical aspect of welfare that is receiving attention is the removal of disincentives to work and the encouragement of people on welfare to find jobs. The Family Support Act of 1988 is an attempt to do just this. Its Job Opportunities and Basic Skills (JOBS) program provides education and training; it provides incentives for young people to complete high school education; it provides benefits to two-parent families to discourage family breakups; and it requires unpaid work—*workfare*—by one member of a two-parent welfare family. It is too early to know whether the 1988 act is achieving its objectives.

REVIEW

Governments redistribute income in the United States using income taxes, income maintenance programs, and provision of goods and services below cost. The income maintenance programs are social security, unemployment compensation, and welfare. The poorest 20 percent of families receive almost two thirds of their income from the government. Existing programs tend to discourage work, encourage family breakup and illegitimacy, create social tensions, and are costly to administer. Proposals for reform include a negative income tax that gives every family a guaranteed annual income but that lowers the disincentives faced by the poor and encourages them to seek work, even if it is low paid. Removing disincentives to work and encouraging people on welfare to find jobs is also the main focus of the Family Support Act of 1988. ◆

Comparing Like with Like

In order to determine just how much inequality there is, it is necessary to compare one person's economic situation with another's. But what is the correct comparison? Should we be looking at income, or should we be looking at wealth? And should we, as we have so far, look at *annual* income, or should we look at income over some other time period—for example, over a family's lifetime?

Wealth versus Income

The main reason wealth is distributed much more unequally than income is that the data on wealth and income measure different things. The wealth data refer only to nonhuman capital—tangible assets that are traded on capital markets (such as those items analyzed in Chapter 16). The data on income distribution refer to income from all sources, not only from nonhuman capital but also from human capital. Let's explore the sources of these differences a bit more closely by looking at an example. We will begin, however, by refreshing our memory of the distinction between *income* and *wealth*.

Income and Wealth: Flow and Stock Income and wealth can be considered different ways of looking at precisely the same thing. *Wealth* is the *stock* of assets owned by an individual. *Income* is the *flow* of earnings received by an individual. It is the *flow of earnings* that results from the *stock of wealth*. It is easiest to see the relationship between income and wealth by considering an example. Suppose that Lee owns assets worth $1 million. Thus Lee's wealth is $1 million. If the rate of return on assets is 5 percent a year, then Lee will receive an income of $50,000 a year from his assets of $1 million. We can describe Lee's economic condition by saying that he has either wealth of $1 million or an income of $50,000. If the rate of return is 5 percent, these two statements are equivalent to each other.

In order to talk about the distribution of income and wealth, let's consider two individuals: Lee, who has wealth of $1 million and income of $50,000, and Peter, who has assets of $500,000. Peter and Lee have the same investment opportunities, and they invest their assets at the same rate of return—5 percent a year. Peter has an income of $25,000 (5 percent of $500,000). We can now talk about the distribution of wealth and income between Peter and Lee. Lee has wealth of $1 million compared with Peter's wealth of $500,000. Thus Lee has twice as much wealth as Peter. Lee has an income of $50,000, and Peter has an income of $25,000.

Again, Lee's income is twice as much as Peter's. Regardless of whether we compare Peter and Lee on the basis of their wealth or their income, we reach the same conclusion: Lee is twice as rich as Peter, in terms of both wealth and income.

Human Capital

So far, we have discussed only the earnings that Peter and Lee receive from their nonhuman wealth. We sometimes refer to physical and financial assets as *tangible assets* or, to contrast them with human capital, as *nonhuman capital.* What about their work effort? The earnings received from work are partly a compensation for giving up leisure time and partly a return on *human capital.* Although human capital represents intangible things like skills, we can put a value on it. We value human capital by looking at the earnings that a person can make from working over and above what would be earned by someone who has had no education or training. The extra earnings are the income from human capital. The value of human capital is the amount of money that a person would have to be given today so that, if invested, it would generate an interest income equal to the income from that individual's human capital.

Consider Peter and Lee again. Suppose now that each of them has no assets other than their productive skills. Lee earns $50,000 a year, and if the interest rate is 5 percent a year, then Lee has $1 million of human capital. A million dollars invested at an interest rate of 5 percent a year will earn $50,000 a year. Peter earns $25,000 a year, and, again, if the interest rate is 5 percent a year, Peter has human capital of $500,000. Lee earns twice as much income as does Peter, and Lee has twice as much human capital.

Human and Nonhuman Capital

We have now considered the distributions of income and wealth in two extreme cases. In the first case, Lee and Peter owned no human capital, so their entire income was generated by their financial and real assets. In the second case, Lee and Peter had only human capital—their productive skills. Most people have both nonhuman and human capital. Wealth, correctly measured, includes both of these types of capital.

No matter what the source of income—whether human capital or nonhuman capital—the distribution of wealth and income is the same when we count both human and nonhuman capital. In both the cases that we have just examined, Lee has twice the wealth and twice the income of Peter. So the distribution of wealth between Lee and Peter is identical to the distribution of income between them.

Let's finally examine the case in which Peter and Lee have both human capital and nonhuman capital. For a reason that will become apparent shortly, however, let's suppose that Peter has much more human capital than does Lee and that Lee has more nonhuman capital than does Peter. Table 18.1 sets out some hypothetical numbers to illustrate this case. As before, Lee has twice the total wealth and twice the total income of Peter. Lee's human capital is only $200,000, so Lee's labor income is just $10,000. But Lee has nonhuman capital of $800,000, which generates an income of $40,000. In contrast, Peter's wealth is almost exclusively human capital. Peter earns $24,950 of income from $499,000 worth of human capital. Peter has only $1,000 worth of tangible assets (nonhuman capital), which generates an annual income of $50.

Suppose that a national wealth and income surveyor is examining this economy comprised of Peter and Lee and observes their incomes of $25,000 and $50,000, respectively. The surveyor concludes that on the basis of income, Lee is twice as rich as Peter. The surveyor then measures their assets. The only assets that are measured are tangible assets. The surveyor observes that Lee owns $800,000 worth of such assets and Peter has $1,000 worth. The assets are listed in a distribution of wealth table, and the

TABLE **18.1**

Capital, Wealth, and Income

	Lee		Peter	
	Wealth	Income	Wealth	Income
Human capital	**$ 200,000**	**$10,000**	**$499,000**	**$24,950**
Nonhuman capital	**800,000**	**40,000**	**1,000**	**50**
Total	**$1,000,000**	**$50,000**	**$500,000**	**$25,000**

When wealth is measured to include the value of human capital as well as nonhuman capital, the distribution of income and the distribution of wealth display the same degree of inequality.

national surveyor concludes that, in terms of assets, Lee is 800 times as wealthy as Peter. The national survey concludes that wealth is much more unevenly distributed than income.

You can see that the national survey techniques measure the distribution of wealth in a way that does not include human capital. The distribution of income takes into account human capital and is the correct measure of the distribution of economic resources. Measured wealth distributions that ignore the distribution of human capital overstate the inequality among individuals.

Annual or Lifetime Income and Wealth

The income distributions that we examined earlier in this chapter are based on annual incomes. And the wealth distributions are based on measuring family wealth in a given year. There are many sources of inequality in annual income and in wealth in a given year, but these do not imply inequality over a family's entire lifetime. For example, young people earn less, on the average, than middle-aged people. Thus in a given year, a young family has a lower income than a middle-aged family. But when the young family becomes middle-aged itself, its income on the average will not differ from the current middle-aged family's income. This is an example of an inequality in annual income that does not reflect an inequality across families over their entire lifetimes. The case of wealth is more extreme. Most young families have few assets and often have debts that exceed those assets. Families with people between middle age and retirement age are at a stage in life when they're building up their assets to provide for a retirement income. Again, the older family looks wealthier than the younger family, but by the time the younger family reaches that same later stage in the life cycle, it will have accumulated assets similar in scale to those of the existing older family.

In order to compare the income and wealth situation of one family with another, it is important that we take into account the family's stage in the life cycle and not be misled by differences arising purely from that factor. To illustrate the importance of this source of inequality, we'll work through an example.

Figure 18.7 shows a family's income, consumption, and wealth over its entire life cycle. The horizontal axis in both parts measures age. The vertical axis measures thousands of dollars of income and consumption in part (a) and of wealth in part (b).

FIGURE 18.7

Life-Cycle Income, Consumption, and Wealth

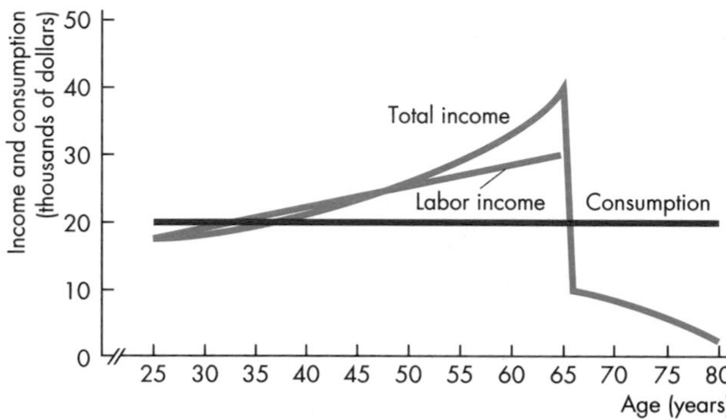

(a) Income and consumption

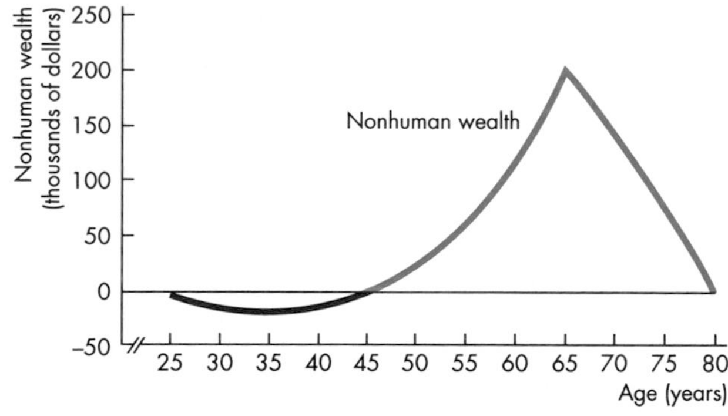

(b) Nonhuman wealth

Part (a) of the figure shows the consumption and income of a household. Consumption is constant at $20,000 a year throughout the lifetime. Labor income starts at $18,000 and gradually increases to $30,000 at retirement. After retirement, the household has no labor income. Total income is labor income plus interest on capital (on nonhuman wealth). Part (b) shows the household's nonhuman wealth. In its early years, the household is consuming more than its income and going into debt. At age 35, the household is at its maximum debt. After that time, the household gradually gets out of debt and begins to accumulate nonhuman wealth up to retirement age. After retirement the household spends its nonhuman wealth throughout the rest of its life. An economy populated by households like this one but with each household at a different stage in its life cycle will have highly unequal distributions of annual income and wealth. The small fraction of the population close to (both before and after) retirement will own almost all the economy's nonhuman wealth.

Part (a) shows the pattern of income and consumption. This family consumes at a steady rate of $20,000 a year throughout its life. The family's income from employment starts out at $18,000 a year. It gradually rises until, just before retirement, the family is earning $30,000 a year. After retirement the family's income from work is zero, but it continues to receive an income in the form of interest on the capital that it has accumulated in the years before retirement. (Some of the transactions of this hypothetical family are being ignored—for example, the purchase of a house, an automobile, and other consumer durable goods. For the purpose of this example, let's imagine that when the family bought these items, it financed their purchase by borrowing. Thus any real assets owned by the family had offsetting financial liabilities and therefore did not change the family's wealth.)

Part (b) shows the family's nonhuman wealth. At first, the family has to borrow to sustain its consumption level. As it does so, it incurs debt and also has to pay interest on the debt. The family is at its deepest point of debt at age 35. After that age, the family gradually gets out of debt and, through its sixties, starts accumulating a great deal of nonhuman wealth. After retirement, that nonhuman wealth is spent on post-retirement consumption.

Now suppose that there are two families identical to the one that we've looked at here but at different stages of the life cycle. One of these families is 25 years old, and the other is 66. If all we look at is income, we will conclude that the 25-year-old family is almost twice as well off as the 66-year-old family. If all we look at is nonhuman wealth, we will conclude that the 66-year-old family, which has accumulated assets worth $200,000, is much better off than the 25-year-old family. Yet from the point of view of consumption, these two families are identical.

If the entire population of this imaginary economy is made up of families that are identical except for their stage of the life cycle, and if there are an equal number of people at each age, we discover some startling facts about the distributions of wealth and annual income. First, let's look at the distribution of nonhuman wealth in this imaginary economy. That distribution is illustrated in Fig. 18.8. For comparison, the wealth distribution in the United States is also shown. As you can see, the Lorenz curve for the imaginary economy's wealth distribution lies inside that for the actual U.S. economy, so wealth in the United States is more unequally distributed than wealth in the imaginary economy. This means that although inequality in wealth arising from measuring different families at different points in the life cycle accounts for some of the inequality in the real world, it does not account for it all.

Second, let's consider the distribution of annual income. The Lorenz curve for the imaginary economy is plotted against that for the U.S. economy, again in Fig. 18.8. As you can see, there is more inequality in the United States than in the imaginary economy, but the difference is smaller than it appears when we do not take account of the differences in the stage of the life cycle.

This example shows that some of the measured inequality in income and wealth arises purely from the fact that different families are at different stages

FIGURE 18.8

Lorenz Curves for Imaginary and Actual Economies

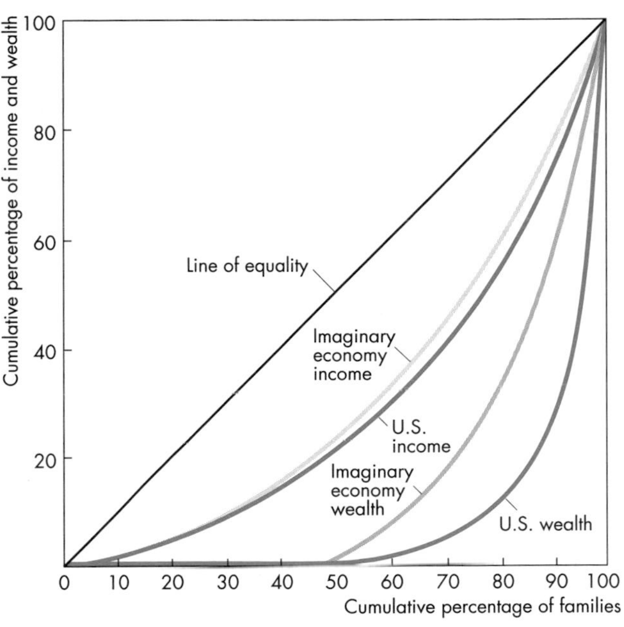

The Lorenz curves for income and wealth in the U.S. economy are shown alongside those for an imaginary economy in which everyone has the same lifetime income and consumption. The degree of lifetime inequality is exaggerated by looking only at the distribution of annual income and the distribution of nonhuman wealth.

in the life cycle. It also shows, however, that there are important remaining inequalities in income and wealth in the United States today. In the next two sections, we're going to explore the sources of those inequalities.

REVIEW

The distribution of wealth is more unequal than the distribution of income because wealth data measure only nonhuman capital—tangible assets—while income data measure income from all sources—nonhuman capital and human capital. The distributions of annual income and wealth in a given year are much more unequal than the distributions of lifetime income and average lifetime wealth. But there remains a great deal of inequality, even when comparisons are made on a lifetime basis. ◆

Factor Prices and Endowments

Each individual owns factors of production and sells the services of those factors to provide an income. A person's income is the price paid for the use of each factor multiplied by the quantity supplied. Factor prices are determined by the forces that we analyzed in Chapters 14 through 16. The amount of each factor service that an individual supplies depends partly on the endowment of the factor owned by the individual and partly on the choices that the individual makes. Let's now examine the extent to which differences in income arise from differences in factor prices and from differences in the quantity of factors that people supply.

Labor Market and Wages

We've seen that the biggest single source of income is labor. To what extent do variations in wage rates account for the unequal distribution of income? Table 18.2 helps answer this question. It sets out the average hourly earnings of private sector employees in seven industry groups in the United States in 1989. Average hourly earnings for all industries is $9.66. As a group, people working in construction earn $13.52, substantially more than the average. Those working in the retail trades earn $6.31, substantially less than the average. Within the seven

TABLE 18.2

Average Hourly Earnings in 1989

Industry	Average hourly earnings (dollars)	
Mining		**13.25**
Coal mining	**16.25**	
Non-metallic minerals	**11.25**	
Manufacturing		**10.49**
Flat glass making	**15.02**	
Children's outerwear	**5.69**	
Construction		**13.52**
Transportation		**12.26**
Pipeline transport	**16.02**	
Local transit	**8.87**	
Retail trade		**6.31**
Furniture stores	**8.36**	
Eating and drinking places	**4.75**	
Finance, insurance, and real estate		**9.54**
Services		**9.39**
Computer and data processing	**14.18**	
Laundry and cleaning	**6.57**	
Average, all industries (private sector)		**9.66**

There is considerable inequality in average hourly earnings across different occupations. But the range of inequality is much lower than the inequality of income. For example, the highest-paid group, coal miners, earn only 3.4 times the income of the lowest-paid group, those who work in eating and drinking places.

Source: Statistical Abstract of the United States: 1991, 111th edition, 408–413.

groups, there is a large variation in individual wage rates. For example, in the mining group the highest-paid work is in coal mining ($16.25 an hour) and the lowest-paid work is in non-metallic minerals ($11.25 an hour). In the lowest-paid industry, retail trades, the highest-paid work is in furniture stores ($8.36 an hour), while the lowest-paid work is in eating and drinking places ($4.75 an hour).

We can measure the spread between the highest- and lowest-paid workers in these employment categories. Take the highest-paid group of workers, coal miners, who earn $16.25 an hour on the average, and divide that wage by the wage of the lowest-paid group, those working in eating and drinking places, who earn $4.75 an hour. That calculation, which we call a wage differential, is 16.25 divided by 4.75, which is (approximately) 3.4. This differential says that the highest-paid group of workers earns 3.4 times as much as the lowest-paid group.

One of the things that wage differentials reflect is differences in skills or human capital. For example, the most highly paid people in manufacturing are the makers of flat glass (glass for windows and mirrors), while the least-paid workers make children's outerwear. The wage differential between those two categories probably reflects, to some degree, differences in training and skill. Similarly, in transportation, operating highly sophisticated pipeline-transport networks requires more skill than driving a local train or bus. Again, the wage differential reflects this difference in human capital. You can see other examples in the table.

Differences in wages are one source of income inequality. Differences in endowments of factors of production are another.

Distribution of Endowments

Although we are all endowed with equal amounts of time, we are not endowed with equal abilities. Physical and mental differences (some inherited, some learned) are such an obvious feature of human life that they hardly need mentioning. But these differences produce differences in earnings and, therefore, differences in income and wealth.

A person's earnings potential is influenced by many physical attributes such as height, weight, strength, and endurance and mental attributes such as memory, vocabulary, mathematical and logical capacity, patience, and motivation. All of these attributes appear to have what is called a normal distribution in the population, and so the distribution of ability and earnings potential is also normally distributed. An example of a normal distribution—the distribution of heights of male students—is shown in Fig. 18.9. The horizontal axis measures those heights in inches. The average height is 70 inches (5′10″). The vertical axis measures the number of students at each height. The curve in the figure traces the percentage of students at each height. The distribution is symmetric. That is, for each person above the average height, there is another person who is below the average by the same amount, so the two are like a mirror image of each other. There are more people at the average and clustered around the average than there are at the two extremes.

The range of individual ability is a major source of differences in income and wealth. But it is not the only source. If it were, the distributions of income and wealth would look like the bell-shaped curve that describes the distribution of heights in Fig. 18.9. In fact, the distribution of income in the

FIGURE 18.9

A Normal Distribution

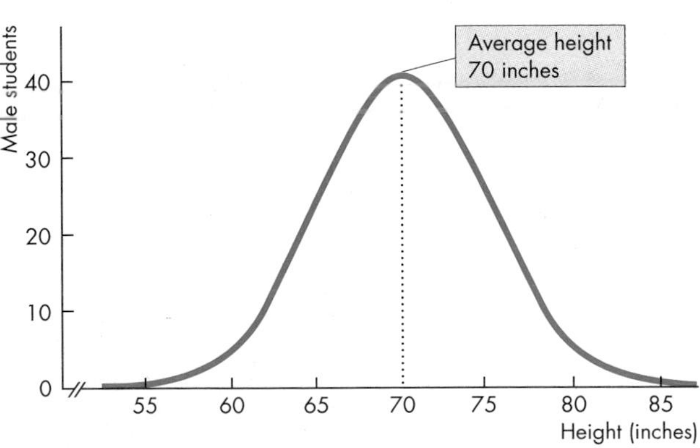

A normal distribution is shaped like a bell and is symmetric around the average. The distribution shown here is the height of a group of male students. The average height is 70 inches. For every person with a height above 70 inches, there is a mirror-image person with a height an equal distance below 70 inches. A symmetric, bell-shaped distribution describes a large number of human characteristics.

United States looks like Fig. 18.10. Figure 18.10 shows different levels of income on the horizontal axis and the percentage of families on the vertical axis. The median income is shown as $34,200. There are many more people with below-average incomes than with above-average incomes, and a relatively small number of people receive extremely high incomes. Because of this, the most common income, $29,000, is below the median, and the average income, $41,500, is above the median.

The distribution of income is skewed. A skewed distribution is one in which there are a larger number of people on one side of the average than on the other. In the case of income distribution, more people have below-average income than above-average income. The asymmetric shape of the distribution of income and wealth has to be explained by something more than the distribution of individual abilities.

FIGURE 18.10

The Distribution of Income

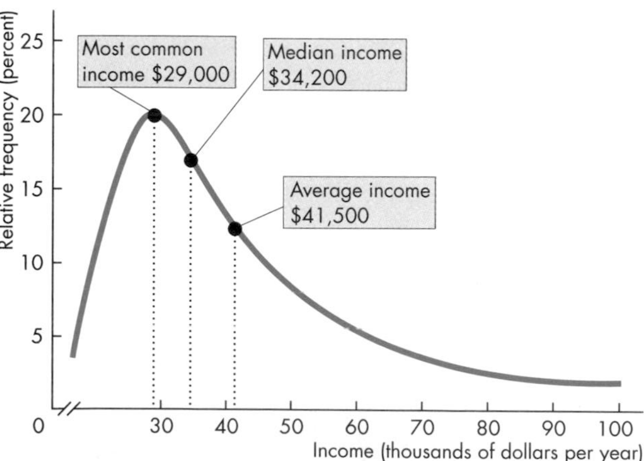

The distribution of income is unequal and is not symmetric around the average. There are many more people below the average than above the average. Also, the distribution has a long, thin upper tail representing a small number of people earning very large incomes. The particular distribution shown here is for 1989, but the features just described are persistent.

Source: Current Population Reports, Consumer Income, Series P-60, Nos. 167 and 168 (1990) and *Money Income and Poverty Status in the United States 1989,* Series P-60, No. 168 (1990) (Washington, D.C.: U.S. Department of Commerce, Bureau of the Census). The mode is my estimate.

Choices and the Distribution of Income and Wealth

A person's income and wealth depend in part on the choices that he or she makes. Households get paid for supplying factors of production—labor services, capital, and natural resources. The income received depends partly on the price of those factors of production and partly on the quantities that the household chooses to supply. In most cases, people can't influence the prices of the factors of production. They can't go to a bank and demand that it pay a higher interest rate or to the New York Stock Exchange and demand that stocks improve their performance. People can't demand higher wages than the equilibrium wage rate for their babysitting, truck driving, car washing, or taxation advice work. An investment banker earns more than a parking lot attendant because of differences in human capital, but the market still determines the wages at which labor is traded.

In contrast, people can and do choose how much of each factor to supply. They also choose whether to babysit or to work in a bank, whether to put their savings in the bank or in stocks. Each individual chooses how much of each factor to supply. So the distribution of income depends not only on factor prices but also on people's choices about supplying factors.

We are going to discover that the choices that people make exaggerate the differences among individuals. Their choices make the distribution of income more unequal than the distribution of abilities and thus make the distribution of income more skewed.

Wages and the Supply of Labor

A family's supply curve of labor shows the relationship between the quantity of labor the household supplies and the wage rate. Suppose that a family has a labor supply curve like the one shown in Fig. 18.11. At a wage rate at or below $1 an hour, the household supplies no labor. As the wage rate increases, the quantity of labor supplied increases, and at a wage rate of $9 an hour, 40 hours a week of labor are supplied. The fact that the quantity of

FIGURE 18.11

The Supply of Labor

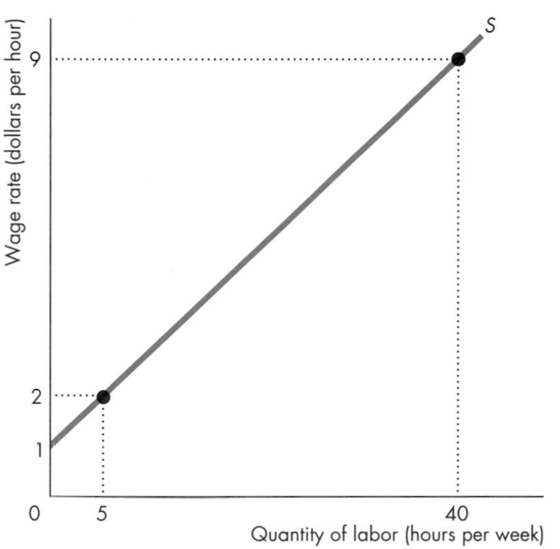

As the wage rate increases, so does the quantity of labor supplied. A person facing a wage rate of $2 an hour works for 5 hours and so earns $10 a week. A person facing a wage rate of $9 an hour works for 40 hours and earns $360 a week. The wage rate of the second person is 4.5 times that of the first, but the second person's income is 36 times larger.

FIGURE 18.12

The Distribution of Wages, Hours, and Income

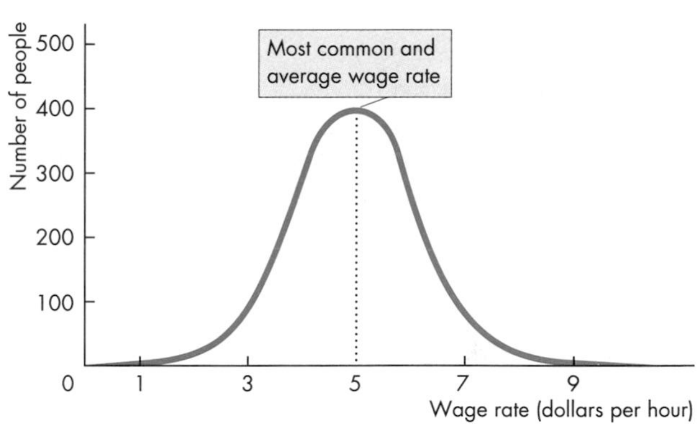

(a) Distribution of wage rates

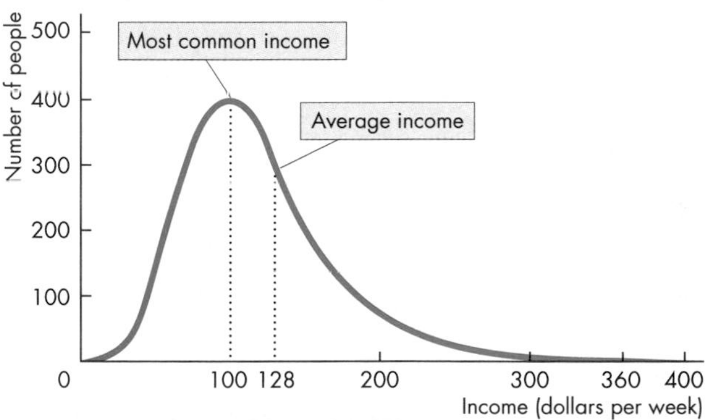

(b) Distribution of weekly incomes

Economic choices create a skewed income distribution. Part (a) graphs the distribution of wages. It is symmetric around the average wage rate of $5 an hour. Part (b) graphs the distribution of weekly income. A majority of the people earn less than the average income. The higher the wage rate, the more labor is a person willing to supply; therefore the distribution of income is more unequal and not symmetric around the average. The range of inequality in wage rates—$1 to $9—is accentuated in the inequality of weekly income—$0 to $360.

labor supplied increases as the wage rate increases results in the distribution of income being more unequal than the distribution of hourly wages. It also results in the distribution of income being skewed even if the distribution of wages is symmetric. To see why these features of the income distribution occur, let's imagine a population of 1,000 people, each one of whom has a labor supply curve like the one shown in Fig. 18.11.

Although everyone has the same labor supply curve, suppose that each person has a different marginal revenue product of labor and so is paid a different wage rate (see pp. 408–410). Figure 18.12 describes this artificial economy. Part (a) shows the distribution of marginal revenue products—and hourly wage rates—for the 1,000 people. This distribution is a normal curve—bell-shaped, like the distribution of students' heights. The average wage rate is $5 an hour, and the wage rate ranges from $1 an hour to $9 an hour.

Choices Skew the Distribution of Income

Choices make the distribution of income skewed. You can see how by looking at Fig. 18.12(b), which shows the distribution of weekly income. Since people who earn a higher hourly wage work longer hours, their weekly income is disproportionately larger than that of people with low hourly wages who work shorter hours. As you can see from Fig. 18.12(b), the most common income is $100 a week, but the average income is $128 a week. People who earn $2 an hour work only 5 hours a week for a weekly wage of $10. Those who earn $9 an hour work 40 hours a week for a wage of $360. Thus the range of income from the highest to the lowest is 36 to 1. In contrast, the wage rate of the highest paid is only 4.5 times that of the lowest paid. This example is artificial, but the point that it illustrates applies in the real world.

Savings and Bequests

Another choice that results in unequal distributions in income and wealth is savings and bequests. A **bequest** is a gift from one generation to the next. The wealthier the family, the more that family tends to save and bequeath to later generations. By making a bequest, a family can spread good and bad luck across the generations.

Savings and bequests are not inevitably a source of increased inequality. Savings that merely redistribute uneven income over the life cycle to enable consumption to be constant are an example of savings having no effect on inequality. A generation that is lucky might make a bequest to a generation that is unlucky, in which case the bequest would be a source of equality, not inequality. But there are two important features of bequests that do make intergenerational transfers of wealth a source of increased inequality:

- Debts cannot be bequeathed.
- Mating is assortative.

Debts Cannot Be Bequeathed Though a person may die with debts in excess of assets, those debts cannot be forced onto the remaining members of the family of the deceased debtor. Also, as a rule, it is difficult to incur debts in excess of assets. It is hard to find anyone willing to lend if there is not some kind of security either in the form of assets that could be seized and sold or in the form of a future earnings potential.

Because a zero inheritance is the smallest inheritance that anyone can receive, savings and bequests can only add to future generations' wealth and income potential. The vast majority of people inherit nothing or a very small amount from the previous generation. A tiny number of people inherit enormous fortunes. As a result of bequests, the distribution of income and wealth is not only more unequal than the distribution of ability and job skills but also more persistent. A family that is poor in one generation is likely to be poor in the next. A family that is enormously wealthy in one generation is likely to be enormously wealthy in the next. But there is a tendency for income and wealth to converge, across the generations, to the average. Though there can be long runs of good luck or bad luck or of good judgment or bad judgment, such long runs are uncommon across the generations. However, one additional feature of human behavior slows down convergence to the average and makes wealth and income inequalities persist—assortative mating.

Assortative Mating **Assortative mating** means that people tend to marry within their own socioeconomic class. In the vernacular, "like attracts like." Although there is a good deal of folklore that "opposites attract," perhaps such Cinderella tales appeal to us because they are so rare in reality. Marriage partners tend to have similar socioeconomic characteristics. Wealthy individuals seek wealthy partners. The consequence of assortative mating is that inherited wealth becomes more unequally distributed. (A further, and in some ways deeper, look at the evolution of the distribution of wealth across the generations is found in Our Advancing Knowledge on pp. 506–507).

Review

The unequal distribution of income arises from unequal wage rates, an unequal distribution of endowments, and the choices that people make. Wage rates are unequal mainly because of differences in skills or human capital. Endowments are unequal for a variety of environmental and biological reasons and are likely to be distributed "normally." The distribution of income is skewed—more people have below-average incomes than above-average incomes—because of the choices people make. Those with greater ability and higher wages choose to work longer hours and make a disproportionately larger income. With higher incomes they save more and bequeath more to the next generation. Marriage among groups with similar wealth reinforces these effects. ◆

We've now completed our positive analysis of inequality in the distribution of income and wealth. We've described the extent of inequality and have identified some of the reasons that it exists. But we have not attempted to make any assessment about fairness or justice in the distribution of income and wealth. Is it fair that some people can be so incredibly rich and others so abjectly poor? In the final section of this chapter, we examine the way in which economists and philosophers have tried to wrestle with this type of question.

Ideas about Fairness

We all have views about fairness and what constitutes a "fair" distribution of income and wealth. These views are diverse, and they are a source of political and philosophical debate. Throughout the ages, moral philosophers have tried to find a satisfactory theory of distributive justice. A **theory of distributive justice** is a set of principles against which we can test whether a particular distribution of economic well-being is fair. There are two broad classes of theories of distributive justice: end-state theories and process theories.

An **end-state theory of distributive justice** focuses on the justice or fairness of the outcomes or ends of economic activity. A **process theory of distributive justice** focuses on the justice or fairness of the *mechanisms* or *means* whereby the ends are achieved. For example, the belief that everyone should have exactly the same income and wealth is an end-state theory. The belief that everyone should have the same *opportunity* to earn and accumulate wealth is a process theory. Equality of income and wealth requires an equality of outcomes or ends. That is, when the process is over, everyone has to have the same income and wealth. Requiring that people have equal opportunity does not imply that they will have equal income and wealth because people will use their opportunities in different ways. Depending on how they use their opportunities and on a variety of chance events (good and bad luck), unequal income and wealth will emerge.

End-State Theories

The two leading end-state theories of distributive justice are the utilitarian and Rawlsian theories.

The **utilitarian theory** is that the fairest outcome is the one that makes the sum of the utilities of all the individuals in a society as large as possible. If Rob gets less utility than does Ian from the last dollar spent, then fairness requires that a dollar be taken from Rob and given to Ian. The reduction in Rob's utility is less than the gain in Ian's utility, so society is better off. Redistribution should take place until the marginal utility of the last dollar spent by each individual is the same. Utilitarian theories of fairness were developed in the eighteenth and nineteenth centuries by such economists as David Hume, Adam Smith, Jeremy Bentham, and John Stuart Mill.

The **Rawlsian theory of fairness** is that the fairest distribution is that which gives the least well-off person the biggest possible income. In the Rawlsian view, if the poorest person can be made better off by taking income from any other person, justice requires that such redistribution take place. The fairest distribution—according to Rawls's criterion—might be one of complete equality but not necessarily so. Because redistribution creates disincentives, too much equality could result in lower average income and a lower income for the least well-off person. The Rawlsian theory of fairness was developed in the 1960s by John Rawls, a contemporary philosopher at Harvard University, and published in his classic work, *A Theory of Justice*, in 1971.[2]

As you can see, the two end-state theories of justice differ in what they regard as the desirable end-state or desirable outcome: for the utilitarian, it is the average or sum of all the individuals that counts; for Rawls, it is the least well-off individual or individuals that count.

How Much Inequality Is Consistent with End-State Theories?

It used to be thought that an end-state theory of justice implied that complete equality in the distribution of income was the best outcome. This conclusion was reached by reasoning along the following lines: First, people are much alike in their capacity for enjoyment. (In the technical language of eco-

[2]John Rawls, *A Theory of Justice* (Cambridge, Mass.: Harvard University Press, 1971).

UNCERTAINTY and the Distribution OF INCOME AND WEALTH

Why is there such vast inequality in income and wealth? The apparently obvious answer is that there is vast inequality in luck. As Simon Kuznets saw it, a major source of good and bad luck is economic growth and the technological change that accompanies it. As technology advances, people who can move to the advancing sectors experience rising incomes, while those who remain in traditional sectors experience low income growth.

But there are many examples of bad luck that do *not* translate into poverty. We *insure* against such misfortunes as fire, earthquake, flood, and sickness. So why don't companies with names like Safety Net, Inc. spring up and do profitable business selling insurance against misfortunes such as an advance in mining technology that wipes out hundreds of jobs in the coalfields of West Virginia?

The main reason is that most poor people are poor for their entire lives and can't afford such insurance. When an advance in mining technology destroys a job, an already poor family becomes even poorer. For poverty insurance to work, the mining family's relatively lucky ancestors—say in seventeenth-century England—would have had to have bought insurance for their less fortunate heirs. With no knowledge of future technological changes and with no guarantee that insurance companies would pay up, those ancestors made no demand for such insurance.

Because we can't buy insurance against poverty, we make other arrangements that act as substitutes. One substitute is redistribution through political institutions. Another substitute is wealth. According to Robert E. Lucas, Jr., the absence of poverty insurance is the key reason why there is so much inequality. By accumulating and bequeathing assets, people spread the effects of good and bad luck across the generations. This response to the risk of poverty decreases inequality within a family but increases inequality across families.

"If the children of Noah had been able and willing to pool risks . . . among themselves and their descendants, then the vast inequality we see today . . . would not exist."

ROBERT E. LUCAS, JR.
"On Efficiency and Distribution"

Social insurance, welfare programs, progressive income taxes and subsidizing of health care, education, and declining industries are some ways in which we pool the risks of poverty. Despite these programs designed to lessen the severity of poverty and bring everyone's living standard up to some minimum level, people fall through the net. And despite advances in knowledge and a great deal of experience with alternative redistribution arrangements—in both the United States and other countries—we have not yet been able to devise and implement programs that help the truly needy, maintain strong incentives to work, and are politically acceptable.

In Western European cities such as Frankfurt, Germany, poverty is virtually invisible. There is a smaller degree of economic inequality in Germany and in other Western European countries than in the United States. Top income tax rates of more than 50 percent pay for generous benefits to the sick and unemployed. How would economic life in the United States change if a redistribution system similar to that of Germany was adopted here? What would be the effect on employment, productivity, and average incomes? Although we have learned a great deal about the effects of alternative tax and redistribution arrangements, we have not yet discovered the answers to questions such as these with sufficient certainty to allow general agreement.

UNDERSTANDING THE *Sources of Inequality*

Born in Kharkov, Russia, in 1901, Simon Kuznets had his first taste of the subjects that were to dominate the rest of his life when he was the teenaged head of the Ukraine government's economic statistics department. Kuznets arrived in the United States in 1922 and immediately enrolled in economics and statistics courses at Columbia University. He went on to a life of relentless work carefully collecting, organizing, and interpreting facts about economic growth and the distribution of income. For this work, in 1971, he became the third recipient of the Nobel Prize in economics.

From his measurements of income distribution, Kuznets discovered that the ravages of the Great Depression of the 1930s took the largest toll, surprisingly, on the richest 5 percent of the population, whose share in the income pie fell. Arguing the case for better economic data, Kuznets once said that the data available during the 1930s "were neither fish nor flesh nor even red herring."

nomics, they have the same marginal utility of income schedule.) Second, marginal utility declines with income. Therefore if a dollar is taken from a rich person and given to a poorer person, the marginal utility lost by the rich person is less than the marginal utility gained by the poorer person. Thus taking from the rich and giving to the poor increases total utility. Maximum utility occurs when each individual has the same marginal utility, a point that is reached only when incomes—after redistribution—are equal. When incomes have been equalized, total utility of the society has been maximized and "fair shares" have been achieved.

The Big Tradeoff

Although it used to be thought that justice implied complete equality, it is now recognized that there exists what has been called a "big tradeoff" between fairness and economic efficiency. The term comes from the title of a book by Arthur Okun, chairman of the Council of Economic Advisors to President Lyndon Johnson.[3]

The big tradeoff is based on the following idea. Greater equality can be achieved only by taxing productive activities. Taxing people's income from their work and savings lowers the after-tax income they receive. This lower income makes them work and save less. In economic terms, lower after-tax factor prices result in reduced factor supplies. Lower factor supplies result in smaller output, and the smaller output results in less consumption not only for the rich but also, possibly, for the poor. According to this line of reasoning, the correct amount of redistribution to undertake depends on the balance between greater equality and lower average level of consumption.

It also must be recognized that taking resources from the rich to give to the poor cannot be achieved without using resources to administer the redistribution. Tax-collecting agencies such as the Internal Revenue Service as well as all the tax accountants, auditors, and lawyers together with the welfare-administering agencies use massive quantities of skilled labor and capital equipment, such as computers, to do their work. A dollar collected from a rich person does not translate into a dollar received by a poor person. The bigger the scale of redistribution, the greater are the costs of administering the process.

When these aspects of redistribution are taken into account, it is not obvious that taking a dollar from a rich person to give to a poor person increases the welfare of the poor person. The wealth available for redistribution could be reduced to the point at which everyone is worse off. Taking account of the disincentive effects of redistribution and the resource costs of administering the redistribution is what produces the "big tradeoff." A more equally shared pie results in a smaller pie.

The Process View of Justice

The process view of distributive justice was given its most recent statement by Harvard philosopher Robert Nozick in his book *Anarchy, State, and Utopia*.[4] Nozick argues that no end-state theory of justice can be valid and that a theory of justice must be based on the justice of the mechanisms through which the distribution of income and wealth arises. Nozick argues for the justice of a system based on private property rights, in which private property can be acquired and transferred only through voluntary exchange. His argument can be illustrated with the following story.

We start out with a distribution of income that you personally regard as the best possible. Now suppose that your favorite rock singer enters into a contract with a recording company and a rock concert organizer. The deal is that she will get 5¢ on every record sold and 50¢ for every ticket sold to her rock concerts. In a given year, she sells 5 million records and 500,000 people attend her concerts. Her total income is half a million dollars. This income is much larger than the average and much larger than she had under the original "ideal" distribution.

Is she entitled to this income? Is the new distribution unfair? The original distribution was fair. You and 5 million other fans contributed 5-cent and 50-cent pieces to the income of this successful singer. Was there something illegitimate about you buying a record and attending a rock concert? Nozick believes that the rock singer is entitled to the income and that there is nothing illegitimate about you and

[3]Arthur Okun, *Equality and Efficiency: The Big Tradeoff* (Washington, D.C.: Brookings Institution, 1975).

[4]Robert Nozick, *Anarchy, State, and Utopia* (New York: Basic Books, 1974).

your friends buying records and attending rock concerts. According to Nozick's definition of fairness, the new distribution is also fair.

The philosophical debate continues and will perhaps never be settled. But this state of affairs is no deterrent to people in the practical world of politics. While moral philosophers continue their disagreement about fairness, federal, state, and local legislators create and implement laws that change the distribution of income in response to the political pressures they face.

◆ ◆ ◆ ◆ We've examined the distributions of income and wealth in the United States and seen that there is a large amount of inequality across families and individuals. Some of that inequality arises from comparing families at different stages in the life cycle. But even taking a lifetime view, there remains a great deal of inequality. Some of that inequality arises from differences in rates of pay. But economic choices accentuate those differences. Also, savings and bequests result in the growth of huge wealth concentrations over the generations. ◆ ◆ The topic of this chapter is highly political, and, as we've seen, governments attempt to redistribute income to alleviate the worst aspects of poverty. In the next three chapters, we're going to undertake a systematic study of a broad range of political economic issues and of the economic behavior of government. We'll return to questions concerning the distribution of income and wealth as part of that broader study.

SUMMARY

Distributions of Income and Wealth in the United States Today

Labor's share in income is the largest, and it has grown slightly over the years. It is approximately three quarters of total income. The distribution of wealth and income among individuals is uneven. The richest 1 percent of Americans own one third of the total wealth in the country. The next 9 percent own another one third, and the remaining 90 percent also own one third. Income is distributed less unevenly than wealth. The income distribution has changed only slightly over time. In the 1960s, inequality declined, and in the 1980s it increased. The poorest people in the United States are most likely to be older, single, black women, with less than eight years of schooling, living in the South. The richest are mostly likely to live in the Northeast and to be college-educated, middle-aged, white families with husband and wife living together. (pp. 486–492)

Income Redistribution

Governments redistribute income in the United States today through income taxes, income maintenance programs, and provision of goods and services below cost. Income taxes are progressive. The poorest families pay no federal income tax, the middle-income families pay 15 percent of their taxable income, and the richest families pay 28 or 33 percent. The income maintenance programs are social security, unemployment compensation, and welfare. The social security programs are OASDHI—Old Age, Survivors, and Disability Health Insurance—and Medicare. Welfare programs provide income maintenance for families and persons who do not qualify for social security or unemployment compensation. The poorest 32 percent of the population receive more benefits than they pay in taxes—they receive net benefits—and the richest 68 percent of the population pay more in taxes than they receive in benefits—they pay net taxes.

The main problems created by the income maintenance programs are the discouragement of work, the encouragement of family breakup, and a high rate of birth of illegitimate children, all of which create a welfare trap. Other problems are social tensions and costly welfare bureaucracy. Reform of income maintenance programs includes the provisions of the Family Support Act of 1988 and the negative income tax proposal. These reforms seek to strengthen the incentives for people on welfare to find work. (pp. 492–496)

Comparing Like with Like

In order to judge the extent of inequality, it is important that we make valid comparisons. The measured distribution of wealth exaggerates the degree of inequality because it fails to take into account the distribution of human capital. The distributions of annual income and wealth exaggerate the degree of lifetime inequality because they do not take into account the family's stage in the life cycle. (pp. 496–500)

Factor Prices and Endowments

Differences in income and wealth arise partly from differences in individual endowments and partly from differences in factor prices. Wage rates vary considerably, depending on skill and other factors. But these differences, on their own, are not enough to account for differences in the distribution of income and wealth. Those differences get exaggerated by the economic choices that people make. (pp. 500–502)

Choices and the Distribution of Income and Wealth

The economic choices that people make have an important influence on income and wealth. Attitudes toward work result in some people taking a larger amount of leisure, earning a smaller income than others, and consuming a smaller amount of goods. Also, savings and bequests affect wealth across the generations. Because of assortative mating, bequests accentuate inequality. (pp. 502–505)

Ideas about Fairness

People disagree on what constitutes a fair distribution of income. Moral philosophers have tried to resolve the issue by finding principles on which we can all agree, but agreement still has not been reached. Two broad groups of theories have been developed: end-state theories and process theories. End-state theories of fairness assert that it is the outcome that matters. Process theories assert that it is equality of opportunity that matters. (pp. 505–509)

KEY ELEMENTS

Key Terms

Assortative mating, 504
Bequest, 504
End-state theory of distributive justice, 505
Lorenz curve, 487
Market income, 493
Negative income tax, 494
Poverty, 489
Process theory of distributive justice, 505
Progressive income tax, 492
Proportional income tax, 492
Rawlsian theory of fairness, 505
Regressive income tax, 492
Theory of distributive justice, 505
Utilitarian theory, 505

Key Figures

Figure 18.2 Lorenz Curves for Income and Wealth, 487
Figure 18.4 Distribution of Income by Selected Family Characteristics in 1989, 489
Figure 18.6 Comparing Current Income Maintenance Programs and a Negative Income Tax, 495

REVIEW QUESTIONS

1 Which of the following statements describe the distributions of personal income and wealth in the United States today?

a The distributions of income and wealth are best represented by normal or bell-shaped curves.

b The richest people are more than 800 times as wealthy as the poorest people, but there is the same percentage of people at each different level of wealth.

c More than 50 percent of the population are wealthier than the average.

d More than 50 percent of the population are poorer than the average.

2 Which is more unequally distributed, income or wealth? In answering this question, pay careful attention both to the way in which income and wealth are measured by official statistics and to the fundamental concepts of income and wealth.

3 How has the distribution of income in the United States changed over the past 20 years? Which groups have gained and which have lost?

4 What is wrong with the way in which the official statistics measure the distribution of wealth?

5 Explain why the work/leisure choices made by individuals can result in a distribution of income and consumption that is more unequal than the distribution of ability. If ability is distributed normally (bell-shaped), will the resulting distribution of income also be bell-shaped?

6 Explain how the distribution of income and wealth is influenced by bequests and assortative mating.

7 What is a Lorenz curve? How does a Lorenz curve illustrate inequality? Explain how the Lorenz curves for the distributions of income and wealth in the United States economy differ from each other.

PROBLEMS

1 Imagine an economy in which there are five people who are identical in all respects. Each lives for 70 years. For the first 14 of those years, they earn no income. For the next 35 years, they work and earn $30,000 a year from their work. For their remaining years, they are retired and have no income from labor. To make the arithmetic easy, let's suppose that the interest rate in this economy is zero; the individuals consume all their income during their lifetime and at a constant annual rate. What are the distributions of income and wealth in this economy if the individuals have the following ages?

a All are 45.

b Their ages are 25, 35, 45, 55, and 65.

Is case (a) one of greater inequality than case (b)?

2 You are given the following information about income and wealth shares:

	Income shares (percent)	Wealth shares (percent)
Lowest 20%	5	0
Second 20%	11	1
Third 20%	17	3
Fourth 20%	24	11
Highest 20%	43	85

Draw the Lorenz curves for income and wealth for this economy. Explain which of the two variables—income or wealth—is more unequally distributed.

3 An economy consists of 10 people, each of whom has the following labor supply schedule:

Hourly wage rate (dollars per hour)	1	2	3	4	5
Hours worked per day	0	1	2	3	4

The people differ in ability and earn different wage rates. The distribution of *wage rates* is as follows:

Wage rate (dollars per hour)	1	2	3	4	5
Number of people	1	2	4	2	1

a Calculate the average wage rate.

b Calculate the ratio of the highest to the lowest wage rate.

c Calculate the average daily income.

d Calculate the ratio of the highest to the lowest daily income.

e Sketch the distribution of hourly wage rates.

f Sketch the distribution of daily incomes.

g What important lesson is illustrated by this problem?

PART 8

MARKETS AND GOVERNMENT

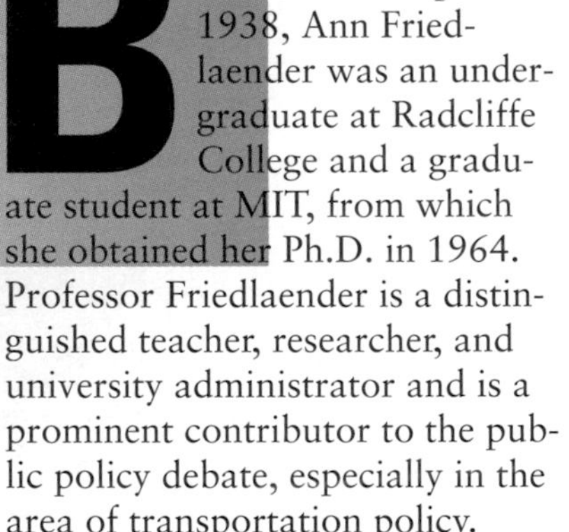

Talking with Ann Friedlaender

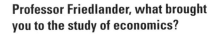

Born in Philadelphia in 1938, Ann Friedlaender was an undergraduate at Radcliffe College and a graduate student at MIT, from which she obtained her Ph.D. in 1964. Professor Friedlaender is a distinguished teacher, researcher, and university administrator and is a prominent contributor to the public policy debate, especially in the area of transportation policy.

Professor Friedlander, what brought you to the study of economics?

My parents were deeply affected by the Great Depression. I consequently grew up in a family in which economic and social issues were very much in the forefront of discussion and concern. As a freshman in college, I took a course in economic principles and was hooked. I liked the combination of analytical rigor and elegance on the one hand and the focus on important social problems on the other. As an economist, I have been primarily interested in normative issues and believe that the discipline provides a powerful analytic framework to address social questions related to distributional equity and economic efficiency.

You are well-known for your work on transportation policy. What is your report card on the deregulation of the trucking and airline industries?

I would give trucking deregulation an A+ and air deregulation a C–. Prior to deregulation, economists argued that both industries were inherently competitive with few barriers to entry or economies of scale. To the extent that rates were propped up by regulatory protection, economists believed that rates would fall and service would improve in a deregulated environment. They were right about the trucking industry. Rates have fallen, service has improved, and shippers have received benefits on the order of several billions of dollars. In the case of airlines, however, economists appear to have been wrong. Not only are there scale economies related to the hub-and-spoke networks that the airlines have adopted, but there also appear to be substantial scale economies associated with passenger reservation systems. The result has been a dramatic increase in the degree of concentration in the industry and in the number of routes served by only one or two carriers, with noncompetitive pricing on these routes as a consequence. Thus while passengers initially benefited from lower rates and increased service competition, as the industry has evolved, it has become relatively noncompetitive.

Have we done all the deregulation that needs doing?

Probably, at least for the time being. During the past 15 years, there has been substantial deregulation of the transportation industries—namely, air, truck, and rail—as well as the telecommunications, cable TV, banking and financial, natural gas, and petroleum industries, to mention just a few. For the most part, the deregulation has been successful, although it has not brought forth all of the benefits expected in the air transportation and financial industries. Although there is some evidence that state-by-state regulation of the insurance industry is not very efficient, we should probably fully digest the deregulation of the past decade before we enter into large-scale deregulation in other areas.

You mentioned cable TV, which has become a highly profitable business in recent years. Does this industry need reregulating?

There are admittedly some troubling aspects of cable TV. For example, most cities are served by a single supplier; cable rates have risen substantially above the rate of inflation; and the industry as a whole is relatively concentrated, raising questions about monopsony power with respect to the programmers. Nevertheless, I think it would be a mistake to reregulate the industry, which was deregulated in 1984. In the last few years, the number of cities with two competing cable carriers has risen substantially, and there is potential for further competition from direct broadcast satellites and microwave television. The best way to ensure that consumers get what they want is to encourage competition rather than to reregulate the industry.

Several economists over the years, including the 1991 Nobel laureate, Ronald Coase, have suggested that the frequency spectrum—the airwaves over which broadcasts and other communications are transmitted—should be allocated to the highest bidder by auction rather than allocated by committee or lottery as they are today. What is your view on this?

I agree. The frequency spectrum has enormous economic value, which will increase as it gets more

"I would give trucking deregulation an A+ and air deregulation a C–."

"The best way to ensure that consumers get what they want is to encourage competition rather than regulate the industry."

"The technology is now being developed to install sensors in automobiles that would measure peak travel in congested zones and bill drivers for their congestion costs."

crowded. Since this is a fixed resource, there is a large economic rent associated with its allocation, which some have estimated to be as large as $50 billion. For the government to give this away freely, either by lottery or by committee allocation, seems to make little sense. An auction not only would ensure that a given slot on the spectrum would go to the use that generated the highest value, but would also ensure that the potential economic rent would be utilized by society rather than accrue to a few lucky firms and their shareholders.

What are the major economic problems in urban transportation today?

The major economic problems in urban transportation are related to congestion and the underutilization of mass transit. Both of these are essentially pricing problems. During peak commuting hours, highways become congested. My use of the roads imposes an additional cost on you, and vice versa. However, other than the additional congestion costs that I incur while driving, the costs of peak and nonpeak travel are the same. Thus the costs of peak travel are too low relative to nonpeak travel, and the costs of driving are too low relative to the costs of mass transit. Consequently, during peak hours, the highway network is overutilized and the mass transit systems are underutilized.

What role can economics and economists play in designing solutions to such problems?

Economics has developed the concept of "externalities" to describe situations in which the private costs of using resources differ from the social costs. Congestion is a classic example of an externality, since in using a highway during peak hours, a given driver imposes additional time and usage costs on all other drivers that he or she does not take into account in personal cost calculations. In such a case, economics indicates that the solution is to impose a congestion charge that would equate an individual's private driving costs with the social costs that he or she imposes on all other drivers. Economists have done considerable work in estimating the difference between private marginal travel costs and social marginal travel costs. The technology is now being developed to install sensors in automobiles that would measure peak travel in congested zones and bill drivers for their congestion costs.

Do you think that the next 30 years are going to provide a set of challenges for the next generation of economists as exciting as those of the past 30 years? What will those challenges be?

During the last 30 years, much of the focus on the interactions between markets and government has been on issues related to regulation. For the most part, economists have successfully argued that markets can do a better job of allocating resources than can government or administrative agencies, and deregulation has occurred in a host of industries that had previously been tightly regulated. With a few notable exceptions, the effects of deregulation have been that rates or prices have fallen, service has improved, and consumers have gained.

Over the next 30 years, I believe that environmental issues will become increasingly important. One of the major challenges facing economists will be to devise marketlike solutions in the environmental and natural resource areas instead of the command and control regulatory solutions that have tended to dominate the debate in the past. Examples of this already exist. The recent acid rain legislation established tradable permits for pollution that can be exchanged between utilities. This seems to be an idea that is long overdue and has clear applications to a whole host of problems related to air and water pollution, hazardous waste disposal, and greenhouse gas emissions. Similarly, market solutions could be applied to fisheries and forests, which are increasingly being subject to excessive exploitation.

Another important area in which the next generation of economists could have a significant impact has to do with competitiveness and growth. Currently, there is a major debate concerning the proper role of government in stimulating research, development, and innovation. The whole question of industrial policy is really one of whether the private market can allocate resources in such a way as to sustain the growth and productivity changes needed to enable the United States to compete in world markets, and thus whether the private gains from investment and innovation fail to reflect their full social gains.

What advice would you give to a student today who is interested in pursuing a career that combines economics with public policy issues?

If you are a student interested in economics and public policy, I would urge you to get a Ph.D. in economics. This would give you a strong analytical framework that could be applied to a host of important policy questions. While a professional degree in law, management, or public policy is certainly useful, on balance, I believe that a Ph.D. in economics would give you the greatest flexibility to pursue a career in government, business, or academia. The potential impact of a career in academic economics on public policy should not be underestimated, since academics often take leaves from their universities and play central policy roles, for example as members of the Council of Economic Advisors or as senior members in the Treasury or Justice Department.

CHAPTER 19

Market Failure

After studying this chapter, you will be able to:

- Describe the range of economic actions governments undertake
- Outline the structure of the government sector of the U.S. economy
- Distinguish between a normative and a positive analysis of government economic behavior
- Define market failure and explain how it might be overcome by government action
- Distinguish between private goods and public goods
- Explain the free-rider problem
- Explain how government provision of public goods avoids the free-rider problem
- Explain how property rights and taxes and subsidies may be used to achieve a more efficient allocation of resources when externalities are present

G OVERNMENT IS BIG BUSINESS—ONE OF THE BIGGEST. IN 1990, the U.S. federal government employed more than 5 million people and spent more than $1 trillion. State and local governments employed a further 14 million people, spending $0.8 trillion between them. Independent government agencies employed yet another million people. What do all these people and all these dollars do for us? Is the government sector of our economy simply too big? Is government, as conservatives often suggest, "the problem"? Or, despite its enormous size, is government too small? Is more government intervention the solution to many outstanding problems? ◆◆ Governments provide an enormous array of goods and services. Some are intangibles like laws and their enforcement; others are tangibles like schools and highways. Why does government supply some goods and not others? You've probably seen a Wells Fargo security truck delivering cash to your local bank. Why does Wells Fargo, a private company, supply security services to banks, while the local police department provides similar services to residential neighborhoods, streets, and highways? What is so special about roads and highways, nuclear weapons, and judicial services that results in such services always being provided by government and never by private firms? ◆◆ We've heard a lot recently about our endangered planet. The massive quantities in which we burn fossil fuels—coal, natural gas, and oil—have immediate effects on the atmosphere that result in acid rain. And there are harder to measure but potentially more serious effects on the chemical balance of the earth's atmosphere, increasing the proportion of carbon dioxide and reducing the proportion of other elements. It is

Government—The Solution or the Problem?

predicted that the continuation of this process will result in a gradual warming of the planet—the so-called greenhouse effect. It is also predicted that the persistent and large-scale use of chlorofluorocarbons (CFCs) will cause irreparable damage to the earth's ozone layer, thereby exposing us to an increased amount of radiation. These environmental issues are simultaneously everybody's problem and nobody's problem. Everyone is put at risk by the continued damage to our atmosphere, and yet no one individual can take the necessary action to protect the environment. What, if anything, might government do to protect our environment? How can the government help us to take account of the damage that we cause others every time we turn on our heating or air conditioning systems?

◆ ◆ ◆ ◆ We've seen that households' and firms' choices are influenced by actions taken by government. For example, rent controls and minimum wage laws influence the way competitive markets operate. We've also seen that many markets are not competitive. They have monopoly elements, and those elements often arise from legal restrictions imposed by government. In this chapter and the next two, we turn our attention to the economic choices that governments make and to the effects of those choices on the economy. ◆ ◆ In this chapter, our main concern is to describe the government sector and explain how the market economy, in the absence of a government, would fail to achieve an efficient allocation of resources. We also provide a brief sketch of the economic theory of government behavior that will be elaborated and applied in the next two chapters.

The Government Sector

We'll begin by describing the anatomy of the government sector.

The Structure and Scale of Government

The government sector of the U.S. economy consists of more than 80,000 separate organizations, some tiny like the Yuma, Arizona, School District and some enormous like the U.S. federal government. The total government sector of the U.S. economy accounts for 35 percent of spending on goods and services and 36 percent of total employment.

There are three levels of government in the United States: federal, state, and local. The federal government spends more than the state and local governments do—about $1 trillion a year—but local government has the highest number of employees—close to 10 million. Each level of government is organized into branches and departments. The branches of government are the legislative, judicial, and executive branches, and the departments are the bureaucracies that take care of the day-to-day business of government. The bulk of the federal government's economic activity takes place in the Departments of Defense, Health and Human Services, and Treasury. Including military personnel, the Defense Department employs almost two thirds of total government-sector employees and spends almost one third of the budget. The Department of Health and Human Services, which administers welfare programs (including social security), spends more than one third of the total budget. Even the Treasury Department spends close to one fifth of the budget (mainly on debt interest and tax collection).

The Scale and Growth of Government

The scale of government has changed dramatically over the years. In 1940, for example, government-sector expenditure accounted for less than 20 percent of the economy's total expenditure, while in 1992 it had reached 35 percent. But the growth of government expenditure over the past 50 years probably understates the growth of the importance of government in economic life. That importance stems partly from the government's expenditure and partly from the extent of the laws and regulations passed by government that affect the economic actions of individual households and firms. We look at this aspect of government in Chapter 21, where we study regulation and antitrust.

Our main task in this chapter is not to describe the anatomy of government and the pace at which it has grown but to analyze the failure of markets to achieve *allocative efficiency* and to explore the role of government in coping with market failure. Before we embark on that main task, we're going to take an overview of the alternative approaches that economists use to study the economic behavior of government.

Economic Theory of Government

We all have opinions on political matters, and some of those opinions are strongly held. As students of economics, our task is to understand, explain, and predict the economic choices that the government sector makes. Although we cannot suppress our political views, it is important, if we are to make progress in studying political behavior, to continually remind ourselves of the important distinction between positive and normative analysis. We first reviewed that distinction in Chapter 1 (pp. 17–18). But because the distinction is so important for the economic study of political behavior, let's remind ourselves of what that distinction is.

Positive and Normative Analysis An economic analysis of government choices may be either *positive* or *normative*. The positive analysis of government seeks to explain the reasons for and effects of government economic choices. A normative analysis seeks to evaluate the desirability of a government action and argues for or against some particular proposal. Positive analysis seeks to understand what *is*; normative analysis seeks to reach conclusions on what *ought* to be. The economic analysis used in both of these activities is similar. But the use to which the analysis is put differs.

Here we undertake a positive study of government action; that is, we seek to understand the reasons for and the effects of the actions that we see being undertaken by governments in the United States today. We do not seek to establish the desirability of any particular course of action or to argue for or against any particular policy.

All government economic action stems from two aspects of economic life:

- Market failure
- Redistribution

Market Failure

One explanation for government intervention in the economy is market failure. **Market failure** is the inability of an unregulated market to achieve, in all circumstances, allocative efficiency. There are three types of situations in which market failure arises:

- The provision of goods and services that we consume in common with everyone else
- The production of goods and services that give rise to *external costs* or *external benefits*
- The restriction of output by monopolies and cartels

In all three cases, the unregulated market produces waste in the sense that a different allocation would result in producing more of some goods without producing less of others and could make someone better off without making anyone worse off. It is important not to take this last statement as being normative. The presence or absence of waste is a positive matter. It is a statement about what *is*. A prediction that government action will (or will not) occur to eliminate such waste is also a positive statement. The proposition that government *ought* (or ought not) to intervene to eliminate waste is normative. In dealing with market failure, it is its positive aspects that will be our concern.

Redistribution

Another explanation for government intervention in the economy is to redistribute income and wealth. Such redistribution is usually justified on the basis of some notion of equity or distributive justice, which we discussed in Chapter 18. But not all redistribution is explained in this way. The creation of monopoly and government protection of cartels also result in the redistribution of income and wealth. And the *rent-seeking* activities that we described in Chapter 12 have an important political dimension.

Again, it is important to keep the distinction between positive and normative aspects of the redistributive role of government clear. The proposition that most people believe that the market distributions of income and wealth are unfair is positive. The proposition that government intervention can redistribute income from the rich to the poor is also positive. The statement that the government *ought* to redistribute income and wealth is normative. We have described the scale of income redistribution in Chapter 18, and we will study it further in Chapter 20. When we do so, our focus will be entirely on its positive aspect.

Public Interest and Public Choice

There are two broad classes of economic theories of government behavior:

- Public interest theories
- Public choice theories

A **public interest theory** of government behavior predicts that government action will take place to eliminate waste and achieve an efficient allocation of resources. A **public choice theory** predicts that the behavior of the government sector is the outcome of individual choices made by voters, politicians, and bureaucrats interacting with each other in a political marketplace. According to public interest theories of government, whenever there is market failure, government action can be designed to eliminate the consequences of that failure and to achieve allocative efficiency. According to public choice theories, matters are not that simple. Not only is there the possibility of market failure (arising in the situations that we have outlined above), but there is also the possibility of "government failure." That is, it is possible that when each voter, politician, and bureaucrat pursues his or her own best interests and interacts in the political "marketplace," the resulting "public choice" no more achieves the elimination of waste and the attainment of allocative efficiency than does an unregulated market. Understanding why not is the main topic of Chapter 20.

In the next section, we're going to explain more fully the economic role of the government arising from two of the sources of market failure—the provision of goods and services that we consume in common with everyone else and the production of goods and services that create external costs or external benefits. The other source of market failure, arising from monopoly and cartels and from the government regulation of such industries, is dealt with in Chapter 21.

Public Goods

Why does the government provide certain goods and services, such as a legal system, a system of national defense, schools and highways, and public health services? Why don't we simply leave the provision of these goods and services to private firms that sell their output in markets? How much national defense would we have if a private firm, Star Wars, Inc., had to compete for our dollars in the marketplace in the same way that McDonald's and Coca-Cola do?

Most of the answers to the above questions lie in the distinction between private goods and public goods.

Private Goods and Public Goods

A **private good** is a good or service each unit of which is consumed by only one individual. An example of a private good is a can of soda. There are two important features of a private good. The first feature is called *rivalry*. Rivalry emphasizes the idea that one person's consumption can take place only at the expense of another person's. If you increase your consumption of soda by one can, other things being equal, someone else has to consume one can less. The second feature of a private good is called *excludability*. Once you have bought a can of soda, the soda is yours to do with as you choose. You can exclude others from using it.

A **pure public good** is a good or service each unit of which is consumed by everyone and from which no one can be excluded. An example of a pure public good is the national defense system. There are two important features of a pure public good that parallel the two features that we identified concerning a private good. The first feature is called *nonrivalry*. One person's consumption of a pure public good does not reduce the amount available for someone else. For example, your consumption of the security provided by a national defense system does not decrease the security of anyone else. The second feature is called *nonexcludability*. No one can be excluded from the additional security that every citizen enjoys from the national defense system.

Many goods lie in between a pure public good and a private good. Such goods are called **mixed goods.** An example of a mixed good is a city street. A city street is like a pure public good until it becomes congested. One more car or truck on a street with plenty of space on it does not reduce the consumption of transportation services of anyone else. But once the street becomes congested, the addition of one more user lowers the quality of the service available for everyone else—it becomes like a private good.

Pure public goods and mixed goods with a large public element—referred to as public goods—give rise to what is called the free-rider problem.

Free Riding

A **free rider** is someone who consumes a good without paying for it. The **free-rider problem** is the tendency for the scale of provision of a public good to be too small if it is produced and sold privately. The free-rider problem arises because there is no incentive for a person to pay for a good if the payment makes no difference to the quantity of the good that the person is able to consume. Public goods are such goods. To see why, let's look at an example.

Imagine that an effective antimissile laser weapon has been developed. One of these new weapons can attack and destroy 400 intercontinental ballistic missiles within seconds of their being launched. The larger the number of antimissile laser weapons deployed, the larger is the number of missiles destroyed. Potential enemies have 1,500 missile launchers, and four of the new weapons can eliminate all of them. Three can do a pretty good job, and even two can severely limit the amount of damage done by missiles that get through the laser defense.

But the new weapons system is very expensive. To build it, resources have to be diverted from peaceful space programs and from the development of other productive uses of lasers in medicine. As a result, the larger the number of weapons installed, the greater is their marginal cost.

Our task is to work out the scale on which to install this new defense system to achieve allocative efficiency. We'll then examine whether private provision can achieve allocative efficiency, and we'll discover that it cannot—that there is a free-rider problem.

Benefits and Costs

The benefits provided by a weapons system are based on the preferences and beliefs of the consumers of the services of that system. The costs are based on technology and the prices of the factors of production used to produce the system. When studying private goods, we observed that the value of a good to an individual is the maximum amount that the person is willing to pay for one more unit of the good. We worked out this value from the individual's demand curve. That is, the demand curve tells us the quantity demanded at a given price or, for a given quantity, the maximum price that is willingly paid for the last unit bought. We can work out the value a person places on a public good in a similar manner. That is, the value that a person places on a public good is the maximum amount willingly paid for one additional unit of the good.

To calculate the maximum amount that a person is willing to pay for one more unit of a public good, we first need to establish that person's total benefit schedule. **Total benefit** is the total dollar value that a person places on a given level of provision of a public good. The greater the scale of provision, the larger is the total benefit. The table in Fig. 19.1 sets out an example of the total benefits to Lisa and Max of different scales of provision of the proposed antimissile lasers. Lisa and Max believe that the weapons system reduces the chance of a nuclear war occurring and, if it does occur, increases the chance of preventing nuclear warheads from reaching their targets. The more lasers there are in place, the greater is the degree of security, but up to a maximum level. Each additional laser is believed to provide less additional security than the previous one. The increase in total benefit resulting from a unit increase in the scale of provision of a public good is called its **marginal benefit.** The marginal benefits to Lisa and Max are calculated in the table in Fig. 19.1. As you can see, the greater the scale of provision, the smaller is the marginal benefit. By the time 4 lasers are deployed, Lisa perceives no additional benefits, and Max perceives only $10 worth. Lisa's and Max's marginal benefits are graphed as MB_L and MB_M, respectively, in parts (a) and (b) of the figure.

The marginal benefit of a public good is the maximum amount that a person is willing to pay for one more unit of the good. This maximum amount varies with the quantity of the good consumed. The greater the quantity, the smaller is the maximum amount that will be paid for one more unit.

Part (c) of the figure shows the economy's marginal benefit curve, *MB* (where the economy has only two people, Lisa and Max). The marginal benefit curve of a public good for an individual is similar to the demand curve for a private good. But there is an important difference between the economy's marginal benefit curve for a public good and the market demand curve for a private good. To obtain the market demand curve for a private good, we add up the quantities demanded by each individual at each price. In other words, we sum the individual

FIGURE 19.1

Benefits of a Public Good

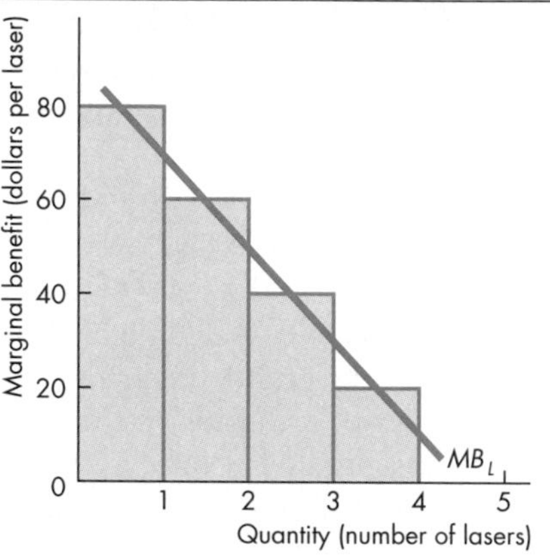

(a) Lisa's marginal benefit curve

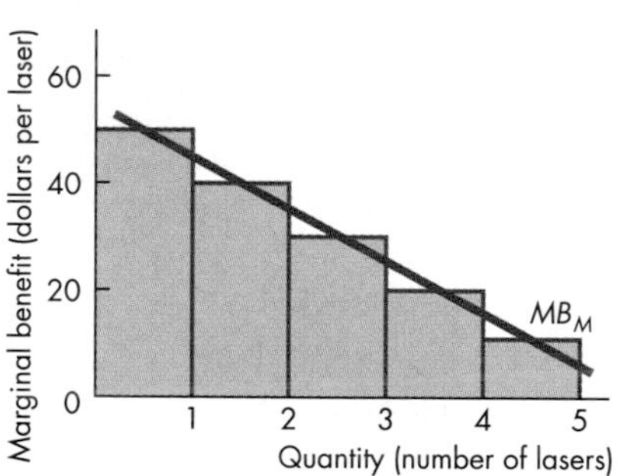

(b) Max's marginal benefit curve

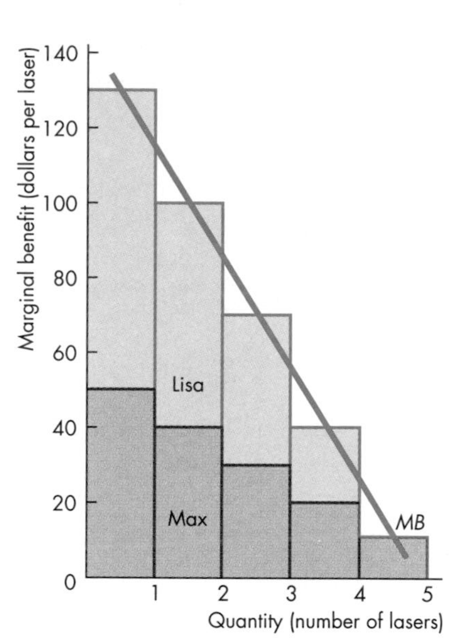

(c) Economy's marginal benefit curve

	Lisa		Max		Economy	
Quantity (number of antimissile lasers)	Total benefit (dollars)	Marginal benefit (dollars per laser)	Total benefit (dollars)	Marginal benefit (dollars per laser)	Total benefit (dollars)	Marginal benefit (dollars per laser)
0	**0**		**0**		**0**	
		80		**50**		**130**
1	**80**		**50**		**130**	
		60		**40**		**100**
2	**140**		**90**		**230**	
		40		**30**		**70**
3	**180**		**120**		**300**	
		20		**20**		**40**
4	**200**		**140**		**340**	
		0		**10**		**10**
5	**200**		**150**		**350**	

The table shows various scales of provision of an antimissile laser defense system. It also lists the total benefits accruing to Lisa, Max, and the economy (comprised of only Lisa and Max) from different scales of provision. The table also calculates the marginal benefit—the change in the total benefit resulting from a unit increase in the scale of provision to Lisa, Max, and the economy. The marginal benefits are graphed in the figure, for Lisa in part (a) and for Max in part (b). The marginal benefit to the economy at each level of provision is the sum of the marginal benefits to each individual and is shown in part (c). The marginal benefit curves are MB_L for Lisa, MB_M for Max, and MB for the economy.

demand curves horizontally (see Fig. 7.1, p. 158). In contrast, to find the economy's marginal benefit curve of a public good, we sum the marginal benefit of each individual at each quantity of provision. That is, we sum the individual marginal benefit curves vertically. The resulting marginal benefit for the economy comprised of just Lisa and Max is calculated in the table, and the economy's marginal benefit curve is graphed in part (c)—the curve labeled *MB*.

An economy with just two people would not buy any antimissile lasers—their total benefits fall far short of their cost. But an economy with 250 million people might. To determine the efficient scale of provision, consider the example set out in Fig. 19.2. The second and third columns of the table show the total and marginal benefits to an entire economy consisting of 250 million people. The next two columns show the total and marginal cost of producing antimissile lasers. These costs are opportunity costs and are derived in exactly the same way as the costs associated with the production of sweaters that we studied in Chapter 10. The final column of the table shows net benefit. **Net benefit** is total benefit minus total cost. The efficient scale of provision is the one that maximizes net benefit.

Total benefit and total cost are graphed as the total benefit curve, *TB*, and total cost curve, *TC*, in part (a). Net benefit is also visible in that part of the figure as the vertical distance between the two curves. Net benefit is maximized when that distance is at its largest, a situation that occurs at a scale of provision of 2 lasers. This is the efficient scale of provision.

Another way of describing the efficient scale of provision is in terms of marginal benefit and marginal cost. The marginal benefit and marginal cost of lasers are graphed as the marginal benefit curve, *MB*, and marginal cost curve, *MC*, in part (b). When marginal benefit exceeds marginal cost, net benefit increases if the quantity produced increases. When marginal cost exceeds marginal benefit, net benefit increases if the quantity produced decreases. When marginal benefit equals marginal cost, net benefit cannot be increased—it is at its maximum possible level. Thus when marginal benefit equals marginal cost, allocative efficiency has been achieved.

Now that we have worked out the efficient scale of provision of a public good, let's go on to see how much of such a good would be provided by a private producer.

Private Provision

We have now worked out the scale of provision of a national defense system that maximizes net benefit. Would a private firm—Star Wars, Inc.—deliver that scale of provision? It would not. To do so, it would have to collect $15 billion to cover its costs—or $60 from each of the 250 million people in the economy. But no one would have any incentive to buy his or her "share" of the laser weapon system. Each person would reason as follows: The number of antimissile lasers provided by Star Wars, Inc. is not going to be affected by my $60. But my own private consumption is going to be affected by whether or not I pay. If I do not pay, I will enjoy the same level of security from the laser weapons and more of other goods. Therefore it pays me to keep my $60 and spend it on other goods, my consumption of which is affected by my spending on them. In other words, it pays me to free ride on the public good and buy private goods.

Since everyone reasons in the same manner, no one pays for a share in the output of Star Wars, Inc. The firm has zero revenue and has no incentive to produce anything. The output of antimissile lasers is zero.

Public Provision

Suppose that the people in this economy have instituted a government that makes the following proposition: the government will collect $60 from each person and will spend the resulting $15 billion to provide 2 antimissile lasers. Will the people vote for this proposition? Clearly, they will. If there is no antimissile system (the output of Star Wars, Inc.), the marginal benefit of installing 1 laser greatly exceeds its marginal cost. By proposing to provide 2 antimissile lasers, the government is offering each voter a level of security that maximizes net benefit. The voters obtain a benefit of $35 billion—$140 each—for a total cost of $15 billion—$60 each. Since the voters recognize this as an improvement over the zero provision by Star Wars, Inc., they will vote for it.

Whether or not actual governments produce public goods on a scale that maximizes net benefit is something that we examine in Chapter 20. But we have established a key proposition: a government is able to provide any public good on a scale larger than that provided by a private producer.

FIGURE 19.2

The Efficient Scale of Provision of a Public Good

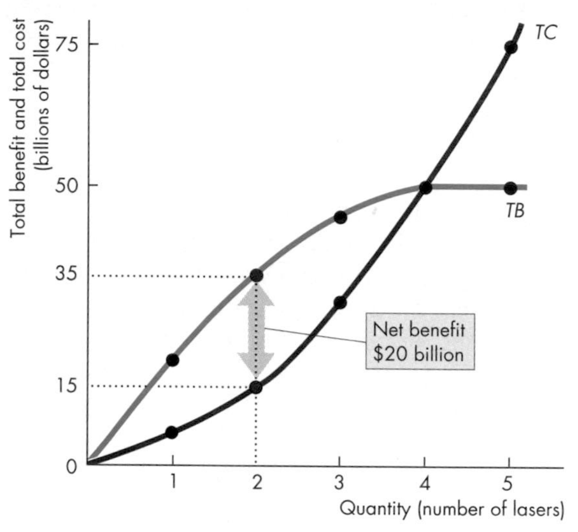

(a) Total benefit and total cost curves

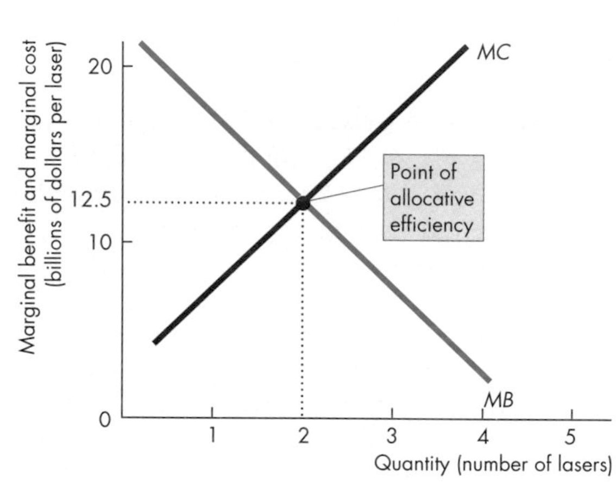

(b) Marginal benefit and marginal cost curves

Quantity (number of antimissile lasers)	Total benefit (billions of dollars)	Marginal benefit (billions of dollars per laser)	Total cost (billions of dollars)	Marginal cost (billions of dollars per laser)	Net benefit (billions of dollars)
0	**0**		**0**		**0**
		20		**5**	
1	**20**		**5**		**15**
		15		**10**	
2	**35**		**15**		**20**
		10		**15**	
3	**45**		**30**		**15**
		5		**20**	
4	**50**		**50**		**0**
		0		**25**	
5	**50**		**75**		**–25**

The table shows the total benefit and marginal benefit to the entire economy of various scales of provision of a laser weapons system. It also shows the total cost and marginal cost of the various scales of provision. Total benefit and total cost are graphed in part (a) as the total benefit curve, *TB*, and the total cost curve, *TC*. Net benefit is visible as the vertical distance between these two curves and is maximized when 2 lasers are installed. Part (b) shows the marginal benefit curve, *MB*, and marginal cost curve, *MC*. When marginal cost equals marginal benefit, net benefit is maximized and allocative efficiency is achieved.

REVIEW

If people make their own decisions about the provision of public goods and buy those goods in private markets, there is a free-rider problem. It is in everyone's individual interest to free ride, with the result that the scale of provision of the goods is smaller than that required for allocative efficiency. A government that balances marginal cost and marginal benefit provides the public good on a scale that achieves allocative efficiency. ◆

Externalities

An **externality** is a cost or a benefit arising from an economic transaction that falls on a third party and that is not taken into account by those who undertake the transaction. For example, when a chemical factory dumps its waste products into a river and kills the fish, it imposes an externality—in this case, an external cost—on the fisherman who lives downstream. Since these costs are not borne by the chemical factory, they are not taken into account in deciding whether to dump waste into the river and, if so, how much. When a person drives a car that burns leaded gasoline and does not have a catalytic converter, an externality—again, an external cost—is imposed on everyone who tries to breathe the unbreathable air. When a homeowner fills her garden with beautiful spring bulbs, she generates an externality—in this case an external benefit—for all the joggers and walkers who pass by. In deciding how much to spend on this lavish display, she takes into account only the benefits accruing to herself.

Two particularly dramatic externalities have received a lot of attention in recent years. The first arises from the use of chlorofluorocarbons (CFCs). These manufactured chemicals are used in a wide variety of products—from coolants in refrigerators and air conditioners to plastic phones to cleaning solvents for computer circuits. Though the precise chemistry of the process is not understood and is even the subject of dispute, many atmospheric physicists believe that CFCs damage the atmosphere's protective ozone layer. Discoveries of depleted ozone over Antarctica in 1983 have heightened fears of extended ozone depletion.

The second externality arises from burning fossil fuels that add carbon dioxide and other gases to the atmosphere, which prevent infrared radiation from escaping, resulting in what has been called the "greenhouse effect." If the greenhouse scenario turns out to be correct, it is predicted that much of the Midwest will become a dustbowl and many eastern and Gulf Coast regions will disappear under an expanded Atlantic Ocean (see Reading Between the Lines, pp. 526–527).

When you take a cold drink from the refrigerator or switch on the air conditioner on a steamy August evening, you do not take into account the consequences of your actions on global atmospheric matters. You compare the private benefits to yourself of drinking the cold can of soda or having a comfortable night's sleep with the cost that *you* have to incur. You do not count the costs of an increase in the incidence of skin cancer as part of the price that has to be paid for the cold soda.

Externalities are not always negative—they are not always external costs. In fact, many activities bring external benefits. Education is a good example. Not only do more highly educated people derive benefits for themselves in the form of higher incomes and the enjoyment of a wider range of artistic and cultural activities, but they also bring benefits to others through social interaction. But in deciding how much schooling to undertake, we make our calculations on the basis of the costs borne by us and the benefits accruing to us as individuals. We do not take into account the extra benefits that we're creating for others.

Health services also create external benefits. The pursuit of good health and personal hygiene reduces the risk that people with whom we come into contact will be infected by transmitted diseases. Again, in making economic choices about the scale of resources to devote to health and hygiene, we take account of the costs borne by ourselves and the benefits accruing to ourselves and not the greater benefit that our actions bring to others.

A Global Externality

TIME, January 2, 1989

Feeling the Heat

by Michael D. Lemonick

For more than a decade, many scientists have warned that cars and factories are spewing enough gases into the atmosphere to heat up the earth in a greenhouse effect that could eventually produce disastrous climatic changes.

Carbon dioxide is released in large quantities when wood and such fossil fuels as coal, oil and natural gas are burned. As society industrialized, coal-burning factories began releasing CO_2 faster than plants and oceans, which absorb the gas, could handle it. In the early 1900s, people began burning oil and gas at prodigious rates. And increasing population led to the widespread cutting of trees in less developed countries. These trees are no longer available to soak up excess CO_2, and whether they are burned or left to rot, they instead release the gas. By the late 1800s atmospheric CO_2 had risen to between 280 and 290 parts per million. Today it stands at 350 p.p.m., and by 2050 it could reach 500 to 700 p.p.m., higher than it has been in millions of years.

By far the most efficient and effective way to spur conservation is to raise the cost of fossil fuels. Current prices fail to reflect the very real environmental costs of pumping carbon dioxide into the air. The answer is a tax on CO_2 emissions—or a CO_2 user fee, if that is a more palatable term. The fee need not raise a country's overall tax burden; it could be offset by reductions in income taxes or other levies.

Imposing a CO_2 fee would not be as difficult as it sounds. It is easy to quantify how much CO_2 comes from burning a gallon of gasoline, a ton of coal or a cubic yard of natural gas. Most countries already have gasoline taxes; similar fees, set according to the amount of CO_2 produced, could be put on all fossil-fuel sources. At the same time, companies could be given credits against their CO_2 taxes if they planted trees to take some of the CO_2 out of the air.

A user fee would have benefits beyond forcing a cutback in CO_2 emissions. The fuels that generate carbon dioxide also generate other pollutants, like soot, along with nitrogen oxides and sulfur dioxide, the primary causes of acid rain. The CO_2 tax would be a powerful incentive for consumers to switch from high-CO_2 fuels, such as coal and oil, to power sources that produce less CO_2, notably natural gas. When burned, methane generates only half as much CO_2 as coal, for example, in producing the same amount of energy. . . .

The Essence of the Story

The amount of carbon dioxide (CO_2) in the earth's atmosphere has been increasing and continues to do so.

In the late nineteenth century, atmospheric carbon dioxide was between 280 and 290 p.p.m.; in the late 1980s, it was 350 p.p.m.; by 2050, it could reach 500 to 700 p.p.m.

The most effective method for controlling the greenhouse effect is to impose a tax on carbon dioxide emissions.

Background and Analysis

The marginal private cost of generating electricity by using fossil fuels is the curve *MPC* in Figs. 1(a) and 2(a). The marginal cost of generating electricity using solar power is the curve *MC* in Figs. 1(b) and 2(b). The supply curve of electricity is *S* and the demand curve is *D* in Figs. 1(c) and 2(c).

The power generated by solar energy has no externalities.

Generating power by using fossil fuel creates a carbon dioxide buildup with a possible greenhouse effect that imposes potentially large social costs. The marginal social cost of generating electricity using fossil fuels, including the external costs of the greenhouse effect, is the curve *MSC* in Figs. 1(a) and 2(a).

With no intervention (Fig. 1), equilibrium occurs at price P_0 and quantity Q_0; only fossil fuels are used; the marginal social cost is MSC_0, which exceeds the price P_0; there is allocative inefficiency—too much electricity is generated.

If a CO_2 tax is imposed equal to the external costs (Fig. 2), fossil fuel producers of electricity face costs shown by the curve labeled *MPC* + *tax* = *MSC*.

The market supply curve becomes the curve labeled *S* + *tax*.

Equilibrium occurs at price P_1 and quantity Q_1; Q_F is produced by fossil fuels and Q_S by solar energy; marginal social cost is MSC_1, which equals the price P_1; allocative efficiency is achieved.

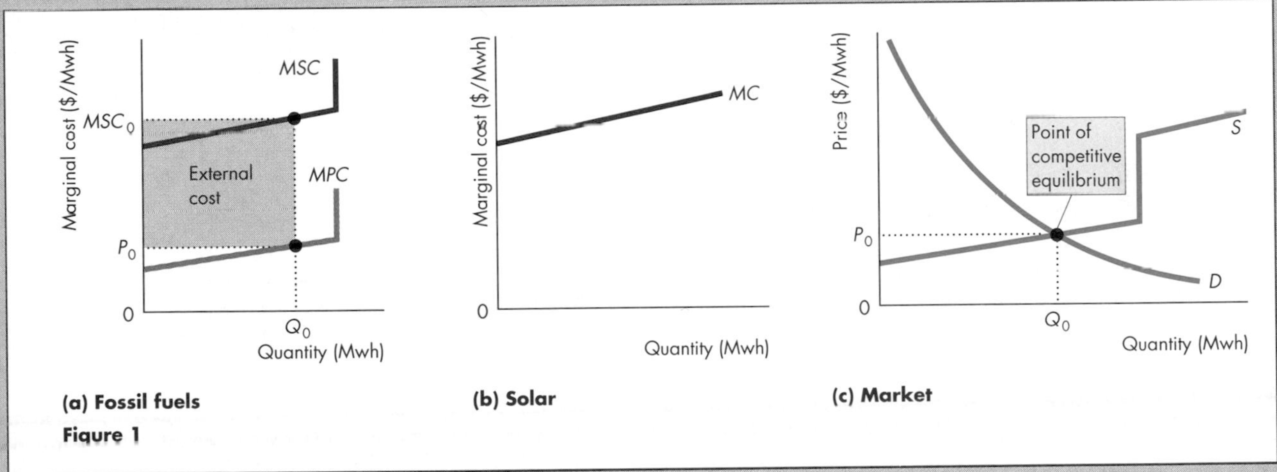

(a) Fossil fuels (b) Solar (c) Market

Figure 1

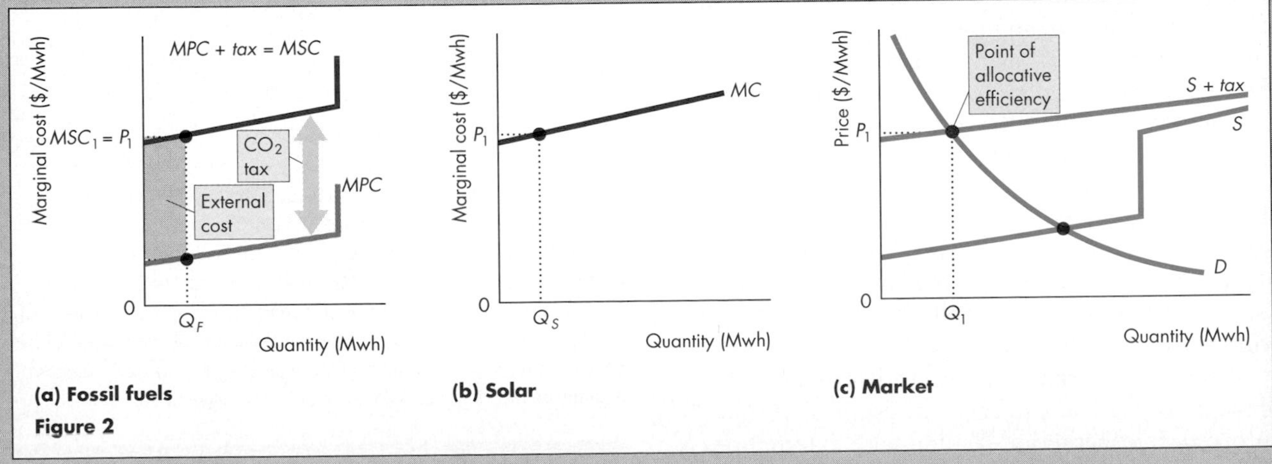

(a) Fossil fuels (b) Solar (c) Market

Figure 2

The existence of externalities—both costs and benefits—is another source of market failure. There are two possible types of action that governments can take to achieve a more efficient allocation of resources in the face of externalities:

- Establish and enforce private property rights
- Tax activities that produce external costs and subsidize those that bring external benefits

The evolution of our understanding of externalities and of the alternative ways of dealing with them is dealt with in Our Advancing Knowledge on pp. 530–531. Let's next consider the use of private property rights for dealing with externalities.

Private Property Rights and Externalities

There are some cases in which externalities arise because of an absence of private property rights. A **private property right** is a legally established title to the sole ownership of a scarce resource. A private property right is enforceable in the courts. The creation of externalities in the absence of private property rights is illustrated well by the example of the chemical factory and a private fishing club. Members of a private fishing club use a particular stretch of a stream that is well stocked with excellent fish. A typical factory opens upstream from the fishing club. It has to make a decision about how it will dispose of some of its waste products.

Consider two different legal situations. In the first, no one owns the stream. If the chemical factory dumps its waste products in the stream, its cost of waste disposal is zero. But the waste kills the fish, and the fishing club goes out of business.

In the second situation, there are property rights established in the stream. The fishing club owns its stretch of the stream and the fish that swim in it. The chemical factory might still dump its waste into the stream, but if it does so, and if it kills the fish, the fishing club will successfully bring a lawsuit against the chemical plant for damages. The damages paid to the fishing club are the cost to the chemical company of disposing of the chemical waste by dumping it in the river. If some other method of waste disposal is available that has a lower cost than killing the fish, the chemical factory will choose that alternative.

Whenever externalities arise from the absence of property rights that can easily be established and enforced, this method of dealing with externalities is a natural one for governments to contemplate. But there are many situations in which private property rights simply cannot be established and enforced. In these cases, governments resort to the alternative method of coping with externalities—using taxes and subsidies. Let's see how these government tools work.

Taxes and External Costs

As we've just noted, every time you burn fossil fuel, you release carbon dioxide into the atmosphere. These carbon dioxide emissions impose unintended costs on others. Let's see how the government might modify your choices and encourage you to take account of the potential costs that you're imposing on others.

FIGURE 19.3

Taxing and Regulating an Externality

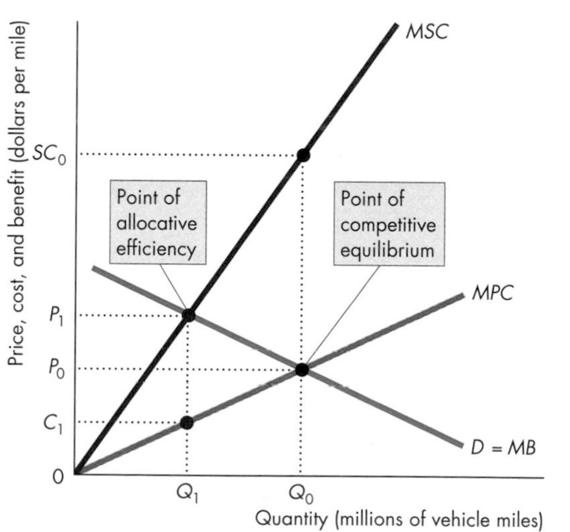

The demand curve for transportation services is also the marginal benefit curve ($D = MB$). The marginal private cost curve is *MPC*. Because of congestion and environmental pollution, the marginal cost of providing transportation services exceeds the marginal private cost. A marginal social cost is shown by curve *MSC*. If the market is competitive, output is Q_0 and the price is P_0. Marginal social cost is SC_0. If a tax is imposed to confront producers of transportation services with their full marginal social cost, the *MSC* curve becomes the relevant marginal cost curve for suppliers' decisions. The price increases to P_1, and the quantity decreases to Q_1. Allocative efficiency is achieved.

One activity that creates carbon dioxide is driving a gasoline-fueled vehicle. To study the demand for this activity, we'll examine the market for transportation services. Figure 19.3 illustrates this market. The demand curve is also the marginal benefit curve, the curve $D = MB$. It tells us how much consumers value each different level of output. Curve *MPC* measures the marginal private cost of producing transportation services. **Marginal private cost** is the marginal cost directly incurred by the producer of a good. Thus the *MPC* curve shows the marginal cost directly incurred by the producers of transportation services. But there are externalities in transportation. The fact that fossil fuels are burned creates atmospheric pollution and contributes to the greenhouse effect. It also causes other, more immediate health problems. Furthermore, one person's decision to use a highway imposes congestion costs on others. These costs are also external costs. When all the external marginal costs are added to the marginal private cost, we obtain the marginal social cost of transportation services. **Marginal social cost** is the marginal cost incurred by the producer of a good together with the marginal cost imposed as an externality on others. Marginal social cost is illustrated by the curve *MSC* in the figure.

Suppose that the transportation market is competitive and unregulated. People will balance the marginal private cost against the marginal benefit and travel Q_0 million miles at a price of P_0 per mile. At this scale of travel, a large amount of external costs will be borne. The marginal social cost is SC_0. The difference between P_0 and SC_0 represents the marginal cost imposed on others—the external marginal cost.

Suppose that the government taxes transportation and that it sets the tax equal to the external marginal cost. By imposing such a tax, the government raises the marginal private cost—the original marginal private cost *plus* the tax—to equal the marginal social cost. The *MSC* curve is now the relevant marginal cost curve for each person's decision, since each person now faces a marginal cost of transportation equal to its marginal social cost. The market supply curve shifts upward to become the *MSC* curve. The price rises to P_1, and the amount of travel falls to Q_1. The marginal cost of the resources used in producing Q_1 million miles of travel is C_1, but the marginal external cost generated is P_1 minus C_1. That external marginal cost is paid by the consumer through the tax.

The situation depicted at the price P_1 and the quantity Q_1 is allocatively efficient. At an output rate above Q_1, marginal social cost exceeds marginal benefit, so net benefit increases by producing less. At an output rate below Q_1, marginal benefit exceeds marginal social cost, so net benefit increases by producing more.

Subsidies and External Benefits

Some goods bring external benefits—benefits to people who do not directly consume the good. In some cases, the government induces additional consumption of such goods by subsidizing them. A **subsidy** is a payment made by the government to producers that depends on the level of output. Figure 19.4 shows how subsidizing education can increase the

FIGURE 19.4

Subsidizing an External Benefit

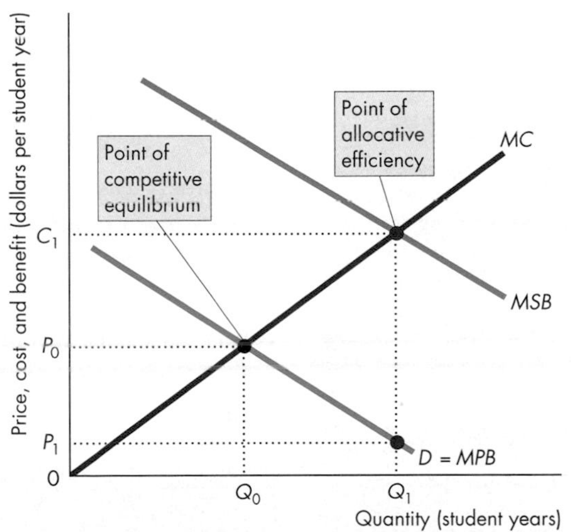

The demand curve for education also measures the marginal private benefit of education ($D = MPB$). The curve *MC* shows the marginal cost of education. If education is provided in a competitive market with no government intervention, the price of education is P_0 and the quantity bought is Q_0. But education produces a social benefit, and the marginal social benefit is shown by the curve *MSB*. Allocative efficiency is achieved if the government provides education services on a scale such that marginal social cost equals marginal social benefit. This scale of provision is Q_1, which is achieved if the government subsidizes education, making it available for a price of P_1. The quantity demanded at price P_1 is Q_1, and at that quantity marginal cost equals marginal social benefit at a level of C_1.

UNDERSTANDING EXTERNALTIES

Whether it's dead fish caused by DDT, acid rain caused by smokestacks, or global warming caused by burning carbon fuels, externalities are easy to see. But solutions have been slow to evolve. Fifty years ago, none of these problems was high on anyone's agenda. Why?

There are two main reasons: as incomes grow, people value the environment more highly; and as technology advances, we discover external effects that were previously unknown. In combination, these two factors have increased the demand (and willingness to pay) for a cleaner and safer environment. And as demand has grown, so has our understanding of alternative economic solutions.

One solution is regulation. For example, DDT was banned and farmers had to substitute more expensive insecticides that were easier on the environment. Were the additional costs of such insecticides lower or higher than the value of reduced toxicity of our rivers and lakes? When regulation is used to control externalities, it is regulators and lawmakers who make judgments about value.

Another solution is taxation. For example, electric power companies could be charged a tax proportional to the volume of pollution they create. Again, lawmakers and bureaucrats make the decisions about comparative values. But given those decisions, firms decide how much pollution to create.

A third solution is establishing property rights over the resources being damaged by external factors. For example, the fishing companies of Lake Erie could be assigned property rights over the lake. They would decide the value of avoiding pollution and charge polluters a price sufficiently high to compensate for lost or lowered incomes resulting from pollution.

Finally, an externality can simply be endured. This is our current "solution" to the problem of global warming. In this case, no one has been able to implement an arrangement at a cost that is sufficiently low to result in a net social gain.

"The question to be decided is: is the value of the fish lost greater or less than the value of the product which contamination of the stream makes possible."

R. H. Coase
The Problem of Social Cost

Chester Jackson, a Lake Erie fisherman, recalls that when he began fishing on the lake, boats didn't carry drinking water. Fishermen drank from the lake. Speaking after World War II, Jackson observed, "Can't do that today. Those chemicals in there would kill you." Ignorant of their external effects, farmers used chemicals such as the insecticide DDT that got carried into the lake by runoff. Industrial waste and trash were also dumped in the lake in large quantities. As a result, Lake Erie became badly polluted during the 1940s and became incapable of sustaining a viable fish stock.

Today, Lake Erie supports a fishing industry, just as it did in the 1930s. No longer treated as a garbage dump for chemicals, the lake is regenerating its ecosystem. Fertilizers and insecticides are now recognized as products that have potential externalities, and their external effects are assessed by the Department of the Environment before new versions are put into widespread use. Dumping industrial waste into rivers and lakes is now subject to much more stringent regulations and penalties. Lake Erie's externalities problems have been solved by one of the methods available: government regulation.

THE *Public Interest and Public Choices*

Externalities are solved by *public choices*. But for a time, economists lost sight of this fact. During the 1920s, Arthur Cecil Pigou (1877–1959), pictured left, of Cambridge, England, pioneered a branch of economics designed to guide public choices—*welfare economics*. Pigou devised rules which, if followed, ensured that decisions about externalities were in the *public interest*. But the rules were not followed.

Not until the 1950s did economists develop *public choice theory* and explain the choices *actually* made by politicians and bureaucrats. Among the leaders in this field was the 1986 Nobel laureate James Buchanan (1919–), pictured right, of George Mason University. Because of the work of Buchanan and others, we now understand that the solutions adopted for externalities depend not on the public interest, but on private interests—on private costs and benefits. We also now appreciate, as a result of the work of Ronald H. Coase, that the transactions costs of organizing alternative solutions are crucial in determining which, if any, of those solutions is pursued.

amount of education and achieve allocative efficiency. Suppose that the marginal cost of producing education is shown by the curve *MC* (assuming there is no difference between marginal private cost and marginal social cost). The demand curve for education tells us the quantity of education demanded at each price when people are free to choose the amount of education that they undertake and pay for it themselves. It also measures the marginal private benefit—the benefit perceived by the individuals undertaking education. That curve is $D = MPB$. A competitive market in private education produces an output of Q_0 at a price of P_0.

Suppose that the external benefit—the benefit derived by people other than those undertaking education—results in marginal social benefits described by the curve *MSB*. Allocative efficiency occurs when marginal cost equals marginal social benefit. The quantity of education at which this equality occurs is Q_1. By providing the quantity of education Q_1 and making it available at the price P_1, the government can achieve allocative efficiency in the education sector. In this case, by producing education at a low price, the government encourages people to undertake the amount of education that makes its marginal social benefit equal to its marginal cost.

We've now looked at two examples of the way in which government action can help market participants take account of external costs and benefits.

REVIEW

When externalities are present, the market allocation is not efficient. Sometimes an efficient allocation can be achieved by establishing private property rights. But in many cases, private property rights simply cannot be established and enforced. In such cases, if the government confronts people with taxes equivalent to the external marginal costs or subsidies equivalent to external marginal benefits, it induces people to produce goods on a scale that achieves allocative efficiency, even in the face of externalities. ◆

◆ ◆ ◆ ◆ We've seen that markets do not always achieve allocative efficiency. When the market fails, we can describe an allocation that is efficient. But showing an efficient allocation is not the same thing as designing institutions to achieve one. Do governments in fact achieve allocative efficiency? Or are there economic problems arising from the functioning of a political system leading to "government failure" and preventing the attainment of an efficient allocation of resources? These questions are dealt with in the next chapter.

SUMMARY

The Government Sector

The government sector of the U.S. economy accounts for 35 percent of all expenditure on goods and services and 36 percent of total employment. The biggest departments of government deal with the provision of defense and health services. The Treasury Department is also a large one. The government share of the economy has grown over the years, increasing from less than 20 percent in 1940 to more than 35 percent in 1990.

But when economists study political behavior, they are careful to maintain the distinction between positive and normative analysis. Their main focus is on positive matters—on what *is* and on how the political system works rather than on what *ought* to be and how the political system *ought* to function.

All government economic actions stem from either market failure or the redistribution of income and wealth. Market failure arises from the provision of public goods and services, from externalities, and from monopolies and cartels. The redistribution of income and wealth arises partly from notions of equity and justice and partly from rent-seeking activities.

There are two broad approaches to the economic analysis of government—public interest theories and public choice theories. Public interest theories emphasize the idea of government as an institution able to eliminate waste and achieve allocative efficiency—an agent that operates with public interest. Public choice theories emphasize the idea that government operates in a political marketplace in which politicians, bureaucrats, and voters interact with each other. According to the public choice view, government failure to achieve allocative efficiency is as real as the possible failure of the market. (pp. 518–520)

Public Goods

Pure public goods have two features: nonrivalry and nonexcludability. One person's consumption does not reduce the amount available for someone else (nonrivalry), and no one can be kept from sharing the consumption of such a good (nonexcludability). An example of a pure public good is the national defense system.

The existence of public goods gives rise to the free-rider problem. This problem is the tendency for the scale of provision of a public good to be too small if it is produced and sold privately. The free-rider problem arises because there is insufficient incentive for a person to pay for a good if that payment has no effect on the quantity of the good the person consumes. Thus it pays everyone to free ride; so with private provision, no revenue can be raised from the sale of a public good. In such a situation, no public goods are produced. In contrast, the government can produce a public good, paying for it out of taxation. People will vote for taxes and a public good provided that the net benefits are positive. The government is able to provide any public good on a scale larger than that provided by a private producer, but it does not necessarily produce an allocatively efficient amount of a public good. (pp. 520–525)

Externalities

An externality is a cost or a benefit arising from an economic transaction that falls on a third party and that is not taken into account by the parties undertaking the transaction. When external costs are present, allocative efficiency requires a reduction in the scale of output below what the market will produce. When external benefits are present, allocative efficiency requires an increase in output. There are two ways in which government can deal with externalities: establishing and enforcing private property rights or using taxes and subsidies. If the government uses taxes and subsidies, it imposes taxes where there are external costs and gives subsidies where there are external benefits. (pp. 525–532)

KEY ELEMENTS

Key Terms

Externality, 525
Free rider, 521
Free-rider problem, 521
Marginal benefit, 521
Marginal private cost, 529
Marginal social cost, 529
Market failure, 519
Mixed good, 520
Net benefit, 523
Private good, 520
Private property right, 528
Public choice theory, 520
Public interest theory, 520
Pure public good, 520
Subsidy, 529
Total benefit, 521

Key Figures

REVIEW QUESTIONS

1 How big is the government sector of the U.S. economy today?

2 Set out the main economic functions of government.

3 Provide an example of each function of government.

4 What is a pure public good?

5 Name examples of three goods: a pure public good, a private good, and a mixed good.

6 What is the free-rider problem, and how does government help overcome it?

7 What is an externality?

8 Give three examples of externalities.

PROBLEMS

1 You are given the following information about a sewage disposal system that a city of 1 million people is considering installing:

Capacity (thousands of gallons a day)	Marginal private benefit to one person (dollars)	Total cost (millions of dollars)
0		0
	100	
1		10
	80	
2		30
	60	
3		60
	40	
4		100
	20	
5		150

a What is the capacity that achieves the maximum net benefit?

b How much will each person have to be taxed to pay for the efficient capacity level?

c What are the total and net benefits?

2 A chemical factory dumps waste in a river. Damage is done to the local fish stock, and membership fees at a nearby fishing club are lowered by the following amounts:

Output of chemical plant (gallons per hour)	Lost fees to fishing club (dollars)
0	0
100	10
200	30
300	70
400	210

a The local government plans to tax the chemical factory. Devise a tax that will achieve allocative efficiency.

b How might private property rights be used in this situation?

3 The demand schedule for education in Brightland is as follows:

Number of students (thousands)	Tuition fee (dollars per year)
0	5,000
100	4,000
200	3,000
300	2,000
400	1,000
500	500
600	250

The marginal cost of providing education is $3,000 per year. There are external benefits of $2,000 per student.

a If the market for education in Brightland is private with no government intervention, how many students enroll in school, and what is the tuition fee?

b If the government wants to achieve allocative efficiency, how many student school places does it make available, and how big is the subsidy per student?

4 Two countries, Greenhaven and Smokehole, have identical marginal private benefit and marginal private cost schedules for electric power generated by burning coal. These schedules are as follows:

Quantity (millions of megawatts a day)	Marginal private benefit (dollars)	Marginal private cost (dollars)
0	14	1
1	12	1
2	10	1
3	8	2
4	6	3
5	5	5
6	4	6
7	3	7
8	2	8
9	1	9
10	0	10

The people of Greenhaven believe that each megawatt generated has a marginal social cost equal to twice its marginal private cost, and the government of Greenhaven imposes an electricity tax that achieves allocative efficiency. The people of Smokehole believe there are no social costs of producing electric power, and there is no government intervention in the market for electricity.

a How much electricity is generated in Greenhaven?
b What is the price of electricity in Greenhaven?
c How much tax revenue does the government of Greenhaven collect on the generation of electricity?
d How much electricity is generated in Smokehole?
e What is the price of electricity in Smokehole?

CHAPTER 20

PUBLIC CHOICE

After studying this chapter, you will be able to:

- Describe the components of the political marketplace
- Define a political equilibrium
- Explain how the main political parties choose their economic policy platforms
- Explain how governments determine the scale of provision of public goods and services
- Explain why we vote for redistributions of income and wealth
- Explain why governments tax some goods at much higher rates than others
- Predict the effects of taxes on prices, production, and profits
- Explain why governments subsidize the producers of some goods
- Predict the effects of subsidies on prices, production, and profits

EMOCRATS AND REPUBLICANS BATTLE TO DOMINATE politics. The Democrats usually advocate increased government spending and intervention. The Republicans generally take the opposite side, promising lower spending and less intervention. Yet when they are in office, the two parties behave in remarkably similar ways. It was Jimmy Carter the Democrat who most effectively kept government spending in check. And it was Ronald Reagan the Republican who allowed spending—especially defense spending—to grow extremely quickly. Voters recognize these patterns. They hear the dramatic differences in the political rhetoric and complain that there really aren't all that many differences in the policies of opposing parties. Why do the two political parties take strongly different positions in what they say and yet deliver such similar policies? ◆◆

Rhetoric and Reality

Government pervades many aspects of our lives. It is present at our birth, supporting the hospitals in which we are born and training the doctors and nurses who deliver us. It is present throughout our education, supporting schools and colleges and training our teachers. It is present throughout our working lives, taxing our incomes, regulating our work environment, and paying us benefits when we are unemployed. It is present throughout our retirement, paying us a small income, and when we die, taxing our bequests. But the government does not make all our economic choices. We decide for ourselves what work to do, how much to save, and what to spend our income on. Why does the government intervene in some aspects of our lives but not others? Why doesn't the government provide more of our health services? Why doesn't it provide less of our education services? ◆◆ Almost everyone, from the poor single mother to the wealthy taxpayer, grumbles about government bureaucracy. Even presidents, senators, and representatives complain that the bureaucracy is too big, too slow, and inefficient. Why is the bureaucracy so unpopular and the target of so much scorn? How do government agencies and departments operate to deliver the many public services for which they are responsible? ◆ ◆ Government taxes almost all the goods and services that we buy. Some goods such as gasoline, alcohol, and tobacco products are taxed heavily. A few items are not taxed at all, and their producers even get subsidies from the government. Examples are milk and wheat. Why does government impose heavy taxes on some goods and subsidies on others? What are the effects of taxes on the amount of revenue raised by the government?

◆ ◆ ◆ ◆ In this chapter, we study the economic interactions of voters, politicians, and bureaucrats and discover how the scale and variety of government economic activity are determined. Our focus here is the provision of public goods and services, the taxes levied to pay for those services, the control of externalities, and the redistribution of income.

The Political Marketplace

Government is not a huge computer that grinds out solutions to resource allocation problems plagued with free riders and externalities. It does not simply calculate and balance marginal social costs and benefits, automatically achieving allocative efficiency. Rather, it is a complex organization made up of thousands of individuals. These individuals have their *own* economic objectives, and government policy choices are the outcomes of the choices made by these individuals. To analyze these choices, economists have developed a theory of the political marketplace that parallels theories of ordinary markets—*public choice theory*.

There are three types of actors in the political marketplace:

- Voters
- Politicians
- Bureaucrats

Voters are the consumers of the outcome of the political process. In ordinary markets for goods and services, people express their demands by their willingness to pay. In the political marketplace, voters express their demands in three principal ways. First, they express them by a willingness to vote, either in an election or on a referendum issue. Second, and less formally, they express their demands through campaign contributions. Third, they express their demands by lobbying. **Lobbying** is the activity of bringing pressure to bear on government agencies or institutions through a variety of informal mechanisms. The pro-life and pro-choice lobbies are two of the most prominent examples of such organizations in the United States today.

Politicians are the elected officials in federal, state, and local government—from the chief executives (the president, state governors, and mayors) to members of the legislatures (state and federal senators and representatives and city councilors). Politicians are chosen by voters.

Bureaucrats are the appointed officials who work at various levels in the many government departments, again at the federal, state, and local levels. The most senior bureaucrats are appointed by politicians. Junior bureaucrats are appointed by senior ones.

Voters, politicians, and bureaucrats make their economic choices in a way that best furthers their own objectives, but each group faces two types of constraints. First, each group is constrained by the preferences of the others. Bureaucrats are constrained by the preferences of politicians; politicians are constrained by the preferences of bureaucrats and voters; and voters are constrained by the preferences of bureaucrats and politicians. Second, voters, bureaucrats, and politicians cannot ignore technological constraints. They can do only things that are technologically feasible. We are going to examine the objectives of voters, politicians, and bureaucrats and the constraints they face when making their choices. We're also going to study the interactions among the three types of actors. In so doing, we are going to discover how the political system actually works.

The predictions of an economic model of voter, politician, and bureaucrat behavior are the equilibrium of the political process—the political equilibrium. A **political equilibrium** is a situation in which the choices of voters, politicians, and bureaucrats are all compatible and in which no one group of agents will be better off by making a different choice. Thus a political equilibrium has the same characteristics as an equilibrium in the markets for goods and services and factors of production.

The theory of public choice that we are about to study is a relatively new branch of economics that has grown rapidly in the past 30 years. It was recently recognized by the awarding of the Nobel Prize for economics to one of its principal architects, James Buchanan.

Let's begin our study of public choice theory by looking at the behavior of politicians and voters.

The Behavior of Politicians and Voters

All kinds of people go into politics. Some have noble ideals and want to make a lasting contribution to improving the conditions of their fellow citizens. Others are single-minded in pursuit of their own self-interest and profit. Most politicians, no doubt, blend these two extremes. Economic models of public choice are based on the assumption that in a democratic political system politicians' central objective is to get enough votes to be elected and to keep enough support to remain in office. Votes, to a politician, are similar to dollars to a private firm. In order to obtain enough votes, politicians form coalitions with each other; we call these coalitions political parties. A political party is simply a collection of politicians who have banded together for the purpose of achieving and maintaining office. A political party attempts to develop policies that appeal to a majority of the voters.

Public choice theory assumes that voters support policies that they believe make them better off and oppose policies that they believe make them worse off. They neither oppose nor support—they are indifferent among—policies that they believe have no effect on them. Voters' *perceptions* rather than reality are what guide their choices.

To obtain the support of voters, a politician (or political party) must offer a package of policies that voters believe will make them better off than the policies proposed by the opposing political parties. There are two ways in which a political program can seek to make a voter better off. One way is to implement policies that make *everyone* better off. Providing national defense and protecting the environment are examples of such policies. Another way is to implement policies that make some voters worse off but at least 50 percent of the voters better off. Redistributing income in such a way that at least one half of the electorate reaps net benefits is one example. Supporting or opposing abortion is another, and supporting or opposing gun control yet another.

Political programs that make everyone better off feature in the platforms of all parties. Policies that favor one group over another differ from party to party and depend on which segment of the population or particular interest group a political party wants to appeal to. Let's see how politicians and voters interact and how the policy platforms of political parties emerge by examining how the political process handles the provision of public goods and external costs and benefits.

Public Goods In Chapter 19, we compared the scale of provision of public goods that achieves allocative efficiency with the scale that would be provided through the private marketplace. Now we want to work out the scale of provision of public goods that a political system will actually deliver.

For the moment, let's ignore differences among individual voters and suppose that people have identical views about the benefits of public goods and externalities. Later we'll consider what happens when people disagree and have different preferences. To be concrete, let's stick with the example of national defense that we studied in Chapter 19.

Suppose that the total costs and total benefits of producing antimissile lasers are the ones shown in Fig. 20.1. (These are the same costs and benefits that we used in Chapter 19, pp. 521–524.) Suppose also that there are two political parties. Let's call one the Hawks and the other the Doves. Suppose that the Hawks and the Doves propose exactly the same policy platform in all respects except for national defense. The Hawks offer a high level of national defense. They propose to provide 4 antimissile lasers at a cost of $50 billion, with benefits of $50 billion and a net benefit of zero. The Doves propose to provide just 1 laser at a cost of $5 billion, with a benefit of $20 billion and a net benefit of $15 billion ($20

FIGURE 20.1

Provision of a Public Good in a Political System

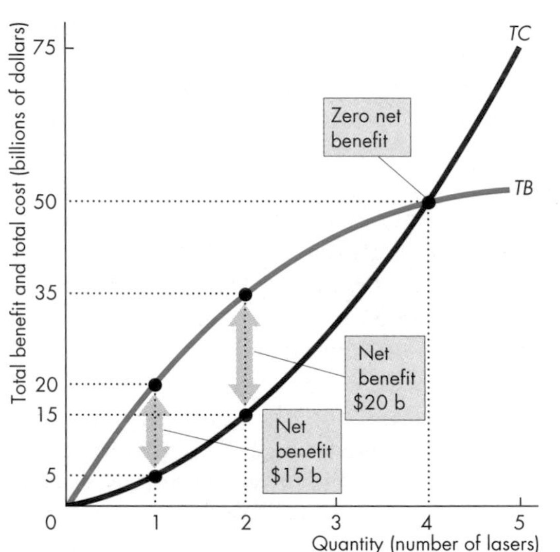

The total benefit curve for an antimissile laser weapon is *TB*, and the total cost curve is *TC*. Net benefit is maximized if 2 antimissile lasers are installed, with a total benefit of $35 billion and a total cost of $15 billion. There are two political parties offering platforms on this defense system: the Doves and the Hawks. Their platforms are identical on all matters except defense. The Doves propose to install 1 antimissile laser, and the Hawks propose 4. In an election, the Doves would win, since their proposal generates a larger net benefit than the Hawks' proposal. But if the Hawks propose to install 2 lasers, they would beat the Doves, since the net benefit resulting from 2 lasers exceeds that from 1. To get even, the Doves would have to match the Hawks. If voters are well informed and in general agreement about the value of a public good, competition between political parties for their votes can achieve an efficient scale of provision.

billion total benefit minus $5 billion total cost).

In an election in which voters are presented with the two platforms just described, the Doves will win. Recall that we assume that both parties are offering identical programs in every respect except for defense. The defense program of the Doves provides the voters with a net benefit of $15 billion over and above the taxes that they are asked to pay, while the Hawks are offering no net benefit; so the Doves will get all the votes.

Now suppose that the Hawks, contemplating the election outcome that we have just described, realize that their party is being too hawkish. It is offering too high a level of defense to get elected. It figures that it has to offer net benefits in excess of $15 billion if it is to beat the Doves. It therefore scales back its plans and proposes to build 2 antimissile lasers. At this level of provision, the total cost is $15 billion and total benefit is $35 billion, so net benefit is $20 billion. The Hawks are now offering a package that the voters prefer to the one offered by the Doves. Now in an election, the Hawks will win.

The Doves, contemplating this outcome, realize that the best they can do is to match the Hawks. They too propose to provide 2 lasers on exactly the same terms as the Hawks. The voters are now indifferent between the proposals of the two parties and are indifferent about which one they vote for.

Competition for votes among political parties, even when there are only two of them, produces a political platform that maximizes the perceived net benefit accruing to the voters. For this outcome to occur, it is necessary that the voters be able to evaluate the alternatives. We'll see below that this condition is not necessarily going to be satisfied.

Externalities

The example that we have just worked through deals with a situation in which the voters are in agreement about and can calculate the benefits arising from different proposals. The same line of reasoning applies to policies concerning the control of externalities. Provided that the voters are in agreement about the benefits and can evaluate them, the political party that offers the level of control of externalities that maximizes net benefits will be the one that wins an election. The political party that proposes a total ban on the production of CFCs or sulfur dioxide emission will lose an election to a party that proposes more limited controls. A party that proposes a free-for-all on CFCs and sulfur dioxide emissions will lose an election to a party that proposes restraint in the production of goods that generate these external costs. Competition for votes will force each party to find the degree of control that maximizes net benefit.

In the examples of public goods and externalities that we have just worked out, we have ignored differences of opinion among the voters. We'll now go on to consider cases in which the preferences of voters differ and in which these differences are crucial in determining the outcome of the political process.

Interest Groups and Redistribution

Most matters decided in the political arena are ones on which people have different opinions. Some people favor a large national defense program while others urge disarmament; some favor a large scale of income redistribution while others urge tax cuts; some want massive government intervention to protect the environment while others want more limited environmental controls. Faced with this diversity of opinion, no political party can propose a platform that pleases everyone. But to attain office, a party must put together a package that attracts a majority of the votes. To do so, each party has to deliver a package that makes a majority of the voters better off (as the voters perceive it) than under the policies proposed by the opposing party (or parties). This search for a majority results in each political party offering policies that are very close to the policies of the others. This tendency toward similar policies is known as the principle of minimum differentiation.

The Principle of Minimum Differentiation The **principle of minimum differentiation** is the tendency for competitors to make themselves almost identical in order to appeal to the maximum number of clients or voters. Let's study the principle of minimum differentiation by looking at a problem that is more familiar and concrete than that faced by political parties.

There are two ice cream vendors on a beach. The beach is one mile long, and it is illustrated in Fig. 20.2 as the distance from *A* to *B*. Sunbathers lounge at equal intervals over the entire beach. One of the ice cream vendors comes along and sets up a stand. Where will she locate? The answer is at position *C*—exactly halfway between *A* and *B*. With the ice cream stand in this position, the farthest that anyone has to walk to buy ice cream is a mile (half a mile to the ice cream stand and half a mile back to the beach towel).

Now suppose that a second ice cream vendor comes along. Where will he place his ice cream stand? The answer is right next to the original one at point *C*. To understand why, imagine that the second vendor locates his stand at point *D*—halfway between *C* and *B*. How many customers will he attract, and how many will go to the stand at *C*? The stand at *D* will pick up all the customers on the beach between *B* and *D*, because this stand is closer for them. It will also pick up all the customers between *D* and *E* (the point halfway between *C* and *D*), because they too will have a shorter trip for an ice cream by going to *D* than by going to *C*. All the people between *A* and *C* and all those between *C* and *E* will go to stand *C*. So the ice cream stand located at *C* will pick up all the people on the beach between *A* and *E*, and the stand located at *D* will pick up all the people located between *E* and *B*.

Now suppose that the vendor with a stand at *D* moves to *C*. There are now two stands at *C*. Half the customers will go to the first vendor and the other half to the second vendor. Only by locating bang in the center of the beach can each pick up half the customers. If either of them moves slightly away from the center, then that vendor picks up less than half the customers and the one remaining at the center picks up a majority of the customers.

This example illustrates the principle of minimum differentiation. By having no differentiation in location, both ice cream vendors do as well as they can and share the market evenly.

FIGURE 20.2

The Principle of Minimum Differentiation

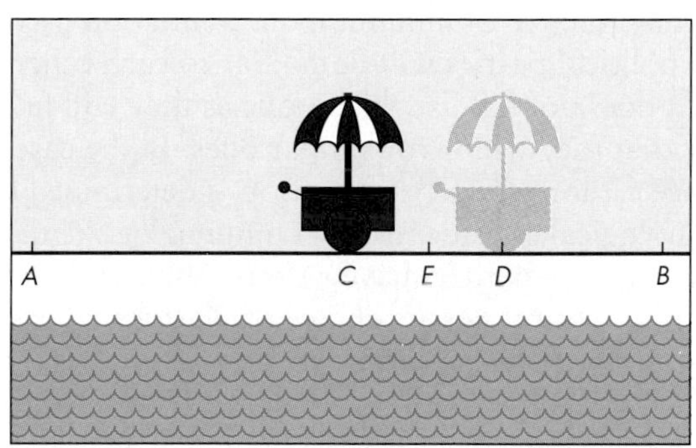

A beach stretches from *A* to *B*. Sunbathers are distributed at even intervals along the whole beach. An ice cream seller sets up a stand at point *C*. The distance that people have to walk for ice cream is the same no matter on which side of the ice cream stand they are located. If a second ice cream seller sets up a stand, it will pay to place it exactly next to *C* in the middle of the beach. If the second stand is placed at *D*, only the customers on the beach between *E* and *B* will buy ice cream at *D*. Those between *A* and *E* will go to *C*. By moving as close to *C* as possible, the second ice cream vendor picks up half the ice cream customers.

The principle of minimum differentiation has been applied to explain a wide variety of choices—how supermarkets choose their locations, how the makers of automobiles and microwave popcorn design their products, and how political parties choose their platforms.

The principle of minimum differentiation predicts that political parties will be similar to each other. But it does not tell us which policies they will favor, only that they will favor similar ones. In the case of the ice cream vendor, the location is determined by technological considerations—minimizing the distance that the bathers have to walk. But what determines a political party's choice of platform? Let's now address this question.

The Median Voter Theorem An interesting proposition about a political party's choice of platform is provided by the median voter theorem. The **median voter theorem** states that political parties will pursue policies that maximize the net benefit of the median voter. (The median of a distribution of, say, student heights is the height of the student in the middle. One half of the students are taller and one half of the students are shorter than the median.) Let's see how the median voter theorem applies to the question of how large a tax to impose on sulfur dioxide emissions that cause acid rain.

Imagine arranging all the voters along a line running from *A* to *B*, as shown in Fig. 20.3. The voter wanting the highest tax is at *A*, the one wanting no tax is at *B*, and all the other voters are arranged along the line based on the level of the tax that they favor. The curve in the figure shows the tax rate favored by each voter between *A* and *B*. As shown, the median voter favors a tax rate of 30 percent.

Suppose that two political parties propose similar but not quite identical taxes on emissions of sulfur dioxide. One party proposes a tax of 61 percent, and the other proposes a tax of 59 percent. All the voters lying between *A* and *C* prefer the higher tax and will vote for it. All the voters lying between *C* and *B* prefer the lower tax and will vote for it. The lower tax party will win the election.

Alternatively, suppose that the two political parties offer a low tax rate—and, again, slightly different rates. One party offers a rate of 11 percent, and the other offers a rate of 9 percent. The voters between *A* and *D* will vote for the higher tax rate and those between *D* and *B* for the lower rate. This time, the higher tax party will win.

FIGURE 20.3

The Median Voter Theorem

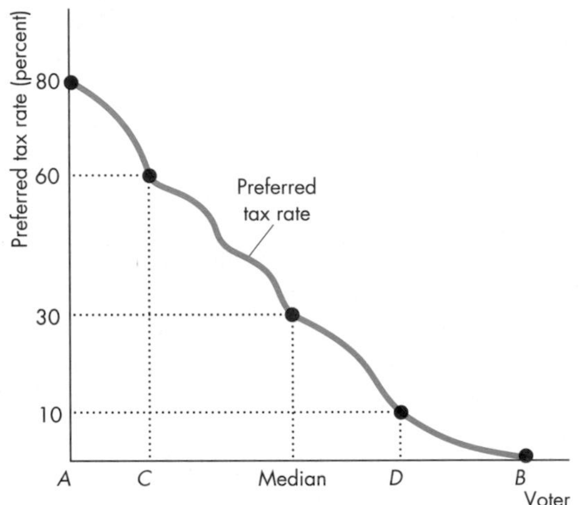

A political party can win an election by proposing policies that appeal to the median voter and to all the other voters on one side of the median. If the median voter mildly favors a policy, that policy will be proposed. In the figure, voters have different preferences concerning the rate at which to tax an externality. They are ranked from *A* to *B* in descending order of their preferred tax. There are two political parties. If one proposes a 61 percent tax and the other a 59 percent tax, the lower tax party will win the election—voters between *A* and *C* will vote for the high tax, and those between *C* and *B* will vote for the low tax. If both parties propose low taxes—11 percent and 9 percent—the party proposing the higher tax will win. It will pick up the votes between *A* and *D*, leaving only the votes between *D* and *B* for the lower tax party. Each party will have an incentive to move toward the tax rate preferred by the median voter, 30 percent. At that point, each party picks up half the votes and neither can improve its share.

But each party, in either of these situations, will see that it can win the election by moving closer to the tax rate preferred by the median voter. Once the two parties are offering that tax rate, however, neither will be able to increase its share of the vote by changing its proposal. One party will get the votes between *A* and the median, and the other the votes between the median and *B*. All the voters except the median will be dissatisfied—for those between *A* and the median the tax rate is too low, and for those between *B* and the median the tax is too high. But no political party can propose a tax other than 30 percent and expect to win the election. Of course, if the two parties propose exactly 30 percent, the voters will be indifferent and either will not bother to vote or will flip a coin to decide which party to vote for.

The principle of minimum differentiation and the median voter theorem seem to imply that all political parties will be identical in all respects. If that is so, it is too bad for the principle and the theorem. The world that we live in has political parties that certainly do differ. Many of us are heated in our support for and opposition to particular parties and policy proposals. It is in the area of the redistribution of income and wealth that one of the major differences in political parties arises. Let's use the principle of minimum differentiation and the median voter theorem to see if we can understand why all political parties favor some redistribution but why, also, there are differences in the parties in this respect.

Voting for Income Redistribution

The first model of redistribution that we'll consider is one that results in voting cycles. Imagine a society with 100 voters. These voters are divided into four different income groups, as set out in Table 20.1. Twenty-five of the voters earn $10,000 a year, another 25 earn $20,000 a year, another 25 earn $40,000 a year, and the richest 25 earn $90,000 a year. The average income in this community is $40,000 a year.

Suppose that a political party proposes to tax the richest 25 people $5,000 and the second richest $3,000. It proposes to make transfers of $5,000 to the poorest 25 people and $3,000 to the next poorest 25. The incomes resulting from the tax and transfers in this proposal are set out in the third column of Table 20.1. The average income is still $40,000. The final column of the table shows the gains and losses to each income group. The poorest gain and the richest lose.

Suppose that there is a second political party in this society that opposes the redistribution scheme just described. Which party will win the election? The answer is that it will be a tie. The party proposing the redistribution scheme will pick up 50 percent of the votes—those of the poorer half of the electorate. The party opposing the redistribution scheme will pick up the other half of the votes (those at the wealthier end of the income distribution).

Now suppose that one of the parties offers the modified scheme set out in Table 20.2. The proposal is to tax the richest quarter of the people not $5,000 but $8,000 and not to tax the second richest quarter at all. Under this scheme, the two poorest groups of people will receive benefits of $5,000 and $3,000, respectively. One party supports these measures, and the other opposes them and proposes no redistribution at all. Which party will win? The answer is the party supporting redistribution. All the people with original incomes of $10,000 and $20,000 will vote for the scheme. Those with incomes of $40,000 will be indifferent between the two parties, so we may suppose that half will vote for one party and half for the other. The party opposing the redistribution

TABLE 20.1

Voting for Income Redistribution: A Tie

	Number of voters		Income before redistribution (thousands of dollars)	Income after redistribution (thousands of dollars)	Gain (+) or loss (–) (thousands of dollars)
	25		10	15	+5
	25		20	23	+3
	25		40	37	–3
	25		90	85	–5
Total:	100	Averages:	40	40	0

TABLE 20.2

Voting for Income Redistribution: The Rich Lose

	Number of voters		Income before redistribution (thousands of dollars)	Income after redistribution (thousands of dollars)	Gain (+) or loss (–) (thousands of dollars)
	25		10	15	+5
	25		20	23	+3
	25		40	40	0
	25		90	82	–8
Total:	100	**Averages:**	40	40	0

scheme will collect the votes of the richest quarter of the people plus half of those in the second richest group.

This example shows one particular redistribution proposal that could gain the support of the majority of voters. But there will be many other proposals that could also gain majority support (but with different people making up the majority in each case). There is no end to the different proposals that could win a majority. As these different schemes are proposed, there are cycles in the voting.

Why do we not observe voting cycles in reality? Why do we see a tendency for redistribution policies to remain in place for very long periods of time? The answer is suggested by a second model of redistribution—a median voter model. A key feature of this model is what has been called the "big tradeoff" (see Chapter 18, p. 508). The greater the amount of income that is redistributed, the smaller is the incentive to work and the lower is the average level of income. As a consequence, redistributive taxes have two effects on the median voter: they raise the median voter's income by taking from those above the median and redistributing to those at and below the median; they also lower the median voter's income by reducing the incentive to work, which lowers average income. Which of these two opposing effects is stronger depends on the scale of redistribution. At low tax rates, the disincentive effects are small, so an increase in taxes makes the median voter better off. The higher income resulting from transfers from the rich is more than enough to offset the lower income resulting from disincentive effects. If tax rates are set too high, a cut in taxes will make the median voter better off. In this case, the lower income resulting from smaller transfers from the rich is more than made up for by the higher average income resulting from improved incentives. But there is a scale of redistribution—level of taxes and transfers—that is exactly right from the point of view of the median voter. This scale of redistribution is the one that balances these two considerations and maximizes the median voter's income. This amount of redistribution is a possible political equilibrium.

Model and Reality

We've now looked at two models of equilibrium redistribution—a voting cycles model and a median voter model. In the voting cycles model, there is a never-ending sequence of different majorities for different directions of redistribution. In the median voter model, there is a unique equilibrium that maximizes the net benefit to the median voter.

Which of these models best fits the facts about income redistribution? The median voter model comes closest. Its strengths lie in its predictions that the political parties will differ in their rhetoric but be very close to each other in the actual redistribution measures for which they vote. In contrast, the voting cycles model predicts a sequence of difference majorities for different directions of redistribution that we do not observe in reality.

REVIEW

Politicians seek to obtain enough votes to achieve and maintain power. They do this by appealing to slightly more than half of the electorate. The key voter is the median voter. To appeal to the median voter, political parties offer programs that favor a majority of the electorate. Each party tries to outdo the other by appealing to the median voter. In part, that appeal results from the political parties proposing income-increasing policies. It also, in part, results from the redistribution of income to the point where no one can invent a way of raising the income of the median voter. ◆

We have analyzed the behavior of politicians but not that of the bureaucrats who translate the choices of the politicians into programs. Let's now turn to an examination of the economic choices of bureaucrats.

The Behavior of Bureaucrats

An interesting model of the behavior of bureaucrats has been suggested by William Niskanen. In that model, bureaucrats aim to maximize the budget of the agency in which they work. The bigger the budget of the agency, the greater is the prestige of the agency chief and the larger is the opportunity for promotion for people farther down the bureaucratic ladder. Thus all the members of an agency have an interest in maximizing the agency's budget. In seeking to obtain the largest budget it can, each government agency and department marshals its best arguments for why it should have more funds to spend. Since each agency does its best to obtain more funds, the net result is upward pressure for expenditure on all publicly provided goods and services.

The constraints on maximizing the budget of a government department or agency are the taxes that politicians have to levy and the implications of those taxes for the politicians' ability to win votes. But government departments and agencies recognize and appreciate the interplay between their own objectives and those of politicians and so do their best to help the politicians appreciate the vote-winning consequences of spending more on their own particular department or agency. Thus budget maximization, to some degree, translates itself into political campaigns designed to explain to voters why they need more defense, more health services, and so on.

Let's examine the consequences of bureaucratic budget maximization for the provision of public goods and their cost by looking again at the example of national defense. We've studied this example twice before. The first time (in Chapter 19, pp. 521–524), our concern was to establish that a government could overcome the free-rider problem and produce a larger quantity of a public good than would be produced by the private market. In this chapter (on pp. 539–540), we examined the way in which political parties competing for votes determine the scale of provision of a public good in a situation in which the voters are in agreement about the benefits of the public good and in which they are able to assess the costs and benefits of different scales of provision. In that example, no bureaucrats intervene in the process.

But the creation and operation of weapons and defense systems require the establishment of a large and complex government bureaucracy. How does the defense bureaucracy influence the scale and cost of the defense program? Let's answer this question by returning to the example of the installation of an antimissile laser defense system.

Take a look at Fig. 20.4. You will recognize it as being similar to Fig. 20.1. The horizontal axis shows the number of antimissile lasers, and the vertical axis shows their total benefit and total cost. The curve labeled *TB* shows the total benefit as perceived by all the individuals in the economy, and the curve labeled *TC* shows the total cost.

We saw earlier that the level of provision that maximizes net benefit is 2 lasers. This level of defense costs $15 billion, and it yields a total benefit of $35 billion and a net benefit of $20 billion. A political party that proposes installing 2 lasers will win an election because there is no higher net benefit possible. But will the Pentagon press Congress to vote for 2 lasers? According to Niskanen's model of bureaucracy, it will not. The Pentagon will push to expand the scale of provision and budget for national defense to the largest possible level. If it is able to increase the number of antimissile lasers to 4, for example, it can increase the budget to $50 billion. In this situation, total benefit equals total cost and net benefit is zero. If the Pentagon is able to increase defense to an even higher level, its budget increases yet further and net benefit becomes negative.

FIGURE 20.4

Bureaucratic Overprovision

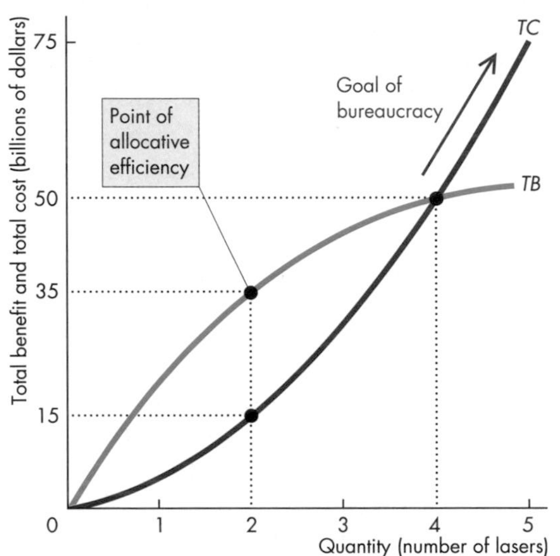

An agency that maximizes its budget will seek to expand output and expenditure as far as possible. For example, the Pentagon prefers 4 antimissile lasers at a cost of $50 billion to the allocatively efficient number—2 at a cost of $15 billion. The goal of the agency is to move as far up the total cost curve as possible, as shown in the figure. If voters are well informed, politicians will not be able to deliver the taxes that enable the agency to get beyond the point of allocative efficiency. But if some voters are rationally ignorant while others are well informed, it is possible that the agency will be able to raise its budget above the allocatively efficient level. In general, the agency will produce a higher quantity than the one that maximizes net benefit.

But how would it be possible for the Pentagon to get away with pressing the politicians for a scale of defense spending in excess of that which maximizes net benefit? Won't it always pay the politicians to take control of the Pentagon and cut back on the scale of military spending?

We've already seen that when there are two political parties competing for votes, the party that gets closest to maximizing net benefit is the one that picks up the most votes. Don't these forces of competition for votes dominate the wishes of the bureaucrats and ensure that the maximum budget allowed to them is that which maximizes net benefit?

If voters are well informed and if their perception of their self-interest is correct, the political party that wins the election is the one that holds the Pentagon budget to the level that provides the efficient amount of defense. But there is another possible equilibrium. It is one based on the principle of voter ignorance and well-informed interest groups.

Voter Ignorance and Well-Informed Interest Groups

One of the major propositions of public choice theory is that it does not pay voters to be well informed about the issues on which they are voting unless those issues have an immediate and direct consequence for their own income. In other words, it pays voters to be rationally ignorant. **Rational ignorance** is the decision *not* to acquire information because the cost of acquiring the information is greater than the benefit derived from having it. For example, each voter knows that he or she can make virtually no difference to the actual defense policy pursued by the U.S. government. Each voter also knows that it would take an enormous amount of time and effort to become even moderately well-informed about alternative defense technologies and the most effective ways of achieving different levels of defense. As a result, voters see it as being in their best interests to remain relatively uninformed about the technicalities of national defense issues. (Though we are using national defense as an example, the same applies to all aspects of government economic activity.)

All voters are consumers of national defense. But not all voters produce it. Only a small number are in this latter category. Those voters who produce national defense, whether they be members of the military or firms and households that work in producing defense equipment, have a direct personal interest in defense because it affects their incomes. Unlike other voters, therefore, it pays these voters to become well informed about national defense issues and to operate a political lobby aimed at furthering their own interests. These voters, in collaboration with the bureaucracies that deliver national defense, will exert a larger influence through the voting process than the relatively uninformed general voters who only consume this public good.

If the rationality of the uninformed voter and the rationality of the informed special interest group are taken into account, a political equilibrium emerges in which the scale of provision of public goods exceeds the one that maximizes net benefit.

REVIEW

Bureaucrats seek the largest possible budgets, and politicians balance the demand for bigger budgets against the cost of losing votes through higher taxes. If voters are well informed, they vote for the budget size that maximizes net benefit. If the consumers of public goods are less well informed about their costs and benefits than are the producers of those goods, the scale of provision of public goods exceeds that which maximizes net benefit. ◆

We've now seen how voters, politicians, and bureaucrats interact to determine the scale of provision of public goods and services and the scale of redistribution and how they deal with external costs and benefits. But public goods and services have to be paid for with taxes. How does the political marketplace determine the scale and variety of taxes that we pay? And why does the government not tax some goods and services, but instead subsidizes them? We've seen one partial answer to some of these questions already—taxes and subsidies might be used as a part of the government's attempt to deal with externalities. But that is not the entire story, as we'll now see.

Taxes and Subsidies

The bulk of the government's revenue arises from income taxes. But more than one fifth of the revenue of the federal, state, and local governments comes from taxes on expenditure. The highest tax rates are levied on such commodities as gasoline, alcoholic beverages, tobacco products, and some imported goods. Why are some goods taxed very highly and others hardly at all? Why are some goods even subsidized?

Excise Taxes

An **excise tax** is a tax on the sale of a particular commodity. The tax may be set as a fixed dollar amount per unit of the commodity, in which case it is called a *specific tax*. Alternatively, the tax may be set as a fixed percentage of the value of the commodity, in which case it is called an *ad valorem tax*. The taxes on gasoline, alcoholic beverages, and tobacco products are all examples of excise taxes.

Let's study the effects of an excise tax by considering the tax on gasoline. We'll assume that the market for gasoline is competitive. The presence of monopolistic elements does affect the answer to the question that we're now examining, and we'll consider what that effect is when we've worked through the competitive case.

Figure 20.5 illustrates the market for gasoline. The quantity of gasoline, measured in millions of gallons a day, is shown on the horizontal axis, and the price of gasoline (measured in cents per gallon) is on the vertical axis. The demand curve for gasoline is D, and the supply curve is S. If there is no tax on gasoline, its price is 60¢ a gallon and 400 million gallons of gasoline a day are bought and sold.

FIGURE 20.5
An Excise Tax

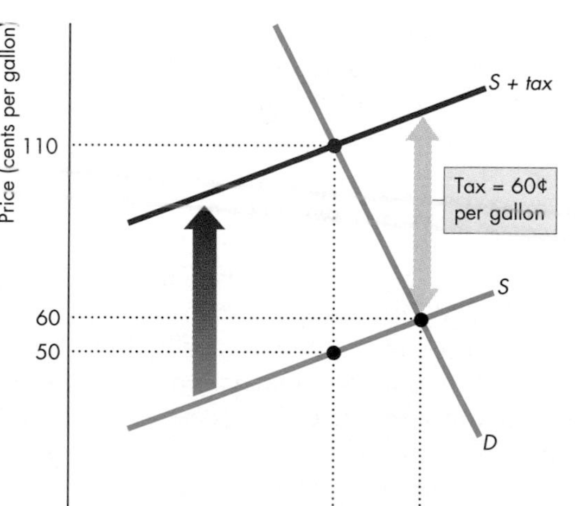

The demand curve for gasoline is D, and the supply curve is S. In the absence of any taxes, gasoline will sell for 60¢ a gallon and 400 million gallons a day will be bought and sold. When a tax of 60¢ a gallon is imposed, the supply curve shifts upward to become the curve $S + tax$. The new equilibrium price is $1.10 a gallon, and 300 million gallons a day are traded.

Let's suppose that a tax is imposed on gasoline at the rate of 60¢ a gallon. If producers are willing to supply 400 million gallons a day for 60¢ when there is no tax, then they will be willing to supply that same quantity in the face of a 60¢ tax only if the price increases to $1.20 a gallon. That is, they will want to get the 60¢ a gallon they received before, plus the additional 60¢ that they now have to hand over to the government in the form of a gasoline tax. As a result of the tax, the supply curve shifts upward by the amount of the tax and becomes the red curve labeled *S + tax*. The new supply curve intersects the demand curve at a quantity of 300 million gallons a day and at a price of $1.10 a gallon. This situation is the new equilibrium after the imposition of the tax.

Although we have just examined the effects of an excise tax on gasoline, the same basic analysis has widespread application. Taxes on alcohol and tobacco, sales taxes, and even taxes imposed in the labor market—for example, personal income taxes and social security taxes—can be analyzed in the same manner. The imposition of a tax shifts the supply curve upward by the amount of the tax. The new equilibrium is determined at a higher price and a lower quantity.

Monopoly Markets A monopoly industry has a higher price and smaller quantity than the same industry would have in competitive conditions. The monopoly determines its profit-maximizing price by making marginal revenue and marginal cost equal. The imposition of a sales tax or excise tax on a monopoly works in a manner similar to the way it works in a competitive industry. The tax represents an increase in the monopoly's marginal cost. Its marginal cost curve shifts upward by the amount of the tax. Monopoly profit is maximized by producing the output at which marginal cost plus tax equals marginal revenue. Thus the imposition of a sales tax or an excise tax on a monopoly industry has the effect of raising the price and lowering output in the same way that it does in a competitive industry.

Why Do Tax Rates Vary?

Why is the structure of taxes the way it is? Why do we tax alcohol, tobacco, and gasoline at a very high rate and some goods not at all? There are two main reasons why some commodities are taxed very highly and others hardly at all. First, the consumption of some goods, as we saw in Chapter 19, imposes external costs. By placing taxes on the purchase and consumption of such goods, people can be made to take into account the external costs they are imposing on others when they make their own consumption choices. Second, taxes create *deadweight losses*, and levying taxes at different rates on different commodities can minimize the deadweight loss arising from raising a given amount of revenue. Let's look at these two explanations for variable tax rates a bit more closely.

External Costs External costs are associated with many goods that are taxed at a high rate. For example, the high tax on gasoline in part enables road users to be confronted with the marginal social cost of the congestion that they impose on others. The high taxes on alcohol and tobacco products in part serve to confront drinkers and smokers with the external costs that their consumption habits impose on others. The impairment of long-term health that results from using these products and the subsequent health-care costs may lead to costs that are borne by others. These costs are not taken into account when a person is deciding whether or not to drink or smoke.

Some goods that have high external costs associated with their consumption are not taxed. Instead, they are made illegal. Marijuana and cocaine are important examples of such goods. Large amounts of these goods are consumed every day in the United States, and the illegal markets in which they are traded generate large external costs. An alternative way of organizing these markets would be to make these drugs legal but to impose heavy taxes on them. Sufficiently high taxes would leave the quantities consumed similar to (and perhaps even smaller than) what they currently are and would confront the users of these drugs with the marginal social cost of their actions. Such taxes would also result in a source of revenue (perhaps a large one) for the government. (Of course, matters relating to drugs have dimensions that go beyond a narrow economic calculation. Some people believe that the consumption of these drugs is so immoral that it would be equally immoral for the government, or anyone else, to legally profit from their production and consumption. These considerations, important though they are, go beyond the scope of economics.)

Let's now look at the deadweight loss that arises from taxes and the way in which this loss can be minimized.

Minimizing the Deadweight Loss of Taxes By returning to the example of the gasoline tax that you studied in Fig. 20.5, it's easy to see that taxes create deadweight loss. The deadweight loss associated with the gasoline tax is illustrated in Fig. 20.6. Without a tax, 400 million gallons of gasoline a day are consumed at a price of 60¢ a gallon. With a 60¢ tax, the price paid by the consumer rises to $1.10 a gallon and the quantity consumed declines to 300 million gallons a day. There is a loss of consumer surplus arising from this price increase and quantity decrease. There is also a loss of producer surplus. Producers now receive 50¢ a gallon for 300 million gallons compared with 60¢ a gallon for 400 million gallons in the absence of taxes. The deadweight loss—the sum of the loss of consumer surplus and the loss of producer surplus—is indicated by the gray triangle in Fig. 20.6. The dollar value of that triangle is 30 million dollars a day.[1] But how much revenue is raised by this tax? Since 300 million gallons of gasoline are sold each day and since the tax is 60¢ a gallon, total revenue from the gasoline tax is $180 million a day (300 million gallons multiplied by 60¢ a gallon). Thus to raise tax revenue of $180 million dollars a day using the gasoline tax, a deadweight loss of $30 million a day—one sixth of the tax revenue—is incurred.

One of the main influences on the deadweight loss arising from a tax is the elasticity of demand for the product. The demand for gasoline is fairly inelastic. As a consequence, when a tax is imposed, the quantity demanded falls by a smaller percentage than the percentage rise in price. In the example that we've just studied, the quantity demanded falls by 25 percent but the price increases by 83.33 percent.

To see the importance of the elasticity of demand, let's consider a different commodity—orange juice. So that we can make a quick and direct comparison, let's assume that the orange juice market is exactly as big as the market for gasoline. Figure 20.7 illustrates this market. The demand curve for orange juice is D, and the supply curve is S. Orange juice is not taxed, and so the price of orange juice is 60¢ a gallon—where the supply curve and the demand curve intersect—and the quantity of orange juice traded is 400 million gallons a day.

Now suppose that the government contemplates abolishing the gasoline tax and taxing orange juice instead. The demand for orange juice is more elastic than the demand for gasoline. It has many more good substitutes in the form of other fruit juices. The government wants to raise $180 million a day so that its total revenue is not affected by this tax change. The government's economists, armed with their statistical estimates of the demand and supply curves for orange juice that appear in Fig. 20.7, work out that a tax of 90¢ a gallon will do the job. With such a tax, the supply curve shifts upward to

FIGURE 20.6

The Deadweight Loss from an Excise Tax

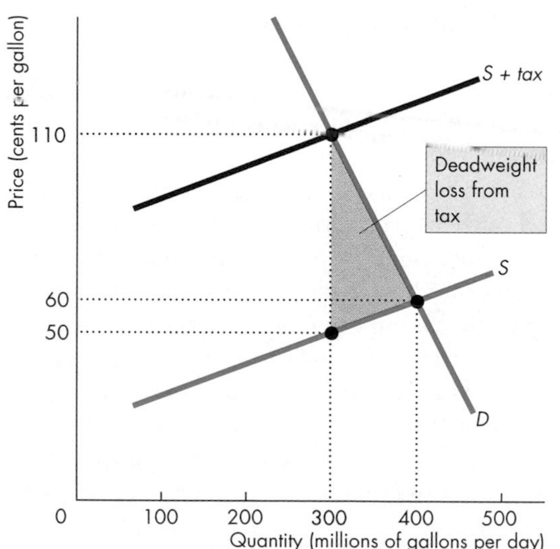

An excise tax creates a deadweight loss represented by the gray triangle. The tax revenue collected is 60¢ a gallon on 300 million gallons, $180 million a day. The deadweight loss from the tax is $30 million a day. That is, to raise tax revenue of $180 million a day, a deadweight loss of $30 million a day is incurred.

[1] You can calculate the area of that triangle by using the formula (base × height)/2. Turn the triangle on its side so that its base is 60¢, the size of the tax. Its height then becomes the reduction in the quantity sold—100 million gallons a day. Multiplying 60¢ by 100 million gallons and then dividing by 2 gives $30 million a day.

FIGURE 20.7

Why We Don't Tax Orange Juice

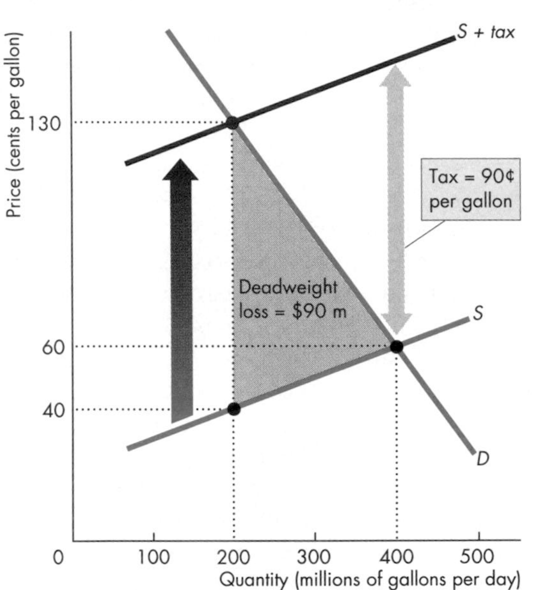

The demand curve for orange juice is *D*, and the supply curve is *S*. The equilibrium price is 60¢ a gallon, and 400 million gallons of juice a day are traded. To raise $180 million of tax revenue, a tax of 90¢ a gallon will have to be imposed. The introduction of this tax shifts the supply curve to *S + tax*. The price rises to $1.30 a gallon, and the quantity traded falls to 200 million gallons a day. The deadweight loss is represented by the gray triangle and equals $90 million a day. The deadweight loss from taxing orange juice is much larger than that from taxing gasoline (Fig. 20.6) because the demand for orange juice is more elastic than the demand for gasoline. Items that have a low elasticity of demand are taxed more heavily than items that have a high elasticity of demand.

the curve labeled *S* + *tax*. This new supply curve intersects the demand curve at a price of $1.30 a gallon and at a quantity of 200 million gallons a day. The price at which suppliers are willing to produce 200 million gallons a day is 40¢ a gallon. The government collects a tax of 90¢ a gallon on 200 million gallons a day, so it collects a total revenue of $180 million dollars a day—exactly the amount that it requires.

But what is the deadweight loss in this case? The answer can be seen by looking at the gray triangle in Fig. 20.7. The magnitude of the deadweight loss is $90 million.[2] Notice how much bigger the deadweight loss is from taxing orange juice than that from taxing gasoline. In the case of orange juice, the deadweight loss is one half the revenue raised, while in the case of gasoline it is only one sixth. The difference between these two markets is the elasticity of demand. The supply curves are identical in each case, and the examples were also set up to ensure that the initial no-tax prices and quantities were identical. The difference between the two cases is the elasticity of demand: In the case of gasoline, the quantity demanded falls by only 25 percent when the price almost doubles. In the case of orange juice, the quantity demanded falls by 50 percent when the price only slightly more than doubles.

You can see why taxing orange juice is not on the political agenda of any of the major parties. Vote-seeking politicians seek out taxes that benefit the median voter. Other things being equal, this means that they try to minimize the deadweight loss of raising a given amount of revenue. Equivalently, they tax items with an inelastic demand more heavily than items with an elastic demand.

Let's now turn to an examination of subsidies.

Subsidies Subsidies do not constitute a large percentage of government expenditure at the federal, state, or local level. Nevertheless, subsidies are important for many individual industries and are particularly important in agriculture. Farms receive subsidies in the form of below-cost inputs such as water—see Reading Between the Lines, pp. 552–553. They also receive subsidies in the form of direct payments related to their production levels. These subsidies bring in more than 10 percent of the total receipts of producers of wheat and other grains. We'll study subsidies by examining the market for wheat.

Suppose that the wheat market is as illustrated in Fig. 20.8. The demand curve is *D*, and the supply curve is *S*. Two billion bushels a year are produced at a price of $3.50 a bushel. Now suppose that the government offers wheat growers a subsidy of $1 a

[2] This deadweight loss is calculated in exactly the same way as the deadweight loss from the gasoline tax. If we turn the deadweight loss triangle on its side, the base is 90¢ and the height is 200 million gallons. Using the formula for the area of the triangle—base multiplied by height divided by 2—we calculate the deadweight loss as 90¢ multiplied by 200 million and then divided by 2, which equals $90 million a day.

FIGURE 20.8

Subsidies

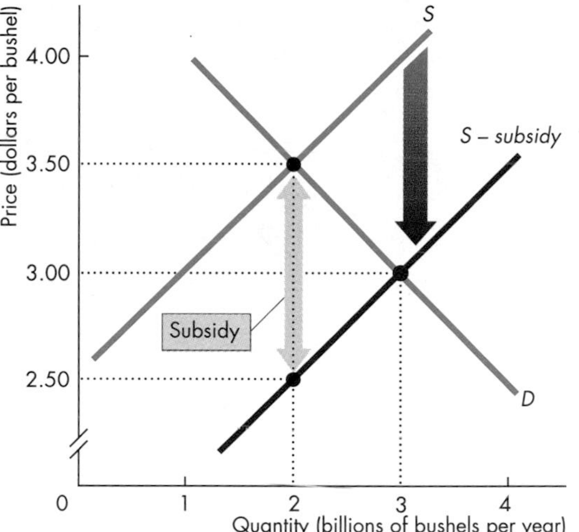

The demand curve for wheat is *D*, and the supply curve is *S*. A competitive market with no taxes or subsidies produces 2 billion bushels of wheat a year at a price of $3.50 a bushel. If the government subsidizes wheat production by $1 a bushel, the supply curve shifts downward to the curve labeled *S – subsidy*. The price of wheat falls to $3 a bushel, and the quantity produced increases to 3 billion bushels a year. Wheat growers receive just enough revenue from the market, along with the subsidy, to cover their costs.

FIGURE 20.9

Subsidies with Quotas

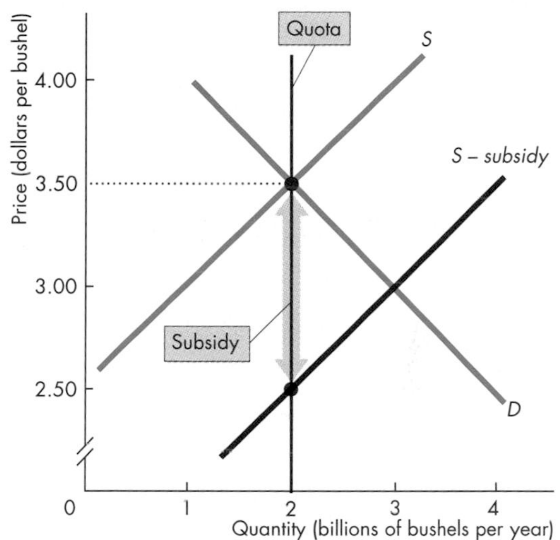

A competitive wheat market with no taxes or subsidies produces 2 billion bushels a year at a price of $3.50 a bushel—the point of intersection of the curves *D* and *S*. A subsidy of $1 a bushel shifts the supply curve to *S – subsidy*. But if a quota is introduced, at the same time as the subsidy, the output of each producer is restricted so that total output stays at 2 billion bushels a year, and the price remains $3.50 a bushel. With the quota, producers receive $3.50 from the market plus $1 from the government. Producers gain from the quota. The revenue from the market covers costs, so the subsidy is like a monopoly profit.

bushel. If suppliers are willing to supply 2 billion bushels a year for $3.50 without a subsidy, then they will be willing to supply that same quantity for $2.50 with a $1 subsidy. The supply curve for wheat, therefore, shifts downward by the amount of the subsidy and becomes the curve that is labeled *S – subsidy*. The equilibrium occurs where the new supply curve intersects the demand curve at a price of $3 a bushel and at a quantity of 3 billion bushels a year. The price of wheat falls by 50¢ a bushel. Consumers pay 50¢ a bushel less, and producers' costs rise by 50¢ a bushel. The 50¢ cost increase and the 50¢ price cut are made up by the $1 subsidy to the producer.

Subsidies with Quotas In the United States, in addition to subsidies on production in the farm sector, there are also quotas. A **quota** is a limit on the quantity that a firm is permitted to produce. When a group of producers can enforce quotas, it is possible to restrict output and thereby obtain monopoly profit. We can see the effects of quotas and subsidies in Fig. 20.9. Suppose that the government establishes and enforces quotas for each producer that result in total output being 2 billion bushels a year (shown by the vertical line marked "Quota" in the figure). At this output level, consumers are willing to pay $3.50 a bushel for the wheat, and so that will be its market price. Producers also get a subsidy of a dollar a bushel on everything they produce, so the supply curve becomes *S – subsidy*. With the subsidy and a market price of $3.50, producers would like to supply 4 billion bushels a year—the quantity on the new (red) supply curve at a price of $3.50. But they're prevented from doing so by the quota.

The Political Economy of Water

THE ECONOMIST, FEBRUARY 22, 1992

Water in California: Wrong Place

The politics of water in California is seldom easy to explain. In the same week that storms, floods and mudslides swept away houses in Los Angeles and San Francisco, the federal government cut off its supplies to California's farmers to save a rare fish. Refreshingly, this time there may be a positive twist: a new, more sensible water policy in the pipeline.

At the heart of California's water problems is agriculture, which accounts for less than 5% of the state's gross product, but 85% of its water use. Farmers have cut back on some of their more extravagant habits such as flood irrigation, but they still grow thirsty crops, like rice and alfalfa. And the farmers receive their water at subsidised prices, sometimes a tenth of the cost to the cities.

California's reservoirs are at only a third of their normal level. The torrential rain that fell on the coast ran off into the sea. Most of the state's water comes from snow in the Rockies and the Sierras—and is carried down by three huge public canals: the State Water Project, the Colorado River Project and the Central Valley Project (CVP). The CVP is run by the federal Bureau of Reclamation and carries water to the farms in the San Joaquin valley.

The federal government turned off the CVP to farmers for the first time in its 40-year history to save a race of the chinook salmon. The fish spawn just below the Shasta dam at the top of the Sacramento River. Their young die if the water gets too warm. That will happen if the water level behind the dam drops too low during summer. . . .

Already the farmers are up in arms, complaining that saving the salmon will cost $1 billion in lost crops. Environmentalists are suspicious of such claims. . . .

The good news is that the bureau's decision may prompt more water trading . . ., now common in other parts of the west. Indeed many California farmers might make more money from selling their water rights than selling their crops. . . .

The Essence of the Story

Agriculture, which accounts for less than 5 percent of California's gross product, uses 85 percent of its water.

Farmers receive water at subsidized prices, sometimes a tenth of those paid by cities.

Most of California's water comes from snow in the Rockies and the Sierras and is carried by three public canals into reservoirs that were at a third of their normal level in 1992.

The federal government turned off the farmers' water from one of the canals (for the first time in its 40-year history) to protect the rare chinook salmon.

Farmers complained that saving the salmon cost $1 billion in lost crops, but environmentalists doubted those claims.

Turning off the water has sparked interest in water trading—selling water rights.

If they were permitted to do so, many California farmers might make larger incomes from selling water rights than from selling crops.

Background and Analysis

The market for water in California is illustrated in the figures. In all three figures, *MC* is the (long-run) marginal cost curve (assumed to be constant).

In Fig. 1, the cities' demand curve for water is D_C. Cities are assumed to pay the full cost of the water they consume. They pay P_C and consume Q_C.

In Fig. 2, the farmers' demand curve for water is D_F. Farmers are subsidized, paying only a tenth of the cost of the water they consume. They pay P_F and consume Q_F.

Figure 3 shows the losses and gains from the subsidy to farmers. Water actually costs *MC*, but farmers pay only P_F and consume Q_F.

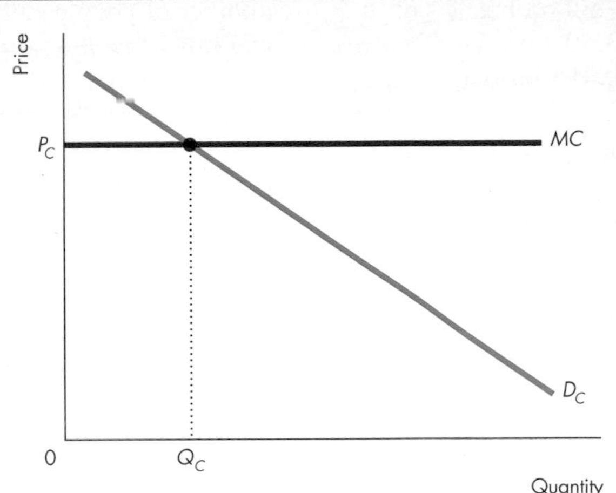

Figure 1

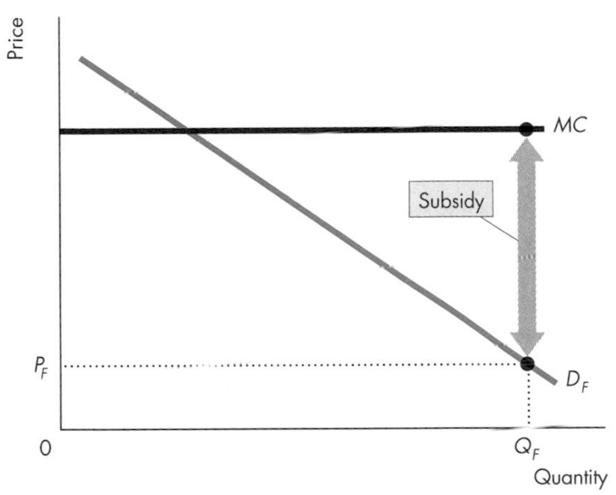

Figure 2

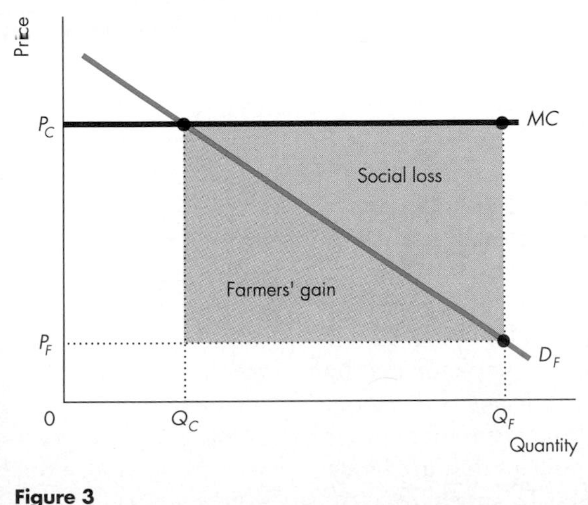

Figure 3

The total amount paid by the government in excess of the amount paid by the farmers is indicated by the two colored triangles in Fig. 3. The blue triangle is the gain to the farmers and the loss to the rest of the community. The gray triangle is the social loss—the loss to the taxpayer that no one gains.

In contrast to the existing state of affairs, if farmers are permitted to sell their water rights to cities, water flows to its highest-value use and the *opportunity cost* of water increases to the price at which farmers can sell it—P_C. Farmers economize and cut their consumption to Q_C. They sell the rights to the rest of their water to the cities at a price of P_C.

With output restricted to 2 billion bushels of wheat, producers' costs are $3.50 a bushel. They are also selling their wheat for $3.50 a bushel. In addition, they are receiving $1 a bushel in subsidies from the government. The subsidy is like a monopoly profit.

It is interesting to contrast this situation with the one in which there is a subsidy but no quota. Without a quota, output is 3 billion bushels and marginal cost is $4 a bushel. The market price is $3 a bushel, so the subsidy of $1 a bushel makes up the difference between the market price and marginal cost. Without a quota, the price plus the subsidy just covers marginal cost. With a quota, price covers marginal cost and the subsidy is a surplus for the producer—an excess revenue over cost.

Subsidies with quotas are clearly a good thing from the point of view of producers. But they are a bad thing from the point of view of consumers. To pay a subsidy, the government has to raise taxes that create deadweight loss. So why do we have subsidies with quotas?

Why Subsidies and Quotas? The existence of quotas and subsidies is explained by the fact that the people who stand to gain from a system of quotas and subsidies are relatively well-defined and easily organized into a political force. Those who stand to lose are highly diffuse and much more difficult and costly to organize. As a result, the political equilibrium that prevails is one in which a relatively small number of people gain a significant per person amount while a relatively large number of people lose an unnoticeable amount each.

◆ ◆ ◆ ◆ We have now reviewed the structure of the government sector, market failure, and the theory of public choice that explains how politicians, bureaucrats, and voters interact to determine the scale of provision of public goods, the extent to which taxes and subsidies are used to cope with externalities, the amount of income redistribution, and the levels of taxes and subsidies. ◆ ◆ We have seen that a political equilibrium emerges in which no individual can improve his or her own situation by proposing or implementing a different policy. Each political party devises a program that appeals as closely as possible to half of the electorate. The parties differ in their rhetoric because of differences in the particular half of the electorate to which they appeal, but their actions are similar to each other. Bureaucrats increase their budgets to the point at which politicians perceive the votes gained from additional public goods and services to be matched by the votes lost from higher taxes. Voters are as well informed as it pays them to be—they are rationally ignorant. ◆ ◆ In the next chapter, we're going to study a further range of government actions—their interventions in markets for goods and services in which there are monopoly and cartel elements.

SUMMARY

The Political Marketplace

There are three types of actors in the political marketplace: voters, politicians, and bureaucrats. Voters are the consumers of the outcome of the political process. They express their demands through their votes, campaign contributions, and lobbying. Public choices are made by politicians and implemented by bureaucrats. The objective of politicians is to win enough votes to be elected and then to remain in office. They do so by offering policies that are likely to appeal to a majority of voters. To appeal to a majority of voters, politicians have to appeal to the median voter. Since politicians aim for the vote of the median voter, their policies will resemble each other—they will be minimally differentiated. For example, in designing income redistribution policies, politicians transfer from the rich not only to the poor but to everyone with incomes at or below the median. Redistribution will be aimed at making the median voter as rich as possible.

Bureaucrats, in pursuing their own objectives, seek to maximize the budget of their own bureau. If voters are well informed, politicians will not be able to collect taxes to enable bureaucrats to achieve budgets in excess of those that maximize net benefit. But if voters are rationally ignorant, producer interests may result in voting to support taxes that in turn support a level of provision of public goods in excess of that which maximizes net benefit. (pp. 538–547)

Taxes and Subsidies

The imposition of a tax on a good shifts the supply curve upward, raises the price of the good, lowers the quantity bought and sold, and creates a deadweight loss. The size of the deadweight loss depends on the elasticity of demand. Taxing goods that have a low elasticity of demand minimizes the deadweight loss of raising a given amount of tax revenue. The highest tax rates are applied to goods with a low elasticity of demand.

Subsidizing a good shifts the supply curve downward, lowers the price of the good, and increases the quantity traded. Subsidies combined with quotas generate additional income for producers at the expense of consumers. (pp. 547–554)

KEY ELEMENTS

Key Terms

Bureaucrats, 538
Excise tax, 547
Lobbying, 538
Median voter theorem, 542
Political equilibrium, 539
Politicians, 538
Principle of minimum differentiation, 541
Quota, 551
Rational ignorance, 546
Voters, 538

Key Figures

Figure 20.1 Provision of a Public Good in a Political System, 540
Figure 20.2 The Principle of Minimum Differentiation, 541
Figure 20.3 The Median Voter Theorem, 542
Figure 20.4 Bureaucratic Overprovision, 546
Figure 20.5 An Excise Tax, 547
Figure 20.8 Subsidies, 551
Figure 20.9 Subsidies with Quotas, 551

REVIEW QUESTIONS

1 What are the three types of actors in the political marketplace?

2 Describe the economic functions of voters, and explain how voters make their economic choices.

3 Describe the economic functions of politicians, and explain how politicians make their economic choices.

4 What is meant by "political equilibrium"?

5 What is the principle of minimum differentiation?

6 How does the principle of minimum differentiation explain political parties' policy platforms?

7 What is the median voter theorem?

8 What features of political choices does the median voter theorem explain?

9 What are the economic functions of bureaucrats, and how do bureaucrats make their economic choices?

10 Describe the ways in which government redistributes income.

11 Why is it rational for voters to be ignorant?

12 Explain why it is likely that the scale of provision of public goods will exceed the allocatively efficient scale.

PROBLEMS

1 Your local city council is contemplating upgrading its system for controlling traffic signals. It reckons that by installing a sophisticated computer with sensing mechanisms at all the major intersections, it can better adjust the timing of the changes in signals and improve the speed of the traffic flow. The bigger the computer the council buys, the better the job it can do, and the more sensors it installs, the more intersections it can monitor and the faster the overall traffic flow that will result. The mayor and the other elected officials who are working on the proposal want to determine the scale and sophistication of the system that will win them the most votes. The city bureaucrats in the traffic department want to maximize the budget. Suppose that you are an economist who is observing this public choice. Your job is to calculate the scale of provision of this public good that maximizes net benefit—that achieves allocative efficiency.

a. What data would you need in order to reach your own conclusions?
b. What does the public choice theory predict will be the scale of provision chosen?
c. How could you, as an informed voter, attempt to influence the choice?

2 Three people—Jan, Jill, and Joyce—have incomes of \$10,000, \$5,000, and \$2,500, respectively. Set up a proposed redistribution of income among these three people that will achieve majority support. Once you've determined the new distribution (after implementing your proposal), set up another scheme that will also command a majority support. Show that you can find a voting cycle.

3 A community of nine people, identified by letters *A* through *I*, have strong views about a local factory that is polluting the atmosphere. Some of them work at the factory and don't want the government to take any action against it, while others want to see the imposition of a huge tax based on the scale of pollution. The preferences of the nine people concerning the scale of the tax that should be imposed are as follows:

A	*B*	*C*	*D*	*E*	*F*	*G*	*H*	*I*
90	80	70	60	50	0	0	0	0

Suppose there are two political parties competing for office in this community. What tax rate would the parties propose?

4 You are given the following information about a perfectly competitive market for cookies:

Price (dollars per pound)	Quantity demanded (pounds per month)	Quantity supplied (pounds per month)
10	0	36
8	3	30
6	6	24
4	9	18
2	12	12
0	15	0

a. What are the competitive equilibrium price and quantity?
b. Suppose that a 10 percent tax is imposed on cookies.
   (1) What is the new price of cookies?
   (2) What is the new quantity bought and sold?
   (3) What is the total amount of tax revenue raised by the government?
   (4) What is the deadweight loss?
c. Now suppose that cookies are not taxed but are instead subsidized by 10 percent.
   (1) What happens to the price of cookies?
   (2) What happens to the quantity bought and sold?
   (3) How much is the subsidy paid out by the government?
   (4) Suppose that along with the 10 percent subsidy, a quota of 12 pounds per month is imposed on cookie producers. What is the level of profit for the producer?

CHAPTER 21

REGULATION AND ANTITRUST LAW

After studying this chapter, you will be able to:

- Define regulation
- Describe the main elements of antitrust law
- Distinguish between the public interest theory and the capture theory of regulation
- State which parts of the economy are subject to regulation
- Describe the main trends in regulation and deregulation
- Explain how regulation of natural monopolies affects prices, outputs, profits, and the gains from trade for consumers and producers
- Explain how regulation of cartels affects prices, outputs, profits, and the gains from trade for consumers and producers
- Explain how antitrust law has been applied in a number of landmark cases

Public Interest or Special Interests?

WHEN YOU CONSUME WATER, ELECTRIC POWER, GAS, cable TV, or local telephone services, you are buying from regulated natural monopolies. Why are the industries that produce these goods and services regulated? How are they regulated? And do the regulations work in the interests of consumers—the public interest—or do they serve the interests of the producer—special interests? ◆◆ Regulation extends beyond natural monopoly to cartels. For example, until 1978, the price of air transportation in the United States and the routes that airlines could fly were regulated by the Civil Aeronautics Board (CAB). But in 1978, domestic air travel was deregulated and the CAB was disbanded, leaving the airlines free to choose their own routes and fares. Interstate trucking and financial services were regulated in the past but in recent years have been deregulated. Why do governments sometimes regulate an industry and at other times deregulate that same industry? Whose interest is served by regulation and deregulation—the consumers' or the producers'? ◆◆ Government also influences the economy with its antitrust laws—laws that block mergers and that result in companies being broken up. For example, until a few years ago, to make a long-distance phone call, you had no choice but to use the American Telephone and Telegraph Company (AT&T). Our antitrust laws were used to break up AT&T and to create a number of independent producers of long-distance telephone service such as MCI and U.S. Sprint. ◆◆ What are the antitrust laws? How have they evolved over the years? How are they used today? Do antitrust laws serve consumer interests or the special interests of producer groups?

◆ ◆ ◆ ◆ This chapter studies the actions taken by government to influence trading in markets for goods and services. The chapter draws on your earlier study of how markets work and on your knowledge of the gains from trade—of consumer surplus and producer surplus. It shows how consumers and producers might redistribute those gains and identifies who stands to gain and who stands to lose from various types of government intervention. Since such intervention is supplied by politicians and bureaucrats, the chapter also looks at the economic behavior of these groups in the "political marketplace."

Market Intervention

There are two main ways in which the government intervenes in monopolistic and oligopolistic markets to influence *what, how,* and *for whom* various goods and services are produced:

- Regulation
- Antitrust law

Regulation

Regulation consists of rules administered by a government agency to restrict economic activity by determining prices, product standards and types, and the conditions under which new firms may enter an industry. In order to implement its regulations, the government establishes agencies to oversee the regulations and ensure their enforcement. The first such agency to be set up in the United States was the Interstate Commerce Commission (ICC), established in 1887. Over the years since then and up to the late 1970s, regulation of the economy grew until, at its peak, almost a quarter of the nation's output was produced by regulated industries. Regulation applied to banking and financial services, telecommunications, gas and electric utilities, railroads, trucking, airlines and buses, and many agricultural products. Since the late 1970s, there has been a tendency to deregulate the U.S. economy.

Deregulation is the process of removing restrictions on prices, product standards and types, and entry conditions. In recent years, deregulation has occurred in domestic air transportation, telephone service, interstate trucking, and banking and financial services.

Antitrust Law

An **antitrust law** is a law that regulates and prohibits certain kinds of market behavior, such as monopoly and monopolistic practices. Antitrust law is enacted by Congress and enforced through the judicial system. Lawsuits under the antitrust laws may be initiated either by government agencies or by privately injured parties.

The main thrust of the antitrust law is the prohibition of monopoly practices and of restricting output in order to achieve higher prices and profits. The first antitrust law—the Sherman Act—was enacted in 1890. Successive acts and amendments have strengthened and refined the body of antitrust law. Antitrust law (like all law) depends as much on decisions of the courts and of the Supreme Court as on the statutes passed by Congress. Over the hundred years since the passage of the Sherman Act, there have been some interesting turns of direction in how the courts have interpreted the law and how vigorously it has been enforced. We'll study these later in this chapter.

To understand why the government intervenes in markets for goods and services and to work out the effects of its interventions, we need to identify the gains and losses that government actions can create. These gains and losses are the consumer surplus and producer surplus associated with different output levels and prices. You've already met these concepts in Chapters 7 (pp. 171–174) and 12 (pp. 330–331). All we need to do here, therefore, is refresh our understanding of these concepts and of the way in which their magnitudes are affected by the price at which a good is sold and the quantity bought.

Surpluses and Their Distribution

Consumer surplus is the difference between the maximum amount that consumers are willing to pay and the amount that they actually do pay for a given quantity of a good. Consumer surplus is the gain from trade accruing to consumers. *Producer surplus* is the difference between the producer's revenue and the opportunity cost of production. Producer surplus is the gain from trade accruing to producers. **Total surplus** is the sum of consumer surplus and producer surplus.

The lower the price and the larger the quantity bought and sold, the larger is consumer surplus. The closer the price and quantity bought to their monopoly profit-maximizing levels, the larger is producer surplus. Total surplus is maximized (in the absence of external costs and benefits) when marginal cost equals price. In this situation, allocative efficiency is achieved.

There is a conflict between maximizing producer surplus and maximizing total surplus. Monopoly firms have an incentive to restrict output below the competitive level, increasing producer surplus but reducing consumer surplus and creating deadweight loss. Thus there is a tension between the public interest of maximization of total surplus and the producer's interest of maximizing monopoly profit and producer surplus. This tension is of central importance in the economic theory of regulation. Let's now examine that theory.

Economic Theory of Regulation

The economic theory of regulation is part of the broader theory of public choice. You have already met that theory in Chapter 20 and seen the main components of a public choice model. We're going to reexamine the main features of such a model but with an emphasis on the regulatory aspects of government behavior. We'll examine the demand for government actions, the supply of those actions, and the political equilibrium—the balancing of demands and supplies.

Demand for Regulation

The demand for regulation is expressed through political institutions. Both consumers and producers vote, lobby, and campaign for regulations that best further their own interests. None of these activities are costless. Voters incur costs in order to acquire information on the basis of which to decide their vote. Lobbying and campaigning cost time, effort, and contributions to the campaign funds of political parties. Individual consumers and producers demand political action only if the benefit that they individually receive from such action exceeds the costs incurred by them in obtaining the action. There are four main factors that affect the demand for regulation:

- Consumer surplus per buyer
- Number of buyers
- Producer surplus per firm
- Number of firms

The larger the consumer surplus per buyer resulting from regulation, the greater is the demand for regulation by buyers. Also, as the number of buyers increases, so does the demand for regulation. But numbers alone do not necessarily translate into an effective political force. The larger the number of buyers, the greater is the cost of organizing them, so the demand for regulation does not increase proportionately with the number of buyers.

The larger the producer surplus per firm arising from a particular regulation, the larger is the demand by firms for that regulation. Also, as the number of firms that might benefit from some regulation increases, so does the demand for that regulation. But again, as in the case of consumers, large numbers do not necessarily mean an effective political force. The larger the number of firms, the greater is the cost of organizing them.

For a given surplus, consumer or producer, the smaller the number of households or firms that share the surplus, the larger is the demand for the regulation that creates it.

The Supply of Regulation

Regulation is supplied by politicians and bureaucrats. As we saw in Chapter 20, politicians choose policies that appeal to a majority of voters, thereby enabling themselves to achieve and maintain office. Bureaucrats support policies that maximize their budgets. Given these objectives of politicians and bureaucrats, the supply of regulation depends on the following factors:

- Consumer surplus per buyer
- Producer surplus per firm
- The number of people affected

The larger the consumer surplus per buyer or producer surplus per firm generated, and the larger the number of people affected by a regulation, the greater is the tendency for politicians to supply that regulation. If regulation benefits a large number of people significantly enough for it to be noticed and if the recipients know who is the source of the benefits, that regulation appeals to politicians and it is supplied. If regulation affects markets that benefit a large number of people but by a small amount per person, and if such benefits do not attract notice, that regulation does not appeal to politicians and it is not supplied. Regulation that bestows clear and large benefits on a small number of people may be attractive to politicians provided that some of those benefits flow back and thus enable the politicians to fight more effective election campaigns.

Equilibrium

In equilibrium, the regulation that exists is such that no interest group feels it is worthwhile to use additional resources to press for changes and no group of politicians feels it is worthwhile to offer different regulations. Being in a political equilibrium is not the same thing as everyone being in agreement. Lobby groups will devote resources to trying to change regulations that are already in place. And others will devote resources to maintaining the existing regulations. But no one will feel it is worthwhile to *increase* the resources they are devoting to such activities. Also, political parties will not agree with each other. Some will support the existing regulations, and others will propose different regulations. In equilibrium, no one wants to change the proposals that they are making.

What will a political equilibrium look like? There are two theories of political equilibrium: one is called the public interest theory, and the other is called the capture theory. Let's look at these two theories.

Public Interest Theory The **public interest theory of regulation** states that regulations are supplied to satisfy the demand of consumers and producers for the maximization of total surplus—or the attainment of allocative efficiency. Public interest theory predicts that the political process will relentlessly seek out deadweight loss and introduce regulations that eliminate it. For example, where monopoly or monopolistic practices by collusive oligopoly exist, the political process will introduce price regulation to ensure that output and price are close to their competitive levels.

Capture Theory The **capture theory of regulation** states that the regulations that exist are those that maximize producer surplus. The key idea of capture theory is that only those regulations that increase the surpluses of small, easily identified groups that have low organization costs will be supplied by the political process. Such regulations will be supplied even if they impose costs on others, provided that those costs are spread thinly and widely enough that they do not have negative effects on votes.

Whichever theory of regulation is correct, the political system delivers regulations that best further the electoral success of politicians. Since we have seen that producer-oriented and consumer-oriented regulation are in direct conflict with each other, it is clear that the political process cannot satisfy both groups in any particular industry. Only one group can win. This makes the regulatory actions of government a bit like a unique product—for example, a painting by Rembrandt. There is only one original, and it will be sold to just one buyer. Normally, a unique commodity is sold through an auction: the highest bidder takes the prize. Equilibrium in the regulatory process can be thought of in much the same way: the suppliers of regulation will satisfy the demands of the higher bidder. If the producer demand offers a bigger return to the politicians, either directly through votes or indirectly through campaign contributions, then the producers' interests will be served. If the consumer demand translates into a larger number of votes, then the consumer interest will be served by regulation.

REVIEW

The demand for regulation is expressed by both consumers and producers who spend scarce resources voting, lobbying, and campaigning for regulations that best further their own interests. Regulation is supplied by politicians and bureaucrats. Politicians choose actions that appeal to a majority of voters, and bureaucrats choose actions that maximize their budgets. The regulation that exists is the equilibrium that balances the opposing demand and supply forces. One possible political equilibrium is regulation that achieves allocative efficiency—the public interest theory of regulation. Another possible equilibrium is regulation that maximizes producer surplus—the capture theory of regulation. ◆

Regulation and Deregulation

The past 20 years have seen dramatic changes in the way in which the U.S. economy is regulated by government. We're going to examine some of the more important changes. To begin, we'll look at what is regulated and also at the scope of regulation. Then we'll turn to the regulatory process itself and examine how regulators control prices and other aspects of market behavior. Finally, we'll tackle the more difficult and controversial questions: Why do we regulate some things but not others? Who benefits from the regulation that we have?

The Scope of Regulation

The first federal regulatory agency, the Interstate Commerce Commission (ICC), was set up in 1887 to control prices, routes, and the quality of service of interstate transportation companies—railroads, trucking lines, bus lines, water carriers, and, in more recent years, oil pipelines. Following the establishment of the ICC, the regulatory environment remained static until the years of the Great Depression. Then, in the 1930s, more agencies were established—the Federal Power Commission, the Federal Communications Commission, the Federal Maritime Commission, and, in 1938, the Civil Aeronautical Agency, which was replaced in 1940 by the Civil Aeronautics Board. There was a further lull until the establishment in the 1970s of the Postal Rate Commission, the Copyright Royalty Tribunal, and finally, the Federal Energy Regulatory Com-

TABLE 21.1

Regulation at Its Peak in 1977

Organization	Year established	Controls and regulates
Interstate Commerce Commission	**1887**	**Prices, routes, and services of railroads, trucks, bus lines, oil pipelines, and domestic water carriers**
Federal Power Commission	**1930**	**Wellhead gas prices and wholesale prices of natural gas and electricity sold for resale in interstate commerce**
Federal Communications Commission	**1934**	**Prices for telephone and telegraph service; entry into telecommunications and broadcasting**
Federal Maritime Commission	**1936**	**Fares and schedules of transoceanic freight shipments**
Civil Aeronautics Board	**1938**	**Airline passenger fares; entry of airlines into city-to-city air routes**
Postal Rate Commission	**1970**	**Classes of mail and rates for those classes; sets fees for other services**
Copyright Royalty Tribunal	**1976**	**Fees and charges on copyright materials**
Federal Energy Regulatory Commission	**1977**	**Wellhead crude-oil prices and refinery, wholesale, and retail prices of petroleum products; allocation levels for wholesalers and retailers of crude oil, residual fuel oil, and most refined petroleum products produced in or imported into the United States during a period of energy emergency**

Source: The Federal Regulatory Directory (Washington, D.C.: Congressional Quarterly, 1991).

mission. Table 21.1 provides a summary of the federal regulatory agencies at the peak of regulation in 1977 and describes their functions.

In the mid-1970s, almost one quarter of the economy was subject to some form of regulation, as seen in Table 21.2(a). The most heavily regulated industries—those subject both to price regulation and to regulation of entry of new firms—were electricity, natural gas, telephones, airlines, highway freight services, and railroads (see Table 21.2b).

Regulation reached its peak in 1977. Since then, there has been a gradual and important deregulation process. Deregulation has had the most significant impact in the telecommunication, banking and finance, railroad, bus, trucking, and airline industries.

What exactly do regulatory agencies do? How do they regulate?

The Regulatory Process

Though regulatory agencies vary in size and scope and in the detailed aspects of economic life that they control, there are certain features common to all agencies.

First, the senior bureaucrats who are the key decision makers in a regulatory agency are appointed by the administration or Congress. In addition, all agencies have a permanent bureaucracy made up of experts in the industry being regulated. These experts are often recruited from the regulated firms. Agencies have financial resources, voted by Congress, to cover the costs of their operations.

Second, each agency adopts a set of practices or operating rules for controlling prices and other aspects of economic performance. These rules and practices are based on well-defined physical and financial accounting procedures that are relatively easy to administer and to monitor.

In a regulated industry, individual firms are free to determine the technology that they will use in production. But they are not free to determine the prices at which they will sell their output, the quantities that they will sell, or the markets that they will serve. The regulatory agency grants certification to a company to serve a particular market with a particular line of products, and it determines the level and structure of prices that will be charged. In some cases, the agency also determines the scale of output permitted.

TABLE 21.2
How Much Regulation?

(a) Regulation as a percentage of total output

	Year	
	1965	1975
Price regulation	5.5	8.8
Financial regulation	2.7	3.0
Health and safety regulation	—	11.9
Total	8.2	23.7

(b) Industries subject to price and entry regulation

Industry	Jurisdiction and extent of regulation
Electricity	**Federal Energy Regulatory Commission and 49 state agencies certify service.**
Natural gas	**Federal Energy Regulatory Commission controls interstate transportation, and 49 state agencies set rates for distribution.**
Telephones	**Federal Communications Commission and 50 state agencies set rates, entry, and service conditions.**
Airlines	**Civil Aeronautics Board regulations set fares and entry conditions before the Airline Deregulation Act of 1978; 21 state agencies set fare and entry conditions interstate.**
Highway freight	**Interstate Commerce Commission and 47 state agencies regulate rates; the ICC and 45 state agencies control entry into common-carrier services.**
Railroads	**Interstate Commerce Commission and 44 state agencies set freight rates; the ICC and 26 state agencies certify entry into the provision of rail services.**

Source: Paul W. MacAvoy, *The Regulated Industries and the Economy* (New York: W.W. Norton, 1979), 18, 25.

To analyze the way in which regulation works, it is convenient to distinguish between the regulation of natural monopoly and the regulation of cartels. Let's begin with natural monopoly.

Regulation of Natural Monopoly

Natural monopoly was defined in Chapter 12 (p. 314) as an industry in which one firm can supply the entire market at a lower price than two or more firms can. As a consequence, a natural monopoly experiences economies of scale, no matter how large an output it produces. Examples of natural monopolies include local distribution of gas and electricity and subway services. It is much more expensive to have two or more competing sets of pipes, wires and train lines serving every neighborhood than it is to have a single set.

Let's consider the example of a subway train service. The demand for the subway service and the subway's cost curves are illustrated in Fig. 21.1. The demand curve is *D*. The marginal cost curve is *MC*. Notice that the marginal cost curve is horizontal at 20¢ a ride—that is, the cost of each additional ride is a constant 20¢. The subway company has a heavy investment in track, trains, and control equipment and so has high fixed costs. These fixed costs feature in the company's average total cost curve, shown as *ATC*. The average total cost curve slopes downward because as the number of rides increases, the fixed cost is spread over a larger number of rides. (If you need to refresh your memory on how the average total cost curve is calculated, take a quick look back at pp. 240–245.)

FIGURE 21.1

Natural Monopoly: Marginal Cost Pricing

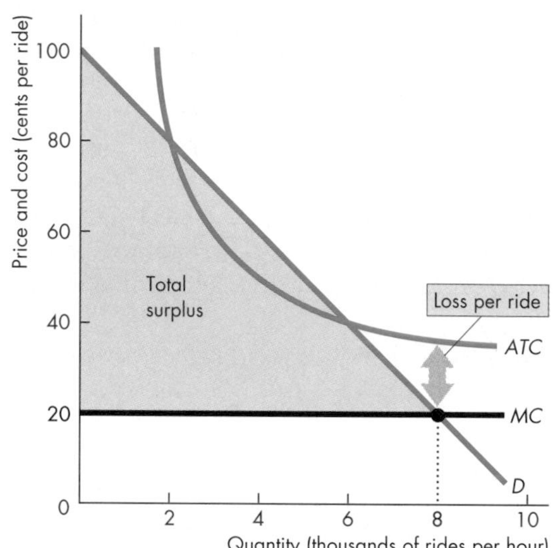

A natural monopoly is an industry in which average total cost is falling even when the entire market demand is satisfied. A natural monopoly for subway rides has a demand curve *D*. Marginal costs are constant at 20¢ a ride, as shown by the curve *MC*. Fixed costs are heavy, and the average total cost curve, which includes average fixed cost, is shown as *ATC*. A marginal cost pricing rule that maximizes total surplus sets the price of a ride at 20¢, with 8,000 rides an hour being taken. The resulting consumer surplus is shown as the green area. The producer makes a loss on each ride, indicated by the arrow. In order to remain in business, the producer must either price discriminate or receive a subsidy.

Regulation in the Public Interest How will this industry be regulated according to the public interest theory? Recall that, in the public interest theory, regulation maximizes total surplus—achieves allocative efficiency. Allocative efficiency occurs when marginal cost equals price. Equivalently, it occurs when total surplus is maximized—when the area above the marginal cost curve and below the demand curve is at a maximum. As you can see in the example in Fig. 21.1, that outcome occurs if the price is regulated at 20¢ a ride and if 8,000 rides an hour are produced. Such a regulation is called a marginal cost pricing rule. A **marginal cost pricing rule** sets price equal to marginal cost. It maximizes total surplus in the regulated industry.

A natural monopoly that is regulated to set price equal to marginal cost makes an economic loss. Because its average total cost curve is falling, marginal cost is below average total cost. Because price equals marginal cost, price is below average total cost. The difference between price and average total cost is the loss per unit produced. It's pretty obvious that a private subway company that is required to use a marginal cost pricing rule will not stay in business for long. How can a company cover its costs and, at the same time, obey a marginal cost pricing rule?

One possibility is price discrimination. Some natural monopolies can fairly easily price discriminate. For example, local telephone companies can charge consumers a monthly fee for being connected to the telephone system and then charge a low price (perhaps even zero) for each local call. A subway company can price discriminate by offering discounts on weekly or monthly season tickets.

But a natural monopoly cannot always price discriminate. When a natural monopoly cannot price discriminate, it can cover its total cost and follow a marginal cost pricing rule only if it receives a subsidy from the government. In such a case, the government would have to raise the revenue for the subsidy by taxing some other activity. But as we saw in Chapter 20, taxes themselves generate deadweight loss. Thus the deadweight loss resulting from additional taxes has to be offset against the allocative efficiency gained by forcing the natural monopoly to adopt a marginal cost pricing rule.

It is possible that deadweight loss will be minimized by permitting the natural monopoly to charge a higher price than marginal cost rather than by taxing some other sector of the economy in order to subsidize the natural monopoly. Such a pricing arrangement is called an average cost pricing rule. An **average cost pricing rule** sets price equal to average total cost. The average cost pricing solution is shown in Fig. 21.2. The subway company charges 40¢ for each ride and sells 6,000 rides an hour. Deadweight loss arises, represented by the gray triangle in the figure. Even though there is a deadweight loss, this situation might well be allocatively efficient. Recall that the subway company goes out of business if it doesn't cover its costs. If a subsidy is required to cover costs and if the subsidy requires a tax that has a deadweight loss larger than the one shown in the figure, then the average cost pricing rule is the best available.

FIGURE 21.2

Natural Monopoly: Average Cost Pricing

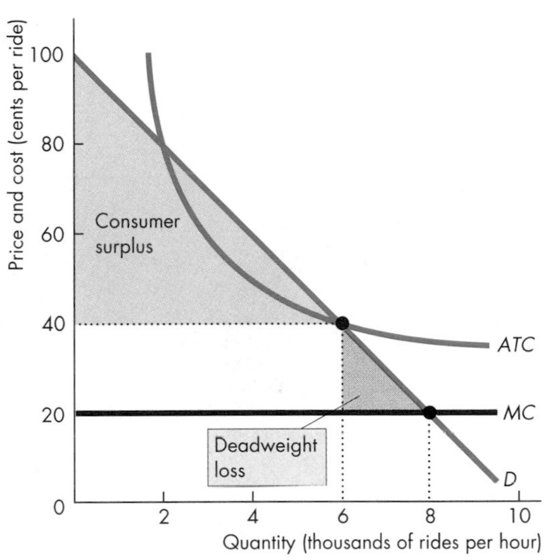

Average cost pricing sets price equal to average total cost. The subway company charges 40¢ a ride and sells 6,000 rides an hour. In this situation the subway company will break even—average total cost equals price. Deadweight loss, shown by the gray triangle, is generated. Consumer surplus is reduced to the green area.

Capturing the Regulator What does the capture theory predict about the regulation of this industry? Recall that according to the capture theory, regulation serves the interests of the producer. The interests of the producer, in this case, are best satisfied by maximizing profit. To work out the price that achieves this goal, we need to look at the relationship between marginal revenue and marginal cost. As you know, a monopoly maximizes profit by producing the output at which marginal revenue equals marginal cost. The monopoly's marginal revenue curve in Fig. 21.3 is the curve *MR*. Marginal revenue equals marginal cost when output is 4,000 rides an hour and the price is 60¢ a ride. Thus a regulation that best serves the interest of the producer will set the price at 60¢ a ride.

But how can a producer go about obtaining regulation that results in this monopoly profit-maximizing outcome? To answer this question, we need to look at the way in which agencies determine the level at which to set a regulated price. The key method used is called rate of return regulation.

Rate of Return Regulation **Rate of return regulation** determines a regulated price by setting the price at a level that enables the regulated firm to earn a specified target percent return on its capital. The target rate of return is determined with reference to what is normal in competitive industries. This rate of return is part of the opportunity cost of the natural monopolist and is included in the firm's average total cost. By examining the firm's total cost, including the normal rate of return on capital, the regulator attempts to determine the price at which average total cost is covered. Thus rate of return regulation is equivalent to average cost pricing.

In the example that we have just been examining—in Fig. 21.2—average cost pricing results in a regulated price of 40¢ a ride with 6,000 rides an hour being sold. Thus rate of return regulation,

FIGURE 21.3

Natural Monopoly: Profit Maximization

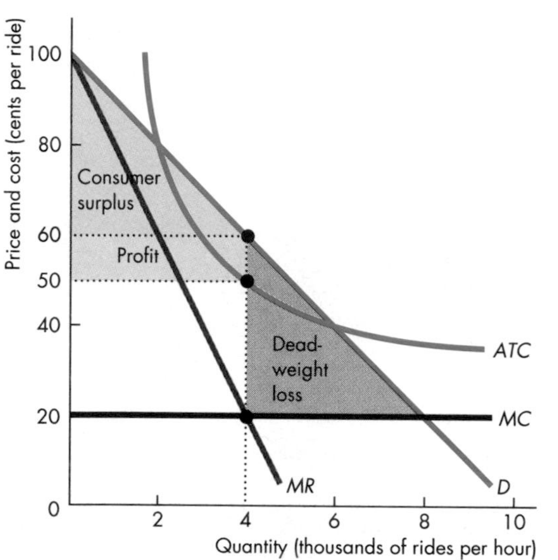

The subway company would like to maximize profit. To do so, marginal revenue (*MR*) is made equal to marginal cost. At a price of 60¢ a ride, 4,000 rides an hour are sold. Consumer surplus is reduced to the green triangle. The deadweight loss increases to the gray triangle. The monopoly makes the profit shown by the blue rectangle. If the producer can capture the regulator, the outcome will be the situation shown here.

FIGURE 21.4

Natural Monopoly: Inflating Costs

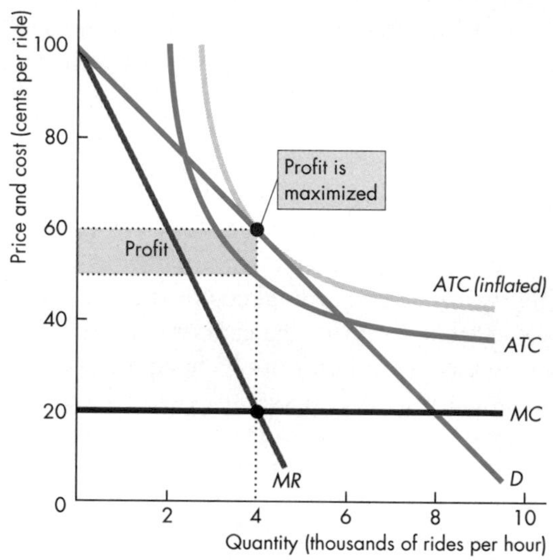

If the subway company is able to inflate its costs to *ATC(inflated)* and persuade the regulator that these are genuine minimum costs of production, rate of return regulation will result in a price of 60¢ a ride—the profit-maximizing price. To the extent that the producer can inflate costs above average total cost, the price will rise, output will fall, and deadweight loss will increase.

based on a correct assessment of the producer's average total cost curve, results in a price and quantity that favors the consumer and does not enable the producer to maximize monopoly profit. The special interest group will have failed to capture the regulator, and the outcome will be closer to that predicted by the public interest theory of regulation.

But there is an important feature of many real-world situations that the above analysis does not take into account—the ability of the monopoly firm to mislead the regulator about its true costs.

Inflating Costs The senior managers of a firm might be able to inflate the firm's costs by spending part of the firm's revenue on inputs that are not strictly required for the production of the good. By this device, the firm's apparent cost curves exceed the true cost curves. The main way in which managers inflate costs is by providing themselves with on-the-job luxury in the form of sumptuous office suites, limousines, free baseball tickets (disguised as public relations expenses), company jets, lavish international travel, and entertainment.

If the subway company manages to inflate its costs and persuade the regulatory agency that its true cost curve is that shown as *ATC(inflated)* in Fig. 21.4, then the regulator, applying the normal rate of return principle, will regulate the price at 60¢ a ride. In this example, the price and quantity will be the same as those under unregulated monopoly. It might be impossible for firms to inflate their costs by as much as the amount shown in the figure. But to the extent that costs can be inflated, the apparent average total cost curve lies somewhere between the true *ATC* curve and *ATC(inflated)*. The greater the ability of the firm to pad its costs in this way, the more closely its profit (measured in economic terms) approaches the maximum possible. The shareholders of this firm don't receive this economic profit. It gets used up by the managers of the firm on the self-serving activities that they have used to inflate the company's costs.

Public Interest or Capture?

It is not clear whether actual regulation produces prices and quantities that correspond more closely with the predictions of capture theory or with those of public interest theory. One thing is clear, however. Price regulation does not require natural monopolies to use the marginal cost pricing rule. If it did, most natural monopolies would make losses and receive hefty government subsidies to enable them to remain in business. But there are even exceptions to this conclusion. For example, many local telephone companies do appear to use marginal cost pricing for local telephone calls. They cover their total cost by charging a flat fee each month for being connected to their telephone system but then permitting each call to be made at its marginal cost—zero or something very close to it.

A test of whether natural monopoly regulation is in the public interest or the interest of the producer is to examine the rates of return earned by regulated natural monopolies. If those rates of return are significantly higher than those in the rest of the economy, then, to some degree, the regulator may have been captured by the producer. If the rates of return in the regulated monopoly industries are similar to those in the rest of the economy, then we cannot tell for sure whether the regulator has been captured or not, since we cannot know the extent to which costs have been inflated by the managers of the regulated firms.

Table 21.3 shows the rates of return in regulated natural monopolies as well as the economy's average rate of return. In the 1960s, rates of return in regulated natural monopolies were somewhat below the economy average; in the 1970s, those returns exceeded the economy average. Overall, the rates of return achieved by regulated natural monopolies were not very different from those in the rest of the economy. We can conclude from these data either that natural monopoly regulation does, to some degree, serve the public interest or that natural monopoly managers inflate their costs by amounts sufficiently large to disguise the fact that they have captured the regulator and that the public interest is not being served.

TABLE 21.3

Rates of Return in Regulated Monopolies

	Years	
	1962–1969	1970–1977
Electricity	3.2	6.1
Gas	3.3	8.2
Railroad	5.1	7.2
Average of above	3.9	7.2
Economy average	6.6	5.1

Source: Paul W. MacAvoy, *The Regulated Industries and the Economy* (New York, W.W. Norton, 1979), 49–60.

We've now examined the regulation of natural monopoly. Let's next turn to regulation in oligopolistic industries—to the regulation of cartels.

Regulation of Cartels

A *cartel* is a collusive agreement among a number of firms designed to restrict output and achieve a higher profit for the members of the cartel. Cartels arise in oligopolistic industries. An oligopoly is an industry in which a small number of firms compete with each other. We studied oligopoly and duopoly in Chapter 14. There we saw that if firms manage to collude and behave like a monopoly, they can set the same price and sell the same total quantity as a monopoly firm would. But we also discovered that in such a situation, each firm will be tempted to "cheat," increasing its own output and profit at the expense of the other firms. The result of such "cheating" on the collusive agreement is the unraveling of the monopoly equilibrium and the emergence of a competitive outcome with zero profit for producers. Such an outcome benefits consumers at the expense of producers.

How is oligopoly regulated? Does regulation prevent monopoly practices, or does it encourage those practices?

According to the public interest theory, oligopoly is regulated to ensure a competitive outcome. Consider, for example, the market for trucking tomatoes from the San Joaquin Valley to Los Angeles, illustrated in Fig. 21.5. The demand curve for trips is *D*. The industry marginal cost curve—and the competitive supply curve—is *MC*. Public interest regulation will regulate the price of a trip at $20, and there will be 300 trips a week.

How would this industry be regulated according to the capture theory? Regulation that is in the producer interest will set the price at $30 a trip and, to ensure that that price is maintained, will restrict the number of trips to 200 a week. Each producer will make a maximum profit, and the industry marginal revenue will be equal to the industry marginal cost. If there are 10 trucking companies, this outcome can be achieved by issuing a production quota to each trucking company restricting it to 20 trips a week so that the total number of trips in a week is 200. Penalties can be imposed to ensure that no single producer violates its quota.

FIGURE 21.5

Collusive Oligopoly

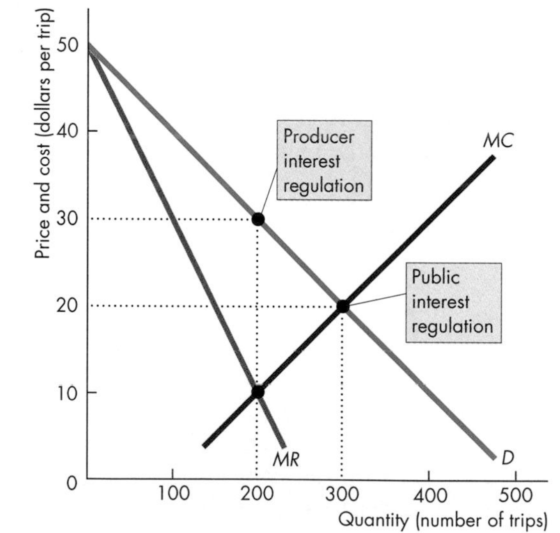

Ten trucking firms transport tomatoes from the San Joaquin Valley to Los Angeles. The demand curve is *D*, and the industry marginal cost curve is *MC*. Under competition, the *MC* curve is the industry supply curve. If the industry is competitive, the price of a trip will be $20 and 300 trips will be made each week. Producers will demand regulation that restricts entry and restricts the output of producers to 200 trips a week. This regulation will raise the price to $30 a trip and result in each producer making maximum profit—as if it is a monopoly. The industry marginal revenue will be equal to industry marginal cost.

What does regulation of oligopoly do in practice? Though there is disagreement about the matter, the consensus view is that regulation tends to favor the producer. Trucking (when it was regulated by the Interstate Commerce Commission), taxicabs (regulated by cities), and airlines (when they were regulated by the Civil Aeronautics Board) are specific examples of industries in which profits of producers increased as a result of regulation. In some cases—and trucking is one of these—the work force, through unionization, also manages to take a large part of the total surplus.

Some further evidence in support of the conclusion that regulation sometimes increases profit is presented in Table 21.4. If regulation ensures a competitive outcome, rates of return in a regulated oligopoly will be no higher than those in the economy as a whole. As the numbers in Table 21.4 show, rates of return in airlines and trucking exceeded twice the economy average rate of return in the 1960s. In the 1970s, the rate of return in trucking remained higher than the economy average (although by a smaller margin than had prevailed in the 1960s). Airline rates of return in the 1970s fell to below the economy average. The overall picture that emerges from examining data on rates of return is mixed. The regulation of oligopoly does not always result in higher profit, but there are many situations in which it does.

Further evidence on cartel and oligopoly regulation can be obtained from the performance of prices and profit following deregulation. If, following deregulation, prices and profit fall, then, to some degree, the regulation must have been serving the interest of the producer. In contrast, if, following deregulation, prices and profits remain constant or increase, then the regulation may be presumed to have been serving the public interest. Since there has been a substantial amount of deregulation in recent years, we may use this test of oligopoly regulation to see which of the two theories better fits the facts. The evidence is mixed, but there are many cases in which deregulation has been accompanied by falling

TABLE 21.4
Rates of Return in Regulated Oligopolies

	Years	
	1962–1969	1970–1977
Airlines	**12.8**	**3.0**
Trucking	**13.6**	**8.1**
Economy average	**6.6**	**5.1**

Source: Paul W. MacAvoy, *The Regulated Industries and the Economy* (New York: W.W. Norton, 1978), 49–60.

prices. Airlines, trucking, railroads, long-distance telephones, and banking and financial services are all industries in which deregulation was, initially at least, associated with more competition, lower prices, and a large increase in the volume of transactions.

Interpreting the deregulation evidence, however, is made difficult by the possibility that firms in oligopolistic industries will find other ways of restricting competition in a deregulated environment. There is evidence, for example, that the big airlines managed to do this in the 1980s through the creation of regional monopolies based on routes that radiate like the spokes of a wheel from hub airports and through their control of computerized reservation systems.

Making Predictions

Most industries have a few producers and many consumers. In these cases, public choice theory predicts that regulation will protect producer interests because a small number of people stand to gain a large amount and so they will be fairly easy to organize as a cohesive lobby. Under such circumstances, politicians will be rewarded with campaign contributions rather than votes. But there are situations in which the consumer interest is sufficiently strong and well organized and thus able to prevail. There are also cases in which the balance switches from producer to consumer, as seen in the deregulation process that began in the late 1970s.

Deregulation raises some hard questions for economists seeking to understand and make predictions about regulation. Why were the transportation and telecommunication sectors deregulated? If producers gained from regulation and if the producer lobby was strong enough to achieve regulation, what happened in the 1970s to change the equilibrium to one in which the consumer interest prevailed? We do not have a complete answer to this question at the present time. But regulation had become so costly to consumers, and the potential benefits to them from deregulation so great, that the cost of organizing the consumer voice became a price worth paying.

An important factor that increased the cost of regulation borne by consumers and brought deregulation in the transportation sector was the large increase in energy prices in the 1970s. These price hikes made route regulation by the ICC extremely costly and changed the balance in favor of consumers in the political equilibrium. Technological change was the main factor at work in the telecommunication sector. New satellite-based, computer-controlled long-distance technologies enabled smaller producers to offer low-cost services. These producers wanted a share of the business—and profit—of AT&T. Furthermore, as communication technology improved, the cost of communication fell and the cost of organizing larger groups of consumers also fell. If this line of reasoning is correct, we can expect to see more consumer-oriented regulation in the future. In practice, more consumer-oriented regulation means deregulation—removing the regulations that are already in place to serve the interests of producer groups.

REVIEW

Agencies regulate natural monopolies by setting their prices at levels that enable them to earn a target percent return on their capital. Such regulation gives firms an incentive to inflate costs and move as closely as possible to maximizing profit instead of producing the output that maximizes total surplus—the sum of consumer surplus and producer surplus. ◆◆ Cartels—collusive agreements among firms to restrict output and increase profit—

are unstable because each firm faces the temptation to increase its own output and profit at the expense of the other firms. The end result of this process is zero profit. Regulation of cartels, by establishing output levels for each firm, can help perpetuate the cartel and work against the public interest. The evidence suggests that cartel regulation tends to operate in the producer's interest. ◆

Let's now leave regulation and turn to the other main method of intervention in markets—antitrust law.

Antitrust Law

Antitrust law provides an alternative way in which the government may influence the marketplace. As in the case of regulation, antitrust law can be formulated in the public interest, to maximize total surplus, or in private interests, to maximize the surpluses of particular special interest groups such as producers.

Landmark Antitrust Cases

The antitrust laws themselves are brief and easily summarized. The first antitrust law, the Sherman Act, was passed in 1890 in an atmosphere of outrage and disgust at the actions and practices of J. P. Morgan, John D. Rockefeller, and W. H. Vanderbilt—the so-called "robber barons."[1] (See Our Advancing Knowledge on pp. 322–323.) The most lurid stories of the actions of these great American capitalists are not of their monopolization and exploitation of consumers but of their sharp practices against each other. Nevertheless, monopolies did emerge—for example, the spectacular control of the oil industry by John D. Rockefeller, Sr. The Sherman Act had little effect until the early part of this century, and by 1914 it was augmented by the more powerful Clayton Act and the creation of the Federal Trade Commission, an agency charged with enforcing the antitrust laws. Table 21.5 gives a summary of the main antitrust laws.

TABLE 21.5

Antitrust Laws

Name of law	Year passed	What the law prohibits
Sherman Act	**1890**	◆ **Combination, trust, or conspiracy to restrict interstate or international trade** ◆ **Monopolization or attempt to monopolize interstate or international trade**
Clayton Act **Robinson-Patman Amendment** **Cellar-Kefauver Amendment**	**1914** **1936** **1950**	◆ **Price discrimination if the effect is to substantially lessen competition or create monopoly and if such discrimination is not justified by cost differences** ◆ **Contracts that force other goods to be bought from same firm** ◆ **Acquisition of competitors' shares or assets if the effect is to reduce competition** ◆ **Interlocking directorships among competing firms**
Federal Trade Commission Act	**1914**	◆ **Unfair methods of competition and unfair or deceptive business practices**

The real force of any law arises from its interpretation. Interpretation of the antitrust laws has ebbed and flowed. At times, it has appeared to favor producers, and at other times, consumers. Let's see how.

Table 21.6 summarizes the landmark antitrust cases. The first important cases were those against the American Tobacco Company and Standard Oil Company, decided in 1911. These two companies were found guilty of violations under the Sherman Act and ordered to divest themselves of large holdings in other companies. The breakup of John D. Rockefeller's Standard Oil Company resulted in the creation of the oil companies that today are household names—such as Exxon.

[1]Business practices of this era are discussed by Matthew Josephson, *The Robber Barons: The Great American Capitalists, 1861–1901* (New York: Harcourt, Brace & Co., 1934).

TABLE 21.6

Landmark Antitrust Cases

Case(s)	Year	Verdict and consequence
American Tobacco Co.* and *Standard Oil Co.	**1911**	***Guilty:* Ordered to divest themselves of large holdings in other companies; "rule of reason" enunciated—only *unreasonable* combinations guilty under Sherman Act.**
U.S. Steel Co.	**1920**	***Not guilty:* Although U.S Steel had a very large market share (near monopoly), mere "size alone is not an offense"; application of the "rule of reason."**
Socony-Vacuum Oil Co.	**1940**	***Guilty:* Combination was formed for purpose of price fixing; no consideration of "reasonableness" applied.**
ALCOA	**1945**	***Guilty:* Too big—had too large a share of the market; end of "rule of reason."**
General Electric, Westinghouse, and others	**1961**	***Guilty:* Price-fixing conspiracy; executives fined and jailed.**
Brown Shoe	**1962**	***Guilty:* Ownership of Kinney, a retail chain, reduced competition; ordered to sell Kinney (Brown supplied 8% of Kinney's shoes, and Kinney sold 2% of nation's shoes).**
Von's Grocery	**1965**	***Guilty:* Merger of two supermarkets in Los Angeles would restrain competition (the merged firm would have had 7½% of the L.A. market).**
IBM	**1982**	***Case dismissed* as being "without merit."**
AT&T	**1983**	***Agreement* between AT&T and government that company would divest itself of all local telephone operating companies—80% of its assets.**

In finding American Tobacco and Standard Oil to be in violation of the provisions of the Sherman Act, the Supreme Court enunciated the "rule of reason." The rule of reason states that monopoly arising from mergers and agreements among firms is not necessarily illegal. Only if there is an unreasonable restraint of trade does the arrangement violate the provisions of the Sherman Act. The rule of reason was widely regarded as removing the force of the Sherman Act itself. This view was reinforced in 1920 when U.S. Steel Company was acquitted of violations under the act even though it had a very large (more than 50 percent) share of the U.S. steel market. Applying the "rule of reason," the court declared that "size alone is not an offense."

Matters remained much as they were in 1920 until 1940, when the *Socony-Vacuum Oil Company* case resulted in the first chink in the armor of the "rule of reason." The court found Socony-Vacuum Oil Company guilty because a combination had been formed for the purpose of price fixing. The court ruled that no consideration of reasonableness should be applied to such a case. But if the purpose of the agreement was price fixing, the automatic interpretation was to be that the agreement was unreasonable.

The "rule of reason" received its death blow in the *ALCOA* case, decided in 1945. ALCOA was judged to be in violation of the law because it was too big. It had too large a share of the aluminum market. A relatively tough interpretation of the law continued through the late 1960s. In 1961, General Electric, Westinghouse, and other electrical component manufacturers were found guilty of a price-fixing conspiracy. This case was the first one in which the executives (as opposed to the company itself) were fined and also jailed.

Tough antimerger decisions were taken in 1962 against Brown Shoe and in 1965 against Von's Grocery. In the first of these cases, Brown Shoe was required to divest itself of ownership of Kinney's shoe retail chain. This case is an example of the court ruling that a vertically integrated firm is capable of restraining competition. **Vertical integration** is the merger of two or more firms operating at different stages in a production process of a single good

Limiting Competition in Chips

The Wall Street Journal, July 1, 1991

FTC Inquiry on Intel's Business Tactics Signals Increased Scrutiny of Industry

by Stephen Kreider Yoder

Intel Corp.'s admission that the Federal Trade Commission is looking into its business tactics hangs a cloud of doubt over the strategies that made Intel one of Silicon Valley's biggest success stories. . . .

Intel's critics have long charged that the chip maker abuses its powerful monopoly of the chips called microprocessors that are the "brains" of popular personal computers. They say the Santa Clara, Calif., chip maker divvies out scarce chips improperly and unfairly crowds competition out of the market. Now, apparently, the FTC plans to test those charges.

Intel last week said it received a letter from the FTC saying the commission was carrying out the "nonpublic" investigation of Intel's business practices to determine whether they violate antitrust laws. . . .

The FTC's initial probe of Intel appears [to be] broad, covering customers and competitors. Intel says the commission's lawyers approached at least one of Intel's PC-making customers for information on Intel. Some PC makers are disgruntled with the way Intel allocates its microprocessors, which are often in short supply, charging that Intel unfairly sells its chips to big customers such as Compaq Computer Corp. while snubbing small newcomers.

"Competitors and customers have been concerned about Intel's ability to allocate market share," says analyst William Tai of Alex. Brown & Sons Inc. Intel's allocation of sought-after chips, in effect, decides which customers gain market share, he says. "Intel's allocations policy creates clear winners and losers, and the non-winners are sure to take issue with Intel's practices," he says. . . .

FTC officials over the past month have also grilled executives and lawyers from at least two companies that have filed antitrust complaints against Intel: chip maker Cyrix Corp. of Richardson, Texas, and Tokyo Cobra Corp., a chip distributor in Irvine, Calif.

Cyrix, which makes chips that mimic the functions of certain Intel chips called "math coprocessors," filed suit last year charging that Intel was conspiring to keep Cyrix out of the business by intimidating Cyrix's customers. Tokyo Cobra sued Intel after Intel cut off the distributor's chip supplies.

Intel's [general counsel, Thomas] Dunlap calls the lawsuits "knee-jerk reactions" to Intel's own suits against both companies. Intel sued Cyrix for alleged patent infringements and charged Tokyo Cobra with not paying bills.

Still, some antitrust lawyers speculate that the FTC may be concerned about what Intel's critics say is the company's pattern of using the courts to batter down potential competitors. Rivals such as Cyrix and Tokyo's NEC Corp. charge that Intel uses drawn-out court proceedings to cast clouds over competing products for years, until the market is gone. Intel denies that it unfairly uses the courts. . . .

The Essence of the Story

The Federal Trade Commission (FTC) is investigating Intel Corp., the profitable maker of the microprocessors used in personal computers.

Critics of Intel charge that the company improperly allocates its chips to big customers while snubbing small newcomers and that it improperly uses court proceedings to discourage competition.

Intel has sued Cyrix Corp., a maker of a math co-processor that performs a similar function to an Intel chip, for alleged patent infringements.

Cyrix has responded that Intel conspired to keep Cyrix out of the chip market by intimidating Cyrix's customers.

Intel has charged Tokyo Cobra, a chip distributor, with not paying its bills.

Tokyo Cobra has sued Intel for cutting off the distributor's chip supplies.

Background and Analysis

Intel makes the microprocessor (chip) that powers IBM and IBM-compatible personal computers, and its market is protected to some degree by patents. But other firms are attempting to enter the profitable chip market.

With limited competition, Intel maximizes profit as illustrated in Fig. 1. The quantity of chips produced, Q_0, is that at which marginal cost, *MC*, equals marginal revenue, *MR*. The price is P_0, and Intel's economic profit is shown by the blue rectangle.

Economic profit encourages entry, which, if unchecked, will eventually put Intel in the situation shown in Fig. 2. Intel still maximizes its profit, but that profit will be zero. The quantity produced will fall to Q_1, and the price will fall to P_1.

It pays Intel to incur costs—such as the costs of establishing and enforcing patents—that create barriers to entry and limit the decrease in the demand for its chips that results from entry.

It pays potential entrants to find ways around Intel's barriers to entry, including using all the available legal moves, such as showing a violation of the antitrust laws.

There is a fine line between legitimate protection of a firm's interests and illegal restriction of competition. The job of the FTC is to investigate cases in which there are allegations or suspicions that the line has been crossed. This is what was happening in the computer chip industry in 1991.

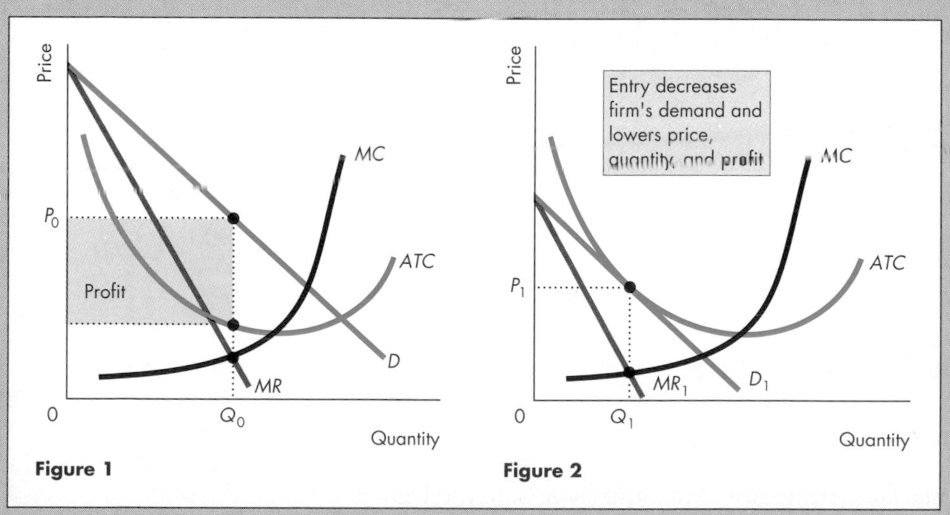

Figure 1

Figure 2

or service. For example, the merger of a firm that produces raw materials, a firm that converts those raw materials into a manufactured good, and a firm that retails the finished product will be a vertically integrated firm. The vertically integrated Brown Shoe and Kinney retail chain was ordered to be broken up even though Brown supplied only 8 percent of Kinney's shoes and Kinney sold only 2 percent of the nation's shoes.

Von's Grocery is an example of a horizontally integrated firm. **Horizontal integration** is a merger of two or more firms providing essentially the same product or service. In the *Von's Grocery* case, the court ruled that the combination of two supermarkets in Los Angeles would restrict competition even though the combined sales of the two firms would have been only 7½ percent of total supermarket sales in the Los Angeles area.

The two most visible recent antitrust cases are those involving AT&T and IBM. Though important and highly visible cases, neither of the two was decided by the courts. The *AT&T* case was resolved by an agreement between AT&T and the Department of Justice, and the *IBM* case, after 13 years of litigation, was dismissed by the government as being "without merit."

The present attitude toward monopoly is pragmatic. AT&T's monopoly on telephone services has gone. IBM's position in the computer industry is much less secure and looks much less like a monopoly today than it did in 1967 when the Justice Department began its proceedings against that firm. Also, increased international competition has reduced monopoly power in the computer industry. Nevertheless, many practices of firms in that industry continue to draw the interest and attention of the FTC, as you can see in Reading Between the Lines on pp. 572–573.

Public or Special Interest?

It is clear from the historical contexts in which antitrust law has evolved that its intent has been to protect and pursue the public interest and restrain the profit-seeking and anticompetitive actions of producers. But it is also clear from the above brief history of antitrust legislation and cases that from time to time the interest of the producer has had an influence on the way in which the law has been interpreted and applied. Nevertheless, the overall thrust of antitrust law appears to have been directed toward achieving allocative efficiency and, therefore, toward serving the public interest.

◆ ◆ ◆ ◆ In this chapter, we've seen how the government intervenes in markets to affect prices, quantities, the gains from trade, and the division of those gains between consumers and producers when there is monopoly or oligopoly. We've seen that there is a conflict between the pursuit of the public interest—achieving allocative efficiency—and the pursuit of the special interests of producers—maximizing monopoly profit. The political and legal arenas are the places in which these conflicts are resolved. We've reviewed the two theories—public interest and capture—concerning the type and scope of government intervention.

SUMMARY

Market Intervention

There are two ways in which the government intervenes to regulate monopolistic and oligopolistic markets: regulation and antitrust law. In the United States, both of these methods are widely used. We seek to understand the reasons for and the effects of regulation.

Government action can influence consumer surplus, producer surplus, and total surplus. Consumer surplus is the difference between what consumers are willing to pay for a given consumption level and what they actually pay. Producer surplus is the difference between a producer's revenue from its sales and the opportunity cost of production. Total surplus is the sum of consumer surplus and producer surplus. Total surplus is maximized under competition. Under monopoly, producer surplus is increased and consumer surplus is decreased, and a deadweight loss is created. (pp. 559–560)

Economic Theory of Regulation

Consumers and producers express their demand for the regulation that influences their surpluses by voting, lobbying, and making campaign contributions. The larger the surplus that can be generated by a particular regulation, and the smaller the number of people affected, the larger is the demand for the regulation. A smaller number of people are easier to organize into an effective political lobby. Regulation is supplied by politicians, who pursue their own best interest. The larger the surplus per head generated and the larger the number of people affected by it, the larger is the supply of regulation. In equilibrium, the regulation that exists is such that no interest group feels it is worthwhile to employ scarce resources to press for further changes. There are two theories of political equilibrium: public interest theory and capture theory. Public interest theory predicts that total surplus will be maximized; capture theory predicts that producer surplus will be maximized. (pp. 560–561)

Regulation and Deregulation

Regulation began with the establishment of the Interstate Commerce Commission in 1887. A further expansion of regulation occurred in the 1930s. There was further steady growth of regulatory activity to the mid-1970s. Since 1978, the transportation, telecommunication, and financial sectors have been deregulated.

Regulation is conducted by regulatory agencies controlled by politically appointed bureaucrats and staffed by a permanent bureaucracy of experts. Regulated firms are required to comply with rules about price, product quality, and output levels. Two types of industries are regulated: natural monopolies and cartels. In both cases, regulation has enabled firms in the regulated industries to achieve profit levels equal to or greater than those attained on the average in the rest of the economy. This outcome is closer to the predictions of the capture theory of regulation than to the predictions of the public interest theory. (pp. 562–570)

Antitrust Law

Antitrust law provides an alternative way in which the government can control monopoly and monopolistic practices. The law itself is brief, and its interpretation has fluctuated between favoring the consumer and favoring the producer.

But the overall thrust of the law has been directed toward serving the public interest. In recent years, increased international competition has reduced the monopoly power. (pp. 570–574)

KEY ELEMENTS

Key Terms

Antitrust law, 559
Average cost pricing rule, 565
Capture theory of regulation, 561
Deregulation, 559
Horizontal integration, 574
Marginal cost pricing rule, 564
Public interest theory of regulation, 561
Rate of return regulation, 565
Regulation, 559
Total surplus, 559
Vertical integration, 571

Key Figures and Tables

REVIEW QUESTIONS

1 What are the two main ways in which the government can intervene in the marketplace?

2 What is consumer surplus? How is it calculated, and how is it represented in a diagram?

3 What is producer surplus? How is it calculated, and how is it represented in a diagram?

4 What is total surplus? How is it calculated, and how is it represented in a diagram?

5 Why do consumers demand regulation? In what kinds of industries are their demands for regulation greatest?

6 Why do producers demand regulation? In what kinds of industries would their demands for regulation be greatest?

7 Explain the public interest and capture theories of the supply of regulation. What does each theory imply about the behavior of politicians?

8 How is oligopoly regulated in the United States? In whose interest is it regulated?

9 What are the main antitrust laws in force in the United States today?

10 What is the "rule of reason"? When was this rule formulated? How has it been applied? When was it abandoned?

PROBLEMS

1 Cascade Springs, Inc. is an unregulated natural monopoly that bottles water from a natural spring high in the Grand Tetons. The total fixed cost incurred by Cascade Springs is $160,000, and its marginal cost is 10¢ a bottle. The demand for bottled water from Cascade Springs is as follows:

Price (cents per bottle)	Quantity demanded (thousands of bottles per year)
100	0
90	200
80	400
70	600
60	800
50	1,000
40	1,200
30	1,400
20	1,600
10	1,800
0	2,000

a What is the price of a bottle of water?
b How many bottles does Cascade Springs sell?
c Does Cascade Springs maximize total surplus or producer surplus?

2 The government regulates Cascade Springs in problem 1 by imposing a marginal cost pricing rule.
a What is the price of a bottle of water?
b How many bottles does Cascade Springs sell?
c What is Cascade Springs' producer surplus?
d What is the consumer surplus?
e Is the regulation in the public interest or in the private interest?

3 The government regulates Cascade Springs in problem 1 by imposing an average cost pricing rule.
a What is the price of a bottle of water?
b How many bottles does Cascade Springs sell?
c What is Cascade Springs' producer surplus?
d What is the consumer surplus?
e Is the regulation in the public interest or in the private interest?

4 The value of the capital invested in Cascade Springs in problem 1 is $2 million. The government introduces a rate of return regulation requiring the firm to sell its water for a price that gives it a rate of return of 5 percent on its capital.
a What is the price of a bottle of water?
b How many bottles does Cascade Springs sell?
c What is Cascade Springs' producer surplus?
d What is the consumer surplus?
e Is the regulation in the public interest or in the private interest?

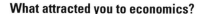

PART 9

INTRODUCTION TO MACROECONOMICS

Talking with Franco Modigliani

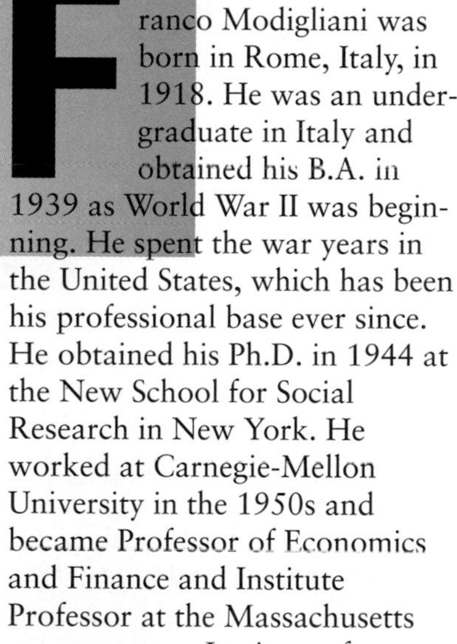

Franco Modigliani was born in Rome, Italy, in 1918. He was an undergraduate in Italy and obtained his B.A. in 1939 as World War II was beginning. He spent the war years in the United States, which has been his professional base ever since. He obtained his Ph.D. in 1944 at the New School for Social Research in New York. He worked at Carnegie-Mellon University in the 1950s and became Professor of Economics and Finance and Institute Professor at the Massachusetts Institute of Technology in 1960. Professor Modigliani was awarded the Nobel Memorial Prize in Economics in 1985 for his pioneering work on consumption and saving—the development of the life-cycle hypothesis—and for his contributions to the theory of finance.

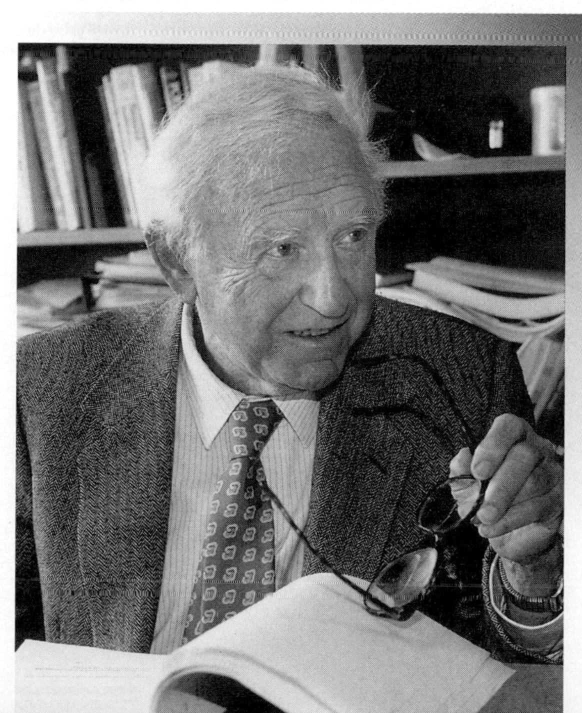

What attracted you to economics?

I studied economics at the University of Rome as part of the requirements for the degree of Doctor in Law. However, the teaching environment under fascism was terrible, and I learned very little, except by studying on my own. I became interested in economics by a fluke: I participated in a national competition in economics and won first prize. I concluded that economics was for me.

What did you study at the New School?

I took advantage of the New School in New York to make up for all that I had not been able to learn in Italy. But my greatest interest was in Keynes and the newly born field of macroeconomics. I also pursued mathematical economics and econometrics—also in its beginning at that time—under the guidance of a great teacher, Jacob Marshack.

> "The differences . . . spring . . . from different value judgments about the cost of unemployment or the dangers of allowing the government to have any discretionary power."

You are an "activist" in contrast to a "monetarist," and you've had many notable verbal battles with the monetarists, especially with Milton Friedman. Yet some of your work and some of Friedman's work are remarkably similar—especially the life-cycle hypothesis and the permanent income hypothesis of consumption expenditure. What is it about economics that unites your work and Friedman's, and what is it that divides you and Friedman on policy questions?

I generally agree with Friedman and other reputable economists on basic economic theory. For instance, we agree on the nature of the mechanism through which money affects the economy or on the way consumers choose to allocate their life resources over their lifetime.

The differences arise, typically, at the level of the economic policies we advocate. They spring to an important extent from different value judgments about the cost of unemployment or the dangers of allowing the government to have any discretionary power. Thus Friedman, who profoundly distrusts government, finds that the system is sufficiently stable when left to itself, that we do not need to take the risk of giving government discretionary power, and indeed that discretionary policies, in the hands of an incompetent government, may be destabilizing.

My value judgments and assessment are very different. I believe that instability is extremely costly, and I find that the economy, when left to itself, is not sufficiently stable. I believe that there exist good governments and central banks and that even an average policymaker can successfully contribute to the stabilization of the economy. Thus, in contrast to Friedman, I conclude that the relevant authorities should be given the discretion necessary for a stabilization policy, but with appropriate checks.

You were one of the pioneers of large-scale econometric models. These models are now routinely used for commercial forecasting but don't appear much in the academic journals. How useful are these models?

I have not followed any of the econometric models from the "inside," that is, in terms of model upkeep and testing, since completing work on the model for the Federal Reserve. However, from what I have been able to observe, the leading models, such as DRI, Wharton, and Michigan, have been quite useful. The forecasting record of these models is, of course, far from perfect, and at times it is outright disappointing. Yet there is considerable evidence to suggest that at least these models perform appreciably better than known alternatives. They have also proved useful in testing hypotheses and in working out the short-run effects of alternative policies.

Suppose you were given carte blanche by the president and Congress to fix the American economy and deliver a prosperous closing decade to the twentieth century. What would you recommend?

In my view, the American economy is not in significantly bad shape for the coming years. At the moment, of course, we are in the midst of a slowdown, but it is of modest magnitude, and it should not take long to get over it. For the longer run, the more serious concerns seem to be the slow growth of productivity, the deterioration in the economic welfare of the lowest income and skill classes, and a continuing substantial balance of payments deficit. All these symptoms bear a relation to one underlying cause: the

"**A**ll these symptoms bear a relation to one underlying cause: the great decline in national saving . . ."

great decline in national saving, initiated by the Reagan administration's fiscal deficit policy. It has hardly been corrected by the Bush administration, with the result that national saving has been reduced to about one fourth of what it used to be for many years. The decline in national saving in turn has contributed to the large decline in domestic investment, which in turn contributed to poor productivity performance and to lower incomes of future generations. These future generations will foot the bill for our failure to pay for what we are consuming now.

The decline in investment also very likely accounts for some of the economic deterioration of the lower economic fringe. To be sure, the decline in investment was not as dramatic as that in national saving because the fiscal deficit served to attract foreign capital; but that is precisely what caused the deterioration of the current account and our growing indebtedness to foreigners.

I would therefore give high priority to eliminating the deficit—exclusive of the current social security surplus—preferably by expenditure cuts but if necessary by higher taxes. Americans pay less taxes than most citizens in other industrialized countries and can certainly afford to pay a little more in favor of future generations. The reduction in deficit could be used to expand investment and reduce the foreign deficit. The expansion of investment should include public investments in infrastructures. This expenditure would not add to the deficit if it were classified as an investment, as would be proper, and as is the prevailing practice in other countries. Productivity growth might also be helped by better education, especially at lower levels, even if it is costly.

"The most basic principle in economics is the postulate of rational behavior."

What other counsel would you give the president and Congress for economic policy?

I would stop the current drift toward protectionism and recommend taking a strong lead in opening up economies to international trade. I would also give high priority to a serious policy of environmental protection, despite its costs. On the other hand, I am not a great believer in government industrial policies and would rather trust the economy to the "invisible hand" except in the case of monetary policy, where, as indicated, I believe that some discretion for the monetary authority is essential to the achievement of macroeconomic stability and stable prices.

What are the major principles of economics that you keep returning to and finding the most useful in your work?

The most basic principle in economics is the postulate of rational behavior. Many of the important propositions in economics rest on that principle. However, it must be used with full awareness of its limitations. For instance, I do not necessarily include in rational behavior "rational expectations" as defined and used by the rational expectations school. More generally, I believe that there are circumstances in which agents' behavior is not adequately described by rationality and one must be prepared to formulate alternative hypotheses.

What advice would you give to students starting out in economics today? What other subjects should they study along with economics?

Anyone interested in becoming a professional economist, whether an academic economist or a business one, should acquire a good preparation in the quantitative methods—mathematics, statistics, and econometrics. Without this background, you will miss much of the interesting literature. There are many other subjects that can be useful, depending on one's long-run interests—for instance, social psychology, law, or political science. From my experience, I can say that whatever "extracurricular" subjects I have been exposed to have turned out to be helpful at some point in my career.

CHAPTER 22

Inflation, Unemployment, Cycles, and Deficits

After studying this chapter, you will be able to:

- Define inflation and explain its effects
- Define unemployment and explain its costs
- Distinguish among the various types of unemployment
- Define gross domestic product (GDP)
- Distinguish between nominal GDP and real GDP
- Explain the importance of increases and fluctuations in real GDP
- Define the business cycle
- Describe how unemployment, stock prices, and inflation fluctuate over the business cycle
- Define the government budget deficit and the country's international deficit

Shopping Cart Blues

A SHOPPING CART OF GROCERIES THAT TODAY COSTS $100 cost only $20 in 1950. An average hour of work in 1950 earned $1.34. The same average hour earns $10.50 today. Higher prices and higher wages mean that firms need more dollars to pay us and we need more dollars to buy the goods and services that we consume. Does this matter? What are the effects of persistently rising prices? ◆◆ In 1991, for every 13 people with jobs, one other person was looking for work but couldn't find it and an unknown number had become discouraged about their chances of finding jobs and had stopped looking. Why can't everyone who wants a job find one? ◆◆ From 1961 to 1991, the value of goods produced in the United States increased tenfold. How much of that growth in the value of our output is real, and how much of it is an illusion created by inflation? ◆◆ Although output has grown, our economy does not follow a smooth and predictable course. Sometimes, such as from 1982 to 1989, it expands—output grows and unemployment falls. At other times, such as in 1990–1991, output sags and unemployment increases. We call these waves of expansion and contraction business cycles. Are business cycles all alike? Do they occur at predictable intervals? ◆◆ We hear a lot these days about deficits—both the U.S. federal government's deficit and the U.S. international deficit. What are these deficits, and just how big are they? Have they been getting bigger? How can we have a deficit with the rest of the world? How do we make up the difference?

◆ ◆ ◆ ◆ These questions are the subject matter of macroeconomics—the branch of economics that seeks to understand rising prices, unemployment, fluctuating output, and government and international deficits. ◆ ◆ The macroeconomic events through which we are now living are as exciting and tumultuous as any in history. Governments here and around the world face a daily challenge to find policies that will give all of us a smoother macroeconomic ride. ◆ ◆ With what you learn in these chapters, you will be better able to understand these macroeconomic policy challenges. We'll begin by looking at inflation.

Inflation

Inflation is an upward movement in the average level of prices. Its opposite is deflation, a downward movement in the average level of prices. The boundary between inflation and deflation is price stability. Price stability occurs when the average level of prices is moving neither up nor down. The average level of prices is called the **price level.** It is measured by a price index. A **price index** measures the average level of prices in one period as a percentage of their average level in an earlier period called the base period.

U.S. price indexes that go all the way back to 1820 have been compiled, and the story they tell is shown in Fig. 22.1. Over the 172-year period shown in that figure, prices have risen nineteenfold—an average annual rate of increase of 1.76 percent. But prices have not moved upward at a constant and steady pace. In some periods, such as the Civil War, World War I, and World War II, the increase was sharp and pronounced—at times exceeding 20 percent a year. In other periods, such as the 1960s and 1970s, the increase was prolonged and steady. At yet other times there have been periods of falling prices—in the 1840s, following the Civil War, and during the Great Depression.

FIGURE 22.1

The Price Level: 1820–1991

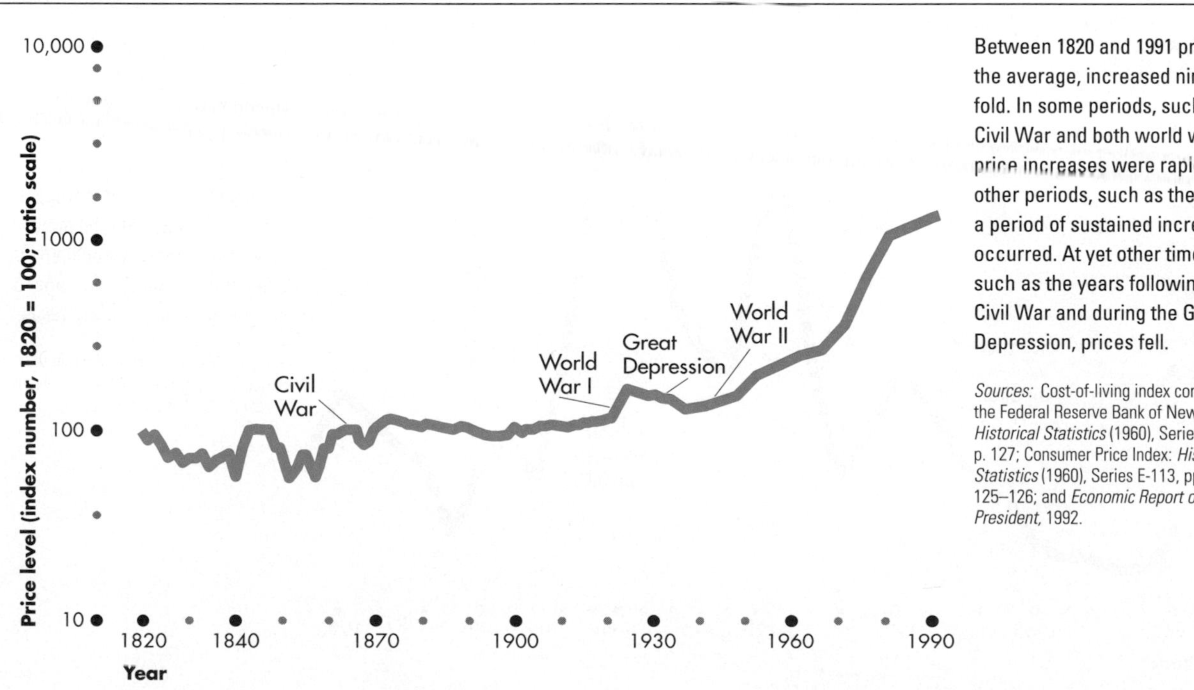

Between 1820 and 1991 prices, on the average, increased nineteenfold. In some periods, such as the Civil War and both world wars, price increases were rapid. In other periods, such as the 1970s, a period of sustained increases occurred. At yet other times, such as the years following the Civil War and during the Great Depression, prices fell.

Sources: Cost-of-living index compiled by the Federal Reserve Bank of New York, *Historical Statistics* (1960), Series E-157, p. 127; Consumer Price Index: *Historical Statistics* (1960), Series E-113, pp. 125–126; and *Economic Report of the President,* 1992.

The Inflation Rate and the Price Level

The **inflation rate** is the percentage change in the price level. The formula for the annual inflation rate is

$$\text{Inflation rate} = \frac{\text{Current year's price level} - \text{Last year's price level}}{\text{Last year's price level}} \times 100.$$

A common way of measuring the price level is to use the *Consumer Price Index,* or simply the CPI. (We'll learn more about the CPI in Chapter 23.) We can illustrate the calculation of the annual inflation rate by using the CPI. In December 1990, the CPI was 133.8. In December 1989, it was 126.1. Substituting these values into the above formula gives the inflation rate for 1990 as

$$\text{Inflation rate} = \frac{133.8 - 126.1}{126.1} \times 100$$

$$= 6.1\%.$$

The Recent Inflation Record

Recent U.S. economic history has seen some dramatic changes in the inflation rate. The inflation rate between 1960 and 1991, as measured by the CPI, is shown in Fig. 22.2.

As you can see, in the early 1960s the inflation rate was low, lying between 1 and 2 percent a year. Its rate began to increase in the late 1960s at the time of the Vietnam War. But the largest increases in inflation occurred in 1974 and again in 1980, years in which the actions of the Organization of Petroleum Exporting Countries (OPEC) resulted in exceptionally large increases in the price of oil. Inflation decreased quickly in the early 1980s at a time when the Federal Reserve chairman, Paul Volcker, pursued a policy of severe monetary restraint, pushing interest rates upward to historically high levels. The inflation rate remained relatively low in the second half of the 1980s, although by the end of the decade, it was beginning to show signs of increasing again.

FIGURE 22.2

Inflation: 1960–1991

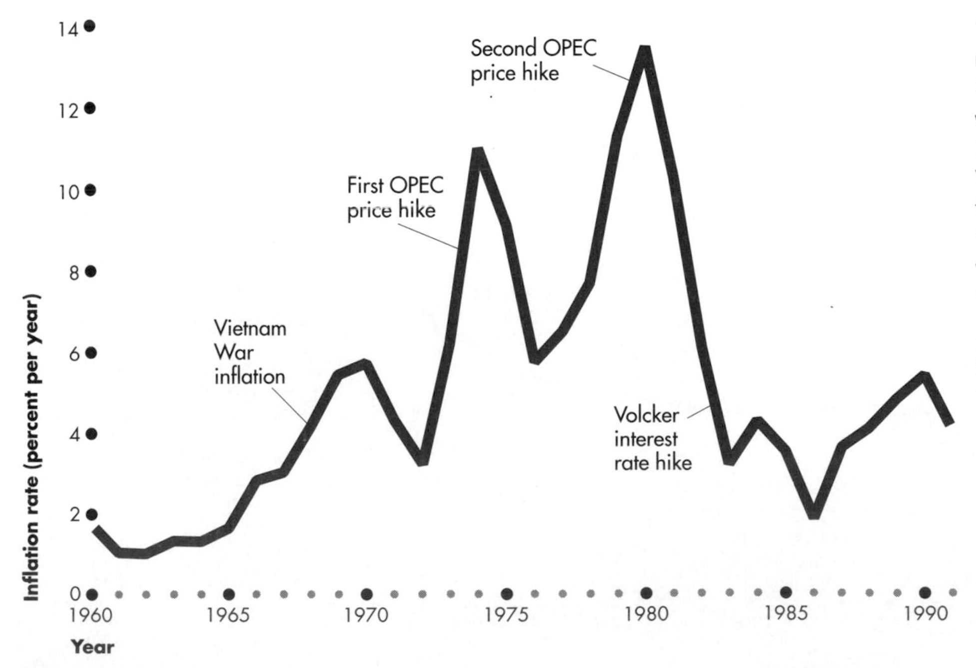

Inflation is a persistent feature of modern economic life in the United States. The inflation rate was low in the first half of the 1960s, but it moved upward in the Vietnam War years. It increased further with the OPEC oil price hikes but eventually declined when the Volcker Fed increased interest rates in the early 1980s.

Sources: Historical Statistics (1960), Series E-113, pp. 125–126; and *Economic Report of the President,* 1992.

The inflation rate rises and falls over the years. But since the 1930s the price level has generally risen (see Fig. 22.1 again). The price level falls only when the inflation rate is negative. Thus even in years such as 1961 and 1986 when the inflation rate was low, the price level was rising.

Inflation and the Value of Money

When inflation is present, money is losing value. The **value of money** is the amount of goods and services that can be bought with a given amount of money. When an economy experiences inflation, the value of money falls—you cannot buy as many groceries with $50 this year as you could last year. The rate at which the value of money falls is equal to the inflation rate. When the inflation rate is high, as it was in 1980, money loses its value at a rapid pace. When inflation is low, as it was in 1961, the value of money falls slowly.

Inflation is a phenomenon that all countries experience. But inflation *rates* vary from one country to another. When inflation rates differ over a prolonged period of time, the result is a change in the foreign exchange value of money. A **foreign exchange rate** is the rate at which one country's money (or currency) exchanges for another country's money. For example, in January 1991, 1 U.S. dollar exchanged for 130 Japanese yen. But in January 1971, you could get 360 yen for a dollar. The value of the U.S. dollar, in terms of the Japanese yen, has gradually fallen over the past 20 years because our inflation rate has been higher than that in Japan. We'll learn more about exchange rates and how they are influenced by inflation in Chapter 36.

Is Inflation a Problem?

Is it a problem if money loses its value and does so at a rate that varies from one year to another? It is, indeed, a problem, but to understand why, we need to distinguish between anticipated and unanticipated inflation. When prices are moving upward, most people are aware of that fact. They also have some notion about the rate at which prices are rising. The rate at which people (on the average) believe that the price level is rising is called the **expected inflation rate.** But expectations may be right or wrong. If they turn out to be right, the actual inflation rate equals the expected inflation rate and inflation is said to be anticipated. That is, an **anticipated inflation** is an inflation rate that has been correctly forecasted (on the average). To the extent that the inflation rate is misforecasted, it is said to be unanticipated. That is, **unanticipated inflation** is the part of the inflation rate that has caught people by surprise.

The problems arising from inflation differ depending on whether its rate is anticipated or unanticipated. Let's begin by looking at the problems arising from unanticipated inflation.

The Problem of Unanticipated Inflation

Unanticipated inflation is a problem because it produces unanticipated changes in the value of money. Money is used as a measuring rod of the value in the transactions that we undertake. Borrowers and lenders, workers and their employers, all make contracts in terms of money. If the value of money varies unexpectedly over time, then the amounts *really* paid and received differ from those that people intended to pay and receive when they signed the contracts. Measuring value with a measuring rod whose units vary is a bit like trying to measure a piece of cloth with an elastic ruler. The size of the cloth depends on how tightly the ruler is stretched.

Let's take a look at the effects of unanticipated inflation by looking at what happens to agreements between borrowers and lenders and between workers and employers.

Borrowers and Lenders People often say that inflation is good for borrowers and bad for lenders. To see how they reach that conclusion—and why it's not always correct—let's consider an example.

Sue is a lender. She lends $5,000 by putting it into a bank deposit for one year at an interest rate of 10 percent. At the end of the year she plans to buy a car that today costs $5,500. She will earn $500 dollars interest on her bank deposit, which she expects will give her just enough to buy the car.

If there is no inflation, Sue can buy her car. But suppose that prices rise during the year and a car that cost $5,500 at the beginning of the year costs $6,000 at the end of the year. Sue can't afford to buy the car at that price. Actually, Sue is as far away from being able to buy the car as she was at the beginning of the year. She's got more money, but everything now costs more. Sue has *really* made no interest income at all, and the bank has *really* paid no interest.

But lenders don't always lose when there is inflation. If Sue and the bank anticipate the inflation, they can adjust the interest rate they agree upon to offset the anticipated fall in the value of money. If the inflation is correctly anticipated, Sue and the bank agree to an interest rate of 20 percent. At the end of the year the bank pays Sue $6,000. Of this amount, $5,000 is the repayment of the initial deposit and $1,000 is interest—at a rate of 20 percent a year. This interest income for Sue consists of $500—the 10 percent rate they agree is appropriate with no inflation—and $500 compensation for the loss in the value of money. Sue *really* receives a 10 percent interest rate, and that's what the bank *really* pays.

If borrowers and lenders correctly anticipate the inflation rate, interest rates are adjusted to cancel out inflation's effect on the interest *really* paid and *really* received. It is only when borrowers and lenders make errors in forecasting the future inflation rate that one of them gains and the other loses. But those gains and losses can go either way. If the inflation rate turns out to be higher than is generally expected, then the borrower gains and the lender loses. Conversely, if the inflation rate turns out to be lower than is generally expected, then the borrower loses and the lender gains.

Thus it is not inflation itself that produces gains and losses for borrowers and lenders. It is an *unanticipated increase* in the *inflation rate* that *benefits borrowers* and hurts lenders. An *unanticipated decrease* in the *inflation rate benefits lenders* and hurts borrowers.

In the United States in the late 1960s and 1970s, the inflation rate kept rising and to some degree the rise was unanticipated, so borrowers tended to gain. In the 1980s, the fall in the inflation rate was also, at least initially, unanticipated and lenders gained. On the international scene, many developing countries, such as Mexico and Brazil, borrowed large amounts of money in the late 1970s and early 1980s at high interest rates in anticipation that an inflation rate above 10 percent a year would persist. But the inflation rate fell. These countries are now stuck with paying the interest on their loans without the extra revenue that they expected to receive from higher prices for their exports.

Workers and Employers Another common belief is that inflation redistributes income between workers and their employers. Some people believe that workers gain at the expense of employers, and others believe the contrary.

The previous discussion concerning borrowers and lenders applies to workers and their employers as well. If inflation increases unexpectedly, then wages will not have been set high enough. Profits will be higher than expected, and wages will buy fewer goods than expected. Employers gain at the expense of workers. Conversely, if the anticipated inflation rate is higher than what the actual inflation rate turns out to be, wages will have been set too high and profits will be squeezed. Workers will be able to buy more with their income than was originally anticipated. In this case, workers gain at the expense of employers.

Large unanticipated changes in the inflation rate that produce fluctuations in the buying power of earnings—fluctuations in the value of paychecks in terms of the goods and services they buy—are not common, but they do occur from time to time. For example, in 1974, when the inflation rate climbed to 10 percent a year, the buying power of earnings fell by 3 percent. In 1980, when the inflation rate rose to 13 percent a year, the buying power of earnings fell by almost 5 percent. These two episodes of higher inflation were largely unanticipated. The *fall* in the inflation rate in 1982 was also to some degree unanticipated and brought a corresponding *rise* in the buying power of earnings.

We've now seen the problems that unanticipated inflation can bring. Let's now turn to anticipated inflation.

The Problem of Anticipated Inflation

At low inflation rates, anticipated inflation is not much of a problem at all. But it becomes more of a problem the higher the anticipated inflation rate is.

At very high inflation rates, people know that money is losing value quickly. The rate at which money is losing value is part of the *opportunity cost* of holding onto money. The higher that opportunity cost, the smaller is the amount of money people want to hold. Instead of having a wallet stuffed with $20 bills and a big checking account balance, people go shopping and spend their incomes as soon as they are received. And the same is true for firms. Instead of hanging onto the money they receive from the sale of their goods and services, they pay it out in wages as quickly as possible.

In Germany, Poland, and Hungary in the 1920s, inflation rates reached extraordinary heights—in excess of 50 percent a month. Such high inflation rates are called *hyperinflations*. At the height of these hyperinflations, firms paid out wages twice a day. As soon as they had been paid, workers rushed off to spend their wages before they lost too much value. To buy a handful of groceries, they needed a shopping cart of currency. People who lingered too long in the coffee shop found that the price of their cup of coffee had increased between the time they placed their order and when the check was presented. Such an anticipated inflation brings economic chaos and disruption.

High and Variable Inflation

Even if inflation is reasonably well anticipated, and even if its rate is not as high as in a hyperinflation, it can still impose very high costs. A high and variable inflation rate causes resources to be diverted from productive activities to forecasting inflation. It becomes more profitable to forecast the inflation rate correctly than to invent a new product. Doctors, lawyers, accountants, farmers—just about everyone—can make themselves better off, not by practicing the profession for which they have been trained, but by becoming amateur economists and inflation forecasters. From a social perspective, this diversion of talent resulting from inflation is like throwing our scarce resources onto the garbage heap. This waste of resources is the main cost of inflation.

Indexing

It is sometimes suggested that the costs of inflation can be avoided by indexing, a technique that links payments made under a contract to the price level. With indexing, Sue and the bank in our example above would not agree to a fixed interest rate; instead, they would agree to an indexing formula for adjusting the interest rate in line with the inflation rate. Similarly, an indexed wage contract does not specify the number of dollars that will be paid to workers; instead, it specifies an indexing formula that takes account of the inflation rate for calculating the number of dollars.

But indexing itself is costly. Reaching agreement on contracts with index clauses is extremely complex, since there are many possible indexes that can be used and the choice of the index has important effects on both parties to a contract.

REVIEW

Inflation is a process in which the average level of prices rises and the value of money falls. The inflation rate is measured as the percentage change in a price index. The inflation rate rises and falls, but, since the 1930s, the *price level* has only risen. The effects of inflation depend on whether it is unanticipated or anticipated. An unanticipated increase in inflation benefits borrowers and hurts lenders; an unanticipated decrease in inflation benefits lenders and hurts borrowers. Anticipated inflation becomes a serious problem when its rate is extremely high. At such times, people spend money as soon as they receive it and there is a severe disruption of economic life. Inflation also becomes a serious problem when its rate is variable because resources get diverted into predicting inflation. Indexing can lower the costs of inflation, but indexing is itself costly. ◆

Unemployment

At many times in the history of the United States, unemployment has been a serious problem. For example, in the recession of 1991, almost 9 million people were seeking jobs. What exactly is unemployment? How is it measured? How has its rate fluctuated? What is full employment? What are the costs of unemployment?

What Is Unemployment?

Unemployment is a state in which there are qualified workers who are available for work at the current wage rate and who do not have jobs. The total number of people who do have jobs—the employed—plus the total number of people who do not have jobs—the unemployed—is called the **labor force**. The **unemployment rate** is the number of people unemployed expressed as a percentage of the labor force.

Measuring Unemployment

Unemployment is measured in the United States every month. The Bureau of Labor Statistics in the U.S. Department of Labor calculates the monthly unemployment figures and publishes them in *Employment and Earnings*. These unemployment figures are based on a survey of households called the Current Population Survey.

To be counted as unemployed in the Current Population Survey, a person must be available for work and must be in one of three categories:

1. Without work, but has made specific efforts to find a job within the previous four weeks
2. Waiting to be called back to a job from which he or she has been laid off
3. Waiting to start a new job within 30 days

Anyone surveyed who satisfies one of these three criteria is counted as unemployed. Part-time workers are counted as being employed.

There are three reasons why the unemployment level as measured by the Current Population Survey may be misleading. Let's examine these.

Unrealistic Wage Expectations If someone is willing to work, but only for a much higher wage than is available, it does not make sense to count that person as unemployed. That is, if someone says that he or she is willing to work at McDonald's, but only for $25 an hour, then that person is not really available for work and, therefore, is not unemployed.

Correcting the unemployment data to take account of wage and job expectations would result in a lower measured unemployment rate. How much lower we do not know. A second factor works in the opposite direction.

Discouraged Workers Many people who still fail to find a suitable job after prolonged and extensive search effort come to believe that there is no work available for them. They become discouraged and stop looking for work. Such people are called discouraged workers. **Discouraged workers** are people who do not have jobs and would like work but have stopped seeking work. Discouraged workers are not counted as unemployed by the Current Population Survey because they have not sought work within the past 30 days. If discouraged workers were added to the unemployment count, the unemployment rate would be higher than what is currently measured.

Part-Time Workers As we have noted, part-time workers are counted as employed. But many part-time workers are available for and seeking full-time work. The measured unemployment rate does not capture this element of part-time unemployment.

The Unemployment Record

The U.S. unemployment record between 1900 and 1991 is set out in Fig. 22.3. The dominant feature of that record is the Great Depression of the early 1930s. During that episode of our history, 25 percent of the labor force was unemployed. Although in recent years we have not experienced anything as devastating as the Great Depression, we have experienced some high unemployment rates. Three such periods are highlighted in the figure—the mid-1970s when oil prices were increased sharply, the early 1980s when the Federal Reserve (under chairman Volcker) increased interest rates sharply, and 1991 when uncertainty and pessimism brought a decrease in spending and recession. The average unemployment rate over this 92-year period was just over 6 percent.

Unemployment is a highly charged topic. We chart the course of the unemployment rate as a measure of U.S. economic health with the intensity with which a physician keeps track of a patient's temperature. What does the unemployment rate tell us? Does all unemployment have the same origin, or are there different types of unemployment? In fact, there are three main sources of variation in unemployment, and they give rise to three types of unemployment. Let's see what they are.

Types of Unemployment

The three types of unemployment are

- Frictional
- Structural
- Cyclical

Frictional Unemployment The unemployment arising from normal labor market turnover is called **frictional unemployment**. Normal labor market turnover arises from two sources. First, people are constantly changing their economic activities—young people are leaving school and joining the labor force; old people are retiring and leaving the labor force; some people are leaving the labor force temporarily, per-

FIGURE 22.3

Unemployment: 1900–1991

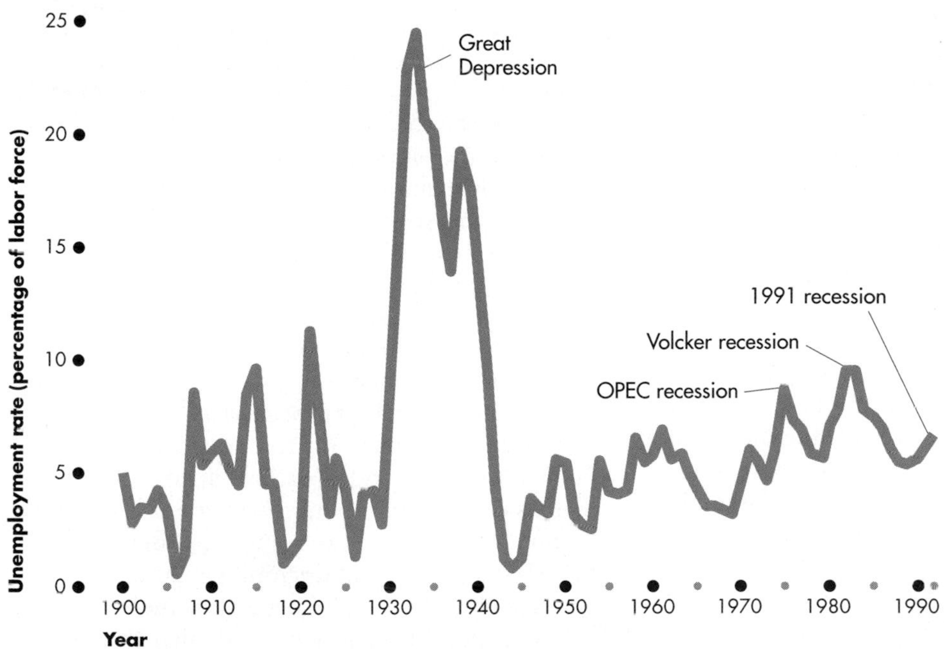

Unemployment is a persistent feature of economic life, but its rate varies considerably. At its worst—during the Great Depression—25 percent of the labor force was unemployed. Even in the recessions following the OPEC price hikes and the Volcker interest rate increases, unemployment climbed toward the 10 percent mark. Between the late 1960s and 1982, there was a general tendency for unemployment to increase. The rate fell between 1983 and 1988 but then increased again through 1991.

Sources: Unemployment, 1900–1946: *Historical Statistics* (1960), Series D-46, p. 73; unemployment, 1946–1988: *Economic Report of the President,* 1992.

haps to raise children or for some other reason, and then rejoining it. Second, the fortunes of businesses are constantly changing—some are closing down and laying off their workers; new firms are starting up and are hiring.

These constant changes result in frictional unemployment. There are always some firms with unfilled vacancies and some people looking for work. Unemployed people don't usually take the first job that comes their way. Instead, they spend time searching out what they believe will be the best job available to them. By doing so, they can match their own skills and interests with the available jobs, finding a satisfying job and income.

It is unlikely that frictional unemployment will ever disappear. The amount of frictional unemployment depends on the rate at which people enter and leave the labor force and on the rate at which jobs are created and destroyed. For example the postwar baby boom of the late 1940s brought a bulge in the number of people entering the labor force in the 1960s and an increase in the amount of frictional unemployment. When a major new shopping mall is built, jobs become available in the mall and a similar number of jobs are lost in the older part of town where shops are struggling to survive. The people who lose jobs aren't always the first to get the new jobs, and while they are between jobs, they are frictionally unemployed.

The length of time that people take to find a job is influenced by unemployment compensation. The more generous the rate of unemployment benefit, the longer is the average time taken in job search and the higher is the rate of frictional unemployment.

Structural Unemployment The unemployment that arises when there is a decline in the number of jobs available in a particular region or industry is called **structural unemployment.** Such a decline might occur because of permanent technological change—for example, the automation of a steel plant. It might also occur because of a permanent change in international competition—for example, the decline of the number of jobs in the U.S. auto industry resulting from Japanese competition.

The distinction between structural and frictional unemployment is not always a sharp one, but some cases are clear. A person who loses a job in a suburban shopping center and gets a job a few weeks later in a new mall has experienced frictional unemployment. An auto worker who loses his or her job and, after a period of retraining and prolonged search, perhaps lasting more than a year, eventually gets a job as an insurance salesperson has experienced structural unemployment.

At some times, the amount of structural unemployment is modest, and at other times it is large. It was especially large during the late 1970s and early 1980s when increases in the price of oil and an increasingly competitive international environment brought a decline in the number of jobs in traditional industries, such as autos and steel, and an increase in the number of jobs in new industries, such as electronics and bio-engineering, as well as in the service industries such as banking and insurance.

Cyclical Unemployment The unemployment arising from a slowdown in the pace of economic expansion is called **cyclical unemployment.** The pace of economic expansion is ever-changing, rapid at some times, slow at others, and even negative on occasion. When the economy is expanding rapidly, cyclical unemployment disappears, and when the economy is expanding slowly or contracting, cyclical unemployment can become extremely high. For example, an auto worker who is laid off because the economy is going through a slow period and who gets rehired some months later when economic activity speeds up has experienced cyclical unemployment.

With frictional and structural unemployment, there are as many job vacancies as there are unemployed workers. The jobs and the workers have simply not found each other. Cyclical unemployment is different. When the level of cyclical unemployment is high, there are fewer job vacancies than unemployed workers. No matter how hard people look for work, they're not all going to find it.

Measuring frictional, structural, and cyclical unemployment and distinguishing one type of unemployment from another are controversial. It is not possible to provide a quantitative breakdown of unemployment among the three types. But we can see the three types in specific real-world situations. Reading Between the Lines on pp. 592–593 gives an example.

Full Employment

At any given time, there are people looking for work and firms looking for people to employ—unemployed people and job vacancies. **Full employment** is a state in which the number of people looking for a job equals the number of job vacancies. Equivalently, full employment occurs when all unemployment is frictional and structural and there is no cyclical unemployment. We've seen that there is always some frictional unemployment and often there is structural unemployment. Thus there is always some unemployment, even at full employment.

The unemployment rate at full employment is called the **natural rate of unemployment**. The natural rate of unemployment fluctuates because of fluctuations in frictional and structural unemployment. But there is controversy about the magnitude of the natural unemployment rate. Some economists believe that the natural rate of unemployment in the United States is between 5 and 6 percent of the labor force. Other economists believe not only that the natural rate of unemployment varies, but that it can be quite high, especially at times when demographic and technological factors point to a high frictional and structural unemployment rate.

What are the costs of unemployment?

The Costs of Unemployment

There are four main costs of unemployment. They are

- Loss of output and income
- Loss of human capital
- Increase in crime
- Loss of human dignity

Loss of Output and Income The most obvious costs of unemployment are the loss of output and the loss of income that the unemployed would have produced if they had jobs. The size of these costs depends on the natural rate of unemployment. If the natural rate of unemployment is between 5 and 6 percent, as economists such as James Tobin of Yale University believe, the lost output from unemployment is enormous.

The late Arthur Okun of the Brookings Institution estimated that for every 1 percentage point rise in the unemployment rate, the nation's output of goods and services falls by 3 percentage points. More recent studies have suggested that each 1 percentage point added to the unemployment rate cuts output by 2 percentage points. If numbers in this range are correct, then the lost output resulting from high unemployment is enormous. One percent of aggregate output in the United States is $55 billion. Thus getting the unemployment rate down from 8 percent to 6 percent raises output between $220 billion and $330 billion. With a U.S. population of 250 million people, the average person could buy additional goods and services each year valued between $880 and $1,320 if this loss could be avoided.

Those economists who believe that the natural rate of unemployment itself varies think that the lost output cost of unemployment is small. They regard the fluctuations in the unemployment rate as arising from fluctuations in structural unemployment. With rapid structural change, people need to find their most productive new jobs. A period of high unemployment is like an investment in the future. It is the price paid today for a larger future income.

Loss of Human Capital A second cost of unemployment is the permanent damage that can be done to an unemployed worker by hindering his or her career development and acquisition of human capital. **Human capital** is the value of a person's education and acquired skills. For example, Jody finishes law school at a time when unemployment is high, and she just can't find a job in a law office. Desperately short of income, she becomes a taxi driver. After a year in this work, she discovers it is impossible to compete with the new crop of law graduates and is stuck with cab driving. Her human capital as a lawyer has been wiped out by high unemployment.

Increase in Crime A high unemployment rate usually leads to a high crime rate. There are two reasons for this relationship. First, when people cannot earn an income from legal work, they sometimes turn to illegal work and the amount of theft increases sharply. Second, with low incomes and increased frustration, family life begins to suffer and there are increases in crimes such as child beating, wife assault, and suicide.

Loss of Human Dignity A final cost that is difficult to quantify, but that is large and very important, is the loss of self-esteem that afflicts many who suffer prolonged periods of unemployment. It is probably this aspect of unemployment that makes it so highly charged with political and social significance.

REVIEW

There have been enormous fluctuations in the unemployment rate, but no matter how low its rate, unemployment never disappears. Some unemployment is frictional, arising from labor market turnover. Some is structural, arising from the decline in certain industries and regions. And some is cyclical, arising from a slowdown in the pace of economic expansion. The natural rate of unemployment is that unemployment rate at which there is a balance between the number of unemployed people and the number of job vacancies. This rate fluctuates with changes in the frictional and structural unemployment rate. The costs of unemployment include lost output and income, loss of human capital, an increase in crime, and a loss of human dignity. ◆

Unemployment is not the only indicator of the state of the nation's economic health. Another is its gross domestic product. Let's now examine that.

Gross Domestic Product

The value of all the final goods and services produced in the economy in a year is called **gross domestic product,** or GDP. **Final goods and services** are goods and services that are not used as inputs in the production of other goods and services but are bought by their final user. Such goods include consumption goods and services and also new durable goods. Examples of final goods are cans of soda and cars. Examples of final services are automobile insurance and haircuts.

Unemployment Hits Auto Workers

TIME, DECEMBER 30, 1991

Major Overhaul

BY WILLIAM MCWHIRTER

The Christmastime speech from the chairman of General Motors traditionally sounds like an address from a head of state. Small wonder: the company is so large (1990 revenues: nearly $127 billion) that if it were an independent nation, its economy would rank among the world's Top 20. By closed-circuit TV from GM headquarters in Detroit, this year's 45-minute broadcast reached 395,000 employees who stopped work and put down their tools in 130 factories across the U.S. But the message from chairman Robert Stempel was like no other in the 83-year history of the giant corporation.

As of Jan. 1, Stempel said, the company would embark on a three-year program that would close 25 North American plants and reduce its current work force by 74,000, or about 19%. GM would abandon for the foreseeable future its hopes to regain its lost share of the U.S. market, which has fallen in the past decade from 45% to just over 35%. According to the plan, which did not specify which plants would be closed, GM would emerge by 1995 only half as large as it was a decade earlier and, as Stempel said, "a much different General Motors."

The announcement was a drastic departure from the company's past benevolent assurances of prosperity and well-being. So was the self-effacing and chastened candor. Stempel conceded that this was not the holiday message he had originally intended. But the severe losses in the company's North American automaking operations, estimated at $450 million a month, had prompted a revolt among GM's directors. They rejected Stempel's reorganization plan and humiliatingly ordered up a more drastic revision. The rebuke left Stempel and his senior management staff publicly lurching. The Christmas message was postponed by a week; a preferred-stock offering to raise $1 billion in cash was halted; even GM's annual Christmas party for the automotive press was cancelled. Then last week Stempel gave workers the overhauled speech: "We are asking you to help remake the world's largest automobile company. We can't wait." . . .

Japanese automakers, whose success in the U.S. has come largely at GM's expense, feared that the Detroit automaker's cutbacks would add fuel to the political backlash against Japan. Toyota, for one, took the remarkable step of publicly expressing sympathy for laid-off GM workers. Next month the chiefs of the Big Three U.S. automakers will accompany President Bush on a trip to East Asia, where they are expected to urge Japan to buy more U.S.-made autos to reduce the trade deficit. But more radical measures are brewing in the U.S. Congress. House of Representatives majority leader Richard Gephardt and Michigan Senator Donald Riegle Jr. introduced a bill last week to limit U.S. sales of Japanese cars and trucks to 2.5 million, a cut of more than one-third from current levels. A few days later Japan suffered another blow when the U.S. Commerce Department indicated it would impose penalty duties on minivans sold in the U.S. by Toyota, Mazda, and other Japanese automakers after ruling that the companies were "dumping" the vehicles in the U.S. at artificially low prices. . . .

The Essence of the Story

General Motors (GM), whose headquarters are in Detroit, had revenues in 1990 of almost $127 billion. At the end of 1991, it had 395,000 employees working in 130 factories across the United States.

But because of competition from Japanese automakers, GM's share of the U.S. car market fell from 45 percent in 1981 to just over 35 percent in 1991, and its North American automaking operations were losing an estimated $450 million a month in 1991.

In his Christmas message to employees, GM chairman Robert Stempel announced a three-year program to close 25 (unspecified) plants and to cut the firm's work force by 74,000 (about 19 percent).

Japanese automakers feared that the GM cutbacks might strengthen an anti-Japan political backlash.

President Bush, with the help of the chiefs of the Big Three U.S. automakers, planned to urge Japan to buy more U.S.-made autos.

House of Representatives majority leader Richard Gephardt and Michigan Senator Donald Riegle Jr. wanted to limit U.S. sales of Japanese cars and trucks to 2.5 million, a cut of more than one third from current levels.

The U.S. Commerce Department said that it would impose penalty duties on minivans sold in the United States by Toyota, Mazda, and other Japanese automakers because the companies were "dumping" the vehicles in the United States at artificially low prices.

Background and Analysis

At the end of 1991, the U.S. auto industry was suffering from two problems: recession in the U.S. economy and fierce competition from foreign automakers, especially Japanese.

GM was suffering especially badly and, losing an estimated $450 million a month, embarked on a large scale cutback of its plants and labor force.

Most of the 74,000 employees whose jobs are expected to disappear between 1991 and 1994 will become unemployed.

Some of the unemployment will be *cyclical.* Some of those who lose their jobs would not have done so if the U.S. economy had not been in a recession in 1991. As the economy begins to recover from the 1991 recession, this component of the unemployment resulting from GM's cutbacks will gradually disappear.

Some of the unemployment will be *frictional.* Some of those who lose their jobs have skills that are directly usable in other industries. They will be unemployed for a period but will quickly find new jobs without even having to relocate.

Some of the unemployment will be *structural.* Some of those who lose their jobs have skills specific to the job that they were doing at GM. To get a new job, they will have to learn new skills and possibly move to a different region of the country. Some will be too old to make this investment worthwhile, and they will do low-paid unskilled work, if they can find it.

Not all goods and services are "final." Some are intermediate goods and services. **Intermediate goods and services** are those used as inputs into the production process of another good or service. Examples of intermediate goods are the windshields, batteries, and gearboxes used by car producers and the paper and ink used by newspaper manufacturers. Examples of intermediate services are the banking and insurance services bought by car producers and news printers. Whether a good or service is intermediate or final depends on who buys it and for what purpose. For example, electric power purchased by a car producer or a printer is an intermediate good. Electric power bought by you is a final good.

When we measure gross domestic product, we do not include the value of intermediate goods and services produced. If we did, we would be counting the same thing more than once. When someone buys a new car from the local Chrysler dealer, that is a final transaction and the value of the car is counted as part of GDP. But we must not also count as part of GDP the amount the dealer paid to Chrysler for the car or the amount paid by Chrysler to all its suppliers for the car's various parts.

If we want to measure GDP, we somehow have to add together all the *final* goods and services produced. Obviously, we can't achieve a useful measure by simply adding together the number of cars, newspapers, kilowatts of electric power, haircuts, and automobile insurance policies. To determine GDP, we first calculate the dollar *value* of the output of each final good or service. This calculation simply involves multiplying the quantity produced of each final good or service by its price. That is, we measure the output of each good and service in the common unit of dollars. We then add up the dollar values of the outputs of the different goods to arrive at their total value, which is GDP. We measure GDP in dollars, but it is a mixture of real quantities—the numbers of final goods and services produced—and dollar quantities—the prices of the goods and services. A change in GDP, therefore, contains a mixture of the effects of changes in prices and changes in the quantities of final goods and services. For many purposes, it is important to distinguish price changes from quantity changes. To do so, we use the concepts of nominal GDP and real GDP. Let's examine these concepts.

FIGURE 22.4

Gross Domestic Product: 1960–1991

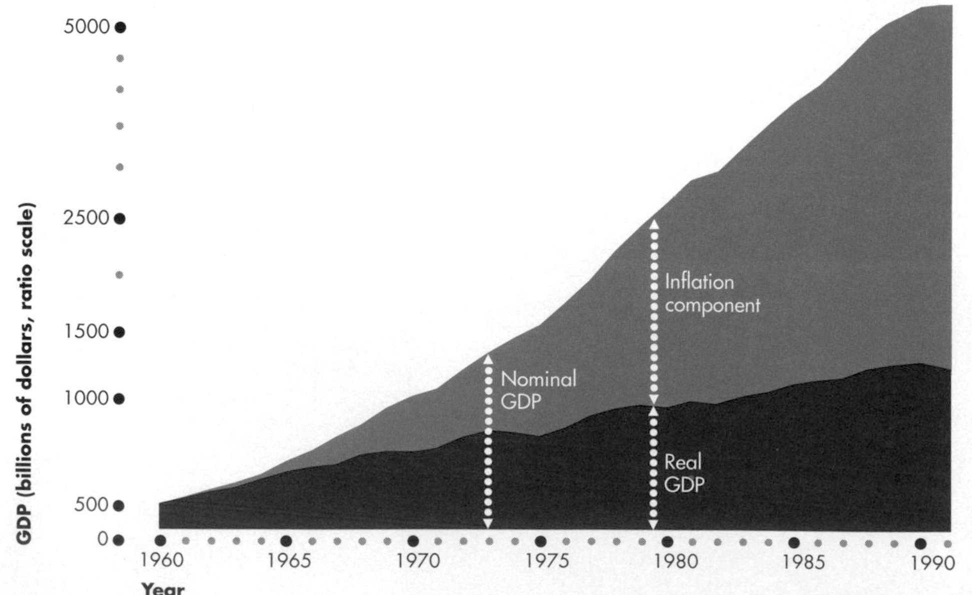

Gross domestic product increased tenfold between 1960 and 1991. But much of that increase was the result of inflation. Real GDP, the increase in GDP attributable to the increase in the volume of goods and services produced, increased but at a more modest pace. The figure shows how real GDP and the inflation component of nominal GDP have evolved. Nominal GDP has increased in every year, but real GDP fell in 1975 and 1982 and again in 1991.

Source: Real and nominal GDP, 1960–1991: *Economic Report of the President,* 1992.

Nominal GDP and Real GDP

Nominal GDP measures the value of the output of final goods and services using *current* prices. It is sometimes called *current dollar GDP.* **Real GDP** measures the value of the output of final goods and services using the prices that prevailed in some base period. An alternative name for real GDP is *constant dollar GDP.*

Comparing real GDP from one year to another enables us to say whether the economy has produced more or fewer goods and services. Comparing nominal GDP from one year to another does not permit us to compare the quantities of goods and services produced in those two years. Nominal GDP may be higher in 1992 than 1991, but that might reflect only higher prices (inflation), not more production. An increase in real GDP means that the production of goods and services expanded.

The importance of the distinction between real GDP and nominal GDP is illustrated in Fig. 22.4. In any year, real GDP is measured by the height of the red area and nominal GDP by the height of the green area. The difference between the height of the green area and the height of the red area shows the inflation component in nominal GDP. In 1960, GDP was $513 billion. By 1991, it had grown to $5,672 billion. But only part of that increase represents an increase in goods and services available—an increase in real GDP. Most of the increase came from inflation. Notice that nominal GDP increases every year in the figure but that real GDP sometimes falls, such as in 1975, 1982, and 1991.

Real GDP—the Record

Estimates of real GDP in the United States go back to 1869. Figure 22.5 illustrates the real GDP record.

FIGURE 22.5

Real GDP: 1869–1991

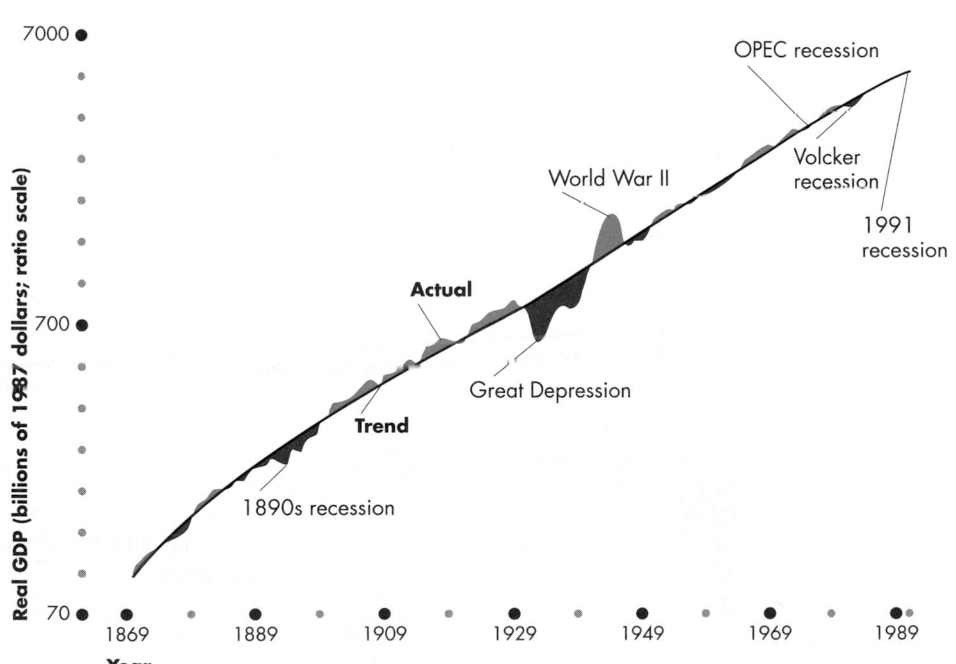

Between 1869 and 1991 real GDP grew at an annual average rate of 3.3 percent. But the growth rate was not the same in each year. In some periods, such as the years during World War II, real GDP expanded quickly. In other periods, such as the Great Depression and, more recently, following the OPEC oil price hikes, the Volcker interest rate increases, and in 1991, real GDP declined. There were several periods of decline in the nineteenth century as well, one of which is marked in the figure.

Source: 1869–1929: Christina D. Romer, "The Prewar Business Cycle Reconsidered: New Estimates of Gross National Product, 1869–1908," *Journal of Political Economy* 97, (1989) 1–37; and Nathan S. Balke and Robert J. Gordon, "The Estimation of Prewar Gross National Product: Methodology and New Evidence," *Journal of Political Economy* 97, (1989) 38–92. The data used are an average of the estimates given in these two sources. 1929–1958: *Economic Report of the President,* 1991. 1959–1991: *Economic Report of the President,* 1992. The data for 1869 to 1958 are GNP and those for 1959 to 1991 are GDP. The difference between these two measures is small and is explained in Chapter 23, pp. 619–620.

Two facts stand out. First, there has been a general tendency for real GDP to increase. Second, the rate of upward movement is not uniform, and sometimes real GDP has actually declined. The most precipitous decline occurred in the early 1930s during the Great Depression. But declines also occurred in recent times during the mid-1970s—the time of the OPEC oil price hikes—during the early 1980s—the time of the Volcker interest rate increases—and in 1991. There were several periods during the nineteenth and early twentieth centuries when real GDP declined, one of which, the 1890s recession, is shown in the figure. There were also periods when real GDP grew extremely quickly—for example, the years during World War II.

In order to obtain a clearer picture of the changes in real GDP, we consider separately the two general tendencies that we've just identified. The first of these tendencies is the general upward movement of real GDP. This feature of real GDP is called trend real GDP. Trend real GDP rises for three reasons:

- Growing population
- Growing stock of capital equipment
- Advances in technology

These forces have produced the general upward tendency that you can see in Fig. 22.5. Trend real GDP is illustrated in Fig. 22.5 as the black thin line passing through the middle of the path followed by real GDP in its meanderings above trend (blue areas) and below trend (red areas).

The second feature of real GDP is its periodic fluctuation around its trend. Real GDP fluctuations are measured as percentage deviations of real GDP from trend. They are illustrated in Fig. 22.6. As you can see, real GDP fluctuations show distinct cycles in economic activity. At times such as during the Great Depression and in the mid-1970s, early 1980s, and 1991, real GDP fluctuates below trend, and during the war years it fluctuates above trend.

The Importance of Real GDP

The upward trend in real GDP is the major source of improvements in living standards. The pace of

FIGURE 22.6

Real GDP Fluctuations: 1869–1991

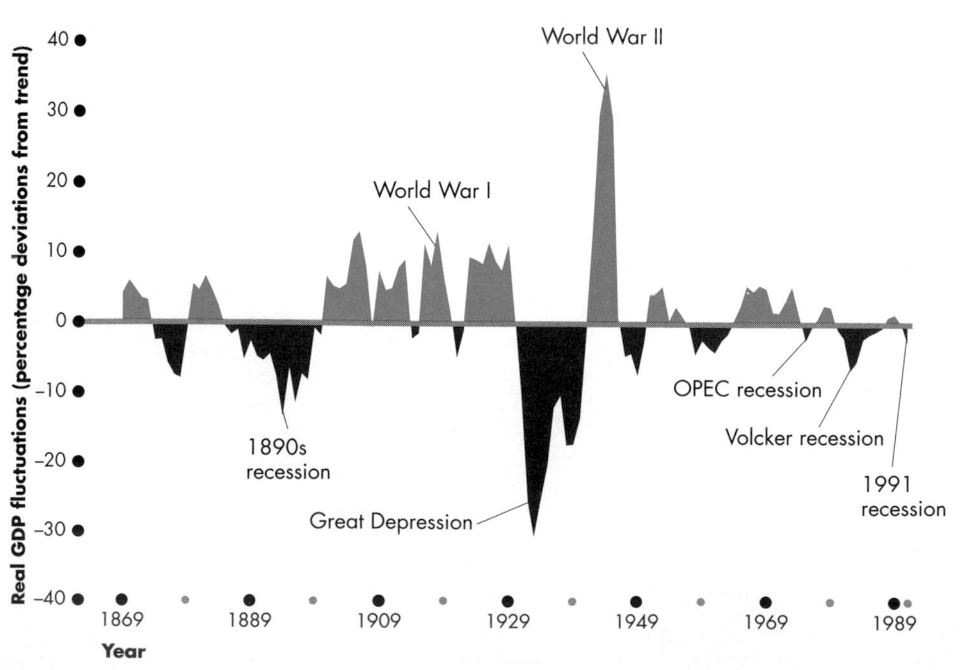

The uneven pace of increase of real GDP is illustrated by tracking its fluctuation measured as the percentage deviation of real GDP from trend. Rapid expansion of real GDP, which occurred during both world wars, puts real GDP above trend. Decreases in real GDP, which occurred during the 1890s recession, the Great Depression, and the three most recent recessions, puts real GDP below trend. The real GDP fluctuations describe the course of the business cycle.

this upward movement has a powerful effect on the standard of living of one generation compared with its predecessor. For example, if real GDP trends upward at 1 percent a year, it takes 70 years for real GDP to double. But a growth trend of 10 percent a year will double real GDP in just 7 years. With an average trend increase of between 2 and 3 percent a year, which is commonly experienced in industrial countries and which has also been the long-term experience of the United States, real GDP doubles approximately every generation (every 25 years or so).

Rapid growth in real GDP brings enormous benefits. It enables us to consume more goods and services of all kinds. It enables us to spend more on health care for the poor and elderly, more on cancer and AIDS research, more on space research and exploration, more on roads, and more on housing. It even enables us to spend more on the environment, cleaning our lakes and protecting our air.

But an upward trend in real GDP has its costs. The more quickly we increase real GDP, the faster are exhaustible resources such as oil and natural gas depleted, and the more severe our environmental and atmospheric pollution problems become. Although we have more to spend on these problems, they become bigger problems requiring higher expenditures. Furthermore, the more quickly real GDP increases, the more we have to accept change, both in what we consume and in the jobs that we do.

The benefits of more rapid growth in real GDP have to be balanced against the costs. The choices that people make to balance these benefits and costs, acting individually and through government institutions, determine the actual pace at which real GDP increases.

As we have seen, real GDP does not increase at an even pace. Are the fluctuations in real GDP important? Economists do not agree on the answer to this question. Some economists believe that real GDP fluctuations are costly. With real GDP below trend, unemployment is above its natural rate and output is lost forever. With real GDP above trend, inflationary bottlenecks and shortages arise. If a downturn can be avoided, average consumption levels can be increased, and if rises above trend can be avoided, inflation can be kept under control.

Other economists believe that fluctuations are the best possible response to the uneven pace and direction of technological change. At some times, technological change is rapid, and at other times it is slow. At some times, new technologies increase the productivity of workers in their existing jobs, and at other times, new technologies increase productivity only after massive structural change has taken place. Real GDP growth fluctuates with the pace of technological change—faster technological change brings faster real GDP growth. But structural change complicates the relationship. Rapid technological and structural changes at first bring structural unemployment and slow real GDP growth. Since we are not able to order the pace and direction of technological change to be smooth, we can smooth the pace of economic growth only by *delaying* the implementation of new technologies. Such delays would result in never-to-be-recovered waste.

Regardless of which position economists take, they all agree that depressions as deep and long as that which occurred in the early 1930s result in extraordinary waste and human suffering. The disagreements concern the more common and gentler ebbs and flows of economic activity that have occurred in the years since World War II, which we saw earlier in Fig. 22.6.

REVIEW

Gross domestic product is the dollar value of all the final goods and services produced in the economy. Nominal GDP measures the value of the output of final goods and services using current prices. Real GDP measures the value of the output using the prices that prevailed in some base period. Nominal GDP rises more quickly than real GDP because of inflation. The general tendency for real GDP to increase is called trend real GDP. Economic fluctuations can be measured by examining departures from trend real GDP. The upward trend in real GDP is the major source of improvements in living standards. However, the upward trend has costs in terms of depletion of exhaustible resources and environmental pollution. ◆

Let's now take a more systematic look at the ebbs and flows of economic activity.

The Business Cycle

The **business cycle** is the periodic but irregular up and down movement in economic activity, measured by fluctuations in real GDP and other macroeconomic variables. As we've just seen, real GDP can be divided into two components:

- Trend real GDP
- Real GDP fluctuations

To identify the business cycle, we focus our attention on the real GDP fluctuations, since this variable gives a direct measure of the uneven pace of economic activity, separate from its underlying trend growth path.

A business cycle is not a regular, predictable, or repeating phenomenon like the swings of the pendulum of a clock. Its timing is random and, to a large degree, unpredictable. A business cycle is identified as a sequence of four phases:

- Contraction
- Trough
- Expansion
- Peak

These four phases are shown in Fig. 22.7. This figure, which is an enlargement of part of Fig. 22.6, shows the business cycle for 1973 to 1991. Notice the four phases of the cycle. A **contraction** is a slowdown in the pace of economic activity, such as occurred between 1979 and 1982. An **expansion** is a speedup in the pace of economic activity, such as occurred between 1983 and 1988. A **trough** is the lower turning point of a business cycle, where a contraction turns into an expansion. A trough occurred in 1982. A **peak** is the upper turning point of a business cycle, where an expansion turns into a contraction. A peak occurred in 1978.

A recession occurs if a contraction is severe enough. A **recession** is a downturn in the level of economic activity in which real GDP declines in two

FIGURE 22.7

The Business Cycle

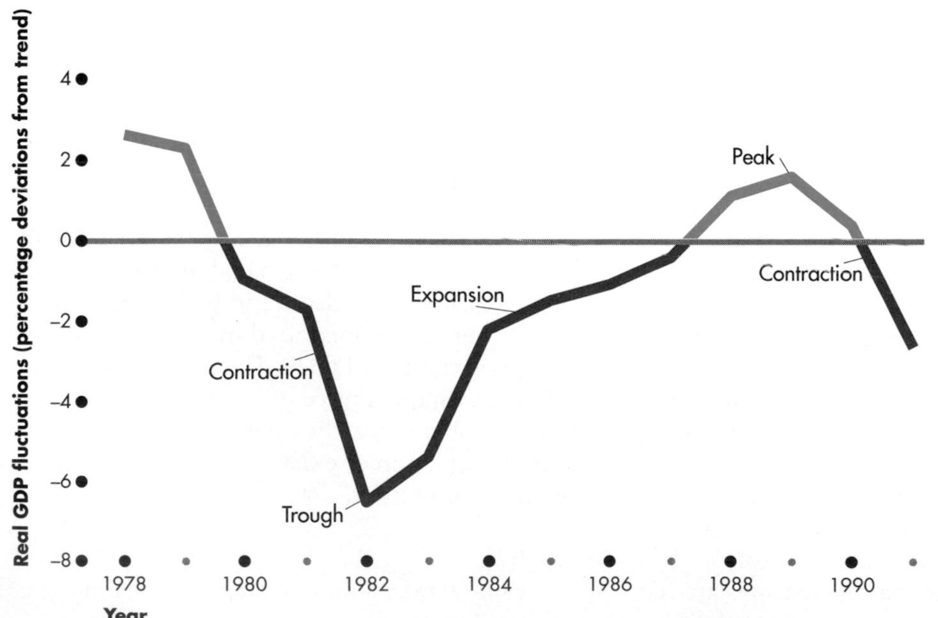

The business cycle has four phases: contraction, trough, expansion, and peak. Our experience in the 1970s and 1980s is used to illustrate these phases. There was a contraction from 1973 to 1975. In 1975, the trough was reached and an expansion began. That expansion reached a peak in 1978, when a new contraction set in that in turn reached a new trough in 1982. From 1982 to 1989, the economy was on a prolonged expansion. In 1989, the expansion reached a peak and a new contraction began.

successive quarters. A deep trough is called a slump or a **depression.**

Unemployment and the Business Cycle

Real GDP is not the only variable that fluctuates over the course of the business cycle. Its fluctuations are matched by related fluctuations in a wide range of other economic variables. One of the most important of these is unemployment. In the contraction phase of a business cycle, unemployment increases; in the expansion phase, unemployment decreases; at the peak, unemployment is at its lowest; at the trough, unemployment is at its highest. This relationship between unemployment and the phases of the business cycle is illustrated in Fig. 22.8.

That figure shows real GDP fluctuations and unemployment in the United States since 1900. The Great Depression, World War II, the OPEC recession, the 1982 recession, and the 1991 recession are highlighted in the figure. The figure also shows the unemployment rate. So that we can see how unemployment lines up with real GDP fluctuations, the unemployment rate has been measured with its scale inverted. That is, as we move down the vertical axis on the right-hand side, the unemployment rate increases. As you can see, fluctuations in unemployment closely follow those in real GDP.

The Stock Market and the Business Cycle

We have defined the business cycle as the ebbs and flows of economic activity and have measured these movements by real GDP fluctuations. We have seen that unemployment fluctuations mirror the business cycle very closely. Another indicator of the state of the economy, and perhaps the most visible of all such indicators, is provided by the stock market. Every weekday evening, newscasts tell us of the day's events on the New York and Tokyo stock exchanges. Movements in share prices attract attention partly for their own sake and also partly for what they may foretell about our *future* economic fortunes.

Do stock prices move in sympathy with fluctuations in real GDP and unemployment? Is a stock

FIGURE **22.8**

Unemployment and the Business Cycle

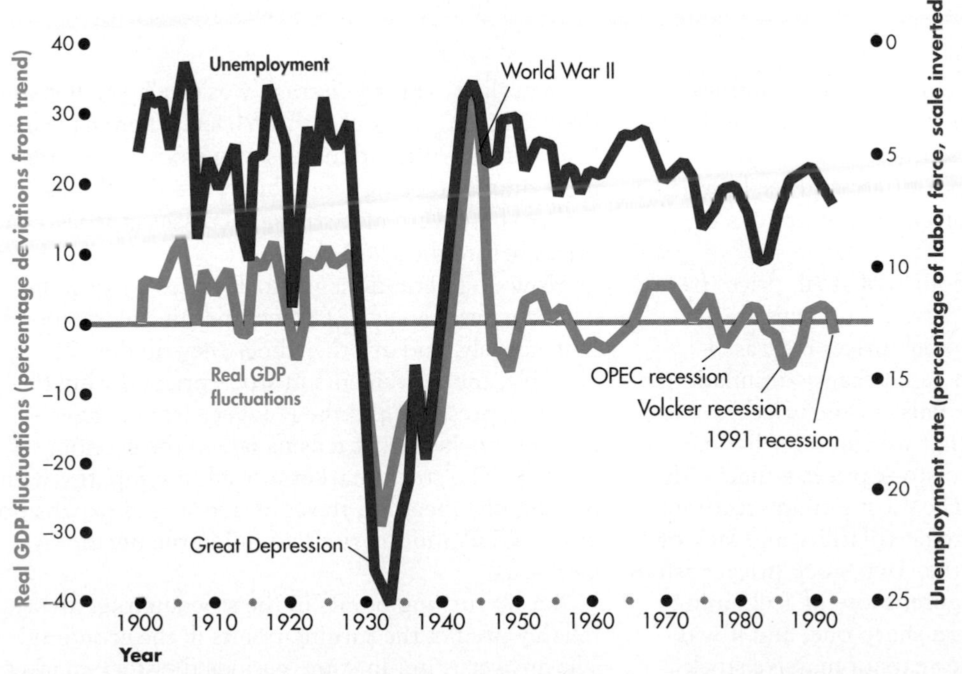

This figure shows the relationship between unemployment and the business cycle. Real GDP fluctuations tell us when the economy is in a contraction or expansion phase. Unemployment is plotted on the same figure but with its scale inverted. The line measuring unemployment is high when unemployment is low, and the line is low when unemployment is high. As you can see, the cycles in real GDP are closely matched by the cycles in unemployment.

FIGURE 22.9

Stock Prices: 1871–1991

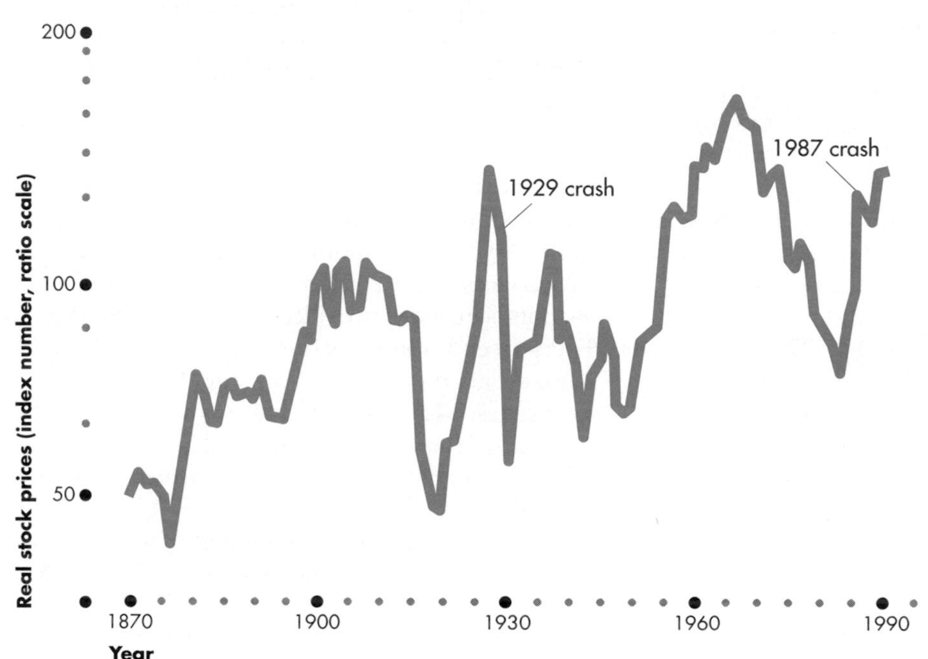

Stock prices are among the most volatile elements of our economy. Here, real stock prices (stock prices measured to take out the effects of changes in the value of money) climbed strongly from 1871 to 1910 but with strong fluctuations. They then fell dramatically through 1920 but increased at a spectacular pace through 1929. Then came the crash that preceded the Great Depression. Stock prices began a new climb after World War II, reaching a peak in 1965. They gradually fell to a trough in 1982, after which they climbed to a new peak before the crash of October 1987. The 1987 crash was short-lived, and real stock prices again increased, even during the 1991 recession.

Sources: 1871–1948: Index of Common Stocks, *Historical Statistics* (1960), Series X-351, p. 657; 1949–1991: The Dow-Jones Industrial Average, *Economic Report of the President,* 1992. The two indexes were linked to form a common index and converted to real terms by using the same price index that converts nominal GDP to real GDP (GNP before 1959). The index is scaled to have an average value between 1871 and 1991 of 100.

price downturn a predictor of economic contraction? Is a stock price boom a predictor of economic expansion? To answer these questions, let's take a look at the behavior of stock prices and see how they relate to the expansions and contractions of economic activity.

Figure 22.9 tracks the course of stock prices from 1871 to 1991. The prices plotted in this figure are inflation-adjusted. Actual stock prices increased much more than indicated here because of inflation, but the purely inflationary parts of the price increases have been removed so that we can see what has "really" been happening to stock prices—that is, the path of real stock prices. The most striking feature of stock prices is their extreme volatility and lack of any obvious cyclical patterns. Two stock price crashes are highlighted in the figure: those of 1929 and 1987. The 1929 crash was a sharp one, and it was followed by two successive years of massive stock price decline. The 1987 crash was much smaller, and the decline in prices was short-lived. There have also been periods of rapid increases in stock prices, the most dramatic being that which preceded the 1929 crash. There were also strong increases in stock prices before the 1987 crash.

How do fluctuations in stock prices correspond with the business cycle? Sometimes they correspond quite closely, and at other times they do not. For example, the movements in stock prices during the Great Depression and the recovery from it suggest that the stock market tells us where the economy is heading. The stock market moved in sympathy with, but slightly ahead of, the contraction and expansion of real GDP and the rise and fall in the unemployment rate.

But do turning points in the stock market always reliably predict the turning points in the economy? The answer is no. In some periods the stock market and real GDP move together, but in others the movements oppose each other. For example, the mini-crash of 1987 occurred at a time when the economy, both in the United States and in the rest of the world, was expanding strongly.

When stock prices collapsed in October 1987, many people drew parallels between that episode and the 1929 stock price crash. In 1930, the economy collapsed. In 1988, the economy continued to grow. Why were the two episodes so different? A key answer—and the key reason for the lack of a strong connection between stock price fluctuations and the business cycle—is our inability to forecast the business cycle. Stock prices are determined by people's expectations about the future profitability of firms. Future profitability, in turn, depends on the state of the economy. Hence stock prices are determined by expectations about the future state of the economy. But those expectations turn out to be wrong about as often as they turn out to be right. Thus the movement in stock prices is not an entirely reliable predictor of the state of the economy.

Inflation and the Business Cycle

We've looked at fluctuations in real variables: real GDP, the unemployment rate, and real stock prices. We've seen that there is a strong and systematic relationship between fluctuations in real GDP and fluctuations in the unemployment rate. We've also seen that there are times when there is a systematic relationship between real stock prices and the business cycle and other times when there isn't. How does inflation behave over the business cycle? Are fluctuations in its rate closely connected with business cycle fluctuations, or does the inflation rate vary independently of the business cycle?

To answer these questions, let's look again at the Great Depression and the two recent recessions and see how inflation varied during those periods. Figure 22.10(a) shows the inflation rate through the Great Depression. The state of the economy is shown by the fluctuations in real GDP. You can see from the figure that as the economy went into the contraction phase of the Great Depression, the inflation rate was also falling. In fact, inflation was negative, so the price level was falling. But the inflation rate reached its low point in 1932, a year before the trough of the business cycle. Thereafter, the inflation rate increased and did so at a much faster pace than the

FIGURE 22.10

Inflation and the Business Cycle

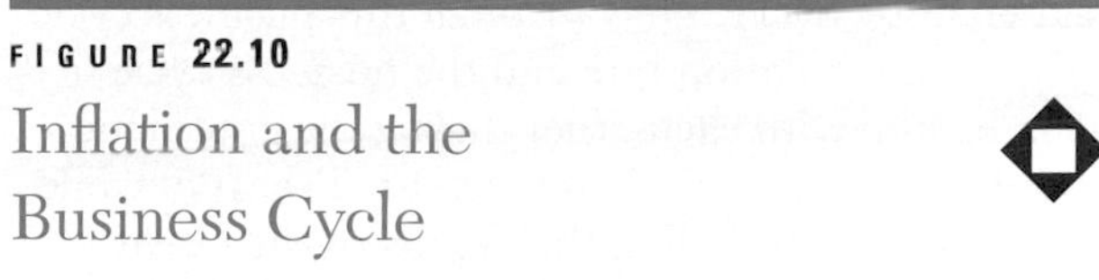

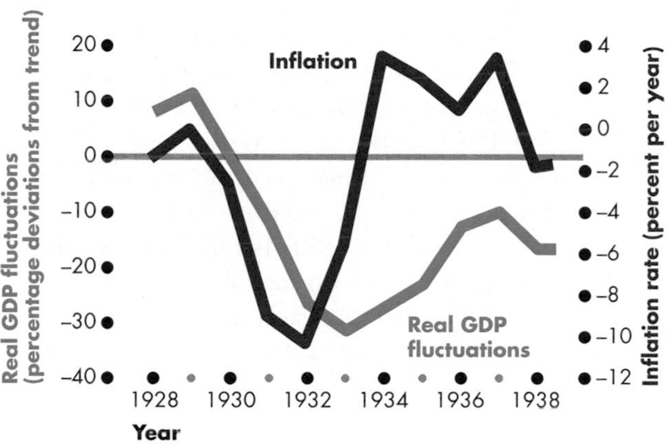

(a) The Great Depression

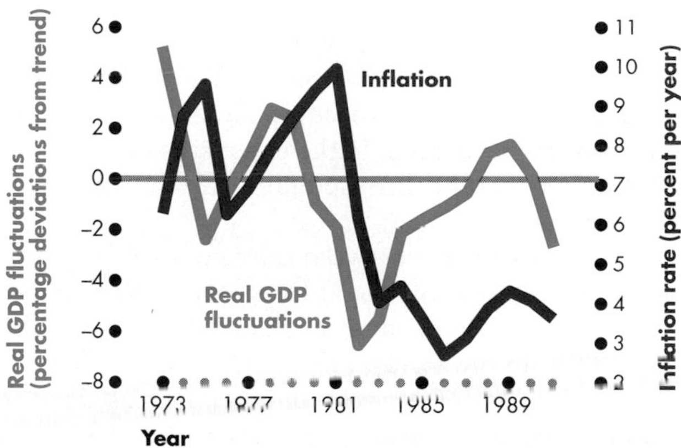

(b) The OPEC, Volcker, and 1991 recessions

Inflation follows the course of the business cycle on some occasions but departs from it on others. As shown in part (a), through the Great Depression, inflation and real GDP moved together during the contraction phase, but in the expansion phase, inflation increased much more strongly than real GDP. As shown in part (b), the inflation rate and real GDP fluctuated together from 1973 to 1982 but with inflation lagging behind real GDP by about a year. From 1982 to 1986, the inflation rate remained moderate as real GDP expanded quickly. From 1986 to 1989, the inflation rate increased as real GDP continued to expand, and after 1989, the inflation rate decreased as real GDP growth slowed down.

real GDP recovery. Thus through this business cycle episode, the inflation rate and the business cycle were in step with each other during the contraction phase, but the inflation rate increased sharply while the economy was still in the depths of the Great Depression.

Part (b) shows the course of inflation and real GDP fluctuations during the years 1973–1991. The cycles in real GDP fluctuations and the inflation rate between 1973 and 1982 look similar, but the inflation cycle lagged behind the real GDP cycle by about a year. After 1982, as the economy went into the expansion phase of the business cycle, the inflation rate remained low. But the inflation rate increased again between 1986 and 1989 as real GDP continued to expand. The inflation rate slowed again as the economy went into recession in 1990–1991.

It is interesting to contrast the course of inflation over these recent cycles with that of the Great Depression. In both cases, there are periods during which the inflation rate fell along with economic contraction and a phase during which the inflation rate increased along with economic expansion. But there are other periods in which the inflation rate and the state of the business cycle went in their own directions. In the recovery from the Great Depression, the inflation rate moved up more quickly than the economy recovered. In the expansion of the 1980s, there was no corresponding increase in the inflation rate.

A further contrast between the two periods is important. During the Great Depression, the average inflation rate was much lower than that of the 1970s and 1980s. In the 1930s, the inflation rate fell from zero to –10 percent per year and then increased to about 3 percent per year. In the 1970s and 1980s, inflation cycled, climbing to a peak of more than 13 percent and then falling to around 2 percent.

These episodes reveal two things about inflation. First, much of the time, inflation moves in sympathy with the business cycle. Second, there are important changes in the inflation rate that are independent of the business cycle—over some cycles the average inflation rate is low, and over others it is high.

REVIEW

The business cycle is the periodic but irregular up and down movement in economic activity. It has four phases: contraction, trough, expansion, and peak. A recession is a contraction in which real GDP declines for at least two quarters. Over the business cycle, real GDP and unemployment fluctuate together. During a contraction, the unemployment rate rises, and during an expansion it falls. Although the stock market sometimes moves in sympathy with the business cycle, it does not reliably predict turning points in the economy. Inflation can also move in sympathy with the business cycle, but there are important fluctuations in the inflation rate that are not related to the business cycle. ◆

We've now studied inflation, unemployment, real GDP fluctuations, and business cycles. Let's turn to our final topic, deficits.

Government Deficit and International Deficit

If you spend more than you earn in a given period, you have a deficit. To cover your deficit, you have to borrow or sell off some of the things that you own. Just as individuals can have deficits, so can governments and so can entire nations. These deficits—the government deficit and the international deficit—have attracted a lot of attention recently.

Government Deficit

The **government deficit** is the total expenditure of the government sector minus the total revenue of that sector in a given period. The government sector is composed of the federal government and the state and local governments. These governments spend on a variety of public and social programs and obtain their revenue from taxes.

Sometimes the government sector is in surplus, and at other times it is in deficit. Occasionally, the deficit is a very large one, as it was in 1975. Since 1980, the government sector has had a persistent deficit, averaging about 3 percent of GDP.

To some degree, the balance of the government budget is related to the business cycle. When the economy is expanding quickly, incomes grow quickly and so do tax receipts. Unemployment decreases, and so do unemployment benefits. The government deficit shrinks through this phase of the business cycle. When the economy is in a contraction phase, tax receipts decline and unemployment benefits increase and the government budget deficit increases. What is significant about the budget deficit in the 1980s is that it persisted despite the fact that the economy experienced strong and prolonged expansion.

We'll study the government deficit more closely and at greater length in Chapter 34. In that chapter, we'll discuss its sources and consequences.

International Deficit

The value of all the goods and services that we sell to other countries (exports) minus the value of all the goods and services that we buy from foreigners (imports) is called our **current account balance.** If we sell more to the rest of the world than we buy from it, we have a current account surplus. If we buy more from the rest of the world than we sell to it, we have a current account deficit.

Most of the time since 1950 we have had a small current account surplus. But in recent years, a current account deficit has emerged. That deficit has been not only persistent but also gradually increasing in magnitude. When we have a current account deficit, we have to borrow from the rest of the world to pay for the goods and services that we are buying in excess of the value of those that we are selling. Mirroring our current account deficit is a current account surplus in some other countries. The most notable country on the opposite side of our international payments balance is Japan. That country has been operating a current account surplus and, in recent years, an increasing surplus. To finance our deficit, we borrow from the rest of the world and the rest of the world lends to us.

The causes of these international surpluses and deficits and their consequences will be discussed at greater length in Chapter 36.

◆ ◆ ◆ ◆ In our study of macroeconomics, we're going to find out what we currently know about the causes of inflation and of variations in its rate; we're also going to discover what we know about the causes of unemployment and business cycle fluctuations. We're going to discover why at certain times the stock market is a good predictor of the state of the economy and at others it is not; we're also going to discover why sometimes inflation and the business cycle move in sympathy with each other and why at times these variables follow separate courses. Finally, we're going to learn more about deficits—the government deficit and the international deficit—and their causes, their importance, and their consequences. ◆ ◆ The next step in our study of macroeconomics is to learn more about macroeconomic measurement—about how we measure GDP, the price level, and inflation.

SUMMARY

Inflation

Inflation is an upward movement in the average level of prices. To measure the average level of prices, we calculate a price index. The inflation rate is the percentage change in the value of a price index.

Inflation is a persistent feature of economic life in the United States, but the rate of inflation fluctuates. In the early 1960s, inflation was between 1 and 2 percent a year. By 1980, its rate exceeded 13 percent a year. There was an upward trend in inflation through the 1960s and 1970s, but inflation has been on a downward trend since 1980.

Inflation is a problem because it brings a fall in the value of money at an unpredictable rate. The more unpredictable the inflation rate, the less useful is money as a measuring rod for conducting transactions. Inflation makes money especially unsuitable for transactions that are spread out over time, such as borrowing and lending or working for an agreed wage rate. A rapid anticipated inflation is a problem because it makes people get rid of money as quickly as possible, disrupting economic life. (pp. 583–587)

Unemployment

Unemployment is a state in which there are qualified workers who are available for work at the current wage rate and who do not have jobs. The labor force is the sum of those who are unemployed and those who are employed. The unemployment rate is the percentage of the labor force that is unemployed. Unemployment is measured each month by a survey of households.

Unemployment in the United States was not regarded as a major problem in the 1960s, when its rate averaged less than 5 percent. Its rate also declined during that decade. Since 1969, unemployment has been on an upward trend and has fluctuated strongly. Its rate reached a peak in 1982 and 1983.

There are three types of unemployment: frictional, structural, and cyclical. Frictional unemployment arises from normal labor market turnover and the fact that people take time to find the job that best matches their skills. Structural unemployment arises when technological change causes a decline in jobs that are concentrated in particular industries or regions. Cyclical unemployment arises when the pace of economic expansion slows down. Full employment is a state in which all unemployment is frictional and structural and the number of job vacancies is equal to the number of unemployed workers. At full employment, the unemployment rate is called the natural rate of unemployment.

The major costs of unemployment are the lost output and earnings that could have been generated if the unemployed had been working. Other major costs include the deterioration of human capital and, when unemployment is prolonged, increased crime and severe social and psychological problems for unemployed workers and their families. (pp. 587–591)

Gross Domestic Product

The nation's total output is measured by gross domestic product (GDP). GDP is the dollar value of all final goods and services produced in the economy in a given time period. Changes in GDP reflect both changes in prices and changes in the quantity of goods and services produced. To separate the effects of prices from real quantities, we distinguish between nominal GDP and real GDP. Nominal GDP is measured by using current prices. Real GDP is measured by using prices for some base year.

Real GDP grows, on average, every year, so the trend of real GDP is upward. But real GDP does not increase at a constant rate. Its rate of expansion fluctuates, so real GDP fluctuates around its trend value. Increases in real GDP bring rising living standards but not without costs. The main costs of fast economic growth are resource depletion, environmental pollution, and the need to face rapid and often costly changes in job type and location. The benefits of higher consumption levels have to be balanced against such costs. (pp. 591–597)

The Business Cycle

The business cycle is the periodic but irregular up and down movement in macroeconomic activity. The cycle has four phases: contraction, trough, expansion, and peak. When real GDP falls for two quarters, the economy is in a recession.

Unemployment fluctuates closely with real GDP fluctuations. When real GDP is above trend, the unemployment rate is low; when real GDP is below trend, the unemployment rate is high. But real stock prices do not fluctuate in a manner similar to business cycle fluctuations. Sometimes a stock market crash precedes a recession, but it does not always do so.

There is no simple relationship between the inflation rate and the business cycle. Sometimes the inflation rate increases in an expansion phase and decreases in a contraction phase. But there are other times when inflation moves independently of the business cycle. Thus there are two types of forces at work generating inflation that have to be investigated—those that are related to the business cycle and those that are not. (pp. 598–602)

Government Deficit and International Deficit

The government deficit is the total expenditure of the government sector minus the total revenue of that sector in a given period. To some degree the government deficit fluctuates over the course of the business cycle. But in the 1980s, the government sector persistently operated with a deficit averaging about 3 percent of GDP while the economy underwent a strong and persistent expansion.

A country's current account balance is the difference between the value of the goods and services that it sells to other countries and the value of the goods and services that it buys from the rest of the world. The United States normally has a current account surplus, but in the 1980s a deficit emerged. Mirroring the U.S. current account deficit is a current account surplus in some other countries. Japan is one of the countries that had a large surplus in the 1980s. (pp. 602–603)

KEY ELEMENTS

Key Terms

Anticipated inflation, 585
Business cycle, 598
Contraction, 598
Current account balance, 603
Cyclical unemployment, 590
Depression, 599
Discouraged workers, 588
Expansion, 598
Expected inflation rate, 585
Final goods and services, 591
Foreign exchange rate, 585
Frictional unemployment, 588
Full employment, 590
Government deficit, 602
Gross domestic product, 591
Human capital, 591
Inflation, 583
Inflation rate, 584
Intermediate goods and services, 594
Labor force, 587
Natural rate of unemployment, 590
Nominal GDP, 595
Peak, 598
Price index, 583
Price level, 583
Real GDP, 595
Recession, 598
Structural unemployment, 589
Trough, 598
Unanticipated inflation, 585
Unemployment, 587
Unemployment rate, 587
Value of money, 585

Key Figures

REVIEW QUESTIONS

1 What is inflation?

2 What are some of the costs of inflation?

3 What, if any, are the benefits from inflation? If there are none, explain why.

4 Why doesn't inflation always benefit borrowers at the expense of lenders?

5 Why might anticipated inflation be a problem?

6 What is the definition of unemployment?

7 How does the U.S. Department of Labor measure the unemployment rate?

8 Why may the measured unemployment rate understate or overstate the true extent of unemployment?

9 What are the different types of unemployment?

10 What are the main costs of unemployment?

11 What makes GDP grow?

12 What are the costs and benefits of a high average increase in real GDP?

13 What are the costs and benefits of fluctuations in real GDP?

14 What is a business cycle? Describe the four phases of a business cycle. What was the phase of the U.S. business cycle in 1975? In 1980? In 1985? In 1991?

15 When the economy is in a recovery phase, what is happening to the unemployment rate? The stock market?

16 How does the inflation rate fluctuate over the business cycle?

17 Compare the fluctuations in inflation and unemployment.

PROBLEMS

1 At the end of 1992 the price index was 150. At the end of 1991 the price index was 125. Calculate the inflation rate in 1992.

2 In a noninflationary world, Joe and Mary are willing to borrow and lend at 2 percent a year. Joe expects that inflation next year will be 5 percent, and Mary expects that it will be 3 percent. Would Joe and Mary be willing to sign a contract in which one of them borrows from the other? Explain why or why not.

3 Lucy operates the Cone-Heads Ice Cream Parlor. She expects that inflation next year will be 3 percent. The students who work at Cone-Heads expect inflation to be only 2 percent. Will Lucy and the students be able to agree now on a wage rate for next summer? Explain your answer.

4 Obtain data on unemployment in your home state. If your school library has the U.S. Department of Labor publication *Employment and Earnings,* you can get the data from there. Otherwise, you might have to call your local newspaper's business desk for the information. Compare the behavior of unemployment in your home state with that in the United States as a whole. Why do you think your state might have a higher or a lower unemployment rate than the U.S. average?

5 Obtain data on inflation in the United States, Japan, Canada, and Germany since 1980. You will find these data in *International Financial Statistics* in your school library. Draw a graph of the data and answer the following questions:

a Which country had the highest inflation rate?

b Which country had the lowest inflation rate?

c Which country had the fastest-rising inflation rate?

d Which country had the fastest-falling inflation rate?

6 On the basis of your discovery in answering problem 5, what do you expect happened to the foreign exchange rates between the U.S. dollar and the Japanese yen, the Canadian dollar, and the German mark? Check your expectation by finding these exchange rates in the *International Financial Statistics* from which you got the inflation rates.

CHAPTER 23

MEASURING OUTPUT AND THE PRICE LEVEL

After studying this chapter, you will be able to:

- Describe the flows of expenditure and income
- Explain why aggregate expenditure and income are equal to each other
- Explain how gross domestic product (GDP) and gross national product (GNP) are measured
- Describe two measures of the price level—the Consumer Price Index (CPI) and the GDP deflator
- Explain how real GDP is measured
- Distinguish between inflation and changes in relative prices
- Explain why real GDP is not a good measure of economic well-being

Economic Barometers

EVERY THREE MONTHS, THE U.S. DEPARTMENT OF Commerce publishes the latest quarterly estimates of the gross domestic product, or GDP—a barometer of our nation's economy. As soon as it is published, analysts pore over the data, trying to understand the past and peer into the future. But how do government accountants add up all the blooming, buzzing economic activity of the country to arrive at the number called GDP? And what exactly *is* GDP? ◆◆ From economists to homemakers, inflation watchers of all types pay close attention to another economic barometer, the Consumer Price Index, or CPI. The Department of Labor publishes new figures each month, and analysts in newspapers and on TV quickly leap to conclusions. How does the government determine the CPI? How well does it measure the consumer's living costs? ◆◆ The pace of expansion of our economy fluctuates and is occasionally interrupted by a period of contraction. We describe these ebbs and flows of economic activity as the business cycle. But to reveal the business cycle, we must remove the effects of inflation on GDP and assess how GDP has changed not because of changing prices but because of changing production. How do we remove the inflation component of GDP? ◆◆ Some people make a living from crime. Others, although doing work that is legal, try to hide the payment they receive in order to evade taxes or other regulations. Most people undertake some economic activity inside their homes. Fixing meals, laundering shirts, and mowing the lawn are all examples. Are these activities taken into account when we measure GDP? If they are not taken into account, how important are they? And does it matter if they don't show up in GDP?

Proprietors' income is a mixture of the elements that we have just reviewed. The proprietor of an owner-operated business supplies labor, capital, and perhaps land and buildings to the business. National income accountants find it difficult to split up the income earned by an owner-operator into its component parts—compensation for labor, payment for the use of capital, rent payments for the use of land or buildings, and profit. As a consequence, the national income accounts lump all these separate factor incomes earned by proprietorships into a single category. **Net domestic income at factor cost** is the sum of all factor incomes. Thus, if we add together the items that we have just reviewed, we arrive at this measure of aggregate income. To measure GDP using the factor incomes approach, we have to make two adjustments to *net domestic income at factor cost.* Let's see what these adjustments are.

Market Price and Factor Cost To calculate GDP using the expenditure approach, we add together expenditures on *final goods and services.* These expenditures are valued at the prices people pay for the various goods and services. The price that people pay for a good or service is called the **market price.**

Another way of valuing a good is factor cost. **Factor cost** is the value of a good measured by adding together the costs of all the factors of production used to produce it. If the only economic transactions were between households and firms, the market price and factor cost methods of measuring value would be identical. But the presence of indirect taxes and subsidies makes these two methods of valuation diverge.

An **indirect tax** is a tax paid by consumers when they purchase goods and services. (In contrast, a *direct* tax is a tax on income.) Examples of indirect taxes are state sales taxes and taxes on alcohol, gasoline, and tobacco products. Indirect taxes result in the consumer paying more than the producer receives for a good. For example, suppose that in your state there is a sales tax of 7 percent. If you buy a $1 chocolate bar, it costs you $1.07. The total cost, including profit, of all the inputs used to produce the chocolate bar is $1. The market price value of the chocolate bar is $1.07. The factor cost value of the chocolate bar is $1.

A **subsidy** is a payment made by the government to producers. Examples are subsidies paid to grain growers and dairy farmers. A subsidy also drives a wedge between the market price value and the factor cost value but in the direction opposite to indirect taxes. A subsidy lowers the market price below the factor cost—consumers pay less for the good than it costs the producer to make the good.

To use the factor incomes approach to measure gross domestic product, we need to add indirect taxes to total factor incomes and to subtract subsidies. Making this adjustment still does not quite get us to GDP. There is one further adjustment needed.

Net Domestic Product and Gross Domestic Product If we total all the factor incomes and add indirect taxes less subsidies to that total, we arrive at **net domestic product at market prices.** What do the words *gross* and *net* mean, and what is the distinction between the two terms *net domestic product* and *gross domestic product*?

The difference between these two terms is accounted for by the depreciation of capital. **Depreciation** is the decrease in the value of the capital stock that results from wear and tear and the passage of time. We've seen that investment is the purchase of new capital equipment. Depreciation is the opposite—the wearing out or destruction of capital equipment. Part of investment represents the purchase of capital equipment to replace equipment that has worn out. That investment does not add to the capital stock; it simply maintains the capital stock. The other part of investment represents additions to the capital stock—the purchase of new additional plant, equipment, and inventories. Total investment is called gross investment. **Gross investment** is the amount spent on replacing depreciated capital and on making net additions to the capital stock. Gross investment minus depreciation is called **net investment.** Net investment is the net addition to the capital stock. Let's illustrate these ideas with an example.

On January 1, 1992, Swanky, Inc. had a capital stock consisting of three knitting machines that had a market value of $7,500. In 1992, Swanky bought a new machine for $3,000. But during the year the machines owned by Swanky depreciated by a total of $1,000. By December 31, 1992, Swanky's stock of knitting machines was worth $9,500. Swanky's purchase of a new machine for $3,000 is the firm's gross investment. The firm's net investment—the difference between gross investment ($3,000) and

TABLE 23.3

Capital Stock, Investment, and Depreciation for Swanky, Inc.

Capital stock on January 1, 1992 (value of knitting machines owned at beginning of year)		**$7,500**
Gross investment (value of new knitting machine bought in 1992)	**+3,000**	
***less* Depreciation (fall in value of knitting machines during year 1992)**	**−1,000**	
***equals* Net investment**		**2,000**
Capital stock on December 31, 1992 (value of knitting machines owned at end of year)		**$9,500**

Swanky, Inc.'s capital stock at the end of 1992 equals its capital stock at the beginning of the year plus net investment. Net investment is equal to gross investment less depreciation. Gross investment is the value of new machines bought during the year, and depreciation is the fall in the value of Swanky's knitting machines over the year.

TABLE 23.4

GDP: The Factor Incomes Approach

Item	Amount in 1990 (billions of dollars)	Percentage of GDP
Compensation of employees	**3,290**	**59.7**
Rental income	**41**	**0.7**
Corporate profits	**319**	**5.8**
Net interest	**490**	**8.9**
Proprietors' income	**350**	**6.3**
Indirect taxes *less* Subsidies	**470**	**8.5**
Capital consumption (depreciation)	**554**	**10.1**
Gross domestic product	**5,514**	**100.0**

The sum of all factor incomes equals net domestic income at factor cost. GDP equals net domestic income at factor cost plus indirect taxes minus subsidies plus capital consumption (depreciation). In 1990, GDP measured by the factor incomes approach was $5,514 billion. The compensation of employees—labor income—was by far the largest part of total factor incomes.

Source: U.S. Department of Commerce, *Survey of Current Business* (January 1992).

depreciation ($1,000)—is $2,000. These transactions and the relationship between gross investment, net investment, and depreciation are summarized in Table 23.3.

Gross domestic product equals net domestic product plus depreciation. (Depreciation is called *capital consumption* by the national income accountants of the Department of Commerce.) Total expenditure *includes* depreciation—because it includes *gross investment.* Total factor incomes plus indirect taxes less subsidies *excludes* depreciation—because when firms calculate their profit, they make an allowance for depreciation and so subtract from their gross profit their estimate of the decrease in the value of their capital stock. As a result, adding up factor incomes gives a measure of domestic product that is net of the depreciation of the capital stock. To reconcile the factor incomes and expenditure approaches, we must add capital consumption (depreciation) to net domestic product. Table 23.4 summarizes these calculations and shows how the factor incomes approach leads to the same estimate of GDP as the expenditure approach. The table also shows the relative importance of the various factor incomes. As you can see, compensation of employees (wages and salaries) is by far the most important factor income.

Valuing the Output of Firms and Sectors

To value the output of an individual firm or sector of the economy, we calculate the value added by that firm or sector. **Value added** is the value of a firm's output minus the value of *intermediate goods* bought from other firms. Equivalently, it is the sum of the incomes (including profits) paid to the factors of production used by a firm to produce its output. Let's illustrate value added by looking at the production of a loaf of bread.

Figure 23.3 takes you through the brief life of a loaf of bread. It starts with the farmer, who grows the wheat. To do so, the farmer hires labor, capital equipment, and land, paying wages, interest, and rent. The farmer also receives a profit. The entire value of the wheat produced is the farmer's value added. The miller buys wheat from the farmer and turns it into flour. To do so, the miller hires labor and uses capital equipment, paying wages and interest, and receives a profit. The miller has now added some value to the wheat bought from the farmer. The baker buys flour from the miller. The price of the flour includes value added by the farmer and by the miller. The baker adds more value by turning the flour into bread. Wages are paid to bakery workers, interest is paid on the capital used by the baker, and the baker makes a profit. The bread is bought from the baker by the grocery store. The bread now has value added by the farmer, the miller, and the baker. At this stage, the value of the loaf is its *wholesale value*. The grocery store adds further value by making the loaf available in a convenient place at a convenient time. The consumer buys the bread for a price—its *retail price*—that includes the value added by the farmer, the miller, the baker, and the grocery store.

FIGURE 23.3

Value Added in the Life of a Loaf of Bread

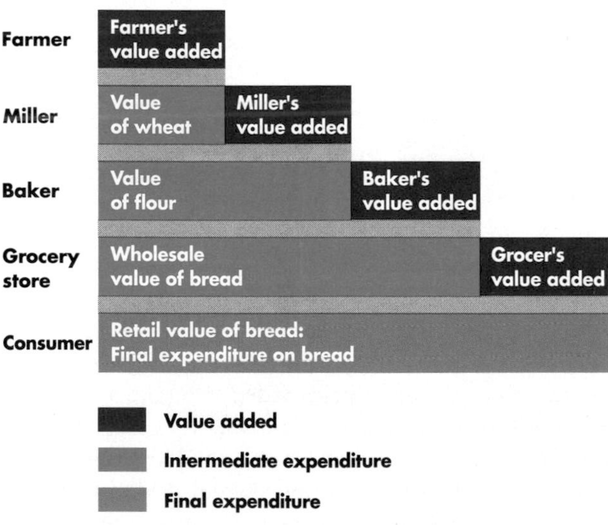

A consumer's expenditure on a loaf of bread is equal to the sum of the value added at each stage in its production. Intermediate expenditure, for example, the purchase of flour by the baker from the miller, already includes the value added by the farmer and the miller. Including intermediate expenditure double counts the value added.

Final Goods and Intermediate Goods In valuing output, we count only *value added.* The sum of the value added at each stage of production equals expenditure on *the final good.* In the above example, the only thing that has been produced and consumed is one loaf of bread. But many transactions occurred in the process of producing the loaf of bread. The miller bought grain from the farmer, the baker bought flour from the miller, and the grocer bought bread from the baker. These transactions were the purchase and sale of *intermediate goods.* To count the expenditure on intermediate goods and services as well as the expenditure on the final good involves counting the same thing twice, or more than twice when there are several intermediate stages, as there are in this example. Counting expenditure on both final goods and intermediate goods is known as **double counting.** Wheat, flour, and even the finished loaf bought by the grocery store are all intermediate goods in the production of a loaf of bread bought by a final consumer.

Many goods are sometimes intermediate goods and sometimes final goods. For example, the electric power used by GM to produce automobiles is an intermediate good, but the electric power that you buy to use in your home is a final good. Whether a good is intermediate or final depends not on what it is, but on what it is used for.

Gross National Product

Until recently, the Department of Commerce focused on a different measure of aggregate economic activity from GDP. This measure is gross national product, or GNP. **Gross national product** is the total value of output *owned by residents* of the United States. Gross *domestic* product measures the value of output *produced in* the United States. The difference between gross *domestic* product and gross *national* product is the net investment income that U.S. residents receive from other parts of the world. For example, Americans own production plants in Japan and Europe. Japanese and European residents own production plants in the United States. Net investment income received from the rest of the world is the total payment of profits and dividends to U.S.

residents on their foreign investments less the payments of interest and dividends to foreigners on their investments in the United States.

The magnitude of the difference between GDP and GNP for the United States is small, but for some countries it is large and important. This difference is explained and illustrated further in Reading Between the Lines on pp. 622–623.

Aggregate Expenditure, Income, and GDP

We've now studied the concepts of aggregate expenditure, aggregate income, and the value of output as well as the measurement of these concepts by the Department of Commerce. The equality of the three concepts and the relative importance of their components are illustrated in Fig. 23.4. This figure provides a snapshot summary of the entire description of the national accounting concepts that you've studied in this chapter.

FIGURE 23.4

Aggregate Expenditure, Output, and Income

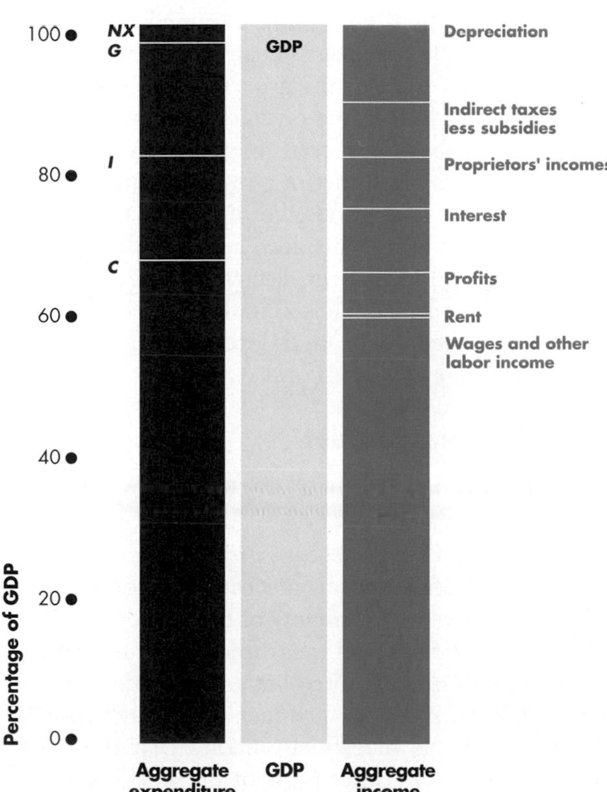

This figure illustrates the relative magnitudes of the main components of aggregate expenditure and aggregate income and also illustrates the equality between aggregate expenditure, aggregate income, and GDP.

REVIEW

GDP is measured by two methods: the *expenditure approach* (the sum of consumption expenditure, investment, government purchases of goods and services, and exports minus imports) and the *factor incomes approach* (the sum of wages, interest, rent, and profit with adjustments for indirect taxes, subsidies, and depreciation). ◆

So far, in our study of GDP and its measurement, we've been concerned with the dollar value of GDP and its components. But GDP can change either because prices change or because there is a change in the volume of goods and services produced—a change in *real* GDP. Let's now see how we measure the price level and distinguish between price changes and changes in real GDP.

The Price Level and Inflation

The *price level* is the average level of prices measured by a *price index*. To construct a price index, we take a basket of goods and services and calculate its value in the current period and in a base period. The price index is the ratio of its value in the current period to its value in the base period. The price index tells us how much more expensive the basket is in the current period than it was in the base period, expressed as a percentage.

Table 23.5 shows you how to calculate a price index for the basket of goods that Tom buys. His basket is a simple one. It contains four movies and two six-packs of soda. The value of Tom's basket,

TABLE 23.5

Calculating a Price Index

Items in the basket	1991 (base period) Quantity bought	Price	Expenditure	1992 (current period) Price	Expenditure
Movies	4	$6	$24	$6.75	$27.00
Six-packs of soda	2	3	6	4.20	8.40
			$30		$35.40

Price Index for 1992 = $\frac{\$35.40}{\$30.00} \times 100 = 118$

A price index for 1992 is calculated in two steps. The first step is to value the goods bought in 1991, the base period, at the prices prevailing in both 1991 and 1992. The second step is to divide the value of those goods in 1992 by their value in 1991 and multiply the result by 100.

shown in the table, in 1991 was $30. The same basket in 1992 cost $35.40. Tom's price index is $35.40 expressed as a percentage of $30. That is,

$$\frac{\$35.40}{\$30} \times 100 = 118.$$

Notice that if the current period is also the base period, the price index is 100.

There are two main price indexes used to measure the price level in the United States today: the Consumer Price Index and the GDP deflator. The **Consumer Price Index** (CPI) measures the average level of prices of the goods and services typically consumed by an urban American family. The **GDP deflator** measures the average level of prices of all the goods and services that are included in GDP. We are now going to study the method used for determining these price indexes. In calculating the actual indexes, the Departments of Commerce and Labor process millions of pieces of information. But we can learn the principles involved in those calculations by working through some simple examples.

Consumer Price Index

The Bureau of Labor Statistics in the U.S. Department of Labor calculates and publishes the *Consumer Price Index* every month. To construct the CPI, the Department of Labor first selects a base period. Currently, the base period is the three-year period from 1982 through 1984. Then, on the basis of surveys of consumer spending patterns, it selects a basket of goods and services—the quantities of approximately 400 different goods and services that were typically consumed by urban households in the base period.

Every month the Department of Labor sends a team of observers to more than 50 urban centers in the United States to record the prices for these 400 items. When all the data are collected, the CPI is calculated by valuing the base-period basket of goods and services at the current month's prices. That value is expressed as a percentage of the value of the same basket in the base period.

To see more precisely how the CPI is calculated, let's work through an example. Table 23.6 summarizes our calculations. Let's suppose that there are only three goods in the typical consumer's basket: oranges, haircuts, and bus rides. The quantities bought and the prices prevailing in the base period are shown in the table. Total expenditure in the base period is also shown: the typical consumer buys 200 bus rides at 70¢ each and so spends $140 on bus rides. Expenditure on oranges and haircuts is worked out in the same way. Total expenditure is the sum of expenditures on the three goods, which is $210.

To calculate the price index for the current period, we need only to discover the prices of the goods

GNP versus GDP

THE ECONOMIST, SEPTEMBER 21-27, 1991

Alphabet soup

Did the American economy start to recover in the second quarter of this year, or was it stuck in recession? America's real gross national product (GNP), the measure that is watched by the government and Wall Street and splashed across newspaper headlines, fell by 0.1% at an annual rate in the second quarter. However, gross domestic product (GDP) rose by 0.8% at an annual rate. By coincidence, the Department of Commerce has just decided that from November, when the third-quarter figures will be released, it will concentrate more on GDP than on GNP.

GDP measures the value of all goods and services produced in America. GNP measures the total income of American residents, regardless of where it comes from; profits from a firm's overseas subsidiary as well as its earnings in America are included. This means that GNP is equal to GDP plus net income from abroad: profits, dividends and interest earned overseas minus income payable to foreigners (the profits of a Japanese car factory in America, for instance). . . .

In most countries it makes little difference, as net income from abroad tends to be small compared with the rest of the economy. America's GNP is only about 1% bigger than its GDP. But in some countries the gap is huge. Kuwait's GNP is a third bigger than its GDP, thanks to its large overseas investments; Ireland's is 13% smaller than its GDP.

GNP is probably more useful in comparing the relative levels of income per head in different countries, but GDP provides a better guide to changes in domestic production—and hence is the better tool for steering economic policy. Because net income from abroad tends to be volatile, the two measures can often move in completely different directions from one quarter to another. Swings in America's GNP sometimes give a misleading picture of domestic economic activity. Over longer periods, however, the two measures usually fall into step. Indeed, since the third quarter of last year, American GDP and GNP have both fallen by exactly the same amount. . . .

Mind the gap

GNP as % of GDP	
Kuwait	135.0
Switzerland	105.3
West Germany	101.7
Britain	100.9
United States	100.8
Japan	100.7
France	99.8
Italy	99.1
Canada	96.6
Jamaica	89.7
Ireland	87.3
Brazil	85.6

Source: IMF

The Essence of the Story

The total income of U.S. residents, regardless of where in the world the income is earned, is U.S. GNP. U.S. GDP measures the value of all goods and services produced in the United States. GNP equals GDP plus net income from the rest of the world.

For most countries the difference between GNP and GDP is small—less than 1 percent for the United States.

For a few countries the difference is large—see the table in the article.

Net income from the rest of the world fluctuates, so over short periods, real GNP and real GDP sometimes move in opposite directions. When they do, movements in GNP give a misleading picture of the change in domestic economic activity.

Such a misleading picture was given in the second quarter of 1991 when U.S. real GNP declined and real GDP increased.

Over longer periods, real GNP and real GDP grow at a similar rate—from the third quarter of 1990 to the second quarter of 1991, U.S. GDP and GNP both fell by the same amount.

Background and Analysis

The value of all the goods and services produced in the United States in a given time period is GDP. It also measures the incomes paid to the factors of production that produced those goods and services.

Real GDP (GDP with the effects of inflation removed) is the broadest measure of economic activity and is used to judge the pace at which the economy is expanding or contracting.

Until the end of 1991, the Commerce Department focused on GNP, a measure of economic activity that adds to GDP the net income received by U.S. residents from the rest of the world. This amount added to GDP is part of the GDP of other countries. Today, the Commerce Department focuses on GDP.

Because U.S. net income from the rest of the world is a small percentage of total income, GDP and GNP tell a similar story, as you can see in Fig. 1.

But over very short periods, as shown in Fig. 2, the two numbers can give different pictures of the growth rate. When they do diverge, as they did during the 1991 recession, it is GDP that tells us where the U.S. economy is heading.

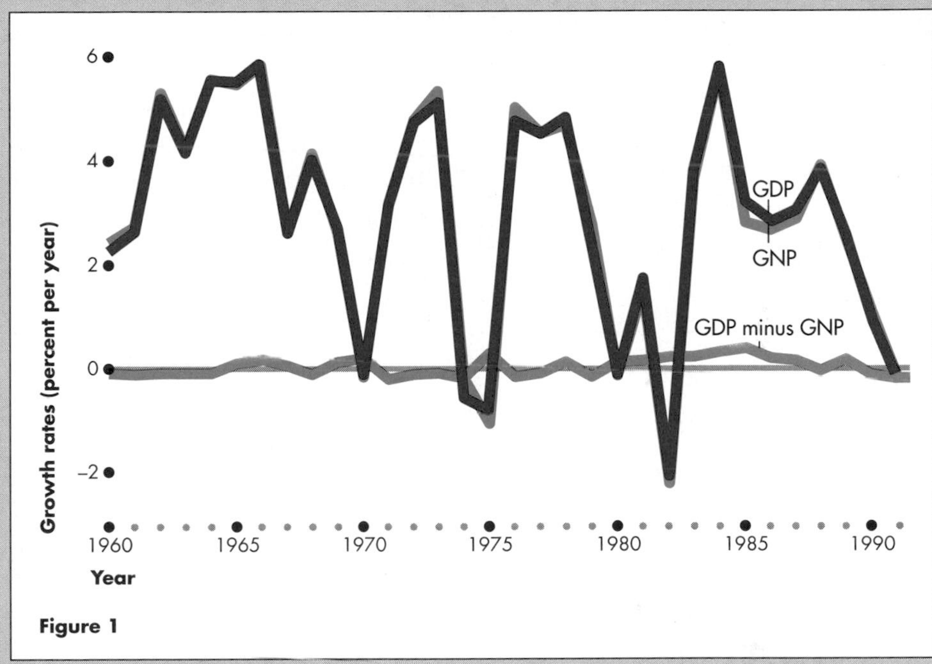

Figure 1

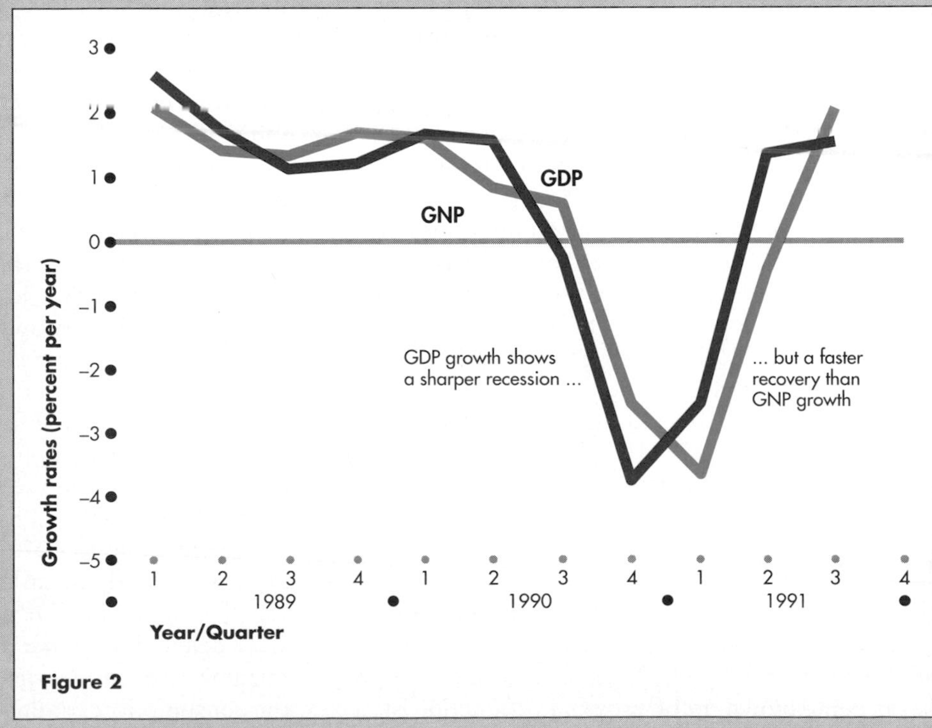

Figure 2

TABLE 23.6

The Consumer Price Index: A Simplified Calculation

	Base period			Current period	
Items in the basket	Quantity	Price	Expenditure	Price	Expenditures on base-period quantities
Oranges	**5 pounds**	**$ 0.80/pound**	**$ 4**	**$ 1.20/pound**	**$ 6**
Haircuts	**6**	**11.00 each**	**66**	**12.50 each**	**75**
Bus rides	**200**	**0.70 each**	**140**	**0.75 each**	**150**
Total expenditure			**$210**		**$231**
CPI		$\frac{\$210.00}{\$210.00} \times 100 = 100$		$\frac{\$231.00}{\$210.00} \times 100 = 110$	

A fixed basket of goods—5 pounds of oranges, 6 haircuts, and 200 bus rides—is valued in the base period at $210. Prices change, and that same basket is valued at $231 in the current period. The CPI is equal to the current-period value of the basket divided by the base-period value of the basket multiplied by 100. In the base period the CPI is 100, and in the current period the CPI is 110.

in the current period. We do not need to know the quantities bought. Let's suppose that the prices are those set out in the table under "Current period." We can now calculate the current period's value of the basket of goods by using the current period's prices. For example, the current price of oranges is $1.20 per pound, so the current period's value of the base-period quantity (5 pounds) is 5 multiplied by $1.20, which is $6. The base-period quantities of haircuts and bus rides are valued at this period's prices in a similar way. The total value in the current period of the base-period basket is $231.

We can now calculate the CPI—the ratio of this period's value of the goods to the base period's value, multiplied by 100. In this example, the CPI for the current period is 110. The CPI for the base period is, by definition, 100.

GDP Deflator

The *GDP deflator* measures the average level of prices of all the goods and services that make up GDP. You can think of GDP as being like a balloon that is being blown up by growing production of goods and services and rising prices. Figure 23.5 illustrates this idea. The purpose of the GDP deflator is to let some air out of the GDP balloon—the contribution of rising prices—so that we can see what has happened to *real* GDP. Real GDP is a measure of the physical volume of output arrived at by valuing the current-period output at prices that prevailed in a *base period.* Currently, the base period for calculating real GDP is 1987. We refer to the units in which real GDP is measured as "1987 dollars." The red balloon for 1987 shows real GDP in that year. The green balloon shows *nominal* GDP in 1992. (We use the term *nominal GDP* because it measures the money value of output.) The red balloon for 1992 shows real GDP for that year. To see real GDP in 1992, we *deflate* nominal GDP using the GDP deflator. Let's see how we calculate real GDP and the GDP deflator.

We are going to learn how to calculate the GDP deflator by studying an imaginary economy. We will calculate nominal GDP and real GDP as well as the GDP deflator. To make our calculations simple, let's imagine an economy that has just three final goods: the consumption good is oranges; the capital good is

FIGURE 23.5

The GDP Balloon

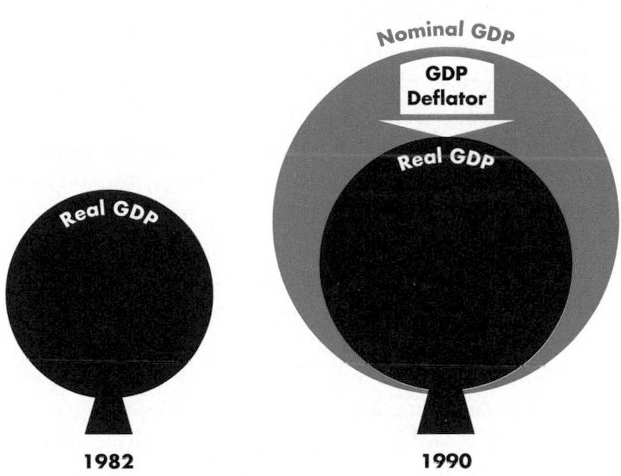

GDP is like a balloon that gets bigger because of growing output and rising prices. The GDP deflator is used to let the air resulting from higher prices out of the balloon so that we can see the extent to which production has grown.

computers; and the government purchases red tape. (Net exports are zero in this example.) Table 23.7 summarizes the calculations of nominal GDP, real GDP, and the GDP deflator in this economy.

Let's focus first on calculating nominal GDP. We'll use the expenditure approach. The table shows the quantities of the final goods and their prices. To calculate nominal GDP, let's work out the expenditure on each good and then total the three expenditures. Consumption expenditure (purchases of oranges) is \$4,452, investment (purchases of computers) is \$10,500, and government purchases of red tape are \$1,060, so nominal GDP is \$16,012.

Next, let's calculate real GDP. This is calculated by valuing the current-period quantities at the base-period prices. The table shows the prices for the base period. Real expenditure on oranges for the current period is 4,240 pounds of oranges valued at \$1 per pound, which is \$4,240. If we perform the same types of calculations for computers and red tape and add up the real expenditures, we arrive at a real GDP of \$15,300.

To calculate the GDP deflator for the current period, we divide nominal GDP (\$16,012) by real GDP (\$15,300) and multiply the result by 100. The GDP deflator that we obtain is 104.7. If the current

TABLE 23.7

Nominal GDP, Real GDP, and the GDP Deflator: Simplified Calculations

	Current period			Base period	
Item	Quantity	Price	Expenditure	Price	Expenditure
Oranges	**4,240 pounds**	**\$1.05/pound**	**\$ 4,452**	**\$1/pound**	**\$ 4,240**
Computers	**5**	**\$2,100 each**	**10,500**	**\$2,000 each**	**\$10,000**
Red tape	**1,060 yards**	**\$1/yard**	**1,060**	**\$1/yard**	**\$ 1,060**
		Nominal GDP	**\$16,012**	**Real GDP**	**\$15,300**

GDP deflator $= \frac{\$16{,}012}{\$15{,}300} \times 100 = 104.7$

An imaginary economy produces only oranges, computers, and red tape. In the current period, nominal GDP is \$16,012. If the current-period quantities are valued at the base-period prices, we obtain a measure of real GDP, which is \$15,300. The GDP deflator in the current period—which is calculated by dividing nominal GDP by real GDP in that period and multiplying by 100—is 104.7.

period is also the base period, nominal GDP equals real GDP and the GDP deflator is 100. Thus the GDP deflator in the base period is 100, just as for the CPI.

Inflation and Relative Price Changes

The inflation rate is calculated as the percentage increase in the price index. For example, in the case that we studied in Table 23.6, the CPI rose by 10 percent from the base period to the current period. Underlying that change in the CPI are the individual changes in the prices of oranges, haircuts, and bus rides. No individual price rose by 10 percent. The price of oranges rose by 50 percent, the price of haircuts by 13.6 percent, and the price of bus rides by 7.1 percent. This example captures a common feature of the world that we live in: it is rarely the case that all prices change by the same percentage amount. When the prices of goods rise by different percentages, there is a change in relative prices. A **relative price** is the ratio of the price of one good to the price of another good. For example, if the price of oranges is 80¢ per pound and the price of a haircut is $11, the relative price of a haircut is 13¾ pounds of oranges. It costs 13¾ pounds of oranges to buy one haircut.

Prices and inflation mean a great deal to people. But many people are confused by the difference between the inflation rate and relative price changes. Inflation and relative price changes are separate and independent phenomena. To see why this is so, we will work through an example showing that, for the same relative price changes, we can have two entirely different inflation rates.

We will first learn how to calculate a change in relative prices. The percentage change in a relative price is the percentage change in the price of one good minus the percentage change in the price of another good. For example, if the price of oranges increases from 80¢ per pound to 88¢ per pound—an increase of 10 percent—and if the price of a haircut remains constant at $11—an increase of zero percent—the relative price of a haircut falls from 13¾ pounds of oranges to 12½ pounds of oranges—a decrease of (approximately) 10 percent.

For practical calculations of relative price changes, we use the inflation rate—the percentage change in prices on the average—as the reference point. That is, we calculate the rate of change of the price of a good minus the inflation rate. Goods whose prices rise at a higher rate than the inflation rate experience a rising relative price, and goods whose prices rise at a rate below the inflation rate experience a falling relative price.

Let's work out some relative price changes, using again the calculations that we worked through in Table 23.6, now presented in Table 23.8(a). The price of oranges rises from 80¢ to $1.20, or by 50 percent. We have already calculated that the inflation rate is 10 percent. That is, prices on the average rise by 10 percent. To calculate the percentage change in the relative price of oranges, we subtract the inflation rate from the percentage change in the price of oranges. The price of oranges increased relative to the price level by 50 percent minus 10 percent, which is 40 percent. The price of bus rides falls relative to the price level by 2.9 percent.

In Table 23.8(b), we see that relative prices can change without inflation. In fact, part (b) illustrates the same changes in relative prices that occur in part (a) but with no inflation. In this case, the price of oranges increases by 40 percent to $1.12, the price of haircuts increases by 3.6 percent to $11.40, and the price of bus rides falls by 2.9 percent to 68¢. If you calculate the current- and base-period values of the basket in part (b), you will find that consumers spend exactly the same at the new prices as they do at the base-period prices. There is no inflation, even though relative prices have changed.

We've now looked at two cases in which the relative price of oranges increases by 40 percent. In one, inflation is 10 percent; in the other, there is no inflation. Clearly, inflation has not been *caused by* the change in the price of oranges. In the first case, the price of each good increases by 10 percent more than it does in the second case. Singling out the good whose relative price has increased most does not help us explain why all prices are rising by 10 percent more in the first case than in the second case.

Any inflation rate can occur with any behavior of relative prices. Relative prices are determined by supply and demand in the markets for the individual goods and services. The price level and the inflation rate are determined independently of *relative* prices. To explain an increase (or decrease) in the inflation rate, we have to explain why all prices are inflating at a different rate and not why some prices are increasing faster than others.

TABLE 23.8

Relative Price Changes With or Without Inflation

(a) 10 percent inflation

Item	Base-period price	New price	Percentage change in price	Percentage change in relative price
Oranges	$ 0.80	$ 1.20	+50.0	+40.0
Haircuts	11.00	12.50	+13.6	+ 3.6
Bus rides	0.70	0.75	+ 7.1	− 2.9

(b) No inflation

Item	Base-period price	New price	Percentage change in price	Percentage change in relative price
Oranges	$ 0.80	$ 1.12	+40.0	+40.0
Haircuts	11.00	11.40	+ 3.6	+ 3.6
Bus rides	0.70	0.68	−2.9	−2.9

A relative price is the price of one good divided by the price of another good. Relative prices change whenever the price of one good changes by a different percentage than the price of some other good. Relative price changes do not cause inflation. They can occur with or without inflation. In part (a), the price index rises by 10 percent. In part (b), the price index remains constant. In both parts, the relative price of oranges increases by 40 percent and that of haircuts by 3.6 percent, and the relative price of bus rides falls by 2.9 percent. The rise in the price of oranges cannot be regarded as the cause of the rise in the price index in part (a) because that same rise in the price of oranges occurs with no change in the price index in part (b).

The Consumer Price Index and the Cost of Living

Does the Consumer Price Index measure the cost of living? Does a 5 percent increase in the CPI mean that the cost of living has increased by 5 percent? It does not, for three reasons. They are

- Substitution effects
- Arrival of new goods and disappearance of old ones
- Quality improvements

Substitution Effects A change in the CPI measures the percentage change in the price of a *fixed* basket of goods and services. The actual basket of goods and services bought depends on relative prices and on consumers' tastes. Changes in relative prices will lead consumers to economize on goods that have become relatively expensive and to buy more of those goods whose relative prices have fallen. If chicken doubles in price but the price of beef increases by only 5 percent, people will substitute the now relatively less expensive beef for the relatively more expensive chicken. Because consumers make such substitutions, a price index based on a fixed basket will overstate the effects of a given price change on the consumer's cost of living.

Arrival and Disappearance of Goods Discrepancies between the CPI and the cost of living also arise from the disappearance of some commodities and the emergence of new ones. For example, suppose that you want to compare the cost of living in 1992 with that in 1892. Using a price index that has horse feed in it will not work. Though that price featured in people's transportation costs in 1892, it plays no role today. Similarly, a price index with gasoline in it will be of little use, since gasoline, while relevant today, did not feature in people's spending in 1892. Even comparisons between 1992 and 1980 suffer from this same problem. Compact discs and microwave popcorn that featured in our budgets in 1992 were not available in 1980.

Quality Improvements The Consumer Price Index can overstate a true rise in prices by ignoring quality improvements. Most goods undergo constant quality improvement. Automobiles, computers, CD players, even textbooks, get better year after year. Part of the increase in price of these items reflects the improvement in the quality of the product. Yet the CPI regards such a price change as inflation. Attempts have been made to assess the importance of this factor, and some economists estimate that it contributes as much as 2 percent a year on the average to the measured inflation rate.

Substitution effects, the arrival of new goods and the departure of old ones, and quality changes make the connection between the CPI and the cost of living imprecise. To reduce the problems that arise from this source, the Bureau of Labor Statistics from time to time updates the weights used for calculating the CPI. Even so, the CPI is of limited value for making comparisons of the cost of living over long periods of time. But for the purpose for which it was devised—calculating month-to-month and year-to-year rates of inflation—the CPI does a pretty good job.

REVIEW

The Consumer Price Index is a price index based on the consumption expenditures of a typical urban family. It is calculated as the ratio of the value of a base-period basket in the current period to its value in the base period (multiplied by 100). The GDP deflator is a price index calculated as the ratio of nominal GDP to real GDP (multiplied by 100). Real GDP values the current period's output at base-period prices. ◆◆ A relative price is the price of one good relative to the price of another good. Relative prices are constantly changing but are independent of the inflation rate. Any pattern of relative price changes can take place at any inflation rate. ◆◆ The CPI has limitations as a means of comparing the cost of living over long periods but does a good job of measuring year-to-year changes in the inflation rate. ◆

Now that we've studied the measurement of GDP and the price level and know how *real* GDP is measured, let's take a look at what real GDP tells us about the aggregate value of economic activity, the standard of living, and economic well-being.

Real GDP, Aggregate Economic Activity, and Economic Well-Being

What does real GDP really measure? How good a measure is it? What does it tell us about aggregate economic activity? And what does it tell us about the standard of living and economic welfare? Some of these questions are discussed further in Our Advancing Knowledge on pp. 630–631.

Economic welfare is a comprehensive measure of the general state of well-being and standard of living. Economic welfare depends on the following factors:

1. The quantity and quality of goods and services available
2. The amount of leisure time available
3. The degree of equality among individuals

Real GDP does not accurately measure all the goods and services that we produce, and it provides no information on the amount of leisure time and the degree of economic equality. Its mismeasurement of production has errors in both directions. We'll examine five factors that limit the usefulness of real GDP as a measure of economic welfare. They are

- Underground real GDP
- Household production
- Environmental damage
- Leisure time
- Economic equality

Underground Real GDP

The **underground economy** is all economic activity that is legal but unreported. Underground economic activity is unreported because participants in the underground economy withhold information to evade taxes or regulations. For example, avoiding safety regulations, minimum wage laws, and social security payments are motives for operating in the underground economy. Attempts have been made to assess the scale of the underground economy, and estimates range between 5 and 15 percent of GDP ($300 billion to $900 billion).

Although not usually regarded as part of the underground economy, a great deal of other unreported activity takes place—economic activity that is illegal. In today's economy, various forms of illegal gambling, prostitution, and drug trading are important omitted components of economic activity. It is impossible to measure the scale of illegal activities, but estimates range between 1 and 5 percent of GDP (between $60 billion and $300 billion).

Household Production

An enormous amount of economic activity that no one is obliged to report takes place every day in our own homes. Changing a light bulb, cutting the grass, washing the car, laundering a shirt, painting a door, and teaching a child to catch a ball are all examples of productive activities that do not involve market transactions and that are not counted as part of GDP.

Household production has become much more capital-intensive over the years. As a result, less labor is used in household production than in earlier periods. For example, a microwave meal that takes just a few minutes to prepare uses a great deal of capital and almost no labor. Because we use less labor and more capital in household production, it is not easy to work out whether this type of production has increased or decreased over time. It is likely, however, that it has decreased as more and more people have joined the labor force.

Household production is almost certainly cyclical. When the economy is in recession, household production increases, since households whose members are unemployed buy fewer goods in the marketplace and provide more services for themselves. When the economy is booming, employment outside the home increases and household production decreases.

Environmental Damage

The environment is directly affected by economic activity. The burning of hydrocarbon fuels is the most visible activity that damages our environment. But it is not the only example. The depletion of exhaustible resources, the mass clearing of forests, and the pollution of lakes and rivers are other important environmental consequences of industrial production.

Resources used to protect the environment are valued as part of GDP. For example, the value of catalytic converters that help to protect the atmosphere from automobile emissions is part of GDP. But if we did not use such pieces of equipment and instead polluted the atmosphere, we would not count the deteriorating air that we were breathing as a negative part of GDP.

It is obvious that an industrial society produces more atmospheric pollution than a primitive or agricultural society. But it is not obvious that such pollution increases as we become wealthier. One of the things that wealthy people value is a clean environment, and they devote resources to protecting it. Compare the pollution that was discovered in East Germany in the late 1980s with pollution in the United States. East Germany, a relatively poor country, polluted its rivers, lakes, and atmosphere in a way that is unimaginable in the United States.

Leisure Time

Leisure time is obviously an economic good that adds to our economic welfare. Other things being equal, the more leisure we have, the better off we are. Our time spent working is valued as part of GDP, but our leisure time is not. Yet from the point of view of economic welfare, that leisure time must be at least as valuable to us as the wage that we earn on the last hour worked. If it was not, we would work instead of taking the leisure.

Economic Equality

A country might have a very large real GDP per person, but with a high degree of inequality. A few people might be extremely wealthy, while the vast majority live in abject poverty. Such an economy would generally be regarded as having less economic welfare than one in which the same amount of real GDP was more equally shared. For example, average GDP per person in the oil-rich countries of the

Our Advancing Knowledge

THE Development of Economic Accounting

National income was first measured in England by William Petty in 1665. But it was not until the 1930s, when it was needed to test and use the new Keynesian theory of economic fluctuations, that national income measurement became a routine part of the operation of the U.S. Department of Commerce.

With one exception, the national income accounts measure only *market transactions.* The exception is owner-occupied housing. National income includes an estimate of the amount that homeowners would have received (and paid) in rent if they had rented their homes rather than owned them. The idea is that regardless of whether a home is rented or owned, it provides a service, and the rent (actual or implicit) measures the value of that service.

> **"To express my self in Terms of Number, Weight, or Measure; to use only Arguments of Sense, and to consider only such Causes as have visible Foundations in Nature"**
>
> Sir William Petty
> *Political Arithmetick*

But owner-occupied housing is not really so exceptional. We produce lots of services at home that are missed by the national accounts. Watching a video is an example. If you go to the movies, the price you pay for the ticket includes the cost of the movie, the rent of the seat, the cost of heating or cooling the theater, the wages of the theater workers, and the profit (or loss) of the theater owner—the full cost of your entertainment. The price of your ticket is measured as part of national income. But if you watch a home video, only the video rental is counted as part of national income. The rental cost of the television, VCR, armchair, and sitting room (you rent them from yourself so there's no market transaction) is not counted.

The amount of home production has increased over the years. Kitchens equipped with microwaves and dishwashers, automated laundries, and living rooms containing more audio and video equipment than a 1970s TV studio have turned the home into a capital-intensive production center.

Partly because of all this capital equipment, women spend more time outside the home earning a wage and what they earn does get counted as part of national income. But both women and men are more productive in the home than ever before, and the value of this production does not get counted as part of national income.

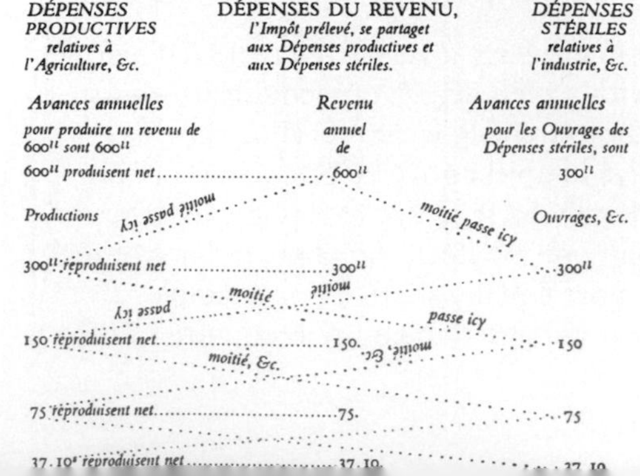

TABLEAU ÉCONOMIQUE.

Objets à considérer, 1°. Trois sortes de dépenses; 2°. leur source; 3°. leurs avances 4°. leur distribution; 5°. leurs effets; 6°. leur reproduction; 7°. leurs rapports entr'elles 8°. leurs rapports avec la population; 9°. avec l'Agriculture; 10°. avec l'industrie 11°. avec le commerce; 12°. avec la masse des richesses d'une Nation.

DÉPENSES PRODUCTIVES *relatives à l'Agriculture, &c.*	DÉPENSES DU REVENU, *l'Impôt prélevé, se partaget aux Dépenses productives et aux Dépenses stériles.*	DÉPENSES STÉRILES *relatives à l'industrie, &c.*
Avances annuelles *pour produire un revenu de 600^{ll} sont 600^{ll}*	*Revenu annuel de*	*Avances annuelles* *pour les Ouvrages des Dépenses stériles, sont*
600^{ll} *produisent net*	600^{ll}	300^{ll}
Productions		*Ouvrages, &c.*
300^{ll} *reproduisent net*	300^{ll}	300^{ll}
150 *reproduisent net*	150	150
75 *reproduisent net*	75	75
37.10 *reproduisent net*	37.10	37.10

One of the earliest national economic accounts was François Quesnay's *Tableau Économique* used to measure economic activity in France in 1758. One of Quesnay's "disciples" was so impressed with this work that he described it as being worthy of being ranked, along with writing and money, as one of the three greatest inventions of the human race. Quesnay's *Tableau* was praised by Karl Marx, the founder of socialism, and is regarded as the forerunner of the types of input-output tables used in the former Soviet Union to construct annual economic plans. Modern national accounts are less like Quesnay's *Tableau* and more like the income and expenditure accounts of large corporations. They record the incomes of factors of production and the expenditures on final goods and services.

Regardless of the method used to wash an automobile, the output is a clean car. And regardless of whether the factors of production are teenagers, rags, a hose, and a bucket or an automated machine, these factors of production have created a good that is valued. Yet the teenagers' efforts are not measured in the national accounts, while that of the automatic car wash is. As do-it-yourself is replaced by purchasing from specialized producers, part of the apparent increase in the value of national production is just an illusion due to the way the books are kept. To avoid this illusion, it is necessary to develop methods of national income accounting that estimate the value of home production by using a method similar to that used to estimate the rental value of owner-occupied homes.

Sir William Petty: A *Pioneer of Economic Statistics*

William Petty was born in England in 1623. He was a cabin boy on a merchant ship at 13, a student in a Jesuit college in France at 14, a successful doctor of medicine in his early 20s, a professor of anatomy at Oxford University at 27, and a professor of music at 28. As chief medical officer of the British army in Ireland at age 29, he managed a topographical survey of that country, from which he emerged as a substantial owner of Irish land! Petty was also an economic thinker and writer of considerable repute. He was the first person to measure national income and one of the first to propose that a government department be established for the collection of reliable and timely economic statistics. He believed that economic policy could only improve economic performance if it was based on an understanding of cause-and-effect relations discovered by the systematic measurement of economic activity—a process he called "Political Arithmetick."

Middle East is similar to that of several countries in Western Europe but much less equally distributed. Economic welfare is higher in those Western European countries.

Are the Omissions a Problem?

If real GDP increases at the expense of other factors that affect economic welfare, there is no change in economic welfare. But if real GDP increases with no reduction (or even an increase) in the other factors, then economic welfare increases. Whether we get the wrong message from changes (or differences) in real GDP depends on the questions being asked. There are two main types of question:

- Business cycle questions
- Standard of living and economic welfare questions

Business Cycle Questions The fluctuations in economic activity measured by real GDP probably overstate the fluctuations in total production and economic welfare. When there is an economic downturn, household production increases and so does leisure time, but real GDP does not record these changes. When real GDP is growing quickly, leisure time and household production probably decline. Again, this change is not recorded as part of real GDP. But the directions of change of real GDP and economic welfare are likely to be the same.

Standard of Living and Economic Welfare Questions For standard of living comparisons, the factors omitted from real GDP are probably very important. For example, in developing countries the underground economy and the amount of household production are a much higher fraction of economic activity than in developed countries. This fact makes comparisons of GDP between countries such as the United States and Nigeria, for example, unreliable measures of comparative living standards unless the GDP data are supplemented with other information.

Using GDP data to gauge changes in living standards over time is also unreliable. Living standards depend only partly on the value of output. They also depend on the composition of that output. For example, two economies may have the same GDP, but one economy may produce more weapons and the other more music. Consumers will not be indifferent as to which of these two economies they live in.

Other factors affecting living standards include the amount of leisure time available, the quality of the environment, the security of jobs and homes, the safety of city streets, and so on. It is possible to construct broader measures that combine the many factors that contribute to human happiness. Real GDP will be one element in that measure, but it will by no means be the whole of it.

◆ ◆ ◆ ◆ In Chapter 22, we examined the macroeconomic performance of the United States in recent years and over a longer sweep of history. In this chapter, we studied in some detail the methods used for measuring the macroeconomy and in particular the average level of prices and the overall level of real economic activity. In the following chapters, we're going to study some macroeconomic models—models designed to explain and predict the behavior of real GDP, the price level, employment and unemployment, the stock market, and other related phenomena. We start this process in the next chapter by examining a macroeconomic model of demand and supply—a model of *aggregate* demand and *aggregate* supply.

SUMMARY

The Circular Flow of Expenditure and Income

All economic agents—households, firms, government, and the rest of the world—interact in the circular flow of income and expenditure. Households sell factors of production to firms and buy consumption goods and services from firms. Firms hire factors of production from households and pay incomes to households in exchange for factor services. Firms sell consumption goods and services to households and capital goods to other firms. Government collects taxes from households and firms, makes transfer payments under various social programs to households, and buys goods and services from firms. Foreigners buy goods from domestic firms and sell goods to them.

The flow of expenditure on final goods and services winds up as somebody's income. Therefore,

$$\text{Aggregate income} = \text{Aggregate expenditure}.$$

Furthermore, expenditure on final goods and services is a method of valuing the output of the economy. Therefore,

$$\text{GDP} = \text{Aggregate expenditure} = \text{Aggregate income}.$$

From the firm's accounts we know that

$$Y = C + I + G + EX - IM,$$

and from the household's accounts we know that

$$Y = C + S + T.$$

Combining these two equations, we obtain

$$I + G + EX = S + T + IM.$$

This equation tells us that injections into the circular flow (left side) equal the leakages from the circular flow (right side). (pp. 609–615)

U.S. National Income and Product Accounts

Because aggregate expenditure, aggregate income, and the value of output are equal, national income accountants can measure GDP using one of two approaches: the expenditure approach and the factor incomes approach.

The expenditure approach adds together consumption expenditure, investment, government purchases of goods and services, and net exports to arrive at an estimate of GDP.

The factor incomes approach adds together the incomes paid to the various factors of production plus profit paid to the owners of firms. To use the factor incomes approach, it is necessary to make an adjustment from the factor cost value of GDP to the market price value by adding indirect taxes and subtracting subsidies. It is also necessary to add capital consumption in order to arrive at GDP.

To value the output of a firm or sector in the economy, we measure value added. The use of value added avoids double counting. (pp. 615–620)

The Price Level and Inflation

There are two major price indexes that measure the price level and inflation: the Consumer Price Index and the GDP deflator.

The CPI measures the average level of prices of goods and services typically consumed by an urban family in the United States. The CPI is the ratio of the value of a base-period basket of commodities at current-period prices to the same basket valued at base-period prices, multiplied by 100.

The GDP deflator is nominal GDP divided by real GDP, multiplied by 100. Nominal GDP is calculated by valuing current-period quantities produced at current-period prices. Real GDP is calculated by valuing the quantities produced in the current period at the prices that prevailed in the base period.

In interpreting changes in prices, we need to distinguish between inflation and relative price changes. A relative price is the price of one good in terms of another good. Relative prices are constantly changing. We cannot tell anything about the sources of inflation by studying which relative prices have changed most. Any relative price changes can occur with any inflation rate.

Because relative prices are constantly changing and causing consumers to substitute less expensive items for more expensive items, because of the disappearance of some goods and the arrival of new goods, and because of quality changes, the CPI is an imperfect measure of the cost of living, especially when comparisons are made across a long time span. (pp. 620–628)

Real GDP, Aggregate Economic Activity, and Economic Well-Being

Real GDP is not a perfect measure of aggregate economic activity or of economic welfare. It excludes production in the underground economy, household production, environmental damage, and the contribution to economic welfare of equality and leisure. (pp. 628–632)

KEY ELEMENTS

Key Terms

Key Figures and Tables

REVIEW QUESTIONS

1 List the components of aggregate expenditure.

2 What are the components of aggregate income?

3 Why does aggregate income equal aggregate expenditure?

4 Why does the value of output (or GDP) equal aggregate income?

5 Distinguish between government purchases of goods and services and transfer payments.

6 What are injections into the circular flow of expenditure and income? What are leakages?

7 Explain why injections into the circular flow of income and expenditure equal leakages from it.

8 How does the Department of Commerce measure GDP?

9 Explain the expenditure approach to measuring GDP.

10 Explain the factor incomes approach to measuring GDP.

11 What is the distinction between expenditure on final goods and expenditure on intermediate goods?

12 What is value added? How is it calculated? What does the sum of value added by all firms equal?

13 What are the two main price indexes used to measure the price level and inflation?

14 How is the Consumer Price Index calculated?

15 How is the basket of goods and services used in constructing the CPI chosen? Is it the same basket

in 1992 as it was in 1952? If not, how is it different?

16 How is the GDP deflator calculated?

17 Explain what a relative price change is.

18 How can relative price changes be identified in periods when the inflation rates are different?

19 Is the CPI a good measure to use to compare the cost of living today with that in the 1930s? If not, why not?

20 Is GDP a good measure of economic welfare? If not, why not?

PROBLEMS

1 The following transactions took place in Ecoland last year:

Item	Value of transaction (billions of dollars)
Wages paid to labor	$800,000
Consumption expenditure	600,000
Taxes paid on wages	200,000
Government transfer payments	50,000
Firms' profits	200,000
Investment	250,000
Taxes paid on profits	50,000
Government purchases of goods and services	200,000
Export earnings	300,000
Saving	250,000
Import payments	250,000

a Calculate Ecoland's GDP.

b Did you use the expenditure approach or the factor incomes approach to answer part (a)?

c Does your answer to part (a) value output in terms of market prices or factor cost? Why?

d What extra information do you need in order to calculate net domestic product?

2 Cindy, the owner of The Great Cookie, spends $100 on eggs, $50 on flour, $45 on milk, $10 on utilities, and $60 on wages to produce 200 great cookies. Cindy sells her cookies for $1.50 each. Calculate the value added per cookie at The Great Cookie.

3 A typical family living on Sandy Island consumes only apple juice, bananas, and cloth. Prices in the base year are $4 a gallon for apple juice, $3 a pound for bananas, and $5 a yard for cloth. The typical family spends $40 on apple juice, $45 on bananas, and $25 on cloth. In the current year, apple juice costs $3 a gallon, bananas cost $4 a pound, and cloth costs $7 a yard. Calculate the Consumer Price Index on Sandy Island in the current year and the inflation rate between the base year and the current year.

4 The newspaper on Sandy Island, commenting on the inflation figures that you calculated in problem 3, runs the headline "Inflation Results from Increases in Cloth Prices." Write a letter to the editor pointing out the weakness in the economic reasoning of that paper's business reporter.

5 An economy has the following real GDP and nominal GDP in 1991 and 1992:

Year	Real GDP	Nominal GDP
1990	$1,000 billion	$1,000 billion
1991	$1,050 billion	$1,200 billion
1992	$1,200 billion	$1,500 billion

a What was the GDP deflator in 1991?

b What was the GDP deflator in 1992?

c What is the inflation rate as measured by the GDP deflator between 1991 and 1992?

d What is the percentage increase in the price level between 1990 and 1992 as measured by the GDP deflator?

CHAPTER 24

AGGREGATE DEMAND AND AGGREGATE SUPPLY

After studying this chapter, you will be able to:

- Define aggregate demand and explain what determines it
- Explain the sources of growth and fluctuations in aggregate demand
- Define aggregate supply and explain what determines it
- Explain the sources of growth and fluctuations in aggregate supply
- Define macroeconomic equilibrium
- Predict the effects of changes in aggregate demand and aggregate supply on real GDP and the price level
- Explain why real GDP grows and why we have recessions
- Explain why we have inflation and why its rate varies, sometimes exploding as it did in the 1970s

IN THE QUARTER CENTURY FROM 1967 TO 1992, U.S. real GDP more than doubled. In fact, a doubling of real GDP every 25 years has been routine. What forces drive our economy to grow? ◆◆ At the same time as real GDP has been growing, we've experienced persistent inflation. Today, you need \$400 to buy what \$100 would have bought in 1960. Most of this inflation occurred in the 1970s, when the price level more than doubled. What causes inflation? And why did it explode in the 1970s? ◆◆ The U.S. economy doesn't grow at a constant pace. Instead, it ebbs and flows over the business cycle. For example, as the 1990s opened, a recession slowed down real GDP growth. What makes real GDP grow unevenly, sometimes speeding up and sometimes slowing down or even shrinking? ◆◆ Sometimes the economy receives a massive shock from some other part of the world. For example, in the summer of 1990 when Saddam Hussein invaded Kuwait, world oil prices increased. But not all the shocks hitting our economy come from abroad. Some are homemade and stem from the actions of the government and the Federal Reserve Board in Washington. How do such foreign and domestic shocks affect prices and production?

What Makes Our Garden Grow

◆◆◆◆ To answer questions like these, we need a model—a macroeconomic model. Our first task in this chapter is to build such a model—the *aggregate demand–aggregate supply model.* Our second task is to use the aggregate demand–aggregate supply model to answer the questions we've just posed. You'll discover that this powerful theory of aggregate demand and aggregate supply enables us to analyze and predict many important economic events that have a major impact on our lives.

Aggregate Demand

The aggregate quantity of goods and services produced is measured as real GDP—GDP valued in constant dollars. The average price of all these goods and services is measured by the GDP deflator. We are going to build a model that determines the values of real GDP and the GDP deflator. The model that we will build is based on the same concepts of demand, supply, and equilibrium that you met in Chapter 4. But here the good is not tapes—it is real GDP—and the price is not the price of tapes—it is the GDP deflator.

The **aggregate quantity of goods and services demanded** is the sum of the quantities of consumption goods and services that households plan to buy, of investment goods that firms plan to buy, of goods and services that governments plan to buy, and of net exports that foreigners plan to buy. Thus the aggregate quantity of goods and services demanded depends on decisions made by households, firms, governments, and foreigners. When we studied the demand for tapes in Chapter 4, we summarized the buying plans of households in a demand schedule and a demand curve. Similarly, when we study the forces influencing aggregate buying plans, we summarize the decisions of households, firms, governments, and foreigners by using an aggregate demand schedule and an aggregate demand curve.

An **aggregate demand schedule** lists the quantity of real GDP demanded at each price level, holding all other influences on buying plans constant. The **aggregate demand curve** plots the quantity of real GDP demanded against the price level. **Aggregate demand** is the entire relationship between the quantity of real GDP demanded and the price level.

Figure 24.1 shows an aggregate demand schedule and an aggregate demand curve. Each row of the table corresponds to a point in the figure. For example, row *c* of the aggregate demand schedule tells us that if the price level (the GDP deflator) is 120, the level of real GDP demanded is 5 trillion 1987 dollars. This row is plotted as point *c* on the aggregate demand curve.

FIGURE 24.1

The Aggregate Demand Curve and Aggregate Demand Schedule

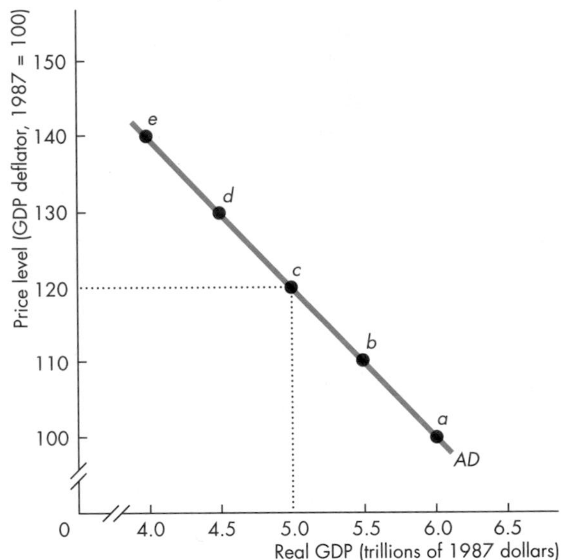

	Price level (GDP deflator)	Real GDP (trillions of 1987 dollars)
a	100	6.0
b	110	5.5
c	120	5.0
d	130	4.5
e	140	4.0

The aggregate demand curve (*AD*) traces the quantity of real GDP demanded as the price level varies, holding everything else constant. The aggregate demand curve is derived from the schedule in the table. Each point *a* through *e* on the curve corresponds to the row in the table identified by the same letter. Thus when the price level is 120, the quantity of real GDP demanded is 5.0 trillion 1987 dollars, as illustrated by point *c* in the figure.

In constructing the aggregate demand schedule and aggregate demand curve, we hold constant all the influences on the quantity of real GDP demanded other than the price level. The effect of a change in the price level is shown as a movement along the aggregate demand curve. A change in any of the other influences on the quantity of real GDP demanded results in a new aggregate demand schedule and a shift in the aggregate demand curve. First, let's concentrate on the effects of a change in the price level on the quantity of real GDP demanded.

You can see from the downward slope of the aggregate demand curve, and from the numbers that describe the aggregate demand schedule, that the higher the price level, the smaller is the quantity of real GDP demanded. Why does the aggregate demand curve slope downward?

Why the Aggregate Demand Curve Slopes Downward

The demand curve for a single good slopes downward because people substitute one good for another as prices change. If the price of Coca-Cola rises, the quantity of Coca-Cola demanded falls because some people switch to drinking Pepsi-Cola and other substitutes. The demand curve for a whole class of goods and services also slopes downward because of substitution effects. If the prices of Coca-Cola, Pepsi-Cola, and all other sodas rise, the quantity of soda demanded falls because some people switch from soda to other substitute drinks and other goods. But why does the demand curve for *all* goods and services slope downward? If the price of all goods increases and people demand less of *all* goods, what do they demand more of? What do they substitute for goods and services?

There are three groups of substitutes for the goods and services that make up current U.S. real GDP. They are

- Money and financial assets
- Goods and services in the future
- Goods and services produced in other countries

People may plan to buy a smaller quantity of the goods and services that make up real GDP and hold a larger quantity of money or other financial assets. They may plan to buy a smaller quantity of goods and services today but a larger quantity at some time in the future. Also, people may decide to buy a smaller quantity of the goods and services made in the United States and buy a larger quantity of the goods and services made in other countries. These decisions are influenced by the price level, and those influences result in the aggregate demand curve sloping downward.

There are three separate effects of the price level on the quantity of real GDP demanded. They are the following:

- Real money balances effect
- Intertemporal substitution effect
- International substitution effect

Real Money Balances Effect The **real money balances effect** is the influence of a change in the quantity of real money on the quantity of real GDP demanded. The **quantity of money** is the quantity of currency, bank deposits, and deposits at other types of financial institutions, such as savings and loan associations and thrift institutions, held by households and firms. **Real money** is a measure of money based on the quantity of goods and services that it will buy. Real money is measured as dollars divided by the price level. For example, suppose that you have $20 in notes and coins in your pocket and $480 in the bank. The quantity of money that you are holding is $500. Suppose that you continue to hold $500 but that the price level increases by 25 percent. Then your real money holdings decrease by 25 percent. That is, the $500 of money that you are holding will now buy what $400 would have bought before the price level increase.

The real money balances effect is the influence of the quantity of real money on the quantity of goods and services bought. Other things being equal, the larger the quantity of real money people are holding, the larger is the quantity of goods and services bought. To understand the real money balances effect, let's think about how the Sony Corporation's spending plans are influenced by its real money holdings.

Suppose that Sony has $20 million in the bank. Furthermore, suppose that Sony has decided that it doesn't want to change the way it's holding its assets. It doesn't want to have less money and more capital equipment in its production and distribution plants. And it doesn't want to sell off some of its productive assets in order to hold more money.

Now suppose that prices fall. Among the prices that fall are those of office buildings, computers, movie studios, and all the other things that Sony owns and operates. The money that Sony is now holding buys more of these and other goods than it would have before. Sony's got *more* real money. But its other equipment is now worth less than before. This fall in the price level has increased Sony's holdings of real money and decreased the value of its holdings of capital equipment. Sony will now take advantage of the fact that it is holding a larger amount of real money to buy some additional capital equipment. But new buildings, plant, and machinery are some of the goods that make up real GDP. Thus Sony's decision to use its extra real money to buy more plant and equipment results in an increase in the quantity of goods and services demanded—an increase in real GDP demanded.

Of course, although Sony is a multinational giant, if only it behaves in this way, real GDP demanded will not increase much. The real money balances effect will be tiny. But if everyone behaves like Sony, the aggregate quantity of goods and services demanded will be larger than before. This increase in the quantity of goods and services demanded results from a fall in the price level.

The real money balances effect is the first reason why the aggregate demand curve slopes downward. A decrease in the price level increases the quantity of real money. The larger the quantity of real money, the larger is the quantity of goods and services demanded.

Intertemporal Substitution Effect The substitution of goods and services now for goods and services later or of goods and services later for goods and services now is called **intertemporal substitution.** An example of intertemporal substitution is your decision to buy a Walkman today instead of waiting until the end of the month. Another example is IBM's decision to speed up its installation of a new computer production plant. Yet another example is your decision to postpone that long-hoped-for vacation.

An important influence on intertemporal substitution is the level of interest rates. Low interest rates encourage people to borrow and change the timing of their spending on capital goods—plant and equipment, houses, and consumer durable goods—shifting some of that spending from the future to the present. High interest rates discourage people from borrowing and change the timing of their spending on goods—shifting some of that spending from the present to the future.

Interest rates, in turn, are influenced by the quantity of real money. We have just seen that the quantity of real money increases if the price level falls. We've also seen that the more real money people have, the larger is the quantity of goods and services they demand. But people do not necessarily have to use all their additional real money to buy other goods. They may lend some of it to others or use some of it to decrease their own borrowing. Some people are borrowers, and others are lenders. Borrowers who have experienced an increase in their real money holdings now need to borrow less and so decrease their demand for loans. Lenders whose real money holdings have increased are now willing to lend even more, and so they increase their supply of loans. A decrease in the demand for loans and an increase in their supply results in a fall in interest rates. And lower interest rates lead to an intertemporal substitution effect—shifting spending plans from the future to the present and increasing the quantity of goods and services demanded.

An increase in the price level decreases the quantity of real money and has the opposite effect on spending plans. With a decrease in the quantity of real money, people to some degree decrease their spending plans (real money balances effect) and decrease their supply of loans or increase their demand for loans. As a consequence, interest rates increase and spending is shifted from the present to the future (intertemporal substitution effect).

This intertemporal substitution effect is the second reason why the aggregate demand curve slopes downward. A lower price level:

- Increases the quantity of real money
- Increases the supply of loans
- Decreases the demand for loans
- Lowers interest rates
- Shifts spending from the future to the present and increases the quantity of goods and services demanded

Let's now look at the third reason why the aggregate demand curve slopes downward.

International Substitution Effect The substitution of domestic goods and services for foreign goods and services, or of foreign goods and services for domestic goods and services, is **international substitution.** An example of international substitution is your decision to buy a Toyota (made in Japan) instead of a General Motors car (made in Detroit). Another example of international substitution is the decision by the British government to equip its armed forces with U.S.-produced weapons rather than weapons made in Great Britain. Yet another example is your decision to take a skiing vacation in the Canadian Rockies instead of Colorado.

If the U.S. price level falls, holding everything else constant, U.S.-made goods become cheaper and therefore more attractive relative to goods made in other countries. Americans will plan to buy more domestically produced goods and fewer imports, and foreigners will plan to buy more U.S.-made goods and fewer of their own domestically produced goods. Thus, at a lower U.S. price level, people and firms will demand a larger quantity of goods and services produced in the United States. International substitution gives us the third reason for the downward slope of the aggregate demand curve.

Changes in the Quantity of Real GDP Demanded

When the price level changes, other things remaining constant, there is a change in the quantity of real GDP demanded. Such a change is illustrated as a movement along the aggregate demand curve. Figure 24.2 illustrates changes in the quantity of real GDP demanded. It also summarizes the three reasons why the aggregate demand curve slopes downward.

REVIEW

The aggregate demand curve traces the effects of a change in the price level—GDP deflator—on the aggregate quantity of goods and services demanded—real GDP demanded. The effect of a change in the price level is shown as a movement along the aggregate demand curve. Other things being equal, the higher the price level, the smaller is the quantity of real GDP demanded—the aggregate demand curve slopes downward. ◆◆ The aggregate demand curve slopes downward for three reasons: money and goods are substitutes (*real money balances effect*); goods today and goods in the future are substitutes (*intertemporal substitution effect*); domestic goods and foreign goods are substitutes (*international substitution effect*). ◆

FIGURE 24.2

Changes in the Quantity of Real GDP Demanded

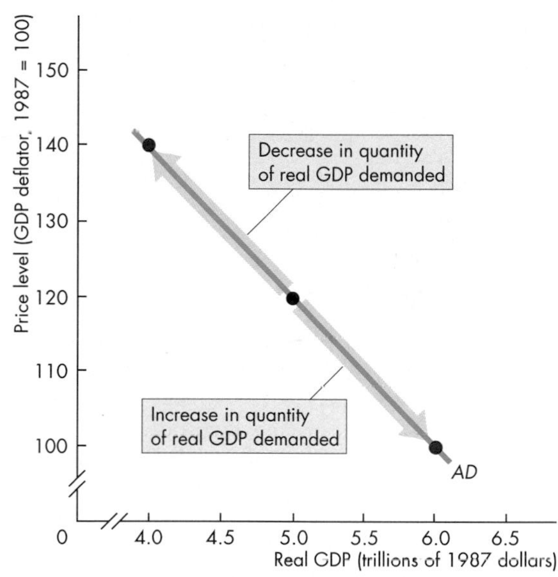

The quantity of real GDP demanded

Decreases if the price level *increases*	*Increases* if the price level *decreases*
because of the:	
Real money balances effect	
◆ An increase in the price level decreases the real money supply	◆ A decrease in the price level increases the real money supply
Intertemporal substitution effect	
◆ An increase in the price level increases interest rates	◆ A decrease in the price level decreases interest rates
International substitution effect	
◆ An increase in the price level increases the cost of domestic goods and services relative to foreign goods and services	◆ A decrease in the price level decreases the cost of domestic goods and services relative to foreign goods and services

Changes in Aggregate Demand

The aggregate demand schedule and aggregate demand curve describe aggregate demand at a point in time. But aggregate demand does not remain constant. It frequently changes. As a consequence, the aggregate demand curve frequently shifts. The main influences on aggregate demand that shift the aggregate demand curve are

- Fiscal policy
- Monetary policy
- International factors
- Expectations

Fiscal Policy

The government's decisions about its purchases of goods and services, taxes, and transfer payments have important effects on aggregate demand. The government's attempt to influence the economy using its spending and taxes is called **fiscal policy.**

Government Purchases of Goods and Services The scale of government purchases of goods and services has a direct effect on aggregate demand. If taxes are held constant, the more weapons, highways, schools, and colleges the government demands, the larger are government purchases of goods and services and so the larger is aggregate demand. The most important changes in government purchases of goods and services that influence aggregate demand arise from the state of international tension and conflict. In times of war, government purchases increase dramatically. In this century, increases in government purchases during World War II, the Korean War, and the Vietnam War and decreases following those episodes exerted a large influence on aggregate demand. Compared with these wars, the increased government purchases during the Gulf War of 1991 were small and had a modest effect on aggregate demand.

Taxes and Transfer Payments A decrease in taxes increases aggregate demand. An increase in transfer payments—unemployment benefits, social security benefits, and other welfare payments—also increases aggregate demand. Both of these influences operate by increasing households' *disposable* income. The higher the level of disposable income, the greater is the demand for goods and services. Since lower taxes and higher transfer payments increase disposable income, they also increase aggregate demand.

This source of changes in aggregate demand has been an important one in recent years. Through the late 1960s, there was a large increase in government payments under various social programs, and these led to a sustained increase in aggregate demand. During the 1980s, Reagan's tax cuts increased aggregate demand.

Monetary Policy

Decisions made by the Federal Reserve Board (the Fed) about the money supply and interest rates have important effects on aggregate demand. The Fed's attempt to influence the economy by varying the money supply and interest rates is called **monetary policy.**

Money Supply The money supply is determined by the Fed and the banks (in a process described in Chapters 27 and 28). The greater the *quantity of money,* the greater is the level of aggregate demand. An easy way to see why money affects aggregate demand is to imagine what would happen if the Fed borrowed the Army's helicopters, loaded them with millions of dollars worth of new $10 bills, and sprinkled the bills like confetti across the nation. We would all stop whatever we were doing and rush out to pick up our share of the newly available money. But we wouldn't just put the money we picked up in the bank. We would spend some of it, so our demand for goods and services would increase. Although this story is pretty extreme, it does illustrate that an increase in the quantity of money increases aggregate demand.

In practice, changes in the quantity of money change interest rates and so have an additional influence on aggregate demand by affecting investment and the demand for consumer durables. When the Fed speeds up the rate at which new money is being injected into the economy, there's a tendency for interest rates to fall. When the Fed slows down the pace at which it is creating money, there's a tendency for interest rates to rise. Thus a change in the quantity of money has a second effect on aggregate demand, operating through its effects on interest rates.

Interest Rates Interest rates change for many reasons. We've already seen that they change when the price level changes and that such changes lead to a movement along the aggregate demand curve. But if the Fed takes actions to increase interest rates *at a given price level,* aggregate demand decreases and there is a shift in the aggregate demand curve. Faced with higher interest rates, firms and households cut back on spending, especially investment, to avoid higher interest costs or to take advantage of higher returns on loans.

Fluctuations in the quantity of money and fluctuations in interest rates induced by those fluctuations have been some of the most important sources of changes in aggregate demand. Sustained increases in the quantity of money through the 1970s increased aggregate demand, contributing to the inflation of those years; decreases in the growth rate of the quantity of money slowed aggregate demand growth, contributing to the recessions of 1981 and 1991.

International Factors

There are two main international factors that influence aggregate demand. They are the foreign exchange rate and foreign income.

The Foreign Exchange Rate We've seen that a change in the U.S. price level, other things being equal, leads to a change in the prices of U.S.-produced goods and services relative to the prices of goods and services produced in other countries. Another important influence on the price of U.S.-produced goods and services relative to those produced abroad is the *foreign exchange rate.* The foreign exchange rate affects aggregate demand because it affects the prices that foreigners have to pay for U.S.-produced goods and services and the prices that we have to pay for foreign-produced goods and services.

Suppose that the dollar is worth 125 Japanese yen. You can buy a Toshiba computer (made in Japan) that costs 125,000 yen for $1,000. What if for $900 you can buy a Zenith computer (made in the United States) that is just as good as the Toshiba, which costs 125,000 yen? In such a case, you will buy the Zenith.

But which computer will you buy if the value of the U.S. dollar rises to 150 yen and everything else remains the same? Let's work out the answer. At 150 yen per dollar, you pay only $833.33 to buy the 125,000 yen needed to buy the Toshiba computer. Since the Zenith computer costs $900, the Toshiba is now cheaper and you will substitute the Toshiba computer for the Zenith. The demand for U.S.-made computers falls as the foreign exchange value of the dollar rises. So as the foreign exchange value of the dollar rises, with everything else held constant, aggregate demand decreases.

There have been huge swings in the foreign exchange value of the dollar through the 1980s, leading to large swings in aggregate demand.

Foreign Income The income of foreigners affects the aggregate demand for domestically produced goods and services. For example, an increase in income in Japan and Germany increases the demand by Japanese and German consumers and producers for U.S.-made consumption goods and capital goods. These sources of change in aggregate demand have been important ones since World War II. The rapid economic growth of Japan and Western Europe and of some of the newly industrializing countries of the Pacific Rim, such as Korea and Singapore, has led to a sustained increase in demand for U.S.-made goods and services.

Expectations

Expectations about all aspects of future economic conditions play a crucial role in determining current decisions. But three expectations are especially important. They are expectations about future inflation, future incomes, and future profits.

Expected Future Inflation An increase in the expected inflation rate, other things being equal, leads to an increase in aggregate demand. The higher the expected inflation rate, the higher is the expected price of goods and services in the future and the lower is the expected real value of money and other assets in the future. As a consequence, when people expect a higher inflation rate, they plan to buy more goods and services in the present and hold smaller quantities of money and other financial assets.

There were changes in inflation expectations during the 1980s. At the beginning of the decade, people expected inflation to persist at close to 10 percent a year. But a severe recession in 1982 reduced those inflation expectations. Other things being equal, the effect of this decrease in inflation expectations was to decrease aggregate demand.

Expected Future Incomes An increase in expected future income, other things being equal, increases the amount that households plan to spend on consumption goods and consumer durables. When households expect slow future income growth, or even a decline in income, they scale back their spending plans.

Expectations about future income growth were pessimistic during 1990, and this factor contributed to the decrease in spending that brought on a recession in 1991.

Expected Future Profits A change in expected future profits changes firms' demands for new capital equipment. For example, suppose that there has been a recent wave of technological change that has increased productivity. Firms will expect that by installing new equipment that uses the latest technology, their future profits will rise. This expectation leads to an increase in demand for new plant and equipment and to an increase in aggregate demand.

Profit expectations were pessimistic in 1981 and led to a decrease in aggregate demand. Expectations were optimistic through most of the mid-1980s, leading to sustained increases in aggregate demand.

Now that we've reviewed the factors that influence aggregate demand, let's summarize their effects on the aggregate demand curve.

Shifts of the Aggregate Demand Curve

We illustrate a change in aggregate demand as a shift in the aggregate demand curve. Figure 24.3 illustrates two changes in aggregate demand and summarizes the factors bringing about such changes. Aggregate demand is initially AD_0, the same as in Fig. 24.1.

The aggregate demand curve shifts to the right, from AD_0 to AD_1, when government purchases of goods and services increase, taxes are cut, transfer payments increase, the money supply increases and interest rates fall, the foreign exchange rate falls, income in the rest of the world increases, expected future profits increase, expected future incomes increase, or the expected inflation rate increases.

The aggregate demand curve shifts to the left, from AD_0 to AD_2, when government purchases of goods and services decrease, taxes are increased, transfer payments decrease, the money supply decreases and interest rates rise, the foreign

FIGURE 24.3

Changes in Aggregate Demand

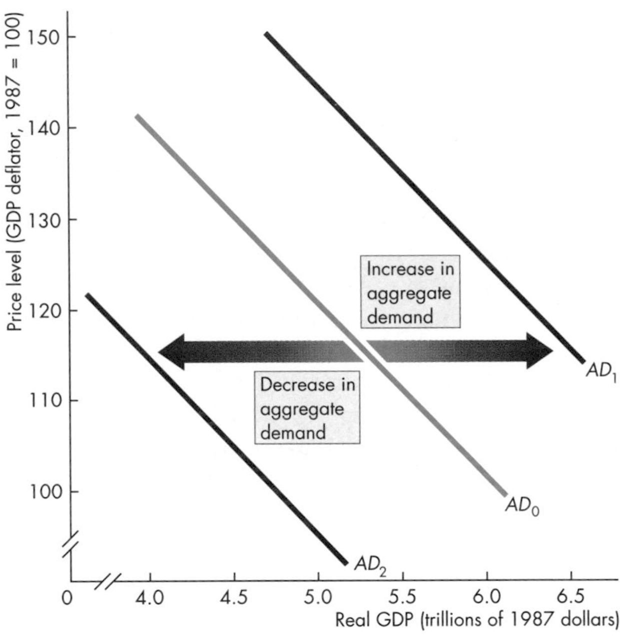

Aggregate demand

Decreases if	*Increases* if
◆ Fiscal policy decreases government spending, increases taxes, or decreases transfer payments	◆ Fiscal policy increases government spending, decreases taxes, or increases transfer payments
◆ Monetary policy decreases the money supply or increases interest rates	◆ Monetary policy increases the money supply or decreases interest rates
◆ The exchange rate increases or foreign income decreases	◆ The exchange rate decreases or foreign income increases
◆ Expected inflation, expected income, or expected profits decrease	◆ Expected inflation, expected income, or expected profits increase

exchange rate rises, income in the rest of the world decreases, expected future profits decrease, expected future incomes decrease, or the expected inflation rate decreases.

Time Lags in Influences on Aggregate Demand

The effects of the influences on aggregate demand that we've considered do not occur instantly. They occur with time lags. A *time lag* is a delay in the response to a stimulus. For example, when you take a pill to cure a headache, the headache doesn't go away immediately—the medication works with a time lag. In a similar way, monetary policy influences aggregate demand with a time lag, one that spreads out over many months. For example, if the Fed increases the money supply, at first there is no change in aggregate demand. A little later, as people reallocate their wealth, there is an increase in the supply of loans and interest rates fall. Later yet, confronted with lower interest rates, households and firms increase their purchases of goods and services. The total effect of the initial change in the quantity of money is spread out over many months.

The next time the Fed takes exactly the same action, there is no guarantee that its effects will take place with exactly the same timing as before. The time lags in the effects of monetary policy on aggregate demand are both spread out and variable and, to a degree, unpredictable.

REVIEW

A change in the price level leads to a change in the aggregate quantity of goods and services demanded. That change is shown as a movement along the aggregate demand curve. A change in any other influence on aggregate demand shifts the aggregate demand curve. These other influences include:

- Fiscal policy
- Monetary policy
- International factors
- Expectations

Aggregate Supply

The **aggregate quantity of goods and services supplied** is the sum of the quantities of all final goods and services produced by all firms in the economy. It is measured as real gross domestic product supplied. In studying aggregate supply, we distinguish between two macroeconomic time frames: the short run and the long run.

Two Macroeconomic Time Frames

The **macroeconomic short-run** is a period during which the prices of goods and services change in response to changes in demand and supply but the prices of factors of production—wage rates and the prices of raw materials—do not change. The short run is an important time frame for two reasons. First, wage rates are determined by labor contracts that run for up to three years. As a result, wage rates change more slowly than prices. Second, the prices of some raw materials, especially oil, are strongly influenced by the actions of a small number of producers that keep the price steady in some periods but change it by a large amount in others.

The **macroeconomic long-run** is a period that is sufficiently long for the prices of all the factors of production—wage rates and other factor prices—to have adjusted to any disturbance so that the quantities demanded and supplied are equal in all markets—goods and services markets, labor markets, and the markets for other factors of production. In the macroeconomic long-run, with wage rates having adjusted to bring equality between the quantities of labor demanded and supplied, there is *full employment.* Equivalently, unemployment is at its *natural rate.*

Short-Run Aggregate Supply

Short-run aggregate supply is the relationship between the aggregate quantity of final goods and services (real GDP) supplied and the price level (the GDP deflator), holding everything else constant. We can represent short-run aggregate supply as either a short-run aggregate supply schedule or a short-run aggregate supply curve. The **short-run aggregate supply schedule** lists the quantity of real GDP supplied at each price level, holding everything else constant. The **short-run aggregate supply curve** plots the relationship between the quantity of real GDP supplied and the price level, holding everything else constant.

Figure 24.4 shows a short-run aggregate supply schedule and the corresponding short-run aggregate supply curve (labeled *SAS*). Part (a) shows the entire curve, and part (b) zooms in on the range of the curve where the economy normally operates. Each row of the aggregate supply schedule corresponds to

FIGURE 24.4

The Aggregate Supply Curves and Aggregate Supply Schedule

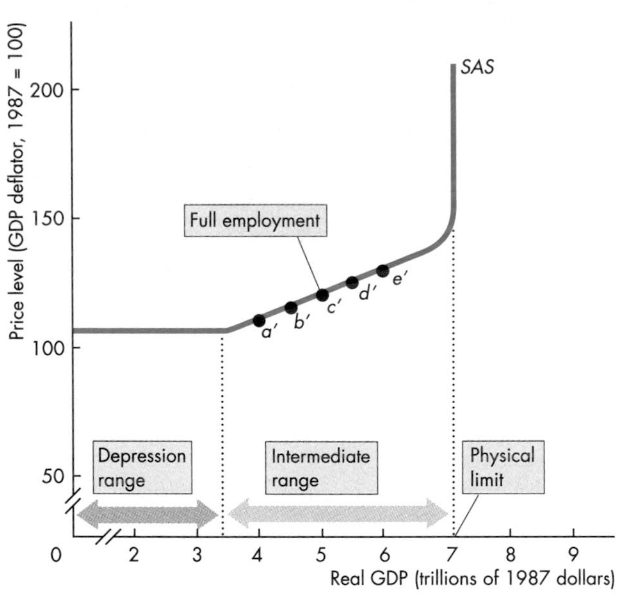

(a) The short-run aggregate supply curve

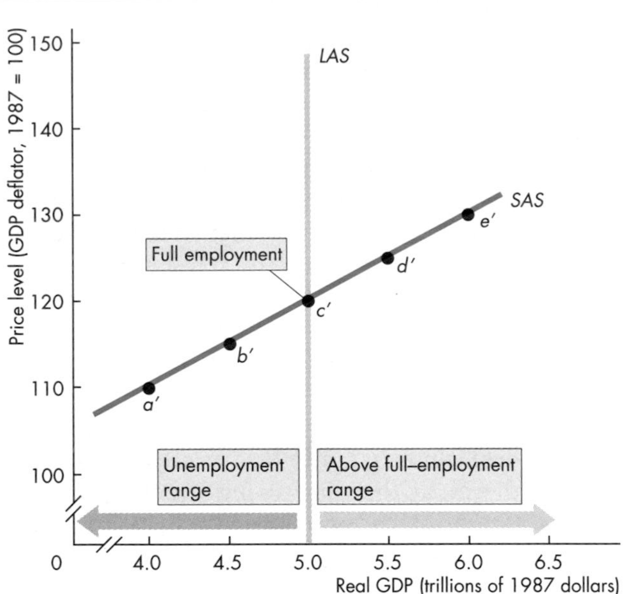

(b) The short-run and long-run aggregate supply curves

	Price level (GDP deflator)	Real GDP (trillions of 1987 dollars)
Depression range	105	0 to 3.5
a′	110	4.0
b′	115	4.5
c′	120	5.0
d′	125	5.5
e′	130	6.0
Physical limit	Above 200	7.0

The short-run aggregate supply curve (*SAS*) traces the quantity of real GDP supplied as the price level varies, holding everything else constant. The short-run aggregate supply curves in this figure are derived from the schedule in the table. Part (a) shows the *SAS* curve over its entire range, and part (b) zooms in on the intermediate range. In a depression, firms are willing to increase the quantity sold with no increase in price and the *SAS* curve is horizontal. At its physical limit, the economy can squeeze out no more production and the *SAS* curve becomes vertical. Normally, the economy operates in the upward-sloping intermediate range. In that range, full employment occurs at *c′*, where real GDP is $5.0 trillion.

The long-run aggregate supply curve (*LAS*) shows the relationship between full-employment real GDP and the price level. This level of real GDP is independent of the price level, so the *LAS* curve is vertical as shown in part (b). At levels of real GDP below the long-run level, unemployment is above the natural rate, and at levels of real GDP above the long-run level, unemployment is below the natural rate.

a point in the figure. For example, row *a*' of the short-run aggregate supply schedule and point *a*' on the curve tell us that if the price level is 110 (GDP deflator is 110), the quantity of real GDP supplied is 4.0 trillion 1987 dollars.

Focus first on the entire short-run aggregate supply curve in Fig. 24.4(a). This curve has three ranges. It is horizontal over the depression range, upward sloping over the intermediate range, and vertical at the physical limit of the economy's ability to produce goods and services. Why is the short-run aggregate curve horizontal in the depression range? Why does it slope upward over the intermediate range? And why does it eventually become vertical?

The Depression Range When the economy is severely depressed, firms have lots of excess capacity and are anxious to sell whatever they can at the going price. They would be glad to be able to sell more and willing to offer it for sale with no inducement from a higher price. Thus each firm has a horizontal supply curve. Since each firm has a horizontal supply curve, the aggregate supply curve is also horizontal. The last time the economy was on the depression range of its *SAS* curve was in the 1930s.

The Intermediate Range Normally, the economy operates in the upward-sloping intermediate range of its *SAS* curve. That's why we've zoomed in on this range in Fig. 24.4(b), and it is this part of the *SAS* curve that we'll use in the rest of the book.

To see why the short-run aggregate supply curve slopes upward, think about the supply curve of tapes. When the price of tapes rises and the wages of the workers in the tape factory remain constant, tape producers offer a larger quantity of tapes for sale. There is an increase in the quantity of tapes supplied. What's true for tape factories is also true for Coke bottling plants, auto assembly lines, and firms producing every other good and service. Thus, when prices rise but factor prices remain constant, the aggregate quantity of goods and services supplied—real GDP supplied—increases.

To increase their output in the short run, firms hire additional labor and work their existing labor force for longer hours. Thus a change in the price level, with wage rates held constant, leads to a change in the aggregate quantity of goods and services supplied and to a change in the level of employment and unemployment. The higher the price level, the greater is the aggregate quantity of goods and services supplied, the higher is the level of employment, and the lower is the level of unemployment.

The Physical Limit to Real GDP At some level of real GDP, the short-run aggregate supply curve becomes vertical because there is a physical limit to the output the economy can produce. If prices increase while wages remain constant, each firm increases its output. It does so by working its labor overtime, hiring more labor, and working its plant and equipment at a faster pace. But there is a limit to the amount of overtime workers are willing to accept. There is also a limit below which the unemployment rate cannot be pushed. And there is a limit beyond which firms are not willing to operate their plant and equipment because of the high cost of wear and tear and breakdowns. Once these limits are reached, no more output is produced, no matter how high prices rise relative to wages. At that output, the short-run aggregate supply curve becomes vertical. In the example in Fig. 24.4, when the economy is operating at its physical limit, real GDP is $7 trillion.

Long-Run Aggregate Supply

Long-run aggregate supply is the relationship between the aggregate quantity of final goods and services (real GDP) supplied and the price level (GDP deflator) when there is full employment.

The Long-Run Aggregate Supply Curve Long-run aggregate supply is represented by the long-run aggregate supply curve. The **long-run aggregate supply curve** plots the relationship between the quantity of real GDP supplied and the price level when there is full employment. The long-run aggregate supply curve is vertical and is illustrated in Fig. 24.4(b) as *LAS*. In this example, full employment occurs when real GDP is $5 trillion. If real GDP is below this amount, a smaller quantity of labor is required and unemployment rises above its natural rate. The economy operates in the unemployment range shown in Fig. 24.4(b). If real GDP is greater than $5 trillion, a larger quantity of labor is required and unemployment falls below its natural rate. The economy operates in the above full-employment range shown in Fig. 24.4(b).

Pay special attention to the *position* of the *LAS* curve. It is a vertical line that intersects the short-run aggregate supply curve at point *c*' on its upward-sloping intermediate range. It does not coincide with the vertical part of the *SAS* curve, where the economy is operating at its physical production limit.

Why is the long-run aggregate supply curve vertical? And why is long-run aggregate supply less than the physical limits to production?

Why the Long-Run Aggregate Supply Curve Is Vertical The long-run aggregate supply curve is vertical because there is only one level of real GDP that can be produced at full employment no matter how high the price level is. As we move along the long-run aggregate supply curve, *two* sets of prices vary: the prices of goods and services and the prices of factors of production. And they vary by the same percentage. You can see why the level of output doesn't vary in these circumstances by thinking about the tape factory again. If the price of tapes increases and the cost of producing them also increases by the same percentage, there is no incentive for tape makers to change their output level. What's true for tape producers is true for the producers of all goods and services, so the aggregate quantity supplied does not change.

Why Long-Run Aggregate Supply Is Less Than the Physical Limit of Production Real GDP cannot be increased above its physical limit. But it can be increased above its long-run level by driving unemployment below its natural rate. When this occurs, there are more unfilled job vacancies than there are people looking for work. Firms compete with each other for labor, wages rise faster than prices, and output eventually falls to its long-run level.

REVIEW

The short-run aggregate supply curve shows the relationship between real GDP supplied and the price level, holding everything else constant. With no change in wage rates or other factor prices, an increase in the price level results in an increase in real GDP supplied. The short-run aggregate supply curve is horizontal in a severe depression, upward sloping in the intermediate range, and vertical when the economy is at the physical limit of its productive capacity. ◆ ◆ The long-run aggregate supply curve shows the relationship between real GDP supplied and the price level when there is full employment. This level of real GDP is independent of the price level, and the long-run aggregate supply curve is vertical. Its position tells us the level of real GDP supplied when the economy is at full employment, which is a lower level of real GDP than the physical production limit. ◆

A change in the price level, with everything else held constant, results in a movement along the short-run aggregate supply curve. A change in the price level, with an accompanying change in wage rates that keeps unemployment at its natural rate, results in a movement along the long-run aggregate supply curve. But there are many other influences on real GDP supplied. These influences result in a change in aggregate supply and shifts in the aggregate supply curves.

Some factors change both short-run aggregate supply and long-run aggregate supply; others affect short-run aggregate supply but leave long-run aggregate supply unchanged. Let's examine these influences on aggregate supply, starting with those that affect only short-run aggregate supply.

Changes in Short-Run Aggregate Supply

The only influences on short-run aggregate supply that do not change long-run aggregate supply are the wage rate and the prices of other factors of production. Factor prices affect short-run aggregate supply through their influence on firms' costs. The higher the level of wage rates and other factor prices, the higher are firms' costs and the lower is the quantity of output that firms want to supply at each price level. Thus an increase in wage rates and other factor prices decreases short-run aggregate supply.

Why do factor prices affect short-run aggregate supply but not long-run aggregate supply? The answer lies in the definition of long-run aggregate supply. Recall that long-run aggregate supply refers to the quantity of real GDP supplied when wages and other factor prices have adjusted by the same percentage amount as the price level has changed.

Faced with the same percentage increase in factor prices and the price of its output, a firm has no incentive to change its output. Thus aggregate output—real GDP—remains constant.

Shift in the Short-Run Aggregate Supply Curve A change in factor prices changes short-run aggregate supply and shifts the short-run aggregate supply curve. Figure 24.5 shows such a shift. The long-run aggregate supply curve is *LAS*, and initially the short-run aggregate supply curve is SAS_0. These curves intersect at the price level 120. Now suppose that labor is the only factor of production and that wage rates increase from $12 an hour to $13 an hour. At the original level of wage rates, firms are willing to supply, in total, $5.0 trillion worth of output at a price level of 120. They will supply that same level of output at the higher wage rate only if prices increase in the same proportion as wages have increased. With wages up from $12 to $13, the price level that will keep the quantity supplied constant is 130. Thus the short-run aggregate supply curve shifts to SAS_1. There is a *decrease* in short-run aggregate supply.

FIGURE 24.5

A Decrease in Short-Run Aggregate Supply

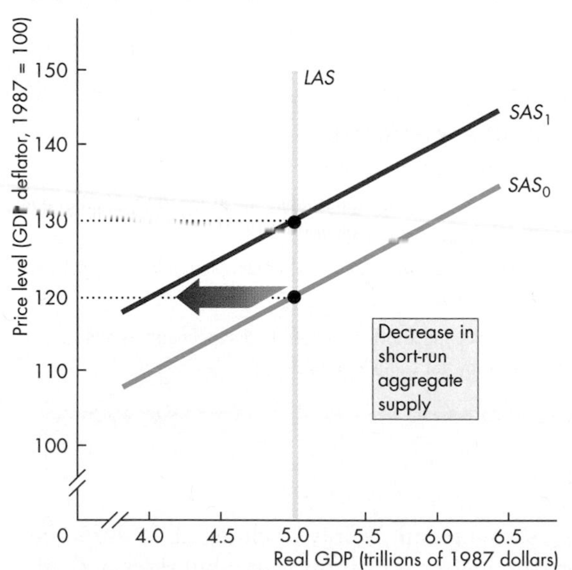

An increase in wage rates or in the prices of other factors of production decreases short-run aggregate supply but does not change long-run aggregate supply. It shifts the short-run aggregate supply curve to the left and leaves the long-run aggregate supply curve unaffected. Such a change is shown here. The original short-run aggregate supply curve is SAS_0, and after the wage rate has increased, the new short-run aggregate supply curve is SAS_1.

Changes in Both Long-Run and Short-Run Aggregate Supply

Four main factors influence both long-run and short-run aggregate supply. They are

- The labor force
- The capital stock
- Technology
- Incentives

The Labor Force The larger the labor force, the larger is the quantity of goods and services produced. Other things being equal, a farm with 10 workers produces more corn than a farm with 1 worker. The same is true for the economy as a whole. With its labor force of more than 125 million people, the United States produces a much larger quantity of goods and services than it would if, everything else remaining the same, it had Canada's labor force of 12.5 million people.

The Capital Stock The larger the stock of plant and equipment, the more productive is the labor force and the greater is the output that it can produce. Also, the larger the stock of *human capital*—the skills that people have acquired in school and through on-the-job training—the greater is the level of output. The capital-rich U.S. economy produces a vastly greater quantity of goods and services than it would if, everything else remaining the same, it had Ethiopia's stock of capital equipment.

Technology Inventing new and better ways of doing things enables firms to produce more from any given amount of inputs. So, even with a constant population and constant capital stock, improvements in technology increase production and increase aggregate supply. Technological advances are by far the most important source of increased production over the past two centuries. As a result of technological advances, in the United States today, one farmer can feed 100 people, and one auto worker can produce almost 14 cars and trucks in a year.

Incentives Aggregate supply is influenced by the incentives that people face. Two examples are unemployment benefits and investment tax credits. In Britain, unemployment benefits are much more generous, relative to wages, than in the United States. There is a greater incentive to find a job in the United States than in Britain. As a result, Britain's natural unemployment rate is higher and its long-run aggregate supply is lower than it would be if Britain had U.S. unemployment compensation arrangements. Investment tax credits are credits that cut business taxes in proportion to the scale of a firm's investment in new plant and equipment. Such credits provide an incentive to greater capital accumulation and, other things being equal, increase aggregate supply.

Shifts in the Short-Run and Long-Run Aggregate Supply Curves If any of the events that change long-run aggregate supply occur, the long-run aggregate supply curve *and the short-run aggregate supply curve* shift. Most of the factors that influence both short-run and long-run aggregate supply bring an *increase* in aggregate supply. This case is summarized in Fig. 24.6.

Initially, the long-run aggregate supply curve is LAS_0 and the short-run aggregate supply curve is SAS_0. These curves intersect at a price level of 120 and a real GDP of 5 trillion 1987 dollars. An increase in productive capacity that increases full-employment real GDP to 6 trillion 1987 dollars shifts the long-run aggregate supply curve to LAS_1 and the short-run aggregate supply curve to SAS_1. Long-run aggregate supply is now 6 trillion 1987 dollars.

FIGURE 24.6

Long-Run Growth in Aggregate Supply

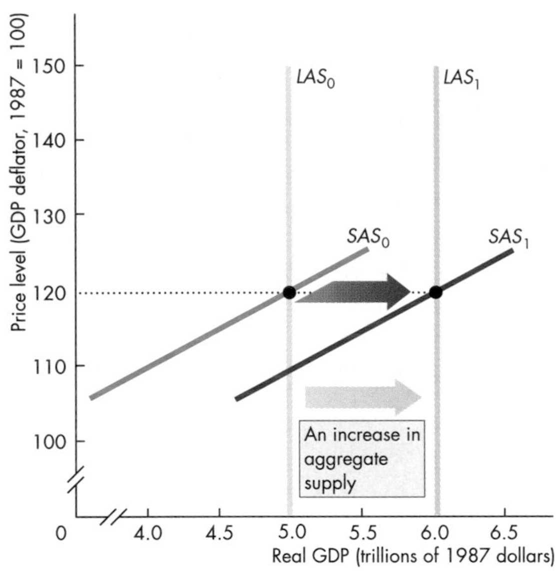

Aggregate supply

Increases in the long run if:

- The labor force increases
- The capital stock increases
- Technological change increases the productivity of labor and capital
- Incentives to work and invest in new plant and equipment are strengthened

Both the long-run and short-run aggregate supply curves shift to the right and do so by the same amount.

REVIEW

A change in wage rates or in other factor prices changes short-run aggregate supply but leaves long-run aggregate supply unchanged. It shifts the short-run aggregate supply curve but does not shift the long-run aggregate supply curve. ◆ ◆ Changes in the size of the labor force and the capital stock, the state of technology, or the incentives households and firms face change both short-run and long-run aggregate supply. Such changes shift both the short-run and long-run aggregate supply curves, and the shifts are in the same direction. ◆

Macroeconomic Equilibrium

The purpose of the aggregate demand–aggregate supply model is to predict changes in real GDP and the price level. To make predictions about real GDP and the price level, we need to combine aggregate demand and aggregate supply and determine macroeconomic equilibrium. **Macroeconomic equilibrium** occurs when the quantity of real GDP demanded equals the quantity of real GDP supplied. Let's see how macroeconomic equilibrium is determined.

Determination of Real GDP and the Price Level

The aggregate demand curve tells us the quantity of real GDP demanded at each price level, and the short-run aggregate supply curve tells us the quantity of real GDP supplied at each price level. There is one and only one price level at which the quantity demanded equals the quantity supplied. Macroeconomic equilibrium occurs at that price level. Figure 24.7 illustrates such an equilibrium at a price level of 120 and a real GDP of 5.0 trillion 1987 dollars (point *c* and *c*').

To see why this position is an equilibrium, let's work out what happens if the price level is something other than 120. Suppose that the price level is 130. In that case, the quantity of real GDP demanded is $4.5 trillion (point *d*), but the quantity of real GDP supplied is $6 trillion (point *e*'). There is an excess of the quantity supplied over the quantity demanded, or a surplus of goods and services. Unable to sell all their output and with inventories piling up, firms cut prices. Prices will be cut until the surplus is eliminated—at a price level of 120.

Next consider what happens if the price level is 110. In this case, the quantity of real GDP that firms supply is $4 trillion worth of goods and services (point *a*') and the quantity of real GDP demanded is $5.5 trillion worth (point *b*). The quantity demanded exceeds the quantity supplied. With inventories running out, firms raise their prices and continue to do so until the quantities demanded and supplied are in balance—again at a price level of 120.

FIGURE 24.7

Macroeconomic Equilibrium 

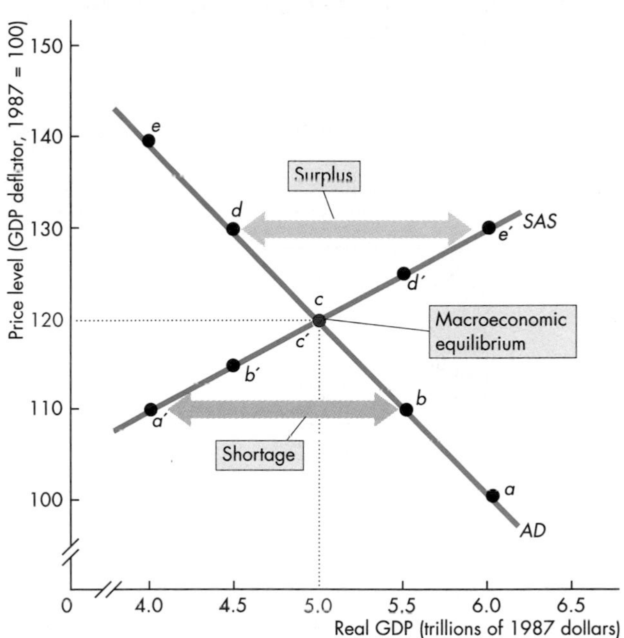

Macroeconomic equilibrium occurs when real GDP demanded equals real GDP supplied. Such an equilibrium is at the intersection of the aggregate demand curve (*AD*) and the short-run aggregate supply curve (*SAS*)—points *c* and *c*'—where the price level is 120 and real GDP is $5.0 trillion 1987 dollars. At price levels above 120, for example, 130, there is an excess of the quantity of goods and services supplied over the quantity demanded—a surplus—and prices fall. At price levels below 120, for example, 110, there is an excess of the quantity of goods and services demanded over the quantity supplied—a shortage—and prices rise. Only when the price level is 120 is the quantity of goods and services demanded equal to the quantity supplied. This is the equilibrium price level.

Macroeconomic Equilibrium and Full Employment

Macroeconomic equilibrium does not necessarily occur at full employment. At full employment, the economy is on its *long-run* aggregate supply curve.

But macroeconomic equilibrium occurs at the intersection of the *short-run* aggregate supply curve and the aggregate demand curve and can occur at, below, or above full employment. We can see this fact most clearly by considering the three possible cases shown in Fig. 24.8.

In Fig. 24.8(a) the fluctuations of real GDP are shown for an imaginary economy over a five-year period. In year 2, real GDP falls below its long-run level to point *b* and there is a recessionary gap. A **recessionary gap** is long-run real GDP minus actual real GDP when actual real GDP is below long-run

FIGURE 24.8

Three Types of Macroeconomic Equilibrium

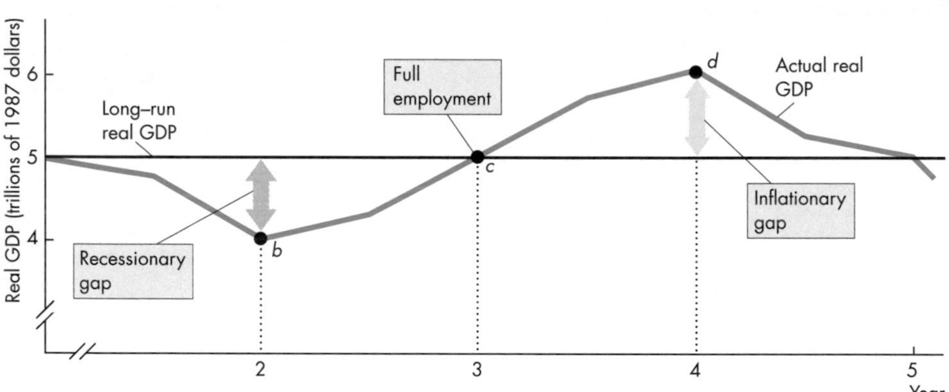

(a) Fluctuations in real GDP

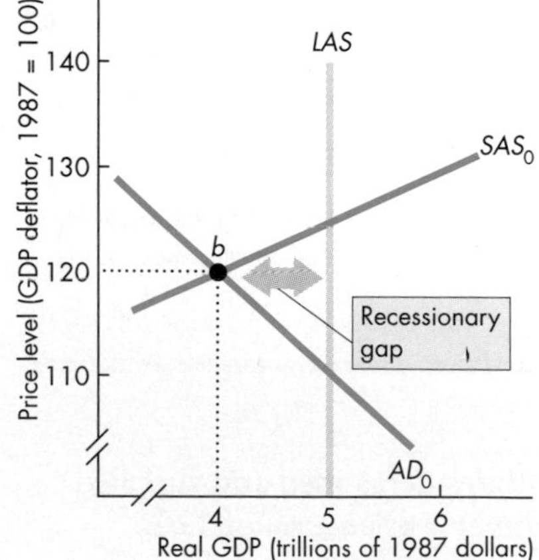

(b) Unemployment equilibrium

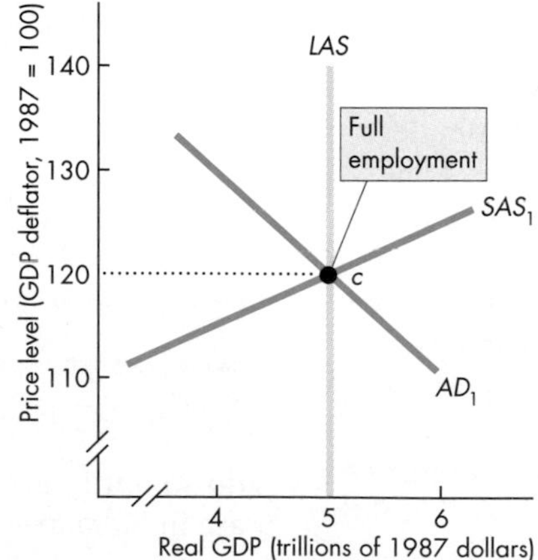

(c) Full-employment equilibrium

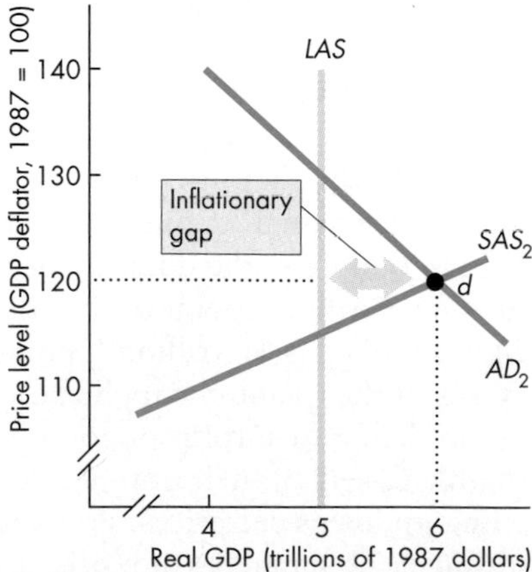

(d) Above full-employment equilibrium

In part (a), real GDP fluctuates around its long-run level. When actual real GDP is below long-run real GDP, there is a recessionary gap (as in year 2). When actual real GDP is above long-run real GDP, there is an inflationary gap (as in year 4). When actual real GDP is equal to long-run real GDP, there is full employment (as in year 3).

In year 2 there is an unemployment equilibrium, as illustrated in part (b). In year 3 there is a full-employment equilibrium, as illustrated in part (c). And in year 4 there is an above full-employment equilibrium, as illustrated in part (d).

real GDP. In year 4, real GDP rises above its long-run level to point *d* and there is an inflationary gap. An **inflationary gap** is actual real GDP minus long-run real GDP when actual real GDP is above long-run real GDP. In year 3, actual real GDP and long-run real GDP are equal and the economy is at full employment, at point *c*.

These situations are illustrated in parts (b), (c), and (d) as the three types of macroeconomic equilibrium. In part (b) there is an unemployment equilibrium. An **unemployment equilibrium** is a situation in which macroeconomic equilibrium occurs at a level of real GDP below long-run GDP. In such an equilibrium, there is a recessionary gap. The unemployment equilibrium illustrated in Fig. 24.8(b) occurs where aggregate demand curve AD_0 intersects short-run aggregate supply curve SAS_0 at a real GDP of 4 trillion 1987 dollars and a price level of 120. There is a recessionary gap of 1 trillion 1987 dollars. The U.S. economy was in a situation similar to that shown in Fig. 24.8(b) in 1982–1983. In those years, unemployment was high and real GDP was substantially below its long-run level.

Figure 24.8(c) is an example of full-employment equilibrium. **Full-employment equilibrium** is a macroeconomic equilibrium in which actual real GDP equals long-run real GDP. In this example, the equilibrium occurs where the aggregate demand curve AD_1 intersects the short-run aggregate supply curve SAS_1 at an actual and long-run real GDP of 5 trillion 1987 dollars. The U.S. economy was in a situation such as that shown in Fig. 24.8(c) in 1987.

Finally, Fig. 24.8(d) illustrates an above full-employment equilibrium. **Above full-employment equilibrium** is a situation in which macroeconomic equilibrium occurs at a level of real GDP above long-run real GDP. In such an equilibrium, there is an inflationary gap. The above full-employment equilibrium illustrated in Fig. 24.8(d) occurs where the aggregate demand curve AD_2 intersects the short-run aggregate supply curve SAS_2 at a real GDP of 6 trillion 1987 dollars and a price level of 120. There is an inflationary gap of 1 trillion 1987 dollars. The U.S. economy was in a situation similar to that depicted in part (d) in 1988–1990.

The economy moves from one type of equilibrium to another as a result of fluctuations in aggregate demand and in short-run aggregate supply. These fluctuations produce fluctuations in real GDP and the price level.

Next, we're going to put the model to work generating macroeconomic fluctuations.

Aggregate Fluctuations and Aggregate Demand Shocks

We're going to work out what happens to real GDP and the price level following a shock to aggregate demand. Let's suppose that the economy starts out at full employment and, as illustrated in Fig. 24.9, is producing \$5 trillion worth of goods and services at a price level of 120. The economy is on the aggregate demand curve AD_0, the short-run aggregate

FIGURE 24.9

The Effects of an Increase in Aggregate Demand

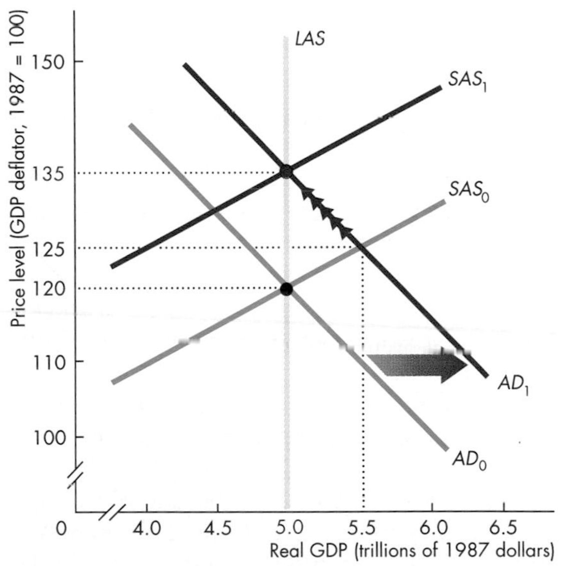

An increase in aggregate demand shifts the aggregate demand curve from AD_0 to AD_1. Real GDP increases from 5.0 trillion to 5.5 trillion 1987 dollars, and the price level increases from 120 to 125. There is an inflationary gap. A higher price level induces higher wage rates, which in turn cause the short-run aggregate supply curve to move leftward. As the *SAS* curve moves leftward from SAS_0 to SAS_1, it intersects the aggregate demand curve AD_1 at higher price levels and lower real GDP levels. Eventually, the price level increases to 135, and real GDP falls back to 5.0 trillion 1987 dollars—its full-employment level.

supply curve SAS_0, and its long-run aggregate supply curve *LAS*.

Now suppose that the Fed takes steps to increase the quantity of money. With more money in the economy, people increase their demand for goods and services—the aggregate demand curve shifts to the right. Suppose that the aggregate demand curve shifts from AD_0 to AD_1 in Fig. 24.9. A new equilibrium occurs where the aggregate demand curve AD_1 intersects the short-run aggregate supply curve SAS_0. Output rises to \$5.5 trillion (1987 dollars), and the price level rises to 125. The economy is now at an above full-employment equilibrium. Real GDP is above its long-run level, and there is an inflationary gap.

The increase in aggregate demand has increased the prices of all goods and services. Faced with higher prices, firms have increased their output rates. At this stage, prices of goods and services have increased but wage rates have not changed. (Recall that as we move along a short-run aggregate supply curve, wage rates are constant.)

The economy cannot stay above its long-run aggregate supply and full-employment levels forever. Why not? What are the forces at work bringing real GDP back to its long-run level and restoring full employment?

If the price level has increased but wage rates have remained constant, workers have experienced a fall in the purchasing power of their wages. Furthermore, firms have experienced a fall in the real cost of labor. In these circumstances, workers demand higher wages, and firms, anxious to maintain their employment and output levels, meet those demands. If firms do not raise wage rates, they either lose workers or have to hire less productive ones.

As wage rates rise, the short-run aggregate supply curve begins to shift upward. It moves from SAS_0 toward SAS_1. The rise in wages and the shift in the *SAS* curve produce a sequence of new equilibrium positions. At each point on the adjustment path, output falls and the price level rises. Eventually, wages will have risen by so much that the *SAS* curve is SAS_1. At this time, the aggregate demand curve AD_1 intersects SAS_1 at a full-employment equilibrium. The price level has risen to 135, and output is back where it started, at its long-run level. Unemployment is again at its natural rate.

Throughout the adjustment process, higher wage rates raise firms' costs and, with rising costs, firms offer a smaller quantity of goods and services for sale at any given price level. By the time the adjustment is over, firms are producing exactly the same amount as initially produced, but at higher prices and higher costs. The level of costs relative to prices will be the same as it was initially.

We've just worked out the effects of an increase in aggregate demand. A decrease in aggregate demand has similar but opposite effects to those that we've just studied. That is, when aggregate demand falls, real GDP falls below its long-run level and unemployment rises above its natural rate. There is a recessionary gap. The lower price level increases the purchasing power of wages and increases firms' costs relative to their output prices. Eventually, as the slack economy leads to falling wage rates, the short-run aggregate supply curve shifts downward. Real GDP gradually returns to its long-run level, and full employment is restored.

Aggregate Fluctuations and Aggregate Supply Shocks

Let's now work out the effects of a change in aggregate supply on real GDP and the price level. Figure 24.10 illustrates the analysis. Suppose that the economy is initially at full-employment equilibrium. The aggregate demand curve is AD_0, the short-run aggregate supply curve is SAS_0, and the long-run aggregate supply curve is *LAS*. Output is 5 trillion 1987 dollars, and the price level is 120.

Now suppose that the price of oil increases sharply, as it did when OPEC used its market power in 1973–1974 and again in 1979–1980. With a higher price of oil, firms are faced with higher costs and they lower their output. Short-run aggregate supply decreases, and the short-run aggregate supply curves shift leftward to SAS_1.

As a result of this decrease in short-run aggregate supply, the economy moves to a new equilibrium where SAS_1 intersects the aggregate demand curve AD_0. The price level rises to 130, and real GDP falls to 4.5 trillion 1987 dollars. Because real GDP falls, the economy experiences recession. Because the price level increases, the economy experiences inflation. Such a combination of recession and inflation—called *stagflation*—actually occurred in the 1970s and 1980s at the times of the OPEC oil price hikes.

FIGURE 24.10

The Effects of an Increase in the Price of Oil

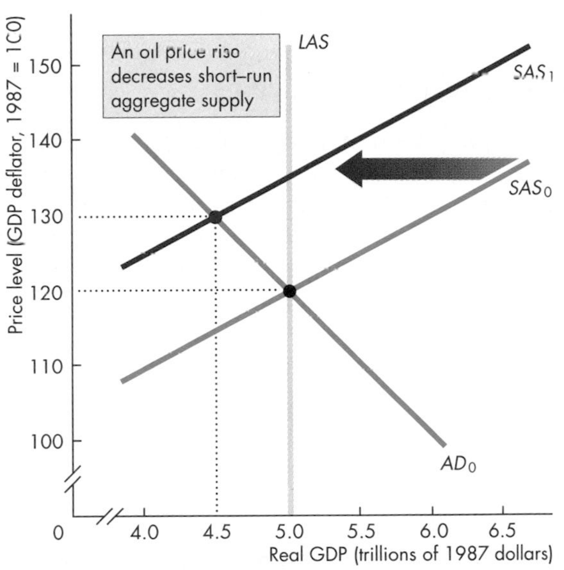

An increase in the price of oil decreases short-run aggregate supply and shifts the short-run aggregate supply curve leftward from SAS_0 to SAS_1. Real GDP falls from 5.0 trillion to 4.5 trillion 1987 dollars, and the price level increases from 120 to 130. The economy experiences both recession and inflation—*stagflation.*

REVIEW

Macroeconomic equilibrium occurs when the quantity of real GDP demanded equals the quantity of real GDP supplied. There are three types of macroeconomic equilibrium—unemployment equilibrium (a situation in which real GDP is below long-run real GDP and there is a recessionary gap), full-employment equilibrium (a situation in which actual real GDP equals long-run real GDP), and above full-employment equilibrium (a situation in which real GDP is above long-run real GDP and there is an inflationary gap). As aggregate demand and aggregate supply fluctuate, the economy moves from one type of macroeconomic equilibrium to another and real GDP and the price level fluctuate. ◆

We've now seen how changes in aggregate demand and aggregate supply influence real GDP and the price level. Let's put our new knowledge to work and see how it helps us understand recent U.S. macroeconomic performance.

Recent Trends and Cycles in the U.S. Economy

We're now going to use our new tools of aggregate demand and aggregate supply to interpret some recent trends and cycles in the U.S. economy. We'll begin by looking at the state of the U.S. economy in 1991–1992.

The Economy in 1991–1992

In 1991, the U.S. economy was in recession. Measured in 1987 dollars, real GDP was $4.85 trillion but long-run real GDP was $5 trillion. The price level was 117. We can illustrate this state of the U.S. economy by using the aggregate demand–aggregate supply model.

In Fig. 24.11, the aggregate demand curve in 1991 is AD_{91} and the short-run aggregate supply curve in 1991 is SAS_{91}. The point at which these curves intersect determines the price level (117) and real GDP ($4.85 trillion) in 1991. The long-run aggregate supply curve in 1991 is LAS_{91} at a real GDP of $5 trillion, and there is a recessionary gap—actual real GDP is below long-run real GDP.

Three forces pushed the economy into recession in 1991. One was the price of oil, which increased sharply in the summer of 1990. This force decreased short-run aggregate supply and produced a leftward shift in the *SAS* curve. The second force was monetary policy. During 1989, the Fed had conducted a policy of restraint that increased interest rates and slowed the growth of aggregate demand. The effects of this restraint were still being felt in 1990. The third force was increased uncertainty and pessimism about future profit and income prospects that lowered spending on new plant and equipment, buildings, and consumer goods. Working in the opposite direction, but with less force than the recessionary

FIGURE 24.11

The U.S. Economy in 1991

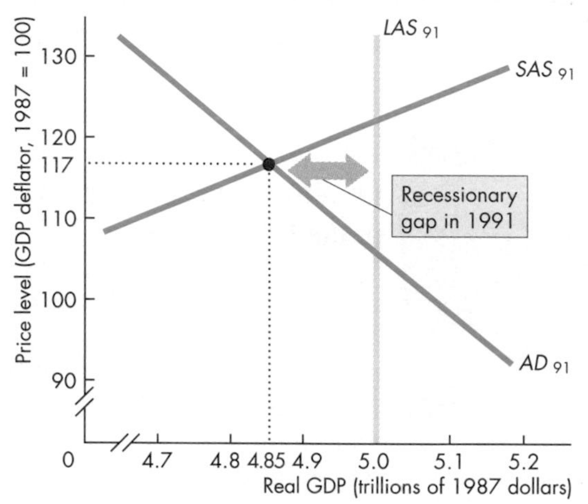

In 1991, the U.S. economy was on the aggregate demand curve AD_{91} and the aggregate supply curve SAS_{91}. The price level was 117, and real GDP was 4.85 trillion 1987 dollars. The long-run aggregate supply curve, LAS_{91}, was at 5 trillion 1987 dollars. There was a recessionary gap of 0.15 trillion 1987 dollars.

forces, fiscal policy was eased. The government's purchases of goods and services increased slightly. The combined effect of these forces led to recession in the winter of 1990–1991.

Through 1991, the economy began to recover from recession but extremely slowly and unemployment remained high throughout the year. The recovery was aided by a decrease in the price of oil. (The increase of the summer of 1990 proved to be short-lived.) It was also aided by a considerable easing of monetary restraint. The Fed engineered successive decreases in interest rates that led to a gradual increase in aggregate demand. But confidence—business confidence about profit prospects and consumer confidence about income growth—remained weak, so aggregate demand did not grow quickly.

The main uncertainty about the economy as it entered 1992 was not whether recovery was underway, but whether it would persist. Some people took the optimistic view that monetary and fiscal policy stimulus would be strong enough to keep aggregate demand growing and maintain the recovery. This view was taken by *Fortune* magazine in its eighteen-month-ahead forecast made in January 1992—see Reading Between the Lines, pp. 658–659. But others (as portrayed in the cartoon) took the pessimistic view that with low confidence, aggregate demand might even fall yet again, causing a "double-dip"—a second recession following quickly on the heels of its predecessor.

Growth, Inflation, and Cycles

The economy is continually changing. If you imagine the economy as a video, then Fig. 24.11 is a freeze-frame. We're going to run the video again—an instant replay—but keep our finger on the freeze-frame button, looking at some important parts of the previous action. Let's run the video from 1960.

Figure 24.12 shows the state of the economy in 1960 at the point of intersection of its aggregate demand curve AD_{60} and short-run aggregate supply curve SAS_{60}. Real GDP was \$2 trillion, and the GDP deflator was 26 (less than one quarter of its 1991 level).

By 1991, the economy had reached the point marked by the intersection of aggregate demand curve AD_{91} and short-run aggregate supply curve SAS_{91}. Real GDP was \$4.85 trillion, and the GDP deflator was 117.

There are three important features of the economy's path traced by the blue and red points:

- Growth
- Inflation
- Cycles

"Please stand by for a series of tones. The first indicates the official end of the recession, the second indicates prosperity, and the third the return of the recession."

Growth Over the years, real GDP grows—shown in Fig. 24.12 by the rightward movement of the points. The main force generating this growth is an increase in long-run aggregate supply. Long-run aggregate supply increases because of labor force growth, the accumulation of capital—both physical plant and equipment and human capital—and the advance of technology.

Inflation The price level rises over the years—shown in Fig. 24.12 by the upward movement of the points. The main force generating this persistent increase in the price level is a tendency for aggregate demand to increase at a faster pace than the increase in long-run aggregate supply. All of the factors that increase aggregate demand and shift the aggregate demand curve influence the pace of inflation. But one factor—the quantity of money—is the most important source of *persistent* increases in aggregate demand and persistent inflation.

Cycles Over the years, the economy grows and shrinks in cycles—shown in Fig. 24.12 by the wave-like pattern made by the points, with recessions highlighted in red. The cycles arise because both the expansion of short-run aggregate supply and the growth of aggregate demand do not proceed at a fixed, steady pace.

FIGURE 24.12

Aggregate Demand and Aggregate Supply: 1960 to 1991

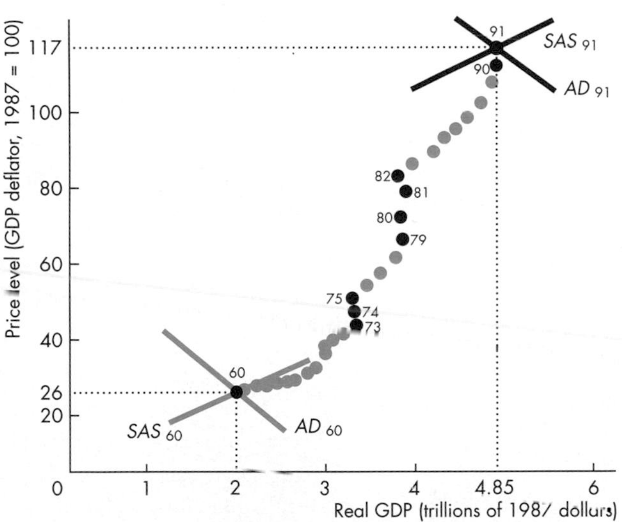

Each point indicates the value of the GDP deflator and real GDP in a given year. In 1960, these variables were determined by the intersection of the aggregate demand curve AD_{60} and the short-run aggregate supply curve SAS_{60}. Each point is generated by the gradual shifting of the *AD* and *SAS* curves. By 1991, the curves were AD_{91} and SAS_{91}. Real GDP grew, and the price level increased. But growth and inflation did not proceed smoothly. Real GDP grew quickly and inflation was moderate in the 1960s; real GDP growth sagged in 1974–1975 and again, more strongly, in 1982. The 1974–1975 slowdown was caused by an unusually sharp increase in oil prices. The 1982 recession was caused by a slowdown in the growth of aggregate demand, which resulted mainly from the Fed's monetary policy. The period from 1982 to 1989 was one of strong, persistent recovery. Inflation was rapid during the 1970s but slowed after the 1982 recession. A recession began in mid-1990.

The Evolving Economy: 1960–1991

During the 1960s, real GDP growth was rapid and inflation was low. This was a period of rapid increases in aggregate supply and of moderate increases in aggregate demand.

The mid-1970s were years of rapid inflation and recession—of stagflation. The major source of these developments was a series of massive oil price increases that shifted the short-run aggregate supply curve leftward and rapid increases in the quantity of money that shifted the aggregate demand curve rightward. Recession occurred because the aggregate supply curve shifted leftward at a faster pace than the aggregate demand curve shifted rightward.

The rest of the 1970s saw high inflation—the price level increased quickly—and only moderate growth in real GDP. This inflation was the product of a battle between OPEC and the Fed. OPEC jacked up the price of oil, and an inflationary recession ensued. Eventually, the Fed gave way and increased the money supply growth rate to stimulate aggregate demand and bring the economy back to full employment. Then OPEC, taking advantage of oil shortages created by a crisis in the relations between the United States and Iran, played a similar hand again, pushing up the price of oil still further. The Fed was faced with a dilemma. Should it stimulate aggregate demand again to restore full employment, notching up the inflation rate yet further, or should it keep the growth of aggregate demand in check?

The answer, delivered by Fed chairman Paul Volcker, was to keep aggregate demand growth in check. You can see the effects of Chairman Volcker's

The Slow 1992 Recovery

FORTUNE, JANUARY 13, 1992

Inching into Recovery

BY VIVIAN BROWNSTEIN

Despite the present gloom, the next 18 months will finish decidedly better than they start out. Growth in the first half of 1992, though barely discernible to most people, will nevertheless be an improvement over the economy's no-growth performance in the last quarter of 1991. As the tempo quickens later in the new year—and it will—businesses and consumers will finally feel that a recovery worthy of the name is under way.

Fortune expects real GDP to move ahead at less than a 2% annual rate during the first and second quarters, helped a bit by the Federal Reserve's full-point cut in the discount rate. For the following 12 months, growth should average 3%. We factor in a relatively small federal stimulus package that should emerge from the current political maneuvering. Unemployment will notch down during the 18 months but will still hover at about 6% in mid-1993. The outlook for inflation is mixed. It will pick up from the recent low rate, but nothing points to a worrisome acceleration. The GDP deflator, the broadest measure of inflation, should average about 4% during the year and a half.

Beyond mid-year, the economy will be moving ahead faster than its long-term potential. Even that will seem mediocre. In the past a quick-start recovery has made up for much of the output lost during a downturn. Without such a surge, some of the pain left by this recession—and the year and a half of subnormal growth that preceded it—will linger. So will corporate restructuring that adds to the anxiety of workers and managers.

Business leaders remain convinced that the recession never ended, regardless of what economists say. Based on the usual statistical data, business cycle expert Geoffrey Moore—who serves on the committee that officially dates expansions and contractions—has concluded that the trough most likely occurred last May. But nearly seven out of ten *Fortune 500* CEOs responding to our latest poll of their views think the country is still in a serious downturn. Small business is equally glum. Economist William Dunkelberg of the National Federation of Independent Business sums up the mood that the 550,000 members expressed in his latest survey: "We're headed nowhere, and we are moving there at a very slow pace." Gallows humor and scare talk reflect a simple fact of life for too many companies: Business is still dismal, seven months into what they had expected would be a period of steady expansion. . . .

The Essence of the Story

In January 1992, *Fortune* forecasted a real GDP growth rate of less than 2 percent a year for the first and second quarters of 1992 and of 3 percent a year for the 12 months from mid-1992 to mid-1993.

Unemployment was forecasted to decline only slightly and to be at 6 percent by mid-1993.

Inflation, measured by the GDP deflator, was forecasted to average 4 percent between January 1992 and mid-1993.

The sources of increased growth were seen as the Federal Reserve's cut in interest rates and a small fiscal policy stimulus.

Beyond mid-1992, real GDP was forecasted to be growing faster than its long-term potential but not fast enough to take up the slack resulting from the recession of 1991.

At the beginning of 1992, economists said the recession was over, but business leaders didn't agree.

Background and Analysis

In 1991, shown in Fig. 1, the aggregate demand curve was AD_{91}, the short-run aggregate supply curve was SAS_{91}, and real GDP and the price level (the GDP deflator) were determined at the intersection of these curves—real GDP was $4.85 (in 1987 dollars), and the price level was 117.

Long-run aggregate supply in 1991 was LAS_{91}, and there was a recessionary gap of $0.15 trillion.

Between mid-1991 and mid-1992, the economy began to recover from recession, but slowly. The Fed's lower interest rates together with a forecasted fiscal policy stimulus were predicted (by *Fortune* magazine) to make real GDP grow by 1.5 percent and the price level to rise by 4 percent.

These forecasts are shown in Fig. 2. They result from an increase in aggregate demand to AD_{92} and a shift in the forecasted short-run aggregate supply curve to SAS_{92}. These changes increase real GDP to $4.92—an increase of 1.5 percent—and increase the price level to 122—an inflation rate of 4 percent.

Because the economy was growing, economists proclaimed the end of recession—a recession is a period of *falling* real GDP that lasts for at least two quarters.

But long-run real GDP grew at a faster rate than the 1.5 percent growth rate of real GDP. In Fig. 2, long-run aggregate supply is assumed to grow at a 3 percent annual rate, with the mid-1992 long-run aggregate supply curve at LAS_{92}.

With full-employment real GDP growing faster than actual real GDP, the recessionary gap actually widened. It is this feature of the economy on which the business community was focused in concluding that we were heading nowhere at a slow pace.

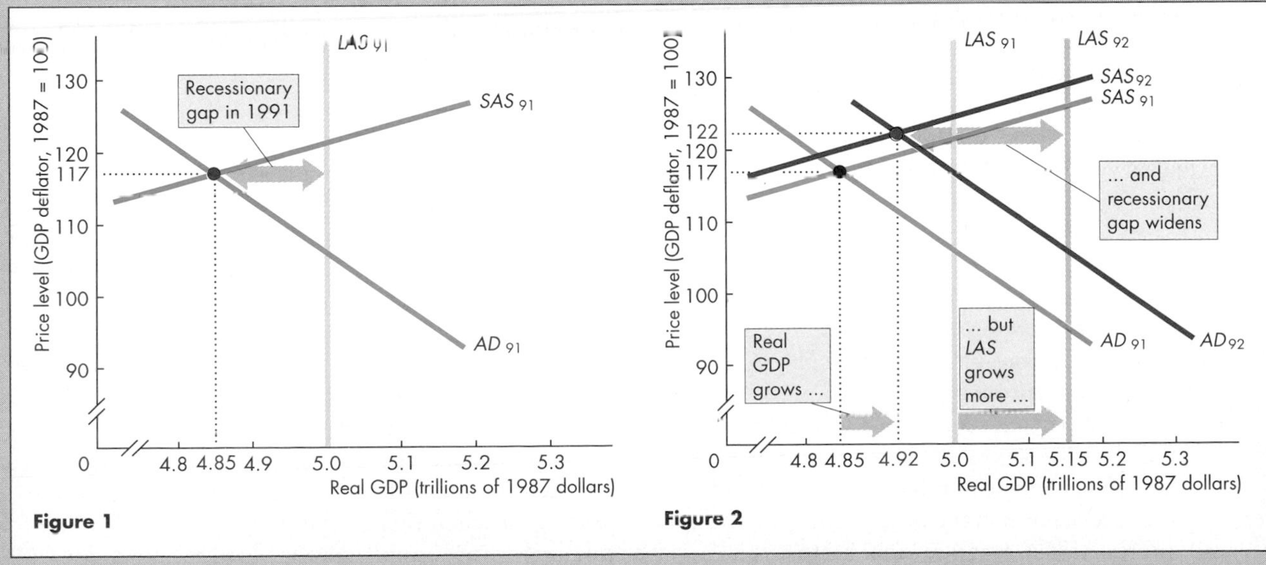

Figure 1

Figure 2

actions in 1979 to 1982. In this period, most people expected high inflation to persist, and wages grew at a rate consistent with those expectations. The short-run aggregate supply curve shifted leftward. Aggregate demand increased, but not at a fast enough rate to create inflation at as fast a pace as most people expected. As a consequence, by 1982 the leftward shift of the short-run aggregate supply curve was so strong relative to the growth of aggregate demand that the economy went into a further deep recession.

During the years 1982 to 1990, capital accumulation and steady technological advance resulted in a sustained rightward shift of the long-run aggregate supply curve. Wage growth was moderate, and the short-run aggregate supply curve also shifted rightward. Aggregate demand growth kept pace with the growth of aggregate supply. Sustained but steady growth in aggregate supply and aggregate demand kept real GDP growing and inflation steady. The economy moved from a recession with real GDP well below its long-run level to above full employment. It was in this condition when the events unfolded (described above) that led to the 1991 recession.

◆ ◆ ◆ ◆ This chapter has provided a model of real GDP and the GDP deflator that can be used to understand the growth, inflation, and cycles that our economy follows. The model is a useful one because it enables us to keep our eye on the big picture—on the broad trends and cycles in inflation and output. But the model lacks detail. It does not tell us as much as we need to know about the components of aggregate demand—consumption, investment, government purchases of goods and services, and exports and imports. It doesn't tell us what determines interest rates or wage rates or even, directly, what determines employment and unemployment. In the following chapters, we're going to start to fill in that detail. ◆ ◆ In some ways, the study of macroeconomics is like doing a large jigsaw puzzle. The aggregate demand–aggregate supply model provides the entire edge of the jigsaw. We know its general shape and size, but we haven't filled in the middle. One block of the jigsaw contains the story of aggregate demand. Another, the story of aggregate supply. And when we place the two together, we place them in the frame of the model developed in this chapter, and the picture is completed.

SUMMARY

Aggregate Demand

Aggregate demand is the relationship between the quantity of real GDP demanded and the price level, holding all other influences constant. Other things held constant, the higher the price level, the smaller is the quantity of real GDP demanded—the aggregate demand curve slopes downward. The aggregate demand curve slopes downward for three reasons: money and goods are substitutes (*real money balances effect*); goods today and goods in the future are substitutes (*intertemporal substitution effect*); domestic goods and foreign goods are substitutes (*international substitution effect*).

The main factors that change aggregate demand—and shift the aggregate demand curve—are fiscal policy (government purchases of goods and services and taxes), monetary policy (the money supply and interest rates), international factors (economic conditions in the rest of the world and the foreign exchange rate), and expectations (especially expectations about future inflation, income, and profits). (pp. 638–645)

Aggregate Supply

Short-run aggregate supply is the relationship between the quantity of real GDP supplied and the price level when wage rates and other factor prices are held constant. The short-run aggregate supply curve is horizontal in a deep depression, vertical at the economy's physical production limit, but generally upward sloping. With factor prices and all other influences on supply held constant, the higher the price level, the more output firms plan to sell.

Long-run aggregate supply is the relationship between the quantity of real GDP supplied and the price level when there is full employment. The long-run aggregate supply curve is vertical—long-run aggregate supply is independent of the price level.

The factors that change short-run aggregate supply shift the short-run aggregate supply curve. The most important of these factors is the average level of wage rates. Factors that change long-run aggregate supply also change short-run aggregate supply. Thus anything that shifts the long-run aggregate supply curve also shifts the short-run aggregate supply curve, and they shift in the same direction. The most important of these factors are the size of the labor force, the capital stock, the state of technology, and incentives. (pp. 645–650)

Macroeconomic Equilibrium

Macroeconomic equilibrium occurs when the quantity of real GDP demanded equals the quantity of real GDP supplied. Macroeconomic equilibrium occurs at the intersection of the aggregate demand curve and the short-run aggregate supply curve. The price level that achieves this equality is the equilibrium price level, and the output level is equilibrium real GDP.

Macroeconomic equilibrium does not always occur at long-run real GDP and full employment—that is, at a point on the long-run aggregate supply curve. Unemployment equilibrium occurs when equilibrium real GDP is less than its long-run level. There is a recessionary gap, and unemployment exceeds its natural rate. When equilibrium real GDP is above its long-run level, there is an inflationary gap and unemployment is below its natural rate.

An increase in aggregate demand shifts the aggregate demand curve to the right and increases both real GDP and the price level. If real GDP is above its long-run level, wage rates begin to increase and, as they do so, the short-run aggregate supply curve shifts to the left. The leftward shift of the short-run aggregate supply curve results in a yet higher price level and a lower real GDP. Eventually, real GDP returns to its long-run level.

An increase in factor prices decreases short-run aggregate supply and shifts the short-run aggregate supply curve to the left. Real GDP decreases, and the price level rises—stagflation occurs. (pp. 651–655)

Recent Trends and Cycles in the U.S. Economy

Growth in the U.S. economy results from labor force growth, capital accumulation, and technological change. Inflation persists in the U.S. economy because of steady increases in aggregate demand largely brought about by increases in the quantity of money. The U.S. economy experiences cycles because the short-run aggregate supply and aggregate demand curves shift at an uneven pace.

Large oil price hikes in 1973 and 1974 resulted in stagflation. Further oil price increases in 1979 intensified the inflationary situation. Restraint in aggregate demand growth in 1980 and 1981 resulted in a severe recession in 1982. This recession resulted in lower output and a lower inflation rate. Moderate increases in wage rates and steady technological advance and capital accumulation resulted in a sustained expansion from 1982 to 1989. But a slowdown in aggregate demand growth brought a recession in mid-1990. (pp. 655–660)

KEY ELEMENTS

Key Terms

Above full-employment equilibrium, 653
Aggregate demand, 638
Aggregate demand curve, 638
Aggregate demand schedule, 638
Aggregate quantity of goods and services demanded, 638
Aggregate quantity of goods and services supplied, 645
Fiscal policy, 642
Full-employment equilibrium, 653
Inflationary gap, 653
International substitution, 641
Intertemporal substitution, 640
Long-run aggregate supply, 647
Long-run aggregate supply curve, 647
Macroeconomic equilibrium, 651
Macroeconomic long-run, 645
Macroeconomic short-run, 645
Monetary policy, 642
Quantity of money, 639

Key Figures

REVIEW QUESTIONS

1 What is aggregate demand?

2 What is the difference between aggregate demand and the aggregate quantity of goods and services demanded?

3 List the main factors that affect aggregate demand. Separate them into those that increase aggregate demand and those that decrease it.

4 Which of the following do not affect aggregate demand?

a Quantity of money
b Interest rates
c Technological change
d Human capital

5 Distinguish between macroeconomic short-run and long-run.

6 What is short-run aggregate supply?

7 What is the difference between short-run aggregate supply and the aggregate quantity of goods and services supplied?

8 Distinguish between short-run aggregate supply and long-run aggregate supply.

9 Consider the following events:

a The labor force increases.
b Technology improves.
c The wage rate increases.
d The quantity of money increases.
e Foreign incomes increase.
f The foreign exchange value of the dollar increases.

Sort these events into the following four categories:

Category A: Those that affect the long-run aggregate supply curve but not the short-run aggregate supply curve.

Category B: Those that affect the short-run aggregate supply curve but not the long-run aggregate supply curve.

Category C: Those that affect both the short-run aggregate supply curve and the long-run aggregate supply curve.

Category D: Those that have no effect on the short-run aggregate supply curve or on the long-run aggregate supply curve.

10 Define macroeconomic equilibrium.

11 Distinguish between an unemployment equilibrium and a full-employment equilibrium.

12 Work out the effect of an increase in the quantity of money on the price level and real GDP.

13 Work out the effect of an increase in the price of oil on the price level and real GDP.

14 What are the main factors generating growth of real GDP in the U.S. economy?

15 What are the main factors generating persistent inflation in the U.S. economy?

16 Why does the U.S. economy experience cycles in aggregate economic activity?

PROBLEMS

1 The economy of Mainland has the following aggregate demand and supply schedules:

Price level (GDP deflator)	Real GDP demanded	Real GDP supplied in the short run
	(trillions of 1987 dollars)	
90	4.5	3.5
100	4.0	4.0
110	3.5	4.5
120	3.0	5.0
130	2.5	5.5
140	2.0	5.5

- a Plot the aggregate demand curve and the short-run aggregate supply curve in a figure.
- b What is Mainland's real GDP? What is Mainland's price level?
- c Mainland's long-run real GDP is 5.0 trillion 1987 dollars. Plot the long-run aggregate supply curve in the same figure with which you answered part (a).
- d Is Mainland at, above, or below its natural rate of unemployment?
- e What is the physical limit of the economy of Mainland?

2 In problem 1, aggregate demand is increased by 1 trillion 1987 dollars. What is the change in real GDP and the price level?

3 In problem 1, aggregate supply decreases by 1 trillion 1987 dollars. What is the new macroeconomic equilibrium?

4 You are the president's economic advisor, and you are trying to figure out where the U.S. economy is headed next year. You have the following forecasts for the *AD*, *SAS*, and *LAS* curves:

Price level (GDP deflator)	Real GDP demanded	Short-run real GDP supplied	Long-run aggregate supply
		(trillions of 1987 dollars)	
115	6.5	3.5	5.2
120	6.0	4.5	5.2
125	5.5	5.5	5.2
130	5.0	6.5	5.2

This year, real GDP is $5.0 trillion and the price level is 120. The president wants answers to the following questions:

- a What is your forecast of next year's real GDP?
- b What is your forecast of next year's price level?
- c What is your forecast of the inflation rate?
- d Will unemployment be above or below its natural rate?
- e Will there be a recessionary gap or an inflationary gap? By how much?

5 Carefully draw some figures similar to those in this chapter and use the information in problem 4 to explain:

- a What has to be done to aggregate demand to achieve full employment
- b What the inflation rate is if aggregate demand is manipulated to achieve full employment

PART 10

AGGREGATE DEMAND FLUCTUATIONS

Talking with Allan Meltzer

Born in Boston, Massachusetts, in 1928, Allan Meltzer is the John M. Olin Professor of Political Economy and Public Policy at Carnegie-Mellon University in Pittsburgh. Professor Meltzer was an undergraduate at Duke University and a graduate student at UCLA, where he obtained his Ph.D. in 1958. Professor Meltzer has made wide-ranging contributions to the theory of money and economic activity and, with the late Karl Brunner, was a co-founder of the Shadow Open Market Committee. More recently, he has been giving some attention to the economic problems of Eastern Europe and the former Soviet Union. Michael Parkin talked with Professor Meltzer about his work as an economist and his views on today's economics problems.

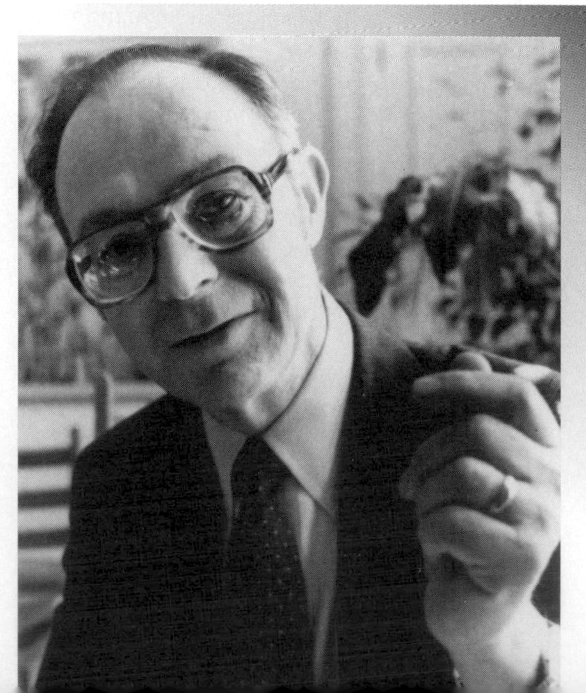

What led you to study economics at UCLA?

I considered graduate school in my last year as an undergraduate majoring in economics, but I wasn't sure that was what I wanted. I started to enroll in Harvard's Ph.D. program but never went through with it. Instead, I moved to California and worked for several different manufacturing companies. After a few years, I realized that I had made the wrong choice and really preferred to study economics. I was married and living in Los Angeles at the time, so I went to UCLA.

What were the earliest economic problems on which you worked?

I was influenced by my teacher at UCLA, Karl Brunner, who had become interested in the money supply while I was a student. My thesis tested money supply theory under conditions of wartime and postwar French inflation. At the time, most of the French economists—and many American economists also—thought money was irrelevant to explaining economic problems. Many economists even considered inflation a non-monetary phenomenon. Soon

"**A**t the time . . . many American economists . . . thought money was irrelevant to explaining economic problems."

after publishing my work on the French money supply, I began a series of papers on the demand for money in the United States.

You are a co-founder with Karl Brunner of the Shadow Open Market Committee. What is the Shadow Open Market Committee, and what does it do?

Karl and I were disturbed by the trend in economic policy. In the early 1970s, inflation was rising. Activist policymakers shifted from expansive to contractive policies and then back again every few years. This produced rising average unemployment and rising inflation. Several countries, including the United States, experimented with price and wage controls. We thought the trend toward controls, rising unemployment, and inflation was based on mistaken ideas about how the economy worked and what policy could or should do.

Looking for a way to improve public discussion of economic policy, Karl and I started the Shadow Open Market Committee in 1973. The committee brought together economists from universities and businesses who wanted to change policies by creating a public demand for more stable policies and lower inflation. At first we concentrated on monetary policy and inflation. Later we broadened our interest to include issues such as growth of the public sector, tax policy, and restrictions on international trade and capital movements.

You and the other members of the Shadow Open Market Committee are generally regarded as "monetarists." What is a monetarist? And do you agree that you are one?

When Karl Brunner coined the term *monetarism* in 1968, he defined it by stating three propositions: First, monetary impulses are important for changes in output, employment, and prices. Second, money growth is the most reliable measure of the monetary impulse. And third, monetary authorities such as central banks can control money growth in an economy like the United States. If being a monetarist means that I accept these propositions, then yes I am a monetarist because they remain true. However, monetarism has been given many meanings that have no connection to money or monetary economics. These political or journalistic usages are an entirely different matter.

In the past decade, some economists have proposed a "real business cycle" theory based on the idea that monetary disturbances are not very important sources of economic fluctuations. What's your view of the new theory?

Real business cycle theorists worked out the often noticed but undeveloped cyclical implications of changes in aggregate supply. This is an important development for theory, but we should not overstate its practical importance. The largest fluctuations that countries experience still appear to result from changes in monetary conditions. I think of the depression of the early 1930s, the decision by Great Britain to return to the gold standard at an overvalued exchange rate in 1925, the decisions by Britain and France in the 1980s to adopt a fixed exchange rate, the Federal Reserve's decision to double reserve requirement ratios in 1937, and the decisions in many countries to reduce inflation in the early 1980s. Each of these monetary disturbances produced relatively severe recessions. Monetary impulses are also important for some mild recessions or for expansions, but real factors like the oil shocks of the 1970s also affect output. These

"Economists had discussed the problems . . . for years, but Congress, the administration, the press, the public, and the regulators ignored the warnings."

"To develop economically, Russia must develop financially . . . A properly functioning financial system . . . encourages people to invest their savings at home."

experiences and many others suggest to me that the factors highlighted by real business cycle theories are a supplement to—not a substitute for—monetary impulses in theories of the cycle. It is also important to distinguish between recessions in which the economy departs from and returns to a long-term growth path and real disturbances like the oil shocks that permanently reduce the level of output.

If the president and Congress gave you carte blanche to fix the economy, what would be your recipe?

I would start by introducing five rules, in some cases constitutional rules, for monetary and fiscal policies to increase certainty, improve economic efficiency, and enhance stability of the domestic and international value of money.

First, the share of government spending relative to total spending would be fixed, except in wartime or declared emergency. Second, to provide for countercyclical changes in fiscal policy, tax revenues would be set to equal government spending on a three- or four-year average. As a result, the government budget—properly measured to include many off-budget items—would have a deficit in recessions and a surplus during expansions or booms but would balance over time. Third, a broad-based consumption tax would replace the income tax to reduce the current bias against saving. Fourth, to maintain domestic price level stability, money would grow at a rate equal to the difference between the three-year moving average growth of real output and the three-year moving average growth of monetary velocity. Fifth, to reduce exchange rate fluctuations, I would try to encourage other countries—principally Germany and Japan—to follow a rule similar to the fourth rule. This should not be difficult, since they have followed a similar strategy in the past. Rules 4 and 5 together would permit smaller countries to fix their exchange rates and get the benefit of more stable internal and external values of money. This is a public good.

These proposals would be just a start. Regulation, international trading rules, and many micro policies deserve attention, too.

Your recipe contains a lot of rules. How would you make sure the rules are followed?

There is an old tradition that in a fixed exchange rate regime, a finance minister resigned if the currency had to be devalued. Devaluation was considered a policy failure. I have often suggested a similar procedure for monetary policy. If the central bank does not follow the agreed-upon rule, the bank's officials would have to resign. I would base fiscal rules on known past magnitudes, not forecasts of future values. Failure to follow the rule would require resignation by the chairpersons of the appropriations committees of Congress and the Director of the Budget. Too much attention is now given to processes and promises and too little to outcomes. Congress should be less concerned about who is appointed and how decisions are made and more concerned about the relation of outcomes to announced program or policy.

Why is the S&L industry in such a mess?

There is no single reason for the S&L problem. Some of the more important contributing causes were inflation, regulation of interest rates, deposit insurance, and regulatory accounting practices. Inflation imposed real losses on the S&Ls' mortgage portfolio and reduced the equity or net worth of most of these firms. Ceilings on the interest rates that S&Ls could pay caused a loss of their deposit base to less regulated institutions. Deposit insurance encouraged some of them to invest in very risky assets once their net worth had fallen to low levels or even to negative values. An S&L with zero or negative net worth got all of the gain if a risky investment succeeded, but the loss went to the deposit insurance fund—that is to say, the taxpayers.

Bankrupt S&Ls had a lot to gain and nothing much to lose if they took big risks. Many of these wild investments failed, adding to the losses. Government regulators, often prodded by Congress, looked away and even changed accounting rules to hide the losses from public view.

The S&L debacle was a major failure of regulation. Economists had discussed the problems of deposit insurance, risk, and accounting practices for years, but Congress, the administration, the press, the public, and the regulators ignored the warnings. There were many papers and conferences about the problem while it was developing, but bad politics overrode careful economic analysis.

What will it cost to clean up the S&L industry?

A best guess about the cost is $200 billion in present value terms, but it is only an informed guess. We won't know until the assets of the failed S&Ls are sold.

You've been studying Russia and Eastern Europe recently, especially their monetary problems and the problems arising from the freeing of markets. What do you think are the main problems for which *monetary* policy is part of the solution?

Monetary policy can provide a stable price level to help people plan rationally for the long term. To develop economically, Russia must develop financially. Stable money is not just a store of value. It is an efficient means of carrying out exchanges at low or minimum transaction and information costs. Low inflation encourages the development of an efficient financial system. A properly functioning financial system with stable prices, free of controls on currency and financial asset markets, encourages people to invest their savings at home. Inflation and currency controls contribute to capital flight, thereby reducing the resources available for investment. Freedom from controls, greater certainty, and price stability contribute to growth and living standards by reducing costs of transacting and costs of information about prices and values.

If a student in a principles of economics course remembers only a few lessons from the course, what should they be?

Three principles constitute the core of economics. First, all demand curves are downward sloping. Less is demanded at a high price than at a low price. Second, supply curves are upward sloping. More is offered at high prices than at low prices. Third, the longer the run or the greater the period of adjustment, the more varied are the alternatives available and the greater is the opportunity to substitute or change. These principles, when properly applied, will help a student to think through many problems correctly, including many that do not at first seem to be economic problems.

CHAPTER 25

EXPENDITURE DECISIONS AND GDP

After studying this chapter, you will be able to:

- Describe the relative magnitudes of the components of aggregate expenditure and their relative volatility
- Explain how households make consumption and saving decisions
- Explain how firms make investment decisions
- Explain what determines exports, imports, and net exports
- Derive the aggregate expenditure schedule and the aggregate expenditure curve
- Explain how aggregate expenditure is determined

Fear and Trembling in the Shopping Aisles

SOME HEADLINES FROM THE WINTER OF 1991: "AUTO Makers Hobble into the New Year with Little Hope for a Robust Recovery," "Consumer Borrowing Flat," "New Home Sales Down," "Consumer Confidence Slips Again," "Little Christmas Cheer for Retailers." Why all the fear and trembling over what happens in the shopping aisles? Besides a few manufacturers and stores, who really cares whether people buy a lot of gifts for the holidays or whether they buy cars and new homes? How does this affect the rest of us? What makes people decide to spend less and save more? ◆◆ It's not only consumer spending that stirs up hope and fear in the economy. At times, firms' orders for new plant and equipment grow to a flood, and at other times they become a trickle. At some times, government purchases of military hardware grows quickly—as it did in the 1980s and during the Gulf War of 1991—but at other times, it falls—as it did at the end of the Cold War. Our exports to the rest of the world ebb and flow with the changing economic fortunes of Europe and Japan. How do business investment, government purchases, and exports affect us? How much of the country's spending do they make up when compared with consumer spending? Are fluctuations in these components of aggregate expenditure sources of fluctuations in our job prospects and living standards?

◆◆◆◆ The spending that people do in shopping aisles spreads out in waves across the economy, affecting millions of people. In this chapter we study the composition of those waves and see why consumption has a big effect outside the stores. We also study the other components of aggregate expenditure—investment, government purchases of goods and services, and net exports. First, we'll learn about their relative magnitudes and volatility. Second, we'll explain how they are determined. Third, we'll see how the private components of aggregate spending along with government purchases interact to determine aggregate expenditure and GDP. ◆ ◆ Let's begin by looking at the components of aggregate expenditure.

The Components of Aggregate Expenditure

The components of aggregate expenditure are

- Consumption expenditure
- Investment
- Government purchases of goods and services
- Net exports (exports minus imports)

Relative Magnitudes

Figure 25.1 shows the relative magnitudes of the components of aggregate expenditure between 1970 and 1991. By far the biggest portion of aggregate expenditure is consumption expenditure, which ranges between 63 and 67 percent and averages 65 percent of total expenditure. The smallest portion is net exports, whose average value is close to zero. Investment ranges between 14 and 18 percent of GDP and averages 16 percent. Government purchases of goods and services are slightly larger than investment, ranging between 18 and 23 percent of GDP and averaging 21 percent.

FIGURE 25.1

The Components of Aggregate Expenditure: 1970–1991

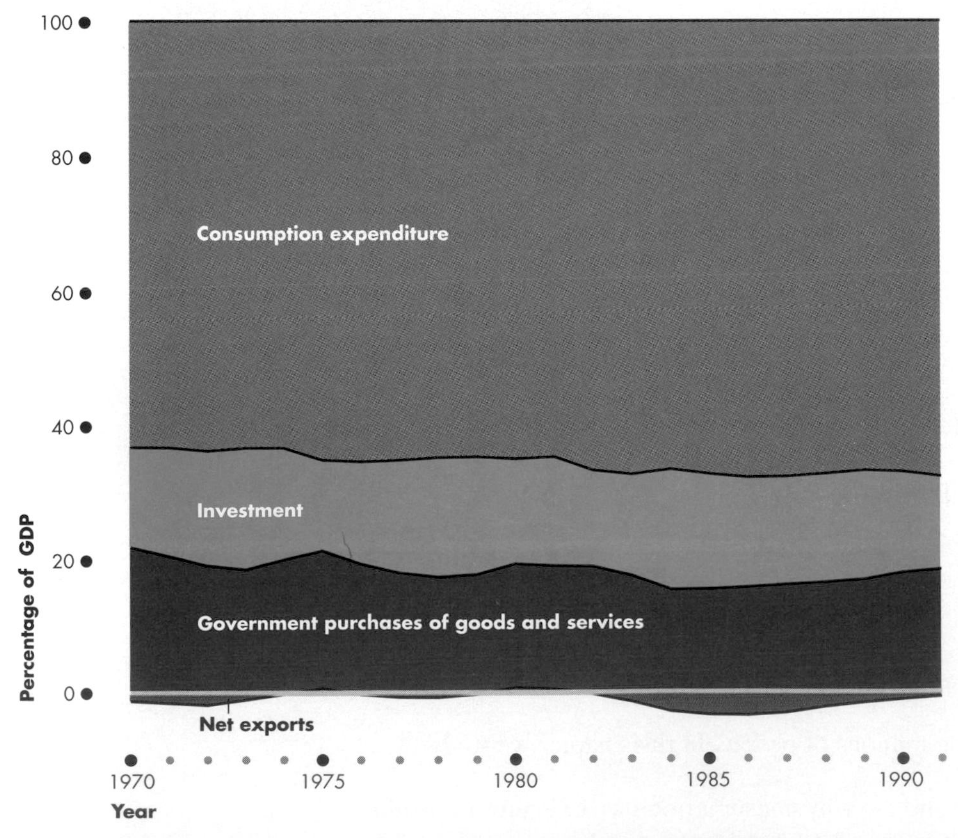

The biggest component of aggregate expenditure is consumption expenditure. It ranges between 63 and 67 percent of GDP and averages 65 percent. Investment averages 16 percent of GDP, fluctuating between 14 and 18 percent. Government expenditure on goods and services ranges between 18 and 23 percent of GDP and averages 21 percent of GDP. The smallest item is net exports and it averages approximately zero.

Relative Volatility

Figure 25.2 shows the relative volatility of the components of aggregate expenditure. The most volatile are investment and net exports. Consumption expenditure and government purchases of goods and services fluctuate much less than these two items.

Notice that although the fluctuations in consumption expenditure have a much smaller range than those in investment, the ups and downs of the two series move in sympathy with each other. Notice also that the three big declines in investment—in 1975, 1982, and 1991—occurred at precisely the time when the economy was in recession (recessions that we saw in Chapter 22, pp. 595–596 and 599, and in Chapter 24, pp. 655–660). Government purchases of goods and services were below trend between 1973 and 1984. But in the second half of the 1980s, they grew quickly and moved above trend. The fluctuations in net exports are similar in magnitude to those in investment, but these two components of aggregate expenditure tend to fluctuate in opposite directions—years of high investment are years of low net exports.

Let's study the choices that determine the size and volatility of the components of aggregate expenditure, beginning with the largest component, consumption expenditure.

FIGURE 25.2

Fluctuations in the Components of Aggregate Expenditure: 1970–1991

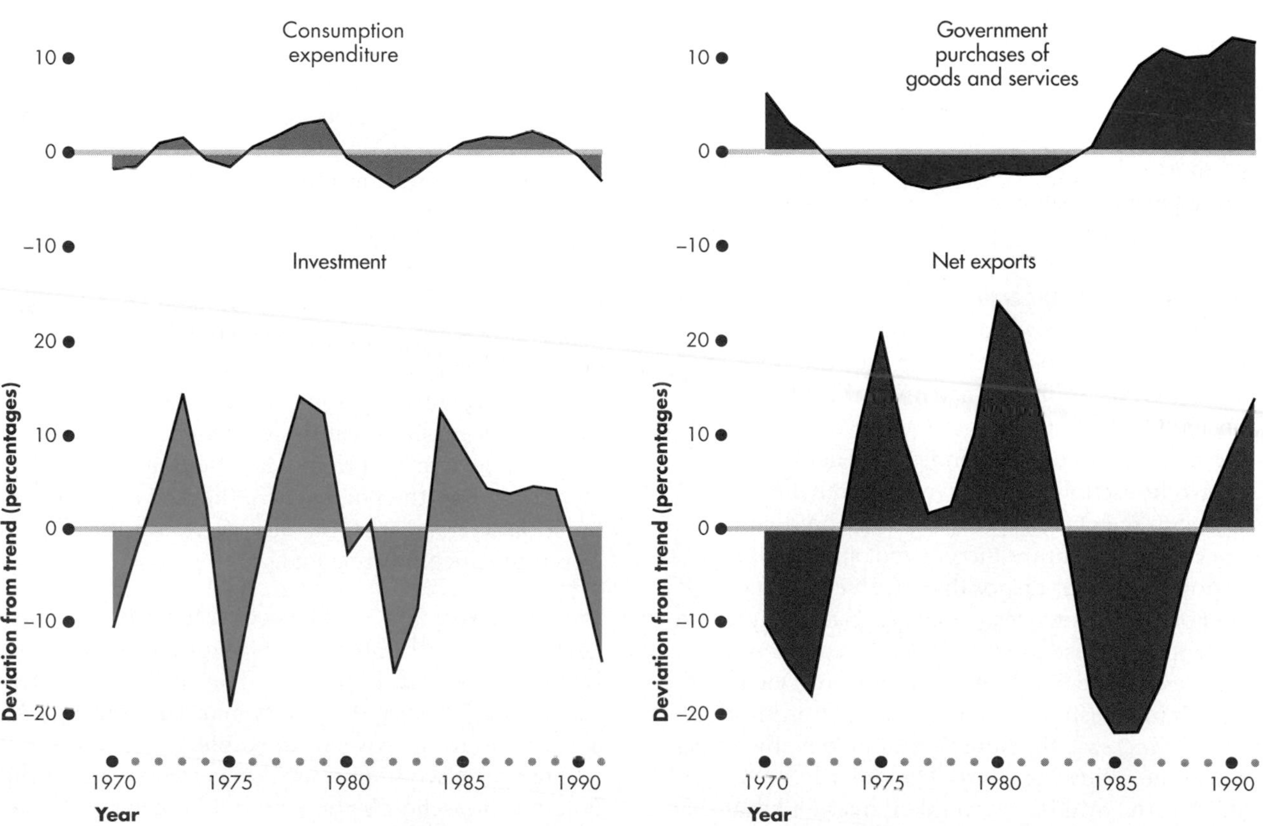

Fluctuations in each component of aggregate expenditure are shown as percentage deviations from trend. Although consumption expenditure is the biggest component of aggregate expenditure, it is the one that fluctuates least in percentage terms. Investment and net exports fluctuate most. Government purchases of goods and services show a strong increase in the 1980s. Net exports fluctuate in the direction opposite to investment.

Consumption Expenditure and Saving

Consumption expenditure is the value of the consumption goods and services bought by households. There are many factors that influence a household's consumption expenditure, but the two most important are

- Disposable income
- Expected future income

1. Disposable Income *Disposable income* is the aggregate income that households receive in exchange for supplying the services of factors of production plus transfers received from the government minus taxes. A household can do only two things with its disposable income: spend it on consumption goods and services or save it.

As a household's disposable income increases, so does its expenditure on food and beverages, clothing, accommodation, transportation, medical care, and most other goods and services. That is, a household's consumption expenditure increases as its income increases.

2. Expected Future Income A household's expected future income depends mainly on the security and income growth prospects of the jobs that its members do. Other things being equal, the higher a household's expected future income, the greater is its current consumption expenditure. That is, if there are two households that have the same disposable income in the current year, the household with the larger expected future income will spend a larger portion of current disposable income on consumption goods and services. Consider, for example, two households whose principal income earner is a senior executive in a large corporation. One executive has just been told of an important promotion that will increase the household's income by 50 percent in the following years. The other has just been told that the firm has been taken over and that there will be no further employment beyond the end of the year. The first household buys a new car and takes an expensive foreign vacation, thereby increasing its current consumption expenditure. The second household sells the family's second car and cancels its winter vacation plans, thereby cutting back on its current consumption expenditure.

The Consumption Function and the Saving Function

The relationship between consumption expenditure and disposable income, other things held constant, is called the **consumption function**. The consumption function has played an important role in macroeconomics over the past 50 years, and the story of its discovery is told in Our Advancing Knowledge on pp. 674–675. The relationship between saving and disposable income, other things held constant, is called the **saving function**. The consumption function and saving function for a typical household—the Polonius household—are shown in Fig. 25.3.

The Consumption Function The Polonius household's consumption function is plotted in Fig. 25.3(a). The horizontal axis measures disposable income, and the vertical axis measures consumption expenditure (both in thousands of dollars). The points labeled *a* through *f* in the figure correspond to the rows having the same letters in the table. For example, point *c* indicates disposable income of $20,000 and consumption of $18,000.

The 45° Line Figure 25.3(a) also contains a line labeled "45° line." This line connects the points at which consumption, measured on the vertical axis, equals disposable income, measured on the horizontal axis. When the consumption function is above the 45° line, consumption exceeds disposable income; when the consumption function is below the 45° line, consumption is less than disposable income; and at the point where the consumption function intersects the 45° line, consumption and disposable income are equal.

The Saving Function The saving function is graphed in Fig. 25.3(b). The horizontal axis is exactly the same as that in part (a). The vertical axis measures saving. Again, the points marked *a* through *f* correspond to the rows of the table.

There are two important things to note about the Polonius household's consumption and saving functions. First, even if the Polonius household has no disposable income, it still consumes. It does so by having a negative level of saving. Negative saving is called **dissaving.** Households that consume more than their disposable income do so either by living

FIGURE 25.3

The Polonius Household's Consumption Function and Saving Function

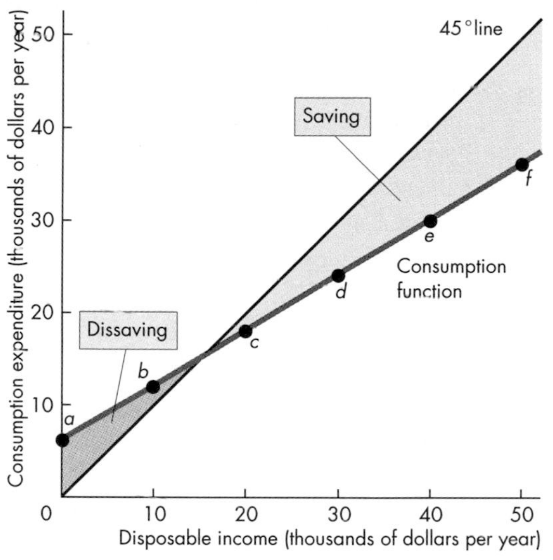

(a) Consumption function

(b) Saving function

	Disposable income	Consumption expenditure	Saving
	(thousands of dollars per year)		
a	0	6	–6
b	10	12	–2
c	20	18	2
d	30	24	6
e	40	30	10
f	50	36	14

The table sets out the consumption and saving plan of the Polonius household at various levels of disposable income. Part (a) of the figure shows the relationship between consumption expenditure and disposable income (the consumption function). Part (b) shows the relationship between saving and disposable income (the saving function). Points *a* through *f* on the consumption and saving functions correspond to the rows in the table.

The 45° line in part (a) is the line of equality between consumption expenditure and disposable income. The Polonius household's consumption expenditure and saving equals its disposable income. When the consumption function is above the 45° line, saving is negative (dissaving occurs) and the saving function is below the horizontal axis. When the consumption function is below the 45° line, saving is positive and the saving function is above the horizontal axis. At the point where the consumption function intersects the 45° line, all disposable income is consumed, saving is zero, and the saving function intersects the horizontal axis.

off assets or by borrowing, a situation that cannot, of course, last forever.

Second, as the Polonius household's disposable income increases, so does the amount that it plans to spend on consumption and the amount that it plans to save. Since a household can only consume or save its disposable income, these two items always add up to disposable income. That is, consumption and saving plans are consistent with disposable income.

This relationship between the consumption function and the saving function can be seen by looking at the two parts of the figure. When the saving function is below the horizontal axis, saving is negative (dissaving) and the consumption function is above the 45° line. When the saving function is above the horizontal axis, saving is positive and the consumption function is below the 45° line. When the saving function intersects the horizontal axis, saving is zero and the consumption function intersects the 45° line.

Other Influences on Consumption Expenditure and Saving Changes in factors other than disposable

ISCOVERING the CONSUMPTION FUNCTION

The theory that consumption is determined by disposable income was proposed by John Maynard Keynes in 1936. With newly available national income data compiled by Simon Kuznets supporting Keynes's theory, it was instantly accepted.

During the 1940s and 1950s, a lot of additional data were collected, some of which revealed shortcomings in Keynes's theory. By the late 1940s, the Keynesian consumption function began to make forecasting errors. The propensity to consume—what Keynes called a "fundamental psychological law"—was revealed to be increasing and to depend on whether a person was young or old, black or white, or from an urban or rural area.

These failings brought forth two new theories—Franco Modigliani's life-cycle hypothesis and Milton Friedman's permanent income hypothesis—based on the proposition that consumption is determined by wealth and wealth depends on current and future income. Other things being equal, the wealthier a person is, the more he or she consumes. But only permanent and previously unexpected changes in income bring changes in wealth and consumption. Temporary changes in income or changes that have been foreseen change wealth by little and bring only small changes in consumption.

The revolution in macroeconomics of the 1970s brought the next reappraisal of consumption and a rational expectations theory of consumption proposed by Robert Hall of Stanford University. Hall started from the same point as Modigliani and Friedman: consumption depends on wealth and wealth depends on future income. But to make consumption decisions, people must form expectations of future income using whatever information is available. Expectations change only as a result of new information, which arrives at random. Therefore people's estimates of how wealthy they are, together with their consumption, change at random. No variable other than current consumption is of any value for predicting future consumption. Consumption and income are correlated, but changes in income do not cause changes in consumption.

"The fundamental psychological law, upon which we are entitled to depend with confidence . . . is that [people] are disposed . . . to increase their consumption as their income increases, but not by as much as the increase in their income."

John Maynard Keynes
General Theory

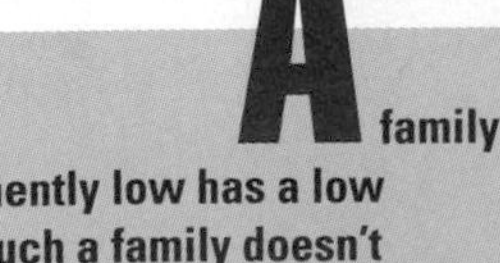

family whose income is permanently low has a low consumption level. But such a family doesn't always spend all its income every week. Instead, it saves a small amount to smooth its consumption between one year and the next. The amount that such a family saves is influenced by its stage in the life cycle. A young family saves a larger fraction of its income than an older family that has exactly the same level of permanent income. For most low-income families, saving does not mean putting money in the bank or in stocks and bonds. It means buying a home, buying life insurance, and paying social security taxes.

College students usually have low incomes. But they consume at a much higher level than most people whose incomes are similar to theirs. They enjoy a higher standard of housing and consume a much wider range of goods and services—from books and compact discs to athletic facilities and live concerts—than other people with similar incomes. The reason: college students have a high expected future income and, therefore, a high *permanent* income. They sustain a high consumption level by consuming all their income and by taking student loans that enable them to consume beyond their current income level.

John Maynard Keynes: A *Macroeconomic Revolutionary*

When John Maynard Keynes (1883–1946) of Cambridge, England, published his *General Theory of Employment, Interest, and Money* in 1936, he set off a revolution. The centerpieces of Keynes's theory of employment and income were the consumption function and the multiplier. Like all intellectual revolutions, this one was rejected by the older generation and embraced eagerly by the young. Many of Keynes's young adherents were in Cambridge, England (among them Joan Robinson), but many were in Cambridge, Massachusetts.

Keynes was one of the chief architects of the International Monetary Fund and visited the United States to finalize arrangements for the world's new monetary order as World War II was ending. He used the occasion to drop in on the Keynesians of Cambridge, Massachusetts. Asked on his return to England what he thought of his American disciples, he reported that they were far more Keynesian than he!

income that influence consumption expenditure shift both the consumption function and the saving function. For example, an increase in expected future income increases consumption expenditure and decreases saving. In such a case, the consumption function shifts upward and the saving function shifts downward. It is common for shifts like these to occur when the economy begins to recover from a recession. Going into the recession, people expect lower future incomes, but when the recovery begins, they expect higher future incomes. The beginning of the recovery from the 1991 recession was such an occasion—see Reading Between the Lines, pp. 678–679.

The Average Propensities to Consume and to Save

The **average propensity to consume** (*APC*) is consumption expenditure divided by disposable income. Table 25.1(a) shows you how to calculate the average propensity to consume. Let's do a sample calculation. At a disposable income of $20,000, the Polonius household consumes $18,000. Its average propensity to consume is $18,000 divided by $20,000, which equals 0.9.

As you can see from the numbers in the table, the average propensity to consume declines as disposable income rises. At a disposable income of $10,000, the household consumes more than its income, so its average propensity to consume is greater than 1. But at a disposable income of $50,000 the household consumes only $36,000, so its average propensity to consume is $36,000 divided by $50,000, which equals 0.72.

The **average propensity to save** (*APS*) is saving divided by disposable income. Table 25.1(a) shows you how to calculate the average propensity to save. For example, when disposable income is $20,000 the Polonius household saves $2,000, so the average propensity to save is $2,000 divided by $20,000, which equals 0.1. When saving is negative, the average propensity to save is negative. As disposable income increases, the average propensity to save increases.

As disposable income increases, the average propensity to consume falls and the average propensity to save rises. Equivalently, as disposable income increases, the fraction of income saved increases and the fraction of income consumed decreases. These patterns in the average propensities to consume and save reflect the fact that people with very low disposable incomes are so poor that their income is not even sufficient to meet their consumption expenditure. Consumption expenditure exceeds disposable income. As people's incomes increase, they are able to meet their consumption requirements with a lower and lower fraction of their disposable income.

The sum of the average propensity to consume and the average propensity to save is equal to 1. These two average propensities add up to 1 because consumption and saving exhaust disposable income. Each dollar of disposable income is either consumed or saved.

You can see that the two average propensities add up to 1 by using the following equation:

$$C + S = YD.$$

Divide both sides of the equation by disposable income to obtain

$$C/YD + S/YD = 1.$$

C/YD is the *average propensity to consume*, and S/YD is *average propensity to save*. Thus

$$APC + APS = 1.$$

The Marginal Propensities to Consume and to Save

The last dollar of disposable income received is called the marginal dollar. Part of that marginal dollar is consumed, and part of it is saved. The allocation of the marginal dollar between consumption expenditure and saving is determined by the marginal propensities to consume and to save.

The **marginal propensity to consume** (*MPC*) is the fraction of the last dollar of disposable income that is spent on consumption goods and services. It is calculated as the change in consumption expenditure divided by the change in disposable income. The **marginal propensity to save** (*MPS*) is the fraction of the last dollar of disposable income that is saved. The marginal propensity to save is calculated as the change in saving divided by the change in disposable income.

Table 25.1(b) shows the calculation of the Polonius household's marginal propensities to consume and to save. Looking at part (a) of the table, you can see that disposable income increases by $10,000 as we move from one row to the next—

TABLE 25.1

Average and Marginal Propensities to Consume and to Save

(a) Calculating average propensities to consume and to save

Disposable income *(YD)*	Consumption expenditure *(C)*	Saving *(S)*	*APC* *(C/YD)*	*APS* *(S/YD)*
	(dollars per year)			
0	**6,000**	**−6,000**	—	—
10,000	**12,000**	**−2,000**	**1.20**	**−0.20**
20,000	**18,000**	**2,000**	**0.90**	**0.10**
30,000	**24,000**	**6,000**	**0.80**	**0.20**
40,000	**30,000**	**10,000**	**0.75**	**0.25**
50,000	**36,000**	**14,000**	**0.72**	**0.28**

(b) Calculating marginal propensities to consume and to save

Change in disposable income	ΔYD = 10,000	
Change in consumption	ΔC = 6,000	
Change in saving	ΔS = 4,000	
Marginal propensity to consume	*MPC* = $\Delta C/\Delta YD$	= 0.6
Marginal propensity to save	*MPS* = $\Delta S/\Delta YD$	= 0.4

Consumption and saving depend on disposable income. At zero disposable income, some consumption is undertaken and saving is negative (dissaving occurs). As disposable income increases, so do both consumption and saving. The average propensities to consume and to save are calculated in part (a). The average propensity to consume—the ratio of consumption to disposable income—declines as disposable income increases; the average propensity to save—the ratio of saving to disposable income—increases as disposable income increases. These two average propensities sum to 1. Each additional—or *marginal*—dollar of disposable income is either consumed or saved. Part (b) calculates the marginal propensities to consume and to save. The marginal propensity to consume is the change in consumption that results from a $1 change in disposable income. The marginal propensity to save is the change in saving that results from a $1 change in disposable income. The marginal propensities to consume and to save sum to 1.

$10,000 is the change in disposable income. You can also see from part (a) that when disposable income increases by $10,000, consumption increases by $6,000. The marginal propensity to consume—the change in consumption divided by the change in disposable income—is therefore $6,000 divided by $10,000, which equals 0.6. The Polonius household's marginal propensity to consume is constant. It is the same at each level of disposable income. Out of a marginal dollar of disposable income, 60¢ is spent on consumption goods and services.

Part (b) of the table also shows the calculation of the marginal propensity to save. You can see from that part of the table that when disposable income increases by $10,000, saving increases by $4,000. The marginal propensity to save—the change in saving divided by the change in disposable income—is therefore $4,000 divided by $10,000, which equals 0.4. The Polonius household's marginal propensity to save is constant. It is the same at each level of disposable income. Out of the last dollar of disposable income, 40¢ is saved.

The Consumption Function in Action

The New York Times, July 30, 1991

June Gains of 0.5% Posted for Income and Spending

(AP)—Personal income and consumer spending both rose five-tenths of 1 percent in June, the Government said today in a report that analysts saw as a sign that the economy would continue to grow in the third quarter.

"It gives consumer spending quite a bit of momentum going into the third quarter," said Laurence H. Meyer, head of a St. Louis economic forecasting firm. "It's another piece of data that the third quarter is locked in as fairly solid." He added that he thought the recovery would be weaker than normal.

Most analysts are projecting a weaker rebound than the average turnaround in the eight previous recessions since World War II.

Mr. Meyer said there was a significant risk that the economy would slow in the fourth quarter. He said a double-dip recession was possible, although he considered a subdued recovery more likely.

Income growth is needed to continue the economic recovery by providing the resources for consumer spending. Personal consumption represents two-thirds of the nation's economic activity.

Fifth Straight Income Rise

The Commerce Department report said personal income in June totaled $4.80 trillion at a seasonally adjusted annual rate, up from $4.78 trillion a month earlier. It was the fifth straight monthly gain.

At the same time, it said consumer spending totaled $3.83 trillion at an annual rate, up from $3.81 trillion in May. It was the second consecutive gain. . . .

The department reported last week that consumer spending from April through June rose at a 3.6 percent annual rate, the first quarterly increase since the July–September period of 1990.

That helped raise the gross national product by an annual rate of four-tenths of 1 percent, the first advance after two quarters of decline—the generally accepted definition of a recession.

Disposable income—income after taxes—rose five-tenths of 1 percent in June, slightly less than the six-tenths of 1 percent increase a month earlier.

The difference between income and spending meant that the savings rate was the same as in May, at 3.5 percent, but down from 4.1 percent in April.

Wages and salaries rose by $26.6 billion after a $17.2 billion gain in the previous month.

The Essence of the Story

The Commerce Department reported the data in the table for June 1991 and revised data for May 1991.

The Commerce Department also reported the following:

- Personal income had increased for five straight months.
- Consumer spending increased at a 3.6 percent annual rate in the second quarter of 1991, the first quarterly increase since the third quarter of 1990.
- The saving rate of 3.5 percent was down from 4.1 percent rate in April.

The increase in consumer spending helped boost the gross national product at a 0.4 percent annual rate, the first advance after two quarters of decline—the definition of a recession. Because consumer spending represents about two thirds of economic activity, its growth boosted GNP growth and was seen as a sign of recovery from recession.

Background and Analysis

When disposable income increases, consumption expenditure increases by an amount determined by the marginal propensity to consume. Such an increase is shown as a movement along a consumption function.

Consumption expenditure also increases when expected future income increases. Such an increase is shown as an upward shift in the consumption function.

The data reported by the Commerce Department in the news story are consistent with this theory of the consumption function.

The increase in disposable income in June induced an increase in consumption expenditure—there was a movement along the May consumption function shown in the figure.

But consumption expenditure increased by the same amount as the increase in disposable income and by a larger amount than implied by the marginal propensity to consume—there was a shift in the consumption function, as shown in the figure.

This additional increase in consumption expenditure resulted from an increase in expected future income—an expectation of continued recovery from recession.

An increase in income and consumption expenditure (as in June 1991) signals that the economy is recovering from recession.

An increase in consumption expenditure in excess of that implied by the marginal propensity to consume signals an expectation of continued recovery.

Item	May 1991	June 1991
Personal incomes	**$4.78 trillion**	**$4.80 trillion**
Consumer spending	**$3.81 trillion**	**$3.83 trillion**
Increase in personal incomes	—	**0.5%**
Increase in consumer spending	—	**0.5%**
Increase in disposable incomes	**0.6%**	**0.5%**
Saving rate	**3.5%**	**3.5%**
Increase in wages and salaries	**$17.2 billion**	**$26.6 billion**

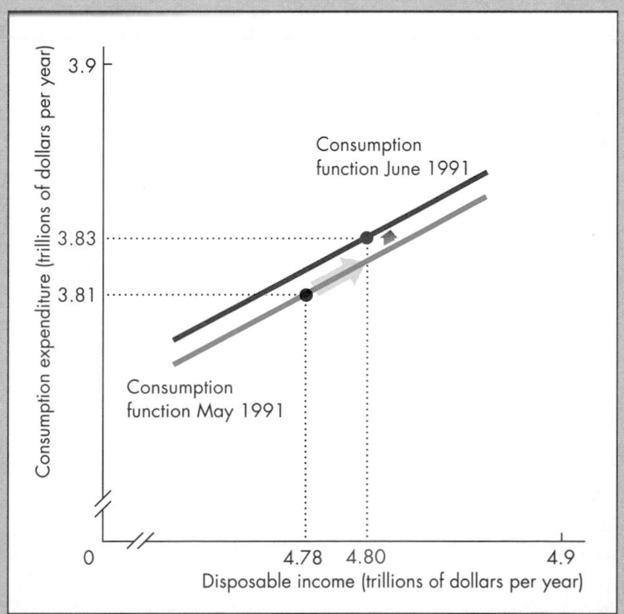

The marginal propensity to consume plus the marginal propensity to save equals 1. Each additional dollar must be either consumed or spent. In this example, when disposable income increases by $1, 60¢ more is spent and 40¢ more is saved. That is,

$$MPC + MPS = 1.$$

Marginal Propensities and Slopes The marginal propensity to consume is equal to the slope of the consumption function. You can see this equality by looking back at Fig. 25.3. In that figure, the consumption function has a constant slope that can be measured as the change in consumption divided by the change in income. For example, when income increases from $20,000 to $30,000—an increase of $10,000—consumption increases from $18,000 to $24,000—an increase of $6,000. The slope of the consumption function is $6,000 divided by $10,000, which equals 0.6—the same value as the marginal propensity to consume that we calculated in Table 25.1.

The marginal propensity to save is equal to the slope of the saving function. You can see this equality by again looking back at Fig. 25.3. In this case, when income increases by $10,000, saving increases by $4,000. The slope of the saving function is $4,000 divided by $10,000, which equals 0.4—the same value as the marginal propensity to save that we calculated in Table 25.1.

REVIEW

Consumption expenditure is influenced by many factors, but the two most important are disposable income and expected future income. Households allocate their disposable income to either consumption expenditure or saving. The relationship between consumption expenditure and disposable income, other things held constant, is the *consumption function*, and the relationship between saving and disposable income, other things held constant, is the *saving function*. Changes in factors other than disposable income that influence consumption expenditure shift the consumption and saving functions. ◆◆ The change in consumption expenditure divided by the change in disposable income, other things held constant, is the *marginal propensity to consume* (*MPC*), and the change in saving divided by the change in disposable income, other things held constant, is the *marginal propensity to save* (*MPS*). Because consumption expenditure plus saving equals disposable income, $MPC + MPS = 1$. ◆

We've studied the consumption function of a household. Let's now look at the U.S. consumption function.

The U.S. Consumption Function

Data for consumption expenditure and disposable income in the United States for the years 1970 to 1991 are shown in Fig. 25.4(a). The vertical axis measures consumption expenditure (in 1987 dollars), and the horizontal axis measures disposable income (also in 1987 dollars). Each point identified by a blue dot represents consumption expenditure and disposable income for a particular year.

The orange line highlights the average relationship between consumption expenditure and disposable income and is an estimate of the U.S. consumption function. It tells us that, on the average, consumption expenditure has been 90 percent of disposable income. The slope of this consumption function—which is also the marginal propensity to consume—is 0.9. The relationship between consumption expenditure and disposable income in any given year does not fall exactly on the orange line. The reason is that the position of the consumption function depends on the other factors that influence consumption expenditure, and as a result the consumption function shifts over time.

Consumption as a Function of GDP Our purpose in developing a theory of the consumption function is to explain the determination of aggregate expenditure and real GDP. To achieve this purpose, we need to establish the relationship between consumption expenditure and real GDP—consumption expenditure as a function of real GDP.

The blue dots in Fig. 25.4(b) show consumption expenditure and real GDP in the United States for each year between 1970 and 1991. The orange line shows consumption expenditure as a function of real GDP. Consumption expenditure is a function of real GDP because disposable income depends on real GDP. Disposable income is real GDP minus net taxes (net taxes are taxes minus transfer payments).

FIGURE 25.4

The U.S. Consumption Function

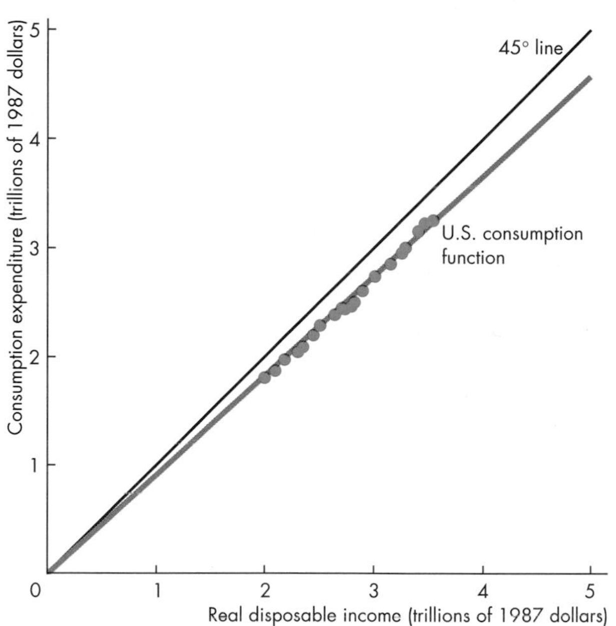

(a) Consumption as a function of disposable income

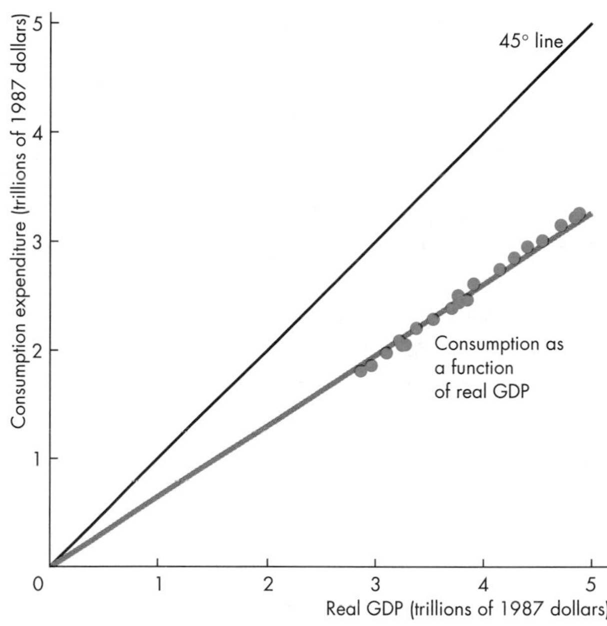

(b) Consumption as a function of real GDP

Real GDP (Y)	Disposable income ($YD = 0.7Y$)	Consumption expenditure ($C = 0.9YD = 0.63Y$)
	(trillions of 1987 dollars)	
1.0	**0.7**	**0.63**
2.0	**1.4**	**1.26**
3.0	**2.1**	**1.89**
4.0	**2.8**	**2.52**

Part (a) shows the U.S. consumption function—the relationship between real consumption expenditure and real disposable income—for each year between 1970 and 1991. Each blue point in the figure represents real consumption expenditure and real disposable income for a particular year. The orange line shows the average relationship between consumption expenditure and disposable income—an estimate of the U.S. consumption function. This consumption function has a slope and a marginal propensity to consume of 0.9.

Part (b) shows the relationship between consumption expenditure and real GDP. This relationship takes into account the fact that as real GDP increases, so do net taxes. The marginal propensity to consume out of real GDP is approximately 0.63. The connection between consumption as a function of disposable income and consumption as a function of real GDP is shown in the table. The tax rate is 30 percent, so real disposable income is 0.7 times real GDP. The marginal propensity to consume is 0.9. Combining a tax rate of 30 percent with a marginal propensity to consume of 0.9 gives a marginal propensity to consume out of real GDP of 0.63.

But net taxes increase as real GDP increases. Almost all the taxes that we pay—personal taxes, corporate taxes, and social security taxes—increase as our incomes increase. Transfer payments, such as social security and welfare benefits, decrease as our incomes increase. (Social security benefits due to retirement do not vary with income, but aggregate transfer payments do vary with income.) Since taxes increase and transfers decrease, net taxes clearly increase as incomes increase. It turns out that there is a tendency for net taxes to be a fairly stable 30 percent of real GDP. If 30 percent of real GDP is paid in net taxes (taxes minus transfers), 70 percent (or 0.7) of real GDP is available as disposable income.

The table in Fig. 25.4 sets out the relationship between real GDP, disposable income, and consumption expenditure. It incorporates the 0.7 relationship between real GDP and disposable income. For example, if real GDP is $3 trillion, disposable income is 0.7 of that amount, which is $2.1 trillion. The table also shows us the amount of consumption expenditure at various levels of disposable income. We have seen that the marginal propensity to consume is 0.9. Thus, if disposable income is $2.1 trillion, consumption expenditure is 0.9 of that amount, which is $1.89 trillion.

The change in consumption expenditure divided by the change in real GDP is the **marginal propensity to consume out of real GDP.** It is measured by the slope of the orange line in Fig. 25.4(b). Since nine tenths (0.9) of disposable income is consumed and since 70 percent (0.7) of real GDP is available as disposable income, the marginal propensity to consume out of real GDP is 0.63 (0.9 × 0.7, which equals 0.63).

REVIEW

Of all the influences on consumption expenditure, disposable income is the most important. Consumption expenditure in the United States is a function of disposable income. Disposable income is, in turn, related to GDP. Therefore consumption expenditure is a function of GDP. In the United States today, each additional dollar of GDP generates, on the average, an additional 63¢ of consumption expenditure. ◆

The theory of the consumption function has an important implication. Because consumption expenditure is determined mainly by disposable income, most of the changes in consumption expenditure result from changes in income and are not causes of those income changes. It is fluctuations in other components of aggregate expenditure that are the most important sources of fluctuations in income. And the most important of these is investment.

Investment

Gross *investment* is the purchase of new buildings, new plant and equipment, and additions to inventories. It has two components: *net investment*—additions to existing capital—and *replacement investment*—purchases to replace worn out or depreciated capital. As we saw in Fig. 25.2, gross investment is a volatile element of aggregate expenditure. What determines gross investment, and why does it fluctuate so much? The answer lies in the investment decisions of firms—in the answers to questions like these: How does Chrysler decide how much to spend on a new car assembly plant? What determines IBM's outlays on new computer designs? How does AT&T choose what it will spend on fiber-optic communications systems? Let's answer such questions.

Firms' Investment Decisions

The main influences on firms' investment decisions are

- Real interest rates
- Profit expectations
- Existing capital

1. Real Interest Rates The **real interest rate** is the interest rate paid by a borrower and received by a lender after taking into account changes in the value of money resulting from inflation. It is approximately equal to the agreed interest rate (called the *nominal* interest rate) minus the inflation rate. To see why, suppose that prices are rising by 10 percent a year. Each dollar borrowed for one year is repaid at the end of the year with a dollar that is worth only 90¢ today. The borrower gains and the lender loses 10¢ on each dollar. This loss must be subtracted from the agreed interest rate to find the interest *really* paid and received—the real interest rate. If the nominal interest rate is 20 percent a year, the real interest rate is only 10 percent a year.

Firms sometimes pay for capital goods with money they have borrowed, and sometimes they use their own funds—called retained earnings. But regardless of the method of financing an investment project, the real interest rate is part of its *opportunity cost*. The real interest paid on borrowed funds is a direct cost. The real interest cost of using retained earnings arises because these funds could be lent to another firm at the going real interest rate, generating income. The real interest income forgone is the opportunity cost of using retained earnings to finance an investment project.

The lower the real interest rate, the lower is the opportunity cost of any given investment project. Some investment projects that are not profitable at a high real interest rate become profitable at a low real interest rate. The lower the real interest rate, the larger is the number of investment projects that are profitable and, therefore, the greater is the amount of investment.

Let's consider an example. Suppose that Chrysler is contemplating building a new automobile assembly line at a cost of $100 million. The assembly line is expected to produce cars for three years, and then it will be scrapped completely and replaced with a new line that produces an entirely new range of models. Chrysler's expected net revenue is $20 million in each of the first two years and $100 million in the third year. Net revenue is the difference between the total revenue from car sales and the costs of producing those cars. In calculating net revenue, we do not take into account the initial cost of the assembly line or the interest that has to be paid on it. We take separate account of these costs. To build the assembly line, Chrysler plans to borrow the initial $100 million and at the end of each year to use its expected net revenue to pay the interest on the loan outstanding along with as much of the loan as it can. Does it pay Chrysler to invest $100 million in this car assembly line? The answer depends on the real interest rate.

Case 1 in Fig. 25.5 shows what happens if the interest rate is 20 percent per year. (We'll assume the expected inflation rate to be zero, so the expected real interest rate is also 20 percent a year. This is an unlikely high rate but makes the numbers work out easily.) Chrysler borrows $100 million and at the end of the first year has to pay $20 million in interest. It has a net revenue of $20 million and so can just meet this interest payment but cannot reduce the size of its outstanding loan. At the end of the second year, it is in exactly the same situation as at the end of the first. It owes another $20 million on its outstanding loan. Again its revenue just covers the interest payment. At the end of the third year, Chrysler owes another $20 million in interest payments plus the $100 million outstanding loan. Therefore it has to pay $120 million. But net revenue in the third year is only $100 million, so Chrysler has a $20 million loss on this project.

Case 2 in Fig. 25.5 shows what happens if the real interest rate is 10 percent per year. (Again, we'll assume that the expected inflation rate is zero, so the expected real interest rate is also 10 percent a year.) In this case, Chrysler owes $10 million in interest at the end of the first year. Since it has $20 million of revenue, it can make this interest payment and reduce its outstanding loan to $90 million. In the second year, the interest owing on the loan is $9 million (10 percent of $90 million). Again, with revenue of $20 million, Chrysler pays the interest and reduces its outstanding loan by $11 million to $79 million. In the third and final year of the project, the interest on the loan is $7.9 million (10 percent of $79 million), so the total amount owing—the outstanding loan plus the interest—is $86.9 million. Chrysler's revenue in year 3 is $100 million, so it repays the loan, pays the interest, and pockets the balance, a profit of $13.1 million. If Chrysler builds the assembly line, it expects to make a profit of $13.1 million.

You can see that at a real interest rate of 20 percent a year, it does not pay Chrysler to invest in this car assembly plant. At a 10 percent real interest rate, it does pay. The lower the real interest rate, the larger is the number of projects, such as the one considered here, that yield a positive net profit. Thus the lower the real interest rate, the larger is the amount of investment.

2. Profit Expectations The higher the expected profitability of new capital equipment, the greater is the amount of investment. Chrysler's assembly line investment decision illustrates this effect. To decide whether or not to build the assembly line, Chrysler has to work out its net revenue. To perform that calculation, it has to work out the total revenue from car sales, which, in turn, are affected by its expectations of car prices and the share of the market that it can attain. Chrysler also has to figure out its operating costs, which include the wages of its assembly workers and the costs of the products that it buys from other producers. The larger the net revenue

FIGURE 25.5

Investment in an Automobile Assembly Line

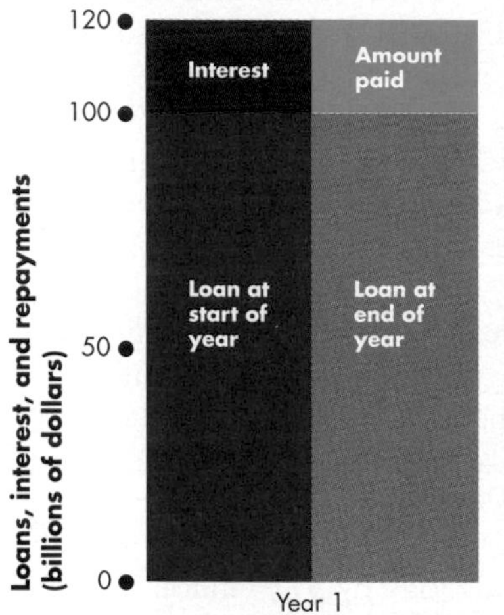

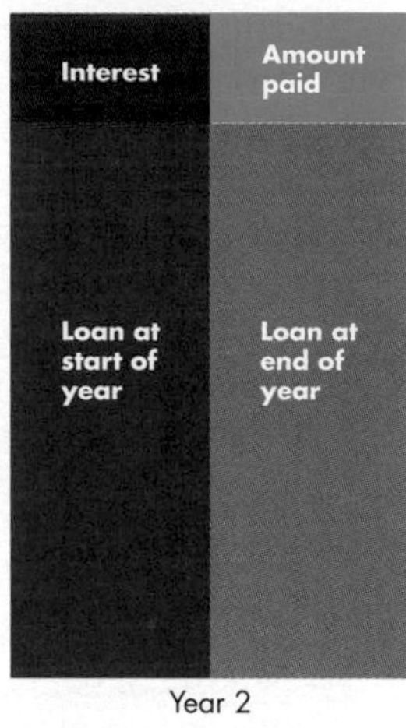

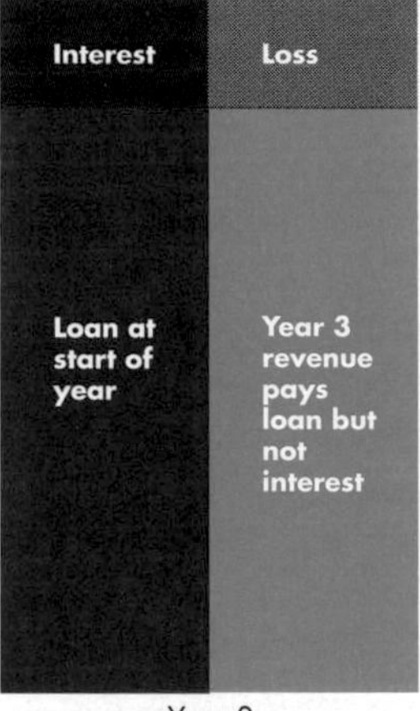

Case 1: Real interest rate is 20 percent

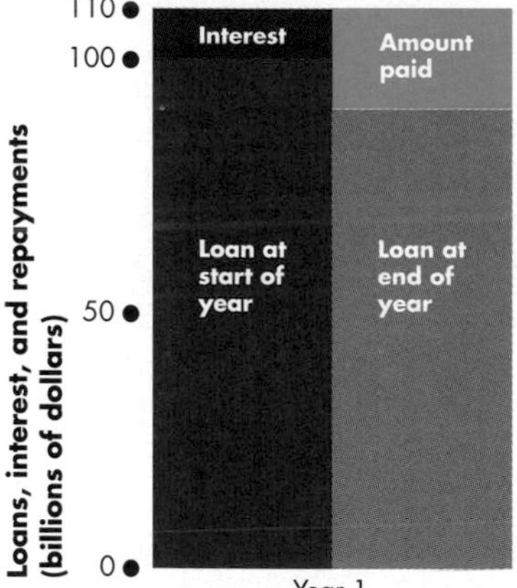

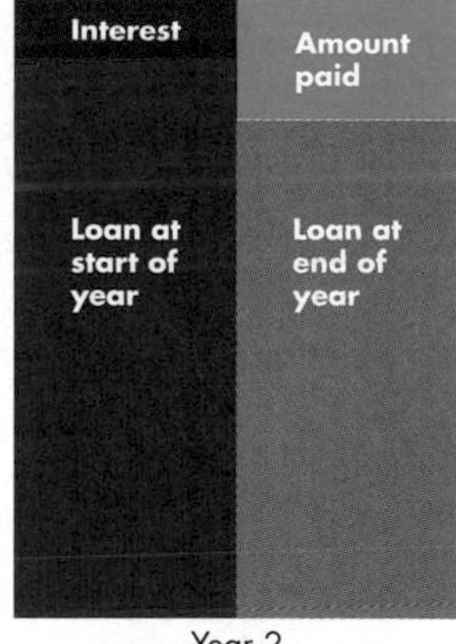

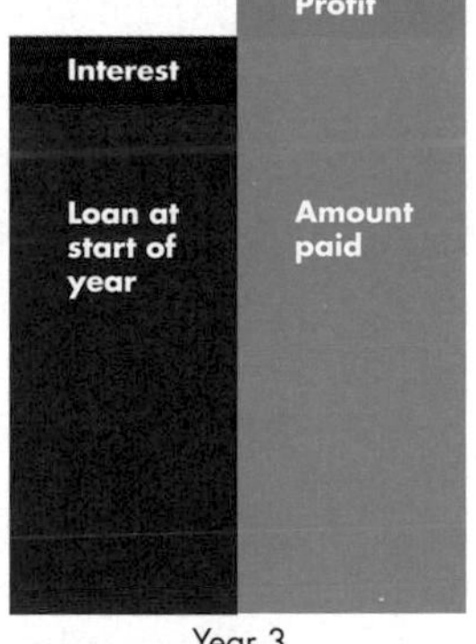

Case 2: Real interest rate is 10 percent

An automobile assembly line costs $100 million to build. It is expected to generate the following revenue:

Year 1	$20 million
Year 2	$20 million
Year 3	$100 million

The line will then be scrapped and replaced by a new one. In case 1, the real interest rate is 20 percent per year. The revenue stream is too low to cover the total expense, and the project is not worth undertaking. In case 2, the real interest rate is 10 percent per year, and the project is profitable. The lower the real interest rate, the larger is the number of projects that are profitable and that are undertaken.

that it anticipates, the more profitable is the investment project that generates those net revenues and the more likely it is that the project will be undertaken.

There are many influences on profit expectations themselves. Among the more important ones are taxes on company profits, the phase of the business cycle through which the economy is passing, and the state of global relations and tensions. For example, the collapse of the Soviet Union and the emergence of the new republics of Eastern Europe are likely to have a large impact on profit expectations in the 1990s—positive in some industries and negative in others.

3. Existing Capital A firm's existing capital influences its investment decisions in two ways. First, the larger the amount of existing capital, other things being equal, the greater is the amount of depreciation and the larger is the amount of replacement investment. But the influence of the amount of existing capital is not a source of volatility in investment.

FIGURE 25.6

Investment Demand Curve and Investment Demand Schedule

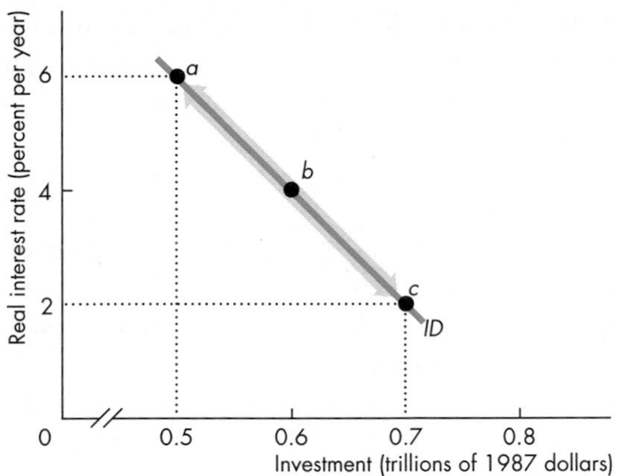

(a) The effect of a change in real interest rate

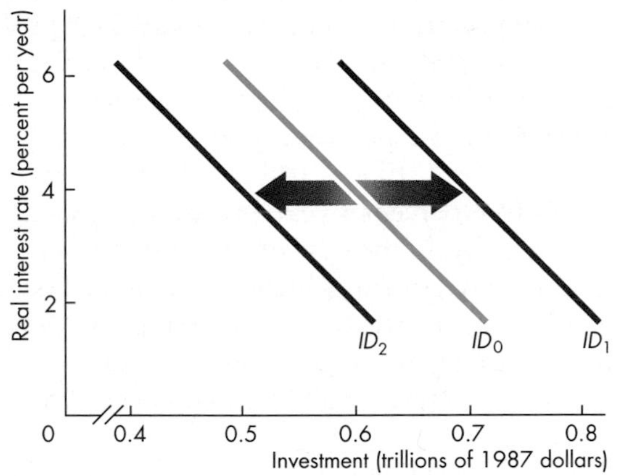

(b) The effect of a change in profit expectations

	Real interest rate (percent per year)	Investment (trillions of 1987 dollars)		
		Optimistic	Average	Pessimistic
a	6	0.6	0.5	0.4
b	4	0.7	0.6	0.5
c	2	0.8	0.7	0.6

An investment demand schedule lists the quantities of aggregate planned investment at each real interest rate. An investment demand curve graphs an investment demand schedule. The table shows the investment demand schedule when expectations are average, optimistic, and pessimistic. Part (a) shows the investment demand curve for average profit expectations. Along that investment demand curve, as the real interest rate rises from 2 percent to 6 percent, planned investment decreases—there is a movement along the investment demand curve from *c* to *a*. Part (b) shows how the investment demand curve changes when expected future profits change. With average profit expectations, the investment demand curve is ID_0—the same curve as in part (a). With optimistic expectations about future profits, planned investment increases at each real interest rate and the investment demand curve shifts to the right to ID_1. With pessimistic expectations about future profits, planned investment decreases at each real interest rate and the investment demand curve shifts to the left to ID_2.

It is a source of steady investment growth. Second, the higher the degree of utilization of existing capital, the larger is the amount of investment. When capital is underutilized, as in a recession, investment falls off. But when capital is overutilized, as in a boom, investment increases.

Investment Demand

Investment demand is the relationship between the level of planned investment and the real interest rate, holding all other influences on investment constant. The **investment demand schedule** lists the quantity of planned investment at each real interest rate, holding all other influences on investment constant. The **investment demand curve** graphs the relationship between the real interest rate and the level of planned investment, holding everything else constant. Some examples of investment demand schedules and investment demand curves appear in Fig. 25.6. The investment demand schedule and the position of the investment demand curve depend on the other influences on investment—expected profit and the existing capital stock.

Sometimes firms are pessimistic about future profits, sometimes they are optimistic, and sometimes their expectations are average. Fluctuations in profit expectations are the main source of fluctuations in investment demand. The three investment demand schedules in the table in Fig. 25.6 give examples of investment demand under the three types of expectations. In the case of average profit expectations, if the real interest rate is 4 percent a year, investment is \$0.6 trillion. If the real interest rate decreases to 2 percent a year, investment increases to \$0.7 trillion. If the real interest rate increases to 6 percent a year, investment decreases to \$0.5 trillion. In the case of optimistic profit expectations, investment is higher at each interest rate than it is when expectations are average. In the case of pessimistic profit expectations, investment is lower at each interest rate than with average expectations.

The investment demand curve is shown in the figure. In part (a), the investment demand curve (*ID*) is that for average expected profit. Each point (*a* through *c*) corresponds to a row in the table. A change in the real interest rate causes a movement along the investment demand curve. Thus, if the real interest rate is 4 percent a year, planned investment is \$0.6 trillion. If the real interest rate rises to 6 percent a year, there is a movement up the investment demand curve (see blue arrow) and planned investment decreases to \$0.5 trillion. If the real interest rate falls to 2 percent a year, there is a movement down the investment demand curve and planned investment increases to \$0.7 trillion.

The effects of profit expectations are shown in part (b). A change in profit expectations shifts the investment demand curve. The demand curve ID_0 represents average expected profit. When profit expectations become optimistic, the investment demand curve shifts to the right, from ID_0 to ID_1. When profit expectations become pessimistic, the investment demand curve shifts to the left, from ID_0 to ID_2.

The investment demand curve also shifts when there is an increase in the amount of investment to replace depreciated capital. This influence leads to a steady rightward shift in the *ID* curve.

FIGURE 25.7

Gross and Net Investment in the United States

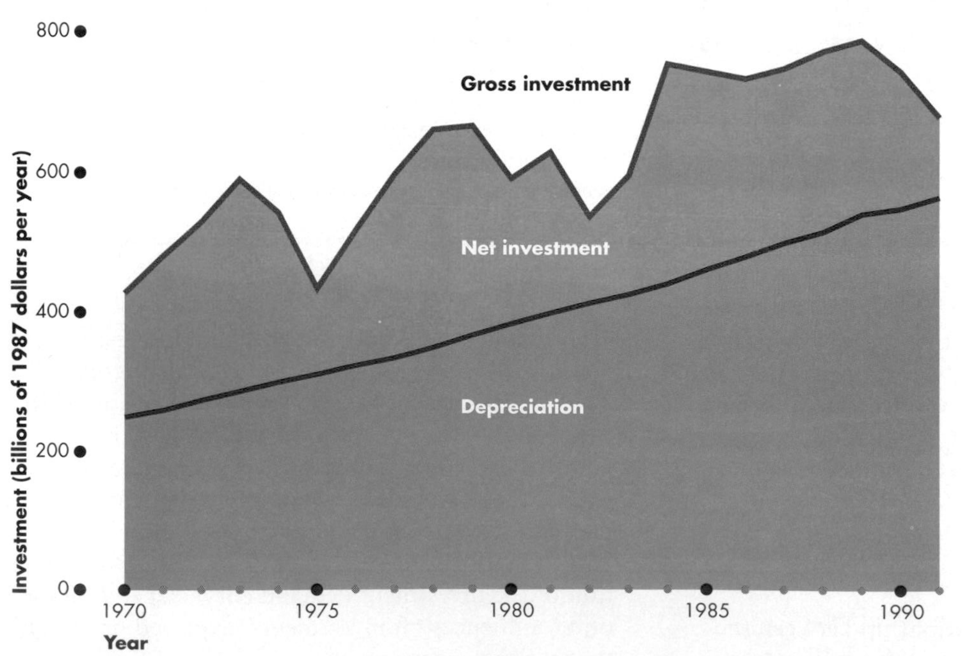

Gross investment is separated into two parts: the replacement of depreciated capital (shaded green) and net investment (shaded blue). Gross investment and depreciation increased steadily between 1970 and 1991. Depreciation follows a very smooth growth path because the capital stock grows steadily and smoothly. Net investment fluctuates.

Source: Economic Report of the President, 1992.

REVIEW

Investment depends on the real interest rate, profit expectations, and the scale of replacement of depreciated capital. Other things held constant, the lower the real interest rate, the larger is the amount of investment. When profit expectations become optimistic, the investment demand curve shifts to the right; when profit expectations become pessimistic, it shifts to the left. Profit expectations are also influenced by taxes, the environment, and the business cycle. When the economy is expanding quickly, profit expectations are optimistic and investment demand is high. When the economy is expanding slowly (or contracting), profit expectations are pessimistic and investment demand is low. Investment to replace depreciated capital grows steadily over time. ◆

We've just studied the *theory* of investment demand. Let's now see how that theory helps us to understand the fluctuations in investment that occur in the U.S. economy.

Investment Demand in the United States

As we saw in Fig. 25.2, investment is one of the most volatile components of aggregate expenditure. In some years, investment is as much as 20 percent below trend, and in others it is more than 10 percent above trend. Let's see how we can interpret these fluctuations in investment with the theory of investment demand we've just been studying.

We'll begin by looking at Fig. 25.7. It shows investment (in billions of 1987 dollars) between 1970 and 1991. It also shows the way in which investment—gross investment—is broken down between net investment and the replacement of depreciated capital—depreciation. As you can see, both depreciation and gross investment increase steadily over time. Depreciation follows a very smooth path. It reflects the fact that the capital stock grows steadily and smoothly. Net investment is the component of investment that fluctuates. You can see that fluctuation as the blue area between gross investment and depreciation.

The theory of investment demand predicts that fluctuations in investment result from fluctuations in the real interest rate and in future profit expectations. What is the relative importance of these two factors? Figure 25.8 answers this question. The points in the figure represent the gross investment and the real interest rate in the United States each year from 1980 to 1991. The figure also shows three U.S. investment demand curves, ID_0, ID_1, and ID_2.

In the early 1980s, the investment demand curve was ID_0. As expected profits increased in 1983 and 1984, the investment demand curve shifted to the right, first to ID_1 and then to ID_2. During the late 1980s, the investment demand curve remained close to ID_2 but began to shift leftward. Then, in 1991,

FIGURE 25.8

The U.S. Investment Demand Curve

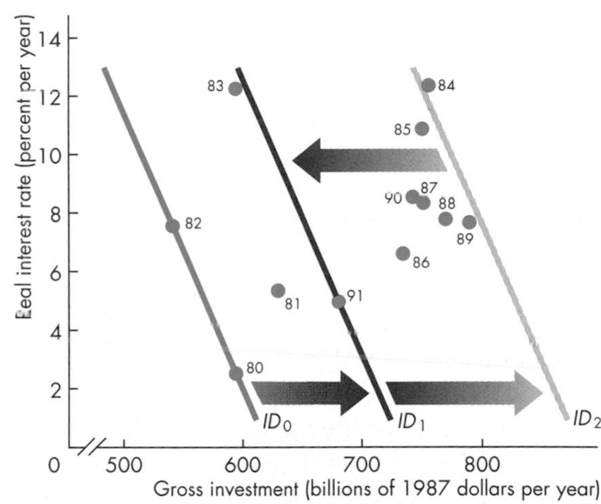

The blue points show the levels of gross investment and the real interest rate in the United States for each year between 1980 and 1991. When expected profits were low in the early 1980s, the investment demand curve was ID_0. As expected profits increased, the investment demand curve shifted rightward. By 1983 it had shifted to ID_1, and by 1984 it had shifted to ID_2. When expected profits declined in 1991, the investment demand curve shifted back to ID_1. Swings in profit expectations are more important than changes in interest rates in creating fluctuations in gross investment.

Source: Economic Report of the President, 1992, and my calculations and assumptions.

expected profits declined as the economy went into recession and the investment demand curve made a large leftward shift to the position it had been in eight years earlier—to ID_1. The fluctuations in investment resulting from changes in expected profits that shift the investment curve are much larger than those resulting from changes in interest rates.

Regardless of whether the fluctuations in investment are generated by shifts in the investment demand curve or movements along it, they have important effects on the economy. We'll learn about some of those effects in Chapter 26.

Let's now turn to the third component of aggregate expenditure, government purchases of goods and services.

Government Purchases of Goods and Services

Government purchases of goods and services cover a wide range of public sector activities. They include goods and services for our national defense, international representation (embassies and delegations in other countries), and domestic programs such as health care, education, and highways.

These expenditures are determined by our political institutions and legislative process. They are influenced by our votes in national, state, and local elections, the views of the members of Congress and state and local legislators we elect, the actions of lobbyists, the political state of the world, and the state of the U.S. and world economies.

Although some components of government purchases do vary with the state of the economy, most do not. Furthermore, government spending decisions are made on a fixed timetable and thus do not respond quickly to the changing economic situation. We will assume, therefore, that government purchases do not vary in a systematic way with the level of GDP. They influence GDP but are not directly influenced by it.

The final component of aggregate expenditure is net exports. Let's now see how they are determined.

Net Exports

Net exports are the expenditure by foreigners on U.S.-made goods and services minus the expenditure by U.S. residents on foreign-made goods and services. That is, net exports are U.S. exports minus U.S. imports. *Exports* are the sale of the goods and services produced in the United States to the rest of the world. *Imports* are the purchase of goods produced in the rest of the world by firms and households in the United States.

Exports

Exports are determined by decisions made in the rest of the world and are influenced by four main factors:

- Real GDP in the rest of the world
- Degree of international specialization
- Prices of U.S.-made goods and services relative to the prices of similar goods and services made in other countries
- Foreign exchange rates

Other things being equal, the higher the level of real GDP in the rest of the world, the greater is the demand by foreigners for U.S.-made goods and services. For example, an economic boom in Japan increases the Japanese demand for U.S.-made goods and services, such as Boeing airplanes, California oranges, Texas beef, and New York investment services, and increases U.S. exports. A recession in Japan cuts the Japanese demand for U.S.-made goods and decreases U.S. exports.

Also, the greater the degree of specialization in the world economy, the larger is the volume of exports, other things being equal. Over time, international specialization has been increasing. For example, the world aircraft industry is now heavily concentrated in the United States. While a small number of transcontinental airliners are built in France, Britain, and Russia, most of the world's major airlines buy their aircraft from either Boeing of McDonnell-Douglas. Also, the United States dominates the world in the manufacture and sale of biotechnology products. But many goods and services, notably in the consumer electronics industry, that were once made in the United States in large quantities are now made almost exclusively in Japan, Hong Kong, and other Asian countries on the Pacific Rim.

Next, other things being equal, the lower the price of U.S.-made goods and services relative to the prices of similar goods and services made in other countries, the greater is the quantity of U.S. exports.

Finally, again other things being equal, the lower the value of the U.S. dollar against other currencies, the larger is the quantity of U.S. exports. For example, as the U.S. dollar fell in value against the German mark and the Japanese yen in 1987, the demand for U.S.-made goods and services by those two countries increased sharply.

Imports

Imports are determined by four main factors:

- U.S. real GDP
- Degree of international specialization
- Prices of foreign-made goods and services relative to the prices of similar goods and services made in the United States
- Foreign exchange rates

Other things being equal, the higher the level of U.S. real GDP, the larger is the quantity of U.S. imports. For example, the long period of sustained income growth in the United States between 1983 and 1987 brought a huge increase in U.S. imports.

Also, the higher the degree of international specialization, the larger is the volume of U.S. imports, other things being equal. For example, there is a high degree of international specialization in the production of VCRs. As a consequence, all the VCRs sold in the United States are now produced in other countries—mainly Japan and Korea.

Finally, again other things being equal, the higher the prices of U.S.-made goods and services relative to the prices of similar foreign-made goods and services, and the higher the value of the U.S. dollar against other currencies, the larger is the quantity of U.S. imports. Though high real GDP growth in the United States in 1985 and 1986 produced an increase in imports, the increase was less severe than it otherwise would have been because of the fall in the value of the U.S. dollar against other currencies. The falling dollar made foreign goods and services more expensive and so slowed down, to some degree, the growth of U.S. imports.

Net Export Function

The **net export function** is the relationship between net exports and U.S. real GDP, holding constant all other influences on U.S. exports and imports. The net export function can also be described by a net export schedule, which lists the level of net exports at each level of real GDP, with everything else held constant. The table in Fig. 25.9 gives an example of a net export schedule.

In the table, exports are a constant $0.5 trillion—they do not depend on U.S. real GDP. Imports increase by $0.15 trillion for each $1.0 trillion increase in U.S. real GDP. Net exports, the difference between exports and imports, are shown in the final column of the table. When real GDP is $1.0 trillion, net exports are $0.35 trillion. Net exports decline as real GDP rises. At a real GDP just above $3 trillion ($3.33 trillion), net exports are zero; and at real GDP levels higher than that, net exports become increasingly negative (imports exceed exports).

Exports and imports are graphed in Fig. 25.9(a), and the net export function is graphed in Fig. 25.9(b). By comparing part (a) and part (b), you can see that when exports exceed imports, net exports are above zero (there is a surplus), and when imports exceed exports, net exports are below zero (there is a deficit). When real GDP is $3.33 trillion, there is a balance between exports and imports.

The data in Fig. 25.9 are based on the U.S. economy in 1988. In that year, real GDP was $4 trillion, exports were $0.5 trillion, imports were $0.6 trillion, and net exports were –$0.1 trillion, highlighted in the figure.

The position of the net export function depends on real GDP in the rest of the world, on the degree of international specialization, and on prices of U.S.-made goods and services compared with the prices of those goods and services made in the rest of the world. If real GDP in the rest of the world increases,

FIGURE 25.9

Net Export Function and Net Export Schedule

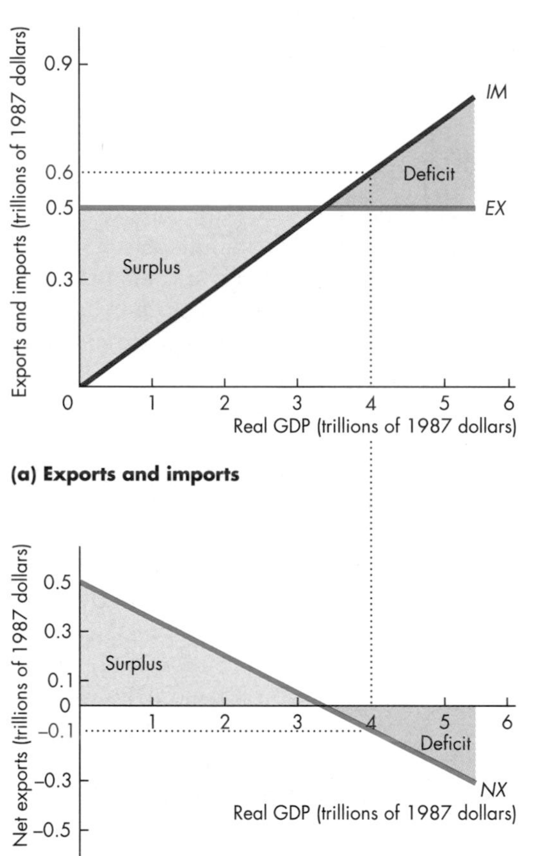

(a) Exports and imports

(b) Net exports

Real GDP (Y)	Exports (EX)	Imports (IM)	Net exports ($EX - IM$)
	(trillions of 1987 dollars)		
0	**0.5**	**0**	**0.5**
1.0	**0.5**	**0.15**	**0.35**
2.0	**0.5**	**0.30**	**0.20**
3.0	**0.5**	**0.45**	**0.05**
4.0	**0.5**	**0.60**	**−0.10**
5.0	**0.5**	**0.75**	**−0.25**

The net export schedule in the table shows the relationship between net exports and real GDP. Net exports are equal to exports (EX) minus imports (IM). Exports are independent of real GDP, but imports rise as real GDP rises. In the table, imports are 15 percent of real GDP. Net exports fall as GDP rises.

Part (a) graphs the export and import schedules. Since exports are independent of real GDP, they are graphed as a horizontal line. Since imports rise as real GDP rises, they appear as an upward-sloping line. The distance between the export curve and the import curve represents net exports. Net exports are graphed in part (b) of the figure. The net export function is downward sloping because the import curve is upward sloping. The real GDP level at which the net export function intersects the horizontal axis in part (b) is the same as that at which the imports curve intersects the exports curve in part (a). That level of real GDP is $3.33 trillion. Below that level of real GDP there is a surplus, and above it there is a deficit. In 1988, when real GDP was $4 trillion, imports exceeded exports and net exports were –$0.1 trillion.

the net export function shifts upward. If U.S.-made goods and services become cheap relative to goods and services made in the rest of the world, the net export function also shifts upward. A change in the degree of international specialization has an ambiguous effect on the position of the net export function. If the United States becomes more specialized in goods and services for which there is an increase in world demand, the net export function shifts upward. If U.S. demand increases for goods and services in which the rest of the world specializes, the net export function shifts downward.

We've now studied the main influences on consumption expenditure, investment, and net exports, and our next task is to see how these components of aggregate expenditure interact with each other and with government purchases of goods and services to determine aggregate expenditure. Our starting point is to establish a relationship between aggregate planned expenditure and real GDP.

Aggregate Expenditure and Real GDP

There is a relationship between aggregate planned expenditure and real GDP. **Aggregate planned expenditure** is the expenditure that economic agents (households, firms, governments, and foreigners) plan to undertake in given circumstances. Aggregate planned expenditure is not necessarily equal to actual aggregate expenditure. We'll see how these two expenditure concepts—planned and actual—differ from each other later in this chapter.

The relationship between aggregate planned expenditure and real GDP may be described by either an aggregate expenditure schedule or an aggregate expenditure curve. The **aggregate expenditure schedule** lists the level of aggregate planned expenditure generated at each level of real GDP. The **aggregate expenditure curve** is a graph of the aggregate expenditure schedule.

Aggregate Expenditure Schedule

The aggregate expenditure schedule is set out in the table in Fig. 25.10. (The data in this figure are examples and do not refer to the real world.) The table shows aggregate planned expenditure as well as its components. To work out the level of aggregate planned expenditure at a given real GDP, we add the various components together. The first column of the table shows real GDP, and the second column shows the consumption expenditure generated by each level of real GDP. When real GDP is $1 trillion, so is consumption expenditure. A $1 trillion increase in real GDP generates a $0.65 trillion increase in consumption expenditure.

The next two columns show investment and government purchases of goods and services. Recall that investment depends on the real interest rate and the state of profit expectations. Suppose that those factors are constant and, at a given point in time, generate a level of investment of $0.5 trillion. This investment level is independent of real GDP. Government purchases of goods and services are also fixed. Their value is $0.7 trillion.

The next three columns show exports, imports, and net exports. Exports are influenced by events in the rest of the world, by our prices compared with prices in other countries, and by the foreign exchange value of our dollar. They are not directly affected by the level of real GDP. In the table, exports appear as a constant $0.45 trillion. In contrast, imports do increase as real GDP increases. In the table, a $1 trillion increase in real GDP generates a $0.15 trillion increase in imports. Net exports—the difference between exports and imports—also vary as real GDP varies. Net exports decrease by $0.15 trillion for each $1 trillion increase in real GDP.

The final column of the table shows aggregate planned expenditure. This amount is the sum of planned consumption expenditure, investment, government purchases of goods and services, and net exports.

Aggregate Expenditure Curve

The aggregate expenditure curve appears in the diagram in Fig. 25.10. Real GDP is shown on the horizontal axis, and aggregate planned expenditure on the vertical axis. The aggregate expenditure curve is the red line labeled *AE*. Points *a* through *f* on that curve correspond to the rows in the table in Fig. 25.10. The *AE* curve is a graph of the last column, "Aggregate planned expenditure," plotted against real GDP.

The figure also shows the components of aggregate expenditure. The constant components—investment, government purchases of goods and services, and exports—are indicated by the horizontal lines in the figure. Consumption is the vertical gap between the line labeled $I + G + EX + C$ and that labeled $I + G + EX$.

To calculate the *AE* curve, we subtract imports from the $I + G + EX + C$ line. Imports are subtracted because they are not expenditure on U.S. real GDP. The purchase of a new car is part of consumption expenditure, but if that car is a Toyota made in Japan, expenditure on it has to be subtracted from consumption expenditure to find out how much is spent on goods and services produced in the United States—on U.S. real GDP. Money paid to Toyota for car imports from Japan does not add to aggregate expenditure in the United States.

FIGURE 25.10

Aggregate Expenditure Curve and Aggregate Expenditure Schedule

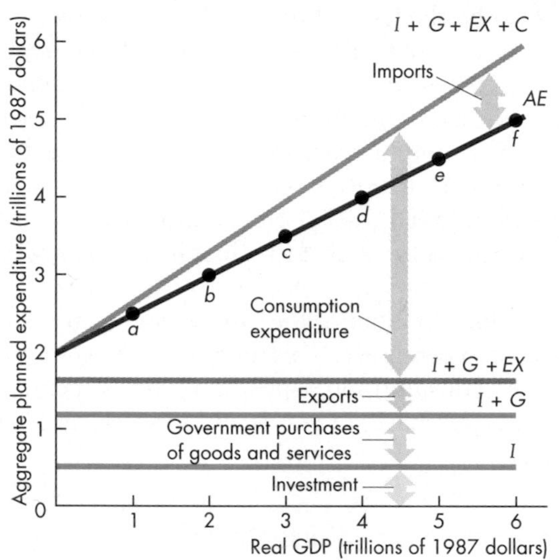

The relationship between aggregate planned expenditure and real GDP may be described by an aggregate expenditure schedule (as shown in the table) or an aggregate expenditure curve (as shown in the diagram). Aggregate planned expenditure is calculated as the sum of planned consumption expenditure, investment, government purchases of goods and services, and net exports. For example, in row *a* of the table, if real GDP is \$1.0 trillion, aggregate planned consumption is \$1.0 trillion, planned investment is \$0.5 trillion, planned government purchases of goods and services are \$0.7 trillion, and planned net exports are \$0.3 trillion. Thus, when real GDP is \$1.0 trillion, aggregate planned expenditure is \$2.5 trillion (\$1.0 + \$0.5 + \$0.7 + \$0.3). The expenditure plans are graphed in the figure as the aggregate expenditure curve *AE*.

		Planned expenditure						
	Real GDP (Y)	Consumption expenditure (C)	Investment (I)	Government purchases (G)	Exports (EX)	Imports (IM)	Net exports ($NX = EX - IM$)	Aggregate planned expenditure ($AE = C + I + G + NX$)
				(trillions of 1987 dollars)				
a	1.0	1.00	0.5	0.7	0.45	0.15	0.30	2.5
b	2.0	1.65	0.5	0.7	0.45	0.30	0.15	3.0
c	3.0	2.30	0.5	0.7	0.45	0.45	0	3.5
d	4.0	2.95	0.5	0.7	0.45	0.60	−0.15	4.0
e	5.0	3.60	0.5	0.7	0.45	0.75	−0.30	4.5
f	6.0	4.25	0.5	0.7	0.45	0.90	−0.45	5.0

We've now seen how to calculate the aggregate expenditure schedule and aggregate expenditure curve and seen that aggregate planned expenditure increases as real GDP increases. This relationship is summarized in the aggregate expenditure curve. But what determines the point on the aggregate expenditure curve at which the economy operates? We're now going to answer this question.

Equilibrium Expenditure

Equilibrium expenditure occurs when aggregate planned expenditure equals real GDP. At levels of real GDP below equilibrium, planned expenditure exceeds real GDP; at levels of real GDP above equilibrium, planned expenditure falls short of real GDP.

To see how equilibrium expenditure is determined, we need to distinguish between actual expenditure and planned expenditure and understand how actual expenditure, planned expenditure, and real GDP are related.

Actual Expenditure, Planned Expenditure, and Real GDP

Actual aggregate expenditure is always equal to real GDP. (We established this fact in Chapter 23, pp. 611 and 613.) But *planned* expenditure is not necessarily equal to actual expenditure and, therefore, is not necessarily equal to actual real GDP. How can actual expenditure and planned expenditure differ from each other? Why don't people implement their plans? The main reason is that firms may end up with unplanned excess inventories or with an unplanned shortage of inventories. People carry out their consumption expenditure plans, the government implements its planned purchases of goods and services, and net exports are as planned. Firms carry out their plans to invest in buildings, plant, and equipment. One component of investment, however, is the change in firms' inventories of goods that have not yet been sold. Inventories change when aggregate planned expenditure differs from real GDP. If real GDP exceeds planned expenditure, inventories rise, and if real GDP is less than planned expenditure, inventories fall.

When aggregate planned expenditure is equal to aggregate actual expenditure and equal to real GDP, the economy is in an expenditure equilibrium. When aggregate planned expenditure and aggregate actual expenditure are unequal, a process of convergence toward an equilibrium expenditure occurs. Let's examine equilibrium expenditure and the process that brings it about.

When Planned Expenditure Equals Real GDP

The table in Fig. 25.11 shows different levels of real GDP. Against each level of real GDP, the second column shows aggregate planned expenditure. Only when real GDP equals $4 billion is aggregate planned expenditure equal to real GDP. This level of expenditure is the equilibrium expenditure.

The equilibrium is illustrated in Fig. 25.11(a). The aggregate expenditure curve is *AE*. Since aggregate planned expenditure on the vertical axis and real GDP on the horizontal axis are measured in the same units and on the same scale, a 45° line drawn in Fig. 25.11(a) shows all the points at which aggregate planned expenditure equals real GDP. Where the aggregate expenditure curve intersects the 45° line, at point *d*, equilibrium expenditure is determined.

Convergence to Equilibrium You will get a better idea of why point *d* is the equilibrium if you consider what is happening when the economy is not at point *d*. Suppose that real GDP is $2 trillion. You can see from Fig. 25.11(a) that in this situation, aggregate planned expenditure is $3 trillion (point *b*). Thus aggregate planned expenditure is larger than real GDP. If aggregate expenditure is actually $3 trillion as planned, then real GDP would also be $3 trillion, since every dollar spent by one person is a dollar of income for someone else. But real GDP is $2 trillion. How can real GDP be $2 trillion if people *plan* to spend $3 trillion? The answer is that *actual* spending is less than *planned* spending. If real GDP is $2 trillion, the value of production is also $2 trillion. The only way that people can buy goods and services worth $3 trillion when the value of production is $2 trillion is if firms' inventories fall by $1 trillion (point *b* in Fig. 25.11b). Since changes in inventories are part of investment, actual investment is less than planned investment.

But this is not the end of the story. Firms have target levels for inventories, and when inventories fall below those targets, firms increase production to restore inventories to their target levels. To restore their inventories, firms hire additional labor and increase production. Suppose that they increase production in the next period by enough to replenish their inventories. Real GDP rises by $1.0 trillion to $3.0 trillion. But again, aggregate planned expenditure exceeds real GDP. When real GDP is $3.0 trillion, aggregate planned expenditure is $3.5 trillion (point *c* in Fig. 25.11a). Again, inventories fall, but this time by less than before. With real GDP of $3.0

FIGURE 25.11

Equilibrium Expenditure and Real GDP

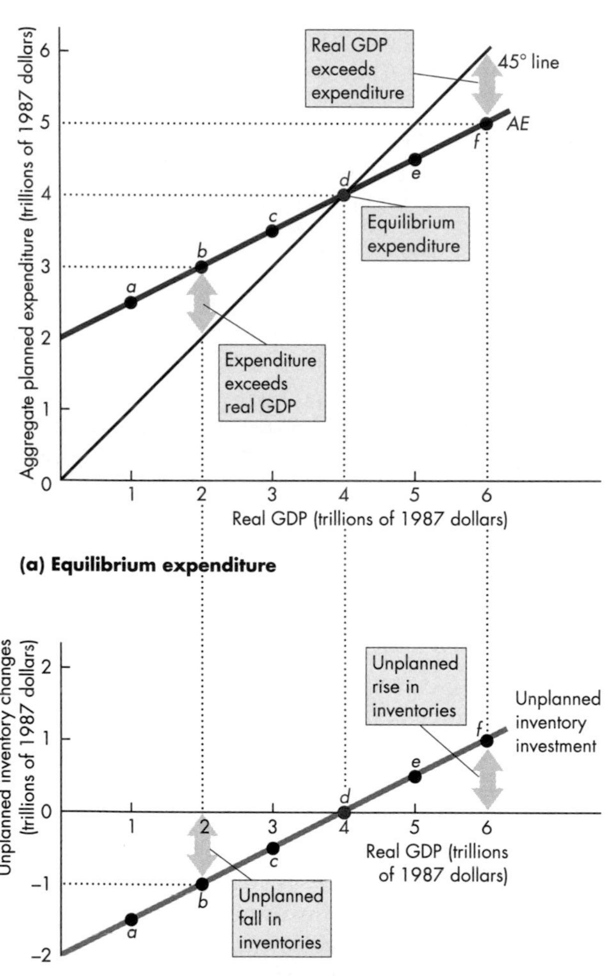

	Real GDP (*Y*)	Aggregate planned expenditure (*AE*)	Unplanned inventory changes (*Y* – *AE*)
		(trillions of 1987 dollars)	
a	**1.0**	**2.5**	**–1.5**
b	**2.0**	**3.0**	**–1.0**
c	**3.0**	**3.5**	**–0.5**
d	**4.0**	**4.0**	**0**
e	**5.0**	**4.5**	**0.5**
f	**6.0**	**5.0**	**1.0**

The table shows the aggregate expenditure schedule. When real GDP is $4 trillion, aggregate planned expenditure equals real GDP. At real GDP levels below $4 trillion, aggregate planned expenditure exceeds real GDP. At real GDP levels above $4 trillion, aggregate planned expenditure is less than real GDP.

The diagram illustrates equilibrium expenditure in part (a). The 45° line shows those points at which aggregate planned expenditure equals real GDP. The aggregate expenditure curve is *AE*. Actual aggregate expenditure equals real GDP. Equilibrium expenditure and real GDP are $4 trillion. That real GDP level generates planned expenditure that equals real GDP—$4 trillion.

The forces bringing the equilibrium about are illustrated in parts (a) and (b). At real GDP levels below $4 trillion, aggregate planned expenditure exceeds real GDP and inventories fall—for example, point *b* in both parts of the figure. In such cases, firms increase output to restore their inventories and real GDP rises. At real GDP levels higher than $4 trillion, aggregate planned expenditure is less than real GDP and inventories rise—for example, point *f* in both parts of the figure. In such a situation, firms decrease output to work off excess inventories and real GDP falls. Only where the aggregate planned expenditure curve cuts the 45° line is planned expenditure equal to real GDP. This position is the equilibrium. There are no unplanned inventory changes, and output remains constant.

trillion and planned expenditure of $3.5 trillion, inventories fall by only $0.5 trillion (point *c* in Fig. 25.11b). Again, firms hire additional labor, and production increases; real GDP increases yet further.

The process that we have just described—planned expenditure exceeds income, inventories fall, and production rises to restore the unplanned inventory reduction—ends when real GDP has reached $4 trillion. At this level of real GDP, there is an equilibrium. There are no unplanned inventory changes, and firms do not change their production.

Next, let's perform a similar experiment, but one starting with a level of real GDP greater than the equilibrium. Suppose that real GDP is $6.0 trillion.

At this level, aggregate planned expenditure is $5.0 trillion (point *f* in Fig. 25.11a), $1.0 trillion less than real GDP. With aggregate planned expenditure less than real GDP, inventories rise by $1.0 trillion (point *f* in Fig. 25.11b)—there is unplanned investment. With unsold inventories on their hands, firms cut back on production and real GDP falls. If they cut back production by the amount of the unplanned increase in inventories, real GDP falls by $1.0 trillion to $5.0 trillion. At that level of real GDP, aggregate planned expenditure is $4.5 trillion (point *e* in Fig. 25.11a). Again, there is an unplanned increase in inventories, but it is only one half of the previous increase (point *e* in Fig. 25.11b). Again, firms will cut back production and lay off yet more workers, reducing real GDP still further. Real GDP continues to fall whenever unplanned inventories increase. As before, real GDP keeps on changing until it reaches its equilibrium level of $4.0 trillion.

You can see, then, that if real GDP is below equilibrium, aggregate planned expenditure exceeds real GDP, inventories fall, firms increase production to restore their inventories, and real GDP rises. If real GDP is above equilibrium, aggregate planned expenditure is less than real GDP, unsold inventories prompt firms to cut back on production, and real GDP falls.

Only if real GDP equals aggregate planned expenditure are there no unplanned inventory changes and no changes in firms' output plans. In this situation, real GDP remains constant.

REVIEW

Equilibrium expenditure occurs when aggregate planned expenditure equals real GDP. If aggregate planned expenditure exceeds real GDP, inventories fall and firms increase output to replenish inventory levels. Real GDP increases, and so does planned expenditure. If aggregate planned expenditure is below real GDP, inventories accumulate and firms cut output to lower inventory levels. Real GDP and aggregate planned expenditure decline. Only when aggregate planned expenditure equals real GDP are there no unplanned changes in inventories and no changes in output. Real GDP remains constant. ◆

◆ ◆ ◆ ◆ In this chapter, we've studied the factors that influence private expenditure decisions, looking at each item of aggregate expenditure—consumption expenditure, investment, and net exports—in isolation from the others. We've also seen how these private components of expenditure interact with each other and with government purchases of goods and services to determine equilibrium aggregate expenditure. In the next chapter, we'll study the sources of *changes* in the equilibrium. In particular, we'll see how changes in investment, exports, and government fiscal policy actions can change equilibrium aggregate expenditure.

SUMMARY

The Components of Aggregate Expenditure

The components of aggregate expenditure are

- Consumption expenditure
- Investment
- Government purchases of goods and services
- Net exports

The main component of aggregate expenditure is consumption expenditure. On the average, 65 percent of total expenditure comes from consumption. Investment accounts for 16 percent, and government purchases of goods and services account for 21 percent of the total. Net exports on the average are close to zero.

The components of aggregate expenditure that fluctuate most are investment and net exports. (pp. 670–671)

Consumption Expenditure and Saving

Consumption expenditure is influenced by many factors, but the most important are

- Disposable income
- Expected future income

As disposable income increases, so do both consumption expenditure and saving. The relationship between consumption expenditure and disposable income is called the *consumption function*. The relationship between saving and disposable income is called the *saving function*. At low levels of disposable income, consumption expenditure exceeds disposable income, which means that saving is negative (dissaving occurs). As disposable income increases, consumption expenditure increases but by less than the increase in disposable income.

The fraction of each additional dollar of disposable income consumed is called the marginal propensity to consume. The fraction of each additional dollar of disposable income saved is called the marginal propensity to save. All influences on consumption and saving, other than disposable income, shift the consumption and saving functions.

Consumption expenditure is a function of real GDP because disposable income and GDP vary together. (pp. 672–682)

Investment

The amount of investment depends on:

- Real interest rates
- Profit expectations
- Existing capital

The lower the real interest rate, the greater is the amount of investment. The higher the expected profit, the greater is the amount of investment. And the larger the amount of existing capital, the larger is the amount of replacement investment and the smaller is the amount of net investment.

The main influence on investment demand is fluctuations in profit expectations. Swings in the degree of optimism and pessimism about future profits lead to shifts in the investment demand curve. Swings in profit expectations are associated with business cycle fluctuations. When the economy is in an expansion phase, profit expectations are optimistic and investment is high. When the economy is in a contraction phase, profit expectations are pessimistic and investment is low. (pp. 682–688)

Government Purchases of Goods and Services

Government purchases are determined by political processes, and the amount of government purchases is determined largely independently of the current level of real GDP. (p. 688)

Net Exports

Net exports are the difference between exports and imports. Exports are determined by decisions made in the rest of the world and are influenced by real GDP in the rest of the world, the degree of international specialization, the prices of U.S.-made goods and services relative to the prices of similar goods and services made in other countries, and the foreign exchange rate. Imports are determined by U.S. real GDP, the degree of international specialization, the prices of foreign-made goods and services relative to the prices of goods and services produced in the United States, and the foreign exchange rate.

The net export function shows the relationship between net exports and U.S. real GDP, holding constant all the other influences on exports and imports. (pp. 688–690)

Aggregate Expenditure and Real GDP

Aggregate planned expenditure is the sum of planned consumption expenditure, planned investment, planned government purchases of goods and services, and planned net exports. The relationship between aggregate planned expenditure and real GDP can be represented by the aggregate expenditure schedule and the aggregate expenditure curve. (pp. 691–692)

Equilibrium Expenditure

Equilibrium expenditure occurs when aggregate planned expenditure equals real GDP. At real GDP levels above the equilibrium, aggregate planned expenditure is below real GDP, and in such a situation, real GDP falls. At levels of real GDP below the equilibrium, aggregate planned expenditure exceeds real GDP and real GDP rises. Only when real GDP equals aggregate planned expenditure is real GDP constant and in equilibrium. The main influence bringing real GDP and aggregate planned expenditure into equality is the behavior of inventories. When aggregate planned expenditure exceeds real GDP, inventories fall. To restore their inventories, firms increase output, and this action increases real GDP. When planned expenditure is below real GDP, inventories accumulate and firms cut back their output. This action lowers the level of real GDP. Only when there are no unplanned inventory changes do firms keep output constant and so real GDP remains constant. (pp. 692–695)

KEY ELEMENTS

Key Terms

Aggregate expenditure curve, 691
Aggregate expenditure schedule, 691
Aggregate planned expenditure, 691
Average propensity to consume, 676
Average propensity to save, 676
Consumption function, 672
Dissaving, 672
Equilibrium expenditure, 692
Investment demand, 685
Investment demand curve, 685
Investment demand schedule, 685
Marginal propensity to consume, 676
Marginal propensity to consume out of real GDP, 682
Marginal propensity to save, 676
Net export function, 689
Real interest rate, 682
Saving function, 672

Key Figures and Tables

REVIEW QUESTIONS

1 What are the components of aggregate expenditure?

2 Which component of aggregate expenditure is the largest?

3 Which components of aggregate expenditure fluctuate the most?

4 What is the consumption function?

5 What is the fundamental determinant of consumption?

6 Distinguish between disposable income and GDP.

7 What is the saving function? What is the relationship between the saving function and the consumption function?

8 What is the meaning of the term *marginal propensity to consume*? Why is the marginal propensity to consume less than 1?

9 Explain the relationship between the marginal propensity to consume and the marginal propensity to save.

10 What determines investment? Why does investment increase as the real interest rate falls?

11 What is the effect of each of the following on U.S. net exports?

a An increase in U.S. real GDP
b An increase in real GDP in Japan
c A rise in the price of Japanese-made cars with no change in the price of U.S.-made cars

12 What is the aggregate expenditure schedule? What is the aggregate expenditure curve?

13 How is equilibrium expenditure determined? What would happen if aggregate planned expenditure exceeded real GDP?

PROBLEMS

1 You are given the following information about the Batman family (Batman and Robin):

Disposable income (dollars per year)	Consumption expenditure (dollars per year)
0	5,000
10,000	10,000
20,000	15,000
30,000	20,000
40,000	25,000

a Calculate the Batman family's marginal propensity to consume.
b Calculate the average propensity to consume at each level of disposable income.
c Calculate how much the Batman family saves at each level of disposable income.
d Calculate their marginal propensity to save.
e Calculate their average propensity to save at each level of disposable income.
f Draw a diagram of the consumption function. Calculate its slope.
g Over what range of income does the Batman family dissave?

2 A car assembly plant can be built for $10 million, and it will have a life of three years. At the end of three years, the plant will have a scrap value of $1 million. The firm will have to hire labor at a cost of $1.5 million a year and will have to buy parts and fuel costing another $1.5 million. If the firm builds the plant, it will be able to produce cars that will sell for $7.5 million each year. Will it pay the firm to invest in this new production line at the following interest rates?

a 2 percent a year
b 5 percent a year
c 10 percent a year

3 You are given the following information about the economy of Dreamland: the marginal propensity to consume is 0.75 and taxes net of transfer payments are a quarter of real GDP. What is the marginal propensity to consume out of real GDP in this economy?

4 You are given the following information about the economy of Happy Isle, an isolated economy with no international trade: When disposable income is zero, consumption is $80 billion. The marginal propensity to consume is 0.75. Investment is $400 billion; government purchases of goods and services are $600 billion; taxes are a constant $500 billion and do not vary as income varies. At the expenditure equilibrium, calculate:

a Real GDP
b Consumption
c Saving
d The average and marginal propensities to consume
e The average and marginal propensities to save

CHAPTER 26

EXPENDITURE FLUCTUATIONS AND FISCAL POLICY

After studying this chapter, you will be able to:

- Explain why changes in investment and exports change consumption expenditure and have multiplier effects on aggregate expenditure
- Define and calculate the multiplier
- Explain why changes in government purchases of goods and services have multiplier effects on aggregate expenditure
- Explain why changes in taxes and transfer payments have multiplier effects on aggregate expenditure
- Explain how the government may use fiscal policy in an attempt to stabilize aggregate expenditure
- Explain the relationship between aggregate expenditure and aggregate demand

Economic Amplifier or Shock Absorber

BONNIE RAITT BREATHES INTO A MICROPHONE AT A BARELY audible whisper. The electronic signal picked up by the sensitive instrument travels along wires to a huge bank of amplifiers and then through high-fidelity speakers to the ears of 10,000 fans spread out across the Red Rocks Amphitheater near Denver. Moving to a louder passage, Raitt increases the volume of her voice and now, through the magic of electronic amplification, booms across the stadium, drowning out every other sound. ◆◆ Coleman Young, the mayor of Detroit, is being driven to a business meeting along one of the city's less well-repaired highways. (There are some pretty badly pot-holed highways in Detroit.) He is dictating notes to a secretary, who is taking down the words in impeccable shorthand. The car's wheels are bouncing and vibrating over some of the worst highway in the nation, but its passengers are completely undisturbed, and the shorthand notes are written without a ripple, thanks to the car's efficient shock absorbers. ◆◆ Investment and exports fluctuate like the volume of Bonnie Raitt's voice and the uneven surface of a Detroit highway. How does the economy react to those fluctuations? Does it react like Coleman Young's limousine, absorbing the shocks and providing a smooth ride for the economy's passengers? Or, does it behave like Bonnie Raitt's amplifier, blowing up the fluctuations and spreading them out to affect the many millions of participants in an economic rock concert? ◆◆ Is the economic machine built to a design that we simply have to live with, or can we modify it, changing its amplification and shock-absorbing powers? And, can the government operate the economic machine in a way that gives us all a smoother ride?

◆ ◆ ◆ ◆ We are now going to explore these questions. We are going to discover that the economy contains an important amplification unit that magnifies the effects of fluctuations in investment and exports, resulting in a larger change in aggregate expenditure than the change in investment or exports that initiated it. We are also going to discover that taxes act as a kind of shock absorber. They don't provide the smooth ride of a Lincoln Continental, but they do a better job than the springs of a stagecoach. Further, we're going to discover that the government can, to some degree, smooth out fluctuations in aggregate expenditure by varying taxes and its purchases of goods and services.

Expenditure Multipliers

We discovered in Chapter 25 that equilibrium expenditure is determined at the point of intersection of the aggregate expenditure curve and the 45° line. We're now going to discover how this equilibrium *changes* when there is a *change* in investment, exports, or government purchases of goods and services. To study the effects of these changes, it is useful to classify the components of aggregate expenditure into two groups:

- Autonomous expenditure
- Induced expenditure

Autonomous Expenditure

The sum of those components of aggregate planned expenditure that are not influenced by real GDP is called **autonomous expenditure.** These components are investment, government purchases of goods and services, exports, and the part of consumption expenditure that does not vary with real GDP. The table in Fig. 26.1 gives an example. In this table, investment is $0.5 trillion, government purchases are $0.7 trillion, and exports are $0.45 trillion. The sum of these items ($I + G + EX$) is $1.65 trillion. The autonomous part of consumption expenditure (C_A) is $0.35 trillion. The sum of all these components is autonomous expenditure (A) and is $2 trillion regardless of the level of real GDP.

Autonomous expenditure is illustrated in both parts of Fig. 26.1 as the point at which the *AE* curve touches the vertical axis—the level of aggregate planned expenditure when real GDP is zero. In part (b), autonomous expenditure is highlighted by the blue arrow.

Induced Expenditure

The part of aggregate planned expenditure on U.S.-produced goods and services that varies as real GDP varies is called **induced expenditure.** Induced expenditure equals the part of consumption expenditure that varies with real GDP minus imports. In the table in Fig. 26.1, induced expenditure (N) is equal to induced consumption expenditure (C_N) minus imports (IM). An increase in real GDP of $1 trillion increases consumption expenditure by $0.65 trillion. This is the induced part of consumption expenditure. But an increase in real GDP of $1 trillion increases imports by $0.15 trillion. You can see that as real GDP increases, both consumption expenditure and imports increase, but consumption expenditure increases by more than imports, so induced expenditure also increases. Thus a $1 trillion increase in real GDP increases aggregate planned expenditure on U.S.-produced goods and services by $0.5 trillion—$0.65 additional consumption expenditure minus $0.15 trillion additional imports. For example, if real GDP increases from $4 trillion to $5 trillion—an increase of $1 trillion—induced expenditure increases from $2 trillion to $2.5 trillion—an increase of $0.5 trillion.

Induced expenditure is illustrated in both parts of Fig. 26.1. In part (a) you can see that as real GDP increases, induced consumption expenditure—the red arrow—increases and imports—the purple arrow—increase, but aggregate planned expenditure also increases. In part (b), induced expenditure is highlighted by the orange arrow.

Slope of the Aggregate Expenditure Curve What determines the slope of the aggregate expenditure curve? The answer is the extent to which expenditure is induced by an increase in real GDP. You can see in Fig. 26.1(b) that if real GDP increases from zero to $2 trillion, an increase of $2 trillion, aggregate planned expenditure increases from $2 trillion to $3 trillion, an increase of $1 trillion. The slope of the aggregate expenditure curve equals the increase in aggregate planned expenditure divided by the

FIGURE 26.1

Aggregate Expenditure

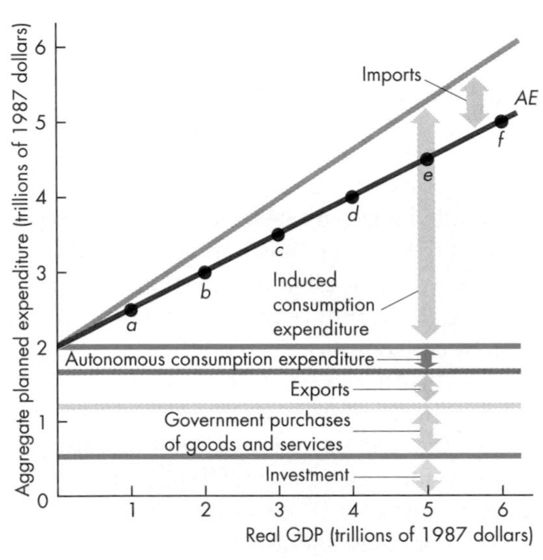

(a) Components of aggregate expenditure

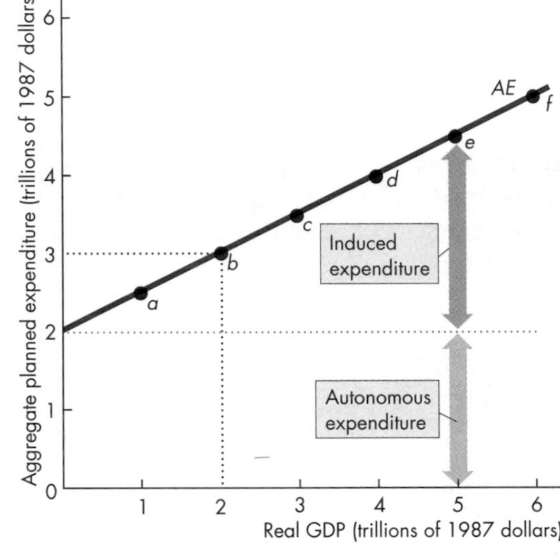

(b) Autonomous and induced expenditure

	Real GDP (Y)	Investment + government purchases + exports ($I + G + EX$)	Autonomous consumption expenditure (C_A)	Autonomous expenditure ($A = I + G + EX + C_A$)	Induced consumption expenditure (C_N)	Imports (IM)	Induced expenditure ($N = C_N - IM$)	Aggregate planned expenditure ($E = A + N$)
	Planned expenditure (trillions of 1987 dollars)							
a	1.0	1.65	0.35	2.0	0.65	0.15	0.5	2.5
b	2.0	1.65	0.35	2.0	1.30	0.30	1.0	3.0
c	3.0	1.65	0.35	2.0	1.95	0.45	1.5	3.5
d	4.0	1.65	0.35	2.0	2.60	0.60	2.0	4.0
e	5.0	1.65	0.35	2.0	3.25	0.75	2.5	4.5
f	6.0	1.65	0.35	2.0	3.90	0.90	3.0	5.0

In the table, autonomous expenditure (A) is $2 trillion regardless of the level of real GDP. It equals investment plus government purchases plus exports ($I + G + EX$) plus the autonomous part of consumption expenditure (C_A). Autonomous expenditure is the point at which the *AE* curve touches the vertical axis—the level of aggregate planned expenditure when real GDP is zero. It is shown in part (a) by the blue line, and its magnitude is highlighted by the blue arrow in part (b). In the table, induced expenditure (N) is equal to induced consumption expenditure (C_N) minus imports (IM). It increases as real GDP increases. In part (a), induced consumption expenditure is shown by the red arrow and imports by the purple arrow. In part (b), induced expenditure is highlighted by the orange arrow.

increase in real GDP—$1 trillion divided by $2 trillion, which equals 0.5.

The increase in induced expenditure is equal to the increase in consumption expenditure minus the increase in imports. Recall that the fraction of the last dollar of real GDP consumed is the *marginal propensity to consume out of real GDP.* In Fig. 26.1, the marginal propensity to consume out of real GDP is 0.65. The fraction of the last dollar of real GDP spent on imports is called the **marginal propensity to import.** In Fig. 26.1, the marginal propensity to import is 0.15. The marginal propensity to consume out of real GDP minus the marginal propensity to import is 0.5 (0.65 – 0.15 = 0.5), which is equal to the slope of the aggregate expenditure curve, *AE*.

A Change in Autonomous Expenditure

There are many possible sources of a change in autonomous expenditure: A fall in the real interest rate might induce firms to increase their planned investment. A major wave of innovation, such as occurred with the spread of computers in the 1980s, might increase expected future profits and lead firms to increase their planned investment. Stiff competition in the auto industry from Japanese and European imports might force GM, Ford, and Chrysler to increase their investment in robotic assembly lines. An economic boom in Western Europe and Japan might lead to a large increase in their expenditure on U.S.-produced goods and services—on U.S. exports. A worsening of international relations might lead the U.S. government to increase its expenditure on armaments—an increase in government purchases of goods and services. These are all examples of increases in autonomous expenditure. What are the effects of such increases on aggregate planned expenditure? And do increases in autonomous expenditure affect consumers? Will they plan to increase their consumption expenditure? Let's answer these questions.

Aggregate planned expenditure is set out in the table in Fig. 26.2. Autonomous expenditure initially is $2 trillion. For each $1 trillion increase in real GDP, induced expenditure increases by $0.5 trillion. Adding induced expenditure and autonomous expenditure together gives aggregate planned expenditure. This aggregate expenditure schedule is shown in the figure as the aggregate expenditure curve AE_0. Initially, equilibrium occurs when real GDP is $4 trillion. You can see this equilibrium in row *d* of the table and in the figure where the curve AE_0 intersects the 45° line at the point marked *d*.

Now suppose that autonomous expenditure increases by $0.5 trillion to $2.5 trillion. What is the new equilibrium? The answer is worked out in the final two columns of the table in Fig. 26.2. When the new level of autonomous expenditure is added to induced expenditure, aggregate planned expenditure increases by $0.5 trillion at each level of real GDP. The new aggregate expenditure curve is AE_1. The new equilibrium, highlighted in the table (row *e'*), occurs where AE_1 intersects the 45° line and is at $5 trillion (point *e'*). At this level of real GDP, aggregate planned expenditure is equal to real GDP. Autonomous expenditure is $2.5 trillion, and induced expenditure is also $2.5 trillion.

The Multiplier Effect

Notice in Fig. 26.2 that an increase in autonomous expenditure of $0.5 trillion increases real GDP by $1 trillion. That is, the change in autonomous expenditure leads, like Bonnie Raitt's music-making equipment, to an amplified change in real GDP. This is the *multiplier effect*—real GDP increases by *more than* the increase in autonomous expenditure. An increase in autonomous expenditure of $0.5 trillion initially increases aggregate expenditure and real GDP by $0.5 trillion. But the increase in real GDP *induces* a further increase in aggregate expenditure—an increase in consumption expenditure minus imports. Aggregate expenditure and real GDP increase by the sum of the initial increase on autonomous expenditure and the increase in induced expenditure. In this example, induced expenditure increases by $0.5 trillion, so real GDP increases by $1 trillion.

Although we have just analyzed the effects of an *increase* in autonomous expenditure, the same analysis applies to a decrease in autonomous expenditure. If autonomous expenditure is initially $2.5 trillion, the initial equilibrium real GDP is $5 trillion. If, in that situation, there is a cut in government purchases, exports, or investment of $0.5 trillion, then the aggregate expenditure curve shifts downward to AE_0. Equilibrium real GDP decreases from $5 trillion to $4 trillion. The decrease in real GDP is larger than the decrease in autonomous expenditure.

FIGURE 26.2

An Increase in Autonomous Expenditure

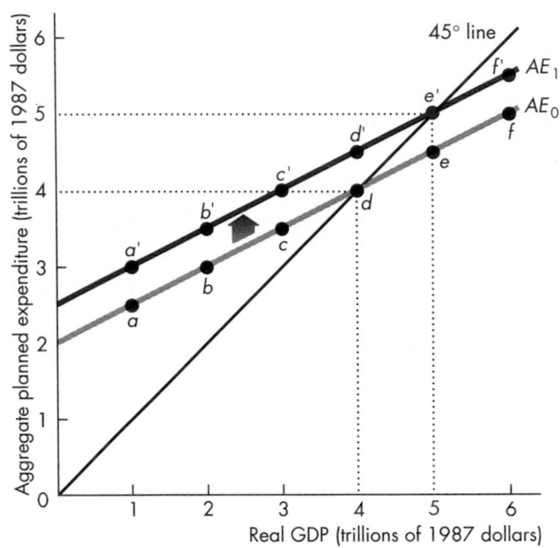

An increase in autonomous expenditure from \$2 trillion to \$2.5 trillion increases aggregate planned expenditure at each level of real GDP by \$0.5 trillion. As shown in the table, the initial equilibrium expenditure of \$4 trillion is no longer the equilibrium. At a real GDP of \$4 trillion, aggregate planned expenditure is now \$4.5 trillion. The new expenditure equilibrium is \$5 trillion, where aggregate planned expenditure equals real GDP. The increase in real GDP is larger than the increase in autonomous expenditure.

The figure illustrates the effect of the increase in autonomous expenditure. At each level of real GDP, aggregate planned expenditure is \$0.5 trillion higher than before. The aggregate planned expenditure curve shifts upward from AE_0 to AE_1. The new AE curve intersects the 45° line at e', where real GDP is \$5 trillion—the new equilibrium.

			Original expenditure			New expenditure	
Real GDP (Y)	Induced expenditure (N)		Autonomous expenditure (A_0)	Aggregate planned expenditure (E_0)		Autonomous expenditure (A_1)	Aggregate planned expenditure (E_1)
			(trillions of 1987 dollars)				
1.0	**0.5**	*a*	**2.0**	**2.5**	*a'*	**2.5**	**3.0**
2.0	**1.0**	*b*	**2.0**	**3.0**	*b'*	**2.5**	**3.5**
3.0	**1.5**	*c*	**2.0**	**3.5**	*c'*	**2.5**	**4.0**
4.0	**2.0**	*d*	**2.0**	**4.0**	*d'*	**2.5**	**4.5**
5.0	**2.5**	*e*	**2.0**	**4.5**	*e'*	**2.5**	**5.0**
6.0	**3.0**	*f*	**2.0**	**5.0**	*f*	**2.5**	**5.5**

The Paradox of Thrift

One possible source of a decrease in autonomous expenditure is a decrease in autonomous consumption expenditure. For example, if households expect lower *future* incomes, they decrease *current* consumption. Such a decrease is represented by a downward shift in the consumption function and a downward shift in the aggregate expenditure curve.

A decrease in autonomous consumption means an increase in saving—the saving function (described in Chapter 25, pp. 672–676) shifts upward. Another word for saving is thrift. The more a household saves, the thriftier it is. Also, the thriftier a household, the wealthier it becomes. By consuming less than its income, a household can increase its income by lending what it saves and earning interest on it. But what happens if we all become thriftier? Does aggregate income increase? We can work out one answer to this question by using the analysis that we've just performed.

Suppose that initially aggregate expenditure is shown by the curve AE_1 in Fig. 26.2. Real GDP is \$5 trillion. Now suppose that there is an increase in thriftiness. As a result, autonomous expenditure decreases by \$0.5 trillion, and, consequently, the aggregate expenditure curve shifts downward from AE_1 to AE_0. Equilibrium expenditure and real GDP fall to \$4 trillion.

An increase in thriftiness has reduced real GDP. The fall in real GDP caused by an increase in saving is called the **paradox of thrift**. It is a paradox because an increase in thriftiness leads to an increase in income for an individual but to a decrease in aggregate income.

The paradox arises in this model because the increase in saving is *not* associated with an increase in investment. Although people save more, no one buys additional capital goods. This combination of events is an unlikely one in reality, so the paradox of thrift, although logically correct, has little to say about the economy in which we live. In the real world, it is possible that when saving increases, investment will also increase. In such a case there is no fall in aggregate income. An increase in saving shifts the AE curve downward, but an increase in investment shifts it upward. If saving and investment change by the same amount, the AE curve does not shift. The result is no change in real GDP. But this is a short-run outcome.

There are further and much more important effects of saving and investment. They result in the accumulation of capital that enables incomes, both of individuals and of the economy as a whole, to grow over time. Thus the paradox of thrift is not paradoxical after all. It is a consequence for current income only if increased saving occurs with unchanged investment. In the long run, increased saving results in more capital and a higher level of real GDP.

We have discovered that a change in autonomous expenditure has a multiplier effect on real GDP. But how big is the multiplier effect?

The Size of the Multiplier

Suppose that the economy is recovering from a recession. Profit prospects look good, and firms are making plans for large increases in investment. The world economy is also heading toward recovery, and exports are rising. The question on everyone's lips is: how strong will the recovery be? This is a hard question to answer. But an important ingredient in the answer is working out the size of the multiplier.

The **autonomous expenditure multiplier** (often abbreviated to simply the **multiplier**) is the amount by which a change in autonomous expenditure is multiplied to determine the change in equilibrium expenditure that it generates. To calculate the multiplier, we divide the change in equilibrium real GDP by the change in autonomous expenditure. Let's calculate the multiplier for the example in Fig. 26.3(a). The economy in recession has a real GDP of \$3 trillion. Autonomous expenditure increases from \$1.5 to \$2.5 trillion, and equilibrium real GDP increases from \$3 trillion to \$5 trillion, an increase of \$2 trillion. That is,

- Autonomous expenditure increases by \$1 trillion.
- Real GDP increases by \$2 trillion.

The multiplier is

$$\text{Multiplier} = \frac{\text{Change in equilibrium real GDP}}{\text{Change in autonomous expenditure}} = \frac{\$2 \text{ trillion}}{\$1 \text{ trillion}} = 2.$$

Thus a change in autonomous expenditure of \$1 trillion produces a change in equilibrium real GDP of \$2 trillion, a change that is twice as big as the initial change in autonomous expenditure.

Next, look at Fig. 26.3(b). Again the economy in recession has a real GDP of \$3 trillion. But now, autonomous expenditure increases from \$1 to \$2 trillion, and equilibrium real GDP increases from \$3 trillion to \$6 trillion, an increase of \$3 trillion. That is,

- Autonomous expenditure increases by \$1 trillion.
- Real GDP increases by \$3 trillion.

The multiplier is

$$\text{Multiplier} = \frac{\text{Change in equilibrium real GDP}}{\text{Change in autonomous expenditure}} = \frac{\$3 \text{ trillion}}{\$1 \text{ trillion}} = 3.$$

FIGURE 26.3

The Multiplier and the Slope of the *AE* Curve

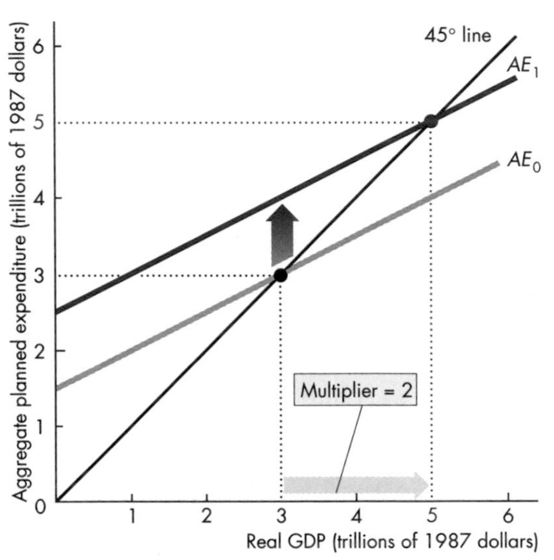

(a) Multiplier is 2

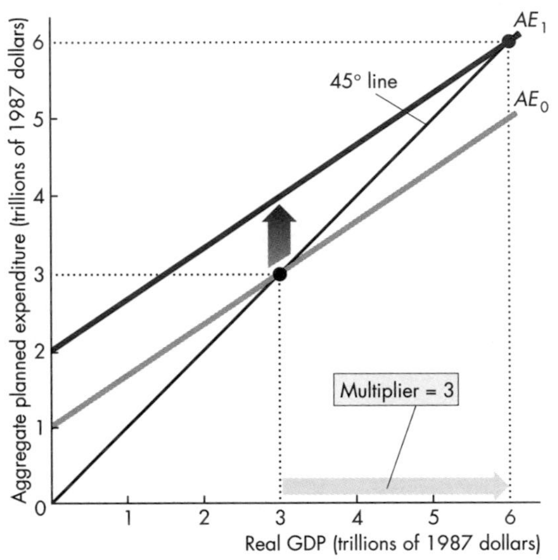

(b) Multiplier is 3

The size of the multiplier depends on the slope of the *AE* curve. The multiplier formula, $1/(1 - g)$, tells us the relationship. If the slope of the *AE* curve (g) is ½, the multiplier is 2. In this case, an increase in autonomous expenditure of $1 trillion shifts the *AE* curve upward from AE_0 to AE_1 in part (a). Real GDP increases from $3 trillion to $5 trillion, twice the increase in autonomous expenditure. If g equals ⅔, the multiplier is 3. In this case, a $1 trillion increase in autonomous expenditure shifts the aggregate expenditure curve upward from AE_0 to AE_1 in part (b). Real GDP increases from $3 trillion to $6 trillion, three times the increase in autonomous expenditure.

Thus a change in autonomous expenditure of $1 trillion produces a change in equilibrium real GDP of $3 trillion, a change that is three times as big as the initial change in autonomous expenditure.

The Multiplier and the Slope of the Aggregate Expenditure Curve

Why is the multiplier in Fig. 26.3(b) bigger than the multiplier in Fig. 26.3(a)? The reason is that the aggregate expenditure curve in part (b) is steeper than that in part (a). The steeper the *AE* curve, the larger is the multiplier. In part (a), the slope of the *AE* curve is ½ and the multiplier is 2. In part (b), the slope of the *AE* curve is ⅔ and the multiplier is 3.

Multiplier Calculations Table 26.1 shows how to calculate the value of the multiplier. Part (a) introduces some definitions. It starts with the change in real GDP, ΔY. Our objective is to calculate the size of this change when there is a given change in autonomous expenditure, ΔA. In the example in Table 26.1, the change in autonomous expenditure is $500 billion. The slope of the aggregate expenditure curve is the marginal propensity to consume out of real GDP minus the marginal propensity to import. Let's call this slope g. In Table 26.1, g is equal to ⅔, the same as in Fig. 26.3(b). The change in aggregate planned expenditure (ΔE) is the sum of the change in autonomous expenditure (ΔA) and the change in induced expenditure (ΔN). Finally, the multiplier is defined as

$$\frac{\Delta Y}{\Delta A}.$$

Part (b) of the table sets out the calculations of the change in real GDP and the multiplier. The change in aggregate planned expenditure (ΔE) is equal to the sum of the change in autonomous

TABLE 26.1

Calculating the Multiplier

	Symbols and formulas*	Numbers
(a) Definitions		
Change in real GDP	ΔY	
Change in autonomous expenditure	ΔA	500
Slope of the *AE* curve	g	⅔
Change in induced expenditure	$\Delta N = g\Delta Y$	$\Delta N = (2/3)\Delta Y$
Change in aggregate planned expenditure	$\Delta E = \Delta A + \Delta N$	
The multiplier (autonomous expenditure multiplier)	$\Delta Y/\Delta A$	
(b) Calculations		
Aggregate planned expenditure	$E = A + gY$	
Change in *AE* curve	$\Delta E = \Delta A + g\Delta Y$	$\Delta E = 500 + (2/3)\Delta Y$
Change in equilibrium expenditure	$\Delta E = \Delta Y$	
Replacing ΔE with ΔY	$\Delta Y = \Delta A + g\Delta Y$	$\Delta Y = 500 + (2/3)\Delta Y$
Subtracting $g\Delta Y$, or $(2/3)\Delta Y$, from both sides and factoring ΔY	$\Delta Y(1 - g) = \Delta A$	$\Delta Y(1 - 2/3) = 500$
Dividing both sides by $(1 - g)$, or $(1 - 2/3)$	$\Delta Y = \frac{1}{1-g}\Delta A$	$\Delta Y = \frac{1}{1-2/3}500$
		or $\Delta Y = \frac{1}{1/3}500$
		or $\Delta Y = 1{,}500$
Dividing both sides by ΔA, or 500, gives the multiplier	$\frac{\Delta Y}{\Delta A} = \frac{1}{1-g}$	$\frac{\Delta Y}{\Delta A} = \frac{1{,}500}{500} = 3$

*The Greek Δ stands for "change in."

expenditure (ΔA) and the change in induced expenditure ($g\Delta Y$). In the example the change in aggregate planned expenditure is equal to \$500 billion plus ⅔ of the change in real GDP. Since in equilibrium the change in aggregate planned expenditure is equal to the change in real GDP, the change in real GDP is

$$\Delta Y = \Delta A + g\Delta Y.$$

Using our numbers,

$$\Delta Y = 500 + (2/3)\Delta Y.$$

This equation has just one unknown, ΔY, and we can find its value as shown in the table. Finally, dividing ΔY by ΔA gives the value of the multiplier, which is:

$$\text{Multiplier} = \frac{1}{(1-g)}.$$

Because g is a fraction—a number lying between 0 and 1—$(1 - g)$ is also a fraction and the multiplier is greater than 1. In the example, g is ⅔, $(1 - g)$ is ⅓, and the multiplier is 3.

You can see that this formula works for the multiplier shown in Fig. 26.3(a). In this case, the slope of the *AE* curve is ½, g is ½, $(1 - g)$ is also ½, and the multiplier is 2.

Why Is the Multiplier Greater Than 1?

The multiplier is greater than 1 because of induced expenditure—an increase in autonomous expenditure *induces* further increases in expenditure. If GM spends $10 million on a new car assembly line, aggregate expenditure and real GDP immediately increase by $10 million. But that is not the end of the story. Engineers and construction workers now have more income, and they spend part of the extra income on cars, microwaves, vacations, and a host of other goods and services. Real GDP now rises by the initial $10 million plus the extra expenditure induced by the $10 million increase in income. The producers of cars, microwaves, vacations, and other goods now have increased incomes, and they, in turn, also spend part of their increase in income on consumption goods and services. Additional income induces additional expenditure, which creates additional income.

This multiplier process is illustrated in Fig. 26.4. In round 1, there is an increase in autonomous

FIGURE 26.4

The Multiplier Process

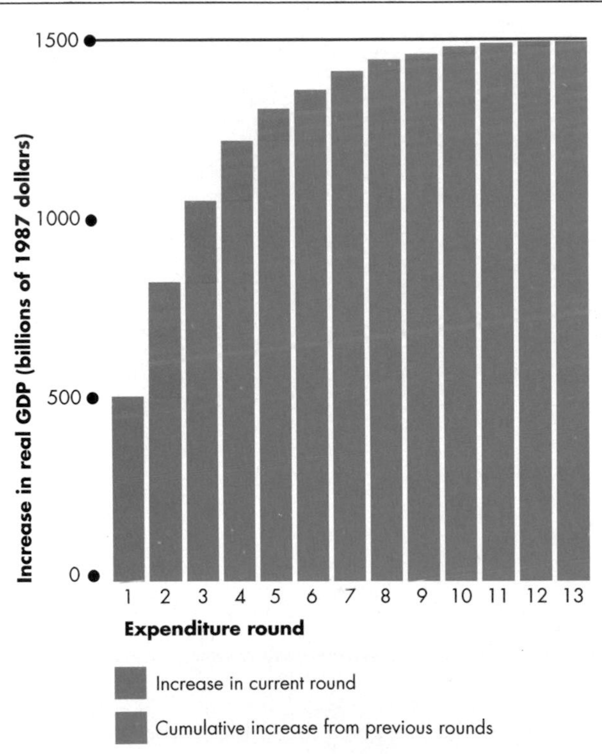

Expenditure round	Increase in aggregate expenditure	Cumulative increase in real GDP
	(billions of 1987 dollars)	
1	500	500
2	333	833
3	222	1,055
4	148	1,203
5	99	1,302
6	66	1,368
7	44	1,412
8	29	1,441
9	20	1,461
10	13	1,474
. . .	. . .	. . .
All others	26	1,500

Autonomous expenditure increases in round 1 by $500 billion. Real GDP also increases by the same amount. Each additional dollar of real GDP induces an additional two thirds of a dollar of aggregate expenditure—the slope of the aggregate expenditure curve is ⅔. In round 2, the round 1 increase in real GDP induces an increase in expenditure of $333 billion. At the end of round 2, real GDP has increased by $833 billion. The extra $333 billion of real GDP in round 2 induces a further increase in expenditure of $222 billion in round 3. Real GDP increases yet further to $1,055 billion. This process continues until real GDP has eventually increased by $1,500 billion. The table stops counting after round 10, since the extra amounts become smaller and smaller. (Perhaps you would like to run the process further on your pocket calculator. As a matter of interest, after 19 rounds you will be within $1 of the $1,500 billion total, and after 30 rounds you will be within 1¢ of that total!) The diagram shows you how quickly the multiplier effect builds up. In this example, the multiplier is 3 because the slope of the *AE* curve is ⅔ (see Table 26.1).

expenditure of $500 billion. At that stage, there is no change in induced expenditure, so aggregate expenditure and real GDP increase by $500 billion. In round 2, the higher real GDP induces higher consumption expenditure. Since, in the example in Fig. 26.4, induced expenditure increases by two thirds the increase in real GDP, the increase in real GDP of $500 billion induces a further increase in expenditure of $333 billion. This change in induced expenditure, when added to the initial change in autonomous expenditure, results in an increase in aggregate expenditure and real GDP of $833 billion. The round 2 increase in real GDP induces a round 3 increase in expenditure. The process repeats through successive rounds recorded in the table. Each increase in real GDP is two thirds the previous increase. The cumulative increase in real GDP gradually approaches $1,500 billion. Even after 10 rounds it has almost reached that level.

It appears, then, that the economy does not operate like the shock absorbers on Coleman Young's car. The economy's potholes and bumps are changes in autonomous expenditure—mainly brought about by changes in investment and exports. These economic potholes and bumps are not smoothed out, but instead are amplified.

REVIEW

Autonomous expenditure is the part of aggregate expenditure that does not respond to changes in real GDP. Induced expenditure is the part of aggregate expenditure that does respond to changes in real GDP. A change in autonomous expenditure changes equilibrium expenditure and real GDP. The magnitude of the change in real GDP is determined by the multiplier. The multiplier, in turn, is determined by the slope of the aggregate expenditure curve, which equals the marginal propensity to consume out of real GDP minus the marginal propensity to import. The steeper the aggregate expenditure curve, the larger is the multiplier. The multiplier acts like an amplifier. ◆

One of the components of autonomous expenditure that the multiplier amplifies is government purchases of goods and services. Because of this fact, the government can take advantage of the multiplier and attempt to smooth out fluctuations in aggregate expenditure. It can also vary transfer payments and taxes for this purpose. Let's see how.

Fiscal Policy Multipliers

Fiscal policy is the government's attempt to smooth the fluctuations in aggregate expenditure by varying its purchases of goods and services, transfer payments, and taxes. If the government foresees a decline in investment or exports, it may attempt to offset the effects of the decline by increasing its own purchases of goods and services, increasing transfer payments, or cutting taxes. But the government must figure out the size of the increase in purchases or transfers or the size of the tax cut needed to achieve its goal. To make this calculation, the government needs to know the multiplier effects of its own actions. Let's study the multiplier effects of changes in government purchases, transfer payments, and taxes.

Government Purchases Multiplier

The **government purchases multiplier** is the amount by which a change in government purchases of goods and services is multiplied to determine the change in equilibrium expenditure that it generates. Government purchases of goods and services are one component of autonomous expenditure. A change in government purchases has the same effect on aggregate expenditure as a change in any other component of autonomous expenditure. It sets up a multiplier effect exactly like the multiplier effect of a change in investment or exports. That is,

$$\text{Government purchases multiplier} = \frac{1}{(1-g)}.$$

By varying government purchases to offset a change in investment or exports, the government can attempt to keep total autonomous expenditure constant (or growing at a steady rate). Because the government purchases multiplier is the same size as the multiplier effect of a change in investment or exports, stabilization of autonomous expenditure can be achieved by increasing government purchases by $1 for each $1 decrease in the other items of autonomous expenditure.

In practice, using variations in government purchases to stabilize aggregate expenditure is not easy because the political decision-making process that changes government purchases of goods and services operates with a long time lag. As a consequence, it is not possible to forecast changes in private expenditure far enough ahead to make this instrument an effective one for macroeconomic stabilization.

A second way in which the government may seek to stabilize aggregate expenditure is by varying transfer payments. Let's see how this type of policy works.

Transfer Payments Multiplier

The **transfer payments multiplier** is the amount by which a change in transfer payments is multiplied to determine the change in equilibrium expenditure that it generates. A change in transfer payments influences aggregate expenditure by changing disposable income, which leads to a change in consumption expenditure. This change in consumption expenditure is a change in autonomous expenditure, and it has a multiplier effect exactly like that of any other change in autonomous expenditure. But how large is the initial change in consumption expenditure? It is equal to the change in transfer payments multiplied by the marginal propensity to consume. If the marginal propensity to consume is b, a $1 increase in transfer payments initially increases consumption expenditure by $$b$. For example, if the marginal propensity to consume is 0.9, a $1 increase in transfer payments initially increases consumption expenditure by 90¢. Therefore the transfer payments multiplier is equal to b times the autonomous expenditure multiplier. That is,

$$\text{Transfer payments multiplier} = \frac{b}{(1 - g)}.$$

For example, if the marginal propensity to consume is 0.9 and the slope of the *AE* curve (g) is 0.5, the transfer payments multiplier is 1.8 (0.9/0.5 = 1.8). Notice that the transfer payments multiplier is b times the government purchases multiplier. Because the marginal propensity to consume (b) is less than 1, the transfer payments multiplier is *smaller* than the government purchases multiplier.

The use of variations in transfer payments to stabilize the economy has the same problems as the use of variations in government purchases of goods and services. The political process does not operate on the time scale required for timely changes in transfer payments to offset fluctuations in other components of autonomous expenditure.

Tax Multipliers

A third type of fiscal stabilization policy is to vary taxes. The **tax multiplier** is the amount by which a change in taxes is multiplied to determine the change in equilibrium expenditure that it generates. An *increase* in taxes leads to a *decrease* in disposable income and a decrease in consumption expenditure. The amount by which consumption expenditure decreases initially is determined by the marginal propensity to consume. This initial response of consumption expenditure to a tax increase is exactly the

FIGURE 26.5
The Tax Multiplier

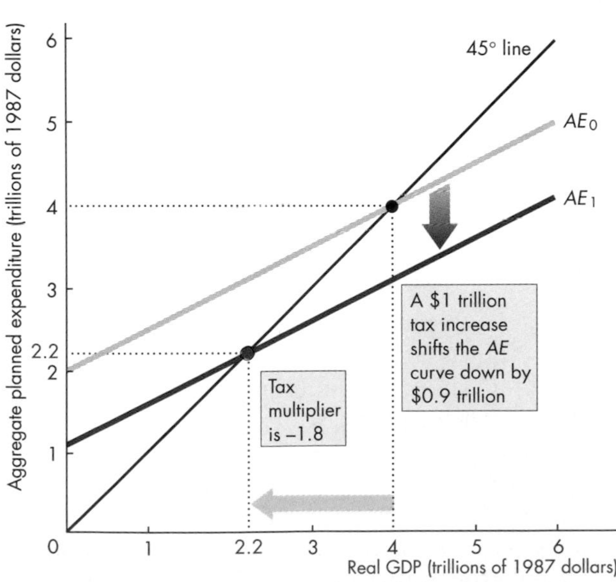

Initially, the aggregate expenditure curve is AE_0, and equilibrium expenditure is $4 trillion. The slope of the *AE* curve is 0.5. Taxes are increased by $1 trillion, so disposable income falls by $1 trillion. The marginal propensity to consume is 0.9, and the aggregate expenditure curve shifts downward by $0.9 trillion to AE_1. Equilibrium expenditure and real GDP decrease by $1.8 trillion—the tax multiplier is –1.8.

same as the response of consumption expenditure to a decrease in transfer payments. Thus a tax change works like a change in transfer payments but in the opposite direction, and the tax multiplier equals the negative of the transfer payments multiplier. Because a tax *increase* leads to a *decrease* in equilibrium expenditure, the tax multiplier is *negative*. It is

$$\text{Tax multiplier} = \frac{-b}{(1-g)}.$$

For example, if the marginal propensity to consume (b) is 0.9 and the slope of the AE curve (g) is 0.5, the tax multiplier is –1.8.

Figure 26.5 illustrates the multiplier effect of a tax increase. Initially, the aggregate expenditure curve is AE_0, and equilibrium expenditure is $4 trillion. The slope of the aggregate expenditure curve AE_0 is 0.5. Taxes increase by $1 trillion, and disposable income falls by that amount. With a marginal propensity to consume of 0.9, consumption expenditure decreases initially by $0.9 trillion and the aggregate expenditure curve shifts downward by that amount to AE_1. Equilibrium expenditure and real GDP fall by $1.8 trillion to $2.2 trillion. The tax multiplier is –1.8.

Balanced Budget Multiplier

A balanced budget fiscal policy action is one that keeps the government budget deficit or surplus unchanged—both government purchases and taxes change by the same amount. The **balanced budget multiplier** is the amount by which a change in government purchases of goods and services is multiplied to determine the change in expenditure equilibrium when taxes are changed by the same amount as the change in government purchases. What is the multiplier effect of this fiscal policy action?

To answer, we must combine the two multipliers that we have just worked out. We've seen that those two separate multipliers are

$$\text{Government purchases multiplier} = \frac{1}{(1-g)}.$$

$$\text{Tax multiplier} = \frac{-b}{(1-g)}.$$

Adding these two multipliers together gives the balanced budget multiplier, which is

$$\text{Balanced budget multiplier} = \frac{(1-b)}{(1-g)}.$$

Because the marginal propensity to consume (b) is bigger than the slope of the AE curve (g), the balanced budget multiplier is less than 1. For example, if the marginal propensity to consume is 0.9 and the slope of the AE curve is 0.5, the balanced budget multiplier is 0.2 (0.1/0.5 = 0.2).

Figure 26.6 illustrates the balanced budget multiplier. Initially, the aggregate expenditure curve is AE_0, and real GDP is $4 trillion. A $1 trillion increase in taxes decreases aggregate planned expenditure by $0.9 trillion and shifts the aggregate expenditure curve downward to AE_0'. A $1 trillion increase in government purchases increases aggregate planned expenditure by the entire $1 trillion and shifts the aggregate expenditure curve upward to AE_1. The net shift in the aggregate expenditure curve is upward by $0.1 trillion. The new equilibrium occurs at the intersection of AE_1 and the 45° line

FIGURE 26.6

The Balanced Budget Multiplier

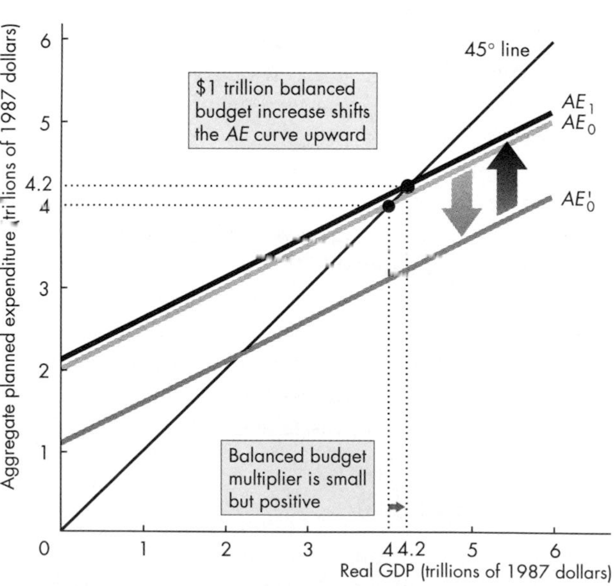

Initially, the aggregate expenditure curve is AE_0. The government increases both taxes and purchases of goods and services by $1 trillion. The $1 trillion tax increase shifts the aggregate expenditure curve downward by $0.9 trillion to AE_0'. The $1 trillion increase in government purchases shifts the aggregate expenditure curve upward by the entire $1 trillion to AE_1. Real GDP increases by $0.2 trillion—the balanced budget multiplier is 0.2.

(highlighted by the red dot). Real GDP increases by \$0.1 trillion times the autonomous expenditure multiplier. Thus the balanced budget multiplier is positive but small. In this example, it is 0.2.

The balanced budget multiplier is important because it means that the government does not have to unbalance its budget and run a deficit in order to stimulate aggregate demand. Reading Between the Lines on pp. 714–715 looks at some fiscal policy proposals being considered in 1992 to change taxes and government purchases by the same amount.

REVIEW

The government purchases multiplier is equal to the autonomous expenditure multiplier. By varying its purchases of goods and services, the government can try to offset fluctuations in investment and exports. The transfer payments multiplier is equal to the marginal propensity to consume multiplied by the government purchases multiplier. A change in transfer payments works through a change in disposable income. Part of the change in disposable income is spent, and part is saved. Only the part that is spent, that is determined by the marginal propensity to consume, has a multiplier effect. The tax multiplier has the same magnitude as the transfer payments multiplier, but it is negative—a tax *increase* leads to a *decrease* in equilibrium expenditure. An equal change in both purchases of goods and services and taxes has a balanced budget multiplier effect on real GDP. The balanced budget multiplier is small but positive. In practice, fiscal actions are difficult to use to stabilize the economy because of time lags in the legislative process. ◆

Automatic Stabilizers

Income taxes and transfer payments act as automatic stabilizers. An **automatic stabilizer** is a mechanism that decreases the fluctuations in *aggregate* expenditure resulting from fluctuations in a *component* of aggregate expenditure. The automatic stabilizing effects of income taxes and transfer payments mean that they act like an economic shock absorber, making the aggregate effects of fluctuations in investment and exports smaller than they otherwise would be.

To see how income taxes and transfer payments act as an economic shock absorber, let's see how a change in investment or exports affects equilibrium expenditure in two economies: in the first economy there are no income taxes and transfer payments, and in the second there are income taxes and transfer payments similar to those in the United States today.

No Income Taxes and Transfer Payments In an economy with no income taxes and transfer payments, the gap between GDP and disposable income is constant—it does not depend on the level of GDP. If the marginal propensity to consume is 0.9, the marginal propensity to consume out of GDP is also 0.9. That is, each extra dollar of GDP is an extra dollar of disposable income and induces an extra 90¢ of consumption expenditure. Suppose that there are no imports, so not only is the marginal propensity to consume 0.9, but so also is the slope of the *AE* curve.

What is the size of the multiplier in this case? You can answer this question by using the formula

$$\text{Multiplier} = \frac{1}{(1 - g)}.$$

The value of g is 0.9, so the value of the multiplier is 10. In this economy, a \$1 million change in autonomous expenditure produces a \$10 million change in equilibrium expenditure. This economy has a very strong amplifier.

Income Taxes and Transfer Payments Contrast the economy that we have just described with one that has income taxes and transfer payments.

The scale of income taxes minus transfer payments is determined by the marginal tax rate. The **marginal tax rate** is the fraction of the last dollar of income paid to the government in net taxes (taxes minus transfer payments).

Let's assume that the marginal tax rate is 0.3. That is, each additional dollar of real GDP generates tax revenue for the government of 30¢ and disposable income of 70¢. If the marginal propensity to consume is 0.9 (the same as in the previous example), a \$1 increase in real GDP increases disposable income by 70¢ and increases consumption expenditure by 63¢ (0.9 of 0.7 equals 0.63). In this economy, the slope of the *AE* curve is 0.63. The value of g is 0.63, so the multiplier is 2.7. The economy still amplifies shocks from changes in exports and investment, but on a much smaller scale than the economy with no income taxes and transfer payments. Thus, to some degree, income taxes and transfer payments absorb the shocks of fluctuations in autonomous expenditure. The higher the marginal tax rate, the greater is the extent to which autonomous expenditure shocks are absorbed.

The existence of taxes and transfer payments that vary with real GDP helps the shock-absorbing capacities of the economy. They don't produce the economic equivalent of the suspension of a Lincoln Continental, but they do produce the economic equivalent of something better than the springs of a stagecoach. As the economy fluctuates, the government's budget fluctuates, absorbing some of the shocks, changing taxes and transfer payments, and smoothing the fluctuations in disposable income and aggregate expenditure.

Let's look at the effects of automatic stabilizers on the government's budget and its deficit.

Automatic Stabilizers and the Government Deficit

Because income taxes and transfer payments fluctuate with real GDP, so does the government's deficit. Figure 26.7 shows how. Government purchases are independent of the level of real GDP. In the figure, they are fixed at $900 billion—shown by the horizontal red line. Income taxes net of transfer payments increase as real GDP increases. In the figure, they are shown by the upward-sloping blue line. There is a particular level of real GDP at which the government's budget is balanced—the deficit is zero. In the figure, that level of real GDP is $4 trillion. When real GDP is below $4 trillion, there is a deficit. And when real GDP is above $4 trillion, there is a surplus.

As investment and exports fluctuate, bringing fluctuations in real GDP, income taxes and the deficit also fluctuate. For example, a large increase in investment increases real GDP, increases income taxes, and reduces the deficit (or creates a surplus). The higher income taxes act as an automatic stabilizer. They decrease disposable income and induce a decrease in consumption expenditure. This decrease dampens the effects of the initial increase in investment and moderates the increase in aggregate expenditure and real GDP.

Conversely, when a large decrease in investment is pushing the economy into recession, income taxes decrease and the deficit increases (or the surplus decreases). The lower income taxes act as an automatic stabilizer. They limit the fall in disposable income and moderate the extent of the decline in aggregate expenditure and real GDP.

FIGURE 26.7

The Government Deficit

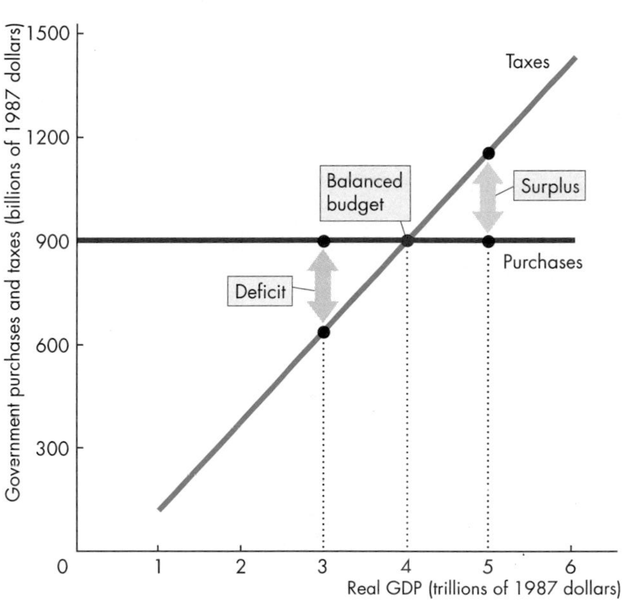

Government purchases (the red line) are independent of the level of real GDP, but income taxes (the blue line) increase as real GDP increases. When real GDP is $4 trillion, the government's budget is balanced. When real GDP is below $4 trillion, there is a deficit, and when real GDP is above $4 trillion, there is a surplus. Fluctuations in taxes act as an automatic stabilizer when the economy is hit by changes in autonomous expenditure.

REVIEW

The presence of income taxes and transfer payments that vary with real GDP reduces the value of the multiplier and acts as an automatic stabilizer. The higher the marginal tax rate, the smaller are the fluctuations in real GDP resulting from fluctuations in autonomous expenditure. ◆

Hoping for a Multiplier

THE BOSTON GLOBE, JANUARY 29, 1992

Bush issues proposal to trim taxes, arms, federal programs

Plan outlined in State of the Union

BY MICHAEL KRANISH

President Bush, with his popularity at a record low and the nation mired in a recession, last night unveiled a modest economic recovery plan that could cut next year's taxes by a few hundred dollars for many families. He also proposed cutting defense spending and eliminating 246 programs.

While vague on many details, Bush sought forcefully to portray himself as a president who is as determined to end the recession as he was in leading the Gulf War. . . .

In the proposal most likely to affect the typical American, Bush proposed a tax break that amounts to a $140 tax cut for each child in a family in the 28 percent tax bracket. That is accomplished by raising the current $2,300 personal exemption by $500. But the break would not take effect until October, meaning that only one-fourth of it would be available on tax returns for 1992. Bush also proposed changing the tax-withholding formula in a way that would allow taxpayers who typically get large refunds to receive a few more dollars a week in their paycheck and a smaller refund at tax time.

Bush also revived many proposals that he has previously failed to get through Congress, but made some of them more controversial than before. For instance, having failed to cut the capital gains tax from 28 percent to 19.6 percent, Bush last night proposed cutting it to 15.4 percent. Similarly, having failed to convince Congress to eliminate more than 100 domestic programs in his three previous budgets, Bush proposed eliminating 246 programs, but he did not name them. . . .

Bush also . . . urged passage of a $5,000 tax credit for first-time home buyers, penalty-free withdrawal from Individual Retirement Accounts and several tax breaks for investors who have lost money in real estate. . . .

Although Bush sought to shift the focus to domestic affairs, many of his most dramatic proposals concerned foreign affairs and defense spending. In moves that are expected to save $50 billion over five years, Bush proposed eliminating all 50 MX long-range multiple-warhead missiles, stopping funding for the Midgetman missile and reducing the B-2 stealth bomber force from a planned force of 132 to 20.

The Essence of the Story

In January 1992, President Bush presented his proposals for helping the economy to recover from recession while keeping the deficit in check.

The package included the following tax changes:

- Increase in personal income tax exemption
- Lower tax withholding from paychecks
- Tax credit for first-time home buyers
- Capital gains tax cut

To cut spending, the president proposed eliminating 246 programs and cutting $50 billion from the defense budget over the next five years.

Background and Analysis

The Omnibus Budget Reconciliation Act of 1990 puts Congress under a constraint to bring the federal deficit down in stages, and there is no scope, under the current law, for using fiscal policy to stimulate the economy if the proposed policy package increases the deficit.

Faced with this constraint, in January 1992 the Bush administration proposed a package of tax cuts balanced by spending cuts.

Other things remaining the same, this type of fiscal policy action has a balanced budget multiplier effect that further depresses the economy. In Fig. 1, a tax cut increases aggregate planned expenditure, shifting the *AE* curve from AE_0 to AE_1. But a decrease in government purchases (the peace dividend) of the same magnitude shifts the *AE* curve from AE_1 to AE_2. Equilibrium expenditure and real GDP decline.

But the intent and hope of the administration is that other things will not remain constant. Its proposed tax cut is aimed mainly at stimulating investment. If the tax cuts bring increased optimism about future profits, investment will increase and, as shown in Fig. 2, the *AE* curve will shift upward to AE_3, increasing real GDP.

Furthermore, with higher investment, the capital stock grows more quickly. As a result, long-run output also grows more quickly. This outcome is the main purpose of the president's "growth package."

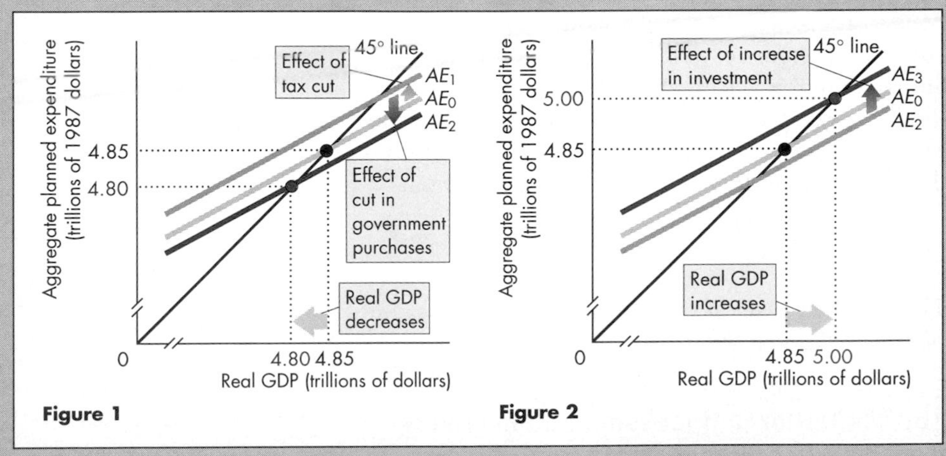

Figure 1

Figure 2

We've now seen what determines the value of the autonomous expenditure multiplier and how the multiplier can be used by the government to influence aggregate planned expenditure by changing government purchases, transfer payments, or taxes. But so far we have studied model economies with hypothetical numbers. Let's now turn to the real world. How big is the multiplier in the U.S. economy?

The Multiplier in the United States

In the model economy that we studied earlier in this chapter, each additional dollar of income induces 50¢ of expenditure. Its multiplier is 2. Let's look at some estimates of the multiplier in the U.S. economy.

The U.S. Multiplier in 1990

In 1990, the marginal propensity to consume in the United States was approximately 0.9 and disposable income was approximately two thirds of GDP. Putting these two pieces of information together, we can calculate that the marginal propensity to consume out of GDP is 0.63 (0.7 of 0.9 equals 0.63). Imports were approximately 15 percent of GDP. Using this percentage as an estimate of the marginal propensity to import gives a value of 0.15; each additional dollar of GDP induces 15¢ of imports. Subtracting the marginal propensity to import from the marginal propensity to consume gives the slope of the *AE* curve, which is 0.48 (that is, 0.63 minus 0.15). The multiplier is 1.92. That is,

$$\text{The multiplier} = \frac{1}{(1 - 0.48)} = \frac{1}{0.42} = 1.92.$$

Thus, on the basis of these estimates, the U.S. multiplier in 1990 was a little under 2.

The Multiplier in Recession and Recovery

Is the multiplier a stable number—a constant—on which we can rely? Does the multiplier take on the same value when the economy is going into a recession as when it is recovering from a recession? Or does its value vary, and if so, does it vary in a systematic way? Answers to questions such as these are important for the design of policies to keep aggregate expenditure steady. How big an increase in government purchases or cut in taxes is needed to avoid a recession? How big a cut in government purchases or increase in taxes is needed to prevent the economy from running into supply bottlenecks?

You can see part of the answers to these questions in Table 26.2, which shows estimates of the value of the U.S. multiplier for selected years between 1960 and 1991. The estimates of the multiplier shown in the table were calculated by dividing the change in real GDP by the change in autonomous expenditure. In these calculations, the change in autonomous expenditure was measured as the change in the sum of investment, government purchases of goods and services, and exports. The

TABLE 26.2

The Multiplier in Selected Years

Period	Change in autonomous expenditure (ΔA)	Change in induced expenditure (ΔN)	Change in real GDP (ΔY)	Multiplier ($\Delta Y/\Delta A$)
	(billions of 1987 dollars)			
1960–1991	**1,255.6**	**1,595.3**	**2,850.8**	**2.27**
1974–1975	**–98.8**	**72.3**	**–26.4**	**0.27**
1981–1982	**–109.6**	**26.8**	**–82.8**	**0.76**
1982–1983	**68.4**	**77.7**	**146.3**	**2.14**
1983–1990*	**560.2**	**436.5**	**996.7**	**1.78**
1990–1991†	**–75.4**	**–3.8**	**–79.3**	**1.05**

*Third quarter of 1990.
†First quarter of 1991.

The average value of the multiplier from 1960 to 1991 was 2.27. In the recessions (shaded red) of 1974–1975 and 1981–1982 the multiplier was less than 1, and in the recession of 1990–1991 the multiplier was close to 1. In the recoveries (shaded blue) of 1982–1983 and 1983–1990 the multiplier was larger than 1. The multiplier was small in recession years because the decrease in income was expected to be temporary. The multiplier was smaller in the 1980s than earlier because the marginal propensity to import increased.

Source: Survey of Current Business, November 1991, pp. 6, 37; and my calculations.

change in induced expenditure is measured as the change in consumption expenditure minus the change in imports.

The first row of the table shows the average value of the multiplier between 1960 and 1991, which is 2.27. The three red rows of the table calculate the multiplier for three recession periods. In 1974–1975, we experienced a sharp cut in investment following the pessimism created by the OPEC oil price hike. In 1981–1982, we experienced a sharp cut in investment caused partly by high interest rates and partly by pessimistic profit expectations. In 1990–1991, investment decreased sharply, mainly because the outlook for profits was bleak. In the first two of these recession periods, despite there being a decrease in autonomous expenditure, induced expenditure increased. As a result, real GDP fell, but by less than the fall in autonomous expenditure. In these two years, the multiplier was less than 1. In the recession of 1991, induced expenditure decreased, but by a tiny amount, and the multiplier was close to 1. The two blue rows of the table calculate the multiplier for recovery periods in the 1980s. As you can see, the multipliers for these periods are larger than the multipliers for the recessions.

Why are multipliers small when the economy goes into recession and larger in recovery? The answer to this question is found in the behavior of the marginal propensity to consume. Consumption expenditure depends on both current disposable income and expected future disposable income. Therefore the effect of a change in current disposable income on consumption expenditure depends on whether the change is expected to be permanent or temporary. A change in current disposable income that is expected to be permanent is larger than the effect of a change that is expected to be temporary. That is, the marginal propensity to consume is larger when there is a permanent change in income than when income changes temporarily. For this reason, the marginal propensity to consume varies and does so in a way that is connected with the business cycle.

At the start of a recovery, income gains are expected to be permanent and the marginal propensity to consume is high. When a business cycle peak is approached and during recessions, income changes are expected to be temporary and the marginal propensity to consume is low. When real GDP fell in 1974–1975 and again in 1981–1982 as the economy went into recession, households expected the income loss they experienced to be temporary. They did not cut their consumption expenditure. Instead, consumption expenditure increased, but by less than it would have done in the absence of the recession. Nevertheless, the increase in consumption expenditure was a rational reaction to events interpreted as a temporary halt to an otherwise ongoing period of economic growth and expansion. Because consumption expenditure did not decline, the recessions were less severe than they otherwise would have been. The multiplier was less than 1, and consumption expenditure acted, to some degree, like a shock absorber.

When a recovery gets under way and real GDP increases, people expect a large part of their increased incomes to be permanent. As a consequence, consumption expenditure increases to reinforce the increase in autonomous expenditure, so the multiplier is larger than 1.

The Declining U.S. Multiplier

Although the multiplier in recovery is larger than that in recession, you can see from the numbers in Table 26.2 that the multiplier has declined over the years. The multiplier is 2.27 for the entire 31 years, 2.14 for the early 1980s, and 1.78 for the late 1980s. Why has the multiplier declined? The answer is the behavior of the *marginal propensity to import.*

We discovered in Chapter 25 that there has been a steady increase in imports as a percentage of GDP over the past 20 years. This steady increase has resulted partly from changes in international relative prices—many goods and services that are produced abroad are produced there at a lower cost than that at which we can produce them in the United States. The increase has also resulted from a steady increase in the degree of international specialization in the production of goods and services. That is, we have become more specialized, increasing our exports, and other countries have also become more specialized, increasing their exports to us. All of these factors have increased the marginal propensity to import. The higher the marginal propensity to import, the lower is the slope of the *AE* curve and the smaller is the multiplier.

We have studied the effects of changes in autonomous expenditure and fiscal policy on real GDP *at a given price level.* We're now going to see how the price level itself responds to changes in autonomous expenditure and fiscal policy. We're also going to see that the autonomous expenditure and fiscal policy multiplier effects on real GDP are smaller when price level changes are taken into account.

Real GDP, the Price Level, and the Multipliers

When firms find unwanted inventories piling up, they cut back on orders and decrease production. They also usually cut prices. Similarly, when firms are having trouble keeping up with sales and their inventories are falling, they increase their orders and step up production. But they also usually increase their prices. So far, we've studied the macroeconomic consequences of firms changing their production levels when their sales change, but we've not looked at the effects of price changes. When firms change their prices, for the economy as a whole the price level changes.

To study the price level, we need to use the *aggregate demand–aggregate supply model*. We also need to work out the relationship between the aggregate demand–aggregate supply model and the aggregate expenditure model that we've used in this chapter. The key to the relationship between these two models is the distinction between the aggregate *expenditure* curve and the aggregate *demand* curve.

Aggregate Expenditure and Aggregate Demand

The aggregate expenditure curve is the relationship between aggregate planned expenditure and real GDP, holding all other influences constant. The aggregate demand curve is the relationship between the aggregate quantity of goods and services demanded and the price level, holding all other influences constant. Let's explore the links between these two relationships.

Aggregate Planned Expenditure and the Price Level

At a given price level, there is a given level of aggregate planned expenditure. But if the price level changes, so does aggregate planned expenditure. Why? There are three main reasons, and they are explained more fully in Chapter 24. They are

- Real money balances effect
- Intertemporal substitution effect
- International substitution effect

A rise in the price level, other things held constant, decreases the real money supply. A lower real money supply decreases aggregate planned expenditure—the *real money balances effect.* A lower real money supply also brings higher interest rates that lead to a decrease in investment—the *intertemporal substitution effect.* A higher price level, other things remaining the same, makes U.S.-produced goods less competitive, increasing imports and decreasing exports—the *international substitution effect.*

All these effects of a higher price level lower aggregate planned expenditure at each level of real GDP. As a result, when the price level rises, the aggregate expenditure curve shifts downward. A decrease in the price level has the opposite effect. When the price level falls, the aggregate expenditure curve shifts upward.

Figure 26.8(a) illustrates these effects. When the price level is 100, the aggregate expenditure curve is AE_0, which intersects the 45° line at point *b*. Equilibrium expenditure and real GDP are $4 trillion. If the price level increases to 150, the aggregate expenditure curve shifts downward to AE_1, which intersects the 45° line at point *a*. Equilibrium expenditure and real GDP are $2 trillion. If the price level decreases to 50, the aggregate expenditure curve shifts upward to AE_2, which intersects the 45° line at point *c*. Equilibrium expenditure and real GDP are $6 trillion.

We've just seen that when the price level changes, other things held constant, the aggregate expenditure curve shifts and a new expenditure equilibrium arises. But when the price level changes, other things held constant, there is a movement along the aggregate demand curve. Figure 26.8(b) illustrates these movements. At a price level of 100, the aggregate quantity of goods and services demanded is $4 trillion—point *b* on the aggregate demand curve *AD*. If the price level increases to 150, the aggregate quantity of goods and services demanded falls to $2 trillion. There is a movement along the aggregate demand curve to point *a*. If the price level decreases to 50, the aggregate quantity of goods and services

FIGURE 26.8

Aggregate Expenditure and Aggregate Demand

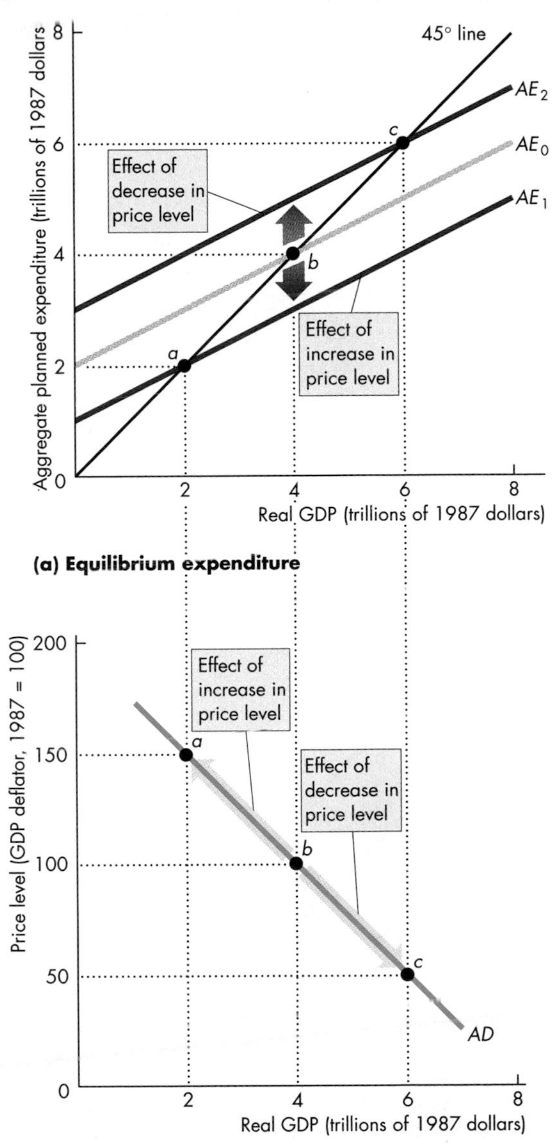

The position of the aggregate expenditure curve depends on the price level—a change in the price level shifts the aggregate expenditure curve. When the price level is 100, the aggregate expenditure curve is AE_0, as shown in part (a). Equilibrium occurs where AE_0 intersects the 45° line, at point *b*. The quantity of real GDP demanded is $4 trillion. When the price level increases to 150, the aggregate expenditure curve shifts downward to AE_1, and equilibrium occurs at point *a*, where the quantity of real GDP demanded is $2 trillion. When the price level falls to 50, the *AE* curve shifts upward to AE_2 and the equilibrium occurs at point *c*, where the quantity of real GDP demanded is $6 trillion. Part (b) shows the aggregate demand curve—the relationship between the price level and the quantity of real GDP demanded. A change in the price level shifts the aggregate expenditure curve but results in a movement along the aggregate demand curve. Thus points *a*, *b*, and *c* on the aggregate demand curve correspond to those same equilibrium points in part (a).

demanded rises to $6 trillion. There is a movement along the aggregate demand curve to point *c*. Each point on the aggregate demand curve corresponds to an expenditure equilibrium. The expenditure equilibrium points *a*, *b*, and *c* in Fig. 26.8(a) correspond to the points *a*, *b*, and *c* on the aggregate demand curve in Fig. 26.8(b).

Now that we've seen the relationship between the aggregate demand curve and equilibrium expenditure, let's work out what happens to aggregate demand, the price level, and real GDP when there are changes in autonomous expenditure and changes in fiscal policy. We'll start by looking at the effects on aggregate demand.

Aggregate Demand, Autonomous Expenditure, and Fiscal Policy

We've just seen that the aggregate expenditure curve shifts when the price level changes. But it also shifts for a thousand other reasons. It is these other sources of shifts in the aggregate expenditure curve that we studied earlier in this chapter—for example, a change in investment, exports, and fiscal policy. Any factor other than the price level that shifts the aggregate expenditure curve also shifts the aggregate demand curve. Figure 26.9 illustrates these shifts.

Initially, the aggregate expenditure curve is AE_0 in part (a) and the aggregate demand curve is AD_0 in part (b). The price level is 100. Now suppose that autonomous expenditure increases by $1 trillion. (This increase could result from an increase in investment, exports, or government purchases of goods and services or a tax cut.) At a constant price level of 100, the aggregate expenditure curve shifts upward to AE_1. This curve intersects the 45° line at an equilibrium expenditure of $6 trillion (point *c'*). This amount is the aggregate quantity of goods and services demanded at a price level of 100, as shown by point *c'* in part (b). Point *c'* lies on a new aggregate demand curve. The aggregate demand curve has shifted to the right to AD_1.

The distance by which the aggregate demand curve shifts to the right is determined by the multiplier. The larger the multiplier, the larger is the shift in the aggregate demand curve resulting from a given change in autonomous expenditure. In this example, a $1 trillion increase in autonomous expenditure produces a $2 trillion increase in the aggregate quantity of goods and services demanded at each price level. The multiplier is 2. That is, a $1 trillion increase in autonomous expenditure shifts the aggregate demand curve to the right by $2 trillion.

A decrease in autonomous expenditure shifts the aggregate expenditure curve downward and shifts the aggregate demand curve to the left. You can see these effects by reversing the change that we've just studied. Suppose that the economy initially is on aggregate expenditure curve AE_1 and aggregate demand curve AD_1. There is then a decrease in autonomous expenditure, and the aggregate planned expenditure curve shifts downward to AE_0. The aggregate quantity of goods and services demanded falls to $4 trillion, and the aggregate demand curve shifts leftward to AD_0.

FIGURE 26.9

Changes in Autonomous Expenditure and Aggregate Demand

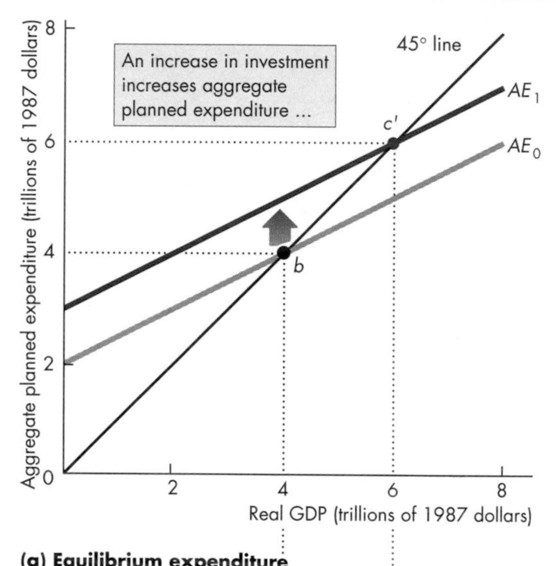

(a) Equilibrium expenditure

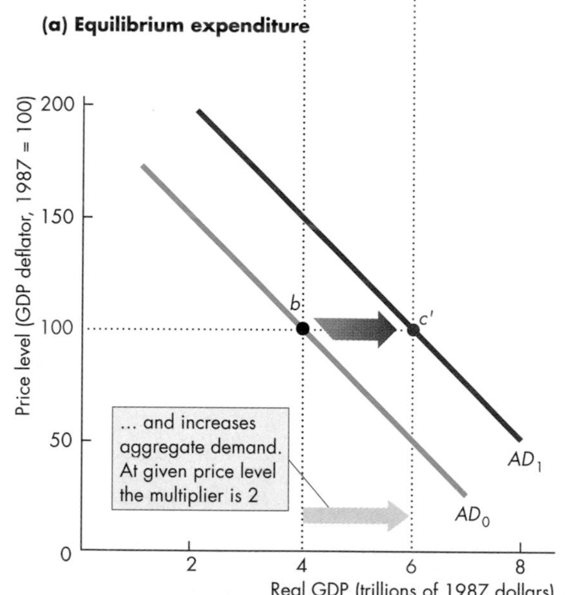

(b) Aggregate demand

The price level is 100. When the aggregate expenditure curve is AE_0 (part a), the aggregate demand curve is AD_0 (part b). An increase in autonomous expenditure shifts the aggregate expenditure upward to AE_1. In the new equilibrium (at *c'*) real GDP is $6 trillion. Since the quantity of real GDP demanded at a price level of 100 increases to $6 trillion, the aggregate demand curve shifts to the right to AD_1.

We can summarize what we have just discovered in the following way: An increase in autonomous expenditure arising from some source other than a change in the price level shifts the *AE* curve upward and shifts the *AD* curve to the right. The size of the shift of the *AD* curve is determined by the change in autonomous expenditure and the size of the multiplier.

Equilibrium GDP and the Price Level

In Chapter 24, we learned how to determine the equilibrium level of real GDP and the price level as the intersection point of the aggregate demand and short-run aggregate supply curves. We've now put aggregate demand under a more powerful microscope and discovered that changes in autonomous expenditure and fiscal policy shift the aggregate demand curve and that the magnitude of the shift depends on the size of the multiplier. But whether a change in autonomous expenditure results ultimately in a change in real GDP or a change in the price level or some combination of the two depends on aggregate supply. We'll look at two cases. First, we'll see what happens in the short run. Then we'll look at the long run.

An Increase in Aggregate Demand in the Short Run

The economy is described in Fig. 26.10. In part (a), the aggregate expenditure curve is AE_0 and equilibrium expenditure and real GDP are $4 trillion—point *b*. In part (b), aggregate demand is AD_0 and the short-run aggregate supply curve is *SAS*. (Check back to Chapter 24 if you need to refresh your understanding of this curve.) Equilibrium is at point *b*, where the aggregate demand and short-run aggregate supply curves intersect. The price level is 100.

Now suppose there is a tax cut that increases autonomous expenditure by $1 trillion. With the price level held constant at 100, the aggregate expenditure curve shifts upward to AE_1. Equilibrium expenditure and real GDP increase to $6 trillion—point *c'* in part (a). In part (b), the aggregate demand curve shifts to the right by $2 trillion, from AD_0 to AD_1. But with this new aggregate demand curve, the price level does not remain constant. It increases to 125, as determined by the point of intersection of the short-run aggregate supply curve and the new aggregate demand curve—point *d*. And real GDP does not increase to $6 trillion, but to $5 trillion.

FIGURE 26.10

Fiscal Policy, Real GDP, and the Price Level

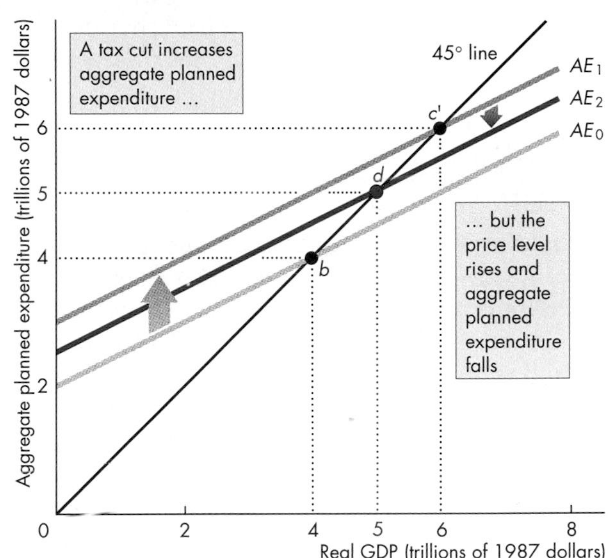

(a) Equilibrium expenditure

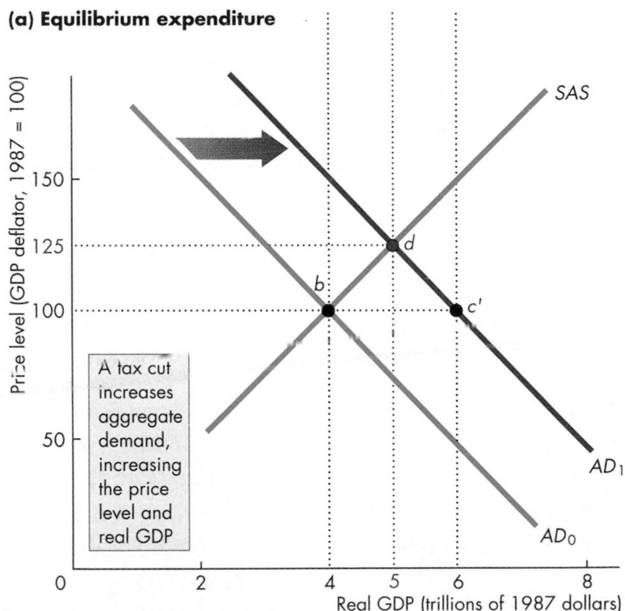

(b) Aggregate demand

A tax cut shifts the *AE* curve upward from AE_0 to AE_1 (part a). The *AD* curve shifts from AD_0 to AD_1 (part b). The economy moves to point c' (parts a and b), and there is excess demand. The price level rises, and the higher price level shifts the *AE* curve downward to AE_2. The economy moves to point *d* in both parts. The steeper the *SAS* curve, the larger is the price level change and the smaller is the change in real GDP.

At a price level of 125, the aggregate expenditure curve does not remain at AE_1 in part (a). It shifts downward to AE_2, which intersects the 45° line at a level of aggregate expenditure and real GDP of $5 trillion (point *d*).

Taking price level effects into account, the tax cut still has a multiplier effect on real GDP, but the effect is smaller than it would be if the price level remained constant. The steeper the short-run aggregate supply curve, the larger is the increase in the price level and the smaller is the multiplier effect on real GDP.

At a Bottling Plant in Kalamazoo The result that we've just worked out might be easier to understand if you think about what happens in a single factory—a bottling plant in Kalamazoo. When taxes are cut and people have more to spend, part of their extra spending is on bottles of soda. Orders increase at the bottling plant, and it increases production. But costs also increase. To produce more bottles of soda, labor must be hired and the plant must be operated for longer hours. The new labor must be trained, and with longer production hours, less time is available for maintenance, so more plant breakdowns occur. Faced with higher costs, the factory increases prices. Thus the bottling factory responds to an increase in demand partly with an increase in production and partly with higher prices. The higher prices result in a decrease in the quantity of soda demanded, and the eventual increase in production is smaller than it would be if prices held steady. Since all firms respond in a similar way to the bottling plant in Kalamazoo, the macroeconomic outcome is the one described in Fig. 26.10.

An Increase in Aggregate Demand in the Long Run In the long run, the economy is at full-employment equilibrium and on its long-run aggregate supply curve. When the economy is at full employment, an increase in aggregate demand has the same initial effect (short-run effect) as we've just worked out, but its long-run effect is different.

To see the long-run effect, suppose that in Fig. 26.10, long-run aggregate supply is $4 trillion. When aggregate demand increases, shifting the aggregate demand curve from AD_0 to AD_1, the equilibrium *d* is an above full-employment equilibrium. When the labor force is more than fully employed, there are shortages of labor and wages increase. Higher wages bring higher costs and a decrease in aggregate supply. The result is a further increase in the price level and a decrease in real GDP. Eventually, when wage rates and the price level have increased by the same percentage, real GDP is again at its full-employment level. The multiplier in the long run is zero.

Back at the bottling plant in Kalamazoo, production and prices have increased, but there's a severe shortage of labor. Wage rates are rising quickly. The bottling plant, facing ever increasing labor costs, keeps pushing up its prices. Eventually, the wage rate paid by the bottling plant increases by the same percentage as the price of a bottle of soda. In this situation, there is no profit in continuing to produce the higher level of output, so the plant returns to its original production level.

◆ ◆ ◆ ◆ We have now studied the forces that influence the components of aggregate expenditure and have analyzed the way the components interact with each other to determine aggregate expenditure and the position of the aggregate demand curve. Fluctuations in the aggregate expenditure curve and in the aggregate demand curve are caused by fluctuations in autonomous expenditure. An important element of autonomous expenditure is investment, which in turn is determined by, among other things, interest rates. But what determines interest rates? That is the question to which we turn in the next two chapters.

SUMMARY

Expenditure Multipliers

Aggregate expenditure is divided into two components: autonomous expenditure and induced expenditure. Autonomous expenditure is the sum of investment, government purchases, exports, and the part of consumption expenditure that does not vary with income. Induced expenditure is the part of consumption expenditure that does vary with income minus imports.

An increase in autonomous expenditure increases aggregate planned expenditure and shifts the aggregate expenditure curve upward. Equilibrium expenditure and real GDP increase by more than the increase in autonomous expenditure. They do so because the increased autonomous expenditure induces an increase in consumption expenditure. Aggregate expenditure increases by the sum of the initial increase in autonomous expenditure and the increase in induced expenditure.

An increase in saving shifts the aggregate expenditure curve downward and decreases real GDP—the paradox of thrift. The paradox arises because the increase in saving does not automatically bring an increase in investment. If investment and saving increase together, the aggregate expenditure curve does not shift and aggregate income does not fall. In the long run, additional saving enables more capital to be accumulated and makes aggregate income grow more quickly.

The autonomous expenditure multiplier (or simply the multiplier) is the change in equilibrium real GDP divided by the change in autonomous expenditure that brought it about. The size of the multiplier depends on the slope of the *AE* curve (g), and its value is given by the formula

$$\text{Multiplier} = \frac{1}{(1-g)}.$$

Because g is a number between 0 and 1, the multiplier is greater than 1. The larger the value of g, the larger is the multiplier. The multiplier is greater than 1 because of induced expenditure—because an increase in autonomous expenditure induces an increase in consumption expenditure. (pp. 701–709)

Fiscal Policy Multipliers

There are three main fiscal policy multipliers:

- Government purchases multiplier
- Transfer payments multiplier
- Tax multiplier

The government purchases multiplier is the amount by which a change in government purchases of goods and services is multiplied to determine the change in equilibrium expenditure that it generates. Because government purchases of goods and services are one of the components of autonomous expenditure, this multiplier is equal to the autonomous expenditure multiplier. That is,

$$\text{Government purchases multiplier} = \frac{1}{(1-g)}.$$

The transfer payments multiplier is the amount by which a change in transfer payments is multiplied to determine the change in equilibrium expenditure that it generates. Because a change in transfer payments influences aggregate expenditure by changing disposable income, this multiplier is equal to the marginal propensity to consume (b) times the autonomous expenditure multiplier. That is,

$$\text{Transfer payments multiplier} = \frac{b}{(1-g)}.$$

The tax multiplier is the amount by which a change in taxes is multiplied to determine the change in equilibrium expenditure that it generates. A tax increase brings a decrease in equilibrium expenditure. The initial response of consumption expenditure to a tax increase is exactly the same as its response to a decrease in transfer payments. Thus a tax change works like a change in transfer payments, but its multiplier is negative. It is

$$\text{Tax multiplier} = \frac{-b}{(1-g)}.$$

If both government purchases of goods and services and taxes are changed together and by the same amount, there is a balanced budget multiplier that combines the two separate multipliers. The balanced budget multiplier is

$$\text{Balanced budget multiplier} = \frac{(1-b)}{(1-g)}.$$

Because the marginal propensity to consume (b) is bigger than the slope of the *AE* curve (g), the balanced budget multiplier is less than 1.

The tax and transfer payments system acts as an automatic stabilizer—a mechanism that decreases the fluctuations in aggregate expenditure. (pp. 709–716)

The Multiplier in the United States

The multiplier in the United States is close to 2. But it fluctuates over the business cycle, rising during a recovery and falling during a recession. Its value has fallen over time because the marginal propensity to import has increased. (pp. 716–718)

Real GDP, the Price Level, and the Multipliers

The aggregate demand curve is the relationship between the quantity of real GDP demanded and the price level, other things held constant. A change in the price level brings a movement along the aggregate demand curve. The aggregate expenditure curve is the relationship between aggregate planned expenditure and real GDP, other things held constant. At a given price level, there is a given aggregate expenditure curve. A change in the price level changes autonomous expenditure and shifts the aggregate expenditure curve. Thus a movement along the aggregate demand curve is associated with a shift in the aggregate expenditure curve. A change in autonomous expenditure not caused by a change in the price level shifts the aggregate expenditure curve and also shifts the aggregate demand curve. The magnitude of the shift in the aggregate demand curve depends on the size of the multiplier and on the change in autonomous expenditure.

Real GDP and the price level are determined by both aggregate demand and aggregate supply. If an increase in aggregate demand occurs at an unemployment equilibrium, both the price level and real GDP increase. But the increase in real GDP is smaller than the increase in aggregate demand. The steeper the short-run aggregate supply curve, the larger is the change in the price level and the smaller is the change in real GDP. If an increase in aggregate demand occurs at full employment, its long-run effect is entirely on the price level. (pp. 718–722)

KEY ELEMENTS

Key Terms

Automatic stabilizer, 712
Autonomous expenditure, 701
Autonomous expenditure multiplier, 705
Balanced budget multiplier, 711
Government purchases multiplier, 709
Induced expenditure, 701
Marginal propensity to import, 703
Marginal tax rate, 712
Multiplier, 705
Paradox of thrift, 705
Tax multiplier, 710
Transfer payments multiplier, 710

Key Figures and Tables

REVIEW QUESTIONS

1 The autonomous expenditure multiplier applies to changes in which components of aggregate expenditure?

2 What is the connection between the autonomous expenditure multiplier and the slope of the *AE* curve?

3 Why is the autonomous expenditure multiplier greater than 1?

4 What is the government purchases multiplier? Is its value greater than 1?

5 What is the transfer payments multiplier?

6 What is the tax multiplier? How does it compare with the autonomous expenditure multiplier?

7 How does the transfer payments multiplier compare with the tax multiplier?

8 What is the balanced budget multiplier? Is its value greater than 1?

9 Explain how income taxes and transfer payments act as automatic stabilizers.

10 What is the size of the multiplier in the United States?

11 What is the relationship between the aggregate expenditure curve and the aggregate demand curve?

12 The price level changes, and everything else is held constant. What happens to the aggregate demand curve and the aggregate expenditure curve?

13 A change in autonomous expenditure occurs that is not produced by a change in the price level. What happens to the aggregate expenditure curve and the aggregate demand curve?

PROBLEMS

1 You are given the following information about the economy of Zeeland: Autonomous consumption expenditure is $100 billion, and the marginal propensity to consume is 0.9. Investment is $460 billion, government purchases of goods and services are $400 billion, and taxes are a constant $400 billion—they do not vary with income. Exports are $350 billion, and imports are 10 percent of income. The government of Zeeland makes no transfer payments.

a Calculate the slope of the *AE* curve.

b The government cuts its purchases of goods and services to $300 billion. What is the change in real GDP? What is the government purchases multiplier?

c The government continues to purchase $400 billion worth of goods and services and cuts taxes to $300 billion. What is the change in real GDP? What is the tax multiplier?

d The government simultaneously cuts both its purchases of goods and services and taxes to $300 billion. What is the change in real GDP? What is the name of the multiplier now at work, and what is its value?

2 Everything in Zeeland remains the same as in problem 1 except that the tax laws are changed. Instead of taxes being a constant $400 billion, they become 10 percent of real GDP.

a Calculate the slope of the *AE* curve.

b Government purchases are cut to $300 billion. What is the change in real GDP? What is the government purchases multiplier?

c What is the change in consumption expenditure? Explain why consumption expenditure changes by more than the change in government purchases.

d The government introduces transfer payments of $50 billion. What is the transfer payments multiplier? What is the change in real GDP?

3 You are given three bits of information about the multiplier in the economy of Alphabeta. Its average value is 2, in year A it is 3½, and in year B it is ½.

a Was year A a recovery year or a recession year? Why?

b Was year B a recovery year or a recession year? Why?

4 Suppose that the price level in the economy of Zeeland, as described in problem 1, is 100.

a Find one point on Zeeland's aggregate demand curve

b If the government of Zeeland increases its purchases of goods and services by $100 billion, what happens to the quantity of real GDP demanded?

c In the short run, does equilibrium real GDP increase by more than, less than, or the same amount as the increase in the quantity of real GDP demanded?

d In the long run, does equilibrium real GDP increase by more than, less than, or the same amount as the increase in the quantity of real GDP demanded?

e In the short run, does the price level in Zeeland rise, fall, or remain unchanged?

f In the long run, does the price level in Zeeland rise, fall, or remain unchanged?

CHAPTER 27

Money, Banking, and Prices

After studying this chapter, you will be able to:

- Define money and state its functions
- Describe the different forms of money
- Explain how money is measured in the United States today
- Describe the balance sheets of the main financial intermediaries
- Explain the economic functions of commercial banks and other financial intermediaries
- Describe some of the important financial innovations of the 1980s
- Explain how banks create money
- Explain why the quantity of money is an important economic magnitude
- Explain the quantity theory of money

Money Makes the World Go Around

ONEY, LIKE FIRE AND THE WHEEL, HAS BEEN AROUND for a very long time. No one knows for sure how long or what its origins are. An incredible array of items have served as money—wampum (beads made from shells) was used by North American Indians; cowries (brightly colored shells) were used in India; whales' teeth were used in Fiji; tobacco was used by early American colonists; cigarettes and liquor have been used in more modern times; and even cakes of salt have served as money in Ethiopia, other parts of Africa, and Tibet. What exactly is money? Why has this rich variety of commodities served as money? ◆◆ Today, when we want to buy something, we use coins or bills, write a check, or present a credit card. Are all these things money? When we deposit some coins or bills into a bank or savings and loan association (S&L), is that still money? And what happens when the bank or the S&L lends the money in our deposit account to someone else? How can we get our money back if it's been lent out? Does lending by banks and S&Ls create money—out of thin air? ◆◆ During the 1980s, banks and other financial institutions introduced new types of deposit accounts—NOW accounts and ATS accounts being the most prominent ones. Why were these new kinds of bank accounts introduced? ◆◆ The S&Ls have been in deep trouble in recent years, and in 1989 the federal government came to their rescue with the largest bailout in U.S. history. Why are the S&Ls in trouble? ◆◆ During the 1970s, the quantity of money in existence in the United States increased quickly, but in the 1980s it increased at a slower pace. In China in the late 1940s, Israel in the early 1980s, and some Latin American countries in the late 1980s, the quantity of money increased at an extremely rapid pace. In Switzerland and Germany, the quantity of money has increased at a modest pace. Does the rate of increase in the quantity of money matter? What are the effects of an increasing quantity of money on our economy?

◆ ◆ ◆ ◆ In this chapter, we'll study that useful invention, money. We'll look at its functions, its different forms, and the way it is defined and measured in the United States today. We'll also study commercial banks and other financial institutions and learn how they create money. Finally, we'll examine the relationship between money and prices.

What Is Money?

What do cowrie shells, whales' teeth, nickels, and dimes have in common? Why are they all examples of money? To answer these questions, we need a definition of money.

The Definition of Money

Money is any commodity or token that is generally acceptable as a means of payment for goods and services. The particular commodities and tokens that have served this purpose have varied enormously. We're going to study money and the institutions of monetary exchange that have evolved in the U.S. economy. But first, let's look at the functions of money.

The Functions of Money

Money has four functions:

- Medium of exchange
- Unit of account
- Store of value
- Standard of deferred payment

Medium of Exchange A **medium of exchange** is a commodity or token that is generally accepted in exchange for goods and services. Money acts as such a medium. Without money, it would be necessary to exchange goods and services directly for other goods and services—an exchange known as **barter.** For example, if you wanted to buy a hamburger, you would offer the paperback novel you've just finished reading or half an hour of your labor in the kitchen in exchange for it. Barter can take place only when there is a double coincidence of wants. A **double coincidence of wants** is a situation that occurs when person A wants to buy what person B is selling and person B wants to buy what person A is selling. That is, to get your hamburger, you'd have to find someone who's selling hamburgers and who wants a paperback novel or your work in the kitchen. The occurrence of a double coincidence of wants is sufficiently rare that barter exchange would leave potential gains from specialization and exchange unrealized.

Money guarantees that there is always a double coincidence of wants. People with something to sell will always accept money in exchange for it, and people who want to buy will always offer money. Money acts as a lubricant that smooths the mechanism of exchange. It lowers the costs of making transactions. The evolution of monetary exchange is a consequence of our economizing activity—of getting the most possible out of limited resources.

Unit of Account An agreed measure for stating the prices of goods and services is a **unit of account.** To get the most out of your budget, you have to figure out, among other things, whether seeing one more movie is worth the price you have to pay, not in dollars and cents, but in terms of the number of ice-cream cones, sodas, and cups of coffee that you have to give up. It's not hard to do such calculations when all these goods have prices in terms of dollars and cents (see Table 27.1). If a movie costs \$6 and a six-pack of soda costs \$3, you know right away that seeing one more movie costs you 2 six-packs of soda. If jelly beans are 50¢ a pack, one more movie costs 12 packs of jelly beans. You need only one calculation to figure out the opportunity cost of any pair of goods and services.

But imagine how troublesome it would be if your local movie theater posted its price as 2 six-packs of soda and if the convenience store posted the price of a six-pack of soda as 2 ice-cream cones and if the ice-cream shop posted the price of a cone as 3 packs of jelly beans and if the candy store priced jelly

TABLE 27.1

The Unit of Account Function of Money Simplifies Price Comparisons

Good	Price in money units	Price in units of another good
Movie	**$6.00 each**	**2 six-packs of soda**
Soda	**$3.00 per six-pack**	**2 ice-cream cones**
Ice cream	**$1.50 per cone**	**3 packs of jelly beans**
Jelly beans	**$0.50 per pack**	**2 cups of coffee**
Coffee	**$0.25 a cup**	**1 local phone call**

Money as a unit of account: One movie costs $6 and a cup of coffee costs 25¢, so one movie costs 24 cups of coffee ($6 ÷ 25¢ = 24).

No unit of account: You go to a movie theater and learn that the price of a movie is 2 six-packs of soda. You go to a candy store and learn that a pack of jelly beans costs 2 cups of coffee. But how many cups of coffee does seeing a movie cost you? To answer that question, you go to the convenience store and find that a six-pack of soda costs 2 ice-cream cones. Now you head for the ice-cream store, where an ice-cream cone costs 3 packs of jelly beans. Now you get out your pocket calculator: 1 movie costs 2 six-packs of soda, or 4 ice-cream cones, or 12 packs of jelly beans, or 24 cups of coffee!

beans as 2 cups of coffee! Now how much running around and calculating would you have to do to figure out how much that movie is going to cost you in terms of the soda, ice cream, jelly beans, or coffee that you must give up to see it? You would get the answer for soda right away from the sign posted on the movie theater, but for all the other goods you would have to visit many different stores to establish the price of each commodity in terms of another and then calculate prices in units that are relevant for your own decision. Cover up the column labeled "Price in money units" in Table 27.1 and see how hard it is to figure out the number of local phone calls it costs to see one movie. It's enough to make a person swear off movies! How much simpler it is for everyone to express their prices in terms of dollars and cents.

Store of Value Any commodity or token that can be held and exchanged later for goods and services is called a **store of value.** Money acts as a store of value. If it did not, it would not be acceptable in exchange for goods and services. The more stable the value of a commodity or token, the better it can act as a store of value and the more useful it is as money. There are no stores of value that are completely safe. The value of a physical object such as a house, a car, or a work of art fluctuates over time. The value of a commodity or token used as money also fluctuates, and when there is inflation, its value persistently falls.

Standard of Deferred Payment An agreed measure that enables contracts to be written for future receipts and payments is called a **standard of deferred payment.** If you borrow money to buy a house or if you save money to provide for retirement, your future commitment or future receipt will be agreed to in dollars and cents. Money is used as the standard for a deferred payment.

Using money as a standard of deferred payment is not entirely without risk because, as we saw in Chapter 22, inflation leads to unpredictable changes in the value of money. But, to the extent that borrowers and lenders anticipate inflation, its rate is reflected in the interest rates paid and received. Lenders in effect protect themselves by charging a higher interest rate, and borrowers, anticipating inflation, willingly pay the higher rate.

Different Forms of Money

Money can take four different forms:

- Commodity money
- Convertible paper money
- Fiat money
- Private debt money

Commodity Money A physical commodity that is valued in its own right and also used as a means of payment is **commodity money.** An amazing array of items have served as commodity money at different times and places, several of which were described in the chapter opener. But the most common commodity monies have been coins made from metals such as gold, silver, and copper. The first known coins were made in Lydia, a Greek city-state, at the beginning of the seventh century B.C. These coins were made of electrum, a natural mixture of gold and silver.

Commodity money has considerable advantages but some drawbacks. Let's look first at the advantages.

Advantages of Commodity Money The main advantage of commodity money is that because the commodity is valued for its own sake, its value as money is readily known. This fact provides a guarantee of the value of money. For example, gold may be used to fill teeth and make rings; its value in these uses determines its value as money. Historically, gold and silver were ideal for use as money because they were in limited supply and in constant demand (by those wealthy enough to use them) for ornaments and jewelry. Further, their quality was easily verified, and they were easily divisible into units small enough to facilitate exchange.

Disadvantages of Commodity Money Commodity money has two main disadvantages. First, there is a constant temptation to cheat on the value of the money. Two methods of cheating have been commonly used—clipping and debasement. *Clipping* is reducing the size of coins by an imperceptible amount, thereby lowering their metallic content. *Debasement* is creating a coin having a lower silver or gold content (the balance being made up of some cheaper metal).

This temptation to lower the value of money led to a phenomenon known as Gresham's Law, after the sixteenth-century English financial expert Sir Thomas Gresham. **Gresham's Law** is the tendency for bad money to drive good money out of circulation. Bad money is debased money; good money is money that has not been debased. It's easy to see why Gresham's Law works. Suppose that a person is paid with two coins, one debased and the other not. Each coin has the same value if used as money in exchange for goods. But one of the coins—the one that's not debased—is more valuable as a commodity than as a coin. It will not, therefore, be used as money. Only the debased coin will be used as money. It is in this way that bad money drives good money out of circulation.

A second major disadvantage of commodity money is that the commodity, valued for its own sake, could be used in ways other than as money—it has an opportunity cost. For example, gold and silver used as money cannot be used to make jewelry or ornaments. This opportunity cost creates incentives to find alternatives to the commodity itself for use in the exchange process. One such alternative is a paper claim to commodity money.

Convertible Paper Money When a paper claim to a commodity circulates as a means of payment, that claim is called **convertible paper money.** The first known example of paper money occurred in China during the Ming dynasty (1368–1399 A.D.). This form of money was also used extensively throughout Europe in the Middle Ages.

The inventiveness of goldsmiths and their clients led to the increase and widespread use of convertible paper money. Because gold was valuable, goldsmiths had well-guarded safes in which to keep their own gold. They also rented space to artisans and others who wanted to put their gold in safekeeping. The goldsmiths issued a receipt entitling the owner of the gold to reclaim his or her "deposit" on demand. These receipts were much like the coat check token that you get at a theater or museum.

Suppose that Isabella has a gold receipt indicating that she has 100 ounces of gold deposited with Samuel Goldsmith. She is going to buy a piece of land valued at 100 ounces of gold from Henry. There are two ways that Isabella might undertake the transaction. The first way is to go to Samuel, hand over her receipt and collect her gold, transport the gold to Henry, and take title to the land. Henry now goes back to Samuel with the gold and deposits it there for safekeeping, leaving with his own receipt. The second way of doing this transaction is for Isabella simply to hand over her gold receipt to Henry, completing the transaction by using the gold receipt as money. Obviously, it is much more convenient to complete the transaction in the second way, provided that Henry can trust Samuel. The gold receipt circulating as a means of payment is money. The paper money is *backed* by the gold held by Goldsmith. Also the paper money is *convertible* into commodity money.

Fractional Backing Once the convertible paper money system is operating and people are using their gold receipts rather than gold itself as the means of payment, goldsmiths notice that their vaults are storing a large amount of gold that is never withdrawn. This gives them a brilliant idea. Why not lend people gold receipts? The goldsmith can charge interest on the loan, and the loan is created just by writing on a piece of paper. As long as the number of such receipts created is not too large in relation to the stock of gold in the goldsmith's safe, the goldsmith is in no danger of not being able to honor the promise to convert receipts into gold on demand. The gold in the goldsmith's safe is a *fraction* of the gold receipts in circulation. By this device, *fractionally backed* convertible paper money was invented.

Between 1879 and 1933, the monetary system of the United States was one based on fractionally backed convertible paper. Until 1933, the U.S. dollar had a guaranteed value in terms of gold and could be converted into gold at a fixed value on demand. Between 1933 and 1971, it was illegal for U.S. citizens to hold gold coins or ingots but the U.S. Treasury stood ready to convert dollars into gold at $35 per ounce of gold for foreign central banks and foreign governments. In 1971, the gold convertibility of the U.S. dollar was finally abandoned, the market price of gold having increased far above $35 an ounce.

Even with fractionally backed paper money, valuable commodities that could be used for other productive activities are tied up in the exchange process. There remains an incentive to find a yet more efficient way of facilitating exchange and of freeing up the commodities used to back the paper money. This alternative is fiat money.

Fiat Money The term *fiat* means "let it be done" or "by order of the authority." **Fiat money** is an intrinsically worthless (or almost worthless) commodity that serves the functions of money. Some of the earliest fiat monies were the continental currency issued during the American Revolution and the "greenbacks" issued during the Civil War, which circulated until 1879. Another early issue of fiat money was that of the so-called *assignats* issued during the French Revolution. These early experiments with fiat money ended in rapid inflation because the amount of fiat money created was allowed to increase at a rapid pace, causing the money to lose value.

However, provided that the quantity of fiat money is not allowed to grow too rapidly, it has a reasonably steady value in terms of the goods and services that it will buy. People are willing to accept fiat money in exchange for the goods and services they sell only because they know it will be honored when they go to buy goods and services. The bills and coins that we use in the United States today—collectively known as **currency**—are examples of fiat money. Because of the creation of fiat money, people are willing to accept a piece of paper with a special watermark, printed in green ink, and worth not more than a few cents as a commodity in exchange for $100 worth of goods and services. The small metal alloy disk that we call a quarter is worth almost nothing as a piece of metal, but it pays for a local phone call and many other small commodities. The replacement of commodity money by fiat money enables the commodities themselves to be used productively.

Private Debt Money In the modern world, there is a fourth important type of money—private debt money. **Private debt money** is a loan that the borrower promises to repay in currency on demand. By transferring the entitlement to be repaid from one person to another, such a loan can be used as money. For example, you give me an IOU for $10; I give the IOU to a bookseller to buy a biography of Adam Smith; you pay the holder of the IOU $10—only now it's the bookseller holding the IOU.

The most important example of private debt money is the checkable deposit at commercial banks and other financial institutions. A **checkable deposit** is a loan by a depositor to a bank, the ownership of which can be transferred from one person to another by writing an instruction to the bank—a check—asking the bank to alter its records. We'll have more to say shortly about this type of money. Before doing so, let's look at the different forms of money and their relative magnitudes in the United States today.

Money in the United States Today

There are three official measures of money in current use: **M1**, **M2**, and **M3**. They are defined in Table 27.2, and the terms used to describe the components of the three measures are set out in the compact glossary in Table 27.3.

Are All the Measures of Money Really Money? The items that make up M1 fit the definition of money fairly closely. Currency (both coins and bills of various denominations) and traveler's checks are universally acceptable in payment for goods and services.

TABLE 27.2

The Three Official Measures of Money

M1 ◆ **Currency held outside banks**
◆ **Traveler's checks**
◆ **Demand deposits**
◆ **Other checkable deposits (OCDs), including NOW accounts and ATS accounts at commercial banks, S&Ls, savings banks, and credit unions**

M2 ◆ **M1**
◆ **Savings deposits**
◆ **Small time deposits**
◆ **Eurodollar deposits, money market mutual fund shares held by individuals, and other M2 deposits**

M3 ◆ **M2**
◆ **Large time deposits**
◆ **Eurodollar time deposits, money market mutual fund shares held by institutions, and other M3 deposits**

M1 consists of currency (pennies, nickels, dimes, and quarters and Federal Reserve bank notes, that is, bills of various denominations) and bank deposits on which a check can be written, including NOW accounts and ATS accounts. The currency component of M1 is only that held outside the banks. Currency held by banks is not part of M1. M2 is M1 plus savings accounts, small time deposits, and other very liquid assets. M3 is M2 plus less liquid assets such as large time deposits and money market mutual fund shares held by institutions.

So also are checkable deposits at commercial banks, S&Ls, savings banks, and credit unions.

The other items that make up M2 and M3 are not quite so clearly money, but they have a high degree of liquidity. **Liquidity** is the degree to which an asset is instantly convertible into money at a known price. Assets vary in their degree of liquidity. Some are not very liquid because some minimum amount of notice has to be given before they can be converted into a means of payment. Others lack liquidity because they are traded on markets and their prices fluctuate, making the amount of money into which they can be converted uncertain. But the savings

TABLE 27.3

A Compact Glossary of the Components of Money

Currency held outside banks

Notes issued by Fed and coins issued by the U.S. Treasury held outside the banking system.

Traveler's check

A bank check convertible into currency on demand.

Checkable deposit

A deposit account on which a check can be written.

Demand deposit

A checkable deposit convertible into currency on demand.

NOW account

Negotiable Order of Withdrawal account—"negotiable order of withdrawal" is another name for a check.

ATS account

Automatic-Transfer Savings account—a checkable deposit the balance on which is maintained at an agreed level by transferring funds to and from a savings account.

Savings deposit

A deposit that technically cannot be withdrawn on demand but in practice can be instantly withdrawn.

Time deposit

A deposit with fixed term to maturity. "Small" deposits are below $100,000; "large" deposits are $100,000 or more.)

Eurodollars

U.S. dollar accounts in banks in other countries, mainly in Europe.

Money market mutual fund

A financial intermediary that obtains funds by issuing shares on which checks may be drawn.

deposits and small time deposits that make up M2 and the large time deposits and other accounts that make up M3 are easily converted into assets that serve as a means of payment. They are highly liquid—or almost money.

The relative magnitudes of the components of the various measures of money are shown in Fig. 27.1. As you can see, the largest components of money in the United States are the deposits in banks and other financial institutions. Even though there is a remarkably large amount of currency in circulation—more than $1,000 per person—currency is only 30 percent of M1. The biggest component of M1 is checkable deposits.

Checkable deposits are money, but the checks people write when they make a payment are not. It is important to understand why.

Checkable Deposits Are Money, but Checks Are Not

The best way to see why checkable deposits are money but checks are not is to consider what happens when someone pays for goods by writing a check. Let's suppose that Barb buys a bike for $200 from Rocky's Mountain Bikes. When Barb goes to Rocky's bike shop, she has $500 in her checkable deposit account at the Laser Bank. Rocky has $1,000 in his checkable deposit account—at the same bank, as it happens. The checkable deposits of these two people total $1,500. On June 11, Barb writes a check for $200. Rocky takes the check to Laser Bank right away and deposits it. Rocky's bank balance rises from $1,000 to $1,200. But the bank not only credits Rocky's account with $200, it also debits Barb's account $200, so her balance falls from $500 to $300. The total checkable deposits of Barb and Rocky are still the same as before, $1,500. Rocky now has $200 more and Barb has $200 less than before. These transactions are summarized in Table 27.4.

This transaction has simply transferred money from one person to another. The check itself was never money. That is, there wasn't an extra $200 worth of money while the check was in circulation. The check simply served as a written instruction to the bank to transfer the money from Barb to Rocky.

In our example, Barb and Rocky use the same bank. Essentially the same story, though with additional steps, describes what happens if Barb and Rocky use different banks. Rocky's bank will credit the check to Rocky's account and then take the check to a check-clearing center. Barb's bank will pay Rocky's bank $200 and then debit Barb's account $200. This process can take a few days, but the principles are the same as when two people use the same bank.

So checks are not money. But what about credit cards? Isn't having a credit card in your wallet and

FIGURE 27.1

The Three Official Measures of Money

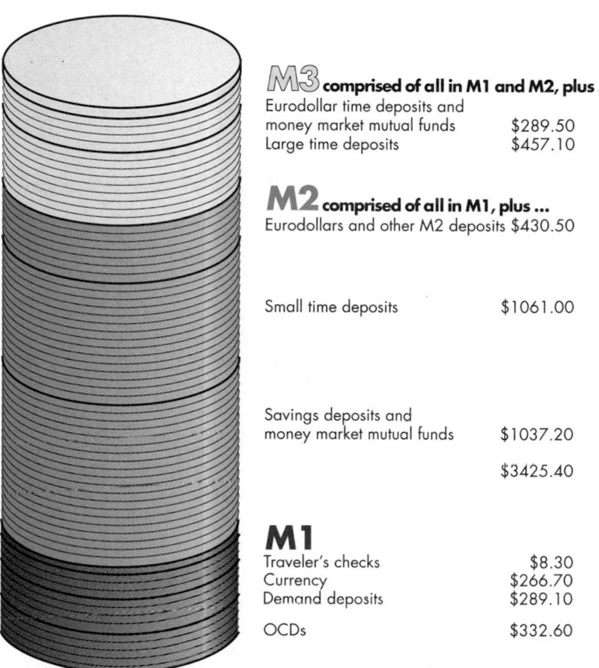

The M1 measure of money consists of all the assets that are a means of payment—currency, traveler's checks, demand deposits, and other checkable deposits. M1 makes up about 26 percent of the M2 measure of the money supply. M2 consists of M1 plus savings deposits and small time deposits as well as money market mutual fund shares held by individuals. M2 constitutes about 82 percent of M3. M3 consists of M2 plus large time deposits, Eurodollar time deposits, and money market mutual fund shares held by institutions.

Source: Economic Report of the President, 1992.

TABLE 27.4

Paying by Check

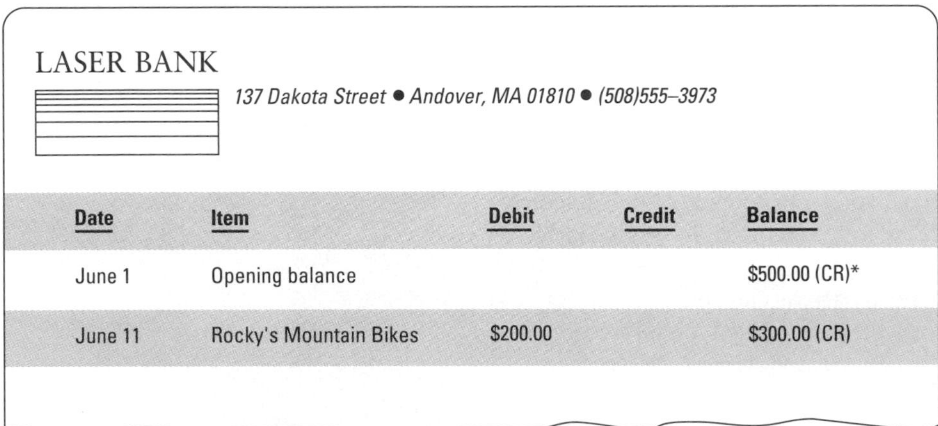

LASER BANK

137 Dakota Street • Andover, MA 01810 • (508)555–3973

Date	Item	Debit	Credit	Balance
June 1	Opening balance			$500.00 (CR)*
June 11	Rocky's Mountain Bikes	$200.00		$300.00 (CR)

Barb's checkable deposit account

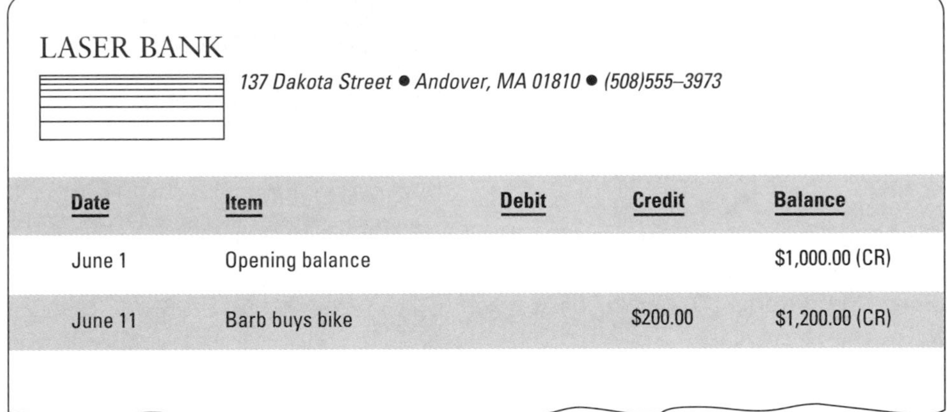

LASER BANK

137 Dakota Street • Andover, MA 01810 • (508)555–3973

Date	Item	Debit	Credit	Balance
June 1	Opening balance			$1,000.00 (CR)
June 11	Barb buys bike		$200.00	$1,200.00 (CR)

Rocky's Mountain Bikes checkable deposit account

*CR means "credit": The bank owes the depositor.

presenting the card to pay for a bike the same thing as using money? Why aren't credit cards somehow valued and counted as part of the quantity of money?

Credit Cards Are Not Money When you pay by check, you are frequently asked to prove your identity by showing your driver's license. It would never occur to you to think of your driver's license as money. Your driver's license is just an ID.

A credit card is also an ID card but one that enables you to borrow money at the instant a purchase is made on the promise of repaying later. When you make a purchase, you sign a credit card sales slip that creates a debt in your name. You are saying: "I agree to pay for these goods when the credit card company bills me." Once you get your statement from the credit card company, you have to make the minimum payment due. To make that payment, you need money—you need to have currency or funds in your checkable deposit so that you can write a check to pay the credit card company. Although you use a credit card to make purchases, it is not money.

REVIEW

Money, a generally acceptable means of payment, has four functions: medium of exchange, unit of account, store of value, and standard of deferred payment. Any durable commodity can serve as money, but modern societies use fiat money and private debt money rather than commodity money. The largest component of money in the United States today is checkable deposits at banks and other financial institutions. Neither checks nor credit cards are money. A check is an instruction to a bank to transfer money from one account to another. Money is the balance in the account itself. A credit card is an ID card that enables a person to borrow at the instant a purchase is made on the promise of repaying later. When repayment is made, money (currency or a checkable deposit) is used for the payment. ◆

We've seen that the most important component of money in the United States is deposits at banks and other financial institutions. Let's take a look at the banking and financial system a bit more closely.

Financial Intermediaries

We are going to study the banking and financial system by first describing the variety of financial intermediaries that operate in the United States today. Then we'll examine the operations of banks and of other financial intermediaries. After describing the main features of financial intermediaries, we'll examine their economic functions, describing what they produce and how they make a profit.

A **financial intermediary** is a firm that takes deposits from households and firms and makes loans to other households and firms. There are five types of financial intermediaries whose deposits are components of the nation's money:

- Commercial banks
- Savings and loan associations
- Savings banks
- Credit unions
- Money market mutual funds

A compact glossary of these financial intermediaries and an indication of their relative size are given in Table 27.5.

Let's begin by examining commercial banks.

Commercial Banks

A **commercial bank** is a private firm, chartered either by the Comptroller of the Currency (in the U.S. Treasury) or by a state agency to receive deposits and make loans. There are close to 13,000 commercial banks in the United States today. The scale and scope of the operations of commercial banks can be seen by examining the balance sheet of the commercial banking sector.

A **balance sheet** is a statement that lists a firm's assets and liabilities. **Assets** are the things of value that a firm owns. **Liabilities** are the things that a firm owes to households and other firms. The liabilities of banks are deposits. Your deposit at a bank is an asset to you but a liability for your bank. The bank has to repay you your deposit (and sometimes interest on it, too) whenever you decide to take your money out of the bank.

The balance sheet for all commercial banks in December 1991 is set out in Table 27.6. The left side—the assets—lists the items *owned* by the banks. The right side—the liabilities—lists the items that the banks *owe* to others. Let's start on the liabilities side. Total liabilities in December 1991 were $3,530 billion. The banks' major liabilities are divided among three types of deposits:

- Checkable deposits
- Savings deposits
- Time deposits

You have met these deposits before in the various definitions of money. The banks' other liabilities

TABLE 27.5

A Compact Glossary of Financial Intermediaries

Type of financial intermediary (approximate number)	Total assets (billions of dollars)	Main functions
Commercial banks (13,000)	**3,530**	**A private firm chartered by either the Comptroller of the Currency (of the U.S. Treasury) or a state agency to receive deposits and make loans.**
Savings and loan associations (2,900)	**1,140**	**Financial institutions that receive savings deposits (sometimes called shares) and checkable deposits and use the funds to make mortgage and other loans.**
Savings banks (500)	**588**	**Financial institutions owned by their depositors that accept deposits and make loans primarily to home buyers.**
Credit unions (13,000)	**197**	**Small cooperative lending institutions often organized in a place of work or by a labor union. They take deposits and make consumer loans.**
Money market mutual funds	**977**	**Financial intermediaries that obtain funds by issuing shares and using the proceeds to buy a portfolio of short-term, liquid assets. Shareholders can write checks on their money market mutual fund share accounts.**

Sources: *Federal Reserve Bulletin* (March 1992), p. A19; *Federal Reserve Bulletin* (March 1991), pp. A26 and A27; *Economic Report of the President* (1991), p. 364; U.S. Bureau of the Census, *Statistical Abstract of the United States 1991,* 111th edition (Washington, D.C., 1991), p. 499.

TABLE 27.6

The Balance Sheet of All Commercial Banks, December 1991

Assets (billions of dollars)			Liabilities (billions of dollars)	
Reserve assets			**Checkable deposits**	**682**
Reserves with Federal Reserve banks	**29**		**Savings deposits**	**653**
Vault cash	**31**		**Time deposits**	**1,155**
Total reserves		**60**	**Other liabilities**	**1,040**
Liquid assets		**205**		
Investment securities		**701**		
Loans		**2,271**		
Other assets		**293**		
Total		**3,530**	**Total**	**3,530**

Source: *Federal Reserve Bulletin* (March 1992), Table 1.25, p. A19.

consist of borrowing by the banks in what is sometimes called the **wholesale deposit market**—the market for deposits among banks and other financial intermediaries.

Why does a bank obligate itself to pay you your money back with interest? Because it wants to use your deposit to make a profit for itself. To achieve this objective, the banks lend the money deposited with them at interest rates higher than the rates they pay for deposits.

The asset side of the balance sheet tells us how the banks do their lending. And the numbers in Table 27.6 tell us what they did with their $3,530 billion worth of borrowed resources in December 1991. The banks kept some of their assets in the form of deposits at Federal Reserve banks and as cash in their vaults. (We'll study the Federal Reserve banks in Chapter 28.) The cash in a bank's vault plus its deposits at Federal Reserve banks are called its **reserves.** You can think of a commercial bank's deposit at the Federal Reserve as being similar to your deposit at your own bank. Commercial banks use these deposits in the same way that you use your bank account. A commercial bank deposits cash into or draws cash out of its account at the Federal Reserve and writes checks on that account to settle debts with other banks.

If the banks kept all their assets in the form of deposits at the Federal Reserve and cash in their vaults, they wouldn't make any profit. But if they didn't keep *some* of their assets as cash in their vaults and as deposits at the Federal Reserve, they wouldn't be able to meet the demands for cash that their customers place on them. Nor would they be able to keep that automatic teller replenished every time you, your friends, and all their other customers raid it for cash for a midnight pizza.

The bulk of a bank's borrowed resources are put to work by making loans. Some of these loans are instantly convertible into cash and with virtually no risk. These are called liquid assets. **Liquid assets,** which take their name from the concept of liquidity, are those assets that are instantly convertible into a means of payment with virtually no uncertainty about the price at which they can be converted. An example of a liquid asset is a U.S. government treasury bond that can be sold at a moment's notice for an almost guaranteed price.

The banks' assets also include investment securities. An **investment security** is a marketable security that a bank can sell at a moment's notice if necessary but at a price that fluctuates. An example of an investment security is a U.S. government long-term bond. Such bonds can be sold instantly, but their prices fluctuate on the bond market. Banks earn a higher interest rate on their investment securities than they do on liquid assets, but investment securities have a higher risk.

Most of the banks' assets are the loans that they have made. A **loan** is a commitment of a fixed amount of money for an agreed period of time. Most of the loans made by banks are used by corporations to finance the purchase of capital equipment and inventories. But banks also make loans to households—personal loans. Such loans are used to buy consumer durable goods such as cars or boats. The outstanding balances on credit card accounts are also bank loans. The interest rates on these balances became a controversial topic in 1991—see Reading Between the Lines, pp. 738–739.

Banks make a profit by earning interest on loans, investment securities, and liquid assets in excess of the interest paid on deposits and other liabilities. Also, banks receive revenue by charging fees for managing accounts.

Money is made up of the various liabilities of the banks. Checkable deposits are an important component of the M1 measure of money—accounting for 32 percent of M1 in 1991. Checkable deposits, savings deposits, and small time deposits are an important part of the M2 measure of money. The commercial banks' total liabilities are an important component of M3. But the deposit liabilities of banks are not the only components of the nation's money. Other financial intermediaries also take deposits that form part—an increasing part—of the nation's money. Let's now examine those financial intermediaries.

Savings and Loan Associations

A **savings and loan association (S&L)** is a financial intermediary that traditionally obtained its funds from savings deposits (called shares) and that made long-term mortgage loans to home buyers. Before 1980, S&Ls were prevented by regulation from offering checking accounts and could make only mortgage loans. Furthermore, the interest rate on these loans was fixed. Many mortgage loans had a term of 30 years, so a large number of mortgages still

High-Cost Card Credit

U.S. NEWS & WORLD REPORT, December 2, 1991

How to play your cards

By Edward C. Baig, with Francesca Lunzer Kritz and David Bowermaster

Consumers may have been disappointed early last week when Congress balked at a bill that would have set a 14 percent ceiling on credit-card interest. The average card rate, after all, has hovered around 19 percent for many months. But that could change—for better and for worse.

The good news: Many card issuers, competing for users, have been lowering rates on their own. AT&T, which ties its Universal Card to the prime, recently dropped the rate for most cardholders to 16.4 percent from 17.4 percent six weeks sooner than it had to. The bad news: the industry's worry over shrinking profits and rising costs. Late payments—and nonpayments—are rising. That trend is making card issuers choosier, especially about which consumers can keep or get lower-rate cards.

Folks who charge often and pay their balances on time might find it easier now to snag lower rates, either from their own bank or from out-of-state institutions. But people who rarely make a due date might find themselves facing a higher rate—or searching for a new card. . . .

Looking low.
Even without pressure from Congress, where there was again a move late last week to push through a cap, creditworthy customers don't seem to be having trouble finding low-interest cards. From January through June, issuers with rates above 18 percent lost about 5 percent of their business, compared with the same period last year. Issuers charging less than 16.5 percent, by contrast, gained 10 percent more new accounts in the same period, according to Ram Research, a credit-card newsletter publisher in Frederick, Md. . . .

Some banks will even waive annual fees for preferred customers who merely ask. You can also inquire about other, less publicized low-rate cards. Citibank's regular cards carry rates of 19.8 percent, but rock-solid customers might qualify for the Bank's 14.9 percent Choice card.

Marginal customers have a better chance of hanging onto their cards if they pay on time and get their finances in order. For example, they might reduce their total available credit by canceling rarely used cards that could conceivably burden them with extra debt. They would have fewer cards in their wallet, but the ones they kept could cost less and let them charge more.

The Essence of the Story

In December 1991, Congress considered but rejected a bill to set a 14 percent ceiling on credit-card interest rates—the average credit-card interest rate had been around 19 percent for many months.

Many credit-card issuers had been lowering interest rates, but a growing incidence of late payments and nonpayments was increasing the costs and shrinking the profits of credit-card issuers.

Banks began to offer regular cards carrying high rates (for example, Citibank's rate was 19.8 percent) and less publicized cards carrying low rates (for example, the rate on Citibank's Choice card, offered only to its "rock-solid customers," was 14.9 percent). Some banks began to waive annual fees for preferred customers.

Card issuers became more careful about which consumers got low-rate cards. People who charge often and pay on time find it easy to get low-rate cards, but those who rarely pay on time face higher interest rates.

Background and Analysis

When a bank or other financial intermediary issues a credit card, it enters into an agreement to make a loan to the card holder up to an agreed limit, to be repaid on an agreed schedule, and at an agreed but variable interest rate.

Borrowing on a credit card is one of several alternative ways of obtaining funds, and, other things being equal, the lower the credit-card interest rate, the greater is the quantity of credit-card loans demanded. The demand curve for credit-card loans is *D* in Fig. 1.

Credit-card issuers obtain their funds from depositors and have alternative uses for those funds. The *opportunity cost* of lending to a credit-card holder is the interest forgone on an alternative type of bank loan. This opportunity cost, assumed to be 10 percent, is illustrated in Fig. 1.

Lending to credit-card holders is costly. Between 2 percent and 3 percent of loans are not repaid. Many more loans that are eventually repaid are costly to collect. Fraud also imposes large costs on card issuers.

The cost of supplying credit-card loans (including the normal rate of economic profit) is equal to the opportunity cost of the funds lent plus these additional costs of credit-card lending. In Fig. 1, these costs make the cost of supplying credit-card loans 19 percent.

The quantity of loans supplied equals the quantity demanded at that interest rate—$250 billion in Fig. 1.

During 1991, most interest rates declined. For example, the prime rate, the rate at which banks lend to their biggest and safest corporate customers, fell from 10 percent to 6.5 percent. This rate decrease lowered the opportunity cost of making loans to credit-card holders—shown in Fig. 2.

Other things being equal, this decline in the prime rate would have lowered the interest rate on credit cards to about 15.5 percent as shown in Fig. 2.

But other things were not equal. In the recession of 1991, the percentage of loans not repaid increased, thus increasing the cost of supplying credit-card loans.

In this situation, credit-card issuers tried to separate their market into high-cost (high-risk) customers and low-cost (low-risk) customers, offering to each group interest rates that reflect their relative costs. Low interest rate business expanded, and high interest rate business declined.

As the news story notes, if Congress puts a cap on the interest rate that card issuers may charge, the trend to weeding out high-cost (high-risk) customers would be intensified, and fewer such customers would be able to obtain credit cards. They would be forced into an even higher-cost segment of the market for loans.

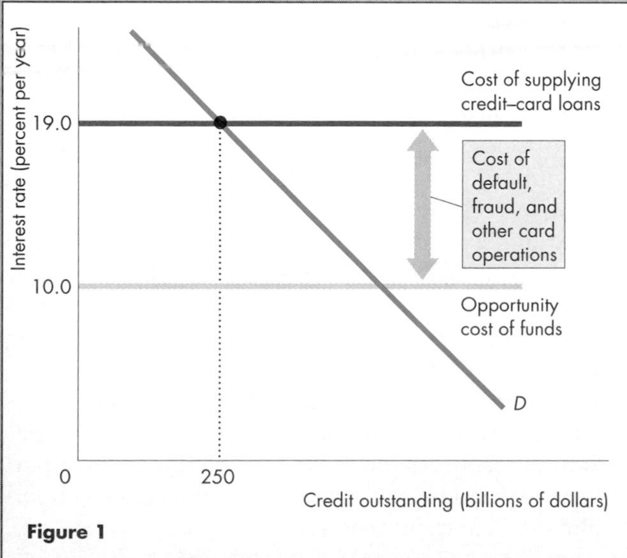

Figure 1

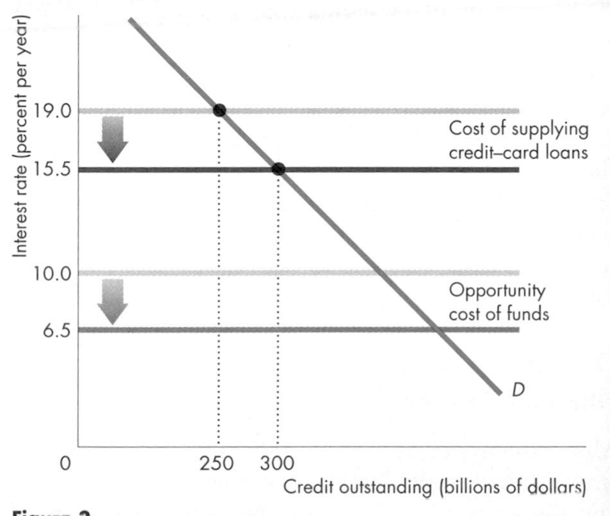

Figure 2

outstanding in the late 1970s had been written in the early 1950s, when the S&Ls were able to borrow at 3 percent a year and lend at 6 percent a year. But by the late 1970s, they had to pay more for deposits than they were making on their older mortgages.

Because of the plight of the S&Ls, Congress loosened the restrictions on them in 1980, permitting them to offer checking accounts and make high-interest consumer and commercial loans. Two years later the Garn–St. Germain Depository Institutions Act loosened the restrictions on the S&Ls yet further, enabling them to invest a larger part of their funds in high-risk commercial real estate ventures. But the way in which they used their greater freedom led the S&Ls to their crisis of the late 1980s.

Savings Banks and Credit Unions

Savings banks are financial intermediaries owned by their depositors that accept savings deposits and make loans, mostly for consumer mortgages. These institutions perform functions similar to those of S&Ls. The key difference is that savings banks, also called *mutual* savings banks, are owned by their depositors. **Credit unions** obtain their funds from checking and savings deposits and make consumer loans. Like savings banks, they are owned by their depositors. The key difference is that credit unions are based on a social or economic group such as a firm's employees.

Money Market Mutual Funds

Money market mutual funds are financial institutions that obtain funds by selling shares and that use these funds to buy highly liquid assets such as U.S. Treasury bills. Money market mutual fund shares act like the deposits at commercial banks and other financial intermediaries. Shareholders can write checks on their money market mutual fund accounts. But there are restrictions on most of these accounts. For example, the minimum deposit accepted might be $2,500, and the smallest check a depositor is permitted to write might be $500.

The Economic Functions of Financial Intermediaries

All financial intermediaries make a profit from a spread between the interest rate they pay on deposits and the interest rate at which they lend. Why can financial intermediaries borrow at a low interest rate and lend at a higher one? What services do they perform that make their depositors willing to put up with a low interest rate and their borrowers willing to pay a higher one?

Financial intermediaries provide four main services:

- Minimizing the cost of obtaining funds
- Minimizing the cost of monitoring borrowers
- Pooling risk
- Creating liquidity

Minimizing the Cost of Obtaining Funds Finding someone from whom to borrow can be a costly business. Imagine how troublesome it would be if there were no financial intermediaries. A firm that was looking for $1 million to buy a new production plant would probably have to hunt around for several dozen people from whom to borrow in order to acquire enough funds for its capital project. Financial intermediaries lower those costs. The firm needing $1 million can go to a single financial intermediary to obtain those funds. The financial intermediary has to borrow from a large number of people, but it's not doing that just for this one firm and the million dollars it wants to borrow. The financial intermediary can establish an organization capable of raising funds from a large number of depositors and can spread the cost of this activity over a large number of borrowers.

Minimizing the Cost of Monitoring Borrowers Lending money is a risky business. There's always a danger that the borrower might not repay. Most of the money lent gets used by firms to invest in projects that they hope will return a profit. But sometimes those hopes are not fulfilled. Checking up on the activities of a borrower and ensuring that the best possible decisions are being made for making a profit and avoiding a loss are costly and specialized activities. Imagine how costly it would be if each and every household that lent money to a firm had to incur the costs of monitoring that firm directly. By depositing funds with a financial intermediary, households avoid those costs. The financial intermediary performs the monitoring activity by using specialized resources that have a much lower cost than what each household would incur if it had to undertake the activity individually.

Pooling Risk As we noted above, lending money is risky. There is always a chance of not being repaid—of default. The risk of default can be reduced by lending to a large number of different individuals. In such a situation, if one person defaults on a loan, it is a nuisance but not a disaster. In contrast, if only one person borrows and that person defaults on the loan, the entire loan is a write-off. Financial intermediaries enable people to pool risk in an efficient way. Thousands of people lend money to any one financial intermediary, and, in turn, the financial intermediary re-lends the money to hundreds, perhaps thousands, of individual firms. If any one firm defaults on its loan, that default is spread across all the depositors with the intermediary and no individual depositor is left exposed to a high degree of risk.

Creating Liquidity Financial intermediaries create liquidity. We defined liquidity earlier as the ease and certainty with which an asset can be converted into money. Some of the liabilities of financial intermediaries are themselves money; others are highly liquid assets that are easily converted into money.

Financial intermediaries create liquidity by borrowing short and lending long. Borrowing short means taking deposits but standing ready to repay them on short notice (and on even no notice in the case of checkable deposits). Lending long means making loan commitments for a prearranged, and often quite long, period of time. For example, when a person makes a deposit with a savings and loan association, that deposit can be withdrawn at any time. But the S&L makes a lending commitment for perhaps more than 20 years to a homebuyer.

REVIEW

Most of the nation's money is made up of deposits in financial intermediaries. Those financial intermediaries are commercial banks, savings and loan associations, savings banks, credit unions, and money market mutual funds. The main economic functions of financial intermediaries are minimizing the cost of obtaining funds, minimizing the cost of monitoring borrowers, pooling risk, and creating liquidity. ◆

Financial Regulation, Deregulation, and Innovation

Financial intermediaries are highly regulated institutions. But regulation is not static, and in the 1980s some important changes in their regulation as well as deregulation took place. Also, the institutions are not static. In their pursuit of profit, they are constantly seeking lower-cost ways of obtaining funds, monitoring borrowers, pooling risk, and creating liquidity. They also are inventive in seeking ways of avoiding the costs imposed on them by financial regulation. Let's take a look at regulation, deregulation, and innovation in the financial sector in recent years.

Financial Regulation

Financial regulation imposes two types of restrictions on financial intermediaries:

- Deposit insurance
- Balance sheet rules

Deposit Insurance The deposits of banks and S&Ls are insured by the Federal Deposit Insurance Corporation (FDIC). The FDIC is a federal agency that receives its income from compulsory insurance premiums paid by commercial banks and other financial intermediaries. The FDIC operates two separate insurance funds, the Bank Insurance Fund (BIF), which insures deposits in commercial banks, and the Saving Association Insurance Fund (SAIF), which insures the deposits of S&Ls. Each of these funds insures deposits of up to $100,000 per depositor.

The existence of deposit insurance provides protection for depositors in the event that a financial intermediary fails. But it also limits the incentive for the owner of a financial intermediary to make safe investments and loans. Some economists believe that deposit insurance played an important role in worsening the problems faced by S&Ls in the 1980s. Savers, knowing that their deposits were being used to make high-risk loans, did not remove their deposits from S&Ls because they knew they had the security of deposit insurance. The S&L owners making high-risk loans knew they were making a one-way bet. If their loans paid off, they made a high rate of return. If they failed and could not meet their obligations to the depositors, the insurance fund would step in. Bad loans were good business!

Because of this type of problem, all financial intermediaries face regulation of their balance sheets.

Balance Sheet Rules The most important balance sheet regulations are

- Capital requirements
- Reserve requirements
- Lending rules

Capital requirements are the minimum amount of an owner's own financial resources that must be put into an intermediary. This amount must be sufficiently large to discourage owners from making loans that are too risky. *Reserve requirements* are rules setting out the minimum percentages of deposits that must be held in currency or other safe, liquid assets. These minimum percentages vary across the different types of intermediaries and deposits; they are largest for checkable deposits and smallest for long-term savings deposits. *Lending rules* are restrictions on the proportions of different types of loans that an intermediary may make. It is these rules that created the sharpest distinctions between the various institutions. Before 1980, commercial banks were the only intermediaries permitted to make commercial loans, and S&Ls and savings banks were restricted to making mortgage loans to home buyers.

To enable S&Ls and savings banks to compete with commercial banks for funds, a ceiling was imposed on the interest rates that could be paid on deposits. This interest ceiling regulation was known as *Regulation Q*. Also, banks were not permitted to pay interest on checkable deposits.

Deregulation in the 1980s

In 1980, Congress passed the Depository Institutions' Deregulation and Monetary Control Act. This legislation removed many of the distinctions between commercial banks and other financial intermediaries. It permitted nonbank financial intermediaries to compete with commercial banks in a wider range of lending business. At the same time it permitted the payment of interest on checkable deposits so that NOW accounts and ATS accounts could be offered by all deposit-taking institutions—banks and nonbanks.

The ability of S&Ls and savings banks to compete for lending business with commercial banks was further strengthened in 1982 with the passage of the Garn–St. Germain Depository Institutions Act. This legislation further eased restrictions on the scale of commercial lending that S&Ls and savings banks could undertake.

Another important regulatory change occurred in 1986—the abolition of Regulation Q. With the abolition of Regulation Q, a fiercely competitive environment was created. In this environment, there was rapid innovation in the types of deposits offered and rapid growth in money market mutual funds.

Financial Innovation

The development of new financial products—of new ways of borrowing and lending—is called **financial innovation.** The aim of financial innovation is to lower the cost of borrowing or to increase the return from lending or, more simply, to increase the profit from financial intermediation. There are three main influences on financial innovation. They are

- Economic environment
- Technology
- Regulation

The pace of financial innovation was remarkable in the 1980s, and all three of these forces played a role.

Economic Environment Some of the innovation of the 1980s was a response to high inflation and high interest rates. An important example is the development of adjustable interest rate mortgages. Traditionally, house purchases have been financed on mortgage loans at a guaranteed interest rate. Rising interest rates brought rising borrowing costs for S&Ls, and since they were committed to fixed interest rates on their mortgages, the industry incurred severe losses. The creation of adjustable interest rate mortgages has taken some of the risk out of long-term lending for house purchases.

Technology Other financial innovations resulted from technological change, most notably that associated with the decreased cost of computing and long-distance communication. The spread of the use of credit cards and the development of international financial markets—for example, the increased importance of Eurodollars—are consequences of technological change.

Regulation A good deal of financial innovation takes place to avoid regulation. The development of NOW accounts and ATS accounts is an example. Regulation that prevented banks from paying interest on checking accounts gave the impetus to devising these new types of deposit accounts, thereby getting around the regulation.

Deregulation, Innovation, and the Money Supply

Deregulation and financial innovation that have led to the development of new types of deposit accounts have brought important changes in the composition of the nation's money. In 1960, M1 consisted of only currency and demand deposits. In the 1980s, other checkable deposits expanded while demand deposits declined. Similar dramatic changes took place in the composition of M2. Savings deposits declined while time deposits, money market mutual fund shares of individuals, and Eurodollar deposits expanded quickly. There have been less dramatic but important changes involving M3. In 1960, M2 and M3 were almost the same concept, but the growth of large time deposits and other types of time deposits included in M3 has gradually expanded.

REVIEW

Financial intermediaries insure their deposits, and their lending is regulated. The 1980s saw a wave of financial deregulation that blurred the distinction between commercial banks and other financial institutions. Financial intermediaries are constantly seeking new ways of making a profit by reacting to the changing economic environment, adopting new technologies, and avoiding the adverse effects of regulations on their activities. Deregulation and innovation in the 1980s brought a whole range of new types of deposit accounts that led to important changes in the composition of the nation's stock of money. ◆

Because financial intermediaries are able to create liquidity and to create assets that are a means of payment—money—they occupy a unique place in our economy and exert an important influence on the quantity of money in existence. Let's see how money gets created.

How Banks Create Money

Money is created by the activities of commercial banks and other financial intermediaries—by all those institutions whose deposits circulate as a means of payment. In this section, we'll use the term *banks* to refer to all these depository institutions.

Actual and Required Reserves

As we saw in Table 27.6, banks don't have $100 in bills for every $100 that people have deposited with them. In fact, a typical bank today has $1.25 in currency and another $1.15 on deposit at a Federal Reserve bank for every $100 deposited in it. No need for panic. Banks have learned, from experience, that these reserve levels are adequate for ordinary business needs. The fraction of a bank's total deposits that are held in reserves is called the **reserve ratio.** The value of the reserve ratio is influenced by the actions of a bank's depositors. If a depositor withdraws currency from a bank, the reserve ratio falls. If a depositor puts currency into a bank, the reserve ratio increases.

The **required reserve ratio** is the ratio of reserves to deposits that banks are required, by regulation, to hold. A bank's **required reserves** are equal to its deposits multiplied by the required reserve ratio. Actual reserves minus required reserves are **excess reserves.** Whenever banks have excess reserves, they are able to create money. When we say that banks create money, we don't mean that they have smoke-filled back rooms in which counterfeiters are busily working. Remember, most money is deposits, not currency. What banks create is deposits, and they do so by making loans. To see how banks create money, we are going to look at a model of the banking system.

Creating Deposits by Making Loans

Let's suppose that the banks have a required reserve ratio of 25 percent. That is, for each dollar deposited, they want to keep 25¢ in the form of reserves. Al, a customer of the Golden Nugget Bank, decides to reduce his holdings of currency and put $100 in his deposit account at the bank. Suddenly, the Golden Nugget Bank has $100 of new deposits and $100 of additional reserves. But with $100 of new deposits the Golden Nugget Bank doesn't want to hold onto $100 of additional reserves. It has excess reserves. Its required reserve ratio is 25 percent, so it plans to lend $75 of the additional $100 to another customer. Amy, a customer at the same bank, borrows $75. At this point, the Golden Nugget Bank has new deposits of $100, new loans of $75, and new reserves of $25. As far as Golden Nugget is concerned, that is the end of the matter. No money has been created. Al has reduced his holdings of currency by $100 and increased his bank deposit by $100, but the total amount of money has remained constant. Although that's the end of the story for the Golden Nugget Bank, it is not the end of the story for the entire banking system. What happens next?

Amy uses the $75 loan to buy a jacket from Barb. To undertake this transaction, she writes a check on her account with the Golden Nugget, and Barb deposits the check in the Laser Bank. The Laser Bank now has new deposits of $75 and an additional $75 of reserves. The total amount of money supply is now $75 higher than before.

The Laser Bank doesn't need to hang on to the entire $75 as reserves: it needs only a quarter of that amount—$18.75. The Laser Bank lends the additional amount, $56.25, to Bob, who buys some used stereo equipment from Carl. Bob writes a check on his account at the Laser Bank, which Carl deposits in his account at the Apollo Bank. The Apollo Bank now has new deposits of $56.25, so the amount of money has increased by a total of $131.25 (the $75 lent to Amy and paid to Barb plus the $56.25 lent to Bob and paid to Carl).

The transactions that we've just described are summarized in Table 27.7. But the story is still incomplete. The process that we're describing continues through the remaining banks and their depositors and borrowers, all the way down the list in that table. By the time we get down to the Pirates Bank, Ken has paid Len $5.63 for a box of computer disks, and so the Pirates Bank has new deposits of $5.63 and additional reserves of that same amount. Since it needs only $1.41 of additional reserves, it makes a loan of $4.22 to Lee, who in turn spends the money. By this time, the total amount of money has increased by $283.11, the new deposits at each stage of the process listed in the first column of numbers in the table less Al's deposit of $100. Remember that when Al made his deposit, he also reduced his holding of currency, so his new deposit did not increase the total amount of money.

This process continues but with amounts that are now getting so tiny that we will not bother to keep track of them. All the remaining stages in the process taken together add up to the numbers in the second to last row of the table. The final tallies appear as the totals at the bottom of the table. Deposits have increased by $400, loans by $300, and reserves by $100. The banks have created money by making loans. The quantity of money created is $300—the same amount as the additional loans made. It's true that deposits have increased by $400, but $100 of that increase is Al's original deposit. That increase in deposits does not increase the quantity of money. The currency that Al deposited was already money. It is only the new deposits created by the lending activity of the banks that have increased the quantity of money in existence.

The Simple Money Multiplier

The ability of banks to create money does not mean that they can create an indefinite amount of money.

TABLE 27.7

Creating Money by Making Loans: Many Banks

Bank	Depositor	Borrower	New deposits	New loans	New reserves	Increase in money	Cumulative increase in money
Golden Nugget	**Al**	**Amy**	**$100.00**	**$ 75.00**	**$ 25.00**	**$ 0.00**	
Laser	**Barb**	**Bob**	**75.00**	**56.25**	**18.75**	**75.00**	**$ 75.00**
Apollo	**Carl**	**Con**	**56.25**	**42.19**	**14.06**	**56.25**	**131.25**
Monty Python	**Di**	**Dan**	**42.19**	**31.64**	**10.55**	**42.19**	**173.44**
Plato	**Ed**	**Eve**	**31.64**	**23.73**	**7.91**	**31.64**	**205.08**
J. R. Ewing	**Fran**	**Fred**	**23.73**	**17.80**	**5.93**	**23.73**	**228.81**
1st Madonna	**Gus**	**Gail**	**17.80**	**13.35**	**4.45**	**17.80**	**246.61**
Rambo	**Holly**	**Hal**	**13.35**	**10.01**	**3.34**	**13.35**	**259.96**
Trump	**Jim**	**Jan**	**10.01**	**7.51**	**2.50**	**10.01**	**269.97**
Disney	**Kym**	**Ken**	**7.51**	**5.63**	**1.88**	**7.51**	**277.48**
Pirates	**Len**	**Lee**	**5.63**	**4.22**	**1.41**	**5.63**	**283.11**
			⋮	⋮	⋮	⋮	⋮
All others			**16.89**	**12.67**	**4.22**	**16.89**	
Total banking system			**$400.00**	**$300.00**	**$100.00**	**$300.00**	**$300.00**

The amount that they can create depends on the size of their reserves and on the required reserve ratio. In this example, in which the required reserve ratio is 25 percent, bank deposits have increased by four times the level of reserves.

The **simple money multiplier** is the amount by which an increase in bank reserves is multiplied to calculate the effect of the increase in reserves on total bank deposits. The simple money multiplier is

$$\text{Simple money multiplier} = \frac{\text{Change in deposits}}{\text{Change in reserves}}.$$

In the example we've just worked through, the simple money multiplier is 4—a \$100 increase in reserves created the \$400 increase in deposits.

The simple money multiplier is related to the required reserve ratio. In our example, that ratio is 25 percent (or ¼). That is,

$$\text{Required reserves} = (\tfrac{1}{4})\text{Deposits}.$$

Whenever required reserves exceed actual reserves (a situation of negative excess reserves), the banks call in loans. When required reserves are below actual reserves (a situation of positive excess reserves), the banks make additional loans. By adjusting their loans, the banks bring their actual reserves into line with their required reserves, eliminating excess reserves. Thus, when banks have changed their loans and reserves to make actual reserves equal required reserves,

$$\text{Actual reserves} = (\tfrac{1}{4})\text{Deposits}.$$

If we divide both sides of this equation by ¼, we obtain

$$\text{Deposits} = (1/\tfrac{1}{4})\text{Actual reserves}.$$

When the banks receive new deposits, actual reserves increase. If the increase in reserves occurs when required reserves and actual reserves are equal, the banks have excess reserves. They lend these excess reserves until bank deposits have increased by enough to increase required reserves by the same amount as the increase in actual reserves. A decrease in deposits lowers reserves and forces the banks to call in some loans. The end result of this process is a decrease in deposits by an amount that decreases required reserves by the same amount as the decrease in actual reserves. When deposits have changed by enough to have eliminated excess reserves, the following change in deposits has taken place:

Change in deposits = (1/¼)Change in reserves.

By definition, (1/¼) is the simple money multiplier. It is the amount by which the change in reserves is multiplied to calculate the change in deposits. In our example, this multiplier equals 4. The relationship between the simple money multiplier and the required reserve ratio is

$$\text{Simple money multiplier} = \frac{1}{\text{Required reserve ratio}}.$$

Real-World Money Multipliers The money multiplier in the real world differs from the simple money multiplier that we have just calculated for two reasons. First, the required reserve ratio of real-world banks is much smaller than the 25 percent we used here. Second, in the real world, not all the loans made by banks return to the banks in the form of reserves. Some of them remain outside the banks in the form of currency in circulation. These two differences between the real-world money multiplier and the simple money multiplier we've just calculated work in opposing directions. The smaller required reserve ratio of real-world banks makes the real-world multiplier larger than the above numerical example. The fact that some currency remains in circulation outside the banks makes the real-world multiplier smaller. We study the actual values of real-world money multipliers in the next chapter.

REVIEW

Banks create money by making loans. The amount that they can lend is determined by their reserves and the required reserve ratio. Each time they make a loan, deposits increase and so do required reserves. When deposits are at a level that makes required reserves equal to actual reserves, the banks cannot increase their lending or deposits any further. An initial change in deposits that changes reserves brings about an eventual change in deposits equal to the change in reserves multiplied by the simple money multiplier. ◆

Concern over the supply of money arises because money has a powerful effect on our economy. Our next task in this chapter is to examine some of these effects.

Money, Real GDP, and the Price Level

We now know what money *is*. We also know that in a modern economy such as that of the United States today, most of the money is made up of deposits at banks and other financial intermediaries. We've seen that these institutions can actually create money by making loans. Does the quantity of money created by the banking and financial system matter? What effects does it have? Does it matter whether the quantity increases quickly or slowly?

We're going to address these questions first by using the aggregate demand–aggregate supply model. Then we're going to consider a special theory of money and prices—the quantity theory of money. Finally, we'll look at some historical and international evidence on the relationship between money and prices. Also, Our Advancing Knowledge on pp. 748–749 looks at the evolution of our understanding of the effects of changes in the quantity of money.

Money in the *AD-AS* Model

Figure 27.2 illustrates the aggregate demand–aggregate supply model. In part (a) there is unemployment, and in part (b) there is full employment. In both parts, the long-run aggregate supply curve is *LAS*.

An Increase in the Money Supply with Unemployment Initially, the aggregate demand curve is AD_0, and the short-run aggregate supply curve is *SAS* (in part a). Equilibrium occurs where the aggregate demand curve AD_0 intersects the short-run aggregate supply curve. The price level is 90, and real GDP is $4.4 trillion. Now suppose there is an increase in the quantity of money. The increase occurs as a result of the process that we've just studied. Banks, flush with excess reserves, make loans, and the loans create money. With more money in their bank accounts, people increase their expenditure, and aggregate demand increases. The aggregate demand curve shifts to the right to become AD_1. The new equilibrium is at the intersection point of AD_1 and *SAS*. The price level rises to 100, and real GDP increases to $4.5 trillion. The economy is now on its long-run aggregate supply curve, and there is full employment. A smaller increase in the money supply would not shift the aggregate demand curve as far to the right, and the economy would remain in an unemployment equilibrium. But the general effect is the same—an increase in both real GDP and the price level.

An Increase in the Money Supply at Full Employment Initially, the aggregate demand curve is AD_1, and the short-run aggregate supply curve is SAS_1 (in part b). Equilibrium occurs where the aggregate demand curve AD_1 intersects the short-run aggregate supply curve SAS_1. The price level is 100 and real GDP is $4.5 trillion. The economy is on its long-run aggregate supply curve and is in full-employment equilibrium. Now suppose there is an increase in the quantity of money that increases aggregate demand and shifts the aggregate demand curve to AD_2. The new equilibrium is at the intersection point of AD_2 and SAS_1. The price level rises to 110, and real GDP increases to $4.6 trillion. But this is the short-run effect. The economy is now at an above full-employment equilibrium, and wages start to increase. As they do so, the short-run aggregate supply curve shifts upward. The price level increases, and real GDP falls. Wages continue to increase until full employment is restored. By this time, the short-run aggregate supply curve is SAS_2 and the price level is 120.

Thus between one full-employment equilibrium and another, an increase in the quantity of money results in an increase in the price level and no change in real GDP. It is this relationship between

FIGURE 27.2

Aggregate Demand, Aggregate Supply, and the Quantity of Money

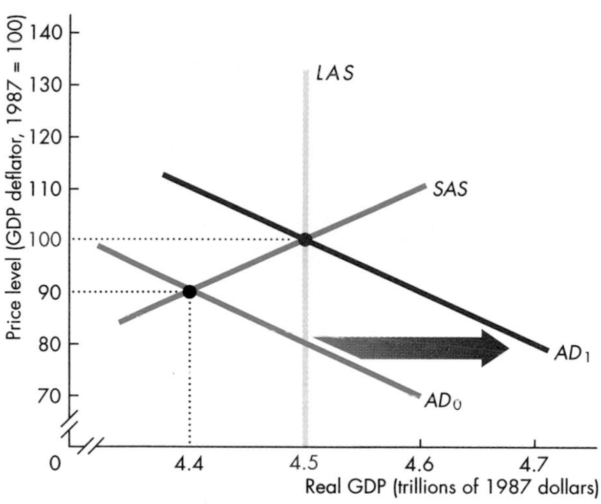

(a) Money supply increase with unemployment

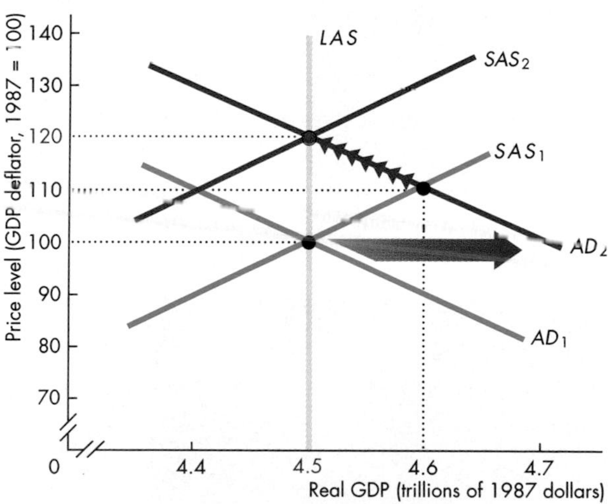

(b) Money supply increase at full employment

In part (a), an increase in the money supply shifts the aggregate demand curve from AD_0 to AD_1, and the price level rises to 100 and real GDP increases to $4.5 trillion, its full-employment level. In part (b), an increase in the quantity of money shifts the aggregate demand curve from AD_1 to AD_2. The price level rises to 110, and real GDP increases to $4.6 trillion. The economy is at an above full-employment equilibrium. Wages rise, and the short-run aggregate supply curve shifts upward to SAS_2. Real GDP falls back to its initial level, and the price level increases to 120.

UNDERSTANDING the Causes of INFLATION

The combination of history and economics has taught us a great deal about the causes of inflation.

Severe inflation—hyperinflation—arises from a breakdown of the normal fiscal policy processes at times of war and political upheaval. Tax revenues fall short of government spending, and the gap between them is filled by printing money. As inflation increases, there is a *shortage* of money, so its rate of creation is increased yet further and prices rise even faster. Eventually, the monetary system collapses. Such was the experience of Germany in the 1920s, and Russia is heading in this direction today.

In earlier times, when commodities were used as money, inflation resulted from the discovery of new sources of money. The most recent occurrence of this type of inflation was in the nineteenth century when gold, then used as money, was discovered in California and Australia.

In modern times, inflation has resulted from increases in the money supply that have accommodated increases in costs. The most dramatic such inflations occurred during the 1970s when oil price increases were accommodated by the Fed and other central banks around the world.

To avoid inflation, money supply growth must be held in check. But at times of severe cost pressure, central banks feel a strong tug in the direction of avoiding recession and accommodating the cost pressure. Yet some countries have avoided inflation more effectively than others. A key source of success is central bank independence. In low-inflation countries, such as Germany and Japan, the central bank decides how much money to create and at what level to set interest rates and does not take instructions from the government. In high-inflation countries, such as the United Kingdom and Italy, the central bank takes direct orders from the government about interest rates and money supply growth. This connection between central bank independence and inflation has been noticed by the architects of a new monetary system for the European Community who are modeling the European Central Bank on Germany's Bundesbank, not on the Bank of England.

"Inflation is always and everywhere a monetary phenomenon."

MILTON FRIEDMAN
The Counter-Revolution in Monetary Theory

When inflation is especially rapid, as it was in Germany in 1923, money becomes almost worthless. In Germany at that time, bank notes were more valuable as kindling than as money, and the sight of people burning Reichmarks was a common one. Because no one wanted to hold money for too long, wages were paid and spent twice a day. Banks took deposits and made loans, but at interest rates that compensated depositors and the bank for the falling value of money—rates that could exceed 100 percent a day. The price of a dinner might double during the course of an evening, making lingering over coffee a very expensive pastime.

Hyperinflation has never occurred in a computer-age economy. But imagine the scene if hyperinflation—an inflation rate of 50 percent a month—did break out. ATMs would have to be refilled several times an hour, and the volume of paper (both money and receipts) they would spew out would grow to astronomical proportions. But most of us would try to avoid using money. Instead, we would buy as much as possible using credit cards. And we'd be eager to pay off our card balances quickly because the interest rate on unpaid balances would be 70 percent a month. Only at such a high interest rate would it pay banks to lend to cardholders, since banks themselves would be paying interest rates of more than 50 percent a month to induce people to deposit their money.

David Hume

And the *Quantity Theory of Money*

Born in Edinburgh, Scotland, in 1711 and a close friend of Adam Smith, David Hume was a philosopher, historian, and economist of extraordinary breadth. His first book, by his own description, "fell dead-born from the press." But his essays—on topics ranging from love and marriage and the immortality of the soul to money, interest, and the balance of payments—were widely read and earned him a considerable fortune.

Hume gave the first clear statement of the quantity theory of money—the theory that an increase in the quantity of money brings a proportional increase in the price level. And his account of the way in which an increase in the quantity of money brings an increase in prices anticipated the discovery, some 220 years later, of the Phillips curve and the Keynesian theory of aggregate demand.

the money supply and the price level at full employment that gives rise to the quantity theory of money.

The Quantity Theory of Money

The **quantity theory of money** is the proposition that an increase in the quantity of money leads to an equal percentage increase in the price level. The original basis of the quantity theory of money is a concept known as the velocity of circulation and an equation called the equation of exchange. The **velocity of circulation** is the average number of times a dollar of money is used annually to buy the goods and services that make up GDP. GDP is equal to the price level (P) multiplied by real GDP (Y). That is,

$$GDP = PY.$$

Call the quantity of money M. The velocity of circulation, V, is determined by the equation

$$V = PY/M.$$

For example, if GDP is $5 trillion and if the quantity of money is $2 trillion, the velocity of circulation is 2.5. On the average, each dollar of money circulates 2.5 times in its use to purchase the final goods and services that make up GDP.

The **equation of exchange** states that the quantity of money (M) multiplied by the velocity of circulation (V) equals GDP, or

$$MV = PY.$$

Given the definition of the velocity of circulation, this equation is always true—it is true by definition. With M equal to $2 trillion and V equal to 2.5, MV is equal to $5 trillion, the value of GDP.

The equation of exchange becomes the quantity theory of money by making two propositions:

- The velocity of circulation is a constant.
- Real GDP is not influenced by the quantity of money.

If these two propositions are true, the equation of exchange tells us that a given percentage change in the quantity of money brings about an equal percentage change in the price level. You can see why by solving the equation of exchange for the price level. Dividing both sides of the equation by real GDP (Y) gives

$$P = (V/Y)M.$$

Because V and Y are constant, the relationship between the change in the price level (ΔP) and the change in the money supply (ΔM) is

$$\Delta P = (V/Y)\Delta M.$$

Dividing this equation by the previous one gives the quantity theory proposition, namely that the percentage increase in the price level ($\Delta P/P$) equals the percentage increase in the money supply ($\Delta M/M$), that is,

$$\Delta P/P = \Delta M/M.$$

The Quantity Theory and the *AD-AS* Model

The quantity theory of money can be interpreted in terms of the aggregate demand–aggregate supply model. The aggregate demand curve is a relationship between the quantity of real GDP demanded (Y) and the price level (P), other things remaining constant. We can obtain such a relationship from the equation of exchange,

$$MV = PY.$$

Dividing both sides of this equation by real GDP (Y) gives

$$P = MV/Y.$$

This equation may be interpreted as describing an aggregate demand curve. For a given money supply (M) and a given velocity of circulation (V), the higher the price level (P), the lower is the quantity of real GDP demanded (Y).

In general, when the quantity of money changes, the velocity of circulation might also change. But the quantity theory asserts that velocity is a constant. If velocity is constant, an increase in the quantity of money increases aggregate demand and shifts the aggregate demand curve upward by the same amount as the percentage change in the quantity of money. For example, in Fig. 27.2(b), the shift in the aggregate demand curve from AD_1 to AD_2, measured by the vertical distance between the two demand curves, is 20 percent. With a given velocity of circulation, this shift is brought about by a 20 percent increase in the quantity of money.

The quantity theory of money also asserts that real GDP is not affected by the money supply. This assertion is true in the aggregate demand–aggregate supply model only at full-employment equilibrium.

As we saw in Fig. 27.2(a), starting out with unemployment, an increase in the quantity of money increases real GDP. In this case, the price level increases by a smaller percentage than the percentage increase in aggregate demand and the money supply. But Fig. 27.2(b) shows what happens at full employment. Here, from the initial full-employment equilibrium to the new one, a 20 percent increase in the quantity of money increases the price level by 20 percent.

According to the aggregate demand–aggregate supply model, the relationship between the quantity of money and the price level is a much looser one than that implied by the quantity theory. First, the aggregate demand–aggregate supply model takes account of influences of the money supply on the velocity of circulation that the quantity theory ignores. We discuss these influences in the next chapter. Second, the aggregate demand–aggregate supply model predicts that changes in the quantity of money change real GDP, an influence that the quantity theory asserts does not occur.

Which theory of the relationship between the quantity of money and the price level is correct? Is the relationship as precise as implied by the quantity theory, or is it a looser relationship as implied by the aggregate demand–aggregate supply model? Let's look at the relationship between money and the price level, both historically and internationally.

Historical Evidence on the Quantity Theory of Money

The quantity theory of money can be tested on the historical data of the United States by looking at the relationship between the growth rate of the quantity of money and the inflation rate. Figure 27.3 shows this relationship for the years between 1875 and

FIGURE 27.3

Money Growth and Inflation in the United States

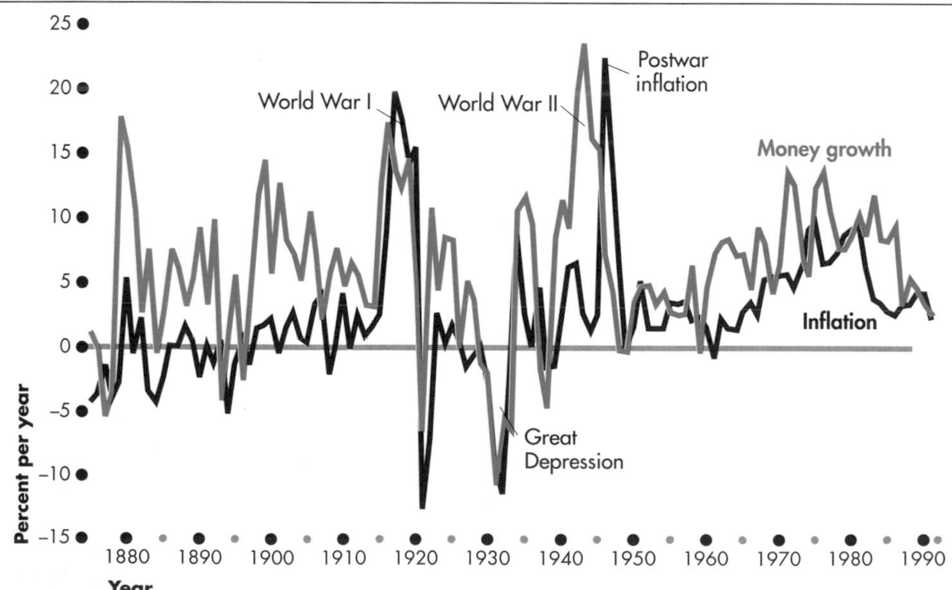

Year-to-year percentage changes in the price level—inflation—and the quantity of money—money growth—are plotted for each year between 1875 and 1991. The figure shows that (1) on the average, money growth exceeds inflation; (2) variations in inflation are correlated with variations in money growth; (3) during World War I, inflation and money growth surged upward together, but during World War II and its aftermath there was a break in the relationship; (4) during the years before 1915 and after 1950, inflation was less volatile than money growth.

Sources: Quantity of money (M2): 1875–1960, Milton Friedman and Anna J. Schwartz, *A Monetary History of the United States* (Princeton, N.J.: Princeton University Press, 1963); 1961–1991, *Economic Report of the President*, 1992. Price level and inflation (GDP deflator): 1875–1929, Nathan S. Balke and Robert J. Gordon, "The Estimation of Prewar Gross National Product: Methodology and New Evidence," *Journal of Political Economy* 97 (February 1989); 1930–1991, *Economic Report of the President*, 1992.

1991. The figure reveals four features of the relationship between money supply growth—measured by M2—and inflation. They are

1. On the average, the quantity of money grows at a rate that exceeds the inflation rate.
2. Variations in the growth rate of the quantity of money are correlated with variations in the inflation rate.
3. During World War I, there was a strong relationship between money growth and inflation, but during World War II and its aftermath, there was a break in that relationship.
4. There is a general tendency, especially clear before 1915 and after 1950, for fluctuations in the inflation rate to be smaller than those in the money growth rate.

1. Average Money Growth and Inflation You can see that the money growth rate is larger than the inflation rate, on the average, by looking at the two lines in Fig. 27.3. Most of the time the money growth line is above the inflation line. The difference in the averages is accounted for by the fact that the economy expands with real GDP growing. Money growth that matches real GDP growth does not add to inflation.

2. Correlation Between Money Growth and Inflation The correlation between money growth and inflation is most evident in the data for the years 1915 to 1940. For example, the massive buildup of inflation between 1915 and 1920 was accompanied by a huge increase in the growth rate of the quantity of money. The falling prices of the early 1920s and the Great Depression were associated with a decrease in the quantity of money. Although the correlation in the post–World War II years has been weak, you can see that the steadily increasing money growth rate through the 1960s and 1970s was associated with steadily rising inflation through those decades.

3. The Effects of Wars During World War I, there was a large increase in the money growth rate and in the inflation rate. There was also a large increase in the money growth rate during World War II. But during World War II, there was no corresponding increase in the inflation rate. Inflation was suppressed by a program of price controls and rationing, but when these measures were lifted at the end of World War II, inflation temporarily exploded even though money growth was, by then, moderate.

4. Relative Volatility of Money Growth and Inflation The quantity theory predicts a closer correlation between money growth and inflation than that visible in the data. In particular, it does not predict the generally observed fact that money growth is more volatile than inflation. You can see this relative volatility both in the years before 1915 and since 1950. This tendency for money growth to fluctuate more than inflation, although not consistent with the quantity theory, is predicted by the aggregate demand–aggregate supply model. The phenomenon arises from fluctuations in real GDP that accompany fluctuations in the quantity of money and from changes in the velocity of circulation.

The year-to-year fluctuations in money supply growth and inflation look very different from the predictions of the quantity theory. But the longer-term fluctuations in money supply growth and inflation are similar to the predictions of the quantity theory.

International Evidence on the Quantity Theory of Money

The international evidence on the quantity theory of money is summarized in Fig. 27.4, which shows the inflation rate and the money growth rate for 60 countries. There is an unmistakable tendency for high money growth to be associated with high inflation.

But like the historical evidence for the United States, these international data also tell us that money supply growth is not the only influence on inflation. Some countries have an inflation rate that exceeds the money supply growth rate, while others have an inflation rate that falls short of the money supply growth rate.

Correlation and Causation

The fact that money growth and inflation are correlated does not mean that we can determine, from that correlation, the direction of causation. Money growth might cause inflation; inflation might cause money growth; or some third variable might simultaneously cause inflation and money growth. In the quantity theory and in the aggregate demand–aggregate supply model, causation runs from money growth to inflation. But neither theory denies the possibility that, at different times and places, causa-

FIGURE 27.4

Money Growth and Inflation in the World Economy

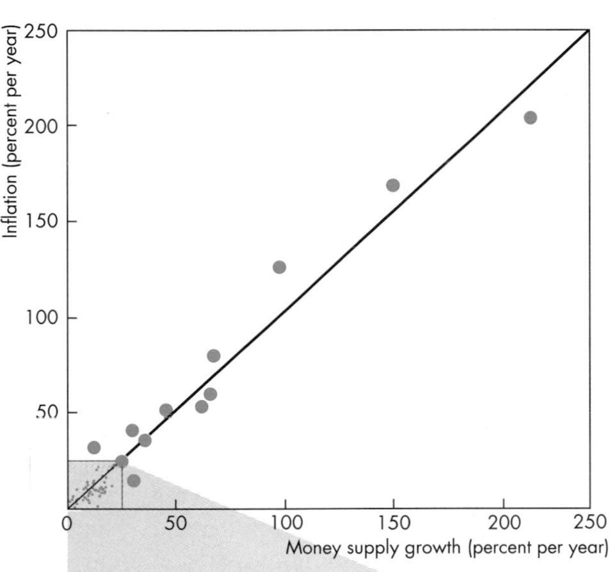

(a) All countries

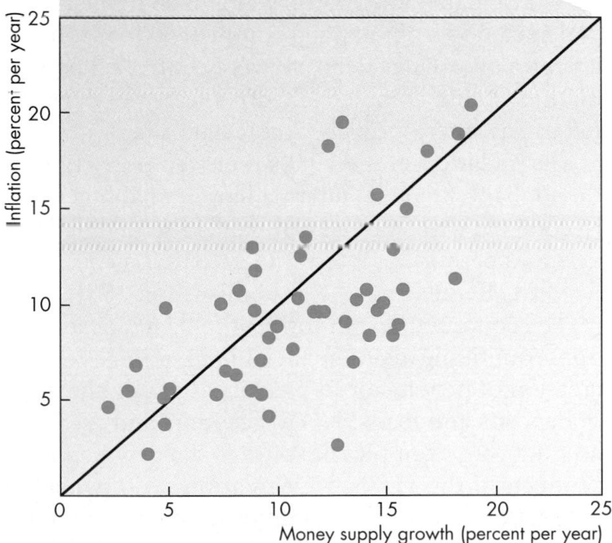

(b) Low-inflation countries

Inflation and money growth in 60 countries (in part a) and low-inflation countries (in part b) show that money growth is an important influence, though not the only influence, on inflation.

Source: Federal Reserve Bank of St. Louis, *Review* (May/June 1988): 15.

tion might run in the other direction or that some third factor, such as a government budget deficit, might be the root cause of both rapid money growth and inflation.

There are some occasions, however, that give us an opportunity to test our assumptions about causation. One of these is World War II and the years immediately following it. Rapid money supply growth during the war years accompanied by price controls almost certainly caused the postwar inflation. The inflationary consequences of the money growth were delayed by the controls but not removed. It is inconceivable that this was an example of reverse causation—of postwar inflation causing wartime money growth.

REVIEW

The quantity of money exerts an important influence on the price level. An increase in the quantity of money increases aggregate demand. In the short run, an increase in aggregate demand increases both the price level and real GDP. But on the average, real GDP fluctuates around its full-employment level and increases in the quantity of money bring increases in the price level. The quantity theory of money predicts that an increase in the quantity of money produces an equivalent percentage increase in the price level. The historical and international evidence on the relationship between the quantity of money and the price level provides broad support for the quantity theory of money as a proposition about long-run tendencies but also reveals important changes in the price level that occur independently of changes in the quantity of money. ◆

◆ ◆ ◆ ◆ In this chapter, we have studied the institutions that make up our banking and financial system. We've seen how the deposit liabilities of commercial banks and other financial institutions comprise our means of payment—our money. Banks and other financial institutions create money by making loans. The quantity of money in existence has important effects on the economy and, in particular, on the price level. ◆ ◆ In the next chapter, we're going to see how the quantity of money is regulated and influenced by the actions of the Federal Reserve System. We're also going to discover how, by its influence on the money supply, the Fed is able to influence interest rates, thereby affecting the level of aggregate demand. It is through its effects on the money supply and interest rates and their wider ramifications that the Fed is able to help steer the course of the economy.

SUMMARY

What Is Money?

Money has four functions. It is a medium of exchange, a unit of account, a standard of deferred payment, and a store of value. The earliest forms of money were commodities. In the modern world, we use a fiat money system. The biggest component of money is private debt money.

There are three official measures of money in the United States today: M1, M2, and M3. M1 consists of currency held outside banks, traveler's checks, demand deposits, and other checkable deposits. M2 includes M1 plus savings deposits, small time deposits, Eurodollar deposits, money market mutual fund shares held by individuals, and other M2 deposits. M3 adds to M2 large time deposits, Eurodollar time deposits, money market mutual fund shares held by institutions, and other M3 deposits. M1 serves the function of the means of payment, but the additional items in M2 and M3 are easily converted into M1 assets—assets that are highly liquid. Checkable deposits are money, but checks and credit cards are not. (pp. 728–735)

Financial Intermediaries

The main financial intermediaries whose liabilities serve as money are commercial banks, savings and loan associations, savings banks, credit unions, and money market mutual funds. These institutions take in deposits, hold cash reserves to ensure that they can meet their depositors' demands for currency, and use the rest of their financial resources either to buy securities or to make loans. Financial intermediaries make a profit by borrowing at a lower interest rate than that at which they lend. All financial intermediaries provide four main economic services: they minimize the cost of obtaining funds, minimize the cost of monitoring borrowers, pool risks, and create liquidity. (pp. 735–741)

Financial Regulation, Deregulation, and Innovation

Financial intermediaries are regulated to protect depositors. Deposits are insured by the FDIC, owners of intermediaries are required to put a certain minimum amount of their own financial resources into the institution, minimum cash and liquid assets reserves are specified, and lending rules are imposed.

Before 1980, S&Ls and savings banks were permitted to make only mortgage loans to home buyers and excluded from making commercial loans. Interest rates on savings deposits were controlled by Regulation Q, and commercial banks were not permitted to pay interest on checkable deposits.

Deregulation in the 1980s removed restrictions on nonbank financial intermediaries, enabling them to compete with commercial banks for lending business and permitting interest to be paid on checkable deposits. Regulation Q was abolished in 1986.

The continual search for profitable financial opportunities leads to financial innovation—to the creation of new financial products such as new types of deposits and loans. NOW accounts and ATS accounts are examples of some of the new financial products of the 1980s. Deregulation and financial innovation have brought important changes in the composition of the nation's money. (pp. 741–743)

How Banks Create Money

Banks create money by making loans. When a loan is made to one person and the amount lent is spent, much of it ends up as someone else's deposit. The total quantity of deposits that can be supported by a given amount of reserves (the simple money multiplier) is equal to 1 divided by the required reserve ratio. (pp. 743–746)

Money, Real GDP, and the Price Level

The quantity of money affects aggregate demand. An increase in the quantity of money increases aggregate demand and, in the short run, increases both the price level and real GDP. Over the long run, real GDP grows and fluctuates around its full-employment level, and increases in the quantity of money bring increases in the price level. The quantity theory of money predicts that an increase in the quantity of money increases the price level by the same percentage amount and leaves real GDP undisturbed. Both historical and international evidence suggests that the quantity theory of money is correct only in a broad average sense. The quantity of money does exert an important influence on the price level but also on real GDP. There are other important influences on the price level. Further, the correlation between money growth and inflation does not tell us the direction of causation. (pp. 746–753)

KEY ELEMENTS

Key Terms

Asset, 735
Balance sheet, 735
Barter, 728
Checkable deposit, 731
Commercial bank, 735
Commodity money, 729
Convertible paper money, 730
Credit union, 740
Currency, 731
Double coincidence of wants, 728
Equation of exchange, 750
Excess reserves, 744
Fiat money, 731
Financial innovation, 742
Financial intermediary, 735
Gresham's Law, 730
Investment security, 737
Liability, 735
Liquid asset, 737
Liquidity, 732
Loan, 737
M1, 731
M2, 731
M3, 731
Medium of exchange, 728
Money, 728
Money market mutual fund, 740
Private debt money, 731
Quantity theory of money, 750
Required reserve ratio, 744
Required reserves, 744
Reserve ratio, 743
Reserves, 737
Savings and loan association, 737
Savings bank, 740
Simple money multiplier, 745
Standard of deferred payment, 729
Store of value, 729
Unit of account, 728
Velocity of circulation, 750
Wholesale deposit market, 737

Key Figures and Tables

REVIEW QUESTIONS

1 What is money? What are its functions?

2 What are the different forms of money?

3 What are the three official measures of money in the United States today?

4 Are checks and credit cards money? Explain your answer.

5 What are financial intermediaries? What are the types of financial intermediaries in the United States? What are the main institutions other than commercial banks that take deposits?

6 What are the main items in the balance sheet of a commercial bank?

7 What are the economic functions of financial intermediaries?

8 How do banks make a profit, and how do they create money?

9 Define the simple money multiplier. Explain why it equals 1 divided by the required reserve ratio.

10 Explain why real-world money multipliers are smaller than the simple money multiplier.

11 What does the aggregate demand–aggregate supply model predict about the effects of a change in the quantity of money on the price level and real GDP?

12 What is the equation of exchange? What is the velocity of circulation? What assumptions are necessary to make the equation of exchange the quantity theory of money?

13 What is the historical and international evidence on the quantity theory of money?

PROBLEMS

1 In the United States today, money includes which of the following items?

a Federal Reserve banknotes in the Bank of America's cash machines
b Your Visa card
c The quarters inside public phones
d Federal Reserve banknotes in your wallet
e The check you have just written to pay for your rent
f The loan you took out last August to pay for your school fees

2 Which of the following items are fiat money? Which are private debt money?

a Checkable deposits at Citicorp
b Shares of IBM stock held by individuals
c Gold bars held by banks
d The Susan B. Anthony dollar
e U.S. government securities
f NOW accounts

3 Sara withdraws $1,000 from her savings deposit at the Lucky S&L, keeps $50 in cash, and deposits the balance in her checkable account, which is a demand deposit at Bank of America. What are the immediate changes in M1, M2, and M3?

4 The commercial banks in Desertland have the following assets and liabilities:

Total reserves	$250 million
Loans	$1,000 million
Deposits	$2,000 million
Total assets	$2,500 million

a Construct the commercial banks' balance sheet. If you are missing any assets, call them "other assets"; if you are missing any liabilities, call them "other liabilities."
b Calculate the commercial banks' reserve ratio.

c If the reserve ratio in part (b) is equal to the commercial banks' desired reserve ratio, calculate the simple money multiplier.

5 An immigrant arrives in New Transylvania with $1,200. The $1,200 is put into a bank deposit. All the banks in New Transylvania have a required reserve ratio of 10 percent.

a What is the initial increase in the quantity of money of New Transylvania?

b What is the initial increase in the quantity of bank deposits when the immigrant arrives?

c How much does the immigrant's bank lend out?

d Using a format similar to that in Table 27.7, calculate the amount lent and the amount of deposits created at each "round," assuming that all the funds lent are returned to the banking system in the form of deposits.

e By how much has the quantity of money increased after 20 rounds of lending?

f What are the ultimate increases in the quantity of money, bank loans, and bank deposits?

6 Quantecon is a country in which the quantity theory of money operates. The country has a constant population, capital stock, and technology. In year 1, real GDP was $400 million, the price level was 200, and the velocity of circulation of money was 20. In year 2, the quantity of money was 20 percent higher than in year 1.

a What was the quantity of money in Quantecon in year 1?

b What was the quantity of money in Quantecon in year 2?

c What was the price level in Quantecon in year 2?

d What was the level of real GDP in Quantecon in year 2?

e What was the velocity of circulation in Quantecon in year 2?

CHAPTER 28

THE FEDERAL RESERVE, MONEY, AND INTEREST RATES

After studying this chapter, you will be able to:

- Describe the structure of the Federal Reserve System (the Fed)
- Describe the tools used by the Fed to influence the money supply and interest rates
- Explain what an open market operation is and how it works
- Explain how an open market operation changes the money supply
- Distinguish between the nominal money supply and the real money supply
- Explain what determines the demand for money
- Explain the effects of financial innovations on the demand for money in the 1980s
- Explain how interest rates are determined
- Explain how the Fed influences interest rates

Fiddling with the Knobs

THE YEAR IS 1983. A YOUNG COUPLE THINKING OF buying a first home has found the perfect place. But mortgage rates are 16 percent a year. Amid much gnashing of teeth, they put off their purchase until interest rates decline, making a home affordable. What determines interest rates? Are they determined by forces of nature? Or is somebody fiddling with the knobs somewhere? ◆◆ You suspect that someone is indeed fiddling with the knobs. You've just read in your newspaper: "Fed nudging interest rates down to spark recovery." And a few months earlier, you read: "The Fed doesn't plan to push interest rates higher unless it sees further rebound of inflation." What is "the Fed"? Why would the Fed want to change interest rates? And how can the Fed influence interest rates? ◆◆ There is enough currency—coins and Federal Reserve bills—circulating in the United States for every single individual to have a wallet stuffed with more than $1,000. There are enough checking deposits in banks and other financial institutions for everyone to have almost $2,500 in these accounts. Of course, not many people hold as much currency and checkable deposits as these averages. But these *are* the averages. Therefore, if most people don't hold this much, some people must be holding a great deal more. What determines the quantity of money that people hold? ◆◆ The 1980s saw a revolution in our banking and financial sector. There was an explosion in the use of credit cards, and many people stopped using cash to buy gasoline, restaurant meals, and many other commonly purchased items. But you can't buy everything with a credit card. For example, you feel like a midnight snack, but your favorite spot doesn't accept credit cards and you're out of cash.

No problem! You head straight for the automatic teller and withdraw what you need tonight and for the next few days as well. While walking out, you wonder to yourself: How much cash would I need to hold if I didn't have quick access to an automatic teller machine? How did people get cash for midnight pizza before such machines existed? How have credit cards and computers affected the amount of money that we hold?

◆ ◆ ◆ ◆ In this chapter, we are going to discover how interest rates are determined by the demand for and supply of money. We are also going to study the Federal Reserve System and learn how the Fed influences the quantity of money and interest rates in an attempt to smooth the business cycle and keep inflation in check.

The Federal Reserve System

The **Federal Reserve System** is the central bank of the United States. A **central bank** is a public authority charged with regulating and controlling a country's monetary and financial institutions and markets. The Fed is also responsible for the nation's monetary policy. *Monetary policy* is the attempt to control inflation and moderate the business cycle by changing the quantity of money in circulation and adjusting interest rates. We are going to study the tools available to the Fed in its conduct of monetary policy and also work out the effects of the Fed's actions on interest rates. But first we'll examine the origins and structure of the Fed.

The Origins of the Federal Reserve System

The Fed was created by the Federal Reserve Act of 1913. Thus, for more than 100 years of our history, we had no central bank. Central banking and a deep hostility to central power—visible in the checks and balances built into our Constitution—just did not seem to mix. As a consequence, we tried to get along without a central bank for the first 137 years of our history. During this period, there was a series of severe national bank panics. In 1907, bank failures and depositors' losses were so severe that the need for a central bank became clear to almost everyone. It was the serious financial turmoil of 1907 that led to the emergence of a consensus on the need for a central bank. That consensus finally found expression in the Federal Reserve Act of 1913.

By the time the Fed was created, most other countries already had a central bank. The first such banks were established in Sweden and England in the seventeenth century. But their origins were very different from that of the Fed. They were set up as private banks designed to solve the financial problems of monarchs. These banks gradually evolved into modern central banks, eventually becoming publicly owned corporations. Central banks, as their name suggests, concentrate the power to control and influence the banking system in a single center. In setting up the Federal Reserve System, care was taken to design a central bank that diffused and decentralized, as far as possible, responsibility for monetary policy. The result was a central bank with a unique structure, unlike all other central banks. Let's examine that structure.

The Structure of the Federal Reserve System

There are three key elements in the structure of the Federal Reserve System:

- Board of Governors
- Regional Federal Reserve banks
- Federal Open Market Committee

Board of Governors The Board of Governors of the Federal Reserve System consists of seven members appointed by the President of the United States and confirmed by the Senate. The board is located in Washington, D.C. Each member is appointed for a 14-year term, and the terms are staggered so that one place on the board becomes vacant every two years. One of the members of the board is named chairman. The length of the term of the chairman is four years.

Regional Federal Reserve Banks There are 12 Federal Reserve banks, one for each of 12 Federal Reserve districts (see Fig. 28.1). Each Federal

FIGURE 28.1
The Federal Reserve System

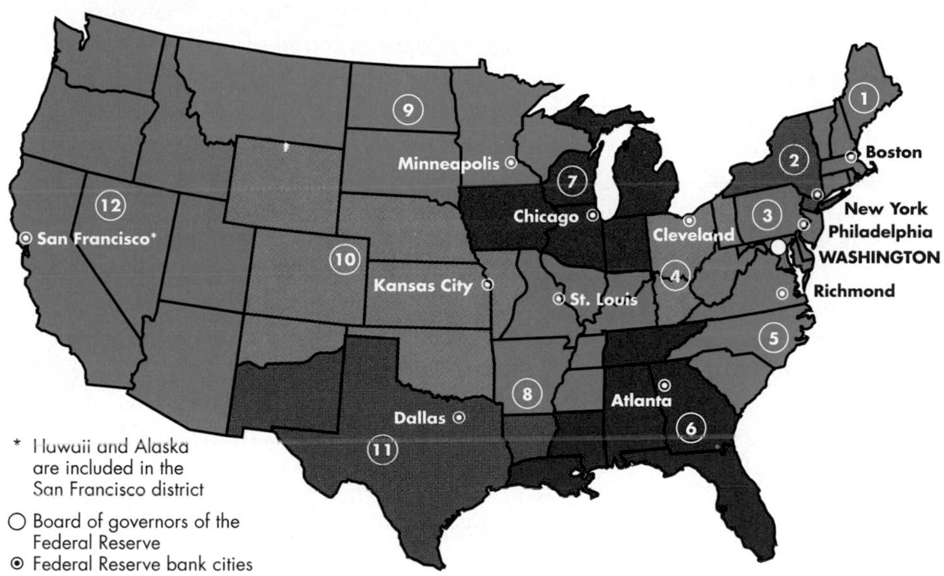

The nation is divided into 12 Federal Reserve districts, each having a Federal Reserve bank. (Some of the larger districts also have branch banks.) The Board of Governors of the Federal Reserve System is located in Washington, D.C.

Source: Federal Reserve Bulletin, published monthly.

Reserve bank has nine directors, three of whom are appointed by the Board of Governors and six of whom are elected by the commercial banks in the Federal Reserve district. The directors of the regional Federal Reserve banks appoint the bank's president and other senior officers.

The Federal Reserve Bank of New York (or the New York Fed as it is often called) occupies a special place in the Federal Reserve System. It is the New York Fed that implements some of the Fed's most important policy decisions.

Federal Open Market Committee The **Federal Open Market Committee** (FOMC) is the main policy-making organ of the Federal Reserve System. The FOMC consists of the following members:

- The chairman of the Board of Governors
- The other six members of the Board of Governors
- The president of the Federal Reserve Bank of New York
- The presidents of four other regional Federal Reserve banks elected to the board on a rotating basis

The FOMC meets once a month to review the state of the economy and to formulate detailed policy actions to be carried out by the New York Fed.

The Fed's Power Center

A description of the formal structure of the Fed gives the impression that power in the Fed resides with the Board of Governors. In practice, it is the chairman of the Board of Governors who has the largest influence on the Fed's monetary policy actions. This position has been held by some remarkable individuals. The current chairman is Alan Greenspan, who was appointed by President Reagan in 1987 and reappointed by President Bush in 1991. His predecessor was Paul Volcker, who was appointed in 1979 by President Carter and reappointed in 1983 by President Reagan.

The chairman's power and influence stem in an important way from his ability to control the agenda at and to dominate the meetings of the FOMC. His influence is yet further enhanced by virtue of his day-to-day contact with and control of a sizable staff of economists and other technical experts who provide the chairman, the Board of Governors, and the FOMC with the detailed background briefings necessary to formulate monetary policy.

The Fed's Policy Tools

The Federal Reserve System has many responsibilities, but we'll examine its single most important one—regulating the amount of money floating around in the United States. How does the Fed control the money supply? It does so by adjusting the reserves of the banking system. It is also by adjusting the reserves of the banking system and by standing ready to make loans to banks that the Fed is able to prevent banking panics and bank failures. The Fed uses three main policy tools to achieve its objectives:

- Required reserve ratios
- Discount rate
- Open market operations

Required Reserve Ratios All depository institutions in the United States are required to hold a minimum percentage of deposits as reserves. This minimum percentage is known as a *required reserve ratio.* The Fed determines a required reserve ratio for each type of deposit, and the ratios in force in 1991 are set out in Table 28.1.

TABLE 28.1

Required Reserve Ratios

Type of deposit	Minimum reserve required (percentage of deposits)
Transactions accounts—$0–42.2 million*	**3**
Transactions accounts—more than $42.2 million	**12**
Nonpersonal time deposits	**0**
Eurodollar deposits	**0**

*Transactions accounts include demand deposits and other checkable deposits.

Source: Federal Reserve Bulletin (January 1992).

By increasing required reserve ratios, the Fed can create a shortage of reserves for the banking system, reducing the amount of bank lending. Reduced lending lowers the money supply by a process similar to that described in Chapter 27. We'll look at this process later in this chapter (see pp. 766–769).

Although changes in required reserve ratios can have an important influence on the money supply, the Fed does not use this policy tool very often. That is, the Fed does not vary required reserve ratios as an active tool for achieving *variations* in the money supply.

Discount Rate The **discount rate** is the interest rate at which the Fed stands ready to lend reserves to commercial banks. The discount rate is proposed by the 12 Federal Reserve banks and determined with the approval of the Board of Governors. By increasing the discount rate, the Fed can make it more costly for banks to borrow reserves, thereby encouraging them to cut back their lending, which reduces the money supply. By lowering the discount rate, the Fed can encourage banks to borrow more reserves, thereby stimulating bank lending, which increases the money supply.

The discount rate can be an effective tool of Federal Reserve policy only if the banking system is short of reserves and needs to borrow some reserves from the Fed. If the banks are not borrowing from the Fed, the level of the discount rate has no immediate impact on the banks' behavior. But the Fed can determine whether or not the banking system has a shortage or a surplus of reserves. It does so by using open market operations.

Open Market Operations An **open market operation** is the purchase or sale of U.S. government securities—U.S. Treasury bills and bonds—by the Federal Reserve System designed to influence the money supply. Decisions to buy or sell government securities are made by the FOMC. They are carried out by the Federal Reserve Bank of New York. When the Fed sells government securities, they are paid for with bank reserves, and tighter monetary and credit conditions are created. With lower reserves, the banks cut their lending, and the money supply decreases. When the Fed buys government securities, the Fed's payment for them puts additional reserves in the hands of the banks and loosens credit conditions. With extra reserves, the banks increase their lending, and the money supply increases.

FIGURE 28.2

The Fed: Structure and Tools

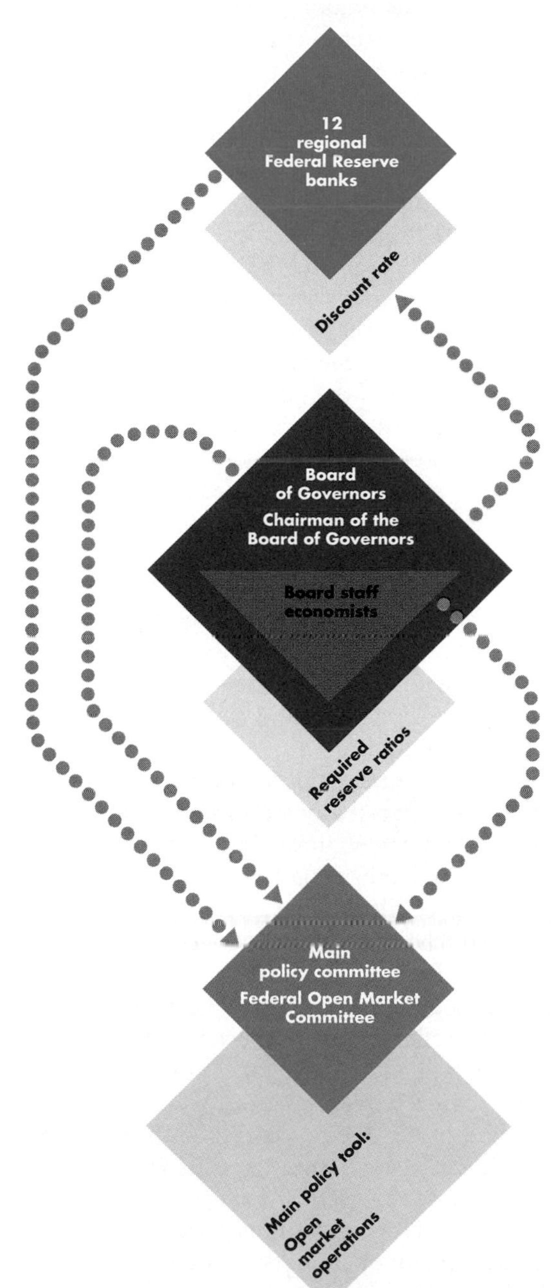

The main organs of the Federal Reserve System are the Board of Governors, the 12 regional Federal Reserve banks, and the Federal Open Market Committee. The Fed's policy tools are required reserve ratios, the discount rate, and open market operations.

The structure and policy tools of the Federal Reserve System are summarized in Fig. 28.2. The most important and powerful of the Fed's policy tools are its open market operations. In order to understand the Fed's open market operations, we first need to examine the structure of the Fed's balance sheet.

The Fed's Balance Sheet

The balance sheet of the Federal Reserve System for December 1991 is set out in Table 28.2. The assets on the left side are what the Fed owns, and the liabilities on the right side are what it owes. Most of the Fed's assets are U.S. government securities. In addition, the Fed holds some gold and foreign exchange—foreign central banks' liabilities. The most important aspect of the Fed's balance sheet is on the liabilities side.

The largest liability of the Fed is Federal Reserve notes in circulation. These are the bank notes that we use in our daily transactions. Some of these bank notes are in circulation with the public, and others are in the tills and vaults of banks and other financial institutions.

You might be wondering why Federal Reserve notes are considered a liability of the Fed. When notes were invented, they gave their owner a claim on the gold reserves of the issuing bank. Such notes were *convertible paper money*. The holder of such a note could convert the note on demand into gold (or some other commodity such as silver) at a guaranteed price. Thus when a bank issued a note, it was holding itself liable to convert that note into a commodity. Modern bank notes are nonconvertible. A **nonconvertible note** is a bank note that is not convertible into any commodity and that obtains its value by government fiat—hence the term fiat money. Such bank notes are considered the legal liability of the bank that issues them, but they are backed not by commodity reserves but by holdings of securities and loans. Federal Reserve notes are backed by the Fed's holdings of U.S. government securities.

The other important liability of the Fed is the deposits held there by banks. We saw these deposits as an asset in the balance sheets of the banks. The remaining liability of the Fed consists of items such as U.S. Treasury deposits (federal government bank accounts at the Fed) and accounts held by foreign central banks (such as the Bank of England and the Bank of Canada).

TABLE 28.2

The Balance Sheet for the Federal Reserve System, December 1991

Assets (billions of dollars)		Liabilities (billions of dollars)	
Gold and foreign exchange	21	**Federal Reserve notes in circulation**	288
U.S. government securities	282	**Banks' deposits**	29
		Monetary base	317
Other assets	50	**Other liabilities**	36
Total	353	**Total**	353

Source: Federal Reserve Bulletin (March 1992).

The two largest items on the liability side of the Fed's balance sheet are Federal Reserve notes in circulation and banks' deposits at the Fed. These two items, together with coins in circulation (coins are issued by the Treasury and are not liabilities of the Fed) are the **monetary base.** The monetary base is so called because it acts like a base that supports the nation's money supply.

By buying or selling government securities, the Fed can directly determine the scale of its own liabilities and change the monetary base. Such purchases and sales of government securities are the Fed's open market operations, its main method of controlling the money supply.

Controlling the Money Supply

The money supply is determined by the actions of the Fed. Let's see how. We begin by looking at what happens when the Fed conducts an open market operation.

How Open Market Operations Work

When the Fed conducts an open market operation in which it buys U.S. government securities, it increases the reserves of the banking system. When it conducts an open market operation in which it sells U.S. government securities, it decreases the reserves of the banking system. Let's study the effects of an open market operation by working out what happens when the Fed buys $100 million of U.S. government securities.

Open market operations affect the balance sheets of the Fed, the banks, and the rest of the economy. Table 28.3 keeps track of the changes in these balance sheets. When the Fed buys securities, there are two possible sellers: the banks or other agents in the economy. Part (a) of the table works out what happens when banks sell the securities that the Fed buys.

When the Fed buys securities from the banks, the Fed pays for the securities by crediting the banks' deposit accounts at the Fed. The changes in the Fed's balance sheet are that its assets increase by $100 million (the additional U.S. government securities bought) and its liabilities also increase by $100 million (the additional bank deposits). The banks' total assets remain constant, but their deposits at the Fed increase by $100 million and their securities decrease by $100 million.

Part (b) of the table deals with the case in which the banks do not sell any securities and the Fed buys securities from agents in the rest of the economy other than the banks. The Fed's holdings of U.S. government securities increase by $100 million, and other agents' holdings of U.S. government securities go down by $100 million. The Fed pays for the securities by giving checks drawn on itself to the sellers. The sellers take the checks to the banks and deposit them. Bank deposits increase by $100 million. The banks in turn present the checks to the Fed, which credits the banks' accounts with the value of the checks. Banks' deposits with the Fed—reserves—increase by $100 million.

Regardless of which of the two cases takes place, by conducting an open market purchase of securities the Fed increases the banks' deposits with itself—increases the banks' reserves.

If the Fed conducts an open market *sale* of securities, the events that we have just traced occur in reverse. The Fed's assets and liabilities will decrease in value, and so will the reserves of the banks.

The effects of an open market operation on the

TABLE 28.3
An Open Market Operation

(a) Banks sell the securities bought by the Fed

Effects on the balance sheet of the Fed (millions of dollars)

Change in assets		Change in liabilities	
U.S. government securities	**+100**	**Banks' deposits (reserves)**	**+100**

Effects on the balance sheet of the banks (millions of dollars)

Change in assets		Change in liabilities	
Banks' deposits (reserves)	**+100**		
U.S. government securities	**–100**		

(b) Agents other than banks sell the securities bought by the Fed

Effects on the balance sheet of the Fed (millions of dollars)

Change in assets		Change in liabilities	
U.S. government securities	**+100**	**Banks' deposits (reserves)**	**+100**

Effects on the balance sheet of the banks (millions of dollars)

Change in assets		Change in liabilities	
Banks' deposits (reserves)	**+100**	**Deposits**	**+100**

Effects on the balance sheet of the other agents (millions of dollars)

Change in assets		Change in liabilities	
Deposits	**+100**		
U.S. government securities	**–100**		

balance sheets of the Fed and the banks that we've traced in Table 28.3 are not the end of the story—they are just the beginning. With an increase in their reserves, the banks are now able to make more loans, and by making loans they create money. We studied this money creation process in Chapter 27, where we learned that the change in the money supply is a multiple of the change in reserves that brings it about. We'll look again at this process. But now that you understand the basic idea, we'll add an element of realism we ignored in Chapter 27: the distinction between the monetary base and bank reserves.

Monetary Base and Bank Reserves

We've defined the *monetary base* as the sum of Federal Reserve notes, coins, and banks' deposits at the Fed. The monetary base is held either by banks as *reserves* or outside the banks as currency in circulation. When the monetary base increases, both bank reserves and currency in circulation increase. Only the increase in bank reserves can be used by banks to make loans and create additional money. An increase in currency held outside the banks is called a **currency drain.** A currency drain reduces the amount of additional money that can be created from a given increase in the monetary base.

The **money multiplier** is the amount by which a change in the monetary base is multiplied to determine the resulting change in the quantity of money. It differs from the simple money multiplier that we studied in Chapter 27. The *simple money multiplier* is the amount by which a change in bank reserves is multiplied to determine the change in the quantity of bank deposits. Since the Fed influences the monetary base (not bank reserves), it is the *money multiplier* that is relevant for determining the effects of the Fed's actions on the money supply.

Let's now look at the money multiplier.

The Multiplier Effect of an Open Market Operation

We'll work out the multiplier effect of an open market operation in which the Fed buys securities from the banks. In this case, although the open market operation increases the banks' reserves, it has no immediate effect on the quantity of money. The banks are holding additional reserves and fewer U.S. government securities. But they have excess reserves. When the banks have excess reserves, the sequence of events shown in Fig. 28.3 takes place. These events are

FIGURE 28.3

A Round in the Multiplier Process Following an Open Market Operation

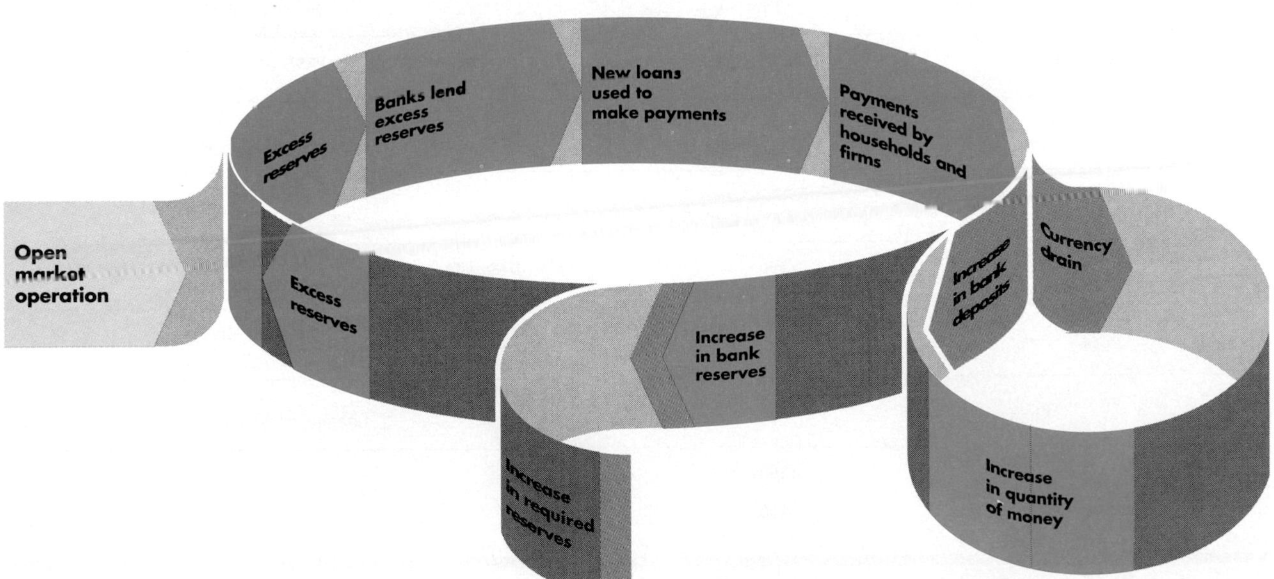

An open market purchase of U.S. government securities increases bank reserves and creates excess reserves. Banks lend the excess reserves, and new loans are used to make payments. Households and firms receiving payments keep some of the receipts in the form of currency—a currency drain—and place the rest on deposit in banks. The increase in bank deposits increases banks' reserves but also increases banks' required reserves. Required reserves increase by less than actual reserves, so the banks still have some excess reserves, though less than before. The process repeats until excess reserves have been eliminated. There are two components to the increase in the quantity of money: the currency drain and the increase in deposits.

- Banks lend excess reserves.
- New loans are used to make payments.
- Households and firms receive payments from new loans.
- Part of the receipts are held as currency—a *currency drain.*
- Part of the receipts are deposited in banks.
- Bank reserves increase (by the same amount as the increase in deposits).
- Required reserves increase (by a fraction—the required reserve ratio—of the increase in deposits).
- Excess reserves decrease but remain positive.
- The quantity of money increases by the amount of the currency drain and the increase in bank deposits.

The sequence just described is similar to the one we studied in Chapter 27 except that there we ignored the currency drain. As before, the sequence repeats in a series of rounds, but each round begins with a smaller quantity of excess reserves than did the previous one. The process continues until excess reserves have finally been eliminated.

Figure 28.4 illustrates the accumulated increase in the quantity of money and in its components, bank

FIGURE **28.4**

The Multiplier Effect of an Open Market Operation

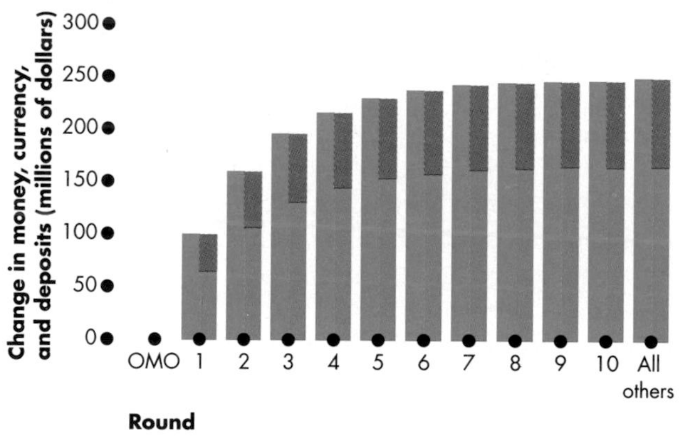

An open market operation (OMO) in which the Fed buys $100 million of government securities from the banks has no immediate effect on the money supply but creates excess reserves in the banking system. When loans are made with these reserves, bank deposits and currency holdings increase. Each time a new loan is made, part of the loan drains out from the banks and is held as currency and part of the loan stays in the banking system in the form of additional deposits and additional reserves. Banks continue to increase their lending until excess reserves have been eliminated. The effects for the first five rounds of lending and money creation are described in the table and the process is illustrated in the figure. The magnitude of the ultimate increase in the money supply is determined by the money multiplier.

Round	Excess reserves at start of round	New loans	Change in deposits	Currency drain	Change in reserves	Change in required reserves	Excess reserves at end of round	Change in quantity of money
	(millions of dollars)							
1	**100.00**	**100.00**	**66.67**	**33.33**	**66.67**	**6.67**	**60.00**	**100.00**
2	**60.00**	**60.00**	**40.00**	**20.00**	**40.00**	**4.00**	**36.00**	**60.00**
3	**36.00**	**36.00**	**24.00**	**12.00**	**24.00**	**2.40**	**21.60**	**36.00**
4	**21.60**	**21.60**	**14.40**	**7.20**	**14.40**	**1.44**	**12.96**	**21.60**
5	**12.96**	**12.96**	**8.64**	**4.32**	**8.64**	**0.86**	**7.78**	**12.96**
	⋮	⋮	⋮	⋮	⋮	⋮	⋮	⋮
All others		**19.44**	**12.96**	**6.48**		**9.63**		**19.44**
Total		**250.00**	**166.67**	**83.33**		**25.00**		**250.00**

deposits and currency, resulting from an open market operation of $100 million. In this figure, the *currency drain* is one third and the *required reserve ratio* is 10 percent. As you can see, when the open market operation takes place (labeled OMO in the figure), there is no initial change in either the quantity of money or its components. Then, after the first round of bank lending, the quantity of money increases by $100 million—the size of the open market operation. In successive rounds, the quantity of money and its components—currency and bank deposits—continue to increase but by successively smaller amounts until, after 10 rounds, the quantities of currency and deposits and their sum, the quantity of money, have almost reached the values to which they are ultimately heading.

The table in Fig. 28.4 keeps track of the magnitudes of new loans, the currency drain, the increases in deposits and reserves, the increase in required reserves, and the change in excess reserves. The initial open market operation increases the banks' reserves, but since deposits do not change, there is no change in required reserves. The banks have excess reserves of $100 million. They lend those reserves. When the money borrowed from the banks is spent, two thirds of it returns as additional deposits and one third drains off as currency. Thus when the banks lend the initial $100 million of excess reserves, $66.67 million comes back to them in the form of deposits and $33.33 million drains off and is held outside the banks as currency. The quantity of money has now increased by $100 million—the increase in deposits plus the increase in currency holdings.

The increased bank deposits of $66.67 million generate an increase in required reserves of 10 percent of that amount, which is $6.67 million. But actual reserves have increased by the same amount as the increase in deposits—$66.67 million. Therefore, the banks now have excess reserves of $60 million. At this stage we have completed round 1. We have gone once around the circle shown in Fig. 28.3. The banks still have excess reserves, but the level has fallen from $100 million at the beginning of the round to $60 million at the end of the round. Round 2 now begins.

The process keeps on repeating. The table in Fig. 28.4 shows the first five rounds and collapses all the remaining ones into the next to last row of the table. At the end of the process, the quantity of money has increased by $250 million.

The U.S. Money Multiplier

The money multiplier is calculated as the ratio of the change in the quantity of money to the change in the monetary base. That is,

$$\text{Money multiplier} = \frac{\text{Change in the quantity of money}}{\text{Change in the monetary base}}.$$

The money multiplier in 1991 (for M1) was 2.9. Its average value between 1960 and 1991 was approximately 2.5. What determines the size of the money multiplier, and what makes it fluctuate?

The size of the money multiplier is determined by two ratios that fluctuate over time. They are

- The ratio of banks' reserves to bank deposits
- The ratio of currency holdings of households and firms to bank deposits

Table 28.4 shows how the money multiplier depends on these two ratios. It also provides numbers that illustrate the M1 money multiplier on the average between 1960 and 1991. Over that period the currency holdings of households and firms were 50 percent (0.5) of the bank deposits that make up M1. Equivalently, currency makes up one third of M1, and deposits make up two thirds. Reserve holdings were approximately 10 percent (0.1) of the deposits in M1. Combining these ratios in the formula derived in the table shows that the M1 money multiplier is 2.5.

Fluctuations in the size of the money multiplier occur because of fluctuations in the two ratios. But it is the currency to deposits ratio that fluctuates most. In determining the effects of its open market operations on the money supply, the Fed must constantly monitor the ratios that determine the money multiplier and adjust the scale of its operations to take into account changes in the size of the multiplier.

Other Policy Tools

The Fed's other policy tools—the required reserve ratio and the discount rate—also affect the quantity of money by changing the excess reserves of the banking system. An increase in the required reserve ratio increases the reserves that the banks must hold at a given level of deposits. With no change in actual reserves, excess reserves fall. An increase in the discount rate also increases the reserves that the banks

TABLE 28.4

Calculating the Money Multiplier

	In general	Numbers
1. The variables		
Reserves	$= R$	
Currency	$= C$	
Monetary base	$= MB$	
Deposits	$= D$	
Quantity of money	$= M$	
Money multiplier	$= mm$	
2. Definitions		
The monetary base is the sum of reserves and currency	$MB = R + C$	
The quantity of money is the sum of deposits and currency	$M = D + C$	
The money multiplier is the ratio of the change in the quantity of money to the change in the monetary base	$mm = \Delta M/\Delta MB$	
3. Ratios		
Change in reserves to change in deposits	$\Delta R/\Delta D$	0.1
Change in currency to change in deposits	$\Delta C/\Delta D$	0.5
4. Calculations		
Begin with the definition	$mm = \Delta M/\Delta MB$	
Use the definitions of *M* and *MB* to give	$mm = \dfrac{\Delta D + \Delta C}{\Delta R + \Delta C}$	
Divide top and bottom by ΔD to give	$mm = \dfrac{1 + \Delta C/\Delta D}{\Delta R/\Delta D + \Delta C/\Delta D}$	$= \dfrac{1 + 0.5}{0.1 + 0.5}$
		$= \dfrac{1.5}{0.6}$
		$= 2.5$

plan to hold. When it costs more to borrow reserves, the banks want to run less risk of being in that position and so plan to hold a larger quantity of reserves to reduce the likelihood of having to borrow from the Fed.

Whatever the source of a change in excess reserves, once it is present, it sets up a chain of events similar to those described earlier, following an open market operation. Thus the Fed's minor policy instruments work in a similar way to its open market operations. By changing excess reserves, they change the amount of bank lending and the quantity of money in circulation.

But required reserve ratios and the discount rate also affect the size of the money multiplier. As we've seen, the required reserve ratio is one of the elements in the money multiplier. The higher the banks' reserve ratio, the smaller is the money multiplier. But because these policy tools are not often used, changes in the money multiplier resulting from these instruments do not often occur.

REVIEW

The Federal Reserve System is the nation's central bank. The Fed influences the quantity of money in circulation by changing the excess reserves of the banking system. It has three instruments at its disposal: changing the required reserve ratio, changing the discount rate, and conducting open market operations. The last of these is the most important and most frequently used. Open market operations not only change the excess reserves of the banking system but also set up a multiplier effect. When excess reserves are lent, some of the loans drain out of the banking system, but others come back in the form of new deposits. The banks continue to lend until the currency drain and the increase in their required reserves have eliminated excess reserves. The multiplier effect of an open market operation depends on the scale of the currency drain and the size of the banks' required reserve ratio. ◆

The Fed's objective in conducting open market operations or taking other actions that influence the quantity of money in circulation is not simply to affect the money supply for its own sake. Its objective is to influence the course of the economy—especially the level of output, employment, and prices. But these effects are indirect. The Fed's immediate objective is to move interest rates up or down. To work out the effects of the Fed's actions on interest rates, we need to work out how and why interest rates change when the quantity of money changes. We'll discover the answer to these questions by studying the demand for money.

The Demand for Money

The amount of money that we *receive* each week in payment for our labor is income—a flow. The amount of money that we hold in our wallet or in a deposit account at the bank is an inventory—a stock. There is no limit to how much income—or flow—we would like to receive each week. But there is a limit to how big an inventory of money each of us would like to hold, on the average.

The Motives for Holding Money

Why do people hold an inventory of money? Why do you carry coins and bills in your wallet, and why do you keep money in a deposit account at your neighborhood bank?

There are three main motives for holding money:

- Transactions motive
- Precautionary motive
- Speculative motive

Transactions Motive The main motive for holding money is to be able to undertake transactions and to minimize the cost of transactions. By carrying an inventory of currency, you are able to undertake small transactions such as buying your lunch at the college cafeteria. If you didn't carry an inventory of currency, you'd have to go to the bank every lunchtime in order to withdraw enough cash. The opportunity cost of these transactions, in terms of your own lost studying or leisure time, would be considerable. You avoid those transactions costs by keeping an inventory of currency large enough to make your normal purchases over a period of perhaps a week in length.

You also keep an inventory of money in the form of deposits at the bank to make transactions such as paying the rent on your apartment or paying your college bookstore bill. Instead of having an inventory of bank deposits for these purposes, you might put all your assets into the stock or bond market—buying IBM stock or U.S. government securities. But if you did that, you would have to call your broker and sell some stocks and bonds each time you needed to pay the rent or the bookstore. Again, you'd have to pay the opportunity cost of such transactions. Instead, those costs can be avoided by holding larger inventories of bank deposits.

Individual holdings of money for transactions purposes fluctuate during any week or month. But aggregate money balances held for transactions purposes do not fluctuate much because what one person is spending, someone else is receiving.

Firms' money holdings are at their peak just before the moment they pay their employees' wages. Households' money holdings are at a peak just after wages have been paid. As households spend their incomes, their money holdings decline and firms' holdings of money increase. Firms' holdings of money are actually quite large, and it is this fact that makes average money holdings appear to be so large. Average money holdings of households are much lower than the economy-wide averages presented in the chapter opener.

Precautionary Motive Money is held as a precaution against unforeseen events that require unplanned purchases to be made. For example, on an out-of-town trip you carry some extra money in case your car breaks down and has to be fixed. Or if you are shopping in the January sales, you take with you more money than you are planning on spending in case you come across a real bargain that you just can't pass up.

Speculative Motive The final motive for holding money is to avoid losses from holding stocks or bonds that are expected to fall in value. Suppose, for example, that a week before the stock market crashes, you predict the crash. On the Friday afternoon before the markets close, you sell all your stocks and put the proceeds into your bank deposit account for the weekend. This temporary holding of money persists until stock prices have fallen. Only then do you reduce your bank deposit and buy stocks again.

The Influences on Money Holding

What determines the quantity of money that households and firms choose to hold? There are three important influences on this quantity:

- Prices
- Real expenditure
- The opportunity cost of holding money

The higher the level of prices, other things being equal, the larger is the quantity of money that people will want to hold. The higher the level of real expenditure, other things being equal, the larger is the quantity of money that people plan to hold. The higher the opportunity cost of holding money, the smaller is the quantity of money that people plan to hold.

These influences on individual decisions about money holding translate into three macroeconomic variables that influence the aggregate quantity of money demanded:

- The price level
- Real GDP
- The interest rate

Price Level and the Quantity of Money Demanded The quantity of money measured in current dollars is called the quantity of **nominal money.** The quantity of nominal money demanded is proportional to the price level. That is, other things being equal, if the price level (GDP deflator) increases by 10 percent, people will want to hold 10 percent more nominal money than before. What matters to people is not the number of dollars that they hold but the buying power of those dollars. Suppose, for example, that to undertake your weekly expenditure on movies and soda, you carry an average of $20 in your wallet. If your income and the prices of movies and soda increased by 10 percent, you would increase your average cash holdings by 10 percent to $22.

The quantity of money measured in constant dollars (for example, in 1987 dollars) is called *real money*. Real money is equal to nominal money divided by the price level. The quantity of real money demanded is independent of the price level. In the above example, you held $20, on the average, at the original price level. When the price level increased by 10 percent, you increased your average cash holding by 10 percent, keeping your *real* cash holding constant. Your $22 at the new price level is the same quantity of *real money* as your $20 at the original price level.

Real GDP and the Quantity of Money Demanded An important determinant of the quantity of money demanded is the level of real income—for the aggregate economy, real GDP. As you know, real GDP and real aggregate expenditure are two sides of the same transaction. The amount of money that households and firms demand depends on the amount that they are spending. The higher the expenditure—the higher the income—the larger is the quantity of money demanded. Again, suppose that you hold an average of $20 to finance your weekly purchases of movies and soda. Now imagine that prices remain constant but that your income increases. As a consequence, you now spend more, and you also keep a larger amount of money on hand to finance your higher volume of expenditure.

The Interest Rate and the Quantity of Money Demanded You already know the fundamental principle that as the opportunity cost of something rises, people try to find substitutes for it. Money is no exception to this principle. The higher the opportunity cost of holding money, other things being equal, the lower is the quantity of real money demanded. But what is the opportunity cost of holding money?

The opportunity cost of holding money is the interest rate. To see why, recall that the opportunity cost of any activity is the value of the best alternative forgone. What is the best alternative to holding money, and what is the value forgone? The best alternative to holding money is holding an interest-earning financial asset such as a savings bond or treasury bill. By holding money instead of such an asset, you forgo the interest that you otherwise would have received. This forgone interest is the opportunity cost of holding money. The higher the interest rate, the higher is the opportunity cost of holding money and the smaller is the amount of money held. At the same time, the quantity of interest-earning assets held increases. Interest-earning assets are substituted for money.

Money loses value because of inflation. Why isn't the inflation rate part of the cost of holding money? It is; other things being equal, the higher the expected inflation rate, the higher are interest rates and the higher, therefore, is the opportunity cost of holding money.

The Demand for Real Money The **demand for real money** is the relationship between the quantity of real money demanded and the interest rate, holding constant all other influences on the amount of money that people wish to hold. To make the demand for real money more concrete, let's consider an example. A household's demand for real money can be represented as a demand schedule for real money. Such a schedule sets out the quantity of real money that a person wants to hold at a given level of real income for different levels of the interest rate.

FIGURE 28.5

The Polonius Household's Demand for Real Money

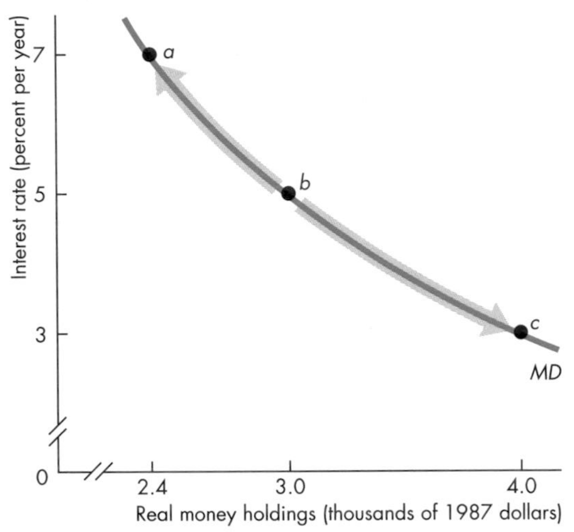

Polonius household's real income is $20,000; price level is 1

	Interest rate (percent per year)	Real money holdings (thousands of 1987 dollars)
a	**7**	**2.4**
b	**5**	**3.0**
c	**3**	**4.0**

The table shows the Polonius household's demand schedule for real money. The lower the interest rate, the larger is the quantity of real money that the household plans to hold. The graph shows the household's demand curve for real money (*MD*). Points *a, b,* and *c* on the curve correspond to the rows in the table. A change in the interest rate leads to a movement along the demand curve. The demand curve for real money slopes downward because the interest rate is the opportunity cost of holding money. The higher the interest rate, the larger is the interest forgone on holding another asset.

Figure 28.5 sets out some numbers for the Polonius household. The household's real income is $20,000 a year. The price level is 1, or the GDP deflator is equal to 100, so the quantity of money is the same whether we measure it in nominal terms or real terms. The table tells us how the quantity of real money demanded by the Polonius household changes as the interest rate changes. For example, in row *a*, when the interest rate is 7 percent a year, the Polonius household holds $2,400 of money, on the average. When the interest rate is 5 percent a year, real money holdings increase to $3,000, and when the interest rate falls to 3 percent a year, real money holdings increase to $4,000.

The figure also graphs the Polonius household's demand curve for real money (*MD*). If the interest rate increases from 5 percent to 7 percent, there is a rise in the opportunity cost of holding money and a decrease in the quantity of real money demanded—illustrated by an upward movement along the demand curve in Fig. 28.5. If the interest rate decreases from 5 percent to 3 percent, there is a fall in the opportunity cost of holding money and an increase in the quantity of real money demanded—illustrated by a downward movement along the demand curve in Fig. 28.5.

Shifts in the Demand Curve for Real Money

The demand curve for real money shifts when:

- Real income changes
- Financial innovation occurs

Changes in Real Income An increase in real income shifts the demand curve for real money to the right, and a decrease shifts it to the left. The effect of real income on the demand curve for real money is shown in Fig. 28.6. The table shows the effects of a change in real income on the quantity of real money demanded when the interest rate is constant at 5 percent. Look first at row *b* of the table. It tells us that when the interest rate is 5 percent and real income is $20,000, the quantity of real money demanded by the Polonius household is $3,000. This row corresponds to point *b* on the demand curve for real money MD_0. If we hold the interest rate constant and real income falls to $12,000, the quantity of real money held falls to $2,400. Thus the demand curve for real money shifts from MD_0 to MD_1 in Fig. 28.6. If the Polonius household's real income increases to $28,000, the quantity of real money held by the household increases to $3,600. In this case, the demand curve shifts to the right from MD_0 to MD_2.

Financial Innovation Financial innovation also results in a change in the demand for real money and a shift in the demand curve for real money. The most important such innovation in recent years has been the development of highly liquid deposits with banks and other financial institutions that makes it possible for people to quickly and easily convert

FIGURE 28.6

Changes in the Polonius Household's Demand for Real Money

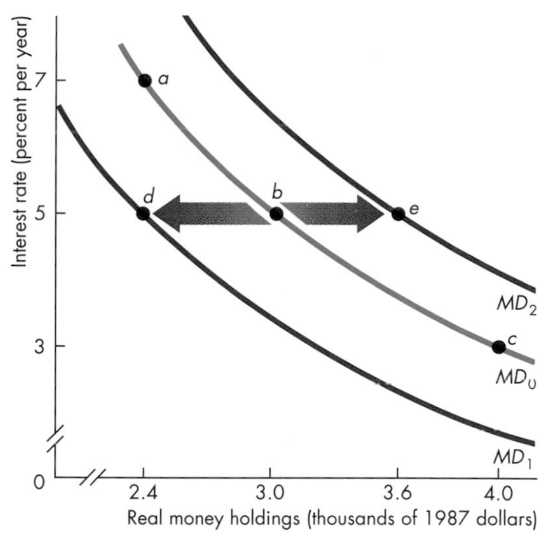

Interest rate is 5 percent; price level is 1

	Real income (thousands of 1987 dollars)	Real money holdings (thousands of 1987 dollars)
d	12	2.4
b	20	3.0
e	28	3.6

A change in real income leads to a change in the demand for real money. The table shows the quantity of real money held by the Polonius household at three different levels of real income when the interest rate is constant at 5 percent. The graph shows the effects of a change in real income on the demand curve for real money. When real income is $20,000 and the interest rate is 5 percent, the household is at point *b* on the demand curve for real money MD_0. When real income falls to $12,000, the demand curve shifts to MD_1, and, at a 5 percent interest rate, the household is at point *d*. When real income rises to $28,000, the demand curve shifts to MD_2. With an interest rate of 5 percent, the household is at point *e*.

such deposits into a medium of exchange—into money. These innovations have been brought about partly as a result of deregulation of the financial sector (see Chapter 27, pp. 742–743) and partly by the availability of low-cost computing power.

Computers are an important part of the story of financial innovation because they have dramatically lowered the cost of keeping records and doing calculations. Interest-bearing checking accounts, for example, have to have balances and interest payments calculated on a daily basis. Doing such calculations by hand, although feasible, would be very costly. Arrangements such as ATS accounts require that funds be transferred to or from a savings account when the balance on a checking account rises above or falls below a certain pre-agreed level. Again, keeping the records that make such bank accounts feasible would have been prohibitively costly in the precomputer age.

Now that banks have access to a vast amount of extremely low-cost computing power, they can offer a wide variety of deposit arrangements that make it convenient to convert non–medium of exchange assets into medium of exchange assets at extremely low cost. The development of these arrangements has led to a decrease in the demand for money—a leftward shift in the demand curve for money.

The availability of low-cost computing power in the financial sector is also responsible, in large degree, for the widespread use of credit cards. Again, keeping the records and calculating the interest and outstanding debt required to operate a credit card system is feasible by hand but too costly to undertake. No one would find it worthwhile to use plastic cards, shuffle sales slips, and keep records if all the calculations had to be done by hand (or even by pre-electronic mechanical calculating machines). This innovation—low-cost computing power—has also lowered the demand for money. By using a credit card to make purchases, people can operate with a much smaller inventory of money. Instead of holding money for transactions purposes through the month, people can charge purchases to a credit card and pay the credit card bill a day or two after payday. As a consequence the average holding of money throughout the month is much smaller.

The financial innovations that we have just considered affect the demand for money. Some financial innovations have changed the composition of our money holdings but not their total amount. One of these is the automatic teller machine. On the average, we can now function efficiently with smaller currency holdings than before, simply because we can easily obtain currency at almost any time or place. Although this innovation has decreased the demand for currency and increased the demand for deposits, it has probably not affected the overall demand for real money.

REVIEW

The quantity of money demanded depends on the price level, real GDP, and the interest rate. The quantity of nominal money demanded is proportional to the price level. Real money is the quantity of nominal money divided by the price level. The quantity of real money demanded increases as real GDP increases. The opportunity cost of holding money is the interest rate. The benefit from holding money is the avoidance of frequent transactions. The higher the interest rate, the smaller is the quantity of real money demanded. ◆◆ The demand curve for real money shows how the quantity of real money demanded varies as the interest rate varies. When the interest rate changes, there is a movement along the demand curve for real money. Other influences on the quantity of real money demanded shift the demand curve for real money. An increase in real income shifts the demand curve to the right; financial innovations that develop convenient near-money deposits shift the demand curve to the left. ◆

Now that we have studied the theory of the demand for real money, let's look at the facts about money holdings in the United States and see how they relate to real income and the interest rate.

The Demand for Money in the United States

We've just seen that the demand curve for real money, which shows how the quantity of real money demanded varies as the interest rate varies, shifts whenever there is a change in real GDP or when there is a financial innovation influencing money holding. Because these factors that shift the demand curve for real money frequently change, it is not easy to "see" the demand curve for real money in a real-world economy.

Instead of examining the demand for money, we'll look at something closely related to it, the *velocity of circulation.* The velocity of circulation is defined as

$$V = PY \div M.$$

Equivalently, it is

$$V = Y \div (M/P),$$

or real GDP divided by the real quantity of money. If the quantity of money demanded equals the quantity supplied, we can study the demand for money by studying the behavior of the velocity of circulation. When the quantity of money demanded falls relative to GDP, the velocity of circulation rises, and when the quantity of money demanded rises relative to GDP, the velocity of circulation falls.

The theory of the demand for money predicts that the higher the interest rate, the lower is the quantity of real money demanded and, therefore, the higher is the velocity of circulation. By examining the velocity of circulation and comparing it with movements in the interest rate, we can check whether the theory of the demand for real money provides a good description of money holding in the United States.

Figure 28.7 shows the relationship between the interest rate and the velocity of circulation of M1 and M2. The interest rate is measured on the left vertical scale of each part of the figure, and the velocity of circulation on the right scale. As you can see, there is a distinct relationship between the interest rate and the velocity of circulation of M1 and M2. The relationship is more pronounced in the case of the velocity of circulation of M2 in part (b). The velocity of circulation of M1 in part (a) is less closely related to the movements in the interest rate than is the velocity of circulation of M2. In fact, the main feature of the velocity of circulation of M1 is its steady increase from 1960 to 1980. Even when interest rates fell, as they did in 1971 and 1972 and again in 1975 and 1976, the velocity of circulation of M1 continued to increase. But the fall in interest rates after 1980 was associated with a decrease in the velocity of circulation of M1 through 1986. And as interest rates fluctuated after 1986, M1 velocity also fluctuated in the same direction.

The fact that the velocities of circulation of M1 and M2 fluctuate in sympathy with fluctuations in interest rates means that the U.S. economy has a demand curve for real money that is similar to that of the Polonius household. As interest rates rise, the economy slides up its demand curve for real money and the quantity of real money demanded decreases, *other things held constant.* But in the real world, other things are not constant. Steadily growing real income has brought an increase in the demand for real money—shifting the demand curve for real money to the right. Financial innovations have slowed that increase.

There is another aspect of the velocities of circulation of M1 and M2 that is interesting and should be noted. It concerns the range of variation in the velocities. The velocity of circulation of M2 is a remarkably stable number. Look at the range of values on the right scale of Fig. 28.7(b). As you can see, the lowest value of the M2 velocity is 1.5, the highest value is 1.7, and the average value is around 1.6. The fact that the M2 velocity varies by only a small amount means that the demand curve for M2 is very steep. Large changes in interest rates bring about only a small change in the quantity of M2 demanded and in its velocity of circulation. In contrast, the variation in the velocity of circulation of M1 is much larger. It ranges from less than 4 to 7. This fact means that the slope of the demand curve for M1 is much less steep than that for M2. An increase in the interest rate produces a much larger decrease in the quantity of M1 demanded and a much larger increase in the velocity of circulation of M1 than it does in the quantity of M2 demanded and the velocity of circulation of M2.

Why does an increase in the interest rate produce a larger decrease in the quantity of M1 demanded than in the quantity of M2 demanded? It is because currency and most of the checkable deposits that make up M1 do not earn interest, while the deposits that are added to M1 to make up M2 do earn interest. There is a tendency for interest rates to vary together. Thus when interest rates in general increase, the interest rate on savings deposits also increases. This increase in interest rates on the deposits in M2 means that people have less incentive to decrease their holdings of such deposits when interest rates in general increase. In contrast, M1, most of which earns no interest, becomes more expensive to hold—its opportunity cost increases—so the quantity of M1 held decreases.

We have now studied the factors that determine the demand for money and discovered that an important determinant of the quantity of real money

FIGURE 28.7

The Interest Rate and the Velocity of Circulation of M1 and M2

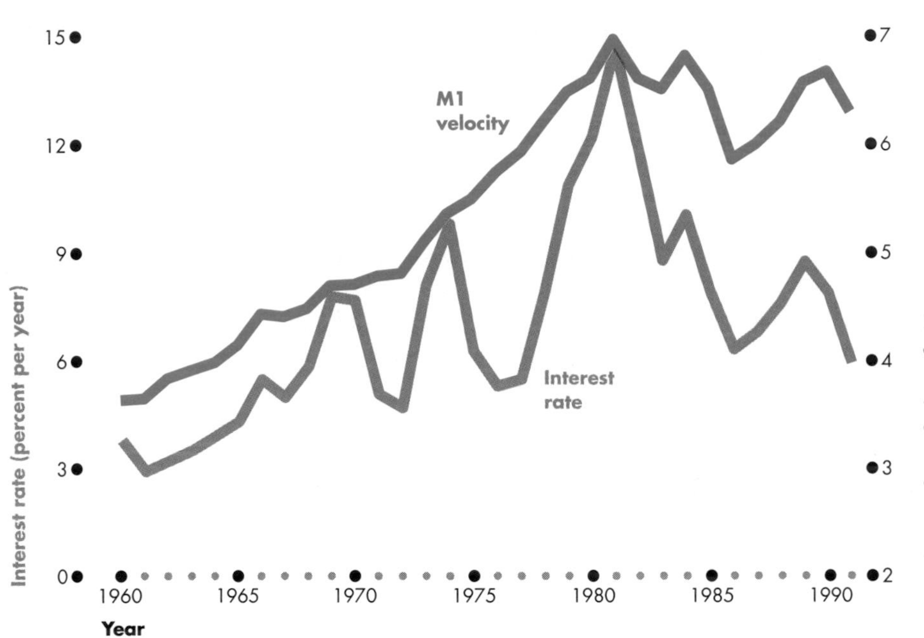

(a) M1 velocity and the interest rate

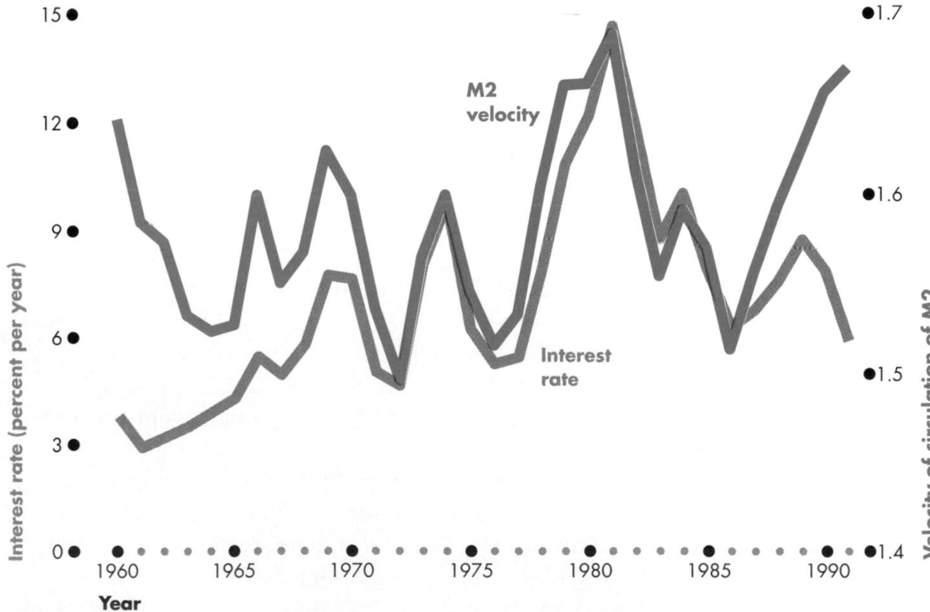

(b) M2 velocity and the interest rate

In part (a), the velocity of circulation of M1 is measured on the right scale and interest rates on the left scale. Both the velocity of circulation of M1 and interest rates increased until 1980 and declined through the 1980s. M1 velocity is much smoother than interest rates and does not have the pronounced cycles visible in interest rates in the 1970s. The two series follow similar trends. In part (b), the velocity of circulation of M2 is measured on the right scale and interest rates on the left scale. These two variables fluctuate remarkably closely together. But the range of variation in the velocity of circulation of M2 is much lower than the range of variation in interest rates (or in the range of variation of the velocity of M1, as seen in part a).

Source: Economic Report of the President, 1992.

demanded is the opportunity cost of holding it—the interest rate. We've also studied the way in which the Fed can influence the quantity of money supplied. We're now going to combine our models of the demand side and the supply side of the money market to see how the interest rate is determined.

TABLE 28.5

The Interest Rate and the Price of a Bond

Formula for interest rate

r = interest rate, c = coupon, p = price of bond

$$r = \frac{c}{p} \times 100$$

Examples

	Price of bond	Coupon	Interest rate (percent per year)
a	$ 50	$10	20
b	100	10	10
c	200	10	5

Interest Rate Determination

An interest rate is the percentage yield on a financial security such as a *bond* or a *stock*. There is an important relationship between the interest rate and the price of a financial asset. Let's spend a moment studying that relationship before analyzing the forces that determine interest rates.

Interest Rates and Asset Prices

A bond is a promise to make a sequence of future payments. There are many different possible sequences, but the simplest one, for our purposes, is the case of a bond called a perpetuity. A **perpetuity** is a bond that promises to pay a certain fixed amount of money each year forever. The issuer of such a bond will never buy the bond back (redeem it); the bond will remain outstanding forever and will earn a fixed dollar payment each year. The fixed dollar payment is called the *coupon*. Since the coupon is a fixed dollar amount, the interest rate on the bond varies as the price of the bond varies. Table 28.5 illustrates this fact.

First, the table shows the formula for calculating the interest rate on a bond. The interest rate (r) is the coupon (c) divided by the price of the bond (p), all multiplied by 100 to convert it into a percentage. The table goes on to show some numerical examples for a bond whose coupon is $10 a year. If the bond costs $100 (row *b* of Table 28.5), the interest rate is 10 percent per year. That is, the holder of $100 worth of bonds receives $10 a year.

Rows *a* and *c* of Table 28.5 show two other cases. In row *a*, the price of the bond is $50. With the coupon at $10, this price produces an interest rate of 20 percent—$10 returned on a $50 bond holding is an interest rate of 20 percent. In row *c*, the bond costs $200 and the interest rate is 5 percent—which gives $10 return on a $200 bond holding.

There is an inverse relationship between the price of a bond and the interest rate earned on the bond. As a bond price rises, the bond's interest rate declines. Understanding this relationship will make it easier for you to understand the process whereby the interest rate is determined. Let's now turn to studying how interest rates are determined.

Money Market Equilibrium

The interest rate is determined at each point in time by equilibrium in the markets for financial assets. We can study that equilibrium in the market for money. We've already studied the determination of the supply of money and the demand for money. We've seen that money is a stock. When the stock of money supplied equals the stock of money demanded, the money market is in equilibrium. *Stock equilibrium* in the money market contrasts with *flow equilibrium* in the markets for goods and services. A **stock equilibrium** is a situation in which the available stock of an asset is willingly held. That is, regardless of what the available stock is, conditions are such that people actually want to hold precisely that stock and neither more nor less. A **flow equilibrium** is a situation in which the quantity of goods or services supplied per unit of time equals the quantity demanded per unit of time. The equilibrium expenditure that we studied in Chapter 26 is an example of a flow equilibrium. So is the equality of aggregate real GDP demanded and supplied.

The quantity of nominal money supplied is determined by the policy decisions of the Fed and by the lending actions of banks and other financial intermediaries. The real quantity of money supplied is equal to the nominal quantity supplied divided by the price level. At a given moment in time, there is a particular price level, and so the quantity of real money supplied is a fixed amount.

The demand curve for real money depends on the level of real GDP. And on any given day, the level of real GDP may be treated as fixed. But the interest rate is not fixed. The interest rate adjusts to achieve stock equilibrium in the money market. If the interest rate is too high, people will try to hold less money than is available. If the interest rate is too low, people will try to hold more than the stock that is available. When the interest rate is such that people want to hold exactly the amount of money that is available, then a stock equilibrium prevails.

Figure 28.8 illustrates an equilibrium in the money market. The quantity of real money supplied is \$3 trillion. This amount is independent of the interest rate, so the money supply curve (*MS*) is vertical. The table sets out the quantity of real money demanded at three different interest rates when real GDP and the price level are constant. These quantities are graphed as the demand curve for real money (*MD*) in the figure.

The equilibrium interest rate is 5 percent, the rate at which the quantity demanded equals the quantity supplied. If the interest rate is above 5 percent, people will want to hold less money than is available. At an interest rate below 5 percent, people will want to hold more money than is available. At a 5 percent interest rate, the amount of money available is willingly held.

How does money market equilibrium come about? To answer this question, let's perform a thought experiment. First, imagine that the interest rate is temporarily at 7 percent. In this situation, people will want to hold only \$2 trillion in real money even though \$3 trillion exists. But since \$3

FIGURE 28.8

Money Market Equilibrium

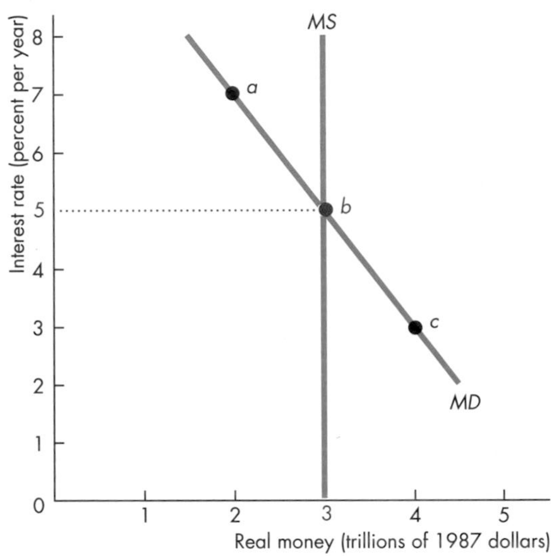

Real GDP is \$4 trillion; price level is 1

	Interest rate (percent per year)	Quantity of real money demanded (trillions of 1987 dollars)	Quantity of real money supplied (trillions of 1987 dollars)
a	**7**	**2**	**3**
b	**5**	**3**	**3**
c	**3**	**4**	**3**

The demand for real money is given by the schedule in the table and the curve *MD*. The supply of real money, shown in the table and by the curve *MS* is \$3 trillion. Adjustments in the interest rate achieve money market equilibrium. Here, equilibrium occurs in row *b* of the table (point *b* in the figure) at an interest rate of 5 percent. At interest rates above 5 percent, the quantity of real money demanded is less than the quantity supplied, so the interest rate falls. At interest rates below 5 percent, the quantity of real money demanded exceeds the quantity supplied, so the interest rate rises. Only at 5 percent is the quantity of real money in existence willingly held.

trillion exists, people must be holding it. That is, people are holding more money than they want to. In such a situation, they will try to get rid of some of their money. Each individual will try to reorganize his or her affairs in order to lower the amount of money held and take advantage of the 7 percent interest rate by buying more financial assets. But everybody will be trying to buy financial assets, and nobody will be trying to sell them at a 7 percent interest rate. There is an excess demand for financial assets such as bonds. When there is an excess demand for anything, its price rises. So with an excess demand for financial assets, the prices of financial assets will rise. We saw earlier that there is an inverse relationship between the price of a financial asset and its interest rate. As the price of a financial asset rises, its interest rate falls.

As long as anyone is holding money in excess of the quantity demanded, that person will try to lower his or her money holdings by buying additional financial assets. Financial asset prices will continue to rise, and interest rates will continue to fall. Only when the interest rate has moved down to 5 percent will the amount of money in existence be held willingly. That is, people's attempts to get rid of unwanted excess money do not result in reducing the amount of money held in aggregate. Instead, those efforts result in a change in the interest rate that makes the amount of money available willingly held.

The thought experiment that we have just conducted can be performed in reverse by supposing that the interest rate is 3 percent. In this situation, people want to hold $4 trillion even though only $3 trillion is available. To acquire more money, people will sell financial assets. There will be an excess supply of financial assets, so their prices will fall. As the prices of financial assets fall, the yield on them—the interest rate—rises. People will continue to sell financial assets and try to acquire money until the interest rate has risen to 5 percent, at which point the amount of money available is the amount that they want to hold.

Changing the Interest Rate

Imagine that the economy is slowing down and the Fed wants to encourage additional aggregate demand and spending. To do so, it wants to lower interest rates and encourage more borrowing and more expenditure on goods and services. What does the Fed do? How does it fiddle with the knobs to achieve lower interest rates?

The Fed undertakes an open market operation, buying government securities from banks, households, and firms. As a consequence, the monetary base increases, and banks start making additional loans. The money supply increases.

Suppose that the Fed undertakes open market operations on a sufficiently large scale to increase the money supply from $3 trillion to $4 trillion. As a consequence, the supply curve of real money shifts to the right, as shown in Fig. 28.9(a), from MS_0 to MS_1, and the thought experiment that we conducted earlier now becomes a real-world event. The interest rate falls as people use some of their new money to buy financial assets. When the interest rate has fallen to 3 percent, people are willing to hold the higher $4 trillion stock of real money that the Fed and the banking system have created.

Conversely, suppose that the economy is overheating and the Fed fears inflation. The Fed decides to take action to slow down spending and cuts the money supply. In this case, the Fed undertakes an open market sale of securities. As it does so, it mops up bank reserves and induces the banks to cut down the scale of their lending. The banks make a smaller quantity of new loans each day until the stock of loans outstanding has fallen to a level consistent with the new lower level of reserves. Suppose that the Fed undertakes an open market sale of securities on a scale big enough to cut the real money supply to $2 trillion. Now the supply of real money curve shifts to the left, as shown in Fig. 28.9(b), from MS_0 to MS_2. With less money available, people attempt to acquire additional money by selling interest-earning assets. As they do so, asset prices fall and interest rates rise. Equilibrium occurs when the interest rate has risen to 7 percent, at which point the new lower real money stock of $2 trillion is willingly held.

The Fed in Action

All this sounds nice in theory, but does it really happen? Indeed, it does happen, sometimes with dramatic effect. Let's look at two episodes in the life of the Fed, one from the turbulent years of the early 1980s and the other from the period since the stock market crash of 1987.

FIGURE 28.9

The Fed Changes Interest Rates

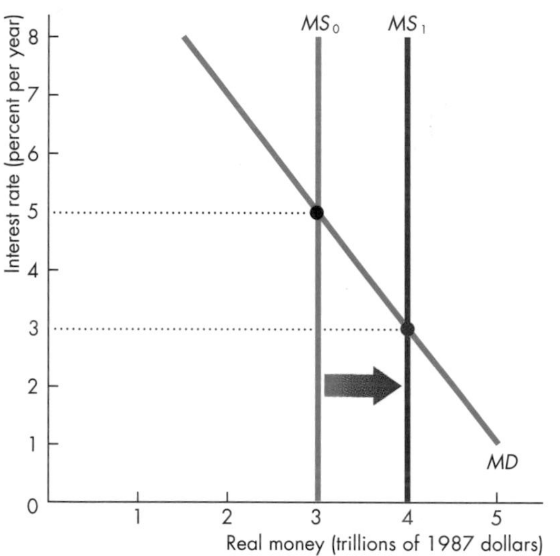

(a) An increase in the money supply

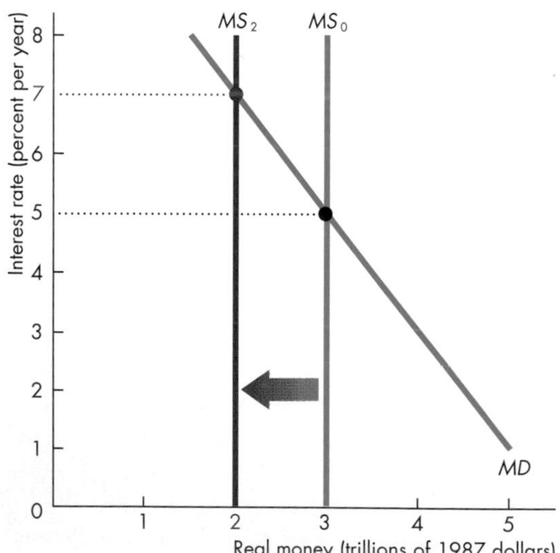

(b) A decrease in the money supply

In part (a), the Fed conducts an open market purchase of securities, increasing the money supply to $4 trillion. The real money supply shifts to the right. The new equilibrium interest rate is 3 percent. In part (b), the Fed conducts an open market sale of securities, decreasing the real money supply to $2 trillion. The money supply curve shifts to the left, and the interest rate rises to 7 percent. By changing the money supply, at a given real GDP and price level, the Fed can adjust interest rates daily or weekly.

Paul Volcker's Fed At the start of Paul Volcker's term of office as chairman of the Fed, which began in August 1979, the United States was locked in the grip of double-digit inflation. Volcker ended that inflation. He did so by forcing interest rates sharply upward from 1979 through 1981. This increase in interest rates resulted from the Fed using open market operations and increases in the discount rate to keep the banks short of reserves, which in turn held back the growth in the supply of loans and of money relative to the growth in their demand.

As we saw in Fig. 28.9(b), to increase interest rates, the Fed has to cut the real money supply. In practice, because the economy is growing and because prices are rising, a *slowdown* in nominal money supply growth is enough to increase interest rates. It is not necessary to actually *cut* the nominal money supply.

When Volcker became chairman of the Fed, the money supply was growing at more than 8 percent a year. Volcker slowed down that money supply growth to 6.5 percent in 1981. As a result, interest rates increased. The treasury bill rate—the rate at which the government borrows—increased from 10 percent to 14 percent. The rate at which big corporations borrow increased from 9 percent to 14 percent. Mortgage rates—the rates at which home buyers borrow—increased from 11 percent to 15 percent. The economy went into recession. The money supply growth slowdown and interest rate hike cut back the growth rate of aggregate demand. Real GDP fell, and the inflation rate slowed down.

Alan Greenspan's Fed Alan Greenspan became chairman of the Fed in August 1987. In the two preceding years the money supply had grown at a rapid pace, interest rates had tumbled, and the stock market had boomed. Then, suddenly and with no warning, stock prices fell, bringing fears of economic calamity and recession. This was Greenspan's first test as Fed chairman.

The Fed's immediate reaction to the new situation was to emphasize the flexibility and sensitivity of the financial system and to make reserves plentiful to avoid any fear of a banking crisis. But as the months passed, it became increasingly clear that the economy was not heading for any kind of a recession. Unemployment continued to fall, income growth continued to be strong, and the fears that emerged were of inflation, not recession.

Seeking to avoid a serious upturn in inflation, the Fed slowed money growth and, just as Paul Volcker had done eight years earlier, forced interest rates sharply upward. Open market operations were targeted toward creating a shortage of reserves in the banking system to slow down the growth rate of the money supply. As a consequence, during the year from May 1988 to May 1989 the M1 measure of the money supply was virtually constant and the M2 measure grew by only 2.4 percent, both down from growth rates of around 5 percent a year earlier and down from around 10 percent a year before the stock market crash. The slowdown in money supply growth had the effect implied by the model that you have been studying in this chapter. Interest rates increased throughout 1988. The interest rate on U.S. government three-month treasury bills increased from less than 6 percent a year at the start of 1988 to almost 9 percent a year by early 1989.

As 1989 advanced, concern about inflation remained, but renewed fears of recession returned as an increasing number of signs of a slowing economy emerged. Interest rates were gradually lowered, and the money supply was permitted to grow more quickly. By 1990, recession had become a reality. At first, the Fed's reaction was to adopt a neutral position, waiting for signs of recovery from an increase in investment and consumption expenditure. But as the months passed and recovery seemed elusive, the Fed eventually began to act vigorously to stimulate spending with a series of interest rate cuts. During 1991, interest rates declined by 3 percentage points as the Fed tried to encourage an increase in borrowing and spending. This episode is further explored in Reading Between the Lines on pp. 782–783.

Profiting by Predicting the Fed

Every day, the Fed influences interest rates by its open market operations. By buying securities and increasing the money supply, the Fed can lower interest rates; by selling securities and lowering the money supply, the Fed can increase interest rates. Sometimes such actions are taken to offset other influences and keep interest rates steady. At other times the Fed moves interest rates up or down. The higher the interest rate, the lower is the price of a bond; the lower the interest rate, the higher is the price of a bond. Thus predicting interest rates is the same as predicting bond prices. Predicting that interest rates are going to fall is the same as predicting that bond prices are going to rise—a good time to buy bonds. Predicting that interest rates are going to rise is the same as predicting that bond prices are going to fall—a good time to sell bonds.

Because the Fed is the major player whose actions influence interest rates and bond prices, predicting the Fed is profitable and a good deal of effort goes into that activity. But people who anticipate that the Fed is about to increase the money supply buy bonds right away, pushing their prices upward and pushing interest rates downward *before* the Fed acts. Similarly, people who anticipate that the Fed is about to decrease the money supply sell bonds right away, pushing their prices downward and pushing interest rates upward before the Fed acts. In other words, bond prices and interest rates change as soon as the Fed's actions are foreseen. By the time the Fed actually takes its actions, if those actions are correctly foreseen, they have no effect. The effects occur in anticipation of the Fed's actions. Only changes in the money supply that are not foreseen change the interest rate at the time that those changes occur.

REVIEW

At any given moment, the interest rate is determined by the demand for and the supply of money. The interest rate makes the quantity of money demanded equal to the quantity of money supplied. Changes in the interest rate occur as a result of changes in the money supply. When the money supply change is unanticipated, interest rates change at the same time as the change in the money supply. When the money supply change is anticipated, interest rates might change ahead of the change in the money supply. ◆

◆ ◆ ◆ ◆ In this chapter, we've studied the determination of interest rates and discovered how the Fed can "fiddle with the knobs" to influence interest rates by its open market operations that change the quantity of money. In Chapter 25 and 26 we discovered that the interest rate has an important influence on investment, aggregate expenditure, and real GDP. In the next chapter, we're going to bring these two aspects of the macroeconomy together and study the wider effects of the Fed's actions—effects on investment and aggregate demand.

The Fed in Action

The New York Times, August 7, 1991

Federal Reserve Moves to Reduce Short-Term Rates

BY MICHAEL QUINT

The Federal Reserve pushed short-term interest rates down a notch yesterday, a move that analysts said was needed to stimulate the economy, which is making only a sluggish recovery from recession.

By continuing to reduce interest rates—a process the Federal Reserve started in mid-1989, when the economy began sliding into recession—officials of the nation's central bank hope to encourage consumers and businesses to spend and borrow more money.

With inflation widely expected to remain below 4 percent, analysts said the Federal Reserve's primary concern now was to make sure that the economy grows more rapidly in coming months. By lowering the Federal funds rate, a closely watched rate for overnight bank loans, the Federal Reserve set the stage for declines in other interest rates including home mortgages, other consumer loans, and yields on certificates of deposit.

'An Insurance Policy'

"This was an insurance policy taken by the Fed to help prevent the economy from sliding back into recession," said Irwin Kellner, chief economist at the Manufacturers Hanover Trust Company. Many economists said the pressure to cut short-term interest rates was increased by last Friday's announcement of a decline of 51,000 workers on payrolls of large companies during July.

The move suggested that some of the optimism expressed by Alan Greenspan, the Federal Reserve's chairman, in mid-July, that a "solid economic recovery" appeared to be on the horizon, had faded. . . .

"The inflation picture looks awfully good, and that gives the Fed more confidence that it can ease," said Donald Fine, chief market strategist for Chase Securities Inc., an affiliate on the Chase Manhattan Bank. . . .

The Essence of the Story

The Federal Reserve embarked on a process of lowering short-term interest rates in mid-1989, as the economy was sliding into recession.

The Fed pushed rates down another notch on August 6, 1992, when the economy was recovering from recession but only sluggishly.

The hope was that lower interest rates would encourage borrowing and spending by consumers and businesses and stimulate a stronger recovery.

Background and Analysis

Throughout the first half of 1991, the Fed had cautiously increased the money supply and pushed interest rates gently downward. The move in the news story was part of this pattern.

In December 1990, the real money supply (real M1) was $721 billion. This money supply is shown in Fig. 1 as MS_0. The demand for money was *MD*, and the interest rate (the average three-month rate) was 7.5 percent, as shown in Fig. 1.

By August 1991 (the time of the news story), real M1 had increased to $741 billion ($MS_1$ in Fig. 1) and the average three-month interest rate had fallen to 6 percent. (These interest rates are higher than the federal funds rate that the news item focuses on.)

The Fed was cautious in the degree to which it wanted to see interest rates decline because it was not sure how strong the recovery would be in the second half of 1991 and the first half of 1992.

The economy was in recession in 1991, as shown in Fig. 2. The aggregate demand curve was AD_{91}, and the short-run aggregate supply curve was SAS_{91}. Real GDP, at $4.85 trillion, was substantially below its long-run level.

By cutting interest rates, the Fed can increase aggregate demand. But if an increase in aggregate demand—with the *AD* curve shifting to AD_a—was going to occur because of an increase in consumer and business confidence, then full employment would be restored without help from the Fed.

Furthermore, if the Fed did take actions to stimulate aggregate demand in such circumstances, the aggregate demand curve might shift to AD_b, taking the economy beyond full employment and bringing renewed inflation.

By the late summer of 1991, it looked increasingly necessary for the Fed to take action to stimulate aggregate demand and encourage the recovery.

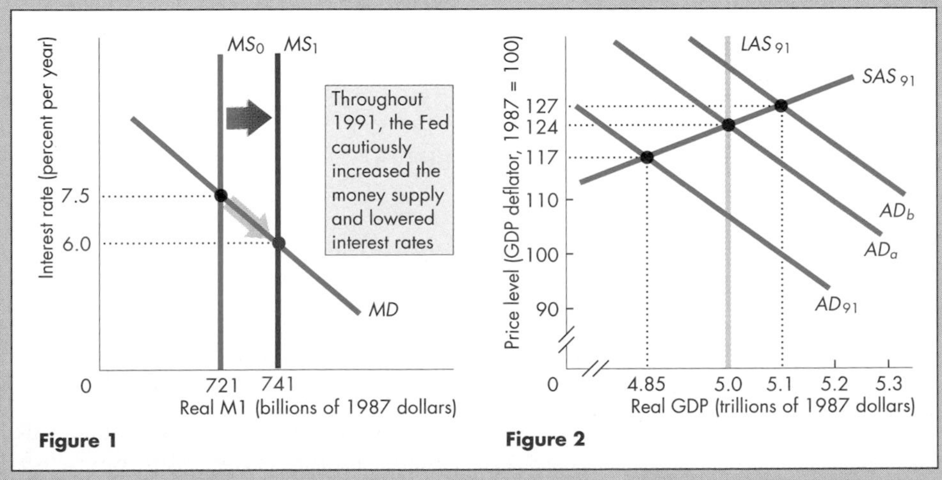

Figure 1

Figure 2

SUMMARY

The Federal Reserve System

The Federal Reserve System is the central bank of the United States. The Fed consists of the Board of Governors and 12 regional Federal Reserve banks. The main policy-making committee is the Federal Open Market Committee. The Fed influences the economy by setting the required reserve ratio for banks and other deposit-taking institutions, by setting the discount rate—the interest rate at which it is willing to lend reserves to the banking system—and by open market operations. (pp. 760–764)

Controlling the Money Supply

By buying government securities in the market (an open market purchase), the Fed is able to increase the monetary base and the reserves available to banks. As a result, there is an expansion of bank lending and the quantity of money increases. By selling government securities, the Fed is able to decrease the monetary base and the reserves of banks and other financial institutions, thereby curtailing loans and decreasing the quantity of money. The overall effect of a change in the monetary base on the money supply is determined by the money multiplier. The value of the money multiplier depends on the ratio of currency to deposits held by households and firms and the ratio of reserves to deposits held by banks and other financial institutions. (pp. 764–770)

The Demand for Money

The quantity of money demanded is the amount of currency, checkable deposits, and other deposits that people hold on the average. The quantity of nominal money demanded is proportional to the price level, and the quantity of real money demanded depends on the interest rate and real GDP. A higher interest rate induces a smaller quantity of real money demanded—a movement along the demand curve for real money. A higher level of real GDP induces a larger demand for real money—a shift in the demand curve for real money. Technological changes in the financial sector also change the demand for money and shift the demand curve for real money. (pp. 770–777)

Interest Rate Determination

Changes in interest rates achieve equilibrium in the markets for money and financial assets. There is an inverse relationship between the interest rate and the price of a financial asset. The higher the interest rate, the lower is the price of a financial asset. Money market equilibrium achieves an interest rate that makes the quantity of real money available willingly held. If the quantity of real money is increased by the actions of the Fed, the interest rate falls and the prices of financial assets rise. (pp. 777–781)

KEY ELEMENTS

Key Terms

Central bank, 760
Currency drain, 766
Demand for real money, 772
Discount rate, 762
Federal Open Market Committee, 761
Federal Reserve System, 760
Flow equilibrium, 778
Monetary base, 764
Money multiplier, 766
Nominal money, 771
Nonconvertible note, 763
Open market operation, 762
Perpetuity, 777
Stock equilibrium, 777

Key Figures and Tables

REVIEW QUESTIONS

1 What are the three main elements in the structure of the Federal Reserve System?

2 What are the three policy tools of the Fed? Which of these is the Fed's main tool?

3 If the Fed wants to cut the quantity of money, does it buy or sell U.S. government securities in the open market?

4 Describe the events that take place when banks have excess reserves.

5 Explain the motives for holding money.

6 What is the money multiplier?

7 What determines the size of the money multiplier, and why has its value changed in the United States in recent years?

8 Distinguish between nominal money and real money.

9 What do we mean by the demand for money?

10 What determines the demand for real money?

11 What is the opportunity cost of holding money?

12 What happens to the interest rate on a bond if the price of the bond increases?

13 How does equilibrium come about in the money market?

14 What happens to the interest rate if real GDP and price level are constant and the money supply increases?

15 Explain why it pays people to try to predict the Fed's actions.

PROBLEMS

1 You are given the following information about the economy of Nocoin: The banks have deposits of $300 billion. Their reserves are $15 billion, two thirds of which is in deposits with the central bank. There is $30 billion in currency outside the banks. There are no coins in Nocoin!

- **a** Calculate the monetary base.
- **b** Calculate the currency drain.
- **c** Calculate the money supply.
- **d** Calculate the money multiplier.

2 Suppose that the Bank of Nocoin, the central bank, undertakes a $0.5 million open market purchase of securities. What happens to the money supply? Explain why the change in the money supply is not equal to the change in the monetary base.

3 You are given the following information about the economy of Miniland: For each $1 increase in real GDP, the demand for real money increases by one quarter of a dollar, other things being equal. Also, if the interest rate increases by 1 percentage point (for example, from 4 percent to 5 percent), the quantity of real money demanded falls by $50. If real GDP is $4,000 and the price level is 1:

- **a** At what interest rate is no money held?
- **b** How much real money is held at an interest rate of 10 percent?
- **c** Draw a graph of the demand for real money.

4 Given the demand for real money in Miniland, if the price level is 1, real GDP is $4,000, and the real money supply is $750, what is the equilibrium in the money market?

5 Suppose that the Bank of Miniland, the central bank, wants to lower the interest rate by 1 percentage point. By how much would it have to change the real money supply to achieve that objective?

CHAPTER 29

FISCAL AND MONETARY INFLUENCES ON AGGREGATE DEMAND

After studying this chapter, you will be able to:

- Explain how fiscal policy—a change in government purchases or taxes—influences interest rates and aggregate demand
- Explain how monetary policy—a change in the money supply—influences interest rates and aggregate demand
- Explain what determines the relative effectiveness of fiscal and monetary policy on aggregate demand
- Describe the Keynesian-monetarist controversy about the influence of fiscal and monetary policy on aggregate demand
- Explain how the mix of fiscal and monetary policy influences the composition of aggregate expenditure
- Explain how fiscal and monetary policy influence real GDP and the price level in both the short run and the long run

Congress, the Fed, and the White House

EACH YEAR, CONGRESS AND THE STATE LEGISLATURES approve budgets that determine the level of government purchases of goods and services, the transfer payments associated with social programs, and the taxes that pay for this spending. By 1991, these spending and tax levels were close to $2 trillion—almost two fifths of GDP. Government purchases, transfer payments, and taxes are the levers of fiscal policy. How do these levers influence the economy? In particular, how do they affect aggregate demand? How do they affect other variables that influence aggregate demand, such as interest rates and the exchange rate? ◆◆ Five city blocks from the White House is the home of the Board of Governors of the Federal Reserve System. Here the Fed pulls the nation's monetary policy levers. Sometimes, such as in 1989, the Fed uses those levers to slow down the economy—slowing money growth, increasing interest rates, and slowing the growth of aggregate demand. At other times, such as in 1991, the Fed uses its monetary policy levers to speed up the economy—speeding up money growth, lowering interest rates, and increasing aggregate demand. We've seen how the Fed's policy levers influence interest rates. But how do the effects of the Fed's actions ripple through from interest rates to the rest of the economy? How do they affect aggregate demand? ◆◆ In the Executive Office Building—part of the White House complex—is the home of the President's Council of Economic Advisors. This council, established by the Employment Act of 1946, monitors both the fiscal policy actions of the Congress and the monetary policy actions of the Fed. It also attempts to keep the president and Cabinet informed about the actions and plans of each branch of macroeconomic policy making and of their likely effects. Both fiscal actions taken by the Congress and monetary actions taken by the Fed can increase or decrease aggregate demand. Are these methods of changing aggregate demand equivalent to each other? Does it matter whether a recession is avoided by having the Fed loosen up its monetary policy or by getting Congress to implement a tax cut? Do changes in taxes and government purchases and changes in the money supply always reinforce each other, or do they sometimes offset each other? For example, when the Fed under Alan Greenspan slowed down money growth and increased interest rates in 1989 to keep the lid on inflation in 1990, could Congress have offset the Fed's actions by taking actions of its own—for example, cutting taxes or increasing government purchases? Or, alternatively, if Congress cuts government purchases, creating fears of recession, could the Fed increase the money supply and keep GDP up, thereby avoiding recession?

◆ ◆ ◆ ◆ We are going to answer these important questions in this chapter. You already know that the effects of fiscal and monetary policy are determined by the interaction of aggregate demand and aggregate supply. And you already know quite a lot about these two concepts. But this chapter gives you an even deeper understanding of aggregate demand and the way it is affected by the monetary policy actions of the Fed and the fiscal policy actions of the federal government.

Money, Interest, and Aggregate Demand

Our goal is to understand how fiscal and monetary policy influence real GDP and the price level (as well as unemployment and inflation). Real GDP and the price level are determined by the interaction of aggregate demand and aggregate supply, as described in Chapter 24. But the main effects of fiscal and monetary policy are on aggregate *demand*. Thus we focus our attention initially on these effects.

To study the effects of fiscal and monetary policy on aggregate demand, we use the aggregate expenditure model of Chapters 25 and 26. This model determines equilibrium expenditure *at a given price level*. Such an equilibrium corresponds to a point on the aggregate demand curve (see Fig. 26.8). When equilibrium expenditure changes, the aggregate demand curve shifts and by the amount of the change in equilibrium expenditure.

The aggregate expenditure model freezes the price level and asks questions about the directions and magnitudes of the shifts of the aggregate demand curve at a given price level. But the price level is not actually fixed. It is determined by aggregate demand and aggregate supply.

We begin our study of fiscal and monetary policy by discovering an important interaction among aggregate expenditure decisions, the interest rate, and the supply of money.

Spending Decisions, Interest, and Money

We discovered in Chapter 25 (pp. 692–695) that equilibrium expenditure depends on the level of autonomous expenditure. We also discovered that one of the components of autonomous expenditure—investment—varies with the interest rate. The higher the interest rate, other things held constant, the lower is investment and hence the lower is autonomous expenditure and the lower is equilibrium expenditure. Therefore equilibrium expenditure and real GDP depend on the interest rate.

In Chapter 28 (pp. 777–779), we saw how the interest rate is determined by equilibrium in the money market. We also saw that the demand for money depends on both real GDP and the interest rate. The higher the level of real GDP, other things held constant, the greater is the demand for money and the higher is the interest rate. Therefore the interest rate depends on real GDP.

We're now going to see how *both* real GDP and the interest rate are determined simultaneously. We'll then go on to see how the Fed's monetary policy and the government's fiscal policy affect both real GDP and the interest rate at a given price level.

Equilibrium Expenditure and the Interest Rate

Let's see how we can link together the money market, in which the interest rate is determined, and the market for goods and services, in which equilibrium expenditure is determined. Figure 29.1 illustrates the

FIGURE 29.1

Equilibrium Interest Rate and Real GDP

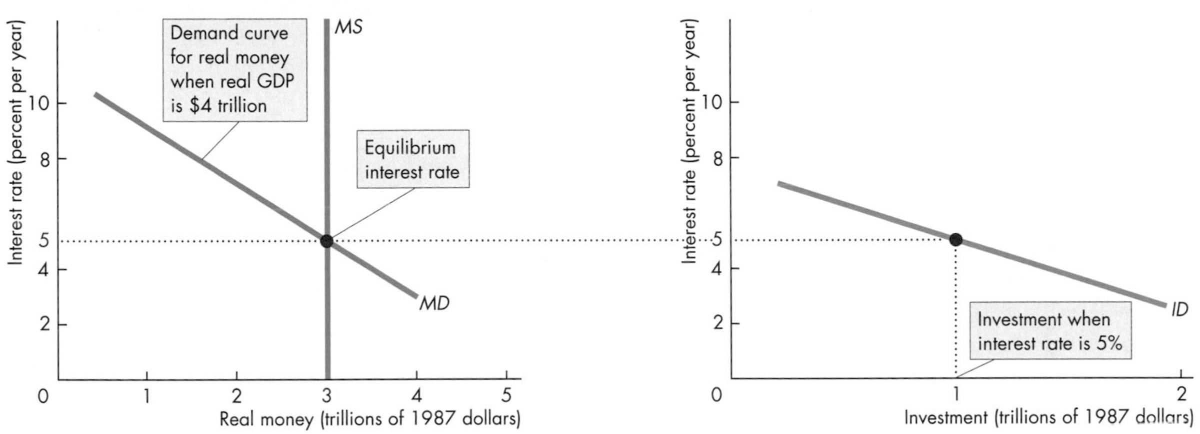

(a) Money and the interest rate

(b) Investment and the interest rate

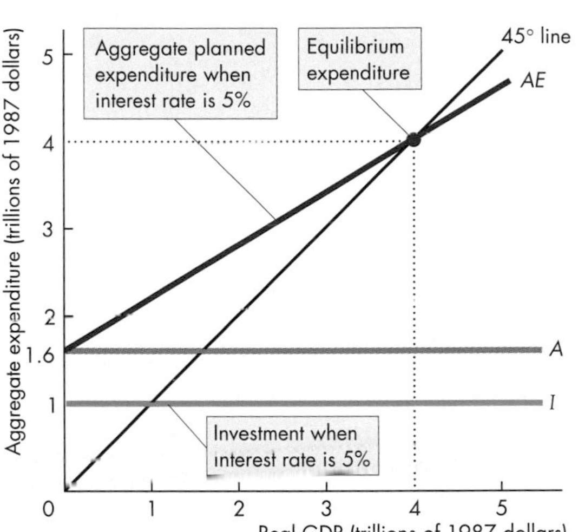

(c) Expenditure and real GDP

Equilibrium in the money market (part a) determines the interest rate. The money supply curve is *MS*, and the demand curve for real money is *MD*. The position of the *MD* curve is determined by real GDP and the curve shown is for a real GDP of $4 trillion. The investment demand curve (*ID*) in part (b) determines investment at the equilibrium interest rate determined in the money market. Investment is part of autonomous expenditure, and its level determines the position of the aggregate expenditure curve (*AE*) shown in part (c). Equilibrium expenditure and real GDP are determined at the point at which the aggregate expenditure curve intersects the 45° line. In equilibrium, real GDP and the interest rate are such that the quantity of real money demanded equals the quantity of real money supplied and aggregate planned expenditure equals real GDP.

determination of equilibrium expenditure and the interest rate. The figure has three parts: part (a) illustrates the money market; part (b) shows investment demand; and part (c) shows aggregate planned expenditure and the determination of equilibrium expenditure. Let's begin in part (a).

The Money Market The curve labeled *MD* is the demand for real money. The position of this curve depends on the level of real GDP. For a given level of real GDP, there is a given demand curve for real money. Suppose that the demand curve shown in the figure describes the demand for real money when real GDP is $4 trillion. If real GDP is higher than $4 trillion, the demand curve for real money is to the right of the one shown; if real GDP is below $4 trillion, the demand curve for real money is to the left of the one shown.

The curve labeled *MS* is the supply curve of real money. Its position is determined by the monetary policy actions of the Fed, the behavior of the banking system, and the price level. At a given point in time, all these influences determine a quantity of money supplied that is independent of the interest rate. Hence the supply curve for real money is vertical.

The interest rate adjusts to achieve equilibrium in the money market—equality between the quantity of real money demanded and the quantity supplied. This equilibrium occurs at the point of intersection of the demand and supply curves of real money. In the economy illustrated in Fig. 29.1, the equilibrium interest rate is 5 percent.

Investment and Interest Rate Next, let's look at part (b), where investment is determined. The investment demand curve is *ID*. The position of the investment demand curve is determined by profit expectations, and as those expectations change, the investment demand curve shifts. For given expectations, there is a given investment demand curve. This curve tells us the level of planned investment at each level of the interest rate. We already know the interest rate from equilibrium in the money market. When the investment demand curve is *ID* and the interest rate is 5 percent, the level of planned investment is $1 trillion.

Equilibrium Expenditure Part (c) shows the determination of equilibrium expenditure. This diagram is similar to the one that you studied in Chapter 25 (Fig. 25.13a). The aggregate expenditure curve (*AE*) tells us aggregate planned expenditure at each level of real GDP. Aggregate planned expenditure is made up of autonomous expenditure and induced expenditure. Investment is part of autonomous expenditure. In this example, investment is $1 trillion and the other components of autonomous expenditure are $0.6 trillion, so autonomous expenditure is $1.6 trillion. These amounts of investment *I* and autonomous expenditure *A* are shown by the horizontal lines in part (c). Induced expenditure is the induced part of consumption expenditure minus imports. In this example, the slope of the *AE* curve is 0.6; therefore induced expenditure equals 0.6 multiplied by real GDP.

Equilibrium expenditure is determined at the point of intersection of the *AE* curve and the 45° line. Equilibrium expenditure occurs when aggregate planned expenditure and real GDP are $4 trillion each. That is, the level of aggregate demand is $4 trillion.

The Money Market Again Recall that the demand curve *MD*, in part (a), is the demand curve for real money when real GDP is $4 trillion. We've just determined in part (c) that when aggregate expenditure is at its equilibrium level, real GDP is $4 trillion. What happens if the level of real GDP that we discover in part (c) is different from the value that we assumed when drawing the demand curve for real money in part (a)? Let's perform a thought experiment to answer this question.

Suppose, when drawing the demand curve for real money, we assume that real GDP is $3 trillion. In this case, the demand curve for real money is to the left of the *MD* curve in part (a). The equilibrium interest rate is lower than 5 percent. With an interest rate below 5 percent, investment is not $1 trillion as determined in part (b), but a larger amount. If investment is larger than $1 trillion, autonomous expenditure is larger and the *AE* curve lies above the one shown in part (c). If the aggregate expenditure curve is above the *AE* curve shown, equilibrium expenditure and real GDP are larger than $4 trillion. Thus if we start with the demand curve for real money for a real GDP less than $4 trillion, equilibrium expenditure occurs at a real GDP that is greater than $4 trillion. There is an inconsistency. The real GDP assumed in drawing the demand curve for real money is too low.

Next, let's reverse the experiment. Assume a level of real GDP of $5 trillion. In this case, the demand curve for real money lies to the right of the *MD* curve in part (a). The equilibrium interest rate is higher than 5 percent. With an interest rate higher than 5 percent, investment is less than $1 trillion and the *AE* curve lies below the one shown in part (c). In this case, equilibrium expenditure occurs at a real GDP that is less than $4 trillion. Again, there is an inconsistency, but now the real GDP assumed in drawing the demand curve for real money is too high.

We've just seen that for a given money supply, money market equilibrium determines an interest rate that varies with real GDP. The higher the level of real GDP, the higher is the equilibrium interest rate. But the interest rate determines investment, which in turn determines equilibrium expenditure. The higher the interest rate, the lower is investment and therefore the lower is equilibrium real GDP.

There is one particular level of both the interest rate and real GDP that simultaneously gives money market equilibrium and equilibrium expenditure. In the example we are studying, that interest rate is 5 percent and real GDP is $4 trillion. Only if we use a real GDP of $4 trillion to determine the position of the demand curve for real money do we get a consistent story in the three parts of this figure. If the demand curve for real money is based on a real GDP of $4 trillion, the interest rate determined (5 percent) delivers investment of $1 trillion, which, in turn, generates equilibrium expenditure at the same level of real GDP that determines the position of the demand curve for real money.

Let's now turn to an examination of the effects of fiscal policy on aggregate demand.

Fiscal Policy and Aggregate Demand

The government is concerned that the economy is slowing down and that a recession looks likely. To head off the recession, the government decides to stimulate aggregate demand by using fiscal policy, increasing its purchases of goods and services by $1 trillion. A fiscal policy that increases aggregate demand is called an *expansionary fiscal policy.*

The effects of the government's actions are similar to those of throwing a pebble into a pond. There's an initial splash followed by a series of ever smaller ripples. The initial splash is the "first round effect" of the fiscal policy action. The ripples are the "second round effects." Let's start by looking at the first round effects of the government's fiscal policy action.

First Round Effects of Fiscal Policy

The economy starts out in the situation shown in Fig. 29.1. The interest rate is 5 percent, investment is $1 trillion, and real GDP is $4 trillion. In this situation, the government increases its purchases of goods and services by $1 trillion.

The first round effects of this action are shown in Fig. 29.2. The increase in government purchases increases autonomous expenditure. This increase is shown in Fig. 29.2 by the shift of the line A_0 to A_1. The increase in autonomous expenditure increases aggregate planned expenditure and shifts the AE curve upward from AE_0 to AE_1. Equilibrium expenditure increases to $6.5 trillion. This increase in aggregate planned expenditure and equilibrium expenditure sets off a multiplier process that starts real GDP increasing. We described this process in Chapter 26, pp. 703–709. These are the first round effects of an expansionary fiscal policy, and they are summarized in Fig. 29.3(a).

FIGURE 29.2

First Round Effects of an Expansionary Fiscal Policy

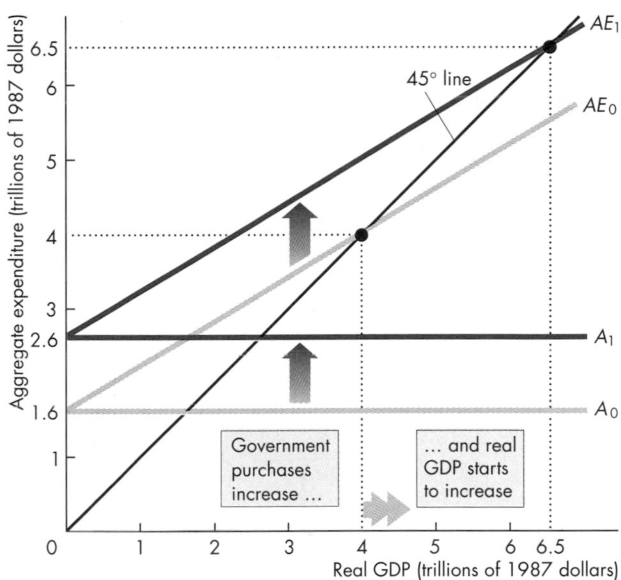

Initially, autonomous expenditure is A_0, the aggregate expenditure curve is AE_0, and real GDP is $4 trillion. An increase in government purchases of goods and services increases autonomous expenditure to A_1. The aggregate expenditure curve shifts upward to AE_1, and equilibrium expenditure increases to $6.5 trillion. A multiplier process is set off in which real GDP starts to increase. These are the first round effects of an expansionary fiscal policy.

Second Round Effects of Fiscal Policy

At the end of the first round that we've just studied, real GDP is rising. The increase in real GDP increases the demand for money. The increase in the

FIGURE 29.3

How the Economy Adjusts to an Expansionary Fiscal Policy

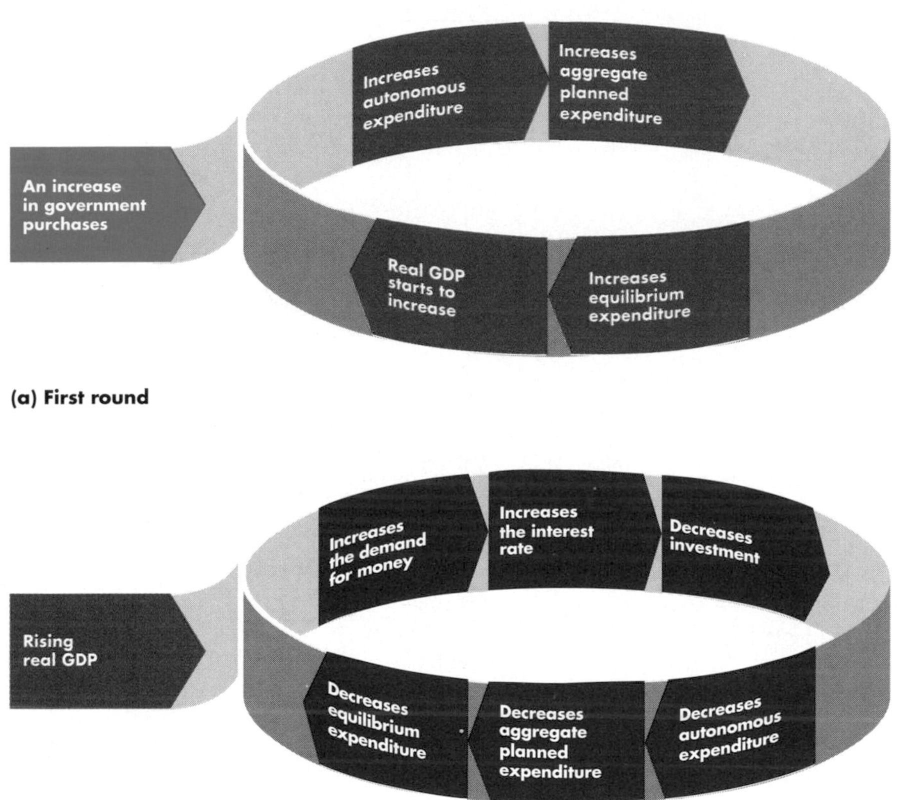

In the first round (part a), an increase in government purchases increases autonomous expenditure. Aggregate planned expenditure and equilibrium expenditure increase. A multiplier process is set off that starts real GDP increasing. In the second round (part b), the rising real GDP increases the demand for money and interest rates rise. The rising interest rate decreases investment, decreases autonomous expenditure, and decreases aggregate planned expenditure and equilibrium expenditure. The second round effects work in the opposite direction to the first round effects but are smaller in magnitude. The outcome of an increase in government purchases is an increase in real GDP, a rise in the interest rate, and a decrease in investment.

demand for money raises the interest rate. The rise in the interest rate decreases investment, and autonomous expenditure decreases. The decrease in autonomous expenditure decreases aggregate planned expenditure, which in turn decreases equilibrium expenditure. These second round effects are summarized in Fig. 29.3(b). These effects go in the opposite direction to the first round effects, but they are smaller. They diminish the magnitude of the first round effects but do not change the direction of the outcome of the fiscal policy action. That outcome is an increase in real GDP, an increase in the interest rate, and a decrease in investment.

When a new equilibrium is arrived at, the new higher real GDP and higher interest rate give simultaneous money market equilibrium and equilibrium expenditure, similar to the situation in Fig. 29.1. This equilibrium is shown in Fig. 29.4. The demand for real money has increased to MD_1, and the interest rate has risen to 6 percent in part (a). The higher interest rate has decreased investment in part (b). The increase in autonomous expenditure is \$0.6 trillion, which is equal to the initial increase in government purchases of \$1 trillion minus the decrease in investment of \$0.4 trillion, shown in part (c). Finally, aggregate planned expenditure has increased to AE_2, and the new equilibrium expenditure is at a real GDP of \$5.5 trillion (also shown in part c).

FIGURE 29.4

The Effects of a Change in Government Purchases

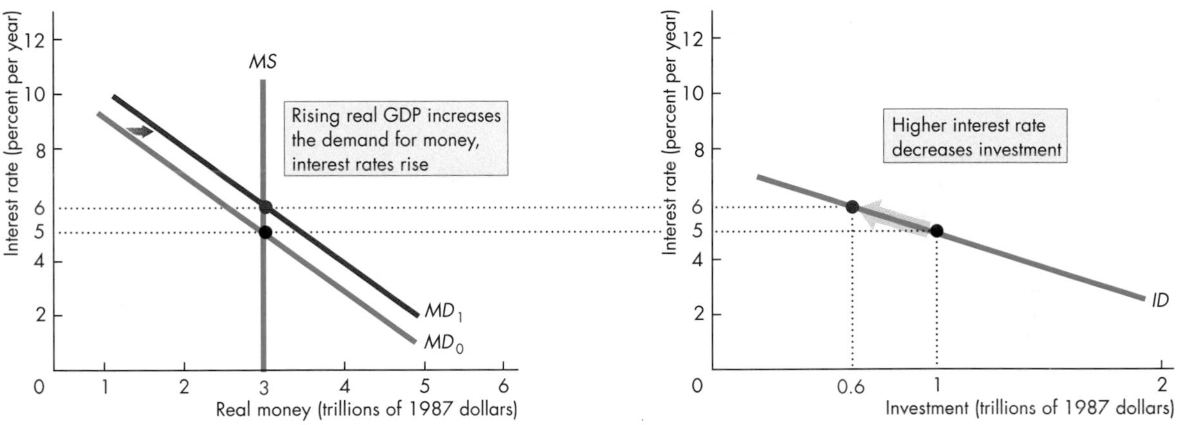

(a) Increase in the demand for money

(b) Decrease in investment

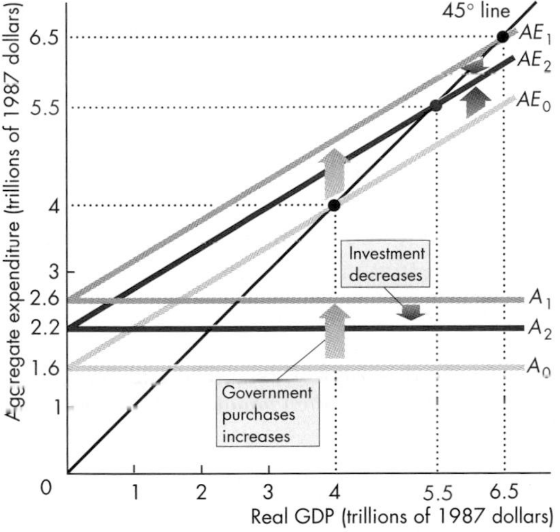

(c) Expenditure and real GDP

Initially, the demand curve for real money is MD_0, the real money supply is *MS*, and the interest rate is 5 percent (part a). With an interest rate of 5 percent, investment is $1 trillion on the investment demand curve *ID* (part b). The aggregate expenditure curve is AE_0, autonomous expenditure is A_0, and equilibrium expenditure and real GDP are $4 trillion (part c). A $1 trillion increase in government purchases increases autonomous expenditure (part c). Real GDP increases, which leads to an increase in the the demand for money. The demand curve for real money shifts rightward to MD_1, raising the interest rate (part a). The higher interest rate decreases investment (part b). Autonomous expenditure decreases to A_2, and aggregate planned expenditure decreases to AE_2 (part c). The new equilibrium expenditure occurs at real GDP of $5.5 trillion.

Other Fiscal Policies A change in government purchases is only one possible fiscal policy action. Others are a change in transfer payments, such as an increase in unemployment compensation or an increase in social security benefits, and a change in taxes. All fiscal policy actions work by changing autonomous expenditure. The magnitude of the change in autonomous expenditure differs for different fiscal actions. But fiscal policy actions that change autonomous expenditure by a given amount and in a given direction have similar effects on equilibrium real GDP and the interest rate regardless of whether they involve changes in purchases of goods and services, transfer payments, or taxes.

REVIEW

An expansionary fiscal policy—an increase in government purchases of goods and services or an increase in transfer payments or a decrease in taxes—affects aggregate demand by increasing autonomous expenditure.

- In the first round, aggregate planned expenditure increases, real GDP increases, the demand for money increases, and the interest rate starts to rise.
- In the second round, the rising interest rate decreases investment, decreases autonomous expenditure, and decreases equilibrium expenditure and real GDP.

The second round effects go in the opposite direction to the first round effects but are smaller. An expansionary fiscal policy increases real GDP, increases the interest rate, and decreases investment. ◆

We've seen that an expansionary fiscal policy raises interest rates and decreases investment. Let's take a closer look at this effect of fiscal policy.

Crowding Out and Crowding In

The tendency for an expansionary fiscal policy to increase interest rates and decrease investment is called **crowding out**. Crowding out may be partial or complete. Partial crowding out occurs when the decrease in investment is less than the increase in government purchases. This is the normal case—and the case we've just seen. Increased government purchases of goods and services increase real GDP, which increases the demand for real money, and so interest rates rise. Higher interest rates decrease investment. However, the effect on investment is smaller than the initial change in government purchases.

Complete crowding out occurs if the decrease in investment equals the initial increase in government purchases. For complete crowding out to occur, a small change in the demand for real money must lead to a large change in the interest rate, and the change in the interest rate must lead to a large change in investment.

Another influence of government purchases on investment that we haven't considered so far works in the opposite direction to the crowding out effect and is called "crowding in." **Crowding in** is the tendency for an expansionary fiscal policy to *increase* investment. This effect works in three ways.

First, in a recession, an expansionary fiscal policy might create expectations of a speedier recovery and bring an increase in expected future profits. With higher expected profits, the investment demand curve shifts to the right and investment increases despite higher interest rates.

The second source of crowding in is increased government purchases of capital. Such expenditure might increase the profitability of privately owned capital and lead to an increase in investment. For example, suppose the government increased its expenditure and built a new highway that cut the cost of transporting a farmer's produce to a market that previously was too costly to serve. The farmer might now purchase a new fleet of refrigerated trucks to take advantage of the newly available profit opportunity.

The third source of crowding in is decreased taxes. If the expansionary fiscal policy cuts the taxes on business profits, firms' after-tax profits increase and additional investment might be undertaken.

As a practical matter, crowding out is probably more common than crowding in, and because of a persistent government deficit, crowding out is a continuing source of uneasiness in the United States. Some of this uneasiness is justified, but some is not, as you can see in Reading Between the Lines on pp. 798–799.

The Exchange Rate and International Crowding Out

We've seen that an expansionary fiscal policy leads to higher interest rates. But a change in interest rates also affects the exchange rate. Higher interest rates make the dollar rise in value against other currencies. With interest rates higher in the United States than in the rest of the world, funds flow into the United States and people around the world demand more U.S. dollars. As the dollar rises in value, foreigners find U.S.-produced goods and services more expensive and Americans find imports less expensive. Exports fall and imports rise—net exports fall. The tendency for an expansionary fiscal policy to decrease net exports is called **international crowding**

out. The decrease in net exports offsets to some degree the initial increase in aggregate expenditure brought about by an expansionary fiscal policy.

REVIEW

Crowding out is the tendency for an expansionary fiscal policy to increase interest rates, thereby reducing investment. Crowding out can be partial or complete. The normal case is partial crowding out—the decrease in investment is less than the initial increase in autonomous expenditure resulting from the fiscal action. ◆ ◆ Crowding in is the tendency for an expansionary fiscal policy to *increase* investment. Crowding in might occur in a recession if fiscal stimulation brings expectations of higher future profits, if the government purchases of capital hasten economic recovery, or if tax cuts stimulate investment. ◆ ◆ International crowding out is the tendency for an expansionary fiscal policy to decrease net exports. International crowding out occurs because fiscal expansion increases interest rates and makes the dollar rise in value against other currencies. A higher dollar increases imports and decreases exports. ◆

Let's now turn to an examination of the effects of monetary policy on aggregate demand.

Monetary Policy and Aggregate Demand

The Fed is concerned that the economy is overheating and that inflation is about to take off. To slow down the economy, the Fed decides to reduce aggregate demand by decreasing the money supply. To work out the consequences of this monetary policy action, we divide its effects into first round and second round effects (just as we did with fiscal policy). Let's look at the first round effects of the Fed's monetary policy action.

First Round Effects of a Change in the Money Supply

The economy is in the situation that we studied in Fig. 29.1. The interest rate is 5 percent, investment is \$1 trillion, and real GDP is \$4 trillion. The Fed now decreases the real money supply by \$1 trillion, from \$3 trillion to \$2 trillion. The first round effects of this action are shown in Fig. 29.5. The immediate effect is shown in part (a). The real money supply curve shifts leftward from MS_0 to MS_1, and the interest rate rises from 5 percent to 7 percent. The effect of the higher interest rate is shown in part (b). Investment decreases from \$1 trillion to \$0.2 trillion—a movement along the investment demand curve. The effect of lower investment is shown in part (c). The fall in investment lowers aggregate planned expenditure—a downward shift in the *AE* curve from AE_0 to AE_1. The fall in aggregate planned expenditure lowers equilibrium expenditure, and real GDP starts to decrease. That is, a multiplier process begins in which real GDP gradually falls toward its equilibrium level. We described such a process in Chapter 26 (pp. 703–709).

We've just described the first round effects of a decrease in the money supply: the interest rate rises, investment decreases, and real GDP starts to decrease. These effects are illustrated in Fig. 29.6(a).

Second Round Effects of a Change in the Money Supply

At the end of the first round that we've just studied, real GDP is decreasing. Decreasing real GDP sets off the second round, which is illustrated in Fig. 29.6(b). A lower real GDP decreases the demand for real money, and the interest rate falls. The lower interest rate brings an increase in investment and an increase in aggregate planned expenditure. With aggregate planned expenditure increasing, equilibrium expenditure is also increasing.

These second round effects go in the opposite direction to the first round effects, but they are smaller. They diminish the magnitude of the first round effects, but they do not change the direction of the outcome of the monetary policy action. That outcome is a decrease in real GDP and an increase in the interest rate. In the new equilibrium, the lower real GDP and higher interest rate give simultaneous money market equilibrium and equilibrium expenditure, similar to the situation shown in Fig. 29.1.

FIGURE 29.5

First Round Effects of a Decrease in the Money Supply

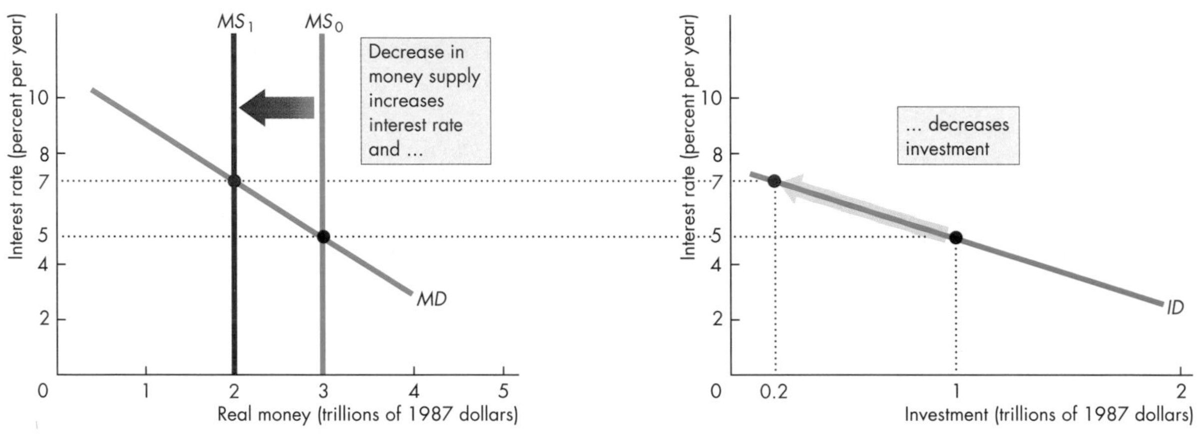

(a) Change in money supply

(b) Change in investment

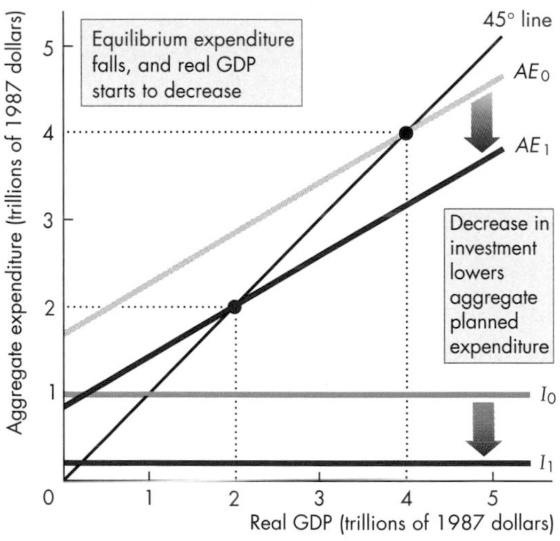

(c) Change in expenditure and real GDP

A decrease in the money supply shifts the supply curve of real money from MS_0 to MS_1 (part a). Equilibrium in the money market is achieved by an increase in the interest rate from 5 percent to 7 percent. At the higher interest rate, investment decreases (part b). The decrease in investment decreases both autonomous expenditure and aggregate planned expenditure (part c). The *AE* curve shifts downward from AE_0 to AE_1. Equilibrium real GDP falls from \$4 trillion to \$2 trillion. And a multiplier process is set up in which real GDP decreases.

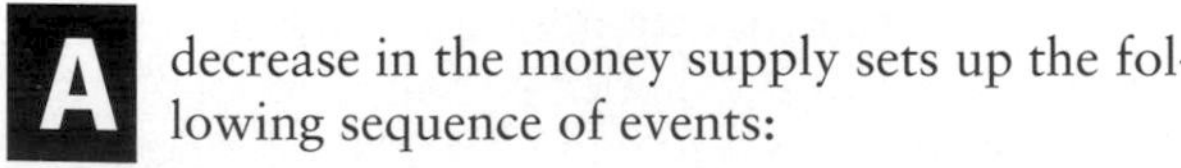

REVIEW

A decrease in the money supply sets up the following sequence of events:

- In the first round, the interest rate increases, investment decreases, and real GDP starts to decrease.
- In the second round, falling real GDP decreases the demand for money, lowers the interest rate, increases investment, and increases equilibrium expenditure.

The second round effects go in the opposite direction to the first round effects but are smaller. A decrease in the money supply decreases real GDP and increases the interest rate. ◆

FIGURE 29.6

How the Economy Adjusts to a Decrease in the Money Supply

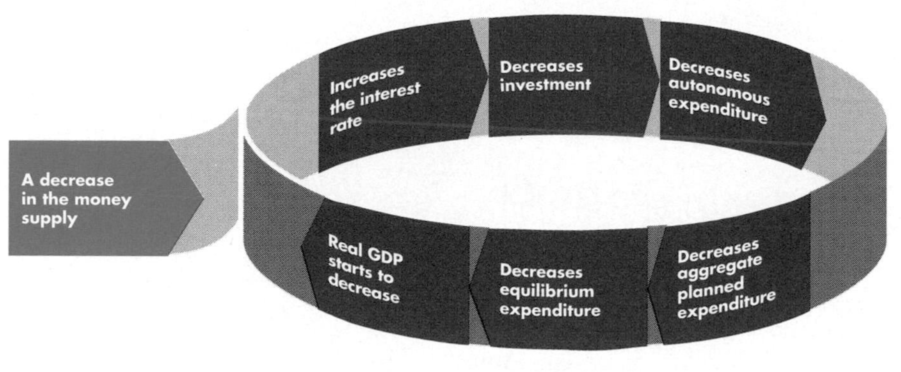

(a) First round

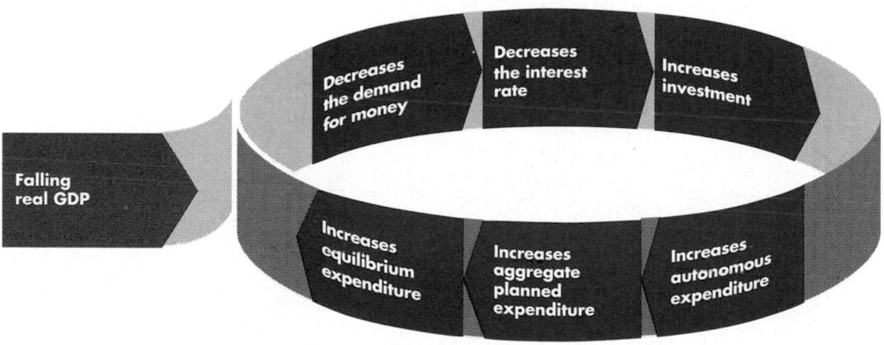

(b) Second round

In the first round (part a), a decrease in the money supply increases the interest rate, decreases investment, autonomous expenditure, aggregate planned expenditure, and equilibrium expenditure, and makes real GDP start to decrease. In the second round (part b), the decreasing real GDP decreases the demand for money, the interest rate falls, and investment increases. The increase in investment increases autonomous expenditure, aggregate planned expenditure, and equilibrium expenditure. The second round effects work in the opposite direction to the first round effects but are smaller in magnitude. The outcome of a decrease in the money supply is a decrease in real GDP and a rise in the interest rate.

So far, we have looked at the effects of monetary policy on the interest rate and investment. There is another important effect—on the foreign exchange rate and exports.

The Exchange Rate and Exports

A decrease in the money supply increases the interest rate. If the interest rate rises in the United States but does not rise in Japan and Western Europe, international investors buy the now higher-yielding U.S. assets and sell the relatively lower-yielding foreign assets. As they undertake these transactions, they buy U.S. dollars and sell foreign currency. These actions increase the demand for U.S. dollars and decrease the demand for foreign currencies. The result is a higher value of the U.S. dollar against other currencies. (This mechanism is discussed in greater detail in Chapter 36, pp. 995–999.)

With the U.S. dollar worth more, foreigners face higher prices for U.S.-produced goods and services and Americans face lower prices for foreign-produced goods and services. Foreigners cut their imports from the United States, and Americans increase their imports from the rest of the world. The result is a net decrease in the demand for U.S.-produced goods and services. The effects of a decrease in net exports are similar to the effects of a decrease in investment that we've described above.

Monetary Policy in Japan

THE ECONOMIST, FEBRUARY 29, 1992

Japan's money supply: Panic stations

Is the Bank of Japan about to be pushed into easing monetary policy? The odds on it are growing, even though the central bank continues to maintain that Japan's slowing economy has entered a stage of "normal adjustment."

This is bunk. Industrial production in January was 4% lower than a year earlier, according to figures released on February 26th. That is the largest decline since October 1982. A survey published in February by the *Nihon Keizai Shimbun*, Japan's leading financial daily, projected an 11% decline in manufacturing firms' capital spending in the 12 months to March 1993 (and of 4.5%, if non-manufacturing companies are included). This prompted Barclays de Zoete Wedd, a British securities firm, to reduce its forecast of GNP growth in that fiscal year, from 2.5% to 1.7%. That is nearly two percentage points below the 3.5% forecast by the government's Economic Planning Agency.

Monetary growth has collapsed, as debt-encumbered banks have stopped lending and companies expecting further interest-rate falls have stopped borrowing. The most closely watched money-supply measure, M2 plus certificates of deposit (CDs), grew by just 1.8% in the year to January, its slowest rate ever. . . .

Despite its official optimism, the Bank of Japan is showing signs of a shift. . . .

The longer the central bank waits to make its move, the bigger the discount-rate cut will have to be to make a difference. Money markets have already discounted a reduction of half a percentage point. With worries about the economy and stockmarket growing, politicians and industrialists calling almost daily for further easing, and an expansionary budget held up in parliament by political scandals, a cut of a full percentage point . . . is no longer out of the question. . . .

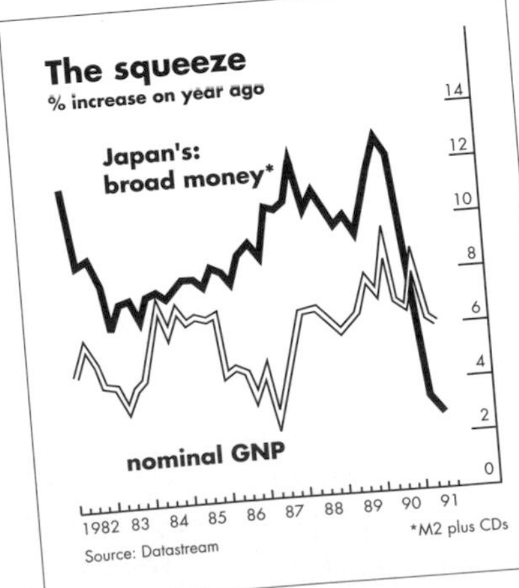

The Essence of the Story

In February 1992, the Bank of Japan and the Japanese government's Economic Planning Agency forecasted a 3.5 percent growth rate of real GNP during fiscal year 1992–93 (March to March).

But this expectation was out of line with other indicators and forecasts. Some reasons for doubt were the following:

- Industrial production in January 1992 was 4 percent lower than a year earlier.
- Japan's leading financial newspaper projected a 4.5 percent decline in capital spending in the fiscal year 1992–93.
- A British securities firm forecasted lower GNP growth in 1992–93.
- In the year to January 1992, the growth rate of Japan's money supply slowed.

Politicians and industrialists were worried about the economy and were calling for an easing of monetary policy, and there were signs that the Bank of Japan would lower interest rates.

Background and Analysis

Monetary policy in Japan is conducted by the Bank of Japan, the country's central bank.

During the year to January 1992, the Bank of Japan had kept a firm grip on the money supply, permitting it to grow by only 1.8 percent.

The money supply growth rate was equal to the inflation rate, so the *real money supply* was constant.

Despite this fact, interest rates fell sharply during 1991. The figures illustrate why.

In Fig. 1, the investment demand curve in 1990 was ID_{90}, the interest rate was 8.5 percent, and the amount of investment (expenditure on new buildings and equipment) was I_0.

During 1991, a large surge of pessimism swept the Japanese business community, and investment demand decreased. The investment demand curve shifted leftward to ID_{91}.

The decrease in investment brought lower spending and a decrease in the demand for money. This decrease is shown in Fig. 2. The (real) money supply was constant at MS_{90}, but the demand for money decreased and the demand for money curve shifted leftward from MD_{90} to MD_{91}. The interest rate decreased to 5.5 percent.

Looking again at Fig. 1, note that the lower interest rate kept investment higher than it would otherwise have been but investment nevertheless did decline—to I_1.

With fiscal policy options unavailable because of political scandals, the Bank of Japan was being urged to increase the money supply. Such an increase might shift the money supply curve rightward to MS_{92}, lowering the interest rate—to 3.5 percent in the example in Fig. 2—and stimulating investment—back up to I_0 in the example in Fig. 1.

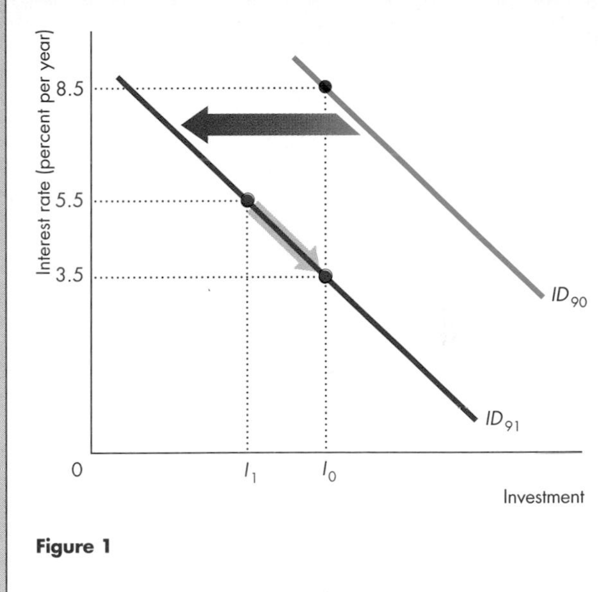

Figure 1

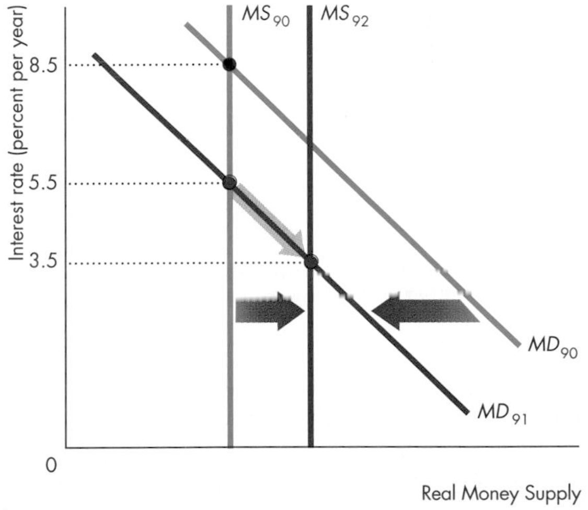

Interest rate (percent per year)
8.5
5.5
3.5
0
MS_{90}
MS_{92}
MD_{90}
MD_{91}
Real Money Supply

Figure 2

The Relative Effectiveness of Fiscal and Monetary Policy

We've now seen that equilibrium aggregate expenditure and real GDP are influenced by both fiscal and monetary policy. But which policy is the more potent? Which has the larger "bang per buck"? This question was once at the center of a controversy among macroeconomists, and later in this section we'll look at that controversy and see how it was settled. Let's begin by discovering what determines the relative effectiveness of fiscal and monetary policy.

The Effectiveness of Fiscal Policy

The effectiveness of fiscal policy is measured by the magnitude of the increase in equilibrium real GDP resulting from a given increase in government purchases of goods and services (or decrease in taxes). The effectiveness of fiscal policy depends on two key factors:

- The sensitivity of investment to the interest rate
- The sensitivity of the quantity of money demanded to the interest rate

We're going to discover how these two factors influence the effectiveness of fiscal policy by studying Fig. 29.7.

Fiscal Policy Effectiveness and Investment Demand

Other things being equal, the more sensitive investment is to the interest rate, the smaller is the effect of a change in fiscal policy on equilibrium real GDP. Figure 29.7(a) shows why.

The figure shows two investment demand curves, ID_A and ID_B. Investment is more sensitive to a change in the interest rate along the demand curve ID_A than along the demand curve ID_B. An increase in government purchases increases real GDP and increases the demand for money. The demand curve for real money shifts from MD_0 to MD_1. This increase in the demand for money increases the interest rate from 5 percent to 6 percent. If the investment demand curve is ID_A, investment decreases from \$1 trillion to \$0.6 trillion. Contrast this outcome with what happens if the investment demand curve is ID_B. The same increase in the interest rate decreases investment from \$1 trillion to \$0.8 trillion.

The decrease in investment decreases autonomous expenditure, offsetting to some degree the increase in government purchases. Therefore the larger the decrease in investment, the smaller is the increase in equilibrium real GDP resulting from a given increase in government purchases. Thus fiscal policy is less effective with the investment demand curve ID_A than with the investment demand curve ID_B.

Fiscal Policy Effectiveness and the Demand for Money

Other things being equal, the more sensitive the quantity of money demanded is to the interest rate, the bigger is the effect of fiscal policy on equilibrium real GDP. Figure 29.7(b) shows why.

The figure shows two alternative initial (blue) demand curves for real money, MD_{A0} and MD_{B0}. The quantity of money demanded is less sensitive to a change in the interest rate along the demand curve MD_A than along the demand curve MD_B.

An increase in government purchases increases real GDP and increases the demand for money, shifting the demand curve for real money to the right. If the initial curve is MD_{A0}, the new curve is MD_{A1}; if the initial curve is MD_{B0}, the new curve is MD_{B1}. Notice that the size of the rightward shift is the same in each case. In the case of MD_A, the increase in the demand for real money increases the interest rate from 5 percent to 6 percent and investment decreases from \$1 trillion to \$0.6 trillion. In the case of MD_B, the increase in the demand for real money increases the interest rate from 5 percent to 5.5 percent and investment decreases from \$1 trillion to \$0.8 trillion.

A decrease in investment decreases autonomous expenditure, offsetting to some degree the increase in government purchases. Therefore the smaller the decrease in investment, the larger is the increase in equilibrium real GDP resulting from a given increase in government purchases. Thus fiscal policy is less effective with the demand for real money curve MD_A than with the demand for real money curve MD_B.

The Effectiveness of Monetary Policy

The effectiveness of monetary policy is measured by the magnitude of the increase in equilibrium real GDP resulting from a given increase in the money

FIGURE 29.7

The Effectiveness of Fiscal Policy

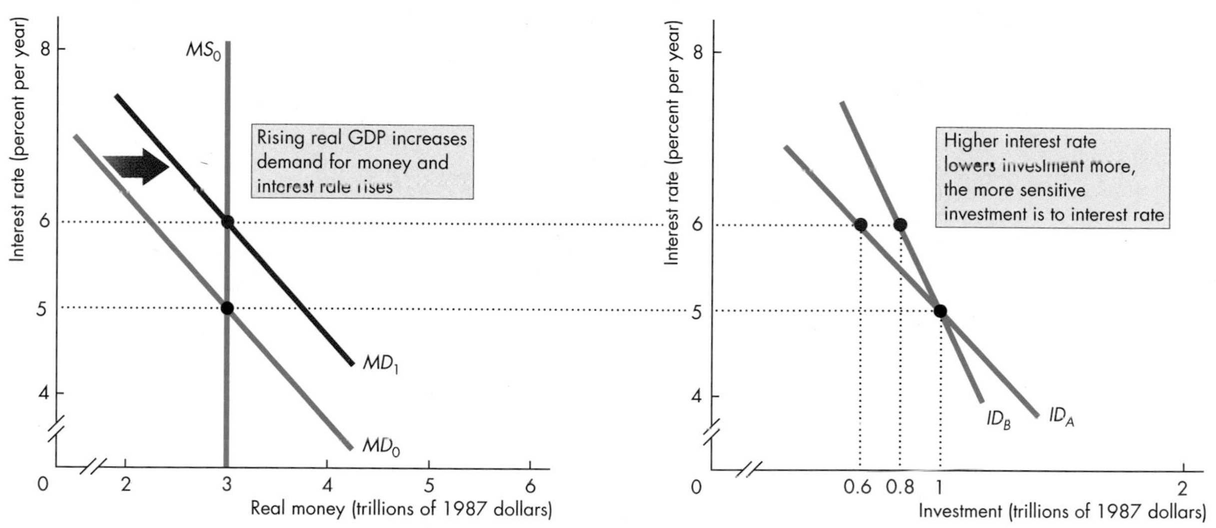

(a) Effectiveness and investment demand

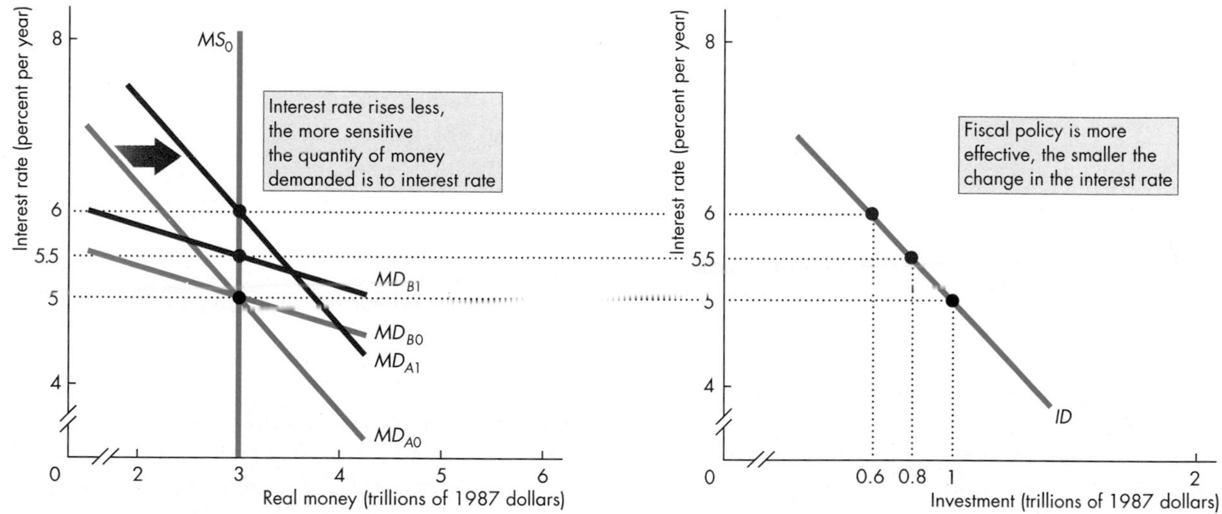

(b) Effectiveness and the demand for money

In part (a), the level of planned investment is more sensitive to a change in the interest rate along ID_A than along ID_B. An increase in government purchases increases real GDP and shifts the demand curve for real money from MD_0 to MD_1, raising the interest rate from 5 percent to 6 percent. With investment demand curve ID_A, investment decreases from \$1 trillion to \$0.6 trillion, but with demand curve ID_B, investment decreases to only \$0.8 trillion. So fiscal policy is less effective with investment demand curve ID_A than with ID_B.

In part (b), the quantity of money demanded is less sensitive to a change in the interest rate along MD_{A0} than along MD_{B0}. An increase in government purchases increases real GDP, and the demand curve for real money shifts to the right—MD_{A0} shifts to MD_{A1} and MD_{B0} shifts to MD_{B1}. The size of the rightward shift is the same in each case. In the case of MD_A, the interest rate rises from 5 percent to 6 percent and investment decreases from \$1 trillion to \$0.6 trillion. In the case of MD_B, the interest rate rises to 5.5 percent and investment decreases to only \$0.8 trillion. So fiscal policy is less effective with the demand curve for real money MD_A than with MD_B.

supply. The effectiveness of monetary policy depends on the same two factors as the effectiveness of fiscal policy:

- The sensitivity of investment to the interest rate
- The sensitivity of the quantity of money demanded to the interest rate

But other things being equal, the more effective is fiscal policy, the less effective is monetary policy. Let's see why by studying Fig. 29.8.

Monetary Policy Effectiveness and Investment Demand Other things being equal, the more sensitive investment is to the interest rate, the bigger is the effect of a change in the money supply on equilibrium real GDP. Figure 29.8(a) shows why.

The figure shows two investment demand curves, ID_A and ID_B. Investment is more sensitive to a change in the interest rate along the demand curve ID_A than along the demand curve ID_B.

With the demand curve for real money *MD*, an increase in the money supply that shifts the real money supply curve from MS_0 to MS_1 decreases the interest rate from 5 percent to 3 percent. If the investment demand curve is ID_A, investment increases from $1 trillion to $1.8 trillion. Contrast this outcome with what happens if the investment demand curve is ID_B. The same decrease in the interest rate increases investment from $1 trillion to $1.4 trillion.

The larger the increase in investment, the larger is the resulting increase in equilibrium real GDP. Thus with the investment demand curve ID_A, monetary policy is more effective than with the investment demand curve ID_B.

Monetary Policy Effectiveness and the Demand for Money Other things being equal, the less sensitive the quantity of money demanded is to the interest rate, the bigger is the effect of a change in the money supply on equilibrium real GDP. Figure 29.8(b) shows why.

The figure shows two demand curves for real money, MD_A and MD_B. The quantity of money demanded is less sensitive to a change in the interest rate along the demand curve MD_A than along the demand curve MD_B.

If the demand curve for real money is MD_A, an increase in the money supply that shifts the real money supply curve from MS_0 to MS_1 decreases the interest rate from 5 percent to 3 percent. Investment increases from $1 trillion to $1.8 trillion. Contrast this outcome with what happens if the demand curve for real money is MD_B. In this case, the same increase in the money supply lowers the interest rate from 5 percent to only 4 percent and investment increases to only $1.4 trillion.

The larger the increase in investment, the larger is the resulting increase in equilibrium real GDP. Thus with the demand curve for real money MD_A, monetary policy is more effective than with the demand curve for real money MD_B.

Interest Sensitivity of Investment and the Quantity of Money Demanded

What determines the degree of sensitivity of investment and the quantity of money demanded to interest rates? The answer is the degree of substitutability between capital and other factors of production and the degree of substitutability between money and other financial assets.

Investment is the purchase of capital—of productive buildings, plant, and equipment. The amount of capital used, and the amount of investment undertaken, decreases as the interest rate increases. The degree to which a change in the interest rate brings a change in investment depends on how easily other factors of production can be substituted for capital.

Money performs a unique function—it facilitates the exchange of goods and services. Therefore money and other financial assets are imperfect substitutes. Holding money has an opportunity cost, which is the interest forgone by not holding other financial assets. The amount of money that we hold decreases as its opportunity cost—the interest rate—increases. The degree to which a change in the interest rate brings a change in the quantity of money held depends on how easily other financial assets can be substituted for money.

The analysis that we have presented in this chapter of the effects of fiscal and monetary policy on aggregate expenditure was for several years in the 1950s and 1960s extremely controversial. It was at the heart of what was called the Keynesian-monetarist controversy. The controversy of today is different from that of the 1950s and 1960s, and we'll consider today's controversy—a controversy about how labor markets work—in Chapter 30. But the Keynesian-monetarist controversy was an interesting and important episode in the development of modern macroeconomics. Let's take a look at the essentials of the dispute and see how it was resolved.

FIGURE 29.8

The Effectiveness of Monetary Policy

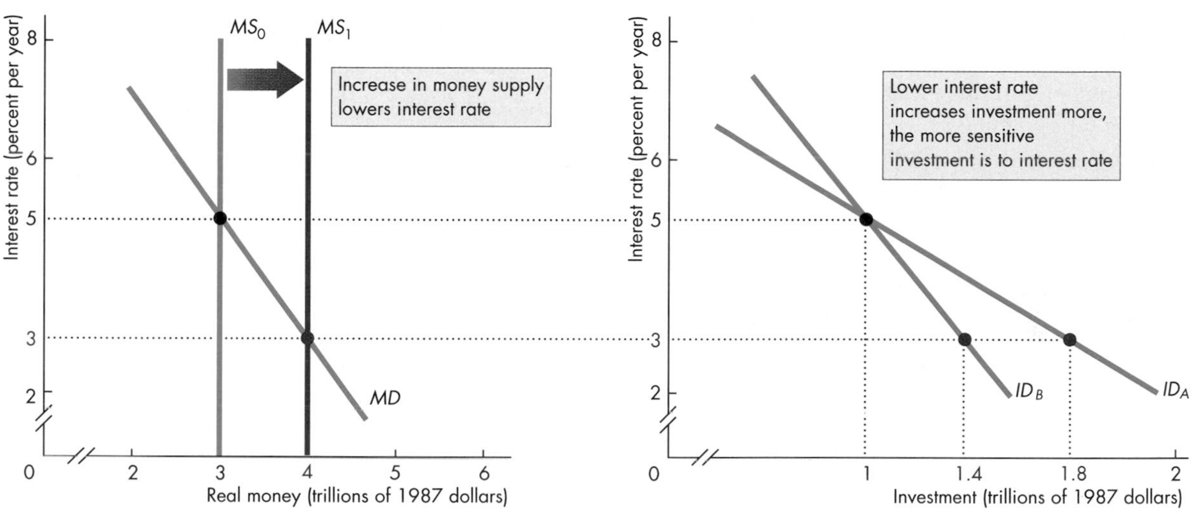

(a) Effectiveness and investment demand

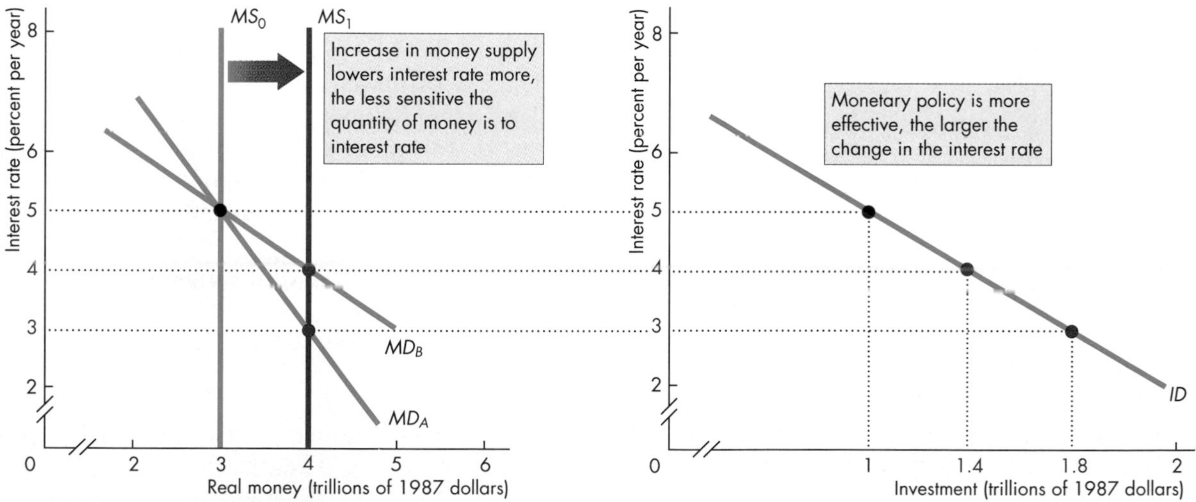

(b) Effectiveness and the demand for money

In part (a), planned investment is more sensitive to a change in the interest rate along the investment demand curve ID_A than along the demand curve ID_B. With the demand curve for real money *MD*, a shift in the real money supply curve from MS_0 to MS_1 lowers the interest rate from 5 percent to 3 percent. With investment demand curve ID_A, investment increases from \$1 trillion to \$1.8 trillion, but with investment demand curve ID_B, investment increases to only \$1.4 trillion. The larger the increase in investment, the larger is the resulting increase in equilibrium real GDP. So monetary policy is more effective with investment demand curve ID_A than with ID_B.

In part (b), the quantity of money demanded is less sensitive to a change in the interest rate along MD_A than along MD_B. With the demand curve MD_A, an increase in the money supply that shifts the real money supply curve from MS_0 to MS_1 lowers the interest rate from 5 percent to 3 percent and increases investment from \$1 trillion to \$1.8 trillion. With demand curve MD_B, the same increase in the money supply lowers the interest rate to only 4 percent and increases investment to only \$1.4 trillion. The larger the increase in investment, the larger is the resulting increase in equilibrium real GDP. So monetary policy is more effective with demand curve MD_A than with MD_B.

The Keynesian-Monetarist Controversy

The Keynesian-monetarist controversy was a dispute in macroeconomics between two broad groups of economists. Keynesians are macroeconomists whose views about the functioning of the economy represent an extension of the theories of John Maynard Keynes, published in his *General Theory* (see Our Advancing Knowledge, pp. 674–675). **Keynesians** regard the economy as being inherently unstable and as requiring active government intervention to achieve stability. They assign a low degree of importance to monetary policy and a high degree of importance to fiscal policy. **Monetarists** are macroeconomists who assign a high degree of importance to variations in the quantity of money as the main determinant of aggregate demand and who regard the economy as inherently stable. The founder of modern monetarism is Milton Friedman (see Our Advancing Knowledge, pp. 918–919).

The Keynesian-monetarist debate in the 1950s and 1960s was a debate about the relative effectiveness of fiscal policy and monetary policy in changing aggregate demand. We can see the essence of that debate by distinguishing three views:

- Extreme Keynesianism
- Extreme monetarism
- Intermediate position

Extreme Keynesianism The extreme Keynesian hypothesis is that a change in the money supply has no effect on the level of aggregate demand and a change in government purchases of goods and services or in taxes has a large effect on aggregate demand.

There are two circumstances in which a change in the money supply has no effect on aggregate demand. They are

- A vertical investment demand curve
- A horizontal demand curve for real money

If the investment demand curve is vertical, investment is completely insensitive to interest rates. In this situation, a change in the money supply changes interest rates but those changes do not affect aggregate planned expenditure. Monetary policy is impotent.

A horizontal demand curve for real money means that people are willing to hold any quantity of money at a given interest rate—a situation called a **liquidity trap.** With a liquidity trap, a change in the money supply affects only the quantity of money held. It does not affect interest rates. With an unchanged interest rate, investment remains constant. Monetary policy is impotent.

Extreme Keynesians assume that both of these conditions prevail. Notice that either one of these circumstances on its own is sufficient for monetary policy to be impotent, but extreme Keynesians suppose that both situations exist in reality.

Extreme Monetarism The extreme monetarist hypothesis is that a change in government purchases of goods and services or in taxes has no effect on aggregate demand and that a change in the money supply has a large effect on aggregate demand. There are two circumstances giving rise to these predictions:

- A horizontal investment demand curve
- A vertical demand curve for real money

If an increase in government purchases of goods and services induces an increase in interest rates that is sufficiently large to reduce investment by the same amount as the initial increase in government purchases, then fiscal policy has no effect on aggregate demand. This outcome is complete crowding out, which we described earlier in this chapter. For this result to occur, either the demand curve for real money must be vertical—a fixed quantity of money is demanded regardless of the interest rate—or the investment demand curve must be horizontal—any amount of investment will be undertaken at a given interest rate.

The Intermediate Position The intermediate position is that both fiscal and monetary policy affect aggregate demand. Crowding out is not complete, so fiscal policy does have an effect. There is no liquidity trap and investment responds to interest rates, so monetary policy does indeed affect aggregate demand. This position is the one that now appears to be correct and is the one that we've spent most of this chapter exploring. Let's see how economists came to this conclusion.

Sorting Out the Competing Claims The dispute between monetarists, Keynesians, and those taking an intermediate position was essentially a disagreement about the magnitudes of two economic parameters:

- The sensitivity of investment to interest rates
- The sensitivity of the quantity of money demanded to interest rates

If investment is highly sensitive to interest rates or the quantity of money demanded is hardly sensitive at all, then monetary policy is powerful and fiscal policy is relatively ineffective. In this case, the world looks similar to the claims of extreme monetarists. If investment is very insensitive to interest rates or the quantity of money demanded is highly sensitive, then fiscal policy is powerful and monetary policy is relatively ineffective. In this case, the world looks similar to the claims of the extreme Keynesians.

By using statistical methods to study the demand for real money and investment demand and by using data from a wide variety of historical and national experiences, economists were able to settle this dispute. Neither extreme position turned out to be supported by the evidence, and the intermediate position won. The demand curve for real money slopes downward. So does the investment demand curve. Neither curve is vertical or horizontal, so the extreme Keynesian and extreme monetarist hypotheses are rejected.

This particular controversy in macroeconomics is now behind us, but other controversies are still around. One concerns the relative magnitudes of the multiplier effects of fiscal and monetary policy. Another concerns the time lags of those effects. But the major unresolved issue that divides economists today concerns the working of the labor market, a controversy that we'll meet in the next chapter.

REVIEW

The relative effectiveness of fiscal and monetary policy depends on the sensitivity to interest rates of investment and the quantity of money demanded. Other things being equal, the more sensitive investment is to interest rates or the less sensitive the quantity of money demanded is, the smaller is the effect of a change in government purchases and the greater is the effect of a change in the money supply on equilibrium expenditure. The less sensitive investment is to interest rates or the more sensitive the quantity of money demanded is, the larger is the effect of a change in government purchases and the smaller is the effect of a change in the money supply on equilibrium expenditure. In the extreme case in which investment is completely insensitive to the interest rate or the quantity of money demanded is infinitely sensitive, fiscal policy is effective and monetary policy is completely ineffective. In the opposite extreme case, in which investment is infinitely sensitive to the interest rate or the quantity of money demanded is completely insensitive, monetary policy is effective and fiscal policy is ineffective. These extremes do not occur in reality. ◆

Influencing the Composition of Aggregate Expenditure

Aggregate expenditure can be increased by either an expansionary fiscal policy or an increase in the money supply. An expansionary fiscal policy increases aggregate expenditure and raises interest rates. Increased expenditure increases income and consumption expenditure, but higher interest rates decrease investment. Hence if aggregate expenditure is increased by an expansionary fiscal policy, consumption expenditure increases and investment decreases. In contrast, an increase in the money supply increases aggregate expenditure and *lowers* interest rates. Again, increased expenditure increases income and consumption expenditure, but in this case lower interest rates also increase investment. Hence if aggregate expenditure is increased by an increase in the money supply, both consumption expenditure and investment increase. Thus the method whereby aggregate expenditure is increased has an important effect on the *composition* of expenditure.

Politics of Fiscal and Monetary Policy

The effects on the composition of aggregate expenditure resulting from different policies for changing aggregate expenditure are a source of tension between the various branches of government and have an important effect on the economy's long-term capacity for growth. Congress and the administration do not want the Fed to tighten monetary policy, which increases interest rates. Instead, they want to see the Fed steadily expanding the money supply, keeping interest rates as low as possible.

The Fed, on the other hand, frequently points to the importance of keeping government purchases of goods and services under control and keeping taxes sufficiently high to pay for those goods and services. It argues that unless Congress increases taxes or cuts its expenditure, then interest rates cannot be lowered.

The choice of monetary or fiscal policy affects our long-term growth prospects because the long-term capacity of the economy to produce goods and services depends on the rate at which capital is accumulated—the level of investment. An expansionary fiscal policy that leads to a decrease in investment slows down the economy's long-term growth. But much government expenditure is on productive capital such as highways and on education and health care that increases human capital. Increases in government purchases of goods and services such as these increase the economy's long-term growth.

FIGURE 29.9

Policy-Induced Changes in Real GDP and the Price Level

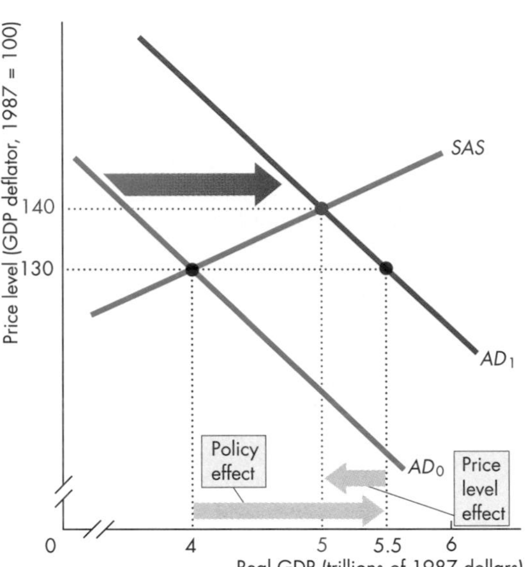

Initially, aggregate demand is AD_0, and the short-run aggregate supply curve is *SAS*. Real GDP is $4 trillion, and the GDP deflator is 130. Fiscal and monetary policy changes shift the aggregate demand curve to AD_1. At the initial price level (GDP deflator equal to 130), real GDP rises to $5.5 trillion. But the price level increases, bringing a decrease in the real money supply. The decrease in the real money supply increases the interest rate, decreases investment, and decreases equilibrium expenditure and real GDP. The increase in real GDP from $4 trillion to $5.5 trillion is the result of the initial policy-induced increase in aggregate demand at a given price level. The decrease in real GDP from $5.5 trillion to $5 trillion is the result of the decrease in the real money supply induced by the higher price level.

Real GDP and the Price Level

We've now studied the effects of fiscal and monetary policy on equilibrium expenditure and real GDP at a given price level. But the effects that we've worked out occur at each and every price level. Thus the fiscal and monetary policy effects that we've studied tell us about changes in aggregate demand and shifts in the aggregate demand curve.

When aggregate demand changes, both real GDP and the price level change. To determine the amounts by which each changes, we need to look at both aggregate demand and aggregate supply. Let's now do this, starting with the short-run effects of fiscal and monetary policy.

The Short-Run Effects on Real GDP and the Price Level

When aggregate demand changes and the aggregate demand curve shifts, there is a movement along the short-run aggregate supply curve and both real GDP and the price level change. Figure 29.9 illustrates the changes in real GDP and the price level that result from an increase in aggregate demand. Initially, the aggregate demand curve is AD_0, and the short-run aggregate supply curve is *SAS*. Real GDP is $4 trillion, and the GDP deflator is 130.

Now suppose that changes in fiscal and monetary policy increase aggregate demand, shifting the aggregate demand curve to AD_1. At the initial price level (GDP deflator equal to 130), the quantity of real GDP demanded increases to $5.5 trillion. This increase is the one we studied earlier in this chapter. But real GDP does not actually increase to this level.

The reason is that the price level increases, bringing a decrease in the quantity of real GDP demanded. The higher level of aggregate demand puts upward pressure on the prices of all goods and services, and the GDP deflator rises to 140. At the higher price level, the real money supply decreases.

A decrease in the real money supply resulting from a rise in the price level has exactly the same effects on real GDP (and the interest rate) as a decrease in the real money supply resulting from a decrease in the *nominal* money supply brought about by the Fed's monetary policy. We've already seen what these effects are. A decrease in the real money supply increases the interest rate, decreases investment, and decreases equilibrium expenditure and real GDP.

The increase in real GDP from $4 trillion to $5.5 trillion is the result of the initial policy-induced increase in aggregate demand at a given price level; and the decrease in real GDP from $5.5 trillion to $5 trillion is the result of the decrease in the real money supply induced by the higher price level.

The exercise that we've just conducted for an increase in aggregate demand can be reversed to see what happens when there is a policy-induced decrease in aggregate demand. In this case, real GDP decreases and the price level falls.

The effects that we've just worked out are short-run effects. Let's now look at the long-run effects of fiscal and monetary policy.

FIGURE 29.10

The Long-Run Effects of Policy-Induced Changes in Real GDP and the Price Level

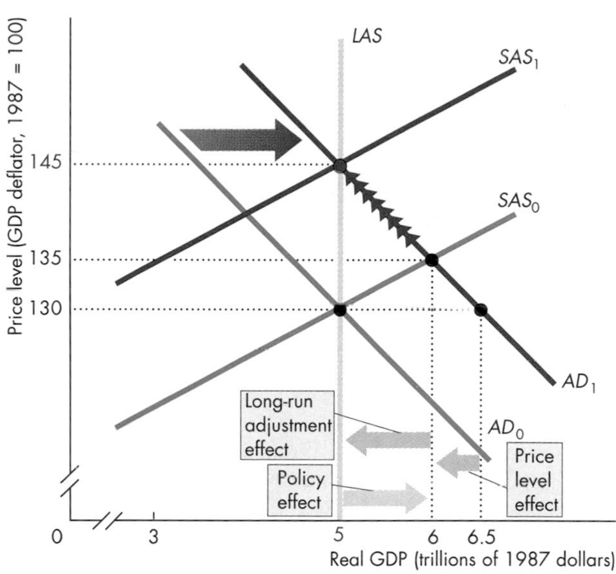

The long-run aggregate supply curve is *LAS*, and initially the aggregate demand curve is AD_0 and the short-run aggregate supply curve is SAS_0. Real GDP is $5 trillion, and the GDP deflator is 130. Fiscal and monetary policy changes shift the aggregate demand curve to AD_1. At the new short-run equilibrium, real GDP is $6 trillion and the GDP deflator is 135. Because real GDP is above its long-run level, wages increase and the short-run aggregate supply curve begins to shift upward to SAS_1. At the new long-run equilibrium, the GDP deflator is 145 and real GDP is back at its original level.

The Long-Run Effects on Real GDP and the Price Level

The long-run effects of fiscal and monetary policy depend on the state of the economy when the policy action is taken. Again, we'll concentrate on the case of an *increase* in aggregate demand. If initially unemployment is above its natural rate and real GDP is below its long-run level, fiscal and monetary policy can be used to restore full employment. We can use the example in Fig. 29.9 to illustrate this case.

Suppose, in Fig. 29.9, that long-run aggregate supply is $5 trillion. The increase in aggregate demand moves the economy from below full employment to full employment, and that is the end of the story. The short-run and long-run adjustments are the same. For example, the tax cuts and expansionary monetary policy of 1982 and 1983 were policy actions used to move the U.S. economy out of a serious recession into a period of sustained expansion.

In contrast, suppose that a policy-induced increase in aggregate demand occurs when the economy is already at full employment with real GDP at its long-run level. The U.S. economy was in such a situation in the late 1960s when spending on social programs and the Vietnam War increased. What then are the long-run effects?

We can see the answers in Fig. 29.10. The long-run aggregate supply curve is *LAS*. Initially, the aggregate demand curve is AD_0, and the short-run aggregate supply curve is SAS_0. Real GDP is $5 trillion, and the GDP deflator is 130.

Suppose that changes in fiscal and monetary policy increase aggregate demand, shifting the aggregate demand curve to AD_1. At the initial price level (GDP deflator equal to 130), the quantity of real GDP demanded increases to $6.5 trillion—the policy effect. But, as we've just seen, real GDP does not actually increase to this level. The higher price level decreases the real money supply and raises the interest rate. As a result, investment, equilibrium expenditure, and real GDP decrease—the price level effect. The new short-run equilibrium occurs at a real GDP of $6 trillion and a GDP deflator of 135.

But real GDP is now above its long-run level, and unemployment is below its natural rate. There is an inflationary gap. A shortage of labor puts upward pressure on wages. And as wages increase, the short-run aggregate supply curve begins to shift to the left. It keeps shifting until it reaches SAS_1. The GDP deflator increases to 145, and real GDP returns to its long-run level—the long-run adjustment effect.

Thus the long-run effect of an expansionary fiscal and monetary policy at full employment brings a rising price level but no change in real GDP. The rising price level during the late 1960s was the result of the increased government spending on social programs and the Vietnam War.

REVIEW

A policy-induced change in aggregate demand changes both real GDP and the price level. The amount by which each changes depends on aggregate supply. In the short run, both real GDP and the price level increase. In the long run, the effects of policy depend on the state of the economy when the policy action is taken. Starting from below long-run real GDP, expansionary policy increases both real GDP and the price level and restores full employment. But starting from full employment, an expansionary policy brings a rise in the price level and no change in real GDP. ◆

◆ ◆ ◆ ◆ We have now studied the effects of fiscal and monetary policy on real GDP, interest rates, and the price level. But we've seen that the effects of these policies on real GDP and the price level depend not only on the behavior of aggregate demand but also on aggregate supply. Our next task is to study the determination of long-run and short-run aggregate supply.

SUMMARY

Money, Interest, and Aggregate Demand

Real GDP and the price level are determined by the interaction of *aggregate demand* and *aggregate supply* (Chapter 24). Fiscal and monetary policy influence *aggregate demand.*

One component of autonomous expenditure, investment, varies with the interest rate. The higher the interest rate, other things held constant, the lower is investment and hence the lower is the quantity of real GDP demanded.

The interest rate is determined by equilibrium in the money market. The demand for real money depends on both real GDP and the interest rate. The higher is real GDP, other things held constant, the greater is the demand for real money and the higher is the interest rate. Therefore the interest rate depends on real GDP.

Real GDP and the interest rate are determined simultaneously. Equilibrium real GDP and the interest rate are such that the money market is in equilibrium and aggregate planned expenditure equals real GDP. (pp. 788–791)

Fiscal Policy and Aggregate Demand

A change in government purchases of goods and services or transfer payments or taxes influences aggregate demand by changing autonomous expenditure. An expansionary fiscal policy increases autonomous expenditure and increases aggregate planned expenditure. The increase in aggregate planned expenditure increases equilibrium expenditure and sets up a multiplier effect that increases real GDP. These are the first round effects. The rising real GDP sets up a second round. The increasing real GDP increases the demand for money, and the interest rate rises. With a rise in the interest rate, investment decreases. A decrease in investment decreases autonomous expenditure and decreases aggregate planned expenditure. These second round effects work in the opposite direction to the first round effects but are smaller in magnitude. The outcome of an increase in government purchases is an increase in real GDP, a rise in the interest rates, and a decrease in investment.

The effect of higher interest rates on investment—the crowding out effect—might, in an extreme situation, be complete. That is, the decrease in investment might be sufficient to offset the initial increase in government purchases. In practice, complete crowding out does not occur. An opposing effect is crowding in, an increase in investment resulting from an increase in government purchases of goods and services. Such an effect may occur in a recession if fiscal stimulation brings expectations of economic recovery and higher future profits, if the government purchases capital that strengthens the economy, or if tax cuts stimulate investment.

Fiscal policy also influences aggregate demand through the foreign exchange rate. An increase in government purchases or a cut in taxes tends to increase interest rates and to make the value of the dollar rise against other currencies. When the dollar strengthens, Americans buy more imports and foreigners buy fewer U.S.-produced goods, so U.S. net exports decline. (pp. 791–795)

Monetary Policy and Aggregate Demand

Monetary policy influences aggregate demand by changing the interest rate. A decrease in the money supply increases the interest rate. The higher interest rate decreases investment, and lower investment reduces aggregate planned expenditure. A decrease in aggregate planned expenditure sets up a multiplier effect in which real GDP starts to decrease. This is the first round effect. Decreasing real GDP sets up a second round effect in which the demand for money decreases and the interest rate falls. A fall in the interest rate increases investment and increases aggregate planned expenditure. The second round effect works in the opposite direction to the first round effect but is smaller in magnitude. The outcome of a decrease in the money supply is a decrease in real GDP and a rise in the interest rate.

Monetary policy also influences aggregate demand through the foreign exchange rate. A decrease in the money supply increases the interest rate and makes the value of the dollar rise against other currencies. When the dollar strengthens, Americans buy more imports and foreigners buy fewer U.S.-produced goods and services, so U.S. net exports decline. (pp. 795–799)

The Relative Effectiveness of Fiscal and Monetary Policy

The relative effectiveness of fiscal and monetary policy depends on two factors: the sensitivity of investment to the interest rate and the sensitivity of the quantity of money demanded to the interest rate. The less sensitive investment is to the interest rate or the more sensitive the quantity of money demanded is to the interest rate, the larger is the effect of a fiscal policy change on aggregate demand. The more sensitive investment is to the interest rate or the less sensitive the quantity of money demanded is to the interest rate, the larger is the effect of a change in the money supply on aggregate demand.

The Keynesian-monetarist controversy concerns the relative effectiveness of fiscal and monetary actions in influencing aggregate demand. The extreme Keynesian position is that only fiscal policy affects aggregate demand and monetary policy is impotent. The extreme monetarist position is the converse—that only monetary policy affects aggregate demand and that fiscal policy is impotent. This controversy was the central one in macroeconomics in the 1950s and 1960s. As a result of statistical investigations, we now know that neither of these extreme positions is correct. The demand curve for real money and the investment demand curve both slope downward, and both fiscal and monetary policy influence aggregate demand.

The mix of fiscal and monetary policy influences the composition of aggregate demand. If aggregate demand increases as a result of an increase in government purchases of goods and services, interest rates rise and investment falls. If aggregate demand increases as a result of an increase in the money supply, interest rates fall and investment increases. These different effects of fiscal and monetary policy on aggregate demand create some political tensions. To keep aggregate demand in check and interest rates moderate, there must be a high enough level of taxes to support the level of government purchases. (pp. 800–806)

Real GDP and the Price Level

When aggregate demand changes, both real GDP and the price level change by amounts determined by both aggregate demand and aggregate supply. A policy-induced increase in aggregate demand shifts the aggregate demand curve to the right. The magnitude of the shift of the aggregate demand curve is equal to the effect of the policy change on aggregate demand at a given price level. In the short run, real GDP and the price level increase. The rise in the price level decreases the real money supply. The decrease in the real money supply increases the interest rate, decreases investment, and decreases real GDP.

The long-run effects of fiscal and monetary policy depend on the state of the economy when the policy action is taken. Starting out with unemployment above its natural rate and real GDP below its long-run level, expansionary fiscal and monetary policy increases real GDP and the price level and restores full employment. But starting out from full employment with real GDP at its long-run level, a policy-induced increase in aggregate demand increases the price level and leaves real GDP unchanged. (pp. 806–808)

KEY ELEMENTS

Key Terms

Key Figures

REVIEW QUESTIONS

1 Explain the link between the money market and the market for goods and services.

2 What are the first round effects of an increase in government purchases of goods and services?

3 What are the second round effects of an increase in government purchases of goods and services?

4 What is the outcome of an increase in government purchases of goods and services?

5 What role does the foreign exchange rate play in influencing aggregate demand when there is an expansionary fiscal policy?

6 What are crowding out, crowding in, and international crowding out? Explain how each occurs.

7 What are the first round effects of a decrease in the money supply?

8 What are the second round effects of a decrease in the money supply?

9 What is the outcome of a decrease in the money supply?

10 What role does the foreign exchange rate play in influencing aggregate demand when there is a change in the money supply?

11 What factors determine the effectiveness of fiscal policy and monetary policy?

12 Under what conditions is fiscal policy more effective than monetary policy in stimulating aggregate demand?

13 Distinguish between the hypotheses of extreme Keynesians and extreme monetarists.

14 Explain the Keynesian-monetarist controversy about the influence of monetary policy and fiscal policy on aggregate demand.

15 Explain how the Keynesian-monetarist controversy in question 14 was settled.

16 Explain how fiscal policy and monetary policy influence the composition of aggregate demand.

17 Explain the effect of an increase in the money supply or an expansionary fiscal policy on the price level and real GDP. Be careful to distinguish between the short-run and long-run effect.

PROBLEMS

1 In the economy described in Fig. 29.1, suppose the government decreases its purchases of goods and services by $1 trillion.

a Work out the first round effects.

b Explain how real GDP and the interest rate change.

c Explain the second round effects that take the economy to a new equilibrium.

2 In the economy described in Fig. 29.1, suppose the Fed increases the money supply by $1 trillion.

a Work out the first round effects.

b Explain how real GDP and the interest rate change.

c Explain the second round effects that take the economy to a new equilibrium.

3 The economies of two countries, Alpha and Beta, are identical in every way except the following: In Alpha, a change in the interest rate of 1 percentage point (for example, from 5 percent to 6 percent) results in a $1 trillion change in the quantity of real money demanded. In Beta, a change in the interest rate of 1 percentage point results in a $0.1 trillion change in the quantity of real money demanded.

a In which economy does an increase in government purchases of goods and services have a larger effect on real GDP?

b In which economy is the crowding out effect weaker?

c In which economy does a change in the money supply have a larger effect on equilibrium real GDP?

4 The economy is in a recession, and the government wants to increase aggregate demand, stimulate exports, and increase investment. It has three policy options: increase government purchases of goods and services, decrease taxes, and increase the money supply.

a Explain the mechanisms at work under each alternative policy.

b What is the effect of each policy on the composition of aggregate demand?

c What are the short-run effects of each policy on real GDP and the price level?

d Which policy would you recommend that the government adopt?

5 The economy is at full employment, but the government is disappointed with the growth rate of real GDP. It wants to stimulate investment and at the same time avoid an increase in the price level. Suggest a combination of fiscal and monetary policies that will achieve the government's objective.

PART 11

AGGREGATE SUPPLY, INFLATION, AND RECESSION

Talking with Edmund Phelps

Edmund S. Phelps was born in Evanston, Illinois, in 1933 and is McVickar Professor of Political Economy at Columbia University. Professor Phelps was an undergraduate at Amherst College and obtained his Ph.D. from Yale in 1959. He was one of the initiators of New Macroeconomics—macroeconomics built on microeconomic foundations—and was the first to formalize the idea of the "natural rate of unemployment." Professor Phelps is a theorist—but a theorist who is driven by the desire to understand and explain the facts of unemployment and inflation and business cycles.

Why did you first study economics?

When I was going into my sophomore year at Amherst, my father prevailed on me to try a course in economics. I had guessed it was a dull subject that didn't get much beyond balance sheets or profit-and-loss statements, but I couldn't refuse my father's sole request. To my surprise, I took to the subject right away. The teacher and the textbook were part of the explanation. My professor, Jim Nelson, had a breezy style and was good at devising brain teasers for the weekly quizzes, and the textbook, by Paul Samuelson, was written in a brilliant style. I did very well, too, which was a reinforcement.

The other important point for me and a lot of students, I think, is that you are vaguely aware that you don't really have down how the various parts of the subject fit together. So you keep deciding to take one more course—until one day you find you've got a Ph.D.

What were the first questions that attracted your attention?

Even as a sophomore, I noticed that the microeconomics chapter on the theory of the firm talked

"...the New Classical models failed one empirical test after another. There are two possible reasons for these failures. The first is that expectations are not generally rational."

about employment levels and relative prices in various industries being determined by supply and demand, while the macroeconomics chapter talked about employment as determined by aggregate demand plus some "story" about rigidity or stickiness of wages and prices. It turned out I spent a big chunk of my career working on that "story."

From thinking about that fundamental theoretical question, I started asking questions about the more applied areas of monetary and fiscal policy and public finance: What difference does it make what kind of inflation targets the monetary authorities adopt? Similarly, what difference does it make what fiscal policy is chosen? Or what tax rate structure is legislated?

These questions appealed to my interest, which went way back, in notions of the just state and the good society or, in economic terms, the optimum economy. The idea of economic justice, of just rewards for contributions to the output of the economy, is a flickering passion of mine. But there are very few economists around who respond to it as I do. It's a minority taste, I guess. Like opera.

How did you hit on the idea that there is a natural rate of unemployment—an equilibrium unemployment rate—that is independent of the inflation rate? Were you driven by the internal logic of the theory or by your observations of events?

I had read enough of earlier scholars—like Lerner and Fellner—to know that the idea of an equilibrium rate of unemployment that is not influenced by inflation had to be good economics. The problem was to develop, or at least sketch, the rudiments of a theory of how the natural rate is actually determined. Then I could develop a concrete, specific explanation of why steady inflation wouldn't affect the equilibrium rate.

How do you rate the predictive power of the natural rate theory?

I kept looking over my shoulder at each month's inflation rate in 1966 and 1967 when the unemployment rate had gotten pretty low. The inflation rate rose so slowly that I worried. Fortunately, the model looked better and better as we got to 1970, and statistical studies over subsequent years have given it mounting support.

The so-called "New Classical" approach of the 1970s in many ways followed your earlier work on wages in a setting of incomplete information. What is your evaluation of the contribution of the New Classicals?

On the one hand, I admired them very much for deriving such beautiful results so clearly. But I was a bit shocked that they accepted the idea of rational expectations so uncritically. And, like a lot of others, I was repelled by the imperious attitude that to be scientific, economics had to be done their way—that you don't question the faith.

Anyway, the New Classical models failed one empirical test after another. For example, they couldn't explain in a plausible way why the economy tends to come out of even short recessions as gradually as it does—what's called the "persistence problem." Also, they couldn't explain why changes in the money supply that are perfectly anticipated by people have about as much effect on output and employment as money supply changes that are presumably unforeseen. There are two possible reasons for these failures. The first is that expectations are not generally rational. The second

is that wages and prices are not all reset simultaneously every month or quarter-year, contrary to the New Classical theory.

You are regarded as one of the founders of the New Keynesian school of macroeconomics. What is New Keynesian macroeconomics, and why do you find it attractive?

The New Keynesian school proposes that prices and wages are *not* all adjusted at the same time. When you introduce that possibility into your model, the average price level can adjust only gradually to monetary and real shocks to the economy. In other words, the effects of a shock are spread out over a long period of time. And even correctly foreseen shocks to the money supply are not offset by anticipatory changes in wages and prices.

At this time the New Keynesian model is still the model of choice for me and many others.

What is your evaluation of the real business cycle school?

The hope was that this school would show how the underlying equilibrium path of employment and output was disturbed by fundamental non-monetary factors. It would be the final achievement rounding out macroeconomic theory.

But it has not gotten as far as it could have because of its insistence on so many of the fetishes of neoclassical theory plus some new self-inflicted constraints.

For example, they can't let go of the neoclassical feature of their models that all unemployment, or nonemployment, is basically voluntary because prices and wages are all market clearing. With only a little exaggeration, you can say that the natural rate of unemployment in their models is zero. Their only way of explaining fluctuations in employment is by explaining fluctuations in the length of the workweek that workers are willing to work.

"The result is a labor market equilibrium in which not all workers can get the jobs they want and meet the qualifications . . ."

> "Any analysis of the consequences of an economic disturbance that focuses just on the short-run or on the long-run . . . runs a big risk of being wrong."

It's a shame, really. Here are these technical wizards who have for some reason decided to turn their backs on the most important development within economic theory of the twentieth century. That is the rise of a modern theory of economic equilibrium based on asymmetric information, or private information. This theory explains that employees inflict damage on their employers, abusing their relationship by quitting frivolously or shirking unconscionably or arriving shamelessly unfit to work. Just about the only thing firms can do about it is to offer any new worker hired a better rate of pay to induce better behavior. But this makes labor too expensive and hence causes some people not to be able to get jobs who otherwise could have. The result is a labor market equilibrium in which not all workers can get the jobs they want and meet the qualifications for because there is no way they can provide convincing information to a firm that they would not quit or shirk or be absent with the same frequency as the firm's existing employees—or be worse if the pay was worse.

What key principle of economics do you keep returning to in your own work?

Well, when I am wondering what economics suggests will be the consequences of some event or other, I keep rediscovering the importance of distinguishing between near-term and far-term effects. In trying to figure out the short-term or medium-term effects, I sooner or later realize I had better focus on the long-run effect first and then work backward to try to see what sort of short-run or medium-term scenario could lead to that long-run outcome. I guess the main principle is that the short term and the long term are distinct, though the one flows into the other. Any analysis of the consequences of an economic disturbance that focuses just on the short run or on the long run is apt to be misleading. And, being incomplete, it runs a big risk of also being wrong.

CHAPTER 30

PRODUCTIVITY, WAGES, AND UNEMPLOYMENT

After studying this chapter, you will be able to:

- Explain why productivity and real GDP grow
- Explain how firms decide how much labor to employ
- Explain how households decide how much labor to supply
- Explain how wages, employment, and unemployment are determined if wages are flexible
- Explain how wages, employment, and unemployment are determined if wages are "sticky"
- Derive the short-run and long-run aggregate supply curves
- Explain what makes aggregate supply and unemployment fluctuate

Incomes and Jobs

OVER THE YEARS, WE BECOME MORE PRODUCTIVE. AS A result, our economy expands and our incomes grow. On the average, in 1991, each hour of work earned us 60 percent more than it did in 1960. But Japanese and German wages have grown even more quickly than our own. What makes our productivity and wages grow over the years, and why do wages in some countries grow faster than those in the United States? ◆◆ Our economy does not expand along a smooth path. It ebbs and flows through the business cycle, sometimes growing quickly and sometimes contracting. As it does so, employment and unemployment and real GDP march in close step with each other. Sometimes the U.S. economy is in a state of recession—as it was in 1991. The official unemployment rate at the end of 1991 was close to 7 percent, up from 5.4 percent a year earlier. Add to the official unemployment rate an allowance for part-time workers who want a full-time job and "discouraged workers"—those who want jobs but have stopped looking—and the rate climbs to more than 10 percent. One third of the unemployed had been without jobs for only four weeks or less, but one third had been without jobs for between one and three months, and one out of six had not worked for more than six months. Why does unemployment occur? And what makes its rate rise and fall? ◆◆ In the eighteen months between the start of a recession in July 1990 and December 1991, 1.9 million jobs were lost in the United States. Three big employers alone—General Motors, Xerox, and IBM—eliminated more than 100,000 jobs. Why, instead of firing workers, didn't these companies cut back on everybody's hours and negotiate pay cuts?

◆ ◆ ◆ ◆ In this chapter we'll take a close look at productivity, wages, and the U.S. labor market. We'll discover what makes our productivity and wages grow, why the unemployment rate is sometimes unusually high, and what brings high unemployment rates down. We'll also take a close look at the major disagreement among macroeconomists—a disagreement about how flexible the labor market is in bringing about changes in wages to keep the quantity of labor supplied equal to the quantity demanded. ◆ ◆ Our study of productivity growth and the labor market completes a further block in the macroeconomic jigsaw puzzle—the aggregate supply block. We'll return to the long-run and short-run aggregate supply curves that you met in Chapter 24 and see how those curves are related to the labor market. We'll also see what makes aggregate supply grow and at a pace that fluctuates, bringing cycles in employment, incomes, and unemployment. ◆ ◆ Let's begin by looking at labor productivity and income growth.

Productivity and Income Growth

When we talk about *productivity,* we usually mean labor productivity—although we can measure the productivity of any factor of production. **Labor productivity** is measured as total output per person employed. To study the growth of labor productivity and its effects on wages, employment, and unemployment, we use the concept of the production function. A **production function** shows how output varies as the employment of inputs is varied. A **short-run production function** shows how output varies when the quantity of labor employed varies, holding constant the quantity of capital and the state of technology. Production functions exist for every kind of economic activity—building dams and highways or baking loaves of bread. But the production function that tells us about the relationship between *aggregate* employment and *aggregate* output is the short-run *aggregate* production function. The **short-run aggregate production function** shows how real GDP varies as the quantity of labor employed is varied, holding constant all other inputs including the capital stock and state of technology.

The table in Fig. 30.1 records part of an economy's short-run aggregate production function. In that table, we look at the aggregate quantity of labor, measured in billions of hours a year, over the range 135 billion to 155 billion. Through that range of employment, real GDP varies between \$4.35 trillion and \$4.53 trillion a year (measured in 1987 dollars). The short-run aggregate production function (*PF*) is illustrated in the graph in Fig. 30.1. The labor input is measured on the horizontal axis, and real GDP is measured on the vertical axis. The short-run production function slopes upward, indicating that more labor input produces more real GDP.

The Marginal Product of Labor

The **marginal product of labor** is the additional real GDP produced by one additional hour of labor input, holding all other inputs and technology constant. We calculate the marginal product of labor as the change in real GDP divided by the change in the quantity of labor employed. Let's do such a calculation, using Fig. 30.1.

When the labor input increases from 135 to 145 billion hours, real GDP increases from \$4.35 trillion to \$4.46 trillion—an increase of \$0.11 trillion, or \$110 billion. The marginal product of labor over this range is \$11 an hour (\$110 billion divided by 10 billion hours). Next, look at what happens at a higher level of labor input. When the labor input increases by the same 10 billion hours but from 145 billion to 155 billion hours, real GDP increases, but by less than in the previous case—by only \$0.07 trillion, or \$70 billion. Now the marginal product of labor is \$7 an hour (\$70 billion divided by 10 billion hours).

The marginal product of labor is measured by the slope of the production function. Figure 30.1 highlights this fact. The slope of the production function at point *b* is \$11 an hour. This slope is calculated as \$110 billion—the change in real GDP from \$4.35 trillion to \$4.46 trillion—divided by 10 billion hours—the change in employment from 135 billion hours to 145 billion hours. Similarly, the slope of the production function at point *d* is \$7 an hour.

FIGURE 30.1

The Short-Run Aggregate Production Function

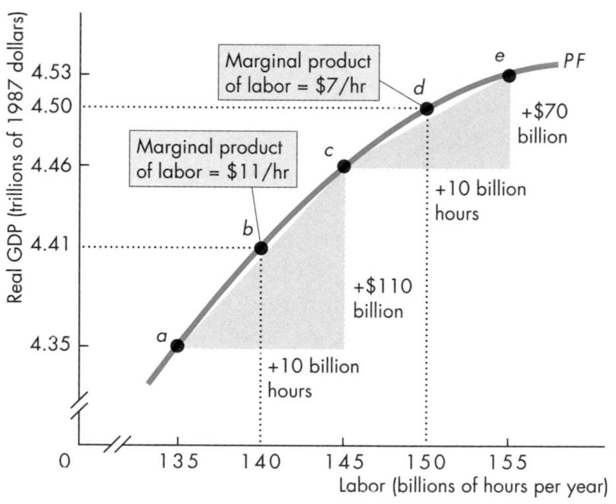

	Labor (billions of hours per year)	Real GDP (trillions of 1987 dollars per year)
a	135	4.35
b	140	4.41
c	145	4.46
d	150	4.50
e	155	4.53

The short-run aggregate production function shows the level of real GDP at each quantity of labor input, holding all other inputs constant. The table lists five points on a short-run aggregate production function. Each row tells us the amount of real GDP that can be produced by a given labor input. Points *a* through *e* in the graph correspond to the rows in the table. The curve passing through these points traces the economy's short-run aggregate production function. The marginal product of labor is highlighted in the diagram. As the labor input increases, real GDP increases but by successively smaller amounts. For example, a 10 billion hour increase in labor from 135 to 145 billion increases real GDP by $0.11 trillion—a marginal product of $11 an hour. But the same 10 billion hour increase in labor from 145 to 155 billion hours increases real GDP by only $0.07 trillion—a marginal product of $7 an hour.

Diminishing Marginal Product of Labor

The most important fact about the marginal product of labor is that it declines as the labor input increases. This phenomenon, apparent from the calculations we've just performed and visible in the figure, is called the diminishing marginal product of labor. The **diminishing marginal product of labor** is the tendency for the marginal product of labor to decline as the labor input increases, holding everything else constant.

Diminishing marginal product of labor arises because we are dealing with a *short-run* production function. As the quantity of labor employed is varied, all other inputs are held constant. Thus, although more labor can produce more output, a larger labor force operates the same capital equipment—machines and tools—as does a smaller labor force. As more people are hired, the capital equipment is worked closer and closer to its physical limits, more breakdowns occur, and bottlenecks arise. As a result, output does not increase in proportion to the amount of labor employed. The marginal product of labor declines as more labor is hired. This feature is present in almost all production processes and also in the relationship between aggregate employment and aggregate output—real GDP.

The fact that the marginal product of labor diminishes has an important influence on the demand for labor, as we shall see shortly. But first, let's look at some of the things that make the production function shift.

Economic Growth and Technological Change

Economic growth is the expansion of the economy's productive capacity. Every year, some of the economy's resources are devoted to developing new technologies to achieve greater output from a given amount of labor input. Also, resources are devoted to building new capital equipment that incorporates the most productive technologies available. Capital accumulation and technology advances shift the short-run aggregate production function upward over time. Figure 30.2 illustrates such a shift. The curve labeled PF_{92} is the same as the production function in Fig. 30.1. During 1992, capital accumulates and new technologies are incorporated into the

FIGURE 30.2

The Growth of Output

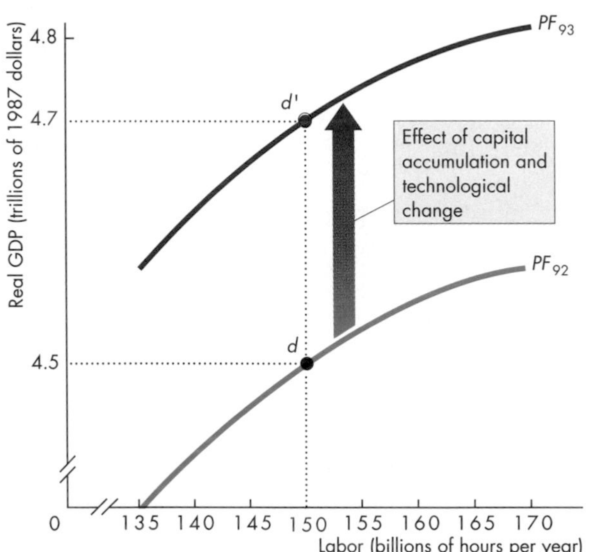

Output grows over time. The accumulation of capital and the adoption of more productive technologies make it possible to achieve a higher level of real GDP for any given labor input. For example, between 1992 and 1993 the production function shifts upward from PF_{92} to PF_{93}. A labor input of 150 billion hours produces \$4.5 trillion of real GDP in 1992 (point *d*) and \$4.7 trillion in 1993 (point *d'*).

new, more productive capital equipment. Some old, less productive capital wears out and is retired to the scrap heap. The net result is an increase in the productivity of the economy that results in an upward movement of the short-run aggregate production function to PF_{93}. When 150 billion hours of labor are employed, the economy can produce a real GDP of \$4.5 trillion in 1992 (point *d*). By 1993, that same quantity of labor can produce \$4.7 trillion (point *d'*). Each level of labor input can produce more output in 1993 than in 1992.

Variable Growth Rates

Capital accumulation and technological change do not proceed at a constant pace. In some years, the level of investment is high and the capital stock grows quickly. In other years—recession years—investment decreases and the capital stock grows slowly. Also, there are fluctuations in the pace of technological change. Technological change has two stages, invention and innovation. **Invention** is the discovery of a new technique; **innovation** is the act of putting a new technique to work. At some times, lots of new things are being discovered but not being put to use—invention is rapid but innovation is slow. It is the pace of innovation that influences the growth rate of productivity. Although the short-run aggregate production function shifts upward over time, occasionally it shifts downward—productivity decreases. Negative influences, or shocks, that make the aggregate production function shift downward are widespread droughts, major disruptions to international trade, civil unrest, or war. A serious disruption of international trade occurred in 1974 when the Organization of Petroleum Exporting Countries (OPEC) placed an embargo on oil exports. This deprived the industrialized world of one of its most crucial raw materials. Firms could not obtain all the fuel they needed, and as a result the labor force was not able to produce as much output as normal. As a consequence, the short-run aggregate production function shifted downward in 1974.

Let's take a closer look at the short-run aggregate production function in the United States and see what it tells about our productivity growth.

U.S. Productivity Growth

We can examine productivity growth in the United States by looking at the U.S. short-run aggregate production function shown in Fig. 30.3. Concentrate first on the blue dots in this figure. There is a dot for each year between 1960 and 1991, and each one represents aggregate employment and real GDP for a particular year. For example, the dot for 1960 tells us that in 1960 labor hours were 132 billion and real GDP was \$2 trillion; in 1991, labor hours were 210 billion and real GDP was \$4.9 trillion.

These two dots together with the other dots in the figure do not all lie on the same short-run aggregate production function. Instead, each dot lies on its own short-run aggregate production function. Each year the stock of capital equipment and the state of technology change, so the economy's productive potential usually is higher than in the year before. The production function for 1960 is PF_{60}, and that for 1991 is PF_{91}.

The 1991 short-run aggregate production function is 88 percent higher than the 1960 short-run aggregate production function. This fact means that

FIGURE 30.3

The U.S. Short-Run Aggregate Production Function

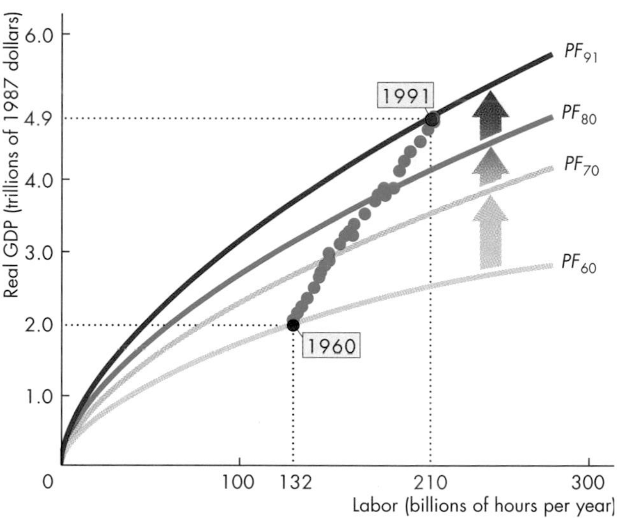

The dots in the figure show real GDP and aggregate hours of labor employed in the United States for each year between 1960 and 1991. For example, in 1960, labor input was 132 billion hours and real GDP was $2 trillion. In 1991, labor input was 210 billion hours and real GDP was $4.9 trillion. The dots do not lie on one short-run aggregate production function. Instead, the short-run aggregate production function shifts from year to year as capital accumulates and technologies change. The figure shows the short-run aggregate production functions for 1960 and 1991—PF_{60} and PF_{91}. The 1991 production function is 88 percent higher than that for 1960. For example, the 132 billion hours of labor that produced $2 trillion of real GDP in 1960 would have produced $3.7 trillion of real GDP in 1991. Similarly, the 210 billion hours of labor that produced $4.9 trillion of real GDP in 1991 would have produced approximately $2.6 trillion of real GDP in 1960.

if employment in 1991 had been the same as it was in 1960, real GDP in 1991 would have been $3.7 trillion. Equivalently, if employment in 1960 had been the same as it was in 1991, real GDP in 1960 would have been $2.6 trillion.

The Productivity Slowdown

The short-run production function shifts upward over time because we become more productive—a given amount of labor produces an increased amount of output. But labor productivity does not grow at an even pace, and during the 1970s we experienced a productivity slowdown. You can see this slowdown in Fig. 30.3. In addition to the production functions for 1960 and 1991 that we've just discussed, the figure shows the production functions for 1970 (PF_{70}) and 1980 (PF_{80}). You can see that there was a large shift in the production function between 1960 and 1970. During that decade, productivity increased by 36 percent. But between 1970 and 1980, the production function shift was smaller. During the 1970s, productivity increased by only 17 percent. Productivity growth increased during the 1980s, but it did not get back to its 1960s performance.

There are several reasons for the slowdown in U.S. productivity growth during the 1970s. Two of the most important are energy price shocks and changes in the composition of output. First, energy prices quadrupled in 1973–1974 and increased sharply again in 1979–1980, forcing firms to find energy-saving, labor-using, and capital-using methods of production. Second, as our economy expanded, the composition of output changed. Agriculture and manufacturing contracted, and services expanded. Productivity growth is the fastest in agriculture and manufacturing and slowest in services; so as the composition of output changed toward a greater emphasis on services, average productivity growth slowed down. Other possible sources of slow productivity growth in the United States compared with some other countries and some possible solutions to the problem are examined in Reading Between the Lines on pp. 822–823.

REVIEW

A production function tells us how the output that can be produced varies as inputs are varied. A short-run production function tells us how the output that can be produced varies as the employment of labor varies, holding everything else constant. The short-run aggregate production function tells us how real GDP varies as total labor hours vary. The marginal product of labor—the increase in real GDP resulting from a one-hour increase of labor input—diminishes as the labor input increases. ◆◆ The short-run production function usually shifts upward from year to year,

The Productivity Slowdown

The New York Times, February 9, 1992

Attention America! Snap Out of It!

BY STEVEN GREENHOUSE

After years of watching Japan increase its manufacturing might, Americans have awakened to the dangers of losing the industrial base that long made their nation the envy of the world. At long last, Americans of all stripes, Democrat and Republican, white collar and blue, are groping for ways to close the competitiveness gap that has allowed Japan to muscle into the lead in such key industries as cars and computer chips.

Some . . . experts say the Federal Reserve should pump $25 billion into the nation's hobbled banks by purchasing their shares, which would enable them to lend some $250 billion to American companies for modernization.

. . . Other experts say the country should adopt the German job-training system in which many high school students spend time in factories learning to master modern technologies and solve problems in teams.

Some say Washington should allow banks to own shares in industrial companies, as they do in Germany and Japan. . . .

A New Cottage Industry

These are just a few of the ideas being churned out by a new cottage industry in which hundreds of economists, think tanks, professors, politicians, columnists, and management consultants ruminate full time on how to improve America's competitiveness.

To a surprising degree, these deep thinkers . . . have reached a consensus on many prescriptions for America's economic ills. They generally agree that the nation needs to take the following steps.

- Increase savings to provide business with more money to invest in buildings and machines that increase productivity. . . .
- Step up efforts to train American workers so they can adapt to the technologies and more flexible factories of tomorrow.
- Get companies to think long-term so they will make the strategic investments in equipment, training, and research. . . .
- Rein in health-care spending, which puts a heavy burden on American industry. . . .
- Spend more on research and development so that industry not only maintains its lead in innovation but also improves its ability to turn ideas into hot-selling products.
- Invest more in public structures like highways, bridges, railways, and airports. . . .

The Essence of the Story

A consensus has emerged on the country's competitiveness problem. It has the following elements:

- Increase saving and invest more in buildings and machines.
- Improve training of American workers.
- Encourage companies to think long-term.
- Cut health care costs.
- Spend more on research and development.
- Invest more in public structures (highways, bridges, railways, and airports).

More controversial proposed solutions are

- Inject Federal Reserve money into banks.
- Put more high school students into factories where they can learn to master modern technologies and solve problems in teams.
- Allow banks to own shares in industrial companies.

Background and Analysis

Between 1960 and 1991, income per person grew in the United States by 82 percent, in Germany by 138 percent, and in Japan by 441 percent.

These *apparently* diverging income levels are shown in Fig. 1.

But in 1960, income per person in the United States was $7,400, in Germany it was $5,200, and in Japan it was $2,200. (These amounts are based on U.S. dollars valued at 1980 prices.)

Because in 1960 the U.S. income level was much higher than Germany's and Japan's, the faster income growth in Germany and Japan has enabled them to close the gap on the United States.

But, as Fig. 2 shows, these countries have not *overtaken* the United States.

During the years 1989–1991, income per person in the United States decreased, while in Germany and Japan it continued to increase.

The U.S. slowdown in 1989–1991 looks more like a business cycle slowdown—similar to that in 1982 (see Fig. 2)—than a permanent change in trend.

The U.S. productivity slowdown is real, but the reactions of the "experts" and their proposed solutions need careful evaluation.

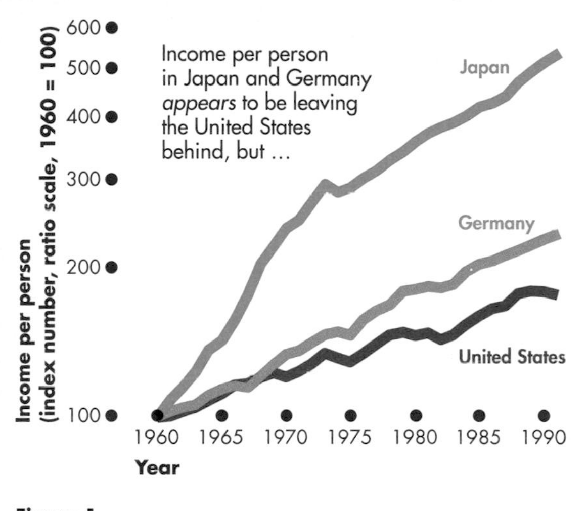

Figure 1

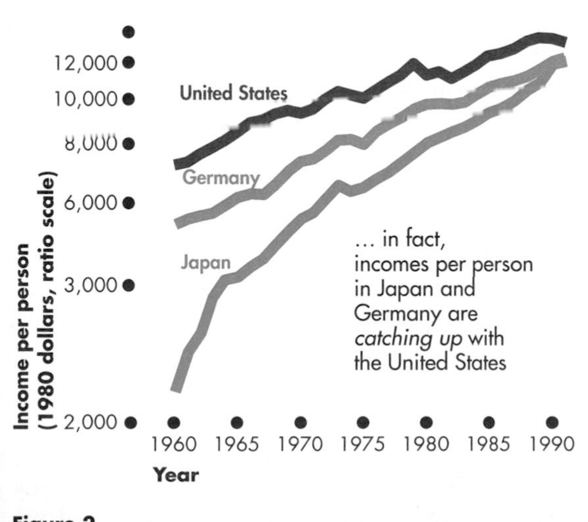

Figure 2

Increasing saving and investment, improving the training of American workers, "thinking long-term," spending more on research and development, and investing more in public structures will pay off only if each individual action passes the market test of delivering a rate of return that is greater than or equal to the next best alternative.

Cutting health care costs is fine if that does not mean cutting health care. But one of the benefits of a high income is a high standard of health care, and, to some degree, high costs in the United States reflect a high standard of care.

The proposal that the Fed pump $25 billion into the banks would increase aggregate *demand*, but it is not clear that aggregate *supply* would increase by much.

The proposal that the banks buy shares in industrial companies would increase the riskiness of the banks, imposing a cost that needs to be weighed against any possible benefits.

but on occasion it shifts downward. Capital accumulation and technological advances shift the short-run aggregate production function upward. Shocks such as droughts, disruptions of international trade, or civil and political unrest shift the production function downward. The short-run aggregate production function in the United States shifted upward by 88 percent between 1960 and 1991. ◆

We've seen that output in any year depends on the position of the short-run aggregate production function and on the quantity of labor employed. Even if the short-run aggregate production function shifts upward, it is still possible for output to fall because of a fall in employment. For example, in 1991, employment and real GDP fell as the economy went into recession. To determine the level of output, we need to understand not only the influences on the short-run aggregate production function but also those on the level of employment. To determine the level of employment, we need to study the demand for and supply of labor and how the market allocates labor to jobs. We'll begin by studying the demand for labor.

The Demand for Labor

The **quantity of labor demanded** is the number of labor hours hired by all the firms in an economy. The **demand for labor** is the quantity of labor demanded at each real wage rate. The **real wage rate** is the wage per hour expressed in constant dollars—for example, the wage per hour expressed in 1987 dollars. The wage rate expressed in *current dollars* is called the **money wage rate.** A real wage rate expressed in 1987 dollars tells us what today's money wage rate would buy if prices today were the same as in 1987. We calculate the real wage rate by dividing the money wage rate by the GDP deflator and multiplying by 100. For example, if the money wage rate is $7 an hour and the GDP deflator is 140, the real wage rate is $5 ($7 divided by 140 and multiplied by 100 equals $5).

We can represent the demand for labor as a schedule or a curve. The table in Fig. 30.4 sets out an example of a demand for labor schedule. Row *b* tells us that at a real wage rate of $11 an hour, 140 billion hours of labor (per year) are demanded. The other rows of the table are read in a similar way. The demand for labor schedule is graphed as the demand for labor curve (*LD*). Each point on the curve corresponds to the row identified by the same letter in the table.

Why is the quantity of labor demanded influenced by the *real* wage rate? Why isn't it the *money* wage rate that affects the quantity of labor demanded? Also, why does the quantity of labor demanded increase as the real wage rate decreases? That is, why does the demand for labor curve slope downward? We're now going to answer these questions.

Diminishing Marginal Product and the Demand for Labor

Firms are in business to maximize profits. Each worker that a firm hires adds to its costs and increases its output. Up to a point, the extra output produced by the worker is worth more to the firm than the wages the firm has to pay. But each additional hour of labor hired produces less output than the previous hour—the marginal product of labor diminishes. As the amount of labor employed increases and the capital equipment employed is constant, more workers have to use the same machines and the plant operates closer and closer to its physical limits. Output increases, but it does not increase in proportion to the increase in labor input. As the firm hires more workers, it eventually reaches the point at which the revenue from selling the extra output produced by an additional hour of labor equals the hourly wage rate. If the firm hires even one more hour of labor, the extra cost incurred will exceed the revenue brought in from selling the extra output. The firm will not employ that additional hour of labor. It hires the quantity of labor such that the revenue brought in by the last hour of labor input equals the money wage rate.

To see why it is the *real* wage rate, rather than the money wage rate, that affects the quantity of labor demanded, let's consider an example.

FIGURE 30.4

Demand for Labor

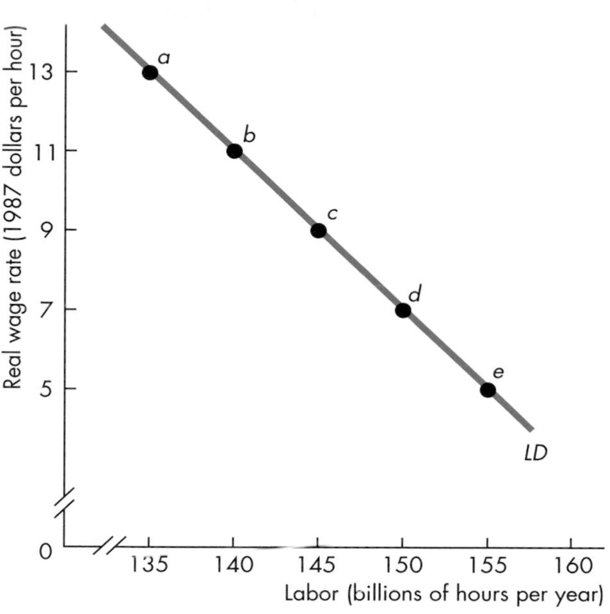

	Real wage rate (1987 dollars per hour)	Quantity of labor demanded (billions of hours per year)
a	13	135
b	11	140
c	9	145
d	7	150
e	5	155

The quantity of labor demanded increases as the real wage rate decreases, as illustrated by the labor demand schedule in the table and the demand for labor curve (*LD*). Each row in the table tells us the quantity of labor demanded at a given real wage rate and corresponds to a point on the labor demand curve. For example, when the real wage rate is $7 an hour, the quantity of labor demanded is 150 billion hours a year (point *d*). The demand for labor curve slopes downward because it pays firms to hire labor as long as the firm's marginal product of labor is greater than or equal to the real wage rate. The lower the real wage rate, the larger is the number of workers whose marginal product exceeds that real wage rate.

The Demand for Labor in a Soda Factory

A soda factory employs 400 hours of labor. The additional output produced by the last hour hired is 11 bottles of soda. That is, the marginal product of labor is 11 bottles of soda per hour. Soda sells for 50¢ a bottle, so the revenue brought in from selling these 11 bottles is $5.50. The money wage rate is also $5.50 an hour. This last hour of labor hired brings in as much revenue as the wages paid out, so it just pays the firm to hire that hour of labor. The firm is paying a real wage rate that is exactly the same as the marginal product of labor—11 bottles of soda. That is, the firm's real wage rate is equal to the money wage rate of $5.50 an hour divided by the price of soda, 50¢ a bottle.

A Change in the Real Wage Rate Let's work out what happens when the real wage rate changes. Suppose the money wage rate increases to $11 an hour while the price of soda remains constant at 50¢ a bottle. The real wage rate has now increased to 22 bottles of soda—equal to the money wage of $11 an hour divided by 50¢ a bottle, the price of a bottle of soda. The last hour of labor hired now costs $11 but brings in only $5.50 of extra revenue. It does not pay the firm to hire this hour of labor. The firm decreases the quantity of labor employed until the marginal product of labor brings in $11 of revenue. This occurs when the marginal product of labor is 22 bottles of soda—that is, 22 bottles at 50¢ a bottle sell for $11. The marginal product of labor is again equal to the real wage rate. But to make the marginal product of labor equal to the real wage rate, the firm has to decrease the quantity of labor employed. Thus, when the real wage rate increases, the quantity of labor demanded decreases.

In the example we've just worked through, the real wage rate increased because the money wage rate increased with a constant output price. But the same outcome occurs if the money wage rate remains constant and the output price decreases. For example, if the wage rate remains at $5.50 an hour while the price of soda falls to 25¢ a bottle, the real wage rate is 22 bottles of soda and the soda bottling factory hires the amount of labor that makes the marginal product of labor equal to 22 bottles.

A Change in the Money Wage Rate with a Constant Real Wage To see why the money wage rate does not affect the quantity of labor demanded, suppose that the money wage rate and all prices double. The money wage rate increases to $11 an hour, and the price of soda increases to $1 a bottle. The soda factory is in the same real situation as before. It pays $11 for the last hour of labor employed and sells the output produced by that labor for $11. The money wage rate has doubled from $5.50 to $11 an hour, but nothing *real* has changed. The real wage rate is still 11 bottles of soda. As far as the firm is concerned, 400 hours is still the right quantity of labor to hire. The money wage rate has changed, but the real wage rate and the quantity of labor demanded have remained constant.

The Demand for Labor in the Economy

The demand for labor in the economy as a whole is determined in the same way as in the soda factory. Thus the quantity of labor demanded depends on the real wage rate, not the money wage rate, and the higher the real wage rate, the smaller is the quantity of labor demanded.

We now know why the quantity of labor demanded depends on the real wage rate and why the demand for labor curve slopes downward, but what makes it shift?

Changes in the Demand for Labor

When the marginal product of each hour of labor changes, the demand for labor changes and the demand for labor curve shifts. The accumulation of capital and the development of new technologies are constantly increasing the marginal product of each hour of labor. We've already seen one effect of such changes. They shift the short-run aggregate production function upward, as shown in Fig. 30.2. At the same time, they make the short-run aggregate production function *steeper*. Anything that makes the short-run production function steeper increases the marginal product of each hour of labor—increases the extra output obtained from one additional hour of labor. At a given real wage rate, firms will increase the amount of labor they hire until the revenue brought in from selling the extra output produced by the last hour of labor input equals the hourly wage. Thus as the short-run aggregate production function shifts upward, the demand for labor curve also shifts to the right.

In general, the demand for labor curve shifts to the right over time. But there are fluctuations in the pace at which the demand for labor curve shifts that match the fluctuations in the short-run aggregate production function. Let's look at the demand for labor in the United States and see how it has changed over the period since 1960.

The U.S. Demand for Labor

Figure 30.5 shows the average real wage rate and the quantity of labor employed in each year between 1960 and 1991. For example, in 1991 the real wage was $13.85 an hour (in 1987 dollars) and 210 billion hours of labor were employed.

FIGURE 30.5

The U.S. Demand for Labor

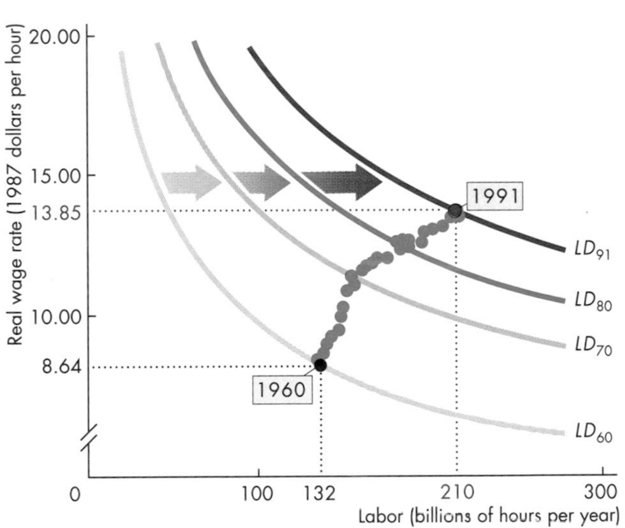

The figure shows the quantity of labor employed and the average real wage rate in the United States from 1960 to 1991. For example, in 1960 the real wage rate was $8.64 an hour and 132 billion hours of labor were employed. In 1991 the real wage rate was $13.85 an hour and 210 billion hours of labor were employed. These two points (and the dots for the years between them) do not lie on a single demand for labor curve. The demand for labor curve has shifted as a result of shifts in the short-run aggregate production function. The figure shows the demand curves for 1960 and 1991—LD_{60} and LD_{91}. Over time, the demand for labor curve has shifted to the right.

The figure shows four demand for labor curves, for 1960, 1970, 1980, and 1991. Between 1960 and 1991, the short-run aggregate production function shifted upward and the marginal product of labor increased. If the quantity of labor employed in 1991 had been the same as in 1960 (132 billion hours), the real wage rate would have been $16.67 per hour. If the quantity of labor employed in 1960 had been as high as that in 1991 (210 billion hours), the real wage rate in that year would have been only $7.10 per hour.

Another View of the Productivity Slowdown

Figure 30.5 also gives another view of the productivity slowdown of the 1970s and 1980s. The demand for labor curve is also the marginal product of labor curve. Thus shifts in the demand curve reflect changes in the marginal productivity of labor. You can see that the productivity of labor increased much more during the 1960s than it did during the two subsequent decades. The demand curve shifted farther between 1960 (LD_{60}) and 1970 (LD_{70}) than it did between and 1970 (LD_{70}) and 1980 (LD_{80}).

REVIEW

The quantity of labor demanded is the quantity of labor hours hired by all firms in the economy. It depends on the real wage rate. For an individual firm, the real wage rate is the money wage rate paid to the worker divided by the price for which the firm's output sells. For the economy as a whole, the real wage rate is the money wage rate divided by the price level. The lower the real wage rate, the greater is the quantity of labor demanded. The demand for labor curve slopes downward. ◆ ◆ The demand for labor curve shifts because of shifts in the short-run aggregate production function. An increase in the capital stock or advances in technology embodied in the capital stock shift the short-run aggregate production function upward and increase the marginal product of labor. The demand for labor curve shifts to the right, but at an uneven pace. ◆

Let's now turn to the other side of the labor market and see how the supply of labor is determined.

The Supply of Labor

The **quantity of labor supplied** is the number of hours of labor services that households supply to firms. The **supply of labor** is the quantity of labor supplied at each real wage rate.

We can represent the supply of labor as a schedule or a curve. The table in Fig. 30.6 shows a supply of labor schedule. For example, row *b* tells us that at a real wage rate of $3 an hour, 140 billion hours of labor (per year) are supplied. The other rows of the table are read in a similar way. The supply of labor schedule is graphed as the supply of labor curve (*LS*). Each point on the *LS* curve represents the row identified by the same letter in the table. As the real wage rate increases, the quantity of labor supplied increases. The supply of labor curve slopes upward.

But why does the quantity of labor supplied increase when the real wage rate increases? There are two reasons:

- Hours per worker increase.
- The labor force participation rate increases.

The Determination of Hours per Worker

In choosing how many hours to work, a household has to decide how to allocate its time between work and other activities. If a household chooses not to work for an hour, it does not get paid for that hour. The opportunity cost of not working an hour is what the household really gives up by not working. It is all the goods and services that the household could buy with the hourly money wage. So the opportunity cost of an hour of time spent not working is the real hourly wage rate.

What happens to people's willingness to work if the real wage rate increases? Such a change has two opposing effects:

- A substitution effect
- An income effect

Substitution Effect The substitution effect of a change in the real wage rate works in exactly the

FIGURE 30.6

The Supply of Labor

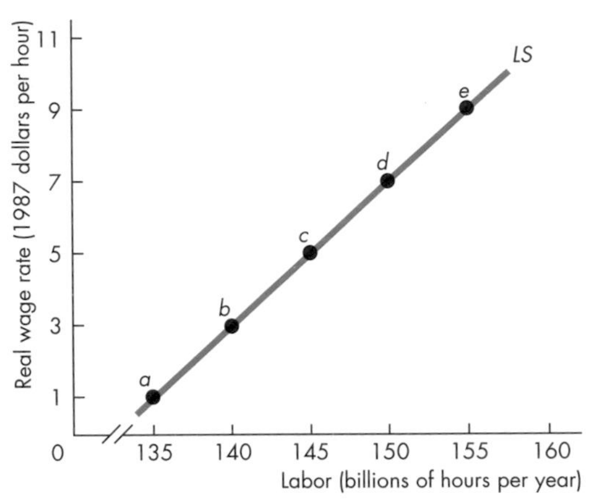

	Real wage rate (1987 dollars per hour)	Quantity of labor demanded (billions of hours per year)
a	1	135
b	3	140
c	5	145
d	7	150
e	9	155

The quantity of labor supplied increases as the real wage rate increases, as illustrated by the labor supply schedule in the table and the supply of labor curve (*LS*). Each row of the table tells us the quantity of labor supplied at a given real wage rate and corresponds to a point on the labor supply curve. For example, when the real wage rate is $7 an hour, the quantity of labor supplied is 150 billion hours a year (point *d*). The supply of labor curve slopes upward because households work longer hours, on the average, at higher real wage rates and more households participate in the labor force. These responses are reinforced by intertemporal substitution—the retiming of work to take advantage of temporarily high wages.

same way that a change in the price of tapes affects the quantity of tapes demanded. Just as tapes have a price, so does time. As we've just noted, the real hourly wage rate is the opportunity cost of an hour spent not working. A higher real wage rate increases the opportunity cost of time and makes time itself a more valuable commodity. This higher opportunity cost of not working encourages people to reduce their nonwork time and increase the time spent working. Thus as the real wage rate increases, more hours of work are supplied.

Income Effect But a higher real wage rate also increases people's incomes. The higher a person's income, the greater is his or her demand for all the different types of goods and services. One such "good" is leisure—the time to do pleasurable things that don't generate an income. Thus a higher real wage rate also makes people want to enjoy longer leisure hours and supply fewer hours of work.

Which of these two effects dominates depends on each individual's attitude toward work and also on the real wage rate. Attitudes toward work, though varying across individuals, do not change much, on the average, over time. But the real wage rate does change and brings changes in the quantity of labor supplied. At a very low real wage rate, the substitution effect is stronger than the income effect. That is, as the real wage rate increases, the inducement to substitute working time for leisure time is stronger than the inducement to spend part of a larger income on more leisure hours. As a consequence, as the real wage rate increases, the quantity of labor supplied increases.

At a high enough real wage rate, the income effect becomes stronger than the substitution effect. As the real wage increases, the inducement to spend more of the additional income on leisure time is stronger than the inducement to economize on leisure time.

Some people undoubtedly receive such a high real wage rate that a further increase would cause them to reduce their hours of work. But for most of us a higher real wage rate coaxes us to work more. Thus, on the average, the higher the real wage rate, the more hours each person works.

The Participation Rate

The **labor force participation rate** is the proportion of the working age population that is either employed or unemployed (but seeking employment). For a variety of reasons, people differ in their willingness to work. Some people have more productive opportunities at home and so need a bigger inducement to quit those activities and work for someone else.

Other individuals place a very high value on leisure, and they require a high real wage to induce them to do any work at all. These considerations suggest each person has a reservation wage. A **reservation wage** is the lowest wage at which a person will supply any labor. Below that wage, a person will not work.

Those people who have a reservation wage below or equal to the actual real wage will be in the labor force, and those who have a reservation wage above the real wage will not be in the labor force. The higher the real wage rate, the larger is the number of people whose reservation wage falls below the real wage rate and hence the larger is the labor force participation rate.

Reinforcing and strengthening the increase in hours worked per household and the labor force participation rate is an intertemporal substitution effect on the quantity of labor supplied.

Intertemporal Substitution

Households have to decide not only whether to work but also *when* to work. This decision is based not just on the current real wage but also on the current real wage relative to expected future real wages.

Suppose that the real wage rate is higher today than it is expected to be later on. How does this fact affect a person's labor supply decision? It encourages more work today and less in the future. Thus the higher is today's real wage rate relative to what is expected in the future (other things being constant), the larger is the supply of labor.

Temporarily high real wages are similar to a high rate of return. If real wages are temporarily high, people can obtain a higher rate of return on their work effort by enjoying a smaller amount of leisure and supplying more labor in such a period. By investing in some work now and taking the return in more leisure time later, they can obtain a higher overall level of consumption of goods and services and of leisure.

REVIEW

The opportunity cost of time is the real wage rate—the goods and services that can be bought with the income from an hour of work. An increase in the real wage rate, other things being equal, increases the supply of hours per worker and increases the labor force participation rate. A higher *current* real wage relative to the expected future real wage encourages people to supply more labor today and less in the future. ◆

We've now seen why, as the real wage rate increases, the quantity of labor supplied increases—why the supply of labor curve slopes upward. Let's next bring the two sides of the labor market together and study the determination of wages and employment.

Wages and Employment

We've discovered that as the real wage rate increases, the quantity of labor demanded declines and the quantity of labor supplied increases. We now want to study how the two sides of the labor market interact to determine the real wage rate, employment, and unemployment.

There is disagreement about how the labor market works, and this disagreement is the main source of current controversy in macroeconomics.

There are two leading theories about the labor market:

- Flexible wage theory
- Sticky wage theory

The flexible wage theory is built on the assumption that the labor market operates in a similar way to the markets for goods and services, with the real wage rate continuously and freely adjusting to keep the quantity demanded equal to the quantity supplied. The sticky wage theory is based on the assumption that wage contracts *fix* the money wage rate—hence the name sticky wages. If the money wage rate is sticky, the real wage rate does not continuously adjust to keep the quantity of labor demanded equal to the quantity supplied. Let's look at these two theories, beginning with the flexible wage theory.

The Flexible Wage Theory

Most people's wages—*money wages*—are determined by wage contracts that run for at least one year and often for two or three years. Doesn't this fact mean that money wages are not flexible? Not necessarily. Money wage rates, even those that are fixed by wage contracts, can and do adjust upward or downward. For example, some workers receive bonus payments in good times and lose those bonuses in bad times. Some workers get overtime at high rates of pay in good times but only get work at the normal hourly wage rate in bad times. Workers often get unusually rapid promotion to jobs with a higher wage rate in good times and get stuck on a lower rung of the promotion ladder in bad times. Thus fluctuations in bonuses, overtime pay, and the pace of promotion result in changes in the average wage rate even when wage rate schedules do not change.

The flexible wage theory of the labor market assumes that these sources of wage adjustment are sufficient to achieve a continuous balance between the quantities of labor supplied and demanded. The economy remains at full employment.

Figure 30.7 illustrates the theory. The demand for labor curve is *LD*, and the supply of labor curve is *LS*. This market determines an equilibrium real wage rate of $7 an hour and a quantity of labor employed of 150 billion hours. If the real wage rate is below its equilibrium level of $7 an hour, the quantity of labor demanded exceeds the quantity supplied. In such a situation, the real wage rate will rise, since firms are willing to offer higher and higher wages in order to overcome their labor shortages. The real wage rate will continue to rise until it reaches $7 an hour, at which point there will be no shortage of labor.

If the real wage rate is higher than its equilibrium level of $7 an hour, the quantity of labor supplied exceeds the quantity demanded. In this situation, households are not able to get all the work they want and firms find it easy to hire labor. Firms will have an incentive to cut the wage, and households will accept the lower wage to get a job. The real wage rate will fall until it reaches $7 an hour, at which point every household is satisfied with the quantity of labor it is supplying.

Changes in Wages and Employment The flexible wage theory makes predictions about wages and employment that are identical to the predictions of the demand and supply model we studied in Chapter 4. An increase in the demand for labor shifts the demand for labor curve to the right and increases both the real wage rate and the quantity of labor employed. A decrease in the demand for labor shifts the demand for labor curve to the left and decreases both the real wage rate and the quantity of labor employed. An increase in the supply of labor shifts the supply of labor curve to the right, lowering the real wage rate and increasing employment. A decrease in the supply of labor shifts the supply of labor curve to the left, raising the real wage rate and decreasing employment.

The demand for labor increases over time because capital accumulation and technological change increase the marginal product of labor. The supply of labor increases over time because the working age population is steadily increasing. Rightward shifts in

FIGURE 30.7

Equilibrium with Flexible Wages

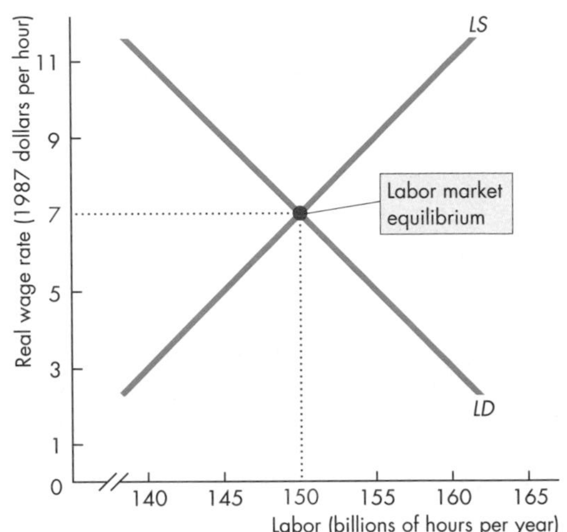

Equilibrium occurs when the real wage rate makes the quantity of labor demanded equal to the quantity supplied. This equilibrium occurs at a real wage rate of $7 an hour. At that real wage rate, 150 billion hours of labor are employed. At real wage rates below $7 an hour, the quantity of labor demanded exceeds the quantity supplied and the real wage rate rises. At real wage rates above $7 an hour, the quantity of labor supplied exceeds the quantity of labor demanded and the real wage rate falls.

the demand for labor curve have generally been larger than shifts in the supply of labor curve, so, over time, both the quantity of labor employed and the real wage rate have increased.

Aggregate Supply with Flexible Wages

The flexible wage theory of the labor market has a remarkable implication for the aggregate supply of goods and services—of real GDP. The quantity of real GDP supplied is independent of the price level.

Recall the definitions of the short-run aggregate supply curve and the long-run aggregate supply curve (Chapter 24, pp. 645–648). The short-run aggregate supply curve tells us how the quantity of real GDP supplied varies as the price level varies, holding everything else constant. The long-run aggregate supply curve tells us how the quantity of real GDP varies as the price level varies when wages change along with the price level to achieve full employment.

According to the flexible wage theory of the labor market, the money wage rate *always* adjusts to determine a real wage rate that brings equality between the quantity of labor demanded and quantity supplied. That is, as the price level changes, the money wage rate adjusts so as to keep the real wage rate constant. The labor market remains in equilibrium—at full employment. The aggregate supply curve generated by the flexible wage model of the labor market is the same as the long-run aggregate supply curve. It is vertical. Let's see why.

Figure 30.8 illustrates the derivation of the long-run aggregate supply curve. Part (a) shows the aggregate labor market. The demand and supply curves shown are exactly the same as those in Fig. 30.7. The equilibrium, a real wage of $7 an hour and employment of 150 billion hours, is exactly the same equilibrium that was determined in that figure.

Figure 30.8(b) shows the short-run aggregate production function. This production function is the one shown in Fig. 30.1. We know from the labor market (part a) that 150 billion hours of labor are employed. Part (b) tells us that when 150 billion hours of labor are employed, real GDP is $4.5 trillion.

Figure 30.8(c) shows the long-run aggregate supply curve. That curve tells us that real GDP is $4.5 trillion regardless of the price level. To see why, look at what happens to real GDP when the price level changes.

Start with a GDP deflator of 100. In this case, the economy is at point *j* in part (c) of the figure. That is, the GDP deflator is 100, and real GDP is $4.5 trillion. We've determined, in part (a), that the real wage rate is $7. With a GDP deflator of 100, the money wage rate (the wage rate in current dollars) is also $7 an hour.

What happens to real GDP if the GDP deflator falls from 100 to 80 (a 20 percent decrease in the price level)? If the money wage rate remains at $7 an hour, the real wage rate rises and the quantity of labor supplied exceeds the quantity demanded. In such a situation, the money wage rate will fall. It falls to $5.60 an hour. With a money wage rate of $5.60 and a GDP deflator of 80, the real wage rate is still $7 ($5.60 divided by 80 and multiplied by 100 equals $7). With the lower money wage rate but a constant real wage rate, employment remains at 150 billion hours (full employment) and real GDP is constant at $4.5 trillion. The economy is at point *k* in Fig. 30.8(c).

What happens to real GDP if the GDP deflator rises from 100 to 120 (a 20 percent increase in the price level)? If the money wage rate stays at $7 an hour, the real wage rate falls and the quantity of labor demanded exceeds the quantity supplied. In such a situation, the money wage rate rises. It will keep rising until it reaches $8.40 an hour. At that money wage rate, the real wage rate is $7 ($8.40 divided by 120 and multiplied by 100 equals $7) and the quantity of labor demanded equals the quantity supplied. Employment remains at 150 billion hours (full employment), and real GDP remains at $4.5 trillion. The economy is at point *l* in Fig. 30.8(c).

Points *j*, *k*, and *l* in part (c) all lie on the long-run aggregate supply curve. We have considered only three price levels. We could have considered any price level, and we would have reached the same conclusion: a change in the price level generates a proportionate change in the money wage rate and leaves the real wage rate unchanged. Employment and real GDP are also unchanged. The long-run aggregate supply curve is vertical.

Fluctuations in Real GDP In the flexible wage theory of the labor market, fluctuations in real GDP arise from shifts in the long-run aggregate supply curve. Technological change and capital accumulation shift the short-run aggregate production function upward and also shift the demand for labor

FIGURE 30.8

Aggregate Supply with Flexible Wages

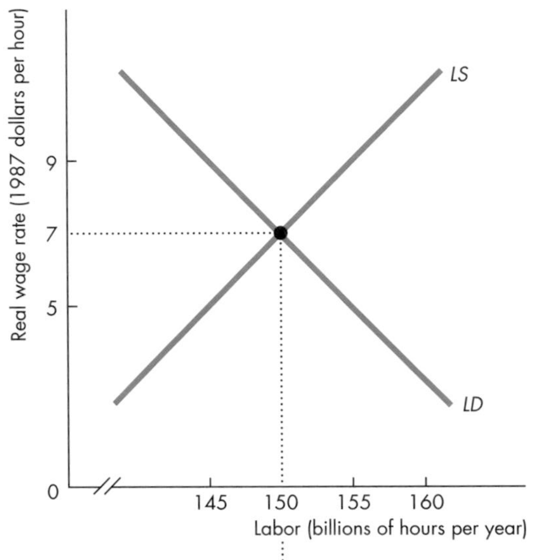

(a) Labor market

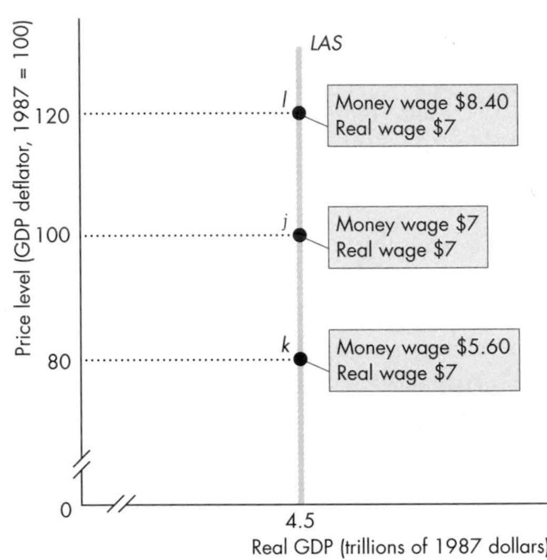

(c) Long-run aggregate supply curve

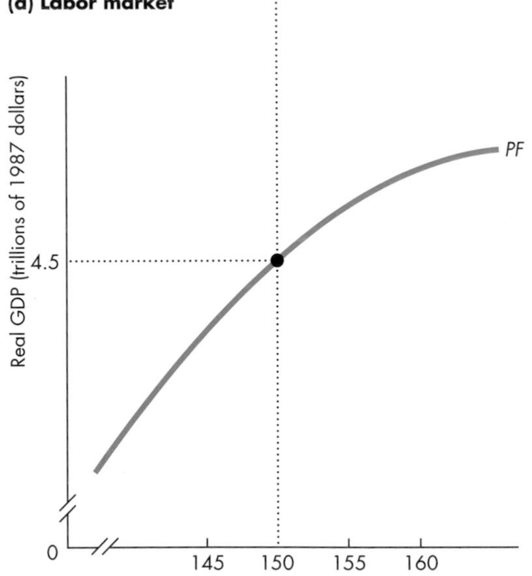

(b) Short-run aggregate production function

Labor market equilibrium determines the real wage rate and employment. The demand for labor curve (*LD*) intersects the supply of labor curve (*LS*) at a real wage rate of $7 an hour and 150 billion hours of employment (part a). The short-run aggregate production function (*PF*) and employment of 150 billion hours determine real GDP at $4.5 trillion (part b). Real GDP supplied is $4.5 trillion regardless of the price level. The long-run aggregate supply curve is the vertical line (*LAS*) in part (c). If the GDP deflator is 100, the economy is at point *j*. If the GDP deflator is 120, the money wage rate rises to keep the real wage rate constant at $7 an hour, employment remains at 150 billion hours, and real GDP is $4.5 trillion. The economy is at point *l*. If the GDP deflator is 80, the money wage rate falls to keep the real wage rate constant at $7 an hour, employment remains at 150 billion hours, and real GDP is $4.5 trillion. The economy is at point *k*.

curve to the right. Growth of the working age population shifts the supply of labor curve to the right. These changes in economic conditions change equilibrium employment and full-employment real GDP and also shift the long-run aggregate supply curve. Most of the time these changes result in the long-run aggregate supply curve moving to the right—increasing real GDP. But the pace at which the long-run aggregate supply curve shifts to the right varies, leading to fluctuations in the growth rate of real

GDP. Occasionally, the short-run aggregate production function shifts downward. When it does so, the demand for labor curve shifts to the left, employment falls, and the long-run aggregate supply curve shifts to the left, decreasing real GDP.

REVIEW

The flexible wage theory of the labor market maintains that the money wage rate adjusts sufficiently freely to maintain continuous equality between the quantity of labor demanded and the quantity of labor supplied. In such an economy, the real wage rate and employment are constant. Therefore as the price level varies, full-employment real GDP remains steady. There is only one aggregate supply curve—the vertical long-run aggregate supply curve. Fluctuations in employment, real wages, and real GDP occur because of fluctuations in the supply of labor and in the short-run aggregate production function that, in turn, bring fluctuations in the demand for labor. The most important source of fluctuations is the uneven pace of technological change, but there are other occasional negative influences on the short-run aggregate production function. ◆

Let's now examine the sticky wage theory of the labor market.

The Sticky Wage Theory

Most economists, while recognizing the scope for flexibility in wages from bonuses and overtime wage rates, believe that these sources of flexibility are insufficient to keep the quantity of labor supplied equal to the quantity demanded. Basic money wage rates rarely adjust more frequently than once a year, so money wage rates are fairly rigid—sticky. Real wage rates change more frequently than do money wage rates because of changes in the price level, but according to the sticky wage theory these adjustments do not make real wages sufficiently flexible to achieve continuous full employment.

The starting point for the sticky wage theory of the labor market is a theory of the determination of the money wage rate.

Money Wage Determination Firms, naturally, like to pay as low a wage as possible. Workers like as high a wage as possible. But workers want to get hired, and firms want to be able to find labor. Firms recognize that if they offer too low a wage, there will be a labor shortage. Workers recognize that if they try to achieve too high a wage, there will be a shortage of jobs—excessive unemployment. The wage that balances these opposing forces is the equilibrium wage—the wage that makes the quantity of labor demanded equal to the quantity supplied. But if money wages are going to be set for a year or more ahead, it will be impossible to achieve a continuous balance between the quantity of labor demanded and the quantity supplied. In such a situation, how is the money wage rate determined? It is set at a level designed to achieve an expectation or belief that, on the average, the quantity of labor demanded will equal the quantity supplied. Let's work out what that money wage rate is.

If the labor demand and supply curves are the same as those we used in Fig. 30.7, the real wage rate that achieves equality between the quantity demanded and quantity supplied is $7 an hour, as shown in Fig. 30.9. The money wage rate that this real wage rate translates into depends on the price level. But when firms and workers agree on a money wage rate for a future contract, they do not know what the price level is going to be. All they can do is base the contract on their best forecast of the future price level. Let's suppose that firms and their workers all have the same expectations about the future. Suppose that they *expect* the GDP deflator for the coming year to be 100. That being the case, firms and workers will be ready to agree to a money wage rate of $7 an hour. That is, with an expected GDP deflator of 100, a money wage rate of $7 an hour translates into an expected real wage rate of $7 an hour.

Real Wage Determination The real wage rate that actually emerges depends on the *actual* price level. If the GDP deflator turns out to be 100, as expected, then the real wage rate is $7 an hour, as expected. But many other outcomes are possible. Let's consider two of them, one in which the price level turns out to be higher than expected and one in which it turns out to be lower than expected.

First, suppose that the GDP deflator turns out to be 140. In this case, the real wage rate is $5 an hour.

FIGURE 30.9

A Labor Market with Sticky Money Wages

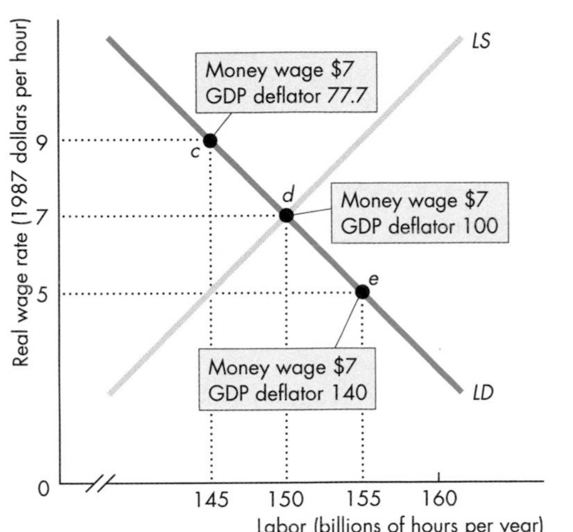

The labor demand curve is *LD* and the labor supply curve is *LS*. The money wage rate is set to achieve an expected balance between the quantity of labor demanded and the quantity supplied. If the GDP deflator is expected to be 100, the money wage rate is set at $7 an hour. The labor market is expected to be at point *d*. The quantity of labor employed is determined by the demand for labor. If the GDP deflator turns out to be 100, then the real wage rate is equal to $7 and the quantity of labor employed is 150 billion hours of labor. The economy operates at point *d*. If the GDP deflator turns out to be 77.7, then the real wage rate is $9 an hour and the quantity of labor employed falls to 145 billion hours. The economy operates at point *c*. If the GDP deflator is 140, then the real wage rate is $5 an hour and the quantity of labor employed increases to 155 billion hours. The economy operates at point *e*.

That is, a money wage rate of $7 an hour and a GDP deflator of 140 enables people to buy the same goods and services that a money wage rate of $5 an hour buys when the GDP deflator is 100. Next, suppose that the GDP deflator turns out to be 77.7 instead of 100. In this case, the real wage rate is $9 an hour. A money wage rate of $7 an hour with a GDP deflator of 77.7 buys the same quantity of goods and services that a money wage rate of $9 an hour buys when the GDP deflator is 100. The three points *c*, *d*, and *e* in Fig. 30.9 illustrate the relationship between the price level, the money wage rate, and the real wage rate. The money wage rate is constant at $7 an hour, and the higher the price level, the lower is the real wage rate. But as the real wage rate varies, what determines the quantity of labor employed?

Employment with Sticky Wages The sticky wage theory assumes that firms determine the level of employment. Provided that firms pay the agreed money wage rate, households supply whatever labor firms demand. These assumptions imply that the level of employment is determined by the demand curve for labor and that households are willing to be "off" their supply curves.

In Fig. 30.9, the money wage rate is $7 an hour. If the GDP deflator turns out to be 100 as expected, the real wage rate is $7 an hour and 150 billion hours of labor are employed (point *d* in the figure). If the GDP deflator turns out to be 77.7, the real wage rate is $9 an hour and the quantity of labor demanded and employed is 145 billion hours (point *c* in the figure). Households supply less labor than they would like to. If the GDP deflator turns out to be 140, the real wage rate is $5 an hour and the quantity of labor demanded and employed is 155 billion hours (point *e* in the figure). In this case, households supply more labor than they would like to.

It is easy to understand why a household might supply less labor, but why would it supply *more* labor than it would like to? In the long run, it would not. But for the duration of the existing contract, the household agrees to supply whatever quantity of labor the firm demands in exchange for a guaranteed money wage rate.

Aggregate Supply with Sticky Wages

When money wages are sticky, the short-run aggregate supply curve slopes upward. Figure 30.10 illustrates why this is so. Let's start by looking at part (a), which describes the labor market. The three equilibrium levels of real wages and employment we discovered in Fig. 30.9 are shown again here. The money wage rate is fixed at $7 an hour. If the price level is 100, the real wage rate is also $7 an hour and 150 billion hours of labor are employed—point *d*. If the price level is 77.7, the real wage rate is $9

FIGURE 30.10

Aggregate Supply with Sticky Wages

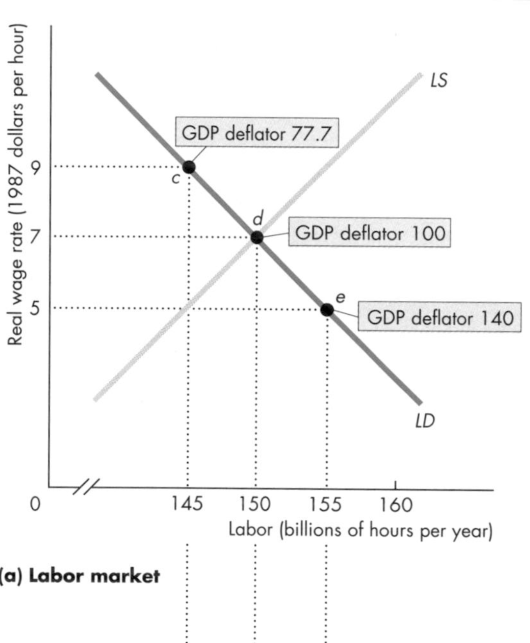

(a) Labor market

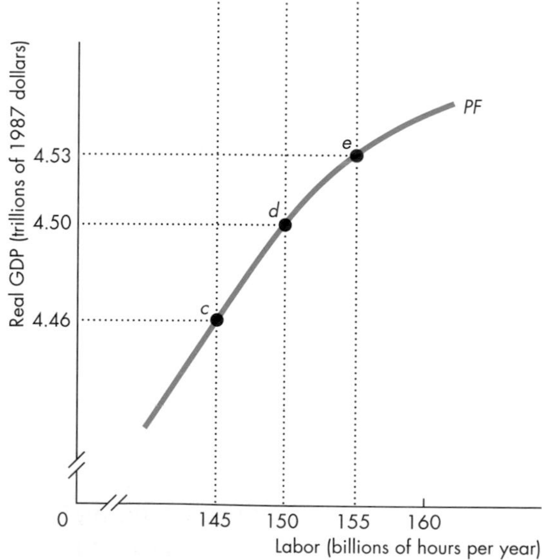

(b) Short-run aggregate production function

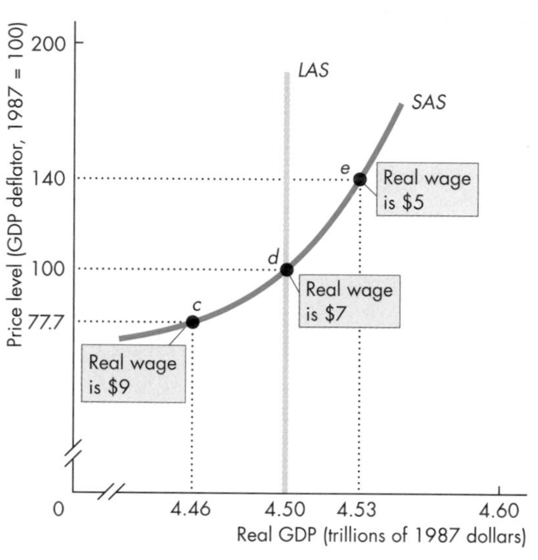

(c) Aggregate supply curves

The money wage rate is fixed at $7 an hour. In part (a), the demand for labor curve (*LD*) intersects the supply of labor curve (*LS*) at a real wage rate of $7 an hour and 150 billion hours of employment. If the GDP deflator is 100, the economy operates at this point—*d.* In part (b), the short-run aggregate production function (*PF*) determines real GDP at $4.5 trillion. This is long-run aggregate supply (*LAS*) in part (c). If the GDP deflator is 77.7, real wages are $9 an hour and the economy is at point *c*—employment is 145 billion hours (part a) and real GDP is $4.46 trillion (part b). The economy is at point *c* on its short-run aggregate supply curve (*SAS*) in part (c). If the GDP deflator is 140, real wages are $5 an hour and the economy is at point *e*—employment is 155 billion hours (part a) and real GDP is $4.53 trillion (part b). The economy is at point *e* on its short-run aggregate supply curve in part (c).

an hour and employment is only 145 billion hours—point *c*. If the price level is 140, the real wage rate is $5 an hour and employment is 155 billion hours—point *e*.

Figure 30.10(b) shows the short-run aggregate production function. We know from the labor market (part a) that at different price levels, different quantities of labor are employed. Part (b) tells us how these employment levels translate into real GDP. For example, when employment is 145 billion hours, real GDP is $4.46 trillion—point *c*. When employment is 150 billion hours, real GDP is $4.5

trillion—point *d*—and when employment is 155 billion hours, real GDP is $4.53 trillion—point *e*.

Figure 30.10(c) shows the aggregate supply curves. The long-run aggregate supply curve, *LAS*, is the one we've already derived in Fig. 30.8. The short-run aggregate supply curve, *SAS*, is derived from the labor market and production function we've just examined. To see why, first focus on point *c* in all three parts of the figure. At point *c*, the price level is 77.7. From the labor market (part a), we know that in this situation the real wage is $9 an hour and 145 billion hours of labor are employed. At this employment level we know from the production function (part b) that real GDP is $4.46 trillion. That's what point *c* in part (c) is telling us—when the price level is 77.7, real GDP supplied is $4.46 trillion. The other two points, *d* and *e*, are interpreted in the same way. At point *e*, the price level is 140 so the real wage rate is $5 an hour and 155 billion hours of labor are employed (part a). This employment level produces a real GDP of $4.53 trillion. Points *c*, *d*, and *e* are all points on the short-run aggregate supply curve. Notice that this curve, like the one in Chapter 24, is *curved*. As the price level rises, real GDP increases but the increments in real GDP become successively smaller. The straight-line *SAS* curve we are using is an approximation to this curve.

The short-run aggregate supply curve intersects the long-run aggregate supply curve at the expected price level—where the GDP deflator is 100. At price levels higher than that expected, the quantity of real GDP supplied exceeds its long-run level, and at price levels lower than that expected, the quantity of real GDP supplied falls short of its long-run level.

Fluctuations in Real GDP All the factors that lead to fluctuations in long-run aggregate supply in the flexible wage theory apply to the long-run aggregate supply curve of the sticky wage theory. They lead to changes in short-run aggregate supply and to shifts in the short-run aggregate supply curve. But in addition, employment and real GDP can fluctuate because of movements along the short-run aggregate supply curve. These movements occur because of changes in real wages. The real wage rate changes in the sticky wage theory when the price level moves, but the contractually determined money wage rate stays constant.

REVIEW

The sticky wage theory assumes that the money wage rate is set on the basis of expectations about the price level over the course of the wage contract to make the expected quantities of labor demanded and supplied equal. The level of employment is determined by the demand for labor and the real wage rate. If the price level equals the expected price level, the quantity of labor demanded equals the quantity supplied. If the price level is lower than expected, the real wage is higher than expected and the quantity of labor demanded decreases. If the price level is higher than expected, the real wage is lower than expected and the quantity of labor demanded increases. Changes in the price level that bring changes in the level of employment result in changes in real GDP—movements along the short-run aggregate supply curve. ◆

So far, although we have been examining models of the labor market, we have used those models to determine the level of employment and wages but have ignored unemployment. How is unemployment determined?

Unemployment

We discovered in Chapter 22 that unemployment is an ever present feature of economic life and that the unemployment rate sometimes rises to a level that poses a massive problem for millions of families (see pp. 587–591). Yet the labor market models that we have just been studying seem to ignore this important phenomenon. They determine the real wage rate and aggregate hours of labor employed, but they don't say anything about *who* supplies the hours. Unemployment arises when some people in the labor force are working zero hours but are seeking work. Why does unemployment exist? Why does its rate vary?

There are four main reasons why unemployment arises.

- To vary employment, it pays firms to vary the number of workers employed rather than the number of hours per worker.
- Firms have imperfect information about people looking for work.
- Households have incomplete information about available jobs.
- Wage contracts prevent the wage adjustments that would be needed to keep the quantity of labor demanded equal to the quantity supplied.

The flexible wage theory places emphasis on the first three of these sources of unemployment. The sticky wage theory acknowledges the importance of these factors but regards the fourth factor as the most significant cause of unemployment and of variations in its rate. First, we'll examine the sources of unemployment that are present regardless of whether wages are flexible or sticky. Then we'll see how wage stickiness generates yet more unemployment.

Indivisible Labor

If it were profitable to do so, firms would vary the amount of labor they employ by varying the hours worked by each person on their payrolls. For example, suppose that a firm employs 400 hours of labor each week and has 10 workers, each working 40 hours. If the firm decides to cut back its production and reduce employment to 360 hours, it might either lay off one worker or cut the hours of each of its 10 workers to 36 hours a week. In most production processes, the profitable reaction for the firm is to lay off one worker and keep the remaining workers' hours constant. There is an optimum or efficient number of hours for each worker. Work hours in excess of the optimum level result in decreased output per hour as workers become tired. Employing a large number of workers for a small number of hours each also lowers output per hour, since workers take time to get started up and there are disruptions to the production process caused by workers leaving and arriving. It is for these reasons that labor is an economically indivisible factor of production. That is, taking account of the output produced per hour, it pays firms to hire labor in indivisible lumps. As a consequence, when the demand for labor changes, the number of people employed changes rather than the number of hours per worker.

Being fired or laid off would not be important if an equally good job could be found right away. But finding a job takes time and effort—it has an opportunity cost. Firms are not fully informed about all the potential workers available to them, and households are not fully informed about all the potential jobs available to them. As a consequence, both firms and workers have to search for a profitable match. Let's examine this source of unemployment.

Job Search and Unemployment

Because households are incompletely informed about available jobs, they find it efficient to devote resources to searching for the best available job. Time spent searching for a job is part of unemployment. Let's take a closer look at this source of unemployment by examining the labor market decisions that people make and the flows that arise from those decisions. Figure 30.11 provides a schematic summary of this discussion.

The working age population is divided into two groups: those in the labor force and those not in the labor force. Those not in the labor force are full-time students, homemakers, and retirees. The labor force consists of two groups: the employed and the unemployed.

Decisions made by the demanders of labor and the suppliers of labor result in five types of flows that change the numbers of people employed and unemployed. The flows resulting from these decisions are shown by the arrows in the figure. Let's look at these decisions and see how the flows that result from them affect the amount of employment and unemployment.

First, there is a flow into the labor force as full-time students decide to quit school and homemakers decide to enter or re-enter the labor force. Initially, when such people enter the labor force, they are unemployed. These decisions result in an increase in the labor force and an increase in unemployment.

Second, there is a flow from employment to unemployment resulting from employers deciding to lay off workers temporarily or fire workers and from workers deciding to quit their current job to

FIGURE 30.11

Labor Market Flows

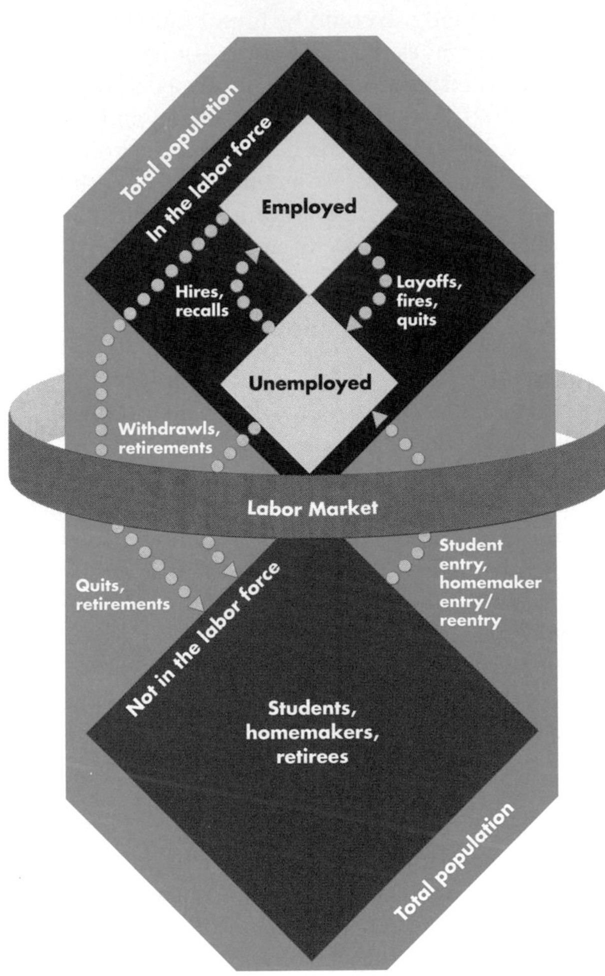

The working age population is divided into two groups: those in the labor force and those not in the labor force. The labor force is comprised of the employed and the unemployed. Flows into and out of the labor force and between employment and unemployment determine the number of people unemployed. New entrants from full-time schooling and re-entrants flow into unemployment. Flows from employment to unemployment result from fires, layoffs, and quits. Flows from unemployment to employment result from hires and recalls. Flows from the labor force occur as people decide to become homemakers, go back to school, or retire. Flows from the labor force also occur as unemployed people get discouraged by their failure to find a job.

find a better one. These decisions result in a decrease in employment and an increase in unemployment, but no change in the labor force.

Third, there is a flow from the labor force as employed people decide to quit their jobs to become homemakers, go back to school, or retire. These decisions result in a decrease in employment and a decrease in the labor force, but no change in unemployment.

Fourth, there is a flow from the labor force as unemployed people give up the search for a job. These people are *discouraged workers* whose job search efforts have been repeatedly unsuccessful. These decisions to leave the labor force result in a decrease in unemployment and a decrease in the labor force.

Fifth, there is a flow from unemployment to employment as firms recall temporarily laid-off workers and hire new workers. These decisions result in an increase in employment, a decrease in unemployment, and no change in the labor force.

At any one moment, there is a stock of employment and unemployment. Over any given period, there are flows into and out of the labor force and between employment and unemployment. In December 1991, for example, there were 127 million people in the labor force—66 percent of the working age population. Of these, 9 million (7 percent of the labor force) were unemployed and 118 million (93 percent of the labor force) were employed. Of the 9 million unemployed, 56 percent had been fired from their previous job or laid off, 24 percent had re-entered the labor force after a period of specializing in household production, 10 percent had voluntarily quit their previous job to seek a better one, and 9 percent were new entrants.

Unemployment with Flexible Wages

According to the flexible wage model of the labor market, all the unemployment that exists arises from the sources we've just reviewed. The unemployment rate is always equal to the natural rate of unemployment. There is a balance between the quantity of labor demanded and the quantity of labor supplied. But the quantity of labor supplied is the number of hours available for work at a given moment without further search for a better job. And the quantity of labor demanded is the number of hours that firms

FIGURE 30.12

Unemployment with Flexible Wages

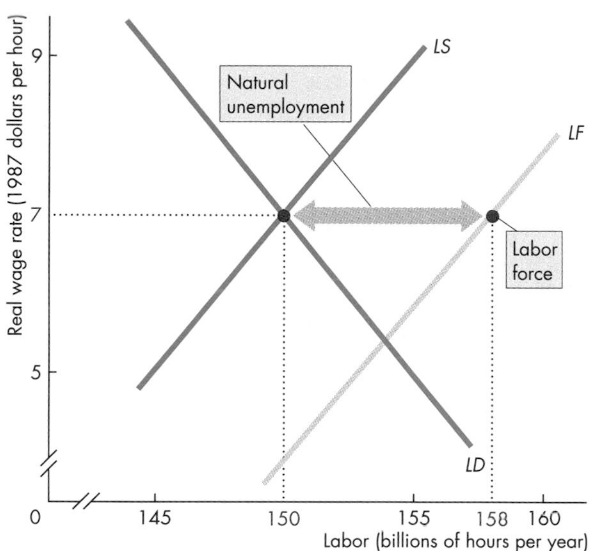

Some members of the labor force are immediately available for work at a given real wage rate, and this amount determines the supply of labor (*LS*). Other members of the labor force are searching for the best available job. Adding this quantity to the supply of labor gives the labor force curve (*LF*). Equilibrium occurs at the real wage rate that makes the quantity of labor supplied equal to the quantity demanded. The economy is at full employment, and unemployment is at its natural rate.

wish to hire at a given moment in time, given their knowledge of the individual skills and talents available. In addition to supplying hours for work, households also supply time for job search. Those people that devote no time to working and specialize in job search are the ones who are unemployed.

Figure 30.12 illustrates such a situation. The labor force—everyone who has a job and all those who are looking for one—is larger than the supply of labor. The supply curve of labor (*LS*) tells us about the quantity of labor available with no further job search. The labor force curve (*LF*) tells us about the quantity of labor available with no further job search plus the quantity of job search. In the figure, the quantity of labor supplied and the labor force increase as the real wage rate increases. But the quantity of job search, measured by the horizontal distance between the *LS* and *LF* curves, is constant. (This is an assumption. In real labor markets, the supply of job search may also increase as the real wage rate increases.)

Equilibrium occurs at the real wage rate that makes the quantity of labor supplied—not the labor force—equal to the quantity of labor demanded. Unemployment arises from the fact that information about jobs and workers is costly and it takes time for people without work to find an acceptable job. Such unemployment is called "natural" because it arises from the normal functioning of the labor market.

According to the flexible wage theory, fluctuations in unemployment are caused by fluctuations in labor market flows that arise on both the supply side and the demand side of the labor market. Changes in these flows lead to shifts in the *LS* and *LF* curves that increase and decrease the natural rate of unemployment.

Supply-Side Events The supply side of the labor market is influenced by the age distribution of the population. A large increase in the proportion of the population of working age brings an increase in the rate of entry into the labor force and a corresponding increase in the unemployment rate as the new entrants take time to find the best available jobs. This factor has been important in the U.S. labor market in recent years. A bulge in the birth rate occurred in the late 1940s and early 1950s, following World War II. This bulge resulted in an increase in the proportion of new entrants into the labor force during the 1970s. It resulted in a rightward shift in the *LS* curve, an even greater rightward shift in the *LF* curve, and an increase in the unemployment rate.

As the birth rate declined, the bulge moved to higher age groups, and the proportion of new entrants into the labor force declined during the 1980s. During this period, the rightward shift in the *LS* curve was larger than the shift in the *LF* curve and the unemployment rate declined.

Demand-Side Events Cycles in unemployment arise from the fact that the scale of hiring, firing, and job quitting ebbs and flows with fluctuations in real GDP—with the business cycle. These labor market flows and the resulting unemployment are also strongly influenced by the pace and direction of technological change. When some firms and sectors of the economy are expanding quickly and others are contracting quickly, labor turnover increases. This means large flows between employment and unemployment, and the pool of those temporarily unemployed increases at such a time. The relative decline of industries in the so-called "Rust Belt" and the rapid expansion of industries in the so-called "Sun Belt" are an important source of large flows of labor and of the rise in unemployment that occurred during the 1970s and early 1980s.

Job Creation and Destruction

The importance of changes in labor market flows can be seen by looking at some newly available data compiled by Steve Davis of the University of Chicago Business School and John Haltiwanger of the University of Maryland. Using data from individual plants in the manufacturing sector of the U.S. economy, they have painted a remarkable picture of the changing U.S. job scene. This picture is shown in Fig. 30.13.

Look first at part (a), which shows the amount of job creation and destruction. On the average, about 5 percent of all jobs disappear each year and a similar number of new jobs are created. Adding together the jobs destroyed and created gives a measure of the total amount of turnover in the labor market arising from this process—shown as the curve labeled "Sum" in the figure. Subtracting jobs destroyed from jobs created gives the change in the number of jobs—shown as the curve labeled "Net" in the figure. As you can see, the scale of job turnover is large and fluctuates a great deal. Part (b) shows how the fluctuations in job creation and destruction correspond with fluctuations in the unemployment rate.

Whether fluctuations in the job creation and destruction rate cause fluctuations in the unemployment rate or whether fluctuations in both the job creation and destruction rate and the unemployment rate have a common cause is not known. According to the sticky wage theory of the labor market, they do have a common cause, which is fluctuations in aggregate demand. Let's see why.

FIGURE 30.13

Job Creation, Job Destruction, and Unemployment

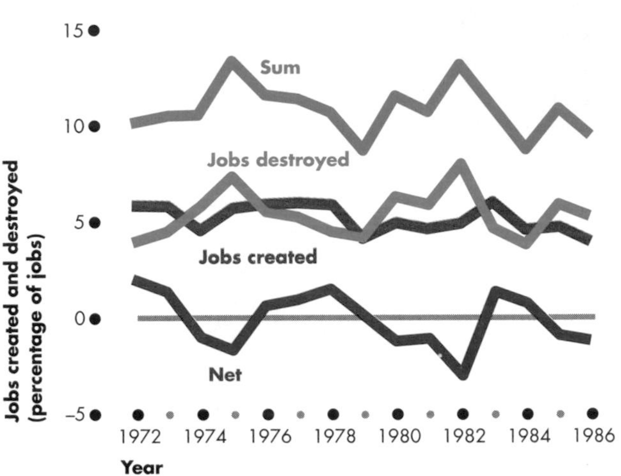

(a) Job creation and destruction rates

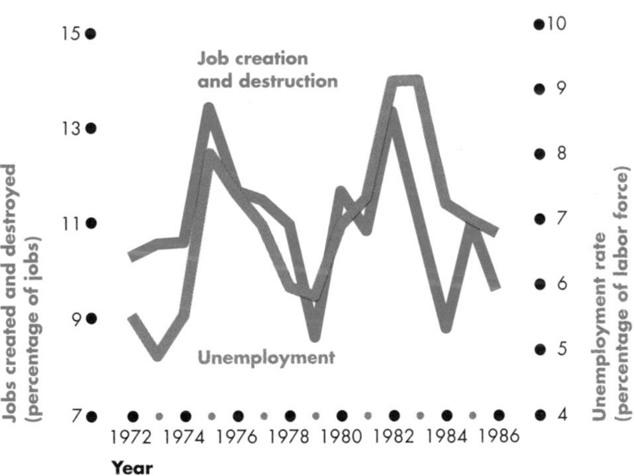

(b) Job creation and destruction and unemployment

On the average, 5 percent of existing jobs disappear each year (the curve labeled "Jobs destroyed" in part a) and a similar number of new jobs are created. The total amount of job creation and destruction (the curve labeled "Sum") and the rate of job creation minus the rate of job destruction (the curve labeled "Net") fluctuate. Those fluctuations follow a similar cycle to that in the unemployment rate (part b).

Source: Data kindly provided by Steve Davis and John Haltiwanger.

Unemployment with Sticky Wages

With sticky money wages, unemployment might rise above or fall below the natural rate. If the real wage rate is above its full-employment level, the quantity of labor employed is less than the quantity supplied and unemployment is above its natural rate. Such a situation is shown in Fig. 30.14. The *LS* and *LF* curves are the same as those in Fig. 30.12, and the amount of natural unemployment is measured by the horizontal distance between those two curves.

The money wage rate is $7 an hour. If the GDP deflator is 87.5, the real wage rate is $8 an hour and the quantity of labor demanded is 147 billion hours. Unemployment is above its natural rate. If the GDP deflator is 116.6, the real wage rate is $6 an hour and the quantity of labor demanded is 153 billion hours. Unemployment is below its natural rate.

Fluctuations in aggregate demand bring fluctuations in the price level. These fluctuations move the economy (upward and downward) along its demand for labor curve. At the same time, unemployment fluctuates around its natural rate. According to the sticky wage theory, fluctuations in unemployment arise primarily from the mechanism just described. Changes in the real wage rate arising from a sticky money wage rate and a changing price level result in movements along the labor demand curve and movements along the short-run aggregate supply curve. The rates of job creation and destruction also fluctuate (as shown in Fig. 30.13), but those fluctuations are the result of aggregate demand fluctuations.

Those economists who emphasize the role of sticky wages in generating fluctuations in unemployment usually regard the natural rate of unemployment as constant—or slowly changing. Fluctuations in the actual unemployment rate are fluctuations around the natural rate. Notice that this interpretation of fluctuations in unemployment contrasts with that of the flexible wage theory. A flexible wage model predicts that *all* changes in unemployment are fluctuations in the natural rate of unemployment.

If most of the fluctuations in unemployment *do* arise from sticky wages, aggregate demand management can moderate those fluctuations in unemployment. If aggregate demand is kept steady so that the price level stays close to its expected level, the economy can be kept close to full employment.

FIGURE 30.14

Unemployment with Sticky Money Wages

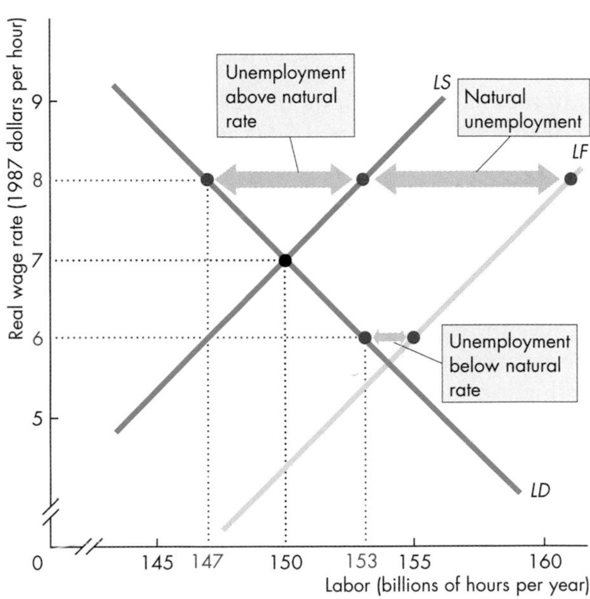

The money wage rate is $7 an hour. If the GDP deflator turns out to be 87.5, the real wage rate is $8 an hour. At this higher real wage rate, the quantity of labor demanded falls short of the quantity of labor supplied and unemployment is above its natural rate. If the GDP deflator turns out to be 116.6, the real wage rate is $6 an hour. At this lower real wage rate, the quantity of labor demanded exceeds the quantity of labor supplied and unemployment is below its natural rate. Fluctuations in the price level, with sticky money wages, cause fluctuations in the level of unemployment.

◆ ◆ ◆ ◆ We have now studied the labor market and the determination of long-run and short-run aggregate supply, employment, wages, and unemployment. We've examined the forces that change aggregate supply, shifting the long-run and short-run aggregate supply curves. We've also examined the sources of productivity growth in the U.S. economy. Our next task is to bring together the aggregate demand and aggregate supply sides of the economy again and see how they interact to determine inflation and business cycles. We are going to pursue these tasks in the next two chapters.

SUMMARY

Productivity and Income Growth

The short-run aggregate production function tells us how real GDP varies as the aggregate quantity of labor employed varies with a given stock of capital equipment and given state of technology. As the labor input increases, real GDP increases but by diminishing marginal amounts. Capital accumulation and technological change lead to productivity growth that causes the short-run aggregate production function to shift upward over time. Occasionally, the production function shifts downward because of negative influences such as restrictions on international trade. The U.S. short-run aggregate production function shifted upward by 88 percent between 1960 and 1991. (pp. 818–824)

The Demand for Labor

Firms choose how much labor to demand. The lower the real wage rate, the larger is the quantity of labor hours demanded. In choosing how much labor to hire, firms aim to maximize their profits. They achieve this objective by ensuring that the revenue brought in by an additional hour of labor equals the hourly wage rate. The more hours of labor that are employed, the lower is the revenue brought in by the last hour of labor. Firms can be induced to increase the quantity of labor hours demanded, either by a decrease in the wage rate or by an increase in the revenue brought in—by an increase in the price of output. Both a decrease in the wage rate and an increase in prices result in a lower real wage rate. Thus the lower the real wage rate, the greater is the quantity of labor demanded.

The relationship between the real wage rate and the quantity of labor demanded is summarized in the demand for labor curve, which slopes downward. The demand for labor curve shifts as a result of shifts in the short-run aggregate production function. (pp. 824–827)

The Supply of Labor

Households choose how much labor to supply. They also choose the timing of their labor supply. A higher real wage rate encourages the substitution of work for leisure—the substitution effect—and encourages the taking of more leisure—the income effect. The substitution effect dominates the income effect, so the higher the real wage rate, the more hours each worker supplies. Also, the higher the real wage rate, the higher is the labor force participation rate. A higher *current* wage relative to the expected future wage encourages more work in the present and less in the future—the intertemporal substitution effect. Taking all these forces together, the higher the real wage rate, the greater is the quantity of labor supplied.

The relationship between the real wage rate and the quantity of labor supplied is summarized in the supply of labor curve, which slopes upward. (pp. 827–829)

Wages and Employment

There are two theories of labor market equilibrium, one based on the assumption that wages are flexible and the other based on the assumption that they are sticky. Under the flexible wage theory, the real wage rate adjusts to ensure that the quantity of labor supplied equals the quantity demanded.

With flexible wages, the aggregate supply curve is vertical—the long-run aggregate supply curve. The quantity of real GDP supplied is independent of the price level. The long-run aggregate supply curve shifts as a result of shifts in the supply of labor curve and shifts in the short-run aggregate production function that lead to shifts in the demand for labor curve.

With sticky money wages, real wages do not adjust to balance the quantity of labor supplied and the quantity demanded. The money wage rate is set to make the expected quantity of labor demanded equal to the expected quantity supplied. The real wage rate depends on the contracted money wage rate and the price level. The level of employment is determined by the demand for labor, with households agreeing to supply the quantity demanded. Fluctuations in the price level relative to what was expected generate fluctuations in the quantity of labor demanded and in employment and real GDP. The higher the price level relative to what was expected, the lower is the real wage rate. The lower the real wage rate, the greater is the quantity of labor demanded, the greater is employment, and the greater is real GDP.

With sticky money wages, the aggregate supply curve slopes upward—the short-run aggregate supply curve. The higher the price level, the higher is the quantity of real GDP supplied. (pp. 829–836)

Unemployment

The labor market is in a constant state of change or labor turnover. Labor turnover creates unemployment. New entrants to the labor force and workers re-entering after a period of household production must take time to find a job. Some people quit an existing job to seek a better one. Some are laid off, and others are fired and forced to find another job. The pace of labor turnover is not constant. When technological change is expanding one sector and leading to a contraction of another sector, labor turnover increases. Finding new jobs takes time, and the process of adjustment may create overtime and unfilled vacancies in the expanding sector but unemployment in the contracting sector.

Even if wages are flexible, unemployment arising from labor-market turnover cannot be avoided. The unemployment rate arising from this source is the natural rate of unemployment. In labor markets with flexible wages, all fluctuations in unemployment are fluctuations in the natural rate arising from changes in the rate of labor turnover. The scale and cycles in the rates of job creation and job destruction are consistent with the flexible wage theory.

If wages are sticky, unemployment arises for all the same reasons as in the case of flexible wages and for one additional reason. With sticky wages the real wage might not move quickly enough to keep the quantity of labor demanded equal to the quantity supplied. In such a case, an increase in the real wage rate can result in unemployment rising above its natural rate and a decrease in real wages can result in unemployment falling below its natural rate. (pp. 836–841)

K E Y   E L E M E N T S

Key Terms

Demand for labor, 824
Diminishing marginal product of labor, 819
Innovation, 820
Invention, 820
Labor force participation rate, 828
Labor productivity, 818
Marginal product of labor, 818
Money wage rate, 824
Production function, 818
Quantity of labor demanded, 824
Quantity of labor supplied, 827
Real wage rate, 824
Reservation wage, 829
Short-run aggregate production function, 818
Short-run production function, 818
Supply of labor, 827

Key Figures

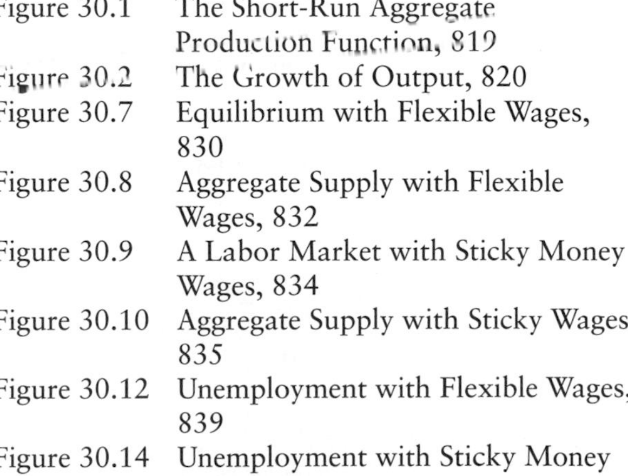

Figure 30.1 The Short-Run Aggregate Production Function, 819
Figure 30.2 The Growth of Output, 820
Figure 30.7 Equilibrium with Flexible Wages, 830
Figure 30.8 Aggregate Supply with Flexible Wages, 832
Figure 30.9 A Labor Market with Sticky Money Wages, 834
Figure 30.10 Aggregate Supply with Sticky Wages, 835
Figure 30.12 Unemployment with Flexible Wages, 839
Figure 30.14 Unemployment with Sticky Money Wages, 841

REVIEW QUESTIONS

1 What is the relationship between output and labor input in the short run? Why does the marginal product of labor diminish?

2 If the short-run production function shifts from 1992 to 1993 by the amount shown in Fig. 30.2, what happens to the marginal product of labor between 1992 and 1993?

3 Explain why the demand for labor curve slopes downward.

4 Given your answer to question 2, does the demand for labor curve shift between 1992 and 1993? If so, in what direction and by how much?

5 Why does the labor force participation rate rise as the real wage rate rises?

6 How is the quantity of labor currently supplied influenced by the wage rate today relative to those expected in the future?

7 Explain what happens in a labor market with flexible wages when technological change increases the marginal product of labor for each unit of labor input.

8 In question 7, explain what happens to the long-run aggregate supply curve.

9 What are sticky wages?

10 Explain what happens in a labor market with sticky wages when technological change increases the marginal product of labor for each unit of labor input.

11 In question 10, explain what happens to the short-run aggregate supply curve.

12 Explain how unemployment can arise if wages are flexible.

13 Describe the main facts about the rates of job creation and job destruction.

14 Explain how unemployment fluctuates around its natural rate.

PROBLEMS

Use the following information about an economy to answer problems 1 through 7. The economy's short-run production function is

Labor (billions of hours per year)	Real GDP (billions of 1987 dollars per year)
1	38
2	54
3	68
4	80
5	90
6	98
7	104
8	108

Its demand and supply schedules for labor are

Real wage rate (1987 dollars per hour)	Quantity of labor demanded (billions of hours per year)	Quantity of labor supplied (billions of hours per year)
3	8	4
5	7	5
7	6	6
9	5	7
11	4	8
13	3	9
15	2	10
17	1	11

1 If real wages are flexible, how much labor is employed, and what is the real wage rate?

2 If the GDP deflator is 120, what is the money wage rate?

3 If the real wage rate is flexible, calculate the aggregate supply curve in this economy.

4 If money wages are sticky and the GDP deflator is expected to be 100, what is the money wage rate in this economy?

5 Find three points on the economy's short-run aggregate supply curve when the money wage rate is at the level determined in problem 4.

6 Calculate the real wage rate at each of the points you used in answering problem 5.

7 At what price level and level of employment do the short-run and long-run aggregate supply curves intersect?

8 There are two economies, each with a *constant* unemployment rate but with a great deal of labor market turnover. In economy A, there is a rapid pace of technological change. Twenty percent of the labor force either is fired or quits its job every year, and 20 percent is hired every year. In economy B, only 5 percent is fired or quits and 5 percent is hired. Which economy has the higher unemployment rate? Why?

9 There are two economies, Flexiland and Fixland. These economies are identical in every way except that in Flexiland, real wages are flexible and maintain equality between the quantities of labor demanded and supplied. In Fixland, wages are sticky but the money wage rate is set so that, *on the average,* the quantity of labor demanded equals the quantity supplied.

a Explain which economy has the higher average unemployment rate.

b Explain which economy has the largest fluctuations in unemployment.

CHAPTER 31

INFLATION

After studying this chapter, you will be able to:

- Explain why inflation is a problem
- Explain how increasing aggregate demand generates a price-wage inflation spiral
- Explain how decreasing aggregate supply generates a cost-price inflation spiral
- Explain why it pays to anticipate inflation accurately
- Explain how inflation expectations are made
- Explain how inflation expectations affect *actual* inflation
- Explain the relationship between inflation and interest rates
- Explain the relationship between inflation and unemployment

Wanted: A Crystal Ball

By a supreme effort of self-discipline you have saved $100 for a rainy day. On January 1, 1992, you put your $100 in a 30-year bond, with an annual yield of 7½ percent. If you reinvest the interest income each year, you could have $875 to spend in 2022. Is that a good deal? Should you run out and buy 30-year bonds? That depends on what $875 will buy in the year 2022. With no inflation, your $100 will have grown into enough to buy a fairly fancy audio-video system. If inflation averages 7½ percent, however, $875 in the year 2022 will buy the same amount of goods as $100 did in 1992. If inflation averages 20 percent, a hamburger lunch at a diner that today costs $3.69 will cost $875 in 2022. No matter how much you like diner food, it would not be a good deal, over 30 years, to shrink $100 into today's equivalent of $3.69. ◆◆ This is an example of the way in which inflation has a big effect on our lives. To make good decisions, we need good forecasts of inflation, not just for next year but for many years into the future. To forecast inflation, we need to know what causes it. Why does the pace of inflation rise and fall? Why do the best-made plans often go awry when it comes to inflation? How do people form expectations about inflation? How do those expectations influence the economy? How do inflation expectations affect interest rates?

◆◆◆◆ This book will not tell you whether 30-year bonds are a good deal today. To do that, we would need a crystal ball. But this chapter will help you to understand the forces that generate inflation. It will also help you to

understand how inflation expectations are formed and how the performance of the economy—real GDP, the GDP deflator, and interest rates—depends on the extent to which inflation is correctly anticipated. ◆ ◆ The forces that determine inflation (and real GDP growth) are studied by using the aggregate demand–aggregate supply model. In that model, inflation—a rising price level—can result from increasing aggregate demand, decreasing aggregate supply, or a combination of the two. Before embarking on a study of the causes of inflation, let's remind ourselves of what inflation is and why it is a problem.

Why Inflation Is a Problem

The inflation rate is the percentage rise in the price level. That is,

$$\text{Inflation rate} = \frac{\text{Current year's price level} - \text{Last year's price level}}{\text{Last year's price level}} \times 100.$$

Let's write this equation in symbols. We'll call this year's price level P_1 and last year's price level P_0, so

$$\text{Inflation rate} = \frac{P_1 - P_0}{P_0} \times 100.$$

This equation shows the connection between the inflation rate and the price level. For a given price level last year, the higher the price level in the current year, the higher is the inflation rate.

The inflation rate is a measure of the rate at which money is losing value, and this fact is the source of the inflation problem. But the nature of the problem depends on whether the inflation is *anticipated* or *unanticipated.*

Anticipated Inflation

If money loses value at a rapid but anticipated rate, it does not function well as a medium of exchange. In such a situation, people try to avoid holding onto money. They spend their incomes as soon as they receive them, and firms pay out incomes—wages and dividends—as soon as they receive revenue from their sales. During the 1920s, when inflation in Germany reached *hyperinflation* levels, rates in excess of 50 percent a month, wages were paid and spent twice in a single day! Also, at high anticipated inflation rates, people seek alternatives to money as a means of payment (for example, cigarettes or foreign currency). During the 1980s, when inflation in Israel reached 1,000 percent a year, the U.S dollar became an important component of that country's money supply. Also, in times of anticipated inflation, barter becomes more common.

The activities that are encouraged by a high anticipated inflation rate use valuable time and other resources. Instead of people concentrating on the activities at which they have a comparative advantage, they find it more profitable to search for ways of avoiding the losses that inflation inflicts.

Anticipated inflation becomes a serious problem only at very high inflation rates. But there are many examples of costly anticipated inflations around the world, especially in South American countries such as Argentina, Bolivia, and Brazil. The closest the United States has come to such a situation was in the late 1970s and early 1980s, when the inflation rate exceeded 10 percent a year.

Unanticipated Inflation

Unanticipated inflation is a problem even at low inflation rates. It redistributes wealth between borrowers and lenders and income between employers and employees. An unanticipated increase in inflation transfers real buying power from lenders to borrowers, and an unanticipated decrease in inflation transfers resources in the opposite direction. An unanticipated increase in inflation also decreases real wages and increases real GDP and employment, while an unanticipated decrease in inflation increases real wages and decreases real GDP and employment. Unanticipated fluctuations in inflation produce fluctuations in the economy—fluctuations in real GDP, employment, and unemployment. Much of this chapter explains why unanticipated inflation has these effects. Let's begin by looking at the unanticipated inflation that results from an increase in aggregate demand.

Demand-Pull Inflation

The inflation resulting from an increase in aggregate demand is called **demand-pull inflation.** Such an inflation may arise from any individual factor that increases aggregate demand. Although there are several such factors, the most important that generate *ongoing* increases in aggregate demand are

- Increases in the money supply
- Increases in government purchases

When aggregate demand increases, the aggregate demand curve shifts to the right. Let's trace the effects of such an increase.

Inflation Effect of an Increase in Aggregate Demand

Suppose that last year the GDP deflator was 120 and real GDP was $5 trillion. Long-run real GDP was also $5 trillion. This situation is shown in Fig. 31.1(a). The aggregate demand curve is AD_0, the short-run aggregate supply curve is SAS_0, and the long-run aggregate supply curve is *LAS*.

In the current year, aggregate demand increases to AD_1. Such a situation arises if, for example, the Fed loosens its grip on the money supply or the government increases its purchases of goods and services. The economy moves to the point where the aggregate demand curve AD_1 intersects the short-run aggregate supply curve SAS_0. The GDP deflator increases to 125, and real GDP increases to $5.5 trillion. The economy experiences 4.2 percent inflation (a GDP deflator of 125 compared with 120 in the previous year) and a rapid expansion of real GDP.

FIGURE 31.1

Demand-Pull Inflation

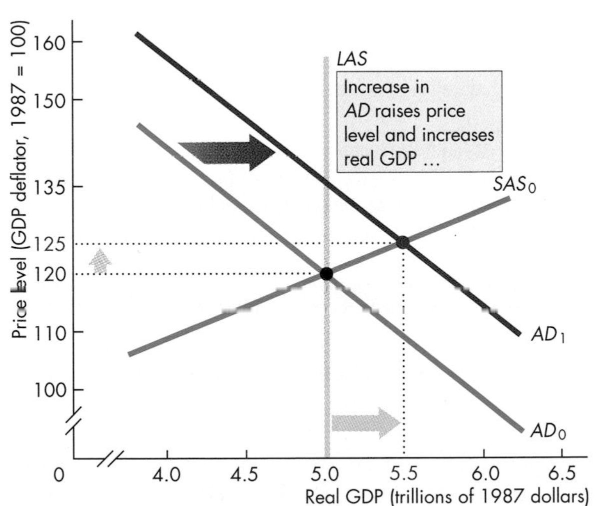

(a) Initial effect

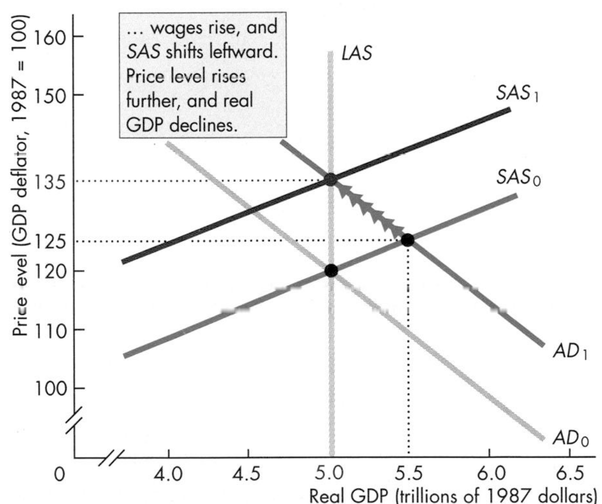

(b) Wages adjust

In part (a), the aggregate demand curve is AD_0, the short-run aggregate supply curve is SAS_0, and the long-run aggregate supply curve is *LAS*. The GDP deflator is 120, and real GDP is $5 trillion, its long-run level. Aggregate demand increases to AD_1 (because the Fed increases the money supply or the government increases its purchases of goods and services). The new equilibrium occurs where AD_1 intersects SAS_0. The economy experiences inflation (the GDP deflator rises to 125), and real GDP increases to $5.5 trillion. In part (b), starting from above full employment, wages begin to rise and the short-run aggregate supply curve shifts to the left toward SAS_1. The price level rises further, and real GDP returns to its long-run level.

The situation that developed in the U.S. economy toward the end of the 1960s is a good example of the process we have just analyzed. In those years, a large increase in government purchases on the Vietnam War and an increase in spending on social programs, together with an increase in the growth rate of the money supply, increased aggregate demand. As a consequence, the aggregate demand curve shifted rightward, the price level increased quickly, and real GDP moved above its long-run or full-employment level. But eventually, wages began to rise to catch up with the rising price level. Let's see why.

Wage Response

The economy cannot produce an above full-employment level of real GDP forever. With unemployment below its natural rate, there is a shortage of labor. Wages begin to increase, and the short-run aggregate supply curve starts to shift to the left. Prices rise further, and real GDP begins to fall. With no further change in aggregate demand—the aggregate demand curve remains at AD_1—this process comes to an end when the short-run aggregate demand curve has moved to SAS_1 in Fig. 31.1(b). At this time, the GDP deflator has increased to 135 and real GDP has returned to its long-run level, the level from which it started.

A Price-Wage Inflation Spiral

The inflation process we've just studied eventually comes to an end when, for a given increase in aggregate demand, wages have adjusted enough to restore the real wage rate to its full-employment level. But suppose that the initial increase in aggregate demand resulted from a large government budget deficit financed by creating more and more money. If such a policy remains in place, aggregate demand will continue to increase year after year. The aggregate demand curve will keep shifting to the right, putting continual upward pressure on the price level. The economy will experience perpetual demand-pull inflation.

Figure 31.2 illustrates a perpetual demand-pull inflation. The starting point is the same as that shown in Fig. 31.1. The aggregate demand curve is AD_0, the short-run aggregate supply curve is SAS_0, and the long-run aggregate supply curve is *LAS*. Real GDP is $5 trillion, and the GDP deflator is 120. Aggregate demand increases, shifting the aggregate demand curve to AD_1. Real GDP increases to $5.5 trillion, and the GDP deflator rises to 125. The economy is at an above full-employment equilibrium. There is a shortage of labor, and the wage rate rises, shifting the short-run aggregate supply curve to SAS_1. The GDP deflator increases to 135, and real GDP returns to its long-run level.

But the money supply increases again by the same percentage as before, and aggregate demand continues to increase. The aggregate demand curve shifts

FIGURE 31.2

A Price-Wage Inflation Spiral

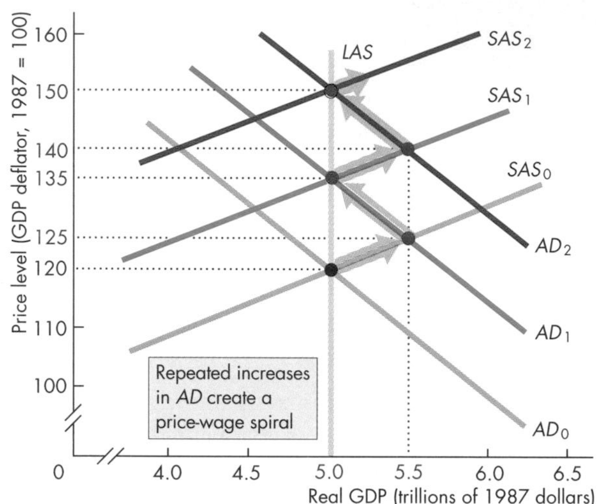

The aggregate demand curve is AD_0, the short-run aggregate supply curve is SAS_0, and the long-run aggregate supply curve is *LAS*. Real GDP is $5 trillion, and the GDP deflator is 120. Aggregate demand increases, shifting the aggregate demand curve to AD_1. Real GDP increases to $5.5 trillion, and the GDP deflator rises to 125. With the economy operating above full employment, the wage rate begins to rise, shifting the short-run aggregate supply curve leftward to SAS_1. The GDP deflator increases to 135, and real GDP returns to its long-run level. As aggregate demand continues to increase, the aggregate demand curve shifts to AD_2. The GDP deflator increases further, real GDP exceeds its long-run level, and the wage rate continues to rise. As the short-run aggregate supply curve shifts leftward to SAS_2, the GDP deflator increases to 150. As aggregate demand continues to increase, the price level rises, generating a perpetual demand-pull inflation. Real GDP fluctuates between $5 trillion and $5.5 trillion. But if aggregate demand increases *at the same time* as wages increase, real GDP remains at $5.5 trillion as the demand-pull inflation occurs.

rightward to AD_2. The GDP deflator increases further, real GDP exceeds its long-run level, and the wage rate continues to rise. As the *SAS* curve shifts to SAS_2, the GDP deflator increases further to 150. As aggregate demand continues to increase, the price level rises continuously, generating a perpetual demand-pull inflation and a price-wage inflation spiral. Real GDP fluctuates between $5 trillion and $5.5 trillion.

In the price-wage inflation spiral that we've just described, aggregate demand increases and wage increases alternate—first aggregate demand increases, then wages, then aggregate demand, and so on. If, after the initial increase in aggregate demand that took real GDP to $5.5 trillion, aggregate demand continues to increase *at the same time* as the wage rate increases, real GDP remains above its long-run level at $5.5 trillion as the demand-pull inflation proceeds.

Demand-Pull Inflation in Kalamazoo You may better understand the inflation process that we've just described by considering what is going on in an individual part of the economy, such as a Kalamazoo soda bottling plant. Initially, when aggregate demand increases, the demand for soda increases and the price of soda rises. Faced with a higher price, the soda plant works overtime and increases production. Conditions are good for workers in Kalamazoo, and the soda factory finds it hard to hang onto its best people. To do so, it has to offer higher wages. As wages increase, so do the costs of the soda factory.

What happens next depends on what happens to aggregate demand. If aggregate demand remains constant (as in Fig. 31.1b), the firm's costs are increasing but the price of soda is not increasing as quickly as its costs. Production is scaled back. Eventually, wages and costs increase by the same amount as the price of soda. In real terms, the soda factory is in the same situation as initially—before the increase in aggregate demand. The bottling plant produces the same amount of soda and employs the same amount of labor.

But if aggregate demand continues to increase, so does the demand for soda, and the price of soda rises at the same rate as wages. The soda factory continues to operate above full employment, and there is a persistent shortage of labor. Prices and wages chase each other upward in an unending price-wage spiral.

REVIEW

Demand-pull inflation results from any initial factor that increases aggregate demand. The most important such factors are an increase in the money supply and an increase in government purchases of goods and services. Initially, the increase in aggregate demand increases the price level and real GDP. With the economy operating at above full employment, the wage rate rises, decreasing short-run aggregate supply. If aggregate demand remains constant at its new level, the price level rises further and real GDP returns to its long-run level. If aggregate demand continues to increase, wages chase prices in an unending price-wage inflation spiral. ◆

Next, let's look at how shocks to aggregate supply can create inflation.

Supply Inflation and Stagflation

Inflation can result from a decrease in aggregate supply. Let's look at the main reasons why aggregate supply might decrease.

Sources of Decreasing Aggregate Supply

There are two main sources of a decrease in aggregate supply. They are

- An increase in wage rates
- An increase in the prices of key raw materials

These sources of a decrease in aggregate supply operate by increasing costs, and such an inflation is called **cost-push inflation.** Other things remaining the same, the higher the cost of production, the smaller is the amount produced. At a given price level, rising wage rates or rising prices of key raw materials such as oil lead firms to decrease the quantity of labor employed and to cut production. This decrease in short-run aggregate supply shifts the short-run aggregate supply curve to the left. Let's see what that does to the price level.

Inflation Effect of a Decrease in Aggregate Supply

Suppose that last year the GDP deflator was 120 and real GDP was $5 trillion. Long-run real GDP was also $5 trillion. This situation is shown in Fig. 31.3. The aggregate demand curve was AD_0, the short-run aggregate supply curve was SAS_0, and the long-run aggregate supply curve was *LAS*. In the current year, a sharp increase in world oil prices decreases short-run aggregate supply. The short-run aggregate supply curve shifts leftward to SAS_1. The GDP deflator increases to 130, and real GDP decreases to $4.5 trillion. The economy experiences 8.3 percent inflation (a GDP deflator of 130 compared with 120 in the previous year) and a contraction of real GDP—*stagflation.*

The situation that developed in the U.S. economy in 1974 was similar to what we've just described. At that time, a fourfold increase in oil prices decreased aggregate supply, bringing a sharp increase in inflation and a decrease in real GDP.

Aggregate Demand Response

When the economy is stuck at an unemployment equilibrium such as that shown in Fig. 31.3, there is often an outcry of concern and a call for action to restore full employment. Such action can include an increase in government purchases of goods and services or a tax cut, but the most likely is a response from the Fed that increases the money supply. If the Fed does respond in this way, aggregate demand increases and the aggregate demand curve shifts rightward. Figure 31.4 shows an increase in aggregate demand that shifts the aggregate demand curve

FIGURE 31.3

Cost-Push Inflation

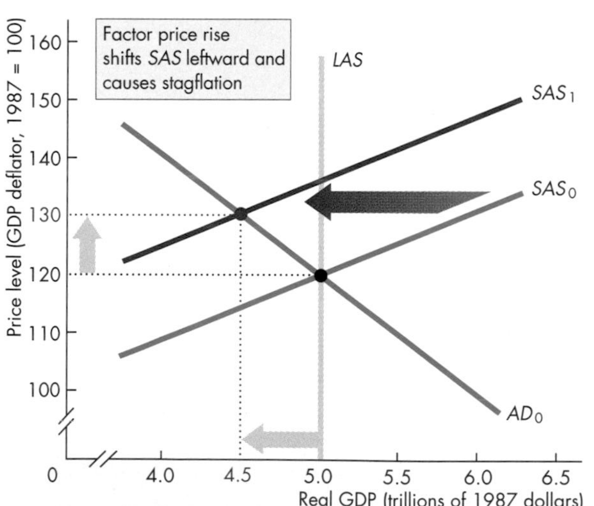

Initially, the aggregate demand curve is AD_0, the short-run aggregate supply curve is SAS_0, and the long-run aggregate supply curve is *LAS*. A decrease in aggregate supply (for example, resulting from an increase in the world price of oil) shifts the short-run aggregate supply curve to SAS_1. The economy moves to the point where the short-run aggregate supply curve SAS_1 intersects the aggregate demand curve AD_0. The GDP deflator increases to 130, and real GDP decreases to $4.5 trillion. The economy experiences inflation and a contraction of real GDP—*stagflation.*

FIGURE 31.4

Aggregate Demand Response to Cost Push

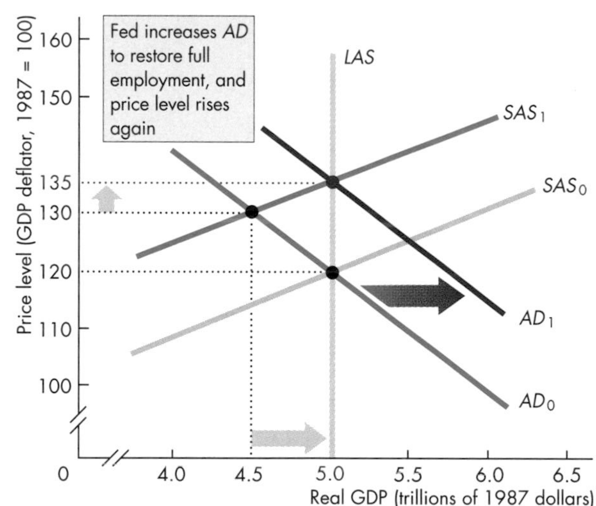

Initially, the aggregate demand curve is AD_0, the short-run aggregate supply curve is SAS_0, and the long-run aggregate supply curve is *LAS*. A decrease in aggregate supply shifts the short-run aggregate supply curve leftward to SAS_1. The GDP deflator rises from 120 to 130, and real GDP decreases from $5 trillion to $4.5 trillion. The economy experiences stagflation. It is stuck at an unemployment equilibrium. If the Fed responds by increasing aggregate demand to restore full employment, the aggregate demand curve shifts to the right to AD_1. The economy returns to full employment, but at the expense of higher inflation. The price level rises to 135.

to AD_1 and restores full employment. But this happens at the expense of a yet higher price level. The price level rises to 135, a 12.5 percent increase over the original price level.

A Cost-Price Inflation Spiral

Suppose now that the oil producers, seeing the prices of everything that they buy increase by 12.5 percent, decide to increase the price of oil yet again. Figure 31.5 continues the story. The short-run aggregate supply curve now shifts to SAS_2, and another bout of stagflation ensues. The price level rises further to 145, and real GDP falls to $4.5 trillion. Unemployment increases above its natural rate. If the Fed responds yet again with an increase in the money supply, aggregate demand increases and the aggregate demand curve shifts to AD_2. The price level rises even higher—to 150—and full employment is again restored. A cost-price inflation spiral results. But if the Fed does not respond, the economy remains below full employment until the initial price increase that triggered the stagflation is reversed.

You can see that the Fed has a dilemma. If it increases the money supply to restore full employment, it invites another oil price hike that will call forth yet a further increase in the money supply. Inflation will rage along at a rate decided by the oil-exporting nations. If the Fed keeps the lid on money supply growth, the economy operates with a high level of unemployment. The Fed faced such a dilemma in 1980 when OPEC again pushed oil prices higher. On that occasion the Fed decided not to respond to the oil price hike with an increase in the money supply. The result was a massive recession but also, eventually, a fall in inflation.

Cost-Push Inflation in Kalamazoo What is going on in the Kalamazoo soda bottling plant when the economy is experiencing cost-push inflation? When the oil price increases, so do the costs of bottling soda. These higher costs decrease the supply of soda, increasing its price and decreasing the quantity produced. The soda plant lays off some workers. This situation will persist until either the Fed increases aggregate demand or the price of oil falls. If the Fed increases aggregate demand, as it did in the mid-1970s, the demand for soda increases and so does its price. The higher price of soda brings higher profits, and the bottling plant increases its production. The soda factory rehires the laid-off workers.

FIGURE 31.5

A Cost-Price Inflation Spiral

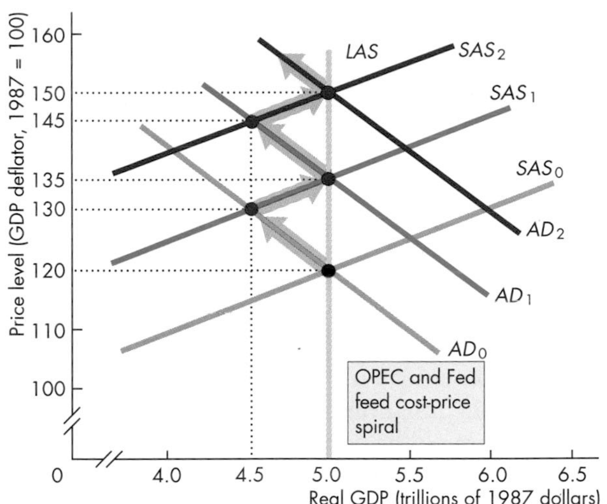

When a cost increase (for example, an increase in the world oil price) decreases short-run aggregate supply from SAS_0 to SAS_1, the GDP deflator rises to 130 and real GDP decreases to $4.5 trillion. The Fed responds with an increase in the money supply that shifts the aggregate demand curve from AD_0 to AD_1. The GDP deflator rises again to 135, and real GDP returns to $5 trillion. The cost increase is applied again, shifting the short-run aggregate supply curve to SAS_2. Stagflation is repeated, and the GDP deflator now rises to 145. The Fed responds again, and the cost-price inflation spiral continues.

REVIEW

Cost-push inflation results from any initial factor, such as an increase in the wage rate or an increase in the price of a key raw material, that decreases aggregate supply. The initial effect of a decrease in aggregate supply is an increase in the price level and a decrease in real GDP—*stagflation.* If monetary or fiscal policy increases aggregate demand to restore full employment, the price level rises further. If aggregate demand remains constant, the economy stays below full employment until the initial price rise is reversed. If the response to stagflation is always an increase in aggregate demand, a freewheeling cost-push inflation takes place at a rate determined by the speed with which costs are pushed upward. ◆

Inflation Expectations

With demand-pull inflation, a persistent increase in the money supply increases aggregate demand and creates a price-wage inflation spiral. With cost-push inflation, a persistent increase in factor prices accommodated by persistent increases in the money supply creates a cost-price inflation spiral. Regardless of whether the inflation is demand pull or cost push, the failure to correctly *anticipate* inflation imposes costs. And these costs create an incentive for people to try to anticipate the inflation.

Let's examine the costs of not anticipating inflation correctly.

The Cost of Wrong Inflation Forecasts

Our inability to know the future combined with our need to make forecasts about it inevitably imposes costs on us. The more wrong we are in assessing the future price level, the more expensive our mistake will be. To see why errors in forecasting inflation are costly, let's review what we've just discovered about the process of unanticipated inflation. And let's do this by returning to the soda bottling plant in Kalamazoo.

Wages When we looked at the effects of demand-pull inflation, we saw that initially the price of soda and of other goods increases but the wage rate doesn't change. The real wage rate falls, and the bottling plant increases production. Workers begin to quit the bottling plant to find jobs that pay a higher real wage rate, one closer to that prevailing before the outburst of inflation. This outcome imposes costs on both the firm and the workers. The firm operates its plant at a high output rate and incurs overtime costs and higher plant maintenance and parts replacement costs. The workers wind up feeling cheated. They have worked overtime to produce the extra output, and when they come to spend their wages, they discover that the prices have increased, so, in reality, their wages buy a smaller quantity of goods and services than was originally anticipated.

Contrast this outcome with what might have happened if the burst of inflation had been correctly anticipated. In this case, the wage rate at the bottling plant increases at the same rate as prices—the price of soda and the price level. The real wage rate, employment, and output remain constant. Anticipated inflation is virtually costless.

Interest Rates Just as firms and workers incur costs from wrong forecasts of the price level, so do borrowers and lenders. Interest rates are agreed upon on the basis of some expectation of the future value of money—which, in turn, depends on the future course of the price level. If inflation turns out to be unexpectedly high, borrowers gain and lenders lose. But neither borrowers nor lenders are as happy as they would have been in the absence of unanticipated inflation. Borrowers would like to have borrowed more and lenders would like to have lent less; so both groups feel that opportunities for extra gain have been lost.

If inflation turns out to be lower than expected, lenders gain and borrowers lose. But again, what lenders gain is less than what borrowers lose. In this case, borrowers would like to have borrowed less and lenders would like to have lent more. Again, both groups feel that they could have made better decisions with greater foresight.

Costs occur regardless of whether inflation expectations turn out to be wrong on the up side or the down side. Wrong expectations impose costs on firms and households, and the larger the forecasting error, the larger are those costs. The costs of wrong forecasts, like any other costs, are something to be minimized. These costs arise from scarcity in the same way that all other costs arise from scarcity. In this case, what is scarce is information about the future. Nevertheless, although the costs of wrong forecasts cannot be entirely avoided, they can be made as small as possible.

Minimizing the Losses from Wrong Forecasts

Lacking crystal balls, people cannot be right about the future all the time. But they can use all the relevant information available to them to make their forecasting errors as small as possible. That is, they can form a rational expectation. A **rational expectation** is a forecast based on all the available relevant information. A rational expectation has two features:

- The expected forecast error is zero.
- The range of the forecast error is as small as possible.

With an expected forecast error of zero, a rational expectation is right *on the average*. But it is not an accurate forecast. There is the same chance that the forecast will be too high as there is that it will be too low. By making a forecast that consciously errs on one side or the other, people avoid being wrong in one direction. But the cost of that is being more wrong in the other direction. Since the costs of wrong forecasts occur regardless of whether expectations are too high or too low, the best that can be done is to make a forecast that has an equal chance of being too high or too low. In making the range of forecast error as small as possible, information has been put to its best possible use. Information is a scarce resource, and none of it has been wasted.

Do people actually forecast by forming rational expectations? Let's see how people in the real world make their forecasts.

How People Forecast in the Real World

People devote different amounts of time and effort to forecasting. Some people specialize in forecasting and even make a living by selling their forecasts. For example, investment advisors forecast the future prices of stocks and bonds. Banks, large stock and commodity brokers, government agencies, and private forecasting firms make macroeconomic forecasts about inflation.

Specialist forecasters stand to lose a great deal from wrong forecasts. They have a strong incentive, therefore, to make their forecasts as accurate as possible—minimizing the range of error and at least making them correct on the average. Furthermore, organizations that stand to lose by having wrong forecasts invest a good deal of effort in checking the forecasts of the professionals. For example, all the large banks, the major labor unions, government departments, and most large private-sector producers of goods and services devote a lot of effort to making their own forecasts and comparing them with the forecasts of others. Specialist forecasters use vast amounts of data, which they analyze with the help of statistical models of the economy. The models they use are based on (but are more detailed than) the aggregate demand–aggregate supply model that you are studying in this book.

In contrast to the specialists, most people devote little time and effort to forecasting. Instead, they either buy their forecasts from specialists or mimic the people who appear to have been successful.

How do economists explain the forecasts that people make?

How Economists Predict People's Forecasts

Economics tries to predict the choices that people make. Because these choices are influenced by people's forecasts of phenomena such as inflation, to predict their choices we must also predict their forecasts. How do economists go about that task?

They assume that people are as rational in their use of information when forming expectations as they are in all their other economic actions. This idea leads economists to the rational expectations hypothesis. The **rational expectations hypothesis** is the proposition that the forecasts that people make are the same as the forecasts made by an economist using the relevant economic theory together with all the information available at the time the forecast is made. For example, to predict people's expectations of the price of orange juice, economists use the economic model of demand and supply together with all the available information about the positions of the demand and supply curves for orange juice. To make a prediction about people's expectations of the price level and inflation, economists use the economic model of aggregate demand and aggregate supply.

Let's see how we can use the model of aggregate demand and aggregate supply to work out the rational expectation of the price level.

A Rational Expectation of Inflation

To form a rational expectation of inflation, we use the model of aggregate demand and aggregate supply to forecast the state of the economy in much the same way that meteorologists use a model of the atmosphere to forecast the weather. But there is an important difference between the meteorologist's model of the atmosphere and the economist's model of aggregate demand and aggregate supply.

Tomorrow's weather will not be affected by our forecast of it. We may forecast a sunny day or a torrential downpour, but the outcome is independent of that forecast. But the consensus forecast of the price level might affect the actual price level. We must take this possibility into account when working out a rational expectation of the price level.

We're going to work out the rational expectation of the price level, using Fig. 31.6 to guide our analysis. The aggregate demand–aggregate supply model predicts that the price level is at the point of intersection of the aggregate demand and short-run aggregate supply curves. To forecast the price level, therefore, we have to forecast the positions of these curves.

Let's begin with aggregate demand. To forecast the position of the aggregate demand curve, we must forecast all the variables that influence aggregate demand. Suppose that we have done this and come up with the forecast of aggregate demand given by the curve *EAD*, the *expected* aggregate demand curve.

Our next task is to forecast the position of the short-run aggregate supply curve, but here we have a problem. We know that the position of the short-run aggregate supply curve is determined by two things:

- Long-run aggregate supply
- The wage rate

The short-run aggregate supply curve intersects the long-run aggregate supply curve at the full-employment price level. So we need a forecast of the position of the long-run aggregate supply curve. To

FIGURE 31.6

Rational Expectation of the Price Level

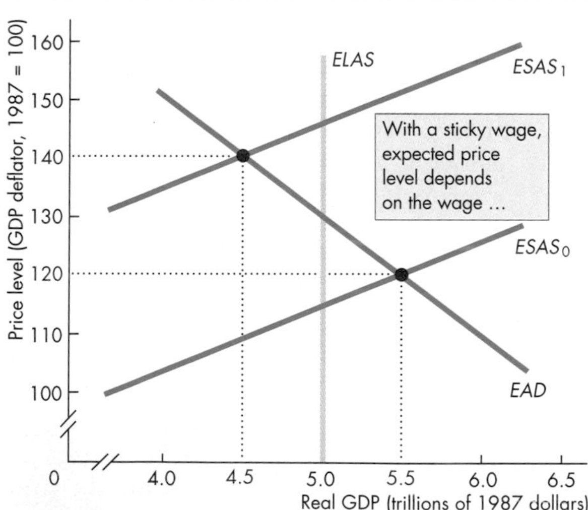

(a) Sticky wages

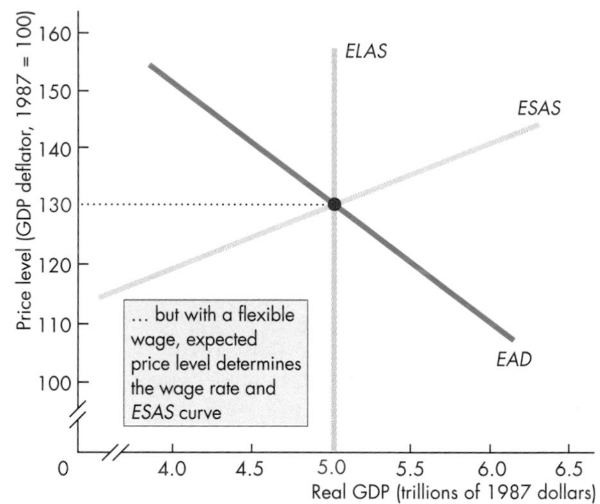

(b) Flexible wages

The rational expectation of the price level is the best available forecast. That forecast is constructed by forecasting the expected aggregate demand curve (*EAD*) and the expected short-run aggregate supply curve (*ESAS*). The rational expectation of the price level occurs at the point of intersection of curves *EAD* and *ESAS*. To forecast the position of *ESAS*, forecasts of the long-run aggregate supply curve *ELAS* and the wage rate are needed. In part (a), wages are sticky and do not respond to price level expectations, so the position of the expected short-run aggregate supply curve depends on *ELAS* and the fixed wage rate. With a low wage rate, the expected short-run aggregate supply curve is $ESAS_0$, and the rational expectation of the price level is 120. With a high wage rate, the expected short-run aggregate supply curve is $ESAS_1$, and the rational expectation of the price level is 140. In part (b), wages are flexible and respond to the expected price level. The rational expectation of the price level is at the point of intersection of *EAD* and *ELAS*. The wage rate is determined by this expected price level, and the expected short-run aggregate supply curve is *ESAS*.

make such a forecast, we must forecast all the factors that determine long-run aggregate supply. Suppose that we have made the best forecast we can of long-run real GDP and that we expect long-run aggregate supply to be $5 trillion. The *expected* long-run aggregate supply curve is *ELAS* in Fig. 31.6.

The final ingredient we need is a forecast of the wage rate. Armed with this information, we have a forecast of the point on the *ELAS* curve at which the short-run aggregate supply intersects it. The forecast of the wage rate depends on the degree of wage flexibility, and we need to look at two cases:

- Sticky wages
- Flexible wages

Rational Expectation with Sticky Wages

With sticky wages the position of the short-run aggregate supply curve is determined by the known and fixed wage rate. Given that fixed wage rate and given the expected long-run aggregate supply curve *ELAS*, there is an expected short-run aggregate supply curve. Figure 31.6(a) illustrates such a curve as $ESAS_0$.

The rational expectation of the price level is the point of intersection of *EAD* and $ESAS_0$, a price level of 120. The rational expectation of inflation is calculated as the percentage amount by which the forecasted future price level exceeds the current price level. For example, if the current price level is 110 and next year's forecasted price level is 120, the expected inflation rate over the year is 9 percent.

There is also a rational expectation of real GDP. Given the wage rate and the expected short-run aggregate supply curve $ESAS_0$, the rational expectation is that real GDP will be $5.5 trillion and the economy will be at an above full-employment equilibrium.

Figure 31.6(a) shows another case—one in which the expected short-run aggregate supply curve is $ESAS_1$. Here, the wage rate is higher. The rational expectation of the price level is determined at the point of intersection of *EAD* and $ESAS_1$, an expected price level of 140. With a current price level of 110, the expected inflation rate over the year is 27 percent. The economy is expected to be at an unemployment equilibrium, with a real GDP of $4.5 trillion.

Rational Expectation with Flexible Wages

When wages are flexible, it is harder to forecast the position of the short-run aggregate supply curve because the wage rate must also be forecasted. Furthermore, the wage rate depends on the expected price level, the variable we are trying to forecast. There seems to be a big problem: to forecast the price level, we need a forecast of the wage rate; and to forecast the wage rate, we need a forecast of the price level.

The problem is solved by finding a forecast of the price level that makes the expected aggregate demand curve and the expected short-run aggregate supply curve intersect at a price level that is the same as the forecasted price level. There is only one such price level. It is the one at which the expected aggregate demand curve intersects the expected long-run aggregate supply curve. This case is shown in Fig. 31.6(b). The wage rate adjusts in response to changes in the expected price level until the expected short-run aggregate supply curve is *ESAS* in Fig. 31.6(b). We forecast the position of the short-run aggregate supply curve and the price level at the same time, and the two forecasts are consistent with each other. Our forecast of the price level is a GDP deflator of 130, and *ESAS* is our forecast of the short-run aggregate supply curve.

Theory and Reality

The analysis we've just conducted shows how economists work out a rational expectation. But do real people form expectations of the price level by using that same analysis? We can imagine that graduates of economics might, but it seems unrealistic to attribute such calculations to most people. Does this make the whole idea of rational expectations invalid?

The answer is no! In performing our calculations, we have been building an economic model. That model does not seek to describe the thought processes of real people. Its goal is to make predictions about *choices,* not mental processes. The *rational expectations hypothesis* states that the forecasts that people make, regardless of how they make them, are on the average the same as those forecasts that an economist makes using the relevant economic theory.

REVIEW

Decisions to produce, work, borrow, and lend are based on forecasts of inflation, but the returns to firms, workers, borrowers, and lenders depend on actual inflation. Wrong inflation forecasts impose costs on firms, workers, borrowers, and lenders. To minimize forecasting errors, people use all available information and form a *rational expectation*. Real-world specialist forecasters use data and statistical models to generate expectations. Others either buy forecasts from specialists or copy people who seem to be successful. Economists use the rational expectations hypothesis to predict people's forecasts. A rational expectation of inflation is the forecast of the future price level made by using the aggregate demand–aggregate supply model. ◆

Now that we know what rational expectations are and how rational expectations of inflation are calculated, let's go on to see how actual real GDP and the actual inflation rate are determined. Let's also compare actual real GDP and actual inflation with people's rational expectations of these variables.

Rational Expectations Equilibrium

So far in this chapter we've studied the process of *unanticipated* inflation and the determination of inflation expectations—the way people try to *anticipate* inflation. Our next task is to bring these two things together and see what happens when there are disturbances to aggregate demand or aggregate supply *and at the same time* people do the best they can to anticipate the consequences of those changes. Such a situation is called a rational expectations equilibrium. A **rational expectations equilibrium** is a macroeconomic equilibrium based on expectations that are the best available forecasts.

Let's look at such situations and see how they come about, using Fig. 31.7. The figure has three parts. Part (a) contains people's *forecasts* of the economy, and parts (b) and (c) show two alternative *outcomes* that differ from the forecast. The forecast in part (a) is exactly the same as that seen in Fig. 31.6(b). The forecasted price level is 130, and real GDP is forecasted to be at its long-run level of $5 trillion.

If the outcome is exactly what was forecasted, then part (a) also describes that outcome. The actual price level is 130, real GDP is $5 trillion, and there is full employment.

Figure 31.7(b) shows what happens when aggregate demand turns out to be less than expected but aggregate supply is the same as expected. The aggregate supply curves (*LAS* and *SAS*) in part (b) are identical to the expected aggregate supply curves (*ELAS* and *ESAS*) in part (a). But the aggregate demand curve (*AD*) is farther to the left in part (b) than the expected aggregate demand curve (*EAD*) in part (a). Such an outcome might arise from an *unexpected* slowdown in the rate at which the Fed is creating money, an *unexpected* fall in foreign demand for U.S. exports, an *unexpected* tax increase, or an *unexpected* reduction in government purchases of goods and services.

Equilibrium is determined where the actual aggregate demand curve intersects the short-run aggregate supply curve. The GDP deflator is 125, and real GDP is $4.5 trillion. With actual aggregate demand less than expected, the price level is lower than expected and real GDP is below its long-run level. There is an unemployment equilibrium.

You can work out, using Fig. 31.7(b), what happens if aggregate demand turns out to be higher than expected. In such a case, the price level is higher than expected and so is real GDP.

Figure 31.7(c) shows what happens when aggregate supply turns out to be less than expected but aggregate demand is the same as expected. The aggregate demand curve (*AD*) in part (c) is identical to the expected aggregate demand curve (*EAD*) in part (a). But the aggregate supply curves (*LAS* and *SAS*) are farther to the left in part (c) than the expected aggregate supply curves (*ELAS* and *ESAS*) in part (a). Such a situation might arise from an *unexpected* slowdown in the pace of technological change or capital accumulation.

Again, the equilibrium occurs where the aggregate demand curve intersects the short-run aggregate supply curve. In this case, the GDP deflator is 135 and real GDP is $4.75 trillion. The actual price level

FIGURE 31.7

Rational Expectations Equilibrium

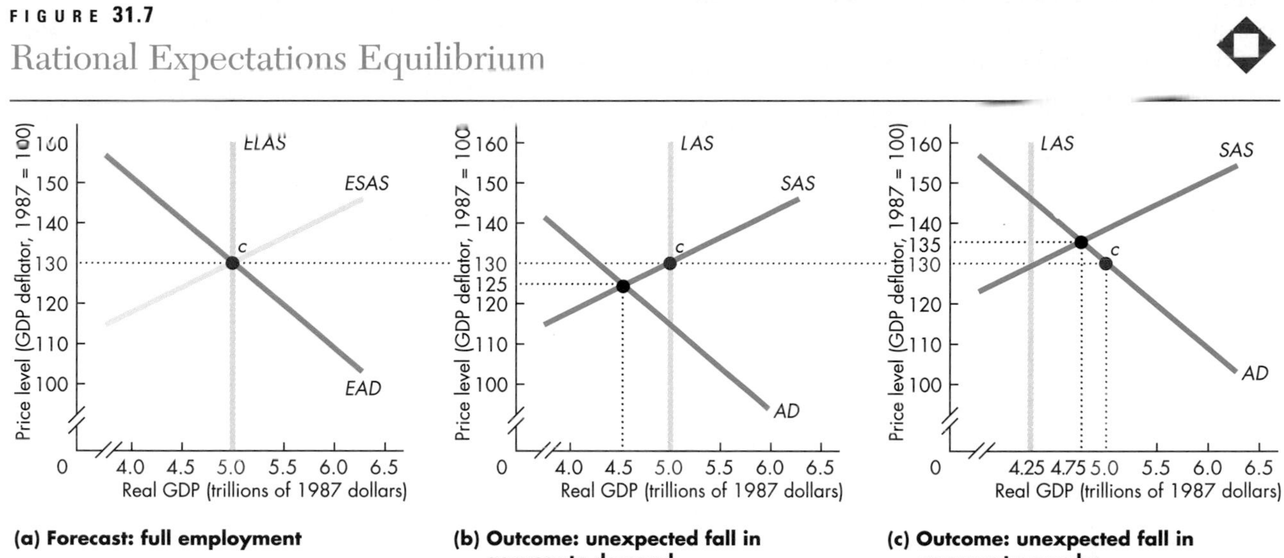

The rational expectation of the price level is calculated in part (a). It occurs at the intersection of curves *EAD* and *ELAS* (point *c*). If long-run aggregate supply turns out to be as expected but aggregate demand is lower than expected, as in part (b), real GDP decreases below its long-run level and the price level falls below that expected. If aggregate demand turns out to be as expected but long-run aggregate supply is lower than expected, as in part (c), the price level rises above its expected level and real GDP decreases.

is higher than expected because short-run aggregate supply is lower than expected. With the price level higher than expected, real GDP is above its long-run level. In this particular case, long-run real GDP has decreased compared with its expected value, and real GDP itself has also decreased but by less than long-run real GDP.

You can work out, using Fig. 31.7(c), what happens if aggregate supply turns out to be higher than expected. In such a case the price level is lower than expected and real GDP is higher than expected.

The outcomes that we've just looked at do not depend on whether wages are sticky or flexible. Even if wages are flexible, they cannot respond to what is not known and not expected. Thus flexible wages do not deliver full employment. In the examples of rational expectations equilibrium that we've just studied, there is unemployment or above full employment.

Individuals in a Rational Expectations Equilibrium

The key characteristic of any economic equilibrium is that all the people in the economy have reached a situation in which they cannot make a reallocation of their resources that they regard as superior to the one they have chosen.

Each household and firm sees itself as a small part of the overall economy. Those firms and households that have sufficient market power to influence prices have exerted that influence to their maximum possible advantage. But most households and firms are not able to exert a significant effect on the prices that they face. Instead, each household and firm does its best to forecast those prices relevant to its own actions.

Armed with its best forecasts, each household works out how many chickens, microwaves, and suits to buy, how much to spend on cars and plumbing, how much money to have in the bank, and how many hours a week to work. These decisions are expressed not as fixed quantities but as demand and supply schedules.

On the other side of the markets, each firm, also armed with its best forecasts, determines how much new capital equipment to install (investment), how much output to supply, and how much labor to demand. Like households, firms don't express their decisions as fixed quantities. Instead, they express them as demand schedules for factors of production and supply schedules of output.

Prices, wages, and interest rates are determined in the markets for goods and services, labor, and money at levels that ensure the mutual consistency of the plans of all the individual households and firms trading in these markets. The quantities demanded and supplied in each market balance.

In a rational expectations equilibrium, each person is satisfied that there is no better action that he or she could currently take. But such an equilibrium is not static. The economy is constantly changing. You could imagine the economy at each point that we observe as a frozen frame in a video: in the frame, the supply and demand curves in the markets for all the different goods, services, and factors of production all intersect, determining their prices and quantities at that moment. Economists try to understand what is happening by stopping the video to take a closer look at it.

We've now seen how unexpected changes in aggregate demand and aggregate supply affect both the price level and real GDP, even when people are doing their best to anticipate these changes. Let's next see how things work out when forecasts are correct—when people get lucky and correctly anticipate the future.

FIGURE 31.8

Anticipated Inflation

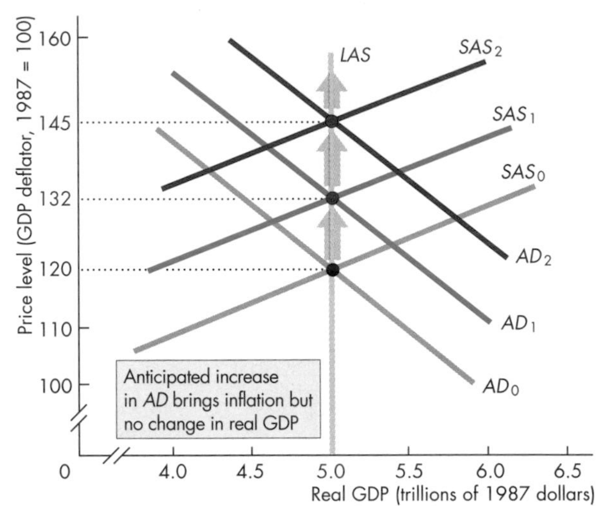

The actual and expected long-run aggregate supply curve (*LAS*) is at a real GDP of \$5 trillion. Last year, aggregate demand was AD_0, and the short-run aggregate supply curve was SAS_0. The actual price level was the same as that expected—a GDP deflator of 120. This year, aggregate demand is expected to rise to AD_1. The rational expectation of the GDP deflator changes from 120 to 132. As a result, the short-run aggregate supply curve shifts up to SAS_1. If aggregate demand actually increases as expected, the actual aggregate demand curve AD_1 is the same as the expected aggregate demand curve. Equilibrium occurs at a real GDP of \$5 trillion and an actual GDP deflator of 132. The inflation is correctly anticipated. Next year, the process continues with aggregate demand increasing as expected to AD_2 and wages rising to shift the short-run aggregate supply curve to SAS_2. Again, real GDP remains at \$5 trillion and the GDP deflator rises, as anticipated, to 145.

Anticipated Inflation

If people could correctly anticipate the future course of inflation, they would never agree to a wage contract in which the wage rate was fixed. Wages would change in line with prices. We'll study anticipated inflation, therefore, using the flexible wage model only.

Let's suppose that last year the GDP deflator was 120 and real GDP was \$5 trillion. Let's also suppose that the economy was at full employment and its long-run real GDP last year was \$5 trillion. Figure 31.8 illustrates the economy last year. The aggregate demand curve last year was AD_0, the aggregate supply curve was SAS_0, and the long-run aggregate supply curve was *LAS*. Since the economy was in equilibrium at long-run real GDP, the actual price level equaled the expected price level.

To simplify our analysis, let's suppose that at the end of last year, long-run real GDP was not expected to change, so this year's expected long-run aggregate supply is the same as last year's. Let's also suppose that aggregate demand was expected to increase, so the expected aggregate demand curve for this year is AD_1. We can now calculate the rational expectation of the price level for this year. It is a GDP deflator of 132, the price level at which the new expected aggregate demand curve intersects the expected long-run aggregate supply curve. The expected inflation rate is 10 percent, the percentage change in the price level from 120 to 132.

Wages increase as a result of the expected inflation, and the short-run aggregate supply curve also shifts to the left. In particular, given that expected inflation is 10 percent, the short-run aggregate supply curve for next year (SAS_1) shifts upward by that same percentage amount (10 percent) and passes through the long-run aggregate supply curve (*LAS*) at the expected price level.

If aggregate demand turns out to be the same as expected, the actual aggregate demand curve is AD_1. The intersection point of AD_1 and SAS_1 determines the actual price level—where the GDP deflator is 132. Between last year and this year, the GDP deflator increased from 120 to 132 and the economy experienced an inflation rate of 10 percent, the same as the inflation rate that was anticipated.

What caused the inflation? The immediate answer is the anticipated and actual increase in aggregate demand. Because aggregate demand was *expected* to increase from AD_0 to AD_1, the short-run aggregate supply curve shifted up from SAS_0 to SAS_1. Because aggregate demand actually did increase by the amount that was expected, the actual aggregate demand curve shifted from AD_0 to AD_1. The combination of the anticipated and actual shifts of the aggregate demand curve to the right produced an increase in the price level that was anticipated.

Only if aggregate demand growth is correctly forecasted does the economy follow the course described in Fig. 31.8. If the expected growth rate of aggregate demand is different from its actual growth rate, the expected aggregate demand curve shifts by an amount different from the actual aggregate demand curve. The inflation rate departs from its expected level, and, to some extent, there is unanticipated inflation. It is this type of inflation that we studied in the first part of this chapter.

Anticipated inflations can be very stubborn and hard to stop. The monetary and fiscal policy that creates inflation also creates expectations of inflation that reinforce the inflationary effects of the policy. Also, people don't like to have their expectations disappointed—so if they anticipate a high inflation rate, they want a high inflation rate. Such was the situation in the United States in the late 1970s and early 1980s. And such is the situation in Brazil today, as you can see in Reading Between the Lines on pp. 862–863.

REVIEW

A *rational expectations equilibrium* is a macroeconomic equilibrium based on expectations that are the best available forecasts. A rational expectations equilibrium describes how real GDP and the price level are determined when people are doing the best they can to anticipate the levels of aggregate demand and aggregate supply. ◆◆ In a rational expectations equilibrium, if aggregate demand is lower than expected, real GDP and the price level are lower than expected. If long-run aggregate supply is lower than expected, the price level is higher and real GDP is lower than expected. These outcomes do not depend on whether wages are sticky or flexible. Even flexible wages cannot respond to the unknown and unexpected, and a rational expectations equilibrium is not always a full-employment equilibrium. ◆◆ If people do correctly anticipate changes in aggregate demand and aggregate supply, the result is anticipated inflation. The price level changes at an anticipated rate, and real GDP and unemployment are unchanged. ◆

Inflation lowers the value of money and changes the real value of amounts borrowed and repaid. Because of this, interest rates are influenced by inflation. Let's see how.

Interest Rates and Inflation

There have been massive fluctuations in interest rates in the U.S. economy in recent years: In the early 1960s, corporations could borrow to finance long-term capital projects at interest rates of 4.5 to 5 percent a year. By the end of the 1960s, that interest rate had almost doubled and stood at 8 percent a year. During the 1970s, the interest rates paid by firms for long-term loans fluctuated between 7.5 and 10.5 percent. In 1981, interest rates hit the high teens. They fell during the rest of the 1980s and by 1991 had returned to the levels of the late 1960s. Why have interest rates fluctuated so much, and why were they so high in the late 1970s and early 1980s?

To answer these questions, it is necessary to distinguish between nominal interest rates and real interest rates. **Nominal interest rates** are those actually paid and received in the marketplace. *Real* interest

Intractable Anticipated Inflation

The Wall Street Journal, March 29, 1991

Brazil's Battle to Curb Inflation Faces Hurdle: A Lot of People Like It

by Thomas Kamm

On March 15, 1990, a new president took office in Brazil and immediately shocked his countrymen with a harsh economic program. President Fernando Collor de Mello's target was wild inflation, long an albatross burdening the country's economy and then soaring at 1,764% a year.

Mr. Collor's radical, enough-is-enough decree seemed finally to be medicine as tough as the disease. He froze about half the money then circulating in the economy, created a new currency and froze all prices.

Yet less than one year later, what was Mr. Collor doing? On Jan. 31 [1991], he was imposing still *another* anti-inflation program for Brazil.

What is it in the economy of this nation—a nation whose economic health deeply concerns its legions of U.S. creditors—that makes runaway inflation so intractable? Why didn't it yield to the recession that was set off by the 1990 program and might have been expected to moderate price increases?

The answer seems to lie, at least partly, in a kind of inflation culture in Brazil. It is a set of expectations that even some of those who call inflation a menace and a curse find curiously comforting.

Consider the experience of Gil Pace. An economist and former government official, he worries that Brazil is "entering chaos as a result of the persistence" of inflation. But as a private citizen, Mr. Pace offers a different view. Inflation allowed him to buy an apartment in Rio's swanky Lagoa district "almost for free."

It worked like this: When Mr. Pace first started making mortgage payments in 1975, both his salary and the mortgage were adjusted annually for inflation, then 30% a year. The state lender continued adjusting the mortgage once a year, but before long inflation was so bad that his employer began raising his salary every month. With inflation totaling more than one million percent between 1985 and 1990, by the time he paid off the mortgage last year, the lagging adjustment on his loan had practically wiped out the debt.

By the end, he was paying the equivalent of a mere $6.50 a month. "It was costing them more than that to send me the mortgage bill," Mr. Pace says. His conclusion: "I'm against inflation, but here, you have to defend inflation." . . .

The Essence of the Story

In March 1990, Brazil's inflation rate was 1,764 percent a year.

The country's new president, Fernando Collor de Mello, froze about half the money then circulating in the economy, created a new currency, and froze all prices.

In January 1991, President Collor introduced another anti-inflation program for Brazil.

Inflation is intractable in Brazil and does not yield to recession, at least partly because people expect inflation and some people, like Gil Pace, gain a great deal from it.

Background and Analysis

Throughout the 1980s, Brazil's inflation rate exceeded 100 percent a year.

By the end of the decade, the rate began to accelerate, reaching 6,000 percent a year in the final quarter of 1989—see the figure.

The government of Brazil persistently spends more than it collects in taxes—has a budget deficit—on a scale that exceeds 10 percent of GDP.

To pay for its deficit, the government of Brazil borrows from the central bank and the money supply grows at a rapid rate.

Brazil's inflation results from this persistent government budget deficit and rapid money supply growth rate. These forces bring a rapid rate of increase in aggregate demand.

The increase in aggregate demand is anticipated, hence wages also increase rapidly, and the inflation is not accompanied by a rise in real GDP.

Also, the inflation is anticipated, so interest rates adjust to compensate lenders for the loss in the value of money—see the figure.

The inflation of the 1980s was *not anticipated* in the 1970s. Hence people (like Gil Pace in the article) borrowed at an interest rate that did not keep up with the inflation of the 1980s and gained from the inflation.

Stopping a persistent and expected inflation is very difficult. Aggregate demand growth must be slowed, and people must *expect* its growth to be slowed.

To achieve this end in Brazil's case, the government budget deficit—which is the source of the rapid money supply growth rate—must be brought under control.

The Collor program did not tackle this cause of inflation. Instead, it tackled the symptom of inflation—rising prices. Without a change in the underlying cause, the symptoms broke out again.

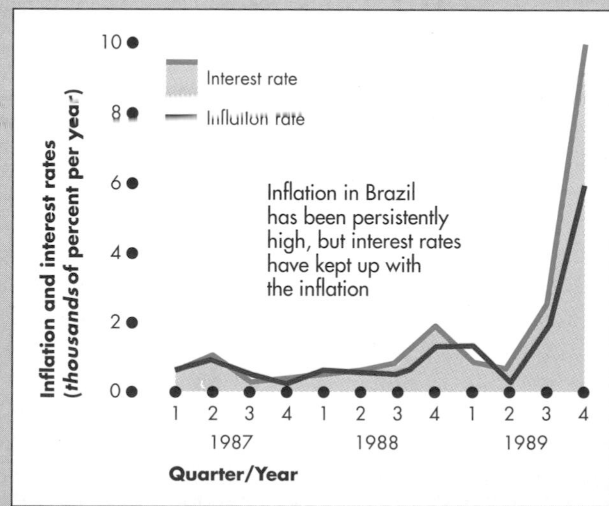

rates are the rates that nominal interest rates translate into when the effects of inflation are taken into account. If the nominal interest rate is 15 percent a year and prices are rising by 10 percent a year, the real interest rate is only 5 percent a year. If you made a loan of $100 on January 1, 1992, it's true you'd have $115 to spend on January 1, 1993. But you'd need $110 to buy the same goods that $100 would have bought a year earlier. All you've really made is $5—the difference between the $110 you need to buy $100 worth of goods and the $115 that you've got.

When we studied the determination interest rates in Chapter 28, we analyzed an economy in which the price level was constant. In such an economy, there is no difference between the nominal and real interest rates. But in the real world, the price level is rarely constant, and most of the time it increases. What are the effects on interest rates of a rising price level and of expectations of the price level continuing to rise?

Expectations of Inflation and Interest Rates

Imagine two economies that are identical in every way except for one: the first economy has no inflation and none is expected; the second economy has an inflation rate of 10 percent a year that is correctly anticipated. In both economies, the real interest rate is 5 percent. What is the difference in the nominal interest rates in these two economies?

In the zero-inflation economy the nominal interest rate is 5 percent a year—the same as the real interest rate. In the second economy the nominal interest rate is 15.5 percent a year. Why?

Lenders in the economy that is inflating at a rate of 10 percent a year recognize that the value of the money that they have lent is falling at a rate of 10 percent a year. They protect themselves against this loss in the value of money by asking for a higher nominal interest rate on the loans that they make. Borrowers in this economy recognize that the money they use to repay their loans is worth 10 percent a year less than money they borrowed. They willingly agree to a higher nominal interest rate. In recognition of the falling value of money, borrowers and lenders agree to add 10 percentage points a year to the interest rate. In addition, they agree to add 10 percent of the interest because they recognize that even the interest buys 10 percent less at the end of the year than at the beginning of the year. Since the real interest rate is 5 percent a year, 10 percent of the interest rate is half a percentage point. So the total amount that borrowers and lenders agree to add to the real interest rate of 5 percent a year is 10.5 percentage points, and the nominal interest rate is 15.5 percent a year.

We've seen that, other things being equal, the higher the expected inflation rate, the higher is the nominal interest rate. Usually, an economy with a high expected inflation rate is one actually experiencing a high inflation rate. We would expect, therefore, that interest rates and inflation rates move up and down together. Let's see if they do.

Inflation and Interest Rates in the United States

The relationship between inflation and nominal interest rates in the United States is illustrated in Fig. 31.9. The interest rate measured on the vertical axis is that paid by large corporations on short-term (6-month) loans. Each point on the graph represents a year in recent U.S. macroeconomic history between 1960 and 1991. The blue line shows the relationship between the nominal interest rate and the inflation rate if the real interest rate is constant at 2.2 percent a year, its actual average value in this period. As you can see, there is a clear relationship between the inflation rate and the interest rate, but it is not exact. As we have just seen, it is only *anticipated* inflation that influences interest rates. Thus only to the extent that a higher inflation rate is anticipated does it result in higher interest rates.

During the 1960s, both actual and expected inflation were moderate and so were nominal interest rates. In the early 1970s, inflation began to increase but it was not expected to increase much and certainly not to persist. As a result, nominal interest rates did not rise very much at that time. By the mid-1970s, there was a burst of unexpectedly high inflation. Interest rates increased somewhat but not by nearly as much as the inflation rate. During the late 1970s and early 1980s, inflation of close to 10 percent a year came to be expected as an ongoing and highly persistent phenomenon. As a result, nominal interest rates increased to around 15 percent a year. Then in 1984 and 1985, the inflation rate

FIGURE 31.9

Inflation and the Interest Rate

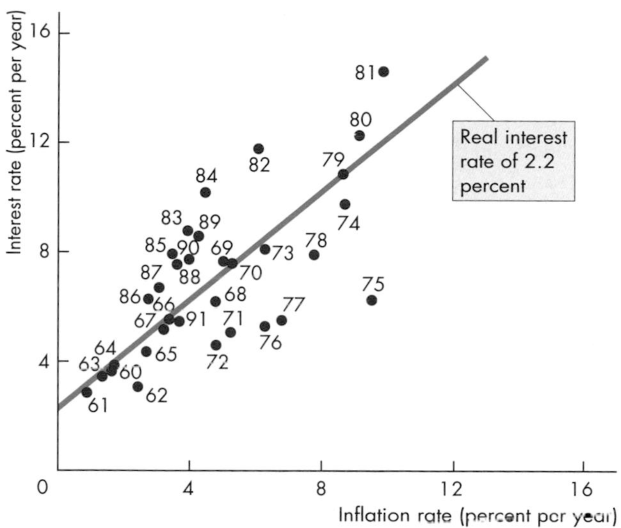

Other things being equal, the higher the expected inflation rate, the higher is the interest rate. A graph showing the relationship between interest rates and the actual inflation rate reveals that the influence of inflation on interest rates is a powerful one. Here, the interest rate is that paid by large corporations on short-term loans (the 6-month commercial paper rate) and the inflation rate is the percentage change in the GDP deflator. Each point represents a year in U.S. macroeconomic history between 1960 and 1991.

Source: Economic Report of the President, 1992.

fell—at first unexpectedly. Interest rates began to fall but not nearly as quickly as the inflation rate. Short-term interest rates fell more quickly than long-term interest rates because, at that time, it was expected that inflation would be lower in the short term but not as low in the longer term.

The relationship between inflation and interest rates is even more dramatically illustrated by international experience. For example, in recent years, Chile has experienced an inflation rate of around 30 percent with nominal interest rates of about 40 percent. Brazil has experienced inflation rates of more than 200 percent a year with nominal interest rates also above 200 percent a year. At the other extreme, such countries as Japan and Belgium have had low inflation and low nominal interest rates.

Money Supply and Interest Rates We have seen that high nominal interest rates and high expected inflation rates go together. We have also seen that high expected inflation is the product of a high anticipated money supply growth rate. Thus a high anticipated growth rate of the money supply brings not only a high anticipated inflation rate but also high nominal interest rates.

In Chapter 28, when we studied the effects of the Fed's actions on interest rates, we concluded that an increase in the quantity of money *lowers* nominal interest rates. How can both of these conclusions be correct? How can an increase in the anticipated growth rate of the money supply increase interest rates while an increase in the quantity of money lowers them?

The answer lies in the time it takes interest rates to adjust to a change in the money supply. If the Fed takes an unexpected action that increases the quantity of money, the immediate effect is lower nominal interest rates. Lower interest rates are needed to make the quantity of money demanded equal the quantity supplied. But if the Fed continues to increase the money supply and keeps on increasing it year after year at a faster pace than real GDP is growing, people come to expect that increase in the money supply and the inflation that goes with it.

In these circumstances, with low interest rates and a high expected inflation rate, people increase their borrowing and increase their spending on goods and services. The inflation rate speeds up and overtakes the growth rate of the money supply. With inflation proceeding at a faster pace than money supply growth, the quantity of real money declines. That is, the fact that the Fed is increasing the money supply but prices are rising even more quickly means that the real money supply is decreasing. The Fed controls the *nominal* money supply but doesn't control the *real* money supply.

Lower quantity of real money brings higher interest rates. Only when interest rates have increased by enough to compensate for the anticipated falling value of money is a long-run equilibrium restored.

Thus an unanticipated increase in the money supply brings a fall in interest rates. An anticipated and ongoing increase in the money supply increases interest rates. The decrease in interest rates following an increase in the money supply is an immediate but temporary response. The increase in interest rates associated with an increase in the growth rate of the money supply is a long-run response.

REVIEW

The nominal interest rate is the rate actually paid and received in the marketplace. The real interest rate is the rate *really* paid and received when the effects of inflation are taken into account. The nominal interest rate is approximately equal to the real interest rate plus the expected inflation rate. The nominal interest rate is also the interest rate that makes the quantity of money demanded equal to the quantity of money supplied. ◆

Inflation over the Business Cycle: The Phillips Curve

We've seen that a speedup in aggregate demand growth that is not fully anticipated increases both inflation and real GDP growth. It also decreases unemployment. Similarly, a slowdown in the growth rate of aggregate demand that is not fully anticipated slows down both inflation and real GDP growth and increases unemployment. We've also seen that a fully anticipated change in the growth rate of aggregate demand changes the inflation rate and has no effect on real GDP or unemployment. Finally, we've seen that a decrease in aggregate supply increases inflation and decreases real GDP growth. In this case, unemployment increases.

The aggregate demand–aggregate supply model that we have used to obtain these results gives predictions about the level of real GDP and the price level. Given these predictions, we can work out how unemployment and inflation have changed. But the aggregate demand–aggregate supply model does not place inflation and unemployment at center stage.

An alternative way of studying inflation and unemployment focuses directly on their joint movements and uses a relationship known as the Phillips curve. The Phillips curve is so named because it was popularized by New Zealand economist A. W. Phillips when working at the London School of Economics in the 1950s. A **Phillips curve** is a curve showing the relationship between inflation and unemployment. There are two time frames for Phillips curves:

- The short run
- The long run

The Phillips Curve in the Short Run

The **short-run Phillips curve** is a curve showing the relationship between inflation and unemployment, holding constant:

1. The expected inflation rate
2. The natural rate of unemployment

Figure 31.10 shows a short-run Phillips curve *SRPC*. Suppose that the expected inflation rate is 10 percent a year and the natural rate of unemployment is 6 percent, point *a* in the figure. The short-run

FIGURE 31.10
The Short-Run Phillips Curve

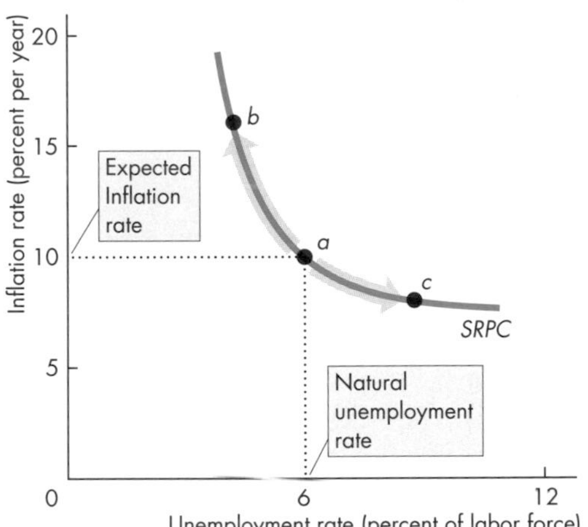

The short-run Phillips curve *SRPC* shows the relationship between inflation and unemployment at a given expected inflation rate and given natural rate of unemployment. With an expected inflation rate of 10 percent a year and a natural rate of unemployment of 6 percent, the short-run Phillips curve passes through point *a*. An unanticipated increase in aggregate demand lowers unemployment and increases inflation—a movement up the short-run Phillips curve. An unanticipated decrease in aggregate demand increases unemployment and lowers inflation—a movement down the short-run Phillips curve.

Phillips curve passes through this point. If the unemployment rate falls below its natural rate, inflation rises above its expected rate. This joint movement in the inflation rate and the unemployment rate is illustrated as a movement up the short-run Phillips curve from point *a* to point *b* in the figure. Similarly, if unemployment rises above the natural rate, inflation falls below its expected rate. In this case, there is movement down the short-run Phillips curve from point *a* to point *c*.

This negative relationship between inflation and unemployment along the short-run Phillips curve is explained by the aggregate demand–aggregate supply model. Suppose that, initially, inflation is anticipated to be 10 percent a year and unemployment is at its natural rate. This situation is illustrated by the aggregate demand–aggregate supply model in Fig. 31.8 and by the Phillips curve approach as point *a* in Fig. 31.10. Suppose that now an unanticipated increase in the growth of aggregate demand occurs. In Fig. 31.8 the aggregate demand curve shifts to the right more quickly than expected. Real GDP increases, the unemployment rate decreases, and the price level starts to increase at a faster rate than expected. There has been a movement from point *a* to point *b* in Fig. 31.10. If the unanticipated increase in aggregate demand is temporary, aggregate demand growth slows to its previous level. When it does so, the process is reversed and the economy moves back to point *a* in Fig. 31.10.

A similar story can be told to illustrate the effects of an unanticipated decrease in the growth of aggregate demand. In this case, an unanticipated slowdown in the growth of aggregate demand reduces inflation, slows real GDP growth, and increases unemployment. There is a movement down the short-run Phillips curve from point *a* to point *c*.

The Phillips Curve in the Long Run

The **long-run Phillips curve** is a curve showing the relationship between inflation and unemployment when the actual inflation rate equals the expected inflation rate. The long-run Phillips curve is vertical at the natural rate of unemployment—the **natural rate hypothesis.** The natural rate hypothesis was proposed independently in the mid-1960s by Edmund Phelps (now at Columbia University but then a young professor at the University of Pennsylvania—see Talking with Edmund Phelps on pp. 812–815) and by Milton Friedman. Sometimes the natural rate hypothesis is given the alternative name the *Phelps-Friedman hypothesis.*

A long-run Phillips curve is shown in Fig. 31.11 as the vertical line *LRPC*. If the expected inflation rate is 10 percent a year, the short-run Phillips curve is $SRPC_0$. If the expected inflation rate falls to 8 percent a year, the short-run Phillips curve shifts downward to $SRPC_1$. At points *a* and *d*, inflation is equal to its expected rate and unemployment is equal to its natural rate. The distance by which the short-run Phillips curve shifts downward when the expected inflation rate falls is equal to the change in the expected inflation rate. Points *a* and *d* lie on the long-run Phillips curve *LRPC*. This curve tells us

FIGURE 31.11

The Short-Run and Long-Run Phillips Curves

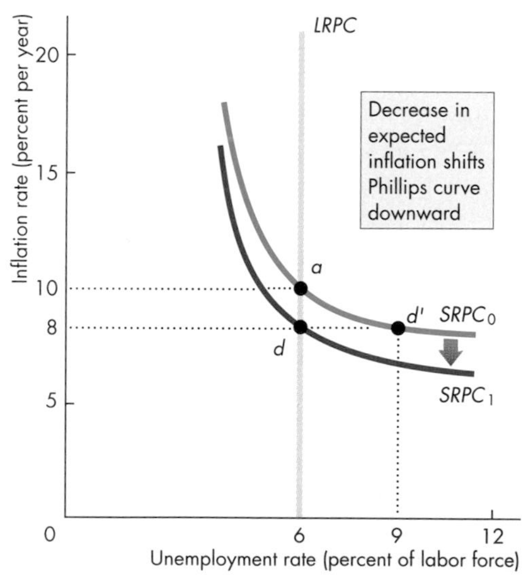

The long-run Phillips curve is *LRPC*, a vertical line at the natural rate of unemployment. A decrease in inflation expectations shifts the short-run Phillips curve down by the amount of the fall in the expected inflation rate. Here, when expected inflation falls from 10 percent a year to 8 percent a year, the short-run Phillips curve shifts from $SRPC_0$ to $SRPC_1$. The new short-run Phillips curve intersects the long-run Phillips curve at the new expected inflation rate at point *d*. With the original expected inflation rate (of 10 percent), an inflation rate of 8 percent a year would occur at an unemployment rate of 9 percent, at point *d'*.

that any inflation rate is possible at the natural rate of unemployment.

To see why the short-run Phillips curve shifts when the expected inflation rate changes, let's do an experiment. The economy is at full employment, and a fully anticipated inflation is raging at 10 percent a year. Now suppose that the Fed and the government begin a permanent attack on inflation by slowing money supply growth and cutting the deficit. Aggregate demand growth slows down, and the inflation rate falls to 8 percent a year. At first, this decrease in inflation is unanticipated, so wages continue to rise at their original rate, shifting the short-run aggregate supply curve to the left at the same pace as before. Real GDP falls, and unemployment increases. In Fig. 31.11, the economy moves from point *a* to point *d'* on the short-run Phillips curve $SRPC_0$.

If the actual inflation rate remains steady at 8 percent a year, eventually this rate will come to be expected. As this happens, wage growth slows down and the short-run aggregate supply curve moves leftward less quickly. Eventually, it shifts to the left at the same pace at which the aggregate demand curve is shifting to the right. When this occurs, the actual inflation rate equals the expected inflation rate and full employment is restored. Unemployment is back at its natural rate. In Fig. 31.11, the short-run Phillips curve has shifted from $SRPC_0$ to $SRPC_1$ and the economy is at point *d*.

FIGURE 31.12

A Change in the Natural Rate of Unemployment

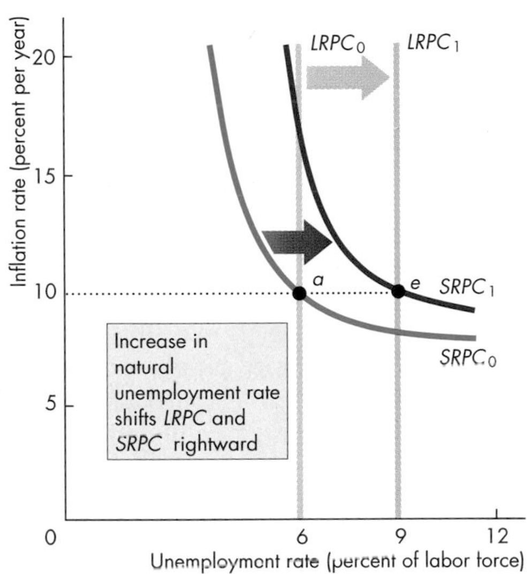

A change in the natural rate of unemployment shifts both the short-run and long-run Phillips curves. Here, the natural rate of unemployment increases from 6 percent to 9 percent, and the two Phillips curves shift right to $SRPC_1$ and $LRPC_1$. The new long-run Phillips curve intersects the new short-run Phillips curve at the expected inflation rate—point *e*

Variable Natural Rate of Unemployment

Until the 1970s, the natural rate of unemployment was regarded as a constant. In recent years, however, it has become clear that the natural rate of unemployment varies. Some of these variations arise from changes in the amount of labor market turnover resulting from technological change, which leads to job switching from firm to firm, sector to sector, and region to region. A change in the natural rate of unemployment shifts both the short-run and long-run Phillips curves. Such shifts are illustrated in Fig. 31.12. If the natural rate of unemployment increases from 6 percent to 9 percent, the long-run Phillips curve shifts from $LRPC_0$ to $LRPC_1$, and if expected inflation is constant at 10 percent a year, the short-run Phillips curve shifts from $SRPC_0$ to $SRPC_1$. Because the expected inflation rate is constant, the short-run Phillips curve $SRPC_1$ intersects the long-run curve $LRPC_1$ (point *e*) at the same inflation rate as that at which the short-run Phillips curve $SRPC_0$ intersects the long-run curve $LRPC_0$ (point *a*).

The Phillips Curve in the United States

Figure 31.13 shows the relationship between inflation and unemployment in the United States. Begin by looking at part (a), a scatter diagram of inflation and unemployment since 1960. Each dot in the figure represents the combination of inflation and unemployment for a particular year. As you can see, there does not appear to be any clear relationship between inflation and unemployment. We certainly cannot see a Phillips curve similar to that shown in Fig. 31.10.

But we can interpret the data in terms of a shifting short-run Phillips curve. Figure 31.13(b) pro-

vides such an interpretation. Four short-run Phillips curves appear in the figure. The short-run Phillips curve of the 1960s (discovered by Paul Samuelson and Robert Solow of MIT—see Talking with Robert Solow, pp. 1–4) is $SRPC_0$. At that time, the expected inflation rate was 2 percent a year and the natural rate of unemployment was 5 percent.

The short-run Phillips curve of the early 1970s and late 1980s is $SRPC_1$. These two periods have a natural rate of unemployment similar to that of the 1960s but an expected inflation rate that is much higher. The short-run Phillips curve of the late 1970s is $SRPC_2$. This period followed the large increase in oil prices that disrupted the economy and had profound effects on both the natural rate of unemployment, which increased to 8 percent, and the expected inflation rate, which increased to around 6 percent a year. The short-run Phillips curve of the early 1980s (and also of 1975) is $SRPC_3$. In these years, both the expected inflation rate and the natural rate of unemployment were high.

Although in the late 1980s the economy was on the same short-run Phillips curve as in the early 1970s ($SRPC_1$), there is an important difference between these two periods. In the early 1970s, the natural rate of unemployment was around 5 percent and the expected inflation rate was around 6 percent a year, while in the late 1980s, the natural rate of unemployment was probably around 6 percent with expected inflation at about 4 percent a year. Thus, although the short-run Phillips curves for these two periods are similar, a different combination of expected inflation and natural rate of unemployment underlies the two curves.

FIGURE 31.13

Phillips Curves in the United States

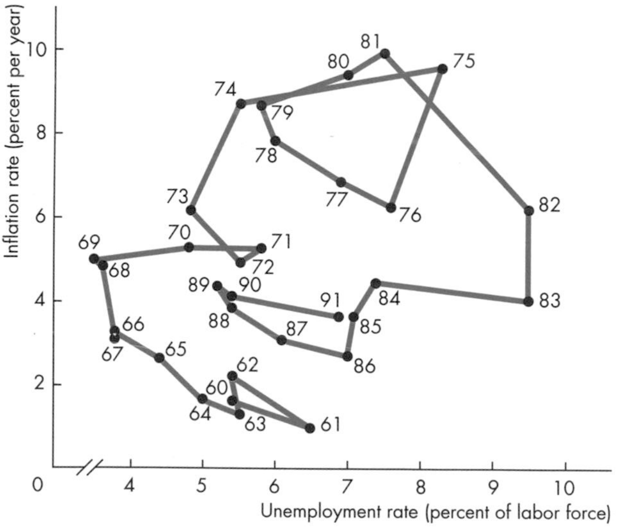

(a) The time sequence

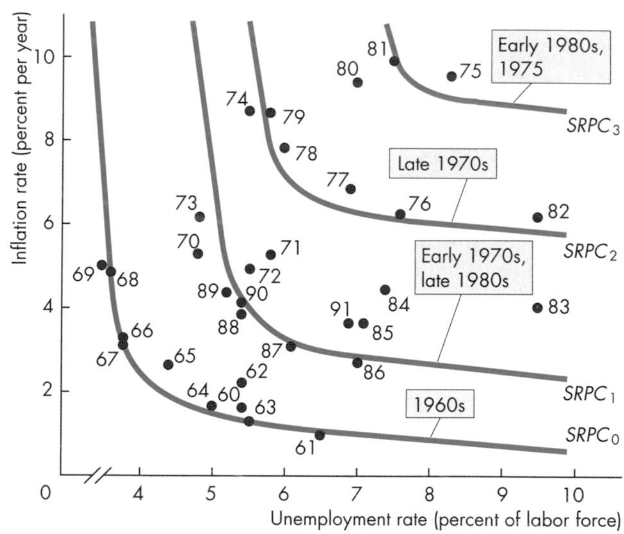

(b) Four Phillips curves

In part (a), each dot represents the combination of inflation and unemployment for a particular year in the United States. There is no clear relationship between the two variables. Part (b) interprets the data in terms of a shifting short-run Phillips curve. The short-run Phillips curve of the 1960s, when the expected inflation rate was 2 percent a year and the natural rate of unemployment was 5 percent, is $SRPC_0$. The short-run Phillips curve of the early 1970s and late 1980s is $SRPC_1$. These two periods have a natural rate of unemployment similar to that of the 1960s but a higher expected inflation rate. The short-run Phillips curve of the late 1970s, when oil price hikes increased both the natural rate of unemployment and the expected inflation rate, is $SRPC_2$. In 1975 and the early 1980s, when oil price increases had their maximum impact on inflation expectations, the short-run Phillips curve is $SRPC_3$.

Source: Economic Report of the President, 1992.

REVIEW

The short-run Phillips curve shows the relationship between inflation and unemployment at a given expected inflation rate and natural rate of unemployment. An unanticipated burst of aggregate demand growth increases inflation and decreases unemployment—a movement up the short-run Phillips curve. An unanticipated slowdown in aggregate demand growth reduces inflation and increases unemployment—a movement down the short-run Phillips curve. ◆◆ The long-run Phillips curve, the relationship between inflation and unemployment when the actual inflation rate equals the expected inflation rate, is vertical at the natural rate of unemployment—the natural rate hypothesis. A change in the expected inflation rate shifts the short-run Phillips curve (up for an increase in inflation and down for a decrease) by an amount equal to the change in the expected inflation rate. ◆◆ A change in the natural rate of unemployment shifts both the short-run and the long-run Phillips curve to the right for an increase in the natural rate and to the left for a decrease. ◆◆ The relationship between inflation and unemployment in the United States can be interpreted in terms of a shifting short-run Phillips curve. ◆

◆◆◆◆ We have now completed our study of inflation and the relationships between the inflation rate, the interest rate, and the unemployment rate. Our next task, which we'll pursue in Chapter 32, is to see how the aggregate demand–aggregate supply model that we have used to study inflation also helps us to explore and interpret fluctuations in real GDP and explain recessions and depressions.

SUMMARY

Why Inflation Is a Problem

Inflation is a problem because it results in a fall in the value of money. The nature of the problem depends on whether inflation is *anticipated* or *unanticipated.* Anticipated inflation reduces the effectiveness of money as a medium of exchange. Unanticipated inflation is a problem because it redistributes wealth between borrowers and lenders and income between employers and employees. Unanticipated fluctuations in the inflation rate produce fluctuations in real GDP, employment, and unemployment. (p. 848)

Demand-Pull Inflation

Demand-pull inflation arises from increasing aggregate demand. Its origin can be any of the factors that shift the aggregate demand curve to the right. The most important of these factors are an increasing money supply and increasing government purchases of goods and services. When the aggregate demand curve shifts to the right, other things remaining the same, both real GDP and the GDP deflator increase and unemployment falls. With a shortage of labor, wages begin to increase and the short-run aggregate supply curve shifts to the left, raising the GDP deflator still more and decreasing real GDP.

If aggregate demand continues to increase, the aggregate demand curve keeps shifting to the right and the price level keeps on rising. Wages respond, aggregate demand increases again, and a price-wage inflation spiral ensues. (pp. 849–851)

Supply Inflation and Stagflation

Cost-push inflation can result from any factor that decreases aggregate supply, but the most important of these are increasing wage rates and increasing prices of key raw materials. These sources of a decreasing aggregate supply bring increasing costs that shift the short-run aggregate supply curve to the left. Firms decrease the quantity of labor employed and cut back production. Real GDP declines, and the price level rises. If no action is taken to increase aggregate demand, the economy remains below full

employment until the initial price increase that triggered the stagflation is reversed.

Action by the Fed or the government to restore full employment (an increase in the money supply or in government purchases of goods and services or a tax cut) increases aggregate demand and shifts the aggregate demand curve to the right, resulting in a yet higher price level and higher real GDP. If the original source of cost-push inflation is still present, costs rise again and the short-run aggregate supply curve shifts to the left again. If the Fed or the government responds again with a further increase in aggregate demand, the price level rises even higher. Inflation proceeds at a rate determined by the cost-push forces. (pp. 851–853)

Inflation Expectations

The decisions made by firms and households to produce and work and to borrow and lend are based on forecasts of inflation. But the real wages and real interest rates they actually pay and receive depend on actual inflation. Errors in forecasting inflation are costly, and people use all available information to minimize these errors.

Specialist forecasters use data and statistical models to generate expectations. Others either buy forecasts from specialists or copy people who are successful. Economists predict people's forecasts by using the rational expectations hypothesis—the hypothesis that inflation forecasts are made by using the aggregate demand–aggregate supply model together with all the available information on the positions of the aggregate demand and aggregate supply curves. (pp. 854–858)

Rational Expectations Equilibrium

A rational expectations equilibrium is a macroeconomic equilibrium based on expectations that are the best available forecasts. The rational expectations equilibrium occurs at the intersection of the aggregate demand and short-run aggregate supply curves. A rational expectations equilibrium might be a full-employment equilibrium, but other possibilities can occur. Aggregate demand and aggregate supply may be higher or lower than expected. The combination of these possibilities means that output may be above or below its long-run level and the price level may be higher or lower than expected. Regardless of which of these states the economy is experiencing, in a rational expectations equilibrium no one would have acted differently, given the state of affairs in which they made their choices.

When changes in aggregate demand and aggregate supply are correctly anticipated, their only effects are on the price level—inflation is anticipated. (pp. 858–861)

Interest Rates and Inflation

Expectations of inflation affect nominal interest rates. The higher the expected inflation rate, the higher is the nominal interest rate. Borrowers will willingly pay more and lenders will successfully demand more as the anticipated inflation rate rises. Borrowing and lending and asset-holding plans are made consistent with each other by adjustments in the real interest rate—the difference between the nominal interest rate and the expected inflation rate. (pp. 861–866)

Inflation over the Business Cycle: The Phillips Curve

Phillips curves describe the relationships between inflation and unemployment. The short-run Phillips curve shows the relationship between inflation and unemployment, holding constant the expected inflation rate and the natural rate of unemployment. The long-run Phillips curve shows the relationship between inflation and unemployment when the actual inflation rate equals the expected inflation rate. The short-run Phillips curve slopes downward—the lower the unemployment rate, the higher is the inflation rate, other things remaining the same. The long-run Phillips curve is vertical at the natural rate of unemployment—the natural rate hypothesis.

Changes in aggregate demand with a constant expected inflation rate and natural rate of unemployment bring movements along the short-run Phillips curve. Changes in expected inflation bring shifts in the short-run Phillips curve. Changes in the natural rate of unemployment bring shifts in both the short-run and long-run Phillips curves.

There is no clear relationship between inflation and unemployment in the United States, but the joint movements in those variables can be interpreted in terms of a shifting short-run Phillips curve. (pp. 866–870)

KEY ELEMENTS

Key Terms

Cost-push inflation, 851
Demand-pull inflation, 849
Long-run Phillips curve, 867
Natural rate hypothesis, 867
Nominal interest rate, 861
Phillips curve, 866
Rational expectation, 854
Rational expectations equilibrium, 858
Rational expectations hypothesis, 855
Short-run Phillips curve, 866

Key Figures

REVIEW QUESTIONS

1 Distinguish between the price level and the inflation rate.

2 Distinguish between anticipated and unanticipated inflation.

3 Distinguish between demand-pull inflation and cost-push inflation.

4 Explain how a price-wage inflation spiral occurs.

5 Explain how a cost-price inflation spiral occurs.

6 Why are wrong inflation expectations costly? Suggest some of the losses that an individual would suffer in labor markets as well as in asset markets.

7 Explain why wrong expectations do more than redistribute between employers and workers and between borrowers and lenders.

8 What is a rational expectation? Explain the two features of a rational expectation.

9 Explain the rational expectations hypothesis.

10 What is the rational expectation of the price in each of the following situations?

a Wages are sticky.
b Wages are flexible.

11 What is a rational expectations equilibrium? Draw three figures to show a rational expectations equilibrium when there is

a Unemployment
b Full employment
c Above full employment

12 Explain how anticipated inflation arises.

13 What are the main factors leading to changes in aggregate demand that produce ongoing and persistent inflation?

14 What is the connection between expected inflation and nominal interest rates?

15 What does the short-run Phillips curve show?

16 What does the long-run Phillips curve show?

17 What were the main shifts in the U.S. short-run Phillips curve during the 1970s and 1980s?

PROBLEMS

1 Work out the effects on the price level of the following unexpected events:

a An increase in the money supply
b An increase in government purchases of goods and services
c An increase in income taxes
d An increase in investment demand
e An increase in the wage rate
f An increase in labor productivity

2 Work out the effects on the price level of the events listed in problem 1 when they are correctly anticipated.

3 An economy in which wages are flexible has a long-run aggregate supply of $3.5 trillion. It has the following expected aggregate demand curve:

Price level (GDP deflator)	Expected GDP demanded (trillions of 1987 dollars)
80	5.0
90	4.5
100	4.0
110	3.5
120	3.0
130	2.5
140	2.0

a What is the expected price level?
b What is expected real GDP?

4 In the economy of problem 3, the expected price level increases to 120.

a What is the new *SAS* curve?
b What would the new *SAS* curve be if wages were sticky?

5 In 1992, the expected aggregate demand schedule for 1993 is as follows:

Price level (GDP deflator)	Expected real GDP demanded (trillions of 1987 dollars)
120	4.0
121	3.9
122	3.8
123	3.7
124	3.6

In 1992, the long-run real GDP is $3.8 trillion, the price level is 110, and the real GDP expected for 1993 is $3.9 trillion. Calculate the 1992 rational expectation of the price level for 1993 if wages are flexible.

6 The economy in problem 5 has the following actual aggregate demand schedule and short-run aggregate supply schedule in 1993:

Price level (GDP deflator)	Real GDP demanded (trillions of 1987 dollars)	Real GDP supplied (trillions of 1987 dollars)
120	4.4	3.2
121	4.3	3.5
122	4.2	3.8
123	4.1	4.1
124	4.0	4.4

a Calculate the actual and expected inflation rate.
b Calculate the level of real GDP.
c Is the economy above or below full employment?

7 An economy has a natural rate of unemployment of 4 percent when its expected inflation is 6 percent. Its inflation and unemployment history is

Inflation rate (percent per year)	Unemployment rate (percent)
8	3
6	4
4	5

a Draw a diagram of this economy's short-run and long-run Phillips curves.
b If the actual inflation rate rises from 6 percent a year to 8 percent a year, what is the change in the unemployment rate? Explain why it occurs.
c Show on your diagram the shifts in the long-run and short-run Phillips curves from:
 (1) A rise in the natural rate of unemployment to 5 percent
 (2) A fall in the expected inflation rate to 4 percent

 Explain these shifts.

CHAPTER 32

RECESSIONS AND DEPRESSIONS

After studying this chapter, you will be able to:

- Describe the origins of the 1991 recession and other recessions of the 1970s and 1980s
- Describe the course of money, interest rates, and expenditure as the economy contracts
- Describe the labor market in recession
- Compare and contrast the flexible and sticky wage theories of the labor market in recession
- Describe the onset of the Great Depression in 1929
- Describe the economy in the depths of the Great Depression between 1929 and 1933
- Compare the economy of the 1930s with that of today and assess the likelihood of another Great Depression

What Goes Up Must Come Down

THE 1920S WERE YEARS OF UNPRECEDENTED PROSPERITY for Americans. After the horrors of World War I, the economic machine was back at work, producing such technological marvels as cars and airplanes, telephones and vacuum cleaners. Houses and apartments were being built at a frantic pace. ◆◆ Then, almost without warning, in October 1929, came an unprecedented stock market crash. Overnight, the values of stocks and shares trading on Wall Street fell by 30 percent. In the four succeeding years, there followed the most severe economic contraction in recorded history. By 1933, real GDP had fallen by 30 percent; unemployment had increased to 25 percent of the labor force; employment was down 20 percent; and prices were down 25 percent. ◆◆ The cost of the Great Depression, in terms of human suffering, will never be fully known. Families were unclothed, hungry, and homeless. But the cost went far beyond the hardship faced by those having no jobs. Social tensions and crime increased, and a polarization of political attitudes occurred that was to dominate the world for the next 50 years. What caused the Great Depression? ◆◆ In October 1987, stock markets in the United States and throughout the world crashed. The crash was so steep and so widespread that it has been dubbed a stock market "meltdown"—conjuring up images of Three Mile Island and Chernobyl. This severe and widespread stock market crash has caused some commentators to draw parallels between 1987 and 1929—the eve of the greatest economic depression in history. Are there similar forces at work in the U.S. and world economies today that might bring about a Great Depression of the 1990s? ◆◆ Although they are not in the same league

as the Great Depression, we have experienced three recessions in recent history. The worst of these, and the most severe recession since the Great Depression, occurred in 1982, a year in which real GDP fell by 2.5 percent and unemployment increased to almost 11 percent. Eight years earlier, in 1974–1975, real GDP fell by 1.8 percent over two years and unemployment almost doubled to 8.5 percent. The most recent recession began in 1990. In the final quarter of that year, real GDP fell at a 2 percent annual rate and unemployment climbed to 6 percent. Throughout 1991, unemployment continued to climb, ending the year at close to 7 percent. What caused these recessions? Are all recessions triggered in the same way, or is there a variety of causes?

◆ ◆ ◆ ◆ In this chapter, we're going to use the macroeconomic tools that we studied in the previous chapters to explain economic contractions. We're going to unravel some of the mysteries of recession and depression and assess the likelihood of a serious depression such as that of the 1930s occurring again. We're going to begin by examining the three most recent recessions in U.S. economic history.

Three Recent Recessions

The three most recent recessions in the United States occurred in 1974–1975, 1982, and 1990–1991. We're going to compare and contrast the origins and mechanisms at work during these episodes of U.S. macroeconomic history. We'll pay special attention to the labor market and to the central disagreement among economists about how the labor market works during an economic contraction. Let's begin with their origins.

The Origins of Recent Recessions

Recessions can be triggered by a variety of forces. Some have their origins in shocks to aggregate supply, some in shocks to aggregate demand, and some in a combination of these shocks. The three recent recessions provide examples of all three cases.

The OPEC Recession In the early 1970s, the U.S. economy was progressing in an unremarkable manner. Real GDP was close to its trend value and growing at a rate similar to its long-run average growth rate. Unemployment ranged between 5 and 6 percent, and inflation ranged between 3 and 6 percent a year. More and more people were enjoying and sharing in the benefits of sustained economic expansion.

Then, toward the end of 1973, the economy was dealt a devastating blow. The price of a barrel of oil, which had cost \$2.60 on January 1, 1973, was increased to \$11.65 by January 1, 1974. This massive 348 percent increase in the price of crude oil was engineered by OPEC (the Organization of Petroleum Exporting Countries), which controlled 68 percent of world oil production (outside the communist countries). The price hike had dramatic macroeconomic effects. For the next two years, the U.S. economy went into a severe recession. The severity of the recession and its immediate cause can be seen in Fig. 32.1. Before the oil price shock, the aggregate demand and short-run aggregate supply curves were AD_{73} and SAS_{73}. Real GDP was \$3.3 trillion, and the GDP deflator was 41. Through the subsequent two years, aggregate demand continued to increase at roughly the same steady pace as it had increased in the previous few years. The aggregate demand curve shifted to the right to AD_{75}. If the prices of inputs—labor and raw materials—had also continued to increase at their normal pace, the short-run aggregate supply curve would have shifted to SAS_n. By 1975, the economy would have moved to point *a*. Inflation would have been about 3 percent a year, and real GDP would have continued to grow at a similar pace.

But that's not how things turned out. When OPEC producers increased the price of crude oil, the prices of other fuels as well as the prices of many other raw materials also increased. The index of all commodity prices excluding fuel (published by the International Monetary Fund) increased by 63 percent in 1973 and 24 percent in 1974. Labor costs also started to increase more quickly. As a result, the short-run aggregate supply curve shifted all the way to SAS_{75}. This shift in the short-run aggregate supply curve, triggered by the oil price increase, was the single most important event producing the OPEC recession. Real GDP fell to \$3.2 trillion, and the GDP deflator increased to 49—an almost 20 percent increase in the price level over the two years of

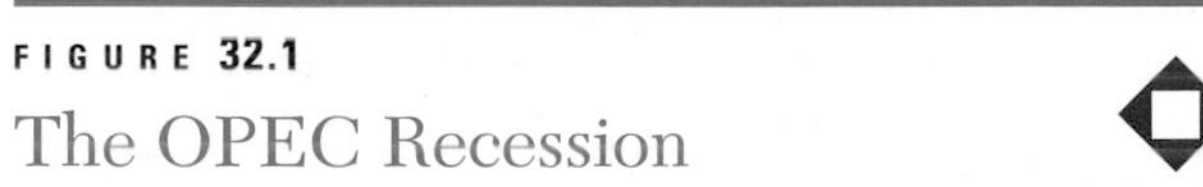

FIGURE 32.1

The OPEC Recession

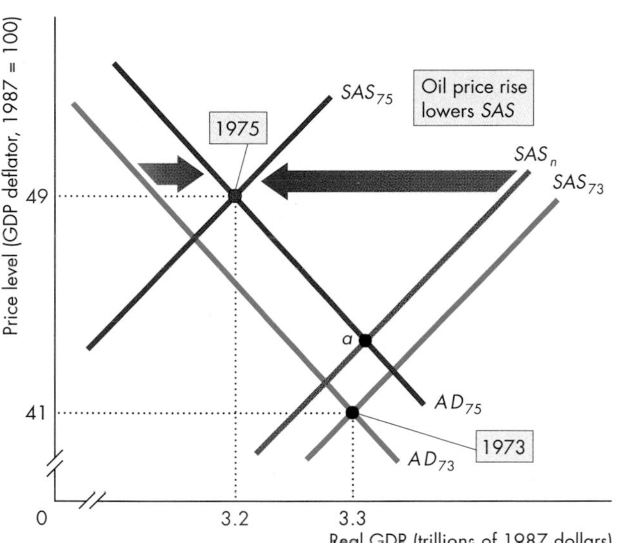

In 1973, the economy was on its aggregate demand curve AD_{73} and its short-run aggregate supply curve SAS_{73}, with real GDP at $3.3 trillion and a GDP deflator of 41. Between 1973 and 1975, aggregate demand continued to increase at a moderate pace and the aggregate demand curve shifted to AD_{75}. In the normal course of events, input prices would have increased at a moderate rate, shifting the short-run aggregate supply curve to SAS_n. The economy would have settled down at point *a* with an increase in real GDP and a continuation of moderate inflation. But in 1974, OPEC increased the price of oil by 348 percent. Other input prices and wages moved up more quickly than in a normal year. The short-run aggregate supply curve shifted to SAS_{75}. The large shift of the *SAS* curve combined with the moderate shift of the *AD* curve led to stagflation—a fall in real GDP and an acceleration of inflation.

recession. Thus during the OPEC recession, real GDP fell but the inflation rate increased. This combination of events gave rise to a new word, *stagflation*, a combination of falling real GDP and rising inflation.

The Volcker Recession The years 1979 to 1981 were not outstanding ones for the U.S. economy. To begin with, the economy had to endure a further series of increases in the price of oil in 1979—to $15 in April, to $19 in June, and finally to $26 by the year's end. Oil prices went on increasing through 1980 and 1981, and by October 1981, crude oil cost $37 a barrel. These large and continued increases in the price of oil put great strain on the U.S. economy. Energy-intensive production activities declined, and research efforts were devoted to finding more energy-efficient methods of production, transportation, and home heating.

Running alongside these energy shocks was a massive revolution in the electronics sector of the economy. Microprocessors of all kinds became cheaper, and affordable computing power found more widespread applications.

The combination of these two forces—continued increases in the price of energy and expanded applications for microprocessors—generated an unusually large reallocation of resources in the U.S. economy. Traditionally strong sectors began to grow more slowly or even to decline, and new sectors emerged with rapid growth. What came to be called the Rust Belt was the scene of relative decline, and the Sun Belt, Silicon Valley, and other areas specializing in electronics and related products (for example, Minneapolis and Massachusetts) became focal points for expansion and growth.

The years 1979 through 1981 were also times of high inflation. The price level increased by close to 10 percent during each of these years. There was a widely held belief that inflation was so entrenched that it could be anticipated to continue at this level into the foreseeable future. This, then, was the scene for the 1982 recession.

The origin of that recession and its magnitude are illustrated in Fig. 32.2. Aggregate demand and short-run aggregate supply in 1980 are shown by AD_{80} and SAS_{80}. Real GDP was $3.80 trillion, and the GDP deflator was 74. Over the next two years to 1982, with a widespread expectation that inflation was going to continue at 10 percent a year, wages and other input prices increased, shifting the short-run aggregate supply curve to SAS_{82}. Aggregate demand was expected to continue increasing at the same pace as in the late 1970s. If it had done so, by 1982 the aggregate demand curve would have shifted to the right to EAD_{82}. The economy would have been at point *a*, with real GDP continuing to grow at its trend rate and inflation remaining at around 10 percent a year.

But events did not turn out like that. Anxious to bring inflation under control, the Federal Reserve Board, under Chairman Paul Volcker, applied a

FIGURE 32.2

The Volcker Recession

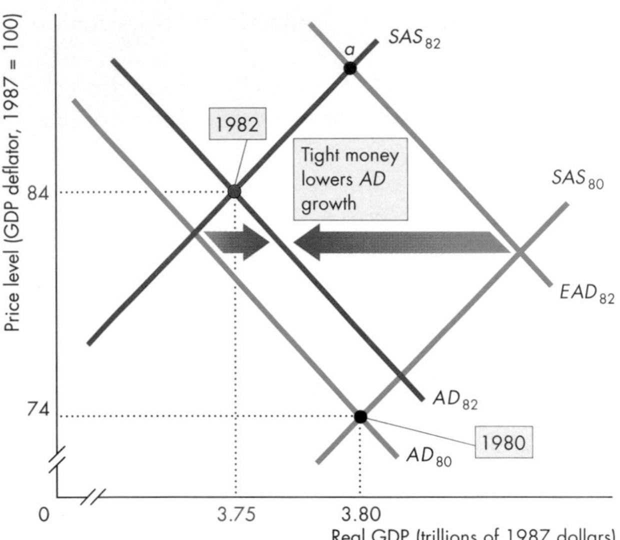

In 1980, the economy was on its aggregate demand curve AD_{80} and its short-run aggregate supply curve SAS_{80}, with real GDP at $3.80 trillion and a GDP deflator of 74. Inflation was raging, and wages and other input prices were increasing at a rapid rate because of strong inflationary expectations. The aggregate supply curve shifted to SAS_{82}. Aggregate demand was expected to increase at the pace of the late 1970s, and the aggregate demand curve was expected to shift to EAD_{82}. The expected equilibrium was point *a*, with inflation at around 10 percent per year. But in 1982, the Fed slowed down money growth and forced interest rates up. The aggregate demand curve shifted to AD_{82}. The combination of continuing high inflation expectations and a slowdown of aggregate demand growth put the economy into recession. Real GDP fell, and inflation moderated.

severe dose of monetary restraint. The Fed forced interest rates up, which slowed the pace of investment. As a result, the aggregate demand curve did not shift to EAD_{82} but to AD_{82}. By slowing the growth of aggregate demand down to below the pace at which the short-run aggregate supply curve was shifting, the Fed put the economy into recession. Real GDP fell to $3.75 trillion, and the inflation rate began to fall.

The 1990–1991 Recession At the beginning of 1990, the economy was at full employment. The unemployment rate was just above 5 percent, and inflation was steady at 4 percent a year. But the events of 1990 disturbed this situation and brought an end to the longest sustained recovery in U.S. history.

The dominant events of that year were the Persian Gulf crisis and the ensuing Gulf War triggered by Saddam Hussein's invasion of Kuwait. The course of the economy was influenced by these events. The Gulf crisis brought shocks to both aggregate demand and aggregate supply. The aggregate demand shocks went in both directions. First, fiscal policy became less restrained as government purchases increased to handle the military consequences of the crisis. The Gulf situation also increased uncertainty and lowered profit expectations, bringing lower investment. With lower investment, aggregate demand decreased. Although fiscal policy was working in the opposite direction, it was not strong enough to prevent aggregate demand from falling.

On the supply side, the Gulf crisis put the world energy markets into turmoil yet again. Between April 1990 and October 1990, the price of crude oil more than doubled. This oil price increase operated in a similar way to that of the 1970s, lowering short-run aggregate supply.

The combined effects of these forces and the onset of the 1990–1991 recession are illustrated in Fig. 32.3. In mid-1990, the economy was on aggregate demand curve AD_{90} and short-run aggregate supply curve SAS_{90} with real GDP at $4.9 trillion and the GDP deflator at 113. By mid-1991, the short-run aggregate supply curve had shifted to SAS_{91}, and investment uncertainty had shifted the aggregate demand curve to AD_{91}. Real GDP had fallen to $4.8 trillion, and inflation had slowed slightly, the GDP deflator having increased to 117, which is an inflation rate of only 3.5 percent over the year.

Origins Compared The OPEC recession was caused by an unexpectedly large increase in the price of oil that shifted the short-run aggregate supply curve to the left. This large shift in the aggregate supply curve, combined with a moderate increase in aggregate demand, lowered real GDP and increased the inflation rate—stagflation.

The Volcker recession was triggered by an unexpectedly sharp slowdown in the pace at which the Fed permitted aggregate demand to grow. Aggregate demand increased by less than expected, leading to a fall in real GDP and a lower inflation rate.

FIGURE 32.3

The 1990–1991 Recession

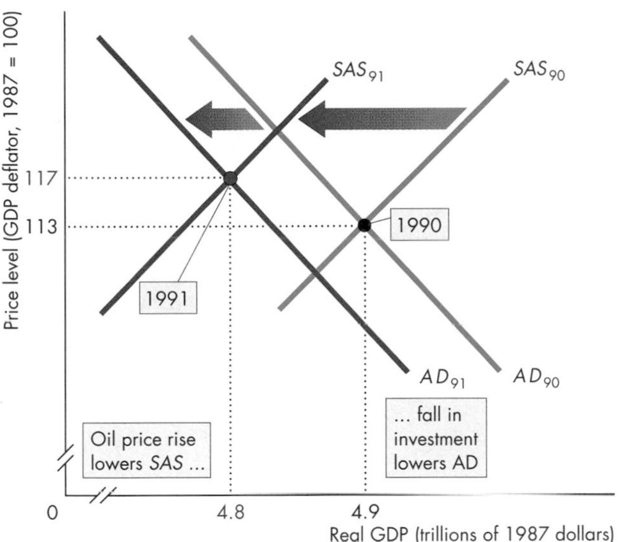

In 1990, the economy was on its aggregate demand curve AD_{90} and its short-run aggregate supply curve, SAS_{90}, with real GDP at $4.9 trillion and a GDP deflator of 113. A large increase in oil prices decreased aggregate supply and shifted the short-run aggregate supply curve to SAS_{91}. Uncertainty surrounding the world economy lowered profit expectations, leading to a fall in investment and a decrease in aggregate demand. The aggregate demand curve shifted to AD_{91}. The combination of a decrease in both aggregate supply and aggregate demand put the economy into recession.

The 1990–1991 recession had the ingredients of *both* of these earlier recessions. Oil price increases again operated to lower aggregate supply, and increased uncertainty about future profits lowered investment, bringing lower aggregate demand. On this occasion, real GDP fell and the inflation rate slowed slightly.

Although recessions have different origins that produce different impacts on inflation, they have some common features. Let's take a look at them, starting with the behavior of interest rates.

Money and Interest Rates in Recession

At the onset of a recession, interest rates may either rise, fall, or remain steady. In both the OPEC and Volcker recessions they increased, and in the 1990–1991 recession they were steady. But once a recession is underway, interest rates begin to fall. By the time real GDP has reached its trough, interest rates have fallen, often to levels lower than those at the onset of the recession. Why do interest rates behave in this way? To find out, let's study the money market in the three recent recessions. Figure 32.4 contains the relevant analysis.

OPEC Recession The OPEC recession is illustrated in Fig. 32.4(a). In 1973, the *real money supply* (M1) was $637 billion. The demand curve for real money in 1973 was MD_{73}, supply curve of real money was MS_{73}, and interest rate was 8 percent.

In 1974, the *real money supply* decreased by about 5 percent, and the supply curve of real money shifted from MS_{73} to MS_{74}. This decrease in the supply of real money occurred because the GDP deflator increased by an amount larger than the increase in the *nominal money supply.* The demand for real money fell in 1974 but only slightly. It fell because real GDP fell. (Recall that the demand for real money depends on real GDP. An increase in real GDP shifts the demand curve for real money to the right, and a decrease in real GDP shifts that curve to the left.) Because real GDP fell only slightly in 1974, the demand curve for real money shifted only slightly to the left. The supply of money curve shifted farther to the left than the demand for money curve. As a consequence, the interest rate increased. In 1974, the interest rate was 10 percent—at the point of intersection of MS_{74} and MD_{74}.

Between 1974 and 1975, the *nominal* money supply continued to increase but at a much slower pace than the price level was rising. As a result, the real money supply continued to decline, shifting the supply curve to MS_{75}. But by 1975, the economy was at the depth of recession. The large fall in real GDP reduced the demand for money. The demand curve shifted to the left to MD_{75}. The interest rate fell to 6 percent a year.

Volcker Recession The money market during the Volcker recession years is illustrated in Fig. 32.4(b). In 1980, interest rates were just over 12 percent a year, at the point of intersection of MS_{80} and MD_{80}.

During 1981, the GDP deflator continued to increase at around 10 percent a year. The Fed slowed the growth rate of the nominal money supply, permitting the quantity of money to increase by only 7 percent. As a consequence, the real money

FIGURE 32.4

Interest Rates and Money in Recession

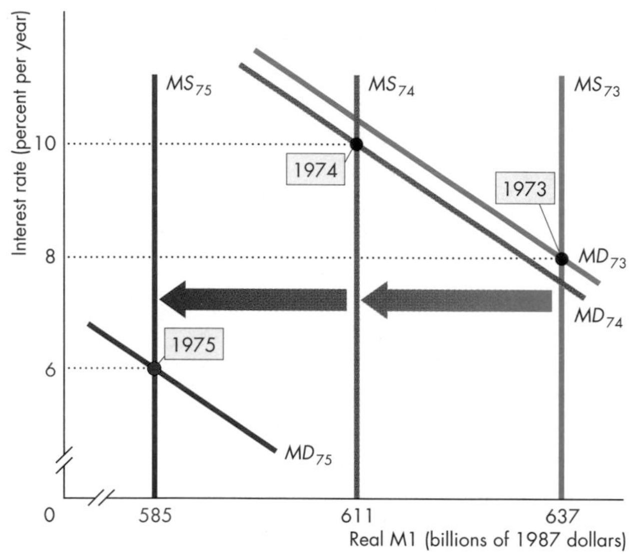

(a) The OPEC recession

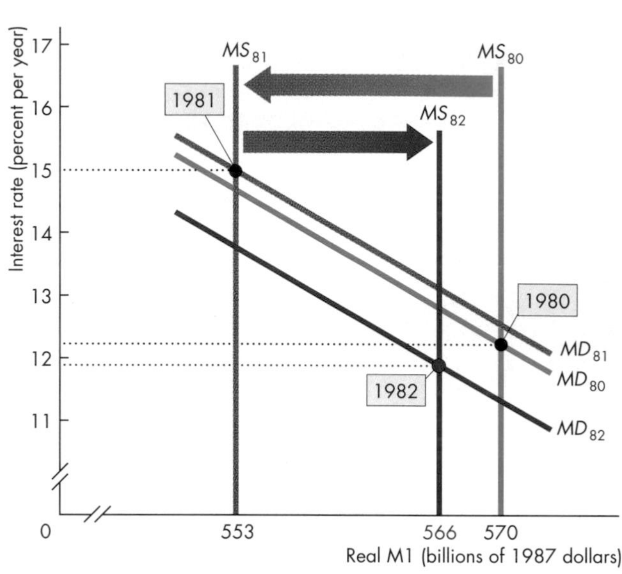

(b) The Volcker recession

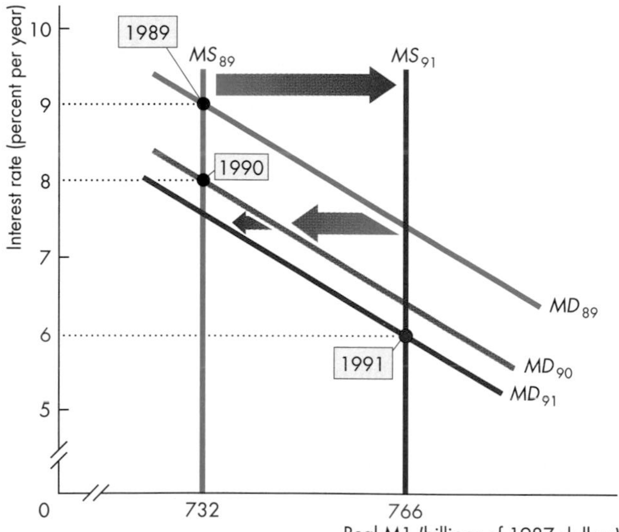

(c) The 1990–1991 recession

In 1973, the interest rate was 8 percent (part a). In 1974, the real money supply decreased, shifting the supply curve to MS_{74}, which, with the demand curve MD_{74}, increased the interest rate to 10 percent. As the recession deepened, the demand for money decreased (to MD_{75}), which, with the supply curve MS_{75}, lowered the interest rate to 6 percent.

In 1980, the interest rate was just above 12 percent (part b). In 1981, the real money supply decreased to MS_{81}, which, with the demand curve MD_{81}, increased the interest rate to 15 percent. As the recession deepened, the demand for money decreased (to MD_{82}), which, with money supply curve MS_{82}, lowered the interest rate to just below 12 percent.

In 1989, the interest rate was 9 percent (part c). In 1990, as the recession deepened, the demand for money decreased to MD_{90}, which, with the supply curve MS_{90}, lowered the interest rate to 8 percent. In 1991, the deepening recession decreased the demand for money further to MD_{91}. At the same time the Fed increased the money supply growth rate above the inflation rate, and the real money supply increased to MD_{91}. Interest rates declined to 6 percent.

supply fell. The fall in the real money supply shifted the supply curve from MS_{80} to MS_{81}. During the same year, real GDP continued to increase. As a result, the demand for real money increased and the demand curve shifted to the right to MD_{81}. The combination of an increased demand for real money and a decreased supply of real money pushed interest rates up to 15 percent a year. These high interest rates began to slow down spending and pushed the economy into its recession.

In 1982, real GDP fell to a level below that of 1980. As a result of the fall in real GDP, the demand for real money decreased and the demand curve shifted to the left to MD_{82}. At the same time, the inflation rate was slowing down. The slowdown in inflation combined with growth in the money supply was sufficient to increase the quantity of real money supplied in 1982, shifting the supply curve to MS_{82}. Money market equilibrium in 1982 occurred at an interest rate of slightly below 12 percent a year.

1990–1991 Recession The money market in the 1990–1991 recession is illustrated in Fig. 32.4(c). In 1989, interest rates were 9 percent a year, at the point of intersection of MS_{89} and MD_{89}.

During 1990, the GDP deflator increased by 4 percent and the Fed kept the growth rate of the nominal money supply close to this rate, holding the real money supply steady. As a consequence, in 1990 the supply curve remained at MS_{89}. At the same time, real GDP growth slowed and real GDP fell in the final quarter of the year. As a result, the demand for real money decreased and the demand curve shifted to the left to MD_{90}. Interest rates fell to 8 percent a year.

During 1991, real GDP continued to fall and the demand for real money decreased further. The demand curve shifted leftward to MD_{91}. At the same time, the Fed increased the money supply quickly in an attempt to get the economy to start a recovery. The real money supply increased to $766 billion, and the money supply curve shifted rightward to MS_{91}. Interest rates declined, and, on the average, during 1991 short-term rates were 6 percent, as shown in Fig. 32.4(c).

Comparing Recessions Comparing the events in the money market in the three recessions reveals some common features. In the first two recessions the interest rate followed a similar path. In both recessions, interest rates rose at first and then declined. But the source of those interest rate movements is different in each case. In the OPEC recession, interest rates increased because a sharp rise in the price level cut the real money supply. Interest rates subsequently fell because of the depth of the recession and the effects of the lower real GDP on the demand for real money. Because of continued strong inflation, the supply of real money continued to decrease through 1975. In the Volcker recession, the initial increase in interest rates was directly induced by Fed policy. Subsequent downward pressure on interest rates came from a fall in the demand for real money, just as in the OPEC recession. In addition, however, the real money supply increased in 1982 and reinforced the effects of the decrease in the demand for real money on interest rates.

Why did the real money supply continue to fall through 1975 but begin to increase in 1982? The key reason is the behavior of the price level in the two recessions. In 1975, inflation continued to be high, higher than the growth rate of the nominal money supply. In 1982, the inflation rate fell substantially below the growth rate of the nominal money supply.

In the 1990–1991 recession, interest rates did not increase initially because the Fed kept the supply of money growing in line with the growth in the demand for money. But interest rates fell, just as they had done in the two earlier recessions, as the economy contracted. And the reason they fell was the same: lower real GDP decreased the demand for money.

Changes in interest rates produce the next step in the recession mechanism—changes in aggregate expenditure.

Expenditure in Recession

When the economy is in a recession, real GDP falls and real aggregate expenditure also falls. (Recall that real GDP and real aggregate expenditure are equal to each other.) But the main component of aggregate expenditure that falls is investment. Investment falls for two reasons. First, interest rates increase. Second, profit expectations worsen.

During the OPEC recession, investment (in 1987 dollars) fell from $592 billion in 1973 to $438 billion by 1975. During the Volcker recession, investment fell from $594 billion in 1980 to $541 billion in 1982. During the 1990–1991 recession, investment fell from $800 billion in 1989 to $656 billion by mid-1991. Such decreases in investment have two effects. First, they decrease aggregate expenditure and aggregate demand. Second, they result in the capital stock growing less quickly, which slows down the pace of innovation of new technologies. This aspect of the investment slowdown feeds back to slow down the growth of aggregate supply. But the effect of decreased investment on aggregate demand dominates.

One of the main reasons people fear recession is because it is associated with a high unemployment rate. What happens in the labor market during a recession? Why does unemployment increase during a recession? Let's now examine these questions.

The Labor Market in Recession

For illustrative purposes, we'll examine the labor market in just one of the three recent recessions—the OPEC recession. Figure 32.5 provides a summary and analysis of the main events.

The starting point to understanding what happens in the labor market during a recession is an examination of the short-run aggregate production function. (Recall that we studied the short-run aggregate production function in Chapter 30.) The short-run aggregate production function, which shows the maximum real GDP that can be produced for a given labor input, is shown in Fig. 32.5(a). Curve PF_{73} is the short-run aggregate production function for 1973, just prior to the OPEC recession. In that year, 164 billion hours of labor produced \$3.3 trillion of real GDP. The effect of the OPEC oil price increase was to shift the short-run production function downward from PF_{73} to PF_{75}. Why did this happen?

There are two aspects of the oil price increase that resulted in the downward shift of the production function. First, to enforce the massive price increase, OPEC severely restricted the output of crude oil. It placed an embargo on oil exports for a period. This disruption of international trade in oil had the direct effect of lowering the availability of a key productive resource. But there was a second and perhaps even more important effect. With such an enormous increase in the price of energy, energy users of all kinds sought ways to economize on their use of this now more expensive commodity. Activities that were intensive in their use of energy were cut back, and other activities were expanded. For example, the cars and airplanes designed with engines that were highly suitable for the cheap fuel that prevailed in the 1960s were scrapped at a much more rapid pace than they otherwise would have been. Research and design efforts were put into making cars, planes, and all kinds of transportation and heating equipment that were more energy-efficient. This redirection of economic activity from fuel-intensive production and consumption to fuel-saving production and consumption created a severe

FIGURE 32.5
Sticky Wages in Recession

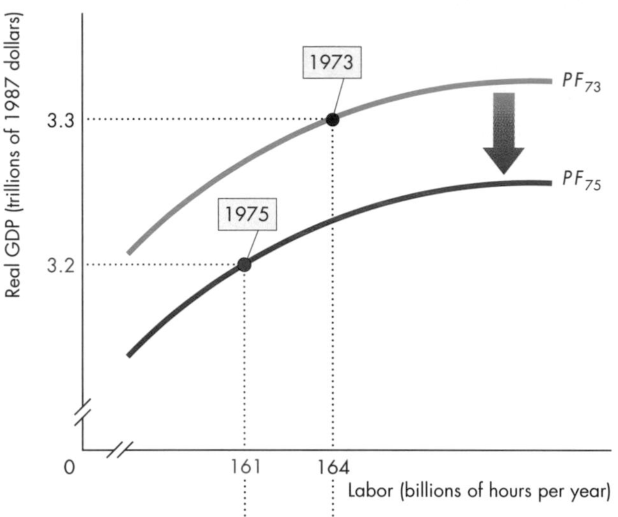

(a) Short-run aggregate production function

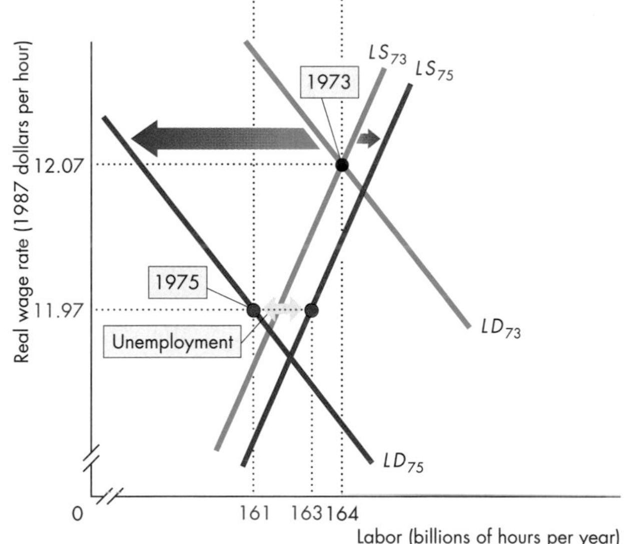

(b) The labor market

The OPEC price hike and embargo lowered the short-run aggregate production function from PF_{73} to PF_{75} in part (a). The marginal product of labor fell, so the demand for labor curve shifted from LD_{73} to LD_{75} in part (b). Assuming quantity of labor demanded equaled quantity supplied in 1973, the real wage rate of \$12.07 and employment of 164 billion hours are at the point of intersection of LD_{73} and LS_{73}. An increase in the labor force shifted the supply curve from LS_{73} to LS_{75}. Real wages fell but not by enough to bring equality to the quantities of labor supplied and demanded. The quantity demanded was 161 billion hours, but the quantity supplied was 163 billion hours. Unemployment increased.

mismatch of people and jobs. More of the labor force, even if it remained employed, had to devote its efforts to retraining and other activities that did not directly, at least initially, produce real GDP. As a consequence of these two related factors, the production function shifted downward as shown in Fig. 32.5(a).

Not only did the production function shift downward, but also the level of employment declined. The economy moved to the point highlighted in Fig. 32.5(a), at which employment was 161 billion hours and real GDP was $3.2 trillion. To see why employment declined, we need to study the labor market.

The downward shift of the production function lowered the marginal product of labor. As we discovered in Chapter 30, the quantity of labor demanded depends on its marginal product. With a lower marginal product of labor, the demand for labor curve shifts to the left. That shift is shown in Fig. 32.5(b) as the shift from LD_{73} to LD_{75}.

Sticky Wage Theory

There is not too much controversy in macroeconomics about the demand side of the labor market. But there is considerable disagreement about the supply side of the labor market and the ability of the labor market to act as a coordination mechanism, bringing about equality of the quantities of labor demanded and supplied. One theory, the sticky wage theory, is that the supply of labor is not very sensitive to changes in real wages and that money wages are sticky—they do not adjust quickly enough to maintain a continuous balance between the quantities of labor demanded and supplied. Let's interpret the labor market in the OPEC recession by using the sticky wage theory.

In 1973, the real wage was $12.07 an hour and 164 billion hours of labor were employed. Let's assume that the actual unemployment rate in 1973 was also the natural rate of unemployment for that year. (This is an assumption, not a fact.) Given this assumption, the real wage rate and employment rate in that year were at the point of intersection of the labor demand and labor supply curves. We'll assume that the supply of labor curve was LS_{73} and the demand for labor curve was LD_{73} in Fig. 32.5(b).

Through 1974 and 1975, the labor force increased, and as a result, the supply of labor curve shifted to the right from LS_{73} to LS_{75}. Money wages continued to increase through the recession but at a slower pace than that at which the price level was rising. As a result, real wages decreased. By 1975, real wages had fallen to $11.97 an hour. But that fall in real wages was insufficient to maintain equality between the quantity of labor supplied and the quantity demanded. The level of employment fell to 161 billion hours—the quantity of labor demanded. That is, at a real wage rate of $11.97 and with the demand for labor curve LD_{75}, the amount of labor that firms wished to hire (to maximize their profits) was 161 billion hours.

Given the assumptions made about the supply of labor curve, the quantity of labor supplied was 163 billion hours. The difference between the amount of labor supplied and the amount employed (and demanded) was unemployment. According to the sticky wage theory of the labor market, this increase in unemployment represents an addition to the natural unemployment that prevailed before the recession's onset.

Flexible Wage Theory

There is an alternative interpretation of the labor market in recession to the one that we have just presented—the flexible wage theory. According to this theory, the supply of labor is highly responsive to a change in real wages, and money wages *do* adjust to maintain equality between the quantity of labor demanded and the quantity supplied. Fluctuations in unemployment are fluctuations in the natural rate of unemployment. Let's examine the OPEC recession again and interpret it in terms of this alternative theory.

Recall that the labor market effects of recession that we've just analyzed are based on an *assumption* about the supply of labor curve. In Fig. 32.5 the labor supply curves LS_{73} and LS_{75} are fairly steep, indicating that a large change in the real wage rate evokes only a small change in the quantity of labor supplied. We are uncertain about the slope of the labor supply curve, but we're reasonably sure that the curve shifted to the right by the amount shown because we know exactly the amount by which the labor force increased over the relevant period. Suppose that the supply of labor curve is less steep than those shown in Fig. 32.5. In particular, suppose that the supply of labor for 1973 and that for 1975 are represented by the curves shown in Fig. 32.6.

Figure 32.6 is identical to Fig. 32.5(b) except that the labor supply curves do not slope upward as

FIGURE 32.6

The Labor Market in Recession: Flexible Wage Theory

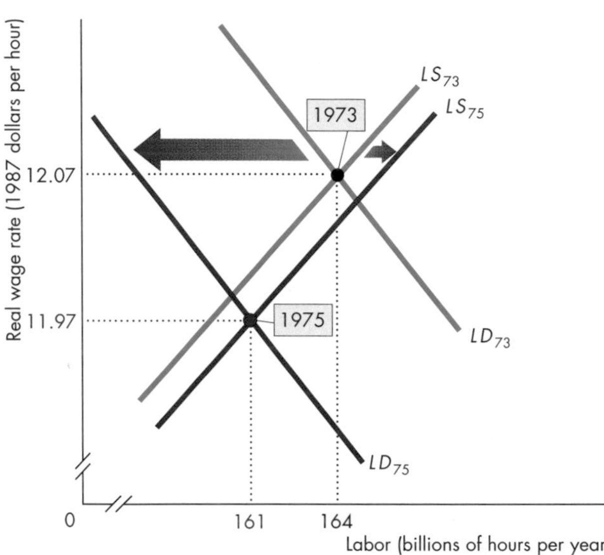

During the OPEC recession, real wages fell from \$12.07 an hour to \$11.97 an hour and employment fell from 164 billion hours to 161 billion hours. These movements of real wages and employment are consistent with the flexible wage theory if the quantity of labor supplied is highly responsive to a change in the real wage as shown by the labor supply curves LS_{73} and LS_{75}. According to the flexible wage theory, the increase in unemployment that occurred between 1973 and 1975 is interpreted as a temporary increase in the natural rate of unemployment.

steeply. Again, the labor market in 1973 is depicted as a situation in which the quantity of labor demanded equals the quantity supplied, so unemployment is at the natural rate. When this supply of labor curve shifts to the right, it moves to LS_{75}. The magnitude of the shift from LS_{73} to LS_{75} is identical in this figure to the magnitude of the shift in Fig. 32.5(b). The demand for labor curve shifts from LD_{73} to LD_{75}. In 1975, the demand for labor curve and the supply of labor curve intersect at a real wage rate of \$11.97 and employment of 161 billion hours, exactly the values that prevailed in 1975. The labor market shown in Fig. 32.6 agrees with the assumptions of the flexible wage theory. Wages fall and employment falls.

But what happens to unemployment? The flexible wage theory of unemployment is that all unemployment arises from job market turnover. During a recession, job market turnover increases because some sectors of the economy decline quickly while others continue to expand. An increase in the amount of labor force reallocation—from the declining sectors to the expanding sectors—results in an increased amount of labor turnover and a temporarily higher natural rate of unemployment. During the 1975 recession, the declining sectors were those sectors that relied heavily on oil and other high-cost energy sources; the expanding sectors were those sectors associated with developing energy-saving technologies.

Which Theory of the Labor Market Is Correct? What exactly do economists agree and disagree about concerning the labor market and why? The essence of the controversy is summarized in Figs. 32.5(b) and 32.6. First, everyone agrees about the facts. Real wages in 1973 were \$12.07 an hour, on the average. In 1975, they had fallen to \$11.97, on the average. Employment in 1973 was 164 billion hours, and it fell to 161 billion hours in 1975.

In addition, there is not much disagreement about the demand for labor. Most economists agree that the quantity of labor actually employed is determined by the profit-maximizing decisions of firms. That quantity depends on the real wage. This means that the level of employment and the real wage in any particular year are a point on the demand for labor curve. If we agree that the employment level and real wage are a point on the demand for labor curve, we can figure out where the demand for labor curve is and work out what makes it shift. Thus there is not much disagreement among economists about the slope and position of the demand for labor curve.

But economists disagree about the supply of labor. Because a large amount of labor is supplied on long-term contracts and on wages and other terms that remain fixed for the duration of the contract, most economists believe that households are not normally operating on their supply of labor curve. Sometimes they are, but much of the time they are not. Furthermore, many economists believe that on the basis of evidence from variations in hours of work and wages, the quantity of labor supplied does not respond much to changes in real wages. In other words, they believe that the supply of labor curve is steep like those shown in Fig. 32.5(b).

Other economists believe that the combination of the real wage rate and the level of employment represents not only a point on the demand for labor curve but also a point on the supply of labor curve. From this assumption they infer that the quantity of labor supplied is highly responsive to wages and that the supply of labor curve looks like those in Fig. 32.6.

No one has yet suggested a test that is sufficiently clear for all economists to agree on. The controversy will be settled only when economists can agree on, and implement, a test of their competing views about the responsiveness of the quantity of labor supplied to a change in real wages. Once such a test has been implemented, we shall be able to put this controversy (like the controversy about monetary and fiscal influences on aggregate demand that you met in Chapter 29) behind us. But until then, economists and students of economics have to live with the fact that we remain ignorant about an important issue at the heart of macroeconomics. This controversy is featured in Our Advancing Knowledge on pp. 892–893.

Determining which of these two theories is correct is not just a matter of academic curiosity. It is a matter of enormous importance in designing an appropriate antirecessionary policy. If the flexible wage theory is correct, there is only one aggregate supply curve—the vertical long-run aggregate supply curve. This fact means that any attempt to bring the economy out of recession by increasing aggregate demand—for example, by lowering interest rates and increasing the money supply or by fiscal policy measures—is doomed to failure and can result only in a higher price level (more inflation). Conversely, if the sticky wage theory is correct, then the short-run aggregate supply curve slopes upward. An increase in aggregate demand, although increasing the price level somewhat, increases real GDP and will bring the economy out of a recession.

From the viewpoint of the unemployed, it matters little whether their unemployment is the result of sticky wages or very costly labor market restructuring with flexible wages. Unemployment is painful, as you can see in Reading Between the Lines on pp. 886–887.

Another Great Depression?

Following the Volcker recession, the U.S. economy moved into a period of long sustained recovery. In fact, that recovery was the longest and strongest on record. Its end was repeatedly (and wrongly) foreseen, and by the fall of 1987 there was widespread fear that the good times were coming to an end, at least for a while. In October 1987, these fears were strengthened by the biggest stock market crash to hit the U.S. economy (and, indeed, the world economy) since that of 1929, which had heralded the Great Depression. The magnitude of the 1987 crash was almost identical to that of the 1929 crash—the range between the high and the low was 34 percent. This similarity was so striking that many commentators concluded that the closing years of the 1980s and the early 1990s would resemble the Great Depression of the early 1930s. But the recovery kept going until the middle of 1990. And when it did end, the recession that followed, although a relatively long one, was not deep.

Yet the question remains: is there going to be another Great Depression? Of course, the answer to this question is that no one knows. But we can try to assess the likelihood of such an event. Let's begin by first asking some questions. What was the Great Depression like? Just how bad did things get in the early 1930s? What would the U.S. economy look like in 1999 if the events of 70 years earlier were to recur? Once we've charted the broad anatomy of the Great Depression, we'll examine why it happened and consider the question of whether it could happen again and how likely such an event would be.

What the Great Depression Was Like

At the beginning of 1929, the U.S. economy was operating at full employment and with only 3.2 percent of the labor force unemployed. But as that eventful year unfolded, increasing signs of economic weakness began to appear. The most dramatic events occurred in October, when the stock market collapsed, losing more than one third of its value in

Unemployment in Recession

The New York Times, July 28, 1991

For Forlorn Millions, the Recession Goes On

BY PETER T. KILBORN

The experts say the economy is growing again after a year in a recession, but tell that to Charles Moreira. A despairing 22-year-old waiting for yet another job counseling session in the New Bedford office of the Massachusetts state employment agency, Mr. Moreira is his family's sole wage earner because his wife stays home with their 3-year-old child.

Mr. Moreira, a mechanic, lost a $6.75-an-hour job in an automobile dealership last December and has been looking fruitlessly for work since. His $170 a week in unemployment benefits has run out. He is vying with scores of similarly strapped contenders for a warehouse job that pays $6 an hour.

"I'm kind of disgusted," he said. "I'm losing all my ambition. I wanted to be the greatest." What about going to a boom town somewhere? "I don't have the money," he said.

Fewer Jobs, Worse Jobs

Nearly nine million people are out of work and looking for jobs. The government does not count several million more among the unemployed because they have given up looking. For all the unemployed, the recession is still going strong. Worse, more of the jobs that are now being offered are inferior to the old ones.

As recessions end, some disappointment is predictable. On getting wind of an improving economy, people who have dropped out of the labor force start looking again. Others look more earnestly with the end of their unemployment benefits, which are often more than $1,000 a month and usually last six months. That makes it harder for all to find jobs.

At the same time, employers put off hiring while they wait to be sure business is truly improving. Instead, they ask the workers whom they have kept on board to work longer and harder.

Mostly for those reasons, economists say, the unemployment rate rose only slightly in June, from 6.9 percent to 7 percent, even as most other gauges of the economy were gaining. In 1983, a whole year after the last, longer and harsher recession ended, the rate was 9.6 percent, hardly different from the high point of 9.7 percent in 1982. . . .

The Essence of the Story

In the summer of 1991, as the economy recovered from a year of recession, unemployment was still rising.

Nearly nine million people were out of work and looking for jobs, and several million more without jobs had given up looking.

As a recession ends, people who have dropped out of the labor force start looking again for work and those whose unemployment benefits have run out search harder for jobs, making it harder for everyone to find jobs.

Employers ask the workers whom they have kept on board to work longer and harder and put off hiring until they are sure business is improving.

Background and Analysis

When real GDP falls in a recession, unemployment increases.

When recovery from a recession begins and real GDP increases, unemployment continues to increase for a while.

You can see this feature of the change in unemployment in the figure.

During the recovery from the OPEC recession, unemployment was still increasing in the second quarter of 1975 (the dot marked 752 in part a of the figure) even though real GDP was increasing at an annual rate of 5 percent.

During the recovery from the Volcker recession, real GDP began to increase in the second quarter of 1982 (the dot marked 822 in part b) but unemployment did not begin to decrease until the first quarter of 1983 (the dot marked 831 in part b).

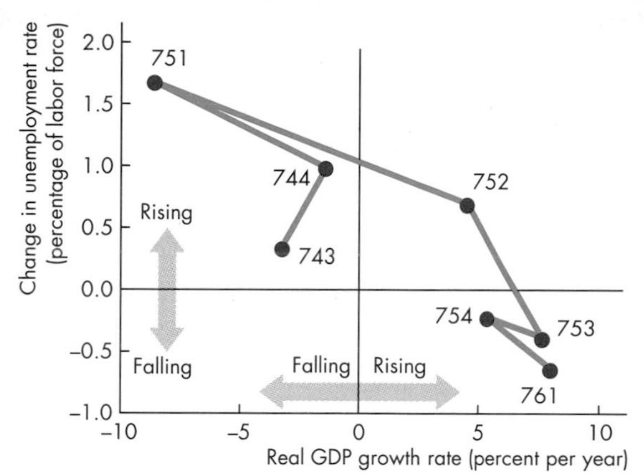

(a) OPEC recession and recovery

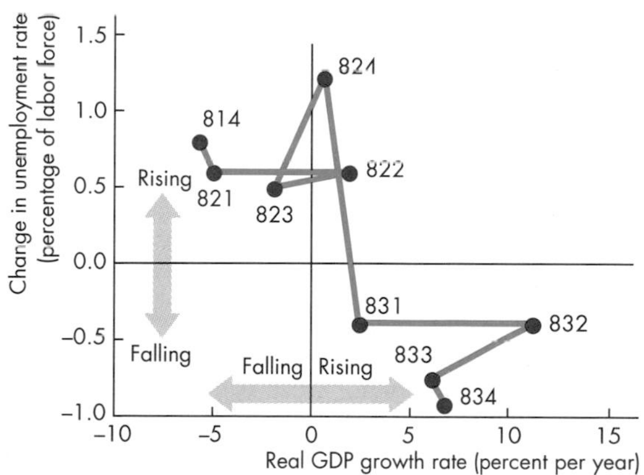

(b) Volcker recession and recovery

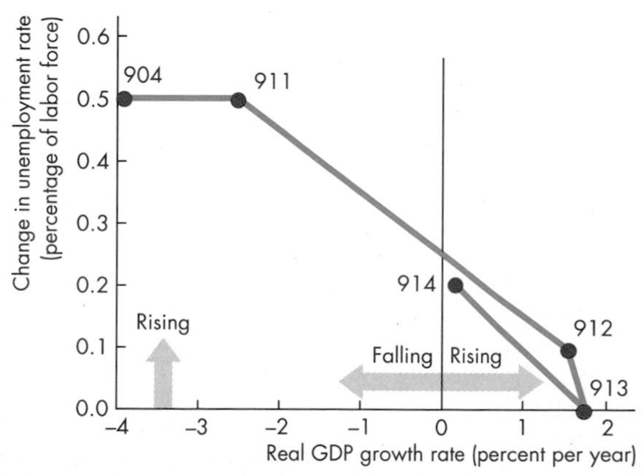

(c) 1991 recession and recovery

During the recovery from the 1991 recession, unemployment was still increasing in the fourth quarter of 1991 (marked 914 in part c), even though real GDP had been growing for three quarters.

Unemployment lags behind real GDP growth for the reasons identified in the article: in the early stages of recovery, firms work their existing labor forces harder, previously discouraged workers start looking for jobs, and workers whose unemployment benefits have run out intensify their job search.

two weeks. The four years that followed were years of monstrous economic depression—depression so severe that it came to be called the Great Depression.

The dimensions of the Great Depression can be seen in Fig. 32.7. That figure shows the situation on the eve of the Great Depression in 1929 when the economy was on its aggregate demand curve AD_{29} and short-run aggregate supply curve SAS_{29}. Real GDP was \$835 billion and the GDP deflator was 18. (Real GDP in 1991 was almost 6 times its 1929 level, and the GDP deflator was more than 8 times its 1929 level.)

In 1930, there was widespread expectation that prices would fall, and wages fell. With lower wages, the short-run aggregate supply curve shifted from SAS_{29} to SAS_{30}. But increased pessimism and uncertainty resulted in a drop in investment and in the demand for durables. Aggregate demand fell, by a larger amount than expected, to AD_{30}. In 1930, the economy went into recession as real GDP fell by about 7 percent. The price level also fell by a similar amount. (It was not unusual at that time for prices occasionally to fall.) When the price level is falling, the economy is experiencing *deflation.*

If the normal course of events had ensued in 1930, the economy might have remained in its depressed state for several months and then started a recovery. But 1930 was not a normal year. In 1930 and the next two years, the economy was further bombarded with huge negative demand shocks (the sources of which we'll look at in a moment). The aggregate demand curve shifted to the left all the way to AD_{33}. With a depressed economy, the price level was expected to fall, and wages fell in line with those expectations. The money wage fell from 55¢ an hour in 1930 to 44¢ an hour by 1933. As a result of lower wages, the aggregate supply curve shifted from SAS_{30} to SAS_{33}. But the size of the shift of the short-run aggregate supply curve was much less than the decrease in aggregate demand. As a result, the aggregate demand curve and the short-run aggregate supply curve intersected in 1933 at a real GDP of \$600 billion and a GDP deflator of 13. Real GDP had fallen by almost 30 percent from its 1929 level, and the price level had fallen by more than 25 percent.

FIGURE 32.7

The Great Depression

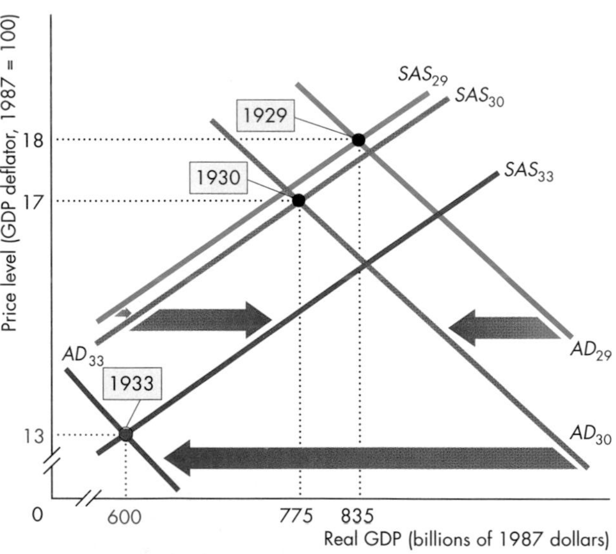

In 1929, real GDP was \$835 billion and the GDP deflator was 18—at the intersection of AD_{29} and SAS_{29}. Increased pessimism and uncertainty resulted in a drop in investment, resulting in a decrease in aggregate demand to AD_{30}. To some degree, this decrease was anticipated and wages fell, so the short-run aggregate supply curve shifted to SAS_{30}. Real GDP and the price level fell. In the next three years, decreases in the money supply and investment lowered aggregate demand, shifting the aggregate demand curve to AD_{33}. Again, to some degree, the decrease in aggregate demand was anticipated, so wages fell and the short-run aggregate supply curve shifted to SAS_{33}. By 1933, real GDP had fallen to \$600 billion (about 70 percent of its 1929 level) and the GDP deflator had fallen to 13 (73 percent of its 1929 level).

Although the Great Depression brought enormous hardship, the distribution of that hardship was very uneven. A quarter of the work force had no jobs at all. Also, at that time there were virtually no organized social security and unemployment programs in place. So for many families there was virtually no income. But the pocketbooks of those who kept their jobs barely noticed the Great Depression. It's true that wages fell (from 57¢ an hour in 1929 to 44¢ an hour in 1933). But at the same time, the price level fell by just about exactly the same percentage amount as the fall in wages. Hence real wages remained constant. Thus those who had jobs continued to be paid a wage rate that had roughly the same buying power at the end of the Great Depression as in 1929.

You can begin to appreciate the magnitude of the Great Depression if you compare it with the three recessions we studied earlier in this chapter. Between

1973 and 1975, real GDP fell by 1.75 percent. From 1981 to 1982, it fell by 2.5 percent. From mid-1990 to mid-1991, it fell by 1.6 percent. In comparison, in 1930 real GDP fell by more than 7 percent, and from 1929 to 1933 it fell by close to 30 percent. A 1999 Great Depression of the same magnitude would lower income per person to its level of more than 20 years earlier.

Why the Great Depression Happened

The late 1920s were years of economic boom. New houses and apartments were built on an unprecedented scale, new firms were created, and the capital stock of the nation expanded. But these were also years of increasing uncertainty. The main source of increased uncertainty was international. The world economy was going through tumultuous times. The patterns of world trade were changing as Britain, the traditional economic powerhouse of the world, began its period of relative economic decline and new economic powers such as Japan began to emerge. International currency fluctuations and the introduction of restrictive trade policies by many countries (see Chapter 35) further increased the uncertainty faced by firms. There was also domestic uncertainty arising from the fact that there had been such a strong boom in recent years, especially in the capital goods sector and housing. No one believed that this boom could continue, but there was great uncertainty as to when it would end and how the pattern of demand would change.

This environment of uncertainty led to a slowdown in consumer spending, especially on new homes and household appliances. By the fall of 1929, the uncertainty had reached a critical level and contributed to the stock market crash. The stock market crash, in turn, heightened people's fears about economic prospects in the foreseeable future. Fear fed fear. Investment collapsed. The building industry almost disappeared. An industry that had been operating flat out just two years earlier was now building virtually no new houses and apartments. It was this drop in investment and a drop in consumer spending on durables that led to the initial leftward shift of the aggregate demand curve from AD_{29} to AD_{30} in Fig. 32.7.

At this stage, what became the Great Depression was no worse than many previous recessions had been. What distinguishes the Great Depression from previous recessions are the events that followed between 1930 and 1933. But economists, even to this day, have not come to agreement on how to interpret those events. One view, argued by Peter Temin, is that spending continued to fall for a wide variety of reasons—including a continuation of increasing pessimism and uncertainty.[1] According to Temin, the continued contraction resulted from a leftward shift in the investment demand curve and a fall in autonomous expenditure. Milton Friedman and Anna J. Schwartz have argued that the continuation of the contraction was almost exclusively the result of the subsequent worsening of financial and monetary conditions.[2] According to Friedman and Schwartz, it was a severe cut in the money supply that lowered aggregate demand, prolonging the contraction and deepening the depression.

Although there is disagreement about the causes of the contraction phase of the Great Depression, the disagreement is not about the elements at work but about the degree of importance attached to each. Everyone agrees that increased pessimism and uncertainty lowered investment demand, and everyone agrees that there was a massive contraction of the real money supply. Temin and his supporters assign primary importance to the fall in autonomous expenditure and secondary importance to the fall in the money supply. Friedman and Schwartz and their supporters assign primary responsibility to the money supply and regard the other factors as being of limited importance.

Let's look at the contraction of aggregate demand a bit more closely. Between 1930 and 1933, there was a massive 20 percent contraction in the nominal money supply. This fall in the money supply was not directly induced by the Fed's actions. The *monetary base* (currency in circulation and bank reserves) hardly fell at all. But the bank deposits component of the money supply suffered an enormous collapse. It did so primarily because a large number of banks failed. The primary source of bank failure was unsound lending during the boom preceding the onset of the Great Depression. Fueled by increasing stock prices and booming business conditions, bank loans expanded. But after the stock market crash

[1]Peter Temin, *Did Monetary Forces Cause the Great Depression?* (New York: W. W. Norton, 1976).

[2]This explanation was developed by Milton Friedman and Anna J. Schwartz in *A Monetary History of the United States 1867–1960* (Princeton, N.J.: Princeton University Press, 1963), Ch. 7.

and the downturn, many borrowers found themselves in hard economic times. They could not pay the interest on their loans, and they could not meet the agreed repayment schedules. Banks had deposits that exceeded the realistic value of the loans that they had made. When depositors withdrew funds from the banks, the banks lost reserves and many of them simply couldn't meet their depositors' demands to be repaid.

Bank failures feed on themselves and create additional failures. Seeing banks fail, people become anxious to protect themselves and so take their money out of the banks. Such were the events of 1930. The quantity of notes and coins in circulation increased, and the volume of bank deposits declined. But the very action of taking money out of the bank to protect one's wealth accentuated the process of banking failure. Banks were increasingly short of cash and unable to meet their obligations.

Bank failure and the massive contraction of the money supply had two effects on the economy. First, the bank failures themselves brought financial hardship to many producers, increasing the business failure rate throughout the economy. At the same time, a sharp drop in the money supply kept interest rates high. Not only did nominal interest rates stay high, but with falling prices, real interest rates increased sharply. The real interest rate is (approximately) the difference between the nominal interest rate and the expected inflation rate. During the Great Depression, inflation was negative—the price level was falling. Thus the real interest rate equaled the nominal interest rate plus the expected rate of deflation. With high real interest rates, investment remained low.

What role did the stock market crash of 1929 play in producing the Great Depression? It certainly created an atmosphere of fear and panic and probably also contributed to the overall air of uncertainty that dampened investment spending. It also reduced the wealth of stockholders, encouraging them to cut back on their consumption spending. But the direct effect of the stock market crash on consumption, although a contributory factor to the Great Depression, was not the major source of the drop in aggregate demand. It was the collapse in investment arising from increased uncertainty that brought the 1930 decline in aggregate demand.

But the stock market crash was a predictor of severe recession. It reflected the expectations of stockholders concerning future profit prospects. As those expectations became pessimistic, the prices of stocks were bid lower and lower (i.e., the behavior of the stock market was a consequence of expectations about future profitability, and those expectations were lowered as a result of increased uncertainty).

Can It Happen Again?

Since, even today, we have an incomplete understanding of the causes of the Great Depression, we are not able to predict such an event or to be sure that it cannot occur again. But there are some important differences between the economy of the 1990s and that of the 1930s that make a severe depression much less likely today than it was 60 years ago. The most important features of the economy that make severe depression less likely today are as follows:

- Bank deposit insurance
- The Fed's role as lender of last resort
- Taxes and government spending
- Multi-income families

Let's examine these in turn.

Bank Deposit Insurance As a result of the Great Depression, the federal government established, in the 1930s, the Federal Deposit Insurance Corporation (FDIC). The FDIC insures bank deposits for up to $100,000 per depositor so that most depositors need no longer fear bank failure. If a bank fails, the FDIC pays the deposit holders. With federally insured bank deposits, the key event that turned a fairly ordinary recession into the Great Depression is most unlikely to occur. It was the fear of bank failure that caused people to withdraw their deposits from banks. The aggregate consequence of these individually rational acts was to cause the very bank failures that were feared. With deposit insurance, most depositors have nothing to lose if a bank fails and so have no incentive to take actions that are likely to give rise to that failure.

Some recent events reinforce this conclusion. With massive failures of S&Ls in the 1980s and with bank failures in New England in 1990 and 1991, there was no tendency for depositors to panic and withdraw their funds in a self-reinforcing run on similar institutions.

Lender of Last Resort The Fed is the lender of last resort in the U.S. economy. If a single bank is short of reserves, it can borrow reserves from other banks. If the entire banking system is short of reserves, banks can borrow from the Fed. By making reserves available (at a suitable interest rate), the Fed is able to make the quantity of reserves in the banking system respond flexibly to the demand for those reserves. Bank failure can be prevented or at least contained to cases in which bad management practices are the source of the problem. Widespread failures of the type that occurred in the Great Depression can be prevented.

But the Fed was around in the Great Depression and was acting as lender of last resort throughout that episode. Why did it not make sufficient bank reserves available? The Fed in fact kept the level of the monetary base roughly constant. And it thought that by so doing it was making an appropriate contribution to economic stability. It was only long after the event, when Friedman and Schwartz examined the contraction years of the Great Depression, that economists came to realize that the Fed would have had to *increase* the monetary base by a sizable amount to have prevented the intensification of the contraction. Now that this lesson has been learned, there is at least some chance that the mistake will not be repeated.

It is interesting to note, in this regard, that during the weeks following the October 1987 stock market crash, Fed Chairman Alan Greenspan used every opportunity available to remind the American banking and financial community of the Fed's ability and readiness to maintain calm financial conditions.

Taxes and Government Spending The government sector was a much less important part of the economy in 1929 than it has become today. On the eve of that earlier recession, government purchases of goods and services were less than 9 percent of GDP. In contrast, today they are more than 20 percent. Government transfer payments were less than 6 percent of GDP in 1929. These items have grown to more than 15 percent of GDP at the present time.

A larger level of government purchases of goods and services means that when recession hits, a large component of aggregate demand does not decline. It is government transfer payments, however, that is the most important economic stabilizer. When the economy goes into recession and depression, more people qualify for unemployment compensation and social security. As a consequence, although disposable income decreases, the extent of the decrease is moderated by the existence of such programs. Consumption expenditure, in turn, does not decline by as much as it would in the absence of such government programs. The limited decline in consumption spending further limits the overall decrease in aggregate expenditure, thereby limiting the magnitude of an economic downturn.

Multi-income Families At the time of the Great Depression, families with more than one wage earner were much less common than they are today. The labor force participation rate in 1929 was around 55 percent. Today, it is 66 percent. Thus, even if the unemployment rate increased to around 25 percent today, close to 50 percent of the adult population would actually have jobs. During the Great Depression, less than 40 percent of the adult population had work. Multi-income families have greater security than single-income families. The chance of both (or all) income earners in a family losing their jobs simultaneously is much lower than the chance of a single earner losing work. With greater family income security, family consumption is likely to be less sensitive to fluctuations in family income that are seen as temporary. Thus when aggregate income falls, it does not induce a cut in consumption. For example, during the OPEC and Volcker recessions, personal consumption expenditure increased.

For the four reasons we have just reviewed, it appears that the economy has better shock-absorbing characteristics today than it had in the 1920s and 1930s. Even if there is a collapse of confidence leading to a fall in investment, the recession mechanism that is now in place will not translate that initial shock into the large and prolonged fall in real GDP and rise in unemployment that occurred more than 60 years ago.

Because the economy is now more immune to severe recession than it was in the 1930s, even a stock market crash of the magnitude that occurred in 1987 had barely noticeable effects on spending. A crash of a similar magnitude in 1929 resulted in the near collapse of housing investment and consumer durable purchases. In the period following the 1987 stock market crash, investment and spending on durable goods hardly changed.

None of this is to say that there might not be a deep recession or even a Great Depression in the 1990s (or beyond). But it would take a very severe shock to trigger one.

UNDERSTANDING Business CYCLES

Economic activity has fluctuated between boom and bust for as long as we've had records, and the range of fluctuations became especially pronounced during the nineteenth and early twentieth centuries. Understanding the sources of economic fluctuations has turned out to be difficult for two reasons.

First, there are no simple patterns. Every new episode of the business cycle is different from its predecessor in some important way. Some cycles are long and some short, some are mild and some severe, some begin in the United States and some abroad. We never know with any certainty when the next turning point (down or up) is coming or what will cause it.

Second, resources are scarce even in a recession or a depression. But at such times, large quantities of scarce resources go unemployed. A satisfactory theory of the business cycle must explain this fact. Why don't scarce resources *always* get fully employed?

There are plenty of simple, but wrong, theories of the business cycle. And when these theories are used to justify policies, they can create severe problems. For example, during the 1960s, recessions were believed to result from insufficient aggregate demand. The solution: increase government spending, cut taxes, and cut interest rates. Countries that pursued such policies most vigorously, such as the United Kingdom, found their economic growth rates sagging, unemployment rising, and inflation accelerating.

Today's new theory—real business cycle theory—predicts that fluctuations in aggregate demand have *no* effect on output and employment and change only the price level and inflation rate. But this theory ignores the *real* effects of financial collapse of the type that occurred in the 1930s. If banks fail on a large scale and people lose their wealth, other firms also begin to fail and jobs are destroyed. Unemployed people cut their spending, and output falls yet further. Demand stimulation may not be called for, but action to ensure that sound banks survive certainly is.

"We don't want to manage the U.S. economy. And we don't think anybody else should take the job either."

ROBERT E. LUCAS, JR.
Personal Interview

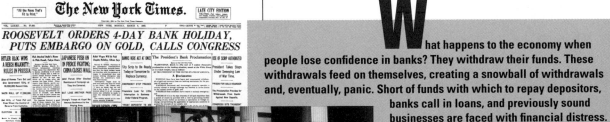

What happens to the economy when people lose confidence in banks? They withdraw their funds. These withdrawals feed on themselves, creating a snowball of withdrawals and, eventually, panic. Short of funds with which to repay depositors, banks call in loans, and previously sound businesses are faced with financial distress. They close down and lay off workers. Recession deepens and turns into depression. Bank failures and the resulting decline in the nation's supply of money and credit were a significant factor in deepening and prolonging the Great Depression. But they taught us the importance of stable financial institutions and gave rise to the establishment of federal deposit insurance to prevent such financial collapse.

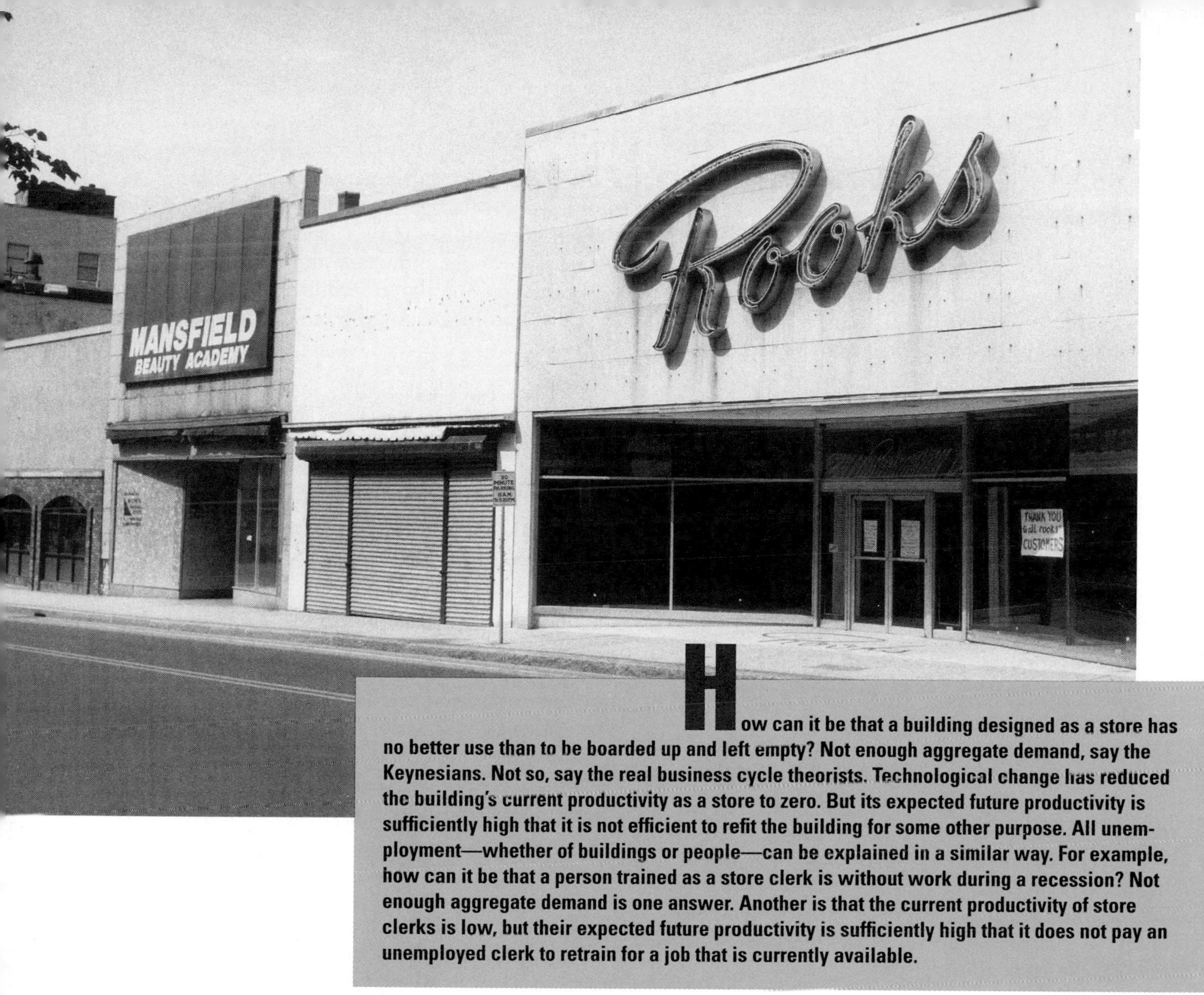

How can it be that a building designed as a store has no better use than to be boarded up and left empty? Not enough aggregate demand, say the Keynesians. Not so, say the real business cycle theorists. Technological change has reduced the building's current productivity as a store to zero. But its expected future productivity is sufficiently high that it is not efficient to refit the building for some other purpose. All unemployment—whether of buildings or people—can be explained in a similar way. For example, how can it be that a person trained as a store clerk is without work during a recession? Not enough aggregate demand is one answer. Another is that the current productivity of store clerks is low, but their expected future productivity is sufficiently high that it does not pay an unemployed clerk to retrain for a job that is currently available.

Robert E. Lucas, Jr.: Today's *Macroeconomic Revolutionary*

Many economists, past and present, have advanced our understanding of business cycles. But one contemporary economist stands out. He is Robert E. Lucas, Jr., of the University of Chicago. In 1970, as a 32-year-old professor at Carnegie-Mellon University, Lucas challenged the Keynesian theories of economic fluctuations and launched a macroeconomic revolution based on two principles: rational expectations and equilibrium. Like all scientific revolutions, the one touched off by Lucas was controversial. Twenty years later, rational expectations (whether right or wrong) is accepted by most economists. But the idea that the business cycle and unemployment can be understood as equilibria remains controversial and, for some economists, even distasteful. Lucas believes that we still know too little about the causes of the business cycle to be able to stabilize the economy.

◆ ◆ ◆ ◆ We have now completed our study of the working of the macroeconomy. We've studied the macroeconomic model of aggregate demand and aggregate supply, and we've learned a great deal about the workings of the markets for goods and services, labor, and money and financial assets. We have applied our knowledge to explain and understand the problems of unemployment, inflation, and business cycle fluctuations. ◆ ◆ In the next part of the book we will study two aspects of macroeconomic policy—the monetary and fiscal policies that governments can take to stabilize the economy and the policy problems posed by the government's budget deficit.

SUMMARY

Three Recent Recessions

The three most recent recessions in U.S. history occurred in 1974–1975, 1982, and 1990–1991. The first recession was caused by the actions of OPEC. At the end of 1973 and the beginning of 1974, OPEC increased the price of oil and, for a period, placed an embargo on the export of oil. These events resulted in a severe decrease in aggregate supply. Aggregate demand also decreased but not by as much as aggregate supply. As a consequence, real GDP fell and the price level increased at an accelerating pace. The phenomenon gave rise to a new economic term—stagflation.

The Volcker recession of 1982 resulted from a fall in the growth of aggregate demand triggered by the monetary policy of the Federal Reserve. In its attempt to beat inflation, the Fed unexpectedly slowed the growth of aggregate demand. Wages increased on the presumption that inflation would continue at close to 10 percent a year, and those wage changes decreased aggregate supply. But the fall in aggregate supply was smaller than the fall in aggregate demand. As a consequence, real GDP declined but the inflation rate moderated.

The 1990–1991 recession resulted from the Persian Gulf crisis, which increased the price of oil—a decrease in aggregate supply—and increased uncertainty, bringing lower investment—a decrease in aggregate demand. The result was a fall in real GDP with a slight moderation in the inflation rate.

In all recessions, interest rates eventually decline as the lower level of real GDP decreases the demand for money.

There is controversy about the behavior of the labor market during a recession. According to the sticky wage theory, the quantity of labor supplied is not very responsive to changes in real wages and wages themselves do not fall much in a recession. As a result, when the economy goes into recession, the quantity of labor supplied exceeds the quantity demanded. According to the flexible wage theory, the quantity of labor supplied is highly responsive to changes in real wages. When the economy goes into recession, real wages fall a little, by enough to keep the quantity of labor demanded equal to the quantity supplied. Unemployment increases, but the increase arises from increased job search activity associated with a higher degree of labor turnover.

Macroeconomists have not yet found the acid test that enables them to resolve their uncertainty about the labor market mechanism in recession. (pp. 876–885)

Another Great Depression?

The Great Depression that began in 1929 lasted longer and was more severe than any before it or since. The Great Depression started with increased uncertainty and pessimism, which brought a fall in investment (especially in housing) and spending on consumer durables. Increased uncertainty and pessimism also brought on the stock market crash. The crash added to the pessimistic outlook, and further spending cuts occurred. There then followed a near total collapse of the financial system. Banks failed and the money supply fell, resulting in a continued fall in aggregate demand. Expectations of falling prices led to falling wages, but the fall in aggregate demand continued to exceed expectations and real GDP continued to decline.

The Great Depression itself produced a series of reforms that make a repeat of such a depression much less likely. The most important of these were the Fed's willingness to act as lender of last resort and the introduction of federal bank deposit insurance, both of which reduced the risk of bank failure and financial collapse. Higher taxes and government spending have given the economy greater resistance against depression, and an increased labor force participation rate provides a greater measure of security, especially for families with more than one wage earner. For these reasons, an initial change in either aggregate demand or aggregate supply is much less likely to translate into an accumulative depression, as it did in the early 1930s. Thus even a stock market crash as severe as the one that occurred in 1987 did not lead to a collapse in aggregate demand. (pp. 885–893)

KEY ELEMENTS

Key Figures

REVIEW QUESTIONS

1 When did the Great Depression, the OPEC recession, and the Volcker recession occur?

2 What triggered each of the following?

a The OPEC recession

b The Volcker recession

c The 1990–1991 recession

3 Which of the three recessions in question 2 was a period of stagflation?

4 Compare the movements in interest rates in the three recessions in question 2.

5 Describe the changes in employment and real wages in the OPEC recession. What is the sticky wage theory of these changes? What is the flexible wage theory of these changes?

6 Describe the changes in real GDP, employment and unemployment, and the price level that occurred during the Great Depression years of 1929 to 1933.

7 What were the main causes of the onset of the Great Depression in 1929?

8 What events in 1931 and 1932 led to the continuation and increasing severity of the fall in real GDP and the rise in employment?

9 What four features of today's economy make it less likely now than in 1929 that a Great Depression will occur? Why do they make it less likely?

PROBLEMS

1 During the OPEC recession, real wages fell from $12.07 an hour to $11.97 an hour. Employment fell from 164 billion hours to 161 billion hours. Illustrate these changes in the labor market by drawing demand and supply curves for labor in 1973 and 1975. Draw two diagrams, one that illustrates these changes in wages and employment if the flexible wage theory is true and one that illustrates these changes if the sticky wage theory is true.

2 Analyze the changes in the interest rate during the Volcker recession by drawing a diagram of the money market showing shifts in the demand and supply curves for real money. What policy changes could have prevented interest rates from rising? What would the effects of such actions have been on real GDP and the price level?

3 During the Volcker recession, real wages did not fall. They held steady at $12.60 an hour. Employment fell from 184 to 180 billion hours. How can these events be explained by the sticky wage theory? By the flexible wage theory?

4 Analyze the changes in the interest rate during the 1990–1991 recession by drawing a diagram of the money market showing shifts in the demand and supply curves for real money. What policy changes could have prevented the recession?

5 During the 1990–1991 recession, real wages increased from $13.78 in 1990 to $13.86 in 1991 and employment decreased from 212 billion hours in 1990 to 209 billion hours in 1991. How can these changes be explained by the sticky and flexible wage theories?

6 Compare and contrast the recessions of 1974–1975, 1982, and 1990–1991. In what ways are they similar, and in what ways do they differ?

7 List all of the features of the U.S. economy today that you can think of that are consistent with a pessimistic outlook for the mid-1990s.

8 List all of the features of the U.S. economy today that you can think of that are consistent with an optimistic outlook for the mid-1990s.

9 How do you think the U.S. economy is going to evolve over the next year or two? Explain your predictions, drawing on the pessimistic and optimistic factors that you listed in the previous two problems and on your knowledge of macroeconomic theory.

PART 12

MACROECONOMIC POLICY

Talking with Andrew F. Brimmer

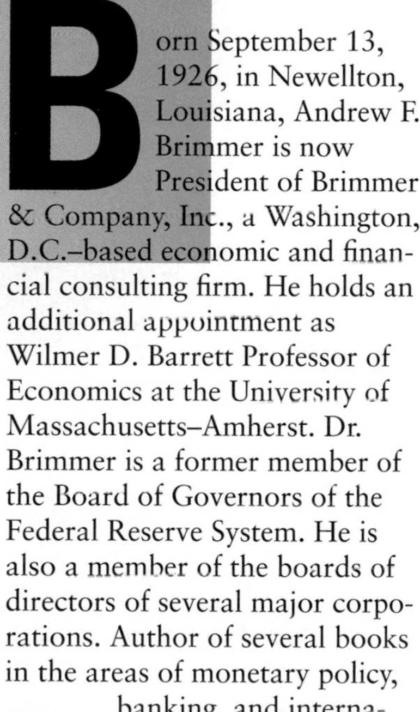

Born September 13, 1926, in Newellton, Louisiana, Andrew F. Brimmer is now President of Brimmer & Company, Inc., a Washington, D.C.–based economic and financial consulting firm. He holds an additional appointment as Wilmer D. Barrett Professor of Economics at the University of Massachusetts–Amherst. Dr. Brimmer is a former member of the Board of Governors of the Federal Reserve System. He is also a member of the boards of directors of several major corporations. Author of several books in the areas of monetary policy, banking, and international finance, he has also published numerous articles in professional journals. Dr. Brimmer has served as vice-president of the American Economic Association and president of the Eastern Economic Association. He has been on the faculties of Harvard University, Michigan State University, and the University of Pennsylvania. He earned his Ph.D. in economics at Harvard.

How did you first become interested in economics?

I was introduced to economics during my second year at the University of Washington. I began my college work as a journalism major, and a survey course in economics was part of the required curriculum. In taking that course, I had a very good teacher. I found that the subject matter dealt with contemporary issues such as the tradeoffs between depression versus prosperity, inflation versus stagnation, and free trade versus protection. I was immediately attracted to the orderly and systematic thinking that lies at the core of economics. At the end of my junior year, I switched my major to economics.

How would you grade the Fed's conduct of monetary policy over the past few years?

I would assign a grade of A–. The main task confronting the Federal Reserve Board until the summer of 1990 was to prevent the resurgence of inflation. To that end, the Federal Reserve adopted a restrictive monetary policy in the spring of 1989. The threat of accelerating inflation became even more pressing after Iraq invaded Kuwait in August 1990, which led to a sharp spurt in oil prices. To limit the spread of these inflationary pressures through the rest of the economy, the Federal Reserve exerted even more restraint on the availability of money and credit. This posture was maintained until the closing months of 1990. By that time, the 1990–91 recession was underway. Although the evidence of declining output was widespread, the Federal Reserve System was reluctant to relax restraint on the growth of bank reserves in order to reduce interest rates. Because of this error in timing the shift to a stimulative monetary policy, the Federal Reserve should get less than a perfect grade.

However, as the recession deepened, the stimulative policy was pursued vigorously. Because the recovery during 1991–92 was exceptionally weak when compared with the record since the end of World War II, the Federal Reserve was generous in supplying bank reserves, and interest rates—particularly short-term rates—remained quite low. This phase of monetary management deserves a grade of A.

Is the Fed doing enough to stimulate full recovery from the 1990–91 recession and to ensure sustained growth in the years ahead?

Yes. The contribution the Fed can make is to supply bank reserves, which will increase liquidity. The latter, in turn, will enable banks to expand loans and purchases of securities. The increased supply of money and credit will lead to a decline in interest rates and a rise in business investment and consumer spending.

The Federal Reserve has pursued these objectives. For example, in 1989, when a restrictive monetary policy was in force, total reserves decreased by 0.8 percent. Monetary restraint continued well into 1990, and total reserves rose by only 2.6 percent for the year. However, as the recession become more evident, a stimulative policy was adopted, and reserves expanded by 5.5 percent in 1991. During 1992, total reserves were projected to increase by 12.9 percent. Reflecting these changes in monetary policy, interest rates decreased appreciably. For instance, the federal funds rate declined from an average of 9.22 percent in 1989 to 8.10 percent in 1990, to 5.69 percent in 1991, and to a projected 4.25 percent in 1992. Parallel—though less dramatic—reductions occurred in the case of long-term interest rates. Yields on 30-year U.S. government bonds decreased from 8.45 percent in 1989 to 8.61 percent in 1990, to 8.14 percent in 1991, and to a projected 7.95 percent in 1992.

In your experience, what are the most effective macroeconomic stabilization policies?

That depends on the nature of the problems the economy is facing at any particular time. There are essentially two types of policies available: (1) fiscal policy and (2) monetary policy. The former focuses on variations in the net position of the federal budget—that is, whether it is in surplus or deficit. The latter focuses on bank reserves and interest rates.

In the simplest case, if the economy is drifting into a recession, the objective should be to stimulate aggregate demand. To achieve this goal, government revenue should decrease while expenditures increase—causing the budget to shift into deficit, or an existing deficit should become larger. The Federal Reserve should expand bank reserves and reduce interest rates. In the opposite case—when excess aggregate demand is pushing the economy toward inflation—both fiscal and monetary policy should become restrictive.

The more difficult problem arises when the economy is suffering from "stagflation"—a mixture of slow growth, a large budget deficit, and inflationary pressures. Under these circumstances, fiscal policy should be restrictive. Perhaps even a budget surplus should be sought. Monetary policy should be less restrictive—which would permit somewhat lower interest rates to promote investment. The fundamental challenges in these more complex cases are to find the right combination of policies and to shift the degree of stimulation and restraint in a timely fashion.

Some people believe that the Fed is too independent and that some of its independence should be removed. What is your opinion?

The Federal Reserve System is an independent agency *within* the federal government, but it is *outside* the executive branch. The Federal Reserve exercises—on delegated authority—the power that the U.S. Constitution vested in Congress "to coin money and determine the value thereof." Congress, in turn, has delegated that authority to the Federal Reserve Board. On four occasions in our history, Congress has debated delegating the "money power" to the president and each time decided against taking that step. Instead, it has tried four different arrangements: the First Bank of the United States (1790), the Second Bank of the United States (1816), the National Banking System (1863), and the Federal Reserve System (1913). In each case, the Congress delegated its authority to control money to an agency outside the executive branch of the government. These were wise decisions.

If the president had control over the power to create money, there would be a strong temptation to use that power to finance the federal budget deficit. This would give the federal government control over goods and services in excess of the tax revenue collected. It would contribute to inflation in the long run.

We occasionally hear reports indicating that the deliberations of the Federal Open Market Committee—the Fed's policymaking arm—get quite heated, with the members of the committee disagreeing with each other concerning the appropriate direction for policy. Are these reports accurate? If so, how does the committee ultimately decide monetary policy?

The appropriate course for monetary policy under different economic conditions is debated vigorously at the periodic meetings of the Federal Open Market Committee (FOMC). However, the discussion is always calm and courteous. Of course, some members are more vocal than others. Yet on most occasions, the chairman can lead the committee to a broadly based consensus that is supported unanimously. Ultimately, the twelve members of the FOMC, which consists of seven Federal Reserve board members and five Federal Reserve bank presidents—four of whom serve on a rotating basis—vote on each proposed change in policy. Dissents are rare; when they do occur, only one or two negative votes are typically cast.

What do you consider the most pressing economic problem facing the United States today?

"The result is a labor market equilibrium in which not all workers can get the jobs they want and meet the qualifications . . ."

The large and persistent federal budget deficit is a matter of great concern. However, the anemic recovery from the 1990–91 recession and the prospect of sub-par growth over the next several years constitute the most pressing problems facing this country. Consequently, the most urgent task is to stimulate investment in the private sector. Measured in real terms, we have suffered a significant decline in spending for plant and equipment and R&D in relation to gross domestic product. We are also lagging significantly in public investment for infrastructure—such as urban transit and water supply systems. Ultimately, these kinds of outlays must be financed by the federal government, and we should press ahead to do it at this time.

Why should we be concerned about the sustained increase in the nation's debt?

There are several reasons why we should be seriously concerned. In the first place, the debt represents the accumulated federal budget deficit incurred in the past. To service the outstanding debt and to cover the new deficits, the federal government has to borrow in the money and capital markets both at home and abroad. Thus the government absorbs savings that would otherwise be available to the private sector. The added competition for funds exerts upward pressure on interest rates. Moreover, an increasing share of the national debt is owned by foreign investors. The amount of interest paid to them provides foreigners with a growing command over U.S. resources and income.

What economic problems await us as we approach the twenty-first century?

Aside from the lag in investment already mentioned, we need to upgrade the nation's labor force. Over the next decade, women, blacks, and members of other minority groups will provide most of the net increase in the civilian labor force. Many of the people from these segments of the population do not have the skills that will be needed to compete successfully in the labor market in the years ahead. Therefore we must substantially increase our investment in education to equip them to undertake the more sophisticated production and management tasks they will be required to perform.

The decline in the competitive position of American industry also has to be reversed. The United States has suffered serious erosion in its world market share in a number of manufactured products for which we once had a significant comparative advantage. Not only are we losing out to advanced industrial countries such as Germany and Japan, but we are also losing market share to a number of the newly industrialized nations such as Hong Kong, South Korea, Singapore, Taiwan, and Thailand. Moreover, imports have taken a sizable share of the U.S. domestic market. Many foreign manufacturers are increasingly able to produce and deliver high-quality products to American consumers at prices below what U.S. firms would require. To counter these trends, U.S. manufacturers will have to increase the productivity of American workers and raise the quality of domestic products.

> "Many foreign manufacturers are increasingly able to produce and deliver high-quality products to American consumers at prices below what U.S. firms would require."

What professional activity provides you with the most satisfaction?

Today, I work primarily as an economic and financial consultant. I spend most of my time preparing analyses and forecasts of interest rates and other developments in money and capital markets at home and abroad. Based on these assessments, I provide advice to clients—who consist mainly of banks, portfolio managers, and other financial institutions. In addition, I serve as a director of several corporations and teach economics on a part-time basis—mainly to graduate students through seminars and workshops. I also write a column for the monthly magazine *Black Enterprise*. All of these activities provide considerable satisfaction.

In your opinion, what is the most important message that college students should take away from a principles of economics course?

Students should take away several important lessons. First, you need to understand the basic tasks that any economy must perform, such as: (1) Given the scarcity of resources, how are decisions made with respect to what is to be produced and by what method of organization? (2) How is the income that is generated from economic activity to be distributed? (3) What is the role of supply and demand in allocating goods and services in the context of a market system?

Also, you need to remember that economics provides citizens with help in making choices among competing claims and the allocation of scarce resources but that economics cannot dictate which choices are to be selected. For example, economics can help to determine the costs and benefits of pollution abatement, but it cannot decide whether a policy of abatement should be adopted. Likewise, economic analysis can show the expected effect of airline deregulation on the volume of air travel, but it cannot decide whether the airline industry should be deregulated.

CHAPTER 33

STABILIZING THE ECONOMY

After studying this chapter, you will be able to:

- Describe the goals of macroeconomic stabilization policy
- Explain how the economy influences government popularity
- Describe the main features of fiscal policy since 1960
- Describe the main features of monetary policy since 1960
- Distinguish between fixed-rule and feedback-rule stabilization policies
- Explain how the economy responds to aggregate demand and aggregate supply shocks under fixed-rule and feedback-rule policies
- Explain why lowering inflation usually brings recession

PEOPLE PANIC WHEN TIMES ARE HARD AND TURN TO their political leaders for action. Thus it was in the depths of the Great Depression that our grandparents turned to Franklin Delano Roosevelt to deliver them from that economic holocaust. Sixty-three years later, with George Bush in the White House, the situation was remarkably similar. The economic ills of 1991 were not as severe as those of 1929, but the economy was again in recession, and for many there was no relief in sight. And so again the cry went out—"Who's in charge?" Who *is* in charge of the U.S. economy? When recession strikes, what can the government do about it? ◆◆ In 1976, with unemployment *and* inflation high by historical standards, the electorate ejected the Republican administration from power and elected Democrat Jimmy Carter as president. Four years later, with unemployment not much lower and inflation substantially higher, the electorate rejected Carter. In 1992, with a stubborn recession dominating the political debate, the stage seemed set for a close call in the presidential race. How important is the economy in determining election outcomes? And what aspects of the economy do voters worry about most—unemployment or inflation or both? ◆◆ The second half of the 1980s was a period of unimagined prosperity and macroeconomic stability. The early 1990s, in contrast, were years of slow income growth, high unemployment, and recession. How were the stability and prosperity of the 1980s achieved? And what can be done to achieve a similar degree of success in the 1990s?

Who's in Charge?

◆ ◆ ◆ ◆ In this chapter, we're going to study the problems of stabilizing the U.S. economy—of avoiding inflation, high unemployment, and wildly fluctuating growth rates of real GDP. At the end of the chapter, you will have a clearer and deeper understanding of the macroeconomic policy problems facing the United States today and of the political debate that surrounds us concerning those problems.

The Stabilization Problem

The stabilization problem is to deliver a macroeconomic performance that is as smooth and predictable as possible. Solving this problem involves specifying targets to be achieved and then devising policies to achieve them. There are two main macroeconomic stabilization policy targets. They are

- Real GDP growth
- Inflation

Real GDP Growth

When real GDP grows less quickly than the economy's ability to produce, output is lost. When real GDP grows more quickly than the economy's ability to produce, bottlenecks arise. Keeping real GDP growth steady and equal to long-run aggregate supply growth avoids these problems.

Fluctuations in real GDP growth also bring fluctuations in unemployment. When unemployment rises above its natural rate, productive labor is wasted and there is a slowdown in the accumulation of human capital. If such unemployment persists, serious psychological and social problems arise for the unemployed workers and their families. When unemployment falls below its natural rate, expanding industries are held back by labor shortages. Keeping real GDP growth steady helps keep unemployment at its natural rate and avoids the waste and shortage of labor.

Fluctuations in real GDP growth contribute to fluctuations in our international trade balance. An international trade deficit enables us to purchase more goods and services than we have produced. But to do so, we must borrow from the rest of the world and pay interest on our borrowing. An international trade surplus enables us to lend to the rest of the world and earn interest. But to do so, we must purchase fewer goods and services than we have produced. Keeping real GDP growth steady helps keep our balance of trade with the rest of the world steady and enables us to consume what we have produced and avoid a buildup of international debt interest.

Inflation

When inflation fluctuates unpredictably, money becomes less useful as a measuring rod for conducting transactions. Borrowers and lenders and employers and workers must take on extra risks. Keeping the inflation rate steady and predictable avoids these problems.

Keeping inflation steady also helps keep the value of the dollar abroad steady. Other things being equal, if the inflation rate goes up by 1 percentage point, the dollar loses 1 percent of its value against the currencies of other countries. Large and unpredictable fluctuations in the foreign exchange rate—the value of the dollar against other currencies—make international trade and international borrowing and lending less profitable and limit the gains from international specialization and exchange. Keeping inflation low and predictable helps avoid such fluctuations in the exchange rate and enables international transactions to be undertaken at minimum risk and on the desired scale.

Policy performance, judged by the two policy targets—real GDP growth and inflation—is shown in Fig. 33.1. Here the red line is real GDP growth, and the green shaded area is inflation. As you can see, our performance has fallen far short of stabilizing the economy. Why has the economy been so unstable? And can policy do better, making the next thirty years more stable than what is shown in Fig. 33.1? Answering these questions will occupy most of the rest of this chapter. Let's begin by identifying the key players and the policy actions they have taken.

FIGURE 33.1

Macroeconomic Performance: Real GDP and Inflation

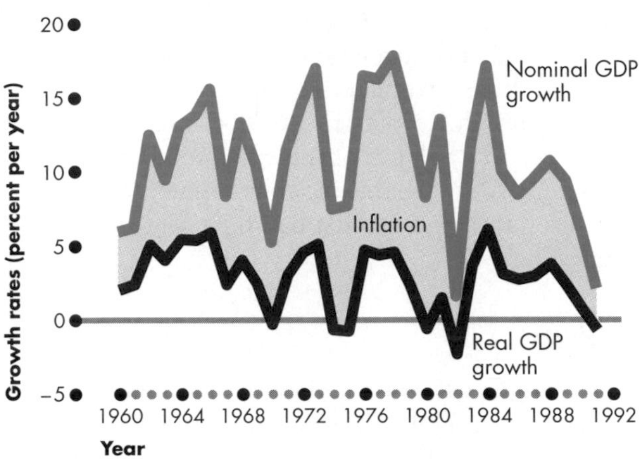

Real GDP growth and inflation fluctuate a great deal. During the 1970s, inflation mushroomed (the green shaded area). This macroeconomic performance falls far short of the goals of a stable real GDP growth rate and moderate and predictable inflation.

Source: The Economic Report of the President, 1992.

Players and Policies

There are three key players that formulate and execute macroeconomic stabilization policy:

- Congress
- The Board of Governors of the Federal Reserve System
- The administration

Congress

The House of Representatives and the Senate and various committees of Congress implement the nation's fiscal policy, summarized in the federal budget. The **federal budget** is a statement of the federal government's financial plan, itemizing programs and their costs, tax revenues, and the proposed budget deficit or surplus.

The timetable for the federal budget process is fairly rigid. The U.S. fiscal year runs from October 1 to September 30. Most of the high-profile political action surrounding the budget takes place in the fall, as Congress and the president attempt to agree on a budget. But the process begins in January when Congress receives the president's proposed budget for the following year. The Congressional Budget Office studies the president's proposals and prepares a report on them for Congress. Then follows a series of long committee sessions and reports. Eventually, the Senate and the House develop a concurrent resolution describing a budget package that both houses are willing to approve. Because of this timetable, fiscal policy, while having an important effect on macroeconomic performance, is not used as a means of fine-tuning the economy.

Fiscal policy has three elements:

- Spending plans
- Tax laws
- Deficit

Spending Plans The expenditure side of the budget is a list of programs with the amount that the government plans to spend on each program and a forecast of the total amount of government expenditure. Some expenditure items in the federal budget are directly controlled by government departments. Others arise from decisions to fund particular programs, the total cost of which depends on actions that Congress can forecast but not directly control. For example, social security expenditure depends on the state of the economy and on how many people qualify for support. Farm subsidies depend on farm costs and prices.

Tax Laws Congress makes decisions about government revenue by enacting tax laws. As in the case of some important items of government expenditure, Congress cannot control with precision the amount of tax revenue it will receive. The amount of tax paid is determined by the actions of the millions of people and firms that make their own choices about how much to work, spend, and save.

Deficit The difference between government spending and taxes is the government deficit. Every year since 1969, the federal government has had a deficit, and in the early 1980s the deficit became unusually large.

The persistence of a federal government deficit has caused alarm and led to a variety of creative ideas on the part of Congress to keep spending in check or to increase revenue. One idea, proposed by Senators Gramm, Rudman, and Hollings and incorporated into the Gramm-Rudman-Hollings Act of 1985, is to impose automatic spending cuts if the deficit does not follow a predetermined path that will ultimately result in a balanced budget by 1993.

Another way of balancing the federal budget is to increase government revenue. But there is disagreement and two competing views about how this objective might be achieved. One, supported by former President Ronald Reagan, is that tax reform and lower tax rates will increase revenue by stimulating economic activity. The incomes on which taxes are paid will increase by enough to ensure that lower tax rates bring in higher revenue. The other view is that revenue can be increased only by increasing tax rates and introducing new taxes.

The Federal Reserve Board

The Federal Reserve System is the nation's central bank. The main features of the Federal Reserve System are described in Chapter 28. Monetary policy actions are formulated and monitored by the Federal Open Market Committee (FOMC) (see p. 761). Each month, the FOMC meets to formulate detailed guidelines for the conduct of monetary policy in the coming month. The minutes of the FOMC are confidential until enough time has elapsed for the actions based on the decisions taken to have already occurred. This confidentiality is regarded as an important means of preventing anyone from benefiting from inside knowledge of the Fed's forthcoming actions.

The Fed influences the economy by trading in markets in which it is one of the major participants. The two most important groups of such markets are those for government debt and for foreign currency. The Fed's decisions to buy and sell in these markets influence interest rates, the value of the dollar in terms of foreign currencies, and the amount of money in the economy. These variables that the Fed can directly influence in turn affect the conditions on which the millions of firms and households in the economy undertake their own economic actions.

Because the Fed's policymaking committee, the FOMC, meets frequently and because the Fed operates daily in financial markets, monetary policy is used in an attempt to fine-tune the economy.

The Administration

The role of the administration in formulating and implementing macroeconomic stabilization policy is to give advice and attempt to persuade. Even the president of the United States has severely limited powers when it comes to stabilizing the economy.

Persuading the Fed The president can attempt to influence the chairman and members of the Board of Governors of the Federal Reserve System, persuading them to take whatever stabilization policy actions the administration deems appropriate. And the president carries some important carrots and sticks that enhance his influence. For example, the president appoints the chairman (for four years) and members of the Federal Reserve Board (for fourteen years). But once they have been appointed, the president cannot remove them until their term of office is complete. This fact means that a president often has to live with a Federal Reserve Board appointed largely by previous presidents.

Influencing Congress The president can also try to influence Congress and the outcome of congressional debates. One source of this influence is the president's power of veto. But in the case of government spending bills, the president has the power only to take the entire bill or to leave it. He does not have a line-item veto as do many state governors. That is, the president cannot decide to veto certain items in a budget proposed by Congress. He either approves the entire package or rejects the entire package. In practical terms, this means that the president does not have a veto on financial bills. To veto a half-billion-dollar dam project would require also vetoing the entire defense budget.

The Economic Report of the President Each year, the president prepares an economic report that reviews the state of the economy and sets out his goals and ambitions for the future. The report is accompanied by the annual report of the president's Council of Economic Advisors. Established in the

Employment Act of 1946, the council consists of a small group of economists who work closely with the president, keeping him informed and advised of economic developments and of policy developments in the Fed and Congress. The Council of Economic Advisors, together with the president, takes a position on the appropriate combination of monetary and fiscal policy actions. It also offers opinions on the actions of the two branches of policymaking, paying special attention to consistency of the policies with each other.

At the head of the Council of Economic Advisors is its chairman. Almost always the chairman is a highly distinguished economist, often with an academic background. The current chairman is Michael Boskin, on leave from his regular job as a professor of economics at Stanford University. Usually, the Council of Economic Advisors and its chairman operate quietly in the background. Occasionally, however, the chairman becomes embroiled in public debate. The most notable such occasion arose in 1984 when Ronald Reagan's Council of Economic Advisors chairman, Martin Feldstein, a Harvard professor, vocally and publicly expressed his concern about the administration's attitude toward the large, and seemingly permanent, federal deficit. But such public disagreements are rare, and most of the time the Council of Economic Advisors works in close harmony with the president.

We've described the key players in the policymaking game. Let's now turn our attention to the policies they have pursued.

Fiscal and Monetary Policy Performance

Macroeconomic stabilization policy is strongly influenced by the constraints on Congress, the Fed, and the president. And the most important constraint is that arising from the effects of economic performance on voters in congressional and presidential elections. To ensure adequate voter support to get re-elected, macroeconomic policy must deliver a macroeconomic performance acceptable to the electorate. What is an acceptable macroeconomic performance?

Macroeconomic Performance and Voter Behavior

The effects of economic performance on voter behavior have been studied most thoroughly by Ray Fair of Yale University. By studying the outcome of all the presidential elections between 1916 and 1984, Fair discovered the following formula:

- For each 1 percentage point *increase* in the real GDP growth rate, the incumbent political party gets a 1 percentage point *increase* in voter share.
- For each 3 percentage point *increase* in the inflation rate, the incumbent political party gets a 1 percentage point *decrease* in voter share.

We can use Fair's discovery to calculate the predicted change in popularity (the change in the percentage of votes that the incumbent is expected to receive in the next election) as follows:

$$\begin{aligned}\text{Percentage of votes} = {} & \text{Real GDP growth} \\ & - \tfrac{1}{3} \times \text{Inflation rate} \\ & + \text{Other influences.}\end{aligned}$$

Politicians take actions that they believe will get them re-elected. That is, they take actions designed to increase the percentage of votes they receive. Among these actions are macroeconomic stabilization policies that increase real GDP growth and lower inflation. But a 1 percentage point increase in real GDP growth brings in as many additional votes as a 3 percentage point decrease in the inflation rate. Therefore politicians tend to favor policies that increase real GDP growth over those that decrease inflation.

Popularity and Economic Performance since 1960

The macroeconomic performance of the United States since 1960, as measured by its predicted effects on the popularity of the incumbent party (but with other influences ignored), is shown in Fig. 33.2. The figure also gives information about the timing of presidential elections and the outcomes of those elections, winners in red and losers in black.

You can see that between 1961 and 1966, economic performance contributed to political popularity. But economic performance then deteriorated through 1971. There followed, through the 1970s and early 1980s, a series of large swings in performance and popularity.

But look closely at the timing of the swings. In every election year except one, the economy was improving and increasing the popularity of the incumbent administration in the year of the election. Only in one year, 1980, did the president (Jimmy

FIGURE 33.2
Election Outcomes and the Economy

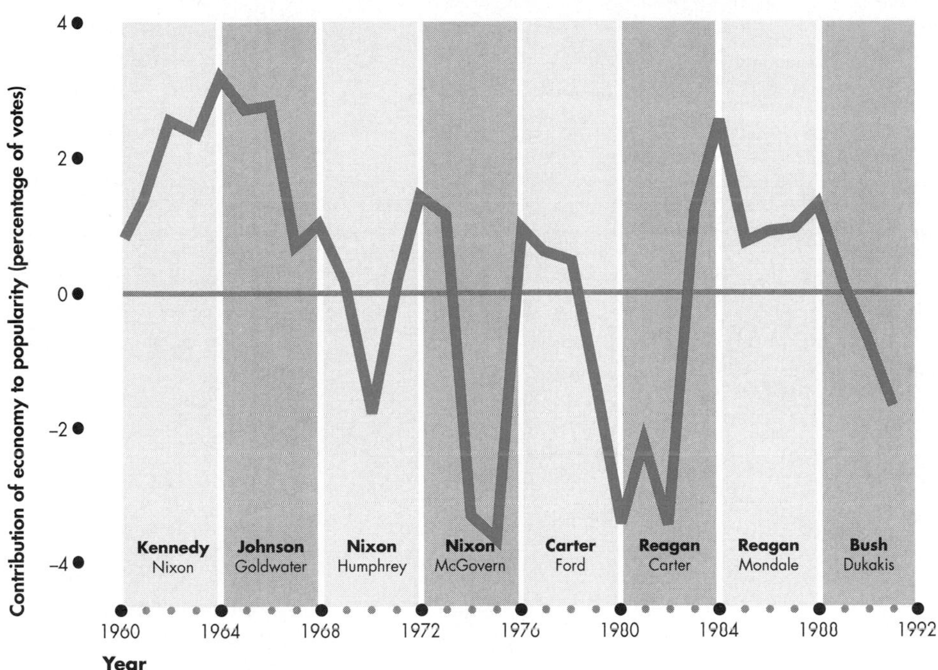

Presidential elections are won or lost depending on the state of the economy. Faster real GDP growth and slower inflation increase the popularity of the incumbent party. Usually, real GDP growth slows after an election and speeds up just before an election, enabling the incumbent to win. Two exceptions are 1976, when the speedup in growth came too late, and 1980, when real GDP growth slowed in the election year.

Source: The Economic Report of the President, 1992, and my calculations based on the work of Ray Fair described in the text. The "predicted popularity" variable is the growth rate of real GDP minus one third of the inflation rate.

Carter) go into an election with a negative economic performance. And, predictably, he lost. Other incumbent administrations that lost were Johnson/Humphrey in 1968 (Johnson withdrew from the race and Humphrey ran as the presidential candidate) and Ford in 1976. In both these cases, economic performance was improving in the election year. But in neither case was economic performance strong enough to get the incumbent party re-elected.

Figure 33.2 shows convincingly that economic performance has been linked to presidential elections, so much so that the cycle has been called a political business cycle. A **political business cycle** is a business cycle whose origins are fluctuations in aggregate demand brought about by policies designed to improve the chance of an administration being re-elected. Is the U.S. business cycle to some extent a political business cycle? And if it is, which policies have caused it, fiscal or monetary? To answer these questions, let's look at fiscal and monetary policy over the years since 1960.

Fiscal Policy since 1960 A broad summary of fiscal policy since 1960 is contained in Fig. 33.3. Here you can see the levels of government spending, taxes, and the deficit (each as a percentage of GDP). You can also see the election years and names of the incumbent presidents.

Fiscal policy was mildly expansionary during the Kennedy years and strongly expansionary during the later Johnson years, when the Vietnam war buildup occurred. During Nixon's presidency, spending growth was kept moderate. But under the pressure of the first OPEC oil shock, spending soared during Ford's presidency. The Carter years were a period of spending cuts, and the first Reagan term was a period of spending growth. The Bush administration worked hard to keep spending in check and was initially committed to "no new taxes" but in mid-term favored a tax increase. As the 1991 recession intensified and the 1992 election drew closer, tax cuts became the rage, especially in Congress (see Reading Between the Lines, pp. 908–909).

Fiscal Policy in Action

TIME, NOVEMBER 4, 1991

Is It a Treat or a Trick?

BY JOHN GREENWALD WITH MICHAEL DUFFY AND HAYS GOREY

What Washington politicians were singing last week sounded like the chorus of a wistful Beach Boys song. Wouldn't it be nice, they all sang, if we could cut taxes? Wouldn't that make voters happy in 1992 and lift the economy too? . . .

Lawmakers hastily crafted programs to appeal to everyone from the super-rich to the working poor. Texas Democrat Lloyd Bentsen, who chairs the U.S. Senate Finance Committee, stirred the most talk by proposing a $72.5 billion tax cut aimed squarely at the middle class. . . . Bentsen would pay for the cuts by reducing defense spending. . . .

Politicians rushed forward with nearly a dozen rival plans, including a move by Democratic Senator Daniel Patrick Moynihan of New York to revive his long-standing proposal to cut Social Security taxes. Not to be outdone by the Democrats, Senate Republican Phil Gramm of Texas and House minority whip Newt Gingrich of Georgia introduced wide-ranging legislation that repeated the Bush Administration's cherished call for reduced capital gains taxes. . . .

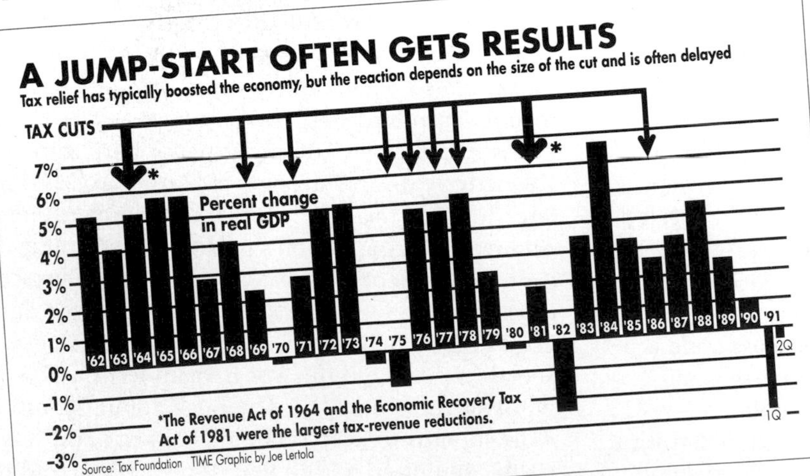

The Essence of the Story

In October 1991, politicians were anxious to speed economic recovery and boost their popularity. They proposed tax cuts aimed at the rich, the middle class, and the poor.

Senator Lloyd Bentsen (Texas Democrat who chairs the U.S. Senate Finance Committee) proposed a $72.5 billion tax cut for the middle class to be paid for by lower defense spending.

Senator Daniel Patrick Moynihan (New York Democrat) proposed a social security tax cut—a proposal he has repeatedly made.

Senator Phil Gramm (Texas Republican) and Representative Newt Gingrich (Georgia Republican and House minority whip) proposed capital gains tax cuts—proposals favored by President Bush.

Background and Analysis

In October 1991, the Commerce Department reported that orders for steel, machinery, aircraft, and other durable goods had fallen by 4.1 percent in August and 3.2 percent in September—the economy appeared stagnant.

In such a situation, feedback fiscal policy can take two forms: automatic or active.

Automatic stabilization occurs because:

- Tax revenues fall as wage and profit incomes fall.
- Transfer payments rise as more people receive unemployment and other benefits.

Active stabilization occurs if Congress passes laws that cut taxes or increase expenditures on programs.

In the 1991 recession, the automatic stabilizers added almost $40 billion to the deficits of the federal, state, and local governments—shown in Fig. 1. But during 1991 the automatic stabilizers began to lose their effect before the economy had recovered. The reason is that corporate taxes began to rise in mid-1991—shown in Fig. 2.

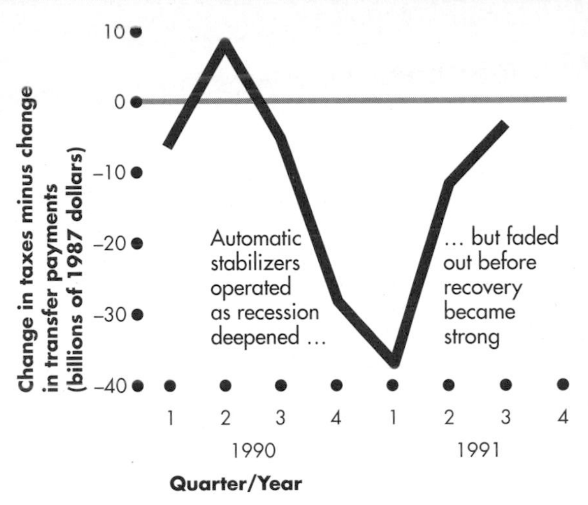

Figure 1

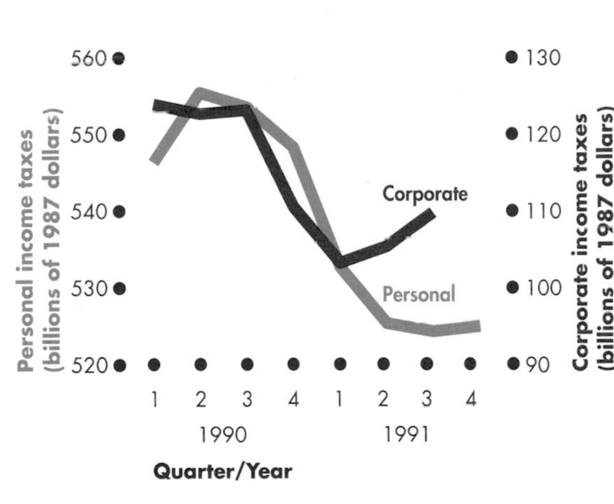

Figure 2

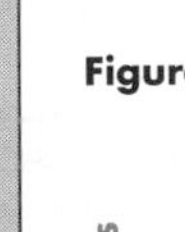

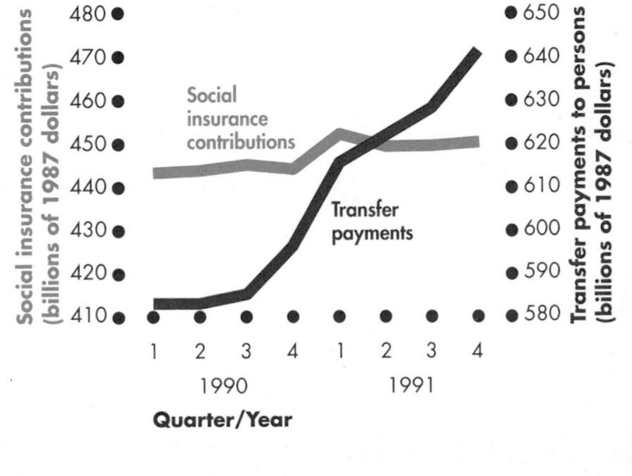

Figure 3

Figure 3 shows an increase in social insurance contributions at the beginning of 1991. (This was not part of stabilization policy, but it had an effect on the economy.) This figure also shows that transfer payments continued to rise during 1991, a sign of continuing high unemployment.

With the economy remaining weak and the steam having gone from the automatic stabilizers, there was a case for additional active stimulus at the beginning of 1992. But some of the proposals in the news article would cut taxes *and* cut spending by the same amount. Such a *balanced budget change* would not be expansionary (see Chapter 26, pp. 711–712). Lower defense spending would decrease aggregate demand by a larger amount than the increase in aggregate demand coming from an equal size tax cut.

The effects of active tax cuts between 1960 and 1991 is mixed, as the chart in the news article makes clear. The Kennedy tax cuts of the early 1960s and the Reagan tax cuts in 1986 were followed by strong economic growth, but for other tax cuts the record is mixed.

FIGURE 33.3

The Fiscal Policy Record: A Summary

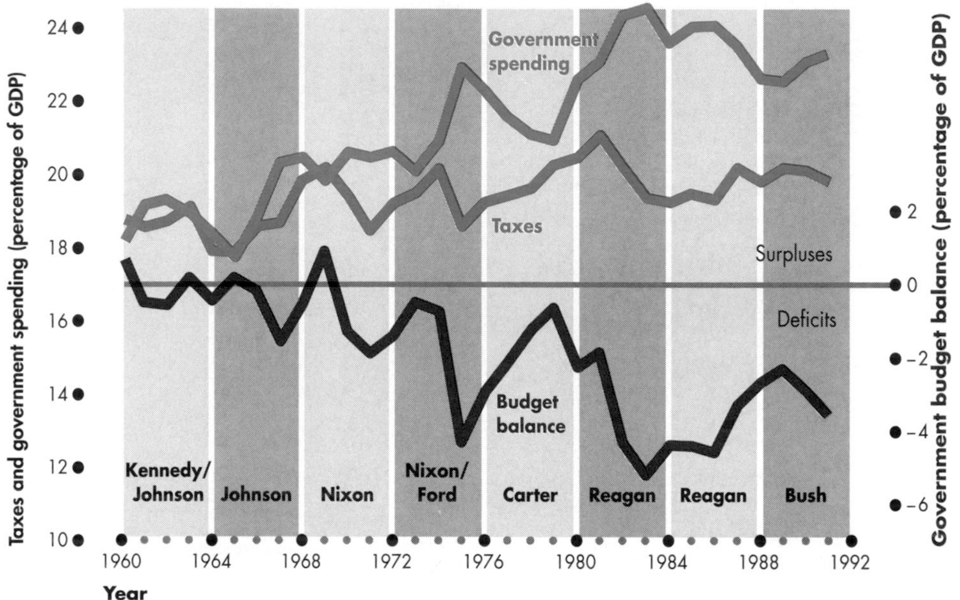

Fiscal policy is summarized here by the performance of government spending, taxes, and the deficit. Both spending and taxes have been on an upward trend, but spending has increased more than taxes, with a deficit emerging. Cycles in spending and taxes have resulted in cycles in the deficit that often have been expansionary in the year before an election and contractionary in the year following an election.

Source: The Economic Report of the President, 1992, and my calculations.

The deficit tells an interesting story. During the terms of Johnson, Nixon, and Ford and the first Reagan term, the deficit decreased in the immediate post-election year and increased as the next election approached. This pattern is consistent with the political business cycle theory. Jimmy Carter inherited a large deficit, brought it under control, and did not permit it to increase during his last year of office. We've seen that the failure of the economy to expand during 1980 was one of the reasons Carter lost the election that year.

Fiscal policy, then, has followed a cycle that has contributed to the political business cycle. But it is not alone. So has monetary policy.

Monetary Policy since 1960 A broad measure of the influence of monetary policy is the growth rate of the money supply. Figure 33.4 shows such a measure, the growth rate of M2. It also identifies the election years, the presidents, and the Fed chairmen. Notice the remarkable tendency for the money supply growth rate to decrease immediately following an election and to increase as the next election approaches. Also notice the only important break in that pattern during the term of Jimmy Carter. Usually, monetary policy has been expansionary a full year before an election, enabling the policy to be effective in the election year.

The performance of monetary policy shown in this figure suggests that the administration is well able to bring sufficient pressure to bear on the independent Fed to ensure that its independence does not get in the way of electoral success too often.

Alternative Stabilization Policies

We've seen that the stabilization policies actually pursued have not brought macroeconomic stability. How might the economy be stabilized? Many different fiscal and monetary policies can be pursued, but they all fall into two broad categories:

- Fixed rules
- Feedback rules

Fixed Rules A **fixed rule** specifies an action to be pursued independently of the state of the economy. There are many examples of fixed rules in everyday

FIGURE 33.4
The Monetary Policy Record: A Summary

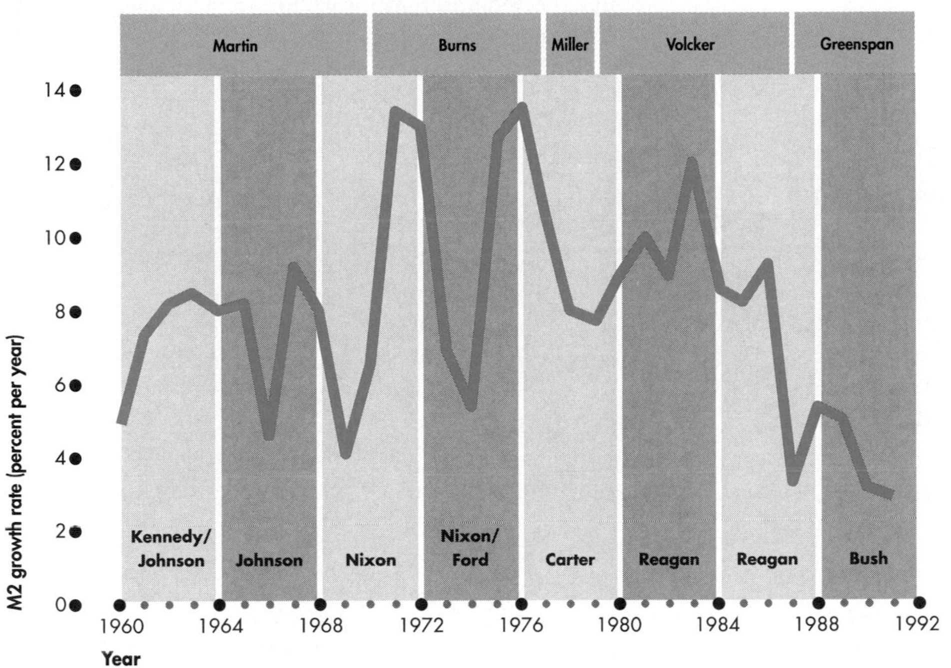

The monetary policy record is summarized here by the growth rate of M2. Fluctuations in M2 growth have coincided with elections, the growth rate usually increasing in the year before an election. An important exception is 1979–1980, when monetary policy did not become expansionary and the incumbent president lost the election.

Source: The Economic Report of the President, 1992.

life. Perhaps the best-known one is the rule that keeps the traffic flowing by having us all stick to the right. The best-known fixed rule for stabilization policy is one that has long been advocated by Milton Friedman. He proposes setting the quantity of money growing at a constant rate year in and year out, regardless of the state of the economy. Inflation persists because continual increases in the money supply increase aggregate demand. Friedman proposes allowing the money supply to grow at a rate that keeps the *average* inflation rate at zero.

Feedback Rules A **feedback rule** specifies how policy actions respond to changes in the state of the economy. An everyday example of a feedback rule is that governing your actions in choosing what to wear and whether to carry an umbrella. You base those actions on the best available forecast of the day's temperature and rainfall. (With a fixed rule, you either always or never carry an umbrella.) A stabilization policy feedback rule is one that changes policy instruments such as the money supply, interest rates, or even taxes, in response to the state of the economy. For example, the Fed pursues a feedback rule if an increase in unemployment causes it to engage in an open market operation aimed at increasing the money supply growth rate and lowering interest rates. The Fed also pursues a feedback rule if an increase in the inflation rate triggers an open market operation aimed at cutting the money supply growth rate and raising interest rates.

REVIEW

Fiscal policy conducted by Congress and the administration and monetary policy conducted by the Fed have generally been cyclical. Policy has usually been restrained following an election and expansionary as another election approaches. Alternative policies based on either fixed rules or feedback rules may be used to stabilize the economy. ◆

We'll study the effects of a fixed rule and a feedback rule for the conduct of stabilization policy by examining how real GDP growth and inflation behave under two alternative rules. We'll begin by studying demand shocks.

Stabilization Policy and Aggregate Demand Shocks

We'll study an economy that starts out at full employment and has no inflation. Figure 33.5 illustrates this situation. The economy is on aggregate demand curve AD_0 and short-run aggregate supply curve *SAS*. These curves intersect at a point on the long-run aggregate supply curve *LAS*. The GDP deflator is 100, and real GDP is $5 trillion. Now suppose that there is an unexpected and temporary fall in aggregate demand. Let's see what happens.

Perhaps investment falls because of a wave of pessimism about the future, or perhaps exports fall because of a recession in the rest of the world. Regardless of the origin of the fall in aggregate demand, the aggregate demand curve shifts to the left, to AD_1 in the figure. Because the fall in aggregate demand is unanticipated, expected aggregate demand remains at AD_0, so the expected GDP deflator remains at 100. The short-run aggregate supply curve stays at *SAS*. Aggregate demand curve AD_1 intersects the short-run aggregate supply curve *SAS* at a GDP deflator of 90 and a real GDP of $4 trillion. The economy is in a depressed state. Real GDP is below its long-run level, and unemployment is above its natural rate.

Recall that we are assuming the fall in aggregate demand from AD_0 to AD_1 to be temporary. As confidence in the future improves, firms' investment picks up, or as economic recovery proceeds in the rest of the world, exports gradually rise. As a result, the aggregate demand curve gradually returns to AD_0, but it takes some time to do so.

We are going to work out how the economy responds during the period in which aggregate demand gradually increases to its original level. To do so, we'll consider two alternative policy rules: a fixed rule and a feedback rule.

FIGURE 33.5

A Fall in Aggregate Demand

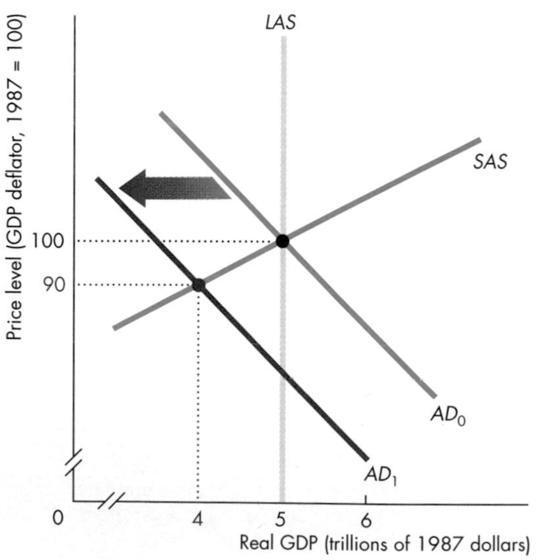

The economy starts out at full employment on aggregate demand curve AD_0 and short-run aggregate supply curve *SAS*, with the two curves intersecting on the long-run aggregate supply curve *LAS*. Real GDP is $5 trillion, and the GDP deflator is 100. A fall in aggregate demand (due to pessimism about future profits, for example) unexpectedly shifts the aggregate demand curve to AD_1. Real GDP falls to $4 trillion, and the GDP deflator falls to 90. The economy is in a recession.

Aggregate Demand Shock with a Fixed Rule

The fixed rule that we'll study here is one in which government purchases of goods and services, taxes, and the deficit remain constant and the money supply remains constant. Neither fiscal policy nor monetary policy responds to the depressed economy.

The response of the economy under this fixed-rule policy is shown in Fig. 33.6(a). When aggregate demand falls to AD_1, no policy measures are taken to bring the economy back to full employment. But recall that we are assuming that the decrease in aggregate demand is temporary and that it gradually increases to AD_0. As it does so, real GDP and the

GDP deflator gradually increase. The GDP deflator gradually returns to 100 and real GDP to its long-run level of $5 trillion. Throughout this process, the economy experiences more rapid growth than usual but beginning from a state of excess capacity. Unemployment remains high until the aggregate demand curve has returned to AD_0.

Let's contrast this adjustment with what occurs under a feedback-rule policy.

Aggregate Demand Shock with a Feedback Rule

The feedback rule that we'll study is one in which government purchases of goods and services increase, taxes decrease, the deficit increases, and the money supply increases when real GDP falls below its long-run level. In other words, both fiscal policy and monetary policy become expansionary when real GDP falls below long-run real GDP. When real GDP rises above its long-run level, both policies operate in reverse, becoming contractionary.

The response of the economy under this feedback-rule policy is shown in Fig. 33.6(b). When aggregate demand falls to AD_1, the expansionary fiscal and monetary policies increase aggregate demand, shifting the aggregate demand curve to AD_0. As the other forces that increase aggregate demand kick in, the fiscal and monetary policies become contractionary, holding the aggregate demand curve steady at AD_0. Real GDP jumps back to its full-employment level, and the GDP deflator jumps back to 100.

FIGURE 33.6

Two Stabilization Policies: Aggregate Demand Shocks

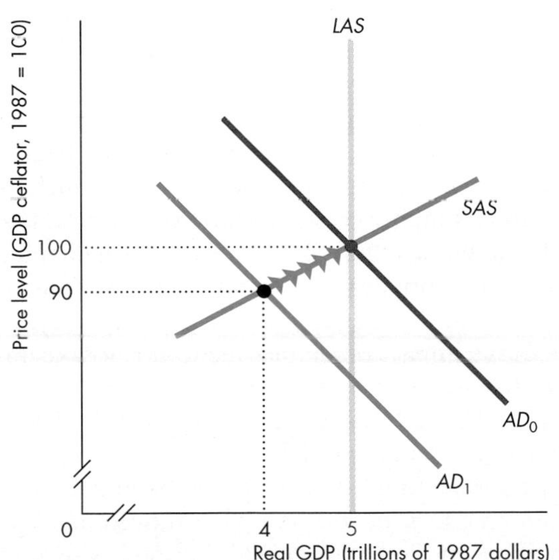

(a) Fixed rule

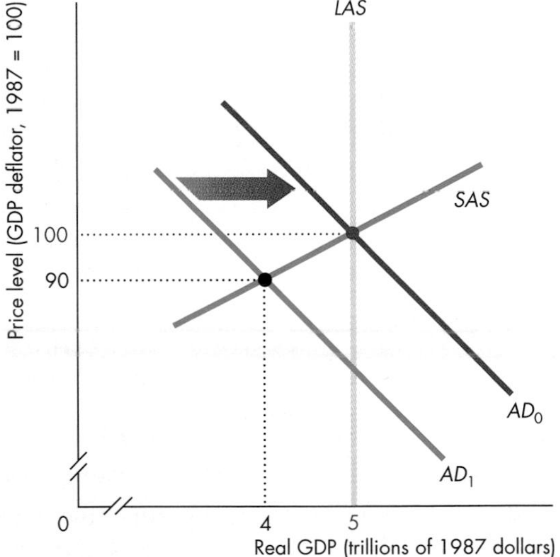

(b) Feedback rule

The economy is in a depressed state with a GDP deflator of 90 and real GDP of $4 trillion. The short-run aggregate supply curve is *SAS*. A fixed-rule stabilization policy (part a) leaves aggregate demand initially at AD_1, so the GDP deflator remains at 90 and real GDP at $4 trillion. As other influences on aggregate demand gradually increase, the aggregate demand curve shifts back to AD_0. As it does, real GDP rises back to $5 trillion and the GDP deflator increases to 100. Part (b) shows a feedback-rule stabilization policy. Expansionary fiscal and monetary policy increases aggregate demand, shifting the aggregate demand curve from AD_1 to AD_0. Real GDP returns to $5 trillion, and the GDP deflator returns to 100. Fiscal and monetary policy becomes contractionary as the other influences on aggregate demand increase its level. As a result, the aggregate demand curve is kept steady at AD_0 and real GDP stays at $5 trillion.

The Two Rules Compared

Under a fixed-rule policy, the economy goes into a recession and stays there for as long as it takes for aggregate demand to increase again under its own steam. Only gradually does the recession come to an end and the aggregate demand curve return to its original position.

Under a feedback-rule policy, the economy is pulled out of its recession by the policy action. Once back at its long-run level, real GDP is held there by a gradual, policy-induced decrease in aggregate demand that exactly offsets the increase in aggregate demand coming from private spending decisions.

The price level and real GDP fall and rise by exactly the same amounts under the two policies, but real GDP stays below its long-run level for longer with a fixed rule than it does with a feedback rule.

So Feedback Rules Are Better? Isn't it obvious that a feedback rule is better than a fixed rule? Can't the government and the Fed use feedback rules to keep the economy close to full employment with a stable price level? Of course, unforecasted events—such as a collapse in business confidence—will hit the economy from time to time. But by responding with a change in tax rates, spending, and money supply, can't the government and the Fed minimize the damage from such a shock? It appears to be so from our analysis.

Despite the apparent superiority of a feedback rule, many economists remain convinced that a fixed rule stabilizes aggregate demand more effectively than a feedback rule. These economists assert that fixed rules are better than feedback rules because:

- Full-employment real GDP is not known.
- Policy lags are longer than the forecast horizon.
- Feedback-rule policies are less predictable than fixed-rule policies.

Let's look at these assertions.

Knowledge of Full-Employment Real GDP

To decide whether a feedback-rule policy needs to stimulate aggregate demand or retard it, it is necessary to determine whether real GDP is currently above or below its full-employment level. But full-employment real GDP is not known with certainty. It depends on a large number of factors, one of which is the level of employment when unemployment is at its natural rate. But there is uncertainty and disagreement about how the labor market works, so we can only estimate the natural rate of unemployment. As a result there is uncertainty about the *direction* in which a feedback-rule policy should be pushing the level of aggregate demand.

Policy Lags and the Forecast Horizon

The effects of policy actions taken today are spread out over the following two years. But no one is able to forecast that far ahead. The forecast horizon of the policymakers is usually less than one year. Further, it is not possible to predict the precise timing and magnitude of the effects of policy itself. Thus feedback-rule policies that react to today's economy might be inappropriate for the state of the economy at that uncertain future date when the policy's effects are felt.

For example, suppose that today the economy is in recession. The Fed reacts with an increase in the money supply growth rate. When the Fed puts on the monetary accelerator, the first reaction is a fall in interest rates. Some time later, lower interest rates produce an increase in investment and the purchases of consumer durable goods. Some time still later, this rise in expenditure increases income, which in turn induces higher consumption expenditure. Later yet, the higher expenditure increases the demand for labor, and eventually wages and prices rise. The sectors in which the spending increases occur vary, and so does the impact on employment. It can take anywhere from nine months to two years for an initial action by the Fed to cause a change in real GDP, employment, and the inflation rate.

By the time the Fed's actions are having their maximum effect, the economy has moved on to a new situation. Perhaps a world economic slowdown has added a new negative effect on aggregate demand that is offsetting the Fed's expansionary actions. Or perhaps a boost in business confidence has increased aggregate demand yet further, adding to the Fed's own expansionary policy. Whatever the situation, the Fed can take the appropriate actions today only if it can forecast those future shocks to aggregate demand.

Thus to smooth the fluctuations in aggregate demand, the Fed needs to take actions today based on a forecast of what will be happening over a period stretching up to two years into the future. It is no use taking actions a year from today to influence the situation that then prevails. It's too late.

If the Fed is good at economic forecasting and bases its policy actions on its forecasts, then the Fed can deliver the type of aggregate demand–smoothing performance that we assumed in the model economy we studied earlier in this chapter. But if the Fed takes policy actions that are based on today's economy rather than based on a forecast of the state of the economy a year in the future, then those actions will often be inappropriate ones.

When unemployment is high and the Fed puts its foot on the accelerator, it speeds the economy back to full employment. But the Fed cannot see far enough ahead to know when to ease off the accelerator and gently tap the brake, holding the economy at its full-employment point. Usually, it keeps its foot on the accelerator for too long, and after the Fed has taken its foot off the accelerator pedal, the economy races through the full-employment point and starts to experience shortages and inflationary pressures. Eventually, when inflation increases and unemployment falls below its natural rate, the Fed steps on the brake, pushing the economy back below full employment.

The Fed's own reaction to the current state of the economy has become one of the major sources of fluctuations in aggregate demand and the major factor that people have to forecast in order to make their own economic choices.

The problems for fiscal policy feedback rules are similar to those for monetary policy but are even more severe because of the lags in the implementation of fiscal policy. The Fed can take actions relatively quickly. But before a fiscal policy action can be taken, the entire legislative process must be completed. Thus even before a fiscal policy action is implemented, the economy may have moved on to a new situation that calls for a different feedback from the one that is in the legislative pipeline.

Predictability of Policies

To make decisions about long-term contracts for employment (wage contracts) and for borrowing and lending, people have to anticipate the future course of prices—the future inflation rate. To forecast the inflation rate, it is necessary to forecast aggregate demand. And to forecast aggregate demand, it is necessary to forecast the policy actions of the government and the Fed.

If the government and the Fed stick to rock-steady, fixed rules for tax rates, spending programs, and money supply growth, then policy itself cannot be a contributor to unexpected fluctuations in aggregate demand.

In contrast, when a feedback rule is being pursued, there is more scope for the policy actions to be unpredictable. The main reason is that feedback rules are not written down for all to see. Rather, they have to be inferred from the behavior of the government and the Fed.

Thus with a feedback-rule policy it is necessary to predict the variables to which the government and Fed react and the extent to which they react. Consequently, a feedback rule for fiscal and monetary policies can create more unpredictable fluctuations in aggregate demand than a fixed rule.

Economists disagree whether those bigger fluctuations offset the potential stabilizing influence of the predictable changes the Fed makes. No agreed measurements have been made to settle this dispute. Nevertheless, the unpredictability of the Fed in its pursuit of feedback-rule policies is an important fact of economic life. And the Fed does not always go out of its way to make its reactions clear. Even in congressional testimony, Federal Reserve Board chairmen are reluctant to make the Fed's actions and intentions entirely plain. (It has been suggested that two former chairmen of the Federal Reserve Board, the pipe-puffing Arthur Burns and the cigar-puffing Paul Volcker, carried their own smokescreens around with them as if to exemplify the mysteriousness and unpredictability of the Fed.)

It is not surprising that the Fed seeks to keep some of its actions behind a smokescreen. First, the Fed wants to maintain as much freedom of action as possible and so does not want to state with too great a precision the feedback rules that it will follow in any given circumstances. Second, the Fed is part of a political process, and, although legally independent of the federal government, it is not immune to subtle influence. For at least these two reasons, the Fed does not specify feedback rules as precisely as the one we've analyzed in this chapter. As a result, the Fed cannot deliver an economic performance that has the stability we generated in the model economy.

To the extent that the Fed's actions are unpredictable, they lead to unpredictable fluctuations in aggregate demand. These fluctuations, in turn, produce fluctuations in real GDP, employment, and unemployment.

If it is difficult for the Fed to pursue a predictable feedback stabilization policy, it is probably impossible for Congress. The stabilization policy of Congress is formulated in terms of spending programs and tax laws. Since these programs and laws are the outcome of a political process that is constrained only by the Constitution, there can be no effective way in which a predictable feedback fiscal policy can be adhered to.

REVIEW

Fixed-rule policies keep fiscal and monetary policy set steady and independent of the state of the economy. Feedback-rule policies cut taxes, increase spending, and speed up money supply growth when the economy is in recession and reverse these measures when the economy is overheating. Feedback rules apparently do a better job, but we are not sure that is the case. Their successful use requires a good knowledge of the current state of the economy, an ability to forecast as far ahead as the policy actions have effects, and clarity and openness about the feedback rules being used. ◆

We have reviewed three reasons why feedback rules might not be more effective than fixed rules in controlling aggregate demand. The evolution of views about aggregate demand stimulation is featured in Our Advancing Knowledge on pp. 918–919. But there is a fourth reason why fixed rules are preferred by some economists—not all shocks to the economy are on the demand side. Advocates of feedback rules believe that most fluctuations do come from aggregate demand. Advocates of fixed rules believe that aggregate supply fluctuations are the dominant ones. Let's now see how aggregate supply fluctuations affect the economy under a fixed rule and a feedback rule. We will also see why those economists who believe that aggregate supply fluctuations are the dominant ones also favor a fixed rather than a feedback rule.

Stabilization Policy and Aggregate Supply Shocks

There are two reasons why aggregate supply fluctuations can cause problems for a stabilization feedback rule:

- Cost-push inflation
- Slowdown in productivity growth

In either of these situations, the economy experiences *stagflation.* Let's study the effects of alternative policies to deal with this problem.

Cost-Push Inflation

Cost-push inflation is inflation that has its origins in cost increases. The two most important potential sources of cost-push inflation are wage increases and increases in raw material prices (such as the increases in the price of oil that occurred in the 1970s and the early 1980s). To proceed, a cost-push inflation must be accommodated by an increase in the money supply—which in turn increases aggregate demand. A monetary policy feedback rule makes cost-push inflation possible. A fixed rule makes such inflation impossible. Let's see why.

Consider the economy that is shown in Fig. 33.7. Aggregate demand is AD_0, short-run aggregate supply is SAS_0, and long-run aggregate supply is LAS. Real GDP is $5 trillion, and the GDP deflator is 100.

Now suppose that a number of labor unions or the key suppliers of an important raw material such as oil try to gain a temporary advantage by increasing the price at which they are willing to sell their services—by increasing wages or by increasing the price of the raw material. To make the exercise interesting, let's suppose that the people in question control a significant portion of the economy. As a consequence, when they increase the wage rate or the price of oil, the short-run aggregate supply curve shifts leftward from SAS_0 to SAS_1.

Fixed Rule Figure 33.7(a) shows what happens if the Fed follows a fixed rule for monetary policy and the government follows a fixed rule for fiscal policy.

FIGURE 33.7

Stabilization Policy and Aggregate Supply: A Factor Price Increase

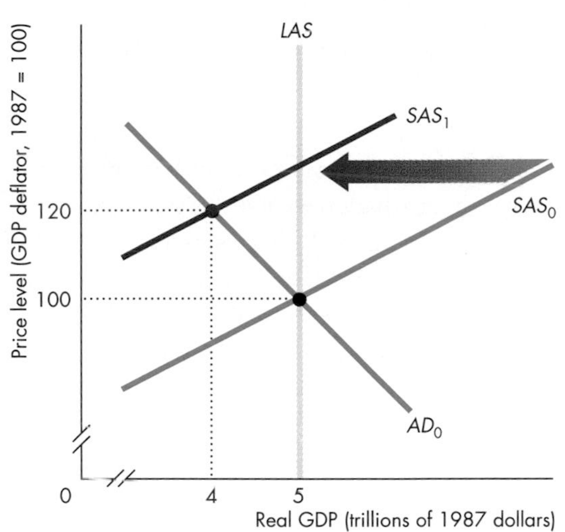

(a) Fixed rule

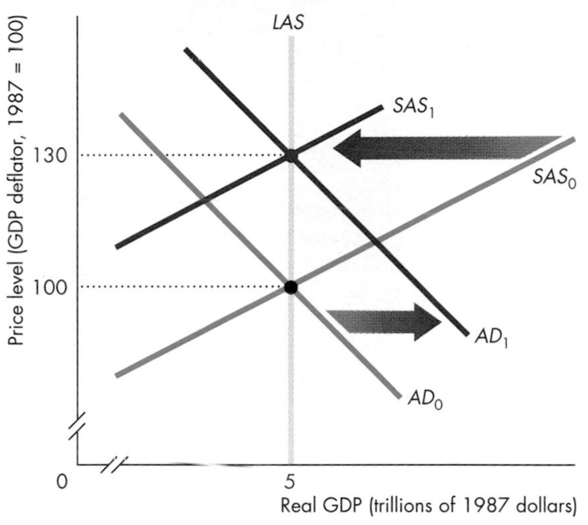

(b) Feedback rule

The economy starts out on AD_0 and SAS_0, with a GDP deflator of 100 and real GDP of $5 trillion. A labor union (or a key supplier of raw materials) forces up the wage rate (or the price of a raw material), shifting the short-run aggregate supply curve to SAS_1. Real GDP falls to $4 trillion and the GDP deflator increases to 120. With a fixed-rule stabilization policy (part a), the Fed and Congress make no change to aggregate demand. The economy stays depressed until wages (or raw material prices) fall again and the economy returns to its original position. With a feedback rule (part b), the Fed injects additional money and/or Congress cuts taxes or increases spending, increasing aggregate demand to AD_1. Real GDP returns to $5 trillion (full employment), but the GDP deflator increases to 130. The economy is set for another round of cost-push inflation.

Suppose that the fixed rule is for zero money growth and no change in taxes or government purchases of goods and services. With these fixed rules, the Fed and the government pay no attention to the fact that there has been an increase in wages or raw material prices. No policy actions are taken. The short-run aggregate supply curve has shifted to SAS_1, but the aggregate demand curve remains at AD_0. The GDP deflator rises to 120, and real GDP falls to $4 trillion. The economy is experiencing stagflation. Until wages or raw material prices fall, the economy will be depressed and will remain depressed. This decrease in wages or raw material prices may take a long time to come about. Eventually, however, the low level of real GDP will bring lower oil prices and wages—those very prices and wages whose increase caused the initial problem. Eventually, the short-run aggregate supply curve will shift back to SAS_0. The GDP deflator will fall to 100, and real GDP will increase to $5 trillion.

Feedback Rule Figure 33.7(b) shows what happens if the Fed and the government operate monetary and fiscal policy feedback rules. The starting point is the same as before—the economy is on SAS_0 and AD_0 with a GDP deflator of 100 and real GDP of $5 trillion. Wages or raw material prices increase, and the short-run aggregate supply curve shifts to SAS_1. The economy goes into a recession with real GDP falling to $4 trillion and the price level increasing to 120. The monetary feedback rule is to increase the money supply growth rate when real GDP is below its long-run level. And the fiscal feedback rule is to cut taxes and increase government purchases when real GDP is below its long-run level. So, with real GDP at $4 trillion, the Fed pumps up

EVOLVING Approaches TO ECONOMIC STABILIZATION

When it comes to stabilizing the economy, people differ in their opinions about what's best. But there was a time when you would have been hard pressed to find an economist who did not believe that active measures taken by a well-informed government could make the market economy function more smoothly. That time was the early 1960s, when President John F. Kennedy was in the White House.

Using the expenditure multiplier model (of Chapter 26), economists believed that setting the levels of government purchases and taxes at the appropriate levels would allow continuous full employment, and steady economic expansion could be maintained indefinitely.

The practice of active stabilization policy worked well until the mid-1960s, but then inflation began to creep upward. Advocates of activist policies blame the Vietnam War and President Lyndon Johnson's unwillingness to finance the war with tax increases. Opponents of activism blame the activist policies themselves, claiming that once an activist policy is anticipated, its effects on output are weak and its main effects are on inflation.

Whichever view is correct, activist policies came into official disrepute during the 1970s, when oil price hikes left no doubt that the main problem (at least for the time being) was not demand fluctuations, but supply shocks. Distrust of activist stabilization became particularly strong during President Ronald Reagan's administration when the prevailing view was that government should set the rules of the game and leave the private sector to get on with the creation of jobs and wealth.

The recession of 1991 saw a return to a more pragmatic approach with attempts to stimulate demand by lowering interest rates, but not too aggressively, especially with such a large and persistent federal deficit. If and when the deficit subsides, there is likely to be renewed enthusiasm for more ambitious fiscal policies to stimulate demand during recessions.

"You have to find a real crackpot to get an economist who doesn't accept the principle of government intervention in the business cycle."

KENNETH ARROW
Time, March 3, 1961

The accumulation of economic data and the development of statistical models of the economy gave a strong boost of confidence to President Kennedy's economic advisors—Kermit Gordon, James Tobin, and Walter Heller. Said Heller, "We simply know a whole lot more about where we are than we ever did before." Using their models and best judgments about where the economy was and where it was heading, Kennedy's economists worked out a program of tax cuts and spending changes designed to keep the economy expanding but with low inflation and high employment.

Today, even in a recession, there is little talk of cutting taxes and increasing spending to lift the economy back to full employment. Instead, people worry about the scale of the deficit. When Budget Director Richard Darman testifies before the Senate, a graph showing the projected decline of the deficit has become a mandatory part of the presentation. But in contrast to the optimism of the projections, the deficit persists, limiting the range of maneuver for fiscal policy. Tax increases and spending cuts would lower the deficit but might intensify the recession. Tax cuts or spending increases would make the deficit higher but might not bring economic recovery. Instead, with a larger deficit, interest rates might rise—bringing a decline in investment.

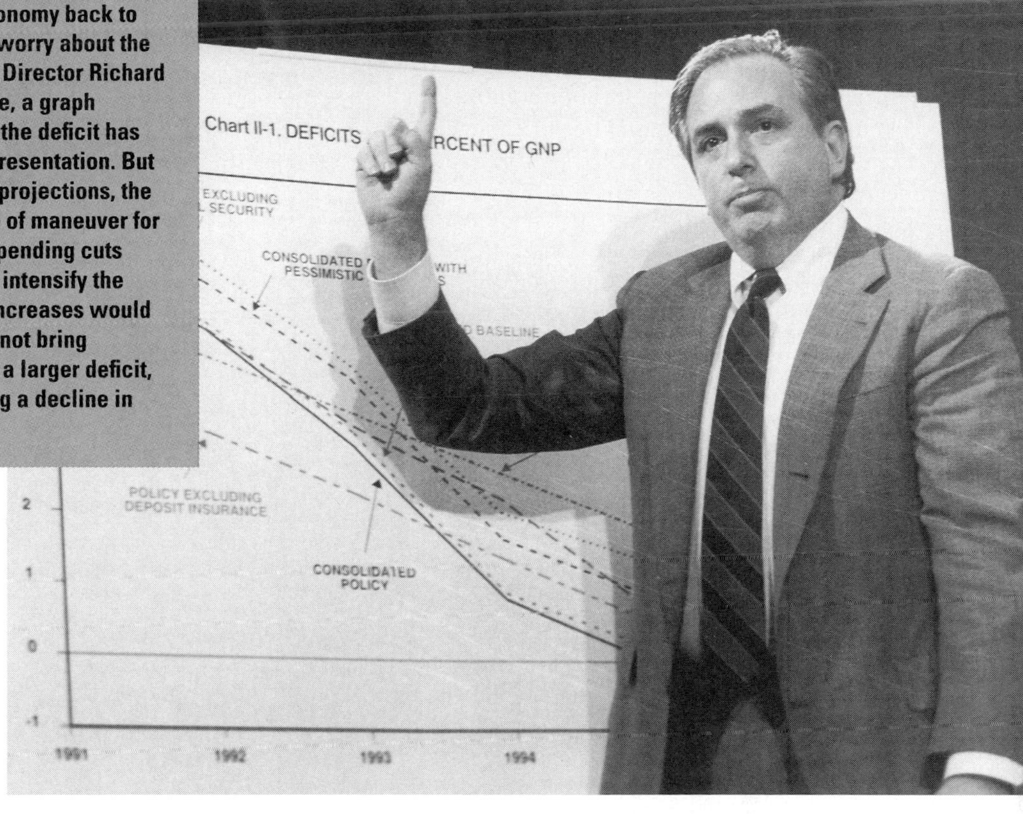

Milton Friedman Versus the Keynesians: *The Rise and Fall of Fine-Tuning*

From 1946 to 1983, Milton Friedman, now a Senior Fellow at the Hoover Institution at Stanford University, was one of the leading members of the Chicago School. This approach to economics was developed at the University of Chicago and based on the views that free markets allocate resources efficiently and that stable and low money supply growth delivers macroeconomic stability. In the early 1960s, these views were in a distinct minority, and many economists placed them in the "crackpot" category. By reasoning from basic economic principles, Friedman predicted that persistent demand stimulation would not increase output but would cause inflation. When output growth slowed and inflation broke out in the 1970s, Friedman seemed like a prophet, and for a time, his policy prescription—known as monetarism—was embraced around the world.

the money supply growth rate, Congress passes a tax cut bill and a series of bills that increase spending, and the aggregate demand curve shifts to AD_1. The price level increases to 130, and real GDP returns to $5 trillion. The economy moves back to full employment but at a higher price level.

The unionized workers or the raw material suppliers, who saw an advantage in forcing up their wages or prices before, see the same advantage again. Thus the short-run aggregate supply curve shifts up once more, and the Fed and the government chase it with increases in aggregate demand. The economy is in a freewheeling inflation.

Incentives to Push Up Factor Prices You can see that there are no checks on the incentives to push up factor prices if the Fed pursues a feedback rule of the type that we've just analyzed. If some group sees a temporary gain from pushing up the price at which it is selling its resources and if the Fed and the government always accommodate to prevent unemployment and slack business conditions from emerging, then cost-push elements will have a free rein.

But when the Fed and the government pursue fixed-rule policies, the incentive to attempt to steal a temporary advantage by increasing wages or prices is severely weakened. The cost of higher unemployment and lower output is a consequence that each group will have to face and recognize.

Thus a fixed rule is capable of delivering a steady inflation rate (or even zero inflation), while a feedback rule, in the face of cost-push pressures, will leave the inflation rate free to rise and fall at the whim of whichever group believes a temporary advantage to be available from pushing up its wage or price.

Slowdown in Productivity Growth

Some economists believe that fluctuations in real GDP (and in employment and unemployment) are caused by fluctuations in productivity growth. These economists have developed a new theory of aggregate fluctuations called real business cycle theory. **Real business cycle theory** is a theory of aggregate fluctuations based on flexible wages and random shocks to the economy's aggregate production function. The word *real* draws attention to the idea that it is real things—random shocks to the economy's real production possibilities—rather than nominal things—the money supply and its rate of growth—that are, according to that theory, the most important sources of aggregate fluctuations.

According to real business cycle theory, there is no useful distinction to be made between the long-run aggregate supply curve and the short-run aggregate supply curve. Because wages are flexible, the labor market is always in equilibrium and unemployment is always at its natural rate. The vertical long-run aggregate supply curve is also the short-run aggregate supply curve. Fluctuations occur because of shifts in the long-run aggregate supply curve. Normally, the long-run aggregate supply curve shifts to the right—the economy expands. But the pace at which the long-run aggregate supply curve shifts to the right varies. Also, on occasion, the long-run aggregate supply curve shifts to the left, bringing a decrease in aggregate supply and a fall in real GDP.

Economic policy that influences aggregate demand has no effect on real GDP. But it does affect the price level. However, if a feedback-rule policy is used to increase aggregate demand every time real GDP falls, and if the real business cycle theory is correct, the feedback-rule policy will make price level fluctuations more severe than they otherwise would be. To see why, consider Fig. 33.8.

Imagine that the economy starts out on aggregate demand curve AD_0 and long-run aggregate supply curve LAS_0 at a GDP deflator of 100 and with real GDP equal to $5 trillion. Now suppose that the long-run aggregate supply curve shifts to LAS_1. An actual decrease in long-run aggregate supply can occur as a result of a severe drought or other natural catastrophe or perhaps as the result of a disruption of international trade such as the OPEC embargo of the 1970s.

Fixed Rule With a fixed rule, the fall in long-run aggregate supply has no effect on the Fed or the government and no effect on aggregate demand. The aggregate demand curve remains AD_0. Real GDP falls to $4 trillion, and the GDP deflator increases to 120.

Feedback Rule Now suppose that the Fed and the government use feedback rules. In particular, suppose that when real GDP falls, the Fed increases the money supply and Congress enacts a tax cut to increase aggregate demand. In this example, the money supply and tax cut shift the aggregate demand curve to AD_1. The policy goal is to bring

FIGURE 33.8

Stabilization Policy and Aggregate Supply: A Decrease in Productivity

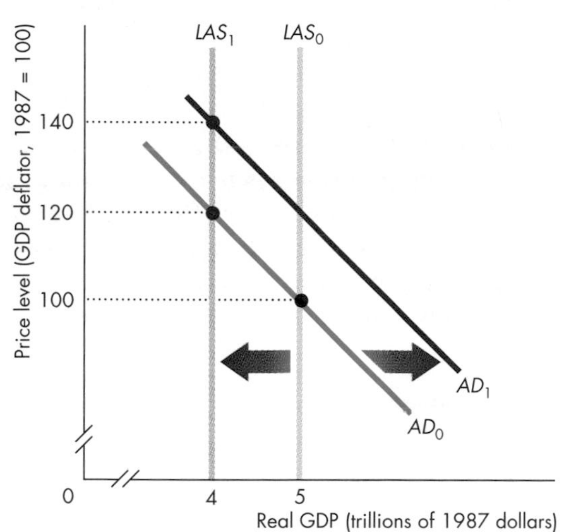

A decrease in productivity shifts the long-run aggregate supply curve from LAS_0 to LAS_1. Real GDP falls to $4 trillion, and the GDP deflator rises to 120. With a fixed rule, there is no change in the money supply, taxes, or government spending, so aggregate demand stays at AD_0, and that is the end of the matter. With a feedback rule, the Fed increases the money supply and/or Congress cuts taxes or increases spending, intending to increase real GDP. Aggregate demand moves to AD_1, but the long-run result is an increase in the price level—the GDP deflator rises to 140—with no change in real GDP.

real GDP back to $5 trillion. But the long-run aggregate supply curve has shifted, and so long-run real GDP has decreased to $4 trillion. The increase in aggregate demand cannot bring forth an increase in output if the economy does not have the capacity to produce that output. So real GDP stays at $4 trillion, but the price level rises still further—the GDP deflator goes to 140. You can see that in this case the attempt to stabilize real GDP by using a feedback-rule policy has no effect on real GDP but generates a substantial price level increase.

We've now seen some of the shortcomings of using feedback rules for stabilization policy. Some economists believe that these shortcomings are serious and want to constrain Congress and the Fed so that they use fixed rules. Others, regarding the potential advantages of feedback rules as greater than their costs, advocate the continued use of such policies but with an important modification that we'll now look at.

Nominal GDP Targeting

Attempting to keep the growth rate of nominal GDP steady is called **nominal GDP targeting.** James Tobin of Yale University and John Taylor of Stanford University have suggested that nominal GDP targeting is a useful operating goal for macroeconomic policy.

The nominal GDP growth equals the real GDP growth rate plus the inflation rate. When nominal GDP grows quickly, it is usually because the inflation rate is high. When nominal GDP grows slowly, it is usually because real GDP growth is negative—the economy is in recession. Thus if nominal GDP growth is kept steady, the excesses of both inflation and recession might be avoided.

Nominal GDP targeting uses feedback rules. Expansionary fiscal and/or monetary actions increase aggregate demand when nominal GDP is below target, and contractionary fiscal and/or monetary actions decrease aggregate demand when nominal GDP is above target. The main problem with nominal GDP targeting is that there are long and variable time lags between the identification of a need to change aggregate demand and the effects of the policy actions taken.

Macroeconomists are still debating the merits of the alternative policies for achieving stability. But they are gradually arriving at a new consensus about what can be achieved.

Taming Inflation

So far, we've concentrated on stabilizing real GDP either directly or indirectly and *avoiding* inflation. But often the problem is not to avoid inflation but to tame it. How can inflation, once it has set in, be cured? Let's look at some alternative ways.

A Surprise Inflation Reduction

To study the problem of lowering inflation, we'll use two equivalent approaches, aggregate demand–aggregate supply and the Phillips curve. You met the Phillips curve in Chapter 31 (pp. 866–869), and it enables us to keep track of what is happening to both inflation and unemployment.

The economy is shown in Fig. 33.9. In part (a), it is on aggregate demand curve AD_0 and short-run aggregate supply curve SAS_0 with real GDP at \$5 trillion and the GDP deflator at 100. With real GDP at its long-run level (on the *LAS* curve), there is full employment. Equivalently, in part (b), the economy is on its long-run Phillips curve *LRPC* and short-run Phillips curve $SRPC_0$. Inflation is raging at 10 percent a year, and unemployment is at its natural rate.

Next year, aggregate demand is *expected* to increase, shifting the aggregate demand curve in Fig. 33.9(a) to AD_1. Expecting this increase in aggregate demand, wages increase to shift the short-run aggregate supply curve to SAS_1. If expectations are fulfilled, the GDP deflator rises to 110 (10 percent inflation), real GDP remains at its long-run level, and unemployment remains at its natural rate.

But suppose the Fed tries to slow down inflation to 4 percent a year. If it simply slows down the growth of aggregate demand, the aggregate demand curve (in part a) shifts to AD_2. With no slowdown in the expected inflation rate, wage increases shift the short-run aggregate supply curve to SAS_1. Real GDP decreases to \$4 trillion, and the GDP deflator rises to 108—an inflation rate of 8 percent a year. In Fig. 33.9(b), there is a movement along the short-run

FIGURE 33.9
Lowering Inflation

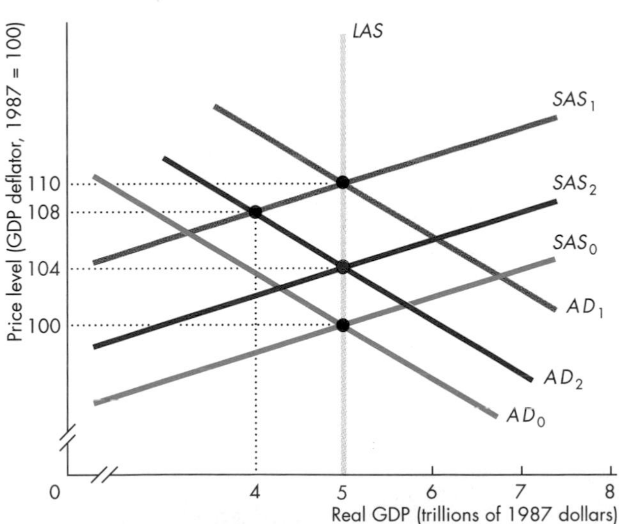

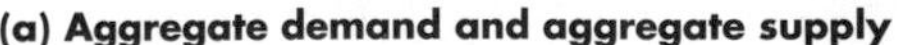
(a) Aggregate demand and aggregate supply

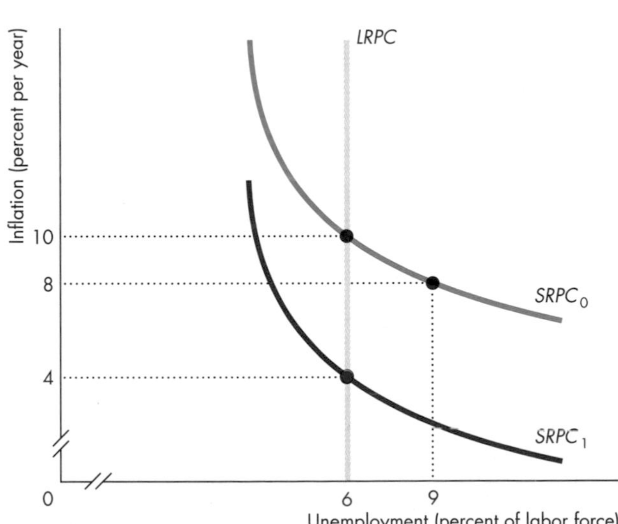

(b) Phillips curves

Initially, aggregate demand is AD_0, and short-run aggregate supply is SAS_0. Real GDP is \$5 trillion (its full-employment level on the long-run aggregate supply curve *LAS*). Inflation is proceeding at 10 percent a year. If it continues to do so, the aggregate demand curve shifts to AD_1 and the short-run aggregate supply curve shifts to SAS_1. The GDP deflator rises to 110. This same situation is shown in part (b) with the economy on the short-run Phillips curve $SRPC_0$.

With an unexpected slowdown in aggregate demand growth, the aggregate demand curve (part a) shifts to AD_2, real GDP falls to \$4 trillion, and inflation slows to 8 percent (a GDP deflator of 108). In part (b), unemployment rises to 9 percent as the economy slides down $SRPC_0$.

If a credibly announced slowdown in aggregate demand growth occurs, the short-run aggregate supply curve (part a) shifts to SAS_2, the short-run Phillips curve (part b) shifts to $SRPC_1$, inflation slows to 4 percent, real GDP remains at \$5 trillion, and unemployment remains at its natural rate of 6 percent.

Phillips curve $SRPC_0$ as unemployment rises to 9 percent and inflation falls to 8 percent a year. The policy has succeeded in slowing inflation but by less than desired and at a cost of recession. Real GDP is below its long-run level, and unemployment is above its natural rate.

A Credibly Announced Inflation Reduction

Suppose that instead of simply slowing down the growth of aggregate demand, the Fed announced its intention ahead of its action and in a credible and convincing way so that its announcement was believed. The lower level of aggregate demand becomes expected. In this case, wages increase at a pace consistent with the lower level of aggregate demand, and the short-run aggregate supply curve (in Fig. 33.9a) shifts to SAS_2. When aggregate demand increases, shifting the aggregate demand curve to AD_2, the GDP deflator rises to 104—an inflation rate of 4 percent a year—and real GDP remains at its full-employment level.

In Fig. 33.9(b), the lower expected inflation rate shifts the short-run Phillips curve downward to $SRPC_1$, and inflation falls to 4 percent a year while unemployment remains at its natural rate.

Inflation Reduction in Practice

When the Fed in fact slowed down inflation in 1981, we all paid a very high price. The Fed's monetary policy action was unpredicted. As a result, it occurred in the face of wages that had been set at too high a level to be consistent with the growth of aggregate demand that the Fed subsequently allowed. The consequence was recession—a decrease in real GDP and a rise in unemployment. Couldn't the Fed have lowered inflation without causing recession by telling people far enough ahead of time that it did indeed plan to slow down the growth rate of aggregate demand?

The answer appears to be no. The main reason is that people form their expectation of the Fed's action (as they form expectations about anyone's actions) on the basis of actual behavior, not on the basis of stated intentions. How many times have you told yourself that it is your firm intention to take off ten unwanted pounds or to keep within the budget and put a few dollars away for a rainy day, only to discover that, despite your very best intentions, your old habits win out in the end?

Forming expectations about the Fed's behavior is no different except, of course, it is more complex than forecasting your own behavior. To form expectations of the Fed's actions, people look at the Fed's past *actions,* not its stated intentions. On the basis of such observations—called Fed-watching—they try to work out what the Fed's policy is, to forecast its future actions, and to forecast the effects of those actions on aggregate demand and inflation.

A Truly Independent Fed

One suggestion for dealing with inflation is to make the Fed more independent and to charge it with the single responsibility of achieving and maintaining price level stability. Some central banks are more independent than the Fed. The German and Swiss central banks are the best examples. Another example is the New Zealand central bank. All these central banks have the responsibility of stabilizing prices but not real GDP and of doing so without interference from the government.

If an arrangement could be devised for making the Fed take a longer-term view concentrated only on inflation, it is possible that inflation could be lowered and kept low at a low cost.

REVIEW

Usually, when inflation is tamed, a recession results. The reason is that people form their expectation about policy on the basis of past policy actions. A more independent Fed pursuing only price stability could possibly achieve price stability with greater credibility and at lower cost. ◆

◆ ◆ ◆ ◆ We've now examined the main issues of stabilization policy. We've looked at the goals of stabilization policy, at the effects of the economy on political popularity, and at the fiscal and monetary policies pursued. We've seen how fixed and feedback rules operate under differing assumptions about the behavior of the economy and why economists take different views on using these rules. We've also seen why lowering inflation usually is accompanied by recession. ◆ ◆ In the next chapter, we examine what many people believe is our economy's single most serious policy problem—the government's budget deficit.

SUMMARY

The Stabilization Problem

The stabilization problem is to keep the growth rate of real GDP steady and keep inflation low and predictable. (pp. 903–904)

Players and Policies

The key macroeconomic policy players are Congress, the Federal Reserve Board, and the administration.

Macroeconomic policy is influenced by the effects of macroeconomic performance on votes in congressional and presidential elections. Both fiscal policy and monetary policy have a cycle that creates a political business cycle.

Fixed-rule policies (such as a constant growth rate of the money supply) are those that do not respond to the state of the economy. Feedback-rule policies do respond to the state of the economy, stimulating activity in recession and holding activity in check in time of inflation. (pp. 904–911)

Stabilization Policy and Aggregate Demand Shocks

In the face of an aggregate demand shock, a fixed-rule policy takes no action to counter the shock. It permits aggregate demand to fluctuate as a result of all the independent forces that influence it. As a result, there are fluctuations in real GDP and the price level. A feedback-rule policy adjusts taxes, government purchases, or the money supply to offset the effects of other influences on aggregate demand. An ideal feedback rule keeps the economy at full employment with stable prices.

Some economists argue that feedback rules make the economy less stable because they require greater knowledge of the state of the economy than we have, operate with time lags that extend beyond the forecast horizon, and introduce unpredictability about policy reactions. (pp. 912–916)

Stabilization Policy and Aggregate Supply Shocks

Two main aggregate supply shocks generate stabilization problems: cost-push inflation and a slowdown in productivity growth. A fixed rule minimizes the threat of and the problems associated with cost-push inflation. A feedback rule reinforces cost-push inflation and leaves the price level and inflation rate free to move to wherever they are pushed. If productivity growth slows down, a fixed rule results in lower output (and higher unemployment) and a higher price level. A feedback rule that increases the money supply or cuts taxes to stimulate aggregate demand results in an even higher price level and higher inflation. Output (and unemployment) follows the same course as with a fixed rule. (pp. 916–921)

Taming Inflation

Inflation can be tamed, at little or no cost in terms of lost output or excessive unemployment, by slowing the growth of aggregate demand in a credible and predictable way. But usually, when inflation is slowed down, a recession occurs. The reason is that people form their expectation about policy on the basis of actual behavior, by looking at past actions, not by believing announced intentions. (pp. 921–923)

KEY ELEMENTS

Key Terms

Federal budget, 904
Feedback rule, 911
Fixed rule, 910
Nominal GDP targeting, 921
Political business cycle, 907
Real business cycle theory, 920

Key Figures

REVIEW QUESTIONS

1 What are the goals of macroeconomic stabilization policy?

2 Describe the key players that formulate and execute macroeconomic policy. Explain the interaction between these players.

3 What is a political business cycle? Explain the evidence for a political business cycle in the United States since 1960.

4 Explain the distinction between a fixed-rule policy and a feedback-rule policy.

5 Analyze the effects of a temporary decrease in aggregate demand if a fixed rule is employed.

6 Analyze the behavior of real GDP and the price level in the face of a permanent decrease in aggregate demand under:

a A fixed rule

b A feedback rule

7 Why do economists disagree with each other on the appropriateness of fixed and feedback rules?

8 Explain the main problems in using fiscal policy for stabilizing the economy.

9 Analyze the effects of a rise in the price of oil on real GDP and the price level if the Fed employs:

a A fixed monetary rule

b A feedback monetary rule

10 Explain nominal GDP targeting and why it reduces real GDP fluctuations and inflation.

11 Explain why the Fed's credibility affects the cost of lowering inflation.

PROBLEMS

1 The economy is experiencing 10 percent inflation and 7 percent unemployment. Set out policies for the Fed and Congress to pursue that will lower both inflation and unemployment. Explain how and why your proposed policies will work.

2 The economy is booming, and inflation is beginning to rise, but it is widely agreed that a massive recession is just around the corner. Weigh the advantages and disadvantages of Congress pursuing a fixed-rule and a feedback-rule fiscal policy.

3 The economy is in a recession, and inflation is falling. It is widely agreed that a strong recovery is just around the corner. Weigh the advantages and disadvantages of the Fed pursuing a fixed-rule and a feedback-rule monetary policy.

4 You have been hired by the president to draw up an economic plan that will maximize the chance of his being re-elected.

a What are the macroeconomic stabilization policy elements in that plan?

b What do you have to make the economy do in an election year?

c What policy actions would help the president achieve his objectives?

(In dealing with this problem, be careful to take into account the effects of your proposed policy on expectations and the effects of those expectations on actual economic performance.)

CHAPTER 34

THE DEFICIT

After studying this chapter, you will be able to:

- Explain why, during the past decade, the federal government spent more each year than it raised in taxes
- Distinguish between debt and the deficit
- Distinguish between the *nominal* deficit and the *real* deficit
- Explain why the deficit appears to be larger than it really is
- Describe the different means available for financing the deficit
- Explain why the deficit makes the Fed's job harder
- Explain why a deficit can cause inflation
- Explain why a deficit can be a burden on future generations
- Describe the measures that are being taken to eliminate the deficit

Spendthrift Uncle Sam

EVERY SINGLE YEAR BETWEEN 1982 AND 1992, THE federal government spent at least $100 billion more than it collected in taxes. In 1982, the total debt of the federal government was just below $1 trillion. Ten years later it stood at more than $3 trillion. Why does the federal government have a deficit and growing debt? Is the deficit really as large as it appears? How can we gauge the size of the deficit when the value of money is steadily falling because of inflation? ◆◆ Some countries, such as Bolivia, Chile, Brazil, and Israel, have had large government deficits and runaway inflation. Do these experiences mean that the United States will eventually be the victim of rapid inflation? Does the deficit somehow make it harder, or even impossible, for the Fed to control the money supply and keep inflation in check? ◆◆ When we incur a personal debt, we accept a self-imposed obligation. When the nation incurs a debt, it imposes an obligation on its taxpayers. But the obligation does not end with the current taxpayers. It is passed onto their children and grandchildren. Does a government deficit impose a burden on future generations? ◆◆ There are two ways in which we can approach any problem: pretend it doesn't exist or try to identify its nature and solve it. How are we approaching the deficit? Are we sticking our heads in the sand like ostriches, or are we taking steps that are likely to eliminate the deficit? What are the prospects for the future of the deficit?

◆ ◆ ◆ ◆ In this chapter, we're going to study what became perhaps the hottest economic topic of the 1980s and remains a hot topic today. We're going to examine the origins of the deficit, gauge its true scale, and explain why deficits are feared and why they constitute a problem. We'll also discuss some of the measures that are being taken to eliminate the deficit. Because the deficit is a hot economic and political topic, the public debate on it has generated more heat and smoke than light. In this chapter, we'll clear away some of the rhetorical smoke, lower the temperature, and try to answer the questions posed above. By the time you're through with this chapter, you'll be able to explain what the deficit is all about.

The Sources of the Deficit

What exactly is the deficit? The federal government's **budget balance** is equal to its total tax revenue minus its total expenditure in a given period of time (normally a year). Thus the government's budget balance is

Budget balance = Revenue – Expenditure.

The government's revenue consists of various types of taxes. Its expenditure is the sum of government purchases of goods and services, transfer payments, and interest on debt. If revenue exceeds expenditure, the budget balance is positive and the federal government has a **budget surplus.** If expenditure exceeds revenue, the budget balance is negative and the federal government has a **budget deficit.** If the budget balance is zero, in other words, if tax revenue and expenditure are equal, the government has a **balanced budget.**

Government debt is the total amount of borrowing that the government has undertaken and the total amount that it owes to households, firms, and foreigners. Government debt is a stock. It is the accumulation of all the past deficits minus all the past surpluses. Thus if the government has a deficit, its debt is increasing. If the government has a surplus, its debt is decreasing. If the government has a balanced budget, its debt is constant.

The Federal Budget since 1975

Figure 34.1 shows the federal government's revenue, expenditure, and deficit since 1975. As the figure

FIGURE 34.1

The Deficit

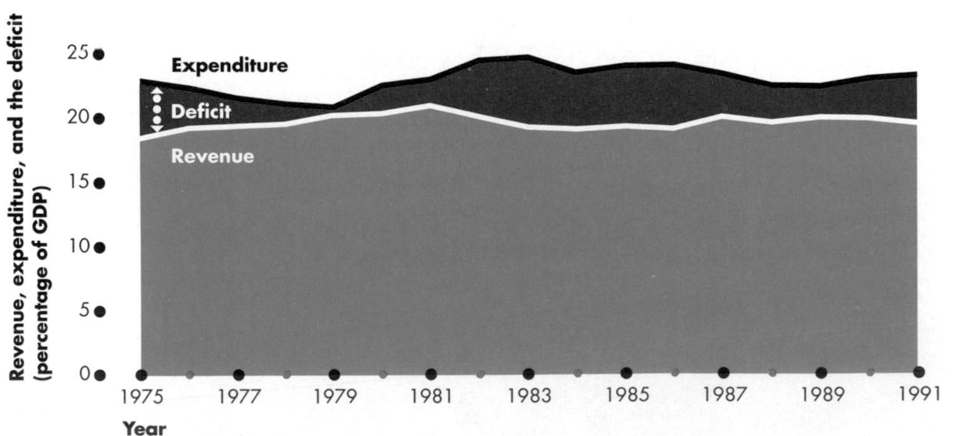

The figure records revenue, expenditure, and the deficit from 1975 to 1991. The deficit was small and falling in the 1970s but became large and persistent during the 1980s. The deficit arose from a combination of a decline in revenue and an increase in spending.

Source: Economic Report of the President, 1992.

illustrates, throughout this period the U.S. federal government had a budget deficit. The deficit was small and falling between 1975 and 1979, and in 1979 the budget was almost balanced. The deficit then climbed to a peak of 5.3 percent of GDP in 1983. It declined from 1983 through 1989 but averaged more than 3½ percent of GDP through the entire decade. The deficit climbed again in the 1991 recession.

The effect of the deficit on the government's debt is shown in Fig. 34.2. So that you can see the government's debt over a slightly longer perspective, this figure begins in 1960. As you can see, federal government debt declined as a percentage of GDP through 1974. The ratio of debt to GDP in this year stood at its lowest point since World War II. The debt-to-GDP ratio increased slightly in the late 1970s and dramatically between 1981 and 1986. In the late 1980s, its growth continued but at a more moderate rate. It grew quickly again in the 1991 recession.

Why did the government deficit grow in the early 1980s and remain high? The immediate answer is that expenditure increased and revenue declined. But which components of expenditure increased and which sources of revenue decreased? Let's answer these questions by looking at revenue and expenditure in a bit more detail.

FIGURE 34.2

The Government Debt

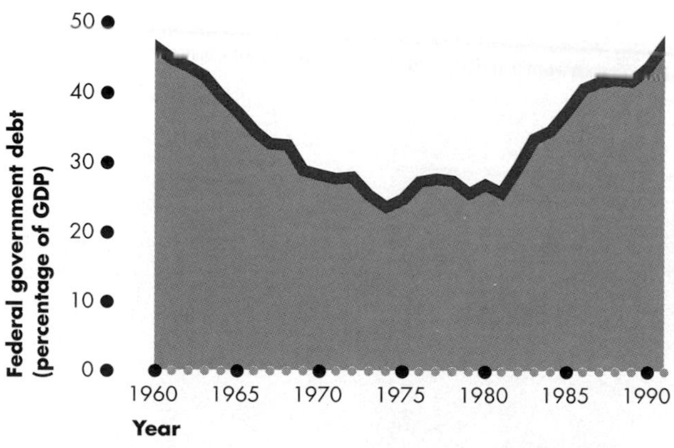

Government debt (the accumulation of past deficits less past surpluses) declined through 1974 but then started to move upward. After a further brief decline in the late 1970s, it exploded in the 1980s.

Source: Economic Report of the President, 1992.

Federal Government Revenue There are four broad categories of federal government revenue:

- ◆ Personal income taxes
- ◆ Corporate income taxes
- ◆ Indirect taxes
- ◆ Social insurance contributions

Personal income taxes are the taxes paid by individuals on their labor and capital incomes. Corporate income taxes are the taxes that companies pay on their profits. Indirect taxes are taxes on the goods and services that we buy and include the customs duties that we pay when we import goods from other countries. Social insurance contributions are the taxes paid by employees and employers to finance social security programs such as Medicare and unemployment insurance.

Figure 34.3(a) shows the levels and fluctuations in these taxes and in total taxes between 1975 and 1991. As you can see, total taxes increased as a percentage of GDP between 1975 and 1981 but then declined through 1986. Most of the decline was in corporate and personal income taxes and resulted from the Economic Recovery Tax Act of 1981. Indirect taxes and social insurance contributions remained relatively stable as percentages of GDP.

Federal Government Expenditure We will examine federal government expenditure by dividing it into three categories:

- ◆ Purchases of goods and services
- ◆ Transfer payments
- ◆ Debt interest payments

The main item in the federal government's shopping basket is the purchase of goods and services for national defense. Other purchases of goods and services include items such as law and order and interstate highways. Transfer payments include payments of social security and welfare benefits to households and subsidies to farms and other producers. Debt interest payments are the amounts paid by the government to the holders of its bonds—its outstanding debt.

FIGURE 34.3

Federal Government Revenue and Expenditure

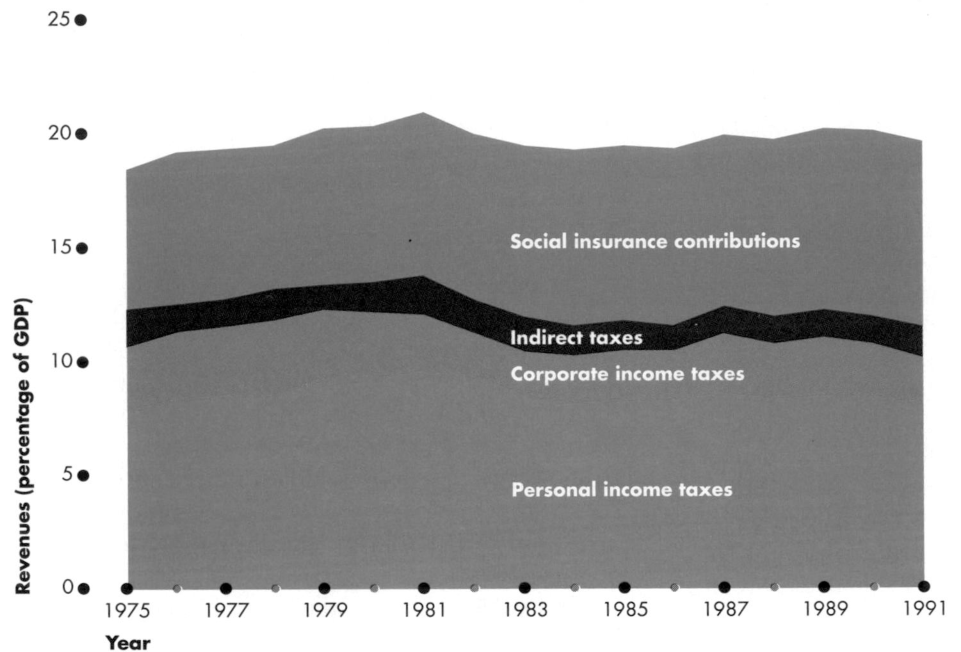

(a) Revenues

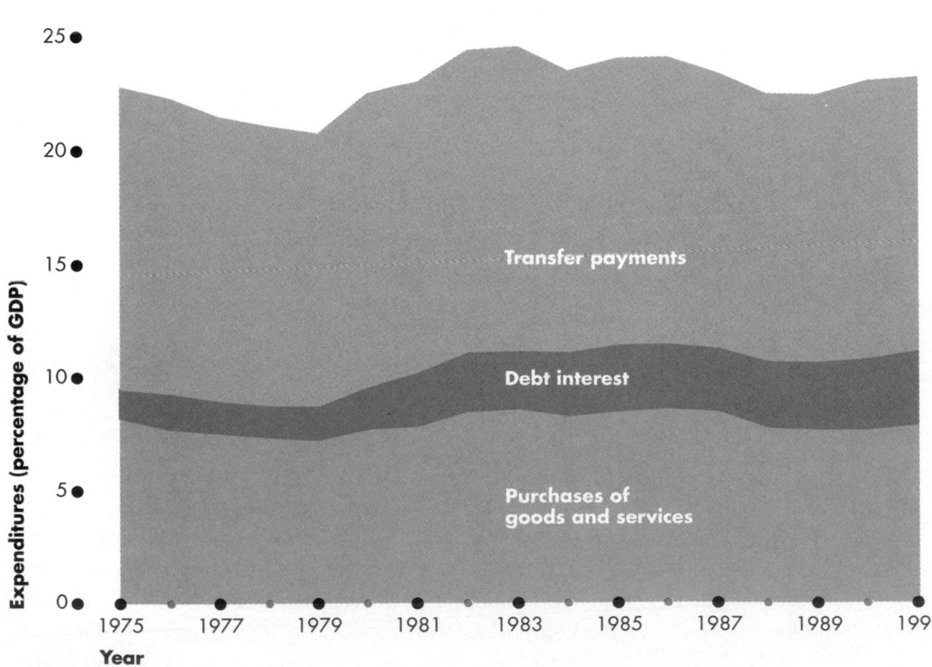

(b) Expenditures

The four categories of federal government revenue shown in part (a) are personal income taxes, corporate income taxes, indirect taxes, and social insurance contributions. Personal and corporate income taxes declined during the early 1980s. The other two revenue components remained steady.

The three categories of federal government expenditure shown in part (b) are purchases of goods and services, debt interest, and transfer payments. Purchases of goods and services have fluctuated but not increased. Transfer payments have fluctuated most and increased especially in the early 1980s. Debt interest has increased steadily as the deficit has fed on itself.

Source: Economic Report of the President, 1992.

Figure 34.3(b) shows the levels and fluctuations in these components of expenditure and in total expenditure between 1975 and 1991. As you can see, total expenditure decreased between 1975 and 1979 but increased between 1979 and 1983. It then declined slightly through 1989 before increasing again. Both the purchase of goods and services and transfer payments fluctuated. But the item that increased most persistently was debt interest. Once a persistent deficit had emerged, that deficit began to feed on itself. The deficit led to increased borrowing; increased borrowing led to higher interest payments; and higher interest payments led to a larger deficit. That is the story of the rising deficit of the 1980s.

A Personal Analogy Perhaps you will see more clearly why the deficit feeds on itself if you think in more personal terms. Suppose that each year you spend more than you earn. Suppose that you keep on doing this. Your debt, let's say at the bank, rises each year. Therefore, you owe the bank more in interest each year as a result of having a bigger debt outstanding. The government is in exactly the same situation. But the government doesn't just borrow from banks. It borrows from anyone who buys the bonds that it issues—households, firms, the Fed, and foreigners. The government has been running a large deficit throughout the 1980s and early 1990s so its outstanding debt has been rising and the interest payments on that debt have also been rising.

The Deficit and the Business Cycle

There is an important relationship between the size of the deficit and the stage of the business cycle through which the economy is passing. This relationship is illustrated in Fig. 34.4. This figure tracks the deficit against the business cycle—measured as the percentage deviations of real GDP from trend. As you can see, the deficit follows the business cycle. The years in which the deficit is especially large are years of severe recession—the OPEC recession of 1975, the Volcker recession of 1981 to 1982, and the 1990–1991 recession.

FIGURE 34.4

The Business Cycle and the Deficit

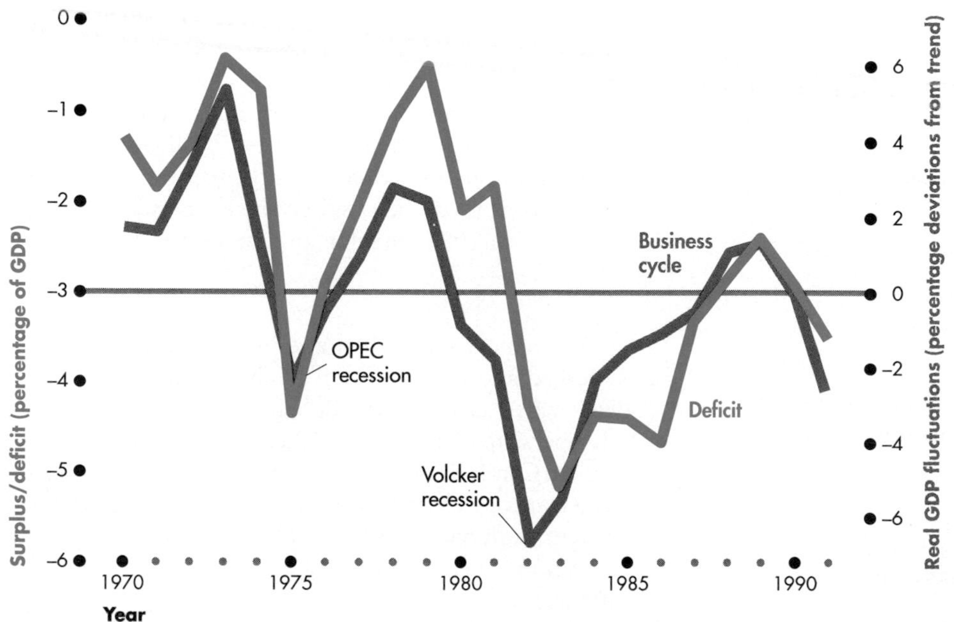

The business cycle—real GDP fluctuations—and the deficit move together. A recession leads to lower taxes, higher transfer payments, and a higher deficit. A recovery leads to higher taxes, lower transfer payments, and a lower deficit.

Source: Economic Report of the President, 1992.

Why docs the deficit become larger when the economy goes into recession? Part of the answer lies on the expenditure side and part on the tax revenue side of the government's account. The scale of government expenditure and tax revenue depends on the state of the economy. The government passes tax laws defining tax *rates*, not *dollars* to be paid in taxes. As a consequence, the tax revenue that the government collects depends on the level of income: if the economy is in a recovery phase of the business cycle, tax collections rise; if the economy is in a recession phase of the business cycle, tax collections fall.

Spending programs behave similarly. Many government programs are related to the state of well-being of individual citizens and firms. For example, when the economy is in a recession, unemployment is high, economic hardship from poverty increases, and a larger number of firms and farms experience hard times. Government transfer payments increase to respond to the increased economic hardship. When the economy experiences boom conditions, expenditure on programs to compensate for economic hardship declines.

In light of both of these factors, the deficit rises when the economy is in a depressed state and falls when the economy is in a state of boom. In order to take into account these facts, economists have developed a modified deficit concept called the cyclically adjusted deficit. The **cyclically adjusted deficit** is the deficit that would occur if the economy were at full employment. To measure the cyclically adjusted deficit, we calculate what tax revenue and expenditures would be if the economy were at full employment.

The formula established by the Department of Commerce for determining the effect of the business cycle on the deficit has two key elements:[1]

- Each 1 percentage point increase in the unemployment rate increases the federal deficit by $30 billion.
- Each $100 billion decrease in current GDP increases the deficit by $35 billion.

[1]Thomas M. Holloway, "The Economy in the Federal Budget: Guides to the Automatic Effects," *Survey of Current Business* 64, 7 (July 1984): 102–5.

The Deficit in Recovery From 1982 to 1989, the economy was in a prolonged and strong recovery. According to the formula for calculating the effect of the business cycle on the deficit, the deficit should have fallen dramatically through these years. But it did not. It persisted at around 3 percent of GDP, and the persistence of a large deficit, even in the face of strong economic recovery, led some observers to express grave concern about the potential effects of an ongoing deficit on the long-term health of the economy.

The Deficit in the 1991 Recession During the 1991 recession, the deficit predictably increased as the growth of tax revenues slowed and spending on unemployment benefits and social programs increased. The deficit climbed from 2½ percent of GDP in 1989 to 3 percent of GDP in 1990 and 3½ percent of GDP in 1991.

Reading Between the Lines on pp. 934–935 takes a further look at the deficit and the features that we've just described.

REVIEW

The federal government deficit grew in the early 1980s because expenditure increased and tax revenue decreased. Because the deficit persisted, debt and interest increased and the deficit fed on itself. A higher deficit led to higher debt, which in turn led to higher interest payments and a yet higher deficit. The deficit is related to the business cycle. Other things being equal, the stronger the economy, the lower is the deficit. When the economy went into recession in 1991, the deficit climbed to 3½ percent of GDP. ◆

We've now seen when and how the deficit emerged and how it relates to the business cycle. We've also seen that the deficit is not only large but also persistent. But is the deficit really as bad as it looks? Can it really be true that in eight years the government debt increased by more than it had in the entire previous history of the nation? These are important questions to which we'll now turn our attention.

The Real Deficit

Inflation distorts many things, not least of which is the deficit. To remove the inflationary distortion from the measured deficit, we need a concept of the real deficit. The **real deficit** is the change in the real value of outstanding government debt. The real value of outstanding government debt is equal to the market value of the debt divided by the price level. We are going to see how we can calculate the real deficit and how such a calculation changes our view of the size of the government's deficit. But before we do that, let's consider real deficits in more personal terms by examining the real deficit of a family.

The Real Deficit of a Family

In 1960, a young couple (perhaps your parents) ran a deficit to buy a new house. The deficit took the form of a mortgage. The amount borrowed to cover the deficit—the difference between the cost of the house and what the family had available to put down as a deposit—was $30,000. Today, the children of that couple are buying their first house. To do so, they also are incurring a deficit. But they're borrowing $120,000 to buy their first house. Is the $120,000 deficit (mortgage) of the 1990 house-buyer really four times as big as the deficit (mortgage) of the 1960 house-buyer? In dollar terms, the 1990 borrowing is indeed four times as big as the 1960 borrowing. But in terms of what money will buy, these two debts are almost equivalent. Inflation in the years between 1960 and 1990 has raised the prices of most things to about four times what they were in 1960. Thus a mortgage of $120,000 in 1990 is really the same as a mortgage of $30,000 in 1960.

When a family buys a new home and finances it on a mortgage, the family has a deficit in the year in which it buys the home. But in all the following years, until the debt has been paid off, the family has a surplus. That is, each year the family pays to the lender a sum of money, part of which covers the interest on the outstanding debt but part of which *reduces* the outstanding debt. The reduction in the outstanding debt is the household's surplus. Inflation has another important effect here. Because inflation brings higher prices, it also brings a lower real value of outstanding debts. Thus the real value of the mortgage declines by the amount paid off each year plus the amount wiped out by inflation. Other things being equal, the higher the inflation rate, the faster is the mortgage really paid off and the larger is the household's real surplus.

The Government's Real Deficit

This line of reasoning applies with equal force to the government. Because of inflation, the government's deficit is not *really* as big as it appears. To see how we can measure the deficit and correct for the distortion of inflation, we'll work through a concrete numerical example. First, look at Case A in Table 34.1—a situation in which there is no inflation. Government expenditure, excluding debt interest, is $17 billion and tax revenue is $20 billion. Thus if the government didn't have interest to pay, it would have a surplus of $3 billion. But the government has outstanding debt of $50 billion, and interest rates are running at 4 percent. Thus the government must pay $2 billion of debt interest (4 percent on $50 billion). When we add the $2 billion of debt interest to the government's other spending, we see that the government's total expenditure is $19 billion, so the government has a $1 billion surplus. The government's debt falls to $49 billion—the $50 billion outstanding at the beginning of the year is reduced by the surplus that the government has run. Ignore the last two rows of Table 34.1 for the moment.

Next, let's look at this same economy with exactly the same expenditure, tax revenue, and debt but in a situation in which there is a 10 percent *anticipated* inflation rate—Case B in Table 34.1. With 10 percent inflation that is anticipated, the market interest rate will not be 4 percent, but 14 percent. The reason why the interest rate is higher by 10 percentage points is that the real value of outstanding debt declines by 10 percent a year. Lenders—the households, firms, and foreigners that are buying government debt—know that the money they'll receive in repayment of the loans they make to the government will be worth less than the money they

The Future of the Deficit

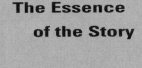

FORTUNE, October 7, 1991

Should You Worry about the Deficit?

By Rob Norton

Is there an economic phenomenon more frustrating than the federal budget deficit? For a decade it has mocked us, defying all efforts to eliminate it—from the Gramm-Rudman-Hollings Act of 1985, which promised a balanced budget by 1991, to last fall's Budget Enforcement Act, which is supposed to trim the deficit to zero by 1996. Now comes the news that not only is the deficit rising, but in the next fiscal year, which starts October 1, it will set a record of $348 billion, far higher than the deficits that had us so worried in the mid-1980s.

Should we start worrying again? After all, the deficit decade produced none of the catastrophes that many experts predicted. Private investment was not crowded out, inflation didn't reignite, and the dollar didn't collapse. But the U.S. did pay a price. Because of those past deficits, real interest rates were higher and national saving and investment lower than they would otherwise have been, which translated into slower productivity growth and less abundant lives for everyone.

If last year's budget act works as advertised, the deficit should soon resume its downward path—but that is an *if* of Himalayan proportions. . . .

But don't fret too much about next year's huge numbers. The deficit's size is distorted by the effects of the Gulf war and the S&L bailout (see chart). . . .

The 1990–91 recession has also swelled the deficit by lowering tax revenues and boosting spending on unemployment insurance.

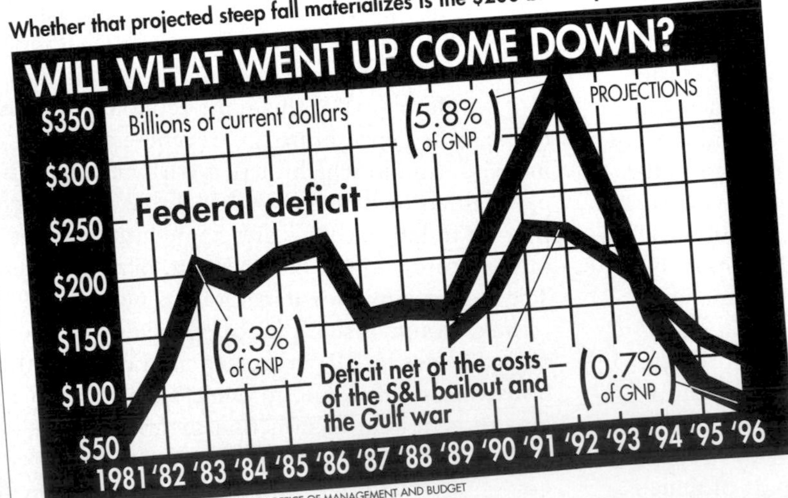

The Essence of the Story

As fiscal year 1991–92 began, the U.S. budget deficit was projected to set a new record at $348 billion.

For a decade, the deficit had defied all efforts to eliminate it—from the Gramm-Rudman-Hollings Act of 1985 to the Budget Enforcement Act of 1991.

We should *not* worry about the deficit because:

- A decade of deficits has not crowded out private investment, increased inflation, or lowered the value of the dollar.
- Its size is distorted by $107 billion because of the effects of the Gulf War, the S&L bailout, and the recession.

We *should* worry about the deficit because:

- It increases real interest rates and decreases saving and investment.
- It slows productivity growth and lowers living standards.

Background and Analysis

The 1991–92 fiscal year (October 1, 1991 to September 30, 1992, also known as "fiscal 1992") had a projected deficit of $348 billion, the highest ever deficit.

Measured in current dollars, the federal deficit has been on an upward trend since 1981 (Fig. 1).

Measured as a percentage of GDP, the deficit has averaged 3.8 percent of GDP and has fluctuated around that average (Fig. 2).

Before 1992, the deficit was farthest above average in the recession of 1982–1983. In the recession year of 1991, the deficit was below average (Fig. 2).

But the deficit of 1991 was $24 billion (about ½ percent of GDP) below what it otherwise would have been because of a one-time payment by allies toward the cost of the Gulf War.

And the deficit in 1992 was temporarily high because of the factors identified in the news article: the recession was keeping tax receipts low and benefits high; the S&L bailout was adding a large amount of spending; and the Gulf War expenses were continuing.

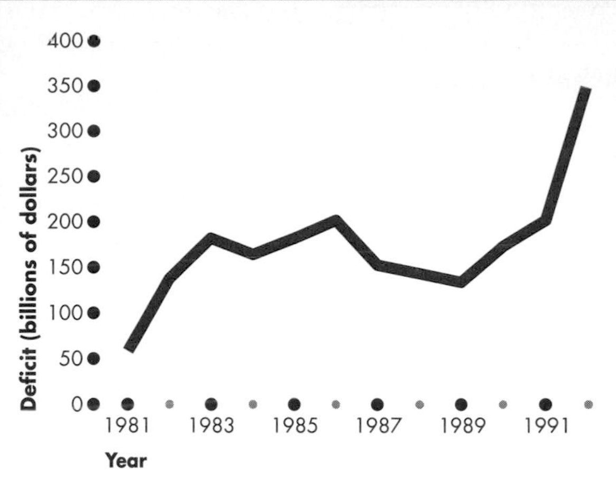

Figure 1

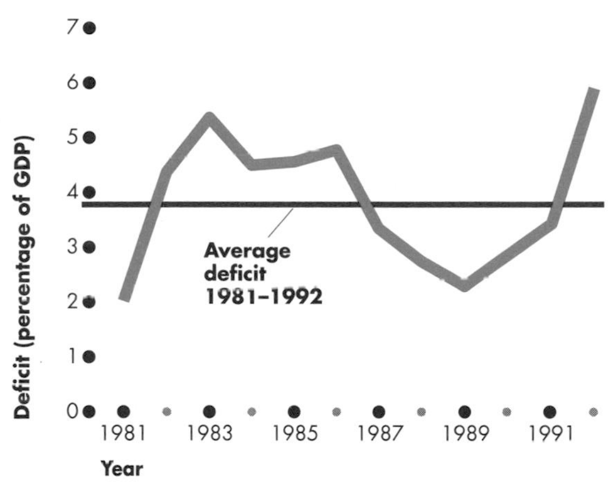

Figure 2

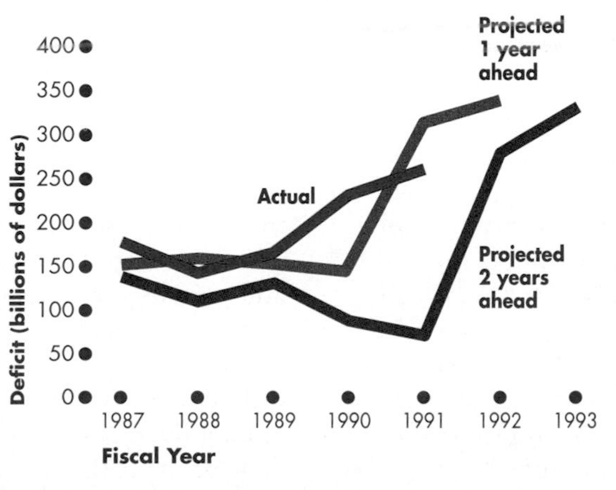

Figure 3

The deficit projects are strongly downward—to less than 1 percent of GDP by 1996. Such projections in the past have been quite accurate for one year ahead but optimistic for the longer term (see Fig. 3).

If the deficit does follow its projected path to less than 1 percent of GNP by 1996, the concerns expressed in the news article will disappear.*

But even if the deficit remains larger than it is currently projected to be, it is not very likely that it will be a major source of higher interest rates. The reason is that there is a *worldwide* capital market and the U.S. federal deficit is a small part of that market.

There is likely to be upward pressure on real interest rates during the 1990s, but that pressure will come from the extremely large-scale capital demands of the rapidly growing Chinese, other Asian, and Eastern European economies. These forces, which dwarf the federal deficit, could raise interest rates in the United States and crowd out some domestic investment.

*This news article was written before the Commerce Department adopted the GDP measure of aggregate income. See pp. 619–620 for an explanation of the distinction between GNP and GDP.

TABLE 34.1

How Inflation Distorts the Deficit

	Case A	Case B
Government expenditure (excluding debt interest)	**$17 billion**	**$17 billion**
Tax revenue	**$20 billion**	**$20 billion**
Government debt	**$50 billion**	**$50 billion**
Market interest rate	**4 percent**	**4 percent**
Inflation rate	**0 percent**	**10 percent**
Real interest rate	**4 percent**	**14 percent**
Debt interest paid	**$ 2 billion**	**$ 7 billion**
Surplus (+) or deficit (–)	**+$ 1 billion**	**–$ 4 billion**
Government debt at end of year	**$49 billion**	**$54 billion**
Real government debt at end of year	**$49 billion**	**$49 billion**
Real surplus (+) or deficit (–)	**+$ 1 billion**	**+$ 1 billion**

Inflation distorts the measured deficit by distorting the debt interest payments made by the government. In this example, the real interest rate is 4 percent and government debt is $50 billion, so debt interest in real terms is $2 billion. With no inflation, Case A, the actual debt interest paid is also $2 billion. At 10 percent inflation, Case B, interest rates rise to 14 percent (in order to preserve a real interest rate of 4 percent) and debt interest increases to $7 billion. The deficit increases by $5 billion from a surplus of $1 billion to a deficit of $4 billion. This deficit is apparent, not real. With 10 percent inflation, the real value of the government's debt falls by $5 billion, offsetting the deficit of $4 billion and resulting in a $1 billion real surplus.

lend out. The government also recognizes that the money it will use to repay its debt will have a lower value than the money it borrows. Thus the government and the people from whom it borrows readily agree to a higher interest rate that compensates for these foreseen changes in the value of money. So with a 14 percent interest rate, the government has to pay $7 billion in debt interest—14 percent of $50 billion. When the $7 billion of debt interest is added to the government's other spending, total expenditure is $24 billion, $4 billion more than tax revenue. Therefore the government has a deficit of $4 billion. At the end of the year, the government's debt will have increased from $50 billion to $54 billion.

The difference between the two situations we've just described is a 10 percent inflation rate. Nothing else is different. Real expenditure by the government and real tax revenue are the same, and the real interest rate is the same in the two cases. But at the end of one year, government debt has increased to $54 billion in Case B and has fallen to $49 billion in Case A. Nevertheless, the real debt is the same in the two cases. You can see this equality by keeping in mind that although government debt increases to $54 billion in Case B, the prices of all things have increased by 10 percent. If we deflate the government debt in Case B to express the debt in constant dollars instead of current dollars, we see that real government debt has actually fallen in Case B to $49 billion. ($54 billion divided by 1.1—1 plus the proportionate inflation rate—equals $49 billion.) Thus even in Case B, the real situation is that there is a surplus of $1 billion. Inflation makes it appear that there is a $4 billion deficit when really there is a $1 billion surplus.

The numbers in Table 34.1 are, of course, hypothetical. They deal with two imaginary situations. But the calculations that we've just done provide us with a method of adjusting the U.S. government deficit to eliminate the effects of inflation and reveal the real deficit. How important is it to adjust the U.S. deficit for inflation in order to obtain an inflation-free view of the deficit?

The Real and Nominal Deficit in the United States

Figure 34.5 provides an answer to the above question. It plots the nominal and real deficits of the United States alongside each other. As you can see, the real deficit has not been as large as the nominal deficit, especially during the 1970s. The reason is that inflation was high during those years. Only when inflation declined in the mid-1980s did a large and persistent real deficit emerge.

You can see, then, that the distinction between the real and nominal deficit is an important practical distinction only when the inflation rate is high. Taking the distinction into account changes our view of the scale and seriousness of the deficit during the 1970s. But it does not change the story much in the second half of the 1980s and the 1990s because by then inflation had subsided.

FIGURE 34.5

The Real Deficit and the Nominal Deficit

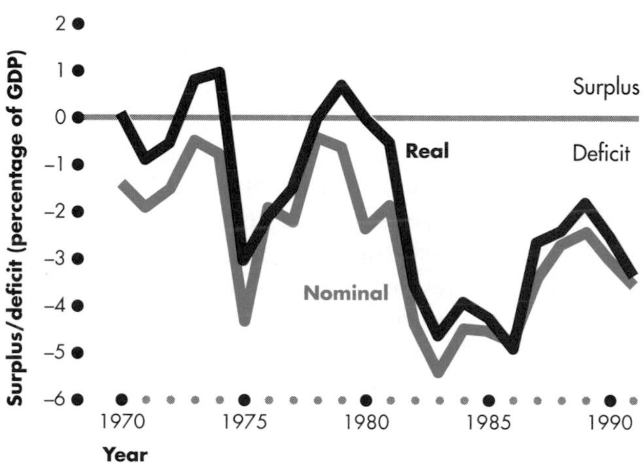

The real deficit removes the effects of inflation from interest rates and from the outstanding value of government debt. The real deficit and the nominal deficit follow a similar path, but the real deficit is smaller than the nominal deficit. Only when inflation declined in the 1980s did the two deficit measures move close together.

Source: Economic Report of the President, 1992, and my calculations.

Deficits and Inflation

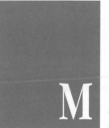

Many people fear government deficits because they believe deficits lead to inflation. Do deficits cause inflation? That depends on how the deficit is financed.

Financing the Deficit

To finance its deficit, the government sells bonds. But the effect of bond sales depends on who buys the bonds. If they are bought by the Fed, they bring an increase in the money supply. But if they are bought by anyone other than the Fed, they do not bring a change in the money supply.

When the Fed buys government bonds, it pays for them by creating new money (see Chapter 28, pp. 764–769). We call such financing of the deficit money financing. **Money financing** is the financing of the government deficit by the sale of bonds to the Federal Reserve System, which results in the creation of additional money. All other financing of the government's deficit is called debt financing. **Debt financing** is the financing of the government deficit by selling bonds to anyone (household, firm, or foreigner) other than the Federal Reserve System.

Let's look at the consequences of these two ways of financing the deficit, starting with debt financing.

Debt Financing First, suppose that the government borrows money by selling treasury bonds to households and firms. In order to sell a bond, the government must offer the potential buyer a sufficiently attractive deal. In other words, the government must offer a high enough rate of return to convince people to lend their money.

Let's suppose that the going interest rate is 10 percent a year. In order to sell a bond worth $100 and cover its deficit of $100, the government must promise not only to pay back the $100 at the end of the year but also to pay the interest of $10 accumulated on that debt. Thus to finance a deficit of $100 today, the government must pay $110 a year from today. In one year's time, in order simply to stand still, the government would have to borrow $110 to cover the cost of repaying, with interest, the bond that it sold a year earlier. Two years from today, the government will have to pay $121—the $110 borrowed plus the 10 percent interest ($11) on that $110. The process continues, with the total amount of debt and total interest payments mushrooming year after year.

Money Financing Next, consider what happens if instead of selling bonds to households and firms, the government sells treasury bonds to the Fed. There are two important differences in this case compared with the case of debt financing. First, the government winds up paying no interest on these bonds; second, additional money gets created.

The government ends up paying no interest on bonds bought by the Fed because the Fed, although an independent agency, pays any profit it makes to the government. Thus, other things being equal, if the Fed receives an extra million dollars from the government in interest payments on government bonds held by the Fed, the Fed's profits increase by that same million dollars and flow back to the government. Second, when the Fed buys bonds from the government, it uses newly created money to do so. This newly created money flows into the banking system in the form of an increase in the monetary base and enables the banks to create yet additional money by making additional loans. (See Chapter 27 and Chapter 28.)

As we studied in Chapter 24 and Chapter 31, an increase in the money supply causes an increase in aggregate demand. And higher aggregate demand eventually brings a higher price level. Persistent money financing leads to a continuously increasing aggregate demand and to inflation.

Debt Financing versus Money Financing In comparing these two methods of financing the deficit, it is clear that debt financing leaves the government with an ongoing obligation to pay interest—an obligation that gets bigger each year if the government keeps running deficits. When the government uses money financing, it pays its bills and that is the end of the matter. (The government pays interest to the Fed, but the Fed pays its profit to the government, so the government has no ongoing interest obligation.) Thus there is a clear advantage, from the government's point of view, to covering its deficit by money financing rather than by debt financing. Unfortunately, this solution causes inflationary problems for everybody else.

But the alternative, debt financing, is not problem-free. Financing the deficit through bond sales to households, firms, and foreigners causes a mushrooming scale of debt and interest payments. The larger the scale of debt and interest payments, the bigger the deficit problem becomes and the greater is the temptation to end the process of debt financing. Thus the temptation increases to finance the deficit by selling bonds to the Fed—money financing. This ever-present temptation is what leads many to fear that deficits are inflationary even when they are not immediately money financed.

Unpleasant Arithmetic

Some economists have argued that debt financing can be even more inflationary than money financing. Because debt financing creates more debt and a bigger interest burden, the amount of money eventually created is greater, the longer the debt financing persists. Anticipating such an outcome, rational people start to dump money—decreasing the demand for money. At the same time they increase the demand for goods, putting upward pressure on prices. Inflation takes off even though no money financing has yet begun.

Thomas Sargent (of the University of Chicago and the Hoover Institution at Stanford University) and Neil Wallace (of the University of Minnesota) first showed this possibility and called their conclusion "unpleasant monetarist arithmetic." It is *unpleasant* arithmetic because postponing money creation worsens the inflation that ensues. It is unpleasant *monetarist* arithmetic because it attacks the central proposition of monetarism—that inflation is caused purely by the growth rate of the money supply. According to monetarism, if the money supply growth rate is contained, inflation will not erupt. According to unpleasant monetarist arithmetic, even if the money supply growth rate is contained, inflation will erupt if the deficit is large enough to create an expectation of its eventual financing by newly created money.

The cure for inflation in an economy with a large and persistent deficit is not merely a slowing in the pace of money creation. The deficit must also be brought under control. Slowing money growth is a necessary part of the process of slowing inflation, but rapid money growth is not the fundamental source of the inflation, and hence it is not the solution.

But for the deficit to have the unpleasant arithmetic effects it must be a persistent phenomenon. A deficit that is large and that lasts even for a decade does not inevitably bring inflation. If the deficit is actually going to be brought under control and the expectation is that it will be brought under control, its presence does not lead to inflation.

International Evidence

We have a large amount of experience from a wide variety of countries on the relationship between inflation and deficits. What does that experience tell us? Are deficits, in fact, inflationary?

This question is answered in Fig. 34.6. It contains data on inflation and deficits for 67 countries covering the 1980s. The countries are in three groups: Latin America (part a), Western Europe (part b), and 48 others (part c). The 67 countries are the only

FIGURE 34.6

Deficits and Inflation

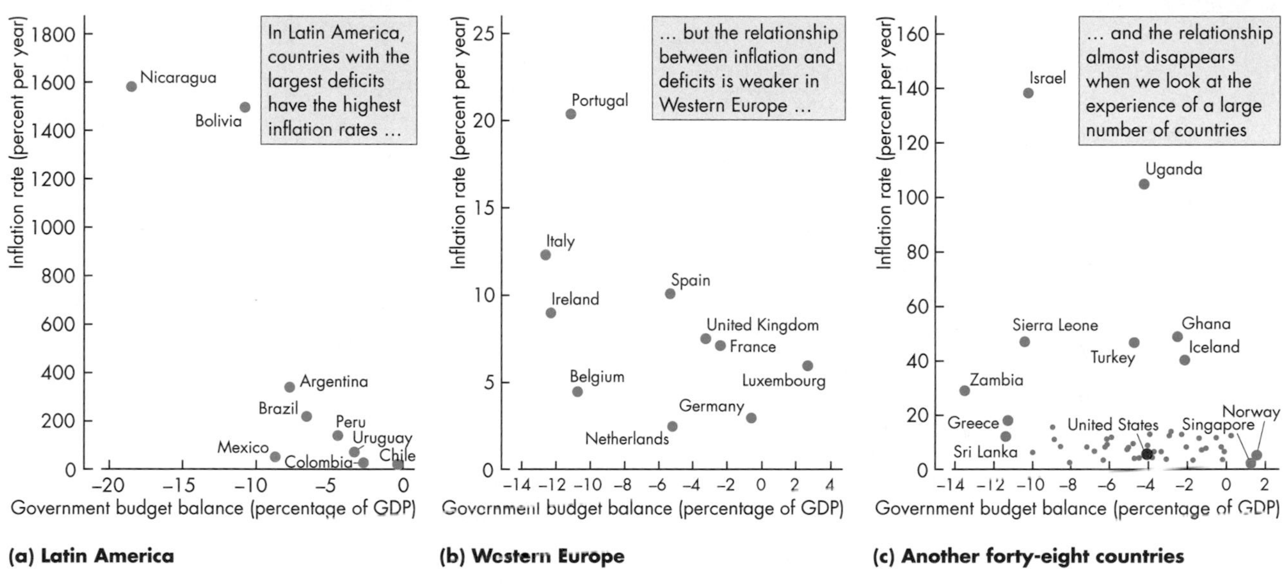

The relationship between the deficit and inflation is shown for 9 Latin American countries (part a), 10 countries in Western Europe (part b), and 48 other countries—including the United States (part c). There is a tendency for large deficit countries to be high inflation countries, but the correlation is weak.

Source: International Financial Statistics Yearbook, 1990. For each country, the dot shows its deficit (as a percentage of GDP) and inflation (GDP deflator) for the 1980s (or part decade where the full decade is not available).

ones for which there are data on both inflation and the deficit for most of the 1980s.

First, notice the tremendous range of experience. The highest inflation rate was almost 1600 percent per year—in Nicaragua (part a). The lowest inflation rate was less than 3 percent—in the Netherlands (part b). The largest deficit was almost 20 percent of GDP—again in Nicaragua. The smallest deficit (actually a surplus) was more than 2 percent of GDP—in Luxembourg.

Second, look at the relationships between deficits and inflation. In the Latin American countries (part a), there is a clear tendency for these two variables to be correlated. The countries with the largest deficits (Nicaragua and Bolivia) have the highest inflation rates. The countries with the smallest deficits (Chile, Colombia, and Uruguay) have the lowest inflation rates. And countries with deficits between these have inflation rates that are intermediate as well (Argentina and Brazil). Only Mexico does not fit the pattern. Its inflation rate is lower than that in countries with much smaller deficits. In Western Europe (part b), there is a similar, although somewhat weaker, relationship between deficits and inflation. And the relationship, although still present, is very loose for the countries shown in part (c).

Third, notice the position of the United States. Its deficit is in the middle of the pack, but its inflation rate is among the lowest.

We have now reviewed the relationship between deficits and inflation. Deficits are not inevitably inflationary. But there is a correlation between deficits and inflation. And the larger the deficit and the longer it persists, the greater are the inflationary pressures.

Another common view about the deficit is that it places a burden on future generations. Let's now examine that view.

A Burden on Future Generations?

It is a common and popular cry that "we owe it to our children to control the deficit." Is this popular view correct? How would the deficit place a burden on future generations?

We've already examined one burden that the deficit might place on future generations—the burden of inflation. But when people talk about the deficit as a burden on future generations, they usually mean something other than inflation. For example, somebody has to pay the interest on the huge national debt that the deficit creates. The government will pay the interest with money it takes from the people as taxes. Taxes will have to be raised. Won't those taxes burden future generations?

Wait, though. Doesn't the interest paid each year get financed with taxes collected each year? So how can the deficit be a burden to *future* generations? It might be a burden to some members of the future generation, but it must be a benefit to others, so in the aggregate it evens out.

Although in the aggregate the interest paid equals the tax revenue collected, there may be important redistribution effects. For example, one feature of our present deficit is that some government debt is being bought not by Americans but by European and Japanese investors. So part of the future burden of the current deficit is that future American taxpayers will have to provide the resources with which to pay interest to foreign holders of U.S. government debt.

There's another way in which today's deficit can make people poorer tomorrow: by slowing today's pace of investment and reducing the stock of productive capital equipment available for future generations. This phenomenon is called crowding out.

Crowding Out

Crowding out is the tendency for an increase in government purchases of goods and services to bring a decrease in investment (see Chapter 29, p. 794). If crowding out does occur, and if government purchases of goods and services are financed by government debt, the economy will have a larger stock of government debt and a smaller stock of capital—plant and equipment. Unproductive government debt replaces productive capital.

Crowding out does *not* occur if:

1. There is unemployment.
2. The deficit arises from the government's purchases of capital on which the return equals (or exceeds) that on privately purchased capital.

Crowding out *does* occur if:

1. There is full employment.
2. The government purchases consumption goods and services or capital on which the return is less than that on privately purchased capital.

The Level of Employment If there is full employment, increased government purchases of goods and services (and an increased deficit) must result in a decrease in the purchases of other goods and services. But if there is unemployment, it is possible that an increase in government purchases (and increased deficit) could result in a decrease in unemployment and an increase in output. In such a case the deficit does not completely crowd out other expenditure. This possibility can occur only for short periods and when the economy is in recession.

Productive Government Purchases Much of what the government purchases is productive capital. Highways, dams, airports, schools, and universities are some obvious examples. But there are some not so obvious examples. Education and health care are investments in productive human capital. Defense expenditure protects our physical and human capital resources and is productive capital expenditure. To the extent that the deficit results from our acquisition of such assets, it does not crowd out productive capital. On the contrary, it contributes to it.

But it is possible for government purchases of consumption goods and services to crowd out productive capital. Let's see how.

How Crowding Out Occurs For crowding out to occur, a deficit must result in less investment, with the consequence that future generations have a smaller capital stock than they otherwise would have had. This drop in the capital stock will lower their income and, in a sense, be a burden to them. (They will still be richer than they were, but not as rich as they would have been if they had had a larger stock of productive machines.)

The scale of investment depends on its opportunity cost. That opportunity cost is the real interest rate. Other things being equal, the higher the real interest rate, the less firms will want to invest in new plant and equipment. For a government deficit to crowd out investment, the deficit must cause real interest rates to rise.

Some people believe that a deficit does increase interest rates because the government's own borrowing represents an increase in the demand for loans with no corresponding increase in the supply of loans. Figure 34.7 shows what happens in this case. Part (a) shows the demand and supply curves for loans. Initially, the demand for loans is D_0, and the supply of loans is S_0. The real interest rate is 3 percent, and the quantity of loans made is $1 trillion. Part (b) shows investment. At a real interest rate of 3 percent, investment is $0.8 trillion. Now suppose that the government runs a deficit. To finance its deficit, the government borrows. The demand for loans increases, and the demand curve for loans shifts from D_0 to D_1. There is no change in the supply of loans, so the real interest rate increases to 4 percent and the quantity of loans increases to $1.2 trillion. Notice that the increase in the quantity of loans made is smaller than the increase in the demand for loans. That is, the demand curve shifts to the right by a larger amount than the increase in loans that actually occurs. The higher interest rate decreases investment and brings a smaller capital stock. Thus the increased stock of government debt crowds out some productive capital.

FIGURE 34.7

The Deficit, Borrowing, and Crowding Out

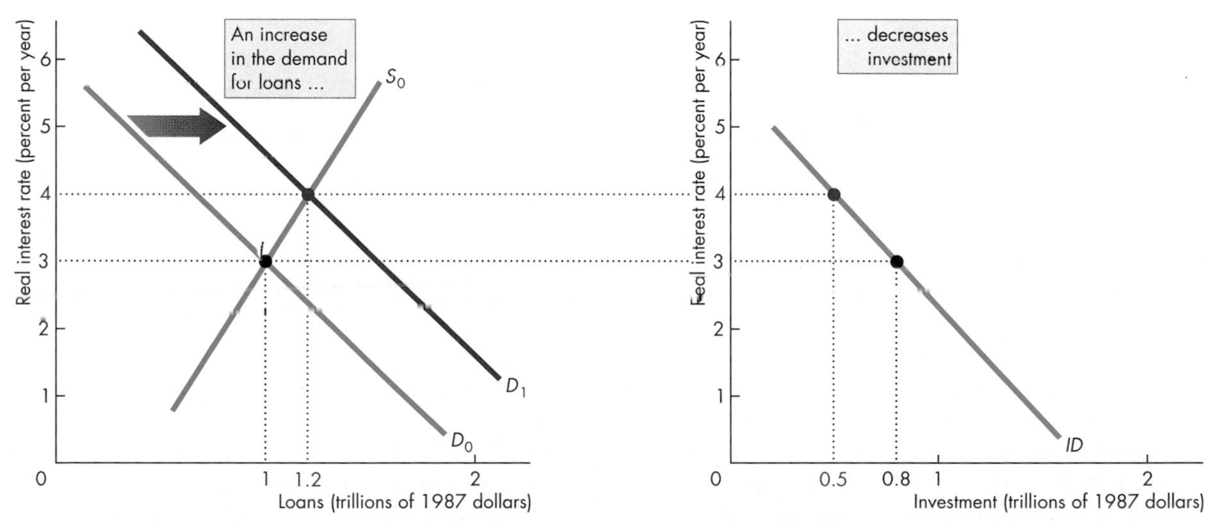

(a) The market for loans

(b) Investment

Part (a) shows the market for loans. The demand for loans is D_0, and the supply is S_0. The quantity of loans made is $1 trillion, and the real interest rate is 3 percent. Part (b) shows the determination of investment. At an interest rate of 3 percent, investment is $0.8 trillion. The government runs a deficit and finances the deficit by borrowing. The government's increase in demand for loans shifts the demand curve to D_1. The interest rate rises to 4 percent, and the equilibrium quantity of loans increases to $1.2 trillion. The higher interest rate leads to a decrease in investment in part (b). The government deficit crowds out capital accumulation.

Does a deficit make real interest rates rise as shown in Fig. 34.7? Many economists believe so, and they have some pretty strong evidence to point to. Real interest rates in the United States in the last decade, in precisely the years in which we have had a large real deficit, have been higher than at any time in history. Furthermore, there is a general tendency for real interest rates and the real deficit to fluctuate in sympathy with each other.

It is this relationship in the data that leads some economists to predict that a higher real deficit means higher real interest rates, lower investment, and a smaller scale of capital accumulation—government debt crowds out productive capital. As a consequence, future output will be lower than it otherwise would have been, and so the deficit burdens future generations.

FIGURE 34.8
Ricardian Equivalence

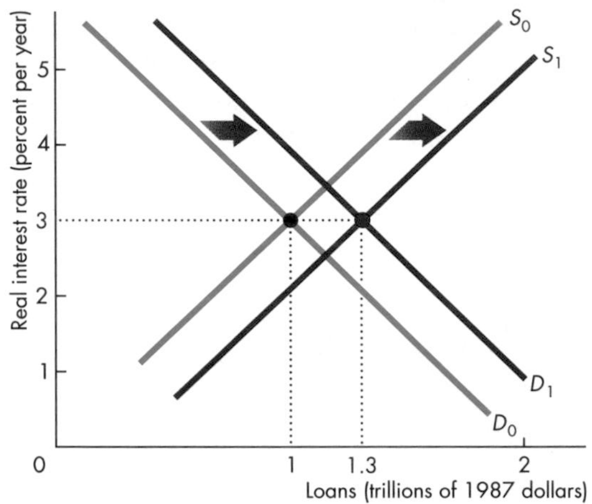

Initially, the demand for loans is D_0, and the supply of loans is S_0. The equilibrium quantity of loans is $1 trillion, and the real interest rate is 3 percent a year. An increase in the government deficit, financed by borrowing, increases the demand for loans, shifting the demand curve to D_1. Households, recognizing that the increased government deficit will bring increased future taxes to pay the additional interest charges, cut their consumption and increase their saving. The supply curve of loans shifts to the right to S_1. The equilibrium quantity of loans increases to $1.3 trillion, but the real interest rate stays constant at 3 percent a year. There is no crowding out of investment.

Ricardian Equivalence

Some economists do not believe that deficits crowd out capital accumulation. On the contrary, they argue, debt financing and paying for government spending with taxes are equivalent. The level of purchases of goods and services matters, but not the way in which it is financed.

The first economist to advance this idea (known as Ricardian equivalence) was the great English economist David Ricardo. Recently, Ricardo's idea has been given a forceful restatement by Robert Barro of Harvard University. Barro argues as follows: If the government increases its purchases of goods and services but does not increase taxes, people are smart enough to recognize that the government will increase taxes later in order to cover the increased spending and interest payments on the debt being issued today. In recognition of having to pay higher taxes later, people will cut their consumption now and save more. They'll increase their saving so that when the higher taxes are finally levied, sufficient wealth has been accumulated to meet those tax liabilities without a further cut in consumption. The scale of increased saving matches the scale of increased government spending.

Figure 34.8 illustrates this case. Initially, the demand for loans is D_0, and the supply of loans is S_0. The real interest rate is 3 percent, and the quantity of loans made is $1 trillion. The government runs a deficit and finances that deficit by borrowing. The demand curve for loans shifts to the right to D_1. At the same time, using the reasoning of Ricardo and Barro, there is a decrease in consumption and an increase in saving. The supply of loans increases, shifting the supply curve to the right to S_1. The quantity of loans increases from $1 trillion to $1.3 trillion, and the real interest rate stays constant at 3 percent. With no change in the real interest rate, there is no crowding out of investment.

Some economists argue that Ricardian equivalence breaks down because people take into account only the future tax liabilities that will be borne by themselves and not by their children and their grandchildren. Proponents of the Ricardian equivalence proposition argue that it makes no difference whether future tax liabilities are going to be borne by those currently alive or by their descendants. If the taxes are going to be borne by children and grandchildren, the current generation takes account of those future taxes and adjusts its own consumption so that it can make bequests on a large enough scale to enable those taxes to be paid.

Laying out the assumptions necessary for Ricardian equivalence leaves most economists convinced that the Ricardian equivalence proposition cannot apply to the real world. Yet there is a surprising amount of evidence in its support. In order to interpret the evidence, it is important to be clear that Ricardian equivalence does *not* imply that real interest rates are not affected by the level of government purchases. A high level of government purchases, other things being equal, brings a higher real interest rate. The Ricardian equivalence proposition implies that real interest rates are not affected by the way in which a given level of government purchases is financed. Regardless of whether government purchases are financed by taxes or by borrowing, real interest rates will be the same.

Whether it is the deficit or the level of government purchases of goods and services that affects real interest rates remains unclear. If people do take into account future tax burdens (and not just their own but their children's and grandchildren's future tax burdens), then saving will respond to offset the deficit. The deficit itself will have little or no effect on real interest rates and capital accumulation. If people ignore the implications of the deficit for their own and their descendants' future consumption possibilities, the deficit will indeed increase real interest rates. The jury remains out on this question.

Eliminating the Deficit

Measures to eliminate the deficit can attack either the revenue side or the expenditure side of the government's budget. That is, there are two ways to eliminate the deficit:

- Reducing expenditure
- Increasing revenue

Reducing Expenditure

Throughout the modern history of most countries, government expenditure has increased as a percentage of GDP. The federal government of the United States has contained the growth of government expenditure more effectively than most governments. In most European countries, governments spend close to 50 percent of GDP, and in the Netherlands, expenditure was more that 53 percent of GDP at its peak in 1983.

Many components of government expenditure have a built-in tendency to increase at a faster pace than GDP. Two such components are education and health care. Even when these items are purchased privately, people spend a larger fraction of their incomes on them as incomes increase. When the government plays a significant role in the provision of these two goods, voter pressure for better provision of services is irresistible and the government has little choice but to increase its expenditures to meet the voter demands. Only by privatizing these activities can the government's share of GDP be prevented from increasing.

In many European countries the government is privatizing a variety of manufacturing operations. The Thatcher government in Britain (in the 1980s) even tried to limit its involvement in health care and health insurance. But there is much less scope for such privatization in the United States. In fact, the political debate appears to be leaning in the direction of expanding the scope of government in the health care insurance business. A major theme in the 1992 presidential campaign was a debate about the desirability of introducing a comprehensive and universal health insurance program similar to that of Canada.

In the early 1990s, one factor working against the tide of ever larger government expenditure is the "peace dividend"—the reduction in defense spending resulting from the end of the Cold War. It is possible that the peace dividend will finance enhanced health and other social programs without an increase in the overall level of government spending. But this dividend is likely to be short-lived. In the long run, growing incomes will bring higher expenditure.

Faced with the general tendency for government spending to increase, there are four main proposals for attempting to keep federal government expenditure under control:

- Cutting revenue to force spending cuts
- Line-item veto
- Budget Enforcement Act of 1990
- Balanced budget amendment

Cutting Revenue to Force Spending Cuts The approach adopted by the Reagan administration toward the deficit, and advocated by Milton Friedman, is based on the view that Congress behaves like an undisciplined child. The child wants more candy. Give the child a dollar, and the child will buy more candy. Take a dollar away from the child, and the child will scream but will eventually find a way of managing without candy. Revenue was certainly reduced in the 1980s. As you can see by looking back at Fig. 34.3, tax revenue as a percentage of GDP declined each year from 1981 through 1984. It increased (again as a percentage of GDP) in subsequent years but did not return to its 1981 peak level. It is impossible to say what the exact effects of these revenue cuts were on spending. It does seem likely, however, that the revenue decrease was in part responsible for keeping the lid on the growth of expenditure and social programs through the 1980s. But, as we have seen, it has not reduced spending to the level of tax revenue. If this method works, it works in a time frame that is more drawn out than most people regard as sensible.

Line-Item Veto In order to give the administration more power to help bring spending under control, it has been suggested that the president be given a line-item veto. A **line-item veto** is a veto power vested in the executive branch to eliminate any specific item in a budget. Many state governors have a line-item veto, but the President of the United States does not. When Congress passes a bill calling for expenditures and taxes, the president must either sign the bill into law in its entirety or veto it in its entirety. He cannot eliminate particular items.

Some people believe that giving the president this power would bring a sharper and more precise scalpel to bear on the process of cutting spending. But it has to be borne in mind that the budget itself emerges as a result of compromise and is Congress's own best attempt to balance competing claims on public resources. If the president had such a veto power, there would likely be an increase in lobbying effort directed at the executive branch itself and there would be no guarantee that the president would be tougher on spending than Congress is.

Budget Enforcement Act of 1990 In an attempt to impose budget discipline on itself, Congress has passed legislation designed to keep total spending growth below the growth of revenue. Its most recent attempt to do this is the Budget Enforcement Act of 1990. This act contains provisions intended to lower the federal budget deficit by more than $0.5 trillion by 1995.

The act contains spending caps and pay-as-you-go rules to prevent new programs from increasing total federal spending. Any spending increase in one program must be offset by a spending decrease in other programs, and if this requirement is violated, across-the-board spending cuts must be made to remain within the cap.

The 1990 act also permits automatic stabilization through an increased deficit during an economic downturn. To facilitate the operation of countercyclical fiscal policy, the law specifies procedures for adjusting the target deficit in light of the state of the economy.

Balanced Budget Amendment Many people want to go further than a congressional self-imposed balanced budget strategy such as the 1990 legislation. They want to amend the Constitution of the United States to include a formula for requiring the federal government to balance its budget. Many economists, including Nobel laureates Milton Friedman and James Buchanan, advocate a balanced budget amendment to the Constitution.

Those favoring a balanced budget amendment argue two things. First, the process of debating and achieving the amendment would itself increase the level of awareness of the importance of financial discipline on the federal government. Second, once such an amendment were in place, Congress would have a cast-iron excuse for not satisfying all the many claims and demands imposed upon it and would, in effect, be able to take refuge behind the balanced budget law. Those who argue against such an amendment argue that it is difficult, if not impossible, to frame the law in such a way as to make it effective.

Because of the difficulty of making significant reductions in government spending, many people take the view that the only way to eliminate the deficit is to increase government revenue. Let's now examine that option.

Increasing Revenue

Two approaches to increasing revenue have been proposed:

- Increase tax rates
- Decrease tax rates

Sound paradoxical? Not really, when you remember that what the government wants to do is to increase its tax *revenue*. *Tax revenue* is the product of the tax rate and the tax base. A **tax rate** is the percentage rate of tax levied on a particular activity. The **tax base** is the activity on which a tax is levied. For example, the tax base for personal income tax is earned income minus some specified allowances. The tax rates on personal income are 15 percent, 28 percent, and 31 percent (depending on income level).

There is ambiguity and disagreement about whether an increase in tax rates increases or decreases tax revenues. The source of the disagreement is something called the Laffer curve. The **Laffer curve** (named after Arthur Laffer, who first proposed it) is a curve that relates tax revenue to the tax rate. Figure 34.9 illustrates a hypothetical Laffer curve. The tax rate ranges between 0 percent and 100 percent on the vertical axis. Tax revenue, measured in billions of dollars, is shown on the horizontal axis. If the tax rate is zero, then no tax revenue is raised. That is why the curve begins at the origin. As the tax rate increases, tax revenue also increases, but only up to some maximum. In this example, once the tax rate has reached 40 percent, tax revenue is at its maximum—point *m* in the figure. If the tax rate increases above 40 percent, tax revenue falls. Why does this happen?

Revenue falls because there is a fall in the scale of the activity that is being taxed. Suppose that the item in question is gasoline. With no tax, lots of people drive gas-guzzling cars and consume billions of gallons a week. If gasoline is taxed, its price increases and the quantity bought declines. At first, the quantity bought decreases by a smaller percentage than the percentage increase in tax, and tax revenue rises. But there comes a point at which the decrease in the quantity demanded rises by a bigger percentage than the rise in taxes. At that point, tax revenue begins to decline. People sell their gas-guzzlers, buy smaller cars, join car pools, and use public transportation. The tax rate goes up, but the tax base goes down and tax revenue declines.

FIGURE 34.9

The Laffer Curve

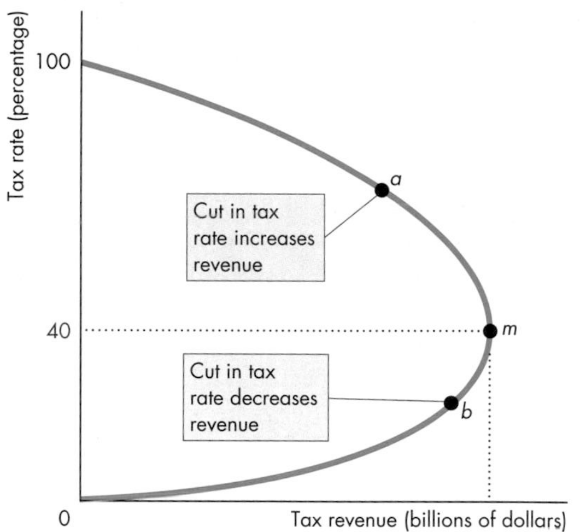

The Laffer curve shows the relationship between a tax rate and tax revenue. If the tax rate is 0 percent, the government collects no tax revenue. As the tax rate increases, the government's tax revenue also increases, but only up to some maximum (point *m*). As the tax rate continues to increase, tax revenue declines. At a tax rate of 100 percent, the government collects no revenue. Higher taxes act as a disincentive. The more heavily taxed is an activity, the less that activity is undertaken. When the percentage decrease in the activity is less than the percentage increase in the tax rate, we are at a point such as *b* and tax revenue rises. When the percentage decrease in the activity exceeds the percentage increase in the tax rate, we are at a point such as *a* and tax revenue decreases.

You can now see that whether a cut in the *tax rate* increases or decreases *tax revenue* depends on where we are on the Laffer curve. If we're at a point such as *a* in Fig. 34.9, a decrease in the tax rate results in an increase in tax revenue. But if we're at point *b*, a decrease in the tax rate results in a decrease in tax revenue. To increase tax revenue from point *b*, we have to increase the tax rate.

Economists and other observers argue about where we are on the Laffer curve for each of the various taxes. Some people suspect that for very highly taxed commodities, such as gasoline, tobacco products, and alcohol, we are on the backward-bending part of the Laffer curve, so an increase in the tax rate would decrease tax revenue. But hardly anyone believes this to be the case for personal income taxes and sales taxes. It is much more likely, in the case of those taxes, that an increase in tax rates would increase tax revenue.

The second approach to increasing revenue is to reform taxes, lowering high marginal tax rates and perhaps introducing new taxes at low rates on activities not previously taxed.

The search for changes in taxes that will bring higher tax revenue is a permanent feature of our economic life and will always be with us, regardless of whether there is a deficit. But in a deficit situation, that search takes on a much greater urgency.

◆ ◆ ◆ ◆ We have now completed our study of macroeconomics and of the challenges and problems of stabilizing the economy. In this study, our main focus has been the economy of the United States. Occasionally, we have taken into account the linkages between the United States and the rest of the world, but international economic relations have not been our main concern. In the remaining chapters we are going to shift our focus and study some vital international issues. First, in Chapter 35, we examine the international exchange of goods and services. Second, in Chapter 36, we study the financing of international trade and the determination of the value of our dollar in terms of other currencies. Third, in Chapter 37, we turn our attention to the problems of the poor developing countries of the Third World. Fourth and finally, in Chapter 38, we examine economic systems that are different from our own, such as those employed in the former Soviet Union and China.

SUMMARY

The Sources of the Deficit

The U.S. federal government deficit grew in the early 1980s because the percentage of GDP spent by the federal government grew and the percentage collected in taxes declined. The deficit, although fluctuating, has tended to get larger. The main items of spending that have increased are transfer payments and debt interest. But the main persistent source of the increasing deficit in the 1980s was the increase in debt interest.

The deficit fluctuates in sympathy with the business cycle. When the economy is in a recovery, tax revenue increases and transfer payments decrease as a percentage of GDP. The deficit declines. When the economy goes into recession, tax revenue decreases and transfer payments increase as a percentage of GDP, and so the deficit increases.

Adjusting the deficit for the effects of the business cycle results in the cyclically adjusted deficit. After cyclical adjustment, the deficit remained large through the expansion of the 1980s. And the deficit increased again in the 1991 recession. (pp. 928–932)

The Real Deficit

Inflation distorts the deficit by overstating the real interest burden carried by the government. Adjusting the deficit for this fact and measuring the real deficit lower the deficit in the 1970s but make little difference in the later 1980s. The cycles in the deficit remain the same, whether measured in real or current dollar terms. (pp. 933–937)

Deficits and Inflation

If deficits are money financed, they cause inflation. If they are debt financed, whether or not they cause inflation depends on how permanent they are. A temporary debt-financed deficit will have no inflationary effects. A permanent debt-financed deficit leads to inflation. It does so because the buildup of debt leads to a buildup of interest payments and a yet higher deficit. At some future date, the deficit will be money financed and the amount of money created will be larger, the longer the deficit persists and the more debt is issued. Fear of future inflation leads to a demand here and now for less government debt and less money. As a consequence, both interest rates and inflation increase in anticipation of a future (and perhaps the distant future) increase in money creation to finance the deficit. (pp. 937–939)

A Burden on Future Generations?

Whether the deficit is a burden on future generations is a controversial issue. Some economists believe that the deficit causes real interest rates to rise, thereby crowding out investment and reducing the amount of capital that we accumulate. As a consequence, future output will be lower than it otherwise would have been and future generations will be burdened with the effects of the deficit.

Other economists argue that government expenditure affects interest rates but the way in which that expenditure is financed does not. They suggest that if government spending is financed by borrowing, people will recognize that future taxes will have to increase to cover both the spending and the interest from the accumulated debt. And in anticipation of those higher future taxes, saving will increase and consumption will decrease in the present. Thus the burden of increased government expenditure—not the burden of the deficit—is spread across all generations. (pp. 940–943)

Eliminating the Deficit

The deficit can be eliminated by reducing expenditure, by increasing revenue, or by a combination of the two. There are four main proposals for reducing expenditure: cut revenue and wait for Congress to gradually bring spending into line; give the president a line-item veto; pursue target spending cuts such as those proposed in the 1990 Budget Enforcement Act; introduce a constitutional amendment requiring Congress to balance the federal budget. Increasing revenue could result from either increasing tax rates (if we are on the upward-sloping part of the Laffer curve) or decreasing tax rates (if we are on the backward-bending part of the Laffer curve). (pp. 943–946)

KEY ELEMENTS

Key Terms

Balanced budget, 928
Budget balance, 928
Budget deficit, 928
Budget surplus, 928
Cyclically adjusted deficit, 932
Debt financing, 937
Government debt, 928
Laffer curve, 945
Line-item veto, 944
Money financing, 937
Real deficit, 933
Tax base, 945
Tax rate, 945

Key Figures

Figure 34.1 The Deficit, 928
Figure 34.4 The Business Cycle and the Deficit, 931
Figure 34.5 The Real Deficit and the Nominal Deficit, 937
Figure 34.9 The Laffer Curve, 945

REVIEW QUESTIONS

1 List the main changes in taxes and government spending that are associated with the emergence of the federal government's deficit.

2 Trace the events between 1980 and 1983 that resulted in an increase in the federal government's deficit.

3 What is meant by the cyclically adjusted deficit?

4 Distinguish between the real deficit and the nominal deficit.

5 In calculating the real deficit, which of the following would you do?

- **a** Value the interest payments in real terms and take into account the change in the real value of government debt
- **b** Calculate the interest payments in nominal terms and take into account the change in the real value of government debt
- **c** Calculate the interest payments in real terms but ignore the change in the real value of outstanding government debt

6 Explain how debt financing of a deficit results in mushrooming interest payments.

7 Explain how the government finances its deficit by creating money.

8 Review the ways in which the deficit can be a burden on future generations.

9 Why do some economists argue that taxes and government debt are equivalent to each other and so the deficit does not matter?

10 What are the four main proposals for reducing government expenditure?

11 Why do some economists think that government revenue can be increased by cutting tax rates?

PROBLEMS

1 You are given the following information about the economy of Spendland. When unemployment is at its natural rate, which is 5.5 percent, government spending and tax revenue are each 10 percent of GDP. There is no inflation. For each 1 percentage point increase in the unemployment rate, government spending increases by 1 percentage point of GDP and tax revenue falls by 1 percentage point of GDP. Suppose that Spendland experiences a cycle in which the unemployment rate takes the following values:

Year	1	2	3	4	5	6	7
Unemployment rate	5	6	7	6	5	4	5

- **a** Calculate the actual deficit (as a percentage of GDP) for each year.
- **b** Calculate Spendland's cyclically adjusted deficit.

2 Government expenditure, excluding debt interest, on Day Dream Island is $8.5 billion. Taxes are $10 billion. The government has a $25 billion outstanding debt. Interest rates are 24 percent, and there is a 20 percent inflation rate. Calculate the following:

- **a** The debt interest that the government pays
- **b** The government's budget surplus or deficit
- **c** The value of the government debt outstanding at the end of the year
- **d** The government's real deficit
- **e** The real value of the government's debt outstanding at the end of the year

3 The rate of return on private capital is 5 percent. The government is planning an increase in public health and welfare programs at an annual cost of $100 billion. These programs are expected to improve health and labor productivity, resulting in an increase in GDP of $50 billion a year. There is full employment.

- **a** What is the opportunity cost of the government program?
- **b** Does it make any difference to the opportunity cost if the program is financed by current taxes, borrowing, or money creation?
- **c** Will the program be a burden or a benefit to future generations if it is financed by borrowing?

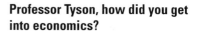

PART 13

International Economics

Talking with Laura Tyson

Laura Tyson was born in New Jersey in 1947. She was an undergraduate at Smith College and obtained her Ph.D. in economics from MIT in 1974. Dr. Tyson is Professor of Economics and Business Administration at the University of California at Berkeley and a consultant to the Council on Competitiveness. Her central area of work has been on the competitiveness and trade performance of the United States.

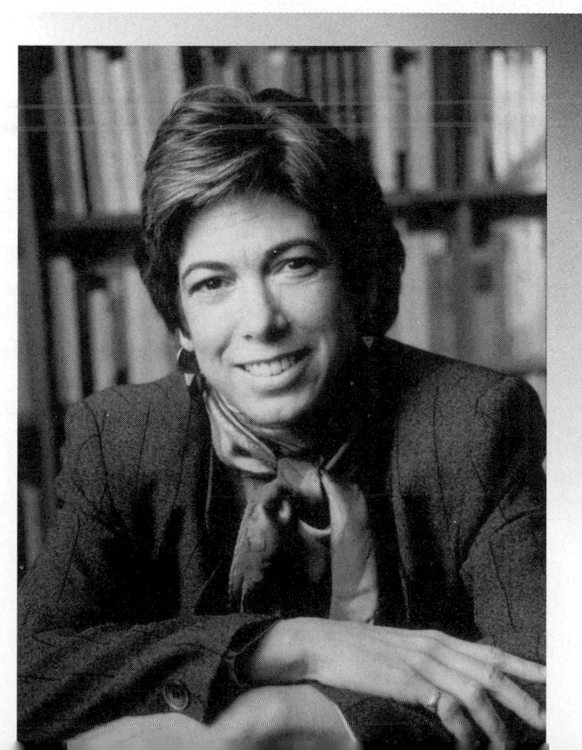

Professor Tyson, how did you get into economics?

I was immediately taken with economics when I first studied it as a sophomore in college. I was fascinated by both the international and public policy aspects: that is to say, how different countries try to solve their basic economic problems and how both the problems and countries relate to one another. I was also looking for a way to combine my analytic instincts with a public policy discipline, and economics was a wonderful match.

Most economists are free traders. But some, perhaps an increasing number, believe some measure of protectionism can help a developing country get off the ground. Where do you stand in the free trade versus protection debate for developing countries?

Like most economists, I consider myself to be a free trader. I believe that GATT has provided significant benefits to the world by breaking down many formal trade barriers. I'd like to see even more free trade. My studies of how countries interact suggest that free trade as an ideal does

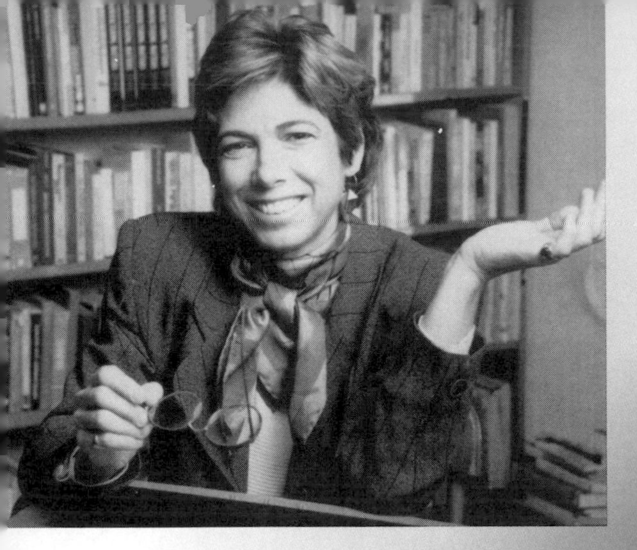

GATT must be overhauled to address the sources of trade friction among the developed countries. Rules about traditional border policies like tariffs and quotas are no longer enough. Deep interdependence among nations requires deep integration—the harmonization of significant national differences and the development of enforceable multilateral rules regulating such nonborder policies as intellectual property protection, competition policy, and industrial targeting.

not exist; we're actually quite far from it. Countries have to push very hard for change at the international level. At the same time, they have to use the domestic policies they have at their disposal to compensate for the fact that free trade doesn't exist.

Trade is of critical importance for bringing developing countries greater prosperity. Developing countries can't depend on aid or investment to the same extent they could in the past. They depend on trading in the world economy to increase their prosperity. They've become extremely dependent on their ability to find markets for their products.

Trade between poor and rich countries is likely to be based on different resource endowments, resulting in differences in comparative advantage. This is the kind of trade that traditional trade theory explains and the kind of trade that benefits both sides. When there exist big differences in development level and resource endowments, countries on both sides of the trading relationship stand to benefit by exploiting these differences and specializing in things that they are good at—their comparative advantage. So you have a powerful argument in favor of freer trade between developed and developing countries.

What about trade between developed countries such as Japan and the United States?

Much of the trade among the developed nations is not based on simple comparative advantage, because all of them are quite similar in underlying resource endowments and technological capabilities. Instead, such trade is often based on differences in product quality, design, reliability, and other non-price characteristics. Such trade takes place in imperfectly competitive markets in which competitive advantage and trade patterns can be manipulated by the market power of individual firms and the policy interventions of individual governments.

For informed national policymaking in such markets, the real choices are not simple choices between free trade and protection but choices about the appropriate combination of liberalization and government intervention that will improve national economic welfare while sustaining an open, international trading system.

There appears to be an increasing tendency toward large regional trading blocs—the European Community and the North American Free Trade Area being the two most important. What are the benefits of large regional trading blocs such as these?

I think the benefits of trading blocs really are twofold. First, because of the benefits of freer trade and specialization, countries within a trading bloc are likely to grow faster. More rapid growth and increased prosperity within the bloc will, in turn, encourage imports from outside the bloc. This is called the "trade creation effect"—there will be new trade opportunities, even for countries that are not members of the bloc itself. Everybody benefits.

Second, a trading bloc can be a model for creating systemic change and establishing new multilateral rules. The politics of forming a free trade area are very complicated. If, over the course of decades, a group of countries such as those in Europe slowly develop a common set of rules and institutions, what they learn "[among the developed countries] Rules about traditional border policies like tariffs and quotas are no longer enough."

in the process can be a rich source of lessons and education for the rest of the world.

What are the dangers that result from the creation of these large regional blocs?

The possible costs of blocs are also, I think, twofold. First of all, there is what economists call "trade diversion," as opposed to trade creation. Trade diversion always occurs when a bloc is formed, because blocs are inherently discriminatory. The bloc by definition breaks down barriers within the bloc nations but not between them and the rest of the world. As a result, the formation of a bloc changes the incentives to trade, encouraging trade among the members of the bloc at the expense of trade between them and the rest of the world. For example, when France and Germany eliminate a barrier to trade between them, they have an incentive to trade more with one another and less with other countries like the United States, with whom trade barriers persist. This is the trade diversion effect.

The trade diversion effect works in conflict with the trade creation effect. On the one hand, the United States will be helped by the trade creation effect—if all of Europe grows faster, there will be a bigger market for the United States. On the other hand, the United States will be hurt by the trade diversion effect because an advantage it had before has now been diminished. Countries forming a bloc can mitigate the diversion effect or make it worse, depending on whether they raise or reduce the common barriers to trade with non-bloc members.

The second basic drawback to the creation of regional trading blocs is what might be called "attention diversion." Countries may expend so much energy and political capital working on their own bloc that they don't have any left to work on the GATT system. The collective effort of the United States, Europe, and Japan is required to improve GATT. But if the Europeans are so heavily engaged in attending to their own regional development, they may not have the political will or energy to commit to the collective problem-solving process.

What will trade barriers between Europe and the rest of the world look like over the next ten years?

That's an open question at this point. There's a big conflict in Europe between the liberalizers who want to see these barriers come down and those who really want to protect Europe for Europeans. It's not clear how that conflict will resolve, but it will be very sensitive to what happens to the world economy. If the world economy stays in a slow growth phase, it's more likely that we will see a protectionist outcome in Europe, as the Europeans strive to keep employment and production at home.

What are the challenges and opportunities created by the emerging new nations of Eastern Europe?

There are three major challenges. The first is macroeconomic stabilization. These economies must be rebuilt on a sound macroeconomic foundation. Fiscal deficits must be controlled, monetary and credit policies must contain inflationary pressure, and outstanding foreign debts must be repaid on a timely basis. Otherwise, macroeconomic crises will undermine the transition, as they have undermined the efforts of developing countries in other parts of the world to build prosperous market economies. The second challenge is restructuring the composition of the economic base. Because the Eastern European countries were inward looking and traded primarily with one another, they have inherited an industrial base that is not competitive by international standards. Many industries have to be scaled back dramatically and some closed down altogether because they simply do not meet the demands of the international marketplace. Additionally, many things must be put into place, such as the appropriate infrastructure of financial services and transportation services that do not exist. These countries do not have a whole series of industries and activities that support modern industrial economies. The last challenge is one of economic reform itself. By that I mean changing the institutions and policy environment in which individ-

"**W**hen perfect markets don't exist, there may be a role for government intervention, since free trade does not always produce welfare-enhancing outcomes."

ual consumers and producers make their decisions. Distinct from the challenge of economic restructuring, which changes the composition of the economy, this third challenge involves changing the basic institutions of the economy—for example, privatizing state-run institutions.

We now see after two years of economic reforms that the process itself is very slow. One can deal with macroeconomic crises rather quickly, although with considerable political risk because of the pain and austerity necessitated by macroeconomic stabilization. Reform and privatization, however, are not changes that can happen quickly. The problems are just too big and the solutions too few.

Now let's consider the opportunities. Many of the Eastern European countries are not that poor by international development standards. It sounds ridiculous when you think about the suffering going on there, but you have to contrast it with the suffering in other parts of the world. Their relative prosperity may permit the Eastern European countries to make a very difficult transition without getting derailed politically. Their second advantage is their location. Trade flows are still disproportionately the greatest between countries that are near one another. Therefore, the Eastern European countries benefit from being near Western Europe, which will shortly become the largest developed market in the world. Finally, these countries have highly educated work forces and are starting out with very high levels of skills. The ability of their workers to learn new skills quickly is enhanced by their high levels of educational achievement.

What are the key principles of economics that you find most useful in your work as an international economist?

I would start with comparative advantage. Students need to understand the benefits of specialization. They need to understand how differences in resource endowments and technologies can lead to differences in cost. Further, they need to recognize that not all countries can do everything well and that countries should specialize in those things they do relatively well.

I would go a step further because I'm a policy-oriented economist and say comparative advantage is to some extent inherited and to some extent created. The trick for national policymakers is to undertake policies that will either enhance the nation's comparative advantage or create new advantage by creating new skills in the work force and new technologies.

It is also important for students and policymakers to understand the role of imperfect competition. Traditional comparative advantage theory is based on the notion of perfectly functioning markets, but almost all of the industries critical to trade among the developed countries have some of the features of imperfectly competitive markets. When perfect markets don't exist, there may be a role for government intervention, since free trade does not always produce welfare-enhancing outcomes.

How would you advise a student who is setting out on the study of economics and is interested in a career that emphasizes the international aspects of our subject?

I would advise students to study comparative economics as well as international economics because it's important to understand how national economies are organized and how they interact with one another. Since how countries organize to solve their economic problems is influenced by their politics, I would also suggest that students take a course or two in political science. They should also regularly read an international economics journal, like *The Economist* or the *Financial Times*. Finally, I strongly recommend that they either work or study abroad sometime during their college career. Studying at home is an imperfect substitute for living abroad when it comes to developing a real feel for differences among nations.

CHAPTER 35

TRADING WITH THE WORLD

After studying this chapter, you will be able to:

- Describe the patterns and trends in international trade
- Explain comparative advantage
- Explain why all countries can gain from international trade
- Explain how prices adjust to bring about balanced trade
- Explain how economies of scale and diversity of taste lead to gains from international trade
- Explain why trade restrictions lower the volume of imports and exports and lower our consumption possibilities
- Explain why we have trade restrictions even though they lower our consumption possibilities

Silk Routes and Rust Belts

SINCE ANCIENT TIMES, PEOPLE HAVE STRIVEN TO EXPAND their trading as far as technology allowed. Roman coins have been found in the ruins of ancient Indian cities, and Marco Polo opened up the silk route between Europe and China in the thirteenth century. Today, container ships laden with cars and machines and Boeing 747s stuffed with farm-fresh foods ply sea and air routes, carrying billions of dollars worth of goods. Why do people go to such great lengths to trade with those in other nations? ◆◆ In recent years, a massive increase in the penetration of the foreign car industry into the United States has brought about a severe contraction of our own car industry. Jobs in Detroit and other car-producing cities have disappeared, creating what has come to be called the Rust Belt. Do the benefits of international trade make up for the cost of jobs displaced by foreign competition? Could we, as politicians often claim, improve our economy by restricting imports? ◆◆ The wages earned by the workers in the textile and electronics factories of Singapore, Taiwan, and Hong Kong are low compared with wages in the United States. Obviously, these countries can make manufactured goods much more cheaply than we can. How can we possibly compete with countries that pay their workers a fraction of U.S. wages? Are there any industries, besides perhaps the Hollywood movie industry, in which we have an advantage? ◆◆ In the 1930s, Congress passed the Smoot-Hawley Act, an act that increased taxes on imports to 60 percent, provoking widespread retaliation from the world's major trading countries. In contrast, after World War II, a process of trade liberalization brought about the creation of the General Agreement on Tariffs and Trade

(GATT) and a gradual reduction of taxes on imports. What are the effects of taxes on international trade? Why don't we have completely unrestricted international trade?

◆ ◆ ◆ ◆ In this chapter, we're going to learn about international trade. We'll discover how *all* nations can gain by specializing in producing the goods and services at which they have an advantage compared with other countries and by exchanging some of their output with each other. We'll discover that all countries can compete, no matter how high their wages. We will also explain why, despite the fact that international trade brings benefits to all, countries restrict trade. We'll discover who suffers and who benefits when international trade is restricted.

TABLE 35.1

U.S. Exports and Imports in 1990

Category	Exports	Imports	Balance
	(billions of dollars)		
Agricultural products	40.2	19.4	20.8
Industrial supplies and materials (excluding agricultural)	105.2	144.6	−39.4
Manufactured goods	244.1	333.7	−89.6
Services	133.3	106.9	26.4
Total	522.8	604.6	−81.8

Source: Survey of Current Business (December 1991), vol. 71.

Patterns and Trends in International Trade

The goods and services that we buy from people in other countries are called **imports.** The goods and services that we sell to people in other countries are called **exports.** What are the most important things that we import and export? Most people would probably guess that a rich nation such as the United States imports raw materials and exports manufactured goods. While that is one feature of U.S. international trade, it is not its most important feature. The vast bulk of our exports *and* imports is manufactured goods. We sell earth-moving equipment, airplanes, supercomputers, and scientific equipment, and we buy TVs, VCRs, blue jeans, and T-shirts. Also, we are a major exporter and importer of agricultural products and raw materials. We also import and export a huge volume of services. Let's look at the international trade of the United States in a recent year.

U.S. International Trade

Table 35.1 classifies U.S. international trade in four major categories of goods—agricultural products, industrial supplies and materials, manufactured goods, and services. The second column gives the value of U.S. exports, and the third column gives the value of U.S. imports. The fourth column tells us the balance of trade in the various categories. The **balance of trade** is the value of exports minus the value of imports. If the balance is positive, then the value of exports exceeds the value of imports and the United States is a **net exporter.** But if the balance is negative, the value of imports exceeds the value of exports and the United States is a **net importer.**

Trade in Goods About 80 percent of U.S. international trade is trade in goods, and 20 percent is trade in services. Of the categories of goods traded, by far the most important is manufactured goods. But the total value of exports of manufactured goods is less than that of imports—the United States is a net importer of manufactured goods. The United States is also a net importer of industrial supplies. It is a net exporter of agricultural products and services.

Table 35.2 highlights some of the major items of U.S. imports and exports of goods. The country's biggest net exports are aircraft, machinery, grains, and chemicals. The country's largest net imports are manufactured consumer goods, fuel, and automobiles (including auto parts).

TABLE 35.2

U.S. Exports and Imports of Goods in 1990: Some Large Individual Items

Item	Exports	Imports	Balance
	(billions of dollars)		
Aircraft	32.3	10.7	21.6
Machinery	119.8	104.6	15.2
Grains	14.9	—	14.9
Chemicals	28.4	14.3	14.1
Automobiles	37.4	87.3	−49.9
Fuels	14.0	65.7	−51.7
Manufactured consumer goods	43.3	105.7	−62.4

Source: *Survey of Current Business* (December 1991), vol. 71.

TABLE 35.3

U.S. Trade in Services in 1990

Category	Exports	Imports	Balance
	(billions of dollars)		
Travel and transportation	75.2	71.1	4.1
Other services	48.2	18.7	29.5
Military services	9.9	17.1	−7.2
Total	133.3	106.9	26.4

Source: *Survey of Current Business* (December 1991), vol. 71.

Trade in Services One fifth of U.S. international trade is not of goods but of services. You might be wondering how a country can "export" and "import" services. Let's look at some examples.

Suppose that you decided to vacation in France, traveling there on an Air France flight from New York. What you buy from Air France is not a good, but a transportation service. Although the concept might sound odd at first, in economic terms you are importing that service from France. Since you pay U.S. money to a French company in exchange for a service, it doesn't matter that most of your flight time is over the Atlantic Ocean. For that matter, the money you spend in France on hotel bills, restaurant meals, and other things is also classified as the import of services. Similarly, the vacation taken by a French student in the United States counts as an export of services to France.

When we import TV sets from South Korea, the owner of the ship that carries those TV sets might be Greek and the company that insures the cargo might be British. The payments that we make for the transportation and insurance to the Greek and British companies are also payments for the import of services. Similarly, when an American shipping company transports California wine to Tokyo, the transportation cost is an export of a service to Japan.

The importance of the various components of trade in services is set out in Table 35.3. As you can see, transportation and travel are the largest items—accounting for more than 50 percent of exports and almost 70 percent of imports.

Geographical Patterns The United States has important trading links with almost every part of the world except for Eastern Europe, where trade is almost nonexistent. As you can see from Table 35.4, our biggest trading partners are Canada and the European Community. Our *imports* from Japan and the newly industrializing countries of Asia such as Hong Kong, Singapore, South Korea, and Taiwan are also very large. Our international trade deficit is almost exclusively with this group of countries.

Trends in Trade

International trade has become an increasingly important part of our economic life. In 1950, we exported less than 5 percent of total output and imported only 4 percent of the goods and services that we consumed ourselves. Over the years since then, that percentage has steadily increased, and today it is more than double its level of 1950.

On the export side, all the major commodity categories have shared in the increased volume of international trade. Machinery, food, and raw materials have remained the most important components of

TABLE 35.4

U.S. Exports and Imports of Goods in 1990: Geographical Patterns

Country or region	Exports	Imports	Balance
	(billions of dollars)		
Canada	83.6	93.0	−9.4
Japan	48.0	89.7	−41.7
European Community	96.3	91.3	5.0
Latin America	54.3	64.3	−10.0
Other Western Europe	15.1	17.9	−2.8
Eastern Europe	4.3	2.3	2.0
Other Asia and Africa	79.2	134.7	−55.5
Australia, New Zealand, and South America	8.7	4.5	4.2
Total	389.5	497.7	−108.2

Source: Survey of Current Business (December 1991), vol. 71.

FIGURE 35.1

The U.S. Balance of Trade

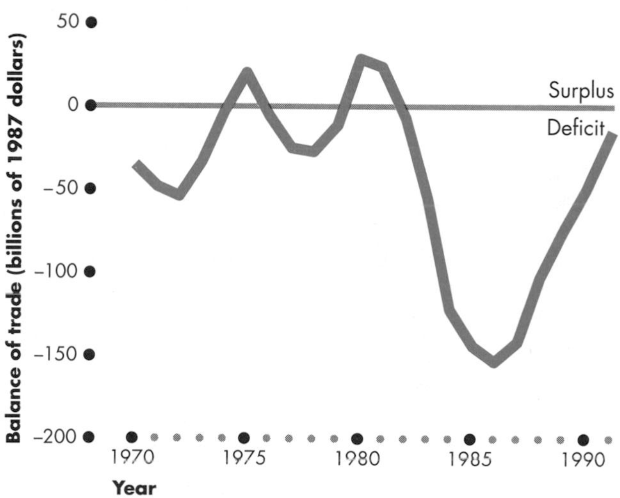

The balance of trade has fluctuated around zero, but since 1982, imports have been higher than exports and a deficit has emerged.

Source: Economic Report of the President, 1992.

exports and have roughly maintained their share in total exports.

But there have been dramatic changes in the composition of imports. Food and raw material imports have declined steadily. Imports of fuel increased dramatically in the 1970s but declined in the 1980s. Imports of machinery of all kinds, after being a fairly stable percentage of total imports until the middle 1980s, now approach 50 percent of total imports.

There have been important trends in the overall balance in U.S. international trade in recent years. That overall *balance of trade* (of goods and services) is shown in Fig. 35.1. As you can see, the balance fluctuates around zero, but in the years since 1982 there has been a large excess of imports over exports (a negative balance of trade).

Balance of Trade and International Borrowing

When people buy more than they sell, they have to finance the difference by borrowing. When they sell more than they buy, they can use the surplus to make loans to others. This simple principle that governs the income and expenditure and borrowing and lending of individuals and firms is also a feature of our balance of trade. If we import more than we export, we have to finance the difference by borrowing from foreigners. When we export more than we import, we make loans to foreigners to enable them to buy goods in excess of the value of the goods they have sold to us.

This chapter does *not* cover the factors that determine the balance of trade and the scale of the international borrowing and lending that finance that balance. It is concerned with understanding the volume, pattern, and directions of international trade rather than its balance. So that we can keep our focus on these topics, we'll build a model in which there is no international borrowing and lending—just international trade in goods and services. We'll find that we are able to understand what determines the volume, pattern, and direction of international trade and also establish its benefits and the costs of trade restrictions within this framework. This model can be expanded to include international borrowing and lending, but such an extension does not change the conclusions that we'll reach here about the factors that determine the volume, pattern, and directions of international trade.

Let's now begin to study those factors.

Opportunity Cost and Comparative Advantage

Let's apply the lessons that we learned in Chapter 3 about the gains from trade between Jane and Joe to the trade between nations. We'll begin by recalling how we can use the production possibility frontier to measure opportunity cost.

Opportunity Cost in Pioneerland

Pioneerland (a fictitious country) can produce grain and cars at any point inside or along the production possibility frontier shown in Fig. 35.2. (We're holding constant the output of all the other goods that Pioneerland produces.) The Pioneers (the people of Pioneerland) are consuming all the grain and cars that they produce, and they are operating at point *a* in the figure. That is, Pioneerland is producing and consuming 15 billion bushels of grain and 8 million cars each year. What is the opportunity cost of a car in Pioneerland?

We can answer that question by calculating the slope of the production possibility frontier at point *a*. As we discovered in Chapter 3 (pp. 54–56), the slope of the frontier measures the opportunity cost of one good in terms of the other. To measure the slope of the frontier at point *a*, place a straight line tangential to the frontier at point *a* and calculate the slope of that straight line. Recall that the formula for the slope of a line is the change in the value of the variable measured on the y-axis divided by the change in the value of the variable measured on the x-axis as we move along the line. Here, the variable measured on the y-axis is billions of bushels of grain, and the variable measured on the x-axis is millions of cars. So the slope (opportunity cost) is

FIGURE 35.2

Opportunity Cost in Pioneerland

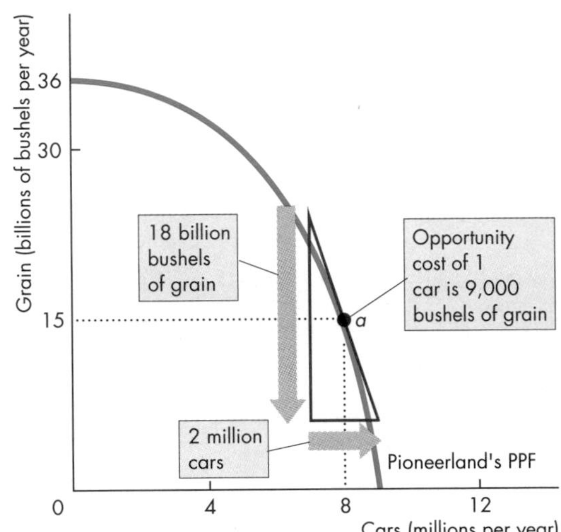

Pioneerland produces and consumes 15 billion bushels of grain and 8 million cars a year. That is, it produces and consumes at point *a* on its production possibility frontier. Opportunity cost is measured as the slope of the production possibility frontier. At point *a*, 2 million cars cost 18 billion bushels of grain. Equivalently, 1 car costs 9,000 bushels of grain or 9,000 bushels cost 1 car.

the change in the number of bushels of grain divided by the change in the number of cars. As you can see from the red triangle at point *a* in the figure, if the number of cars produced increases by 2 million, grain production decreases by 18 billion bushels. Therefore the slope is 18 billion divided by 2 million, which equals 9,000. To get one more car, the people of Pioneerland must give up 9,000 bushels of grain. Thus the opportunity cost of 1 car is 9,000 bushels of grain. Equivalently, 9,000 bushels of grain cost 1 car.

Opportunity Cost in Magic Empire

Now consider the production possibility frontier in Magic Empire (another fictitious country and the only other country in our model world). Figure 35.3 illustrates its production possibility frontier. Like the Pioneers, the Magicians (the people in Magic Empire) consume all the grain and cars that they produce. Magic Empire consumes 18 billion bushels of grain a year and 4 million cars, at point *a*'.

FIGURE 35.3

Opportunity Cost in Magic Empire

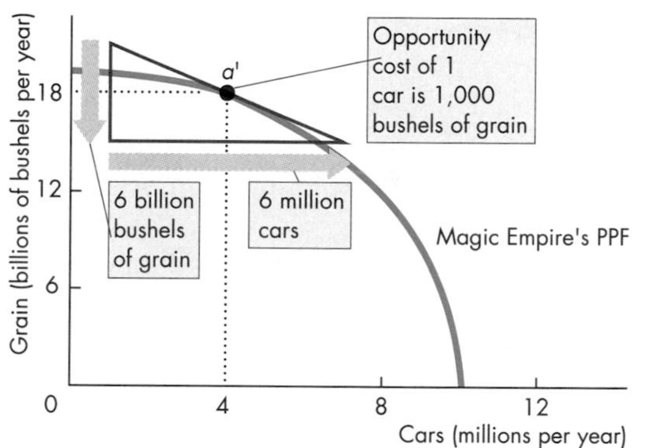

Magic Empire produces and consumes 18 billion bushels of grain and 4 million cars a year. That is, it produces and consumes at point *a*' on its production possibility frontier. Opportunity cost is measured as the slope of the production possibility frontier. At point *a*', 6 million cars cost 6 billion bushels of grain. Equivalently, 1 car costs 1,000 bushels of grain or 1,000 bushels cost 1 car.

We can do the same kind of calculation of opportunity cost for Magic Empire as we have just done for Pioneerland. At point *a*', 1 car costs 1,000 bushels of grain, or, equivalently, 1,000 bushels of grain costs 1 car.

Comparative Advantage

Cars are cheaper in Magic Empire than in Pioneerland. One car costs 9,000 bushels of grain in Pioneerland but only 1,000 bushels of grain in Magic Empire. But grain is cheaper in Pioneerland than in Magic Empire—9,000 bushels of grain cost only 1 car in Pioneerland, while that same amount of grain costs 9 cars in Magic Empire.

Magic Empire has a comparative advantage in car production. Pioneerland has a comparative advantage in grain production. A country has a **comparative advantage** in producing a good if it can produce that good at a lower opportunity cost than any other country can. Let's see how opportunity cost differences and comparative advantage generate gains from international trade.

The Gains from Trade

If Magic Empire bought grain for what it costs Pioneerland to produce it, then Magic Empire could buy 9,000 bushels of grain for 1 car. That is much lower than the cost of growing grain in Magic Empire, since there it costs 9 cars to produce 9,000 bushels of grain. If the Magicians buy at the low Pioneerland price, they will reap some gains.

If the Pioneers buy cars for what it costs Magic Empire to produce them, they will be able to obtain a car for 1,000 bushels of grain. Since it costs 9,000 bushels of grain to produce a car in Pioneerland, the Pioneers would gain from such an activity.

In this situation, it makes sense for Magicians to buy their grain from Pioneers and for Pioneers to buy their cars from Magicians. Let's see how such profitable international trade comes about.

Reaping the Gains from Trade

We've seen that the Pioneers would like to buy their cars from the Magicians and that the Magicians would like to buy their grain from the Pioneers. Let's see how the two groups do business with each other, concentrating attention on the international market for cars.

Figure 35.4 illustrates such a market. The quantity of cars traded internationally is measured on the horizontal axis. On the vertical axis we measure the price of a car, but it is expressed as its opportunity cost—the number of bushels of grain that a car costs. If no international trade takes place, that price in Pioneerland is 9,000 bushels of grain, indicated by point *a* in the figure. Again, if no trade takes place, that price is 1,000 bushels of grain in Magic Empire, indicated by point *a*' in the figure.

The points *a* and *a*' in Fig. 35.4 correspond to the points identified by those same letters in Figs. 35.2 and 35.3. The lower the price of a car (in terms of bushels of grain), the greater is the quantity of cars that the Pioneers import from the Magicians. This fact is illustrated in the downward-sloping curve that shows Pioneerland's import demand for cars.

FIGURE 35.4

International Trade in Cars

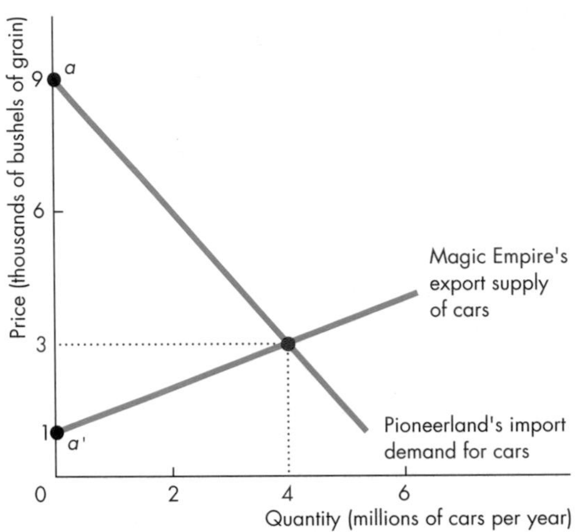

As the price of a car decreases, the quantity of imports demanded by Pioneerland increases—Pioneerland's import demand curve for cars is downward-sloping. As the price of a car increases, the quantity of cars supplied by Magic Empire for export increases—Magic Empire's export supply curve of cars is upward-sloping. Without international trade, the price of a car is 9,000 bushels of grain in Pioneerland (point *a*) and 1,000 bushels of grain in Magic Empire (point *a'*). With free international trade, the price of a car is determined where the export supply curve intersects the import demand curve—a price of 3,000 bushels of grain. At that price, 4 million cars a year are imported by Pioneerland and exported by Magic Empire. The value of grain exported by Pioneerland and imported by Magic Empire is 12 billion bushels a year, the quantity required to pay for the cars imported.

The Magicians respond in the opposite direction. The higher the price of cars (in terms of bushels of grain), the greater is the quantity of cars that Magicians export to Pioneers. This fact is reflected in Magic Empire's export supply of cars—the upward-sloping line in the figure.

The international market in cars determines the equilibrium price and quantity traded. This equilibrium occurs where the import demand curve intersects the export supply curve. In this case, the equilibrium price of a car is 3,000 bushels of grain. Four million cars a year are exported by Magic Empire and imported by Pioneerland. Notice that the price at which cars are traded is lower than the initial price in Pioneerland but higher than the initial price in Magic Empire.

Balanced Trade

Notice that the number of cars exported by Magic Empire—4 million a year—is exactly equal to the number of cars imported by Pioneerland. How does Pioneerland pay for its cars? By exporting grain. How much grain does Pioneerland export? You can find the answer by noticing that for 1 car, Pioneerland has to pay 3,000 bushels of grain. Hence for 4 million cars they have to pay 12 billion bushels of grain. Thus Pioneerland's exports of grain are 12 billion bushels a year. Magic Empire imports this same quantity of grain.

Magic Empire is exchanging 4 million cars for 12 billion bushels of grain each year, and Pioneerland is doing the opposite, exchanging 12 billion bushels of grain for 4 million cars. Trade is balanced between these two countries. The value received from exports equals the value paid out for imports.

Changes in Production and Consumption

We've seen that international trade makes it possible for Pioneers to buy cars at a lower price than that at which they can produce them for themselves. It also enables Magicians to sell their cars for a higher price, which is equivalent to saying that Magicians can buy grain for a lower price. Thus everybody seems to gain. Magicians buy grain at a lower price, and Pioneers buy cars at a lower price. How is it possible for everyone to gain? What are the changes in production and consumption that accompany these gains?

An economy that does not trade with other economies has identical production and consumption possibilities. Without trade, the economy can consume only what it produces. But with international trade, an economy can consume different quantities of goods from those that it produces. The production possibility frontier describes the limit of what a country can produce, but it does not describe the limits to what it can consume. Figure 35.5 will help you to see the distinction between production possibilities and consumption possibilities when a country trades with other countries.

First of all, notice that the figure has two parts, part (a) for Pioneerland and part (b) for Magic Empire. The production possibility frontiers that you saw in Figs. 35.2 and 35.3 are reproduced here. The slopes of the two black lines in the figure represent the opportunity costs in the two countries when

FIGURE 35.5

Expanding Consumption Possibilities

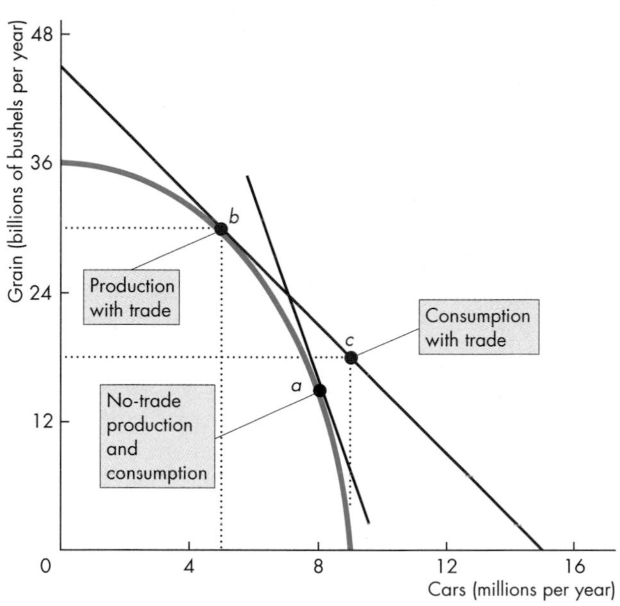

(a) Pioneerland

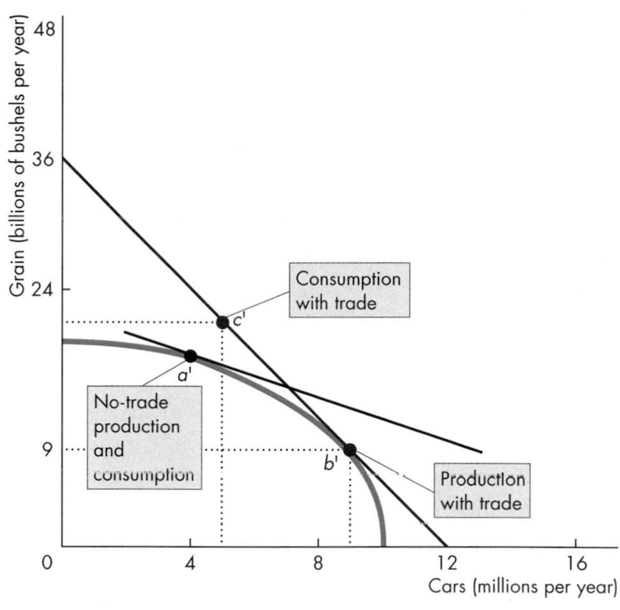

(b) Magic Empire

With no international trade, the Pioneers produce and consume at point *a* and the opportunity cost of a car is 9,000 bushels of grain (the slope of the black line in part a). Also, with no international trade, the Magicians produce and consume at point *a*' and the opportunity cost of 1,000 bushels of grain is 1 car (the slope of the black line in part b).

Goods can be exchanged internationally at a price of 3,000 bushels of grain for 1 car along the red line. In part (a), Pioneerland decreases its production of cars and increases its production of grain, moving from *a* to *b*. It exports grain and imports cars, and it consumes at point *c*. The Pioneers have more of both cars and grain than they would if they produced all their own consumption goods—at point *a*. In part (b), Magic Empire increases car production and decreases grain production, moving from *a*' to *b*'. Magic Empire exports cars and imports grain, and it consumes at point *c*'. The Magicians have more of both cars and grain than they would if they produced all their own consumption goods—at point *a*'.

there is no international trade. Pioneerland produces and consumes at point *a*, and Magic Empire produces and consumes at *a*'. Cars cost 9,000 bushels of grain in Pioneerland and 1,000 bushels of grain in Magic Empire.

Consumption Possibilities The countries' consumption possibilities with international trade are shown by the two red lines in Fig. 35.5. These lines in both parts of the figure have the same slope, and that slope is the opportunity cost of a car in terms of grain on the world market—3,000 bushels per car. The *slope* of the consumption possibilities line is common to both countries because it is determined by the *world* price. But the position of a country's consumption possibilities line depends on its production possibilities. A country cannot produce outside its production possibility curve, so its consumption possibilities curve touches its production possibility curve. Thus Pioneerland could choose to consume what it produces, at point *b*, and not trade internationally or to trade internationally and consume at a point on its red consumption possibilities line.

Free Trade Equilibrium With international trade, the producers of cars in Magic Empire can get a higher price for their output. As a result, they increase the quantity of car production. At the same time, grain producers in Magic Empire are getting a lower price for their grain and so they reduce production. Producers in Magic Empire adjust their output until the opportunity cost in Magic Empire equals the opportunity cost in the world market. This situation arises when Magic Empire is producing at point *b*' in Fig. 35.5(b).

But the Magicians do not consume at point *b*'. That is, they do not increase their consumption of cars and decrease their consumption of grain. They sell some of the cars they produce to Pioneerland in exchange for some of Pioneerland's grain. But to see how that works out, we first need to check in with Pioneerland to see what's happening there.

In Pioneerland, cars are now less expensive and grain more expensive than before. As a consequence, producers in Pioneerland decrease car production and increase grain production. They do so until the opportunity cost of a car in terms of grain equals the cost on the world market. They move to point *b* in part (a). But the Pioneers do not consume at point *b*. They exchange some of the additional grain they produce for the now cheaper cars from Magic Empire.

The figure shows us the quantities consumed in the two countries. We saw in Fig. 35.4 that Magic Empire exports 4 million cars a year and Pioneerland imports those cars. We also saw that Pioneerland exports 12 billion bushels of grain a year and Magic Empire imports that grain. Thus Pioneerland's consumption of grain is 12 billion bushels a year less than it produces, and its consumption of cars is 4 million a year more than it produces. Pioneerland consumes at point *c* in Fig. 35.5(a).

Similarly, we know that Magic Empire consumes 12 billion bushels of grain more than it produces and 4 million cars fewer than it produces. Thus Magic Empire consumes at *c*' in Fig. 35.5(b).

Calculating the Gains from Trade

You can now literally "see" the gains from trade in Fig. 35.5. Without trade, Pioneers produce and consume at *a* (part a)—a point on Pioneerland's production possibility frontier. With international trade, Pioneers consume at point *c* in part (a)—a point *outside* the production possibility frontier. At point *c*, Pioneers are consuming 3 billion bushels of grain a year and 1 million cars a year more than before. These increases in consumption of cars and grain, beyond the limits of the production possibility frontier, are the gains from international trade.

But Magicians also gain. Without trade, they consume at point *a*' in part (b)—a point on Magic Empire's production possibility frontier. With international trade, they consume at point *c*'—a point outside the production possibility frontier. With international trade, Magic Empire consumes 3 billion bushels of grain a year and 1 million cars a year more than without trade. These are the gains from international trade for Magic Empire.

Gains for All

When Pioneers and Magicians trade with each other, potentially everyone can gain. Domestic sellers add the net demand of foreigners to their domestic demand, and so their market expands. Buyers are faced with domestic supply plus net foreign supply and so have a larger total supply available to them. As you know, prices increase when there is an increase in demand and they decrease when there is an increase in supply. Thus the increased demand (from foreigners) for exports increases their price and the increased supply (from foreigners) of imports decreases their price. Gains in one country do not bring losses in another. Everyone, in this example, gains from international trade.

Absolute Advantage

Suppose that in Magic Empire, fewer workers are needed to produce any given output of either grain or cars than in Pioneerland—productivity is higher in Magic Empire than in Pioneerland. In this situation, Magic Empire has an *absolute advantage* over Pioneerland. We defined absolute advantage in Chapter 3 in terms of an individual. If one person has greater productivity than another in the production of all goods, that person is said to have an absolute advantage. A country has an absolute advantage if it has greater productivity than another country in the production of all goods. With an absolute advantage, isn't it the case that Magic Empire can outsell Pioneerland in all markets? Why, if Magic Kingdom has greater productivity than Pioneerland, does it pay Magic Empire to buy *anything* from Pioneerland?

The answer is that the cost of production in terms of the factors of production employed is irrelevant for determining the gains from trade. It does not matter how much labor, land, and capital are required to produce 1,000 bushels of grain or a car.

What matters is how many cars must be given up to produce more grain or how much grain must be given up to produce more cars. That is, what matters is the opportunity cost of one good in terms of the other good. Magic Empire may have an absolute advantage in the production of all things, but it cannot have a comparative advantage in the production of all goods. The statement that the opportunity cost of cars in Magic Empire is lower than in Pioneerland is identical to the statement that the opportunity cost of grain is higher in Magic Empire than that in Pioneerland. Thus *whenever opportunity costs diverge, everyone has a comparative advantage in something*. All countries can potentially gain from international trade.

The story of the discovery of the logic of the gains from international trade is presented in Our Advancing Knowledge on pp. 964–965.

REVIEW

When countries have divergent opportunity costs, they can gain from international trade. Each country can buy goods and services from another country at a lower opportunity cost than that at which it can produce them for itself. Gains arise when each country increases its production of those goods and services in which it has a comparative advantage (of goods and services that it can produce at an opportunity cost that is lower than that of other countries) and exchanges some of its production for that of other countries. All countries gain from international trade. Everyone has a comparative advantage at something. ◆

Gains from Trade in Reality

The gains from trade that we have just studied between Pioneerland and Magic Empire in grain and cars are taking place in a model economy—in an economy that we have imagined. But these same phenomena are occurring every minute of every day in real-world economies. We buy cars made in Japan, and American producers of grain and lumber sell large parts of their output to Japanese households and firms. We buy cars and machinery from European producers and sell airplanes and computers to Europeans in return. We buy shirts and fashion goods from the people of Hong Kong and sell them machinery in return. We buy TV sets and VCRs from South Korea and Taiwan and sell them financial and other services as well as manufactured goods in return.

Thus much of the international trade that we see in the real world takes precisely the form of the trade that we have studied in our model of the world economy. But as we discovered earlier in this chapter, a great deal of world trade is heavily concentrated among industrial countries and primarily involves the international exchange of manufactured goods. Thus the type of trade that we have just analyzed—exchanging cars for grain—although an important and clearly profitable type of trade, is not the most prominent type. Why do countries exchange manufactured goods with each other? Can our model of international trade explain such exchange?

Trade in Similar Goods

At first thought, it seems puzzling that countries would trade manufactured goods. Consider, for example, America's trade in automobiles and auto parts. Why does it make sense for the United States to produce automobiles for export and at the same time to import large quantities of them from Canada, Japan, Korea, and Western Europe? Wouldn't it make more sense to produce all the cars that we buy here in the United States? After all, we have access to the best technology available for producing cars. Auto workers in the United States are surely as productive as their fellow workers in Canada, Western Europe, and the Pacific countries. Capital equipment, production lines, robots, and the like used in the manufacture of cars are as available to American car producers as they are to any others. This line of reasoning leaves a puzzle concerning the sources of international exchange of similar commodities produced by similar people using similar equipment. Why does it happen?

Diversity of Taste The first part of the answer to the puzzle is that people have a tremendous diversity of taste. Let's stick with the example of cars. Some people prefer a sports car, some prefer a limousine, some prefer a regular, full-size car, and some prefer a compact. In addition to size and type of car, there are many other dimensions on which cars vary.

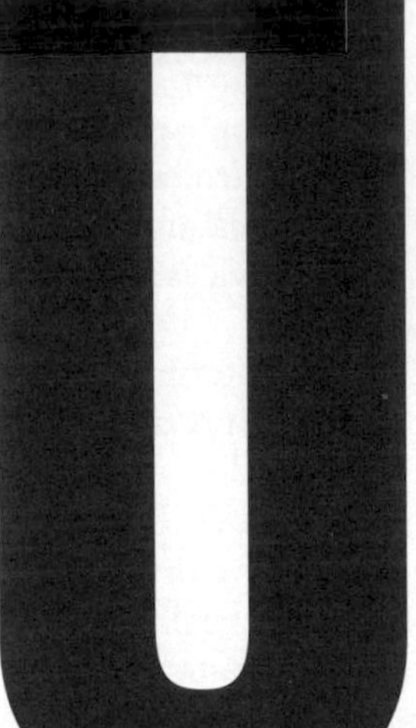

NDERSTANDING the Gains from INTERNATIONAL TRADE

Until the mid-eighteenth century, it was generally believed that the purpose of international trade was to keep exports above imports and pile up gold. If gold was accumulated, it was believed, the nation would prosper; and if gold was lost through an international deficit, the nation would be drained of money and be impoverished. These beliefs are called *mercantilism,* and the *mercantilists* were pamphleteers who advocated with missionary fervor the pursuit of an international surplus. If exports did not exceed imports, the mercantilists wanted imports restricted.

In the 1740s, David Hume explained that as the quantity of money (gold) changes, so also does the price level, and the nation's *real* wealth is unaffected. In the 1770s, Adam Smith explained that restricting imports lowers the gains from specialization and makes a nation poorer. Mercantilism was intellectually bankrupt.

Gradually, through the nineteenth century, the mercantilists' influence waned, and North America and Western Europe prospered in an environment of increasingly free international trade. But despite remarkable advances in economic understanding, mercantilism never quite died. It had a brief and devastating revival in the 1920s and 1930s, when tariff hikes brought about the collapse of international trade and accentuated the Great Depression. It subsided again after World War II with the establishment of the General Agreement on Tariffs and Trade (GATT).

But mercantilism lingers on. The often expressed view that the United States should restrict Japanese imports and reduce its deficit with Japan is a modern manifestation of mercantilism. It would be interesting to have Hume and Smith commenting on these views. But we know what they would say—the same things that they said to the eighteenth-century mercantilists. And they would still be right.

"Free trade, one of the greatest blessings which a government can confer on a people, is in almost every country unpopular."

THOMAS MACAULAY
Essay on Mitford's History of Greece

Merchants' Express Line of Clipper Ships for San Francisco.
Despatching the greatest number of vessels, and only those standing in the first-class in all respects.
THE SPLENDID A I CLIPPER SHIP
W. B. DINSMORE
FOSTER Commander,
IS LOADING AT PIER 13 EAST RIVER.
As this very fine vessel was BUILT for the trade, it is scarcely necessary to say that she combines all of the necessary qualifications, viz. :—strength, speed and good ventilation. Early despatch may be relied upon.
D. S. STETSON & CO.,
112 North Wharves, Philadelphia.
Agents in San Francisco,
Messrs. De Witt, Kittle & Co.

In the eighteenth century, when mercantilists and economists were debating the pros and cons of free international exchange, the transportation technology available severely limited the gains from international trade. Sailing ships with tiny cargo holds took close to a month to cross the Atlantic Ocean. But the potential gains were large and so was the incentive to cut shipping costs. By the 1850s, the clipper ship had been developed, cutting the time for the journey from Boston to Liverpool to only 12¼ days. Half a century later, 10,000-ton steamships were sailing between America and England in just 4 days. As sailing times and costs declined, the gains from international trade increased and the volume of trade expanded.

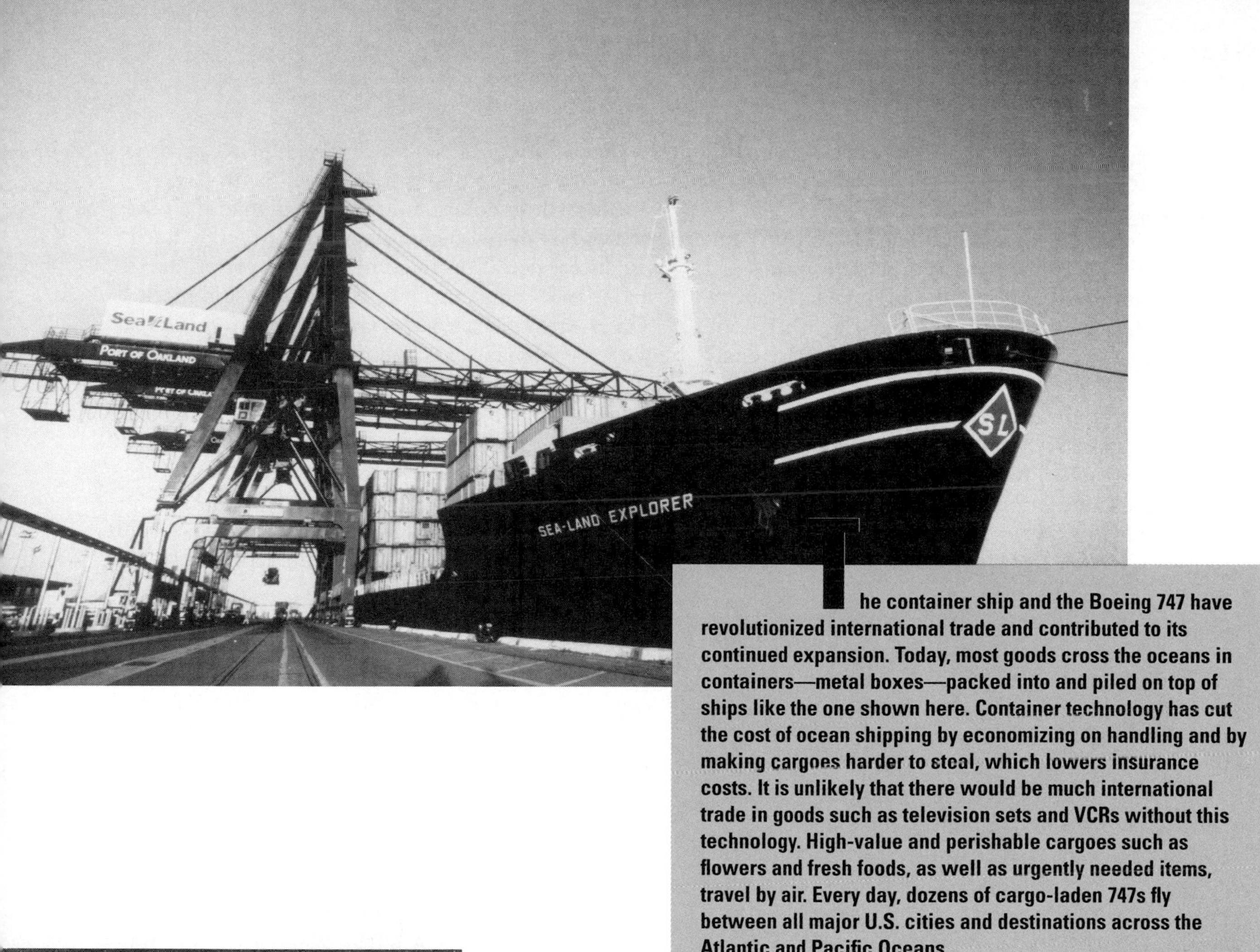

The container ship and the Boeing 747 have revolutionized international trade and contributed to its continued expansion. Today, most goods cross the oceans in containers—metal boxes—packed into and piled on top of ships like the one shown here. Container technology has cut the cost of ocean shipping by economizing on handling and by making cargoes harder to steal, which lowers insurance costs. It is unlikely that there would be much international trade in goods such as television sets and VCRs without this technology. High-value and perishable cargoes such as flowers and fresh foods, as well as urgently needed items, travel by air. Every day, dozens of cargo-laden 747s fly between all major U.S. cities and destinations across the Atlantic and Pacific Oceans.

From Smith & Ricardo To GATT

David Ricardo (1772–1832) was a highly successful 27-year-old stockbroker when he stumbled on a copy of Adam Smith's *Wealth of Nations* on a weekend visit to the country. He was immediately hooked and went on to become the most celebrated economist of his age and one of the greatest economists of all time. One of his many contributions was to develop the principle of comparative advantage, the foundation on which the modern theory of international trade is built. The example he used to illustrate this principle was the trade between England and Portugal in cloth and wine.

The General Agreement on Tariffs and Trade (GATT) was established as a reaction against the devastation wrought by beggar-my-neighbor tariffs imposed during the 1920s. But it is also a triumph for the logic first worked out by Smith and Ricardo.

Some have low fuel consumption, some have high performance, some are spacious and comfortable, some have a large trunk, some have four-wheel drive, some have front-wheel drive, some have manual transmission, some have automatic transmission, some are durable, some are flashy, some have a radiator grill that looks like a Greek temple, others look like a wedge. People's preferences across these many dimensions vary.

The tremendous diversity in tastes for cars means that people would be dissatisfied if they were forced to consume from a limited range of standardized cars. People value variety and are willing to pay for it in the marketplace.

Economies of Scale The second part of the answer to the puzzle is economies of scale. *Economies of scale* are the tendency, present in many production processes, for the average cost of production to be lower, the larger the scale of production. In such situations, larger and larger production runs lead to ever lower average production costs. Many manufactured goods, including cars, experience economies of scale. For example, if a car producer makes only a few hundred (or perhaps a few thousand) cars of a particular type and design, the producer has to use production techniques that are much more labor-intensive and much less automated than those actually employed to make hundreds of thousands of cars in a particular model. With low production runs and labor-intensive production techniques, costs are high. With very large production runs and automated assembly lines, production costs are much lower. But to obtain lower costs, the automated assembly lines have to produce a large number of cars.

It is the combination of diversity of taste and economies of scale that produces such a large amount of international trade in similar commodities. Diversity of taste and the willingness to pay for variety do not guarantee that variety will be available. It could simply be too expensive to provide a highly diversified range of different types of cars, for example. If every car bought in the United States today was made in the United States and if the present range of diversity and variety was available, production runs would be remarkably short. Car producers would not be able to reap economies of scale. Although the current variety of cars could be made available, it would be at a very high price, perhaps at a price that no one would be willing to pay.

But with international trade, each manufacturer of cars has the whole world market to serve. Each producer specializes in a limited range of products and then sells its output to the entire world market. This arrangement enables large production runs on the most popular cars and feasible production runs even on the most customized cars demanded by only a handful of people.

The situation in the market for cars is also present in many other industries, especially those producing specialized machinery and specialized machine tools. Thus international exchange of similar but slightly differentiated manufactured products is a highly profitable activity.

This type of trade can be understood with exactly the same model of international trade that we studied earlier. Although we normally think of cars as a single commodity, we simply have to think of sports cars, sedans, and so on as different goods. Different countries, by specializing in a few of these "goods," are able to enjoy economies of scale and, therefore, a comparative advantage in their production.

You can see that comparative advantage and international trade bring gains regardless of the goods being traded. When the rich countries of the European Community, Japan, and the United States import raw materials from the Third World and from Australia and Canada, the rich importing countries gain and so do the exporting countries. When we buy cheap TV sets, VCRs, shirts, and other goods from low-wage countries, both we and the exporters gain from the exchange. It's true that if we increase our imports of cars and produce fewer cars ourselves, jobs in our car industry disappear. But jobs in other industries, industries in which we have a comparative advantage and supply to other nations, expand. After the adjustment is completed, people whose jobs have been lost find employment in the expanding industries. They buy goods produced in other countries at even lower prices than those at which the goods were available before. The gains from international trade are not gains for some at the expense of losses for others.

But changes in comparative advantage that lead to changes in international trade patterns can take a long time to adjust to. For example, the increase in automobile imports and the corresponding relative decline in domestic car production have not brought increased wealth for displaced auto workers. Good new jobs take time to find, and often people go through a period of prolonged search, putting up with inferior jobs and lower wages than they had before. Thus only in the long run does everyone potentially gain from international specialization and exchange. Short-run adjustment costs that can be large and relatively prolonged are borne by the people who have lost their comparative advantage. Some of the people who lose their jobs may be too old for it to be worth their while to make the move to another region of the country or industry, and so they never share in the gains.

Partly because of the costs of adjustment to changing international trade patterns, but partly also for other reasons, governments intervene in international trade, restricting its volume. Let's examine what happens when governments restrict international trade. We'll contrast restricted trade with free trade. We'll see that free trade brings the greatest possible benefits. We'll also see why, in spite of the benefits of free trade, governments sometimes restrict trade.

Trade Restrictions

Governments restrict international trade in order to protect domestic industries from foreign competition. The restriction of international trade is called **protectionism.** There are two main protectionist methods employed by governments:

- Tariffs
- Nontariff barriers

A **tariff** is a tax that is imposed by the importing country when a good crosses an international boundary. A **nontariff barrier** is any action other than a tariff that restricts international trade. Examples of nontariff barriers are quantitative restrictions and licensing regulations limiting imports. We'll consider nontariff barriers in more detail below. First, let's look at tariffs.

The History of Tariffs

Average tariff levels in the United States today are quite modest compared with their historical levels. As you can see from Fig. 35.6, tariff levels averaged around 40 percent before World War II. During the 1930s, with the passage of the Smoot-Hawley Act, they reached 60 percent. Today, average tariffs are only 4 percent of total imports and 6 percent of the value of those imports that are subject to a tariff.

The reduction in tariffs followed the establishment of the General Agreement on Tariffs and Trade (GATT). The **General Agreement on Tariffs and Trade** is an international agreement designed to limit government intervention to restrict international trade. It was negotiated immediately following World War II and was signed in October 1947. Its goal is to liberalize trading activity and to provide an organization to administer more liberal trading arrangements. GATT itself is a small organization located in Geneva, Switzerland.

Since the formation of GATT, several rounds of negotiations have taken place that have resulted in general tariff reductions. One of these, the Kennedy Round, which began in the early 1960s, resulted in large tariff cuts in the late 1960s. Yet further tariff cuts resulted from the Tokyo Round, which took place between 1973 and 1979, and the Uruguay Round of the late 1980s and early 1990s.

In addition to the agreements under the GATT, the United States is a party to several important trade agreements with individual countries. One of these is the Canada–United States free trade agreement that became effective on January 1, 1989. Under this agreement, barriers to international trade between Canada and the United States will be virtually eliminated after a ten-year phasing-in period. Another important development is an attempt to work out a free trade deal with Mexico that could create a large North American free trade area embracing Mexico, Canada, and the United States. Within Western Europe, trade barriers among the member countries of the European Community were virtually eliminated by 1992, creating the largest unified tariff-free market in the world.

The benefits of free trade, both in theory and in the recent experience of the countries of the European Community, have given impetus to a series of talks among the countries of Central and South America aimed at creating a series of free-trade

FIGURE 35.6

U.S. Tariffs: 1900–1990

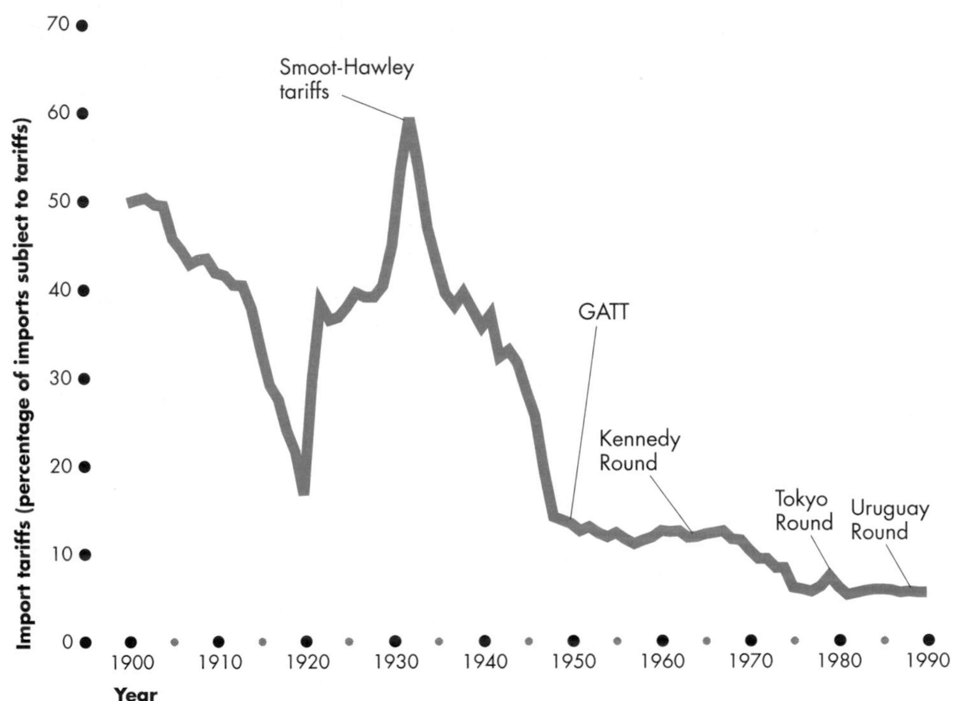

Tariffs in the United States averaged around 40 percent before World War II. In the early 1930s, they increased to 60 percent with the passage of the Smoot-Hawley Act. Since the establishment of GATT following World War II, tariffs have steadily declined in a series of negotiating rounds and are now at the lowest level they have ever been.

Sources: U.S. Bureau of the Census, *Historical Statistics of the United States, Colonial Times to 1970, Bicentennial Edition, Part 1* (Washington D.C.: 1975); Series U-212: *Statistical Abstract of the United States: 1986,* 106th edition (Washington, D.C.: 1985); and *Statistical Abstract of the United States: 1991,* 111th edition (Washington, D.C.: 1991).

agreements among these countries and, even more ambitiously, free-trade American continents. This movement is discussed in Reading Between the Lines on pp. 970–971.

The talks taking place among the countries of North and South America underline the fact that despite a steady process of tariff reductions, trade among some countries and trade in some goods are still subject to extremely high tariffs. The highest tariffs faced by U.S. buyers are those on textiles and footwear. A tariff of more than 10 percent (on the average) is imposed on almost all our imports of textiles and footwear. For example, when you buy a pair of blue jeans for $20, you pay about $5 more than you would if there were no tariffs on textiles. Other goods protected by tariffs are agricultural products, automobiles, energy and chemicals, minerals, and metals. Almost all the meat and cheese that you consume costs significantly more because of protection than it would with free international trade.

The temptation for governments to impose tariffs is a strong one. First, tariffs provide revenue to the government. Second, they enable the government to satisfy special interest groups in import-competing industries. But, as we'll see, free international trade brings enormous benefits that are reduced when tariffs are imposed. Let's see how.

How Tariffs Work

To analyze how tariffs work, let's return to the example of trade between Pioneerland and Magic Empire. Suppose that these two countries are trading cars and grain in exactly the same way that we analyzed before. Magic Empire exports cars, and Pioneerland exports grain. The volume of car imports into Pioneerland is 4 million a year, and cars are selling on the world market for 3,000 bushels of grain. Let's suppose that grain costs $1 a bushel, so, equivalently, cars are selling for $3,000. Figure 35.7 illustrates this situation. The volume of trade in cars and their price are determined at the point of intersection of Magic Empire's export supply curve of cars and Pioneerland's import demand curve for cars.

Now suppose that the government of Pioneerland, perhaps under pressure from car producers, decides to impose a tariff on imported cars. In particular, suppose that a tariff of $4,000 per car is imposed. (This is a huge tariff, but the car producers of Pioneerland are pretty fed up with competition from Magic Empire.) What happens?

The first part of the answer is obtained by studying the effects on the supply of cars in Pioneerland. Cars are no longer going to be available at the Magic Empire export supply price. The tariff of $4,000 must be added to that price—the amount paid to the government of Pioneerland on each car imported. As a consequence, the supply curve in Pioneerland shifts upward as shown in Fig. 35.7. The new supply curve becomes that labeled "Magic Empire's export supply of cars plus tariff." The vertical distance between Magic Empire's export supply curve and the new supply curve is the tariff imposed by the government of Pioneerland.

The next part of the answer is found by determining the new equilibrium. Imposing a tariff has no effect on the demand for cars in Pioneerland and so has no effect on Pioneerland's import demand for cars. The new equilibrium occurs where the new supply curve intersects Pioneerland's import demand curve for cars. That equilibrium is at a price of $6,000 a car with 2 million cars a year being imported. Imports fall from 4 million to 2 million cars a year. At the higher price of $6,000 a car, domestic car producers increase their production. Domestic grain production decreases to free up the resources for the expanded car industry.

The total expenditure on imported cars by the Pioneers is $6,000 a car multiplied by the 2 million cars imported ($12 billion). But not all of that money goes to the Magicians. They receive $2,000 a car, or $4 billion for the 2 million cars. The difference—$4,000 a car, or a total of $8 billion for the 2 million cars—is collected by the government of Pioneerland as tariff revenue.

Obviously, the government of Pioneerland is happy with this situation. It is now collecting $8 billion that it didn't have before. But what about the Pioneers? How do they view the new situation? The demand curve tells us the maximum price that a buyer is willing to pay for one more unit of a good. As you can see from Pioneerland's import demand curve for cars, if one more car could be imported, someone would be willing to pay almost $6,000 for it. Magic Empire's export supply curve of cars tells us the minimum price at which additional cars are available. As you can see, one additional car would be supplied by Magic Empire for a price only slightly more than $2,000. Thus, since someone is willing to pay almost $6,000 for a car and someone is willing to supply one for little more than $2,000, there is obviously a gain to be had from trading an extra car. In fact, there are gains to be had—willingness to pay exceeds the minimum supply price—all the way up to 4 million cars a year. Only when 4 million cars are being traded is the maximum price that a Pioneer is willing to pay equal to the minimum price that is acceptable to a Magician. Thus restricting

FIGURE 35.7

The Effects of a Tariff

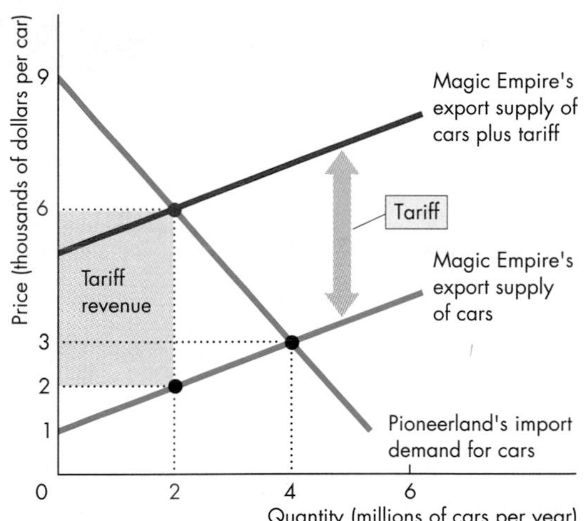

Pioneerland imposes a tariff on car imports from Magic Empire. The tariff increases the price that Pioneers have to pay for cars. It shifts the supply curve of cars in Pioneerland upward. The distance between the original supply curve and the new one is the amount of the tariff. The price of cars in Pioneerland increases, and the quantity of cars imported decreases. The government of Pioneerland collects a tariff revenue of $4,000 per car—a total of $8 billion on the 2 million cars imported. Pioneerland's exports of grain decrease, since Magic Empire now has a lower income from its exports of cars.

The Gains from Trade in Action

THE ECONOMIST, JANUARY 4, 1992

Free-trade free-for-all

Having spent the 1950s and 1960s building the non-communist world's most impenetrable trade barriers, Latin America is pulling them down as fast as it can . . ., preparing the way for a single Latin American trade block. In fact the dream of most Latin American countries is to join, together or alone, with a North American Free-Trade Area of Mexico, Canada and the United States. . . .

The first pillar in this ambitious and hurried edifice is this month's free-trade pact between Venezuela, Colombia and Bolivia. Peru and Ecuador will join the pact in six months' time. . . .

[A] . . . free-trade agreement [is] being forged by Argentina, Brazil, Uruguay and Paraguay. Called Mercosur, it originated in 1988 as a free-trade pact between Brazil and Argentina and was expanded to embrace Uruguay and Paraguay last March. By the end of 1994 it is supposed to enshrine a completely free market in goods, services and labour for Argentina and Brazil, with Uruguay and Paraguay following a year later. . . .

Two other pacts are in the offing. Central America is trying to revive its common market, which was set up in the 1960s. It collapsed in 1969, when war broke out between Honduras and El Salvador. . . .

Lastly, there is the customs union that . . . the English-speaking Caribbean countries under the auspices of the Caribbean Community (Caricom) [are attempting to establish]. . . .

The real prize is . . . the establishment of a pan-American free-trade area. . . . Since 1987 the United States has signed 16 "framework" agreements with Latin American countries. In theory these are agreements merely to talk about trade. In practice, they are paving the way for a trade block embracing all the Americas.

Achieving such a goal depends almost entirely upon success of the free-trade agreement that the United States is negotiating with Mexico. Once this is approved by Congress, other Latin American governments might accede to it, just as new members join the EC. A stampede to join is expected. . . .

The Essence of the Story

Among Latin American countries, trade barriers are high, but a movement is underway to lower them.

Four agreements are being forged:

- The Andean Pact between Bolivia, Colombia, Ecuador, Peru, and Venezuela
- Mercosur, a free-trade area embracing Argentina, Brazil, Uruguay, and Paraguay
- The Central American common market embracing Costa Rica, El Salvador, Guatemala, Honduras, and Nicaragua
- Caricom, a customs union among the English-speaking Caribbean countries

Since 1987 the United States has signed 16 "framework" agreements to talk about trade with Latin American countries. These agreements are paving the way for a trade block embracing all the Americas.

Achieving such a goal depends crucially on the success of the United States–Mexico free-trade agreement. Once this agreement is approved by Congress, there could be a stampede of other Latin American governments seeking to join the group—just like countries joining the European Community.

Background and Analysis

With the exception of the Caricom countries, international trade plays a much smaller part in the nations of North and South America than it does in Western Europe—see Fig. 1.

The move to open up the countries of the Americas to greater international competition will bring increased specialization as countries seek to gain from exporting the goods and services in which they have a comparative advantage.

The evidence from Western Europe is that lower trade barriers bring a larger amount of international trade and more rapidly growing real incomes—see Fig. 2.

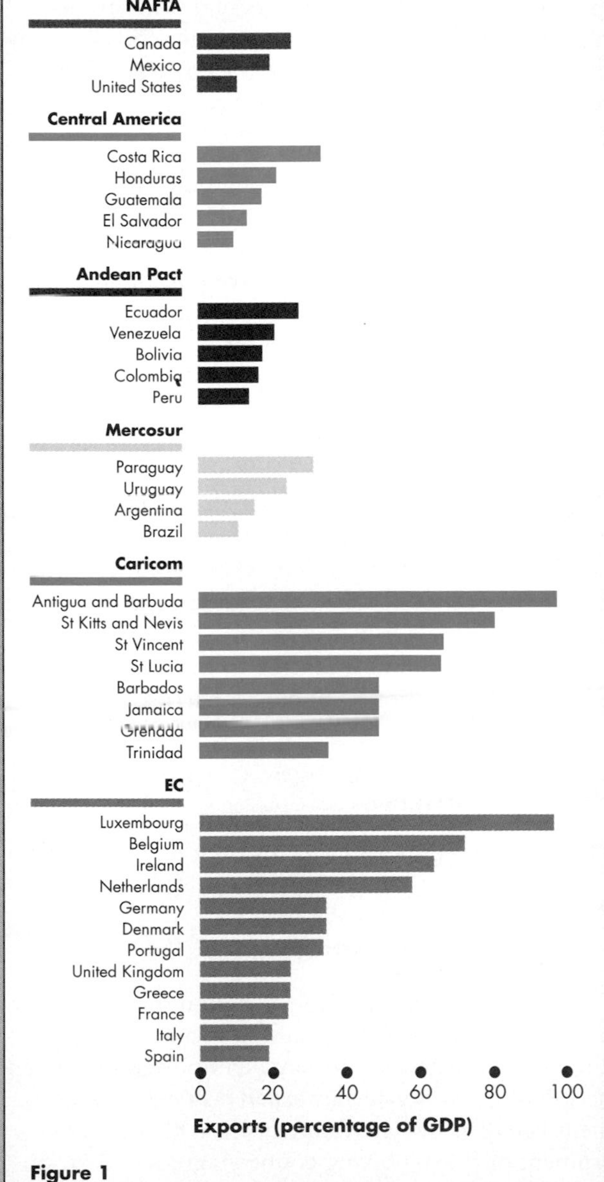

Figure 1

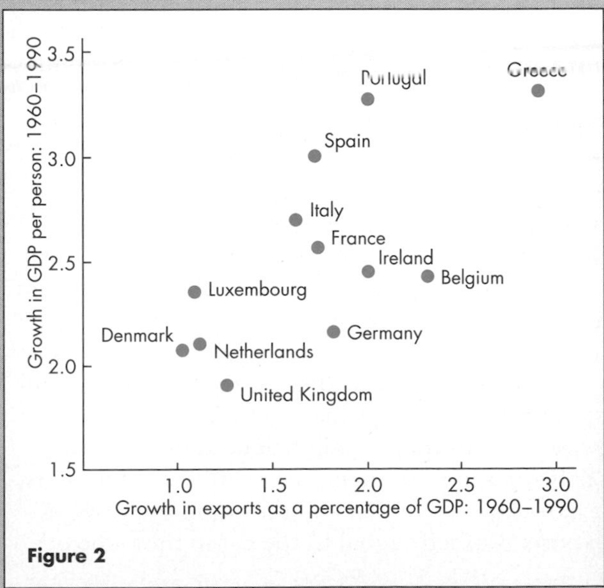

Figure 2

international trade reduces the gains from international trade.

It is easy to see that the tariff has lowered Pioneerland's total import bill. With free trade, Pioneerland was paying $3,000 a car and buying 4 million cars a year from Magic Empire. Thus the total import bill was $12 billion a year. With a tariff, Pioneerland's imports have been cut to 2 million cars a year and the price paid to Magic Empire has also been cut to only $2,000 a car. Thus the import bill has been cut to $4 billion a year. Doesn't this fact mean that Pioneerland's balance of trade has changed? Is Pioneerland now importing less than it is exporting?

To answer that question, we need to figure out what's happening in Magic Empire. We've just seen that the price that Magic Empire receives for cars has fallen from $3,000 to $2,000 a car. Thus the price of cars in Magic Empire has fallen. But if the price of cars has fallen, the price of grain has increased. With free trade, the Magicians could buy 3,000 bushels of grain for one car. Now they can buy only 2,000 bushels for a car. With a higher price of grain, the quantity demanded by the Magicians decreases. As a result, Magic Empire's import of grain declines. But so does Pioneerland's export of grain. In fact, Pioneerland's grain industry suffers from two sources. First, there is a decrease in the quantity of grain sold to Magic Empire. Second, there is increased competition for inputs from the now expanded car industry. Thus the tariff leads to a contraction in the scale of the grain industry in Pioneerland.

It seems paradoxical at first that a country imposing a tariff on cars would hurt its own export industry, lowering its exports of grain. It might help to think of it this way: Foreigners buy grain with the money they make from exporting cars. If they export fewer cars, they cannot afford to buy as much grain. In fact, in the absence of any international borrowing and lending, Magic Empire has to cut its imports of grain by exactly the same amount as the loss in revenue from its export of cars. Grain imports into Magic Empire will be cut back to a value of $4 billion, the amount that can be paid for by the new lower revenue from Magic Empire's car exports. Thus trade is still balanced in this post-tariff situation. Although the tariff has cut imports, it has also cut exports, and the cut in the value of exports is exactly equal to the cut in the value of imports. The tariff, therefore, has no effect on the balance of trade—it reduces the volume of trade.

The result that we have just derived is perhaps one of the most misunderstood aspects of international economics. On countless occasions, politicians and others have called for tariffs in order to remove a balance of trade deficit or have argued that lowering tariffs would produce a balance of trade deficit. They reach this conclusion by failing to work out all the implications of a tariff. Because a tariff raises the price of imports and cuts imports, the easy conclusion is that the tariff strengthens the balance of trade. But the tariff also changes the *volume* of exports. The equilibrium effects of a tariff are to reduce the volume of trade in both directions and by the same value on each side of the equation. The balance of trade itself is left unaffected.

Learning the Hard Way Although the analysis that we have just worked through leads to the clear conclusion that tariffs cut both imports and exports and make everyone worse off, we have not found that conclusion easy to accept. Time and again in our history, we have imposed high tariff barriers on international trade (as Fig. 35.6 illustrates). Whenever tariff barriers are increased, trade collapses. The most vivid historical example of this interaction of tariffs and trade occurred during the Great Depression years of the early 1930s when, in the wake of the Smoot-Hawley tariff increases and the retaliatory tariff changes that other countries introduced as a consequence, world trade almost dried up.

Let's now turn our attention to the other range of protectionist weapons—nontariff barriers.

Nontariff Barriers

There are two important forms of nontariff barriers:

- ◆ Quotas
- ◆ Voluntary export restraints

A **quota** is a quantitative restriction on the import of a particular good. It specifies the maximum amount of the good that may be imported in a given period of time. A **voluntary export restraint** is an agreement between two governments in which the government of the exporting country agrees to restrain the volume of its own exports. Voluntary export restraints are often called VERs.

Nontariff barriers have become important features of international trading arrangements in the period since World War II, and there is now general agreement that nontariff barriers are a more severe impediment to international trade than tariffs.

It is difficult to quantify the effects of nontariff barriers in a way that makes them easy to compare with tariffs, but some studies have attempted to do just that. Such studies attempt to assess the tariff rate that would restrict trade by the same amount as the nontariff barriers do. With such calculations, nontariff barriers and tariffs can be added together to assess the total amount of protection. When we add nontariff barriers to tariffs for the United States, the overall amount of protection increases more than threefold. Even so, the United States is the least protectionist country in the world. Total protection is higher in the European Community and higher still in other developed countries and Japan. The less developed countries and the so-called newly industrializing countries have the highest protection rates.

Quotas are especially important in the textile industries, in which there exists an international agreement called the Multifiber Agreement, which establishes quotas on a wide range of textile products. Agriculture is also subject to extensive quotas. Voluntary export restraints are particularly important in regulating the international trade in cars between Japan and the United States.

FIGURE 35.8

The Effects of a Quota

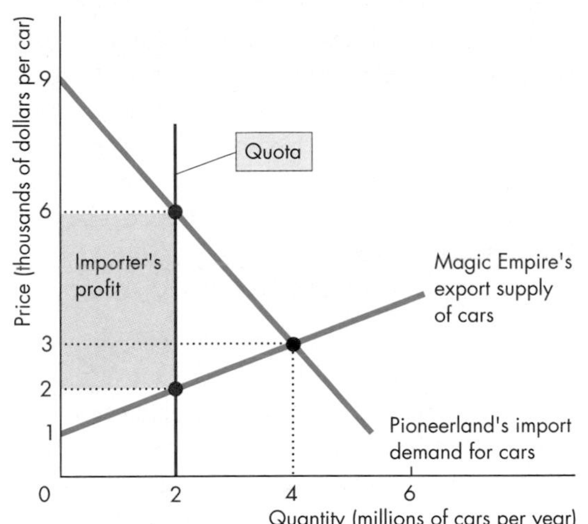

Pioneerland imposes a quota of 2 million cars a year on car imports from Magic Empire. That quantity appears as the vertical line labeled "Quota." Since the quantity of cars supplied by Magic Empire is restricted to 2 million, the price at which those cars will be traded increases to \$6,000. Importing cars is profitable, since Magic Empire is willing to supply cars at \$2,000 each. There is competition for import quotas—rent seeking.

How Quotas and VERs Work

To understand how nontariff barriers affect international trade, let's return to the example of trade between Pioneerland and Magic Empire. Suppose that Pioneerland imposes a quota on car imports. Specifically, suppose that the quota restricts imports to not more than 2 million cars a year. What are the effects of this action?

The answer is found in Fig. 35.8. The quota is shown by the vertical red line at 2 million cars a year. Since it is illegal to import more than that number of cars, car importers buy only that quantity from Magic Empire producers. They pay \$2,000 a car to the Magic Empire producer. But what do they sell their cars for? The answer is \$6,000 each. Since the import supply of cars is restricted to 2 million cars a year, people with cars for sale will be able to get \$6,000 each for them. The quantity of cars imported equals the quantity determined by the quota.

Importing cars is now obviously a profitable business. An importer gets \$6,000 for an item that costs only \$2,000. Thus there is severe competition among car importers for the available quotas. The pursuit of the profits from quotas is called "rent seeking."

The value of imports—the amount paid to Magic Empire—declines to \$4 billion, exactly the same as in the case of the tariff. Thus with lower incomes from car exports and with a higher price of grain, Magicians cut back on their imports of grain in exactly the same way they did under a tariff.

The key difference between a quota and a tariff lies in who gets the profit represented by the difference between the import supply price and the domestic selling price. In the case of a tariff, that difference goes to the government. In the case of a quota, that difference goes to the person who has the right to import under the import-quota regulations.

A voluntary export restraint is like a quota arrangement in which quotas are allocated to each exporting country. The effects of voluntary export restraints are similar to those of quotas but differ from them in that the gap between the domestic price and the export price is captured not by domestic importers but by the foreign exporter. The government of the exporting country has to establish procedures for allocating the restricted volume of exports among its producers.

Paying with Your Shirt! Two of the most heavily protected industries in the United States today are apparel and textiles. It has been estimated that the total protection on these industries, most of which takes the form of quotas, costs the average American family between $200 and $400 a year. Despite this fact, the House of Representatives passed a new act (the Textile and Apparel Trade Act) in 1975 that, if it had become law, would have increased protection in those industries even further, adding $300 to $400 a year in additional costs for the average household.[1] Taking all protection together, it has been estimated that the cost per year to an individual U.S. family is more than $1,000.[2]

Another way of looking at the cost of protection is to calculate the cost per job saved. It has been estimated, for example, that to protect one job in the textile industry costs $46,000 a year; one job in the footwear industry costs close to $80,000 a year; and one job in the carbon, steel, and auto industries costs more than $80,000 a year. In all these cases, it costs many times more to save a job through international trade barriers than the wages of the workers involved.[3]

[1]For more on this topic, see "Expanding Trade and Avoiding Protectionism," *Economic Report of the President* (1988), pp. 127–162.

[2]Murray Weidenbaum and N. Munger, "Protection at Any Price?" *Regulation* (July/August 1983): 14–18.

[3]Keith E. Maskus, "Rising Protectionism and U.S. International Trade Policy," *Economic Review of the Federal Reserve Bank of Kansas City* (July/August 1984): 3–17.

REVIEW

When a country opens itself up to international trade and trades freely at world market prices, it expands its consumption possibilities. When trade is restricted, some of the gains from trade are lost. A country may be better off with restricted trade than with no trade but not as well off as it could be if it engaged in free trade. A tariff reduces the volume of imports, but it also reduces the volume of exports. Under both free trade and restricted trade (and without international borrowing and lending), the value of imports equals the value of exports. With restricted trade, both the total value of exports and the total value of imports are lower than under free trade, but trade is still balanced. ◆

Why Quotas and VERs Might Be Preferred to Tariffs

At first sight, it seems puzzling that countries would ever want to use quotas and even more puzzling that they would want to use voluntary export restraints. We have seen that the same domestic price and the same quantity of imports can be achieved by using any of the three devices for restricting trade. However, a tariff provides the government with a source of revenue; a quota provides domestic importers with a profit; and a voluntary export restraint provides the foreigner with a profit. Why, then, would a country use a quota or a voluntary export restraint rather than a tariff?

There are three possible reasons. First, a government can use quotas to reward its political supporters. Under a quota, licenses to import become tremendously profitable. So the government bestows riches on the people to whom it gives licenses to import.

Second, quotas are more precise instruments for holding down imports. As demand fluctuates, the domestic price of the good fluctuates but not the quantity of imports. You can see this implication of a quota by going back to Fig. 35.8. Suppose that the demand for imports fluctuates. With a quota, these demand fluctuations simply produce fluctuations in the domestic price of the import but no change in the volume of imports. With a tariff, fluctuations in demand lead to no change in the domestic price but to large changes in the volume of imports. Thus if for some reason the government wants to control the quantity of imports and does not care about fluctuations in the domestic price, it will use a quota.

Third, different branches of government have jurisdiction over different aspects of international trade restriction. Congress has the power to impose tariffs. The administration has the power to impose nontariff barriers. Thus changing tariffs is a slow and cumbersome matter requiring the passage of an act of Congress. In contrast, nontariff barriers can be changed quickly, provided that the administration is persuaded of the need for the change.

Why would a government use voluntary export restraints rather than a tariff or quota? The government might want to avoid a tariff or quota war with another country. If one country imposes a tariff or a quota, that might encourage another country to impose a similar tariff or quota on the exports of the first country. Such a tariff or quota war would result in a much smaller volume of trade and a much worse outcome for both countries. A voluntary export restraint can be viewed as a way of achieving trade restrictions to protect domestic industries but with some kind of compensation to encourage the foreign country to accept that situation and not retaliate with its own restrictions. Finally, VERs are often the only form of trade restriction that can be legally entered into under the terms of the General Agreement on Tariffs and Trade.

Dumping and Countervailing Duties

Dumping is the selling of a good in a foreign market for a lower price than in the domestic market or for a lower price than its cost of production. Such a practice can arise from a discriminating monopoly seeking to maximize profit. An example of alleged dumping has occurred with Japanese sales of pickup trucks to the United States. Under current U.S. law and under GATT, dumping is illegal and antidumping duties may be imposed on foreign producers if U.S. producers can show that they have been injured by dumping.

Countervailing duties are tariffs that are imposed to enable domestic producers to compete with subsidized foreign producers. Often, foreign governments subsidize some of their domestic industries. Two examples are the Canadian pork and lumber industries. Under current U.S. law, if American producers can show that a foreign subsidy has damaged their market, a countervailing duty may be imposed.

Why Is International Trade Restricted?

There are many reasons why international trade is restricted. We've just seen two reasons—to offset the effects of dumping and of foreign subsidies. Even in these cases, it does not obviously benefit a country to protect itself from cheap foreign imports. However, more generally, we've seen that international trade benefits a country by raising its consumption possibilities. Why do we restrict international trade when such restrictions lower our consumption possibilities?

The key reason is that consumption possibilities increase *on the average* but not everyone shares in the gain and some people even lose. Free trade brings benefits to some and costs to others, with total benefits exceeding total costs. It is the uneven distribution of costs and benefits that is the principal source of impediment to achieving more liberal international trade.

Returning to our example of international trade in cars and grain between Pioneerland and Magic Empire, the benefits from free trade accrue to all the producers of grain and to those producers of cars who would not have to bear the costs of adjusting to a smaller car industry. The costs of free trade are borne by those car producers and their employees who have to move and become grain producers. The number of people who gain will, in general, be enormous compared with the number who lose. The gain per person will, therefore, be rather small. The loss per person to those who bear the loss will be large. Since the loss that falls on those who bear it is large, it will pay those people to incur considerable expense in order to lobby against free trade. On the other hand, it will not pay those who gain to organize to achieve free trade. The gain from trade for any one individual is too small for that individual to spend much time or money on a political organization to achieve free trade. The loss from free trade will be seen as being so great by those bearing that loss that they *will* find it profitable to join a political organization to prevent free trade. Each group is optimizing—weighing benefits against costs and choosing the best action for themselves. The anti–free-trade group will, however, undertake a larger quantity of political lobbying than the pro–free-trade group.

Compensating Losers

If, in total, the gains from free international trade exceed the losses, why don't those who gain compensate those who lose so that everyone is in favor of free trade? To some degree, such compensation does take place. It also takes place indirectly as a consequence of unemployment compensation arrangements. But, as a rule, only limited attempts are made to compensate those who lose from free international trade. The main reason why full compensation is not attempted is that the costs of identifying the losers would be enormous. Also, it would never be clear whether a person who has fallen on hard times is suffering because of free trade or for other reasons, perhaps reasons largely under the control of the individual. Furthermore, some people who look like losers at one point in time may, in fact, wind up gaining. The young auto worker who loses his job in Michigan and becomes an insurance salesperson in Chicago resents the loss of work and the need to move. But a year or two later, looking back on events, he counts himself fortunate. He's made a move that has increased his income and given him greater job security.

It is because we do not, in general, compensate the losers from free international trade that protectionism is such a popular and permanent feature of our national economic and political life.

Political Outcome

The political outcome that emerges from this activity is one in which a modest amount of restriction on international trade occurs and is maintained. Politicians react to constituencies pressing for protection and find it necessary, in order to get re-elected, to support legislative programs that protect those constituencies. The producers of protected goods are far more vocal and much more sensitive swing-voters than the consumers of those goods. The political outcome, therefore, leans in the direction of maintaining protection.

The politics of trade can be seen easily today. The United States restricts imports of sugar by quota. Who profits from the quotas? Not the foreign exporters. Whereas voluntary export restraints give exporters like Toyota and Honda big profits, quotas do not help foreign producers. In this case, the quotas have brought real economic and political suffering to Central American and Caribbean countries that produce sugar. The U.S. sugar growers, on the other hand, who benefit from the quotas, are extremely active in their support for politicians who can see their point of view. Similarly, the auto producers and unions are extremely active in their attempts to further limit the intrusion of Japanese imports.

◆ ◆ ◆ ◆ You've now seen how free international trade enables everyone to gain from increased specialization and exchange. By producing goods in which we have a comparative advantage and exchanging some of our own production for that of others, we expand our consumption possibilities. Placing impediments on that exchange when it crosses national borders restricts the extent to which we can gain from specialization and exchange. When we open our country up to free international trade, the market for the things that we sell expands and the price rises. The market for the things that we buy also expands, and the price falls. All countries gain from free international trade. As a consequence of price adjustments, and in the absence of international borrowing and lending, the value of imports adjusts to equal the value of exports. ◆ ◆ In the next chapter, we're going to study the ways in which international trade is financed and also learn why the international borrowing and lending that permits unbalanced international trade arises. We'll discover the forces that determine the U.S. balance of payments and the value, in terms of foreign currency, of our dollar.

SUMMARY

Patterns and Trends in International Trade

Large flows of trade take place between rich and poor countries. Resource-rich countries exchange natural resources for manufactured goods, and resource-poor countries import their resources in exchange for their own manufactured goods. However, by far the biggest volume of trade is in manufactured goods exchanged among the rich industrialized countries. The biggest single U.S. export item is machinery. However, the biggest single U.S. net export is grain. Trade in services has grown in recent years. Total trade has also grown over the years. The U.S. balance of trade fluctuates around zero, but since 1982 the United States has had a balance of trade deficit. (pp. 955–958)

Opportunity Cost and Comparative Advantage

When opportunity costs differ between countries, the country with the lowest opportunity cost of producing a good is said to have a comparative advantage in that good. Comparative advantage is the source of the gains from international trade. A country can have an absolute advantage, but not a comparative advantage, in the production of all goods. Every country has a comparative advantage in something. (pp. 958–959)

The Gains from Trade

Countries can gain from trade if their opportunity costs differ. Through trade, each country can obtain goods at a lower opportunity cost than it could if it produced all goods at home. International trade allows a country to consume outside its production possibilities. By specializing in producing the good in which it has a comparative advantage and then trading some of that good for imports, a country can consume at points outside its production possibility frontier. Each country can consume at such a point.

In the absence of international borrowing and lending, trade is balanced as prices adjust to reflect the international supply of and demand for goods. The world price is established at the level that balances the production and consumption plans of the trading parties. At the equilibrium price, trade is balanced and domestic consumption plans exactly match a combination of domestic production and international trade.

Comparative advantage explains the enormous volume and diversity of international trade that takes place in the world. But much trade takes the form of exchanging similar goods for each other—one type of car for another. Such trade arises because of economies of scale in the face of diversified tastes. By specializing in producing a few goods, having long production runs, and then trading those goods internationally, consumers in all countries can enjoy greater diversity of products at lower prices. (pp. 959–967)

Trade Restrictions

A country can restrict international trade by imposing tariffs or nontariff barriers—quotas and voluntary export restraints. All trade restrictions raise the domestic price of imported goods, lower the volume of imports, and reduce the total value of imports. They also reduce the total value of exports by the same amount as the reduction in the value of imports.

All trade restrictions create a gap between the domestic price and the foreign supply price of an import. In the case of a tariff, that gap is the tariff revenue collected by the government. But the government raises no revenue from a quota. Instead, domestic importers who have a license to import increase their profit. A voluntary export restraint resembles a quota except that a higher price is received by the foreign exporter.

Governments restrict trade because restrictions help the producers of the protected commodity and the workers employed by those producers. Because their gain is sufficiently large and the loss per consumer is sufficiently small, the political equilibrium favors restricted trade. Politicians pay more attention to the vocal concerns of the few who stand to lose than to the less strongly expressed views of the many who stand to gain. (pp. 967–976)

KEY ELEMENTS

Key Terms

Balance of trade, 955
Comparative advantage, 959
Countervailing duties, 975
Dumping, 975
Exports, 955
General Agreement on Tariffs and Trade, 967
Imports, 955
Net exporter, 955
Net importer, 955
Nontariff barrier, 967
Protectionism, 967
Quota, 972
Tariff, 967
Voluntary export restraint, 972

Key Figures

Figure 35.2 Opportunity Cost in Pioneerland, 958
Figure 35.3 Opportunity Cost in Magic Empire, 959
Figure 35.4 International Trade in Cars, 960
Figure 35.5 Expanding Consumption Possibilities, 961
Figure 35.7 The Effects of a Tariff, 969
Figure 35.8 The Effects of a Quota, 973

REVIEW QUESTIONS

1 What are the main exports and imports of the United States?

2 How does the United States trade services internationally?

3 Which items of international trade have been growing the most quickly in recent years?

4 What is comparative advantage? Why does it lead to gains from international trade?

5 Explain why international trade brings gains to all countries.

6 Distinguish between comparative advantage and absolute advantage.

7 Explain why all countries have a comparative advantage in something.

8 Explain why we import and export such large quantities of certain goods that are similar—for example, cars.

9 What are the main ways in which we restrict international trade?

10 What are the effects of a tariff?

11 What are the effects of a quota?

12 What are the effects of a voluntary export restraint?

13 Describe the main trends in tariffs and nontariff barriers.

14 Which countries have the largest restrictions on their international trade?

15 Why do countries restrict international trade?

PROBLEMS

1 Using Fig. 35.2, calculate the opportunity cost of cars in Pioneerland at the point on the production possibility frontier at which 4 million cars are produced.

2 Using Fig. 35.3, calculate the opportunity cost of a car in Magic Empire when it produces 8 million cars.

3 With no trade, Pioneerland produces 4 million cars and Magic Empire produces 8 million cars. Which country has a comparative advantage in the production of cars?

4 If there is no trade between Pioneerland and Magic Empire, how much grain is consumed and how many cars are bought in each country?

5 Suppose that the two countries in problems 1–4 trade freely.

a What country exports grain?

b What adjustments will be made to the amount of each good produced by each country?

c What adjustment will be made to the amount of each good consumed by each country?

d What can you say about the price of a car under free trade?

6 Compare the total production of each good produced in problems 1–5.

7 Compare the situation in problems 1–5 with that analyzed in this chapter (pp. 958–962). Why does Magic Empire export cars in the chapter but import them in problem 5?

8 The following figure depicts the international market for soybeans (there are only two countries in the world).

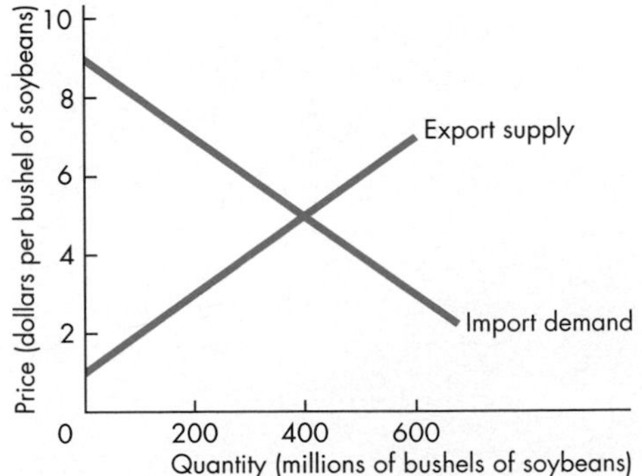

a What is the world price of soybeans if there is free trade between these countries?

b If the country that imports soybeans imposes a tariff of $2 per bushel, what is the world price of soybeans and what quantity of soybeans gets traded internationally? What is the price of soybeans in the importing country? Calculate the tariff revenue.

9 If the importing country in problem 8(a) imposes a quota of 300 million bushels, what is the price of soybeans in the importing country? What is the revenue from the quota, and who gets this revenue?

10 If the exporting country in problem 8(a) imposes a VER of 300 million bushels of soybeans, what is the world price of soybeans? What is the revenue of soybean growers in the exporting country? Which country gains from the VER?

11 Suppose that the exporting country in problem 8(a) subsidizes production by paying its farmers $1 a bushel for soybeans harvested.

a What is the price of soybeans in the importing country?

b What action might soybean growers in the importing country take? Why?

CHAPTER 36

THE BALANCE OF PAYMENTS AND THE DOLLAR

After studying this chapter, you will be able to:

- Explain how international trade is financed
- Describe a country's balance of payments accounts
- Explain what determines the amount of international borrowing and lending
- Explain why the United States changed from being a lender to being a borrower in the mid-1980s
- Explain how the foreign exchange value of the dollar is determined
- Explain why the foreign exchange value of the dollar fluctuated in the 1980s
- Explain the effects of changes in the exchange rate
- Explain what determines interest rates and why they vary so much from one country to another

For Sale: America

F OREIGN ENTREPRENEURS ARE ROAMING THE UNITED States with a giant shopping cart and loading it up with everything in sight, from high-rise buildings in Manhattan to movie studios in Los Angeles. The Rockefeller Center and Columbia Pictures are just two small examples of an enormous buying spree. What is causing this foreign invasion of the United States? Why are foreigners finding U.S. real estate and businesses such attractive investments? ◆◆ In 1971, one U.S. dollar was enough to buy 360 Japanese yen. At the end of 1991, that same dollar bought only 130 yen. But the slide from 360 to 130 yen was not a smooth one. At some times, the dollar held its own or even rose in value against the Japanese currency, as it did, for example, in 1982. But at other times, the dollar's slide was precipitous, as in the period between 1985 and 1988. The dollar has fallen in value not only against the Japanese currency. It has fallen against the German mark and the Swiss franc. But the dollar has gained in value in terms of the Canadian dollar, the British pound, and the French franc. What makes our dollar fluctuate in value against other currencies? Why have the fluctuations been particularly extreme in recent years? Is there anything we can do to stabilize the value of the dollar? ◆◆ The world capital market is becoming ever more integrated. As the Wall Street stock market rises and falls, so also do the stock markets around the globe—such as those in London, Paris, Tokyo, and Toronto. But despite the fact that the world is getting smaller, there are enormous differences in the interest rates at which people borrow and lend around the world. For example, in early

1992, the U.S. government was paying just under 8 percent a year on its long-term borrowing. At that same time, governments in Australia, Italy, and Spain were paying more than 10 percent. In Japan, the government was borrowing for only 5½ percent. How can interest rates diverge so widely? Why don't loans dry up in low-interest-rate countries with all the money flooding to countries where interest rates are high? Why aren't interest rates made the same everywhere by the force of such movements?

◆ ◆ ◆ ◆ During the 1980s, the issues of international economics became important matters for almost every American. We're going to study these issues in this chapter. We're going to discover why the U.S. economy has become such an attractive target for foreign investors, why the dollar fluctuates against the values of other currencies, and why interest rates vary from country to country.

Financing International Trade

When 47th Street Photo in New York City imports Minolta cameras, it does not pay for those cameras with U.S. dollars—it uses Japanese yen. When Saks Fifth Avenue imports Fila track suits, it pays for them using Italian lire. And when a French construction company buys an earth mover from Caterpillar, Inc., it uses U.S. dollars. Whenever we buy things from another country, we use the currency of that country in order to make the transaction. It doesn't make any difference what the item being traded is—it might be a consumer good or a capital good, a building, or even a firm.

We're going to study the markets in which transactions in money—in different types of currency—take place. But first we're going to look at the scale of international trading and borrowing and lending and at the way in which we keep our records of these transactions. Such records are called the balance of payments accounts.

Balance of Payments Accounts

A country's **balance of payments accounts** records its international trading, borrowing, and lending. There are in fact three balance of payments accounts:

- Current account
- Capital account
- Official settlements account

The **current account** records the receipts from the sale of goods and services to foreigners, the payments for goods and services bought from foreigners, and gifts and other transfers (such as foreign aid

TABLE 36.1
U.S. Balance of Payments Accounts in 1990

	Billions of dollars
Current account	
Import of goods and services	**–604.5**
Export of goods and services	**522.8**
Net factor incomes	**11.9**
Net transfers	**–22.3**
Current account balance	**–92.1**
Capital account	
Foreign investment in the United States	**88.5**
U.S. investment abroad	**–57.7**
Statistical discrepancy	**63.5**
Capital account balance	**94.3**
Official settlements account	
Increase (–) in official U.S. reserves	**–2.2**

Source: Survey of Current Business (December 1991), vol. 71.

FIGURE 36.1

The Balance of Payments

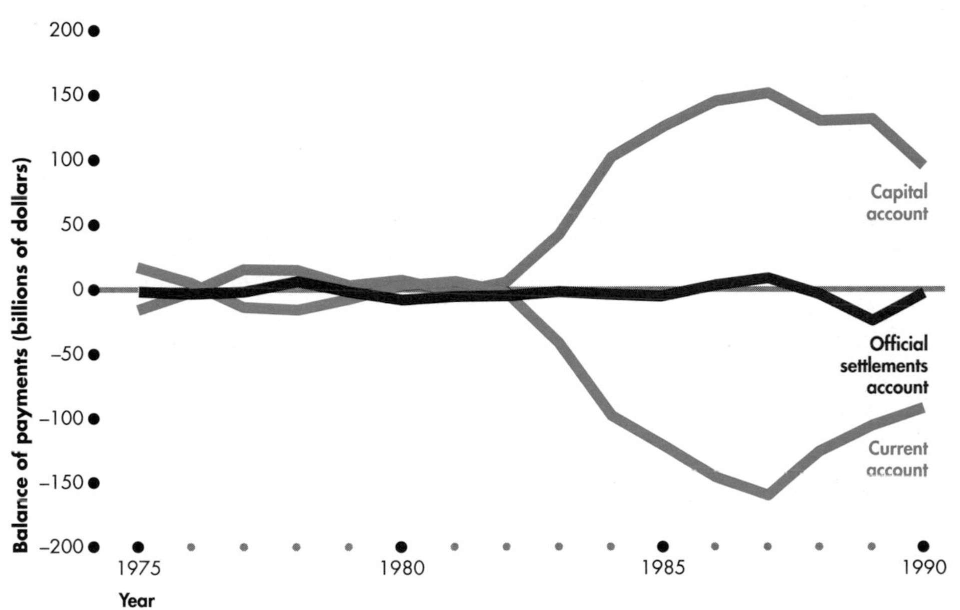

During the 1970s, fluctuations in the balance of payments were small. In the 1980s, an enormous current account deficit arose. The capital account balance mirrors the current account balance. When the current account balance is positive, the capital account balance is negative—we lend to the rest of the world—and when the current account balance is negative, the capital account balance is positive—we borrow from the rest of the world. Fluctuations in the official settlements balance are small compared with fluctuations in the current account balance and the capital account balance.

Source: Economic Report of the President, 1992.

payments) received from and paid to foreigners. By far the largest items in the current account are the receipts from the sale of goods and services to foreigners (the value of exports) and the payments made for goods and services bought from foreigners (the value of imports). Net transfers are relatively small items. The **capital account** records all the international borrowing and lending transactions. The capital account balance records the difference between the amounts that a country lends to and borrows from the rest of the world. The **official settlements account** shows the net increase or decrease in a country's holdings of foreign currency.

Table 36.1 shows the U.S. balance of payments accounts in 1990. As you can see from the table, the United States had a current account deficit of $92.1 billion in 1990. How do we pay for our current account deficit? That is, how do we pay for imports that exceed the value of our exports? We pay by borrowing from abroad. The capital account tells us by how much. We borrowed $88.5 billion but made loans of $57.7 billion. Thus our identified net foreign borrowing was $30.8 billion. There is also a statistical discrepancy in the capital account of $63.5 billion.[1] Actually, this discrepancy represents a combination of capital and current account transactions such as unidentified borrowing from abroad, illegal international trade—for example, the import of illegal drugs—and transactions not reported in order to illegally evade tariffs or other international trade protection measures.

Our net borrowing from abroad minus our current account deficit is the change in U.S. official reserves. **Official reserves** are the government's holdings of foreign currency. In 1990, those reserves increased by $2.2 billion (net borrowing from foreigners was $94.3 billion, the current account deficit was $92.1 billion, and the difference, $2.2 billion, was the increase in official reserves).

The numbers in Table 36.1 give a snapshot of the balance of payments accounts in 1990. Figure 36.1 puts that snapshot into perspective by showing the

[1]The statistical discrepancy in 1990 was particularly large. Usually, it is much smaller than this.

balance of payments between 1975 and 1990. As you can see, the current account balance is almost a mirror image of the capital account balance, and the official settlements balance is very small compared with the balances on these other two accounts. A large current account deficit (and capital account surplus) emerged during the 1980s but was declining after 1987.

You will perhaps obtain a better understanding of the balance of payments accounts and the way in which they are linked together if you consider the income and expenditure, borrowing and lending, and bank account of an individual.

Individual Analogy An individual's current account records the income from supplying the services of factors of production and the expenditure on goods and services. Consider, for example, Joanne. She earned an income in 1992 of $25,000. Joanne has $10,000 worth of investments that earned her an income of $1,000. Joanne's current account shows an income of $26,000. Joanne spent $18,000 buying goods and services for consumption. She also bought a new house, which cost her $60,000. So Joanne's total expenditure was $78,000. The difference between her expenditure and income is $52,000 ($78,000 minus $26,000). This amount is Joanne's current account deficit.

To pay for expenditure of $52,000 in excess of her income, Joanne has to either use the money that she has in the bank or take out a loan. In fact, Joanne took a mortgage of $50,000 to help buy her house. This was the only borrowing that Joanne did, so her capital account surplus was $50,000. With a current account deficit of $52,000 and a capital account surplus of $50,000, Joanne is still $2,000 short. She got that $2,000 from her own bank account. Her cash holdings decreased by $2,000.

Joanne's supply of factors of production is analogous to a country's supply of exports. Her purchases of goods and services, including her purchase of a house, are analogous to a country's imports. Joanne's mortgage—borrowing from someone else—is analogous to a country's foreign borrowing. Joanne's purchase of the house is analogous to a country's foreign investment. The change in her own bank account is analogous to the change in the country's official reserves.

Later in this chapter, we will study the factors that influence the official settlements balance, but for now we'll concentrate on the current account and the capital account.

Borrowers and Lenders, Debtors and Creditors

A country that is borrowing more from the rest of the world than it is lending to it is called a **net borrower.** Similarly, a **net lender** is a country that is lending more to the rest of the world than it is borrowing from it. A net borrower might be going deeper into debt or might simply be reducing its net assets held in the rest of the world. The total stock of foreign investment determines whether a country is a debtor or a creditor. A **debtor nation** is a country that, during its entire history, has borrowed more from the rest of the world than it has lent to it. It has a stock of outstanding debt to the rest of the world that exceeds the stock of its own claims on the rest of the world. The United States became a debtor nation in the mid-1980s. A **creditor nation** is a country that has invested more in the rest of the world than other countries have invested in it. The largest creditor nation is Japan. A creditor nation is one whose net receipts of interest on debt are positive—payments made to it exceed the payments that it makes.

At the heart of the distinction between a net borrower/net lender and a debtor/creditor nation is the distinction between flows and stocks. Borrowing and lending are flows. They are amounts borrowed or lent per unit of time. Debts are stocks. They are amounts owed at a point in time. The flow of borrowing and lending changes the stock of debt. But the outstanding stock of debt depends mainly on past flows of borrowing and lending, not on the current period's flows. The current period's flows determine the *change* in the stock of debt outstanding.

The United States is a newcomer to the ranks of net borrower nations. Throughout the 1960s and most of the 1970s, it had a surplus on its current account and a deficit on its capital account. Thus the country was a net lender to the rest of the world. It was not until 1983 that it became a significant net borrower. Since then, borrowing has increased each year and, by the end of the 1980s, exceeded $100 billion a year. The United States is not only a net borrower nation. It is also a debtor nation. That is, its total stock of borrowing from the rest of the world exceeds its lending to the rest of the world.

The largest debtor nations are the capital-hungry developing countries. The international debt of these countries grew from less than a third to more than a half of their gross domestic product during the 1980s, giving rise to what has been called the "Third World debt crisis."

The majority of countries are net borrowers. But a small number of countries are huge net lenders. Examples of net lenders are the oil-rich countries, such as Kuwait and Venezuela, and successful developed economies, such as Japan and Germany.

Should the United States be concerned about the switch from being a net lender to being a net borrower? The answer to this question depends mainly on what the net borrower is doing with the borrowed money. If borrowing is financing investment that in turn is generating economic growth and higher income, borrowing is not a problem. If the borrowed money is being used to finance consumption, then higher interest payments are being incurred, and, as a consequence, consumption will eventually have to be reduced. The more the borrowing and the longer it goes on, the greater is the reduction in consumption that will eventually be necessary. We'll explore whether the United States is borrowing for investment or for consumption.

Current Account Balance

What determines the current account balance and the scale of a country's net foreign borrowing or lending?

To answer that question, we need to begin by recalling and using some of the things that we learned about the national income accounts. Table 36.2 is going to refresh your memory and summarize the necessary calculations for you. Part (a) lists the national income variables that are needed, with their symbols. Their values in the United States in 1990 are also shown.

Part (b) presents two key national income equations. First, equation (1) reminds us that aggregate expenditure is the sum of consumption expenditure, investment, government purchases of goods and services, and net exports (the difference between exports and imports). Equation (2) reminds us that aggregate income is used in three different ways. It can be consumed, saved, or paid to the government in the form of taxes (net of transfer payments). Equation (1) tells us how our expenditure generates our income. Equation (2) tells us how we dispose of that income.

Part (c) of the table takes you into some new territory. It examines surpluses and deficits. We'll look at three surpluses/deficits—those of the current account, the government's budget, and the private sector. To get at these surpluses and deficits, first subtract equation (2) from equation (1) in Table 36.2. The result is equation (3). By rearranging equation (3), we obtain a relationship for the current account—exports minus imports—that appears as equation (4) in the table.[2]

Notice that the current account, in equation (4), is made up of two components. The first is taxes minus government spending, and the second is saving minus investment. These items are the surpluses/deficits of the government and private sectors. Taxes (net of transfer payments) minus government purchases of goods and services equals the budget surplus or deficit. If that number is positive, the government's budget is a surplus, and if the number is negative, it is a deficit. The **private sector surplus or deficit** is the difference between saving and investment. If saving exceeds investment, the private sector has a surplus to lend to other sectors. If investment exceeds saving, the private sector has a deficit that has to be financed by borrowing from other sectors. As you can see from our calculations, the current account deficit is equal to the sum of the other two deficits—the government's budget deficit and the private sector deficit. In the United States in 1990, the most important of these other two deficits was the government budget deficit. The private sector was almost in balance, and the $95 billion current account deficit was accounted for almost exclusively by the $104 billion government budget deficit.

Part (d) of Table 36.2 shows you how investment is financed. To increase investment, either private saving, the government surplus, or the current account deficit must increase.

The calculations that we've just performed are really nothing more than bookkeeping. We've manipulated the national income accounts and dis-

[2]In the national income accounts, the difference between exports and imports is called *net exports*. There are some slight differences in the way these numbers are calculated in the national income accounts and the balance of payments accounts, but for most purposes you can regard net exports and the current account balance as meaning the same thing.

TABLE 36.2

The Current Account Balance, Net Foreign Borrowing, and the Financing of Investment

	Symbols and equations	U.S. values in 1990 (billions of dollars)
(a) Variables		
Gross domestic product (GDP)	Y	5,514
Consumption expenditure	C	3,743
Investment	I	803
Government purchases of goods and services	G	1,043
Exports of goods and services	EX	550
Imports of goods and services	IM	625
Saving	S	868
Taxes, net of transfer payments	T	903
(b) Domestic income and expenditure		
Aggregate expenditure	(1) $Y = C + I + G + EX - IM$	
Uses of income	(2) $Y = C + S + T$	
Subtracting (1) from (2)	(3) $0 = I - S + G - T + EX - IM$	
(c) Surpluses and deficits		
Current account	(4) $EX - IM = (T - G) + (S - I) =$	550 – 625 = –75
Government budget	(5) $T - G =$	903 – 1,043 = –140
Private sector	(6) $S - I =$	868 – 803 = 65
(d) Financing investment		
Investment is financed by		
the sum of private saving,	S,	868
net government saving,	$T - G$,	–140
and net foreign saving,	$IM - EX$,	75
that is:	(7) $I = S + (T - G) + (IM - EX)$	803 = 868 – 140 + 75

Source: Economic Report of the President, 1992.

covered that the current account deficit is just the sum of the deficits of the government and private sectors. But these calculations do reveal a fundamental fact—our international balance of payments can change only if either our government budget balance changes or our private sector financial balance changes. This fact is often lost sight of in popular discussions of our international deficit—see Reading Between the Lines, pp. 988–989.

We've seen that our international deficit is equal to the sum of the government deficit and the private sector deficit. But what determines those two deficits? Why isn't the private sector in a surplus equal to the government's budget deficit so that the current account deficit is zero? Does an increase in the government budget deficit bring an increase in the current account deficit?

The Twin Deficits

You can see the answer to this question by looking at Fig. 36.2. In that figure, the government sector (federal, state, and local governments) budget balance is plotted alongside the current account balance. As you can see, these two balances moved in close sympathy with each other during the 1980s. This tendency for the two deficits to move together has given rise to the term *twin deficits*. The **twin deficits** are the government budget deficit and current account deficit. But the twin deficits are not identical. There are independent variations in the two deficits that are accommodated by variations in the private sector deficit. Let's see why.

Effects of Government Deficit on Private Surplus

As we've just seen, the private sector surplus/deficit is the gap between saving and investment. One of the main influences on the level of saving is disposable income. Anything that increases disposable income, other things being equal, increases saving and increases the private sector surplus. The main influences on investment are the interest rate and expectations of future profits. Other things being equal, anything that lowers interest rates or increases expected future profits increases investment and decreases the private sector surplus.

Changes in taxes or government spending change the budget deficit and influence income and interest rates. These changes, in turn, influence private sector saving and investment and hence change the private sector surplus/deficit. An increase in government purchases of goods and services or a tax cut—either

FIGURE 36.2

The Twin Deficits

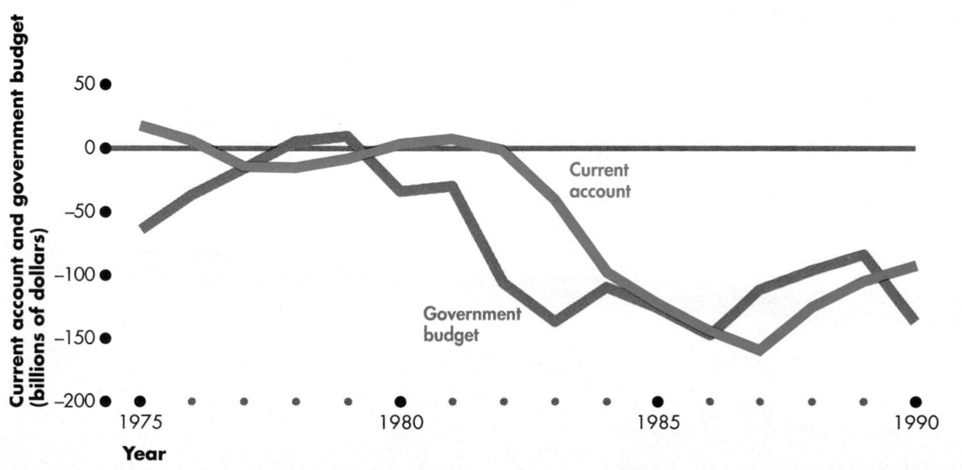

The twin deficits are the current account deficit and the government budget deficit, which move in sympathy with each other. As the government budget deficit grew larger during the 1980s, so did the current account deficit.

Source: Economic Report of the President, 1992.

The U.S.-Japan Trade Gap

THE ECONOMIST, JANUARY 11, 1992

A poor match in Tokyo

The president arrived in Japan on January 7th hoping to depart three days later with a list of goodies that would help him get re-elected in November. . . .

. . . With 8.5 million Americans out of work, and America's trade deficit with Japan nosing back towards $42 billion, this was, his advisers advised, the time to get tough. Bashing Japan for not buying enough goods made in America should, it was argued, go down well in Detroit. . . .

What have the Americans gained? Two dozen Japanese companies have been bullied into buying more manufactured goods from abroad. . . .The Japanese may or may not chip in something towards an $8.25 billion atom-smashing machine that American scientists want to build in Texas. Nine Japanese car manufacturers have outlined plans for buying $19 billion-worth of components from America by 1994. . . .

Though they are already widely known, the import targets for American cars ($6.4 billion worth by 1994) have not been put in the plan. No one in Japan wants to be blamed for breaking a written promise—as happened when the Semi-conductor Accord of 1986 recklessly guaranteed American chip makers 20% of the Japanese market. Mr Miyazawa has also offered to relax import-inspection standards that have irked the Americans on more than 50 items. . . .

The Americans will gain access to $5 billion-worth of trade insurance covering the next five years. The cash is for underwriting Japanese overseas projects in which American firms take part, such as building power stations in Latin America and drilling for oil in Siberia. The scheme came into effect last May and has so far provided some $700 million of Japanese government insurance for six overseas projects—helping American firms export $2 billion-worth of goods.

On the tricky issue of rice, the Americans have been urging Japan to accept GATT proposals for replacing import restrictions on agricultural products with tariffs. This would help bring the Uruguay round of multilateral trade talks to a successful conclusion. But the ruling Liberal Democrats are afraid of offending Japan's farmers before July's election. . . .

When they are added up, the measures announced this week will buy few jobs for Americans. They may even backfire on Mr Bush in the months ahead. Expectations have been rising in Washington that Japan's latest market-opening measures are somehow different from the dozens that have gone before. All have helped, bit by bit, to make the Japanese market more accessible to foreigners, but none has allowed Japan's trading partners to eliminate their deficits. Mr Bush's efforts will be no different. . . .

The Essence of the Story

With a recession in the United States (8.5 million unemployed), a trade deficit with Japan ($42 billion), and an upcoming election (in November 1992), President Bush visited Tokyo in January 1992 hoping to return with agreements that would boost U.S. exports to Japan and limit Japanese imports into the United States.

The outcome:

- Two dozen Japanese companies agreed to buy more manufactured goods from abroad.
- The Japanese agreed to consider making a contribution toward the cost of the $8.25 billion supercollider to be built in Texas.
- Nine Japanese car manufacturers outlined plans for buying components from U.S. auto makers ($19 billion worth by 1994).
- Import inspection standards on more than 50 items were to be relaxed.
- $5 billion worth of trade insurance underwriting was to be bought from U.S. companies over a five-year period.
- There was to be no relaxation of restrictions on rice imports into Japan.

The bottom line: few jobs for Americans and little change in the U.S. trade deficit with Japan.

Background and Analysis

In 1991, U.S. exports of goods and services were 10 percent of GDP, and imports were 11 percent of GDP. Japan's exports of goods and services were 11 percent of GDP, and its imports were 10 percent of GDP.

A large part of the U.S. deficit was in its trade with Japan.

To decrease the U.S. trade deficit with Japan, a number of measures have been proposed to limit U.S. imports of specific Japanese manufacturers and to increase U.S. exports of specific goods and services to Japan. The measures have not worked.

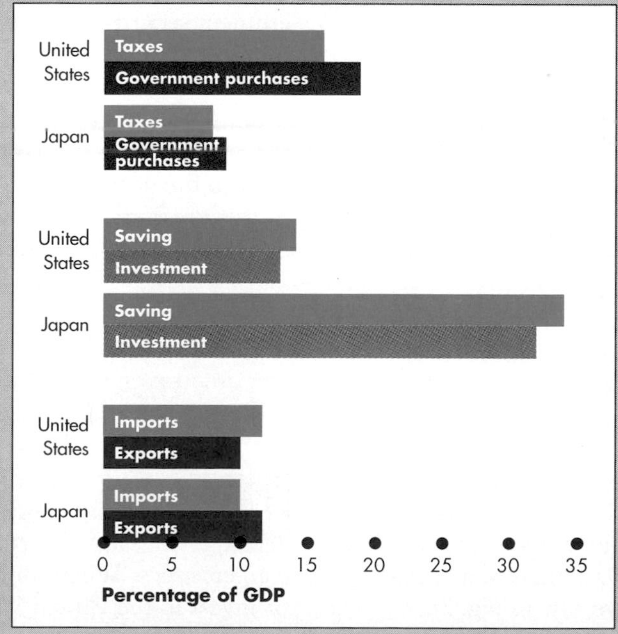

It is not surprising that the measures have not worked. A decrease in Japanese car exports to the United States does not necessarily lower the U.S.-Japan trade deficit. It could lower Japanese imports from the United States or increase U.S. imports of other Japanese manufactures.

Net exports *NX* are linked to the government and private sector surpluses by the equation

$$NX = (T - G) + (S - I).$$

The main difference between the United States and Japan is in the levels of taxes, government purchases, saving, and investment—shown in the figure. Japan has smaller government purchases and larger saving and investment than the United States.

Only if U.S. saving or taxes increase or government purchases or investment decreases can U.S. net exports increase.

Measures that boost U.S. saving, other things being equal, will increase U.S. net exports. Measures aimed at changing the volume of trade in specific goods and services will increase net exports only if they also change the level of saving in the United States.

of which increases the budget deficit—tends to increase GDP and the interest rate. The higher GDP stimulates additional saving, and the higher interest rate dampens investment plans. Thus, to some degree, an increased government budget deficit induces an increased private sector surplus.

For an increase in the government budget deficit to lead to an increase in the private sector surplus, the government's actions must stimulate higher income and/or induce higher interest rates. There are two factors that tend to limit these channels of influence. First, when the economy is operating close to full employment, as it is much of the time, a higher budget deficit does not produce a higher level of real GDP. Second, internationally mobile capital lessens the effect of increased government spending on interest rates. Thus the two mechanisms by which an increase in the budget deficit increases the private sector surplus can be weak.

Effects of Government Deficit on Current Account Deficit

Since the three deficits—the government budget deficit, the current account deficit, and the private sector deficit—add up to zero, any change in the government budget deficit that does not influence the private sector deficit must affect the current account deficit. But how does this effect come about? The easiest way of seeing the effect is to consider what happens when there is full employment. An increase in government purchases of goods and services or a tax cut leads to an increase in aggregate demand. But with the economy at full employment there is no spare capacity to generate a comparable increase in output. Part of the increased aggregate demand, therefore, spills over into the rest of the world, and imports increase. Also, part of the domestic production going for export is diverted to satisfy domestic demand. Exports decrease. The rise in imports and the fall in exports increase the current account deficit. The excess of imports over exports leads to a net increase in borrowing from the rest of the world.

Of course, the economy is not always at full employment. Nor does foreign capital flow in at a fixed interest rate. Thus the link between government budget deficit and the current account deficit is not a mechanical one. It is, nevertheless, a remarkably strong relationship, as we saw in Fig. 36.2.

Is U.S. Borrowing for Consumption or Investment?

We noted above that whether international borrowing is a problem or not depends on what that borrowing is used for. You've seen that in recent years the United States has borrowed internationally to finance the purchase of goods and services provided by the government. Private sector saving has been sufficient to pay for investment in plant and equipment, but it has not been sufficient to pay for the spending by the government in excess of its tax revenue. Does the fact that the government deficit has been similar to the amount of foreign borrowing mean that we're borrowing to consume?

It probably does not. There is no sure way to determine the extent to which government spending is consumption or investment. Some items, such as the purchase of improved highways, are investment. But what about expenditure on education and health care? Are these expenditures consumption or investment? A good case can be made that they are investment—investment in human capital—and that they earn a rate of return at least equal to the interest rate that we pay on our foreign debt.

Another reason for believing that most foreign lending is used to finance productive investment in the United States is that foreign investors do not buy a large volume of government bonds. In fact, in 1990, less than a third of the government's deficit was *directly* financed by foreigners buying U.S. government securities. Most of the foreign investment in the United States is in the private sector and is undertaken in the pursuit of the highest available profit. Foreigners diversify their lending to spread their risk. We do the same. Some of our saving is used to finance investment in U.S. firms, some is lent to the government, and some is used to finance U.S. investment in other countries.

REVIEW

When we buy goods from the rest of the world or invest in the rest of the world, we use foreign currency. When foreigners buy goods from us or invest in the United States, they use U.S. currency.

We record international transactions in the balance of payments accounts. The current account shows our exports and imports of goods and services and net transfers to the rest of the world. The capital account shows our net foreign borrowing or lending. The official settlements account shows the change in the country's holdings of a foreign currency. In the late 1980s, the U.S. current account moved into a large deficit, and the capital account moved into a large surplus—the country became a net borrower. The current account deficit is equal to the sum of the government budget deficit and the private sector deficit. During the 1980s, the U.S. current account deficit fluctuated in a similar way to the government budget deficit—the phenomenon of the twin deficits. We borrow from the rest of the world to purchase goods and services provided by the government in excess of the taxes that we pay. ◆

Foreign Exchange and the Dollar

When we buy foreign goods or invest in another country, we have to obtain some of that country's currency to make the transaction. When foreigners buy U.S.-produced goods or invest in the United States, they have to obtain some U.S. dollars. We get foreign currency, and foreigners get U.S. dollars in the foreign exchange market. The **foreign exchange market** is the market in which the currency of one country is exchanged for the currency of another. The foreign exchange market is not a place like a downtown flea market or produce market. The market is made up of thousands of people—importers and exporters, banks, and specialists in the buying and selling of foreign exchange called foreign exchange brokers. The foreign exchange market opens on Monday morning in Hong Kong, which is still Sunday evening in New York. As the day advances, markets open in Singapore, Tokyo, Bahrain, Frankfurt, London, New York, Chicago, and San Francisco. As the West Coast markets close, Hong Kong is only an hour away from opening for the next day of business. As Fig. 36.3 shows, the sun barely sets on the foreign exchange market. Dealers around the world are continually in contact by telephone, and on any given day, billions of dollars change hands.

The price at which one currency exchanges for another is called a **foreign exchange rate.** For example, in March 1992, one U.S. dollar bought 133 Japanese yen. The exchange rate between the U.S. dollar and the Japanese yen was 133 yen per dollar. Exchange rates can be expressed either way. We've just expressed the exchange rate between the yen and the dollar as a number of yen per dollar. Equivalently, we could express the exchange rate in terms of dollars per yen. That exchange rate in March 1992 was $0.0075 per yen. (In other words, a yen was worth ¾ of a penny.)

The actions of the foreign exchange brokers make the foreign exchange market highly efficient. Exchange rates are almost identical no matter where in the world the transaction is taking place. If U.S. dollars were cheap in London and expensive in Tokyo, within a flash someone would have placed a buy order in London and a sell order in Tokyo, thereby increasing the demand in one place and increasing the supply in another, moving the prices to equality.

Foreign Exchange Regimes

Foreign exchange rates are of critical importance for millions of people. They affect the costs of our foreign vacations and our imported cars. They affect the number of dollars that we end up getting for the oranges and beef that we sell to Japan. Because of its importance, governments pay a great deal of attention to what is happening in foreign exchange markets and, more than that, take actions designed to achieve what they regard as desirable movements in exchange rates. There are three ways in which the government can operate the foreign exchange market—three regimes. They are

- Fixed exchange rate
- Flexible exchange rate
- Managed exchange rate

A **fixed exchange rate** is an exchange rate the value of which is held steady by the country's central bank. For example, the U.S. government could adopt a fixed exchange rate by defining the U.S.

FIGURE 36.3
The Global Foreign Exchange Market

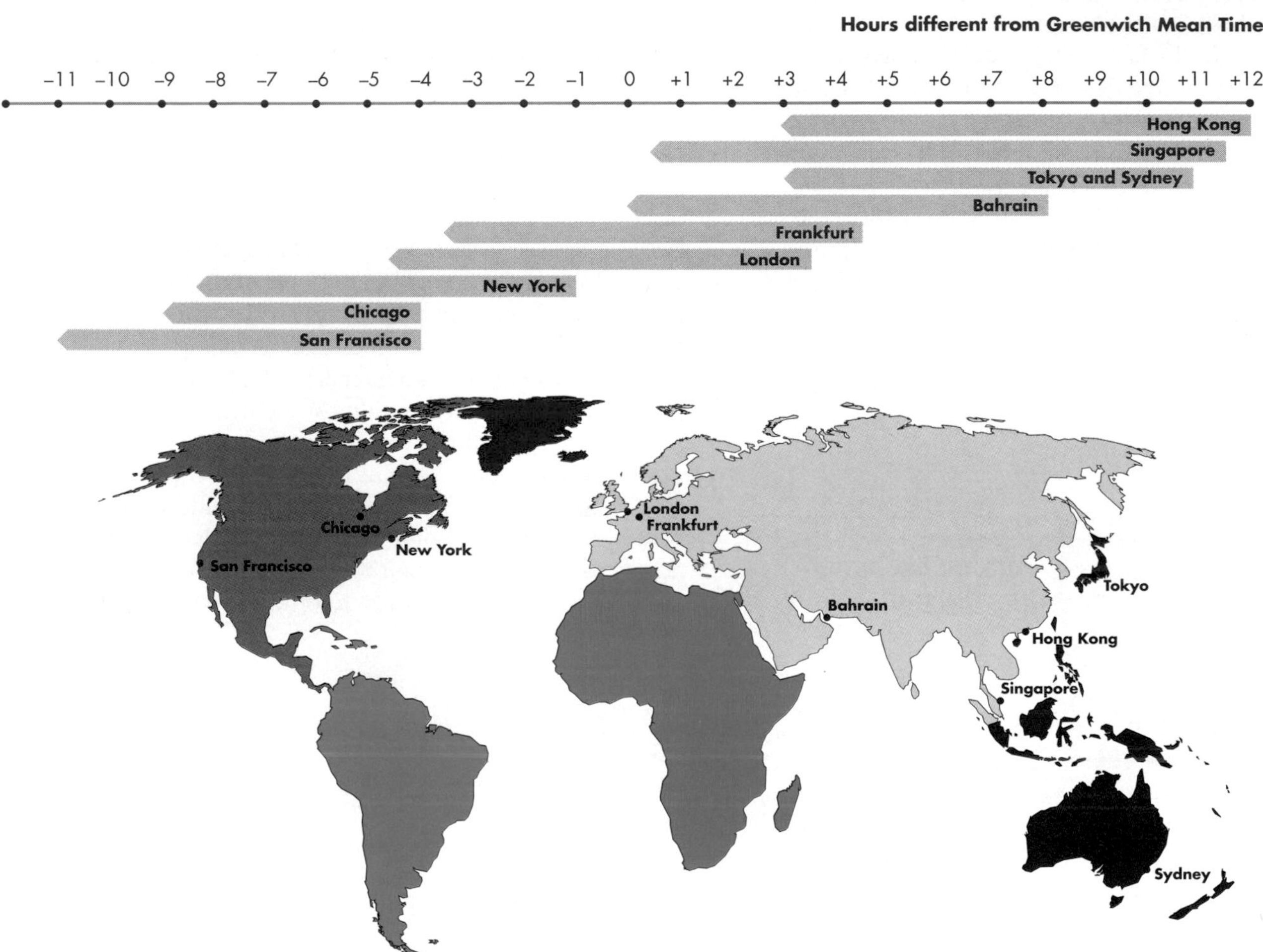

The foreign exchange market barely closes. The day begins in Hong Kong, and as the globe spins, markets open up in Singapore, Tokyo, Sydney, Bahrain, Zurich, Frankfurt, London, New York, Chicago, and San Francisco. By the time the West Coast markets close, Hong Kong is almost ready to begin another day.

Source: Based on a similar map in Steven Husted and Michael Melvin, *International Economics* (New York: Harper & Row, 1989), and data from *Euromoney,* April 1979, p. 14.

dollar to be worth a certain number of units of some other currency and having the Fed take actions designed to maintain that announced value. We'll study what those actions are below.

A **flexible exchange rate** is an exchange rate the value of which is determined by market forces in the absence of central bank intervention. A **managed exchange rate** is an exchange rate the value of which

FIGURE 36.4

Exchange Rates

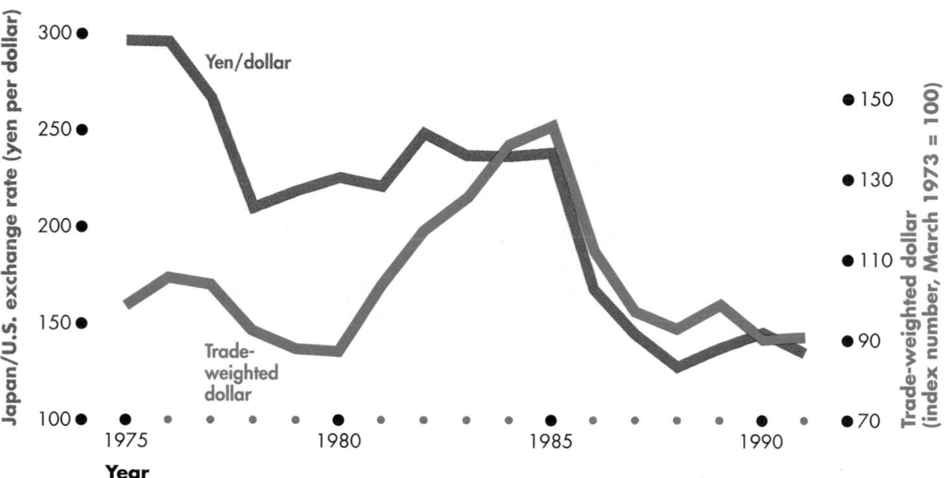

The exchange rate is the price at which two currencies can be traded. The yen-dollar exchange rate, expressed as yen per dollar, shows that the dollar has fallen in value—depreciated—against the yen. An index of the value of the U.S. dollar against all currencies shows that the U.S. dollar appreciated on the average against all currencies between 1980 and 1985 and depreciated between 1985 and 1990.

Source: Economic Report of the President, 1992.

is influenced by central bank intervention in the foreign exchange market. Under a managed exchange rate regime, the central bank's intervention does not seek to keep the exchange rate fixed at a preannounced level.

Recent Exchange Rate History

At the end of World War II, the major countries of the world set up the International Monetary Fund (IMF). The **International Monetary Fund** is an international organization that monitors balance of payments and exchange rate activities. The IMF is located in Washington, D.C. It came into being as a result of negotiations between the United States and the United Kingdom during World War II. In July 1944, at Bretton Woods, New Hampshire, 44 countries signed the Articles of Agreement of the IMF. At the centerpiece of those agreements was the establishment of a worldwide system of fixed exchange rates between currencies. The anchor for this fixed exchange rate system was gold. One ounce of gold was defined to be worth 35 U.S. dollars. All other currencies were pegged to the U.S. dollar at a fixed exchange rate. For example, the Japanese yen was set at 360 yen per dollar; the British pound was set to be worth $4.80. Although the fixed exchange rate system established in 1944 served the world well during the 1950s and early 1960s, it came under increasing strain in the late 1960s, and by 1971 the order had almost collapsed. In the period since 1971, the world has operated a variety of flexible and managed exchange rate arrangements. Some currencies have increased in value, and others have declined. The U.S. dollar is among the currencies that have declined. The Japanese yen is the currency that has had the most spectacular increase in value.

Figure 36.4 shows what happened to the exchange rate of the U.S. dollar between 1975 and 1991. The red line shows the value of the dollar against the Japanese yen. As you can see, the value of the dollar has fallen against the yen—the dollar has depreciated. **Currency depreciation** is the fall in the value of one currency in terms of another currency.

Although the dollar has depreciated in terms of the Japanese yen, it has not depreciated, on the average, in terms of all other currencies. To calculate the value of the U.S. dollar in terms of other currencies on the average, a trade-weighted index is calculated. The **trade-weighted index** is the value of a basket of currencies when the weight placed on each currency is related to its importance in U.S. international trade. An example of the calculation of the trade-weighted index is set out in Table 36.3. In this example, we suppose that the United States trades with only three countries: Canada, Japan, and Great Britain. Fifty percent of the trade is with Canada, 30 percent with Japan, and 20 percent with Great Britain. In year 1, the U.S. dollar is worth either 1.25 Canadian dollars, 100 Japanese yen, or 0.50 British pound. Imagine putting these three currencies into a "basket" worth 100 U.S. dollars, in which 50 percent of the value of the basket is in Canadian dollars, 30 percent in Japanese yen, and 20 percent in British pounds. In year 1, the index number for the basket is 100. Suppose that in year 2, the exchange rates change in the way shown in the table. The Canadian dollar stays constant; the Japanese yen goes up in value, so only 90 Japanese yen can be bought for 1 U.S. dollar; and the British pound goes down in value, so 1 U.S. dollar buys 0.55 British pound. What is the change in the value of the basket? The percentage changes in the value of the U.S. dollar against each currency are calculated in the table. The dollar goes down against the Japanese yen by 10 percent and up against the British pound by 10 percent. Applying the trade weights to these percentage changes, we can calculate the weighted average change in the value of the U.S. dollar. Since the weight on the Japanese yen is 0.3 and that on the British pound is 0.2, the yen is more important than the pound. That is, a larger fraction of the basket's value consists of yen than of pounds. The weighted average value of the basket falls by 1 percent. The trade-weighted index declines by 1 percent and is 99. In this example, the U.S. dollar has depreciated on the average against the other three currencies.

The calculations that we have just worked through used hypothetical numbers. How the U.S. dollar has actually fluctuated against other currencies on the average in the period 1975 to 1991 is shown in Fig. 36.4. As you can see, during the 1970s the value of the U.S. dollar fluctuated but on the average remained steady against other currencies; from 1980 to 1985 it appreciated very strongly; and after 1985 it depreciated almost equally strongly.

TABLE 36.3

Trade-Weighted Index Calculation

Currency	Trade weights	Exchange rates (units of foreign currency per U.S. dollar) Year 1	Year 2	Percentage changes Unweighted	Weighted
Canadian dollar	**0.5**	**1.25**	**1.25**	**0**	**0**
Japanese yen	**0.3**	**100**	**90**	**–10**	**–3**
British pound	**0.2**	**0.50**	**0.55**	**+10**	**+2**
Total	**1.0**				**–1**

Trade-weighted index: year 1 = 100
year 2 = 99

Exchange Rate Determination

What determines the foreign currency value of the dollar? The foreign exchange value of the dollar is a price and, like any other price, is determined by demand and supply. But what exactly do we mean by the demand for and supply of dollars? And what is the quantity of dollars?

The Quantity of U.S. Dollar Assets The **quantity of U.S. dollar assets** (which we'll call the **quantity of dollars**) is the *stock* of financial assets denominated in U.S. dollars minus the *stock* of financial liabilities denominated in U.S. dollars. In other words, it is the *stock of net financial assets denominated in U.S. dollars.* There are three things about the quantity of dollars that need to be emphasized and explained a bit more fully.

First, the quantity of dollars is a *stock,* not a *flow.* People make decisions about the quantity of dollars to hold and about the quantities to buy or sell. But it is the decision about how many dollars to hold that determines whether people plan to buy or sell dollars.

Second, the quantity of dollars is a stock *denominated in U.S. dollars.* The denomination of an asset defines the units in which a debt must be repaid. It is possible to make a loan using any currency of denomination. The U.S. government could borrow Japanese yen. If it did borrow in yen, it would issue a bond denominated in yen. Such a bond would be a promise to pay an agreed number of yen on an agreed date. It would not be a dollar debt and, even though issued by the U.S. government, would not be part of the supply of dollars. Many governments actually do issue bonds in currencies other than their own. The Canadian government, for example, issues bonds denominated in U.S. dollars, British pounds, German marks, and Swiss francs.

Third, the supply of dollars is a *net* supply—the quantity of assets *minus* the quantity of liabilities. This fact means that the quantity of dollars supplied does not include dollar assets created by private households, firms, financial institutions, or foreigners. The reason is that when a private debt is created, there is both an asset (for the holder) and a liability (for the issuer), so the *net* financial asset is zero. The quantity of dollars includes only the dollar liabilities of the federal government *plus* those of the Fed. This quantity is equal to the government debt held outside the Fed plus the dollar liabilities of the Fed—the monetary base (see p. 766). That is,

Quantity of dollars = Government debt held outside the Fed + Monetary base.

Changes in the Quantity of Dollar Assets There are two ways in which the quantity of dollar assets can change:

- The federal government has a deficit or surplus.
- The Fed buys or sells assets denominated in foreign currency.

When the federal government has a deficit, it borrows by issuing bonds. These bonds, denominated in U.S. dollars, are held by households, firms, financial institutions, foreigners, and the Fed. Bonds bought by the Fed are not part of the stock of dollar assets. But to buy the bonds, the Fed creates additional monetary base, and this equivalent amount *is* part of the quantity of dollar assets. Thus when the Fed buys U.S. government debt, there is no change in the quantity of dollar assets, just a change in its composition.

The Fed can increase the quantity of dollars by buying assets denominated in foreign currency. If the Fed buys Japanese yen in the foreign exchange market, the monetary base increases by the amount paid for the yen.

We've now seen what dollar assets are and how their quantity can change. Let's now study the demand for these assets.

The Demand for Dollar Assets

The law of demand applies to dollar assets just as it does to anything else that people value. The quantity of dollar assets demanded increases when the price of dollars in terms of foreign currency falls and decreases when the price of dollars in terms of foreign currency rises. There are two separate reasons why the law of demand applies to dollars.

First, there is a transactions demand. The lower the value of the dollar, the larger is the demand for U.S. exports and the lower is our demand for imports, so the larger also is the amount of trade financed by dollars. Foreigners demand more dollars to buy U.S. exports, and we demand fewer units of foreign currency and more dollars as we switch from importing to buying U.S.-produced goods.

Second, there is a demand arising from expected capital gains. Other things being equal, the lower the value of the dollar today, the higher is its expected rate of appreciation (or the lower is its expected rate of depreciation), so the higher is the expected gain from holding dollar assets relative to the expected gain from holding foreign currency assets. Suppose that you expect the dollar to be worth 110 Japanese yen at the end of one year. If today the dollar is worth 120 yen, you're expecting the dollar to depreciate by 10 yen.

Other things being equal, you will not plan to hold dollar assets in this situation. Instead, you will plan to hold yen assets. But if today's value of the dollar is 100 yen, then you're expecting the dollar to appreciate by 10 yen. In this situation, you will plan to hold dollar assets and take advantage of the expected rise in their value. Holding assets in a particular currency in anticipation of a gain in their value arising from a change in the exchange rate is one of the most important influences on the quantity demanded of dollar assets and of foreign currency assets. The more a currency is expected to appreciate, the greater is the quantity of assets in that currency that people want to hold.

Figure 36.5 shows the relationship between the price of the U.S. dollar in yen and the quantity of dollar assets demanded—the demand curve for dollar assets. When the foreign exchange rate changes, other things being equal, there is a movement along the demand curve.

Any other influence on the quantity of dollar assets that people want to hold results in a shift in the demand curve. Demand either increases or decreases. These other influences are

- The volume of dollar-financed trade
- The interest rates on dollar assets
- The interest rates on foreign currency assets
- The expected future value of the dollar

Table 36.4 summarizes the above discussion of the influences on the quantity of dollar assets that people demand.

FIGURE 36.5

The Demand for Dollar Assets

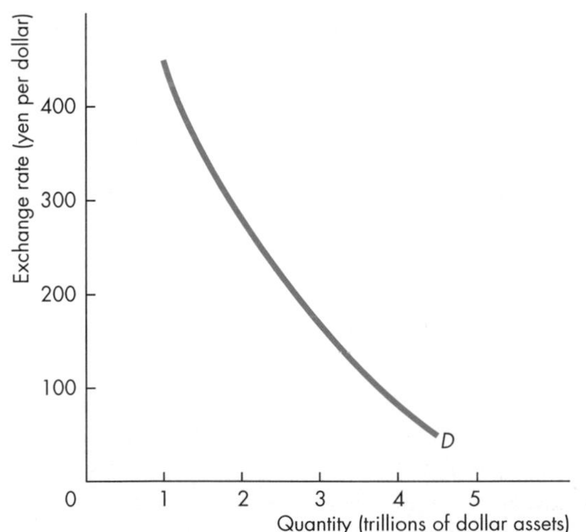

The quantity of dollar assets that people demand, other things held constant, depends on the exchange rate. The lower the exchange rate (the smaller the number of yen per dollar), the larger is the quantity of dollar assets demanded. The increased quantity demanded arises from an increase in the volume of dollar trade (the Japanese buy more American goods and we buy fewer Japanese goods) and an increase in the expected appreciation (or decrease in the expected depreciation) of dollar assets.

TABLE 36.4

The Demand for Dollar Assets

The law of demand

The quantity of dollar assets demanded	
Increases if:	***Decreases if:***
The foreign currency value of the dollar falls	**The foreign currency value of the dollar rises**

Changes in demand

The demand for dollar assets	
Increases if:	***Decreases if:***
Dollar-financed trade increases	**Dollar-financed trade decreases**
Interest rates on dollar assets rise	**Interest rates on dollar assets fall**
Interest rates on foreign currency assets fall	**Interest rates on foreign currency assets rise**
The dollar is expected to appreciate	**The dollar is expected to depreciate**

The Supply of Dollar Assets

The supply of dollar assets is determined by the actions of the government and the Federal Reserve. We've seen that the quantity of dollars is equal to government debt plus the monetary base. Of these two items, the monetary base is by far the smallest. But it plays a crucial role in determining the supply of dollars, since the behavior of the monetary base itself depends crucially on the foreign exchange rate regime in operation.

Under a fixed exchange rate regime, the supply curve of dollar assets is horizontal at the chosen exchange rate. The Fed stands ready to supply whatever quantity of dollar assets is demanded at the fixed exchange rate. Under a managed exchange rate regime, the government wants to smooth fluctuations in the exchange rate, so the supply curve of dollar assets is upward-sloping. The higher the foreign exchange rate, the larger is the quantity of dollar assets supplied. Under a flexible exchange rate regime, a fixed quantity of dollar assets is supplied, regardless of their price. As a consequence, under a flexible exchange rate regime, the supply curve of dollar assets is vertical.

The supply of dollar assets changes over time as a result of the following:

- The government's budget
- The Fed's monetary policy

If the government has a budget deficit, the supply of dollar assets increases. If the government has a budget surplus, the supply of dollar assets decreases. The supply of dollar assets increases whenever the Fed increases the monetary base and decreases whenever the Fed reduces the monetary base.

The above discussion of the influences on the supply of dollar assets is summarized in Table 36.5.

The Market for Dollar Assets

Let's now bring the demand and supply sides of the market for dollar assets together and determine the exchange rate. Figure 36.6 illustrates the analysis.

Fixed Exchange Rate First, consider a fixed exchange rate regime such as that from 1944 to 1971. This case is illustrated in Fig. 36.6(a). The supply curve of dollars is horizontal at the fixed exchange rate of 200 yen per dollar. If the demand curve is D_0, the quantity of dollar assets is Q_0. An increase in demand to D_1 results in an increase in the quantity of dollar assets from Q_0 to Q_1 but no change in the yen price of dollars.

Flexible Exchange Rate Next look at Fig. 36.6(b), which shows what happens under a flexible exchange rate regime. In this case, the quantity of dollar assets supplied is fixed at Q_0, so the supply curve of dollar assets is vertical. If the demand curve for dollars is D_0, the exchange rate is 200 yen per dollar. If the demand for dollars increases from D_0 to D_1, the exchange rate increases to 300 yen per dollar.

Managed Exchange Rate Finally, consider a managed exchange rate regime, which appears in Fig. 36.6(c). Here, the supply curve is upward-sloping. When the demand curve is D_0, the exchange rate is 200 yen per dollar. If demand increases to D_1, the yen value of the dollar rises, but only to 225 yen per dollar. Compared with the flexible exchange rate case, the same increase in demand results in a smaller increase in the exchange rate when it is managed.

TABLE 36.5
The Supply of Dollar Assets

Supply

Fixed exchange rate regime

The supply curve of dollar assets is horizontal at the fixed exchange rate.

Managed exchange rate regime

In order to smooth fluctuations in the price of the dollar, the quantity of dollar assets supplied by the Fed increases if the foreign currency price of the dollar rises and decreases if the foreign currency price of the dollar falls. The supply curve of dollar assets is upward-sloping.

Flexible exchange rate

The supply curve of dollar assets is vertical.

Changes in supply

The supply of dollar assets

Increases if:	*Decreases if:*
◆ **The U.S. government has a deficit**	◆ **The U.S. government has a surplus**
◆ **The Fed increases the monetary base**	◆ **The Fed decreases the monetary base**

FIGURE 36.6

Three Exchange Rate Regimes

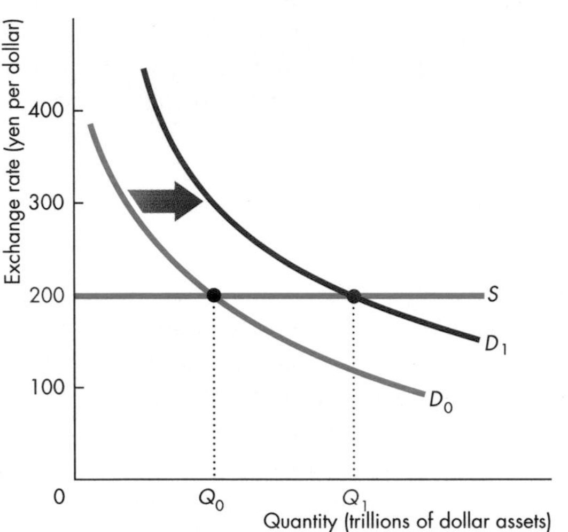

(a) Fixed exchange rate

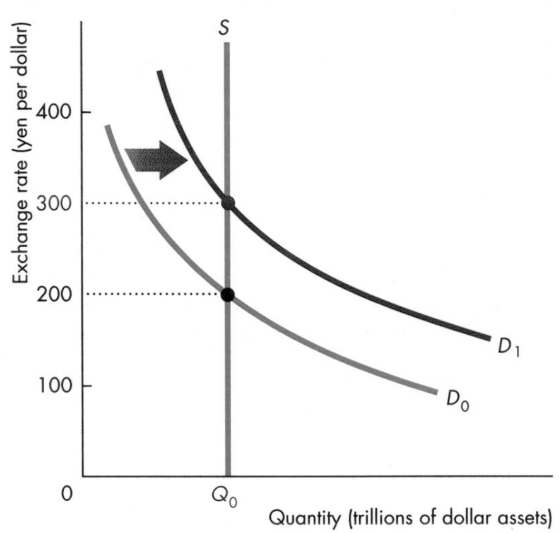

(b) Flexible exchange rate

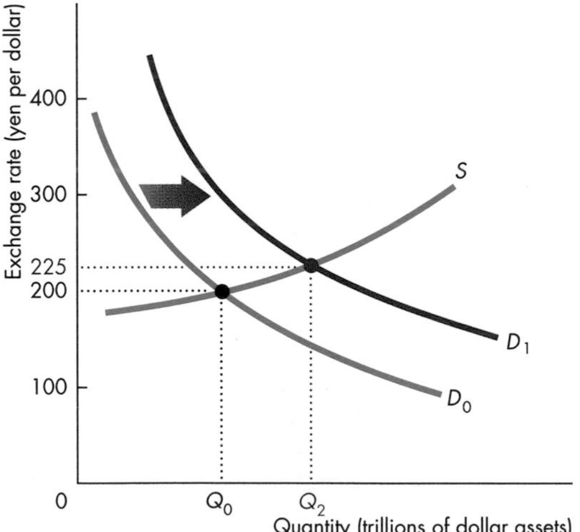

(c) Managed exchange rate

Under a fixed exchange rate regime (part a), the Fed stands ready to supply dollar assets or to take dollar assets off the market (supplying foreign currency in exchange) at a fixed exchange rate. The supply curve for dollar assets is horizontal. Fluctuations in demand lead to fluctuations in the quantity of dollar assets outstanding and to fluctuations in the nation's official holdings of foreign exchange. If demand increases from D_0 to D_1, the quantity of dollar assets increases from Q_0 to Q_1. Under a flexible exchange rate regime (part b), the Fed fixes the quantity of dollar assets so that their supply curve is vertical. An increase in the demand for dollar assets from D_0 to D_1 results only in an increase in the value of the dollar—the exchange rate rises from 200 to 300 yen per dollar. The quantity of dollar assets remains constant at Q_0. Under a managed exchange rate regime (part c), the Fed has an upward-sloping supply curve of dollar assets, so if demand increases from D_0 to D_1, the dollar appreciates but the quantity of dollar assets supplied also increases—from Q_0 to Q_2. The increase in the quantity of dollar assets supplied moderates the rise in the value of the dollar but does not completely prevent it as in the case of fixed exchange rates.

The reason for this is that the quantity supplied increases in the managed exchange rate case.

Exchange Rate Regime and Official Settlements Balance There is an important connection between the foreign exchange rate regime and the balance of payments. The official settlements account of the balance of payments records the change in the country's official holdings (by the government and the Fed) of foreign currency. Under fixed exchange rates (as shown in Fig. 36.6a), every time there is a change in the demand for dollar assets, the Fed must change the quantity of dollar assets supplied to match it. When the Fed has to increase the quantity of dollar assets supplied, it does so by offering dollar assets (bank deposits) in exchange for foreign currency (foreign bank deposits). In this case, the official holdings of foreign exchange increase. If the demand for dollar assets decreases, the Fed has to decrease the quantity of dollar assets supplied. The Fed does so by buying dollars back, using its foreign exchange holdings to do so. In this case, official holdings of foreign exchange decrease. Thus with a fixed exchange rate, fluctuations in the demand for dollar assets result in fluctuations in official holdings of foreign exchange.

Under a flexible exchange rate regime, there is no government or Fed intervention in the foreign exchange market. Regardless of what happens to the demand for dollars, no action is taken to change the quantity of dollars supplied. Therefore there are no changes in the country's official holdings of foreign exchange. In this case, the official settlements balance is zero.

With a managed exchange rate, official holdings of foreign exchange have to be adjusted to meet fluctuations in demand but in a less extreme manner than under fixed exchange rates. As a consequence, fluctuations in the official settlements balance are smaller under a managed floating regime than in a fixed exchange rate regime.

Up to 1970, the United States operated a fixed exchange rate, but so did all the other countries in the world. Furthermore, the United States was the largest country in the system. The task of keeping exchange rates fixed under that system was left to the individual smaller countries. Thus it was the Japanese government and the Bank of Japan that were charged with the responsibility of maintaining the yen-dollar exchange rate; the British government and the Bank of England were charged with maintaining the exchange rate of the British pound. Since 1971, the United States has been on a managed exchange rate regime, but on occasion it has come close to having a flexible exchange rate.

Why Is the Exchange Rate So Volatile?

We've seen times, especially recently, when the dollar-yen exchange rate has moved dramatically. On most of these occasions, the dollar has depreciated spectacularly, but on some occasions it has appreciated strongly.

The main reason why the exchange rate fluctuates so remarkably is that fluctuations in supply and demand are not always independent of each other. Sometimes a change in supply will trigger a change in demand that reinforces the effect of the change in supply. Let's look at two episodes to see how these effects work.

1981 to 1982 Between 1981 and 1982, the dollar appreciated against the yen, rising from 220 to 250 yen per dollar. Figure 36.7(a) explains why this happened. In 1981, the demand and supply curves were those labeled D_{81} and S_{81}. The foreign exchange value of the dollar was 220 yen—where these supply and demand curves intersect. The period between 1981 and 1982 was one of severe recession. This recession was brought about in part by the Fed pursuing a very restrictive monetary policy. The Fed permitted interest rates to rise sharply, cutting back on the monetary base and thus on the supply of dollar assets. The direct effect was a shift in the supply curve from S_{81} to S_{82}—a decrease in the supply of dollars. But higher U.S. interest rates induced an increase in demand for dollars to take advantage of the higher interest rates. As a result, the demand curve shifted from D_{81} to D_{82}. These two shifts reinforced each other, increasing the yen price of the dollar to 250 yen.

1985 to 1986 There was a spectacular depreciation of the dollar in terms of yen from 240 yen per dollar in 1985 to 170 yen per dollar in 1986. This fall came about in the following way. First, in 1985, the demand and supply curves were those labeled D_{85} and S_{85} in Fig. 36.7(b). The yen price of the dollar—the price at which these two curves intersect—was 240 yen per dollar. From 1982 to 1985, the U.S. economy had been on a recovery. But it was a recovery through which a budget deficit of increasing severity was emerging. Thus with a large government deficit, the supply of dollar assets was increasing. The Fed was also loosening up its monetary policy, permitting money supply growth rates to be rapid enough to keep the recovery going. The direct effect of these actions was an increase in the supply of dollar assets from S_{85} to S_{86}. But interest rates in the United States began to fall, and expectations of future declines in the value of the dollar also became widely held. As a consequence, the demand for dollar assets decreased from D_{85} to D_{86}. The result of this combined increase in supply and decrease in demand was a dramatic fall in the value of the dollar to 170 yen in 1986.

FIGURE 36.7

Why the Exchange Rate Is So Volatile

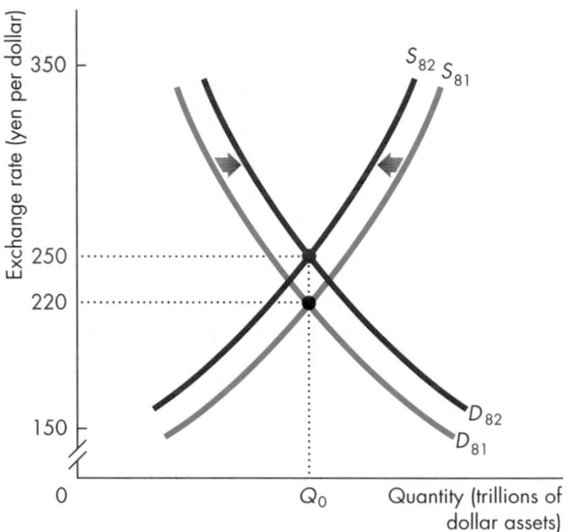

(a) 1981 to 1982

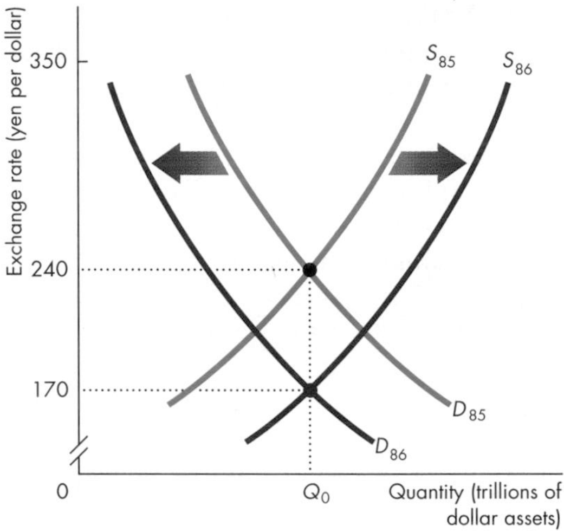

(b) 1985 to 1986

The exchange rate is volatile because shifts in the demand and supply curves for dollar assets are not independent of each other. Between 1981 and 1982 (part a), the dollar appreciated from 220 to 250 yen per dollar. This appreciation arose because the supply curve of dollar assets shifted to the left and higher interest rates induced an increase in demand for dollar assets, shifting the demand curve to the right. The result was a large increase in the foreign exchange value of the dollar.

Between 1985 and 1986 (in part b), the Fed permitted the quantity of dollar assets to increase to sustain the long economic recovery. The supply curve shifted to the right. At the same time, interest rates decreased and expectations of further declines in the value of the dollar shifted the demand curve to the left. The result was a steep fall in the exchange rate, from 240 yen to 170 yen per dollar between 1985 and 1986.

REVIEW

There are three possible foreign exchange rate regimes: fixed, flexible, and managed. Under a fixed exchange rate regime, the government and the Fed hold the exchange rate steady but the official settlements account of the balance of payments has to carry the burden of holding the exchange rate constant. A decrease in the demand for U.S. dollar assets is met by lowering the country's official holdings of foreign currency. Under a flexible exchange rate regime, the government and the Fed do not intervene in the foreign exchange markets. The official settlements balance is zero, and the country's official holdings of foreign currency remain constant. Under a managed exchanged rate regime, the Fed smooths exchange rate fluctuations to a degree but less strongly than under fixed exchange rates. Under a flexible or managed exchange rate regime, the exchange rate is determined by the demand for and supply of dollar assets. Fluctuations in supply often induce reinforcing fluctuations in demand, bringing severe fluctuations in the exchange rate. ◆

Arbitrage, Prices, and Interest Rates

Arbitrage is the activity of buying low and selling high in order to make a profit on the margin between the two prices.

Arbitrage has important effects on exchange rates, prices, and interest rates. An increase in the quantity of purchases forces the buying price up. A decrease in the quantity of sales forces the selling price down. The prices move until they are equal and there is no arbitrage profit available. An implication of arbitrage is the law of one price. The **law of one price** states that any given commodity will be available at a single price.

The law of one price has no respect for national borders or currencies. If the same commodity is being bought and sold on either side of the Detroit River, it doesn't matter that one of these transactions is being undertaken in Canada and the other in the United States and that one is using U.S. dollars and the other Canadian dollars. The forces of arbitrage bring about one price. Let's see how.

Arbitrage

Consider the price of a floppy disk that can be bought in either the United States or Canada. We will ignore taxes, tariffs, and transportation costs in order to keep the calculations simple, since these factors do not affect the fundamental issue.

Suppose that we can buy floppy disks in the United States for US$10 a box. Suppose that this same box of disks is available in Canada for C$15 a box. (The symbol US$ stands for the U.S. dollar and C$ for the Canadian dollar.) Where would it pay to buy disks—in Canada or in the United States? The answer depends on the relative costs of Canadian and U.S. money. If a U.S. dollar costs C$1.50, then it is clear that the price of the disks is the same in both countries. Americans can buy a box of disks in the United States for US$10, or they can use US$10 to buy C$15 and then buy the disks in Canada. The cost will be the same either way. The same is true for Canadians. Canadians can use C$15 to buy a box of disks in Canada, or they can use C$15 to buy US$10 and then buy the disks in the United States. Again, there is no difference in the price of the disks.

Suppose, however, that a U.S. dollar is less valuable than in the above example. In particular, suppose that a U.S. dollar costs C$1.40. In this case, it will pay to buy the disks in the United States. Canadians can buy US$10 for C$14 and therefore can buy the disks in the United States for C$14 a box compared with C$15 in Canada. The same comparison holds for Americans. Americans can use US$10 to buy C$14, but that would not be enough to buy the disks in Canada since the disks cost C$15 there. It therefore pays Americans also to buy the disks in the United States.

If the situation described above did prevail, there would be an advantage in switching the purchases of disks from Canada to the United States. Canadians would cross the border to buy their disks in the United States and keep on doing so until the Canadian price had fallen to C$14. Once that had happened, Canadians would be indifferent between buying their disks in Canada and in the United States. Arbitrage would have eliminated the difference in prices in the two countries.

Perhaps you are thinking that this is a pretty crazy example, since Canadians don't rush down to the United States every time they want to buy a box of floppy disks. But the fact that there is a profit to be made means that it would pay someone to organize the importing of disks into Canada from the United States, thereby increasing the number of disks available there and lowering their price. The incentive to undertake such a move would be present as long as disks were selling for a higher price in Canada than in the United States.

Purchasing Power Parity

Purchasing power parity occurs when money has equal value across countries. (The word *parity* simply means equality. The phrase *purchasing power* refers to the *value of money.* Thus *purchasing power parity* directly translates to *equal value of money.*) Purchasing power parity is an implication of arbitrage and of the law of one price. In the floppy disk example, when US$1 is worth C$1.40, US$10 will buy the same box of floppy disks that C$14 will buy. The value of money, when converted to common prices, is the same in both countries. Purchasing power parity thus prevails in that situation.

Purchasing power parity theory predicts that purchasing power parity applies to all goods and to price indexes, not just to a single good such as the floppy disk that we considered above. That is, if any goods are cheaper in one country than in another, it will pay to convert money into the currency of that country, buy the goods in that country, and sell them in another. By such an arbitrage process, all prices are brought to equality.

One test of the purchasing power parity theory that has been proposed is to calculate the prices of goods in different countries converted to a common currency. One such good that has been used is the Big Mac, sold by McDonald's in all the major countries. It is claimed that if purchasing power parity holds, the Big Mac will cost the same everywhere. In fact, the Big Mac is more expensive in Tokyo than in Toronto and more expensive in Toronto than in Buenos Aires. These facts have led some people to conclude that purchasing power parity does not hold.

There is an important problem with this test of purchasing power parity. Big Macs are not easily traded internationally. In fact, they are not even easily traded across cities within the United States. For example, it's lunch time in Provo, you are hungry, and Big Macs are your thing. You don't have much choice but to buy your Big Mac right there. You can't take advantage of the fact that Big Macs are cheaper in Houston and begin an arbitrage operation. Big Macs are examples of nontraded goods. A **nontraded good** is one that cannot be traded over long distances. Sometimes it is technically possible to undertake such a trade but prohibitively costly. In other cases, it is simply not possible to undertake the trade.

There are many examples of nontraded goods. Almost all the public services provided by the government are nontraded. You can't buy cheap street-sweeping services in Seoul and sell them at a profit in San Francisco. Location-specific services, such as fast food, are also in this category. When goods cannot be traded over long distances, the goods are strictly different goods. A Big Mac in Provo is as different from a Big Mac in Houston as it is from a pancake across the street.

"On the foreign-exchange markets today, the dollar fell against all major currencies and the doughnut."

Arbitrage operates to bring about equality in prices of identical goods, not different goods. It does not operate to bring about equality between prices of similar-looking goods in widely differing locations. For this reason, tests of the purchasing power parity theory based on the prices of nontraded goods are faulty. In fact, for nontraded goods to have identical prices in different countries, every time the exchange rate changes, the prices of all goods will also have to change—the dollar will have to fall against all currencies, the Big Mac, and the doughnut!

Arbitrage does not occur only in markets for goods and services. It also occurs in markets for assets. As a result, it brings about another important equality or parity—interest rate parity.

Interest Rate Parity

Interest rate parity occurs when interest rates are equal across countries once the differences in risk are taken into account. Interest rate parity is a condition brought about by arbitrage in the markets for assets—markets in which borrowers and lenders operate.

At the beginning of this chapter, we noted that there are large differences in the interest rates at which people borrow and lend in different countries. For example, in the United States, interest rates are much lower than in England. Suppose that it is possible to borrow in New York at an interest rate of 6 percent a year and lend in London at an interest rate of 12 percent a year. Isn't it possible, in this situation, to make a huge profit on such a transaction? In fact, it is not. Interest rates in New York and London are actually equal—interest rate parity prevails.

The key to understanding why the interest rates are equal is to realize that when you borrow in New York, you borrow *dollars,* and when you lend money in England—such as by placing it on deposit in a bank—you are lending *pounds.* You are obliged to repay *dollars,* but you will be repaid in *pounds.* It's a bit like borrowing apples and lending oranges. But if you're borrowing apples and lending oranges, you've got to convert the apples to oranges. When the loans become due, you've got to convert oranges back into apples. The prices at which you do these transactions affect the interest rates that you pay and receive. How many dollars you get for your pounds depends on the exchange rate when the loan is repaid. If the pound has fallen in value, you'll get fewer dollars per pound than you paid in the first place.

The difference between the interest rates in New York and London reflects the change in the exchange rate between the dollar and the pound that, on the average, people are expecting. In this example, the average expectation is that the pound will fall against the dollar by 6 percent a year. So when you sell pounds to repay your dollar loan, you can expect to get 6 percent fewer dollars than you needed by buy the pounds. This 6 percent foreign exchange loss must be subtracted from the 12 percent interest income you earn in London. Thus your return from lending in London, when you convert your money back into dollars, is the same 6 percent that you must pay for the funds in New York. Your profit is zero. Actually, you would incur a loss because you would pay commissions on your foreign exchange transactions.

In the situation that we've just described, interest rate parity prevails. The interest rate in New York, when the expected change in the price of the dollar is taken into account, is almost identical to that in London. If interest rate parity did *not* prevail, it would be possible to profit, without risk, by borrowing at low interest rates and lending at high interest rates. Such *arbitrage* actions would increase the demand for loans in countries with low interest rates, and their interest rates would rise. And these actions would increase the supply of loans in countries with high interest rates, and their interest rates would fall. Such movements would restore interest rate parity very quickly.

A World Market

Arbitrage in asset markets operates on a worldwide scale and keeps the world capital markets linked in a single global market. This market is an enormous one. It involves borrowing and lending through banks, in bond markets, and in stock markets. The scale of this international business has been estimated by Salomon Brothers, an investment bank, at more than $1 trillion. It is because of international arbitrage in asset markets that the fortunes of the stock markets around the world are so closely linked. A stock market crash in New York makes its new low-priced stocks look attractive compared with high-priced stocks in Tokyo, Hong Kong, Zurich, Frankfurt, and London. As a consequence, investors make plans to sell high in these other markets and buy low in New York. But before many such transactions can be put through, the prices in the other markets fall to match the fall in New York. Conversely, if the Tokyo market experiences rapid price increases and markets in the rest of the world stay constant, investors seek to sell high in Tokyo and buy low in the rest of the world. Again, these trading plans will induce movements in the prices in the other markets to bring them into line with the Tokyo market. The action of selling high in Tokyo will lower the prices there, and the action of buying low in Frankfurt, London, and New York will raise the prices there.

◆ ◆ ◆ ◆ You've now discovered what determines a country's current account balance and the value of its currency. The most important influence on the current account balance is the government budget deficit. A country in which taxes are less than government spending is likely to be one that has a deficit in its trade with the rest of the world. The value of a country's currency is determined by the demand for and supply of that currency and is strongly influenced by monetary actions. A rapid increase in the supply of a currency will result in a decline in its value relative to other currencies. ◆ ◆ You've also learned how international arbitrage links prices and interest rates together in different countries. International arbitrage does not occur in markets for nontraded goods. But arbitrage operates in markets for traded goods and is especially powerful in markets for assets. Arbitrage in asset markets keeps interest rates equal around the world. Differences in national interest rates reflect the expectations of changes in exchange rates. Once these differences in exchange rates are taken into account, interest rates are equal across countries. ◆ ◆ In the final two chapters, we're going to look at some further global economic issues. First, in Chapter 37, we'll examine the problems faced by developing countries as they seek to grow. Then, in Chapter 38, we'll look at the countries of Eastern Europe and China as they make the transition from planned economies to market economies.

Summary

Financing International Trade

International trade, borrowing, and lending are financed by using foreign currency. A country's international transactions are recorded in its balance of payments accounts. The current account records receipts and expenditures connected with the sale and purchase of goods and services, as well as net transfers to the rest of the world; the capital account records international borrowing and lending transactions; the official settlements account shows the increase or decrease in the country's foreign currency holdings.

Historically, the United States has been a net lender to the rest of the world, but in the mid-1980s that situation changed and it became a huge net borrower and a net debtor. Nevertheless, the stock of U.S. investment in the rest of the world exceeds foreign investment here.

The current account deficit is equal to the government budget deficit plus the private sector deficit. The private sector deficit is small, and fluctuations in the trade balance arise mainly from fluctuations in the government's budget. As the government budget deficit has grown, so the trade deficit has also grown. (pp. 982–991)

Foreign Exchange and the Dollar

Foreign currency is obtained in exchange for domestic currency in the foreign exchange market. There are three types of foreign exchange rate regimes: fixed, flexible, and managed. When the exchange rate is fixed, the government declares a value for the currency in terms of some other currency and the Fed takes actions to ensure that that price is maintained. To fix the exchange rate, the Fed has to stand ready to supply dollars and take in foreign currency or to remove dollars from circulation in exchange for foreign currency. The country's reserves of foreign currency fluctuate to maintain the fixed exchange rate.

A flexible exchange rate is one in which the central bank takes no actions to influence the value of its currency in the foreign exchange market. The country's holdings of foreign currencies remain constant, and fluctuations in demand and supply lead to fluctuations in the exchange rate.

A managed exchange rate is one in which the central bank takes actions to smooth fluctuations that would otherwise arise but does so less strongly than under a fixed exchange rate regime.

In a flexible or managed exchange rate regime, the exchange rate is determined by the demand for and supply of dollars. The demand for dollars depends on the volume of dollar trade financed, the interest rates on dollar assets, the interest rates on foreign currency assets, and expected changes in the value of the dollar.

The supply of dollars depends on the exchange rate regime. Under fixed exchange rates, the supply curve is horizontal; under flexible exchange rates, the supply curve is vertical; under managed exchange rates, the supply curve is upward-sloping. The position of the supply curve depends on the government's budget and the Fed's monetary policy. The larger the budget deficit or the more rapidly the Fed permits the monetary base to grow, the further to the right the supply curve moves. Fluctuations in the exchange rate occur because of fluctuations in demand and supply, and sometimes these fluctuations are large. Large fluctuations arise from interlinked changes in demand and supply. A shift in the supply curve often produces an induced change in the demand curve that reinforces the effect on the exchange rate. (pp. 991–1000)

Arbitrage, Prices, and Interest Rates

Arbitrage—buying low and selling high—keeps the prices of goods and services that are traded internationally close to equality across all countries. Arbitrage also keeps the different interest rates in line with each other.

Interest rates around the world look unequal, but the appearance arises from the fact that loans are contracted in different currencies in different countries. To compare interest rates across countries, we have to take into account changes in the values of currencies. Countries whose currencies are appreciating have low interest rates; countries whose currencies are depreciating have high interest rates. If the rate of currency depreciation is taken into account, interest rates are nearly equal. (pp. 1000–1003)

Key Elements

Key Terms

Arbitrage, 1000
Balance of payments accounts, 982
Capital account, 983
Creditor nation, 984
Currency depreciation, 994
Current account, 982
Debtor nation, 984
Fixed exchange rate, 991
Flexible exchange rate, 992
Foreign exchange market, 991
Foreign exchange rate, 991
Interest rate parity, 1002
International Monetary Fund, 993
Law of one price, 1001
Managed exchange rate, 992
Net borrower, 984
Net lender, 984
Nontraded good, 1002
Official reserves, 983
Official settlements account, 983
Private sector surplus or deficit, 985
Purchasing power parity, 1001
Quantity of U.S. dollar assets (quantity of dollars), 995
Trade-weighted index, 994
Twin deficits, 987

Key Figures and Tables

Review Questions

1 What are the transactions recorded in a country's current account, capital account, and official settlements account?

2 What is the relationship between the balance on the current account, the capital account, and the official settlements account?

3 Distinguish between a country that is a net borrower and one that is a creditor. Are net borrowers always creditors? Are creditors always net borrowers?

4 What is the connection between a country's current account balance, the government's budget deficit, and the private sector deficit?

5 Why do fluctuations in the government budget balance lead to fluctuations in the current account balance?

6 Distinguish among the three exchange rate regimes: fixed, flexible, and managed.

7 Review the main influences on the quantity of dollars that people demand.

8 Review the influences on the supply of dollars.

9 How does the supply curve of dollars differ under the three exchange rate regimes?

10 Why does the dollar fluctuate so much?

11 What is arbitrage?

12 How does arbitrage lead to purchasing power parity?

13 What is interest rate parity?

14 How does interest rate parity come about?

PROBLEMS

1 The citizens of Silecon, whose currency is the grain, conducted the following transactions in 1990:

	Billions of grains
Imports of goods and services	350
Exports of goods and services	500
Borrowing from the rest of the world	60
Lending to the rest of the world	200
Increase in official holdings of foreign currency	10

a Set out the three balance of payments accounts for Silecon.
b Does Silecon have a flexible exchange rate?

2 You are told the following about Ecflex, a country with a flexible exchange rate whose currency is the band:

	Billions of bands
GDP	100
Consumption expenditure	60
Government purchases of goods and services	24
Investment	22
Exports of goods and services	20
Government budget deficit	4

Calculate the following for Ecflex:
a Imports of goods and services
b Current account balance
c Capital account balance
d Taxes (net of transfer payments)
e Private sector deficit or surplus

3 A country's currency appreciates, and its official holdings of foreign currency increase. What can you say about the following?
a The exchange rate regime being pursued by the country
b The country's current account
c The country's official settlements account

4 The average annual interest rate in Japan is 4 percent; in the United States it is 6 percent; in Germany it is 9 percent; and in England it is 13 percent. What is the expected percentage change over the coming year in each of the following?
a The U.S. dollar against the Japanese yen
b The British pound against the German mark
c The U.S. dollar against the British pound
d The Japanese yen against the German mark
e The U.S. dollar against the German mark

PART 14

Growth, Development, and Reform

Talking with Jeffrey Sachs

Jeffrey Sachs was born in Detroit in 1954 and has spent his entire university career at Harvard, first as an undergraduate and eventually as a professor. Today, however, Professor Sachs spends most of his time on airplanes or in Eastern Europe. He first began advising foreign governments on economic policy by helping Bolivia with hyperinflation in 1985. His name burst before the public with his work on Poland, but now he is increasingly associated with the economic reforms of Boris Yeltsin and the Russian Federation.

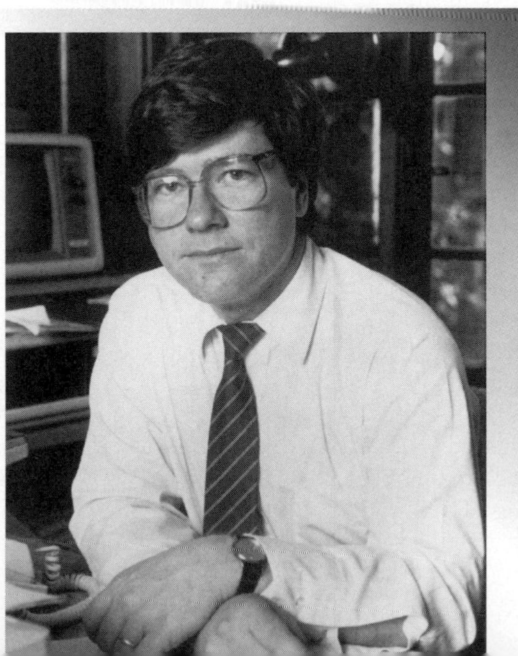

How did you get drawn into the Eastern European reform area?

I started my work in Eastern Europe in Poland at the time that Solidarity was legalized in the spring of 1989. I had been invited by the Communist government to give advice to them about their financial troubles. Events obviously went very fast because soon after legalization there was an election, which Solidarity won overwhelmingly. From that point on, I became an economic advisor to believers in Solidarity and helped them draft an outline of a radical economic reform program. Soon after that, a Solidarity government actually came to power, and I began to work on the implementation of economic reforms, which were widely viewed as the first and most comprehensive reforms in Eastern Europe. From there, I got to know reformers in all of the countries in the region and began to work closely with some Russian economists who are now senior members of the Yeltsin government. As democratization proceeded in Russia, these people invited me to help them develop their reform strategy.

Your name has been associated with the "big bang" or "cold turkey" approach to reform. Can you describe that approach and explain why you favor it over a more gradual and tentative one?

The basic idea is to start with the goal of the reform, such as to put in place a working capitalist system. Of course, it'll be a capitalist system that reflects the particular culture, history, tradition, and resources of the country. It is an attempt not to find a so-called "third way in" between the old system and the new system but to go fully toward the working capitalist model. In the case of Eastern Europe, the goal is even more explicit: to implement reforms that will make these countries harmonize with the economies of Western Europe so that in a short period of time—within a decade is their hope—they can actually become members of the European Community.

The essence of "big bang" is that it's important to move comprehensively and quickly toward the goal of a working capitalist economy because various aspects of the market economy are all interrelated. If one does just a piece of the reform but leaves much of the old system intact, the conflicts of the old and the new are likely to make things considerably worse rather than better.

What are the major pieces of the radical reform strategy that you're recommending to governments in Eastern Europe?

The reform strategy comes down to four components. The first is macroeconomic stabilization, because usually these countries start out in a deep macroeconomic crisis characterized by high inflation and intense shortages. Second is economic liberalization, which means ending central planning, trade quotas, and other barriers that cut the country off from the world market. The third part of the reform is privatization, which is the transfer of state property back to private owners. Those private owners could be individuals or they could be, as in the West, financial intermediaries like mutual funds or banks or pension funds that are in turn owned by individuals. When I say privatization, I use the word "transfer" rather than "sell" because selling state property is only one way to privatize. There are other ways, such as giving away the state property to workers, managers, or the public. The Eastern European countries are privatizing through a mix of sales and direct giveaways. The fourth part of the radical reform is the introduction of social safety nets, which provide protection for the most vulnerable parts of the society that are perhaps hardest hit by the reform or are already suffering even irrespective of the reform. That means putting in place unemployment benefits, an adequate retirement system and health care system, job training, public works spending, and so forth. Those are the four main pillars.

It's called "big bang" because you must move quickly on this. Probably the most dramatic part of all is the stabilization and liberalization phase, where subsidies are cut very quickly and price controls are eliminated. The result is usually a very dramatic one-time jump in prices. That starts off the reform.

How long does the reform process generally take?

Certain things can be done quickly, and others take more time. Stabilization and liberalization can be accomplished fast, or most parts of them. Freeing price controls, eliminating trade barriers, and cutting subsidies, for example, can all be done on the first day of the program, which is why it's sometimes called "shock therapy" or "cold turkey." Privatization, though, takes much longer. Some aspects of the fourth component of the reform strategy, the social safety net, can be done quickly. For example, pensions of retirees can be protected through budgetary allocation. An unemployment insurance system was started up very quickly in Poland, and it has worked adequately. Other parts of the social safety net, for instance, real reform of the health care system, are very complex and take a considerable amount of time to effect.

Even if the reforms go very quickly, the process of change that those reforms set loose will take years or even decades to work themselves out. What do I mean? The socialist system wasn't just messed up in terms of the organization of production and the ways that prices were set. It was also systematically misusing resources by putting tremendous overemphasis on heavy industrial production while neglecting other important parts of the economy, such as services and wholesale and retail trade. When you free up market forces, the market doesn't demand all the heavy industrial production that was built up in the past. This leads to unemployment, a drop in demand, and people voluntarily

quitting those industries to move into areas that were starved for people, resources, and capital in the past. You get a great boom in retail trade, for example, with tens of thousands of new shops opening up. The reforms set loose that process, but the corresponding shift of resources could take five, ten, fifteen, even twenty years to adjust.

Even within a big bang approach, presumably you can't literally do everything at once. What are the highest priorities?

The highest priority is to avoid real financial chaos. Poland, Yugoslavia, and Russia all fell into hyperinflation at the end of the Communist system. That meant that the new democratic governments' highest priority was to end the underlying conditions that were feeding the hyperinflation. If you can accomplish the financial stability, then I think the next highest priority is to have the rudiments of the private property system in place, such as a commercial code and laws for corporate enterprises, contracts, and protection of private property. Then the next priority is rapid privatization because until the enterprises are with real owners facing proper incentives, one has to be skeptical that they'll be managed in an efficient and sensible way.

What are the earliest indicators of whether the reforms are beginning to take hold?

Of course, different things happen at different times. The first thing one looks for if an economy is trying to emerge from hyperinflation is stability of prices. After freeing prices and experiencing a significant one time jump in the price level, this should not turn into ongoing high inflation but rather be followed by price stability.

Can the countries of Eastern Europe and the former Soviet Union evolve into democratic nations with market economies without economic aid from the West?

The whole history of radical economic change underscores the importance of financial assistance during the first critical years of reform. It takes many years for the real fruits of the reform to be widely evident in the society. Certain costs of the reform, however, such as closing down old inefficient enterprises, can become evident very quickly. It's during that crucial period between the introduction of the reforms and the time when they really are bearing fruit that lie the greatest dangers and also the greatest need for international assistance to help provide a cushion to living standards and a bolstering of the reform effort until the reforms really take hold.

The foreign assistance does not actually pay for the reconstruction of the country. It's never big enough. The Marshall Plan was not enough to really rebuild Europe, but what the Marshall Plan did was to give the new democratic postwar governments time to put in place market-based policies so that they could take hold.

Whether it's postwar Germany or Japan, Mexico's turnaround in the 1980s, or Poland at the beginning of the 1990s, countries on the path to economic and political reform need help at the beginning. For Russia and the other states of the former Soviet Union, it will be the same. They will definitely need some years of Western and foreign help to keep their reforms on track and to make the living conditions tolerable.

What form will that aid take? Free-trading opportunities? Private investment? Government loans?

The form of aid has to be linked to the timetable of the reform process. At the beginning, say in the first year, the aid is inevitably of two sorts. First, humanitarian emergency assistance to make sure that food is getting to the table and that medical supplies are available. Second, stabilization assistance, or various kinds of financial support to help make the currency strong and to increase the flow of basic imports, which are needed just to keep the economy functioning. Russia has suffered a sharp decline in its own capacity to buy imports because its export earnings have fallen sharply in the past few years. They need help just to keep basic imports going, and by doing that you help strengthen the currency.

In later years, you want to get away from that kind of emergency stabilization support and put much more attention on project financing to get new enterprises going. One hopes these will become the major engine of economic growth in the future. Private investment, of course, is to be desired, but it will take many years to attract. Private investors first want to know the market, and then they wait to see signs that the reforms are working and that political stability is being achieved. The official support from government has to come first. Then the private money will flow in.

What are the economic principles that you find most valuable in dealing with the acute problems of Russia today?

The starting point for me is to recognize that all of the successful economies in the world have a shared core set of institutions. There are, of course, major differences across countries, but all of the advanced industrial economies share certain features—such as a currency that trades, that can be used to buy goods without facing fixed prices or shortages, and that is convertible internationally; an open trading system in which, with some exceptions, goods can be bought and sold from abroad on normal market terms; an economy based on private ownership not state ownership; a legal infrastructure that supports private ownership so that property rights are clearly defined and defensible. Things like that. It's that core of institutions that is so important to put into place.

What are the undergraduates studying economics in Russia today actually studying? Are they learning about demand and supply, competition and monopoly, aggregate demand and aggregate supply, and the role of money in creating inflation?

Of course, things are changing very fast. It was only a few years ago that ideas like market economy and private property were unfamiliar. What one sees now is incredible hunger to study and analyze the basic properties of market economies. There is no doubt, I think, in the minds of virtually everybody that the old system was a terrible failure and that what Russia should have is a normal economy like that which is in place in Western Europe, the United States, and Japan. The curricula are being revised with incredible speed to teach the standard economics that we also learn. Of course, students' attention is focused not just on the well-functioning system but also on the problems of transitions.

What do you see as the major obstacles to economic development in Eastern Europe?

The major obstacle is that this is a time of great upheaval. The collapse of communism occurred, in part, because the old system had failed so thoroughly and people were in economic misery. So all this transformation is starting in the midst of a real economic crisis—a crisis that breeds confusion, fear, and anxiety. That confusion, fear, and anxiety can lead a whole country astray from its basic path of building up democratic market institutions. There are politicians waiting with messages attacking democracy, trying to take advantage of the anxieties of the people to win power. This could derail the reforms. If the new governments cannot deliver economic improvement, then I think risks to democracy will certainly exist. And once there is doubt about the basic direction of these changes, then things become unpredictable, but very hazardous results are possible. I don't think that's the likely outcome, but it's one of the reasons why I underscored the need for support, understanding, and a financial cushion from the West during this very critical and complicated stage of implementing the reforms.

Assuming that Russia does develop rapidly and solves its economic problems in the decade ahead, what are the major implications for the United States?

The overwhelming implication is that the chance for us to live in a peaceful world is enormously improved. We should not underestimate the difference that will mean to our own quality of life. The success of Russian democracy will make a huge difference to our security and, in financial terms, to our ability to divert our own resources from military spending to civilian use. Now, Russia's success with democracy depends a great deal on its success in overcoming this economic crisis. We know all too well that economic instability is one of the great dangers to a young democracy.

There are many, many other implications. The whole world will change, and I think vastly for the better. There will be a huge trading and investment opportunity when a country that covers one sixth of the world's land mass, spanning over eleven time zones, becomes closely integrated with the rest of the world economy after having been cut off for seventy-five years. There will be important changes in trade patterns, investment opportunities, and global cooperation.

CHAPTER 37

GROWTH AND DEVELOPMENT

After studying this chapter, you will be able to:

- Describe the international distribution of income
- Explain the importance of economic growth
- Explain how the accumulation of capital and technological progress bring higher per capita incomes
- Describe the obstacles to economic growth in poor countries
- Explain the possible effects of population control, foreign aid, free trade, and demand stimulation on economic growth and development
- Evaluate policies designed to stimulate economic growth and development

Feed the World

OST COUNTRIES OF AFRICA, ASIA, AND CENTRAL America have much lower living standards than our own. Some countries, such as Ethiopia, are so poor that people die from an inadequate diet. Why are some countries, like Ethiopia, chained to poverty? Why are there such differences in income between the poorest and richest countries? In 1946, as World War II ended, Hong Kong emerged from occupation by the Japanese as a poor colony of Britain. Occupying a cluster of overcrowded rocky islands, Hong Kong today is a city of vibrant, hardworking, and increasingly wealthy people. A similar story can be told of Singapore. Two and a half million people crowded into an island city-nation have, by their dynamism, transformed their economy, increasing their average income more than sixfold since 1960. How do some countries manage to unshackle themselves from poverty? What do they have that other poor countries lack? Can their lessons be applied elsewhere? ◆◆ The world's population has passed 5 billion inhabitants. These billions of people are unevenly distributed over the earth's surface. More than 4 billion live in the world's poor countries, and only 1 billion live in the rich industrial countries. It is estimated that by the year 2020, world population will exceed 8 billion, with close to 7 billion living in the poor countries and only 1.4 billion in the industrial countries. Why is the population growth rate so rapid in poor countries? What are the effects of rapid population growth on economic growth and development? ◆◆ In a typical year in the 1980s, $85 billion worth of aid was given by rich countries to developing countries. The United States provided more than a third of this aid. Does foreign aid help poor countries? Why hasn't it alleviated their poverty? ◆◆ Some poor countries try to encourage growth and development by protecting their industries from international trade and foreign competition. Other countries are outward-looking and engage in free trade with the rest of the world. What kind of international trade policy gives a developing country the best chance of rapid and sustained economic growth?

◆◆◆◆ In this chapter, we'll study the questions just posed. They are all aspects of one of the big economic questions posed in Chapter 1: what causes differences in wealth among nations, making the people in some countries rich and those in others poor? We don't fully understand the answer to this question. But there are some things that we do know. We'll review that knowledge in this chapter. We'll also review some of the ideas people have advanced about what can be done to speed up the growth of poor countries. Some strategies truly help poor countries, but others have mixed results and may even hurt their development.

The International Distribution of Income

When we studied the distribution of U.S income, we discovered that there is a great deal of inequality. As we will see, the differences in income within a country, large though they are, look insignificant when compared with the differences among the nations. Let's see how income is distributed among the nations of the world.

Poorest Countries

The poorest countries are sometimes called underdeveloped countries. An **underdeveloped country** is a country in which there is little industrialization, limited mechanization of the agricultural sector, very little capital equipment, and low per capita income. In many underdeveloped countries, large numbers of people live on the edge of starvation. Such people devote their time to producing the supplies of food and clothing required for themselves and their families. They have no surplus to trade with others or to invest in new tools and capital equipment. One of the most publicized of the poor countries is Ethiopia, where thousands of people spend their lives trekking across parched landscapes in search of meager food supplies.

Just how poor are the poorest countries? Twenty-seven percent of the world's population lives in countries whose per capita incomes range between 4 and 9 percent of those in the United States. Although these countries contain 27 percent of the world's people, they earn only 6 percent of world income. These poorest of countries are located mainly in Africa.

Developing Countries

A **developing country** is one that is poor but is accumulating capital and developing an industrial and commercial base. The developing countries have a large and growing urban population and have steadily growing incomes. The per capita income level in such countries ranges between 10 and 30 percent of that in the United States. These countries are located in all parts of the world, but many are found in Asia, the Middle East, and Central America. Seventeen percent of the world's people live in these countries and earn 11 percent of world income.

Newly Industrialized Countries

Newly industrialized countries (often called NICs) are countries in which there is a rapidly developing broad industrial base and per capita income is growing quickly. Today their per capita income levels approach 50 percent of those in the United States. Examples of such countries are Trinidad, Israel, and South Korea. Three percent of the world's people live in the newly industrialized countries and earn 3 percent of world income.

Industrial Countries

Industrial countries are countries that have a large amount of capital equipment and in which people undertake highly specialized activities, enabling them to earn high per capita incomes. These are the countries of Western Europe, the United States and Canada, Japan, and Australia and New Zealand. Seventeen percent of the world's people live in these countries, and they earn 49 percent of world income.

Oil-Rich Countries

A small number of oil-rich countries have very high per capita incomes despite the fact that they are, in most other respects, similar to the poorest countries or developing countries. These countries have little industry, and indeed little of anything of value to sell to the world, except oil. Four percent of the world's people live in these countries, and they earn 4 percent of world income. But that income is very unequally distributed within the countries: most of the people in these countries have incomes similar to those in the poorest countries, but a small number of people are extremely rich—indeed, among the richest people in the world.

Communist and Former Communist Countries

Close to 33 percent of the world's people live in communist countries or in countries that were formerly communist and are now making a transition toward capitalism. These countries earn 28 percent of world income. A **communist country** is a country in which there is limited private ownership of productive capital and of firms, there is limited reliance on the market as a means of allocating resources, and government agencies plan and direct the production and distribution of most goods and services. Rapid changes are taking place in many of these countries at the present time. We describe the economies of these countries, and the changes that are taking place as they move toward market economies, in Chapter 38.

Per capita incomes in these countries vary enormously. In China, per capita income is around 15 percent of that in the United States. China is a developing country. Per capita income in the former East Germany—now part of a reunited Germany—is almost 70 percent of that of the United States. Other countries in this category are Czechoslovakia, Poland, Hungary, and the former Soviet Union. Some formerly communist countries, such as Rumania, Yugoslavia, and Bulgaria, have per capita incomes similar to those of the newly industrialized countries. Thus within the communist and formerly communist countries, there is a great deal of variety in income levels and the degree of economic development.

The World Lorenz Curve

A **Lorenz curve** plots the cumulative percentage of income against the cumulative percentage of population. If income is equally distributed, the Lorenz curve is a 45° line running from the origin. The degree of inequality is indicated by the extent to which the Lorenz curve departs from the 45° line of equality. Figure 37.1 shows two Lorenz curves: one curve depicts the distribution of income among families in the United States, and the other depicts the distribution of average per capita income across countries.

FIGURE 37.1
The World Lorenz Curve, 1985

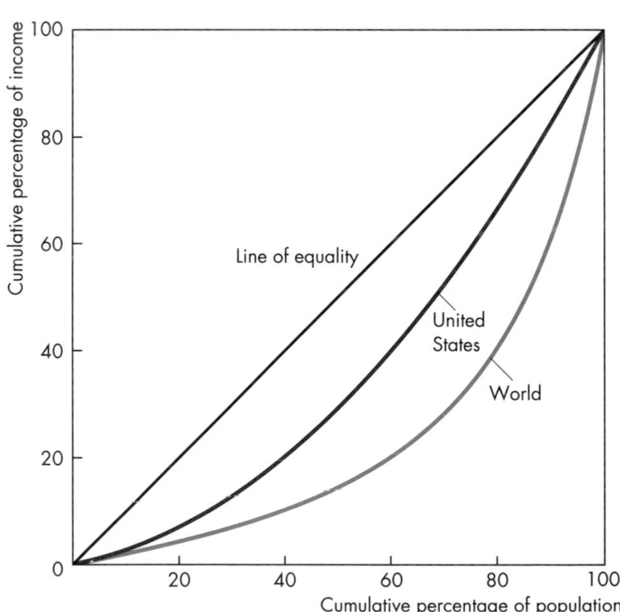

The cumulative percentage of income is plotted against the cumulative percentage of population. If income were distributed equally across countries, the Lorenz curve would be a straight diagonal line. The distribution of per capita income across countries is even more unequal than the distribution of income among families in the United States.

Source: Robert Summers and Alan Heston, "A New Set of International Comparisons of Real Product and Price Levels; Estimates for 130 Countries, 1950–1985," *Review of Income and Wealth,* Series 34 (1988): 207–262; and *Current Population Reports, Consumer Income,* Series P-60, Nos. 167 and 168 (Washington, D.C.: U.S. Department of Commerce, Bureau of the Census, 1990).

As you can see, the distribution of income among countries is more unequal than the distribution of income among families within the United States. Forty percent of the world's people live in countries whose incomes account for less than 10 percent of the world's total. The richest 20 percent of the world's people live in countries whose incomes account for 55 percent of the world's total income. Inequality in income is even more severe than that apparent in Fig. 37.1, because the world Lorenz curve tells us only how unequal average incomes are among countries. Inequality within countries is not revealed by the world Lorenz curve.

Such numbers provide a statistical description of the enormity of the world's poverty problem. And they are *real* numbers. That is, the effects of differences in prices have been removed. To better appreciate the severity of the problem, imagine that your family has an income of 30 cents a day for each person. That 30 cents has to buy housing, food, clothing, transportation, and all the other things consumed. Such is the lot of more than a quarter of the world's people.

Although there are many poor people in the world, there are also many whose lives are undergoing dramatic change. They live in countries in which rapid economic growth is taking place. As a result of economic growth and development, millions of people now enjoy living standards undreamt of by their parents and inconceivable to their grandparents. Let's look at the connection between income levels and the rate of economic growth.

Growth Rates and Income Levels

Poor countries can and do grow into rich countries. Poor countries become rich countries by achieving high growth rates of real per capita income over prolonged periods of time. Over the years, a small increase in the growth rate, like compound interest, pays large dividends. A slowdown in the growth rate, maintained over a number of years, can result in a huge loss of real income.

The importance of economic growth and its effects on income levels are vividly illustrated by our own recent experience. In the United States in the early 1960s, aggregate income, measured by real GDP, was growing at around 4 percent a year. After 1965, GDP growth slowed down. The path actually followed by U.S. GDP growth is shown in Fig. 37.2(a). The path that would have been followed if the pre-1965 growth trend had been maintained is also shown in that figure. By 1991, U.S. real GDP was approximately $2 trillion below—40 percent below—what it would have been if the 1965 growth rate had been maintained.

When poor countries have a slow growth rate and rich countries have a fast growth rate, the gap between the rich and the poor widens. Figure 37.2(b) shows how the gap between the United States and many poor countries, such as Ethiopia, has widened over the years.

For a poor country to catch up to a rich country, it is necessary for its growth rate to exceed that of the rich country. In 1980, per capita income in China was 14 percent of that in the United States. In the 1980s, the United States experienced an average per capita income growth rate of 1.5 percent a year. If that growth rate is maintained and if per capita income in China also grows at 1.5 percent a year, China will remain at 14 percent of U.S. income levels forever. The gap will remain constant. If per capita income in the United States were to grow at 1.5 percent and if China could maintain a per capita income growth rate at twice that level—3 percent per year—China would catch up to the United States in per capita income levels in the first part of the *twenty-second* century, around 2115. If China could do even twice as well as that—maintaining a 6 percent per year growth rate in per capita incomes—the people of China would have income levels as high as those in the United States within your own lifetime—in the mid-2030s. If China could pull off a miracle and make per capita income grow at 12 percent a year, it would take just 20 years to catch up to the United States.

Growth rates as high as 10 or 12 percent are not unknown. Japan's per capita income grew in excess of 10 percent a year, on the average, for almost 20 years following World War II. Recently, China has indeed experienced per capita income growth of 12 percent a year, a rate that, if sustained, doubles per capita income every six years. Even the poorest

FIGURE 37.2

Growth Rates and Income Levels

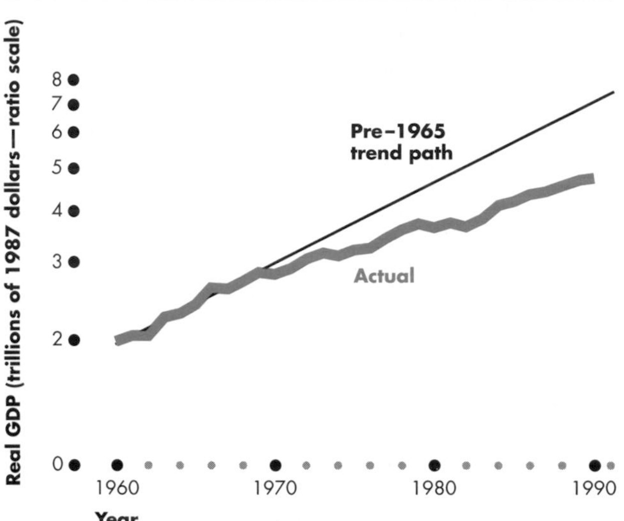

(a) U.S. output loss from growth slowdown

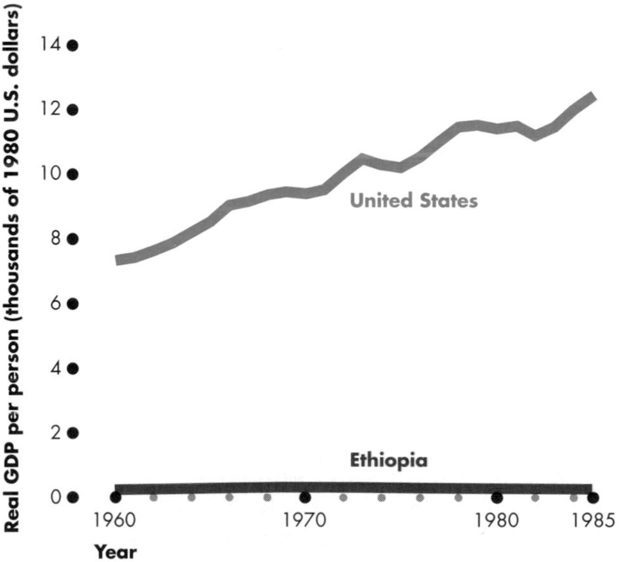

(b) The gap widens between rich and poor

A fall in the U.S. growth rate after 1965 (part a) has resulted in real GDP being some $2 trillion (40 percent) below its pre-1965 trend path. But with almost no growth, Ethiopia has fallen further behind the United States (part b).

Source: Robert Summers and Alan Heston, "A New Set of International Comparisons of Real Product and Price Levels; Estimates for 130 Countries, 1950–1985," *Review of Income and Wealth,* Series 34 (1988): 207–262; and *Economic Report of the President,* 1992.

countries in the world—those with per capita incomes of only 4 percent of those of the United States—would catch up to the United States in a matter of 30 or 40 years if they could achieve and maintain growth rates of this level.

The key, then, to achieving high per capita income is to attain and maintain a high rate of economic growth. That is how today's rich countries attained their high living standards. The poor countries of today will join the rich countries of tomorrow only if they can find ways of attaining and maintaining rapid growth.

Clearly, the question of what determines a country's economic growth rate is a vital one. What does determine a country's economic growth rate? Let's turn to an examination of this crucial question.

Resources, Technological Progress, and Economic Growth

In the aggregate, income equals the value of output. Thus to increase average income, a country has to increase its output. A country's output depends on its resources and the techniques it employs for transforming these resources into outputs. This relationship between resources and outputs is the *production function.* There are three types of resource:

- Land
- Labor
- Capital

Land includes all the natural, nonproduced resources such as land itself, the minerals under it, and all other nonproduced inputs. The quantity of these resources is determined by nature, and countries have no choice but to put up with whatever natural resources they happen to have. Countries cannot achieve rapid and sustained economic growth by increasing their stock of natural resources. But countries can and do experience fluctuations in income as a result of fluctuations in the prices of their natural resources. Furthermore, there are times when those prices are rising quickly, and such periods bring temporary income growth. The late 1970s is an example of a period in which resource-rich countries experienced rapid income growth as a result of rising commodity prices. But to achieve long-run, sustained income growth, countries have to look beyond their natural resources.

One such source of increased output is a sustained increase in *labor* resources. That is, a country can produce more output over the years simply because its population of workers grows. But for each successively larger generation of workers to have a higher *per capita* income than the previous generation, per capita output must increase. Population growth, on its own, does not lead to higher per capita output.

The resource most responsible for rapid and sustained economic growth is capital. There are two broad types of capital—physical and human. *Physical capital* includes such things as highways and railways, dams and irrigation systems, tractors and plows, factories, trucks and cars, and buildings of all kinds. *Human capital* is the accumulated knowledge and skills of the working population. As individuals accumulate more capital, their incomes grow. As nations accumulate more capital per worker, labor productivity and output per capita grow.

To study the behavior of per capita output, we use the per capita production function. The **per capita production function** shows how per capita output varies as the per capita stock of capital varies in a given state of knowledge about alternative technologies. Figure 37.3 illustrates the per capita production function. Per capita output is measured on the vertical axis, and the per capita stock of capital is measured on the horizontal axis. Curve *PF* shows how per capita output varies as the amount of per capita capital varies. A rich country such as the United States has a large amount of per capita capital and a large per capita output. A poor country such as Ethiopia has hardly any capital and a very low per capita output.

FIGURE 37.3

The Per Capita Production Function

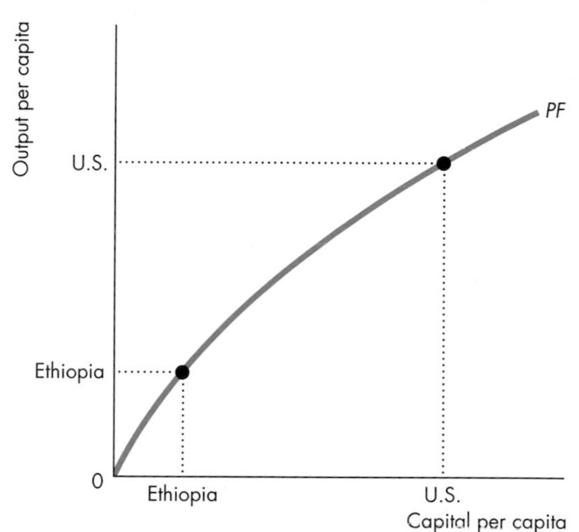

The per capita production function (*PF*) traces how per capita output varies as the stock of per capita capital varies. If two countries use the same technology but one country has a larger capital stock, that country will also have a higher per capita income level. For example, suppose that Ethiopia and the United States use the same technology. Ethiopia has a low per capita capital stock and low level of output per capita. The United States has a large per capita capital stock and a large per capita output rate.

Capital Accumulation

By accumulating capital, a country can grow and move along its per capita production function. The greater the amount of capital (per capita), the greater is output (per capita). But the fundamental *law of diminishing returns* applies to the per capita production function. That is, as capital per capita increases, output per capita also increases but by decreasing increments. Thus there is a limit to the extent to which a country can grow merely by accumulating capital. Eventually, the country reaches the point at which the extra output from extra capital is simply not worth the effort of accumulating more capital. At such a point, it pays the country to consume rather than to increase its capital stock.

But no country has yet reached such a point because the per capita production function is constantly shifting upward as a result of improvements in technology. Let's see how technological change affects output and growth.

Technological Change

Although rich countries have much more capital per capita than poor countries, that is not the only difference between them. Typically, rich countries use more productive technologies than do poor countries. That is, even if they have the same per capita capital, the rich country produces more output than the poor country. For example, a farmer in a rich

FIGURE 37.4
Technological Change

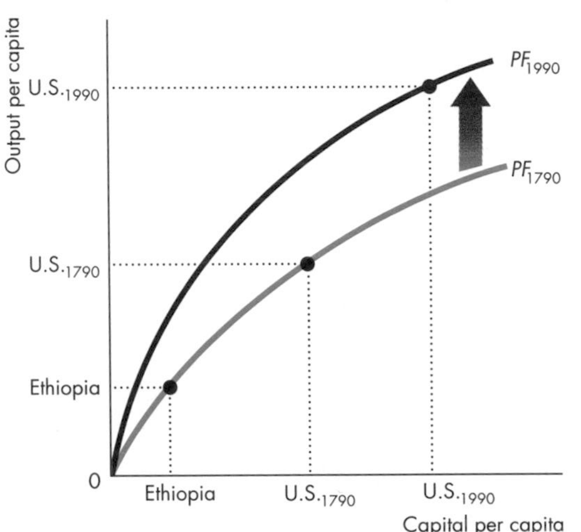

In 1790, the United States and Ethiopia have the same production function, PF_{1790}. By 1990, technological change has shifted the production function upward in the United States to PF_{1990}. Per capita income in the United States has increased from $U.S._{1790}$ to $U.S._{1990}$, partly because of an increase in the per capita capital stock and partly because of an increase in productivity arising from the adoption of better technology.

country might use a ten-horsepower tractor, whereas a farmer in a poor country might literally use ten horses. Each has the same amount of "horsepower," but the output achieved by using the tractor is considerably more than that produced by using ten horses. The combination of better technology and more per capita capital accentuates still further the difference between the rich and poor countries.

Figure 37.4 illustrates the importance of the difference that technological progress makes. Imagine that the year is 1790 and both the United States and Ethiopia (then called Abyssinia) use the same techniques of production and have the same per capita production function, PF_{1790}. With a larger per capita stock of capital, the United States produces a higher level of per capita output in 1790 than does Ethiopia. By 1990, technological advances adopted in the United States, but not in Ethiopia, enable the United States to produce more output from given inputs. The per capita production function in the United States shifts upward to PF_{1990}. Output per capita in the United States in 1990 is much higher than it was in 1790 for two reasons. First, the per capita stock of capital equipment has increased dramatically; second, the techniques of production have improved, resulting in an upward shift in the production function.

The faster the pace of technological progress, the faster the production function shifts upward. The faster the pace of capital accumulation, the more quickly a country moves along its production function. Both of these forces lead to increased per capita output. A poor country becomes a rich country partly by moving along its production function and partly by adopting better technology, thereby shifting its production function upward.

The importance of the connection between capital accumulation and output growth is illustrated in Fig. 37.5. Capital accumulation is measured by the percentage of output represented by investment. (Recall that investment is the purchase of new capital equipment.) The figure shows what has been happening to investment over time in developing countries and industrial countries and in the two extreme cases of Singapore and Ethiopia. As you can see in part (a), the percentage of income invested by developing countries increased through 1981 and then began to decline. In the industrial countries, the percentage of income invested has persistently declined, the fall being especially sharp in 1975. Fast-growing Singapore invests more than 40 percent of its income. Slow-growing Ethiopia invests less than 15 percent of its income. The source of Singapore's dramatic growth and of Ethiopia's almost static income level can be seen in part (b).

REVIEW

There is enormous inequality in the world. The poorest people in the poorest countries live on the edge of starvation. The poorest fifth of the world's people consume less than one twentieth of total output, and the richest fifth consume more than half of total output. Nations become rich by establishing and maintaining high rates of economic growth over prolonged periods. Economic growth results from the accumulation of capital and the adoption of increasingly efficient technologies. The more rapidly capital is accumulated and the more rapid is the pace of technological change, the higher

FIGURE 37.5

Investment Trends

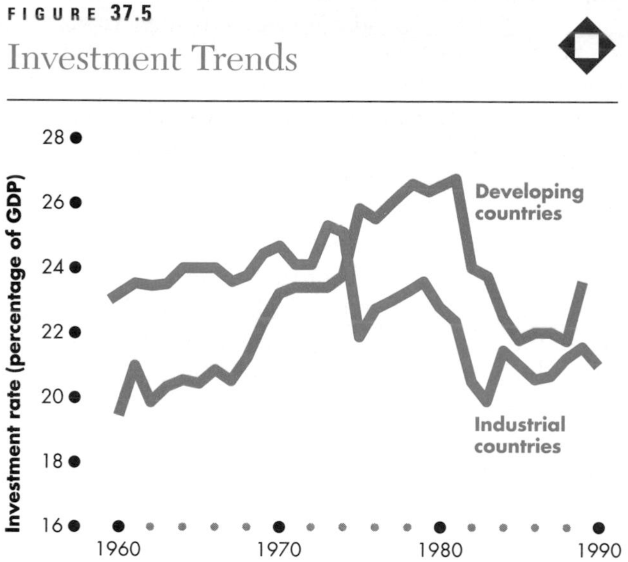

(a) Investment rates in developing and industrial countries

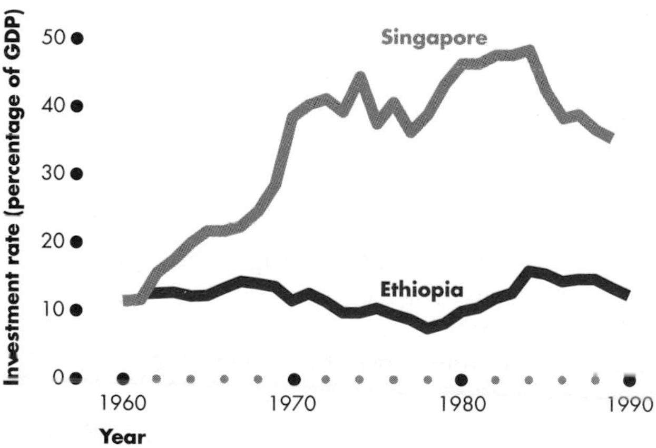

(b) Investment rates in Singapore and Ethiopia

The rate of investment in developing countries increased from 1960 to 1981 and subsequently decreased. Investment in industrial countries was steady during the 1960s and early 1970s but fell after 1974 (part a). Investment in Singapore has increased dramatically, while that in Ethiopia has been almost constant (part b). High investment in Singapore has led to rapid growth, while low investment in Ethiopia has led to low growth.

Source: International Monetary Fund, *International Financial Statistics Yearbook*, 1991.

is the rate of growth of output. Small changes in growth rates maintained over a long period of time make large differences in income levels. ◆

Obstacles to Economic Growth

The prescription for economic growth seems straightforward: poor countries can become wealthy by accumulating capital and adopting the most productive technologies. But if the cure for abject poverty is so simple, why haven't more poor countries become rich? Why are there so many poor people in the world today?

We do not know the answers to these questions. If we did, we would be able to solve the problem of economic underdevelopment and there wouldn't be any poor countries. But we do understand some of the reasons for poverty and underdevelopment. Let's see what they are.

Population Growth

One of the obstacles to economic development and rapid and sustained growth in per capita income is rapid population growth. In the past 20 years, world population has been growing at an average rate of 2 percent per year. At a population growth rate this high, world population doubles every 37 years. That population is now more than 5 billion. But the pattern of population growth is uneven. Rich industrial countries have relatively low population growth rates—often less than half a percent a year—while the poor, underdeveloped countries have high population growth rates—in some cases exceeding 3 percent a year.

Why is fast population growth an impediment to economic growth and development? Doesn't a larger population give a country more productive resources and permit more specialization, more division of labor, and therefore yet greater output? These benefits do indeed stem from a large population. But when the population is growing at a rapid rate and a country is poor, there are two negative effects on economic growth and development that outweigh the benefits of a larger population. They are

- An increase in the proportion of dependents to workers
- An increase in the amount of capital devoted to supporting the population rather than producing goods and services

Some facts about the relationship between the number of dependents and population growth are shown in Fig. 37.6. The number of dependents is measured on the vertical axis as the percentage of the population under 15 years of age. As you can see, the higher the population growth rate, the larger is the percentage of the population under 15. In countries such as the United States, where the population growth rate is less than 1 percent per year, about one person in five (20 percent) is under the age of 15. In countries such as Ethiopia that have rapid population growth rates (3 percent per year or higher), close to one half (50 percent) of the population is under the age of 15.

FIGURE 37.6

Population Growth and Number of Dependents

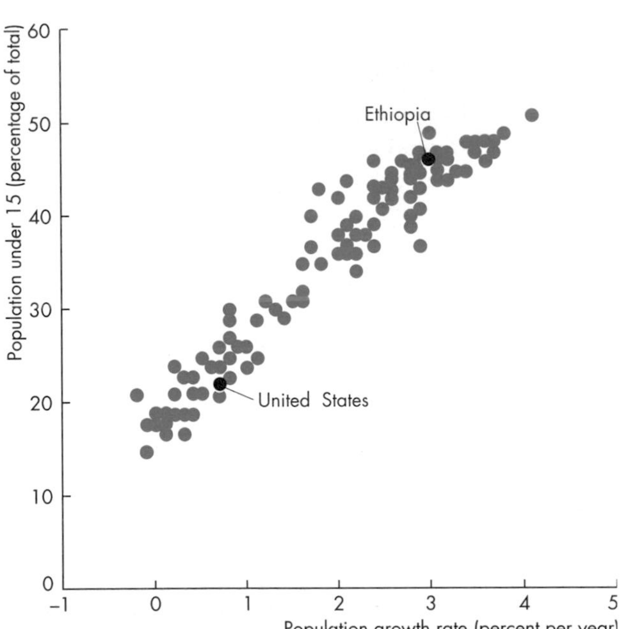

Each point represents a country. It shows the percentage of the population that is under 15 years of age (measured on the vertical axis) and the population growth rate (measured on the horizontal axis). The number of young people in the population is strongly influenced by the population growth rate. In slow-growing countries such as the United States, about a fifth of the population is under the age of 15, while in fast-growing countries such as Ethiopia, more than 40 percent of the population is under the age of 15.

Source: Population Reference Bureau Inc., *World Population Data Sheet* (Washington, D.C.: 1988).

Let's see why there is a connection between the population growth rate and the percentage of young people in the population. A country might have a steady population because it has a high birth rate and an equally high death rate. But the same steady population growth could occur with a low birth rate and a low death rate. Population growth rates increase when either the birth rate increases or the death rate decreases. Historically, it is a fall in the death rate with a relatively constant birth rate that has led to population explosions. The fall in the death rate mainly takes the form of a fall in the infant mortality rate, and it is this phenomenon that results in an enormous increase in the proportion of young people in the population.

In a country with a large number of young people, capital resources are directed toward providing schools, hospitals, roads, and housing rather than irrigation schemes and industrial capital projects. Such a use of scarce capital resources is obviously not wasteful and does bring great benefits, but it does not add to the economy's capacity to produce goods and services out of which yet additional capital accumulation can be provided.

Low Saving Rate

There is a further obstacle to rapid and sustained economic growth and development. It is the fact that poor people have such a low level of income that they consume most of it, undertaking a tiny volume of saving. Saving is the source of finance for capital accumulation, and, as we have seen, capital accumulation is itself one of the main engines of economic growth. Let's investigate the connection between capital accumulation and saving.

There are just three things that people can do with their income: consume it, save it, or pay it in taxes. That is,

$$\text{Income} = \text{Consumption} + \text{Saving} + \text{Taxes}.$$

An economy's output consists of consumption goods, capital goods, goods and services bought by the government, and net exports (exports minus imports). Expenditure on capital goods is investment, and expenditure on goods and services bought by the government is called government purchases of goods and services. Thus,

Income = Consumption + Investment
+ Government purchases
+ Net exports.

The first of the above equations tells us that income minus consumption is equal to saving plus taxes. The second equation tells us that income minus consumption is equal to the value of investment plus government purchases plus net exports. Using these two equations, then, we see that

Saving + Taxes = Investment
+ Government purchases
+ Net exports.

The difference between government purchases and taxes is the government budget deficit. Net exports are the balance of payments current account surplus—known more simply as the current account surplus. We can rearrange the last equation, therefore, as

Investment = Saving – Current account surplus
– Government budget deficit.

There are three influences on the pace at which a country can accumulate capital (can invest): saving, the government budget, and the current account surplus. Other things being equal, the larger the volume of saving, the smaller the government budget deficit (the larger the government budget surplus), and the smaller the current account surplus (the larger the current account deficit), the faster is the pace of capital accumulation.

The fraction of income that people save depends on the income level. Very poor people save nothing. As income rises, some part of income is saved. The higher the income level, the higher is the proportion of income saved. These patterns in the relationship between income and saving crucially affect the pace at which a country can grow.

Saving is by far the most important component in the sources of financing investment. But, in general, the larger the amount of saving, the larger also is the amount of resources available from the rest of the world through the country's current account deficit. Furthermore, the countries with the least resources are those in which the government runs a deficit, thereby restricting yet further the amount available for capital accumulation through investment.

Let's now look at a third obstacle to rapid growth and development, the burden of international debt.

International Debt

Poor countries often go into debt with the rest of the world. Loans have to be repaid, and interest has to be paid on the loans outstanding. To make debt repayments and interest payments, poor countries need a net export surplus. That is, a country needs a current account surplus. As we have just seen, when a country has a current account deficit, that deficit provides additional financial resources to domestic saving, enabling the country to accumulate capital at a faster pace than would otherwise be possible. A country that has a current account surplus is one that is accumulating capital at a slower pace than its domestic saving permits. Such a country uses part of its saving to accumulate capital—and thereby increases productivity—and uses the other part to pay interest on or repay loans from the rest of the world.

A poor country that borrows heavily from the rest of the world and uses the borrowing to invest in productive capital will not become overburdened by debt, provided that the growth rate of income exceeds the interest rate on the debt. In such a situation, debt interest can be paid out of the higher income and there is still some additional income leftover for additional domestic consumption or capital accumulation. Countries that borrow from the rest of the world and use the resources for consumption or invest in projects that have a low rate of return—lower than the interest rate on the debt—are the ones that become overburdened by debt.

The burden of international debt became particularly onerous for many developing countries during the 1980s. For example, the Latin American countries have accumulated external debts of almost half a trillion dollars. Many of these debts were incurred during the 1970s when raw material prices were rising quickly. From 1973 to 1980, the prices of most raw materials increased on the average by close to 20 percent per year—a rate much higher than the interest rates on the foreign debt being accumulated. In such a situation, countries producing raw materials, hungry for capital, borrowed on an enormous scale. In the 1980s, raw material prices collapsed. Huge debts had been incurred, but the revenue with which to repay those debts was not coming in. To add a further burden, interest rates increased sharply during the 1980s. Today, because of the combination of sagging raw material prices and higher interest rates, many poor countries have a crippling burden of international debt.

The Underdevelopment Trap

The obstacles to economic development are so severe that some economists have suggested that there is a kind of poverty trap that applies to countries—the underdevelopment trap. The **underdevelopment trap** is a situation in which a country is locked into a low per capita income situation that reinforces itself. A low level of capital per worker (both physical and human capital) results in low output per worker. Low productivity in turn produces low per capita income. Low per capita income results in low saving. With low saving, there is a low rate of capital accumulation. Capital accumulation can barely keep up with population growth, so the stock of capital per worker remains low and the cycle repeats itself.

Overcoming the Obstacles to Economic Development

A variety of ways of breaking out of the underdevelopment trap have been suggested. They are

- Population control
- Foreign aid
- Removal of trade restrictions
- Aggregate demand stimulation

Let's look at each of these in turn.

Population Control

Almost all developing countries use population control methods as part of their attempt to break out of the underdevelopment trap. Population control programs have two key elements: the provision of low-cost birth control facilities and the provision of incentives encouraging people to have a small number of children. These methods meet with some, but limited, success. One of the most highly publicized programs of population control is that employed in China. In that country, families are strongly discouraged from having more than one child. Despite this policy, the population of China continues to grow, and forecasts suggest that by the year 2000 the population will have grown above its target level by an amount equal to one half of the entire population of the United States.

Thus important though they are, population control methods are not the most likely to yield success in the fight against underdevelopment and poverty.

Foreign Aid

The idea that foreign aid helps economic development arises from a simple consideration. If a poor country is poor because it has too little capital, then by obtaining aid, it can accumulate more capital and achieve a higher per capita output. Repeated applications of foreign aid year after year can enable a country to grow much more quickly than it could if it had to rely exclusively on its own domestic saving. By this line of reasoning, the greater the flow of foreign aid to a country, the faster it will grow.

Some economists suggest that foreign aid will not necessarily make a country grow faster. They argue that such aid consolidates the position of corrupt and/or incompetent politicians and that these politicians and their policies are two of the main impediments to economic development. Most people who administer foreign aid do not take this view. The consensus is that foreign aid does indeed help economic development. But it is also agreed that foreign aid is not a major factor in influencing the pace of development of poor countries. Its scale is simply too small to make a decisive difference.

A factor that has made a decisive difference in many countries is international trade policy. Let's now turn to an examination of the effects of international trade on growth and development.

Removal of Trade Restrictions

There is steady political pressure in the rich countries in support of protection from imports produced with "cheap labor" in the underdeveloped countries. Some people also complain that buying from underdeveloped countries exploits low-wage workers. As a consequence, countries introduce tariffs, quotas, and voluntary restrictions on trade (see Chapter 35). How do such restrictions affect underdeveloped countries, and how does the removal of such restrictions affect their growth and development? To

FIGURE 37.7

International Trade and Economic Development

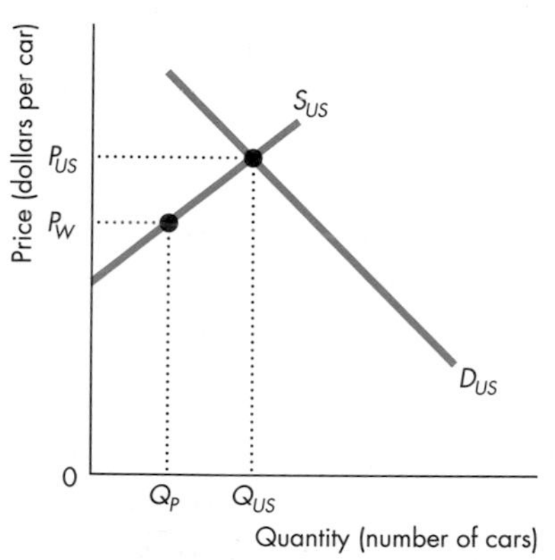

(a) U.S. production and demand

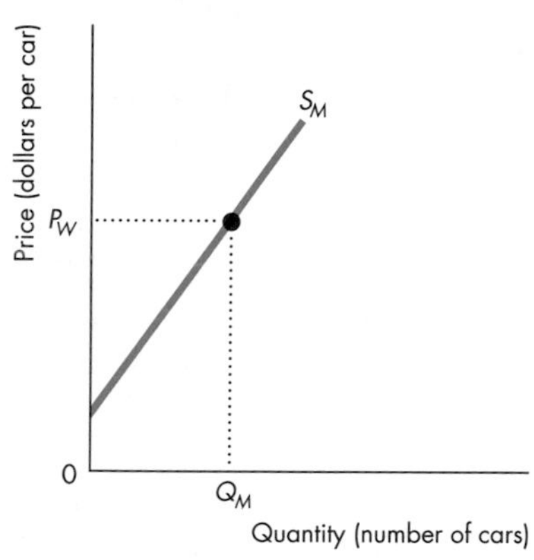

(b) Mexican production

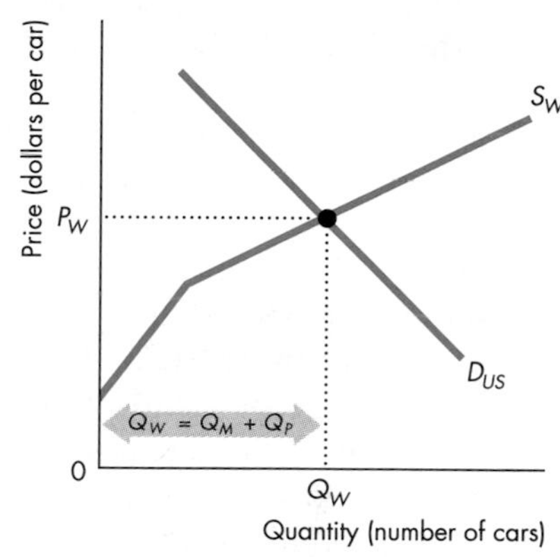

(c) U.S. car market with free trade

The market for cars in the United States (part a) has demand curve D_{US} and supply curve S_{US}. The price of cars is P_{US} and the quantity produced and bought is Q_{US}. Mazda builds an automobile plant in Mexico, and the supply curve of cars from that plant is S_M (part b). If the United States prohibits the import of cars from Mexico, the U.S. automobile market remains unchanged and Mexican output is zero. If the United States permits free international trade in cars with Mexico, the price in the U.S. market is P_W (part c) and the total quantity of cars bought in the United States is Q_W (W stands for "with trade"). Parts (a) and (b) show that at price P_W, Q_M cars are produced in Mexico and Q_P (P stands for "production") in the United States. Free international trade permits poor countries to sell their output for a price higher than they would otherwise receive and rich countries to buy goods for a price lower than they would otherwise pay.

answer this question, consider the following example (which is illustrated in Fig. 37.7). Imagine a situation (such as that prevailing in the 1950s) in which the United States produces virtually all its cars. The automobile market in the United States is shown in part (a). The demand for cars is shown by curve D_{US}, and the supply is shown by curve S_{US}. The price of cars is P_{US}, and the quantity produced and bought is Q_{US}.

Suppose that Mazda builds an automobile production plant in Mexico. The supply curve of cars produced in Mexico is shown in Fig. 37.7(b) as the curve S_M. What happens in the United States depends on U.S. international trade policy.

First, suppose that the United States restricts the import of cars from Mexico. To make things as clear as possible, let's suppose that there is a complete ban on such imports. In this case, Mexico produces no cars for export to the United States. The price of cars in the United States remains at P_{US}, and the quantity traded remains at Q_{US}.

In contrast, let's see what happens if the United States engages in free trade with Mexico. (A trade accord between the United States and Mexico has, in fact, recently been negotiated.) To determine the price of cars, the quantities produced and consumed in the United States, and the quantity produced in Mexico for export to the United States, we need to consider Fig. 37.7(c). The demand curve for cars in the United States remains D_{US}, but the supply curve becomes S_W. This supply curve is made up of the sum of the quantities supplied in both the United States and Mexico at each price. Equilibrium is achieved in the U.S. market at a price of P_W and a quantity traded of Q_W. To see where these cars are produced, go back to parts (a) and (b) of the figure. Mexico produces Q_M, the United States produces Q_P, and these two production levels sum to Q_W.

Mazda's Mexican plant increases its output of cars, and its workers generate an income. The output of cars is decreased in the United States. By permitting unrestricted trade with underdeveloped countries, rich countries gain by being able to consume goods that are imported at lower prices than would be possible if only domestic supplies were available. Developing countries gain by being able to sell their output for a higher price than would prevail if they had only the domestic market available to them.

Some of the most dramatic economic growth and development success stories have been based on reaping the gains from relatively unrestricted international trade. Countries such as Hong Kong and Singapore have opened their economies to free trade with the rest of the world and dramatically increased their living standards by specializing and producing goods and services at which they have a *comparative advantage*—which they can produce at a lower opportunity cost than other countries. The potential economic development that can result from specialization and trade is discussed further in Reading Between the Lines on pp. 1026–1027.

Aggregate Demand Stimulation

It is often suggested that growth and development can be stimulated by expanding aggregate demand. The suggestion takes two forms. Sometimes it is suggested that if the rich countries stimulate their own aggregate demand, their economies will grow more quickly, and, as a consequence, commodity prices will remain high. High commodity prices help poor countries and so stimulate their income growth and economic development. It is also often suggested that poor countries can make themselves grow faster by stimulating their own level of aggregate demand.

Can stimulating aggregate demand in the rich countries help the poor countries? Can aggregate demand stimulation in poor countries help them grow? The answers to both of these questions are almost certainly no, but let's see why. As we discovered when we studied the theory of aggregate demand and aggregate supply in Chapter 24, changes in aggregate income can occur as a result of either a change in aggregate demand or a change in aggregate supply. But aggregate demand changes affect output and income in the short run only. That is, when wages and other input prices are fixed, a change in aggregate demand changes both output and the price level. But in the long run, a change in aggregate demand leads to a change in the prices of goods and services and of factors of production. Once input prices have adjusted in response to a change in aggregate demand, income returns to its long-run level. Changes in per capita long-run aggregate supply can be brought about only by changes in per capita productivity—which in turn are brought about by changes in the stock of per capita capital and in the state of technology.

This macroeconomic model of aggregate demand and aggregate supply applies to all countries, rich and poor alike. If rich countries stimulate aggregate demand by persistently permitting aggregate demand to grow at a pace faster than the growth rate of long-run aggregate supply, they will generate inflation. If they permit aggregate demand to grow at a pace similar to the growth rate of long-run aggregate supply, prices will be stable. In recent history, we have seen rich countries generating rapid inflation and moderate inflation. The 1970s were a decade of rapid inflation. During that decade, commodity prices also increased quickly, enabling many developing countries to increase the pace of capital accumulation and income growth. The 1980s were a decade of moderate inflation. It is this decade that brought falling raw material prices and the burden of large international debt to many developing countries.

Don't the facts of the 1970s and 1980s support the conclusion that rapid aggregate demand growth and inflation in the rich countries help the poor countries? They do not. Rather, they provide an example of what can happen, over a limited time period, when there is a previously unexpected increase or decrease in the growth rate of aggregate demand. In the 1970s, there was an unexpectedly rapid increase in aggregate demand. As a consequence, many countries experienced increasing inflation and increasing output growth. In the 1980s, there was an unexpectedly severe contraction of aggregate demand in the rich countries, notably in the United States, resulting in falling inflation and a slowdown in output growth (and in some countries, including the United States, a fall in output). Unexpected fluctuations in the inflation rate can produce fluctuations in output growth—precisely what happened in the 1970s and 1980s. But sustained aggregate demand growth and sustained steady inflation are not capable of producing sustained growth in output.

FIGURE 37.8

Inflation and Economic Growth

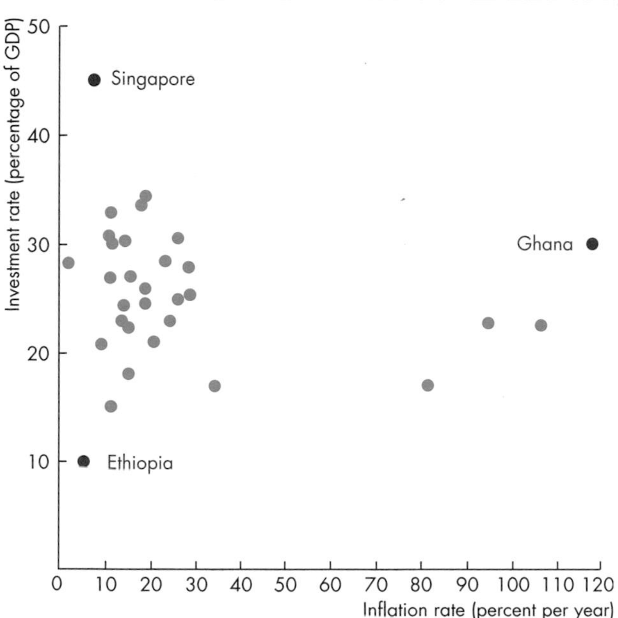

Each point in the figure represents a country. It shows the country's investment level (as a percentage of GDP) plotted against the annual inflation rate. The data are for 1960 to 1990. There is no discernible connection between a country's inflation rate and its pace of investment and economic growth. Fast-growing Singapore has a low inflation rate, as does slow-growing Ethiopia. Medium-growth Ghana has the highest inflation rate in the developing world.

Source: International Monetary Fund, *International Financial Statistics,* 1991.

Developing countries can make aggregate demand grow at a rapid or a moderate rate. The more rapidly aggregate demand grows, relative to the growth of long-run aggregate supply, the higher is the inflation rate. Some developing countries inflate quickly, and others inflate slowly. But there is virtually no connection between the pace of their development and the rate of inflation. As Fig. 37.8 illustrates, fast-growing Singapore, which invests more than 40 percent of its income in capital equipment each year, has a moderate inflation rate, while average-growing Ghana has the highest inflation rate of the developing countries—a rate in excess of 100 percent a year. Slow-growing Ethiopia, which invests only 10 percent of its income, has a moderate inflation rate. Each blue dot in the figure shows the investment percentage and inflation rate in a developing country. As you can see, the dots do not form a clear relationship between these variables. Thus the pace at which a developing country stimulates aggregate demand, while affecting its inflation rate, has no appreciable effect on the growth rate of real income or the pace of economic development.

We've seen that to grow quickly, a country must accumulate capital at a rapid pace. To do so, it must achieve a high saving rate and undertake foreign borrowing that is used in high-return activities. The most rapidly growing developing countries have a high pace of capital accumulation and obtain a high return on their capital by pursuing a free trade policy, thereby ensuring that they produce those goods and services in which they have a comparative advantage.

S U M M A R Y

The International Distribution of Income

There is enormous inequality in the international distribution of income. The poorest countries have average per capita income levels of 4 percent to 9 percent of that in the United States. Half of the world's population earns only 15 percent of world income, and the richest 20 percent of the world's population earns 55 percent of world income. (pp. 1013–1015)

Growth Rates and Income Levels

Poor countries become rich by achieving and maintaining for prolonged periods high rates of per capita income growth. Rich countries grow at about 1.5 percent per year. Poor countries that have a growth rate lower than 1.5 percent fall further behind. Poor countries that achieve a growth rate higher than 1.5 percent close the gap on the rich countries. High and sustained growth makes a dramatic difference in a

Capital, Trade, and Economic Development

THE ECONOMIST, MARCH 21, 1992

Hard sell

The names hardly trip off the tongue. But if all goes as planned, by the end of the 1990s the sleepy backwaters of Najin in North Korea, Hunchun in China and Posyet in Russia's far east will be the whirring hub of a larger circle of prosperity that will stretch from Vladivostok down to North Korea's Chongjin and west to Yanji in China's north-eastern Jilin province.

The plan is for a huge duty-free shipping and processing zone, on the Tumen River close to the point where the borders of Russia, China and North Korea meet. These three plus South Korea, Japan and Mongolia are the unlikely partners in the venture, which calls for an unaccustomed degree of co-operation and, for now, improbable amounts of cash: the necessary roads, railways, ports and airports are expected to cost at least $30 billion over 15–20 years. The United Nations Development Programme has promised the $2m–3m needed for the feasibility study. The planners next meet in Beijing in April.

The economies of the region could complement one another. Japan and South Korea have the capital to invest, along with modern industrial technologies and management and marketing skills. North Korea and China can provide the labour. Between them the three closest neighbours, North Korea, China and Russia, have the coal, timber, minerals and other raw materials to supply new manufacturing industries.

There is flat land for building and fresh water in abundance. There is also biting winter cold, with temperatures plunging to the minus-30s. For industrialists wanting to take a look there is an arduous day-or-more-long train journey from Harbin, the nearest Chinese metropolis worthy of the name. . . .

Hence the importance of all those new transport links. Once in place they would greatly facilitate trade across the Sea of Japan and dramatically improve prospects for the neglected eastern reaches of both China and Russia. At present China's Japan-bound cargoes sail from the more southerly port of Dalian and around the Korean peninsula. Russian and Chinese trade with South Korea could be done directly, rather than via intermediaries. And all this bustle, it is hoped, will help tempt hermit-like North Korea out of its economic isolation. With extra rail links, distant, land-locked Mongolia, desperate to win new outlets for its minerals, wool and livestock, would benefit from quicker access to ports. . . .

The Essence of the Story

Russia, China, North Korea, South Korea, Japan, and Mongolia are the partners in a planned venture that, if implemented, will create a huge duty-free shipping and processing zone on the Tumen River close to the point where the borders of Russia, China, and North Korea meet.

The area has abundant flat land and fresh water and is ideally situated to open up trade links with the landlocked regions of eastern Russia, China, and Mongolia and to speed and ease the flow of trade across the Sea of Japan.

But the region has extreme winters and is currently almost inaccessible. A priority, therefore, is establishing communication links. The cost of the necessary roads, railways, ports, and airports is expected to be at least $30 billion over 15–20 years.

Background and Analysis

The economies of the region complement one another. Japan and South Korea have capital, modern technologies, and management and marketing skills. North Korea and China have labor. North Korea, China, and Russia (between them) have the coal, timber, minerals, and other raw materials.

If the plan succeeds, by the end of the 1990s a large region that currently has almost no economic activity will become a prosperous industrial and commercial region.

Economic development occurs in a variety of ways, but there are two essential ingredients of any development project likely to succeed:

- Capital
- Specialization and exchange

The Tumen River project in northeast Asia (see the maps) is an outstanding example of the applications of these ingredients.

The capital required for this project includes:

- Transportation infrastructure—roads, railroads, airports, and seaports (estimated cost $30 billion)
- Buildings, plant, and equipment for hundreds (perhaps thousands) of factories, processing plants, warehouses, and offices
- Housing, schools, hospitals, and retail and commercial buildings

The financing of this huge amount of investment will likely come from the capital markets of Japan, Europe, and North America, together with some government funding from the countries involved.

The project also requires human capital—the skills of technicians, managers, and marketers. These will likely come, initially, from Japan and South Korea.

This massive accumulation of capital will push the *production possibility frontier* for the region outward and bring higher living standards.

But the most crucial ingredient in this project is the removal of political barriers to economic activity, specialization, and exchange. By creating a *duty-free* shipping and processing zone, the countries involved in this project are creating (albeit on a limited scale) *free trade* in a wide range of goods and services.

By permitting individuals and firms in the six countries involved to specialize in the activities at which they have a comparative advantage and freely exchange their products, the Tumen River project will allow all the countries in the region to share in the gains from trade.

This aspect of the project will enable the people of the region to consume at a point outside their new expanded production possibility frontier and bring even greater prosperity both to the region and to the people who trade with it.

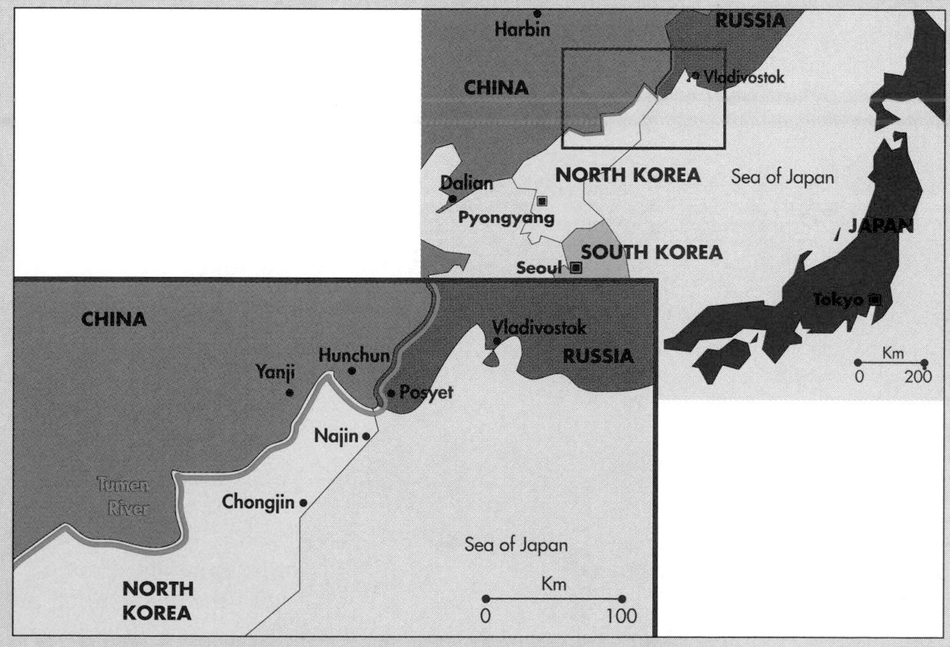

short time span. If China can achieve and maintain a per capita income growth rate of 6 percent per year, the per capita income of China will catch up with that of the United States by the mid-2030s. (pp. 1015–1016)

Resources, Technological Progress, and Economic Growth

Per capita income growth results from growth in per capita capital and technological change. The greater the fraction of income invested in new capital equipment and the faster the pace of technological change, the higher is the rate of economic growth. (pp. 1016–1019)

Obstacles to Economic Growth

There are three major obstacles to sustained economic growth and development: rapid population growth, a low saving rate, and an international debt burden. Rapid population growth results in there being a large proportion of young dependents in the population. A low saving rate results in a low rate of capital accumulation. A large international debt burden results in some saving having to be used to pay debt interest rather than to accumulate capital and improve productivity.

Low income results in low saving, which in turn results in low investment and thus low income growth. Many poor countries are caught in what appears to be an underdevelopment trap. (pp. 1019–1022)

Overcoming the Obstacles to Economic Development

The main techniques for overcoming the obstacles to economic development are the implementation of population control measures, foreign aid, and the removal of trade restrictions. Of these, the most dramatic success stories have almost always involved rapid expansion of international trade.

The stimulation of aggregate demand, by either rich or poor countries, cannot contribute, in the long run, to economic growth and development. If aggregate demand grows at the same rate as long-run aggregate supply, prices are stable; if aggregate demand grows at a faster rate than long-run aggregate supply, prices rise—there is inflation. The rate of inflation does not appear to have a major influence on the rate of economic growth and development. (pp. 1022–1027)

KEY ELEMENTS

Key Terms

Communist country, 1014
Developing country, 1013
Industrial country, 1013
Lorenz curve, 1014
Newly industrialized country, 1013
Per capita production function, 1017
Underdeveloped country, 1013
Underdevelopment trap, 1022

Key Figures

REVIEW QUESTIONS

1 Describe the main differences between the richest and poorest countries.

2 Compare the distribution of income among families in the United States with the distribution of income among countries in the world. Which distribution is more unequal?

3 What determines a country's per capita income level? What makes the per capita income level change?

4 Give an example of a country in which rapid economic growth has occurred and one in which slow economic growth has occurred. Which country has the higher investment rate?

5 Review the obstacles to economic growth.

6 Why is rapid population growth an obstacle to economic growth?

7 Describe the underdevelopment trap.

8 What are the main ways in which poor countries try to overcome their poverty?

9 Why does free trade stimulate economic growth and development?

10 Why does demand stimulation not improve a country's rate of economic growth and its development?

PROBLEMS

1 A poor country has 10 percent of the income of a rich country. The poor country achieves a growth rate of 10 percent per year. The rich country is growing at 5 percent per year. How many years will it take income in the poor country to catch up with that in the rich country?

2 Silecon is a poor country with no natural resources except sand. Per capita income is $500 a year, and this entire income is consumed. Per capita income is constant—there is no economic growth. The government has a balanced budget, and there are no exports or imports. Then, one day, the price of silicon increases, and Silecon is able to export sand at a huge profit. Exports soar from zero to $400 (per capita). Per capita income increases to $1,000 a year, and per capita consumption increases to $600 a year. There are still no imports, and Silecon has a balance of payments current account surplus of $400 per capita.

- **a** What happens to investment and the growth rate in Silecon?
- **b** If Silecon imports capital goods equal in value to its exports, what will be its investment?
- **c** What will be Silecon's current account balance?
- **d** If the government of Silecon runs a budget deficit of $100 (per capita), what will be its investment?

3 The per capita production function in Machecon is illustrated in the figure, and in year 1, Machecon has 1 machine per person.

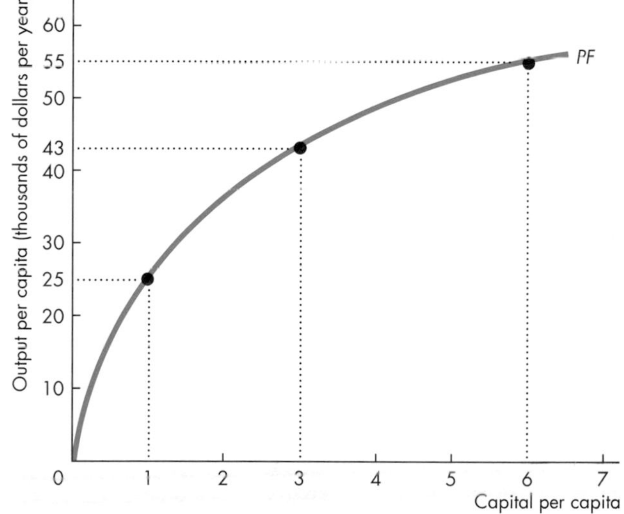

- **a** What is per capita output in Machecon?
- **b** If Machecon adds 1 machine per person to its capital stock during year 2, what is its new level of output and what is its output growth rate in year 2?
- **c** In year 3, Machecon adds 1 more machine per person to its capital stock. What now is its output, and what is its growth rate in year 3?
- **d** If in year 4 Machecon adds no new machines to its capital stock, but a new technology becomes available that increases the productivity of each machine by 20 percent, what is the level of output in Machecon in year 4?

CHAPTER 38

ECONOMIC SYSTEMS IN TRANSITION

After studying this chapter, you will be able to:

- Describe the fundamental economic problem that confronts all nations
- Describe the alternative systems that have been used to solve the economic problem
- Describe the Soviet-style system of central planning
- Describe the economic problems confronting the former Soviet Union
- Describe the economic problems of Eastern European countries
- Describe the process of economic change in China
- Describe and evaluate the alternative strategies for making the transition from a centrally planned economy to a market economy

EXTRAORDINARY EVENTS ARE TAKING PLACE IN EASTERN Europe. The Berlin Wall has fallen, and Germany is reunited. The centrally planned economy of East Germany has been replaced by the market economic system of West Germany. Poland, Hungary, Czechoslovakia, Bulgaria, and Rumania have embraced democratic political institutions and are creating market economies. The Soviet Union has disintegrated. Some of its former republics are now independent nations, and the others are loosely linked in a Commonwealth of Independent States. These nations have abandoned central economic planning and are moving toward a market economy. And the process of adopting the market economic system does not end with Eastern Europe. The People's Republic of China, although remaining a communist dictatorship, is undergoing massive economic change, gradually replacing its system of central planning with the market. ◆◆ Why are so many countries abandoning central economic planning and jumping on the market bandwagon? What are the problems that a country faces as it makes the transition to a market economy?

The Market Bandwagon

◆ ◆ ◆ ◆ This chapter brings you full circle. In Chapter 1 you studied the fundamental economic problem of scarcity and considered the alternative ways in which people attempt to solve that problem. In the rest of the book you studied the way in which our own economy (and the similar economies of Western Europe, Japan, and most of the world) solves the economic problem. But a significant number of countries, in which more than a quarter of the human population lives, have employed an economic system that relies on the state to direct the economy through a central planning system. We are going to look at this alternative system and also at the extraordinary—perhaps revolutionary—process of change that is taking place during the 1990s as the centrally planned economies make the transition toward market economies.

FIGURE 38.1

The Fundamental Economic Problem

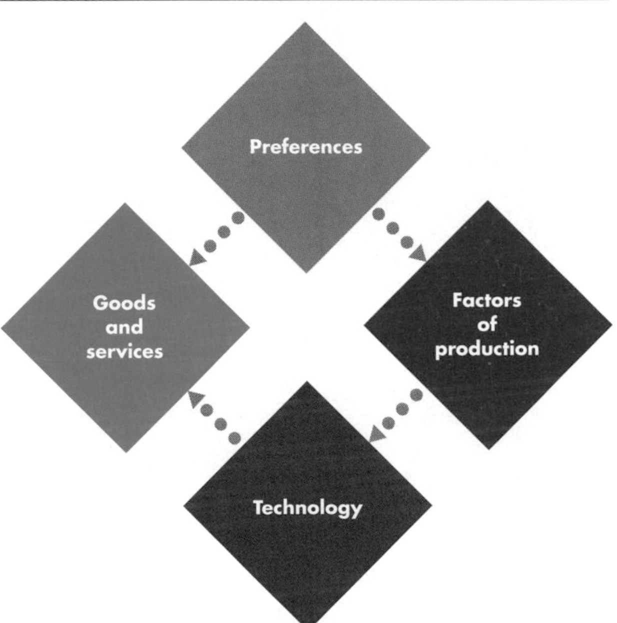

People have preferences about goods and services and the use of factors of production. Technologies are available for transforming factors of production into goods and services. People want to consume more goods and services than can be produced with the available factors of production and technology. The fundamental economic problem is to choose *what* goods and services to produce, *how* to produce them, and *for whom* to produce them. Different economic systems deliver different solutions to this problem.

The Economic Problem and Its Alternative Solutions

The economic problem is the universal fact of scarcity—we want to consume more goods and services than the available resources make possible. The economic problem is illustrated in Fig. 38.1. People have preferences about the goods and services they would like to consume and about how they would like to use the factors of production that they own or control. Techniques of production—technologies—convert factors of production into goods and services. The economic problem is to choose the quantities of goods and services to produce—*what*—the ways to produce them—*how*—and the distribution of goods and services to each individual—*for whom.*

The production of goods and services is the objective of the economic system. But *what, how,* and *for whom* goods and services are produced depend on the way the economy is organized—on who makes which decisions. Different systems deliver different outcomes. Let's look at the main alternatives that have been used.

Alternative Economic Systems

Economic systems vary in two dimensions:

- Ownership of capital and land
- Incentive structure

Ownership of Capital and Land Capital and land may be owned entirely by individuals, entirely by the state, or by a mixture of the two. The private ownership of capital and land enables individuals to create and operate their own firms. It also enables them to buy and sell capital, land, and firms freely at their going market prices. State ownership of capital and land enables individuals to control the use of these resources in state-owned firms but does not permit this control to be passed to others in a market transaction.

In practice, no economy has pure private ownership or pure and exclusive state ownership. For example, in an economy with widespread private ownership, the freedom to buy and sell firms is modified by the antitrust laws. Also, national defense or the public interest may be invoked to limit private ownership. Such limitations operate to restrict the private ownership of beaches and areas of natural scenic beauty.

In an economy that has predominantly state ownership, individuals sometimes own small plots of land and their homes. Also, in many economies, private ownership and state ownership exist side by side. In such cases, the state acts like a private individual and buys capital, land, or even a production enterprise from its existing owner.

Incentive Structure An **incentive structure** is a set of arrangements that induce people to take certain actions. Incentives may be created by market prices, by administered prices and administrative sanctions, or by a mixture of the two.

An incentive system based on market prices is one in which people respond to the price signals they receive and the price signals themselves respond to people's actions. For example, suppose a severe frost wipes out the Florida orange crop one year. The supply of orange juice falls. As a result, the price of orange juice rises. Faced with the higher price, people have an *incentive* to economize on orange juice and they decrease the quantity demanded. At the same time, the higher price of orange juice induces an increase in the demand for apple juice, a substitute for orange juice. As a result, the price of apple juice also rises. With higher prices for orange juice and apple juice, orange and apple growers in other parts of the country and in other countries have an *incentive* to increase the quantity supplied.

An incentive system based on administered prices is one in which administrators set prices to achieve their own objectives. For example, a government might want everyone to have access to low-cost bread. As a result, bread might be priced at, say, a penny a loaf. Under these circumstances, people have an *incentive* to buy lots of bread. Poor children might even use stale loaves as footballs! (This use of bread apparently did actually occur in the former Soviet Union.) An incentive system based on administrative sanctions is one in which people are rewarded or punished in a variety of non-monetary ways to induce them to take particular actions. For example, a manager might reward a salesperson for achieving a sales goal with more rapid promotion or with a bigger office. Alternatively, a salesperson might be punished for failing to achieve a sales goal by being moved to a less desirable sales district. When an entire economy is operated on administrative incentives, everyone, from the highest political authority to the lowest rank of workers, faces non-monetary rewards and punishments from immediate superiors.

Types of Economic System Economic systems differ in the ways in which they combine ownership and incentive arrangements. The range of alternatives is illustrated in Fig. 38.2. One type of economic

FIGURE **38.2**

Alternative Economic Systems

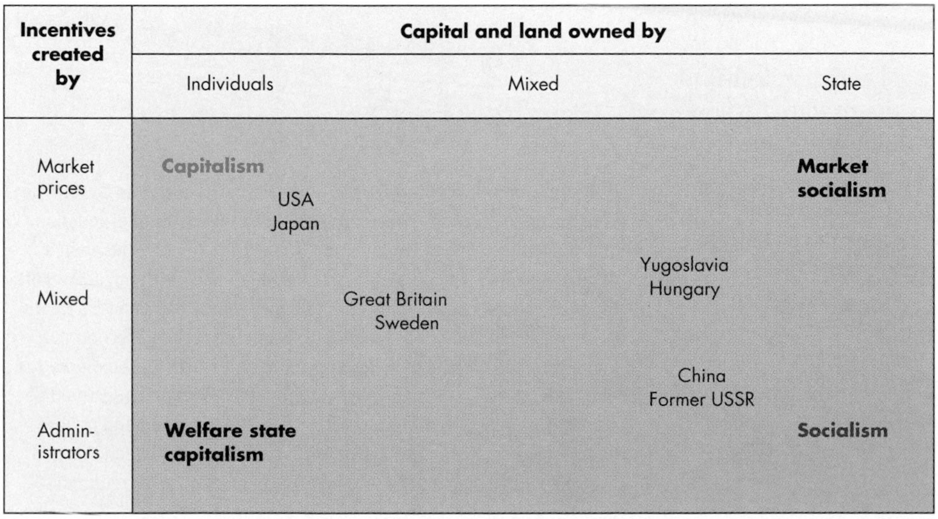

Incentives created by	Capital and land owned by		
	Individuals	Mixed	State
Market prices	**Capitalism** USA Japan		**Market socialism**
Mixed		Great Britain Sweden	Yugoslavia Hungary
Administrators	**Welfare state capitalism**		China Former USSR **Socialism**

Under capitalism, individuals own capital—farms and factories, plant and equipment—and incentives are created by market prices. Under socialism, the state owns capital, and incentives are created by administrated prices and administrative sanctions. Market socialism combines state ownership of capital with incentives based on market prices. Welfare state capitalism combines private capital ownership with a high degree of state intervention in the incentive structure.

system is **capitalism,** a system based on the private ownership of capital and land and on an incentive system based on market prices. Another type of economic system is **socialism,** a system based on state ownership of capital and land and on an incentive system based on administered prices or sanctions arising from a central economic plan. **Central planning** is a method of allocating resources *by command.* A central plan for action is drawn up, and the plan is implemented by creating a set of sanctions and rewards that ensure that the commands are carried out.

No country has used an economic system that precisely corresponds to one of these extreme types, but the United States and Japan come closest to being capitalist economies and the former Soviet Union and China before the 1980s came closest to being socialist economies. Socialism evolved from the ideas of Karl Marx (see Our Advancing Knowledge on pp. 1038–1039).

Some countries combine private ownership with state ownership, and some combine market price incentives with administrative incentives and central planning. **Market socialism** (also called **decentralized planning**) is an economic system that combines state ownership of capital and land with incentives based on a mixture of market and administered prices. Hungary and Yugoslavia have had market socialist economies. In such economies, planners set the prices at which the various production and distribution organizations are able to buy and sell and then leave those organizations free to choose the quantities of inputs and outputs. But the prices set by the planners responded to the forces of demand and supply.

Another combination is welfare state capitalism. **Welfare state capitalism** combines the private ownership of capital and land with state intervention in markets that change the price signals that people respond to. Sweden, Great Britain, and other Western European countries are examples of such economies.

Alternative Systems Compared

Since all economic systems are made up of a combination of the two extreme special cases—capitalism and socialism—let's examine these two extreme types a bit more closely.

Capitalism Figure 38.3 shows how capitalism solves the economic problem of scarcity. Households

FIGURE 38.3

Capitalism's Solution to the Economic Problem

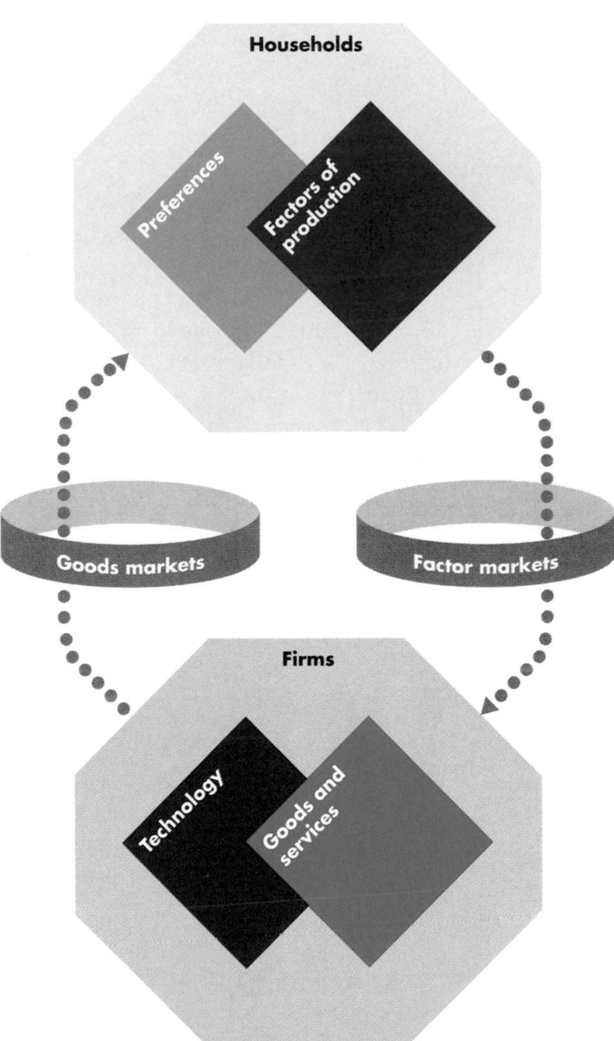

Under capitalism, the preferences of individual households dictate the choices that are made. Households own all the factors of production and sell the services of those factors in factor markets. Households decide which goods and services to consume and buy them in markets for goods and services. Firms decide which goods and services to produce and which factors of production to employ, selling their output and buying their inputs in the goods and factor markets. The markets determine the prices that bring the quantities demanded and quantities supplied into equality for each factor of production and good or service. Capitalism economizes on information because households and firms need to know only the prices of various goods and factors that they buy and sell.

own the factors of production and are free to use those factors, and the incomes they receive from the sale of their services, in any way they choose. These choices are governed by their preferences. The preferences of households are all-powerful in a capitalist economy.

Households choose the quantity of each factor of production to sell, and firms, which organize production, choose the quantity of each factor to buy. These choices respond to the prices prevailing in the factor markets. An increase in a factor price gives households an incentive to increase the quantity supplied and gives firms an incentive to decrease the quantity demanded. Factor prices adjust to bring the quantity of each factor supplied into equality with the quantity of each factor demanded.

Households choose the quantity of each good or service to buy, and firms choose the quantity of each to produce and sell. These choices respond to the prices confronting households and firms in the goods markets. An increase in the price of a good gives firms an incentive to increase the quantity supplied of that good and gives households an incentive to decrease the quantity demanded. Prices adjust to bring the quantities demanded and supplied into equality with each other.

Resources and goods and services flow in a clockwise direction from households to firms and back to households through the factors and goods markets. *What* is produced, *how* it is produced, and *for whom* it is produced are determined by the preferences of the households, the resources that they own, and the technologies available to the firms.

Nobody *plans* the capitalist economy. Doctors perform nearly miraculous life-saving surgery by using sophisticated computer-controlled equipment. The equipment is designed by medical and electronic engineers, programmed by mathematicians, financed by insurance companies and banks, and bought and installed by hospital administrators. Each individual household and firm involved in this process allocates the resources that it controls in the way that seems best for it. The firms try to maximize profit, and the households try to maximize utility. And these plans are coordinated in the markets for health care equipment, computers, engineers, computer programmers, insurance, hospital services, nurses, doctors, and hundreds of other items that range from anaesthetic chemicals to apple juice.

When a surgeon performs an operation, an incredible amount of information is used. Yet no one possesses this information. It is not centralized in one place. The capitalist economic system economizes on information. Each household or firm needs to know very little about the other households and firms with which it does business. The reason is that *prices convey most of the information it needs.* By comparing the prices of factors of production, households choose the quantity of each factor to supply. And by comparing the prices of goods and services, they choose the quantity of each to buy. Similarly, by comparing the prices of factors of production, firms choose the quantity of each factor to use, and by comparing the prices of goods and services, they choose the quantity of each to supply.

Socialism Figure 38.4 shows how socialism solves the economic problem of scarcity. In this case the planners' preferences carry the most weight. Those preferences dictate the activities of the production enterprises. The planners control capital and natural resources, directing them to the uses that satisfy their priorities. The planners also decide what types of jobs will be available, and the state plays a large role in the allocation of the only factor of production owned by households—labor.

The central plan is communicated to state-owned enterprises, which use the factors of production and the available technologies to produce goods and services. These goods and services are supplied to households in accordance with the central plan. The purchases by each household are determined by household preferences, but the total amount available is determined by the central planners.

A centrally planned economy has prices, but prices do not adjust to make quantity demanded and quantity supplied equal. Instead, they are set to achieve social objectives. For example, the prices of staple food products are set at low levels so that even the poorest families can afford an adequate basic diet. The effect of setting such prices at low levels is chronic shortages. The incentives that people respond to are the penalties and rewards that superiors can impose on and give to their subordinates.

REVIEW

he economic problem—*what, how,* and *for whom* to produce the various goods and

FIGURE 38.4

Socialism's Solution to the Economic Problem

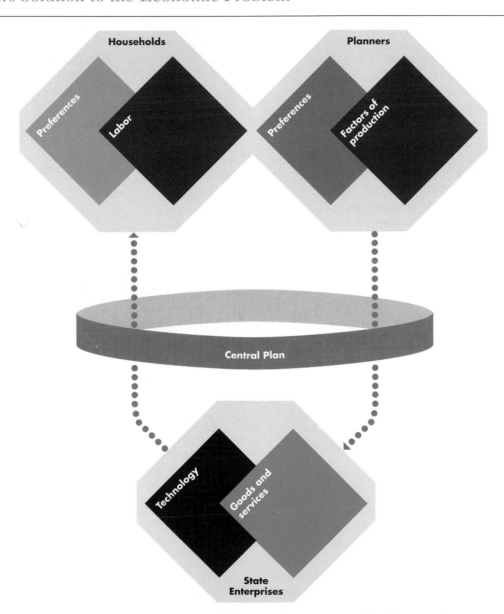

Under socialism, the preferences of the planners dictate the choices that are made. The planners control all the capital and natural resources owned by the state. They draw up plans and issue orders that determine how these resources will be used in the production of goods and services. Households decide which goods and services to consume and buy them from state-owned shops. State enterprises produce the goods and services and employ the factors of production required by the central plan. The output of state enterprises is shipped to other enterprises in accordance with the plan or sold in the state-owned shops. Prices are set by the planners to achieve social objectives and bear no relation to the quantities demanded and quantities supplied. Prices set at low levels for social reasons—as in the case of basic food products—result in chronic shortages.

services—is solved in different ways by different economic systems. Capitalism solves it by permitting households and firms to exchange factors of production and goods and services in markets. Firms produce the items that maximize their profits, households buy the goods that maximize their utility, and markets adjust prices to make buying and selling plans compatible. Socialism solves the economic problem by setting up a central planning system. The planners decide what will be produced and communicate their plans to state-owned enterprises. Incentives to fulfill the plan are created by a series of non-monetary rewards and sanctions. Each household decides what it wants to buy, but the total amount available is determined by the planners. Shortages, especially of basic staple food products, frequently arise. ◆

Let's now take a closer look at some socialist economies. We'll begin with the country that invented central planning and "exported" its system to the other socialist countries, the former Soviet Union.

Economic Change in the Former Soviet Union

The Soviet Union, or the Union of Soviet Socialist Republics (USSR), was founded in 1917 following the Bolshevik revolution led by Vladimir Ilyich Lenin. The union collapsed and was replaced by the Commonwealth of Independent States (CIS) in 1991. The republics that make up the Commonwealth are resource-rich and diverse. Their land area is three times that of the United States; their population is approaching 300 million, 20 percent larger than the United States; they have vast reserves of coal, oil, iron ore, natural gas, timber, and almost every other mineral resource. They are republics of enormous ethnic diversity with Russians making up 50 percent of the population and many European, Asian, and Arabic ethnic groups making up the other 50 percent.

Economic History of the Soviet Union

A compact economic history of the Soviet Union appears in Table 38.1. Although the nation was founded in 1917, its economic management system was not put in place until the 1930s. The architect of this system was Joseph Stalin. The financial,

TABLE 38.1

A Compact Summary of Key Periods in the Economic History of the Soviet Union

Period	Main economic events/characteristics
1917–1921 (Lenin)	◆ Bolshevik Revolution ◆ Nationalization of banking, industry, and transportation ◆ Forced requisitioning of agricultural output
1921–1924 (Lenin)	◆ New Economic Policy (NEP), 1921 ◆ Market allocation of most resources
1928–1953 (Stalin)	◆ Abolition of market ◆ Introduction of command planning and five-year plans ◆ Collectivization of farms ◆ Emphasis on capital goods and economic growth ◆ Harsh conditions
1953–1970 (Khrushchev to Brezhnev)	◆ Steady growth ◆ Increased emphasis on consumer goods
1970–1985 (Brezhnev to Chernenko)	◆ Deteriorating productivity in agriculture and industry ◆ Slowdown in growth
1985–1991 (Gorbachev)	◆ Perestroika—reforms based on increased accountability
1991	◆ Breakup of the Soviet Union
1992	◆ Creation of the Commonwealth of Independent States

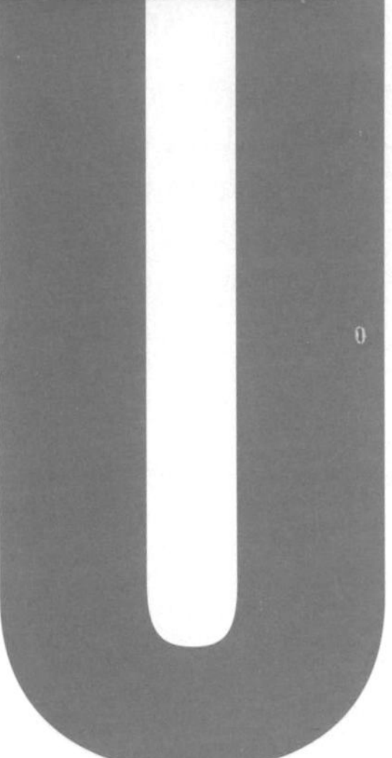

UNDERSTANDING the Limits of CENTRAL PLANNING

Our economy is a highly planned one. But it is not *centrally* planned. The planning takes place inside corporations—some of them huge. General Motors, for example, is bigger than many countries. If it makes sense to plan GM's economy, why doesn't it make sense to plan a national economy?

This question has puzzled and divided economists for many years. The answer given by Friedrich von Hayek is that an economy produces billions of different goods and services, while a corporation, even a very large one, produces only a limited range of items. As a consequence, central planning requires the centralization of vast amounts of information that it is extremely costly to collect. The market economizes on this information. Each household or firm needs to know only the prices of the range of goods and services that it buys and sells. No household or firm needs to know every price. And none needs to know the technologies for producing anything beyond its area of specialization. Markets find the prices that make the plans of producers and consumers consistent.

But Hayek's answer leaves open another question. Why does GM plan? Why isn't the market used to allocate resources inside GM? This question was answered by Ronald H. Coase. Planning, he explained, economizes on transactions costs, while the market economizes on information costs. There is an optimal size of the planning unit (firm) and an optimal extent of the market for each activity.

The poor economic performance of the former Soviet Union, the communist countries of Eastern Europe, and China before 1978 suggests that planning was taken too far in those countries and that the scope of the market was too restricted. These countries were run like big firms, but the firms were too big.

"The more complicated the whole, the more dependent we become on that division of knowledge between individuals whose separate efforts are coordinated by the impersonal . . . price system."

Friedrich von Hayek
The Road to Serfdom

Before 1978, the farms of China were operated as part of the national economic plan. The planners decided what would be produced and how the food would be distributed. Peasant farmers received an allocation of food, but their rewards were unrelated to their efforts. Food production and living standards were low. In 1978, Deng Xiaoping reformed the farms. Families were permitted to take long-term leases on their land and to decide what to produce and where to sell it. The result was a massive increase in food production and a rapid increase in the standard of living. By 1984, the farms had become so productive that China became an *exporter* of grain.

Deng Xiaoping's 1978 economic reforms have had dramatic effects on China's large cities and urban population. New laws that permitted the creation of private firms resulted in massive numbers of new private enterprises springing up—manufacturing a wide range of consumer goods and providing employment for people who were no longer needed on the increasingly efficient farms. By 1990, real income per person had increased to 2½ times its 1978 level. Between 1982 and 1988, real income per person grew at a staggering 9.7 percent a year, almost doubling in six years. Many of the new private firms sell on world markets, and China's exports grew at a much faster rate than GDP during the 1980s. By 1990, they stood at 17 percent of GDP.

Karl Marx: An Alternative Economic Vision

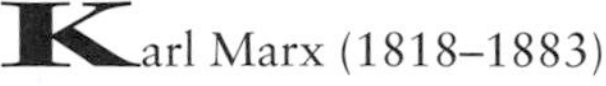

Karl Marx (1818–1883) was a social scientist (political scientist, sociologist, and economist) of extraordinary breadth and influence. Born in Germany, he spend most of his adult life in London, using the British Museum as his workplace. With little income, life was harsh for Marx and his wife (his childhood sweetheart to whom he was devoted). Marx's major work in economics was *Das Kapital,* in which he argued that capitalism was self-destructive and would be replaced by a system in which private property was abolished and a central plan replaced the market—a system he called "communism." Events have rejected Marx's theory, and his lasting contribution to modern economics is negligible. But his contribution to modern politics is substantial. Marxism, a political creed based on his ideas, thrives throughout much of the world today.

manufacturing, and transportation sectors of the economy had been taken under state ownership and control by Lenin. Stalin added the farms to this list. He abolished the market and introduced a command planning mechanism, initiating a series of five-year plans that placed their major emphasis on setting and attaining goals for the production of capital goods. The production of consumer goods was given a secondary place, and personal economic conditions were harsh. With emphasis on the production of capital goods, the Soviet economy grew quickly.

By the 1950s, after Stalin's death, steady economic growth continued, but the emphasis in economic planning gradually shifted away from capital goods production toward consumer goods production. In the 1960s, the growth rate began to sag, and by the 1970s and early 1980s, the Soviet economy was running into serious problems. Productivity was actually declining, especially in agriculture but also in industry. Growth slowed, and, by some estimates, per capita income in the Soviet Union began to fall. It was in this situation that Mikhail Gorbachev came to power with plans to restructure the Soviet economy, based on the idea of increased individual accountability and rewards based on performance.

As a unified political entity, the Soviet Union effectively disintegrated following an unsuccessful coup to topple former President Gorbachev in August 1991. What emerged from that coup in 1992 was a more loosely federated Commonwealth of Independent States. Political freedoms began to be enjoyed in the late 1980s under President Gorbachev's programs of *perestroika* (restructuring) and *glasnost* (openness). These political freedoms released nationalist and ethnic feelings that had been held in check for 50 years and created a virtual explosion of political activity. At the same time, the economies of the now independent republics underwent tumultuous change.

We are going to look at that change. But you will better appreciate the severity and nature of the problems posed by economic change if we first look at the way the Soviet Union operated before it abandoned its central planning system.

Soviet-Style Central Planning

Soviet-style central planning is a method of economic planning and control that has four key elements:

- Administrative hierarchy
- Iterative planning process
- Legally binding commands
- Taut and inflexible plans

Administrative Hierarchy A large and complex hierarchy implements and controls the central economic plan that determines almost every aspect of economic activity. A **hierarchy** is an organization arranged in ranks, each rank being subordinate to the one above it. At the top of an economic planning hierarchy is the highest *political* authority. Immediately below it is the economic planning ministry, the senior of a large number of ministries. Below the planning ministry are a large number of ministries that are responsible for the detailed aspects of production. For example, one ministry deals with engineering production, another with fruit and vegetables, and another with railroad transportation. Responsibility for production processes is divided and subdivided yet further down to the level of the individual factories that carry out the production processes. For example, engineering is divided into light, heavy, electrical, and civil divisions. Light engineering is divided into departments that deal with individual product groups, such as ball bearings. And finally, ball bearings are manufactured in a number of factories. At each level of the hierarchy, there are superiors and subordinates. Superiors have absolute and arbitrary power over their subordinates.

Iterative Planning Process Central planning is an iterative planning process. An iterative process is a repetitive series of calculations that get closer and closer to a solution. A plan is proposed, and adjustments are repeatedly made until all the elements of the plan are consistent with each other. But a plan is not arrived at as the result of a set of neat calculations performed on a computer. Rather, the process involves a repeated sequence of communications of proposals and reactions down and up the administrative hierarchy.

The process begins with the issue of a big picture set of objectives or directives by the highest political authority. These directives are translated into targets by the planning ministry and retranslated into ever more detailed targets as they are passed down the hierarchy. Tens of millions of raw materials and intermediate goods featured in the detailed plans of the Soviet Union, which filled 70 volumes, or 12,000 pages, each year.

When the targets are specified as production plans for individual products, the factories react with their own assessments of what is feasible. Reactions as to feasibility are passed back up the hierarchy, and the central planning ministry makes the targets and reports of feasibility consistent. A good deal of bargaining takes place in this process, the superiors demanding the impossible and subordinates claiming requests to be infeasible.

Legally Binding Commands Once a consistent (even if infeasible) plan has been determined by the planning ministry, the plan is given the force of law in a set of binding commands from the political authority. The commands are translated into increasing detail as they pass down the chain of command and are implemented by the production units in a way that most nearly satisfies the superiors of each level.

Taut and Inflexible Plans In the Soviet Union, the targets set by superiors for their subordinates were infeasible. The idea was that in the attempt to do the impossible, more would be achieved than if an easily attained task was set. The outcome of this planning process was a set of taut and inflexible plans. A taut plan is one that has no slack built into it. If one unit fails to meet its planned targets, all the other units that rely on the output of the first unit will fail to meet their targets also. An inflexible plan is one that has no capacity for reactions to changing circumstances.

Faced with impossible targets, factories produced a combination of products that enabled their superiors to report plan fulfillment, but the individual items produced did not meet the needs of the other parts of the economy. No factory received exactly the quantity and types of inputs needed, and the economy was unable to respond to changes in circumstances. In practice, the plan for the current year was the outcome of the previous year plus a wished for but unattainable increment.

The Market Sector

Although the economy of the Soviet Union was a planned one, a substantial amount of economic activity took place outside the planning and command economy. The most important component of the market sector was in agriculture. It has been estimated that during the 1980s there were 35 million private plots worked by rural households in the Soviet Union. These private plots constituted less than 3 percent of the agricultural land of the Soviet Union but produced close to 25 percent of total agricultural output and a third of all the meat and milk. Some estimates suggested that the productivity on private plots was 40 times that of state enterprise farms and collective farms. Other economic activities undertaken by Soviet citizens outside the planning system were illegal.

Money in the Soviet Union

Money played a minor role in the economy of the Soviet Union. It was used in the market sector and in the state sector to pay wages and buy consumer goods and services. But all the transactions among state enterprises and between state enterprises and government took place as part of the *physical* plan, and money was used only as a means of keeping records. International trade was undertaken by the direct exchange of goods for goods—barter.

Soviet Economic Decline

Table 38.2 describes the growth performance of the Soviet economy between 1928 and 1990. The economy performed extraordinarily well before 1970. Growth rates of output in excess of 5 percent a year were achieved on the average for the entire period between 1928 and 1970, bringing an eightfold increase in aggregate output over these years. Then the growth rate began to fall. During the 1970s, output expanded by 3.2 percent a year, and in the 1980s, growth collapsed to 2 percent a year between 1980 and 1986 and then to only 1 percent a year between 1986 and 1990. In 1990, the economy shrank by 4 percent.

Why did the economy perform well before 1970 and then begin to deliver successively slower growth rates? What brought the decline of the Soviet economy during the 1980s? The combination and interaction of three features were responsible. They are

- Transition from investment to consumption economy
- External shocks
- Taut and inflexible plans

TABLE 38.2

Economic Growth Rates in the Soviet Union

Years	Growth rates (percent per year)
1928–1937	**5.4**
1940–1960	**5.7**
1960–1970	**5.1**
1970–1979	**3.2**
1980–1986	**2.0**
1987	**1.6**
1988	**4.4**
1989	**2.5**
1990	**−4.0**

Economic growth in the Soviet Union was rapid between 1928 and 1970. During the 1970s, growth began to slow down, and the growth rate became successively lower until the early 1990s, when the economy began to contract.

Sources: Paul R. Gregory and Robert C. Stuart, *Soviet Economic Structure and Performance*, 2nd edition (New York: Harper and Row, 1981); U.S. Central Intelligence Agency, *USSR: Measures of Economic Growth and Development, 1950–1980*, U.S. Congress, Joint Economic Committee (Washington, D.C.: U.S. Government Printing Office, 1982); U.S. Central Intelligence Agency, "Gorbachev's Economic Program," Report to U.S. Congress, Subcommittee on National Security Economics, April 13, 1989 (Washington, D.C.: U.S. Government Printing Office, 1989); and The World Bank, *The Economy of the USSR* (Washington, D.C.: 1990).

Transition from Investment to Consumption Economy Before 1960, the Soviet economic planners concentrated on producing capital goods and maintaining a rapid rate of investment in new buildings, plant, and equipment. They ran the Soviet economy like a large corporation intent on rapid growth that puts all its profits into yet more growth. The central planning system is at its best when implementing such a strategy. The planners know exactly which types of capital they need to remove or reduce bottlenecks and can achieve a high rate of growth.

During the 1960s, the orientation of the Soviet economy began to change with a relative increase in the production of consumer goods and services. By the 1970s and 1980s, this process had gone much further. A centrally planned economy does a very bad job of handling the complexities of producing a large variety of types, sizes, colors, designs, and styles of consumer goods. The planners need to collect and take into account more information than their computers can handle.

As a result, the planners order the wrong goods to be produced, creating surpluses of some and chronic shortages of others. Easy-to-produce plain white bread is available in excessive quantities at give-away prices, and hard-to-produce blueberry muffins can't be found at any price. Surplus goods get wasted or used inefficiently, and increasing amounts of the resources that could be used to add to the economy's productive capital get diverted to meeting ever more desperate consumer demands. Gradually, economic growth vanishes.

External Shocks As the world's largest producer of crude oil, the Soviet Union benefited enormously, during the 1970s, from the massive oil price increases. The extra revenue obtained from oil exports helped, during those years, to mask the problems just described. But the 1980s brought *falling* oil prices and exposed the problems of the Soviet Union in a sharp light.

During the late 1980s, the countries of Eastern Europe that had been the Soviet Union's traditional trading partners embarked on their own transitions to market economies and began to look to the West for trading opportunities. As a consequence, the Soviet Union's sources of international trade collapsed.

Taut and Inflexible Plans A flexible economic system might have been able to deal with the switch to consumption goods production and the consequences of a changing world economic environment. But the Soviet economy was not flexible. On the contrary, with its system of taut planning and its unresponsive command structure, it was only able to attempt to produce the same bundle of goods as it had produced in the previous year. With less revenue from oil and other raw material exports, fewer imported inputs could be obtained. Imbalances in the central plan rippled through the entire economy, disrupting the production of all goods and putting the system itself under enormous strain.

Living Standards in the Late 1980s

The problems of the Soviet economy are put in sharp focus in Fig. 38.5. In this figure, the productivity and consumption levels of the Soviet Union in the mid-1980s are compared with those of the United States, Western Europe (Germany, France, and Italy), Japan, and Portugal. As you can see from the figure, average worker productivity in the Soviet Union, measured by GDP per worker, was less than 40 percent of real GDP per worker in the United States and lagged considerably behind that in the other Western European countries and Japan. A similar picture is painted by comparing consumption per worker and consumption per person. The capitalist country whose level of productivity and consumption was most similar to that of the Soviet Union was Portugal.

FIGURE 38.5

GDP and Consumption in the Soviet Union and Other Countries

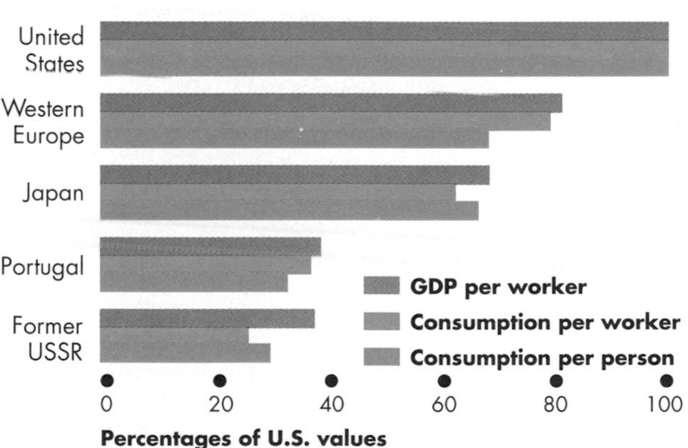

GDP per worker in the Soviet Union in the mid-1980s was less than 40 percent of its level in the United States and similar to the level in Portugal. Consumption per worker and consumption per person were even lower at less than 30 percent of the U.S. level. The Soviet Union lagged considerably behind Western Europe and Japan in GDP and consumption level.

Source: Abram Bergson, "The USSR Before the Fall: How Poor and Why," *Journal of Economic Perspectives* 5, 4 (Fall 1991): 29–44.

Market Economy Reforms

By the end of the 1980s, there was widespread dissatisfaction throughout the Soviet Union with the economic planning system, and a process of transition toward a market economy began. This process had three main elements:

1. Relaxing central plan enforcement
2. Deregulating prices
3. Permitting limited private ownership of firms

The transition in all three areas was one of gradual change. But the relaxation of central plan enforcement was the fastest and most far-reaching element of the transition. The idea was that by relaxing central control over the annual plan and permitting the managers of state enterprises greater freedom to act like the managers of private firms, enterprises would be able to respond to changing circumstances without having to wait for orders from the center.

Price deregulation was gradual and covered a limited range of products. Here, the idea was that with the removal of price controls, the price mechanism would allocate scarce resources to their highest-value uses. Shortages would disappear and be replaced by available but sometimes expensive goods and services. High prices would strengthen the inducement for producers to increase the quantities supplied. The move toward private ownership of firms was extremely gradual. The idea here was that enterprising individuals would move quickly to seize profit opportunities by responding to price signals much more rapidly than the replaced planning system could respond to shortages and bottlenecks.

But the transition process ran into problems. One of these problems was that of unlearning the old methods of the centrally planned economy. Reading Between the Lines on pp. 1044–1045 looks at an example of this problem in the Moscow market for bread. But deeper transition problems arose from the nature of the system being replaced.

Transition Problems

There are three major problems confronting the republics of the former Soviet Union that complicate

The Market Comes to Moscow

The Wall Street Journal, January 21, 1992

Moscow's 'Capitalists' Decide the Best Price Is a Firmly Fixed One

by Laurie Hays and Adi Ignatius

Late last month, on the eve of Russia's historic plunge into a market economy, Vladimir Grechanik, the top financial planner of Moscow's Bread Factory No. 14, went into a panic.

After 70 years of government control of everything from the cost of raw materials to salaries, the factory suddenly would be able to set its own prices. He and his fellow producers anxiously tried to calculate how much flour would cost, how much transportation might rise and what consumers would be willing to pay.

Just before prices were freed Jan. 2, Mr. Grechanik and executives from Moscow's other bread factories were called to a meeting at the Moscow Bread Consortium, the de facto ministry of bread. They eyed one another nervously, suspicious that, after years of mandated equality, the system might make rivals of former comrades. The bread consortium suggested raising the free-market bread price to 3½ times the old price, but not a kopeck more. The factory men were confused. In the old days, such a "suggestion" carried the full weight of a decree. But there were no certainties anymore. The new freedom was unbearable.

An Old Reflex

Left to his own devices, Mr. Grechanik returned to his office and got on the phone. For the next two days he and the other factory directors discussed their fears. Finally, they came to a decision: If the state was no longer to set prices, the factories themselves would jointly fix them—to ensure their mutual survival.

"We all agreed on a single price," says Mr. Grechanik, as he walks past huge vats of flour on the factory floor. Lowering his voice, he confides, "I've heard that Bread Factory No. 26 is charging a little less, but I hope it's just a rumor."...

The Essence of the Story

In Russia, the prices of many items, including bread, were deregulated on January 2, 1992.

In December 1991, in preparation for this event, the executives of Moscow's bread factories attended a meeting at the Moscow Bread Consortium (the de facto ministry of bread).

The consortium suggested that producers increase the price of bread to 3½ times the old price. This "suggestion" did not, as in the formerly planned economy, have the force of law.

The bread producers were confused, anxious, nervous, and suspicious.

For two days the factory directors discussed their fears by telephone and eventually decided to jointly fix the price of bread.

There was a rumor that one bread factory (No. 26) was charging a lower price.

Background and Analysis

When the central planning system operated, the price and quantity of bread were determined by the planners.

Figure 1 illustrates this situation. The plan quantity is Q_0, and the plan price is 0.50 ruble (50 kopecks). The average cost of producing bread was higher than this price, and bread factories were subsidized. In this example (the numbers are hypothetical) the subsidy is 50 kopecks per loaf.

The move toward the market economy that began in January 1992 resulted in:

- The removal of the subsidy to bread producers
- Increased cost of flour and other raw materials and salaries

Increases in incomes (increases in ruble incomes, not increases in real incomes) and increases in other prices also led to an increase in the demand for bread.

The combination of these changes is illustrated in Fig. 2. There was uncertainty in the minds of the executives of the bread factories about the magnitude of these changes.

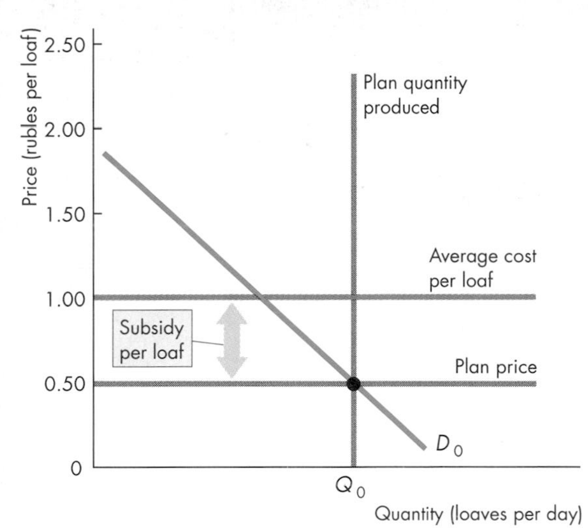

Figure 1

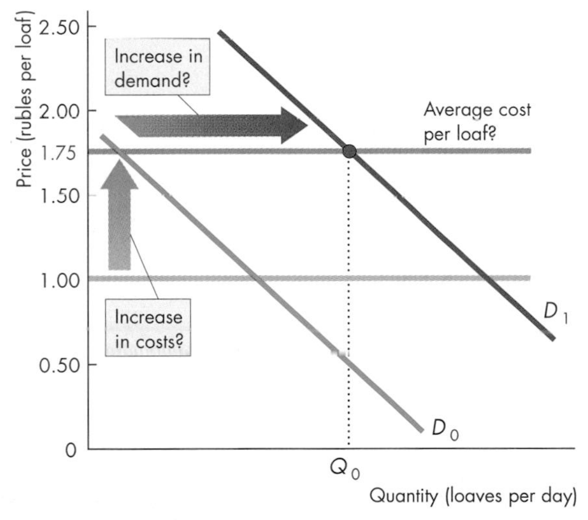

Figure 2

Adding to these uncertainties, each producer was uncertain about the prices that the other producers would charge for bread.

To remove the last-mentioned uncertainty, the producers pooled their information and fixed a single price. This price is based on the assumption that the costs of production—the opportunity cost of bread—would increase to 1.75 rubles a loaf.

If the demand for bread increased to D_1, the quantity produced would remain at its previous level of Q_0.

If the bread producers overestimated the opportunity cost of producing bread, the free market would result in new firms entering to compete with them and the price would fall below the level they had fixed.

If the bread producers underestimated the opportunity cost of bread, some of them would begin to incur losses and might eventually go out of business. In this event, the supply of bread would decrease and its price would rise until it covered its opportunity cost.

their transition to the capitalist market economic system. They are

- Value and legal systems alien to capitalism
- Collapse of traditional trade flows
- Fiscal crisis

Value and Legal Systems More than 60 years of socialist dictatorship have left a legacy of values and memories alien to the rapid and successful establishment of a capitalist, market economy. The political leaders and people of the former Soviet Union have no personal memories of free political institutions and markets. And they have been educated, both formally and informally, to believe in a political creed in which traders and speculators are not just shady characters, but criminals. Unlearning these values will be a slow and perhaps painful process.

The legal system is also unsuited to the needs of a market economy in two ways. First, there are no well-established property rights and methods of protecting those rights. Second, and more important, there is no tradition of government behaving like individuals and firms before the rule of law. In the Soviet system, the government *was* the law. Its economic plan and the arbitrary decisions made by superiors at each level in the hierarchy were the only law that counted. Rational, self-promoting actions taken outside the plan were illegal. It will take a long time to establish a legal system based on private property rights and the rule of law.

Collapse of Traditional Trade Flows A centrally administered empire has collapsed, and its constituent republics have decided to create a loose federation. Such a political reorganization can have devastating economic consequences. The most serious of these is the collapse of traditional trade flows. The Soviet Union was a highly interdependent grouping of republics organized on a wheel-hub basis with Moscow (and to a lesser degree Leningrad—now St. Petersburg) at its center. This view of the Soviet economy is shown in Fig. 38.6. The figure also shows the magnitude of the flows of goods from the republics through the Moscow hub.

The most heavily dependent republic, Belorussia, delivered 70 percent of its output to other republics and received a similar value of goods from the other republics. Even the least dependent republic, Kazakhstan, traded 30 percent of its production with the other republics. The vast amount of interrepublic trade, managed by the central planners and channeled through the Moscow hub, meant that individual enterprise managers had (and still have) little knowledge of where their products end up being used or their inputs originate.

With the collapse of the central plan, managers must search for supplies and for markets. Until they have built new networks of information, shortages of raw materials and other material inputs will be

FIGURE 38.6
The Wheel-Hub Economy of the Soviet Union

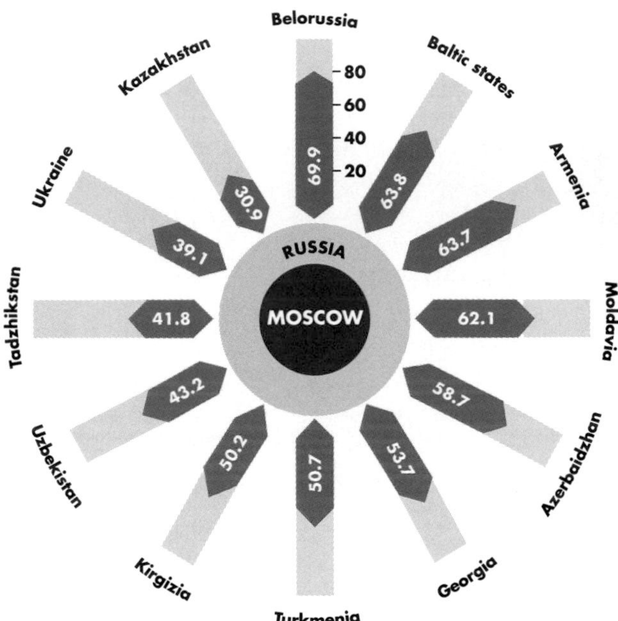

The Soviet economy was organized on a wheel-hub model. Vast amounts of goods and services were traded among the republics but mainly through the Moscow hub. The percentages of production in each republic exported to other republics are shown along the spokes of the wheel.

Source: The World Bank, *The Economy of the USSR* (Washington, D.C.: 1990), p. 51.

Note: The names of the republics in this figure are the ones used in the former Soviet Union. With the breakup of the Soviet Union, Belorussia became Belarus, Moldavia became Moldova, Turkmenia became Turkmenistan, Kirgizia became Kyrgyzstan, and Talzhikstan became Tajikistan.

common and a lack of markets will stunt production. This problem can be solved by the activities of specialist traders and speculators, but the emergence of this class of economic agent is likely to be slow because of political attitudes toward this activity.

The collapse of an economic empire does not inevitably lead to a collapse of traditional trade flows and an associated decline in production. But it usually has done so. The most similar collapse this century was that of the Austro-Hungarian Empire in 1919. Like the Soviet Union, the Austro-Hungarian Empire was a centralized economic system organized with Vienna and Budapest as its hubs with a single currency and free trade. The empire was a great economic success, achieving rapid improvements in living standards for its people. Following the collapse of the empire, tariffs were introduced, each country established its own currency, trade flows dried up, and economic growth declined.

Fiscal Crisis Under the central planning system of the Soviet Union, the central government collected taxes in an arbitrary way. One source of revenue was a tax on consumer goods. But the major source of revenue was the profits of the state enterprises. Since the state owned these enterprises, it also received the profits. Money played virtually no role in the centrally planned system. Workers received their wages in currency and used it to purchase consumer goods and services. But for the state enterprises and the government, money was just a unit for keeping records.

With the collapse of central planning, money has become more important, especially for the government. With the loss of its traditional sources of revenue and with little change in its spending, the government has a large budget deficit. It covers this deficit by printing money, and the result is inflation. The inflation rate during the final six months of the life of the Soviet Union—the first half of 1991—reached close to 200 percent and was on a rising path.

Inflation is not an inevitable accompaniment of the collapse of an economic empire, but like the collapse of trade flows, it has happened before. The rates of growth of the newly created currencies of Austria, Hungary, Poland, Rumania, and Yugoslavia following the disintegration of the Austro-Hungarian Empire were extremely rapid and led to hyperinflation. In Poland, the hyperinflation reached an annual rate of 250 million percent.

REVIEW

The Soviet Union's system of central economic planning and state ownership was established in the 1930s. Under this system, a hierarchical administrative structure engaged in an iterative planning process to arrive at a consistent economic plan. The plan was implemented by the political authority issuing legally binding commands that were translated into ever greater detail as they were passed down the chain of command. In practice, the plans were infeasible and inflexible. The system performed well before 1970 but became steadily less effective during the 1970s and 1980s. The system's inflexibility could not cope with the transition from an investment to a consumption economy and with a series of external shocks. As a result, its growth rate slowed, and eventually output began to decrease. A market reform process was begun that deregulated prices, permitted limited private ownership of firms, and relaxed the enforcement of the central plan. But the value and legal systems, the collapse of traditional trade flows, the loss of tax revenue, and inflation are making the transition extremely costly. ◆

Economic Transition in Eastern Europe

The formerly planned economies of Eastern Europe—Czechoslovakia, East Germany, Hungary, and Poland—are also making transitions to market economies. The processes being followed and the problems faced are similar to those of the former Soviet Union. But their problems, although severe, take different forms from those of the Soviet Union. The major differences arise from political factors. Let's take a brief look at the transition process in these countries.

East Germany

For East Germany, the transition from a centrally planned economy has been the most dramatic and the most complete. On October 3, 1990, East

Germany united with West Germany. East Germany was a country with 16 million people, 26 percent of the population of West Germany, and with a GDP per person of less than 80 percent of that of West Germany. Even before the formal reunification of the two parts of Germany, East Germany had begun to dismantle its Soviet-style planning system and replace it with a market economy.

The former East Germany adopted the monetary system of West Germany, deregulated its prices, and opened itself up to free trade with its western partner. State enterprises were permitted to fail in the competition with western private firms, private firms were permitted to open up in the former East Germany, and a massive sell-off of state enterprises was embarked upon.

The process of selling state enterprises began by the creation of a state corporation called Treuhandanstalt (which roughly translates as "Trust Corporation") that took over the assets of the almost 11,000 state enterprises. The idea was to then sell off these enterprises in an orderly way over a period of a few years. By November 1991, Treuhandanstalt had disposed of more than 4,000 firms. Most of these firms had been sold to the private sector, but about 900 firms were closed down or merged with other firms.

The loss of jobs resulting from this rapid shakeout of state enterprises was large. Even by July 1990, before the two Germanies were reunited, unemployment in East Germany had reached one third of the labor force. The unemployment rate in the east will remain high for some years, but the safety net of the West German social security system will cushion the blow to individual workers and their families.

East Germany has no fiscal policy crisis and no inflation problem. It has adopted the West German taxation and monetary systems and has assured financial stability. But the transition for East Germany will last for several years, even though it will be the most rapid transition imaginable.

Czechoslovakia, Hungary, and Poland

The problems facing Czechoslovakia, Hungary, and Poland differ in important ways but share some common features. And these common features are similar to some of the problems faced by the former Soviet Union that we've already seen. The most severe of these are the collapse of traditional trade flows and the loss of traditional sources of government revenue.

Czechoslovakia Czechoslovakia removed its communist government in what has been called the "Velvet Revolution" in November 1989 and almost immediately embarked on a program of economic reforms aimed at replacing its centrally planned economy with a market system.

The first step in the transition was the freeing of wages, prices, and interest rates. This step was accomplished quickly, but the emergence of well-functioning markets did not immediately follow. Financial markets were especially nervous, and a shortage of liquidity created a financial crisis.

The second step in the transition was privatization. Czechoslovakia is pursuing a so-called two-track policy of "little privatization" and "big privatization." "Little privatization" is the sale or, where possible, the return to their former owners of small businesses and shops. "Big privatization" is the sale of shares in the large industrial enterprises. One feature of this privatization process is the issue of vouchers to citizens that may be used to buy shares in formerly state-owned enterprises.

Czechoslovakia's transition has not yet reached the point of a positive economic payoff. Real GDP is growing, but very slowly, and unemployment is high.

Hungary Hungary has been in a long transition toward a capitalist, market economy. The process began in the 1960s when central planning was replaced by decentralized planning based on a price system. Hungary has also established a taxation system similar to that in the market economies. But the privatization of large-scale industry began only in the 1990s and is proceeding slowly.

Because of its extreme gradualism, Hungary's transition is much less disruptive than those in the other countries. But it is feeling the repercussions of the economic restructuring of the other Eastern European countries with which it has traditionally had the strongest trade links, so its rate of economic expansion has slowed substantially in recent years.

Poland Severe shortages, black markets, and inflation were the jumping off point for Poland's journey toward a market economy. This journey began in September 1989 when a non-communist government that included members of the trade union Solidarity took office. The new government has deregulated prices, and black markets have disappeared. It has also pursued a policy of extreme financial restraint, bringing the state budget and inflation under control.

Privatization has also been put on a fast track in Poland. In mid-1991, the government announced its Mass Privatization Scheme. Under this scheme, the shares of 400 state enterprises were to be transferred to a Privatization Fund, the shares in which were to be distributed freely to the entire adult population. This method of privatization is like creating a giant insurance company that owns most of the production enterprises and that is in turn owned by private shareholders.

Although the transition to the market economy is the most dynamic in Eastern Europe and the former Soviet Union, it has been going on for longer and has had more dramatic effects on living standards in China. Let's now look at this country.

Economic Transition in China

China is the world's largest nation. In 1990, its population was 1.2 billion—almost a quarter of the world's population. Chinese civilization is ancient and has a splendid history, but the modern nation—the People's Republic of China—dates only from 1949. A compact summary of key periods in the economic history of the People's Republic is presented in Table 38.3.

Modern China began when a revolutionary Communist movement, led by Mao Zedong, captured control of China, forcing the country's previous leader, Chiang Kai-shek (Jiang Jie-shi) onto the island of Formosa—now Taiwan. Like the Soviet Union, China is a socialist country. But unlike the Soviet Union, China is largely nonindustrialized—it is a developing country.

During the early years of the People's Republic, the country followed the Soviet model of economic planning and command. Urban manufacturing industry was taken over and operated by the state, and the farms were collectivized. Also, following the Stalin model of the 1930s, primary emphasis was placed on the production of capital equipment.

TABLE 38.3

A Compact Summary of Key Periods in the Economic History of the People's Republic of China

Period	Main economic events/characteristics
1949	◆ People's Republic of China established under Mao Zedong
1949–1952	◆ Economy centralized under a new communist government
	◆ Emphasis on heavy industry and "socialist transformation"
1952–1957	◆ First five-year plan
1958–1960	◆ The Great Leap Forward: an economic reform plan based on labor-intensive production methods
	◆ Massive failure
1966	◆ Cultural Revolution: revolutionary zealots
1976	◆ Death of Mao Zedong
1978	◆ Deng's reforms: under leadership of Deng Xiaoping, liberalization of agriculture and introduction of individual incentives
	◆ Growth rates accelerated
1989	◆ Democracy movement, government crackdown

The Great Leap Forward

In 1958, Mao Zedong set the Chinese economy on a sharply divergent path from that which the Soviet Union had followed. Mao called his new path the Great Leap Forward. The **Great Leap Forward** was an economic plan based on small-scale, labor-intensive production. The Great Leap Forward paid little or no attention to linking individual pay to individual effort. Instead, a revolutionary commitment to the success of collective plans was relied upon. The Great Leap Forward was an economic failure. Productivity increased, but so slowly that living standards hardly changed. In the agricultural sector, massive injections of modern high-yield seeds, improved irrigation, and chemical fertilizers were insufficient to enable China to feed its population. The country became the largest importer of grains, edible vegetable oils, and even raw cotton.

The popular explanation within China for poor performance, especially in agriculture, was that the country had reached the limits of its arable land and that its population explosion was so enormous that agriculture was being forced to use substandard areas for farming. But the key problem was that the revolutionary and ideological motivation for the Great Leap Forward degenerated into what came to be called the Cultural Revolution. Revolutionary zealots denounced productive managers, engineers, scientists, and scholars and banished them to the life of the peasant. Schools and universities were closed, and the accumulation of human capital was severely disrupted.

The 1978 Reforms

By 1978, two years after the death of Mao Zedong, the new Chinese leader, Deng Xiaoping, proclaimed major economic reforms. Collectivized agriculture was abolished. Agricultural land was distributed among households on long-term leases. In exchange for a lease, a household agreed to pay a fixed tax and contracted to sell part of its output to the state. But the household made its own decisions on cropping patterns and the quantity and types of fertilizers and other inputs to use, and it also hired its own workers. Private farm markets were liberalized, and farmers received a higher price for their produce. Also, the state increased the price that it paid to farmers, especially for cotton and other nongrain crops.

The results of the reforms of Deng Xiaoping were astounding. Annual growth rates of output of cotton and oil-bearing crops increased a staggering fourteenfold. Soybean production, which had been declining at an annual rate of 1 percent between 1957 and 1978, started to grow at 4 percent a year. Growth rates of yields per acre also increased dramatically. By 1984, a country that six years earlier had been the world's largest importer of agricultural products became a food exporter!

The reforms led to more than a massive expansion in the agricultural sector. Increased rural incomes brought an expanding rural industrial sector that, by the mid-1980s, was employing a fifth of the rural population.

China has gone even further and is encouraging foreign investment and joint ventures. In addition, China is experimenting with formal capital markets and now has a stock market.

Motivated partly by political considerations, China is proclaiming the virtues of what it calls the "one country, two systems" approach to economic management. The political source of this movement is the existence of two capitalist enclaves in which China has a close interest—Taiwan and Hong Kong. China claims sovereignty over Taiwan and wants to create an atmosphere in which it becomes possible for China to be "reunified" at some future date. Hong Kong, a British crown colony, is currently leased by Britain from China, and that lease terminates in 1997. When the lease expires, Hong Kong will become part of China. Anxious not to damage the economic prosperity of Hong Kong, China is proposing to continue operating Hong Kong as a capitalist economy. With Hong Kong and Taiwan as part of the People's Republic of China, the stage will be set for the creation of other capitalist "islands" in such dynamic cities as Shanghai.

The results of this move toward capitalism in China are dramatically summarized in the country's real GDP growth statistics. Between 1978 and 1990, real GDP per person grew at an average rate of 7.2 percent a year—a 2.3-fold increase in income per person over the twelve-year period. Between 1982 and 1988, real GDP per person grew at a staggering 9.7 percent a year, almost doubling in a six-year period. To see how staggering these growth rates are, look at Fig. 38.7. It shows the consequences of China and the United States maintaining their post-1978 average growth rates of real GDP per person. For the United States, that growth rate was a little over 1 percent a year, and for China it was almost 8 percent a year. If they maintain these growth rates, China will catch up with the United States in a single generation, by 2010. Even if China's growth slackens off to 5 percent a year, with no change in the U.S. growth rate, China will catch up by 2030.

China is not only experiencing rapid growth of real income per person but is also increasing its international competitiveness. Its exports have grown during the 1980s at a much faster rate than GDP and, by 1990, stood at 17 percent of GDP.

How has China achieved this dramatic success?

FIGURE 38.7

Economic Growth in China

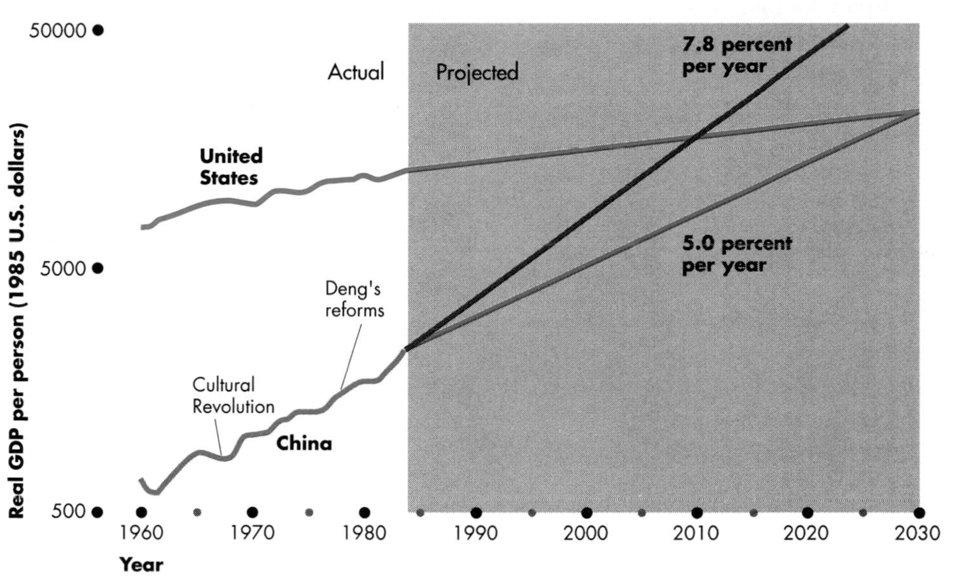

Source: Alan Heston and Robert Summers, "A New Set of International Comparisons of Real Product and Price Levels: Estimates for 130 Countries, 1950–1985," *Review of Income and Wealth,* series 34, vol. 1, 1988, pp. 1–25, Appendix B.

The growth of per capita income in China has been strongly influenced by the economic system. During the Cultural Revolution, per capita income fell. Under a central planning and command mechanism in the early 1970s, per capita income grew at a moderate pace. Under capitalist methods of production in agriculture following the 1978 reforms, per capita income growth increased dramatically. If China continues to grow at the pace it has achieved since 1978, and if the United States also maintains its post-1978 growth rate, China will catch up with the United States in 2010. Even if China slows to a 5 percent growth rate, it will catch up with the United States in 2030.

China's Success

China's success in achieving a high rate of economic growth has resulted from four features of its reforms.[1] They are

- Massive rate of entry of new non-state firms
- Increases in the productivity and profitability of state firms
- An efficient taxation system
- Gradual price deregulation

Entry of Non-State Firms The most rapidly growing sector of the Chinese economy during the 1980s was non-state industrial firms located typically in rural areas. This sector grew at an annual rate of 17½ percent between 1978 and 1990. In 1978 this sector produced 22 percent of the nation's industrial output. By 1990 it was producing 45 percent of total industrial output. By contrast, the state-owned firms—the firms organized by the state under its national plan—shrank (relatively) from producing 78 percent of total output in 1978 to 55 percent in 1990.

The entry of new firms created a dramatic increase in competition both among the new firms and between the new firms and the state firms. This competition spurred both non-state and state firms into greater efficiency and productivity.

Increases in the Productivity and Profitability of State Firms China has not privatized its economy by selling off state firms. Instead, privatization has come from the entry of new firms. The state firms have continued to operate. But the government has a strong incentive to ensure that the state firms are profitable. If state firms make no profit, the government collects no taxes from them.

To achieve the greatest possible level of profit and tax revenue, the Chinese economic planners have changed the incentives faced by the managers of

[1]This section is based on John McMillan and Barry Naughton, *How to Reform a Planned Economy: Lessons from China,* Graduate School of International Relations and Pacific Studies, University of California, San Diego, 1991.

state enterprises to resemble those of the market incentives faced by the non-state sector. Managers of state-owned firms are paid according to the firm's performance—similar to managers in private firms.

The Chinese system gives incentives for managers of state enterprises to be extremely enterprising and productive. As a result of this new system the Chinese government is now able to auction off top management jobs. Potential managers bid for the right to be manager. The manager offering the best promise of performance is the one who gets the job.

Efficient Taxation System Firms (both private and state firms) are taxed, but the tax system is unusual and different from that in our own economy. Firms are required to pay a fixed amount of profit to the government. Once that fixed amount of tax has been paid, the firm keeps any additional profit beyond that point. In contrast, the U.S. corporate tax system requires firms to pay a fixed percentage of their profits in tax. Thus in the United States, more profit means higher taxes, while in China, taxes are set independently of a firm's profit level. The Chinese system creates much stronger incentives than does our own system for firms to seek out and pursue profitable ventures.

Gradual Price Deregulation China has not abandoned planning its prices. The socialist planning system keeps the prices of manufactured goods fairly high and keeps domestic prices higher than world prices. This pricing arrangement makes private enterprise production in China extremely profitable. In 1978, when the non-state sector was small, the profit rate in that sector was almost 40 percent—for every dollar invested, 40¢ a year was earned. With such high profits there was a tremendous incentive for enterprising people to find niches and engage in creative and productive activity. The forces of competition have gradually lowered prices; by 1990, rates of return had fallen to 10 percent. But the price movements were gradual. There was no "big bang" adjustment of prices—no abandonment of the planning mechanism and introduction of a rip-roaring free market system.

Growing Out of the Plan

As a result of the reforms adopted in the 1970s and pursued vigorously since that time, the Chinese economy has gradually become a much more market-oriented economy and is, in effect, growing out of its central plan.[2] The proportion of the economy accounted for by private enterprise and market-influenced prices has gradually increased, and the proportion accounted for by state enterprises and planned and regulated prices has gradually decreased.

To sustain this process, changes in fiscal policy and monetary policy have been necessary. The reform of the economy has entailed the redesigning of the tax system. In a centrally planned economy the government's tax revenues come directly through its pricing policy. Also, the government, as the controller of all financial institutions, receives all of the nation's saving. When the central planning system is replaced by the market, the government must establish a tax collection agency similar to the Internal Revenue Service of the United States. Also, it must establish financial markets so that the savings of households can be channeled into the growing private firms to finance their investment in new buildings, plant, and equipment.

Despite the reform of its tax system, the government of China spends more than it receives in tax revenue and covers its deficit by the creation of money. The result is a steady rate of inflation. But the inflation in China is not out of control, as it is in the former Soviet Union, because the rapidly growing level of economic activity absorbs a great deal of the new money.

Whether China has found a way of making the transition from socialism to capitalism in a relatively painless way is a controversial issue. The violent suppression of the democracy movement in Tiananmen Square in the summer of 1989 suggests that China might have bought economic gains at the expense of political freedoms. Because China has retained a strong central government and only gradually changed its system, its experience is not directly useful to the struggling countries of Eastern Europe. But the experiment in comparative *economic* systems currently going on in China is one of the most exciting that the world has seen. Economists of all political shades of opinion will closely watch its outcome, and its lessons will be of enormous value for future generations—whatever those lessons turn out to be.

[2]Barry Naughton, *Growing Out of the Plan: Chinese Economic Reform, 1978–90,* Graduate School of International Relations and Pacific Studies, University of California, San Diego, 1992.

The Transition from Central Plan to Market

As the countries of Eastern Europe and China abandon their central planning systems, they must make a series of important choices. The key ones are these:

- The style of market economy to adopt
- The sequencing of reforms
- The speed of reforms

Styles of Market Economy

There is no unique type of market economy, and countries that formerly relied on central planning must choose from an array of possible models. The three main ones are

1. U.S.-style capitalism
2. Japanese-style capitalism
3. Welfare state capitalism

U.S.-Style Capitalism No country relies on a pure, unregulated market mechanism to solve its economic problem. But the United States comes closer than any other country to doing so. In this country, individuals own the factors of production and decide how to use their factors to earn an income. They decide how much of their incomes to save to add to their capital resources and how much to spend, and on which goods and services. These decisions by more than 250 million individuals are coordinated in markets. Governments (federal, state, and local) regulate these markets, provide public goods and services, and tax income and expenditure. Command mechanisms similar in kind to those used in the centrally planned economies are used in the government sector and by firms in their internal planning processes.

The other types of capitalism depart from the U.S. model mainly in the degree and nature of state intervention in the economy. But there are two distinct styles.

Japanese-Style Capitalism Japan's economic performance since World War II has been called the "Japanese economic miracle." Emerging from war with an average income per person that was less than one fifth of that in the United States, Japan has transformed itself into an economic giant whose income per person now approaches our own. The most spectacular growth period occurred in the 25 years from 1945 to 1970, when per capita income increased eightfold. Today, Japan has a dominant position in world markets for cars and computers, audio and video equipment, and a whole range of high-tech commodities. The Japanese tourist is now as common a sight in London, Paris, and Rome as the U.S. tourist. And there are more Japanese visitors to the United States than U.S. visitors to Japan. What has led to this transformation of Japan into one of the world's most powerful and richest economies?

Three features of the Japanese economy have contributed to its dramatic success: reliance on free-market, capitalist methods; the small scale of government; and pro-business government intervention.

The economic system in Japan is like that in the United States. People are free to pursue their ideas, to own firms, to hire labor and other inputs, and to sell their outputs in relatively free markets.

The Japanese government is the smallest in the capitalist world. Average taxes and government spending account for slightly less than one fifth of GDP. This contrasts with close to 30 percent in the United States and more than 40 percent in some Western European capitalist countries. A small scale of government means that taxes are low and therefore do not constitute a discouragement to work and to saving and accumulating capital.

But the Japanese government does intervene in the economy, and its intervention is pro-business. The main vehicle for intervention is the Ministry of International Trade and Industry (MITI)—a government agency responsible for stimulating Japanese industrial development and international trade. In the years immediately following World War II, MITI encouraged the development of basic industries such as coal, electric power, shipbuilding, and steel. It used tariffs and quotas to protect these industries in their early stages of development, subsidized them, and ensured that capital resources were abundantly available for them. MITI is almost entrepreneurial in its activities. During the 1960s, with the basic industries in place, MITI turned its attention to helping the chemical and lighter manufacturing industries. In the 1980s, it helped Japanese industry dominate the world computer market.

MITI not only fosters the growth and development of industries. It also helps speed the decline of those industries that are not contributing to rapid income growth. For example, in the mid-1970s, when the price of oil increased dramatically, the smelting of bauxite to create aluminum became inefficient in Japan. Within two years, Japan's bauxite-smelting industry had been closed down, and Japan was importing all its aluminum from Australia. By identifying industries for profitable growth and those for profitable decline, MITI helps speed the adjustment process in reallocating resources to take maximum advantage of technological change and trends in prices.

The result of Japan's economic system and government economic intervention has been a high rate of capital accumulation. There has also been a high rate of accumulation of human capital, especially in the applied sciences. Going along with a high rate of capital accumulation—both physical and human—has been a high rate of technological advance with no inhibitions about using the best technologies available, wherever in the world they might have been developed.

Welfare State Capitalism Capitalism in Western Europe is more heavily tinged with socialism than in either the United States or Japan. It is welfare state capitalism. The countries of Western Europe, many of which now belong to the European Community, are basically capitalist market economies in the sense that most productive resources are owned by private individuals and most resources are allocated by individuals trading freely in markets for both goods and services and factors of production. But the scale of government and the degree and direction of government intervention are much larger in these countries than in the United States and Japan.

Government expenditure and taxes range between 40 and 50 percent of GDP in European countries. Tax rates this high create disincentives that result, other things being equal, in less effort and lower saving rates than in countries with lower taxes. The European countries also have a large, nationalized industry sector. A **nationalized industry** is an industry owned and operated by a publicly owned authority that is directly responsible to the government. Railways, airlines, gas, electricity, telephones, radio and television broadcasting, coal, steel, banking and finance, and even automobiles are among the industries that are either wholly or partly publicly owned in some European countries. Nationalized industries are often managed on a command rather than a market principle and usually are less efficient than privately owned, competitive firms.

Increasingly in recent years, European governments have been selling state-owned enterprises. The process of selling state-owned enterprises is called **privatization.** There has also been a retreat, in some countries, from very high tax rates. European countries, impressed by the economic success of Japan and the United States, have reached the conclusion that the greater reliance on capitalism in those economies is, in part, responsible for their economic success, and they are seeking to emulate the more successful economies.

The Sequence of Reform

We've seen that socialism and capitalism differ along two dimensions: the ownership of capital and land and the incentive structure. The features of a capitalist economy that must be adopted by a socialist economy if it is to make the transition are

- Private ownership of capital and natural resources
- Market-determined prices

In making the transition from socialism to capitalism, a country must choose the order in which to adopt these capitalist features.

By placing firms in private ownership, a formerly socialist economy gets the benefits of strengthened incentives to put resources to work at their most profitable uses. Also, by permitting the free entry of new firms, the economy is able to reap the benefits of increased competition. Both the existing firms and new firms become more efficient. At the same time, the state loses its major source of revenue—the profits of state enterprises. Thus, as industry is privatized, a taxation system must be set up to enable the state to raise the revenue needed to provide public goods and services.

By freeing markets and allowing prices to be determined by supply and demand, a formerly socialist economy gets the benefits of price signals that reflect the relative scarcity of different goods and services. These signals get translated into changes in production. Those items whose prices rise most become highly profitable, so their production increases fastest.

But often, the prices that rise the fastest are those on such basic staples as bread and milk. Because food items such as these are a very important part of the budget of the poorest families, when their prices increase sharply, there is great hardship. There is also likely to be political opposition to the reform process.

The Speed of Reform

Since reform brings turmoil, there is a case for doing it slowly—gradualism—and a case for doing it quickly—in a "big bang." The case for gradualism is that the adverse effects of reform are minimized and the transition can be managed and made smooth. The case for a big bang is that the socialist economy is a complete organism and that it cannot function unless it is left intact. Remove one piece of the system and the rest ceases to function.

◆ ◆ ◆ ◆ The countries that we've studied in this chapter—the former Soviet Union, the countries of Eastern Europe, and China—are undergoing enormous political and economic change. These changes will have repercussions throughout the world economy of the 1990s of historical proportions. No one can foresee what the world economy of the mid-1990s will look like. ◆ ◆ But the world has seen change of historical proportions before. The transformation of the economies of formerly war-torn Germany and Japan into the economic powerhouses of today is one example. Throughout all this change—past and present—our knowledge and understanding of the economic forces that produce the change and are unleashed by it have been gradually getting better. There remains a great deal that we do not understand. But we have made a great deal of progress. The economic principles presented in this book summarize this progress and the current state of knowledge. As the world continues to change, you will need a compass to guide you into unknown terrain. The principles of economics are that compass!

SUMMARY

The Economic Problem and Its Alternative Solutions

The economic problem is the universal fact of scarcity. Different economic systems deliver different solutions to the economic problem of determining *what, how,* and *for whom* goods and services are produced. Alternative economic systems vary in two dimensions: ownership of capital and land and the incentives people face. Capital and land may be owned by individuals, by the state, or by a mixture of the two. Incentives may be created by market prices, by administered prices and administrative sanctions, or by a mixture of the two. Economic systems differ in the ways in which they combine ownership and incentive arrangements. Capitalism is based on the private ownership of capital and land and on market price incentives. Socialism is based on state ownership of capital and land and on administrative incentives and a central economic plan. Market socialism combines state ownership of capital and land with incentives based on a mixture of market and administered prices. Welfare state capitalism combines the private ownership of capital and land with state intervention in markets that change the price signals that people respond to. (pp. 1032–1037)

Economic Change in the Former Soviet Union

The Soviet Union was founded in 1917 and collapsed in 1991. The economy of the Soviet Union was based on a system of central planning that had four key elements: an administrative hierarchy, an iterative planning process, legally binding commands, and taut and inflexible plans. The Soviet Union had a market sector in which a substantial amount of economic activity took place, especially in agriculture. Money played only a minor role in the economy of the Soviet Union.

The Soviet economy grew extraordinarily quickly before 1970—in excess of 5 percent a year—but during the 1970s, and more especially during the 1980s, output growth declined. By the early 1990s, the economy was shrinking. A combination of three features of the Soviet economy caused this deterioration in economic performance: the economy made a transition from being an investment economy to being a consumption economy; the economy was hit by serious external shocks; and its taut and inflexible planning system was incapable of coping with these events.

By the end of the 1980s, the Soviet Union began a process of transition toward a market economy. This process had three main elements: the relaxation of central plan enforcement, the deregulation of prices, and the introduction of limited private ownership of firms. The transition was a process of gradual change, but it ran into severe problems. The most important were value and legal systems alien to capitalism, the collapse of traditional trade flows, and the emergence of a large state budget deficit and inflation. (pp. 1037–1047)

Economic Transition in Eastern Europe

The formerly planned economies of East Germany, Czechoslovakia, Hungary, and Poland are also making transitions to market economies. East Germany's transition has been the most dramatic and the most complete. It has taken the form of a reunification of the two Germanies and the adoption by the former East Germany of West Germany's monetary and taxation system. Price deregulation and privatization have been rapid. Czechoslovakia has deregulated wages, prices, and interest rates and is privatizing its industry by returning small businesses and shops to their former owners and by issuing vouchers to its citizens that they may use to buy shares in formerly state-owned enterprises. Hungary began the process of moving toward a market economy during the 1960s when central planning was replaced by decentralized planning. Hungary has established a taxation system similar to that in the market economies. But the privatization of large-scale industry began only in the 1990s and is proceeding slowly. Poland has deregulated prices, pursued a policy of financial restraint that has brought inflation under control, and put privatization on a fast track. (pp. 1047–1049)

Economic Transition in China

Since the foundation of the People's Republic of China, economic management has been through turbulent changes. At first, China used the Soviet system of central planning. It then introduced the Great Leap Forward, which in turn degenerated into the Cultural Revolution. China at first grew quickly with heavy reliance on state planning and capital accumulation, but growth slowed, and, at times, per capita income actually fell. In 1978, China revolutionized its economic management, placing greater emphasis on private incentives and markets. As a consequence, productivity grew at a rapid rate and per capita income increased.

China's success in achieving a high rate of economic growth has resulted from four features of its reforms: a massive rate of entry of new non-state firms, large increases in the productivity and profitability of state firms, an efficient taxation system, and gradual price deregulation. Whether China has found a way of making the transition from socialism to capitalism in a relatively painless way is a controversial issue. (pp. 1049–1052)

The Transition from Central Plan to Market

In the transition from central planning to the market economy, three important choices must be made: the style of market economy to adopt, the sequencing of reforms, and the speed of reforms.

There are three main types of market economy to choose from: U.S.-style capitalism, Japanese-style capitalism, and welfare state capitalism. Two features of Japanese capitalism distinguish it from U.S. capitalism: its smaller scale of government and its pro-business government intervention. The capitalism of Western Europe, welfare state capitalism, is more heavily tinged with socialism than is that of either the United States or Japan. Government expenditure and taxes are much higher there—between 40 and 50 percent of GDP—and more of the manufacturing sector is state-owned, or nationalized.

The main issue in the sequencing of reform is the order in which to privatize the ownership of capital and land and to deregulate prices. The main issue concerning the speed of reform is whether to go slowly—gradualism—or quickly—in a "big bang." (pp. 1053–1055)

Key Elements

Key Terms

Capitalism, 1034
Central planning, 1034
Decentralized planning, 1034
Great Leap Forward, 1049
Hierarchy, 1040
Incentive structure, 1033
Market socialism, 1034
Nationalized industry, 1054
Privatization, 1054
Socialism, 1034
Welfare state capitalism, 1034

Key Figures and Tables

Figure 38.1 The Fundamental Economic Problem, 1032
Figure 38.2 Alternative Economic Systems, 1033
Figure 38.3 Capitalism's Solution to the Economic Problem, 1034
Figure 38.4 Socialism's Solution to the Economic Problem, 1036
Table 38.1 A Compact Summary of Key Periods in the Economic History of the Soviet Union, 1037
Table 38.3 A Compact Summary of Key Periods in the Economic History of the People's Republic of China, 1049

Review Questions

1 What is the fundamental economic problem that any economic system must solve?

2 What are the main economic systems? Set out the key features of each.

3 Give examples of countries that are capitalist, socialist, market socialist, and welfare state capitalist. (Name some countries other than those in Fig. 38.2.)

4 How does capitalism solve the economic problem? What determines how much of each good to produce?

5 How does socialism solve the economic problem? What determines how much of each good to produce?

6 How does market socialism determine the price and quantity of each good?

7 Why did the Soviet economy begin to fail in the 1980s?

8 What are the main features of the transition program in the former Soviet Union?

9 What are the main problems faced by the republics of the former Soviet Union?

10 What are the problems faced by the Eastern European countries as they make the transition to a market economy?

11 Review the main episodes in China's economic management since 1949.

12 Compare the economic growth performance of the United States and China. What do we learn from this comparison?

13 What are the lessons of the economic experiment that is going on in China?

GLOSSARY

Above full-employment equilibrium A situation in which macroeconomic equilibrium occurs at a level of real GDP above long-run real GDP.

Absolute advantage A person has an absolute advantage in production if that person has greater productivity than anyone else in the production of all goods. A country has an absolute advantage if its output per unit of inputs of all goods is larger than that of another country.

Adverse selection The tendency for the people who accept contracts to be those with private information that they plan to use to their own advantage and to the disadvantage of the less informed party.

Agency relationship The relationship between a firm and its owners, managers, and workers and between a firm and other firms.

Agent A person (or firm) hired by a firm (or another person) to do a specific job.

Aggregate demand The relationship between the aggregate quantity of goods and services demanded—real GDP demanded—and the price level—the GDP deflator—holding everything else constant.

Aggregate demand curve A curve showing real GDP demanded at each price level, holding everything else constant.

Aggregate demand schedule A list showing the quantity of real GDP demanded at each price level, holding everything else constant.

Aggregate expenditure curve A graph of the aggregate expenditure schedule.

Aggregate expenditure schedule A list of the level of aggregate planned expenditure generated at each level of real GDP.

Aggregate income The amount received by households in payment for the services of factors of production.

Aggregate planned expenditure The expenditure that economic agents (households, firms, governments, and foreigners) plan to undertake in given circumstances.

Aggregate quantity of goods and services demanded The sum of the quantities of consumption goods and services that households plan to buy, of investment goods that firms plan to buy, of goods and services that governments plan to buy, and of net exports that foreigners plan to buy.

Aggregate quantity of goods and services supplied The sum of the quantities of all final goods and services produced by all firms in the economy.

Allocative efficiency The situation that occurs when no resources are wasted—when no one can be made better off without someone else being made worse off.

Anticipated inflation An inflation rate that has been correctly forecasted (on the average).

Antitrust law A law that regulates and prohibits certain kinds of market behavior, such as monopoly and monopolistic practices.

Arbitrage The activity of buying low and selling high in order to make a profit on the margin between the two prices.

Asset Anything of value that a household, firm, or government owns.

Assortative mating Marrying within one's own socioeconomic group.

Assumptions The foundation on which a model is built.

Automatic stabilizer A mechanism that decreases the fluctuations in aggregate expenditure resulting from fluctuations in a component of aggregate expenditure.

Autonomous expenditure The sum of those components of aggregate planned expenditure that are not influenced by real GDP.

Autonomous expenditure multiplier The amount by which a change in autonomous expenditure is multiplied to determine the change in equilibrium expenditure that it generates.

Average cost pricing rule A rule that sets the price equal to average total cost.

Average fixed cost Total fixed cost per unit of output—total fixed cost divided by output.

Average product Total product per unit of variable input.

Average propensity to consume The ratio of consumption expenditure to disposable income.

Average propensity to save The ratio of saving to disposable income.

Average revenue Total revenue divided by the quantity sold. Average revenue also equals price.

Average revenue product Total revenue divided by the quantity of the factor hired.

Average revenue product curve A curve that shows the average revenue product of a factor at each quantity of the factor hired.

Average total cost Total cost per unit of output—total cost divided by output.

Average variable cost Total variable cost per unit of output—total variable cost divided by output.

Axes The scale lines on a graph.

Balanced budget A government budget in which tax revenue and expenditure are equal.

Balanced budget multiplier The amount by which a change in government purchases of goods and services is multiplied to determine the change in expenditure equilibrium when taxes are changed by the same amount as the change in government purchases.

Balance of payments accounts A country's record of international trading, borrowing, and lending.

Balance of trade The value of exports minus the value of imports.

Balance sheet A list of assets and liabilities.

Barriers to entry Legal or natural impediments protecting a firm from competition from potential new entrants.

Barter The direct exchange of goods and services for other goods and services.

Bequest A gift from one generation to the next.

Bilateral monopoly A market structure in which a single buyer and a single seller confront each other.

Binding arbitration A process in which a third party—an arbitrator—determines wages and other employment conditions on behalf of the negotiating parties and the decision is final.

Black market An illegal trading arrangement in which buyers and sellers do business at a price higher than the legally imposed price ceiling.

Bond A legally enforceable obligation to pay specified sums of money at specified future dates.

Bond market The market in which the bonds issued by firms and governments are traded.

Bond yield The interest on a bond expressed as a percentage of the price of the bond.

Break-even point The output at which total revenue equals total cost (and at which profit is zero).

Budget balance Total tax revenue minus the government's total expenditure in a given period of time (normally a year).

Budget deficit A government's budget balance that is negative—expenditure exceeds tax revenue.

Budget equation An equation that states the limits to consumption for a given income and given prices.

Budget line The limits to a household's consumption choices.

Budget surplus A government's budget balance that is positive—tax revenue exceeds expenditure.

Bureaucrats Appointed officials who work at various levels in government departments.

Business cycle The periodic but irregular up-and-down movement in economic activity, measured by fluctuations in real GDP and other macroeconomic variables.

Buyer's reservation price The highest price that the buyer is willing to pay for the good.

Capacity The output rate at which a plant's average total cost is at a minimum.

Capital The real assets—the equipment, buildings, tools, and other manufactured goods used in production—owned by a household, firm, or government.

Capital account A record of a country's international borrowing and lending transactions.

Capital accumulation The growth of capital resources.

Capital goods Goods that are added to our capital resources.

Capital-intensive technique A method of production that uses a relatively large amount of capital and a relatively small amount of labor to produce a given quantity of output.

Capital stock The stock of plant, equipment, buildings (including residential housing), and inventories.

Capitalism An economic system that permits private ownership of capital and land used in production and market allocation of resources.

Capture theory of regulation A theory of regulation that states that the regulations that exist are those that maximize producer surplus.

Cartel A group of producers that enter into a collusive agreement to restrict output in order to raise prices and profits.

Central bank A public authority charged with regulating and controlling a country's monetary and financial institutions and markets.

Central planning A method of allocating resources by command.

Ceteris paribus Other things being equal, or other things remaining constant.

Change in demand A shift of the entire demand curve that occurs when some influence on buyers' plans, other than the good's price, changes.

Change in quantity demanded A movement along a demand curve that results from a change in the price of the good.

Change in quantity supplied A movement along a supply curve that results from a change in the price of the good.

Change in supply A shift of the entire supply curve that occurs when some influence on producers' plans, other than the good's price, changes.

Checkable deposit A loan by a depositor to a bank, the ownership of which can be transferred from one person to another by writing an instruction to the bank—a check—asking the bank to alter its records.

Choke price The price at which it no longer pays to use a natural resource.

Closed economy An economy that has no links with any other economy.

Closed shop An arrangement (illegal since the passage of the Taft-Hartley Act in 1947) in which only union members may be hired.

Collective bargaining A process of negotiation between representatives of employers and unions.

Collusive agreement An agreement between two or more producers to restrict output in order to raise prices and profits.

Command economy An economy that relies on a command mechanism.

Command mechanism A method of determining *what*, *how*, and *for whom* goods and services are produced, based on the authority of a ruler or ruling body.

Commercial bank A private firm, chartered either by the Comptroller of the Currency (in the U.S. Treasury) or by a state agency to receive deposits and make loans.

Commodity money A physical commodity valued in its own right and also used as a means of payment.

Communist country A country in which there is limited private ownership of productive capital and firms, there is limited reliance on the market as a means of allocating resources, and government agencies plan and direct the production and distribution of most goods and services.

Comparable worth The payment of equal wages for different jobs that are judged to be comparable.

Comparative advantage A person has a comparative advantage in producing a good if he or she can produce that good at a lower opportunity cost than anyone else. A country has a comparative advantage in producing a good if it can produce that good at a lower opportunity cost than any other country.

Competition A contest for command over scarce resources.

Complement A good that is used in conjunction with another good.

Constant returns to scale Technological conditions under which the percentage increase in a firm's output is equal to the percentage increase in its inputs.

Consumer equilibrium A situation in which a consumer has allocated his or her income in the way that maximizes utility.

Consumer Price Index An index that measures the average level of prices of the goods and services typically consumed by an urban American family.

Consumer surplus The difference between the value of a good and its price.

Consumption The process of using up goods and services.

Consumption expenditure The total payment made by households on consumption goods and services.

Consumption function The relationship between consumption expenditure and disposable income, other things held constant.

Consumption goods Goods that are used up as soon as they are produced.

Contraction A business cycle phase in which there is a slowdown in the pace of economic activity.

Convertible paper money A paper claim to a commodity (such as gold) that circulates as a means of payment.

Cooperation People working with others to achieve a common end.

Cooperative equilibrium An equilibrium resulting from each player responding rationally to the credible threat of the other player to inflict heavy damage if the agreement is broken.

Coordinates Lines running from a point on a graph perpendicularly to the axes.

Corporation A firm owned by one or more limited liability stockholders.

Cost-push inflation Inflation that results from a decrease in aggregate supply, which increases costs.

Countervailing duty A tariff that is imposed to enable domestic producers to compete with subsidized foreign producers.

Craft union A group of workers who have a similar range of skills but work for different firms and industries.

Credit union A financial intermediary based on a social or economic group that obtains its funds from checking and savings deposits and makes consumer loans.

Creditor nation A country that has invested more in the rest of the world than other countries have invested in it.

Cross elasticity of demand The percent change in the quantity demanded of a good divided by the percent change in the price of another good (a substitute or complement).

Crowding in The tendency for an expansionary fiscal policy to increase investment.

Crowding out The tendency for an expansionary fiscal policy to increase interest rates, thereby reducing—crowding out—investment.

Currency The bills and coins that we use today.

Currency appreciation The increase in the value of one currency in terms of another currency.

Currency depreciation The fall in the value of one currency in terms of another currency.

Currency drain The tendency for some of the funds lent by banks and financial institutions to remain outside the banking system and circulate as currency in the hands of the public.

Current account A record of receipts from the sale of goods and services to foreigners, the payments for goods and services bought from foreigners, and gifts and other transfers (such as foreign aid payments) received from and paid to foreigners.

Current account balance The value of all the goods and services that we sell to other countries minus the value of goods and services that we buy from foreigners.

Curve Any relationship between two variables plotted on a graph, even a linear relationship.

Cyclical unemployment The unemployment arising from the slowdown in the pace of economic expansion.

Cyclically adjusted deficit The deficit that would occur if the economy were at full employment.

Deadweight loss A measure of allocative inefficiency as the reduction in consumer and producer surplus resulting from a restriction of output below its efficient level.

Debt financing The financing of the government deficit by selling bonds to anyone (household, firm, or foreigner) other than the Federal Reserve System.

Debtor nation A country that, during its entire history, has borrowed more from the rest of the world than it has lent to it. It has a stock of outstanding debt to the rest of the world that exceeds the stock of its own claims on the rest of the world.

Decentralized planning An economic system that combines state ownership of capital and land with incentives based on a mixture of market and administered prices.

Decreasing returns to scale Technological conditions under which the percentage change in a firm's output is less than the percentage change in the scale of inputs; sometimes called diseconomies of scale.

Demand The entire relationship between the quantity demanded of a good and its price.

Demand curve A graph showing the relationship between the quantity demanded of a good and its price, holding everything else constant.

Demand for labor The quantity of labor demanded at each level of the real wage rate.

Demand for real money The relationship between the quantity of real money demanded and the interest rate, holding constant all other influences on the amount of money that people wish to hold.

Demand-pull inflation Inflation that results from an increase in aggregate demand.

Demand schedule A list of the quantities demanded at different prices, holding everything else constant.

Depreciation The decrease in the value of capital stock or the value of a durable input that results from wear and tear and the passage of time.

Depression A deep business cycle trough.

Deregulation The process of removing restrictions on prices, product standards and types, and entry conditions.

Derived demand Demand for an input not for its own sake but in order to use it in the production of goods and services.

Developing country A country that is poor but is accumulating capital and developing an industrial and commercial base.

Diminishing marginal product of labor The tendency for the marginal product of labor to decline as the labor input increases, holding everything else constant.

Diminishing marginal rate of substitution The general tendency for the marginal rate of substitution to diminish as the consumer moves along an indifference curve, increasing the consumption of good x and decreasing the consumption of good y.

Diminishing marginal returns A situation in which the marginal product of the last worker hired falls short of the marginal product of the second last worker hired.

Diminishing marginal utility The decline in marginal utility that occurs as more and more of the good is consumed.

Discount rate The interest rate at which the Fed stands ready to lend reserves to commercial banks.

Discounting The conversion of a future amount of money to its present value.

Discouraged workers People who do not have jobs and would like to work but have stopped seeking work.

Diseconomies of scale Technological conditions under which the percentage change in a firm's output is less than the percentage change in the scale of inputs; sometimes called decreasing returns to scale.

Disposable income Income plus transfer payments minus taxes.

Dissaving Negative saving; a situation in which consumption expenditure exceeds disposable income.

Dominant strategy A strategy in a game that is the unique best action regardless of the action taken by the other player.

Dominant strategy equilibrium A Nash equilibrium in which there is a dominant strategy for each player in a game.

Double coincidence of wants A situation that occurs when person A wants to buy what person B is selling and person B wants to buy what person A is selling.

Double counting Counting the expenditure on both the final good and the intermediate goods and services used in its production.

Dumping The sale of a good in a foreign market for a lower price than in the domestic market or for a lower price than its cost of production.

Duopoly A market structure in which two producers of a commodity compete with each other.

Durable input A factor of production that is not entirely used up in a single production period.

Economic activity What people do to cope with scarcity.

Economic depreciation The change in the market price of a durable input over a given period.

Economic efficiency A state in which the cost of producing a given output is as low as possible.

Economic growth The expansion of our production possibilities.

Economic information Data on prices, quantities, and qualities of goods and services and factors of production.

Economic profit Revenue minus cost when the opportunity costs of production are included in cost.

Economic rent An income received by the owner of a factor over and above the amount required to induce that owner to offer the factor for use.

Economic theory A rule or principle that enables us to understand and predict economic choices.

Economic welfare A comprehensive measure of the general state of well-being and standard of living.

Economics The study of how people use their limited resources to try to satisfy unlimited wants.

Economies of scale Technological conditions under which the percent increase in a firm's output exceeds the percent increase in its inputs; sometimes called increasing returns to scale.

Economies of scope Decreases in average total cost made possible by increasing the number of different goods produced.

Economizing Making the best use of scarce resources.

Economy A mechanism that allocates scarce resources among competing uses.

Efficient market A market in which the actual price embodies all currently available relevant information.

Elastic demand Elasticity of demand is greater than 1; the quantity demanded of a good decreases by a larger percentage than its price increases.

Elasticity of demand The absolute value of the price elasticity of demand.

Elasticity of supply The percentage change in the quantity supplied of a good divided by the percentage change in its price.

Endowment The resources that people have.

End-state theory of distributive justice A theory of distributive justice that examines the fairness of the outcome of economic activity.

Entry The act of setting up a new firm in an industry.

Equation of exchange An equation that states that the quantity of money multiplied by the velocity of circulation of money equals GDP—the price level multiplied by real GDP.

Equilibrium A situation in which everyone has economized—that is, all individuals have made the best possible choices in the light of their own preferences and given their endowments, technologies, and information—and in which those choices have been coordinated and made compatible with the choices of everyone else. Equilibrium is the solution or outcome of an economic model.

Equilibrium expenditure The level of aggregate planned expenditure that equals real GDP.

Equilibrium price The price at which the quantity demanded equals the quantity supplied.

Equilibrium quantity The quantity bought and sold at the equilibrium price.

Equity or equity capital The owner's stake in a business.

Excess capacity A state in which output is below that at which average total cost is a minimum.

Excess reserves A bank's actual reserves minus its required reserves.

Excise tax A tax on the sale of a particular commodity.

Exhaustible natural resources Natural resources that can be used only once and cannot be replaced.

Exit The act of closing down a firm and leaving an industry.

Expansion A business cycle phase in which there is a speedup in the pace of economic activity.

Expected inflation rate The rate at which people, on the average, believe that the price level is rising.

Expected utility The average utility arising from all possible outcomes.

Expenditure approach A measure of GDP obtained by adding together consumption expenditure, investment, government purchases of goods and services, and net exports.

Exports The goods and services that we sell to people in other countries.

External benefits Those benefits accruing to people other than the buyer of a good.

External costs Those costs not borne by the producer but borne by other members of society.

External diseconomies Factors outside the control of a firm that raise its average total cost as industry output rises.

External economies Factors beyond the control of a firm that lower its average total cost as industry output rises.

Externality A cost or a benefit arising from an economic transaction that falls on a third party and that is not taken into account by those who undertake the transaction.

Factor cost The value of a good measured by adding together the costs of all the factors of production used to produce it.

Factor incomes approach A measure of GDP obtained by adding together all the incomes paid by firms to households for the services of the factors of production they hire—wages, interest, rent, and profits.

Factor market A market in which the factors of production are bought and sold.

Factors of production The economy's productive resources—land, labor, and capital.

Fair Labor Standards Act An act making it illegal to hire an adult worker for less than $4.25 an hour.

Federal budget A statement of the federal government's financial plan, itemizing programs and their costs, tax revenues, and the proposed deficit or surplus.

Federal Open Market Committee The main policymaking organ of the Federal Reserve System.

Federal Reserve System The central bank of the United States.

Feedback rule A rule that states how policy actions respond to changes in the state of the economy.

Fiat money An intrinsically worthless (or almost worthless) commodity that serves the functions of money.

Final goods and services Goods and services that are not used as inputs in the production of other goods and services but are bought by their final user.

Financial assets Paper claims of the holder against another household or firm.

Financial innovation The development of new financial products—of new ways of borrowing and lending.

Financial intermediary A firm that takes deposits from households and firms and makes loans to other households and firms.

Firm An institution that buys or hires factors of production and organizes them to produce and sell goods and services.

Fiscal policy The government's attempt to influence the economy by varying its purchases of goods and services and taxes to smooth the fluctuations in aggregate expenditure.

Fixed cost A cost that is independent of the output level.

Fixed exchange rate An exchange rate, the value of which is held steady by the country's central bank.

Fixed inputs Those inputs whose quantity used cannot be varied in the short run.

Fixed rule A rule that specifies an action to be pursued independently of the state of the economy.

Flexible exchange rate An exchange rate, the value of which is determined by market forces in the absence of central bank intervention.

Flow equilibrium A situation in which the quantity of goods or services supplied per unit of time equals the quantity demanded per unit of time.

Foreign exchange market The market in which the currency of one country is exchanged for the currency of another.

Foreign exchange rate The rate at which one country's money (or currency) exchanges for another country's money.

Forward market A market in which a commitment is made at a price agreed here and now to exchange a specified quantity of a particular commodity at a specified future date.

Four-firm concentration ratio The percentage of the value of sales accounted for by the largest four firms in an industry.

Free rider Someone who consumes a good without paying for it.

Free-rider problem The tendency for the scale of provision of a public good to be too small—to be allocatively inefficient—if it is produced and sold privately.

Frictional unemployment Unemployment arising from normal labor turnover—new entrants are constantly coming into the labor market, and firms are constantly laying off workers and hiring new workers.

Full employment A situation in which the number of people looking for a job equals the number of job vacancies.

Full-employment equilibrium A macroeconomic equilibrium in which real GDP equals long-run real GDP.

Futures market An organized market operated on a futures exchange in which large-scale contracts for the future delivery of goods can be exchanged.

Game theory A method of analyzing strategic behavior.

GDP deflator A price index that measures the average level of the prices of all the goods and services that make up GDP.

General Agreement on Tariffs and Trade An international agreement that limits government intervention to restrict international trade.

Goods and services All the valuable things that people produce. Goods are tangible; services are intangible.

Goods market A market in which goods and services are bought and sold.

Government An organization that provides goods and services to households and firms and redistributes income and wealth.

Government debt The total amount of borrowing that the government has undertaken and the total amount that it owes to households, firms, and foreigners.

Government deficit The total expenditure of the government sector less the total revenue of that sector in a given period.

Government license A license that controls entry into particular occupations, professions, or industries.

Government purchases multiplier The amount by which a change in government purchases of goods and services is multiplied to determine the change in equilibrium expenditure that it generates.

Great Leap Forward An economic plan for postrevolutionary China based on small-scale, labor-intensive production.

Gresham's Law The tendency for bad money to drive good money out of circulation.

Gross domestic product The value of all final goods and services produced in the economy in a year.

Gross investment The amount spent on replacing depreciated capital and on net additions to the capital stock.

Gross national product The total value of output owned by residents of the United States.

Herfindahl-Hirschman Index An index calculated as the square of the market share (percentage) of each firm summed over the largest 50 firms (or all firms if there are fewer than 50 firms) in the market.

Hierarchy An organization arranged in ranks, each rank being subordinate to the one above.

Historical cost Cost that values factors of production at the prices actually paid for them.

Horizontal integration The merger of two or more firms providing essentially the same product or service.

Hotelling Principle The proposition that the market for a stock of a natural resource is in equilibrium when the price of the resource is expected to rise at a rate equal to the interest rate.

Household Any group of people living together as a decision-making unit.

Household production The production of goods and services for consumption within the household.

Human capital The accumulated skill and knowledge of human beings; the value of a person's education and acquired skills.

Implications The outcome of a model that follows logically from its assumptions.

Implicit rental rate The rent that a firm implicitly pays to itself for the use of the durable inputs that it owns.

Imports The goods and services that we buy from people in other countries.

Imputed cost An opportunity cost that does not require an actual expenditure of cash.

Incentive structure A set of arrangements that induce people to take certain actions.

Income effect The effect of a change in income on consumption.

Income elasticity of demand The percentage change in the quantity demanded divided by the percentage change in income.

Increasing marginal returns A situation in which the marginal product of the last worker hired exceeds the marginal product of the second last worker hired.

Increasing returns to scale Technological conditions under which the percentage increase in a firm's output exceeds the percentage increase in its inputs; sometimes called economies of scale.

Indifference curve A line showing all possible combinations of two goods that give the consumer equal satisfaction.

Indirect tax A tax paid by consumers when they purchase goods and services.

Individual demand The relationship between the quantity of a good demanded by a single individual and its price.

Induced expenditure The part of aggregate planned expenditure on U.S.-produced goods and services that varies as real GDP varies.

Industrial country A country that has a large amount of capital equipment and in which people undertake highly specialized activities, enabling them to earn high per capita incomes.

Industrial union A group of workers who have a variety of skills and job types but who work for the same firm or industry.

Inelastic demand Elasticity of demand is between 0 and 1; the quantity demanded of a good decreases by a smaller percentage than its price increases.

Inferior good A good the demand for which decreases when income increases.

Inflation An upward movement in the average level of prices.

Inflation rate The percentage change in the price level.

Inflationary gap Actual real GDP minus long-run real GDP when actual real GDP is above long-run real GDP.

Information costs The cost of acquiring information on prices, quantities, and qualities of goods and services and factors of production—the opportunity cost of economic information received.

Injections Expenditures that add to the circular flow of expenditure and income—investment, government purchases, and exports.

Innovation The act of putting a new technique to work.

Intellectual property The intangible product of creative effort, protected by copyrights and patents. This type of property includes books, music, computer programs, and inventions of all kinds.

Interest rate parity A situation in which interest rates are equal across all countries once the differences in risk are taken into account.

Intermediate goods and services Goods and services that are used as inputs into the production process of another good or service.

International crowding out The tendency for an expansionary fiscal policy to decrease net exports.

International Monetary Fund An international organization that monitors the balance of payments and exchange rate activities.

International substitution The substitution of domestic goods and services for foreign goods and services or of foreign goods and services for domestic goods and services.

Intertemporal substitution The substitution of goods and services now for goods and services later or of goods and services later for goods and services now.

Invention The discovery of a new technique.

Inventories The stocks of raw materials, semi-finished products, and unsold final goods held by firms.

Investment The purchase of new plant, equipment, and buildings and additions to inventories.

Investment demand The relationship between the level of planned investment and the real interest rate, holding all other influences on investment constant.

Investment demand curve A curve showing the relationship between the real interest rate and the level of planned investment, holding everything else constant.

Investment demand schedule The list showing the quantity of planned investment at each real interest rate, holding everything else constant.

Investment security A marketable security that a bank can sell at a moment's notice if necessary but at a price that fluctuates.

Keynesian A macroeconomist who regards the economy as being inherently unstable and as requiring active government intervention to achieve stability.

Labor The brain power and muscle power of human beings.

Labor force The total number of employed and unemployed workers.

Labor force participation rate The proportion of the working age population that is either employed or unemployed (but seeking employment).

Labor-intensive technique A method of production that uses a relatively large amount of labor and a relatively small amount of capital to produce a given quantity of output.

Labor productivity Total output per person employed.

Labor union An organized group of workers whose purpose is to increase wages and influence other job conditions.

Laffer curve A curve that relates tax revenue to the tax rate.

Land Natural resources of all kinds.

Law of diminishing returns The general tendency for marginal product to eventually diminish as more of the variable input is employed, holding the quantity of fixed inputs constant.

Law of one price A law stating that any given commodity will be available at a single price.

Leakages Income that is not spent on domestically produced goods and services—saving, taxes (net of transfer payments), and imports.

Legal monopoly A monopoly that occurs when a law, license, or patent restricts competition by preventing entry.

Liability A debt—something that a household, firm, or government owes.

Line-item veto A veto power vested in the executive branch of the government to eliminate any specific item in a budget.

Linear relationship The relationship between two variables depicted by a straight line on a graph.

Liquid asset An asset that is instantly convertible into a means of payment with virtually no uncertainty about the price at which it can be converted.

Liquidity The degree to which an asset is instantly convertible into cash at a known price.

Liquidity trap A situation in which people are willing to hold any amount of money at a given interest rate—the demand curve for real money is horizontal.

Loan A commitment of a fixed amount of money for an agreed period of time.

Loans market The market in which households and firms borrow and lend.

Lobbying The activity of bringing pressure to bear on government agencies or institutions through a variety of informal mechanisms.

Local A subunit of a union that organizes individual workers.

Lockout The refusal by a firm to operate its plant and employ its workers.

Long run A period of time in which the quantities of all inputs can be varied.

Long-run aggregate supply The relationship between the aggregate quantity of final goods and services (GDP) supplied and the price level (GDP deflator) when there is full employment.

Long-run aggregate supply curve A curve showing the quantity of real GDP supplied and the price level when there is full employment.

Long-run average cost curve A curve that traces the relationship between the lowest attainable average total cost and output when all inputs can be varied.

Long-run cost The cost of production when a firm uses the economically efficient plant size.

Long-run demand curve The demand curve that describes the response of buyers to a change in price after all possible adjustments have been made.

Long-run demand for labor The relationship between the wage rate and the quantity of labor demanded when all inputs can be varied.

Long-run elasticity of demand for labor The magnitude of the percentage change in the quantity of labor demanded divided by the percentage change in the wage rate when all inputs are varied.

Long run Phillips curve A curve showing the relationship between inflation and unemployment when the actual inflation rate equals the expected inflation rate.

Long-run supply curve The supply curve that describes the response of the quantity supplied to a change in price after all technologically possible adjustments to supply have been exploited.

Lorenz curve A curve that shows the cumulative percentage of income or wealth against the cumulative percentage of families or population.

M1 A measure of money that sums currency held outside banks, traveler's checks, demand deposits, and other checkable deposits such as NOW and ATS accounts.

M2 A measure of money that sums M1, savings deposits, small time deposits, Eurodollar deposits, money market mutual fund shares held by individuals, and other M2 deposits.

M3 A measure of money that sums M2, large time deposits, Eurodollar time deposits, institutional money market mutual fund shares, and other M3 deposits.

Macroeconomic equilibrium A situation in which the quantity of real GDP demanded equals the quantity of real GDP supplied.

Macroeconomic long-run A period that is sufficiently long for the prices of all the factors of production to have adjusted to any disturbance.

Macroeconomic short-run A period during which the prices of goods and services change in response to changes in demand and supply but the prices of factors of production do not change.

Macroeconomics The branch of economics that studies the economy as a whole. Macroeconomics is concerned with the overall level of economic activity rather than with detailed individual choices.

Managed exchange rate An exchange rate, the value of which is influenced by bank intervention in the foreign exchange market.

Marginal benefit The increase in total benefit resulting from a one-unit increase in the scale of provision of a public good.

Marginal cost The increase in total cost resulting from a one-unit increase in output.

Marginal cost pricing rule The rule that sets price equal to marginal cost.

Marginal private cost The marginal cost directly incurred by the producer of a good.

Marginal product The increase in total product resulting from a one-unit increase in a variable input.

Marginal product of capital The change in total product resulting from a one-unit increase in the quantity of capital employed, holding the quantity of labor constant.

Marginal product of labor The change in total product (output) resulting from a one-unit increase in the quantity of labor employed, holding the quantity of all other inputs constant.

Marginal propensity to consume The fraction of the last dollar of disposable income that is spent on consumption goods and services.

Marginal propensity to consume out of real GDP The change in consumption expenditure divided by the change in real GDP.

Marginal propensity to import The fraction of the last dollar of real GDP spent on imports.

Marginal propensity to save The fraction of the last dollar of disposable income that is saved.

Marginal rate of substitution The rate at which a person will give up one good in order to get more of another good and at the same time remain indifferent.

Marginal revenue The change in total revenue resulting from a one-unit increase in the quantity sold.

Marginal revenue product The change in total revenue resulting from employing one more unit of a factor.

Marginal revenue product curve A curve that shows the marginal revenue product of a factor at each quantity of the factor hired.

Marginal social benefit The dollar value of the benefit from one additional unit of consumption, including the benefit to the buyer and any indirect benefits accruing to other members of society.

Marginal social cost The cost of producing one additional unit of output, including the costs borne by the producer and any other costs indirectly incurred by any other member of society; the marginal cost incurred by the producer of a good together with the marginal cost imposed as an externality on others.

Marginal tax rate The fraction of the last dollar of income paid to the government in net taxes (taxes minus transfer payments).

Marginal utility The change in total utility resulting from a one-unit increase in the quantity of a good consumed.

Marginal utility per dollar spent The marginal utility obtained from the last unit of a good consumed divided by the price of the good.

Market Any arrangement that facilitates buying and selling of a good, service, factor of production, or future commitment.

Market activity The supplying of labor through the market.

Market constraints The conditions under which a firm can buy its inputs and sell its output.

Market demand The relationship between the total quantity of a good demanded and its price.

Market economy An economy that determines *what*, *how*, and *for whom* goods and services are produced by coordinating individual choices through markets.

Market failure The inability of an unregulated market to achieve, in all circumstances, allocative efficiency.

Market income A person's income in the absence of government redistribution.

Market price The price that people pay for a good or service.

Market socialism An economic system that combines state ownership of capital and land with incentives based on a mixture of market and administered prices.

Median voter theorem The proposition that political parties will pursue policies that maximize the net benefit of the median voter.

Medium of exchange Anything that is generally acceptable in exchange for goods and services.

Merger The combining of the assets of two firms to form a single, new firm.

Microeconomics The branch of economics that studies the decisions of individual households and firms and the way in which individual markets work. Microeconomics also studies the way in which taxes and government regulation affect our economic choices.

Minimum wage law A regulation that makes trading labor below a specified wage illegal.

Mixed economy An economy that relies partly on markets and partly on a command mechanism to coordinate economic activity.

Mixed good A good that lies between a private good and a pure public good.

Momentary supply curve The supply curve that describes the immediate response of the quantity supplied to a change in price.

Monetarist A macroeconomist who assigns a high degree of importance to variations in the quantity of money as the main determinant of aggregate demand and who regards the economy as inherently stable.

Monetary base The sum of the Federal Reserve notes in circulation, banks' deposits at the Fed, and coins in circulation.

Monetary exchange A system in which some commodity or token serves as the medium of exchange.

Monetary policy The Fed's attempt to influence the economy by varying the money supply and interest rates.

Money Any commodity or token that is generally acceptable as a means of payment for goods and services.

Money financing The financing of the government deficit by the sale of bonds to the Federal Reserve System, which results in the creation of additional money.

Money market mutual fund A financial institution that obtains funds by selling shares and that uses the funds to buy highly liquid assets such as U.S. Treasury bills.

Money multiplier The amount by which a change in the monetary base is multiplied to determine the resulting change in the quantity of money.

Money wage rate The wage rate expressed in current dollars.

Monopolistic competition A market type in which a large number of firms compete with each other by making similar but slightly different products.

Monopoly The sole supplier of a good, service, or resource that has no close substitutes and in which there is a barrier preventing the entry of new firms.

Monopsony A market structure in which there is just a single buyer.

Moral hazard When one of the parties to an agreement has an incentive, after the agreement is made, to act in a manner that benefits himself or herself at the expense of the other party.

Multiplier The change in equilibrium real GDP divided by the change in autonomous expenditure.

Nash equilibrium The outcome of a game in which player A takes the best possible action given the action of player B and player B takes the best possible action given the action of player A.

Nationalized industry An industry owned and operated by a publicly owned authority that is directly responsible to the government.

Natural monopoly A monopoly that occurs when there is a unique source of supply of a raw material or when one firm can supply the entire market at a lower price than two or more firms can.

Natural rate hypothesis The proposition that the long-run Phillips curve is vertical at the natural rate of unemployment.

Natural rate of unemployment The unemployment rate when the economy is at full employment.

Natural resources The nonproduced factors of production with which we are endowed—all the gifts of nature, including land, water, air, and all the minerals that they contain.

Negative income tax A redistribution scheme that gives every family a *guaranteed annual income* and decreases the family's benefit at a specified *benefit loss rate* as its market income increases.

Negative relationship A relationship between two variables that move in opposite directions.

Net benefit Total benefit minus total cost.

Net borrower A country that is borrowing more from the rest of the world than it is lending to it.

Net domestic income at factor cost The sum of all factor incomes.

Net domestic product at market prices The sum of all factor income plus indirect taxes less subsidies.

Net export function The relationship between net exports and U.S. real GDP, holding constant all other influences on U.S. exports and imports.

Net exporter A country whose value of exports exceeds its value of imports—its balance of trade is positive.

Net exports The expenditure by foreigners on U.S.-produced goods minus the expenditure by U.S. residents on foreign-produced goods—exports minus imports.

Net financial assets Financial assets minus financial liabilities.

Net importer A country whose value of imports exceeds its value of exports—its balance of trade is negative.

Net investment Net additions to the capital stock—gross investment minus depreciation.

Net lender A country that is lending more to the rest of the world than it is borrowing from it.

Net present value The sum of the present values of payments spread over several years.

Net present value of an investment The present value of a stream of marginal revenue product generated by the investment minus the cost of the investment.

Newly industrialized country A country in which there is a rapidly developing broad industrial base and per capita income is growing quickly.

Nominal GDP The output of final goods and services valued at current prices.

Nominal GDP targeting The attempt to keep the growth of nominal GDP steady.

Nominal interest rate The interest rate actually paid and received in the marketplace.

Nominal money The quantity of money measured in current dollars.

Nonconvertible note A bank note that is not convertible into any commodity and that obtains its value by government fiat.

Nonexhaustible natural resources Natural resources that can be used repeatedly without depleting what is available for future use.

Nonmarket activity Leisure and nonmarket production activities, including housework, education, and training.

Nontariff barriers Any action other than a tariff that restricts international trade.

Nontraded good A good that cannot be traded over long distances.

Normal good A good the demand for which increases when income increases.

Normative statement A statement about what *ought* to be. An expression of an opinion that cannot be verified by observation.

Official reserves The government's holdings of foreign currency.

Official settlements account An account showing the net increase or decrease in a country's holdings of foreign currency.

Oligopoly A market type in which a small number of producers compete with each other.

Open economy An economy that has economic links with other economies.

Open market operation The purchase or sale of government securities by the Federal Reserve System designed to influence the money supply.

Open shop An arrangement in which no requirement is placed on an individual worker to join a union.

Opportunity cost The best forgone alternative.

Optimal search rule A rule that says that the buyer searches until an item is found at or below the buyer's reservation price and then stops searching and buys.

Optimizing The process of balancing benefits against costs and doing the best within the limits of what is possible.

Origin The zero point that is common to both axes on a graph.

Overutilized capacity When a plant produces more than the output at which average total cost is a minimum.

Paradox of thrift The fact that an increase in thriftiness leads to an increase in the income of an individual but to a decrease in aggregate income. The paradox arises because an increase in saving occurs with no increase in investment.

Partnership A firm with two or more owners who have unlimited liability.

Patent An exclusive right granted by the government to the inventor of a product or service.

Payoff The score of each player in a game.

Payoff matrix A table that shows the payoffs resulting from every possible action by each player for every possible action by each other player.

Peak The upper turning point of a business cycle, where an expansion turns into a contraction.

Per capita production function A curve showing how per capita output varies as the per capita stock of capital varies in a given state of knowledge about alternative technology.

Perfect competition A state that occurs in markets in which a large number of firms sell an identical product; there are many buyers; there are no restrictions on entry; firms have no advantage over potential new entrants; and all firms and buyers are fully informed about the prices of each and every firm.

Perfect price discrimination The practice of charging a different price for each unit sold and of charging each consumer the maximum price that he or she is willing to pay for each unit bought.

Perfectly competitive firm's supply curve A curve that shows how a perfectly competitive firm's output varies as the market price varies, other things remaining constant.

Perfectly elastic demand Elasticity of demand is infinite; the quantity demanded becomes zero if the price rises by the smallest amount, and the quantity demanded becomes infinite if the price falls by the smallest amount.

Perfectly inelastic demand Elasticity of demand is zero; the quantity demanded does not change as the price rises.

Perpetuity A bond that promises to pay a certain fixed amount of money each year forever.

Phillips curve A curve showing the relationship between inflation and unemployment.

Physical assets Buildings, plant and equipment, inventories, and consumer durable goods.

Physical limits The maximum output that a plant can produce.

Political business cycle A business cycle whose origins are fluctuations in aggregate demand brought about by policies designed to improve the chance of the government being reelected.

Political equilibrium A situation in which the choices of voters, politicians, and bureaucrats are all compatible and in which no one group of agents will be better off by making a different choice.

Politicians Elected officials in federal, state, and local government—from chief executives (the president, state governors, and mayors) to members of the legislature (state and federal senators and representatives and city councilors).

Portfolio choice A choice concerning which assets and liabilities to hold.

Positive relationship A relationship between two variables that move in the same direction.

Positive statement A statement about what *is*. Something that can be verified by careful observation.

Poverty An income level measured by a poverty index first calculated by the Social Security Administration in 1964.

Preferences People's likes and dislikes and the intensity of those likes and dislikes.

Present value The value in the present of a future amount of money; equal to the amount that, if invested today, will grow as large as that future amount, taking into account the interest that it will earn.

Price discrimination The practice of charging some customers a higher price than others for an identical good or of charging an individual customer a higher price on a small purchase than on a large one.

Price effect The effect of a change in the price on the quantity of a good consumed.

Price elasticity of demand The responsiveness of the quantity demand of a good to a change in its price. It is measured by the percentage change in the quantity demanded of a good divided by the percentage change in its price.

Price index A measure of the average level of prices in one period as a percentage of their level in an earlier period.

Price level The average level of prices as measured by a price index.

Price taker A firm that cannot influence the price of its product.

Principal A firm (or person) that hires a person (or firm) to undertake a specific job.

Principle of minimum differentiation The tendency for competitors to make themselves almost identical in order to appeal to the maximum number of clients or voters.

Private debt money A loan that the borrower promises to repay in currency on demand.

Private enterprise An economic system that permits individuals to decide on their own economic activities.

Private good A good or service, each unit of which is consumed by only one individual.

Private information Information that is available to one person but is too costly for anyone else to obtain.

Private property right A legally established title to the sole ownership of a scarce resource.

Private sector surplus or deficit The difference between saving and investment.

Privatization The process of selling state-owned enterprises to private individuals and firms.

Probability A number between 0 and 1 that measures the chance of some possible event occurring.

Process theory of distributive justice A theory of distributive justice that examines the fairness of the *mechanism* or *process* that results in a given distribution.

Producer surplus The difference between a producer's revenue and the opportunity cost of production.

Product differentiation Making a product slightly different from that of a competing firm.

Production The conversion of natural, human, and capital resources into goods and services.

Production function A relationship showing how output varies as the employment of inputs is varied.

Production possibility frontier The boundary between attainable and unattainable levels of production.

Productivity The amount of output produced per unit of inputs used to produce it.

Professional association An organized group of professional workers such as lawyers, dentists, or doctors that seeks to influence the compensation and other labor market conditions affecting its members.

Profit maximization Making the largest possible profit.

Progressive income tax An income tax at a marginal rate that rises with the level of income.

Property Anything of value that is owned.

Property rights Social arrangements that govern the ownership, use, and disposal of economic resources.

Proportional income tax An income tax that is at a constant rate regardless of the level of income.

Proprietorship A firm with a single owner who has unlimited liability.

Protectionism The restriction of international trade.

Public choice theory A theory predicting the behavior of the government sector of the economy as the outcome of the individual choices made by voters, politicians, and bureaucrats interacting with each other in a political marketplace.

Public franchise An exclusive right granted to a firm to supply a good or service.

Public interest theory A theory predicting that government action will take place to eliminate waste and achieve an efficient allocation of resources.

Public interest theory of regulation A theory of regulation that states that regulations are supplied to satisfy the demand of consumers and producers for the maximization of total surplus—or the attainment of allocative efficiency.

Purchasing power parity A situation that occurs when money has equal value across countries.

Pure public good A good each unit of which is consumed by everyone and from which no one can be excluded.

Quantity demanded The amount of a good or service that consumers plan to buy in a given period of time at a particular price.

Quantity of labor demanded The number of labor hours hired by all the firms in an economy.

Quantity of labor supplied The number of hours of labor services that households supply to firms.

Quantity of money The quantity of currency, bank deposits, and deposits at other types of financial institutions such as savings and loan associations and thrift institutions held by households and firms.

Quantity of U.S. dollar assets The stock of financial assets denominated in U.S. dollars minus the stock of financial liabilities denominated in U.S. dollars.

Quantity supplied The amount of a good or service that producers plan to sell in a given period of time at a particular price.

Quantity theory of money The proposition that an increase in the quantity of money leads to an equal percentage increase in the price level.

Quota A restriction on the quantity of a good that a firm is permitted to produce or that a country is permitted to import.

Rate of return regulation A regulation that sets the price at a level that enables the regulated firm to earn a specified target percent return on its capital.

Rational choice The choice that, among all possible choices, best achieves the goals.

Rational expectation A forecast that uses all of the relevant information available about past and present events and that has the least possible error.

Rational expectations equilibrium A macroeconomic equilibrium based on expectations that are the best available forecasts.

Rational expectations hypothesis The proposition that the forecasts people make, regardless of how they make them, are the same as the forecasts made by an economist using the relevant economic theory together with all information available at the time the forecast is made.

Rational ignorance The decision not to acquire information because the cost of acquiring it is greater than the benefit derived from having it.

Rawlsian theory of fairness A theory of distributive justice that gives the biggest income possible to the least well-off.

Real business cycle theory A theory of aggregate fluctuations based on flexible wages and random shocks to the economy's aggregate production function.

Real deficit The change in the real value of outstanding government debt.

Real GDP The output of final goods and services valued at prices prevailing in the base period.

Real income Income expressed in units of goods. Real income in terms of a particular good is income divided by the price of that good.

Real interest rate The interest rate paid by a borrower and received by a lender after taking into account the change in the value of money resulting from inflation.

Real money A measure of money based on the quantity of goods and services it will buy.

Real money balances effect The influence of a change in the quantity of real money on the quantity of real GDP demanded.

Real wage rate The wage rate per hour expressed in constant dollars.

Recession A downturn in the level of economic activity in which real GDP falls in two successive quarters.

Recessionary gap Long-run real GDP minus actual real GDP when actual real GDP is below long-run real GDP.

Regressive income tax An income tax at a marginal rate that falls with the level of income.

Regulation Rules administered by a government agency to restrict economic activity by determining prices, product standards and types, and the conditions under which new firms may enter an industry.

Relative price The ratio of the price of one good to the price of another.

Rent ceiling A regulation making it illegal to charge a rent higher than a specified level.

Rent seeking The activity of attempting to create a monopoly.

Required reserve ratio The ratio of reserves to deposits that banks are required, by regulation, to hold.

Required reserves The minimum reserves that a bank is permitted to hold—its deposits multiplied by the required reserve ratio.

Reservation wage The lowest wage rate at which a person or household will supply labor to the market. Below that wage, a person will not work.

Reserve ratio The fraction of a bank's total deposits that are held in reserves.

Reserves Cash in a bank's vault plus the bank's deposits with the Federal Reserve banks.

Returns to scale Increases in output that result from increasing all the inputs by the same percentage.

Right-to-work law A law allowing an individual to work at any firm without joining a union.

Risk A state in which more than one outcome may occur and the probability of each possible outcome can be estimated.

Saving Income minus consumption. Saving is measured in the national income accounts as disposable income (income less taxes) minus consumption expenditure.

Saving function The relationship between saving and disposable income, other things held constant.

Savings and loan association A financial intermediary that traditionally obtained its funds from savings deposits and that made long-term mortgage loans to home buyers.

Savings bank A financial intermediary owned by its depositors that accepts deposits and makes loans, mostly for consumer mortgages.

Scarcity The universal state in which wants exceed resources.

Scatter diagram A diagram that plots values of one economic variable associated with values of another.

Search activity The time and effort spent in searching for someone with whom to do business.

Self-sufficiency A state that occurs when people produce only enough for their own consumption.

Short run A period of time in which the quantity of at least one input is fixed and the quantities of the other inputs can be varied.

Short-run aggregate production function The relationship showing how real GDP varies as the quantity of labor employed varies, holding constant the inputs, including the capital stock and state of technology.

Short-run aggregate supply The relationship between the aggregate quantity of goods and services (real GDP) supplied and the price level (the GDP deflator), holding everything else constant.

Short-run aggregate supply curve A curve showing the relationship between the quantity of real GDP supplied and the price level, holding everything else constant.

Short-run aggregate supply schedule A list showing the quantity of real GDP supplied at each price level, holding everything else constant.

Short-run demand curve The demand curve that describes the initial response of buyers to a change in the price of a good.

Short-run demand for labor The relationship between the wage rate and the quantity of labor demanded when the firm's capital input is fixed and labor is the only variable input.

Short-run elasticity of demand for labor The magnitude of the percentage change in the quantity of labor demanded divided by the percentage change in the wage rate when labor is the only variable input.

Short-run industry supply curve A curve that shows how the total quantity supplied in the short run by all firms in an industry varies as the market price varies.

Short-run Phillips curve A curve showing the relationship between inflation and unemployment, holding constant the expected inflation rate and the natural rate of unemployment.

Short-run production function The relationship showing how output varies when the quantity of labor employed varies, holding constant the quantity of capital and the state of technology.

Short-run supply curve The supply curve that describes the response of the quantity supplied to a change in price when only *some* of the technologically possible adjustments have been made.

Shutdown point The quantity and price at which the firm is just covering its total variable cost.

Signal An action taken outside a market that conveys information that can be used by that market.

Simple money multiplier The amount by which an increase in bank reserves is multiplied to calculate the effect of that increase on total bank deposits when there are no losses of currency from the banking system.

Single-price monopoly A monopoly that charges the same price for each and every unit of output.

Slope The change in the value of the variable measured on the y-axis divided by the change in the value of the variable measured on the x-axis.

Socialism An economic system based on state ownership of capital and land and on an incentive system based on administered prices or sanctions arising from a central economic plan.

Specialization The production of only one good or a few goods.

Standard of deferred payment An agreed measure that enables contracts to be written for future receipts and payments.

Stock equilibrium A situation in which the available stock of an asset is willingly held.

Stock exchange An organized market for trading in stock.

Stock market The market in which the equities of firms are traded.

Stock yield The income from a share in the stock of a firm expressed as a percentage of the share's price.

Store of value Any commodity or token that can be held and exchanged later for goods and services.

Strategic behavior Acting in a way that takes into account the expected behavior of others and the mutual recognition of interdependence.

Strategies All the possible actions of each player.

Strike The refusal of a group of workers to work under the prevailing conditions.

Structural unemployment The unemployment that arises when there is a decline in the number of jobs available in a particular region or industry.

Subsidy A payment made by the government to producers that depends on the level of output.

Substitute A good that may be used in place of another good.

Substitution effect The effect of a change in price on the quantities consumed when the consumer remains indifferent between the original and the new combinations of goods consumed.

Sunk costs The historical cost of buying plant and machinery that have no current resale value.

Supply The entire relationship between the quantity supplied of a good and its price.

Supply curve A graph showing the relationship between the quantity supplied and the price of a good, holding everything else constant.

Supply of labor The quantity of labor supplied at each real wage rate.

Supply schedule A list of quantities supplied at different prices, holding everything else constant.

Takeover The purchase of the stock of one firm by another firm.

Tariff A tax on an import by the government of the importing country.

Tax base The activity on which a tax is levied.

Tax multiplier The amount by which a change in taxes is multiplied to determine the change in equilibrium expenditure that it generates.

Tax rate The percentage rate at which a tax is levied on a particular activity.

Team production A production process in which individuals work in a group and each individual specializes in mutually supportive tasks.

Technique Any feasible way of converting inputs into output.

Technological efficiency A state in which it is not possible to increase output without increasing inputs.

Technological progress The development of new and better ways of producing goods and services.

Technology The method for converting resources into goods and services.

Theory of distributive justice A set of principles against which we can test whether a particular distribution of economic well-being is fair.

Time-series graph A graph showing the value of a variable on the y-axis plotted against time on the x-axis.

Tit-for-tat strategy A strategy in which a player cooperates in the current period if the other player cooperated in the previous period but cheats in the current period if the other player cheated in the previous period.

Total benefit The total dollar value that a person places on a given level of provision of a public good.

Total cost The sum of the costs of all the inputs used in production.

Total fixed cost The cost of all the fixed inputs.

Total product The total quantity produced by a firm in a given period of time.

Total product curve A graph showing the maximum output attainable with a given amount of capital as the amount of labor employed is varied.

Total surplus The sum of consumer surplus and producer surplus.

Total utility The total benefit or satisfaction that a person gets from the consumption of goods and services.

Total variable cost The cost of variable inputs.

Trade-weighted index The value of a basket of currencies when the weight placed on each currency is related to its importance in U.S. international trade.

Transactions costs The costs arising from finding someone with whom to do business, of reaching an agreement about the price and other aspects of the exchange, and of ensuring that the terms of the agreement are fulfilled.

Transfer earnings The income required to induce the owner to offer the factor of production for use.

Transfer payments Payments made by the government to households under social programs.

Transfer payments multiplier The amount by which a change in transfer payments is multiplied to determine the change in equilibrium expenditure that it generates.

Trend A general tendency for a variable to rise or fall.

Trigger strategy A strategy in which a player cooperates if the other player cooperates but plays the Nash equilibrium strategy forever thereafter if the other player cheats.

Trough The lower turning point of a business cycle, where a contraction turns into an expansion.

Twin deficits The government budget deficit and the current account deficit.

Unanticipated inflation Inflation that catches people by surprise.

Uncertainty A state in which more than one event may occur but we don't know which one.

Underdeveloped country A country in which there is little industrialization, limited mechanization of the agricultural sector, very little capital equipment, and low per capita income.

Underdevelopment trap A situation in which a country is locked into a low per capita income situation that reinforces itself.

Underground economy All economic activity that is legal but unreported.

Unemployment A state in which there are qualified workers who are available for work at the current wage rate and who do not have jobs.

Unemployment equilibrium A situation in which macroeconomic equilibrium occurs at a level of real GDP below long-run real GDP.

Unemployment rate The number of people unemployed expressed as a percentage of the labor force.

Union shop An arrangement in which a firm may hire nonunion workers but, in order for such workers to remain employed, they must join the union within a brief period specified by the union.

Unit elastic demand An elasticity of demand of 1; the quantity demanded of a good and its price change in equal proportions.

Unit of account An agreed measure for stating the prices of goods and services.

Utilitarian theory The theory that the fairest outcome is the one that maximizes the sum of the utilities of all individuals in a society.

Utility The benefit or satisfaction that a person obtains from the consumption of a good or service.

Utility of wealth schedule (or curve) A schedule or curve that describes how much utility a person attaches to each level of wealth.

Utility maximization The attainment of the greatest possible utility.

Value The maximum amount that a person is willing to pay for a good.

Value added The value of a firm's output minus the value of the intermediate goods bought from other firms.

Value of money The amount of goods and services that can be bought with a given amount of money.

Variable cost A cost that varies with the output level.

Variable inputs Those inputs whose quantity used can be varied in the short run.

Velocity of circulation The average number of times a dollar of money is used annually to buy the goods and services that make up GDP.

Vertical integration The merger of two or more firms operating at different stages in the production process of a single good or service.

Voluntary export restraint A self-imposed restriction by an exporting country on the volume of its exports of a particular good. Voluntary export restraints are often called VERs.

Voters The consumers of the outcome of the political process.

Wants The unlimited desires or wishes that people have for goods and services.

Wealth Total assets of a household, firm, or government minus its total liabilities.

Welfare state capitalism An economic system that combines the private ownership of capital and land with state interventions in markets that change the price signals that people respond to.

Wholesale deposit market The market for deposits among banks and other financial institutions.

***x*-axis** The horizontal scale on a graph.

***x*-coordinate** A line running from a point on a graph horizontally to the *y*-axis. It is called the *x*-coordinate because its length is the same as the value marked off on the *x*-axis.

***y*-axis** The vertical scale on a graph.

***y*-coordinate** A line running from a point on a graph vertically to the *x*-axis. It is called the *y*-coordinate because its length is the same as the value marked off on the *y*-axis.

INDEX

Key concepts and pages on which they are defined appear in boldface.

Credits

(continued from p. ii)

Part 1: Robert Solow (pp. 1–4), © **L. Barry Hetherington.**

Chapter 1: Pin factory (p. 22), **Culver Pictures.** Woman holding silicon wafer (p. 23), **Tony Stone Worldwide.** Adam Smith (p. 23), **The Bettmann Archive.**

Chapter 4: The railroad suspension bridge near Niagara Falls, anonymous (p. 86), **gift of Maxim Karolik for the M. and M. Karolik Collection of American Paintings, 1815–1865; courtesy Museum of Fine Arts, Boston.** Crowded airport (p. 87), **Steve Proehl/The Image Bank.** Antoine-Augustin Cournot (p. 87), **Historical Pictures/Stock Montage.** Alfred Marshall (p. 87), **Historical Pictures/Stock Montage.**

Part 2: Herbert Stein (pp. 97–100), **American Enterprise Institute for Public Policy Research.**

Chapter 6: Boston tea party (p. 140), **American Antiquarian Society.** Gas pump (p. 141), **Lightstream.** Fleeming Jenkins (p. 141), **Mary Evans Picture Library.**

Part 3: Richard Easterlin (pp. 152–154), **Irene Fertik/USC Periodicals.**

Chapter 7: Women workers canning peaches (p. 172), **Keystone-Mast Collection, California Museum of Photography, University of California at Riverside.** Modern businesswoman (p. 173), **Richard Wood/The Picture Cube.** Jeremy Bentham (p. 173), **Mary Evans Picture Library.** William Stanley Jevons (p. 173), **MacMillan Press.**

Part 4: Ronald H. Coase (pp. 203–204), **David Joel, Randy Tunnell/The University of Chicago.**

Chapter 10: Ford assembly line (p. 256), **Brown Brothers.** Michael Dell (p. 257), **Will Van Overbeek.** Jacob Viner (p. 257), **Seeley G. Mudd Library, Princeton University.** Ronald H. Coase (p. 257), **David Joel/The University of Chicago.**

Part 5: Kenneth Arrow (pp. 274–277), **Stanford University.**

Chapter 12: Puck monopoly cartoon (p. 322), **Culver Pictures.** Cable TV worker (p. 323), © **1992 John Lidington, Continental Cablevision.** Joan Robinson (p. 323), **Ramsey & Muspratt Archives.**

Part 6: Claudia Goldin (pp. 372–375), **Jane Reed/Harvard University.**

Chapter 14: Chicago city scene (p. 398), **Chicago Historical Society.** Cartoon of stacked cars (p. 399), *The Economist*, **9/14/91; reprinted by permission of Robert Hunt.** Harold Hotelling (p. 399), **Photography by Wootten-Moulio.** Thomas Robert Malthus (p. 399), **The Bettmann Archive.**

Part 7: Anthony Atkinson (pp. 454–457), **Carlo Faulds/Cambridge University.**

Chapter 18: Homeless man on Fifth Avenue (p. 506), **AP/Wide World Photos.** Frankfurt crowd (p. 507), **Mike Mazzaschi/Stock Boston.** Simon Kuznets (p. 507), **Harvard University News Office.**

Part 8: Anne Friedlaender (pp. 512–515), © **L. Barry Hetherington.**

Chapter 19: Great Lakes pollution (p. 530), **Jim Baron/© 1992 Image Finders.** Lake Erie fishing boat (p. 531), **Pat Mullen.** James Buchanan (p. 531), **George Mason University, photo by Carl Zitzman.** Arthur Pigou (p. 531), **Y. H. Mottram/National Portrait Gallery, London.**

Part 9: Franco Modigliani (pp. 577–580), © **L. Barry Hetherington.**

Chapter 23: Four teens washing car (p. 631), **Jeffrey Meyers/Stock Boston.** Automatic car wash (p. 631), **Lightstream.** William Petty (p. 631), **The Bettmann Archive.**

Part 10: Allan Meltzer (pp. 664–667), **AP/Wide World Photos.**

Chapter 25: Young couple in kitchen (p. 674), **Peter Menzel/Stock Boston.** College students buying CDs (p. 675), © **John Coletti/The Picture Cube.** John Maynard Keynes (p. 675), **Historical Pictures/Stock Montage.**

Chapter 27: Woman burning marks (p. 748), **UPI/Bettmann.** Woman at ATM (p. 749), **Stock Boston © Doug Cooke.** David Hume (p. 749), **The Bettmann Archive.**

Part 11: Edmund Phelps (pp. 812–815), **Joe Pineiro/Columbia University.**

Chapter 32: NYT headlines, March 6, 1933 (p. 892), **The New York Times.** Crowd outside bank (p. 892), **Franklin D. Roosevelt Library Collection/UPI (ACME)/ The Bettmann Archive.** Boarded-up contemporary businesses (p. 893), **Lightstream.** Robert Lucas (p. 893), **Marshall Henrichs/Addison-Wesley.**

Part 12: Andrew F. Brimmer (pp. 897–898), **Brooks Photographers.**

Chapter 33: Kennedy and economic advisors (p. 918), **Walter Bennett/TIME Magazine.** Richard Darman and chart (p. 919), **AP/Wide World Photos.** Milton Friedman (p. 919), **Marshall Henrichs/Addison-Wesley.**

Part 13: Laura Tyson (pp. 949–950), **Jane Scherr/University of California.**

Chapter 35: Nineteenth-century clipper ship card (p. 964), **Museum of the City of New York.** Container ship (p. 965), **Sea-Land Corporation.** David Ricardo (p. 965), **Historical Pictures/Stock Montage.**

Part 14: Jeffrey Sachs (pp. 1007–1009), **Hank Morgan.**

Chapter 38: Chinese peasant farmers (p. 1038), **Mark Riboud/Magnum.** Affluent contemporary Chinese couple (p. 1039) **Owen Franken/Stock Boston.** Karl Marx (p. 1039), **The Bettmann Archive.**

Macroeconomic data for the United States: 1959–1991

Year	Gross domestic product (Y)	Personal consumption expenditures (C)	Gross private domestic investment (I)	Government purchases of goods and services (G)	Net exports (NX)	Growth rate of GDP (percent change)	Unemployment rate (percentage of all workers)
1959	1,931.3	1,178.9	296.4	477.8	–21.8	0.0	5.3
1960	1,973.2	1,210.8	290.8	479.2	–7.7	2.2	5.4
1961	2,025.6	1,238.4	289.4	503.3	–5.4	2.7	6.5
1962	2,129.8	1,293.3	321.2	525.9	–10.5	5.1	5.4
1963	2,218.0	1,341.9	343.3	538.7	0.1	4.1	5.5
1964	2,343.3	1,417.2	371.8	551.7	2.5	5.6	5.0
1965	2,473.5	1,497.0	413.0	569.9	–6.4	5.6	4.4
1966	2,622.3	1,573.8	438.0	628.5	–18.0	6.0	3.7
1967	2,690.3	1,622.4	418.6	673.0	–23.7	2.6	3.7
1968	2,801.0	1,707.5	440.1	691.0	–37.5	4.1	3.5
1969	2,877.1	1,771.2	461.3	686.1	–41.4	2.7	3.4
1970	2,875.8	1,813.5	429.7	667.8	–35.1	0.0	4.8
1971	2,965.1	1,873.7	481.5	655.8	–45.9	3.1	5.8
1972	3,107.1	1,978.4	532.2	653.0	–56.5	4.8	5.5
1973	3,268.6	2,066.7	591.7	644.2	–34.1	5.2	4.8
1974	3,248.1	2,053.8	543.0	655.4	–4.0	–0.6	5.5
1975	3,221.7	2,097.5	437.6	663.5	23.1	–0.8	8.3
1976	3,380.8	2,207.3	520.6	659.2	–6.3	4.9	7.6
1977	3,533.2	2,296.6	600.4	664.1	–27.8	4.5	6.9
1978	3,703.5	2,391.8	664.6	677.0	–29.9	4.8	6.0
1979	3,796.8	2,448.4	669.7	689.3	–10.6	2.5	5.8
1980	3,776.3	2,447.1	594.4	704.2	30.6	–0.5	7.0
1981	3,843.1	2,476.9	631.1	713.2	22.0	1.8	7.6
1982	3,760.3	2,503.7	540.5	723.6	–7.4	–2.2	9.5
1983	3,906.6	2,619.4	599.5	743.8	–56.2	3.9	9.5
1984	4,148.5	2,746.1	757.5	766.9	–122.0	6.2	7.4
1985	4,279.8	2,865.8	745.9	813.4	–145.4	3.2	7.1
1986	4,404.5	2,969.1	735.1	855.4	–155.1	2.9	6.9
1987	4,540.0	3,052.2	749.3	881.5	–143.1	3.1	6.1
1988	4,718.6	3,162.4	773.4	886.8	–104.1	3.9	5.4
1989	4,836.9	3,223.1	789.2	900.4	–75.7	2.5	5.2
1990	4,884.9	3,262.6	744.5	929.1	–51.3	1.0	5.4
1991	4,848.4	3,256.7	672.6	936.7	–17.6	-0.7	6.6

Sources: GDP: 1959–1991, *Economic Report of the President, 1992,* Table B-2; unemployment: 1959–1991, *Economic Report of the President, 1992,* Table B-37;

Macroeconomic data for the United States: 1959–1991

Year	GDP deflator (1987 = 100)	GDP deflator (percent change)	Consumer Price Index (1982–1984) = 100)	Consumer Price Index (percent change)	M1 (billions of dollars)	M2 (billions of dollars)	M1 (percent change)	M2 (percent change)
1959	**25.6**		**29.1**		**140.0**	**297.8**		
1960	**26.0**	**1.6**	**29.6**	**1.7**	**140.7**	**312.4**	**0.5**	**4.9**
1961	**26.3**	**1.2**	**29.9**	**1.0**	**145.2**	**335.5**	**3.2**	**7.4**
1962	**26.8**	**1.9**	**30.2**	**1.0**	**147.9**	**362.7**	**1.9**	**8.1**
1963	**27.2**	**1.5**	**30.6**	**1.3**	**153.4**	**393.3**	**3.7**	**8.4**
1964	**27.7**	**1.8**	**31.0**	**1.3**	**160.4**	**424.8**	**4.6**	**8.0**
1965	**28.4**	**2.5**	**31.5**	**1.6**	**167.9**	**459.4**	**4.7**	**8.1**
1966	**29.4**	**3.5**	**32.4**	**2.9**	**172.1**	**480.0**	**2.5**	**4.5**
1967	**30.3**	**3.1**	**33.4**	**3.1**	**183.3**	**524.4**	**6.5**	**9.3**
1968	**31.7**	**4.6**	**34.8**	**4.2**	**197.5**	**566.4**	**7.7**	**8.0**
1969	**33.3**	**5.0**	**36.7**	**5.5**	**204.0**	**589.6**	**3.3**	**4.1**
1970	**35.1**	**5.4**	**38.8**	**5.7**	**214.5**	**628.1**	**5.1**	**6.5**
1971	**37.0**	**5.4**	**40.5**	**4.4**	**228.4**	**712.7**	**6.5**	**13.5**
1972	**38.8**	**4.9**	**41.8**	**3.2**	**249.3**	**805.2**	**9.2**	**13.0**
1973	**41.3**	**6.4**	**44.4**	**6.2**	**262.9**	**861.0**	**5.5**	**6.9**
1974	**44.9**	**8.7**	**49.3**	**11.0**	**274.4**	**908.6**	**4.4**	**5.5**
1975	**49.2**	**9.6**	**53.8**	**9.1**	**287.6**	**1,023.3**	**4.8**	**12.6**
1976	**52.3**	**6.3**	**56.9**	**5.8**	**306.4**	**1,163.7**	**6.5**	**13.7**
1977	**55.9**	**6.9**	**60.6**	**6.5**	**331.3**	**1,286.7**	**8.1**	**10.6**
1978	**60.3**	**7.9**	**65.2**	**7.6**	**358.4**	**1,389.0**	**8.2**	**8.0**
1979	**65.5**	**8.6**	**72.6**	**11.3**	**382.8**	**1,497.1**	**6.8**	**7.8**
1980	**71.7**	**9.5**	**82.4**	**13.5**	**408.8**	**1,629.8**	**6.8**	**8.9**
1981	**78.9**	**10.0**	**90.9**	**10.3**	**436.4**	**1,793.3**	**6.8**	**10.0**
1982	**83.8**	**6.2**	**96.5**	**6.2**	**474.4**	**1,952.9**	**8.7**	**8.9**
1983	**87.2**	**4.1**	**99.6**	**3.2**	**521.2**	**2,186.3**	**9.9**	**12.0**
1984	**91.0**	**4.4**	**103.9**	**4.3**	**552.2**	**2,374.7**	**5.9**	**8.6**
1985	**94.4**	**3.7**	**107.6**	**3.6**	**619.9**	**2,569.7**	**12.3**	**8.2**
1986	**96.9**	**2.6**	**109.6**	**1.9**	**724.3**	**2,811.6**	**16.8**	**9.4**
1987	**100.0**	**3.2**	**113.6**	**3.6**	**749.7**	**2,910.1**	**3.5**	**3.5**
1988	**103.9**	**3.9**	**118.3**	**4.1**	**786.4**	**3,069.9**	**4.9**	**5.5**
1989	**108.4**	**4.3**	**124.0**	**4.8**	**793.6**	**3,223.1**	**0.9**	**5.0**
1990	**112.9**	**4.2**	**130.7**	**5.4**	**825.4**	**3,327.8**	**4.0**	**3.2**
1991	**117.0**	**3.6**	**136.2**	**4.2**	**896.7**	**3,425.4**	**8.6**	**2.9**

Sources: GDP deflator: 1959–1991, *Economic Report of the President, 1992,* Table B-3; Consumer Price Index: 1959–1991, *Economic Report of the President, 1992,* Table B-58, money supply: *Economic Report of the President, 1992,* Table B-65.